JAN 1 3 2025

ProQuest Statistical Abstract of the United States 2025

ProQuest Statistical Abstract of the United States 2025

Part of **Clarivate**

Published by Rowman & Littlefield
An imprint of The Rowman & Littlefield Publishing Group, Inc.
4501 Forbes Boulevard, Suite 200, Lanham, Maryland 20706
www.rowman.com, 800-462-6420
86-90 Paul Street, London, EC2A 4NE

ISBN 13: 979-8-89205-059-3

Suggested Citation:
ProQuest LLC. ProQuest Statistical Abstract of the United States, 2025. (13th ed.) 2024

Preface

The *Statistical Abstract of the United States,* published since 1878, is the best-known statistical reference publication in the country. As a comprehensive collection of statistics on the social, political, and economic conditions of the United States, it is a snapshot of America and its people. In the spring of 2011, the Census Bureau terminated their Statistical Compendia program and production of the *Statistical Abstract.* Since 2012, ProQuest, now part of Clarivate, has taken responsibility for curating the data found in this valuable statistical reference tool and publishing it in this print edition and an expanded online edition.

The *ProQuest Statistical Abstract of the United States* is designed to serve as a convenient volume for statistical reference and as a guide to other statistical publications and sources. The latter function is served by the introductory text to each section; source citations appearing below each table; and Appendix I, which is comprised of the Guide to Sources of Statistics, including a list of international statistical abstracts, and the Guide to State Statistical Abstracts.

Contents—This volume includes a selection of data from many statistical sources, both government and private, as indicated in the source citations at the bottom of every table. Data are obtained from a variety of resources, including PDF documents, Excel data packages, and complex databases. Publications cited as source reports usually contain additional statistical detail and more comprehensive discussions of definitions and concepts. Data not available in written publications issued by the contributing agency but obtained from data files available on the internet or unpublished records are also identified in the source notes. More information on the subjects covered in the tables may generally be obtained from the source.

Except as indicated, figures are for the United States as presently constituted. Although emphasis in the *ProQuest Statistical Abstract* is primarily given to national data, many tables present data for regions and individual states and a smaller number for metropolitan areas and cities. "Appendix II, Metropolitan and Micropolitan Statistical Areas: Concepts, Components, and Population," presents explanatory text, a complete current listing, and 2023 population data for metropolitan and micropolitan areas delineated as of July 2023. Statistics for the Commonwealth of Puerto Rico and for Island Areas of the United States are included in many state tables and are supplemented by information in Section 29.

Statistics in this edition are generally for the most recent year or period available, as of early September 2024. Each year over 1,400 tables are reviewed and evaluated, new tables of current interest are added, continuing series are updated, and less timely data are condensed or eliminated. Text notes and appendices are revised as appropriate.

Changes in this edition—This year ProQuest introduces 41 new tables presenting data on topics that include state to state geographic mobility, religious congregations and adherents, life expectancy projections, nursery and primary school enrollment, financial aid received by undergraduate and graduate students, murder victims by circumstance and victim characteristics, crime rates by geographic area and state, household use of community food and nutrition assistance, labor law compliance and payment of back wages, fishery landings by port and species, crude oil and natural gas reserves, solar energy generation, household energy consumption and expenditures, and aging-ready housing units. For a complete list of new tables, see "New Tables," p. xi.

Online edition—*ProQuest Statistical Abstract* is also available in an electronic format. This dynamic edition features table-specific capabilities for narrowing search results by source, data date, subject, and type of data breakdown. The online edition is updated with new statistical content on a monthly basis, enabling users to access new and revised data in advance of the annual publication of this printed edition. The online product functions as a repository for additional historical trends that cannot fit into the print publication. Users will find spreadsheets that correspond to each table in the book. In many cases, these spreadsheets present expanded coverage of the data shown in print. The online edition is available as a stand-alone product or as a part of ProQuest's Statistical Premium Collection (see inside back cover for details).

Limitations of the data—The contents of this volume were taken from many sources. All data from censuses, surveys, and administrative records are subject to error arising from a number of factors including the following: sampling variability (for statistics based on samples), reporting errors in the data for individual units, incomplete coverage, nonresponse, and imputation and processing errors (see also Appendix III). ProQuest cannot accept responsibility for the accuracy or limitations of the data presented here; however, selection of the material and its proper presentation is the responsibility of ProQuest.

For additional information on data presented—Please consult the source publications available in local libraries and on the internet, or contact the agency or organization indicated in the source notes.

Contents

[Numbers following subject are page numbers]

New and Deleted Tables for the 2025 Edition

New Tables for 2025

Tables Deleted Since the 2024 Edition of the Statistical Abstract

[Tables are deleted for several reasons, including: source data has been discontinued, source data were monographic and new data are not expected to be available, data are no longer reliable, and data were previously unpublished and cannot be replicated. Some tables have been replaced with tables illustrating similar content. Where applicable, please see reference to new table number]

2024 Table	Section and Table Title	Replaced by...
	Section 2: Births, Deaths, Marriages, and Divorces	
Table 94........	Contraceptive Use Among Women by Age, Race/Ethnicity, Educational Attainment, and Method: 2017 to 2019	Table 101
Table 112.......	Coronavirus Disease 2019 (COVID-19) Deaths by Sex and State: Through September 2, 2023	
	Section 3: Health and Nutrition	
Table 187......	Average Cost to Community Hospitals Per Patient: 1990 to 2021	
Table 190......	Cosmetic Plastic Surgical and Nonsurgical Procedures: 2018 and 2019	
Table 199......	Coronavirus Disease 2019 (COVID-19) Vaccinations by Week: 2022 to 2023	
Table 200......	Coronavirus Disease 2019 (COVID-19) Vaccinations by State, Territory, and Federal Entity: As of May 10, 2023	
	Section 4: Education	
Table 257......	Preprimary School Enrollment—Summary: 1970 to 2021	Table 258
Table 306......	Federal Student Financial Assistance: 1995 to 2017	
Table 312......	Financial Aid for Graduate Students by Degree Type and Source of Aid: 2016	Table 314
	Section 5: Law Enforcement, Courts, and Prisons	
Table 348......	Rape and Sexual Assault Rates Among College-Age Females: 1998 to 2013	
Table 351......	Robbery and Property Crimes by Type, Location, and Average Value Lost: 2010 to 2020	
	Section 6: Geography and Environment	
Table 421......	Generation and Recovery of Selected Materials in Municipal Solid Waste: 1980 to 2018	
Table 422......	Municipal Solid Waste—Generation, Recycling, and Landfill Disposal by Selected Type of Product: 2018	
Table 431......	Number of Earthquakes in the United States: 2000 to 2012	
	Section 10: National Security and Veterans Affairs	
Table 565......	Federal Arrests for Immigration Offenses by Sex, Age, Citizenship Status, and Country and World Region of Citizenship: 1998 to 2018	
	Section 11: Social Insurance and Human Services	
Table 596......	Household Use of Food Pantries and Emergency (Soup) Kitchens: 2021	Table 598
Table 615......	Charitable Giving by Source and Type of Recipient Organization: 1990 to 2019	
	Section 12: Labor Force, Employment, and Earnings	
Table 632......	Employment Status of Women by Marital Status and Presence and Age of Children: 1970 to 2018	
Table 633......	Labor Force Participation Rates for Wives, Spouse Present, by Age of Own Youngest Child: 1990 to 2018	Table 635
Table 638......	Class of Worker by Sex and Selected Characteristics: 2016	
	Section 13: Income, Expenditures, Poverty, and Wealth	
Table 718......	Personal Income in Current and Constant (2012) Dollars by State: 2000 to 2021	Table 719
Table 719......	Personal Income Per Capita in Current and Constant (2012) Dollars by State: 2000 to 2021	Table 720
Table 724......	Personal Income by Source Including Federal COVID-19 Pandemic Response Programs: 2021 to 2022	
Table 725......	Consumer Spending Using Payment Card Transactions—Monthly Growth Rates by Type of Business: 2021 to October 2022	
	Section 15: Business Enterprise	
Table 814......	Patents and Trademarks: 2000 to 2020	Table 814
Table 815......	Patents by State and Island Areas: 2020	Table 815
Table 821......	Firms Utilizing Selected Digital Technology by Industry: 2018	
	Section 18: Forestry, Fishing, and Mining	
Table 956......	Crude Oil and Natural Gas—Reserves by State: 2010 to 2021	Table 959
	Section 23: Transportation	
Table 1142.....	Use of Ride Hailing Services by Age Group: 2017	
Table 1147.....	Commuters Who Ride Bicycles or Walk to Work—Selected Large Cities: 2016	
Table 1151.....	Petroleum Pipeline Companies—Characteristics: 1980 to 2019	
	Section 24: Information and Communications	
Table 1176.....	Electronic Device Ownership by Device Type and Owner Characteristics: 2021	
Table 1182.....	Adult Internet Users and Home Internet Connection by Selected Characteristics: 2000 to 2021	
	Section 26: Arts, Recreation, and Travel	
Table 1248.....	Arts and Culture Production—Real Value Added In Chained (2012) Dollars and Employment by Industry: 2010 to 2021	Table 1252
	Section 30: International Statistics	
Table 1367.....	Selected Indexes of Manufacturing Productivity, Unit Labor Costs, Employment, and Hours Worked by Country: 2000 to 2018	
Table 1368.....	Indexes of Hourly Compensation Costs for Employees in Manufacturing by Country: 2000 to 2016	
Table 1379.....	Labor Force, Employment, and Unemployment by Country: 1990 to 2018	
Table 1397.....	Average Temperatures and Precipitation—Selected International Cities	
Table 1400.....	Patents by Country: 2020	Table 1402
Table 1409.....	International Tourism Arrivals, Expenditures, and Receipts—Leading Countries: 2005 to 2020	

Guide to Tabular Presentation

Example of Table Structure

Table 1288. Top 20 U.S. Gateway Airports for Nonstop International Air Travel Passengers: 2023

[237,345 represents 237,345,000. International passengers are residents of any country traveling nonstop to and from the United States on U.S. and foreign carriers. The data cover all passengers arriving and departing from U.S. airports on nonstop commercial international flights with 60 seats or more]

Gateway airport	Airport code	Passengers (1,000)	Gateway airport	Airport code	Passengers (1,000)
Total, all airports	(X)	**237,345**	Dallas-Fort Worth, TX	DFW	10,866
Total, top 20 airports	(X)	210,551	Washington, DC (Dulles)	IAD	9,235
Top 20, percentage of total	(X)	88.7	Boston, MA	BOS	7,763
			Fort Lauderdale, FL	FLL	7,511
New York, NY	JFK	32,934	Orlando, FL	MCO	6,793
Miami, FL	MIA	21,765	Seattle, WA	SEA	5,579
Los Angeles, CA	LAX	21,686	Charlotte, NC	CLT	4,189
Newark, NJ	EWR	14,460	Denver, CO	DEN	3,972
San Francisco, CA	SFO	13,811	Philadelphia, PA	PHL	3,555
Chicago, IL	ORD	13,164	Las Vegas, NV	LAS	3,220
Atlanta, GA	ATL	12,479	Honolulu, HI	HNL	3,191
Houston, TX	IAH	11,337	Detroit, MI	DTW	3,041

X Not applicable.

Source: U.S. Department of Transportation, Research and Innovative Technology Administration, Bureau of Transportation Statistics, Office of Airline Information, "T-100 International Segment data," <www.transtats.bts.gov/Fields.asp?gnoyr_VQ=FJE>, accessed June 2024.

Headnotes immediately below table titles provide information important for correct interpretation or evaluation of the table as a whole or for a major segment of it.

Footnotes below the bottom rule of tables give information relating to specific items or figures within the table.

Unit indicators show the *specified quantities* in which data items are presented. They are used for two primary reasons. Sometimes data are not available in absolute form and are estimates (as in the case of many surveys). In other cases we round the numbers in order to save space to show more data, as in the case above.

When a table presents data with more than one unit indicator, they are found in the headnotes and column headings (Tables 5 and 23), spanner (Table 37), stub (Table 60), or unit column (Table 246). When the data in a table are shown in the same unit indicator, it is shown as the first part of the headnote (Table 2). If no unit indicator is shown, data presented are in absolute form (Table 1).

Vertical rules are used to separate independent sections of a table (Table 1), or in tables where the stub is continued into one or more additional columns (Table 2).

Averages—An average is a single number or value that is often used to represent the "typical value" of a group of numbers. It is regarded as a measure of "location" or "central tendency" of a group of numbers.

The *arithmetic mean* is the type of average used most frequently. It is derived by summing the individual item values of a particular group and dividing the total by the number of items. The arithmetic mean is often referred to as simply the "mean" or "average."

The *median* of a group of numbers is the middle number or value when each item in the group is arranged according to size (lowest to highest or vice versa); it generally has the same number of items above it as well as below it. If there is an even number of items in the group, the median is taken to be the average of the two middle numbers.

Per capita (or per person) quantities—a per capita figure represents an average computed for every person in a specified group (or population). It is derived by taking the total for an item (such as income, taxes, or retail sales) and dividing it by the number of persons in the specified population.

Index numbers—An index number is the measure of difference or change, usually expressed as a percent, relating one quantity (the variable) of a specified kind to another quantity of the same kind. Index numbers are widely used to express changes in prices over periods of time, but may also be used to express differences between related subjects for a single point in time.

To compute a price index, a base year or period is selected. The base year price (of the commodity or service) is then designated as the base or reference price to which the prices for other years or periods are related. Many price indexes use the year 1982 as the base year; in tables, this is shown as "1982 = 100." A method expressing the price relationship is: The price of a set of one or more items for a related year (e.g. 1990) **divided by** the price of the same set of items for the base year (e.g. 1982). The result multiplied by 100 provides the index number. When 100 is subtracted from the index number, the result equals the percent change in price from the base year.

Average annual percent change—Unless otherwise stated in the *Abstract* (as in Section 1, Population), average annual percent change is computed by use of a *compound interest formula*. This formula assumes that the rate of change is constant throughout a specified compounding period (1 year for average annual rates of change). The formula is similar to that used to compute the balance of a savings account that receives compound interest. According to this formula, at the end of a compounding period the amount of accrued change (e.g., school enrollment or bank interest) is added to the amount that existed at the beginning of the period. As a result, over time (e.g., with each year or quarter), the same rate of change is applied to a larger and larger figure.

The *exponential formula,* which is based on continuous compounding, is often used to measure population change. It is preferred by population experts because they view population and population-related subjects as changing without interruption, ever ongoing. Both exponential and compound interest formulas assume a constant rate of change. The former, however, applies the amount of change continuously to the base rather than at the end of each compounding period. When the average annual rates are small (e.g., less than 5 percent), both formulas give virtually the same results. For an explanation of these two formulas as they relate to population, see U.S. Census Bureau, *The Methods and Materials of Demography,* Vol. 2, 3rd printing (rev.), 1975.

Current and constant dollars—Statistics in some tables in a number of sections are expressed in both current and constant dollars (see, e.g., Table 705 in Section 13, Income, Expenditures, Poverty, and Wealth). Current dollar figures reflect actual prices or costs prevailing during the specified year(s). Constant dollar figures are estimates representing an effort to remove the effects of price changes from statistical series reported in dollar terms. In general, constant dollar series are derived by dividing current dollar estimates by the appropriate price index for the appropriate period (e.g., the Consumer Price Index). The result is a series as it would presumably exist if prices were the same throughout, as in the base year—in other words, as if the dollar had constant purchasing power. Any changes in this constant dollar series would reflect only changes in real volume of output, income, expenditures, or other measure.

Explanation of Symbols

The following symbols, used in the tables throughout this book, are explained in condensed form in footnotes to the tables where they appear:

— Represents zero or rounds to less than half the unit of measurement shown.

B Base figure too small to meet statistical standards for reliability of a derived figure.

D Figure withheld to avoid disclosure pertaining to a specific organization or individual.

NA Data not enumerated, tabulated, or otherwise available separately.

P Data are preliminary or projected.

S Figure does not meet publication standards for reasons other than that covered by symbol B, above.

X Figure not applicable because column heading and stub line make entry impossible, absurd, or meaningless.

Z Entry would amount to less than half the unit of measurement shown.

In many tables, details will not add to the totals shown because of rounding.

Section 1
Population

This section presents statistics on the growth, distribution, and characteristics of the U.S. population. The principal source of these data is the U.S. Census Bureau, which conducts a decennial census of population, a monthly population survey, a program of population estimates and projections, and a number of other periodic surveys.

Decennial censuses—The U.S. Constitution provides for a census of the population every 10 years, primarily to establish a basis for apportionment of members of the House of Representatives among the states. For over a century after the first census in 1790, the census organization was a temporary one, created only for each decennial census. In 1902, the Census Bureau was established as a permanent federal agency, responsible for enumerating the population and also for compiling statistics on other population and housing characteristics.

Historically, the enumeration of the population has been a complete (100 percent) count. That is, an attempt is made to account for every person, for each person's residence, and for other characteristics (sex, age, family relationships, etc.). In the twentieth century, the questions were divided between a short form and a long form. Only a subset of the population was required to answer the long-form questions. Starting in 2010, the census consisted only of a short form, which included basic questions about age, sex, race, Hispanic origin, household relationship, and owner/renter status. After the 2000 Census, the long form became the American Community Survey (ACS) and continues to collect long-form-type information. The ACS includes not only the basic short-form questions, but also detailed questions about population and housing characteristics. It is a nationwide, continuous sample survey designed to provide communities with reliable and timely demographic, housing, social, and economic data every year. Since its start, the ACS has been providing a continuous stream of updated information for states and local areas. Sample data may be used with confidence where large numbers are involved and assumed to indicate trends and relationships where small numbers are involved.

Current Population Survey (CPS)—The CPS sample is a probability sample designed primarily to produce national and state estimates of labor force characteristics of the civilian non-institutional population 16 years of age and older. The sample consists of independent samples in each state and the District of Columbia, and each state sample is specifically tailored to the demographic and labor market conditions that prevail in that particular state. About 70,000 housing units are required in order to meet the national and State reliability criteria, drawn from approximately 826 sample areas.

The CPS also serves as a vehicle for inquiries on other subjects. Using CPS data, the Census Bureau issues a series of publications under the general title of *Current Population Reports*.

Estimates of population characteristics based on the CPS will not agree with the counts from the census because the CPS and the census use different procedures for collecting and processing the data for racial groups, the Hispanic population, and other topics. Caution should also be used when comparing estimates for various years because of the periodic introduction of changes into the CPS. Beginning in January 1994, a number of changes were introduced into the CPS that affect all data comparisons with prior years. These changes included the results of a major redesign of the survey questionnaire and collection methodology and the introduction of 1990 census population controls, adjusted for the estimated undercount. Data estimates from the March 2002 through March 2011 CPS supplements are based on civilian population benchmarks consistent with Census 2000. In 2003, the name of the March supplement was changed to Annual Social and Economic Supplement (ASEC). Data estimates from the 2012 through 2021 March CPS ASEC supplements are based on Census 2010 population controls. Beginning with the March 2022 CPS ASEC supplement, estimates are based on Census 2020 population controls. Ideally, the same population controls should be used when comparing any estimates. However, the use of the same population controls is not practical when comparing trend data over a period of 10 to 20 years. Therefore, when it is necessary to combine or compare data based on different controls or different designs, data users should be aware that changes in weighting controls or weighting procedures could create small differences between estimates.

In 2002, the ASEC incorporated a significant sample expansion. The sample was expanded primarily to improve state estimates of children's health insurance coverage (CHIP). This sample increase of 19,000 households, added to the regular sample of 72,500 households and the Hispanic sample of 6,500 households, gives a total sample size of about 98,000 households. The 2014 CPS ASEC included redesigned questions for income and health insurance coverage. All of the approximately 98,000 addresses were selected to receive the improved set of health insurance coverage items. The improved income questions were implemented using a split panel design. Approximately 68,000 addresses were selected to receive a set of income questions similar to those used in the 2013 CPS ASEC. The remaining 30,000 addresses were selected to receive the redesigned income questions.

Population estimates and projections—The Census Bureau produces and publishes estimates of the population for the nation, states, counties, state/county equivalents, and Puerto Rico. With each annual release of population estimates, the Population Estimates Program (PEP) revises and updates the entire time series of estimates from April 1, 2020 to July 1 of the current year, which is referred to as the vintage year. "Vintage" denotes an entire time series created with a consistent population starting point and methodology. The release of a new vintage of estimates supersedes any previous series and incorporates the most up-to-date input data and methodological improvements. PEP annually utilizes current data on births, deaths, and migration to calculate population change since the most recent decennial census and produce a time series of estimates of population, demographic components of change, and housing units. The annual time series of estimates begins with the most recent decennial census data and extends to the vintage year.

Registered births and deaths are estimated from data supplied by the National Center for Health Statistics and the Federal-State Cooperative for Population Estimates (FSCPE). The net international migration component consists of four parts: (1) the net international migration of the foreign born, (2) the net migration of natives to and from the United States, (3) the net migration between the United States and Puerto Rico, and (4) the net overseas movement of the Armed Forces population. Data from the ACS are used to estimate the annual net migration of the foreign-born population. The estimated net migration of the native-born population is produced using the foreign-census method, which utilizes data from over 80 countries. This method compares estimates of the U.S.-born or U.S. citizen population living overseas, as measured by population registers and censuses in other countries, at two consecutive time periods. The residual is used to develop estimates of net native migration. Estimates for net migration between Puerto Rico and the U.S. are derived from the ACS and the Puerto Rico Community Survey. Estimates of the net overseas movement of the Armed Forces are derived from data collected by the Defense Manpower Data Center.

Estimates for state and county areas are based on the same components of change data and sources as the national estimates, with the addition of net internal migration. Estimates of net internal migration are derived from federal income tax returns from the Internal Revenue Service; group quarters data from the branches of the military, the Department of Veterans Affairs, and the FSCPE; and Medicare data from the Centers for Medicare and Medicaid Services.

Population estimates and projections are available on the Census Bureau Web site; see <www.census.gov>. These estimates and projections are consistent with official decennial census figures, with no adjustment for estimated net census coverage. For details on methodology, see "Methodology for the United States Population Estimates: Vintage 2023," <www.census.gov/programs-surveys/popest/ technical-documentation/methodology.html>.

Immigration—Immigration (migration to a country) is one component of international migration; the other component is emigration (migration *from* a country). In its simplest form, international migration is defined as any movement across a national border. In the United States, federal statistics on international migration are produced primarily by the U.S. Census Bureau and the Office of Homeland Security Statistics (OHSS) of the U.S. Department of Homeland Security (DHS).

The Census Bureau collects data used to estimate international migration through its decennial censuses and numerous surveys of the U.S. population.

The OHSS publishes immigration data in annual flow reports and the *Yearbook of Immigration Statistics.* Data for these publications are collected from several administrative data sources, including the DS-230 *Application for Immigrant Visa and Alien Registration*, the DS-260 *Electronic Application for Immigrant Visa and Alien Registration* of the U.S. Department of State (used by applicants living abroad), and the I-485

Application to Register Permanent Residence or Adjust Status of the U.S. Citizenship and Immigration Services (USCIS) for applicants living in the United States.

An immigrant, or lawful permanent resident (LPR), is a foreign national who has been granted lawful permanent residence in the United States. New arrivals are foreign nationals living abroad who apply for an immigrant visa at a consular office of the Department of State, while individuals adjusting status are already living in the United States and file an application for adjustment of status to lawful permanent residence with USCIS. Individuals adjusting status include refugees, asylees, and various classes of nonimmigrants. A refugee is a person outside their country of nationality who is unable or unwilling to return to their country of nationality because of persecution or a well-founded fear of persecution. An asylee is a person who meets the definition of refugee and is already present in the United States or is seeking admission at a port of entry. Refugees are required to apply for LPR ("green card") status one year after being admitted, and asylees may apply for green card status one year after their grant of asylum.

Nonimmigrants are foreign nationals granted temporary entry into the United States. The major activities for which nonimmigrant admission is authorized include temporary visits for business or pleasure, academic or vocational study, temporary employment, and to act as a representative of a foreign government or international organization. DHS collects information on the characteristics of a proportion of nonimmigrant admissions, those recorded on the I-94/I-94W arrival and departure records.

U.S. immigration law gives preferential immigration status to persons with a close family relationship with a U.S. citizen or legal permanent resident, persons with needed job skills, persons who qualify as refugees or asylees, and persons who are from countries with relatively low levels of immigration to the United States (diversity immigrants). Immigration to the United States can be divided into two general categories: (1) classes of admission subject to the annual worldwide limitation and (2) classes of admission exempt from worldwide limitations. Numerical limits are imposed on visas issued and not on admissions. In fiscal year (FY) 2023, the annual limit for family-sponsored preferences was 226,000 and the limit for employment-based preferences was 197,091, which included unused family-based visas from FY2022.

The Diversity Visa Program is available to nationals of countries with fewer than 50,000 persons granted LPR status during the preceding five years in the employment-based and family-sponsored preferences and immediate relative classes of admission. In FY2023, the diversity visa limit was 54,833.

The number of persons who may be admitted to the United States as refugees each year is established by the President in consultation with Congress. Admissions ceilings for FY2022-2024 were set at 125,000. There is no numerical limit on the number of persons who can be granted asylum status in a year.

Classes of admission exempt from the worldwide limitation include immediate relatives of U.S. citizens, refugees and asylees adjusting to permanent residence, and other various classes of special immigrants.

Metropolitan and micropolitan areas—Metropolitan and micropolitan statistical areas (metro and micro areas) are geographic entities delineated by the U.S. Office of Management and Budget (OMB) for use by Federal statistical agencies in collecting, tabulating, and publishing Federal statistics. These areas are the result of the application of published standards to Census Bureau data. Generally, the areas are delineated using the most recent set of standards following each decennial census. Between censuses, the delineations are updated annually to reflect the most recent Census Bureau population estimates. The metropolitan and micropolitan statistical areas appearing in this edition of the Statistical Abstract are based on the 2020 standards published in the Federal Register July 16, 2021, and adhere to delineations of statistical areas issued by the OMB in July 2023.

The term "Core Based Statistical Area" (CBSA) is a collective term for both metro and micro areas. A metro area contains a core urban area of 50,000 or more population, and a micro area contains an urban core of at least 10,000 (but less than 50,000) population. Each metro or micro area consists of one or more counties and includes the counties containing the core urban area, as well as any adjacent counties that have a high degree of social and economic integration (as measured by commuting to work) with the urban core.

Urban and rural—The Census Bureau's urban-rural classification is fundamentally a delineation of geographical areas, identifying both individual urban areas and the rural areas of the nation. The Census Bureau's urban areas represent densely developed territory, and encompass residential, commercial, and other non-residential urban land uses. Rural encompasses all population, housing, and territory not included within an urban area.

The 2020 Census introduced major changes to the definition of urban areas that include the use of housing unit density instead of population density when delineating urban areas. For the 2020 Census, each urban area must encompass at least 2,000 housing units or at least 5,000 people. This is a change from the previous minimum of 2,500 persons that had been in place since 1910. Urban areas are defined primarily based on housing unit density measured at the census block level. In addition to the change in minimum thresholds for qualification and the change to use of housing unit density, the Census Bureau will no longer distinguish between urbanized areas of 50,000 or more people and urban clusters of less than 50,000 people.

Residence—In determining residence, the Census Bureau counts each person as an inhabitant of a usual place of residence (i.e., the place where one lives and sleeps most of the time). While this place is not necessarily a person's legal residence or voting residence, the use of these different bases of classification would produce the same results in the vast majority of cases.

Race—Beginning with Census 2000, collection and presentation of data on race and ethnicity adhere to federal standards established by the OMB in October 1997. The OMB requires federal agencies to use a minimum of five race categories: White, Black or African American, American Indian or Alaska Native, Asian, and Native Hawaiian or Other Pacific Islander. Additionally, to collect data on individuals of mixed race parentage, respondents were allowed to select

one or more races. For respondents who did not identify with any of these five race categories, the OMB approved and included a sixth category—"Some other race" on Census 2000, 2010, and 2020 questionnaires. The OMB standard requires two separate questions, one for Hispanic or Latino origin and one for race. The 2020 Census implemented improvements to the two questions design and updated data processing and coding procedures to enable a more thorough and accurate depiction of how people self-identify. The response categories and write-in answers for the race question can be combined to create the five minimum OMB race categories plus "Some other race." People who responded to the question on race by indicating only one race are referred to as the *race alone* population, or the group that reported only one race category. Six categories make up this population: White alone, Black or African American alone, American Indian and Alaska Native alone, Asian alone, Native Hawaiian and Other Pacific Islander alone, and Some other race alone. Individuals who chose more than one of the six race categories are referred to as the *Two or More Races* population, or as the group that reported more than one race. Additionally, respondents who reported one race together with those who reported the same race plus one or more other races are combined to create the *race alone or in combination* categories. For example, the *White alone or in combination* group consists of those respondents who reported only White or who reported White combined with one or more other race groups, such as "White and Black or African American," or "White and Asian and American Indian and Alaska Native." Another way to think of the group who reported *White alone or in combination* is as the total number of people who identified entirely or partially as White. This group is also described as people who reported White, whether or not they reported any other race.

The *alone or in combination* categories are tallies of *responses* rather than *respondents*. That is, the alone or in combination categories are not mutually exclusive. Individuals who reported two races were counted in two separate and distinct alone or in combination race categories, while those who reported three races were counted in three categories, and so on. Consequently, the sum of all alone or in combination categories equals the number of races reported, which exceeds the total population.

The racial categories included in the census questionnaire generally reflect a social definition of race recognized in this country and not an attempt to define race biologically, anthropologically, or genetically. It is also recognized that the categories of the race item include racial and national origin or sociocultural groups. For example, data are available for the American Indian and Alaska Native tribes. A detailed explanation of race can be found at <www.census.gov/topics/population/race/about.html>.

In the CPS and other household sample surveys conducted through personal interview, respondents are asked to classify their race as: (1) White; (2) Black or African American; (3) American Indian or Alaska Native; (4) Asian; or (5) Native Hawaiian or Other Pacific Islander. Beginning January 2003, respondents were allowed to report more than one race to indicate their mixed racial heritage.

Hispanic population—People who identify with the terms "Hispanic" or "Latino" are those who classify themselves in one of the specific Hispanic or Latino categories listed on the decennial census questionnaire and various Census Bureau survey questionnaires – "Mexican, Mexican American, Chicano" or "Puerto Rican" or "Cuban" – as well as those who indicate that they are of "another Hispanic, Latino, or Spanish origin." Origin can be viewed as the heritage, nationality group, lineage, or country of birth of the person or the person's ancestors before their arrival in the United States.

Traditional and current data collection and classification treat race and Hispanic origin as two separate and distinct concepts in accordance with guidelines from the OMB. People who are Hispanic may be of any race and people in each race group may be either Hispanic or Not Hispanic. Also, each person has two attributes, their race (or races) and whether or not they are Hispanic. The overlap of race and Hispanic origin is the main comparability issue. For example, Black Hispanics (Hispanic Blacks) are included in both the number of Blacks and in the number of Hispanics.

Foreign-born and native populations—The Census Bureau separates the U.S. resident population into two groups based on whether or not a person was a U.S. citizen or U.S. national at the time of birth. Anyone born in the United States, Puerto Rico, or a U.S. Island Area (such as Guam), or born abroad to a U.S. citizen parent, is a U.S. citizen at the time of birth and consequently included in the *native population*. The term *foreign-born population* refers to anyone who is not a U.S. citizen or a U.S. national at birth. This includes naturalized U.S. citizens, legal permanent resident aliens (immigrants), temporary migrants (such as foreign students), humanitarian migrants (such as refugees), and people illegally present in the United States. The Census Bureau provides a variety of demographic, social, economic, geographic, and housing information on the foreign-born population in the United States at <www.census.gov/topics/population/foreign-born.html>.

Mobility status—The U.S. population is classified according to mobility status on the basis of a comparison between the place of residence of each individual at the time of the survey or census and the place of residence at a specified earlier date. Nonmovers are all persons who were living in the same house or apartment at the end of the period as at the beginning of the period. Movers are all persons who were living in a different house or apartment at the end of the period than at the beginning of the period. Movers are further classified as to whether they were living in the same or different county, state, or region, or were movers from abroad. Movers from abroad include all persons whose place of residence was outside the United States (including Puerto Rico, other U.S. Island Area, or a foreign country) at the beginning of the period.

Living arrangements—Living arrangements refer to residency in households or in group quarters. A "household" comprises all persons who occupy a "housing unit," that is, a house, an apartment or other group of rooms, or a single room that constitutes "separate living quarters." A household includes the related family members and all the unrelated persons, if any, such as lodgers, foster children, or employees who share the housing unit. A person living alone or a group of unrelated persons sharing the same housing unit is also counted as a household. See text, Section 20, Construction and Housing, for definition of housing unit.

All persons not living in housing units are classified as living in group quarters. These individuals may be institutionalized, e.g., under care or custody in juvenile facilities, jails, correctional centers, hospitals, or nursing homes; or they may be residents in noninstitutional group quarters such as college dormitories, group homes, or military barracks.

Householder—The householder is the person, or one of the people, in whose name the home is owned, being bought, or rented. If a home is owned or rented jointly by a married couple, either spouse may be listed first. Two types of householders are distinguished: a family householder and a nonfamily householder. A family householder is a householder living with one or more people related to him or her by birth, marriage, or adoption. The householder and all people in the household related to him or her are family members. A family household may contain people not related to the householder, but those people are not included as part of the householder's family in census tabulations. Thus, the number of family households is equal to the number of families, but family households may include more members than do families.

Nonfamily—A nonfamily householder is a householder living alone or with nonrelatives only.

Subfamily—A subfamily is a married couple with or without children, or a single parent with one or more own never-married children under 18 years old, who does not maintain their own household, but lives in the home of someone else (the householder). Subfamilies are divided into "related" and "unrelated" subfamilies. A related subfamily is related to, but does not include, the householder or the spouse of the householder. Members of a related subfamily are also members of the family with whom they live. The number of related subfamilies, therefore, is not included in the count of families. An unrelated subfamily may include persons such as guests, lodgers, or resident employees and their spouses and/or children; none of whom is related to the householder. The number of unrelated subfamily members is included in the total number of household members, but is not included in the count of family members.

Married couple—A married couple live together in the same household, with or without children and other relatives.

Statistical reliability—For a discussion of statistical collection and estimation, sampling procedures, and measures of statistical reliability applicable to Census Bureau data, see Appendix III.

Percent Change in Resident Population for the 50 States, the District of Columbia, and Puerto Rico: 2010 to 2020

Percent Change

- 14.9 to 18.4 — *Twice the U.S. percent change*
- 7.5 to 14.8 — ***U.S. percent change (7.4)***
- 0 to 7.4
- -7.4 to -0.1 — *No change*
- -11.8 to -7.5

PR -11.8

ME 2.6
NH 4.6
MA 7.4
RI 4.3
CT 0.9
NJ 5.7
DE 10.2
MD 7.0
DC 14.6
VT 2.8
NY 4.2
PA 2.4
VA 7.9
NC 9.5
SC 10.7
FL 14.6
WV -3.2
GA 10.6
OH 2.3
KY 3.8
TN 8.9
AL 5.1
MI 2.0
IN 4.7
MS -0.2
WI 3.6
IL -0.1
MO 2.8
AR 3.3
LA 2.7
MN 7.6
IA 4.7
OK 5.5
TX 15.9
ND 15.8
SD 8.9
NE 7.4
KS 3.0
NM 2.8
MT 9.6
WY 2.3
CO 14.8
UT 18.4
AZ 11.9
ID 17.3
NV 15.0
WA 14.6
OR 10.6
CA 6.1
AK 3.3
HI 7.0

Mean Center of Population for the United States: 1790 to 2020

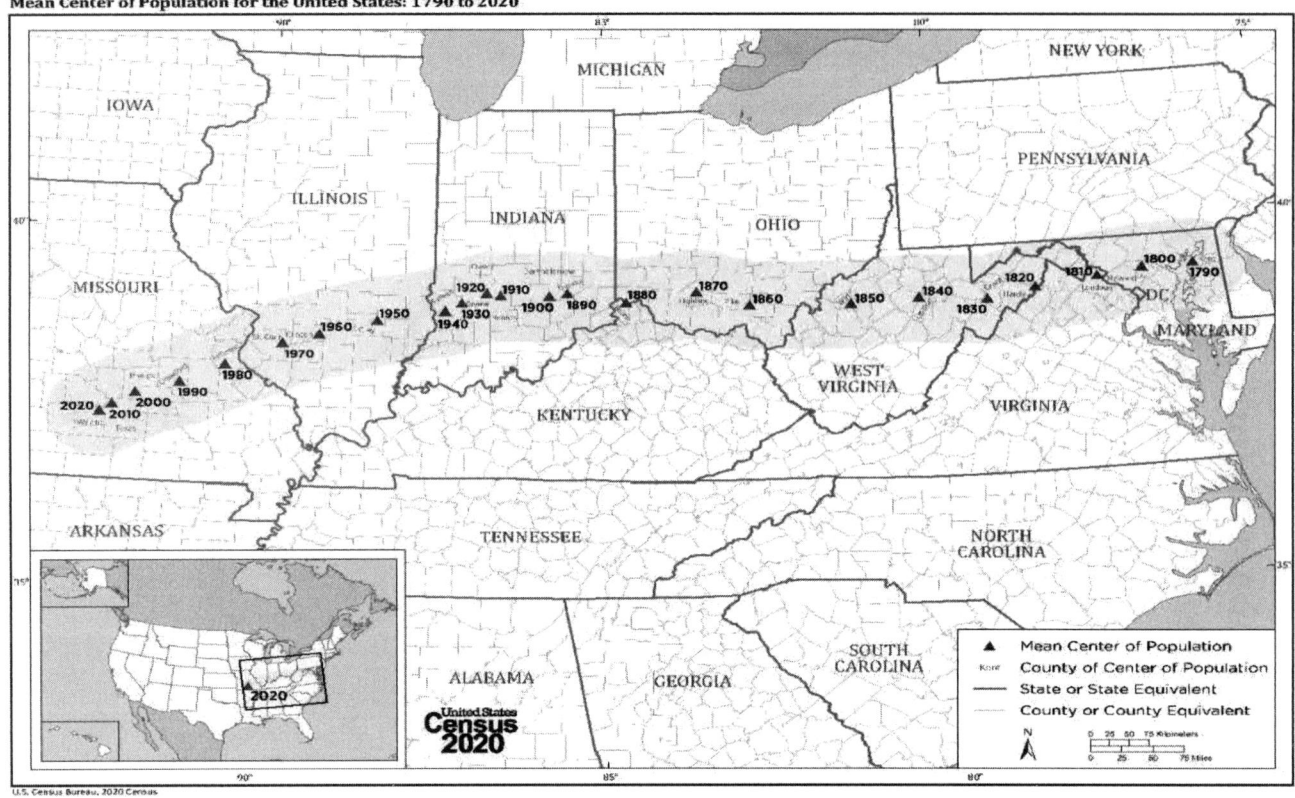

U.S. Census Bureau, 2020 Census

Median Center of Population for the United States: 1880 to 2020

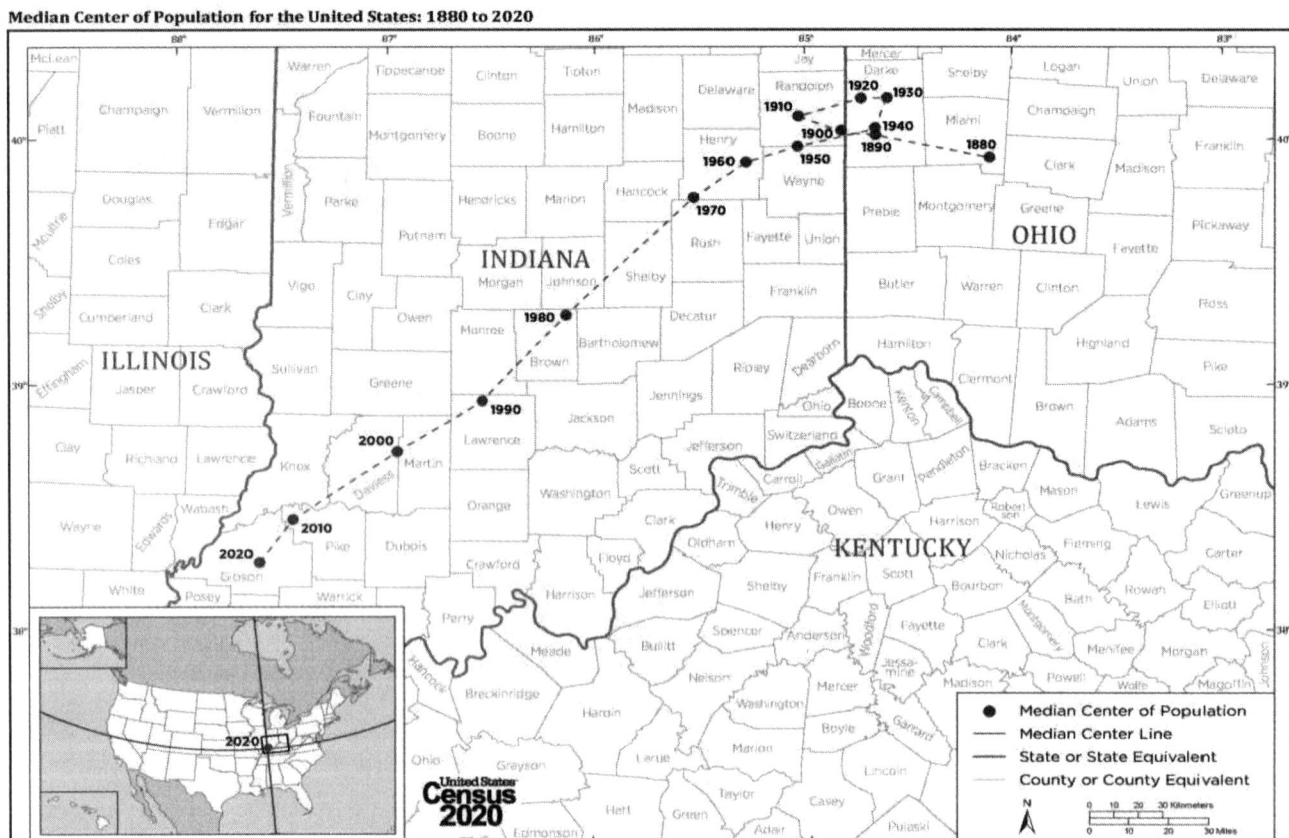

U.S. Census Bureau, 2020 Census

Table 1. Population and Area: 1790 to 2020

[Area figures represent area on indicated date including in some cases considerable areas not then organized or settled, and not covered by the census. Area data include Alaska beginning in 1870 and Hawaii beginning in 1900. Total area figures for 1790 to 1970 have been recalculated on the basis of the remeasurement of states and counties for the 1980 census, but not on the basis of subsequent censuses. The land and water area figures for past censuses have not been adjusted and are not strictly comparable with the total area data for comparable dates because the land areas were derived from different base data, and these values are known to have changed with the construction of reservoirs, draining of lakes, etc. Density figures are based on land area measurements as reported in earlier censuses]

Census date	Resident population				Area (square miles)		
	Number	Per square mile of land area	Increase over preceding census		Total	Land	Water [1]
			Number	Percent			
1790 (Aug. 2)	3,929,214	4.50	(X)	(X)	891,364	864,746	24,065
1800 (Aug. 4)	5,308,483	6.10	1,379,269	35.1	891,364	864,746	24,065
1810 (Aug. 6)	7,239,881	4.30	1,931,398	36.4	1,722,685	1,681,828	34,175
1820 (Aug. 7)	9,638,453	5.50	2,398,572	33.1	1,792,552	1,749,462	38,544
1830 (June 1)	12,866,020	7.40	3,227,567	33.5	1,792,552	1,749,462	38,544
1840 (June 1)	17,069,453	9.80	4,203,433	32.7	1,792,552	1,749,462	38,544
1850 (June 1)	23,191,876	7.90	6,122,423	35.9	2,991,655	2,940,042	52,705
1860 (June 1)	31,443,321	10.60	8,251,445	35.6	3,021,295	2,969,640	52,747
1870 (June 1)	[2] 39,818,449	[2] 11.2	8,375,128	26.6	3,612,299	3,540,705	68,082
1880 (June 1)	50,189,209	14.20	10,370,760	26.0	3,612,299	3,540,705	68,082
1890 (June 1)	62,979,766	17.80	12,790,557	25.5	3,612,299	3,540,705	68,082
1900 (June 1)	76,212,168	21.50	13,232,402	21.0	3,618,770	3,547,314	67,901
1910 (Apr. 15)	92,228,531	26.00	16,016,363	21.0	3,618,770	3,547,045	68,170
1920 (Jan. 1)	106,021,568	29.90	13,793,037	15.0	3,618,770	3,546,931	68,284
1930 (Apr. 1)	123,202,660	34.70	17,181,092	16.2	3,618,770	3,554,608	60,607
1940 (Apr. 1)	132,165,129	37.20	8,962,469	7.3	3,618,770	3,554,608	60,607
1950 (Apr. 1)	151,325,798	42.60	19,160,669	14.5	3,618,770	3,552,206	63,005
1960 (Apr. 1)	179,323,175	50.60	27,997,377	18.5	3,618,770	3,540,911	74,212
1970 (Apr. 1)	203,211,926	57.50	23,888,751	13.3	3,618,770	3,536,855	78,444
1980 (Apr. 1)	226,545,805	64.10	23,333,879	11.5	3,618,770	3,539,289	79,481
1990 (Apr. 1)	248,709,873	70.40	22,164,068	9.8	[3] 3,717,796	3,536,278	[3] 181,518
2000 (Apr. 1)	281,421,906	79.70	32,712,033	13.2	3,794,083	3,537,438	256,645
2010 (Apr. 1)	308,745,538	87.40	27,323,632	9.7	3,796,742	3,531,905	264,837
2020 (Apr. 1)	331,449,281	93.80	22,703,743	7.4	(NA)	3,533,038	(NA)

X Not applicable. NA Not available. [1] Data for 1790 to 1980 cover inland water only. Data for 1990 comprise Great Lakes, inland, and coastal water. Data for 2000 and 2010 comprise Great Lakes, inland, territorial, and coastal water. [2] Revised to include adjustments for underenumeration in southern states; unrevised number is 38,558,371 (10.9 per square mile). [3] Data reflect corrections made after publication of the results.

Source: U.S. Census Bureau, *Areas of the United States: 1940*; Area data for 1990: unpublished data from TIGER ®; and "Fast Facts," <www.census.gov/history/www/through_the_decades/fast_facts/>, "QuickFacts," <www.census.gov/quickfacts/>, and "Historical Population Change Data (1910-2020)" and "Historical Population Density Data (1910-2020)," <www.census.gov/programs-surveys/decennial-census/data /tables.2020.html>, accessed August 2023.

Table 2. Population: 1970 to 2023

[In thousands (205,052 represents 205,052,000). Estimates as of July 1. Civilian population excludes Armed Forces. Estimates for 2010-2019 are based on the 2010 Census; beginning 2020, estimates are developed from a base that incorporates the 2020 Census, Vintage 2020 estimates, and 2020 Demographic Analysis estimates]

Year	Resident population, including Armed Forces overseas	Resident population	Civilian population	Year	Resident population, including Armed Forces overseas	Resident population	Civilian population
1970	205,052	203,984	201,895	2000	(NA)	282,162	(NA)
1975	215,973	215,465	213,789	2001	(NA)	284,969	(NA)
1978	222,585	222,095	220,467	2002	(NA)	287,625	(NA)
1979	225,055	224,567	222,969	2003	(NA)	290,108	(NA)
1980	227,726	227,225	225,621	2004	(NA)	292,805	(NA)
1981	229,966	229,466	227,818	2005	(NA)	295,517	(NA)
1982	232,188	231,664	229,995	2006	(NA)	298,380	(NA)
1983	234,307	233,792	232,097	2007	(NA)	301,231	(NA)
1984	236,348	235,825	234,110	2008	(NA)	304,094	(NA)
1985	238,466	237,924	236,219	2009	(NA)	306,772	(NA)
1986	240,651	240,133	238,412	2010	309,747	309,327	308,092
1987	242,804	242,289	240,550	2011	312,001	311,583	310,366
1988	245,021	244,499	242,817	2012	314,214	313,878	312,638
1989	247,342	246,819	245,131	2013	316,361	316,060	314,817
1990	250,132	249,623	247,983	2014	318,662	318,386	317,160
1991	253,493	252,981	251,370	2015	320,975	320,739	319,542
1992	256,894	256,514	254,929	2016	323,291	323,072	321,869
1993	260,255	259,919	258,446	2017	325,343	325,122	323,932
1994	263,436	263,126	261,714	2018	327,075	326,838	325,651
1995	266,557	266,278	264,927	2019	328,566	328,330	327,143
1996	269,667	269,394	268,108	2020	331,773	331,527	330,412
1997	272,912	272,647	271,394	2021	332,299	332,049	330,919
1998	276,115	275,854	274,633	2022	333,521	333,271	332,184
1999	279,295	279,040	277,841	2023	335,161	334,915	333,850

NA Not available.

Source: U.S. Census Bureau, Population Division, data prior to 2010, <www.census.gov/programs-surveys/popest.html>; National Population by Characteristics: 2010 to 2020, "Monthly National Population Estimates by Age, Sex, Race, Hispanic Origin, and Population Universe for the United States: April 1, 2010 to December 1, 2020," <www.census.gov/programs-surveys/popest/technical-documentation/ research/evaluation-estimates/2020-evaluation-estimates.html>; and National Population Totals and Components of Change: 2020-2023, "Monthly Population Estimates for the United States: April 1, 2020 to December 1, 2024 (NA-EST2023-POP)," <www.census.gov/data/tables/ time-series/demo/popest/2020s-national-total.html>, accessed February 2024.

Table 3. Resident Population Projections and Components of Change: 2025 to 2100

[In thousands, except as indicated (338,016 represents 338,016,000). As of July 1. The 2023 National Projections are based on July 1, 2022 population estimates, which are derived from the Census Bureau's Vintage 2022 Population Estimates and partially based on the 2020 Census through the blended base method. The projections were produced using a cohort-component method and are based on assumptions about future births, deaths, and net international migration. More information on methodology and assumptions is available at <www.census.gov/programs-surveys/popproj/technical-documentation.html>]

Year	Population			Components of change			
	Total	Numeric change	Percent change [1]	Natural change	Births	Deaths	Net international migration [2]
2025...............	338,016	1,534	0.5	676	3,637	2,960	858
2030...............	345,074	1,320	0.4	441	3,653	3,212	879
2040...............	355,309	779	0.2	-133	3,592	3,725	912
2050...............	360,639	392	0.1	-549	3,431	3,979	940
2060...............	364,287	378	0.1	-578	3,372	3,950	956
2070...............	367,913	303	0.1	-667	3,331	3,999	971
2080...............	369,363	7	0.0	-969	3,239	4,208	976
2090...............	368,120	-206	-0.1	-1,171	3,176	4,348	965
2100...............	365,558	-283	-0.1	-1,227	3,125	4,352	944

[1] Percent change from immediate preceding year. For 2025, change from 2024. [2] Net international migration includes the international migration of both native and foreign-born populations.

Source: U.S. Census Bureau, 2023 National Population Projections Tables: Main Series, "Table 1. Projected population and Components of Change," November 2023, <www.census.gov/programs-surveys/popproj/data/tables.html>, accessed March 2024.

Table 4. Resident Population Projections and Components of Change Under High, Low, and Zero Immigration Scenarios: 2025 to 2100

[In thousands (338,016 represents 338,016,000). As of July 1. The 2023 National Projections are based on July 1, 2022 population estimates, which are derived from the Census Bureau's Vintage 2022 Population Estimates and partially based on the 2020 Census through the blended base method. The projections were produced using a cohort-component method and are based on assumptions about future births, deaths, and net international migration. More information on methodology and assumptions is available at <www.census.gov/programs-surveys/popproj/technical-documentation.html>]

Year and scenario	Population	Births	Deaths	Natural change [2]	Net international migration [3]	Year and scenario	Population	Births	Deaths	Natural change [2]	Net international migration [3]
MAIN SERIES [1]						HIGH IMMIGRATION					
2025...............	338,016	3,637	2,960	676	858	2025...............	340,326	3,686	2,965	720	1,586
2030...............	345,074	3,653	3,212	441	879	2030...............	351,303	3,794	3,227	567	1,546
2040...............	355,309	3,592	3,725	-133	912	2040...............	369,865	3,861	3,761	100	1,543
2050...............	360,639	3,431	3,979	-549	940	2050...............	384,054	3,785	4,045	-260	1,553
2060...............	364,287	3,372	3,950	-578	956	2060...............	396,954	3,831	4,056	-226	1,550
2070...............	367,913	3,331	3,999	-667	971	2070...............	410,209	3,888	4,161	-273	1,545
2080...............	369,363	3,239	4,208	-969	976	2080...............	421,213	3,864	4,445	-582	1,528
2090...............	368,120	3,176	4,348	-1,171	965	2090...............	429,130	3,868	4,670	-802	1,494
2100...............	365,558	3,125	4,352	-1,227	944	2100...............	435,346	3,878	4,751	-873	1,452
LOW IMMIGRATION						ZERO IMMIGRATION					
2025...............	336,476	3,604	2,957	647	372	2025...............	333,396	3,539	2,951	589	-598
2030...............	340,921	3,559	3,202	357	434	2030...............	332,615	3,372	3,183	189	-455
2040...............	345,605	3,413	3,701	-289	491	2040...............	326,196	3,054	3,653	-600	-351
2050...............	345,029	3,195	3,936	-741	532	2050...............	313,807	2,722	3,848	-1,126	-286
2060...............	342,510	3,066	3,878	-812	560	2060...............	298,951	2,454	3,736	-1,282	-232
2070...............	339,715	2,960	3,890	-930	588	2070...............	283,313	2,218	3,674	-1,456	-178
2080...............	334,795	2,822	4,050	-1,228	608	2080...............	265,650	1,988	3,733	-1,745	-128
2090...............	327,447	2,715	4,132	-1,417	613	2090...............	246,084	1,792	3,702	-1,910	-91
2100...............	319,032	2,623	4,086	-1,463	605	2100...............	225,961	1,619	3,555	-1,935	-72

[1] Current expected projections. [2] Total births minus total deaths. [3] Includes the international migration of both native and foreign-born populations.

Source: U.S. Census Bureau, 2023 National Population Projections Tables: Alternative Scenarios, "Comparison Tables," November 2023, <www.census.gov/programs-surveys/popproj/data/tables.html>, accessed March 2024.

Table 5. Components of Population Change: 2020 to 2023

[In thousands except as indicated (331,465 represents 331,465,000). Resident population. Estimates base incorporates the 2020 Census, Vintage 2020 estimates, and 2020 Demographic Analysis estimates. See <www.census.gov/programs-surveys/popest/technical-documentation/methodology.html> for details]

Period	Population as of beginning of period	Net increase		Births	Deaths	Net international migration [2]	Population as of end of period
		Total	Percent [1]				
April 1, 2020 to July 1, 2020....................	331,465	62	(Z)	894	852	20	331,527
July 1, 2020 to July 1, 2021....................	331,527	522	0.2	3,584	3,438	376	332,049
July 1, 2021 to July 1, 2022....................	332,049	1,222	0.4	3,679	3,456	999	333,271
July 1, 2022 to July 1, 2023....................	333,271	1,643	0.5	3,653	3,149	1,139	334,915

Z represents less than 0.05%. [1] Net increase as percent of population at beginning of period. [2] Net international migration includes the international migration of both native and foreign-born populations. Specifically, it includes: (a) the net international migration of the foreign born, (b) the net migration between the United States and Puerto Rico, (c) the net migration of natives to and from the United States, and (d) the net movement of the Armed Forces population between the United States and overseas.

Source: U.S. Census Bureau, Population Division, National Population Totals and Components of Change: 2020-2023, "Annual Population Estimates, Estimated Components of Resident Population Change, and Rates of the Components of Resident Population Change for the United States, States, District of Columbia, and Puerto Rico: April 1, 2020 to July 1, 2023 (NST-EST2023-ALLDATA)," <www.census.gov/data/tables/time-series/demo/popest/2020s-national-total.html>, accessed February 2024.

Table 6. Resident Population by Sex, Race, and Hispanic Origin: 2000 to 2023

[281,425 represents 281,425,000. Data shown are modified race counts; see text, this section. Estimates for 2020-2023 are developed from a base that incorporates the 2020 Census, Vintage 2020 estimates, and 2020 Demographic Analysis estimates]

Characteristic	Number (1,000)					Percent change	
	2000 [1,2] (April)	2010 [1,2] (April)	2020 [2] (April)	2022 (July)	2023 (July)	2000 to 2010	2010 to 2020
BOTH SEXES							
Total	**281,425**	**308,758**	**331,465**	**333,271**	**334,915**	**9.7**	**7.4**
One race	277,527	301,774	321,938	323,212	324,596	8.7	6.7
White	228,106	241,945	251,724	251,616	252,066	6.1	4.0
Black or African American	35,705	40,254	44,888	45,398	45,757	12.7	11.5
American Indian and Alaska Native	2,664	3,740	4,292	4,413	4,486	40.4	14.8
Asian	10,589	15,160	20,184	20,903	21,387	43.2	33.1
Native Hawaiian and Other Pacific Islander	463	675	849	882	900	45.9	25.9
Two or more races	3,898	6,984	9,527	10,060	10,319	79.2	36.4
Race alone or in combination with one or more races:							
White	(NA)	248,076	260,198	260,585	261,275	(NA)	4.9
Black or African American	(NA)	43,217	49,262	50,075	50,579	(NA)	14.0
American Indian and Alaska Native	(NA)	6,139	7,093	7,293	7,407	(NA)	15.6
Asian	(NA)	17,677	23,698	24,622	25,208	(NA)	34.1
Native Hawaiian and Other Pacific Islander	(NA)	1,333	1,680	1,746	1,780	(NA)	26.1
Not Hispanic	246,118	258,279	269,401	269,211	269,696	4.9	4.3
One race	242,712	252,675	261,825	261,224	261,513	4.1	3.6
White	195,577	197,326	197,551	195,894	195,433	0.9	0.1
Black or African American	34,314	37,926	41,712	42,048	42,313	10.5	10.0
American Indian and Alaska Native	2,097	2,263	2,410	2,424	2,433	7.9	6.5
Asian	10,357	14,662	19,534	20,219	20,685	41.6	33.2
Native Hawaiian and Other Pacific Islander	367	497	618	638	649	35.4	24.3
Two or more races	3,406	5,605	7,577	7,988	8,183	64.5	35.2
Race alone or in combination with one or more races:							
White	(NA)	202,237	204,286	203,014	202,734	(NA)	1.0
Black or African American	(NA)	40,287	45,159	45,730	46,103	(NA)	12.1
American Indian and Alaska Native	(NA)	4,042	4,408	4,462	4,490	(NA)	9.1
Asian	(NA)	16,795	22,511	23,367	23,918	(NA)	34.0
Native Hawaiian and Other Pacific Islander	(NA)	1,020	1,272	1,315	1,337	(NA)	24.6
Hispanic [3]	35,306	50,479	62,064	64,060	65,219	43.0	23.0
One race	34,815	49,099	60,113	61,988	63,083	41.0	22.4
White	32,530	44,619	54,173	55,722	56,633	37.2	21.4
Black or African American	1,391	2,328	3,176	3,350	3,444	67.4	36.4
American Indian and Alaska Native	566	1,476	1,882	1,988	2,054	160.6	27.5
Asian	232	498	651	684	701	114.2	30.7
Native Hawaiian and Other Pacific Islander	95	177	232	244	251	85.9	30.5
Two or more races	491	1,380	1,950	2,072	2,136	180.8	41.3
Race alone or in combination with one or more races:							
White	(NA)	45,839	55,912	57,571	58,541	(NA)	22.0
Black or African American	(NA)	2,930	4,103	4,345	4,476	(NA)	40.0
American Indian and Alaska Native	(NA)	2,097	2,686	2,831	2,918	(NA)	28.1
Asian	(NA)	881	1,187	1,255	1,290	(NA)	34.6
Native Hawaiian and Other Pacific Islander	(NA)	312	409	431	443	(NA)	30.9
MALE							
Total	**138,056**	**151,789**	**164,196**	**164,963**	**165,749**	**9.9**	**8.2**
One race	136,146	148,362	159,464	159,963	160,618	9.0	7.5
White	112,478	119,703	125,556	125,403	125,606	6.4	4.9
Black or African American	16,972	19,208	21,596	21,827	22,001	13.2	12.4
American Indian and Alaska Native	1,333	1,890	2,170	2,229	2,265	41.8	14.8
Asian	5,128	7,219	9,710	10,056	10,289	40.8	34.5
Native Hawaiian and Other Pacific Islander	235	343	432	448	456	45.8	26.0
Two or more races	1,910	3,426	4,731	5,000	5,131	79.4	38.1
Race alone or in combination with one or more races:							
White	(NA)	122,721	129,776	129,873	130,198	(NA)	5.7
Black or African American	(NA)	20,635	23,745	24,130	24,377	(NA)	15.1
American Indian and Alaska Native	(NA)	3,055	3,543	3,640	3,697	(NA)	16.0
Asian	(NA)	8,468	11,473	11,922	12,207	(NA)	35.5
Native Hawaiian and Other Pacific Islander	(NA)	668	847	879	895	(NA)	26.8
Not Hispanic	119,894	126,169	132,755	132,560	132,774	5.2	5.2
Hispanic [3]	18,162	25,620	31,441	32,403	32,975	41.1	22.7
FEMALE							
Total	**143,368**	**156,969**	**167,269**	**168,308**	**169,165**	**9.5**	**6.6**
One race	141,381	153,411	162,473	163,248	163,978	8.5	5.9
White	115,628	122,242	126,168	126,212	126,459	5.7	3.2
Black or African American	18,733	21,047	23,292	23,570	23,756	12.4	10.7
American Indian and Alaska Native	1,331	1,850	2,122	2,184	2,221	39.0	14.7
Asian	5,461	7,941	10,475	10,847	11,098	45.4	31.9
Native Hawaiian and Other Pacific Islander	227	332	417	434	444	45.9	25.8
Two or more races	1,987	3,558	4,796	5,060	5,187	79.0	34.8
Race alone or in combination with one or more races:							
White	(NA)	125,355	130,422	130,712	131,077	(NA)	4.0
Black or African American	(NA)	22,582	25,517	25,945	26,202	(NA)	13.0
American Indian and Alaska Native	(NA)	3,084	3,550	3,653	3,710	(NA)	15.1
Asian	(NA)	9,209	12,225	12,700	13,001	(NA)	32.8
Native Hawaiian and Other Pacific Islander	(NA)	665	834	867	885	(NA)	25.4
Not Hispanic	126,224	132,110	136,647	136,652	136,921	4.7	3.4
Hispanic [3]	17,144	24,859	30,622	31,656	32,244	45.0	23.2

NA Not available. [1] The April 1, 2000 and 2010 population estimates base reflect changes to the Census 2000 and 2010 population from the Count Question Resolution program and geographic program revisions. [2] Estimates base. [3] Persons of Hispanic origin may be of any race.

Source: U.S. Census Bureau, Population and Housing Unit Estimates Tables, National Population by Characteristics: 2020-2023, "Annual Estimates of the Resident Population by Sex, Race, and Hispanic Origin for the United States: April 1, 2020 to July 1, 2023 (NC-EST2023-SR11H)," June 2024 and earlier releases, <www.census.gov/programs-surveys/popest/data/tables.html>.

Table 7. Resident Population Projections by Sex and Age: 2025 to 2070

[In thousands, except as indicated (338,016 represents 338,016,000). As of July 1. The 2023 National Projections are based on July 1, 2022 population estimates, which are derived from the Census Bureau's Vintage 2022 Population Estimates and partially based on the 2020 Census through the blended base method. The projections were produced using a cohort-component method and are based on assumptions about future births, deaths, and net international migration. More information on methodology and assumptions is available at <www.census.gov/programs-surveys/popproj/technical-documentation.html>]

Age	2025 Total	2025 Male	2025 Female	2030	2035	2040	2050	2060	2070	Percent distribution 2025	2030	2040	2050	2060	2070
Total	338,016	167,544	170,473	345,074	350,861	355,309	360,639	364,287	367,913	100.0	100.0	100.0	100.0	100.0	100.0
FIVE-YEAR AGE GROUPS															
Under 5 years	18,303	9,358	8,945	18,422	18,454	18,299	17,535	17,132	16,992	5.4	5.3	5.2	4.9	4.7	4.6
5 to 9 years	19,364	9,901	9,463	18,630	18,770	18,815	18,311	17,640	17,499	5.7	5.4	5.3	5.1	4.8	4.8
10 to 14 years	20,350	10,416	9,934	19,647	18,924	19,076	18,987	18,247	17,863	6.0	5.7	5.4	5.3	5.0	4.9
15 to 19 years	21,758	11,140	10,618	20,728	20,039	19,330	19,557	19,076	18,425	6.4	6.0	5.4	5.4	5.2	5.0
20 to 24 years	22,438	11,450	10,988	22,370	21,385	20,725	20,233	20,197	19,500	6.6	6.5	5.8	5.6	5.5	5.3
25 to 29 years	22,664	11,578	11,087	23,159	23,134	22,200	20,920	21,235	20,823	6.7	6.7	6.2	5.8	5.8	5.7
30 to 34 years	23,225	11,824	11,401	23,291	23,817	23,839	22,350	21,956	21,993	6.9	6.7	6.7	6.2	6.0	6.0
35 to 39 years	22,992	11,653	11,339	23,561	23,668	24,230	23,429	22,237	22,617	6.8	6.8	6.8	6.5	6.1	6.1
40 to 44 years	22,108	11,167	10,941	23,046	23,652	23,799	24,470	23,073	22,735	6.5	6.7	6.7	6.8	6.3	6.2
45 to 49 years	20,441	10,264	10,177	21,995	22,965	23,603	24,394	23,694	22,559	6.0	6.4	6.6	6.8	6.5	6.1
50 to 54 years	19,905	9,944	9,960	20,131	21,689	22,689	23,574	24,329	23,021	5.9	5.8	6.4	6.5	6.7	6.3
55 to 59 years	20,151	10,010	10,141	19,447	19,708	21,272	22,994	23,899	23,322	6.0	5.6	6.0	6.4	6.6	6.3
60 to 64 years	20,993	10,244	10,748	19,463	18,827	19,138	21,753	22,782	23,652	6.2	5.6	5.4	6.0	6.3	6.4
65 to 69 years	19,610	9,386	10,224	19,890	18,500	17,947	19,856	21,677	22,729	5.8	5.8	5.1	5.5	6.0	6.2
70 to 74 years	16,332	7,593	8,738	18,099	18,409	17,194	17,142	19,716	20,884	4.8	5.2	4.8	4.8	5.4	5.7
75 to 79 years	12,639	5,723	6,916	14,401	16,015	16,363	15,014	16,882	18,679	3.7	4.2	4.6	4.2	4.6	5.1
80 to 84 years	7,698	3,304	4,394	10,234	11,726	13,114	12,743	12,988	15,214	2.3	3.0	3.7	3.5	3.6	4.1
85 to 89 years	4,237	1,669	2,568	5,339	7,164	8,286	9,678	9,134	10,600	1.3	1.5	2.3	2.7	2.5	2.9
90 to 94 years	2,032	700	1,332	2,314	2,959	4,027	5,392	5,471	5,833	0.6	0.7	1.1	1.5	1.5	1.6
95 to 99 years	672	195	477	773	899	1,174	1,949	2,403	2,397	0.2	0.2	0.3	0.5	0.7	0.7
100 years and over	107	24	82	134	158	189	357	519	573	(Z)	(Z)	0.1	0.1	0.1	0.2
SPECIAL AGE CATEGORIES															
5 to 13 years	35,613	18,213	17,400	34,178	33,952	34,061	33,457	32,183	31,760	10.5	9.9	9.6	9.3	8.8	8.6
14 to 17 years	17,019	8,719	8,301	16,487	15,494	15,386	15,498	15,021	14,551	5.0	4.8	4.3	4.3	4.1	4.0
18 to 24 years	31,278	15,975	15,302	30,710	29,673	28,499	28,133	27,956	26,975	9.3	8.9	8.0	7.8	7.7	7.3
16 years and over	275,812	135,724	140,088	284,239	290,864	295,281	301,944	307,534	311,936	81.6	82.4	83.1	83.7	84.4	84.8
18 years and over	267,081	131,254	135,827	275,986	282,962	287,563	294,149	299,951	304,609	79.0	80.0	80.9	81.6	82.3	82.8
15 to 44 years	135,184	68,811	66,373	136,155	135,695	134,123	130,960	127,775	126,093	40.0	39.5	37.8	36.3	35.1	34.3
55 years and over	104,471	48,848	55,620	110,094	114,365	118,704	126,878	135,471	143,883	30.9	31.9	33.4	35.2	37.2	39.1
65 years and over	63,327	28,595	34,731	71,183	75,828	78,294	82,130	88,788	96,910	18.7	20.6	22.0	22.8	24.4	26.3
75 years and over	27,385	11,615	15,769	33,195	38,921	43,153	45,133	47,397	53,296	8.1	9.6	12.1	12.5	13.0	14.5
85 years and over	7,047	2,588	4,459	8,560	11,179	13,676	17,375	17,526	19,403	2.1	2.5	3.9	4.8	4.8	5.3
Median age (years) [1]	39.5	38.4	40.7	40.6	41.6	42.3	43.9	45.3	46.2	(X)	(X)	(X)	(X)	(X)	(X)

X Not applicable. Z Less than 0.05 percent. [1] For definition of median, see Guide to Tabular Presentation.

Source: U.S. Census Bureau, 2023 National Population Projections Tables: Main Series, "Table 2. Projected Population by Age Group and Sex" and "Table 3. Projected Population by Five-Year Age Group and Sex," November 2023, <www.census.gov/programs-surveys/popproj/popproj.html>, accessed March 2024.

Table 8. Resident Population by Race, Hispanic Origin, and Age: 2020 and 2023

[In thousands (331,465 represents 331,465,000), except as indicated. 2020 data are as of April 1. 2023 data are as of July 1. Estimates are developed from a base that incorporates the 2020 Census, Vintage 2020 estimates, and 2020 Demographic Analysis estimates. For definition of median, see Guide to Tabular Presentation]

Age	Total		White alone		Black or African American alone		American Indian, Alaska Native alone		Asian alone		Native Hawaiian, Other Pacific Islander alone		Two or more races		Hispanic origin [1]		Not Hispanic White alone	
	2020	2023	2020	2023	2020	2023	2020	2023	2020	2023	2020	2023	2020	2023	2020	2023	2020	2023
Total	331,465	334,915	251,724	252,066	44,888	45,757	4,292	4,486	20,184	21,387	849	900	9,527	10,319	62,064	65,219	197,551	195,433
FIVE-YEAR AGE GROUPS																		
Under 5 years	19,400	18,511	13,529	12,751	3,034	2,999	350	344	1,176	1,110	72	71	1,240	1,236	5,044	5,004	9,384	8,696
5 to 9 years	20,367	20,153	14,385	14,074	3,126	3,123	346	357	1,210	1,266	68	73	1,231	1,261	5,235	5,247	10,000	9,731
10 to 14 years	21,749	20,835	15,684	14,785	3,305	3,194	346	349	1,169	1,217	65	67	1,180	1,223	5,650	5,440	10,834	10,189
15 to 19 years	21,558	22,075	15,785	15,979	3,196	3,310	330	354	1,204	1,242	61	66	982	1,124	5,252	5,692	11,222	11,076
20 to 24 years	21,472	21,811	15,690	15,878	3,260	3,258	320	335	1,290	1,338	59	62	854	940	4,892	5,238	11,419	11,326
25 to 29 years	22,889	22,018	16,525	15,913	3,640	3,361	337	328	1,572	1,529	67	63	748	824	4,897	4,960	12,244	11,585
30 to 34 years	22,821	23,524	16,706	16,892	3,385	3,713	321	345	1,742	1,796	73	72	595	706	4,690	4,957	12,605	12,572
35 to 39 years	22,211	22,507	16,552	16,559	3,070	3,199	303	312	1,706	1,809	70	72	510	556	4,625	4,691	12,487	12,450
40 to 44 years	20,569	21,884	15,430	16,312	2,839	3,023	274	295	1,534	1,694	60	68	433	491	4,310	4,589	11,624	12,278
45 to 49 years	20,436	19,817	15,530	14,895	2,748	2,683	258	260	1,486	1,528	51	55	363	396	3,937	4,147	12,013	11,217
50 to 54 years	20,768	20,677	16,150	15,845	2,725	2,726	244	250	1,287	1,455	48	50	314	349	3,450	3,759	13,062	12,486
55 to 59 years	22,096	20,606	17,549	16,124	2,787	2,668	242	235	1,177	1,236	45	46	297	297	2,982	3,234	14,877	13,228
60 to 64 years	20,982	21,248	16,908	16,983	2,519	2,591	209	225	1,052	1,129	37	42	257	279	2,344	2,681	14,806	14,580
65 to 69 years	17,885	19,151	14,668	15,541	1,951	2,170	157	183	887	995	28	33	193	228	1,727	2,032	13,109	13,717
70 to 74 years	14,436	15,535	12,073	12,812	1,400	1,597	113	132	690	804	21	24	140	165	1,235	1,445	10,951	11,505
75 to 79 years	9,613	11,387	8,143	9,590	865	1,024	68	88	437	555	12	16	88	113	791	978	7,420	8,699
80 to 84 years	6,135	6,981	5,199	5,906	545	603	41	51	288	344	7	9	54	68	521	593	4,721	5,364
85 years and over	6,081	6,195	5,218	5,225	493	516	34	44	280	340	6	8	49	62	482	533	4,773	4,734
SPECIAL AGE CATEGORIES																		
Under 18 years	74,416	72,832	53,044	51,228	11,362	11,340	1,241	1,265	4,270	4,325	242	251	4,258	4,423	19,118	19,176	36,896	35,237
Under 5 years	19,400	18,511	13,529	12,751	3,034	2,999	350	344	1,176	1,110	72	71	1,240	1,236	5,044	5,004	9,384	8,696
5 to 13 years	37,784	36,679	26,917	25,773	5,784	5,656	623	636	2,148	2,245	120	127	2,192	2,242	9,777	9,556	18,638	17,800
14 to 17 years	17,232	17,642	12,598	12,704	2,544	2,685	268	284	946	970	50	53	826	945	4,297	4,617	8,875	8,741
18 to 64 years	202,899	202,835	153,378	151,763	28,272	28,507	2,637	2,724	13,333	14,024	533	558	4,745	5,259	38,190	40,462	119,680	116,176
18 to 24 years	30,130	30,553	22,029	22,239	4,560	4,543	451	474	1,779	1,848	83	88	1,228	1,361	6,954	7,444	15,962	15,780
25 to 44 years	88,489	89,933	65,212	65,677	12,934	13,296	1,234	1,279	6,553	6,828	269	276	2,286	2,577	18,522	19,197	48,960	48,885
45 to 64 years	84,281	82,348	66,137	63,847	10,779	10,668	953	970	5,001	5,348	181	194	1,231	1,321	12,714	13,821	54,759	51,511
65 years and over	54,149	59,248	45,302	49,075	5,254	5,910	413	498	2,582	3,038	74	91	524	636	4,756	5,581	40,974	44,020
85 years and over	6,081	6,195	5,218	5,225	493	516	34	44	280	340	6	8	49	62	482	533	4,773	4,734
16 years and over	265,654	270,944	204,992	207,245	34,789	35,756	3,182	3,365	16,393	17,548	632	675	5,667	6,354	45,056	48,354	165,133	164,614
18 years and over	257,049	262,083	198,680	200,838	33,526	34,417	3,050	3,222	15,915	17,062	607	649	5,269	5,895	42,946	46,043	160,654	160,195
15 to 44 years	131,519	133,820	96,687	97,533	19,390	19,863	1,884	1,969	9,046	9,409	390	404	4,121	4,641	28,666	30,127	71,601	71,287
Median age (years)	38.5	39.1	40.3	41.0	34.2	34.9	31.8	32.5	37.1	38.3	32.2	33.3	20.7	21.6	30.1	31.0	43.6	44.1

[1] Hispanic origin is considered an ethnicity, not a race. Persons of Hispanic origin may be of any race.

Source: U.S. Census Bureau, National Population by Characteristics: 2020-2023, "Annual Estimates of the Resident Population by Sex, Age, Race, and Hispanic Origin for the United States: April 1, 2020 to July 1, 2023 (NC-EST2023-ASR6H)," June 2024, <www.census.gov/data/tables/time-series/demo/popest/2020s-national-detail.html>, accessed July 2024.

Table 9. Resident Population by Race, Hispanic Origin, and Single Years of Age: 2023

[In thousands (334,915 represents 334,915,000). As of July 1. Estimates are developed from a base that incorporates the 2020 Census, Vintage 2020 estimates, and 2020 Demographic Analysis estimates]

Age	Total	Race						Hispanic origin [1]	Non-Hispanic White alone
		White alone	Black or African American alone	American Indian, Alaska Native alone	Asian alone	Native Hawaiian and Other Pacific Islander alone	Two or more races		
Total.........................	334,915	252,066	45,757	4,486	21,387	900	10,319	65,219	195,433
Under 5 years old............	18,511	12,751	2,999	344	1,110	71	1,236	5,004	8,696
Under 1 year old............	3,649	2,515	597	67	208	14	248	1,004	1,703
1 year old..................	3,694	2,540	603	68	217	15	252	1,018	1,718
2 years old.................	3,612	2,471	597	67	218	14	245	983	1,676
3 years old.................	3,748	2,589	598	70	231	14	245	989	1,784
4 years old.................	3,809	2,636	605	72	235	14	246	1,009	1,814
5 to 9 years old..............	20,153	14,074	3,123	357	1,266	73	1,261	5,247	9,731
5 years old.................	3,896	2,695	618	73	246	15	250	1,022	1,859
6 years old.................	3,973	2,759	618	72	258	15	251	1,040	1,902
7 years old.................	4,076	2,860	622	71	254	15	254	1,065	1,975
8 years old.................	4,110	2,881	632	71	258	15	254	1,065	1,995
9 years old.................	4,098	2,878	632	71	251	14	251	1,055	2,000
10 to 14 years old............	20,835	14,785	3,194	349	1,217	67	1,223	5,440	10,189
10 years old................	4,083	2,868	629	70	255	14	247	1,050	1,991
11 years old................	4,090	2,886	629	72	246	14	244	1,059	2,000
12 years old................	4,134	2,934	633	69	240	13	244	1,085	2,018
13 years old................	4,219	3,011	642	68	239	13	246	1,116	2,061
14 years old................	4,308	3,086	661	69	237	13	242	1,131	2,119
15 to 19 years old............	22,075	15,979	3,310	354	1,242	66	1,124	5,692	11,076
15 years old................	4,472	3,210	686	72	247	14	244	1,175	2,203
16 years old................	4,466	3,221	680	73	243	13	236	1,171	2,215
17 years old................	4,395	3,186	659	71	243	13	223	1,140	2,204
18 years old................	4,357	3,165	644	70	251	13	214	1,112	2,205
19 years old................	4,385	3,196	641	69	259	13	207	1,094	2,249
20 to 24 years old............	21,811	15,878	3,258	335	1,338	62	940	5,238	11,326
20 years old................	4,344	3,171	635	68	260	13	197	1,074	2,240
21 years old................	4,323	3,153	643	67	257	12	191	1,056	2,236
22 years old................	4,402	3,202	659	67	273	12	189	1,054	2,285
23 years old................	4,405	3,198	668	68	275	12	184	1,041	2,292
24 years old................	4,337	3,154	652	66	273	12	179	1,012	2,274
25 to 29 years old............	22,018	15,913	3,361	328	1,529	63	824	4,960	11,585
25 years old................	4,330	3,141	655	66	284	12	173	997	2,272
26 years old................	4,340	3,145	653	65	296	12	169	990	2,283
27 years old................	4,369	3,165	654	65	308	13	164	985	2,306
28 years old................	4,444	3,206	683	65	315	13	161	990	2,341
29 years old................	4,536	3,256	716	67	326	13	157	999	2,383
30 to 34 years old............	23,524	16,892	3,713	345	1,796	72	706	4,957	12,572
30 years old................	4,607	3,300	738	69	335	14	151	1,002	2,424
31 years old................	4,709	3,375	752	71	348	14	149	1,013	2,490
32 years old................	4,776	3,423	759	70	365	15	144	1,000	2,554
33 years old................	4,785	3,442	752	69	373	15	135	990	2,580
34 years old................	4,648	3,353	713	66	375	15	126	951	2,524
35 to 39 years old............	22,507	16,559	3,199	312	1,809	72	556	4,691	12,450
35 years old................	4,563	3,323	673	65	367	15	120	948	2,496
36 years old................	4,509	3,305	651	63	361	14	115	938	2,484
37 years old................	4,515	3,329	638	62	361	15	110	942	2,504
38 years old................	4,508	3,334	630	61	361	15	107	940	2,510
39 years old................	4,412	3,267	607	60	359	14	104	923	2,456
40 to 44 years old............	21,884	16,312	3,023	295	1,694	68	491	4,589	12,278
40 years old................	4,473	3,322	614	61	357	14	104	938	2,499
41 years old................	4,461	3,321	611	60	353	14	101	938	2,497
42 years old................	4,393	3,283	603	59	336	14	99	920	2,473
43 years old................	4,370	3,258	612	59	330	14	97	923	2,447
44 years old................	4,188	3,128	583	55	319	12	91	870	2,362
45 to 49 years old............	19,817	14,895	2,683	260	1,528	55	396	4,147	11,217
45 years old................	4,092	3,071	560	54	308	12	87	861	2,311
46 years old................	4,037	3,031	551	53	307	12	84	849	2,280
47 years old................	3,896	2,925	526	51	304	11	79	828	2,191
48 years old................	3,935	2,963	529	51	306	11	75	817	2,235
49 years old................	3,857	2,906	516	50	302	10	72	791	2,200
50 to 54 years old............	20,677	15,845	2,726	250	1,455	50	349	3,759	12,486
50 years old................	3,905	2,943	530	50	302	10	71	778	2,248
51 years old................	4,090	3,110	549	50	300	10	71	771	2,420
52 years old................	4,330	3,330	571	52	294	10	73	767	2,644
53 years old................	4,258	3,286	555	50	287	10	70	741	2,623
54 years old................	4,094	3,177	522	48	273	10	65	701	2,550
55 to 59 years old............	20,606	16,124	2,668	235	1,236	46	297	3,234	13,228
55 years old................	4,002	3,103	522	47	261	9	61	682	2,492
56 years old................	4,011	3,135	519	46	242	9	59	656	2,548
57 years old................	4,065	3,172	535	47	244	9	58	646	2,594
58 years old................	4,216	3,309	548	48	243	9	59	637	2,738
59 years old................	4,311	3,404	544	48	246	9	59	614	2,855

See footnotes at end of table.

Table 9. Resident Population by Race, Hispanic Origin, and Single Years of Age: 2023-Continued.

See headnote on page 12.

Age	Total	Race						Hispanic origin [1]	Non-Hispanic White alone
		White alone	Black or African American alone	American Indian, Alaska Native alone	Asian alone	Native Hawaiian and Other Pacific Islander alone	Two or more races		
60 to 64 years old............	21,248	16,983	2,591	225	1,129	42	279	2,681	14,580
60 years old.................	4,306	3,412	534	47	246	9	58	585	2,888
61 years old.................	4,313	3,445	528	46	227	9	58	564	2,939
62 years old.................	4,297	3,448	519	45	220	8	56	533	2,971
63 years old.................	4,211	3,364	515	44	224	8	55	519	2,899
64 years old.................	4,122	3,313	495	42	212	8	52	479	2,884
65 to 69 years old............	19,151	15,541	2,170	183	995	33	228	2,032	13,717
65 years old.................	4,077	3,293	474	40	212	7	50	451	2,889
66 years old.................	3,993	3,234	461	39	204	7	48	431	2,847
67 years old.................	3,807	3,083	435	37	200	7	46	407	2,718
68 years old.................	3,709	3,014	414	35	196	6	44	387	2,666
69 years old.................	3,565	2,917	386	32	184	6	40	355	2,597
70 to 74 years old............	15,535	12,812	1,597	132	804	24	165	1,445	11,505
70 years old.................	3,405	2,800	356	30	175	5	38	329	2,503
71 years old.................	3,264	2,695	335	28	166	5	35	305	2,419
72 years old.................	3,094	2,551	323	26	157	5	33	289	2,290
73 years old.................	2,935	2,411	304	25	159	5	31	272	2,164
74 years old.................	2,837	2,355	279	23	146	4	29	250	2,128
75 to 79 years old............	11,387	9,590	1,024	88	555	16	113	978	8,699
75 years old.................	2,754	2,306	259	22	136	4	28	236	2,091
76 years old.................	2,878	2,453	244	22	128	4	28	226	2,248
77 years old.................	2,013	1,684	185	16	104	3	21	188	1,513
78 years old.................	1,910	1,599	176	15	97	3	20	172	1,443
79 years old.................	1,832	1,547	161	14	89	3	18	156	1,405
80 to 84 years old............	6,981	5,906	603	51	344	9	68	593	5,364
80 years old.................	1,820	1,555	153	13	81	2	17	146	1,422
81 years old.................	1,529	1,294	131	11	76	2	15	128	1,177
82 years old.................	1,343	1,132	118	10	68	2	13	116	1,026
83 years old.................	1,201	1,008	108	9	63	2	12	107	910
84 years old.................	1,086	917	93	8	56	1	11	96	829
85 to 89 years old............	3,807	3,210	327	28	200	5	37	338	2,898
85 years old.................	985	832	84	7	51	1	9	87	752
86 years old.................	850	716	73	6	45	1	8	76	646
87 years old.................	756	636	66	6	40	1	7	67	574
88 years old.................	667	563	57	5	35	1	7	60	508
89 years old.................	549	463	47	4	30	1	5	49	418
90 to 94 years old............	1,763	1,494	140	12	98	2	17	149	1,356
90 years old.................	484	409	40	3	27	1	5	41	371
91 years old.................	414	352	33	3	22	1	4	35	319
92 years old.................	349	297	27	2	19	(Z)	3	30	270
93 years old.................	289	244	22	2	17	(Z)	3	24	222
94 years old.................	226	192	17	1	13	(Z)	2	18	175
95 to 99 years old............	541	456	41	4	34	1	6	40	419
95 years old.................	180	153	14	1	11	(Z)	2	14	140
96 years old.................	138	116	10	1	8	(Z)	1	10	107
97 years old.................	100	84	8	1	6	(Z)	1	7	77
98 years old.................	73	61	6	1	5	(Z)	1	5	56
99 years old.................	50	42	4	(Z)	4	(Z)	1	3	39
						(Z)			
100 years old and over.......	84	67	7	1	8	(Z)	1	5	62

Z Less than 500. [1] Persons of Hispanic origin may be of any race.

Source: U.S. Census Bureau, National Population by Characteristics: 2020-2023, "Monthly Population Estimates by Age, Sex, Race and Hispanic Origin for the United States: April 1, 2020 to July 1, 2023 (NC-EST2023-ALLDATA)," <www.census.gov/data/tables/time-series/demo/popest/2020s-national-detail.html>, accessed July 2024.

Table 10. Resident Population by Sex and Age: 2000 to 2023

[In thousands (281,425 represents 281,425,000), except as indicated. Census years as of April 1; all others as of July 1. Estimates for 2020-2023 are developed from a base that incorporates the 2020 Census, Vintage 2020 estimates, and 2020 Demographic Analysis estimates. Excludes Armed Forces overseas]

Age	2000 [1]			2010 [1]			2020, estimates base			2023		
	Total	Male	Female	Total	Male	Female	Total	Male	Female	Total	Male	Female
Total................	281,425	138,056	143,368	308,758	151,789	156,969	331,465	164,196	167,269	334,915	165,749	169,165
Under 5 years........	19,176	9,811	9,365	20,201	10,319	9,882	19,400	9,919	9,482	18,511	9,459	9,052
5 to 9 years..........	20,550	10,523	10,026	20,349	10,390	9,959	20,367	10,423	9,944	20,153	10,305	9,848
10 to 14 years........	20,528	10,520	10,008	20,677	10,580	10,097	21,749	11,136	10,613	20,835	10,668	10,167
15 to 19 years........	20,219	10,391	9,828	22,042	11,305	10,737	21,558	11,016	10,541	22,075	11,297	10,779
20 to 24 years........	18,963	9,688	9,275	21,588	11,015	10,572	21,472	10,949	10,523	21,811	11,127	10,684
25 to 29 years........	19,382	9,799	9,583	21,103	10,637	10,467	22,889	11,618	11,270	22,018	11,176	10,842
30 to 34 years........	20,511	10,322	10,189	19,963	9,997	9,966	22,821	11,549	11,272	23,524	11,883	11,641
35 to 39 years........	22,707	11,319	11,388	20,180	10,043	10,138	22,211	11,215	10,996	22,507	11,364	11,143
40 to 44 years........	22,442	11,130	11,313	20,892	10,395	10,497	20,569	10,315	10,253	21,884	10,998	10,886
45 to 49 years........	20,093	9,890	10,203	22,709	11,210	11,500	20,436	10,221	10,214	19,817	9,886	9,931
50 to 54 years........	17,586	8,608	8,978	22,299	10,934	11,365	20,768	10,362	10,405	20,677	10,301	10,376
55 to 59 years........	13,469	6,509	6,961	19,665	9,524	10,141	22,096	10,888	11,208	20,606	10,166	10,440
60 to 64 years........	10,806	5,137	5,669	16,818	8,078	8,741	20,982	10,203	10,779	21,248	10,337	10,911
65 to 74 years........	18,391	8,303	10,088	21,714	10,097	11,617	32,320	15,246	17,074	34,685	16,335	18,350
75 to 84 years........	12,361	4,879	7,482	13,062	5,477	7,585	15,748	6,956	8,792	18,368	8,162	10,206
85 years and over. ..	4,240	1,227	3,013	5,495	1,790	3,705	6,081	2,178	3,903	6,195	2,284	3,911
5 to 13 years.........	37,026	18,964	18,062	36,860	18,834	18,026	37,784	19,343	18,441	36,679	18,767	17,912
14 to 17 years........	16,093	8,285	7,808	17,121	8,792	8,329	17,232	8,810	8,422	17,642	9,033	8,609
18 to 24 years........	27,141	13,873	13,268	30,674	15,663	15,011	30,130	15,371	14,758	30,553	15,596	14,957
18 years and over. ..	209,130	100,996	108,133	234,576	113,843	120,733	257,049	126,124	130,925	262,083	128,490	133,593
55 years and over. ..	59,267	26,055	33,212	76,755	34,966	41,789	97,227	45,471	51,756	101,103	47,285	53,817
65 years and over. ..	34,992	14,410	20,582	40,271	17,364	22,907	54,149	24,380	29,769	59,248	26,782	32,467
75 years and over. ..	16,601	6,106	10,495	18,557	7,267	11,290	21,829	9,134	12,694	24,563	10,446	14,117
Median age (years)..	35.3	34.0	36.5	37.2	35.8	38.5	38.5	37.4	39.5	39.1	38.0	40.2

[1] The April 1, 2000 and April 1, 2010 population estimates bases reflect changes to the Census 2000 and Census 2010 population from the Count Question Resolution program and geographic program revisions.

Source: U.S. Census Bureau, Current Population Reports, P25-1095; "Intercensal Estimates of the United States Population by Age and Sex, 1990-2000: All Months," September 2002, <www.census.gov/data/tables/time-series/demo/popest/intercensal-national.html>; National Population by Characteristics: 2010-2020, "Annual Estimates of the Resident Population by Single Year of Age and Sex: April 1, 2010 to July 1, 2020," <www.census.gov/programs-surveys/popest/technical-documentation/research/evaluation-estimates/2020-evaluation-estimates.html>; and National Population by Characteristics: 2020-2023, "Annual Estimates of the Resident Population for Selected Age Groups by Sex for the United States: April 1, 2020 to July 1, 2023 (NC-EST2023-AGESEX)," <www.census.gov/data/tables/time-series/demo/popest/2020s-national-detail.html>, accessed July 2024.

Table 11. Resident Population Projections for Native and Foreign-Born Populations by Age Group: 2025 to 2100

[In thousands (338,016 represents 338,016,000). As of July 1. The 2023 National Projections are based on July 1, 2022 population estimates, which are derived from the Census Bureau's Vintage 2022 Population Estimates and partially based on the 2020 Census through the blended base method. The projections were produced using a cohort-component method and are based on assumptions about future births, deaths, and net international migration. More information on methodology and assumptions is available at <www.census.gov/programs-surveys/popproj/technical-documentation.html>]

Nativity and age group	2025	2030	2040	2050	2060	2070	2080	2090	2100
Total population.................	338,016	345,074	355,309	360,639	364,287	367,913	369,363	368,120	365,558
Under 18 years.....................	70,935	69,087	67,746	66,490	64,336	63,304	62,403	61,008	59,903
Under 5 years.....................	18,303	18,422	18,299	17,535	17,132	16,992	16,565	16,216	15,977
5 to 13 years.....................	35,613	34,178	34,061	33,457	32,183	31,760	31,364	30,586	30,056
14 to 17 years.....................	17,019	16,487	15,386	15,498	15,021	14,551	14,474	14,205	13,871
18 to 64 years.....................	203,755	204,803	209,269	212,019	211,163	207,698	203,682	201,928	199,320
18 to 24 years.....................	31,278	30,710	28,499	28,133	27,956	26,975	26,556	26,357	25,762
25 to 44 years.....................	90,988	93,057	94,068	91,169	88,502	88,168	86,639	85,038	84,277
45 to 64 years.....................	81,489	81,036	86,702	92,716	94,705	92,555	90,487	90,533	89,281
65 years and over..................	63,327	71,183	78,294	82,130	88,788	96,910	103,277	105,184	106,335
Native population.................	289,854	294,212	299,798	301,378	302,064	303,190	302,317	298,863	294,386
Under 18 years.....................	68,280	66,440	64,996	63,577	61,299	60,178	59,221	57,800	56,698
Under 5 years.....................	17,971	18,131	17,987	17,207	16,792	16,644	16,211	15,861	15,623
5 to 13 years.....................	34,260	32,745	32,604	31,913	30,575	30,106	29,680	28,889	28,360
14 to 17 years.....................	16,050	15,564	14,405	14,456	13,932	13,428	13,330	13,050	12,715
18 to 64 years.....................	167,756	168,201	171,980	174,016	171,857	166,805	161,306	158,425	155,069
18 to 24 years.....................	28,454	27,993	25,692	25,219	24,898	23,811	23,319	23,078	22,471
25 to 44 years.....................	75,025	77,384	78,475	74,991	71,553	70,537	68,458	66,493	65,543
45 to 64 years.....................	64,277	62,825	67,813	73,806	75,406	72,458	69,530	68,854	67,055
65 years and over..................	53,818	59,571	62,822	63,785	68,908	76,206	81,789	82,639	82,619
Foreign-born population.......	48,162	50,862	55,511	59,261	62,223	64,722	67,046	69,257	71,172
Under 18 years.....................	2,654	2,648	2,750	2,913	3,037	3,125	3,182	3,208	3,205
Under 5 years.....................	332	291	311	328	340	349	354	356	354
5 to 13 years.....................	1,353	1,433	1,458	1,543	1,608	1,654	1,684	1,697	1,695
14 to 17 years.....................	969	924	981	1,042	1,089	1,123	1,145	1,155	1,155
18 to 64 years.....................	35,999	36,601	37,289	38,002	39,305	40,893	42,376	43,504	44,250
18 to 24 years.....................	2,824	2,717	2,807	2,915	3,058	3,164	3,238	3,279	3,291
25 to 44 years.....................	15,963	15,673	15,593	16,178	16,949	17,632	18,181	18,545	18,733
45 to 64 years.....................	17,212	18,211	18,889	18,910	19,299	20,097	20,957	21,679	22,226
65 years and over..................	9,508	11,613	15,472	18,345	19,881	20,704	21,488	22,545	23,717

Source: U.S. Census Bureau, 2023 National Population Projections Tables, "Table 2. Projected Population by Age Group and Sex," "Table 9. Projected Native-Born Population for Selected Age Groups," and "Table 10. Projected Foreign-Born Population for Selected Age Groups," November 2023, <www.census.gov/programs-surveys/popproj.html>, accessed March 2024.

Table 12. Resident Population Projections by Race, Hispanic Origin, and Age: 2030

[In thousands (345,074 represents 345,074,000). As of July 1. The 2023 National Projections are based on July 1, 2022 population estimates, which are derived from the Census Bureau's Vintage 2022 Population Estimates and partially based on the 2020 Census through the blended base method. The projections were produced using a cohort-component method and are based on assumptions about future births, deaths, and net international migration. More information on methodology and assumptions is available at <www.census.gov/programs-surveys/popproj/technical-documentation.html>]

Age group	Total	White alone	Black or African American alone	American Indian/ Alaska Native alone	Asian alone	Native Hawaiian/ Other Pacific Islander alone	Two or more races	Hispanic origin [1]	Not Hispanic, White alone
Total	345,074	255,570	47,622	4,593	24,051	973	12,264	71,677	193,347
Under 5 years	18,422	12,616	2,779	274	1,210	58	1,484	5,098	8,320
5 to 9 years	18,630	12,787	2,926	299	1,238	63	1,316	5,070	8,560
10 to 14 years	19,647	13,620	3,062	350	1,300	73	1,243	5,238	9,299
15 to 19 years	20,728	14,556	3,164	346	1,352	71	1,239	5,449	9,978
20 to 24 years	22,370	15,918	3,366	345	1,477	70	1,194	5,913	10,823
25 to 29 years	23,159	16,625	3,376	342	1,713	69	1,034	5,799	11,563
30 to 34 years	23,291	16,686	3,464	334	1,829	68	910	5,495	11,865
35 to 39 years	23,561	16,774	3,676	335	1,930	72	775	5,181	12,229
40 to 44 years	23,046	16,699	3,400	314	1,948	75	610	4,778	12,512
45 to 49 years	21,995	16,303	3,012	290	1,808	70	512	4,570	12,278
50 to 54 years	20,131	15,060	2,748	260	1,571	59	431	4,184	11,362
55 to 59 years	19,447	14,736	2,574	238	1,493	51	354	3,751	11,386
60 to 64 years	19,463	15,105	2,478	220	1,310	46	303	3,237	12,207
65 to 69 years	19,890	15,799	2,407	209	1,157	42	275	2,699	13,381
70 to 74 years	18,099	14,631	2,049	173	981	34	230	2,059	12,786
75 to 79 years	14,401	11,849	1,469	122	774	24	163	1,438	10,552
80 to 84 years	10,234	8,564	934	78	536	16	106	931	7,720
85 to 89 years	5,339	4,520	458	38	262	7	53	483	4,079
90 to 94 years	2,314	1,954	202	17	116	3	23	219	1,753
95 to 99 years	773	654	67	5	38	1	7	71	590
100 years and over	134	114	11	1	7	(Z)	1	11	104
SPECIAL CATEGORIES									
5 to 13 years	34,178	23,533	5,366	580	2,271	121	2,306	9,221	15,894
14 to 17 years	16,487	11,554	2,516	277	1,078	58	1,004	4,332	7,930
18 to 24 years	30,710	21,793	4,636	484	2,018	98	1,682	8,117	14,837
16 years and over	284,239	213,652	38,224	3,600	20,031	764	7,968	55,182	165,183
18 years and over	275,986	207,867	36,961	3,462	19,492	735	7,470	53,025	161,204
16 to 64 years	213,055	155,568	30,626	2,956	16,160	637	7,110	47,270	114,217
55 years and over	110,093	87,926	12,650	1,103	6,675	224	1,515	14,901	74,558
65 years and over	71,183	58,084	7,598	644	3,872	127	858	7,912	50,965
75 years and over	33,195	27,654	3,142	261	1,733	51	353	3,154	24,798
85 years and over	8,560	7,242	738	61	423	11	85	784	6,526

Z Less than 500. [1] Hispanic origin is considered an ethnicity, not a race. Persons of Hispanic origin may be of any race.

Source: U.S. Census Bureau, 2023 National Population Projections Datasets, "Table 1. Projected Population by Single Year of Age, Sex, Race, and Hispanic Origin for the United States: 2022 to 2100," November 2023, <www.census.gov/programs-surveys/popproj/data/datasets.html>, accessed March 2024.

Table 13. Resident Population Projections by Race and Hispanic Origin: 2025 to 2060

[In thousands, except as indicated (338,016 represents 338,016,000). As of July 1. The 2023 National Projections are based on July 1, 2022 population estimates, which are derived from the Census Bureau's Vintage 2022 Population Estimates and partially based on the 2020 Census through the blended base method. The projections were produced using a cohort-component method and are based on assumptions about future births, deaths, and net international migration. More information on methodology and assumptions is available at <www.census.gov/programs-surveys/popproj/technical-documentation.html>]

Characteristic	2025	2030	2035	2040	2045	2050	2055	2060
Total..	338,016	345,074	350,861	355,309	358,438	360,639	362,450	364,287
One race...................................	327,158	332,809	337,083	339,936	341,424	341,955	342,058	342,122
White....................................	253,416	255,570	256,548	256,274	254,811	252,546	249,976	247,459
Black or African American..........................	46,248	47,622	48,881	50,032	51,087	52,068	53,024	53,997
American Indian and Alaska Native..............	4,464	4,593	4,713	4,820	4,911	4,979	5,023	5,046
Asian...................................	22,115	24,051	25,914	27,729	29,485	31,183	32,810	34,357
Native Hawaiian/Other Pacific Islander..........	915	973	1,027	1,080	1,132	1,180	1,225	1,263
Two or more races...........................	10,858	12,264	13,778	15,374	17,014	18,683	20,392	22,165
Race alone or in combination: [1]								
White....................................	263,126	266,610	269,023	270,268	270,371	269,706	268,778	267,970
Black or African American..........................	51,383	53,572	55,728	57,838	59,890	61,903	63,930	66,030
American Indian and Alaska Native..............	7,455	7,749	8,028	8,286	8,513	8,706	8,866	9,001
Asian...................................	26,166	28,671	31,149	33,615	36,051	38,445	40,784	43,069
Native Hawaiian/Other Pacific Islander..........	1,845	1,989	2,134	2,282	2,428	2,573	2,713	2,850
Not Hispanic................................	**271,359**	**273,397**	**274,142**	**273,659**	**272,155**	**270,115**	**268,046**	**266,293**
One race...................................	262,751	263,691	263,257	261,537	258,765	255,438	252,055	248,939
White....................................	195,478	193,347	190,048	185,644	180,364	174,664	168,993	163,630
Black or African American..........................	42,764	43,880	44,876	45,759	46,543	47,265	47,981	48,736
American Indian and Alaska Native..............	2,435	2,453	2,462	2,458	2,440	2,410	2,373	2,332
Asian...................................	21,409	23,299	25,116	26,880	28,584	30,229	31,805	33,306
Native Hawaiian/Other Pacific Islander..........	665	711	754	795	834	870	904	935
Two or more races...........................	8,608	9,706	10,885	12,123	13,390	14,677	15,992	17,354
Race alone or in combination: [1]								
White....................................	203,179	202,092	199,916	196,696	192,632	188,171	183,771	179,728
Black or African American..........................	46,803	48,559	50,260	51,891	53,452	54,975	56,520	58,147
American Indian and Alaska Native..............	4,528	4,623	4,703	4,759	4,791	4,802	4,803	4,800
Asian...................................	24,832	27,202	29,532	31,840	34,106	36,322	38,479	40,580
Native Hawaiian/Other Pacific Islander........	1,382	1,489	1,596	1,703	1,806	1,905	2,001	2,095
Hispanic [2]................................	**66,657**	**71,677**	**76,719**	**81,650**	**86,283**	**90,524**	**94,404**	**97,994**
One race...................................	64,407	69,118	73,826	78,399	82,659	86,517	90,003	93,183
White....................................	57,938	62,223	66,500	70,630	74,446	77,882	80,983	83,829
Black or African American..........................	3,484	3,742	4,004	4,274	4,544	4,803	5,044	5,262
American Indian and Alaska Native..............	2,029	2,141	2,251	2,362	2,471	2,569	2,650	2,714
Asian...................................	705	751	798	848	900	954	1,005	1,051
Native Hawaiian/Other Pacific Islander..........	250	261	273	285	298	310	321	328
Two or more races...........................	2,250	2,558	2,893	3,251	3,624	4,007	4,400	4,811
Race alone or in combination: [1]								
White....................................	59,947	64,518	69,107	73,573	77,739	81,534	85,007	88,242
Black or African American..........................	4,580	5,013	5,468	5,947	6,439	6,928	7,409	7,882
American Indian and Alaska Native..............	2,928	3,126	3,326	3,527	3,723	3,903	4,063	4,201
Asian...................................	1,334	1,469	1,616	1,775	1,945	2,123	2,305	2,489
Native Hawaiian/Other Pacific Islander........	463	500	538	579	623	667	712	755
PERCENT DISTRIBUTION								
Total..	**100.0**	**100.0**	**100.0**	**100.0**	**100.0**	**100.0**	**100.0**	**100.0**
One race...................................	96.8	96.5	96.1	95.7	95.3	94.8	94.4	93.9
White....................................	75.0	74.1	73.1	72.1	71.1	70.0	69.0	67.9
Black or African American..........................	13.7	13.8	13.9	14.1	14.3	14.4	14.6	14.8
American Indian and Alaska Native..............	1.3	1.3	1.3	1.4	1.4	1.4	1.4	1.4
Asian...................................	6.5	7.0	7.4	7.8	8.2	8.7	9.1	9.4
Native Hawaiian/Other Pacific Islander..........	0.3	0.3	0.3	0.3	0.3	0.3	0.3	0.4
Two or more races...........................	3.2	3.6	3.9	4.3	4.8	5.2	5.6	6.1
Not Hispanic................................	**80.3**	**79.2**	**78.1**	**77.0**	**75.9**	**74.9**	**74.0**	**73.1**
One race...................................	77.7	76.4	75.0	73.6	72.2	70.8	69.5	68.3
White....................................	57.8	56.0	54.2	52.3	50.3	48.4	46.6	44.9
Black or African American..........................	12.7	12.7	12.8	12.9	13.0	13.1	13.2	13.4
American Indian and Alaska Native..............	0.7	0.7	0.7	0.7	0.7	0.7	0.7	0.6
Asian...................................	6.3	6.8	7.2	7.6	8.0	8.4	8.8	9.1
Native Hawaiian/Other Pacific Islander........	0.2	0.2	0.2	0.2	0.2	0.2	0.3	0.3
Two or more races...........................	2.6	2.8	3.1	3.4	3.7	4.1	4.4	4.8
Hispanic [2]................................	**19.7**	**20.8**	**21.9**	**23.0**	**24.1**	**25.1**	**26.1**	**26.9**
One race...................................	19.1	20.0	21.0	22.1	23.1	24.0	24.8	25.6
White....................................	17.1	18.0	19.0	19.9	20.8	21.6	22.3	23.0
Black or African American..........................	1.0	1.1	1.1	1.2	1.3	1.3	1.4	1.4
American Indian and Alaska Native..............	0.6	0.6	0.6	0.7	0.7	0.7	0.7	0.7
Asian...................................	0.2	0.2	0.2	0.2	0.3	0.3	0.3	0.3
Native Hawaiian/Other Pacific Islander........	0.1	0.1	0.1	0.1	0.1	0.1	0.1	0.1
Two or more races...........................	0.7	0.7	0.8	0.9	1.0	1.1	1.2	1.3

[1] In combination with one or more other races. The sum of the five race groups adds to more than the total population because individuals may report more than one race. [2] Persons of Hispanic origin may be of any race.

Source: U.S. Census Bureau, 2023 National Population Projections Datasets, "Table 1. Projected Population by Single Year of Age, Sex, Race, and Hispanic Origin for the United States: 2022 to 2100," November 2023, <www.census.gov/programs-surveys/popproj/data/datasets.html>, accessed March 2024.

Table 14. Resident Population by Region and State: 1990 to 2023

[In thousands (248,791 represents 248,791,000). 1990, 2000, 2010, and 2020 data as of April 1; data for other years as of July 1. Data for 2010-2019 are based on the 2010 Census; beginning 2020, estimates are developed from a base that incorporates the 2020 Census, Vintage 2020 estimates, and 2020 Demographic Analysis estimates. Insofar as possible, population shown for all years is that of present area of state. See Appendix III]

State and region	1990, (April) estimates base [1]	2000, (April) estimates base [2]	2010, (April) estimates base [3]	2015 (July)	2020, (April) estimates base	2020 (July)	2021 (July)	2022 (July)	2023 (July)
United States	**248,791**	**281,425**	**308,758**	**320,739**	**331,465**	**331,527**	**332,049**	**333,271**	**334,915**
Northeast	50,828	53,595	55,318	56,053	57,614	57,430	57,243	57,027	56,984
Midwest	59,669	64,397	66,930	67,886	68,987	68,970	68,850	68,783	68,909
South	85,456	100,235	114,563	121,049	126,269	126,465	127,353	128,702	130,125
West	52,837	63,199	71,947	75,751	78,595	78,661	78,602	78,760	78,897
Alabama	4,040	4,447	4,780	4,855	5,024	5,032	5,050	5,074	5,108
Alaska	550	627	710	738	733	733	735	733	733
Arizona	3,665	5,130	6,392	6,833	7,158	7,187	7,272	7,366	7,431
Arkansas	2,351	2,673	2,916	2,980	3,011	3,014	3,028	3,046	3,068
California	29,811	33,872	37,255	38,904	39,538	39,503	39,145	39,041	38,965
Colorado	3,294	4,302	5,029	5,454	5,774	5,785	5,812	5,841	5,878
Connecticut	3,287	3,406	3,574	3,589	3,606	3,578	3,604	3,609	3,617
Delaware	666	784	898	942	990	992	1,005	1,019	1,032
District of Columbia	607	572	602	677	690	671	669	671	679
Florida	12,938	15,983	18,805	20,219	21,538	21,591	21,831	22,246	22,611
Georgia	6,478	8,187	9,689	10,183	10,714	10,732	10,790	10,913	11,029
Hawaii	1,108	1,211	1,360	1,423	1,455	1,451	1,447	1,439	1,435
Idaho	1,007	1,294	1,568	1,652	1,839	1,849	1,905	1,939	1,965
Illinois	11,431	12,420	12,832	12,860	12,813	12,790	12,690	12,583	12,550
Indiana	5,544	6,081	6,484	6,611	6,785	6,789	6,814	6,832	6,862
Iowa	2,777	2,927	3,047	3,123	3,190	3,191	3,198	3,200	3,207
Kansas	2,478	2,689	2,853	2,911	2,938	2,938	2,938	2,937	2,941
Kentucky	3,687	4,042	4,339	4,429	4,506	4,508	4,508	4,512	4,526
Louisiana	4,222	4,469	4,534	4,667	4,658	4,652	4,627	4,588	4,574
Maine	1,228	1,275	1,328	1,329	1,363	1,365	1,379	1,389	1,396
Maryland	4,781	5,297	5,774	5,989	6,177	6,174	6,175	6,164	6,180
Massachusetts	6,016	6,349	6,548	6,797	7,033	6,998	6,992	6,983	7,001
Michigan	9,295	9,939	9,884	9,934	10,078	10,071	10,038	10,033	10,037
Minnesota	4,376	4,920	5,304	5,484	5,707	5,711	5,718	5,714	5,738
Mississippi	2,575	2,845	2,968	2,990	2,961	2,958	2,950	2,939	2,940
Missouri	5,117	5,597	5,989	6,075	6,155	6,154	6,170	6,177	6,196
Montana	799	902	989	1,031	1,084	1,087	1,106	1,123	1,133
Nebraska	1,578	1,711	1,826	1,892	1,962	1,963	1,964	1,968	1,978
Nevada	1,202	1,998	2,701	2,869	3,105	3,116	3,147	3,177	3,194
New Hampshire	1,109	1,236	1,316	1,337	1,378	1,379	1,387	1,399	1,402
New Jersey	7,748	8,415	8,792	8,870	9,289	9,272	9,269	9,261	9,291
New Mexico	1,515	1,819	2,059	2,090	2,118	2,118	2,117	2,113	2,114
New York	17,991	18,977	19,378	19,657	20,202	20,105	19,855	19,673	19,571
North Carolina	6,632	8,046	9,536	10,037	10,439	10,454	10,567	10,696	10,835
North Dakota	639	642	673	756	779	780	778	779	784
Ohio	10,847	11,353	11,537	11,622	11,799	11,798	11,765	11,760	11,786
Oklahoma	3,146	3,450	3,752	3,911	3,959	3,965	3,992	4,019	4,054
Oregon	2,842	3,422	3,831	4,019	4,237	4,245	4,256	4,239	4,233
Pennsylvania	11,883	12,281	12,703	12,790	13,003	12,995	13,014	12,972	12,962
Rhode Island	1,003	1,048	1,053	1,057	1,097	1,096	1,097	1,094	1,096
South Carolina	3,486	4,012	4,625	4,896	5,118	5,132	5,194	5,283	5,374
South Dakota	696	755	814	855	887	888	896	910	919
Tennessee	4,877	5,689	6,346	6,595	6,911	6,926	6,964	7,049	7,126
Texas	16,986	20,851	25,146	27,469	29,145	29,234	29,561	30,030	30,503
Utah	1,723	2,233	2,764	2,984	3,272	3,284	3,339	3,381	3,418
Vermont	563	609	626	626	643	643	647	647	647
Virginia	6,189	7,079	8,001	8,367	8,631	8,637	8,657	8,679	8,716
Washington	4,867	5,894	6,725	7,167	7,705	7,725	7,741	7,784	7,813
West Virginia	1,793	1,808	1,853	1,843	1,794	1,792	1,785	1,774	1,770
Wisconsin	4,892	5,364	5,687	5,763	5,894	5,897	5,880	5,891	5,911
Wyoming	454	494	564	586	577	578	580	582	584

[1] The April 1, 1990 census counts include corrections processed through August 1997, results of special censuses and test censuses, and do not include adjustments for census coverage errors. [2] The April 1, 2000 population estimates base reflects changes to the Census 2000 population from the Count Question Resolution program, legal boundary updates, and other geographic program revisions. [3] The April 1, 2010 population estimates base reflects changes to the Census 2010 population from the Count Question Resolution program and geographic program revisions.

Source: U.S. Census Bureau, 1990 Census of Population and Housing, Population and Housing Unit Counts (CPH-2); Current Population Reports, P25-1106; "Table CO-EST2001-12-00 - Time Series of Intercensal State Population Estimates: April 1, 1990 to April 1, 2000," April 2002, <www2.census.gov/programs-surveys/popest/tables/1990-2000/intercensal/st-co/co-est2001-12-00.pdf>; "Table 1. Intercensal Estimates of the Resident Population for the United States, Regions, States, and Puerto Rico: April 1, 2000 to July 1, 2010 (ST-EST00INT-01)," September 2011, <www.census.gov/data/tables/time-series/demo/popest/intercensal-2000-2010-state.html>; "Annual Estimates of the Resident Population for the United States, Regions, States, and the District of Columbia: April 1, 2010 to July 1, 2020 (NST-EST2020)," December 2020, <www.census.gov/programs-surveys/popest/technical-documentation/research/evaluation-estimates. html>; and "Annual Estimates of the Resident Population for the United States, Regions, States, District of Columbia, and Puerto Rico: April 1, 2020 to July 1, 2023 (NST-EST2023-POP)," December 2023, <www.census.gov/data/tables/time-series/demo/popest/2020s-national-total. html>.

Table 15. State Population—Rank, Percent Change, and Population Density: 2000 to 2023

[As of April 1, except 2023 as of July 1. Insofar as possible, population shown for all years is that of present area of state. For land area by State, see Table 404. Minus sign (-) indicates decrease. See Appendix III]

State	Rank				Percent change			Population per square mile of land area [1]		
	2000	2010	2020	2023	2000 to 2010	2010 to 2020 [2]	2020 to 2023	2010	2020	2023
United States.........	(X)	(X)	(X)	(X)	**9.7**	**7.4**	**1.0**	**87.4**	**93.8**	**94.8**
Alabama................	23	23	24	24	7.5	5.1	1.7	94.4	99.2	100.9
Alaska.................	48	47	48	48	13.3	3.3	(Z)	1.2	1.3	1.3
Arizona................	20	16	14	14	24.6	12.0	3.8	56.2	63.0	65.4
Arkansas...............	33	32	33	33	9.1	3.3	1.9	56.1	57.9	59.0
California.............	1	1	1	1	10.0	6.1	-1.4	239.0	253.7	250.0
Colorado...............	24	22	21	21	16.9	14.8	1.8	48.5	55.7	56.7
Connecticut............	29	29	29	29	4.9	0.9	0.3	738.1	744.7	747.0
Delaware...............	45	45	45	45	14.6	10.2	4.2	460.8	508.0	529.6
District of Columbia....	(X)	(X)	(X)	(X)	5.2	14.6	-1.5	9,843.3	11,280.0	11,107.0
Florida................	4	4	3	3	17.6	14.5	5.0	350.4	401.4	421.4
Georgia................	10	9	8	8	18.3	10.6	2.9	167.8	185.6	191.1
Hawaii.................	42	40	40	40	12.3	7.0	-1.4	211.8	226.6	223.5
Idaho..................	39	39	38	38	21.1	17.3	6.8	19.0	22.3	23.8
Illinois...............	5	5	6	6	3.3	-0.1	-2.1	231.1	230.8	226.1
Indiana................	14	15	17	17	6.6	4.6	1.1	181.0	189.4	191.5
Iowa...................	30	30	31	31	4.1	4.7	0.5	54.5	57.1	57.4
Kansas.................	32	33	35	34	6.1	3.0	0.1	34.9	35.9	36.0
Kentucky...............	25	26	26	26	7.4	3.8	0.4	109.9	114.1	114.6
Louisiana..............	22	25	25	25	1.4	2.7	-1.8	104.9	107.8	105.8
Maine..................	40	41	42	42	4.2	2.6	2.4	43.1	44.2	45.2
Maryland...............	19	19	18	19	9.0	7.0	(Z)	594.5	636.1	636.4
Massachusetts..........	13	14	15	16	3.1	7.4	-0.4	839.3	901.5	897.5
Michigan...............	8	8	10	10	-0.6	2.0	-0.4	174.6	178.0	177.3
Minnesota..............	21	21	22	22	7.8	7.6	0.5	66.6	71.7	72.1
Mississippi............	31	31	34	35	4.3	-0.2	-0.7	63.2	63.1	62.6
Missouri...............	17	18	19	18	7.0	2.8	0.7	87.1	89.5	90.1
Montana................	44	44	44	43	9.7	9.6	4.5	6.8	7.4	7.8
Nebraska...............	38	38	37	37	6.7	7.4	0.8	23.8	25.5	25.8
Nevada.................	35	35	32	32	35.1	15.0	2.9	24.6	28.3	29.1
New Hampshire..........	41	42	41	41	6.5	4.6	1.8	147.0	153.8	156.6
New Jersey.............	9	11	11	11	4.5	5.7	(Z)	1,195.4	1,263.0	1,263.2
New Mexico.............	36	36	36	36	13.2	2.8	-0.1	17.0	17.5	17.4
New York...............	3	3	4	4	2.1	4.3	-3.1	411.2	428.7	415.3
North Carolina.........	11	10	9	9	18.5	9.5	3.8	196.1	214.7	222.8
North Dakota...........	47	48	47	47	4.7	15.8	0.6	9.7	11.3	11.4
Ohio...................	7	7	7	7	1.6	2.3	-0.1	282.4	288.8	288.5
Oklahoma...............	27	28	28	28	8.7	5.5	2.4	54.7	57.7	59.1
Oregon.................	28	27	27	27	12.0	10.6	-0.1	39.9	44.1	44.1
Pennsylvania...........	6	6	5	5	3.4	2.4	-0.3	283.9	290.6	289.7
Rhode Island...........	43	43	43	44	0.4	4.2	-0.1	1,018.1	1,061.4	1,060.0
South Carolina.........	26	24	23	23	15.3	10.7	5.0	153.8	170.2	178.7
South Dakota...........	46	46	46	46	7.9	8.9	3.7	10.7	11.7	12.1
Tennessee..............	16	17	16	15	11.5	8.9	3.1	153.9	167.6	172.8
Texas..................	2	2	2	2	20.6	15.9	4.7	96.2	111.6	116.8
Utah...................	34	34	30	30	23.8	18.4	4.5	33.6	39.7	41.5
Vermont................	49	49	49	49	2.8	2.8	0.7	67.9	69.8	70.2
Virginia...............	12	12	12	12	13.0	7.9	1.0	202.6	218.6	220.8
Washington.............	15	13	13	13	14.1	14.6	1.4	101.2	115.9	117.6
West Virginia..........	37	37	39	39	2.5	-3.2	-1.3	77.1	74.6	73.6
Wisconsin..............	18	20	20	20	6.0	3.6	0.3	105.0	108.8	109.1
Wyoming................	50	50	50	50	14.1	2.3	1.2	5.8	5.9	6.0

X Not applicable. Z less than 0.05 percent. [1] Persons per square mile were calculated on the basis of 2020 land area data. [2] Based on 2010 population estimates base that reflects changes to the Census 2010 population from the Count Question Resolution program and geographic program revisions.

Source: U.S. Census Bureau, *2000 Census of Population and Housing, PHC-3-1, United States Summary*, 2004, <www.census.gov/prod/cen2000/phc3-us-pt1.pdf>; *2010 Census Briefs, Population Distribution and Change: 2000 to 2010*, March 2011, <www.census.gov/prod/cen2010/briefs/c2010br-01.pdf>; "QuickFacts," <www.census.gov/quickfacts/>, accessed August 2023; and "Annual and Cumulative Estimates of Resident Population Change for the United States, Regions, States, District of Columbia, and Puerto Rico and Region and State Rankings: April 1, 2020 to July 1, 2023 (NST-EST2023-CHG)," December 2023, <www.census.gov/data/tables/time-series/demo/popest/2020s-state-total.html>.

Table 16. State and Region Resident Population—Components of Change: 2020 to 2023

[Covers period April 1, 2020 to July 1, 2023. Minus sign (-) indicates net decrease or net outflow]

State and region	Numeric population change [1]	Births	Deaths	Natural change (births minus deaths)	Net migration Total	Inter-national [2]	Domestic
United States............	**3,449,947**	**11,811,192**	**10,895,395**	**915,797**	**2,534,150**	**2,534,150**	**(X)**
Northeast...................	-630,624	1,889,402	1,842,927	46,475	-661,666	520,034	-1,181,700
Midwest....................	-78,013	2,438,549	2,420,819	17,730	-111,617	368,719	-480,336
South.....................	3,856,761	4,740,236	4,402,589	337,647	3,508,262	1,071,260	2,437,002
West......................	301,823	2,743,005	2,229,060	513,945	-200,829	574,137	-774,966
Alabama...................	84,174	187,408	211,321	-23,913	108,227	11,689	96,538
Alaska....................	32	30,481	18,422	12,059	-12,060	5,296	-17,356
Arizona...................	273,442	251,434	248,900	2,534	270,441	52,194	218,247
Arkansas..................	56,242	115,300	125,490	-10,190	66,041	8,751	57,290
California.................	-573,019	1,353,681	1,040,617	313,064	-874,952	322,998	-1,197,950
Colorado..................	103,903	202,910	153,093	49,817	53,082	26,501	26,581
Connecticut...............	11,264	112,936	114,184	-1,248	15,968	37,453	-21,485
Delaware..................	41,944	34,361	36,572	-2,211	44,124	5,656	38,468
District of Columbia......	-10,576	26,721	18,433	8,288	-15,161	13,291	-28,452
Florida....................	1,072,510	703,817	798,173	-94,356	1,168,132	349,370	818,762
Georgia...................	315,456	402,386	342,499	59,887	253,772	68,020	185,752
Hawaii....................	-20,136	50,277	41,182	9,095	-28,964	12,706	-41,670
Idaho.....................	125,609	72,191	56,525	15,666	111,512	7,199	104,313
Illinois...................	-263,780	422,189	407,527	14,662	-280,776	83,667	-364,443
Indiana...................	76,757	256,969	248,835	8,134	67,089	39,751	27,338
Iowa......................	16,577	118,737	112,362	6,375	9,309	20,367	-11,058
Kansas....................	2,711	111,993	103,411	8,582	-6,819	11,654	-18,473
Kentucky..................	19,857	168,707	186,981	-18,274	36,533	13,942	22,591
Louisiana.................	-84,036	183,333	178,649	4,684	-89,834	20,875	-110,709
Maine.....................	32,545	38,541	54,795	-16,254	48,601	5,783	42,818
Maryland..................	3,000	221,460	187,253	34,207	-33,517	66,062	-99,579
Massachusetts............	-31,534	221,010	208,755	12,255	-38,502	110,964	-149,466
Michigan..................	-40,413	335,709	370,139	-34,430	-9,343	49,036	-58,379
Minnesota.................	31,111	207,857	167,489	40,368	-11,352	34,624	-45,976
Mississippi................	-21,616	112,921	128,144	-15,223	-6,904	7,040	-13,944
Missouri..................	41,267	223,250	236,234	-12,984	53,416	22,111	31,305
Montana..................	48,568	36,078	38,942	-2,864	51,602	3,158	48,444
Nebraska.................	16,414	78,825	62,001	16,824	-860	11,156	-12,016
Nevada...................	89,559	108,125	102,156	5,969	83,038	18,194	64,844
New Hampshire...........	24,530	39,525	46,128	-6,603	30,472	6,323	24,149
New Jersey................	1,802	327,246	277,066	50,180	-49,614	103,579	-153,193
New Mexico...............	-3,154	68,639	77,977	-9,338	5,810	11,898	-6,088
New York.................	-631,104	676,026	592,082	83,944	-701,412	181,264	-882,676
North Carolina............	396,032	388,209	367,758	20,451	376,420	66,231	310,189
North Dakota.............	4,847	32,070	23,852	8,218	-3,152	4,040	-7,192
Ohio......................	-13,396	418,233	460,941	-42,708	26,900	61,616	-34,716
Oklahoma.................	94,413	155,246	158,333	-3,087	96,467	16,403	80,064
Oregon...................	-3,921	129,508	141,143	-11,635	7,358	14,324	-6,966
Pennsylvania..............	-41,105	424,237	491,580	-67,343	21,873	62,322	-40,449
Rhode Island.............	-1,409	32,968	36,233	-3,265	1,445	9,589	-8,144
South Carolina............	255,133	184,396	202,464	-18,068	272,176	24,121	248,055
South Dakota.............	32,650	36,588	29,581	7,007	25,245	5,734	19,511
Tennessee................	215,703	263,010	281,168	-18,158	231,466	24,369	207,097
Texas.....................	1,357,842	1,227,704	820,137	407,567	947,383	291,163	656,220
Utah......................	146,120	149,901	71,496	78,405	67,362	17,921	49,441
Vermont..................	4,387	16,913	22,104	-5,191	9,503	2,757	6,746
Virginia...................	84,325	309,542	269,795	39,747	43,207	80,621	-37,414
Washington...............	107,613	270,104	218,608	51,496	57,413	80,910	-23,497
West Virginia..............	-23,642	55,715	89,419	-33,704	9,730	3,656	6,074
Wisconsin.................	17,242	196,129	198,447	-2,318	18,726	24,963	-6,237
Wyoming.................	7,207	19,676	19,999	-323	7,529	838	6,691
Puerto Rico..............	-80,183	61,842	109,878	-48,036	-32,147	-32,147	(X)

X Not applicable. [1] Total population change includes a residual. This residual represents the change in population that cannot be attributed to any specific demographic component. [2] Net international migration for the United States includes the international migration of both native and foreign-born populations. Specifically, it includes: (a) the net international migration of the foreign born, (b) the net migration of natives to and from the United States, (c) the net migration between the United States and Puerto Rico, and (d) the net movement of the Armed Forces population between the United States and overseas.

Source: U.S. Census Bureau, Population Division, State Population Totals and Components of Change: 2020-2023, "Annual and Cumulative Estimates of the Components of Resident Population Change for the United States, Regions, States, District of Columbia, and Puerto Rico: April 1, 2020 to July 1, 2023 (NST-EST2023-COMP)," December 2023, <www.census.gov/data/tables/time-series/demo/popest/2020s-state-total.html>.

Table 17. Resident Population by Age and State: 2023

[In thousands (334,915 represents 334,915,000), unless otherwise noted. As of July 1. Estimates are developed from a base that incorporates the 2020 Census, Vintage 2020 estimates, and 2020 Demographic Analysis estimates]

State	Total	Under 5 years	5 to 14 years	15 to 24 years	25 to 34 years	35 to 44 years	45 to 54 years	55 to 64 years	65 to 74 years	75 to 84 years	85 years and over	Median age (years)	Percent 65 years old and over
United States	**334,915**	**18,511**	**40,987**	**43,887**	**45,543**	**44,391**	**40,494**	**41,854**	**34,685**	**18,368**	**6,195**	**39.1**	**17.7**
Alabama	5,108	293	632	686	661	631	619	654	551	291	90	39.5	18.3
Alaska	733	46	100	96	112	106	83	85	69	29	7	36.1	14.4
Arizona	7,431	394	892	1,002	1,027	944	859	880	805	480	149	39.2	19.3
Arkansas	3,068	181	396	415	400	388	362	376	320	175	56	38.7	18.0
California	38,965	2,098	4,779	5,131	5,672	5,450	4,847	4,676	3,661	1,947	704	38.2	16.2
Colorado	5,878	309	681	765	924	864	714	677	575	282	86	37.9	16.0
Connecticut	3,617	181	403	474	453	465	444	507	395	216	80	41.3	19.1
Delaware	1,032	54	119	126	128	127	116	143	132	68	20	41.9	21.3
District of Columbia	679	39	70	85	147	114	72	63	51	27	11	34.9	13.1
Florida	22,611	1,125	2,457	2,614	2,835	2,875	2,762	3,027	2,673	1,660	583	42.8	21.7
Georgia	11,029	636	1,427	1,521	1,525	1,475	1,404	1,345	1,021	524	151	37.7	15.4
Hawaii	1,435	78	168	163	186	193	169	176	166	95	41	41.3	21.1
Idaho	1,965	113	266	282	255	257	225	226	205	106	30	37.6	17.4
Illinois	12,550	665	1,531	1,648	1,690	1,675	1,553	1,584	1,292	669	243	39.4	17.6
Indiana	6,862	406	892	950	901	870	819	844	703	355	121	38.2	17.2
Iowa	3,207	186	410	454	400	404	362	396	346	178	71	38.9	18.6
Kansas	2,941	175	393	426	377	379	330	348	303	153	58	37.7	17.5
Kentucky	4,526	264	569	591	595	566	554	580	484	247	76	39.4	17.8
Louisiana	4,574	279	597	607	599	608	524	566	479	240	75	38.4	17.4
Maine	1,396	62	140	158	169	173	167	206	190	99	32	44.8	23.0
Maryland	6,180	350	766	765	800	848	767	817	623	330	114	39.7	17.3
Massachusetts	7,001	344	748	931	971	924	847	943	753	398	142	40.3	18.5
Michigan	10,037	530	1,191	1,314	1,319	1,224	1,193	1,339	1,154	584	188	40.4	19.2
Minnesota	5,738	328	736	743	738	781	662	725	603	304	116	39.1	17.8
Mississippi	2,940	174	376	413	376	365	351	367	309	158	51	38.7	17.6
Missouri	6,196	352	772	815	813	799	720	789	668	349	120	39.3	18.3
Montana	1,133	58	134	146	148	147	126	142	141	70	22	40.5	20.5
Nebraska	1,978	124	271	281	253	260	221	230	201	101	38	37.4	17.2
Nevada	3,194	171	388	381	458	446	399	395	331	178	47	39.3	17.4
New Hampshire	1,402	63	141	168	179	177	170	214	175	87	29	43.4	20.8
New Jersey	9,291	519	1,125	1,138	1,190	1,234	1,187	1,249	950	512	187	40.4	17.7
New Mexico	2,114	107	257	288	277	273	236	258	246	133	40	39.6	19.8
New York	19,571	1,039	2,220	2,442	2,736	2,546	2,362	2,592	2,078	1,123	433	40.1	18.6
North Carolina	10,835	606	1,302	1,451	1,458	1,384	1,353	1,373	1,133	597	178	39.3	17.6
North Dakota	784	49	105	118	110	103	79	87	78	38	18	36.0	17.0
Ohio	11,786	659	1,450	1,514	1,552	1,485	1,397	1,520	1,314	669	227	39.8	18.7
Oklahoma	4,054	244	548	572	547	536	463	470	398	208	67	37.2	16.6
Oregon	4,233	202	473	514	589	596	523	505	491	261	77	40.6	19.6
Pennsylvania	12,962	666	1,480	1,647	1,663	1,649	1,523	1,737	1,507	796	292	41.1	20.0
Rhode Island	1,096	52	114	147	151	142	128	151	123	64	24	40.8	19.3
South Carolina	5,374	292	641	698	689	671	641	702	620	329	90	40.4	19.3
South Dakota	919	58	125	124	115	117	98	113	103	47	19	38.2	18.4
Tennessee	7,126	411	875	919	987	912	877	903	742	387	113	39.0	17.4
Texas	30,503	1,937	4,267	4,324	4,401	4,308	3,739	3,339	2,534	1,262	392	35.7	13.7
Utah	3,418	231	527	575	509	465	385	309	254	127	37	32.3	12.2
Vermont	647	27	65	86	77	81	76	92	86	44	13	43.4	22.1
Virginia	8,716	486	1,056	1,141	1,171	1,186	1,075	1,102	877	472	150	39.2	17.2
Washington	7,813	421	934	949	1,184	1,133	933	922	800	410	127	38.5	17.1
West Virginia	1,770	87	199	221	214	210	222	235	224	120	37	42.9	21.5
Wisconsin	5,911	310	704	788	740	749	689	802	680	336	114	40.6	19.1
Wyoming	584	31	74	78	73	78	66	72	69	32	10	39.7	19.2

Source: U.S. Census Bureau, State Population by Characteristics: 2020-2023, "Annual Estimates of the Resident Population for Selected Age Groups by Sex: April 1, 2020 to July 1, 2023 (SC-EST2023-AGESEX)," <www.census.gov/data/tables/time-series/demo/popest/2020s-state-detail.html>, accessed July 2024.

Table 18. Age Dependency Ratios by State: 2010 to 2023

[2010 and 2020, as of April. 2023 as of July. Estimates for 2020 and 2023 are developed from a base that incorporates the 2020 Census, Vintage 2020 estimates, and 2020 Demographic Analysis estimates]

State	Age dependency ratio [1]			Child dependency ratio [2]			Old-age dependency ratio [3]		
	2010	2020	2023	2010	2020	2023	2010	2020	2023
United States.........	**58.9**	**63.4**	**65.1**	**38.2**	**36.7**	**35.9**	**20.7**	**26.7**	**29.2**
Alabama...............	59.9	65.7	67.7	37.9	37.3	37.1	22.0	28.4	30.6
Alaska................	51.8	59.5	62.0	40.0	39.3	38.8	11.7	20.2	23.3
Arizona...............	64.7	68.1	68.4	42.0	37.6	35.9	22.7	30.5	32.5
Arkansas.............	63.4	68.3	69.4	39.9	39.5	39.0	23.5	28.7	30.4
California.............	57.1	59.5	61.0	39.2	36.1	34.9	17.9	23.4	26.1
Colorado..............	54.6	57.5	58.0	37.7	34.4	32.7	16.9	23.1	25.4
Connecticut..........	58.8	61.6	64.2	36.3	33.3	32.8	22.5	28.3	31.4
Delaware.............	59.5	68.0	71.8	36.6	35.7	35.3	23.0	32.4	36.5
District of Columbia....	39.3	43.9	46.4	23.3	26.4	27.3	15.9	17.6	19.1
Florida................	62.9	68.3	69.8	34.7	33.4	32.9	28.2	34.8	36.9
Georgia...............	57.2	61.4	62.3	40.4	38.4	37.4	16.7	22.9	25.0
Hawaii................	57.9	67.3	71.0	35.3	35.4	35.0	22.7	31.9	36.1
Idaho.................	66.1	69.8	69.9	45.5	42.2	40.4	20.6	27.5	29.5
Illinois................	58.6	62.5	64.3	38.7	36.6	35.4	19.9	26.0	28.8
Indiana...............	60.7	65.7	67.5	39.9	39.2	38.8	20.9	26.5	28.8
Iowa..................	63.3	68.5	70.5	39.0	39.3	38.8	24.3	29.2	31.7
Kansas...............	63.0	67.8	69.7	41.5	40.8	40.1	21.5	27.0	29.6
Kentucky..............	58.5	65.1	67.5	37.4	37.7	37.6	21.1	27.4	29.9
Louisiana.............	58.6	65.4	68.6	39.1	39.3	39.3	19.5	26.1	29.3
Maine.................	57.6	66.2	69.0	32.6	31.0	30.2	25.0	35.2	38.9
Maryland..............	55.5	61.8	64.7	36.4	36.4	36.3	19.1	25.4	28.4
Massachusetts.........	54.9	57.9	60.4	33.6	31.3	30.7	21.4	26.6	29.6
Michigan..............	60.0	64.6	67.3	37.9	35.7	35.2	22.0	28.9	32.1
Minnesota............	59.0	65.5	68.1	38.5	38.6	38.1	20.5	26.8	30.0
Mississippi............	62.0	66.7	68.7	41.2	39.5	39.0	20.8	27.3	29.7
Missouri...............	60.8	65.9	68.1	38.3	37.6	37.3	22.5	28.3	30.8
Montana..............	59.8	68.8	70.3	36.1	36.4	35.4	23.7	32.4	34.9
Nebraska.............	63.0	69.0	70.9	41.0	42.1	41.5	22.0	26.9	29.3
Nevada...............	57.8	62.9	63.6	38.9	36.6	35.1	19.0	26.3	28.5
New Hampshire........	54.7	60.1	63.3	33.8	30.2	29.4	20.9	29.9	34.0
New Jersey............	58.7	62.6	65.0	37.3	36.0	35.7	21.4	26.6	29.3
New Mexico............	62.4	68.9	69.9	40.9	38.2	36.3	21.5	30.7	33.6
New York..............	55.8	60.6	63.4	34.8	33.6	33.1	21.1	27.0	30.3
North Carolina.........	58.4	63.0	64.4	37.9	36.2	35.5	20.5	26.8	29.0
North Dakota..........	58.2	65.6	68.3	35.2	39.6	39.7	22.9	26.0	28.6
Ohio..................	60.6	65.8	68.4	38.0	37.1	36.8	22.6	28.8	31.6
Oklahoma.............	62.1	67.0	68.0	40.2	40.7	40.0	21.9	26.4	27.9
Oregon...............	57.6	63.1	64.6	35.6	33.7	32.3	21.9	29.4	32.2
Pennsylvania..........	59.8	64.9	67.5	35.1	34.4	34.0	24.6	30.6	33.5
Rhode Island..........	55.5	58.7	61.0	33.1	30.7	30.0	22.5	28.0	31.1
South Carolina........	58.8	66.3	68.4	37.1	36.3	35.9	21.7	29.9	32.5
South Dakota..........	64.5	72.1	73.9	41.0	42.5	42.0	23.6	29.5	31.9
Tennessee.............	58.8	63.8	65.2	37.4	36.9	36.4	21.4	26.9	28.8
Texas.................	60.4	62.5	62.6	43.8	41.6	40.3	16.6	20.8	22.3
Utah..................	68.2	67.6	65.3	53.0	48.7	45.1	15.2	18.9	20.2
Vermont...............	54.3	62.7	66.1	31.9	30.1	29.4	22.5	32.6	36.7
Virginia...............	54.7	61.1	63.4	35.9	35.7	35.3	18.9	25.4	28.1
Washington...........	55.8	60.6	61.9	36.6	35.4	34.1	19.2	25.2	27.7
West Virginia..........	58.6	68.0	70.7	33.2	34.0	34.0	25.5	34.0	36.7
Wisconsin.............	59.3	64.9	67.4	37.5	36.2	35.4	21.8	28.7	32.0
Wyoming..............	57.4	68.1	70.5	37.8	39.0	37.8	19.6	29.1	32.6

[1] The age dependency ratio is derived by dividing the sum of populations age under 18 and age 65 and over by the population age 18-64, and multiplying by 100. [2] The child dependency ratio is derived by dividing the population under age 18 by the population age 18-64, and multiplying by 100. [3] The old-age dependency ratio is derived by dividing the population age 65 and over by the population age 18-64, and multiplying by 100.

Source: U.S. Census Bureau, Census 2010 Briefs, "Age and Sex Composition: 2010," May 2011; and State Population by Characteristics: 2020-2023, "Annual Estimates of the Resident Population for Selected Age Groups by Sex: April 1, 2020 to July 1, 2023 (SC-EST2023-AGESEX)," <www.census.gov/data/tables/time-series/demo/popest/2020s-state-detail.html>, accessed July 2024.

Table 19. Resident Population by Hispanic Origin and State: 2023

[In thousands, except as indicated (334,915 represents 334,915,000). As of July 1. The estimates are developed from a base that incorporates the 2020 Census, Vintage 2020 estimates, and 2020 Demographic Analysis estimates. Hispanic origin is considered an ethnicity, not a race. Persons of Hispanic origin may be of any race]

State	Number (1,000)				Percent of total		
	Total population	Hispanic or Latino	Total Non-Hispanic	Non-Hispanic White alone	Hispanic or Latino	Total Non-Hispanic	Non-Hispanic White alone
United States.........	**334,915**	**65,219**	**269,696**	**195,433**	**19.5**	**80.5**	**58.4**
Alabama..............	5,108	290	4,818	3,275	5.7	94.3	64.1
Alaska................	733	55	679	433	7.5	92.5	59.0
Arizona..............	7,431	2,347	5,085	3,966	31.6	68.4	53.4
Arkansas.............	3,068	284	2,784	2,155	9.2	90.8	70.2
California.............	38,965	15,760	23,205	13,362	40.4	59.6	34.3
Colorado.............	5,878	1,336	4,541	3,882	22.7	77.3	66.1
Connecticut...........	3,617	673	2,944	2,288	18.6	81.4	63.3
Delaware.............	1,032	115	917	608	11.1	88.9	58.9
District of Columbia....	679	81	598	256	12.0	88.0	37.7
Florida................	22,611	6,197	16,413	11,743	27.4	72.6	51.9
Georgia..............	11,029	1,228	9,801	5,466	11.1	88.9	49.6
Hawaii...............	1,435	145	1,290	309	10.1	89.9	21.5
Idaho................	1,965	272	1,693	1,577	13.8	86.2	80.3
Illinois...............	12,550	2,383	10,166	7,378	19.0	81.0	58.8
Indiana...............	6,862	602	6,260	5,217	8.8	91.2	76.0
Iowa.................	3,207	239	2,968	2,665	7.4	92.6	83.1
Kansas...............	2,941	404	2,537	2,168	13.7	86.3	73.7
Kentucky.............	4,526	228	4,298	3,728	5.0	95.0	82.4
Louisiana.............	4,574	332	4,242	2,591	7.3	92.7	56.6
Maine................	1,396	32	1,364	1,281	2.3	97.7	91.8
Maryland.............	6,180	781	5,399	2,921	12.6	87.4	47.3
Massachusetts.........	7,001	944	6,057	4,819	13.5	86.5	68.8
Michigan.............	10,037	600	9,437	7,393	6.0	94.0	73.7
Minnesota............	5,738	371	5,367	4,412	6.5	93.5	76.9
Mississippi............	2,940	114	2,826	1,636	3.9	96.1	55.6
Missouri..............	6,196	331	5,865	4,827	5.3	94.7	77.9
Montana..............	1,133	54	1,079	964	4.7	95.3	85.1
Nebraska.............	1,978	256	1,722	1,507	12.9	87.1	76.2
Nevada...............	3,194	956	2,238	1,452	29.9	70.1	45.4
New Hampshire........	1,402	68	1,334	1,241	4.8	95.2	88.5
New Jersey...........	9,291	2,105	7,185	4,834	22.7	77.3	52.0
New Mexico...........	2,114	1,027	1,087	777	48.6	51.4	36.8
New York.............	19,571	3,873	15,698	10,577	19.8	80.2	54.0
North Carolina.........	10,835	1,238	9,597	6,573	11.4	88.6	60.7
North Dakota..........	784	38	746	648	4.9	95.1	82.6
Ohio.................	11,786	571	11,215	9,044	4.8	95.2	76.7
Oklahoma.............	4,054	523	3,531	2,539	12.9	87.1	62.6
Oregon...............	4,233	632	3,602	3,083	14.9	85.1	72.8
Pennsylvania..........	12,962	1,154	11,808	9,600	8.9	91.1	74.1
Rhode Island..........	1,096	197	899	759	18.0	82.0	69.2
South Carolina........	5,374	401	4,973	3,379	7.5	92.5	62.9
South Dakota..........	919	47	873	740	5.1	94.9	80.5
Tennessee............	7,126	536	6,591	5,130	7.5	92.5	72.0
Texas................	30,503	12,136	18,368	12,089	39.8	60.2	39.6
Utah.................	3,418	547	2,871	2,588	16.0	84.0	75.7
Vermont..............	647	17	630	592	2.6	97.4	91.5
Virginia..............	8,716	975	7,741	5,151	11.2	88.8	59.1
Washington...........	7,813	1,142	6,671	5,015	14.6	85.4	64.2
West Virginia..........	1,770	40	1,730	1,610	2.2	97.8	90.9
Wisconsin.............	5,911	478	5,433	4,700	8.1	91.9	79.5
Wyoming.............	584	63	521	485	10.8	89.2	83.1

Source: U.S. Census Bureau, State Population by Characteristics: 2020-2023, Datasets, "Age, Sex, Race, and Hispanic Origin - 6 race groups," <www.census.gov/data/tables/time-series/demo/popest/2020s-state-detail.html>, accessed July 2024.

Table 20. Resident Population by Race and State: 2023

[334,915 represents 334,915,000. As of July 1. The estimates are developed from a base that incorporates the 2020 Census, Vintage 2020 estimates, and 2020 Demographic Analysis estimates]

State	Total population	Number (1,000)						Percent distribution					
		White [1]	Black [1]	American Indian [1,2]	Asian [1]	Native Hawaiian [1,3]	Two or more races	White [1]	Black [1]	American Indian [1,2]	Asian [1]	Native Hawaiian [1,3]	Two or more races
U.S.	334,915	252,066	45,757	4,486	21,387	900	10,319	75.3	13.7	1.3	6.4	0.3	3.1
AL	5,108	3,519	1,360	38	82	6	103	68.9	26.6	0.7	1.6	0.1	2.0
AK	733	470	27	114	50	12	59	64.2	3.7	15.6	6.8	1.7	8.1
AZ	7,431	6,056	423	384	304	22	243	81.5	5.7	5.2	4.1	0.3	3.3
AR	3,068	2,406	478	35	58	15	76	78.4	15.6	1.1	1.9	0.5	2.5
CA	38,965	27,428	2,528	677	6,438	205	1,689	70.4	6.5	1.7	16.5	0.5	4.3
CO	5,878	5,052	283	99	225	13	205	86.0	4.8	1.7	3.8	0.2	3.5
CT	3,617	2,822	474	28	188	4	101	78.0	13.1	0.8	5.2	0.1	2.8
DE	1,032	697	248	8	46	1	32	67.6	24.1	0.7	4.4	0.1	3.1
DC	679	316	301	5	33	1	22	46.6	44.4	0.7	4.9	0.2	3.3
FL	22,611	17,333	3,829	129	728	29	561	76.7	16.9	0.6	3.2	0.1	2.5
GA	11,029	6,474	3,662	65	537	15	276	58.7	33.2	0.6	4.9	0.1	2.5
HI	1,435	362	31	6	536	148	353	25.2	2.2	0.4	37.3	10.3	24.6
ID	1,965	1,817	20	34	34	5	56	92.5	1.0	1.7	1.7	0.2	2.8
IL	12,550	9,541	1,836	81	794	9	289	76.0	14.6	0.6	6.3	0.1	2.3
IN	6,862	5,743	715	32	197	6	169	83.7	10.4	0.5	2.9	0.1	2.5
IA	3,207	2,875	145	20	87	9	71	89.6	4.5	0.6	2.7	0.3	2.2
KS	2,941	2,524	182	37	94	5	98	85.9	6.2	1.3	3.2	0.2	3.3
KY	4,526	3,923	396	15	81	6	105	86.7	8.8	0.3	1.8	0.1	2.3
LA	4,574	2,861	1,491	41	88	3	90	62.6	32.6	0.9	1.9	0.1	2.0
ME	1,396	1,308	30	10	19	1	28	93.7	2.1	0.7	1.4	(Z)	2.0
MD	6,180	3,534	1,951	48	438	8	202	57.2	31.6	0.8	7.1	0.1	3.3
MA	7,001	5,530	675	39	551	8	198	79.0	9.6	0.6	7.9	0.1	2.8
MI	10,037	7,899	1,416	76	358	5	284	78.7	14.1	0.8	3.6	(Z)	2.8
MN	5,738	4,720	450	81	317	2	165	82.3	7.9	1.4	5.5	0.1	2.9
MS	2,940	1,726	1,112	19	35	2	45	58.7	37.8	0.7	1.2	0.1	1.5
MO	6,196	5,105	725	39	144	13	169	82.4	11.7	0.6	2.3	0.2	2.7
MT	1,133	1,005	7	73	12	1	35	88.7	0.6	6.4	1.1	0.1	3.1
NE	1,978	1,726	108	33	56	3	52	87.3	5.5	1.7	2.8	0.1	2.6
NV	3,194	2,284	351	55	311	29	166	71.5	11.0	1.7	9.7	0.9	5.2
NH	1,402	1,297	29	5	44	1	27	92.5	2.1	0.3	3.1	0.1	1.9
NJ	9,291	6,541	1,443	72	989	14	232	70.4	15.5	0.8	10.6	0.1	2.5
NM	2,114	1,707	60	241	43	4	60	80.7	2.8	11.4	2.0	0.2	2.8
NY	19,571	13,409	3,457	209	1,904	29	563	68.5	17.7	1.1	9.7	0.1	2.9
NC	10,835	7,565	2,392	173	399	17	290	69.8	22.1	1.6	3.7	0.2	2.7
ND	784	678	29	41	14	1	20	86.4	3.8	5.3	1.7	0.1	2.6
OH	11,786	9,503	1,582	41	331	9	323	80.6	13.4	0.3	2.8	0.1	2.7
OK	4,054	2,954	321	387	107	10	274	72.9	7.9	9.5	2.6	0.3	6.8
OR	4,233	3,624	101	81	220	21	186	85.6	2.4	1.9	5.2	0.5	4.4
PA	12,962	10,441	1,589	61	542	13	316	80.6	12.3	0.5	4.2	0.1	2.4
RI	1,096	903	101	14	41	2	34	82.4	9.3	1.3	3.7	0.2	3.1
SC	5,374	3,709	1,395	33	110	6	122	69.0	26.0	0.6	2.0	0.1	2.3
SD	919	774	24	78	16	1	25	84.2	2.6	8.5	1.8	0.1	2.8
TN	7,126	5,585	1,178	41	151	8	164	78.4	16.5	0.6	2.1	0.1	2.3
TX	30,503	23,436	4,158	331	1,819	50	709	76.8	13.6	1.1	6.0	0.2	2.3
UT	3,418	3,069	55	54	98	40	103	89.8	1.6	1.6	2.9	1.2	3.0
VT	647	606	10	3	14	(Z)	14	93.6	1.6	0.4	2.1	(Z)	2.2
VA	8,716	5,955	1,744	54	645	12	306	68.3	20.0	0.6	7.4	0.1	3.5
WA	7,813	5,963	365	157	840	68	420	76.3	4.7	2.0	10.8	0.9	5.4
WV	1,770	1,643	67	5	16	1	38	92.8	3.8	0.3	0.9	(Z)	2.1
WI	5,911	5,110	392	73	196	4	136	86.4	6.6	1.2	3.3	0.1	2.3
WY	584	539	7	16	7	1	14	92.3	1.2	2.8	1.2	0.1	2.4

Z Less than 500 or 0.05 percent. [1] Data shown for each race alone. [2] Includes Alaska Natives. [3] Includes Other Pacific Islanders.

Source: U.S. Census Bureau, State Population by Characteristics: 2020-2023, Datasets, "Age, Sex, Race, and Hispanic Origin - 6 race groups," <www.census.gov/data/tables/time-series/demo/popest/2020s-state-detail.html>, accessed July 2024.

Table 21. Large Metropolitan Statistical Areas—Population: 2020 to 2023

[Covers metropolitan statistical areas with population of 250,000 and over in 2023, as delineated by the U.S. Office of Management and Budget as of July 2023. Estimates are developed from a base that incorporates the 2020 Census, Vintage 2020 estimates, and 2020 Demographic Analysis estimates. For definitions and components of all metropolitan and micropolitan areas, see Appendix II. Minus sign (-) indicates decrease]

Metropolitan statistical area	2020 estimates base (April)	2020 (July)	2022 (July)	2023 (July)	Cumulative change, April 2020 to July 2023		Rank, 2023
					Number	Percent	
Akron, OH.	702,225	701,674	697,511	698,398	-3,827	-0.5	85
Albany-Schenectady-Troy, NY.	899,247	899,724	903,595	904,682	5,435	0.6	64
Albuquerque, NM.	916,545	917,579	920,138	922,296	5,751	0.6	61
Allentown-Bethlehem-Easton, PA-NJ.	861,910	861,557	870,570	873,555	11,645	1.4	67
Amarillo, TX.	268,683	269,029	270,589	272,395	3,712	1.4	184
Anchorage, AK.	398,312	398,397	400,455	401,314	3,002	0.8	137
Ann Arbor, MI.	372,258	371,834	366,504	365,536	-6,722	-1.8	153
Asheville, NC.	406,933	407,563	413,969	417,202	10,269	2.5	131
Atlanta-Sandy Springs-Roswell, GA.	6,106,847	6,120,849	6,238,676	6,307,261	200,414	3.3	6
Atlantic City-Hammonton, NJ.	369,798	369,234	370,787	369,823	25	(Z)	151
Augusta-Richmond County, GA-SC.	610,978	612,172	623,985	629,429	18,451	3.0	92
Austin-Round Rock-San Marcos, TX.	2,283,379	2,300,135	2,423,170	2,473,275	189,896	8.3	26
Bakersfield-Delano, CA.	909,229	905,910	916,751	913,820	4,591	0.5	62
Baltimore-Columbia-Towson, MD.	2,844,523	2,842,668	2,834,813	2,834,316	-10,207	-0.4	20
Baton Rouge, LA.	870,580	870,286	872,347	873,661	3,081	0.4	66
Beaumont-Port Arthur, TX.	397,566	397,237	394,489	395,479	-2,087	-0.5	140
Bend, OR.	247,497	248,974	258,184	260,919	13,422	5.4	192
Birmingham, AL.	1,180,632	1,181,776	1,180,786	1,184,290	3,658	0.3	47
Boise City, ID.	764,714	770,223	811,355	824,657	59,943	7.8	74
Boston-Cambridge-Newton, MA-NH.	4,944,611	4,933,650	4,903,026	4,919,179	-25,432	-0.5	11
Boulder, CO.	330,759	330,938	327,339	326,831	-3,928	-1.2	162
Bremerton-Silverdale-Port Orchard, WA.	275,612	275,823	277,813	277,658	2,046	0.7	181
Bridgeport-Stamford-Danbury, CT.	946,293	942,755	949,982	951,558	5,265	0.6	59
Brownsville-Harlingen, TX.	421,020	421,480	424,911	426,710	5,690	1.4	127
Buffalo-Cheektowaga, NY.	1,166,897	1,164,468	1,158,890	1,155,604	-11,293	-1.0	50
Canton-Massillon, OH.	401,580	401,224	399,471	399,474	-2,106	-0.5	138
Cape Coral-Fort Myers, FL.	760,814	765,547	822,391	834,573	73,759	9.7	72
Cedar Rapids, IA.	276,524	276,621	275,631	275,668	-856	-0.3	182
Charleston-North Charleston, SC.	799,636	803,475	830,352	849,417	49,781	6.2	71
Charlotte-Concord-Gastonia, NC-SC.	2,660,348	2,669,651	2,754,657	2,805,115	144,767	5.4	22
Chattanooga, TN-GA.	562,648	563,952	574,461	580,971	18,323	3.3	99
Chicago-Naperville-Elgin, IL-IN.	9,450,304	9,435,217	9,279,427	9,262,825	-187,479	-2.0	3
Cincinnati, OH-KY-IN.	2,249,781	2,251,974	2,258,625	2,271,479	21,698	1.0	30
Clarksville, TN-KY.	320,518	321,827	335,522	340,495	19,977	6.2	159
Cleveland, OH.	2,185,727	2,184,115	2,160,701	2,158,932	-26,795	-1.2	33
College Station-Bryan, TX.	268,244	268,953	277,751	281,445	13,201	4.9	178
Colorado Springs, CO.	755,112	757,128	765,456	768,832	13,720	1.8	79
Columbia, SC.	829,466	830,137	848,112	858,302	28,836	3.5	70
Columbus, GA-AL.	328,887	329,196	323,826	323,768	-5,119	-1.6	164
Columbus, OH.	2,138,941	2,141,895	2,162,066	2,180,271	41,330	1.9	32
Corpus Christi, TX.	445,758	446,171	446,640	448,323	2,565	0.6	121
Crestview-Fort Walton Beach-Destin, FL.	286,973	288,026	299,868	304,818	17,845	6.2	170
Dallas-Fort Worth-Arlington, TX.	7,637,398	7,666,418	7,947,439	8,100,037	462,639	6.1	4
Daphne-Fairhope-Foley, AL.	231,768	233,227	246,531	253,507	21,739	9.4	194
Davenport-Moline-Rock Island, IA-IL.	384,318	383,768	379,439	379,441	-4,877	-1.3	148
Dayton-Kettering-Beavercreek, OH.	814,050	814,209	812,714	814,363	313	(Z)	76
Deltona-Daytona Beach-Ormond Beach, FL.	668,909	671,804	706,423	721,796	52,887	7.9	83
Denver-Aurora-Centennial, CO.	2,963,814	2,970,119	2,986,190	3,005,131	41,317	1.4	19
Des Moines-West Des Moines, IA.	709,512	711,200	729,303	737,164	27,652	3.9	81
Detroit-Warren-Dearborn, MI.	4,392,390	4,385,248	4,348,636	4,342,304	-50,086	-1.1	14
Duluth, MN-WI.	280,719	280,619	280,328	281,603	884	0.3	177
Durham-Chapel Hill, NC.	588,911	585,020	602,827	608,879	19,968	3.4	94
El Paso, TX.	868,862	869,802	870,655	873,331	4,469	0.5	68
Erie, PA.	270,892	270,578	268,840	267,571	-3,321	-1.2	187
Eugene-Springfield, OR.	382,983	383,308	382,181	381,181	-1,802	-0.5	147
Evansville, IN.	269,238	269,517	269,892	270,717	1,479	0.5	185
Fargo, ND-MN.	249,833	250,220	258,573	262,620	12,787	5.1	189
Fayetteville, NC.	386,807	387,706	390,472	392,336	5,529	1.4	142
Fayetteville-Springdale-Rogers, AR.	546,725	549,937	576,967	590,337	43,612	8.0	98
Flint, MI.	406,217	405,777	401,923	401,522	-4,695	-1.2	136
Fort Collins-Loveland, CO.	359,074	359,923	367,577	370,771	11,697	3.3	149
Fort Wayne, IN.	447,744	448,587	454,519	457,842	10,098	2.3	118
Fresno, CA.	1,164,904	1,165,897	1,175,688	1,180,020	15,116	1.3	48
Gainesville, FL.	339,241	340,678	348,296	352,126	12,885	3.8	157
Grand Rapids-Wyoming-Kentwood, MI.	1,149,996	1,151,502	1,157,285	1,162,950	12,954	1.1	49
Greeley, CO.	328,987	331,458	350,266	359,442	30,455	9.3	156
Green Bay, WI.	328,273	328,591	330,417	331,882	3,609	1.1	161
Greensboro-High Point, NC.	776,548	774,941	784,619	789,842	13,294	1.7	78
Greenville-Anderson-Greer, SC.	928,212	930,762	958,918	975,480	47,268	5.1	57
Gulfport-Biloxi, MS.	416,249	416,640	420,054	421,916	5,667	1.4	130
Hagerstown-Martinsburg, MD-WV.	293,845	294,483	302,071	305,902	12,057	4.1	168
Harrisburg-Carlisle, PA.	591,711	592,793	603,332	606,055	14,344	2.4	95
Hartford-West Hartford-East Hartford, CT.	1,150,500	1,135,704	1,148,050	1,151,543	1,043	0.1	51
Hickory-Lenoir-Morganton, NC.	365,270	365,594	367,802	370,030	4,760	1.3	150
Houston-Pasadena-The Woodlands, TX.	7,149,604	7,168,723	7,370,464	7,510,253	360,649	5.0	5

See footnotes at end of table.

Table 21. Large Metropolitan Statistical Areas—Population: 2020 to 2023-Continued.

See headnote on page 24.

Metropolitan statistical area	2020 estimates base (April)	2020 (July)	2022 (July)	2023 (July)	Cumulative change, April 2020 to July 2023		Rank, 2023
					Number	Percent	
Huntington-Ashland, WV-KY-OH....................	376,141	375,689	369,974	368,261	-7,880	-2.1	152
Huntsville, AL..	491,719	494,706	514,473	527,254	35,535	7.2	108
Indianapolis-Carmel-Greenwood, IN...............	2,089,636	2,092,745	2,120,661	2,138,468	48,832	2.3	34
Jackson, MS...	619,989	618,896	610,703	610,257	-9,732	-1.6	93
Jacksonville, FL...	1,605,844	1,612,981	1,676,329	1,713,240	107,396	6.7	38
Kalamazoo-Portage, MI................................	261,677	261,796	260,892	262,215	538	0.2	190
Kansas City, MO-KS...................................	2,192,065	2,195,218	2,208,782	2,221,343	29,278	1.3	31
Kennewick-Richland, WA..............................	303,616	304,569	311,411	314,253	10,637	3.5	166
Killeen-Temple, TX.....................................	475,371	477,093	494,449	501,333	25,962	5.5	110
Kingsport-Bristol, TN-VA..............................	307,610	307,750	311,040	313,025	5,415	1.8	167
Kiryas Joel-Poughkeepsie-Newburgh, NY.........	698,336	696,887	704,100	704,620	6,284	0.9	84
Knoxville, TN..	903,322	905,896	932,921	946,264	42,942	4.8	60
Lafayette, LA..	408,082	408,213	412,641	414,288	6,206	1.5	132
Lakeland-Winter Haven, FL...........................	725,048	730,158	788,382	818,330	93,282	12.9	75
Lancaster, PA...	552,989	552,821	556,660	558,589	5,600	1.0	104
Lansing-East Lansing, MI.............................	473,202	473,020	471,983	473,177	-25	(-Z)	114
Laredo, TX...	267,113	267,363	267,619	269,148	2,035	0.8	186
Las Vegas-Henderson-North Las Vegas, NV......	2,265,475	2,274,887	2,322,535	2,336,573	71,098	3.1	29
Lexington-Fayette, KY..................................	516,820	517,407	517,748	520,045	3,225	0.6	109
Lincoln, NE..	340,221	340,783	342,059	344,387	4,166	1.2	158
Little Rock-North Little Rock-Conway, AR..........	748,038	748,990	757,768	764,045	16,007	2.1	80
Longview, TX..	286,179	286,350	290,575	293,498	7,319	2.6	173
Los Angeles-Long Beach-Anaheim, CA............	13,200,973	13,178,547	12,870,137	12,799,100	-401,873	-3.0	2
Louisville/Jefferson County, KY-IN..................	1,362,145	1,362,955	1,361,300	1,365,557	3,412	0.3	43
Lubbock, TX...	351,261	352,167	356,789	360,104	8,843	2.5	155
Lynchburg, VA...	261,597	261,643	263,209	264,590	2,993	1.1	188
Madison, WI...	680,805	681,902	686,829	694,345	13,540	2.0	87
Manchester-Nashua, NH..............................	422,938	422,913	427,493	427,354	4,416	1.0	126
McAllen-Edinburg-Mission, TX.......................	870,787	872,856	888,286	898,471	27,684	3.2	65
Memphis, TN-MS-AR..................................	1,345,436	1,346,172	1,338,667	1,335,674	-9,762	-0.7	45
Merced, CA..	281,205	281,830	290,210	291,920	10,715	3.8	174
Miami-Fort Lauderdale-West Palm Beach, FL......	6,138,356	6,133,365	6,139,812	6,183,199	44,843	0.7	9
Milwaukee-Waukesha, WI............................	1,574,713	1,574,476	1,559,128	1,560,424	-14,289	-0.9	40
Minneapolis-St Paul-Bloomington, MN-WI.........	3,690,271	3,694,114	3,691,666	3,712,020	21,749	0.6	16
Mobile, AL...	414,809	414,377	411,398	411,640	-3,169	-0.8	133
Modesto, CA..	552,882	553,257	551,226	551,430	-1,452	-0.3	105
Montgomery, AL..	386,062	385,403	385,410	385,480	-582	-0.2	143
Myrtle Beach-Conway-North Myrtle Beach, SC....	351,032	353,765	383,147	397,478	46,446	13.2	139
Naples-Marco Island, FL..............................	375,760	377,310	397,516	404,310	28,550	7.6	135
Nashville-Davidson--Murfreesboro--Franklin, TN...	2,014,420	2,021,744	2,071,019	2,102,573	88,153	4.4	35
New Haven, CT..	570,455	564,076	568,402	568,158	-2,297	-0.4	101
New Orleans-Metairie, LA.............................	1,007,286	1,005,281	973,385	962,165	-45,121	-4.5	58
New York-Newark-Jersey City, NY-NJ..............	20,081,990	19,990,547	19,563,798	19,498,249	-583,741	-2.9	1
North Port-Bradenton-Sarasota, FL.................	833,724	837,856	891,721	910,108	76,384	9.2	63
Norwich-New London-Willimantic, CT...............	280,428	278,342	279,257	279,634	-794	-0.3	179
Ocala, FL..	375,904	377,472	396,437	409,959	34,055	9.1	134
Ogden, UT...	637,207	639,141	652,184	658,133	20,926	3.3	88
Oklahoma City, OK.....................................	1,425,703	1,429,940	1,459,957	1,477,926	52,223	3.7	42
Olympia-Lacey-Tumwater, WA.......................	294,792	295,998	298,639	299,003	4,211	1.4	172
Omaha, NE-IA...	967,606	969,146	976,309	983,969	16,363	1.7	56
Orlando-Kissimmee-Sanford, FL.....................	2,673,391	2,680,491	2,763,017	2,817,933	144,542	5.4	21
Oxnard-Thousand Oaks-Ventura, CA...............	843,840	843,371	832,871	829,590	-14,250	-1.7	73
Palm Bay-Melbourne-Titusville, FL..................	606,621	608,775	630,707	643,979	37,358	6.2	91
Pensacola-Ferry Pass-Brent, FL.....................	509,899	511,579	522,059	530,090	20,191	4.0	107
Peoria, IL..	368,789	367,917	362,771	362,240	-6,549	-1.8	154
Philadelphia-Camden-Wilmington, PA-NJ-DE-MD....................................	6,245,020	6,241,967	6,242,746	6,246,160	1,140	(Z)	8
Phoenix-Mesa-Chandler, AZ..........................	4,851,102	4,875,246	5,020,870	5,070,110	219,008	4.5	10
Pittsburgh, PA..	2,457,036	2,455,323	2,432,532	2,422,725	-34,311	-1.4	27
Port St Lucie, FL.......................................	487,660	490,112	520,873	536,901	49,241	10.1	106
Portland-South Portland, ME.........................	551,737	552,577	563,159	566,329	14,592	2.6	102
Portland-Vancouver-Hillsboro, OR-WA.............	2,512,843	2,518,160	2,508,928	2,508,050	-4,793	-0.2	25
Providence-Warwick, RI-MA..........................	1,676,579	1,673,216	1,673,586	1,677,803	1,224	0.1	39
Provo-Orem-Lehi, UT..................................	671,172	675,414	715,278	732,197	61,025	9.1	82
Raleigh-Cary, NC.......................................	1,413,967	1,417,455	1,480,080	1,509,231	95,264	6.7	41
Reading, PA...	428,851	428,671	431,573	432,821	3,970	0.9	124
Reno, NV...	549,829	551,283	562,773	564,782	14,953	2.7	103
Richmond, VA...	1,314,424	1,316,646	1,338,238	1,349,732	35,308	2.7	44
Riverside-San Bernardino-Ontario, CA..............	4,599,842	4,606,384	4,669,149	4,688,053	88,211	1.9	12
Roanoke, VA...	315,246	315,217	314,150	314,314	-932	-0.3	165
Rochester, NY...	1,065,398	1,062,841	1,054,829	1,052,087	-13,311	-1.2	53
Rockford, IL...	338,788	338,259	334,610	334,124	-4,664	-1.4	160
Sacramento-Roseville-Folsom, CA..................	2,397,388	2,400,029	2,417,259	2,420,608	23,220	1.0	28
Salem, OR...	433,341	434,306	436,312	436,546	3,205	0.7	123
Salinas, CA..	439,035	438,322	432,884	430,723	-8,312	-1.9	125
Salt Lake City-Murray, UT............................	1,257,939	1,260,338	1,266,524	1,267,864	9,925	0.8	46
San Antonio-New Braunfels, TX......................	2,558,115	2,568,526	2,655,928	2,703,999	145,884	5.7	24

See footnotes at end of table.

Metropolitan statistical area	2020 estimates base (April)	2020 (July)	2022 (July)	2023 (July)	Cumulative change, April 2020 to July 2023		Rank, 2023
					Number	Percent	
San Diego-Chula Vista-Carlsbad, CA...............	3,298,648	3,295,298	3,277,176	3,269,973	-28,675	-0.9	18
San Francisco-Oakland-Fremont, CA..............	4,748,982	4,740,838	4,578,135	4,566,961	-182,021	-3.8	13
San Jose-Sunnyvale-Santa Clara, CA..............	2,000,489	1,995,698	1,945,978	1,945,767	-54,722	-2.7	36
San Luis Obispo-Paso Robles, CA..................	282,443	281,884	282,046	281,639	-804	-0.3	176
Santa Cruz-Watsonville, CA.........................	270,870	270,474	264,240	261,547	-9,323	-3.4	191
Santa Maria-Santa Barbara, CA.....................	448,220	448,424	443,915	441,257	-6,963	-1.6	122
Santa Rosa-Petaluma, CA...........................	488,850	488,282	482,669	481,812	-7,038	-1.4	112
Savannah, GA.......................................	404,803	405,301	418,277	424,935	20,132	5.0	129
Scranton--Wilkes-Barre, PA.........................	567,603	566,788	568,270	569,413	1,810	0.3	100
Seattle-Tacoma-Bellevue, WA.......................	4,018,797	4,027,804	4,032,242	4,044,837	26,040	0.6	15
Shreveport-Bossier City, LA.........................	393,409	392,511	384,943	383,295	-10,114	-2.6	145
Sioux Falls, SD-MN..................................	286,400	287,364	299,079	304,555	18,155	6.3	171
Slidell-Mandeville-Covington, LA....................	264,571	265,000	273,237	275,583	11,012	4.2	183
South Bend-Mishawaka, IN-MI.......................	324,513	324,241	323,759	324,490	-23	(-Z)	163
Spartanburg, SC.....................................	355,232	356,560	372,687	383,327	28,095	7.9	144
Spokane-Spokane Valley, WA........................	585,790	587,766	598,023	600,292	14,502	2.5	96
Springfield, MA......................................	465,839	464,311	460,758	460,291	-5,548	-1.2	117
Springfield, MO.....................................	475,433	476,371	486,931	491,053	15,620	3.3	111
St Louis, MO-IL.....................................	2,820,285	2,819,212	2,800,245	2,796,999	-23,286	-0.8	23
Stockton-Lodi, CA...................................	779,230	780,617	794,293	800,965	21,735	2.8	77
Syracuse, NY..	662,068	659,556	655,021	652,956	-9,112	-1.4	89
Tallahassee, FL.....................................	384,301	385,658	390,913	392,645	8,344	2.2	141
Tampa-St Petersburg-Clearwater, FL...............	3,175,291	3,187,828	3,291,341	3,342,963	167,672	5.3	17
Toledo, OH..	606,241	605,761	600,519	600,141	-6,100	-1.0	97
Trenton-Princeton, NJ...............................	387,328	386,466	380,779	381,671	-5,657	-1.5	146
Tucson, AZ..	1,043,435	1,045,175	1,057,476	1,063,162	19,727	1.9	52
Tulsa, OK...	1,015,338	1,017,350	1,034,048	1,044,757	29,419	2.9	54
Tuscaloosa, AL......................................	268,686	272,988	277,490	278,290	9,604	3.6	180
Urban Honolulu, HI..................................	1,016,507	1,012,399	994,828	989,408	-27,099	-2.7	55
Utica-Rome, NY.....................................	292,257	291,119	287,942	287,039	-5,218	-1.8	175
Vallejo, CA..	453,491	452,723	448,885	449,218	-4,273	-0.9	120
Virginia Beach-Chesapeake-Norfolk, VA-NC.......	1,780,062	1,781,712	1,785,390	1,787,169	7,107	0.4	37
Visalia, CA..	473,116	473,914	477,884	479,468	6,352	1.3	113
Waco, TX...	295,788	296,405	301,825	304,865	9,077	3.1	169
Washington-Arlington-Alexandria, DC-VA-MD-WV..................................	6,278,594	6,260,311	6,265,891	6,304,975	26,381	0.4	7
Waterbury-Shelton, CT..............................	450,435	449,285	453,590	456,128	5,693	1.3	119
Wichita, KS...	647,607	648,526	649,687	652,939	5,332	0.8	90
Wilmington, NC.....................................	422,601	425,133	454,390	467,337	44,736	10.6	115
Winston-Salem, NC.................................	675,986	677,134	688,799	695,630	19,644	2.9	86
Worcester, MA......................................	862,116	859,669	862,873	866,866	4,750	0.6	69
Yakima, WA...	256,738	256,733	257,019	256,643	-95	(-Z)	193
York-Hanover, PA...................................	456,441	456,720	461,049	464,640	8,199	1.8	116
Youngstown-Warren, OH............................	430,676	429,690	426,648	425,969	-4,707	-1.1	128

Z Less than 0.05%.

Source: U.S. Census Bureau, Metropolitan and Micropolitan Statistical Areas Totals: 2020-2023, "Annual and Cumulative Estimates of Resident Population Change for Metropolitan Statistical Areas in the United States and Puerto Rico and Metropolitan Statistical Area Rankings: April 1, 2020 to July 1, 2023 (CBSA-MET-EST2023-CHG)," <www.census.gov/programs-surveys/popest/data/tables.html>, accessed March 2024.

Table 22. The 50 Largest Metropolitan Statistical Areas in 2023—Components of Population Change: 2020 to 2023

[Covers period April 1, 2020 to July 1, 2023. Covers metropolitan statistical areas (MSAs) as delineated by the U.S. Office of Management and Budget as of July 2023. Top 50 MSAs ranked by July 2023 population. Estimates developed from a base that incorporates the 2020 Census, Vintage 2020 estimates, and 2020 Demographic Analysis estimates. For definitions and components of all metropolitan and micropolitan areas, see Appendix II. Minus sign (-) indicates decrease]

Metropolitan statistical area	Number							Percent change
	Total change [1]	Natural change			Net migration			
		Total	Births	Deaths	Total	International [2]	Domestic migration	
Atlanta-Sandy Springs-Roswell, GA	200,414	68,229	226,979	158,750	131,924	55,252	76,672	3.3
Austin-Round Rock-San Marcos, TX	189,896	47,227	91,541	44,314	143,186	24,775	118,411	8.3
Baltimore-Columbia-Towson, MD	-10,207	9,984	103,042	93,058	-21,465	18,637	-40,102	-0.4
Birmingham, AL	3,658	-3,637	43,708	47,345	7,006	2,622	4,384	0.3
Boston-Cambridge-Newton, MA-NH	-25,432	24,007	159,265	135,258	-49,100	88,322	-137,422	-0.5
Buffalo-Cheektowaga, NY	-11,293	-6,279	37,534	43,813	-5,685	5,612	-11,297	-1.0
Charlotte-Concord-Gastonia, NC-SC	144,767	25,698	104,000	78,302	118,382	26,048	92,334	5.4
Chicago-Naperville-Elgin, IL-IN	-187,479	45,227	314,340	269,113	-234,239	71,189	-305,428	-2.0
Cincinnati, OH-KY-IN	21,698	7,630	84,374	76,744	13,642	14,300	-658	1.0
Cleveland, OH	-26,795	-15,097	71,198	86,295	-11,963	10,559	-22,522	-1.2
Columbus, OH	41,330	19,671	84,075	64,404	21,713	23,315	-1,602	1.9
Dallas-Fort Worth-Arlington, TX	462,639	138,239	320,639	182,400	325,602	92,983	232,619	6.1
Denver-Aurora-Centennial, CO	41,317	35,092	107,759	72,667	6,024	17,835	-11,811	1.4
Detroit-Warren-Dearborn, MI	-50,086	-7,646	150,860	158,506	-44,385	29,471	-73,856	-1.1
Fresno, CA	15,116	18,429	51,708	33,279	-3,934	4,658	-8,592	1.3
Grand Rapids-Wyoming-Kentwood, MI	12,954	10,167	42,993	32,826	2,208	4,810	-2,602	1.1
Houston-Pasadena-The Woodlands, TX	360,649	131,792	302,703	170,911	229,159	118,487	110,672	5.0
Indianapolis-Carmel-Greenwood, IN	48,832	16,780	83,661	66,881	32,362	18,834	13,528	2.3
Jacksonville, FL	107,396	4,543	59,717	55,174	102,717	12,764	89,953	6.7
Kansas City, MO-KS	29,278	14,506	83,100	68,594	13,833	10,173	3,660	1.3
Las Vegas-Henderson-North Las Vegas, NV	71,098	10,758	81,299	70,541	59,432	15,519	43,913	3.1
Los Angeles-Long Beach-Anaheim, CA	-401,873	72,471	410,090	337,619	-468,472	114,778	-583,250	-3.0
Louisville/Jefferson County, KY-IN	3,412	-1,816	49,639	51,455	4,792	7,371	-2,579	0.3
Memphis, TN-MS-AR	-9,762	4,637	55,541	50,904	-14,708	4,652	-19,360	-0.7
Miami-Fort Lauderdale-West Palm Beach, FL	44,843	12,914	205,821	192,907	32,594	186,544	-153,950	0.7
Milwaukee-Waukesha, WI	-14,289	4,706	57,002	52,296	-18,524	9,667	-28,191	-0.9
Minneapolis-St Paul-Bloomington, MN-WI	21,749	43,187	137,709	94,522	-22,860	25,337	-48,197	0.6
Nashville-Davidson-Murfreesboro-Franklin, TN	88,153	18,259	80,288	62,029	70,297	12,899	57,398	4.4
New York-Newark-Jersey City, NY-NJ	-583,741	159,846	695,546	535,700	-732,334	242,585	-974,919	-2.9
Oklahoma City, OK	52,223	9,628	56,521	46,893	42,099	6,759	35,340	3.7
Orlando-Kissimmee-Sanford, FL	144,542	19,238	93,832	74,594	124,338	58,588	65,750	5.4
Philadelphia-Camden-Wilmington, PA-NJ-DE-MD	1,140	13,201	217,917	204,716	-15,069	39,139	-54,208	–
Phoenix-Mesa-Chandler, AZ	219,008	28,025	178,048	150,023	191,042	38,708	152,334	4.5
Pittsburgh, PA	-34,311	-31,064	72,749	103,813	-4,258	7,638	-11,896	-1.4
Portland-Vancouver-Hillsboro, OR-WA	-4,793	10,104	78,997	68,893	-15,660	12,710	-28,370	-0.2
Providence-Warwick, RI-MA	1,224	-5,523	51,071	56,594	6,680	14,217	-7,537	0.1
Raleigh-Cary, NC	95,264	22,611	53,758	31,147	73,246	13,455	59,791	6.7
Richmond, VA	35,308	3,405	48,108	44,703	31,677	9,458	22,219	2.7
Riverside-San Bernardino-Ontario, CA	88,211	42,313	174,519	132,206	43,609	12,432	31,177	1.9
Sacramento-Roseville-Folsom, CA	23,220	14,415	81,682	67,267	7,180	22,817	-15,637	1.0
Salt Lake City-Murray, UT	9,925	24,871	52,053	27,182	-15,271	10,621	-25,892	0.8
San Antonio-New Braunfels, TX	145,884	28,680	103,817	75,137	115,908	13,404	102,504	5.7
San Diego-Chula Vista-Carlsbad, CA	-28,675	38,417	121,030	82,613	-65,280.0	22,067	-87,347	-0.9
San Francisco-Oakland-Fremont, CA	-182,021	38,137	148,141	110,004	-214,106	68,367	-282,473	-3.8
San Jose-Sunnyvale-Santa Clara, CA	-54,722	26,133	64,489	38,356	-77,756	45,623	-123,379	-2.7
Seattle-Tacoma-Bellevue, WA	26,040	46,041	142,553	96,512	-18,637	64,683	-83,320	0.6
St Louis, MO-IL	-23,286	-9,057	94,365	103,422	-15,150	10,743	-25,893	-0.8
Tampa-St Petersburg-Clearwater, FL	167,672	-20,442	101,855	122,297	187,640	36,314	151,326	5.3
Virginia Beach-Chesapeake-Norfolk, VA-NC	7,107	10,527	68,262	57,735	-3,937	8,484	-12,421	0.4
Washington-Arlington-Alexandria, DC-VA-MD-WV	26,381	97,521	233,311	135,790	-68,842	110,394	-179,236	0.4

– Represents zero or rounds to zero. [1] Total population change includes residual. This residual represents the change in population that cannot be attributed to any specific demographic component of change. [2] Net international migration for the United States includes the international migration of both U.S.-born and non-U.S.-born populations. Specifically, it includes: (a) the net international migration of the non-U.S. born, (b) the net migration of U.S. born to and from the United States, (c) the net migration between the United States and Puerto Rico, and (d) the net movement of the Armed Forces population between the United States and overseas.

Source: U.S. Census Bureau, Metropolitan and Micropolitan Statistical Areas Totals: 2020-2023, "Annual and Cumulative Estimates of the Components of Resident Population Change for Metropolitan Statistical Areas in the United States: April 1, 2020 to July 1, 2023 (CBSA-MET-EST2023-COMP)" and "Annual and Cumulative Estimates of Resident Population Change for Metropolitan Statistical Areas in the United States and Puerto Rico and Metropolitan Statistical Area Rankings: April 1, 2020 to July 1, 2023 (CBSA-MET-EST2023-CHG)," <www.census.gov/programs-surveys/popest/data/tables.html>, March 2024.

Table 23. Population by Core Based Statistical Area (CBSA) Status and State: 2023

[334,915 represents 334,915,000. As of July 1. Covers core based statistical areas (metropolitan and micropolitan statistical areas) as delineated by the U.S. Office of Management and Budget as of July 2023. Estimates were developed from a base that incorporates the 2020 Census, Vintage 2020 estimates, and 2020 Demographic Analysis estimates. For definitions and components of all metropolitan and micropolitan statistical areas, see Appendix II. Minus sign (-) indicates decrease]

State	Total population, 2023 (1,000)	Inside Core-Based Statistical Area, 2023				Outside CBSA, 2023		Percent change, 2020–2023		
		Total		Metro-politan (1,000)	Micro-politan (1,000)	Number (1,000)	Percent	Metro-politan	Micro-politan	Outside CBSAs
		Number (1,000)	Percent							
United States.........	**334,915**	**316,997**	**94.7**	**288,911**	**28,087**	**17,918**	**5.3**	**1.1**	**0.5**	**0.3**
Alabama................	5,108	4,704	92.1	3,988	716	405	7.9	2.1	0.9	-1.2
Alaska.................	733	541	73.8	496	45	192	26.2	0.4	-2.0	-0.6
Arizona................	7,431	7,340	98.8	7,088	252	91	1.2	3.9	2.3	-1.1
Arkansas..............	3,068	2,492	81.2	1,883	609	576	18.8	3.5	-0.6	-0.5
California..............	38,965	38,707	99.3	38,120	587	258	0.7	-1.4	-2.2	-0.3
Colorado..............	5,878	5,599	95.3	5,160	439	279	4.7	1.9	0.5	1.2
Connecticut...........	3,617	3,617	100.0	3,407	210	–	–	0.3	1.1	(X)
Delaware..............	1,032	1,032	100.0	768	264	–	–	2.1	11.0	(X)
District of Columbia....	679	679	100.0	679	–	–	–	-1.5	(X)	(X)
Florida.................	22,611	22,298	98.6	21,935	363	312	1.4	5.1	3.4	1.7
Georgia................	11,029	10,293	93.3	9,199	1,094	736	6.7	3.0	2.9	1.8
Hawaii.................	1,435	1,435	100.0	1,154	281	–	–	-2.3	2.8	(X)
Idaho..................	1,965	1,815	92.4	1,448	367	150	7.6	7.1	5.6	6.9
Illinois.................	12,550	11,943	95.2	10,949	995	606	4.8	-2.1	-2.0	-2.3
Indiana................	6,862	6,405	93.3	5,373	1,033	457	6.7	1.4	0.1	0.1
Iowa...................	3,207	2,465	76.9	1,988	478	742	23.1	1.5	-1.0	-1.2
Kansas................	2,941	2,528	86.0	2,081	447	413	14.0	0.8	-1.2	-1.9
Kentucky..............	4,526	3,730	82.4	2,804	926	796	17.6	0.7	0.4	-0.2
Louisiana..............	4,574	4,271	93.4	3,856	415	303	6.6	-1.6	-2.5	-3.5
Maine..................	1,396	963	69.0	835	127	433	31.0	2.5	2.2	2.2
Maryland..............	6,180	6,099	98.7	5,907	192	81	1.3	0.0	0.8	(Z)
Massachusetts.........	7,001	7,001	100.0	6,895	106	–	–	-0.5	0.2	(X)
Michigan..............	10,037	9,323	92.9	8,367	956	714	7.1	-0.6	0.1	1.2
Minnesota.............	5,738	5,251	91.5	4,470	781	487	8.5	0.6	0.7	0.2
Mississippi............	2,940	2,375	80.8	1,460	915	565	19.2	0.4	-1.9	-1.7
Missouri...............	6,196	5,367	86.6	4,679	688	829	13.4	0.7	(-Z)	1.4
Montana...............	1,133	776	68.5	626	150	357	31.5	4.3	7.6	3.5
Nebraska..............	1,978	1,651	83.4	1,304	347	328	16.6	1.6	-0.3	-0.7
Nevada................	3,194	3,164	99.0	2,959	204	30	1.0	3.0	2.5	-2.8
New Hampshire........	1,402	1,318	94.0	881	437	84	6.0	1.5	2.1	3.0
New Jersey............	9,291	9,291	100.0	9,291	–	–	–	(Z)	(X)	(X)
New Mexico............	2,114	2,021	95.6	1,424	597	93	4.4	0.8	-2.1	-1.9
New York..............	19,571	19,191	98.1	18,201	990	380	1.9	-3.3	-1.3	-1.4
North Carolina.........	10,835	10,136	93.5	8,609	1,527	700	6.5	4.4	1.6	0.9
North Dakota..........	784	596	76.0	481	115	188	24.0	2.5	-2.2	-2.2
Ohio...................	11,786	11,312	96.0	9,665	1,647	474	4.0	(Z)	-0.7	-0.6
Oklahoma..............	4,054	3,501	86.4	2,752	749	553	13.6	3.1	1.1	0.8
Oregon................	4,233	4,170	98.5	3,591	579	63	1.5	-0.2	0.2	0.7
Pennsylvania..........	12,962	12,599	97.2	11,206	1,393	363	2.8	-0.2	-1.1	-1.3
Rhode Island..........	1,096	1,096	100.0	1,096	–	–	–	-0.1	(X)	(X)
South Carolina........	5,374	5,063	94.2	4,644	419	311	5.8	5.8	1.3	-1.3
South Dakota..........	919	708	77.0	468	240	211	23.0	6.2	2.2	0.1
Tennessee.............	7,126	6,566	92.1	5,615	951	560	7.9	3.2	3.6	1.9
Texas..................	30,503	29,174	95.6	27,552	1,622	1,329	4.4	5.0	1.4	2.5
Utah...................	3,418	3,271	95.7	3,003	268	147	4.3	4.3	6.9	4.0
Vermont...............	647	520	80.2	228	292	128	19.8	1.1	0.3	0.8
Virginia................	8,716	7,888	90.5	7,645	243	828	9.5	1.1	-0.6	0.4
Washington............	7,813	7,658	98.0	7,012	646	155	2.0	1.3	2.2	4.6
West Virginia..........	1,770	1,342	75.8	1,085	257	428	24.2	-0.5	-1.7	-3.1
Wisconsin.............	5,911	5,258	89.0	4,404	854	653	11.0	0.3	(-Z)	1.0
Wyoming..............	584	455	77.9	181	274	129	22.1	0.2	1.5	2.1

– Represents zero. Z less than 500 or .05 percent. X Not applicable.

Source: U.S. Census Bureau, Metropolitan and Micropolitan Statistical Areas Totals: 2020-2023, "Annual Resident Population Estimates and Estimated Components of Resident Population Change for Metropolitan and Micropolitan Statistical Areas and Their Geographic Components for the United States: April 1, 2020 to July 1, 2023," <www.census.gov/programs-surveys/popest/data/tables.html>, accessed March 2024.

Table 24. Population of Incorporated Places With 175,000 or More Inhabitants in 2023: 2020 to 2023

[Number except as noted. Estimates are based on the 2020 Census and reflect changes to the April 1, 2020 population due to the Count Question Resolution and Post-Census Group Quarters Review programs, geographic program revisions, and the application of disclosure avoidance to protect confidentiality. For population estimates methodology, see <www.census.gov/programs-surveys/popest/technical-documentation/methodology.html>. Geographic boundaries as of January 1, 2023. Minus sign (-) indicates decrease. See Appendix III]

City or place	Population					Population change, 2020 to 2023		Rank, 2023
	2020 (April, estimates base)	2020 (July)	2021 (July)	2022 (July)	2023 (July)	Number	Percent	
Akron, Ohio....................	190,418	190,146	188,619	188,472	188,701	-1,717	-0.9	137
Albuquerque, New Mexico..............	564,584	564,888	563,354	561,368	560,274	-4,310	-0.8	32
Amarillo, Texas.................	200,378	200,526	200,798	201,366	202,408	2,030	1.0	120
Anaheim, California.............	346,816	346,658	345,039	342,777	340,512	-6,304	-1.8	56
Anchorage municipality, Alaska..........	291,244	290,893	289,169	286,983	286,075	-5,169	-1.8	74
Arlington, Texas................	394,265	394,248	393,373	394,747	398,431	4,166	1.1	50
Atlanta, Georgia................	498,736	499,896	492,690	498,771	510,823	12,087	2.4	37
Augusta-Richmond County, Georgia [1]...	202,077	201,999	200,754	201,805	200,884	-1,193	-0.6	124
Aurora, Colorado................	386,325	386,773	390,516	393,794	395,052	8,727	2.3	52
Aurora, Illinois.................	180,530	180,215	179,397	177,931	177,563	-2,967	-1.6	149
Austin, Texas..................	961,893	965,827	969,608	975,418	979,882	17,989	1.9	11
Bakersfield, California..............	404,448	405,280	409,782	412,269	413,381	8,933	2.2	47
Baltimore, Maryland..............	585,690	583,157	576,578	569,107	565,239	-20,451	-3.5	30
Baton Rouge, Louisiana.............	226,916	226,264	224,048	221,244	219,573	-7,343	-3.2	107
Birmingham, Alabama.............	200,657	200,375	197,875	196,887	196,644	-4,013	-2.0	129
Boise City, Idaho................	235,719	236,034	238,150	236,727	235,421	-298	-0.1	95
Boston, Massachusetts.............	678,617	675,466	657,283	653,243	653,833	-24,784	-3.7	25
Brownsville, Texas................	186,719	187,004	187,737	189,236	190,158	3,439	1.8	135
Buffalo, New York................	278,290	277,551	277,707	275,762	274,678	-3,612	-1.3	81
Cape Coral, Florida................	193,994	195,422	204,023	216,915	224,455	30,461	15.7	102
Cary town, North Carolina..............	174,784	174,778	176,886	179,867	180,010	5,226	3.0	145
Chandler, Arizona...............	276,011	277,345	279,615	280,778	280,167	4,156	1.5	78
Charlotte, North Carolina.............	874,629	875,752	883,012	895,704	911,311	36,682	4.2	15
Chattanooga, Tennessee.............	181,057	181,568	181,167	184,038	187,030	5,973	3.3	139
Chesapeake, Virginia..............	249,369	249,781	251,763	252,459	253,886	4,517	1.8	89
Chicago, Illinois.................	2,746,352	2,743,329	2,704,101	2,672,660	2,664,452	-81,900	-3.0	3
Chula Vista, California.............	275,499	275,809	275,774	274,823	274,333	-1,166	-0.4	82
Cincinnati, Ohio.................	309,567	309,601	308,661	309,405	311,097	1,530	0.5	64
Clarksville, Tennessee..............	166,742	167,509	170,824	176,747	180,716	13,974	8.4	144
Cleveland, Ohio.................	372,596	371,806	365,329	362,806	362,656	-9,940	-2.7	54
Colorado Springs, Colorado.............	479,021	480,331	483,369	486,304	488,664	9,643	2.0	39
Columbus, Georgia...............	206,919	207,006	205,060	202,432	201,877	-5,042	-2.4	123
Columbus, Ohio.................	905,939	906,418	903,184	908,238	913,175	7,236	0.8	14
Corpus Christi, Texas..............	317,863	318,065	317,877	316,147	316,595	-1,268	-0.4	62
Dallas, Texas..................	1,304,182	1,303,212	1,289,705	1,297,358	1,302,868	-1,314	-0.1	9
Denver, Colorado................	715,524	717,606	711,467	713,453	716,577	1,053	0.1	19
Des Moines, Iowa................	214,124	213,826	212,625	211,048	210,381	-3,743	-1.7	112
Detroit, Michigan................	639,475	638,300	633,738	631,366	633,218	-6,257	-1.0	26
Durham, North Carolina..............	283,662	284,444	289,378	292,587	296,186	12,524	4.4	70
El Paso, Texas..................	678,862	679,255	678,271	677,788	678,958	96	(Z)	23
Elk Grove, California..............	176,138	176,569	177,964	178,009	178,444	2,306	1.3	146
Eugene, Oregon.................	177,225	177,428	178,013	177,873	177,899	674	0.4	148
Fayetteville, North Carolina............	208,473	209,170	210,527	209,321	209,749	1,276	0.6	113
Fontana, California..............	208,402	209,177	212,489	214,317	215,465	7,063	3.4	109
Fort Lauderdale, Florida.............	182,777	182,892	181,997	183,118	184,255	1,478	0.8	140
Fort Wayne, Indiana...............	263,909	264,380	266,417	268,067	269,994	6,085	2.3	83
Fort Worth, Texas................	918,907	923,602	937,590	957,103	978,468	59,561	6.5	12
Fremont, California...............	230,494	230,430	227,953	226,305	226,208	-4,286	-1.9	99
Fresno, California...............	542,248	542,710	544,175	545,253	545,716	3,468	0.6	34
Frisco, Texas..................	200,537	202,754	211,102	219,641	225,007	24,470	12.2	101
Garland, Texas.................	246,121	246,311	244,290	245,795	243,470	-2,651	-1.1	94
Gilbert town, Arizona..............	267,931	269,173	273,179	275,255	275,411	7,480	2.8	79
Glendale, Arizona...............	248,403	248,949	249,884	252,061	253,855	5,452	2.2	90
Glendale, California...............	196,523	195,934	192,153	189,175	187,050	-9,473	-4.8	138
Grand Prairie, Texas...............	196,139	196,255	197,345	201,539	202,134	5,995	3.1	122
Grand Rapids, Michigan..............	198,890	198,707	197,708	197,192	196,608	-2,282	-1.1	130
Greensboro, North Carolina..............	299,182	296,345	298,249	300,805	302,296	3,114	1.0	69
Henderson, Nevada...............	317,321	319,072	322,445	331,313	337,305	19,984	6.3	57
Hialeah, Florida.................	223,123	222,408	220,921	220,205	221,300	-1,823	-0.8	106
Houston, Texas.................	2,300,833	2,299,269	2,291,020	2,302,488	2,314,157	13,324	0.6	4
Huntington Beach, California..............	198,721	198,405	196,427	194,195	192,129	-6,592	-3.3	133
Huntsville, Alabama..............	215,120	216,407	218,778	222,030	225,564	10,444	4.9	100
Indianapolis city, Indiana [1]............	887,648	887,177	882,325	880,397	879,293	-8,355	-0.9	16
Irvine, California................	307,675	308,411	304,258	312,820	314,621	6,946	2.3	63
Irving, Texas..................	256,691	256,807	254,392	254,209	254,373	-2,318	-0.9	88
Jacksonville, Florida..............	949,618	951,880	957,410	971,777	985,843	36,225	3.8	10
Jersey City, New Jersey..............	292,751	291,949	285,105	289,772	291,657	-1,094	-0.4	72
Kansas City, Missouri..............	507,978	508,220	509,080	509,129	510,704	2,726	0.5	38
Knoxville, Tennessee..............	190,682	191,446	192,718	196,748	198,162	7,480	3.9	127
Laredo, Texas.................	255,208	255,489	255,665	256,027	257,602	2,394	0.9	87
Las Vegas, Nevada...............	644,883	646,794	650,827	656,191	660,929	16,046	2.5	24
Lexington-Fayette county, Kentucky [1]....	322,564	322,627	320,519	320,281	320,154	-2,410	-0.7	59
Lincoln, Nebraska................	291,138	291,633	291,497	292,380	294,757	3,619	1.2	71
Little Rock, Arkansas..............	202,564	202,634	202,229	203,176	203,842	1,278	0.6	119
Long Beach, California..............	466,772	465,585	455,449	452,931	449,468	-17,304	-3.7	44
Los Angeles, California..............	3,898,841	3,895,848	3,832,573	3,822,782	3,820,914	-77,927	-2.0	2
Louisville/Jefferson County, Kentucky [1]..	631,976	631,912	627,031	623,630	622,981	-8,995	-1.4	28

See footnotes at end of table.

Table 24. Population of Incorporated Places With 175,000 or More Inhabitants in 2023: 2020 to 2023-Continued.

See headnote on page 29.

City or place	2020 (April, estimates base)	Population 2020 (July)	2021 (July)	2022 (July)	2023 (July)	Population change, 2020 to 2023 Number	Percent	Rank, 2023
Lubbock, Texas	257,179	258,013	261,255	264,083	266,878	9,699	3.8	84
Madison, Wisconsin	274,644	275,204	272,520	277,414	280,305	5,661	2.1	77
McKinney, Texas	195,329	197,497	203,479	207,603	213,509	18,180	9.3	110
Memphis, Tennessee	635,425	635,225	629,493	623,840	618,639	-16,786	-2.6	29
Mesa, Arizona	504,296	505,890	509,287	512,264	511,648	7,352	1.5	36
Miami, Florida	442,260	442,827	441,869	450,014	455,924	13,664	3.1	42
Milwaukee, Wisconsin	577,893	577,207	566,557	563,632	561,385	-16,508	-2.9	31
Minneapolis, Minnesota	429,988	430,710	427,806	422,003	425,115	-4,873	-1.1	46
Mobile, Alabama	187,043	186,621	185,176	183,290	182,595	-4,448	-2.4	142
Modesto, California	218,487	218,691	218,827	218,344	218,915	428	0.2	108
Montgomery, Alabama	200,591	200,041	198,460	196,944	195,287	-5,304	-2.6	132
Moreno Valley, California	208,640	208,868	211,072	211,648	212,392	3,752	1.8	111
Nashville-Davidson, Tennessee [1]	689,454	689,700	675,578	682,130	687,788	-1,666	-0.2	21
New Orleans, Louisiana	383,997	383,241	377,346	369,917	364,136	-19,861	-5.2	53
New York, New York	8,804,199	8,740,292	8,462,216	8,335,798	8,258,035	-546,164	-6.2	1
Newark, New Jersey	311,553	310,645	307,368	304,552	304,960	-6,593	-2.1	66
Newport News, Virginia	186,245	186,047	184,691	183,980	183,118	-3,127	-1.7	141
Norfolk, Virginia	238,003	237,789	234,862	232,558	230,930	-7,073	-3.0	96
North Las Vegas, Nevada	259,525	261,214	271,104	280,404	284,771	25,246	9.7	75
Oakland, California	440,669	440,943	436,850	434,568	436,504	-4,165	-0.9	45
Oklahoma City, Oklahoma	681,091	683,078	688,531	695,178	702,767	21,676	3.2	20
Omaha, Nebraska	491,870	492,758	488,626	485,132	483,335	-8,535	-1.7	40
Ontario, California	175,265	175,712	178,272	180,500	182,457	7,192	4.1	143
Orlando, Florida	307,763	307,834	309,883	315,859	320,742	12,979	4.2	58
Overland Park, Kansas	197,249	197,734	197,610	197,705	197,089	-160	-0.1	128
Oxnard, California	202,071	201,911	201,807	200,193	198,488	-3,583	-1.8	126
Peoria, Arizona	190,991	191,997	194,981	197,786	198,750	7,759	4.1	125
Philadelphia, Pennsylvania	1,603,793	1,600,684	1,589,623	1,566,836	1,550,542	-53,251	-3.3	6
Phoenix, Arizona	1,608,215	1,612,459	1,625,187	1,643,899	1,650,070	41,855	2.6	5
Pittsburgh, Pennsylvania	302,955	302,779	305,400	302,799	303,255	300	0.1	68
Plano, Texas	285,465	286,408	288,792	289,750	290,190	4,725	1.7	73
Port St. Lucie, Florida	204,855	206,815	217,864	231,852	245,021	40,166	19.6	92
Portland, Oregon	652,521	653,344	643,179	634,668	630,498	-22,023	-3.4	27
Providence, Rhode Island	190,931	190,745	190,169	189,567	190,792	-139	-0.1	134
Raleigh, North Carolina	467,867	465,354	470,813	473,423	482,295	14,428	3.1	41
Reno, Nevada	264,146	264,981	270,019	273,547	274,915	10,769	4.1	80
Richmond, Virginia	226,548	226,936	227,140	228,367	229,247	2,699	1.2	98
Riverside, California	315,015	315,067	313,350	318,991	318,858	3,843	1.2	61
Rochester, New York	211,314	210,862	210,581	208,546	207,274	-4,040	-1.9	117
Sacramento, California	524,925	525,528	525,502	525,297	526,384	1,459	0.3	35
Salem, Oregon	175,478	175,942	178,171	177,523	177,432	1,954	1.1	150
Salt Lake City, Utah	199,708	200,660	201,125	207,677	209,593	9,885	4.9	114
San Antonio, Texas	1,434,306	1,439,257	1,454,003	1,473,325	1,495,295	60,989	4.3	7
San Bernardino, California	222,073	222,090	220,691	221,111	223,728	1,655	0.7	104
San Diego, California	1,386,972	1,386,292	1,376,142	1,387,378	1,388,320	1,348	0.1	8
San Francisco, California	873,950	870,518	811,935	807,774	808,988	-64,962	-7.4	17
San Jose, California	1,013,241	1,009,319	981,214	972,082	969,655	-43,586	-4.3	13
Santa Ana, California	310,557	311,244	311,166	310,648	310,539	-18	(-Z)	65
Santa Clarita, California	232,804	232,406	229,753	227,123	224,028	-8,776	-3.8	103
Santa Rosa, California	178,123	177,959	177,412	176,078	175,845	-2,278	-1.3	151
Scottsdale, Arizona	241,340	241,883	242,759	242,972	244,394	3,054	1.3	93
Seattle, Washington	737,018	740,565	731,757	749,134	755,078	18,060	2.5	18
Shreveport, Louisiana	187,601	186,848	183,269	180,086	177,959	-9,642	-5.1	147
Sioux Falls, South Dakota	192,718	193,437	196,807	202,016	206,410	13,692	7.1	118
Spokane, Washington	228,978	229,205	230,150	230,405	229,447	469	0.2	97
St. Louis, Missouri	301,565	300,496	293,622	286,193	281,754	-19,811	-6.6	76
St. Paul, Minnesota	311,516	311,140	307,677	304,436	303,820	-7,696	-2.5	67
St. Petersburg, Florida	258,354	259,266	259,578	261,722	263,553	5,199	2.0	86
Stockton, California	320,806	320,976	322,004	320,831	319,543	-1,263	-0.4	60
Tacoma, Washington	219,185	219,719	219,652	221,731	222,906	3,721	1.7	105
Tallahassee, Florida	196,180	197,933	200,233	201,718	202,221	6,041	3.1	121
Tampa, Florida	384,662	387,924	392,929	398,325	403,364	18,702	4.9	49
Tempe, Arizona	184,213	185,328	184,690	189,520	189,834	5,621	3.1	136
Toledo, Ohio	270,880	270,276	268,821	266,350	265,304	-5,576	-2.1	85
Tucson, Arizona	542,658	542,638	541,217	546,500	547,239	4,581	0.8	33
Tulsa, Oklahoma	413,144	413,651	412,856	411,748	411,894	-1,250	-0.3	48
Urban Honolulu CDP, Hawaii [2]	350,963	348,438	346,478	343,664	341,778	-9,185	-2.6	55
Vancouver, Washington	190,888	191,278	192,770	194,500	196,442	5,554	2.9	131
Virginia Beach, Virginia	459,476	459,684	458,569	455,069	453,649	-5,827	-1.3	43
Washington, District of Columbia	689,548	670,839	669,037	670,949	678,972	-10,576	-1.5	22
Wichita, Kansas	397,547	398,024	396,638	396,063	396,119	-1,428	-0.4	51
Winston-Salem, North Carolina	249,558	249,804	251,042	251,746	252,975	3,417	1.4	91
Worcester, Massachusetts	206,519	205,056	205,839	205,676	207,621	1,102	0.5	116
Yonkers, New York	211,584	210,994	210,075	208,406	207,657	-3,927	-1.9	115

Z represents less than 0.05%. [1] Represents the portion of a consolidated city that is not within one or more separately incorporated places. [2] CDP=Census Designated Place.

Source: U.S. Census Bureau, City and Town Population Totals: 2020-2023, "Annual Estimates of the Resident Population for Incorporated Places of 20,000 or More, Ranked by July 1, 2023 Population: April 1, 2020 to July 1, 2023 (SUB-IP-EST2023-ANNRNK)," <www.census.gov/data/tables/time-series/demo/popest/2020s-total-cities-and-towns.html>, accessed May 2024.

Table 25. Incorporated Places by Population Size: 2000 to 2023

[173.5 represents 173,500,000]

Population size	Number of incorporated places				Population (mil.)				Percent of total population			
	2000	2010	2020 [1]	2023	2000	2010	2020 [1]	2023	2000	2010	2020 [1]	2023
Total....................	**19,452**	**19,540**	**19,494**	**19,484**	**173.5**	**192.0**	**207.5**	**210.7**	**100.0**	**100.0**	**100.0**	**100.0**
1,000,000 or more........	9	9	10	9	22.9	23.6	25.9	24.4	13.2	12.3	12.5	11.6
500,000 to 999,999........	20	24	27	29	12.9	16.1	18.9	20.3	7.4	8.4	9.1	9.6
250,000 to 499,999........	37	40	52	53	13.3	14.0	17.4	17.6	7.7	7.3	8.4	8.4
100,000 to 249,999........	172	200	228	242	25.5	30.2	33.4	35.1	14.7	15.7	16.1	16.7
50,000 to 99,999..........	363	432	468	468	24.9	30.1	32.7	32.7	14.4	15.7	15.8	15.5
25,000 to 49,999..........	644	723	746	779	22.6	25.2	25.9	27.2	13.0	13.1	12.5	12.9
10,000 to 24,999..........	1,435	1,542	1,564	1,599	22.6	24.2	24.7	25.2	13.0	12.6	11.9	11.9
Under 10,000..............	16,772	16,570	16,399	16,305	28.7	28.7	28.5	28.1	16.5	14.9	13.8	13.4

[1] Data reflect incorporated places as of January 1, 2020 and population estimates available at that time, which do not incorporate 2020 Census results.

Source: U.S. Census Bureau, *1990 Census of Population and Housing, Population and Housing Unit Counts (CPH-2-1)*; *Census 2000 PHC-3, Population and Housing Unit Counts; 2010 Census Redistricting Data (Public Law 94-171) Summary File*; City and Town Population Totals: 2010-2020, "Subcounty Resident Population Estimates: April 1, 2010 to July 1, 2020 (SUB-EST2020)"; and City and Town Population Totals: 2020-2023, "Subcounty Resident Population Estimates: April 1, 2020 to July 1, 2023 (SUB-EST2023)," <www.census.gov/data/tables/time-series/demo/popest/2020s-total-cities-and-towns.html>, accessed May 2024.

Table 26. Urban and Rural Population by State: 2000 to 2020

[222,361 represents 222,361,000. As of April 1. Resident population. Based on current urban definitions, see text, this section]

State	2000			2010			2020		
	Urban population		Rural population (1,000)	Urban population		Rural population (1,000)	Urban population		Rural population (1,000)
	Number (1,000)	Percent		Number (1,000)	Percent		Number (1,000)	Percent	
United States..........	**222,361**	**79.0**	**59,061**	**249,253**	**80.7**	**59,492**	**265,149**	**80.0**	**66,300**
Alabama..................	2,466	55.4	1,981	2,822	59.0	1,958	2,901	57.7	2,123
Alaska....................	411	65.6	216	469	66.0	241	476	64.9	257
Arizona..................	4,524	88.2	607	5,741	89.8	651	6,385	89.3	766
Arkansas.................	1,404	52.5	1,269	1,638	56.2	1,278	1,671	55.5	1,341
California................	31,990	94.4	1,882	35,374	95.0	1,880	37,259	94.2	2,279
Colorado.................	3,633	84.5	668	4,333	86.2	696	4,967	86.0	807
Connecticut..............	2,988	87.7	418	3,145	88.0	429	3,110	86.3	496
Delaware.................	628	80.1	156	748	83.3	150	818	82.6	172
District of Columbia......	572	100.0	–	602	100.0	–	690	100.0	–
Florida...................	14,270	89.3	1,712	17,140	91.2	1,661	19,715	91.5	1,823
Georgia..................	5,864	71.6	2,322	7,272	75.1	2,416	7,934	74.1	2,778
Hawaii...................	1,108	91.5	103	1,250	91.9	110	1,252	86.1	203
Idaho....................	859	66.4	434	1,106	70.6	461	1,273	69.2	566
Illinois..................	10,910	87.8	1,510	11,354	88.5	1,477	11,138	86.9	1,675
Indiana..................	4,304	70.8	1,776	4,697	72.4	1,787	4,830	71.2	1,956
Iowa.....................	1,787	61.1	1,139	1,950	64.0	1,096	2,015	63.2	1,176
Kansas...................	1,921	71.4	768	2,117	74.2	736	2,124	72.3	814
Kentucky.................	2,254	55.8	1,788	2,533	58.4	1,806	2,645	58.7	1,861
Louisiana................	3,246	72.6	1,223	3,318	73.2	1,216	3,332	71.5	1,326
Maine....................	513	40.2	762	514	38.7	815	526	38.6	836
Maryland.................	4,559	86.1	738	5,034	87.2	739	5,289	85.6	888
Massachusetts............	5,801	91.4	548	6,022	92.0	526	6,417	91.3	613
Michigan.................	7,419	74.7	2,519	7,370	74.6	2,514	7,404	73.5	2,673
Minnesota................	3,490	70.9	1,429	3,886	73.3	1,418	4,102	71.9	1,605
Mississippi...............	1,387	48.8	1,457	1,464	49.4	1,503	1,371	46.3	1,590
Missouri.................	3,883	69.4	1,712	4,218	70.4	1,771	4,276	69.5	1,879
Montana..................	488	54.1	414	553	55.9	436	579	53.4	505
Nebraska.................	1,194	69.8	518	1,336	73.1	491	1,432	73.0	530
Nevada...................	1,829	91.5	170	2,544	94.2	157	2,921	94.1	183
New Hampshire..........	732	59.3	503	794	60.3	523	803	58.3	574
New Jersey..............	7,939	94.4	475	8,324	94.7	468	8,709	93.8	580
New Mexico.............	1,364	75.0	456	1,594	77.4	465	1,579	74.5	539
New York...............	16,603	87.5	2,374	17,028	87.9	2,350	17,665	87.4	2,536
North Carolina...........	4,849	60.2	3,200	6,302	66.1	3,234	6,965	66.7	3,475
North Dakota............	359	55.9	283	403	59.9	270	475	61.0	304
Ohio.....................	8,782	77.4	2,571	8,990	77.9	2,547	9,001	76.3	2,798
Oklahoma................	2,255	65.3	1,196	2,485	66.2	1,266	2,559	64.6	1,401
Oregon..................	2,694	78.7	727	3,104	81.0	727	3,411	80.5	826
Pennsylvania............	9,464	77.1	2,817	9,991	78.7	2,711	9,941	76.5	3,062
Rhode Island............	953	90.9	95	955	90.7	98	999	91.1	98
South Carolina...........	2,427	60.5	1,585	3,068	66.3	1,558	3,478	67.9	1,641
South Dakota............	391	51.9	363	461	56.7	353	507	57.2	379
Tennessee...............	3,620	63.6	2,069	4,213	66.4	2,133	4,577	66.2	2,334
Texas....................	17,204	82.5	3,648	21,298	84.7	3,848	24,401	83.7	4,745
Utah.....................	1,970	88.2	263	2,504	90.6	260	2,937	89.8	334
Vermont.................	232	38.2	376	243	38.9	382	226	35.1	417
Virginia.................	5,170	73.0	1,909	6,037	75.5	1,964	6,528	75.6	2,103
Washington..............	4,831	82.0	1,063	5,652	84.1	1,073	6,424	83.4	1,281
West Virginia............	833	46.1	976	903	48.7	950	801	44.6	993
Wisconsin................	3,664	68.3	1,700	3,990	70.2	1,697	3,954	67.1	1,940
Wyoming.................	321	65.1	172	365	64.8	199	358	62.0	219

– Represents zero.

Source: U.S. Census Bureau, 2000 Census of Population and Housing, Population and Housing Unit Counts PHC-3; 2010 Census of Population and Housing, Population and Housing Unit Counts, CPH-2-1, United States Summary; "Percent Urban and Rural in 2010 by State," <www.census.gov/programs-surveys/geography/guidance/geo-areas/urban-rural/2010-urban-rural.html>; and Table P2, "Urban and Rural," <data.census.gov> accessed August 2023.

Table 27. Geographic Mobility Status of the Population by Selected Characteristics: 1950 to 2022

[Numbers in thousands (148,400 represents 148,400,000). For persons 1 year old and over. Based on comparison of place of residence in year of survey vs. 1 year earlier. Movers are all people who were living in a different home at the end of the period rather than at the beginning. Excludes members of the Armed Forces except those living off post or with their families on post. Movers from Puerto Rico and the United States Island Areas are counted as movers from abroad. Based on Current Population Survey, Annual Social and Economic Supplement. See text, this section and Appendix III]

Mobility period	Number (1,000)			Percent distribution					
						Movers (different house in U.S.)			
							Different county		Movers from abroad
	Total persons	Non-movers	Movers	Non-movers	Total movers	Same county	Same state	Different state	
1950-1951.............	148,400	116,936	31,464	78.8	21.2	13.9	3.6	3.5	0.2
1960-1961.............	177,354	140,821	36,533	79.4	20.6	13.7	3.1	3.2	0.6
1970-1971.............	201,506	163,800	37,705	81.3	18.7	11.4	3.1	3.4	0.8
1975-1976.............	208,069	171,276	36,793	82.3	17.7	10.8	3.4	3.0	0.6
1980-1981.............	221,641	183,442	38,200	82.8	17.2	10.4	3.4	2.8	0.6
1985-1986.............	232,998	189,760	43,237	81.4	18.6	11.3	3.7	3.0	0.5
1990-1991.............	244,884	203,345	41,539	83.0	17.0	10.3	3.2	2.9	0.6
1995-1996.............	260,406	217,868	42,537	83.7	16.3	10.3	3.1	2.5	0.5
2000-2001 [1]........	275,611	236,605	39,007	85.8	14.2	8.0	2.7	2.8	0.6
2001-2002.............	278,160	237,049	41,111	85.2	14.8	8.5	2.9	2.8	0.6
2002-2003.............	282,556	242,463	40,093	85.8	14.2	8.3	2.7	2.7	0.4
2003-2004 [2]........	284,367	245,372	38,995	86.3	13.7	7.9	2.8	2.6	0.4
2004-2005 [3]........	287,148	247,261	39,888	86.1	13.9	7.9	2.7	2.6	0.6
2005-2006.............	289,781	249,945	39,837	86.3	13.7	8.6	2.8	2.0	0.4
2006-2007.............	292,749	254,068	38,681	86.8	13.2	8.6	2.5	1.7	0.4
2007-2008.............	294,851	259,685	35,167	88.1	11.9	7.8	2.1	1.6	0.4
2008-2009.............	297,182	260,077	37,105	87.5	12.5	8.4	2.1	1.6	0.4
2009-2010 [4]........	300,419	262,975	37,445	87.5	12.5	8.6	2.1	1.4	0.3
2010-2011 [4]........	302,640	267,602	35,038	88.4	11.6	7.7	1.9	1.6	0.4
2011-2012.............	304,924	268,436	36,488	88.0	12.0	7.7	2.2	1.7	0.4
2012-2013.............	307,243	271,325	35,918	88.3	11.7	7.5	2.3	1.6	0.3
2013-2014 [5]........	309,601	273,920	35,681	88.5	11.5	7.6	2.1	1.5	0.4
2014-2015.............	312,295	275,971	36,324	88.4	11.6	7.3	2.1	1.6	0.5
2015-2016.............	314,992	279,854	35,138	88.8	11.2	6.9	2.4	1.5	0.4
2016-2017.............	316,550	281,647	34,902	89.0	11.0	6.8	2.1	1.7	0.4
2017-2018.............	319,319	286,967	32,352	89.9	10.1	6.2	2.0	1.5	0.4
2018-2019.............	320,667	289,296	31,371	90.2	9.8	5.9	2.1	1.5	0.4
2019-2020 [6]........	324,002	294,065	29,938	90.8	9.2	5.4	2.2	1.3	0.3
2020-2021 [6]........	324,591	297,373	27,217	91.6	8.4	4.9	1.9	1.4	0.2
2021-2022.............	325,303	297,124	28,179	91.3	8.7	4.6	2.1	1.5	0.4

[1] State Children's Health Insurance Program (SCHIP) sample expansion; population controls consistent with 2000 Census. [2] The migration question wording changed in 2004. Before 2004, it asked about Residence on March 1 of the previous year. As of 2004, it asked about residence one year ago. See <www.census.gov/topics/population/migration/guidance/user-notes.html> for more information. [3] Caution should be used when comparing numbers/rates of movers within the same county and from a different county between the 1999-2000 to 2004-2005 period with other periods. For more information see <www.census.gov/topics/population/migration/guidance/impact-of-processing-on-cps-interstate-migration-rates.html>. [4] Population controls consistent with 2010 Census. [5] The source of 2014 data for this table is the CPS ASEC sample of 98,000 addresses. The 2014 CPS ASEC included redesigned questions for income and health insurance coverage. For more information, see <www.census.gov/topics/population/migration/guidance/user-notes.html>. [6] Population controls consistent with 2020 Census.

Source: U.S. Census Bureau, "CPS Historical Migration/Geographic Mobility Tables," August 2023, <www.census.gov/data/tables/time-series/demo/geographic-mobility/historic.html>.

Table 28. Movers by Type of Move and Reason for Moving: 2022

[28,179 represents 28,179,000. As of March. For persons 1 year old and over. Based on comparison of place of residence in 2022 vs. 2021. Excludes members of the Armed Forces except those living off post or with their families on post. Based on Current Population Survey, Annual Social and Economic Supplement. See text, this section and Appendix III]

Reason for move	All movers	Intra-county	Inter-county	From abroad	Reason for move	All movers	Intra-county	Inter-county	From abroad
Total (1,000).....................	28,179	15,068	11,741	1,369	Housing–related reasons......	41.6	52.3	30.8	15.3
					Wanted to own home/not rent.....	8.5	9.9	7.4	2.8
PERCENT DISTRIBUTION					New/better/larger housing [1].......	14.4	19.0	9.6	5.1
Total..............................	100.0	100.0	100.0	100.0	Better neighborhood/less crime...	4.7	5.2	4.4	2.3
Family–related reasons........	26.5	27.1	26.1	22.8	Cheaper housing..................	7.7	9.7	5.8	2.8
Change in marital status...........	6.0	6.7	5.0	7.6	Foreclosure/eviction..............	0.7	1.1	0.3	(S)
To establish own household.......	11.2	13.7	8.8	4.3	Other housing.....................	5.5	7.4	3.3	2.3
Other family reasons..............	9.2	6.7	12.3	10.8					
Employment–related					Other reasons....................	15.9	12.0	18.7	34.3
reasons........................	16.1	8.6	24.4	27.6	Unmarried partner relationship. ..	4.4	4.5	4.6	1.4
New job/job transfer................	9.2	2.3	17.0	18.8	Attend/leave college..............	2.9	1.2	4.0	13.0
To look for work/lost job...........	1.3	0.7	1.4	7.0	Change of climate.................	0.9	0.1	2.0	(S)
Closer to work/easier commute...	4.2	4.6	4.0	1.4	Health reasons....................	1.5	1.5	1.7	(S)
Retired..............................	0.8	0.6	1.2	(S)	Natural disaster...................	0.3	0.3	0.2	1.5
Other job–related reason..........	0.5	0.3	0.8	0.4	Other reason......................	5.8	4.4	6.2	17.9

S Data do not meet publication standards. [1] In 2020, this reason was expanded from "wanted new or better house/apartment" to "wanted newer/better/larger house or apartment."

Source: U.S. Census Bureau, "Geographic Mobility: 2022," August 2023, <www.census.gov/topics/population/migration/data/tables.html>.

Table 29. Geographic Mobility Status of the Population by Selected Characteristics: 2022

[325,303 represents 325,303,000. As of March. For persons 1 year old and over, unless otherwise noted. Based on comparison of place of residence in 2022 vs. 2021. Excludes members of the Armed Forces except those living off post or with their families on post. Based on Current Population Survey, Annual Social and Economic Supplement. See text, this section and Appendix III. For composition of regions, see map, inside front cover]

Characteristic	Total persons (1,000)	Percent distribution by geographic mobility						
		Non–movers	Movers (different house in United States)					Movers from abroad
			Total	Same county	Different county			
					Total	Same state	Different state	
2021 to 2022, total	325,303	91.3	8.2	4.6	3.6	2.1	1.5	0.4
By age:								
1 to 4 years old	15,120	88.3	11.0	6.4	4.5	2.7	1.8	0.7
5 to 9 years old	20,228	91.2	8.5	4.8	3.7	2.3	1.4	0.3
10 to 14 years old	21,231	91.9	7.8	4.6	3.2	1.8	1.4	0.3
15 to 17 years old	13,468	93.4	6.1	3.7	2.4	1.4	1.0	0.5
18 to 19 years old	7,946	90.8	8.5	4.8	3.6	2.2	1.4	0.7
20 to 24 years old	21,035	82.0	17.1	9.9	7.2	4.4	2.8	0.8
25 to 29 years old	21,747	80.9	18.2	9.7	8.5	5.1	3.4	0.9
30 to 34 years old	22,836	86.8	12.4	7.0	5.3	3.0	2.3	0.8
35 to 39 years old	21,992	90.8	8.8	5.0	3.9	2.2	1.6	0.3
40 to 44 years old	21,198	92.0	7.4	4.5	2.9	1.6	1.3	0.6
45 to 49 years old	19,430	93.7	6.0	3.2	2.7	1.6	1.2	0.3
50 to 54 years old	20,700	93.9	5.7	3.2	2.5	1.5	1.1	0.4
55 to 59 years old	21,004	94.0	5.9	3.0	2.9	1.7	1.2	0.2
60 to 64 years old	21,174	95.1	4.7	2.5	2.2	1.2	1.0	0.2
65 to 74 years old	33,704	96.6	3.3	1.8	1.5	0.8	0.7	0.1
75 years old and over	22,489	96.8	3.1	1.7	1.4	0.9	0.6	(Z)
By region:								
Northeast	55,571	94.0	5.7	2.9	2.8	1.7	1.1	0.3
Midwest	67,400	91.4	8.3	4.7	3.6	2.3	1.3	0.3
South	125,066	90.6	8.8	4.8	4.0	2.3	1.7	0.5
West	77,266	90.5	9.1	5.5	3.5	1.9	1.6	0.4
By housing tenure:								
Owner occupied units	222,682	94.8	5.0	2.6	2.4	1.5	1.0	0.2
Renter occupied units	102,621	83.8	15.2	9.0	6.2	3.5	2.7	1.0
Persons 16 years old and over	264,356	91.4	8.1	4.5	3.6	2.1	1.5	0.4
Civilian labor force	163,997	90.0	9.6	5.4	4.1	2.5	1.6	0.4
Employed	157,723	90.1	9.5	5.4	4.1	2.5	1.6	0.4
Unemployed	6,274	86.9	12.1	6.0	6.1	3.3	2.8	0.9
Armed Forces	915	77.6	20.9	7.2	13.7	3.4	10.3	1.5
Not in labor force	99,445	93.9	5.6	3.0	2.6	1.4	1.2	0.4
By occupation:								
Employed civilians, 16 years old and over	157,723	90.1	9.5	5.4	4.1	2.5	1.6	0.4
Management, business, science, & arts	67,522	89.9	9.8	5.3	4.5	2.6	1.9	0.4
Management, business, & financial	28,687	90.7	9.0	4.9	4.0	2.2	1.8	0.3
Professional	38,835	89.2	10.4	5.5	4.9	2.9	2.0	0.4
Service	25,154	90.0	9.5	5.9	3.6	2.4	1.2	0.5
Sales & office occupations	30,995	89.8	9.8	5.5	4.2	2.6	1.7	0.4
Sales	14,467	89.5	10.0	5.5	4.5	2.8	1.7	0.4
Office & administrative support	16,528	90.1	9.5	5.5	4.0	2.4	1.6	0.4
Natural resources, construction, & maintenance	14,061	90.6	8.9	5.2	3.8	2.4	1.4	0.5
Production, transportation, & material moving	19,992	91.2	8.5	5.4	3.1	2.2	0.9	0.3

Z Represents less than 0.05%.

Source: U.S. Census Bureau, "Geographic Mobility: 2022," August 2023, <www.census.gov/topics/population/migration/data/tables.html>.

Table 30. Geographic Mobility Status of Households by Household Income: 2022

[131,221 represents 131,221,000. As of March. Covers householders 15 years old and over. Based on comparison of place of residence in 2022 vs. 2021. Excludes members of the Armed Forces except those living off post or with their families on post. Based on Current Population Survey, Annual Social and Economic Supplement. See text, this section and Appendix III]

Household income in 2021	Total (1,000)	Percent distribution						
		Non–movers	Movers (different home in United States)					Movers from abroad
			Total	Same county	Different county			
					Total	Same state	Different state	
Householders, 15 years and over	131,221	91.2	8.5	4.8	3.7	2.1	1.5	0.3
Under $10,000 or loss	6,956	89.0	9.4	5.5	3.9	2.2	1.7	1.6
$10,000 to $19,999	10,515	92.2	7.5	4.8	2.7	1.8	0.9	0.3
$20,000 to $29,999	10,479	91.2	8.6	5.4	3.1	2.0	1.2	0.2
$30,000 to $39,999	10,130	90.2	9.4	5.7	3.7	2.1	1.6	0.4
$40,000 to $49,999	9,422	89.2	10.4	5.9	4.4	2.5	1.9	0.4
$50,000 to $69,999	17,417	90.6	9.2	5.7	3.6	2.1	1.5	0.2
$70,000 to $84,999	10,845	91.3	8.5	5.0	3.5	2.3	1.2	0.2
$85,000 to $99,999	8,535	90.3	9.4	4.7	4.8	2.6	2.2	0.3
$100,000 and over	46,920	92.2	7.5	3.9	3.7	2.1	1.6	0.2

Source: U.S. Census Bureau, "Geographic Mobility: 2022," August 2023, <www.census.gov/topics/population/migration/data/tables.html>.

Table 31. Geographic Mobility Status of Resident Population by State: 2022

[In percent, except as indicated (329,821 represents 328,821,000). Based on comparison of place of residence in 2022 vs. 2021. The American Community Survey universe includes the household population and the population living in institutions, college dormitories, and other group quarters. Based on a sample and subject to sampling variability. See text, this section and Appendix III]

| State | Population 1 year old and over (1,000) | Same house in 2021 | Different house in United States in 2021 | | | | | Abroad in 2021 |
| | | | Total | Same county | Different county | | | |
					Total	Same state	Different state	
United States............	**329,821**	**87.4**	**11.9**	**6.2**	**5.7**	**3.2**	**2.5**	**0.6**
Alabama....................	5,022	87.6	12.2	6.4	5.8	3.0	2.8	0.3
Alaska......................	724	84.8	14.5	7.3	7.2	2.1	5.0	0.7
Arizona....................	7,285	86.0	13.4	7.9	5.5	1.6	3.9	0.6
Arkansas..................	3,008	87.0	12.7	6.1	6.5	3.7	2.9	0.3
California..................	38,629	88.9	10.3	6.3	4.0	2.8	1.2	0.8
Colorado..................	5,781	83.6	15.8	6.7	9.1	5.1	4.0	0.6
Connecticut...............	3,589	88.4	10.9	4.9	6.0	1.9	4.0	0.7
Delaware..................	1,008	89.2	10.3	5.0	5.3	0.7	4.6	0.5
District of Columbia.......	661	78.0	20.1	10.3	9.8	(X)	9.8	1.9
Florida.....................	22,044	86.3	12.5	6.1	6.4	3.1	3.4	1.2
Georgia....................	10,791	86.6	12.8	5.2	7.6	4.6	3.0	0.6
Hawaii.....................	1,426	87.8	11.4	6.9	4.5	0.6	3.9	0.8
Idaho......................	1,919	85.1	14.4	6.8	7.7	3.1	4.6	0.5
Illinois.....................	12,455	88.3	11.1	6.6	4.4	2.6	1.8	0.6
Indiana....................	6,757	87.1	12.5	6.6	5.8	3.6	2.2	0.4
Iowa.......................	3,167	87.2	12.5	6.6	5.9	3.6	2.3	0.3
Kansas....................	2,907	85.3	14.3	7.5	6.8	3.5	3.2	0.4
Kentucky..................	4,462	87.2	12.4	6.4	5.9	3.4	2.5	0.4
Louisiana.................	4,537	88.3	11.3	6.5	4.8	3.1	1.7	0.4
Maine......................	1,372	89.7	10.0	4.6	5.4	2.3	3.0	0.3
Maryland..................	6,100	88.5	10.7	5.4	5.3	3.0	2.3	0.9
Massachusetts............	6,918	87.7	11.2	5.6	5.6	3.1	2.5	1.1
Michigan..................	9,937	88.4	11.1	6.1	5.1	3.5	1.6	0.4
Minnesota.................	5,655	87.4	12.2	5.7	6.5	4.4	2.1	0.5
Mississippi................	2,907	88.9	10.6	5.1	5.5	3.1	2.4	0.5
Missouri...................	6,111	87.1	12.6	6.3	6.3	3.7	2.7	0.3
Montana...................	1,112	86.7	13.0	5.8	7.2	2.8	4.3	0.3
Nebraska..................	1,943	87.4	12.0	6.3	5.8	3.2	2.5	0.5
Nevada....................	3,146	86.4	13.1	8.3	4.8	0.8	4.1	0.5
New Hampshire............	1,385	89.8	9.9	4.1	5.8	2.2	3.6	0.3
New Jersey................	9,174	90.4	8.8	4.4	4.4	2.5	1.9	0.9
New Mexico...............	2,093	88.2	11.3	5.8	5.5	2.0	3.4	0.5
New York..................	19,474	89.6	9.7	5.3	4.4	2.8	1.5	0.7
North Carolina............	10,589	87.3	12.2	5.2	6.9	3.7	3.2	0.6
North Dakota..............	770	84.2	15.2	7.2	8.0	3.5	4.5	0.7
Ohio.......................	11,632	87.8	11.7	6.6	5.1	3.4	1.7	0.4
Oklahoma..................	3,974	85.5	14.1	7.1	7.0	4.0	3.0	0.5
Oregon....................	4,201	85.5	14.1	7.2	6.9	3.9	3.1	0.4
Pennsylvania..............	12,845	89.3	10.3	5.7	4.6	2.5	2.0	0.4
Rhode Island..............	1,084	89.3	9.9	4.8	5.1	1.4	3.7	0.8
South Carolina............	5,228	86.5	13.0	5.5	7.5	3.3	4.2	0.4
South Dakota..............	899	86.6	13.0	6.1	6.9	3.5	3.5	0.4
Tennessee.................	6,977	87.0	12.5	6.1	6.5	3.2	3.2	0.4
Texas......................	29,671	85.7	13.5	7.3	6.2	4.0	2.3	0.8
Utah.......................	3,337	85.7	13.7	7.9	5.9	3.1	2.7	0.6
Vermont...................	642	88.2	11.2	5.4	5.8	1.7	4.1	0.6
Virginia....................	8,591	86.6	12.7	4.5	8.1	5.0	3.1	0.7
Washington................	7,710	85.2	14.0	7.8	6.2	2.9	3.2	0.7
West Virginia..............	1,758	89.6	10.2	5.0	5.2	2.8	2.5	0.2
Wisconsin.................	5,835	87.7	11.9	6.3	5.5	3.5	2.1	0.4
Wyoming..................	576	84.7	15.1	7.4	7.6	2.6	5.0	0.3

X Not applicable.

Source: U.S. Census Bureau, 2022 American Community Survey, B07003, "Geographical Mobility in the Past Year by Sex for Current Residence in the United States," <data.census.gov>, accessed November 2023.

Table 32. Geographic Mobility—State to State Migration Flows: 2022

[Based on a comparison of place of residence in 2022 vs. 2021. Data are shown for 15 States with the highest number of movers. Estimates are from the American Community Survey. Based on a sample and subject to sampling variability; see text, this section and Appendix III]

Current state of residence	Total	Movers by state of residence 1 year ago														
		California	New York	Texas	Florida	Illinois	Virginia	Pennsylvania	New Jersey	North Carolina	Washington	Georgia	Colorado	Massachusetts	Maryland	Arizona
United States	8,230,953	817,669	545,598	494,077	489,905	344,027	282,050	278,699	267,106	259,422	257,785	253,275	239,200	214,644	205,406	204,734
Alabama	139,263	8,012	3,827	10,102	18,236	4,328	3,654	3,330	1,207	3,320	1,639	23,155	3,329	599	1,517	1,202
Alaska	36,563	3,855	2,430	3,135	1,575	130	345	160	40	3,305	3,076	834	665	285	142	1,645
Arizona	282,729	74,157	5,071	17,404	4,471	10,623	3,791	4,273	3,626	3,300	21,242	3,046	12,232	3,143	1,955	(X)
Arkansas	86,375	7,783	666	17,105	7,065	2,383	978	267	113	451	2,703	497	2,562	145	1,212	1,776
California	475,803	(X)	31,255	42,279	28,557	24,559	15,373	13,544	13,162	13,302	31,866	11,002	19,970	15,540	7,903	27,412
Colorado	229,876	33,213	8,526	25,466	11,107	9,281	6,727	4,557	3,928	6,165	6,796	3,360	(X)	3,976	3,033	7,386
Connecticut	145,315	7,097	50,670	2,920	7,476	3,290	3,481	2,298	8,087	3,897	1,670	3,478	1,992	21,256	2,460	1,267
Delaware	46,162	660	4,603	692	1,339	1,256	1,990	11,392	5,312	2,250	171	293	123	384	9,709	949
District of Columbia	64,506	4,539	5,647	2,788	2,932	2,548	7,496	2,493	3,093	1,519	1,216	2,289	1,187	1,401	13,093	712
Florida	738,969	50,701	91,101	38,207	(X)	35,262	32,932	35,384	47,000	24,601	11,804	39,990	20,980	20,320	23,422	11,901
Georgia	327,795	25,960	16,535	23,754	51,380	11,096	14,204	9,223	8,295	23,175	8,761	(X)	5,419	3,299	6,706	1,798
Hawaii	56,209	10,562	982	5,966	1,442	1,133	1,775	903	383	1,931	4,090	2,823	2,750	397	1,269	2,750
Idaho	87,949	26,887	880	2,868	1,109	314	415	267	173	815	14,387	1,548	1,655	577	1,426	3,633
Illinois	228,308	20,573	12,072	19,949	14,078	(X)	3,866	4,475	3,576	5,384	3,965	7,424	6,720	5,625	2,260	5,377
Indiana	149,331	7,769	4,124	8,276	7,474	31,015	2,315	2,209	1,907	2,157	2,282	2,326	3,586	1,308	1,739	4,953
Iowa	72,231	2,349	1,865	3,856	3,546	16,504	291	923	795	804	786	289	1,932	3	653	2,264
Kansas	94,208	5,520	2,200	7,767	4,694	2,766	2,314	373	108	655	3,475	3,284	7,359	803	192	1,519
Kentucky	113,197	5,985	2,946	7,630	8,062	6,821	851	1,348	36	3,392	3,235	4,941	2,182	904	903	2,618
Louisiana	75,330	4,847	2,885	17,663	5,089	1,223	1,824	597	2,288	1,272	2,021	3,215	1,332	211	912	315
Maine	41,618	3,552	9,453	861	2,911	517	1,198	1,711	759	675	1,514	358	1,148	8,663	114	138
Maryland	139,784	7,198	21,186	4,917	8,425	3,134	19,478	12,481	6,151	4,152	1,774	3,193	2,186	2,686	(X)	1,439
Massachusetts	171,077	18,543	6,161	7,517	11,098	4,060	4,232	8,009	7,670	3,934	3,006	2,024	4,589	(X)	3,404	2,251
Michigan	157,955	13,939	3,196	8,529	17,557	10,942	4,323	3,165	3,290	5,852	1,983	3,404	3,620	1,791	1,513	3,772
Minnesota	117,016	6,908	113	6,506	4,521	7,131	3,401	3,524	829	2,300	2,255	892	2,701	1,005	2,514	4,234
Mississippi	69,948	1,638	900	8,312	6,611	847	1,506	335	106	1,715	2,090	3,094	1,905	402	394	1,848
Missouri	163,254	12,107	2,742	9,168	9,758	20,646	3,701	2,726	2,037	1,162	4,333	3,395	8,042	1,239	864	3,576
Montana	48,165	4,660	441	1,357	1,993	617	180	176	62	1,507	5,225	563	912	158	69	2,415
Nebraska	49,159	1,535	554	4,285	1,203	1,295	1,436	698	318	538	1,630	447	6,422	800	236	3,661
Nevada	127,406	48,836	3,795	6,946	2,360	3,845	529	2,167	829	2,053	6,212	842	4,522	748	317	6,888
New Hampshire	49,782	2,974	1,939	1,239	1,938	412	4,689	1,247	699	1,016	58	416	726	23,605	726	430
New Jersey	175,023	6,543	75,103	5,690	9,627	2,484	4,299	31,300	(X)	3,264	1,179	961	3,905	4,383	3,249	1,077
New Mexico	72,095	8,897	2,467	16,986	2,164	1,261	1,749	1,114	844	1,114	2,468	1,162	7,846	364	457	6,862
New York	301,461	34,681	(X)	12,233	21,300	8,679	11,990	28,184	38,771	10,915	3,962	8,889	4,849	20,673	7,787	4,661
North Carolina	341,582	22,891	25,024	16,332	34,920	7,931	33,919	11,683	10,750	(X)	1,040	22,551	5,902	6,781	12,924	5,619
North Dakota	34,536	1,989	526	1,745	675	458	113	128	52	23	535	433	0	51	94	535
Ohio	200,809	11,924	8,431	10,239	16,831	8,652	7,309	11,399	6,277	5,592	2,929	4,155	4,827	3,523	3,284	5,224
Oklahoma	117,788	15,200	1,840	26,440	3,478	3,052	2,152	757	60	2,613	3,811	2,576	3,840	604	213	4,822
Oregon	128,359	36,429	3,712	3,534	3,501	3,266	539	624	833	775	25,457	1,230	5,000	2,062	687	6,108
Pennsylvania	262,700	16,336	44,807	8,544	16,014	5,659	11,888	(X)	40,517	9,687	2,687	2,982	3,700	7,541	22,247	5,561
Rhode Island	40,311	919	2,324	2,684	3,951	355	786	1,543	1,330	468	662	369	400	12,606	1,143	662
South Carolina	219,707	15,035	15,537	8,811	14,769	5,342	11,446	9,377	7,926	36,324	5,097	19,121	2,472	5,109	7,891	2,628
South Dakota	31,300	957	52	832	328	29	373	129	66	441	1,001	2,134	700	76	0	1,446
Tennessee	225,969	22,565	5,821	12,862	25,318	12,602	9,450	6,568	3,517	7,391	4,661	14,770	4,105	2,424	2,635	4,584
Texas	668,338	102,442	30,890	(X)	41,747	25,272	20,705	12,578	12,949	17,975	21,083	22,324	24,511	9,565	13,711	22,634
Utah	91,341	18,669	2,236	7,070	3,025	1,456	1,675	1,366	563	1,348	8,845	398	5,327	1,391	1,030	5,357
Vermont	26,151	855	3,196	1,128	873	404	1,215	873	1,659	996	646	143	230	4,760	842	264
Virginia	266,970	19,036	17,516	13,359	23,766	5,881	(X)	16,830	11,155	21,395	6,877	6,689	4,485	4,709	28,470	3,478
Washington	248,355	49,968	4,732	19,245	8,368	4,772	7,406	3,789	2,943	5,849	(X)	5,574	9,396	5,773	2,038	7,237
West Virginia	43,493	879	949	580	3,418	806	8,279	4,299	290	2,217	0	2,903	210	877	5,246	240
Wisconsin	120,434	7,537	1,626	6,088	6,762	27,369	1,360	1,761	704	3,591	4,207	1,064	2,564	548	548	3,474
Wyoming	28,948	1,558	463	2,211	1,063	319	337	133	21	845	1,225	425	5,076	91	253	2,132

X Not applicable.

Source: U.S. Census Bureau, Migration, Migration/Geographic Mobility Data, "State-to-State Migration Flows," <www.census.gov/topics/population/migration/data/tables.html>, accessed May 2024.

Table 33. Persons 65 Years Old and Over—Characteristics by Sex: 2010 to 2023

[In percent except as noted (38.6 represents 38,600,000). As of March, except as noted. Covers civilian noninstitutional population. Excludes members of Armed Forces except those living off post or with their families on post. Based on Current Population Survey. See text, this section]

Characteristic	Total				Male				Female			
	2010	2020	2022	2023	2010	2020	2022	2023	2010	2020	2022	2023
Total (million).................	**38.6**	**54.6**	**56.1**	**57.7**	**16.8**	**24.9**	**25.6**	**26.3**	**21.8**	**29.7**	**30.5**	**31.5**
PERCENT DISTRIBUTION												
Marital status:												
Never married...........................	4.3	5.8	6.6	6.7	4.1	6.0	6.7	6.7	4.5	5.6	6.4	6.7
Married......................................	57.6	60.5	58.9	59.0	74.5	72.5	70.8	70.3	44.5	50.2	49.0	49.4
Spouse present........................	55.2	58.1	56.5	56.4	71.7	69.9	67.9	67.5	42.4	48.2	46.9	47.1
Spouse absent [1].....................	2.4	2.4	2.4	2.6	2.8	2.6	2.9	2.8	2.1	2.0	2.1	2.3
Widowed....................................	28.1	20.9	21.2	20.6	12.7	10.4	10.9	11.1	39.9	29.7	29.9	28.5
Divorced....................................	10.0	12.9	13.3	13.8	8.7	11.1	11.6	11.8	11.1	14.5	14.7	15.4
Educational attainment:												
Less than 9th grade..................	10.2	5.2	5.0	(NA)	10.2	5.0	4.9	(NA)	10.1	5.3	5.0	(NA)
Completed 9th to 12th grade, but no high school diploma............	10.3	6.3	5.8	(NA)	9.7	5.7	5.9	(NA)	10.8	6.7	5.7	(NA)
High school graduate...................	36.4	30.5	31.3	(NA)	32.0	27.9	28.2	(NA)	39.8	32.6	33.8	(NA)
Some college or associate's degree....................................	20.6	25.3	25.4	(NA)	19.7	24.2	24.8	(NA)	21.2	26.2	26.0	(NA)
Bachelor's or advanced degree.........	22.5	32.8	32.5	(NA)	28.4	37.1	36.1	(NA)	18.0	29.1	29.5	(NA)
Labor force status: [2]												
Employed....................................	16.2	18.0	18.6	18.7	20.5	22.3	23.0	22.5	12.9	14.5	15.0	15.5
Unemployed...............................	1.2	1.5	0.6	0.5	1.6	1.6	0.7	0.6	0.9	1.3	0.4	0.5
Not in labor force......................	82.6	80.6	80.8	80.8	77.9	76.1	76.3	76.8	86.2	84.2	84.5	84.0
Percent below poverty level [3]............	8.9	8.9	10.3	10.2	6.6	7.2	8.8	9.0	10.7	10.3	11.6	11.2

NA Not available. [1] Includes separated. [2] Annual averages of monthly figures. Source: U.S. Bureau of Labor Statistics, "Labor Force Statistics from the Current Population Survey," <www.bls.gov/cps/tables.htm>. [3] Poverty status based on income in preceding year.

Source: Except as noted, U.S. Census Bureau, Current Population Reports, P20-546, and earlier reports; series P-23, No. 59; series P-60, No. 226; "The Older Population in the United States: March 2002 Detailed Tables (PPL-167)," May 2003; and "Educational Attainment," <www.census.gov/topics/education/educational-attainment.html>, "America's Families and Living Arrangements," <www.census.gov/topics/families/families-and-households/data/tables.html>, and "Poverty," <www.census.gov/data/tables/time-series/demo/income-poverty/cps-pov.html>, accessed August 2024.

Table 34. Persons 65 Years Old and Over by Living Arrangement: 2010 to 2022

[In thousands (40,434 represents 40,434,000), except as indicated. Based on the American Community Survey (ACS). Based on a sample and subject to sampling variability; see text, this section and Appendix III]

Relationship by household type	2010		2019		2021		2022	
	Number	Percent distribution	Number	Percent distribution	Number	Percent distribution	Number	Percent distribution
Total..............................	**40,434**	**100.0**	**54,074**	**100.0**	**55,892**	**100.0**	**57,822**	**100.0**
In households........................	38,869	96.1	52,561	97.2	54,481	97.5	56,090	97.0
In family households..............	26,809	66.3	36,512	67.5	38,002	68.0	38,965	67.4
Householder.....................	13,379	33.1	17,967	33.2	18,813	33.7	19,412	33.6
Spouse...........................	9,563	23.7	13,483	24.9	14,338	25.7	14,768	25.5
Parent.............................	2,208	5.5	2,680	5.0	2,589	4.6	2,531	4.4
Parent-in-law...................	661	1.6	803	1.5	773	1.4	754	1.3
Other relatives.................	807	2.0	1,218	2.3	1,139	2.0	1,140	2.0
Nonrelatives....................	191	0.5	362	0.7	349	0.6	360	0.6
In nonfamily households........	12,060	29.8	16,050	29.7	16,479	29.5	17,125	29.6
Householder.....................	11,495	28.4	15,029	27.8	15,469	27.7	16,066	27.8
Male.............................	3,417	8.5	5,104	9.4	5,380	9.6	5,575	9.6
Living alone.................	3,124	7.7	4,560	8.4	4,814	8.6	4,988	8.6
Female..........................	8,078	20.0	9,925	18.4	10,089	18.1	10,491	18.1
Living alone.................	7,784	19.3	9,424	17.4	9,539	17.1	9,911	17.1
Nonrelatives....................	565	1.4	1,021	1.9	1,009	1.8	1,058	1.8
In group quarters..................	1,565	3.9	1,513	2.8	1,411	2.5	1,732	3.0

Source: U.S. Census Bureau, American Community Survey, B09020, "Relationship by Household Type (Including Living Alone) for the Population 65 Years and Over," <data.census.gov>, accessed November 2023.

Table 35. Persons 65 Years Old and Over with a Disability by Type and Sex: 2022

[In thousands (18,664 represents 18,664,000). Based on data from the American Community Survey (ACS). Disability data limited to civilian noninstitutionalized population. Based on a sample and subject to sampling variability; see text in this section, and Appendix III]

Type of disability	Number					Percent				
	Total age 65 and over	Males		Females		Total age 65 and over	Males		Females	
		Age 65 to 74	Age 75 and over	Age 65 to 74	Age 75 and over		Age 65 to 74	Age 75 and over	Age 65 to 74	Age 75 and over
Persons with any disability...	**18,664**	**3,961**	**4,374**	**4,168**	**6,162**	**33.1**	**25.2**	**45.2**	**23.5**	**46.4**
Hearing difficulty....................	7,646	1,836	2,503	1,009	2,297	13.6	11.7	25.9	5.7	17.3
Vision difficulty.......................	3,336	680	736	758	1,162	5.9	4.3	7.6	4.3	8.8
Cognitive difficulty..................	4,530	855	1,051	901	1,723	8.0	5.4	10.9	5.1	13.0
Ambulatory difficulty...............	11,741	2,067	2,458	2,865	4,351	20.8	13.1	25.4	16.1	32.8
Self-care difficulty..................	4,028	644	930	752	1,703	7.1	4.1	9.6	4.2	12.8
Independent living difficulty.......	7,519	1,034	1,648	1,470	3,367	13.3	6.6	17.0	8.3	25.4

Source: U.S. Census Bureau, 2022 American Community Survey, Tables B18101, B18102, B18103, B18104, B18105, B18106, and B18107, <data.census.gov>, accessed November 2023.

Table 36. Selected Characteristics of Racial Groups and Hispanic or Latino Population: 2022

[In thousands (229,707 represents 229,707,000), except as indicated. The American Community Survey universe includes the household population and the population living in institutions, college dormitories, and other group quarters. Based on a sample and subject to sampling variability; see text, this section and Appendix III]

Characteristic	Total population	White alone	Black or African American alone	American Indian, Alaska Native alone	Asian alone	Native Hawaiian and other Pacific Islander alone	Some other race alone	Two or more races	Hispanic or Latino origin [1]	White alone, not Hispanic or Latino
EDUCATIONAL ATTAINMENT										
Persons 25 years old and over, total	**229,707**	**147,734**	**26,714**	**2,013**	**14,185**	**422**	**14,991**	**23,648**	**37,371**	**141,836**
Less than 9th grade	10,694	3,142	901	216	1,024	23	2,993	2,396	5,937	2,559
9th to 12th grade, no diploma	13,131	6,152	2,214	225	647	30	1,838	2,025	4,099	5,625
High school graduate (includes equivalency)	59,909	38,299	8,270	621	1,982	154	4,407	6,177	10,517	36,711
Some college, no degree	43,842	28,801	6,138	435	1,493	97	2,369	4,509	6,479	27,609
Associate's degree	20,223	13,781	2,405	176	897	36	974	1,953	2,734	13,259
Bachelor's degree	49,641	35,030	4,063	223	4,402	57	1,650	4,217	5,080	34,060
Graduate degree	32,267	22,528	2,724	116	3,742	27	760	2,371	2,525	22,013
OCCUPATION										
Employed civilian population, 16 years old and over, total	**162,590**	**100,836**	**18,660**	**1,447**	**10,477**	**306**	**12,048**	**18,815**	**30,228**	**95,871**
Management, business, science, and arts occupations	69,122	47,096	6,416	396	6,061	91	2,683	6,379	8,159	45,428
Management, business, and financial occupations	28,675	20,057	2,544	168	1,997	43	1,153	2,712	3,532	19,356
Computer, engineering, and science occupations	11,754	7,403	862	52	2,017	14	388	1,019	1,196	7,149
Education, legal, community service, arts, and media occupations	18,334	12,744	1,886	125	986	23	792	1,778	2,354	12,268
Healthcare practitioners and technical occupations	10,359	6,892	1,125	51	1,060	11	349	869	1,077	6,654
Service occupations	26,256	13,654	3,999	339	1,531	63	2,876	3,793	6,712	12,675
Sales and office occupations	32,236	20,433	3,920	269	1,616	67	2,197	3,735	5,863	19,344
Natural resources, construction, and maintenance occupations	13,767	8,211	852	210	273	23	2,040	2,160	4,406	7,674
Farming, fishing, and forestry occupations	934	438	39	22	14	1	228	192	463	388
Construction and extraction occupations	7,952	4,489	437	136	113	14	1,384	1,379	2,924	4,152
Installation, maintenance, and repair occupations	4,882	3,284	376	52	146	8	427	589	1,019	3,134
Production, transportation, and material moving occupations	21,208	11,443	3,474	233	997	62	2,252	2,748	5,087	10,750
Production occupations	8,712	4,971	1,130	105	496	23	910	1,078	2,038	4,701
Transportation occupations	6,116	3,296	1,159	57	256	15	557	777	1,326	3,107
Material moving occupations	6,380	3,176	1,185	71	245	25	785	892	1,723	2,942
FAMILY INCOME IN THE PAST 12 MONTHS										
Total families	**83,304**	**54,339**	**9,172**	**714**	**4,911**	**141**	**5,385**	**8,643**	**13,872**	**51,955**
Less than $10,000	2,811	1,315	665	47	134	6	283	361	666	1,201
$10,000 to $29,999	7,305	3,731	1,390	98	343	14	730	999	1,775	3,452
$30,000 to $34,999	2,493	1,361	410	33	105	6	239	340	597	1,267
$35,000 to $39,999	2,461	1,387	387	31	101	5	246	304	566	1,297
$40,000 to $44,999	2,695	1,568	409	33	106	6	246	326	592	1,477
$45,000 to $49,999	2,566	1,528	360	30	105	4	225	313	555	1,441
$50,000 to $59,999	5,312	3,282	676	57	224	10	435	627	1,084	3,104
$60,000 to $74,999	7,777	4,976	928	72	320	14	603	864	1,500	4,727
$75,000 to $99,999	11,596	7,759	1,183	100	527	18	789	1,220	2,011	7,419
$100,000 to $124,999	9,587	6,691	864	73	504	16	535	904	1,414	6,432
$125,000 to $149,999	7,116	5,063	580	46	413	13	349	654	963	4,881
$150,000 to $199,999	9,138	6,561	677	51	652	13	385	799	1,092	6,358
$200,000 or more	12,448	9,118	643	43	1,377	16	319	932	1,057	8,899
Median family income in the past 12 months (in dollars) [2]	92	101	64	66	124	81	67	78	71	102
POVERTY STATUS IN THE PAST 12 MONTHS [3]										
Persons below poverty level	40,952	19,544	8,317	676	1,938	114	4,304	6,060	10,465	17,808
Families below poverty level	284,570	178,842	30,737	2,434	17,331	531	19,746	34,949	51,920	170,128
HOUSING TENURE										
Total households	**129,871**	**86,508**	**15,699**	**1,038**	**6,792**	**198**	**7,101**	**12,536**	**18,824**	**83,085**
Owner-occupied	84,649	62,505	6,923	572	4,298	88	3,339	6,925	9,610	60,632
Renter-occupied	45,222	24,003	8,776	466	2,495	110	3,761	5,611	9,214	22,453

[1] Persons of Hispanic origin may be of any race. [2] For definition of median, see Guide to Tabular Presentation. [3] For explanation of poverty level, see text, Section 13.

Source: U.S. Census Bureau, 2022 American Community Survey, Tables B15002, B17001, B17010, B19101, B19113, B24010, and B25003, <data.census.gov>, accessed December 2023.

Table 37. Hispanic Population Social and Economic Characteristics: 2023

[63,956 represents 63,956,000, except as noted. As of March, except for labor force status which is annual average. Excludes members of the Armed Forces except those living off post or with their families on post. Estimates are developed from a base that incorporates the 2020 Census, 2020 Demographic Analysis estimates, and Vintage 2020 postcensal population estimates. Based on Current Population Survey, Annual Social and Economic Supplement; see text, this section, and Appendix III]

Characteristic	Number (1,000)						Percent distribution					
	Hispanic, total [1]	Mexican	Puerto Rican	Cuban	Central American [2]	South American	Hispanic, total [1]	Mexican	Puerto Rican	Cuban	Central American [2]	South American
Total persons	**63,956**	**38,448**	**5,573**	**2,630**	**7,197**	**4,960**	**100.0**	**100.0**	**100.0**	**100.0**	**100.0**	**100.0**
Under 5 years old	4,934	3,105	419	155	556	334	7.7	8.1	7.5	5.9	7.7	6.7
5 to 14 years old	10,523	6,538	847	310	1,334	670	16.4	17.0	15.2	11.8	18.6	13.6
15 to 44 years old	29,584	18,273	2,364	1,066	3,507	2,225	46.3	47.5	42.4	40.5	48.7	44.8
45 to 64 years old	13,489	7,770	1,289	655	1,398	1,194	21.1	20.2	23.1	24.9	19.4	24.1
65 years old and over	5,426	2,761	653	445	404	537	8.5	7.2	11.7	16.9	5.6	10.8
EDUCATIONAL ATTAINMENT												
Persons 25 years old and over	**37,691**	**21,847**	**3,449**	**1,833**	**4,136**	**3,248**	**100.0**	**100.0**	**100.0**	**100.0**	**100.0**	**100.0**
Less than high school graduate	9,251	6,183	420	258	1,594	260	24.6	28.3	12.2	14.1	38.6	8.0
High school graduate	12,356	7,506	1,155	510	1,245	969	32.8	34.4	33.5	27.8	30.1	29.8
Some college or associate degree	7,987	4,571	992	343	629	694	21.2	20.9	28.8	18.7	15.2	21.4
Bachelor's degree or more	8,097	3,588	881	722	667	1,324	21.5	16.4	25.6	39.4	16.1	40.8
NATIVITY AND CITIZENSHIP STATUS												
Total	**63,956**	**38,448**	**5,573**	**2,630**	**7,197**	**4,960**	**100.0**	**100.0**	**100.0**	**100.0**	**100.0**	**100.0**
Native	41,275	26,917	5,541	1,084	2,806	1,688	64.5	70.0	99.4	41.2	39.0	34.0
Foreign born	22,681	11,530	32	1,546	4,391	3,273	35.5	30.0	0.6	58.8	61.0	66.0
Naturalized citizen	8,157	3,718	28	887	1,195	1,429	12.8	9.7	0.5	33.7	16.6	28.8
Not a citizen	14,524	7,812	4	658	3,196	1,843	22.7	20.3	0.1	25.0	44.4	37.2
LABOR FORCE STATUS [3]												
Civilians 16 years old and over	**47,532**	**28,167**	**4,223**	**2,230**	**(NA)**	**(NA)**	**100.0**	**100.0**	**100.0**	**100.0**	**(NA)**	**(NA)**
Civilian labor force	31,818	18,890	2,553	1,427	(NA)	(NA)	66.9	67.1	60.5	64.0	(NA)	(NA)
Employed	30,343	18,014	2,421	1,379	(NA)	(NA)	63.8	64.0	57.3	61.8	(NA)	(NA)
Unemployed	1,475	876	133	48	(NA)	(NA)	3.1	3.1	3.1	2.2	(NA)	(NA)
Not in labor force	15,714	9,277	1,670	803	(NA)	(NA)	33.1	32.9	39.5	36.0	(NA)	(NA)
HOUSEHOLDS [4]												
Total	**19,319**	**10,880**	**1,923**	**1,026**	**2,059**	**1,655**	**100.0**	**100.0**	**100.0**	**100.0**	**100.0**	**100.0**
Family households	14,241	8,332	1,288	646	1,623	1,169	73.7	76.6	67.0	63.0	78.8	70.6
Married-couple families	8,960	5,293	770	435	985	756	46.4	48.7	40.1	42.4	47.8	45.7
Male householder, no spouse present	1,895	1,180	143	70	246	148	9.8	10.8	7.5	6.8	12.0	9.0
Female householder, no spouse present	3,386	1,858	374	141	392	264	17.5	17.1	19.5	13.8	19.1	16.0
Nonfamily households [5]	5,078	2,549	635	380	436	486	26.3	23.4	33.0	37.0	21.2	29.4
Male householder	2,658	1,415	324	181	229	238	13.8	13.0	16.8	17.7	11.1	14.4
Female householder	2,420	1,134	311	199	207	248	12.5	10.4	16.2	19.4	10.1	15.0
MONEY INCOME IN 2022												
Total families	**14,241**	**8,332**	**1,288**	**646**	**1,623**	**1,169**	**100.0**	**100.0**	**100.0**	**100.0**	**100.0**	**100.0**
Under $10,000	601	313	81	48	61	39	4.2	3.8	6.3	7.4	3.7	3.3
$10,000 to $19,999	713	417	62	21	105	44	5.0	5.0	4.8	3.3	6.5	3.8
$20,000 to $24,999	539	304	36	31	73	45	3.8	3.7	2.8	4.8	4.5	3.9
$25,000 to $34,999	1,144	657	107	34	165	72	8.0	7.9	8.3	5.2	10.2	6.2
$35,000 to $49,999	1,738	1,036	152	87	215	135	12.2	12.4	11.8	13.5	13.3	11.5
$50,000 to $74,999	2,763	1,644	238	97	346	234	19.4	19.7	18.5	15.1	21.3	20.0
$75,000 to $99,999	2,063	1,263	208	84	181	169	14.5	15.2	16.1	13.0	11.1	14.4
$100,000 and over	4,680	2,697	404	244	476	431	32.9	32.4	31.4	37.7	29.4	36.9
POVERTY STATUS IN 2022												
Total persons [6]	**63,795**	**38,366**	**5,539**	**2,630**	**7,169**	**4,947**	**100.0**	**100.0**	**100.0**	**100.0**	**100.0**	**100.0**
Below poverty level	10,776	6,499	849	437	1,555	586	16.9	16.9	15.3	16.6	21.7	11.8
At or above poverty level	53,019	31,867	4,690	2,193	5,614	4,361	83.1	83.1	84.7	83.4	78.3	88.2

NA Not available. [1] Includes other Hispanic groups not shown separately. [2] Central American totals exclude Mexican. [3] Source: U.S. Bureau of Labor Statistics, "Labor Force Statistics from the Current Population Survey," <www.bls.gov/cps/tables.htm>. [4] Hispanic origin of the householder. [5] Includes a single householder living alone or sharing a home with unrelated persons. [6] Persons for whom poverty level determined. Excludes unrelated individuals under 15 years old.

Source: U.S. Census Bureau, Hispanic Origin Data Tables, "The Hispanic Population in the United States: 2023," <www.census.gov/topics/population/hispanic-origin/data/tables.html>, accessed May 2024.

Table 38. Native and Foreign-Born Population by State: 2022

[287,105 represents 287,105,000. The term foreign-born refers to anyone who is not a U.S. citizen at birth. This includes naturalized U.S. citizens, legal permanent residents (immigrants), temporary migrants (such as foreign students), humanitarian migrants (such as refugees), and persons illegally present in the United States. The American Community Survey universe includes the household population and the population living in institutions, college dormitories, and other group quarters. Based on a sample and subject to sampling variability; see text, this section and Appendix III]

State	Native population (1,000)	Foreign-born population			State	Native population (1,000)	Foreign-born population		
		Number (1,000)	Percent of total population	Percent entered 2010 or later			Number (1,000)	Percent of total population	Percent entered 2010 or later
U.S.	**287,105**	**46,182**	**13.9**	**31.4**	MO	5,925	253	4.1	39.7
AL	4,883	191	3.8	40.6	MT	1,097	(NA)	(NA)	(NA)
AK	679	55	7.5	35.4	NE	1,825	143	7.2	39.4
AZ	6,397	963	13.1	27.7	NV	2,577	601	18.9	23.5
AR	2,890	156	5.1	32.6	NH	1,308	87	6.2	33.2
CA	28,601	10,428	26.7	23.0	NJ	7,081	2,181	23.5	31.3
CO	5,282	558	9.5	30.9	NM	1,916	197	9.3	23.6
CT	3,058	568	15.7	31.4	NY	15,217	4,460	22.7	28.4
DE	917	101	9.9	33.2	NC	9,782	917	8.6	35.9
DC	572	100	14.9	40.1	ND	741	(NA)	(NA)	(NA)
FL	17,428	4,817	21.7	36.6	OH	11,170	586	5.0	43.3
GA	9,745	1,168	10.7	34.3	OK	3,777	243	6.0	33.2
HI	1,194	247	17.1	25.8	OR	3,819	421	9.9	28.7
ID	1,823	116	6.0	31.1	PA	11,994	978	7.5	38.4
IL	10,772	1,810	14.4	26.2	RI	936	158	14.4	35.0
IN	6,419	415	6.1	42.0	SC	5,009	273	5.2	35.4
IA	3,010	191	6.0	45.9	SD	878	(NA)	(NA)	(NA)
KS	2,730	208	7.1	34.3	TN	6,659	392	5.6	41.9
KY	4,331	181	4.0	50.3	TX	24,860	5,169	17.2	34.3
LA	4,397	193	4.2	42.7	UT	3,089	292	8.6	34.0
ME	1,329	56	4.1	40.2	VT	620	27	4.2	31.6
MD	5,135	1,030	16.7	35.7	VA	7,579	1,105	12.7	33.6
MA	5,722	1,260	18.0	38.8	WA	6,597	1,188	15.3	36.7
MI	9,339	695	6.9	38.4	WV	1,743	32	1.8	31.6
MN	5,218	499	8.7	38.4	WI	5,598	295	5.0	35.8
MS	2,875	65	2.2	43.1	WY	564	(NA)	(NA)	(NA)

NA Not available.

Source: U.S. Census Bureau, 2022 American Community Survey, B05002, "Place of Birth by Nativity and Citizenship Status"; and B05007, "Place of Birth by Year of Entry by Citizenship Status for the Foreign-Born Population"; <data.census.gov>, accessed November 2023.

Table 39. Nativity and Place of Birth of Resident Population—25 Largest Cities: 2022

[The American Community Survey universe includes the household population and the population living in institutions, college dormitories, and other group quarters. Based on a sample and subject to sampling variability; see text, this section and Appendix III. See headnote, Table 38]

City	Total population	Native population			Foreign born			
					Total		Entered 2010 or later	
		Total	Born in United States	Born outside United States [1]	Number	Percent of total population	Number	Percent of foreign-born population
Austin, TX	975,335	802,151	779,632	22,519	173,184	17.8	84,057	48.5
Boston, MA	649,768	470,164	448,636	21,528	179,604	27.6	72,898	40.6
Charlotte, NC	897,720	746,539	732,728	13,811	151,181	16.8	65,988	43.6
Chicago, IL	2,665,064	2,116,612	2,060,309	56,303	548,452	20.6	143,319	26.1
Columbus, OH	908,372	774,405	762,907	11,498	133,967	14.7	73,279	54.7
Dallas, TX	1,299,553	989,495	972,527	16,968	310,058	23.9	112,832	36.4
Denver, CO	713,252	614,685	602,856	11,829	98,567	13.8	33,637	34.1
El Paso, TX	677,469	522,183	506,134	16,049	155,286	22.9	40,572	26.1
Fort Worth, TX	961,160	801,177	780,687	20,490	159,983	16.6	54,203	33.9
Houston, TX	2,304,414	1,627,702	1,585,617	42,085	676,712	29.4	299,320	44.2
Indianapolis, IN [2]	876,564	769,947	759,990	9,957	106,617	12.2	54,200	50.8
Jacksonville, FL	971,315	849,052	820,133	28,919	122,263	12.6	48,654	39.8
Las Vegas, NV	656,302	518,596	506,221	12,375	137,706	21.0	35,232	25.6
Los Angeles, CA	3,822,224	2,456,023	2,394,377	61,646	1,366,201	35.7	304,635	22.3
Nashville–Davidson, TN [2]	683,639	595,109	585,964	9,145	88,530	12.9	43,259	48.9
New York, NY	8,335,897	5,270,761	4,973,105	297,656	3,065,136	36.8	887,127	28.9
Oklahoma City, OK	694,768	614,137	602,892	11,245	80,631	11.6	23,977	29.7
Philadelphia, PA	1,567,258	1,320,679	1,261,913	58,766	246,579	15.7	106,976	43.4
Phoenix, AZ	1,644,403	1,321,728	1,296,604	25,124	322,675	19.6	88,429	27.4
San Antonio, TX	1,472,904	1,261,316	1,226,837	34,479	211,588	14.4	71,331	33.7
San Diego, CA	1,381,182	1,041,606	1,008,366	33,240	339,576	24.6	94,490	27.8
San Francisco, CA	808,437	540,240	519,011	21,229	268,197	33.2	73,208	27.3
San Jose, CA	971,265	565,549	548,925	16,624	405,716	41.8	128,456	31.7
Seattle, WA	749,267	596,810	580,118	16,692	152,457	20.3	68,280	44.8
Washington, DC	671,803	571,905	558,085	13,820	99,898	14.9	40,077	40.1

[1] Includes persons born in Puerto Rico, Guam, the Northern Marianas, or the U.S. Virgin Islands, as well as those born abroad of at least one U.S. citizen parent. [2] Represents the portion of a consolidated city that is not within one or more separately incorporated places.

Source: U.S. Census Bureau, 2022 American Community Survey, C05002, "Place of Birth by Nativity"; and C05005, "Period of Entry by Nativity and Citizenship Status in the United States"; <data.census.gov>, accessed January 2024.

Table 40. Native and Foreign-Born Populations by Selected Characteristics: 2023

[In thousands (330,632 represents 330,632,000), except as noted. As of March. The foreign-born population includes anyone who is not a U.S. citizen at birth. This includes legal permanent residents (immigrants), temporary migrants (such as foreign students), humanitarian migrants (such as refugees), and persons illegally present in the United States. Estimates are developed from a base that incorporates the 2020 Census, 2020 Demographic Analysis estimates, and Vintage 2020 postcensal population estimates. Based on Current Population Survey, Annual Social and Economic Supplement, which includes the civilian noninstitutional population plus Armed Forces living in housing units on or off post with at least one other civilian adult; see text, this section, and Appendix III]

Characteristic	Total population	Native population	Foreign-born population Total	Natural-ized citizen	Not a U.S. citizen	Year of entry: 2010 or later
Total	**330,632**	**281,854**	**48,778**	**23,935**	**24,843**	**17,491**
Under 5 years old	18,473	18,201	273	52	221	273
5 to 9 years old	19,929	19,274	655	97	558	655
10 to 14 years old	20,698	19,642	1,056	220	836	1,020
15 to 19 years old	21,577	20,082	1,495	441	1,053	1,094
20 to 24 years old	22,281	19,792	2,489	692	1,797	1,652
25 to 29 years old	21,788	18,545	3,243	923	2,321	2,209
30 to 34 years old	23,126	18,921	4,205	1,323	2,882	2,671
35 to 39 years old	22,178	17,149	5,029	1,885	3,144	2,077
40 to 44 years old	21,309	16,457	4,852	2,050	2,802	1,648
45 to 49 years old	19,537	14,503	5,033	2,487	2,546	1,284
50 to 54 years old	20,465	15,935	4,530	2,529	2,001	897
55 to 59 years old	20,380	16,252	4,127	2,471	1,656	713
60 to 64 years old	21,007	17,542	3,465	2,297	1,168	454
65 to 69 years old	18,417	15,676	2,741	2,061	680	328
70 to 74 years old	15,599	13,405	2,195	1,672	523	225
75 to 79 years old	10,851	9,309	1,542	1,208	334	153
80 to 84 years old	6,970	6,035	935	770	165	78
85 years and over	6,047	5,134	913	756	156	59
Median age (years)	39	37	46	54	39	33
MARITAL STATUS						
Persons 15 years old and over	**271,531**	**224,737**	**46,794**	**23,566**	**23,228**	**15,543**
Married	133,159	104,415	28,744	15,418	13,326	8,727
Widowed	15,210	13,019	2,190	1,519	671	290
Divorced	26,016	22,601	3,414	2,214	1,200	643
Separated	4,628	3,281	1,347	540	807	352
Never married	92,519	81,421	11,098	3,874	7,224	5,531
EDUCATIONAL ATTAINMENT						
Persons 25 years old and over	**227,674**	**184,863**	**42,810**	**22,432**	**20,378**	**12,796**
Less than high school diploma	19,526	10,207	9,320	3,152	6,168	2,203
High school graduate	64,107	52,663	11,444	5,910	5,534	3,060
Some college or associate's degree	56,728	50,464	6,264	3,983	2,281	1,678
Bachelor's degree	53,611	44,742	8,868	5,521	3,347	3,201
Advanced degree	33,702	26,788	6,914	3,866	3,048	2,654
EMPLOYMENT STATUS						
Persons 16 years old and over	**166,395**	**135,577**	**30,818**	**14,880**	**15,938**	**10,734**
Employed	160,206	130,491	29,715	14,462	15,254	10,260
Unemployed	6,189	5,086	1,103	418	684	474
EARNINGS IN 2022 [1]						
Persons 15 years old and over with earnings	**121,355**	**98,916**	**22,439**	**11,367**	**11,072**	**7,304**
$1 to $14,999 or loss	2,516	1,826	690	233	457	282
$15,000 to $29,999	12,666	9,305	3,361	1,164	2,197	1,288
$30,000 to $39,999	15,812	12,346	3,467	1,376	2,091	1,207
$40,000 to $49,999	15,119	12,349	2,770	1,301	1,470	847
$50,000 to $74,999	31,432	26,528	4,905	2,800	2,105	1,426
$75,000 to $99,999	16,287	13,952	2,336	1,462	874	738
$100,000 and over	27,522	22,612	4,910	3,032	1,879	1,517
Median earnings (dollars)	60,073	60,727	51,736	61,611	43,692	50,166
HOUSEHOLD SIZE [2]						
Total households	**131,434**	**110,289**	**21,145**	**11,770**	**9,375**	**5,938**
One person	38,097	33,826	4,272	2,617	1,654	1,031
Two people	45,959	40,192	5,767	3,527	2,241	1,522
Three people	19,771	15,847	3,924	2,082	1,842	1,288
Four people	16,038	12,143	3,894	2,011	1,883	1,204
Five or more people	11,568	8,280	3,288	1,533	1,755	893
INCOME IN 2022 [2]						
Total family households	**84,334**	**68,527**	**15,807**	**8,755**	**7,052**	**4,421**
$1 to $14,999 or loss	3,816	2,951	866	358	508	298
$15,000 to $29,999	5,460	4,044	1,416	631	784	417
$30,000 to $39,999	5,048	3,935	1,113	546	567	316
$40,000 to $49,999	5,051	3,959	1,092	533	559	330
$50,000 to $74,999	13,338	10,680	2,658	1,317	1,341	705
$75,000 to $99,999	11,386	9,333	2,053	1,161	892	590
$100,000 and over	40,236	33,626	6,610	4,210	2,400	1,765
Median income (dollars)	95,453	97,877	82,462	96,442	70,546	79,567
POVERTY STATUS IN 2022 [3]						
Persons below poverty level	37,923	30,995	6,928	2,257	4,671	3,166
Persons at or above poverty level	292,154	250,347	41,808	21,666	20,141	14,283
HOUSEHOLD TENURE [2]						
Total households	**131,433**	**110,288**	**21,145**	**11,770**	**9,376**	**5,938**
Owner occupied unit	86,784	75,413	11,371	7,914	3,457	1,982
Renter occupied unit [4]	44,649	34,875	9,774	3,855	5,919	3,956

[1] Covers only year-round full-time workers. [2] Based on citizenship of householder. [3] Persons for whom poverty status is determined. Excludes unrelated individuals under 15 years old. [4] Includes occupiers who paid no cash rent.

Source: U.S. Census Bureau, "Foreign Born CPS Data Tables," <www.census.gov/topics/population/foreign-born/data/tables.html>, accessed May 2024.

Table 41. Foreign-Born Population by Selected Characteristics and Region of Origin: 2023

[In thousands (48,778 represents 48,778,000), except as noted. As of March. Foreign-born refers to anyone who is not a U.S. citizen at birth. This includes naturalized U.S. citizens, legal permanent residents (immigrants), temporary migrants (such as foreign students), humanitarian migrants (such as refugees), and persons illegally present in the United States. Estimates are developed from a base that incorporates the 2020 Census, 2020 Demographic Analysis estimates, and Vintage 2020 postcensal population estimates. Based on Current Population Survey, Annual Social and Economic Supplement; see text, this section and Appendix III]

Characteristic	Total foreign-born	Asia	Europe	Latin America Total	Mexico	Other Latin America	Other areas [1]
Total............................	**48,778**	**14,734**	**4,374**	**25,746**	**11,702**	**14,044**	**3,924**
0 to 9 years old........................	928	285	79	449	92	357	114
10 to 14 years old.......................	1,056	278	73	586	111	474	119
15 to 19 years old.......................	1,495	426	97	756	217	539	215
20 to 24 years old.......................	2,489	714	124	1,422	559	863	228
25 to 29 years old.......................	3,243	997	187	1,826	768	1,058	232
30 to 34 years old.......................	4,205	1,322	265	2,214	1,027	1,187	404
35 to 39 years old.......................	5,029	1,512	300	2,743	1,331	1,412	474
40 to 44 years old.......................	4,852	1,349	364	2,720	1,404	1,316	419
45 to 49 years old.......................	5,033	1,373	410	2,860	1,445	1,415	390
50 to 54 years old.......................	4,530	1,376	341	2,503	1,350	1,153	310
55 to 59 years old.......................	4,127	1,211	370	2,240	1,139	1,100	308
60 to 64 years old.......................	3,465	1,098	342	1,787	839	949	238
65 to 69 years old.......................	2,741	912	363	1,328	558	770	138
70 to 74 years old.......................	2,195	824	328	914	324	591	128
75 to 79 years old.......................	1,542	483	277	685	285	400	98
80 to 84 years old.......................	935	342	159	382	156	226	51
85 years old and over....................	913	234	293	328	96	232	57
Median age (years) [2]....................	46.1	46.8	54.2	45.3	46.2	44.3	42.1
EDUCATIONAL ATTAINMENT							
Persons 25 years old and over..........	**42,810**	**13,031**	**4,001**	**22,532**	**10,722**	**11,810**	**3,247**
Less than high school diploma...........	9,319	1,086	211	7,787	5,034	2,753	235
High school graduate....................	11,444	2,410	935	7,413	3,515	3,897	687
Some college or associate's degree.......	6,264	1,535	718	3,235	1,193	2,042	776
Bachelor's degree.......................	8,868	4,132	1,062	2,768	754	2,014	907
Advanced degree........................	6,914	3,868	1,075	1,329	226	1,104	642
INCOME IN 2022 [3]							
Total family households.................	**15,807**	**4,855**	**(NA)**	**8,349**	**3,959**	**4,391**	**2,602**
$1 to $29,999 or loss....................	2,281	442	(NA)	1,616	772	844	223
$30,000 to $49,999......................	2,205	424	(NA)	1,529	797	732	252
$50,000 to $74,999......................	2,658	572	(NA)	1,668	844	824	418
$75,000 to $99,999......................	2,053	490	(NA)	1,190	587	603	373
$100,000 and over......................	6,610	2,927	(NA)	2,347	959	1,388	1,336
Median income (dollars) [2]..............	82,462	122,526	(NA)	64,609	61,142	68,789	101,597
POVERTY STATUS IN 2022 [4]							
Persons below poverty level..............	6,928	1,433	435	4,610	2,080	2,530	450
Persons at or above poverty level.........	41,808	13,298	3,935	21,102	9,620	11,483	3,472

NA Not available. [1] Africa, Oceania, Northern America, and born at sea, except as noted. [2] For definition of median, see Guide to Tabular Presentation. [3] Data for other areas includes data for the European-born population. [4] Persons for whom poverty status is determined. Excludes unrelated individuals under age 15.

Source: U.S. Census Bureau, "Foreign Born CPS Data Tables," <www.census.gov/topics/population/foreign-born/data/tables.html>, accessed May 2024.

Table 42. Foreign-Born Population by Citizenship Status and Place of Birth: 2022

[The term foreign-born refers to anyone who is not a U.S. citizen at birth. This includes naturalized U.S. citizens, legal permanent residents (immigrants), temporary migrants (such as foreign students), humanitarian migrants (such as refugees), and persons illegally present in the United States. The American Community Survey universe includes the household population and the population living in institutions, college dormitories, and other group quarters. Based on a sample and subject to sampling variability; see text, this section and Appendix III]

Region and country	Foreign-born population, total	Naturalized citizens	Not a U.S. citizen Number	Percent of foreign-born
Total [1]................................	**46,182,177**	**24,509,131**	**21,673,046**	**46.9**
Latin America............................	23,233,834	10,089,255	13,144,579	56.6
Caribbean [2]............................	4,627,494	2,934,877	1,692,617	36.6
Cuba.................................	1,312,510	(NA)	(NA)	(NA)
Dominican Republic...................	1,279,900	(NA)	(NA)	(NA)
Central America........................	14,635,414	5,112,970	9,522,444	65.1
Mexico...............................	10,678,502	3,759,287	6,919,215	64.8
Other Central America [2]...............	3,956,912	1,353,683	2,603,229	65.8
El Salvador.........................	1,407,622	(NA)	(NA)	(NA)
South America.........................	3,970,926	2,041,408	1,929,518	48.6
Asia [2].................................	14,349,080	9,010,035	5,339,045	37.2
China, excluding Hong Kong and Taiwan....	2,217,894	(NA)	(NA)	(NA)
India..................................	2,839,618	(NA)	(NA)	(NA)
Philippines............................	1,982,333	(NA)	(NA)	(NA)
Vietnam...............................	1,331,192	(NA)	(NA)	(NA)
Europe.................................	4,728,948	3,187,081	1,541,867	32.6
Africa..................................	2,752,965	1,680,079	1,072,886	39.0
North America...........................	828,702	425,758	402,944	48.6
Oceania................................	288,560	116,835	171,725	59.5

NA Not available. [1] Includes persons born at sea. [2] Includes other countries not shown separately.

Source: U.S. Census Bureau, 2022 American Community Survey, B05002, "Place of Birth by Nativity and Citizenship Status"; B05006, "Place of Birth for the Foreign-Born Population in the United States"; and B05007, "Place of Birth by Year of Entry by Citizenship Status for the Foreign-Born Population"; <data.census.gov>, accessed November 2023.

Table 43. American Indian and Alaska Native Population by Selected Tribal Grouping: 2015 to 2022

[Based on the American Community Survey (ACS). The ACS universe includes the household population and the population living in institutions, college dormitories, and other group quarters. Based on a sample and subject to sampling variability; see text, this section and Appendix III]

Tribal grouping	American Indian and Alaska Native Alone [1,2]				American Indian and Alaska Native Alone or in combination [3]			
	2015	2019	2021	2022	2015	2019	2021	2022
Total	2,597,249	2,847,336	3,158,694	3,205,331	5,637,061	5,869,109	9,269,322	9,024,511
American Indian tribes, specified	1,996,821	2,185,088	2,446,491	2,496,239	4,282,161	4,422,243	6,388,042	6,268,029
Apache	68,715	78,041	72,153	73,085	141,134	158,127	194,715	191,823
Arapaho	8,511	8,015	5,905	5,688	12,467	12,950	11,000	9,540
Blackfeet	24,904	30,996	26,225	32,727	158,584	144,569	295,812	288,255
Canadian & French American Indian	6,576	8,064	3,668	5,132	19,558	19,519	45,725	47,518
Central American Indian	11,107	15,869	276,591	315,313	38,191	28,908	588,949	634,503
Cherokee	284,858	289,234	227,856	239,224	1,135,770	1,005,636	1,550,003	1,449,888
Cheyenne	9,660	12,189	11,347	8,027	19,434	24,001	28,197	21,713
Chickasaw	26,560	28,024	25,605	23,670	69,234	76,870	75,237	72,601
Chippewa	115,280	126,987	89,481	87,888	201,486	223,869	209,362	206,224
Choctaw	93,810	103,063	82,503	90,321	240,019	255,554	285,711	295,373
Colville	8,318	9,540	8,082	4,736	12,195	13,833	12,042	10,577
Comanche	12,270	16,834	10,059	8,128	29,062	35,648	35,869	31,546
Cree	1,669	2,231	1,895	2,811	8,232	11,428	17,236	16,569
Creek	39,752	47,906	40,596	36,446	100,793	112,485	120,978	119,850
Crow	12,444	14,463	11,024	12,903	17,796	19,427	20,431	26,349
Delaware	6,692	8,658	4,445	5,201	21,147	24,546	24,470	30,494
Hopi	16,841	17,679	14,173	12,871	24,627	26,698	26,522	25,185
Houma	10,197	11,274	6,523	5,727	16,590	17,301	13,750	11,772
Iroquois	38,504	44,532	28,202	30,095	106,211	100,248	100,875	107,839
Kiowa	8,233	8,995	7,379	4,539	15,016	14,600	13,487	12,162
Lumbee	71,967	74,140	59,608	58,226	90,764	92,515	82,594	81,645
Menominee	8,371	10,751	5,142	7,520	13,747	16,778	11,482	13,207
Mexican American Indian	127,696	152,778	548,959	548,717	200,167	246,009	905,271	875,183
Navajo	323,757	340,669	328,370	328,434	390,606	418,100	449,318	434,910
Osage	8,750	9,057	8,514	6,249	23,802	25,031	26,518	23,938
Ottawa	5,538	5,774	4,422	6,494	12,998	13,213	12,931	19,082
Paiute	10,138	11,025	7,883	8,635	19,496	17,730	18,314	16,656
Pima	22,398	26,411	27,153	15,967	29,866	34,578	36,627	24,976
Potawatomi	19,683	22,143	17,593	14,704	39,415	44,398	40,113	37,640
Pueblo	58,813	60,274	45,064	49,201	75,833	81,491	79,262	81,419
Puget Sound Salish	15,696	20,798	13,964	12,957	24,532	31,566	23,734	22,233
Seminole	11,873	15,289	8,800	9,580	35,908	42,039	42,572	41,710
Shoshone	9,024	11,029	7,459	7,719	16,987	18,411	18,556	17,149
Sioux	117,019	119,004	106,145	100,575	202,109	206,781	234,434	220,739
South American Indian	30,325	38,547	26,686	28,813	88,889	121,279	86,286	91,508
Spanish American Indian	6,122	8,678	5,019	2,903	9,611	16,728	11,200	9,125
Tohono O'Odham	24,721	22,224	20,790	17,704	30,532	28,457	30,033	24,638
Ute	8,467	8,984	5,853	6,289	16,597	14,575	17,148	16,040
Yakama	8,750	7,632	7,544	7,159	12,920	11,169	11,528	11,243
Yaqui	26,534	30,451	24,299	35,442	46,509	50,748	58,050	71,063
Yuman	9,038	8,514	5,377	8,891	11,948	11,376	8,623	14,195
All other American Indian tribes (with only one tribe reported) [4]	267,240	298,322	208,135	209,528	501,379	553,054	513,077	509,949
American Indian tribes, not specified [5]	69,361	96,715	134,102	141,879	179,008	229,320	1,312,413	1,178,535
Alaska Native tribes, specified	110,676	117,473	103,729	96,830	172,399	176,710	171,365	177,631
Alaskan Athabascan	16,931	18,778	13,014	12,456	28,509	28,612	25,334	25,748
Aleut	10,380	11,153	12,353	9,304	20,945	21,082	23,650	22,187
Inupiat	28,117	30,744	27,729	25,321	43,958	44,054	47,813	48,294
Tlingit-Haida	16,838	14,750	12,906	9,288	30,231	29,864	27,837	26,161
Tsimshian	2,364	2,422	2,608	2,134	5,105	5,133	4,951	5,358
Yup'ik	36,046	39,626	35,119	38,327	43,651	47,965	41,780	49,883
Alaska Native tribes, not specified [6]	10,926	16,809	17,152	11,047	18,353	24,218	33,421	28,323
American Indian or Alaska Native tribes, not specified [7]	344,191	361,256	340,205	351,958	985,140	1,016,618	1,364,081	1,371,993
Two or more American Indian or Alaska Native Tribes [8]	65,274	69,995	117,015	107,378	(X)	(X)	(X)	(X)

X Not applicable. [1] Data shown are for people who are American Indian and Alaska Native alone and people with no tribe reported. [2] Total includes people who reported American Indian or Alaska Native only, regardless of whether they reported one or more American Indian or Alaska Native tribes or tribal groupings. [3] The numbers by American Indian and Alaska Native tribal grouping do not add to the total population because the American Indian and Alaska Native tribal groupings are tallies of the number of American Indian and Alaska Native responses rather than the number of American Indian and Alaska Native respondents. Responses that include more than one race and/or American Indian and Alaska Native tribal grouping are counted several times. For example, a respondent reporting "Apache, Blackfeet, and White" would be included in the Apache as well as Blackfeet numbers. [4] Includes respondents who provide a response of another American Indian tribe not shown separately, such as Abenaki, Catawba, Eastern Tribes, Kickapoo, Mattaponi, Quapaw, Shawnee, or Yuchi. [5] Includes people who provide a generic term such as "American Indian" or tribal groupings not elsewhere classified. [6] Includes people who provide a generic term such as "Alaska Indian" or "Alaska Native" or tribal groupings not elsewhere classified. [7] Includes respondents who checked the American Indian or Alaska Native response category on the ACS questionnaire and did not write in a specific group. [8] Includes respondents who provided multiple American Indian or Alaska Native Tribes responses such as Blackfeet and Pueblo; or Alaskan Athabascan and Tlingit-Haida; or Paiute and Aleut.

Source: U.S. Census Bureau, American Community Survey, Tables B02014 and B02017, <data.census.gov>, accessed January 2024.

Table 44. Refugee Arrivals and Individuals Granted Asylum by Country of Nationality: 2013 to 2022

[For year ending September 30. Persons admitted to the U.S. as refugees or granted asylum in the United States in the year shown. For definitions of refugee and asylee, see text, this section. Refugee data were derived from data on refugee admissions that are maintained in the Worldwide Refugee Admissions Processing System (WRAPS) of the Bureau of Population, Refugees, and Migration (PRM) of the U.S. Department of State. Asylee data were derived from data obtained from Global, a cloud-based platform of the U.S. Citizenship and Immigration Services (USCIS) of the U.S. Department of Homeland Security that replaced the Refugee, Asylum, and Parole System (RAPS), and also data obtained from the Executive Office for Immigration Review (EOIR) of the U.S. Department of Justice]

Country of nationality	2013	2014	2015	2016	2017	2018	2019	2020	2021	2022
REFUGEE ARRIVALS										
Total	69,909	69,975	69,920	84,989	53,691	22,405	29,916	11,840	11,454	25,519
Congo, Democratic Republic	2,545	4,502	7,823	16,279	9,325	7,841	12,875	2,863	4,876	7,742
Syria	48	132	1,693	12,583	6,566	62	560	486	1,255	4,562
Burma	16,295	14,578	18,323	12,294	5,047	3,525	4,928	2,112	769	2,141
Sudan	2,137	1,307	1,576	1,444	962	74	376	258	510	1,665
Afghanistan	622	758	914	2,743	1,315	802	1,197	603	874	1,619
Ukraine	235	493	1,454	2,526	4,254	2,637	4,432	1,935	802	1,586
Guatemala	–	–	–	8	50	42	117	249	64	1,084
El Salvador	–	–	–	364	1,124	724	311	362	200	524
Moldova	115	141	323	464	293	197	116	352	75	511
Iraq	19,331	19,651	12,608	9,837	6,857	140	462	541	500	501
Somalia	7,579	9,011	8,852	9,032	6,122	257	230	149	196	491
Eritrea	1,763	1,445	1,576	1,924	1,912	1,260	1,750	475	185	317
Ethiopia	859	754	646	1,147	791	387	258	119	75	266
Iran	2,579	2,833	3,099	3,736	2,575	41	198	135	182	258
Cuba	4,205	4,063	1,526	354	178	–	(D)	7	(D)	–
Bhutan	9,045	8,316	5,563	5,455	3,340	2,016	28	7	3	12
ASYLEES										
Total	24,631	23,038	25,946	20,311	26,382	37,702	45,805	30,736	16,628	36,615
China	8,526	7,866	6,176	4,488	5,556	6,809	7,414	4,749	1,870	4,589
Venezuela	673	386	492	342	539	5,796	6,591	4,013	1,916	3,691
El Salvador	245	366	2,153	2,134	3,448	2,905	3,181	1,981	1,422	2,639
Guatemala	358	486	2,054	1,900	2,948	2,317	2,579	1,847	1,300	2,329
India	391	473	472	471	672	1,305	2,261	1,335	704	2,203
Honduras	191	237	1,404	1,477	2,035	1,992	1,800	1,257	988	1,829
Afghanistan	111	118	169	107	118	103	107	57	107	1,493
Turkey	[1] 25	[1] 5	31	[1] 11	28	499	1,746	1,556	912	1,228
Russia	531	337	403	280	335	852	1,390	971	555	1,158
Mexico	327	570	851	898	1,030	1,354	1,591	1,205	665	975
Nicaragua	20	22	53	39	58	67	666	544	249	974
Egypt	3,358	2,825	1,660	830	1,147	1,546	2,244	1,409	667	893

– Represents zero. D Data withheld to limit disclosure. [1] Asylum affirmatively granted only. The affirmative asylum process applies to persons who are not in removal proceedings.

Source: U.S. Department of Homeland Security, Office of Homeland Security Statistics, *Refugees and Asylees: 2022*, November 2023; and "2022 Yearbook of Immigration Statistics," <www.dhs.gov/ohss/topics/immigration/yearbook>, accessed February 2024.

Table 45. Nonimmigrant Admissions by Class of Admission: 2015 to 2022

[In thousands (181,300 represents 181,300,000). Fiscal years ending September 30. Nonimmigrants are foreign nationals granted temporary admission to the U.S. Admissions represent counts of events, i.e., arrivals, not unique individuals; multiple entries of an individual on the same day are counted as one admission. The majority of short-term admissions from Canada and Mexico are excluded. The major purposes for which nonimmigrant admissions are authorized include temporary visits for business or pleasure, academic or vocational study, temporary employment, and to act as a representative of a foreign government or international organization. U.S. Department of Homeland Security (DHS) collects information regarding nonimmigrant admissions at ports of entry and from DHS Form I-94/I-94W arrival records]

Class of admission	2015	2016	2017	2018	2019	2020	2021	2022
Total all admissions [1]	**181,300**	**178,700**	**181,100**	**186,200**	**186,200**	**86,100**	**35,300**	**96,800**
Total I-94 admissions	**76,638**	**77,112**	**77,643**	**81,280**	**81,563**	**37,176**	**13,623**	**44,898**
Temporary workers and families	3,723	3,938	3,969	3,920	4,106	2,573	1,844	3,177
Temporary workers and trainees	2,307	2,446	2,447	2,379	2,559	1,792	1,449	2,335
Intracompany transferees	918	965	977	993	988	471	182	478
Treaty traders and investors	450	478	497	503	516	292	201	338
Representatives of foreign information media	48	48	49	44	44	19	12	25
Students	1,991	1,992	1,940	1,958	1,907	918	799	1,264
Academic students (F1 visa)	1,887	1,893	1,846	1,863	1,818	876	758	1,199
Spouses and children of F1 (F2 visa)	83	79	74	75	70	32	32	55
Vocational students (M1 visa)	20	19	19	19	18	9	8	10
Spouses and children of M1 (M2 visa)	1	1	1	1	1	(Z)	(Z)	1
Exchange visitors	576	586	594	611	620	226	174	432
Diplomats and other representatives	438	442	450	458	454	219	161	331
Temporary visitors for pleasure	61,017	61,029	61,600	64,820	64,865	28,732	9,055	34,946
Temporary visitors for business	8,009	8,291	8,456	8,967	9,060	4,209	1,346	4,235
Transit individuals	690	635	498	454	463	252	211	447
Commuter students [2]	100	68	35	19	9	3	1	1
Noncitizen fiancé(e)s of U.S. citizens and children	35	44	41	29	40	23	19	26
Legal Immigration Family Equity (LIFE) Act	2	1	1	1	(Z)	(Z)	(NA)	(NA)
Other	(Z)	(Z)	(Z)	(Z)	(Z)	(Z)	(Z)	(Z)
Unknown	57	86	58	44	39	21	12	38

Z represents less than 500. NA Not available. [1] Estimated admission totals rounded to the nearest hundred thousand. Excludes sea and air crew admissions (D1 and D2 visas). [2] Canadian or Mexican national academic and vocational commuter students.

Source: U.S. Department of Homeland Security, Office of Homeland Security Statistics, *U.S. Nonimmigrant Admissions: 2022*, November 2023; and "2022 Yearbook of Immigration Statistics," <www.dhs.gov/ohss/topics/immigration/yearbook>, accessed February 2024.

Table 46. Immigrants, Refugees, and Asylees by State of Residence: 2022

[Data are for fiscal year ending September 30. Includes persons receiving lawful permanent residence status, becoming naturalized citizens, and admitted as refugees or granted asylum in the current year]

State	Lawful permanent residents [1]				Naturalizations [2]		Refugees		Asylees [3]	
	Total	Rank	New arrivals	Adjust- ments	Total	Rank	Total	Rank	Total	Rank
U.S. total [4]	1,018,349	(X)	465,718	552,631	969,380	(X)	25,519	(X)	36,541	(X)
Alabama	3,747	34	1,655	2,092	3,998	32	36	44	31	43
Alaska	673	49	386	287	1,184	45	21	46	18	45
Arizona	16,984	15	7,156	9,828	16,396	13	1,029	10	325	19
Arkansas	3,391	35	1,419	1,972	2,528	39	65	39	59	35
California	182,921	1	78,493	104,428	181,995	1	2,182	1	9,638	1
Colorado	11,410	17	5,266	6,144	9,523	21	625	16	359	16
Connecticut	11,219	18	5,159	6,060	11,070	18	142	32	287	21
Delaware	2,385	40	902	1,483	2,416	41	46	43	59	36
District of Columbia	2,595	39	1,074	1,521	2,424	40	0	(D)	80	31
Florida	113,653	2	53,855	59,798	105,528	3	749	13	2,302	3
Georgia	26,312	11	11,666	14,646	28,440	8	820	12	195	23
Hawaii	2,706	38	1,550	1,156	4,397	29	0	(D)	40	42
Idaho	2,050	42	728	1,322	2,545	38	453	24	13	47
Illinois	34,551	6	17,428	17,123	32,519	6	907	11	1,567	7
Indiana	8,681	21	3,594	5,087	8,330	22	538	19	430	15
Iowa	4,737	30	2,324	2,413	4,097	31	501	21	42	41
Kansas	4,449	32	1,980	2,469	3,758	33	345	26	50	38
Kentucky	6,476	25	2,960	3,516	6,380	24	1,300	4	168	26
Louisiana	4,819	29	2,025	2,794	3,246	34	22	45	439	14
Maine	1,363	45	597	766	1,240	44	103	34	150	27
Maryland	24,233	12	11,486	12,747	22,657	12	495	23	1,590	6
Massachusetts	32,885	7	14,406	18,479	27,008	10	507	20	1,074	8
Michigan	16,881	16	8,464	8,417	16,077	14	1,143	7	352	17
Minnesota	9,762	20	4,829	4,933	13,491	17	541	18	309	20
Mississippi	1,721	44	754	967	1,086	46	3	48	61	33
Missouri	7,178	24	3,193	3,985	4,872	26	606	17	60	34
Montana	486	51	171	315	349	51	47	42	(D)	(D)
Nebraska	3,755	33	2,017	1,738	3,197	35	318	27	49	40
Nevada	8,587	22	4,843	3,744	10,573	19	157	31	173	25
New Hampshire	2,086	41	923	1,163	1,716	42	86	36	50	39
New Jersey	54,958	5	23,264	31,694	54,952	5	248	30	1,071	9
New Mexico	3,327	37	1,459	1,868	2,973	37	105	33	135	29
New York	111,309	3	56,898	54,411	104,052	4	1,399	3	8,214	2
North Carolina	21,868	13	10,284	11,584	13,626	16	1,152	6	344	18
North Dakota	1,164	46	677	487	984	47	57	41	8	48
Ohio	18,057	14	9,182	8,875	15,867	15	1,128	8	442	12
Oklahoma	4,631	31	2,257	2,374	4,242	30	70	38	73	32
Oregon	8,143	23	3,426	4,717	9,799	20	306	29	187	24
Pennsylvania	28,381	10	13,233	15,148	26,747	11	1,101	9	657	11
Rhode Island	3,381	36	1,803	1,578	3,014	36	72	37	112	30
South Carolina	5,854	28	2,565	3,289	4,789	27	318	28	52	37
South Dakota	683	48	316	367	651	50	61	40	16	46
Tennessee	10,821	19	5,496	5,325	6,717	23	500	22	250	22
Texas	109,720	4	46,847	62,873	106,123	2	2,109	2	1,706	5
Utah	6,053	27	2,340	3,713	4,787	28	452	25	441	13
Vermont	523	50	218	305	706	48	91	35	4	50
Virginia	28,902	9	14,141	14,761	27,324	9	636	15	1,809	4
Washington	31,835	8	10,127	21,708	31,041	7	1,243	5	672	10
West Virginia	814	47	274	540	660	49	13	47	6	49
Wisconsin	6,109	26	2,468	3,641	6,125	25	645	14	137	28
Wyoming	357	52	161	196	298	52	0	(D)	(D)	(D)

X Not applicable. D Data withheld to avoid individual disclosure. [1] There are two paths to lawful permanent residence (LPR) (also known as the "green card"), depending on whether the applicant is seeking LPR status from within the U.S. or applying for an immigrant visa from abroad. Persons who gain LPR status from within the U.S. are referred to as "adjustments of status." [2] Immigrants aged 18 and over who become citizens of the U.S. [3] Includes affirmative and defensive asylees. [4] Includes American Samoa, Guam, Northern Mariana Islands, Puerto Rico, U.S. Virgin Islands, and U.S. Armed Forces posts, not shown separately.

Source: U.S. Department of Homeland Security, Office of Homeland Security Statistics, "2022 Yearbook of Immigration Statistics," and "State Immigration Data Sheets," <www.dhs.gov/immigration-statistics/readingroom/state-immigration-data-sheets>, accessed March 2024.

Table 47. Immigrants Obtaining Legal Permanent Resident Status: 1820 to 2022

[152 represents 152,000. For fiscal years ending in year shown, except as noted. For 1820-1867, alien passengers arriving; 1868-1891 and 1895-1897, immigrants arriving; 1892-1894 and 1898 to the present, persons obtaining legal permanent residence. Rates based on Census Bureau resident population estimates as of July 1 through 1929, and for total population thereafter]

Period/year	Number (1,000)	Rate [1]	Period/year	Number (1,000)	Rate [1]	Period/year	Number (1,000)	Rate [1]
1820 to 1830 [2]	152	1.2	1901 to 1910	8,795	10.4	1981 to 1990	7,256	3.0
1831 to 1840 [3]	599	3.9	1911 to 1920	5,736	5.7	1991 to 2000	9,081	3.4
1841 to 1850 [4]	1,713	8.4	1921 to 1930	4,107	3.5	2001 to 2010	10,501	3.5
1851 to 1860 [4]	2,598	9.3	1931 to 1940	528	0.4	2011 to 2020	10,298	3.2
1861 to 1870 [5]	2,315	6.4	1941 to 1950	1,035	0.7	2021 to 2022	1,758	2.6
1871 to 1880	2,812	6.2	1951 to 1960	2,515	1.5	2020	707	2.1
1881 to 1890	5,247	9.2	1961 to 1970	3,322	1.7	2021	740	2.2
1891 to 1900	3,688	5.3	1971 to 1980	4,399	2.0	2022	1,018	3.1

[1] Annual rate per 1,000 U.S. population. Rate computed by dividing sum of annual immigration totals by sum of annual U.S. population totals for same number of years. [2] October 1, 1819 to September 30, 1830. [3] October 1, 1830 to December 31, 1840. [4] Calendar years. [5] January 1, 1861 to June 30, 1870.

Source: U.S. Department of Homeland Security, Office of Homeland Security Statistics, "2022 Yearbook of Immigration Statistics," <www.dhs.gov/ohss/topics/immigration/yearbook>, accessed February 2024.

Table 48. Petitions for Naturalization Filed, Persons Naturalized, and Petitions Denied: 1920 to 2022

[For years ending September 30. Naturalizations refer to immigrants aged 18 and over who become citizens of the United States]

| Year | Petitions filed | Persons naturalized | | | | Petitions denied |
		Total	Civilian	Military	Not reported	
1920............	218,732	177,683	125,711	51,972	–	15,586
1930............	113,151	169,377	167,637	1,740	–	9,068
1940............	278,028	235,260	232,500	2,760	–	6,549
1950............	66,038	66,346	64,279	2,067	–	2,276
1960............	127,543	119,442	117,848	1,594	–	2,277
1970............	114,760	110,399	99,783	10,616	–	1,979
1980............	192,230	156,627	152,073	4,554	–	4,370
1990............	233,843	267,586	245,410	1,618	20,558	6,516
2000............	460,916	886,026	812,579	836	72,611	399,670
2005............	602,972	604,280	589,269	4,614	10,397	108,247
2006............	730,642	702,589	684,484	6,259	11,846	120,722
2007............	1,382,993	660,477	648,005	3,808	8,664	89,683
2008............	525,786	1,046,539	1,032,281	4,342	9,916	121,283
2009............	570,442	743,715	726,043	7,100	10,572	109,832
2010............	710,544	619,913	604,410	9,122	6,381	56,994
2011............	756,008	694,193	677,385	8,373	8,435	57,065
2012............	899,162	757,434	745,932	7,257	4,245	65,874
2013............	772,623	779,929	769,073	6,652	4,204	83,112
2014............	773,824	653,416	642,431	7,468	3,517	66,767
2015............	783,062	730,259	720,645	7,234	2,380	75,810
2016............	972,151	753,060	742,090	8,885	2,085	86,033
2017............	986,851	707,265	695,718	6,883	4,664	83,176
2018............	837,168	761,901	750,771	4,495	6,635	92,631
2019............	830,560	843,593	823,490	3,760	16,343	97,789
2020............	967,755	628,254	615,773	2,588	9,893	80,609
2021............	789,119	813,861	797,105	4,462	12,294	85,170
2022............	781,075	969,380	951,985	5,412	11,983	111,637

– Represents zero.

Source: U.S. Department of Homeland Security, Office of Homeland Security Statistics, "2022 Yearbook of Immigration Statistics," <www.dhs.gov/ohss/topics/immigration/yearbook>, accessed February 2024.

Table 49. Estimated Unauthorized Immigrants by Selected Country of Birth and State of Residence: 2000 to 2022

[In thousands (8,460 represents 8,460,000). As of January. The unauthorized resident immigrant population is defined as all foreign-born non-citizens who are not legal U.S. residents; most entered the U.S. without inspection or were admitted temporarily and stayed past the date they were required to leave. Unauthorized immigrants applying for adjustment to legal permanent resident status under the Immigration and Nationality Act are unauthorized until they have been granted lawful permanent residence, though they may have been authorized to work. These estimates were calculated using a "residual method," whereby estimates of the legally resident foreign-born population were subtracted from the total foreign-born population. All of these component populations were resident in the United States on January 1 and entered during the period from 1980 to the year prior to the year shown. Persons who entered the U.S. prior to 1980 were assumed to be legally resident. Estimates of the legally resident foreign-born population were based primarily on administrative data of the Department of Homeland Security, while estimates of the total foreign-born population were obtained from the American Community Survey of the U.S. Census Bureau]

Country of birth	2000	2005	2010 [1]	2015 [2]	2016	2017	2018 [2]	2019	2020	2021	2022
Total......................	8,460	10,490	11,590	11,440	11,750	11,410	11,570	11,110	10,510	(NA)	10,990
By country of birth:											
Mexico.....................	4,680	5,970	6,830	6,200	5,970	5,860	5,540	5,350	4,970	(NA)	4,810
Guatemala................	290	370	520	600	610	610	620	670	780	(NA)	750
El Salvador...............	430	470	670	720	750	750	730	750	750	(NA)	710
Honduras..................	160	180	380	420	430	500	450	450	550	(NA)	560
Philippines................	200	210	290	350	410	300	370	360	340	(NA)	350
Venezuela [3]............	(NA)	(NA)	50	80	100	120	190	220	260	(NA)	320
Colombia [3]..............	100	110	120	130	140	130	210	190	190	(NA)	240
Brazil [3]..................	100	170	150	100	110	150	190	180	190	(NA)	230
India.......................	120	280	270	450	560	490	480	390	340	(NA)	220
China [4]..................	190	230	300	320	420	410	390	330	270	(NA)	210
Other countries...........	2,180	2,500	2,020	2,080	2,260	2,090	2,400	2,220	1,870	(NA)	2,600
By State of residence:											
California..................	2,510	2,770	2,910	2,760	2,860	2,790	2,640	2,620	2,410	(NA)	2,600
Texas......................	1,090	1,360	1,780	1,860	1,910	1,870	1,950	1,950	1,900	(NA)	2,060
Florida.....................	800	850	730	540	610	610	680	650	610	(NA)	590
New Jersey...............	350	380	440	420	420	450	460	390	400	(NA)	490
Illinois.....................	440	520	550	440	520	440	460	440	370	(NA)	420
New York..................	540	560	690	630	630	620	600	510	370	(NA)	410
North Carolina............	260	360	390	370	360	320	360	340	360	(NA)	360
Georgia....................	220	470	430	370	400	400	390	360	360	(NA)	340
Washington...............	170	(NA)	260	260	280	280	310	330	340	(NA)	340
Arizona....................	330	480	350	360	330	340	340	330	340	(NA)	290
Other states..............	1,750	2,750	3,040	3,420	3,430	3,300	3,380	3,200	3,040	(NA)	3,090

NA Not available. [1] Revised to be consistent with estimates derived from the 2010 Census. [2] Revised to reflect updated methodology. [3] Estimates shown for Colombia 2000-2013, Brazil 2010-2015, and Venezuela 2007-2015 are approximations based on historical estimation and project notes. [4] Beginning 2018, estimates for China include Hong Kong and Macau.

Source: U.S. Department of Homeland Security, Office of Homeland Security Statistics, *Estimates of the Unauthorized Immigrant Population Residing in the United States, January 2018-January 2022*, April 2024. See also <www.dhs.gov/ohss/topics/immigration/unauthorized-immigrants>.

Table 50. Immigrants Obtaining Legal Permanent Resident Status by Class of Admission: 2010 to 2022

[For years ending September 30. For definition of immigrants, see text, this section]

Class of admission	2010	2015	2019	2020	2021	2022
Total	**1,042,625**	**1,051,031**	**1,031,765**	**707,362**	**740,002**	**1,018,349**
New arrivals	476,049	505,031	453,718	268,153	227,206	465,718
Adjustments	566,576	546,000	578,047	439,209	512,796	552,631
Immediate relatives of U.S. citizens	476,414	465,068	505,765	321,148	385,396	428,268
Spouses	271,909	265,367	304,334	195,718	251,825	238,632
Children [1]	88,297	66,740	61,303	37,379	53,056	57,131
Parents	116,208	132,961	140,128	88,051	80,515	132,505
Family-sponsored preferences	214,589	213,910	204,139	121,560	65,690	166,041
Unmarried sons/daughters of U.S. citizens and their children	26,998	24,533	24,497	11,383	6,837	17,763
Spouses, children, and unmarried sons/daughters of lawful permanent residents	92,088	104,892	93,398	51,701	39,126	89,856
Married sons/daughters of U.S. citizens [2]	32,817	24,271	25,213	13,930	6,625	17,449
Brothers or sisters of U.S. citizens age 21 and older [2]	62,686	60,214	61,031	44,546	13,102	40,973
Employment-based preferences	148,343	144,047	139,458	148,959	193,338	270,284
Priority workers [2]	41,055	41,688	39,471	47,388	61,451	53,433
Professionals with advanced degrees or persons of exceptional ability [2]	53,946	44,344	39,506	43,666	59,834	109,081
Skilled workers, professionals, unskilled workers [2]	39,762	37,243	41,787	43,218	54,099	79,362
Certain special immigrants [2]	11,100	10,584	9,609	10,704	15,315	20,526
Employment creation (investors) [2]	2,480	10,188	9,085	3,983	2,639	7,882
Diversity (lottery) [3]	49,763	47,934	43,463	25,028	15,145	43,233
Refugees	92,741	118,431	80,908	44,404	35,847	29,423
Asylees	43,550	33,564	26,003	19,471	20,550	53,659
Parolees	1,592	23	16	13	13	14
Children born abroad to noncitizen residents	716	403	60	30	75	85
Nicaraguan Adjustment and Central American Relief Act	248	49	(NA)	(NA)	(NA)	(NA)
Haitian Refugee Immigration Fairness Act (HRIFA)	386	9	(NA)	(NA)	(NA)	(NA)
Certain Iraqis and Afghans employed by U.S. Government [2]	2,575	7,048	8,081	9,727	8,303	11,911
Cancellation of removal	8,180	4,713	4,033	3,685	5,017	4,160
Victims of human trafficking	511	970	818	866	942	712
Victims of crimes and their immediate relatives	2,165	14,138	18,442	11,937	9,257	9,952
Other	852	724	579	534	429	607

NA Not available. [1] Includes orphans. [2] Includes spouses and children. [3] The Diversity Visa Program is a lottery available to nationals of countries with fewer than 50,000 persons granted legal permanent residency status within family- and employment-based categories during the preceding 5 years. Includes categories of immigrants admitted under three laws intended to diversify immigration: P.L. 99-603, P.L. 100-658, and P.L. 101-649. Additional rules and adjustments apply; see source for more information.

Source: U.S. Department of Homeland Security, Office of Homeland Security Statistics, "2022 Yearbook of Immigration Statistics," <www.dhs.gov/ohss/topics/immigration/yearbook>, accessed February 2024.

Table 51. Immigrants Obtaining Legal Permanent Resident Status by Selected Country of Birth and Selected Characteristics: 2022

[For year ending September 30]

Age, marital status, occupation, class of admission	All countries [1]	Mexico	India	China	Dominican Republic	Cuba	Philippines	El Salvador	Vietnam
Total	**1,018,349**	**138,772**	**127,012**	**67,950**	**40,152**	**36,642**	**35,998**	**30,876**	**24,425**
AGE									
Under 18 years old	(NA)	14,888	12,807	6,641	9,384	6,286	5,932	5,918	3,858
18 to 24 years old	(NA)	14,128	4,508	3,676	5,608	4,756	3,000	7,082	3,122
25 to 34 years old	237,655	30,163	18,895	22,919	7,840	6,710	10,191	5,260	4,136
35 to 44 years old	240,932	31,309	64,518	14,691	6,174	4,925	8,385	5,265	2,805
45 to 54 years old	137,863	31,542	14,923	9,437	5,692	4,497	3,849	4,616	4,451
55 to 64 years old	81,864	11,723	5,586	6,828	3,616	5,430	3,036	1,886	4,273
65 years old and over	52,299	5,019	5,775	3,758	1,838	4,038	1,605	849	1,780
MARITAL STATUS									
Married	625,325	96,356	102,967	47,410	20,488	15,815	20,876	12,070	15,146
Single	333,313	32,820	20,195	16,829	17,343	15,922	13,730	16,120	7,641
Other	48,655	6,365	3,454	3,360	2,217	4,785	1,292	1,345	1,607
Unknown	11,056	3,231	396	351	104	120	100	1,341	31
OCCUPATION [2]									
Management, professional, and related	133,637	7,848	32,241	11,057	1,882	1,989	8,949	1,160	1,059
Service	28,182	5,493	1,090	3,065	643	1,172	968	1,336	240
Sales and office	50,878	6,581	4,824	4,793	2,143	1,033	1,258	905	2,652
Farming, fishing, and forestry	11,294	4,088	1,467	926	256	(D)	121	556	439
Construction, extraction, maintenance and repair	12,104	6,662	95	170	284	385	63	(D)	(D)
Production, transportation, and material moving	39,087	14,697	2,258	1,548	1,408	1,533	1,745	1,252	443
MAJOR CLASS OF ADMISSION									
Immediate relatives of U.S. citizens	428,268	94,101	20,396	16,698	28,966	11,432	15,034	10,541	11,446
Family-sponsored preferences	166,041	25,148	8,055	11,738	10,679	9,958	3,573	10,719	9,749
Employment-based preferences	270,284	8,356	96,335	30,514	302	38	17,127	4,509	2,995
Diversity program (lottery)	43,233	15	56	33	3	663	12	0	4
Refugees and asylees	83,082	1,392	1,829	8,861	109	14,548	35	3,995	89
Other	27,441	9,760	341	106	93	3	217	1,112	142

NA Not available. D Data withheld to avoid disclosure. [1] Includes other countries not shown separately. [2] Not shown are persons in the military, without an occupation or not working outside of home (e.g. homemakers, students), and with an unknown occupation.

Source: U.S. Department of Homeland Security, Office of Homeland Security Statistics, "Profiles on Lawful Permanent Residents: Fiscal Year 2022," <www.dhs.gov/ohss/topics/immigration/lpr/profiles>, and "2022 Yearbook of Immigration Statistics," <www.dhs.gov/ohss/topics/immigration/yearbook>; accessed February 2024.

Table 52. Immigrants Obtaining Legal Permanent Resident Status by Country of Birth: 2001 to 2022

[In thousands (10,501.1 represents 10,501,100). For years ending September 30]

Region and country of birth	2001-2010	2011-2020	2021-2022	2022	Region and country of birth	2001-2010	2011-2020	2021-2022	2022
All countries [1]	**10,501.1**	**10,298.2**	**1,758.4**	**1,018.3**	Vietnam	306.1	333.9	40.7	24.4
Europe	**1,263.9**	**835.7**	**137.1**	**75.6**	Yemen	24.6	46.8	10.0	5.6
Albania	50.5	44.1	8.6	5.9	**Africa**	**860.4**	**1,041.6**	**155.8**	**89.6**
France	39.6	44.0	8.5	4.4	Algeria	10.7	17.7	5.0	3.1
Germany	77.7	52.2	8.0	4.1	Cameroon	23.2	41.8	9.5	5.9
Italy	26.5	33.0	6.5	3.5	Congo, Dem. Rep. of the	7.9	60.6	8.6	4.7
Poland	116.8	53.4	6.2	3.2	Egypt	73.1	98.0	12.7	8.3
Russia	139.7	90.2	14.4	8.9	Ethiopia	109.7	120.7	9.4	5.7
Spain	15.8	27.6	5.5	2.9	Ghana	65.3	79.9	9.4	5.5
Ukraine	149.3	94.0	19.2	11.6	Kenya	59.7	63.9	8.1	5.0
United Kingdom	153.5	115.9	18.4	9.1	Liberia	45.2	35.3	4.9	2.4
Asia	**3,784.6**	**4,053.1**	**710.3**	**415.0**	Morocco	44.4	37.2	8.6	4.8
Afghanistan	24.3	90.8	23.7	14.2	Nigeria	111.2	133.8	25.5	12.4
Armenia	29.9	29.7	4.9	3.0	South Africa	32.9	28.5	6.3	3.5
Bangladesh	106.7	145.3	17.3	10.9	**Oceania**	**58.1**	**50.2**	**9.3**	**5.1**
Burma	45.0	113.6	5.0	2.9	Australia	26.4	27.9	5.5	2.9
Cambodia	35.6	27.0	5.2	3.4	**North America**	**3,605.1**	**3,520.9**	**573.1**	**332.7**
China	662.7	713.5	117.8	68.0	Canada	168.2	118.3	21.3	11.3
India	662.5	631.7	220.5	127.0	Cuba	318.4	468.6	59.7	36.6
Iran	125.9	118.0	15.1	9.4	Dominican Republic	329.1	481.2	64.7	40.2
Iraq	65.0	147.6	4.5	2.8	El Salvador	252.8	214.4	49.5	30.9
Israel	46.6	39.4	6.5	3.4	Guatemala	160.7	116.8	25.9	17.0
Japan	76.1	51.7	8.1	4.2	Haiti	213.8	190.9	21.9	10.4
Jordan [2]	38.7	45.9	8.2	4.8	Honduras	65.4	102.0	27.2	17.1
Korea, South [3]	221.5	197.8	28.5	16.2	Jamaica	180.7	196.6	29.8	16.5
Lebanon	39.5	28.1	5.7	3.4	Mexico	1,693.2	1,480.9	246.0	138.8
Nepal	33.1	114.3	19.3	12.0	Nicaragua	60.9	31.7	8.0	3.8
Pakistan	157.0	157.1	21.5	11.8	Trinidad and Tobago	61.8	36.4	4.3	2.4
Philippines	587.2	496.4	63.5	36.0	**South America**	**906.0**	**783.1**	**170.4**	**99.0**
Saudi Arabia	11.6	18.4	4.5	2.8	Argentina	50.5	38.4	7.4	4.1
Sri Lanka	17.6	17.7	3.8	2.6	Brazil	123.8	136.9	42.5	24.2
Syria	25.9	51.1	5.0	3.2	Colombia	251.3	186.1	37.0	21.7
Taiwan	87.9	52.1	9.3	5.1	Ecuador	112.5	102.2	19.4	11.9
Thailand	68.3	69.3	8.7	4.6	Guyana	76.2	54.8	6.9	3.5
Turkey	41.1	45.7	11.5	7.0	Peru	145.7	106.6	13.1	8.0
Uzbekistan	36.0	40.3	6.0	5.0	Venezuela	84.4	107.9	35.4	21.0

[1] Includes other countries not shown separately. [2] Prior to 2003, includes Palestine; beginning in 2003, Palestine included in Unknown (not shown separately). [3] Prior to 2009, includes a small number of cases from North Korea.

Source: U.S. Department of Homeland Security, Office of Homeland Security Statistics, "2022 Yearbook of Immigration Statistics," and earlier releases, <www.dhs.gov/ohss/topics/immigration/yearbook>, accessed February 2024.

Table 53. Refugees and Asylees Obtaining Legal Permanent Resident Status by Country of Birth: 2001 to 2022

[For years ending September 30]

Country of birth	2001-2010	2011-2020	2021	2022	Country of birth	2001-2010	2011-2020	2021	2022
All countries [1]	**1,325,365**	**1,385,064**	**56,397**	**83,082**	Egypt	7,987	19,170	1,025	2,409
Europe	**296,794**	**46,140**	**3,603**	**4,997**	Cameroon	7,564	8,034	310	1,222
Ukraine	57,186	16,255	1,927	2,116	Eritrea	4,534	13,555	912	1,186
Russia	32,819	6,922	566	908	Tanzania	3,503	10,294	956	1,143
Soviet Union [2]	6,794	3,127	256	458	Liberia	28,808	6,109	1,294	1,086
Moldova	10,813	4,215	127	331	Ethiopia	31,900	33,852	717	1,031
Albania	10,905	1,762	(D)	296	Nigeria	3,358	1,547	366	797
Asia	**389,469**	**599,826**	**13,869**	**24,156**	Uganda	2,482	7,380	523	657
China	111,632	125,465	5,187	8,861	Rwanda	2,939	6,823	470	622
Turkey	985	1,792	377	1,882	Burundi	3,387	4,828	584	550
India	24,010	9,965	1,009	1,829	Guinea	4,467	4,351	84	371
Burma	32,904	98,900	1,427	1,500	Sudan	23,580	11,694	218	371
Nepal	6,000	42,850	518	1,262	Burkina Faso	256	1,169	57	271
Syria	2,223	25,065	613	1,032	Kenya	15,351	15,970	274	264
Pakistan	8,339	8,190	440	1,027	Somalia	59,069	40,980	254	252
Iraq	40,789	116,207	578	817	Cote d'Ivoire	4,404	2,865	79	223
Bangladesh	3,382	1,669	173	752	**Oceania**	**1,453**	**361**	**12**	**14**
Afghanistan	13,533	8,042	426	609	**North America**	**326,846**	**456,534**	**23,625**	**26,889**
Iran	45,515	31,439	493	555	Cuba	276,331	402,832	19,354	14,548
Thailand	22,405	27,288	474	527	El Salvador	4,061	[3] 10,218	1,124	3,995
Malaysia	1,125	12,955	476	332	Guatemala	7,399	11,608	1,116	2,932
Sri Lanka	1,852	2,522	58	287	Honduras	1,684	5,708	593	2,597
Kyrgyzstan	1,649	1,781	144	279	Mexico	2,780	8,751	959	1,392
Saudi Arabia	929	1,850	141	257	Haiti	29,824	11,790	116	573
Kazakhstan	3,964	1,440	134	253	**South America**	**65,912**	**32,959**	**3,495**	**10,175**
Uzbekistan	14,047	2,850	93	243	Venezuela	10,726	13,044	2,419	8,100
Bhutan	6,762	54,459	80	63	Colombia	40,321	9,991	475	983
Africa	**242,839**	**248,486**	**11,768**	**16,806**	Ecuador	1,125	(D)	163	427
Congo, Dem. Rep. of the	5,643	33,531	2,822	2,464	Brazil	1,680	2,001	178	301

D Data withheld to avoid disclosure. [1] Includes other countries and unknown not shown separately. [2] Data are for unknown republics only. [3] Omits data for 2017 that was withheld to avoid disclosure.

Source: U.S. Department of Homeland Security, Office of Homeland Security Statistics, "2022 Yearbook of Immigration Statistics," and earlier releases, <www.dhs.gov/ohss/topics/immigration/yearbook>, accessed February 2024.

Table 54. Population by Selected Ancestry Group and Region: 2022

[In thousands (333,288 represents 333,288,000), except percent. Covers single and multiple ancestries; includes all people who reported each ancestry. Ancestry refers to a person's ethnic origin, heritage, descent, or "roots," which may reflect their place of birth or that of previous generations of their family. The American Community Survey universe includes the household population and the population living in institutions, college dormitories, and other group quarters. Based on a sample and subject to sampling variability; see text, this section]

Ancestry group	Total, (1,000)	Percent distribution by region North-east	Mid-west	South	West
Total population [1]	**333,288**	**17**	**21**	**39**	**24**
Afghan	189	11	9	39	40
Albanian	224	50	26	18	6
American	17,786	13	18	53	15
Arab [1]	2,238	24	24	30	22
Egyptian	335	36	11	30	23
Iraqi	165	11	37	24	28
Jordanian	87	21	21	28	30
Lebanese	584	22	27	32	20
Moroccan	140	34	10	40	15
Palestinian	172	18	29	31	22
Syrian	203	32	20	23	25
Arab	215	15	26	33	26
Armenian	459	21	8	11	60
Assyrian [3]	94	3	61	3	33
Australian	89	17	16	25	42
Austrian	585	26	24	26	24
Belgian	316	11	51	19	19
Brazilian	547	41	6	37	15
British	1,196	14	16	40	30
Bulgarian	107	22	28	27	23
Cajun	92	4	5	83	9
Canadian	542	24	16	30	30
Croatian	389	22	37	17	24
Czech	1,189	10	43	29	17
Czechoslovakian	227	19	34	27	20
Danish	1,128	9	30	17	44
Dutch	3,019	14	37	25	24
Eastern European	951	34	17	26	23
English	31,381	14	21	42	24
European	4,820	12	23	33	33
Finnish	606	11	43	17	29
French (except Basque)	6,311	23	21	35	21
French Canadian	1,626	42	18	25	14
German	41,137	15	38	28	19
Greek	1,201	32	20	27	21
Guyanese	250	72	2	23	2
Hungarian	1,247	32	29	23	17
Iranian	520	11	8	27	55

Ancestry group	Total, (1,000)	Percent distribution by region North-east	Mid-west	South	West
Irish	30,656	25	24	33	19
Israeli	144	35	8	30	28
Italian	16,010	41	16	26	17
Lithuanian	599	35	27	21	17
Northern European	434	12	20	28	41
Norwegian	3,937	6	46	15	33
Pennsylvania German	229	51	30	13	6
Polish	8,249	30	36	21	13
Portuguese	1,350	42	4	19	35
Romanian	451	22	25	26	26
Russian	2,099	33	16	24	26
Scandinavian	935	7	30	25	37
Scotch-Irish	2,525	12	17	51	20
Scottish	5,352	14	20	40	26
Serbian	192	18	40	19	23
Slavic	141	29	22	26	23
Slovak	603	39	32	19	10
Slovene	154	13	52	20	16
Sub-Saharan African [1]	4,177	19	20	46	15
Cape Verdean	105	81	2	11	6
Ethiopian	388	9	16	51	25
Ghanaian	217	40	13	38	10
Kenyan	122	23	22	35	20
Liberian	93	34	29	27	10
Nigerian	712	18	17	52	13
Somali	165	4	70	10	16
African	1,721	16	20	50	14
Swedish	3,317	13	36	19	32
Swiss	847	16	31	22	30
Turkish	240	35	10	33	22
Ukrainian	1,165	34	19	22	25
Welsh	1,522	18	21	34	28
West Indian [1,2]	3,155	39	5	50	5
Haitian	1,139	32	5	60	3
Jamaican	1,234	42	5	47	6
Trinidadian and Tobagonian	244	55	3	36	6
West Indian	246	48	6	38	9
Yugoslavian	199	18	31	25	25

[1] Includes other groups, not shown separately. [2] Excludes Hispanic-origin groups. [3] Assyrian, Chaldean, and Syriac.

Source: U.S. Census Bureau, 2022 American Community Survey, B04006, "People Reporting Ancestry," <data.census.gov>, accessed November 2023.

Table 55. Language Spoken at Home and English Speaking Ability: 2022

[314,929 represents 314,929,000. The American Community Survey universe includes the household population and the population living in institutions, college dormitories, and other group quarters. Based on a sample and subject to sampling variability]

Language	Number of speakers of language at home (1,000)	Percent who speak English less than "very well"
Total population age 5 and over	**314,929**	**(X)**
Speak only English	245,688	(X)
Spanish	42,033	39.9
French (including Cajun)	1,223	21.1
Haitian	910	37.1
Italian	522	24.6
Portuguese	998	36.8
German	876	15.5
Yiddish, Pennsylvania Dutch [1]	620	32.8
Greek	263	23.2
Russian	975	40.2
Polish	483	37.3
Serbo-Croatian	247	31.8
Ukrainian or other Slavic languages	434	39.1
Armenian	240	38.3
Persian (including Farsi, Dari)	515	38.0
Gujarati	457	31.9
Hindi	881	16.6
Urdu	519	27.7
Punjabi	343	39.0

Language	Number of speakers of language at home (1,000)	Percent who speak English less than "very well"
Bengali	416	41.1
Nepali, Marathi, or other Indic	510	32.2
Other Indo-European	652	31.9
Telugu	506	18.3
Tamil	341	15.8
Malayalam, Kannada, or other Dravidian	294	20.5
Chinese (including Mandarin, Cantonese)	3,507	51.1
Japanese	432	39.7
Korean	1,111	51.0
Hmong	234	38.7
Vietnamese	1,538	57.1
Khmer	198	54.3
Thai, Lao, or other Tai-Kadai	302	49.1
Tagalog (including Filipino)	1,758	30.3
Ilocano, Samoan, Hawaiian [2]	485	35.1
Arabic	1,428	33.5
Hebrew	221	16.3
Amharic, Somali, or other Afro-Asiatic	624	39.0
Yoruba, Twi, Igbo [3]	673	20.1
Swahili and other African [4]	342	31.0
Navajo	143	24.3

X Not applicable. [1] Includes other West Germanic. [2] Includes other Austronesian. [3] Includes other West African. [4] Other languages of Central, Eastern, and Southern Africa.

Source: U.S. Census Bureau, 2022 American Community Survey, B16001, "Language Spoken at Home by Ability to Speak English for the Population 5 Years and Over," <data.census.gov>, accessed November 2023.

Table 56. Language Spoken at Home by State: 2022

[In thousands (314,929 represents 314,929,000), except percent. The American Community Survey universe includes the household population and the population living in institutions, college dormitories, and other group quarters. Based on a sample and subject to sampling variability; see text, this section, and Appendix III]

| State | Population 5 years old and over (1,000) | English only (1,000) | Language other than English | | State | Population 5 years old and over (1,000) | English only (1,000) | Language other than English | |
			Number (1,000)	Percent of population 5 years and over				Number (1,000)	Percent of population 5 years and over
U.S.	**314,929**	**245,688**	**69,242**	**22.0**	MO.	5,828	5,456	372	6.4
AL.	4,790	4,514	276	5.8	MT.	1,066	1,017	49	4.6
AK.	687	580	107	15.6	NE.	1,847	1,634	213	11.5
AZ.	6,966	5,143	1,823	26.2	NV.	3,005	2,108	897	29.9
AR.	2,868	2,634	234	8.1	NH.	1,333	1,229	104	7.8
CA.	36,911	20,540	16,370	44.4	NJ.	8,748	5,922	2,827	32.3
CO.	5,535	4,639	895	16.2	NM.	2,008	1,387	621	30.9
CT.	3,448	2,645	803	23.3	NY.	18,622	12,909	5,713	30.7
DE.	964	834	130	13.5	NC.	10,114	8,825	1,289	12.7
DC.	633	503	130	20.6	ND.	731	679	52	7.1
FL.	21,143	14,759	6,385	30.2	OH.	11,095	10,236	859	7.7
GA.	10,292	8,761	1,531	14.9	OK.	3,780	3,365	415	11.0
HI.	1,361	1,032	329	24.2	OR.	4,041	3,422	619	15.3
ID.	1,827	1,626	201	11.0	PA.	12,303	10,787	1,516	12.3
IL.	11,908	9,067	2,841	23.9	RI.	1,042	813	229	22.0
IN.	6,434	5,789	645	10.0	SC.	5,001	4,613	388	7.8
IA.	3,021	2,750	270	8.9	SD.	853	790	63	7.4
KS.	2,760	2,438	322	11.7	TN.	6,649	6,129	520	7.8
KY.	4,252	3,999	253	5.9	TX.	28,148	18,257	9,891	35.1
LA.	4,319	3,989	330	7.6	UT.	3,152	2,654	499	15.8
ME.	1,324	1,245	79	6.0	VT.	619	586	33	5.4
MD.	5,815	4,612	1,204	20.7	VA.	8,202	6,806	1,396	17.0
MA.	6,640	4,979	1,661	25.0	WA.	7,364	5,807	1,557	21.1
MI.	9,497	8,531	966	10.2	WV.	1,688	1,645	43	2.5
MN.	5,389	4,733	656	12.2	WI.	5,583	5,096	487	8.7
MS.	2,771	2,657	114	4.1	WY.	551	516	35	6.3

Source: U.S. Census Bureau, 2022 American Community Survey, C16005, "Nativity by Language Spoken at Home by Ability to Speak English for the Population 5 Years and Over," <data.census.gov>, accessed November 2023.

Table 57. Language Spoken at Home—25 Largest Cities: 2022

[In thousands (925 represents 925,000), except percent. Data shown for population aged 5 and over. The American Community Survey universe includes the household population and the population living in institutions, college dormitories, and other group quarters. Based on a sample and subject to sampling variability; see text, this section, and Appendix III]

| City | Population 5 years old and over (1,000) | English only (1,000) | Language other than English, total [1] | | | Spanish (1,000) | Other Indo-European language (1,000) | Asian and Pacific Island language (1,000) |
			Number (1,000)	Percent	Speak English less than "very well" (1,000)			
Austin, TX.	925	651	274	29.6	95	190	32	39
Boston, MA.	618	403	215	34.8	92	100	60	40
Charlotte, NC.	841	657	184	21.9	83	109	35	29
Chicago, IL.	2,520	1,615	905	35.9	369	612	155	104
Columbus, OH.	851	696	154	18.1	65	44	41	20
Dallas, TX.	1,207	693	514	42.6	220	438	29	23
Denver, CO.	675	508	167	24.7	57	111	22	17
El Paso, TX.	633	209	424	67.0	161	406	10	6
Fort Worth, TX.	897	602	294	32.8	111	224	28	26
Houston, TX.	2,150	1,107	1,043	48.5	504	836	73	94
Indianapolis, IN [2]	815	673	141	17.3	65	74	27	21
Jacksonville, FL.	910	751	159	17.5	61	75	43	28
Las Vegas, NV.	617	407	209	34.0	81	155	16	33
Los Angeles, CA.	3,632	1,597	2,035	56.0	916	1,431	254	297
Nashville–Davidson, TN [2].	641	534	107	16.7	60	55	16	13
New York, NY.	7,863	4,093	3,771	48.0	1,781	1,813	1,004	710
Oklahoma City, OK.	649	516	133	20.5	51	98	7	20
Philadelphia, PA.	1,474	1,108	366	24.9	184	171	82	85
Phoenix, AZ.	1,546	968	578	37.4	205	473	39	36
San Antonio, TX.	1,379	818	561	40.7	180	507	22	23
San Diego, CA.	1,311	793	518	39.5	181	277	73	151
San Francisco, CA.	775	440	335	43.3	147	81	53	194
San Jose, CA.	923	382	541	58.6	220	201	76	246
Seattle, WA.	722	548	174	24.1	50	34	40	81
Washington, DC.	633	503	130	20.6	32	60	33	15

[1] Includes other language groups, not shown separately. [2] Represents the portion of a consolidated city that is not within one or more separately incorporated places.

Source: U.S. Census Bureau, 2022 American Community Survey, C16005, "Nativity by Language Spoken at Home by Ability to Speak English for the Population 5 Years and Over," <data.census.gov>, accessed November 2023.

Table 58. Marital Status of the Population by Sex, Race, and Hispanic Origin: 2010 to 2023

[In millions, except percent (242.0 represents 242,000,000). As of March. Data are shown for persons aged 15 years and over. Excludes members of Armed Forces except those living off post or with their families on post. Data for 2010 based on population controls from Census 2000; data for 2020 based on population controls from Census 2010; and, beginning 2021, data based on population controls from Census 2020. Based on Current Population Survey; see text, this section and Appendix III]

Marital status, race and Hispanic origin	Total				Male				Female			
	2010	2020	2022	2023	2010	2020	2022	2023	2010	2020	2022	2023
Total [1]	**242.0**	**264.7**	**268.6**	**271.3**	**117.7**	**128.5**	**131.3**	**133.1**	**124.4**	**136.2**	**137.3**	**138.2**
Never married	74.2	86.8	91.5	92.4	40.2	46.0	48.8	49.5	34.0	40.9	42.7	43.0
Married [2]	129.7	137.8	136.3	137.8	64.5	68.4	67.9	68.7	65.2	69.3	68.4	69.0
Widowed	14.3	14.7	15.2	15.1	3.0	3.5	3.7	3.8	11.4	11.3	11.5	11.3
Divorced	23.7	25.3	25.6	26.0	10.0	10.7	11.0	11.1	13.8	14.7	14.6	14.9
Percent of total	100.0	100.0	100.0	100.0	100.0	100.0	100.0	100.0	100.0	100.0	100.0	100.0
Never married	30.7	32.8	34.1	34.1	34.2	35.8	37.1	37.2	27.4	30.0	31.1	31.1
Married [2]	53.6	52.0	50.7	50.8	54.8	53.2	51.7	51.6	52.4	50.9	49.9	50.0
Widowed	5.9	5.6	5.7	5.6	2.5	2.7	2.8	2.8	9.1	8.3	8.4	8.2
Divorced	9.8	9.6	9.5	9.6	8.5	8.3	8.4	8.3	11.1	10.8	10.7	10.8
White, total [3]	**195.5**	**204.9**	**206.9**	**207.7**	**96.2**	**100.6**	**102.4**	**102.9**	**99.3**	**104.2**	**104.5**	**104.7**
Never married	54.7	60.5	63.8	64.1	30.6	32.9	35.0	35.2	24.1	27.6	28.8	28.9
Married [2]	109.6	112.2	110.3	110.6	54.7	56.2	55.4	55.6	54.8	56.1	55.0	55.0
Widowed	11.8	11.8	12.2	12.2	2.5	2.9	3.0	3.1	9.3	8.9	9.2	9.1
Divorced	19.4	20.3	20.6	20.7	8.3	8.7	9.0	9.0	11.1	11.6	11.6	11.7
Percent of total	100.0	100.0	100.0	100.0	100.0	100.0	100.0	100.0	100.0	100.0	100.0	100.0
Never married	28.0	29.5	30.8	30.9	31.8	32.7	34.2	34.2	24.3	26.5	27.5	27.6
Married [2]	56.1	54.8	53.3	53.3	56.9	55.8	54.1	54.0	55.2	53.8	52.6	52.5
Widowed	6.0	5.8	5.9	5.9	2.6	2.8	3.0	3.0	9.3	8.6	8.8	8.7
Divorced	9.9	9.9	9.9	10.0	8.7	8.7	8.8	8.8	11.2	11.1	11.1	11.2
Black, total [3]	**29.4**	**33.9**	**34.8**	**35.3**	**13.3**	**15.6**	**16.1**	**16.4**	**16.0**	**18.3**	**18.7**	**18.9**
Never married	13.7	16.7	17.5	17.5	6.5	8.0	8.4	8.5	7.2	8.7	9.1	9.0
Married [2]	10.6	11.8	11.9	12.3	5.2	5.8	5.8	6.1	5.4	5.9	6.0	6.2
Widowed	1.8	1.9	2.0	1.9	0.4	0.4	0.5	0.5	1.5	1.5	1.5	1.4
Divorced	3.2	3.6	3.5	3.6	1.2	1.3	1.4	1.4	2.0	2.2	2.1	2.2
Percent of total	100.0	100.0	100.0	100.0	100.0	100.0	100.0	100.0	100.0	100.0	100.0	100.0
Never married	46.8	49.3	50.4	49.6	48.8	51.4	52.3	51.7	45.2	47.5	48.8	47.9
Married [2]	36.1	34.7	34.0	34.8	39.4	37.3	36.3	37.0	33.4	32.4	32.1	32.9
Widowed	6.2	5.6	5.6	5.4	2.7	2.6	3.0	2.7	9.1	8.1	7.9	7.6
Divorced	10.9	10.5	9.9	10.2	9.1	8.6	8.5	8.6	12.4	12.1	11.2	11.6
Asian, total [3]	**11.2**	**16.7**	**17.1**	**18.0**	**5.3**	**7.9**	**8.2**	**8.7**	**5.9**	**8.8**	**9.0**	**9.3**
Never married	3.2	5.0	5.2	5.6	1.7	2.6	2.8	3.1	1.4	2.3	2.4	2.5
Married [2]	7.0	10.4	10.5	11.0	3.3	4.9	5.0	5.2	3.7	5.5	5.5	5.8
Widowed	0.5	0.7	0.7	0.7	0.1	0.1	0.1	0.1	0.5	0.6	0.6	0.5
Divorced	0.5	0.7	0.7	0.7	0.2	0.2	0.3	0.2	0.3	0.4	0.5	0.5
Percent of total	100.0	100.0	100.0	100.0	100.0	100.0	100.0	100.0	100.0	100.0	100.0	100.0
Never married	28.3	29.8	30.6	31.3	32.8	33.4	34.3	35.9	24.2	26.7	27.3	27.1
Married [2]	62.8	62.1	61.1	61.0	62.6	62.0	61.0	59.9	62.9	62.3	61.2	62.1
Widowed	4.7	4.1	3.9	3.7	1.3	1.5	1.5	1.5	7.7	6.4	6.2	5.7
Divorced	4.3	4.0	4.3	4.0	3.3	3.1	3.2	2.7	5.2	4.7	5.3	5.2
Hispanic, total [4]	**34.3**	**45.0**	**47.1**	**48.5**	**17.7**	**22.5**	**23.6**	**24.4**	**16.6**	**22.6**	**23.5**	**24.1**
Never married	13.3	18.9	20.0	20.6	7.7	10.3	10.9	11.3	5.6	8.6	9.1	9.4
Married [2]	17.2	21.2	21.9	22.6	8.6	10.3	10.7	11.1	8.6	10.9	11.2	11.5
Widowed	1.2	1.4	1.6	1.7	0.3	0.3	0.5	0.5	0.9	1.1	1.2	1.2
Divorced	2.6	3.5	3.6	3.6	1.1	1.5	1.5	1.5	1.5	2.0	2.1	2.1
Percent of total	100.0	100.0	100.0	100.0	100.0	100.0	100.0	100.0	100.0	100.0	100.0	100.0
Never married	38.7	42.0	42.4	42.5	43.4	46.0	46.2	46.2	33.7	38.1	38.6	38.8
Married [2]	50.1	47.0	46.5	46.5	48.7	45.7	45.3	45.5	51.7	48.3	47.6	47.5
Widowed	3.5	3.2	3.5	3.5	1.7	1.5	1.9	1.9	5.4	4.8	5.1	5.1
Divorced	7.7	7.8	7.7	7.4	6.2	6.8	6.6	6.3	9.2	8.8	8.8	8.6

[1] Includes persons of other races not shown separately. [2] Includes persons who are married with spouse present, married with spouse absent, and separated. Beginning 2019, estimates for married individuals include same-sex married couples. [3] Beginning 2003, data represent persons who selected this race group only and exclude persons reporting more than one race. Prior to 2003, the CPS allowed respondents to report only one race group. See also comments on race in the text for this section. [4] Hispanic persons may be of any race.

Source: U.S. Census Bureau, Families and Living Arrangements, Historical Marital Status Tables, "Table MS-1. Marital Status of the Population 15 Years Old and Over, by Sex, Race and Hispanic Origin: 1950 to Present," <www.census.gov/data/tables/time-series/demo/families/marital.html>, accessed January 2024.

Table 59. Marital Status of the Population by Sex and Age: 2023

[133,050 represents 133,050,000. As of March. Data are shown for population aged 15 and older. Excludes members of Armed Forces except those living off post or with their families on post. Population controls based on Census 2020. Based on Current Population Survey; see text, this section, and Appendix III]

Sex and age	Number of persons (1,000)					Percent distribution				
	Total	Never married	Married [1]	Widowed	Divorced	Total	Never married	Married [1]	Widowed	Divorced
MALE										
Total....................	**133,050**	**49,473**	**68,713**	**3,782**	**11,082**	**100.0**	**37.2**	**51.6**	**2.8**	**8.3**
15 to 64 years old.............	106,790	47,706	50,235	872	7,976	100.0	44.7	47.1	0.8	7.5
15 to 24 years old...........	22,202	21,091	985	16	111	100.0	95.0	4.0	–	–
25 to 34 years old...........	22,668	13,637	8,450	48	534	100.0	60.2	37.3	–	2.4
35 to 44 years old...........	21,819	6,405	13,607	100	1,707	100.0	29.4	62.4	–	7.8
45 to 54 years old...........	19,898	3,679	13,511	229	2,478	100.0	18.5	67.9	1.2	12.5
55 to 64 years old...........	20,202	2,894	13,683	478	3,147	100.0	14.3	67.7	2.4	15.6
65 years old and over.........	26,260	1,767	18,477	2,910	3,106	100.0	6.7	70.3	11.1	11.8
65 to 74 years old...........	15,997	1,365	11,302	1,071	2,261	100.0	8.5	70.6	6.7	14.1
75 years old and over........	10,263	403	7,176	1,839	846	100.0	3.9	69.9	17.9	8.2
FEMALE										
Total....................	**138,217**	**42,963**	**69,044**	**11,328**	**14,882**	**100.0**	**31.1**	**50.0**	**8.2**	**10.8**
15 to 64 years old.............	106,750	40,864	53,492	2,373	10,021	100.0	38.3	50.2	2.2	9.4
15 to 24 years old...........	21,637	19,967	1,531	31	107	100.0	92.3	7.1	–	–
25 to 34 years old...........	22,235	11,112	10,225	124	773	100.0	50.0	45.9	0.6	3.5
35 to 44 years old...........	21,661	4,788	14,517	245	2,110	100.0	22.1	67.0	1.1	9.7
45 to 54 years old...........	20,075	2,758	13,723	505	3,090	100.0	13.7	68.3	2.5	15.4
55 to 64 years old...........	21,141	2,239	13,494	1,468	3,940	100.0	10.6	63.8	6.9	18.6
65 years old and over.........	31,468	2,099	15,551	8,955	4,862	100.0	6.7	49.4	28.5	15.4
65 to 74 years old...........	17,997	1,497	10,424	2,914	3,162	100.0	8.3	58.0	16.2	17.6
75 years old and over........	13,471	602	5,128	6,041	1,700	100.0	4.5	38.0	44.8	12.6

– Represents or rounds to zero. [1] Includes persons who are married with spouse present, married with spouse absent, and separated.

Source: U.S. Census Bureau, America's Families and Living Arrangements, Adult (A table series), "Table A1. Marital Status of People 15 Years and Over, by Age and Sex: 2023," <www.census.gov/topics/families/families-and-households/data/tables.html>, accessed January 2024.

Table 60. Living Arrangements of Persons 18 Years Old and Over by Age and Sex: 2023

[In thousands (257,871 represents 257,871,000), except percent. As of March. Excludes members of Armed Services except those living off post or with their families on post. Population controls based on Census 2020 and an expanded sample of households. Based on Current Population Survey (CPS); see text, this section, and Appendix III]

Living arrangement	Total	18 to 24 years old	25 to 34 years old	35 to 64 years old	65 to 74 years old	75 years old and over
NUMBER (1,000)						
Total................................	**257,871**	**30,442**	**44,903**	**124,798**	**33,994**	**23,734**
Male..................................	126,325	15,477	22,668	61,920	15,997	10,263
Female................................	131,546	14,965	22,235	62,878	17,997	13,471
PERCENT DISTRIBUTION						
Male, total..........................	**100.0**	**100.0**	**100.0**	**100.0**	**100.0**	**100.0**
Alone.................................	(NA)	5.6	12.6	13.0	20.8	23.0
With spouse [1].........................	(NA)	4.4	35.0	61.8	67.4	67.6
Child of householder [2]..................	(NA)	57.7	18.8	6.4	(NA)	(NA)
Living with partner......................	(NA)	8.4	15.3	7.0	3.9	2.1
Other relatives.........................	(NA)	15.5	10.4	8.5	[3] 5.9	[3] 6.2
Nonrelatives...........................	(NA)	8.4	7.9	3.3	1.9	1.1
Female, total........................	**100.0**	**100.0**	**100.0**	**100.0**	**100.0**	**100.0**
Alone.................................	(NA)	4.3	10.3	11.5	27.1	41.8
With spouse [1].........................	(NA)	7.8	42.7	62.3	55.5	35.9
Child of householder [2]..................	(NA)	54.1	11.4	3.0	(NA)	(NA)
Living with partner......................	(NA)	11.7	16.4	6.3	2.6	1.2
Other relatives.........................	(NA)	13.9	14.5	15.5	[3] 13.6	[3] 20.1
Nonrelatives...........................	(NA)	8.2	4.6	1.5	1.3	1.0

NA Not available. [1] Includes only adults who are married, spouse present in the household. This living arrangement supersedes the others shown in the table. For example, people living with their parents and a spouse are counted as living with a spouse, not as a child of the householder. [2] Children of the householder are not living with a spouse or unmarried partner and are residing in the household of a parent. In CPS, unmarried college students living in dormitories are counted as living in the parental home. [3] Includes children of the householder who are not living with a spouse or unmarried partner, and are residing in the household of a parent.

Source: U.S. Census Bureau, America's Families and Living Arrangements, Historical Living Arrangements of Adults, "Table AD-3. Living Arrangements of Adults 18 and Over, 1967 to Present," <www.census.gov/data/tables/time-series/demo/families/adults.html>, accessed January 2024.

Table 61. Households, Families, Subfamilies, and Married Couples: 2000 to 2023

[In thousands (104,705 represents 104,705,000), except as indicated. As of March. Excludes members of the Armed Services except those living off post or with their families on post. Beginning 2001, based on an expanded sample of households. Data for 2010 based on Census 2000 population controls; data for 2015 to 2021 based on Census 2010 population controls; and, beginning 2022, data based on Census 2020 population controls. Based on Current Population Survey (CPS), see text, this section and Appendix III. Minus sign (-) indicates decrease]

Type of unit	2000	2010	2015	2020	2022	2023	Percent change 2000 to 2010	Percent change 2010 to 2020	Percent change 2020 to 2023
Households	**104,705**	**117,538**	**124,587**	**128,451**	**131,202**	**131,434**	**12.3**	**9.3**	**2.3**
Persons per household	2.62	2.59	2.54	2.53	2.50	2.51	(X)	(X)	(X)
White [1]	87,671	95,489	98,679	100,568	102,057	101,420	8.9	5.3	0.8
Black [1]	12,849	14,730	16,437	17,054	17,698	18,077	14.6	15.8	6.0
Asian [1]	(NA)	4,687	6,040	6,853	7,276	7,609	(NA)	46.2	11.0
Hispanic [2]	9,319	13,298	16,239	17,667	19,230	19,319	42.7	32.9	9.4
Family households	72,025	78,833	81,716	83,677	84,265	84,334	9.5	6.1	0.8
Married couple	55,311	58,410	60,010	62,342	61,435	62,175	5.6	6.7	-0.3
Male householder [3]	4,028	5,580	6,162	6,503	7,212	7,128	38.5	16.5	9.6
Female householder [3]	12,687	14,843	15,544	14,832	15,618	15,032	17.0	-0.1	1.3
Nonfamily households	32,680	38,705	42,871	44,774	46,937	47,099	18.4	15.7	5.2
Male householder	14,641	18,263	20,143	21,304	22,716	22,738	24.7	16.7	6.7
Female householder	18,039	20,442	22,728	23,470	24,221	24,361	13.3	14.8	3.8
One person	26,724	31,399	34,866	36,198	37,887	38,097	17.5	15.3	5.2
Families	**72,025**	**78,833**	**81,716**	**83,677**	**84,265**	**84,334**	**9.5**	**6.1**	**0.8**
Persons per family	3.17	3.16	3.14	3.15	3.13	3.15	(X)	(X)	(X)
With own children under age 18	34,605	35,218	34,979	33,464	33,924	33,289	1.8	-5.0	-0.5
Without own children under age 18	37,420	43,615	46,737	50,213	50,340	51,045	16.6	15.1	1.7
Married couple	55,311	58,410	60,010	62,342	61,435	62,175	5.6	6.7	-0.3
With own children under age 18	25,248	24,575	24,040	23,618	23,345	23,523	-2.7	-3.9	-0.4
Without own children under age 18	30,062	33,835	35,970	38,724	38,090	38,652	12.6	14.4	-0.2
Male householder [3]	4,028	5,580	6,162	6,503	7,212	7,128	38.5	16.5	9.6
With own children under age 18	1,786	2,224	2,388	2,374	2,673	2,476	24.5	6.7	4.3
Without own children under age 18	2,242	3,356	3,774	4,130	4,540	4,652	49.7	23.1	12.6
Female householder [3]	12,687	14,843	15,544	14,832	15,618	15,032	17.0	-0.1	1.3
With own children under age 18	7,571	8,419	8,551	7,472	7,906	7,291	11.2	-11.2	-2.4
Without own children under age 18	5,116	6,424	6,993	7,359	7,711	7,741	25.6	14.6	5.2
Unrelated subfamilies [4]	**571**	**484**	**566**	**372**	**379**	**356**	**-15.2**	**-23.1**	**-4.3**
Married couple	37	93	76	70	62	77	(B)	(B)	(B)
Male reference persons [3]	57	44	63	47	71	41	(B)	(B)	(B)
Female reference persons [3]	477	347	428	255	246	238	-27.3	-26.5	-6.7
Related subfamilies [4]	**2,984**	**4,300**	**4,508**	**4,697**	**4,457**	**4,488**	**44.1**	**9.2**	**-4.4**
Married couple	1,149	1,881	2,144	2,437	2,397	2,374	63.7	29.6	-2.6
Father-child [3]	201	313	308	506	430	417	55.7	61.7	-17.6
Mother-child [3]	1,634	2,106	2,056	1,754	1,630	1,697	28.9	-16.7	-3.2
Married couples	**56,497**	**60,384**	**62,230**	**64,849**	**63,894**	**64,626**	**6.9**	**7.4**	**-0.3**
With own household	55,311	58,410	60,010	62,342	61,435	62,175	5.6	6.7	-0.3
Without own household	1,186	1,974	2,220	2,507	2,459	2,451	66.4	27.0	-2.2
Percent without own household	2.1	3.2	3.6	3.9	3.8	3.8	(X)	(X)	(X)

B Base less than 75,000. NA Not available. X Not applicable. [1] Beginning with the 2003 CPS, respondents could choose more than one race. Beginning in 2003, data represent persons who selected this race group only and exclude persons reporting more than one race. The CPS in prior years allowed respondents to report only one race group. See also comments on race in text for this section. [2] Persons of Hispanic origin may be of any race. [3] No spouse present. [4] A subfamily is a married couple or parent/child group that does not maintain its own household. A subfamily may be related to the householder or unrelated to the householder.

Source: U.S. Census Bureau, America's Families and Living Arrangements, Tables F2, FG7, and H1, and Historical Households Tables, Table HH-6, <www.census.gov/topics/families/families-and-households.html>, accessed January 2024, and earlier releases.

Table 62. Married Couples by Difference in Race and Hispanic Origin of Spouses: 2005 to 2023

[In thousands (59,373 represents 59,373,000). As of March. Persons 15 years old and over. Data are shown for opposite-sex married couples only. Persons of Hispanic origin may be of any race. Based on the Current Population Survey; see headnote Table 61]

Race and origin of spouses	2005	2010	2015	2020	2021	2022	2023
Married couples, total	**59,373**	**60,384**	**62,230**	**64,248**	**63,131**	**63,191**	**63,869**
SAME RACE COUPLES							
Both White alone [1]	42,819	42,611	41,641	41,589	40,406	40,206	39,892
Both Black alone [1]	3,799	3,869	3,994	4,176	4,076	4,102	4,346
Both other race alone or any combination [1]	2,819	3,231	4,066	4,621	4,557	4,612	4,891
DIFFERENT RACE AND HISPANIC ORIGIN COUPLES							
Husband White alone [1]; wife Black alone [1]	106	147	147	244	195	244	268
Husband White alone [1]; wife Hispanic	973	1,043	1,280	1,663	1,655	1,661	1,604
Husband White alone [1]; wife other race alone or any combination [1]	892	940	1,254	1,355	1,439	1,439	1,453
Husband Black alone [1]; wife White alone [1]	247	357	308	312	400	371	409
Husband Black alone [1]; wife Hispanic	71	92	166	200	214	178	195
Husband Black alone [1]; wife other race alone or any combination [1]	84	103	119	133	118	88	120
Husband Hispanic; wife White alone [1]	891	962	1,056	1,247	1,296	1,249	1,336
Husband Hispanic; wife Black alone [1]	68	37	54	69	77	102	87
Husband Hispanic; wife other race alone or any combination [1]	82	88	140	152	158	188	198
Husband other race alone or any combination [1]; wife White alone [1]	623	644	653	737	713	758	756
Husband other race alone or any combination [1]; wife Black alone [1]	52	25	41	65	42	41	56
Husband other race alone or any combination [1]; wife Hispanic	87	69	135	151	129	156	195
HISPANIC ORIGIN OF COUPLES							
Both Hispanic	5,760	6,166	7,176	7,533	7,657	7,795	8,063
One Hispanic; one non-Hispanic	2,172	2,289	2,830	3,483	3,529	3,535	3,615
Neither Hispanic	51,442	51,928	52,224	53,232	51,946	51,860	52,191

[1] Non-Hispanic.

Source: U.S. Census Bureau, America's Families and Living Arrangements, Family groups (FG table series), Table FG3, <www.census.gov/topics/families/families-and-households/data/tables.html>, accessed January 2024.

Table 63. Households and Persons Per Household by Type of Household: 2010 to 2023

[117,538 represents 117,538,000. As of March. See headnote, Table 61]

Type of household	Households						Persons per household		
	Number (1,000)			Percent distribution					
	2010	2020	2023	2010	2020	2023	2010	2020	2023
Total households..........................	**117,538**	**128,451**	**131,434**	**100.0**	**100.0**	**100.0**	**2.59**	**2.53**	**2.51**
Family households..............................	78,833	83,677	84,334	67.1	65.1	64.2	3.24	3.22	3.22
Married couple family........................	58,410	62,342	62,175	49.7	48.5	47.3	3.24	3.20	3.19
Male householder, no spouse present........	5,580	6,503	7,128	4.7	5.1	5.4	3.24	3.21	3.22
Female householder, no spouse present.....	14,843	14,832	15,032	12.6	11.5	11.4	3.23	3.29	3.33
Nonfamily households..........................	38,705	44,774	47,099	32.9	34.9	35.8	1.26	1.25	1.25
Living alone................................	31,399	36,198	38,097	26.7	28.2	29.0	1.00	1.00	1.00
Male householder...........................	18,263	21,304	22,738	15.5	16.6	17.3	1.35	1.31	1.31
Living alone................................	13,971	16,256	17,434	11.9	12.7	13.3	1.00	1.00	1.00
Female householder..........................	20,442	23,470	24,361	17.4	18.3	18.5	1.18	1.19	1.19
Living alone................................	17,428	19,942	20,663	14.8	15.5	15.7	1.00	1.00	1.00

Source: U.S. Census Bureau, Current Population Reports, P20-537, 2001, and earlier reports; and America's Families and Living Arrangements, Table AVG1 and Table H1, <www.census.gov/topics/families/families-and-households/data/tables.html>, accessed January 2024, and earlier releases.

Table 64. Households by Age of Householder and Size of Household: 1990 to 2023

[In millions (93.3 represents 93,300,000). As of March. Based on Current Population Survey; see headnote, Table 61]

Age of householder and size of household	1990	2000	2005	2010	2015	2019	2020	2021	2022	2023
Total..........................	**93.3**	**104.7**	**113.3**	**117.5**	**124.6**	**128.6**	**128.5**	**129.9**	**131.2**	**131.4**
Age of householder:										
15 to 24 years old................	5.1	5.9	6.7	6.2	6.4	6.2	5.4	5.5	6.1	6.1
25 to 29 years old................	9.4	8.5	9.2	9.4	9.4	10.0	9.5	9.4	9.5	9.4
30 to 34 years old................	11.0	10.1	10.1	9.8	10.7	10.6	10.9	11.2	11.5	11.4
35 to 44 years old................	20.6	24.0	23.2	21.5	21.1	21.4	21.4	22.1	22.6	22.5
45 to 54 years old................	14.5	20.9	23.4	24.9	23.6	22.1	21.7	21.7	21.6	21.5
55 to 64 years old................	12.5	13.6	17.5	20.4	23.5	24.2	24.6	24.3	24.1	23.4
65 to 74 years old................	11.7	11.3	11.5	13.2	16.9	19.7	20.0	20.5	21.0	21.4
75 years old and over.............	8.4	10.4	11.6	12.1	13.1	14.5	14.9	15.2	14.9	15.7
Size of household:										
One person.......................	23.0	26.7	30.1	31.4	34.9	36.5	36.2	37.0	37.9	38.1
Male.............................	9.0	11.2	12.8	14.0	15.5	16.5	16.3	16.7	17.3	17.4
Female...........................	14.0	15.5	17.3	17.4	19.4	20.0	19.9	20.3	20.6	20.7
Two persons......................	30.1	34.7	37.4	39.5	41.9	44.4	44.7	45.5	45.5	46.0
Three persons....................	16.1	17.2	18.3	18.6	19.3	19.4	19.3	19.5	19.8	19.8
Four persons.....................	14.5	15.3	16.4	16.1	16.5	16.4	16.3	16.1	16.2	16.0
Five persons or more.............	9.6	10.8	11.1	11.9	12.1	11.9	11.9	11.8	11.8	11.6
Five persons.....................	6.2	7.0	7.2	7.4	7.5	7.4	7.4	7.6	(NA)	(NA)
Six persons......................	2.1	2.4	2.5	2.8	2.8	2.9	2.9	2.6	(NA)	(NA)
Seven persons or more..........	1.3	1.4	1.4	1.7	1.7	1.6	1.5	1.6	(NA)	(NA)

NA Not available.

Source: U.S. Census Bureau, Current Population Reports, P20-537, and earlier reports; and America's Families and Living Arrangements, Households (H table series), Tables H1 and H2, <www.census.gov/topics/families/families-and-households/data/tables.html>, accessed January 2024.

Table 65. Family Households With Own Children Under 18 Years of Age by Type of Family, 2000 to 2023, and by Educational Attainment of Householder, 2023

[34,605 represents 34,605,000. As of March. See headnote, Table 66]

Educational attainment of householder	Family households with children		Married couple households with children		Male householder with children [1]		Female householder with children [1]	
	Number (1,000)	Percent of all family households	Number (1,000)	Percent of all married couple households	Number (1,000)	Percent of all male householder families	Number (1,000)	Percent of all female householder families
2000, total........................	34,605	48	25,248	46	1,786	44	7,571	60
2010, total........................	35,218	45	24,575	42	2,224	40	8,419	57
2015, total........................	34,979	43	24,040	40	2,388	39	8,551	55
2020, total........................	33,464	40	23,618	38	2,374	37	7,472	50
2023, total........................	**33,289**	**39**	**23,523**	**38**	**2,476**	**35**	**7,291**	**49**
Less than high school............	2,495	39	1,546	39	251	30	699	43
High school graduate.............	7,503	35	4,472	32	858	34	2,172	48
Some college.....................	8,821	39	5,464	35	774	37	2,584	52
Bachelor's degree or higher.....	14,470	42	12,041	42	593	35	1,835	47

[1] No spouse present.

Source: U.S. Census Bureau, Current Population Reports, P20-537, 2001 and earlier reports; and America's Families and Living Arrangements, Family households (F table series), "Table F2. Family Households, by Type, Age of Own Children, and Educational Attainment of Householder: 2023," <www.census.gov/topics/families/families-and-households/data/tables.html>, accessed January 2024, and earlier releases.

Table 66. Family Groups With Children Under 18 Years of Age by Race and Hispanic Origin: 2000 to 2023

[In thousands (37,496 represents 37,496,000). As of March. Family groups are family households, related subfamilies, and unrelated subfamilies; each married couple or parent/child group is counted separately, even if they reside in the same household. Excludes members of Armed Forces except those living off post or with their families on post. Beginning 2005, based on an expanded sample of households. Data for 2001 to 2011 based on Census 2000 population controls; data for 2012 to 2021 based on Census 2010 population controls; and, beginning 2022, data based on Census 2020 population controls. Based on Current Population Survey, Annual Social and Economic Supplement]

Race and Hispanic origin of householder or reference person	Number (1,000)					Percent distribution				
	2000	2010	2020	2022	2023	2000	2010	2020	2022	2023
All races, total [1]	37,496	39,947	37,891	37,938	37,312	100	100	100	100	100
Two-parent family groups [2]	25,771	27,082	26,062	25,968	25,911	69	68	69	68	69
One-parent family groups	11,725	11,686	10,719	10,889	10,279	31	29	28	29	28
Maintained by mother	9,681	9,924	8,625	8,657	8,242	26	25	23	23	22
Maintained by father	2,044	1,762	2,094	2,232	2,037	5	4	6	6	5
Grandparent householder [3]	(NA)	1,179	1,110	1,081	1,122	(NA)	3	3	3	3
White, total [4]	30,079	30,933	28,265	28,063	27,572	100	100	100	100	100
Two-parent family groups [2]	22,241	22,457	20,632	20,541	20,427	74	73	73	73	74
One-parent family groups	7,838	7,729	6,901	6,856	6,449	26	25	24	24	23
Maintained by mother	6,216	6,396	5,341	5,260	4,956	21	21	19	19	18
Maintained by father	1,622	1,333	1,560	1,596	1,493	5	4	6	6	5
Grandparent householder [3]	(NA)	747	732	666	696	(NA)	2	3	2	3
Black, total [4]	5,530	5,903	5,544	5,686	5,631	100	100	100	100	100
Two-parent family groups [2]	2,135	2,275	2,255	2,267	2,375	39	39	41	40	42
One-parent family groups	3,396	3,280	2,976	3,083	2,913	61	56	54	54	52
Maintained by mother	3,060	2,977	2,622	2,661	2,512	55	50	47	47	45
Maintained by father	335	303	354	422	401	6	5	6	7	7
Grandparent householder [3]	(NA)	348	313	336	343	(NA)	6	6	6	6
Asian, total [4]	1,469	2,025	2,586	2,585	2,554	100	100	100	100	100
Two-parent family groups [2]	1,184	1,694	2,286	2,203	2,239	81	84	88	85	88
One-parent family groups	285	292	285	353	299	19	14	11	14	12
Maintained by mother	236	235	229	272	249	16	12	9	11	10
Maintained by father	49	57	56	81	50	3	3	2	3	2
Grandparent householder [3]	(NA)	39	15	29	16	(NA)	2	1	1	1
Hispanic, total [5]	5,503	7,572	8,258	8,403	8,119	100	100	100	100	100
Two-parent family groups [2]	3,625	4,856	5,381	5,523	5,302	66	64	65	66	65
One-parent family groups	1,877	2,499	2,674	2,672	2,584	34	33	32	32	32
Maintained by mother	1,565	2,186	2,234	2,204	2,150	28	29	27	26	26
Maintained by father	313	313	440	468	434	6	4	5	6	5
Grandparent householder [3]	(NA)	217	203	208	233	(NA)	3	2	2	3
Non-Hispanic White, total [4]	24,847	23,911	20,885	20,683	20,375	100	100	100	100	100
Two-parent family groups [2]	18,750	17,911	15,760	15,618	15,647	75	75	75	76	77
One-parent family groups	6,096	5,457	4,576	4,576	4,236	25	23	22	22	21
Maintained by mother	4,766	4,404	3,400	3,379	3,146	19	18	16	16	15
Maintained by father	1,331	1,053	1,176	1,197	1,090	5	4	6	6	5
Grandparent householder [3]	(NA)	543	549	489	492	(NA)	2	3	2	2

NA Not available. [1] Includes other race/ethnicities, not shown separately. [2] Beginning 2007, includes children living with married and unmarried parents. Does not include children of married same-sex couples. [3] With grandchild(ren) under age 18. [4] Beginning with the 2003 Current Population Survey (CPS), respondents could choose more than one race. Beginning 2003, data represent persons who selected this race group only and exclude persons reporting more than one race. The CPS prior to 2003 allowed respondents to report only one race group. [5] Hispanic persons may be of any race.

Source: U.S. Census Bureau, Families and Living Arrangements, Current Population Reports, P20-537, 2001; and America's Families and Living Arrangements, Family groups (FG table series), "Table FG10. Family Groups: 2023," <www.census.gov/topics/families/families-and-households/data/tables.html>, accessed January 2024, and earlier releases.

Table 67. Parents and Children in Stay-At-Home Parent Family Groups: 1995 to 2023

[In thousands (22,973 represents 22,973,000), except percent. Family groups with children include those families that maintain their own household (family households with own children); those that live in the home of a relative (related subfamilies); and those that live in the home of a nonrelative (unrelated subfamilies). Stay-at-home family groups are opposite-sex married-couple family groups with children under age 15 where one parent is in the labor force all of the previous year and the other parent is out of the labor force for the entire year with the reason 'taking care of home and family.' Based on Current Population Survey; see Appendix III]

Year	Married-couple family groups with children under 15 years old					Children under 15 years old in married-couple family groups				
	Number			Percent		Number			Percent	
	Total	With stay-at-home mothers	With stay-at-home fathers	With stay-at-home mothers	With stay-at-home fathers	Total	With stay-at-home mothers	With stay-at-home fathers	With stay-at-home mothers	With stay-at-home fathers
1995	22,973	4,440	64	19.3	0.3	41,008	9,106	125	22.2	0.3
2000	22,953	4,785	93	20.8	0.4	41,860	10,087	180	24.1	0.4
2005	23,305	5,584	142	24.0	0.6	41,111	11,224	247	27.3	0.6
2010	22,138	5,020	154	22.7	0.7	41,026	10,833	287	26.4	0.7
2015	21,586	5,210	199	24.1	0.9	39,621	10,758	368	27.2	0.9
2020	21,327	4,777	215	22.4	1.0	40,249	10,176	404	25.3	1.0
2021 [1]	20,879	4,415	205	21.1	1.0	39,687	9,497	416	23.9	1.0
2022	20,930	4,549	239	21.7	1.1	39,426	9,653	507	24.5	1.3
2023	20,883	4,271	231	20.5	1.1	39,356	9,138	456	23.2	1.2

[1] Begin use of Census 2020 population controls.

Source: U.S. Census Bureau, Families and Households, Historical Families Tables, "Table SHP-1. Parents and Children in Stay-At-Home Parent Family Groups: 1994 to Present," <www.census.gov/data/tables/time-series/demo/families/families.html>, accessed January 2024.

Table 68. Children Under 18 Years of Age Living with Both Parents, One Parent, and No Parents by Race and Hispanic Origin: 1990 to 2023

[64,137 represents 64,137,000. As of March. Excludes persons under 18 years old who maintained households or family groups and their spouses. Based on Current Population Survey; see headnote, Table 66]

Race, Hispanic origin, and year	Number (1,000)	Both parents [1]	Percent living with—				
			One parent			No parents	
			Total	Mother only	Father only	Other relative	Non-relative
ALL RACES [2]							
1990	64,137	72.5	24.7	21.6	3.1	2.2	0.5
2000	72,012	69.1	26.7	22.4	4.2	3.0	1.2
2005	73,494	67.3	28.2	23.4	4.8	3.4	1.0
2010	74,718	69.4	26.6	23.1	3.4	3.2	0.9
2015	73,623	69.2	26.8	23.1	3.7	3.3	0.6
2020	72,901	70.4	25.5	21.0	4.5	3.2	0.9
2021	73,817	69.7	26.5	21.5	4.9	3.0	0.8
2022	73,289	70.2	26.2	21.5	4.7	2.7	0.9
2023	72,296	71.1	25.1	20.9	4.2	2.9	0.9
WHITE [3]							
1990	51,390	79.0	19.2	16.2	3.0	1.4	0.4
2000	56,455	75.3	21.6	17.3	4.3	2.0	1.1
2005	56,234	73.5	23.1	18.4	4.7	2.4	1.0
2010	56,416	74.9	21.8	18.3	3.5	2.5	0.9
2015	53,621	74.9	21.9	18.2	3.7	2.6	0.5
2020	52,652	75.8	20.8	16.3	4.5	2.6	0.8
2021	52,505	74.8	21.8	17.0	4.8	2.6	0.8
2022	51,907	75.6	21.3	16.7	4.6	2.3	0.8
2023	50,921	76.3	20.2	16.1	4.1	2.5	0.9
BLACK [3]							
1990	10,018	37.7	54.7	51.2	3.5	6.5	1.0
2000	11,412	37.6	53.3	49.0	4.2	7.7	1.5
2005	11,293	35.0	55.2	50.2	5.0	8.4	1.4
2010	11,272	39.2	53.3	49.7	3.6	6.6	0.9
2015	11,091	38.7	53.6	49.4	4.2	6.6	1.2
2020	10,913	41.2	50.8	46.3	4.5	6.6	1.4
2021	11,272	42.6	50.6	44.8	5.8	5.5	1.3
2022	11,272	43.0	51.2	45.6	5.6	4.6	1.2
2023	11,227	44.6	49.7	44.2	5.5	4.7	1.0
HISPANIC [4]							
1990	7,174	66.8	30.0	27.1	2.9	2.5	0.8
2000	11,613	65.1	29.5	25.1	4.4	3.7	1.7
2005	14,241	64.7	30.2	25.4	4.8	3.8	1.4
2010	16,941	67.0	29.0	26.3	2.7	3.2	0.8
2015	17,981	67.0	28.9	25.9	3.0	3.3	0.7
2020	18,655	67.9	28.1	24.0	4.1	3.1	0.9
2021	18,799	67.5	29.1	24.8	4.3	2.6	0.8
2022	18,750	67.5	28.8	24.5	4.3	2.5	1.2
2023	18,781	67.4	28.3	24.5	3.8	3.3	1.0

[1] Beginning in 2007, includes children living with married and unmarried parents. [2] Includes other races and non-Hispanic groups, not shown separately. [3] Beginning with the 2003 Current Population Survey (CPS), respondents could choose more than one race. Data represents persons who selected this race group only and exclude persons reporting more than one race. Prior to 2003, the CPS allowed respondents to report only one race group. See also comments on race in the text for this section. [4] Hispanic persons may be of any race.

Source: U.S. Census Bureau, Families and Households Data Tables, "Historical Living Arrangements of Children," <www.census.gov/data/tables/time-series/demo/families/children.html>, accessed January 2024.

Table 69. Grandparents Living With Grandchildren by Race, Hispanic Origin, and Sex: 2022

[In thousands (6,483 represents 6,483,000), except percent. Covers both grandparents living in own home with grandchildren present and grandparents living in grandchildren's home. The American Community Survey universe includes the household population and the population living in institutions, college dormitories, and other group quarters. Based on a sample and subject to sampling variability; see Appendix III]

Race, Hispanic origin, and sex	Grandparents living with own grandchildren, total	Grandparents responsible for grandchildren		
		Total	30 to 59 years old	60 years old and over
Grandparents living with own grandchildren under 18 years old (1,000)	**6,483**	**2,064**	**1,001**	**1,063**
PERCENT DISTRIBUTION				
Total	100.0	100.0	100.0	100.0
One race	85.9	87.5	85.9	88.9
White alone	46.6	52.6	49.1	55.9
Black or African American alone	15.7	19.7	21.3	18.3
American Indian and Alaska Native alone	1.7	2.2	2.1	2.2
Asian alone	9.3	4.0	2.2	5.6
Native Hawaiian and Other Pacific Islander alone	0.5	0.4	0.6	0.4
Some other race alone	12.3	8.6	10.6	6.7
Two or more races	14.1	12.5	14.1	11.1
Hispanic origin [1]	27.4	20.9	25.5	16.5
White alone, not Hispanic	43.3	49.7	45.4	53.7
Male	37.0	36.6	33.1	39.9
Female	63.0	63.4	66.9	60.1

[1] Persons of Hispanic origin may be of any race.

Source: U.S. Census Bureau, 2022 American Community Survey, S1002, "Grandparents," <data.census.gov>, accessed November 2023.

Table 70. Group Quarters Population by Type of Group Quarter and Selected Resident Characteristics: 2022

[In percent, except as indicated. The American Community Survey universe includes the household population and the population living in institutions, college dormitories, and other group quarters. Based on a sample and subject to sampling variability]

Characteristic	Total group quarters population [1]	Institutionalized group quarters population			Noninstitutionalized group quarters population	
		Total [1]	Adult correctional facilities	Nursing facilities/ skilled nursing facilities	Total [1]	College/ university housing
Total population (number).................	8,152,893	3,608,768	1,849,176	1,603,598	4,544,125	2,856,057
PERCENT DISTRIBUTION						
Male...	58.6	66.8	91.1	38.5	52.0	44.7
Female...	41.4	33.2	8.9	61.5	48.0	55.3
Under 15 years old............................	0.6	0.6	(X)	(X)	0.6	(X)
15 to 17 years old.............................	1.2	1.6	0.1	(X)	0.9	1.0
18 to 24 years old.............................	40.7	5.3	8.9	0.2	68.7	96.6
25 to 34 years old.............................	11.2	16.0	29.8	0.7	7.4	2.0
35 to 44 years old.............................	10.1	16.4	30.2	1.5	5.1	0.3
45 to 54 years old.............................	7.2	10.7	17.2	3.6	4.4	0.1
55 to 64 years old.............................	7.8	10.6	10.0	11.5	5.6	–
65 to 74 years old.............................	6.9	11.5	3.1	21.8	3.4	–
75 to 84 years old.............................	6.7	12.7	0.6	27.7	2.0	(X)
85 years old and over........................	7.6	14.7	0.1	32.9	1.9	(X)
Median age (years)...........................	31.8	54.4	38.5	78.9	20.7	19.7
One race..	100.0	100.0	100.0	100.0	100.0	100.0
White..	65.0	62.2	47.1	78.8	67.3	68.7
Black..	22.6	29.4	42.0	15.7	17.2	14.9
American Indian and Alaska Native........	1.3	1.7	2.7	0.6	1.0	0.5
Asian..	5.9	1.6	0.9	2.2	9.3	12.4
Native Hawaiian/Pacific Islander............	0.3	0.2	0.3	0.2	0.3	0.2
Some other race..............................	4.9	4.9	7.0	2.5	4.9	3.3
Hispanic origin [2].............................	13.9	13.9	19.9	6.7	13.9	11.2
Not Hispanic....................................	86.1	86.1	80.1	93.3	86.1	88.8
White alone, not Hispanic....................	55.7	53.5	36.2	74.1	57.5	59.2

– Represents or rounds to zero. X Not applicable or not available. [1] Includes other types of group quarters, not shown separately. [2] Persons of Hispanic origin may be of any race.

Source: U.S. Census Bureau, 2022 American Community Survey, S2601A, "Characteristics of the Group Quarters Population"; and S2602, "Characteristics of the Group Quarters Population by Group Quarters Type (3 Types)"; <data.census.gov>, accessed November 2023.

Table 71. Population in Group Quarters by State: 2010 to 2023

[In thousands (7,999 represents 7,999,000). Census years as of April; all others as of July. All persons not living in housing units are classified as living in group quarters. These individuals may be institutionalized, e.g., under care or custody in juvenile facilities, jails, correctional centers, hospitals, or nursing homes; or they may be residents in noninstitutional group quarters such as college dormitories, group homes, or military barracks. Estimates for 2020-2023 are developed from a base that incorporates the 2020 Census, Vintage 2020 estimates, and 2020 Demographic Analysis estimates]

State	2010 [1]	2020	2022	2023	State	2010 [1]	2020	2022	2023
United States........	**7,999**	**8,255**	**8,170**	**8,213**	Missouri.............	174	169	164	163
Alabama.................	116	128	142	144	Montana.............	29	29	29	29
Alaska...................	26	30	30	30	Nebraska............	51	50	47	47
Arizona..................	140	167	161	163	Nevada...............	36	37	35	35
Arkansas................	79	82	84	85	New Hampshire....	40	43	42	42
California................	820	918	886	892	New Jersey.........	187	180	168	168
Colorado................	116	127	123	125	New Mexico.........	43	43	43	43
Connecticut............	118	108	103	103	New York............	586	610	613	617
Delaware................	24	23	24	24	North Carolina......	257	286	282	282
District of Columbia....	40	41	37	38	North Dakota.......	25	26	29	29
Florida..................	425	465	480	480	Ohio..................	306	300	289	296
Georgia.................	254	257	252	255	Oklahoma............	112	117	117	117
Hawaii..................	43	41	40	40	Oregon...............	87	97	97	97
Idaho...................	29	50	50	50	Pennsylvania.......	427	404	433	434
Illinois..................	302	276	278	278	Rhode Island.......	43	46	45	44
Indiana.................	187	178	178	178	South Carolina.....	139	139	139	139
Iowa....................	99	99	98	98	South Dakota......	34	32	32	32
Kansas.................	79	87	87	87	Tennessee..........	154	156	145	148
Kentucky...............	126	125	120	121	Texas................	582	606	605	605
Louisiana...............	128	124	124	124	Utah..................	46	55	54	55
Maine...................	36	37	42	42	Vermont.............	25	25	25	25
Maryland...............	139	126	125	125	Virginia..............	240	237	236	236
Massachusetts........	239	248	240	241	Washington.........	139	160	153	153
Michigan...............	230	222	213	216	West Virginia.......	49	52	52	52
Minnesota.............	135	139	134	140	Wisconsin...........	151	151	137	137
Mississippi.............	93	94	94	94	Wyoming............	14	13	14	14

[1] The April 1, 2010 population estimates base reflects changes to the Census 2010 population from the Count Question Resolution program and geographic program revisions.

Source: U.S. Census Bureau, "CO-EST2009-ALLDATA" and "CO-EST2020-ALLDATA," <www2.census.gov/programs-surveys/popest/datasets/>; and "Annual Resident Population Estimates, Estimated Components of Resident Population Change, and Rates of the Components of Resident Population Change for States and Counties: April 1, 2020 to July 1, 2023 (CO-EST2023-ALLDATA)," <www.census.gov/data/tables/time-series/demo/popest/2020s-counties-total.html>, accessed March 2024.

Table 72. Opposite-Sex and Same-Sex Couple Households by Selected Characteristics: 2022

[In percent, except as indicated (60,180 represents 60,180,000). The American Community Survey universe includes the household population and the population living in institutions, college dormitories, and other group quarters. Based on a sample and subject to sampling variability. See text, this section and Appendix III]

Characteristic	Married opposite-sex couples	Unmarried opposite-sex couples	Married and unmarried same-sex couples			Married same-sex couples
			Total	Male-male couples	Female-female couples	
Total households (1,000)..........................	**60,180**	**8,985**	**1,277**	**608**	**669**	**741**
Age of householder:						
15 to 24 years old..	1.2	11.9	6.1	4.4	7.7	2.3
25 to 34 years old..	12.3	35.0	25.4	22.3	28.2	19.1
35 to 44 years old..	20.3	21.0	21.5	21.4	21.7	22.9
45 to 54 years old..	20.1	13.7	16.3	17.9	14.9	19.2
55 to 64 years old..	20.5	10.4	17.3	19.8	15.0	20.7
65 years old and over..................................	25.6	7.9	13.3	14.3	12.4	15.9
Average age of householder (years)...............	52.9	39.8	45.4	47.0	43.9	48.6
Average age of spouse/partner (years).............	52.4	39.2	44.0	45.0	43.1	47.4
Race of householder:						
White alone...	71.0	64.5	71.1	72.0	70.2	72.3
Black or African American alone.................	7.0	10.1	8.2	6.4	9.8	7.1
American Indian or Alaska Native alone...........	0.7	1.3	1.0	0.8	1.1	1.0
Asian alone...	6.6	3.2	3.5	3.9	3.2	3.8
Native Hawaiian or Pacific Islander alone..........	0.1	0.2	0.2	0.2	0.3	0.3
Some other race alone................................	5.3	8.2	4.5	4.4	4.6	4.6
Two or more races.....................................	9.3	12.5	11.5	12.3	10.7	10.9
Percent of couples interracial...........................	18.6	28.6	32.2	38.0	26.9	30.8
Hispanic origin of householder:						
Hispanic [1]...	14.2	21.2	15.4	17.0	14.0	14.8
White alone, not Hispanic............................	68.5	60.4	67.4	68.1	66.8	69.1
Children in the household:						
Children in the household [2]...........................	38.1	34.5	14.6	5.7	22.6	18.2
Own children in the household......................	38.0	32.9	13.7	5.5	21.2	17.7
Household income:						
Less than $35,000.......................................	8.7	13.6	9.2	6.9	11.3	7.4
$35,000 to $49,999.....................................	7.2	10.2	6.7	5.7	7.6	5.1
$50,000 to $74,999.....................................	14.3	19.1	14.1	11.6	16.3	12.3
$75,000 to $99,999.....................................	14.4	16.7	14.4	13.0	15.8	13.3
$100,000 or more..	55.4	40.3	55.7	62.9	49.1	61.9
Median household income (dollars).................	109,700	84,740	110,600	127,900	98,420	123,500
Housing tenure:						
Owner occupied...	81.9	47.9	62.6	65.0	60.5	72.7
Renter occupied...	18.1	52.1	37.4	35.0	39.5	27.3

[1] Persons of Hispanic origin may be of any race. [2] Includes biological children, stepchildren, adopted children, and nonrelatives of the householder under 18 years old.

Source: U.S. Census Bureau, 2022 American Community Survey, "Characteristics of Same-Sex Couple Households: 2005 to Present," <www.census.gov/topics/families/same-sex-couples/data/tables.html>, accessed November 2023.

Table 73. Opposite Sex Unmarried Couples by Presence of Biological Children, Sex, and Age: 2023

[In thousands (9,481 represents 9,481,000), except percent. As of March. Excludes members of Armed Forces except those living off post or with their families on post. All opposite-sex unmarried couples are included, regardless of householder status. Unmarried couples of the opposite sex with children under 18 years old are included in the estimates if either partner had at least one never-married biological child living with them. Population controls based on Census 2020. Based on Current Population Survey; see text, this section and Appendix III]

Sex and age of partner	Unmarried couples, total	Without children under 18 years old	With children under 18 years old	
			Number	Percent of total
Total...	**9,481**	**6,471**	**3,010**	**31.7**
Age of male partner:				
15 to 24 years old..	1,264	963	302	23.9
25 to 29 years old..	1,738	1,276	462	26.6
30 to 34 years old..	1,534	926	608	39.6
35 to 39 years old..	1,080	502	578	53.5
40 to 44 years old..	891	390	501	56.2
45 to 49 years old..	602	322	280	46.5
50 to 54 years old..	613	457	157	25.6
55 to 59 years old..	481	413	67	13.9
60 years old and over..................................	1,278	1,223	56	4.4
Age of female partner:				
15 to 24 years old..	1,665	1,260	405	24.3
25 to 29 years old..	1,979	1,389	590	29.8
30 to 34 years old..	1,478	782	695	47.0
35 to 39 years old..	951	392	559	58.8
40 to 44 years old..	795	378	417	52.5
45 to 49 years old..	599	400	199	33.2
50 to 54 years old..	611	486	125	20.5
55 to 59 years old..	435	423	13	3.0
60 years old and over..................................	969	960	9	0.9

Source: U.S. Census Bureau, America's Families and Living Arrangements, Unmarried couples (UC table series), "Table UC3. Opposite Sex Unmarried Couples by Presence of Biological Children under 18, and Age, Earnings, Education, and Race and Hispanic Origin of Both Partners," <www.census.gov/topics/families/families-and-households.html>, accessed January 2024.

Table 74. Opposite and Same-Sex Coupled Households by Marital Status and Region: 2022

[129,871 represents 129,871,000. The American Community Survey universe includes the household population and the population living in institutions, college dormitories, and other group quarters. For composition of regions, see map inside front cover. Based on a sample and subject to sampling variability; see text, this section and Appendix III]

Household type	Total (1,000s)					Percent distribution				
	Total	North-east	Mid-west	South	West	Total	North-east	Mid-west	South	West
Total households.....................	**129,871**	**22,703**	**28,095**	**50,111**	**28,962**	**100.0**	**100.0**	**100.0**	**100.0**	**100.0**
Married couple households.............	60,922	10,324	13,066	23,596	13,936	46.9	45.5	46.5	47.1	48.1
Opposite-sex............................	60,181	10,177	12,940	23,330	13,734	46.3	44.8	46.1	46.6	47.4
Same-sex................................	741	147	126	265	202	0.6	0.6	0.4	0.5	0.7
Male householder and male spouse..................	348	72	55	121	100	0.3	0.3	0.2	0.2	0.3
Female householder and female spouse.................	392	75	71	144	103	0.3	0.3	0.3	0.3	0.4
Cohabiting couple households..........	9,522	1,739	2,106	3,368	2,309	7.3	7.7	7.5	6.7	8.0
Opposite-sex............................	8,985	1,632	2,012	3,167	2,174	6.9	7.2	7.2	6.3	7.5
Same-sex................................	537	107	94	201	135	0.4	0.5	0.3	0.4	0.5
Male householder and male partner.................	260	56	40	98	65	0.2	0.2	0.1	0.2	0.2
Female householder and female partner...............	277	51	54	102	69	0.2	0.2	0.2	0.2	0.2
All other households....................	59,427	10,640	12,923	23,147	12,717	45.8	46.9	46.0	46.2	43.9

Source: U.S. Census Bureau, 2022 American Community Survey, B11009, "Coupled Households by Type," <data.census.gov>, accessed November 2023.

Table 75. Young Adults Living in Parental Home by Sex and Age: 1990 to 2023

[In thousands (12,450 represents 12,450,000), except percent. As of March. Excludes members of Armed Forces except those living off post or with their families on post. Unmarried college students living in dormitories are counted as living in the home of their parent(s). Beginning 2005, based on an expanded sample of households. Population controls for 2005 and 2010 based on Census 2000; for 2015 and 2020 based on Census 2010; and, beginning 2021, based on Census 2020. Based on Current Population Survey; see text, this section and Appendix III]

Year	Male young adults			Female young adults		
		Child of householder living at home			Child of householder living at home	
	Total	Number	Percent of total	Total	Number	Percent of total
18 TO 24 YEARS OLD						
1990...............................	12,450	7,232	58.1	12,860	6,135	47.7
2000...............................	13,291	7,593	57.1	13,242	6,232	47.1
2010...............................	14,824	8,501	57.3	14,469	7,123	49.2
2015...............................	15,123	8,808	58.2	14,893	7,714	51.8
2020...............................	14,634	8,792	60.1	14,418	8,122	56.3
2021...............................	14,655	8,818	60.2	14,413	7,978	55.4
2022...............................	14,557	8,258	56.7	14,405	7,855	54.5
2023...............................	15,477	9,013	58.2	14,965	8,177	54.6
25 TO 34 YEARS OLD						
1990...............................	21,462	3,213	15.0	21,779	1,774	8.1
2000...............................	18,563	2,387	12.9	19,222	1,602	8.3
2010...............................	20,685	3,387	16.4	20,383	2,133	10.5
2015...............................	21,417	3,896	18.2	21,574	2,613	12.1
2020...............................	22,778	5,021	22.0	22,451	3,011	13.4
2021...............................	22,549	4,586	20.3	22,348	2,950	13.2
2022...............................	22,322	4,182	18.7	22,251	2,759	12.4
2023...............................	22,668	4,466	19.7	22,235	2,728	12.3

Source: U.S. Census Bureau, Families and Households, Historical Living Arrangements of Adults, "Table AD-1. Young Adults, 18-34 Years Old, Living At Home: 1960 to Present," <www.census.gov/data/tables/time-series/demo/families/adults.html>, accessed January 2024.

Table 76. Children in Households by Relationship to Householder: 2010 to 2022

[In thousands (73,904 represents 73,904,000). Data shown for population under age 18 in households, excluding householders, spouses, and unmarried partners. Based on a sample and subject to sampling variability; see text this section and Appendix III]

Type of relationship	2010	2015	2016	2017	2018	2019	2021	2022
NUMBER								
Total children in households..............	**73,904**	**73,386**	**73,399**	**73,403**	**73,106**	**72,746**	**73,262**	**72,142**
Own child...........................	65,472	64,445	64,392	64,367	63,987	63,307	64,361	63,440
Biological child...................	61,540	60,632	60,564	60,518	60,180	59,488	60,545	59,718
Adopted child.....................	1,582	1,423	1,428	1,439	1,440	1,422	1,402	1,366
Stepchild..........................	2,351	2,391	2,400	2,410	2,367	2,396	2,413	2,356
Grandchild............................	5,397	5,887	5,964	5,957	6,038	6,179	5,794	5,668
Other relatives........................	1,826	1,793	1,762	1,803	1,807	1,842	1,859	1,841
Foster child or other unrelated child.......	1,209	1,261	1,280	1,276	1,274	1,419	1,248	1,191
PERCENT DISTRIBUTION								
Total children in households................	100.0	100.0	100.0	100.0	100.0	100.0	100.0	100.0
Own child...........................	88.6	87.8	87.7	87.7	87.5	87.0	87.9	87.9
Biological child...................	83.3	82.6	82.5	82.4	82.3	81.8	82.6	82.8
Adopted child.....................	2.1	1.9	1.9	2.0	2.0	2.0	1.9	1.9
Stepchild..........................	3.2	3.3	3.3	3.3	3.2	3.3	3.3	3.3
Grandchild............................	7.3	8.0	8.1	8.1	8.3	8.5	7.9	7.9
Other relatives........................	2.5	2.4	2.4	2.5	2.5	2.5	2.5	2.6
Foster child or other unrelated child.......	1.6	1.7	1.7	1.7	1.7	2.0	1.7	1.7

Source: U.S. Census Bureau, American Community Survey, B09018, "Relationship to Householder for Children Under 18 in Households," <data.census.gov>, accessed November 2023.

Table 77. Religious Congregations and Adherents by State: 2020

[Based on the U.S. Religion Census (USRC) conducted by the Association of Statisticians of American Religious Bodies (ASARB). The USRC focuses on congregations and the individuals affiliated with them, and not on religious individuals directly; therefore, it does not include all U.S. religious adherents. The 2020 USRC includes congregations for 372 religious bodies. For 217 of these 372 bodies, the 2020 USRC provides data on affiliated adherents. Congregations may be churches, mosques, temples, or other meeting places. A congregation is generally defined as a group of people who meet regularly (typically weekly or monthly) at a pre-announced time and location for a religious purpose. Adherents may include all those with an affiliation to a congregation (including children, members, and other regular participants who are not members). The number of adherents in the 2020 USRC represents 48.6% of the 2020 U.S. Census population]

State	Congregations Total	Congregations Per 100,000 population	Adherents Total	Adherents As a percent of total population	State	Congregations Total	Congregations Per 100,000 population	Adherents Total	Adherents As a percent of total population
United States	**356,642**	**108**	**161,224,088**	**48.6**	Missouri	9,058	147	2,979,494	48.4
Alabama	10,756	214	3,195,509	63.6	Montana	1,766	163	377,713	34.8
Alaska	1,264	172	258,020	35.2	Nebraska	2,856	146	966,578	49.3
Arizona	5,244	73	3,151,361	44.1	Nevada	1,540	50	1,291,778	41.6
Arkansas	7,428	247	1,739,575	57.8	New Hampshire	1,048	76	374,948	27.2
California	23,567	60	17,726,437	44.8	New Jersey	6,071	65	4,846,460	52.2
Colorado	4,333	75	2,044,440	35.4	New Mexico	2,405	114	1,111,977	52.5
Connecticut	2,889	80	1,708,179	47.4	New York	13,828	68	10,347,548	51.2
Delaware	966	98	409,412	41.4	North Carolina	16,200	155	5,443,737	52.1
Dist. of Columbia	751	109	389,241	56.4	North Dakota	1,452	186	428,647	55.0
Florida	17,511	81	10,140,053	47.1	Ohio	13,906	118	5,646,238	47.9
Georgia	12,891	120	5,439,946	50.8	Oklahoma	7,166	181	2,422,123	61.2
Hawaii	1,424	98	603,730	41.5	Oregon	4,072	96	1,405,973	33.2
Idaho	2,534	138	969,901	52.7	Pennsylvania	15,135	116	6,097,345	46.9
Illinois	12,153	95	6,510,363	50.8	Rhode Island	708	65	565,251	51.5
Indiana	9,028	133	2,859,439	42.1	South Carolina	8,205	160	2,695,900	52.7
Iowa	4,822	151	1,431,349	44.9	South Dakota	1,944	219	491,026	55.4
Kansas	4,624	157	1,352,241	46.0	Tennessee	13,397	194	3,844,957	55.6
Kentucky	8,143	181	2,226,288	49.4	Texas	29,750	102	16,045,479	55.1
Louisiana	6,600	142	2,949,420	63.3	Utah	6,018	184	2,489,571	76.1
Maine	1,574	116	419,523	30.8	Vermont	823	128	242,017	37.6
Maryland	5,715	93	2,685,338	43.5	Virginia	10,465	121	3,970,305	46.0
Massachusetts	4,357	62	3,419,370	48.6	Washington	6,196	80	3,184,751	41.3
Michigan	9,694	96	3,998,585	39.7	West Virginia	4,072	227	677,633	37.8
Minnesota	5,970	105	2,824,374	49.5	Wisconsin	6,183	105	2,831,594	48.0
Mississippi	7,182	243	1,759,935	59.4	Wyoming	958	166	233,016	40.4

Source: Association of Statisticians of American Religious Bodies (ASARB). Clifford Grammich, Erica J. Dollhopf, Mary L. Gautier, Richard Houseal, Dale E. Jones, Alexei Krindatch, Richie Stanley, and Scott Thumma. 2023. © 2020 U.S. Religion Census: Religious Congregations & Adherents Study. See also <www.usreligioncensus.org> and <www.asarb.org>.

Table 78. Religious Congregations and Adherents by Religious Tradition: 2020

[Based on the U.S. Religion Census (USRC) conducted by the Association of Statisticians of American Religious Bodies (ASARB). The USRC focuses on congregations and the individuals affiliated with them, and not on religious individuals directly; therefore, it does not include all U.S. religious adherents. The 2020 USRC includes congregations for 372 religious bodies. For 217 of these 372 bodies, the 2020 USRC provides data on affiliated adherents. Congregations may be churches, mosques, temples, or other meeting places. A congregation is generally defined as a group of people who meet regularly (typically weekly or monthly) at a pre-announced time and location for a religious purpose. Adherents may include all those with an affiliation to a congregation (including children, members, and other regular participants who are not members). The number of adherents in the 2020 USRC represents 48.6% of the 2020 U.S. Census population]

Religious tradition	Total congregations	Adherents Total	Adherents As a percent of 2020 population	Adherents As a percent of total adherents
Total	**356,642**	**161,224,088**	**48.6**	**100.0**
Protestant—Conservative	199,694	54,652,238	16.5	33.9
Protestant—Mainline	69,865	17,184,424	5.2	10.7
Protestant—Black	23,483	7,404,653	2.2	4.6
Catholic	19,522	61,858,937	18.7	38.4
Orthodox Christian	2,921	1,164,594	0.4	0.7
Latter-day Saints	14,631	6,721,031	2.0	4.2
Jehovah's Witnesses	12,285	3,016,924	0.9	1.9
Other Christian	2,764	210,685	0.1	0.1
Buddhism	1,984	1,040,796	0.3	0.6
Hinduism	1,811	1,268,344	0.4	0.8
Islam	2,771	4,453,908	1.3	2.8
Judaism	3,306	2,068,827	0.6	1.3
Other	1,605	178,727	0.1	0.1

Source: Association of Statisticians of American Religious Bodies (ASARB). Clifford Grammich, Erica J. Dollhopf, Mary L. Gautier, Richard Houseal, Dale E. Jones, Alexei Krindatch, Richie Stanley, and Scott Thumma. 2023. © 2020 U.S. Religion Census: Religious Congregations & Adherents Study. See also <www.usreligioncensus.org> and <www.asarb.org>.

Section 2
Births, Deaths, Marriages, and Divorces

This section presents vital statistics data on births, deaths, life expectancy, marriages, and divorces, as well as factors that help explain fertility, such as use of contraception, sexual activity, and prevalence of abortions and fetal deaths. Vital statistics are collected and disseminated for the nation through the National Vital Statistics System by the National Center for Health Statistics (NCHS) and published annually in *Vital Statistics of the United States, National Vital Statistics Reports (NVSR),* and other selected publications. Reports are also issued by various state bureaus participating in the National Vital Statistics System. Factors influencing fertility are collected in NCHS's National Survey of Family Growth and the U.S. Census Bureau's American Community Survey and Current Population Reports (published in *Fertility of American Women*).

Additionally, data on births, deaths, and other public health topics can be accessed via the Centers for Disease Control and Prevention's (CDC) WONDER Online databases at <wonder.cdc.gov>. Data on abortions are collected by CDC's Abortion Surveillance System and published in selected issues of *Morbidity and Mortality Weekly Report (MMWR) Surveillance Summaries*.

Registration of vital events—The registration of births, deaths, fetal deaths, and other vital events in the United States is primarily a state and local function. There are 57 vital registration jurisdictions in the United States: the 50 states, five territories (Puerto Rico, the U.S. Virgin Islands, Guam, American Samoa, and the Commonwealth of the Northern Mariana Islands), District of Columbia, and New York City. Each of the 57 jurisdictions has a direct statistical reporting relationship with NCHS. Vital events occurring to U.S. residents outside the United States are not included in the data.

Births and deaths—The live-birth, death, and fetal-death statistics prepared by NCHS are based on vital records filed in the registration offices of all states, New York City, and the District of Columbia. The annual collection of death statistics on a national basis began in 1900 with a national death-registration area of ten states and the District of Columbia; a similar annual collection of birth statistics for a national birth-registration area began in 1915, also with ten reporting states and the District of Columbia. Since 1933, the birth- and death-registration areas have comprised the entire United States, including Alaska (beginning 1959) and Hawaii (beginning 1960). National statistics on fetal deaths were first compiled for 1918 and annually since 1922. Prior to 1951, birth statistics came from a complete count of records received by the Public Health Service (now received in NCHS). From 1951 through 1971, they were based on a 50-percent sample of all registered births (except for a complete count in 1955 and a 20- to 50-percent sample in 1967). Beginning in 1972, they have been based on a complete count for states participating in the Vital Statistics Cooperative Program (VSCP) (for details, see the technical appendix in *U.S. Vital Statistics System: Major Activities and Developments, 1950-95*) and on a 50-percent sample of all other areas. Beginning in 1985, all 50 States and the District of Columbia participate in the VSCP. Mortality data

have been based on a complete count of records for each area (except for a 50-percent sample in 1972). Beginning in 1970, births to and deaths of nonresident aliens of the United States and U.S. citizens outside the United States have been excluded from the data. Fetal deaths and deaths among Armed Forces abroad are excluded. Data based on samples are subject to sampling error; for details, see annual issues of *National Vital Statistics Reports*.

Mortality statistics by cause of death are compiled in accordance with World Health Organization regulations according to the *International Classification of Diseases* (ICD). The ICD is revised approximately every 10 years. The tenth revision of the ICD was employed beginning in 1999. Deaths for prior years were classified according to the revision of the ICD in use at the time. Each revision of the ICD introduces a number of discontinuities in mortality statistics; for more information, see *Deaths: Final Data for 2020, National Vital Statistics Report*, Vol. 72, No. 10. Information on tests of statistical significance, differences between death rates, and standard errors can also be found in the aforementioned report.

Some of the tables present age-adjusted death rates in addition to crude death rates. Age-adjusted death rates shown in this section were prepared using the direct method, in which age-specific death rates for a population of interest are applied to a standard population distributed by age. Age adjustment eliminates the differences in observed rates between points in time or among compared population groups that result from age differences in population composition.

Fertility and life expectancy—The total fertility rate, defined as the number of births that 1,000 women would have in their lifetime if at each year of age they experienced the birth rates occurring in the specified year, is compiled and published by NCHS. See *Births: Final Data for 2022, National Vital Statistics Reports*, Vol. 73, No. 2. Data on life expectancy, the average remaining lifetime in years for persons who attain a given age, are also computed and published by NCHS. See *Deaths: Final Data for 2020, National Vital Statistics Reports*, Vol. 72, No. 10 and <www.cdc.gov/nchs/nvss/deaths.htm> for details.

Marriage and divorce—In 1957 and 1958 respectively, the National Office of Vital Statistics established marriage- and divorce-registration areas consisting of an increasing number of States over time. Procedures for estimating the number of marriages and divorces in the registration States are discussed in *Vital Statistics of the United States, Vol. III—Marriage and Divorce*. Total counts of events for registration and nonregistration states are gathered by collecting already summarized data on marriages and divorces reported by state offices of vital statistics and by county offices of registration. The collection and publication of detailed marriage and divorce statistics was suspended beginning in January 1996. For additional information, visit the National Center for Health Statistics online at <www.cdc.gov/nchs/nvss/marriage-divorce.htm>.

With the suspension of detailed data collection by the NCHS, data on marriage and divorce can be found in the Census Bureau's American Community Survey data tables. See <www.census.gov/programs-surveys/acs/> for information and data access.

Vital statistics rates—Except as noted, vital statistics rates computed by NCHS are based on decennial census population figures as of April 1 for census years; and on midyear population figures for other years, as estimated by the Census Bureau (see text, Section 1).

Race—Data by race for births, deaths, marriages, and divorces from NCHS are based on information contained in the certificates of registration. The Census Bureau's Current Population Survey obtains information on race by asking respondents to classify their race as (1) White, (2) Black, (3) American Indian or Alaska Native, (4) Native Hawaiian or Other Pacific Islander, or (5) Asian. Beginning with the 1989 data year, NCHS has tabulated birth data primarily by race of the mother. In 1988 and prior years, births were tabulated by race of the child, which was determined from the race of the parents as entered on the birth certificate. Trend data by race shown in this section are by race of mother beginning with the 1980 data.

Persons of Hispanic origin may be of any race; therefore, Hispanic origin of the mother is reported and tabulated independently of race. The majority of women of Hispanic origin are reported as White.

Race categorizations found in the *National Vital Statistics Reports* are variously shown according to either 1977 or 1997 Office of Management and Budget (OMB) standards. The NCHS has transitioned from the use of OMB 1977 standards, which provide for collecting data by four race categories, to OMB 1997 standards, which expand the race categories to five and also allow for reporting multiple race categories. The reporting of Hispanic-origin ethnicity was not affected by the change to 1997 OMB standards. States reporting multiple-race data according to new 1997 OMB standards has varied widely. In some cases, to provide a comparison of data by race between the 1977 and 1997 OMB standards, the responses of those reporting more than one race were "bridged" to a single race. See headnotes of individual tables and respective source reports for additional information.

Statistical reliability—For a discussion of statistical collection, estimation, and sampling procedures and measures of reliability applicable to data from NCHS and the Census Bureau, see Appendix III.

Table 79. Live Births, Deaths, Marriages, and Divorces: 1960 to 2022

[4,258 represents 4,258,000. Beginning 1970, excludes births to and deaths of nonresidents of the United States. See Appendix III]

Year	Number (1,000)					Rate per 1,000 population				
	Births	Deaths		Mar-riages [2]	Divorces [3]	Births	Deaths		Mar-riages [2]	Divorces [3]
		Total	Infant [1]				Total	Infant [1]		
1960..............	4,258	1,712	111	1,523	393	23.7	9.5	26.0	8.5	2.2
1965..............	3,760	1,828	93	1,800	479	19.4	9.4	24.7	9.3	2.5
1970..............	3,731	1,921	75	2,159	708	18.4	9.5	20.0	10.6	3.5
1971..............	3,556	1,928	68	2,190	773	17.2	9.3	19.1	10.6	3.7
1972..............	3,258	1,964	60	2,282	845	15.6	9.4	18.5	10.9	4.0
1973..............	3,137	1,973	56	2,284	915	14.8	9.3	17.7	10.8	4.3
1974..............	3,160	1,934	53	2,230	977	14.8	9.1	16.7	10.5	4.6
1975..............	3,144	1,893	51	2,153	1,036	14.6	8.8	16.1	10.0	4.8
1976..............	3,168	1,909	48	2,155	1,083	14.6	8.8	15.2	9.9	5.0
1977..............	3,327	1,900	47	2,178	1,091	15.1	8.6	14.1	9.9	5.0
1978..............	3,333	1,928	46	2,282	1,130	15.0	8.7	13.8	10.3	5.1
1979..............	3,494	1,914	46	2,331	1,181	15.6	8.5	13.1	10.4	5.3
1980..............	3,612	1,990	46	2,390	1,189	15.9	8.8	12.6	10.6	5.2
1981..............	3,629	1,978	43	2,422	1,213	15.8	8.6	11.9	10.6	5.3
1982..............	3,681	1,975	42	2,456	1,170	15.9	8.5	11.5	10.6	5.1
1983..............	3,639	2,019	41	2,446	1,158	15.6	8.6	11.2	10.5	5.0
1984..............	3,669	2,039	40	2,477	1,169	15.6	8.6	10.8	10.5	5.0
1985..............	3,761	2,086	40	2,413	1,190	15.8	8.8	10.6	10.1	5.0
1986..............	3,757	2,105	39	2,407	1,178	15.6	8.8	10.4	10.0	4.9
1987..............	3,809	2,123	38	2,403	1,166	15.7	8.8	10.1	9.9	4.8
1988..............	3,910	2,168	39	2,396	1,167	16.0	8.9	10.0	9.8	4.8
1989..............	4,041	2,150	40	2,403	1,157	16.4	8.7	9.8	9.7	4.7
1990..............	4,158	2,148	38	2,443	1,182	16.7	8.6	9.2	9.8	4.7
1991..............	4,111	2,170	37	2,371	1,187	16.2	8.6	8.9	9.4	4.7
1992..............	4,065	2,176	35	2,362	1,215	15.8	8.5	8.5	9.3	4.8
1993..............	4,000	2,269	33	2,334	1,187	15.4	8.7	8.4	9.0	4.6
1994..............	3,953	2,279	31	2,362	1,191	15.0	8.7	8.0	9.1	4.6
1995..............	3,900	2,312	30	2,336	1,169	14.6	8.7	7.6	8.9	4.4
1996..............	3,891	2,315	28	2,344	1,150	14.4	8.6	7.3	8.8	4.3
1997..............	3,881	2,314	28	2,384	1,163	14.2	8.5	7.2	8.9	4.3
1998..............	3,942	2,337	28	2,244	[4] 1,135	14.3	8.5	7.2	8.4	[4] 4.2
1999..............	3,959	2,391	28	2,358	(NA)	14.2	8.6	7.1	8.6	[4] 4.1
2000..............	4,059	2,403	28	2,315	[5] 944	14.4	8.5	6.9	8.2	[5] 4.0
2001..............	4,026	2,416	28	2,326	[5] 940	14.1	8.5	6.9	8.2	[5] 4.0
2002..............	4,022	2,443	28	2,290	[6] 955	14.0	8.5	7.0	8.0	[6] 3.9
2003..............	4,090	2,448	28	2,245	[7] 927	14.1	8.4	6.9	7.7	[7] 3.8
2004..............	4,112	2,398	28	2,279	[8] 879	14.0	8.2	6.8	7.8	[8] 3.7
2005..............	4,138	2,448	28	2,249	[9] 847	14.0	8.3	6.9	7.6	[9] 3.6
2006..............	4,266	2,426	29	[10] 2,193	[9] 872	14.3	8.1	6.7	[10] 7.5	[9] 3.7
2007..............	4,316	2,424	29	2,197	[9] 856	14.3	8.0	6.8	7.3	[9] 3.6
2008..............	4,248	2,472	28	2,157	[9] 844	14.0	8.1	6.6	7.1	[9] 3.5
2009..............	4,131	2,437	26	2,080	[9] 840	13.5	7.9	6.4	6.8	[9] 3.5
2010..............	3,999	2,468	25	2,096	[9] 872	13.0	8.0	6.2	6.8	[9] 3.6
2011..............	3,954	2,515	24	2,118	[9] 877	12.7	8.1	6.1	6.8	[9] 3.6
2012..............	3,953	2,543	24	2,131	[9] 851	12.6	8.1	6.0	6.8	[9] 3.4
2013..............	3,932	2,597	23	[11] 2,081	[12] 832	12.4	8.2	6.0	[11] 6.8	[12] 3.3
2014..............	3,988	2,626	23	[11] 2,140	[12] 814	12.5	8.2	5.8	[11] 6.9	[12] 3.2
2015..............	3,978	2,713	23	2,222	[12] 801	12.4	8.4	5.9	6.9	[12] 3.1
2016..............	3,946	2,744	23	2,251	[13] 776	12.2	8.5	5.9	7.0	[13] 3.0
2017..............	3,856	2,814	22	2,236	[14] 787	11.8	8.6	5.8	6.9	[14] 2.9
2018..............	3,792	2,839	21	2,133	[14] 782	11.6	8.7	5.7	6.5	[14] 2.9
2019..............	3,748	2,855	21	2,016	[14] 747	11.4	8.7	5.6	6.1	[14] 2.7
2020..............	3,614	3,384	20	1,677	[14] 631	10.9	10.3	5.4	5.1	[14] 2.3
2021..............	3,664	3,464	20	1,985	[14] 689	11.0	10.4	5.4	6.0	[14] 2.5
2022..............	3,668	3,280	21	2,066	[14] 674	11.0	9.8	5.6	6.2	[14] 2.4

NA Not available. [1] Infant mortality rate; infants under 1 year of age, excluding fetal deaths. [2] Marriages and marriage rates are by place of occurrence. Beginning 1991, data are provisional. Includes estimates for some States through 1965 and for 1976-1977, and marriage licenses for some states for all years except 1973 and 1975. Beginning 1978, includes nonlicensed marriages in California. [3] Divorces and divorce rates are by place of occurrence. Includes reported annulments and some estimated state figures for all years. Beginning 1991, data are provisional. [4] Excludes data for California, Colorado, Indiana, and Louisiana. [5] Excludes data for California, Indiana, Louisiana, and Oklahoma. [6] Excludes data for California, Indiana, New York City, and Oklahoma. [7] Excludes data for California, Hawaii, Indiana, and Oklahoma. [8] Excludes data for California, Georgia, Hawaii, Indiana, and Louisiana. [9] Excludes data for California, Georgia, Hawaii, Indiana, Louisiana, and Minnesota. [10] Excludes data for Louisiana. [11] Excludes data for Georgia. [12] Excludes data for California, Georgia, Hawaii, Indiana, and Minnesota. [13] Excludes data for California, Georgia, Hawaii, Indiana, Minnesota, and New Mexico. [14] Excludes data for California, Hawaii, Indiana, Minnesota, and New Mexico.

Source: U.S. National Center for Health Statistics, *Births: Final Data for 2022*, Vol. 73, No. 2, April 2024; and CDC WONDER Online Database, "Multiple Cause of Death, 2018-2022," <wonder.cdc.gov/>, and "National Marriage and Divorce Rate Trends," <www.cdc.gov/nchs/nvss/marriage-divorce.htm>, accessed May 2024.

Table 80. Births, Birth Rates, and Fertility Rates by Sex and Mother's Race and Age: 1980 to 2022

[Births in thousands (3,612 represents 3,612,000). Beginning 2016, all States and the District of Columbia reported race data according to 1997 Office of Management and Budget (OMB) standards. To maintain comparability of 2016 data with earlier data, data for mothers reporting multiple-race were bridged to single-race categories. Beginning with 2003, data shown here for race/ethnicity of mother are from the CDC WONDER database and are calculated differently than in other natality published reports. In computing birth and fertility rates by race and Hispanic origin, the National Center for Health Statistics includes births with origin of mother not stated with non-Hispanic births, according to the race of mother. See Technical Notes, source. For population bases used to derive these data, see text this section, and Appendix III]

Item	1980	1990	2000	2010	2015	2017	2018	2019	2020	2021	2022
Live births [1]	**3,612**	**4,158**	**4,059**	**3,999**	**3,978**	**3,856**	**3,792**	**3,748**	**3,614**	**3,664**	**3,668**
Male	1,853	2,129	2,077	2,047	2,036	1,973	1,938	1,917	1,848	1,873	1,874
Female	1,760	2,029	1,982	1,952	1,942	1,883	1,854	1,830	1,766	1,791	1,793
Males per 100 females (sex ratio)	105	105	105	105	105	105	105	105	105	105	105
Race/ethnicity of mother:											
Non-Hispanic	(NA)	(NA)	(NA)	3,027	3,022	2,924	2,872	2,825	2,713	2,742	2,695
White alone	(NA)	(NA)	(NA)	(NA)	(NA)	1,992	1,956	1,916	1,843	1,888	1,841
Black or African American alone	(NA)	(NA)	(NA)	(NA)	(NA)	561	552	548	530	518	511
American Indian or Alaska Native alone	(NA)	(NA)	(NA)	(NA)	(NA)	30	29	28	27	26	26
Asian alone	(NA)	(NA)	(NA)	(NA)	(NA)	249	241	239	219	214	219
Native Hawaiian or Other Pacific Islander alone	(NA)	(NA)	(NA)	(NA)	(NA)	9	9	10	10	10	10
Hispanic	(NA)	595	816	945	924	899	886	886	867	886	937
Bridged race estimates: [2]											
White	2,936	3,290	3,194	3,069	3,013	2,858	2,835	2,790	(NA)	(NA)	(NA)
Black	568	684	623	636	640	658	634	635	(NA)	(NA)	(NA)
American Indian or Alaska Native	29	39	42	47	44	42	42	42	(NA)	(NA)	(NA)
Asian or Pacific Islander	74	142	201	247	281	298	281	281	(NA)	(NA)	(NA)
Age of mother:											
Under 20 years old	562	533	478	372	232	196	182	173	160	149	146
20 to 24 years old	1,226	1,094	1,018	952	851	765	726	704	666	648	639
25 to 29 years old	1,108	1,277	1,088	1,134	1,152	1,124	1,099	1,078	1,024	1,024	1,013
30 to 34 years old	550	886	929	962	1,095	1,092	1,091	1,089	1,070	1,115	1,119
35 to 39 years old	141	318	452	465	528	555	567	573	564	592	607
40 to 44 years old	(NA)	(NA)	90	107	112	115	117	120	121	126	134
45 to 54 years old	(NA)	(NA)	4	8	9	9	10	10	9	9	11
Mean age of mother at first birth (years)	22.7	24.2	24.9	25.4	26.4	26.8	26.9	27.0	27.1	27.3	27.4
Birth rate per 1,000 population	**15.9**	**16.7**	**14.4**	**13.0**	**12.4**	**11.8**	**11.6**	**11.4**	**10.9**	**11.0**	**11.0**
Race/ethnicity of mother:											
Non-Hispanic	(NA)	(NA)	(NA)	11.7	11.4	11.0	10.7	10.6	10.1	10.2	10.0
White alone	(NA)	(NA)	(NA)	(NA)	(NA)	10.1	9.9	9.7	9.4	9.6	9.4
Black or African American alone	(NA)	(NA)	(NA)	(NA)	(NA)	13.8	13.5	13.3	12.8	12.4	12.2
American Indian or Alaska Native alone	(NA)	(NA)	(NA)	(NA)	(NA)	12.5	12.0	11.7	11.0	10.7	10.6
Asian alone	(NA)	(NA)	(NA)	(NA)	(NA)	13.6	12.9	12.6	11.3	10.9	10.8
Native Hawaiian or Other Pacific Islander alone	(NA)	(NA)	(NA)	(NA)	(NA)	16.3	16.2	16.4	15.7	15.2	15.9
Hispanic	23.5	26.7	23.1	18.7	16.3	15.3	14.8	14.6	14.1	14.1	14.7
Bridged race estimates: [2]											
White	15.1	15.8	13.9	12.5	12.0	11.3	11.1	10.9	(NA)	(NA)	(NA)
Black	21.3	22.4	17.0	15.1	14.3	14.3	13.7	13.6	(NA)	(NA)	(NA)
American Indian or Alaska Native	20.7	18.9	14.0	11.0	9.7	8.9	8.9	8.7	(NA)	(NA)	(NA)
Asian or Pacific Islander	19.9	19.0	17.1	14.5	14.0	14.0	13.0	12.9	(NA)	(NA)	(NA)
Age of mother:											
10 to 14 years old	1.1	1.4	0.9	0.4	0.2	0.2	0.2	0.2	0.2	0.2	0.2
15 to 19 years old	53.0	59.9	47.7	34.2	22.3	18.8	17.4	16.7	15.0	13.9	13.6
20 to 24 years old	115.1	116.5	109.7	90.0	76.8	71.0	68.0	66.6	63.3	61.5	57.5
25 to 29 years old	112.9	120.2	113.5	108.3	104.3	98.0	95.3	93.7	90.9	93.0	93.5
30 to 34 years old	61.9	80.8	91.2	96.5	101.5	100.3	99.7	98.3	94.9	97.6	97.5
35 to 39 years old	19.8	31.7	39.7	45.9	51.8	52.3	52.6	52.8	51.3	53.7	55.3
40 to 44 years old	3.9	5.5	8.0	10.2	11.0	11.6	11.8	12.0	11.8	12.0	12.6
45 to 54 years old [3]	0.2	0.2	0.5	0.7	0.8	0.9	0.9	0.9	0.9	0.9	1.1
Fertility rate per 1,000 women [4]	**68.4**	**70.9**	**65.9**	**64.1**	**62.5**	**60.3**	**59.1**	**58.3**	**55.7**	**56.3**	**56.0**
Race/ethnicity of mother:											
Non-Hispanic	(NA)	(NA)	(NA)	59.8	59.6	57.7	56.6	55.7	53.4	53.7	52.6
White alone	(NA)	(NA)	(NA)	(NA)	(NA)	56.6	55.7	54.6	52.6	53.7	52.5
Black or African American alone	(NA)	(NA)	(NA)	(NA)	(NA)	62.7	61.5	60.9	58.6	56.8	55.6
American Indian or Alaska Native alone	(NA)	(NA)	(NA)	(NA)	(NA)	58.9	56.9	55.4	51.9	50.1	49.8
Asian alone	(NA)	(NA)	(NA)	(NA)	(NA)	56.9	54.2	53.7	49.4	48.1	48.0
Native Hawaiian or Other Pacific Islander alone	(NA)	(NA)	(NA)	(NA)	(NA)	71.4	71.1	72.2	70.5	68.9	72.2
Hispanic	95.4	107.7	95.9	80.2	71.7	67.6	65.9	65.3	63.1	63.4	65.7
Bridged race estimates: [2]											
White	65.6	68.3	65.3	64.4	63.1	59.8	59.2	58.2	(NA)	(NA)	(NA)
Black	84.7	86.8	70.0	66.3	64.0	64.9	62.2	61.9	(NA)	(NA)	(NA)
American Indian or Alaska Native	82.7	76.2	58.7	48.6	43.9	40.8	40.7	40.0	(NA)	(NA)	(NA)
Asian or Pacific Islander	73.2	69.6	65.8	59.2	58.5	59.3	55.2	54.9	(NA)	(NA)	(NA)

NA Not available. [1] Includes other races not shown separately. [2] Bridged race categories consistent with 1977 Office of Management and Budget standards. [3] Birth rates computed by relating births to women age 45 and over (includes mothers up to age 64) to women age 45-49. [4] Number of live births per 1,000 women aged 15 to 44 years in specified group.

Source: U.S. National Center for Health Statistics, National Vital Statistics Reports, *Births: Final Data for 2022*, Vol. 73, No. 2, April 2024, and earlier reports; and CDC WONDER Online Database, "Natality for 2016-2022 (expanded)," <wonder.cdc.gov/natality.html>, accessed April 2024.

Table 81. Births—Number and Rate by Race and Hispanic Origin and State and Island Area: 2022

[For registered births by place of residence. Excludes births to nonresidents of the United States. Based on race and Hispanic origin of mother. Race categories are consistent with 1997 Office of Management and Budget standards; see Technical Notes in source. Race alone is defined as only one race reported on the birth certificate. See Appendix III]

State and Island Area	All races [1]	White alone [2]	Black alone [2]	American Indian or Alaska Native alone [2]	Asian alone [2]	Native Hawaiian or Other Pacific Islander alone [2]	Hispanic [3]	Birth rate [4]	Fertility rate [5]
United States [6]	3,667,758	1,840,739	511,439	25,721	218,994	10,122	937,421	11.0	56.0
Alabama	58,149	33,725	16,067	131	782	56	6,231	11.5	58.7
Alaska	9,359	4,639	249	1,727	563	311	794	12.8	64.9
Arizona	78,547	30,499	4,425	3,436	2,748	205	34,839	10.7	54.9
Arkansas	35,471	22,539	6,301	194	777	545	4,227	11.6	60.2
California	419,104	110,370	20,050	1,297	56,915	1,601	203,312	10.7	52.8
Colorado	62,383	35,076	2,981	336	2,450	203	18,982	10.7	51.5
Connecticut	35,332	18,681	4,298	30	1,878	3	9,597	9.7	50.7
Delaware	10,816	5,035	2,853	13	553	6	1,996	10.6	57.3
District of Columbia	8,075	2,602	3,495	11	393	3	1,348	12.0	44.9
Florida	224,433	91,763	47,635	231	6,592	155	74,864	10.1	55.6
Georgia	126,130	53,638	42,042	104	5,640	110	21,202	11.6	56.0
Hawaii	15,535	2,896	326	30	3,854	1,486	2,701	10.8	59.3
Idaho	22,391	16,894	258	194	378	66	4,002	11.5	58.4
Illinois	128,350	68,107	19,296	87	8,277	39	29,710	10.2	51.8
Indiana	79,649	55,178	10,119	50	2,458	76	9,939	11.7	59.7
Iowa	36,506	27,527	2,562	136	1,032	323	4,172	11.4	59.9
Kansas	34,401	23,669	2,208	163	1,055	78	6,309	11.7	60.3
Kentucky	52,315	40,484	5,043	59	1,151	92	4,291	11.6	61.1
Louisiana	56,479	28,105	20,229	302	1,045	29	5,936	12.3	61.8
Maine	12,093	10,640	679	76	163	6	338	8.7	49.7
Maryland	68,782	27,333	20,438	77	4,480	36	14,398	11.2	56.9
Massachusetts	68,584	37,682	7,125	57	5,630	21	15,383	9.8	48.7
Michigan	102,321	70,340	17,235	394	3,989	40	7,127	10.2	54.0
Minnesota	64,015	42,246	7,923	774	4,931	95	6,040	11.2	58.2
Mississippi	34,675	17,703	14,035	231	396	15	1,930	11.8	59.7
Missouri	68,985	49,846	9,188	160	1,684	265	5,224	11.2	57.7
Montana	11,175	8,995	63	946	134	15	678	10.0	53.2
Nebraska	24,345	16,120	1,597	261	816	37	4,815	12.4	63.6
Nevada	33,193	10,961	4,334	218	2,548	358	13,019	10.4	53.2
New Hampshire	12,077	10,318	267	8	441	8	812	8.7	47.9
New Jersey	102,893	47,356	12,911	34	10,561	51	29,931	11.1	58.7
New Mexico	21,614	5,531	403	2,221	412	19	12,617	10.2	53.1
New York	207,774	104,103	27,935	327	20,652	70	50,131	10.6	53.6
North Carolina	121,562	62,762	26,375	1,401	4,824	144	22,568	11.4	57.6
North Dakota	9,567	6,965	585	613	183	30	671	12.3	62.0
Ohio	128,231	90,671	20,380	89	3,923	115	9,062	10.9	57.3
Oklahoma	48,332	26,224	3,689	4,355	1,310	232	8,462	12.0	60.4
Oregon	39,493	23,034	1,007	370	2,151	374	8,510	9.3	47.3
Pennsylvania	130,252	85,031	16,616	162	6,212	40	18,118	10.0	53.3
Rhode Island	10,269	5,673	842	38	418	3	2,965	9.4	47.5
South Carolina	57,820	32,323	15,333	124	1,176	74	7,073	10.9	57.0
South Dakota	11,201	8,008	362	1,463	191	20	726	12.3	66.5
Tennessee	82,265	52,818	14,514	87	1,877	72	11,048	11.7	59.3
Texas	389,741	121,868	47,804	685	20,794	579	190,889	13.0	61.9
Utah	45,768	32,461	606	303	1,210	575	8,920	13.5	61.3
Vermont	5,316	4,754	116	13	145	–	163	8.2	44.3
Virginia	95,630	51,085	18,543	151	7,140	114	15,943	11.0	55.6
Washington	83,333	44,084	3,797	861	9,159	1,284	17,190	10.7	53.3
West Virginia	16,929	15,300	566	14	178	2	412	9.5	54.0
Wisconsin	60,049	42,455	5,688	499	2,661	34	6,971	10.2	54.2
Wyoming	6,049	4,622	46	178	64	7	835	10.4	55.4
Puerto Rico	19,112	311	45	4	24	–	18,707	5.9	31.1
Virgin Islands	868	88	503	3	4	–	181	8.2	46.8
Guam	2,518	166	31	3	594	1,595	26	14.9	76.9
American Samoa	(NA)	(NA)	(NA)	(NA)	(NA)	(NA)	(NA)	(NA)	(NA)
Northern Marianas	467	5	–	–	152	271	1	9.1	51.5

– Represents zero. NA Not available. [1] Includes persons of other racial/ethnic groups, not shown separately. [2] Non-Hispanic. [3] Persons of Hispanic origin may be of any race. [4] Per 1,000 estimated population. [5] Number of births per 1,000 women aged 15 to 44 years. [6] Does not include data for the Island Areas.

Source: U.S. National Center for Health Statistics, National Vital Statistics Reports, *Births: Final Data for 2022*, Vol. 73, No. 2, April 2024. See also <www.cdc.gov/nchs/nvss/births.htm>.

Table 82. Births, Twin Births, and Triplet and Higher-order Multiple Births by Race and Hispanic Origin: 2010 to 2022

[Represents registered births. Excludes births to nonresidents of the United States. Data are based on Hispanic origin and race of mother. Persons of Hispanic origin may be of any race. Race categories are consistent with 1997 Office of Management and Budget standards; see source for details. See Appendix III]

Year and race and Hispanic origin	Number			Rate		
	Total births	Twin births	Triplet and higher-order births	Multiple births, total [1]	Twin births [2]	Triplet and higher-order births [3]
All races and origins: [4]						
2010.............................	3,999,386	132,562	5,503	34.5	33.1	137.6
2015.............................	3,978,497	133,155	4,123	34.5	33.5	103.6
2019.............................	3,747,540	120,291	3,286	33.0	32.1	87.7
2020.............................	3,613,647	112,437	2,875	31.9	31.1	79.6
2021.............................	3,664,292	114,161	2,933	32.0	31.2	80.0
2022.............................	3,667,758	114,483	2,895	32.0	31.2	78.9
White alone, non-Hispanic :						
2019.............................	1,915,912	64,011	1,865	34.4	33.4	97.3
2020.............................	1,843,432	60,082	1,664	33.5	32.6	90.3
2021.............................	1,887,656	61,438	1,762	33.5	32.5	93.3
2022.............................	1,840,739	59,969	1,549	33.4	32.6	84.2
Black alone, non-Hispanic:						
2019.............................	548,075	22,397	589	41.9	40.9	107.5
2020.............................	529,811	21,554	521	41.7	40.7	98.3
2021.............................	517,889	21,047	424	41.5	40.6	81.9
2022.............................	511,439	21,163	556	42.5	41.4	108.7
Hispanic: [5]						
2019.............................	886,467	21,811	590	25.3	24.6	66.6
2020.............................	866,713	20,709	488	24.5	23.9	56.3
2021.............................	885,916	21,401	554	24.8	24.2	62.5
2022.............................	937,421	22,992	575	25.1	24.5	61.3

[1] Number of live births in all multiple deliveries per 1,000 live births. [2] Number of births in twin deliveries per 1,000 live births. [3] Number of births in greater than twin deliveries per 100,000 live births. [4] Includes other races not shown separately. [5] Persons of Hispanic origin may be of any race.

Source: U.S. National Center for Health Statistics, National Vital Statistics Reports, *Births: Final Data for 2022*, Vol. 73, No. 2, April 2024. See also <www.cdc.gov/nchs/nvss/births.htm>.

Table 83. Births by Method of Delivery and Race and Hispanic Origin: 2010 to 2022

[In thousands (3,999 represents 3,999,000), except rate. Race categories are consistent with 1997 Office of Management and Budget standards. Data are based on race and Hispanic origin of mother. Persons of Hispanic origin may be of any race. See Appendix III]

Method of delivery	2010	2017	2018	2019	2020	2021	2022			
							Total [1]	White alone, non-Hispanic	Black alone, non-Hispanic	Hispanic
Births, total..................	**3,999**	**3,856**	**3,792**	**3,748**	**3,614**	**3,664**	**3,668**	**1,841**	**511**	**937**
Vaginal.........................	2,681	2,621	2,582	2,559	2,463	2,487	2,487	1,268	323	640
Cesarean.......................	1,309	1,232	1,208	1,186	1,149	1,175	1,178	571	188	297
Not stated......................	9	2	2	2	2	3	3	1	(Z)	(Z)
Cesarean delivery rate [2]......	32.8	32.0	31.9	31.7	31.8	32.1	32.1	31.1	36.8	31.7
Rate of vaginal birth after previous Cesarean [3].........	(NA)	12.8	13.3	13.8	13.9	14.2	14.6	14.7	14.6	14.3

Z Represents less than 500. NA Not available. [1] Includes other races not shown separately. [2] Percent of all live births by cesarean delivery. [3] Number of births to women having a vaginal delivery per 100 births to women with a previous cesarean delivery.

Source: U.S. National Center for Health Statistics, National Vital Statistics Reports, *Births: Final Data for 2022*, Vol. 73, No. 2, April 2024, and earlier reports. See also <www.cdc.gov/nchs/nvss/births.htm>.

Table 84. Births Delivered by Physicians, Midwives, and Other Attendants by Place of Delivery: 2022

[Number, except as noted]

Place of delivery	Total births [1]	Physician			Midwife			Other
		Total	Doctor of medicine	Doctor of osteopathy	Total	Certified nurse or midwife	Other midwife	
Total............................	**3,667,758**	**3,175,650**	**2,830,551**	**345,099**	**443,504**	**398,976**	**44,528**	**45,916**
Percent.........................	100.0	86.6	77.2	9.4	12.1	10.9	1.2	1.3
In hospital [2]........................	3,584,633	3,172,777	2,827,950	344,827	379,497	373,535	5,962	31,339
Not in hospital.....................	83,007	2,817	2,549	268	63,994	25,432	38,562	14,542
Freestanding birthing center.	23,945	474	459	15	22,003	12,004	9,999	1,444
Clinic or doctor's office..........	562	77	67	10	455	307	148	28
Residence.......................	54,071	1,638	1,480	158	39,669	12,577	27,092	11,450
Other...........................	4,429	628	543	85	1,867	544	1,323	1,620
Not specified.....................	118	56	52	4	13	9	4	35

[1] Includes unspecified attendants, not shown separately. [2] Includes births occurring en route to or upon arrival at hospital.

Source: U.S. National Center for Health Statistics, National Vital Statistics Reports, *Births: Final Data for 2022, Supplemental Tables*, Vol. 73, No. 2, April 2024. See also <www.cdc.gov/nchs/nvss/births.htm>.

Table 85. Total Fertility Rate by Race and Hispanic Origin: 2010 to 2022

[Based on race and Hispanic origin of mother. Excludes births to nonresidents of the United States. The total fertility rate estimates the number of births that a hypothetical cohort of 1,000 women would have if they experienced throughout their childbearing years the same age-specific birth rates observed in a given year. The rate can be expressed as the average number of children that would be born per woman. A total fertility rate of 2,100 represents "replacement level" fertility for the total population under current mortality conditions (assuming no net immigration). Race categories are consistent with 1997 Office of Management and Budget standards. See Appendix III]

Race and Hispanic origin	2010	2016	2017	2018	2019	2020	2021	2022
Total.................................	**1,931**	**1,821**	**1,766**	**1,730**	**1,706**	**1,642**	**1,664**	**1,657**
Non-Hispanic:								
White alone........................	(NA)	1,719	1,667	1,640	1,611	1,551	1,599	1,568
Black alone........................	(NA)	1,833	1,825	1,792	1,776	1,714	1,675	1,639
American Indian or Alaska Native alone..........	(NA)	1,795	1,702	1,651	1,612	1,521	1,477	1,470
Asian alone........................	(NA)	1,691	1,597	1,525	1,511	1,379	1,352	1,353
Native Hawaiian or other Pacific Islander alone...	(NA)	2,077	2,086	2,107	2,178	2,135	2,131	2,238
Hispanic [1].................................	2,350	2,093	2,007	1,959	1,940	1,880	1,899	1,970

NA Not available. [1] Persons of Hispanic origin may be of any race.

Source: U.S. National Center for Health Statistics, National Vital Statistics Reports, *Births: Final Data for 2022*, Vol. 73, No. 2, April 2024. See also <www.cdc.gov/nchs/nvss/births.htm>.

Table 86. Teenagers—Births and Birth Rates by Age, Race, and Hispanic Origin: 2019 to 2022

[Birth rates per 1,000 women in specified group. Based on race and Hispanic origin of mother. Race categories are consistent with 1997 Office of Management and Budget (OMB) standards. See source for details]

Age, race, and Hispanic origin	Number of births				Birth rates			
	2019	2020	2021	2022	2019	2020	2021	2022
All races, 15 to 19 years [1]...................	**171,674**	**158,043**	**146,973**	**143,789**	**16.7**	**15.0**	**13.9**	**13.6**
15 to 17 years............................	41,081	38,587	35,542	35,422	6.7	6.1	5.6	5.6
18 to 19 years............................	130,593	119,456	111,431	108,367	31.1	28.2	26.6	25.8
Non-Hispanic:								
White alone................................	60,484	54,426	50,203	48,060	11.4	10.1	9.4	9.1
Black alone................................	36,696	34,147	31,231	29,194	25.8	23.7	21.8	20.3
American Indian or Alaska Native alone.....	2,516	2,189	2,117	1,924	29.2	25.2	24.2	22.5
Asian alone................................	1,357	1,127	971	982	2.7	2.2	2.0	1.9
Native Hawaiian or other Pacific Islander alone....................	520	452	447	431	26.2	22.2	21.9	20.5
Hispanic [2].................................	62,654	58,752	55,263	56,566	25.3	23.0	21.1	21.3

[1] Includes other racial/ethnic groups, not shown separately. [2] Persons of Hispanic origin may be of any race.

Source: U.S. National Center for Health Statistics, National Vital Statistics Reports, *Births: Final Data for 2022*, Vol. 73, No. 2, April 2024. See also <www.cdc.gov/nchs/nvss/births.htm>.

Table 87. Births to Unmarried Women by Age, Race, and Hispanic Origin: 2022

[Data are based on Hispanic origin and race of mother. Race categories are consistent with 1997 Office of Management and Budget standards; see source for details. See also Appendix III]

Race and Hispanic origin		Age of mother						
	Total	Under 15 years old	15 to 19 years old	20 to 24 years old	25 to 29 years old	30 to 34 years old	35 to 39 years old	40 years and over
NUMBER								
Total.................................	**1,461,305**	**1,816**	**131,713**	**433,087**	**413,703**	**296,005**	**145,178**	**39,803**
Non-Hispanic:								
White alone........................	498,291	404	41,984	152,945	139,390	99,909	50,212	13,447
Black alone........................	354,351	481	28,682	99,618	104,305	77,822	34,498	8,945
American Indian or Alaska Native alone......................	17,511	32	1,863	5,453	4,674	3,607	1,518	364
Asian alone........................	26,942	4	740	3,845	7,224	7,917	5,368	1,844
Native Hawaiian or other Pacific Islander alone.............	5,295	4	384	1,849	1,530	939	464	125
Hispanic [1].................................	498,971	791	51,867	150,477	139,886	94,827	47,710	13,413
PERCENT OF TOTAL BIRTHS								
Total.................................	**39.8**	**99.5**	**91.6**	**67.8**	**40.8**	**26.5**	**23.9**	**27.5**
Non-Hispanic:								
White alone........................	27.1	99.3	87.4	55.4	27.1	16.2	15.8	20.1
Black alone........................	69.3	99.8	98.2	89.9	73.3	58.1	46.9	42.2
American Indian or Alaska Native alone......................	68.1	100.0	96.8	81.0	64.2	58.2	52.8	53.6
Asian alone........................	12.3	(S)	75.4	38.4	17.2	8.8	8.8	12.3
Native Hawaiian or other Pacific Islander alone.............	52.3	(S)	89.1	70.9	52.5	38.6	33.7	35.4
Hispanic [1].................................	53.2	99.4	91.7	72.7	51.7	39.9	36.8	37.9

S Figure does not meet standards of reliability. [1] Persons of Hispanic origin may be of any race.

Source: U.S. National Center for Health Statistics, National Vital Statistics Reports, *Births: Final Data for 2022*, Vol. 73, No. 2, April 2024. See also <www.cdc.gov/nchs/nvss/births.htm>.

Table 88. Percent of Births to Teenage Mothers, Unmarried Women, and Births with Low Birth Weight by State: 2020 and 2022

[In percent. By place of residence. Excludes nonresidents of the United States]

State	Births to teenage mothers [1] 2020	2022	Births to unmarried women 2020	2022	Births with low birth weight [2] 2020	2022	State	Births to teenage mothers [1] 2020	2022	Births to unmarried women 2020	2022	Births with low birth weight [2] 2020	2022
U.S.	4.4	3.9	40.5	39.8	8.2	8.6	MO.	5.1	4.7	41.1	39.1	8.7	9.1
AL.	6.6	5.9	48.4	45.3	10.8	10.4	MT.	3.8	3.6	33.9	31.5	7.7	7.6
AK.	4.0	3.8	36.5	36.7	6.6	7.0	NE.	4.1	3.8	33.4	34.1	7.4	7.9
AZ.	5.1	4.5	45.2	45.0	7.4	7.8	NV.	4.5	3.9	48.8	48.1	9.0	9.3
AR.	7.6	6.9	46.8	45.2	9.6	9.3	NH.	2.3	1.5	32.1	29.3	6.8	6.7
CA.	3.2	2.9	38.6	38.8	6.9	7.4	NJ.	2.5	2.2	33.9	33.4	7.7	7.8
CO.	3.6	3.2	23.2	23.3	9.3	9.9	NM.	6.8	6.3	53.2	52.6	8.9	9.9
CT.	2.6	2.2	38.1	37.1	7.8	8.0	NY.	2.7	2.4	38.1	37.9	8.2	8.6
DE.	4.2	4.3	48.1	47.3	8.9	9.0	NC.	5.0	4.3	41.9	40.7	9.5	9.4
DC.	3.4	3.0	46.7	46.6	9.6	9.9	ND.	3.2	3.2	32.8	31.2	6.9	7.1
FL.	4.3	3.6	47.2	46.1	8.7	9.1	OH.	5.0	4.4	43.6	42.3	8.5	8.7
GA.	5.4	4.9	46.3	45.5	9.9	10.6	OK.	6.8	5.9	44.4	43.8	8.4	8.5
HI.	3.0	2.8	39.4	39.6	8.1	8.5	OR.	3.0	3.1	36.7	37.6	6.5	7.1
ID.	4.2	3.6	27.7	26.4	6.9	7.1	PA.	3.7	3.3	40.9	38.9	8.3	8.5
IL.	4.0	3.5	40.5	39.4	8.3	8.7	RI.	3.2	2.9	44.7	42.9	7.7	7.9
IN.	5.2	4.7	43.6	42.6	8.1	8.7	SC.	5.5	5.0	46.6	45.0	9.8	10.0
IA.	3.8	3.7	36.3	35.2	6.9	7.2	SD.	4.9	4.6	36.0	35.8	6.9	7.1
KS.	5.1	4.7	36.8	36.0	7.2	7.8	TN.	6.1	5.5	44.6	42.4	8.9	9.0
KY.	6.4	5.8	43.1	42.5	8.5	8.9	TX.	6.1	5.5	41.7	41.7	8.2	8.7
LA.	6.4	6.2	54.5	54.7	10.9	11.5	UT.	3.0	2.6	19.3	20.3	7.0	7.6
ME.	3.4	2.6	38.4	36.0	7.5	8.2	VT.	2.7	2.2	38.9	36.8	7.0	7.6
MD.	3.5	3.0	40.8	40.7	8.5	8.7	VA.	3.7	3.2	35.8	34.8	8.3	8.4
MA.	2.0	1.9	33.0	32.7	7.4	7.8	WA.	3.0	2.6	31.6	31.6	6.7	7.0
MI.	4.0	3.5	41.2	39.4	8.9	9.2	WV.	6.6	6.0	46.8	45.1	9.3	10.0
MN.	2.5	2.3	32.6	32.2	6.7	7.2	WI.	3.5	3.1	37.9	36.8	7.7	8.0
MS.	7.6	7.7	55.8	54.3	11.8	12.7	WY.	5.3	5.0	34.1	32.5	9.7	9.5

[1] Defined as teenage mothers aged 15 to 19. [2] Less than 2,500 grams (5 pounds, 8 ounces).

Source: U.S. National Center for Health Statistics, National Vital Statistics Reports, *Births: Final Data for 2022, Supplemental Tables*, Vol. 73, No. 2, April 2024, and earlier reports; and CDC WONDER Online Database, "Natality, 2016-2022 (expanded)," <wonder.cdc.gov>, accessed April 2024. See also <www.cdc.gov/nchs/nvss/births.htm>.

Table 89. Rate of Pregnancy Risk Factors, Labor and Delivery Characteristics, and Birth Defects by Age of Mother: 2022

[Rates are number of live births with specified risk factor or characteristic per 1,000 live births in specified group, except as noted; birth defects are per 100,000 live births. In 2022, total number of births to residents in reporting areas is 3,667,758]

Factor/characteristic	Births with factor reported (number)	Rates by age All ages	Under 20 years	20 to 24 years	25 to 29 years	30 to 34 years	35 to 39 years	40 to 54 years
RISK FACTORS IN CURRENT PREGNANCY (rates per 1,000 live births)								
Diabetes:								
Prepregnancy (diagnosis prior to pregnancy)	42,803	11.7	4.2	7.3	10.0	12.1	17.0	25.7
Gestational (diagnosis in current pregnancy)	296,451	81.0	25.1	44.6	69.2	90.1	118.8	150.5
Hypertension:								
Prepregnancy (chronic)	106,772	29.2	9.6	18.4	24.4	30.5	42.8	61.9
Gestational (pregnancy-induced, preeclampsia)	348,420	95.2	93.3	95.6	94.4	91.8	98.3	113.2
Eclampsia [1]	9,923	2.7	3.7	2.8	2.6	2.4	2.9	3.7
Previous preterm birth	142,381	38.9	7.9	26.3	37.3	42.3	51.0	59.2
Pregnancy resulted from infertility treatment	88,977	24.3	0.3	2.3	9.9	25.7	52.0	119.2
Mother had previous cesarean delivery [2]	560,801	224.7	92.7	156.4	202.0	235.7	273.7	293.9
LABOR AND DELIVERY CHARACTERISTICS								
Induction of labor (rate per 1,000 live births)	1,169,221	319.0	361.7	345.2	326.8	304.3	296.7	313.7
Breech presentation (rate per 100 live births)	158,073	4.3	2.7	3.1	3.9	4.7	5.4	6.7
BIRTH DEFECTS (CONGENITAL ANOMALIES) (rates per 100,000 live births)								
Anencephaly	387	10.6	17.9	12.7	10.1	9.9	8.4	11.8
Meningomyelocele or spina bifida	499	13.6	15.1	13.5	14.2	14.5	11.4	11.1
Cyanotic congenital heart disease	2,424	66.2	66.0	62.0	63.0	65.0	70.7	98.4
Gastroschisis	586	16.0	75.7	34.0	15.5	6.2	4.1	5.5
Cleft lip with or without cleft palate	1,861	50.8	61.9	56.2	50.2	47.7	50.6	45.7
Down syndrome	1,857	50.7	24.1	27.3	27.1	32.7	93.8	305.6

[1] Excludes data for South Carolina. [2] Excludes women who have not had a previous pregnancy and from whom total birth order is unknown.

Source: U.S. National Center for Health Statistics, National Vital Statistics Reports, *Births: Final Data for 2022, Supplemental Tables*, Vol. 73, No. 2, April 2024. See also <www.cdc.gov/nchs/nvss/births.htm>.

Table 90. Percent of Premature Births by Whether Early or Late Preterm and by Age, Race, and Hispanic Origin of Mother: 2022

[Preterm/premature births are those with less than 37 completed weeks of gestation based on obstetric estimates. Based on race and Hispanic origin of mother. Race categories are consistent with 1997 Office of Management and Budget standards. See source for details]

Characteristic	Total births (number)	Total under 37 weeks	Percent preterm			
			Early preterm			Late preterm
			Under 28 weeks	28 to 31 weeks	32 to 33 weeks	34 to 36 weeks
Total [1]	**3,667,758**	**10.4**	**0.6**	**0.9**	**1.2**	**7.6**
Age of mother:						
Under 15 years............	1,825	16.5	1.5	1.9	2.4	10.6
15 to 19 years............	143,789	10.7	0.9	1.1	1.2	7.5
20 to 24 years............	638,685	9.9	0.7	0.9	1.1	7.2
25 to 29 years............	1,013,417	9.7	0.6	0.8	1.1	7.2
30 to 34 years............	1,118,787	10.0	0.6	0.9	1.2	7.4
35 to 39 years............	606,598	11.6	0.7	1.0	1.4	8.5
40 to 44 years............	134,115	14.1	0.8	1.3	1.7	10.3
45 to 54 years............	10,542	20.7	1.2	1.9	3.3	14.3
Race and Hispanic origin of mother:						
White alone, non-Hispanic..........	1,840,739	9.4	0.4	0.8	1.1	7.2
Black alone, non-Hispanic..........	511,439	14.6	1.5	1.6	1.9	9.7
Hispanic [2]...............	937,421	10.1	0.6	0.9	1.1	7.5

[1] Total includes those with gestational age not stated and races other than White and Black, not shown separately. [2] Persons of Hispanic origin may be of any race.

Source: U.S. National Center for Health Statistics, National Vital Statistics Reports, *Births: Final Data for 2022*, Vol. 73, No. 2, April 2024. See also <www.cdc.gov/nchs/nvss/births.htm>.

Table 91. Women Who Had a Birth in the Past 12 Months by Selected Characteristics: 2022

[For women aged 15 to 50 years old. Based on the 2022 American Community Survey (ACS). The ACS sample includes the household population and the population living in institutions, dormitories, and other group quarters. Based on a sample and subject to sampling variability. See Appendix III for details]

Characteristic	Total women (number)	Women who had a birth in the past 12 months			
		Number	Percent distribution	Rate per 1,000 women	Percent unmarried
Total, aged 15 to 50 years................	**77,449,729**	**4,036,894**	**(X)**	**52**	**30.8**
Age:					
15 to 19 years................	10,618,136	82,852	2.1	8	85.9
20 to 34 years................	33,160,377	2,792,759	69.2	84	33.2
35 to 50 years................	33,671,216	1,161,283	28.8	34	21.3
Race/ethnicity:					
One race................	67,155,115	3,496,326	86.6	52	29.6
White................	43,777,271	2,235,487	55.4	51	22.7
Black or African American................	10,425,771	556,897	13.8	53	58.4
American Indian and Alaska Native................	834,963	46,300	1.1	55	51.7
Asian................	5,408,497	272,956	6.8	50	10.7
Native Hawaiian and Other Pacific Islander................	173,425	11,152	0.3	64	42.2
Some other race................	6,535,188	373,534	9.3	57	39.0
Two or more races................	10,294,614	540,568	13.4	53	38.5
Hispanic origin:					
Hispanic or Latino origin (of any race)................	16,647,830	946,385	23.4	57	39.4
White alone, not Hispanic or Latino................	40,825,475	2,056,093	50.9	50	21.4
Nativity:					
Native................	64,926,623	3,242,060	80.3	50	33.0
Foreign born [1]................	12,523,106	794,834	19.7	63	21.7
Education:					
Less than high school graduate................	12,019,033	390,149	9.7	32	48.4
High school graduate (includes equivalency)................	16,164,267	930,380	23.0	58	47.8
Some college or associate's degree................	22,437,503	1,138,882	28.2	51	37.0
Bachelor's degree................	17,066,788	972,072	24.1	57	14.1
Graduate or professional degree................	9,762,138	605,411	15.0	62	8.6
Poverty status in past 12 months:					
Women 15 to 50 years old with poverty status determined...	75,618,474	4,027,788	(X)	53	30.7
Below 100 percent of poverty level................	10,823,152	796,620	19.8	74	65.3
100 to 199 percent of poverty level................	12,073,881	757,503	18.8	63	38.5
200 percent or more above poverty level................	52,721,441	2,473,665	61.4	47	17.2
Labor force status:					
In labor force [2]................	56,099,673	2,688,129	66.6	48	30.9
Public assistance status in past 12 months:					
Women 15 to 50 years old with public assistance status determined................	77,449,729	4,036,894	(X)	52	30.8
Received public assistance income................	1,490,074	143,232	3.5	96	64.3
Did not receive public assistance income................	75,959,655	3,893,662	96.5	51	29.6

X Not applicable. [1] Excludes persons born outside of the United States to a parent who is a U.S. citizen. [2] Data are shown for women aged 16 to 50 years old.

Source: U.S. Census Bureau, 2022 American Community Survey, S1301, "Fertility," <data.census.gov>, accessed November 2023.

Table 92. Women by Number of Children Ever Born by Age, Marital Status, and Race/Ethnicity: 2022

[76,920 represents 76,920,000. As of June. Data shown are for women aged 15 to 50. Based on the Current Population Survey; for more information, see <www.census.gov/programs-surveys/cps.html>]

Characteristic	Total women (1,000)	Percent distribution by number of children ever born					
		None	One	Two	Three	Four	Five or more
Total women: [1]	**76,920**	**46.9**	**16.3**	**20.2**	**10.4**	**3.9**	**2.3**
By age:							
15 to 19 years old	10,570	97.4	1.7	0.3	0.3	(D)	(D)
20 to 24 years old	10,470	82.2	11.7	4.6	1.1	0.2	0.2
25 to 29 years old	10,760	60.2	17.6	13.3	5.9	2.3	0.8
30 to 34 years old	11,450	38.2	22.7	21.9	11.2	3.5	2.4
35 to 39 years old	10,980	22.2	20.8	30.6	15.4	7.2	3.8
40 to 44 years old	10,630	17.7	19.0	32.4	20.1	6.7	4.1
45 to 50 years old	12,060	16.5	19.3	35.7	17.3	6.8	4.4
By marital status:							
Women ever married	39,650	19.0	21.6	33.1	16.5	6.2	3.6
Women never married	37,270	76.5	10.7	6.6	3.8	1.5	1.0
By race and Hispanic origin:							
White alone	56,140	47.0	15.4	20.8	10.8	3.9	2.2
White alone, non-Hispanic	41,670	48.3	15.1	21.1	10.4	3.2	1.8
Black alone	11,470	44.3	19.5	17.2	10.8	4.4	3.8
Asian alone	5,635	48.0	18.8	24.0	6.6	1.8	0.9
Hispanic [2]	16,500	43.4	16.6	19.5	11.5	5.8	3.2

D Suppressed to avoid individual disclosure. [1] Includes women of other races, not shown separately. [2] Persons of Hispanic origin may be of any race.

Source: U.S. Census Bureau, "Fertility of Women in the United States: 2022," <www.census.gov/topics/health/fertility/data/tables.html>, accessed February 2024.

Table 93. Women's Relationship Status and Age at First Birth by Current Age and Race/Ethnicity: 2022

[In percent, except as noted (40,870 represents 40,870,000). As of June. Data are from the Current Population Survey; for more information, see <www.census.gov/programs-surveys/cps.html>]

Current age and race/ethnicity	Total mothers, 1,000	Married at first birth			Not married at first birth					
					Living with unmarried partner			Neither married nor living with unmarried partner		
		Under age 20 at first birth	Age 20 to 25 at first birth	Over age 25 at first birth	Under age 20 at first birth	Age 20 to 25 at first birth	Over age 25 at first birth	Under age 20 at first birth	Age 20 to 25 at first birth	Over age 25 at first birth
TOTAL										
15 to 50 years old	**40,870**	**4.9**	**19.0**	**36.9**	**6.1**	**11.2**	**5.6**	**6.0**	**7.7**	**2.7**
15 to 19 years old	273	6.3	(X)	(X)	47.4	(X)	(X)	46.2	(X)	(X)
20 to 24 years old	1,868	8.4	16.0	(X)	15.7	27.4	(X)	18.0	14.6	(X)
25 to 29 years old	4,287	5.4	22.1	12.3	11.5	21.4	3.6	9.8	11.7	2.3
30 to 34 years old	7,080	5.3	18.0	31.0	7.3	12.3	7.0	5.9	9.6	3.7
35 to 39 years old	8,549	5.0	19.4	39.9	5.2	10.3	6.2	5.3	5.9	2.9
40 to 44 years old	8,743	4.7	18.5	45.9	4.3	7.5	6.1	4.6	5.5	2.8
45 to 50 years old	10,070	3.7	19.8	48.9	2.3	7.2	5.8	2.8	6.9	2.6
WHITE ALONE										
15 to 50 years old	29,730	5.3	21.4	39.3	5.8	11.0	5.4	4.7	5.3	1.8
15 to 19 years old	194	4.7	(X)	(X)	54.0	(X)	(X)	41.4	(X)	(X)
20 to 24 years old	1,317	9.4	18.2	(X)	15.8	28.9	(X)	18.0	9.8	(X)
25 to 29 years old	3,002	6.2	26.3	14.0	10.7	20.9	3.0	9.3	8.2	1.4
30 to 34 years old	5,052	6.0	20.1	33.3	7.4	12.6	7.0	4.7	6.7	2.2
35 to 39 years old	6,246	4.9	22.2	43.2	4.7	10.2	5.8	3.9	3.1	2.0
40 to 44 years old	6,448	5.4	20.4	47.1	4.4	7.3	5.7	3.0	4.7	2.0
45 to 50 years old	7,475	4.0	21.6	51.4	1.9	6.9	5.7	1.8	4.9	1.8
BLACK ALONE										
15 to 50 years old	6,391	3.8	9.2	17.2	8.5	14.5	7.2	12.7	19.7	7.2
15 to 19 years old	33	(D)	(X)	(X)	(D)	(X)	(X)	(D)	(X)	(X)
20 to 24 years old	379	(D)	(D)	(X)	16.4	25.0	(X)	18.6	33.7	(X)
25 to 29 years old	841	3.3	5.7	3.5	14.0	23.2	5.3	13.9	26.0	5.3
30 to 34 years old	1,198	3.9	10.4	10.6	8.0	14.9	7.0	12.8	22.3	10.2
35 to 39 years old	1,258	6.2	8.0	13.4	9.0	13.6	8.1	13.1	19.2	9.4
40 to 44 years old	1,273	3.1	10.3	29.1	6.1	11.3	8.7	12.1	11.9	7.3
45 to 50 years old	1,410	2.8	12.0	28.9	4.4	10.4	8.3	9.6	18.1	5.6
HISPANIC [1]										
15 to 50 years old	9,344	8.5	21.0	23.2	9.3	14.2	6.3	7.6	7.6	2.5
15 to 19 years old	100	(D)	(X)	(X)	(D)	(X)	(X)	47.9	(X)	(X)
20 to 24 years old	636	14.7	15.8	(X)	12.3	28.6	(X)	14.1	14.4	(X)
25 to 29 years old	1,146	7.9	19.9	7.2	11.8	23.1	4.0	13.6	11.4	1.1
30 to 34 years old	1,649	8.3	17.9	19.4	12.2	15.8	6.8	7.3	8.7	3.5
35 to 39 years old	1,824	10.4	21.0	24.2	9.7	12.2	6.8	8.1	5.9	1.7
40 to 44 years old	1,880	7.2	23.0	30.7	7.7	9.2	7.3	4.6	7.6	2.6
45 to 50 years old	2,111	6.9	24.6	35.3	3.8	10.4	7.9	2.7	4.5	3.8

X Not applicable. D Suppressed to avoid disclosure of individuals. [1] Persons of Hispanic origin may be of any race.

Source: U.S. Census Bureau, "Fertility of Women in the United States: 2022," <www.census.gov/topics/health/fertility/data/tables.html>, accessed February 2024.

Table 94. Women Who Had a Birth in the Past Year Who Are in the Labor Force by Educational Attainment: 2010 to 2021

[In thousands (2,562 represents 2,562,000), except percent. For women aged 16 to 50 years old. Due to the COVID-19 pandemic, 2020 data were not released. Based on the American Community Survey (ACS). The ACS universe includes the household population and population living in institutions, college dormitories, and other group quarters. Based on a sample and subject to sampling variability, see Appendix III]

Year	Number of women who had a birth in the past year who are in the labor force					Percent of women who had a birth in the past year who are in the labor force				
	Total	Less than high school diploma	High school diploma or GED	Some college	Bachelor's degree or higher	Total	Less than high school diploma	High school diploma or GED	Some college	Bachelor's degree or higher
2010........	2,562	278	589	859	836	61.6	39.7	57.9	66.4	72.7
2015........	2,447	196	509	816	927	62.4	38.2	56.0	65.1	74.2
2017........	2,534	182	532	794	1,027	63.5	39.6	56.7	64.3	75.4
2018........	2,560	179	537	792	1,053	64.8	40.4	57.9	65.9	76.4
2019........	2,549	171	519	785	1,073	65.8	41.0	57.7	66.8	77.8
2021........	2,603	155	510	752	1,186	66.5	40.2	56.4	66.4	79.3

Source: U.S. Census Bureau, "Fertility: Historical Time Series Tables," <www.census.gov/topics/health/fertility/data/tables.html>, accessed February 2024.

Table 95. Women Who Had a Birth in the Past 12 Months by Nativity, Educational Attainment, and Poverty Status by State: 2022

[In percent, except for total. For women 15 to 50 years old. Based on the 2022 American Community Survey. See headnote, Table 94]

State	Total (number)	Nativity		Educational attainment					Below poverty [3]
		Native born	Foreign born [1]	Less than high school graduate	High school graduate [2]	Some college or associate's degree	Bachelor's degree	Graduate or professional degree	
United States.......	**4,036,894**	**80.3**	**19.7**	**9.7**	**23.0**	**28.2**	**24.1**	**15.0**	**19.8**
Alabama.............	61,506	90.4	9.6	8.3	28.9	32.1	19.2	11.6	25.6
Alaska..............	10,125	86.5	13.5	6.2	29.3	29.7	20.1	14.7	25.4
Arizona.............	86,548	78.8	21.2	12.2	25.7	31.4	20.7	9.9	20.8
Arkansas............	39,688	90.6	9.4	9.6	25.5	40.4	15.8	8.7	25.7
California...........	453,850	70.2	29.8	11.4	20.5	28.5	24.3	15.3	18.0
Colorado............	70,204	85.3	14.7	6.4	15.7	28.7	30.5	18.8	10.6
Connecticut..........	37,999	71.8	28.2	8.3	18.8	22.5	25.3	25.0	18.8
Delaware............	12,915	84.8	15.2	6.2	17.8	34.1	24.4	17.5	10.5
District of Columbia...	8,309	82.8	17.2	5.2	10.1	19.9	32.3	32.6	10.3
Florida.............	237,974	70.8	29.2	9.3	24.3	30.4	24.1	11.9	21.3
Georgia.............	151,128	83.0	17.0	10.4	24.8	31.1	21.2	12.5	21.1
Hawaii..............	15,928	78.4	21.6	2.4	25.9	32.8	26.4	12.6	13.7
Idaho...............	25,329	86.9	13.1	7.5	24.6	31.2	28.9	7.7	15.2
Illinois.............	147,198	81.7	18.3	7.1	20.2	27.1	26.0	19.5	19.9
Indiana.............	90,329	88.9	11.1	10.7	24.7	26.8	26.4	11.4	20.8
Iowa................	41,204	88.5	11.5	9.7	18.9	28.7	26.6	16.1	15.1
Kansas..............	36,787	86.0	14.0	8.6	21.9	28.0	24.7	16.8	21.4
Kentucky............	56,396	93.9	6.1	10.1	28.7	29.3	19.4	12.5	28.1
Louisiana...........	61,980	94.1	5.9	8.9	30.5	32.7	17.2	10.7	29.6
Maine...............	16,407	92.9	7.1	5.9	18.0	31.2	24.8	20.2	15.2
Maryland............	71,827	70.0	30.0	10.6	17.8	24.4	24.1	23.1	15.1
Massachusetts........	71,722	69.3	30.7	8.1	15.4	18.8	31.0	26.7	13.8
Michigan............	111,639	87.7	12.3	8.2	23.6	30.3	21.3	16.7	21.8
Minnesota...........	69,168	81.4	18.6	8.8	17.4	28.4	29.6	15.7	11.7
Mississippi..........	40,116	95.5	4.5	15.3	24.8	35.1	14.8	9.9	30.7
Missouri............	74,145	92.4	7.6	10.7	24.2	28.9	24.0	12.2	22.6
Montana.............	16,895	92.7	7.3	9.6	32.3	24.5	24.5	9.0	11.6
Nebraska............	27,111	83.6	16.4	8.7	18.0	31.0	29.5	12.8	15.0
Nevada..............	41,310	75.8	24.2	17.6	27.2	29.5	17.5	8.2	18.3
New Hampshire.......	14,072	89.2	10.8	4.7	28.0	25.5	23.5	18.5	14.5
New Jersey..........	105,942	65.7	34.3	8.1	22.0	20.7	27.3	21.9	13.6
New Mexico..........	24,681	84.5	15.5	9.1	24.3	31.8	20.7	14.2	23.4
New York............	232,961	70.6	29.4	10.6	21.9	21.6	24.0	21.8	22.2
North Carolina........	129,267	84.2	15.8	9.7	21.1	30.3	25.3	13.7	21.5
North Dakota........	10,748	88.0	12.0	8.5	16.6	37.0	26.0	11.8	15.7
Ohio................	144,549	89.3	10.7	10.2	26.0	27.5	22.2	14.2	24.2
Oklahoma............	54,326	89.7	10.3	9.1	30.2	33.1	18.5	9.2	22.0
Oregon..............	44,166	80.2	19.8	12.5	16.9	27.5	28.5	14.6	18.8
Pennsylvania.........	149,542	85.3	14.7	9.4	22.4	26.0	23.8	18.4	19.3
Rhode Island.........	11,327	75.1	24.9	4.8	16.4	27.7	24.9	26.1	15.0
South Carolina........	63,426	91.0	9.0	8.6	20.9	33.8	24.4	12.4	19.4
South Dakota.........	14,399	87.6	12.4	7.3	24.8	28.3	30.8	8.9	19.1
Tennessee...........	82,884	91.7	8.3	9.3	27.7	26.0	23.5	13.5	20.9
Texas...............	420,463	77.1	22.9	11.1	26.3	29.1	23.0	10.5	21.5
Utah................	50,803	87.6	12.4	5.7	21.3	33.8	32.8	6.4	15.1
Vermont.............	6,908	97.0	3.0	9.7	29.9	18.2	25.7	16.5	22.0
Virginia............	104,539	79.6	20.4	6.0	22.3	24.5	26.6	20.5	16.8
Washington..........	92,565	74.5	25.5	7.5	23.0	27.1	24.7	17.7	14.2
West Virginia.........	19,540	96.4	3.6	6.2	34.5	26.6	20.0	12.8	29.3
Wisconsin...........	66,580	90.4	9.6	10.5	19.4	28.8	27.8	13.5	16.2
Wyoming.............	7,469	99.5	0.5	10.1	27.4	23.0	24.9	14.6	20.6

[1] Foreign born excludes people born outside the U.S. to a parent who is a U.S. citizen. [2] Includes equivalency. [3] The population universe used when determining poverty status excludes people institutionalized, in military group quarters, and in college dormitories, and unrelated individuals under 15 years old.

Source: U.S. Census Bureau, 2022 American Community Survey, Tables B13008, B13010, and B13014, <data.census.gov>, accessed November 2023.

Table 96. Women Who Had a Birth in the Past 12 Months by Household Income and Marital Status: 2021

[In thousands (3,205 represents 3,205,000), except percent. Data shown for women aged 15 to 50 years old; does not include women living in group quarters. Based on the American Community Survey (ACS). Based on a sample and subject to sampling variability]

Annual household income	Total women	Women with a birth in the past 12 months			Percent of total women	Percent of women with a birth in the past 12 months		
		Total	Married [1]	Unmarried [2]		Total	Married [1]	Unmarried [2]
Under $10,000..............	3,205	201	57	144	4.3	5.2	2.2	11.1
$10,000-$14,999..............	1,595	83	27	57	2.1	2.1	1.0	4.4
$15,000-$24,999..............	3,627	205	81	123	4.8	5.2	3.1	9.5
$25,000-$34,999..............	4,473	263	125	138	5.9	6.7	4.8	10.6
$35,000-$49,999..............	7,205	380	211	169	9.6	9.7	8.1	13.0
$50,000-$74,999..............	12,110	642	414	229	16.1	16.5	15.9	17.6
$75,000-$99,999..............	10,450	551	391	160	13.9	14.1	15.0	12.4
$100,000-$149,999..............	15,080	752	593	159	20.0	19.3	22.7	12.3
$150,000-$199,999..............	7,959	370	309	61	10.6	9.5	11.8	4.7
$200,000 or more..............	9,605	457	401	56	12.8	11.7	15.4	4.3

[1] Includes women who are married, spouse present. [2] Includes women who are widowed, divorced, separated, and never married.

Source: U.S. Census Bureau, "Fertility of Women in the United States: 2022," <www.census.gov/topics/health/fertility/data/tables.html>, accessed February 2024.

Table 97. Sexually Active High School Students and Birth Control Use by Sex, Race/Ethnicity, and Grade: 2021

[In percent. For public and private school students in grades 9 to 12. Current sexual activity defined as having had sexual intercourse with at least one person during the 3 months before the survey. Based on the Youth Risk Behavior Survey; see source for details]

Item	Total	Race/ethnicity			Grade level			
		White [1]	Black [1]	Hispanic	9th	10th	11th	12th
Ever had sexual intercourse.......................	30.0	30.4	33.9	30.6	15.9	22.6	34.6	48.4
Currently sexually active...........................	20.7	21.9	23.0	20.6	9.2	14.6	24.9	35.4
Condom use [2]......................................	51.8	54.6	48.8	49.7	53.4	59.8	55.0	46.4
Condom and other birth control use [3]...........	10.2	13.2	4.9	6.0	5.1	9.0	12.0	10.7
Birth control use [4]................................	32.7	38.3	20.5	24.6	14.4	20.9	33.3	41.9
No pregnancy prevention method [2].............	13.7	9.6	22.2	19.6	23.9	17.1	11.6	10.8
MALE								
Ever had sexual intercourse.......................	29.3	28.0	39.4	29.8	16.4	20.7	34.8	47.3
Currently sexually active...........................	18.8	19.3	25.6	17.9	8.7	12.4	23.9	31.9
Condom use [2]......................................	57.7	58.1	55.0	59.6	58.4	67.1	59.8	52.4
Condom and other birth control use [3]...........	8.8	10.4	2.7	6.7	4.3	8.3	10.8	9.0
Birth control use [4]................................	27.4	32.9	15.8	16.7	12.1	16.1	28.4	36.0
No pregnancy prevention method [2].............	11.8	9.5	20.4	13.7	23.7	14.6	10.4	8.1
FEMALE								
Ever had sexual intercourse.......................	30.6	32.8	28.7	31.1	15.0	24.4	34.4	49.5
Currently sexually active...........................	22.6	24.7	20.7	22.6	9.5	16.7	25.9	38.8
Condom use [2]......................................	47.3	52.0	41.4	42.1	47.1	54.8	50.8	41.7
Condom and other birth control use [3]...........	11.4	15.5	7.6	5.7	5.9	9.7	13.3	12.1
Birth control use [4]................................	37.2	42.5	26.1	31.3	17.0	23.9	37.5	46.8
No pregnancy prevention method [2].............	15.2	9.8	24.4	23.5	25.1	19.0	12.9	13.0

[1] Non-Hispanic. [2] During last sexual intercourse. [3] Includes use of both a condom during last sexual intercourse and another birth control method (birth control pills, IUD or implant, or a shot, patch, or birth control ring) before last sexual intercourse to prevent pregnancy. [4] Includes use of birth control pills, an IUD or implant, or a shot, patch, or birth control ring.

Source: U.S. Centers for Disease Control and Prevention, Youth Risk Behavior Surveillance System (YRBSS), "YRBS Explorer," <yrbs-explorer.services.cdc.gov/#/>, accessed May 2023. See also <www.cdc.gov/healthyyouth/data/yrbs/>.

Table 98. Assisted Reproductive Technology (ART) Procedures and Outcomes: 2000 to 2021

[Covers ART procedures with the intent to transfer at least one embryo; excludes freezing/banking cycles. In 1996, Centers for Disease Control (CDC) initiated data collection regarding Assisted Reproductive Technology (ART) procedures performed in the United States, as mandated by the Fertility Clinic Success Rate and Certification Act. ARTs include those infertility treatments in which both eggs and sperm are handled in the laboratory for the purpose of establishing a pregnancy (i.e., in vitro fertilization and related procedures)]

Year	Procedures started [1]	Number of pregnancies [2]	Live birth deliveries [3]	Live born infants	Year	Procedures started [1]	Number of pregnancies [2]	Live birth deliveries [3]	Live born infants
2000.......	99,629	30,557	25,228	35,025	2015.......	186,157	72,870	60,778	72,913
2005.......	134,260	47,651	38,910	52,041	2016.......	197,737	80,971	65,969	76,897
2010.......	147,260	57,773	47,090	61,564	2017.......	196,454	84,340	68,908	78,052
2011.......	151,923	59,132	47,818	61,610	2018.......	203,119	89,688	73,831	81,478
2012.......	157,662	62,977	51,267	65,160	2019.......	209,687	95,030	77,998	83,946
2013.......	163,209	65,580	54,323	67,996	2020.......	203,164	91,453	75,023	79,942
2014.......	173,198	68,988	57,323	70,354	2021.......	246,087	112,088	91,906	97,128

[1] Excludes procedures for which new treatments were being evaluated. [2] Beginning in 2012, excludes pregnancies from procedures performed in U.S. territories other than Puerto Rico; and, beginning in 2013, excludes pregnancies resulting from oocyte thaw procedures. [3] A live birth delivery is defined as the delivery of one or more live born infants.

Source: U.S. Centers for Disease Control and Prevention, *2021 Assisted Reproductive Technology, Fertility Clinic and National Summary Report*, 2023 and earlier reports; and *Assisted Reproductive Technology Surveillance - United States, 2018*, MMWR Surveillance Summaries, Vol. 71, No. 4, February 2022 and earlier reports.

Table 99. Abortions Reported and Rates by Age: 2012 to 2021

[Data on abortions are voluntarily provided to the CDC by the central health agencies of 47 reporting areas (New York City and 46 states, excluding California, the District of Columbia, Maryland, New Hampshire, and New Jersey). Data by age are from 43 reporting areas (excludes California, District of Columbia, Florida, Maine, Maryland, New Hampshire, New Jersey, Tennessee, and Wyoming that did not report, did not report by age, or did not meet reporting standards for 1 year or more)]

Age	2012	2015	2016	2017	2018	2019	2020	2021	Percent change, 2012 to 2021
Total (number) [1]......................	673,634	613,911	599,001	587,611	591,884	603,168	592,939	622,108	-7.6
Rate per 1,000 women aged 15-44....	13.1	11.8	11.5	11.2	11.2	11.4	11.1	11.6	-11.5
BY AGE									
Total (number).........................	574,314	520,602	508,565	497,249	500,974	508,955	502,481	514,695	-10.4
Percent distribution:									
Under 15 years old......................	0.4	0.3	0.3	0.2	0.2	0.2	0.2	0.2	−50.0
15 to 19 years old......................	12.3	9.8	9.4	9.1	8.8	8.7	8.3	8.2	−33.3
20 to 24 years old......................	32.8	31.2	30.1	29.4	28.6	27.9	28.2	28.5	−13.1
25 to 29 years old......................	25.3	27.6	28.5	28.9	29.3	29.3	29.3	28.7	13.4
30 to 34 years old......................	16.4	17.7	18.0	18.3	18.8	19.4	19.7	20.2	23.2
35 to 39 years old......................	9.1	10.0	10.3	10.5	10.7	10.8	10.6	10.6	16.5
40 years old and over...................	3.7	3.6	3.6	3.6	3.5	3.7	3.6	3.5	−5.4
Abortion rate: [2]									
Under 15 years old......................	0.8	0.5	0.4	0.4	0.4	0.4	0.4	0.4	−50.0
15 to 19 years old......................	9.2	6.7	6.2	5.9	5.8	5.8	5.5	5.4	−41.3
20 to 24 years old......................	23.2	19.9	19.0	18.3	18.1	18.1	18.1	18.6	−19.8
25 to 29 years old......................	18.8	17.8	17.7	17.3	17.5	17.8	17.7	18.3	−2.7
30 to 34 years old......................	12.3	11.7	11.6	11.5	11.8	12.3	12.1	12.5	1.6
35 to 39 years old......................	7.3	7.0	6.9	6.7	6.8	7.0	6.7	6.8	−6.8
40 years old and over...................	2.8	2.5	2.5	2.5	2.5	2.6	2.4	2.4	−14.3

[1] Data shown for continuously reporting areas during 2012-2021 period. [2] Number of abortions obtained by women in a given age group per 1,000 women in that same age group. Adolescents aged 13–14 years were used as the denominator for the group of women aged under 15 years, and women aged 40–44 years were used as the denominator for the group of women aged 40 and older. Abortions for women of unknown age were distributed according to the distribution of abortions among women of known age.

Source: U.S. Centers for Disease Control and Prevention, *Morbidity and Mortality Weekly Report, Surveillance Summaries*, 72:9, November 24, 2023, "Abortion Surveillance—United States, 2021." See also <www.cdc.gov/mmwr/index.html>.

Table 100. Abortions Reported and Those Obtained by Out-of-State Residents by State and Reporting Area of Occurrence: 2021

[Data are presented by the State or reporting area in which abortions were performed, not by residence of the person obtaining the abortion. Data are voluntarily provided to the CDC by the central health agencies of 48 reporting areas (New York City, the District of Columbia, and 46 states, excluding California, Maryland, New Hampshire, and New Jersey)]

State and area of occurrence	Abortions reported			Abortions obtained by out-of-state residents	State and area of occurrence	Abortions reported			Abortions obtained by out-of-state residents
	Total	Abortions per 1,000 women age 15-44	Abortions per 1,000 live births			Total	Abortions per 1,000 women age 15-44	Abortions per 1,000 live births	
Total [1]...............	625,978	(NA)	(NA)	(X)	Montana..........	1,798	8.8	160	252
Alabama...............	6,489	6.6	112	1,143	Nebraska..........	2,360	6.2	96	292
Alaska................	1,227	8.5	131	11	Nevada............	8,751	14.2	260	545
Arizona...............	13,998	10.0	180	83	New Mexico.......	4,891	12.1	229	1,973
Arkansas..............	3,133	5.4	87	387	New York.........	63,487	16.3	301	[2] 3,755
Colorado..............	11,580	9.7	184	1,559	New York City....	37,813	21.0	404	3,368
Connecticut...........	10,146	14.8	284	493	New York State...	25,674	12.2	219	2,354
Delaware..............	1,825	9.8	174	162	North Carolina....	32,454	15.7	269	5,346
District of Columbia. ..	3,870	21.8	447	2,740	North Dakota......	1,153	7.6	114	313
Florida................	79,817	20.3	369	4,873	Ohio..............	21,813	9.7	168	1,097
Georgia...............	41,833	18.8	337	7,013	Oklahoma.........	7,287	9.3	151	2,887
Hawaii................	2,214	8.4	142	58	Oregon............	7,109	8.5	174	695
Idaho.................	1,553	4.2	69	99	Pennsylvania......	33,206	13.7	250	2,352
Illinois................	51,797	20.8	392	11,307	Rhode Island......	2,175	10.0	208	352
Indiana...............	8,414	6.3	105	465	South Carolina....	6,279	6.3	110	327
Iowa..................	3,761	6.2	102	598	South Dakota.....	192	1.2	17	17
Kansas................	7,845	13.8	226	3,912	Tennessee.........	12,182	8.9	149	2,501
Kentucky..............	4,441	5.2	85	653	Texas..............	51,860	8.4	139	1,076
Louisiana..............	7,444	8.1	130	1,744	Utah................	3,129	4.3	67	151
Maine.................	1,915	8.0	160	121	Vermont............	1,033	8.6	192	215
Massachusetts.........	16,795	11.9	243	792	Virginia...........	16,139	9.4	168	1,428
Michigan..............	30,074	15.9	286	1,664	Washington........	16,349	10.6	195	988
Minnesota.............	10,136	9.2	157	1,008	West Virginia......	1,375	4.4	80	222
Mississippi............	3,817	6.6	109	680	Wisconsin.........	6,579	5.9	106	107
Missouri..............	150	0.1	2	34	Wyoming..........	103	0.9	17	32

NA Not available. X Not applicable. [1] Includes those with known and unknown residence status. [2] Residents of New York State who had abortions in New York City and residents of New York City who had abortions in New York State were excluded from the number and percentage of abortions obtained by out-of-area residents in New York.

Source: U.S. Centers for Disease Control and Prevention, *Morbidity and Mortality Weekly Report, Surveillance Summaries*, 72:9, November 24, 2023, "Abortion Surveillance—United States, 2021." See also <www.cdc.gov/mmwr/index.html>.

Table 101. Contraceptive Methods Ever Used Among Women Aged 15 to 49 by Race/Ethnicity and Method: 2015 to 2019

[Percent, except as noted (63,703 represents 63,703,000). Data are for the 2015-2019 period and show methods of contraception ever used by women aged 15 to 49 who ever had vaginal intercourse with a male partner, defined here as sexually experienced women. Estimates are based primarily on data collected from 10,122 sexually experienced women during in-person interviews conducted as part of the 2015-2019 National Survey of Family Growth]

Contraceptive method	Total [1]	Asian, non-Hispanic	Black, non-Hispanic	White, non-Hispanic	Hispanic [2]
All sexually experienced women (1,000s)..........	**63,703**	**2,806**	**8,710**	**35,768**	**12,588**
PERCENT					
Any method.......................	99.2	96.8	99.1	99.5	98.6
Male sterilization [3]........................	14.6	(S)	7.7	18.7	8.6
Female sterilization [3].....................	21.3	12.8	23.4	21.1	22.8
Any most or moderately effective reversible method....	87.8	69.1	86.0	92.4	79.5
Long-acting reversible contraception..................	24.9	12.8	23.3	25.1	28.3
Contraceptive implant (Norplant or Implanon)........	5.7	1.8	7.4	5.2	6.6
Intrauterine device (IUD)........................	20.4	11.3	16.9	21.1	23.5
Injectable.............................	24.5	7.2	41.2	20.3	27.5
Pill (oral contraceptive).......................	79.8	65.6	73.1	87.5	65.7
Contraceptive patch........................	8.2	(S)	11.8	7.1	9.8
Contraceptive ring............................	10.4	3.5	8.8	11.6	9.3
Condom...........................	94.5	87.5	95.5	96.5	89.2
Withdrawal............................	65.7	65.0	66.7	67.2	60.0
Emergency contraception......................	23.5	22.2	20.8	22.1	28.0
Fertility awareness-based methods.....................	18.5	31.2	18.0	17.1	20.2

S Figure does not meet publication standards. [1] Includes women of other or multiple race and origin groups, not shown separately. [2] Persons of Hispanic origin may be of any race. [3] Male sterilization includes vasectomy or any other operation that makes it impossible to father a baby. Female sterilization includes tubal sterilization, hysterectomy, ovary removal, and any other operation that makes it impossible to have a baby.

Source: U.S. National Center for Health Statistics, *Contraceptive Methods Women Have Ever Used: United States, 2015-2019*, National Health Statistics Reports, No. 195, December 2023. See also <www.cdc.gov/nchs/nsfg/index.htm>.

Table 102. Percent of Children Ever and Exclusively Breastfed by Selected Characteristics of Child and Mother: 2016 to 2021

[Data are for children born in year shown. Exclusive breastfeeding is defined as only breast milk – no solids, water, or other liquids. Data are from the National Immunization Survey - Child, which uses random-digit cell phone dialing to survey households with children aged 19-35 months]

Year of birth and characteristic	Any breastfeeding			Exclusive breastfeeding	
	Ever breastfed	Breastfed at age 6 months	Breastfed at age 12 months	Through age 3 months	Through age 6 months
2016...............................	83.8	57.3	36.2	47.5	25.4
2017...............................	84.1	58.3	35.3	46.9	25.6
2018...............................	83.9	56.7	35.0	46.3	25.8
2019...............................	83.2	55.8	35.9	45.3	24.9
2020...............................	83.1	58.2	37.6	45.3	25.4
2021					
Total.............................	**84.1**	**59.8**	**39.5**	**46.5**	**27.2**
SEX					
Male..............................	83.8	59.3	39.0	45.8	26.5
Female............................	84.4	60.3	40.1	47.3	27.9
RACE/ETHNICITY					
White, non-Hispanic.............................	86.2	63.4	42.5	50.3	29.2
Black, non-Hispanic.............................	75.4	51.7	31.0	39.0	24.4
Asian, non-Hispanic.............................	92.7	73.9	50.8	46.0	30.2
Two or more races.............................	85.2	58.4	38.9	43.2	23.2
Hispanic [1]..............................	83.4	56.1	37.0	45.6	25.9
MOTHER'S EDUCATION					
Less than high school............................	72.5	47.6	34.1	38.4	23.3
High school graduate............................	75.8	46.4	27.6	39.1	22.1
Some college or technical school................	84.0	54.8	37.0	45.8	25.6
College graduate.............................	92.4	74.1	50.0	53.9	32.3
MOTHER'S AGE					
Under 20 years old..............................	(NA)	(NA)	(NA)	(NA)	(NA)
20 to 29 years old.............................	80.0	49.8	32.7	43.9	25.2
30 years old and over.............................	86.1	64.8	42.9	47.8	28.1
MOTHER'S MARITAL STATUS					
Married.............................	90.1	69.9	47.3	51.9	31.3
Unmarried [2].............................	74.6	44.0	27.4	38.2	20.7

NA Not available. [1] Persons of Hispanic origin may be of any race. [2] Unmarried includes never married, widowed, separated, divorced and living with partners.

Source: U.S. Centers for Disease Control and Prevention, "Results: Breastfeeding Rates," <www.cdc.gov/breastfeeding/data/nis_data/results.html>, accessed August 2024.

Table 103. Life Expectancy at Birth: 1940 to 2021

[In years. Beginning 2001, life table data are based on revised life table methodology. For 1940-2017, Race and Hispanic-origin categories are consistent with 1977 Office of Management and Budget (OMB) standards. From 2003-2017, the number of states reporting multiple-race data according to new 1997 OMB standards varied widely. To provide a comparison of data by race between the 1977 and 1997 OMB standards, multiple race data were race were "bridged" to single-race categories. Beginning 2018, all states and DC reported data based on 1997 OMB standards. Life expectancies by single-race categories are not completely comparable with life expectancies by bridged-race categories and should be interpreted accounting for the change from bridged- to single-race categories. Life tables are based on death rates that have been adjusted for race and Hispanic-origin misclassification on death certificates. For more information, see Technical notes, source]

Year	Total [1]			White, non-Hispanic			Black, non-Hispanic			Hispanic [2]		
	Total	Male	Female	Total	Male	Female	Total	Male	Female	Total	Male	Female
Bridged race												
1940............	62.9	60.8	65.2	(NA)	(NA)	(NA)	(NA)	(NA)	(NA)	(NA)	(NA)	(NA)
1950............	68.2	65.6	71.1	(NA)	(NA)	(NA)	(NA)	(NA)	(NA)	(NA)	(NA)	(NA)
1960............	69.7	66.6	73.1	(NA)	(NA)	(NA)	(NA)	(NA)	(NA)	(NA)	(NA)	(NA)
1970............	70.8	67.1	74.7	(NA)	(NA)	(NA)	(NA)	(NA)	(NA)	(NA)	(NA)	(NA)
1980............	73.7	70.0	77.4	(NA)	(NA)	(NA)	(NA)	(NA)	(NA)	(NA)	(NA)	(NA)
1990............	75.4	71.8	78.8	(NA)	(NA)	(NA)	(NA)	(NA)	(NA)	(NA)	(NA)	(NA)
2000............	76.8	74.1	79.3	(NA)	(NA)	(NA)	(NA)	(NA)	(NA)	(NA)	(NA)	(NA)
2001............	77.0	74.3	79.5	(NA)	(NA)	(NA)	(NA)	(NA)	(NA)	(NA)	(NA)	(NA)
2002............	77.0	74.4	79.6	(NA)	(NA)	(NA)	(NA)	(NA)	(NA)	(NA)	(NA)	(NA)
2003............	77.2	74.5	79.7	(NA)	(NA)	(NA)	(NA)	(NA)	(NA)	(NA)	(NA)	(NA)
2004............	77.6	75.0	80.1	(NA)	(NA)	(NA)	(NA)	(NA)	(NA)	(NA)	(NA)	(NA)
2005............	77.6	75.0	80.1	(NA)	(NA)	(NA)	(NA)	(NA)	(NA)	(NA)	(NA)	(NA)
2006............	77.8	75.2	80.3	78.2	75.7	80.6	73.1	69.5	76.4	80.3	77.5	82.9
2007............	78.1	75.5	80.6	78.4	75.9	80.8	73.5	69.9	76.7	80.7	77.8	83.2
2008............	78.2	75.6	80.6	78.4	76.0	80.7	73.9	70.5	77.0	80.8	78.0	83.3
2009............	78.5	76.0	80.9	78.7	76.3	81.0	74.4	71.0	77.4	81.1	78.4	83.5
2010............	78.7	76.2	81.0	78.8	76.4	81.1	74.7	71.5	77.7	81.7	78.8	84.3
2011............	78.7	76.3	81.1	78.7	76.4	81.1	75.0	71.8	77.8	81.8	79.2	84.2
2012............	78.8	76.4	81.2	78.9	76.5	81.2	75.1	71.9	78.1	81.9	79.3	84.3
2013............	78.8	76.4	81.2	78.8	76.5	81.2	75.1	71.9	78.1	81.9	79.2	84.2
2014............	78.9	76.5	81.3	78.8	76.5	81.2	75.3	72.2	78.2	82.1	79.4	84.5
2015............	78.7	76.3	81.1	78.7	76.3	81.0	75.1	71.9	78.1	81.9	79.3	84.3
2016............	78.7	76.2	81.1	78.6	76.2	81.0	74.9	71.6	78.0	81.8	79.1	84.3
2017............	78.6	76.1	81.1	78.5	76.1	81.0	74.9	71.5	78.1	81.8	79.1	84.3
Single race												
2018............	78.7	76.2	81.2	78.6	76.2	81.1	74.7	71.3	78.0	81.8	79.1	84.3
2019............	78.8	76.3	81.4	78.8	76.3	81.3	74.8	71.3	78.1	81.9	79.1	84.4
2020............	77.0	74.2	79.9	77.4	74.8	80.1	71.5	67.8	75.4	77.9	74.6	81.3
2021............	76.4	73.5	79.3	76.7	74.0	79.5	71.2	67.6	75.0	77.8	74.6	81.1

NA Not available. [1] Includes races and origins not shown separately. [2] Persons of Hispanic origin may be of any race.

Source: U.S. National Center for Health Statistics, National Vital Statistics Reports (NVSR), *United States Life Tables, 2021*, Vol. 72, No. 12, November 2023. See also <www.cdc.gov/nchs/nvss/life-expectancy.htm>.

Table 104. Life Expectancy by Sex, Age, and Race and Hispanic Origin: 2021

[Average number of years of life remaining. Excludes deaths of nonresidents of the United States. Race categories are consistent with 1997 Office of Management and Budget (OMB) standards. Race and Hispanic origin data are based on death rates that have been adjusted for misclassification on death certificates. For more information, see Technical Notes, source]

Age	Total [1]			White alone, Non-Hispanic			Black alone, Non-Hispanic			Hispanic [2]		
	Total	Male	Female	Total	Male	Female	Total	Male	Female	Total	Male	Female
0.............	76.4	73.5	79.3	76.7	74.0	79.5	71.2	67.6	75.0	77.8	74.6	81.1
1.............	75.8	73.0	78.7	76.0	73.4	78.8	71.0	67.4	74.7	77.2	74.0	80.5
5.............	71.9	69.1	74.8	72.1	69.4	74.8	67.1	63.5	70.8	73.3	70.1	76.5
10.............	66.9	64.1	69.8	67.1	64.5	69.9	62.2	58.6	65.9	68.3	65.1	71.5
15.............	62.0	59.2	64.9	62.1	59.5	64.9	57.3	53.7	61.0	63.4	60.2	66.6
20.............	57.1	54.4	60.0	57.3	54.7	60.0	52.7	49.2	56.1	58.5	55.4	61.7
25.............	52.5	49.8	55.2	52.6	50.1	55.2	48.2	44.9	51.4	53.8	50.8	56.9
30.............	47.8	45.4	50.4	47.9	45.6	50.4	43.8	40.7	46.8	49.2	46.3	52.1
35.............	43.3	41.0	45.7	43.4	41.2	45.7	39.5	36.6	42.3	44.6	41.9	47.3
40.............	38.8	36.6	41.1	38.9	36.8	41.1	35.3	32.5	37.8	40.1	37.5	42.6
45.............	34.4	32.3	36.5	34.5	32.5	36.5	31.1	28.6	33.5	35.6	33.2	37.9
50.............	30.1	28.2	32.1	30.2	28.3	32.1	27.1	24.8	29.3	31.2	28.9	33.3
55.............	26.0	24.2	27.8	26.0	24.3	27.8	23.3	21.1	25.3	27.0	24.9	28.9
60.............	22.1	20.5	23.7	22.1	20.5	23.7	19.8	17.8	21.6	23.0	21.1	24.7
65.............	18.4	17.0	19.7	18.4	17.0	19.7	16.7	14.9	18.1	19.3	17.6	20.6
70.............	14.9	13.7	16.0	14.9	13.7	15.9	13.7	12.3	14.9	15.8	14.4	16.8
75.............	11.6	10.6	12.5	11.5	10.6	12.4	11.0	9.8	11.8	12.4	11.3	13.2
80.............	8.7	7.9	9.4	8.7	7.8	9.3	8.5	7.6	9.1	9.4	8.5	9.9
85.............	6.3	5.6	6.7	6.2	5.6	6.6	6.4	5.6	6.7	6.9	6.1	7.1
90.............	4.4	3.9	4.6	4.3	3.8	4.5	4.7	4.2	4.9	4.8	4.3	4.9
95.............	3.0	2.7	3.2	3.0	2.6	3.1	3.4	3.1	3.5	3.4	3.0	3.3
100..........	2.2	1.9	2.2	2.1	1.9	2.2	2.6	2.4	2.6	2.4	2.2	2.3

[1] Includes other races and origins not shown separately. [2] Persons of Hispanic origin may be of any race.

Source: U.S. National Center for Health Statistics, National Vital Statistics Reports (NVSR), *United States Life Tables, 2021*, Vol. 72, No. 12, November 2023. See also <www.cdc.gov/nchs/nvss/life-expectancy.htm>.

Table 105. Life Expectancy at Birth and Age 65 By Sex and State: 2021

[Average number of years of life remaining, except rank. Life expectancies shown are rounded; rankings are based on unrounded life expectancies. Excludes deaths of nonresidents of the United States. Based on state-specific final numbers of deaths for 2021 collected from death certificates filed in state vital statistics offices and reported to the National Center for Health Statistics (NCHS)]

State	Life expectancy at birth				Life expectancy at age 65			
	Rank	Average years			Rank	Average years		
		Total	Male	Female		Total	Male	Female
United States.................	(X)	**76.4**	**73.5**	**79.3**	(X)	**18.4**	**17.0**	**19.7**
Alabama.........................	49	72.0	68.9	75.3	49	16.4	14.9	17.7
Alaska...........................	39	74.5	72.2	77.3	33	17.9	16.7	19.2
Arizona..........................	34	75.0	72.0	78.3	31	18.1	16.6	19.5
Arkansas........................	45	72.5	69.7	75.6	45	16.6	15.2	18.1
California........................	10	78.3	75.3	81.4	8	19.3	17.8	20.7
Colorado........................	15	77.7	75.0	80.6	11	19.1	17.8	20.4
Connecticut.....................	3	79.2	76.3	82.0	2	19.9	18.4	21.2
Delaware........................	26	76.3	73.3	79.4	21	18.6	17.1	20.0
District of Columbia............	32	75.3	71.9	78.5	28	18.3	16.5	19.8
Florida...........................	27	76.1	73.1	79.3	19	18.7	17.2	20.2
Georgia..........................	41	74.3	71.6	77.1	43	17.1	15.7	18.3
Hawaii...........................	1	79.9	77.0	83.1	1	20.6	18.9	22.2
Idaho............................	20	77.2	74.8	79.7	25	18.4	17.2	19.5
Illinois...........................	21	77.1	74.2	80.0	23	18.6	17.1	19.9
Indiana..........................	38	74.6	71.8	77.5	42	17.3	16.0	18.6
Iowa.............................	16	77.7	75.2	80.4	24	18.6	17.1	19.9
Kansas..........................	28	76.0	73.4	78.7	32	18.0	16.5	19.4
Kentucky........................	47	72.3	69.6	75.3	47	16.4	15.1	17.6
Louisiana........................	48	72.2	68.8	75.9	44	16.8	15.3	18.3
Maine............................	23	76.7	73.8	79.8	22	18.6	17.3	19.8
Maryland........................	19	77.2	74.3	79.9	18	18.7	17.4	19.9
Massachusetts..................	2	79.6	76.9	82.2	3	19.6	18.1	20.9
Michigan.........................	30	75.7	72.9	78.6	34	17.9	16.5	19.1
Minnesota.......................	6	78.8	76.3	81.4	4	19.4	18.1	20.7
Mississippi......................	51	70.9	67.7	74.3	51	16.1	14.6	17.5
Missouri.........................	37	74.6	71.6	77.8	37	17.6	16.2	18.8
Montana.........................	29	75.8	73.1	78.8	26	18.4	17.1	19.6
Nebraska........................	13	77.8	75.4	80.3	17	18.8	17.2	20.2
Nevada..........................	33	75.1	72.4	78.2	38	17.5	16.1	19.0
New Hampshire..................	7	78.5	76.1	81.1	13	19.0	17.8	20.2
New Jersey......................	5	79.0	76.3	81.6	7	19.4	17.9	20.6
New Mexico......................	43	73.0	69.4	77.0	27	18.3	16.9	19.6
New York........................	4	79.0	76.3	81.6	5	19.4	17.9	20.7
North Carolina..................	36	74.9	72.0	77.9	36	17.7	16.3	18.9
North Dakota....................	17	77.6	75.0	80.5	10	19.1	17.6	20.6
Ohio..............................	40	74.5	71.7	77.5	41	17.3	15.9	18.6
Oklahoma........................	44	72.7	70.0	75.6	48	16.4	15.0	17.7
Oregon..........................	18	77.4	74.8	80.2	20	18.6	17.3	19.9
Pennsylvania....................	25	76.4	73.6	79.3	30	18.2	16.7	19.6
Rhode Island....................	8	78.5	75.9	81.0	14	19.0	17.6	20.3
South Carolina..................	42	73.5	70.4	76.7	40	17.4	16.0	18.8
South Dakota...................	24	76.6	74.1	79.3	9	19.2	17.8	20.6
Tennessee.......................	46	72.4	69.4	75.5	46	16.6	15.3	17.8
Texas............................	31	75.4	72.7	78.3	39	17.5	16.1	18.7
Utah.............................	12	78.2	76.3	80.2	16	18.8	17.9	19.7
Vermont.........................	9	78.4	75.7	81.2	6	19.4	18.2	20.5
Virginia..........................	22	76.8	74.2	79.4	29	18.2	16.9	19.4
Washington......................	11	78.2	75.8	80.8	12	19.1	17.7	20.3
West Virginia....................	50	71.0	68.1	74.2	50	16.1	14.8	17.3
Wisconsin.......................	14	77.8	75.2	80.5	15	18.9	17.5	20.2
Wyoming.........................	35	75.0	72.5	77.7	35	17.8	16.7	18.9

X Not applicable.

Source: U.S. National Center for Health Statistics, National Vital Statistics Reports (NVSR), *U.S. State Life Tables, 2021*, Vol. 73, No. 7, August 2024. See also <www.cdc.gov/nchs/nvss/life-expectancy.htm>.

Table 106. Life Expectancy Projections by Race/Ethnicity and Sex: 2030 to 2100

[In years. Race and Hispanic-origin categories are consistent with 1977 Office of Management and Budget (OMB) standards. Due to concerns about the quality of race reporting in death data over the time series, non-Hispanic race groups with similar mortality patterns are collapsed into two categories. For more on methodology, see <www2.census.gov/programs-surveys/popproj/technical-documentation/methodology/methodstatement23.pdf>]

Year	Total population			White and Asian or Pacific Islander, non-Hispanic			Black and American Indian and Alaska Native, non-Hispanic			Hispanic [1]		
	Total	Male	Female	Total	Male	Female	Total	Male	Female	Total	Male	Female
2030....	80.7	78.5	83.0	81.0	78.8	83.2	77.6	74.6	80.5	83.0	80.7	85.3
2040....	82.0	79.9	84.1	82.2	80.2	84.3	79.5	76.8	82.1	83.9	81.8	86.1
2050....	83.2	81.3	85.2	83.3	81.5	85.3	81.2	78.8	83.6	84.8	82.8	86.7
2060....	84.3	82.5	86.1	84.4	82.6	86.2	82.8	80.6	84.9	85.6	83.7	87.4
2070....	85.2	83.5	87.0	(NA)	(NA)	(NA)	(NA)	(NA)	(NA)	(NA)	(NA)	(NA)
2080....	86.2	84.5	87.9	(NA)	(NA)	(NA)	(NA)	(NA)	(NA)	(NA)	(NA)	(NA)
2090....	87.0	85.5	88.7	(NA)	(NA)	(NA)	(NA)	(NA)	(NA)	(NA)	(NA)	(NA)
2100....	87.8	86.3	89.4	(NA)	(NA)	(NA)	(NA)	(NA)	(NA)	(NA)	(NA)	(NA)

NA Not available. [1] Persons of Hispanic origin may be of any race.

Source: U.S. Census Bureau, 2023 National Population Projections Datasets, "Projected Life Expectancy at Birth by Nativity, Sex, Race, and Hispanic Origin for the United States: 2023 to 2100," <www.census.gov/data/datasets/2023/demo/popproj/2023-popproj.html>, accessed May 2024.

Table 107. Survivors Out of 100,000 Population Born Alive by Age, Sex, and Race/Ethnicity: 2021

[Number of persons from the original hypothetical cohort of 100,000 live births who survive to the beginning of each age interval. Data are based on final numbers of deaths for the year 2021; July 1, 2021 population estimates; and age-specific death and population counts for Black and White Medicare beneficiaries aged 66–99 for the year 2021 from the Centers for Medicare & Medicaid Services. Excludes deaths of nonresidents of the United States. Race categories are consistent with 1997 Office of Management and Budget standards. See Technical Notes, source]

SURVIVORS

Age	All races Total	Male	Female	White, non-Hispanic Total	Male	Female	Black, non-Hispanic Total	Male	Female	American Indian or Alaska Native, non-Hispanic Total	Male	Female	Asian, non-Hispanic Total	Male	Female	Hispanic Total	Male	Female
Age 0	100,000	100,000	100,000	100,000	100,000	100,000	100,000	100,000	100,000	100,000	100,000	100,000	100,000	100,000	100,000	100,000	100,000	100,000
Age 1	99,455	99,417	99,496	99,562	99,532	99,594	98,949	98,849	99,051	99,257	99,247	99,259	99,632	99,599	99,668	99,520	99,488	99,552
Age 5	99,355	99,308	99,404	99,475	99,426	99,526	98,744	98,652	98,864	99,042	98,979	99,099	99,576	99,539	99,615	99,439	99,408	99,472
Age 10	99,296	99,242	99,352	99,423	99,363	99,487	98,625	98,527	98,765	98,937	98,715	98,835	99,537	99,494	99,582	99,390	99,357	99,427
Age 15	99,214	99,147	99,283	99,349	99,270	99,433	98,478	98,360	98,658	98,777	98,437	98,577	99,491	99,444	99,542	99,317	99,278	99,360
Age 20	98,906	98,711	99,109	99,092	98,921	99,273	97,836	97,379	98,365	98,057	97,826	98,279	99,339	99,285	99,453	99,047	98,907	99,197
Age 25	98,335	97,896	98,795	98,606	98,239	98,992	96,769	95,813	97,815	96,607	95,946	97,258	99,030	98,930	99,334	98,523	98,163	98,907
Age 30	97,566	96,811	98,357	97,889	97,246	98,566	95,498	94,028	97,081	94,408	93,064	95,777	98,744	98,551	99,155	97,817	97,108	98,569
Age 35	96,577	95,472	97,733	96,914	95,942	97,933	93,979	91,989	96,090	91,275	89,191	93,442	98,428	98,125	98,990	96,945	95,870	98,103
Age 40	95,363	93,895	96,897	95,697	94,385	97,074	92,065	89,489	94,752	87,185	84,388	90,109	98,059	97,614	98,751	95,905	94,418	97,520
Age 45	93,824	91,958	95,776	94,167	92,492	95,929	89,657	86,488	92,916	82,828	79,181	86,662	97,538	96,888	98,373	94,573	92,601	96,720
Age 50	91,803	89,467	94,245	92,158	90,060	94,371	86,602	82,746	90,522	76,675	71,977	81,660	96,737	95,788	97,873	92,779	90,306	95,481
Age 55	89,000	86,044	92,099	89,388	86,725	92,213	82,552	77,867	87,290	70,188	64,669	76,110	95,456	94,024	97,018	90,281	87,132	93,745
Age 60	85,017	81,235	88,984	85,464	82,013	89,127	77,026	71,389	82,721	62,572	56,019	69,683	93,672	91,552	95,829	86,669	82,602	91,146
Age 65	79,571	74,780	84,604	80,137	75,722	84,833	69,672	62,902	76,517	54,466	47,020	62,648	90,892	87,756	93,912	81,570	76,387	87,249
Age 70	72,671	66,772	78,857	73,392	67,896	79,235	60,702	52,730	68,729	46,513	38,920	54,950	86,649	82,352	90,673	75,031	68,505	82,059
Age 75	63,810	57,001	70,967	64,531	58,093	71,381	50,597	41,890	59,355	37,780	30,541	46,011	80,516	75,035	85,558	66,603	58,966	74,730
Age 80	51,702	44,313	59,493	52,197	45,115	59,748	38,950	30,316	47,649	28,343	21,952	35,734	71,187	64,510	77,321	55,311	46,928	64,080
Age 85	36,667	29,498	44,237	36,832	29,850	44,270	26,312	18,890	33,750	19,186	14,220	24,994	56,955	49,432	63,756	40,842	32,479	49,262
Age 90	20,222	14,623	26,100	20,105	14,643	25,909	14,248	9,043	19,484	11,142	7,868	14,889	37,174	30,193	43,111	24,301	17,447	30,641
Age 95	7,260	4,407	10,201	7,035	4,252	9,919	5,528	2,984	8,014	5,181	3,467	6,962	16,428	11,992	19,438	9,981	6,053	12,958
Age 100	1,390	657	2,127	1,283	587	1,985	1,355	601	2,027	1,826	1,162	2,372	3,873	2,462	4,372	2,383	1,134	3,011

PERCENT SURVIVING

Age	All races Total	Male	Female	White, non-Hispanic Total	Male	Female	Black, non-Hispanic Total	Male	Female	American Indian or Alaska Native, non-Hispanic Total	Male	Female	Asian, non-Hispanic Total	Male	Female	Hispanic Total	Male	Female
Age 0	100.0	100.0	100.0	100.0	100.0	100.0	100.0	100.0	100.0	100.0	100.0	100.0	100.0	100.0	100.0	100.0	100.0	100.0
Age 1	99.5	99.4	99.5	99.6	99.5	99.6	98.9	98.8	99.1	99.3	99.2	99.3	99.6	99.6	99.7	99.5	99.5	99.6
Age 5	99.4	99.3	99.4	99.5	99.4	99.5	98.7	98.7	98.9	99.0	99.0	99.1	99.6	99.5	99.6	99.4	99.4	99.5
Age 10	99.3	99.2	99.4	99.4	99.4	99.5	98.6	98.5	98.8	98.9	98.7	98.8	99.5	99.5	99.6	99.4	99.4	99.4
Age 15	99.2	99.1	99.3	99.3	99.3	99.4	98.5	98.4	98.7	98.8	98.4	98.6	99.5	99.4	99.5	99.3	99.3	99.4
Age 20	98.9	98.7	99.1	99.1	98.9	99.3	97.8	97.4	98.4	98.1	97.8	98.3	99.3	99.3	99.5	99.0	98.9	99.2
Age 25	98.3	97.9	98.8	98.6	98.2	99.0	96.8	95.8	97.8	96.6	95.9	97.3	99.0	98.9	99.3	98.5	98.2	98.9
Age 30	97.6	96.8	98.4	97.9	97.2	98.6	95.5	94.0	97.1	94.4	93.1	95.8	98.7	98.6	99.2	97.8	97.1	98.6
Age 35	96.6	95.5	97.7	96.9	95.9	97.9	94.0	92.0	96.1	91.3	89.2	93.4	98.4	98.1	99.0	96.9	95.9	98.1
Age 40	95.4	93.9	96.9	95.7	94.4	97.1	92.1	89.5	94.8	87.2	84.4	90.1	98.1	97.6	98.8	95.9	94.4	97.5
Age 45	93.8	92.0	95.8	94.2	92.5	95.9	89.7	86.5	92.9	82.8	79.2	86.7	97.5	96.9	98.4	94.6	92.6	96.7
Age 50	91.8	89.5	94.2	92.2	90.1	94.4	86.6	82.7	90.5	76.7	72.0	81.7	96.7	95.8	98.0	92.8	90.3	95.5
Age 55	89.0	86.0	92.1	89.4	86.7	92.2	82.6	77.9	87.3	70.2	64.7	76.1	95.5	94.0	97.0	90.3	87.1	93.7
Age 60	85.0	81.2	89.0	85.5	82.0	89.1	77.0	71.4	82.7	62.6	56.0	69.7	93.7	91.6	95.8	86.7	82.6	91.1
Age 65	79.6	74.8	84.6	80.1	75.7	84.8	69.7	62.9	76.5	54.5	47.0	62.6	90.9	87.8	93.9	81.6	76.4	87.2
Age 70	72.7	66.8	78.9	73.4	67.9	79.2	60.7	52.7	68.7	46.5	38.9	55.0	86.6	82.4	90.7	75.0	68.5	82.1
Age 75	63.8	57.0	71.0	64.5	58.1	71.4	50.6	41.9	59.4	37.8	30.5	46.0	80.5	75.0	85.6	66.6	59.0	74.7
Age 80	51.7	44.3	59.5	52.2	45.1	59.7	39.0	30.3	47.6	28.3	22.0	35.7	71.2	64.5	77.3	55.3	46.9	64.1
Age 85	36.7	29.5	44.2	36.8	29.9	44.3	26.3	18.9	33.8	19.2	14.2	25.0	57.0	49.4	63.8	40.8	32.5	49.3
Age 90	20.2	14.6	26.1	20.1	14.6	25.9	14.2	9.0	19.5	11.1	7.9	14.9	37.2	30.2	43.1	24.3	17.4	30.6
Age 95	7.3	4.4	10.2	7.0	4.3	9.9	5.5	3.0	8.0	5.2	3.5	7.0	16.4	12.0	19.4	10.0	6.1	13.0
Age 100	1.4	0.7	2.1	1.3	0.6	2.0	1.4	0.6	2.0	1.8	1.2	2.4	3.9	2.5	4.4	2.4	1.1	3.0

Source: U.S. National Center for Health Statistics, National Vital Statistics Reports (NVSR), United States Life Tables, 2021, Vol. 72, No. 12, November 2023. See also <www.cdc.gov/nchs/products/life_tables.htm>.

Table 108. Deaths and Death Rates by Sex, Race, and Hispanic Origin: 2018 to 2022

[Rates per 100,000 population for specified groups. Excludes deaths of nonresidents of the United States and fetal deaths. Rates are based on population estimated as of July 1. Beginning 2018, all 50 states and the District of Columbia reported race and Hispanic origin data according to 1997 Office of Management and Budget (OMB) standards. Data for Hispanic origin and specified races other than non-Hispanic White and non-Hispanic Black should be interpreted with caution due to inconsistencies between reporting these items on death certificates and on censuses and surveys. See source for details]

Sex, race, and Hispanic origin	2018	2019	2020	2021	2022
Deaths [1]	**2,839,205**	**2,854,838**	**3,383,729**	**3,464,231**	**3,279,857**
Male [1]	1,458,469	1,473,823	1,769,884	1,838,108	1,719,250
Female [1]	1,380,736	1,381,015	1,613,845	1,626,123	1,560,607
White alone, non-Hispanic	2,182,552	2,183,844	2,484,072	2,548,809	2,448,093
Male	1,108,848	1,115,767	1,278,612	1,337,385	1,267,526
Female	1,073,704	1,068,077	1,205,460	1,211,424	1,180,567
Black alone, non-Hispanic	341,408	346,677	449,213	449,764	411,934
Male	177,958	181,363	237,703	238,599	219,538
Female	163,450	165,314	211,510	211,165	192,396
American Indian or Alaska Native alone, non-Hispanic	17,790	18,057	24,725	26,972	23,613
Male	9,678	9,732	13,431	14,724	12,721
Female	8,112	8,325	11,294	12,248	10,892
Asian alone, non-Hispanic	68,768	70,532	91,175	92,432	89,591
Male	35,089	35,914	47,699	48,386	46,137
Female	33,679	34,618	43,476	44,046	43,454
Native Hawaiian or other Pacific Islander alone, non-Hispanic	3,277	3,491	4,439	5,223	4,592
Male	1,786	1,938	2,489	2,906	2,461
Female	1,491	1,553	1,950	2,317	2,131
More than one race, non-Hispanic	12,704	12,897	15,523	17,316	16,904
Male	7,020	6,959	8,565	9,636	9,367
Female	5,684	5,938	6,958	7,680	7,537
Hispanic origin [2]	204,719	212,397	305,708	315,664	275,684
Male	113045	117683	175585	181195	155240
Female	91,674	94,714	130,123	134,469	120,444
Death rates [1]	**867.8**	**869.7**	**1,027.0**	**1,043.8**	**984.1**
Male [1]	905.2	911.7	1,090.8	1,118.2	1,040.2
Female [1]	831.6	829.0	965.1	970.8	928.9
White alone, non-Hispanic	1,104.8	1,106.8	1,262.4	1,294.9	1,247.6
Male	1,138.2	1,146.6	1,317.7	1,368.8	1,299.7
Female	1,072.3	1,068.1	1,208.6	1,222.1	1,196.1
Black alone, non-Hispanic	834.7	842.5	1,084.3	1,074.5	979.2
Male	909.8	921.8	1,200.0	1,185.8	1,085.4
Female	765.9	769.9	978.4	971.4	880.8
American Indian or Alaska Native alone, non-Hispanic	735.9	741.6	1,016.5	1,100.0	975.4
Male	813.5	812.1	1,123.4	1,216.0	1,062.4
Female	660.8	673.3	913.2	986.2	890.2
Asian, non-Hispanic	367.2	373.1	470.8	469.5	441.9
Male	393.4	398.7	515.8	511.7	472.3
Female	343.3	349.8	429.6	430.5	413.6
Native Hawaiian or other Pacific Islander alone, non-Hispanic	558.9	585.8	723.5	834.0	722.1
Male	605.4	646.5	804.6	917.5	765.3
Female	511.8	524.4	641.1	748.6	677.9
More than one race, non-Hispanic	178.6	177.3	205.4	222.3	211.5
Male	199.9	193.7	229.2	249.6	235.9
Female	157.8	161.3	182.1	195.4	187.4
Hispanic origin [2]	341.9	350.7	498.6	503.9	433.0
Male	373.9	384.9	567.8	571.3	481.0
Female	309.3	315.7	428.2	434.7	383.7
Age-adjusted death rates [1,3]	**723.6**	**715.2**	**835.4**	**879.7**	**798.8**
Male [1]	855.5	846.7	998.3	1,048.0	954.5
Female [1]	611.3	602.7	695.1	733.3	666.1
White alone, non-Hispanic	748.7	739.9	834.7	893.9	822.2
Male	878.0	868.8	985.0	1,055.6	972.1
Female	636.5	627.4	703.1	751.4	692.7
Black alone, non-Hispanic	892.6	884.0	1,119.0	1,118.0	1,002.8
Male	1,102.8	1,092.8	1,399.0	1,374.0	1,257.5
Female	733.7	724.9	905.2	917.2	809.0
American Indian or Alaska Native alone, non-Hispanic	790.8	782.5	1,036.2	1,109.2	947.9
Male	918.7	901.9	1,205.9	1,282.7	1,084.3
Female	673.1	673.3	881.5	946.6	816.1
Asian, non-Hispanic	381.2	372.8	457.7	461.7	417.5
Male	454.1	442.4	557.4	554.9	501.7
Female	324.1	317.2	378.5	386.3	350.7
Native Hawaiian or other Pacific Islander alone, non-Hispanic	675.7	679.0	821.3	924.3	782.0
Male	758.1	769.0	947.9	1,042.8	859.5
Female	597.3	589.5	699.8	806.0	705.4
More than one race, non-Hispanic	338.1	326.5	376.9	406.0	366.8
Male	403.0	379.6	445.5	479.3	433.0
Female	283.0	280.7	317.4	341.5	308.2
Hispanic origin [2]	524.1	523.8	723.6	724.7	614.7
Male	633.1	633.2	903.8	884.9	748.8
Female	431.7	430.7	570.1	582.7	498.4

[1] Includes other races not shown separately. [2] Persons of Hispanic origin may be of any race. [3] Age-adjusted death rates are better indicators than crude death rates for showing changes in the risk of death over time when the age distribution of the population is changing, and for comparing the mortality of population subgroups that have different age compositions. All age-adjusted death rates are standardized to the year 2000 population.

Source: U.S. National Center for Health Statistics, National Vital Statistics Reports (NVSR), *Deaths: Final Data*, annual; and CDC WONDER Online Database, "Multiple Cause of Death, 2018-2022," <wonder.cdc.gov>, accessed June 2024.

Table 109. Death Rates by Age, Sex, and Race and Hispanic Origin: 2019 to 2022

[Rates per 100,000 population. Beginning 2018, all States and the District of Columbia reported race and Hispanic origin data according to 1997 Office of Management and Budget (OMB) standards. Death rates for specified races other than non-Hispanic White and non-Hispanic Black should be interpreted with caution because of inconsistencies between reporting race on death certificates and censuses and surveys. See source for details]

Characteristic	All ages [1]	Under 1 year	1 to 4 years	5 to 14 years	15 to 24 years	25 to 34 years	35 to 44 years	45 to 54 years	55 to 64 years	65 to 74 years	75 to 84 years	85 years and over
MALE												
Total:												
2019	912	603	25	15	100	177	257	490	1,112	2,179	5,074	14,230
2020	1,091	569	26	16	122	221	326	602	1,323	2,582	5,937	16,355
2021	1,118	599	27	16	127	251	373	668	1,398	2,640	6,032	17,191
2022	1,040	604	31	17	113	226	332	566	1,230	2,420	5,527	16,140
Non-Hispanic:												
White alone												
2020	1,318	472	23	15	101	214	320	576	1,252	2,455	5,929	17,096
2021	1,369	496	25	15	105	237	365	655	1,362	2,587	6,169	18,353
2022	1,300	510	29	16	91	211	331	573	1,234	2,409	5,695	17,191
Black alone												
2020	1,200	1,191	48	30	248	370	540	980	2,133	4,172	7,864	16,563
2021	1,186	1,232	53	32	258	416	609	1,051	2,118	3,936	7,252	15,909
2022	1,085	1,171	59	31	233	374	545	900	1,867	3,600	6,723	15,380
Asian alone												
2020	516	275	13	8	47	64	115	254	651	1,462	3,689	10,626
2021	512	357	15	10	53	75	120	266	633	1,400	3,637	10,593
2022	472	338	16	9	46	69	105	228	532	1,250	3,257	10,082
American Indian or Alaska Native alone												
2020	1,123	781	59	28	216	524	839	1,248	1,915	3,064	5,656	10,263
2021	1,217	761	58	23	254	631	1,002	1,457	2,182	2,964	5,451	9,996
2022	1,062	933	59	37	242	582	930	1,210	1,741	2,515	4,366	7,885
Native Hawaiian or other Pacific Islander alone												
2020	805	805	(S)	(S)	138	294	410	939	1,645	2,889	4,909	7,883
2021	918	1,097	(D)	(S)	206	364	587	1,205	1,754	3,077	4,566	8,113
2022	765	1,167	(S)	(S)	155	275	429	809	1,491	2,497	4,307	6,935
More than one race												
2020	229	415	18	10	66	141	198	345	668	1,187	2,527	5,196
2021	250	420	20	9	74	148	242	416	743	1,276	2,454	5,551
2022	236	403	21	12	67	152	218	379	678	1,150	2,208	4,777
Hispanic:												
2020	568	478	20	13	116	186	274	538	1,221	2,562	5,616	13,436
2021	571	503	21	14	119	227	324	579	1,213	2,374	5,209	12,927
2022	481	514	23	15	109	210	271	432	906	1,900	4,369	12,380
FEMALE												
Total:												
2019	829	500	21	12	38	79	142	297	670	1,402	3,711	12,666
2020	965	478	20	11	45	96	171	349	773	1,627	4,261	14,560
2021	971	517	23	12	49	109	201	394	848	1,716	4,396	14,915
2022	929	510	25	13	44	98	177	340	762	1,586	4,061	13,439
Non-Hispanic:												
White alone												
2020	1,209	402	18	10	42	99	176	350	749	1,587	4,304	15,276
2021	1,222	433	19	11	45	109	207	402	839	1,698	4,511	15,884
2022	1,196	434	22	12	42	100	185	359	784	1,611	4,220	14,302
Black alone												
2020	978	1,006	37	18	76	149	287	569	1,240	2,443	5,336	14,425
2021	971	1,023	47	21	84	178	333	628	1,302	2,459	5,201	13,781
2022	881	960	46	23	73	156	289	523	1,122	2,174	4,610	12,446
Asian alone												
2020	430	233	13	8	24	28	51	132	318	807	2,459	9,611
2021	431	297	13	7	24	32	57	139	328	829	2,526	9,549
2022	414	272	12	7	21	30	54	125	284	734	2,333	8,690
American Indian or Alaska Native alone												
2020	913	608	48	24	105	327	526	791	1,257	2,108	4,655	10,208
2021	986	682	37	25	132	362	638	935	1,397	2,312	4,526	10,116
2022	890	730	61	31	122	348	538	800	1,216	1,926	3,946	8,292
Native Hawaiian or other Pacific Islander alone												
2020	641	777	(D)	(D)	54	128	257	628	1,146	2,099	3,888	7,838
2021	749	582	(D)	(D)	77	155	385	815	1,344	2,287	4,385	8,028
2022	678	1,029	(D)	(S)	48	136	266	650	1,133	2,163	4,132	6,546
More than one race												
2020	182	303	13	7	30	65	100	203	433	847	1,838	5,072
2021	195	379	14	9	35	67	125	229	457	867	2,003	5,292
2022	187	373	19	10	32	68	121	212	413	828	1,724	4,558
Hispanic:												
2020	428	394	16	11	37	67	115	250	615	1,440	3,777	11,448
2021	435	441	20	11	43	79	140	282	655	1,475	3,683	11,396
2022	384	439	21	12	38	69	114	218	500	1,194	3,183	10,428

D Withheld due to confidentiality constraints. S Figure does not meet publication standards; based on fewer than 20 deaths. [1] Figures for age not stated are included in "All ages" but not distributed among age groups.

Source: U.S. National Center for Health Statistics, CDC WONDER Online Database, "Multiple Cause of Death, 2018-2022," <wonder.cdc.gov>, accessed June 2024. See also <www.cdc.gov/nchs/nvss/deaths.htm>.

Table 110. Deaths and Death Rates by Age, Sex, Race, and Hispanic Origin: 2022

[Rates per 100,000 population in specified group. Beginning 2018, all States and the District of Columbia reported race and Hispanic origin data according to 1997 Office of Management and Budget (OMB) standards. Data shown here are consistent with the 1997 OMB standards. Data for specified race or Hispanic-origin groups other than non-Hispanic White and non-Hispanic Black should be interpreted with caution because of inconsistencies in reporting these items on death certificates and surveys; see Technical Notes, source]

Age	Total [1]			White alone, non-Hispanic			Black alone, non-Hispanic			American Indian or Alaska Native alone, non-Hispanic			Asian or Pacific Islander alone, non-Hispanic			Hispanic [2]		
	Total	Male	Female	Total	Male	Female	Total	Male	Female	Total	Male	Female	Total	Male	Female	Total	Male	Female
DEATHS																		
All ages	3,279,857	1,719,250	1,560,607	2,448,093	1,267,526	1,180,567	411,934	219,538	192,396	23,613	12,721	10,892	89,591	46,137	43,454	275,684	155,240	120,444
Under 1 year	20,553	11,371	9,182	8,075	4,469	3,606	5,800	3,230	2,570	210	120	90	624	356	268	4,765	2,612	2,153
1 to 4 years	4,156	2,353	1,803	1,795	1,044	751	1,116	634	482	64	32	32	120	70	50	869	466	403
5 to 9 years	2,567	1,423	1,144	1,120	619	501	660	365	295	43	25	18	86	44	42	556	314	242
10 to 14 years	3,672	2,164	1,508	1,690	1,001	689	842	509	333	67	36	31	107	66	41	830	473	357
15 to 19 years	12,745	9,180	3,565	5,400	3,665	1,735	3,484	2,715	769	253	155	98	300	208	92	2,994	2,227	767
20 to 24 years	22,487	16,457	6,030	10,005	7,089	2,916	5,882	4,465	1,417	411	292	119	523	361	162	5,041	3,813	1,228
25 to 29 years	31,295	22,477	8,818	15,313	10,696	4,617	7,626	5,514	2,112	693	465	228	640	454	186	6,290	4,836	1,454
30 to 34 years	43,074	30,034	13,040	22,928	15,669	7,259	9,757	6,768	2,989	1,036	632	404	940	643	297	7,501	5,706	1,795
35 to 39 years	50,472	33,877	16,595	28,608	18,855	9,753	10,485	6,867	3,618	1,132	721	411	1,131	766	365	8,182	6,059	2,123
40 to 44 years	61,133	39,609	21,524	35,068	22,516	12,552	12,749	7,973	4,776	1,170	740	430	1,464	895	569	9,612	6,816	2,796
45 to 49 years	73,143	46,125	27,018	42,719	26,600	16,119	14,685	8,965	5,720	1,277	779	498	2,029	1,272	757	11,200	7,731	3,469
50 to 54 years	110,141	68,722	41,419	69,430	43,227	26,203	20,691	12,533	8,158	1,504	884	620	2,913	1,799	1,114	13,943	9,224	4,719
55 to 59 years	168,323	103,522	64,801	111,814	68,499	43,315	30,631	18,308	12,323	1,969	1,128	841	3,718	2,339	1,379	17,863	11,730	6,133
60 to 64 years	249,218	150,756	98,462	173,886	105,322	68,564	42,744	25,037	17,707	2,329	1,314	1,015	5,253	3,223	2,030	21,885	13,846	8,039
65 to 69 years	306,165	180,725	125,440	220,861	130,893	89,968	48,502	27,931	20,571	2,312	1,239	1,073	7,069	4,171	2,898	23,891	14,281	9,610
70 to 74 years	362,416	204,260	158,156	273,137	155,019	118,118	48,355	26,131	22,224	2,400	1,252	1,148	9,224	5,205	4,019	25,889	14,651	11,238
75 to 79 years	407,592	218,209	189,383	323,137	174,686	148,451	42,188	21,254	20,934	2,128	1,033	1,095	10,338	5,468	4,870	26,803	14,096	12,707
80 to 84 years	417,311	209,298	208,013	335,058	170,536	164,522	37,998	17,256	20,742	1,925	890	1,035	12,290	6,278	6,012	27,542	13,067	14,475
85 years and over	933,291	368,601	564,690	768,010	307,090	460,920	67,734	23,078	44,656	2,690	984	1,706	30,822	12,519	18,303	60,018	23,283	36,735
DEATH RATES																		
All ages	984.1	1,040.2	928.9	1,247.6	1,299.7	1,196.1	979.2	1,085.4	880.8	975.4	1,062.4	890.2	441.9	472.3	413.6	433.0	481.0	383.7
Under 1 year	558.0	603.9	510.0	472.8	509.9	433.8	1,066.7	1,170.5	959.6	833.5	932.8	729.8	306.0	338.1	271.7	477.4	514.1	439.4
1 to 4 years	28.0	31.0	24.8	25.4	28.8	21.8	52.8	59.2	46.2	60.0	58.9	61.1	14.1	16.0	12.2	22.2	23.4	21.0
5 to 9 years	12.8	13.9	11.7	11.5	12.4	10.6	24.0	26.2	21.7	27.5	31.3	(S)	7.3	7.3	7.4	10.8	12.0	9.6
10 to 14 years	17.6	20.2	14.8	16.4	18.9	13.8	29.2	34.7	23.5	39.4	41.5	37.1	9.6	11.5	7.5	15.3	17.1	13.5
15 to 19 years	58.9	82.8	33.8	49.0	64.6	32.4	118.9	182.9	53.2	143.3	172.7	112.9	25.9	35.5	16.1	55.0	79.8	28.8
20 to 24 years	99.0	141.8	54.3	84.1	116.1	50.4	186.1	280.3	90.4	220.4	308.1	129.8	40.0	54.8	24.9	94.2	139.3	47.0
25 to 29 years	141.0	198.0	81.3	130.2	176.9	80.8	238.9	342.4	133.6	381.9	502.9	256.1	43.2	61.3	25.1	128.6	192.3	61.2
30 to 34 years	184.8	253.7	113.7	181.6	244.0	117.1	289.6	404.3	176.3	548.3	657.0	435.5	54.3	75.8	33.7	155.7	227.2	77.9
35 to 39 years	226.7	299.7	151.3	230.2	297.9	159.9	363.1	488.1	244.4	692.7	878.1	505.5	65.8	91.9	41.2	177.6	249.5	97.4
40 to 44 years	285.3	366.1	202.9	290.1	365.7	211.6	464.7	605.9	334.5	780.5	986.9	573.9	92.5	119.2	68.4	215.6	293.2	131.0
45 to 49 years	372.7	468.5	276.3	382.0	467.7	293.3	594.1	765.3	439.9	936.5	1,150.2	725.6	137.9	182.5	97.7	277.7	374.3	176.3
50 to 54 years	529.3	658.6	399.3	543.2	665.7	416.7	805.5	1,029.2	603.8	1,067.6	1,267.3	871.8	212.1	276.8	154.0	383.0	496.2	264.9
55 to 59 years	802.8	997.9	611.7	816.9	1,000.4	633.2	1,197.9	1,528.3	906.7	1,343.9	1,588.9	1,113.5	313.9	420.7	219.4	572.3	745.5	396.3
60 to 64 years	1,180.1	1,463.9	910.0	1,184.9	1,454.1	922.5	1,751.4	2,227.4	1,345.0	1,591.6	1,897.9	1,316.6	493.5	657.3	353.7	862.7	1,108.0	624.5
65 to 69 years	1,643.3	2,036.6	1,285.6	1,640.7	2,009.4	1,294.9	2,430.7	3,164.6	1,848.6	1,895.1	2,195.8	1,636.4	754.4	993.2	560.5	1,251.8	1,580.9	956.1
70 to 74 years	2,391.1	2,902.8	1,947.7	2,412.8	2,895.3	1,979.7	3,279.3	4,220.8	2,598.0	2,598.4	2,938.6	2,307.1	1,220.4	1,575.7	944.6	1,902.8	2,365.9	1,515.9
75 to 79 years	3,752.8	4,444.5	3,182.2	3,862.5	4,533.6	3,289.5	4,584.1	5,765.5	3,794.7	3,476.6	3,699.2	3,289.8	2,058.6	2,478.4	1,729.7	2,951.9	3,592.9	2,464.2
80 to 84 years	6,266.4	7,408.4	5,424.9	6,554.7	7,722.6	5,666.5	6,827.9	8,451.1	5,887.2	5,228.8	5,519.4	5,002.4	3,780.8	4,482.1	3,249.8	4,851.1	5,694.8	4,278.9
85 years and over	14,389.6	16,139.6	13,438.5	15,332.2	17,191.0	14,301.9	13,311.4	15,380.3	12,446.1	8,138.4	7,885.2	8,292.0	9,206.1	10,082.0	8,689.8	11,107.1	12,379.5	10,427.8

S Does not meet standards of reliability; based on fewer than 20 deaths. [1] Includes deaths for other race groups and those with unstated age, not shown separately. [2] Persons of Hispanic origin may be of any race.

Source: U.S. National Center for Health Statistics, National Vital Statistics Reports (NVSR), *Deaths: Final Data*, annual; and CDC WONDER Online Database, "Multiple Cause of Death, 2018-2022," <wonder.cdc.gov>, accessed June 2024. See also <www.cdc.gov/nchs/nvss/deaths.htm>.

Table 111. Deaths and Death Rates by State: 2000 to 2022

[2,403 represents 2,403,000; rates per 1,000 population. By state of residence. Excludes deaths of nonresidents of the United States. Caution should be used in comparing death rates by state; rates are affected by the population composition of the area. See also Appendix III]

State	Number of deaths (1,000)						Death rate [1]						Age-adjusted death rate, 2022 [1,2]
	2000	2010	2019	2020	2021	2022	2000	2010	2019	2020	2021	2022	
United States.........	2,403	2,468	2,855	3,384	3,464	3,280	8.5	8.0	8.7	10.3	10.4	9.8	8.0
Alabama................	45	48	54	65	69	62	10.1	10.1	11.0	13.2	13.7	12.3	9.9
Alaska..................	3	4	5	5	6	6	4.6	5.2	6.3	7.1	8.5	7.8	8.2
Arizona.................	41	47	60	76	81	74	7.9	7.3	8.3	10.2	11.2	10.1	7.9
Arkansas...............	28	29	33	38	40	38	10.6	9.9	10.9	12.6	13.2	12.4	10.0
California...............	230	234	270	320	333	313	6.8	6.3	6.8	8.1	8.5	8.0	6.9
Colorado................	27	31	39	47	48	47	6.3	6.3	6.8	8.1	8.3	8.0	7.4
Connecticut............	30	29	32	38	34	35	8.8	8.0	8.9	10.6	9.5	9.5	7.2
Delaware...............	7	8	9	11	11	11	8.8	8.6	9.6	11.2	11.3	11.1	8.3
District of Columbia....	6	5	5	6	6	5	10.5	7.8	7.0	8.7	8.7	8.0	7.9
Florida.................	164	174	207	240	261	239	10.3	9.2	9.6	11.0	12.0	10.7	7.1
Georgia................	64	71	86	103	112	102	7.8	7.4	8.1	9.6	10.4	9.4	8.7
Hawaii.................	8	10	12	12	13	13	6.8	7.1	8.2	8.6	8.9	9.2	6.2
Idaho..................	10	11	14	16	18	17	7.4	7.3	8.1	9.0	9.7	8.9	7.7
Illinois.................	107	100	109	133	125	123	8.6	7.8	8.6	10.5	9.9	9.8	7.8
Indiana................	55	57	66	78	78	75	9.1	8.8	9.8	11.6	11.5	11.0	9.2
Iowa...................	28	28	31	36	34	34	9.6	9.1	9.8	11.4	10.7	10.6	8.0
Kansas................	25	25	28	32	32	32	9.2	8.6	9.5	11.0	10.9	10.7	8.7
Kentucky..............	40	42	49	56	60	57	9.8	9.7	11.0	12.5	13.4	12.6	10.4
Louisiana..............	41	41	46	57	58	52	9.2	9.0	9.9	12.2	12.4	11.4	9.7
Maine.................	12	13	15	16	17	17	9.7	9.6	11.2	11.7	12.6	12.5	8.4
Maryland..............	44	43	51	60	58	56	8.3	7.5	8.4	9.9	9.4	9.2	7.5
Massachusetts........	57	53	59	68	63	63	8.9	8.0	8.5	9.9	9.0	9.1	6.9
Michigan..............	87	88	99	117	118	110	8.7	8.9	9.9	11.7	11.7	11.0	8.6
Minnesota.............	38	39	46	52	52	51	7.7	7.3	8.1	9.3	9.0	9.0	7.1
Mississippi............	29	29	33	40	41	38	10.1	9.8	11.1	13.5	13.9	12.9	10.7
Missouri...............	55	55	62	74	74	72	9.8	9.2	10.2	12.0	12.0	11.6	9.2
Montana...............	8	9	10	12	13	12	9.0	8.9	9.7	11.1	11.5	10.4	7.9
Nebraska..............	15	15	17	20	19	19	8.8	8.3	8.8	10.1	9.6	9.5	7.7
Nevada................	15	20	26	31	33	31	7.6	7.3	8.3	9.8	10.5	9.7	8.4
New Hampshire.......	10	10	13	14	14	15	7.8	7.7	9.4	10.0	10.2	10.4	7.5
New Jersey............	75	69	75	96	84	81	8.9	7.9	8.4	10.8	9.1	8.8	6.8
New Mexico...........	13	16	20	24	25	24	7.4	7.7	9.3	11.3	12.0	11.2	9.0
New York..............	158	146	156	203	181	174	8.3	7.6	8.0	10.5	9.1	8.8	6.6
North Carolina.........	72	79	96	109	118	113	8.9	8.3	9.1	10.3	11.2	10.6	8.8
North Dakota..........	6	6	7	8	7	7	9.1	8.8	8.8	10.5	9.4	9.0	7.4
Ohio...................	108	109	124	144	148	138	9.5	9.4	10.6	12.3	12.5	11.8	9.2
Oklahoma.............	35	37	41	48	51	48	10.2	9.7	10.3	12.0	12.8	11.9	10.3
Oregon................	30	32	37	40	45	45	8.6	8.3	8.9	9.5	10.6	10.5	8.1
Pennsylvania..........	131	125	134	156	155	147	10.7	9.8	10.5	12.2	12.0	11.3	8.2
Rhode Island..........	10	10	10	12	11	11	9.6	9.1	9.7	11.2	10.3	9.8	7.1
South Carolina........	37	42	51	61	65	61	9.2	9.0	9.9	11.7	12.6	11.6	9.2
South Dakota..........	7	7	8	10	9	9	9.3	8.7	9.3	11.0	10.3	9.9	8.0
Tennessee.............	55	60	72	84	91	85	9.7	9.4	10.5	12.2	13.1	12.1	10.1
Texas..................	150	167	203	250	268	241	7.2	6.6	7.0	8.5	9.1	8.0	8.2
Utah...................	12	15	19	21	23	22	5.5	5.3	5.8	6.6	6.8	6.5	7.6
Vermont...............	5	5	6	6	7	7	8.4	8.6	9.5	10.4	10.7	10.8	7.6
Virginia................	56	59	70	81	86	83	8.0	7.4	8.2	9.4	9.9	9.6	7.9
Washington............	44	48	58	63	69	69	7.5	7.2	7.7	8.2	8.9	8.9	7.6
West Virginia..........	21	21	23	26	30	28	11.7	11.5	13.1	14.6	16.5	15.5	11.2
Wisconsin.............	46	47	54	63	61	61	8.7	8.3	9.3	10.8	10.3	10.3	7.9
Wyoming..............	4	4	5	6	7	6	7.9	7.9	8.8	10.3	11.4	10.2	8.3

[1] Rates based on enumerated resident population as of April 1 for 2000 and 2010; estimated resident population as of July 1 for all other years. [2] Age-adjusted death rates are better indicators than crude death rates for showing changes in the risk of death over time when the age distribution of the population is changing, and for comparing the mortality of population subgroups that have different age compositions. See text this section.

Source: U.S. National Center for Health Statistics, National Vital Statistics Reports (NVSR), *Deaths: Final Data*, annual; and CDC WONDER Online Database, "Multiple Cause of Death 2018-2022," <wonder.cdc.gov>, accessed June 2024.

Table 112. Deaths and Death Rates by Urban-Rural Status: 2000 to 2022

[Rates per 100,000 population. Rates are based on population enumerated as of April 1 for 2000 and 2010 and estimated as of July 1 for all other years]

Year	Number		Crude rate		Age-adjusted rate [1]	
	Urban	Rural	Urban	Rural	Urban	Rural
2000.................	1,931,159	472,192	816.1	1,054.4	858.3	918.1
2005.................	1,972,266	475,751	788.8	1,046.1	800.3	885.7
2010.................	1,989,099	479,336	757.9	1,035.4	728.7	837.6
2015.................	2,196,111	516,519	797.9	1,118.8	711.6	846.0
2017.................	2,285,463	528,040	817.3	1,145.9	710.7	845.8
2018.................	2,308,265	530,940	821.3	1,151.7	702.5	837.5
2019.................	2,320,231	534,607	822.3	1,160.6	693.4	834.0
2020.................	2,763,553	620,176	975.0	1,347.2	(NA)	(NA)
2021.................	2,810,394	653,837	983.3	1,418.8	(NA)	(NA)
2022.................	2,668,273	611,584	940.4	1,331.8	(NA)	(NA)

NA Not available. [1] See footnote 2, Table 111.

Source: U.S. National Center for Health Statistics, *Trends in Death Rates in Urban and Rural Areas: United States, 1999–2019*, September 2021; and CDC WONDER Online Database, "Multiple Cause of Death, 2018-2022," <wonder.cdc.gov>, accessed June 2024.

Table 113. Fetal and Infant Deaths: 1990 to 2022

[The term "fetal death," defined on an all inclusive basis to end confusion arising from the use of such terms as stillbirth, spontaneous abortion, and miscarriage, has been adopted by the National Center for Health Statistics (NCHS) as the nationally recommended standard. Fetal deaths do not include induced terminations of pregnancy. In 2014, the NCHS transitioned to the use of the obstetric estimate of gestational age (OE) rather than the last normal menses (LMP) estimate, introducing a discontinuity in perinatal measures for earlier years]

Year	Fetal deaths [1,6]			Infant deaths		Fetal mortality rate [2,6]			Perinatal mortality rate [6]	
	Total [1]	20 to 27 weeks [3]	28 weeks or more [3]	Less than 7 days	Less than 28 days	Total [1]	20 to 27 weeks [3]	28 weeks or more [3]	Defi-nition I [4]	Defi-nition II [5]
1990.....	31,386	13,427	17,959	19,439	23,591	7.5	3.2	4.3	9.0	13.1
1995.....	27,294	13,043	14,251	15,483	19,186	7.0	3.3	3.6	7.6	11.8
2000.....	27,003	13,497	13,506	14,893	18,733	6.6	3.3	3.3	7.0	11.2
2005.....	25,894	13,326	12,568	15,013	18,782	6.2	3.2	3.0	6.6	10.7
2010.....	24,258	12,388	11,870	12,900	16,193	6.0	3.1	3.0	6.2	10.1
2011.....	24,289	12,432	11,857	12,960	16,065	6.1	3.1	3.0	6.3	10.1
2012.....	24,073	12,334	11,739	12,911	15,887	6.1	3.1	3.0	6.2	10.0
2013.....	23,595	11,874	11,721	12,900	15,893	6.0	3.0	3.0	6.2	10.0
2014.....	23,980	12,579	11,263	12,772	15,737	6.0	3.1	2.8	6.0	9.9
2015.....	23,776	12,351	11,317	12,579	15,672	5.9	3.1	2.8	6.0	9.9
2016.....	23,880	12,422	11,336	12,354	15,303	6.0	3.1	2.9	6.0	9.9
2017.....	22,827	11,792	10,903	11,971	14,844	5.9	3.0	2.8	5.9	9.7
2018.....	22,459	11,782	10,559	11,577	14,328	5.9	3.1	2.8	5.8	9.6
2019.....	21,478	11,159	10,209	11,124	13,834	5.7	3.0	2.7	5.7	9.4
2020.....	20,854	10,693	10,023	10,348	12,866	5.7	3.0	2.8	5.6	9.3
2021.....	21,105	10,747	10,208	10,082	12,797	5.7	2.9	2.8	5.5	9.2
2022.....	20,202	10,173	9,886	10,304	13,158	5.5	2.8	2.7	5.5	9.0

[1] Fetal deaths with stated or presumed gestation of 20 weeks or more. [2] Rate per 1,000 live births and fetal deaths in specified age group. [3] Prior to 2014, not stated gestational age proportionally distributed. Beginning 2014, unknown gestational age not shown. [4] Infant deaths of less than 7 days and fetal deaths with stated or presumed period of gestation of 28 weeks or more, per 1,000 live births and fetal deaths. [5] Infant deaths of less than 28 days and fetal deaths with stated or presumed period of gestation of 20 weeks or more, per 1,000 live births and fetal deaths. [6] Prior to 2014, based on LMP (last normal menses) measure of gestational age. Beginning 2014, based on the OE (obstetric estimate) of gestational age.

Source: U.S. National Center for Health Statistics, National Vital Statistics Reports (NVSR), *Fetal Mortality, United States*, annual report; and CDC WONDER Online Database, "Linked Birth / Infant Death Records for 2007-2022," and "Fetal Deaths for 2014-2022 (expanded)," <wonder.cdc.gov/>, accessed August 2024.

Table 114. Infant Deaths and Death Rates and Maternal Mortality Rates by Race/Ethnicity: 2000 to 2022

[Infant deaths are for those under 1 year of age, neonatal are infant deaths at less than 28 days, and postneonatal are infant deaths at 28 days or more. Infant deaths are based on birth and infant death certificates registered in all 50 states and D.C. Race categories are consistent with 1997 Office of Management and Budget (OMB) standards. Based on race and Hispanic origin of the mother. See source for details]

Race/ethnicity and year	Number of deaths			Deaths per 1,000 live births			Maternal mortality rate [1]
	Infant	Neonatal	Postneonatal	Infant	Neonatal	Postneonatal	
ALL RACES							
2000.........................	27,961	18,733	9,227	6.9	4.6	2.3	(NA)
2010.........................	24,572	16,193	8,379	6.1	4.1	2.1	(NA)
2015.........................	23,458	15,672	7,786	5.9	3.9	2.0	(NA)
2016.........................	23,157	15,303	7,854	5.9	3.9	2.0	(NA)
2017.........................	22,341	14,844	7,497	5.8	3.9	1.9	(NA)
2018.........................	21,498	14,329	7,169	5.7	3.8	1.9	17.4
2019.........................	20,927	13,834	7,093	5.6	3.7	1.9	20.1
2020.........................	19,578	12,866	6,712	5.4	3.6	1.9	23.8
2021.........................	19,928	12,797	7,131	5.4	3.5	2.0	32.9
2022.........................	20,577	13,158	7,419	5.6	3.6	2.0	22.3
BY RACE/ETHNICITY							
White, non-Hispanic:							
2017.........................	9,306	6,061	3,246	4.7	3.0	1.6	(NA)
2018.........................	9,059	5,873	3,186	4.6	3.0	1.6	14.9
2019.........................	8,603	5,589	3,014	4.5	2.9	1.6	17.9
2020.........................	8,115	5,290	2,825	4.4	2.9	1.5	19.1
2021.........................	8,236	5,251	2,984	4.4	2.8	1.6	26.6
2022.........................	8,324	5,318	3,006	4.5	2.9	1.6	19.0
Black, non-Hispanic:							
2017.........................	6,152	4,012	2,140	11.0	7.2	3.8	(NA)
2018.........................	5,933	3,897	2,037	10.8	7.1	3.7	37.3
2019.........................	5,821	3,754	2,067	10.6	6.9	3.8	44.0
2020.........................	5,501	3,472	2,028	10.4	6.6	3.8	55.3
2021.........................	5,463	3,291	2,172	10.6	6.4	4.2	69.9
2022.........................	5,573	3,296	2,277	10.9	6.4	4.5	49.5
Hispanic:							
2017.........................	4,583	3,198	1,383	5.1	3.6	1.5	(NA)
2018.........................	4,303	3,036	1,267	4.9	3.4	1.4	11.8
2019.........................	4,462	3,091	1,371	5.0	3.5	1.6	12.6
2020.........................	4,063	2,828	1,235	4.7	3.3	1.4	18.2
2021.........................	4,246	2,899	1,347	4.8	3.3	1.5	28.0
2022.........................	4,581	3,138	1,442	4.9	3.4	1.5	16.9

NA Not available. [1] Number of maternal deaths per 100,000 live births. A maternal death is defined by the World Health Organization as "the death of a woman while pregnant or within 42 days of termination of pregnancy, irrespective of the duration and the site of the pregnancy, from any cause related to or aggravated by the pregnancy or its management, but not from accidental or incidental causes."

Source: U.S. National Center for Health Statistics, *Infant Mortality in the United States, 2022: Data From the Period Linked Birth/Infant Death File*, July 2024; and *Maternal Mortality Rates in the United States, 2022*, May 2024. See also <www.cdc.gov/nchs/nvss/linked-birth.htm> and <www.cdc.gov/nchs/maternal-mortality/index.htm>.

Table 115. Infant Deaths and Mortality Rates by Race/Ethnicity and State: 2022

[Rates are for infant (under 1 year old) deaths per 1,000 live births in specified group. Based on race or Hispanic origin of mother. Race and Hispanic-origin categories are consistent with 1997 Office of Management and Budget (OMB) standards]

State	Total [1]		White alone, non-Hispanic		Black alone, non-Hispanic		Hispanic	
	Number	Rate	Number	Rate	Number	Rate	Number	Rate
United States........	**20,577**	**5.6**	**8,324**	**4.5**	**5,573**	**10.9**	**4,581**	**4.9**
Alabama.................	389	6.7	155	4.6	195	12.1	31	5.0
Alaska..................	62	6.6	26	5.6	(D)	(D)	(D)	(D)
Arizona.................	485	6.2	153	5.0	47	10.6	212	6.1
Arkansas...............	272	7.7	149	6.6	80	12.7	25	5.9
California..............	1,724	4.1	350	3.2	173	8.6	821	4.0
Colorado...............	283	4.5	119	3.4	29	9.7	96	5.1
Connecticut............	150	4.3	43	2.3	33	7.7	60	6.3
Delaware...............	81	7.5	25	5.0	38	13.3	(D)	(D)
District of Columbia....	44	5.5	(D)	(D)	28	8.0	(D)	(D)
Florida.................	1,342	6.0	426	4.6	530	11.1	333	4.5
Georgia................	893	7.1	270	5.0	445	10.6	123	5.8
Hawaii.................	90	5.8	(D)	(D)	(D)	(D)	21	7.8
Idaho..................	118	5.3	83	4.9	(D)	(D)	24	6.0
Illinois.................	718	5.6	265	3.9	239	12.4	146	4.9
Indiana................	570	7.2	325	5.9	138	13.6	71	7.1
Iowa...................	190	5.2	120	4.4	28	10.9	26	6.2
Kansas................	200	5.8	132	5.6	18	(B)	36	5.7
Kentucky..............	302	5.8	211	5.2	45	8.9	33	7.7
Louisiana..............	416	7.4	139	5.0	231	11.4	32	5.4
Maine.................	77	6.4	64	6.0	(D)	(D)	(D)	(D)
Maryland..............	415	6.0	87	3.2	206	10.1	80	5.6
Massachusetts........	228	3.3	94	2.5	46	6.5	61	4.0
Michigan..............	657	6.4	330	4.7	231	13.4	39	5.5
Minnesota.............	288	4.5	144	3.4	84	10.6	23	3.8
Mississippi............	316	9.1	126	7.1	168	12.0	10	(B)
Missouri...............	467	6.8	294	5.9	112	12.2	34	6.5
Montana...............	52	4.7	36	4.0	0	0.0	(D)	(D)
Nebraska..............	142	5.8	87	5.4	18	(B)	25	5.2
Nevada................	149	4.5	27	2.5	39	9.0	59	4.5
New Hampshire........	42	3.5	33	3.2	0	0.0	(D)	(D)
New Jersey............	367	3.6	113	2.4	108	8.4	104	3.5
New Mexico............	127	5.9	32	5.8	(D)	(D)	73	5.8
New York..............	885	4.3	333	3.2	239	8.6	221	4.4
North Carolina.........	825	6.8	325	5.2	318	12.1	116	5.1
North Dakota...........	42	4.4	29	4.2	(D)	(D)	(D)	(D)
Ohio...................	912	7.1	520	5.7	266	13.1	55	6.1
Oklahoma..............	333	6.9	164	6.3	48	13.0	43	5.1
Oregon................	177	4.5	90	3.9	(D)	(D)	47	5.5
Pennsylvania..........	741	5.7	381	4.5	164	9.9	102	5.6
Rhode Island..........	40	3.9	11	(B)	(D)	(D)	26	8.8
South Carolina.........	391	6.8	160	5.0	180	11.7	28	4.0
South Dakota..........	87	7.8	50	6.2	(D)	(D)	(D)	(D)
Tennessee.............	544	6.6	304	5.8	177	12.2	47	4.3
Texas.................	2,228	5.7	610	5.0	495	10.4	981	5.1
Utah..................	230	5.0	146	4.5	(D)	(D)	52	5.8
Vermont...............	26	4.9	20	4.2	(D)	(D)	(D)	(D)
Virginia................	594	6.2	234	4.6	225	12.1	86	5.4
Washington............	362	4.3	148	3.4	33	8.7	82	4.8
West Virginia..........	124	7.3	109	7.1	(D)	(D)	(D)	(D)
Wisconsin..............	348	5.8	199	4.7	66	11.6	49	7.0
Wyoming..............	34	5.6	23	5.0	0	0.0	(D)	(D)

B Does not meet standards of reliability or precision. D Suppressed to avoid disclosure. [1] Includes other races, not shown separately.

Source: U.S. National Center for Health Statistics, National Vital Statistics Reports (NVSR), CDC WONDER Online Database, "Linked Birth/Infant Death Records for 2017-2022 with ICD codes (expanded)," <wonder.cdc.gov>, accessed August 2024.

Table 116. Maternal Mortality—Number and Rate by Race, Hispanic Origin, and Age: 2020 to 2022

[Rates per 100,000 live births. Maternal mortality is deaths of women that occur while pregnant or within 42 days of being pregnant, from any cause related to or aggravated by the pregnancy or its management, but not from accidental or incidental causes. Data are shown for maternal causes using the International Classification of Diseases, Tenth Revision (ICD-10)]

Race/ethnicity and age	Live births (number)			Maternal deaths (number)			Maternal mortality rate		
	2020	2021	2022	2020	2021	2022	2020	2021	2022
Total [1].....................	**3,613,647**	**3,664,292**	**3,667,758**	**861**	**1,205**	**817**	**23.8**	**32.9**	**22.3**
Under 25 years old.......	825,403	797,334	784,299	114	163	113	13.8	20.4	14.4
25 to 39 years old........	2,658,445	2,731,223	2,738,802	607	854	578	22.8	31.3	21.1
40 years and over........	129,799	135,735	144,657	140	188	126	107.9	138.5	87.1
Black alone [2]...............	529,811	517,889	511,439	293	362	253	55.3	69.9	49.5
Under 25 years old.......	159,541	149,435	140,498	46	62	44	28.8	41.5	31.3
25 to 39 years old........	351,648	349,170	349,740	198	242	172	56.3	69.3	49.2
40 years and over........	18,622	19,284	21,201	49	58	37	263.1	300.8	174.5
White alone [2]...............	1,843,432	1,887,656	1,840,739	352	503	350	19.1	26.6	19.0
Under 25 years old.......	348,666	336,792	324,604	40	57	35	11.5	16.9	10.8
25 to 39 years old........	1,433,839	1,486,249	1,449,365	253	364	259	17.6	24.5	17.9
40 years and over........	60,927	64,615	66,770	59	82	56	96.8	126.9	83.9
Hispanic [3]..................	866,713	885,916	937,421	158	248	158	18.2	28.0	16.9
Under 25 years old.......	258,635	255,806	264,310	20	36	25	7.7	14.1	9.5
25 to 39 years old........	576,690	597,703	637,735	111	184	108	19.2	30.8	16.9
40 years and over........	31,388	32,407	35,376	27	28	25	86.0	86.4	70.7

[1] Includes other race/ethnicities not shown separately. [2] Non-Hispanic. [3] Persons of Hispanic origin may be of any race.

Source: U.S. National Center for Health Statistics, *Maternal Mortality Rates in the United States, 2022*, May 2024.

Table 117. Age-Adjusted Death Rates by Major Cause: 1960 to 2022

[Age-adjusted rates per 100,000 population. Age-adjusted death rates were prepared using the direct method, in which age specific death rates for a population of interest are applied to a standard population distributed by age. Age adjustment eliminates the differences in observed rates between points in time or among compared population groups that result from age differences in population composition. Beginning 1999, deaths classified according to International Classification of Diseases, Tenth Revision (ICD-10); for earlier years, causes of death were classified according to the revisions then in use. Changes in classification of causes of death due to these revisions may result in discontinuities in cause-of-death trends. See Appendix III]

Year	Diseases of the heart	Malignant neoplasms (cancer)	Accidents [1]	Coronavirus disease 2019, COVID-19	Cerebrovascular diseases	Chronic lower respiratory diseases	Alzheimer's disease	Diabetes mellitus	Intentional self-harm (suicide)	Nephritis, nephrotic syndrome and nephrosis
1960	559.0	193.9	63.1	(X)	177.9	12.5	(NA)	22.5	12.5	10.6
1970	492.7	198.6	62.2	(X)	147.7	21.3	(NA)	24.3	13.1	5.5
1980	412.1	207.9	46.4	(X)	96.4	28.3	(NA)	18.1	12.2	9.1
1990	321.8	216.0	36.3	(X)	65.3	37.2	6.3	20.7	12.5	9.3
1995	293.4	209.9	34.4	(X)	63.1	40.1	8.4	23.2	11.8	9.5
2000	257.6	199.6	34.9	(X)	60.9	44.2	18.1	25.0	10.4	13.5
2001	249.5	196.5	35.7	(X)	58.4	43.9	19.3	25.4	10.7	14.1
2002	244.6	194.3	37.1	(X)	57.2	43.9	20.8	25.6	10.9	14.4
2003	236.3	190.9	37.6	(X)	54.6	43.7	22.1	25.5	10.8	14.7
2004	221.6	186.8	38.1	(X)	51.2	41.6	22.6	24.7	11.0	14.5
2005	216.8	185.1	39.5	(X)	48.0	43.9	24.0	24.9	10.9	14.7
2006	205.5	181.8	40.2	(X)	44.8	41.0	23.7	23.6	11.0	14.8
2007	196.1	179.3	40.4	(X)	43.5	41.4	23.8	22.8	11.3	14.9
2008	192.1	176.4	39.2	(X)	42.1	44.7	25.8	22.0	11.6	15.1
2009	182.8	173.5	37.5	(X)	39.6	42.7	24.2	21.0	11.8	15.1
2010	179.1	172.8	38.0	(X)	39.1	42.2	25.1	20.8	12.1	15.3
2011	173.7	169.0	39.1	(X)	37.9	42.5	24.7	21.6	12.3	13.4
2012	170.5	166.5	39.1	(X)	36.9	41.5	23.8	21.2	12.6	13.1
2013	169.8	163.2	39.4	(X)	36.2	42.1	23.5	21.2	12.6	13.2
2014	167.0	161.2	40.5	(X)	36.5	40.5	25.4	20.9	13.0	13.2
2015	168.5	158.5	43.2	(X)	37.6	41.6	29.4	21.3	13.3	13.4
2016	165.5	155.8	47.4	(X)	37.3	40.6	30.3	21.0	13.5	13.1
2017	165.0	152.5	49.4	(X)	37.6	40.9	31.0	21.5	14.0	13.0
2018	163.6	149.1	48.0	(X)	37.1	39.7	30.5	21.4	14.2	12.9
2019	161.5	146.2	49.3	(X)	37.0	38.2	29.8	21.6	13.9	12.7
2020	168.2	144.1	57.6	85.0	38.8	36.4	32.4	24.8	13.5	12.7
2021	173.8	146.6	64.7	104.1	41.1	34.7	31.0	25.4	14.1	13.6
2022	167.2	142.3	64.0	44.5	39.5	34.3	28.9	24.1	14.2	13.8

NA Not available. X Not applicable. [1] Unintentional injuries.

Source: U.S. National Center for Health Statistics, National Vital Statistics Reports (NVSR), *Deaths: Final Data*, annual report; and CDC WONDER Online Database, "Multiple Cause of Death, 1999-2020," and "Multiple Cause of Death, 2018-2022," <wonder.cdc.gov>, accessed June 2024. See also <www.cdc.gov/nchs/nvss/deaths.htm>.

Table 118. Deaths by Leading Cause, Race, and Hispanic Origin: 2022

[Rank based on number of deaths. Data shown here are consistent with 1997 Office of Management and Budget (OMB) standards for reporting race and Hispanic origin. Race and Hispanic origin are reported separately on death certificates. Persons of Hispanic origin may be any race. Data for racial and ethnic groups other than non-Hispanic White and non-Hispanic Black should be interpreted with caution because of misreporting of Hispanic origin and race on the death certificate. Cause of death is based on International Classification of Diseases, Tenth Revision (ICD-10). See Appendix III]

Cause of death	White, Non-Hispanic Rank	White, Non-Hispanic Deaths	Black, Non-Hispanic Rank	Black, Non-Hispanic Deaths	American Indian or Alaska Native, Non-Hispanic Rank	American Indian or Alaska Native, Non-Hispanic Deaths	Asian, Non-Hispanic Rank	Asian, Non-Hispanic Deaths	Hispanic Rank	Hispanic Deaths
All causes	(X)	2,448,093	(X)	411,934	(X)	23,613	(X)	89,591	(X)	275,684
Diseases of heart	1	537,969	1	88,964	1	3,753	2	18,091	1	47,715
Malignant neoplasms (cancer)	2	462,834	2	70,698	3	3,137	1	19,864	2	47,021
Accidents (unintended injuries)	3	152,647	3	34,644	2	3,146	5	4,046	3	28,699
Coronavirus disease 2019 (COVID-19)	4	135,484	5	21,896	4	1,690	4	5,450	4	20,499
Chronic lower respiratory diseases	5	127,003	8	10,990	7	761	10	1,785	9	5,615
Cerebrovascular diseases	6	119,929	4	22,656	8	747	3	6,482	5	14,224
Alzheimer's disease	7	96,899	10	9,284	13	337	7	3,448	7	9,552
Diabetes mellitus	8	64,701	6	17,954	6	1,219	6	3,709	6	12,508
Nephritis, nephrotic syndrome and nephrosis	9	38,813	9	10,921	10	434	8	1,985	10	5,299
Chronic liver disease and cirrhosis	10	38,779	14	4,017	5	1,579	15	910	8	8,933
Intentional self-harm (suicide)	11	37,481	15	3,826	9	650	12	1,459	11	5,122
Influenza and pneumonia	12	34,951	13	5,335	11	392	11	1,766	13	4,166
Parkinson disease	13	33,969	20	1,919	17	113	13	1,232	16	2,508
Septicemia	14	30,197	12	7,134	14	316	14	968	15	3,259
Essential hypertension and hypertensive renal disease	15	29,296	11	7,673	15	219	9	1,903	14	3,806
Assault (homicide)	21	5,980	7	13,236	12	386	21	310	12	4,482

X Not applicable.

Source: U.S. National Center for Health Statistics, National Vital Statistics Reports (NVSR), *Deaths: Leading Causes*, annual; and CDC WONDER Online database, "Multiple Cause of Death, 2018-2022," <wonder.cdc.gov>, accessed July 2024. See also <www.cdc.gov/nchs/nvss/deaths.htm>.

ProQuest Statistical Abstract of the United States: 2025

Table 119. Deaths and Death Rates by Selected Causes: 2021 and 2022

[Rates per 100,000 population. Figures are weighted data rounded to the nearest individual, so categories may not add to total or subtotal. Excludes deaths of nonresidents of the United States. Deaths are classified according to the International Classification of Diseases, Tenth Revision (ICD-10). See also Appendix III]

Cause of death	2021			2022		
	Number	Rate	Age-adjusted rate [1]	Number	Rate	Age-adjusted rate [1]
All causes [2]................	**3,464,231**	**1,043.8**	**879.7**	**3,279,857**	**984.1**	**798.8**
Major cardiovascular diseases [2]................	925,923	279.0	231.8	936,436	281.0	223.0
Diseases of heart................	695,547	209.6	173.8	702,880	210.9	167.2
Acute rheumatic fever and chronic rheumatic heart disease................	3,907	1.2	1.0	4,294	1.3	1.0
Hypertensive heart disease................	67,774	20.4	17.1	72,070	21.6	17.3
Hypertensive heart and renal disease................	13,918	4.2	3.5	16,091	4.8	3.9
Ischemic heart disease................	375,476	113.1	92.8	371,506	111.5	87.6
Acute myocardial infarction................	109,097	32.9	26.8	103,905	31.2	24.5
Other heart diseases................	234,472	70.6	59.4	238,919	71.7	57.4
Heart failure................	85,037	25.6	21.6	87,941	26.4	21.0
Essential (primary) hypertension and hypertensive renal disease................	42,816	12.9	10.7	43,293	13.0	10.3
Cerebrovascular diseases................	162,890	49.1	41.1	165,393	49.6	39.5
Atherosclerosis................	4,214	1.3	1.1	3,936	1.2	0.9
Malignant neoplasms (cancer) [2]................	605,213	182.4	146.6	608,371	182.5	142.3
Malignant neoplasms of lip, oral cavity, and pharynx................	11,394	3.4	2.7	11,884	3.6	2.7
Malignant neoplasms of esophagus................	15,743	4.7	3.7	16,016	4.8	3.7
Malignant neoplasms of stomach................	10,894	3.3	2.7	10,853	3.3	2.6
Malignant neoplasms of colon, rectum and anus................	54,121	16.3	13.4	54,268	16.3	13.0
Malignant neoplasms of liver and intrahepatic bile ducts................	28,719	8.7	6.7	28,937	8.7	6.6
Malignant neoplasms of pancreas................	47,906	14.4	11.4	48,323	14.5	11.1
Malignant neoplasms of trachea, bronchus and lung................	134,592	40.6	31.7	131,982	39.6	30.1
Malignant melanoma of skin................	8,224	2.5	2.0	8,243	2.5	2.0
Malignant neoplasm of breast................	42,810	12.9	10.6	42,672	12.8	10.3
Malignant neoplasm of ovary................	13,430	4.0	3.3	13,214	4.0	3.1
Malignant neoplasm of prostate................	32,563	9.8	8.0	33,363	10.0	7.7
Malignant neoplasms of kidney and renal pelvis................	14,163	4.3	3.4	14,488	4.3	3.4
Malignant neoplasms of bladder................	16,840	5.1	4.1	17,334	5.2	4.1
Malignant neoplasms of meninges, brain and other parts of central nervous system................	17,857	5.4	4.4	17,937	5.4	4.3
Malignant neoplasms of lymphoid, hematopoietic and related tissue [2]................	57,375	17.3	14.2	56,959	17.1	13.6
Non-Hodgkin's lymphoma................	20,020	6.0	5.0	19,794	5.9	4.7
Leukemia................	23,271	7.0	5.8	23,324	7.0	5.6
Accidents (unintentional injuries)................	224,935	67.8	64.7	227,039	68.1	64.0
Transport accidents [2]................	49,845	15.0	14.6	49,178	14.8	14.2
Motor vehicle accidents................	46,980	14.2	13.8	46,027	13.8	13.3
Nontransport accidents [2]................	175,090	52.8	50.1	177,861	53.4	49.8
Falls................	44,686	13.5	11.4	46,630	14.0	11.2
Accidental discharge of firearms................	549	0.2	0.2	463	0.1	0.2
Accidental drowning and submersion................	4,337	1.3	1.3	4,168	1.3	1.2
Accidental exposure to smoke, fire and flames................	3,389	1.0	0.9	3,478	1.0	0.9
Accidental poisoning and exposure to noxious substances................	102,001	30.7	31.0	102,958	30.9	31.1
Chronic lower respiratory diseases [2]................	142,342	42.9	34.7	147,382	44.2	34.3
Bronchitis, chronic and unspecified................	335	0.1	0.1	358	0.1	0.1
Emphysema................	7,336	2.2	1.8	7,905	2.4	1.8
Asthma................	3,517	1.1	1.0	3,602	1.1	1.0
Pneumonitis due to solids and liquids................	19,969	6.0	5.0	20,052	6.0	4.8
Coronavirus disease 2019 (COVID-19)................	416,893	125.6	104.1	186,552	56.0	44.5
Influenza and pneumonia [2]................	41,917	12.6	10.5	47,052	14.1	11.3
Influenza................	608	0.2	0.1	5,944	1.8	1.5
Pneumonia................	41,309	12.4	10.4	41,108	12.3	9.8
Septicemia (blood poisoning)................	41,281	12.4	10.2	42,261	12.7	10.1
Viral hepatitis................	3,589	1.1	0.8	3,107	0.9	0.7
Human immunodeficiency virus (HIV) disease................	4,977	1.5	1.3	4,941	1.5	1.3
Anemias................	5,987	1.8	1.5	6,021	1.8	1.5
Diabetes mellitus................	103,294	31.1	25.4	101,209	30.4	24.1
Nutritional deficiencies................	17,505	5.3	4.5	21,020	6.3	5.0
Malnutrition................	17,106	5.2	4.4	20,552	6.2	4.9
Parkinson's disease................	38,536	11.6	9.8	39,915	12.0	9.5
Alzheimer's disease................	119,399	36.0	31.0	120,122	36.0	28.9
Chronic liver disease and cirrhosis................	56,585	17.0	14.5	54,803	16.4	13.8
Alcoholic liver disease................	33,098	10.0	8.7	30,910	9.3	8.1
Nephritis, nephrotic syndrome, and nephrosis [2]................	54,358	16.4	13.6	57,937	17.4	13.8
Renal failure................	53,261	16.0	13.3	56,756	17.0	13.5
Intentional self-harm (suicide)................	48,183	14.5	14.1	49,476	14.8	14.2
Intentional self-harm (suicide) by discharge of firearms................	26,328	7.9	7.5	27,032	8.1	7.6
Assault (homicide)................	26,031	7.8	8.2	24,849	7.5	7.7
Assault (homicide) by discharge of firearms................	20,958	6.3	6.7	19,651	5.9	6.2
Events of undetermined intent................	6,259	1.9	1.9	5,604	1.7	1.7
Complications of medical and surgical care................	6,051	1.8	1.5	3,726	1.1	0.9
Enterocolitis due to Clostridium difficile [3]................	4,105	1.2	1.0	4,231	1.3	1.0
Drug-induced deaths [3]................	111,219	33.5	33.6	112,109	33.6	33.8
Alcohol-induced deaths [3]................	54,258	16.3	14.4	51,191	15.4	13.5
Injury by firearms [3]................	48,830	14.7	14.6	48,204	14.5	14.2

[1] See text, this section. [2] Includes other causes, not shown separately. [3] Also included in selected other categories.

Source: U.S. National Center for Health Statistics, National Vital Statistics Reports, *Deaths: Final Data*, annual report; and CDC WONDER Online database, "Multiple Cause of Death, 2018-2022," <wonder.cdc.gov>, accessed June 2024. See also <www.cdc.gov/nchs/nvss/deaths.htm>.

Table 120. Deaths by Age and Selected Cause: 2022

[Deaths are classified according to the International Classification of Diseases, Tenth Revision (ICD-10). See Appendix III]

Cause of death	All ages[1]	Under 1 year	1 to 4 years	5 to 14 years	15 to 24 years	25 to 34 years	35 to 44 years	45 to 54 years	55 to 64 years	65 to 74 years	75 to 84 years	85 years and over
All causes[2]	3,279,857	20,553	4,156	6,239	35,232	74,369	111,605	183,284	417,541	668,581	824,903	933,291
Septicemia	42,261	123	60	59	113	447	1,024	2,488	6,167	10,623	11,723	9,433
Human immunodeficiency virus (HIV) disease	4,941	(D)	(D)	0	43	481	777	1,002	1,407	902	271	57
Malignant neoplasms (cancer)[2]	608,371	40	266	835	1,421	3,641	11,177	33,363	105,133	178,860	171,573	102,057
Malignant neoplasm of esophagus	16,016	0	0	(D)	(D)	33	226	1,040	3,456	5,524	4,099	1,629
Malignant neoplasms of colon, rectum, and anus	54,268	0	0	(D)	35	349	1,647	5,072	10,491	13,981	12,751	9,941
Malignant neoplasms of liver and intrahepatic bile ducts	28,937	(D)	(D)	16	26	122	373	1,354	6,098	10,692	7,237	3,006
Malignant neoplasms of pancreas	48,323	(D)	(D)	(D)	(D)	70	490	2,403	8,783	15,445	14,239	6,886
Malignant neoplasms of trachea, bronchus, and lung	131,982	0	0	(D)	12	118	771	4,484	24,394	44,583	40,755	16,863
Malignant neoplasm of breast	42,672	0	0	0	(D)	383	1,856	4,083	8,165	10,747	9,864	7,567
Malignant neoplasm of ovary	13,214	0	0	(D)	33	104	287	1,061	2,717	3,835	3,549	1,626
Malignant neoplasm of prostate	33,363	0	0	0	(D)	(D)	21	357	2,777	8,385	11,604	10,215
Malignant neoplasms of kidney and renal pelvis	14,488	(D)	12	29	22	57	198	919	2,633	4,214	4,012	2,390
Malignant neoplasm of bladder	17,334	0	0	(D)	(D)	20	100	330	1,640	3,910	5,870	5,462
Malignant neoplasms of meninges, brain and other parts of central nervous system	17,937	(D)	56	302	243	446	823	1,692	3,881	5,365	3,708	1,412
Malignant neoplasms of lymphoid, hematopoietic and related tissue[2]	56,959	14	98	206	383	594	996	2,180	6,551	14,392	18,901	12,644
Non-Hodgkin's lymphoma	19,794	0	(D)	20	55	150	320	776	2,335	5,058	6,670	4,407
Leukemia	23,324	14	95	184	313	384	526	873	2,437	5,620	7,561	5,317
Diabetes mellitus	101,209	(D)	(D)	48	324	1,188	2,879	7,364	17,410	26,963	26,388	18,634
Parkinson's disease	39,915	0	0	0	0	(D)	12	86	879	6,424	17,886	14,621
Alzheimer's disease	120,122	0	0	0	0	(D)	(D)	111	1,480	9,000	36,133	73,387
Major cardiovascular diseases[2]	936,436	340	156	335	1,078	4,765	15,656	40,956	107,984	182,806	242,054	340,276
Diseases of heart[2]	702,880	241	103	218	848	3,789	12,258	32,298	85,733	140,475	178,108	248,782
Hypertensive heart disease	72,070	0	(D)	(D)	58	539	2,146	4,701	10,137	13,199	14,820	26,465
Ischemic heart diseases	371,506	11	(D)	(D)	102	990	4,956	17,223	50,365	83,121	97,826	116,879
Acute myocardial infarction	103,905	(D)	0	(D)	47	394	1,877	6,109	16,744	25,801	27,512	25,409
Heart failure	87,941	13	0	(D)	43	247	714	1,962	5,820	12,599	22,750	43,779
Essential (primary) hypertension and hypertensive renal disease[2]	43,293	87	49	100	24	175	697	1,832	4,982	8,315	10,790	16,472
Cerebrovascular diseases	165,393	154	129	131	157	599	2,150	5,563	14,173	28,384	46,421	67,708
Influenza and pneumonia	47,052	154	53	76	168	490	985	1,905	5,067	9,408	12,774	15,840
Influenza	5,944	12	76	55	61	112	217	310	771	1,147	1,475	1,710
Pneumonia	41,108	142	39	106	107	378	768	1,595	4,296	8,261	11,299	14,130
Chronic lower respiratory diseases[2]	147,382	10	(D)	(D)	197	368	732	2,987	17,138	38,712	49,746	37,345
Pneumonitis due to solids and liquids[2]	20,052	(D)	(D)	(D)	49	132	278	599	1,763	3,647	5,892	7,672
Chronic liver disease and cirrhosis[2]	54,803	0	(D)	(D)	58	1,786	5,501	9,401	16,484	13,178	6,428	1,959
Alcoholic liver disease	30,910	(D)	0	0	46	1,508	4,335	6,688	10,362	6,017	1,683	270
Nephritis, nephrotic syndrome, and nephrosis[2]	57,937	38	(D)	11	64	358	1,029	2,679	6,668	12,948	17,003	17,135
Renal failure	56,756	36	(D)	(D)	57	340	995	2,608	6,535	12,718	16,661	16,798
Accidents (unintentional injuries)[2]	227,039	1,354	1,288	1,652	14,669	33,058	36,972	31,394	34,017	23,150	22,392	27,074
Transport accidents[2]	49,178	80	386	945	7,215	8,797	7,586	6,545	7,273	5,482	3,435	1,431
Motor vehicle accidents	46,027	79	366	900	6,997	8,406	7,084	6,080	6,567	4,949	3,219	1,377
Nontransport accidents[2]	177,861	1,274	902	707	7,454	24,261	29,386	24,849	26,744	17,668	18,957	25,643
Falls	46,630	(D)	21	21	149	383	682	1,200	3,247	6,698	13,396	20,825
Accidental poisoning and exposure to noxious substances[2]	102,958	28	75	99	6,205	22,295	26,767	21,364	19,334	5,924	697	159
Intentional self-harm (suicide)[2]	49,476	0	0	502	6,040	8,663	8,185	7,781	7,864	5,396	3,549	1,493
Assault (homicide)[2]	24,849	252	343	546	6,262	6,712	4,765	2,740	1,824	877	399	127
Assault (homicide) by discharge of firearms	19,651	16	77	395	5,814	5,836	3,861	1,947	1,080	422	163	40
Coronavirus disease 2019 (COVID-19)	186,552	141	101	131	447	1,640	3,841	9,678	24,252	42,062	51,188	53,070

D Data representing fewer than 10 persons are suppressed due to confidentiality restraints. [1] Includes persons with age not stated, not shown separately. [2] Includes other causes, not shown separately.

Source: U.S. National Center for Health Statistics, National Vital Statistics Reports (NVSR), Deaths: Final Data, annual report; and CDC WONDER Online Database, "Multiple Cause of Death, 2018-2022," <wonder.cdc.gov>, accessed June 2024. See also <www.cdc.gov/nchs/nvss/deaths.htm>.

Table 121. Deaths and Death Rates by Leading Cause and Age: 2022

[Rates per 100,000 population in specified group. Data are based on the International Classification of Diseases, Tenth Revision (ICD-10)]

Age and cause of death	Number	Rate	Age and cause of death	Number	Rate
ALL AGES [1]			**25 TO 34 YEARS (continued)**		
All causes	**3,279,857**	**984.1**	Malignant neoplasms (cancer)	3,641	8.0
Diseases of heart	702,880	210.9	Chronic liver disease and cirrhosis	1,786	3.9
Malignant neoplasms (cancer)	608,371	182.5	COVID-19	1,640	3.6
Accidents (unintentional injuries)	227,039	68.1	Diabetes mellitus	1,188	2.6
Coronavirus disease 2019 (COVID-19)	186,552	56.0	Cerebrovascular diseases	599	1.3
Cerebrovascular diseases	165,393	49.6	Pregnancy, childbirth and the puerperium	591	1.3
Chronic lower respiratory diseases	147,382	44.2	**35 TO 44 YEARS**		
Alzheimer's disease	120,122	36.0	All causes	**111,605**	**255.4**
Diabetes mellitus	101,209	30.4	Accidents (unintentional injuries)	36,972	84.6
Nephritis, nephrotic syndrome and nephrosis	57,937	17.4	Diseases of heart	12,258	28.1
Chronic liver disease and cirrhosis	54,803	16.4	Malignant neoplasms (cancer)	11,177	25.6
1 TO 4 YEARS			Intentional self-harm (suicide)	8,185	18.7
All causes	**4,156**	**28.0**	Chronic liver disease and cirrhosis	5,501	12.6
Accidents (unintentional injuries)	1,288	8.7	Assault (homicide)	4,765	10.9
Congenital malformations [2]	441	3.0	COVID-19	3,841	8.8
Assault (homicide)	343	2.3	Diabetes mellitus	2,879	6.6
Malignant neoplasms (cancer)	266	1.8	Cerebrovascular diseases	2,150	4.9
Influenza and pneumonia	129	0.9	Nephritis, nephrotic syndrome and nephrosis	1,029	2.4
Diseases of heart	103	0.7	**45 TO 54 YEARS**		
COVID-19	101	0.7	All causes	**183,284**	**453.3**
Certain conditions originating in			Malignant neoplasms (cancer)	33,363	82.5
the perinatal period	62	0.4	Diseases of heart	32,298	79.9
Septicemia	60	0.4	Accidents (unintentional injuries)	31,394	77.6
Cerebrovascular diseases	49	0.3	COVID-19	9,678	23.9
5 TO 9 YEARS			Chronic liver disease and cirrhosis	9,401	23.3
All causes	**2,567**	**12.8**	Intentional self-harm (suicide)	7,781	19.2
Accidents (unintentional injuries)	726	3.6	Diabetes mellitus	7,364	18.2
Malignant neoplasms (cancer)	393	2.0	Cerebrovascular diseases	5,563	13.8
Congenital malformations [2]	241	1.2	Chronic lower respiratory diseases	2,987	7.4
Assault (homicide)	180	0.9	Assault (homicide)	2,740	6.8
Influenza and pneumonia	77	0.4	**55 TO 64 YEARS**		
Diseases of heart	73	0.4	All causes	**417,541**	**992.1**
COVID-19	62	0.3	Malignant neoplasms (cancer)	105,133	249.8
Chronic lower respiratory diseases	48	0.2	Diseases of heart	85,733	203.7
Cerebrovascular diseases	45	0.2	Accidents (unintentional injuries)	34,017	80.8
Septicemia	33	0.2	COVID-19	24,252	57.6
			Diabetes mellitus	17,410	41.4
10 TO 14 YEARS			Chronic lower respiratory diseases	17,138	40.7
All causes	**3,672**	**17.6**	Chronic liver disease and cirrhosis	16,484	39.2
Accidents (unintentional injuries)	926	4.4	Cerebrovascular diseases	14,173	33.7
Intentional self-harm (suicide)	493	2.4	Intentional self-harm (suicide)	7,864	18.7
Malignant neoplasms (cancer)	442	2.1	Nephritis, nephrotic syndrome and nephrosis	6,668	15.8
Assault (homicide)	366	1.8	**65 to 74 YEARS**		
Congenital malformations [2]	205	1.0	All causes	**668,581**	**1,978.7**
Diseases of heart	145	0.7	Malignant neoplasms (cancer)	178,860	529.4
COVID-19	69	0.3	Diseases of heart	140,475	415.7
Chronic lower respiratory diseases	58	0.3	COVID-19	42,062	124.5
Cerebrovascular diseases	55	0.3	Chronic lower respiratory diseases	38,712	114.6
Influenza and pneumonia	54	0.3	Cerebrovascular diseases	28,384	84.0
15 TO 19 YEARS			Diabetes mellitus	26,963	79.8
All causes	**12,745**	**58.9**	Accidents (unintentional injuries)	23,150	68.5
Accidents (unintentional injuries)	4,762	22.0	Chronic liver disease and cirrhosis	13,178	39.0
Assault (homicide)	2,781	12.9	Nephritis, nephrotic syndrome and nephrosis	12,948	38.3
Intentional self-harm (suicide)	2,164	10.0	Septicemia	10,623	31.4
Malignant neoplasms (cancer)	631	2.9	**75 TO 84 YEARS**		
Diseases of heart	286	1.3	All causes	**824,903**	**4,708.2**
Congenital malformations [2]	216	1.0	Diseases of heart	178,108	1,016.6
COVID-19	161	0.7	Malignant neoplasms (cancer)	171,573	979.3
Diabetes mellitus	75	0.3	COVID-19	51,188	292.2
Chronic lower respiratory diseases	72	0.3	Chronic lower respiratory diseases	49,746	283.9
Influenza and pneumonia	63	0.3	Cerebrovascular diseases	46,421	265.0
20 TO 24 YEARS			Alzheimer's disease	36,133	206.2
All causes	**22,487**	**99.0**	Diabetes mellitus	26,388	150.6
Accidents (unintentional injuries)	9,907	43.6	Accidents (unintentional injuries)	22,392	127.8
Intentional self-harm (suicide)	3,876	17.1	Parkinson's disease	17,886	102.1
Assault (homicide)	3,481	15.3	Nephritis, nephrotic syndrome and nephrosis	17,003	97.0
Malignant neoplasms (cancer)	790	3.5	**85 YEARS AND OVER**		
Diseases of heart	562	2.5	All causes	**933,291**	**14,389.6**
COVID-19	286	1.3	Diseases of heart	248,782	3,835.8
Diabetes mellitus	249	1.1	Malignant neoplasms (cancer)	102,057	1,573.5
Congenital malformations [2]	196	0.9	Alzheimer's disease	73,387	1,131.5
Pregnancy, childbirth and the puerperium	132	0.6	Cerebrovascular diseases	67,708	1,043.9
Chronic lower respiratory diseases	125	0.6	COVID-19	53,070	818.2
25 TO 34 YEARS			Chronic lower respiratory diseases	37,345	575.8
All causes	**74,369**	**163.4**	Accidents (unintentional injuries)	27,074	417.4
Accidents (unintentional injuries)	33,058	72.7	Diabetes mellitus	18,634	287.3
Intentional self-harm (suicide)	8,663	19.0	Nephritis, nephrotic syndrome and nephrosis	17,135	264.2
Assault (homicide)	6,712	14.8	Essential hypertension and		
Diseases of heart	3,789	8.3	hypertensive renal disease	16,472	254.0

[1] Includes deaths under 1 year of age and deaths with age not stated, not shown separately. [2] Congenital malformations, deformations and chromosomal abnormalities.

Source: U.S. National Center for Health Statistics, *Deaths: Leading Causes*, annual; and CDC WONDER Online database, "Multiple Cause of Death, 2018-2022," <wonder.cdc.gov>, accessed July 2024. See also <www.cdc.gov/nchs/nvss/deaths.htm>.

Table 122. Age-Adjusted Death Rates for Major Causes of Death by State: 2022

[Age-adjusted rates per 100,000 resident population as of July 1. Excludes nonresidents of the United States. Causes of death are classified according to the International Classification of Diseases, Tenth Revision (ICD-10)]

State	All causes of death	Diseases of heart	Malignant neoplasms (cancer)	Accidents Total	Accidents Motor vehicle accidents	Coronavirus disease 2019 (COVID-19)	Cerebrovascular diseases	Chronic lower respiratory disease	Alzheimer's disease	Diabetes mellitus	Intentional self-harm (suicide)
U.S........	798.8	167.2	142.3	64.0	13.3	44.5	39.5	34.3	28.9	24.1	14.2
AL.........	989.1	234.2	154.4	68.3	20.0	54.6	51.1	46.9	42.2	25.4	16.3
AK.........	821.3	145.7	145.3	77.6	15.6	38.3	35.1	30.2	33.1	25.6	27.6
AZ.........	784.6	148.5	132.9	75.6	17.8	47.4	34.5	35.1	28.4	25.1	20.6
AR.........	999.7	224.1	168.1	64.9	20.9	54.4	46.0	59.7	41.0	36.0	18.0
CA.........	686.0	142.4	129.8	51.0	12.4	37.8	39.8	25.8	37.5	25.0	10.4
CO.........	736.3	131.4	124.5	69.7	13.7	34.8	33.8	38.0	31.4	18.5	21.1
CT.........	716.8	137.8	133.6	66.5	10.2	40.8	30.1	24.3	21.5	15.2	10.6
DE.........	829.1	156.8	160.7	83.8	14.9	43.7	56.9	32.0	31.5	25.1	11.4
DC.........	789.6	182.6	141.8	90.9	8.4	33.1	42.1	17.3	10.2	18.2	6.1
FL.........	714.7	140.9	135.8	68.9	15.9	34.4	45.1	30.6	17.0	22.3	14.1
GA.........	871.6	183.9	147.0	58.9	17.1	47.1	44.0	39.6	39.3	21.9	14.6
HI.........	615.9	128.4	122.4	40.9	7.3	20.3	39.5	15.6	22.0	17.2	16.6
ID.........	771.4	156.3	133.7	57.9	13.6	36.3	34.4	41.6	39.5	20.5	22.2
IL.........	784.9	166.6	145.1	55.9	10.4	45.5	41.4	32.2	25.6	21.8	11.7
IN.........	923.4	185.0	162.5	71.6	14.5	54.9	41.9	53.0	27.8	29.8	16.4
IA.........	798.0	176.8	146.1	49.8	11.3	39.7	32.0	39.0	29.4	24.0	18.5
KS.........	873.2	173.2	148.8	63.8	15.3	56.1	35.8	44.4	25.2	26.2	20.5
KY.........	1,043.8	208.6	177.3	91.5	16.7	72.9	42.9	55.8	28.4	29.4	18.0
LA.........	974.7	224.0	160.3	93.9	20.5	43.1	50.2	38.8	40.0	29.9	15.6
ME.........	844.3	167.1	154.3	93.5	13.7	37.2	29.4	40.0	24.9	28.2	17.7
MD........	746.5	155.8	136.8	48.8	9.8	40.2	43.8	24.5	15.5	23.1	9.5
MA.........	693.5	132.3	132.2	61.6	6.3	34.0	25.6	25.0	17.0	16.1	8.3
MI.........	855.4	206.3	154.4	59.2	11.7	45.1	44.2	38.5	32.4	25.6	14.7
MN.........	710.3	124.1	139.0	61.1	9.3	31.3	31.8	29.1	31.6	20.5	14.8
MS.........	1,073.3	248.0	178.4	78.4	25.8	63.8	54.2	59.5	48.5	34.7	14.0
MO.........	916.7	199.8	159.6	75.6	17.3	53.8	39.1	45.9	32.5	23.5	19.1
MT.........	795.9	165.9	142.2	65.4	19.8	33.6	26.5	39.6	22.5	22.0	28.7
NE.........	773.5	154.3	142.2	46.8	14.2	35.5	35.1	37.4	30.0	22.1	15.6
NV.........	842.1	196.8	138.9	62.8	13.4	58.3	40.0	42.8	25.3	23.4	21.0
NH.........	749.7	147.5	141.4	66.7	9.8	30.3	30.3	36.3	23.9	22.3	16.6
NJ.........	683.6	152.8	125.3	49.7	7.3	40.6	30.0	21.8	18.8	17.3	7.7
NM.........	901.4	156.8	127.5	98.4	23.4	61.8	38.1	38.6	26.6	31.2	24.7
NY.........	664.5	159.2	122.4	50.2	6.6	41.4	24.5	22.6	11.7	18.2	8.5
NC.........	877.1	165.8	149.0	80.0	16.7	47.4	47.7	38.7	33.9	28.8	14.4
ND.........	739.2	155.0	128.4	54.0	13.5	34.2	32.8	30.7	31.6	25.1	22.5
OH.........	917.2	193.9	155.5	78.5	11.5	60.1	46.5	42.6	32.3	27.6	15.0
OK.........	1,025.6	257.1	171.6	81.4	18.9	71.9	39.5	62.3	34.7	33.8	21.4
OR.........	811.3	145.4	147.0	67.9	13.7	34.1	47.1	34.4	37.0	25.4	19.3
PA.........	818.2	173.4	148.7	70.4	9.8	47.5	36.6	30.8	20.9	22.6	14.2
RI.........	714.0	152.6	136.5	67.6	6.4	35.0	29.2	27.4	29.8	18.9	10.6
SC.........	918.8	177.7	153.2	88.2	21.4	51.0	45.6	39.7	37.4	25.8	15.4
SD.........	801.0	158.2	144.7	60.7	18.3	39.4	33.1	35.3	36.5	29.4	21.6
TN.........	1,009.2	218.3	162.3	98.4	18.5	62.0	46.4	47.0	36.0	31.2	16.7
TX.........	816.9	172.3	140.8	51.1	15.1	49.0	42.3	34.0	38.8	25.6	14.4
UT.........	755.0	159.4	116.1	50.2	9.7	33.3	34.6	30.3	39.8	25.4	22.1
VT.........	757.6	165.1	150.2	81.4	11.5	25.2	27.1	29.6	34.5	18.9	18.0
VA.........	794.1	159.2	144.8	57.1	11.8	44.4	41.2	29.6	24.4	26.9	13.3
WA.........	757.9	142.7	140.9	66.2	10.4	31.6	36.7	30.7	41.6	23.3	14.9
WV.........	1,115.6	209.5	176.3	121.6	15.1	71.5	43.4	61.9	29.5	41.1	18.3
WI.........	791.5	166.6	145.3	74.9	10.5	36.7	35.3	33.7	30.3	19.1	15.1
WY.........	826.8	157.1	143.0	65.3	18.7	40.0	29.8	45.4	34.7	24.5	25.6

Source: U.S. National Center for Health Statistics, National Vital Statistics Reports (NVSR), *Deaths: Final Data*, annual; and CDC WONDER Online database, "Multiple Cause of Death, 2018-2022," <wonder.cdc.gov>, accessed July 2024.

Table 123. Death Rates For Heart Disease by Selected Characteristics: 1980 to 2022

[Rates per 100,000 population. Beginning 2018, all 50 states and the District of Columbia report race and Hispanic origin data according to 1997 Office of Management and Budget (OMB) standards, which allows for reporting multiple races (previous standards permitted only single race reporting). To maintain comparability of data during the transition to the new standards, 2018-2020 multiple-race data were bridged to single-race categories. Excludes deaths of nonresidents of the United States. Beginning 1999, deaths are classified according to the International Classification of Diseases, Tenth Revision (ICD-10); for earlier years, causes of death were classified according to the revisions then in use. Changes due to these revisions may result in discontinuities in cause-of-death trends. See source for details]

Characteristic	1980	1990	2000	2010	2015	2019	2020	2021	2022
All ages, age-adjusted [1].........	**412.1**	**321.8**	**257.6**	**179.1**	**168.5**	**161.5**	**168.2**	**173.8**	**167.2**
All ages, crude rate...............	**336.0**	**289.5**	**252.6**	**193.6**	**197.2**	**200.8**	**211.5**	**209.6**	**210.9**
Under 1 year.........................	22.8	20.1	13.0	8.3	7.3	7.1	6.5	7.4	6.5
1 to 4 years.........................	2.6	1.9	1.2	1.0	0.9	0.8	0.7	0.8	0.7
5 to 14 years........................	0.9	0.9	0.7	0.5	0.5	0.4	0.4	0.5	0.5
15 to 24 years.......................	2.9	2.5	2.6	2.4	2.3	2.0	2.0	2.2	1.9
25 to 34 years.......................	8.3	7.6	7.4	7.8	8.0	7.6	8.6	9.1	8.3
35 to 44 years.......................	44.6	31.4	29.2	25.8	25.6	25.2	28.9	29.4	28.1
45 to 54 years.......................	180.2	120.5	94.2	81.6	79.3	76.2	84.6	84.9	79.9
55 to 64 years.......................	494.1	367.3	261.2	186.6	188.1	190.4	208.8	208.7	203.7
65 to 74 years.......................	1,218.6	894.3	665.6	409.2	389.5	388.8	414.2	416.6	415.7
75 to 84 years.......................	2,993.1	2,295.7	1,780.3	1,172.0	1,071.6	991.2	1,017.2	1,044.2	1,016.6
85 years and over...................	7,777.1	6,739.9	5,926.1	4,285.2	3,986.5	3,798.3	3,822.1	4,078.7	3,835.8
MALE									
All ages, age-adjusted [1].........	**538.9**	**412.4**	**320.0**	**225.1**	**211.8**	**204.8**	**214.2**	**219.5**	**213.5**
Non-Hispanic, single-race:									
American Indian, Alaska Native....	(NA)	(NA)	(NA)	(NA)	(NA)	180.3	191.0	197.7	183.9
Asian.................................	(NA)	(NA)	(NA)	(NA)	(NA)	101.6	112.2	108.6	109.1
Black.................................	(NA)	(NA)	(NA)	(NA)	(NA)	267.5	297.4	289.9	281.3
Native Hawaiian, other Pacific Islander.............................	(NA)	(NA)	(NA)	(NA)	(NA)	213.8	209.8	228.7	201.8
White.................................	(NA)	(NA)	(NA)	(NA)	(NA)	210.7	217.3	226.7	220.5
Non-Hispanic, more than one race...	(NA)	(NA)	(NA)	(NA)	(NA)	86.2	98.8	94.7	93.0
Hispanic origin [2]...................	(NA)	270.0	238.2	165.1	146.4	141.9	157.5	149.9	147.8
Bridged race estimates: [3]									
American Indian, Alaska Native....	320.5	264.1	222.2	158.7	148.0	137.9	144.0	(NA)	(NA)
Asian, Pacific Islander..............	286.9	220.7	185.5	127.2	109.7	106.0	116.5	(NA)	(NA)
Black.................................	561.4	485.4	392.5	280.6	258.6	256.0	284.5	(NA)	(NA)
White.................................	539.6	409.2	316.7	222.9	211.2	203.9	211.3	(NA)	(NA)
Non-Hispanic, White [2]..............	(NA)	413.6	319.9	226.9	216.3	209.8	216.5	(NA)	(NA)
All ages, crude rate...............	**368.6**	**297.6**	**249.8**	**202.5**	**211.7**	**221.3**	**235.9**	**234.1**	**234.0**
Under 1 year.........................	25.5	21.9	13.3	9.8	7.5	7.6	6.1	8.0	6.8
1 to 4 years.........................	2.8	1.9	1.4	1.1	1.0	0.9	0.7	0.7	0.8
5 to 14 years........................	1.0	0.9	0.8	0.5	0.5	0.4	0.4	0.5	0.5
15 to 24 years.......................	3.7	3.1	3.2	3.2	3.0	2.4	2.5	2.8	2.4
25 to 34 years.......................	11.4	10.3	9.6	10.7	10.3	10.0	11.4	11.9	11.1
35 to 44 years.......................	68.7	48.1	41.4	36.0	35.1	34.6	39.7	40.3	37.8
45 to 54 years.......................	282.6	183.0	140.2	117.8	112.1	109.0	120.8	120.0	112.0
55 to 64 years.......................	746.8	537.3	371.7	269.5	269.4	272.7	301.1	296.4	285.9
65 to 74 years.......................	1,728.0	1,250.0	898.3	553.0	529.7	537.2	571.3	568.8	567.4
75 to 84 years.......................	3,834.3	2,968.2	2,248.1	1,475.7	1,354.4	1,261.2	1,301.0	1,320.2	1,292.9
85 years and over...................	8,752.7	7,418.4	6,430.0	4,833.6	4,495.1	4,302.4	4,325.4	4,640.3	4,504.6
FEMALE									
All ages, age-adjusted [1].........	**320.8**	**257.0**	**210.9**	**143.3**	**133.6**	**126.2**	**130.2**	**135.6**	**129.5**
Non-Hispanic, single race:									
American Indian, Alaska Native....	(NA)	(NA)	(NA)	(NA)	(NA)	107.9	112.0	118.1	116.2
Asian.................................	(NA)	(NA)	(NA)	(NA)	(NA)	61.6	66.9	66.8	64.6
Black.................................	(NA)	(NA)	(NA)	(NA)	(NA)	165.0	182.6	177.8	169.5
Native Hawaiian, other Pacific Islander.............................	(NA)	(NA)	(NA)	(NA)	(NA)	124.7	138.8	138.6	143.7
White.................................	(NA)	(NA)	(NA)	(NA)	(NA)	129.6	131.7	140.1	133.9
Non-Hispanic, more than one race...	(NA)	(NA)	(NA)	(NA)	(NA)	55.5	58.6	57.8	55.4
Hispanic origin [2]...................	(NA)	177.2	163.7	107.8	93.0	86.4	94.3	92.9	87.7
Bridged race estimates: [3]									
American Indian, Alaska Native....	175.4	153.1	143.6	103.5	94.0	79.9	83.6	(NA)	(NA)
Asian, Pacific Islander..............	132.3	149.2	115.7	81.2	68.5	63.6	69.1	(NA)	(NA)
Black.................................	378.6	327.5	277.6	185.3	165.7	158.5	175.1	(NA)	(NA)
White.................................	315.9	250.9	205.6	140.4	132.4	125.3	127.8	(NA)	(NA)
Non-Hispanic, White [2]..............	(NA)	252.6	206.8	142.5	135.6	129.1	131.2	(NA)	(NA)
All ages, crude rate...............	**305.1**	**281.8**	**255.3**	**184.9**	**183.1**	**180.9**	**187.9**	**185.5**	**188.2**
Under 1 year.........................	20.0	18.3	12.5	6.8	7.2	6.5	6.9	6.8	6.3
1 to 4 years.........................	2.5	1.9	1.0	0.9	0.9	0.8	0.7	0.8	0.6
5 to 14 years........................	0.9	0.8	0.5	0.4	0.5	0.5	0.4	0.5	0.5
15 to 24 years.......................	2.1	1.8	2.1	1.5	1.5	1.7	1.5	1.5	1.4
25 to 34 years.......................	5.3	5.0	5.2	4.9	5.6	5.2	5.8	6.3	5.4
35 to 44 years.......................	21.4	15.1	17.2	15.6	16.2	15.9	18.1	18.3	18.1
45 to 54 years.......................	84.5	61.0	49.8	46.5	47.4	44.2	49.4	49.8	47.6
55 to 64 years.......................	272.1	215.7	159.3	109.3	112.3	113.6	122.5	124.6	124.4
65 to 74 years.......................	828.6	616.8	474.0	284.2	266.2	258.9	276.9	280.9	280.8
75 to 84 years.......................	2,497.0	1,893.8	1,475.1	952.7	855.9	780.5	795.0	825.4	798.2
85 years and over...................	7,350.5	6,478.1	5,720.9	4,020.3	3,717.6	3,515.0	3,535.8	3,757.1	3,472.2

NA Not available. [1] See footnote 1, Table 125. [2] Persons of Hispanic origin may be of any race. Prior to 1997, excludes data from states lacking a Hispanic-origin item on their death certificates. [3] Consistent with 1977 OMB standards.

Source: U.S. National Center for Health Statistics, *Health, United States*, annual; and CDC WONDER Online database, "Multiple Cause of Death, 2018-2022," <wonder.cdc.gov>, accessed July 2024. See also <www.cdc.gov/nchs/nvss/deaths.htm>.

Table 124. Death Rates For Cerebrovascular Diseases (Stroke) by Sex and Age: 2000 to 2022

[Rates per 100,000 population. Excludes deaths of nonresidents of the United States. Deaths are classified according to the International Classification of Diseases, Tenth Revision (ICD-10). For explanation of age adjustment, see text, this section]

Age	Total				Male				Female			
	2000	2010	2020	2022	2000	2010	2020	2022	2000	2010	2020	2022
All ages, age-adjusted [1]	60.9	39.1	38.8	39.5	62.4	39.3	39.8	40.5	59.1	38.3	37.4	38.2
All ages, crude rate	59.6	41.9	48.6	49.6	46.9	34.5	42.9	43.5	71.8	49.1	54.2	55.7
Under 1 year	3.3	3.3	2.8	2.4	3.8	3.2	2.9	2.8	2.7	3.4	2.7	1.9
1 to 4 years	0.3	0.3	0.4	0.3	(B)	0.3	0.4	0.4	0.4	0.3	0.3	(B)
5 to 14 years	0.2	0.2	0.2	0.2	0.2	0.3	0.2	0.3	0.2	0.2	0.2	0.2
15 to 24 years	0.5	0.4	0.4	0.4	0.5	0.5	0.4	0.4	0.5	0.4	0.5	0.3
25 to 34 years	1.5	1.3	1.3	1.3	1.5	1.3	1.4	1.4	1.5	1.2	1.2	1.2
35 to 44 years	5.8	4.6	4.8	4.9	5.8	5.0	5.7	5.5	5.7	4.2	3.8	4.3
45 to 54 years	16.0	13.1	14.1	13.8	17.5	14.9	16.6	15.7	14.5	11.4	11.6	11.8
55 to 64 years	41.0	29.3	33.4	33.7	47.2	34.7	40.8	40.3	35.3	24.3	26.4	27.2
65 to 74 years	128.6	81.7	81.0	84.0	145.0	92.0	93.0	96.1	115.1	72.8	70.5	73.3
75 to 84 years	461.3	288.3	262.9	265.0	490.8	295.2	277.8	273.5	442.1	283.4	251.3	258.2
85 years and over	1,589.2	993.8	1,017.9	1,043.9	1,484.3	892.0	911.8	965.6	1,632.0	1,043.0	1,078.3	1,086.5

B Figure too small to meet statistical standards for reliability. [1] See footnote 1, Table 123.

Source: U.S. National Center for Health Statistics, *Health, United States*, annual; and CDC WONDER Online database, "Multiple Cause of Death, 2018-2022," <wonder.cdc.gov>, accessed July 2024. See also <www.cdc.gov/nchs/nvss/deaths.htm>.

Table 125. Death Rates For All and Selected Types of Malignant Neoplasms (Cancer) by Age: 1990 to 2022

[Rates per 100,000 population. Excludes deaths of nonresidents of the United States. Beginning 1999, deaths are classified according to the International Classification of Diseases, Tenth Revision (ICD-10); for earlier years, causes of death were classified according to the revisions then in use. Changes in classification of causes of death due to these revisions may result in discontinuities in cause-of-death trends. For explanation of age adjustment, see text, this section. See Appendix III]

Item	1990	2000	2010	2015	2019	2020	2021	2022
ALL MALIGNANT NEOPLASMS								
All ages, age-adjusted [1]	216.0	199.6	172.8	158.5	146.2	144.1	146.6	142.3
All ages, crude rate	203.2	196.5	186.2	185.4	182.7	182.8	182.4	182.5
Under 1 year	2.3	2.4	1.6	1.3	1.5	1.4	1.5	1.1
1 to 4 years	3.5	2.7	2.1	2.2	1.8	2.0	1.8	1.8
5 to 14 years	3.1	2.5	2.2	2.1	1.9	1.9	1.9	2.0
15 to 24 years	4.9	4.4	3.7	3.4	3.3	3.1	3.1	3.2
25 to 34 years	12.6	9.8	8.8	8.4	7.8	7.8	7.9	8.0
35 to 44 years	43.3	36.6	28.8	26.9	25.7	25.5	25.8	25.6
45 to 54 years	158.9	127.5	111.6	99.7	87.1	85.7	82.5	82.5
55 to 64 years	449.6	366.7	300.1	284.1	263.3	260.0	252.4	249.8
65 to 74 years	872.3	816.3	666.1	594.3	543.3	539.1	532.1	529.4
75 to 84 years	1,348.5	1,335.6	1,202.2	1,100.8	1,005.9	990.0	1,017.2	979.3
85 years old and over	1,752.9	1,819.4	1,729.5	1,628.6	1,571.0	1,538.1	1,712.9	1,573.5
MALIGNANT NEOPLASM OF BREAST FOR FEMALES								
All ages, age-adjusted [1]	33.3	26.8	22.1	20.3	19.4	19.1	19.4	18.8
All ages, crude rate	34.0	29.2	26.1	25.4	25.4	25.3	25.3	25.1
Under 25 years	(B)	(B)	(B)	(B)	(B)	(B)	(B)	(B)
25 to 34 years	2.9	2.3	1.6	1.8	1.9	1.7	1.6	1.7
35 to 44 years	17.8	12.4	9.8	9.0	9.2	8.4	8.6	8.6
45 to 54 years	45.4	33.0	25.7	23.7	22.2	22.1	20.3	20.1
55 to 64 years	78.6	59.3	47.7	43.3	40.4	39.1	38.4	37.8
65 to 74 years	111.7	88.3	73.9	66.7	62.1	61.1	60.3	59.3
75 to 84 years	146.3	128.9	109.1	101.7	96.9	98.2	102.9	99.3
85 years old and over	196.8	205.7	185.8	173.3	173.5	173.9	198.1	178.3
MALIGNANT NEOPLASM OF TRACHEA, BRONCHUS, AND LUNG								
All ages, age-adjusted [1]	59.3	56.1	47.6	40.5	33.4	31.9	31.7	30.1
All ages, crude rate	56.8	55.3	51.3	47.9	42.6	41.3	40.6	39.6
Under 25 years	(Z)	(Z)	(Z)	(Z)	(Z)	(B)	(B)	(B)
25 to 34 years	0.7	0.5	0.4	0.3	0.2	0.3	0.3	0.3
35 to 44 years	6.8	6.1	3.3	2.5	1.9	1.8	1.8	1.8
45 to 54 years	46.8	31.6	26.9	20.5	13.6	12.5	11.9	11.1
55 to 64 years	160.6	122.4	85.4	76.8	64.8	62.9	60.5	58.0
65 to 74 years	288.4	284.2	223.9	181.0	144.3	140.0	134.5	131.9
75 to 84 years	333.3	370.8	357.2	306.4	260.9	246.3	248.9	232.6
85 years old and over	242.5	302.1	332.4	316.1	281.3	262.2	289.5	260.0

B Base figure too small to meet statistical standards for reliability of a derived figure. Z Less than 0.05. [1] Age-adjusted death rates were prepared using the direct method, in which age specific death rates for a population of interest are applied to a standard population distributed by age. Age adjustment eliminates the differences in observed rates between points in time or among compared population groups that result from age differences in population composition.

Source: U.S. National Center for Health Statistics, *Health, United States*, annual; and CDC WONDER Online database, "Multiple Cause of Death, 2018-2022," <wonder.cdc.gov>, accessed July 2024. See also <www.cdc.gov/nchs/nvss/deaths.htm>.

Table 126. Deaths and Death Rates for Coronavirus Disease 2019 (COVID-19) by Sex, Age, and Race/Ethnicity: 2022

[Rates per 100,000 population; based on resident population as of July 1. Data are shown for underlying cause of death classified as U07.1 (COVID-19) under the International Classification of Diseases, Tenth Revision (ICD-10)]

Characteristic	Number			Crude rate			Age-adjusted rate [1]		
	Total	Male	Female	Total	Male	Female	Total	Male	Female
Total [2]...............................	**186,552**	**102,660**	**83,892**	**56.0**	**62.1**	**49.9**	**44.5**	**56.7**	**35.4**
AGE									
Under 1 year....................	141	81	60	3.8	4.3	3.3	(X)	(X)	(X)
1 to 4 years......................	101	60	41	0.7	0.8	0.6	(X)	(X)	(X)
5 to 14 years....................	131	69	62	0.3	0.3	0.3	(X)	(X)	(X)
15 to 24 years..................	447	268	179	1.0	1.2	0.8	(X)	(X)	(X)
25 to 34 years..................	1,640	1,005	635	3.6	4.3	2.8	(X)	(X)	(X)
35 to 44 years..................	3,841	2,240	1,601	8.8	10.1	7.4	(X)	(X)	(X)
45 to 54 years..................	9,678	5,732	3,946	23.9	28.3	19.6	(X)	(X)	(X)
55 to 64 years..................	24,252	14,194	10,058	57.6	68.7	47.0	(X)	(X)	(X)
65 to 74 years..................	42,062	24,492	17,570	124.5	153.9	98.3	(X)	(X)	(X)
75 to 84 years..................	51,188	29,033	22,155	292.2	375.4	226.4	(X)	(X)	(X)
85 years and over.............	53,070	25,485	27,585	818.2	1,115.9	656.5	(X)	(X)	(X)
RACE/ETHNICITY									
Non-Hispanic, single-race:									
American Indian, Alaska Native..............	1,690	861	829	69.8	71.9	67.8	65.9	73.1	60.1
Asian...............................	5,450	3,120	2,330	26.9	31.9	22.2	25.3	34.5	18.6
Black..............................	21,896	10,778	11,118	52.0	53.3	50.9	53.9	66.5	46.2
Native Hawaiian, other Pacific Islander.....	285	157	128	44.8	48.8	40.7	48.9	58.7	41.2
White..............................	135,484	75,114	60,370	69.0	77.0	61.2	43.9	55.9	34.8
Non-Hispanic, more than one race...........	778	410	368	9.7	10.3	9.1	18.5	21.4	16.0
Hispanic [3]...........................	20,499	11,923	8,576	32.2	36.9	27.3	47.2	62.8	35.6

X Not applicable. [1] Age-adjusted death rates were prepared using the direct method, in which age specific death rates for a population of interest are applied to a standard population distributed by age. Age adjustment eliminates the differences in observed rates between points in time or among compared population groups that result from age differences in population composition. [2] Total counts and rates include deaths for persons with age and race/ethnicity "not stated." [3] Persons of Hispanic origin may be of any race.

Source: U.S. National Center for Health Statistics, CDC WONDER Online database, "Multiple Cause of Death, 2018-2022," <wonder.cdc.gov>, accessed July 2024. See also <www.cdc.gov/nchs/nvss/deaths.htm>.

Table 127. Firearm Deaths and Death Rates by Sex and Race/Ethnicity: 2018 to 2022

[Rates per 100,000 population. Beginning 2018, all 50 states and the District of Columbia report race and Hispanic origin data according to 1997 Office of Management and Budget (OMB) standards. Deaths are those attributable to injury by firearms. See source for details]

Sex and race/ethnicity	Number of deaths					Age-adjusted rates				
	2018	2019	2020	2021	2022	2018	2019	2020	2021	2022
Total [1].................................	**39,740**	**39,707**	**45,222**	**48,830**	**48,204**	**11.9**	**11.9**	**13.6**	**14.6**	**14.2**
Male..............................	33,955	34,041	38,981	41,866	41,302	20.7	20.7	23.8	25.3	24.6
Female...........................	5,785	5,666	6,241	6,964	6,902	3.4	3.4	3.8	4.2	4.1
Non-Hispanic, single-race:										
American Indian, Alaska Native.........	361	336	449	466	530	15.0	13.8	18.1	19.1	22.2
Male...........................	298	272	381	390	452	24.8	22.5	31.2	32.1	37.7
Female........................	63	64	68	76	78	5.4	5.3	5.3	6.3	6.7
Asian alone......................	492	513	516	576	583	2.5	2.5	2.6	2.9	2.7
Male...........................	396	424	435	469	474	4.2	4.4	4.5	4.8	4.6
Female........................	96	89	81	107	109	1.0	0.8	0.8	1.0	1.0
Black alone......................	9,713	10,288	13,974	15,290	14,203	23.2	24.5	33.1	36.0	33.2
Male...........................	8,567	9,198	12,416	13,349	12,410	42.0	44.8	59.9	64.0	59.0
Female........................	1,146	1,090	1,558	1,941	1,793	5.4	5.1	7.3	9.0	8.3
Native Hawaiian, other Pacific Islander....................	54	54	58	68	65	8.8	8.6	9.1	10.4	9.8
Male...........................	48	45	52	63	58	15.6	14.0	15.7	18.9	17.1
Female........................	(D)	(D)	(D)	(D)	(D)	(D)	(D)	(D)	(D)	(D)
White alone......................	24,643	23,964	24,664	26,054	26,323	11.4	11.1	11.6	12.3	12.2
Male...........................	20,745	20,173	20,838	22,068	22,285	19.5	19.0	19.9	21.0	20.7
Female........................	3,898	3,791	3,826	3,986	4,038	3.7	3.6	3.7	3.9	3.9
Non-Hispanic, more than one race.......	372	416	477	556	563	6.1	6.6	7.1	7.9	8.0
Male...........................	305	352	389	447	471	10.6	11.7	11.9	13.2	13.8
Female........................	67	64	88	109	92	2.1	1.9	2.6	3.0	2.5
Hispanic [2].........................	4,018	4,058	5,003	5,741	5,853	6.6	6.6	7.9	8.9	8.9
Male...........................	3,521	3,503	4,395	5,014	5,081	11.6	11.2	13.8	15.3	15.2
Female........................	497	555	608	727	772	1.7	1.9	1.9	2.3	2.4

D Data withheld due to confidentiality constraints. [1] Includes deaths for other race and origin combinations and those not stated, not shown separately. [2] Persons of Hispanic origin may be of any race.

Source: U.S. National Center for Health Statistics, National Vital Statistics Reports (NVSR), *Deaths: Final Data, Supplemental Tables,* annual; and CDC WONDER Online database "Multiple Cause of Death, 2018-2022," <wonder.cdc.gov>, accessed July 2024. See also <www.cdc.gov/nchs/nvss/deaths.htm>.

Table 128. Death Rates For Suicide by Selected Characteristics: 1990 to 2022

[Rates per 100,000 population. Beginning 2018, all 50 states and the District of Columbia report race and Hispanic origin data according to 1997 Office of Management and Budget (OMB) standards, which allow for reporting multiple races (previous standards permitted only single race reporting). To maintain comparability of data during the transition to the new standards, 2018-2020 multiple-race data were bridged to single-race categories. Beginning 2021, only data consistent with the 1997 OMB standards are available. Excludes deaths of nonresidents of the United States. Beginning 1999, deaths are classified according to the International Classification of Diseases, Tenth Revision (ICD-10)]

Characteristic	1990	2000	2005	2010	2015	2019	2020	2021	2022
All ages, age-adjusted [1]	**12.5**	**10.4**	**10.9**	**12.1**	**13.3**	**13.9**	**13.5**	**14.1**	**14.2**
All ages, crude rate	**12.4**	**10.4**	**11.0**	**12.4**	**13.7**	**14.5**	**14.0**	**14.5**	**14.8**
5 to 14 years	0.8	0.7	0.7	0.7	1.0	1.3	1.5	1.5	1.2
15 to 24 years	13.2	10.2	9.9	10.5	12.5	13.9	14.2	15.2	13.6
25 to 34 years	15.2	12.0	12.7	14.0	15.7	17.5	18.4	19.5	19.0
35 to 44 years	15.3	14.5	15.1	16.0	17.1	18.1	17.4	18.1	18.7
45 to 54 years	14.8	14.4	16.5	19.6	20.3	19.6	18.0	18.2	19.2
55 to 64 years	16.0	12.1	13.7	17.5	18.9	19.4	16.9	17.0	18.7
65 to 74 years	17.9	12.5	12.4	13.7	15.2	15.5	14.5	15.3	16.0
75 to 84 years	24.9	17.6	16.8	15.7	17.9	18.6	18.4	19.6	20.3
85 years and over	22.2	19.6	18.3	17.6	19.4	20.1	20.9	22.4	23.0
AGE-ADJUSTED RATES [1]									
Male	**21.5**	**17.7**	**18.1**	**19.8**	**21.1**	**22.4**	**22.0**	**22.8**	**23.0**
Non-Hispanic, single-race:									
American Indian, Alaska Native	(NA)	(NA)	(NA)	(NA)	(NA)	33.0	36.4	42.6	39.6
Asian	(NA)	(NA)	(NA)	(NA)	(NA)	10.1	9.5	9.9	10.1
Black	(NA)	(NA)	(NA)	(NA)	(NA)	12.5	13.1	14.6	14.9
Native Hawaiian, other Pacific Islander	(NA)	(NA)	(NA)	(NA)	(NA)	22.1	20.0	19.5	22.1
White	(NA)	(NA)	(NA)	(NA)	(NA)	28.0	27.2	28.0	28.1
Non-Hispanic, more than one race	(NA)	(NA)	(NA)	(NA)	(NA)	14.2	14.5	15.3	16.8
Hispanic [2]	13.7	10.3	9.6	9.9	9.9	11.6	12.3	12.8	13.0
Bridged race estimates: [3]									
American Indian, Alaska Native	20.1	16.0	17.3	15.5	18.8	20.3	22.5	(NA)	(NA)
Asian, Pacific Islander	9.6	8.6	7.3	9.5	9.1	10.7	10.1	(NA)	(NA)
Black	12.8	10.0	9.2	9.1	9.6	11.8	12.4	(NA)	(NA)
White	22.8	19.1	19.8	22.0	23.6	24.9	24.3	(NA)	(NA)
Non-Hispanic, White [2]	23.5	20.2	21.4	24.2	26.6	27.9	27.0	(NA)	(NA)
Female	**4.8**	**4.0**	**4.4**	**5.0**	**6.0**	**6.0**	**5.5**	**5.7**	**5.9**
Non-Hispanic, single-race:									
American Indian, Alaska Native	(NA)	(NA)	(NA)	(NA)	(NA)	12.1	11.7	13.8	14.6
Asian	(NA)	(NA)	(NA)	(NA)	(NA)	3.7	3.7	3.9	3.9
Black	(NA)	(NA)	(NA)	(NA)	(NA)	2.9	2.9	3.3	3.5
Native Hawaiian, other Pacific Islander	(NA)	(NA)	(NA)	(NA)	(NA)	(B)	(B)	(B)	6.1
White	(NA)	(NA)	(NA)	(NA)	(NA)	7.7	6.9	7.1	7.3
Non-Hispanic, more than one race	(NA)	(NA)	(NA)	(NA)	(NA)	3.9	5.0	4.6	4.7
Hispanic [2]	2.3	1.7	1.8	2.1	2.6	3.0	2.8	3.0	3.1
Bridged race estimates: [3]									
American Indian, Alaska Native	3.6	3.8	4.2	6.1	6.5	6.9	6.6	(NA)	(NA)
Asian, Pacific Islander	4.1	2.8	3.2	3.4	4.0	3.8	3.8	(NA)	(NA)
Black	2.4	1.8	1.8	1.8	2.0	2.8	2.8	(NA)	(NA)
White	5.2	4.3	4.9	5.6	6.9	6.8	6.1	(NA)	(NA)
Non-Hispanic, White [2]	5.4	4.7	5.3	6.2	7.8	7.6	6.9	(NA)	(NA)

B Base figure too small to meet statistical standards for reliability of a derived figure. NA Not available. [1] Age-adjusted death rates were prepared using the direct method, in which age-specific death rates for a population of interest are applied to a standard population distributed by age. Age adjustment eliminates the differences in observed rates between points in time or among compared population groups that result from age differences in population composition. [2] Persons of Hispanic origin may be of any race. Excludes data from states lacking a Hispanic-origin item on their death certificates. [3] Bridged race categories consistent with 1977 Office of Management and Budget standards.

Source: U.S. National Center for Health Statistics, *Health, United States*, annual; and CDC WONDER Online database, "Multiple Cause of Death, 2018-2022," <wonder.cdc.gov>, accessed July 2024. See also <www.cdc.gov/nchs/nvss/deaths.htm>.

Table 129. Suicide Deaths by Age, Sex, and Method: 2022

[It is generally accepted that children under 5 years of age cannot commit suicide. Deaths are based on the International Classification of Diseases, Tenth Revision (ICD-10)]

Method	Total	Age								
		5-14 years	15-24 years	25-34 years	35-44 years	45-54 years	55-64 years	65-74 years	75-84 years	85+ years
Total [1]	**49,476**	**502**	**6,040**	**8,663**	**8,185**	**7,781**	**7,864**	**5,396**	**3,549**	**1,493**
MEN										
Total [1]	**39,273**	**311**	**4,779**	**6,928**	**6,462**	**5,977**	**6,098**	**4,320**	**3,075**	**1,320**
Knife or other sharp object	802	0	41	113	147	142	175	99	52	33
Drowning	331	0	45	78	66	38	48	26	22	(D)
Fall or jump from high place	939	10	162	195	179	137	111	79	39	27
Fire/flame	144	(D)	10	30	15	30	27	26	(D)	(D)
Firearm	23,538	148	2,872	3,642	3,151	3,219	3,782	3,136	2,500	1,088
Poisoning	3,114	(D)	282	444	530	592	598	374	215	70
Hanging, suffocation, strangulation	9,542	141	1,214	2,219	2,194	1,685	1,253	523	226	85
WOMEN										
Total [1]	**10,203**	**191**	**1,261**	**1,735**	**1,723**	**1,804**	**1,766**	**1,076**	**474**	**173**
Knife or other sharp object	168	0	(D)	19	29	30	42	28	(D)	(D)
Drowning	171	0	20	28	26	28	25	29	10	(D)
Fall or jump from high place	306	(D)	40	61	44	49	60	29	13	(D)
Fire/flame	49	0	(D)	(D)	13	10	(D)	(D)	(D)	0
Firearm	3,494	32	374	588	608	619	630	400	186	57
Poisoning	3,036	33	287	363	433	612	639	404	194	71
Hanging, suffocation, strangulation	2,705	119	480	611	522	407	318	162	58	28

D Data withheld due to confidentiality constraints. [1] Includes other methods not shown separately and deaths with age not stated.

Source: U.S. National Center for Health Statistics, CDC WONDER Online database, "Multiple Cause of Death, 2018-2022," <wonder.cdc.gov>, accessed July 2024.

Table 130. Drug Overdose/Poisoning Deaths and Those Involving Opioids: 1999 to 2022

[Rates are age-adjusted and per 100,000 population. Deaths may involve more than one drug and are classified according to the International Classification of Diseases, Tenth Revision (ICD-10). Opioids include opium, heroin, natural and semisynthetic opioids, methadone, synthetic opioids other than methadone, and other and unspecified narcotics]

Year	Total [1]		Opioids					
			Total [1]		Heroin		Synthetic opioids including fentanyl [2]	
	Number	Rate	Number	Rate	Number	Rate	Number	Rate
1999............	16,849	6.1	8,050	2.9	1,960	0.7	730	0.3
2000............	17,415	6.2	8,407	3.0	1,842	0.7	782	0.3
2001............	19,394	6.8	9,496	3.3	1,779	0.6	957	0.3
2002............	23,518	8.2	11,920	4.1	2,089	0.7	1,295	0.4
2003............	25,785	8.9	12,940	4.5	2,080	0.7	1,400	0.5
2004............	27,424	9.4	13,756	4.7	1,878	0.6	1,664	0.6
2005............	29,813	10.1	14,918	5.1	2,009	0.7	1,742	0.6
2006............	34,425	11.5	17,545	5.9	2,088	0.7	2,707	0.9
2007............	36,010	11.9	18,516	6.1	2,399	0.8	2,213	0.7
2008............	36,450	11.9	19,582	6.4	3,041	1.0	2,306	0.8
2009............	37,004	11.9	20,422	6.6	3,278	1.1	2,946	1.0
2010............	38,329	12.3	21,089	6.8	3,036	1.0	3,007	1.0
2011............	41,340	13.2	22,784	7.3	4,397	1.4	2,666	0.8
2012............	41,502	13.1	23,166	7.4	5,925	1.9	2,628	0.8
2013............	43,982	13.8	25,052	7.9	8,257	2.7	3,105	1.0
2014............	47,055	14.7	28,647	9.0	10,574	3.4	5,544	1.8
2015............	52,404	16.3	33,091	10.4	12,989	4.1	9,580	3.1
2016............	63,632	19.8	42,249	13.3	15,469	4.9	19,413	6.2
2017............	70,237	21.7	47,600	14.9	15,482	4.9	28,466	9.0
2018............	67,367	20.7	46,802	14.6	14,996	4.7	31,335	9.9
2019............	70,630	21.6	49,860	15.5	14,019	4.4	36,359	11.4
2020............	91,799	28.3	68,630	21.4	13,165	4.1	56,516	17.8
2021............	106,699	32.4	80,411	24.7	9,173	2.8	70,601	21.8
2022............	107,941	32.6	81,806	25.0	5,871	1.8	73,838	22.7

[1] Includes deaths due to other drug types not shown separately. [2] Synthetic opioids other than methadone. Includes drugs such as fentanyl, fentanyl analogs, and tramadol.

Source: U.S. National Center for Health Statistics, *Drug Overdose Deaths in the United States, 2002-2022*, March 2024 and earlier reports.

Table 131. Drug Overdose Deaths and Age-adjusted Death Rates by Drug and Sex, Age, and Race/Ethnicity: 2016 to 2021

[Age-adjusted rates per 100,000 population. Deaths may involve other drugs in addition to the referent drug. Deaths involving more than one drug are counted in all relevant categories. Drug overdose deaths were identified using International Classification of Diseases, Tenth Revision (ICD-10) underlying cause-of-death codes X40–X44 (unintentional), X60–X64 (suicide), X85 (homicide), and Y10–Y14 (undetermined intent); drugs involved in deaths were identified from the literal text fields in death certificate records held in the National Vital Statistics System database. See Appendix III]

Year and characteristic	Fentanyl		Methamphetamine		Cocaine		Heroin		Oxycodone	
	Number	Rate	Number	Rate	Number	Rate	Number	Rate	Number	Rate
2016........................	18,499	5.7	6,830	2.1	11,404	3.5	16,005	4.9	6,238	1.9
2017........................	27,530	8.8	9,438	3.0	15,050	4.7	16,047	5.1	6,094	1.8
2018........................	30,286	9.6	11,784	3.7	15,689	4.9	15,496	4.9	5,070	1.5
2019........................	35,436	11.2	15,049	4.7	16,985	5.2	14,517	4.5	4,624	1.4
2020........................	55,785	17.4	22,523	6.9	21,071	6.4	13,636	4.2	5,121	1.5
2021										
Total........................	**69,943**	**21.6**	**31,170**	**9.6**	**26,198**	**7.9**	**9,471**	**2.9**	**5,060**	**1.5**
SEX										
Female......................	19,096	11.9	8,661	5.4	7,317	4.5	2,439	1.5	2,194	1.3
Male.........................	50,847	31.3	22,509	13.8	18,881	11.3	7,032	4.2	2,866	1.7
AGE										
Under 25 years old........	6,100	5.9	1,395	1.4	1,273	1.2	387	0.4	188	0.2
25 to 34 years old..........	18,573	40.8	7,006	15.4	5,224	11.5	2,236	4.9	840	1.9
35 to 44 years old..........	18,899	43.5	8,828	20.3	6,474	14.9	2,474	5.7	1,046	2.4
45 to 54 years old..........	13,298	32.7	7,082	17.4	6,088	15.0	1,975	4.9	1,220	3.0
55 to 64 years old..........	10,595	24.8	5,554	13.0	5,726	13.4	1,858	4.3	1,216	2.8
65 years old and over......	2,469	4.4	1,298	2.3	1,412	2.5	539	1.0	550	1.0
RACE/ETHNICITY										
American Indian/Alaska Native [1]...................	792	33.1	649	27.4	183	7.4	114	4.7	57	2.4
Black [1].......................	13,552	31.3	2,926	7.0	9,045	20.6	1,675	3.7	714	1.7
White [1].......................	45,033	24.6	22,709	12.0	12,773	6.8	5,983	3.2	3,786	1.8
Asian [1].......................	464	2.3	291	1.4	206	1.0	58	0.3	38	0.2
Hispanic [2]....................	8,818	14.1	3,768	6.2	3,544	5.8	1,418	2.4	401	0.7

[1] Non-Hispanic. [2] Persons of Hispanic origin may be of any race.

Source: National Center for Health Statistics, National Vital Statistics System, *Estimates of Drug Overdose Deaths Involving Fentanyl, Methamphetamine, Cocaine, Heroin, and Oxycodone: United States, 2021*, May 2023. See also <www.cdc.gov/nchs/nvss/vsrr/reports.htm>.

Table 132. Drug Overdose Death Rates by Age, Sex, and Race/Ethnicity: 2000 to 2022

[Rates per 100,000 resident population. Drug overdose deaths include those resulting from accidental or intentional overdose of a drug, being given the wrong drug, taking the wrong drug in error, taking a drug inadvertently, or other misuses of drugs. These deaths are from all manners and intents, including unintentional, suicide, homicide, legal intervention, operations of war, and undetermined intent. Deaths are classified according to the International Classification of Diseases, Tenth Revision (ICD-10). Beginning with 2018 data, all States and the District of Columbia reported race according to 1997 OMB standards, which allows for reporting multiple races (previous standards permitted only single race reporting). See source for details]

Characteristic	2000	2005	2010	2015	2017	2018	2019	2020	2021	2022
ALL PERSONS										
All ages, age-adjusted [1]	**6.2**	**10.1**	**12.3**	**16.3**	**21.7**	**20.7**	**21.6**	**28.3**	**32.4**	**32.6**
All ages, crude	**6.2**	**10.1**	**12.4**	**16.3**	**21.6**	**20.6**	**21.5**	**27.9**	**32.1**	**32.4**
Under 15 years old	0.1	0.2	0.2	0.2	0.2	0.2	0.3	0.4	0.5	0.7
15 to 24 years old	3.7	6.9	8.2	9.7	12.6	10.8	11.2	16.7	17.2	15.1
25 to 34 years old	7.9	13.6	18.4	26.9	38.4	35.5	35.6	47.3	52.9	50.6
35 to 44 years old	14.3	19.6	20.8	28.3	39.0	38.3	40.5	53.9	62.0	63.1
45 to 54 years old	11.6	21.1	25.1	30.0	37.7	35.3	36.9	46.9	53.8	55.3
55 to 64 years old	4.2	9.0	15.0	21.8	28.0	28.3	30.4	37.3	45.3	48.1
65 to 74 years old	2.0	3.2	4.7	7.2	9.2	10.2	11.3	13.2	16.8	19.0
75 to 84 years old	2.4	3.1	3.4	3.6	3.6	3.9	4.2	4.0	4.9	5.3
85 years old and over	4.4	4.1	4.7	4.4	4.0	3.8	3.6	3.9	4.3	3.7
AGE-ADJUSTED RATES [1]										
MALE										
Total	**8.3**	**12.8**	**15.0**	**20.8**	**29.1**	**27.9**	**29.6**	**39.5**	**45.1**	**45.6**
Non-Hispanic, single-race:										
American Indian, Alaska Native	(NA)	(NA)	(NA)	(NA)	(NA)	33.1	36.6	51.2	69.3	83.4
Asian	(NA)	(NA)	(NA)	(NA)	(NA)	4.4	5.2	7.2	7.2	8.4
Black	(NA)	(NA)	(NA)	(NA)	(NA)	32.4	37.7	54.8	67.3	73.3
Native Hawaiian/other Pacific Islander	(NA)	(NA)	(NA)	(NA)	(NA)	17.7	13.4	20.8	30.0	28.3
White	(NA)	(NA)	(NA)	(NA)	(NA)	33.8	34.5	44.5	49.4	47.6
Non-Hispanic, more than one race	(NA)	(NA)	(NA)	(NA)	(NA)	16.3	16.0	26.2	29.3	31.1
Hispanic [2]	7.1	8.4	7.6	10.9	15.9	16.6	19.5	27.3	32.4	35.2
FEMALE										
Total	**4.1**	**7.3**	**9.6**	**11.8**	**14.4**	**13.6**	**13.7**	**17.1**	**19.6**	**19.4**
Non-Hispanic, single-race:										
American Indian, Alaska Native	(NA)	(NA)	(NA)	(NA)	(NA)	20.7	24.5	34.0	44.1	47.1
Asian	(NA)	(NA)	(NA)	(NA)	(NA)	1.8	1.6	2.2	2.3	2.4
Black	(NA)	(NA)	(NA)	(NA)	(NA)	11.6	13.4	18.9	23.5	24.5
Native Hawaiian/other Pacific Islander	(NA)	(NA)	(NA)	(NA)	(NA)	(B)	(B)	6.6	9.9	8.9
White	(NA)	(NA)	(NA)	(NA)	(NA)	18.0	17.6	21.5	23.8	23.3
Non-Hispanic, more than one race	(NA)	(NA)	(NA)	(NA)	(NA)	8.9	9.6	12.1	14.2	15.6
Hispanic [2]	2.0	3.0	3.6	4.4	5.1	5.2	5.7	7.5	9.4	9.5

NA Not available. B Base figure too small to meet statistical standards for reliability of a derived figure. [1] Age-adjusted rates are calculated using the year 2000 standard population and were prepared using the direct method, in which age specific death rates for a population of interest are applied to a standard population distributed by age. Age adjustment eliminates the differences in observed rates between points in time or among compared population groups that result from age differences in population composition. [2] Persons of Hispanic origin may be of any race.

Source: U.S. National Center for Health Statistics, "Health, United States—Data Finder," <www.cdc.gov/nchs/hus/index.htm>; and CDC WONDER Online Database, "Multiple Cause of Death, 2018-2022," <wonder.cdc.gov>; accessed July 2024.

Table 133. Percent of First Marriages Reaching Stated Anniversary by Sex and Year of Marriage: 2014

[In percent except number of marriages (6,609 represents 6,609,000). For currently married couples aged 15 years and over. Based on the 2014 Social Security Administration Supplement to the Survey of Income and Program Participation (SIPP)]

Sex and year of marriage	Marriages (1,000)	Anniversary						
		5th	10th	15th	20th	25th	30th	35th
MEN								
1970 to 1974	6,609	86.4	73.6	64.3	58.0	54.8	51.1	50.0
1975 to 1979	6,668	84.9	71.3	63.4	57.4	52.3	50.7	(X)
1980 to 1984	7,133	88.1	74.3	62.7	57.2	54.6	(X)	(X)
1985 to 1989	6,683	84.3	69.2	59.3	54.1	(X)	(X)	(X)
1990 to 1994	7,996	83.9	70.9	62.1	(X)	(X)	(X)	(X)
1995 to 1999	7,678	88.2	73.6	(X)	(X)	(X)	(X)	(X)
2000 to 2004	7,174	87.0	(X)	(X)	(X)	(X)	(X)	(X)
WOMEN								
1970 to 1974	7,526	86.4	71.5	64.2	56.5	52.3	48.7	46.6
1975 to 1979	7,122	82.9	70.4	63.0	57.6	52.8	49.7	(X)
1980 to 1984	8,081	84.1	73.2	62.4	58.0	52.8	(X)	(X)
1985 to 1989	7,503	85.0	69.0	57.8	50.8	(X)	(X)	(X)
1990 to 1994	7,705	85.8	73.5	67.2	(X)	(X)	(X)	(X)
1995 to 1999	7,711	88.3	75.6	(X)	(X)	(X)	(X)	(X)
2000 to 2004	7,653	87.5	(X)	(X)	(X)	(X)	(X)	(X)

X Not applicable.

Source: U.S. Census Bureau, Current Population Reports, *Number, Timing, and Duration of Marriages and Divorces: 2016*, P70-167, April 2021. See also <www.census.gov/newsroom/press-releases/2021/marriages-and-divorces.html>.

Table 134. People Who Got Married and Divorced in the Past 12 Months by State: 2022

[For 12-month period prior to interview date, which occurred for each month in calendar year. For example, a person interviewed in January 2022 could report they got married between January 2021 and January 2022. Data shown for persons 15 years old and over. Vital event is counted in state in which respondent lived at the time of survey. Based on the 2022 American Community Survey (ACS). The ACS universe includes the household population and the group quarters population. Based on a sample and subject to sampling variability. See Appendix III]

State	People who got married in the past 12 months				People who got divorced in the past 12 months			
	Males	Marriage rate per 1,000 men	Females	Marriage rate per 1,000 women	Males	Divorce rate per 1,000 men	Females	Divorce rate per 1,000 women
United States............	**2,419,384**	**17.9**	**2,322,727**	**16.7**	**888,129**	**6.6**	**990,301**	**7.1**
Alabama...................	38,969	19.6	38,022	17.5	16,699	8.4	19,709	9.1
Alaska....................	7,097	22.9	5,104	18.5	1,821	5.9	1,508	5.5
Arizona...................	50,148	16.6	51,736	17.0	22,221	7.4	22,297	7.3
Arkansas..................	24,523	20.2	23,737	18.9	13,516	11.2	14,921	11.9
California.................	270,661	16.9	254,338	15.8	85,119	5.3	94,652	5.9
Colorado..................	52,127	21.2	50,056	20.9	17,774	7.2	20,303	8.5
Connecticut...............	23,180	15.7	22,567	14.5	7,883	5.3	9,989	6.4
Delaware..................	6,648	16.3	6,347	14.4	3,513	8.6	3,992	9.1
District of Columbia.......	6,023	22.7	7,287	24.4	1,480	5.6	783	2.6
Florida...................	159,935	17.5	150,076	15.7	63,454	6.9	69,400	7.3
Georgia...................	84,781	19.8	81,133	17.7	35,960	8.4	39,910	8.7
Hawaii....................	9,283	15.5	8,048	13.6	3,403	5.7	4,221	7.1
Idaho.....................	13,934	17.8	14,034	18.1	5,406	6.9	7,165	9.2
Illinois...................	86,492	17.0	80,428	15.3	27,238	5.3	30,122	5.7
Indiana...................	49,554	18.1	47,137	16.7	22,157	8.1	25,343	9.0
Iowa......................	21,116	16.2	21,764	16.7	7,855	6.0	9,061	6.9
Kansas....................	22,644	19.1	21,188	17.8	6,404	5.4	9,829	8.3
Kentucky..................	29,729	16.4	30,540	16.3	14,439	8.0	18,616	9.9
Louisiana.................	29,717	16.5	27,800	14.5	14,023	7.8	16,228	8.5
Maine....................	8,789	15.1	8,634	14.3	4,016	6.9	3,858	6.4
Maryland..................	42,004	17.3	41,377	15.8	17,607	7.2	21,962	8.4
Massachusetts.............	47,679	16.7	45,487	15.0	13,595	4.8	17,978	5.9
Michigan..................	64,559	15.8	67,523	16.0	23,237	5.7	26,110	6.2
Minnesota.................	37,016	15.9	37,136	15.9	12,956	5.6	13,228	5.7
Mississippi................	21,044	18.4	21,442	17.2	7,452	6.5	10,371	8.3
Missouri..................	44,633	18.0	49,004	19.0	17,755	7.2	19,359	7.5
Montana..................	7,892	16.8	8,080	17.6	2,839	6.0	3,105	6.7
Nebraska.................	16,610	21.1	16,412	20.8	5,922	7.5	5,604	7.1
Nevada...................	24,416	18.6	25,657	19.7	10,605	8.1	10,183	7.8
New Hampshire............	9,309	15.7	11,175	18.7	3,543	6.0	3,765	6.3
New Jersey................	59,933	16.1	55,946	14.3	21,115	5.7	20,104	5.2
New Mexico...............	11,404	13.2	10,648	12.1	4,521	5.3	7,996	9.1
New York.................	138,265	17.4	123,941	14.7	43,326	5.5	48,203	5.7
North Carolina.............	87,565	20.5	83,022	18.3	30,121	7.1	37,073	8.2
North Dakota..............	5,964	18.6	5,671	18.5	866	2.7	2,520	8.2
Ohio......................	75,949	16.0	74,337	15.1	30,115	6.4	33,206	6.7
Oklahoma.................	30,489	19.0	30,522	18.7	14,653	9.2	15,259	9.3
Oregon...................	28,978	16.4	29,054	16.2	13,153	7.4	13,140	7.3
Pennsylvania..............	92,437	17.4	85,590	15.5	30,779	5.8	32,766	5.9
Rhode Island..............	8,597	19.0	8,643	18.1	2,637	5.8	3,181	6.7
South Carolina.............	45,701	21.7	46,606	20.6	13,929	6.6	17,009	7.5
South Dakota.............	5,391	14.6	5,606	15.7	2,234	6.0	2,853	8.0
Tennessee.................	54,137	19.2	50,485	17.0	24,405	8.7	26,961	9.1
Texas.....................	240,585	20.2	229,790	19.1	84,520	7.1	89,194	7.4
Utah......................	26,703	20.2	25,504	19.7	10,435	7.9	10,481	8.1
Vermont..................	5,115	18.6	4,761	17.0	1,876	6.8	1,302	4.6
Virginia...................	69,555	19.8	64,767	17.8	21,678	6.2	28,809	7.9
Washington...............	68,321	21.1	61,701	19.3	21,184	6.6	22,342	7.0
West Virginia..............	10,845	14.7	10,925	14.5	8,167	11.1	7,256	9.7
Wisconsin.................	38,473	15.8	37,348	15.3	16,429	6.7	14,519	5.9
Wyoming.................	4,465	18.4	4,591	19.8	2,094	8.6	2,555	11.0

Source: U.S. Census Bureau, 2022 American Community Survey, B12501, "Marriage in the Last Year by Sex by Marital Status for the Population 15 Years and Over," and B12503, "Divorces in the Last Year by Sex by Marital Status for the Population 15 Years and Over"; <data.census.gov>, accessed November 2023.

Table 135. Marriage and Divorce Rates by State: 1990 to 2022

[Rate per 1,000 population residing in area. Population enumerated as of April 1 for Census years; estimated as of July 1 for all other years. Rates are based on provisional counts by state of occurrence. See Appendix III]

State	Marriage rates						Divorce rates [1]					
	1990	2000	2010	2020	2021	2022	1990	2000	2010	2020	2021	2022
United States [2]	**9.8**	**8.2**	**6.8**	**5.1**	**6.0**	**6.2**	**4.7**	**4.0**	**3.6**	**2.3**	**2.5**	**2.4**
Alabama.................	10.6	10.1	8.2	7.2	7.6	7.3	6.1	5.5	4.4	3.7	3.6	3.2
Alaska..................	10.2	8.9	8.0	5.7	6.3	6.5	5.5	3.9	4.7	3.2	3.1	3.0
Arizona.................	10.0	7.5	5.9	4.9	5.4	5.8	6.9	4.6	3.5	2.9	2.7	2.3
Arkansas...............	15.3	15.4	10.8	7.8	8.2	7.9	6.9	6.4	5.7	3.6	3.6	3.5
California [3]	7.9	5.8	5.8	3.2	5.2	5.7	4.3	(NA)	(NA)	(NA)	(NA)	(NA)
Colorado...............	9.8	8.3	6.9	6.7	7.4	7.5	5.5	4.7	4.3	2.9	3.0	2.9
Connecticut.............	7.9	5.7	5.6	4.3	5.4	6.0	3.2	3.3	2.9	1.6	2.5	2.8
Delaware...............	8.4	6.5	5.2	4.4	4.9	5.1	4.4	3.9	3.5	2.3	2.6	2.3
District of Columbia......	8.2	4.9	7.6	6.5	7.3	8.3	4.5	3.2	2.8	2.1	2.6	2.0
Florida..................	10.9	8.9	7.3	5.7	6.8	7.1	6.3	5.1	4.4	3.0	3.4	3.1
Georgia.................	10.3	6.8	7.3	5.1	5.5	6.1	5.5	3.3	(NA)	1.9	2.2	2.1
Hawaii..................	16.4	20.6	17.6	7.4	12.8	14.4	4.6	3.9	(NA)	(NA)	(NA)	(NA)
Idaho...................	13.9	10.8	8.8	7.3	7.4	7.4	6.5	5.5	5.2	3.4	3.4	3.3
Illinois..................	8.8	6.9	5.7	3.9	4.7	4.9	3.8	3.2	2.6	1.6	1.3	1.1
Indiana.................	9.6	7.9	6.3	5.8	6.0	6.1	(NA)	(NA)	(NA)	(NA)	(NA)	(NA)
Iowa....................	9.0	6.9	6.9	4.9	5.3	5.5	3.9	3.3	2.4	2.1	2.3	2.0
Kansas.................	9.2	8.3	6.4	4.9	5.4	5.5	5.0	3.6	3.7	1.8	1.9	1.9
Kentucky...............	13.5	9.8	7.4	4.9	6.3	6.2	5.8	5.1	4.5	3.1	3.3	3.0
Louisiana...............	9.6	9.1	6.9	3.4	4.4	3.7	(NA)	(NA)	(NA)	1.4	2.2	0.7
Maine..................	9.7	8.8	7.1	5.8	7.3	7.5	4.3	5.0	4.2	2.4	2.7	2.4
Maryland...............	9.7	7.5	5.7	4.3	5.2	5.0	3.4	3.3	2.8	1.7	2.6	2.6
Massachusetts...........	7.9	5.8	5.6	4.0	4.6	5.1	2.8	2.5	2.5	1.0	1.0	1.4
Michigan................	8.2	6.7	5.5	4.2	5.2	5.3	4.3	3.9	3.5	2.1	2.3	2.3
Minnesota..............	7.7	6.8	5.3	4.4	4.8	5.2	3.5	3.2	(NA)	(NA)	(NA)	(NA)
Mississippi..............	9.4	6.9	4.9	5.7	6.0	5.9	5.5	5.0	4.3	3.3	3.3	3.0
Missouri................	9.6	7.8	6.5	5.6	6.0	5.8	5.1	4.5	3.9	2.7	2.9	2.7
Montana................	8.6	7.3	7.4	10.4	11.0	9.9	5.1	4.2	3.9	2.3	2.5	2.0
Nebraska...............	8.0	7.6	6.6	5.0	5.3	5.6	4.0	3.7	3.6	2.8	2.6	2.6
Nevada.................	99.0	72.2	38.3	21.0	26.2	25.9	11.4	9.9	5.9	3.0	4.2	4.2
New Hampshire..........	9.5	9.4	7.3	6.1	6.7	7.0	4.7	4.8	3.8	2.4	2.6	2.5
New Jersey.............	7.6	6.0	5.1	4.1	5.1	5.1	3.0	3.0	3.0	1.7	2.2	2.3
New Mexico.............	8.8	8.0	7.7	3.4	5.9	4.2	4.9	5.1	4.0	(NA)	(NA)	(NA)
New York...............	8.6	7.1	6.5	4.5	5.2	6.3	3.2	3.0	2.9	1.8	2.2	2.3
North Carolina..........	7.8	8.2	6.6	5.5	6.2	6.3	5.1	4.5	3.8	2.8	3.2	2.7
North Dakota...........	7.5	7.2	6.5	5.3	5.2	5.4	3.6	3.4	3.1	2.4	2.9	2.7
Ohio....................	9.0	7.8	5.8	4.8	5.2	5.3	4.7	4.2	3.4	2.5	2.6	2.4
Oklahoma...............	10.6	(NA)	7.2	5.9	6.1	6.1	7.7	(NA)	5.2	3.5	3.8	3.7
Oregon.................	8.9	7.6	6.5	5.2	5.7	5.5	5.5	4.8	4.0	2.6	2.7	2.8
Pennsylvania............	7.1	6.0	5.3	4.6	5.4	5.6	3.3	3.1	2.7	2.3	2.4	2.2
Rhode Island............	8.1	7.6	5.8	4.5	5.8	6.4	3.7	2.9	3.2	1.9	2.7	2.4
South Carolina..........	15.9	10.6	7.4	5.7	6.5	6.5	4.5	3.8	3.1	2.0	2.4	2.4
South Dakota...........	11.1	9.4	7.3	6.0	6.3	6.4	3.7	3.5	3.4	2.5	2.5	2.3
Tennessee..............	13.9	15.5	8.8	7.3	7.6	7.3	6.5	5.9	4.2	3.2	3.3	3.0
Texas..................	10.5	9.4	7.1	5.3	5.8	5.8	5.5	4.0	3.3	1.5	1.4	1.9
Utah...................	11.2	10.8	8.5	8.4	9.1	9.9	5.1	4.3	3.7	3.3	3.3	2.9
Vermont................	10.9	10.0	9.3	6.0	7.4	7.8	4.5	4.1	3.8	2.1	2.3	2.3
Virginia.................	11.4	8.8	6.8	5.3	5.9	6.0	4.4	4.3	3.8	2.6	3.1	2.9
Washington.............	9.5	6.9	6.0	4.8	5.5	5.8	5.9	4.6	4.2	2.8	2.9	2.8
West Virginia...........	7.2	8.7	6.7	5.6	6.0	6.1	5.3	5.1	5.1	3.1	2.9	3.2
Wisconsin..............	7.9	6.7	5.3	4.5	5.0	5.3	3.6	3.2	3.0	2.0	2.1	2.1
Wyoming...............	10.7	10.0	7.6	6.8	7.4	7.3	6.6	5.8	5.1	3.8	3.7	3.3

NA Not available. [1] Includes annulments. Includes divorce petitions filed or legal separations for some counties or States. [2] Beginning 2000, rates based solely on the combined counts and populations for reporting states and the District of Columbia. [3] Marriage data includes nonlicensed marriages registered.

Source: U.S. National Center for Health Statistics, National Vital Statistics System, "Marriages and Divorces, Detailed State Tables," <www.cdc.gov/nchs/nvss/marriage-divorce.htm>, accessed April 2024.

Table 136. People Who Got Married or Divorced in the Past 12 Months by Selected Characteristics: 2022

[In units, as indicated (273,939 represents 273,939,000). For 12-month period prior to interview date, which occurred for each month in calendar year. For example, a person interviewed in January 2022 could report they got married between January 2021 and January 2022. Data shown for persons 15 years old and over. Based on the 2022 American Community Survey (ACS). The ACS universe includes the household population and the group quarters population. Based on a sample and subject to sampling variability. See Appendix III]

Characteristic	Total population	Married in the past 12 months		Divorced in the past 12 months	
		Males	Females	Males	Females
Population 15 years old and over (1,000)	**273,939**	**2,419**	**2,323**	**888**	**990**
AGE					
Median age	45.9	32.2	30.6	46.1	44.6
EDUCATIONAL ATTAINMENT					
Population 18 years and over (1,000)	260,962	2,380	2,288	887	989
Bachelor's degree or higher (percent)	33.0	37.2	44.4	28.0	32.4
LABOR FORCE PARTICIPATION					
Population 16 years and over (1,000)	269,555	2,400	2,304	888	990
In labor force (percent)	63.5	88.8	80.1	79.0	78.1
Not in labor force (percent)	36.5	11.2	19.9	21.0	21.9
POVERTY STATUS IN PAST 12 MONTHS					
Population for whom poverty status is determined (1,000)	267,168	2,388	2,313	863	985
Below poverty (percent)	11.7	6.2	7.2	11.6	19.3
PRESENCE OF OWN CHILD UNDER 18 YEARS					
Population in households (1,000)	265,834	2,379	2,306	860	982
With own child under 18 years (percent)	22.7	27.2	29.6	20.0	36.4
HOUSING TENURE					
Population 15 years and over in occupied housing units (1,000)	265,834	2,379	2,306	860	982
Owner-occupied housing units (percent)	69.1	55.9	55.4	57.0	53.2
Renter-occupied housing units (percent)	30.9	44.1	44.6	43.0	46.8

Source: U.S. Census Bureau, 2022 American Community Survey, S1251, "Characteristics of People with a Marital Event in the Last 12 Months," <data.census.gov>, accessed November 2023.

Table 137. Marital Status of Population and Number of Times Married by Sex, and Median Duration of Marriage: 2010 to 2022

[248,056 represents 248,056,000. Data shown for persons age 15 years old and over. Based on the American Community Survey (ACS). The ACS universe includes the household population and the group quarters population. Based on a sample and subject to sampling variability. See Appendix III]

Characteristic	2010	2015	2016	2017	2018	2019	2021	2022
NUMBER (1,000)								
Population aged 15 years and over	**248,056**	**260,415**	**262,140**	**264,697**	**266,322**	**267,721**	**271,400**	**273,939**
Male	120,743	127,013	127,864	129,186	129,974	130,629	133,358	134,830
Never married	42,741	46,677	47,195	47,654	48,052	48,481	49,530	50,164
Ever married	78,001	80,336	80,669	81,532	81,921	82,148	83,828	84,666
Once	58,734	60,648	60,898	61,580	61,927	62,106	63,756	64,568
Two times	15,183	15,381	15,438	15,592	15,635	15,649	15,791	15,747
Three or more times	4,085	4,307	4,333	4,359	4,359	4,393	4,281	4,351
Female	127,313	133,402	134,277	135,511	136,349	137,092	138,042	139,109
Never married	36,899	40,667	41,143	41,442	41,880	42,292	43,215	43,916
Ever married	90,414	92,734	93,134	94,070	94,469	94,800	94,827	95,193
Once	68,330	70,088	70,419	71,248	71,413	71,632	72,166	72,494
Two times	17,449	17,776	17,838	17,945	18,110	18,191	17,796	17,801
Three or more times	4,636	4,871	4,876	4,876	4,945	4,977	4,865	4,898
PERCENT DISTRIBUTION								
Male:								
Never married	35.4	36.7	36.9	36.9	37.0	37.1	37.1	37.2
Ever married	64.6	63.3	63.1	63.1	63.0	62.9	62.9	62.8
Once	48.6	47.7	47.6	47.7	47.6	47.5	47.8	47.9
Two times	12.6	12.1	12.1	12.1	12.0	12.0	11.8	11.7
Three or more times	3.4	3.4	3.4	3.4	3.4	3.4	3.2	3.2
Female:								
Never married	29.0	30.5	30.6	30.6	30.7	30.8	31.3	31.6
Ever married	71.0	69.5	69.4	69.4	69.3	69.2	68.7	68.4
Once	53.7	52.5	52.4	52.6	52.4	52.3	52.3	52.1
Two times	13.7	13.3	13.3	13.2	13.3	13.3	12.9	12.8
Three or more times	3.6	3.7	3.6	3.6	3.6	3.6	3.5	3.5
Median duration of marriage (years) [1]	19.0	19.6	19.7	19.7	19.7	19.8	20.0	20.0

[1] Data shown for current marriage.

Source: U.S. Census Bureau, American Community Survey, B12504, "Median Duration of Current Marriage in Years By Sex By Marital Status for the Married Population 15 years and Over," and B12505, "Number of Times Married by Sex By Marital Status for the Population 15 Years and Over"; <data.census.gov>, accessed November 2023.

Health and Nutrition

This section presents statistics on numerous indicators of the nation's health care system, the health care industry and its institutions, and the health of the population. Data in this section cover national and personal health expenditures, health insurance coverage, Medicare and Medicaid, medical personnel, hospitals, nursing homes and other health care facilities, injuries, diseases, vaccinations, disability status, substance use (including alcohol, tobacco, and illicit drug use), exercise, food consumption, and nutrition. This section also includes data on selected health conditions and indicators among children.

Also appearing in this section are data on weekly trends in testing for and hospitalizations due to the coronavirus disease, COVID-19, as available during the time of production of this *Statistical Abstract*. The data presented here are an illustration of the progression of the pandemic in the U.S.; please see the sources noted in the relevant tables for revised and up-to-date data.

Data on national health expenditures, medical costs, and insurance coverage are compiled by the U.S. Centers for Medicare & Medicaid Services (CMS) and are available at <www.cms.gov/data-research/ statistics-trends-and-reports/national-health-expenditure-data>. Medicare data are available on the CMS website under "CMS Program Statistics." Internet users can find data on Medicare enrollment, utilization, and expenditures, and also data on Medicare-certified institutional and noninstitutional health care providers. Another key source of information on Medicare is the annual report to Congress from the Boards of Trustees for Medicare. The Trustees' report covers the financial operations and actuarial status of Medicare. Selected data on Medicaid and the Children's Health Insurance Program (CHIP) are available from <Medicaid.gov>, the U.S. National Center for Health Statistics (NCHS), and the Medicaid and CHIP Payment and Access Commission, a nonpartisan legislative branch agency that provides analysis to the states, Congress, and the Secretary of the Department of Health and Human Services.

Summary statistics showing recent trends in health care and health indicators of the population, and discussions of selected health issues are published annually by the NCHS in *Health, United States*. Statistics on health insurance are collected by surveys conducted by the Census Bureau. The NCHS also collects health insurance data and other detailed data on the population's health status annually in its National Health Interview Survey. Data from past and the most recent National Health Interview Surveys are available in online data tools and various reports, including the Early Release Program, accessible at <www.cdc.gov/nchs/nhis/index.htm>. Please note that the NHIS went through a questionnaire redesign that was implemented in 2019; therefore users should exercise caution in comparing trends before and after the questionnaire redesign. NCHS also operates the National Health and Nutrition Examination Survey to track various health indicators, such as food and nutrition, exercise, body weight, and incidence of conditions such as diabetes, high blood cholesterol, and high blood pressure (hypertension).

Statistics on hospitals are published annually by the Health Forum, LLC, an affiliate of the American Hospital Association (AHA), in *AHA Hospital Statistics*. As a proxy for actual food consumption, the U.S. Dept of Agriculture's Economic Research Service provides data on food availability online at <www.ers.usda.gov/ data-products/food-availability-per-capita-data-system/>. Available from the USDA's Agricultural Research Service are data on nutrient and energy consumption, compiled by the Food Surveys Research Group for the *What We Eat In America* program.

National health expenditures—CMS compiles estimates of national health expenditures (NHE) to measure spending for health care in the United States. The NHE accounts are structured to show spending by type of expenditure: hospital care, physician and clinical care, dental care, and other professional care; home health care; retail sales of prescription drugs, durable medical equipment, and other nondurable medical goods; nursing care facilities and continuing care retirement communities; expenditures for public health activities, administration, and the net cost of private health insurance; and medical sector investment, which is the sum of noncommercial medical research and capital formation in medical sector structures and equipment. The NHE also shows spending by source of funding (e.g., private health insurance, Medicare, Medicaid, out-of-pocket payments, and other third party payers and programs).

Data used to estimate health expenditures come from numerous public and private sources. The expenditure type estimates rely upon statistics produced by such groups as the AHA, the Census Bureau, and the U.S. Department of Health and Human Services (HHS). Funding source estimates are constructed using administrative and statistical records from the Medicare and Medicaid programs, the U.S. Department of Defense and Veterans Affairs medical programs, the Social Security Administration, the Census Bureau, state and local governments, other HHS agencies, and other nongovernment sources.

The Health Care Satellite Account (HCSA), developed by the Bureau of Economic Analysis (BEA), measures health care spending as the cost to treat specific diseases and medical conditions (such as cancer, or diseases of the circulatory system), as opposed to spending on specific types of health care services and goods (such as doctor's visits and prescription drugs). The HCSA can help answer questions regarding whether changes in medical expenditures are due to changes in costs of treatments or changes in number of persons receiving care, which medical conditions account for larger portions of spending, and which medical conditions experience the greatest changes in treatment costs. The BEA presents two versions of the HCSA. One version, the "MEPS Account," uses data from the Medical Expenditure Panel Survey; the other version, the "Blended Account," combines data from multiple sources, including large claims databases that cover millions of health insurance enrollees and billions of claims. The table in this section presents data from the Blended Account. See <www.bea.gov/data/special-topics/health-care> for detailed information about how the Health Care Satellite Account is constructed.

Medicare, Medicaid, and Children's Health Insurance Program (CHIP)—Medicare is health insurance for people age 65 and older. Certain individuals under age 65 with a disability can also participate in Medicare, including those with ALS (amyotrophic lateral sclerosis, also known as Lou Gehrig's disease) and end-stage renal disease. Persons under age 65 also automatically get Medicare after receiving 24 months of disability benefits from Social Security or the Railroad Retirement Board; persons who receive retirement or disability benefits from social security at least 4 months before they reach the age of 65 will also automatically get Medicare upon turning 65. The Original Medicare program (also known as fee-for-service) has two components: Medicare Part A, Hospital Insurance; and Medicare Part B, Medical Insurance. Medicare Part A generally has no premium for those who paid Medicare taxes while working, and helps pay for in-patient hospital stays, care in a skilled nursing facility, hospice care, and home health care after hospital stays. Medicare Part B is optional; it helps pay for physician and outpatient care services, durable medical equipment, and preventive services such as screenings, vaccines, and annual checkups. An additional component of Medicare, Part D, provides subsidized access to prescription drug insurance coverage on a voluntary basis for all beneficiaries, with premium and cost-sharing subsidies for low-income enrollees. Participants in Parts B and D pay monthly premiums. Medicare consists of two separate but coordinated trust funds: Hospital Insurance (HI, or Part A) and Supplementary Medical Insurance (SMI). The SMI trust fund comprises two separate accounts: the Part B account and the Part D account.

Medicare also has an alternative option to Original Medicare coverage, the Medicare Advantage Plan (also known as Part C). Medicare Advantage plans are offered by private companies and organizations, are required to provide at least services covered by Medicare Parts A and B (except hospice services), and are financed from both Medicare's Hospital Insurance (HI) trust fund and the Part B account within the Supplementary Medical Insurance (SMI) trust fund in proportion to the relative weights of Part A and Part B benefits to the total benefits paid by the Medicare program.

Title XIX of the Social Security Act established Medicaid in 1965, a health insurance program for certain low-income people, families and children, pregnant women, the elderly, and people with disabilities. There are special rules for those who live in nursing homes and for disabled children living at home. Medicaid is funded and administered through a federal-state partnership. Although there are broad federal requirements for Medicaid, states have a wide degree of flexibility to design their programs. Eligibility criteria, services, and payments for Medicaid varies from state to state.

Title XXI of the Social Security Act, the Children's Health Insurance Program (CHIP), was originally signed into law in 1997 and funded through fiscal year 2007. Since then, several pieces of legislation have extended CHIP funding, including the Children's Health Insurance Program Reauthorization Act of 2009, The Affordable Care Act of 2010, the Medicare Access and CHIP Reauthorization Act of 2015; and the Bipartisan Budget Act of 2018. CHIP is a federal-state partnership, similar to Medicaid, that expands health insurance to children whose families earn too much money to be eligible for Medicaid, but not enough money to purchase private health insurance. States also have the option to provide prenatal, delivery, and postpartum care to low-income pregnant women without health insurance. Under CHIP, states can operate their programs as an expansion of Medicaid or as a program entirely separate from Medicaid, or a combination of both approaches. Most states have either expanded Medicaid or run a combination of both types of programs. Only two states, Connecticut and Washington, run separate programs without Medicaid expansions.

Health care resources and utilization—Hospital statistics based on data from AHA's yearly survey are published annually in *AHA Hospital Statistics* and cover all hospitals accepted for registration by the Association. Up until fiscal year 2016, the AHA used its own detailed criteria for recognizing hospitals for registration. Beginning with fiscal year 2017, the AHA uses the following definition: an institution is a hospital if it is licensed as a general or specialty hospital by the appropriate state agency and accredited by one of the following organizations: The Joint Commission, Healthcare Facilities Accreditation Program (HFAP), DNV Health Accreditation, Center for Improvement in Healthcare Quality Accreditation, or Medicare certified as a provider of acute services under Title 18 of the Social Security Act.

Ambulatory care data, including emergency room visits, are presented here from the National Hospital Ambulatory Medical Care Survey (NHAMCS). Data on physicians generally come from the professional organizations that collect data on medical school graduates and physicians. Statistics on patient visits to health care providers come from the National Health Interview Survey and the National Ambulatory Medical Care Survey.

Disability and illness, mental health, and substance use—General health statistics, including morbidity, disability, injuries, preventive care, and findings from physiological testing are collected by NCHS in its National Health Interview Survey and its National Health and Nutrition Examination Surveys. The Centers for Disease Control and Prevention in Atlanta, Georgia collects and publishes data on nationally notifiable diseases. Data are collected from State health departments and territories under the National Notifiable Diseases Surveillance System (NNDSS), which is operated by the CDC in collaboration with the Council of State and Territorial Epidemiologists. The list of diseases is revised annually. The Substance Abuse and Mental Health Services Administration, an agency within HHS, studies and provides data regarding mental health disorders and treatment (including mental health treatment facilities and clients), and substance use (including tobacco, alcohol, and prescription and illicit drugs).

Statistical reliability—For discussions of statistical collections, including methodologies and sources of information on measures of reliability and other technical issues for data from the NCHS and CMS, see Appendix III.

Table 138. National Health Expenditures by Type of Service: 1960 to 2022

[In billions of dollars (27.1 represents $27,100,000,000). Excludes Puerto Rico and Island Areas. For definitions, methodology, and related information, see <www.cms.gov/files/document/definitions-sources-and-methods.pdf>]

Year	Total expenditures [1]	Health consumption expenditures, total [2]	Personal health care expenditures Total [3]	Hospital care	Physician and clinical services	Dental services	Other professional services [4]	Home health care [5]	Nursing care facilities [6]	Prescription drugs	Durable medical equipment [7]	Non-durable medical equipment [8]
1960....	27.1	24.6	23.1	9.0	5.6	2.0	0.4	0.1	0.8	2.7	0.7	1.5
1961....	29.1	26.2	24.6	9.8	5.8	2.1	0.4	0.1	0.8	2.7	0.8	1.6
1962....	31.8	28.3	26.5	10.4	6.3	2.2	0.4	0.1	0.9	3.0	0.9	1.8
1963....	34.6	30.8	29.0	11.5	7.1	2.4	0.5	0.1	1.0	3.2	0.9	1.8
1964....	38.2	33.9	31.8	12.5	8.1	2.6	0.5	0.1	1.2	3.3	1.0	1.9
1965....	41.6	36.9	34.4	13.5	8.6	2.8	0.5	0.1	1.4	3.7	1.1	1.9
1966....	45.8	40.8	38.0	15.3	9.3	3.0	0.6	0.1	1.7	4.0	1.2	2.0
1967....	51.2	46.0	43.0	17.8	10.4	3.4	0.6	0.2	2.2	4.2	1.1	2.0
1968....	58.0	52.2	48.6	20.5	11.3	3.7	0.6	0.2	2.9	4.7	1.3	2.2
1969....	65.4	58.4	54.9	23.4	12.7	4.2	0.7	0.3	3.4	5.1	1.5	2.3
1970....	74.1	66.3	62.4	27.2	14.3	4.7	0.7	0.2	4.0	5.5	1.7	2.6
1971....	82.4	73.6	68.7	30.2	15.9	5.2	0.8	0.2	4.6	5.9	1.8	2.7
1972....	92.4	82.5	76.4	33.8	17.7	5.6	0.9	0.2	5.2	6.3	2.0	2.9
1973....	102.7	92.2	85.3	37.9	19.6	6.4	1.0	0.3	6.0	6.8	2.2	3.1
1974....	116.3	104.9	97.8	44.1	22.2	7.2	1.2	0.4	6.9	7.4	2.5	3.5
1975....	132.7	119.9	112.1	51.2	25.3	8.0	1.3	0.6	8.0	8.1	2.8	3.8
1976....	152.0	138.0	128.1	59.4	28.7	9.0	1.6	0.9	9.1	8.7	3.0	4.2
1977....	172.7	158.3	145.1	67.0	33.1	10.1	2.1	1.1	10.3	9.2	3.2	4.5
1978....	194.0	178.1	162.4	75.6	35.8	11.0	2.4	1.6	11.8	9.9	3.4	5.3
1979....	219.7	202.2	184.9	86.2	41.2	12.0	2.8	1.9	13.3	10.7	3.8	6.2
1980....	253.2	232.7	214.3	100.5	47.7	13.3	3.5	2.4	15.3	12.0	4.1	7.1
1981....	293.6	270.1	248.6	117.5	55.6	15.7	4.3	2.9	17.3	13.4	4.3	8.1
1982....	330.9	304.2	279.5	133.6	61.6	17.0	4.9	3.5	19.5	15.0	4.6	9.0
1983....	364.8	335.5	308.0	144.7	68.7	18.3	5.7	4.2	21.7	17.3	5.3	10.1
1984....	401.9	371.0	337.9	154.4	77.4	19.9	7.3	5.1	23.7	19.6	6.1	11.2
1985....	439.9	408.7	372.6	164.6	90.9	21.7	8.1	5.6	26.2	21.8	7.1	12.2
1986....	472.3	440.0	405.4	175.8	100.7	23.2	9.3	6.4	28.6	24.3	8.1	13.4
1987....	514.5	478.8	444.4	189.7	112.9	25.3	11.3	6.6	30.6	26.9	9.5	14.7
1988....	576.6	536.8	495.1	206.5	128.6	27.4	13.7	8.4	34.2	30.6	11.1	15.7
1989....	642.2	598.5	547.0	226.0	143.3	29.4	14.5	10.2	38.6	34.8	11.9	17.0
1990....	718.7	670.2	611.9	250.4	159.0	31.6	17.3	12.5	44.7	40.3	13.8	18.5
1991....	786.0	733.9	672.6	275.8	176.6	33.4	18.6	15.1	49.2	44.4	13.1	19.2
1992....	852.2	795.1	728.3	298.5	191.3	37.2	20.9	18.7	52.8	47.0	13.5	19.1
1993....	914.9	854.0	775.5	315.7	202.7	39.0	23.0	22.7	55.8	49.6	14.1	19.4
1994....	966.4	902.8	817.7	328.4	212.7	41.6	24.0	27.3	58.4	53.0	15.3	19.8
1995....	1,020.3	954.7	866.5	339.3	222.2	44.6	26.7	32.3	64.2	59.8	15.9	20.4
1996....	1,073.6	1,006.5	914.6	350.8	230.8	47.0	28.9	35.7	69.2	68.1	17.4	21.1
1997....	1,132.9	1,061.3	965.6	363.4	241.6	50.3	31.3	36.9	74.1	77.6	19.2	21.6
1998....	1,198.4	1,119.9	1,019.2	374.9	256.5	53.6	33.4	34.1	79.1	88.5	21.3	22.5
1999....	1,273.2	1,188.8	1,078.8	393.6	269.5	57.3	34.6	32.8	80.6	105.3	22.2	24.1
2000....	1,366.0	1,280.3	1,156.5	415.5	288.2	62.1	36.6	32.3	85.0	122.0	26.0	25.2
2001....	1,483.4	1,393.4	1,256.5	449.4	312.7	67.7	40.3	34.3	90.8	140.6	25.4	26.1
2002....	1,631.0	1,529.6	1,365.5	486.5	337.7	73.6	43.3	36.5	94.5	159.8	29.6	27.9
2003....	1,770.4	1,661.8	1,475.9	525.9	364.3	76.3	46.5	40.2	100.1	179.7	30.7	30.3
2004....	1,894.7	1,777.8	1,582.4	565.3	384.6	82.2	50.2	44.6	105.1	195.6	33.2	32.7
2005....	2,026.6	1,901.0	1,693.8	608.6	409.8	87.2	52.8	49.3	111.4	208.6	36.2	35.5
2006....	2,165.1	2,032.1	1,806.5	651.2	433.0	91.8	55.3	52.1	115.9	228.1	39.6	38.7
2007....	2,305.5	2,159.3	1,921.5	691.9	457.3	97.7	60.1	57.5	124.9	239.3	43.4	41.7
2008....	2,402.4	2,246.1	2,007.2	721.6	481.5	102.8	64.5	62.2	130.4	244.3	42.6	45.3
2009....	2,492.7	2,345.5	2,105.5	771.0	497.5	103.4	67.0	67.0	135.2	254.3	41.4	47.6
2010....	2,589.6	2,437.5	2,180.5	808.8	512.4	105.9	69.9	70.5	140.5	253.4	40.0	51.8
2011....	2,676.5	2,517.8	2,253.9	833.2	535.8	108.0	72.8	74.6	145.3	256.3	40.6	56.6
2012....	2,783.3	2,620.1	2,346.2	878.0	557.1	109.7	76.4	78.1	147.3	257.0	43.3	61.2
2013....	2,855.7	2,692.6	2,404.6	906.8	568.0	111.4	78.0	81.0	148.7	259.4	44.2	63.5
2014....	3,001.7	2,842.2	2,526.2	940.5	598.2	114.7	82.4	84.7	152.5	290.7	45.0	66.2
2015....	3,163.8	3,000.6	2,672.9	989.0	637.3	120.0	87.3	89.6	156.8	312.2	46.3	70.3
2016....	3,305.3	3,139.1	2,793.7	1,035.4	676.7	126.2	92.1	93.8	162.0	313.3	46.7	73.3
2017....	3,443.7	3,263.0	2,901.5	1,077.6	709.4	131.1	96.9	99.4	163.4	315.7	47.5	76.3
2018....	3,601.2	3,411.6	3,017.1	1,122.7	736.2	137.4	104.5	105.6	167.6	322.7	49.9	80.7
2019....	3,756.4	3,562.3	3,171.2	1,193.6	767.8	143.7	110.9	112.4	174.1	335.7	53.4	84.8
2020....	4,156.3	3,962.2	3,375.3	1,268.0	818.5	139.4	118.1	125.1	196.4	350.6	53.8	94.7
2021....	4,289.1	4,081.6	3,561.5	1,325.2	861.8	164.8	133.8	125.4	181.1	374.5	63.8	106.4
2022....	4,464.6	4,246.8	3,704.8	1,355.0	884.9	165.3	140.6	132.9	191.3	405.9	67.1	115.4

[1] Includes Health Consumption Expenditures plus, not shown here, expenditures for noncommercial medical research, and medical structures and equipment. [2] Includes Personal Health Expenditures plus, not shown, expenditures for government administration, net cost of health insurance, and government public health activities. [3] Includes other health, residential, and personal services, not shown separately. [4] Includes health practitioners other than physicians and dentists, such as, but not limited to, chiropractors, optometrists, podiatrists, private-duty nurses, and physical, occupational and speech therapists. [5] Services delivered by freestanding home health care facilities only. [6] Care provided in nursing care facilities (NAICS 6231), continuing care retirement communities (623311), state and local government nursing facilities, and nursing facilities operated by the Department of Veterans Affairs. [7] Retail sales of items such as contact lenses, eyeglasses and other ophthalmic products, surgical and orthopedic products, medical equipment rental, oxygen, and hearing aids. Durable products generally last over 3 years. [8] Non-prescription drugs and sundry medical items.

Source: U.S. Centers for Medicare and Medicaid Services, Office of the Actuary, National Health Statistics Group, "National Health Expenditure Data, Historical," <www.cms.gov/data-research/statistics-trends-and-reports/national-health-expenditure-data>, accessed January 2024.

Table 139. National Health Expenditures by Source of Funds: 1990 to 2022

[In billions of dollars (718.7 represents $718,700,000,000), except percent. Excludes Puerto Rico and Island Areas. For definitions and related information, see <www.cms.gov/files/document/definitions-sources-and-methods.pdf>]

Source of funds	1990	2000	2010	2015	2019	2020 [8]	2021 [8]	2022 [8]
National health expenditure, total.........	**718.7**	**1,366.0**	**2,589.6**	**3,163.8**	**3,756.4**	**4,156.3**	**4,289.1**	**4,464.6**
Annual percent change [1]......................	11.9	7.3	3.9	5.4	4.3	10.6	3.2	4.1
Percent of gross domestic product...........	12.1	13.3	17.2	17.3	17.5	19.5	18.2	17.3
Consumer out of pocket........................	133.8	193.6	301.5	352.7	402.3	398.3	442.2	471.4
Health insurance...............................	431.1	902.0	1,832.6	2,288.3	2,718.0	2,807.4	3,011.8	3,211.5
Private health insurance.....................	225.9	441.0	820.2	976.5	1,155.7	1,146.2	1,218.3	1,289.8
Medicare......................................	110.2	224.8	519.5	647.7	802.3	832.2	892.1	944.3
Medicaid (Title XIX)...........................	73.7	200.4	397.4	543.0	615.0	672.0	735.4	805.7
CHIP (Title XIX and Title XXI).................	(X)	3.0	11.5	14.7	19.9	21.2	22.3	23.5
Department of Defense.......................	10.4	13.7	38.3	41.6	42.8	43.7	43.9	46.2
Department of Veterans Affairs...............	10.9	19.1	45.7	64.7	82.3	92.2	99.9	102.0
Other third party payers and programs........	85.3	141.7	227.7	274.1	333.6	514.6	417.1	355.5
Worksite health care........................	2.2	3.5	4.7	6.1	7.5	7.4	8.0	8.7
Other private revenues [2]...................	37.5	74.1	124.3	154.0	205.5	210.0	226.6	217.7
Indian health services.......................	1.0	1.9	3.5	3.7	4.2	4.6	5.9	7.0
Workers' compensation.......................	17.5	27.3	37.6	49.4	49.0	43.1	44.9	45.8
General assistance...........................	5.0	3.9	7.1	6.7	6.3	6.5	6.8	7.0
Maternal and Child health....................	1.6	2.3	2.5	1.9	1.9	1.9	1.9	2.0
Vocational rehabilitation.....................	0.3	0.4	0.6	0.5	0.5	0.5	0.5	0.6
Other federal programs [3]...................	1.6	4.5	7.7	12.6	14.0	193.6	72.3	17.2
Substance Abuse and Mental Health Services Administration......................	1.4	2.6	3.4	3.5	5.6	6.7	8.5	6.3
Other state and local programs [4]...........	15.9	18.7	32.1	30.8	32.9	33.9	34.9	36.0
School health...............................	1.3	2.5	4.3	4.9	6.2	6.5	6.9	7.3
Public health activity [5].......................	20.0	43.1	75.7	85.5	108.4	241.9	210.6	208.4
Investment...................................	**48.6**	**85.7**	**152.1**	**163.1**	**194.0**	**194.2**	**207.5**	**217.8**
Research [6]...................................	12.7	25.5	49.1	46.4	56.6	60.1	61.9	64.8
Structures & equipment [7]....................	35.9	60.2	103.0	116.7	137.5	134.1	145.5	153.0

X Not applicable. [1] Average percent change from prior year. [2] Includes the medical portion of property and casualty insurance, philanthropic support, and non-patient revenue. [3] Includes federal general hospital/medical; pre-existing conditions insurance plans (2010-2014) created under the Affordable Care Act; and the Provider Relief Fund and the Paycheck Protection Program, both established under the Coronavirus Aid, Relief and Economic Security (CARES) Act of 2020. [4] Includes temporary disability insurance, and state and local subsidies to providers. [5] Government health services such as epidemiological surveillance, inoculations, immunization/vaccination services, disease prevention programs, and public health laboratories. In the National Health Expenditure Accounts, spending for these activities is reported in government public health activity. [6] Non-profit or government entities. Excludes R&D expenditures by drug and medical supply and equipment manufacturers. [7] Structures are defined as the value of new construction by the medical sector. Equipment includes the value of new capital equipment (including software). Includes establishments that provide health care, and excludes retail establishments that sell non-durable or durable medical goods. Excludes maintenance and repairs. [8] For information on federal spending during the COVID-19 pandemic, see <www.cms.gov/files/document/accounting-federal-covid-expenditures-national-health-expenditure-accounts.pdf>.

Source: U.S. Centers for Medicare and Medicaid Services, Office of the Actuary, National Health Statistics Group, "National Health Expenditure Data, Historical," <www.cms.gov/data-research/statistics-trends-and-reports/national-health-expenditure-data>, accessed January 2024.

Table 140. National Health Expenditure Projections by Source of Funds and Type of Expenditure: 2023 to 2031

[In billions of dollars (4,799.3 represents $4,799,300,000,000). For calendar years. Projections are constructed using a current-law framework, and do not assume any potential legislative changes over the projection period nor do they speculate on possible deviations from current law. Excludes Puerto Rico and Island areas]

Funding source and expenditure type	2023	2024	2025	2026	2027	2028	2029	2030	2031
Total......................................	**4,799.3**	**5,048.8**	**5,295.2**	**5,560.3**	**5,890.0**	**6,215.5**	**6,575.0**	**6,931.9**	**7,307.4**
SOURCE OF FUNDS									
Consumer out-of-pocket......................	508.6	542.4	562.7	583.5	609.6	635.7	662.1	689.8	718.8
Health insurance.............................	3,498.2	3,669.7	3,862.6	4,069.7	4,336.1	4,596.0	4,887.1	5,171.7	5,471.0
Private health insurance [1].................	1,433.5	1,550.3	1,631.8	1,671.9	1,753.0	1,837.1	1,926.1	2,019.4	2,116.8
Medicare...................................	1,023.9	1,086.0	1,147.5	1,246.1	1,357.8	1,455.5	1,581.2	1,691.9	1,809.5
Medicaid...................................	851.9	833.5	872.5	930.4	991.6	1,057.4	1,120.7	1,187.8	1,257.6
Other health insurance programs [2]........	189.0	199.9	210.5	221.9	233.8	246.1	259.2	272.7	287.0
Other third party payers and programs [3].....	394.1	425.3	446.3	468.0	489.8	512.2	535.5	559.5	584.7
TYPE OF EXPENDITURE									
Health consumption expenditures [4]..........	4,565.2	4,802.7	5,036.5	5,288.3	5,605.3	5,917.5	6,263.1	6,605.3	6,965.8
Personal health care........................	4,038.2	4,251.2	4,460.3	4,687.4	4,972.5	5,253.0	5,563.5	5,868.9	6,190.9
Hospital care..............................	1,491.7	1,559.6	1,634.3	1,709.4	1,809.7	1,912.6	2,023.2	2,132.2	2,245.8
Physician and clinical services.............	959.1	1,006.5	1,055.3	1,105.1	1,171.1	1,230.7	1,302.9	1,371.9	1,445.1
Dental services............................	176.1	185.2	193.6	201.4	211.3	221.1	231.7	242.8	254.4
Other professional services [5].............	157.8	168.6	176.5	184.2	194.8	204.2	215.7	226.6	238.1
Home health care [6].......................	145.2	154.8	164.4	177.5	192.2	207.6	224.5	242.1	261.3
Nursing care facilities and continuing care retirement communities....................	209.3	216.3	225.2	237.6	253.0	268.3	284.4	300.6	318.1
Prescription drugs.........................	434.1	463.6	484.7	516.5	551.0	585.8	622.6	656.4	692.0
Durable medical equipment.................	70.9	75.3	79.6	84.1	88.8	93.5	98.5	103.7	109.1
Nondurable medical products...............	127.2	137.2	143.9	149.3	157.0	164.2	171.5	179.0	186.6
Other health, residential, and personal care [7]......	266.6	284.1	302.8	322.4	343.8	365.1	388.8	413.7	440.3
Government public health activity [8]........	164.3	165.2	164.9	167.1	169.8	173.5	178.3	184.4	191.2
Research [9]................................	68.0	71.3	74.7	78.3	82.0	85.9	89.9	94.1	98.4
Structures [10].............................	76.5	79.1	83.6	87.7	91.8	96.2	100.9	105.9	111.0
Equipment [10].............................	89.6	95.7	100.4	105.9	111.0	116.0	121.1	126.6	132.3

[1] Includes employer sponsored insurance and other private insurance, which also includes marketplace plans. [2] Children's Health Insurance Program (Titles XIX and XXI), Department of Defense, and Department of Veterans' Affairs. [3] See Table 139. [4] See footnote 2, Table 138. [5] See footnote 4, Table 138. [6] See footnote 5, Table 138. [7] See footnote 4, Table 141. [8] See footnote 5, Table 139. [9] See footnote 6, Table 139. [10] See footnote 7, Table 139.

Source: U.S. Centers for Medicare and Medicaid Services, Office of the Actuary, National Health Statistics Group, "National Health Expenditure Data, Projected," <www.cms.gov/nationalhealthexpenddata>, accessed June 2024.

Table 141. Health Consumption Expenditures—Per Capita Spending by Type of Expenditure: 2000 to 2022

[In dollars, except percent. Based on U.S. Census Bureau estimates of total U.S. resident population. Health consumption expenditures include all personal health care spending, government administration and the net cost of private health insurance, and public health activities. Excludes investment in research, structures, and equipment. Excludes Puerto Rico and Island Areas]

Type of expenditure	2000	2005	2010	2015	2018	2019	2020	2021	2022
Total [1]	**4,541**	**6,446**	**7,889**	**9,364**	**10,449**	**10,862**	**12,039**	**12,383**	**12,835**
Annual percent change [2]	(NA)	6.0	3.1	4.8	4.0	4.0	10.8	2.9	3.7
Hospital care	1,474	2,064	2,618	3,086	3,438	3,639	3,853	4,020	4,095
Physician and clinical services	1,022	1,390	1,658	1,989	2,255	2,341	2,487	2,615	2,674
Dental services	220	296	343	374	421	438	424	500	500
Other professional services [3]	130	179	226	272	320	338	359	406	425
Other health, residential, and personal care [4]	225	320	412	512	582	594	640	682	745
Home health care	115	167	228	280	323	343	380	380	402
Nursing care facilities and continuing care retirement communities	302	378	455	489	513	531	597	549	578
Prescription drugs	433	707	820	974	988	1024	1,065	1,136	1,227
Durable medical equipment [5]	92	123	129	144	153	163	163	194	203
Other nondurable medical products [6]	89	120	168	219	247	259	288	323	349
Public health activities [7]	153	194	245	267	304	330	735	639	630

NA Not available. [1] Includes other items, not shown separately. [2] Average annual growth from previous year. [3] See footnote 4, Table 138. [4] Mostly services in non-traditional settings, including school health, worksite health care, Medicaid home and community based waivers, some ambulance services, residential mental health and substance abuse facilities, and residential intellectual and developmental disability facilities. [5] See footnote 7, Table 138. [6] See footnote 8, Table 138. [7] See footnote 5, Table 139.

Source: U.S. Centers for Medicare and Medicaid Services, Office of the Actuary, National Health Statistics Group, "National Health Expenditure Data, Historical," <www.cms.gov/data-research/statistics-trends-and-reports/national-health-expenditure-data>, accessed January 2024.

Table 142. Health Consumption Expenditures by Type of Expenditure and Source of Funds: 2022

[In billions of dollars (4,246.8 represents $4,246,800,000,000). Excludes Puerto Rico and Island Areas. Excludes investment in research, structures, and equipment]

Type of expenditure	Total	Out-of-pocket	Health insurance Total	Private health insurance	Medicare	Medicaid	Other health insurance programs [1]	Other third party payers and programs [2]
Total	**4,246.8**	**471.4**	**3,211.5**	**1,289.8**	**944.3**	**805.7**	**171.6**	**355.5**
Personal health care [3]	3,704.8	471.4	2,904.1	1,158.5	873.3	709.9	162.4	329.3
Hospital care	1,355.0	35.4	1,188.9	485.9	353.2	262.6	87.2	130.7
Physician and clinical services	884.9	67.3	731.6	342.0	234.1	110.1	45.4	86.0
Dental services	165.3	66.6	96.2	68.0	6.2	17.0	5.0	2.4
Other health, residential, and personal care [4]	246.5	7.8	172.6	15.9	4.2	149.3	3.2	66.1
Home health care	132.9	15.4	114.0	18.6	47.5	46.9	1.0	3.5
Nursing care facilities and continuing care retirement communities	191.3	48.3	125.2	18.2	42.2	58.5	6.3	17.8
Prescription drugs	405.9	56.7	343.5	155.0	129.8	45.3	13.4	5.7
Durable medical equipment	67.1	27.8	38.0	13.9	14.1	9.7	0.2	1.3
Government administration [5]	54.2	(X)	51.3	(X)	13.4	30.9	6.4	2.9
Net cost of health insurance [5]	279.4	(X)	256.1	131.3	57.6	64.9	2.2	23.3
Public health activities [6]	208.4	(X)	(X)	(X)	(X)	(X)	(X)	(X)

X Not applicable. [1] Includes Children's Health Insurance Program (CHIP) Titles XIX and XXI, Department of Defense, and Department of Veterans Affairs. [2] Includes worksite health care, other private revenues, Indian Health Service, workers' compensation, general assistance, maternal and child health, vocational rehabilitation, other federal programs, Substance Abuse and Mental Health Services Administration, other state and local programs, and school health. [3] Comprises all medical goods and services that are rendered to treat or prevent a specific disease or condition in a specific person. Includes expenditures for items not shown separately. [4] See footnote 4, Table 141. [5] See source for definitions. [6] See footnote 5, Table 139.

Source: U.S. Centers for Medicare and Medicaid Services, Office of the Actuary, National Health Statistics Group, "National Health Expenditure Data, Historical," <www.cms.gov/data-research/statistics-trends-and-reports/national-health-expenditure-data>, accessed January 2024.

Table 143. Personal Health Care Expenditures by Source of Funds: 2000 to 2022

[In billions of dollars (1,156.5 represents $1,156,500,000,000). Excludes Puerto Rico and Island Areas]

Source of funds	2000	2005	2010	2015	2018	2019	2020	2021	2022
Personal health care expenditures	**1,156.5**	**1,693.8**	**2,180.5**	**2,672.9**	**3,017.1**	**3,171.2**	**3,375.3**	**3,561.5**	**3,704.8**
Out-of-pocket	193.6	264.5	301.5	352.7	385.7	402.3	398.3	442.2	471.4
Health insurance	832.9	1,261.5	1,670.2	2,075.6	2,347.5	2,466.6	2,494.0	2,732.5	2,904.1
Private health insurance	394.8	587.1	725.4	869.8	989.0	1,028.0	996.5	1,096.6	1,158.5
Medicare	216.3	326.3	488.8	606.1	696.7	746.9	760.6	832.2	873.3
Medicaid	186.9	287.6	365.7	484.5	531.9	553.6	587.7	646.2	709.9
Other health insurance [1]	34.9	60.5	90.3	115.2	129.9	138.1	149.2	157.4	162.4
Other third party payers and programs [2]	130.1	167.9	208.8	244.6	283.9	302.3	482.9	386.9	329.3

[1] Includes Children's Health Insurance Program (Titles XIX and XXI), Department of Defense, and Department of Veterans Affairs. [2] See footnote 2, Table 142.

Source: U.S. Centers for Medicare and Medicaid Services, Office of the Actuary, National Health Statistics Group, "National Health Expenditure Data, Historical," <www.cms.gov/data-research/statistics-trends-and-reports/national-health-expenditure-data>, accessed January 2024.

Table 144. National Health Expenditures by Sponsor: 2000 to 2022

[In billions of dollars (1,366.0 represents $1,366,000,000,000). Excludes Puerto Rico and Island Areas. Type of sponsor is defined as the entity that is ultimately responsible for financing the health care bill. These sponsors pay health insurance premiums and out-of-pocket costs, or finance health care through dedicated taxes and/or general revenues. See source for sponsor inclusion and exclusion details]

Type of sponsor	2000	2005	2010	2015	2019	2020 [5]	2021 [5]	2022 [5]
Total.	**1,366.0**	**2,026.6**	**2,589.6**	**3,163.8**	**3,756.4**	**4,156.3**	**4,289.1**	**4,464.6**
Business, households and other private revenues.	878.0	1,223.4	1,432.3	1,711.9	2,045.1	2,041.4	2,188.9	2,308.0
Private business [1]	336.4	469.8	512.2	596.9	708.5	690.5	742.8	787.3
Household [2]	437.5	616.3	746.0	901.1	1,063.5	1,078.6	1,151.7	1,231.6
Other private revenues.	104.1	137.3	174.1	214.0	273.0	272.3	294.4	289.1
Governments.	488.0	803.2	1,157.4	1,451.8	1,711.3	2,114.9	2,100.3	2,156.6
Federal government [3]	263.2	456.5	739.7	915.8	1,104.5	1,519.9	1,468.3	1,483.5
State and local government [4]	224.7	346.7	417.7	536.0	606.8	595.0	631.9	673.1

[1] Includes employer contributions to employer-sponsored health insurance premiums, employer Medicare Hospital Insurance (HI) Trust Fund payroll taxes, workers' compensation, temporary disability insurance, and worksite health care. [2] Includes employee contributions to employer-sponsored health insurance premiums, directly purchased health insurance, the medical portion of property and casualty insurance premiums, employee and self-employment payroll taxes and premiums paid to the Medicare HI Trust Fund, premiums paid to the Medicare Supplementary Medical Insurance (SMI) Trust Fund, premiums paid for the Pre-existing Condition Insurance Program (PCIP) for 2010-2014, and out-of-pocket health spending. [3] Includes employer contributions to employer-sponsored health insurance premiums, employer Medicare HI payroll taxes, federal general revenue and Medicare net Trust Fund expenditures, federal Medicaid expenditures, the federal portion of Medicaid buy-ins for the Medicare premiums of people eligible for both Medicaid and Medicare (dual eligibles), Medicare Retiree Drug Subsidy (RDS) payments to private business and state and local government employer plans beginning in 2006, Marketplace tax credits and subsidies, and other federal health programs. [4] Includes employer contributions to employer-sponsored health insurance premiums, employer Medicare HI payroll taxes, state and local Medicaid expenditures, the state and local portion of Medicaid buy-ins for the Medicare premiums of people eligible for both Medicaid and Medicare (dual eligibles), and other programs. [5] For information on federal spending during the COVID-19 pandemic, see <www.cms.gov/files/document/accounting-federal-covid-expenditures-national-health-expenditure-accounts.pdf>.

Source: U.S. Centers for Medicare and Medicaid Services, Office of the Actuary, National Health Statistics Group, "National Health Expenditure Data, Historical," <www.cms.gov/data-research/statistics-trends-and-reports/national-health-expenditure-data>, accessed January 2024.

Table 145. Hospital Care, Physician and Clinical Services, Nursing Care Facilities and Continuing Care Retirement Communities, and Prescription Drug Expenditures by Source of Funds: 2000 to 2022

[In billions of dollars (415.5 represents $415,500,000,000). Excludes Puerto Rico and Island Areas]

Expense type and payment source	2000	2005	2010	2015	2019	2020 [3]	2021 [3]	2022 [3]
Hospital care, total	**415.5**	**608.6**	**808.8**	**989.0**	**1,193.6**	**1,268.0**	**1,325.2**	**1,355.0**
Out-of-pocket.	13.3	19.5	27.0	30.6	36.4	32.3	34.2	35.4
Health insurance.	355.6	528.1	698.7	862.1	1,034.0	1,027.0	1,136.7	1,188.9
Private health insurance.	138.2	212.2	284.4	350.3	433.2	403.5	456.6	485.9
Medicare.	123.5	176.6	220.8	261.7	319.1	322.2	349.0	353.2
Medicaid.	70.9	103.8	142.2	186.1	207.4	221.4	245.6	262.6
CHIP [1]	0.9	2.7	3.2	3.7	5.1	5.3	5.6	5.7
Dept. of Defense.	7.6	12.0	16.5	15.8	16.6	16.3	15.9	16.4
Veterans Affairs.	14.3	20.8	31.7	44.5	52.5	58.4	64.0	65.1
Other third party payers and programs [2]	46.7	60.9	83.1	96.2	123.2	208.6	154.3	130.7
Physician and clinical services, total	**288.2**	**409.8**	**512.4**	**637.3**	**767.8**	**818.5**	**861.8**	**884.9**
Out-of-pocket.	31.5	40.6	47.6	55.5	61.9	60.0	65.8	67.3
Health insurance.	216.8	318.5	406.2	511.4	620.6	629.7	688.9	731.6
Private health insurance.	131.7	190.0	223.7	263.8	304.1	305.7	326.8	342.0
Medicare.	59.1	86.4	118.2	149.3	194.3	194.0	219.2	234.1
Medicaid.	19.3	30.1	43.4	70.1	83.9	87.3	99.3	110.1
CHIP [1]	0.7	1.7	3.1	3.5	4.7	4.8	4.9	4.8
Dept. of Defense.	4.7	7.9	12.1	14.8	17.4	18.2	18.5	19.7
Veterans Affairs.	1.3	2.5	5.8	9.9	16.3	19.8	20.2	20.9
Other third party payers and programs [2]	39.9	50.7	58.6	70.5	85.3	128.8	107.1	86.0
Nursing care facilities and continuing care retirement communities, total	**85.0**	**111.4**	**140.5**	**156.8**	**174.1**	**196.4**	**181.1**	**191.3**
Out-of-pocket.	26.9	32.4	37.1	40.2	46.1	45.0	43.9	48.3
Health insurance.	51.9	71.6	93.3	105.1	113.0	116.5	116.8	125.2
Private health insurance.	7.2	6.9	10.6	13.4	16.7	16.6	16.3	18.2
Medicare.	10.9	20.5	32.3	37.0	38.1	39.9	39.6	42.2
Medicaid.	31.9	41.3	46.3	49.8	52.2	53.5	54.1	58.5
Veterans Affairs.	1.9	2.8	4.0	5.0	6.0	6.5	6.8	6.3
Other third party payers and programs [2]	6.3	7.4	10.1	11.5	15.1	35.0	20.5	17.8
Prescription drugs, total	**122.0**	**208.6**	**253.4**	**312.2**	**335.7**	**350.6**	**374.5**	**405.9**
Out-of-pocket.	34.7	55.8	47.7	51.8	47.2	47.8	50.8	56.7
Health insurance.	83.4	146.6	200.2	255.9	284.0	298.6	318.5	343.5
Private health insurance.	59.9	99.5	114.3	130.7	136.6	140.3	147.8	155.0
Medicare.	1.6	3.2	56.3	86.4	104.6	111.6	118.7	129.8
Medicaid.	19.8	36.5	20.4	27.7	31.7	34.4	39.6	45.3
CHIP [1]	0.3	1.1	1.4	1.6	2.1	2.2	2.3	2.6
Dept. of Defense.	0.7	3.6	4.7	6.3	4.8	5.1	5.2	5.8
Veterans Affairs.	1.1	2.7	3.0	3.3	4.1	4.8	4.9	5.1
Other third party payers and programs [2]	3.9	6.3	5.5	4.5	4.5	4.3	5.1	5.7

[1] Children's Health Insurance Program (Titles XIX and XXI), effective beginning 1998. [2] Includes worksite health care, other private revenues, Indian Health Service, workers' compensation, general assistance, maternal and child health, vocational rehabilitation, other federal programs (including the Provider Relief Fund and the Paycheck Protection Program, both established under the Coronavirus Aid, Relief and Economic Security (CARES) Act of 2020), Substance Abuse and Mental Health Services Administration, other state and local programs, and school health. [3] For information on federal spending during the COVID-19 pandemic, see <www.cms.gov/files/document/accounting-federal-covid-expenditures-national-health-expenditure-accounts.pdf>.

Source: U.S. Centers for Medicare and Medicaid Services, Office of the Actuary, National Health Statistics Group, "National Health Expenditure Data, Historical," <www.cms.gov/data-research/statistics-trends-and-reports/national-health-expenditure-data>, accessed January 2024.

Table 146. Medical Care Consumer Price Indexes: 1990 to 2023

[Indexes with base of 1982-1984=100, except as noted. Indexes are annual averages of monthly data based on components of consumer price index for all urban consumers; for explanation, see text, Section 14 and Appendix III]

Year	Medical care, total	Medical care services						Medical care commodities		Annual percent change [2]		
		Total	Professional services			Hospital and related services	Health insur- ance [3]	Total [1]	Pre- scription drugs	Medical care, total	Medical care services	Medical care com- modities
			Total [1]	Physi- cians	Dental							
1990......	162.8	162.7	156.1	160.8	155.8	178.0	(NA)	163.4	181.7	9.0	9.3	8.4
2000......	260.8	266.0	237.7	244.7	258.5	317.3	(NA)	238.1	285.4	4.1	4.3	3.2
2005......	323.2	336.7	281.7	287.5	324.0	439.9	(NA)	276.0	349.0	4.2	4.8	2.5
2010......	388.4	411.2	328.2	331.3	398.8	607.7	106.6	314.7	407.8	3.4	3.5	3.1
2015......	446.8	476.2	361.5	366.1	452.2	761.9	123.6	354.6	479.3	2.6	2.4	3.3
2016......	463.7	494.8	371.5	378.1	465.0	795.1	131.8	366.8	502.5	3.8	3.9	3.4
2017......	475.3	506.8	375.1	380.1	472.6	831.7	133.9	377.0	519.6	2.5	2.4	2.8
2018......	484.7	517.8	378.4	380.5	485.5	866.9	135.5	381.4	528.0	2.0	2.2	1.2
2019......	498.4	536.1	382.6	383.2	496.2	885.2	155.2	381.3	526.8	2.8	3.5	–
2020......	518.9	562.7	389.9	389.9	511.1	921.1	179.8	383.2	532.1	4.1	4.9	0.5
2021......	525.3	573.1	401.9	406.5	522.5	950.0	172.0	377.1	522.4	1.2	1.9	-1.6
2022......	546.6	597.7	411.8	411.9	543.7	985.5	196.0	388.1	533.9	4.1	4.3	2.9
2023......	549.1	595.6	419.1	412.6	574.3	1,028.0	151.3	404.3	549.5	0.5	-0.3	4.2

– Represents or rounds to zero. NA Not available. [1] Includes other services or commodities not shown separately. [2] Percent change from the immediate prior year. [3] Index on a December 2005=100 basis.

Source: U.S. Bureau of Labor Statistics, "Consumer Price Index Databases," <www.bls.gov/cpi/data.htm>, accessed July 2024.

Table 147. Consumer Expenditures per Consumer Unit for Health Care: 2022

[In dollars, except percent. Expenditures are direct out-of-pocket expenditures. Consumers units may be all members in a housing unit (families), a person living alone or sharing a household with others and financially independent, or 2 or more unrelated persons living together who share expenses. See also text for Section 13, and source. For composition of regions, see map, inside front cover]

Consumer characteristic	Health care, total		Health insur- ance	Medical services	Drugs and medical sup- plies [1]	Percent distribution		
	Amount	Percent of total expendi- tures				Health insur- ance	Medical services	Drugs and medical sup- plies [1]
Total.............................	**5,850**	**8.0**	**3,843**	**1,184**	**824**	**65.7**	**20.2**	**14.1**
Age of reference person:								
Under 25 years old...........................	1,353	2.9	821	342	118	60.7	25.3	8.7
25 to 34 years old...........................	3,560	5.2	2,325	842	393	65.3	23.7	11.0
35 to 44 years old...........................	5,329	6.2	3,516	1,254	559	66.0	23.5	10.5
45 to 54 years old...........................	6,081	6.7	3,819	1,449	814	62.8	23.8	13.4
55 to 64 years old...........................	6,699	8.6	4,075	1,444	259	60.8	21.6	3.9
65 years old and older.......................	7,540	13.0	5,277	1,142	1,121	70.0	15.1	14.9
Race of reference person:								
White and other [2].........................	6,183	8.3	4,002	1,271	910	64.7	20.6	14.7
Asian.........................	5,643	6.4	3,943	1,148	552	69.9	20.3	9.8
Black.........................	3,869	6.7	2,813	654	402	72.7	16.9	10.4
Origin of reference person:								
Hispanic...........................	3,964	6.2	2,575	955	434	65.0	24.1	10.9
Non-Hispanic...........................	6,173	8.3	4,060	1,222	891	65.8	19.8	14.4
Region of residence:								
Northeast...........................	6,069	7.6	3,934	1,424	711	64.8	23.5	11.7
Midwest...........................	6,569	9.4	4,176	1,265	265	63.6	19.3	4.0
South...........................	5,376	8.2	3,671	1,005	700	68.3	18.7	13.0
West...........................	5,828	7.0	3,758	1,230	839	64.5	21.1	14.4
Size of consumer unit:								
One person...........................	3,770	8.5	2,434	796	540	64.6	21.1	14.3
Two or more persons...........................	6,785	7.9	4,476	1,358	951	66.0	20.0	14.0
Two persons...........................	6,878	9.0	4,684	1,226	968	68.1	17.8	14.1
Three persons...........................	6,660	7.7	4,583	1,259	817	68.8	18.9	12.3
Four persons...........................	7,288	7.2	4,254	1,742	239	58.4	23.9	3.3
Five persons or more...........................	6,045	6.2	3,908	1,466	671	64.6	24.3	11.1
Income before taxes, by quintile:								
Lowest 20 percent...........................	3,355	10.3	2,253	663	439	67.2	19.8	13.1
Second 20 percent...........................	4,441	9.3	3,097	651	693	69.7	14.7	15.6
Third 20 percent...........................	5,951	9.6	3,699	1,182	183	62.2	19.9	3.1
Fourth 20 percent...........................	6,694	8.2	4,515	1,379	800	67.4	20.6	12.0
Highest 20 percent...........................	8,814	6.3	5,654	2,042	1,118	64.1	23.2	12.7
Education: [3]								
Less than a high school graduate............	2,993	8.1	2,022	(B)	309	67.6	(NA)	10.3
High school graduate.........................	3,956	8.6	2,829	662	465	71.5	16.7	11.8
High school graduate with some college....	4,928	8.7	3,243	976	710	65.8	19.8	14.4
Associate's degree.........................	5,516	8.7	3,753	1,085	679	68.0	19.7	12.3
Bachelor's degree...........................	6,992	8.1	4,369	1,535	1,089	62.5	22.0	15.6
Master's, professional, or doctoral degree...	7,889	7.2	5,181	1,616	1,091	65.7	20.5	13.8

B Data suppressed due to relative standard error being equal to or greater than 25 percent. NA Not available. [1] Includes prescription, vitamins, and nonprescription drugs. [2] All other races includes Native Hawaiian or other Pacific Islander, American Indian or Alaska Native, and respondents reporting more than one race. [3] Highest education level of any member of the consumer unit.

Source: U.S. Bureau of Labor Statistics, Consumer Expenditure Surveys, "Calendar year tables by demographic characteristics," <www.bls.gov/cex/tables.htm>, accessed November 2023.

Table 148. Medical Expenditures by Health Condition in Current and Chained (2017) Dollars and Per Capita: 2020 and 2021

[In billions of dollars (2,792.28 represents $2,792,280,000,000), except as noted. Health conditions are classified according to the International Classification of Diseases, 10th revision (ICD-10). Estimates reflect deductions for manufacturer rebates from prescription drug spending. Based on Bureau of Economic Analysis' Health Care Satellite Account, Blended Account. The Blended Account combines data from multiple sources, including large claims databases. The BEA also has available health expenditure data based on the Medical Expenditure Panel Survey. See source for details]

Health expense item	Current dollars (billions)		Chained (2017) dollars (billions)		Per capita (dollars)	
	2020	2021	2020	2021	2020	2021
Total health	**2,792.28**	**3,076.95**	**2,532.17**	**2,720.42**	**8,451.29**	**9,298.69**
Health services	2,631.03	2,891.65	2,372.67	2,536.87	7,963.24	8,738.70
Medical services by disease	2,324.61	2,556.06	2,094.46	2,238.09	7,035.81	7,724.53
Infectious and parasitic diseases	204.82	230.81	153.81	171.85	619.92	697.52
Neoplasms	159.98	171.99	140.55	151.51	484.21	519.76
Endocrine, nutritional, and metabolic diseases and immunity disorders	145.01	158.67	131.38	141.43	438.90	479.51
Mental illness	127.26	139.61	109.06	120.42	385.17	421.91
Diseases of the nervous system and sense organs	175.26	191.41	161.40	172.40	530.45	578.45
Diseases of the circulatory system	245.86	265.74	235.29	249.78	744.14	803.08
Diseases of the respiratory system	147.53	148.31	135.03	124.46	446.52	448.20
Diseases of the digestive system	123.90	136.25	107.69	116.96	375.00	411.75
Diseases of the genitourinary system	114.15	122.68	108.19	115.19	345.49	370.74
Complications of pregnancy, childbirth, and the puerperium	50.75	53.97	49.46	52.10	153.60	163.10
Diseases of the skin and subcutaneous organs	57.66	65.23	53.27	57.10	174.52	197.13
Diseases of the musculoskeletal system and connective tissue	215.14	240.48	203.38	218.49	651.16	726.74
Injury and poisoning	131.64	144.81	117.62	125.18	398.43	437.62
Symptoms, signs, and ill-defined conditions	332.28	386.00	293.63	314.91	1,005.70	1,166.51
Other diseases	93.37	100.10	88.65	98.61	282.60	302.51
Diseases of blood and blood-forming organs	25.22	26.84	21.97	23.56	76.33	81.11
Congenital anomalies	7.82	8.58	6.52	7.38	23.67	25.93
Conditions originating in perinatal period	12.34	11.34	9.32	10.62	37.35	34.27
Residual codes, unclassified, all E codes [1]	47.99	53.34	51.37	57.73	145.25	161.20
Medical services by provider	306.42	335.59	278.29	298.89	927.43	1,014.17
Dental services	119.08	145.94	110.15	131.97	360.42	441.04
Nursing homes	187.35	189.65	167.97	167.11	567.05	573.13
Proprietary and government nursing homes	125.90	128.69	112.88	113.40	381.06	388.91
Nonprofit nursing homes services to households	61.45	60.95	55.09	53.71	185.99	184.19
Medical products, appliances and equipment	161.25	185.30	161.16	186.91	488.05	559.99
Pharmaceutical and other medical products	94.71	106.36	95.62	108.18	286.66	321.42
Pharmaceutical products (excl. prescription drugs) [2]	88.84	99.58	89.72	101.17	268.89	300.94
Nonprescription drugs	88.84	99.58	89.72	101.17	268.89	300.94
Other medical products	5.87	6.78	5.90	7.02	17.77	20.49
Therapeutic appliances and equipment	66.54	78.95	65.66	78.81	201.39	238.59
Corrective eyeglasses and contact lenses	33.90	41.57	32.89	40.13	102.60	125.63
Therapeutic medical equipment	32.65	37.38	32.80	38.68	98.82	112.96

[1] E codes cover external causes of injury or poisoning. [2] Excludes prescription drugs; prescription drug expenses have been allocated by health condition.

Source: U.S. Bureau of Economic Analysis, Health Care Satellite Account, "Blended Account, 2000-2021," <www.bea.gov/data/special-topics/health-care>, accessed January 2024.

Table 149. Federal Budget Outlays For Health Programs: 1980 to 2024

[In billions of dollars (65.4 represents $65,400,000,000), except percent. For fiscal years ending September 30]

Year	Total [1]	Defense health program	Medicare (excluding premiums)	Medicaid	Veterans medical care	Federal employee health benefits	Health insurance assistance	Other health	Health program outlays as percent of: Total outlays	GDP
1980	65.4	3.7	35.0	14.0	6.5	3.6	(NA)	9.2	11.1	2.3
1990	180.4	12.4	109.7	41.1	12.1	11.0	(NA)	17.8	14.4	3.1
2000	388.9	17.8	219.0	117.9	19.5	19.6	(NA)	36.7	21.7	3.8
2005	614.1	36.1	336.9	181.7	28.8	29.6	0.1	70.5	24.8	4.8
2010	916.3	49.8	516.8	272.8	45.7	39.0	4.1	93.1	26.5	6.2
2012	922.5	53.3	544.6	250.5	50.6	42.6	3.8	94.5	26.2	5.7
2013	955.3	46.7	575.1	265.4	52.5	43.9	2.4	92.6	27.7	5.7
2014	1,026.3	48.9	592.4	301.5	56.2	46.1	13.7	94.5	29.3	5.9
2015	1,138.4	48.0	629.6	349.8	61.9	48.4	27.3	104.7	30.8	6.3
2016	1,218.8	47.7	684.9	368.3	65.2	50.1	30.9	112.9	31.6	6.5
2017	1,249.2	49.0	696.9	374.7	69.7	50.6	39.2	121.6	31.4	6.4
2018	1,264.4	50.5	700.1	389.2	73.9	53.2	46.0	117.3	30.8	6.2
2019	1,366.7	50.6	770.8	409.4	80.3	55.3	48.7	127.0	30.7	6.4
2020	1,667.8	53.4	904.4	458.5	90.6	56.1	51.5	238.2	25.4	7.8
2021	1,644.4	51.7	830.8	520.6	99.9	59.0	64.7	210.8	24.1	7.2
2022	1,835.3	55.4	905.6	591.9	110.7	61.0	79.5	242.0	29.3	7.3
2023	1,919.2	57.6	1,004.7	615.8	125.5	65.1	82.7	188.4	31.3	7.1
2024 [2]	1,911.1	58.4	1,019.0	567.2	147.2	69.7	101.6	187.9	27.5	6.8

NA Not available. [1] Total outlays are net of Medicare premiums and income from Federal employee health benefits, not shown separately. [2] Estimated.

Source: U.S. Office of Management and Budget, *Budget of the U.S. Government, Fiscal Year 2025: Historical Tables*, March 2024. See also <www.whitehouse.gov/omb/budget>.

Table 150. Medicare Enrollment by State: 2020 and 2021

[In thousands (62,840.3 represents 62,840,300). Covers Medicare beneficiaries enrolled in either Hospital Insurance and/or Supplementary Medical Insurance. Enrollment counts are determined by using a person-year methodology; for each calendar year, total person-year counts are determined by summing the total number of months that each beneficiary is enrolled during the year and dividing by 12 (see source for more information). Numbers may not add to totals because of rounding]

State	2020			2021		
	Total Medicare	Original Medicare [1]	Medicare Advantage [2]	Total Medicare	Original Medicare [1]	Medicare Advantage [2]
Total...............	62,840.3	37,776.3	25,063.9	63,892.6	36,356.4	27,536.2
United States [3]...............	61,551.9	37,094.4	24,457.5	62,590.5	35,681.3	26,909.1
Alabama......................	1,062.6	576.7	485.9	1,070.5	529.0	541.5
Alaska.......................	104.5	102.6	1.8	108.1	105.8	2.3
Arizona......................	1,370.1	788.0	582.1	1,400.2	767.5	632.6
Arkansas.....................	646.9	453.9	193.0	653.3	430.7	222.6
California....................	6,411.1	3,503.9	2,907.2	6,499.2	3,436.7	3,062.5
Colorado.....................	938.9	527.9	411.1	961.6	518.8	442.8
Connecticut..................	692.0	382.1	309.9	702.4	363.4	339.0
Delaware.....................	215.7	174.8	40.9	222.8	171.1	51.7
District of Columbia...........	94.1	73.3	20.8	94.1	70.2	23.8
Florida......................	4,680.1	2,411.9	2,268.3	4,803.8	2,359.9	2,443.9
Georgia......................	1,773.1	1,012.1	761.1	1,808.9	954.0	855.0
Hawaii.......................	281.2	148.1	133.0	288.5	145.6	142.8
Idaho.......................	349.2	219.6	129.6	361.6	215.7	145.9
Illinois......................	2,265.9	1,582.6	683.3	2,287.3	1,507.0	780.3
Indiana......................	1,284.0	823.6	460.4	1,301.3	775.3	526.0
Iowa........................	637.4	477.4	160.0	646.9	465.6	181.3
Kansas......................	546.4	429.9	116.5	555.8	414.9	140.9
Kentucky....................	943.2	578.9	364.3	952.2	537.0	415.2
Louisiana....................	884.2	513.0	371.3	893.6	473.6	420.1
Maine.......................	347.6	202.7	144.9	356.2	187.4	168.8
Maryland....................	1,058.2	920.1	138.1	1,075.1	898.9	176.1
Massachusetts................	1,352.8	989.5	363.3	1,374.2	973.1	401.2
Michigan....................	2,100.4	1,096.7	1,003.7	2,130.1	1,024.1	1,105.9
Minnesota...................	1,046.4	540.0	506.4	1,068.6	509.9	558.6
Mississippi..................	609.8	464.5	145.3	614.6	431.5	183.1
Missouri.....................	1,248.4	748.3	500.1	1,263.8	707.2	556.6
Montana.....................	237.7	189.0	48.8	244.1	188.1	56.0
Nebraska....................	353.8	282.6	71.2	360.4	272.2	88.2
Nevada......................	549.4	329.3	220.1	561.9	317.0	244.9
New Hampshire................	307.6	240.2	67.4	316.6	234.8	81.7
New Jersey...................	1,637.1	1,109.3	527.8	1,656.8	1,075.7	581.1
New Mexico..................	432.5	262.0	170.5	439.4	252.5	186.9
New York....................	3,672.6	2,069.6	1,603.0	3,705.6	1,996.2	1,709.4
North Carolina................	2,035.6	1,211.4	824.2	2,078.0	1,149.0	929.0
North Dakota.................	134.3	107.6	26.7	137.2	105.9	31.2
Ohio........................	2,381.2	1,279.4	1,101.9	2,407.8	1,227.3	1,180.5
Oklahoma....................	753.5	563.3	190.2	763.7	528.4	235.3
Oregon......................	886.2	468.7	417.5	901.9	459.1	442.8
Pennsylvania.................	2,776.1	1,539.9	1,236.2	2,805.4	1,493.9	1,311.5
Rhode Island.................	224.7	117.5	107.2	228.1	112.0	116.2
South Carolina...............	1,106.0	737.9	368.1	1,134.0	712.0	421.9
South Dakota.................	180.2	138.7	41.5	184.6	136.5	48.1
Tennessee...................	1,385.3	796.8	588.4	1,406.2	766.8	639.4
Texas.......................	4,286.1	2,456.1	1,829.9	4,386.9	2,347.9	2,038.9
Utah........................	415.0	248.8	166.1	427.6	242.4	185.2
Vermont.....................	151.3	129.5	21.9	155.1	124.4	30.7
Virginia.....................	1,545.6	1,157.3	388.3	1,575.5	1,112.7	462.8
Washington..................	1,398.9	888.9	510.0	1,431.9	865.2	566.7
West Virginia.................	442.7	275.1	167.6	444.3	254.2	190.1
Wisconsin....................	1,200.5	645.4	555.1	1,225.5	622.4	603.0
Wyoming....................	113.8	108.2	5.6	117.4	110.5	6.9
American Samoa..............	4.7	4.4	0.3	4.8	4.5	0.3
Guam.......................	17.8	17.7	0.1	18.2	18.1	0.1
Northern Mariana Islands......	2.7	2.6	(Z)	2.8	2.8	(Z)
Puerto Rico..................	750.4	149.2	601.2	754.8	138.2	616.6
U.S. Virgin Islands............	20.1	19.6	0.5	20.4	14.8	5.6
Foreign and other outlying areas........................	492.3	488.1	4.3	501.0	496.5	4.5

Z Less than 50. [1] Original Medicare consists of Part A (Hospital Insurance) and Part B (Supplementary Medical Insurance). Enrollment in Original Medicare includes beneficiaries enrolled in either Part A and/or Part B. [2] Medicare Advantage is also known as Medicare Part C. Medicare Part C includes both Part A and Part B coverage. Medicare Advantage enrollees are Medicare beneficiaries who are enrolled in health plans offered by private companies approved by Medicare. Also includes enrollees in Medicare-Medicaid plans, Medicare cost plans, and Program of All-Inclusive Care for the Elderly (PACE) plans. [3] U.S. total excludes territories, possessions, foreign countries or outlying areas, and unknown.

Source: U.S. Centers for Medicare and Medicaid Services, CMS Program Statistics, "Medicare Monthly Enrollment," <data.cms.gov/collection/cms-program-statistics>, accessed March 2023.

Table 151. Medicare Enrollment by Type: 2015 to 2021

[In thousands (55,496 represents 55,496,000), except as noted. Based on person-year methodology; see source for details. Medicare Advantage, an alternative option to traditional Medicare, allows beneficiaries to receive health care services through private sector health plans. Medicare Advantage plans are required to provide at least services covered by Medicare Parts A and B (except hospice services), and are financed from both Medicare's Hospital Insurance (HI) trust fund and the Part B account within the Supplementary Medical Insurance (SMI) trust fund in proportion to the relative weights of Part A and Part B benefits to the total benefits paid by the Medicare program]

Enrollment by type	2015	2016	2017	2018	2019	2020	2021
Total Medicare enrollment [1]	**55,496**	**56,981**	**58,457**	**59,990**	**61,515**	**62,840**	**63,893**
Aged	46,631	48,143	49,678	51,304	52,991	54,532	55,851
Disabled [2]	8,865	8,838	8,779	8,686	8,523	8,308	8,041
Part A, Hospital insurance	55,153	56,639	58,115	59,650	61,167	62,499	63,557
Aged	46,289	47,802	49,338	50,964	52,644	54,191	55,517
Disabled [2]	8,865	8,837	8,778	8,686	8,523	8,308	8,041
Part B, Medical insurance	50,758	52,086	53,350	54,690	56,002	57,308	58,377
Aged	42,741	44,074	45,394	46,813	48,269	49,732	51,024
Disabled [2]	8,017	8,012	7,956	7,877	7,732	7,576	7,353
Original Medicare enrollment [1]	**38,025**	**38,610**	**38,668**	**38,665**	**38,577**	**37,776**	**36,356**
Percent of total	68.5	67.8	66.2	64.5	62.7	60.1	56.9
Aged	31,479	32,204	32,471	32,745	33,046	32,753	31,894
Disabled [2]	6,547	6,406	6,197	5,920	5,531	5,024	4,463
Part A, Hospital insurance	37,708	38,288	38,348	38,352	38,258	37,465	36,052
Aged	31,162	31,883	32,152	32,432	32,728	32,442	31,589
Disabled [2]	6,546	6,406	6,196	5,919	5,531	5,023	4,462
Part B, Medical insurance	33,287	33,715	33,562	33,366	33,077	32,246	30,843
Aged	27,589	28,136	28,188	28,255	28,333	27,954	27,068
Disabled [2]	5,698	5,580	5,374	5,111	4,745	4,291	3,774
Medicare Advantage enrollment [1,3]	**17,471**	**18,371**	**19,789**	**21,325**	**22,937**	**25,064**	**27,536**
Percent of total	31.5	32.2	33.9	35.6	37.3	39.9	43.1
Part A, Hospital insurance	17,445	18,351	19,768	21,298	22,908	25,034	27,506
Aged	15,127	15,919	17,186	18,532	19,917	21,749	23,927
Disabled [2]	2,319	2,432	2,582	2,766	2,992	3,285	3,578
Part B, Medical insurance	17,471	18,370	19,788	21,324	22,924	25,063	27,534
Aged	15,152	15,939	17,206	18,558	19,937	21,778	23,956
Disabled [2]	2,318	2,432	2,582	2,766	2,988	3,285	3,578

[1] Enrollment in Medicare Part A and/or Part B. [2] Persons enrolled due to end stage renal disease-only are included in the disabled enrollee counts. [3] Includes enrollees in Medicare-Medicaid plans, Medicare cost plans, and Program of All-Inclusive Care for the Elderly (PACE) plans.

Source: U.S. Centers for Medicare & Medicaid Services, CMS Program Statistics: Medicare Enrollment, <data.cms.gov/collection/cms-program-statistics>, accessed March 2023.

Table 152. Medicare Utilization—Persons Utilizing Medicare, Program Payments, and Cost Sharing: 2016 to 2021

[38,610 represents 38,610,000. Covers all Original Medicare, which consists of Part A (Hospital Insurance), and Part B (Supplementary Medical Insurance). Persons utilizing Medicare do not include beneficiaries who received services but for whom no program payments were reported. Counting methodology may result in persons with utilization counts being greater than enrollee counts. Persons with utilization are counted using a whole-person methodology; enrollees are counted using a person-year methodology. Amounts do not sum to totals because beneficiaries may have used more than one type of service during a year, and for payments and costs, due to rounding]

Item	2016	2017	2018	2019	2020	2021
ORIGINAL MEDICARE ENROLLEES (1,000)						
Total, Part A and/or Part B	**38,610**	**38,668**	**38,665**	**38,577**	**37,776**	**36,356**
Part A	38,288	38,348	38,352	38,258	37,465	36,052
Part B	33,715	33,562	33,366	33,077	32,246	30,843
UTILIZATION (1,000)						
Medicare Part A and/or Part B	**34,827**	**34,790**	**34,822**	**34,335**	**33,406**	**33,296**
Part A	7,680	7,719	7,627	7,491	6,904	6,656
Inpatient hospital services	6,619	6,609	6,460	6,264	5,391	5,149
Skilled nursing facility services	1,803	1,764	1,705	1,624	1,468	1,395
Hospice services [1]	1,441	1,505	1,564	1,622	1,728	1,737
Home health agency services	1,642	1,610	1,572	1,515	1,373	1,323
Part B	34,241	34,170	34,168	33,654	32,682	32,680
Physician and other medical services	33,713	33,609	33,601	33,184	32,163	32,138
Outpatient services	25,711	25,715	25,687	25,357	23,334	23,918
Home health agency services	1,982	1,953	1,964	1,932	1,833	1,826
PAYMENTS AND COSTS (mil. dol.)						
Medicare Part A and/or Part B	**368,728**	**376,990**	**389,526**	**400,240**	**379,601**	**396,122**
Part A	185,493	188,093	190,702	193,251	187,446	187,713
Inpatient hospital services	133,380	135,274	136,996	138,525	130,157	131,317
Skilled nursing facility services	28,409	28,064	27,652	27,132	28,555	27,223
Hospice services	16,847	17,922	19,251	20,899	22,445	23,066
Home health agency services	6,857	6,833	6,802	6,695	6,288	6,107
Part B	183,235	188,896	198,824	206,989	192,156	208,409
Physician and other medical services	103,806	105,610	109,928	114,813	106,549	117,391
Outpatient services	68,169	72,288	77,764	81,021	74,813	80,253
Home health agency services	11,260	10,998	11,132	11,156	10,794	10,766
BENEFICIARY COST SHARING [2] (mil. dol.)						
Medicare Part A and/or Part B	**63,045**	**64,488**	**66,402**	**67,866**	**61,742**	**64,282**
Part A	16,210	16,171	15,908	15,525	14,360	14,275
Part B	46,835	48,317	50,493	52,340	47,382	50,007

[1] The total Medicare Part A enrollee counts are based on enrollees in Original Medicare and Medicare Advantage/Other Health Plans combined, because once a beneficiary enrolled in Medicare Advantage/Other Health Plans elects the hospice benefit, his or her Medicare benefits revert to fee-for-service. [2] Includes costs for copayments, coinsurance, deductibles, and out-of-pocket payments for balanced billing (the difference between Medicare allowed charges and physicians' submitted charges). Excludes monthly premium for Part B coverage, Part D coverage, voluntary hospital insurance coverage, and other supplemental insurance.

Source: U.S. Centers for Medicare and Medicaid Services, CMS Program Statistics: Medicare Use and Payment, "Medicare Part A & Part B - All Types of Service," <data.cms.gov/collection/cms-program-statistics>, accessed March 2023.

Table 153. Medicare and Medicaid Dual Enrollment by Type of Eligibility: 2011 to 2021

[In thousands (8,972.1 represents 8,972,100). Covers Medicare beneficiaries who have low incomes and limited resources who also receive Medicaid program benefits. Services that are covered by Medicare are paid for by the Medicare program first before any payments are made by Medicaid. Based on person-year methodology; see source for details. Includes Puerto Rico and Island areas and enrollees in foreign countries and unknown areas. See headnote, Table 151. Numbers may not sum to totals due to rounding]

Year	Total Medicare-Medicaid dual enrollment	Type of eligibility							
		Full benefit enrollment				Partial benefit enrollment			
		Total	Qualified Medicare beneficiary plus [1]	Specified low-income Medicare beneficiary plus [2]	Other full-benefit enrollee with Medicaid	Total	Qualified Medicare beneficiary [1]	Specified low-income Medicare beneficiary [2]	Qualified disabled & working individual [3]
Total Medicare:									
2011	8,972.1	6,603.6	4,829.3	230.5	1,543.7	2,368.5	1,096.3	821.8	450.3
2012	9,329.6	6,769.1	4,958.0	242.6	1,568.5	2,560.5	1,184.0	879.7	496.7
2013	9,586.4	6,902.3	5,080.4	245.2	1,576.7	2,684.1	1,255.4	911.1	517.5
2014	9,913.8	7,131.2	5,188.1	251.1	1,691.9	2,782.6	1,329.1	922.7	530.7
2015	10,192.6	7,317.9	5,302.7	256.9	1,758.3	2,874.7	1,383.0	940.6	551.0
2016	10,415.7	7,464.6	5,394.7	263.1	1,806.8	2,951.1	1,447.9	961.8	541.4
2017	10,632.6	7,602.3	5,491.3	270.5	1,840.6	3,030.3	1,520.4	976.8	533.0
2018	10,822.7	7,709.7	5,612.8	286.3	1,810.6	3,112.9	1,552.5	1,002.5	558.0
2019	10,959.8	7,787.5	5,740.9	290.8	1,755.8	3,172.2	1,567.4	1,023.9	580.9
2020	11,218.0	7,959.9	5,916.8	304.3	1,738.8	3,258.1	1,654.2	1,026.5	577.4
2021	11,751.8	8,419.2	6,204.4	331.2	1,883.5	3,332.6	1,709.0	1,038.0	585.6
Original Medicare:									
2011	7,165.9	5,527.5	4,019.6	195.9	1,312.1	1,638.4	828.8	537.2	272.3
2012	7,260.4	5,546.9	4,033.0	202.1	1,311.8	1,713.5	862.9	557.0	293.6
2013	7,219.8	5,494.4	4,002.0	200.5	1,292.0	1,725.4	875.1	555.1	295.1
2014	7,178.2	5,453.4	3,911.9	200.3	1,341.2	1,724.8	890.1	541.3	293.4
2015	7,025.4	5,312.3	3,777.7	196.6	1,338.0	1,713.1	889.6	529.7	293.9
2016	6,994.9	5,296.6	3,753.8	196.6	1,346.2	1,698.3	900.5	520.2	277.6
2017	6,889.5	5,222.5	3,689.1	195.4	1,338.0	1,667.0	898.4	506.4	262.3
2018	6,675.7	5,083.3	3,611.2	199.9	1,272.2	1,592.5	845.1	487.9	259.5
2019	6,342.0	4,861.8	3,477.1	191.4	1,193.2	1,480.2	771.3	458.7	250.2
2020	5,942.9	4,609.6	3,305.4	184.9	1,119.4	1,333.2	713.8	400.7	218.7
2021	5,578.2	4,431.7	3,132.0	181.0	1,118.7	1,146.5	620.2	339.5	186.8
Medicare Advantage:									
2011	1,806.1	1,076.0	809.7	34.7	231.6	730.1	267.5	284.6	178.0
2012	2,069.2	1,222.2	925.0	40.5	256.7	847.0	321.1	322.7	203.2
2013	2,366.6	1,407.9	1,078.5	44.7	284.7	958.7	380.3	356.0	222.4
2014	2,735.6	1,677.8	1,276.2	50.9	350.8	1,057.8	439.0	381.4	237.3
2015	3,167.2	2,005.6	1,524.9	60.3	420.3	1,161.5	493.4	411.0	257.2
2016	3,420.8	2,168.0	1,640.8	66.5	460.6	1,252.8	547.5	441.6	263.8
2017	3,743.0	2,379.8	1,802.2	75.1	502.6	1,363.2	622.0	470.5	270.7
2018	4,146.9	2,626.5	2,001.7	86.4	538.3	1,520.5	707.4	514.6	298.5
2019	4,617.8	2,925.8	2,263.8	99.4	562.6	1,692.1	796.1	565.2	330.8
2020	5,275.2	3,350.3	2,611.4	119.3	619.5	1,924.9	940.4	625.8	358.7
2021	6,173.6	3,987.5	3,072.5	150.2	764.8	2,186.1	1,088.8	698.5	398.9

[1] A qualified Medicare beneficiary (QMB) has Medicare Part A, income less than or equal to 100 percent of the Federal poverty level, and resources below twice the value allowed under supplemental security income (SSI). The Medicaid program pays Medicare Part A premiums (if applicable), Part B premiums, and Medicare deductibles and coinsurance amounts for Medicare covered services depending on the Medicaid state plan. An individual qualifying for full Medicaid benefits is sometimes referred to as "QMB plus". [2] A specified low-income Medicare beneficiary (SLMB) has Medicare Part A, income above 100 percent but less than 120 percent of the Federal poverty level, and resources below twice the value allowed under SSI. For those who qualify, the Medicaid program pays only the Medicare Part B premium. An individual who qualifies for full Medicaid benefits is sometimes referred to as "SLMB plus". [3] Data are combined for qualified disabled and working individuals (QDWIs) and qualifying individuals; total counts for QDWIs are less than 100. For QDWIs, Medicaid pays Medicare Part A premiums for certain disabled individuals who lost Medicare coverage because they returned to work. These individuals have incomes below 200 percent of the Federal Poverty Level, resources not more than twice the value allowed under SSI, and are not otherwise eligible for Medicaid. Qualifying individuals are entitled to Medicare Part A, have income of at least 120% but less than 135% of the Federal Poverty Level, resources that do not exceed twice the limit for SSI eligibility, and are not otherwise eligible for Medicaid. Medicaid pays their Medicare Part B premiums only. There is an annual cap on the amount of money available, which may limit the number of individuals in the group.

Source: U.S. Centers for Medicare and Medicaid Services, CMS Program Statistics: Medicare Enrollment, "Medicare-Medicaid Dual Enrollment," <data.cms.gov/collection/cms-program-statistics>, accessed March 2023.

Table 154. Medicare Hospital Insurance and Supplementary Medical Insurance (SMI)—Average Costs per Beneficiary: 1970 to 2033

[In dollars. See headnote, Table 155]

Year	Total	Hospital Insurance	SMI Part B	SMI Part D	Year	Total	Hospital Insurance	SMI Part B	SMI Part D
1970........	385	270	115	(X)	2016........	12,925	5,095	5,673	2,156
1980........	1,352	929	423	(X)	2017........	13,136	5,147	5,869	2,120
1990........	3,334	1,979	1,355	(X)	2018........	13,616	5,222	6,254	2,139
2000........	5,844	3,348	2,496	(X)	2019........	14,228	5,400	6,653	2,175
2002........	6,788	3,813	2,975	(X)	2020........	14,414	5,498	6,718	2,198
2003........	7,144	3,922	3,221	(X)	2021........	15,188	5,625	7,357	2,206
2004........	7,722	4,162	3,561	(X)	2022........	15,840	5,859	7,694	2,287
2005........	8,278	4,439	3,839	(X)	2023........	16,698	6,030	8,223	2,445
2006........	10,179	4,602	4,116	1,461	2024 (P).....	17,364	6,160	8,531	2,673
2007........	10,702	4,759	4,313	1,630	2025 (P).....	17,906	6,280	9,019	2,606
2008........	11,232	4,996	4,574	1,662	2026 (P).....	18,938	6,527	9,599	2,811
2009........	11,696	5,174	4,792	1,730	2027 (P).....	20,105	6,878	10,229	2,998
2010........	11,902	5,193	4,901	1,808	2028 (P).....	21,024	7,247	10,667	3,110
2011........	12,167	5,276	5,032	1,858	2029 (P).....	22,342	7,652	11,467	3,223
2012........	12,204	5,195	5,169	1,839	2030 (P).....	23,462	8,037	12,150	3,275
2013........	12,199	5,155	5,170	1,874	2031 (P).....	24,719	8,474	12,901	3,344
2014........	12,433	5,010	5,392	2,031	2032 (P).....	26,122	8,949	13,771	3,402
2015........	12,734	5,027	5,554	2,153	2033 (P).....	27,890	9,544	14,843	3,502

X Not applicable. P Projected.

Source: U.S. Centers for Medicare and Medicaid Services, Trustees Report & Trust Funds, "2024 Expanded and Supplementary Tables and Figures," May 2024, <www.cms.gov/data-research/statistics-trends-and-reports/trustees-report-trust-funds>.

Table 155. Medicare Insurance Trust Funds: 1990 to 2023

[In billions of dollars (126.3 represents $126,300,000,000), on cash basis, for calendar years. The Medicare program has two trust funds, the Hospital Insurance (HI) trust fund, and the Supplementary Medical Insurance (SMI) trust fund, which correspond to the components of the Medicare program. The SMI trust fund covers Part B (medical insurance) and Part D (prescription drug coverage). See text, this section, for details]

Type of trust fund	1990	2000	2005	2010	2015	2020	2021	2022	2023
TOTAL MEDICARE									
Total income [1]...........................	126.3	257.1	357.5	486.1	644.4	899.9	887.7	988.5	1,024.6
Total expenditures......................	111.0	221.8	336.4	522.9	647.6	925.8	839.4	905.1	1,037.0
Net change in assets....................	15.3	35.3	21.0	-36.8	-3.2	-25.9	48.3	83.4	-12.4
Assets, end of year......................	114.4	221.5	309.8	344.0	263.2	277.4	325.7	409.1	396.7
HOSPITAL INSURANCE, PART A									
Net contribution income [2]...............	71.9	155.5	183.3	199.5	265.3	335.0	332.4	390.7	407.4
Interest and other income [3, 4]...........	8.5	11.7	16.1	16.1	10.1	6.7	5.1	5.9	7.9
Benefit payments [4, 5, 11]..................	66.2	128.5	180.0	244.5	273.4	397.7	323.6	337.4	397.5
Trust fund balance, end of year..........	98.9	177.5	285.8	271.9	193.8	134.1	142.7	196.6	208.8
SMI, PART B									
Premiums from enrollees [1]................	11.3	20.6	37.5	52.0	69.4	111.2	111.0	130.9	131.2
Government contributions [1, 6, 12].........	33.0	65.9	118.1	153.5	203.9	336.0	318.6	329.7	342.1
Interest and other income [3, 4]..............	1.6	3.5	1.4	3.3	5.7	5.1	6.0	6.9	7.6
Benefit payments [1, 4, 5]....................	42.5	88.9	149.2	209.7	275.8	414.1	400.5	431.6	497.4
Trust fund balance, end of year..........	15.5	44.0	24.0	71.4	68.2	133.3	163.3	194.2	172.2
SMI, PART D									
Premiums from enrollees [7]...............	(X)	(X)	–	6.5	12.7	15.8	17.0	17.6	18.6
Government contributions [8]...............	(X)	(X)	1.1	51.1	68.4	77.7	85.3	92.4	93.7
Transfers from states [9].....................	(X)	(X)	(X)	4.0	8.9	11.6	12.1	13.7	15.8
Interest and other income.................	(X)	(X)	–	(Z)	(Z)	0.7	0.3	0.7	0.2
Benefit payments [10].......................	(X)	(X)	1.1	61.7	89.4	104.6	104.5	125.2	130.5
Trust fund balance, end of year..........	(X)	(X)	–	0.7	1.3	10.0	19.7	18.3	15.7

– Represents zero. X Not applicable. Z Less than $50 million. [1] Includes adjustments for benefit checks issued at the end of the year instead of the following January; see source for details on this and other adjustments. [2] Includes income from payroll taxes, taxation of benefits, railroad retirement account transfers, reimbursement for uninsured persons, premiums from voluntary enrollees, and payments for military wage credits. [3] Includes recoveries of amounts reimbursed from the trust fund, receipts from fraud and abuse control program, and other miscellaneous income. [4] Values after 2005 include additional premiums for Medicare Advantage (MA) plans that are deducted from beneficiaries' Social Security checks; see source for details. [5] Includes monies transferred to the SMI trust fund in 1998-2003 for home health agency costs. [6] Matching payments from the general fund, plus certain interest-adjustment items. See also footnote 1. [7] Premiums include both amounts withheld from Social Security benefit checks (and other certain Federal benefit payments) and amounts paid directly to Part D plans. [8] Includes, net of transfers from States, all government transfers required to fund benefit payments, administrative expenses, and State expenses for making low-income eligibility determinations. [9] With the availability of Part D drug coverage and low-income subsidies beginning in 2006, Medicaid is no longer the primary payer for full-benefit dual Medicare and Medicaid eligibles. States are subject to a contribution requirement and must pay the Part D account in the SMI trust fund a portion of their estimated forgone drug costs for this population. [10] Includes payments to plans, subsidies to employer-sponsored retiree prescription drug plans, payments to States for making low-income eligibility determinations, Part D drug premiums collected from beneficiaries and transferred to Medicare Advantage plans and private drug plans, and premium amounts paid directly by enrollees to plans. Includes amounts for transitional assistance benefits in 2004-2007. [11] Beginning 2020, includes net payments made through the Medicare Accelerated and Advance Payments Program; see source for details. [12] Includes a transfer made in 2020 from the Treasury to Part B for the outstanding balance of the Medicare Accelerated and Advance Payments Program, and subsequent recoveries from providers that were transferred from Part B to the Treasury; see source for details.

Source: U.S. Centers for Medicare and Medicaid Services, Trustees Report & Trust Funds, "2024 Expanded and Supplementary Tables and Figures," May 2024, <www.cms.gov/OACT/TR>.

Table 156. Medicaid Benefit Spending by Source of Funds and Per Enrollee by State and Island Area: 2022

[In units as indicated (792,734.4 represents $792,734,400,000). For the fiscal year 2022. Data exclude spending for program administration and Medicaid-expansion Children's Health Insurance Program enrollees. Data are based on analysis of administrative data submitted to the Centers for Medicare & Medicaid Services (CMS) via CMS-64 records, as of May 30, 2023 for expenditures and as of October 25, 2023 for enrollment. All states had certified their CMS-64 financial management report (FMR) submissions as of May 30, 2023. Data may change if states revise their expenditure data after this date]

State and Island Area	Medicaid benefit spending (million dollars)			Medicaid full year equivalent enrollment [1] (1,000)	Total spending per enrollee (dollars)
	Total	Federal funds	State funds		
Total [2]	792,734.4	565,788.2	226,946.2	94,124.7	8,422
U.S. total [3]	787,190.5	562,025.4	225,165.2	92,545.6	8,506
Alabama	7,166.5	5,685.2	1,481.3	1,263.2	5,673
Alaska	2,435.5	1,911.0	524.5	251.3	9,692
Arizona	20,257.9	16,932.5	3,325.4	2,325.6	8,711
Arkansas	8,533.1	7,022.1	1,510.9	1,018.0	8,382
California	117,884.6	80,358.0	37,526.6	14,339.7	8,221
Colorado	11,873.7	7,966.0	3,907.7	1,599.5	7,423
Connecticut	9,671.7	6,285.0	3,386.7	1,126.6	8,585
Delaware	3,136.9	2,254.6	882.4	273.2	11,480
District of Columbia	3,647.7	2,902.4	745.3	291.8	12,501
Florida	32,667.5	22,212.3	10,455.2	5,186.8	6,298
Georgia	14,339.6	10,664.0	3,675.6	2,464.3	5,819
Hawaii	2,990.0	2,130.2	859.8	446.7	6,694
Idaho	3,195.3	2,550.9	644.4	440.4	7,255
Illinois	25,956.0	17,224.7	8,731.3	3,276.6	7,922
Indiana	16,850.9	13,042.3	3,808.6	1,937.9	8,695
Iowa	6,614.1	4,905.8	1,708.3	754.2	8,770
Kansas	4,301.3	2,956.9	1,344.5	444.6	9,676
Kentucky	14,590.5	12,164.0	2,426.4	1,514.7	9,633
Louisiana	14,674.0	11,790.1	2,883.9	2,511.1	5,844
Maine	3,785.8	2,879.3	906.5	371.8	10,182
Maryland	14,343.5	9,608.9	4,734.7	1,851.5	7,747
Massachusetts	20,864.8	13,427.7	7,437.1	2,079.4	10,034
Michigan	21,023.3	16,123.1	4,900.2	2,945.5	7,137
Minnesota	16,158.8	10,707.8	5,451.0	1,316.7	12,272
Mississippi	5,943.7	5,062.4	881.3	806.9	7,367
Missouri	13,013.1	10,303.0	2,710.1	1,234.2	10,544
Montana	2,343.6	1,929.1	414.5	294.3	7,962
Nebraska	3,295.9	2,353.8	942.1	366.3	8,997
Nevada	5,052.7	3,976.5	1,076.2	799.6	6,319
New Hampshire	2,460.9	1,600.5	860.3	229.9	10,706
New Jersey	20,872.6	14,229.2	6,643.4	1,997.1	10,451
New Mexico	8,258.0	7,073.9	1,184.1	967.8	8,533
New York	80,518.4	52,155.4	28,363.0	7,436.1	10,828
North Carolina	18,403.7	13,966.5	4,437.2	2,737.5	6,723
North Dakota	1,524.1	1,076.1	448.1	123.0	12,395
Ohio	30,024.8	23,179.3	6,845.6	3,432.0	8,748
Oklahoma	7,523.2	6,353.5	1,169.8	1,121.4	6,709
Oregon	13,083.2	10,174.1	2,909.1	1,240.2	10,550
Pennsylvania	41,178.3	28,126.4	13,051.9	3,484.1	11,819
Rhode Island	3,392.6	2,394.1	998.5	343.1	9,888
South Carolina	7,544.3	5,887.1	1,657.2	1,514.4	4,982
South Dakota	1,246.3	886.1	360.2	129.1	9,655
Tennessee	11,264.6	8,322.9	2,941.7	1,793.6	6,280
Texas	54,941.9	37,497.4	17,444.5	5,675.5	9,681
Utah	4,211.5	3,304.2	907.2	479.8	8,778
Vermont	1,884.4	1,303.6	580.8	197.9	9,522
Virginia	17,823.7	12,251.9	5,571.8	1,819.3	9,797
Washington	17,140.7	12,133.4	5,007.4	2,082.5	8,231
West Virginia	5,183.9	4,389.2	794.7	634.6	8,169
Wisconsin	11,429.1	7,981.7	3,447.5	1,495.3	7,643
Wyoming	668.4	409.5	258.8	79.2	8,437
American Samoa	68.5	58.6	9.9	31.4	2,178
Guam	167.1	149.6	17.5	38.9	4,291
Northern Mariana Islands	73.3	65.6	7.7	18.0	4,076
Puerto Rico	5,097.8	3,368.2	1,729.5	1,454.5	3,505
Virgin Islands	137.3	120.9	16.4	36.3	3,781

[1] Full year equivalent enrollment may also be referred to as average monthly enrollment. [2] Total includes 50 states, DC, and Island Areas. [3] Includes 50 states and DC.

Source: Medicaid and CHIP Payment and Access Commission, *MACStats: Medicaid and CHIP Data Book,* December 2023. See also <www.macpac.gov/macstats/>.

Table 157. Children's Health Insurance Program (CHIP) by State—Expenditures and Enrollment: 2021 and 2022

[21,161.6 represents $21,161,600,000. For fiscal year. Components may not add to total due to rounding. CHIP is a federal-state program that provides health benefits coverage to children without health insurance and living in families whose incomes are too high to qualify for Medicaid. States may create CHIP programs as an expansion of Medicaid, a program separate from Medicaid, or a combination of both approaches. Based on analysis of CHIP data from the Centers for Medicare & Medicaid Services; see source for details. Minus (-) sign indicates negative spending; see source for details]

| State | Expenditures [1] (million dollars) | | | | | | Children enrolled [2] (number) | |
| | 2021 | | | 2022 | | | | |
	Total	Federal	State [3]	Total	Federal	State [3]	2021	2022
Total [4]....................	**21,161.6**	**15,953.7**	**5,207.9**	**22,268.9**	**16,858.3**	**5,410.6**	**(NA)**	**(NA)**
United States...............	**20,999.7**	**15,815.3**	**5,184.3**	**22,019.3**	**16,645.0**	**5,374.3**	**8,601,162**	**8,274,189**
Alabama.....................	403.8	343.2	60.7	462.4	392.9	69.5	204,696	201,869
Alaska......................	25.5	17.6	7.8	26.3	18.4	7.9	14,951	13,363
Arizona.....................	356.9	298.2	58.7	407.9	339.0	68.8	134,122	141,427
Arkansas....................	221.1	185.1	36.0	232.1	196.0	36.0	92,956	83,146
California...................	4,047.1	2,876.9	1,170.1	4,265.9	2,973.9	1,292.0	1,601,751	1,556,216
Colorado....................	337.5	226.9	110.7	344.9	240.0	104.9	(NA)	143,145
Connecticut.................	47.6	53.5	-5.9	50.4	57.3	-6.9	20,410	18,199
Delaware....................	52.5	39.3	13.2	34.8	26.0	8.9	12,814	10,968
District of Columbia..........	59.9	49.9	10.0	61.1	50.9	10.2	17,062	16,490
Florida......................	771.8	600.2	171.5	787.3	606.4	180.8	399,577	332,812
Georgia.....................	520.1	422.8	97.3	581.3	469.5	111.8	283,844	304,701
Hawaii......................	67.7	49.1	18.6	71.5	51.3	20.3	25,533	24,208
Idaho.......................	92.1	77.1	15.1	109.3	91.2	18.1	39,980	42,807
Illinois......................	760.9	532.2	228.7	712.3	499.6	212.7	336,655	344,143
Indiana.....................	270.2	219.0	51.2	269.3	217.5	51.8	105,116	121,342
Iowa........................	175.3	136.0	39.4	171.0	132.6	38.4	91,640	82,784
Kansas......................	171.4	130.6	40.8	180.2	137.9	42.3	65,275	62,043
Kentucky....................	327.3	276.1	51.2	412.9	350.3	62.6	123,953	128,336
Louisiana...................	451.3	363.9	87.4	509.2	418.2	91.0	181,891	200,397
Maine.......................	43.5	34.4	9.1	45.3	35.8	9.5	32,771	33,507
Maryland....................	402.1	279.0	123.1	444.7	308.4	136.3	118,616	126,971
Massachusetts...............	869.3	610.5	258.7	884.4	614.4	270.0	222,537	221,280
Michigan....................	308.9	248.7	60.3	337.8	270.9	66.9	96,739	130,716
Minnesota...................	16.5	62.3	-45.8	20.0	73.4	-53.4	3,268	3,881
Mississippi..................	249.7	212.5	37.2	207.7	176.7	31.1	80,058	82,878
Missouri....................	381.6	305.3	76.3	366.3	294.1	72.2	99,958	107,395
Montana.....................	99.0	79.4	19.6	111.8	89.2	22.6	30,652	29,465
Nebraska....................	112.9	83.1	29.8	111.6	83.1	28.5	57,523	58,137
Nevada......................	81.9	64.4	17.5	107.0	83.6	23.4	183,875	76,358
New Hampshire..............	48.9	40.8	8.1	58.3	48.6	9.6	20,261	23,479
New Jersey..................	779.3	535.8	243.5	833.8	580.7	253.1	250,049	268,245
New Mexico.................	127.3	108.0	19.3	131.0	111.3	19.8	6,830	11,036
New York....................	1,768.8	1,229.4	539.4	1,816.9	1,260.1	556.7	631,404	623,678
North Carolina..............	693.1	565.3	127.7	763.9	624.2	139.7	305,646	302,481
North Dakota................	30.1	21.6	8.5	26.7	19.1	7.6	(NA)	7,063
Ohio........................	628.3	496.8	131.4	694.1	552.5	141.5	220,188	238,100
Oklahoma...................	272.3	220.4	51.9	284.5	233.8	50.7	237,437	241,232
Oregon......................	487.3	374.2	113.2	604.0	461.9	142.1	217,105	251,411
Pennsylvania................	819.2	580.6	238.5	706.0	502.9	203.1	295,698	270,486
Rhode Island................	110.6	79.8	30.8	130.6	94.9	35.7	33,974	33,978
South Carolina..............	220.0	184.3	35.7	223.5	187.5	36.1	107,946	104,623
South Dakota................	33.2	24.8	8.4	37.1	28.0	9.1	19,262	19,065
Tennessee...................	390.0	314.2	75.8	403.6	326.2	77.4	68,238	68,780
Texas.......................	1,603.6	1,243.8	359.8	1,667.5	1,280.9	386.5	799,975	657,566
Utah........................	119.0	96.0	23.0	128.4	104.3	24.2	42,338	37,451
Vermont.....................	14.9	14.9	0.1	16.6	15.8	0.8	4,823	4,877
Virginia.....................	479.3	333.2	146.1	523.3	362.3	161.0	221,231	173,697
Washington..................	280.2	180.0	100.2	240.3	224.8	15.5	81,870	81,985
West Virginia................	85.2	72.5	12.8	88.4	75.1	13.3	34,417	33,701
Wisconsin...................	274.9	215.8	59.2	305.3	245.4	60.0	108,981	117,193
Wyoming....................	8.8	6.1	2.7	9.2	6.3	2.8	44,622	5,078

NA Not available. [1] Expenditure data for FY2021 as of August 2022, and for FY2022 as of October 9, 2023. [2] Enrollment data for FY2021 as of September 2022, and for FY2022 as of August 14, 2023, and subject to revision. [3] Section 2105(g) of the Social Security Act permits 11 qualifying states to use CHIP funds to pay the difference between the regular Medicaid matching rate and the enhanced CHIP matching rate for Medicaid-enrolled, Medicaid-financed children whose family income exceeds 133 percent of the federal poverty level. Although these are CHIP funds, they effectively reduce state spending on children in Medicaid and do not require a state match within the CHIP program. In cases in which the sum of 2105(g) federal CHIP spending (for Medicaid enrollees) and regular federal CHIP spending (for CHIP enrollees) exceeds total spending for CHIP enrollees, states are shown in this table as having negative state CHIP spending. [4] Total includes the 50 states, DC, and American Samoa, Guam, Northern Mariana Islands, Puerto Rico, and Virgin Islands.

Source: Medicaid and CHIP Payment and Access Commission, "MACStats: Program Enrollment and Spending: CHIP," <www.macpac.gov/macstats/>, accessed February 2024.

Table 158. Medicaid Managed Care Enrollment by State and Other Areas: 2000 to 2021

[In thousands except as noted (33,690 represents 33,690,000). Through 2010, for year ending June 30; thereafter, as of July 1. Medicaid managed care provides Medicaid health benefits and additional services through contracted arrangements between state Medicaid agencies and managed care entities. The unduplicated Medicaid enrollment figures, shown here, include Medicare-Medicaid dual enrollees and individuals in state health care reform programs that expand eligibility beyond traditional Medicaid eligibility standards. The data include enrollees in any Medicaid managed care program, including comprehensive managed care organizations (MCOs), limited benefit plans such as prepaid inpatient and ambulatory health plans, primary care case management (PCCM) programs, and PCCM entities]

State and other areas	Total enroll-ment	Managed care enrollment		State and other areas	Total enroll-ment	Managed care enrollment		State and other areas	Total enroll-ment	Managed care enrollment	
		Number	Percent of total			Number	Percent of total			Number	Percent of total
2000.......	33,690	18,786	55.8	GA.........	2,539	2,229	87.8	NM........	942	782	83.0
2010.......	54,612	39,020	71.5	HI.........	420	420	100.0	NY [4].......	7,146	5,620	78.7
2015.......	77,847	62,373	80.1	ID.........	422	391	92.8	NC.........	2,558	2,054	80.3
2016.......	80,264	65,034	81.0	IL.........	3,468	2,681	77.3	ND.........	125	86	68.7
2017.......	80,243	65,796	82.0	IN.........	1,870	1,474	78.8	OH [5].......	3,239	2,783	85.9
2018.......	79,899	66,164	82.8	IA.........	750	711	94.9	OK [5]......	1,065	1,050	98.5
2019.......	78,738	65,745	83.5	KS.........	461	407	88.3	OR.........	1,286	1,165	90.6
2020.......	80,815	67,837	83.9	KY.........	1,585	1,582	99.8	PA.........	3,292	3,156	95.9
2021				LA.........	1,895	1,759	92.9	RI.........	339	336	99.1
Total [1]...	**90,520**	**77,212**	**85.3**	ME.........	331	327	98.6	SC.........	1,446	1,446	100.0
U.S........	89,018	75,710	85.0	MD.........	1,781	1,521	85.4	SD.........	137	84	61.1
AL.........	1,199	951	79.4	MA.........	2,092	1,388	66.3	TN.........	1,718	1,596	92.9
AK [2]......	242	–	–	MI.........	2,901	2,692	92.8	TX.........	4,929	4,771	96.8
AZ.........	2,244	1,920	85.6	MN.........	1,254	1,150	91.7	UT [6]......	425	402	94.7
AR.........	1,070	964	90.1	MS.........	776	475	61.2	VT.........	191	131	68.5
CA.........	14,150	11,675	82.5	MO.........	1,048	811	77.4	VA.........	1,853	1,692	91.3
CO [3]......	1,499	1,423	94.9	MT.........	310	245	79.2	WA.........	2,009	2,009	100.0
CT [2]......	1,106	–	–	NE.........	336	335	99.6	WV.........	599	488	81.4
DE.........	276	245	88.6	NV.........	848	792	93.5	WI.........	1,485	1,082	72.9
DC.........	285	268	94.0	NH.........	239	219	91.3	WY.........	73	–	–
FL.........	4,871	4,099	84.1	NJ.........	1,892	1,821	96.2	PR.........	1,502	1,502	100.0

– Represents zero. [1] Includes enrollment for Puerto Rico. [2] Alaska and Connecticut total Medicaid enrollment as of July 1, 2021 was taken from the July-September 2021 enrollment data collected through the Medicaid Budget and Expenditure System (MBES), updated January 2023, and accessed April 2, 2023. [3] Colorado reported plan level enrollment as 0 for plans that had less than 30 beneficiaries. [4] New York's total Medicaid Section VIII expansion count is higher than expected as compared to MBES. New York's Medicaid Section VIII expansion count includes many people with New York State of Health enrollment who are not actually in the Medicaid Section VIII expansion population. [5] Oklahoma expanded Medicaid coverage to childless adults effective July 1, 2021. [6] Utah expanded Medicaid in 2020.

Source: U.S. Centers for Medicare and Medicaid Services, Medicaid Managed Care Enrollment Report, "2021 Managed Care Enrollment Data," <www.medicaid.gov/medicaid/managed-care/enrollment-report/index.html>, accessed January 2024; and earlier releases and reports.

Table 159. Medicaid Benefit Spending by Service Category: 2016 to 2022

[In millions of dollars (550,880 represents $550,880,000,000). For fiscal years. Covers the 50 states, DC, and the territories. Includes federal and state funds. Service category definitions and spending amounts shown here may differ from other Centers for Medicare & Medicaid (CMS) sources. The specific services included in each category have changed over time and therefore may not be directly comparable over the years. Data shown here are subject to revisions because States may revise their expenditure data after an initial submission date]

Spending category	2016	2017	2018	2019	2020	2021	2022
Total benefit spending...................	**550,880**	**572,244**	**588,213**	**597,385**	**652,931**	**717,143**	**792,734**
Fee for service:							
Hospital services....................	88,607	77,790	78,862	79,077	81,939	77,847	84,544
Physician and surgical services................	9,935	8,752	8,968	8,113	8,645	8,489	8,668
Dental services.....................	3,929	3,951	3,420	4,305	3,739	4,598	5,183
Other practitioner services................	2,599	1,892	1,784	1,848	1,799	1,918	4,119
Clinic and health centers...............	10,624	11,134	11,156	12,648	12,499	13,869	14,694
Other acute services [1]...............	36,541	45,622	45,430	40,968	43,138	46,334	46,193
Drugs [2]............................	8,480	3,218	9,981	4,727	4,210	6,148	12,764
Institutional long-term services and supports (LTSS) [3]......	60,070	58,001	56,652	56,505	55,486	54,545	57,206
Home and community LTSS [4]...............	62,052	63,987	71,485	76,622	84,129	88,002	100,964
Managed care and premium assistance......................	258,551	285,653	288,219	301,727	347,756	406,915	448,983
Medicare premiums and coinsurance....................	17,159	19,209	19,884	20,599	21,890	23,176	26,281
Collections [5]............................	-7,667	-6,966	-7,628	-9,754	-12,299	-14,697	-16,865

[1] Other acute services include laboratory or x-ray services; early periodic screening, diagnostic, and treatment (EPSDT) screenings; emergency services for unauthorized aliens; physical, occupational, speech, and hearing therapy; prosthetics, dentures, and eyeglasses; preventive services and vaccines; school-based services; rehabilitative services; hospice; and various other services. [2] Spending for drugs are net of rebates. [3] Institutional LTSS includes nursing facility, intermediate care facility for individuals with intellectual disabilities, and mental health facility. [4] Home- and community-based LTSS includes home health, waiver and state plan services, personal care, and certified community behavioral health clinic. [5] Collections includes third-party liability, estate, and other recoveries.

Source: Medicaid and CHIP Payment and Access Commission, *MACStats: Medicaid and CHIP Data Book*, December 2020, and previous editions; and "MACStats, Program Enrollment and Spending: Medicaid Benefits," <www.macpac.gov/2023-macstats/>, accessed February 2024. See also <www.macpac.gov/publication/macstats-archive/>.

Table 160. Medicare Hospital Insurance and Supplemental Medical Insurance Expenditures, Total and as a Percent of GDP: 1980 to 2040

[In units as noted (2,857 represents $2,857,000,000,000). Incurred amounts relate to the expenditures for services performed in a given year, even if payment for those expenditures occurs in a later year. The Medicare program has two components: Medicare Part A Hospital Insurance (HI); and Supplementary Medical Insurance (SMI), consisting of Part B Medical Insurance, and Part D Prescription Drug Coverage. See text in this section for details]

Year	GDP (billion dollars)	Medicare expenditures (million dollars)				Medicare expenditures as percent of GDP			
		Total	HI Part A	SMI Part B	SMI Part D	Total	HI Part A	SMI Part B	SMI Part D
ACTUAL									
1980.............	2,857	37,556	26,008	11,548	(X)	1.31	0.91	0.40	(X)
1990.............	5,963	110,903	66,785	44,118	(X)	1.86	1.12	0.74	(X)
2000.............	10,251	224,629	131,449	93,180	(X)	2.19	1.28	0.91	(X)
2010.............	15,049	523,912	245,985	215,070	62,857	3.48	1.63	1.43	0.42
2015.............	18,295	649,564	277,697	281,918	89,949	3.55	1.52	1.54	0.49
2020.............	21,323	835,957	343,866	385,097	106,993	3.92	1.61	1.81	0.50
2021.............	23,594	897,856	357,999	429,609	110,249	3.81	1.52	1.82	0.47
2022.............	25,744	954,917	379,680	457,714	117,522	3.71	1.47	1.78	0.46
2023.............	27,358	1,029,520	400,047	500,242	129,232	3.76	1.46	1.83	0.47
PROJECTED [1]									
2024.............	28,599	1,094,827	416,792	529,624	148,411	3.83	1.46	1.85	0.52
2025.............	29,710	1,158,498	434,174	572,712	151,612	3.90	1.46	1.93	0.51
2026.............	30,942	1,256,752	462,541	625,294	168,916	4.06	1.49	2.02	0.55
2027.............	32,271	1,367,606	498,945	683,060	185,601	4.24	1.55	2.12	0.58
2028.............	33,709	1,463,861	537,387	729,053	197,420	4.34	1.59	2.16	0.59
2029.............	35,143	1,588,624	578,974	800,572	209,078	4.52	1.65	2.28	0.59
2030.............	36,589	1,699,139	618,680	864,150	216,310	4.64	1.69	2.36	0.59
2031.............	38,095	1,817,338	661,419	931,780	224,138	4.77	1.74	2.45	0.59
2032.............	39,666	1,946,032	706,953	1,008,118	230,962	4.91	1.78	2.54	0.58
2033.............	41,286	2,102,080	761,908	1,099,651	240,521	5.09	1.85	2.66	0.58
2034.............	42,966	2,235,957	808,793	1,178,986	248,178	5.20	1.88	2.74	0.58
2035.............	44,714	2,371,076	853,059	1,261,494	256,522	5.30	1.91	2.82	0.57
2040.............	54,472	3,077,007	1,083,477	1,692,737	300,793	5.65	1.99	3.11	0.55

X Not applicable. [1] Projections are a projected baseline, and are based on current law; that is, they assume that laws on the books will be implemented and adhered to with respect to scheduled taxes, premium revenues, and payments to providers and health plans. The one exception is that the projections disregard payment reductions that would result from the projected depletion of the Medicare Hospital Insurance trust fund (Part A), thus allowing the size of deficits to become apparent. To date, Congress has not allowed the assets of the Medicare Hospital Insurance trust fund to become depleted. For additional information, see <www.cms.gov/oact/tr/2024>.

Source: U.S. Centers for Medicare and Medicaid Services, Trustees Report & Trust Funds, "2024 Expanded and Supplementary Tables and Figures," May 2024, <www.cms.gov/OACT/TR>.

Table 161. Persons With and Without Health Insurance Coverage by State: 2022

[301,942 represents 301,942,000. Data are based on a sample of the civilian noninstitutionalized population. Data are from the American Community Survey (ACS) and measures population without health insurance coverage at the time of the interview. See source for more information]

State	Total persons covered (1,000)	Total persons not covered		Children not covered [1]		State	Total persons covered (1,000)	Total persons not covered		Children not covered [1]	
		Number (1,000)	Percent of total	Number (1,000)	Percent of total			Number (1,000)	Percent of total	Number (1,000)	Percent of total
U.S.........	301,942	26,368	8.0	3,932	5.1	MO.........	5,551	521	8.6	83	5.8
AL...........	4,551	437	8.8	37	3.1	MT.........	1,014	91	8.3	17	6.9
AK...........	625	77	11.0	15	8.4	NE.........	1,810	130	6.7	23	4.6
AZ...........	6,503	749	10.3	142	8.4	NV.........	2,791	349	11.1	55	7.6
AR...........	2,739	252	8.4	44	5.9	NH.........	1,312	68	4.9	9	3.4
CA...........	36,057	2,492	6.5	287	3.2	NJ.........	8,541	627	6.8	82	3.9
CO...........	5,334	409	7.1	62	4.8	NM.........	1,904	170	8.2	18	3.8
CT...........	3,397	185	5.2	25	3.2	NY.........	18,530	945	4.9	111	2.6
DE...........	949	57	5.6	7	3.4	NC.........	9,508	973	9.3	118	4.8
DC...........	642	19	2.9	2	1.4	ND.........	714	49	6.4	10	5.5
FL...........	19,457	2,448	11.2	336	7.4	OH.........	10,905	683	5.9	122	4.5
GA...........	9,467	1,251	11.7	166	6.2	OK.........	3,469	461	11.7	73	7.3
HI...........	1,335	49	3.5	9	3.0	OR.........	3,947	252	6.0	27	3.0
ID...........	1,755	157	8.2	28	5.7	PA.........	12,109	681	5.3	145	5.2
IL...........	11,600	813	6.6	99	3.4	RI.........	1,032	45	4.2	5	2.1
IN...........	6,268	469	7.0	91	5.5	SC.........	4,715	470	9.1	56	4.7
IA...........	3,013	141	4.5	28	3.7	SD.........	817	72	8.1	14	6.2
KS...........	2,629	247	8.6	38	5.2	TN.........	6,304	647	9.3	86	5.3
KY...........	4,181	247	5.6	46	4.3	TX.........	24,641	4,899	16.6	854	10.9
LA...........	4,182	312	6.9	39	3.5	UT.........	3,081	273	8.1	61	6.1
ME...........	1,278	90	6.6	12	4.6	VT.........	616	25	3.9	3	2.6
MD...........	5,705	368	6.1	60	4.2	VA.........	7,901	545	6.5	87	4.4
MA...........	6,751	168	2.4	22	1.5	WA.........	7,199	468	6.1	48	2.8
MI...........	9,478	451	4.5	60	2.7	WV.........	1,638	103	5.9	11	2.8
MN...........	5,403	254	4.5	45	3.3	WI.........	5,529	303	5.2	60	4.5
MS...........	2,561	312	10.8	39	5.5	WY.........	505	66	11.5	11	7.9

[1] Children under age 19, who may be eligible for health insurance coverage under Medicaid and the Children's Health Insurance Program.

Source: U.S. Census Bureau, 2022 American Community Survey, S2701 "Selected Characteristics of Health Insurance Coverage in the United States," <data.census.gov/>, accessed November 2023.

Table 162. Health Insurance Coverage Status by Selected Characteristics: 2022

[330,000 represents 330,000,000. Data for coverage during all or part of 2022; people not covered had no health insurance for the entire year. Based on the Current Population Survey, Annual Social and Economic Supplement (CPS ASEC); see text, Section 1, and Appendix III. Private health insurance includes coverage provided through an employer or union, coverage purchased directly from an insurance company or through a federal or state marketplace, or TRICARE (uniformed services health care program). Public (government) health insurance coverage includes Medicaid, Medicare, CHAMPVA (Civilian Health and Medical Program of the Department of Veterans Affairs), and care provided by the Department of Veterans Affairs and the military. People covered only through the Indian Health Service are considered uninsured]

Characteristic	Number (1,000)							Percent			
	Total persons	Not covered by health insurance	Covered by private or public health insurance					Not covered by health insurance	Total covered [1]	Employer based coverage	Medicaid coverage
			Total [1]	Private		Public					
				Total	Employer based	Medicare	Medicaid				
Total..................	330,000	25,940	304,000	216,500	179,800	61,570	62,050	7.9	92.1	54.5	18.8
Sex:											
Male.....................	163,100	14,590	148,500	107,500	89,980	27,970	29,400	8.9	91.1	55.2	18.0
Female.................	166,900	11,350	155,600	109,000	89,790	33,600	32,650	6.8	93.2	53.8	19.6
Race:											
White alone [2]...........	248,700	19,540	229,200	166,900	137,000	50,190	41,620	7.9	92.1	55.1	16.7
Black alone [2]...........	44,540	3,714	40,820	25,230	21,760	6,903	12,390	8.3	91.7	48.9	27.8
Asian alone [2]...........	21,550	1,275	20,270	15,560	13,350	3,054	3,401	5.9	94.1	62.0	15.8
Hispanic origin [3].........	63,790	10,950	52,840	31,510	26,180	5,720	19,340	17.2	82.8	41.0	30.3
Age:											
Under 19 years........	76,200	4,079	72,120	47,100	41,890	475	27,050	5.4	94.6	55.0	35.5
19 to 25 years..........	30,430	4,247	26,190	20,940	17,920	434	5,541	14.0	86.0	58.9	18.2
26 to 34 years..........	40,580	5,061	35,520	28,790	25,550	821	7,019	12.5	87.5	63.0	17.3
35 to 44 years..........	43,490	4,884	38,600	32,220	28,690	873	6,729	11.2	88.8	66.0	15.5
45 to 64 years..........	81,390	7,022	74,370	60,940	52,210	4,863	11,720	8.6	91.4	64.2	14.4
65 years and over......	57,880	643	57,240	26,540	13,520	54,110	3,983	1.1	98.9	23.4	6.9
Household income:											
Less than $25,000......	35,520	4,684	30,830	8,509	4,541	12,740	15,400	13.2	86.8	12.8	43.4
$25,000 to $49,999.....	50,020	6,147	43,880	20,020	13,050	14,860	16,570	12.3	87.7	26.1	33.1
$50,000 to $74,999.....	50,720	5,137	45,580	29,310	22,580	10,800	12,270	10.1	89.9	44.5	24.2
$75,000 to $99,999.....	42,720	3,518	39,210	29,720	24,820	7,246	7,021	8.2	91.8	58.1	16.4
$100,000 to $124,999..	36,250	2,283	33,970	28,020	24,140	4,715	4,437	6.3	93.7	66.6	12.2
$125,000 to $149,999..	26,690	1,141	25,550	22,270	19,670	3,150	2,390	4.3	95.7	73.7	9.0
$150,000 or more.......	88,050	3,026	85,020	78,680	70,970	8,055	3,962	3.4	96.6	80.6	4.5
Below poverty...........	37,820	6,238	31,580	8,949	5,501	7,451	19,220	16.5	83.5	14.5	50.8

[1] Includes other private and public insurance, not shown separately. Persons with coverage counted only once in total, even if covered by more than one type of policy. [2] Refers to people who reported specified race and no other race category. [3] Persons of Hispanic origin may be of any race.

Source: U.S. Census Bureau, *Health Insurance Coverage in the United States: 2022,* Current Population Reports, P60-281, September 2023; and "Health Insurance Data Tables, Health Insurance: Tables 2018-forward," Table H-01, <www.census.gov/topics/health/health-insurance/data/tables.html>, accessed November 2023.

Table 163. People Without Health Insurance for the Entire Year by Age, Sex, Race/Ethnicity, and Marital Status: 2021 and 2022

[In thousands (328,074 represents 328,074,000), except as noted. Based on the Current Population Survey, Annual Social and Economic Supplement (CPS ASEC); see text, Section 1]

Characteristic	2021			2022		
	Total persons	Uninsured persons		Total persons	Uninsured persons	
		Number	Percent of total persons		Number	Percent of total persons
Total [1].....................	328,074	27,187	8.3	330,000	25,940	7.9
Male............................	161,758	15,154	9.4	163,100	14,590	8.9
Female.........................	166,316	12,033	7.2	166,900	11,350	6.8
White alone [2].................	248,776	20,434	8.2	248,700	19,540	7.9
Black alone [2].................	43,963	3,959	9.0	44,540	3,714	8.3
Asian alone [2].................	20,681	1,274	6.2	21,550	1,275	5.9
Hispanic [3]....................	62,515	11,410	18.3	63,790	10,950	17.2
Under age 19 [4]...............	77,026	3,886	5.0	76,200	4,079	5.4
Age 19 to 25 [4]...............	29,045	4,318	14.9	30,430	4,247	14.0
Age 26 to 34 years............	40,312	5,426	13.5	40,580	5,061	12.5
Age 35 to 44 years............	43,190	5,154	11.9	43,490	4,884	11.2
Age 45 to 64 years............	82,308	7,748	9.4	81,390	7,022	8.6
Age 65 and older.............	56,193	655	1.2	57,880	643	1.1
Married........................	99,078	8,065	8.1	99,680	7,726	7.8
Widowed.......................	3,267	402	12.3	3,239	444	13.7
Divorced.......................	18,138	2,273	12.5	17,960	2,021	11.3
Separated......................	3,898	739	19.0	3,802	730	19.2
Never married..................	70,474	11,166	15.8	71,200	10,290	14.5

[1] Includes other races not shown separately. [2] Refers to people who reported specified race and no other race category. [3] Persons of Hispanic origin may be of any race. [4] Children under age 19 may be eligible for Medicaid/CHIP (Children's Health Insurance Program). Individuals age 19-25 may be eligible to participate as a dependent on a parent's health insurance plan.

Source: U.S. Census Bureau, *Health Insurance Coverage in the United States: 2022,* Current Population Reports, P60-281, September 2023; and "Health Insurance Data Tables, Health Insurance: Tables 2018-forward," Table H-01, <www.census.gov/topics/health/health-insurance/data/tables.html>, accessed November 2023.

Table 164. Health Insurance Coverage—Public, Private, and Exchange-Based Coverage by Selected Characteristics: 2021 to 2023

[In percent, except as noted (11.6 represents 11,600,000). Covers persons age 18 to 64, except as indicated. Based on the National Health Interview Survey. Data are estimates that have been released prior to final data editing and final weighting; see source for details. Data are based on a sample of the civilian noninstitutionalized population and are subject to sampling error. In 2019, the NCHS redesigned the NHIS questionnaire and made other methodological changes]

Year and characteristic	No insurance [1]	Public health plan [2]	Private health insurance [3]	Exchange-based private health insurance [4]	
				Total (millions)	Percent
Total age 64 and under:					
2021 [8]	11.0	27.7	63.2	11.6	4.3
2022	10.1	27.8	64.2	11.6	4.3
2023	9.1	28.6	64.4	13.0	4.8
Age 17 and under:					
2021 [8]	4.1	44.3	53.8	1.5	2.1
2022	4.2	43.7	54.3	1.6	2.2
2023	3.9	44.2	54.0	2.1	2.8
Age 18 to 64:					
2021 [8]	13.5	21.7	66.6	10.1	5.1
2022	12.2	22.0	67.8	10.0	5.0
2023	10.9	23.0	68.1	11.0	5.5
Male:					
2021 [8]	15.8	18.4	67.5	5.2	3.9
2022	14.2	19.0	68.7	5.3	3.9
2023	12.8	19.6	69.6	6.0	4.4
Female:					
2021 [8]	11.3	24.8	65.7	6.5	4.8
2022	10.2	25.0	66.9	6.3	4.6
2023	9.1	26.4	66.6	7.0	5.1
Black only, non-Hispanic:					
2021 [8]	14.1	32.6	55.4	1.3	3.9
2022	13.3	33.0	56.1	1.3	3.8
2023	10.4	34.4	57.7	1.6	4.7
White only, non-Hispanic:					
2021 [8]	8.7	18.5	74.8	6.4	4.2
2022	7.4	18.8	76.1	6.4	4.2
2023	6.8	19.6	75.9	7.1	4.7
Hispanic or Latino: [5]					
2021 [8]	30.1	23.7	47.4	2.5	4.4
2022	27.6	23.7	49.7	2.7	4.7
2023	24.8	27.5	48.8	3.1	5.2
Income less than 100% FPL: [6]					
2021 [8]	24.5	54.1	22.9	1.3	3.6
2022	22.7	57.0	22.3	1.0	3.3
2023	20.2	59.2	22.9	1.5	4.6
Income 100% to less than 200% FPL: [6]					
2021 [8]	23.7	39.0	40.1	3.5	6.4
2022	22.3	42.5	37.9	3.1	6.0
2023	19.1	43.9	39.8	3.0	5.9
Income 200% to 400% FPL: [6]					
2021 [8]	14.2	17.6	69.8	4.2	5.3
2022	14.2	19.3	68.7	4.0	5.2
2023	11.5	19.6	71.1	4.9	6.5
In states with Medicaid expansion: [7]					
2021 [8]	10.1	23.8	67.8	7.2	4.0
2022	9.1	24.2	68.8	7.2	3.9
2023	8.3	25.2	68.6	7.8	4.1
In states without Medicaid expansion: [7]					
2021 [8]	20.4	17.4	64.1	4.4	4.9
2022	19.2	17.0	65.6	4.4	5.2
2023	16.8	18.1	67.0	5.2	6.2

[1] Also includes persons with only Indian Health Service coverage or only a private plan covering one type of service, such as accidents or dental care. [2] Includes Medicaid, Children's Health Insurance Program (CHIP), state-sponsored or other government-sponsored health plan, Medicare, and military plans. A small number of persons covered by both public and private plans are included in both categories. [3] Includes plans obtained through an employer, purchased directly, purchased through local or community programs, or purchased through the Health Insurance Marketplace or a state-based exchange. Excludes plans that cover only one type of service, such as accidents or dental care. A small number of persons covered by both public and private plans are included in both categories. [4] For persons under age 65, except for the age groups below. Covers persons who purchased a private health insurance plan through the Health Insurance Marketplace or state-based exchanges established under the Affordable Care Act of 2010. These persons are also included under "private health insurance." [5] Persons of Hispanic or Latino origin may be of any race or combination of races. [6] FPL is federal poverty level. Not shown are data for greater than 400% FPL. Income categories are based on the ratio of the family's income in the previous year to the appropriate poverty threshold (given family size and number of children) defined by the U.S. Census Bureau. Excludes persons with unknown poverty status. [7] The Affordable Care Act gave states the option to expand Medicaid coverage to adults with incomes up to and including 138 percent of the federal poverty level. As of 2019, Medicaid had been expanded in 33 states and DC; states with no Medicaid expansion included Alabama, Florida, Georgia, Idaho, Kansas, Mississippi, Missouri, Nebraska, North Carolina, Oklahoma, South Carolina, South Dakota, Tennessee, Texas, Utah, Wisconsin, and Wyoming. After 2019, States expanded Medicaid as follows: 2020, Idaho and Utah; 2021, Nebraska; 2022, Missouri and Oklahoma. [8] Due to the COVID-19 pandemic, National Health Interview Survey data collection switched from personal interviews to a telephone-only mode beginning March 19, 2020. Personal visits (with telephone attempts first) resumed in September 2020. The "telephone first" data collection approach ran from July 2020 to April 2021. Prepandemic interviewing procedures (personal visit first) resumed in May 2021.

Source: U.S. National Center for Health Statistics, National Health Interview Survey Early Release Program, *Health Insurance Coverage: Early Release of Estimates From the National Health Interview Survey, 2023,* June 2024. See also <www.cdc.gov/nchs/nhis/releases.htm>.

Table 165. Worker Participation in Employer-Sponsored Health Insurance and Benefit Programs, and Participant Contributions: 2023

[Based on the March 2023 National Compensation Survey; survey drew responses from 6,990 private industry establishments of all sizes, representing about 126.23 million workers. Excludes federal government workers, the military, agricultural workers, private household workers, and the self-employed. For more information, see Appendix III, and the Bureau of Labor Statistics (BLS) Handbook of Methods, National Compensation Measures, online at <www.bls.gov/opub/hom/ncs/home.htm>]

Characteristic	Percent of workers participating				Single coverage medical plans		Family coverage medical plans	
	Medical care	Dental care	Vision care	Out-patient prescription drug coverage	Share of premiums paid by employees (percent)	Average monthly contribution [1] (dol.)	Share of premiums paid by employees (percent)	Average monthly contribution [1] (dol.)
Total....................................	**46**	**31**	**20**	**45**	**21**	**152.45**	**33**	**633.48**
Management, professional, and related...	61	46	26	61	21	146.53	32	621.03
Management, business, and financial...	67	50	27	66	21	155.40	32	642.67
Professional and related.................	58	44	26	58	20	140.75	32	607.05
Service....................................	24	12	9	23	22	161.24	38	712.48
Sales and office...........................	40	27	19	40	21	146.71	34	648.45
Sales and related........................	31	19	15	31	22	149.68	36	692.30
Office and administrative support.......	48	33	21	47	20	145.06	32	624.30
Natural resources, construction, and maintenance.............................	55	32	23	54	23	168.87	35	668.11
Production, transportation, and material moving..........................	53	34	25	52	22	156.15	30	581.13
Production................................	57	40	30	56	22	149.99	30	554.24
Transportation, and material moving....	50	30	23	49	22	160.70	31	601.71
Full-time [2]..............................	57	39	25	56	21	151.68	33	633.23
Part-time [2]..............................	13	7	6	13	22	162.49	33	636.94
Union [3].................................	78	59	47	76	20	177.15	21	487.42
Nonunion.................................	43	28	18	43	22	148.70	35	655.39
Average hourly wage percentile: [4]								
Lowest 25 percent.........................	21	11	8	21	23	157.21	39	702.63
Lowest 10 percent.........................	14	6	5	13	23	145.04	43	707.27
Second 25 percent.........................	45	27	19	44	22	150.10	35	642.70
Third 25 percent..........................	59	41	26	58	21	155.94	33	643.03
Highest 25 percent........................	67	51	31	66	20	149.14	29	590.21
Highest 10 percent........................	69	56	33	68	20	150.08	29	606.29

[1] The average is for all workers with medical care benefits, and covers plans that have a flat monthly cost. [2] Employees are classified as working either a full-time or part-time schedule based on the definition used by each establishment. [3] Union workers are those whose wages are determined through collective bargaining. [4] Tenth percentile, $14.00; 25th, $17.00; 50th (median), $22.57; 75th, $35.64; and 90th, $55.29. See "Technical Note" in source, <www.bls.gov/ebs/publications/employee-benefits-in-the-united-states-march-2023.htm>.

Source: U.S. Bureau of Labor Statistics, National Compensation Survey, Annual Summaries on Benefit Coverage, "Employee Benefits in the United States, March 2023," <www.bls.gov/ebs/home.htm>, accessed February 2024.

Table 166. Employer-Sponsored Health Insurance Enrollment by Type of Plan and Employer Size: 2021

[In millions (178.3 represents 178,300,000). Based on the Current Population Survey, Annual and Social Economic Supplement, and Agency for Healthcare Research and Quality's Medical Expenditure Panel Surveys. For persons and their dependents covered by health insurance sponsored by a current or former employer. Abbreviations: HMO = health maintenance organization; PPO = preferred provider organization; POS = point-of-service plan; and HDED = high deductible health plan (including but not limited to IRS-qualified high deductible health plans)]

Employer sector and size	Total					Self-insured plans [1]					Fully insured plans [2]				
	Total	HMO	PPO	POS	HDED	Total	HMO	PPO	POS	HDED	Total	HMO	PPO	POS	HDED
TOTAL															
Total employee size.....	**178.3**	**29.3**	**88.0**	**14.0**	**47.1**	**99.5**	**9.3**	**53.1**	**5.0**	**32.1**	**78.8**	**19.9**	**34.8**	**9.0**	**15.0**
Less than 25.............	27.2	3.6	12.2	5.1	6.2	4.7	0.3	2.7	0.4	1.2	22.5	3.3	9.5	4.8	5.0
25 to 99.................	10.4	1.4	5.0	1.9	2.2	2.2	0.2	1.3	0.1	0.5	8.2	1.1	3.7	1.7	1.6
100 to 499...............	23.5	2.4	11.4	1.5	8.2	10.8	0.4	6.3	0.3	3.8	12.7	2.0	5.1	1.2	4.4
500 to 999...............	11.9	1.3	6.1	0.7	3.8	6.6	0.3	4.0	0.1	2.1	5.2	0.9	2.1	0.5	1.7
1,000 or more...........	105.4	20.7	53.3	4.8	26.6	75.3	8.1	38.8	4.0	24.4	30.1	12.6	14.5	0.8	2.2
PRIVATE SECTOR [3]															
Total employee size.....	**134.1**	**20.8**	**62.8**	**12.5**	**38.0**	**78.1**	**7.4**	**41.3**	**4.2**	**25.3**	**55.9**	**13.4**	**21.4**	**8.3**	**12.8**
Less than 25.............	26.0	3.4	11.6	5.0	6.0	4.0	0.3	2.4	0.3	1.1	21.9	3.2	9.2	4.6	4.9
25 to 99.................	9.3	1.2	4.3	1.8	2.0	1.7	0.2	1.0	0.1	0.4	7.6	1.1	3.3	1.6	1.5
100 to 499...............	19.7	2.0	9.5	1.3	6.8	9.0	0.3	5.3	0.3	3.1	10.7	1.7	4.2	1.0	3.7
500 to 999...............	9.5	1.0	4.8	0.6	3.1	5.2	0.3	3.1	0.1	1.7	4.2	0.8	1.7	0.5	1.3
1,000 or more...........	69.7	13.1	32.5	3.9	20.2	58.1	6.4	29.5	3.3	18.9	11.5	6.7	3.0	0.5	1.3

[1] Self-insured plans are those in which the employer directly assumes some or all medical claim and administrative costs. [2] Fully insured plans are those in which the employer contracts with another organization to assume financial responsibility for the enrollees' medical claims and administrative costs. [3] Private sector includes self-employed.

Source: U.S. Department of Labor, Employee Benefits Security Administration, *Health Insurance Coverage Bulletin: Abstract of Auxiliary Data for the March 2022 Annual Social and Economic Supplement to the Current Population Survey*, August 2023. See also <www.dol.gov/agencies/ebsa/researchers/data/auxiliary-data>.

Table 167. Revenue for Health Care Industries: 2020 to 2022

[In millions of dollars (2,822,900 represents $2,822,900,000,000). Data are based on the 2012 North American Industry Classification System (NAICS). Estimates have been adjusted using results of the 2017 Economic Census where applicable. For a description of benchmarking methods and exceptions, see <www.census.gov/programs-surveys/sas/technical-documentation/methodology/benchmarkprocess.html>. Based on Service Annual Survey and administrative data; see Appendix III]

Kind of business	NAICS code [1]	Total, all firms [2]			Taxable employer firms		
		2020	2021	2022	2020	2021	2022
Health care and social assistance [3]	**62**	**2,822,900**	**3,099,433**	**3,263,306**	**1,379,760**	**1,520,043**	**1,624,432**
Ambulatory health care services [3]	**621**	**1,133,361**	**1,255,294**	**1,334,439**	**1,010,819**	**1,124,905**	**1,196,882**
Offices of physicians (except mental health specialists)	621111	506,496	551,925	590,856	506,496	551,925	590,856
Offices of physicians, mental health specialists	621112	7,672	8,656	10,068	7,672	8,656	10,068
Offices of dentists	6212	125,931	152,382	157,906	125,931	152,382	157,906
Offices of chiropractors	62131	14,655	16,431	17,658	14,655	16,431	17,658
Offices of optometrists	62132	15,746	17,996	18,213	15,746	17,996	18,213
Offices of mental health practitioners (except physicians)	62133	13,074	16,234	20,102	13,074	16,234	20,102
Offices of PT/OT/speech therapists and audiologists [4]	62134	33,046	37,143	40,900	33,046	37,143	40,900
Offices of podiatrists	621391	4,939	5,654	5,872	4,939	5,654	5,872
Outpatient care centers	6214	192,796	206,976	217,722	109,465	118,243	123,754
Family planning centers	62141	3,274	3,575	3,891	1,327	1,477	1,577
Outpatient mental health and substance abuse centers	62142	26,051	28,083	30,799	10,017	11,328	13,075
HMO medical centers [5]	621491	40,726	42,166	42,430	26,636	27,780	27,415
Kidney dialysis centers	621492	28,869	28,150	28,191	26,975	26,293	26,397
Freestanding ambulatory surgical and emergency centers	621493	34,589	40,154	43,138	30,163	35,427	37,968
All other outpatient care centers	621498	59,287	64,848	69,273	14,347	15,938	17,322
Medical laboratories and diagnostic imaging	6215	62,049	72,142	70,820	62,049	72,142	70,820
Home health care services	6216	99,794	104,703	113,264	76,694	80,296	88,197
Ambulance services	62191	15,757	16,760	17,842	12,356	13,242	14,217
Blood and organ banks	621991	14,197	15,432	16,297	5,213	5,658	6,562
Hospitals	**622**	**1,208,499**	**1,326,282**	**1,369,548**	**136,821**	**150,885**	**154,725**
General medical and surgical hospitals, government	622118	244,668	267,467	285,691	(X)	(X)	(X)
General medical and surgical hospitals, private	622119	885,997	973,620	995,172	110,219	122,429	123,625
Psychiatric and substance abuse hospitals, government	622218	13,336	13,790	14,300	(X)	(X)	(X)
Psychiatric and substance abuse hospitals, private	622219	14,069	15,124	16,026	8,594	9,380	9,981
Specialty hospitals, government	622318	10,220	11,924	10,528	(X)	(X)	(X)
Specialty hospitals, private	622319	40,209	44,357	47,831	18,008	19,076	21,119
Nursing and residential care facilities [3]	**623**	**260,514**	**264,631**	**286,027**	**168,068**	**171,371**	**190,233**
Nursing care facilities (skilled nursing facilities)	6231	128,617	128,690	139,663	105,054	105,569	116,677
Residential intellectual/developmental disability facilities	62321	30,809	32,071	34,845	10,167	10,872	12,549
Residential mental health and substance abuse facilities	62322	19,377	21,911	24,321	8,609	10,242	11,946
Continuing care retirement communities	623311	39,783	39,278	41,119	14,392	14,346	15,800
Assisted living facilities for the elderly	623312	33,430	34,022	37,274	28,576	29,037	31,746

X Not applicable. [1] 2012 North American Industry Classification System (NAICS); see text, Section 15. [2] Includes taxable and tax-exempt employer firms. [3] Includes other kinds of business, not shown separately. See Table 611 for data on NAICS 624 Social assistance industries. [4] Offices of physical, occupational, and speech therapists, and audiologists. [5] HMO is health maintenance organization.

Source: U.S. Census Bureau, Service Annual Survey, "Service Annual Survey Latest Data (NAICS-basis): 2022," <www.census.gov/programs-surveys/sas/data/tables.html>, accessed February 2024.

Table 168. Revenue for Selected Health Care Industries by Source: 2022

[In millions of dollars (600,924 represents $600,924,000,000). For all employer firms regardless of tax status. See headnote, Table 167. Based on Service Annual Survey and administrative data; see Appendix III]

Source of revenue	Offices of physicians (NAICS 6211)	Offices of dentists (NAICS 6212)	Outpatient care centers (NAICS 6214)	Home health care services (NAICS 6216)	Hospitals (NAICS 622)	Nursing and residential care facilities (NAICS 623) [1]
Revenue, total	**600,924**	**157,906**	**217,722**	**113,264**	**1,369,548**	**286,027**
Medicare [2]	97,731	1,154	25,333	42,306	297,205	39,857
Medicaid (fee for service only)	22,611	8,297	23,837	23,659	117,999	88,316
Workers' compensation	5,442	62	2,939	564	6,881	(S)
All other government programs	9,990	2,089	12,722	4,331	(S)	19,481
Revenue from health care providers for patient care	39,987	3,900	4,728	(S)	(S)	(NA)
Private health insurance [3]	272,224	67,390	70,494	23,730	666,199	34,722
Property, auto, and casualty insurance	1,401	(S)	658	(S)	3,076	193
Patient out-of-pocket from patients and their families	47,407	64,914	9,705	5,572	27,352	50,240
All other sources of revenue for patient care	58,931	8,455	37,446	7,023	(S)	22,376
Contributions, gifts, and grants received	(NA)	(NA)	12,752	795	25,237	6,829
Investment and property income	(NA)	(NA)	631	166	16,569	1,228
Revenue from health care providers for non-patient care [4]	20,792	778	6,296	(S)	10,289	(NA)
All other non-patient care revenue	24,408	[5] 841	10,181	901	70,412	19,492

NA Not available. S Figure does not meet publication standards. [1] Total revenue for NAICS 623 also includes $3,118 million in revenue from social security benefits—direct payments of social security on behalf of patients. [2] Fee for service, Medicare Part A hospital insurance, Part B medical insurance, and Part D prescription drug coverage. [3] Also includes Medicare Part C (Medicare Advantage plans providing coverage from private insurance companies), and Medicaid managed care plans. [4] Includes revenue from medical administration and other administrative services, incentive payments, management fees, medical director fees, etc. [5] Estimated coefficient of variation is between 30 and 40 percent.

Source: U.S. Census Bureau, Service Annual Survey, "Service Annual Survey Latest Data (NAICS-basis): 2022," <www.census.gov/programs-surveys/sas/data/tables.html>, accessed February 2024.

Table 169. Medical Record Confidentiality Breaches Reported—Incidents and Persons Affected by Type and Location of Breach: 2020 to 2023

[Individuals affected in thousands (35,000 represents 35,000,000). Data for breaches by date of submission to the Secretary of Health and Human Services (HHS) for those affecting 500 or more individuals. As required by section 13402(e)(4) of the Health Information Technology for Economic and Clinical Health (HITECH) Act, the Secretary of HHS must post a list of breaches of unsecured protected health information affecting 500 or more individuals. The Privacy Rule of the Health Insurance Portability and Accountability Act of 1996 (HIPAA) provides federal protections for individually identifiable health information held by covered entities and their business associates. Covered entities include health care providers, health plans, and health care clearinghouses. Data are subject to revision]

Breach type and location	2020		2021		2022		2023	
	Incidents (number)	Individuals affected (1,000)	Incidents (number)	Individuals affected (1,000)	Incidents (number)	Individuals affected (1,000)	Incidents (number)	Individuals affected (1,000)
Total............................	**663**	**35,000**	**715**	**59,742**	**721**	**56,975**	**742**	**139,955**
TYPE OF BREACH								
Hacking/information technology incident.....	457	32,318	547	57,783	571	49,112	597	131,444
Improper disposal.............................	15	584	5	191	4	7	5	12
Loss...	13	55	10	33	11	18	3	15
Theft..	39	820	24	108	21	382	12	29
Unauthorized access/disclosure.............	139	1,222	129	1,627	114	7,456	125	8,455
LOCATION OF INFORMATION BREACHED [1]								
Desktop computer............................	17	475	13	248	6	87	14	730
Electronic medical record....................	32	308	32	506	66	6,536	26	1,189
E-mail...	241	12,445	204	7,717	170	5,710	136	2,718
Laptop computer..............................	10	688	8	64	11	75	4	12
Network server................................	255	19,729	391	50,829	407	43,979	516	134,447
Other portable electronic device.............	10	109	9	29	16	201	5	12
Paper/films...................................	86	1,006	46	177	42	229	39	142
Other [2]......................................	12	239	12	172	3	159	2	705

[1] Location of information breaches can include a combination of other locations within the categories specified. For example, incidents involving desktop computers can also include electronic medical record, network server, email, and other locations. Incidents are categorized according to the first type as listed in the source. [2] Other locations of information breached can include various other media and methods, including capturing images of protected health information (PHI), publishing PHI on the internet, mailings (postal and electronic) and other methods of sending or delivering information, and other miscellaneous materials and locations.

Source: U.S. Department of Health and Human Services, Office for Civil Rights, HIPAA for Professionals—Breach Notification Rule, "Breaches Affecting 500 or More Individuals," <www.hhs.gov/hipaa/for-professionals/breach-notification/index.html>, accessed June 2024.

Table 170. Employment in the Health Service Industries: 2000 to 2023

[In thousands (12,861 represents 12,861,000). Covers persons on establishment payrolls who worked or received pay for any part of the pay period that includes the 12th day of the month. Excludes proprietors, the unincorporated self-employed, unpaid volunteer or family employees, farm employees, domestic employees, and military personnel. Based on the 2022 North American Industry Classification System (NAICS)]

Industry	NAICS code	2000	2010	2015	2019	2020	2021	2022	2023
Health care and social assistance [1]......	**62**	**12,861**	**16,820**	**18,557**	**20,421**	**19,796**	**20,065**	**20,579**	**21,525**
Health care................................	**621,2,3**	**10,858**	**13,777**	**15,042**	**16,269**	**15,850**	**15,997**	**16,306**	**16,953**
Ambulatory health care services [1]...............	621	4,320	5,975	6,856	7,704	7,498	7,858	8,130	8,461
Offices of physicians............................	6211	1,801	2,264	2,471	2,673	2,632	2,732	2,813	2,921
Office of physicians, except mental health...	621111	1,764	2,218	2,420	2,615	2,574	2,668	2,742	2,842
Office of mental health physicians...........	621112	37	46	51	58	58	64	71	79
Offices of dentists.............................	6212	688	828	905	974	889	988	1,012	1,027
Offices of other health practitioners...........	6213	438	671	813	974	926	1,012	1,090	1,155
Outpatient care centers........................	6214	425	649	806	969	970	1,000	1,032	1,061
Medical and diagnostic laboratories...........	6215	162	228	260	283	282	309	320	321
Home health care services....................	6216	633	1,085	1,315	1,519	1,495	1,504	1,535	1,627
Hospitals.......................................	622	3,954	4,679	4,896	5,190	5,137	5,117	5,167	5,338
General medical and surgical hospitals........	6221	3,745	4,357	4,498	4,767	4,715	4,695	4,739	4,886
Psychiatric and substance abuse hospitals. ..	6222	86	109	138	152	153	149	150	158
Specialty hospitals [2].........................	6223	123	213	260	271	270	273	278	294
Nursing and residential care facilities [1].........	623	2,583	3,124	3,291	3,375	3,214	3,022	3,009	3,154
Skilled nursing care facilities..................	6231	1,514	1,657	1,648	1,596	1,499	1,374	1,355	1,417

[1] Includes other industries not shown separately. [2] Excluding psychiatric and substance abuse hospitals.

Source: U.S. Bureau of Labor Statistics, Current Employment Statistics, "Employment, Hours, and Earnings—National," <www.bls.gov/ces/data/>, accessed April 2024.

Table 171. Physicians by Sex, Osteopathic Physicians, and International Medical Graduates by Specialty: 2021

[Covers federal and nonfederal physicians working 20 or more hours per week in specialties in which there are over 2,500 active physicians. Active physicians include those working in direct patient care, administration, medical teaching, research, or other non-patient care activities. Physicians selected their specialties on the American Medical Association's Census of Physicians]

Specialty	Total [1]	By sex			By type		
		Male	Female	Percent female	Patient care physicians	Osteopathic physicians	International graduates [2]
All specialties [3]............................	**949,658**	**595,673**	**351,117**	**37.1**	**819,007**	**78,904**	**236,940**
Allergy and immunology....................	5,009	2,849	2,158	43.1	4,264	190	1,146
Anatomic/clinical pathology...............	12,180	7,433	4,738	38.9	8,295	321	3,761
Anesthesiology.............................	42,264	31,188	11,032	26.1	39,195	2,953	8,515
Cardiovascular disease....................	22,262	18,795	3,448	15.5	20,146	914	6,896
Child and adolescent psychiatry..........	9,966	4,520	5,441	54.6	8,772	599	3,099
Clinical cardiac electrophysiology.........	2,632	2,360	266	10.1	2,295	86	910
Critical care medicine.....................	14,159	10,281	3,861	27.3	11,895	782	5,837
Dermatology...............................	12,767	6,091	6,665	52.2	11,865	781	585
Emergency medicine.......................	46,857	33,257	13,565	29.0	42,633	5,561	2,935
Endocrinology, diabetes, & metabolism...	8,246	3,867	4,367	53.0	6,603	255	3,480
Family medicine/general practice.........	118,641	68,411	50,053	42.3	109,035	19,415	28,686
Gastroenterology...........................	15,678	12,576	3,083	19.7	14,116	669	4,580
General surgery............................	24,881	19,234	5,627	22.6	21,451	1,181	4,641
Geriatric medicine.........................	6,149	2,761	3,382	55.1	5,124	356	3,154
Hematology and oncology.................	16,673	10,826	5,828	35.0	13,701	501	6,256
Infectious disease.........................	9,913	5,657	4,242	42.9	7,579	367	3,508
Internal medicine..........................	120,342	73,016	47,115	39.2	105,468	6,955	47,881
Internal medicine/pediatrics...............	5,701	2,655	3,044	53.4	5,054	306	594
Interventional cardiology..................	4,736	4,338	390	8.2	4,220	207	2,184
Neonatal-perinatal medicine..............	6,056	2,771	3,281	54.2	5,056	269	2,273
Nephrology.................................	11,554	8,153	3,388	29.4	10,073	518	5,889
Neurological surgery.......................	5,748	5,193	551	9.6	5,204	116	675
Neurology..................................	13,853	9,499	4,340	31.4	11,684	735	4,364
Neuroradiology............................	4,311	3,471	834	19.4	3,653	188	605
Obstetrics and gynecology................	42,496	16,777	25,682	60.5	39,531	3,083	5,813
Ophthalmology.............................	18,948	13,786	5,152	27.2	17,528	473	1,281
Orthopedic surgery........................	18,469	17,374	1,090	5.9	17,526	1,085	836
Otolaryngology............................	9,616	7,798	1,812	18.9	8,990	396	520
Pain medicine and pain management....	6,240	5,007	1,220	19.6	5,725	623	1,631
Pediatric anesthesiology..................	2,843	1,381	1,455	51.3	2,269	181	513
Pediatric cardiology.......................	2,993	1,858	1,131	37.8	2,426	74	775
Pediatric critical care medicine...........	2,774	1,398	1,374	49.6	2,195	130	756
Pediatric hematology/oncology...........	3,179	1,408	1,768	55.7	2,296	111	789
Pediatrics..................................	60,305	21,063	39,189	65.0	54,302	2,882	14,616
Physical medicine and rehabilitation......	9,724	6,224	3,474	35.8	8,859	1,416	2,157
Plastic surgery.............................	7,228	5,949	1,275	17.6	6,832	123	727
Preventive medicine.......................	6,555	4,192	2,359	36.0	4,125	562	861
Psychiatry..................................	38,424	22,690	15,711	40.9	33,217	1,883	11,606
Pulmonary disease........................	4,867	4,250	616	12.7	4,265	193	1,499
Radiation oncology........................	5,376	3,884	1,489	27.7	4,865	86	524
Radiology and diagnostic radiology.......	27,197	19,876	7,304	26.9	24,002	1,080	2,924
Rheumatology..............................	6,420	3,373	3,034	47.4	5,416	356	2,264
Sports medicine...........................	3,208	2,320	881	27.5	2,865	633	529
Sports medicine (orthopedic surgery)....	3,065	2,848	217	7.1	2,887	204	125
Thoracic surgery...........................	4,449	4,079	369	8.3	4,042	103	884
Urology....................................	10,081	9,074	1,003	10.0	9,483	262	989
Vascular and interventional radiology.....	4,011	3,611	399	10.0	3,534	151	536
Vascular surgery...........................	4,039	3,414	623	15.4	3,632	168	705

[1] Includes active physicians with unknown sex and type of medical degree. [2] All physicians, including U.S. citizens, who completed their medical education in a school outside the U.S., Puerto Rico, and Canada. [3] Includes data for specialties not shown separately.

Source: Association of American Medical Colleges, *2022 Physician Specialty Data Report* ©. See also <www.aamc.org/data-reports/workforce-studies>.

Table 172. Physicians, Doctors of Osteopathy, and Female Physicians by State: 2020

[As of year end. Rates per 100,000 resident population, based on U.S. Census Bureau estimates as of July 1, 2019. Covers active federal and nonfederal physicians who work at least 20 hours per week]

State	Active physicians [1] Total (number)	Female Number	Female Percent [2]	Active physicians in patient care Total [3] Number	Total [3] Rate	Osteopathic physicians Number	Osteopathic physicians Rate	Primary care physicians [4] Number	Primary care physicians [4] Rate
U.S. [5]	940,254	344,329	36.7	812,492	247.5	68,910	21.0	277,466	84.5
AL	10,983	3,212	29.3	9,853	201.0	550	11.2	3,563	72.7
AK	2,101	806	38.4	1,945	265.9	252	34.4	812	111.0
AZ	18,343	6,003	33.2	16,787	230.6	2,074	28.5	5,452	74.9
AR	6,500	1,885	29.0	5,843	193.6	346	11.5	2,328	77.1
CA	113,718	44,030	38.8	98,607	249.6	5,514	14.0	35,136	88.9
CO	16,956	6,723	39.7	15,562	270.2	1,591	27.6	5,217	90.6
CT	12,977	5,033	38.8	11,092	311.1	480	13.5	3,414	95.8
DE	2,850	1,138	40.0	2,532	260.0	329	33.8	880	90.4
DC	6,147	2,967	48.3	4,449	630.4	113	16.0	1,304	184.8
FL	58,822	18,604	31.7	52,947	246.5	5,017	23.4	17,508	81.5
GA	25,072	9,177	36.6	22,140	208.5	1,098	10.3	7,818	73.6
HI	4,557	1,651	36.3	3,965	280.0	221	15.6	1,546	109.2
ID	3,504	949	27.1	3,285	183.8	484	27.1	1,235	69.1
IL	37,122	14,567	39.3	31,194	246.2	2,294	18.1	11,182	88.2
IN	15,918	5,205	32.7	14,456	214.7	1,157	17.2	5,088	75.6
IA	7,056	2,383	33.8	6,239	197.7	1,290	40.9	2,503	79.3
KS	6,874	2,335	34.0	6,224	213.6	752	25.8	2,409	82.7
KY	10,528	3,385	32.2	9,718	217.5	718	16.1	3,286	73.6
LA	12,557	4,076	32.5	11,082	238.4	255	5.5	3,664	78.8
ME	4,459	1,691	38.0	4,103	305.2	714	53.1	1,599	119.0
MD	23,791	9,984	42.0	18,707	309.4	742	12.3	5,927	98.0
MA	32,116	13,885	43.3	24,956	362.1	854	12.4	7,947	115.3
MI	30,040	10,820	36.1	25,841	258.8	4,969	49.8	9,049	90.6
MN	17,617	6,711	38.1	15,342	272.0	822	14.6	5,502	97.6
MS	5,857	1,653	28.3	5,316	178.6	426	14.3	1,859	62.5
MO	18,297	6,051	35.1	14,806	241.2	2,143	34.9	4,900	79.8
MT	2,750	899	32.7	2,620	245.1	267	25.0	988	92.4
NE	4,820	1,609	33.4	4,309	222.8	257	13.3	1,590	82.2
NV	6,731	1,956	29.8	5,859	190.2	781	25.4	2,031	65.9
NH	4,391	1,637	37.3	3,990	293.4	370	27.2	1,343	98.8
NJ	27,832	10,487	37.8	24,409	274.8	2,869	32.3	7,860	88.5
NM	5,269	2,096	39.8	4,586	218.7	307	14.6	1,771	84.5
NY	75,749	30,131	39.8	60,446	310.7	3,558	18.3	18,799	96.6
NC	27,650	10,138	36.7	24,113	229.9	1,435	13.7	8,305	79.2
ND	1,826	571	31.3	1,655	217.2	94	12.3	618	81.1
OH	35,333	12,630	35.8	29,798	254.9	4,005	34.3	9,887	84.6
OK	8,293	2,548	30.8	7,548	190.8	1,627	41.1	2,717	68.7
OR	13,127	5,269	40.2	11,720	277.9	950	22.5	4,288	101.7
PA	42,051	15,484	36.9	35,571	277.9	5,351	41.8	11,425	89.2
RI	4,063	1,723	42.4	3,505	330.9	236	22.3	1,139	107.5
SC	12,197	3,901	32.0	10,844	210.6	728	14.1	3,814	74.1
SD	2,214	713	32.2	2,028	229.2	180	20.3	777	87.8
TN	17,687	5,552	31.4	15,638	229.0	859	12.6	5,325	78.0
TX	67,182	24,199	36.1	59,332	204.6	4,542	15.7	19,578	67.5
UT	7,198	1,821	25.4	6,631	206.8	643	20.1	2,038	63.6
VT	2,410	1,031	42.8	2,106	337.5	91	14.6	810	129.8
VA	22,874	8,768	38.4	20,038	234.8	1,306	15.3	7,000	82.0
WA	21,731	8,643	39.8	19,099	250.8	1,327	17.4	7,057	92.7
WV	4,914	1,507	30.7	4,198	234.2	715	39.9	1,606	89.6
WI	15,975	5,770	36.1	14,289	245.4	1,070	18.4	5,117	87.9
WY	1,225	322	26.3	1,169	202.0	137	23.7	455	78.6
PR	9,813	3,717	38.0	8,059	252.3	2	0.1	3,396	106.3

[1] Active physicians work in direct patient care, administration, medical teaching, research, or other nonpatient care activities. [2] Excludes physicians whose sex was not reported. [3] Includes physicians with Doctor of Medicine degrees, and unknown degree type. [4] Primary care physicians include physicians in the following specialties: adolescent medicine (pediatrics), family medicine, general practice, geriatric medicine (family practice and internal medicine), internal medicine, and pediatrics. [5] U.S. totals exclude Puerto Rico (PR).

Source: Association of American Medical Colleges, *2021 State Physician Workforce Data Report*, January 2022 ©. See also <www.aamc.org/data-reports>.

Table 173. Registered Nurses, Nurse Practitioners, and Licensed Practical and Licensed Vocational Nurses by State: 2023

[Covers nurses working in the health care and social assistance industry (North American Industry Classification System code 62), as of May. Rates per 100,000 resident population, based on U.S. Census Bureau estimates as of July 1 for year shown]

State	Registered nurses (RNs)		Nurse practitioners		Licensed practical and licensed vocational nurses	
	Total	Rate [2]	Total	Rate [2]	Total	Rate [2]
United States [1]	2,675,320	798.8	256,870	76.7	533,180	159.2
Alabama	43,700	855.4	3,770	73.8	8,700	170.3
Alaska	5,740	782.6	580	79.1	190	25.9
Arizona	52,310	703.9	6,040	81.3	4,020	54.1
Arkansas	22,860	745.2	3,030	98.8	9,580	312.3
California	285,520	732.8	20,270	52.0	66,080	169.6
Colorado	46,630	793.3	3,420	58.2	4,140	70.4
Connecticut	30,240	836.0	3,110	86.0	7,310	202.1
Delaware	9,910	960.4	1,100	106.6	1,450	140.5
District of Columbia	8,750	1,288.7	560	82.5	1,040	153.2
Florida	177,780	786.3	21,260	94.0	30,840	136.4
Georgia	76,520	693.8	10,240	92.8	20,300	184.1
Hawaii	10,380	723.3	500	34.8	580	40.4
Idaho	11,920	606.7	1,080	55.0	1,910	97.2
Illinois	122,580	976.8	8,740	69.6	18,490	147.3
Indiana	62,040	904.1	6,640	96.8	12,120	176.6
Iowa	28,870	900.2	2,340	73.0	4,910	153.1
Kansas	26,120	888.3	2,740	93.2	5,660	192.5
Kentucky	40,160	887.3	4,440	98.1	8,390	185.4
Louisiana	30,940	676.5	3,780	82.6	15,660	342.4
Maine	12,310	882.0	1,320	94.6	660	47.3
Maryland	40,720	658.9	4,520	73.1	6,360	102.9
Massachusetts	73,430	1,048.8	7,560	108.0	11,920	170.3
Michigan	91,100	908.4	7,630	76.0	8,890	88.6
Minnesota	56,900	991.6	5,050	88.0	11,300	196.9
Mississippi	23,680	805.5	3,630	123.5	8,070	274.5
Missouri	62,830	1,014.0	6,310	101.8	11,240	181.4
Montana	8,250	728.3	790	69.7	1,470	129.8
Nebraska	19,550	988.2	1,630	82.4	4,070	205.7
Nevada	21,630	677.2	1,830	57.3	2,230	69.8
New Hampshire	11,490	819.5	1,730	123.4	1,830	130.5
New Jersey	71,630	771.0	5,440	58.6	14,240	153.3
New Mexico	12,000	567.5	1,430	67.6	1,550	73.3
New York	149,120	761.9	14,270	72.9	29,700	151.8
North Carolina	89,210	823.3	6,700	61.8	14,490	133.7
North Dakota	8,650	1,103.4	670	85.5	2,150	274.3
Ohio	113,370	961.9	11,410	96.8	31,250	265.1
Oklahoma	26,600	656.2	2,580	63.6	9,700	239.3
Oregon	27,130	640.9	2,100	49.6	3,240	76.5
Pennsylvania	121,700	938.9	8,880	68.5	26,930	207.8
Rhode Island	9,740	888.7	980	89.4	850	77.6
South Carolina	40,230	748.7	5,020	93.4	7,640	142.2
South Dakota	12,320	1,340.1	860	93.5	1,810	196.9
Tennessee	52,380	735.0	12,730	178.6	16,670	233.9
Texas	211,870	694.6	17,730	58.1	50,640	166.0
Utah	21,560	630.8	2,250	65.8	1,190	34.8
Vermont	6,010	928.2	640	98.8	890	137.5
Virginia	58,870	675.4	6,680	76.6	14,290	164.0
Washington	53,440	684.0	4,180	53.5	5,050	64.6
West Virginia	17,280	976.2	1,710	96.6	5,030	284.2
Wisconsin	53,100	898.3	4,530	76.6	5,970	101.0
Wyoming	4,140	708.8	430	73.6	490	83.9
Guam	630	(NA)	80	(NA)	70	(NA)
Puerto Rico	16,390	511.3	(NA)	(NA)	2,420	75.5

NA Not available. [1] U.S. total excludes Puerto Rico and Guam. [2] Rates are calculated using data from the U.S. Census Bureau, "Annual Estimates of the Resident Population for the United States, Regions, States, District of Columbia, and Puerto Rico: April 1, 2020 to July 1, 2023 (NST-EST2023-POP)," <www.census.gov/data/tables/time-series/demo/popest/2020s-state-total.html>, accessed May 2024. The population estimates are developed from a base that incorporates the 2020 Census.

Source: U.S. Bureau of Labor Statistics, Occupational Employment and Wage Statistics, OEWS Data, "All data," and "Research Estimates by State and Industry," <www.bls.gov/oes/tables.htm>, accessed May 2024.

Table 174. Coronavirus Disease 2019 (COVID-19) Testing and Hospitalizations by Week: June 2022 to August 2024

[Data through August 24, 2024. Data are provisional and subject to change. The coronavirus virus disease 2019 (COVID-19) federal Public Health Emergency ended May 11, 2023. The CDC instituted changes in the collection and reporting of indicators of COVID-19, most notably discontinuing the reporting of the number of cases of COVID-19; for more information, see <archive.cdc.gov/#/details?url=https://www.cdc.gov/coronavirus/2019-ncov/covid-data/covidview/index.html> and <www.cdc.gov/mmwr/volumes/72/wr/mm7219e1.htm>. Data are presented here as an illustration of the progression of COVID-19 in the U.S. See source for more information regarding data sources and limitations]

Week ending	New test results reported [1]		New hospital admissions for COVID-19 [2]	Week ending	New test results reported [1]		New hospital admissions for COVID-19 [2]
	Weekly tests	Percent of tests positive			Weekly tests	Percent of tests positive	
June 11, 2022	299,605	10.3	29,115	July 22, 2023	45,896	7.4	7,795
June 18, 2022	286,749	10.4	30,009	July 29, 2023	47,458	9.0	8,889
June 25, 2022	269,708	11.5	32,309	August 5, 2023	47,280	10.6	10,432
July 2, 2022	255,329	13.1	35,281	August 12, 2023	52,862	12.3	12,678
July 9, 2022	263,621	13.5	38,387	August 19, 2023	60,011	13.3	14,763
July 16, 2022	281,178	13.7	42,006	August 26, 2023	70,310	14.5	17,054
July 23, 2022	281,142	14.3	44,081	September 2, 2023	77,345	14.1	18,669
July 30, 2022	265,063	14.0	43,412	September 9, 2023	81,910	13.9	20,160
August 6, 2022	247,194	13.8	42,241	September 16, 2023	87,127	12.6	19,423
August 13, 2022	239,182	12.8	40,553	September 23, 2023	89,369	12.0	19,001
August 20, 2022	236,375	11.9	37,694	September 30, 2023	87,458	10.9	17,914
August 27, 2022	234,470	11.7	36,396	October 7, 2023	85,271	10.0	16,718
September 3, 2022	229,216	11.0	34,104	October 14, 2023	83,458	9.2	15,709
September 10, 2022	221,337	9.6	31,160	October 21, 2023	86,631	9.4	15,504
September 17, 2022	222,454	8.5	28,549	October 28, 2023	87,611	9.6	15,822
September 24, 2022	233,980	7.7	26,518	November 4, 2023	87,152	9.3	14,686
October 1, 2022	204,423	6.9	23,989	November 11, 2023	96,096	10.1	16,262
October 8, 2022	193,072	6.9	23,267	November 18, 2023	111,184	9.5	17,362
October 15, 2022	194,264	7.1	22,605	November 25, 2023	95,828	11.2	18,695
October 22, 2022	199,584	6.8	22,491	December 2, 2023	116,294	11.7	22,339
October 29, 2022	205,124	6.9	22,989	December 9, 2023	121,831	11.6	22,836
November 5, 2022	227,947	6.5	23,271	December 16, 2023	131,686	11.9	24,587
November 12, 2022	210,676	6.8	23,446	December 23, 2023	140,574	12.5	28,800
November 19, 2022	223,638	6.7	23,762	December 30, 2023	141,276	13.1	34,128
November 26, 2022	204,316	7.6	26,076	January 6, 2024	128,838	12.9	34,334
December 3, 2022	248,811	8.6	33,400	January 13, 2024	122,350	11.9	30,426
December 10, 2022	237,920	8.7	34,438	January 20, 2024	106,580	10.9	25,325
December 17, 2022	230,153	9.4	35,973	January 27, 2024	110,685	10.4	22,755
December 24, 2022	196,678	9.8	38,176	February 3, 2024	114,801	9.9	20,886
December 31, 2022	178,063	10.6	44,207	February 10, 2024	117,913	9.5	19,758
January 7, 2023	177,334	10.2	43,434	February 17, 2024	114,407	8.4	18,968
January 14, 2023	168,828	8.8	36,687	February 24, 2024	111,295	7.7	17,366
January 21, 2023	157,646	8.4	31,067	March 2, 2024	106,291	6.7	15,301
January 28, 2023	157,515	8.2	27,670	March 9, 2024	101,245	5.5	13,346
February 4, 2023	149,167	8.0	25,856	March 16, 2024	91,173	4.7	10,663
February 11, 2023	152,534	8.0	25,784	March 23, 2024	84,122	4.1	9,262
February 18, 2023	143,612	8.1	24,891	March 30, 2024	78,137	3.8	7,954
February 25, 2023	136,330	7.9	23,516	April 6, 2024	75,413	3.5	7,317
March 4, 2023	133,779	7.3	21,858	April 13, 2024	70,716	3.4	6,449
March 11, 2023	129,512	6.8	19,724	April 20, 2024	63,932	3.1	5,626
March 18, 2023	122,499	6.8	17,689	April 27, 2024	62,999	3.1	5,098
March 25, 2023	118,506	6.8	16,764	May 4, 2024	59,279	3.3	3,605
April 1, 2023	111,169	6.5	15,487	May 11, 2024	57,438	3.1	2,319
April 8, 2023	104,818	6.2	14,074	May 18, 2024	56,009	3.5	2,208
April 15, 2023	99,713	5.7	13,029	May 25, 2024	54,232	4.1	2,273
April 22, 2023	90,617	5.0	11,527	June 1, 2024	50,074	4.8	2,331
April 29, 2023	86,890	4.9	9,915	June 8, 2024	49,891	5.6	2,558
May 6, 2023	81,935	5.0	9,474	June 15, 2024	48,171	7.0	2,897
May 13, 2023	75,721	4.8	9,050	June 22, 2024	46,625	8.6	3,414
May 20, 2023	69,189	4.6	8,233	June 29, 2024	46,216	9.5	3,748
May 27, 2023	62,949	4.6	7,641	July 6, 2024	42,094	11.3	4,709
June 3, 2023	58,341	4.2	7,253	July 13, 2024	48,270	13.1	5,280
June 10, 2023	55,967	4.1	6,783	July 20, 2024	48,870	14.8	5,884
June 17, 2023	49,714	4.3	6,488	July 27, 2024	52,949	16.4	6,947
June 24, 2023	46,953	4.4	6,111	August 3, 2024	53,166	17.8	7,312
July 1, 2023	43,984	4.9	6,314	August 10, 2024	54,250	18.1	7,619
July 8, 2023	42,752	5.9	6,264	August 17, 2024	56,605	17.8	7,698
July 15, 2023	45,568	6.6	6,991	August 24, 2024	52,445	17.0	7,523

[1] Data as of August 29, 2024. Data are subject to change. The data represent SARS-CoV-2 Nucleic Acid Amplification Test (NAAT) results, which include reverse transcriptase-polymerase chain reaction (RT-PCR) tests from a sentinel network of laboratories reporting to the National Respiratory and Enteric Virus Surveillance System (NREVSS). The sentinel network includes clinical, public health, and commercial laboratories providing test results from the 50 states, DC, Puerto Rico, and U.S. Virgin Islands. Data do not include all test results in the U.S. The data represent laboratory test totals, not individual people, and exclude antigen, antibody, and at-home test results. On May 11, 2023, CDC discontinued the COVID electronic laboratory reporting platform for collecting COVID testing data. See source for more information. [2] Data as of August 30, 2024. Data are subject to change. Data are from the CDC's National Healthcare Safety Network (NHSN). As of December 15, 2022, COVID-19 hospital data are required to be reported to CDC's NHSN, which monitors national and local trends in the healthcare system for approximately 6,000 hospitals in the U.S. Mandatory reporting ended April 30, 2024. Beginning May 1, 2024, data are reported voluntarily and may not be complete or representative of all hospitals. Includes data reported by hospitals in selected U.S. territories. Psychiatric, rehabilitation, and religious non-medical hospital types are excluded. Prior to December 15, 2022, COVID-19 hospital data were collected by the Department of Health and Human Services (HHS) Unified Hospital Data Surveillance System (UHDSS). See source for more information.

Source: U.S. Centers for Disease Control and Prevention, COVID Data Tracker, "Trends in United States COVID-19 Deaths, Emergency Department (ED) Visits, and Test Positivity by Geographic Area," as of August 29, 2024 and posted August 30, 2024; and "Hospital Inpatient and ICU Bed Occupancy and Reporting Trends – CDC's National Healthcare Safety Network (NHSN)," updated August 30, 2024; <covid.cdc.gov/covid-data-tracker/#datatracker-home>, accessed September 3, 2024.

Table 175. Long-Term and Post-Acute Care Facilities, Staff, and Clients by Provider Type and Selected Characteristics: 2020

[Based on the National Post-acute and Long-term Care Study (formerly named the National Study of Long-term Care Providers). The study collects survey data from adult day services and residential care community facilities, and administrative data for federally regulated facilities. Numbers are rounded to nearest hundred or whole number. Percentages are based on unrounded numbers]

Item	Adult day services center	Home health agency	Hospice	Inpatient rehabilita-tion facility	Nursing home	Residential care community
Number of providers	**4,130**	**11,400**	**5,200**	**1,200**	**15,300**	**30,600**
Number of beds or licensed maximum capacity [1]	294,000	(X)	(X)	335,000	1,632,900	1,197,600
Average capacity [1]	71	(X)	(X)	291	107	39
Average number of people served [2]	40	376	349	321	84	27
Provider ownership type (percent):						
For profit	45.5	83.5	70.4	35.2	70.3	81.9
Not for profit	50.8	13.4	18.4	46.9	23.4	17.1
Government and other	3.7	3.1	11.2	17.9	6.3	1.1
Services provided (percent):						
Hospice	25.9	4.4	(X)	(X)	(NA)	76.0
Mental health or counseling	36.1	(NA)	97.3	(NA)	(NA)	57.0
Pharmacy or pharmacist	28.5	4.3	(NA)	98.9	(NA)	86.3
Skilled nursing or nursing	55.8	100.0	100.0	(NA)	(NA)	64.6
Social work	45.3	81.0	99.9	97.2	(NA)	50.6
Physical, occupational, or speech therapy	36.0	95.7	97.4	(D)	(NA)	74.8
Dementia care specialty or unit	14.3	(X)	(X)	(X)	13.2	20.5
Total nursing and social work FTE employees [3]	**17,600**	**135,300**	**90,500**	**252,200**	**(NA)**	**376,400**
Percent of total nursing & social work FTE employees:						
Aide	53.0	24.8	31.6	(NA)	(NA)	75.4
Licensed practical nurse or licensed vocational nurse	9.4	21.7	8.6	8.2	(NA)	11.6
Registered nurse	27.0	51.0	48.2	92.7	(NA)	12.5
Total clients [4]	**237,400**	**2,977,900**	**1,534,600**	**345,200**	**1,294,800**	**818,800**
Percent by age:						
Under 65	36.7	10.3	4.8	10.7	17.9	5.8
65 and over	63.3	89.7	95.2	89.3	82.1	94.2
65 to 74	23.7	27.9	18.0	33.0	22.0	13.4
75 to 84	24.9	32.5	30.2	34.6	27.3	30.9
85 and over	14.6	29.3	47.0	21.7	32.8	49.9
Percent by sex:						
Men	43.3	40.5	42.0	47.5	37.8	30.5
Women	56.7	59.5	58.0	52.5	62.2	69.5
Percent with selected conditions:						
Diagnosed with Alzheimer's or other dementia	24.7	35.6	45.2	36.7	45.6	42.1
Diagnosed with depression	25.3	42.5	23.7	50.7	49.6	28.6

NA Not available. X Not applicable. D Data withheld to avoid disclosure. [1] For adult day services, capacity is licensed maximum capacity. For nursing homes, inpatient rehabilitation facilities, and residential care communities, capacity is number of licensed or certified beds. [2] For adult day services, nursing homes, and residential care communities, data are average daily people served on any given day in 2020. For home health agencies, based on number of patients who started and ended care at any time in 2020. For hospices, inpatient rehabilitation facilities, and long-term care hospitals, based on patients receiving care at any time in 2020. [3] FTE is full-time equivalent. [4] For adult day services centers, clients refer to the total number of enrolled participants and for nursing homes and residential care communities it is the current number of residents on any given day in 2020. For home health agencies, hospices, inpatient rehabilitation facilities, and long-term care hospitals, clients refer to number who received care at any time in 2020.

Source: U.S. Centers for Disease Control and Prevention, National Center for Health Statistics, "Biennial Overview of Post-acute and Long-term Care in the United States," <www.cdc.gov/nchs/npals/webtables/overview.htm> accessed February 2024.

Table 176. Mental Health Treatment Facilities, Clients, and Beds by Service Setting and Facility Type: 2022

[Based on the 2022 National Substance Use and Mental Health Services Survey (N-SUMHSS). Covers 9,586 facilities (82 percent of 11,647 eligible facilities) that provide mental health services in the 50 states, the District of Columbia, and U.S. territories. Facilities can offer treatment in more than one service setting. Client data are not annual averages but for a date meant to indicate levels for an average day or month. The N-SUMHSS is a census of all known facilities, public and private, that provide substance use and mental health treatment services. Survey excludes: (1) Department of Defense (DoD) military treatment facilities, (2) individual private practitioners or small group practices not licensed as a mental health clinic or center, and (3) jails or prisons. See source for more information]

Facility type	24-hour hospital inpatient care			24-hour residential care			Outpatient, day treatment, or partial hospitalization	
	Facilities	Clients [1]	Beds [1]	Facilities	Clients [1]	Beds [1]	Facilities	Clients [1]
Total [2]	**1,305**	**93,156**	**61,346**	**1,713**	**27,736**	**33,660**	**7,785**	**1,675,337**
Psychiatric hospitals	442	44,093	34,380	87	4,366	5,118	211	28,429
Public	118	12,525	14,843	25	1,872	2,757	16	4,552
Private	324	31,568	19,537	62	2,494	2,361	195	23,877
General hospitals [3]	612	38,715	15,209	37	572	626	215	19,550
State hospitals	32	5,148	6,635	7	578	1,905	2	0
Residential treatment centers for children	12	266	363	443	8,278	10,419	99	887
Residential treatment centers for adults	18	432	505	689	6,970	7,181	100	12,055
Other types of residential facilities	3	11	76	68	1,385	1,723	21	4,047
Veterans Affairs medical centers	65	1,595	982	57	629	778	387	87,119
Community mental health centers	27	506	598	62	953	791	1,815	574,178
Certified community behavioral health clinics	3	179	62	9	48	74	479	178,967
Partial hospitalization or day treatment facilities	12	301	419	9	85	88	333	12,005
Outpatient mental health facilities	28	295	443	28	284	291	3,508	632,591
Multi-setting mental health facilities [4]	18	499	578	163	2,862	3,715	294	81,548

[1] On March 31, 2022. [2] Total includes data for other unspecified type of facilities not shown separately. [3] Nonfederal general hospitals with separate psychiatric units. [4] Includes non-hospital residential, plus either outpatient and/or partial hospitalization/day treatment.

Source: U.S. Substance Abuse and Mental Health Services Administration, *National Substance Use and Mental Health Services Survey (N-SUMHSS), 2022: Annual Detailed Tables*, September 2023.

Table 177. Mental Health Treatment Facilities by Type: 2022

[Based on the 2022 National Substance Use and Mental Health Services Survey (N-SUMHSS). Covers 9,586 facilities (82 percent of 11,647 eligible facilities) that provide mental health services in the 50 states, the District of Columbia, and U.S. territories. Facilities can offer treatment in more than one service setting. The N-SUMHSS is a census of all known facilities, public and private, that provide substance use and mental health treatment services. Survey excludes: (1) Department of Defense (DoD) military treatment facilities, (2) individual private practitioners or small group practices not licensed as a mental health clinic or center, and (3) jails or prisons. See source for more information on methodology]

Characteristic	Total [1]	Psychi-atric hos-pitals	General hos-pitals [2]	RTCs for children [3]	RTCs for adults [3]	Veterans Affairs medical centers	Com-munity mental health centers [4]	Certified community behavioral health clinics	Out-patient facilities [5]
Total (number)	**9,586**	**448**	**618**	**448**	**699**	**393**	**1,835**	**481**	**3,516**
Percent	100.0	4.7	6.4	4.7	7.3	4.1	19.1	5.0	36.7
SERVICE SETTING [6]									
24-hour hospital inpatient	1,305	442	612	12	18	65	27	3	28
24-hour residential	1,713	87	37	443	689	57	62	9	28
Less than 24-hour day treatment or partial hospitalization	1,395	162	103	64	50	28	213	26	209
Less than 24-hour outpatient [5]	7,505	167	184	81	85	387	1,807	478	3,504
FACILITY CONTROL									
Private for-profit	1,834	221	88	182	179	3	94	9	770
Private non-profit	5,966	108	457	251	488	–	1,352	382	2,209
Public [7]	1,771	118	73	13	32	390	388	90	536
AGE OF PATIENTS ACCEPTED [6]									
All ages	2,531	33	25	1	–	–	928	257	1,130
Children age 5 and younger	3,344	53	43	22	1	–	1,070	279	1,615
Children age 6 to 12	5,182	146	83	214	2	–	1,429	367	2,446
Children age 13 to 17	6,181	222	137	432	8	–	1,551	410	2,754
Young adults age 18 to 25	8,537	384	508	62	664	392	1,785	472	3,309
Adults age 26 to 64	8,057	397	565	5	681	393	1,690	460	3,011
Senior adults age 65 and older	7,700	383	555	2	622	393	1,650	452	2,842

– Represents zero. [1] Total includes other types of facilities not shown separately. [2] Nonfederal general hospitals with separate psychiatric units. [3] Residential treatment centers. [4] Community mental health centers provide outpatient services, 24-hour emergency care, day treatment or partial hospitalization or psychosocial rehabilitation services, or patient screening for admission to state facilities. [5] Outpatient mental health facilities and settings provide services to clients, usually in under 3 hours per visit. [6] Sums to more than the total because a facility could offer treatment in more than one service setting and to more than one age group. [7] Includes facilities operated by state and local/county/municipal governments, tribal governments, Indian Health Service, Department of Veterans Affairs, and Department of Defense.

Source: U.S. Substance Abuse and Mental Health Services Administration, *National Substance Use and Mental Health Services Survey (N-SUMHSS), 2022: Annual Detailed Tables*, September 2023. See also <www.samhsa.gov/data/data-we-collect/n-sumhss-national-substance-use-and-mental-health-services-survey>.

Table 178. Mental Health Care Client Characteristics by Treatment Setting: 2022

[Client data are for March 31, 2022, which is meant to indicate levels for an average day or month. Based on the 2022 National Substance Use and Mental Health Services Survey (N-SUMHSS). Not all facilities reported demographic data for all clients. See headnote, Table 177]

Client characteristic	24-hour hospital inpatient treatment		24-hour residential treatment		Outpatient, day treatment, or partial hospitalization [1]	
	Number	Percent	Number	Percent	Number	Percent
Total clients	**93,874**	**100.0**	**29,126**	**100.0**	**1,665,187**	**100.0**
SEX						
Male	49,380	55.3	16,501	58.7	747,298	47.1
Female	39,948	44.7	11,604	41.3	840,655	52.9
AGE						
17 years old and under	13,711	15.5	11,855	43.2	450,526	28.4
18 to 64 years old	58,645	66.4	13,758	50.1	993,886	62.6
65 years old and over	15,945	18.1	1,844	6.7	144,099	9.1
RACE						
American Indian or Alaska Native	3,753	4.4	507	1.9	19,880	1.3
Asian	1,426	1.7	394	1.5	21,583	1.4
Black or African American	12,830	14.9	4,745	17.8	217,829	14.1
Native Hawaiian or Other Pacific Islander	5,174	6.0	154	0.6	8,005	0.5
White	30,329	35.2	11,856	44.6	830,924	53.9
Two or more races	1,930	2.2	1,052	4.0	61,502	4.0
Unknown or not collected	30,746	35.7	7,878	29.6	382,504	24.8
HISPANIC ORIGIN [2]						
Hispanic or Latino	9,943	11.7	2,288	8.6	201,882	13.0
Not Hispanic or Latino	47,726	56.1	15,440	58.3	937,678	60.6
Unknown or not collected	27,361	32.2	8,737	33.0	407,730	26.4
LEGAL STATUS [3]						
Voluntary	44,215	50.8	19,905	73.1	1,493,574	97.6
Involuntary, non-forensic	34,081	39.2	4,837	17.8	25,299	1.7
Involuntary, forensic	8,685	10.0	2,470	9.1	11,434	0.7

[1] Less than 24-hour care provided to ambulatory patients. Outpatient care typically involves care for less than 3 hours per visit. Day treatment and partial hospitalization programs typically involve care lasting more than 3 hours per visit, on a regular schedule. [2] Persons of Hispanic origin may be of any race. [3] Clients may voluntarily admit themselves to receive mental health treatment, or be admitted involuntarily with a forensic (criminal) or non-forensic (noncriminal) status.

Source: U.S. Substance Abuse and Mental Health Services Administration, *National Substance Use and Mental Health Services Survey (N-SUMHSS), 2022: Annual Detailed Tables*, September 2023. See also <www.samhsa.gov/data/data-we-collect/n-sumhss-national-substance-use-and-mental-health-services-survey>.

Table 179. Opioid Treatment and Medication-Assisted Therapy—Clients and Facilities: 2022

[Facility data for 2022; client data for March 31, 2022. Based on the 2022 National Substance Use and Mental Health Services Survey (N-SUMHSS). Covers 14,854 facilities (86 percent of 17,353 eligible facilities) that provide substance use treatment services. Medication-assisted opioid therapy includes the use of methadone or buprenorphine for the treatment of opioid addiction or dependence, and the use of naltrexone for preventing a relapse in opioid addiction. Methadone is available only at opioid treatment programs (OTPs) certified by the Substance Abuse and Mental Health Services Administration (SAMHSA). Buprenorphine is prescribed by medical practitioners who have Drug Addiction Treatment Act of 2000 (DATA 2000) specific training and a waiver to prescribe the medication for treating opioid use disorder. Naltrexone is prescribed by any medical practitioner with prescribing privileges. See headnote, Table 177]

Facilities by type of therapy	Total	Private for-profit	Private non-profit	State government	Local, county, or community government	Tribal government	Federal government [1]
Clients receiving medication-assisted opioid therapy, total [2]	**698,890**	**447,819**	**209,573**	**10,170**	**15,055**	**3,042**	**12,910**
Methadone [3]	401,939	264,183	120,259	5,524	8,776	1,342	1,856
Buprenorphine [4]	257,900	164,395	74,351	4,008	5,099	1,471	8,286
Naltrexone [4]	39,051	19,241	14,963	638	1,180	229	2,768
Substance abuse treatment facilities	**14,854**	**6,311**	**7,170**	**297**	**598**	**210**	**252**
Facilities offering detoxification from opioids	3,071	1,766	1,036	54	98	13	103
Facilities providing medication-assisted therapy	8,468	3,992	3,689	175	310	85	213
Buprenorphine	6,904	3,188	3,075	127	253	60	198
Naltrexone	6,283	2,693	2,925	149	246	65	201
Opioid treatment program (OTP) [5]	**2,072**	**1,347**	**578**	**40**	**49**	**19**	**39**
Outpatient treatment	1,889	1,246	512	30	46	18	37
Regular	1,570	992	457	24	42	18	37
Intensive	606	324	225	9	10	7	31
Detoxification	696	518	134	9	8	6	21
Day treatment or partial hospitalization	171	100	60	1	0	0	10
Methadone/buprenorphine maintenance or naltrexone treatment	1,838	1,216	495	26	46	18	37
Residential, non-hospital	264	143	92	8	3	1	17
Hospital inpatient	172	77	63	10	4	1	17

[1] Includes Department of Veterans Affairs, Department of Defense, Indian Health Service, and other, not shown separately. [2] Client data are for a point in time (reference date noted above), and are not annual totals. [3] Clients in facilities SAMHSA certified to use methadone. [4] Clients in all substance abuse treatment facilities that provide opioid medication-assisted therapy. Excludes clients of independent physicians. [5] Facilities that have opioid treatment programs certified by SAMHSA. Methadone is available only at these facilities.

Source: U.S. Substance Abuse and Mental Health Services Administration, *National Substance Use and Mental Health Services Survey (N-SUMHSS), 2022: Annual Detailed Tables*, September 2023.

Table 180. Community Health Centers, Patients, and Medical Personnel: 2022

[Patient and patient visit data in thousands (30,517 represents 30,517,000). Community health centers are community-based and patient-directed organizations that provide primary health care services to underserved populations with limited access to health care. Populations served include low-income persons, the uninsured, those with limited English proficiency, migratory and seasonal agricultural workers and their families, people experiencing homelessness, and residents of public housing. Most health centers receive Health Center Program federal grant funding. Some health centers that meet all Health Center Program requirements do not receive Federal award funding; these are called health center program look-alikes]

Item	Health Center Program grantees	Health Center Program look-alikes	Item	Health Center Program grantees	Health Center Program look-alikes
Health centers, total (number)	**1,370**	**117**	Insurance source:		
PATIENTS (1,000s)			None/uninsured	5,681	95
Total patients	30,517	1,039	Regular Medicaid (Title XIX)	15,087	550
Male	12,981	446	CHIP Medicaid [2]	139	6
Female	17,537	593	Dual eligible (Medicare and Medicaid)	1,281	53
Age 17 and under	8,824	299	Medicare [3]	3,330	129
Age 18 to 64	18,138	616	Other public insurance [4]	209	10
Age 65 and older	3,555	124	Private insurance	6,071	248
			PERSONNEL (FTEs) [5]		
Non-Hispanic, total [1]	17,960	649	Total physicians [6]	15,206	594
White	10,424	375	Family, general practice, and internist	9,627	372
Black/African American	5,028	161	Obstetrician/gynecologists	1,366	75
American Indian/Alaska Native	251	4	Pediatricians	3,248	104
Asian	1,043	64	Nurse practitioners	12,178	431
Native Hawaiian/Other Pacific Islander	203	3	Physician assistants	3,766	144
Multiracial	369	13	Certified nurse midwives	727	23
Hispanic	11,039	323	PATIENT VISITS (1,000s) [7]		
Unreported race and ethnicity	1,519	67	By type of practitioner seen:		
			Total physicians [6]	41,255	1,425
Income as percent of poverty level:			Family, general practice, and internist	25,230	871
100% and under	13,629	373	Obstetrician/gynecologists	3,542	131
101 to 150%	3,095	109	Pediatricians	9,560	334
151 to 200%	1,702	56	Nurse practitioners	29,376	1,073
Over 200%	2,126	74	Physician assistants	10,036	398
Unknown	9,966	428	Certified nurse midwives	1,465	51

[1] Includes unknown/unreported race, not shown separately. [2] CHIP, Children's Health Insurance Program. [3] Includes dual eligible and other Title XVIII beneficiaries. [4] CHIP and non-CHIP. [5] FTE, full-time equivalent. [6] Includes data for other specialty physicians not shown separately. [7] Includes clinic and virtual visits.

Source: U.S. Health Resources & Services Administration, Bureau of Primary Health Care, "Data & Reporting: National Health Center Program Uniform Data System (UDS) Awardee and Look-Alike Data," <bphc.hrsa.gov/data-reporting>, accessed February 2024.

Table 181. Health Care Visits—Percent Distribution by Selected Patient Characteristics: 2010 and 2018

[Covers visits to hospital emergency departments, home health care visits, and visits to doctor's offices, clinics, or some other place during a 12-month period. Excludes dental visits. Based on the National Health Interview Survey. See source, and Appendix III]

Characteristic	Percent distribution of health care visits							
	None		1–3 visits		4–9 visits		10 or more visits	
	2010	2018	2010	2018	2010	2018	2010	2018
All persons [1,2]	**15.6**	**14.5**	**45.4**	**49.2**	**25.8**	**23.4**	**13.2**	**12.9**
SEX [2]								
Male	20.4	18.7	46.4	49.7	22.7	21.2	10.5	10.3
Female	10.9	10.3	44.4	48.8	28.8	25.6	15.9	15.4
AGE								
Under 18 years	8.1	7.4	55.6	60.3	28.2	25.4	8.2	6.9
Under 6 years	3.7	4.9	48.9	52.7	36.8	33.9	10.6	8.4
6 to 17 years	10.4	8.6	59.1	63.9	23.6	21.4	6.9	6.2
18 to 44 years	24.2	21.9	43.9	47.6	20.6	18.7	11.3	11.7
45 to 64 years	14.8	14.2	42.8	45.5	26.1	24.7	16.4	15.7
65 years and over	5.3	5.5	33.8	38.0	36.7	32.5	24.2	24.0
75 years and over	4.1	4.1	31.0	34.8	38.0	33.6	27.0	27.6
RACE [2,3]								
White	15.3	14.0	44.9	48.5	26.1	24.0	13.7	13.4
Black or African American	15.7	13.8	47.2	51.9	24.7	22.1	12.4	12.2
American Indian or Alaska Native	19.4	16.5	40.3	41.5	28.1	25.9	12.2	16.1
Asian	20.4	19.9	49.9	53.3	22.1	18.8	7.6	8.0
Native Hawaiian or Other Pacific Islander only	(B)	20.9	(B)	53.2	(B)	15.7	(B)	(B)
Two or more races	13.9	15.3	42.3	47.1	25.2	23.5	18.6	14.1
HISPANIC ORIGIN AND RACE [2,3,4]								
Hispanic or Latino	23.5	20.3	43.2	48.1	22.6	21.0	10.7	10.6
Not Hispanic or Latino	14.0	13.1	45.8	49.4	26.5	24.0	13.7	13.5
White, non-Hispanic	13.2	12.1	45.3	48.5	27.1	25.1	14.4	14.3
Black, non-Hispanic	15.6	13.7	47.3	51.8	24.9	22.2	12.2	12.3
HEALTH INSURANCE STATUS [5,6]								
Insured	12.3	13.0	48.5	51.8	26.1	23.1	13.1	12.1
Private	12.4	13.2	51.0	53.6	25.5	22.7	11.1	10.4
Medicaid	10.9	12.2	38.2	44.5	28.0	24.3	23.0	19.0
Uninsured	37.2	36.8	42.2	44.9	15.2	13.2	5.4	5.1
Insured continuously 12 months prior to interview	12.1	12.9	48.6	51.9	26.2	23.1	13.0	12.1
Uninsured for any period during the 12 months prior to interview	18.5	21.2	47.8	48.4	22.0	20.9	11.6	9.5
Uninsured more than 12 months prior to interview	43.8	45.3	39.7	41.6	12.6	9.9	3.9	3.1

B Estimates are considered unreliable. [1] Includes other categories not shown separately. [2] Age adjusted to the year 2000 standard population. [3] Race groups include persons of Hispanic and non-Hispanic origin. Race-specific estimates are for persons reporting one race only. [4] Persons of Hispanic or Latino origin may be of any race. [5] For persons under age 65, at time of interview. Estimates are age-adjusted to the year 2000 standard population. [6] Health insurance categories are mutually exclusive. Persons who reported both Medicaid and private coverage are classified as having private coverage. Medicaid coverage includes State-sponsored health plans and the Children's Health Insurance Program (CHIP). The insured category also includes military plans, other government-sponsored health plans, and Medicare, not shown separately. Persons not covered by private insurance, Medicaid, CHIP, state-sponsored or other government-sponsored health plans, Medicare, or military plans are considered to have no health insurance coverage. Persons with only Indian Health Service coverage are considered to have no health insurance coverage.

Source: U.S. National Center for Health Statistics, "Health, United States—Data Finder," <www.cdc.gov/nchs/hus/index.htm>, accessed July 2024.

Table 182. Physician Office Visits by Leading Reason for Visit by Patient Sex: 2019

[1,036,484 represents 1,036,484,000. Based on the 2019 National Ambulatory Medical Care Survey (NAMCS). NAMCS is an annual nationally representative sample survey of visits to nonfederal office-based patient care physicians, excluding anesthesiologists, radiologists, and pathologists. The 2019 NAMCS sampling design selected physicians from the master files maintained by the American Medical Association and the American Osteopathic Association. Data are subject to sampling and nonsampling errors. Users should exercise caution when comparing 2018 and 2019 NAMCS estimates. The overall estimate of visits to office-based physicians in 2019 is 20.5 percent higher than the 2018 estimate. The 2019 survey includes a greater number of physicians and a higher number of patients seen by physicians; see source for details]

Leading reason for visit	Number of visits (1,000)	Percent distribution		Leading reason for visit	Number of visits (1,000)	Percent distribution	
		Male [1]	Fe-male [2]			Male [1]	Fe-male [2]
All visits [3]	**1,036,484**	**100.0**	**100.0**	Diabetes mellitus	13,393	1.3	1.3
Progress visit [4]	221,258	22.6	20.5	Prenatal exam, routine	12,565	(X)	2.1
General medical exam	60,352	6.4	5.4	For test results	[5] 12,465	1.2	1.2
Postoperative visit	28,479	3.2	2.4	Cancer, breast	([5])	([5])	([5])
Gynecological exam	25,218	(X)	4.2	Knee symptoms	10,370	1.1	0.9
Counseling, [4]	22,685	2.2	2.2	Skin lesion	[5] 10,295	1.3	0.8
Medication	18,491	1.4	2.1	Diagnostic endoscopies	[5] 10,264	1.3	0.7
Shoulder symptoms	16,436	1.6	1.5	Stomach & abdominal pain, cramps, spasms	10,098	1.0	1.0
Hypertension	15,194	1.2	1.7	Other special exam	[5] 9,939	1.5	0.5
Well baby exam	15,141	1.6	1.4	Preoperative visit surgery	9,328	0.6	1.1
Cough	15,048	1.5	1.4	All other reasons	488,995	49.1	45.8

X Not applicable. [1] Based on 431,439,000 visits made by males. [2] Based on 605,045,000 visits made by females. [3] Numbers may not sum to totals due to rounding. [4] Not otherwise specified. [5] Estimate does not meet NCHS standards of reliability.

Source: U.S. National Center for Health Statistics, *National Ambulatory Medical Care Survey: 2019 National Summary Tables*, January 2023. See also <www.cdc.gov/nchs/ahcd/index.htm>.

Table 183. Hospital Emergency Department Visits by Wait Time and Total Time Spent: 2019 to 2021

[150,650 represents 150,650,000. Based on the National Hospital Ambulatory Medical Care Survey (NHAMCS). Data cover visits to hospital emergency departments; excludes federal, military, and Veterans Administration hospitals]

Visit characteristic	Number of visits (1,000)			Percent distribution of visits		
	2019	2020	2021	2019	2020	2021
Total visits [1]	**150,650**	**131,297**	**139,781**	**100.0**	**100.0**	**100.0**
WAIT TIME TO SEE MEDICAL PROFESSIONAL [2]						
Fewer than 15 minutes	64,345	66,243	58,442	42.7	50.5	41.8
15 to 59 minutes	41,217	34,929	43,213	27.4	26.6	30.9
1 hour, but less than 2 hours	11,983	7,400	11,960	8.0	5.6	8.6
2 hours, but less than 3 hours	4,721	2,492	4,573	3.1	1.9	3.3
3 hours, but less than 4 hours	2,069	1,118	1,799	1.4	0.9	1.3
4 hours, but less than 6 hours	1,468	805	1,331	1.0	0.6	1.0
6 hours or more	999	[3] 613	483	0.7	0.5	0.3
TIME SPENT IN EMERGENCY DEPARTMENT						
Less than 1 hour	14,868	11,791	11,435	9.9	9.0	8.2
1 hour, but less than 2 hours	30,942	25,935	24,394	20.5	19.8	17.5
2 hours, but less than 4 hours	52,104	44,853	48,147	34.6	34.2	34.4
4 hours, but less than 6 hours	21,833	20,921	25,408	14.5	15.9	18.2
6 hours, but less than 10 hours	12,532	12,298	15,600	8.3	9.4	11.2
10 hours, but less than 14 hours	2,484	2,659	3,140	1.6	2.0	2.2
14 hours, but less than 24 hours	2,567	2,654	2,933	1.7	2.0	2.1
24 hours or more	2,274	1,716	2,846	1.5	1.3	2.0

[1] Totals include nonresponse and nonapplicable categories. [2] Medical professional may be a physician, physician assistant, or advanced practice registered nurse. [3] Estimate does not meet National Center for Health Statistics standards of reliability.

Source: U.S. National Center for Health Statistics, *National Hospital Ambulatory Medical Care Survey: 2021 Emergency Department Summary Tables*, August 2023 and earlier reports. See also <www.cdc.gov/nchs/ahcd/index.htm>.

Table 184. Emergency Departments by Patient and Other Characteristics: 2020 and 2021

[131,297 represents 131,297,000. Covers emergency departments (EDs) in noninstitutional general and short-stay hospitals, excluding Federal, military, and Veterans Administration hospitals. Based on the National Hospital Ambulatory Medical Care Survey (NHAMCS) and subject to sampling error; see sources for details]

Characteristic	2020		2021	
	Number (1,000)	Per 100 persons [1]	Number (1,000)	Per 100 persons [1]
Total	**131,297**	**40.5**	**139,781**	**42.7**
PATIENT AGE				
Under 15 years old	18,487	30.7	24,644	40.7
15 to 24 years old	17,372	41.8	17,604	41.8
25 to 44 years old	36,978	42.9	38,561	44.3
45 to 64 years old	31,639	38.6	31,863	38.5
65 years and over	26,822	49.3	27,109	49.6
65 to 74 years old	12,875	39.8	13,191	39.4
75 years old and over	13,947	63.2	13,918	65.5
PATIENT SEX				
Male	61,220	38.6	64,173	39.9
Female	70,077	42.3	75,609	45.5
PATIENT RACE/ETHNICITY [2]				
White	95,434	38.7	99,266	40.0
Black or African American	29,267	67.7	34,808	79.5
Other	6,596	19.2	5,708	16.2
Hispanic or Latino	20,716	34.1	22,105	35.6
EXPECTED PAYMENT SOURCE [3]				
Private insurance	39,824	(X)	45,097	(X)
Medicaid/CHIP/state-based program [4]	48,043	(X)	52,083	(X)
Medicare	28,433	(X)	27,791	(X)
Medicare and Medicaid [5]	4,988	(X)	4,996	(X)
No insurance: [6]	10,442	(X)	9,345	(X)
Self pay	10,101	(X)	9,076	(X)
No charge or charity	361	(X)	410	(X)
Worker's compensation	764	(X)	665	(X)

X Not applicable. [1] Rates are based on July 1 Census Bureau estimates of the civilian noninstitutional population for the same year as data are shown. [2] Race groups White, Black or African American, and Other include persons of Hispanic origin. Persons of Hispanic origin may be of any race. See source for information on missing and imputed data. [3] Estimates include all expected sources of payment. Other and unknown sources are not shown separately. [4] Children's Health Insurance Program (CHIP). [5] Visits for patients with dual Medicare and Medicaid coverage are also included in the Medicare and Medicaid/CHIP/state-based program categories. [6] "No insurance" is having only self-pay, no charge, or charity as payment sources.

Source: U.S. National Center for Health Statistics, Ambulatory Health Care Data, "2021 NHAMCS Emergency Department Summary Tables," October 2023 and earlier reports, <www.cdc.gov/nchs/ahcd/new_ahcd.htm>.

Table 185. Medicare-Certified Hospitals, Institutions, and Physicians by Provider Type: 2010 to 2021

[Inpatient hospitals and other institutional providers are active and Medicare-certified in the reporting year. Physician provider counts originate from Medicare fee-for-service Part B claims, and reflect services provided by participating and non-participating physicians]

Providers by type	2010	2016	2017	2018	2019	2020	2021
INPATIENT HOSPITALS							
Total hospitals [1]	**6,169**	**6,146**	**6,123**	**6,072**	**6,023**	**6,214**	**6,266**
Beds	927,535	933,209	934,197	931,555	932,559	927,342	929,459
Beds per 1,000 enrollees [2]	19.6	16.5	16.1	15.6	15.2	14.8	14.6
Short stay	3,566	3,419	3,392	3,334	3,283	3,481	3,506
Psychiatric units	1,180	1,113	1,092	1,063	1,027	998	970
Rehabilitation units	938	911	890	864	840	832	822
Swing bed hospitals	510	474	467	455	445	662	676
Psychiatric	511	570	586	598	604	613	622
Rehabilitation	235	277	282	296	306	314	332
Children's	77	99	97	96	95	93	91
Long term care	438	420	401	382	367	347	344
Critical access	1,325	1,343	1,347	1,351	1,353	1,351	1,358
SELECTED INSTITUTIONAL PROVIDERS							
Skilled nursing facilities	15,084	15,274	15,268	15,218	15,103	15,015	14,908
Beds	1,572,511	1,607,056	1,605,515	1,602,222	1,592,041	1,588,755	1,574,485
Beds per 1,000 enrollees [2]	33.2	28.4	27.6	26.9	26.0	25.4	24.8
Home health agencies	10,914	11,956	11,593	11,317	11,157	11,221	11,353
Hospices	3,509	4,473	4,650	4,775	4,970	5,260	5,966
Independent and clinical labs	224,684	254,133	258,473	262,524	265,057	284,414	311,775
Outpatient physical therapy/speech pathology	2,536	2,080	2,043	2,016	2,032	2,044	2,023
End stage renal disease	5,631	6,843	7,082	7,429	7,629	7,755	7,834
Rural health clinics	3,845	4,153	4,233	4,402	4,482	4,736	5,009
Ambulatory surgical centers	5,316	5,529	5,598	5,718	5,812	5,905	6,055
Federally qualified health centers	4,308	7,723	8,289	8,836	9,467	10,000	10,509
PHYSICIAN PROVIDERS							
All physician specialties [1,3]	**595,783**	**665,772**	**675,579**	**684,790**	**692,846**	**698,164**	**702,691**
Primary care	212,849	228,907	229,946	227,587	227,255	225,008	223,561
Family practice	84,982	93,893	94,703	95,031	95,358	95,263	94,830
General practice	13,401	9,492	9,225	8,849	8,648	8,215	7,845
Internal medicine	106,343	115,335	115,792	113,155	112,362	110,443	109,202
Pediatric medicine	8,123	10,187	10,226	10,552	10,887	11,087	11,684
Surgical specialties	108,093	111,439	112,390	112,839	113,541	113,522	113,432
Radiology	36,656	38,736	39,419	39,903	40,434	40,828	41,179
Obstetrics/gynecology	32,881	35,092	35,439	35,556	35,605	35,433	35,451
Psychiatry	27,550	28,150	28,224	28,200	28,277	27,925	27,684

[1] Includes other provider types not shown separately. [2] Beds per 1,000 enrollees based on Medicare Part A enrollee counts. [3] Physicians may be counted in more than one specialty.

Source: U.S. Centers for Medicare & Medicaid Services, "CMS Program Statistics – Medicare Providers," <data.cms.gov/collection/cms-program-statistics>, accessed February 2023.

Table 186. Medicare Certified Skilled Nursing Facilities, Home Health Agencies, and Hospices by State and Other Area: 2021

[Represents Medicare-certified institutional providers active during the reporting calendar year]

State and other area	Skilled nursing facilities Number of facilities	Skilled nursing facilities Number of beds	Home health agencies	Hospices	State and other area	Skilled nursing facilities Number of facilities	Skilled nursing facilities Number of beds	Home health agencies	Hospices
Total [1]	**14,908**	**1,574,485**	**11,353**	**5,966**	MT	70	6,217	24	30
U.S. [2]	**14,901**	**1,574,232**	**11,309**	**5,915**	NE	180	13,524	66	34
AL	225	26,567	118	89	NV	64	6,983	159	83
AK	20	826	15	5	NH	70	7,095	28	22
AZ	142	15,578	177	206	NJ	353	51,573	41	63
AR	218	23,547	99	46	NM	66	6,764	78	50
CA	1,147	113,845	1,828	1,746	NY	609	112,505	117	41
CO	212	19,080	207	73	NC	424	43,894	173	80
CT	208	25,095	80	27	ND	77	5,421	17	13
DE	41	4,571	26	11	OH	954	86,610	774	144
DC	16	2,403	35	3	OK	291	27,767	239	120
FL	699	84,310	970	49	OR	121	10,193	53	54
GA	358	38,566	105	234	PA	678	84,866	426	180
HI	43	4,123	15	10	RI	76	8,244	25	7
ID	80	6,046	52	48	SC	188	20,042	73	85
IL	682	77,333	558	127	SD	92	5,025	27	14
IN	518	50,718	202	89	TN	308	34,663	130	55
IA	417	28,021	137	73	TX	1,186	129,204	2,084	872
KS	286	18,456	112	80	UT	92	8,107	93	86
KY	280	26,271	92	23	VT	35	3,077	11	10
LA	268	33,329	186	125	VA	278	31,495	240	106
ME	90	6,453	20	15	WA	195	18,392	65	37
MD	222	27,651	55	24	WV	116	10,006	55	18
MA	365	42,475	273	73	WI	339	26,593	106	76
MI	431	44,962	458	148	WY	33	2,838	31	18
MN	353	26,443	166	78	PR	6	211	36	44
MS	184	16,622	45	94	VI	–	–	2	3
MO	501	49,843	143	121	All other	1	42	6	4

– Represents zero. [1] Includes 50 states, DC, Puerto Rico, Virgin Islands, and all other. [2] Includes 50 states and DC.

Source: U.S. Centers for Medicare & Medicaid Services, "CMS Program Statistics – Medicare Providers," <data.cms.gov/collection/cms-program-statistics>, accessed June 2023.

Table 187. Hospital Emergency Department Visits by Leading Reason for Visit by Patient Age and Sex: 2021

[139,781 represents 139,781,000. Based on the annual National Hospital Ambulatory Medical Care Survey and subject to sampling error; see source for details. Data may not sum due to rounding]

Principal reason for visit	Visits (1,000)	Percent of visits	Principal reason for visit	Visits (1,000)	Percent of visits
Total, all ages	**139,781**	**100.0**	Problems of pregnancy	1,465	1.7
			Back symptoms	1,357	1.5
Stomach & abdominal pain, cramps, spasms	12,441	8.9	Pain [2]	1,326	1.5
Chest pain & related symptoms [1]	7,811	5.6	Cough	1,183	1.3
Shortness of breath	5,918	4.2	Nausea	954	1.1
Cough	4,655	3.3	Symptoms referable to throat	879	1.0
Fever	4,650	3.3	All other reasons [4]	28,540	32.4
Headache, pain in head	3,893	2.8	**Male**	**38,987**	**44.3**
Pain [2]	3,365	2.4	Stomach & abdominal pain, cramps, spasms	3,170	3.6
Back symptoms	3,050	2.2	Chest pain & related symptoms [1]	2,620	3.0
Vomiting	2,810	2.0	Shortness of breath	1,608	1.8
Relating to psychological & mental disorders	2,429	1.7	Pain [2]	1,389	1.6
All other reasons [4]	88,759	63.5	Relating to psychological & mental disorders	993	1.1
Patients under age 15 years	**24,644**	**100.0**	Back symptoms	892	1.0
Female	**11,516**	**46.7**	Headache, pain in head	821	0.9
Fever	1,809	7.3	Cough	740	0.8
Cough	1,191	4.8	Laceration or cut of upper extremity	722	0.8
Stomach & abdominal pain, cramps, spasms	660	2.7	Foot and toe symptoms	608	0.7
Vomiting	633	2.6	All other reasons [4]	25,424	28.9
Earache, or ear infection	338	1.4	**Patients age 65 years and over**	**27,109**	**100.0**
Symptoms referable to throat	(B)	1.1	**Female**	**15,051**	**55.5**
Injury [3]—head, neck, and face	(B)	0.9	Shortness of breath	1,225	4.5
Shortness of breath	(B)	0.9	Stomach & abdominal pain, cramps, spasms	940	3.5
Skin rash	(B)	0.8	Chest pain & related symptoms [1]	840	3.1
Nasal congestion	(B)	0.8	General weakness	499	1.8
All other reasons [4]	5,756	23.4	Back symptoms	425	1.6
Male	**13,128**	**53.3**	Leg symptoms	402	1.5
Fever	1,593	6.5	Vertigo—dizziness	401	1.5
Cough	1,163	4.7	Headache, pain in head	384	1.4
Stomach & abdominal pain, cramps, spasms	652	2.6	Accident, not otherwise specified	376	1.4
Vomiting	579	2.4	Nausea	(B)	1.3
Skin rash	516	2.1	All other reasons [4]	9,207	34.0
Laceration or cut of facial area	352	1.4	**Male**	**12,058**	**44.5**
Injury [3]—head, neck, and face	351	1.4	Shortness of breath	928	3.4
Labored or difficult breathing (dyspnea)	(B)	1.3	Stomach & abdominal pain, cramps, spasms	834	3.1
Nasal congestion	285	1.2	Chest pain and related symptoms [1]	761	2.8
Injury [3]—hand and finger(s)	(B)	1.0	General weakness	394	1.5
All other reasons [4]	7,065	28.7	Vertigo—dizziness	288	1.1
Patients age 15 to 64 years	**88,029**	**100.0**	Back symptoms	285	1.1
Female	**49,041**	**55.7**	Relating to psychological & mental disorders	(B)	1.0
Stomach & abdominal pain, cramps, spasms	6,184	7.0	Fainting (syncope)	(B)	0.9
Chest pain & related symptoms [1]	3,337	3.8	Abnormalities of urine	(B)	0.9
Headache, pain in head	2,111	2.4	Pain [2]	246	0.9
Shortness of breath	1,706	1.9	All other reasons [4]	7,553	27.9

B Based on fewer than 30 cases and does not meet statistical standards for reliability. [1] Not referable to body systems. [2] Site not referable to a specific body system. [3] Injury, other and unspecified type. [4] Includes all other reasons not listed above, and unknown and blank responses.

Source: U.S. National Center for Health Statistics, *National Hospital Ambulatory Medical Care Survey, 2021 Emergency Department Summary Tables*, August 2023. See also <www.cdc.gov/nchs/ahcd/index.htm>.

Table 188. Hospital Utilization Rates by Type of Hospital: 1990 to 2022

[In units, as indicated (21.9 represents 21,900,000)]

Type of hospital	1990	2000	2005	2010	2015	2019 [4]	2020	2021	2022
Community hospitals: [1]									
Admissions per 1,000 population [2]	125	117	119	114	105	104	95	96	95
Admissions per bed	34	40	44	44	42	43	40	41	40
Average length of stay (days) [3]	7.2	5.8	5.6	5.4	5.5	5.4	5.6	5.8	5.9
Outpatient visits per admission	9.7	15.8	16.6	18.5	21.6	23.0	22.8	24.6	25.3
Outpatient visits per 1,000 population [2]	1,207	1,852	1,976	2,108	2,274	2,392	2,177	2,367	2,399
Surgical operations (million)	21.9	26.1	27.5	27.3	27.3	28.4	25.0	26.9	27.4
Number per admission	0.7	0.8	0.8	0.8	0.8	0.8	0.8	0.8	0.9
Nonfederal psychiatric:									
Admissions per 1,000 population [2]	2.9	2.4	2.5	2.5	2.6	3.8	3.6	3.8	3.7
Days in hospital per 1,000 population [2]	190	93	89	77	67	78	73	72	70

[1] See headnote, Table 190. [2] Based on Census Bureau estimated resident population as of July 1. Data for 1990, 2000, and 2010 based on enumerated resident population as of April 1. [3] Number of inpatient days divided by number of admissions. [4] Beginning with data from the 2017 annual survey, the American Hospital Association (AHA) discontinued using its own methodology to classify hospitals as registered and began including hospitals under a more generally known and accepted definition, which resulted in an increase in the number of hospitals covered in AHA Hospital Statistics.

Source: Health Forum LLC, an affiliate of the American Hospital Association, Chicago, IL, *AHA Hospital Statistics 2024 Edition* ©, and previous editions. See also <guide.prod.iam.aha.org/stats/>.

Table 189. Hospitals—Summary Characteristics: 2000 to 2022

[In units indicated (984 represents 984,000). Covers hospitals accepted for registration by the American Hospital Association; see text, this section. Short-term hospitals have an average patient stay of less than 30 days; long-term, an average stay of longer duration. Beginning with the 2019 edition of *AHA Hospital Statistics* presenting data from the 2017 annual survey, the AHA discontinued using its own methodology to classify hospitals as registered and began including hospitals under a more generally known and accepted definition, which resulted in an increase in the number of hospitals covered in *AHA Hospital Statistics*]

Item	2000	2005	2010	2015	2018 [8]	2019	2020	2021	2022
NUMBER									
All hospitals.................................	5,810	5,756	5,754	5,564	6,146	6,090	6,093	6,129	6,120
With 100 beds or more...................	3,102	2,942	2,832	2,682	2,730	2,692	2,672	2,655	2,621
Nonfederal [1].................................	5,565	5,530	5,541	5,352	5,937	5,882	5,886	5,923	5,913
Community hospitals [2].................	4,915	4,936	4,985	4,862	5,198	5,141	5,139	5,157	5,129
Nongovernmental nonprofit..............	3,003	2,958	2,904	2,845	2,937	2,946	2,960	2,978	2,987
For profit..................................	749	868	1,013	1,034	1,296	1,233	1,228	1,235	1,219
State and local government..............	1,163	1,110	1,068	983	965	962	951	944	923
Long term general and special.............	131	115	109	77	109	102	98	92	110
Psychiatric...................................	496	456	435	401	616	625	645	659	659
Tuberculosis & other respiratory diseases...............................	4	3	2	2	2	2	2	3	3
Federal.......................................	245	226	213	212	209	208	207	206	207
BEDS (1,000) [3]									
All hospitals..................................	984	947	942	898	924	920	921	920	917
Rate per 1,000 population [4]...............	3.5	3.2	3.0	2.8	2.8	2.8	2.8	2.8	2.8
Beds per hospital..........................	169	165	164	160	150	151	151	150	150
Nonfederal [1].................................	931	901	897	859	887	882	884	883	880
Community hospitals [2]..................	824	802	805	782	792	788	789	788	784
Rate per 1,000 population [4]............	2.9	2.7	2.6	2.4	2.4	2.4	2.4	2.4	2.4
Nongovernmental nonprofit.............	583	561	556	531	543	546	548	548	549
For profit..................................	110	114	125	135	140	131	130	130	127
State and local government..............	131	128	125	117	110	110	112	110	108
Long term general and special..............	18	15	15	8	11	9	9	8	9
Psychiatric...................................	87	82	76	68	82	84	87	85	85
Federal.......................................	53	46	45	39	38	38	37	37	37
AVERAGE DAILY CENSUS (1,000) [5]									
All hospitals..................................	650	656	627	588	612	611	600	607	610
Community hospitals [2]...................	526	540	520	497	508	507	485	514	518
Nongovernmental nonprofit..............	382	388	368	346	356	358	340	364	369
For profit..................................	61	68	71	77	81	78	75	80	78
State and local government..............	83	85	80	74	71	71	70	71	71
EXPENSES (bil. dol.) [6, 9]									
All hospitals..................................	395.4	570.5	750.6	936.5	1,112.2	1,161.0	1,213.9	(NA)	(NA)
Nonfederal [1].................................	371.5	533.7	698.2	872.0	1,037.2	1,083.7	1,131.9	(NA)	(NA)
Community hospitals [2]..................	356.6	515.7	678.0	851.5	1,010.0	1,056.5	1,102.3	(NA)	(NA)
Nongovernmental nonprofit..............	267.1	386.0	510.7	636.0	755.8	794.7	830.0	(NA)	(NA)
For profit..................................	35.0	51.8	67.2	88.8	108.0	106.9	106.8	(NA)	(NA)
State and local government..............	54.5	77.9	100.1	126.7	146.0	154.9	165.5	(NA)	(NA)
Long term general and special.............	2.8	3.6	4.2	3.2	4.1	3.6	4.1	(NA)	(NA)
Psychiatric...................................	11.9	13.9	15.8	16.8	22.2	23.0	24.9	(NA)	(NA)
Federal.......................................	23.9	36.8	52.4	64.5	75.0	77.4	82.0	(NA)	(NA)
PERSONNEL (1,000) [7]									
All hospitals..................................	4,454	4,790	5,184	5,397	5,903	5,989	6,002	6,001	6,084
Nonfederal [1].................................	4,157	4,479	4,825	5,056	5,484	5,563	5,562	5,573	5,623
Community hospitals [2]..................	3,911	4,260	4,600	4,859	5,239	5,315	5,317	5,331	5,393
Nongovernmental nonprofit..............	2,919	3,154	3,388	3,562	3,848	3,929	3,927	3,937	4,001
For profit..................................	378	421	474	534	594	573	560	557	551
State and local government..............	614	681	738	762	797	813	830	837	840
Long term general and special.............	41	38	39	23	32	27	28	29	30
Psychiatric...................................	200	182	182	172	211	218	215	208	199
Federal.......................................	297	311	359	341	419	426	440	428	461
OUTPATIENT VISITS (mil.)									
Total...	592.7	673.7	750.4	832.3	879.6	900.7	834.0	903.8	930.7
Emergency visits.............................	106.9	118.9	131.5	145.3	147.4	147.5	126.9	130.5	141.3

NA Not available. [1] Includes hospital units of institutions; and tuberculosis hospitals, not shown separately. [2] Short-term (average stay less than 30 days) general and specialty (e.g., obstetrics and gynecology, rehabilitation, etc. except psychiatric, tuberculosis, alcoholism, and chemical dependency). Excludes hospital units of institutions. [3] Number of beds at end of reporting period. [4] See footnote 2, Table 188. [5] The average number of people served on an inpatient basis on a single day during the reporting period. [6] Excludes new construction. [7] Includes full-time equivalents of part-time personnel. [8] Beginning with data from the 2017 annual survey, the AHA discontinued using its own methodology to classify hospitals as registered and began including hospitals under a more generally known and accepted definition, which resulted in an increase in the number of hospitals covered in *AHA Hospital Statistics*. [9] Beginning with *AHA Hospital Statistics 2023 edition,* source no longer publishes expense data.

Source: Health Forum LLC, an affiliate of the American Hospital Association, Chicago, IL, *AHA Hospital Statistics 2024 Edition* ©, and previous editions. See also <guide.prod.iam.aha.org/stats/>.

Table 190. Community Hospital Summary Data by State: 2020 and 2022

[In units indicated (789.4 represents 789,400). Community hospitals are defined as all nonfederal, short-term general, and other specialty hospitals. Other specialty hospitals include obstetrics and gynecology; eye, ear, nose, and throat; rehabilitation; orthopedic; and other individually described specialty services. Community hospitals include academic medical centers or other teaching hospitals if they are nonfederal short-term hospitals. Excluded are hospitals not accessible by the general public, such as prison hospitals or college infirmaries]

State	Number of hospitals		Beds (1,000)		Patients admitted (1,000)		Average daily census [1] (1,000)		Outpatient visits (mil.)		Average cost per day (dol.)	
	2020	2022	2020	2022	2020	2022	2020	2022	2020	2022	2020	2022 [2]
United States..........	5,139	5,129	789.4	784.1	31,393	31,556	484.5	517.5	717.2	799.7	2,873	(NA)
Alabama.................	101	102	15.4	15.6	589	602	9.6	10.5	7.8	8.8	1,786	(NA)
Alaska...................	20	20	1.6	1.6	37	51	1.0	1.1	1.7	1.3	2,233	(NA)
Arizona.................	81	87	14.3	14.7	623	640	8.8	9.4	8.0	6.6	3,131	(NA)
Arkansas................	90	93	9.5	9.5	343	352	4.9	5.3	5.7	6.2	1,947	(NA)
California...............	353	355	72.6	73.9	3,100	3,169	46.2	50.3	52.5	56.0	4,098	(NA)
Colorado................	91	92	11.1	11.2	419	435	6.2	6.8	8.7	11.9	3,302	(NA)
Connecticut.............	31	31	7.5	7.5	356	362	5.6	6.2	7.9	10.2	3,290	(NA)
Delaware................	7	8	2.2	2.3	95	102	1.5	1.9	2.0	2.4	3,364	(NA)
District of Columbia.......	10	10	3.2	3.4	114	108	2.4	2.4	2.4	2.9	3,648	(NA)
Florida..................	214	213	55.0	55.1	2,435	2,545	34.8	37.6	27.7	32.5	2,586	(NA)
Georgia.................	144	141	25.1	24.6	971	957	17.4	17.7	19.1	21.2	2,100	(NA)
Hawaii..................	22	23	2.7	2.9	108	106	1.9	2.0	2.7	3.1	2,945	(NA)
Idaho...................	46	47	3.5	3.6	134	128	1.7	1.8	6.3	6.8	2,683	(NA)
Illinois.................	184	181	31.8	30.7	1,218	1,196	17.7	18.6	34.2	39.7	2,939	(NA)
Indiana.................	129	130	18.4	18.0	686	708	10.1	11.0	20.4	21.6	2,814	(NA)
Iowa....................	116	118	9.1	8.7	287	262	4.8	4.7	12.0	14.9	1,786	(NA)
Kansas..................	135	135	9.4	9.3	299	287	4.9	4.9	8.7	10.0	2,191	(NA)
Kentucky................	104	104	14.3	14.0	506	499	8.0	8.3	14.4	15.0	2,303	(NA)
Louisiana...............	159	159	15.1	14.6	541	513	8.2	8.1	10.7	11.9	2,371	(NA)
Maine...................	34	34	3.5	3.5	117	109	2.3	2.6	6.8	8.0	2,902	(NA)
Maryland................	49	47	11.2	11.2	509	483	7.6	8.1	8.0	7.3	3,336	(NA)
Massachusetts...........	74	73	15.8	16.0	716	731	11.1	12.1	21.6	23.7	3,462	(NA)
Michigan................	141	140	24.5	24.6	1,013	1,004	14.8	15.7	34.2	37.8	2,681	(NA)
Minnesota...............	125	124	13.8	13.7	489	455	8.4	8.6	11.8	11.9	2,568	(NA)
Mississippi..............	97	99	11.8	11.5	347	301	6.7	6.4	6.9	7.8	1,311	(NA)
Missouri................	118	115	18.5	17.8	718	715	10.9	11.6	24.8	26.7	2,668	(NA)
Montana................	56	59	3.8	3.6	91	94	1.9	2.0	4.4	5.3	2,050	(NA)
Nebraska................	93	93	6.6	6.7	189	184	3.5	3.6	5.7	6.8	2,473	(NA)
Nevada.................	46	46	6.5	6.5	263	256	4.2	4.4	3.0	2.9	2,397	(NA)
New Hampshire..........	28	28	2.8	2.9	115	115	1.7	1.9	5.5	6.3	3,247	(NA)
New Jersey..............	81	79	21.9	21.8	958	874	13.8	14.6	13.3	16.1	3,232	(NA)
New Mexico.............	42	43	3.8	3.7	181	173	2.3	2.4	3.6	4.0	3,150	(NA)
New York...............	162	160	50.7	49.7	1,970	2,030	36.3	38.5	53.3	61.6	3,676	(NA)
North Carolina..........	112	111	21.7	22.1	971	976	14.5	16.3	19.5	20.7	2,528	(NA)
North Dakota............	41	43	3.4	3.3	88	87	1.8	2.0	3.0	2.8	1,808	(NA)
Ohio....................	193	187	32.2	31.5	1,284	1,290	18.3	19.1	41.3	47.3	3,226	(NA)
Oklahoma...............	122	125	11.1	11.2	402	393	6.1	6.3	7.5	7.9	2,207	(NA)
Oregon.................	61	61	7.0	7.0	324	320	4.2	4.8	12.2	12.1	3,986	(NA)
Pennsylvania............	186	185	35.4	34.7	1,416	1,410	21.7	23.6	38.0	41.9	2,810	(NA)
Rhode Island............	11	11	2.2	2.1	105	98	1.5	1.5	2.0	2.4	3,019	(NA)
South Carolina..........	73	70	11.2	11.8	490	507	7.4	8.1	10.0	10.3	2,341	(NA)
South Dakota............	57	57	4.3	4.2	102	108	2.4	2.7	3.1	3.4	1,642	(NA)
Tennessee...............	111	112	19.2	18.9	785	766	12.0	12.7	12.9	14.3	2,350	(NA)
Texas...................	523	509	66.6	66.1	2,632	2,765	38.7	42.1	41.7	49.0	2,923	(NA)
Utah....................	53	54	5.9	5.7	236	235	3.2	3.3	8.4	9.0	3,350	(NA)
Vermont................	14	14	1.3	1.3	47	46	0.8	0.9	2.9	3.3	3,114	(NA)
Virginia.................	95	94	18.2	17.5	727	759	11.4	11.7	16.2	18.7	2,549	(NA)
Washington..............	91	92	12.2	12.4	504	525	7.6	8.9	15.5	17.7	3,945	(NA)
West Virginia............	52	54	6.3	6.4	223	222	3.9	4.0	7.3	7.6	2,104	(NA)
Wisconsin...............	133	133	12.2	11.5	480	465	6.9	7.4	18.5	21.1	2,732	(NA)
Wyoming................	28	28	1.9	1.9	40	38	1.0	0.9	1.3	1.3	1,466	(NA)

NA Not available. [1] The average number of people served on an inpatient basis on a single day during the reporting period. [2] Beginning with *AHA Hospital Statistics 2023 Edition,* source no longer publishes cost data.

Source: Health Forum LLC, an affiliate of the American Hospital Association, Chicago, IL, *AHA Hospital Statistics 2024 Edition* ©, and previous editions. See also <guide.prod.iam.aha.org/stats/>.

Table 191. Household Medical Debt—Incidence and Value by Selected Characteristics: 2022

[In units as indicated. Based on the Survey of Income and Program Participation, a survey of a sample of households and subject to sampling variability. Presence of medical debt was determined by asking respondents whether they had medical bills that they were unable to pay in full]

Characteristic	Percent with medical debt	Median value of medical debt (dollars)	Mean value of medical debt (dollars)	Characteristic	Percent with medical debt	Median value of medical debt (dollars)	Mean value of medical debt (dollars)
Total [1]......	**14.3**	**2,000**	**15,670**	Highest education in household:			
Race/ethnicity of householder:				No high school diploma.........	14.2	2,000	11,520
White alone......	13.4	2,000	14,890	High school graduate only.......	16.3	2,000	14,700
White alone, not Hispanic......	12.8	2,000	14,180	Some college, no degree........	19.4	2,000	27,340
Black alone......	22.6	2,000	18,500	Associate's degree...............	17.7	2,000	10,400
Asian alone......	6.3	2,000	24,370	Bachelor's degree...............	12.8	1,800	9,229
Other race group......	15.9	3,000	8,857	Graduate/professional degree...	8.7	1,700	15,690
Hispanic origin [2]......	16.5	2,000	16,160	Household poverty status:			
Not of Hispanic origin......	13.9	2,000	15,570	Below poverty threshold.........	14.0	2,000	22,280
Age of householder:				Above poverty threshold........	14.3	2,000	14,910
Less than 35 years......	12.6	1,600	8,094	Health insurance coverage:			
35 to 44 years......	16.2	2,010	12,190	Coverage for all of household			
45 to 54 years......	16.6	2,000	15,630	all year............................	12.7	1,740	13,490
55 to 64 years......	17.7	2,120	23,530	No coverage for part or all of			
65 years and over......	10.6	1,500	16,160	household during the year......	22.7	2,500	22,280

[1] Includes persons of other race groups not shown separately. [2] Persons of Hispanic origin may be of any race.

Source: U.S. Census Bureau, Survey of Income and Program Participation, Wealth and Asset Ownership, "Wealth, Asset Ownership, & Debt of Households Detailed Tables: 2022," <www.census.gov/topics/income-poverty/wealth/data/tables.html>, accessed July 2024.

Table 192. Medical and Mental Health Care Delay or Nonreceipt During the Past 12 Months Due to Cost: 2021 to 2023

[Data shown as percent of population. For adults age 18 and over. Based on the National Health Interview Survey, a sample survey of the civilian noninstitutionalized population. Respondents reported delaying or not getting needed medical and mental health care due to cost in the past 12 months, and for those taking prescription medications, not taking medication as prescribed to save money in the past 12 months. Unknowns were not included in the denominators when calculating percentages. For information on data source, methods, and definitions, see *Technical Notes for Interactive Summary Health Statistics—2019-2023: National Health Interview Survey*, <wwwn.cdc.gov/NHISDataQueryTool/SHS_adult/SHS_Tech_Notes.pdf>]

Characteristic	Delayed medical care			Did not get needed medical care			Did not get needed mental health care			Did not take medication as prescribed [1]		
	2021 [5]	2022	2023	2021 [5]	2022	2023	2021 [5]	2022	2023	2021 [5]	2022	2023
Total..........	**7.1**	**7.0**	**7.2**	**6.1**	**6.3**	**6.3**	**4.2**	**5.0**	**5.5**	**6.8**	**6.8**	**7.8**
Sex:												
Male......	6.3	6.2	6.4	5.4	5.4	5.5	2.7	3.4	3.6	5.8	5.9	6.7
Female......	7.9	7.8	7.9	6.7	7.1	7.1	5.6	6.5	7.2	7.5	7.5	8.7
Age group:												
18 to 34 years......	8.7	8.3	8.7	7.0	7.0	7.0	8.0	9.0	9.4	8.5	8.3	9.2
35 to 49 years......	8.3	9.4	9.0	7.4	8.4	8.3	4.4	5.9	6.7	8.7	8.8	9.9
50 to 64 years......	8.4	7.1	7.8	7.2	6.7	7.4	2.5	3.0	3.4	7.6	7.0	8.6
65 years and over......	2.5	2.7	2.5	2.2	2.6	2.2	1.0	1.2	1.4	3.7	4.0	4.5
Race and Hispanic origin: [2]												
American Indian/Alaska Native alone......	10.3	(B)	(B)	7.8	(B)	8.3	(B)	(B)	(B)	(B)	(B)	9.6
Asian alone......	3.1	4.3	3.3	2.6	3.8	3.6	1.7	3.2	3.6	5.1	4.3	4.9
Black or African American alone......	7.0	6.9	8.7	7.2	7.2	8.1	4.2	5.3	5.5	9.3	8.2	11.1
White alone......	7.2	6.8	7.0	5.8	5.9	5.9	4.4	5.0	5.6	6.3	6.4	7.2
Hispanic or Latino......	8.7	10.9	9.6	8.0	10.3	9.3	4.1	5.2	5.2	8.5	9.5	9.7
Not Hispanic or Latino......	6.8	6.2	6.7	5.7	5.4	5.7	4.2	5.0	5.5	6.5	6.3	7.5
Health insurance status: [3]												
Private......	6.6	5.7	6.4	5.2	4.8	5.3	4.7	5.4	6.4	6.6	6.4	7.5
Medicaid or other public........	5.4	6.6	7.1	5.3	7.1	6.9	4.6	6.6	6.5	8.1	9.6	9.7
Other coverage......	8.3	7.7	9.2	6.6	6.9	9.4	4.4	6.8	7.5	11.5	9.4	13.3
Uninsured......	22.2	24.8	24.7	20.6	22.1	22.6	9.3	9.7	9.6	23.1	20.5	26.1
Disability status: [4]												
With disability......	12.3	12.2	13.0	11.8	12.4	12.8	7.3	8.5	9.8	13.0	12.7	13.9
Without disability......	6.6	6.5	6.6	5.5	5.7	5.7	3.9	4.7	5.0	5.9	6.0	6.9

B Estimate does not meet standards of reliability. [1] Respondents were asked in separate questions if during the past 12 months any of the following were true: they skipped medication doses, they took less medication, or they delayed filling a prescription, to save money. [2] Persons who indicated only a single race group, regardless of Hispanic or Latino origin. Persons of Hispanic or Latino origin may be of any race or combination of races. [3] For adults age 18 to 64, at time of interview. Based on a hierarchy of mutually exclusive categories. Adults with more than one type of health insurance were assigned to the first appropriate category in the following hierarchy: private, Medicaid or other public, other coverage, or uninsured. "Uninsured" includes adults who had no coverage, or who had only Indian Health Service coverage, or had only a private plan that paid for one type of service such as dental or vision care. [4] Respondents considered to have a disability reported "a lot of difficulty" or "cannot do at all" regarding at least one of six functioning domains: seeing (even if wearing glasses), hearing (even if wearing hearing aids), mobility (walking or climbing stairs), communication (understanding or being understood by others), cognition (remembering or concentrating), and self-care (such as washing all over or dressing). [5] Due to the COVID-19 pandemic, NHIS data collection switched from in-person to telephone interviews; personal visits resumed in September 2020 but cases were still attempted by telephone first through April 2021. Starting May 2021, NHIS returned to regular in-person interview procedures, with follow-up allowed by telephone.

Source: U.S. National Center for Health Statistics, National Health Interview Survey, "Interactive Summary Health Statistics for Adults," <www.cdc.gov/nchs/nhis/SHS.htm>, accessed July 2024.

Table 193. Top 15 Cancers Among Men and Women by Race/Ethnicity: 2017 to 2021

[Rates per 100,000 population, age-adjusted to the 2000 U.S. standard population. Based on November 2023 data submission. Includes top 15 cancers for each racial/ethnic group. Cancer incidence measures the number of newly diagnosed cases occurring in a specified population during a year. Data are for cancers diagnosed during 2017-2021 period, based on cancer registries in 22 areas monitored by the National Cancer Institute's Surveillance, Epidemiology, and End Results (SEER) Program. See source for more information]

Cancer by site and sex	All race/ethnicities		White, non-Hispanic		Black, non-Hispanic		Asian/Pacific Islander, non-Hispanic		Hispanic [1]	
	Rank	Rate	Rank	Rate	Rank	Rate	Rank	Rate	Rank	Rate
TOTAL										
All sites	(X)	440.5	(X)	471.8	(X)	452.1	(X)	304.2	(X)	351.0
Female breast [2]	1	129.4	1	139.0	2	129.3	1	110.3	1	101.2
Prostate [2]	2	116.5	2	114.9	1	188.7	2	61.4	2	88.1
Lung and bronchus	3	49.1	3	55.4	3	52.5	3	33.7	5	26.0
Colon and rectum	4	36.5	4	36.9	4	42.1	4	29.4	3	33.5
Corpus and uterus, NOS [2,3]	5	28.0	6	27.7	5	30.2	5	23.4	4	26.9
Melanoma of the skin	6	21.2	5	30.8	31	0.9	27	1.2	20	4.4
Non-Hodgkin lymphoma	7	18.6	8	20.0	9	14.2	7	13.4	7	17.4
Urinary bladder, invasive & in situ	8	18.2	7	21.9	11	11.0	14	8.4	13	10.0
Kidney and renal pelvis	9	17.2	9	17.7	6	18.4	12	8.7	6	18.5
Leukemia	10	14.1	10	15.5	10	11.1	15	8.2	11	11.2
Pancreas	11	13.5	12	13.8	7	16.2	9	10.1	10	12.1
Thyroid	12	13.5	11	14.5	17	8.0	6	14.8	9	13.2
Oral cavity and pharynx	13	11.5	13	13.4	16	8.3	13	8.5	16	7.1
Ovary [2]	14	10.3	14	10.5	14	8.9	10	9.4	12	10.0
Liver and IBD [4]	15	9.4	15	7.5	12	10.3	8	11.4	8	15.0
Cervix uteri	16	7.6	18	6.9	15	8.7	16	6.1	15	9.8
Myeloma	17	7.2	19	6.4	8	14.6	17	4.1	17	6.7
Stomach	18	7.0	20	5.4	13	10.0	11	9.2	14	9.9
MEN										
All sites	(X)	478.7	(X)	510.7	(X)	526.5	(X)	299.8	(X)	367.0
Prostate	1	116.5	1	114.9	1	188.7	1	61.4	1	88.1
Lung and bronchus	2	54.9	2	60.0	2	66.5	2	41.4	3	31.0
Colon and rectum	3	41.8	3	42.0	3	49.4	3	34.5	2	39.5
Urinary bladder, invasive & in situ	4	31.6	5	37.7	5	18.9	6	14.8	7	17.0
Melanoma of the skin	5	27.1	4	38.1	26	1.0	23	1.3	17	4.5
Kidney and renal pelvis	6	23.4	6	24.2	4	25.3	7	12.1	4	23.9
Non-Hodgkin lymphoma	7	22.5	7	24.2	7	17.1	5	16.1	6	20.0
Leukemia	8	17.9	9	19.8	10	13.7	11	10.2	8	13.3
Oral cavity and pharynx	9	17.1	8	20.1	12	12.7	9	12.0	11	10.2
Pancreas	10	15.4	10	16.0	6	17.7	10	10.9	9	13.0
Liver and IBD [4]	11	14.0	11	11.2	9	16.6	4	17.4	5	21.5
Stomach	12	9.1	16	7.5	11	13.2	8	12.1	10	11.9
Myeloma	13	8.7	15	8.1	8	17.1	13	5.1	12	7.9
Brain & other nervous system	14	7.3	12	8.6	15	4.8	14	4.6	15	5.7
Thyroid	15	7.2	13	8.4	19	3.5	12	7.3	14	5.8
Esophagus	16	7.1	14	8.4	14	5.2	15	3.6	16	4.7
Larynx	19	4.5	19	4.8	13	6.5	20	1.9	18	3.8
Testis	17	5.9	17	7.2	24	1.6	18	2.4	13	6.2
WOMEN										
All sites	(X)	416.7	(X)	447.0	(X)	403.2	(X)	313.2	(X)	347.8
Female breast	1	129.4	1	139.0	1	129.3	1	110.3	1	101.2
Lung and bronchus	2	44.8	2	52.2	2	43.2	2	27.8	4	22.6
Colon and rectum	3	32.0	3	32.4	3	36.8	3	25.3	2	28.7
Corpus and uterus, NOS [3]	4	28.0	4	27.7	4	30.2	4	23.4	3	26.9
Thyroid	5	19.8	6	20.9	9	11.9	5	21.7	5	20.6
Melanoma of the skin	6	16.9	5	25.6	29	0.9	23	1.1	18	4.5
Non-Hodgkin lymphoma	7	15.5	7	16.5	8	12.0	6	11.3	6	15.3
Pancreas	8	12.0	9	11.9	5	15.1	8	9.4	8	11.4
Kidney and renal pelvis	9	11.9	10	11.8	6	13.0	13	5.8	7	13.9
Leukemia	10	11.0	8	12.0	10	9.2	10	6.6	11	9.4
Ovary	11	10.3	11	10.5	11	8.9	7	9.4	9	10.0
Urinary bladder, invasive & in situ	12	7.8	12	9.3	14	5.8	15	3.5	15	4.7
Cervix uteri	13	7.6	14	6.9	12	8.7	12	6.1	10	9.8
Oral cavity and pharynx	14	6.4	13	7.2	16	4.9	14	5.6	17	4.5
Myeloma	15	5.9	16	5.1	7	13.0	16	3.3	14	5.8
Stomach	16	5.4	19	3.7	13	8.0	9	6.9	13	8.4
Liver and IBD [4]	17	5.4	17	4.3	15	5.5	11	6.4	12	9.4
Brain & other nervous system	18	5.2	15	6.1	18	3.5	17	3.2	16	4.6

X Not applicable. [1] Persons of Hispanic origin may be of any race. [2] For cancer sites that occur in only one sex, the sex-specific population (e.g., females for cervical cancer) is used. [3] NOS, not otherwise specified. [4] IBD, intrahepatic bile duct.

Source: National Institutes of Health, National Cancer Institute, Surveillance, Epidemiology, and End Results Program, "SEER*Explorer: SEER Incidence," <seer.cancer.gov/statistics-network/>, accessed April 2024.

Table 194. Cancer Incidence for Total and Top 5 Cancers by State: 2021

[For invasive cancer sites. Top five cancers are ranked by total number of new cases. Data are produced by the Centers for Disease Control and Prevention (CDC) and the National Cancer Institute]

State	Total cases (number)	Rate per 100,000 population					
		All cancers [1]	Breast [1]	Prostate	Lung and bronchus	Colon and rectum	Melanoma of the skin
Total [2].............................	**1,793,976**	**546.1**	**84.4**	**147.3**	**64.0**	**43.7**	**27.6**
Alabama.............................	27,395	542.5	84.9	145.0	76.7	49.7	26.4
Alaska...............................	3,267	445.0	63.3	119.2	53.3	39.8	18.1
Arizona..............................	34,437	474.0	73.5	93.4	52.6	36.7	42.1
Arkansas............................	16,379	540.9	79.7	109.5	86.9	46.8	22.9
California............................	180,858	462.0	77.2	118.7	40.0	38.6	27.6
Colorado............................	25,385	436.8	79.9	102.9	39.4	35.2	24.5
Connecticut.........................	23,548	649.9	105.0	206.5	76.5	43.6	23.4
Delaware............................	6,295	626.5	102.4	188.6	82.0	42.0	28.9
District of Columbia................	2,917	436.2	79.1	130.9	43.4	34.5	12.1
Florida..............................	147,442	675.5	95.7	167.0	80.7	50.7	37.0
Georgia.............................	58,576	543.0	83.7	171.4	61.9	45.5	27.7
Hawaii...............................	8,015	553.8	89.7	152.1	54.7	52.9	33.2
Idaho...............................	9,971	523.6	77.6	143.2	51.4	44.0	38.2
Illinois..............................	72,620	572.4	87.5	153.9	72.3	46.3	29.4
Indiana..............................	(NA)	(NA)	(NA)	(NA)	(NA)	(NA)	(NA)
Iowa................................	20,367	636.9	87.2	174.4	79.7	48.8	42.0
Kansas..............................	15,835	539.0	85.4	150.4	63.4	44.0	29.9
Kentucky............................	28,974	642.9	85.7	155.7	106.4	54.5	35.7
Louisiana...........................	27,170	587.2	82.9	186.3	74.5	52.9	21.7
Maine...............................	9,952	722.6	107.3	185.8	102.8	51.3	36.5
Maryland............................	33,665	545.2	91.7	174.8	59.5	41.2	30.0
Massachusetts......................	35,253	504.4	92.6	143.3	62.8	36.8	15.6
Michigan............................	55,710	555.0	86.0	156.3	74.2	42.1	24.3
Minnesota...........................	34,257	599.8	89.4	159.2	67.0	44.0	45.2
Mississippi..........................	17,177	582.4	80.5	175.0	86.4	54.5	22.5
Missouri............................	35,092	568.8	87.1	129.1	83.4	48.8	25.4
Montana............................	6,655	601.6	84.1	190.0	65.3	49.1	32.4
Nebraska............................	10,300	524.6	74.5	128.6	65.8	43.5	35.3
Nevada..............................	14,445	459.1	69.5	117.7	52.0	39.3	27.8
New Hampshire.....................	8,886	640.4	100.8	176.1	82.0	43.3	37.3
New Jersey..........................	56,819	613.1	93.1	190.9	61.4	49.5	27.2
New Mexico.........................	9,899	467.7	75.5	120.8	41.7	40.8	22.2
New York............................	119,678	602.7	91.0	183.0	68.9	45.3	22.4
North Carolina......................	62,489	591.4	94.3	167.0	76.3	42.6	35.3
North Dakota........................	4,195	539.2	74.2	143.2	64.1	45.2	38.2
Ohio................................	71,924	611.4	91.3	164.3	83.9	48.1	35.0
Oklahoma...........................	21,407	536.4	77.2	127.5	76.2	49.4	23.9
Oregon..............................	21,589	507.2	81.4	126.6	58.4	38.2	25.4
Pennsylvania........................	77,139	592.8	90.1	154.8	76.2	46.4	23.0
Rhode Island........................	6,337	577.7	96.8	134.8	77.5	40.3	21.6
South Carolina......................	28,910	556.7	93.6	155.8	74.1	43.8	28.2
South Dakota........................	5,045	563.0	78.7	158.6	66.6	45.5	36.9
Tennessee...........................	38,668	554.9	81.3	135.0	81.7	45.3	23.0
Texas...............................	129,511	438.1	67.7	108.1	44.0	39.1	16.0
Utah................................	13,327	399.1	59.2	125.0	22.6	26.4	39.0
Vermont.............................	4,061	627.7	82.2	184.1	81.6	43.0	48.1
Virginia.............................	42,412	489.9	83.7	133.5	61.6	39.7	23.4
Washington.........................	41,272	533.2	87.6	136.3	58.6	40.0	29.2
West Virginia........................	12,647	708.3	95.3	158.4	115.1	60.7	35.6
Wisconsin...........................	36,420	619.4	91.2	183.0	72.4	43.3	34.5
Wyoming............................	2,974	513.2	86.1	155.6	46.2	43.3	31.9
Puerto Rico.........................	16,410	503.0	79.5	207.7	24.3	54.7	4.5

NA Not available. [1] Excludes data for in situ breast cancers. [2] Total includes Puerto Rico.

Source: U.S. Centers for Disease Control and Prevention, CDC WONDER Online Database, "Cancer Incidence 1999-2021," 2023 submission, 2024 release, <wonder.cdc.gov/cancer.html>, accessed August 2024.

Table 195. Cancer Survival Rates by Type/Body Site and Race and Year of Diagnosis: 2002 to 2020

[For invasive cancer, unless otherwise noted. For leading cancers ranked by incidence rates per 100,000 persons for 1990-2021 period. Based on follow-up of patients into 2021. The 5-year relative survival rate represents the proportion of patients alive 5 years after their cancer diagnosis, compared to similar persons among the general population without cancer. Based on information collected as part of the National Cancer Institute's Surveillance, Epidemiology and End Results (SEER) program, from a collection of population-based registries in 8 areas]

Cancer site	5-year relative survival rates by year of diagnosis (percent)									
	White					Black				
	2002 to 2004	2005 to 2007	2008 to 2010	2011 to 2013	2014 to 2020	2002 to 2004	2005 to 2007	2008 to 2010	2011 to 2013	2014 to 2020
All types [1].....................	**68.7**	**70.3**	**70.9**	**70.8**	**72.8**	**60.5**	**63.7**	**65.7**	**65.6**	**68.9**
Female breast.....................	91.8	92.6	92.6	93.1	94.2	79.9	81.0	83.4	84.6	86.1
Prostate...........................	99.8	99.8	99.6	98.8	98.5	98.0	98.8	98.4	97.1	98.2
Lung and bronchus..............	16.4	18.1	19.6	20.8	28.2	13.9	14.1	18.4	19.7	27.7
Colon and rectum...............	67.3	68.0	68.0	67.4	68.1	56.1	60.5	62.3	60.4	63.7
Corpus and uterus..............	85.7	86.1	85.8	85.5	85.9	61.6	67.1	67.6	66.1	66.6
Melanoma of skin...............	93.0	93.7	94.3	95.6	96.8	76.5	75.7	65.3	68.6	71.4
Urinary bladder [2]...............	81.0	80.5	78.7	79.7	81.8	65.5	67.2	67.7	65.1	67.7
Non-Hodgkin's lymphoma [3].....	71.6	72.9	75.4	76.2	78.5	63.4	62.4	69.1	72.8	73.2
Kidney and renal pelvis.........	69.4	74.6	75.2	76.0	79.3	64.0	74.4	76.6	78.9	79.8
Leukemia [3].......................	59.9	64.5	66.5	69.4	71.2	52.7	58.5	57.4	63.6	66.7
Ovary..............................	43.9	44.9	47.5	49.7	51.3	39.4	39.5	34.8	47.0	40.9
Pancreas..........................	5.7	7.4	8.5	11.0	12.8	5.0	6.0	7.9	11.5	12.4
Oral cavity and pharynx.........	66.3	68.2	69.9	71.5	74.2	50.9	47.2	52.2	53.5	61.5
Thyroid............................	97.4	98.1	98.7	98.7	98.7	97.3	96.6	98.3	96.7	96.3
Liver & intrahepatic bile duct....	14.0	16.9	18.1	18.2	22.2	9.1	12.8	13.7	18.3	24.3

[1] Includes other sites, not shown separately. [2] Invasive and in situ. [3] All types combined.

Source: U.S. National Institutes of Health, National Cancer Institute, Surveillance Epidemiology and End Results Program, "Cancer Query System: SEER Survival Statistics," <seer.cancer.gov/canques/survival.html>, accessed April 2024.

Table 196. HIV Diagnoses and Chlamydia and Lyme Disease Cases Reported by State: 2021

[Data reported through March 29, 2023. Data reflect impacts of the coronavirus disease 2019 (COVID-19) pandemic]

State	HIV [1]	Chla-mydia [1]	Lyme disease [2]	State	HIV [1]	Chla-mydia [1]	Lyme disease [2]
U.S. [3].....................	**31,269**	**1,613,840**	**24,610**	Montana.....................	21	4,029	13
Alabama.....................	386	31,500	51	Nebraska.....................	85	8,897	10
Alaska.......................	22	5,571	([5])	Nevada.....................	450	16,348	17
Arizona......................	726	41,498	3	New Hampshire...........	30	3,027	397
Arkansas....................	337	17,936	11	New Jersey.................	902	33,425	3,518
California...................	3,538	191,542	106	New Mexico.................	143	12,441	2
Colorado....................	356	26,747	([5])	New York [4].................	492	39,719	2,187
Connecticut................	200	14,750	541	New York City.............	1,353	61,938	819
Delaware....................	81	4,880	140	North Carolina.............	1,298	63,659	338
District of Columbia.......	97	6,952	91	North Dakota.............	21	3,964	34
Florida.......................	4,443	104,400	193	Ohio.........................	822	56,520	590
Georgia.....................	1,689	67,941	35	Oklahoma.................	261	20,709	([5])
Hawaii.......................	58	6,078	([6])	Oregon.....................	193	15,596	74
Idaho........................	36	6,318	6	Pennsylvania..............	830	53,124	2,900
Illinois.......................	844	71,836	540	Rhode Island..............	51	5,199	980
Indiana......................	485	34,755	314	South Carolina............	527	36,477	76
Iowa.........................	120	15,620	359	South Dakota..............	24	4,853	16
Kansas......................	155	14,851	22	Tennessee.................	783	39,227	57
Kentucky....................	351	18,392	41	Texas.......................	3,627	149,636	32
Louisiana...................	957	33,759	4	Utah.........................	119	11,221	18
Maine........................	30	3,372	1,510	Vermont....................	6	910	115
Maryland....................	636	(NA)	916	Virginia.....................	766	40,409	705
Massachusetts.............	269	26,950	27	Washington...............	471	29,632	43
Michigan....................	628	45,473	862	West Virginia..............	131	5,226	1,792
Minnesota..................	286	22,573	1,902	Wisconsin.................	230	27,841	2,193
Mississippi..................	390	22,126	1	Wyoming...................	6	2,078	2
Missouri.....................	507	31,915	7	Island areas..............	350	6,419	1

[1] Total diagnoses reported to the National Center for HIV/AIDS, Viral Hepatitis, STD, and TB Prevention. [2] Confirmed and probable. [3] Excludes Island areas. [4] Data for New York state excludes New York City. [5] No cases reported. [6] Not reportable.

Source: U.S. Centers for Disease Control and Prevention, National Notifiable Diseases Surveillance System, "WONDER Annual Tables of Infectious Diseases and Conditions (2016 to present)," <www.cdc.gov/nndss/data-statistics/index.html>, accessed April 2024.

Table 197. Selected Notifiable Diseases—Cases Reported: 1990 to 2021

[Number except as indicated (21,150 represents 21,150,000). Interpret figures with caution. Although reporting of some of these diseases is incomplete, the figures are of value in indicating trends of disease incidence. Includes cases imported from outside the U.S.]

Disease	1990	2000	2005	2010	2015	2018	2019[13]	2020[13]	2021[13]
Babesiosis	(¹)	(¹)	(¹)	(¹)	2,100	2,160	2,420	1,820	2,674
Botulism[2]	92	138	135	112	195	225	196	189	236
Campylobacteriosis	(¹)	(¹)	(¹)	(¹)	54,556	70,200	71,509	51,764	63,409
Coccidioidomycosis	(¹)	2,867	6,542	(¹)	11,072	15,611	18,407	19,220	20,201
Coronavirus disease 2019 (1,000)[3]	(¹)	(¹)	(¹)	(¹)	(¹)	(¹)	(¹)	21,150	36,096
Cryptosporidiosis	(¹)	3,128	5,659	8,944	9,735	12,533	13,975	7,648	9,155
Cyclosporiasis	(¹)	60	543	179	645	3,519	4,703	2,689	2,424
Dengue virus infections[14]	(¹)	(¹)	(¹)	700	951	474	1,487	450	193
Anaplasma phagocytophilum	(¹)	(¹)	(¹)	1,761	3,656	4,008	5,655	3,637	6,729
Giardiasis	(¹)	(¹)	19,733	19,811	14,485	15,548	14,860	9,453	11,643
Haemophilus influenza	(¹)	1,398	2,304	3,151	4,138	5,573	6,143	2,996	3,042
Hepatitis virus, acute: A	31,441	13,397	4,488	1,670	1,390	12,474	18,846	9,946	5,726
Hepatitis virus, acute: B	21,102	8,036	5,119	3,374	3,370	3,322	3,544	2,155	2,044
Hepatitis virus, acute: C	2,553	3,197	652	849	2,447	4,768	5,479	6,025	6,028
HIV diagnoses[4]	(X)	(X)	(X)	35,741	33,817	32,999	31,723	25,007	31,269
Invasive pneumococcal disease[5]	(¹)	(¹)	(¹)	16,569	16,163	19,857	19,951	11,946	12,098
Legionellosis	1,370	1,127	2,301	3,346	6,079	9,933	8,890	6,310	8,442
Listeriosis	(¹)	755	896	821	768	864	928	780	977
Lyme disease	(¹)	17,730	23,305	30,158	38,069	33,666	34,945	18,000	24,610
Malaria	1,292	1,560	1,494	1,773	1,390	1,748	1,936	603	1,503
Measles	27,786	86	66	63	188	375	1,275	12	48
Meningococcal disease	2,451	2,256	1,245	833	372	327	371	242	208
Mumps	5,292	338	314	2,612	1,329	2,515	3,780	694	189
Pertussis (whooping cough)	4,570	7,867	25,616	27,550	20,762	15,609	18,617	6,124	2,116
Rabies, animal	4,826	6,934	5,915	4,331	5,491	4,984	4,645	4,457	3,641
Rubella[6]	1,125	176	11	5	5	4	6	6	7
Salmonella Typhi infection[7]	552	377	324	467	367	401	409	182	234
Salmonellosis[8]	48,603	39,574	45,322	54,424	55,108	60,999	58,371	45,442	49,249
Shiga toxin-producing E. coli (STEC)	(¹)	(¹)	(¹)	5,476	7,059	15,996	16,939	9,922	13,943
Shigellosis	27,077	22,922	16,168	14,786	23,590	16,333	18,574	9,108	9,999
Spotted fever rickettsiosis	(¹)	495	1,936	1,985	4,198	5,544	5,207	1,175	1,257
Streptococcal toxic-shock syndrome	(¹)	83	129	142	335	371	416	224	145
Tetanus	64	35	27	26	29	23	26	17	28
Toxic-shock syndrome	322	135	90	82	64	33	44	24	15
Tuberculosis[9]	25,701	16,377	14,097	11,182	9,557	9,025	8,916	7,174	7,882
Varicella (chickenpox) morbidity[10]	173,099	27,382	32,242	15,427	9,789	8,201	8,297	2,927	3,496
Vibriosis	(¹)	(¹)	(¹)	846	1,323	2,964	2,851	1,852	2,853
West Nile virus, neuroinvasive[11]	(¹)	(¹)	1,309	629	1,455	1,657	636	558	2,007
West Nile virus, nonneuroinvasive[11]	(¹)	(¹)	1,691	392	720	989	338	172	899
Zika virus disease and infections[12]	(¹)	(¹)	(¹)	(¹)	(¹)	334	205	23	3
Sexually transmitted diseases:									
Chlamydia trachomatis (1,000)	(¹)	702	976	1,308	1,527	1,759	1,809	1,580	1,614
Gonorrhea (1,000)	690	359	340	309	395	583	616	678	700
Syphilis (1,000)	134	32	33	46	75	115	130	134	174

X Not applicable. [1] Disease was not notifiable. [2] Includes foodborne, infant, wound, and unspecified cases. [3] In thousands; total cases (confirmed and probable). [4] Human immunodeficiency virus diagnoses, including cases of AIDS (classified as HIV stage III). Cases reported to the Division of HIV/AIDS Prevention, National Center for HIV/AIDS, Viral Hepatitis, STD, and TB Prevention. In 2008, CDC revised the HIV case definition to cover HIV infection and AIDS into a single case definition. [5] Data for 2010, 2011, and 2015 reported as Streptococcus pneumoniae invasive disease. [6] German measles, excluding congenital syndrome. [7] Prior to 2019, cases were reported as typhoid fever. Beginning January 2019, cases reported as Salmonella Typhi infection. [8] Excludes typhoid fever. Beginning 2018, excludes paratyphoid fever. [9] Totals reported to the Division of Tuberculosis Elimination, NCHHSTP. [10] Varicella (chickenpox) was removed from the nationally notifiable disease list in 1981; it became notifiable again in 2003. [11] Totals reported to the Division of Vector-Borne Diseases (DVBD), National Center for Emerging and Zoonotic Infectious Diseases (NCEZID) (ArboNET Surveillance). [12] Includes Zika virus diseases and infections, congenital and noncongenital. [13] Data reflect impacts of the COVID-19 pandemic. [14] Totals reported to the DVBD, NCEZID (ArboNET Surveillance). The national surveillance case definitions for arboviral diseases were revised in 2005, and nonneuroinvasive arboviral diseases were added to the list of nationally notifiable infectious diseases. Beginning 2015, dengue includes "dengue," "dengue-like illness," and "severe dengue" cases; these categories are based on World Health Organization dengue case definitions.

Source: U.S. Centers for Disease Control and Prevention, "Summary of Notifiable Infectious Diseases and Conditions—United States, 2015," *Morbidity and Mortality Weekly Report*, 64:53, August 11, 2017, and earlier reports; and "WONDER Annual Tables of Infectious Diseases and Conditions (2016 to present)," <www.cdc.gov/nndss/data-statistics/infectious-tables/index.html>, accessed April 2024.

Table 198. HIV (Human Immunodeficiency Virus) Infection Diagnoses and Persons Living With HIV by Selected Characteristics: 2019 to 2022

[For all HIV infections, regardless of stage of disease. Data reported to the Centers for Disease Control and Prevention's National HIV Surveillance System as of December 31, 2023. Covers the 50 states, the District of Columbia, and 6 U.S. territories and freely associated states. As of April 2008, all jurisdictions had implemented confidential name-based HIV infection reporting. Data may not be representative of all persons with HIV. The completeness of HIV infection reporting, as of December 2023, is estimated to be at least 85% in all but one jurisdiction. See source for more information. Users should interpret 2020 data with caution due to the impact of the coronavirus disease 2019 (COVID-19) pandemic on access to HIV testing, care-related services, and case surveillance activities, and also consider the effects of the pandemic on data for 2021 and 2022]

Characteristic	Diagnoses [10]				Persons living with HIV			
	2019	2020	2021	2022	2019	2020	2021	2022 (P)
Total [1]	**36,826**	**30,688**	**36,149**	**38,043**	**1,054,699**	**1,067,316**	**1,085,619**	**1,109,418**
GENDER IDENTITY [2]								
Man/boy	29,097	24,466	28,607	30,041	794,983	805,905	821,160	840,579
Woman/girl	6,928	5,433	6,561	7,008	246,324	247,412	249,640	253,150
Transgender woman/girl	722	722	874	869	12,545	13,095	13,808	14,565
Transgender man/boy	45	41	60	59	516	546	604	656
Additional gender identity	34	26	47	66	329	356	405	466
AGE AT DIAGNOSIS								
Under 13 years	58	58	53	62	1,674	1,445	1,268	1,126
13 to 14 years	21	14	15	22	663	648	599	526
15 to 19 years	1,660	1,289	1,475	1,360	4,276	3,841	3,738	3,652
20 to 24 years	6,063	4,921	5,581	5,717	26,353	24,546	24,081	23,909
25 to 29 years	7,459	6,131	6,805	7,255	70,038	66,222	63,331	61,688
30 to 34 years	5,693	5,260	6,389	6,905	93,842	97,870	101,569	104,866
35 to 39 years	4,128	3,421	4,429	4,812	96,265	97,464	101,027	105,859
40 to 44 years	2,957	2,490	3,177	3,555	99,078	101,357	104,056	106,793
45 to 49 years	2,605	2,065	2,316	2,452	118,179	110,322	105,939	104,955
50 to 54 years	2,301	1,858	2,140	2,124	152,129	146,717	140,228	134,381
55 to 59 years	1,862	1,592	1,790	1,767	161,715	164,385	164,168	160,708
60 to 64 years	1,127	891	1,125	1,119	113,338	121,492	129,130	137,329
65 to 69 years	516	430	554	515	66,272	72,621	80,084	87,691
70 to 74 years	240	171	194	239	31,194	35,986	40,742	45,822
75 and over	136	97	106	139	19,683	22,400	25,659	30,113
RACE/ETHNICITY [3]								
American Indian/Alaska Native	181	178	211	217	2,902	2,999	3,132	3,274
Asian [4]	725	599	732	796	15,208	15,796	16,525	17,406
Black/African American	15,169	12,572	14,341	14,589	417,639	422,282	428,620	436,028
Native Hawaiian/other Pacific Islander	60	61	73	83	819	869	932	1,010
White	8,900	7,656	8,993	9,120	298,515	300,554	303,523	307,118
Multiple races	1,466	1,144	1,241	1,061	59,562	59,437	59,220	58,916
Hispanic/Latino	10,325	8,478	10,558	12,177	259,399	264,725	273,015	285,014
TRANSMISSION CATEGORY [5]								
Males age 13 and over, total	29,818	25,187	29,499	30,935	807,036	818,647	834,755	855,052
Male-to-male sexual contact	24,064	20,662	24,041	25,422	589,335	602,436	619,204	639,235
Injection drug use	1,393	1,210	1,458	1,490	69,143	67,887	66,941	66,335
Male-to-male sexual contact and injection drug use	1,629	1,244	1,439	1,327	59,507	59,067	58,763	58,439
Heterosexual contact [6]	2,694	2,047	2,535	2,660	81,121	81,269	81,782	82,897
Perinatal [7]	20	9	11	19	5,145	5,224	5,308	5,383
Other [8]	17	14	16	17	2,785	2,764	2,756	2,764
Females age 13 and over, total	6,950	5,443	6,597	7,046	245,989	247,224	249,596	253,240
Injection drug use	1,195	889	1,098	1,161	49,629	49,020	48,626	48,407
Heterosexual contact [6]	5,720	4,523	5,464	5,835	188,727	190,437	193,073	196,775
Perinatal [7]	30	27	30	46	5,939	6,063	6,185	6,339
Other [8]	5	5	5	4	1,694	1,704	1,712	1,719
Children under age 13 at diagnosis	58	58	53	62	1,674	1,445	1,268	1,126
Perinatal	48	49	43	54	1,389	1,210	1,069	958
Other [8]	10	9	10	8	285	235	199	168
REGION								
Northeast	5,324	4,273	4,898	5,080	233,982	233,477	234,065	236,341
Midwest	4,784	4,125	4,837	4,903	124,253	126,159	128,618	131,602
South	18,856	15,498	18,628	19,822	473,420	481,441	492,500	506,546
West	7,444	6,479	7,361	7,858	206,814	210,074	214,201	218,658
U.S. dependent areas [9]	418	313	425	380	16,230	16,165	16,235	16,271

P Preliminary [1] Total may include persons of unknown gender and unknown racial/ethnic category, not shown separately. [2] Man/boy and woman/girl represent persons who identify with their sex assigned at birth. Transgender woman/girl was assigned "male" sex at birth and identify as "woman" or "girl." Transgender man/boy was assigned "female" sex at birth and identify as "man" or "boy." Additional gender identity includes persons who do not identify as male, female, transgender woman, or transgender man; includes "nonbinary," "gender queer," and "two-spirit." [3] Persons by race are not Hispanic or Latino, but may include persons whose Hispanic ethnicity was not reported. Persons of Hispanic/Latino ethnicity can be of any race. [4] For persons living with HIV, the Asian category includes Asian/Pacific Islander legacy cases. See source for more information. [5] Transmission category is classified based on a hierarchy of the risk factors most likely responsible for HIV transmission; see technical notes in source for details. Classification is determined based on the person's sex assigned at birth regardless of gender identity. Data have been statistically adjusted to account for missing transmission category; therefore, values may not sum to column subtotals and total. [6] Heterosexual contact with a person known to have, or be at high risk for, HIV infection. [7] Persons were age 13 and over at the time of diagnosis of HIV infection. [8] Includes hemophilia, blood transfusion, and risk factor not reported or not identified. [9] American Samoa, Guam, Northern Mariana Islands, Puerto Rico, Republic of Palau, and the U.S. Virgin Islands. [10] Numbers less than 12 should be interpreted with caution.

Source: U.S. Centers for Disease Control and Prevention, *HIV Surveillance Report, 2022*, Vol. 35, May 2024. See also <www.cdc.gov/hiv-data/nhss/estimated-hiv-incidence-and-prevalence.html>.

Table 199. AIDS Classifications and Persons Living with HIV Infection Ever Classified as Stage 3 (AIDS) by Selected Characteristics: 2019 to 2022

[Covers persons age 13 and over. Data reported to the Centers for Disease Control and Prevention's National HIV Surveillance System as of December 31, 2023. HIV infection is classified as stage 3 (AIDS) when the immune system of a person infected with human immunodeficiency virus becomes severely compromised. Data cover the 50 states, DC, and 6 U.S. dependent areas. Data may not be representative of all persons with HIV. See headnote, Table 198]

Characteristic	AIDS classifications				Persons living with HIV ever classified as stage 3			
	2019	2020 [6]	2021	2022	2019	2020 [6]	2021	2022 (P)
Total [1]............................	16,410	14,353	15,992	16,687	529,196	529,066	530,044	532,646
SEX [2]								
Male...........................	12,594	11,097	12,388	13,040	403,691	403,759	404,755	406,948
Female.........................	3,816	3,256	3,604	3,647	125,505	125,307	125,289	125,698
AGE								
13 to 24 years...................	1,100	928	1,025	1,145	4,682	4,057	3,796	3,690
25 to 34 years...................	4,634	4,052	4,452	4,803	44,101	42,486	40,991	39,697
35 to 44 years...................	3,980	3,430	4,043	4,311	81,743	80,397	80,102	79,840
45 to 54 years...................	3,337	2,952	3,025	3,052	151,068	140,568	131,243	124,201
55 to 64 years...................	2,476	2,161	2,467	2,369	172,005	177,300	180,211	180,973
65 years and over...............	883	830	980	1,007	75,597	84,258	93,701	104,245
RACE/ETHNICITY [3]								
American Indian/Alaska Native..............	59	74	86	84	1,342	1,360	1,391	1,421
Asian [4]........................	266	260	277	332	6,556	6,738	6,915	7,168
Black/African American............	7,269	6,271	6,811	6,975	212,222	212,230	212,640	213,645
Native Hawaiian/Other Pacific Islander.....	19	12	31	28	362	363	382	404
White...........................	3,837	3,422	3,812	3,941	148,805	147,972	147,303	146,953
Multiple races...................	897	786	842	782	33,002	32,718	32,374	32,036
Hispanic/Latino..................	4,063	3,528	4,133	4,545	126,876	127,654	129,008	130,988
TRANSMISSION CATEGORY [5]								
Male transmission:								
Heterosexual contact..............	1,703	1,397	1,535	1,594	47,224	47,129	47,040	47,275
Injection drug use................	863	716	789	886	43,302	42,145	41,082	40,278
Male-to-male sexual contact..........	9,076	8,203	9,245	9,698	273,729	275,693	278,431	281,684
Male-to-male sexual contact and injection drug use..................	875	726	759	774	34,971	34,361	33,775	33,253
Female transmission:								
Heterosexual contact..............	2,975	2,592	2,855	2,871	92,282	92,630	93,081	93,852
Injection drug use................	770	605	695	691	29,193	28,640	28,175	27,771

P Preliminary. [1] HIV prevalence data may include persons of unknown racial/ethnic category, not shown separately. [2] Sex assigned at birth. [3] Race categories are non-Hispanic. Persons of Hispanic/Latino origin may be of any race. [4] For persons living with HIV ever classified as stage 3 (AIDS), Asian category includes Asian/Pacific Islander legacy cases. [5] Data by transmission category are based on sex assigned at birth and are adjusted for missing transmission category. [6] Interpret 2020 data with caution due to the impact of the COVID-19 pandemic.

Source: U.S. Centers for Disease Control and Prevention, National Center for HIV, Viral Hepatitis, STD, and Tuberculosis Prevention, "NCHHSTP AtlasPlus," <www.cdc.gov/nchhstp/about/atlasplus.html>, accessed June 2024. See also *HIV Surveillance Report, 2022*, <www.cdc.gov/hiv-data/nhss/hiv-diagnoses-deaths-prevalence.html>.

Table 200. Youth and Adult Vaccinations by Selected Type: 2015 to 2022

[In percent. Data for youth are from the National Immunization Survey-Teen, which monitors vaccines received by adolescents age 13-17 across the U.S. and its territories. Youth vaccination coverage estimates are based on provider-reported information, except for the influenza vaccination, which is parent-reported. Data for adults are from the Behavioral Risk Factor Surveillance Survey, and excludes U.S. territories. Abbreviations: Td = tetanus diphtheria toxoid vaccine; Tdap = tetanus, diphtheria, and acellular pertussis vaccine; MenACWY = quadrivalent meningococcal conjugate vaccine; HPV = human papillomavirus]

Vaccination	2015	2016	2017	2018	2019	2020	2021	2022
YOUTH, AGE 13 to 17								
Tdap, ≥ 1 dose......................	86.4	88.0	88.7	88.9	90.2	90.1	89.6	89.9
MenACWY, ≥ 1 dose.....................	81.3	82.2	85.1	86.6	88.9	89.3	89.0	88.6
HPV vaccine:								
Total, ≥ 1 dose...................	(NA)	60.4	65.5	68.1	71.5	75.1	76.9	76.0
Total, up-to-date [1]..................	(NA)	43.4	48.6	51.1	54.2	58.6	61.7	62.6
Males, ≥ 1 dose..................	49.8	56.0	62.6	66.3	69.8	73.1	75.4	74.4
Males, up-to-date [1]................	(NA)	37.5	44.3	48.7	51.8	56.0	59.8	60.6
Males, ≥ 3 doses................	28.1	31.5	34.8	32.1	26.6	(NA)	(NA)	(NA)
Females, ≥ 1 dose.................	62.8	65.1	68.6	69.9	73.2	77.1	78.5	77.8
Females, up-to-date [1].............	(NA)	49.5	53.1	53.7	56.8	61.4	63.8	64.6
Females, ≥ 3 doses..................	41.9	43.0	44.0	37.9	28.5	(NA)	(NA)	(NA)
Influenza [2]........................	46.8	48.8	47.3	52.1	53.3	50.8	49.8	49.0
ADULTS								
Pneumococcal (pneumonia) vaccine:								
Age 18 to 64 at increased risk [3]........	33.5	33.3	36.1	30.1	33.2	29.2	29.7	30.5
Age 65 and over.....................	71.9	72.4	74.7	71.8	71.7	70.3	70.1	70.0
Tetanus (Td or Tdap) vaccine [4]								
Age 18 and over.....................	(NA)	60.3	(NA)	(NA)	70.5	(NA)	(NA)	64.2
Age 65 and over.....................	(NA)	48.7	(NA)	(NA)	65.1	(NA)	(NA)	59.8
Herpes zoster (shingles) vaccine								
Age 60 and over.....................	(NA)	(NA)	39.4	(NA)	(NA)	40.5	(NA)	(NA)
Age 65 and over.....................	(NA)	(NA)	44.4	(NA)	(NA)	45.7	(NA)	(NA)
Influenza, age 18 and over [2].............	41.7	43.3	37.1	45.3	48.4	50.2	49.4	46.9

NA Not available. [1] HPV up-to-date measure assesses completion of the HPV vaccine series. Beginning 2016, includes those with ≥3 doses, and those with 2 doses when the first HPV vaccine dose was initiated before age 15 and there was at least 5 months minus 4 days between the 1st and 2nd dose. [2] For the season beginning in the year shown. Excludes U.S. territories. [3] Self-reported risk. [4] Tetanus vaccination is determined by asking respondents if they received a tetanus shot in the past 10 years. During 2013-2017, tetanus vaccination was determined by asking respondents if they had received a tetanus shot since 2005.

Source: U.S. Centers for Disease Control and Prevention, Vaccines & Immunizations, "TeenVaxView," "AdultVaxView," and "FluVaxView," <www.cdc.gov/vaccines/vaxview/index.html>, accessed January 2024.

Table 201. Organ Transplants: 1990 to 2023

[As of year end. Based on Organ Procurement and Transplantation Network data; data are from work supported in part by Health Resources and Services Administration contract HHSH250-2019-00001C]

Organ [1]	1990	1995	2000	2005	2010	2015	2020	2021	2022	2023
NUMBER OF TRANSPLANTS										
Total [2]	**15,001**	**19,396**	**23,274**	**28,119**	**28,668**	**30,974**	**39,036**	**41,356**	**42,889**	**46,630**
Kidney	9,416	11,084	13,631	16,485	16,900	17,878	22,817	24,670	25,500	27,332
Liver	2,690	3,934	5,001	6,444	6,291	7,127	8,906	9,236	9,528	10,660
Pancreas	69	109	439	542	349	228	135	143	108	102
Kidney-pancreas	459	919	915	903	828	719	827	820	810	812
Heart	2,107	2,363	2,199	2,125	2,332	2,804	3,658	3,818	4,111	4,545
Lung	203	872	959	1,406	1,769	2,057	2,539	2,524	2,692	3,026
Heart-lung	52	69	48	35	42	15	58	45	51	54
Intestine	5	46	82	178	151	141	91	96	82	95
Multiple organ [3]	71	127	222	521	559	892	1,200	1,256	1,339	1,417
PATIENTS ON WAITLIST [4]										
Total	**20,481**	**41,203**	**74,078**	**90,526**	**110,375**	**122,071**	**108,605**	**106,937**	**105,209**	**103,353**
Kidney	16,833	29,603	47,758	64,833	87,757	100,916	91,760	90,483	89,594	88,823
Liver	1,232	5,649	16,832	17,356	16,146	14,832	12,049	11,611	10,841	9,998
Pancreas	464	283	1,025	1,686	1,418	1,033	883	848	873	841
Kidney-pancreas	(NA)	1,210	2,466	2,502	2,224	1,956	1,689	1,806	1,940	1,988
Heart	1,780	3,460	4,148	2,994	3,189	4,170	3,526	3,502	3,344	3,327
Lung	302	1,887	3,636	3,162	1,805	1,529	983	1,051	973	919
Heart-lung	217	205	207	141	70	49	42	41	36	35
Intestine	(NA)	83	150	205	265	262	219	200	212	207

NA Not available. [1] Kidney-pancreas and heart-lung transplants are each counted as one procedure. All other multi-organ transplants are included in the multi-organ row. [2] Total may include other types of organ transplants not shown separately. [3] Excludes kidney-pancreas and heart-lung transplants. [4] Number of patients on the National Transplant Waiting List, at year end, December 31; data as of January 26, 2024. A patient who is waiting at more than one center, or for multiple organs, would be counted as only one candidate. Totals may be less than the sums of organs due to patients included in multiple categories.

Source: U.S. Department of Health and Human Services, Health Resources and Services Administration, Organ Procurement and Transplantation Network (OPTN), <optn.transplant.hrsa.gov/data/>, accessed May 2024; and unpublished data, based on OPTN data as of January 26, 2024.

Table 202. Disability Rates Among Adults Age 18 and Over by Type of Disability and Selected Characteristics: 2022

[As percent of total population. Data are from the Behavioral Risk Factor Surveillance System, a state-based telephone survey of noninstitutionalized adults age 18 and over in the 50 states, DC, Puerto Rico, Guam, and the U.S. Virgin Islands. Disability is defined as having serious difficulty with cognition (concentration, memory, making decisions), hearing, mobility, vision, self-care activities (such as dressing or bathing), and independent living activities (such as doing errands alone). Estimates are age-adjusted to the 2000 U.S. standard population, except for estimates stratified by age. Survey respondents could report more than one type of disability]

Characteristic	No disability	Any disability	Cognitive disability	Hearing disability	Mobility disability	Vision disability	Self-care disability	Independent living disability
Total	**71.3**	**28.7**	**13.9**	**6.2**	**12.2**	**5.5**	**3.6**	**7.7**
Male	73.3	26.7	12.3	7.7	10.6	5.0	3.4	5.9
Female	69.4	30.6	15.5	4.9	13.7	6.0	3.7	9.4
Age 18 to 44	76.4	23.6	16.2	2.9	4.7	4.0	1.9	6.5
Age 45 to 64	70.9	29.1	11.7	6.2	16.8	6.7	5.2	8.0
Age 65 and over	56.1	43.9	10.4	16.4	27.5	8.2	5.9	10.7
Non-Hispanic:								
White	72.6	27.4	13.7	6.2	10.9	4.0	3.0	7.4
Black	69.4	30.6	13.7	4.8	16.0	7.6	5.4	8.7
Asian	81.9	18.1	7.3	3.7	6.5	3.9	1.7	3.4
Native Hawaiian or Other Pacific Islander	68.4	31.6	17.1	7.7	13.2	8.6	4.8	7.3
American Indian or Alaska Native	61.3	38.7	21.6	10.2	18.4	7.5	6.5	12.3
Other/multiracial	61.3	38.7	21.2	8.1	17.2	7.9	5.9	12.8
Hispanic	66.6	33.4	15.9	6.5	15.3	9.4	4.6	9.0
Veteran	66.1	33.9	16.4	12.2	14.2	4.8	5.2	8.1
Non-veteran	71.9	28.1	13.7	5.5	12.1	5.6	3.4	7.7
Have health care coverage	91.5	88.9	89.0	88.5	89.1	86.8	(NA)	(NA)
No health care coverage	8.5	11.1	11.0	11.5	10.9	13.2	(NA)	(NA)
Self-reported fair or poor health	8.8	37.7	42.5	34.7	55.7	42.3	(NA)	(NA)

NA Not available.

Source: U.S. Centers for Disease Control and Prevention, Disability and Health Data System, "Comparison Report," <www.cdc.gov/ncbddd/disabilityandhealth/dhds/index.html>, accessed July 2024.

Table 203. Population With a Disability by Age Group and State: 2022

[In thousands (44,147 represents 44,147,000). Disability data limited to civilian noninstitutionalized population. Covers children under age 5 with a hearing or vision difficulty. Covers children age 5 to 14 with a hearing, vision, cognitive, ambulatory, or self-care difficulty. For people age 15 and older, also covers independent living difficulty. American Community Survey (ACS) disability data should not be compared with disability estimates from more detailed measures of disability from sources such as the National Health Interview Survey and the Survey of Income and Program Participation. Based on a sample and subject to sampling variability; see Appendix III]

State	Total	Under age 18	18 to 64 years	65 years and over	State	Total	Under age 18	18 to 64 years	65 years and over
U.S...................	44,147	3,475	22,007	18,664	Missouri...........	914	68	470	375
Alabama..............	841	59	440	342	Montana..........	160	11	79	70
Alaska...............	93	7	52	34	Nebraska.........	244	19	121	104
Arizona..............	985	80	470	435	Nevada...........	449	37	229	184
Arkansas.............	540	45	286	210	New Hampshire...	182	11	92	79
California............	4,527	339	2,164	2,025	New Jersey.......	1,031	87	472	472
Colorado.............	664	48	354	263	New Mexico.......	356	26	176	154
Connecticut..........	446	37	217	192	New York.........	2,508	186	1,197	1,125
Delaware.............	139	10	66	63	North Carolina....	1,438	106	723	608
District of Columbia...	72	5	40	27	North Dakota.....	93	8	47	38
Florida...............	3,016	211	1,332	1,473	Ohio..............	1,668	137	849	682
Georgia..............	1,429	131	739	558	Oklahoma.........	686	61	363	262
Hawaii...............	186	11	80	95	Oregon...........	662	45	337	280
Idaho................	270	24	141	106	Pennsylvania.....	1,863	150	929	784
Illinois...............	1,522	103	749	670	Rhode Island.....	142	10	74	59
Indiana..............	959	82	502	374	South Carolina....	751	55	378	318
Iowa.................	403	34	200	169	South Dakota.....	117	11	56	50
Kansas...............	395	33	198	165	Tennessee........	1,042	75	534	433
Kentucky.............	801	66	433	302	Texas.............	3,665	366	1,895	1,405
Louisiana.............	753	59	395	300	Utah..............	355	38	197	121
Maine................	216	15	108	93	Vermont..........	96	6	51	40
Maryland.............	724	63	352	310	Virginia...........	1,070	87	538	445
Massachusetts.......	869	65	434	369	Washington.......	1,037	70	532	435
Michigan.............	1,425	107	733	585	West Virginia......	338	20	167	150
Minnesota...........	659	50	331	277	Wisconsin........	726	52	365	309
Mississippi...........	534	44	279	210	Wyoming.........	84	6	41	37

Source: U.S. Census Bureau, 2022 American Community Survey, S1810, "Disability Characteristics," <data.census.gov>, accessed November 2023.

Table 204. Diabetes, Chronic Kidney Disease, and End-Stage Renal Disease by Selected Characteristics: 2017 to 2021

[38.1 represents 38,100,000. Data on diabetes and chronic kidney disease are for adults aged 18 and over and are based on the National Health and Nutrition Examination Survey (NHANES), which involves interviews, physical examinations, and laboratory testing. Data on end-stage renal disease (ESRD) cover persons of all ages with ESRD in treatment; estimates are based on validated submissions of the ESRD Medical Evidence Report (form CMS 2728)]

Characteristic	Number of adults with diabetes (millions), 2021 [1]			Percent of adults with diabetes, 2017-2020 period [1]			Percent of adults with chronic kidney disease, 2017-2020 [2]	Rate of persons with end-stage renal disease, 2021 [4,5]
	Total	Diag-nosed	Undiag-nosed	Total	Diag-nosed	Undiag-nosed		
Total...................	38.1	29.4	8.7	14.7	11.3	3.4	[3] 14.0	2,219.3
By age:								
18 to 44 years.........	5.8	3.5	2.2	4.8	3.0	1.9	6.3	923.5
45 to 64 years.........	15.8	12.0	3.8	18.9	14.5	4.5	12.3	3,990.6
65 years and over.....	16.5	13.8	2.7	29.2	24.4	4.7	33.7	([6])
By sex:								
Men....................	19.8	16.1	3.7	15.4	12.6	2.8	11.8	2,769.4
Women.................	18.3	13.3	5.0	14.1	10.2	3.9	14.4	1,750.5
By race/ethnicity:								
White, non-Hispanic...	22.1	17.8	4.3	13.6	11.0	2.7	11.7	1,441.9
Black, non-Hispanic...	5.4	4.0	1.4	17.4	12.7	4.7	19.5	6,195.6
Asian, non-Hispanic...	2.7	1.8	0.9	16.7	11.3	5.4	13.7	2,376.3
Hispanic...............	6.9	5.0	1.9	15.5	11.1	4.4	13.7	3,244.7

[1] Estimated numbers for 2021 were derived from percentages for January 2017–March 2020 period applied to July 1, 2021 U.S. resident population estimates from the U.S. Census Bureau. Data in percent cover January 2017-March 2020 period. Diagnosed diabetes is based on self-report. Undiagnosed diabetes is based on fasting plasma glucose and A1C levels among people self-reporting no diabetes. [2] Percent of adults with chronic kidney disease (CKD) stages 1 to 4 using data from the 2017-March 2020 NHANES based on the 2021 CKD Epidemiology Collaboration GFR estimating equation. Excludes CKD stage 5 (kidney failure). Estimates are based on a single measure of albuminuria or serum creatinine, and do not account for persistence of albuminuria or levels of creatinine that are higher than normal as indicated by the Kidney Disease Improving Global Outcomes recommendations. Estimates might be overestimated. [3] Data are rounded. [4] Prevalence of end-stage renal disease is per one million population. Data are adjusted to the age, sex, race, and Hispanic ethnicity distribution of the 2015 U.S. population; rates omit patients with unknown sex and other/unknown race/ethnicity. [5] Total persons with end-stage renal disease in 2021 is 808,536. [6] Prevalence for population age 65-74 is 6,873.55 per million; prevalence for persons age 75 and over is 7,744.25 per million.

Source: U.S. Centers for Disease Control and Prevention, "National Diabetes Statistics Report," <www.cdc.gov/diabetes/php/data-research/index.html>; "Chronic Kidney Disease in the United States, 2023," <www.cdc.gov/kidney-disease/php/data-research/index.html>; and U.S. Renal Data System, "2023 USRDS Annual Data Report," <usrds-adr.niddk.nih.gov/2023>; accessed July 2024.

Table 205. Circulatory Diseases Among Persons Age 18 and Over by Selected Characteristics: 2022 and 2023

[In percent. Based on the National Health Interview Survey (NHIS), a household survey of a sample of the civilian noninstitutionalized population. In separate questions, respondents were asked if they had ever been told by a doctor or other health professional that they had: high cholesterol, hypertension (or high blood pressure), coronary heart disease, angina (or angina pectoris), or heart attack (or myocardial infarction). A person may be represented in more than one column. Unknowns were not included in the denominators when calculating percentages. For information on data source, methods, and definitions, see *Technical Notes for Interactive Summary Health Statistics — 2019-2023: National Health Interview Survey,* <wwwn.cdc.gov/NHISDataQueryTool/SHS_adult/SHS_Tech_Notes.pdf>]

Characteristic	2022					2023				
	High choles- terol [1]	Hyper- tension [2]	Coronary heart disease	Angina	Heart attack	High choles- terol [1]	Hyper- tension [2]	Coronary heart disease	Angina	Heart attack
Total....................	**22.0**	**27.2**	**4.9**	**1.6**	**3.0**	**23.3**	**27.5**	**4.8**	**1.6**	**3.0**
SEX										
Male................................	22.7	27.9	6.4	1.9	4.1	23.8	28.3	6.0	1.8	3.8
Female.............................	21.4	26.5	3.6	1.4	1.8	22.8	26.7	3.7	1.4	2.3
AGE										
18 to 44 years....................	5.7	7.2	0.5	0.4	0.4	6.5	7.4	0.5	0.4	0.5
45 to 64 years....................	27.5	34.0	4.1	1.5	3.1	30.5	35.1	4.2	1.8	3.1
65 to 74 years....................	47.4	54.6	12.3	4.3	7.0	47.8	54.3	11.4	3.2	6.9
75 years and over.................	49.1	64.4	19.7	4.9	9.9	47.2	62.7	19.3	4.5	9.9
RACE/ETHNICITY										
Single race: [3]										
American Indian or Alaska Native...........................	17.8	19.1	4.6	(B)	(B)	16.8	25.1	2.6	2.1	2.5
Asian.............................	21.1	21.1	3.8	1.4	1.8	23.7	22.3	2.7	0.8	1.3
Black or African American.......	18.1	34.4	4.2	1.1	2.5	19.7	34.8	3.7	1.2	2.3
Native Hawaiian or Other Pacific Islander..........	14.7	14.5	(B)	–	(B)	(B)	25.7	(B)	–	(B)
White.............................	23.6	27.4	5.4	1.8	3.3	24.7	27.7	5.4	1.8	3.5
Hispanic or Latino [4]...........	16.6	19.7	3.0	1.2	1.6	17.7	19.9	3.0	1.3	1.4
Not Hispanic or Latino...........	23.2	28.7	5.3	1.7	3.2	24.4	29.1	5.2	1.7	3.4
DISABILITY										
With disability [5]................	40.6	51.7	15.8	6.3	9.6	40.9	52.3	14.7	5.7	9.6
Without disability.................	20.2	24.7	3.8	1.2	2.3	21.5	24.9	3.8	1.2	2.4

– Represents zero. B Estimate does not meet NCHS standards of reliability. [1] Among respondents who had been told they had high cholesterol, respondents classified as having high cholesterol were told they had high cholesterol or were taking prescription medication to help lower their cholesterol, within the past 12 months. [2] Among respondents who had ever been told on two or more different physician visits that they had high blood pressure, respondents classified as having diagnosed hypertension were told they had hypertension or were taking prescription medication for high blood pressure, within the past 12 months. [3] Persons who indicated only a single race group, regardless of Hispanic or Latino origin. [4] Persons of Hispanic or Latino origin may be of any race or combination of races. [5] Represents adults who responded "a lot of difficulty" or "cannot do at all" to questions regarding at least one of six functional areas: seeing (even if wearing glasses), hearing (even if wearing hearing aids), mobility (walking or climbing stairs), communication (understanding or being understood by others), cognition (remembering or concentrating), and self-care (such as washing all over or dressing).

Source: U.S. National Center for Health Statistics, National Health Interview Survey, "Interactive Summary Health Statistics for Adults," <www.cdc.gov/nchs/nhis/SHS.htm>, accessed July 2024.

Table 206. Yoga, Meditation, and Chiropractor Use Among Children and Adults: 2017

[In percent. Covers use within the past 12 months. Data are from the National Health Interview Survey of the civilian noninstitutional population. Data are age-adjusted using the projected 2000 U.S. population as the standard population and age groups 4-11 and 12-17 for children, and age groups 18-44, 45-64, and 65 and over for adults. Data shown by age are not age-adjusted]

Characteristic	Children			Characteristic	Adults		
	Yoga	Medi- tation	Chiro- practor		Yoga	Medi- tation	Chiro- practor
Total......................	**8.4**	**5.4**	**3.4**	Total.....................	**14.3**	**14.2**	**10.3**
				Men........................	8.6	11.8	9.4
Boys........................	5.6	4.9	3.0	Women.....................	19.8	16.3	11.1
Girls........................	11.3	6.0	3.7	Age 18 to 44...............	17.9	13.4	9.9
Age 4 to 11.................	8.7	4.7	2.1	Age 45 to 64...............	12.2	15.9	11.4
Age 12 to 17...............	8.0	6.5	5.1	Age 65 and over...........	6.7	13.4	9.5
White, non-Hispanic.......	10.5	5.9	5.1	White, non-Hispanic.......	17.1	15.2	12.7
Black, non-Hispanic.......	4.6	4.7	1.0	Black, non-Hispanic.......	9.3	13.5	5.5
Hispanic....................	5.9	4.7	1.4	Hispanic....................	8.0	10.9	6.6

Source: U.S. National Center for Health Statistics, *Use of Yoga, Meditation, and Chiropractors Among U.S. Children Aged 4–17 Years,* NCHS Data Brief No. 324, November 2018; and *Use of Yoga, Meditation, and Chiropractors Among U.S. Adults Aged 18 and Over,* NCHS Data Brief No. 325, November 2018. See also <www.cdc.gov/nchs/nhis/nhis_db.htm>.

Table 207. Selected Indicators of Health Status and Access to Health Care Among Adults: 2019 to 2023

[In percent. Covers experiences in the past 12 months, for adults age 18 and over. The National Health Interview Survey (NHIS) surveys a sample of the civilian noninstitutionalized population living in households and group quarters (e.g. homeless shelters, group homes) in the 50 states and DC. Unknowns were not included in the denominators when calculating percentages. The NHIS questionnaire was redesigned in 2019. For more information, see <www.cdc.gov/nchs/nhis/2019_quest_redesign.htm>. See also Appendix III]

Indicator	2019	2020 [9]	2021 [9]	2022	2023 (P)
HEALTH STATUS					
Having a disability [1]	9.0	8.8	8.8	9.3	9.4
Missing 6 or more workdays due to illness, injury, or disability	11.2	11.9	15.6	18.2	15.3
Asthma episode	3.4	3.5	3.3	3.7	3.8
Hypertension (high blood pressure) diagnosis	27.0	26.6	26.9	27.2	27.6
Chronic pain, regularly	20.5	21.8	20.9	(NA)	24.5
Feelings of worry, nervousness, or anxiety, regularly [2]	11.1	11.2	11.3	12.7	12.5
Feelings of depression, regularly [2]	4.7	4.4	4.5	5.1	5.0
HEALTH CARE SERVICES USED					
Doctor visit	84.9	83.4	82.3	83.4	84.6
Hospital emergency department visit	21.8	19.0	18.0	19.9	20.6
Counseling with a mental health professional	9.5	10.1	11.1	12.6	13.3
Blood pressure check	88.1	(NA)	84.0	(NA)	87.0
Dental exam or cleaning	65.3	63.0	(NA)	63.3	65.5
Receipt of influenza vaccination	46.8	47.9	48.7	47.2	48.0
HEALTH CARE ACCESS					
Did not get needed medical care due to cost	8.3	6.6	6.1	6.3	6.4
Did not get needed mental health care due to cost	4.4	4.3	4.2	5.0	5.4
Did not take medication as prescribed to save money [3]	9.6	8.3	6.8	6.8	7.8
HEALTH INSURANCE [4]					
No health insurance at time of interview [5]	14.5	13.9	12.6	12.4	10.9
Covered by private health insurance at time of interview [6]	67.5	67.7	69.2	67.5	68.1
Covered by public health insurance at time of interview [7]	20.4	20.7	20.4	22.6	23.0
Covered by an exchange-based health plan at time of interview [8]	4.8	4.7	5.3	5.4	5.5
HEALTH BEHAVIORS					
Current cigarette smoking	14.0	12.5	11.5	11.6	10.9
Current electronic cigarette (e-cigarette) use	4.5	3.7	4.5	6.0	6.6

NA Not available. P Preliminary. [1] Represents adults who responded "a lot of difficulty" or "cannot do at all" regarding at least one of six functional areas: seeing (even if wearing glasses), hearing (even if wearing hearing aids), mobility (walking or climbing stairs), communication (understanding or being understood by others), cognition (remembering or concentrating), and self-care (such as bathing or dressing). [2] Adults responded having these feelings a) daily and describing the level of these feelings as "somewhere in between a little and a lot" or "a lot," or b) weekly and describing the level of these feelings as "a lot." [3] Skipping doses of medication, taking less medicine, or delaying filling a prescription, to save money. [4] For persons age 18-64 only. A small number of people with both public and private plans are included in both categories. [5] No health insurance includes only Indian Health Service or only a private plan that covers one type of service such as dental or vision care. [6] Includes any comprehensive private insurance plan obtained through an employer, or purchased through local or community programs, the Health Insurance Marketplace, or a state-based exchange. Excludes plans that cover only one type of service such as dental or vision care. [7] Includes Medicaid, Children's Health Insurance Program (CHIP), state-sponsored or other government-sponsored health plan, Medicare, and military plans. [8] Covered by a private health insurance plan purchased through the Health Insurance Marketplace or state-based exchanges established as part of the Affordable Care Act of 2010. [9] Due to the coronavirus disease (COVID-19) pandemic, NHIS data collection switched from in-person interviews to a telephone-only mode on March 19, 2020. Personal visits resumed in September 2020 but interviews were first attempted by telephone. In May 2021, NHIS resumed regular survey procedures. See *Technical Notes for Early Release of Selected Estimates Based on Data from the National Health Interview Survey,* <www.cdc.gov/nchs/data/nhis/earlyrelease/earlyrelease202405_tech.pdf>.

Source: U.S. National Center for Health Statistics, National Health Interview Survey, *Early Release of Selected Estimates Based on Data from the 2023 National Health Interview Survey,* May 2024, <www.cdc.gov/nchs/nhis/releases.htm>; and "Interactive Summary Health Statistics for Adults," <www.cdc.gov/nchs/nhis/SHS.htm>, accessed July 2024.

Table 208. Nonfatal Injury and Poisoning Episodes by Cause, Sex, and Age: 2021

[Data are from the National Electronic Injury Surveillance System–All Injury Program, which collects data on nonfatal injuries and poisonings treated in participating hospital emergency departments]

Cause of injury	Total		Male	Female	Under age 1	Age 1 to 14	Age 15 to 24	Age 25 to 64	Age 65 and over
	Number [1]	Percent							
Total [2]	23,455,654	100.0	12,941,093	10,512,110	171,410	3,144,220	3,496,466	12,248,476	4,387,291
UNINTENTIONAL									
Fall	6,981,390	29.8	3,180,796	3,800,280	92,571	1,120,703	479,128	2,397,501	2,890,680
Struck by or against [3]	2,373,706	10.1	1,431,070	942,516	18,061	583,254	475,604	1,055,864	240,923
Motor vehicle occupant	1,876,520	8.0	910,225	966,195	3,011	87,552	469,944	1,149,061	166,277
Poisoning	1,734,576	7.4	1,148,652	585,636	3,438	43,505	223,014	1,335,165	128,234
Overexertion	1,612,781	6.9	826,631	786,134	3,502	193,835	309,379	928,402	177,663
Cut/pierce/stab	1,540,617	6.6	981,682	558,873	3,539	197,640	303,685	890,646	145,056
Bite or sting excl. dog bites [4]	611,729	2.6	303,274	308,454	4,800	130,867	68,926	324,330	82,806
Foreign object [5]	483,703	2.1	278,060	205,459	7,643	172,856	52,753	193,701	56,750
Dog bite	312,876	1.3	156,387	156,488	1,447	80,282	49,699	155,579	25,869
Fire/burn/smoke inhalation	273,138	1.2	144,990	128,142	6,365	52,358	43,476	145,682	25,211
VIOLENCE RELATED									
Assault (all)	1,392,061	5.9	842,751	549,195	5,285	76,079	304,416	958,828	45,663
Legal intervention	74,269	0.3	64,159	10,109	(NA)	(S)	14,761	58,044	(S)
Self-harm	491,943	2.1	187,350	303,701	(X)	74,016	179,565	224,583	13,758

NA Not available. S Estimate is unstable due to small sample size or coefficient of variation is greater than 30 percent. X Not applicable. [1] Total number may include injuries with unknown sex and age of victim. [2] Total includes injuries from various other causes not shown separately and for injuries with unknown age of victim. [3] Injury from being struck, hit, or crushed by, or hitting against, another person, animal, object or force; excludes vehicles and machinery. [4] Include bites and stings from another person or any insect, animal, or plant; excludes dogs. [5] Injury resulting from the entrance of a foreign object into or through the eye or other natural body opening; excludes objects blocking an airway or causing suffocation.

Source: U.S. Centers for Disease Control and Prevention, National Center for Injury Prevention and Control, "WISQARS (Web-based Injury Statistics Query and Reporting System)," <www.cdc.gov/injury/wisqars/index.html>, accessed January 2024.

Table 209. Injuries Associated With Selected Consumer Products: 2022

[Estimates are based on a national probability sample of hospitals in the U.S. and its territories. Patient information is collected from each participating hospital for every emergency visit involving an injury associated with consumer products. From this sample, the total number of product-related injuries treated in hospital emergency rooms nationwide is estimated. A person's injury may be represented in up to three product groups. Products are associated with injuries, not necessarily the cause of injuries]

Product type	Number	Rate [1]	Product type	Number	Rate [1]
Items for infants/children:			**Household & other items:**		
All nursery equipment	94,358	28.3	Cans, other containers	257,292	77.3
Baby strollers	11,054	(NA)	Cleaning equipment,		
High chairs	14,554	(NA)	noncaustic detergents	45,172	13.6
Toys	180,953	54.4	Glass bottles, jars	31,187	9.4
Sports & recreational equipment:			Soaps, detergents	47,891	14.4
All terrain vehicles, mopeds,			Fireworks, flares	10,292	3.1
minibikes, etc	242,347	72.8	**Tools & garden equipment:**		
Baseball, softball	136,874	41.1	Chain saws	25,853	7.8
Basketball	313,924	94.3	Hand garden tools	42,765	12.8
Bicycles & accessories	405,411	121.8	Lawn and garden equipment	85,199	25.6
Exercise, exercise equipment	445,642	133.9	Lawn mowers	70,712	21.2
Football	265,747	79.8	Power home workshop saws	68,000	20.4
Lacrosse, rugby, misc. ball games	66,882	20.1	Workshop manual tools	113,561	34.1
Playground equipment	208,257	62.6	**Household appliances:**		
Skateboards, scooters, hoverboards	230,506	69.3	Cooking ranges, ovens, etc	47,384	14.2
Skating (excluding in-line)	76,505	23.0	Heating stoves, space heaters	21,564	6.5
Snowskiing, snowboarding	66,633	20.0	Refrigerators, freezers	50,804	15.3
Soccer	179,284	53.9	Small kitchen appliances	51,144	15.4
Swimming, pools, equipment	187,465	56.3	**Home furnishings & fixtures:**		
Trampolines	123,014	37.0	Bathroom structures & fixtures	535,200	160.8
Home entertainment equipment:			Beds, mattresses, pillows	906,231	272.3
Sound recording equipment	56,780	17.1	Carpets, rugs	202,542	60.9
Television sets & stands	34,456	10.4	Chairs, sofas, sofa beds	597,128	179.4
Personal use items:			Desks, cabinets, shelves, racks	256,815	77.2
Clothing	374,646	112.6	Glass doors, windows, panels	102,975	30.9
Grooming devices	43,548	13.1	Ladders, stools	226,362	68.0
Razors, shavers, razor blades	42,543	12.8	Tables [2]	300,097	90.2

NA Not available. [1] Estimated rates are calculated using the Census Bureau's July 1, 2022 U.S. resident population estimates. [2] Excludes baby-changing tables, billiard or pool tables, and television tables or stands.

Source: Consumer Product Safety Commission, National Electronic Injury Surveillance System (NEISS), *2022 NEISS Data Highlights;* and "NEISS Estimates Query Builder," <www.cpsc.gov/cgibin/NEISSQuery/home.aspx>, accessed January 2024. See also <www.cpsc.gov/Research--Statistics/NEISS-Injury-Data/>.

Table 210. Food Security Status of Households and Households with Children: 2000 to 2022

[106,043 represents 106,043,000. Food security status of households is measured through a series of questions about experiences and behaviors that characterize households having difficulty meeting basic food needs. All questions refer to the previous 12 months and remind respondents to report only conditions resulting from inadequate financial resources; survey excludes voluntary fasting and dieting to lose weight. *Food-secure* households report 0-2 food-insecure conditions. *Food-insecure* households report 3 or more conditions. Low and very low food security differ in the extent and character of the adjustments the household makes to its eating patterns and food intake. Households classified as having *low food security* report multiple indications of food access problems, but typically report few, if any, indications of reduced food intake. Households classified as having *very low food security* report multiple indications of reduced food intake and disrupted eating patterns due to inadequate resources for food. Prior to 2006, households with very low food security were described as "food insecure with hunger." The omission of homeless persons biases the statistics downward. Data are from the Food Security Supplement to the Current Population Survey (CPS); for details about the CPS, see text, Section 1 and Appendix III]

Household food security status	Number (1,000)					Percent distribution				
	2000	2010	2020	2021	2022	2000	2010	2020	2021	2022
Households, total [1]	**106,043**	**118,756**	**130,459**	**132,043**	**132,730**	**100.0**	**100.0**	**100.0**	**100.0**	**100.0**
Food-secure	94,942	101,527	116,705	118,533	115,750	89.5	85.5	89.5	89.8	87.2
Food-insecure	11,101	17,229	13,754	13,510	16,980	10.5	14.5	10.5	10.2	12.8
With low food security	7,786	10,872	8,613	8,428	10,187	7.3	9.1	6.6	6.4	7.7
With very low food security	3,315	6,357	5,141	5,082	6,793	3.1	5.4	3.9	3.8	5.1
Adult members [2]	**201,922**	**229,129**	**251,953**	**253,092**	**255,297**	**100.0**	**100.0**	**100.0**	**100.0**	**100.0**
In food-secure households	181,586	196,505	225,388	228,510	224,541	89.9	85.8	89.5	90.3	88.0
In food-insecure households	20,336	32,624	26,565	24,582	30,756	10.1	14.2	10.5	9.7	12.0
With low food security	14,763	21,357	17,174	16,007	19,034	7.3	9.3	6.8	6.3	7.4
With very low food security	5,573	11,267	9,391	8,575	11,722	2.8	4.9	3.7	3.4	4.6
Child members [2, 3]	**71,763**	**74,905**	**72,837**	**72,416**	**72,595**	**100.0**	**100.0**	**100.0**	**100.0**	**100.0**
In food-secure households	58,867	58,697	61,115	63,154	59,201	82.0	78.4	83.9	87.2	81.5
In food-insecure households	12,896	16,208	11,722	9,262	13,394	18.0	21.6	16.1	12.8	18.5
In households with food insecure children	7,018	8,458	6,142	4,959	7,263	9.8	11.3	8.4	6.8	10.0
With very low food security among children	562	976	584	521	783	0.8	1.3	0.8	0.7	1.1

[1] Total excludes households for which food security status is unknown. [2] The food security survey measures food security status at the household level. Not all individuals and children residing in food-insecure households were directly affected by the households' food insecurity. Similarly, not all individuals and children in households classified as having very low food security were subject to the reductions in food intake and disruptions in eating patterns that characterize this condition. Young children, in particular, are often protected from effects of the households' food insecurity. [3] Percents among only households with children.

Source: U.S. Department of Agriculture, Economic Research Service, *Household Food Security in the United States in 2022,* Economic Research Report Number 325, October 2023. See also <www.ers.usda.gov/topics/food-nutrition-assistance/food-security-in-the-us.aspx>.

Table 211. Mammography Use Among Women Age 40 and Over by Patient Characteristics: 2000 to 2019

[Percent of women having a mammogram within the past 2 years. Covers civilian noninstitutional population. Based on National Health Interview Survey; see Appendix III]

Characteristic	2000	2003	2005	2008	2010	2013	2015	2018	2019 [7]
Women age 40 and over, total [1].............	**70.4**	**69.7**	**66.8**	**67.6**	**67.1**	**66.8**	**65.3**	**66.7**	**69.1**
AGE									
40 to 49 years....................................	64.3	64.4	63.5	61.5	62.3	59.6	58.3	61.5	60.2
50 to 64 years....................................	78.7	76.2	71.8	74.2	72.6	71.4	71.3	71.8	75.7
65 years and over...............................	67.9	67.7	63.8	65.5	64.4	66.9	63.3	64.8	68.1
65 to 74 years..................................	74.0	74.6	72.5	72.6	71.9	75.3	72.2	75.0	78.1
75 years and over.............................	61.3	60.6	54.7	57.9	55.7	56.5	51.5	50.6	54.2
RACE AND ETHNICITY [2]									
White only..	71.4	70.1	67.4	67.9	67.4	66.8	65.3	67.3	69.2
Black only..	67.8	70.4	64.9	68.0	67.9	67.1	69.8	68.1	71.1
American Indian or Alaska Native only..........	47.4	63.1	72.8	62.7	71.2	62.6	51.5	65.3	61.3
Asian only..	53.5	57.6	54.6	66.1	62.4	66.6	59.7	57.8	63.7
Two or more races..............................	69.2	65.3	63.7	55.2	51.4	65.4	62.7	59.8	65.6
Hispanic or Latina [3]...........................	61.2	65.0	58.8	61.2	64.2	61.4	60.9	62.7	69.4
Not Hispanic or Latina..........................	71.1	70.1	67.5	68.3	67.4	67.5	65.9	67.3	69.1
EDUCATION									
No high school diploma nor GED [4]..............	57.7	58.1	52.8	53.8	53.0	53.6	51.7	54.0	59.8
High school diploma or GED.....................	69.7	67.8	64.9	65.2	64.4	63.4	60.1	63.2	65.7
Some college or more...........................	76.2	75.1	72.7	73.4	72.1	71.6	70.5	70.9	72.7
POVERTY STATUS [5]									
Below 100% poverty.............................	54.8	55.4	48.5	51.4	51.4	49.9	52.2	51.7	59.0
100% to 199% poverty...........................	58.1	60.8	55.3	55.8	53.8	56.7	54.9	56.8	61.3
200% to 399% poverty...........................	68.8	69.9	67.2	64.4	66.2	66.0	63.4	65.3	66.7
400% and over poverty..........................	81.5	77.7	76.6	79.0	78.1	77.2	74.7	75.4	77.3
HEALTH INSURANCE STATUS [6]									
Insured..	76.0	75.1	72.5	73.4	74.1	72.1	69.7	71.1	73.3
Private insurance................................	77.1	76.3	74.5	74.2	75.6	73.4	72.2	73.2	74.4
Medicaid..	61.7	63.5	55.6	64.2	64.4	63.5	57.7	58.0	66.6
Uninsured...	40.7	41.5	38.1	39.7	36.0	37.3	30.0	37.5	40.6

[1] Includes other races not shown separately and unknown education, poverty, and health insurance status. [2] Race groups include persons of Hispanic and non-Hispanic origin. [3] Persons of Hispanic origin may be of any race. [4] GED is General Educational Development high school equivalency diploma. [5] Poverty as percent of Federal poverty level based on family income and family size and composition using U.S. Census Bureau poverty thresholds. [6] Health insurance status at time of interview, only for women age 40 to 64. Health insurance categories are mutually exclusive. Persons who reported both Medicaid and private coverage are classified as having private coverage. Persons with only Indian Health Service coverage are considered to have no health insurance coverage. [7] In 2019, the NHIS questionnaire was redesigned and other changes were made to weighting and design methodology. Data have not been fully evaluated for comparability with earlier years.

Source: U.S. National Center for Health Statistics, "Health, United States—Data Finder," <www.cdc.gov/nchs/hus/index.htm>, accessed July 2024.

Table 212. Current Cigarette Smoking Among Adults: 2000 to 2019

[In percent. A current smoker is a person who has smoked at least 100 cigarettes and who now smokes every day or some days. Excludes unknown smoking status. Race groups White and Black include persons of Hispanic and non-Hispanic origin. For definition of age adjustment, see text, Section 2. Based on National Health Interview Survey; for details, see Appendix III]

Sex, age, and race	2000	2010	2015	2019 [4]	Sex, age, and race	2000	2010	2015	2019 [4]
Total smokers, age-adjusted [1]............	**23.1**	**19.3**	**15.3**	**14.2**	Black, total....................	26.2	24.3	20.6	17.2
Male.............................	25.2	21.2	16.8	15.5	18 to 24 years................	20.9	18.8	[3] 15.9	(B)
Female..........................	21.1	17.5	13.8	13.0	25 to 34 years................	23.2	25.7	26.0	21.5
					35 to 44 years................	30.7	22.6	17.9	23.6
White male.....................	25.4	21.4	16.8	15.6	45 to 64 years................	32.2	31.8	22.8	21.0
Black male.....................	25.7	23.3	20.3	17.7	65 years and over............	14.2	10.0	16.0	9.4
					Female, total....................	**20.9**	**17.3**	**13.6**	**12.7**
White female...................	22.0	18.3	14.8	14.5	18 to 24 years................	24.9	17.4	11.0	8.2
Black female...................	20.7	16.6	13.2	12.8	25 to 34 years................	22.3	20.6	15.0	14.4
					35 to 44 years................	26.2	19.0	16.5	14.7
					45 to 64 years................	21.7	19.1	16.1	16.2
Total smokers [2]............	**23.2**	**19.3**	**15.1**	**14.0**	65 years and over............	9.3	9.3	7.3	7.3
Male, total.......................	**25.6**	**21.5**	**16.7**	**15.3**	White, total....................	21.4	17.9	14.3	14.0
18 to 24 years................	28.1	22.8	15.0	7.8	18 to 24 years................	28.5	18.4	11.2	9.0
25 to 34 years................	28.9	26.1	21.3	19.1	25 to 34 years................	24.9	22.0	16.3	16.4
35 to 44 years................	30.2	22.5	18.3	18.5	35 to 44 years................	26.6	20.5	18.3	17.2
45 to 64 years................	26.4	23.2	17.9	17.9	45 to 64 years................	21.4	19.5	17.1	17.9
65 years and over............	10.2	9.7	9.7	9.4	65 years and over............	9.1	9.4	7.5	7.5
White, total....................	25.7	21.4	16.5	15.3	Black, total....................	20.8	17.0	13.1	12.9
18 to 24 years................	30.4	23.8	15.6	9.0	18 to 24 years................	14.2	14.2	[3] 8.6	(B)
25 to 34 years................	29.7	26.6	20.9	19.6	25 to 34 years................	15.5	19.3	14.9	14.0
35 to 44 years................	30.6	23.1	19.1	17.9	35 to 44 years................	30.2	17.2	15.4	15.5
45 to 64 years................	25.8	22.5	17.3	17.9	45 to 64 years................	25.6	19.8	14.5	14.5
65 years and over............	9.8	9.6	9.3	9.4	65 years and over............	10.2	9.4	9.7	9.6

B Estimates are considered unreliable. [1] Data are age-adjusted to the year 2000 standard population using five age groups: 18–24 years, 25–34 years, 35–44 years, 45–64 years, 65 years and over. Includes persons of unknown race and sex. [2] Crude, not age-adjusted. Includes persons of unknown race and sex. [3] Estimate has a relative standard error of 20%–30%. [4] In 2019, the NHIS questionnaire was redesigned and other changes were made to weighting and design methodology. Data for 2019 have not been fully evaluated for comparability with earlier years. For more information, see <www.cdc.gov/nchs/nhis/2019_quest_redesign.htm>.

Source: U.S. National Center for Health Statistics, "Health, United States—Data Finder," <www.cdc.gov/nchs/hus/index.htm>, accessed July 2024.

Table 213. Current Cigarette Smoking by Sex and State: 2015 to 2022

[In percent. Current cigarette smoking is defined as persons age 18 and older who reported having smoked 100 or more cigarettes during their lifetime and who currently smoke every day or some days. Based on the Behavioral Risk Factor Surveillance System (BRFSS), a telephone survey of health behaviors of the civilian, noninstitutionalized U.S. population, age 18 and over]

State	2015			2020			2022		
	Total	Male	Female	Total	Male	Female	Total	Male	Female
United States [1]......	**17.5**	**19.3**	**15.8**	**15.5**	**(NA)**	**(NA)**	**14.0**	**(NA)**	**(NA)**
Alabama...............	21.4	23.8	19.2	18.5	20.5	16.6	15.6	16.9	14.4
Alaska................	19.1	19.6	18.6	18.0	17.9	18.1	15.9	17.9	13.8
Arizona...............	14.0	16.2	12.0	13.1	15.9	10.4	12.7	14.2	11.2
Arkansas..............	24.9	27.8	22.1	20.5	22.2	18.8	18.7	21.6	16.0
California.............	11.7	15.2	8.3	8.9	11.1	6.7	9.7	12.6	7.0
Colorado..............	15.7	17.1	14.2	12.4	13.4	11.4	10.7	12.4	8.9
Connecticut...........	13.5	16.3	10.9	11.8	13.3	10.5	10.0	11.8	8.4
Delaware..............	17.4	20.9	14.2	15.1	18.0	12.6	12.9	14.4	11.6
District of Columbia. . .	16.0	15.8	16.1	11.3	11.6	11.2	10.6	12.5	9.0
Florida...............	15.8	17.4	14.3	14.7	17.6	12.0	11.3	13.0	9.7
Georgia...............	17.7	20.0	15.5	15.8	18.3	13.5	12.5	12.6	12.5
Hawaii................	14.1	17.3	10.8	11.6	12.1	11.1	10.0	11.6	8.3
Idaho.................	13.8	14.7	13.0	13.6	14.3	13.0	11.9	12.7	11.0
Illinois...............	15.1	17.6	12.8	12.7	14.0	11.5	12.4	14.4	10.5
Indiana...............	20.6	21.9	19.3	19.4	20.8	18.1	16.2	17.3	15.2
Iowa..................	18.1	19.5	16.7	15.8	17.1	14.5	14.7	16.6	12.9
Kansas................	17.7	19.3	16.1	16.6	18.2	15.1	14.5	15.7	13.3
Kentucky..............	26.0	26.4	25.5	21.4	22.3	20.5	17.4	19.4	15.5
Louisiana.............	21.9	24.7	19.3	18.3	20.5	16.3	16.7	18.9	14.7
Maine.................	19.5	21.0	18.1	16.5	17.3	15.8	15.0	16.0	14.1
Maryland..............	15.1	16.9	13.4	10.9	13.2	8.8	9.6	11.2	8.2
Massachusetts.........	14.0	16.4	11.9	11.1	12.8	9.5	10.4	11.6	9.2
Michigan..............	20.7	22.4	19.1	18.4	19.7	17.2	15.2	16.0	14.5
Minnesota............	16.2	17.6	14.8	13.8	15.0	12.8	13.0	13.6	12.4
Mississippi...........	22.6	27.0	18.4	20.1	23.4	17.1	17.4	20.6	14.4
Missouri..............	22.3	23.6	21.0	17.8	18.6	16.9	16.8	17.3	16.2
Montana..............	18.9	19.3	18.5	16.4	16.6	16.2	15.2	14.8	15.6
Nebraska..............	17.1	18.4	15.8	13.9	15.6	12.4	13.0	13.8	12.2
Nevada................	17.6	20.5	14.6	14.2	16.6	11.9	14.8	15.0	14.6
New Hampshire........	15.9	16.5	15.4	13.9	15.1	12.7	11.2	11.4	11.0
New Jersey............	13.5	15.7	11.5	10.8	13.2	8.6	10.4	11.9	9.0
New Mexico...........	17.5	19.1	16.0	16.1	18.9	13.4	15.0	17.0	12.9
New York..............	15.2	17.7	12.9	12.0	14.2	10.0	11.2	12.9	9.7
North Carolina........	19.0	21.9	16.3	16.5	18.8	14.4	14.5	15.4	13.6
North Dakota..........	18.7	21.9	15.4	17.4	18.9	15.8	15.1	14.8	15.5
Ohio..................	21.6	23.1	20.2	19.3	19.8	18.8	17.1	17.7	16.5
Oklahoma.............	22.2	24.0	20.4	19.1	20.6	17.6	15.6	16.6	14.6
Oregon...............	17.1	18.0	16.3	13.4	14.6	12.1	12.4	13.5	11.3
Pennsylvania..........	18.1	19.8	16.6	15.8	16.7	14.8	14.9	15.9	14.0
Rhode Island..........	15.5	18.5	12.8	13.5	14.1	12.8	11.8	12.6	11.0
South Carolina........	19.7	23.4	16.2	18.1	20.2	16.2	15.4	17.3	13.6
South Dakota..........	20.1	19.6	20.6	17.8	17.6	17.9	14.0	14.5	13.5
Tennessee.............	21.9	22.8	21.1	19.5	20.5	18.5	18.5	20.5	16.7
Texas.................	15.2	18.2	12.4	13.2	17.2	9.3	11.8	13.0	10.7
Utah..................	9.1	11.2	7.0	8.2	9.4	7.0	6.7	8.4	4.9
Vermont..............	16.0	18.0	14.0	13.3	14.8	11.8	13.0	13.6	12.5
Virginia...............	16.5	18.8	14.4	13.6	16.1	11.3	12.1	14.2	10.1
Washington...........	15.0	16.6	13.4	11.5	12.3	10.7	10.0	10.9	9.1
West Virginia..........	25.7	25.8	25.7	22.6	22.7	22.4	21.0	20.9	21.1
Wisconsin.............	17.3	19.8	14.9	15.5	17.2	13.8	14.2	15.4	13.1
Wyoming..............	19.1	20.6	17.5	18.5	19.4	17.5	15.5	16.5	14.4
Guam.................	27.4	32.5	22.3	20.0	24.7	15.2	19.8	24.4	14.9
Puerto Rico...........	10.8	14.6	7.4	9.9	14.2	6.2	9.4	12.6	6.6

NA Not available. [1] Represents median value among the states and DC. For definition of median, see Guide to Tabular Presentation.

Source: U.S. Centers for Disease Control and Prevention, Behavioral Risk Factors Data Portal, "Behavioral Risk Factor Surveillance System: Table of Tobacco Use (updated November 17, 2023)," <chronicdata.cdc.gov/browse?category=Behavioral+Risk+Factors>, accessed February 2024.

Table 214. Substance Abuse Treatment Facilities and Clients: 2022

[Facility data for 2022; client data for March 31, 2022. Based on the 2022 National Substance Use and Mental Health Services Survey (N-SUMHSS). Covers 14,854 facilities (85.6 percent of 17,353 eligible facilities) that provide substance use treatment services. The N-SUMHSS is a census of all known facilities, public and private, that provide substance use and mental health treatment services across the U.S and associated jurisdictions. Survey excludes: (1) Department of Defense (DoD) military treatment facilities, (2) individual private practitioners or small group practices not licensed as a mental health clinic or center, and (3) jails or prisons. See source for more information on methodology]

Facility characteristic	Facilities	Clients	Facility characteristic	Facilities	Clients
Total...............................	**14,854**	**1,623,647**	TYPE OF CARE OFFERED/RECEIVED [2]		
FACILITY OPERATIONAL STRUCTURE			Outpatient...........................	12,308	1,509,934
Private for-profit.................................	6,311	699,345	Regular...........................	11,434	748,996
Private non-profit...............................	7,170	770,253	Intensive...........................	6,508	106,315
State government...........................	297	26,132	Detoxification...........................	1,700	10,570
Local, county, or community government.....	598	64,343	Day treatment/partial hospitalization........	2,092	26,228
Tribal government...........................	210	11,254	Medication-assisted treatment [3]............	6,108	618,012
Federal government...........................	252	51,316			
Dept. of Veterans Affairs....................	184	45,050	Residential (non-hospital)......................	3,587	81,239
Dept. of Defense...........................	40	5,381	Detoxification...........................	1,306	7,645
Indian Health Service.........................	17	452	Short-term treatment (30 days or fewer)....	2,346	32,723
Other, unspecified federal agencies.........	8	433	Long-term treatment (more than 30 days)...	2,700	40,871
TREATMENT FOR SUBSTANCE ABUSE [1]					
Alcohol and other substance use..............	9,037	529,909	Hospital inpatient...........................	1,111	32,474
Substance (except alcohol) use only.........	9,047	820,334	Detoxification...........................	707	11,987
Alcohol use only...........................	7,757	237,406	Treatment...........................	760	20,487
Substance use and mental health disorders..	9,588	810,173			

[1] Number of facilities may sum to more than the total because a facility could treat more than one type of substance abuse problem. 10,943 facilities responded to the questions on treatment by substance use problem and for diagnosed co-occurring mental and substance use disorders. Client counts also may not sum to total due to lack of response data. [2] Facilities may provide more than one type of care. [3] Methadone/buprenorphine maintenance or naltrexone treatment. Methadone is available only at facilities that have opioid treatment programs certified by the Substance Abuse and Mental Health Services Administration.

Source: U.S. Substance Abuse and Mental Health Services Administration, *National Substance Use and Mental Health Services Survey (N-SUMHSS), 2022: Annual Detailed Tables*, September 2023.

Table 215. Drug Use by Type of Drug and Age Group: 2022

[In percent. Data are from the National Survey on Drug Use and Health (NSDUH). Based on a representative sample of the U.S. noninstitutionalized population age 12 and older, including persons living in households, in noninstitutional group quarters such as dormitories and homeless shelters, and civilians on military bases. The final 2022 sample consists of 71,369 completed interviews, including 41,121 completed in person, and 30,248 completed online. Data are subject to sampling variability]

Age and type of drug	Lifetime (ever) use	Past year use	Past month use	Age and type of drug	Lifetime (ever) use	Past year use	Past month use
AGE 12 YEARS AND OLDER				AGE 18 TO 25 YEARS			
Any illicit drug [1]....................	**50.7**	**24.9**	**16.5**	Any illicit drug [1]....................	55.0	40.9	27.2
Marijuana...........................	46.9	22.0	15.0	Marijuana...........................	51.9	38.2	25.9
Cocaine...........................	15.0	1.9	0.7	Cocaine...........................	9.0	3.7	1.2
Heroin...........................	2.3	0.4	0.3	Heroin...........................	0.6	0.2	−
Hallucinogens...........................	17.3	3.0	0.8	Hallucinogens...........................	16.9	7.7	1.6
Inhalants...........................	9.7	0.8	0.3	Inhalants...........................	8.8	1.9	0.6
Methamphetamine...........................	5.9	1.0	0.6	Methamphetamine...........................	2.0	0.5	0.2
Opioids [2]...........................	(NA)	3.2	1.0	Opioids [2]...........................	(NA)	3.2	0.6
Opioids and illegal fentanyl [3].....	(NA)	3.2	1.1	Opioids and illegal fentanyl [3]...	(NA)	3.3	0.7
Tobacco products [4]...................	57.2	22.5	18.1	Tobacco products [4]...................	41.6	24.8	15.4
Cigarettes...........................	51.8	17.8	14.6	Cigarettes...........................	35.0	18.2	10.7
Smokeless tobacco..............	13.8	2.9	2.2	Smokeless tobacco..............	10.6	4.2	2.4
Cigars...........................	30.0	6.8	3.7	Cigars...........................	23.0	11.3	5.3
Nicotine vaping...........................	23.9	12.4	8.3	Nicotine vaping...........................	49.6	33.4	24.0
Alcohol...........................	78.5	62.8	48.7	Alcohol...........................	74.0	67.9	50.2
"Binge" alcohol use [5]..............	(NA)	(NA)	21.7	"Binge" alcohol use [5]...........	(NA)	(NA)	29.5
AGE 12 TO 17 YEARS				AGE 26 YEARS AND OLDER			
Any illicit drug [1]....................	20.9	14.3	7.3	Any illicit drug [1]....................	53.6	23.7	15.9
Marijuana...........................	13.5	11.5	6.4	Marijuana...........................	50.0	20.6	14.3
Cocaine...........................	0.3	0.2	−	Cocaine...........................	17.6	1.8	0.7
Heroin...........................	−	−	(B)	Heroin...........................	2.9	0.4	0.3
Hallucinogens...........................	2.1	1.4	0.4	Hallucinogens...........................	19.2	2.5	0.7
Inhalants...........................	7.5	2.2	0.7	Inhalants...........................	10.0	0.5	0.2
Methamphetamine...........................	0.1	0.1	−	Methamphetamine...........................	7.2	1.1	0.7
Opioids [2]...........................	(NA)	1.6	0.5	Opioids [2]...........................	(NA)	3.3	1.2
Opioids and illegal fentanyl [3].....	(NA)	1.6	0.5	Opioids and illegal fentanyl [3]...	(NA)	3.4	1.2
Tobacco products [4]...................	8.7	4.8	2.0	Tobacco products [4]...................	65.2	24.2	20.4
Cigarettes...........................	6.6	3.4	1.2	Cigarettes...........................	59.7	19.4	16.7
Smokeless tobacco..............	1.5	0.7	0.2	Smokeless tobacco..............	15.7	3.0	2.4
Cigars...........................	2.8	1.6	0.7	Cigars...........................	34.2	6.7	3.8
Nicotine vaping...........................	18.9	13.8	6.9	Nicotine vaping...........................	20.5	9.0	6.0
Alcohol...........................	22.3	16.7	6.8	Alcohol...........................	85.7	67.3	53.4
"Binge" alcohol use [5]..............	(NA)	(NA)	3.2	"Binge" alcohol use [5]...........	(NA)	(NA)	22.6

− Represents or rounds to zero. NA Not available. B Low precision; data are deemed unreliable. [1] Illicit drugs include marijuana, cocaine, heroin, hallucinogens, inhalants, methamphetamine, and the misuse of prescription psychotherapeutic drugs. [2] Includes use of heroin and/or misuse of prescription pain relievers. Excludes illegally made fentanyl. [3] Includes illegally made fentanyl. [4] Includes pipe tobacco, not shown separately. Tobacco product use in the past year excludes past year pipe tobacco use, but includes past month pipe tobacco use. [5] Binge alcohol use is defined as drinking five or more drinks (for males) or four or more drinks (for females) on the same occasion (i.e., at the same time or within a couple of hours of each other) on at least 1 day in the past 30 days.

Source: U.S. Substance Abuse and Mental Health Services Adminstration, *Results from the 2022 National Survey on Drug Use and Health: Detailed Tables*, November 2023. See also <www.samhsa.gov/data/data-we-collect/nsduh-national-survey-drug-use-and-health>.

Table 216. Drug, Alcohol, and Cigarette Estimated Users by State and Region: 2021 to 2022

[In units as indicated (43,582 represents 43,582,000). Data in this table are annual averages for a 2-year period. Data are based on the National Survey on Drug Use and Health (NSDUH). Covers persons age 12 years and over who indicated current use of a substance (use within the 30 days prior to the interview). Based on a representative sample of the U.S. population in the 50 states and the District of Columbia, including persons living in households, noninstitutional group quarters such as dormitories and homeless shelters, and civilians living on military bases. The 2021 and 2022 NSDUH used a multimode data collection; the surveys collected data through in-person interviews and via the internet from 141,219 respondents. Estimates based on multimode data collection since 2021 are not comparable with estimates from prior years. For methodology information, see "2021-2022 National Survey on Drug Use and Health: Guide to State Tables and Summary of Small Area Estimation Methodology" at <www.samhsa.gov/data/nsduh/state-reports-NSDUH-2022>]

State and region	Estimated current users (1,000)					Current users as percent of population				
	Illicit drug use [1]	Mari-juana	Any illicit drug other than mari-juana [2]	Binge alcohol use [3]	Cigarette use	Illicit drug use [1]	Mari-juana	Any illicit drug other than mari-juana [2]	Binge alcohol use [3]	Cigarette use
United States............	**43,582**	**39,632**	**9,334**	**60,889**	**42,912**	**15.5**	**14.1**	**3.3**	**21.7**	**15.3**
Northeast..................	8,346	7,654	1,690	11,080	6,699	17.0	15.6	3.5	22.6	13.7
Midwest...................	9,302	8,608	1,938	13,595	10,257	16.0	14.8	3.3	23.4	17.7
South.....................	13,686	12,175	3,200	22,048	17,948	12.7	11.3	3.0	20.5	16.7
West......................	12,247	11,195	2,506	14,166	8,008	18.4	16.8	3.8	21.3	12.0
Alabama...................	469	370	136	799	826	11.0	8.7	3.2	18.7	19.4
Alaska....................	134	129	19	124	109	22.8	21.9	3.2	21.1	18.6
Arizona...................	1,241	1,166	196	1,376	917	20.0	18.8	3.2	22.2	14.8
Arkansas..................	319	284	90	486	520	12.6	11.2	3.5	19.2	20.5
California................	5,524	5,024	1,222	6,977	3,332	16.7	15.2	3.7	21.1	10.1
Colorado..................	1,031	956	216	1,218	653	20.8	19.3	4.4	24.6	13.2
Connecticut...............	511	464	96	683	390	16.4	14.9	3.1	21.9	12.5
Delaware..................	135	122	29	183	135	15.6	14.1	3.4	21.2	15.7
District of Columbia......	126	120	27	186	73	22.1	20.9	4.8	32.5	12.7
Florida...................	2,512	2,296	438	3,829	2,622	13.3	12.1	2.3	20.2	13.8
Georgia...................	1,187	1,094	285	1,732	1,600	13.1	12.1	3.1	19.1	17.7
Hawaii....................	173	142	38	246	136	14.6	12.0	3.2	20.7	11.5
Idaho.....................	202	184	56	337	227	12.6	11.5	3.5	21.0	14.2
Illinois..................	1,845	1,724	354	2,483	1,640	17.2	16.1	3.3	23.2	15.3
Indiana...................	758	704	181	1,180	1,123	13.3	12.3	3.2	20.7	19.7
Iowa......................	358	314	96	636	461	13.3	11.7	3.6	23.7	17.2
Kansas....................	328	296	78	568	428	13.5	12.2	3.2	23.4	17.6
Kentucky..................	469	394	136	722	861	12.4	10.4	3.6	19.1	22.8
Louisiana.................	575	500	149	932	825	15.1	13.1	3.9	24.4	21.6
Maine.....................	265	253	39	236	214	22.0	21.0	3.3	19.5	17.7
Maryland..................	824	733	193	1,053	722	15.9	14.1	3.7	20.3	13.9
Massachusetts.............	1,259	1,195	227	1,403	737	20.8	19.7	3.7	23.1	12.2
Michigan..................	1,660	1,589	253	1,870	1,406	19.4	18.5	2.9	21.8	16.4
Minnesota.................	799	743	166	1,156	729	16.6	15.4	3.5	24.0	15.1
Mississippi...............	308	273	71	460	498	12.6	11.1	2.9	18.8	20.3
Missouri..................	888	835	183	1,085	1,118	17.1	16.1	3.5	20.9	21.5
Montana...................	186	175	34	243	150	19.7	18.5	3.6	25.6	15.8
Nebraska..................	192	166	51	409	242	11.8	10.2	3.1	25.2	14.9
Nevada....................	597	544	114	627	447	22.3	20.3	4.3	23.4	16.7
New Hampshire.............	197	175	48	286	165	16.2	14.4	4.0	23.5	13.6
New Jersey................	1,110	1,044	242	1,781	850	14.1	13.3	3.1	22.6	10.8
New Mexico................	420	381	70	409	319	23.5	21.3	3.9	22.9	17.8
New York..................	2,913	2,714	572	3,998	2,397	17.2	16.1	3.4	23.7	14.2
North Carolina............	1,071	930	269	1,715	1,565	12.0	10.4	3.0	19.2	17.5
North Dakota..............	77	72	21	170	115	12.1	11.3	3.3	26.7	18.1
Ohio......................	1,614	1,476	368	2,423	2,099	16.2	14.8	3.7	24.4	21.1
Oklahoma..................	617	594	109	667	693	18.7	18.0	3.3	20.2	21.0
Oregon....................	880	800	161	818	527	24.0	21.8	4.4	22.3	14.4
Pennsylvania..............	1,754	1,500	407	2,298	1,691	15.8	13.5	3.7	20.7	15.3
Rhode Island..............	188	171	39	244	158	19.9	18.1	4.1	25.7	16.7
South Carolina............	538	478	140	935	798	12.1	10.8	3.2	21.1	18.0
South Dakota..............	87	80	26	171	133	11.8	10.8	3.5	23.0	17.9
Tennessee.................	704	601	223	1,189	1,193	11.9	10.2	3.8	20.1	20.2
Texas.....................	2,520	2,213	610	5,358	3,627	10.3	9.0	2.5	21.9	14.8
Utah......................	311	259	105	374	258	11.3	9.4	3.8	13.7	9.4
Vermont...................	149	137	20	152	98	26.2	24.2	3.5	26.8	17.2
Virginia..................	1,071	957	234	1,551	991	14.8	13.2	3.2	21.4	13.7
Washington................	1,493	1,385	259	1,309	844	22.7	21.1	3.9	19.9	12.8
West Virginia.............	242	217	61	253	397	15.9	14.2	4.0	16.6	26.0
Wisconsin.................	695	610	162	1,444	764	13.8	12.1	3.2	28.7	15.2
Wyoming...................	55	49	18	107	91	11.2	10.1	3.6	21.8	18.6

[1] "Illicit drug use" includes the misuse of prescription psychotherapeutics or the use of marijuana (including vaping), cocaine (including crack), heroin, hallucinogens, inhalants, or methamphetamine. Misuse of prescription psychotherapeutics is defined as use in any way not directed by a doctor, including use without a prescription of one's own; use in greater amounts, more often, or longer than told; or use in any other way not directed by a doctor. Prescription psychotherapeutics do not include over-the-counter drugs. [2] "Illicit drug use other than marijuana" includes the misuse of prescription psychotherapeutics or the use of cocaine (including crack), heroin, hallucinogens, inhalants, or methamphetamine. Excludes persons who use marijuana only, but includes persons who use marijuana in addition to other illicit drugs. [3] "Binge alcohol use" is defined as drinking 5/more drinks (for males) or 4/more drinks (for females) on the same occasion (i.e., at the same time or within a couple of hours of each other) on at least 1 day in the past 30 days.

Source: U.S. Substance Abuse and Mental Health Services Administration, National Survey on Drug Use and Health, "State Data Tables and Reports From the 2021-2022 NSDUH," <www.samhsa.gov/data/data-we-collect/nsduh-national-survey-drug-use-and-health>, accessed February 2024.

Table 217. Prescription Psychotherapeutic Drug Use and Misuse by Drug Type and User Characteristics: 2022

[In percent. Data are from the National Survey on Drug Use and Health, and cover persons age 12 and older. Misuse of prescription drugs is defined as use in any way not directed by a physician, including use without a prescription of one's own; use in greater amounts, more often, or longer than instructed to take a drug; or use in any other way not directed by a physician. Excludes over-the-counter drugs. See also headnote, Table 215]

User characteristics	Any use in past year				Misuse in past year			
	Pain relievers	Stimu-lants	Tranquil-izers	Seda-tives	Pain relievers	Stimu-lants	Tranquil-izers	Seda-tives
Total.............................	**26.2**	**7.0**	**11.6**	**5.5**	**3.0**	**1.5**	**1.5**	**0.3**
SEX								
Male...........................	24.2	6.8	8.6	4.3	3.1	1.8	1.3	0.3
Female.........................	28.1	7.1	14.5	6.5	2.9	1.3	1.6	0.4
AGE								
12 to 17 years....................	12.4	7.2	2.8	2.0	1.6	0.9	0.4	0.1
18 years and over.................	27.6	7.0	12.5	5.8	3.1	1.6	1.6	0.4
18 to 25 years...................	18.7	10.9	7.5	3.1	3.2	3.7	2.2	0.3
26 years and over................	29.0	6.3	13.3	6.2	3.1	1.3	1.5	0.4
RACE AND ETHNICITY								
Not Hispanic......................	27.1	7.3	12.5	5.8	2.9	1.5	1.5	0.3
American Indian or Alaska Native........	33.7	5.6	6.0	5.1	5.1	0.9	1.1	0.4
Asian...........................	16.8	2.6	4.9	2.4	1.4	0.7	0.7	0.0
Black or African American..............	28.4	4.8	7.0	4.3	3.8	0.9	1.0	0.1
Native Hawaiian or Other Pacific Islander......................	24.9	4.2	(B)	(B)	1.8	(B)	(B)	(B)
White............................	27.7	8.2	14.4	6.5	2.8	1.7	1.7	0.4
Two or more races.................	31.8	10.1	14.2	5.8	4.4	2.3	2.1	0.5
Hispanic or Latino.................	22.0	5.6	7.7	3.9	3.3	1.4	1.3	0.4
REGION								
Northeast........................	22.0	6.2	11.1	4.6	2.6	1.5	1.5	0.2
Midwest.........................	27.5	8.0	12.6	5.2	2.8	1.7	1.3	0.4
South...........................	27.8	7.2	12.3	5.9	3.2	1.4	1.6	0.4
West............................	25.6	6.3	10.0	5.5	3.2	1.5	1.4	0.3
METRO STATUS								
Large metro [1]...................	24.9	6.8	10.5	5.4	3.0	1.6	1.4	0.3
Small metro [2]...................	26.7	7.5	12.8	5.6	3.1	1.5	1.6	0.3
Nonmetro........................	30.3	6.4	13.6	5.5	2.9	1.1	1.6	0.5

B Figure does not meet standards of reliability or precision. [1] Over 1 million population. [2] Less than 1 million population.

Source: U.S. Substance Abuse and Mental Health Services Administration, *Results From the 2022 National Survey on Drug Use and Health: Detailed Tables*, November 2023. See also <www.samhsa.gov/data/data-we-collect/nsduh-national-survey-drug-use-and-health>.

Table 218. Prescription Drug Use in Past 30 Days by Sex, Race/Ethnicity, and Age: 1999 to 2018

[Data shown as percent of population using prescription drugs in past 30 days. Based on the National Health and Nutrition Examination Survey, covering a sample of the civilian noninstitutionalized population]

Sex, race/ethnicity, and age	Use of 1 or more prescription drugs			Use of 3 or more prescription drugs			Use of 5 or more prescription drugs		
	1999-2002	2007-2010	2015–2018	1999-2002	2007-2010	2015–2018	1999-2002	2007-2010	2015–2018
Both sexes, age adjusted [1,2]..........	**45.2**	**47.5**	**45.7**	**17.8**	**20.8**	**21.3**	**7.5**	**10.1**	**11.2**
Male..........................	39.8	42.8	41.7	14.8	19.1	20.0	6.1	9.2	10.8
Female........................	50.3	52.0	49.5	20.4	22.5	22.6	8.7	11.0	11.6
White alone [3]...................	48.7	52.8	49.7	18.9	22.4	22.8	7.8	10.7	12.0
Male..........................	43.0	47.5	45.5	15.9	20.6	21.4	6.3	9.8	11.7
Female........................	54.3	57.9	53.9	21.8	24.3	24.3	9.2	11.6	12.2
Black or African American alone [3]...........	40.1	42.3	43.3	16.5	20.7	21.1	7.7	10.8	12.4
Male..........................	35.4	36.7	39.8	14.5	17.7	19.1	6.4	9.1	10.9
Female........................	43.8	46.8	46.1	18.1	22.9	22.7	8.7	12.0	13.5
Asian alone [3]..................	(NA)	(NA)	35.4	(NA)	(NA)	14.7	(NA)	(NA)	6.6
Male..........................	(NA)	(NA)	32.9	(NA)	(NA)	15.4	(NA)	(NA)	6.9
Female........................	(NA)	(NA)	37.6	(NA)	(NA)	14.1	(NA)	(NA)	6.3
Hispanic or Latino [4]............	(NA)	35.2	37.7	(NA)	15.7	17.9	(NA)	8.4	9.0
Male..........................	(NA)	31.7	33.1	(NA)	14.0	17.0	(NA)	7.3	8.3
Female........................	(NA)	38.8	42.3	(NA)	17.4	18.7	(NA)	9.5	9.7
Both sexes, crude..............	**45.0**	**48.5**	**48.6**	**17.6**	**21.7**	**24.0**	**7.4**	**10.6**	**12.8**
Male..........................	38.6	43.0	43.8	13.9	19.0	21.7	5.6	9.1	11.8
Under 18 years.................	25.7	24.5	23.3	4.3	4.4	3.9	(B)	0.8	1.2
18 to 44 years.................	27.1	29.5	27.0	6.7	7.1	8.2	1.7	2.1	3.4
45 to 64 years.................	55.6	61.3	62.9	23.6	30.4	33.8	9.5	14.4	17.4
65 years and over...............	80.1	88.8	87.9	46.3	66.8	65.5	24.7	39.5	42.0
Female........................	51.1	53.8	53.1	21.1	24.2	26.1	9.1	12.1	13.7
Under 18 years.................	21.7	23.5	19.6	3.9	3.1	2.9	[5] 0.8	[5] 0.7	0.7
18 to 44 years.................	44.6	47.6	44.2	10.2	12.2	11.9	2.8	4.0	5.0
45 to 64 years.................	72.0	70.8	71.0	37.5	38.1	38.9	16.8	19.1	18.7
65 years and over...............	88.1	90.4	88.9	55.9	66.4	67.1	28.9	39.8	41.9

NA Not available. B Estimate has a relative standard error greater than 30%. [1] Estimates are age-adjusted to the year 2000 standard population using four age groups: under 18 years, 18-44 years, 45-64 years, and 65 years and over. [2] Includes persons of other race/ethnicities not shown separately. [3] Not Hispanic or Latino. [4] Persons of Hispanic or Latino origin may be of any race. [5] Estimate has a relative standard error (RSE) of 20% to 30% and is considered unreliable.

Source: U.S. National Center for Health Statistics, "Health, United States—Data Finder," <www.cdc.gov/nchs/hus/index.htm>, accessed July 2024.

Table 219. Height of Population Age 20 and Over by Sex, Age, and Race/Ethnicity: 2015 to 2018

[In inches. Data cover the 2015 to 2018 period. Based on National Health and Nutrition Examination Survey (NHANES), a sample of the civilian noninstitutional population. Data are collected through household interviews, and through health examinations conducted in mobile examination centers by health technicians following a standard protocol. Standing height is measured with a wall-mounted stadiometer and recorded automatically. Measurements are done in the metric system; conversions are made to U.S. customary units. Survey oversampled persons age 80 and over, Hispanic persons, black persons, Asian persons, and persons with low income; see source for more information]

Age and race/ethnicity	Males, height in inches						Females, height in inches					
	Mean	Percentile					Mean	Percentile				
		10th	25th	50th	75th	90th		10th	25th	50th	75th	90th
Total: [1]												
20 years and over......	69.0	65.3	67.0	69.1	71.0	72.7	63.5	60.0	61.6	63.5	65.3	67.0
20 to 29 years..........	69.2	65.8	67.3	69.3	71.0	72.8	64.0	60.5	62.2	64.1	65.8	67.2
30 to 39 years..........	69.4	65.6	67.4	69.6	71.4	73.3	64.1	60.7	62.2	64.0	66.0	67.5
40 to 49 years..........	69.4	65.4	67.5	69.5	71.4	72.8	63.9	60.2	62.1	64.0	65.6	67.5
50 to 59 years..........	69.0	65.0	67.0	69.0	71.1	72.8	63.5	60.2	61.6	63.4	65.3	67.0
60 to 69 years..........	68.7	64.9	66.7	68.6	70.4	72.3	63.3	60.1	61.4	63.3	65.1	66.5
70 to 79 years..........	68.1	64.8	66.4	68.1	69.9	71.8	62.3	59.3	60.6	62.2	64.0	65.3
80 years and over......	67.1	63.4	65.3	67.1	69.0	70.7	61.3	57.9	59.6	61.3	62.9	64.4
White, non to Hispanic:												
20 years and over......	69.5	66.0	67.6	69.6	71.4	73.0	63.9	60.5	62.1	63.9	65.7	67.3
20 to 39 years..........	70.1	66.7	68.2	70.1	71.7	73.5	64.7	61.6	63.3	64.7	66.4	67.6
40 to 59 years..........	69.8	66.4	67.9	69.9	71.5	73.0	64.3	60.8	62.6	64.2	65.9	67.4
60 years and over......	68.7	65.4	66.8	68.6	70.3	72.2	62.9	59.8	61.0	62.9	64.7	66.2
Black, non to Hispanic:												
20 years and over......	69.3	65.8	67.4	69.3	71.1	72.8	64.0	60.6	62.3	64.0	65.6	67.1
20 to 39 years..........	69.4	66.0	67.6	69.2	71.3	72.9	64.3	60.9	62.6	64.4	66.1	67.5
40 to 59 years..........	69.6	66.2	67.7	69.7	71.2	72.9	64.1	60.7	62.6	64.1	65.6	67.2
60 years and over......	68.4	64.9	66.6	68.5	70.1	71.8	63.2	60.2	61.6	63.0	64.7	66.1
Hispanic:												
20 years and over......	67.1	63.3	65.1	67.0	69.1	70.8	62.0	58.8	60.2	61.8	63.7	65.4
20 to 39 years..........	67.4	63.7	65.6	67.4	69.3	70.9	62.5	59.3	60.7	62.3	64.3	66.0
40 to 59 years..........	67.0	63.0	64.9	66.9	69.1	70.7	61.9	58.6	60.1	61.8	63.5	65.2
60 years and over......	66.2	62.8	64.5	66.2	67.8	69.6	60.9	58.1	59.4	60.8	62.3	63.5

[1] Total includes persons of other race/ethnicities not shown separately.

Source: U.S. Centers for Disease Control and Prevention, National Health and Nutrition Examination Survey, *Anthropometric Reference Data For Children and Adults: United States, 2015-2018*, Series 3, No. 46, January 2021. See also <www.cdc.gov/nchs/nhanes/index.htm>.

Table 220. Weight of Population Age 20 and Over by Sex, Age, and Race/Ethnicity: 2015 to 2018

[In pounds. Data are for 2015 to 2018 period. Based on National Health and Nutrition Examination Survey (NHANES). Weight is measured using a digital floor scale and values are recorded automatically. Measurements are done in the metric system; conversions are made to U.S. customary units. For persons age 20 and over. Excludes pregnant females. See headnote, Table 219]

Age and race/ethnicity	Males, weight in pounds						Females, weight in pounds					
	Mean	Percentile					Mean	Percentile				
		10th	25th	50th	75th	90th		10th	25th	50th	75th	90th
Total: [1]												
20 years and over.......	199.8	146.9	166.1	192.6	224.6	263.2	170.8	118.9	137.1	161.2	195.3	232.1
20 to 29 years..........	188.6	135.6	152.8	179.1	216.5	255.7	165.0	113.3	128.7	153.2	190.5	236.0
30 to 39 years..........	208.1	154.9	171.1	197.7	230.6	273.0	174.9	118.6	139.9	161.5	201.6	244.2
40 to 49 years..........	206.9	154.5	176.2	199.5	229.2	263.6	178.1	125.7	142.4	165.7	203.0	249.5
50 to 59 years..........	202.5	151.1	169.1	197.5	224.8	273.2	173.5	121.6	140.5	164.4	198.7	231.0
60 to 69 years..........	201.2	149.1	168.7	197.2	226.8	257.3	172.4	124.5	141.7	165.5	196.9	228.5
70 to 79 years..........	193.4	147.8	167.0	188.0	216.1	239.7	164.6	119.8	138.4	161.4	184.9	209.6
80 years and over.......	177.5	136.7	152.6	175.6	198.4	218.6	149.7	110.2	126.3	146.2	168.2	190.2
White, non-Hispanic:												
20 years and over.......	203.4	150.3	169.9	197.6	227.6	264.7	170.9	120.3	138.3	161.3	194.7	231.2
20 to 39 years..........	201.9	142.8	163.2	191.2	230.2	270.4	170.0	116.8	133.0	157.5	194.9	238.1
40 to 59 years..........	207.5	155.3	175.7	200.7	230.9	269.6	176.1	127.1	144.9	165.3	201.6	235.1
60 years and over.......	200.3	152.1	170.9	195.6	226.2	253.1	166.6	120.3	137.5	161.0	188.1	220.6
Black, non-Hispanic:												
20 years and over.......	200.1	140.7	162.7	190.6	229.0	272.7	188.5	128.9	150.6	180.0	215.3	262.0
20 to 39 years..........	195.3	138.5	154.2	182.8	216.0	274.3	183.9	120.8	142.8	175.4	212.1	255.8
40 to 59 years..........	211.8	155.4	176.2	204.1	241.1	277.9	199.4	134.1	157.7	193.5	229.1	278.1
60 years and over.......	189.6	137.7	157.7	184.6	214.4	246.3	179.2	133.1	151.2	170.1	199.0	234.2
Hispanic:												
20 years and over.......	193.7	147.0	165.0	187.6	216.2	245.4	168.0	121.1	138.4	159.1	189.1	224.3
20 to 39 years..........	193.9	143.4	164.1	188.1	218.7	244.4	169.0	118.4	134.2	156.4	192.4	233.7
40 to 59 years..........	196.9	151.2	169.0	189.7	218.3	251.6	169.3	126.0	141.9	161.6	191.0	220.7
60 years and over.......	185.3	145.0	159.1	180.5	206.7	233.6	162.9	124.3	138.4	158.0	182.4	207.1

[1] Total includes persons of other race/ethnicities not shown separately.

Source: U.S. Centers for Disease Control and Prevention, National Health and Nutrition Examination Survey, *Anthropometric Reference Data For Children and Adults: United States, 2015-2018*, Series 3, No. 46, January 2021. See also <www.cdc.gov/nchs/nhanes/index.htm>.

Table 221. Body Mass Index of Population Age 20 and Over by Sex, Age, and Race/Ethnicity: 2015 to 2018

[Data are for 2015 to 2018 period. Body Mass Index (BMI) is a measure that adjusts body weight for height, and is calculated as weight in kilograms divided by the square of height in meters. For both men and women, BMI weight categories are: below 18.5 underweight, 18.5-24.9 normal, 25.0-29.9 overweight, and 30.0 and higher obese. Data are based on National Health and Nutrition Examination Survey (NHANES), a sample of the civilian noninstitutional population. Data are collected through household interviews and health examinations. Measurements are conducted by health technicians following a standard protocol and are recorded automatically. Excludes pregnant women. Survey oversampled persons age 80 and over, Hispanic persons, black persons, Asian persons, and persons with low income; see source for more information]

Age and race/ethnicity	Males, BMI Mean	Males Percentile 10th	15th	25th	50th	75th	85th	90th	Females, BMI Mean	Females Percentile 10th	15th	25th	50th	75th	85th	90th
Total: [1]																
20 years and over	29.4	22.4	23.3	25.0	28.5	32.8	35.3	37.1	29.8	21.2	22.1	23.9	28.4	33.9	37.5	40.3
20 to 29 years	27.6	20.0	21.0	22.6	26.5	31.6	34.4	36.8	28.3	19.6	20.4	21.9	26.2	32.9	37.4	39.6
30 to 39 years	30.3	23.0	23.8	25.4	28.9	33.7	36.4	38.3	29.9	21.2	22.0	23.6	28.3	34.2	38.2	41.1
40 to 49 years	30.1	23.5	24.7	26.2	29.1	32.8	35.5	38.1	30.7	22.0	22.8	24.4	28.6	34.8	39.3	43.1
50 to 59 years	29.8	22.6	24.0	25.2	29.1	32.8	35.5	37.4	30.3	21.5	22.5	24.3	29.1	34.2	37.7	41.5
60 to 69 years	29.9	23.2	23.9	25.8	28.9	33.3	35.3	37.1	30.3	22.2	23.2	24.9	29.2	34.7	37.2	39.5
70 to 79 years	29.2	22.9	24.1	25.9	28.2	32.8	34.5	35.6	29.8	22.0	23.3	25.3	28.8	33.3	35.7	37.9
80 years and over	27.6	22.3	22.9	24.3	27.2	30.2	32.3	34.0	28.0	20.8	22.2	23.8	27.5	30.8	33.5	35.5
White, non-Hispanic:																
20 years and over	29.5	22.4	23.3	25.1	28.6	32.9	35.3	37.1	29.4	21.2	22.0	23.6	27.9	33.5	37.1	39.7
20 to 39 years	28.8	21.2	22.4	23.7	27.3	32.7	36.0	37.9	28.5	19.9	21.0	22.2	26.2	33.0	37.3	39.8
40 to 59 years	29.9	22.8	24.0	25.6	29.2	32.7	35.3	37.1	30.0	21.8	22.4	24.0	28.4	33.9	38.1	42.2
60 years and over	29.8	23.2	24.1	26.0	28.7	33.3	35.1	36.4	29.6	21.8	22.9	24.6	28.4	33.5	36.1	38.4
Black, non-Hispanic:																
20 years and over	29.2	21.2	22.2	24.2	27.9	33.1	36.2	38.4	32.3	22.2	23.5	26.1	31.1	37.1	40.7	43.6
20 to 39 years	28.4	20.4	21.2	22.4	26.6	31.9	36.4	38.5	31.1	20.8	21.9	24.0	30.1	36.5	40.0	42.6
40 to 59 years	30.6	22.8	24.1	26.0	30.0	34.6	36.8	39.1	34.1	23.8	25.1	27.2	32.9	38.8	43.5	46.8
60 years and over	28.4	21.3	22.4	24.2	27.7	31.6	33.8	36.0	31.6	23.2	24.6	26.5	30.2	35.4	38.5	40.4
Asian, non-Hispanic:																
20 years and over	26.1	21.5	22.2	23.3	25.5	28.4	29.7	31.2	25.1	19.8	20.4	21.3	24.2	27.9	30.1	31.8
20 to 39 years	26.7	21.4	22.4	23.3	25.8	28.9	31	32.1	24.8	19.4	20	20.8	23.9	27.7	30.1	31.9
40 to 59 years	26.2	21.9	22.5	23.7	25.8	28.5	29.4	30.9	25.1	20.1	20.7	21.8	24.2	28.1	29.7	31.3
60 years and over	24.8	21.0	21.8	22.7	24.2	26.9	28.3	29.1	25.6	20.0	20.8	22.0	24.9	27.9	30.2	31.9
Hispanic:																
20 years and over	30.2	23.8	25.0	26.5	29.2	33.0	35.7	37.1	30.7	22.1	23.4	25.4	29.4	34.5	38.0	40.6
20 to 39 years	30.0	22.4	24.0	26.1	29.1	33.3	35.5	37.0	30.4	21.1	22.0	24.4	28.5	34.1	38.9	41.4
40 to 59 years	30.7	25.1	25.9	27.1	29.5	33.0	36.2	37.9	31.0	23.1	24.0	26.2	29.9	34.7	37.4	40.3
60 years and over	29.6	23.9	24.7	26.1	29.0	32.1	34.3	35.8	30.9	23.8	25.0	26.6	29.8	34.7	37.4	39.4
Mexican American:																
20 years and over	30.5	23.7	25.0	26.6	29.9	33.4	35.9	37.2	31.6	23.0	24.2	26.4	30.1	35.9	39.1	41.6
20 to 39 years	30.4	22.3	24.3	26.4	29.9	33.7	35.9	37.2	31.5	21.6	23.2	25.6	29.7	36.0	39.8	42.7
40 to 59 years	31.0	25.1	25.9	27.2	30.1	33.2	36.2	38.6	31.8	23.6	24.8	26.8	30.4	36.0	38.9	41.2
60 years and over	29.6	23.9	24.8	26.3	29.2	31.9	34.3	35.7	31.7	24.5	25.3	27.0	30.0	35.2	38.4	40.5

[1] Total includes persons of other race/ethnicities not shown separately.

Source: U.S. Centers for Disease Control and Prevention, National Health and Nutrition Examination Survey, *Anthropometric Reference Data For Children and Adults: United States, 2015-2018*, Series 3, No. 46, January 2021. See also <www.cdc.gov/nchs/nhanes/index.htm>.

Table 222. Overweight and Obesity Prevalence Among Adults Age 20 and Over by Sex, Age, and Race/Ethnicity: 1988 to 2018

[Shown as percent of population age 20 and over. Weight status is determined by body mass index (BMI), which is calculated as weight in kilograms divided by the square of height in meters. Excludes pregnant women. Data are based on the National Health and Nutrition Examination Survey (NHANES). Measurements are conducted by health technicians following a standard protocol and are recorded automatically. Percents do not sum to 100 because data for persons with BMI under 18.5 are not shown, and percent of persons with obesity are included in the overweight or obese category. See headnote, Table 221]

Characteristic	Normal weight [1]			Overweight or obese [2]			Obese [3]		
	1988 to 1994	2001 to 2004	2015 to 2018	1988 to 1994	2001 to 2004	2015 to 2018	1988 to 1994	2001 to 2004	2015 to 2018
Total, age-adjusted [4]	**41.6**	**32.3**	**26.0**	**56.0**	**66.0**	**72.5**	**22.9**	**31.4**	**41.1**
Male	37.9	28.3	22.5	60.9	70.5	76.4	20.2	29.5	40.5
Female	45.0	36.1	29.4	51.4	61.6	68.8	25.5	33.2	41.5
Total, crude	**42.6**	**32.2**	**25.9**	**54.9**	**66.1**	**72.6**	**22.3**	**31.5**	**41.2**
Male	39.4	28.4	22.7	59.4	70.4	76.0	19.5	29.5	40.5
Female	45.7	35.8	28.8	50.7	61.9	69.4	25.0	33.3	41.8
White, non-Hispanic	43.6	33.2	26.8	53.8	65.1	71.6	21.3	30.9	40.7
Male	38.2	27.4	22.8	60.6	71.6	76.0	19.8	30.5	41.7
Female	48.8	38.8	30.6	47.4	58.7	67.4	22.7	31.2	39.7
Black or African American, non-Hispanic	35.9	24.8	22.8	61.8	73.3	75.7	29.5	41.9	48.1
Male	41.5	31.5	27.3	56.7	66.3	70.9	20.7	30.7	38.7
Female	31.2	19.3	19.0	66.0	79.1	79.6	36.7	51.1	55.9
Asian, non-Hispanic	(NA)	(NA)	47.9	(NA)	(NA)	49.6	(NA)	(NA)	15.1
Male	(NA)	(NA)	41.5	(NA)	(NA)	56.8	(NA)	(NA)	14.2
Female	(NA)	(NA)	53.6	(NA)	(NA)	43.3	(NA)	(NA)	16.0
Hispanic [5]	(NA)	(NA)	17.1	(NA)	(NA)	82.0	(NA)	(NA)	45.8
Male	(NA)	(NA)	13.8	(NA)	(NA)	85.4	(NA)	(NA)	44.8
Female	(NA)	(NA)	20.5	(NA)	(NA)	78.6	(NA)	(NA)	46.8
Male by age:									
20 to 34 years	51.1	38.3	32.3	47.5	59.0	65.2	14.1	23.2	37.2
35 to 44 years	33.4	26.5	18.7	65.5	72.9	81.0	21.3	33.8	42.5
45 to 54 years	33.6	21.2	16.2	66.1	78.5	83.0	23.2	31.8	42.9
55 to 64 years	28.6	22.2	21.5	70.5	77.3	77.5	27.2	36.0	43.9
65 to 74 years	30.1	23.1	15.6	68.5	76.1	83.7	24.1	32.1	41.9
75 years and over	40.9	32.1	24.7	56.5	66.8	74.6	13.2	19.9	31.8
Female by age:									
20 to 34 years	57.9	44.2	36.6	37.0	51.6	60.0	18.5	28.6	35.6
35 to 44 years	47.1	38.3	28.3	49.6	60.1	70.7	25.5	33.3	45.0
45 to 54 years	37.2	31.0	27.1	60.3	67.4	71.3	32.4	38.0	43.1
55 to 64 years	31.5	29.2	25.6	66.3	69.9	72.7	33.7	39.0	46.2
65 to 74 years	37.0	27.0	20.9	60.3	71.5	78.9	26.9	37.9	45.9
75 years and over	43.0	34.6	29.0	52.3	63.7	69.9	19.2	23.2	36.1

NA Not available. [1] Normal weight status is a BMI of 18.5 to 24.9. [2] Overweight or obese is a BMI of 25.0 or more. [3] Obese is a BMI of 30.0 or more. [4] Estimates are age-adjusted to the year 2000 standard population using five age groups: 20–34 years, 35–44 years, 45–54 years, 55–64 years, and 65 years and over. [5] Persons of Hispanic origin may be of any race.

Source: U.S. National Center for Health Statistics, "Health, United States—Data Finder," <www.cdc.gov/nchs/hus/index.htm>, accessed July 2024.

Table 223. Dental Care Visit in the Past Year—Percent of Population by Age and Selected Characteristics: 2000 to 2019

[In percent. Covers civilian noninstitutionalized population who had a dental care visit in the past year. Based on the National Health Interview Survey; see Appendix III]

Characteristic	Age 2 to 17 years				Age 18 to 64 years				Age 65 years and over			
	2000	2010	2018	2019 [5]	2000	2010	2018	2019 [5]	2000	2010	2018	2019 [5]
Total [1]	**74.1**	**78.9**	**85.9**	**86.9**	**65.1**	**61.1**	**65.9**	**65.5**	**56.6**	**57.7**	**65.6**	**64.5**
Sex:												
Male	73.7	78.3	86.1	87.0	60.7	56.8	61.5	61.5	56.1	56.2	64.4	61.5
Female	74.6	79.6	85.7	86.7	69.4	65.4	70.2	69.3	56.9	58.9	66.5	67.0
Race/ethnicity: [2]												
White alone	75.8	79.2	85.6	87.0	67.2	62.4	66.6	66.8	58.4	59.3	67.6	67.2
Black or African American alone	70.0	79.0	87.5	88.3	57.1	53.1	63.0	61.2	38.2	40.6	54.6	49.8
American Indian/Alaska Native alone	71.3	73.2	93.5	[6] 83.8	55.0	49.8	56.7	64.9	(B)	72.2	42.9	49.8
Asian alone	72.8	74.8	85.5	85.2	65.6	64.6	67.1	70.1	60.6	61.9	59.0	69.8
Two or more races	71.4	77.9	84.6	88.2	60.5	54.7	63.2	57.8	57.4	48.1	51.0	47.5
Hispanic or Latino [3]	60.6	74.8	85.1	85.7	48.6	48.5	58.5	58.7	44.5	42.1	55.9	49.2
Not Hispanic or Latino	76.8	80.1	86.2	87.3	67.5	63.4	67.6	67.0	57.2	59.0	66.5	66.0
Percent of poverty level: [4]												
Below 100%	62.4	73.2	83.9	84.0	46.8	41.0	48.8	49.8	33.3	32.8	39.6	36.3
100% to 199%	66.1	73.4	82.2	83.6	48.4	44.1	50.0	50.6	43.0	43.8	46.9	45.5
200% to 399%	75.5	79.0	85.0	86.5	62.2	59.6	62.9	62.8	62.8	57.9	64.7	64.1
400% or more	85.9	88.0	90.5	91.6	78.5	77.5	78.7	78.8	73.8	77.2	82.3	82.6

B Estimates are considered unreliable. [1] Includes persons of other race and ethnic groups not shown separately, and those with unknown sex. [2] Race groups include persons of Hispanic and non-Hispanic origin. [3] Persons of Hispanic origin may be of any race. [4] Poverty level is based on family income and family size and composition using Census Bureau poverty thresholds. Missing family income data are imputed. [5] In 2019, the NHIS questionnaire was redesigned and other changes were made to weighting and design methodology. Data for 2019 have not been fully evaluated for comparability with earlier years. For more information, see <www.cdc.gov/nchs/nhis/2019_quest_redesign.htm>. Beginning 2019, dental visits in past year were identified by asking respondents "About how long has it been since [child of respondent or adult respondent] last had a dental examination or cleaning?" [6] Estimate meets National Center for Health Statistics (NCHS) standards of reliability, but its complement does not. See source for more information.

Source: U.S. National Center for Health Statistics, "Health, United States—Data Finder," <www.cdc.gov/nchs/hus/index.htm>, accessed July 2024.

Table 224. Depression and Receipt of Mental Health Treatment in the Past Year Among Adults Age 18 and Over by Selected Characteristics: 2021 and 2022

[In thousands (21,553 represents 21,553,000), except percent. Based on the National Survey on Drug Use and Health. Covers adults who had a major depressive episode (MDE) as defined in the 5th edition of the *Diagnostic and Statistical Manual of Mental Disorders* (DSM-5), which specifies a period of as least 2 weeks when a person experienced a depressed mood or loss of interest or pleasure in daily activities and had a majority of specified depression symptoms. Treatment is defined as seeing or talking to a professional or using prescription medication for depression in the past year; respondents with unknown treatment data were excluded]

Characteristic	Had major depressive episode (MDE)				Those with an MDE who received treatment for depression			
	2021		2022		2021		2022	
	Number (1,000)	Percent of population	Number (1,000)	Percent of population	Number (1,000)	Percent	Number (1,000)	Percent
Total..........................	**21,553**	**8.5**	**22,475**	**8.8**	**12,932**	**60.8**	**14,088**	**63.7**
AGE								
18 to 25 years old...........................	6,442	19.3	6,990	20.1	3,192	50.3	3,766	54.8
26 to 49 years old...........................	9,810	9.6	9,975	9.7	6,121	63.1	6,542	66.5
50 years old and older......................	5,301	4.5	5,510	4.6	3,619	69.5	3,780	70.1
SEX AND AGE								
Male...	7,844	6.4	8,780	7.0	4,184	53.5	4,725	55.6
18 to 25 years old...........................	2,139	12.8	2,633	15.1	755	35.6	1,202	46.2
26 to 49 years old...........................	3,928	7.7	4,227	8.2	2,280	58.5	2,377	57.8
50 years old and older......................	1,777	3.2	1,919	3.4	1,149	63.9	1,146	64.3
Female......................................	13,709	10.5	13,695	10.4	8,748	65.1	9,363	68.8
18 to 25 years old...........................	4,303	25.7	4,357	25.2	2,437	57.7	2,564	60.0
26 to 49 years old...........................	5,881	11.4	5,748	11.2	3,841	66.2	4,165	72.8
50 years old and older......................	3,525	5.7	3,590	5.7	2,470	72.4	2,634	73.0
RACE AND HISPANIC ORIGIN								
Not Hispanic or Latino......................	18,074	8.6	18,573	8.8	10,975	61.3	12,098	66.1
American Indian or Alaska Native........	177	10.8	94	7.6	(B)	(B)	(B)	(B)
Asian..	746	5.0	963	6.3	(B)	(B)	(B)	(B)
Black or African American................	2,121	6.9	2,038	6.6	1,030	49.6	1,118	56.1
Native Hawaiian or other Pacific Islander.....................................	44	4.3	(B)	(B)	(B)	(B)	(B)	(B)
White..	14,342	9.1	14,574	9.2	9,131	64.0	9,824	68.4
Two or more races..........................	644	14.1	825	16.4	374	58.6	529	66.2
Hispanic or Latino..........................	3,479	8.1	3,902	8.8	1,957	58.3	1,990	52.2

B Low precision; does not meet statistical standards for reliability of a derived figure.

Source: U.S. Substance Abuse and Mental Health Services Administration, *Results from the 2022 National Survey on Drug Use and Health: Detailed Tables*, November 2023. See also <www.samhsa.gov/data/data-we-collect/nsduh-national-survey-drug-use-and-health>.

Table 225. Allergies Diagnosed Among Children and Adults by Selected Characteristics: 2021

[In percent. Respondents were considered to have an allergic condition if they were diagnosed with one or more of three selected conditions. In 2021, 31.8% of adults and 27.2% of children were diagnosed with any allergic condition. Based on the National Health Interview Survey, a household survey of a sample of the of the civilian noninstitutionalized population]

Characteristic	Adults			Characteristic	Children		
	Seasonal allergy	Eczema	Food allergy		Seasonal allergy	Eczema	Food allergy
Total [1]......................	**25.7**	**7.3**	**6.2**	**Total** [1]......................	**18.9**	**10.8**	**5.8**
Male..........................	21.1	5.7	4.6	Male..........................	20.0	10.8	5.9
Female........................	29.9	8.9	7.8	Female........................	17.7	10.8	5.8
Age 18 to 44..................	24.7	8.4	6.6				
Age 45 to 64..................	27.9	6.5	6.7	Age 5 and under.............	10.4	10.4	4.4
Age 65 to 74..................	26.4	6.8	5.1	Age 6 to 11...................	21.3	12.1	5.8
Age 75 and over.............	21.7	5.5	4.5	Age 12 to 17..................	24.2	9.8	7.1
White alone, non-Hispanic..	28.4	7.7	6.2	White alone, non-Hispanic..	20.4	10.2	5.3
Black alone, non-Hispanic...	24.0	8.6	8.5	Black alone, non-Hispanic...	21.3	14.2	7.6
Asian alone, non-Hispanic...	17.0	6.5	4.5	Asian alone, non-Hispanic...	11.0	9.0	6.6
Hispanic [2].....................	18.8	4.8	4.4	Hispanic [2].....................	15.3	9.5	5.0

[1] Includes data for persons of other races and multiple races, not shown separately. [2] Persons of Hispanic origin may be of any race or combination of races.

Source: U.S. National Center for Health Statistics, *Diagnosed Allergic Conditions in Children Aged 0–17 Years: United States, 2021*, NCHS Data Brief No. 459, January 2023; and *Diagnosed Allergic Conditions in Adults: United States, 2021*, NCHS Data Brief No 460, January 2023. See also <www.cdc.gov/nchs/products/databriefs.htm>.

Table 226. Learning Disability and Attention Deficit Hyperactivity Disorder Among Children Age 3 to 17 by Selected Characteristics: 2020 to 2023

[In percent. Learning disability is based on the question, "Has a representative from a school or a health professional ever told you that [child's name] had a learning disability?" Attention deficit hyperactivity disorder is based on the question, "Has a doctor or other health professional ever told you that [child's name] had attention deficit hyperactivity disorder (ADHD) or attention deficit disorder (ADD)?" Data based on responses about the survey sample child, not all children in the family. Unknowns were not included in the denominators when calculating percentages. For information on data source, methods, and definitions, see <wwwn.cdc.gov/NHISDataQueryTool/SHS_child/SHS_Tech_Notes.pdf>]

Characteristic	Learning disability				Attention deficit hyperactivity disorder			
	2020 [4]	2021 [4]	2022	2023	2020 [4]	2021 [4]	2022	2023
Total	**8.6**	**7.3**	**8.2**	**8.6**	**10.3**	**9.5**	**10.2**	**12.0**
SEX								
Male	9.8	9.2	9.3	10.9	13.0	12.2	13.2	15.0
Female	7.3	5.4	7.0	6.1	7.4	6.8	7.0	8.8
AGE								
3 to 4 years	2.9	3.4	2.4	2.7	1.0	1.2	1.1	1.7
5 to 11 years	8.3	6.9	7.9	7.9	9.1	8.2	8.6	9.9
12 to 17 years	10.6	9.1	10.3	11.0	14.4	13.7	14.7	17.2
RACE AND HISPANIC ORIGIN								
Single race: [1]								
Asian	2.7	2.5	3.0	4.2	3.2	2.1	2.8	5.0
Black	10.1	10.0	9.5	11.0	9.4	10.6	9.4	9.7
White	9.4	7.3	7.9	8.5	11.4	10.7	11.4	13.7
Black and White	(B)	11.8	12.0	12.2	(B)	11.1	13.7	15.3
Hispanic or Latino [2]	7.6	7.1	9.4	8.1	8.3	7.3	7.9	8.1
Not Hispanic or Latino	8.9	7.4	7.8	8.7	11.0	10.3	11.0	13.4
FAMILY STRUCTURE [3]								
Single parent, never married	8.4	9.7	11.9	12.6	11.6	11.3	10.3	11.6
Single parent, ever married	12.6	10.7	10.1	13.5	15.8	12.9	12.6	19.3
Married parents	7.1	5.6	6.5	6.7	8.1	7.5	9.0	10.0
Cohabiting parents	(B)	5.3	8.6	8.8	(B)	8.9	7.4	7.4
At least one related or unrelated adult (not a parent)	17.8	10.9	13.9	12.7	21.3	17.4	14.9	19.5

B Estimate is considered unreliable. [1] Persons indicating a single race group only, and includes those of Hispanic or Latino origin. [2] Persons of Hispanic or Latino origin may be of any race or combination of races. [3] Refers to parents living in the household. "Parent" can include biological, adoptive, or step. Legal guardians and foster relationships are classified in "At least 1 related or unrelated adult (not a parent)." [4] Due to the COVID-19 pandemic, NHIS data collection switched to a telephone-only mode beginning March 19, 2020. Personal visits resumed in all areas in September 2020, but cases were still attempted by telephone first through April 2021. Starting in May 2021, the NHIS resumed regular survey interviewing procedures, whereby first contact attempts to households were made in person. See source for more information.

Source: U.S. National Center for Health Statistics, National Health Interview Survey, "Interactive Summary Health Statistics for Children," <www.cdc.gov/nchs/nhis/shs.htm>, accessed July 2024.

Table 227. Depression and Receipt of Mental Health Treatment in the Past Year Among Youth Age 12 to 17 by Selected Characteristics: 2021 and 2022

[In percent. Data from the National Survey on Drug Use and Health, and covers youth who had a major depressive episode (MDE) as defined in the *Diagnostic and Statistical Manual of Mental Disorders* (DSM-5), which specifies a period of at least 2 weeks when a person experienced a depressed mood or loss of interest or pleasure in daily activities and had a majority of specified depression symptoms. Treatment is defined as seeing or talking to a medical doctor or other professional, or using prescription medication in the past year for depression. Respondents with unknown incidence of major depressive episode and unknown treatment data were excluded. Estimates are not comparable to earlier surveys due to changes in methodology; see <www.samhsa.gov/data/report/2021-methodological-summary-and-definitions>]

Characteristic	Youth with major depressive episode (MDE)		Youth with an MDE receiving treatment for depression	
	2021	2022	2021	2022
Total [1]	**20.8**	**19.5**	**40.0**	**47.8**
Sex:				
Male	12.0	11.5	38.6	41.3
Female	30.1	28.0	40.5	50.6
Age:				
12 to 13 years	13.5	13.0	33.0	46.9
14 to 15 years	21.3	21.4	41.5	45.6
16 to 17 years	27.5	23.8	42.2	50.5
Race, non-Hispanic:				
American Indian or Alaska Native	(B)	14.1	(B)	(B)
Asian	15.0	14.9	(B)	(B)
Black or African American	14.1	16.7	41.2	34.5
White	21.4	21.0	46.5	54.1
Two or more races	27.9	19.1	(B)	(B)
Hispanic [2]	23.1	19.5	29.7	44.3
Poverty status: [3]				
Below 100% poverty	18.4	16.6	34.9	41.7
100% to 199% poverty	21.6	20.7	38.4	45.6
200% poverty and above	21.4	20.1	42.1	50.4

B Data do not meet statistical standards for reliability of a derived figure. [1] Includes persons of other races, not shown separately. [2] Persons of Hispanic origin may be of any race. [3] Based on a definition of poverty level that incorporates information on family income, size, and composition and is calculated as a percentage of the U.S. Census Bureau's poverty thresholds.

Source: U.S. Substance Abuse and Mental Health Services Administration, *Results From the 2022 National Survey on Drug Use and Health: Detailed Tables,* November 2023. See also <www.samhsa.gov/data/data-we-collect/nsduh-national-survey-drug-use-and-health>.

Table 228. Children and Youth With Disabilities Receiving Special Education and Related Services by Type of Disability: 2000 to 2022

[In thousands (5,773.9 represents 5,773,900). As of Fall. For children and youth age 6 to 21, except as noted, receiving special education and related services in all educational settings under the Individuals with Disabilities Education Act (IDEA) Part B. Includes outlying areas]

Disability	2000	2005	2010	2015	2019	2020 [2]	2021 [2]	2022 [2]
Total................................	**5,773.9**	**6,109.6**	**5,834.9**	**6,050.7**	**6,472.1**	**6,712.0**	**6,881.4**	**7,095.1**
Autism...............................	79.6	193.6	370.6	550.4	704.4	768.2	828.4	909.1
Deaf-blindness....................	1.3	1.6	1.3	1.3	1.5	1.6	1.7	1.7
Developmental delay [1]..........	28.6	79.1	109.4	149.3	178.0	255.8	267.4	277.3
Emotional disturbance.............	474.3	472.4	388.2	346.5	345.2	345.4	327.6	320.8
Hearing impairment...............	70.8	72.4	69.9	67.4	63.4	65.0	65.6	64.7
Intellectual disability..............	613.4	545.5	445.8	418.5	416.1	408.5	414.0	420.9
Multiple disabilities...............	122.9	133.9	123.8	125.2	126.1	123.7	122.2	123.0
Orthopedic impairment............	73.0	63.1	55.8	41.2	30.9	30.4	29.9	28.7
Other health impairment...........	294.0	561.0	706.1	907.2	1,074.2	1,097.3	1,128.1	1,162.0
Specific learning disability.........	2,881.6	2,780.2	2,420.0	2,348.9	2,377.7	2,319.7	2,351.9	2,406.5
Speech or language impairment...	1,093.4	1,157.2	1,093.7	1,044.3	1,043.7	1,183.3	1,230.6	1,265.8
Traumatic brain injury..............	14.9	23.5	24.7	25.5	24.9	24.2	24.1	23.9
Visual impairment..................	26.0	26.0	25.7	24.9	23.9	24.0	24.1	23.7

[1] "Developmental delay" applies only to children ages 3 to 9. [2] Data cover school-age children age 5 (in kindergarten) to age 21.

Source: U.S. Department of Education, Office of Special Education Programs, "IDEA Section 618 Data Products: State Level Data Files," <ideadata.org/idea-section-618-data-products>, accessed January 2024.

Table 229. Children Under Age 18 Receiving Special Education or Early Intervention Services: 2021 to 2023

[In percent. Based on the National Health Interview Survey (NHIS), a household survey of a sample of the civilian noninstitutionalized population. Receiving special education or early intervention services is based on the question, "Does [child's name] currently have a special education or early intervention plan? (Consider special education or early intervention plans received during the past school year.)" Estimates are based on responses about the sample child, not all children in the family. Unknowns were not included in the denominators when calculating percentages. For more information, see <wwwn.cdc.gov/NHISDataQueryTool/SHS_child/SHS_Tech_Notes.pdf>]

Characteristic	2021 [6]	2022	2023	Characteristic	2021 [6]	2022	2023
Total.........................	**8.5**	**9.8**	**10.6**	FAMILY STRUCTURE [3]			
SEX and AGE				Single parent, never married........	11.7	11.3	15.5
Male..............................	10.8	12.0	12.7	Single parent, ever married...........	12.0	14.6	17.0
Female...........................	6.1	7.6	8.4	Married parents.....................	7.2	8.4	8.4
4 years and under.................	3.8	4.4	5.2	Cohabiting parents..................	4.1	8.4	9.1
5 to 11 years......................	9.4	11.0	12.1	At least 1 related or unrelated adult			
12 to 17 years.....................	11.0	12.4	12.9	(not a parent).....................	12.8	15.2	15.5
RACE AND ETHNICITY				DISABILTY STATUS [4]			
Single race: [1]				With a disability....................	36.5	37.2	46.2
American Indian/Alaska Native...	19.0	(B)	(B)	Without a disability.................	6.1	7.2	6.9
Asian.............................	3.0	5.1	6.0	HEALTH INSURANCE COVERAGE [5]			
Black.............................	10.2	10.6	13.0	Private............................	7.4	8.6	8.7
White.............................	8.5	10.1	10.5	Medicaid or other public..............	10.6	12.7	13.8
Hispanic [2]........................	7.6	9.3	10.1	Other..............................	9.4	5.8	9.5
Not Hispanic or Latino.............	8.8	10.0	10.8	Uninsured..........................	3.3	(B)	5.1

B Estimate is unreliable. [1] Persons indicating a single race group, and includes those of Hispanic origin. [2] Persons of Hispanic origin may be of any race. [3] Refers to parents living in the household. "Parent" includes biological, adoptive, or step. Legal guardians and foster relationships are classified in "At least 1 related or unrelated adult (not a parent)." [4] Based on questions asking the level of difficulty the child has with various types of activities and skills indicating a physical, learning, emotional, or behavioral disability. [5] Children with more than one type of health insurance were assigned to the first appropriate category in the following hierarchy: private, Medicaid or other public, other coverage, or uninsured. "Uninsured" includes children with no coverage, only Indian Health Service coverage, or only a private plan that paid for one type of service such as dental or vision care. [6] Due to the COVID-19 pandemic, NHIS data collection switched to a telephone-only mode beginning March 19, 2020. Personal visits resumed in all areas in September 2020, but cases were still attempted by telephone first through April 2021. Starting in May 2021, regular interviewing procedures resumed, whereby first contact attempts were made in person.

Source: U.S. National Center for Health Statistics, National Health Interview Survey, "Interactive Summary Health Statistics for Children," <www.cdc.gov/nchs/nhis/shs.htm>, accessed July 2024.

Table 230. Autism Spectrum Disorder Among Children Age 8: 2000 to 2020

[Covers children age 8. Data are from the Centers for Disease Control and Prevention's Autism and Developmental Disabilities Monitoring (ADDM) Network. The ADDM network collects data from health, special education, or administrative or billing records of children living in communities that identify and treat or provide services to children with autism spectrum disorder (ASD). The ADDM method is population-based; the network attempts to identify all children with ASD from the entire population of children within each geographic area. The ADDM is not a representative sample of the United States. More information is available at <www.cdc.gov/autism>]

Year	Number of ADDM sites reporting data	Birth year of children	Prevalence of ASD per 1,000 children	Approximate prevalence (1 child in X children)	2020 Sex and race/ethnicity	2020 Prevalence of ASD per 1,000 children
2000.......	6	1992	6.7	1 in 150	By sex:	
2006.......	11	1998	9.0	1 in 110	Male........................	43.0
2008.......	14	2000	11.3	1 in 88	Female......................	11.4
2010.......	11	2002	14.7	1 in 68	By race/ethnicity:	
2012.......	11	2004	14.5	1 in 69	White, non-Hispanic...............	24.3
2014.......	11	2006	16.8	1 in 59	Black, non-Hispanic...............	29.3
2016.......	11	2008	18.5	1 in 54	Asian/Pacific Islander, non-Hispanic...	33.4
2018.......	11	2010	23.0	1 in 44	Two or more races...............	22.9
2020.......	11	2012	27.6	1 in 36	Hispanic......................	31.6

Source: U.S. Centers for Disease Control and Prevention, "Data & Statistics on Autism Spectrum Disorder," <www.cdc.gov/autism/data-research/index.html>, accessed May 2023; and Maenner, Matthew J. et al., *Prevalence and Characteristics of Autism Spectrum Disorder Among Children Aged 8 Years — Autism and Developmental Disabilities Monitoring Network, 11 Sites, United States, 2020*, Morbidity and Mortality Weekly Report, Surveillance Summaries, Vol 72:2, March 24, 2023.

Table 231. Immunization of Children Born in 2019 and 2020 by Vaccine Type and State: 2020 to 2022

[In percent. Data cover children born in 2019 and 2020 who received the recommended doses of each vaccine by age 24 months, except as noted. Based on estimates from the National Immunization Survey (NIS), which includes a survey of the parents and guardians of children age 19-35 months, and a survey of health care providers of the children to verify and/or complete vaccination information. Data for the 2019 birth year are from survey years 2020, 2021, and 2022; data for the 2020 birth year are considered preliminary and are from survey years 2021 and 2022. Abbreviations: DTaP = diphtheria, tetanus toxoids, and pertussis vaccine; MMR = measles, mumps, and rubella vaccine; HepB = hepatitis B vaccine; HepA = hepatitis A vaccine; Hib = Haemophilus influenzae type b conjugate vaccine; PCV = pneumococcal conjugate vaccine]

State	DTaP, ≥3 doses [1]	DTaP, ≥4 doses [1]	Polio, ≥3 doses	MMR, ≥1 dose [2]	Hib, primary series [3]	Hib, full series [3]	HepB, birth dose [4]	HepB, ≥3 doses	Varicella, ≥1 dose	PCV, ≥3 doses	PCV, ≥4 doses	HepA, ≥2 doses [5]	Rotavirus [6]	Combined series [7]
U.S.....	93.8	81.0	93.0	91.6	93.4	79.1	81.5	92.1	91.1	92.8	82.7	80.0	76.6	69.1
AL......	96.8	82.6	95.3	95.3	97.0	76.3	80.4	93.2	96.7	96.9	83.6	75.6	77.3	64.8
AK.....	86.1	74.7	84.7	84.5	87.1	72.2	78.6	85.9	77.4	84.4	72.7	68.5	64.4	59.4
AZ.....	90.1	77.5	88.2	87.1	89.6	74.9	77.9	87.6	87.9	89.6	76.2	86.8	69.1	66.2
AR.....	87.9	76.1	87.7	87.5	86.9	79.6	81.1	87.3	87.9	87.7	76.9	74.8	76.5	67.0
CA.....	94.9	79.5	94.6	92.1	94.6	78.7	79.2	93.7	90.7	93.1	81.9	79.2	79.6	67.6
CO.....	96.4	81.3	95.0	92.9	95.3	81.0	81.8	94.4	91.2	94.8	84.9	76.9	79.5	71.2
CT.....	96.2	86.9	95.8	93.7	94.7	87.4	84.4	94.3	96.9	95.8	90.7	89.6	84.5	77.3
DE.....	93.0	84.4	92.7	93.3	92.7	81.3	80.2	91.3	91.3	92.9	85.9	92.2	77.4	75.7
DC.....	92.0	80.2	91.8	88.2	91.7	80.1	76.6	90.0	88.6	91.4	84.9	77.1	76.5	69.7
FL......	92.5	82.5	90.9	92.2	92.9	81.4	76.4	90.6	91.6	92.4	81.1	76.1	69.4	67.6
GA.....	93.5	81.1	92.3	89.7	91.5	73.9	81.1	93.4	90.1	94.2	83.2	82.6	77.2	68.6
HI......	91.6	79.4	90.8	88.5	92.1	78.6	83.2	90.0	91.2	90.8	80.8	70.9	79.1	73.0
ID......	92.9	80.6	89.4	89.0	93.0	82.6	80.3	92.9	88.1	92.1	85.8	79.1	79.0	71.7
IL......	94.4	83.3	94.2	89.9	93.9	78.5	80.6	92.2	90.7	91.8	83.0	76.2	78.6	70.5
IN......	93.0	81.7	91.3	88.9	92.2	81.0	87.3	90.7	89.6	92.2	84.5	81.4	73.9	71.0
IA......	94.4	85.1	93.8	92.7	95.2	84.7	87.3	94.7	91.7	94.4	88.3	78.3	83.1	77.0
KS.....	92.4	75.5	91.3	87.1	92.6	77.2	81.9	91.3	87.4	92.2	78.5	78.0	78.3	63.0
KY.....	92.3	84.2	92.3	89.5	93.2	77.3	83.0	91.6	89.3	91.2	83.4	83.6	68.5	67.6
LA.....	94.8	77.8	94.7	90.2	93.6	76.8	75.4	93.3	92.2	93.2	77.0	75.0	70.3	67.5
ME.....	96.9	86.9	96.8	94.4	96.3	85.5	85.5	92.2	94.3	96.0	88.9	90.9	80.0	76.5
MD.....	96.1	85.5	95.6	94.0	95.4	81.4	81.4	93.9	94.4	94.8	87.0	82.5	78.3	76.0
MA.....	95.5	85.5	95.8	95.9	95.8	86.6	83.7	95.2	95.2	95.8	87.9	91.2	82.1	79.4
MI......	96.1	82.5	95.9	95.4	94.4	83.5	83.2	94.2	95.3	95.3	86.9	87.3	82.4	73.6
MN.....	95.5	86.8	94.3	92.8	94.0	79.1	82.9	92.3	93.0	94.6	86.1	78.2	84.1	72.7
MS.....	89.2	76.3	89.1	91.0	90.3	73.0	75.5	87.8	91.7	90.0	79.8	49.7	62.9	64.7
MO.....	89.4	77.3	89.0	88.5	89.9	74.1	82.2	91.2	88.5	89.3	79.5	77.6	71.8	66.0
MT.....	94.0	74.8	93.7	89.8	93.9	77.0	75.7	92.1	85.8	91.7	79.0	70.1	75.4	66.4
NE.....	96.7	87.5	96.3	94.5	95.9	73.1	84.9	95.6	94.4	96.8	90.1	79.0	79.8	66.5
NV.....	92.7	80.3	92.8	90.0	92.4	79.5	83.5	92.1	90.0	93.1	83.4	75.0	75.9	73.8
NH.....	96.1	82.6	96.1	93.2	96.1	82.5	84.9	93.5	91.3	93.3	86.1	77.8	83.3	75.8
NJ......	94.8	78.7	91.4	93.9	93.6	79.0	81.5	92.2	90.8	92.3	75.7	72.4	70.7	64.2
NM.....	95.5	83.4	95.8	91.0	94.3	85.2	76.2	94.1	91.1	94.1	85.1	87.3	81.6	76.4
NY.....	92.5	81.6	91.5	91.4	92.3	78.8	80.4	90.4	91.8	92.0	80.8	79.6	76.9	68.6
NC.....	97.3	84.3	97.5	94.3	96.4	84.0	87.8	93.6	93.2	96.6	92.0	79.0	81.0	72.3
ND.....	94.5	81.6	94.4	91.4	94.9	83.8	89.0	96.4	90.9	92.0	85.4	84.6	80.4	76.4
OH.....	94.0	83.0	93.3	90.7	93.4	77.1	85.1	90.7	90.4	94.0	81.9	86.0	76.2	67.2
OK.....	93.3	74.5	93.0	86.3	92.5	74.6	74.8	91.4	85.2	89.9	75.5	76.2	72.0	61.6
OR.....	92.1	77.5	90.2	88.4	89.6	77.5	85.2	90.6	89.0	91.0	79.0	72.5	73.9	66.1
PA......	93.1	80.1	93.1	93.0	93.6	77.8	85.2	93.2	92.0	92.9	85.1	81.1	79.7	71.0
RI......	98.1	88.5	97.8	96.3	96.7	87.7	77.1	97.5	95.2	98.0	93.0	86.3	92.0	78.5
SC.....	93.2	80.4	93.2	92.5	93.8	76.5	85.3	92.5	89.9	94.3	84.8	84.3	79.5	70.8
SD.....	93.9	72.1	93.1	92.6	93.5	72.4	87.3	94.2	91.9	93.4	79.7	78.2	80.3	63.7
TN.....	94.7	81.5	93.8	92.7	94.8	75.9	74.6	94.3	93.7	95.6	84.2	79.5	72.8	67.5
TX.....	92.3	77.4	91.5	89.9	91.4	77.7	82.3	89.2	90.0	89.5	80.2	81.3	74.5	65.4
UT.....	96.4	87.0	96.3	95.5	96.3	84.9	84.4	92.9	93.1	94.7	88.7	81.7	81.7	76.4
VT.....	97.3	88.2	96.9	94.6	97.2	87.1	78.7	94.6	93.2	97.3	90.8	82.7	82.8	77.6
VA.....	93.4	83.7	92.1	93.1	94.5	79.9	81.0	91.1	91.6	94.5	85.2	86.8	80.1	73.1
WA.....	96.1	81.8	94.8	91.0	96.0	84.3	84.5	95.5	91.3	95.3	84.6	78.8	77.9	72.3
WV.....	90.3	75.5	89.3	88.4	88.6	68.6	78.9	90.0	88.7	88.2	80.1	82.8	71.2	59.1
WI.....	91.7	81.1	90.8	91.8	92.4	80.9	85.0	93.1	88.0	91.2	82.4	82.1	74.2	67.5
WY.....	93.2	80.1	91.8	88.9	92.0	81.4	80.5	92.4	87.5	92.1	82.7	74.4	80.9	72.1
GU.....	84.8	66.6	84.5	81.2	85.9	68.8	89.0	81.7	81.6	84.6	67.1	66.4	59.3	52.5
PR.....	78.7	57.9	76.7	68.5	76.4	56.6	67.9	72.7	71.5	74.7	57.4	56.5	55.0	43.4

[1] Includes children who might have received diphtheria and tetanus toxoids vaccine or diphtheria, tetanus toxoids, and pertussis vaccine. [2] Includes children who might have received measles, mumps, rubella, and varicella combination vaccine. [3] Hib primary series: receipt of ≥2 or ≥3 doses, depending on product type received. Full series (by age 24 months): primary series and booster dose, which includes receipt of ≥3 or ≥4 doses, depending on product type received. [4] HepB administered from birth through age 3 days. [5] ≥2 doses of Hepatitis A vaccine administered by age 35 months. [6] ≥2 or ≥3 doses of Rotavirus vaccine, depending on product type received, administered through age 8 months. [7] The combined 7 vaccine series (4:3:1:3*:3:1:4) includes ≥4 doses of DTaP, ≥3 doses of poliovirus vaccine, ≥1 dose of measles-containing vaccine, full series of Hib vaccine (3 or 4 doses, depending on product type), ≥3 doses of HepB, ≥1 dose of varicella vaccine, and ≥4 doses of PCV.

Source: U.S. Centers for Disease Control and Prevention, ChildVaxView, "ChildVaxView Interactive!," <www.cdc.gov/vaccines/imz-managers/coverage/childvaxview/index.html>, accessed January 2024. See also Hill, Holly A. et al, "Vaccination Coverage by Age 24 Months Among Children Born in 2019 and 2020 — National Immunization Survey–Child, United States, 2020-2022," *Morbidity and Mortality Weekly Report*, 72:44, November 3, 2023.

Table 232. Immunization of Children Born in 2019 and 2020 by Vaccine, Race/Ethnicity, Poverty Status, and Health Insurance Coverage: 2020 to 2022

[In percent. Data cover children born in 2019 and 2020 who received the recommended doses of each vaccine by age 24 months, except as noted. Based on estimates from the National Immunization Survey (NIS), which includes a survey of the parents and guardians of children age 19-35 months, and a survey of health care providers of the children to verify and/or complete vaccination information. See headnote, Table 231. Abbreviations: DTaP = diphtheria, tetanus toxoids, and acellular pertussis vaccine; MMR = measles, mumps, and rubella vaccine; HepB = hepatitis B vaccine; HepA = hepatitis A vaccine; Hib = Haemophilus influenzae type b conjugate vaccine; PCV = pneumococcal conjugate vaccine]

Vaccination	Total [1]	Race/ethnicity [2]				Poverty		Health insurance		
		White	Black	His-panic	Asian	At or above poverty	Below poverty	Private only	Any Med-icaid	Unin-sured
DTaP, ≥4 doses [3]	81.0	83.2	76.3	79.1	88.4	84.5	71.0	87.3	76.6	61.3
Poliovirus, ≥3 doses	93.0	93.9	91.9	92.4	93.8	94.4	89.0	95.6	91.3	80.0
MMR, ≥1 dose [4]	91.6	92.6	88.7	91.2	93.8	92.5	88.7	94.6	89.6	78.3
Hib, Full series [5]	79.1	80.8	73.1	78.5	83.2	82.3	69.7	84.4	75.1	61.9
HepB, birth dose [6]	81.5	81.1	78.9	82.1	82.8	81.6	81.5	83.0	81.6	63.7
HepB, ≥ 3 doses	92.1	92.8	91.4	91.7	93.3	92.9	89.2	93.7	91.3	76.2
Varicella (chickenpox), ≥1 dose [4]	91.1	92.0	90.0	90.6	93.4	92.0	88.5	94.0	89.5	76.5
PCV, ≥4 doses	82.7	85.4	76.3	81.0	86.1	86.3	72.7	89.3	78.1	55.3
HepA, ≥1 dose	88.4	89.1	86.8	88.1	91.0	89.4	85.2	91.2	86.7	72.3
HepA, ≥2 doses	47.7	48.8	42.9	47.6	52.1	50.3	40.7	51.9	44.7	36.6
Rotavirus [7]	76.6	79.1	71.0	75.1	82.1	80.5	66.1	84.1	71.2	52.0
Influenza, ≥ 2 doses [8]	61.3	66.7	46.1	58.0	75.3	67.1	45.3	75.5	49.2	37.8
Combined 7 series [9]	69.1	71.6	63.3	66.7	75.6	73.2	57.9	76.6	63.6	42.5
No vaccinations	1.0	1.0	1.1	0.9	1.2	0.9	1.3	0.6	1.2	6.0

[1] Includes other racial/ethnic and health insurance coverage categories not shown separately. [2] Children identified as White, Black, and Asian are Non-Hispanic. Children of Hispanic origin may be of any race. [3] Includes diphtheria and tetanus toxoids vaccine or diphtheria, tetanus toxoids, and pertussis vaccine. [4] May include measles, mumps, rubella, and varicella vaccine. [5] Hib full series: primary series and booster dose, which includes receipt of ≥3 or ≥4 doses, depending on product type. [6] One dose given from birth through age 3 days. [7] Includes ≥2 doses of Rotarix monovalent rotavirus vaccine, or ≥3 doses of RotaTeq pentavalent rotavirus vaccine (RV5). Maximum age for the final dose is 8 months. [8] Doses must be at least 24 days apart, and could be received during two influenza seasons. [9] The combined 7 vaccine series (4:3:1:3*:3:1:4) includes ≥4 doses of DTaP, ≥3 doses of poliovirus vaccine, ≥1 dose of measles-containing vaccine, Hib full series vaccine (≥3 or ≥4 doses, depending on product type), ≥3 doses of HepB, ≥1 dose of varicella vaccine, and ≥4 doses of PCV.

Source: U.S. Centers for Disease Control and Prevention, Immunization Managers, Hill, Holly A. et al, "Vaccination Coverage by Age 24 Months Among Children Born in 2019 and 2020 — National Immunization Survey–Child, United States, 2020-2022," *Morbidity and Mortality Weekly Report,* 72:44, November 3, 2023. See also <www.cdc.gov/vaccines/imz-managers/coverage/childvaxview/pubs-presentations.html>.

Table 233. Asthma Incidence Among Children Under Age 18 by Selected Characteristics: 2021 to 2023

[In percent. Based on the National Health Interview Survey (NHIS), a household survey of a sample of the civilian noninstitutionalized population. Based on the questions: "Has a doctor or other health professional ever told you that [child's name] had asthma?" and "Does [child's name] still have asthma?" Estimates are based on responses about the sample child, not all children in the family. Unknowns were not included in the denominators when calculating percentages. For more information on data source, methods, and definitions, see *Technical Notes for Interactive Summary Health Statistics—2019-2023: National Health Interview Survey,* <wwwn.cdc.gov/NHISDataQueryTool/SHS_child/SHS_Tech_Notes.pdf>]

Characteristic	Ever told had asthma			Still have asthma		
	2021 [3]	2022	2023	2021 [3]	2022	2023
Total	**10.2**	**9.9**	**10.3**	**6.5**	**6.2**	**6.7**
SEX						
Male	12.2	11.4	12.1	7.3	7.0	7.6
Female	8.1	8.2	8.5	5.6	5.4	5.7
AGE						
4 years and under	2.6	3.2	3.9	1.9	2.7	3.0
5 to 11 years	11.0	10.6	9.8	7.5	7.0	7.1
12 to 17 years	15.0	13.9	15.6	8.7	7.9	8.8
RACE AND HISPANIC ORIGIN						
Single race: [1]						
American Indian or Alaska Native	(B)	(B)	(B)	(B)	(B)	(B)
Asian	7.0	6.0	5.8	3.0	3.0	2.8
Black or African American	16.9	15.9	15.1	12.5	11.2	11.5
Native Hawaiian or Other Pacific Islander	(B)	(B)	(B)	(B)	(B)	(B)
White	8.9	8.9	9.6	5.5	5.8	6.0
Hispanic or Latino [2]	8.9	9.8	11.5	5.4	5.5	7.1
Not Hispanic or Latino	10.6	9.9	9.9	6.8	6.5	6.6

B Estimate is considered unreliable. [1] Persons indicating a single race group only, and includes those of Hispanic or Latino origin. [2] Persons of Hispanic or Latino origin may be of any race or combination of races. [3] Due to the COVID-19 pandemic, NHIS data collection switched to a telephone-only mode beginning March 19, 2020. Personal visits resumed in all areas in September 2020, but cases were still attempted by telephone first through April 2021. Starting in May 2021, the NHIS resumed regular survey interviewing procedures, whereby first contact attempts to households were made in person, with follow-up allowed by telephone. See source for more information.

Source: U.S. National Center for Health Statistics, National Health Interview Survey, "Interactive Summary Health Statistics for Children,," <www.cdc.gov/nchs/nhis/shs.htm>, accessed July 2024.

Table 234. Child Obesity by Age, Sex, and Race/Ethnicity: 1976 to 2020

[In percent. For children age 6 to 17. Data are from U.S. National Center for Health Statistics, National Health and Nutrition Examination Surveys, a program of studies that combines interviews and physical examinations to assess the health and nutritional status of adults and children. Children classified as obese have a body mass index (BMI) at or above the sex- and age-specific 95th percentile]

Selected characteristic	1976 to 1980	1988 to 1994	1999 to 2002	2003 to 2006	2007 to 2010	2011 to 2014	2017 to 2020 [4]
Total [1]	**5.7**	**11.2**	**16.0**	**17.3**	**18.6**	**19.5**	**21.3**
RACE AND HISPANIC ORIGIN							
White, non-Hispanic	4.9	10.5	13.2	15.5	16.0	17.1	17.8
Black, non-Hispanic	8.2	14.0	20.7	21.5	24.0	22.5	27.4
Asian, non-Hispanic	(NA)	(NA)	(NA)	(NA)	(NA)	9.8	11.1
Hispanic origin [2,3]	(NA)	(NA)	(NA)	(NA)	23.7	24.3	27.6
Mexican-American [2,3]	(NA)	15.4	23.0	22.7	23.8	25.2	30.2
SEX AND AGE							
Male	5.5	11.8	17.2	18.1	20.4	18.9	22.9
Female	5.8	10.6	14.7	16.3	16.7	20.0	19.8
Age 6 to 11	6.5	11.3	15.8	17.0	18.8	17.5	20.9
Male	6.7	11.6	16.9	18.0	20.7	17.6	23.0
Female	6.4	11.0	14.7	15.8	16.9	17.5	18.7
Age 12 to 17	4.9	11.1	16.1	17.5	18.4	21.3	21.8
Male	4.5	12.0	17.5	18.2	20.1	20.1	22.7
Female	5.4	10.2	14.7	16.8	16.6	22.5	20.8

NA Not available. [1] Includes other races not shown separately. [2] Persons of Hispanic and Mexican origin may be of any race. [3] From 1976 to 2006, the survey sample was designed to provide estimates specifically for persons of Mexican origin. Beginning in 2007, the survey allows for reporting of both total Hispanics and Mexican Americans. [4] Data collection for 2019-2020 was suspended in March 2020 due to the COVID-19 pandemic. Data collected 2019 to March 2020 were combined with data from the 2017-2018 collection cycle to provide a nationally representative sample. Data not strictly comparable to data from earlier years. See source for more information.

Source: Federal Interagency Forum on Child and Family Statistics, "America's Children: Key National Indicators of Well-Being, 2023," <www.childstats.gov/>, accessed January 2024.

Table 235. High School Students Engaged in Physical Activity by Sex and Race/Ethnicity: 2021

[In percent. Data are based on questions regarding selected activities in the past seven days before the survey, except as noted. For students in grades 9 to 12. Based on the Youth Risk Behavior Survey, a biennial survey of students in grades 9-12 conducted in public and private schools, and subject to sampling error; see source for details]

Characteristic	No physical activity for 60+ min. on any day [1]	Physically active for 60+ min. on 5 of last 7 days [2]	Physically active for 60+ min. on all 7 days [2]	Exercise to strengthen or tone muscle on 3+ days [3]	Played on at least one sports team [4]	Attended physical education class [5]		Spent 3+ hours per day on a screen [6]
						Total	Attended daily	
All students	**15.8**	**45.3**	**23.9**	**44.9**	**49.1**	**46.8**	**19.0**	**75.9**
Female	19.2	35.9	15.7	32.4	46.4	43.0	16.7	78.7
Male	12.4	54.7	31.7	56.6	52.1	50.3	21.1	73.4
White, non-Hispanic	12.1	51.6	27.7	47.0	55.3	43.4	19.0	75.6
Female	14.4	43.0	18.7	35.7	55.0	39.3	16.3	78.7
Male	9.8	59.7	35.9	56.7	56.3	46.9	21.3	72.7
Black, non-Hispanic	24.5	35.2	19.7	40.7	47.2	48.9	19.6	74.1
Female	28.9	25.1	12.4	27.5	41.6	46.0	17.7	77.7
Male	20.3	44.8	26.6	53.2	53.0	52.3	21.8	70.8
Asian, non-Hispanic	16.2	41.3	19.4	41.7	45.0	48.3	9.6	75.2
Female	19.9	30.0	12.4	28.5	43.8	48.3	7.4	73.4
Male	12.9	52.9	26.5	56.5	46.8	48.1	12.2	77.5
Multiple race, non-Hispanic	14.6	41.9	21.3	39.4	48.8	40.0	16.5	80.0
Female	18.3	33.7	14.3	27.0	46.5	38.0	14.1	81.5
Male	10.3	52.0	29.7	54.6	51.7	42.1	18.8	78.1
Hispanic	18.7	39.2	18.9	44.2	39.4	53.3	21.0	77.8
Female	24.2	29.0	12.1	29.8	34.4	48.2	19.1	80.4
Male	13.5	49.6	25.6	58.4	44.1	58.3	22.7	75.1
Male	**12.4**	**54.7**	**31.7**	**56.6**	**52.1**	**50.3**	**21.1**	**73.4**
Grade 9	9.6	57.1	33.1	58.3	57.3	67.6	29.4	70.6
Grade 10	11.8	57.0	33.4	59.9	51.6	55.2	24.5	71.5
Grade 11	12.9	52.4	32.1	55.0	51.8	39.9	15.1	77.2
Grade 12	15.6	51.8	27.6	53.1	46.7	36.0	14.1	74.6
Female	**19.2**	**35.9**	**15.7**	**32.4**	**46.4**	**43.0**	**16.7**	**78.7**
Grade 9	15.7	38.6	17.5	36.4	49.2	66.3	28.9	77.3
Grade 10	17.2	39.4	16.8	37.9	49.3	47.8	19.0	78.5
Grade 11	20.9	34.0	14.8	28.7	46.4	29.9	9.9	80.2
Grade 12	23.0	31.2	13.7	26.5	40.7	28.3	9.1	79.0

[1] Did not participate for 60 or more minutes in any physical activity that increased their heart rate and made them breathe hard some of the time for at least 1 day. [2] Did any kind of physical activity that increased their heart rate and made them breathe hard some of the time. [3] Performed muscle strengthening or toning exercises such as push-ups, sit-ups, or weight-lifting. [4] Any team run by the school or community groups, during the 12 months before the survey. [5] In an average week when student was in school. [6] Includes time on an average school day spent in front of a TV, computer, smartphone, or other electronic device watching shows or videos, playing games, accessing the internet, or using social media, not counting time spent doing school work.

Source: U.S. Centers for Disease Control and Prevention, Youth Risk Behavior Surveillance System (YRBSS), "Youth Online Data Analysis Tool: Physical Activity," <www.cdc.gov/healthyyouth/data/yrbs/index.htm>, accessed April 2023.

Table 236. High School Students Who Had a Concussion by Sex, Race/Ethnicity, and Grade: 2017 to 2021

[In percent. Based on the Youth Risk Behavior Survey. Covers students reporting having a concussion one or more times in the past 12 months from playing a sport or being physically active. Survey defined concussion as a blow or jolt to the head that causes problems such as headaches, dizziness, being dazed or confused, difficulty remembering or concentrating, vomiting, blurred vision, or being knocked out]

Characteristic	2017			2019			2021		
	Total	Male	Female	Total	Male	Female	Total	Male	Female
Total	**15.1**	**17.2**	**13.0**	**15.1**	**17.0**	**13.3**	**11.9**	**13.2**	**10.4**
Race/ethnicity: [1]									
American Indian or Alaska Native	19.1	24.3	10.7	41.8	44.7	36.3	22.3	17.7	28.2
Asian	13.0	11.9	14.0	10.2	11.0	9.4	8.4	10.6	6.2
Black	17.0	20.1	13.9	16.7	19.0	14.5	14.2	17.0	11.3
Native Hawaiian, Other Pacific Islander	18.6	11.5	24.9	21.4	(NA)	(NA)	20.3	18.6	22.5
White	14.6	16.7	12.6	15.2	16.7	13.6	11.5	12.5	10.3
Multiple race	14.0	19.0	9.6	13.9	15.0	12.9	9.7	9.0	10.4
Hispanic	15.0	16.5	13.5	14.7	16.9	12.5	12.3	14.0	10.2
Grade:									
9th	17.0	18.6	15.5	15.8	18.2	13.4	13.3	14.7	11.6
10th	15.2	18.6	11.9	14.4	15.2	13.7	12.2	13.5	11.0
11th	15.3	17.1	13.6	16.1	17.9	14.3	12.3	13.5	10.9
12th	12.2	13.9	10.6	13.9	16.6	11.2	9.5	10.6	8.0

NA Not available. [1] Race groups are non-Hispanic.

Source: U.S. Centers for Disease Control and Prevention, Youth Risk Behavior Surveillance System, "Youth Online Data Analysis Tool," <www.cdc.gov/healthyyouth/data/yrbs/index.htm>, accessed April 2023.

Table 237. High School Student Use of Tobacco and Nicotine Products by Sex and Race/Ethnicity: 2023

[In percent, except as noted (1,970 represents 1,970,000). Data represent current use of tobacco and nicotine products, defined as use within the past 30 days. Data are based on the National Youth Tobacco Survey, an internet-based and self-administered survey of students in public and private middle schools (grade 6-8) and high schools (grades 9-12). The 2023 results are based on responses from 22,069 students attending 179 schools; overall response rate was 30.5 percent. Only results from high school students are presented below]

Tobacco and nicotine product	Total		Sex		Race and ethnicity			
	Number [1] (1,000)	Percent	Male	Female	White, non-Hispanic	Black or African-American, non-Hispanic	Multiracial, non-Hispanic	Hispanic [2]
Use of any tobacco product [3]	**1,970**	**12.6**	**11.2**	**14.1**	**13.6**	**9.8**	**17.2**	**12.4**
Electronic cigarettes (vaping)	1,560	10.0	8.0	12.2	11.3	5.6	14.2	9.7
Cigarettes	290	1.9	2.3	1.5	2.2	(B)	(B)	2.2
Cigars	280	1.8	2.3	1.4	1.4	1.9	(B)	2.3
Nicotine pouch	260	1.7	2.6	(B)	2.2	(B)	(B)	1.6
Smokeless tobacco [4]	230	1.5	2.1	(B)	1.7	(B)	(B)	1.7
Other oral nicotine products	180	1.2	1.5	0.9	1.3	(B)	(B)	1.6
Hookah	170	1.1	0.9	1.4	(B)	(B)	(B)	1.0
Heated tobacco product [5]	150	1.0	1.4	0.7	(B)	(B)	(B)	1.6
Pipe tobacco	90	0.6	0.7	0.5	0.6	(B)	(B)	(B)
Any combustible tobacco product [6]	600	3.9	4.3	3.6	3.8	4.5	5.3	3.8
Use of 2 or more tobacco products	610	3.9	4.3	3.5	4.3	(B)	6.1	3.9

B Statistically unreliable. Sample size less than 50 or relative standard error greater than 0.3. [1] Estimates are rounded down to nearest 10,000. [2] Persons of Hispanic origin may be of any race. [3] Any tobacco product use is defined as current use of one or more of the following tobacco products: e-cigarettes, cigars, cigarettes, smokeless tobacco (chewing tobacco, snuff, dip, or snus), hookahs, nicotine pouches, heated tobacco products, pipe tobacco, or bidis (small brown cigarettes wrapped in a leaf). [4] Includes chewing tobacco, snuff, dip, or snus. [5] Heated tobacco products heat processed tobacco leaf to produce a vapor. They are different from e-cigarettes, which heat a liquid containing nicotine to produce a vapor. [6] Includes cigarettes, cigars, hookahs, pipe tobacco, and/or bidis.

Source: U.S. Centers for Disease Control and Prevention, Birdsey, Jan et al., "Tobacco Product Use Among U.S. Middle and High School Students—National Youth Tobacco Survey, 2023," *Morbidity and Mortality Weekly Report,* 72:44, November 3, 2023. See also <www.cdc.gov/tobacco/data_statistics/fact_sheets/youth_data/tobacco_use/index.htm>.

Table 238. Fruit and Vegetable Availability for Consumption Per Capita by Commodity: 1990 to 2022

[In pounds, farm weight. Available supply of fresh fruits and vegetables at the farm level or early stage of processing for domestic consumption after subtracting measurable uses such as farm inputs (feed and seed), exports, ending stocks, and industrial uses. Food availability is a proxy for actual food consumption. Based on Census Bureau estimated resident population plus Armed Forces overseas for most commodities]

Commodity	1990	2000	2005	2010	2015	2018	2019	2020	2021	2022
Fruits and vegetables, total [1]	**662.5**	**711.9**	**684.3**	**652.8**	**633.7**	**648.3**	**625.9**	**627.4**	**621.6**	**(NA)**
Fruits, total	**270.8**	**286.7**	**268.8**	**253.7**	**249.7**	**240.2**	**237.3**	**231.4**	**237.7**	**(NA)**
Fresh fruits	117.1	127.3	123.3	126.3	133.8	139.6	138.4	139.4	138.7	(NA)
Noncitrus [2]	95.6	103.8	101.7	104.8	111.0	115.6	112.7	112.5	112.6	(NA)
Apples	19.8	17.6	16.8	15.4	17.6	16.9	17.7	16.3	15.8	(NA)
Apricots	0.2	0.2	0.1	0.1	0.1	0.1	0.1	0.1	0.1	(NA)
Avocados	1.4	2.3	3.5	4.0	7.2	8.5	8.2	9.3	8.4	(NA)
Bananas	24.3	28.4	25.2	25.6	27.9	28.3	27.4	27.2	26.9	(NA)
Blueberries	0.1	0.3	0.4	1.1	1.6	2.0	2.3	2.3	2.5	(NA)
Cantaloupes	9.2	11.1	9.6	8.5	6.8	7.1	5.7	5.4	5.2	(NA)
Cherries	0.4	0.6	0.9	1.3	1.1	1.3	1.2	1.2	1.4	(NA)
Grapes	7.9	7.5	8.7	8.0	7.9	8.1	8.4	8.2	8.5	(NA)
Honeydew melons	2.1	2.3	1.9	1.7	1.7	1.7	1.3	1.2	1.4	(NA)
Kiwifruit	0.5	0.6	0.4	0.5	0.6	0.6	0.6	0.7	0.8	(NA)
Mangoes	0.5	1.8	1.9	2.2	2.6	3.2	3.3	3.6	3.7	(NA)
Papayas	0.2	0.7	0.9	1.2	1.3	1.3	1.3	1.3	1.3	(NA)
Peaches and nectarines	5.5	5.3	4.8	4.7	2.9	2.2	2.1	2.4	2.4	(NA)
Pears	3.3	3.4	2.9	2.9	2.7	2.9	2.7	2.9	3.1	(NA)
Pineapples	2.0	3.2	4.9	5.7	7.0	7.8	7.6	7.3	7.9	(NA)
Plums and prunes	1.5	1.2	1.1	0.8	0.6	0.6	0.6	0.6	0.5	(NA)
Raspberries	(NA)	0.1	0.1	0.2	0.9	0.8	0.9	1.0	0.9	(NA)
Strawberries	3.2	3.4	3.9	5.0	5.5	6.3	6.0	7.1	7.3	(NA)
Watermelons	13.3	13.8	13.5	15.7	14.9	15.9	15.2	14.4	14.4	(NA)
Fresh citrus	21.5	23.5	21.6	21.6	22.7	24.0	25.7	27.0	26.2	24.9
Oranges and temples	12.4	11.7	11.4	9.7	8.7	8.2	8.5	9.4	8.1	8.2
Tangerines and tangelos	1.3	2.9	2.5	3.8	5.2	5.9	6.8	6.7	7.0	6.0
Grapefruit	4.6	5.1	2.6	2.8	2.2	1.6	1.4	1.7	1.5	1.1
Lemons	2.6	2.4	2.9	2.8	3.6	4.2	4.9	4.9	4.9	4.9
Limes	0.7	1.4	2.1	2.6	3.0	4.1	4.1	4.3	4.7	4.6
Processed fruit [2]	153.6	159.4	145.5	127.3	115.9	100.6	98.9	92.0	99.0	(NA)
Canned fruit [3]	21.1	17.6	16.7	15.0	14.4	12.1	12.5	10.9	11.3	(NA)
Fruit juice [4]	115.8	126.5	112.9	97.2	84.8	80.0	77.4	72.2	79.0	(NA)
Frozen fruit [5]	4.3	4.5	5.2	5.1	5.6	4.9	5.1	5.0	5.0	(NA)
Dried fruit [6]	12.2	10.5	10.1	9.3	10.2	2.8	3.2	3.1	3.0	(NA)
Vegetables, total	**391.8**	**425.2**	**415.5**	**399.2**	**384.0**	**408.1**	**388.6**	**396.0**	**383.9**	**373.8**
Fresh vegetables [7]	176.4	200.7	196.4	190.7	186.4	189.7	181.6	180.6	176.2	171.4
Asparagus	0.6	1.0	1.1	1.4	1.5	1.8	1.8	1.8	2.0	1.7
Bell peppers (all uses)	5.9	8.2	9.2	10.3	10.7	11.2	10.9	10.7	11.2	11.1
Broccoli	3.4	5.9	5.3	6.0	7.4	5.9	5.9	5.9	5.1	5.2
Brussels sprouts	0.3	0.3	0.3	0.3	0.7	0.9	1.0	1.3	1.0	1.1
Cabbage	8.3	8.9	7.8	7.5	6.3	5.7	6.4	6.1	5.9	6.2
Carrots	8.3	9.2	8.7	7.8	8.8	12.2	8.3	8.1	8.1	8.4
Cauliflower	2.2	1.7	1.8	1.3	1.6	2.5	3.0	2.6	2.3	2.1
Celery (all uses)	7.2	6.3	5.9	6.1	5.1	4.9	5.2	5.1	4.7	4.1
Collard greens	(NA)	0.8	0.7	1.3	1.2	1.3	1.3	1.3	1.3	1.3
Corn, sweet	6.7	9.0	8.7	9.2	8.6	6.8	5.1	4.3	4.3	4.1
Cucumbers	4.7	6.4	6.2	6.7	7.6	8.0	7.8	7.5	8.0	8.2
Eggplant	0.4	0.8	0.8	0.7	0.8	0.8	0.8	1.0	1.0	1.0
Garlic (all uses)	1.4	2.2	2.4	2.3	2.4	2.4	1.8	1.7	1.7	2.4
Kale	(NA)	0.4	0.3	0.4	0.5	0.7	0.7	0.7	1.1	1.0
Lettuce, head	27.7	23.5	20.9	15.9	13.6	12.3	12.8	11.7	10.6	10.3
Lettuce, Romaine and leaf	3.8	8.4	9.7	12.0	11.9	12.1	12.3	14.3	12.5	12.7
Mushrooms	2.0	2.6	2.6	2.6	3.0	2.8	2.8	2.6	2.5	(NA)
Onions	15.1	18.9	20.9	19.6	18.3	20.6	19.9	20.8	20.8	19.2
Potatoes	46.7	47.1	41.3	36.8	34.2	33.0	30.1	30.3	28.6	28.4
Pumpkin (all uses)	4.4	4.6	4.8	4.4	3.2	5.4	5.0	5.7	6.2	5.6
Radishes (all uses)	0.7	0.5	0.5	0.5	0.5	0.5	0.5	0.7	0.8	0.8
Snap beans	1.1	2.0	1.8	1.9	1.6	1.6	1.4	1.3	1.3	1.2
Spinach	0.8	1.4	2.3	1.7	1.7	1.9	2.4	1.8	1.8	2.1
Squash (all uses)	3.5	4.4	4.4	4.3	4.6	5.6	5.8	5.6	5.7	5.3
Sweet potatoes (all uses)	4.4	4.2	4.5	6.3	7.6	5.6	7.1	6.5	6.4	5.7
Tomatoes	15.5	19.0	20.2	20.6	20.6	20.2	18.3	18.2	18.8	19.0
Processed vegetables [12]	215.3	224.5	219.1	208.4	197.6	218.4	207.0	215.4	207.7	202.4
Canned vegetables [8]	110.3	103.2	104.8	99.4	82.0	91.5	88.4	(NA)	(NA)	(NA)
Frozen vegetables [9]	66.7	79.7	76.4	71.0	70.2	75.8	72.3	(NA)	(NA)	(NA)
Dehydrated vegetables [10]	14.9	17.6	14.8	14.1	17.3	20.2	18.1	18.3	18.8	18.9
Chips, potato	16.3	15.6	16.0	15.0	19.6	17.8	17.9	17.6	17.5	16.9
Pulses [11]	7.2	8.5	6.9	8.9	8.6	13.1	10.3	11.2	10.8	10.3

NA Not available. [1] Excludes wine grapes. [2] Includes other fruits not shown separately. [3] Canned fruit include apples, apricots, cherries, olives, peaches, pears, pineapples, plums, and prunes. [4] Fruit juice includes apple, cranberry, grape, grapefruit, lemon, lime, orange, pineapple, and prune juice. [5] Frozen fruit include apples, apricots, blackberries, blueberries, boysenberries, cherries, loganberries, peaches, plums, prunes, raspberries, strawberries, and other miscellaneous fruit and berries. [6] Dried fruit include apples, apricots, dates, figs, peaches, pears, prunes, and raisins. [7] Includes other vegetables not shown separately. [8] Canned vegetables include asparagus, lima beans, snap beans, beets, cabbage, carrots, sweet corn, cucumbers, mushrooms, green peas, chile peppers, potatoes, spinach, tomatoes, and other miscellaneous vegetables. [9] Frozen vegetables include asparagus, lima beans, snap beans, broccoli, carrots, cauliflower, sweet corn, green peas, potatoes, spinach and other miscellaneous vegetables. [10] Onions and potatoes. [11] Dry peas, beans, and lentils. [12] Estimates for several individual vegetables and total vegetables for canning and freezing are not available after 2019.

Source: U.S. Department of Agriculture, Economic Research Service, "Food Availability (Per Capita) Data System," <www.ers.usda.gov/data-products/food-availability-per-capita-data-system/>, accessed June 2024.

Table 239. Food Availability for Consumption Per Capita by Major Food Commodity: 1980 to 2021

[In pounds, retail weight, except as indicated. Available supply for domestic consumption after subtracting measurable uses, such as farm inputs (feed and seed), exports, ending stocks, and industrial uses. Food availability is a proxy for actual food consumption. Based on Census Bureau estimated resident population plus Armed Forces overseas for most commodities. For commodities not shipped overseas in substantial amounts, such as fluid milk and cream, the resident population is used]

Commodity	Unit	1980	1990	2000	2010	2019	2020	2021
Red meat, total (boneless, trimmed weight) [1]	Pounds	126.4	112.2	113.7	102.0	105.2	105.1	104.8
Beef	Pounds	72.1	63.9	64.5	56.7	55.4	55.7	56.2
Veal	Pounds	1.3	0.9	0.5	0.3	0.2	0.1	0.1
Pork	Pounds	52.1	46.4	47.8	44.4	48.8	48.4	47.5
Lamb	Pounds	1.0	1.0	0.8	0.7	0.8	0.9	1.0
Poultry (boneless, trimmed weight)	Pounds	40.8	56.2	67.9	70.9	79.6	80.3	80.2
Chicken	Pounds	32.7	42.4	54.2	58.0	67.0	67.9	68.1
Turkey	Pounds	8.1	13.8	13.7	12.9	12.6	12.4	12.1
Fish and shellfish (boneless, trimmed weight)	Pounds	12.3	16.7	16.6	17.4	19.1	(NA)	(NA)
Eggs (farm weight)	Number	271.1	234.1	250.7	246.2	293.0	286.3	279.6
Shell	Number	236.2	186.2	178.0	172.1	206.9	210.9	201.5
Processed	Number	34.9	48.0	72.7	74.1	86.1	75.4	78.1
Dairy products, total [2]	Pounds	543.1	568.0	591.1	604.1	651.4	653.6	661.3
Beverage milks [3]	Gallons	27.6	25.7	22.8	20.6	16.4	16.3	15.6
Plain whole milk	Gallons	16.5	10.2	7.8	5.5	5.7	5.9	5.6
Plain reduced-fat milk (2%)	Gallons	6.3	9.1	7.2	7.2	5.4	5.6	5.1
Plain reduced-fat milk (1%)	Gallons	1.8	2.3	2.6	2.8	2.1	2.0	1.9
Plain skim milk	Gallons	1.3	2.6	3.4	3.1	1.2	1.1	0.9
Flavored whole milk	Gallons	0.6	0.3	0.4	0.2	0.3	0.3	0.3
Flavored milk, low-fat and skim	Gallons	0.6	0.8	1.1	1.5	1.3	1.0	1.2
Buttermilk	Gallons	0.5	0.4	0.3	0.2	0.2	0.1	0.2
Yogurt (excl. frozen)	Gallons	0.3	0.5	0.8	1.6	1.5	1.6	1.7
Sour cream	Gallons	0.2	0.3	0.4	0.5	0.5	0.5	0.5
Fluid cream products [4]	Gallons	0.4	0.5	0.7	(NA)	(NA)	(NA)	(NA)
Condensed and evaporated milks	Pounds	7.0	7.9	5.8	7.2	6.7	6.9	6.5
Whole milk	Pounds	3.8	3.1	2.0	2.0	1.9	2.1	2.0
Skim milk	Pounds	3.3	4.8	3.8	5.2	4.8	4.8	4.5
Butter (product weight)	Pounds	4.5	4.3	4.5	4.9	6.2	6.3	6.5
Cheese [5]	Pounds	17.5	24.6	29.8	32.9	38.6	38.4	39.4
American [6]	Pounds	9.6	11.1	12.7	13.3	15.5	15.5	16.1
Cheddar	Pounds	6.8	9.1	9.9	10.1	11.2	11.2	11.4
Italian [6]	Pounds	4.4	8.9	11.4	13.5	15.9	15.6	15.8
Mozzarella	Pounds	3.0	6.9	9.1	10.6	12.5	12.3	12.3
Other [6]	Pounds	3.5	4.6	5.4	5.9	6.9	6.9	7.2
Swiss	Pounds	1.3	1.3	1.0	1.2	1.1	1.0	1.0
Cream and Neufchatel	Pounds	1.0	1.7	2.4	2.3	2.6	2.8	2.9
Cottage cheese, total	Pounds	4.4	3.3	2.6	2.3	2.1	2.0	1.9
Low-fat	Pounds	0.8	1.2	1.3	1.3	1.0	0.9	0.9
Frozen dairy products [7]	Pounds	25.8	28.2	27.5	23.9	22.7	22.3	22.0
Ice cream	Pounds	17.1	15.4	16.1	14.0	12.3	12.8	12.0
Low-fat ice cream	Pounds	6.1	6.6	6.6	6.5	6.8	6.6	6.5
Sherbet	Pounds	1.2	1.2	1.1	1.0	0.8	0.7	0.8
Frozen yogurt	Pounds	(NA)	2.8	2.0	1.0	1.0	0.7	0.9
Flour and cereal products [8]	Pounds	146.4	181.1	199.5	194.2	173.9	173.8	170.0
Wheat flour	Pounds	116.9	135.6	146.3	134.8	131.0	132.3	129.3
Rice, milled	Pounds	11.0	16.2	19.2	20.4	(NA)	(NA)	(NA)
Corn products	Pounds	12.9	21.4	28.4	33.1	36.8	35.5	35.5
Oat products	Pounds	3.9	6.5	4.4	4.7	4.9	4.7	4.8
Caloric sweeteners, total [9]	Pounds	120.2	132.5	150.8	133.8	126.5	126.7	127.3
Sugar, refined cane and beet	Pounds	83.6	64.4	65.5	65.9	68.4	68.8	69.7
Corn sweeteners [10]	Pounds	35.3	66.8	83.6	66.1	56.0	55.9	55.3
High-fructose corn syrup	Pounds	19.0	49.6	64.4	50.6	40.1	40.2	39.5
Honey	Pounds	0.8	0.8	1.1	1.0	1.3	1.3	1.5
Other:								
Cocoa, bean equivalent	Pounds	3.4	5.4	5.9	5.5	(NA)	(NA)	(NA)
Coffee, green bean equivalent	Pounds	10.3	10.3	10.3	9.2	(NA)	(NA)	(NA)
Tea, dry leaf equivalent	Pounds	0.8	0.7	0.8	1.0	(NA)	(NA)	(NA)
Peanuts, total	Pounds	5.1	6.5	6.0	7.2	7.7	8.0	(NA)
Tree nuts, total	Pounds	1.8	2.5	2.6	3.9	5.5	5.8	(NA)

NA Not available. [1] Excludes edible offal. [2] Milk-fat milk-equivalent basis. Includes fluid milk and cream, sour cream, yogurt, butter, cheese, frozen and dry dairy products, and evaporated and condensed milk. [3] Includes eggnog and other miscellaneous milk products not shown separately. [4] Heavy cream, light cream, and half-and-half. Includes total fluid cream sales and volume consumed where produced. [5] Natural equivalent of cheese and cheese products. Excludes full-skim American, cottage, pot, and baker's cheese. [6] Includes other cheeses, not shown separately. [7] Includes other frozen dairy products made with dairy ingredients, and mellorine mix for 1980 to 1990, not shown separately. Excludes whipped cream products. [8] Includes rye flour and barley products, not shown separately. Excludes wheat not ground into flour. [9] Dry weight. Includes edible syrups (maple, molasses, etc.), not shown separately. [10] Includes glucose and dextrose, not shown separately.

Source: U.S. Department of Agriculture, Economic Research Service, "Food Availability (Per Capita) Data System," <www.ers.usda.gov/data-products/food-availability-per-capita-data-system/>, accessed February 2023.

Table 240. Nutrient Consumption From Food and Beverages by Sex, Age, and Race and Hispanic Origin: 2017 to March 2020

[In units as indicated. Covers population age 2 years and older, except as noted. Data are mean amounts per person estimated from Day 1 dietary recall interviews conducted in the What We Eat in America, National Health and Nutrition Examination Survey (NHANES). The NHANES 2019-2020 cycle was interrupted in March 2020 due to the coronavirus 2019 (COVID-19) pandemic, and is not nationally representative. Data from the 2017-2018 and the 2019-2020 cycles of the NHANES were combined to produce nationally representative data for the 2017 to March 2020 period. Data are based on consumption of food and beverages, including water, and exclude intake from dietary supplements and medications. What We Eat in America is a joint project of the USDA and the U.S. Department of Health and Human Services]

Nutrient	Unit	Total	Male	Female	Age 2 to 19	Age 20 and over	White, non-Hispanic	Black, non-Hispanic	Asian, non-Hispanic	Hispanic
Total energy intake......	kcal [1]	2,089	2,379	1,812	1,911	2,144	2,097	2,055	1,921	2,107
Protein......................	g	77.7	89.2	66.8	66.9	81.0	77.8	72.7	78.3	80.4
Carbohydrate..............	g	244	275	214	244	244	241	240	242	254
Sugars, total..............	g	107	119	95	111	105	108	107	86	106
Dietary fiber..............	g	16.0	17.2	14.9	14.1	16.6	15.7	13.5	19.5	17.8
Fats, total.................	g	85.4	96.4	75.0	76.5	88.2	87.4	84.7	71.0	83.0
Saturated fat..............	g	28.1	31.8	24.6	26.4	28.6	29.1	26.7	22.1	27.1
Monounsaturated fat....	g	28.9	32.9	25.2	25.0	30.1	29.5	29.0	24.9	28.0
Polyunsaturated fat......	g	19.9	22.1	17.8	17.4	20.7	20.2	20.7	16.9	19.3
Cholesterol.................	mg	294	334	256	229	314	289	292	269	323
Vitamin A, RAE [2].........	mcg	613	645	583	562	629	640	518	593	576
Thiamin.....................	mg	1.6	1.8	1.3	1.5	1.6	1.6	1.4	1.6	1.6
Riboflavin...................	mg	2.0	2.3	1.7	1.8	2.1	2.1	1.6	1.7	1.9
Niacin.......................	mg	24.7	29.3	20.4	21.2	25.8	25.0	23.5	23.3	25.1
Vitamin B6.................	mg	2.0	2.4	1.7	1.7	2.1	2.1	1.8	1.9	2.1
Folic acid [3]..............	mcg	165	192	140	187	159	163	155	172	172
Folate [3]..................	mcg	198	215	182	151	213	197	171	239	209
Choline.....................	mg	316	361	273	248	337	316	290	314	336
Vitamin B12...............	mcg	4.6	5.6	3.7	4.3	4.8	4.7	4.1	4.0	4.8
Vitamin C..................	mg	75.9	79.5	72.5	71.4	77.3	71.8	77.9	91.0	85.8
Vitamin D..................	mcg	4.4	5.0	3.9	4.8	4.3	4.4	3.8	5.1	4.8
Vitamin E [4]..............	mg	9.0	9.8	8.3	7.8	9.4	9.2	8.5	8.3	8.7
Vitamin K..................	mcg	113.8	111.9	115.7	72.2	126.7	116.2	115.1	135.3	100.9
Calcium.....................	mg	953	1,059	852	978	945	981	818	814	980
Phosphorus................	mg	1,342	1,522	1,171	1,254	1,369	1,362	1,204	1,268	1,381
Magnesium.................	mg	287	318	259	236	303	291	247	304	295
Iron.........................	mg	13.7	15.5	12.0	13.2	13.9	13.7	12.6	13.8	14.2
Zinc.........................	mg	10.4	12.0	8.9	9.2	10.8	10.5	9.2	9.8	10.8
Copper......................	mg	1.1	1.2	1.0	0.9	1.2	1.2	1.0	1.3	1.1
Selenium....................	mcg	108.0	124.8	92.1	93.7	112.5	106.8	104.4	111.6	112.8
Potassium..................	mg	2,475	2,735	2,229	2,088	2,595	2,515	2,177	2,597	2,509
Sodium.....................	mg	3,346	3,824	2,891	2,968	3,463	3,337	3,259	3,454	3,387
Caffeine....................	mg	134.9	150.1	120.4	25.7	168.7	169.0	55.6	81.2	88.9

[1] A kilocalorie is equal to the amount of energy (heat) required to raise the temperature of 1 kilogram of water 1 degree centigrade. The "Calorie" commonly used to measure food energy is actually the kilocalorie. One kilocalorie is the same as one Calorie (upper case C), and represents 1,000 true calories of energy. [2] RAE, retinol activity equivalent. [3] Folate occurs naturally in foods, and covers several forms of vitamin B9. Folic acid is the synthetic form of folate and is added in the manufacturing process of food and supplements. [4] Alpha-tocopherol.

Source: U.S. Department of Agriculture, Agricultural Research Service, Food Surveys Research Group: Beltsville, MD, "What We Eat in America, Data Tables," <www.ars.usda.gov/northeast-area/beltsville-md-bhnrc/beltsville-human-nutrition-research-center/food-surveys-research-group/>, accessed August 2022.

Table 241. Energy Consumption from Food and Beverages: 2005 to 2020

[In units as indicated. Data cover population age 2 years and older, except as noted. See headnote, Table 240]

Energy and component	2005-2006	2007-2008	2009-2010	2011-2012	2013-2014	2015-2016	2017-2018	2017-2020 [4]
Energy (kcal) [1].....................	2,157	2,070	2,081	2,139	2,079	2,048	2,093	2,089
GRAMS								
Protein..........................	81.8	78.1	79.5	79.9	80.3	78.8	78.3	77.7
Carbohydrate......................	265.0	256.0	259.0	266.0	251.0	243.0	247.0	244.0
Sugar...........................	124.0	120.0	119.0	120.0	112.0	106.0	108.0	107.0
Fiber...........................	15.1	15.2	16.2	17.2	16.3	16.5	16.2	16.0
Total fat.............................	81.9	78.3	76.8	80.0	80.0	81.4	85.0	85.4
Saturated fat.....................	27.8	26.3	25.5	26.2	26.3	27.1	28.0	28.1
Monounsaturated fat..............	30.1	28.8	27.5	28.4	27.6	28.4	28.8	28.9
Polyunsaturated fat..............	17.0	16.4	16.8	18.9	18.6	18.6	19.9	19.9
Alcohol [2].........................	(NA)	(NA)	(NA)	12.1	11.0	9.9	10.0	10.6
PERCENT [3]								
Protein..........................	15	15	16	15	16	16	15	15
Carbohydrate......................	50	50	51	51	49	48	48	47
Total fat.............................	34	33	33	33	34	35	36	36
Saturated fat.....................	11	11	11	11	11	12	12	12
Monounsaturated fat..............	12	12	12	12	12	12	12	12
Polyunsaturated fat..............	7	7	7	8	8	8	8	8
Alcohol [2].........................	(NA)	(NA)	(NA)	3	3	3	3	3

NA Not available. [1] See footnote 1, Table 240. [2] Data for alcohol are shown for population age 20 and over. [3] Percents are estimated as a ratio of each person's energy intake of protein, carbohydrate, fat, and alcohol, divided by the individual's total food energy intake. [4] The NHANES 2019-2020 cycle was interrupted in March 2020 due to the COVID-19 pandemic, and is not nationally representative. Data from the 2017-2018 and 2019-2020 cycles of the NHANES were combined to produce nationally representative data for the 2017 to March 2020 period.

Source: U.S. Department of Agriculture, Agricultural Research Service, Food Surveys Research Group: Beltsville, MD, "What We Eat in America, Data Tables," <www.ars.usda.gov/northeast-area/beltsville-md-bhnrc/beltsville-human-nutrition-research-center/food-surveys-research-group/>, accessed August 2022.

Table 242. Foodborne Disease Outbreaks, Illnesses, and Hospitalizations: 1998 to 2022

[Covers outbreaks of foodborne disease, commonly known as food poisoning. A foodborne disease outbreak occurs when two or more people get the same illness from the same contaminated food or drink. Covers only those illnesses for which people seek treatment; local and state health departments get notified of these cases, and investigate and report them into the CDC's National Outbreak Reporting System (NORS). Excludes outbreaks from an exposure outside the U.S., including an illness that occurs after a person returns to the U.S. after having consumed contaminated food outside the U.S. Some outbreaks are not identified nor investigated]

Etiology	1998 to 2022				2022			
	Outbreaks	Illnesses	Hospital-izations	Deaths	Outbreaks	Illnesses	Hospital-izations	Deaths
Total [1].............................	**23,987**	**455,238**	**21,319**	**512**	**371**	**5,647**	**376**	**2**
Selected leading etiologies: [2]								
Bacillus..................................	756	10,778	141	5	10	91	0	0
Campylobacter...........................	629	9,915	449	1	22	391	12	0
Ciguatoxin...............................	373	1,389	162	1	3	8	0	0
Clostridium..............................	1,276	38,622	454	38	19	202	1	0
Cyclospora...............................	156	5,693	172	0	11	283	13	0
Escherichia coli (E. coli), Shiga toxin-producing.................	714	12,930	2,867	49	22	243	55	0
Norovirus................................	6,861	167,493	1,682	18	137	2,150	14	1
Salmonella...............................	3,250	87,273	11,493	118	79	1,860	258	1
Scombroid toxin..........................	481	1,781	52	0	5	15	0	0
Staphylococcus aureus..................	726	11,421	583	5	7	64	4	0
Vibrio...................................	258	2,344	120	3	4	11	0	0

[1] Total includes data for outbreaks with other, unknown, and unidentified etiologies, not shown separately. [2] Includes suspected and confirmed etiologies.

Source: U.S. Centers for Disease Control and Prevention, National Center for Emerging and Zoonotic Infectious Diseases (NCEZID), "BEAM (Bacteria, Enterics, Amoeba, and Mycotics) Dashboard, NORS View," <www.cdc.gov/ncezid/dfwed/beam-dashboard.html>, accessed August 2024.

Education

This section presents data primarily concerning formal education as a whole, at various levels, and for public and private schools. Data shown relate to the school-age population and school enrollment, educational attainment, education personnel, and financial aspects of education. In addition, data are shown for charter schools, homeschooling, post-secondary education, security measures used in schools, and academic libraries. The chief sources are the decennial census of population and the Current Population Survey (CPS), both conducted by the U.S. Census Bureau (see text, Section 1, Population); annual, biennial, and other periodic surveys conducted by the National Center for Education Statistics (NCES), a part of the U.S. Department of Education; and surveys conducted by the National Education Association.

The censuses of population have included data on school enrollment since 1840 and on educational attainment since 1940. The CPS has reported on school enrollment annually and on educational attainment periodically since 1947.

The NCES is continuing the pattern of statistical studies and surveys conducted by the U.S. Office of Education since 1870. The annual *Digest of Education Statistics*, found at <nces.ed.gov/programs/digest>, provides data on pupils, staff, finances (including government expenditures), and organization at the elementary, secondary, and higher education levels. It is also a primary source for detailed information on federal funds for education, projections of enrollment, graduates, and teachers. The *Condition of Education*, issued annually and found at <nces.ed.gov/programs/coe>, presents a summary of information on education of particular interest to policymakers. NCES also conducts special studies periodically.

The Census of Governments, conducted by the Census Bureau every 5 years (for the years ending in "2" and "7"), provides data on school district finances and state and local government expenditures for education. Reports published by the Bureau of Labor Statistics contain data relating civilian labor force experience to educational attainment (see also Tables 627, 653, and 660 in Section 12, Labor Force, Employment, and Earnings).

Types and sources of data—The statistics in this section are of two general types. One type, exemplified by data from the Census Bureau, is based on direct interviews with individuals to obtain information about their own and their family members' education. Data of this type relate to school enrollment and level of education attained, classified by age, sex, and other characteristics of the population. The school enrollment statistics reflect attendance or enrollment in any regular school within a given period; educational attainment statistics reflect the highest grade completed by an individual, or beginning 1992, the highest diploma or degree received.

Beginning in 2012, CPS estimates reflect population controls based on Census 2010. From 2000–2011, the CPS used Census 2000 population controls. From 1994 to 2000, the CPS used 1990 census population controls plus adjustment for undercount. Also beginning 1994, the survey is conducted through computer-assisted technology rather than by paper forms. For years 1981 through 1993, 1980 census population controls were used; 1971 through 1980, 1970 census population controls had been used. These changes had little impact on summary measures (e.g., medians) and proportional measures (e.g., enrollment rates); however, use of the controls may have significant impact on absolute numbers.

The second type of data, generally exemplified by data from the NCES and the National Education Association, is based on reports from administrators of educational institutions and of state and local agencies having jurisdiction over education. Data of this type relate to enrollment, attendance, staff, and finances for the nation, individual states, and local areas.

Unlike the NCES, the Census Bureau does not regularly include specialized vocational, trade, business, or correspondence schools in its surveys. The NCES includes nursery schools and kindergartens that are part of regular grade schools in their enrollment figures. The Census Bureau includes all nursery schools and kindergartens. At the higher education level, the statistics of both agencies are concerned with institutions granting degrees or offering work acceptable for degree-credit, such as junior colleges.

School attendance—All states require that children attend school. While state laws vary as to the ages and circumstances of compulsory attendance, generally they require that formal schooling begin by age 6 and continue to age 16.

Schools—The NCES defines a school as "a division of the school system consisting of students composing one or more grade groups or other identifiable groups, organized as one unit with one or more teachers to give instruction of a defined type, and housed in a school plant of one or more buildings. More than one school may be housed in one school plant, as is the case when the elementary and secondary programs are housed in the same school plant."

Regular schools are those which advance a person toward a diploma or degree. They include public and private nursery schools, kindergartens, graded schools, colleges, universities, and professional schools.

Public schools are schools controlled and supported by local, state, or federal governmental agencies.

Private schools are those controlled and supported mainly by religious organizations or by private persons or organizations.

The Census Bureau defines *elementary* schools as including grades 1 through 8; *high* schools as including grades 9 through 12; and *colleges* as including junior or community colleges, regular 4-year colleges, and universities and graduate or professional schools. Statistics reported by the NCES and the National Education Association by type of organization, such as elementary level and secondary level, may not be strictly comparable with those from the Census Bureau because the grades included at the two levels vary, depending on the level assigned to the middle or junior high school by the local school systems.

School year—Except as otherwise indicated in the tables, data refer to the school year which, for elementary and secondary schools, generally begins in August or September of the preceding year and ends in June of the year stated. For the most part, statistics concerning school finances are for a 12-month period, usually July 1 to June 30. Enrollment data generally refer to a specific point in time, such as Fall, as indicated in the tables.

Statistical reliability—For a discussion of statistical collection, estimation, and sampling procedures and measures of statistical reliability applicable to the Census Bureau and the NCES data, see Appendix III.

Table 243. Federal Funds for Education and Related Programs: 2010 to 2022

[In millions of dollars (179,560.2 represents $179,560,200,000), except percent. For fiscal years ending in September. Figures represent on-budget funds (appropriations or outlays)]

Level, agency, and program	2010	2020	2022
Total, all programs	**179,560.2**	**374,619.3**	**726,068.6**
Percent of federal budget outlays	5.2	5.7	11.6
Elementary/secondary education programs [1]	**75,155.8**	**103,159.2**	**96,177.4**
Department of Education [1]	39,646.5	55,245.7	44,675.7
Education for the disadvantaged [1]	15,864.7	16,996.8	18,229.8
Impact aid program [2]	1,276.2	1,486.1	1,557.1
School improvement programs	6,999.9	6,718.8	7,257.6
Indian education	127.3	180.7	189.2
Special education	12,587.0	13,885.2	14,519.1
Vocational and adult education	2,016.4	1,960.7	2,091.4
Department of Agriculture [1]	18,336.1	25,543.0	28,629.0
Child nutrition programs [3]	16,891.0	23,615.0	26,850.0
Agricultural Marketing Service commodities [3]	1,053.0	1,708.0	1,549.0
Department of Defense [1]	1,981.3	2,213.8	2,455.6
Junior Reserve Officers Training Corps (JROTC)	359.7	392.7	425.8
Overseas dependents schools [4]	1,186.6	1,235.0	1,381.9
Domestic schools [4]	435.1	586.1	647.9
Department of Health and Human Services	7,234.0	10,613.1	10,748.1
Head Start	7,234.0	10,613.1	10,748.1
Department of the Interior [1]	781.1	1,075.6	1,143.2
Mineral Leasing Act and other funds [5]	73.0	73.8	107.5
Indian Education	707.1	1,001.8	1,035.7
Department of Justice	137.5	157.0	210.5
Department of Labor	4,845.7	5,354.9	5,411.9
Job Corps	1,017.2	1,743.7	1,748.7
Department of Veterans Affairs [6]	760.5	1,581.2	1,491.3
Vocational rehabilitation for disabled veterans	760.5	1,559.1	1,463.2
Social Security student benefits	1,281.7	1,219.0	1,168.0
Higher education programs [1]	**58,198.9**	**213,450.0**	**577,519.1**
Department of Education [1]	35,518.2	179,320.4	542,808.4
Student financial assistance	24,596.6	31,663.8	29,676.8
Direct loan program [6]	3,481.9	114,143.5	474,121.3
Federal Family Education Loans [6]	4,274.4	16,599.4	34,896.4
Department of Agriculture	80.7	100.5	109.5
Department of Defense	2,550.7	2,569.7	2,774.1
Tuition assistance for military personnel	669.9	555.7	580.1
Service academies	402.6	256.3	283.4
Senior ROTC	885.5	991.3	988.4
Professional development education	592.6	766.4	922.2
Department of Health and Human Services [1]	10,372.6	16,277.7	19,618.2
Health professions training programs	406.0	734.5	799.1
Medicare medical education benefits	9,080.0	14,500.0	17,700.0
National Health Service Corps scholarships [7]	41.0	38.0	31.4
National Institutes of Health training grants [7]	775.2	909.9	983.6
Department of Homeland Security	45.8	13.7	15.8
Department of the Interior	143.0	60.0	70.2
Indian programs	126.8	41.0	42.5
Department of State	657.7	730.7	740.3
Department of Transportation	90.0	427.7	513.8
Department of Veterans Affairs [1]	8,034.5	12,763.4	9,646.9
Post-Vietnam veterans	1.5	0.1	8.5
All-volunteer-force educational assistance	1,854.9	300.6	253.0
National Endowment for the Humanities	47.9	33.0	37.6
National Science Foundation	618.8	996.4	1,014.7
Other education programs [1]	**9,212.2**	**12,782.7**	**10,790.5**
Department of Education [1] Administration	5,062.7	8,909.1	6,531.4
Rehabilitative services and disability research	1,531.2	2,391.9	2,628.4
Department of Agriculture	3,506.9	3,534.7	3,862.6
Department of Health and Human Services	565.4	618.1	639.9
Department of Homeland Security	339.7	459.4	466.8
Department of Justice	341.1	351.2	355.6
Department of Labor	47.9	8.0	14.6
Department of State	143.5	284.1	291.8
Job Corps	542.7	(NA)	(NA)
Agency for International Development	857.0	806.5	865.4
Corporation for National and Community Service	510.9	551.9	618.3
Library of Congress	339.0	377.8	476.5
National Archives and Records Administration	2.9	2.9	4.6
National Endowment for the Arts	94.6	63.1	69.9
Research programs at universities & related institutions [1,8]	**36,993.3**	**45,227.4**	**41,581.7**
Department of Agriculture	737.2	883.7	1,190.0
Department of Defense	3,154.3	4,988.0	4,778.0
Department of Energy	3,402.6	5,062.8	1,765.0
Department of Health and Human Services	21,796.2	23,948.6	24,637.7
National Aeronautics and Space Administration	1,585.5	3,345.3	1,242.0
National Science Foundation	4,914.7	5,500.3	6,294.9

NA Not available. [1] Includes other programs and agencies, not shown separately. [2] Includes funds used to support school districts with concentrations of children who reside on Indian lands, military bases, low-rent housing properties, and other federal properties, or who have parents in the uniformed services or employed on eligible federal properties. [3] Purchased under Section 32 of the Agricultural Adjustment Act of 1935 (Public Law 74-320) for use in child nutrition programs. [4] The DoD Domestic Dependent Elementary and Secondary Schools (DDESS) program supports students in military communities in the United States, Guam, and Puerto Rico. [5] Data for 2014 through 2022 are estimated. [6] The U.S. Department of Education periodically reestimates the subsidy costs of the Direct Loan Program and Federal Family Education Loan (FFEL) Program to reflect changes in collection and technical assumptions or other changing circumstances. The Federal Family Education Loan (FFEL) Program eliminated the authorization to originate new FFEL loans after June 30, 2010; all new loans are originated through the Direct Loan Program. In 2022, the net upward reestimates were $13.0 billion for the Direct Loan Program and $9.8 billion for the FFEL program. In 2022, there was a large increase in the appropriations of upward modification of existing loans. [7] Includes alcohol, drug abuse, and mental health training programs. [8] Data prior to FY2022 include federal obligations for research and development centers and R&D plant administered by colleges and universities. However, data for this funding are not available for FY2022. Data for 2022 are estimated.

Source: U.S. National Center for Education Statistics, *Digest of Education Statistics*, "Latest version of all Digest tables," <nces.ed.gov/programs/digest>, accessed June 2024.

Table 244. School Expenditures by Level of Instruction in Current and Constant (2021-2022) Dollars: 1980 to 2022

[In millions of dollars (160,075 represents $160,075,000,000). For school years ending in year shown. Data shown reflect historical revisions. Total expenditures for public elementary and secondary schools include current expenditures, interest on school debt, and capital outlay. Based on surveys of state education agencies and higher education institutions; see source for details]

Year	Current dollars			Constant 2021-2022 dollars [1]			
	Total	Elementary and secondary schools	Colleges and universities [2]	Total	Elementary and secondary schools		Colleges and universities [2]
					Total	Public	
1980...............	160,075	103,162	56,914	581,521	374,765	348,609	206,756
1990...............	365,825	231,170	134,656	812,537	513,452	472,584	299,084
2000...............	649,322	412,538	236,784	1,081,712	687,251	636,107	394,461
2005...............	875,988	540,969	335,019	1,288,788	795,895	734,986	492,893
2010...............	1,100,897	654,418	446,479	1,432,535	851,558	789,879	580,978
2011...............	1,124,352	652,356	471,997	1,434,257	832,164	770,934	602,092
2012...............	1,136,876	648,794	488,083	1,408,949	804,060	746,060	604,889
2013...............	1,153,874	655,013	498,861	1,406,607	798,481	739,724	608,126
2014...............	1,192,886	675,818	517,067	1,431,797	811,171	750,197	620,626
2015...............	1,241,626	706,135	535,491	1,479,525	841,433	775,895	638,092
2016...............	1,296,371	736,905	559,466	1,534,412	872,217	802,028	662,196
2017...............	1,352,197	768,623	583,574	1,571,580	893,325	821,499	678,255
2018...............	1,404,183	798,580	605,603	1,596,022	907,682	834,938	688,341
2019...............	1,468,533	836,125	632,409	1,635,276	931,061	856,454	704,215
2020...............	1,517,125	861,719	655,406	1,663,364	944,782	870,227	718,582
2021...............	1,529,000	[3] 874,000	655,292	1,639,000	[3] 937,000	[3] 863,000	702,000
2022 [3].............	1,643,000	945,000	698,000	1,643,000	945,000	870,000	698,000

[1] Constant dollars based on the Consumer Price Index, prepared by the Bureau of Labor Statistics, U.S. Department of Labor, adjusted to a school-year basis. [2] Postsecondary data through 1996 are for institutions of higher education; thereafter, data are for degree-granting institutions. See source for details. [3] Estimated by the National Center for Education Statistics based on teacher and enrollment data and actual expenditures for prior years.

Source: U.S. National Center for Education Statistics, *Digest of Education Statistics*, "Latest version of all Digest tables," <nces.ed.gov/programs/digest/>, accessed December 2023.

Table 245. School Enrollment: 1990 to 2031

[In thousands (60,683 represents 60,683,000). As of Fall]

Year	All levels			Pre-kindergarten through grade 8		Grades 9 through 12		College [3]	
	Total	Public	Private	Public	Private [1,2]	Public	Private [1]	Public	Private
1990.....................	60,683	52,061	8,622	29,876	4,512	11,341	1,136	10,845	2,974
1995.....................	65,020	55,933	9,087	32,338	4,756	12,502	1,163	11,092	3,169
2000.....................	68,685	58,956	9,729	33,686	4,906	13,517	1,264	11,753	3,560
2001.....................	69,920	59,905	10,014	33,936	5,023	13,736	1,296	12,233	3,695
2002.....................	71,015	60,935	10,080	34,114	4,915	14,069	1,306	12,752	3,860
2003.....................	71,551	61,399	10,152	34,201	4,788	14,339	1,311	12,859	4,053
2004.....................	72,154	61,776	10,379	34,178	4,756	14,618	1,331	12,980	4,292
2005.....................	72,674	62,135	10,539	34,204	4,724	14,909	1,349	13,022	4,466
2006.....................	73,061	62,491	10,570	34,235	4,631	15,081	1,360	13,175	4,579
2007.....................	73,459	62,791	10,667	34,204	4,546	15,086	1,364	13,501	4,757
2008.....................	74,055	63,236	10,818	34,286	4,365	14,980	1,342	13,971	5,111
2009.....................	75,163	64,172	10,991	34,409	4,179	14,952	1,309	14,811	5,503
2010.....................	75,886	64,626	11,260	34,625	4,084	14,860	1,299	15,142	5,877
2011.....................	75,800	64,638	11,162	34,773	3,977	14,749	1,291	15,116	5,894
2012.....................	75,748	64,656	11,092	35,018	4,031	14,753	1,302	14,885	5,760
2013.....................	75,817	64,791	11,026	35,251	4,084	14,794	1,312	14,747	5,630
2014.....................	76,097	64,967	11,130	35,370	4,202	14,943	1,373	14,655	5,554
2015.....................	76,177	65,011	11,166	35,388	4,304	15,050	1,446	14,573	5,415
2016.....................	76,216	65,201	11,015	35,477	4,293	15,138	1,460	14,586	5,261
2017.....................	76,184	65,257	10,926	35,496	4,252	15,190	1,468	14,572	5,206
2018.....................	75,955	65,233	10,722	35,498	4,167	15,196	1,443	14,539	5,112
2019.....................	75,912	65,300	10,612	35,551	4,066	15,246	1,420	14,504	5,127
2020, [4]................	74,405	63,259	11,145	34,061	4,496	15,314	1,506	13,884	5,143
2021, [4]................	74,153	62,977	11,176	33,998	4,544	15,436	1,516	13,544	5,116
2022, projection...........	74,162	63,126	11,036	33,724	4,399	15,539	1,540	13,864	5,098
2023, projection...........	73,774	62,874	10,900	33,484	4,278	15,528	1,544	13,861	5,079
2024, projection...........	73,591	62,795	10,796	33,267	4,151	15,441	1,486	14,088	5,160
2025, projection...........	73,305	62,546	10,759	33,037	4,044	15,190	1,466	14,318	5,249
2026, projection...........	72,802	62,134	10,668	32,722	3,890	14,923	1,460	14,490	5,318
2027, projection...........	72,614	61,973	10,641	32,633	3,818	14,737	1,459	14,603	5,365
2028, projection...........	72,441	61,860	10,580	32,542	3,715	14,642	1,466	14,676	5,399
2029, projection...........	72,256	61,742	10,514	32,522	3,561	14,505	1,535	14,714	5,418
2030, projection...........	72,097	61,677	10,420	32,313	3,546	14,627	1,444	14,736	5,431
2031, projection...........	72,026	61,675	10,351	32,225	3,545	14,664	1,357	14,785	5,449

[1] Since the biennial Private School Universe Survey (PSS) is collected in the fall of odd numbered years, data for even numbered years are estimated. [2] Excludes preprimary students in private schools that do not offer kindergarten or higher grades. [3] Postsecondary data through 1995 are for institutions of higher education, while later data are for degree-granting institutions. Degree-granting institutions grant associate's or higher degrees and participate in Title IV federal financial aid programs. The degree-granting classification is very similar to the earlier higher education classification, but it includes more 2-year colleges and excludes a few higher education institutions that did not grant degrees. [4] Data for private school enrollment pre-K through 12 are projections.

Source: U.S. National Center for Education Statistics, *Digest of Education Statistics*, "Latest version of all Digest tables," <nces.ed.gov/programs/digest>, accessed November 2023.

Table 246. School Enrollment, Faculty, Graduates, and Finances—Projections: 2021 to 2031

[In units as indicated (55,493 represents 55,493,000). As of the fall for the academic years indicated below, except as noted. Data for higher education are for degree-granting institutions that grant associate's or higher degrees and participate in Title IV federal financial aid programs]

Item	Unit	2021[1]	2022	2023	2024	2025	2030	2031
ELEMENTARY AND SECONDARY SCHOOLS								
School enrollment, total	1,000	55,493	55,201	54,834	54,344	53,737	51,930	51,792
Pre-kindergarten through grade 8	1,000	38,542	38,123	37,762	37,417	37,081	35,860	35,771
Grades 9 through 12	1,000	16,951	17,078	17,072	16,927	16,656	16,071	16,021
Public	1,000	49,433	49,262	49,012	48,707	48,228	46,940	46,890
Pre-kindergarten through grade 8	1,000	33,998	33,724	33,484	33,267	33,037	32,313	32,225
Grades 9 through 12	1,000	15,436	15,539	15,528	15,441	15,190	14,627	14,664
Private	1,000	6,060	5,939	5,822	5,636	5,510	4,990	4,902
Pre-kindergarten through grade 8	1,000	4,544	4,399	4,278	4,151	4,044	3,546	3,545
Grades 9 through 12	1,000	1,516	1,540	1,544	1,486	1,466	1,444	1,357
Classroom teachers, total FTE[2]	1,000	3,698	3,656	3,662	3,684	3,688	3,672	3,676
Public	1,000	3,214	3,176	3,181	3,200	3,203	3,186	3,188
Private	1,000	483	480	481	484	485	486	487
High school graduates, total	1,000	3,670	3,684	3,733	3,798	3,793	3,549	(NA)
Public	1,000	3,343	3,358	3,343	3,457	3,444	3,216	(NA)
Private	1,000	327	326	391	341	349	333	(NA)
Public schools:								
Constant (2022-2023) dollars:[3]								
Current school expenditure	Bil. dol.	794.5	780.0	780.8	783.6	783.3	776.2	775.7
Per pupil in fall enrollment	Dollar	16,065	15,833	15,930	16,089	16,242	16,535	16,544
HIGHER EDUCATION								
Enrollment, total	1,000	18,660	18,961	18,940	19,248	19,568	20,167	20,234
Full-time	1,000	11,330	11,548	11,511	11,694	11,907	12,171	12,177
Males	1,000	4,889	4,937	4,915	5,003	5,106	5,257	5,262
Females	1,000	6,442	6,611	6,596	6,691	6,801	6,914	6,914
Part-time	1,000	7,330	7,413	7,428	7,554	7,661	7,996	8,057
Males	1,000	2,881	2,877	2,878	2,935	2,987	3,148	3,177
Females	1,000	4,449	4,536	4,550	4,618	4,674	4,848	4,880
Public	1,000	13,544	13,864	13,861	14,088	14,318	14,736	14,785
Four-year institutions	1,000	9,066	9,143	9,128	9,275	9,432	9,716	9,739
Two-year institutions	1,000	4,478	4,721	4,733	4,813	4,887	5,020	5,046
Private	1,000	5,116	5,098	5,079	5,160	5,249	5,431	5,449
Four-year institutions	1,000	4,912	4,890	4,872	4,950	5,036	5,214	5,232
Two-year institutions	1,000	205	207	207	210	214	216	217
Undergraduate	1,000	15,448	15,870	15,887	16,145	16,407	16,790	16,823
Postbaccalaureate	1,000	3,211	3,183	3,052	3,103	3,161	3,377	3,411
Full-time equivalent	1,000	14,030	14,277	14,245	14,474	14,726	15,115	15,143
Public	1,000	9,766	10,049	10,035	10,196	10,372	10,625	10,643
2-year	1,000	2,468	2,657	2,658	2,701	2,746	2,803	2,813
4-year	1,000	7,298	7,393	7,377	7,495	7,626	7,822	7,830
Private	1,000	4,264	4,228	4,210	4,278	4,355	4,490	4,500
2-year	1,000	197	199	198	201	205	207	207
4-year	1,000	4,068	4,030	4,012	4,077	4,150	4,283	4,293
Degrees conferred, total	1,000	4,155	4,211	4,221	4,264	4,356	4,768	4,833
Associate's	1,000	999	1,013	1,019	1,029	1,047	1,126	1,139
Bachelor's	1,000	2,075	2,114	2,136	2,168	2,217	2,434	2,464
Master's	1,000	883	882	860	864	886	983	1,000
Doctoral[4]	1,000	197	202	206	203	205	225	230

NA Not available. [1] Data are projected except for public elementary and secondary education enrollment, higher education enrollment, and classroom teachers. [2] Full-time equivalent. [3] Based on the Consumer Price Index (CPI) for all urban consumers, U.S. Bureau of Labor Statistics. CPI adjusted to a school year basis by NCES. [4] Doctoral degrees include Ph.D., Ed.D., and comparable degrees at the doctoral level. Includes most degrees formerly classified as first-professional, such as M.D., D.D.S., and law degrees.

Source: U.S. National Center for Education Statistics, *Digest of Education Statistics*, "Latest version of all Digest Tables," <nces.ed.gov/programs/digest/>, accessed February 2024. See also <nces.ed.gov/programs/pes/>.

Table 247. School Enrollment by Control and Level: 1990 to 2023

[In thousands (60,683 represents 60,683,000). As of Fall. Data below college level are for regular day schools and exclude subcollegiate departments of colleges, federal schools, and home-schooled children. Based on survey of state education agencies; see source for details. For more projections, see Table 245 and Table 246]

Control of school and level	1990	2000	2005	2010	2015	2019	2020	2021	2022, proj.	2023, proj.
Total	60,683	68,685	72,674	75,886	76,177	75,912	74,405	74,153	74,162	73,774
Public	52,061	58,956	62,135	64,626	65,011	65,300	63,259	62,977	63,126	62,874
Private	8,622	9,729	10,539	11,260	11,166	10,612	11,145	11,176	11,036	10,900
Pre-kindergarten through 8	34,388	38,592	38,928	38,708	39,692	39,617	38,557	38,542	38,123	37,762
Public	29,876	33,686	34,204	34,625	35,388	35,551	34,061	33,998	33,724	33,484
Private[1]	4,512	4,906	4,724	4,084	4,304	4,066	4,496	4,544	4,399	4,278
Grades 9 through 12	12,476	14,781	16,258	16,159	16,496	16,665	16,820	16,951	17,078	17,072
Public	11,341	13,517	14,909	14,860	15,050	15,246	15,314	15,436	15,539	15,528
Private[1]	1,136	1,264	1,349	1,299	1,446	1,420	1,506	1,516	1,540	1,544
College[2]	13,819	15,312	17,487	21,019	19,988	19,630	19,027	18,660	18,961	18,940
Public	10,845	11,753	13,022	15,142	14,573	14,504	13,884	13,544	13,864	13,861
Private	2,974	3,560	4,466	5,877	5,415	5,127	5,143	5,116	5,098	5,079
Not-for-profit	2,760	3,109	3,455	3,854	4,066	4,135	4,101	4,113	(NA)	(NA)
For profit	214	450	1,011	2,023	1,349	991	1,042	1,003	(NA)	(NA)

NA Not available. [1] Private school data for even numbered years are estimated; 2020 and 2021 data are projected. [2] Beginning 2000, reflects new classification system. See footnote 3, Table 245.

Source: U.S. National Center for Education Statistics, *Digest of Education Statistics*, "Latest version of all Digest tables," <nces.ed.gov/programs/digest>, accessed December 2023.

Table 248. School Enrollment by Age: 1970 to 2022

[Enrollment in thousands (60,357 represents 60,357,000); rate as percent of total population in each age group. As of October. Covers civilian noninstitutional population enrolled in nursery school and above. Based on Current Population Survey; see text, Section 1 and Appendix III]

Age	1970	1980	1990	2000	2010	2016	2019	2020	2021	2022
ENROLLMENT (1,000)										
Total, 3 to 34 years old...........	60,357	57,348	60,588	69,560	75,148	74,672	73,571	70,868	71,487	72,753
3 and 4 years old...................	1,461	2,280	3,292	4,097	4,706	4,289	4,334	3,189	3,870	4,041
5 and 6 years old...................	7,000	5,853	7,207	7,648	7,955	7,507	7,506	7,268	7,314	7,385
7 to 13 years old...................	28,943	23,751	25,016	28,296	27,984	28,381	28,212	27,573	27,653	28,040
14 and 15 years old...............	7,869	7,282	6,555	7,885	7,736	8,107	8,141	8,159	8,196	8,612
16 and 17 years old...............	6,927	7,129	6,098	7,341	7,963	7,879	7,778	7,671	7,826	8,141
18 and 19 years old...............	3,322	3,788	4,044	4,926	5,904	5,741	5,586	5,484	5,177	5,324
20 and 21 years old...............	1,949	2,515	2,852	3,314	4,552	4,597	4,641	4,621	4,288	4,381
22 to 24 years old.................	1,410	1,931	2,231	2,731	3,602	3,841	3,537	3,236	3,249	3,396
25 to 29 years old.................	1,011	1,714	2,013	2,030	3,088	2,966	2,517	2,366	2,621	2,282
30 to 34 years old.................	466	1,105	1,281	1,292	1,658	1,364	1,319	1,301	1,293	1,151
35 years old and over............	(NA)	1,290	2,439	2,653	3,372	2,561	2,520	2,353	2,347	2,418
ENROLLMENT RATE										
Total, 3 to 34 years old...........	56.4	49.7	50.2	55.9	56.5	55.2	54.1	52.4	53.1	53.8
3 and 4 years old...................	20.5	36.7	44.4	52.1	53.2	53.8	53.7	40.3	50.4	53.3
5 and 6 years old...................	89.5	95.7	96.5	95.6	94.5	93.3	93.6	89.2	91.2	93.0
7 to 13 years old...................	99.2	99.3	99.6	98.2	98.0	98.2	97.8	96.4	97.0	97.5
14 and 15 years old...............	98.1	98.2	99.0	98.7	98.1	98.0	97.9	97.8	97.8	97.5
16 and 17 years old...............	90.0	89.0	92.5	92.8	96.1	93.0	92.7	92.3	93.7	92.8
18 and 19 years old...............	47.7	46.4	57.3	61.2	69.2	69.5	67.3	66.5	63.9	63.9
20 and 21 years old...............	31.9	31.0	39.7	44.1	52.4	55.5	53.5	52.8	51.4	51.4
22 to 24 years old.................	14.9	16.3	21.0	24.6	28.9	28.8	28.6	26.6	26.1	27.4
25 to 29 years old.................	7.5	9.3	9.7	11.4	14.6	13.2	11.0	10.5	11.9	10.7
30 to 34 years old.................	4.2	6.5	5.8	6.7	8.3	6.4	6.0	5.8	5.7	5.1
35 years old and over............	(NA)	1.6	2.1	1.9	2.1	1.5	1.4	1.3	1.3	1.3

NA Not available.

Source: U.S. Census Bureau, Current Population Reports, P-20, and earlier reports; and "School Enrollment Tables," <www.census.gov/topics/education/school-enrollment/data/tables.html>, accessed November 2023.

Table 249. School Enrollment by Race, Hispanic Origin, and Age: 2010 to 2022

[Enrollment in thousands (56,776 represents 56,776,000); rate as percent of total population in each age group. As of October. Covers civilian noninstitutional population enrolled in nursery school and above. Based on Current Population Survey; see text, Section 1 and Appendix III]

Age	White alone			Black alone			Hispanic [1]		
	2010	2020	2022	2010	2020	2022	2010	2020	2022
ENROLLMENT (1,000)									
Total, 3 to 34 years old............	**56,776**	**50,905**	**51,499**	**11,272**	**10,568**	**11,042**	**15,235**	**17,097**	**17,753**
3 and 4 years old...................	3,439	2,266	2,741	776	491	729	1,025	674	938
5 and 6 years old...................	5,956	5,172	5,145	1,207	1,152	1,138	1,961	1,821	1,896
7 to 13 years old....................	21,201	19,857	19,832	4,108	4,114	4,321	6,241	7,165	7,199
14 and 15 years old................	5,907	5,913	6,196	1,157	1,224	1,312	1,555	2,075	2,234
16 and 17 years old................	6,059	5,628	5,832	1,245	1,115	1,160	1,448	1,815	1,962
18 and 19 years old................	4,566	3,949	3924	837	867	766	1,171	1,289	1,346
20 and 21 years old................	3,432	3,338	3195	678	551	588	582	1,000	852
22 to 24 years old..................	2,720	2,285	2398	514	471	441	559	578	670
25 to 29 years old..................	2,289	1,636	1466	462	339	374	462	494	470
30 to 34 years old..................	1,207	861	770	288	244	213	231	186	186
35 years old and over..............	2,462	1,603	1,600	697	445	502	435	426	481
ENROLLMENT RATE									
Total, 3 to 34 years old.............	**55.8**	**51.8**	**52.8**	**58.4**	**52.2**	**54.1**	**55.1**	**53.4**	**54.7**
3 and 4 years old...................	52.1	40.0	52.1	56.2	40.1	60.6	44.2	32.9	47.4
5 and 6 years old...................	94.2	89.2	92.7	94.4	90.0	93.6	94.3	87.0	92.6
7 to 13 years old...................	97.9	96.4	97.3	98.0	95.9	97.9	97.8	95.8	97.0
14 and 15 years old...............	98.1	97.5	97.3	98.5	98.8	97.8	97.9	98.1	97.6
16 and 17 years old...............	96.2	92.7	92.7	95.5	93.2	91.0	96.0	91.3	93.7
18 and 19 years old...............	70.0	65.1	63.2	62.7	71.6	62.9	66.2	62.7	60.9
20 and 21 years old...............	51.6	53.2	51.3	50.2	41.5	45.9	37.0	47.8	42.1
22 to 24 years old.................	28.1	25.3	26.3	29.0	26.9	24.7	23.8	21.2	22.9
25 to 29 years old.................	13.9	10.0	9.4	16.0	9.8	11.7	11.4	10.2	10.0
30 to 34 years old.................	7.8	5.3	4.7	10.9	7.5	6.1	5.7	4.0	3.9
35 years old and over..............	1.9	1.1	1.1	4.0	2.1	2.3	2.3	1.6	1.7

[1] Persons of Hispanic origin may be of any race.

Source: U.S. Census Bureau, Current Population Reports, P-20, and earlier reports; and "School Enrollment Tables," <www.census.gov/topics/education/school-enrollment/data/tables.All.html>, accessed November 2023.

Table 250. Enrollment in Public and Private Schools: 1970 to 2022

[In millions (52.2 represents 52,200,000), except percent. As of October. For civilian noninstitutional population. Prior to 1995, total enrolled does not include the population age 35 and over. For enrollment of population age 35 and over, see Table 248. Based on Current Population Survey]

Year	Public						Private					
	Total	Nursery	Kinder-garten	Elemen-tary	High school	College	Total	Nursery	Kinder-garten	Elemen-tary	High school	College
1970...........	52.2	0.3	2.6	30.0	13.6	5.7	8.1	0.8	0.5	3.9	1.2	1.7
1980...........	(NA)	0.6	2.7	24.4	(NA)	(NA)	(NA)	1.4	0.5	3.1	(NA)	(NA)
1990 [1]......	51.8	1.2	3.3	26.6	11.8	8.9	8.7	2.2	0.6	2.7	0.9	2.4
2000...........	61.2	2.2	3.2	29.4	14.4	12.0	11.0	2.2	0.7	3.5	1.3	3.3
2005...........	64.3	2.5	3.3	29.1	15.9	13.4	11.5	2.1	0.6	3.4	1.4	4.0
2010...........	67.9	2.8	3.8	29.8	15.3	16.2	10.6	2.1	0.4	2.8	1.2	4.1
2011...........	68.2	2.9	3.7	30.0	15.4	16.1	10.9	2.0	0.5	2.9	1.2	4.3
2012...........	67.8	2.7	3.7	29.9	15.7	15.8	10.7	1.9	0.5	2.8	1.3	4.2
2013...........	67.4	2.6	3.7	30.2	15.5	15.5	10.3	2.1	0.4	2.7	1.1	4.0
2014...........	66.8	2.7	3.6	29.8	15.4	15.3	10.4	2.0	0.5	2.8	1.3	3.9
2015...........	67.0	2.6	3.6	30.2	15.4	15.2	10.1	1.9	0.4	2.7	1.2	3.9
2016...........	66.7	2.8	3.7	30.0	15.3	15.0	10.5	1.9	0.4	2.6	1.3	4.2
2017...........	66.6	2.8	3.5	29.9	15.6	14.8	9.9	1.9	0.4	2.7	1.3	3.6
2018...........	66.7	2.8	3.5	29.7	15.5	15.2	10.1	2.1	0.4	2.8	1.2	3.7
2019...........	65.9	2.6	3.5	29.8	15.2	14.8	10.2	2.1	0.5	2.9	1.2	3.5
2020...........	62.7	2.1	3.1	28.6	15.0	13.9	10.5	1.5	0.6	3.4	1.3	3.8
2021...........	63.7	2.5	3.6	28.7	15.1	13.8	10.1	1.8	0.5	3.1	1.2	3.5
2022...........	65.1	2.5	3.5	29.4	15.8	14.0	10.0	1.9	0.5	3.0	1.4	3.3
Percent White:												
1970...........	84.5	59.5	84.4	83.1	85.6	90.7	93.4	91.1	88.2	94.1	96.1	92.8
1980...........	(NA)	68.2	80.7	80.9	(NA)	(NA)	(NA)	89.0	87.0	90.7	(NA)	(NA)
1990...........	79.5	71.7	78.3	78.9	79.3	83.4	87.5	89.6	83.2	88.2	89.4	85.1
2000...........	77.0	69.4	77.3	76.7	78.0	78.0	83.5	84.8	82.7	85.9	84.6	79.8
2005 [2].......	75.7	71.3	78.0	75.2	76.0	76.6	81.4	83.6	79.0	83.0	83.6	78.4
2010 [2].......	74.9	71.8	72.9	75.1	75.2	75.4	78.9	81.0	79.4	80.9	84.5	74.7
2015 [2].......	72.3	68.1	72.2	72.2	72.9	72.7	75.5	75.5	79.4	78.7	79.4	71.9
2016 [2].......	72.3	70.7	70.6	72.7	71.9	72.5	74.3	75.3	77.2	74.1	78.7	72.3
2017 [2].......	71.6	67.8	72.8	71.6	72.7	71.0	75.8	75.5	80.1	76.3	75.3	75.2
2018 [2].......	71.2	70.3	71.1	71.5	72.0	70.1	75.9	75.5	84.7	76.8	82.8	72.2
2019 [2].......	70.9	67.2	71.7	71.0	72.8	69.3	74.8	75.5	69.0	78.8	73.3	72.5
2020 [2].......	71.3	68.2	71.5	71.4	72.0	70.9	74.0	77.5	72.5	75.7	77.6	69.9
2021 [2].......	70.3	69.5	69.8	70.2	71.6	69.6	74.5	72.1	69.6	77.5	81.5	71.2
2022 [2].......	70.1	64.0	70.6	69.7	71.5	70.3	74.1	74.9	74.2	76.8	80.5	68.3

NA Not available. [1] Beginning 1990, based on a revised edit and tabulation package. [2] Beginning in 2003, represents persons who selected this race group only. See footnote 4, Table 252.

Source: U.S. Census Bureau, Current Population Reports, P-20, and earlier reports; and "School Enrollment: CPS Historical Time Series Tables on School Enrollment," <www.census.gov/topics/education/school-enrollment/data/tables.All.html>, accessed November 2023.

Table 251. School Enrollment by Sex and Level: 1970 to 2022

[In millions (60.4 represents 60,400,000). As of October. For the civilian noninstitutional population. Prior to 1980, data cover persons age 3 to 34; beginning 1980, age 3 and over. Elementary includes kindergarten and grades 1–8; high school, grades 9–12; and college, 2-year and 4-year colleges, universities, and graduate and professional schools. Data for college represent degree-credit enrollment. Based on Current Population Survey; see text, Section 1 and Appendix III]

Year	All levels [1]			Elementary			High school			College		
	Total	Male	Female	Total	Male	Female	Total	Male	Female	Total	Male	Female
1970...........	60.4	31.4	28.9	37.1	19.0	18.1	14.7	7.4	7.3	7.4	4.4	3.0
1980...........	58.6	29.6	29.1	30.6	15.8	14.9	14.6	7.3	7.3	11.4	5.4	6.0
1990 [2]........	63.0	31.5	31.5	33.2	17.1	16.0	12.8	6.5	6.4	13.6	6.2	7.4
2000...........	72.2	35.8	36.4	36.7	18.9	17.9	15.8	8.1	7.7	15.3	6.7	8.6
2001...........	73.1	36.3	36.9	36.9	19.0	17.9	16.1	8.2	7.8	15.9	6.9	9.0
2002...........	74.0	36.8	37.3	36.7	18.9	17.8	16.4	8.3	8.0	16.5	7.2	9.3
2003...........	74.9	37.3	37.6	36.3	18.7	17.6	17.1	8.6	8.4	16.6	7.3	9.3
2004...........	75.5	37.4	38.0	36.5	19.0	17.6	16.8	8.4	8.4	17.4	7.6	9.8
2005...........	75.8	37.4	38.4	36.4	18.6	17.7	17.4	8.9	8.5	17.5	7.5	9.9
2006...........	75.2	37.2	38.0	36.1	18.5	17.6	17.1	8.8	8.4	17.2	7.5	9.7
2007...........	76.0	37.6	38.4	36.3	18.6	17.7	17.1	8.8	8.3	18.0	7.8	10.1
2008...........	76.4	37.8	38.6	36.4	18.7	17.7	16.7	8.5	8.2	18.6	8.3	10.3
2009...........	77.3	38.0	39.3	36.4	18.6	17.7	16.4	8.4	8.1	19.8	8.6	11.1
2010...........	78.5	38.7	39.8	36.8	18.8	18.1	16.6	8.5	8.1	20.3	9.0	11.3
2011...........	79.0	39.2	39.8	37.1	19.0	18.1	16.6	8.6	8.1	20.4	9.1	11.3
2012...........	78.4	38.5	39.9	36.8	19.0	17.9	17.0	8.6	8.5	19.9	8.6	11.3
2013...........	77.8	38.3	39.5	37.0	19.0	18.0	16.6	8.4	8.2	19.5	8.5	10.9
2014...........	77.2	38.2	39.0	36.7	18.8	17.9	16.7	8.4	8.2	19.2	8.6	10.5
2015...........	77.1	38.2	38.9	36.9	18.9	18.0	16.5	8.4	8.1	19.1	8.5	10.6
2016...........	77.2	38.4	38.9	36.6	18.7	17.9	16.7	8.5	8.1	19.2	8.6	10.6
2017...........	76.4	37.8	38.6	36.5	18.7	17.8	16.8	8.6	8.3	18.4	8.1	10.3
2018...........	76.8	38.0	38.8	36.4	18.6	17.8	16.7	8.6	8.1	18.9	8.4	10.5
2019...........	76.1	37.8	38.3	36.7	18.8	17.9	16.4	8.4	8.0	18.3	8.1	10.2
2020...........	73.2	35.9	37.3	35.7	18.4	17.4	16.3	8.2	8.1	17.7	7.6	10.1
2021...........	73.8	36.1	37.7	35.9	18.4	17.5	16.3	8.2	8.1	17.3	7.3	10.1
2022...........	75.2	37.1	38.1	36.4	18.7	17.7	17.2	8.8	8.3	17.3	7.3	10.0

[1] Includes nursery schools, not shown separately. [2] For data beginning 1990, based on a revised edit and tabulation package.

Source: U.S. Census Bureau, Current Population Reports, P-20, and earlier reports; and "School Enrollment Tables," <www.census.gov/topics/education/school-enrollment/data/tables.All.html>, accessed November 2023.

Table 252. Educational Attainment by Race and Hispanic Origin: 1970 to 2022

[In percent. For persons 25 years old and over. 1970 and 1980 data as of April 1 and based on sample data from the censuses of population. Other years as of March and based on the Current Population Survey; see text, Section 1 and Appendix III. See Table 253 for data by sex]

Year	High school graduate or more [1]					College graduate or more [2]				
	Total [3]	White [4]	Black [4]	Asian [4]	His-panic [5]	Total [3]	White [4]	Black [4]	Asian [4]	His-panic [5]
1970	55.2	57.4	33.7	(NA)	(NA)	11.0	11.6	4.5	(NA)	(NA)
1980	68.6	70.5	51.2	(NA)	45.3	17.0	17.8	7.9	(NA)	7.9
1990	77.6	79.1	66.2	(NA)	50.8	21.3	22.0	11.3	(NA)	9.2
2000	84.1	84.9	78.5	(NA)	57.0	25.6	26.1	16.5	(NA)	10.6
2010	87.1	87.6	84.2	88.9	62.9	29.9	30.3	19.8	52.4	13.9
2011	87.6	88.1	84.5	88.6	64.3	30.4	31.0	19.9	50.3	14.1
2012	87.6	88.1	85.0	88.9	65.0	30.9	31.3	21.2	51.0	14.5
2013	88.2	88.6	85.1	90.1	66.2	31.7	32.0	21.8	53.2	15.1
2014	88.3	88.8	85.8	89.5	66.5	32.0	32.3	22.2	52.3	15.2
2015	88.4	88.8	87.0	89.1	66.7	32.5	32.8	22.5	53.9	15.5
2016	89.1	89.5	87.1	90.3	68.5	33.4	33.7	23.3	55.9	16.4
2017	89.6	90.1	87.3	90.9	70.5	34.2	34.5	23.9	54.8	17.2
2018	89.8	90.2	87.9	90.5	71.6	35.0	35.2	25.2	56.5	18.3
2019	90.1	90.5	87.9	91.2	71.8	36.0	36.3	26.1	58.1	18.8
2020	90.9	91.3	89.4	91.6	74.3	37.5	37.5	27.8	61.1	20.8
2021	91.1	91.2	90.3	92.9	74.2	37.9	37.9	28.1	61.0	20.6
2022	91.2	91.4	90.1	92.3	75.2	37.7	37.9	27.6	59.3	20.9

NA Not available. [1] Through 1991, completed 4 years of high school or more. [2] Through 1991, completed 4 years of college or more. [3] Includes other races not shown separately. [4] The 2003 Current Population Survey (CPS) allowed respondents to choose more than one race. Beginning 2003, data represent persons who selected this race group only and exclude persons reporting more than one race. Before 2003, the CPS permitted respondents to report only one race group. See also comments on race in the text for Section 1, Population. [5] Persons of Hispanic origin may be of any race.

Source: U.S. Census Bureau, U.S. Census of Population,1960, 1970, and 1980, Summary File 3; Current Population Reports, P20-550, and earlier reports; and "Educational Attainment in the United States: CPS Historical Time Series Tables," <www.census.gov/topics/education/educational-attainment.html>, accessed March 2023.

Table 253. Educational Attainment by Race, Hispanic Origin, and Sex: 1970 to 2022

[In percent. See Table 252 for headnote and totals for both sexes]

Year	All races [1]		White [2]		Black [2]		Asian [2]		Hispanic [3]	
	Male	Female	Male	Female	Male	Female	Male	Female	Male	Female
HIGH SCHOOL GRADUATE OR MORE [4]										
1970	55.0	55.4	57.2	57.6	32.4	34.8	(NA)	(NA)	(NA)	(NA)
1980	69.2	68.1	71.0	70.1	51.1	51.3	(NA)	(NA)	46.4	44.1
1990	77.7	77.5	79.1	79.0	65.8	66.5	(NA)	(NA)	50.3	51.3
2000	84.2	84.0	84.8	85.0	78.7	78.3	(NA)	(NA)	56.6	57.5
2010	86.6	87.6	86.9	88.2	83.6	84.6	91.2	87.0	61.4	64.4
2011	87.1	88.0	87.4	88.6	83.8	85.0	90.4	87.1	63.6	65.1
2012	87.3	88.0	87.6	88.5	84.3	85.5	90.4	87.6	64.0	66.0
2013	87.6	88.6	88.0	89.2	84.1	86.0	91.5	89.0	64.6	67.9
2014	87.7	88.9	88.0	89.6	85.3	86.2	91.9	87.4	65.1	67.9
2015	88.0	88.8	88.3	89.3	86.4	87.6	91.0	87.4	65.5	67.8
2016	88.5	89.6	88.8	90.1	86.4	87.7	91.9	89.0	67.2	69.7
2017	89.1	90.0	89.5	90.6	86.5	87.9	92.6	89.4	69.5	71.6
2018	89.4	90.2	89.6	90.8	87.7	88.1	92.7	88.6	70.7	72.5
2019	89.6	90.5	89.9	91.0	87.1	88.6	92.8	89.8	70.8	72.8
2020	90.6	91.3	90.8	91.7	88.6	90.0	92.6	90.7	73.8	74.8
2021	90.5	91.6	90.5	91.8	89.8	90.7	94.0	91.9	72.6	75.9
2022	90.6	91.8	90.7	92.1	89.2	90.8	93.5	91.1	74.0	76.4
COLLEGE GRADUATE OR MORE [4]										
1970	14.1	8.2	15.0	8.6	4.6	4.4	(NA)	(NA)	(NA)	(NA)
1980	20.9	13.6	22.1	14.0	7.7	8.1	(NA)	(NA)	9.7	6.2
1990	24.4	18.4	25.3	19.0	11.9	10.8	(NA)	(NA)	9.8	8.7
2000	27.8	23.6	28.5	23.9	16.3	16.7	(NA)	(NA)	10.7	10.6
2010	30.3	29.6	30.8	29.9	17.7	21.4	55.6	49.5	12.9	14.9
2011	30.8	30.1	31.5	30.5	18.0	21.4	53.4	47.7	13.1	15.2
2012	31.4	30.6	31.9	30.8	19.2	22.9	53.7	48.8	13.3	15.8
2013	32.0	31.4	32.4	31.6	19.8	23.3	56.1	50.8	13.9	16.2
2014	31.9	32.0	32.3	32.3	20.4	23.7	54.7	50.3	14.2	16.1
2015	32.3	32.7	32.6	32.9	20.6	24.0	56.8	51.5	14.3	16.6
2016	33.2	33.7	33.4	34.0	21.7	24.6	58.8	53.4	15.4	17.4
2017	33.7	34.6	34.0	35.0	22.1	25.4	56.6	53.2	15.8	18.6
2018	34.6	35.3	34.9	35.5	23.2	26.9	59.3	54.0	16.6	20.1
2019	35.4	36.6	35.7	36.8	24.1	27.7	60.4	56.1	16.9	20.8
2020	36.7	38.3	36.8	38.2	24.7	30.5	63.0	59.4	19.4	22.3
2021	36.6	39.1	36.6	39.1	24.9	30.8	63.5	58.9	18.9	22.3
2022	36.2	39.0	36.4	39.3	24.6	30.1	61.7	57.1	18.9	22.9

NA Not available. [1] Includes other races not shown separately. [2] Beginning 2003, for persons who selected this race group only. See footnote 4, Table 252. [3] Persons of Hispanic origin may be of any race. [4] Through 1990, completed 4 years of high school or more and 4 years of college or more.

Source: U.S. Census Bureau, U.S. Census of Population, 1960, 1970, and 1980, Summary File 3; Current Population Reports, P20-550, and earlier reports; and "Educational Attainment in the United States: CPS Historical Time Series Tables," <www.census.gov/topics/education/educational-attainment.html>, accessed March 2023.

Table 254. Educational Attainment by Selected Characteristics: 2022

[226,274 represents 226,274,000. For persons 25 years old and over. As of March. Based on the Current Population Survey; see text, Section 1 and Appendix III]

Characteristic	Population (1,000)	Percent of population—					
		Not a high school graduate	High school graduate	Some college, but no degree	Associate's degree[1]	Bachelor's degree	Advanced degree
Total persons............................	**226,274**	**8.8**	**28.5**	**14.6**	**10.5**	**23.4**	**14.2**
Age:							
25 to 34 years old.........................	44,583	6.0	27.1	15.6	10.2	28.6	12.5
35 to 44 years old.........................	43,190	8.4	24.8	13.6	10.2	25.9	17.1
45 to 54 years old.........................	40,130	9.1	27.0	13.2	10.6	24.2	16.0
55 to 64 years old.........................	42,178	9.3	31.4	14.5	11.6	21.1	12.0
65 to 74 years old.........................	33,704	9.2	29.2	16.5	11.1	19.9	14.1
75 years old or over......................	22,489	13.1	34.5	14.1	8.1	17.0	13.2
Sex:							
Male..	109,979	9.4	30.1	14.6	9.7	22.9	13.3
Female.......................................	116,296	8.2	27.0	14.5	11.2	24.0	15.1
Race:							
White[2]......................................	175,898	8.6	28.4	14.5	10.6	23.9	14.0
Black[2]......................................	28,565	9.9	33.6	17.8	11.0	17.1	10.5
Asian[2]......................................	14,657	7.7	18.8	7.8	6.4	32.6	26.7
Hispanic origin:							
Hispanic.....................................	36,824	24.8	32.7	13.0	8.6	4.8	6.4
Non-Hispanic white......................	143,248	4.8	27.4	14.9	11.1	6.4	15.7
Marital status:							
Never married..............................	51,663	9.4	31.3	15.7	9.4	23.6	10.6
Married, spouse present................	125,973	7.2	25.6	13.3	10.6	26.0	17.3
Married, spouse absent[3]..............	3,562	15.9	30.3	13.5	8.3	20.0	12.0
Separated...................................	4,413	19.7	32.5	16.0	10.5	13.8	7.4
Widowed.....................................	15,182	15.1	38.1	15.4	9.3	13.7	8.5
Divorced.....................................	25,482	8.8	30.4	18.0	13.2	18.4	11.2
Civilian labor force status:							
Employed....................................	138,881	6.1	25.1	14.0	11.0	27.0	16.8
Unemployed................................	4,534	12.5	36.0	15.4	9.4	19.1	7.6
Not in the labor force....................	82,859	13.2	33.8	15.5	9.6	17.7	10.2

[1] Includes occupational and academic degrees. [2] For persons who selected this race group only. See footnote 4, Table 252. [3] Excludes those separated.

Source: U.S. Census Bureau, "Educational Attainment in the United States: 2022," <www.census.gov/topics/education/educational-attainment.html>, accessed March 2023.

Table 255. Mean Earnings of Persons by Highest Level of Education or Degree and Selected Characteristics: 2022

[In dollars. For persons 18 years old and over with earnings. Persons as of March 2022. Based on Current Population Survey, Annual Social and Economic Supplement; see text, Section 1 and Appendix III. For definition of mean, see Guide to Tabular Presentation]

Characteristic	Mean earnings, total[1]	Mean earnings by highest level of education or degree (dollars)							
		9th to 12th grade, non-graduate	High school graduate only[2]	Some college, no degree	Asso-ciate's	Bach-elor's	Master's	Profes-sional	Doctorate
All persons[3]...................	**67,010**	**34,430**	**45,410**	**49,220**	**57,470**	**84,340**	**102,200**	**162,900**	**140,300**
Age:									
25 to 34 years old...............	60,860	36,100	42,860	46,990	53,600	73,700	86,370	121,400	106,800
35 to 44 years old...............	76,620	42,050	50,440	55,860	60,150	91,540	112,300	166,500	154,300
45 to 54 years old...............	82,280	45,380	53,620	66,550	63,930	100,900	113,200	213,400	159,900
55 to 64 years old...............	77,130	39,940	54,100	63,660	64,490	98,970	110,200	187,300	157,300
65 years old and over..........	58,600	39,070	40,420	53,320	49,130	64,910	75,130	106,600	108,600
Sex:									
Male..........................	76,460	39,210	51,500	58,080	67,600	101,200	123,800	187,300	157,100
Female.......................	56,360	26,660	36,510	39,390	48,360	67,540	85,210	137,000	119,600
White[4]...........................	67,670	34,510	46,640	51,480	58,510	85,770	100,500	163,500	138,100
Male..........................	77,500	39,650	52,670	61,290	68,970	104,200	121,500	190,800	155,500
Female.......................	56,150	25,590	37,160	40,260	48,740	66,920	84,010	132,900	116,000
Black[4]...........................	55,230	34,690	41,380	41,510	52,260	72,680	86,920	160,100	130,700
Male..........................	60,090	36,220	46,980	45,350	62,800	81,670	103,200	(B)	144,900
Female.......................	50,880	32,940	35,040	37,830	45,190	65,470	78,090	143,700	120,700
Asian[4]...........................	88,570	39,900	44,300	44,220	51,120	87,390	125,000	176,000	156,300
Male..........................	100,700	48,790	51,270	53,420	55,890	98,140	144,700	175,500	166,300
Female.......................	74,880	26,120	37,140	33,520	45,670	76,200	102,700	176,600	140,000
Hispanic[5].......................	48,440	34,350	40,070	45,230	48,850	66,300	85,050	113,100	138,500
Male..........................	53,260	38,140	44,710	50,840	58,360	79,650	99,150	109,100	166,600
Female.......................	42,270	27,420	32,770	39,460	40,690	54,000	73,570	116,700	116,100

B Reporting standards not met; base less than 75,000. [1] Includes persons with less than 9th grade education, not shown separately. [2] Includes persons with General Education Development credential. [3] Includes persons age 18 to 24, and persons of other races, not shown separately. [4] For persons who selected this race group only. [5] Persons of Hispanic origin may be of any race.

Source: U.S. Census Bureau, *Income in the United States: 2022,* Current Population Reports, P60-279, September 2023; and "Current Population Survey Tables for Personal Income: Table PINC-04," <www.census.gov/data/tables/time-series/demo/income-poverty/cps-pinc/pinc-04.html>, accessed November 2023.

Table 256. Educational Attainment by State: 2010 to 2022

[In percent. For persons 25 years old and over. Based on the American Community Survey, which includes the household population and the population living in institutions, college dormitories, and other group quarters. See text, Section 1 and Appendix III]

State	2010			2021			2022		
	High school graduate or more	Bachelor's degree or more	Advanced degree or more	High school graduate or more	Bachelor's degree or more	Advanced degree or more	High school graduate or more	Bachelor's degree or more	Advanced degree or more
United States.............	**85.6**	**28.2**	**10.4**	**89.4**	**35.0**	**13.8**	**89.6**	**35.7**	**14.0**
Alabama......................	82.1	21.9	8.0	87.9	27.4	10.9	88.8	28.8	11.3
Alaska.......................	91.0	27.9	9.4	93.3	32.8	11.9	93.3	30.6	11.3
Arizona......................	85.6	25.9	9.2	89.0	32.4	12.6	89.2	33.0	12.5
Arkansas.....................	82.9	19.5	6.3	88.7	25.3	9.4	89.1	25.4	9.7
California....................	80.7	30.1	11.0	84.4	36.2	14.0	84.7	37.0	14.4
Colorado.....................	89.7	36.4	13.0	92.4	44.4	17.0	93.0	45.9	17.1
Connecticut..................	88.6	35.5	15.3	91.1	42.1	18.9	91.5	41.9	18.9
Delaware.....................	87.7	27.8	11.3	91.4	35.6	15.0	92.0	36.5	15.5
District of Columbia..........	87.4	50.1	26.9	92.8	63.0	37.8	93.7	65.4	38.9
Florida......................	85.5	25.8	9.2	89.8	33.2	12.6	89.9	34.3	12.9
Georgia......................	84.3	27.3	9.8	89.0	34.6	13.7	89.5	34.7	14.0
Hawaii.......................	89.9	29.5	9.6	92.9	35.3	13.1	92.9	35.4	13.3
Idaho........................	88.3	24.4	7.7	91.3	30.7	10.5	92.0	32.3	10.8
Illinois......................	86.9	30.8	11.5	90.2	37.1	15.0	90.4	37.7	15.2
Indiana......................	87.0	22.7	8.1	90.6	28.9	10.4	90.2	29.6	10.6
Iowa.........................	90.6	24.9	7.9	93.3	30.5	9.9	93.5	32.3	10.8
Kansas.......................	89.2	29.8	10.5	91.9	35.4	13.4	92.1	35.6	13.7
Kentucky.....................	81.9	20.5	8.1	88.0	27.0	11.1	89.0	27.9	11.4
Louisiana....................	81.9	21.4	7.0	86.7	26.4	9.7	87.3	27.1	10.2
Maine........................	90.3	26.8	9.5	94.5	36.0	13.8	94.6	36.1	13.8
Maryland.....................	88.1	36.1	16.4	91.1	42.5	20.2	91.4	43.8	20.6
Massachusetts................	89.1	39.0	16.7	91.1	46.6	21.3	91.3	46.6	21.3
Michigan.....................	88.7	25.2	9.6	92.0	31.7	12.5	91.8	32.1	12.6
Minnesota....................	91.8	31.8	10.3	94.1	38.9	13.4	94.0	39.1	13.7
Mississippi...................	81.0	19.5	7.1	86.5	24.8	9.3	87.6	24.8	9.6
Missouri.....................	86.9	25.6	9.5	91.6	31.7	12.2	91.6	32.2	12.5
Montana......................	91.7	28.8	9.0	94.4	34.8	12.4	94.0	34.6	11.7
Nebraska.....................	90.4	28.6	9.0	92.2	34.4	12.3	92.8	34.7	12.1
Nevada.......................	84.7	21.7	7.4	87.2	27.6	9.6	87.4	27.0	9.5
New Hampshire...............	91.5	32.8	12.4	94.4	40.2	15.7	94.5	41.3	16.7
New Jersey...................	88.0	35.4	13.3	91.0	43.1	17.4	90.7	43.5	17.6
New Mexico..................	83.3	25.0	10.8	87.5	30.1	14.1	88.0	30.5	13.5
New York.....................	84.9	32.5	14.0	88.0	39.9	17.7	87.9	40.0	17.7
North Carolina...............	84.7	26.5	8.7	89.7	34.9	13.2	90.2	35.9	13.2
North Dakota.................	90.3	27.6	7.9	93.6	31.7	9.4	93.9	31.8	9.5
Ohio.........................	88.1	24.6	8.9	91.7	30.7	11.8	91.8	32.0	12.6
Oklahoma....................	86.2	22.9	7.5	88.7	27.9	9.6	89.6	28.5	9.9
Oregon.......................	88.8	28.8	10.5	91.9	36.3	13.9	91.6	36.3	14.1
Pennsylvania.................	88.4	27.1	10.4	91.9	34.5	13.9	92.2	35.1	14.3
Rhode Island.................	83.5	30.2	12.2	89.1	36.5	15.6	90.5	39.6	15.7
South Carolina...............	84.1	24.5	8.8	89.6	31.5	11.9	90.5	32.6	12.8
South Dakota.................	89.6	26.3	7.7	93.1	31.7	10.1	93.2	31.6	9.9
Tennessee....................	83.6	23.1	8.5	89.7	30.5	11.3	90.4	31.1	11.4
Texas........................	80.7	25.9	8.6	85.4	33.1	11.9	86.1	33.9	12.3
Utah.........................	90.6	29.3	9.4	93.2	36.8	12.7	93.0	37.9	13.2
Vermont......................	91.0	33.6	13.3	94.5	44.4	18.4	95.0	44.2	19.7
Virginia......................	86.5	34.2	14.2	91.4	41.8	18.3	91.5	42.2	18.6
Washington...................	89.8	31.1	11.1	92.3	39.0	15.1	92.2	39.5	15.7
West Virginia.................	83.2	17.5	6.6	88.8	24.1	9.9	89.1	24.8	9.8
Wisconsin....................	90.1	24.1	9.0	93.3	32.5	11.0	93.5	33.2	11.6
Wyoming.....................	92.3	22.3	8.4	93.6	29.2	10.7	93.7	29.6	11.6

Source: U.S. Census Bureau, American Community Survey, S1501, "Educational Attainment," <data.census.gov>, accessed November 2023.

Table 257. Children Who Speak a Language Other Than English at Home by Region: 2022

[In thousands (11,572 represents 11,572,000), except percent. For children 5 to 17 years old. For more on languages spoken at home, see Table 56 and Table 57. Based on the American Community Survey; see text Section 1, and Appendix III. For composition of regions, see map inside front cover]

Item	U.S.	Northeast	Midwest	South	West
Children who speak another language at home..............................	**11,572**	**1,993**	**1,405**	**4,278**	**3,896**
Percent of children 5 to 17 years old..................................	**21.4**	**23.4**	**12.5**	**20.1**	**30.2**
Speak Spanish...	7,973	1,053	764	3,267	2,888
Speak English "very well"..	6,183	793	588	2,505	2,297
Speak English less than "very well".................................	1,790	260	176	763	591
Speak other Indo-European languages...............................	1,681	558	297	485	341
Speak English "very well"..	1,297	400	227	391	279
Speak English less than "very well".................................	384	158	70	94	62
Speak Asian and Pacific Island languages.........................	1,256	240	166	331	519
Speak English "very well"..	959	179	125	259	397
Speak English less than "very well".................................	296	61	41	72	122
Speak other languages..	662	141	179	194	148
Speak English "very well"..	537	117	139	155	126
Speak English less than "very well".................................	125	24	40	39	22
Have difficulty speaking English [1]......................................	2,595	503	327	968	798
Language spoken at home in limited English speaking households [2].........	2,265	474	271	893	626
Speak only English...	234	52	33	80	70
Speak Spanish...	1,442	257	125	656	404
Speak other Indo-European languages..............................	233	89	38	68	39
Speak Asian and Pacific Island languages.........................	258	56	40	63	99
Speak other languages..	98	20	36	28	14

[1] Children age 5 to 17 who speak English less than "very well." [2] A household in which no person age 14 or over speaks English at least "very well."

Source: U.S. Census Bureau, 2022 American Community Survey, B16003, "Age by Language Spoken at Home for the Population 5 Years and Over" and B16004, "Age by Language Spoken at Home by Ability to Speak English for the Population 5 Years and Over," <data.census.gov>, accessed November 2023.

Table 258. Nursery and Primary School Enrollment by Selected School and Child Characteristics: 2010 to 2022

[17,269 represents 17,269,000. As of October. Covers children aged 3 to 6 years old. Includes public and private preschool (or nursery school), kindergarten programs, and elementary schools. Based on Current Population Survey. See text, Section 1 and Appendix III]

School type and child characteristic	2010	2015	2020	2021	2022
NUMBER OF CHILDREN (1,000)					
Total population, 3 to 6 years old...................................	17,269	15,944	16,058	15,697	15,530
Total enrolled in school [1].....................................	**12,661**	**11,710**	**10,457**	**11,184**	**11,429**
Preschool (or nursery school).....................................	4,835	4,532	3,545	4,285	4,357
Public...	2,776	2,610	2,094	2,513	2,460
Private..	2,059	1,922	1,451	1,772	1,897
Kindergarten...	4,101	4,024	3,646	4,009	3,961
Public...	3,698	3,600	3,079	3,531	3,502
Private..	404	424	568	478	459
Elementary school...	3,725	3,155	3,266	2,890	3,108
Public...	3,415	2,903	2,842	2,601	2,791
Private..	309	252	424	289	317
By race and Hispanic origin:					
White alone...	9,395	8,428	7,438	7,844	7,884
White alone, non-Hispanic.....................................	6,715	5,966	5,294	5,593	5,514
Black alone...	1,983	1,751	1,642	1,730	1,868
Asian alone..	645	613	587	729	773
Hispanic [2]...	2,986	2,817	2,495	2,634	2,834
By age:					
3 years old...	1,718	1,512	1,143	1,419	1,533
4 years old...	2,988	2,691	2,047	2,451	2,508
5 years old...	3,787	3,626	3,327	3,498	3,409
6 years old...	4,169	3,881	3,941	3,816	3,977
PERCENT ENROLLED					
Total enrolled [1]..	**73.3**	**73.4**	**65.1**	**71.2**	**73.6**
By race and Hispanic origin:					
White alone...	72.7	73.3	64.9	71.2	72.9
White alone, non-Hispanic.....................................	75.1	75.3	67.1	73.5	74.5
Black alone...	74.5	72.8	65.6	69.6	77.2
Asian alone..	79.8	74.2	64.8	76.7	73.1
Hispanic [2]...	67.9	68.7	60.3	66.1	70.3
By age:					
3 years old...	38.2	38.4	29.7	37.5	40.8
4 years old...	68.6	66.7	50.3	62.9	65.5
5 years old...	92.4	91.0	84.3	86.3	89.0
6 years old...	96.5	97.3	93.8	96.2	96.7

[1] Includes children of other races not shown separately. [2] Persons of Hispanic origin may be of any race.

Source: U.S. Census Bureau, Educational Attainment Tables, "Educational Attainment in the United States," <www.census.gov/topics/education/educational-attainment.html>, accessed February 2024.

Table 259. Public Elementary and Secondary School Finances by Enrollment-Size Group: 2022

[In units, as indicated (878,244 represents $878,244,000,000). For school fiscal year ending in 2022. Enrollment as of Fall 2021. Data are based on the 2022 Census of Governments: Survey of School System Finances. For details, see source. See also Appendix III]

Item	All school systems	\>50,000 or more	25,000 to 49,999	15,000 to 24,999	7,500 to 14,999	5,000 to 7,499	3,000 to 4,999	Under 3,000
TOTAL (millions of dollars)								
General revenue	**878,244**	**184,409**	**110,252**	**89,791**	**124,218**	**74,614**	**95,214**	**199,746**
From federal sources	119,089	26,203	16,444	12,582	16,295	8,520	11,115	27,930
Through state [1]	113,386	25,169	15,839	12,179	15,677	8,222	10,615	25,685
Child nutrition programs	28,621	5,759	4,011	3,114	4,348	2,430	3,021	5,938
Direct	5,703	1,035	605	403	618	298	500	2,245
From state sources [1]	383,943	69,312	47,086	45,458	58,481	32,910	41,051	89,646
General formula assistance	254,902	44,599	33,385	32,106	40,640	21,784	26,329	56,059
Compensatory programs	6,964	1,863	1,003	799	1,023	461	679	1,137
Special education	24,515	6,176	2,644	2,452	2,809	1,790	2,287	6,357
From local sources	375,212	88,893	46,722	31,751	49,443	33,184	43,048	82,171
Taxes [1]	258,703	43,727	33,367	24,035	38,200	25,259	33,099	61,016
Property taxes	245,222	40,580	30,463	22,820	36,411	24,369	31,744	58,835
Contributions from parent government	67,498	33,199	7,317	3,505	5,113	4,388	5,828	8,147
From other local governments	11,753	870	2,069	1,225	1,827	979	1,050	3,734
Current charges [1]	11,455	1,472	1,246	942	1,535	1,006	1,232	4,022
School lunch	1,570	148	144	138	246	182	238	475
Other	25,802	9,625	2,723	2,044	2,767	1,552	1,839	5,251
General expenditure	**857,278**	**180,102**	**107,404**	**87,034**	**121,999**	**73,361**	**93,803**	**193,576**
Current spending [2]	746,937	156,344	93,214	75,616	105,662	63,957	81,920	170,224
By function:								
Instruction	446,911	98,833	54,642	44,748	63,306	38,965	49,523	96,893
Support services	264,596	50,594	33,861	27,111	37,263	22,144	28,850	64,773
Other current spending [2]	35,431	6,916	4,710	3,757	5,093	2,848	3,547	8,559
By object:								
Total salaries and wages	403,376	81,579	53,124	42,322	58,652	34,637	44,203	88,859
Total employee benefits	175,102	33,504	20,541	17,655	25,679	16,009	20,653	41,060
Capital outlay	84,214	17,968	10,637	8,740	12,474	7,025	9,271	18,100
Interest on debt	21,324	4,674	2,928	2,350	3,307	2,002	2,284	3,779
Payments to other governments	4,803	1,117	626	328	556	378	327	1,472
Debt outstanding	543,854	115,095	71,774	62,687	87,928	49,505	56,625	100,241
Long-term	539,409	114,713	71,694	62,571	87,436	49,091	55,722	98,182
Short-term	4,445	381	81	116	492	414	903	2,059
Long-term debt issued	70,420	12,037	9,835	7,949	12,083	5,768	7,043	15,706
Long-term debt retired	50,334	9,965	7,447	5,481	7,696	4,003	5,205	10,536
Fall enrollment (1,000s)	46,441	9,462	6,513	5,093	7,104	3,972	4,988	9,309
PER PUPIL (dollars)								
General revenue	**18,911**	**19,490**	**16,928**	**17,630**	**17,485**	**18,786**	**19,089**	**21,457**
From federal sources	2,564	2,769	2,525	2,470	2,294	2,145	2,228	3,000
From state sources [1]	8,267	7,325	7,229	8,925	8,232	8,286	8,230	9,630
General formula assistance	5,489	4,714	5,126	6,304	5,720	5,485	5,279	6,022
Special education	528	653	406	481	395	451	458	683
From local sources [1]	8,079	9,395	7,174	6,234	6,959	8,355	8,630	8,827
Taxes [1]	5,571	4,621	5,123	4,719	5,377	6,359	6,636	6,554
Property taxes	5,280	4,289	4,677	4,481	5,125	6,135	6,364	6,320
Contributions from parent government	1,453	3,509	1,123	688	720	1,105	1,168	875
Current charges [1]	247	156	191	185	216	253	247	432
School lunch	34	16	22	27	35	46	48	51
General expenditure [1]	**18,009**	**18,351**	**16,159**	**16,700**	**16,861**	**18,006**	**18,399**	**20,342**
Current spending [2]	15,633	15,840	13,980	14,458	14,561	15,638	16,017	17,834
By function:								
Instruction	9,348	9,928	8,215	8,570	8,754	9,501	9,658	10,197
Support services	5,697	5,347	5,199	5,323	5,245	5,575	5,784	6,958
By object:								
Total salaries and wages	8,686	8,622	8,157	8,310	8,256	8,721	8,862	9,545
Total employee benefits	3,770	3,541	3,154	3,467	3,615	4,031	4,141	4,411
Capital outlay	1,813	1,899	1,633	1,716	1,756	1,769	1,859	1,944
Interest on debt	459	494	449	461	466	504	458	406
Debt outstanding	11,711	12,164	11,020	12,308	12,377	12,464	11,352	10,768
Long-term	11,615	12,124	11,008	12,285	12,307	12,360	11,171	10,547

[1] Includes other sources not shown separately. [2] Expenditures for adult education, community services, and other non-elementary/secondary programs are included in total "Current spending" and "Other current spending" but excluded under pupil amounts.

Source: U.S. Census Bureau, Annual Survey of School System Finances Tables, "2022 Public Elementary-Secondary Education Finance Data," April 2024 release, <www.census.gov/programs-surveys/school-finances/data/tables.html>, accessed April 2024.

Table 260. Public Elementary and Secondary School Estimated Finances by State: 2022

[In millions of dollars (878,244 represents $878,244,000,000), except as noted. For the school fiscal year. Includes finances of charter schools whose charters are held directly by a government or government agency; excludes charters schools whose charters are held by nongovernmental entities]

State	Revenue receipts Total	Source Federal	Source State	Source Local	Expenditures Total [1]	Per capita [2] (dol.)	Current expenditures Total current spending [3]	Average per pupil [4] Amount [5] (dol.)	Average per pupil [4] Rank
Total....................	878,244	119,089	383,943	375,212	857,278	2,582	746,937	15,633	(X)
Alabama.....................	10,656	1,849	5,526	3,282	10,108	2,001	8,989	11,819	41
Alaska......................	2,769	571	1,604	594	2,875	3,913	2,633	20,191	8
Arizona.....................	12,026	2,364	4,934	4,728	11,425	1,571	9,470	10,315	49
Arkansas....................	6,641	1,356	4,446	839	6,538	2,159	5,692	12,159	40
California..................	116,324	16,298	61,309	38,718	106,865	2,730	92,975	17,049	18
Colorado....................	14,105	1,490	5,455	7,160	14,291	2,459	11,599	13,422	33
Connecticut.................	13,300	1,066	4,722	7,512	12,850	3,566	11,866	24,453	5
Delaware....................	2,665	341	1,492	832	2,575	2,563	2,387	19,357	10
District of Columbia..........	1,597	221	(X)	1,376	1,663	2,485	1,398	27,425	2
Florida.....................	37,243	6,598	12,021	18,623	35,638	1,632	31,805	11,076	46
Georgia.....................	27,872	4,403	11,076	12,394	25,670	2,379	23,195	13,619	30
Hawaii......................	3,565	517	3,020	28	3,356	2,320	3,034	17,420	16
Idaho.......................	3,307	601	1,938	768	2,981	1,565	2,791	9,670	50
Illinois....................	42,890	4,571	17,128	21,191	40,433	3,186	35,826	18,927	12
Indiana.....................	15,164	1,881	8,726	4,557	14,673	2,153	12,320	12,322	38
Iowa........................	8,339	1,107	4,156	3,076	8,191	2,561	6,809	13,259	36
Kansas......................	7,709	778	5,023	1,909	8,098	2,756	6,987	14,408	27
Kentucky....................	10,625	2,109	5,021	3,494	10,123	2,246	8,951	13,549	32
Louisiana...................	10,799	1,943	3,801	5,055	9,882	2,136	9,087	14,928	25
Maine.......................	3,498	358	1,406	1,733	3,357	2,435	3,166	17,885	14
Maryland....................	18,693	2,141	7,574	8,978	17,637	2,856	15,669	17,753	15
Massachusetts...............	20,859	1,959	8,772	10,129	22,492	3,217	20,370	21,906	6
Michigan....................	24,041	3,812	12,616	7,613	23,240	2,315	19,882	15,719	21
Minnesota...................	15,003	1,761	8,938	4,303	15,710	2,748	12,878	15,441	23
Mississippi.................	5,723	1,334	2,508	1,881	5,457	1,850	4,835	10,984	47
Missouri....................	13,604	2,028	4,734	6,841	13,119	2,126	11,123	12,631	37
Montana.....................	2,355	493	932	930	2,336	2,112	2,033	13,582	31
Nebraska....................	5,348	648	1,606	3,094	5,480	2,790	4,675	14,285	28
Nevada......................	6,196	993	4,293	910	5,921	1,882	5,056	11,677	43
New Hampshire...............	3,647	321	1,071	2,254	3,699	2,666	3,486	21,605	7
New Jersey..................	37,941	2,809	16,991	18,141	36,752	3,965	34,934	25,099	3
New Mexico..................	5,017	880	3,238	898	4,627	2,186	3,970	13,260	35
New York....................	85,194	6,175	30,778	48,241	84,692	4,266	76,055	29,873	1
North Carolina..............	18,722	3,811	10,448	4,462	19,044	1,802	17,182	12,298	39
North Dakota................	2,205	402	1,082	721	2,191	2,816	1,869	15,843	19
Ohio........................	28,504	3,977	9,740	14,787	28,045	2,384	24,595	15,583	22
Oklahoma....................	8,357	1,632	3,483	3,241	7,959	1,994	6,998	10,890	48
Oregon......................	10,655	1,161	5,628	3,867	11,187	2,628	9,092	15,754	20
Pennsylvania................	37,598	4,669	13,345	19,584	36,308	2,790	32,573	19,186	11
Rhode Island................	2,869	335	1,136	1,399	2,893	2,637	2,711	19,962	9
South Carolina..............	12,555	1,913	5,433	5,210	11,747	2,262	9,975	13,387	34
South Dakota................	1,999	433	612	954	1,935	2,159	1,651	11,564	44
Tennessee...................	13,414	2,555	5,429	5,430	12,515	1,797	11,226	11,317	45
Texas.......................	74,262	13,387	23,047	37,828	78,693	2,662	60,151	11,803	42
Utah........................	7,124	907	3,401	2,816	6,903	2,067	5,907	9,552	51
Vermont.....................	2,287	240	1,999	48	2,257	3,487	2,171	24,608	4
Virginia....................	20,909	2,547	8,138	10,224	20,726	2,394	18,898	15,059	24
Washington..................	21,849	2,694	13,822	5,333	22,620	2,922	18,540	17,119	17
West Virginia...............	4,022	747	1,895	1,380	3,858	2,161	3,545	13,858	29
Wisconsin...................	14,151	1,635	7,385	5,131	13,781	2,344	12,186	14,505	26
Wyoming.....................	2,050	266	1,068	716	1,864	3,216	1,725	18,529	13

X Not applicable. [1] Includes interest on school debt and payments to state and local governments, not shown separately. [2] Based on U.S. Census Bureau estimated resident population, as of July 1, 2021. [3] Includes expenditures for adult education, community services, and other nonelementary-secondary programs. [4] Based on Fall 2021 enrollment, National Center for Education Statistics, Common Core of Data. [5] Per pupil amounts exclude expenditures for payments to other school systems, adult education, community services, and other nonelementary-secondary programs.

Source: U.S. Census Bureau, Annual Survey of School System Finances Tables, "2022 Public Elementary-Secondary Education Finance Data," April 2024 release, <www.census.gov/programs-surveys/school-finances/data/tables.html>, accessed April 2024.

Table 261. Public Elementary and Secondary Schools—Summary: 2000 to 2024

[In units as indicated (52,811 represents 52,811,000). For school year ending in year shown, except as indicated]

Item	Unit	2000	2010	2015	2020	2022	2023	2024, estimates
School districts, total	**Number**	**15,403**	**16,340**	**16,638**	**16,391**	**16,432**	**16,431**	**16,423**
ENROLLMENT								
Population 5-17 years old [1]	1,000	52,811	53,890	53,691	53,462	54,780	54,568	54,321
Percent of resident population	Percent	18.9	17.6	16.9	16.3	16.5	16.4	16.2
Fall enrollment [2]	**1,000**	**46,577**	**49,104**	**49,923**	**50,229**	**48,878**	**49,033**	**48,921**
Percent of population 5-17 years old	Percent	88.2	91.1	93.0	94.0	89.2	89.9	90.1
Average daily attendance	1,000	43,313	45,835	46,779	46,947	45,604	45,635	45,446
INSTRUCTIONAL STAFF								
Total [3]	**1,000**	**3,273**	**3,644**	**3,654**	**3,753**	**3,775**	**3,831**	**3,843**
Classroom teachers	1,000	2,891	3,182	3,149	3,180	3,187	3,222	3,229
Average salaries:								
Instructional staff	Dollar	43,837	56,995	59,712	66,134	68,726	71,518	73,841
Classroom teachers	Dollar	41,807	55,370	57,737	64,179	66,805	69,544	71,699
REVENUES								
Revenue receipts	**Mil. dol.**	**369,754**	**586,995**	**650,246**	**788,322**	**881,738**	**911,940**	**930,728**
Federal	Mil. dol.	26,346	75,592	53,793	58,178	116,858	120,578	115,078
State	Mil. dol.	183,986	258,396	305,920	375,629	391,150	405,444	421,357
Local	Mil. dol.	159,421	253,006	290,533	354,515	373,730	385,919	394,293
Percent of total:								
Federal	Percent	7.1	12.9	8.3	7.4	13.3	13.2	12.4
State	Percent	49.8	44.0	47.1	47.7	44.4	44.5	45.3
Local/other	Percent	43.1	43.1	44.68	45.0	42.4	42.3	42.4
EXPENDITURES								
Total	**Mil. dol.**	**374,782**	**615,210**	**653,729**	**799,015**	**885,722**	**917,403**	**941,401**
Current expenditures	Mil. dol.	320,954	526,146	572,350	688,361	772,689	798,302	818,087
Other current expenditures [4]	Mil. dol.	6,618	10,621	13,842	9,613	11,619	12,103	12,639
Capital outlay	Mil. dol.	37,552	53,052	48,193	77,778	77,504	82,477	85,444
Interest on school debt	Mil. dol.	9,659	25,391	19,344	23,263	23,910	24,520	25,230
Percent of total:								
Current expenditures	Percent	85.6	85.5	87.6	86.2	87.2	87.0	86.9
Other current expenditures [4]	Percent	1.8	1.7	2.1	1.2	1.3	1.3	1.3
Capital outlay	Percent	10.0	8.6	7.4	9.7	8.8	9.0	9.1
Interest on school debt	Percent	2.6	4.1	3.0	2.9	2.7	2.7	2.7
Current expenditures per pupil enrolled	Dollar	6,891	10,715	11,465	13,704	15,808	16,281	16,722

[1] Based on Census Bureau estimated resident population as of July 1 of the previous year, except 2000, 2010 and 2020 population enumerated as of April 1. [2] Enrollment in fall of the previous year. [3] Full-time equivalent. [4] Current expenses for summer schools, adult education, post-high-school vocational education, personnel retraining, and community services; and services to private school pupils, community centers, recreational activities, and public libraries, and so on, when operated by local school districts and not part of regular public elementary and secondary day-school programs.

Source: National Education Association, Washington, DC. Data from *Rankings of the States 2023 and Estimates of School Statistics 2024*, used with permission of the National Education Association © 2024. All rights reserved.

Table 262. Public Elementary and Secondary School Enrollment by Grade: 1980 to 2022

[In thousands (40,877 represents 40,877,000). As of Fall of year shown. Covers the 50 states and DC. Based on a survey of state education agencies; see source for details]

Grade	1980	1990	1995	2000	2005	2010	2015	2019	2020	2021	2022
Pupils enrolled [1]	**40,877**	**41,217**	**44,840**	**47,204**	**49,113**	**49,484**	**50,438**	**50,796**	**49,375**	**49,433**	**49,618**
Pre-kindergarten to 8 [1]	27,647	29,876	32,338	33,686	34,204	34,625	35,388	35,551	34,061	33,998	34,071
Pre-kindergarten [2]	96	303	637	776	1,036	1,279	1,402	1,586	1,242	1,411	1,528
Kindergarten	2,593	3,306	3,536	3,382	3,619	3,682	3,713	3,716	3,378	3,554	3,526
First	2,894	3,499	3,671	3,636	3,691	3,754	3,768	3,647	3,522	3,458	3,590
Second	2,800	3,327	3,507	3,634	3,606	3,701	3,842	3,638	3,529	3,519	3,502
Third	2,893	3,297	3,445	3,676	3,586	3,686	3,869	3,686	3,552	3,542	3,573
Fourth	3,107	3,248	3,431	3,711	3,578	3,711	3,793	3,706	3,607	3,550	3,561
Fifth	3,130	3,197	3,438	3,707	3,633	3,718	3,733	3,801	3,646	3,611	3,591
Sixth	3,038	3,110	3,395	3,663	3,670	3,682	3,731	3,896	3,748	3,650	3,643
Seventh	3,085	3,067	3,422	3,629	3,777	3,676	3,732	3,918	3,860	3,756	3,685
Eighth	3,086	2,979	3,356	3,538	3,802	3,659	3,719	3,865	3,889	3,859	3,783
Ungraded	924	541	500	334	205	77	87	92	89	88	88
Grades 9 to 12 [1]	13,231	11,341	12,502	13,517	14,909	14,860	15,050	15,246	15,314	15,436	15,547
Ninth	3,377	3,169	3,704	3,963	4,287	4,008	4,019	4,044	4,014	4,169	4,142
Tenth	3,368	2,896	3,237	3,491	3,866	3,800	3,846	3,868	3,894	3,862	3,992
Eleventh	3,195	2,612	2,826	3,083	3,454	3,538	3,598	3,671	3,700	3,693	3,709
Twelfth	2,925	2,381	2,487	2,803	3,180	3,472	3,537	3,621	3,664	3,670	3,663
Ungraded	366	284	247	177	121	42	49	41	42	41	42

[1] Includes unclassified students, not shown separately. [2] Data for 2019 includes imputations for nonreported prekindergarten enrollment in California; data for 2020 includes imputations for Oregon; data for 2021 and 2022 includes imputations for California and Oregon.

Source: U.S. National Center for Education Statistics, *Digest of Education Statistics*, "Latest version of all Digest tables," <nces.ed.gov/programs/digest>, accessed May 2024.

Table 263. Selected Statistics for the Largest Public School Districts: 2021

[For the 50 largest districts by enrollment size. For school year ending in 2021. Data from the Common Core of Data Program; see source for details. School district boundaries are not necessarily the same as city or county boundaries]

School district	City	County	Number of students [1]	Number of full-time equivalent (FTE) teachers [2]	Number of schools [3]	Total expenditures per pupil
New York City Public Schools, NY [4]	New York	(X)	912,994	70,202	1,525	37,461
Los Angeles Unified School District, CA	Los Angeles	Los Angeles	460,633	21,873	782	21,493
City of Chicago School District 299, IL	Chicago	Cook	341,382	(NA)	649	21,914
Miami-Dade County Public School District, FL	Miami	Miami-Dade	334,261	16,758	516	12,440
Clark County School District, NV	Las Vegas	Clark	315,646	14,395	374	12,103
Broward County School District, FL	Fort Lauderdale	Broward	260,235	13,737	331	12,217
Hillsborough County School District, FL	Tampa	Hillsborough	218,943	13,711	303	11,103
Orange County School District, FL	Orlando	Orange	199,089	11,757	264	13,197
Houston Independent School District, TX	Houston	Harris	196,943	11,750	276	13,304
Palm Beach County School District, FL	West Palm Beach	Palm Beach	187,057	11,696	236	13,485
Fairfax County Public Schools, VA	Falls Church	Fairfax	180,028	13,150	222	18,256
Gwinnett County School District, GA	Lawrenceville	Gwinnett	177,401	11,361	139	12,574
Hawaii Department Of Education, HI	Honolulu	Honolulu	176,441	12,145	294	17,656
Montgomery County Public Schools, MD	Rockville	Montgomery	160,564	11,511	209	19,824
Wake County Schools, NC	Cary	Wake	159,802	10,516	192	11,914
Dallas Independent School District, TX	Dallas	Dallas	145,113	10,266	233	16,695
Charlotte-Mecklenburg Schools, NC	Charlotte	Mecklenburg	142,733	9,284	176	14,569
Prince George's County Public Schools, MD	Upper Marlboro	Prince George's	131,646	9,368	209	19,580
Duval County School District, FL	Jacksonville	Duval	126,815	6,539	204	10,682
Philadelphia City School District, PA	Philadelphia	Philadelphia	124,111	7,856	217	31,422
Cypress-Fairbanks Independent School District, TX	Houston	Harris	114,881	7,659	90	13,772
Baltimore County Public Schools, MD	Towson	Baltimore	111,084	7,821	178	17,380
Memphis-Shelby County Schools, TN	Memphis	Shelby	110,780	6,546	221	12,482
Cobb County School District, GA	Marietta	Cobb	107,379	7,348	109	13,562
Northside Independent School District, TX	San Antonio	Bexar	103,151	6,845	121	13,035
Polk County School District, FL	Bartow	Polk	100,495	5,865	164	12,889
San Diego Unified School District, CA	San Diego	San Diego	97,968	4,267	176	22,937
Pinellas County School District, FL	Largo	Pinellas	96,068	6,829	157	12,820
Jefferson County, KY	Louisville	Jefferson	95,911	6,236	172	16,716
Lee County School District, FL	Fort Myers	Lee	94,927	5,156	119	12,129
Dekalb County School District, GA	Decatur	Dekalb	93,470	7,109	131	14,583
Fulton County Schools, GA	Atlanta	Fulton	90,300	6,261	107	14,692
Prince William County Public Schools, VA	Manassas	Prince William	89,548	5,650	95	14,678
Denver Public Schools, CO	Denver	Denver	89,081	6,121	205	17,893
Katy Independent School District, TX	Katy	Fort Bend	84,176	5,882	73	12,931
Anne Arundel County Public Schools, MD	Annapolis	Anne Arundel	83,044	5,957	125	17,648
Albuquerque Public Schools, NM	Albuquerque	Bernalillo	83,031	6,050	174	14,476
Alpine School District, UT	American Fork	Utah	82,800	(NA)	91	9,907
Loudoun County Public Schools, VA	Ashburn	Loudoun	81,066	6,115	96	18,921
Davidson County Schools, TN	Nashville	Davidson	80,494	5,246	162	15,097
Jefferson County School District No. R-1, CO	Golden	Jefferson	80,099	4,701	165	14,748
Baltimore City Public Schools, MD	Baltimore	Baltimore City	77,856	5,063	159	20,673
Pasco County School District, FL	Land O Lakes	Pasco	77,125	4,790	103	12,038
Fort Worth Independent School District, TX	Fort Worth	Tarrant	76,858	5,488	146	16,504
Fort Bend Independent School District, TX	Sugar Land	Fort Bend	76,735	5,055	82	15,190
Austin Independent School District, TX	Austin	Travis	74,871	5,508	126	26,732
Greenville County School District, SC	Greenville	Greenville	74,094	4,990	91	13,280
Davis School District, UT	Farmington	Davis	72,082	(NA)	95	9,782
Milwaukee School District, WI	Milwaukee	Milwaukee	71,510	4,345	158	17,506
Brevard County School District, FL	Viera	Brevard	70,996	4,397	114	10,991

X Not applicable. NA Not available. [1] Number of students receiving educational services from the school district. [2] Full-time equivalent is the amount of time required to perform an assignment stated as a proportion of a full-time position. [3] Totals for number of schools may differ from published estimates since they exclude closed, inactive, and future schools. [4] Represents New York City Geographic Districts 1-32. Data for per pupil expenditures are from the NYC Chancellor's Office.

Source: U.S. Department of Education, National Center for Education Statistics, "Elementary/Secondary Information System," <www.nces.ed.gov/ccd/elsi>, accessed June 2024.

Table 264. Public Elementary and Secondary School Enrollment by State: 2000 to 2022

[In thousands (33,686 represents 33,686,000). As of Fall. Includes unclassified/ungraded students. Based on survey of state education agencies; see source for details]

State	Pre-kindergarten through grade 8					Grades 9 through 12				
	2000	2010	2020	2021	2022	2000	2010	2020	2021	2022
United States............	**33,686**	**34,625**	**34,059**	**34,004**	**34,071**	**13,517**	**14,860**	**15,316**	**15,449**	**15,547**
Alabama........................	539	534	518	528	529	201	222	217	220	222
Alaska..........................	94	92	92	92	92	39	40	38	38	39
Arizona.........................	641	752	761	769	763	237	320	355	365	369
Arkansas.......................	318	346	342	344	345	132	136	144	146	149
California.......................	4,407	4,294	4,093	4,004	3,994	1,734	1,996	1,970	1,956	1,937
Colorado.......................	517	601	605	601	591	208	242	279	280	280
Connecticut....................	406	387	345	346	349	156	173	164	163	165
Delaware.......................	81	90	95	94	96	34	39	43	44	45
District of Columbia...........	54	54	71	69	70	15	18	19	20	21
Florida..........................	1,760	1,858	1,929	1,959	1,976	675	785	861	874	894
Georgia.........................	1,060	1,202	1,199	1,203	1,205	385	475	531	538	546
Hawaii..........................	132	128	124	121	118	52	52	52	52	52
Idaho...........................	170	194	212	217	218	75	82	95	97	99
Illinois..........................	1,474	1,455	1,286	1,265	1,256	575	637	606	603	596
Indiana.........................	703	729	710	712	710	286	318	323	324	326
Iowa............................	334	348	355	356	355	161	148	152	154	156
Kansas.........................	323	343	337	340	341	147	141	145	146	147
Kentucky.......................	471	480	458	455	459	194	193	201	200	201
Louisiana.......................	547	512	492	483	505	197	184	201	200	213
Maine...........................	146	129	117	118	118	61	60	55	56	55
Maryland........................	609	588	615	610	613	244	264	268	271	276
Massachusetts.................	703	666	628	628	630	273	289	294	293	293
Michigan........................	1,222	1,076	971	979	980	498	511	463	461	454
Minnesota......................	578	570	594	591	589	277	268	278	280	281
Mississippi.....................	364	351	313	311	308	134	140	130	131	132
Missouri........................	645	643	614	618	619	268	276	269	271	273
Montana........................	105	98	103	106	105	50	43	44	45	45
Nebraska.......................	195	210	227	230	230	91	88	98	98	99
Nevada.........................	251	307	335	336	332	90	130	148	151	152
New Hampshire................	147	132	114	115	115	61	63	55	55	54
New Jersey.....................	968	981	950	947	955	346	421	424	426	429
New Mexico.....................	225	239	217	216	213	95	99	100	101	102
New York.......................	2,029	1,869	1,787	1,747	1,737	853	866	815	801	796
North Carolina.................	945	1,058	1,050	1,054	1,058	348	432	464	471	483
North Dakota...................	72	66	82	83	84	37	30	33	33	34
Ohio............................	1,294	1,223	1,142	1,148	1,145	541	531	503	505	536
Oklahoma......................	445	483	498	499	497	178	176	197	200	205
Oregon.........................	379	393	397	394	394	167	178	181	182	183
Pennsylvania...................	1,258	1,210	1,156	1,148	1,141	556	584	548	592	552
Rhode Island...................	114	98	94	94	93	44	46	45	45	45
South Carolina.................	493	516	538	546	549	184	210	229	235	240
South Dakota..................	88	88	99	100	100	41	38	41	42	42
Tennessee.....................	668	702	690	698	706	241	286	295	298	301
Texas...........................	2,943	3,587	3,762	3,792	3,851	1,117	1,349	1,611	1,637	1,669
Utah............................	333	425	473	480	477	148	161	208	211	215
Vermont........................	70	68	58	59	59	32	29	24	25	24
Virginia.........................	816	871	856	854	860	329	380	394	396	400
Washington....................	694	714	744	743	741	310	330	343	347	349
West Virginia...................	201	201	177	175	174	85	81	77	77	77
Wisconsin......................	595	598	569	566	560	285	274	261	263	263
Wyoming.......................	60	63	65	64	63	30	26	28	29	29

Source: U.S. National Center for Education Statistics, *Digest of Education Statistics*, "Latest version of all Digest tables," and earlier releases, <nces.ed.gov/programs/digest>, accessed February 2024.

Table 265. Parent Participation in School-Related Activities by Selected School, Student, and Family Characteristics: 2019

[In percent, except as noted (51,498 represents 51,498,000). For school year ending in year shown. Covers parents with children in kindergarten through grade 12. Homeschooled students are excluded. Based on the Parent and Family Involvement in Education Survey, a component of the National Household Education Surveys Program]

Characteristic	Number of students in grades K through 12 (1,000)	Participation in school activities by parent or other household member				
		Attended a general school or PTO/PTA meeting [1]	Attended regularly scheduled parent-teacher conference	Attended a school or class event	Volunteered or served on school committee	Participated in school fundraising
Total............................	**51,498**	**89**	**75**	**79**	**43**	**57**
School type: [2]						
Public, assigned............................	39,830	88	73	78	39	54
Public, chosen............................	6,036	90	77	79	45	57
Private, religious............................	3,736	95	86	91	73	79
Private, nonreligious............................	916	95	91	92	74	75
Student's sex:						
Male............................	26,633	88	76	78	41	56
Female............................	24,865	89	74	81	45	57
Student's race/ethnicity:						
White, non-Hispanic............................	24,906	90	76	85	49	64
Black, non-Hispanic............................	7,032	88	77	76	35	49
Asian or Pacific Islander, non-Hispanic............	3,166	83	73	70	41	55
Other, non-Hispanic [3]............................	3,268	90	79	83	45	58
Hispanic [4]............................	13,126	87	73	72	35	46
Student's grade level:						
Kindergarten to 2nd grade............................	12,229	94	90	83	57	66
3rd to 5th grade............................	12,173	93	88	86	49	61
6th to 8th grade............................	12,263	89	72	80	36	53
9th to 12th grade............................	14,833	80	54	70	32	48
Parents' highest education level:						
Less than high school............................	5,291	82	68	61	25	36
High school graduate or equivalent.............	9,745	82	71	69	28	44
Vocational/technical or some college.............	13,082	88	75	79	38	56
Bachelor's degree............................	13,609	92	78	86	54	66
Graduate or professional school...............	9,772	94	80	90	58	68
Parents' language at home:						
Both/only parent(s) speak(s) English.............	43,935	90	76	82	45	59
One of two parents speaks English...............	1,932	89	75	76	38	43
No parent speaks English............................	5,631	81	67	62	26	38

[1] Parent Teacher Organization (PTO) or Parent Teacher Association (PTA) meeting. [2] School type classifies the school currently attended as either public or private. Public schools are further classified according to whether the school was chosen or assigned. Private schools are classified as being religious or nonreligious. [3] Includes persons of all other races and multiple races, non-Hispanic. [4] Persons of Hispanic ethnicity may be of any race.

Source: U.S. Department of Education, National Center for Education Statistics, *Parent and Family Involvement in Education: 2019, First Look*, July 2020, NCES 2020-076. See also <nces.ed.gov/nhes>.

Table 266. School Enrollment Below Postsecondary—Summary by Sex, Race, and Hispanic Origin: 2022

[In thousands (75,170 represents 75,170,000), except percent. As of October. Covers civilian noninstitutional population enrolled in nursery school through high school. Based on Current Population Survey, see text, Section 1 and Appendix III]

Characteristic	Total			Race and Hispanic origin				
				White [2]				
	Number [1]	Male	Female	Total	Non-Hispanic	Black [2]	Asian [2]	Hispanic [3]
All students............................	**75,170**	**37,100**	**38,070**	**53,090**	**37,640**	**11,540**	**5,142**	**18,240**
Nursery............................	4,357	2,236	2,121	2,996	2,207	714	304	939
Full day............................	1,786	(NA)	(NA)	1,383	1,040	178	103	374
Part day............................	2,571	(NA)	(NA)	1,613	1,167	535	201	566
Public schools............................	2,460	(NA)	(NA)	1,575	1,017	565	128	663
Full day............................	1,049	(NA)	(NA)	762	512	152	65	280
Part day............................	1,411	(NA)	(NA)	813	506	414	62	383
Private schools............................	1,897	(NA)	(NA)	1,421	1,189	148	176	276
Full day............................	737	(NA)	(NA)	621	528	27	38	93
Part day............................	1,160	(NA)	(NA)	799	661	121	138	183
Kindergarten............................	4,026	2,051	1,975	2,861	1,944	624	220	1,075
Elementary............................	32,370	16,680	15,700	22,780	15,830	5,085	1,912	8,346
High school............................	17,160	8,835	8,323	12,390	8,554	2,487	973	4,440
Population 18 to 24 years old.......	29,254	14,591	14,662	21,548	15,229	4,287	1,770	7,160
Percent dropouts [4]...............	5.0	5.8	4.2	4.9	3.8	5.7	1.3	7.6
Percent high school graduates....	89.2	87.5	90.9	89.1	90.7	88.8	94.8	85.1
Percent enrolled in college........	39.0	34.2	43.8	38.2	40.7	36.4	59.9	32.8

NA Not available. [1] Includes other races not shown separately. [2] For persons who selected this race group only. See footnote 4, Table 252. [3] Persons of Hispanic origin may be of any race. [4] For persons not in regular school and who have not completed the 12th grade nor received a general equivalency degree.

Source: U.S. Census Bureau, "School Enrollment Tables," <www.census.gov/topics/education/school-enrollment.html>, accessed November 2023.

Table 267. Elementary and Secondary Schools—Teachers, Enrollment, and Pupil-Teacher Ratio: 1960 to 2021

[In thousands (1,600 represents 1,600,000), except ratios. As of Fall. Data are for full-time equivalent teachers. Based on surveys of state education agencies and private schools; see source for details. Data may not sum due to rounding]

Year	Teachers			Enrollment			Pupil-teacher ratio		
	Total	Public	Private [1]	Total	Public	Private [1]	Total	Public	Private [1]
1960	1,600	1,408	192	42,181	36,281	5,900	26.4	25.8	30.7
1970	2,292	2,059	233	51,257	45,894	5,363	22.4	22.3	23.0
1980	2,485	2,184	301	46,208	40,877	5,331	18.6	18.7	17.7
1990	2,759	2,398	361	46,864	41,217	5,648	17.0	17.2	15.6
2000	3,366	2,941	424	53,373	47,204	6,169	15.9	16.0	14.5
2005	3,593	3,143	450	55,187	49,113	6,073	15.4	15.6	13.5
2010	3,529	3,099	429	54,867	49,484	5,382	15.5	16.0	12.5
2011	3,524	3,103	421	54,790	49,522	5,268	15.5	16.0	12.5
2012	3,540	3,109	431	55,104	49,771	5,333	15.6	16.0	12.4
2013	3,555	3,114	441	55,440	50,045	5,396	15.6	16.1	12.2
2014	3,594	3,132	461	55,888	50,313	5,575	15.6	16.1	12.1
2015	3,633	3,151	482	56,189	50,438	5,751	15.5	16.0	11.9
2016	3,653	3,169	483	56,369	50,615	5,754	15.4	16.0	11.9
2017	3,652	3,170	482	56,406	50,686	5,720	15.4	16.0	11.9
2018	3,652	3,170	482	56,304	50,694	5,610	15.4	16.0	11.6
2019	3,679	3,198	481	56,282	50,796	5,486	15.3	15.9	11.4
2020	3,677	3,196	[2] 481	55,377	49,375	[2] 6,002	15.1	15.4	[2] 12.5
2021	3,698	3,214	[2] 483	55,493	49,433	[2] 6,060	15.0	15.4	[2] 12.5

[1] Private school data are estimated based on the Private School Universe Survey, conducted biennially 1990-2020. [2] Projected. Projections were made after the onset of the coronavirus disease 2019 (COVID-19) pandemic and account for the impact of the pandemic.

Source: U.S. National Center for Education Statistics, *Digest of Education Statistics*, "Latest version of all Digest tables," <nces.ed.gov/programs/digest>, accessed August 2023.

Table 268. Private Schools—Number, Students, and Teachers by School Characteristics: 2022

[In thousands where indicated (4,731 represents 4,731,000). For school year ending in year shown. Based on the Private School Survey, conducted every 2 years; see source for details. For composition of regions, see map inside front cover]

Characteristic	Schools (number)	Students (1,000)	Teachers (1,000) [1]	Average enrollment by school level				Student to teacher ratio by school level			
				Total	Elementary & middle [2]	Secondary & high [3]	Combined	Total	Elementary & middle [2]	Secondary & high [3]	Combined
Total	**29,727**	**4,731**	**483**	**159.2**	**110.3**	**250.2**	**223.0**	**9.8**	**10.1**	**10.2**	**9.3**
School type:											
Catholic	6,122	1,665	135	272.0	212.9	488.6	369.0	12.3	12.7	12.5	10.0
Parochial	1,789	410	32	229.4	216.6	432.8	331.0	12.7	12.9	12.5	10.3
Diocesan	3,247	884	69	272.4	218.0	493.1	423.0	12.8	13.0	13.0	11.1
Private	1,086	370	34	341.0	167.6	492.3	330.8	11.1	10.3	12.0	8.8
Other religious	13,507	1,963	194	145.3	88.2	158.1	216.5	10.1	9.9	9.2	10.4
Conservative Christian	3,549	705	63	198.7	118.3	154.8	233.3	11.2	11.0	11.5	11.3
Other affiliated	3,441	651	69	189.2	128.4	189.5	296.0	9.4	9.1	8.5	9.8
Unaffiliated	6,516	606	62	93.1	62.5	130.2	150.2	9.8	10.3	9.4	9.6
Nonsectarian	10,099	1,103	154	109.3	57.0	132.4	215.1	7.2	6.6	7.2	7.5
Regular	4,729	747	96	157.9	67.2	221.7	399.9	7.8	7.3	7.5	8.2
Special emphasis	3,597	239	35	66.5	44.9	84.4	158.4	6.7	5.8	8.0	8.1
Special education	1,773	118	23	66.3	56.6	42.2	76.8	5.2	5.5	4.7	5.2
Program emphasis:											
Regular	20,186	4,177	399	206.9	150.2	323.9	266.3	10.5	11.1	10.7	9.8
Montessori	2,441	98	18	40.3	35.8	(B)	94.5	5.6	5.4	(B)	7.0
Special program emphasis	918	144	17	156.9	98.8	177.6	237.8	8.3	7.4	8.7	9.0
Special education	2,011	131	26	65.3	56.9	41.8	75.2	5.2	5.2	4.7	5.2
Vocational/technical	28	5	(Z)	177.3	(B)	216.6	(B)	14.0	(B)	15.6	(B)
Alternative	1,439	129	15	89.9	59.4	64.0	131.4	8.8	7.3	8.0	9.8
Early childhood	2,705	47	8	17.3	17.2	(X)	14.0	5.5	5.6	(X)	2.8
Enrollment size:											
Less than 50	11,878	257	46	21.6	19.8	24.1	26.4	5.5	6.0	4.3	5.2
50 to 149	8,075	741	93	91.8	93.1	87.5	90.6	8.0	8.6	6.7	7.4
150 to 299	5,260	1,114	108	211.7	208.9	217.5	215.8	10.3	11.3	9.0	9.1
300 to 499	2,536	969	90	382.1	376.9	391.8	384.1	10.8	11.9	10.6	9.7
500 to 749	1,139	691	62	606.7	588.9	610.8	613.1	11.1	13.8	11.3	10.1
750 or more	839	959	83	1,143.9	1,070.2	1,089.1	1,183.9	11.6	12.7	13.1	10.8
Region:											
Northeast	6,370	976	113	153.3	109.3	240.6	198.8	8.6	9.6	8.9	7.5
Midwest	6,928	1,072	97	154.8	118.0	301.8	217.4	11.1	11.5	11.8	10.0
South	10,562	1,746	182	165.3	98.8	235.5	231.5	9.6	9.2	10.6	9.6
West	5,867	937	90	159.7	117.6	238.8	229.6	10.4	10.4	10.5	10.3
Urban/rural status:											
City	10,119	2,054	210	203.0	138.1	305.8	304.3	9.8	9.9	10.6	9.2
Suburban	11,259	1,867	187	165.8	117.0	265.2	236.1	10.0	10.4	10.4	9.4
Town	2,590	281	29	108.5	85.5	137.8	136.8	9.7	10.0	9.6	9.4
Rural	5,760	529	57	91.9	52.1	126.3	142.9	9.3	10.1	8.1	9.4

Z Less than 500. X Not applicable. B Reporting standards not met. There are fewer than 15 sample cases. [1] Full-time equivalents. [2] Schools enrolling the majority of students in either grades kindergarten to 4 or grades 5 to 8. [3] Schools enrolling the majority of students in grades 9 to 12.

Source: U.S. National Center for Education Statistics, Private School Universe Survey, "Data Tables," <nces.ed.gov/surveys/pss>, accessed March 2024.

Table 269. Public Elementary and Secondary Schools by Type and Size of School: 2022

[Total enrollment in thousands (49,090 represents 49,090,000). For school year ending in 2022. Data reported by schools rather than school districts. Based on the Common Core of Data Survey; see source for details]

Enrollment size of school	Number of schools					Enrollment				
	Total [1]	Elemen-tary	Middle	Second-ary	Other [2]	Total [1]	Elemen-tary	Middle	Second-ary	Other [2]
Total..................	**99,239**	**52,450**	**16,300**	**23,742**	**5,212**	**49,090**	**22,545**	**9,216**	**15,318**	**1,823**
PERCENT [3]										
Total..................	100.00	100.00	100.00	100.00	100.00	100.00	100.00	100.00	100.00	100.00
Under 100 students.......	9.96	4.46	5.93	19.39	32.99	0.87	0.54	0.53	1.13	2.97
100 to 199 students.......	9.41	8.12	7.71	11.41	15.71	2.77	2.89	2.08	2.41	5.00
200 to 299 students.......	12.62	14.93	9.83	9.36	11.16	6.20	8.76	4.34	3.33	6.05
300 to 399 students......	15.35	20.22	11.40	8.73	7.62	10.49	16.43	7.00	4.37	5.79
400 to 499 students.......	14.15	19.27	10.94	6.64	5.85	12.38	19.99	8.64	4.27	5.84
500 to 599 students.......	10.88	13.94	10.94	5.30	4.96	11.61	17.63	10.56	4.17	5.95
600 to 699 students.......	7.71	8.85	10.32	4.31	3.54	9.73	13.24	11.76	4.01	5.05
700 to 799 students.......	5.18	4.82	9.51	3.57	2.91	7.56	8.33	12.51	3.84	4.80
800 to 999 students.......	5.73	3.86	13.06	5.40	4.18	9.91	7.84	20.39	6.96	8.33
1,000 to 1,499 students...	5.11	1.41	9.42	10.87	6.03	11.96	3.75	19.29	19.27	16.26
1,500 to 1,999 students...	2.02	0.08	0.83	7.55	2.42	6.82	0.32	2.40	18.86	9.06
2,000 to 2,999 students...	1.53	0.02	0.10	6.29	1.20	7.03	0.11	0.41	21.38	6.36
3,000 or more students. ..	0.34	0.02	0.01	1.18	1.44	2.66	0.18	0.09	6.01	18.55

[1] Excludes special education schools, vocational schools, and alternative schools. Totals include data for prekindergarten schools, not shown separately. [2] Other includes ungraded, and not applicable or not reported. [3] Percent distribution calculations include data only for schools reporting enrollments greater than zero.

Source: U.S. National Center for Education Statistics, *Digest of Education Statistics*, "Latest version of all Digest tables," <nces.ed.gov/programs/digest>, accessed November 2023.

Table 270. Public Elementary and Secondary Schools—Number and Average Salary of Classroom Teachers: 1990 to 2022, and by State, 2023

[Estimates for school year ending in June of year shown]

Year and state	Teachers [1]	Average salary (dollars)	Year and state	Teachers [1]	Average salary (dollars)	Year and state	Teachers [1]	Average salary (dollars)
1990.........	2,361,588	31,367	HI.............	10,969	70,947	NM............	23,094	63,580
2000.........	2,891,071	41,807	ID.............	17,922	56,365	NY............	215,761	92,696
2010.........	3,182,220	55,370	IL.............	134,897	73,916	NC............	92,681	56,559
2015.........	3,152,710	57,748	IN.............	61,323	57,015	ND............	9,244	56,792
2020.........	3,194,190	64,172	IA.............	38,190	61,231	OH............	102,323	66,390
2021.........	3,178,463	65,456	KS.............	34,821	56,481	OK............	42,763	55,505
2022.........	3,187,113	66,805	KY.............	40,180	56,296	OR............	31,781	72,476
2023			LA.............	48,299	54,248	PA............	122,324	74,945
U.S. total. ..	**3,222,170**	**69,544**	ME.............	14,714	59,964	RI............	10,785	79,289
AL.............	47,386	60,441	MD.............	62,686	79,420	SC............	54,569	57,778
AK.............	7,030	76,371	MA.............	76,978	92,307	SD............	10,038	53,153
AZ.............	49,565	60,275	MI.............	82,718	67,011	TN............	65,781	55,369
AR.............	31,138	54,309	MN.............	57,057	70,005	TX............	371,802	60,716
CA.............	292,378	95,160	MS.............	32,092	53,354	UT............	31,087	63,481
CO.............	58,083	60,775	MO.............	73,653	53,999	VT............	7,924	66,536
CT.............	42,184	83,400	MT.............	11,036	55,909	VA............	105,025	63,103
DE.............	10,144	68,787	NE.............	24,929	58,763	WA............	63,629	86,804
DC.............	8,052	84,882	NV.............	19,059	61,719	WV............	19,250	52,870
FL.............	138,399	53,098	NH.............	15,609	64,169	WI............	56,429	62,524
GA.............	120,414	64,461	NJ.............	116,698	81,102	WY............	7,277	61,979

[1] Full-time equivalent.

Source: National Education Association, Washington, DC. Data from *Rankings of the States 2023 and Estimates of School Statistics 2024*, April 2024, used with permission of the National Education Association © 2024, and earlier reports. All rights reserved.

Table 271. Public School Employment by Occupation, Sex, and Race/Ethnicity: 2022

[In thousands (5,557 represents 5,557,000). Covers all public elementary-secondary school districts with 100 or more full-time employees]

Occupation	Total [1]	Male	Female	White non-Hispanic	Black non-Hispanic	Asian non-Hispanic	Hispanic [2]
All occupations........................	**5,557**	**1,367**	**4,190**	**3,835**	**692**	**136**	**779**
Officials, administrators, managers.......	122	51	71	87	16	3	14
Principals and assistant principals........	162	61	100	108	27	5	17
Classroom teachers [3]......................	2,869	676	2,193	2,184	258	68	304
Elementary schools......................	1,296	147	1,150	993	105	29	145
Secondary schools......................	1,156	442	714	890	103	28	114
Other professional staff [4].................	593	96	496	410	78	16	76
Nonprofessional staff [5]...................	1,812	483	1,329	1,046	313	45	369
Teachers aides...........................	621	70	551	376	106	17	110

[1] Includes other races/ethnicities not shown separately. [2] Persons of Hispanic origin may be of any race. [3] Includes other classroom teachers not shown separately. [4] Includes guidance, psychological, librarians/audiovisual staff, and consultants and supervisors of instruction. [5] Includes technicians, administrative support workers, service workers, skilled crafts, and unskilled laborers, not shown separately.

Source: U.S. Equal Employment Opportunity Commission, "Job Patterns for Minorities and Women in Elementary-Secondary Public Schools (EEO-5)," <www.eeoc.gov/statistics/job-patterns-minorities-and-women-elementary-secondary-public-schools-eeo-5>, accessed August 2023.

Table 272. Public School Teachers, Base Salary, and Additional Income by Selected Characteristics: 2021

[3,537 represents 3,537,000. Salary and income shown in current dollars. For school year ending in 2021. Data shown for regular full-time teachers only; excludes other staff even when they have full-time teaching duties. Based on the 2020-2021 National Teacher and Principal Survey and subject to sampling error; for details, see <nces.ed.gov/surveys/ntps>]

Characteristic	Number of full-time teachers (1,000)	Base teacher salary (dollars)	Total income from school and nonschool sources [1,2] (dollars)	Teachers with additional income					
				Job outside the school system during the school year		Supplemental school system contract during summer [3]		Employed in a non-school job during the summer	
				Percent of teachers	Average income (dollars)	Percent of teachers	Average income (dollars)	Percent of teachers	Average income (dollars)
Total.......................	3,537	61,600	65,400	16.8	6,090	17.1	2,840	16.1	3,550
Sex:									
Male........................	835	63,050	69,420	22.4	7,190	19.7	3,530	22.3	4,770
Female....................	2,701	61,140	64,160	15.0	5,580	16.3	2,580	14.2	2,960
Race/ethnicity: [4]									
White........................	2,820	61,560	65,430	17.3	6,000	16.7	2,820	16.9	3,520
Black........................	217	58,980	62,610	17.0	5,940	20.4	2,830	14.0	3,440
Asian........................	83	70,250	73,000	9.2	6,820	16.8	3,610	8.8	3,910
Pacific Islander.............	6	60,120	63,160	[6] 11.4	(S)	27.3	(S)	15.1	(S)
American Indian or Alaska Native.............	15	52,100	55,830	12.3	(S)	15.0	2,930	16.9	3,030
Two or more races.........	58	60,240	63,980	22.8	4,330	17.9	2,330	17.2	3,300
Hispanic.....................	339	62,120	65,820	13.0	7,540	18.4	2,900	12.0	4,000
Age:									
Under 30 years old........	510	49,230	52,580	18.0	4,370	22.4	2,400	24.3	2,580
30 to 39 years old..........	961	57,150	60,780	17.5	5,740	17.6	2,630	17.0	3,110
40 to 49 years old..........	1,008	65,210	68,930	17.2	6,320	16.1	2,840	14.7	3,970
50 years old or over.......	1,058	68,150	72,420	15.1	7,190	15.1	3,390	12.6	4,530
Years of full- and part-time teaching experience:									
1 year or less...............	97	45,880	50,140	16.0	6,040	18.7	4,170	34.9	4,310
2 to 4 years.................	470	49,280	52,750	17.3	6,140	20.6	2,580	19.9	2,840
5 to 9 years.................	729	53,980	57,420	17.8	5,330	19.1	2,510	17.6	2,960
10 to 14 years..............	591	59,820	63,350	16.7	5,730	17.3	2,560	15.3	3,420
15 to 19 years..............	585	66,300	70,020	16.1	6,450	15.0	2,780	13.4	3,900
20 to 24 years..............	531	71,770	75,350	16.1	6,200	14.9	2,880	13.5	3,790
25 to 29 years..............	295	72,670	77,300	17.1	7,570	16.7	4,160	14.4	4,950
30 years or more...........	239	72,000	77,750	15.5	6,400	13.8	3,190	12.8	4,350
Highest degree held:									
Less than bachelor's........	26	54,680	62,140	30.5	9,660	14.1	4,100	32.9	7,320
Bachelor's...................	1,379	52,540	56,050	16.0	5,710	16.7	2,680	17.4	3,370
Master's.....................	1,794	66,960	70,870	16.9	6,250	17.1	2,870	15.3	3,590
Education specialist........	292	70,480	74,310	17.5	5,640	18.9	3,070	13.8	3,600
Doctorate...................	46	71,280	77,620	22.2	8,970	20.3	4,040	13.7	3,480
Instructional level: [5]									
Elementary..................	1,741	60,490	63,080	14.2	5,510	16.3	2,440	14.4	3,000
Secondary..................	1,795	62,670	67,650	19.2	6,500	17.9	3,200	17.8	3,980
School locale:									
City..........................	984	63,460	67,020	15.7	6,260	18.6	2,840	14.4	3,580
Suburban...................	1,364	66,930	70,650	16.9	6,060	17.1	2,980	15.2	3,370
Town........................	423	54,260	58,280	17.0	5,670	15.9	2,650	18.6	3,360
Rural........................	766	53,750	57,920	17.7	6,150	16.0	2,690	18.5	3,890

S Figure does not meet publication standards. [1] Includes retirement pension funds paid during the school year. [2] Includes types of income not shown separately. [3] Includes teaching summer sessions and other non-teaching jobs at any school. [4] Race categories exclude those of Hispanic ethnicity. [5] Teachers were classified as elementary or secondary on the basis of the grades they taught, rather than on the level of the school in which they taught. In general, elementary teachers include those teaching pre-kindergarten through grade 6 and those teaching multiple grades with a preponderance of grades taught being kindergarten through grade 6. In general, secondary teachers include those teaching grades 7 through 12 and those teaching multiple grades with a preponderance of grades taught being grades 7 through 12 and usually no grade taught being lower than grade 5. [6] Interpret data with caution. The coefficient of variation is between 30 and 50 percent.

Source: U.S. National Center for Education Statistics, *Digest of Education Statistics*, "Latest version of all Digest tables," <nces.ed.gov/programs/digest>, accessed May 2023.

Table 273. Education and Teaching Experience of Public Elementary and Secondary School Teachers by Selected Characteristics: 2021

[3,764 represents 3,764,000. For school year ending in 2021. Excludes prekindergarten teachers. Data are based on a head count of full-time and part-time teachers. Based on the National Teacher and Principal Survey (NTPS); see source for details]

Characteristic	Number of teachers (1,000s)	Percent of teachers by highest degree earned					Percent of teachers by years of teaching experience [1]			
		Less than bachelor's	Bach-elor's	Master's	Education specialist [2]	Doctor's	Less than 3	3 to 9	10 to 20	Over 20
Total...................	**3,764**	**0.8**	**38.2**	**51.2**	**8.4**	**1.4**	**7.3**	**29.1**	**37.3**	**26.3**
Sex:										
Male.......................	873	1.9	37.7	51.4	6.8	2.2	7.5	28.8	36.5	27.2
Female.....................	2,890	0.5	38.3	51.2	8.9	1.1	7.2	29.2	37.6	26.1
Race/ethnicity: [3]										
White......................	3,007	0.8	37.4	52.4	8.3	1.1	6.8	28.1	37.7	27.4
Black......................	228	0.7	34.0	51.5	10.5	3.3	8.5	30.9	37.1	23.5
Asian......................	89	(S)	30.5	54.1	10.9	3.8	11.1	34.3	33.9	20.8
Pacific Islander..............	6	(S)	43.8	46.0	[5] 6.7	(S)	[5] 4.5	27.4	45.1	23.0
American Indian/Alaska Native.	16	[5] 3.8	44.0	42.4	9.2	(S)	[5] 5.4	35.7	35.7	23.2
Two or more races...........	62	[5] 1.2 0.0	40.6	46.3	10.2	[5] 1.7 0.0	8.2 0.0	39.5	33.1	19.3
Hispanic....................	355	1.0	48.3	41.7	7.3	1.6	9.4	32.9	35.5	22.3
Age:										
Under age 30.................	535	0.5	65.0	32.5	1.9	(S)	32.9	67.0	(S)	(S)
Age 30 to 39.................	1,016	0.4	38.0	53.5	7.3	0.7	4.9	46.9	48.2	(S)
Age 40 to 49.................	1,073	0.8	31.4	56.7	9.8	1.4	2.9	14.8	54.2	28.1
Age 50 to 59.................	841	1.0	31.1	54.5	11.2	2.2	1.5	9.6	29.1	59.9
Age 60 and over.............	300	2.3	34.8	48.2	11.2	3.5	1.3	7.0	29.5	62.2
Level of instruction: [4]										
Elementary.................	1,884	0.3	41.0	49.3	8.5	0.8	7.3	29.7	37.2	25.9
Secondary.................	1,880	1.3	35.3	53.1	8.3	2.0	7.3	28.5	37.4	26.8

S Figure does not meet publication standards. [1] Includes full- and part-time teaching experience. [2] Education specialist degrees or certificates are generally awarded for 1 year of work beyond the master's degree level. Includes certificate of advanced graduate studies. [3] Data for race categories exclude persons of Hispanic origin. [4] Teachers were classified as elementary or secondary on the basis of the grades they taught, rather than on the level of the school in which they taught. Elementary teachers generally include those teaching prekindergarten through grade 5 and those teaching multiple grades with a preponderance of grades taught being kindergarten through grade 6. Secondary teachers generally include those teaching grades 7 through 12 and those teaching multiple grades with a preponderance of grades taught being grades 7 through 12. [5] Interpret data with caution. The coefficient of variation (CV) is between 30 and 50 percent.

Source: U.S. National Center for Education Statistics, *Digest of Education Statistics*, "Latest version of all Digest Tables," <nces.ed.gov/programs/digest>, accessed November 2023.

Table 274: Teachers Who Moved to a Different School or Left Teaching by Selected Characteristics: 2022

[In percent. For school year ending in year shown. Based on comparisons of teaching status in current school year vs. previous school year. Movers are teachers who are teaching in a different school compared to the previous school year. Leavers are teachers who are no longer teaching in the current school year. Data are from the Teacher Follow-up Survey conducted during the school year ended 2022 of teachers participating in the National Teacher and Principal Survey conducted during the 2021 school year; see source for details]

Item	Movers		Leavers	
	Public	Private	Public	Private
Total...	**7.9**	**6.4**	**7.9**	**11.7**
Age:				
Less than 30 years old............................	13.5	12.0	7.1	17.0
30 to 49 years old...............................	7.7	7.4	5.9	9.1
50 to 54 years old...............................	7.1	[2] 4.4	6.8	7.4
55 years old or older............................	5.0	[2] 3.1	16.1	15.8
Sex:				
Male...	7.4	8.1	7.1	12.2
Female...	8.1	5.9	8.2	11.5
Race/ethnicity:				
Black or African American, Non-Hispanic.............	8.9	[2] 7.3	10.7	[2] 9.2
White, Non-Hispanic.............................	7.8	6.0	7.8	11.3
Hispanic..	9.3	8.9	6.5	12.1
Highest degree:				
Bachelor's degree or less.........................	9.3	5.7	6.0	12.6
Master's degree.................................	7.2	7.7	8.6	10.1
Higher than a master's degree [1]...................	6.9	[2] 4.5	11.6	14.2
Years of experience at 2020-21 school:				
3 years or less..................................	11.3	8.6	8.3	12.9
4 to 9 years....................................	8.5	7.3	7.1	9.6
10 to 14 years..................................	4.4	[2] 3.2	6.6	7.5
15 or more years................................	3.5	[2] 2.4	9.1	15.4
Years of experience at any school:				
3 years or less..................................	13.0	11.0	7.1	15.4
4 to 9 years....................................	10.1	9.2	7.7	11.3
10 to 14 years..................................	7.7	4.0	6.3	7.3
15 or more years................................	5.6	4.0	8.8	12.0
Teaching status:				
Full time.......................................	8.1	6.8	7.0	9.5
Part time.......................................	6.1	[2] 4.6	20.4	22.1
Changed schools or left teaching involuntarily.....................	19.0	15.7	3.3	9.5

NA Not available. [1] Completed an educational specialist or professional diploma, a certificate of advanced graduate studies, or a doctorate or first professional degree. [2] Interpret data with caution. The coefficient of variation (CV) is between 30 percent and 50 percent.

Source: U.S. National Center for Education Statistics, *Teacher Attrition and Mobility Results From the 2021-22 Teacher Follow-up Survey to the National Teacher and Principal Survey*, NCES 2024-039, December 2023. See also <nces.ed.gov/surveys/ntps/>.

Table 275. Private School Teachers, Base Salary, and Additional Income by Selected Characteristics: 2021

[387.1 represents 387,100. For school year ending in 2021. Data shown for regular full-time teachers only; excludes other staff even when they have full-time teaching duties. Based on the 2020-2021 National Teacher and Principal Survey and subject to sampling error; for details, see <nces.ed.gov/surveys/ntps/>]

Characteristic	Number of full-time teachers (1,000)	Base teacher salary (dollars)	Total income [1,2] (dollars)	Teachers with additional income					
				Job outside the school system during the school year		Supplemental school system contract during summer [3]		Employed in a non-school job during the summer	
				Percent of teachers	Average income (dollars)	Percent of teachers	Average income (dollars)	Percent of teachers	Average income (dollars)
Total [4]	387.1	46,400	50,500	17.2	6,080	19.6	3,750	16.0	3,600
SEX									
Male	93.1	52,590	60,110	23.8	8,110	25.3	5,210	23.2	5,080
Female	293.9	44,440	47,450	15.1	5,070	17.8	3,090	13.7	2,800
RACE/ETHNICITY									
Non-Hispanic:									
White	320.4	46,530	50,730	17.6	6,090	19.0	3,810	16.4	3,710
Black	14.8	42,570	47,620	19.2	(S)	24.1	3,860	13.4	(S)
Asian	10.0	51,670	55,370	12.1	(S)	34.6	3,670	[6]10.9	(S)
Two or more races	7.9	48,150	51,770	22.4	(S)	33.0	(S)	24.5	(S)
Hispanic	32.8	45,330	48,330	13.2	6,630	15.9	3,090	12.6	3,040
AGE									
Less than 30 years old	55.7	37,680	41,300	17.1	4,760	27.8	3,520	25.4	3,560
30 to 39 years old	91.9	45,770	50,050	20.7	5,590	24.0	4,110	19.4	3,720
40 to 49 years old	97.4	47,980	51,220	15.7	6,330	16.9	3,100	15.7	3,130
50 or more years old	142.1	49,150	53,890	16.0	6,880	15.4	4,030	10.2	3,960
YEARS OF TEACHING EXPERIENCE									
1 year or less	30.2	35,510	39,600	15.3	7,100	26.7	4,180	24.2	5,390
2 to 4 years	51.8	39,430	42,900	20.4	5,480	23.4	3,860	22.9	2,570
5 to 9 years	76.2	43,060	46,500	17.1	5,160	24.2	2,980	17.6	3,510
10 to 14 years	62.7	48,050	52,610	20.0	7,090	20.3	5,040	16.9	4,160
15 to 19 years	53.5	49,890	52,930	14.8	5,320	15.6	3,350	11.7	2,860
20 to 24 years	42.3	52,200	55,480	15.8	5,550	14.4	2,580	12.1	3,010
25 to 29 years	28.4	51,760	56,370	18.0	7,510	18.2	3,330	12.0	2,810
30 or more years	42.1	52,520	59,660	14.5	6,600	11.6	4,850	9.3	[6]4,760
HIGHEST DEGREE HELD									
Less than bachelor's	16.4	29,720	34,650	17.5	(S)	19.1	(S)	18.4	(S)
Bachelor's	178.9	40,740	44,150	16.2	5,370	18.5	3,620	16.0	3,290
Master's	157.6	52,760	57,150	17.9	6,570	20.0	3,580	16.0	3,170
Education specialist	22.1	51,560	57,600	19.9	6,110	21.9	4,040	13.8	3,130
Doctorate	12.1	60,570	66,320	16.9	9,340	25.3	4,500	16.4	(S)
INSTRUCTIONAL LEVEL [5]									
Elementary	199.6	41,770	44,650	14.4	4,870	18.3	3,290	15.3	2,780
Secondary	187.5	51,340	56,720	20.1	7,000	20.9	4,180	16.8	4,380

S Figure does not meet publication standards. [1] Includes retirement pension funds paid during the school year. [2] Income from school and non-school sources. Includes sources of income not shown separately. [3] Includes teaching summer sessions and other non-teaching jobs at any school. [4] Includes race/ethnicities not shown separately. [5] Teachers were classified as elementary or secondary on the basis of the grades they taught, rather than on the level of the school in which they taught. In general, elementary teachers include those teaching prekindergarten through grade 6 and those teaching multiple grades with a preponderance of grades taught being kindergarten through grade 6. In general, secondary teachers include those teaching any of grades 7 through 12 and those teaching multiple grades with a preponderance of grades taught being grades 7 through 12 and usually with no grade taught being lower than grade 5. [6] Interpret data with caution. The coefficient of variation is between 30 and 50 percent.

Source: U.S. National Center for Education Statistics, *Digest of Education Statistics,* "Latest version of all Digest Tables," <nces.ed.gov/programs/digest/>, accessed March 2023.

Table 276. Public and Private Schools Reporting Changes to Instruction During COVID-19 Pandemic by Selected School Characteristics and Type of Change: 2020

[Percent of schools reporting changes to instruction delivery during spring 2020. Data are preliminary. Respondents could select more than one way in which the pandemic affected instruction. Based on data from the 2020-21 National Teacher and Principal Survey]

Characteristics	All or some classes were cancelled	All or some classes moved to online distance-learning format	All or some classes moved to paper-based distance-learning format	Instruction changed in some other way	No change
PUBLIC SCHOOLS					
Total	**9**	**77**	**41**	**9**	**3**
School classification:					
Traditional public	9	77	41	9	3
Charter school	8	82	38	9	4
Region:					
Northeast	6	84	33	11	[1] 1
Midwest	10	76	40	10	4
South	10	73	44	9	3
West	8	80	43	6	2
School level:					
Primary	10	76	47	9	2
Middle	8	80	30	11	2
High	7	81	30	8	2
Combined	10	72	43	10	8
PRIVATE SCHOOLS					
Total	**10**	**73**	**48**	**10**	**5**
School classification:					
Catholic	8	84	44	8	3
Other religious	11	64	52	12	6
Nonsectarian	11	78	45	11	6
Region:					
Northeast	11	73	38	13	4
Midwest	8	71	55	10	5
South	9	73	46	9	8
West	13	78	52	11	[1] 3
School level:					
Elementary	11	72	54	10	5
Secondary	6	77	16	11	8
Combined	9	74	48	10	6

[1] Interpret data with caution. The coefficient of variation (CV) for this estimate is between 30 and 50 percent.

Source: U.S. National Center for Education Statistics, *Impact of the Coronavirus (COVID-19) Pandemic on Public and Private Elementary and Secondary Education in the United States (Preliminary Data): Results from the 2020–21 National Teacher and Principal Survey (NTPS) First Look*, February 2022. See also <nces.ed.gov/surveys/ntps/>.

Table 277. Elementary and Secondary Schools—English Language Learner Student Enrollment by Home Language and Grade: 2012 to 2021

[4,850.3 represents 4,850,300. Data cover the academic year beginning with year shown. Data for 2013 and earlier years include all English Language Learner (ELL) students enrolled at any time during the school year; beginning 2014, data shown as of fall. Includes all students identified as English language learners (ELL), both those participating in ELL programs and those not participating in ELL programs. Data exclude U.S. territories, and the Bureau of Indian Education]

Home language and grade	2012	2013	2014	2015	2016	2017	2018 [3]	2019	2020	2021
Total	**4,850.3**	**4,930.0**	**4,813.7**	**4,854.3**	**4,949.4**	**5,010.5**	**5,024.2**	**5,115.9**	**4,963.4**	**5,263.6**
HOME LANGUAGE										
Spanish, Castilian	3,718.0	3,770.8	3,709.8	3,741.1	3,790.9	3,749.3	3,777.9	3,872.2	3,745.5	4,023.3
Arabic	98.0	109.2	109.2	114.4	129.4	136.5	135.9	131.6	128.6	130.9
English [1]	90.7	91.7	83.2	80.3	70.0	94.9	99.5	105.3	124.9	116.8
Chinese	104.8	107.8	104.3	101.3	104.1	106.5	102.8	100.1	93.3	95.6
Vietnamese	92.6	89.7	85.3	81.2	78.7	77.8	76.5	75.6	73.1	75.1
Portuguese	17.1	19.1	19.8	23.7	28.2	33.3	37.5	44.8	43.4	50.2
Russian	33.7	33.8	32.5	33.1	34.8	36.8	38.2	39.7	37.2	39.4
Haitian, Haitian Creole	38.8	37.4	31.4	30.2	31.6	32.7	32.8	31.5	30.1	31.1
Hmong	41.4	39.9	37.4	34.8	33.1	32.2	31.3	30.8	28.7	30.2
Urdu	22.6	22.5	22.3	22.9	24.7	25.3	25.5	25.3	25.2	26.6
GRADE										
Kindergarten	667.8	667.7	629.0	606.4	600.2	587.5	555.7	555.6	435.3	522.5
Grade 1	665.3	665.6	640.0	621.1	603.8	588.5	571.9	554.6	526.6	519.6
Grade 2	609.8	630.5	614.7	614.8	599.1	574.7	557.8	549.0	520.1	524.6
Grade 3	540.4	558.9	567.1	564.8	576.1	551.3	527.4	521.5	511.6	510.6
Grade 4	428.1	439.5	436.6	461.0	457.5	505.0	494.2	475.8	479.4	492.9
Grade 5	367.1	361.7	364.2	372.8	389.3	400.1	426.3	430.4	409.3	445.9
Grade 6	288.1	293.8	287.8	305.5	318.7	329.3	346.3	372.6	370.8	383.2
Grade 7	255.4	267.4	260.5	267.1	286.3	291.9	308.2	332.9	348.8	364.9
Grade 8	227.8	239.8	242.5	245.6	258.2	265.2	278.7	299.0	315.5	346.3
Grade 9	255.0	261.6	263.1	269.7	286.2	280.4	291.1	326.4	307.5	369.5
Grade 10	202.8	202.4	197.5	214.0	232.7	255.0	251.4	269.6	288.0	292.5
Grade 11	170.8	168.4	157.4	162.3	184.0	202.4	219.0	219.1	235.4	255.6
Grade 12	159.4	161.2	143.2	138.8	146.4	167.1	185.7	199.1	204.6	224.7
Ungraded [2]	11.8	11.4	10.1	10.2	11.0	11.8	10.0	10.5	10.5	10.5

[1] Examples of situations in which English might be reported as an English learner's home language include students who live in multilingual households and students adopted from other countries who speak English at home but also have been raised speaking another language. [2] Includes students reported in grade 13. [3] Data for Vermont were not available.

Source: U.S. National Center for Education Statistics, *Digest of Education Statistics*, "Latest version of all Digest tables," <nces.ed.gov/programs/digest/> and earlier reports, accessed May 2024.

Table 278. Public and Private School Start Times by Selected Characteristics: 2021

[For academic year ending in 2021. Data are from the National Teacher and Principal Survey]

School characteristic	Average start time	Percent distribution of start times				
		Before 7:30 a.m.	7:30 a.m. to 7:59 a.m.	8:00 a.m. to 8:29 a.m.	8:30 a.m. to 8:59 a.m.	9:00 a.m. or later
All schools...................	**8:13**	**3.8**	**23.0**	**40.5**	**22.4**	**10.2**
Public schools................	**8:13**	**4.5**	**24.8**	**37.5**	**21.9**	**11.3**
School classification:						
Traditional public...............	8:13	4.6	25.4	36.7	21.9	11.3
Charter school.................	8:11	3.0	19.7	44.5	22.0	10.7
School level:						
Primary.........................	8:16	2.6	22.7	36.7	26.2	11.7
Middle.........................	8:11	5.7	28.9	35.6	17.1	12.7
High...........................	8:07	8.9	27.6	35.5	17.6	10.5
Combined......................	8:08	2.7	23.6	52.5	14.0	7.2
Private schools..............	**8:12**	**1.1**	**16.0**	**52.3**	**24.4**	**6.3**
School classification:						
Catholic.......................	8:00	[1] 2.6	34.7	54.0	6.2	[1] 2.5
Other religious.................	8:14	[1] 0.5	10.2	55.9	28.0	5.4
Nonsectarian...................	8:21	(S)	7.4	43.4	36.6	11.9
School level:						
Elementary.....................	8:15	(S)	10.7	46.2	37.8	4.5
Secondary......................	8:14	[1] 1.8	22.1	46.8	16.7	12.7

S Figure does not meet publication standards. [1] Interpret data with caution. The coefficient of variation (CV) for this estimate is between 30 percent and 50 percent.

Source: U.S. National Center for Education Statistics, National Teacher and Principal Survey, "2020-2021 NTPS Tables," <nces.ed.gov/surveys/ntps/tables_list.asp>, accessed May 2023.

Table 279. Homeschooled Students by Selected Characteristics: 2012 to 2019

[1,773 represents 1,773,000. For students age 5 to 17 with a grade equivalent of K–12. Homeschoolers are students whose parents reported them to be schooled at home instead of in a public or private school. Excludes students who were enrolled in school for more than 25 hours a week in 2012 and 2016 or for more than 24 hours a week in 2019, or who were homeschooled due to a temporary illness. Based on the Parent and Family Involvement in Education Survey of the National Household Education Surveys Program]

Characteristic	2012 [1]		2016		2019	
	Home-schooled (1,000)	Percent home-schooled	Home-schooled (1,000)	Percent home-schooled	Home-schooled (1,000)	Percent home-schooled
Total.............................	**1,773**	**3.4**	**1,690**	**3.3**	**1,457**	**2.8**
Sex:						
Male...........................	875	3.3	807	3.0	725	2.7
Female.........................	898	3.6	882	3.5	732	2.9
Race/ethnicity: [2]						
White, non-Hispanic.............	1,205	4.5	998	3.8	1,014	4.0
Black, non-Hispanic.............	140	2.0	132	1.9	84	1.2
Hispanic [3].....................	265	2.3	444	3.5	250	1.9
Grade equivalent: [4]						
Kindergarten to grade 5...........	833	3.2	767	3.0	703	2.8
Kindergarten..................	212	4.0	181	3.5	115	2.6
Grades 1 to 3.................	353	2.9	300	2.4	322	2.7
Grades 4 to 5.................	268	3.2	287	3.4	267	3.2
Grades 6 to 8..................	424	3.5	398	3.3	429	3.4
Grades 9 to 12.................	516	3.8	525	3.8	325	2.3
Number of children in the household:						
One child......................	418	3.4	338	2.7	276	2.2
Two children...................	493	2.5	475	2.3	475	2.3
Three or more children..........	862	4.5	877	4.7	706	3.9
Number of parents in the household:						
Two parents....................	1,354	3.8	1,358	3.7	1,214	3.3
One parent.....................	342	2.5	293	2.3	206	1.6
Nonparental guardians..........	[5] 77	[5] 4.0	38	2.0	[5] 37	[5] 2.1
Parent/guardian participation in the labor force:						
Two parents/guardians—both in labor force.................	588	2.5	427	1.7	399	1.6
Two parents/guardians—one in labor force.................	719	6.2	935	7.2	839	6.6
One parent/guardian in labor force..........................	247	2.2	189	1.8	127	1.2
No parent/guardian in labor force............................	130	4.8	139	4.0	93	3.1
Highest education of parents/guardians:						
High school diploma or less......	560	3.4	510	3.3	330	2.2
Vocational/technical degree or some college...............	525	3.4	418	3.1	376	2.9
Bachelor's degree or some graduate school..............	434	3.7	501	3.6	449	3.3
Graduate/professional school.....	255	3.3	260	3.0	302	3.1
Household income:						
$20,000 or less................	219	2.9	184	2.9	150	3.0
$20,001 to 50,000.............	528	3.8	483	3.7	292	2.5
$50,001 to 75,000.............	370	3.9	435	4.8	302	3.6
$75,001 to 100,000.............	288	4.2	268	3.8	223	3.2
$100,000 or more...............	367	2.7	319	1.9	490	2.5

[1] The NCES uses a statistical adjustment for estimates of total homeschoolers in 2012; therefore, data will not add to total. [2] Includes other race/ethnicities not shown separately. [3] Persons of Hispanic origin may be of any race. [4] Excludes those ungraded. [5] Interpret data with caution.

Source: U.S. National Center for Education Statistics, *Digest of Education Statistics,* "Latest version of all Digest tables," <nces.ed.gov/programs/digest>, accessed May 2022.

Table 280. Average Class Size in Public and Private Schools by Selected School Characteristics: 2021

[Data are average number of students per class. For school year ending in year shown. In self-contained classes, teachers give instruction to the same group of students all or most of the day in multiple subjects. Departmentalized instruction is instruction to several classes of different students most or all of the day in one or more subjects. Data are from the National Teacher and Principal Survey (NTPS)]

School characteristic	Public schools						School characteristic	Private schools			
	Self-contained classes			Departmentalized education				Self-contained classes		Departmentalized education	
	Primary	Middle	High	Primary	Middle	High		Elementary	Secondary	Elementary	Secondary
All schools.......	**19.1**	**16.9**	**17.2**	**20.7**	**22.0**	**21.0**	**All schools........**	**14.2**	**16.1**	**14.5**	**15.8**
School type:							School type:				
Traditional.........	19.0	16.6	16.1	20.5	22.0	21.0	Catholic...........	17.4	33.5	17.9	19.0
Charter school....	20.8	26.2	27.5	22.4	22.2	20.2	Other religious.....	12.3	17.3	13.5	16.0
							Nonsectarian......	14.6	6.9	12.2	9.7
Community type:							Community type:				
City................	19.6	17.1	19.3	21.4	22.6	22.4	City................	14.3	[1] 15.2	15.3	16.9
Suburban..........	19.4	15.5	16.9	21.5	22.5	22.4	Suburban..........	14.8	[1] 18.2	17.4	15.4
Town..............	18.9	17.9	18.0	20.2	20.3	18.7	Town..............	14.6	(S)	10.4	16.5
Rural..............	18.0	18.7	14.3	18.9	21.2	18.3	Rural..............	12.2	14.0	6.9	12.1
Enrollment size:							Enrollment size:				
Less than 100.....	12.6	(S)	18.7	11.9	14.8	12.2					
100–199...........	16.7	17.3	13.9	17.7	18.9	12.9	Less than 100.....	12.1	9.4	9.1	6.2
200–499...........	18.6	17.7	21.1	19.1	19.2	17.0	100–199...........	15.6	19.5	13.1	11.6
500–749...........	19.9	16.7	18.5	22.7	21.8	19.0	200–499...........	17.3	[1] 18.8	17.3	16.6
750–999...........	20.5	16.8	14.2	23.6	22.9	19.9	500–749...........	(S)	(S)	45.3	18.0
1,000 or more.....	20.5	15.9	15.9	25.8	24.0	23.3	750 or more.......	(S)	(S)	(S)	20.6

S Data does not meet publication standards. [1] Interpret data with caution. The coefficient of variation (CV) for this estimate is between 30 percent and 50 percent.

Source: U.S. National Center for Education Statistics, National Teacher and Principal Survey, "2020-2021 NTPS Tables," <nces.ed.gov/surveys/ntps/tables_list.asp>, accessed May 2023.

Table 281. Enrollment in Public Schools by School Type, Level, and Charter, Magnet, and Virtual Status: 2010 to 2022

[As of Fall. Covers the 50 states and the District of Columbia. Based on the Common Core of Data, Public Elementary/Secondary School Universe Survey]

School characteristic	2010	2015	2018	2019	2020 [4]	2021 [5]	2022
Total, all schools..........................	**49,177,617**	**50,115,178**	**50,330,883**	**50,437,821**	**49,038,443**	**49,089,640**	**48,860,517**
School type:							
Regular.................................	48,259,245	49,313,134	49,534,589	49,629,390	48,241,988	48,216,636	48,044,450
Special education........................	190,910	180,155	180,523	173,348	154,165	150,280	152,781
Vocational..............................	164,013	146,321	158,088	152,961	161,495	193,189	193,612
Alternative [1]............................	563,449	475,568	457,683	482,122	480,795	529,535	469,674
School level:							
Prekindergarten.........................	159,013	186,614	211,861	[6] 217,022	168,694	[6] 187,555	[6] 208,086
Elementary..............................	23,725,686	24,154,981	23,898,171	23,808,079	22,442,665	22,545,068	22,596,733
Middle..................................	9,391,287	9,392,450	9,603,188	9,693,590	9,422,643	9,215,744	9,016,934
Secondary and high......................	14,842,780	15,050,043	15,174,601	15,227,541	15,240,146	15,318,119	15,274,019
Other, ungraded, and not applicable.........	1,058,851	1,331,090	1,443,062	1,491,589	1,764,295	1,823,154	1,764,745
SCHOOL STATUS AND LEVEL							
Charter schools, total [2].....................	1,787,091	2,845,322	3,290,149	3,431,230	3,680,294	3,674,712	3,717,857
Prekindergarten.........................	5,884	5,857	5,219	5,365	3,421	3,057	3,071
Elementary..............................	771,063	1,235,990	1,443,839	1,512,281	1,563,961	1,568,732	1,584,854
Middle..................................	156,606	235,177	249,027	256,721	272,808	258,718	241,330
Secondary and high......................	430,332	657,256	747,380	771,361	810,186	806,729	804,670
Other, ungraded, and not applicable.........	423,206	711,042	844,684	885,502	1,029,918	1,037,476	1,083,932
Magnet schools, total [2].....................	2,055,133	2,604,145	2,672,473	2,694,281	2,207,082	2,220,219	(NA)
Prekindergarten.........................	1,488	1,203	591	1,184	875	1,278	(NA)
Elementary..............................	707,591	838,514	882,526	886,750	696,181	719,658	(NA)
Middle..................................	374,297	505,172	552,592	560,470	491,772	481,276	(NA)
Secondary and high......................	943,492	1,220,936	1,207,307	1,215,852	993,982	988,480	(NA)
Other, ungraded, and not applicable.........	28,265	38,320	29,457	30,025	24,272	29,527	(NA)
Virtual schools, total [2, 3]....................	(NA)	234,148	289,614	293,689	590,267	566,188	562,659
Prekindergarten.........................	(NA)	–	–	–	–	–	–
Elementary..............................	(NA)	15,972	11,208	12,757	71,972	65,579	58,962
Middle..................................	(NA)	3,384	5,442	7,854	22,777	22,993	14,945
Secondary and high......................	(NA)	47,373	65,749	64,444	110,016	111,703	105,676
Other, ungraded, and not applicable.........	(NA)	167,419	207,215	208,634	385,502	365,913	383,076

– Represents zero. NA Not available. [1] Includes schools that provide nontraditional education, address needs of students that typically cannot be met in regular schools, serve as adjuncts to regular schools, or fall outside the categories of regular, special education, or vocational education. [2] Magnet, charter, and virtual schools are also included under regular, special education, vocational, or alternative schools as appropriate. [3] Virtual schools provide instruction during which students and teachers are separated by time and/or location and interact via internet-connected computers or other electronic devices. [4] Data for magnet and virtual schools are missing for California, Illinois, and Utah. [5] Data for magnet and virtual schools are missing for California. [6] Data are missing for California.

Source: U.S. National Center for Education Statistics, *Digest of Education Statistics,* "Latest version of all Digest tables," <nces.ed.gov/programs/digest>, accessed May 2024.

Table 282. Public Charter and Traditional Schools by Selected Characteristics: 2020 and 2022

[49,038 represents 49,038,000. As of Fall. A public charter school is a public school that, in accordance with an enabling state statute, has been granted a charter exempting it from selected state and local rules and regulations]

Characteristic	2020 Total	2020 Traditional	2020 Public charter	2022 Total	2022 Traditional	2022 Public charter
Enrollment (1,000)	**49,038**	**45,358**	**3,680**	**48,861**	**45,143**	**3,718**
PERCENT DISTRIBUTION OF STUDENTS						
Race/ethnicity	100.0	100.0	100.0	100.0	100.0	100.0
White, non-Hispanic	45.7	47.0	30.8	44.8	46.1	28.6
Black, non-Hispanic	15.0	14.3	24.3	15.0	14.2	24.4
Hispanic	28.0	27.5	35.1	28.5	27.8	36.8
Asian	5.4	5.5	4.2	5.5	5.6	4.3
Pacific Islander	0.4	0.4	0.4	0.4	0.4	0.4
American Indian/Alaska Native	0.9	0.9	0.7	0.9	0.9	0.7
Two or more races	4.5	4.5	4.6	5.0	5.0	4.8
Number of teachers (1,000) [1]	2,984	2,808	176	3,172	2,975	197
Pupil/teacher ratio	15.5	15.3	18.3	15.4	15.3	17.3
Total number of schools	**98,577**	**90,936**	**7,641**	**99,388**	**91,390**	**7,998**
PERCENT DISTRIBUTION OF SCHOOLS						
School level	100.0	100.0	100.0	100.0	100.0	100.0
Prekindergarten	1.5	1.6	0.3	1.6	1.7	0.3
Elementary	53.1	53.6	47.2	52.8	53.3	47.0
Middle	16.5	17.0	10.5	16.4	16.9	10.2
Secondary and high	23.9	23.6	27.5	24.0	23.6	27.5
Other	5.1	4.3	14.5	5.3	4.4	15.0
Size of enrollment	100.0	100.0	100.0	100.0	100.0	100.0
Less than 300 students	31.9	30.9	42.7	31.9	30.9	43.4
300 to 499 students	29.4	29.8	24.6	29.2	29.7	24.3
500 to 999 students	29.6	30.0	24.8	29.8	30.3	24.4
1,000 students or more	9.2	9.3	7.9	9.0	9.1	7.9
Region	100.0	100.0	100.0	100.0	100.0	100.0
Northeast	15.1	15.5	10.1	15.0	15.4	9.9
Midwest	25.8	26.3	19.7	26.0	26.6	20.0
South	34.9	34.9	34.5	34.8	34.8	35.4
West	24.2	23.2	35.7	24.2	23.3	34.6

[1] For 2020, data are missing for Illinois and Utah.

Source: U.S. National Center for Education Statistics, *Digest of Education Statistics,* "Latest version of all Digest tables," <nces.ed.gov/programs/digest>, accessed May 2024.

Table 283. Public Charter Schools and Enrollment by State: 2022

[3,717.9 represents 3,717,900. As of Fall]

State	Number of charter schools	Number of students (1,000)	Charter schools as a percent of public schools	Charter school enrollment as a percent of public school enrollment	State	Number of charter schools	Number of students (1,000)	Charter schools as a percent of public schools	Charter school enrollment as a percent of public school enrollment
United States	**7,998**	**3,717.9**	**8.0**	**7.6**	Missouri	82	25.3	3.3	2.8
Alabama	17	5.7	1.1	0.8	Montana	–	–	–	–
Alaska	32	8.4	6.4	6.4	Nebraska	–	–	–	–
Arizona	576	232.4	23.7	20.5	Nevada	101	68.7	13.8	14.2
Arkansas	102	41.7	9.3	8.4	New Hampshire	40	5.5	8.0	3.3
California	1,284	645.7	12.4	11.9	New Jersey	85	58.5	3.3	4.3
Colorado	269	131.8	13.9	15.1	New Mexico	101	31.0	11.3	9.9
Connecticut	21	10.9	2.1	2.2	New York	342	175.7	7.1	7.0
Delaware	23	18.2	10.0	12.9	North Carolina	206	139.5	7.6	9.0
Dist. of Columbia	126	41.2	51.6	45.3	North Dakota	–	–	–	–
Florida	740	382.4	17.5	13.3	Ohio	334	115.6	9.2	6.9
Georgia	97	69.9	4.2	4.0	Oklahoma	63	50.7	3.5	7.2
Hawaii	37	12.1	12.5	7.1	Oregon	132	41.3	10.3	7.6
Idaho	77	28.6	9.7	9.0	Pennsylvania	177	161.7	6.0	9.7
Illinois	134	60.1	3.0	3.3	Rhode Island	41	12.1	13.0	8.9
Indiana	121	51.1	6.3	4.9	South Carolina	88	49.5	7.0	6.3
Iowa	4	0.3	0.3	–	South Dakota	–	–	–	–
Kansas	9	2.5	0.7	0.5	Tennessee	114	44.4	6.0	4.4
Kentucky	–	–	–	–	Texas	1,039	468.9	11.3	8.5
Louisiana	150	95.1	11.2	13.2	Utah	140	78.6	12.7	11.4
Maine	13	2.7	2.2	1.6	Vermont	–	–	–	–
Maryland	48	24.0	3.4	2.7	Virginia	7	1.3	0.3	0.1
Massachusetts	76	48.0	4.1	5.3	Washington	16	4.7	0.6	0.4
Michigan	378	150.2	10.8	10.8	West Virginia	4	1.2	0.6	0.5
Minnesota	300	67.9	11.2	7.8	Wisconsin	239	49.0	10.7	6.0
Mississippi	8	3.2	0.8	0.7	Wyoming	5	0.7	1.4	0.7

– Represents or rounds to zero.

Source: U.S. National Center for Education Statistics, *Digest of Education Statistics,* "Latest version of all Digest tables," <nces.ed.gov/programs/digest>, accessed May 2024.

Table 284. Proficiency Levels on Selected NAEP Tests for Students in Public Schools by State: 2022

[Represents percent of public school students scoring at or above basic and proficient levels. Basic denotes partial mastery of the knowledge and skills that are fundamental for proficient work at a given grade level. Proficient represents solid academic performance. Students reaching this level demonstrated competency over challenging subject matter. For more detail, see <nationsreportcard.gov>. Based on the National Assessment of Educational Progress (NAEP) tests which are administered to a representative sample of students in public schools, private schools, and Department of Defense schools]

State	Grade 4 Math		Grade 8 Math		Grade 4 Reading		Grade 8 Reading	
	At or above Basic	At or above Proficient	At or above Basic	At or above Proficient	At or above Basic	At or above Proficient	At or above Basic	At or above Proficient
U.S. average....................	**74**	**35**	**60**	**26**	**61**	**32**	**68**	**29**
Alabama.........................	71	27	53	19	59	28	61	22
Alaska..........................	65	28	59	23	51	24	63	26
Arizona.........................	70	32	58	24	61	31	68	28
Arkansas.......................	69	28	55	19	58	30	64	26
California.......................	67	30	56	23	58	31	67	30
Colorado........................	75	36	63	28	68	38	73	34
Connecticut.....................	74	37	63	30	64	35	72	35
Delaware.......................	64	26	51	18	53	25	62	24
District of Columbia.............	57	24	46	16	50	26	57	22
Florida..........................	81	41	58	23	71	39	69	29
Georgia.........................	75	34	59	24	61	32	69	31
Hawaii..........................	77	37	58	22	64	35	68	31
Idaho...........................	76	36	71	32	61	32	74	32
Illinois..........................	76	38	62	27	62	33	71	32
Indiana.........................	78	40	66	30	63	33	70	31
Iowa............................	80	40	67	28	64	33	71	29
Kansas..........................	75	35	61	23	60	31	67	26
Kentucky........................	75	33	57	21	62	31	68	29
Louisiana........................	69	27	53	19	57	28	66	27
Maine...........................	75	32	61	24	60	29	66	29
Maryland........................	65	31	54	25	56	31	67	33
Massachusetts..................	79	43	70	35	70	43	77	40
Michigan........................	71	32	60	25	58	28	68	28
Minnesota.......................	78	41	69	32	61	32	72	30
Mississippi......................	74	32	54	18	63	31	63	22
Missouri.........................	72	34	61	24	60	30	67	28
Montana.........................	80	38	68	29	65	34	72	29
Nebraska........................	80	43	68	31	65	34	70	29
Nevada..........................	69	28	56	21	57	27	68	29
New Hampshire..................	80	40	70	29	67	37	73	33
New Jersey......................	77	39	67	33	67	38	77	42
New Mexico.....................	60	19	45	13	48	21	57	18
New York........................	66	28	60	28	58	30	70	32
North Carolina...................	75	35	61	25	61	32	66	26
North Dakota....................	81	40	69	28	65	31	69	27
Ohio............................	76	40	64	29	65	35	71	33
Oklahoma.......................	71	27	52	16	55	24	62	21
Oregon..........................	66	29	57	22	56	28	67	28
Pennsylvania....................	76	40	62	27	64	34	68	31
Rhode Island....................	74	34	58	24	62	34	68	31
South Carolina..................	74	34	56	22	61	32	63	27
South Dakota....................	80	40	72	32	65	32	73	31
Tennessee.......................	76	36	60	25	59	30	67	28
Texas...........................	78	38	61	24	58	30	66	23
Utah............................	78	42	70	35	67	37	75	36
Vermont.........................	74	34	66	27	62	34	73	34
Virginia.........................	75	38	65	31	60	32	69	31
Washington......................	74	35	64	28	61	34	71	32
West Virginia....................	67	23	48	15	52	22	60	22
Wisconsin.......................	79	43	70	33	63	33	72	32
Wyoming........................	84	44	72	31	71	38	71	30

Source: U.S. National Center for Education Statistics, "NAEP Data Explorer," <www.nationsreportcard.gov/ndecore/xplore/nde>, accessed March 2023.

Table 285. Public High School Graduates by State: 1980 to 2030

[In thousands (2,747.7 represents 2,747,700). For school year ending in year shown. Data include regular diploma recipients, and exclude students receiving a certificate of attendance and persons receiving high school equivalency certificates]

State	1980	1990	2000	2010	2015 [1]	2020 (P)	2025 (P)	2030 (P)
United States...............	2,747.7	[2] 2,320.3	2,553.8	3,128.0	3,209.6	3,371.0	3,524.5	3,255.5
Alabama......................	45.2	40.5	37.8	43.2	45.4	46.9	50.1	47.8
Alaska........................	5.2	5.4	6.6	8.2	8.0	8.2	8.6	8.6
Arizona.......................	28.6	32.1	38.3	61.1	66.7	72.1	78.8	74.4
Arkansas.....................	29.1	26.5	27.3	28.3	30.8	32.6	34.3	32.0
California.....................	249.2	236.3	309.9	405.0	430.1	436.4	429.3	387.1
Colorado.....................	36.8	33.0	38.9	49.3	51.8	58.9	61.2	54.4
Connecticut..................	37.7	27.9	31.6	34.5	38.0	37.6	38.3	34.9
Delaware.....................	7.6	5.6	6.1	8.1	8.3	9.0	10.3	9.5
District of Columbia [3].........	5.0	3.6	2.7	3.6	3.8	3.7	4.2	4.4
Florida........................	87.3	88.9	106.7	156.1	166.7	185.2	197.7	194.7
Georgia......................	61.6	56.6	62.6	91.6	99.5	114.3	122.2	113.8
Hawaii........................	11.5	10.3	10.4	11.0	10.7	11.2	11.8	10.5
Idaho.........................	13.2	12.0	16.2	17.8	17.7	19.5	21.6	21.8
Illinois........................	135.6	108.1	111.8	139.0	138.8	134.4	136.4	125.3
Indiana.......................	73.1	60.0	57.0	64.6	65.9	65.6	67.3	63.7
Iowa..........................	43.4	31.8	33.9	34.5	32.6	33.7	36.4	33.8
Kansas.......................	30.9	25.4	29.1	31.6	31.9	33.3	34.9	32.7
Kentucky.....................	41.2	38.0	36.8	42.7	43.3	46.3	47.1	38.8
Louisiana.....................	46.3	36.1	38.4	36.6	38.4	43.2	43.9	37.6
Maine.........................	15.4	13.8	12.2	14.1	12.2	11.4	11.4	10.3
Maryland.....................	54.3	41.6	47.8	59.1	57.3	59.3	63.5	56.5
Massachusetts...............	73.8	55.9	53.0	64.5	65.9	67.9	68.4	62.4
Michigan.....................	124.3	93.8	97.7	110.7	101.3	97.7	94.8	86.0
Minnesota....................	64.9	49.1	57.4	59.7	58.0	60.3	64.3	62.4
Mississippi...................	27.6	25.2	24.2	25.5	26.7	28.0	28.7	24.1
Missouri......................	62.3	49.0	52.8	64.0	60.8	60.9	64.3	59.4
Montana......................	12.1	9.4	10.9	10.1	9.4	9.2	10.2	10.1
Nebraska.....................	22.4	17.7	20.1	19.4	20.3	21.8	21.9	22.7
Nevada.......................	8.5	9.5	14.6	21.0	25.1	31.4	34.8	32.9
New Hampshire...............	11.7	10.8	11.8	15.0	13.5	12.9	12.8	11.4
New Jersey...................	94.6	69.8	74.4	96.2	94.6	95.3	99.8	91.3
New Mexico...................	18.4	14.9	18.0	18.6	19.7	20.1	21.7	18.2
New York.....................	204.1	143.3	141.7	183.8	179.6	182.8	173.5	152.4
North Carolina................	70.9	64.8	62.1	88.7	97.4	106.8	113.5	104.3
North Dakota.................	9.9	7.7	8.6	7.2	7.0	6.9	7.9	8.1
Ohio..........................	144.2	114.5	111.7	123.4	120.5	121.5	122.7	114.6
Oklahoma....................	39.3	35.6	37.6	38.5	38.9	43.6	48.1	46.5
Oregon.......................	29.9	25.5	30.2	34.7	36.2	38.1	39.1	35.0
Pennsylvania.................	146.5	110.5	114.0	131.2	125.0	124.3	142.7	132.3
Rhode Island.................	10.9	7.8	8.5	9.9	9.6	9.9	10.0	8.8
South Carolina...............	38.7	32.5	31.6	40.4	43.7	48.6	54.4	51.4
South Dakota.................	10.7	7.7	9.3	8.2	8.2	8.2	9.7	9.2
Tennessee....................	49.8	46.1	41.6	62.4	62.0	63.5	67.7	64.9
Texas.........................	171.4	172.5	212.9	280.9	312.1	356.9	396.0	373.1
Utah..........................	20.0	21.2	32.5	31.5	35.3	42.5	48.3	46.8
Vermont......................	6.7	6.1	6.7	7.2	6.0	5.2	5.3	4.9
Virginia.......................	66.6	60.6	65.6	81.5	83.8	91.7	94.5	85.3
Washington...................	50.4	45.9	57.6	66.0	67.3	68.9	72.2	65.7
West Virginia.................	23.4	21.9	19.4	17.7	17.7	17.6	18.3	16.1
Wisconsin....................	69.3	52.0	58.5	64.7	60.6	60.7	63.0	56.7
Wyoming.....................	6.1	5.8	6.5	5.7	5.6	5.8	6.5	5.9

P Projected. [1] Estimated. [2] U.S. total includes estimates for nonreporting states. [3] Beginning in 1989-90, graduates from adult programs are excluded.

Source: U.S. National Center for Education Statistics, *Digest of Education Statistics*, "Latest version of all Digest tables," and earlier releases, <nces.ed.gov/programs/digest>, accessed April 2024.

Table 286. School Enrollment Status of Persons Age 18 to 21 by Race, Hispanic Origin, and Sex: 2020 and 2022

[16,995 represents 16,995,000. As of October. For persons 18 to 21 years old. For the civilian noninstitutional population. Based on the Current Population Survey; see text, Section 1 and Appendix III]

Characteristic	Total persons 18 to 21 years old (1,000)		Percent distribution							
			Enrolled in high school		High school graduates				Not high school graduates, not enrolled in high school	
					Total		In college			
	2020	2022	2020	2022	2020	2022	2020	2022	2020	2022
Total [1]	**16,995**	**16,854**	**9.4**	**9.4**	**85.3**	**85.2**	**50.0**	**48.1**	**5.3**	**5.3**
White	12,341	12,444	8.9	9.7	85.5	85.1	50.1	47.4	5.5	5.1
Black	2,538	2,499	12.7	8.8	83.5	84.7	43.2	45.4	3.7	6.6
Asian	1,070	912	4.7	7.1	91.9	92.0	77.2	74.8	3.5	0.9
Hispanic [2]	4,146	4,237	9.8	11.6	83.2	80.3	45.4	40.2	7.0	8.0
Male [1]	**8,584**	**8,403**	**10.8**	**11.2**	**83.0**	**82.6**	**44.5**	**41.5**	**6.1**	**6.1**
White	6,254	6,277	10.2	11.0	83.1	82.3	43.8	40.8	6.6	6.6
Black	1,257	1,214	14.1	12.0	81.1	82.9	39.3	39.3	4.7	5.2
Asian	540	438	5.2	9.1	90.4	89.0	74.3	68.0	4.3	1.8
Hispanic [2]	2,026	2,156	11.3	13.6	80.2	76.4	39.0	31.7	8.5	10.0
Female [1]	**8,412**	**8,451**	**8.0**	**7.7**	**87.7**	**87.8**	**55.7**	**54.7**	**4.4**	**4.5**
White	6,087	6,167	7.6	8.4	88.0	87.9	56.5	54.1	4.4	3.6
Black	1,281	1,285	11.3	5.8	85.9	86.4	47.0	51.1	2.8	7.9
Asian	530	474	4.2	5.3	93.4	94.7	80.0	81.0	2.6	0.0
Hispanic [2]	2,120	2,081	8.4	9.5	85.9	84.2	51.4	49.0	5.5	6.1

[1] Includes other races not shown separately. [2] Persons of Hispanic origin may be of any race.

Source: U.S. Census Bureau, Current Population Reports, P-20, and earlier reports; and "School Enrollment Tables," <www.census.gov/topics/education/school-enrollment/data/tables.All.html>, accessed November 2023.

Table 287. High School Graduates Earning Career and Technical Education (CTE) Credits by Selected Characteristics: 2019

[In percent. For public and private high school students who earned at least one Carnegie credit (120 hours of class instruction) in selected career and technical education courses. Based on the 2019 National Assessment of Educational Progress High School Transcript Study; for details, see <nces.ed.gov/nationsreportcard/hsts/>]

Student or school characteristic	Any career/ technical education courses	Agriculture, food, and natural resources	Business and marketing	Communi- cation and audio/video technology	Engineer- ing and technology	Health care sciences	Hospitality and tourism	Human services	Infor- mation tech- nology
All students	**84.6**	**10.8**	**21.3**	**17.4**	**13.6**	**11.8**	**8.2**	**28.0**	**28.7**
Sex:									
Male	87.4	12.1	23.9	16.4	20.2	7.4	7.2	22.2	33.9
Female	81.7	9.6	18.6	18.4	6.8	16.4	9.2	34.0	23.2
Race and ethnicity: [1]									
White	85.9	13.0	22.4	17.2	14.5	10.3	7.2	30.1	27.8
Black	86.4	8.4	26.4	17.7	12.5	14.4	11.1	32.8	32.4
Asian	77.4	2.3	15.1	12.9	16.2	11.5	3.6	15.8	37.2
Pacific Islander	84.3	[2] 7.2	12.5	21.7	12.5	10.2	[2] 8.9	28.4	25.3
American Indian or Alaska Native	87.4	14.6	16.4	21.0	9.9	11.8	10.5	37.0	32.5
Two or more races	82.4	7.9	17.5	18.0	12.0	13.5	7.2	28.9	27.6
Hispanic	82.8	9.8	18.5	18.3	12.0	13.4	9.5	23.8	26.7
English learner	82.8	8.5	17.4	13.4	11.3	9.5	7.9	24.5	29.4
Non-English learner (EL)	84.6	11.0	21.5	17.5	13.6	11.9	8.2	28.2	28.5
Enrollment size of school:									
Under 500	85.6	21.2	20.5	17.9	10.0	7.9	6.6	33.0	33.8
500 to 999	82.6	11.8	22.0	17.4	12.9	10.7	6.5	25.1	29.0
1,000 to 1,499	86.2	8.4	22.6	16.1	15.7	12.5	8.5	30.5	27.4
1,500 to 1,999	85.6	8.2	22.3	18.2	16.6	14.3	9.6	27.4	26.4
2,000 or more	83.4	7.0	19.6	17.5	12.7	12.9	9.0	25.4	27.6
School location:									
City	79.6	4.7	19.0	17.8	11.9	11.3	7.3	21.5	28.0
Suburban	83.0	5.6	20.5	16.3	15.3	11.0	7.7	25.6	26.2
Town	91.3	21.4	26.0	17.1	12.3	14.1	9.9	38.3	30.2
Rural	91.6	25.0	23.8	19.2	13.3	12.9	9.5	37.1	33.9
School region:									
Northeast	76.9	2.5	19.1	12.5	16.2	4.7	4.6	21.4	22.3
Midwest	87.5	11.7	23.6	14.1	12.0	7.4	7.4	36.1	21.5
South	91.0	15.1	26.5	21.8	15.8	16.4	10.0	33.3	40.2
West	76.4	8.2	12.1	16.2	9.5	12.6	8.1	16.5	19.8

[1] Data for race categories exclude persons of Hispanic origin. [2] Interpret data with caution. The coefficient of variation (CV) for this estimate is between 30 and 50 percent.

Source: U.S. National Center for Education Statistics, *Digest of Education Statistics*, "Latest version of all Digest tables," <www.nces.ed.gov/programs/digest>, accessed April 2023. See also <www.nationsreportcard.gov/hstsreport/>.

Table 288. High School Dropouts by Selected Characteristics: 2010 to 2022

[3,294 represents 3,294,000. As of October. Data are for status dropouts, youth age 16 to 24 who are not enrolled in school and who have not completed a high school program, regardless of when they left school and whether they ever attended school in the United States. People who have received equivalency credentials, such as the GED, are counted as high school completers. Based on the American Community Survey; see Appendix III]

Characteristic	2010	2014	2015	2016	2017	2018	2019	2020 [3]	2021	2022
Total dropouts (1,000).............	**3,294**	**2,497**	**2,397**	**2,279**	**2,125**	**2,079**	**1,970**	**(NA)**	**2,019**	**2,115**
PERCENT										
Total..................................	**8.3**	**6.3**	**6.0**	**5.8**	**5.4**	**5.3**	**5.1**	**(NA)**	**5.2**	**5.3**
Male..................................	10.0	7.2	7.0	6.8	6.4	6.2	6.0	(NA)	6.1	6.3
Female................................	6.6	5.2	5.0	4.7	4.4	4.4	4.2	(NA)	4.2	4.3
Race/ethnicity:										
American Indian/Alaska Native......	15.4	11.5	13.2	11.0	10.1	9.5	9.6	(NA)	10.2	9.9
Asian.................................	2.8	2.5	2.4	2.0	2.1	1.9	1.8	(NA)	2.1	1.9
Black.................................	10.3	7.9	7.2	7.0	6.5	6.4	5.6	(NA)	5.9	5.7
Hispanic..............................	16.7	10.7	9.9	9.1	8.2	8.0	7.7	(NA)	7.8	7.9
Pacific Islander.......................	4.8	10.6	5.4	6.9	3.9	8.1	8.0	(NA)	7.6	9.1
White.................................	5.3	4.4	4.5	4.5	4.3	4.2	4.1	(NA)	4.1	4.3
Some other race [1]...................	9.2	5.6	7.5	5.1	5.2	4.5	3.9	(NA)	7.1	5.8
Two or more races....................	6.1	5.0	4.7	4.8	4.5	5.2	5.1	(NA)	4.9	4.5
Nativity:										
Native-born...........................	7.0	5.6	5.5	5.3	5.0	5.0	4.7	(NA)	4.8	4.8
Foreign-born..........................	20.3	12.6	11.3	10.5	9.4	9.3	9.5	(NA)	10.3	11.6
Disability status: [2]										
With a disability......................	17.4	13.9	12.6	12.4	12.1	11.7	10.7	(NA)	10.4	9.7
Without a disability...................	7.8	5.8	5.6	5.3	5.0	4.9	4.7	(NA)	4.8	4.9

NA Not available. [1] Respondents who wrote in some other race that was not included as an option on the questionnaire. [2] Disability status identifies individuals who have serious difficulty with one or more of four basic areas of functioning (hearing, vision, cognition, and ambulation) or with self-care or independent living. [3] Data was not collected for the year 2020 due to disruptions to the American Community Survey caused by the COVID-19 pandemic. For more information, refer to Appendix III.

Source: U.S. National Center for Education Statistics, *Digest of Education Statistics*, "Latest version of all Digest tables," <nces.ed.gov/programs/digest>, accessed April 2024.

Table 289. High School Dropouts by Age, Race, and Hispanic Origin: 2000 to 2022

[3,883 represents 3,883,000. As of October. For persons 14 to 24 years old. Dropouts are persons not in regular school and who have not completed the 12th grade nor received a general equivalency degree. Based on Current Population Survey; see text, Section 1 and Appendix III]

Age and race	Number of dropouts (1,000)					Percent of population				
	2000	2010	2020	2021	2022	2000	2010	2020	2021	2022
Total dropouts [1,2]......	**3,883**	**2,952**	**2,161**	**2,079**	**2,095**	**9.1**	**6.4**	**4.7**	**4.6**	**4.5**
16 to 17 years.............	460	227	473	390	424	5.8	2.7	5.7	4.7	4.8
18 to 21 years.............	2,005	1,445	893	935	897	12.9	8.4	5.3	5.7	5.3
22 to 24 years.............	1,310	1,144	614	589	569	11.8	9.2	5.1	4.7	4.6
White [2,3]..................	3,065	2,232	1,671	1,623	1,533	9.1	6.3	5.0	4.9	4.5
16 to 17 years.............	366	181	347	298	317	5.8	2.9	5.7	4.9	5.0
18 to 21 years.............	1,558	1,048	614	732	638	12.6	8.0	5.5	6.0	5.1
22 to 24 years.............	1,040	893	493	465	420	11.7	9.2	5.5	5.1	4.6
Black [2,3]..................	705	498	238	247	339	10.9	7.2	3.5	3.7	4.9
16 to 17 years.............	84	30	49	46	67	7.0	2.3	4.1	3.8	5.3
18 to 21 years.............	383	283	95	120	164	16.0	10.5	3.7	5.0	6.6
22 to 24 years.............	232	167	79	70	80	14.3	9.4	4.5	3.8	4.5
Hispanic [2,4].............	1,499	1,122	693	783	696	23.5	12.8	6.3	7.1	6.0
16 to 17 years.............	121	40	129	133	99	11.0	2.7	6.5	6.5	4.7
18 to 21 years.............	733	506	290	341	341	30.0	15.2	7.0	8.3	8.0
22 to 24 years.............	602	543	234	257	205	35.5	23.2	8.6	9.3	7.0

[1] Includes other race groups, not shown separately. [2] Includes persons age 14 to 15, not shown separately. [3] Beginning 2003, for persons who selected this race only. See footnote 4, Table 252. [4] Persons of Hispanic origin may be of any race.

Source: U.S. Census Bureau, Current Population Reports, series PPL and P-20; and "School Enrollment Tables," <www.census.gov/topics/education/school-enrollment/data/tables.All.html>, accessed November 2023.

Table 290. ACT Program Scores and Characteristics of College-Bound Students: 1990 to 2023

[For academic year ending in year shown. Data based on all ACT tested seniors graduating in year shown. Beginning 1990, not comparable with previous years because a new version of the ACT was introduced]

Type of test and characteristic	Unit	1990	2000	2010	2015	2018	2019	2020	2021	2022	2023
TEST SCORES [1]											
Composite	Point	**20.6**	**21.0**	**21.0**	**21.0**	**20.8**	**20.7**	**20.6**	**20.3**	**19.8**	**19.5**
Male	Point	21.0	21.2	21.2	21.1	20.8	20.6	20.5	20.3	19.7	19.4
Female	Point	20.3	20.9	20.9	21.0	20.9	20.8	20.8	20.6	20.0	19.7
Other responses [2]	Point	(NA)	(NA)	(NA)	(NA)	(NA)	(NA)	17.8	18.5	18.3	18.2
English	Point	20.5	20.5	20.5	20.4	20.2	20.1	19.9	19.6	19.0	18.6
Male	Point	20.1	20.0	20.1	20.0	19.7	19.6	19.3	19.1	18.5	18.2
Female	Point	20.9	20.9	20.8	20.8	20.7	20.6	20.5	20.2	19.6	19.2
Other responses [2]	Point	(NA)	(NA)	(NA)	(NA)	(NA)	(NA)	16.8	17.4	17.5	17.2
Math	Point	19.9	20.7	21.0	20.8	20.5	20.4	20.2	19.9	19.3	19.0
Male	Point	20.7	21.4	21.6	21.3	20.9	20.8	20.6	20.4	19.7	19.4
Female	Point	19.3	20.2	20.5	20.4	20.2	20.0	20.0	19.7	19.1	18.8
Other responses [2]	Point	(NA)	(NA)	(NA)	(NA)	(NA)	(NA)	17.8	18.2	17.8	17.6
Reading [2]	Point	(NA)	21.4	21.3	21.4	21.3	21.2	21.2	20.9	20.4	20.1
Male	Point	(NA)	21.2	21.1	21.2	21.0	20.7	20.8	20.6	20.0	19.7
Female	Point	(NA)	21.5	21.4	21.6	21.7	21.7	21.6	21.5	20.9	20.6
Other responses [2]	Point	(NA)	(NA)	(NA)	(NA)	(NA)	(NA)	18.2	19.0	19.2	19.1
Science	Point	(NA)	21.0	20.9	20.9	20.7	20.6	20.6	20.4	19.9	19.6
Male	Point	(NA)	21.6	21.4	21.3	20.9	20.8	20.7	20.6	20.0	19.8
Female	Point	(NA)	20.6	20.5	20.6	20.6	20.5	20.5	20.4	19.9	19.6
Other responses [2]	Point	(NA)	(NA)	(NA)	(NA)	(NA)	(NA)	18.0	18.8	18.4	18.4
PARTICIPANTS [3]											
Total [4]	1,000	**817**	**1,065**	**1,569**	**1,924**	**1,915**	**1,783**	**1,670**	**1,295**	**1,350**	**1,386**
Male	Percent	46	43	45	47	47	46	46	46	47	46
White	Percent	73	72	62	55	52	52	52	54	53	52
Black	Percent	9	10	14	13	13	12	12	12	11	12
Obtaining composite scores of:											
27 or above	Percent	12	14	16	18	15	15	15	14	12	12
18 or below	Percent	35	32	35	37	40	35	42	44	48	53

NA Not available. [1] Minimum score, 1; maximum score, 36. [2] Includes "another gender," "prefer not to respond," and missing values. [3] Data by race are for those responding to the race question. [4] 817 represents 817,000.

Source: ACT, Inc., Iowa City, IA. Most recent score reported in the *The ACT® Profile Report - National*, annual ©. Reproduced with permission.

Table 291. SAT Scores and Characteristics of High School Graduates: 2023

[Data reflect 2023 high school graduates who took the new SAT during high school. If a student took the SAT more than once, the most recent score and self-reported SAT questionnaire responses are summarized. Maximum total score is 1600]

Characteristic	Test takers		Mean score			Percent with benchmarks met			
	Number	Percent	Total	ERW [1]	Math	Both	ERW [1]	Math	None
Total	**1,913,742**	**(X)**	**1,028**	**520**	**508**	**40**	**62**	**42**	**35**
Took essay [2]	264,011	14	979	497	482	31	54	33	44
Race/ethnicity:									
White	752,632	39	1,082	550	532	51	76	53	22
Black	225,954	12	908	466	441	17	42	19	57
Hispanic/Latino	462,186	24	943	482	461	24	49	25	50
Asian	194,108	10	1,219	593	626	74	84	78	11
American Indian/Alaska Native	15,384	1	901	458	443	17	37	19	60
Native Hawaiian/Other Pacific Islander	3,791	(Z)	925	473	452	21	44	23	54
Two or more races	69,410	4	1,091	556	535	51	76	52	23
Gender:									
Female	966,726	51	1,023	523	500	38	64	39	34
Male	936,481	49	1,032	517	515	42	61	45	37
Another gender or no response	10,535	1	1,058	552	506	45	69	46	30
First language learned:									
English only	1,047,520	55	1,054	537	517	45	70	46	28
English and another language	323,387	17	1,058	530	529	44	65	47	33
Another language	200,762	10	1,052	517	534	44	60	49	34
Highest level of parental education:									
No high school diploma	116,796	6	910	460	451	18	39	21	58
High school diploma	384,502	20	966	492	473	27	54	29	43
Associate degree	89,393	5	1,004	513	491	33	64	35	34
Bachelor's degree	493,158	26	1,107	558	549	55	80	58	18
Graduate degree	408,482	21	1,181	594	588	68	86	70	12

X Not applicable. Z Represents less than 0.5%. [1] Evidence-based reading and writing. [2] Reflects test takers who completed the SAT essay at any point, not necessarily on the most recent test administration date.

Source: The College Board, *2023 SAT Suite of Assessments Annual Report*, © 2023. Reproduced with permission. See also <www.collegeboard.org>.

Table 292. Higher Education—Institutions and Enrollment: 1990 to 2022

[13,819 represents 13,819,000. As of Fall. Covers universities, colleges, professional schools, and junior and teachers' colleges, both publicly and privately controlled, regular session. Includes estimates for institutions not reporting. Data for 1990 cover institutions of higher education; beginning 2000, data cover degree-granting institutions. Degree-granting institutions grant associate's or higher degrees and participate in Title IV federal financial aid programs. The degree-granting classification includes more 2-year colleges and excludes a few higher education institutions that did not grant degrees. Data are based on the Integrated Postsecondary Education Data System. See also Appendix III]

Item	Unit	1990	2000	2010	2015	2019	2020	2021 [5]	2022 [5]
ALL INSTITUTIONS									
Number of institutions [1]	**Number**	**3,559**	**4,182**	**4,599**	**4,583**	**3,982**	**3,931**	**3,899**	**3,896**
4-year	Number	2,141	2,450	2,870	3,004	2,679	2,637	2,619	2,628
2-year	Number	1,418	1,732	1,729	1,579	1,303	1,294	1,280	1,268
Instructional staff—									
lecturer or above [2]	**1,000**	**(NA)**	**(NA)**	**(NA)**	**1,552**	**1,549**	**1,490**	**1,499**	**1,508**
Percent full-time	Percent	(NA)	(NA)	(NA)	52	54	56	56	56
Total enrollment [3]	**1,000**	**13,819**	**15,312**	**21,019**	**19,988**	**19,630**	**19,027**	**18,659**	**18,580**
Male	1,000	6,284	6,722	9,046	8,724	8,364	7,885	7,768	7,815
Female	1,000	7,535	8,591	11,974	11,264	11,266	11,142	10,891	10,765
4-year institutions	1,000	8,579	9,364	13,336	13,489	14,038	14,096	13,977	13,923
2-year institutions	1,000	5,240	5,948	7,684	6,499	5,599	4,932	4,683	4,657
Full-time	1,000	7,821	9,010	13,087	12,288	11,954	11,609	11,326	11,286
Part-time	1,000	5,998	6,303	7,932	7,701	7,676	7,418	7,332	7,294
Public	1,000	10,845	11,753	15,142	14,573	14,504	13,884	13,546	13,494
Private	1,000	2,974	3,560	5,877	5,415	5,127	5,143	5,113	5,086
Not-for-profit	1,000	2,760	3,109	3,854	4,066	4,135	4,101	4,112	4,108
For profit	1,000	214	450	2,023	1,349	991	1,042	1,001	978
Undergraduate	1,000	11,959	13,155	18,082	17,047	16,558	15,885	15,448	15,397
Men	1,000	5,380	5,778	7,836	7,502	7,149	6,665	6,524	6,573
Women	1,000	6,579	7,377	10,246	9,544	9,408	9,219	8,924	8,824
Full-time	1,000	6,976	7,923	11,457	10,603	10,210	9,843	9,497	9,425
Part-time	1,000	4,983	5,232	6,625	6,444	6,348	6,041	5,951	5,972
First-time freshmen [4]	1,000	2,257	2,428	3,157	2,883	2,857	2,603	2,664	2,749
Postbaccalaureate	1,000	1,860	2,157	2,937	2,942	3,073	3,143	3,211	3,183
Men	1,000	904	944	1,209	1,222	1,214	1,220	1,244	1,241
Women	1,000	955	1,213	1,728	1,720	1,858	1,923	1,967	1,941
2-YEAR INSTITUTIONS									
Number of institutions [1]	Number	1,418	1,732	1,729	1,579	1,303	1,294	1,280	1,268
Public	Number	972	1,076	978	910	853	835	826	817
Private	Number	446	656	751	669	450	459	454	451
Instructional staff—									
lecturer or above [2]	1,000	(NA)	(NA)	(NA)	372	315	281	274	265
Enrollment [3]	1,000	5,240	5,948	7,684	6,499	5,599	4,932	4,683	4,657
Public	1,000	4,996	5,697	7,218	6,224	5,398	4,721	4,478	4,454
Private	1,000	244	251	466	275	201	211	205	203
Male	1,000	2,233	2,559	3,266	2,818	2,374	1,987	1,922	1,957
Female	1,000	3,007	3,390	4,418	3,681	3,225	2,944	2,760	2,701
4-YEAR INSTITUTIONS									
Number of institutions [1]	Number	2,141	2,450	2,870	3,004	2,679	2,637	2,619	2,628
Public	Number	595	622	678	710	772	752	756	782
Private	Number	1,546	1,828	2,192	2,294	1,907	1,885	1,863	1,846
Instructional staff—									
lecturer or above [2]	1,000	(NA)	(NA)	(NA)	1,181	1,234	1,209	1,225	1,242
Enrollment [3]	1,000	8,579	9,364	13,336	13,489	14,038	14,096	13,977	13,923
Public	1,000	5,848	6,055	7,924	8,349	9,103	9,164	9,066	9,040
Private	1,000	2,730	3,308	5,412	5,140	4,935	4,932	4,912	4,882
Male	1,000	4,051	4,163	5,780	5,906	5,989	5,898	5,847	5,858
Female	1,000	4,527	5,201	7,556	7,583	8,049	8,198	8,130	8,065

NA Not available. [1] Number of institutions includes count of branch campuses. Includes schools accredited by the National Association of Trade and Technical Schools. [2] Beginning in 2007, includes institutions with fewer than 15 full-time employees; prior to 2007, these institutions did not report staff. [3] Branch campuses counted according to actual status, e.g., 2-year branch in 2-year category. May include unclassified students taking courses for credit but not towards a degree. [4] Students seeking certificates or degrees. [5] Enrollment data for 2- and 4-year institutions are provisional.

Source: U.S. National Center for Education Statistics, *Digest of Education Statistics*, "Latest version of all Digest tables," and earlier releases, <nces.ed.gov/programs/digest/>, accessed June 2024.

Table 293. Degree-Granting Higher Education Institutions—Number and Enrollment by State and Selected Characteristics: 2020

[18,992 represents 18,992,000. Number of institutions at the beginning of the academic year. Fall enrollment of resident and extension students attending full-time or part-time. Based on data from the Integrated Postsecondary Education Data System (IPEDS)]

State	Num-ber of institu-tions [1]	Enrollment (1,000)							Minority			Non-resi-dent alien
		Total	Male	Female	Public	Private	Full-time	White [2]	Total [3]	Black [2]	His-panic	
United States........	**3,736**	**18,992**	**7,870**	**11,122**	**13,867**	**5,125**	**11,591**	**9,798**	**8,346**	**2,382**	**3,690**	**849**
Alabama.............	60	292	121	171	246	46	195	183	102	72	13	8
Alaska.................	8	22	8	14	21	1	9	13	9	1	2	(Z)
Arizona...............	62	600	224	376	359	241	334	287	299	78	154	15
Arkansas............	49	149	60	90	133	16	94	100	45	22	12	4
California.............	384	2,580	1,092	1,488	2,124	456	1,437	679	1,774	154	1,079	127
Colorado.............	61	362	150	212	270	92	203	219	134	30	67	9
Connecticut..........	37	187	74	112	103	84	125	102	74	24	30	10
Delaware.............	8	59	22	37	41	17	35	32	23	12	6	4
District of Columbia....	19	97	37	61	4	94	63	41	47	24	11	10
Florida.................	163	1,027	417	610	763	264	604	433	552	172	299	42
Georgia.................	108	547	219	329	443	104	334	250	272	165	52	25
Hawaii.................	17	60	23	37	50	10	33	9	47	1	8	3
Idaho.................	14	123	52	71	75	48	61	90	24	1	12	9
Illinois.................	152	682	279	403	416	266	401	350	295	83	135	37
Indiana.................	66	411	178	233	323	88	262	279	112	41	36	21
Iowa.................	56	208	94	114	155	53	132	157	42	12	16	8
Kansas.................	60	193	85	108	164	29	113	127	55	15	23	11
Kentucky.............	57	261	107	154	192	70	156	194	54	24	13	13
Louisiana.............	51	244	92	152	211	32	162	131	106	74	15	6
Maine.................	29	70	28	42	47	23	41	57	11	3	3	2
Maryland.............	49	348	150	198	287	61	178	149	180	96	37	20
Massachusetts........	107	474	199	274	191	282	331	256	162	41	59	56
Michigan.............	88	490	213	277	424	66	306	336	131	52	30	24
Minnesota.............	82	396	143	252	234	162	209	253	130	60	28	13
Mississippi.............	34	163	62	101	144	19	115	90	70	58	5	3
Missouri.................	91	343	143	200	213	130	210	242	87	37	22	13
Montana.................	23	45	20	25	42	4	31	36	9	(Z)	2	1
Nebraska.................	33	135	58	77	97	38	86	98	33	8	16	4
Nevada.................	20	117	47	70	107	10	64	46	69	9	36	2
New Hampshire........	24	189	71	117	35	153	82	127	57	25	20	5
New Jersey.............	72	392	174	218	308	84	261	179	194	53	88	20
New Mexico............	35	110	43	67	106	4	54	33	74	3	55	3
New York.............	283	1,182	499	683	647	536	841	543	544	155	222	95
North Carolina..........	132	558	222	336	454	103	345	319	222	119	54	17
North Dakota...........	20	51	24	27	45	7	34	41	9	2	2	2
Ohio...................	155	655	276	378	513	142	395	465	164	76	38	25
Oklahoma...............	46	189	78	111	165	24	121	107	74	15	20	7
Oregon.................	51	204	88	116	175	29	123	128	68	6	33	7
Pennsylvania............	187	668	281	387	370	297	481	433	195	71	54	39
Rhode Island...........	13	77	32	45	38	39	59	49	25	6	12	4
South Carolina........	62	235	94	142	193	42	163	149	81	53	14	5
South Dakota...........	21	51	23	28	42	8	31	41	8	2	2	1
Tennessee...............	82	316	125	191	217	99	221	213	97	57	18	7
Texas...................	218	1,601	657	944	1,419	183	847	549	998	191	645	54
Utah...................	27	396	164	232	189	207	301	288	101	23	45	7
Vermont.................	17	40	18	22	24	16	28	32	7	1	2	1
Virginia.................	108	556	233	323	377	179	347	311	229	107	52	16
Washington.............	72	334	143	191	289	46	235	180	135	16	50	19
West Virginia...........	42	138	68	69	75	63	68	100	35	14	11	3
Wisconsin.............	67	319	135	183	262	57	197	238	70	17	27	10
Wyoming.............	9	31	14	17	30	1	17	25	5	(Z)	3	1
U.S. military [4]...........	5	16	11	4	16	(X)	16	10	5	1	2	(Z)

X Not applicable. Z Fewer than 500. [1] Branch campuses counted as separate institutions. [2] Non-Hispanic. [3] Includes other races not shown separately. [4] Service academies.

Source: U.S. National Center for Education Statistics, *Digest of Education Statistics*, "Latest version of all Digest tables," <nces.ed.gov/programs/digest>, accessed September 2023.

Table 294. Historically Black Colleges and Universities (HBCUs) Enrollment, Degrees Conferred, and Finances by Selected Characteristics: 2022

[In units as indicated (10,692,638 represents $10,692,638,000). Institutions and enrollment for Fall 2022. Degrees conferred and financial statistics for 2021-2022 academic year. Data in this table represent the 50 states, the District of Columbia, and the U.S. Virgin Islands. Historically Black colleges and universities are degree-granting institutions established prior to 1964 with the principal mission of educating Black Americans. Excludes HBCUs not participating in Title IV programs. Totals include persons of other racial and ethnic groups not shown separately. Totals may not sum due to rounding. Data are from the Integrated Postsecondary Education Data System]

Item	Total	Public			Private		
		Total	4-year	2-year	Total	4-year	2-year
Number of institutions...............	**100**	**51**	**41**	**10**	**49**	**48**	**1**
FALL ENROLLMENT (Number)							
Total enrollment.....................	**289,426**	**221,450**	**185,770**	**35,680**	**67,976**	**67,655**	**321**
Males, total...........................	104,109	78,096	64,318	13,778	26,013	25,887	126
Black................................	76,518	54,436	49,718	4,718	22,082	21,991	91
Females, total........................	185,317	143,354	121,452	21,902	41,963	41,768	195
Black................................	142,809	107,060	97,103	9,957	35,749	35,601	148
Full-time.............................	217,437	156,919	145,340	11,579	60,518	60,226	292
Male...............................	78,888	55,899	50,950	4,949	22,989	22,876	113
Female.............................	138,549	101,020	94,390	6,630	37,529	37,350	179
Part-time.............................	71,989	64,531	40,430	24,101	7,458	7,429	29
Male...............................	25,221	22,197	13,368	8,829	3,024	3,011	13
Female.............................	46,768	42,334	27,062	15,272	4,434	4,418	16
DEGREES CONFERRED (Number)							
Associate's.............................	5,298	5,135	1,282	3,853	163	134	29
Males, total...........................	1,809	1,745	276	1,469	64	57	7
Black................................	577	522	152	370	55	48	7
Females, total........................	3,489	3,390	1,006	2,384	99	77	22
Black................................	1,754	1,672	645	1,027	82	64	18
Bachelor's.............................	32,842	23,744	23,744	(X)	9,098	9,098	(X)
Males, total...........................	10,878	7,854	7,854	(X)	3,024	3,024	(X)
Black................................	8,480	5,920	5,920	(X)	2,560	2,560	(X)
Females, total........................	21,964	15,890	15,890	(X)	6,074	6,074	(X)
Black................................	18,086	12,714	12,714	(X)	5,372	5,372	(X)
Master's..............................	7,598	6,268	6,268	(X)	1,330	1,330	(X)
Males, total...........................	2,214	1,830	1,830	(X)	384	384	(X)
Black................................	1,483	1,190	1,190	(X)	293	293	(X)
Females, total........................	5,384	4,438	4,438	(X)	946	946	(X)
Black................................	3,873	3,131	3,131	(X)	742	742	(X)
Doctorate [1]...........................	3,041	1,614	1,614	(X)	1,427	1,427	(X)
Males, total...........................	1,095	570	570	(X)	525	525	(X)
Black................................	598	246	246	(X)	352	352	(X)
Females, total........................	1,946	1,044	1,044	(X)	902	902	(X)
Black................................	1,262	610	610	(X)	652	652	(X)
FINANCIAL STATISTICS ($1,000) [2]							
Total revenue.......................	**10,692,638**	**7,010,468**	**6,499,228**	**511,239**	**3,682,170**	**3,666,269**	**15,901**
Student tuition and fees..............	1,896,051	1,004,302	965,048	39,254	891,748	888,595	3,154
Federal government [3]................	3,613,767	2,312,020	2,058,452	253,567	1,301,748	1,291,864	9,884
State governments [3].................	2,397,382	2,278,233	2,130,367	147,866	119,149	116,501	2,648
Local governments [3].................	142,779	104,920	53,608	51,311	37,859	37,859	–
Private gifts and grants [4]............	946,336	261,849	258,881	2,968	684,487	684,487	–
Investment return (gain or loss).....	-374,061	-69,798	-69,555	-242	-304,263	-304,263	–
Auxiliary enterprises [5]...............	918,050	596,806	590,542	6,264	321,244	321,244	–
Hospitals and other sources.........	1,152,334	522,135	511,885	10,250	630,199	629,984	215
Total expenditures....................	**9,896,952**	**6,492,075**	**6,055,545**	**436,530**	**3,404,877**	**3,393,983**	**10,893**
Instruction..........................	2,326,063	1,547,664	1,414,274	133,390	778,399	774,841	3,559
Research............................	601,983	404,118	404,118	–	197,866	197,866	–
Academic support....................	833,236	579,204	551,742	27,462	254,031	253,033	999
Institutional support.................	1,981,585	1,102,536	1,016,135	86,401	879,049	873,173	5,876
Auxiliary enterprises.................	1,121,727	839,216	830,062	9,154	282,511	282,511	–
Other expenditures..................	3,032,358	2,019,338	1,839,215	180,122	1,013,021	1,012,560	460

– Represents zero. X Not applicable. [1] Includes Ph.D., Ed.D., and comparable degrees at the doctoral level, as well as such degrees as M.D., D.D.S., and law degrees. [2] Most public institutions reported data using the Government Accounting Standards Board form. Private institutions and some public institutions reported data using the Financial Accounting Standards Board form. Combined totals are approximate. [3] Federal government includes independent operations. Federal, state, and local governments include appropriations, grants, and contracts. [4] Includes contributions from affiliated entities. [5] Essentially self-supporting.

Source: U.S. National Center for Education Statistics, *Digest of Education Statistics*, "Latest version of all Digest tables," <nces.ed.gov/programs/digest>, accessed February 2024.

Table 295. College Enrollment of Recent High School Completers: 1970 to 2022

[2,758 represents 2,758,000. For persons 16 to 24 years old who graduated from high school in the preceding 12 months. Includes persons who completed a General Educational Development (GED) or other high school equivalency credential. Based on sample surveys and subject to sampling error; data not comparable with that in other tables]

Year	Number of high school completers (1,000)						Percent enrolled in college [5]					
	Total [1]	Male	Female	White [2]	Black [2,3]	Hispanic [3,4]	Total [1]	Male	Female	White [2]	Black [2,3]	Hispanic [3,4]
1970	2,758	1,343	1,415	2,461	(NA)	(NA)	51.7	55.2	48.5	52.0	(NA)	(NA)
1975	3,185	1,513	1,672	2,701	302	132	50.7	52.6	49.0	51.1	41.7	58.0
1980	3,088	1,498	1,589	2,554	350	130	49.3	46.7	51.8	49.8	42.7	52.3
1985	2,668	1,287	1,381	2,104	332	141	57.7	58.6	56.8	60.1	42.2	51.0
1990	2,362	1,173	1,189	1,819	331	121	60.1	58.0	62.2	63.0	46.8	42.7
1991	2,276	1,140	1,136	1,727	310	154	62.5	57.9	67.1	65.4	46.4	57.2
1992	2,397	1,216	1,180	1,724	354	198	61.9	60.0	63.8	64.3	48.2	55.0
1993	2,342	1,120	1,223	1,719	304	201	62.6	59.9	65.2	62.9	55.6	62.2
1994	2,517	1,244	1,273	1,915	316	178	61.9	60.6	63.2	64.5	50.8	49.1
1995	2,599	1,238	1,361	1,861	349	288	61.9	62.6	61.3	64.3	51.2	53.7
1996	2,660	1,297	1,363	1,875	406	227	65.0	60.1	69.7	67.4	56.0	50.8
1997	2,769	1,354	1,415	1,909	384	336	67.0	63.6	70.3	68.2	58.5	65.6
1998	2,810	1,452	1,358	1,980	386	314	65.6	62.4	69.1	68.5	61.9	47.4
1999	2,897	1,474	1,423	1,978	436	329	62.9	61.4	64.4	66.3	58.9	42.3
2000	2,756	1,251	1,505	1,938	393	300	63.3	59.9	66.2	65.7	54.9	52.9
2001	2,549	1,277	1,273	1,834	381	241	61.8	60.1	63.5	64.3	55.0	51.7
2002	2,796	1,412	1,384	1,903	382	344	65.2	62.1	68.4	69.1	59.4	53.6
2003	2,677	1,306	1,372	1,832	327	314	63.9	61.2	66.5	66.2	57.5	58.6
2004	2,752	1,327	1,425	1,854	398	286	66.7	61.4	71.5	68.8	62.5	61.8
2005	2,675	1,262	1,414	1,799	345	390	68.6	66.5	70.4	73.2	55.7	54.0
2006	2,692	1,328	1,363	1,805	318	382	66.0	65.8	66.1	68.5	55.5	57.9
2007	2,955	1,511	1,444	2,043	416	355	67.2	66.1	68.3	69.5	55.7	64.0
2008	3,151	1,640	1,511	2,091	416	458	68.6	65.9	71.6	71.7	55.7	63.9
2009	2,937	1,407	1,531	1,863	415	459	70.1	66.0	73.8	71.3	69.5	59.3
2010	3,160	1,679	1,482	1,937	461	507	68.1	62.8	74.0	70.5	62.0	59.7
2011	3,079	1,611	1,468	1,747	464	623	68.2	64.7	72.2	68.3	67.1	66.6
2012	3,203	1,622	1,581	(NA)	(NA)	(NA)	66.2	61.3	71.3	65.7	56.4	70.3
2013	2,977	1,524	1,453	(NA)	(NA)	(NA)	65.9	63.5	68.4	68.8	56.7	59.8
2014	2,868	1,423	1,445	(NA)	(NA)	(NA)	68.4	64.0	72.6	67.7	70.2	65.2
2015	2,965	1,448	1,516	(NA)	(NA)	(NA)	69.2	65.8	72.5	71.3	55.6	68.9
2016	3,137	1,517	1,620	(NA)	(NA)	(NA)	69.8	67.5	71.9	69.7	57.3	72.0
2017	2,870	1,345	1,525	(NA)	(NA)	(NA)	66.7	61.1	71.7	69.1	59.4	61.0
2018	3,212	1,614	1,598	(NA)	(NA)	(NA)	69.1	66.9	71.4	70.9	64.5	65.4
2019	3,178	1,486	1,693	(NA)	(NA)	(NA)	66.2	62.0	69.8	68.0	49.8	63.4
2020	3,118	1,581	1,537	(NA)	(NA)	(NA)	62.7	59.3	66.2	65.0	57.5	56.2
2021	2,731	1,444	1,287	(NA)	(NA)	(NA)	61.8	54.9	69.5	62.3	59.2	58.6
2022	2,987	1,355	1,632	(NA)	(NA)	(NA)	62.0	57.2	66.0	64.0	60.9	58.0

NA Not available. [1] Includes persons of other racial/ethnic groups, not shown separately. [2] Beginning 2003, for persons of this race group only. [3] Due to small sample size, data are subject to relatively large sampling errors. [4] Persons of Hispanic origin may be of any race. [5] As of October.

Source: U.S. National Center for Education Statistics, *Digest of Education Statistics*, "Latest version of all Digest tables," <nces.ed.gov/programs/digest/>, accessed January 2024.

Table 296. College Enrollment by Sex and Attendance Status: 2010 to 2022

[In thousands (21,019 represents 21,019,000). As of Fall. Data cover enrollment in degree-granting institutions that grant associate's or higher degrees and participate in Title IV federal financial aid programs]

Sex and age	2010		2015		2019		2021		2022 (P)	
	Total	Part-time	Total	Part-time	Total	Part-time	Total	Part-time	Total	Part-time
Total [1]	**21,019**	**7,932**	**19,988**	**7,701**	**19,630**	**7,676**	**18,660**	**7,330**	**18,961**	**7,413**
Male [1]	**9,046**	**3,207**	**8,724**	**3,165**	**8,364**	**3,088**	**7,769**	**2,881**	**7,814**	**2,877**
Under 18 years old	94	23	435	352	592	492	603	505	539	448
18 to 19 years old	1,820	245	1,955	342	2,002	347	1,816	320	1,878	321
20 to 21 years old	1,948	362	1,849	378	1,812	358	1,702	324	1,708	334
22 to 24 years old	1,723	508	1,541	507	1,372	455	1,271	419	1,297	428
25 to 29 years old	1,410	695	1,227	545	1,085	496	977	444	983	452
30 to 34 years old	731	430	644	348	571	318	536	298	540	304
35 years old and over	1,320	944	1,056	683	921	617	856	567	862	585
Female [1]	**11,974**	**4,725**	**11,264**	**4,535**	**11,266**	**4,587**	**10,890**	**4,449**	**11,147**	**4,536**
Under 18 years old	108	9	618	495	863	708	884	730	836	686
18 to 19 years old	2,237	316	2,387	387	2,509	410	2,332	390	2,473	402
20 to 21 years old	2,155	377	2,230	459	2,251	454	2,179	431	2,230	450
22 to 24 years old	2,036	666	1,784	661	1,676	620	1,597	581	1,675	616
25 to 29 years old	1,844	953	1,552	792	1,490	767	1,424	720	1,438	739
30 to 34 years old	1,074	630	867	514	832	502	848	504	841	507
35 years old and over	2,520	1,774	1,802	1,214	1,633	1,118	1,613	1,086	1,642	1,127

P Projection. [1] Beginning with data for 2015, totals may include data for "age unknown," not shown separately.

Source: U.S. National Center for Education Statistics, *Digest of Education Statistics*, "Latest version of all Digest Tables," <www.nces.ed.gov/programs/digest>, accessed May 2023.

Table 297. College Enrollment by Selected Characteristics: 1990 to 2022

[In thousands (13,818.6 represents 13,818,600). As of Fall. Nonresident (foreign) students are not distributed among racial/ethnic groups. Beginning in 2000, data reflect a new classification of institutions; this includes more 2-year colleges and excludes a few institutions that did not award degrees. Includes institutions that were eligible to participate in Title IV federal financial aid programs and schools accredited by the National Association of Trade and Technical Schools. Based on data from the Integrated Postsecondary Education Data System (IPEDS)]

Characteristic	1990	2000	2010	2015	2019	2020	2021	2022
Total	**13,818.6**	**15,312.3**	**21,019.4**	**19,988.2**	**19,630.2**	**19,027.4**	**18,658.8**	**18,580.0**
Male	6,283.9	6,721.8	9,045.8	8,723.8	8,363.9	7,885.0	7,767.9	7,814.5
Female	7,534.7	8,590.5	11,973.7	11,264.4	11,266.3	11,142.4	10,890.9	10,765.5
Public	10,844.7	11,752.8	15,142.2	14,572.8	14,503.6	13,884.5	13,545.7	13,494.3
Private	2,973.9	3,559.5	5,877.3	5,415.4	5,126.5	5,143.0	5,113.1	5,085.7
2-year	5,240.1	5,948.4	7,683.6	6,499.5	5,590.7	4,931.7	4,683.8	4,657.5
4-year	8,578.6	9,363.9	13,335.8	13,488.7	14,039.5	14,095.7	13,974.9	13,922.6
Undergraduate	11,959.1	13,155.4	18,082.4	17,046.7	16,557.5	15,884.6	15,447.6	15,397.5
Postbaccalaureate	1,859.5	2,156.9	2,937.0	2,941.5	3,072.6	3,142.9	3,211.2	3,182.5
White [1]	**10,722.5**	**10,462.1**	**12,720.8**	**10,939.2**	**10,139.8**	**9,817.2**	**9,498.8**	**9,207.7**
Male	4,861.0	4,634.6	5,605.8	4,848.5	4,395.5	4,165.9	4,035.2	3,934.7
Female	5,861.5	5,827.5	7,115.0	6,090.7	5,744.3	5,651.3	5,463.6	5,273.0
Public	8,385.4	7,963.4	9,182.1	7,910.7	7,368.8	7,059.8	6,810.6	6,611.5
Private	2,337.0	2,498.7	3,538.7	3,028.5	2,771.0	2,757.4	2,688.2	2,596.1
2-year	3,954.3	3,804.1	4,321.3	3,225.8	2,583.2	2,328.3	2,200.1	2,127.5
4-year	6,768.1	6,658.0	8,399.5	7,713.4	7,556.6	7,488.9	7,298.7	7,080.2
Undergraduate	9,272.6	8,983.5	10,895.9	9,303.8	8,497.8	8,133.6	7,831.0	7,636.6
Postbaccalaureate	1,449.8	1,478.6	1,824.9	1,635.4	1,641.9	1,683.6	1,667.8	1,571.1
Black [1]	**1,247.0**	**1,730.3**	**3,039.0**	**2,681.0**	**2,467.3**	**2,389.4**	**2,329.1**	**2,322.9**
Male	484.7	635.3	1,089.0	998.9	894.3	834.6	823.7	831.9
Female	762.3	1,095.0	1,949.9	1,682.1	1,573.1	1,554.8	1,505.4	1,491.0
Public	976.4	1,319.2	1,988.8	1,775.1	1,695.7	1,604.7	1,574.1	1,568.3
Private	270.6	411.1	1,050.2	906.0	771.7	784.7	755.0	754.6
2-year	524.3	734.9	1,198.9	940.5	776.8	670.4	653.2	653.1
4-year	722.8	995.4	1,840.0	1,740.5	1,690.5	1,719.0	1,676.0	1,669.8
Undergraduate	1,147.2	1,548.9	2,677.1	2,316.5	2,100.2	2,004.3	1,947.1	1,953.6
Postbaccalaureate	99.8	181.4	361.9	364.5	367.2	385.1	382.1	369.2
Hispanic	**782.4**	**1,461.8**	**2,748.8**	**3,297.7**	**3,785.9**	**3,696.8**	**3,667.7**	**3,780.3**
Male	353.9	627.1	1,157.6	1,389.2	1,549.0	1,446.2	1,445.7	1,515.3
Female	428.5	834.7	1,591.2	1,908.5	2,236.9	2,250.6	2,222.0	2,265.0
Public	671.4	1,229.3	2,163.8	2,694.5	3,126.6	3,000.6	2,948.0	3,039.3
Private	111.0	232.5	585.0	603.2	659.2	696.2	719.7	741.0
2-year	424.2	843.9	1,393.0	1,555.6	1,533.8	1,302.4	1,239.5	1,281.4
4-year	358.2	617.9	1,355.9	1,742.1	2,252.1	2,394.4	2,428.2	2,498.9
Undergraduate	724.6	1,351.0	2,551.0	3,055.0	3,478.4	3,355.4	3,309.4	3,421.9
Postbaccalaureate	57.9	110.8	197.8	242.7	307.5	341.4	358.3	358.3
Asian/Pacific Islander [1]	**572.4**	**978.2**	**1,281.6**	**1,284.3**	**1,378.0**	**1,391.2**	**1,400.4**	**1,415.6**
Male	294.9	465.9	600.6	602.9	634.6	629.2	633.2	645.7
Female	277.5	512.3	681.0	681.5	743.4	762.1	767.2	769.8
Public	461.0	770.5	968.7	970.1	1,043.1	1,043.7	1,035.8	1,046.8
Private	111.5	207.7	312.8	314.2	334.9	347.6	364.6	368.7
2-year	215.2	401.9	463.1	401.9	358.7	329.1	304.3	304.3
4-year	357.2	576.3	818.5	882.5	1,019.3	1,062.1	1,096.1	1,111.2
Undergraduate	500.5	845.5	1,087.3	1,084.0	1,147.3	1,144.7	1,139.8	1,154.5
Postbaccalaureate	72.0	132.7	194.3	200.3	230.7	246.6	260.6	261.1
American Indian/ Alaska Native [1]	**102.8**	**151.2**	**196.2**	**146.1**	**129.7**	**120.8**	**120.6**	**121.1**
Male	43.1	61.4	78.7	58.2	49.2	43.4	43.4	44.2
Female	59.7	89.7	117.5	88.0	80.4	77.4	77.2	76.9
Public	90.4	127.3	150.8	113.7	102.4	93.2	92.8	93.7
Private	12.4	23.9	45.5	32.5	27.2	27.6	27.8	27.4
2-year	54.9	74.7	87.2	62.8	49.3	42.1	42.1	42.8
4-year	47.9	76.5	109.0	83.4	80.3	78.7	78.6	78.4
Undergraduate	95.5	138.5	179.1	132.2	116.2	107.1	106.6	107.7
Postbaccalaureate	7.3	12.6	17.1	13.9	13.4	13.7	14.0	13.4
Nonresident (foreign)	**391.5**	**528.7**	**707.7**	**982.3**	**974.6**	**848.5**	**885.2**	**967.9**
Male	246.3	297.3	379.6	548.6	528.6	457.7	478.3	527.9
Female	145.2	231.4	328.0	433.7	446.0	390.8	406.8	440.0
Public	260.0	343.1	453.0	626.8	596.3	511.2	522.5	566.6
Private	131.4	185.6	254.7	355.5	378.3	337.3	362.6	401.3
2-year	67.1	89.0	99.3	104.2	79.1	60.8	52.3	55.7
4-year	324.3	439.7	608.3	878.1	895.5	787.7	832.9	912.2
Undergraduate	218.7	288.0	398.4	565.1	548.6	468.8	451.8	454.6
Postbaccalaureate	172.7	240.7	309.3	417.2	426.1	379.8	433.4	513.3

[1] Non-Hispanic.

Source: U.S. National Center for Education Statistics, *Digest of Education Statistics*, "Latest version of all Digest tables," and earlier releases, <nces.ed.gov/programs/digest>, accessed Febrary 2024.

Table 298. College Enrollment by Sex, Age, and Race/Ethnicity: 1980 to 2022

[In thousands (11,387 represents 11,387,000). As of October for the civilian noninstitutional population 14 years old and over. Based on the Current Population Survey; see text, Section 1 and Appendix III]

Characteristic	1980	1990 [1]	2000	2005	2010	2015	2018	2019	2020	2021	2022
Total [2]	**11,387**	**13,621**	**15,314**	**17,472**	**20,275**	**19,101**	**18,908**	**18,289**	**17,674**	**17,323**	**17,260**
Male [3]	5,430	6,192	6,682	7,539	9,007	8,484	8,373	8,067	7,577	7,262	7,298
18 to 24 years	3,604	3,922	4,342	4,972	5,698	5,694	5,587	5,442	5,187	4,817	4,995
25 to 34 years	1,325	1,412	1,361	1,486	2,055	1,803	1,842	1,641	1,514	1,554	1,401
35 years old and over	405	772	918	1,019	1,161	878	859	880	785	767	805
Female [3]	5,957	7,429	8,631	9,933	11,268	10,617	10,534	10,223	10,097	10,059	9,959
18 to 24 years	3,625	4,042	5,109	5,859	6,515	6,460	6,510	6,492	6,477	6,170	6,416
25 to 34 years	1,378	1,749	1,846	2,115	2,569	2,372	2,358	2,104	2,096	2,282	1,959
35 years old and over	802	1,546	1,589	1,838	2,049	1,672	1,541	1,477	1,443	1,462	1,442
White [3, 4]	9,925	11,488	11,999	13,467	15,258	13,859	13,323	12,783	12,497	12,115	12,070
18 to 24 years	6,334	6,635	7,566	8,499	9,324	8,969	8,770	8,602	8,419	7,824	8,225
25 to 34 years	2,328	2,698	2,339	2,647	3,414	2,966	2,737	2,411	2,459	2,562	2,187
35 years old and over	1,051	2,023	1,978	2,206	2,365	1,776	1,647	1,613	1,522	1,534	1,486
Male	4,804	5,235	5,311	5,844	6,883	6,253	5,980	5,661	5,343	5,141	5,061
Female	5,121	6,253	6,689	7,624	8,375	7,607	7,343	7,123	7,154	6,973	7,006
Black [3, 4]	1,163	1,393	2,164	2,297	3,083	2,826	3,009	2,848	2,591	2,717	2,634
18 to 24 years	688	894	1,216	1,229	1,692	1,637	1,670	1,587	1,549	1,568	1,559
25 to 34 years	289	258	567	520	715	627	807	699	573	630	563
35 years old and over	156	207	361	448	642	537	517	517	415	466	473
Male	476	587	815	864	1,185	1,147	1,183	1,171	1,055	995	1,078
Female	686	807	1,349	1,435	1,898	1,679	1,826	1,676	1,536	1,721	1,557
Asian [3, 4]	(NA)	(NA)	(NA)	1,184	1,322	1,616	1,691	1,768	1,759	1,627	1,735
18 to 24 years	(NA)	(NA)	(NA)	696	811	1,026	1,079	1,132	1,174	1,045	1,060
25 to 34 years	(NA)	(NA)	(NA)	341	354	426	466	468	390	432	468
35 years old and over	(NA)	(NA)	(NA)	130	125	143	127	133	181	136	186
Male	(NA)	(NA)	(NA)	605	647	752	846	870	821	754	822
Female	(NA)	(NA)	(NA)	579	676	864	844	898	938	871	912
Hispanic origin [3, 5]	443	748	1,426	1,942	2,879	3,374	3,574	3,555	3,553	3,430	3,434
18 to 24 years	315	435	899	1,216	1,814	2,369	2,431	2,469	2,460	2,301	2,350
25 to 34 years	118	168	309	438	652	648	780	714	665	729	638
35 years old and over	(NA)	130	195	257	372	315	305	332	392	340	400
Male	222	364	619	804	1,302	1,484	1,613	1,559	1,436	1,469	1,394
Female	221	384	807	1,139	1,576	1,890	1,960	1,996	2,116	1,961	2,040

NA Not available. [1] Beginning 1990, based on a revised edit and tabulation package. [2] Includes other races, not shown separately. [3] Includes persons 14 to 17 years old, not shown separately. [4] Beginning 2003, for persons who selected this race group only. See footnote 4, Table 252. [5] Persons of Hispanic origin may be of any race.

Source: U.S. Census Bureau, Current Population Reports, P-20, and earlier reports; and "School Enrollment Tables," <www.census.gov/topics/education/school-enrollment/data/tables.All.html>, accessed November 2023.

Table 299. College Enrollment by Type of College, Sex, and Selected Characteristics: 2022

[In thousands (17,260 represents 17,260,000). As of October. Covers civilian noninstitutional population 15 years old and over enrolled in colleges and graduate schools. Based on Current Population Survey. See text, Section 1 and Appendix III]

Characteristic	Total				Male		Female	
	Total enrolled	Two-year college	Four-year college	Graduate school	Total enrolled [1]	Four-year college	Total enrolled [1]	Four-year college
Total enrollment [2]	**17,260**	**3,457**	**10,067**	**3,732**	**7,298**	**4,293**	**9,959**	**5,773**
Age:								
15 to 19 years old	4,115	1,173	2,894	48	1,707	1,132	2,408	1,762
20 to 24 years old	7,535	1,230	5,276	1,029	3,385	2,408	4,150	2,868
25 to 34 years old	3,360	599	1,182	1,579	1,401	484	1,959	698
35 years old and over	2,246	456	716	1,076	804	269	1,442	446
Race/ethnicity:								
White [3]	12,070	2,502	7,174	2,391	5,061	3,082	7,006	4,093
White, non-Hispanic [3]	9,113	1,590	5,558	1,965	3,880	2,448	5,232	3,109
Black [3]	2,634	601	1,457	577	1,078	581	1,557	875
Asian [3]	1,735	146	952	637	822	439	912	513
Hispanic [4]	3,434	1,044	1,914	477	1,394	747	2,040	1,167
Control of school:								
Public	13,990	3,196	8,271	2,525	5,970	3,536	8,023	4,736
Private	3,263	261	1,795	1,207	1,328	757	1,935	1,037
Employment status:								
Employed full-time	4,321	927	1,710	1,685	1,811	733	2,510	976
Employed part-time	4,706	1,013	2,866	827	1,918	1,128	2,788	1,739
Not employed	8,230	1,519	5,491	1,220	3,569	2,433	4,661	3,058
Enrollment status:								
Full time students	13,440	2,383	8,693	2,359	5,822	3,749	7,613	4,944
15 to 19 years old	3,848	1,046	2,753	48	1,583	1,082	2,265	1,671
20 to 24 years old	6,555	864	4,797	895	2,980	2,209	3,574	2,588
25 to 34 years old	2,081	302	723	1,056	913	310	1,168	413
35 years old and over	952	173	420	359	346	148	606	272
Part time students	3,821	1,074	1,374	1,374	1,476	545	2,345	829
15 to 19 years old	267	127	141	–	124	50	143	91
20 to 24 years old	981	366	478	135	405	199	576	280
25 to 34 years old	1,279	298	459	522	488	174	791	285
35 years old and over	1,294	283	296	716	459	122	836	174

– Represents or rounds to zero. [1] Includes enrollment in two-year colleges and graduate school, not shown separately. [2] Includes other race groups, not shown separately. [3] For persons who selected this race group only. [4] Persons of Hispanic origin may be of any race.

Source: U.S. Census Bureau, "School Enrollment Tables," <www.census.gov/topics/education/school-enrollment/data/tables.All.html>, accessed November 2023.

Table 300. Higher Education Institutions—Admission Selection Criteria by Control and Level of Institution: 2010 to 2022

[For school year beginning in fall of year shown. Data shown for degree-granting institutions that grant associate's or higher degrees and participate in Title IV federal financial aid programs. Excludes institutions not enrolling any first-time degree/certificate-seeking undergraduates. Data are from the Integrated Postsecondary Education Data System (IPEDS)]

Item	All institutions			Public institutions			Private institutions		
	Total	4-year	2-year	Total	4-year	2-year	Total	4-year	2-year
NUMBER OF INSTITUTIONS									
2010..	4,209	2,487	1,722	1,614	637	977	2,595	1,850	745
2015..	4,147	2,584	1,563	1,578	669	909	2,569	1,915	654
2022..	3,548	2,287	1,261	1,566	750	816	1,982	1,537	445
PERCENT OF INSTITUTIONS									
Open admissions									
2010..	47.2	22.5	82.9	65.6	17.6	96.9	35.8	24.2	64.6
2015..	51.0	27.5	89.8	64.3	19.0	97.7	42.8	30.4	78.9
2022..	48.9	25.1	92.1	65.1	28.8	98.4	36.1	23.2	80.4
Some admission requirements [1]									
2010..	52.1	76.6	16.8	34.4	82.4	3.1	63.2	74.6	34.8
2015..	48.3	71.9	9.3	35.4	81.0	1.9	56.3	68.8	19.7
2022..	51.0	74.8	7.9	34.9	71.2	1.6	63.8	76.6	19.6
Secondary grades									
2010..	33.3	54.2	3.2	27.8	67.8	1.7	36.7	49.5	5.1
2015..	35.4	55.3	2.4	30.4	69.8	1.3	38.5	50.2	4.0
2022..	41.8	63.1	3.0	31.8	65.1	1.2	49.6	62.2	6.3
Secondary class rank									
2010..	8.4	13.9	0.4	9.2	22.9	0.3	7.8	10.8	0.5
2015..	6.0	9.5	0.3	7.8	18.2	0.1	4.9	6.4	0.6
2022..	3.4	5.0	0.4	4.4	9.1	0.1	2.6	3.1	0.9
Recommendations									
2010..	18.1	29.2	2.1	3.3	8.3	0.1	27.2	36.3	4.7
2015..	17.9	27.8	1.7	4.5	10.5	0.1	26.2	33.8	3.8
2022..	16.6	24.7	1.8	4.0	8.4	–	26.5	32.7	5.2
Test scores [2]									
2010..	37.6	55.1	12.2	30.5	74.1	2.0	42.0	48.6	25.5
2015..	34.3	51.0	6.7	32.4	74.7	1.3	35.5	42.7	14.2
2022..	7.0	8.4	4.4	5.0	10.1	0.4	8.6	7.6	11.9
No admission requirements, only recommendations:									
2010..	0.6	0.9	0.3	–	–	–	1.0	1.2	0.7
2015..	0.7	0.6	0.8	0.3	–	0.4	0.9	0.8	1.4
2022..	0.1	0.1	–	–	–	–	0.2	0.2	–

– Represents zero. [1] Institutions may have more than one admission requirement. Includes other kinds of admissions requirements, not shown separately. [2] Includes SAT, ACT, or other admission tests.

Source: U.S. National Center for Education Statistics, *Digest of Education Statistics*, "Latest version of all Digest Tables," <www.nces.ed.gov/programs/digest/>, accessed May 2024. See also <nces.ed.gov/ipeds/>.

Table 301. College Students Reporting Disability Status by Selected Characteristic: 2020

[16,936 represents 16,936,000. For academic year ending in year shown. Students with disabilities are those who reported having deafness or serious difficulty hearing; blindness or serious difficulty seeing; serious difficulty concentrating, remembering, or making decisions because of a physical, mental, or emotional condition; or serious difficulty walking or climbing stairs. Based on the 2019-2020 National Postsecondary Student-Aid Study]

Student characteristic	Undergraduate			Graduate and first-professional		
	All students	Disabled students	Nondisabled students	All students	Disabled students	Nondisabled students
Total students (1,000).............................	16,936	3,478	13,457	3,600	385	3,215
PERCENT DISTRIBUTION						
Total..	100.0	20.5	79.5	100.0	10.7	89.3
Age:						
15 to 23 years old.................................	100.0	20.3	79.7	100.0	8.9	91.1
24 to 29 years old.................................	100.0	21.3	78.7	100.0	10.9	89.1
30 years or older..................................	100.0	20.7	79.3	100.0	11.0	89.0
Gender:						
Male..	100.0	17.6	82.4	100.0	8.5	91.5
Female..	100.0	21.9	78.1	100.0	11.7	88.3
Nonbinary [1]......................................	100.0	53.7	46.3	100.0	39.8	60.2
Race/ethnicity of student:						
Non-Hispanic:						
White..	100.0	21.1	78.9	100.0	11.0	89.0
Black..	100.0	18.0	82.0	100.0	10.1	89.9
Asian..	100.0	13.9	86.1	100.0	6.8	93.2
Pacific Islander.................................	100.0	22.1	77.9	100.0	(S)	89.1
American Indian/Alaska Native..................	100.0	23.7	76.3	100.0	(S)	90.8
Two or more races..............................	100.0	25.4	74.6	100.0	14.9	85.1
Hispanic [2].......................................	100.0	21.3	78.7	100.0	14.0	86.0
Attendance status:						
Full-time, full-year................................	100.0	17.7	82.3	100.0	11.1	88.9
Part-time or part-year............................	100.0	22.5	77.5	100.0	10.3	89.7

S Reporting standards not met. The coefficient of variation (CV) for this estimate is 50% or greater. [1] Nonbinary includes genderqueer, gender nonconforming, or a different identity. [2] Persons of Hispanic origin may be of any race.

Source: U.S. National Center for Education Statistics, *Digest of Education Statistics*, "Latest version of all Digest tables," <nces.ed.gov/programs/digest>, accessed December 2023.

Table 302. Foreign (Nonimmigrant) Student Enrollment in U.S. Colleges and Universities by World Region and Selected Country of Origin: 1980 to 2023

[In thousands (286 represents 286,000). For Fall of the previous year]

Region of origin	1980	1990	1995	2000	2005	2010	2015	2016	2017	2018	2019	2020	2021	2022	2023
All regions.........	286	387	453	515	565	691	975	1,044	1,079	1,095	1,095	1,075	914	949	1,057
Africa [1].............	36	25	21	30	36	37	40	43	45	47	47	49	45	49	57
Nigeria.............	16	4	2	4	6	7	9	11	12	13	13	14	13	14	18
Asia [1,2,3]...........	165	245	292	315	356	469	724	790	827	842	842	823	697	705	793
China.............	1	33	39	54	63	128	304	329	351	363	370	373	317	290	290
Taiwan............	18	31	36	29	26	27	21	21	22	22	23	24	20	20	22
Hong Kong.........	10	11	13	8	7	8	8	8	8	7	7	7	6	6	6
India...............	9	26	34	42	80	105	133	166	186	196	202	193	167	199	269
Indonesia...........	2	9	12	11	8	7	8	9	9	9	8	8	7	8	8
Iran.................	51	7	3	2	2	5	11	12	13	13	12	11	10	9	11
Japan.............	12	30	45	47	42	25	19	19	19	19	18	18	12	13	16
Saudi Arabia........	10	4	4	5	3	16	60	61	53	44	37	31	22	18	16
South Korea........	5	22	34	41	53	72	64	61	59	55	52	50	39	41	44
Europe [4].........	23	46	65	78	72	85	91	92	93	93	91	90	68	83	90
Latin America [1,5].....	42	48	47	62	68	66	86	85	80	80	81	80	73	78	82
Mexico.............	6	7	9	11	13	13	17	17	17	15	15	14	13	15	16
Venezuela..........	10	3	4	5	5	5	8	8	9	8	8	7	6	5	4
North America [6]......	16	19	23	24	29	29	27	27	27	26	26	26	25	27	28
Canada.............	15	18	23	24	28	28	27	27	27	26	26	26	25	27	28
Oceania.............	4	4	4	5	4	5	6	7	7	7	8	8	6	6	7

[1] Includes countries not shown separately. [2] Includes the Middle East. [3] Beginning 2006, excludes Cyprus and Turkey. [4] Beginning 2006, includes Cyprus and Turkey. [5] Includes Mexico, Central America, Caribbean, and South America. Prior to 2011, excludes Bermuda. [6] Prior to 2011, includes Bermuda.

Source: Institute of International Education, New York, NY, *Open Doors Report on International Educational Exchange* ©, annual (2023). See also <opendoorsdata.org>.

Table 303. Higher Education Enrollment in Languages Other Than English: 1970 to 2021

[1,153.2 represents 1,153,200. As of Fall. For credit enrollment]

Language other than English	1970	1980	1990	1998	2006	2009	2013	2016	2021
Enrollment, total [1] (1,000).............	1,153.2	924.3	1,185.5	1,186.6	1,575.8	1,673.6	1,561.2	1,418.6	1,182.6
By selected language (1,000):									
Spanish........................	386.6	379.0	534.1	649.2	822.1	861.0	789.9	713.0	584.5
French.........................	358.5	248.3	273.1	199.1	206.0	215.2	197.7	175.7	135.1
American Sign Language.................	(NA)	(NA)	1.6	11.4	79.7	92.1	109.6	107.1	107.9
Japanese.......................	6.6	11.5	45.8	43.1	65.4	72.4	66.8	68.8	65.7
German........................	201.8	127.0	133.6	89.0	94.1	95.6	86.8	80.6	53.5
Chinese........................	6.1	11.4	19.4	28.5	51.4	61.6	62.0	54.2	46.5
Italian.........................	34.2	34.8	49.8	49.3	78.2	80.3	71.0	56.7	45.2
Arabic.........................	1.3	3.5	3.7	5.5	24.0	35.2	33.5	31.6	22.9
Latin..........................	28.4	25.0	28.2	26.1	32.2	32.4	27.2	24.8	19.5
Korean........................	0.1	0.4	2.4	4.5	7.1	8.4	12.3	13.9	19.3
Russian........................	36.4	24.0	44.5	23.8	24.8	26.7	22.0	20.4	17.6
Hebrew........................	16.6	19.3	13.0	15.8	23.8	22.1	19.3	15.1	14.6
Index (1965 = 100).............	111.5	89.3	114.6	114.7	152.3	161.8	150.9	137.1	114.3

NA Not available. [1] Includes other languages, not shown separately.

Source: Modern Language Association, Lusin, Natalia, et al., *Enrollments in Languages Other Than English in United States Institutions of Higher Education*, November 2023 ©. For 1970 to 2009, consult Association of Departments of Foreign Languages (ADFL) Bulletins. For 2002 to 2021 reports, see: <www.mla.org/Resources/Guidelines-and-Data/Reports-and-Professional-Guidelines>.

Table 304. COVID-19 Pandemic Impact on Higher Education Students: 2020

[In percent. Data are based on responses from approximately 61,000 undergraduate students participating in the 2019-2020 National Postsecondary Student Aid Study. Data are preliminary, and cover students attending higher education institutions in the 50 states, DC, and Puerto Rico. Data represent percent of undergraduate students who experienced disruptions at their higher education institution due to the COVID-19 pandemic between January 1 and June 30, 2020]

Student experiences	Total	Public			Private, nonprofit	
		Less than 2-year	2-year	4-year	Less than 4-year	4-year
Experienced enrollment disruption or change.........................	87.5	88.6	87.8	92.2	82.6	85.7
Withdrew from school.................................	4.4	6.9	6.8	2.7	6.3	2.9
Took leave of absence from school......................	3.8	9.3	4.1	2.5	[2] 5.0	2.7
Some or all classes canceled...........................	9.5	31.7	9.8	9.1	13.6	9.1
School break extended............................	35.0	25.1	31.7	39.9	(S)	40.4
Some or all in-person classes moved to online only instruction.....	84.1	73.2	81.5	89.2	75.2	84.8
Experienced housing disruption or change.........................	27.5	[2] 11.0	8.3	34.7	6.9	50.1
Experienced financial disruption or change.........................	39.6	25.2	35.4	43.0	39.0	40.4
Received emergency financial assistance from school.............	14.6	[2] 7.4	10.3	17.6	16.2	16.2
Lost job or lost income due to reduced work hours..................	28.6	18.6	26.4	31.0	23.4	28.8
Received full or partial tuition refund [1].....................	27.3	13.3	26.3	30.6	[2] 28.7	24.0
Received full or partial room and board refund [1]......................	38.3	[2] 8.2	6.1	45.5	(S)	60.3

S Reporting standards not met. [1] Excludes credit for future enrollment costs. Housing refunds include only students who lived on campus or in college-owned housing. [2] Interpret data with caution. Standard error is between 30 and 50 percent.

Source: U.S. National Center for Education Statistics, *2019-20 National Postsecondary Student Aid Study (NPSAS:20): First Look at the Impact of the Coronavirus (COVID-19) Pandemic on Undergraduate Student Enrollment, Housing, and Finances (Preliminary Data)*, June 2021.

Table 305. Employed Undergraduate Students by Enrollment Status and Selected Characteristics: 2021

[In percent. Students were classified as full time if they were taking at least 12 hours of classes during an average school week and as part time if they were taking fewer hours. Data are from the Current Population Survey; based on sample surveys of the civilian noninstitutionalized population]

Characteristic	Full-time undergraduates						Part-time undergraduates	
	Percent of all full-time under-graduates	Percent employed					Percent of all full-time under-graduates	Percent employed [1]
		Total [1]	Hours worked per week [2]					
			Less than 10	10 to 19	20 to 34	35 or more		
Total	**100.0**	**40.9**	**5.4**	**9.3**	**15.4**	**10.7**	**100.0**	**77.4**
Sex:								
Male	42.8	37.0	3.5	8.6	14.2	10.8	38.6	79.0
Female	57.2	43.8	6.9	9.9	16.4	10.6	61.4	76.4
Race/ethnicity: [3]								
White, non-Hispanic	54.1	42.9	6.6	10.1	16.6	9.6	44.9	79.3
Black, non-Hispanic	14.4	37.2	5.2	4.8	13.5	13.7	16.2	77.6
Asian, non-Hispanic	7.8	27.7	[6] 3.3	14.0	7.1	[6] 3.3	4.5	66.5
Two or more races	2.5	43.2	(S)	[6] 12.3	16.5	[6] 9.8	2.5	(S)
Hispanic	19.9	43.3	[6] 3.3	8.4	17.2	14.4	30.3	76.5
Age:								
16 to 24 years old	85.2	39.0	5.3	10.1	15.8	7.9	42.9	79.1
25 to 29 years old	7.2	45.4	[6] 5.1	6.7	13.0	20.6	22.6	78.7
30 to 39 years old	5.2	55.7	[6] 6.3	[6] 3.2	16.0	30.2	20.3	69.7
40 to 49 years old	1.8	60.4	[6] 9.2	(S)	[6] 8.0	39.9	9.6	84.4
50 to 64 years old	0.7	(S)	(S)	(S)	(S)	(S)	4.6	73.3
Level of institution:								
2-year	20.8	46.5	5.5	7.3	20.1	13.6	46.3	74.2
4-year	79.2	39.4	5.4	9.9	14.2	9.9	53.7	80.1
Householder status: [4]								
Non-householder	78.8	36.4	4.9	8.9	15.1	7.6	51.4	75.1
Householder	21.2	57.6	7.5	10.9	16.7	22.4	48.6	79.8
Presence of own children under 18 in household: [5]								
Child or children present	6.4	55.5	[6] 5.9	[6] 3.6	14.8	31.1	23.2	77.7
No children present	93.6	39.9	5.4	9.7	15.5	9.3	76.8	77.3

S Figure does not meet publication standards. [1] Includes those who were employed but not at work during the survey week. [2] Excludes those who were employed but not at work during the survey week; therefore, detail may not sum to total percent employed. [3] Includes other races not shown separately. [4] Householders are persons in whose name the housing unit is owned or rented. Never-married students living away from home in college dormitories are not considered householders. [5] Includes stepchildren and adopted children. [6] Use data with caution. The coefficient of variation for this estimate is between 30 and 50 percent.

Source: U.S. National Center for Education Statistics, *Digest of Education Statistics*, "Latest version of all Digest tables," <nces.ed.gov/programs/digest>, accessed November 2023.

Table 306. Residence and Migration of College Freshmen by State: 2020

[As of Fall. Includes first-time postsecondary students who had graduated from high school in the previous 12 months and were enrolled at public and private nonprofit 4-year degree-granting institutions that participated in Title IV federal financial aid programs. Excludes respondents for whom state residence and/or migration are unknown. Based on data from the Integrated Postsecondary Education Data System (IPEDS). See source for more information]

State	Total freshmen enrollment in institutions located in the state	Ratio of in-state students to freshmen enrollment	Ratio of in-state students to residents enrolled in any state [1]	State	Total freshmen enrollment in institutions located in the state	Ratio of in-state students to freshmen enrollment	Ratio of in-state students to residents enrolled in any state [1]
U.S. [2]	**1,592,602**	**0.72**	**0.74**	MO	25,712	0.65	0.71
AL	26,392	0.59	0.83	MT	5,647	0.54	0.75
AK	1,313	0.91	0.48	NE	11,889	0.71	0.79
AZ	32,175	0.55	0.79	NV	11,941	0.87	0.77
AR	15,573	0.68	0.84	NH	7,537	0.39	0.43
CA	151,420	0.86	0.79	NJ	29,597	0.86	0.46
CO	28,333	0.72	0.69	NM	6,247	0.76	0.73
CT	19,738	0.52	0.45	NY	110,047	0.70	0.73
DE	6,935	0.56	0.64	NC	49,085	0.73	0.82
DC	8,638	0.05	0.19	ND	5,653	0.50	0.77
FL	106,346	0.85	0.86	OH	68,718	0.76	0.83
GA	59,787	0.83	0.80	OK	18,263	0.68	0.83
HI	4,132	0.59	0.45	OR	14,263	0.57	0.66
ID	10,095	0.52	0.71	PA	78,013	0.62	0.76
IL	43,929	0.73	0.52	RI	10,759	0.25	0.53
IN	44,849	0.66	0.84	SC	25,556	0.64	0.82
IA	18,337	0.54	0.79	SD	5,646	0.55	0.72
KS	14,263	0.65	0.74	TN	31,242	0.68	0.75
KY	23,029	0.71	0.83	TX	131,950	0.93	0.84
LA	25,629	0.78	0.86	UT	21,832	0.64	0.90
ME	6,963	0.51	0.62	VT	4,998	0.22	0.42
MD	18,879	0.68	0.47	VA	42,409	0.70	0.72
MA	48,596	0.51	0.58	WA	29,101	0.78	0.71
MI	48,476	0.81	0.85	WV	11,044	0.58	0.87
MN	23,207	0.73	0.58	WI	33,179	0.68	0.76
MS	10,180	0.55	0.77	WY	1,832	0.62	0.62

[1] Students residing in a particular state when admitted to an institution anywhere, either in their home state or another state. [2] Includes U.S. Service Academies (Air Force Academy, Coast Guard Academy, Merchant Marine Academy, Military Academy, and Naval Academy), not shown separately.

Source: U.S. National Center for Education Statistics, *Digest of Education Statistics*, "Latest version of all Digest tables," <nces.ed.gov/programs/digest>, accessed December 2023.

Table 307. Higher Education Public and Private Institutions—Average Charges: 1990 to 2023

[In current dollars. Estimated. For the entire academic year ending in year shown. Figures are average charges per full-time equivalent student. Room and board are based on full-time students]

Academic control and year	Tuition and required fees [1]			Dormitory room charges			Board rates [2]		
	All institutions	4 year institutions	2 year institutions	All institutions	4 year institutions	2 year institutions	All institutions	4 year institutions	2 year institutions
PUBLIC									
1990................	1,356	1,780	756	1,513	1,557	962	1,635	1,638	1,581
1995................	2,057	2,681	1,192	1,959	2,023	1,232	1,949	1,967	1,712
2000................	2,504	3,349	1,348	2,440	2,519	1,549	2,364	2,406	1,834
2005................	3,629	5,027	1,849	3,304	3,418	2,174	2,931	2,981	2,353
2010................	4,763	6,717	2,283	4,401	4,564	2,854	3,655	3,755	2,571
2015................	6,370	8,543	2,955	5,504	5,677	3,559	4,313	4,412	3,072
2020................	7,410	9,349	3,377	6,483	6,655	4,105	4,943	5,031	3,578
2021................	7,635	9,374	3,503	6,630	6,774	4,408	5,107	5,189	3,649
2022................	7,869	9,596	3,563	6,798	6,944	4,428	5,207	5,292	3,613
2023................	7,998	9,750	3,598	7,017	7,167	4,566	5,386	5,472	3,790
PRIVATE									
1990................	8,147	8,396	5,196	1,923	1,935	1,663	1,948	1,953	1,811
1995................	11,111	11,481	6,914	2,587	2,601	2,233	2,509	2,520	2,023
2000................	14,100	14,616	8,225	3,236	3,242	3,067	2,877	2,879	2,753
2005................	18,154	18,604	12,122	4,178	4,173	4,475	3,485	3,483	3,700
2010................	21,764	22,269	14,862	5,248	5,248	5,211	4,329	4,329	4,390
2015................	26,182	26,739	14,261	6,221	6,228	5,506	5,019	5,021	4,560
2020................	32,411	32,764	15,831	7,397	7,401	6,326	5,756	5,760	4,587
2021................	32,351	32,728	15,473	7,573	7,580	5,571	5,903	5,907	4,619
2022................	33,700	34,051	16,588	7,824	7,830	5,942	6,046	6,049	4,819
2023................	34,923	35,248	17,408	8,118	8,124	6,236	6,279	6,282	5,148

[1] Public institution's data are for in-state students. [2] Beginning 1990, rates reflect 20 meals per week, rather than meals served 7 days a week.

Source: U.S. National Center for Education Statistics, *Digest of Education Statistics*, "Latest version of all Digest tables," <nces.ed.gov/programs/digest>, accessed February 2024.

Table 308. Financial Aid Received by Undergraduate Students by Type of Aid and Selected Characteristics: 2020

[In units as indicated. For school year ending in 2020. Covers students enrolled in Title IV eligible postsecondary institutions in the 50 states, DC, and Puerto Rico. Based on the National Postsecondary Student Aid Study; see source for details]

Characteristic	Average total aid (dollars)	Average amount (dollars)					Percent of students receiving—		
		Total grants [1]	Total student loans [2]	Total work-study	Federal veterans education benefits [3]	Direct PLUS Loans to parents	Any aid	Any grants [1]	Any student loans [2]
Total.......................	**14,100**	**9,300**	**7,900**	**2,500**	**17,900**	**16,300**	**71.5**	**63.9**	**36.1**
Public institutions:									
Less than 2-year....................	6,700	4,800	6,300	(S)	(S)	(S)	56.1	47.0	[5] 17.5
2-year............................	5,400	4,100	4,800	2,800	13,500	5,700	56.7	51.9	12.4
4-year............................	13,200	8,400	7,700	2,700	17,200	15,300	74.8	65.4	39.9
Private nonprofit institutions:									
Less than 4-year....................	13,500	6,300	8,400	(S)	(S)	(S)	93.7	87.0	71.0
4-year............................	28,100	20,600	9,200	2,300	24,300	18,700	83.5	77.1	53.7
Private for-profit institutions:									
Less than 2-year....................	10,100	4,400	6,900	(S)	18,500	7,000	84.6	78.0	62.6
2-year............................	14,800	5,400	9,800	(S)	29,100	13,100	89.4	80.8	73.3
4-year............................	13,300	5,700	9,500	[5] 2,500	20,200	17,200	88.3	76.8	62.4
Attended more than one institution. ..	13,500	7,700	8,100	2,400	19,100	15,300	74.3	64.5	45.3
Non-Hispanic:									
American Indian or Alaska Native. ...	11,600	8,900	7,600	(S)	(S)	(S)	73.6	66.7	26.3
Asian.............................	17,300	13,000	8,900	2,700	22,300	20,800	65.5	59.7	26.3
Black.............................	13,700	8,300	7,400	2,500	13,900	14,300	80.6	73.8	48.9
Native Hawaiian or other Pacific Islander............................	10,300	6,200	7,400	(S)	(S)	(S)	73.9	64.7	35.8
White............................	14,500	9,300	8,200	2,400	17,900	16,200	70.4	61.0	38.2
Two or more races.................	15,700	9,800	8,200	2,300	20,300	18,600	67.9	60.1	36.2
Hispanic or Latino..................	11,900	8,500	7,500	2,500	19,100	15,500	72.1	67.2	27.4
Attendance:									
Full-time, full-year..................	19,900	13,600	9,000	2,500	23,700	17,300	81.3	72.9	45.5
Part-time or part-year...............	8,700	5,300	6,800	2,600	13,600	13,000	64.6	57.4	29.3
Dependency status: [4]									
Dependent students.................	20,900	14,900	8,400	2,400	23,300	17,300	80.9	73.4	44.8
Independent students...............	16,500	8,800	10,900	2,700	23,800	(X)	82.5	71.2	48.3

X Not applicable. S Reporting standards not met. [1] Includes grants, scholarships, or tuition wavers. [2] Student loans include only loans to students and may be from federal, state, institution, or private sources. Student loans do not include Direct PLUS Loans to parents or other forms of financing such as credit cards, home equity loans, or loans from individuals. [3] Federal veterans education benefits includes benefits to dependents. Amounts are based on Veterans Benefits Administration data. [4] Data shown for full-time, full year undergraduates. Independent students include those who are age 24 and over, as well as those who are under age 24 and who are married, have dependents, are veterans or on active duty, are orphans or wards of the courts, are homeless or at risk of homelessness, or were determined to be independent by a financial aid officer using professional judgment. Other students under the age of 24 are considered to be dependent. [5] Interpret data with caution. The coefficient of variation is between 30 and 50 percent.

Source: U.S. Department of Education, National Center for Education Statistics, *2019-20 National Postsecondary Student Aid Study (NPSAS:20): First Look at Student Financial Aid Estimates for 2019-20*, July 2023. See also <nces.ed.gov/surveys/npsas>.

Table 309. Average Cost of Attendance for Undergraduate Education by Control of Institution, Living Arrangement, and Type of Cost: 2020 and 2023

[In current dollars. For school year ending in year shown. Data shown are for first time, full-time undergraduate students in degree-granting postsecondary institutions. Based on data from the Integrated Postsecondary Education Data System (IPEDS). See source for more information]

Level of institution, living arrangement, and type of cost	2020				2023			
	All institutions	Public, in-state [1]	Private, non-profit	Private, for-profit	All institutions	Public, in-state [1]	Private, non-profit	Private, for-profit
4-YEAR INSTITUTIONS								
By living arrangement:								
On campus	34,830	25,145	53,457	33,349	38,270	27,146	58,628	33,574
Off campus, living with family	24,186	14,726	42,415	23,443	26,527	15,708	46,280	23,885
Off campus, not living with family	34,534	25,242	53,308	31,778	38,197	27,756	57,519	34,071
By type of cost:								
Tuition and required fees	18,595	9,102	36,927	17,853	20,727	9,834	40,713	18,241
Books and supplies	1,276	1,296	1,250	1,063	1,212	1,220	1,215	990
Room, board, and other expenses:								
On campus								
Room and board	11,780	11,291	12,543	9,363	12,917	12,302	13,842	9,151
Other	3,180	3,457	2,738	5,069	3,413	3,790	2,858	5,192
Off campus, living with family								
Other	4,315	4,328	4,239	4,527	4,588	4,654	4,352	4,654
Off campus, not living with family								
Room and board	10,227	10,580	10,019	8,368	11,464	11,983	10,876	9,564
Other	4,437	4,264	5,112	4,493	4,794	4,720	4,715	5,276
2-YEAR INSTITUTIONS								
By living arrangement:								
On campus	16,265	15,674	33,992	27,076	17,439	16,641	36,026	26,640
Off campus, living with family	9,983	9,589	24,570	21,114	10,748	10,199	25,200	22,208
Off campus, not living with family	19,542	19,162	34,129	30,250	21,430	20,910	36,426	32,352
By type of cost:								
Tuition and required fees	4,196	3,799	18,656	15,510	4,584	4,027	19,517	16,301
Books and supplies	1,545	1,552	1,007	1,427	1,463	1,467	930	1,501
Room, board, and other expenses:								
On campus								
Room and board	7,240	6,989	11,893	9,220	7,717	7,420	12,732	7,920
Other	3,284	3,335	2,437	919	3,675	3,728	2,847	918
Off campus, living with family								
Other	4,242	4,239	4,907	4,177	4,701	4,705	4,753	4,406
Off campus, not living with family								
Room and board	9,478	9,519	9,904	8,262	10,667	10,738	10,397	9,434
Other	4,323	4,292	4,562	5,051	4,716	4,678	5,582	5,116

[1] Tuition and fees at public institutions are the lower of either in-district or in-state tuition and fees.

Source: U.S. National Center for Education Statistics, *Digest of Education Statistics*, "Latest version of all Digest tables," <nces.ed.gov/programs/digest/>, accessed May 2024.

Table 310. Bachelor's Degree Recipients with Loans and Amount Borrowed in Constant (2009) Dollars by Selected Characteristics: 2001 to 2017

[For first-time Bachelor's degree recipients 1 year after they complete their degrees. Estimates cover students who were enrolled in Title IV eligible postsecondary institutions in the 50 states, D.C., and Puerto Rico. Based on Baccalaureate and Beyond Longitudinal Studies]

Characteristic	Percent with loans			Average cumulative amount borrowed for undergraduate education (2009 dollars)		
	2001 [2]	2009	2017	2001 [2]	2009	2017
Total loans	**63.5**	**65.6**	**67.4**	**21,800**	**24,700**	**30,500**
Sex:						
Male	62.5	62.9	63.7	21,300	23,900	29,800
Female	64.3	67.6	70.3	22,100	25,200	31,000
Race/ethnicity: [1]						
White	62.2	64.6	66.8	21,700	24,500	30,500
Black	78.8	80.3	85.9	25,200	28,700	36,900
Hispanic	66.7	67.0	69.7	19,900	22,800	26,900
Asian	55.5	53.4	45.4	19,100	21,000	24,600
Other	62.8	68.8	70.4	21,500	25,600	30,300
Age at receipt of bachelor's degree:						
18 to 23	60.0	61.0	62.4	20,800	23,700	27,400
24 to 29	71.3	76.8	73.4	23,100	24,900	33,100
30 and older	65.7	72.5	82.0	23,000	28,300	37,700
Institution type:						
2-year or less:						
Public 2-year	67.8	67.5	71.1	21,500	24,500	30,600
Other 2-year or less	64.6	85.0	85.6	24,500	31,600	38,300
4-year:						
Public	59.5	62.1	64.1	20,100	21,900	28,600
Private nonprofit	69.0	69.4	66.4	24,100	27,900	31,200
For-profit	77.3	87.7	84.1	27,400	36,000	42,700

[1] Asian includes Pacific Islander and Native Hawaiian. Other includes American Indian, Alaska Native, and graduates of two or more races or a race not listed. Excludes persons of Hispanic origin, unless specified. [2] Includes loans from family and friends.

Source: National Center for Education Statistics, *Trends in Debt for Bachelor's Degree Recipients a Year After Graduation: 1994, 2001, and 2009*, December 2012; and *Baccalaureate and Beyond (B&B:16/17): A First Look at the Employment and Educational Experiences of College Graduates, 1 Year Later*, June 2019. See also <nces.ed.gov/surveys/b&b>.

Table 311. Voluntary Financial Support of Higher Education: 1990 to 2023

[9,800 represents $9,800,000,000. For school years ending in years shown. Voluntary support, as defined in Gift Reporting Standards, excludes income from endowment and other invested funds as well as all support received from federal, state, and local governments and their agencies, and contract research]

Item	Unit	1990	2000	2010	2015	2020	2021	2022 [1]	2023 [1]
Estimated support, total....................	**Mil. dol.**	**9,800**	**23,200**	**28,000**	**40,300**	**49,500**	**52,900**	**59,500**	**58,000**
SOURCES OF SUPPORT									
Individuals, total.............................	Mil. dol.	4,770	12,220	12,020	18,850	19,690	21,050	23,000	20,500
Alumni...	Mil. dol.	2,540	6,800	7,100	10,850	11,060	12,250	13,500	12,000
Nonalumni individuals......................	Mil. dol.	2,230	5,420	4,920	8,000	8,630	8,800	9,500	8,500
Organizations, total........................	Mil. dol.	5,030	10,980	15,675	21,450	29,810	31,850	36,500	37,500
Corporations................................	Mil. dol.	2,170	4,150	4,730	5,750	6,630	7,000	(NA)	(NA)
Foundations.................................	Mil. dol.	1,920	5,080	8,400	11,600	16,440	17,500	(NA)	(NA)
Other organizations........................	Mil. dol.	940	1,750	2,545	4,100	6,740	7,350	(NA)	(NA)
PURPOSES OF SUPPORT									
Current operations, total....................	Mil. dol.	5,440	11,270	17,000	24,650	30,500	32,300	34,250	35,000
Capital purposes............................	Mil. dol.	4,360	11,930	11,000	15,650	19,000	20,600	25,250	23,000
Institutions reporting support.................	Number	1,056	945	996	983	873	864	826	757
Total support reported......................	Mil. dol.	8,214	19,419	23,487	35,082	38,263	41,481	45,844	42,791
Private 4-year institutions.................	Mil. dol.	5,072	11,047	12,189	17,944	19,709	20,854	22,852	21,946
Public 4-year institutions.................	Mil. dol.	3,056	8,254	11,114	14,876	18,365	20,314	22,712	20,643
2-year colleges.............................	Mil. dol.	85	117	185	192	189	314	280	201

NA Not available. [1] Implementation of new Council for Advancement and Support of Education (CASE) Global Reporting Standards; use caution when comparing data to prior years. See source for details.

Source: Council for Advancement and Support of Education, Washington, DC, *CASE Insights on Voluntary Support of Education* ©, annual. See also <www.case.org>.

Table 312. Undergraduate Students Who Received a Pell Grant by Selected Characteristics: 2008 to 2020

[In units as indicated. For school year ending in year shown. Data shown for students enrolled in Title IV eligible postsecondary institutions in the 50 States, the District of Columbia, and Puerto Rico. Based on the National Postsecondary Student-Aid Study; see source for details]

Institutional and student characteristics	2008		2012 [1]		2016		2020	
	Percent	Average amount (dollars)	Percent	Average amount (dollars)	Percent	Average amount (dollars)	Percent	Average amount (dollars)
Total.................................	**27.8**	**2,500**	**41.3**	**3,400**	**39.1**	**3,700**	**40.2**	**4,100**
SEX								
Male......................................	21.9	2,600	36.5	3,400	34.0	3,700	34.2	4,100
Female....................................	32.2	2,500	44.8	3,400	43.1	3,700	44.6	4,100
Genderqueer, non-conforming, or different gender identity..........	(NA)	(NA)	(NA)	(NA)	(NA)	(NA)	34.1	4,000
RACE/ETHNICITY [2]								
White......................................	20.9	2,400	33.5	3,300	31.5	3,600	32.1	3,900
Black......................................	46.0	2,600	61.9	3,400	57.7	3,700	59.5	4,200
Asian/Pacific Islander...................	23.3	2,800	33.8	3,800	(NA)	(NA)	(NA)	(NA)
Asian.....................................	(NA)	(NA)	(NA)	(NA)	30.9	4,200	33.7	4,700
Native Hawaiian/ Other Pacific Islander..............	(NA)	(NA)	(NA)	(NA)	35.6	4,100	39.0	3,900
American Indian/Alaska Native......	36.0	2,500	54.0	3,400	51.1	3,500	45.3	4,100
Other or two or more races..........	31.1	2,600	45.2	3,500	42.2	3,800	38.9	4,000
Hispanic.................................	39.8	2,700	50.0	3,500	46.9	3,900	49.5	4,200
ATTENDANCE STATUS								
Full-time, full-year......................	33.6	3,300	47.1	4,400	44.7	4,700	38.8	5,300
Part-time, full-year......................	(NA)	(NA)	(NA)	(NA)	44.0	3,500	(NA)	(NA)
Part-time or part-year..................	24.4	1,900	37.6	2,600	(NA)	(NA)	41.3	3,300
TYPE OF INSTITUTION								
Public 4-year............................	26.2	2,800	38.0	3,800	38.2	4,100	39.1	4,400
Private nonprofit 4-year...............	26.8	2,900	35.8	3,700	36.4	4,000	36.1	4,400
Public 2-year............................	21.1	2,300	37.7	3,000	33.5	3,300	36.9	3,600
EMPLOYMENT STATUS [3]								
Not employed............................	31.0	2,700	44.7	3,500	41.7	3,900	(NA)	(NA)
Employed part-time....................	29.2	2,600	41.4	3,500	38.3	3,800	(NA)	(NA)
Employed full-time.....................	23.4	2,200	36.2	3,000	36.4	3,300	(NA)	(NA)

NA Not available. [1] 2012 excludes Puerto Rico. [2] Data by race are for persons of non-Hispanic origin. Persons of Hispanic origin may be of any race. [3] For 2000 to 2012, employment also includes work-study, assistantships, and traineeships. Data for 2016 exclude students who worked in school-related jobs such as work-study and assistantships, and jobs worked while not enrolled in classes. Full-time work is defined as 35 or more hours per week, and part-time work is defined as less than 35 hours.

Source: U.S. Department of Education, National Center for Education Statistics, *Trends in Pell Grant Receipt and the Characteristics of Pell Grant Recipients: Selected Years, 1999–2000 to 2011–12*, September 2015; *Student Financing of Undergraduate Education in 2015-16: Financial Aid by Types and Source*, March 2019; and *First Look at Student Financial Aid Estimates for 2019-20*, July 2023. See also <nces.ed.gov/surveys/npsas>.

Table 313. Undergraduate Student Receipt of Financial Aid by Source and Type of Institution Attended: 2020

[In percent. For school year ending in 2020. Covers students enrolled in Title IV eligible postsecondary institutions in the 50 states, DC, and Puerto Rico. Based on the National Postsecondary Student-Aid Study; see source for details]

Type of institution	Total [1]	Source of aid							
		Federal [2]				State [3]		Institutional [4]	
		Any aid	Any grants	Any student loans	Any work-study	Any aid	Any grants	Any aid	Any grants
Total	**71.5**	**55.0**	**40.7**	**34.3**	**4.4**	**22.9**	**22.5**	**27.7**	**27.5**
Institution attended:									
Public 2-year	56.7	41.6	37.2	11.3	1.4	22.8	22.4	8.8	8.8
Public 4-year	74.8	56.9	39.6	38.2	4.1	29.2	28.9	33.5	33.4
Private nonprofit 4-year	83.5	62.8	36.7	51.3	14.0	18.3	18.1	57.1	57.0
Private for-profit less-than-2-year	84.6	81.3	75.7	59.7	(S)	[5] 8.5	[5] 7.4	[5] 7.4	[5] 7.2
Private for-profit 2-year	89.4	85.1	76.1	70.3	(S)	9.7	9.6	[5] 11.6	[5] 9.5
Private for-profit 4-year	88.3	73.3	59.2	60.3	[5] 0.7	[5] 3.4	[5] 3.1	26.9	26.6

S Does not meet publication standards. [1] Excludes aid from parents, friends, or relatives, and federal tax credits for education. Includes Direct PLUS Loans to parents and aid from Veterans' benefits and job training grants. Excludes emergency aid related to COVID-19 pandemic. [2] Includes federal grants, loans, work-study awards, and federal loans including Direct PLUS loans to parents. Includes aid from programs in Title IV of the Higher Education Act, and aid from other federal sources. Excludes federal veterans' benefits and education tax credits and tax deduction benefits. [3] Includes all grants and scholarships, loans, and work-study provided by state governments, including vocational rehabilitation and job training grants funded by the federal Workforce Investment Opportunity Act (WIOA). [4] Includes all institution need- and merit-based grants, scholarships, tuition waivers, loans, and work-study assistance. [5] Interpret data with caution. The standard error is between 30 and 50 percent.

Source: U.S. Department of Education, National Center for Education Statistics, *2019-20 National Postsecondary Student Aid Study (NPSAS:20): First Look at Student Financial Aid Estimates for 2019-20,* July 2023. See also <nces.ed.gov/surveys/npsas>.

Table 314. Graduate Students Receiving Financial Aid and Amount Received by Type of Aid and Selected Institutional and Student Characteristics: 2020

[For school year ending in 2020. Students may receive more than one type of aid. Estimates include students enrolled in Title IV eligible postsecondary institutions in the 50 states, the District of Columbia, and Puerto Rico. Based on the National Postsecondary Student-Aid Study (NPSAS); see source for details]

Program and student characteristics	Percent of graduate students receiving aid							Total aid received per student [1] (dollars)
	Any aid [1]	Grants			Any graduate assistant-ships [4]	Student loans		
		Any grants [2]	Employer aid [3]			Any loans [5]	Direct Unsub-sidized Loans	Direct PLUS Loans
Total	**73.9**	**43.0**	**13.0**	**12.0**	**42.2**	**39.1**	**11.1**	**25,300**
Graduate program type:								
Master's degree	72.0	40.7	16.4	5.7	45.5	42.1	7.9	19,700
Doctoral, research/scholarship	78.9	50.8	8.0	40.4	19.1	16.7	4.1	27,300
Doctoral, professional practice	85.2	47.0	3.6	2.1	71.6	68.8	39.6	47,500
Doctoral, other	74.7	34.0	10.3	8.3	52.0	47.7	19.5	27,200
Other and nondegree	54.6	35.7	18.6	[9] 1.8	25.4	21.6	1.7	11,100
Control and level of institution:								
Public 4-year	73.7	46.7	12.2	18.3	36.4	33.6	8.2	22,000
Non-doctorate-granting	57.2	31.8	14.5	3.4	35.9	34.6	[9] 1.2	11,400
Doctorate-granting	75.0	47.8	12.1	19.4	36.5	33.6	8.7	22,700
Private nonprofit 4-year	74.0	41.4	13.7	8.5	43.6	40.4	15.2	30,800
Non-doctorate-granting	71.7	43.1	18.8	[9] 3.0	45.2	42.2	5.3	15,200
Doctorate-granting	74.3	41.1	13.0	9.2	43.4	40.2	16.4	32,800
Private for-profit 4-year	74.4	37.5	13.8	(S)	58.8	54.0	6.4	16,700
Attended more than one institution [6]	73.0	34.6	12.9	5.9	52.3	49.2	12.4	22,400
Attendance pattern: [7]								
Full-time/full-year	83.3	48.0	7.4	18.2	49.5	46.3	18.1	33,900
Part-time or part-year	64.6	38.2	18.5	5.9	35.2	32.1	4.4	14,400
Race/ethnicity: [8]								
American Indian or Alaska Native	62.8	[9] 39.5	(S)	(S)	[9] 39.5	[9] 35.8	(S)	19,000
Asian	66.8	41.8	7.6	20.2	27.2	21.4	10	31,400
Black	80.8	39.8	12.2	7.6	60.3	57.2	13	23,700
Native Hawaiian or Other Pacific Islander	59.9	[9] 41.0	[9] 12.2	(S)	38.5	38.5	(S)	25,700
White	73.2	43.7	15.5	10.7	40.8	38.2	11.4	24,100
Hispanic or Latino	82.4	45.5	12.3	12.2	52.0	49.3	10.6	23,600

S Figure does not meet publication standards. [1] Includes all types of financial aid from any source except parents, friends, or relatives. Types of aid such as federal veterans education benefits and job training funds are included, but federal tax credits for education are not included. [2] Includes grants, scholarships, or tuition waivers from federal, state, institution, or private sources, including employers. [3] Excludes tuition waivers to students holding assistantships. [4] Teaching assistantships are funded by institutions, but research assistantship funds may come from any source. [5] Includes only loans to students and may be from any source but exclude other forms of financing such as credit cards, home equity loans, and loans from individuals. [6] Students who attended more than one institution during the 2019–20 academic year are included in a separate category because they may have received financial aid from an institution other than the NPSAS sample institution. [7] Full-time/full-year students were enrolled full time for 9 or more months between July 1, 2019, and June 30, 2020. Part-time or part-year students may have been enrolled full time for fewer than 9 months (full-time/part-year), enrolled for 9 or more months part time (part-time/full-year), or enrolled part time for fewer than 9 months (part-time/part-year). [8] Data by race are for persons of non-Hispanic origin. Persons of Hispanic origin may be of any race. [9] Interpret data with caution. Standard error is between 30% and 50%.

Source: U.S. Department of Education, National Center for Education Statistics, *2019–20 National Postsecondary Student Aid Study (NPSAS:20): First Look at Student Financial Aid Estimates for 2019–20,* July 2023. See also <nces.ed.gov/surveys/npsas>.

Table 315. State and Local Financial Support for Higher Education by State: 2023

[10,245.3 represents 10,245,300. For fiscal year ending in 2023. Educational appropriations include State and local appropriations for general operating expenses of public postsecondary education. Includes state-funded financial aid to students attending in-state public institutions and federal stimulus funds. Excludes appropriations for independent institutions, financial aid for students attending independent institutions, research, hospitals, and medical education. FTE is full-time equivalent]

State	FTE enroll- ment [2] (1,000)	Educational appropri- ations per FTE enrollment [3] (dollars)	Net tuition revenue per FTE enrollment [3, 4] (dollars)	State	FTE enroll- ment [2] (1,000)	Educational appropri- ations per FTE enrollment [3] (dollars)	Net tuition revenue per FTE enrollment [3, 4] (dollars)
Total U.S. [1] ...	10,245.3	11,040	7,353	MO.............	143.4	9,688	8,838
AL.............	197.4	14,549	15,062	MT.............	33.8	7,213	7,878
AK.............	12.1	20,160	5,140	NE.............	71.2	13,046	7,034
AZ.............	305.0	7,103	9,769	NV.............	74.0	8,590	2,980
AR.............	103.6	9,859	8,036	NH.............	30.0	3,990	9,961
CA.............	1,547.9	11,801	2,717	NJ.............	242.3	9,635	7,671
CO.............	176.0	6,603	12,123	NM.............	73.1	21,953	3,395
CT.............	89.3	14,862	9,067	NY.............	445.7	14,816	6,457
DE.............	36.1	6,816	19,338	NC.............	393.8	12,961	5,301
DC.............	2.9	25,834	4,115	ND.............	32.2	8,813	10,326
FL.............	561.0	10,029	2,461	OH.............	349.1	7,669	10,404
GA.............	348.5	13,911	5,309	OK.............	119.5	8,500	9,738
HI.............	31.9	16,672	4,846	OR.............	123.7	8,412	9,704
ID.............	54.3	12,655	8,912	PA.............	291.7	7,327	11,264
IL.............	278.5	22,590	8,896	RI.............	28.5	6,900	9,991
IN.............	238.2	7,201	11,768	SC.............	170.2	7,728	11,143
IA.............	115.1	6,981	11,319	SD.............	30.7	9,644	9,745
KS.............	118.9	9,859	7,344	TN.............	175.7	15,422	7,181
KY.............	135.4	10,236	9,472	TX.............	1,007.0	10,335	7,985
LA.............	159.0	7,628	6,034	UT.............	129.1	10,956	7,139
ME.............	32.3	9,453	6,122	VT.............	19.3	5,649	16,728
MD.............	216.0	11,452	8,028	VA.............	289.8	9,112	9,134
MA.............	139.1	11,972	5,636	WA.............	201.5	11,233	6,690
MI.............	324.7	10,490	16,644	WV.............	57.7	7,654	8,314
MN.............	159.0	9,746	10,637	WI.............	195.1	9,814	7,922
MS.............	117.3	9,159	8,787	WY.............	20.9	18,531	4,308

[1] Does not include data for the District of Columbia. [2] Full-time equivalent enrollment converts student credit hours to full-time, academic year students, and excludes medical students. Data for Arkansas, Oklahoma, and Pennsylvania are estimated. [3] State and local appropriations for general operating expenses of public postsecondary education. Includes state-funded financial aid to students attending in-state public institutions and federal stimulus funding. Excludes appropriations for independent institutions, financial aid for students attending independent institutions, research, hospitals, and medical education. [4] Net tuition revenue is the gross amount of tuition and fees, less financial aid, tuition waivers or discounts, and medical student tuition and fees. Includes revenue used for capital debt service.

Source: State Higher Education Executive Officers, Boulder, CO, *State Higher Education Finance: FY2023* ©, 2024. See also <shef.sheeo.org/>.

Table 316. Higher Education Price Indexes: 2010 to 2023 ©

[1983=100. For years ending June 30. The Higher Education Price Index (HEPI), calculated for the July-June academic fiscal year, reflects prices paid by colleges and universities for the following eight cost factors: faculty salaries, administrative salaries, clerical and service employees, fringe benefits, miscellaneous services, supplies and materials, and utilities. In 2015, the American Association of University Professors (AAUP) began using a new methodology to calculate salary and total compensation that was not directly comparable with the past. Further adjustments were made to the data for FY2022 and data for fiscal years 2015-2022 have been restated to account for the change and make the data compatible with past reporting. Minus sign (-) indicates decrease]

Item and year	Total	Personnel compensation					Contracted services, supplies, and equipment		
		Faculty salaries	Admin- istrative salaries	Clerical salaries	Service employ- ees salaries	Fringe benefits	Miscel- laneous services	Supplies and materials	Utilities
INDEXES									
2010......................	281.8	280.6	337.6	255.2	230.0	402.8	255.8	179.3	193.6
2015......................	312.9	306.4	381.9	280.4	248.4	484.0	279.8	190.7	183.5
2017......................	327.4	326.0	405.2	297.3	262.7	501.6	290.7	180.1	167.8
2018......................	336.1	333.6	414.1	305.9	271.6	516.3	297.8	187.9	170.7
2019......................	346.0	342.2	424.1	316.6	282.5	534.1	304.8	195.6	172.3
2020......................	352.7	351.4	430.3	326.6	293.9	549.6	313.2	188.8	145.3
2021......................	362.3	354.7	437.2	335.7	306.6	572.2	319.3	195.4	167.0
2022......................	381.1	362.1	449.8	353.2	332.9	587.3	332.9	237.5	239.0
2023 [1]	396.2	376.8	468.1	370.7	354.2	603.6	349.2	257.3	230.1
ANNUAL PERCENT CHANGE [2]									
2010......................	0.9	1.2	2.0	1.4	1.4	2.1	1.1	-1.3	-9.5
2015......................	2.0	1.8	4.2	2.1	2.6	5.6	2.1	-4.8	-13.2
2017......................	3.0	2.5	3.0	2.8	3.7	2.8	1.7	0.3	14.5
2018......................	2.6	2.3	2.2	2.9	3.4	2.9	2.4	4.3	1.7
2019......................	3.0	2.6	2.4	3.5	4.0	3.5	2.4	4.1	0.9
2020......................	1.9	2.7	1.5	3.2	4.0	2.9	2.8	-3.5	-15.7
2021......................	2.7	1.0	1.6	2.8	4.3	4.1	2.0	3.5	15.0
2022......................	5.2	2.1	2.9	5.2	8.6	2.6	4.3	21.5	43.1
2023 [1]	4.0	4.0	4.1	5.0	6.4	2.8	4.9	7.3	-3.7

[1] As of FY2023, HEPI incorporates an amended materials category. [2] Percent change from immediate prior year.

Source: The Commonfund Institute, Wilton, CT ©. See also <www.commonfund.org>.

Table 317. Average Salaries for College Faculty Members: 2022 to 2024

[In dollars. For academic year ending in year shown. Figures are for 9 months teaching for full-time faculty members in 2-year and 4-year institutions. Data are based on the American Association of University Professors (AAUP) Faculty Compensation Survey; the number of institutions reporting salary data varies from year to year]

Type of control and academic rank	2022	2023	2024	Type of control and academic rank	2022	2023	2024
Public: All ranks [1]	**98,745**	**103,190**	**106,726**	**Private: All ranks [1,2]**	**127,366**	**132,225**	**137,889**
Professor	134,580	140,426	145,112	Professor	181,490	188,375	196,353
Associate professor	95,764	100,126	104,179	Associate professor	110,651	115,557	120,631
Assistant professor	83,562	87,287	90,309	Assistant professor	96,657	100,610	105,491
Instructor	58,064	62,538	65,742	Instructor	74,566	76,925	79,079

[1] Includes other ranks not shown separately. [2] Excludes religiously-affiliated colleges and universities.

Source: American Association of University Professors, Washington, DC, *The Annual Report on the Economic Status of the Profession* © 2024. See also <www.aaup.org>.

Table 318. Employees in Higher Education Institutions by Employment Status, Sex, and Occupation: 2021

[In thousands (3,817.2 represents 3,817,200). As of Fall. Covers institutions that grant associate's or higher degrees and that participate in Title IV federal financial aid programs. Includes institutions with fewer than 15 full-time employees. Detail may not sum to totals because of rounding. Based on Integrated Postsecondary Education Data System data]

Primary occupation	Full-time and part-time				Full-time		Part-time	
	Total	Male	Female		Male	Female	Male	Female
			Total	Percent				
All institutions	**3,817.2**	**1,690.6**	**2,126.6**	**55.7**	**1,109.8**	**1,420.8**	**580.8**	**705.9**
Faculty	1,499.2	732.4	766.8	51.1	435.1	402.0	297.3	364.8
Instruction	1,370.2	663.4	706.9	51.6	374.2	350.9	289.2	355.9
Research	95.9	53.5	42.4	44.3	48.3	37.5	5.1	5.0
Public service	33.1	15.6	17.5	52.9	12.6	13.6	2.9	3.9
Graduate assistants [1]	392.3	194.2	198.1	50.5	(X)	(X)	194.2	198.1
Librarians, curators, and archivists	37.3	11.2	26.1	69.9	9.8	22.4	1.4	3.7
Student and academic affairs, and other education services	172.9	53.5	119.4	69.1	34.9	88.3	18.6	31.2
Management	266.0	111.7	154.4	58.0	109.2	150.7	2.5	3.6
Business and financial operations	227.8	61.8	166.0	72.9	58.7	157.9	3.0	8.1
Computer, engineering, and science	239.2	140.8	98.4	41.1	133.7	89.3	7.1	9.1
Community, social service, legal, arts, design, entertainment, sports, and media	191.7	84.0	107.7	56.2	68.6	91.8	15.4	15.9
Healthcare practitioners and technicians	115.2	33.3	81.9	71.1	29.1	69.3	4.2	12.5
Service occupations	218.1	123.8	94.3	43.2	108.0	80.8	15.8	13.5
Sales and related occupations	10.4	3.6	6.9	65.9	3.0	5.8	0.5	1.1
Office and administrative support	363.2	65.0	298.2	82.1	48.5	255.7	16.5	42.5
Natural resources, construction, and maintenance	67.0	61.5	5.5	8.2	59.2	4.5	2.3	1.0
Production, transportation, and material moving	16.9	13.9	3.0	17.9	11.9	2.3	2.0	0.7

X Not applicable. [1] By definition, all graduate assistants are part time.

Source: U.S. National Center for Education Statistics, *Digest of Education Statistics*, "Latest version of all Digest tables," <nces.ed.gov/programs/digest>, accessed December 2023.

Table 319. Faculty in Institutions of Higher Education: 1980 to 2022

[In thousands (686 represents 686,000), except percent. As of Fall. Beginning in 1997, data reflect a new classification of institutions; this classification includes some additional, primarily 2-year, colleges and excludes a few institutions that did not award degrees. Includes institutions that were eligible to participate in Title IV federal financial aid programs. Includes schools accredited by the National Association of Trade and Technical Schools. Based on complete census; see source]

Year	Total	Employment status		Control		Level		Percent		
		Full-time	Part-time	Public	Private	4-year	2-year or less	Part-time	Public	2-year or less
1980 [1]	686	450	236	495	191	494	192	34.4	72.2	28.0
1985 [1]	715	459	256	503	212	504	211	35.8	70.3	29.5
1991 [2]	826	536	291	581	245	591	235	35.2	70.3	28.4
1995	932	551	381	657	275	647	285	40.9	70.5	30.6
1999	1,038	593	444	719	319	719	318	42.8	69.3	30.7
2001	1,113	618	495	771	342	764	349	44.5	69.3	31.4
2003	1,174	630	544	792	382	814	359	46.3	67.5	30.6
2005	1,290	676	615	841	449	917	373	47.6	65.2	28.9
2007 [3]	1,372	704	668	877	495	992	379	48.7	63.9	27.6
2009	1,439	729	710	914	525	1,038	401	49.3	63.5	27.8
2011	1,524	762	762	954	570	1,116	409	50.0	62.6	26.8
2013	1,545	791	754	969	577	1,152	394	48.8	62.7	25.5
2015	1,552	807	745	971	581	1,181	372	48.0	62.6	23.9
2016	1,546	814	732	974	572	1,197	349	47.4	63.0	22.6
2017	1,546	823	723	973	573	1,209	337	46.8	62.9	21.8
2018	1,543	832	711	982	561	1,216	327	46.1	63.6	21.2
2019	1,549	844	705	984	565	1,234	315	45.5	63.5	20.3
2020	1,490	837	653	941	548	1,209	281	43.8	63.2	18.8
2021	1,499	837	662	945	554	1,225	274	44.2	63.0	18.3
2022	1,508	842	665	947	561	1,242	265	44.1	62.8	17.6

[1] Estimated on the basis of enrollment. [2] Beginning 1987, data are not comparable to prior years. [3] Beginning in 2007, data include institutions with fewer than 15 full-time employees; these institutions did not report staff data prior to 2007.

Source: U.S. National Center for Education Statistics, *Digest of Education Statistics*, "Latest version of all Digest tables," <nces.ed.gov/programs/digest>, accessed May 2024.

Table 320. Starting Salaries for New College Graduates by Degree and Field of Study: 2015 to 2023

[In dollars. Data are actual starting base salaries. Data are reported by a representative sample of colleges throughout the United States]

Field of study	Bachelor's			Master's [1]			Doctorate		
	2015	2020	2023	2015	2020	2023	2015	2020	2023
Accounting..................	51,426	54,809	65,086	54,721	56,791	68,052	(NA)	(NA)	[3] 84,680
Business administration/ management [2]..............	49,494	54,392	63,535	73,951	82,372	95,808	[3] 123,162	118,429	104,982
Marketing..................	43,678	48,610	56,571	66,537	59,238	67,555	(NA)	(NA)	(NA)
Engineering:									
Civil...........................	57,368	62,249	69,106	58,290	68,415	77,175	[3] 60,464	72,632	87,604
Chemical....................	65,782	72,713	75,980	64,140	74,399	86,307	75,743	95,334	118,994
Computer....................	68,820	85,996	95,892	87,546	109,343	117,738	[3] 105,400	134,111	131,877
Electrical....................	67,593	80,819	87,513	86,218	99,769	108,475	95,373	115,013	119,827
Mechanical.................	[3] 62,239	69,278	75,512	66,786	82,459	91,725	79,664	97,206	111,759
Nuclear [4]..................	54,351	[3] 68,742	[3] 79,167	[3] 56,643	[3] 82,867	[3] 94,769	[3] 73,480	[3] 100,824	[3] 87,572
Petroleum..................	74,996	87,989	95,229	(NA)	[3] 84,600	[3] 74,800	(NA)	[3] 110,000	(NA)
Chemistry...................	41,832	44,981	54,406	[3] 51,908	60,485	[3] 56,944	63,091	70,518	93,341
Mathematics...............	56,440	64,244	73,307	72,976	70,513	[3] 67,928	[3] 79,250	76,050	73,802
Physics......................	56,403	63,600	67,728	[3] 65,875	58,715	[3] 105,908	66,601	72,758	85,569
Humanities.................	52,990	52,010	62,216	[3] 47,583	66,858	77,226	68,216	[3] 62,579	95,430
Social sciences [5]...............	40,964	50,298	60,343	50,705	62,185	71,202	65,101	85,458	93,246
Computer science.......	75,191	85,766	102,033	90,934	107,193	118,284	100,726	129,821	144,633

NA Not available. [1] Candidates with 1 year or less of full-time nonmilitary employment. [2] For master's degree, starting salaries are after nontechnical undergraduate degree. [3] Fewer than 50 salaries reported. [4] Includes engineering physics. [5] Excludes economics.

Source: National Association of Colleges and Employers, Bethlehem, PA ©. Reprinted with permission from Fall 2010-2014, Spring 2015-2019, and Summer 2020-2024 Salary Surveys. All rights reserved.

Table 321. Degrees Earned by Level and Sex: 1960 to 2022

[In thousands (477 represents 477,000), except percent. Based on data from the Integrated Postsecondary Education Data System (IPEDS)]

Year ending	All degrees		Associate's		Bachelor's		Master's		Doctoral [1]	
	Total	Percent male	Male	Female	Male	Female	Male	Female	Male	Female
1960..............	477	65.8	(NA)	(NA)	[2] 254	[2] 138	51	24	9	1
1970..............	1,271	59.2	117	89	451	341	131	83	54	6
1975..............	1,666	56.0	191	169	505	418	166	131	71	14
1980..............	1,731	51.1	184	217	474	456	157	148	70	26
1990..............	1,940	46.6	191	264	492	560	158	172	64	40
1991..............	2,025	45.8	199	283	504	590	161	182	64	41
1992..............	2,108	45.6	207	297	521	616	166	192	67	43
1993..............	2,167	45.5	212	303	533	632	173	202	67	45
1994..............	2,206	45.1	215	315	532	637	181	212	67	46
1995..............	2,218	44.9	218	321	526	634	183	221	67	47
1996..............	2,248	44.2	220	336	522	642	183	229	67	48
1997..............	2,288	43.6	224	347	521	652	185	240	68	50
1998..............	2,298	43.2	218	341	520	664	189	247	67	52
1999..............	2,330	42.7	221	344	520	682	190	256	65	51
2000..............	2,385	42.6	225	340	530	708	196	267	65	54
2001..............	2,416	42.4	232	347	532	712	198	276	64	55
2002..............	2,494	42.2	238	357	550	742	203	285	63	57
2003..............	2,623	42.1	253	381	573	776	215	304	63	59
2004..............	2,757	41.8	260	406	596	804	233	331	64	62
2005..............	2,852	41.6	268	429	613	827	237	343	67	67
2006..............	2,936	41.3	270	443	631	855	242	358	69	69
2007..............	3,008	41.2	275	453	650	875	242	368	71	73
2008..............	3,094	41.2	283	467	668	896	250	381	73	76
2009..............	3,205	41.3	298	489	685	916	264	399	76	79
2010..............	3,351	41.2	323	526	707	943	275	418	77	82
2011..............	3,554	41.3	361	582	734	982	292	439	80	84
2012..............	3,740	41.3	393	628	766	1,026	302	453	83	88
2013..............	3,775	41.4	389	618	787	1,053	302	450	85	90
2014..............	3,807	41.5	391	614	802	1,068	303	452	86	92
2015..............	3,847	41.6	397	618	813	1,082	307	452	85	94
2016..............	3,893	41.6	392	616	822	1,099	321	465	84	94
2017..............	3,948	41.6	394	612	836	1,120	327	478	85	97
2018..............	3,996	41.4	399	613	845	1,136	327	493	85	98
2019..............	4,071	41.2	407	629	858	1,155	326	508	86	102
2020..............	4,091	40.7	393	626	861	1,177	326	518	85	105
2021..............	4,165	39.9	383	654	861	1,206	331	536	85	109
2022..............	4,107	39.6	375	633	835	1,180	329	551	88	116

NA Not available. [1] Includes Ph.D., Ed.D., and comparable degrees at the doctoral level. Includes most degrees formerly classified as first-professional, such as M.D., D.D.S., and law degrees. [2] Includes some degrees classified as master's or doctor's degrees in later years.

Source: U.S. National Center for Education Statistics, *Digest of Education Statistics*, "Latest version of all Digest tables," <nces.ed.gov/programs/digest>, accessed May 2024.

Table 322. Degrees Earned by Level and Race and Hispanic Ethnicity: 2000 to 2022

[For school year ending in year shown. Race groups exclude persons of Hispanic ethnicity. Covers postsecondary institutions participating in Title IV federal financial aid programs. Based on Integrated Postsecondary Education Data System surveys; see Appendix III]

Degree and race and Hispanic ethnicity	Total					Percent distribution		
	2000	2010	2020	2021	2022	2010	2020	2022
Associate's degrees, total...............	**564,933**	**848,856**	**1,019,038**	**1,037,331**	**1,008,285**	**100.0**	**100.0**	**100.0**
White..	408,822	552,376	509,581	509,377	488,066	66.3	51.2	49.3
Black..	60,208	113,867	119,892	124,001	121,611	13.7	12.0	12.3
Asian..	(NA)	(NA)	61,790	65,173	64,688	(NA)	6.2	6.5
Native Hawaiian or Pacific Islander.......	(NA)	(NA)	2,870	3,067	2,887	(NA)	0.3	0.3
American Indian/Alaska Native..........	6,474	10,101	8,449	8,160	8,171	1.2	0.8	0.8
Two or more races.........................	(NA)	(NA)	37,811	39,063	40,038	(NA)	3.8	4.0
Hispanic......................................	51,563	112,403	255,047	266,178	264,301	13.5	25.6	26.7
Nonresident alien...........................	10,088	16,083	23,598	22,312	18,523	(NA)	(NA)	(NA)
Bachelor's degrees, total................	**1,237,875**	**1,649,919**	**2,038,682**	**2,066,463**	**2,015,035**	**100.0**	**100.0**	**100.0**
White..	929,102	1,167,322	1,184,082	1,172,068	1,129,570	72.9	61.3	58.8
Black..	108,018	164,789	197,491	206,530	199,962	10.3	10.2	10.4
Asian..	(NA)	(NA)	157,085	164,870	170,278	(NA)	8.1	8.9
Native Hawaiian or Pacific Islander.......	(NA)	(NA)	4,383	4,419	4,323	(NA)	0.2	0.2
American Indian/Alaska Native..........	8,717	12,405	9,154	9,542	8,912	0.8	0.5	0.5
Two or more races.........................	(NA)	(NA)	77,621	81,386	81,658	(NA)	4.0	4.3
Hispanic......................................	75,063	140,426	302,663	324,901	325,929	8.8	15.7	17.0
Nonresident alien...........................	39,066	47,586	106,203	102,747	94,403	(NA)	(NA)	(NA)
Master's degrees, total..................	**463,185**	**693,313**	**843,531**	**866,932**	**880,249**	**100.0**	**100.0**	**100.0**
White..	324,990	445,158	448,447	460,270	470,784	72.8	63.5	61.6
Black..	36,606	76,472	92,778	98,239	99,068	12.5	13.1	13.0
Asian..	(NA)	(NA)	53,033	56,716	62,427	(NA)	7.5	8.2
Native Hawaiian or Pacific Islander.......	(NA)	(NA)	1,655	1,670	1,716	(NA)	0.2	0.2
American Indian/Alaska Native..........	2,263	3,965	3,549	3,783	3,719	0.6	0.5	0.5
Two or more races.........................	(NA)	(NA)	22,132	23,205	24,969	(NA)	3.1	3.3
Hispanic......................................	19,379	43,603	84,570	93,344	101,343	7.1	12.0	13.3
Nonresident alien...........................	56,424	81,595	137,367	129,705	116,223	(NA)	(NA)	(NA)
Doctoral degrees, total [1]...............	**118,736**	**158,590**	**190,133**	**194,052**	**203,884**	**100.0**	**100.0**	**100.0**
White..	82,984	104,419	107,823	108,057	112,595	74.4	64.9	63.1
Black..	7,078	10,413	15,719	17,042	18,490	7.4	9.5	10.4
Asian..	(NA)	(NA)	21,308	22,254	22,577	(NA)	12.8	12.6
Native Hawaiian or Pacific Islander.......	(NA)	(NA)	301	275	276	(NA)	0.2	0.2
American Indian/Alaska Native..........	708	952	674	690	724	0.7	0.4	0.4
Two or more races.........................	(NA)	(NA)	5,498	5,769	6,222	(NA)	3.3	3.5
Hispanic......................................	5,042	8,085	14,865	16,486	17,662	5.8	8.9	9.9
Nonresident alien...........................	12,242	18,161	23,945	23,479	25,338	(NA)	(NA)	(NA)

NA Not available. [1] Includes Ph.D., Ed.D., and comparable degrees at the doctoral level, as well as M.D., D.D.S., and law degrees that were formerly classified as first-professional degrees prior to 2010-2011.

Source: U.S. National Center for Education Statistics, *Digest of Education Statistics*, "Latest version of all Digest tables," <nces.ed.gov/programs/digest>, accessed August 2024.

Table 323. Bachelor's Degrees Earned by Field: 1971 to 2022

[For school year ending in year shown. Data are based on the 2020 Classification of Instructional Programs. Data for previous years have been reclassified where necessary to conform to the new classifications. Based on data from the Integrated Postsecondary Education Data System (IPEDS)]

Field of study	1971	1981	1991	2001	2011	2021	2022
Total [1]...	**839,730**	**935,140**	**1,094,538**	**1,244,171**	**1,716,053**	**2,066,463**	**2,015,035**
Agriculture and natural resources............................	12,674	21,886	13,363	23,766	29,203	41,921	40,675
Architecture and related services............................	5,570	9,455	9,781	8,480	9,831	9,296	9,462
Area, ethnic, cultural, gender, and group studies.............	2,579	2,887	4,776	6,160	8,955	7,390	6,658
Biological and biomedical sciences...........................	35,705	43,078	39,482	60,576	89,984	131,515	131,462
Business [2]...	115,396	200,521	249,165	263,515	365,133	391,352	375,418
Communication, journalism, and related programs..........	10,324	29,428	51,650	58,013	83,231	90,761	86,043
Communications technologies................................	478	1,854	1,397	1,178	4,858	4,556	4,851
Computer and information sciences and support services...	2,388	15,121	25,159	44,142	43,066	104,883	108,503
Education..	176,307	108,074	110,807	105,458	104,008	89,477	89,410
Engineering...	45,034	63,642	62,448	58,209	76,356	126,042	123,017
Engineering technologies....................................	5,148	11,713	17,303	14,660	16,741	19,004	18,405
English language and literature/letters......................	63,914	31,922	51,064	50,569	52,754	35,764	33,429
Family and consumer sciences/human sciences..............	11,167	18,370	13,920	16,421	22,438	22,319	20,630
Foreign languages, literatures, and linguistics..............	20,988	11,638	13,937	16,128	21,705	15,514	13,912
Health professions and related programs....................	25,221	63,665	59,636	75,537	142,890	267,993	263,765
Homeland security, law enforcement, and firefighting.......	2,045	13,707	16,806	25,211	47,600	58,006	56,901
Legal professions and studies...............................	545	776	1,827	1,991	4,429	4,585	4,444
Liberal arts/sciences, general studies, and humanities......	7,481	21,643	30,526	37,962	46,717	41,827	37,887
Mathematics and statistics..................................	24,801	11,078	14,393	11,171	17,182	27,106	26,212
Multi/interdisciplinary studies...............................	6,324	12,986	17,774	26,478	42,473	54,615	52,573
Parks, recreation, leisure, fitness, and kinesiology..........	1,621	5,729	4,315	17,948	35,934	54,268	52,776
Philosophy and religious studies............................	8,149	6,776	7,423	9,442	14,336	11,989	11,230
Physical sciences and science technologies.................	21,410	23,936	16,334	18,025	24,705	29,236	28,301
Psychology..	38,187	41,068	58,655	73,645	100,906	126,950	129,609
Public administration and social services....................	5,466	16,707	14,350	19,447	26,799	34,817	33,429
Social sciences and history.................................	155,324	100,513	125,107	128,036	177,169	160,851	151,109
Theology and religious vocations............................	3,720	5,808	4,799	6,220	7,567	6,735	6,394
Transportation and materials moving........................	–	263	2,622	3,748	4,941	5,993	6,540
Visual and performing arts..................................	30,394	40,479	42,186	61,148	93,939	90,027	90,241

– Represents zero. [1] Includes other fields of study, not shown separately. [2] Includes business, management, marketing, and related support services; and culinary, entertainment, and personal services.

Source: U.S. National Center for Education Statistics, *Digest of Education Statistics*, "Latest version of all Digest tables," <nces.ed.gov/programs/digest>, accessed February 2024.

Table 324. Associate's Degrees by Field of Study and Sex: 2015 to 2022

[For school year ending in year shown. Covers associate's degrees conferred by degree-granting institutions. Data are based on the 2020 Classification of Instructional Programs. Data for previous years have been reclassified where necessary to conform to the new classifications. Based on data from the Integrated Postsecondary Education Data System (IPEDS); see Appendix III]

Field of study	2015	2019	2020	2021	2022 Total	2022 Male	2022 Female
Total [1]	**1,014,341**	**1,036,640**	**1,019,038**	**1,037,331**	**1,008,285**	**375,498**	**632,787**
Agriculture and natural resources, total	13,759	13,229	12,740	11,847	11,965	4,429	7,536
Architecture and related services	491	585	631	615	678	384	294
Area, ethnic, cultural, gender, and group studies	382	713	673	936	995	322	673
Biological and biomedical sciences	4,883	7,299	7,454	9,218	8,862	2,420	6,442
Business [1]	132,374	116,799	112,191	116,138	113,070	44,553	68,517
Business, management, marketing, and support services [1]	113,681	105,588	102,585	106,733	103,401	41,360	62,041
Accounting and related services	16,080	12,114	11,468	11,372	11,182	3,098	8,084
Business administration, management, and operations	52,668	56,307	56,291	59,628	58,049	25,342	32,707
Culinary, entertainment, and personal services	18,693	11,211	9,606	9,405	9,669	3,193	6,476
Communication, journalism, and related programs	6,034	8,548	9,019	8,997	7,974	3,452	4,522
Communications technologies	4,628	4,256	4,104	3,910	3,867	2,406	1,461
Computer and information sciences and support services	36,420	32,001	32,037	34,184	34,758	27,012	7,746
Education	17,178	16,210	16,179	18,160	18,498	1,847	16,651
Engineering	4,875	6,367	6,518	6,319	5,971	4,834	1,137
Engineering technologies	56,585	53,252	49,423	48,750	50,201	44,413	5,788
English language and literature/letters	2,324	3,340	3,434	3,604	3,404	1,077	2,327
Family and consumer sciences/human sciences	8,750	9,365	9,281	9,773	9,739	476	9,263
Foreign languages, literatures, and linguistics	2,102	2,798	2,917	2,877	2,818	638	2,180
Health professions and related programs	193,952	177,506	172,294	181,138	177,413	27,151	150,262
Dental assisting	7,762	7,129	5,623	7,135	7,074	418	6,656
Emergency medical technician (EMT paramedic)	3,456	3,648	3,527	3,583	3,631	2,285	1,346
Clinical/medical lab science	3,143	3,037	3,116	3,528	2,744	532	2,212
Medical and other health assisting	30,825	22,689	17,954	20,012	17,819	3,321	14,498
Nursing and patient care assistant	50	58	79	79	58	11	47
Practical nursing	1,858	1,274	1,297	1,624	1,869	210	1,659
Nursing, registered nurse and other	82,904	81,070	82,860	84,119	81,611	10,873	70,738
Health sciences, other	63,954	58,601	57,838	61,058	62,607	9,501	53,106
Homeland security, law enforcement, and firefighting [1]	43,041	35,197	34,913	35,027	33,382	17,138	16,244
Criminal justice and corrections	36,213	29,758	29,751	29,708	27,805	12,725	15,080
Legal professions and studies	9,095	5,646	5,547	5,809	5,644	868	4,776
Liberal arts and sciences, general studies, and humanities	367,852	410,632	402,888	401,092	383,286	137,517	245,769
Library science	170	195	202	171	217	36	181
Mathematics and statistics	2,697	4,632	4,851	4,844	4,248	2,878	1,370
Military technologies and applied sciences	1,229	1,202	992	1,106	1,133	861	272
Multi/interdisciplinary studies	29,139	33,390	33,791	32,916	32,950	12,528	20,422
Parks, recreation, leisure, fitness, and kinesiology	4,669	5,634	5,674	5,955	6,254	3,208	3,046
Philosophy and religious studies	697	1,417	1,625	1,616	1,530	975	555
Physical sciences and science technologies	7,568	10,557	10,753	10,196	9,219	4,824	4,395
Physical sciences	5,040	7,066	6,762	6,425	5,470	2,959	2,511
Science technologies/technicians	2,528	3,491	3,991	3,771	3,749	1,865	1,884
Precision production	4,382	5,386	4,763	4,837	5,036	4,518	518
Psychology	8,780	14,486	16,207	18,801	19,305	4,296	15,009
Public administration and social services	8,436	6,822	6,321	6,768	6,743	850	5,893
Social sciences and history	17,916	25,974	28,241	28,824	26,847	9,980	16,867
Social sciences	16,631	23,561	25,729	26,267	24,309	8,433	15,876
History	1,285	2,413	2,512	2,557	2,538	1,547	991
Theology and religious vocations	1,135	1,131	1,079	982	884	421	463
Transportation and materials moving	1,810	1,926	1,720	1,999	1,964	1,651	313
Visual and performing arts	20,988	20,145	20,576	19,922	19,430	7,535	11,895
Fine and studio arts	2,866	4,060	4,267	4,206	4,329	1,335	2,994
Music and dance	1,886	2,621	2,647	2,498	2,345	1,382	963
Visual and performing arts, other	16,236	13,464	13,662	13,218	12,756	4,818	7,938

[1] Includes other fields of study, not shown separately.

Source: U.S. National Center for Education Statistics, *Digest of Education Statistics*, "Latest version of all Digest tables," <nces.ed.gov/programs/digest>, accessed February 2024.

Table 325. Education Certificates Awarded by Field of Study and Sex: 2021

[For school year ending in 2021. Covers certificates below the associate's degree level based on postsecondary curriculums of less than 4 years in degree- and nondegree-granting institutions of higher education. Based on Integrated Postsecondary Education Data System (IPEDS) survey; see Appendix III]

Field of study	Less than 1-year awards			1- to less than 4-year awards		
	Total	Male	Female	Total	Male	Female
Total	**544,467**	**242,013**	**302,454**	**446,914**	**167,246**	**279,668**
Agriculture and natural resources	6,145	2,626	3,519	4,467	1,400	3,067
Agricultural, animal, plant, veterinary science, and related fields	4,938	1,998	2,940	4,283	1,278	3,005
Natural resources and conservation	1,207	628	579	184	122	62
Architecture and related services	231	104	127	81	34	47
Area, ethnic, cultural, gender, and group studies	1,915	432	1,483	93	17	76
Biological and biomedical sciences	2,208	471	1,737	395	104	291
Business, management, marketing, and support services	88,544	34,230	54,314	18,768	5,645	13,123
Accounting and related services	13,071	3,465	9,606	4,229	964	3,265
Business/commerce, general	2,748	1,132	1,616	1,434	624	810
Business administration, management, and operations	31,191	12,805	18,386	4,803	1,677	3,126
Management information systems and services	751	475	276	68	49	19
Business operations support and assistant services	11,059	4,948	6,111	4,160	861	3,299
Business and management, other	29,724	11,405	18,319	4,074	1,470	2,604
Culinary, entertainment, and personal services	53,593	3,764	49,829	59,506	9,165	50,341
Communication, journalism, and related programs	3,179	1,376	1,803	1,365	759	606
Communications technologies	2,890	1,801	1,089	2,375	1,628	747
Computer and information sciences and support services	39,196	29,580	9,616	9,753	7,583	2,170
Education	11,066	1,058	10,008	3,753	319	3,434
Engineering	1,280	951	329	698	540	158
Engineering technologies [1]	69,784	63,102	6,682	65,781	61,427	4,354
English language and literature/letters	2,145	709	1,436	477	178	299
Family and consumer sciences/human sciences	15,593	635	14,958	3,864	133	3,731
Foreign languages, literatures, and linguistics	3,120	706	2,414	676	146	530
Health professions and related programs	128,278	24,703	103,575	138,986	16,458	122,528
Dental assisting	4,950	413	4,537	10,975	828	10,147
Emergency medical technician (EMT paramedic)	17,138	10,101	7,037	5,185	3,669	1,516
Clinical/medical lab science	8,844	1,073	7,771	1,317	183	1,134
Medical and other health assisting	17,342	2,907	14,435	43,870	3,522	40,348
Nursing and patient care assistant	32,858	3,689	29,169	1,308	135	1,173
Practical nursing	5,571	603	4,968	41,883	4,028	37,855
Nursing, registered nurse and other	2,084	227	1,857	2,412	310	2,102
Health sciences, other	39,491	5,690	33,801	32,036	3,783	28,253
Homeland security, law enforcement, and firefighting	27,329	18,439	8,890	6,141	4,043	2,098
Criminal justice and corrections	18,053	11,331	6,722	4,808	2,951	1,857
Fire control and safety	7,055	6,205	850	1,073	960	113
Homeland security and related protective services, other	1,207	626	581	73	42	31
Security science and technology	1,014	277	737	187	90	97
Legal professions and studies	2,378	429	1,949	2,656	407	2,249
Liberal arts and sciences, general studies, and humanities	15,944	4,913	11,031	93,672	34,167	59,505
Library science	276	42	234	43	6	37
Mathematics and statistics	376	236	140	30	20	10
Military technologies and applied sciences	186	134	52	12	10	2
Multi/interdisciplinary studies	4,532	1,584	2,948	3,010	1,214	1,796
Parks, recreation, leisure, fitness, and kinesiology	1,583	675	908	458	248	210
Philosophy and religious studies	504	44	460	51	27	24
Physical sciences and science technologies	1,446	629	817	867	571	296
Physical sciences	220	131	89	47	15	32
Science technologies/technicians	1,226	498	728	820	556	264
Precision production	29,408	26,890	2,518	18,121	16,617	1,504
Psychology	389	86	303	55	12	43
Public administration and social services	1,820	376	1,444	498	90	408
Social sciences and history	2,405	1,092	1,313	329	130	199
Social sciences	2,284	1,054	1,230	324	128	196
History	121	38	83	5	2	3
Theology and religious vocations	398	210	188	549	227	322
Transportation and materials moving	18,964	16,670	2,294	1,131	1,024	107
Visual and performing arts	7,362	3,316	4,046	8,253	2,897	5,356
Fine and studio arts	459	158	301	4,923	1,589	3,334
Music and dance	511	297	214	217	119	98
Visual and performing arts, other [2]	6,392	2,861	3,531	3,113	1,189	1,924

[1] Includes engineering-related fields; construction trades; and mechanic and repair technologies/technicians. [2] Includes design and applied arts, drama and theatre arts, film and photographic arts, and all other arts not included under "Fine and studio arts" or "Music and dance."

Source: U.S. National Center for Education Statistics, *Digest of Education Statistics*, "Latest version of all Digest tables," <www.nces.ed.gov/programs/digest>, accessed May 2023.

Table 326. Master's and Doctoral Degrees Earned by Field: 1971 to 2022

[For school years ending in years shown. Data are based on the 2020 Classification of Instructional Programs. Data for previous years have been reclassified where necessary to conform to the new classifications. Based on data from the Integrated Postsecondary Education Data System (IPEDS)]

Field of study	1971	1981	1991	2001	2011	2021	2022
MASTER'S DEGREES							
Total [1]	**235,564**	**302,637**	**342,863**	**473,502**	**730,922**	**866,932**	**880,249**
Agriculture and natural resources	2,546	4,150	3,402	4,430	6,023	7,404	8,056
Architecture and related services	1,705	3,153	3,490	4,302	7,788	6,321	6,702
Area, ethnic, cultural, gender, and group studies	1,032	802	1,233	1,555	1,913	1,447	1,465
Biological and biomedical sciences	5,625	5,766	4,834	7,017	11,324	19,434	20,629
Business	26,490	57,888	78,255	115,602	187,178	202,350	205,751
Communication, journalism, and related programs	1,770	2,896	4,123	5,218	8,302	10,819	12,168
Communications technologies	86	209	204	427	502	517	578
Computer and information sciences and support services	1,588	4,218	9,324	16,911	19,516	54,174	51,338
Education	87,666	96,713	87,352	127,829	185,127	153,745	151,707
Engineering	16,813	16,893	24,454	25,174	38,664	47,277	42,997
Engineering technologies	134	323	996	2,013	4,515	6,375	6,342
English language and literature/letters	10,441	5,742	6,784	6,763	9,475	7,850	8,073
Family and consumer sciences/human sciences	1,452	2,570	1,541	1,838	2,918	3,137	2,948
Foreign languages, literatures, and linguistics	5,480	2,934	3,049	3,035	3,727	2,885	2,837
Health professions and related programs	5,241	16,029	21,247	43,465	75,314	141,978	147,035
Homeland security, law enforcement, and firefighting	194	1,538	1,108	2,514	7,433	11,325	11,580
Legal professions and studies	955	1,832	2,057	3,829	6,475	7,038	12,077
Liberal arts and sciences, general studies, and humanities	885	2,375	2,213	3,193	3,997	2,044	1,862
Library science	7,001	4,859	4,763	4,727	7,729	5,477	5,856
Mathematics and statistics	5,191	2,567	3,549	3,209	5,866	12,583	11,761
Parks, recreation, leisure, fitness, and kinesiology	218	643	483	2,354	6,546	9,880	10,118
Philosophy and religious studies	1,326	1,231	1,471	1,534	2,257	2,073	2,197
Physical sciences and science technologies	6,336	5,246	5,281	5,134	6,386	6,778	6,904
Psychology	5,717	10,223	11,349	16,539	25,062	31,818	33,661
Public administration and social services	7,785	17,803	17,905	25,268	38,614	49,391	50,051
Social sciences and history	16,539	11,945	12,233	13,791	21,085	19,846	20,614
Theology and religious vocations	7,747	11,061	10,498	9,728	12,752	13,228	12,592
Transportation and materials moving	−	−	406	756	1,390	670	674
Visual and performing arts	6,675	8,629	8,657	11,404	16,277	15,748	15,729
DOCTORAL DEGREES							
Total [1]	**64,998**	**98,016**	**105,547**	**119,585**	**163,827**	**194,052**	**203,884**
Agriculture and natural resources	2,384	3,062	3,319	3,483	4,028	4,868	4,973
Architecture and related services	36	93	135	153	205	255	252
Area, ethnic, cultural, gender, and group studies	143	161	159	216	278	269	358
Biological and biomedical sciences	3,603	3,640	4,152	5,225	7,693	7,486	8,550
Business	774	808	1,185	1,180	2,286	3,711	4,485
Communication, journalism, and related programs	145	171	259	368	577	532	601
Computer and information sciences and support services	128	252	676	768	1,588	2,573	2,790
Education	6,041	7,279	6,189	6,284	9,642	13,642	14,839
Engineering	3,687	2,598	5,316	5,485	8,369	10,893	12,075
English language and literature/letters	1,554	1,040	1,056	1,330	1,344	1,079	1,192
Foreign languages, literatures, and linguistics	1,084	931	889	1,078	1,158	985	1,026
Health professions and related programs	14,690	27,600	27,708	36,663	57,439	85,569	87,750
Legal professions and studies	17,441	36,391	38,035	38,190	44,853	35,977	36,401
Mathematics and statistics	1,199	728	978	997	1,586	1,958	2,209
Philosophy and religious studies	555	411	464	612	835	627	649
Physical sciences and science technologies	4,324	3,105	4,248	3,968	5,295	5,709	6,530
Psychology	2,144	3,576	3,932	5,091	5,851	6,365	6,685
Public administration and social services	174	362	430	574	851	1,437	1,568
Social sciences and history	3,660	3,122	3,012	3,930	4,390	4,161	4,480
Theology and religious vocations	312	1,273	1,076	1,449	2,343	2,100	2,347
Visual and performing arts	621	654	838	1,167	1,646	1,669	1,762

− Represents zero. [1] Includes other fields of study, not shown separately.

Source: U.S. National Center for Education Statistics, *Digest of Education Statistics*, "Latest version of all Digest tables," <nces.ed.gov/programs/digest>, accessed February 2024.

Table 327. First Professional Degrees Earned in Selected Professions: 1970 to 2021

[First professional degrees include degrees which require at least 6 years of college work for completion (including at least 2 years of preprofessional training). Based on Integrated Postsecondary Education Data System surveys; see Appendix III]

Type of degree and sex of recipient	1970	1980	1990	2000	2010	2015	2018	2019	2020	2021
Medicine (M.D.):										
Institutions conferring degrees	86	112	124	118	120	127	133	134	137	139
Degrees conferred, total	8,314	14,902	15,075	15,286	16,356	18,302	19,142	19,423	19,774	20,265
Percent to women	8.4	23.4	34.2	42.7	48.2	47.8	47.5	48.2	49.7	50.5
Dentistry (D.D.S. or D.M.D.):										
Institutions conferring degrees	48	58	57	54	55	60	63	63	64	64
Degrees conferred, total	3,718	5,258	4,100	4,250	5,062	5,816	6,267	6,321	6,542	6,689
Percent to women	0.9	13.3	30.9	40.1	45.8	47.9	49.5	50.7	51.0	51.6
Law (LL.B. or J.D.):										
Institutions conferring degrees	145	179	182	190	205	212	211	211	209	207
Degrees conferred, total	14,916	35,647	36,485	38,152	44,346	40,024	34,128	34,133	34,194	35,766
Percent to women	5.4	30.2	42.2	45.9	47.3	48.0	49.7	51.6	52.4	53.2
Theological (B.D., M.Div., M.H.L.):										
Institutions conferring degrees	(NA)	(NA)	(NA)	198	(NA)	(NA)	(NA)	(NA)	(NA)	(NA)
Degrees conferred, total	5,298	7,115	5,851	6,129	5,825	6,300	5,842	5,774	5,670	5,875
Percent to women	2.3	13.8	24.8	29.2	(NA)	31.4	30.1	31.6	31.8	32.5

NA Not available.

Source: U.S. National Center for Education Statistics, *Digest of Education Statistics*, "Latest version of all Digest tables," <nces.ed.gov/programs/digest>, accessed November 2023.

Table 328. College Student Participation in Distance Education Courses by Institution Type: 2020 and 2021

[In percent, except as noted (19,027 represents 19,027,000). As of Fall. Data shown for students enrolled in degree-granting institutions. Distance education is education that uses one or more types of technology to deliver instruction to students who are separated from the instructor and to support regular and substantive interaction between the students and the instructor synchronously or asynchronously. Data are from the Integrated Postsecondary Education Data System (IPEDS)]

Item	Number of students (1,000s)	Percent taking no distance education courses	Percent taking any distance education courses					
			Any distance education courses	At least one, but not all of student's courses	Exclusively distance education courses by location of student			
					Total [1]	Same state as school	Different state than school	Outside of the U.S.
All students, 2020	**19,027**	**25.3**	**74.7**	**28.0**	**46.7**	**33.8**	**10.3**	**1.1**
Public	13,884	23.0	77.0	29.9	47.1	40.5	4.2	0.9
Private	5,143	31.7	68.3	23.0	45.4	15.9	26.7	1.7
Nonprofit	4,101	34.5	65.5	26.0	39.5	16.4	20.1	1.8
For-profit	1,042	20.4	79.6	11.2	68.4	13.7	53.0	1.2
All students, 2021	**18,660**	**39.9**	**60.1**	**29.7**	**30.3**	**20.6**	**8.7**	**0.5**
4-year	13,977	41.7	58.3	31.1	27.2	15.2	10.8	0.6
2-year	4,683	34.8	65.2	25.6	39.7	36.8	2.2	0.2
Public	13,544	37.2	62.8	33.8	28.9	24.8	3.2	0.4
Private	5,116	47.1	52.9	19.0	33.9	9.7	23.0	0.8
Nonprofit	4,113	53.6	46.4	20.0	26.4	9.3	15.9	0.8
For-profit	1,003	20.4	79.6	14.9	64.7	11.1	52.0	1.0
Undergraduate	**15,448**	**39.2**	**60.8**	**32.6**	**28.2**	**21.0**	**6.4**	**0.3**
Public	11,945	36.0	64.0	36.0	28.0	25.0	2.2	0.3
Private	3,504	50.2	49.8	21.0	28.8	7.3	20.7	0.6
Nonprofit	2,726	57.5	42.5	21.9	20.5	6.2	13.6	0.6
For-profit	777	24.3	75.7	17.8	57.9	11.0	45.8	0.5
Postbaccalaureate	**3,211**	**43.6**	**56.4**	**16.1**	**40.3**	**18.9**	**19.4**	**1.4**
Public	1,599	46.9	53.1	17.4	35.7	23.0	10.7	1.5
Private	1,613	40.4	59.6	14.7	44.9	14.9	28.0	1.4
Nonprofit	1,387	45.9	54.1	16.3	37.8	15.4	20.6	1.2
For-profit	226	6.8	93.2	5.0	88.1	11.7	73.4	2.6

[1] Includes students for whom the place of residence is not known or not reported, not shown separately.

Source: U.S. National Center for Education Statistics, *Digest of Education Statistics*, "Latest version of all Digest Tables," <www.nces.ed.gov/programs/digest>, accessed November 2023.

Table 329. College and University Libraries by Selected Characteristics: 2018 to 2020

[In units as indicated (700,352 represents 700,352,000). As of Fall of year shown. Data shown for degree-granting postsecondary institution libraries. FTE is full-time equivalent. Based on data from the Integrated Postsecondary Education Data System (IPEDS)]

Item	Unit	2018	2019	2020			
				Total	Public	Private non-profit	Private for-profit
Number of libraries	Number	3,697	3,654	3,631	1,547	1,542	542
Percent of institutions with libraries	Percent	92.8	93.0	93.1	97.8	94.8	78.4
Circulation transactions	1,000	700,352	1,028,996	1,074,154	682,420	311,469	80,266
Physical transaction	1,000	46,054	31,405	13,480	6,626	6,673	181
Electronic transaction	1,000	654,298	997,592	1,060,674	675,793	304,796	80,085
Circulation transactions per FTE student	Number	47	70	75	68	90	100
ENROLLMENT							
Total enrollment	1,000	19,651	19,630	19,027	13,884	4,101	1,042
FTE enrollment	1,000	14,786	14,762	14,340	10,068	3,472	800
COLLECTIONS							
Total number of physical and electronic materials	1,000	2,567,446	2,746,699	2,889,335	1,560,992	1,089,658	238,685
Number of books	1,000	1,798,225	1,956,845	2,078,928	1,091,293	839,665	147,970
Physical books	1,000	731,008	728,004	715,070	429,930	283,173	1,967
Electronic books	1,000	1,067,217	1,228,841	1,363,858	661,363	556,492	146,003
Number of media (incl. audiovisual materials)	1,000	767,710	788,307	808,942	469,115	249,414	90,413
Number of databases [1]	1,000	1,511	1,547	1,464	584	579	302
OPERATING EXPENDITURES (CURRENT DOLLARS)							
Total operating expenditures [2,3]	1,000 dol.	8,386,070	8,322,052	7,908,508	4,734,820	3,101,663	72,025
Salaries and wages [4]	1,000 dol.	3,555,572	3,548,072	3,317,580	2,093,322	1,197,063	27,196
Fringe benefits	1,000 dol.	816,903	829,550	793,183	525,318	265,659	2,206
Information resources	1,000 dol.	3,196,130	3,184,815	3,126,299	1,778,974	1,313,098	34,228
Operating expenditures per FTE student	Dol.	567	564	552	470	893	90

[1] Electronic databases only. [2] Excludes capital outlay. Expenditure data are reported only by degree-granting institutions with total expenditures over $100,000. [3] Includes other expenditures not shown separately. [4] Includes student hourly wages.

Source: U.S. National Center for Education Statistics, *Digest of Education Statistics*, "Latest version of all Digest tables," <nces.ed.gov/programs/digest>, accessed December 2023.

Table 330. College Campus Crime—Incidents and Rates by Type of Crime and Institution: 2005 to 2021

[For school year ending in year shown. Data are from Department of Education's Campus Safety and Security Reporting System. Data are for degree-granting institutions and U.S. service academies. Degree-granting institutions grant associate's or higher degrees and participate in Title IV federal financial aid programs. Some institutions that report data as mandated by the Clery Act, specifically, non-degree-granting institutions and institutions outside of the 50 states and the District of Columbia, are excluded from this table. Crimes, arrests, and referrals include incidents involving students, staff, and on-campus guests. Excludes off-campus crimes and arrests even if they involve college students or staff]

Control and level of institution and type of crime	Total, in residence halls and other locations						2021[8]		
	2005	2010	2015	2018	2019	2020[8]	Total	In residence halls	At other locations
NUMBER OF INCIDENTS									
Selected crimes against persons and property	**42,710**	**32,097**	**27,532**	**28,324**	**27,156**	**21,257**	**23,426**	**10,607**	**12,819**
Murder[1]	11	15	28	12	20	13	13	3	10
Negligent manslaughter[2]	2	1	2	2	5	2	5	4	1
Sex offenses, forcible[3]	2,674	2,927	8,022	12,249	11,708	9,392	10,364	7,018	3,346
Sex offenses, nonforcible[4]	42	33	63	61	74	74	39	20	19
Robbery	1,551	1,392	1,044	827	799	477	524	95	429
Aggravated assault	2,656	2,221	2,258	2,216	2,136	1,515	2,076	574	1,502
Burglary	29,256	21,335	12,320	9,504	8,910	6,857	6,453	2,679	3,774
Motor vehicle theft	5,531	3,441	3,218	3,045	3,053	2,482	3,522	63	3,459
Arson	987	732	577	408	451	445	430	151	279
Arrests[5]	**49,024**	**51,519**	**40,299**	**31,288**	**26,744**	**14,768**	**13,819**	**6,006**	**7,813**
Illegal weapons possession	1,316	1,112	1,183	1,171	1,137	802	972	221	751
Drug law violations	13,707	18,589	19,431	17,794	13,761	8,017	6,463	2,335	4,128
Liquor law violations	34,001	31,818	19,685	12,323	11,846	5,949	6,384	3,450	2,934
Referrals for disciplinary action[5]	**202,816**	**230,269**	**241,687**	**198,199**	**185,946**	**122,842**	**127,278**	**117,312**	**9,966**
Illegal weapons possession	1,882	1,314	1,425	1,217	1,058	584	890	639	251
Drug law violations	25,356	42,022	56,037	53,060	45,906	27,023	23,715	20,082	3,633
Liquor law violations	175,578	186,933	184,225	143,922	138,982	95,235	102,673	96,591	6,082
INCIDENTS PER 10,000 FTE STUDENTS[6,7]									
Selected crimes against persons and property	**32.9**	**20.9**	**18.7**	**19.7**	**18.8**	**15.0**	**16.9**	**21.0**	**5.5**
By type of crime:									
Murder[1]	–	–	–	–	–	–	–	–	–
Negligent manslaughter[2]	–	–	–	–	–	–	–	–	–
Sex offenses, forcible[3]	2.1	1.9	5.4	8.5	8.1	6.6	7.5	9.9	0.7
Sex offenses, nonforcible[4]	–	–	–	–	0.1	0.1	–	–	–
Robbery	1.2	0.9	0.7	0.6	0.6	0.3	0.4	0.4	0.2
Aggravated assault	2.0	1.4	1.5	1.5	1.5	1.1	1.5	1.7	1.1
Burglary	22.5	13.9	8.4	6.6	6.2	4.8	4.7	5.6	2.1
Motor vehicle theft	4.3	2.2	2.2	2.1	2.1	1.8	2.5	3.0	1.2
Arson	0.8	0.5	0.4	0.3	0.3	0.3	0.3	0.4	0.2
By type of institution:									
Public 4-year	34.3	23.4	19.7	21.2	21.2	17.9	18.7	20.2	6.5
Nonprofit 4-year	54.2	35.2	31.1	31.0	27.3	19.1	23.7	24.8	14.0
For-profit 4-year	17.0	6.5	4.4	5.3	5.4	4.2	5.3	20.7	2.0
Public 2-year	16.4	10.2	8.4	6.7	6.8	4.8	5.4	9.3	4.4
Nonprofit 2-year	91.3	48.4	20.0	8.8	7.2	11.3	7.0	21.2	4.0
For profit-2-year	17.9	8.2	6.9	6.1	5.2	2.5	6.2	19.9	5.9
Arrests[5]	**37.7**	**33.5**	**27.4**	**21.7**	**18.5**	**10.4**	**10.0**	**12.9**	**1.9**
Illegal weapons possession	1.0	0.7	0.8	0.8	0.8	0.6	0.7	0.9	0.3
Drug law violations	10.5	12.1	13.2	12.4	9.5	5.7	4.7	5.9	1.3
Liquor law violations	26.2	20.7	13.4	8.6	8.2	4.2	4.6	6.2	0.3
By type of institution:									
Public 4-year	66.6	63.5	47.3	34.0	28.7	15.7	15.7	17.4	2.0
Nonprofit 4-year	25.8	17.2	13.6	10.6	8.3	5.3	3.9	4.0	2.8
For-profit 4-year	0.6	1.9	1.5	3.0	7.2	3.9	1.3	5.0	0.5
Public 2-year	9.4	8.8	7.9	9.5	8.6	4.4	4.1	11.1	2.1
Nonprofit 2-year	22.1	19.8	12.1	6.3	8.2	2.2	3.3	11.8	1.5
For profit-2-year	2.0	1.1	1.5	2.1	1.1	0.6	0.4	6.6	0.3
Referrals for disciplinary action[5]	**156.1**	**149.7**	**164.1**	**137.6**	**129.0**	**86.9**	**91.8**	**124.6**	**0.9**
Illegal weapons possession	1.4	0.9	1.0	0.8	0.7	0.4	0.6	0.8	0.1
Drug law violations	19.5	27.3	38.0	36.8	31.8	19.1	17.1	23.1	0.4
Liquor law violations	135.1	121.5	125.1	99.9	96.4	67.4	74.1	100.6	0.4
By type of institution:									
Public 4-year	175.5	175.5	184.1	141.5	132.5	87.9	91.4	102.4	0.7
Nonprofit 4-year	336.1	329.7	314.4	259.7	239.1	156.7	162.5	180.4	3.4
For-profit 4-year	10.9	8.8	11.9	14.8	18.3	15.2	19.9	112.7	0.1
Public 2-year	12.8	18.6	20.4	20.2	21.2	14.9	16.2	71.4	0.8
Nonprofit 2-year	149.4	152.2	206.4	90.4	46.3	60.1	60.5	342.3	1.5
For profit-2-year	9.5	3.8	9.5	4.6	2.0	0.5	1.8	86.2	0.2

– Represents or rounds to zero. [1] Excludes suicides, fetal deaths, traffic fatalities, accidental deaths, and justifiable homicide (such as the killing of a felon by a law enforcement officer in the line of duty). [2] Defined as the killing of another person through gross negligence (excludes traffic fatalities). [3] Any sexual act directed against another person forcibly and/or against that person's will. [4] Includes only statutory rape or incest. [5] If an individual is both arrested and referred to college officials for disciplinary action for a single offense, only the arrest is counted. [6] FTE is full-time equivalent. Although crimes, arrests, and referrals include incidents involving students, staff, and campus guests, they are expressed as a ratio to FTE students because comprehensive FTE counts of all these groups are not available. [7] Data on incidents per 10,000 FTE students are shown for institutions with and without residence halls. [8] Use caution when comparing on-campus data for 2020 and 2021 with data from other years due to the switch to online learning in many institutions during the 2019 coronavirus pandemic.

Source: U.S. National Center for Education Statistics, *Digest of Education Statistics*, "Latest version of all Digest tables," <nces.ed.gov/programs/digest>, accessed April 2024.

Table 331. Public Schools Reporting Incidents of Crime by Incident Type and Selected School Characteristics: 2022

[For school year ending in year shown. Includes incidents that happen in school buildings, on school grounds, on school buses, and at places that hold school-sponsored events or activities, before, during, or after normal school hours or when school activities or events were in session. Based on the School Survey on Crime and Safety (SSOCS). Based on sample; see source for details]

School characteristic	Total number of schools	Number of incidents		Percent of schools with—		Rate per 1,000 students	
		Violent incidents [1]	Serious violent incidents [2]	Violent incidents [1]	Serious violent incidents [2]	Violent incidents [1]	Serious violent incidents [2]
All public schools..............	**85,300**	**857,500**	**70,000**	**67.3**	**19.7**	**18.0**	**1.5**
Level: [3]							
Elementary.........................	51,200	335,300	23,400	55.2	12.6	14.7	1.0
Middle.............................	15,200	295,800	23,500	89.7	30.4	31.9	2.5
High school........................	16,900	207,500	21,600	84.6	32.1	14.2	1.5
Combined..........................	2,000	18,900	[4] 1,500	61.1	17.1	18.3	[4] 1.5
Enrollment size:							
Less than 300.....................	19,700	[4] 104,000	[4] 8.800	54.9	12.7	[4] 23.4	[4] 2.0
300 to 499.........................	26,000	168,300	13,100	64.2	15.2	16.1	1.3
500 to 999.........................	30,500	382,700	31,400	70.8	22.2	19.6	1.6
1,000 or more.....................	9,000	202,400	16,600	92.0	39.8	15.3	1.3
Percent minority enrollment:							
Zero to 25 percent.................	27,900	186,900	19,000	64.7	21.3	13.9	1.4
26 to 50 percent...................	18,400	146,500	11,700	60.5	17.5	13.3	1.1
51 to 75 percent...................	15,400	236,000	13,800	72.0	20.6	24.3	1.4
76 percent or more................	23,500	288,000	25,500	72.7	19.0	21.2	1.9

[1] Violent incidents include rape or attempted rape, sexual battery other than rape, physical attack or fight with or without a weapon, threat of physical attack with or without a weapon, and robbery with or without a weapon. [2] Serious violent incidents include rape or attempted rape, sexual battery other than rape, physical attack or fight with a weapon, threat of physical attack with a weapon, and robbery with or without a weapon. [3] Elementary schools are defined as schools that enroll more students in grades K through 4 than in higher grades. Middle schools are defined as schools that enroll more students in grades 5 through 8 than in higher or lower grades. High schools are defined as schools that enroll more students in grades 9 through 12 than in lower grades. Combined schools include all other combinations of grades, including K–12 schools. [4] Interpret data with caution. The coefficient of variation (CV) for this estimate is between 30 and 50 percent.

Source: U.S. National Center for Education Statistics, *Digest of Education Statistics*, "Latest version of all Digest tables," <nces.ed.gov/programs/digest>, accessed May 2024; and *Report on Indicators of School Crime and Safety*, annual. See also <nces.ed.gov/surveys/ssocs>.

Table 332. Disciplinary Problems Reported at Public Schools by Selected School Characteristics: 2022

[In percent. For school year ending in 2022. "At school" includes activities that happen in school buildings, on school grounds, on school buses, and at places that hold school-sponsored events or activities. Based on the School Survey on Crime and Safety (SSOCS); responses were provided by the principal or the person most knowledgeable about crime and safety issues at the school. Based on sample; see source for details]

School characteristic	Happens at least once a week						Happens at all
	Student racial tensions	Student bullying	Student sexual harassment of other students [1]	Student verbal abuse of teachers	Widespread disorder in classrooms	Student acts of disrespect for teachers	Gang activities [2]
All public schools.........	**4.7**	**14.3**	**1.6**	**7.6**	**5.0**	**14.5**	**11.9**
Level: [3]							
Elementary....................	2.3	10.0	(S)	6.3	4.8	12.8	4.8
Middle.........................	12.0	27.6	4.6	12.2	7.1	21.1	21.7
Secondary/high school.......	5.5	15.2	2.7	6.9	3.4	13.8	24.8
Combined.....................	[4] 5.3	15.2	(S)	[4] 11.1	[4] 7.6	13.9	10.3
Enrollment size:							
Less than 300.................	1.6	12.4	[4] 0.7	4.5	[4] 3.1	10.7	5.2
300 to 499.....................	4.3	13.8	1.4	7.7	6.3	14.2	7.9
500 to 999.....................	5.8	14.7	1.8	8.7	5.7	16.1	13.1
1,000 or more.................	9.3	18.6	3.9	10.3	3.3	18.3	34.1
Percent minority enrollment:							
Zero to 25 percent...........	5.2	12.7	1.1	4.4	3.1	11.0	3.5
26 to 50 percent..............	4.7	12.7	1.3	6.5	4.3	13.5	8.6
51 to 75 percent..............	5.5	14.7	2.9	11.8	7.1	18.2	19.0
76 percent or more..........	3.6	17.2	1.6	9.5	6.4	17.1	19.8

S Figure does not meet publication standards. [1] Defined as conduct that is unwelcome, sexual in nature, and denies or limits a student's ability to participate in or benefit from a school's education program. The conduct can be carried out by school employees, other students, and non-employee third parties. Both male and female students can be victims of sexual harassment, and the harasser and the victim can be of the same sex. The conduct can be verbal, nonverbal, or physical. [2] Gang includes an "ongoing loosely organized association of three or more persons, whether formal or informal, that has a common name, signs, symbols or colors, whose members engage, either individually or collectively, in violent or other forms of illegal behavior." [3] Elementary schools are defined as schools that enroll more students in grades K through 4 than in higher grades. Middle schools are defined as schools that enroll more students in grades 5 through 8 than in higher or lower grades. Secondary or high schools are defined as schools that enroll more students in grades 9 through 12 than in lower grades. Combined schools include all other combinations of grades, including K–12 schools. [4] Interpret data with caution.

Source: U.S. National Center for Education Statistics, *Digest of Education Statistics*, "Latest version of all Digest tables," <nces.ed.gov/programs/digest>, accessed May 2024; and *Report on Indicators of School Crime and Safety*, annual. See also <nces.ed.gov/surveys/ssocs>.

Table 333. Students Who Reported Being Threatened or Injured With a Weapon on School Property by Selected Student Characteristics: 2005 to 2021

[In percent. Based on the Centers for Disease Control and Prevention's Youth Risk Behavior Surveillance System, which surveys students in public and private schools, in grades 9 to 12. Data are for previous 12 months. "On school property" was not defined for survey respondents. "Weapon" was defined as a gun, knife, or club for survey respondents]

Characteristic	2005	2009	2011	2013	2015	2017	2019	2021
Total..........................	**7.9**	**7.7**	**7.4**	**6.9**	**6.0**	**6.0**	**7.4**	**6.6**
Sex:								
Male..........................	9.7	9.6	9.5	7.7	7.0	7.8	8.0	7.0
Female........................	6.1	5.5	5.2	6.1	4.6	4.1	6.5	5.9
Race/ethnicity: [1]								
White.........................	7.2	6.4	6.1	5.8	4.9	5.0	7.1	6.2
Black.........................	8.1	9.4	8.9	8.4	[2] 7.9	7.8	8.8	7.9
Asian.........................	4.6	5.5	7.0	5.3	[2] 3.6	4.3	3.2	3.2
Native Hawaiian/other Pacific Islander..................	[2] 14.5	12.5	11.3	[2] 8.7	[2] 20.5	[2] 7.0	[2] 12.3	(S)
American Indian/Alaska Native.......	9.8	16.5	8.2	18.5	[2] 8.2	13.7	12.6	[2] 8.3
More than one race................	10.7	9.2	9.9	7.7	8.0	8.0	11.4	8.5
Hispanic......................	9.8	9.1	9.2	8.5	6.6	6.1	6.9	6.5
Grade:								
9th...........................	10.5	8.7	8.3	8.5	7.2	6.8	8.1	6.2
10th..........................	8.8	8.4	7.7	7.0	6.2	6.8	8.0	7.4
11th..........................	5.5	7.9	7.3	6.8	5.5	5.1	7.1	7.3
12th..........................	5.8	5.2	5.9	4.9	4.4	4.6	5.9	5.0
Sexual identity: [3]								
Heterosexual..................	(NA)	(NA)	(NA)	(NA)	5.1	5.4	6.3	5.7
Gay or lesbian................	(NA)	(NA)	(NA)	(NA)	13.4	9.0	15.5	8.7
Bisexual......................	(NA)	(NA)	(NA)	(NA)	8.9	9.5	10.9	8.1
Not sure, other, or questioning.......	(NA)	(NA)	(NA)	(NA)	12.6	11.1	12.9	8.3

NA Not available. S Reporting standards not met. [1] Race categories exclude persons of Hispanic ethnicity. [2] Interpret data with caution. [3] Students were asked "which of the following best describes you: heterosexual (straight), gay or lesbian, bisexual, or not sure." Beginning 2021, they were asked "which of the following best describes you: heterosexual, gay or lesbian, bisexual, I describe my sexual identity some other way, I am not sure about my sexual identity (questioning), or I do not know what this question is asking." Excludes students who selected "I do not know what this question is asking." Caution should be used in comparing data on sexual identity from 2021 with data from earlier years.

Source: U.S. National Center for Education Statistics, *Digest of Education Statistics,* "Latest version of all Digest tables," <nces.ed.gov/programs/digest>, accessed January 2024. See also <www.cdc.gov/healthyyouth/data/yrbs/>.

Table 334. Public Schools Using Selected Safety and Security Measures by Type: 2000 to 2022

[In percent. For school year ending in year shown. Based on the School Survey on Crime and Safety and subject to sampling error; see source for details]

Measure	2000	2010	2016	2018	2020 [5]	2022
Controlled access during school hours:						
Buildings (locked or monitored doors).............................	74.6	91.7	94.1	95.4	97.1	97.1
Grounds (locked or monitored gates)............................	33.7	46.0	49.9	50.8	58.9	61.1
Visitors required to sign or check in and wear badges [1]...................	96.6	99.3	93.5	94.6	98.1	97.1
Classrooms equipped with doors that lock from the inside................	(NA)	(NA)	66.7	64.8	73.1	76.1
Student dress, IDs, and school supplies:						
Required students to wear uniforms..............................	11.8	18.9	21.5	19.8	18.8	16.4
Enforced a strict dress code.....................................	47.4	56.9	53.1	48.8	43.7	36.6
Required students to wear badges or picture IDs...................	3.9	6.9	7.0	9.2	10.1	9.2
Required faculty and staff to wear badges or picture IDs.............	25.4	62.9	67.9	69.9	76.8	70.7
Required clear book bags or banned book bags on school grounds......	5.9	5.5	3.9	3.5	4.4	3.7
Provided school lockers to students...............................	46.5	52.1	50.4	49.0	49.4	43.0
Drug testing:						
Students participating in athletics or other extracurricular activities.......	(NA)	6.2	7.7	8.9	9.5	9.0
Athletes...	(NA)	6.0	7.2	(NA)	(NA)	(NA)
Students in non-athletic extracurricular activities..........................	(NA)	4.6	6.0	(NA)	(NA)	(NA)
Any other students.....................................	(NA)	3.0	(NA)	(NA)	(NA)	(NA)
Metal detectors and sweeps:						
Random metal detector checks on students.............................	7.2	5.2	4.5	4.9	6.0	6.2
Students required to pass through metal detectors daily..................	0.9	1.4	1.8	2.2	2.7	2.4
Random sweeps for contraband [2].....................	25.3	27.7	28.2	27.4	28.7	23.1
Communications systems and technology:						
Provided telephones in most classrooms.................................	44.6	74.0	79.3	(NA)	(NA)	(NA)
Provided electronic notification system for school wide emergencies.....	(NA)	63.1	73.0	71.6	70.4	69.4
Provided structured anonymous threat reporting system [3]................	(NA)	35.9	43.9	49.3	65.7	62.4
Had silent alarms directly connected to law enforcement.................	(NA)	(NA)	27.1	29.1	40.0	43.0
Used security cameras to monitor the school.............................	19.4	61.1	80.6	83.5	91.1	92.6
Provided two-way radios to any staff.............................	(NA)	73.3	73.3	77.8	83.2	83.3
Limited access to social networking sites from school computers........	(NA)	93.4	89.1	(NA)	(NA)	(NA)
Prohibited non-academic use of cell phones or smartphones [4]...........	(NA)	90.9	65.8	70.3	76.9	76.1

NA Not available. [1] Prior to the 2015-2016 survey, the survey asked only if visitors were required to sign or check in, and did not include the requirement to wear badges. [2] May include locker checks and/or random dog sniffs for items such as drugs and weapons. [3] For example, a system for reporting threats through online submission, telephone hotline, or written submission via drop box. [4] Prior to the 2017-2018 survey, the survey asked about prohibiting the use of cell phones and text messaging devices during school hours, and did not refer to "non-academic" use of such devices, nor the use of smartphones. [5] The coronavirus pandemic affected 2020 data collection activities. Use caution when comparing 2020 estimates with those from other years.

Source: U.S. National Center for Education Statistics, *Digest of Education Statistics*, "Latest version of all Digest tables," <nces.ed.gov/programs/digest>, accessed June 2024; and *Indicators of School Crime and Safety*, annual. See also <nces.ed.gov/surveys/ssocs>.

Table 335. Students Who Reported Being Bullied at School or Cyber-Bullied by Student Characteristics: 2022

[In percent. For school year ending in 2022. For students aged 12 through 18. Excludes students who received any homeschooling education during the school year, or who only attended virtual schools. Beginning in 2022, students were asked to report their experiences "during school," which includes in the school building, on school property, on a school bus, going to and from school, and via the phone, internet, or social media. The 2022 survey included changes in the definition and types of bullying; use caution when comparing 2022 estimates to those from earlier surveys. See source for more information]

Characteristic	Total bullying at school [1]	Made fun of, called names, or insulted	Subject of rumors	Private information, photos, or videos shared	Threatened with harm	Purposefully excluded	Pushed, shoved, tripped, or spit on	Online or by text
Total	**19.2**	**11.9**	**13.1**	**2.5**	**3.3**	**3.7**	**4.9**	**21.6**
Sex:								
Male	16.7	10.6	9.7	1.8	3.7	2.6	6.1	14.1
Female	21.8	13.4	16.6	3.2	2.9	4.9	3.7	27.7
Race/ethnicity: [2]								
Asian/Pacific Islander	8.6	[3] 5.1	6.3	(S)	(S)	[3] 2.2	(S)	(S)
Black	17.0	10.5	10.9	3.2	4.3	[3] 2.7	3.9	[3] 14.9
Hispanic	16.4	9.5	11.2	2.4	2.1	2.2	4.5	20.1
White	21.6	13.5	14.9	2.5	3.7	4.8	5.6	23.2
Two or more races	30.1	24.2	20.2	[3] 2.6	[3] 7.6	[3] 4.6	[3] 9.3	[3] 17.0
Grade:								
6th	26.9	18.4	16.6	2.6	4.6	4.1	12.0	[3] 11.1
7th	26.3	20.7	15.5	4.2	5.5	5.2	8.5	15.2
8th	25.1	16.1	17.4	2.2	3.5	3.7	8.4	18.9
9th	17.7	9.9	12.0	3.2	3.1	3.5	2.7	24.5
10th	15.8	7.9	12.5	2.5	3.3	2.1	3.4	33.2
11th	10.4	6.2	7.0	1.4	1.8	3.3	[3] 0.9	27.6
12th	14.8	6.8	11.6	[3] 1.5	[3] 1.9	4.5	[3] 1.2	28.7

S Reporting standards not met. [1] Students who reported more than one type of bullying were counted only once for the total. [2] Race categories exclude persons of Hispanic ethnicity. [3] Interpret data with caution. The coefficient of variation (CV) for this estimate is between 30 and 50 percent.

Source: U.S. National Center for Education Statistics, *Digest of Education Statistics*, "Latest version of all Digest tables," <nces.ed.gov/programs/digest>, accessed March 2024; and *Indicators of School Crime and Safety*, annual. See also <nces.ed.gov/surveys/ssocs>.

Table 336. Cyberbullying Among Students in Grades 9 to 12 by Student Characteristics: 2011 to 2021

[In percent. Covers students in grades 9 to 12 who reported being electronically bullied during the previous 12 months. Data are based on the U.S. Centers for Disease Control and Prevention's Youth Risk Behavior Surveillance System. Electronic bullying, or cyberbullying, for 2011-2015 includes "being bullied through e-mail, chat rooms, instant messaging, websites, or texting," and for 2017 onward, "being bullied through texting, Instagram, Facebook, or other social media"]

Student characteristic	2011	2013	2015	2017	2019	2021
Total	**16.2**	**14.8**	**15.5**	**14.9**	**15.7**	**15.9**
Sex:						
Male	10.8	8.5	9.7	9.9	10.9	11.2
Female	22.1	21.0	21.7	19.7	20.4	20.5
Race/ethnicity: [1]						
American Indian/Alaska Native	16.2	18.0	18.7	13.2	[2] 21.3	20.9
Asian	14.4	12.9	13.9	10.0	12.1	13.3
Black	8.9	8.7	8.6	10.9	8.6	9.5
Pacific Islander	19.6	15.7	[2] 11.8	15.0	[2] 19.0	9.7
White	18.6	16.9	18.4	17.3	18.6	18.8
Two or more races	21.0	18.9	20.4	16.0	19.2	16.9
Hispanic ethnicity	13.6	12.8	12.4	12.3	12.7	13.2
Sexual identity: [3]						
Heterosexual	(NA)	(NA)	14.2	13.3	14.1	12.7
Gay or lesbian	(NA)	(NA)	20.0	18.4	28.1	24.8
Bisexual	(NA)	(NA)	30.7	29.6	26.1	28.4
Not sure or other	(NA)	(NA)	22.5	22.0	19.4	24.8
Grade:						
9th	15.5	16.1	16.5	16.7	16.5	16.6
10th	18.1	14.5	16.6	14.8	16.0	16.5
11th	16.0	14.9	14.7	14.2	14.4	15.5
12th	15.0	13.5	14.3	13.5	15.4	14.4

NA Not available. [1] Race categories exclude persons of Hispanic ethnicity. [2] Interpret data with caution. The coefficient of variation (CV) for this estimate is between 30 and 50 percent. [3] Students were asked "which of the following best describes you: heterosexual (straight), gay or lesbian, bisexual, or not sure." Beginning 2021, they were asked "which of the following best describes you: heterosexual, gay or lesbian, bisexual, I describe my sexual identity some other way, I am not sure about my sexual identity (questioning), or I do not know what this question is asking." Excludes students who selected "I do not know what this question is asking." Because the response categories changed in 2021, caution should be used in comparing data on sexual identity from 2021 with data from earlier years.

Source: U.S. National Center for Education Statistics, *Digest of Education Statistics*, "Latest version of all Digest tables," <nces.ed.gov/programs/digest>, accessed January 2024.

Table 337. Violent Deaths Occurring at Schools by Type; and Homicides and Suicides of Youth Aged 5 to 18, Total and School-Associated: 2000 to 2021

[For school year ending in year shown. A school-associated violent death is defined as a homicide, suicide, or legal intervention (involving a law enforcement officer) in which the fatal injury occurred on the campus of a functioning elementary or secondary school in the United States, while the victim was on the way to or from regular sessions at school, or while the victim was attending or traveling to or from an official school-sponsored event. Victims include students, staff members, and others who are not students. Data from school year 2000 onward are subject to change until interviews with school and law enforcement officials have been completed. The details learned during interviews can occasionally change the classification of a case. Based on data from U.S. Centers for Disease Control and Prevention, and Federal Bureau of Investigation and Bureau of Justice Statistics]

Year	School-associated violent deaths				Homicides of youth aged 5 to 18		Suicides of youth aged 5 to 18	
	Total [1]	Homicides	Suicides [2]	Legal inter-ventions	Total	At school	Total [2]	At school
2000	37	26	11	0	1,694	14	1,420	8
2005	52	40	10	2	1,720	22	1,484	8
2006	44	37	6	1	1,859	21	1,311	3
2007	63	48	13	2	1,906	32	1,243	9
2008	48	39	7	2	1,858	21	1,256	5
2009	44	29	15	0	1,720	18	1,425	7
2010	35	27	5	3	1,551	19	1,441	2
2011	32	26	6	0	1,436	11	1,559	3
2012	45	26	14	5	1,360	15	1,541	5
2013	53	41	11	1	1,310	31	1,608	6
2014	48	26	20	1	1,160	12	1,638	8
2015	47	28	17	2	1,273	20	1,882	9
2016	38	30	7	1	1,478	18	1,941	3
2017	42	28	13	1	1,587	18	2,186	6
2018	56	46	9	1	1,502	35	2,408	8
2019	39	29	10	0	1,508	10	2,233	3
2020	25	23	1	1	1,855	11	2,047	1
2021	41	20	17	3	2,436	11	2,346	6

[1] Total includes unintentional firearm-related deaths and undetermined violent deaths, not shown separately. [2] Excludes self-inflicted deaths among children age 5 to 9. The number of self-inflicted deaths among children age 5 to 9 was generally less than 7 per year during the period covered by this table.

Source: U.S. National Center for Education Statistics, *Digest of Education Statistics*, "Latest version of all Digest tables," <nces.ed.gov/programs/digest>, accessed May 2024; and *Report on Indicators of School Crime and Safety*, annual. See also <nces.ed.gov/surveys/ssocs>.

Table 338. School Shootings and Casualties by Type of Casualty and School Level: 2001 to 2022

[For school year ending in year shown. School shootings include all incidents in which a gun is brandished or fired or a bullet hits school property for any reason, regardless of the number of victims (including zero), time, day of the week, or reason (e.g., planned attack, accidental, domestic violence, gang-related). Deaths and injuries include both shooters and victims. Data are from the School Shooting Database Project of the Department of Defense, Naval Postgraduate School's Center for Homeland Defense and Security]

Year	Casualties			School shootings							
					Type of casualty			School level [1]			
	Total	Deaths	Injuries	Total	With deaths	With injuries only	With no casualties	Elementary schools	Middle or junior high schools	High schools [2]	Other [3]
2001	47	18	29	30	16	7	7	4	3	23	0
2002	18	5	13	17	5	8	4	2	1	14	0
2003	29	13	16	24	12	7	5	2	6	16	0
2004	45	16	29	34	12	16	6	5	3	26	0
2005	63	22	41	44	12	27	5	9	1	32	2
2006	55	13	42	51	12	30	9	5	6	39	0
2007	91	28	63	64	21	35	8	9	12	42	1
2008	23	10	13	16	8	6	2	2	2	11	1
2009	61	19	42	52	19	22	11	11	6	31	4
2010	15	5	10	15	5	6	4	1	2	12	0
2011	32	8	24	18	7	10	1	4	2	12	0
2012	21	9	12	16	6	8	2	3	3	9	1
2013	55	42	13	26	14	8	4	7	5	13	1
2014	55	19	36	46	15	22	9	7	3	32	4
2015	65	20	45	43	15	20	8	13	4	24	2
2016	45	9	36	38	8	19	11	7	4	25	2
2017	61	14	47	48	13	26	9	8	9	31	0
2018	185	52	133	89	22	37	30	14	8	64	3
2019	116	34	82	115	33	45	37	35	14	60	4
2020 [4]	126	32	94	116	27	51	38	33	11	70	2
2021 [4]	118	46	72	146	43	50	53	59	21	57	8
2022	350	81	269	327	57	131	139	82	37	189	11

[1] Schools that had multiple shootings in a single year are counted only once in that year's total. [2] Includes other school types which end in grade 12. [3] Includes schools for which school-level information was unknown or unspecified as well as those whose school level was "other." [4] Due to school closures caused by the COVID-19 pandemic, caution should be used when comparing 2020 and 2021 data with data from earlier years.

Source: U.S. National Center for Education Statistics, *Digest of Education Statistics*, "Latest version of all Digest tables," <nces.ed.gov/programs/digest>, accessed May 2023.

Section 5
Law Enforcement, Courts, and Prisons

This section presents data on crimes committed, victims of crimes, arrests, and data related to criminal violations and the criminal justice system. The major sources of these data are the Bureau of Justice Statistics (BJS), the Federal Bureau of Investigation (FBI), and the Administrative Office of the U.S. Courts. BJS issues many reports—see Appendix I: Guide to Sources for a complete listing. The Federal Bureau of Investigation presents data on reported crimes as gathered from state and local law enforcement agencies.

Legal jurisdiction and law enforcement—Law enforcement is, for the most part, a function of state and local officers and agencies. The U.S. Constitution reserves general police powers to the states. By act of Congress, federal offenses include only offenses against the U.S. government and against or by its employees while engaged in their official duties, and offenses which involve the crossing of state lines or an interference with interstate commerce. Excluding the military, there are 52 separate criminal law jurisdictions in the United States: one in each of the 50 states, one in the District of Columbia, and the federal jurisdiction. Each of these has its own criminal laws and procedures and its own law enforcement agencies. While the systems of law enforcement are quite similar among the states, there are often substantial differences in the penalties for like offenses.

Law enforcement can be divided into three parts: Investigation of crimes and arrests of persons suspected of committing them; prosecution of those charged with crime; and the punishment or treatment of persons convicted of crime.

Crime—The U.S. Department of Justice administers two statistical programs to measure the magnitude, nature, and impact of crime in the nation: the Uniform Crime Reporting (UCR) Program and the National Crime Victimization Survey (NCVS). Each of these programs produces valuable information about aspects of the nation's crime problem. Because the UCR and NCVS programs are conducted for different purposes, use different methods, and focus on somewhat different aspects of crime, the information they produce together provides a more comprehensive panorama of the nation's crime problem than either could produce alone.

Uniform Crime Reporting (UCR) Program—The FBI's UCR Program, which began in 1929, collects information on the crimes reported to law enforcement authorities. The latest UCR releases are available on the FBI's Crime Data Explorer. UCR definitions of criminal offenses can be found at <cde.ucr.cjis.gov>.

The UCR Program compiles data from monthly law enforcement reports or individual crime incident records transmitted directly to the FBI or to centralized state agencies that then report to the FBI. The UCR Program presents crime counts for the nation as a whole, as well as for regions, states, counties, cities, towns, tribal law enforcement, and colleges and universities. This permits studies among neighboring jurisdictions and among those with similar populations and other common characteristics.

In addition to crime counts and trends, this program includes data on persons arrested, with detail by age, sex, and race; law enforcement personnel, including the number of sworn officers killed or assaulted; and the characteristics of homicides including age, sex, and race of victims and offenders.

In 2021, the FBI's UCR Program transitioned from its long-time Summary Reporting System (SRS), a simple collection of counts of crimes and arrests, to the more comprehensive National Incident-Based Reporting System (NIBRS). The NIBRS provides more information about offenses, victims, offenders, and demographic and other characteristics of crime incidents. There are two categories of offenses reported in the NIBRS: Group A and Group B. Group A offenses are used to report all incidents committed within a law enforcement agency's jurisdiction, whereas Group B offenses are used only to report arrest data. With these groupings, NIBRS expands on the offense types measured in the SRS and collects incident and arrest information from law enforcement agencies for 22 categories of offenses in Group A, as well as arrest information only for 10 Group B offense categories.

National Crime Victimization Survey (NCVS)—A second perspective on crime is provided by this survey of the Bureau of Justice Statistics (BJS). The NCVS is an annual data collection (interviews of persons aged 12 or older) conducted by the U.S. Census Bureau for the BJS. As an ongoing survey of households, the NCVS measures crimes of violence and property both reported and not reported to police. It produces national rates and levels of personal and property victimization. No attempt is made to validate the information against police records or any other source.

The NCVS measures rape/sexual assault, robbery, assault, pocket-picking, purse snatching, burglary, and motor vehicle theft. Murder and kidnaping are not covered. The so-called victimless crimes, such as drunkenness, drug abuse, and prostitution, also are excluded, as are crimes for which it is difficult to identify knowledgeable respondents or to locate data records.

Crimes of which the victim may not be aware also cannot be measured effectively. Buying stolen property may fall into this category, as may some instances of embezzlement. Attempted crimes of many types probably are under-recorded for this reason. Events in which the victim has shown a willingness to participate in illegal activity also are excluded.

A *victimization*, the basic measure of the occurrence of crime, is a specific criminal act as it affects a single victim. The number of victimizations is determined by the number of victims of such acts. Victimization counts serve as key elements in computing rates of victimization. For crimes against persons, the rates are based on the total number of individuals aged 12 and over or on a portion of that population sharing a particular characteristic or set of traits. As general indicators of the danger of having been victimized during the reference period, the rates are not sufficiently refined to represent true measures of risk for specific individuals or households.

An *incident* is a specific criminal act involving one or more victims; therefore the number of incidents of personal crimes is lower than that of victimizations.

In any encounter involving a personal crime, more than one criminal act can be committed against an individual. For example, a rape may be associated with a robbery, or a household property offense, such as a burglary, can escalate into something more serious in the event of a personal confrontation. Each criminal incident has been counted only once, by the most serious act that took place during the incident, and ranked in accordance with the seriousness classification system used by the FBI. The order of seriousness for crimes against persons is as follows: rape, robbery, assault, and larceny. Personal crimes take precedence over household offenses.

Courts—Statistics on criminal offenses and the outcome of prosecutions are incomplete for the country as a whole, although data are available for many states individually.

State courts handle the majority of civil and criminal litigation in the country. Only when the U.S. Constitution and acts of Congress specifically confer jurisdiction upon the federal courts may civil or criminal litigation be heard and decided by them. Generally, the federal courts have jurisdiction over the following types of cases: suits or proceedings by or against the United States; civil actions between private parties arising under the Constitution, laws, or treaties of the United States; civil actions between private litigants who are citizens of different states; civil cases involving admiralty, maritime, or private jurisdiction; and all matters in bankruptcy.

There are several types of courts with varying degrees of legal jurisdiction. These jurisdictions include original, appellate, general, and limited or special. A court of original jurisdiction is one having the authority initially to try a case and pass judgment on the law and the facts; a court of appellate jurisdiction is one with the legal authority to review cases and hear appeals; a court of general jurisdiction is a trial court of unlimited original jurisdiction in civil and/or criminal cases, also called a "major trial court"; a court of limited or special jurisdiction is a trial court with legal authority over only a particular class of cases, such as probate, juvenile, or traffic cases.

The 94 federal courts of original jurisdiction are known as the U.S. district courts. One or more of these courts is established in every state and one each in the District of Columbia, Puerto Rico, the Virgin Islands, the Northern Mariana Islands, and Guam. Appeals from the district courts are taken to intermediate appellate courts of which there are 13, known as U.S. courts of appeals and the United States Court of Appeals for the Federal Circuit. The Supreme Court of the United States is the final and highest appellate court in the federal system of courts.

Juvenile offenders—For statistical purposes, the FBI and most states classify as juvenile offenders persons under the age of 18 years who have committed a crime or crimes.

Delinquency cases are all cases of youths referred to a juvenile court for violation of a law or ordinance or for seriously "antisocial" conduct. Several types of

facilities are available for those adjudicated delinquents, ranging from short-term physically unrestricted to long-term very restrictive supervision.

Prisoners and jail inmates—BJS started to collect annual data in 1979 on prisoners in federal and state prisons and reformatories. Adults convicted of criminal activity may be given a prison or jail sentence. A *prison* is a confinement facility having custodial authority over adults sentenced to confinement of more than 1 year. A *jail* is a facility, usually operated by a local law enforcement agency, holding persons detained pending adjudication and/or persons committed after adjudication for 1 year or less.

Data on inmates in local jails were collected by the BJS for the first time in 1970. Jail censuses are taken periodically. For details, see <bjs.ojp.gov/data-collection/census-jails-coj>.

Statistical reliability—For discussion of statistical collection, estimation and sampling procedures, and measures of statistical reliability pertaining to the National Crime Victimization Survey and Uniform Crime Reporting Program, see Appendix III.

Table 339. Crimes and Crime Rates by Type of Offense: 2005 to 2022

[11,875 represents 11,875,000. Data include offenses reported to law enforcement, and offense estimations for nonreporting and partially reporting agencies within each state. Rates are based on Census Bureau estimated resident population as of July 1, except 2000 and 2010, which are enumerated as of April 1. See source for details]

Item and year	All crimes	Violent crime						Property crime			
		Total	Murder [1]	Rape [2]	Rape legacy def. [2]	Robbery	Aggra-vated assault	Total	Burglary	Larceny/theft	Motor vehicle theft
NUMBER OF OFFENSES (1,000)											
2005	11,875	1,461	17.8	(NA)	92.0	453	898	10,414	2,209	6,917	1,288
2006	11,457	1,433	17.2	(NA)	89.6	452	875	10,023	2,198	6,626	1,199
2007	11,406	1,438	17.4	(NA)	87.6	456	877	9,969	2,214	6,645	1,110
2008	11,231	1,398	16.6	(NA)	85.6	448	848	9,832	2,249	6,617	966
2009	10,739	1,333	15.5	(NA)	86.3	414	817	9,406	2,223	6,380	803
2010	10,502	1,271	14.9	(NA)	87.4	376	793	9,231	2,197	6,277	756
2011	10,287	1,213	14.8	(NA)	84.6	357	757	9,074	2,197	6,154	723
2012	10,198	1,218	15.0	(NA)	84.9	355	763	8,981	2,111	6,146	723
2013	9,845	1,171	14.3	114.9	80.8	347	729	8,674	1,936	6,034	704
2014	9,415	1,159	14.2	118.5	83.6	325	736	8,256	1,725	5,837	694
2015	9,172	1,197	15.9	125.4	88.9	327	766	7,975	1,580	5,685	710
2016	9,233	1,260	17.4	132.2	98.5	335	809	7,973	1,525	5,676	773
2017	8,923	1,230	18.2	137.1	95.9	311	805	7,693	1,397	5,526	769
2018	8,620	1,222	16.9	146.5	103.9	282	819	7,398	1,268	5,364	767
2019	8,195	1,195	17.0	144.6	101.8	263	812	7,000	1,112	5,162	725
2020	7,740	1,269	22.4	131.9	92.7	241	913	6,471	1,026	4,629	816
2021	7,338	1,254	22.5	140.9	109.7	218	904	6,084	899	4,335	850
2022	7,746	1,232	21.2	133.3	96.8	220	894	6,514	899	4,672	942
RATE PER 100,000 POPULATION											
2005	4,006	493	6.0	(NA)	31.0	153	303	3,513	745	2,334	434
2006	3,827	479	5.8	(NA)	29.9	151	292	3,348	734	2,213	400
2007	3,782	477	5.8	(NA)	29.1	151	291	3,305	734	2,203	368
2008	3,694	460	5.4	(NA)	28.1	147	279	3,234	740	2,176	318
2009	3,498	434	5.1	(NA)	28.1	135	266	3,064	724	2,078	261
2010	3,402	412	4.8	(NA)	28.3	122	257	2,990	712	2,033	245
2011	3,302	389	4.7	(NA)	27.2	115	243	2,912	705	1,975	232
2012	3,249	388	4.8	(NA)	27.1	113	243	2,861	673	1,958	230
2013	3,114	370	4.5	36.4	25.6	110	231	2,744	612	1,909	223
2014	2,953	364	4.5	37.2	26.2	102	231	2,589	541	1,831	218
2015	2,854	372	4.9	39.0	27.7	102	238	2,481	492	1,769	221
2016	2,857	390	5.4	40.9	30.5	104	250	2,468	472	1,757	239
2017	2,740	378	5.6	42.1	29.5	96	247	2,362	429	1,697	236
2018	2,635	373	5.2	44.8	31.7	86	250	2,261	388	1,639	234
2019	2,497	364	5.2	44.1	31.0	80	248	2,133	339	1,573	221
2020	2,349	385	6.8	40.0	28.1	73	277	1,964	312	1,405	248
2021	2,210	378	6.8	42.4	33.0	66	272	1,832	271	1,306	256
2022	2,324	370	6.3	40.0	29.1	66	268	1,954	270	1,402	283

NA Not available. [1] Includes nonnegligent manslaughter. [2] Beginning 2013, the FBI introduced a revised definition of rape. For more information, see <ucr.fbi.gov/recent-program-updates/new-rape-definition-frequently-asked-questions>.

Source: U.S. Department of Justice, Federal Bureau of Investigation, Crime Data Explorer, Documents & Downloads, "Crime in the United States Annual Reports," <cde.ucr.cjis.gov/LATEST/webapp/#/pages/downloads>, accessed April 2024.

Table 340. Crimes and Crime Rates by Offense Type and Geographic Area: 2022

[In thousands (940.4 represents 940,400), except rate. Rate per 100,000 population. For area definitions, see source. See headnote, Table 339]

Type of crime	Cities		Metropolitan counties [1]		Nonmetropolitan counties [1]		Suburban areas [2]	
	Total	Rate	Total	Rate	Total	Rate	Total	Rate
Violent crime	940.4	485.5	189.2	261.9	47.8	216.5	313.3	252.4
Murder [3]	15.1	7.8	3.1	4.3	1.1	4.8	4.8	3.9
Rape [4]	88.9	45.9	22.6	31.2	9.0	40.8	39.9	32.2
Robbery	186.0	96.0	22.5	31.1	1.7	7.5	39.7	32.0
Aggravated assault	650.4	335.8	141.0	195.2	36.1	163.5	228.9	184.4
Property crime	4,812.4	2,484.8	906.7	1,255.4	189.4	857.6	1,816.9	1,463.8
Burglary	634.9	327.8	142.6	197.4	46.0	208.2	250.8	202.1
Larceny-theft	3,440.1	1,776.2	643.2	890.5	119.0	538.9	1,338.6	1,078.4
Motor vehicle theft	737.4	380.7	121.0	167.5	24.4	110.5	227.4	183.2

[1] Includes state police agencies that report aggregately for the entire state. [2] Suburban areas include law enforcement agencies in cities with less than 50,000 inhabitants and county law enforcement agencies within a Metropolitan Statistical Area. Excludes all metropolitan agencies associated with a principal city. Agencies associated with suburban areas also appear in other groups within this table. [3] Includes nonnegligent manslaughter. [4] Estimated using the revised FBI Uniform Crime Reporting (UCR) definition of rape. For more information, see <ucr.fbi.gov/recent-program-updates/new-rape-definition-frequently-asked-questions>.

Source: U.S. Department of Justice, Federal Bureau of Investigation, Crime Data Explorer, Documents & Downloads, "Crime in the United States Annual Reports, Offenses Known to Law Enforcement," <cde.ucr.cjis.gov/LATEST/webapp/#/pages/downloads>, accessed June 2024.

Table 341. Crimes Against Persons and Property by Type of Offense and State: 2022

[Number, except as noted (256,188 represents 256,188,000). For year ending December 31. Offenses reported to law enforcement. Based on Census Bureau estimated resident population as of July 1. Beginning 2021, the FBI's Uniform Crime Reporting (UCR) program transitioned from its long-time Summary Reporting System (SRS) to the more comprehensive National Incident-Based Reporting System (NIBRS). See source for details]

State	Agencies reporting	Population covered (1,000s)	Crimes against persons				Crimes against property				
			Total [1]	Assault	Homicide	Sex offenses [2]	Total [1]	Burglary/ breaking and entering	Larceny/ theft offenses	Motor vehicle theft	Robbery
United States....	**13,293**	**256,188**	**3,456,189**	**3,187,575**	**18,785**	**204,055**	**7,849,624**	**672,139**	**3,618,452**	**721,157**	**149,862**
Alabama.............	404	4,520	76,654	73,898	482	1,900	130,599	12,056	60,400	8,757	1,513
Alaska..............	32	444	6,681	5,826	45	760	8,399	760	3,452	637	99
Arizona.............	89	4,572	58,118	53,000	293	3,949	127,557	10,138	61,878	7,667	1,387
Arkansas...........	294	2,986	64,358	60,242	337	3,117	119,718	13,732	54,872	7,436	1,208
California...........	559	20,451	184,079	165,486	762	12,857	543,624	52,995	227,300	65,460	14,283
Colorado............	234	5,826	72,319	63,021	448	6,536	284,165	22,374	119,556	45,599	4,320
Connecticut........	107	3,626	31,418	29,074	168	1,830	88,162	4,645	43,041	7,009	1,630
Delaware...........	63	1,018	16,578	15,790	71	530	38,855	2,132	16,794	1,658	584
Dist. of Columbia. ..	2	672	21,196	20,235	197	716	45,536	1,376	19,002	3,907	2,404
Florida [3].............	73	7,025	74,044	70,914	394	2,540	136,827	8,632	77,091	8,361	2,780
Georgia.............	454	9,959	134,475	122,238	886	8,675	264,972	19,996	124,775	19,699	4,217
Hawaii..............	3	1,234	13,870	12,829	35	791	38,681	3,145	22,110	4,621	887
Idaho...............	111	1,939	19,073	16,597	56	2,128	32,343	3,003	13,436	1,734	160
Illinois [3].............	520	10,011	163,645	155,025	924	6,528	313,085	20,294	122,857	31,339	11,258
Indiana..............	209	5,604	74,029	66,875	483	4,827	125,037	12,344	67,178	11,678	2,777
Iowa................	228	2,969	29,140	26,733	66	2,082	64,022	6,355	29,204	4,285	621
Kansas.............	327	2,676	45,701	41,377	146	2,745	97,016	6,578	40,300	6,204	797
Kentucky...........	431	4,510	44,610	39,877	343	3,235	100,000	10,519	46,499	9,486	1,654
Louisiana...........	148	3,428	60,879	57,358	390	2,434	126,599	16,487	63,632	8,128	1,577
Maine...............	131	1,384	13,056	12,059	54	901	26,621	1,583	14,562	980	141
Maryland [3].........	95	4,898	59,862	56,010	502	3,164	141,602	9,647	61,563	11,711	6,248
Massachusetts......	384	6,948	74,878	69,888	159	4,243	137,461	9,989	60,288	6,986	2,647
Michigan............	603	9,617	164,531	151,275	811	11,562	252,945	20,657	105,229	26,155	3,667
Minnesota..........	408	5,711	49,649	43,792	252	4,919	177,765	12,166	84,856	16,534	3,266
Mississippi..........	152	1,792	23,446	22,172	148	964	46,673	5,681	21,510	2,898	433
Missouri............	498	6,077	86,566	80,256	726	4,676	217,981	17,381	97,588	30,218	3,397
Montana............	110	1,121	15,469	13,322	58	1,763	33,707	2,180	17,725	2,509	266
Nebraska...........	261	1,460	17,645	15,871	49	1,549	37,642	2,220	15,986	2,021	240
Nevada.............	55	3,162	66,653	61,511	245	3,871	121,232	13,886	48,477	15,654	2,748
New Hampshire.....	213	1,379	15,448	13,400	40	1,777	28,486	960	12,182	902	221
New Jersey.........	309	5,630	43,739	40,919	171	2,384	123,401	8,111	61,952	9,341	2,573
New Mexico........	95	1,813	39,872	36,610	229	2,045	99,041	11,159	38,343	10,859	2,245
New York...........	149	4,588	50,087	47,124	201	2,107	117,908	7,875	58,611	6,324	2,392
North Carolina......	407	10,236	149,418	139,683	919	7,031	345,497	36,551	160,189	20,366	5,774
North Dakota........	111	779	12,417	11,127	45	1,086	24,848	2,600	11,109	1,994	217
Ohio................	637	10,917	163,545	151,500	710	9,207	305,310	27,901	144,278	26,339	6,146
Oklahoma...........	461	4,020	66,170	60,354	328	4,739	144,894	19,172	63,269	12,736	1,649
Oregon..............	212	4,080	41,715	37,219	244	3,741	186,210	14,587	86,671	22,816	2,865
Pennsylvania [3]......	132	5,229	67,815	61,606	767	5,148	161,382	9,984	71,539	14,367	6,237
Rhode Island........	48	1,092	9,334	8,560	18	714	25,159	1,448	11,083	1,717	268
South Carolina......	462	5,271	96,360	90,929	641	3,849	190,908	17,643	91,615	12,726	2,133
South Dakota.......	107	830	13,812	12,497	67	1,099	23,632	2,021	11,746	2,114	230
Tennessee..........	399	7,048	143,204	134,516	688	6,009	253,273	21,927	116,528	25,562	4,755
Texas...............	1,063	29,644	467,425	437,755	2,369	23,246	999,574	94,689	496,659	98,026	21,219
Utah................	135	3,326	39,497	32,918	85	5,290	105,136	6,331	50,492	6,631	977
Vermont.............	86	647	4,224	3,791	27	317	15,882	1,004	9,408	595	88
Virginia.............	410	8,683	109,467	100,568	732	6,182	252,769	10,886	124,772	13,673	3,353
Washington..........	246	7,730	89,785	82,011	454	5,807	402,332	42,473	179,545	49,693	6,785
West Virginia........	214	1,542	13,813	12,453	92	1,126	27,946	2,894	14,630	1,383	168
Wisconsin..........	362	5,610	50,315	43,989	401	4,856	126,511	8,163	57,313	13,033	2,326
Wyoming............	50	454	6,105	5,495	27	503	10,699	809	5,357	629	32

[1] Includes other crimes not shown separately. [2] Any sexual act including rape, sodomy, sexual assault with an object, fondling, and incest directed against another person without the consent of the victim, including instances where the victim is incapable of giving consent. [3] Interpret with caution; limited data available.

Source: U.S. Department of Justice, Federal Bureau of Investigation, Crime Data Explorer, Documents & Downloads, "National Incident-Based Reporting System (NIBRS) Tables, State," <cde.ucr.cjis.gov/LATEST/webapp/#/pages/downloads>, accessed June 2024.

Table 342. Crime Rates by State, 2021 and 2022, and by Type of Offense, 2022

[For year ending December 31. Rates per 100,000 population. Offenses reported to law enforcement. Based on Census Bureau estimated resident population as of July 1. Beginning 2021, the FBI's Uniform Crime Reporting (UCR) program transitioned from its long-time Summary Reporting System (SRS) to the more comprehensive National Incident-Based Reporting System (NIBRS)]

State	Violent crime						Property crime				
	2021, total [4]	2022					2021, total [4]	2022			
		Total	Murder	Rape [1]	Robbery	Aggravated assault		Total	Burglary	Larceny/ theft	Motor vehicle theft
United States............	**387.0**	**380.7**	**6.3**	**40.0**	**66.1**	**268.2**	**1,832.3**	**1,954.4**	**269.8**	**1,401.9**	**282.7**
Alabama...................	348.3	409.1	10.9	29.6	34.5	334.1	1,470.8	1,739.0	283.9	1,252.7	202.3
Alaska....................	759.1	758.9	9.5	134.0	75.1	540.2	1,832.8	1,789.0	269.0	1,274.6	245.5
Arizona...................	425.6	431.5	6.8	44.1	70.1	310.5	2,114.8	2,057.6	271.0	1,542.4	244.2
Arkansas..................	702.4	645.3	10.2	76.0	39.7	519.4	2,529.0	2,451.5	466.4	1,734.4	250.7
California................	481.2	499.5	5.7	37.4	123.5	332.8	2,165.3	2,343.2	371.9	1,499.3	471.9
Colorado..................	480.4	492.5	6.4	63.4	72.6	350.1	3,146.5	3,147.6	395.2	1,966.7	785.7
Connecticut...............	168.6	150.0	3.8	18.1	44.9	83.3	1,518.4	1,494.0	130.1	1,168.1	195.8
Delaware..................	419.2	383.5	4.8	22.0	57.0	299.8	1,881.4	1,964.1	203.1	1,591.1	169.9
District of Columbia [2]......	951.3	812.3	29.3	41.5	357.5	383.9	4,137.2	3,561.5	201.2	2,783.0	577.3
Florida [3].................	337.3	258.9	5.0	30.2	33.6	190.1	1,517.6	1,566.2	173.5	1,254.7	138.0
Georgia...................	349.8	367.0	8.2	36.4	43.6	278.8	1,601.4	1,690.8	217.8	1,266.5	206.5
Hawaii....................	274.0	259.6	2.1	37.9	66.1	153.5	2,533.2	2,434.7	260.0	1,767.7	407.0
Idaho.....................	240.8	241.4	2.7	48.7	8.2	181.7	964.7	926.9	158.6	677.1	91.2
Illinois [3]................	344.8	287.3	7.8	48.1	84.7	146.7	1,393.3	1,682.7	208.5	1,192.7	281.6
Indiana...................	332.6	306.2	6.2	32.8	43.0	224.2	1,553.0	1,544.2	226.1	1,118.6	199.4
Iowa......................	295.0	286.5	1.7	42.5	21.6	220.7	1,508.3	1,331.5	218.6	965.4	147.4
Kansas....................	444.9	414.6	4.6	45.5	29.2	335.4	2,247.2	1,992.2	273.4	1,488.7	230.2
Kentucky..................	269.0	214.1	6.8	33.8	38.1	135.4	1,623.7	1,448.8	244.8	989.8	214.2
Louisiana.................	662.7	628.6	16.1	43.0	67.3	502.1	2,528.9	2,748.2	497.8	1,940.0	310.3
Maine.....................	112.9	103.3	2.2	32.0	10.0	59.0	1,134.2	1,213.5	115.9	1,026.8	70.9
Maryland [3]...............	435.1	398.5	8.5	30.6	114.2	245.2	1,522.0	1,635.4	190.2	1,225.4	219.8
Massachusetts.............	301.1	322.0	2.1	29.1	37.7	253.1	1,000.3	1,070.1	142.8	827.6	99.7
Michigan..................	491.1	461.0	6.9	64.8	36.6	352.7	1,366.9	1,536.8	214.3	1,055.3	267.2
Minnesota.................	308.9	280.6	3.2	40.7	57.0	179.7	2,045.6	1,966.8	214.2	1,464.8	287.9
Mississippi...............	255.4	245.0	7.8	33.7	25.6	178.0	1,860.4	1,746.8	350.2	1,222.6	173.9
Missouri..................	524.3	488.0	10.1	48.9	54.8	374.2	2,346.8	2,340.1	295.8	1,557.2	487.1
Montana...................	469.8	417.9	4.5	54.4	23.3	335.7	2,029.3	1,918.6	200.3	1,495.7	222.6
Nebraska..................	297.0	282.8	3.2	55.3	29.1	195.2	1,818.6	1,888.8	182.5	1,431.4	275.0
Nevada....................	432.0	454.0	6.8	58.9	86.1	302.3	2,232.3	2,380.1	436.1	1,453.5	490.5
New Hampshire.............	129.7	125.6	1.8	39.6	16.1	68.1	1,037.5	1,010.9	73.5	871.0	66.5
New Jersey................	183.5	202.9	3.1	16.8	47.6	135.4	1,109.4	1,416.7	148.0	1,109.1	159.6
New Mexico................	820.8	780.5	12.0	54.6	110.6	603.3	2,772.4	2,984.0	604.0	1,838.4	541.7
New York..................	308.3	429.3	4.0	29.5	112.0	283.8	1,047.8	1,721.6	162.5	1,422.0	137.1
North Carolina............	419.5	405.1	8.1	30.5	54.9	311.6	2,087.2	2,064.1	370.8	1,494.0	199.3
North Dakota..............	276.4	279.6	3.5	56.7	27.6	191.8	2,144.8	1,994.8	357.9	1,381.3	255.6
Ohio......................	317.4	293.6	6.1	48.4	53.1	185.9	1,720.1	1,782.7	255.3	1,292.9	234.5
Oklahoma..................	438.0	419.7	6.7	57.5	40.6	314.8	2,628.5	2,332.4	482.6	1,535.7	314.0
Oregon....................	341.3	342.4	4.5	40.6	68.6	228.7	2,690.9	2,935.3	360.7	2,023.0	551.5
Pennsylvania [3]...........	281.8	279.9	7.9	29.5	68.1	174.5	1,246.3	1,482.5	148.2	1,171.2	163.0
Rhode Island..............	200.5	172.3	1.5	38.0	24.6	108.3	1,228.3	1,285.3	128.1	997.6	159.6
South Carolina............	513.8	491.3	11.2	38.2	40.6	401.3	2,493.8	2,308.2	352.7	1,706.3	249.2
South Dakota..............	391.8	377.4	4.3	55.8	25.3	292.0	1,678.0	1,737.0	263.0	1,231.8	242.2
Tennessee.................	671.8	621.6	8.6	38.2	67.1	507.6	2,255.8	2,302.3	319.1	1,620.9	362.3
Texas.....................	453.0	431.9	6.7	50.0	70.5	304.7	2,171.9	2,299.9	334.3	1,634.4	331.2
Utah......................	259.1	241.8	2.0	59.5	29.6	150.7	2,099.2	1,895.1	201.7	1,485.1	208.4
Vermont...................	194.0	221.9	3.4	36.8	13.3	168.5	1,383.8	1,671.1	152.1	1,425.5	93.5
Virginia..................	225.5	234.0	7.3	30.2	38.4	158.1	1,449.4	1,695.7	124.6	1,410.4	160.7
Washington................	335.7	375.6	5.0	39.2	86.8	244.7	3,035.5	3,356.4	563.0	2,154.0	639.3
West Virginia.............	291.5	277.9	4.6	44.4	10.0	218.9	1,356.7	1,230.1	190.2	951.2	88.7
Wisconsin.................	325.4	297.0	5.3	38.6	39.4	213.7	1,537.5	1,385.0	153.7	981.0	250.3
Wyoming...................	223.8	201.9	2.6	62.8	7.9	128.7	1,685.8	1,636.8	209.5	1,264.9	162.4

[1] Beginning in 2013, the FBI has revised the definition of rape as used in Uniform Crime Reporting (UCR) Program. For more information, see <ucr.fbi.gov/recent-program-updates/new-rape-definition-frequently-asked-questions>. [2] Includes offenses reported by the Metro Transit Police and the District of Columbia Fire and Emergency Medical Services: Arson Investigation Unit. [3] Limited data for 2022 were available. [4] Limited data for 2021 were available for California, District of Columbia, Florida, Illinois, Maryland, New Jersey, New Mexico, New York, and Pennsylvania]

Source: U.S. Department of Justice, Federal Bureau of Investigation, Crime Data Explorer, Documents & Downloads, "Crime in the United States Annual Reports, Expanded Homicide Tables," <cde.ucr.cjis.gov/LATEST/webapp/#/pages/downloads>, accessed June 2024.

Table 343. Crime Rates by Type—Selected Large Cities: 2022

[For year ending December 31. Rates per 100,000 population. Offenses reported to law enforcement. Limited data were available for Florida, Illinois, Maryland, and Pennsylvania]

Cities ranked by population size, 2022	Population	Violent crime					Property crime			
		Total	Murder & nonnegligent manslaughter	Rape	Robbery	Aggravated assault	Total	Burglary	Larceny/ theft	Motor vehicle theft
New York, NY	8,236,567	744	5	32	212	495	2,141	177	1,795	170
Los Angeles, CA	3,809,182	834	10	55	240	530	2,708	394	1,645	669
Chicago, IL	2,652,124	540	23	52	337	128	3,133	288	2,046	799
Houston, TX	2,276,533	1,142	19	50	306	767	4,582	656	3,164	762
Las Vegas, NV	1,667,961	516	9	62	97	347	2,918	560	1,721	637
Phoenix, AZ	1,637,902	825	13	67	196	549	2,902	383	2,053	466
Philadelphia, PA	1,555,812	1,041	33	50	370	587	4,321	417	3,090	815
San Antonio, TX	1,465,608	883	16	106	116	645	5,069	637	3,588	844
San Diego, CA	1,377,838	431	4	30	93	303	1,818	239	1,096	482
Dallas, TX	1,286,121	778	12	38	166	562	3,813	528	2,245	1,040
Honolulu, HI	994,799	253	3	30	84	137	2,578	264	1,850	465
Austin, TX	965,234	540	7	55	97	381	3,590	499	2,536	555
San Jose, CA	956,814	527	4	93	132	298	2,651	406	1,569	676
Charlotte-Mecklenburg, NC	955,466	746	11	28	145	562	3,375	429	2,549	397
Fort Worth, TX	948,605	502	11	62	73	357	2,740	421	1,944	375
Columbus, OH	907,196	450	14	111	141	185	3,484	473	2,208	804
Indianapolis, IN	886,455	1,028	23	64	183	757	3,377	542	2,307	528
San Francisco, CA	764,693	696	7	40	310	339	6,246	778	4,646	822
Seattle, WA	729,691	838	7	43	240	548	5,721	1,201	3,568	951
Denver, CO	705,264	1,070	13	107	184	765	6,428	733	3,540	2,155
Oklahoma City, OK	692,726	642	9	73	93	467	3,059	553	2,078	428
Nashville, TN	679,562	1,102	12	57	180	853	3,825	511	2,874	440
El Paso, TX	678,232	313	3	43	39	227	1,379	143	1,028	208
Washington, DC	671,803	745	29	41	324	351	3,484	201	2,719	565
Boston, MA	638,925	619	7	28	121	464	1,802	190	1,427	185
Portland, OR	630,129	751	15	56	203	477	6,324	760	3,841	1,723
Detroit, MI	626,757	2,028	49	114	223	1,642	4,478	770	2,201	1,507
Memphis, TN	624,944	2,421	43	64	372	1,942	7,166	964	4,454	1,748
Baltimore, MD	570,546	1,553	50	45	556	901	3,277	584	2,093	600
Milwaukee, WI	561,743	1,509	38	76	281	1,114	3,507	397	1,429	1,681
Albuquerque, NM	560,557	1,380	22	61	295	1,002	4,796	813	2,931	1,052
Fresno, CA	546,871	865	11	44	176	634	3,449	728	2,148	573
Sacramento, CA	526,671	902	10	35	236	620	3,167	526	1,961	681
Mesa, AZ	513,116	427	5	48	61	314	1,770	214	1,348	208
Kansas City, MO	508,856	1,481	33	74	220	1,155	4,715	567	2,952	1,196
Atlanta, GA	495,707	841	34	32	143	632	3,748	371	2,711	666
Colorado Springs, CO	487,728	643	9	91	75	467	3,400	551	2,289	560
Omaha, NE	483,462	561	6	62	69	424	3,468	260	2,514	694
Raleigh, NC	470,829	500	9	37	93	360	2,335	256	1,823	255
Virginia Beach, VA	457,556	87	5	12	30	41	1,611	77	1,359	175
Long Beach, CA	447,528	549	8	44	158	338	2,599	478	1,435	686
Oakland, CA	428,374	1,521	28	77	639	777	6,475	629	4,049	1,797
Minneapolis, MN	421,690	1,226	19	78	420	709	5,262	605	3,201	1,456
Bakersfield, CA	411,873	546	9	31	161	345	3,972	773	2,020	1,179
Tulsa, OK	410,135	929	14	90	115	710	4,272	875	2,632	765
Wichita, KS	394,286	931	8	69	77	777	3,524	428	2,697	399
Aurora, CO	392,134	1,077	14	75	211	777	4,229	464	2,030	1,735
Arlington, TX	391,591	580	4	86	70	420	2,525	261	1,947	316
Tampa, FL	390,145	497	11	34	81	371	1,674	194	1,298	182
New Orleans, LA	370,128	1,444	72	119	281	972	4,641	496	3,009	1,135
Cleveland, OH	363,764	1,614	40	125	426	1,023	4,317	826	2,399	1,092
Anaheim, CA	344,795	766	3	36	110	616	2,769	491	1,756	522
Henderson, NV	325,332	303	1	30	72	200	1,919	292	1,359	268
Stockton, CA	323,501	1,157	15	55	303	784	2,744	544	1,742	458
Lexington, KY	320,983	270	10	55	70	135	2,716	342	1,992	382
Riverside, CA	319,889	516	5	43	136	332	3,240	489	2,206	546
Corpus Christi, TX	317,694	791	13	76	112	591	3,121	501	2,354	266
Irvine, CA	311,696	75	1	11	13	49	1,479	267	1,119	93
Orlando, FL	310,713	836	10	73	137	616	4,028	450	3,174	405
Cincinnati, OH	307,761	842	24	84	208	526	3,751	610	2,487	653
Newark, NJ	304,311	520	17	28	154	320	1,820	176	943	701
Greensboro, NC	298,719	819	13	26	156	624	3,785	556	2,817	412
Lincoln, NE	293,937	382	4	81	49	248	2,842	299	2,257	286
Plano, TX	289,847	158	0	31	30	97	1,896	235	1,481	180
Durham, NC	286,377	687	15	51	205	417	3,317	511	2,502	304
St. Louis, MO	286,053	1,472	70	53	281	1,069	7,254	806	3,898	2,550
Anchorage, AK	285,821	1,151	10	172	153	816	2,764	412	1,961	390
North Las Vegas, NV	284,422	422	9	46	128	238	1,774	291	837	646
Chandler, AZ	281,373	182	4	34	26	119	1,808	170	1,481	157
Chula Vista, CA	277,976	351	3	12	106	230	1,277	187	732	358
St. Paul, MN	277,533	766	12	87	149	518	4,648	542	2,957	1,149
Gilbert, AZ	277,123	117	1	27	11	78	1,017	100	842	76
Jersey City, NJ	276,300	220	4	14	32	170	1,384	22	1,131	231
Buffalo, NY	275,710	736	24	40	193	479	3,211	480	2,178	552

Source: U.S. Department of Justice, Federal Bureau of Investigation, Crime Data Explorer, Documents & Downloads, "Crime in the United States Annual Reports, Offenses Known to Law Enforcement," <cde.ucr.cjis.gov/LATEST/webapp/#/pages/downloads>, accessed June 2024.

Table 344. Homicide Trends: 1990 to 2020

[Based on Federal Bureau of Investigation's Uniform Crime Reports Supplementary Homicide Reports. Homicide includes murder and nonnegligent manslaughter, which is the willful killing of one human being by another. Excludes deaths caused by negligence, suicide, or accident; justifiable homicides; and attempts to murder. Justifiable homicides based on the reports of law enforcement agencies are analyzed separately. Deaths from the terrorist attacks of September 11, 2001 are not included. Data based on criminal homicides handled by state and local law enforcement, and as determined solely by police investigation, and not by the determination of a court, medical examiner, coroner, jury, or other non-law enforcement body. Excludes homicides handled by Federal law enforcement]

Year	Number of victims							Rate [1]						
	Total [2]	Male	Female	White	Black	American Indian/ Alaskan Native	Asian [3]	Total [2]	Male	Female	White	Black	American Indian/ Alaska Native	Asian [3]
1990...	23,438	18,303	5,115	11,278	11,487	150	250	9.4	15.0	4.0	5.4	37.5	7.3	3.3
1995...	21,606	16,549	5,021	10,374	10,442	160	421	8.1	12.7	3.7	4.7	30.9	6.6	4.4
1998...	16,974	12,756	4,140	8,391	7,933	141	252	6.2	9.4	2.9	3.7	22.3	5.2	2.3
1999...	15,522	11,704	3,800	7,777	7,139	160	298	5.6	8.6	2.7	3.4	19.7	5.6	2.6
2000...	15,586	11,818	3,733	7,560	7,425	119	280	5.5	8.6	2.6	3.3	20.3	4.0	2.4
2001...	16,037	12,232	3,775	7,884	7,522	105	319	5.6	8.7	2.6	3.4	20.2	3.4	2.6
2002...	16,229	12,429	3,770	7,796	7,770	130	308	5.6	8.8	2.6	3.3	20.6	4.1	2.4
2003...	16,528	12,792	3,707	7,944	7,883	117	351	5.7	9.0	2.5	3.4	20.6	3.5	2.6
2004...	16,148	12,553	3,555	7,939	7,570	134	282	5.5	8.7	2.4	3.4	19.5	3.9	2.0
2005...	16,740	13,149	3,565	8,045	8,016	131	312	5.7	9.1	2.4	3.4	20.4	3.7	2.2
2006...	17,309	13,605	3,661	8,063	8,548	123	343	5.8	9.3	2.4	3.4	21.4	3.3	2.3
2007...	17,128	13,411	3,678	8,017	8,450	104	302	5.7	9.1	2.4	3.3	20.9	2.7	1.9
2008...	16,465	12,844	3,573	7,953	7,860	124	250	5.4	8.6	2.3	3.3	19.1	3.1	1.6
2009...	15,399	11,846	3,535	7,450	7,374	119	290	5.0	7.9	2.3	3.0	17.7	2.9	1.7
2010...	14,722	11,371	3,328	6,851	7,322	117	260	4.8	7.5	2.1	2.8	17.4	2.7	1.5
2011...	14,661	11,354	3,281	6,786	7,277	111	284	4.7	7.4	2.1	2.7	17.1	2.6	1.6
2012...	14,856	11,518	3,318	6,834	7,481	101	285	4.7	7.5	2.1	2.8	17.3	2.3	1.6
2013...	14,319	11,116	3,178	6,519	7,268	104	257	4.5	7.1	2.0	2.6	16.6	2.3	1.4
2014...	14,164	10,939	3,188	6,421	7,196	122	249	4.4	7.0	2.0	2.6	16.2	2.7	1.3
2015...	15,883	12,499	3,354	6,938	8,293	183	253	4.9	7.9	2.1	2.8	18.5	4.0	1.3
2016...	17,413	13,648	3,719	7,628	9,084	169	298	5.4	8.6	2.3	3.0	20.0	3.6	1.5
2017...	17,294	13,545	3,695	7,574	8,922	214	302	5.3	8.4	2.2	3.0	19.4	4.6	1.4
2018...	16,374	12,618	3,722	7,117	8,516	184	289	5.0	7.8	2.2	2.8	18.4	3.9	1.3
2019...	16,669	13,061	3,573	6,912	8,971	199	304	5.1	8.1	2.1	2.7	19.3	4.2	1.4
2020...	21,570	17,185	4,341	8,526	12,035	293	328	6.5	10.6	2.6	3.3	25.5	6.0	1.5

[1] Rate is per 100,000 inhabitants. [2] Includes unknown sex, race, or ethnicity. [3] Includes Native Hawaiian and Pacific Islanders.

Source: U.S. Department of Justice, Office of Justice Programs, "Easy Access to the FBI's Supplementary Homicide Reports (EZASHR)," <ojjdp.gov/ojstatbb/ezashr/>; and U.S. Centers for Disease Control and Prevention, WONDER Online Database, "Multiple Cause of Death, 1999-2020," <wonder.cdc.gov/>; accessed May 2022.

Table 345. Homicide Victims by Race and Sex: 1990 to 2022

[Excludes deaths to nonresidents of the United States. Through 2017, data by race are consistent with 1977 Office of Management and Budget (OMB) standards. Beginning 2018, all 50 states and the District of Columbia reported race and Hispanic origin data according to 1997 Office of Management and Budget (OMB) standards. Beginning 1999, causes of death are classified by the International Classification of Diseases, Tenth Revision (ICD-10), replacing the Ninth Revision (ICD-9) used for 1979–1998 data. In ICD-9, the category Homicide also includes death as a result of legal intervention. ICD-10 differentiates between homicides due to assault and deaths due to legal intervention. Caution should be used in comparing data. See text, Section 2]

Year	Homicide victims					Homicide rate [2]				
	Total [1]	White		Black		Total [1]	White		Black	
		Male	Female	Male	Female		Male	Female	Male	Female
1990............	24,932	9,147	3,006	9,981	2,163	10.0	9.0	2.8	69.2	13.5
1995............	22,895	8,336	3,028	8,847	1,936	8.7	7.8	2.7	56.3	11.1
1999............	16,889	6,162	2,466	6,214	1,434	6.1	5.5	2.1	36.1	7.6
2000............	16,765	5,925	2,414	6,482	1,385	6.0	5.2	2.1	37.2	7.2
2001............	20,308	8,254	3,074	6,780	1,446	7.1	7.2	2.6	38.2	7.4
2002............	17,638	6,282	2,403	6,896	1,391	6.1	5.4	2.0	38.4	7.0
2003............	17,732	6,337	2,372	7,083	1,309	6.1	5.5	2.0	38.9	6.5
2004............	17,357	6,302	2,341	6,839	1,296	5.9	5.4	2.0	37.0	6.4
2005............	18,124	6,457	2,313	7,412	1,257	6.1	5.5	1.9	39.6	6.1
2006............	18,573	6,514	2,346	7,677	1,355	6.2	5.5	1.9	40.4	6.5
2007............	18,361	6,541	2,373	7,584	1,286	6.1	5.5	1.9	39.3	6.1
2008............	17,826	6,556	2,337	7,148	1,187	5.9	5.5	1.9	36.5	5.5
2009............	16,799	5,983	2,340	6,715	1,159	5.5	4.9	1.9	33.8	5.3
2010............	16,259	5,648	2,215	6,704	1,114	5.3	4.7	1.8	33.4	5.1
2011............	16,238	5,569	2,199	6,739	1,119	5.2	4.6	1.8	33.0	5.0
2012............	16,688	5,639	2,197	7,129	1,112	5.3	4.6	1.8	34.5	4.9
2013............	16,121	5,393	2,130	6,937	1,122	5.1	4.4	1.7	33.1	4.9
2014............	15,872	5,304	2,093	6,823	1,080	5.0	4.3	1.7	32.1	4.7
2015............	17,793	5,798	2,209	8,021	1,152	5.5	4.6	1.7	37.3	4.9
2016............	19,362	6,325	2,343	8,650	1,345	6.0	5.1	1.8	39.8	5.7
2017............	19,510	6,274	2,496	8,776	1,297	6.0	5.0	1.9	39.8	5.4
2018 [3].......	18,830	5,987	2,348	8,184	1,424	5.8	4.8	1.9	39.0	6.2
2019 [3].......	19,141	5,828	2,268	8,737	1,353	5.8	4.7	1.8	41.4	5.9
2020 [3].......	24,576	7,286	2,532	11,845	1,809	7.5	5.9	2.0	55.5	7.8
2021 [3].......	26,031	7,760	2,573	12,476	2,078	7.8	6.2	2.0	57.5	8.9
2022 [3].......	24,849	7,538	2,620	11,528	1,918	7.5	6.0	2.1	52.7	8.2

[1] Includes other races not shown separately. [2] Rates per 100,000 resident population in specified group. Based on enumerated population figures as of April 1 for 1990, 2000, and 2010; estimated resident population as of July 1 for other years. [3] Beginning 2018, data by race not directly comparable with previous years due to implementation of new OMB race reporting standards.

Source: U.S. National Center for Health Statistics, through 2014, National Vital Statistics Reports (NVSR), *Deaths: Final Data for 2014*, Vol. 65, No. 4, June 2016 and earlier reports; thereafter, CDC WONDER Online Database, "Multiple Cause of Death, 1999-2020," and "Multiple Cause of Death, 2018-2022," <wonder.cdc.gov>, accessed August 2024.

Table 346. Murder Victims by Age, Sex, and Race/Ethnicity: 2022

[For year ending December 31. The FBI's Uniform Crime Reporting (UCR) Program defines murder and nonnegligent manslaughter as the willful (nonnegligent) killing of one human being by another. The classification of this offense is based solely on police investigation as opposed to the determination of a court, medical examiner, coroner, jury, or other judicial body. The UCR Program does not include the following situations in this offense classification: deaths caused by negligence, suicide, or accident; justifiable homicides; and attempts to murder, which are scored as aggravated assaults]

Age	Total [1]	Sex		Race			Ethnicity [2]	
		Male	Female	White	Black	Other [3]	Hispanic or Latino	Not Hispanic or Latino
Murders, total [1].............	**19,196**	**14,993**	**4,118**	**7,704**	**10,470**	**568**	**3,206**	**11,933**
Percent of total [4].............	100.0	78.1	21.5	40.1	54.5	3.0	19.0	70.5
Under 18 years old [1]..........	1,800	1,295	490	694	1,001	61	353	1,065
18 years old and over [1].......	17,211	13,588	3,592	6,962	9,400	500	2,834	10,802
Infant (under 1 year old).......	163	89	68	87	66	4	26	94
1 to 4 years old................	251	141	106	103	116	15	25	156
5 to 8 years old................	127	70	56	64	54	8	18	78
9 to 12 years old...............	125	63	61	70	45	8	43	65
13 to 16 years old..............	683	556	124	230	423	19	152	400
17 to 19 years old..............	1,628	1,382	246	513	1,059	30	335	972
20 to 24 years old..............	2,720	2,219	499	796	1,818	56	445	1,702
25 to 29 years old..............	2,604	2,130	472	820	1,678	54	465	1,623
30 to 34 years old..............	2,667	2,179	484	970	1,569	80	450	1,663
35 to 39 years old..............	1,997	1,585	408	829	1,050	75	399	1,206
40 to 44 years old..............	1,624	1,285	337	715	835	51	274	1,022
45 to 49 years old..............	1,116	866	248	555	503	31	193	699
50 to 54 years old..............	927	721	202	464	409	37	138	578
55 to 59 years old..............	774	561	206	406	305	34	82	497
60 to 64 years old..............	607	437	170	343	228	22	58	419
65 to 69 years old..............	413	281	132	253	128	22	32	293
70 to 74 years old..............	242	149	91	168	59	7	28	160
75 years old and over..........	343	169	172	270	56	8	24	240

[1] Includes unknown victim categories not shown separately. [2] Not all agencies provide ethnicity data; therefore, data will not sum to total. [3] Includes American Indian or Alaska Native, Asian, and Native Hawaiian or Pacific Islander. [4] Percentages rounded, may not add to 100.

Source: U.S. Department of Justice, Federal Bureau of Investigation, Crime Data Explorer, Documents & Downloads, "Crime in the United States Annual Reports, Expanded Homicide Tables," <cde.ucr.cjis.gov/LATEST/webapp/#/pages/downloads>, accessed June 2024.

Table 347. Murder Victims—Circumstances and Weapons Used or Cause of Death: 2000 to 2022

[For year ending December 31. The FBI's Uniform Crime Reporting (UCR) Program defines murder and nonnegligent manslaughter as the willful (nonnegligent) killing of one human being by another. See headnote, Table 346]

Characteristic	2000	2010	2015	2018	2019	2020	2021	2022
Murders, total [1].........................	**13,230**	**13,164**	**13,847**	**14,378**	**14,372**	**18,788**	**16,259**	**19,196**
CIRCUMSTANCES								
Felonies, total [1]........................	2,229	1,974	1,930	2,181	2,082	2,153	1,217	1,534
Rape [2]..............................	58	41	14	14	12	20	8	25
Robbery.............................	1,077	803	596	548	520	553	252	369
Burglary.............................	76	85	87	87	86	105	83	86
Larceny-theft.......................	23	21	18	23	33	51	49	43
Motor vehicle theft.................	25	35	34	62	39	60	76	63
Arson...............................	81	35	19	67	74	96	94	123
Prostitution and commercialized vice.	6	5	7	13	15	7	2	5
Other sex offenses..................	10	14	15	5	9	12	3	5
Narcotic drug laws..................	589	474	452	609	645	670	434	454
Gambling...........................	12	7	5	6	3	5	0	0
Suspected felony type...............	60	68	103	206	118	86	0	38
Other than felony type [1]............	6,871	6,485	5,831	6,362	6,225	8,267	6,871	8,329
Domestic violence..................	122	90	103	143	84	113	4	30
Child killed by babysitter...........	30	36	42	32	20	11	8	8
Brawl due to influence of alcohol....	188	122	117	67	46	33	2	9
Brawl due to influence of narcotics..	99	60	72	20	29	63	1	5
Argument over money or property....	206	187	181	201	131	140	11	49
Other arguments....................	3,589	3,280	2,932	3,304	3,506	4,356	4,046	4,715
Gangland killings...................	65	181	181	315	282	500	178	279
Juvenile gang killings...............	653	675	576	309	294	418	41	316
Institutional killings................	10	17	24	24	32	35	53	88
Unknown.............................	4,070	4,637	5,983	5,629	5,947	8,282	8,171	9,295
TYPE OF WEAPON OR CAUSE OF DEATH [1]								
Total firearms............................	8,661	8,874	9,143	10,379	10,503	14,369	12,702	14,789
Handguns...........................	6,778	6,115	6,194	6,604	6,526	8,576	6,500	7,936
Rifles...............................	411	367	215	298	367	486	455	541
Shotguns...........................	485	366	248	232	212	212	169	186
Other guns..........................	53	93	152	162	48	111	292	422
Firearms, type not stated...........	934	1,933	2,334	3,083	3,350	4,984	5,286	5,704
Knives or cutting instruments............	1,782	1,732	1,533	1,540	1,520	1,796	1,189	1,630
Blunt objects (club, hammer, etc.)........	617	549	438	453	413	417	279	367
Personal weapons (hands, fists, feet, pushed, etc.)..........	927	769	651	719	646	722	552	665
Fire.....................................	134	78	63	80	86	114	88	94
Narcotics................................	20	45	70	106	115	166	160	187
Drowning................................	15	10	12	9	7	5	0	3
Strangulation............................	166	122	96	74	62	58	3	20
Asphyxiation.............................	92	90	105	93	91	77	62	98

[1] Includes items not shown separately. [2] Rape figures in this table are an aggregate total of data submitted using both the revised and legacy UCR definitions.

Source: U.S. Department of Justice, Federal Bureau of Investigation, Crime Data Explorer, Documents & Downloads, "Crime in the United States Annual Reports, Expanded Homicide Tables," <cde.ucr.cjis.gov/LATEST/webapp/#/pages/downloads>, accessed June 2024.

Table 348. Criminal Victimizations and Victimization Rates: 2010 to 2022

[4,936 represents 4,936,000. A victimization refers to a single victim or household that experienced a criminal incident. Includes victimizations reported and not reported to the police. Criminal incidents or crimes are distinguished from victimizations in that one criminal incident may have multiple victims or victimizations. Based on the National Crime Victimization Survey (NCVS). See source for more information]

Type of crime	Number of victimizations (1,000)				Victimization rates [1]			
	2010	2015	2020	2022	2010	2015	2020	2022
Violent victimization [2]	**4,936**	**5,007**	**4,558**	**6,625**	**19.3**	**18.6**	**16.4**	**23.5**
Not Injured	3,646	3,703	3,397	5,213	14.2	13.7	12.2	18.5
Injured:								
Treated	591	622	365	555	2.3	2.3	1.3	2.0
Not treated	696	678	794	857	2.7	2.5	2.9	3.0
Serious violent victimization [3]	1,695	1,827	1,569	2,767	6.6	6.8	5.6	9.8
Rape/sexual assault	269	432	320	532	1.0	1.6	1.2	1.9
Robbery	569	579	437	695	2.2	2.1	1.6	2.5
Not Injured	370	370	265	466	1.4	1.4	1.0	1.7
Injured:								
Treated	97	100	92	112	0.4	0.4	0.3	0.4
Not treated	101	108	81	116	0.4	0.4	0.3	0.4
Aggravated assault	858	817	812	1,540	3.4	3.0	2.9	5.5
Not Injured	538	526	556	1,133	2.1	1.9	2.0	4.0
Injured:								
Treated	192	173	118	255	0.8	0.6	0.4	0.9
Not treated	127	116	136	153	0.5	0.4	0.5	0.5
Simple assault	3,241	3,179	2,989	3,858	12.7	11.8	10.7	13.7
Not Injured	2,619	2,534	2,451	3,289	10.2	9.4	8.8	11.7
Injured:								
Treated	198	271	120	154	0.8	1.0	0.4	0.5
Not treated	420	374	418	415	1.6	1.4	1.5	1.5
Personal theft/larceny [4]	138	89	77	147	0.5	0.3	0.3	0.5
Property crimes	**15,412**	**14,611**	**12,085**	**13,373**	**125.4**	**110.7**	**94.5**	**101.9**
Motor vehicle theft	607	564	546	717	4.9	4.3	4.3	5.5
Theft [5]	11,628	11,142	9,798	10,737	94.6	84.4	76.6	81.8
Burglary	2,338	2,021	1,211	1,324	19.0	15.3	9.5	10.1
Trespassing	838	884	531	596	6.8	6.7	4.1	4.5

[1] Per 1,000 persons age 12 or older for violent victimization and personal theft/larceny; per 1,000 households for property crime. [2] Excludes homicide because the NCVS is based on interviews with victims and therefore cannot measure murder. [3] Includes rape, sexual assault, personal robbery, and aggravated assault, attempted and completed crimes. [4] Includes pocket picking, completed purse snatching, and attempted purse snatching. [5] The taking or attempted unlawful taking of property or cash without personal contact with the victim. Incidents involving theft of property from within a household are classified as theft if the offender has a legal right to be in the house (such as a maid, delivery person, or guest).

Source: U.S. Department of Justice, Bureau of Justice Statistics, "National Crime Victimization Survey (NCVS) Dashboard (N-DASH) Tool," <ncvs.bjs.ojp.gov/>, accessed July 2024.

Table 349. Victimization Rates by Type of Crime and Characteristics of the Victim: 2022

[Rate per 1,000 persons age 12 years or older. Based on the National Crime Victimization Survey. See text, this section and Appendix III]

Victim characteristics	Violent victimization						Personal theft [2]
	Total	Serious violent victimization [1]	Rape/ sexual assault	Robbery	Aggravated assault	Simple assault	
Total	**23.5**	**9.8**	**1.9**	**2.5**	**5.5**	**13.7**	**0.5**
Male	23.5	9.5	0.6	2.6	6.3	14.0	0.6
Female	23.4	10.0	3.1	2.3	4.6	13.4	0.4
12 to 14 years old	30.4	8.2	[4] 1.5	[4] 2.5	4.2	22.1	[4] 0.4
15 to 17 years old	24.4	8.6	[4] 3.6	[4] 1.1	4.0	15.7	[4] 0.4
18 to 20 years old	35.0	21.8	6.6	[4] 2.3	12.8	13.2	[4] 2.7
21 to 24 years old	38.1	16.5	3.7	2.9	9.8	21.6	[4] 0.7
25 to 34 years old	34.2	13.4	2.8	3.4	7.1	20.9	[4] 0.6
35 to 49 years old	25.8	10.6	1.5	2.6	6.4	15.2	[4] 0.3
50 to 64 years old	17.3	8.0	0.9	1.9	5.2	9.3	[4] 0.4
65 years old and over	10.5	4.1	[4] 0.7	2.3	1.0	6.5	[4] 0.4
White, non-Hispanic	24.0	9.7	1.8	2.2	5.8	14.3	0.4
Black, non-Hispanic	21.8	9.0	1.5	2.4	5.0	12.8	[4] 0.4
Hispanic	22.6	11.0	2.6	3.8	4.6	11.7	0.9
Other [3]	23.7	9.5	1.8	2.0	5.7	14.3	[4] 0.5
Household income:							
Less than $7,500	54.1	29.5	6.1	8.1	15.2	24.6	7.2
$7,500 to $14,999	55.7	24.9	9.3	5.3	10.3	30.8	(Z)
$15,000 to $24,999	28.9	11.2	2.6	3.0	5.5	17.7	[4] 0.5
$25,000 to $34,999	35.6	17.5	2.3	3.3	12.0	18.1	[4] 0.8
$35,000 to $49,999	20.9	9.3	1.6	3.3	4.4	11.7	[4] 0.3
$50,000 to $74,999	20.3	8.1	1.5	2.3	4.3	12.3	[4] 0.1
$75,000 or more	17.7	6.5	1.0	1.5	4.0	11.2	0.3

Z Rounds to less than .05 victimizations per 1,000. [1] Includes rape, sexual assault, personal robbery, and aggravated assault, attempted and completed crimes. [2] Includes pocket picking and purse snatching. [3] Other includes Asian, Native Hawaiian and Other Pacific Islander, American Indian and Alaska Native, and persons of two or more races; all non-Hispanic. [4] Based on 10 or fewer sample cases or the coefficient of variation is greater than 50%.

Source: U.S. Department of Justice, Bureau of Justice Statistics, "National Crime Victimization Survey (NCVS) Dashboard (N-DASH) Tool," <ncvs.bjs.ojp.gov>, accessed July 2024.

Table 350. Violent Crime Between Intimate Partners by Sex of Victims: 1993 to 2022

[Intimate partners are defined as current and former spouses, boyfriends, and girlfriends. Based on the National Crime Victimization Survey (NCVS); see text this section, and source]

Year	Female victims				Male victims			
	Total intimate partner violence	Rate per 1,000 [1]			Total intimate partner violence	Rate per 1,000 [1]		
		Overall intimate partner violence	Serious violence [3]	Simple assault [4]		Overall intimate partner violence	Serious violence [3]	Simple assault [4]
1993............	1,689,687	15.5	5.7	9.9	347,924	3.4	1.5	1.9
1994............	1,843,713	16.8	6.1	10.7	258,990	2.5	0.7	1.8
1995............	1,727,462	15.5	3.7	11.8	285,907	2.8	1.0	1.8
1996............	1,626,516	14.5	4.7	9.8	194,647	1.9	0.8	1.1
1997............	1,661,683	14.7	4.8	9.8	176,651	1.7	0.5	1.2
1998............	1,336,585	11.7	3.6	8.0	228,793	2.1	0.6	1.5
1999............	1,164,554	10.0	3.5	6.5	230,230	2.1	0.5	1.6
2000............	783,762	6.7	1.9	4.8	116,152	1.1	[5] 0.2	0.9
2001............	981,671	8.3	2.9	5.4	108,740	1.0	0.5	0.5
2002............	797,805	6.7	2.0	4.7	131,956	1.2	[5] 0.5	0.7
2003............	906,628	7.4	3.6	3.8	133,657	1.2	0.5	0.7
2004............	816,139	6.6	2.3	4.3	215,582	1.8	0.5	1.4
2005............	621,041	4.9	1.6	3.4	194,966	1.6	[5] 0.9	0.7
2006 [2].........	1,063,775	8.4	3.2	5.2	241,475	2.0	1.1	0.9
2007............	780,979	6.1	2.1	4.0	124,831	1.0	[5] 0.4	0.7
2008............	914,422	7.1	2.5	4.6	188,970	1.5	0.7	0.9
2009............	914,529	7.0	1.6	5.4	125,121	1.0	0.3	0.7
2010............	636,770	4.9	1.7	3.2	136,663	1.1	0.4	0.7
2011............	604,645	4.6	1.6	3.0	246,127	2.0	[5] 0.4	1.6
2012............	682,417	5.1	1.7	3.4	128,378	1.0	0.4	0.6
2013............	619,357	4.6	2.1	2.5	129,438	1.0	0.6	0.4
2014............	500,920	3.7	1.4	2.2	133,692	1.0	0.6	0.5
2015............	741,645	5.4	2.2	3.1	64,403	0.5	[5] 0.2	0.3
2016............	513,494	3.7	1.6	2.0	83,705	0.6	0.3	0.4
2017............	602,902	4.3	1.7	2.6	63,407	0.5	0.2	0.2
2018............	754,842	5.3	2.4	2.9	92,384	0.7	0.3	0.4
2019............	627,635	4.4	2.0	2.4	67,424	0.5	[5] 0.1	0.4
2020............	408,038	2.9	1.3	1.6	76,789	0.6	0.3	0.3
2021............	406,221	2.8	1.2	1.7	67,501	0.5	[5] 0.1	0.4
2022............	844,776	5.9	3.3	2.5	107,150	0.8	0.3	0.5

[1] Rates are per 1,000 persons age 12 and older. [2] Due to methodological changes, use caution when comparing 2006 National Crime Victimization Survey criminal victimization estimates to other years. See *Criminal Victimization, 2007*, NCJ 224390, <bjs.ojp.gov/content/pub/pdf/cv07.pdf>. [3] Rape or sexual assault, robbery, and aggravated assault. [4] Attack or attempted attack without a weapon that results in no injury, minor injury, or an undetermined injury requiring less than two days of hospitalization. [5] Interpret data with caution.

Source: U.S. Department of Justice, Bureau of Justice Statistics, "National Crime Victimization Survey (NCVS) Dashboard (N-DASH) Tool," <ncvs.bjs.ojp.gov/>, accessed July 2024.

Table 351. Stalking Victimization by Type of Stalking and Selected Victim Characteristics: 2019

[Data shown for persons age 16 or older who experienced stalking victimization in the past year. Stalking is repeated unwanted contacts or behaviors that either cause the victim to experience fear or substantial emotional distress or that would cause a reasonable person to experience fear or substantial emotional distress]

Characteristic	Number of victims	Percent of all persons	Characteristic	Number of victims	Percent of all persons
Total stalking victims [1]............	**3,419,710**	**1.3**	SEX		
Traditional stalking [2]....................	2,300,830	0.9	Male...	982,080	0.8
Traditional stalking only................	681,240	0.3	Female..	2,437,630	1.8
			MARITAL STATUS		
Stalking with technology [3]..............	2,738,470	1.1	Never married................................	1,394,440	1.7
Stalking with technology only.........	1,118,890	0.4	Married..	973,100	0.8
Both traditional and with technology...	1,619,580	0.6	Widowed..	126,680	0.8
			Divorced..	719,900	2.5
AGE			Separated......................................	197,250	3.8
			RACE AND ETHNICITY		
16 to 19 years old.......................	239,650	1.5	White [4]..	2,188,360	1.3
20 to 24 years old.......................	426,840	2.0	Black [4]..	342,430	1.1
25 to 34 years old.......................	796,270	1.7	Hispanic..	515,110	1.2
35 to 49 years old.......................	942,610	1.5	Asian/Native Hawaiian/Other Pacific Islander [4]....	179,840	1.1
50 to 64 years old.......................	690,500	1.1	American Indian/Alaska Native [4].....................	48,940	3.3
65 years old and over...................	323,830	0.6	Two or more races..........................	145,030	3.9

[1] Victims may experience more than one type of stalking. [2] Includes the following unwanted behaviors: following; sneaking into, waiting at, or showing up at a place; leaving or sending unwanted items; and harassing friends or family about the victim's whereabouts. [3] Includes the following unwanted behaviors: making unwanted phone calls, leaving voice messages, or sending text messages; spying using technology; tracking the victim's whereabouts with an electronic tracking device or application; posting or threatening to post unwanted information on the internet; sending emails or messages using the internet; and monitoring activities using social media. [4] Non-Hispanic.

Source: U.S. Department of Justice, Bureau of Justice Statistics, *Stalking Victimization, 2019*, NCJ 301735, February 2022. See also <bjs.ojp.gov/library>.

Table 352. Hate Crimes—Number of Incidents, Offenses, Victims, and Known Offenders by Bias Motivation: 2010 to 2022

[3,109 law enforcement agencies submitted data on hate crimes. 14,631 law enforcement agencies covering over 305 million people participated in the Hate Crime Statistics Program in 2022. Hate crime offenses cover incidents motivated by race, ethnicity/national origin, religion, sexual orientation, gender identity, and disability. See source and Appendix III]

Bias motivation	Incidents reported	Offenses	Victims [1]	Known offenders [2]
2010.........	6,628	7,699	8,208	6,008
2020.........	7,759	10,532	10,861	6,431
2022, total [3].........	**11,634**	**13,337**	**13,711**	**10,299**
Race/ethnicity/ancestry, total.........	**6,567**	**7,677**	**7,852**	**5,980**
Anti-White.........	966	1,102	1,126	892
Anti-Black or African American.........	3,421	4,000	4,075	3,017
Anti-American Indian/Alaska native.........	194	209	217	196
Anti-Asian.........	499	579	602	466
Anti-Native Hawaiian or Other Pacific Islander.........	26	29	30	23
Anti-multiple races, group.........	232	271	287	175
Anti-Arab.........	92	105	105	82
Anti-Hispanic or Latino.........	738	937	958	778
Anti-Other race/ethnicity/ancestry.........	399	445	452	351
Religion, total [3].........	**2,042**	**2,199**	**2,293**	**1,527**
Anti-Jewish.........	1,122	1,194	1,217	769
Anti-Catholic.........	107	110	113	77
Anti-Protestant.........	63	68	71	59
Anti-Islamic (Muslim).........	158	179	200	136
Anti-Sikh.........	181	192	198	150
Sexual orientation, total.........	**1,944**	**2,210**	**2,289**	**1,842**
Anti-gay (male homosexual).........	1,075	1,194	1,217	1,115
Anti-lesbian (female homosexual).........	190	211	216	162
Anti-lesbian, gay, bisexual, or transgender.........	622	745	796	509
Anti-heterosexual.........	22	23	23	23
Anti-bisexual.........	35	37	37	33
Disability, total.........	**171**	**191**	**194**	**179**
Anti-physical.........	74	83	83	72
Anti-mental.........	97	108	111	107
Gender identity.........	**469**	**515**	**527**	**437**
Anti-transgender.........	338	374	382	335
Anti-gender non-conforming.........	131	141	145	102
Multiple bias [4].........	**346**	**424**	**433**	**253**

[1] "Victim" may refer to an individual, business/financial institution, government entity, religious organization, or society/public as a whole. [2] "Known offender" does not imply that the identity of the suspect is known, but only that an attribute of the suspect has been identified that distinguishes him/her from an unknown offender. [3] Includes other motivation types not shown separately. [4] Incident in which one or more offense types are motivated by two or more biases.

Source: U.S. Department of Justice, Federal Bureau of Investigation, Crime Data Explorer, "Hate Crime Statistics Annual Reports," <cde.ucr.cjis.gov/LATEST/webapp/#/pages/downloads>, accessed November 2023.

Table 353. Hate Crimes by Bias Motivation and Location of Incident: 2022

[See headnote, Table 352]

Location	Total incidents	Race/ ethnicity/ ancestry	Religion	Sexual orientation	Disability	Gender	Gender identity	Multiple- bias incidents [1]
Total [2].........	**11,634**	**6,567**	**2,042**	**1,944**	**171**	**95**	**469**	**346**
Air/bus/train terminal.........	181	112	18	29	2	2	8	10
Bar/nightclub.........	172	75	15	65	2	0	9	6
Church/synagogue/temple/mosque.........	419	45	332	20	0	0	3	19
Commercial office building.........	241	145	41	31	6	2	6	10
Community center.........	46	14	20	7	2	1	1	1
Construction site.........	40	26	9	2	0	0	1	2
Convenience store.........	205	143	22	26	2	1	8	3
Cyberspace.........	122	48	23	28	2	1	13	7
Department/discount store.........	146	91	21	19	8	0	6	1
Drug store/doctor's office/hospital.........	165	111	15	15	4	3	9	8
Field/woods.........	58	29	15	6	0	3	2	3
Government/public building.........	180	119	25	20	2	4	6	4
Grocery/supermarket.........	153	107	21	16	1	0	5	3
Highway/road/alley/street/sidewalk.........	1,823	1,146	208	313	19	14	91	32
Hotel/motel/etc.........	115	80	10	12	0	4	5	4
Jail/prison/penitentiary/corrections facility...	147	88	9	34	5	1	6	4
Park/playground.........	386	197	85	55	2	6	10	31
Parking lot/garage.........	676	445	70	103	5	5	28	20
Residence/home.........	3,115	1,729	415	666	53	33	147	72
Restaurant.........	314	208	22	58	4	1	10	11
School/college [3].........	129	72	25	24	1	0	6	1
School—college/university.........	274	124	52	63	2	3	12	18
School—elementary/secondary.........	788	469	120	109	27	0	21	42
Service/gas station.........	146	107	14	16	1	0	5	3
Shopping mall.........	43	30	4	3	1	0	3	2
Specialty store (TV, fur, etc.).........	122	81	16	16	1	0	3	5
Other/unknown.........	1,428	726	415	188	19	11	45	24

[1] An incident in which one or more offense types are motivated by two or more biases. [2] Includes other locations not shown separately. [3] The location designation school/college has been retained for agencies that have not updated their records to include the new location designations of school, which allow for more specificity in reporting.

Source: U.S. Department of Justice, Federal Bureau of Investigation, Crime Data Explorer, "Hate Crime Statistics Annual Reports," <cde.ucr.cjis.gov/LATEST/webapp/#/pages/downloads>, accessed November 2023.

Table 354. Property Crime by Selected Household Characteristics: 2022

[131,260 represents 131,260,000. For crimes against households, each household affected by a crime is counted as a single victimization. Based on National Crime Victimization Survey (NCVS); see text, this section and Appendix III]

Characteristic	Number of house-holds (1,000)	Property crime									
		Number of victimizations (1,000)					Victimization rate per 1,000 households				
		Total	Bur-glary [1]	Motor vehicle theft	Tres-passing [2]	Other theft [3]	Total	Bur-glary [1]	Motor vehicle theft	Tres-passing [2]	Other theft [3]
Total......................	131,260	13,373	1,324	717	596	10,737	101.9	10.1	5.5	4.5	81.8
Household income:											
Less than $7,500........	5,166	686	77	18	35	555	132.8	15.0	3.6	6.8	107.4
$7,500–$14,999.........	6,582	954	128	49	123	654	145.0	19.4	7.5	18.7	99.3
$15,000–$24,999.......	10,123	1,164	167	54	75	868	115.0	16.5	5.4	7.4	85.8
$25,000–$34,999.......	12,224	1,216	173	60	64	920	99.5	14.2	4.9	5.2	75.2
$35,000–$49,999.......	18,109	1,823	248	94	63	1,418	100.6	13.7	5.2	3.5	78.3
$50,000–$74,999.......	22,513	2,225	193	135	104	1,794	98.8	8.6	6.0	4.6	79.7
$75,000 or more.........	56,543	5,305	338	307	131	4,528	93.8	6.0	5.4	2.3	80.1
Northeast.................	22,868	1,980	184	63	78	1,654	86.6	8.1	2.8	3.4	72.3
Midwest..................	28,240	2,516	276	117	148	1,976	89.1	9.8	4.1	5.2	70.0
South.....................	50,658	4,118	470	206	230	3,212	81.3	9.3	4.1	4.5	63.4
West......................	29,493	4,759	394	330	141	3,894	161.4	13.4	11.2	4.8	132.0
Number of persons in household:											
1.........................	46,106	4,232	606	210	290	3,125	91.8	13.1	4.6	6.3	67.8
2 or 3....................	63,189	6,217	521	327	222	5,147	98.4	8.2	5.2	3.5	81.5
4 or 5....................	18,860	2,378	152	150	73	2,003	126.1	8.1	8.0	3.9	106.2
6 or more................	3,105	546	45	29	10	462	176.0	14.5	9.3	3.4	148.7

[1] Includes unlawful or forcible entry or attempted entry of places, including a permanent residence, other residence (e.g., a hotel room or vacation residence), or other structure (e.g., a garage or shed). Includes only crimes where the offender committed or attempted a theft. [2] Includes unlawful or forcible entry or attempted entry of places, including a permanent residence, other residence (e.g., a hotel room or vacation residence), or other structure (e.g., a garage or shed). Includes only crimes where the offender did not commit or attempt a theft. Excludes trespassing on land. [3] Includes other unlawful taking or attempted unlawful taking of property or cash without personal contact with the victim.

Source: U.S. Department of Justice, Bureau of Justice Statistics, "National Crime Victimization Survey (NCVS) Dashboard (N-DASH) Tool," <ncvs.bjs.ojp.gov/>, accessed July 2024.

Table 355. Internet Crime Complaints—Victims and Value of Loss by Crime Type: 2021 to 2023

[Data shown are suspected criminal internet activities reported by victims to the FBI's Internet Crime Complaint Center (IC3). Victims are encouraged and often directed by law enforcement to file a complaint online at <www.ic3.gov> along with documentation and other information necessary to support the complaint. Complaints are reviewed by an IC3 analyst and categorized according to crime type. See source for full description of crime types and additional information]

Crime	2021		2022		2023	
	Victims (number)	Loss (dollars)	Victims (number)	Loss (dollars)	Victims (number)	Loss (dollars)
Phishing/vishing/smishing/pharming.............	323,972	44,213,707	300,497	52,089,159	[3] 298,878	[3] 18,728,550
Personal data breach..............................	51,829	517,021,289	58,859	742,438,136	55,851	744,219,879
Non-payment/non-delivery........................	82,478	337,493,071	51,679	281,770,073	50,523	309,648,416
Extortion..	39,360	60,577,741	39,416	54,335,128	48,223	74,821,835
Investment..	20,561	1,455,943,193	30,529	3,311,742,206	39,570	4,570,275,683
Tech support......................................	23,903	347,657,432	32,538	806,551,993	37,560	924,512,658
BEC/EAC (email) [1]...............................	19,954	2,395,953,296	21,832	2,742,354,049	21,489	2,946,830,270
Identity theft......................................	51,629	278,267,918	27,922	189,205,793	19,778	126,203,809
Confidence/romance fraud........................	24,299	956,039,739	19,021	735,882,192	17,823	652,544,805
Employment.......................................	15,253	47,231,023	14,946	52,204,269	15,443	70,234,079
Government impersonation.......................	11,335	142,643,253	11,554	240,553,091	14,190	394,050,518
Credit card/check fraud...........................	16,750	172,998,385	22,985	264,148,905	13,718	173,627,614
Harassment/stalking..............................	(NA)	(NA)	11,779	5,621,402	9,587	9,677,332
Real estate/rental property.......................	11,578	350,328,166	11,727	396,932,821	9,521	145,243,348
Advanced fee.....................................	11,034	98,694,137	11,264	104,325,444	8,045	134,516,577
Lottery/sweepstakes/inheritance.................	5,991	71,289,089	5,650	83,602,376	4,168	94,502,836
Overpayment......................................	6,108	33,407,671	6,183	38,335,772	4,144	27,955,195
Corporate data breach............................	1,287	151,568,225	2,795	459,321,859	3,727	534,397,222
Ransomware [2]....................................	3,729	49,207,908	2,385	34,353,237	2,825	59,641,384
Crimes against children...........................	2,167	198,950	2,587	577,464	2,361	2,031,485
Threats of violence...............................	(NA)	(NA)	2,224	4,972,099	1,697	13,531,178
Intellectual property rights, copyright & counterfeit..	4,270	16,365,011	2,183	4,591,177	1,498	7,555,329
SIM Swap...	(NA)	(NA)	2,026	72,652,571	1,075	48,798,103
Malware/scareware/virus.........................	810	5,596,889	762	9,326,482	659	1,213,317
Botnet...	(NA)	(NA)	568	17,099,378	540	22,422,708
Spoofing [3]..	18,522	82,169,806	20,649	107,926,252	(3)	(3)
Denial of service (DoS)/telephony DoS..........	2,018	512,127	(NA)	(NA)	(NA)	(NA)
Health care related...............................	1,383	29,042,515	(NA)	(NA)	(NA)	(NA)
Re-shipping.......................................	883	3,095,265	(NA)	(NA)	(NA)	(NA)
Misrepresentation.................................	24,276	19,707,242	(NA)	(NA)	(NA)	(NA)
False charity......................................	659	4,428,766	(NA)	(NA)	(NA)	(NA)

NA Not available. [1] Business email compromise/email account compromise are scams carried out in order to conduct unauthorized transfer of funds. [2] Does not include estimates of lost business, time, wages, files, or equipment, or any third party remediation services acquired by a victim. In some cases victims do not report any loss amount to the FBI, thereby creating an artificially low overall ransomware loss rate. Represents what victims report to the FBI via the IC3 and does not account for victim direct reporting to FBI field offices and agents. [3] Phishing and spoofing are combined in the 2023 Internet Crime Report.

Source: U.S. Department of Justice, Federal Bureau of Investigation, 2023 Internet Crime Report, and earlier reports. See also <www.ic3.gov>.

Table 356. Fraud and Identity Theft—Consumer Complaints by State: 2023

[Rate per 100,000 population. As of December 31. Rates based on U.S. Census Bureau's 2021 population estimates. The Consumer Sentinel Network is a secure online database of consumer complaints available only to law enforcement. Based on unverified complaints reported by consumers. Excludes complaints from state-specific data contributors]

State	Fraud and other complaints		Identity theft victims		State	Fraud and other complaints		Identity theft victims	
	Number	Rate	Number	Rate		Number	Rate	Number	Rate
AL........	55,182	1,104	12,228	245	MO.......	61,131	995	9,873	161
AK........	6,456	877	839	114	MT.......	8,375	777	1,354	126
AZ........	86,066	1,216	18,539	262	NE.......	14,994	768	2,673	137
AR........	24,291	808	5,071	169	NV.......	46,840	1,531	12,362	404
CA........	405,354	1,027	119,929	304	NH.......	12,576	917	1,892	138
CO........	61,433	1,073	12,729	222	NJ.......	102,041	1,105	26,136	283
CT........	33,892	940	13,848	384	NM.......	18,118	859	2,825	134
DE........	14,733	1,500	3,523	359	NY.......	209,039	1,039	51,484	256
DC........	12,877	1,885	3,268	478	NC.......	117,231	1,131	25,142	243
FL........	333,570	1,563	93,547	438	ND.......	4,685	606	913	118
GA........	166,229	1,564	48,606	457	OH.......	107,556	914	34,616	294
HI........	11,947	822	1,773	122	OK.......	30,833	781	6,032	153
ID........	14,424	796	2,223	123	OR.......	41,706	991	7,444	177
IL........	141,330	1,102	39,314	307	PA.......	148,998	1,149	40,778	314
IN........	57,865	857	11,870	176	RI.......	9,170	840	2,357	216
IA........	19,673	619	4,468	141	SC.......	59,444	1,170	14,931	294
KS........	22,052	752	4,405	150	SD.......	5,183	588	833	94
KY........	33,525	746	5,340	119	TN.......	73,244	1,068	12,709	185
LA........	49,020	1,053	12,816	275	TX.......	327,936	1,136	101,002	350
ME........	11,098	818	1,714	126	UT.......	26,263	813	5,345	165
MD........	84,353	1,372	18,327	298	VT.......	5,314	828	620	97
MA........	62,481	894	24,540	351	VA.......	97,746	1,139	19,211	224
MI........	94,683	941	23,621	235	WA.......	76,832	1,009	12,582	165
MN........	44,428	783	8,063	142	WV.......	13,720	762	1,977	110
MS........	26,774	902	6,663	225	WI.......	46,121	785	8,301	141
					WY.......	4,516	783	609	106

Source: U.S. Federal Trade Commission, *Consumer Sentinel Network Data Book 2023,* February 2024. See also <www.ftc.gov/enforcement/consumer-sentinel-network/reports>.

Table 357. Victims of Identity Theft by Type of Account and Selected Victim Characteristics: 2021

[Data shown are for persons age 16 or older who experienced at least one identity theft incident during the past 12 months. Excludes respondents who discovered the most recent incident prior to the reference period. Estimates are based on the most recent identity theft incident. Please note that the survey questionnaire for 2021 was redesigned and data cover only successful incidents of identity theft; previous surveys included successful and attempted identity theft. Details do not sum to totals because persons could experience more than one type of identity theft. Based on the National Crime Victimization Survey's Identity Theft Supplement. See source for methodology]

Theft type and victim characteristics	Number of victims	Percent of all persons [1]	Theft type and victim characteristics	Number of victims	Percent of all persons [1]
Total.....................................	**23,928,600**	**9.1**	By sex:		
By type of theft:			Male..	10,996,850	8.6
Misused one type of existing account.....	18,175,200	6.9	Female......................................	12,931,750	9.6
Credit card...............................	7,289,970	2.8	By race/Hispanic origin:		
Bank......................................	5,662,590	2.2	White, non-Hispanic.................	16,786,460	10.3
Email/social media.......................	3,856,390	1.5	Black, non-Hispanic......................	2,584,720	8.2
Other....................................	1,366,250	0.5	Hispanic..................................	2,776,650	6.1
Opened new account only.................	759,330	0.3	Asian, Native Hawaiian, or		
Other misuse of personal information [2]...	1,639,600	0.6	other Pacific Islander, non-Hispanic...	1,181,550	6.5
Multiple types of identity theft.............	3,354,470	1.3	Other, non-Hispanic [4]..................	599,220	13.0
Existing account only......................	2,125,130	0.8	By age:		
Other [3].................................	1,229,350	0.5	16 to 17 years old.......................	108,610	1.4
By household income:			18 to 24 years old........................	2,048,000	7.0
$24,999 or less...........................	2,932,100	7.4	25 to 34 years old........................	4,045,430	8.9
$25,000-$49,999...........................	4,244,230	7.1	35 to 49 years old........................	6,090,210	9.9
$50,000-$99,999...........................	7,703,790	9.2	50 to 64 years old........................	6,772,050	10.9
$100,000-$199,999.........................	6,407,310	10.9	65 years or older.........................	4,864,310	8.6
$200,000 or more..........................	2,641,170	12.5			

[1] For data by characteristic, percent based on number of persons in each category. [2] Includes misuse of personal information for other fraudulent purposes other than opening a new account or the misuse of an existing account, such as filing a fraudulent income tax return, getting medical treatment, applying for a job, concealing the offender's identity from police or other government authority, applying for government benefits, or other fraudulent purpose. [3] Includes victims who experienced two or more of the following: misuse of an existing account, personal information to open a new account, or personal information for other fraudulent purposes. [4] Includes American Indian or Alaska Native persons, and persons of two or more races.

Source: U.S. Department of Justice, Bureau of Justice Statistics, *Victims of Identity Theft, 2021*, NCJ 306474, October 2023. See also <bjs.ojp.gov/library/publications/victims-identity-theft-2021>.

Table 358. Firearm Violence Victimizations by Selected Characteristics: 2010 to 2022

[In units as indicated. Includes violent crimes in which the offender possessed, showed, or used a firearm]

Characteristic	2010	2015	2016	2017	2018	2019	2020	2021	2022
Total violent victimizations (number).....	4,935,983	5,006,615	5,353,816	5,612,667	6,385,515	5,813,408	4,558,154	4,598,306	6,624,953
Firearm victimizations (number) [1]	**415,003**	**284,910**	**486,591**	**456,269**	**470,843**	**481,947**	**350,458**	**326,894**	**640,706**
Rate of firearm victimization [2]...	1.6	1.1	1.8	1.7	1.7	1.7	1.3	1.2	2.3
By race/ethnicity:									
White, non-Hispanic..........	1.1	0.7	1.6	1.4	1.4	1.3	1.2	1.1	2.1
Black, non-Hispanic..........	3.2	2.8	3.1	2.0	2.6	2.9	3.2	2.0	2.7
Hispanic....................	2.3	1.2	2.1	2.4	2.0	2.5	0.6	1.2	3.1
Firearm victimizations reported to police:									
Number.........................	211,383	217,850	314,502	254,913	310,306	290,785	212,475	237,983	389,588
Percent.........................	50.9	76.5	64.6	55.9	65.9	60.3	60.6	72.8	60.8

[1] Each victimization represents one person involved in an incident. [2] Rate is per 1,000 persons age 12 or older.

Source: U.S. Department of Justice, Bureau of Justice Statistics, "National Crime Victimization Survey (NCVS) Dashboard (N-DASH) Tool," <ncvs.bjs.ojp.gov>, accessed July 2024.

Table 359. Nonfatal Firearm and Nonfirearm Violence by Victim-Offender Relationship and Location of Crime: 2014 to 2018

[Data are for victimizations and whether the offender did or did not have, show, or use a firearm. Covers period from 2014 to 2018. Detail may not sum to total due to rounding. Data from National Crime Victimization Survey]

Characteristic	Total nonfatal violence		Firearm violence		Nonfirearm violence	
	Number	Percent	Number	Percent	Number	Percent
RELATIONSHIP TO VICTIM						
Any.................	**9,179,700**	**100.0**	**1,907,300**	**100.0**	**7,272,400**	**100.0**
Nonstranger..................	5,211,900	56.8	768,800	40.3	4,443,100	61.1
Intimate [1].................	1,517,800	16.5	175,300	9.2	1,342,600	18.5
Other relative..............	716,600	7.8	125,900	6.6	590,700	8.1
Friend/acquaintance........	2,977,500	32.4	467,600	24.5	2,509,800	34.5
Stranger...................	3,967,800	43.2	1,138,500	59.7	2,829,300	38.9
LOCATION						
Any.................	**10,032,400**	**100.0**	**2,164,700**	**100.0**	**7,867,600**	**100.0**
Victim's home or lodging........	2,660,200	26.5	372,600	17.2	2,287,600	29.1
Near victim's home.............	1,495,400	14.9	453,800	21.0	1,041,500	13.2
In, at, or near a friend, neighbor, or relative's home......	1,009,000	10.1	218,500	10.1	790,500	10.0
Commercial place..............	811,200	8.1	189,300	8.7	621,900	7.9
Parking lot or garage...........	704,700	7.0	239,600	11.1	465,000	5.9
School [2].....................	611,300	6.1	[3] 33,700	[3] 1.6	577,600	7.3
Open area, on street, or public transportation..............	1,877,200	18.7	503,400	23.3	1,373,900	17.5
Other location.................	863,400	8.6	153,800	7.1	709,600	9.0

[1] Includes current or former spouses, boyfriends, or girlfriends. [2] Includes inside a school building or on school property. [3] Interpret with caution. Estimate based on 10 or fewer sample cases, or coefficient of variation is greater than 50%.

Source: Department of Justice, Bureau of Justice Statistics, *Trends and Patterns in Firearm Violence, 1993-2018*, NCJ 251663, April 2022. See also <bjs.ojp.gov/library>.

Table 360. Active Shooter Incidents and Casualties: 2000 to 2023

[The Federal Bureau of Investigation (FBI) defines active shooters as "one or more individuals actively engaged in killing or attempting to kill people in a populated area." This definition encompasses shootings that happen in schools, workplaces, and other public spaces. A shooting can be categorized as an active shooter incident even if no one is killed or wounded. Excluded from this report are gang- and drug-related shootings and gun-related incidents that appeared not to have put other people in peril (e.g., the accidental discharge of a firearm in a bar)]

Year and location	Active shooter incidents	Casualties		
		Total	Fatal	Injury
2000.................................	3	18	16	2
2010.................................	27	91	38	53
2015.................................	20	134	56	78
2016.................................	20	214	83	131
2017.................................	31	734	143	591
2018.................................	30	225	86	139
2019.................................	30	258	102	156
2020.................................	40	164	38	126
2021.................................	61	243	103	140
2022.................................	50	313	100	213
2023.................................	48	244	105	139
BY LOCATION 2000-2023				
Total.................	**532**	**3,815**	**1,408**	**2,407**
Place of commerce..................	231	1,517	653	864
Education facility..................	71	504	218	286
Open space........................	130	1,185	261	924
Government........................	38	236	99	137
Residence..........................	24	138	57	81
Place of worship...................	18	156	84	72
Health care facility................	19	77	35	42
Other location.....................	1	2	1	1

Source: U.S. Department of Justice, Federal Bureau of Investigation, *Active Shooter Incidents in the United States 2023*, June 2024 and earlier reports. See also <www.fbi.gov/how-we-can-help-you/safety-resources/active-shooter-safetyresources>.

Table 361. Persons Experiencing Nonfatal Threats or Use of Force During Police Contact: 2018 and 2020

[Data shown for persons age 16 and older. Includes persons reporting threats or use of force during the most recent contact or any earlier contacts with police in the last 12 months. Details may not sum to totals due to rounding. Data from the Police-Public Contact Survey]

Characteristics	2018			2020		
	Persons with any police contact	Experienced threats or use of force [2]		Persons with any police contact	Experienced threats or use of force [2]	
		Number	Percent		Number	Percent
Total...............	61,542,300	1,254,300	2.0	53,836,600	1,045,600	1.9
SEX						
Male.................	30,467,400	917,900	3.0	26,751,200	721,200	2.7
Female...............	31,074,900	336,400	1.1	27,085,400	324,400	1.2
RACE/ETHNICITY						
White, non-Hispanic.........	42,525,700	647,100	1.5	36,677,800	560,200	1.5
Black, non-Hispanic.........	6,545,700	250,700	3.8	5,656,300	241,800	4.3
Hispanic.................	8,238,400	280,100	3.4	7,283,900	172,900	2.4
Asian, non-Hispanic.........	2,419,500	30,900	1.3	2,595,000	26,600	1.0
Other [1].................	1,813,000	45,500	2.5	1,623,600	44,000	2.7
AGE						
16 to 17 years old.........	1,143,500	39,200	3.4	1,025,400	(B)	(B)
18 to 24 years old.........	8,859,700	280,000	3.2	7,513,500	229,800	3.1
25 to 44 years old.........	23,518,700	625,500	2.7	20,787,400	513,500	2.5
45 to 64 years old.........	19,160,700	274,400	1.4	16,634,300	213,500	1.3
65 years or older.........	8,859,600	35,200	0.4	7,876,000	69,200	0.9

B Sample size is below the minimum threshold or coefficient of variation is greater than 50%. [1] Includes non-Hispanic Native Hawaiians, other Pacific Islanders, American Indians, Alaska Natives, and persons of two or more races. [2] Includes residents whom police threatened with force, handcuffed, pushed or grabbed, hit or kicked, used chemical or pepper spray, used an electroshock weapon, pointed or fired a gun, or used another type of physical force.

Source: Department of Justice, Bureau of Justice Statistics, *Contacts Between Police and the Public, 2020*, NCJ 304527, November 2022. See also <bjs.ojp.gov/library>.

Table 362. Background Checks for Firearm Transfers: 2010 to 2020

[In thousands (10,643 represents 10,643,000), except as noted. The Brady Handgun Violence Prevention Act (Brady Act) P.L. 103–159, 1993 requires a background check on an applicant for a firearm purchase from a dealer who is a Federal Firearms Licensee. The period beginning November 30, 1998 is the effective date for the Brady Act. The National Instant Criminal Background Check System (NICS) began operations in 1998. Checks on handgun and long gun transfers are conducted by the FBI, and by state and local agencies. Totals combine Firearm Inquiry Statistics (FIST) estimates for state and local agencies with transactions and denials reported by the FBI]

Inquiries and rejections	2010	2012	2013	2014	2015	2016	2017	2018	2019	2020
Applications received...........	10,643	15,718	17,602	14,993	16,610	19,203	17,163	16,765	16,706	24,994
Applications denied.............	153	192	193	193	226	265	237	230	243	398
Denied (percent).............	*1.4*	*1.2*	*1.1*	*1.3*	*1.4*	*1.4*	*1.4*	*1.4*	*1.5*	*1.6*
Selected reasons for rejection: [1]										
Felony indictment/conviction...	62	82	(NA)	82	100	111	108	108	(NA)	201
Other..........................	91	110	(NA)	111	126	154	129	122	(NA)	197
Felony denials per 1,000 applications..........	6.0	5.2	(NA)	5.5	6.0	5.8	6.3	6.4	(NA)	8.0

NA Not available. [1] Beginning in 2008, the FBI instituted a new classification system; therefore, data prior to 2008 aren't comparable to previously published estimates.

Source: U.S. Department of Justice, Bureau of Justice Statistics, *Background Checks for Firearm Transfers, 2019-2020*, NCJ 306971, November 2023. See also <bjs.ojp.gov/library>.

Table 363. Denials of Firearm Transfer Applications by Reason and Agency Type: 2018 to 2020

[In percent. Reasons for denials are based on The Brady Handgun Violence Prevention Act, pursuant to 18 U.S.C. 922 and state laws. Denial occurs when an applicant is prohibited from receiving a firearm or a permit that can be used to receive a firearm because a disqualifying factor was found during a background check. Application for firearm transfer is information submitted by a person to a state or local checking agency to purchase a firearm or obtain a permit that can be used for a purchase. Information may be submitted directly to a checking agency or forwarded by a prospective seller. Totals were based on federal and state agencies that reported counts on reasons for denial. Reasons for denial for local agencies were estimated]

Reason for denial	2018			2019			2020		
	FBI	State	Local	FBI	State	Local	FBI	State	Local
Felony indictment/conviction.....................	53.0	27.7	23.5	52.2	23.5	(NA)	59.0	27.5	17.5
Felony conviction................................	45.1	20.9	14.9	44.5	21.8	(NA)	50.2	25.2	13.8
Felony indictment/information..................	7.9	6.8	8.6	7.7	1.7	(NA)	8.8	2.3	3.7
Felony arrest with no disposition...............	(X)	14.5	2.5	(X)	18.1	(NA)	(X)	16.7	2.6
Fugitive..	5.8	3.8	3.3	7.6	6.1	(NA)	5.5	4.9	2.7
Domestic violence...............................	10.6	10.5	16.1	10.5	9.2	(NA)	9.1	10.6	11.7
Misdemeanor conviction........................	7.6	5.4	12.9	7.5	5.4	(NA)	6.8	5.6	8.8
Protection/restraining order....................	3.0	5.1	3.2	3.0	3.8	(NA)	2.3	5.0	2.9
Drug use/addiction..............................	13.7	7.5	6.6	13.7	8.3	(NA)	10.4	6.3	6.6
Mental health commitment/adjudication........	6.1	6.8	6.1	5.8	5.4	(NA)	5.6	6.0	5.0
Illegal/unlawful alien...........................	3.0	1.5	1.0	2.7	0.7	(NA)	3.4	1.7	0.9
State law prohibition [1]........................	7.5	16.7	17.1	7.4	16.7	(NA)	6.8	15.7	37.8
Local law prohibition [1]........................	(X)	(X)	3.7	(X)	(X)	(NA)	(X)	(X)	4.8
Other prohibitions [2]...........................	0.2	11.0	20.2	0.1	11.9	(NA)	0.1	10.6	10.3

NA Not available. X Not applicable. [1] State and local laws may impose prohibitions based on juvenile offense records, adjudications of delinquency, misdemeanor convictions for an offense other than domestic violence, and mental health orders that do not cause a federal prohibition. [2] Includes juveniles, persons dishonorably discharged from the Armed Services, persons who have renounced their U.S. citizenship, and other unspecified persons.

Source: U.S. Department of Justice, Bureau of Justice Statistics, *Background Checks For Firearm Transfers, 2019-2020*, NCJ 306971, November 2023, and earlier reports. See also <bjs.ojp.gov/library>.

Table 364. Employment by State and Local Law Enforcement Agencies by Type of Agency and Employee: 2020

[As of December 31. Excludes agencies that did not employ the equivalent of at least one full-time sworn officer. Data are from the Law Enforcement Management and Administrative Statistics survey]

Type of agency	Number of agencies	Full-time employees (number)			Part-time employees (number)		
		Total	Sworn	Civilian [1]	Total	Sworn	Civilian [1]
Total..........................	**14,726**	**1,056,038**	**708,153**	**347,885**	**85,716**	**37,734**	**47,981**
Local police......................	11,788	598,620	473,102	125,518	59,182	28,117	31,066
Sheriffs' offices [2]...............	2,889	364,533	173,899	190,634	25,267	9,400	15,867
Primary State [3].................	49	92,886	61,153	31,733	1,266	217	1,048

[1] Includes officers and deputies with limited or no arrest powers and nonsworn employees. [2] Excludes sheriffs' offices without primary law enforcement jurisdiction in the counties they serve. [3] Hawaii's Department of Public Safety is excluded from the LEMAS survey.

Source: U.S. Bureau of Justice Statistics, *Primary State Law Enforcement Agencies: Personnel, 2020,* NCJ 307507, January 2024. See also <bjs.ojp.gov/library>.

Table 365. Full-time Sworn Officers in Primary State Law Enforcement Agencies by Selected Characteristics: 2020

[In percent, except total. Estimates are as of December 31, 2020. Details may not sum to totals due to rounding. Data are from the Law Enforcement Management and Administrative Statistics (LEMAS) survey. Estimates reflect an adjustment factor that accounts for nonresponse and preserves comparability of the national estimate of personnel with other reports in the LEMAS series. Data by sex and race/ethnicity exclude agencies in New Hampshire and South Dakota that did not respond to the survey or provide counts of officers by those characteristics]

Region and agency size	Full-time sworn officers, total	Sex		Race and Hispanic origin				
		Male	Female	White, non-Hispanic	Black, non-Hispanic	Hispanic	Other [1]	Unknown
Total......................	**61,153**	**93.0**	**7.0**	**80.2**	**6.5**	**10.4**	**2.4**	**0.6**
REGION								
South.........................	20,070	93.6	6.4	75.3	11.3	11.0	2.3	0.2
Northeast......................	16,631	92.0	8.0	87.4	4.5	6.1	1.7	0.2
West..........................	13,579	93.8	6.2	71.5	2.7	20.4	3.8	1.6
Midwest.......................	10,873	92.2	7.8	89.0	5.0	3.5	1.9	0.5
AGENCY SIZE [2]								
1,500 or more.................	36,985	92.6	7.4	77.6	6.0	13.5	2.4	0.5
750 to 1,499..................	12,986	94.6	5.4	84.5	9.1	4.1	1.9	0.4
450 to 749....................	8,023	92.7	7.3	80.8	5.9	8.5	3.5	1.4
449 or fewer..................	3,159	91.6	8.4	91.0	2.2	4.2	2.4	0.2

[1] Includes Asians, Native Hawaiians, or Other Pacific Islanders; American Indians or Alaska Natives; and persons of two or more races. [2] Size of agency is based on the number of full-time-equivalent (FTE) sworn officers (i.e., the number of full-time sworn officers plus half the number of part-time sworn officers).

Source: U.S. Bureau of Justice Statistics, *Primary State Law Enforcement Agencies: Personnel, 2020*, NCJ 307507, January 2024. See also <bjs.ojp.gov/library>.

Table 366. State and Local Government Criminal Justice Expenditures Per Capita by State: 2021

[In dollars. Based on Census Bureau's Annual Survey of State and Local Government Finances]

State	Total justice system	Police protec-tion	Judicial and legal	Correc-tions	State	Total justice system	Police protec-tion	Judicial and legal	Correc-tions
Total..................	**826**	**406**	**158**	**262**	Missouri.................	587	339	104	144
Alabama.................	559	287	88	184	Montana.................	795	338	198	258
Alaska...................	1,409	552	341	516	Nebraska................	692	283	105	303
Arizona..................	800	398	144	258	Nevada..................	918	466	177	275
Arkansas................	506	241	87	178	New Hampshire.........	632	350	126	155
California................	1,332	636	236	460	New Jersey.............	846	455	173	218
Colorado................	848	420	172	257	New Mexico.............	915	355	179	381
Connecticut.............	796	363	189	244	New York...............	1,095	539	249	307
Delaware................	966	392	199	375	North Carolina..........	666	359	95	211
District of Columbia.....	1,759	1,000	346	412	North Dakota...........	801	354	156	290
Florida..................	843	485	122	236	Ohio....................	686	333	164	189
Georgia.................	641	299	146	196	Oklahoma...............	572	296	91	186
Hawaii..................	766	400	213	153	Oregon.................	979	388	214	377
Idaho...................	677	281	137	259	Pennsylvania............	845	383	172	290
Illinois..................	784	471	125	188	Rhode Island...........	795	451	139	206
Indiana.................	535	251	102	183	South Carolina..........	526	272	99	154
Iowa....................	572	296	122	154	South Dakota...........	655	274	123	258
Kansas..................	718	391	133	195	Tennessee..............	633	331	125	177
Kentucky................	563	232	130	200	Texas...................	677	332	131	213
Louisiana................	684	345	143	196	Utah....................	579	267	128	184
Maine...................	541	256	93	192	Vermont................	842	437	174	231
Maryland................	1,003	510	172	321	Virginia.................	814	336	129	349
Massachusetts..........	751	352	165	233	Washington.............	794	347	168	278
Michigan................	688	291	154	243	West Virginia...........	682	263	154	265
Minnesota..............	796	450	143	204	Wisconsin..............	743	339	124	280
Mississippi..............	561	268	104	189	Wyoming................	970	383	221	366

Source: U.S. Census Bureau, "2021 State and Local Government Finance Historical Datasets and Tables," <www.census.gov/programs-surveys/gov-finances.html>, accessed November 2023; and "Annual Estimates of the Resident Population for the United States, Regions, States, the District of Columbia, and Puerto Rico: April 1, 2020 to July 1, 2023 (NST-EST2023-POP)," December 2023, <www.census.gov/programs-surveys/popest/technical-documentation/research/evaluation-estimates.html>.

Table 367. Equal Employment Opportunity Commission (EEOC) Discrimination Charges Filed by Type and Litigation: 2010 to 2023

[Number, except as noted (85.1 represents $85,100,000). For fiscal years ending in year shown. The EEOC enforces federal laws making it illegal to discriminate against a job applicant or employee for charges listed below. Most employers with at least 15 employees, labor unions, and employment agencies are covered by EEOC laws. If the EEOC does not resolve charges through conciliation or other informal methods, the Commission may pursue litigation against private sector employers, employment agencies, labor unions and, in cases alleging age discrimination or equal pay violations, against state and local governments. The number for total charges reflects the number of individual charge filings. Charge data do not sum to total because individuals often file charges claiming multiple types of discrimination. See <www.eeoc.gov> for more information]

Discrimination charges and litigation	2010	2015	2017	2018	2019	2020	2021	2022	2023
CHARGES FILED									
Total charges filed with EEOC......	**99,922**	**89,385**	**84,254**	**76,418**	**72,675**	**67,448**	**61,331**	**73,485**	**81,055**
Race.....................................	35,890	31,027	28,528	24,600	23,976	22,064	20,908	20,992	27,505
Sex......................................	29,029	26,396	25,605	24,655	23,532	21,398	18,762	19,805	25,473
National origin..........................	11,304	9,438	8,299	7,106	7,009	6,377	6,213	5,500	6,963
Religion.................................	3,790	3,502	3,436	2,859	2,725	2,404	2,111	[5] 13,814	4,341
Color (skin complexion).................	2,780	2,833	3,240	3,166	3,415	3,562	3,516	4,088	5,819
Retaliation, all statutes................	36,258	39,757	41,097	39,469	39,110	37,632	34,332	37,898	46,047
Retaliation, Title VII only [1]..............	30,948	31,893	32,023	30,556	30,117	27,997	25,121	28,462	31,972
Age.....................................	23,264	20,144	18,376	16,911	15,573	14,183	12,965	11,500	14,144
Disability (ADA) [2].......................	25,165	26,968	26,838	24,605	24,238	24,324	22,843	25,004	29,160
Equal Pay Act..........................	1,044	973	996	1,066	1,117	980	885	955	1,012
GINA [3]...................................	201	257	206	220	209	440	242	444	361
Pregnant Workers Fairness Act........	(X)	(X)	(X)	(X)	(X)	(X)	(X)	(X)	188
LITIGATION [4]									
Suits filed...............................	271	174	201	217	157	97	124	93	158
Resolutions.............................	315	171	125	156	180	176	140	100	105
Monetary benefits (mil. dol.)...........	85.1	65.3	42.4	53.6	39.1	106.1	34.0	39.7	22.6

X Not applicable [1] Title VII of the Civil Rights Act of 1964. [2] Americans with Disabilities Act. [3] Genetic Information Non-Discrimination Act. [4] Suits filed and resolved in federal district courts. [5] Significant increase in vaccine-related charges filed on the basis of religion.

Source: U.S. Equal Employment Opportunity Commission, "Enforcement and Litigation Statistics," <www.eeoc.gov/data/data-and-statistics>, accessed May 2024.

Table 368. Asset Forfeiture Fund—Net Deposits by State: 2020 to 2023

[In thousands of dollars (1,758,166 represents $1,758,166,000). For fiscal years ending September 30. Transactions to or from the Department of Justice Asset Forfeiture Fund (AFF), which encompasses the seizure and forfeiture of assets that represent the proceeds of or were used to facilitate federal crimes. They do not reflect total forfeiture activity for any jurisdiction. See source for more details. Minus (-) sign indicates refunds]

State or territory	2020	2022	2023	State or territory	2020	2022	2023
Total......................	**1,758,166**	**1,788,303**	**3,454,786**	Montana...................	–	–	–
				Nebraska..................	4,603	6,371	5,362
Investment income [1]......	68,865	40,501	277,286	Nevada....................	8,068	6,047	7,063
Alabama...................	2,846	2,858	1,362	New Hampshire...........	699	1,283	1,399
Alaska....................	329	23	82	New Jersey................	32,125	32,830	15,167
Arizona...................	5,874	8,134	4,928	New Mexico...............	2,076	3,731	1,763
Arkansas..................	2,703	1,682	1,060	New York..................	72,729	223,083	2,393,246
California.................	718,338	291,253	86,505	North Carolina............	15,073	42,598	29,496
Colorado..................	22,516	28,414	12,477	North Dakota.............	72	46	169
Connecticut...............	5,548	6,669	44,936	Ohio......................	20,914	22,469	23,217
Delaware.................	–	58	–	Oklahoma.................	2,339	6,560	12,739
District of Columbia.......	356,894	164,264	79,627	Oregon...................	5,295	20,338	8,441
Florida...................	59,339	146,625	71,071	Pennsylvania..............	23,018	97,484	31,682
Georgia...................	10,259	19,227	19,338	Rhode Island..............	2	28	43
Hawaii....................	7	3,257	1,272	South Carolina............	2,851	8,540	4,080
Idaho.....................	–	–	32	South Dakota.............	–	–	–
Illinois....................	28,803	28,003	48,117	Tennessee.................	6,859	15,422	8,112
Indiana...................	4,772	9,143	14,318	Texas.....................	43,306	125,702	87,258
Iowa.....................	21	–	–	Utah......................	2,788	5,352	6,115
Kansas...................	4,964	1,247	1,213	Vermont..................	2,023	988	802
Kentucky.................	7,582	9,442	15,098	Virginia...................	65,959	79,089	30,767
Louisiana.................	7,652	7,511	4,457	Washington...............	9,281	13,786	8,336
Maine....................	36	64	–	West Virginia.............	464	49	-16
Maryland.................	18,319	14,566	7,446	Wisconsin.................	11,212	8,943	7,373
Massachusetts............	20,923	30,110	20,555	Wyoming.................	-1	–	–
Michigan.................	15,909	221,060	33,070	Guam....................	123	796	1,195
Minnesota................	5,638	5,507	3,121	Puerto Rico...............	25,461	19,100	12,236
Mississippi...............	24,294	9,865	9,612	Virgin Islands.............	33	–	-21
Missouri..................	21,890	12,905	19,238	Other [2]..................	-13,529	-14,720	-17,456

– Represents or rounds to zero. [1] Idle funds invested in U.S. Treasury Securities. [2] Comprised of transactions made to the AFF where a district has not been identified, where Federal reimbursements were made for services rendered, or summary estimates for financial reporting purposes where details by state were not available.

Source: U.S. Department of Justice, Asset Forfeiture Program, "Annual Reports to Congress," <www.justice.gov/afp>, accessed February 2024.

Table 369. Arrests by Type of Offense, Age, and Sex: 2022

[For year ending December 31. Beginning 2021, the FBI's Uniform Crime Reporting (UCR) program transitioned from its long-time Summary Reporting System (SRS) to the more comprehensive National Incident-Based Reporting System (NIBRS). Data are not strictly comparable to data from earlier years. See source for details]

Offense	Total	Age			Sex	
		18 years and over	Under 18 years	Unknown Age	Male	Female
Total	5,407,860	5,038,017	367,777	2,066	3,926,238	1,481,622
Crimes against persons	978,368	872,658	105,389	321	706,956	271,412
Assault offenses	928,239	828,612	99,328	299	660,733	267,506
Homicide offenses	9,540	8,583	953	4	8,321	1,219
Human trafficking offenses	483	471	12	–	410	73
Kidnapping/abduction	12,842	12,454	385	3	11,321	1,521
Sex offenses	27,264	22,538	4,711	15	26,171	1,093
Crimes against property [1]	868,990	783,439	85,232	319	597,730	271,260
Arson	6,301	5,340	961	–	4,846	1,455
Burglary/breaking & entering	81,142	73,081	8,032	29	66,122	15,020
Counterfeiting/forgery	20,773	20,399	359	15	14,247	6,526
Destruction/damage/vandalism	112,568	95,258	17,279	31	86,223	26,345
Embezzlement	7,013	6,696	315	2	3,542	3,471
Fraud offenses	59,332	57,396	1,907	29	38,796	20,536
Larceny/theft offenses	434,206	399,127	34,919	160	265,259	168,947
Motor vehicle theft	52,718	44,221	8,474	23	41,247	11,471
Robbery	37,135	29,871	7,249	15	31,577	5,558
Stolen property offenses	57,095	51,404	5,676	15	45,326	11,769
Crimes against society	928,385	870,101	58,080	204	695,949	232,436
Animal cruelty	3,944	3,829	111	4	2,412	1,532
Drug/narcotic offenses	787,347	744,324	42,846	177	573,727	213,620
Gambling offenses	765	741	24	–	571	194
Pornography/obscene material	5,844	4,181	1,660	3	5,164	680
Prostitution offenses	8,682	8,625	55	2	3,966	4,716
Weapon law violations	121,803	108,401	13,384	18	110,109	11,694
Group B offenses [1]	2,632,117	2,511,819	119,076	1,222	1,925,603	706,514
Curfew/loitering/vagrancy violations	17,414	11,853	5,512	49	12,933	4,481
Disorderly conduct	190,491	163,854	26,520	117	135,045	55,446
Driving under the influence	581,518	577,497	3,878	143	431,735	149,783
Family offenses, nonviolent	37,168	35,589	1,564	15	24,043	13,125
Liquor law violations	76,186	64,760	11,397	29	51,900	24,286
Trespass of real property	188,159	180,098	7,978	83	139,340	48,819

– Represents zero. [1] Includes other offenses not shown separately.

Source: U.S. Department of Justice, Federal Bureau of Investigation, Crime Data Explorer, Documents and Downloads, "National Incident-Based Reporting System (NIBRS) Tables, Arrestees," <cde.ucr.cjis.gov/LATEST/webapp/#/pages/downloads>, accessed June 2024.

Table 370. Arrests by Type of Offense and Race: 2022

[See headnote Table 369]

Offense	Total	White	Black or African American	American Indian or Alaska Native	Asian	Native Hawaiian or Other Pacific Islander	Unknown race
Total	5,407,860	3,560,196	1,507,203	128,397	65,585	22,060	124,419
Crimes against persons	978,368	590,086	329,430	20,817	13,764	4,285	19,986
Assault offenses	928,239	559,424	313,102	19,959	12,937	4,096	18,721
Homicide offenses	9,540	3,826	5,313	141	94	31	135
Human trafficking offenses	483	222	201	3	23	4	30
Kidnapping/abduction	12,842	8,052	4,119	230	190	28	223
Sex offenses	27,264	18,562	6,695	484	520	126	877
Crimes against property [1]	868,990	544,927	277,421	16,057	10,073	3,153	17,359
Arson	6,301	4,421	1,502	135	108	21	114
Burglary/breaking & entering	81,142	53,603	23,695	1,403	761	266	1,414
Counterfeiting/forgery	20,773	13,330	6,418	196	293	59	477
Destruction/damage/vandalism	112,568	72,813	33,086	2,692	1,266	371	2,340
Embezzlement	7,013	3,938	2,742	52	93	10	178
Fraud offenses	59,332	36,555	19,468	997	779	177	1,356
Larceny/theft offenses	434,206	279,463	131,249	8,196	5,041	1,369	8,888
Motor vehicle theft	52,718	32,794	17,348	1,034	480	228	834
Robbery	37,135	15,153	20,377	464	374	230	537
Stolen property offenses	57,095	32,323	21,389	879	868	422	1,214
Crimes against society	928,385	603,520	278,767	15,675	9,091	2,205	19,127
Animal cruelty	3,944	2,836	891	54	40	25	98
Drug/narcotic offenses	787,347	538,346	209,288	14,338	6,959	1,853	16,563
Gambling offenses	765	378	230	4	106	15	32
Pornography/obscene material	5,844	4,598	967	36	95	5	143
Prostitution offenses	8,682	4,389	3,398	42	691	27	135
Weapon law violations	121,803	52,973	63,993	1,201	1,200	280	2,156
Group B offenses [1]	2,632,117	1,821,663	621,585	75,848	32,657	12,417	67,947
Curfew/loitering/vagrancy violations	17,414	10,218	4,424	2,133	191	141	307
Disorderly conduct	190,491	123,606	51,508	8,494	2,051	633	4,199
Driving under the influence	581,518	443,355	87,244	13,058	11,278	2,298	24,285
Family offenses, nonviolent	37,168	24,916	9,028	1,974	347	99	804
Liquor law violations	76,186	56,256	11,222	3,765	1,179	475	3,289
Trespass of real property	188,159	119,880	56,552	4,580	2,814	1,204	3,129

[1] Includes other offenses not shown separately.

Source: U.S. Department of Justice, Federal Bureau of Investigation, Crime Data Explorer, Documents and Downloads, "National Incident-Based Reporting System (NIBRS) Tables, Arrestees," <cde.ucr.cjis.gov/LATEST/webapp/#/pages/downloads>, accessed June 2024.

Table 371. Law Enforcement Officers Killed and Assaulted: 2000 to 2023

[The statistics presented in this table are based on information collected by the staff of the FBI's Law Enforcement Officers Killed and Assaulted Program from law enforcement agencies throughout the U.S. and U.S. Territories. It contains statistics on line-of-duty felonious deaths, accidental deaths, and assaults of duly sworn local, state, tribal, and federal law enforcement officers]

Item	2000	2010	2015	2017	2018	2019	2020	2021	2022	2023
OFFICERS KILLED										
Total killed	**134**	**127**	**86**	**94**	**107**	**89**	**92**	**129**	**118**	**94**
By region and area:										
Northeast	13	11	9	9	10	4	3	7	13	11
Midwest	32	24	11	20	23	17	18	21	17	19
South	67	61	48	51	53	49	52	70	66	44
West	19	28	14	12	19	17	19	26	22	17
Puerto Rico	3	3	4	2	2	2	–	5	–	3
Total feloniously killed	**51**	**55**	**41**	**46**	**57**	**48**	**46**	**73**	**61**	**60**
By type of weapon:										
Firearms	47	54	38	42	52	44	41	61	49	45
Handgun	33	38	29	32	39	34	21	16	13	9
Rifle	10	15	7	9	10	7	10	12	6	5
Shotgun	4	1	1	1	2	1	–	2	–	1
Multiple firearms [1]	(NA)	(NA)	–	–	–	–	–	–	–	–
Type of firearm unknown	(NA)	–	1	–	–	1	1	2	1	1
Firearm type not reported	–	–	–	–	1	1	9	29	29	29
Knife/cutting instrument [2]	1	–	–	1	–	–	–	2	–	–
Knife [2]	(NA)	(NA)	–	1	–	–	–	2	–	–
Personal weapons [3]	–	–	–	–	1	–	1	4	8	2
Vehicle	3	1	3	3	4	4	4	6	3	11
Total accidentally killed	**83**	**72**	**45**	**48**	**50**	**41**	**46**	**56**	**57**	**34**
OFFICERS ASSAULTED										
Population covered (1,000) [4]	204,599	248,727	265,100	191,249	270,458	201,405	252,827	193,474	247,169	(NA)
Number of:										
Reporting agencies	8,940	11,826	12,695	7,686	11,897	7,972	10,409	8,735	10,125	(NA)
Officers employed	452,531	557,884	579,746	406,104	604,629	442,381	562,022	394,406	530,278	(NA)
Total assaulted	**58,398**	**56,491**	**52,442**	**49,620**	**61,264**	**56,009**	**66,335**	**46,539**	**66,415**	**(NA)**
By type of weapon:										
Firearm	1,749	1,925	2,095	2,215	2,264	2,247	3,095	2,343	3,061	(NA)
Knife/cutting instrument	1,015	918	956	892	1,201	1,074	1,313	1,041	1,411	(NA)
Other dangerous weapon	8,132	7,413	8,042	8,723	9,876	8,509	12,934	8,567	11,306	(NA)
Personal weapons [3]	47,502	46,235	41,349	37,790	47,923	44,179	48,993	34,588	50,637	(NA)

– Represents zero. NA Not available. [1] Multiple firearms used by offender(s), unable to determine which caused fatal injury. [2] Prior to 2011, the type of weapon categories Knife and Other cutting instrument were combined. [3] Includes hands, fists, feet, etc. [4] Represents the number of persons covered by reporting agencies.

Source: U.S. Department of Justice, Federal Bureau of Investigation, Crime Data Explorer, "Law Enforcement Officers Killed and Assaulted Annual Reports," <cde.ucr.cjis.gov/LATEST/webapp/#/pages/downloads>, accessed July 2024.

Table 372. Presidential Pardons and Commutations: 1961 to 2024

[For fiscal years shown. Not shown are petitions pending at the beginning of the fiscal year, or in the case of a change of administration, the number of cases pending at the time of the new President's inauguration]

Period	President	Petitions received	Petitions granted [1]			Petitions denied or closed without presidential action
			Pardon	Commutation	Remission	
1961 to 2024 [2]	**Total**	**95,968**	**4,644**	**2,465**	**17**	**80,721**
1961 to 1964	John F. Kennedy	1,749	472	100	3	831
1964 to 1969	Lyndon B. Johnson	4,537	960	226	1	2,830
1969 to 1975	Richard M. Nixon	2,591	863	60	3	2,614
1975 to 1977	Gerald R. Ford	1,527	382	22	5	900
1977 to 1981	Jimmy Carter	2,627	534	29	3	2,056
1981 to 1989	Ronald W. Reagan	3,404	393	13	–	2,804
1989 to 1993	George H.W. Bush	1,466	74	3	–	1,621
1993 to 2001	William J. Clinton	7,489	396	61	2	4,554
2001 to 2009	George W. Bush	11,074	189	11	–	11,914
2009 to 2017	Barack Obama	36,544	212	1,715	–	25,217
2017 to 2021	Donald J. Trump	12,078	144	94	–	8,303
2021 to 2024 [2]	Joseph R. Biden	10,882	25	131	–	17,077

– Represents zero. [1] Petitions granted are taken from a count of clemency warrants maintained by the Office of the Pardon Attorney. Cases in which multiple forms of relief were granted are counted in only one category. Cases in which clemency was granted to a person who did not file an application with the Office of the Pardon Attorney are counted as "petitions granted" but have not been counted as "petitions pending" or "petitions received" since at least FY1990. Excludes individual members of a class of persons granted pardons by proclamation. [2] As of August 7, 2024.

Source: U.S. Department of Justice, Office of the Pardon Attorney, "Clemency Statistics," <www.justice.gov/pardon/clemency-statistics>, accessed August 2024.

Table 373. Forensic Services Requests and Backlog by Type of Request: 2020

[Numbers are rounded to the nearest thousand or hundred. Data are from the 2020 Census of Publicly Funded Forensic Crime Laboratories, covering 326 federal, state, and local crime laboratories; response rate was 89.9 percent. Totals exclude requests outsourced to other laboratories. Request is classified as backlogged if it has been submitted to a crime lab and has not yet been examined and reported to the submitting agency within 30 days. See source for methodology]

Type of request	Received		Completed		Backlogged requests	
	Number	Percent	Number	Percent	Number	Percent
All requests...	**3,346,000**	**100.0**	**3,218,000**	**100.0**	**710,900**	**100.0**
Controlled substances...................................	1,088,000	32.5	1,026,000	31.9	260,600	36.7
Crime scene..	144,000	4.3	144,000	4.5	(X)	(X)
Digital evidence..	27,000	0.8	26,000	0.8	1,900	1.0
DNA databasing of offender/arrestee samples [1].............	671,000	20.1	650,000	20.2	121,000	17.0
Firearms/toolmarks......................................	225,000	6.7	199,000	6.2	101,000	14.2
Forensic biology casework [1]............................	339,000	10.1	318,000	9.9	126,100	17.7
Impressions..	7,000	(Z)	[2] 8,000	(Z)	600	(Z)
Latent prints...	180,000	5.4	172,000	5.3	43,900	6.2
Questioned documents...................................	2,000	(Z)	2,000	(Z)	300	(Z)
Toxicology..	629,000	18.8	643,000	20.0	46,400	6.5
Trace evidence...	34,000	1.0	31,000	1.0	9,200	1.3

X Not applicable. Z Less than 0.5%. [1] Includes biology screening and DNA analysis. [2] Interpret with caution. Estimate is based on 10 or fewer sample cases, or coefficient of variation is greater than 50%.

Source: U.S. Bureau of Justice Statistics, *Publicly Funded Forensic Crime Laboratories, 2020*, NCJ 306473, December 2023. See also <bjs.ojp.gov/library>.

Table 374. Freedom of Information Act (FOIA) Requests Received, Processed, Granted and Denied by Federal Department and Selected Agency: 2023

[For year ending September 30. Freedom of Information Act (FOIA) provides the public the right to request access to records from any executive federal agency. Agencies are required to disclose any information requested under the FOIA unless it falls under one of nine exemptions; see <www.foia.gov/faq.html#exemptions> for full listing. Each agency is required to file an annual report with the Department of Justice detailing their administration of the FOIA. Data are compiled from those reports]

Department or agency	Requests pending from prior year	Requests received	Requests processed	Requests pending at year end	Disposition		
					Requests granted in full	Requests granted in part	Full denials [2]
Total [1]..................................	**298,449**	**1,199,644**	**1,122,166**	**375,927**	**180,065**	**432,298**	**509,803**
Department of Agriculture............................	2,387	16,605	16,242	2,750	10,931	2,284	3,027
Department of Commerce............................	1,133	2,241	2,093	1,281	442	290	1,361
Department of Defense..............................	25,357	60,109	55,731	29,735	14,933	17,148	23,650
Department of Education.............................	1,730	2,816	2,385	2,161	228	1,096	1,061
Department of Energy................................	1,011	2,156	1,790	1,377	349	364	1,077
Department of Health and Human Services........	13,461	46,530	47,038	12,953	14,609	5,618	26,811
Department of Homeland Security...................	104,434	674,856	580,205	199,085	37,713	245,237	297,255
Department of Housing and Urban Development...	802	1,909	1,932	779	318	385	1,229
Department of Justice................................	83,369	110,934	144,065	50,238	62,264	11,348	70,453
Department of Labor..................................	2,325	14,282	14,219	2,388	2,493	4,641	7,085
Department of the Interior............................	5,261	7,085	7,388	4,958	1,666	1,736	3,986
Department of State...................................	20,982	15,713	12,576	24,119	372	5,676	6,528
Department of the Treasury..........................	3,036	10,782	10,550	3,268	2,902	2,281	5,367
Department of Transportation.......................	6,657	17,136	16,458	7,335	6,443	6,470	3,545
Department of Veterans Affairs......................	2,427	79,590	72,403	9,614	7,301	52,477	12,625
Central Intelligence Agency..........................	3,162	2,426	1,567	4,021	79	184	1,304
Commodity Futures Trading Commission...........	6	290	291	5	53	47	191
Consumer Financial Protection Bureau.............	81	510	537	54	76	96	365
Consumer Product Safety Commission.............	517	601	844	274	174	175	495
Court Services and Offender Supervision Agency...	11	354	342	23	16	126	200
Environmental Protection Agency...................	1,956	6,588	6,777	1,767	2,149	1,139	3,489
Equal Employment Opportunity Commission.......	508	15,929	14,703	1,734	846	10,285	3,572
Federal Communications Commission..............	65	586	535	116	106	179	250
Federal Deposit Insurance Corporation............	37	826	685	178	54	83	548
Federal Labor Relations Authority...................	31	222	158	95	17	56	85
Federal Reserve System.............................	52	772	739	85	233	67	439
Federal Trade Commission..........................	88	1,820	1,812	96	536	448	828
General Services Administration....................	327	1,723	1,510	540	216	349	945
National Aeronautics and Space Administration....	79	1,005	1,003	81	113	191	699
National Archives and Records Administration.....	9,969	62,505	66,064	6,410	899	54,428	10,737
National Labor Relations Board.....................	95	2,198	2,236	57	310	1,403	523
National Railroad Passenger Corporation...........	361	364	550	175	150	85	315
National Science Foundation........................	503	339	158	684	18	97	43
National Transportation Safety Board...............	183	558	601	140	34	95	472
Nuclear Regulatory Commission....................	91	236	207	120	45	61	101
Office of Management and Budget..................	610	315	362	563	22	52	288
Office of Personnel Management....................	153	581	586	148	80	135	371
Office of the Director of National Intelligence.......	570	386	269	687	16	120	133
Peace Corps...	110	265	301	74	42	70	189
Pension Benefit Guaranty Corporation.............	73	2,682	2,643	112	1,835	320	488
Securities and Exchange Commission..............	977	9,481	9,022	1,436	1,286	526	7,210
Small Business Administration......................	956	4,381	4,133	1,204	1,645	717	1,771
Social Security Administration.......................	637	10,130	10,305	462	4,694	1,995	3,616
U.S. Agency for International Development.........	428	338	334	432	34	103	197
United States Postal Service........................	266	4,168	4,104	330	447	749	2,908

[1] Includes other agencies not shown below. [2] Denials due to FOIA exemptions and other nonexemption reasons, including no records available, incorrect agency, duplicate, and not reasonably descriptive.

Source: U.S. Department of Justice, Office of Information Policy, "Agency FOIA data: Annual FOIA Reports," <www.foia.gov/reports.html>, accessed April 2024. See also <www.justice.gov/oip/reports-1>.

Table 375. Drug Enforcement Administration Arrests by Type of Drug: 2010 to 2022

[For fiscal year ending in year shown. Includes federal and state arrests. Data are from Drug Enforcement Administration's (DEA) Defendant Statistical System]

Fiscal year	Total arrested	Powder cocaine	Crack cocaine	Heroin [1]	Other opioids [2]	Marijuana	Metham- phetamine	Other nonopioids [3]
2010.........	31,517	8,231	2,640	3,029	1,582	8,215	5,527	2,293
2011.........	32,379	7,664	2,726	3,575	2,379	7,723	5,547	2,765
2012.........	31,628	7,386	2,653	3,664	2,269	6,787	6,000	2,869
2013.........	30,532	6,346	2,113	4,181	2,227	5,862	6,858	2,945
2014.........	29,549	5,582	1,782	4,852	2,048	5,082	7,005	3,197
2015.........	31,593	6,017	1,567	6,340	1,918	4,741	8,023	2,932
2016.........	29,486	5,484	1,455	5,926	1,553	4,213	8,068	2,787
2017.........	27,223	5,495	1,152	5,452	1,790	3,541	7,280	2,513
2018.........	27,348	5,198	1,103	5,078	2,170	3,266	8,088	2,445
2019.........	27,543	4,899	970	4,837	2,598	2,597	9,076	2,566
2020.........	26,696	4,474	1,217	3,707	2,925	2,576	8,783	3,014
2021.........	28,224	5,049	1,118	2,661	3,744	2,615	9,412	3,625
2022.........	26,233	5,065	1,048	1,523	5,375	2,136	8,083	3,003

[1] Includes heroin, morphine, and opium base. [2] Synthetic compounds that emulate the effects of natural compounds found in the opium poppy. Synthetic opioids are commonly available by prescription but can also be manufactured in labs. Includes fentanyl, oxycodone, hydrocodone, opioid treatment pharmaceuticals, hydromorphone, palladone, and oxymorphone. [3] Includes nonopioid pharmaceutical controlled substances, other depressants, sedatives, ephedrine, pseudoephedrine, hallucinogens, synthetic cannabinoids, other steroids, equipment to manufacture controlled substances, and drug-use paraphernalia.

Source: U.S. Department of Justice, Bureau of Justice Statistics, *Federal Justice Statistics, 2022*, NCJ 307553, January 2024, and earlier releases. See also <bjs.ojp.gov/library>.

Table 376. Missing Person Reports by Selected Characteristics: 2021 to 2023

[Data shown are missing person records entered into the National Crime Information Center's (NCIC) Missing Person File during the year shown and do not include records removed (canceled, cleared, and located). The NCIC contained 96,955 active missing person records remaining in the database as of December 31, 2023; this figure includes entries from earlier years. For more information, see source]

Characteristic	2021			2022			2023		
	All ages [8]	Under age 18	Age 18 and older	All ages [8]	Under age 18	Age 18 and older	All ages [8]	Under age 18	Age 18 and older
Total missing person entries....................	**521,705**	**337,195**	**184,068**	**546,568**	**359,094**	**187,003**	**563,389**	**375,304**	**187,623**
By type:									
Juvenile [1].........................	317,869	316,757	1,112	340,573	339,543	1,030	356,908	355,931	977
Endangered [2].........................	41,855	8,632	33,137	41,111	8,538	32,501	43,176	8,837	34,244
Involuntary [3].........................	13,621	4,680	8,907	11,884	3,778	8,072	8,401	2,984	5,396
Disability [4].........................	29,393	4,093	25,253	29,749	4,283	25,412	29,254	4,486	24,713
Catastrophe [5].........................	346	75	264	220	58	159	260	58	195
Other [6].........................	118,621	2,958	115,395	123,031	2,894	119,829	125,390	3,008	122,098
By sex:									
Female.........................	257,385	183,684	73,541	271,493	196,025	75,302	280,031	205,171	74,681
Male.........................	264,160	153,383	110,495	274,939	162,966	111,668	283,185	170,014	112,888
Unknown.........................	160	128	32	136	103	33	173	119	54
By race/ethnicity:									
White [7].........................	305,249	186,321	118,639	313,017	193,087	119,658	320,225	200,163	119,768
Black.........................	177,530	126,607	50,815	193,151	141,015	52,016	202,097	149,472	52,505
Asian.........................	10,805	5,040	5,763	11,349	5,452	5,893	11,959	5,909	6,042
American Indian.........................	9,572	6,630	2,938	10,123	6,907	3,204	10,650	7,374	3,269
Unknown.........................	18,549	12,597	5,913	18,928	12,633	6,232	18,458	12,386	6,039

[1] A person not declared emancipated as defined by the laws of state of residence and does not meet any of the entry criteria set forth in the disability, endangered, involuntary, or catastrophe victim categories. [2] Indicating that physical safety may be in danger. [3] Disappearance may not have been voluntary, i.e. abduction or kidnapping. [4] Proven physical/mental disability or senile and subjecting themselves or others to personal and immediate danger. [5] Missing after a catastrophe. [6] A person not meeting the criteria for entry in any other category who is missing and (1) for whom there is a reasonable concern for their safety or (2) a person who is under age 21 and declared emancipated by the laws of state of residence. [7] Includes Hispanic ethnicity or origin. [8] Includes persons of unknown age.

Source: U.S. Department of Justice, Federal Bureau of Investigation, "2023 NCIC Missing Person and Unidentified Person Statistics," and earlier releases, <le.fbi.gov/informational-tools/ncic>, accessed May 2024.

Table 377. Federal Prosecutions of Public Corruption by Prosecution Status: 2010 to 2022

[As of December 31. Prosecution of persons who have corrupted public office in violation of Federal Criminal Statutes]

Type of official	2010			2020			2021			2022		
	Charged	Con- victed	Await- ing trial	Charged	Con- victed	Await- ing trial	Charged	Con- victed	Await- ing trial	Charged	Con- victed	Await- ing trial
Total....................	**1,184**	**1,036**	**554**	**628**	**469**	**561**	**646**	**598**	**555**	**466**	**589**	**401**
Federal officials.........	422	397	103	242	207	154	246	228	153	183	205	128
State officials...........	168	108	105	55	30	48	52	43	60	50	68	36
Local officials............	296	280	146	135	110	129	167	138	150	122	149	107
Others involved [1].......	298	251	200	196	122	230	181	189	192	111	167	130

[1] Includes individuals who are neither public officials nor employees, but were involved with public officials or employees in violating the law.

Source: U.S. Department of Justice, Criminal Division, *Report to Congress on the Activities and Operations of the Public Integrity Section for 2022*, and earlier reports. See also <www.justice.gov/criminal/pin>.

Table 378. U.S. Supreme Court—Cases on Docket, Disposed of, and Remaining: 2000 to 2022

[Statutory term of court begins first Monday in October. Often the Court grants or denies cases after the Court recesses but before the next statutory term]

Action	2000	2010	2015	2017	2018	2019	2020	2021	2022
NUMBER OF CASES ON DOCKET									
Total	**8,965**	**9,066**	**7,535**	**7,390**	**7,626**	**6,534**	**6,129**	**5,797**	**4,882**
Original	9	4	8	8	9	10	10	5	4
Paid	2,305	1,895	1,839	2,062	1,915	1,818	2,137	1,996	1,529
In Forma Pauperis	6,651	7,167	5,688	5,320	5,702	4,706	3,982	3,796	3,349
CASES DISPOSED OF									
Total	**7,762**	**7,827**	**6,506**	**6,192**	**6,528**	**5,712**	**5,232**	**5,071**	**4,179**
Original	2	2	1	1	2	2	6	1	3
Paid	2,024	1,580	1,539	1,728	1,583	1,509	1,752	1,716	1,274
In Forma Pauperis	5,736	6,245	4,966	4,463	4,943	4,201	3,474	3,354	2,912
NUMBER REMAINING ON DOCKET									
Total	**1,203**	**1,239**	**1,029**	**1,198**	**1,094**	**822**	**897**	**726**	**703**
Original	7	2	7	7	7	8	4	4	1
Paid	281	315	300	334	327	309	385	280	255
In Forma Pauperis	915	922	722	857	760	505	508	442	437
Cases argued during term	86	86	82	69	73	73	72	70	68
Number disposed of by full opinions	83	83	70	63	69	69	69	63	66
Number disposed of by per curiam opinions	4	3	12	6	2	4	3	7	2
Number set for re-argument next term	0	0	0	0	2	0	0	0	0
Total cases granted plenary review	99	90	81	78	86	60	72	74	61
Cases reviewed and decided without oral argument	127	84	145	103	56	105	91	97	57
Total cases available for argument at start of next term	49	43	31	38	50	37	31	0	23

Source: Administrative Office of the U.S. Courts, "Judicial Business of the United States Courts, Table A-1–Supreme Court of the United States Judicial Business," September 2023, and earlier reports, <www.uscourts.gov/data-table-topics/us-supreme-court>. See also <www.supremecourt.gov/orders/journal.aspx>.

Table 379. Federal Judiciary Caseloads: 2000 to 2023

[For 12-month periods ending June 30]

Judicial caseload	2000	2010	2015	2019	2020	2021	2022	2023
U.S. Courts of Appeals: [1]								
Cases filed	54,642	56,097	53,032	47,783	49,044	45,790	42,094	40,713
Cases terminated	56,509	59,343	53,934	47,832	48,514	47,842	45,910	41,537
Cases pending	40,815	46,816	40,913	38,433	38,973	36,921	33,138	32,432
U.S. District Courts Civil:								
Cases filed	263,049	289,630	280,037	293,520	421,082	374,250	293,762	295,215
Cases terminated	260,277	295,908	273,562	325,920	281,742	272,609	290,998	313,736
Cases pending	247,973	285,071	340,401	363,532	503,329	604,970	607,720	589,144
U.S. District Courts Criminal (includes transfers):								
Cases filed	62,523	78,213	60,866	72,926	64,853	59,500	55,220	54,366
Defendants filed	84,147	100,031	79,154	90,411	79,122	75,407	69,466	67,651
Cases terminated	57,543	77,633	61,299	66,307	66,034	48,912	55,971	57,740
Cases pending	46,796	80,506	72,094	84,687	82,894	93,437	92,766	89,895
U.S. Bankruptcy Courts:								
Cases filed	1,276,922	1,572,597	879,736	773,361	682,363	462,309	380,634	418,724
Cases terminated	1,271,300	1,441,419	1,024,504	791,523	760,297	609,855	492,439	453,121
Cases pending	1,396,916	1,659,399	1,316,672	1,032,572	954,786	807,243	694,287	660,128
Post-conviction supervision:								
Persons under supervision	99,577	126,642	133,428	128,649	127,680	124,249	124,167	123,852
Pretrial services:								
Total cases activated	86,067	110,666	95,538	106,019	90,069	77,065	73,147	74,045
Pretrial services cases activated	84,107	109,711	94,757	105,579	89,685	76,709	72,783	73,762
Pretrial diversion cases activated	1,960	955	781	440	384	356	364	283
Total released on supervision	31,607	29,748	24,429	25,392	23,357	26,867	24,072	21,901
Pretrial supervision	31,927	28,440	23,368	24,738	22,779	26,290	23,571	21,492
Diversion supervision	2,166	1,308	1,061	654	578	577	501	409

[1] Excludes the U.S. Court of Appeals for the Federal Circuit.

Source: Administrative Office of the United States Courts, "Statistical Tables for the Federal Judiciary," <www.uscourts.gov/statistics-reports/analysis-reports/statistical-tables-federal-judiciary>, accessed November 2023.

Table 380. U.S. District Courts—Civil Cases Filed by Basis of Jurisdiction and Nature of Suit: 2010 to 2023

[For 12-month periods ending June 30]

Type of case	2010	2015	2019	2020	2021	2022	2023
Total cases filed [1].........................	**285,215**	**280,037**	**293,520**	**421,082**	**374,250**	**293,762**	**295,215**
BASIS OF JURISDICTION							
U.S. cases:							
U.S. plaintiff................................	8,427	6,182	4,237	3,630	3,322	2,876	2,990
U.S. defendant.............................	34,306	35,651	37,135	41,278	43,803	34,085	42,685
Private cases:							
Federal question...........................	137,776	151,330	151,513	142,089	136,546	130,132	133,534
Diversity of citizenship....................	104,703	86,865	100,629	234,084	190,578	126,669	116,005
Local jurisdiction..........................	3	9	6	1	1	0	1
NATURE OF SUIT							
Contract actions [1].........................	31,461	26,506	25,216	26,012	26,661	26,112	31,469
Insurance..................................	9,236	9,923	10,749	11,071	13,294	14,298	18,174
Recovery of overpayments [2]...............	3,079	2,307	1,043	743	534	484	651
Real property actions [1].....................	6,809	8,963	6,966	5,689	3,325	3,751	4,249
Foreclosure...............................	3,836	4,043	2,983	2,324	1,035	1,190	1,391
Tort actions................................	87,256	69,875	81,089	213,392	169,073	105,267	90,357
Personal injury............................	82,057	62,318	77,297	209,489	165,253	101,241	86,049
Personal injury product liability...........	66,958	41,607	53,456	188,878	147,013	84,410	66,428
Other personal injury [1]...................	15,099	20,711	23,841	20,611	18,240	16,831	19,621
Motor vehicle.........................	3,574	3,763	4,993	5,352	5,558	5,480	5,719
Medical malpractice....................	1,120	1,097	1,209	1,069	1,120	1,015	1,063
Personal property damage.................	5,199	7,557	3,792	3,903	3,820	4,026	4,308
Actions under statutes [1]....................	159,683	174,693	180,249	175,989	175,191	158,632	169,140
Bankruptcy suits..........................	2,615	2,688	2,233	2,146	1,984	1,598	1,502
Civil rights [1].............................	34,427	37,015	43,223	42,053	43,272	39,592	39,700
Employment............................	14,343	12,258	12,572	12,252	11,264	10,218	11,476
Environmental matters.....................	826	578	659	439	489	442	392
Prisoner petitions.........................	52,450	52,844	54,445	56,823	49,658	45,778	49,995
Forfeiture and penalty.....................	2,297	1,620	1,148	1,024	1,138	1,052	853
Labor laws...............................	18,878	19,047	16,840	15,479	14,039	13,180	13,447
Immigration..............................	1,262	1,244	2,017	2,387	3,971	6,611	10,657
Protected property rights [3]..............	8,519	14,145	13,185	10,178	11,161	12,411	13,694
Securities, commodities, and exchanges...	1,442	1,012	1,655	1,835	2,301	2,173	1,565
Social security laws.......................	13,725	19,102	17,903	18,259	23,615	13,347	14,911
RICO [4]..................................	793	689	1,957	1,196	775	741	1,147
Tax suits.................................	1,171	1,005	773	587	528	540	557
Consumer credit..........................	8,249	9,474	10,978	10,507	10,091	9,714	8,159
Freedom of information....................	315	481	819	799	690	711	906
Cases terminated..........................	**295,909**	**273,562**	**325,920**	**281,742**	**272,609**	**290,998**	**313,736**
Cases pending.............................	**285,071**	**340,401**	**363,532**	**503,329**	**604,970**	**607,720**	**589,144**

[1] Includes other types not shown separately. [2] Includes enforcement of judgments in student loan cases, and overpayments of veterans' benefits. [3] Includes copyright, patent, and trademark rights. [4] Racketeer Influenced and Corrupt Organizations Act.

Source: Administrative Office of the United States Courts, "Statistical Tables for the Federal Judiciary," <www.uscourts.gov/statistics-reports/analysis-reports/statistical-tables-federal-judiciary>, accessed November 2023.

Table 381. U.S. Courts of Appeals—Nature of Suit or Offense in Cases Arising from the U.S. District Courts: 2010 to 2023

[For 12-month periods ending June 30. Excludes data for the U.S. Court of Appeals for the Federal Circuit. Includes appeals reopened, remanded, and reinstated (after being terminated due to procedural defaults) as well as original appeals]

Nature of suit and offense	2010	2015	2017	2018	2019	2020	2021	2022	2023
Total cases............................	**43,880**	**40,234**	**38,594**	**37,487**	**36,596**	**36,186**	**34,141**	**32,677**	**31,740**
Criminal cases...............................	12,863	10,902	10,216	9,614	9,895	9,577	10,756	10,078	9,860
Civil cases...................................	31,017	29,332	28,378	27,873	26,701	26,609	23,385	22,599	21,880
U.S cases....................................	7,772	7,471	7,609	7,660	6,778	6,634	5,779	5,224	4,848
U.S. plaintiff.............................	435	353	305	261	206	226	182	211	228
U.S. defendant............................	7,337	7,118	7,304	7,399	6,572	6,408	5,597	5,013	4,620
Private cases................................	23,245	21,861	20,769	20,213	19,923	19,975	17,606	17,375	17,032
Federal question..........................	20,599	18,821	17,918	17,423	17,133	16,865	15,049	14,635	14,424
Diversity of citizenship...................	2,646	3,040	2,851	2,790	2,789	3,109	2,557	2,740	2,608
General local jurisdiction.................	–	–	–	–	1	1	–	–	–
Criminal cases...............................	12,863	10,902	10,216	9,614	9,895	9,577	10,756	10,078	9,860
Violent offenses..........................	621	483	570	512	523	546	661	648	700
Property offenses.........................	1,624	1,420	1,271	1,212	1,241	931	950	915	982
Drug offenses............................	5,066	3,843	3,578	3,207	3,371	3,562	4,292	3,444	3,227
Firearms and explosives offenses..........	1,927	1,560	1,860	1,888	1,967	2,011	2,298	2,350	2,291
Sex offenses.............................	651	786	769	762	765	746	874	896	905
Justice system offenses...................	142	169	147	134	133	140	133	169	170
Immigration offenses.....................	1,787	1,491	957	897	929	725	548	672	549
General offenses.........................	411	289	253	235	279	231	261	245	277
Other [1].................................	634	861	811	767	687	685	739	739	759

– Represents zero. [1] Other includes regulatory, traffic, and unclassified offenses.

Source: Administrative Office of the United States Courts, "Statistical Tables for the Federal Judiciary," <www.uscourts.gov/statistics-reports/analysis-reports/statistical-tables-federal-judiciary>, accessed November 2023.

Table 382. U.S. District Courts—National Petit and Grand Juror Service: 2010 to 2023

[For years ending September 30. Includes data on jury selection days only. Data on juror service after the selection day are not included]

Juror service	2010	2015	2018	2019	2020	2021	2022	2023
PETIT JUROR SERVICE								
Jurors present for jury selection								
or orientation.............	262,376	195,206	189,504	192,595	102,531	104,270	180,553	171,099
Percent selected...........................	22.7	22.6	22.0	22.0	21.9	23.7	22.0	22.4
Percent challenged........................	38.5	40.6	40.5	39.4	38.4	36.9	36.9	36.8
Percent not selected or challenged........	38.7	36.8	37.5	38.6	39.8	39.4	41.1	40.8
Voir Dire [1]........................	24.9	23.7	24.0	24.8	25.0	26.3	27.1	27.3
Non-Voir Dire [2].........................	13.9	13.1	13.4	13.8	14.8	13.1	14.0	13.5
Total juries selected......................	5,332	4,149	3,660	3,718	1,916	2,098	3,506	3,508
GRAND JUROR SERVICE								
Juries serving.............................	784	749	755	749	651	698	649	707
Sessions convened........................	9,277	8,087	8,258	8,374	5,449	5,686	6,348	6,650
Jurors in session..........................	186,020	161,493	163,859	167,310	107,489	110,954	123,770	130,757
Average per session......................	20.1	20.0	19.8	20.0	19.7	19.5	19.5	19.7
Hours in session..........................	44,845	36,098	36,458	36,706	24,940	27,086	26,932	27,244
Average hours per session.................	4.8	4.5	4.4	4.4	4.6	4.8	4.2	4.1
Proceedings filed by indictment:								
Cases...................................	49,654	(NA)	(NA)	(NA)	(NA)	(NA)	(NA)	(NA)
Defendants..............................	70,433	56,164	63,877	70,078	55,233	57,816	53,388	50,397
Average defendants indicted per session...	7.6	6.9	7.7	8.4	10.1	10.2	8.4	7.6

NA Not available. [1] Jurors who completed pre-screening questionnaires or were in the courtroom during the conducting of voir dire. [2] Other jurors not selected or challenged who were not called to the courtroom or otherwise did not participate in the actual voir dire.

Source: Administrative Office of the United States Courts, "Judicial Business of the United States Courts 2023," <www.uscourts.gov/Statistics/JudicialBusiness.aspx>, accessed March 2024.

Table 383. Incoming Caseloads in State Trial Courts by Case Category: 2022

[States reporting incomplete data or data not conforming to reporting guidelines are not shown. Represents new filings, plus reopened and reactivated cases when provided, as reported to the Court Statistics Project. Cases should only be viewed in the context of each state's court structure; comparisons of the data reported here should not be made without additional information, see source]

State	Total	Civil [1]	Domestic relations [2]	Criminal [3]	Juvenile [4]	Traffic/other violations [5]
Alabama....................	844,033	154,695	61,097	225,005	34,139	369,097
Alaska.....................	94,958	18,873	10,141	24,067	2,551	39,326
Arizona....................	1,503,128	261,087	78,291	375,894	9,274	778,582
California..................	4,599,967	822,700	311,060	808,600	52,264	2,605,343
Colorado..................	623,864	248,000	36,797	226,138	10,075	102,854
Connecticut...............	441,472	168,393	53,242	79,669	13,549	126,619
Delaware..................	316,952	46,527	25,100	79,003	3,142	163,180
District of Columbia.......	41,312	24,959	10,352	4,942	1,059	(NA)
Florida....................	3,265,020	1,160,984	211,400	558,651	33,200	1,300,785
Georgia...................	2,890,400	726,037	117,945	1,702,092	46,011	298,315
Hawaii....................	427,563	31,145	11,066	57,014	4,409	323,929
Idaho.....................	313,087	61,188	20,801	78,634	7,106	145,358
Illinois....................	1,459,782	336,880	114,654	190,370	15,591	802,287
Indiana...................	1,052,416	326,954	91,051	265,989	36,970	331,452
Iowa......................	631,360	115,344	27,672	115,557	8,635	364,152
Kentucky..................	756,867	194,031	55,054	247,219	24,011	236,552
Louisiana..................	958,383	184,526	71,390	184,690	22,594	495,183
Maine.....................	120,855	19,574	11,660	36,331	1,906	51,384
Maryland..................	1,286,598	640,692	85,725	219,136	6,935	334,110
Massachusetts............	496,297	227,962	71,053	138,154	13,583	45,545
Michigan..................	2,824,078	547,103	99,769	705,956	32,912	1,438,338
Minnesota................	939,238	155,308	49,076	150,811	19,907	564,136
Missouri..................	1,245,253	261,722	104,244	191,684	10,563	677,040
Montana..................	263,674	41,538	14,429	57,955	2,394	147,358
Nebraska.................	358,865	93,946	26,030	128,290	15,314	95,285
Nevada...................	811,004	188,775	57,009	170,392	9,099	385,729
New Hampshire...........	108,059	42,370	11,533	28,892	3,351	21,913
New Jersey................	6,199,698	662,333	164,627	555,537	16,450	4,800,751
New Mexico...............	308,851	61,667	27,060	118,170	2,795	99,159
New York..................	2,072,719	766,322	391,335	478,533	40,775	395,754
North Carolina............	2,190,142	494,764	111,957	1,236,817	16,793	329,811
Ohio......................	2,403,031	501,027	171,037	571,675	73,402	1,085,890
Pennsylvania..............	2,970,208	346,086	364,798	347,990	28,970	1,882,364
Rhode Island..............	150,710	38,927	9,477	27,975	4,560	69,771
Texas.....................	8,699,945	1,581,818	302,287	1,975,978	30,380	4,809,482
Utah......................	598,942	90,270	24,360	166,376	17,829	300,107
Vermont...................	81,518	14,332	6,651	19,170	1,893	39,472
West Virginia..............	41,286	19,597	2,216	11,331	8,142	(NA)
Wyoming..................	112,280	22,420	5,709	24,639	1,152	58,360

NA Not available. [1] Includes tort, contract, real property, small claims, probate/estate, mental health, and civil appeals cases. [2] Includes divorce/dissolution, paternity, custody, support, visitation, adoption, and civil protection/restraining order cases. [3] Includes felony, misdemeanor, and appeals from limited jurisdiction courts. [4] Includes delinquency, dependency, and status offense petitions. [5] Includes non-criminal traffic violations (infractions), parking violations, and ordinance violations.

Source: National Center for State Courts, Court Statistics Project, "CSP Stat, Overview Trial Courts ©," <www.courtstatistics.org>, accessed August 2024.

Table 384. U.S. Sentencing Commission Summary—Cases Reviewed by Disposition and Primary Offense: 2023

[In numbers, except as noted. For fiscal year ending in year shown. Covers federal felony and Class A misdemeanor cases reported to the U.S. Sentencing Commission by federal courts as required under the Sentencing Reform Act. See source for details]

Characteristic	Total [1]	Immi-gration	Drug traffick-ing	Firearms	Fraud, theft, embezzle-ment	Robbery	Child sexual abuse material	Money laun-dering	All other
Total cases...........................	64,124	19,226	19,007	8,832	5,205	1,503	1,408	1,312	7,631
CASES INVOLVING PRISON									
Total receiving prison...................	59,268	18,452	18,475	8,257	3,857	1,491	1,395	1,172	6,169
Prison only.................................	57,579	18,108	17,862	8,078	3,656	1,450	1,381	1,122	5,922
Prison term ordered:									
Up to 12 months........................	15,344	10,831	1,253	604	1,086	28	31	159	1,352
13 to 60 months.........................	24,990	7,125	7,118	5,088	2,184	383	324	537	2,231
61 to 120 months.......................	10,140	138	5,572	2,032	314	533	576	228	747
Over 120 months.......................	7,104	13	3,919	354	72	506	450	198	1,592
Prison & alternatives [2].....................	1,689	344	613	179	201	41	14	50	247
Mean sentence (in months) [3]............	52	12	82	49	22	110	115	63	81
Median sentence (in months) [3]..........	24	8	63	40	12	96	97	36	24
CASES INVOLVING PROBATION									
Total receiving probation..............	4,563	774	530	567	1,305	12	13	138	1,224
Probation only.............................	3,808	681	417	458	1,076	12	13	101	1,050
Probation & alternatives [2]................	755	93	113	109	229	–	–	37	174
CASES INVOLVING FINES & RESTITUTION									
Total receiving fines & restitution..........	[4] 11,960	822	1,294	677	4,127	866	771	467	2,936
Median amount (in dollars).................	11,000	1,500	1,500	1,500	127,966	4,502	18,000	422,695	(NA)
Fine only.....................................	293	–	2	8	43	–	–	2	238

NA Not available. – Represents zero. [1] Details may not sum to total due to rounding. [2] Includes additional conditions of a term of community confinement, home detention, or intermittent confinement. [3] Sentences greater than 470 months are included in these calculations as 470 months. [4] 1,165 cases are excluded due to missing information.

Source: U.S. Sentencing Commission, "2023 Sourcebook of Federal Sentencing Statistics," <www.ussc.gov/research/sourcebook-2023>, accessed March 2024.

Table 385. Mandatory Minimum Sentencing Summary: 2015 to 2022

[For fiscal year ending in year shown for cases reported to the U.S. Sentencing Commission (USSC). Relief from mandatory minimum sentencing may be provided through a safety valve provision and/or by providing the government with substantial assistance; see source]

Item	2015	2016	2017	2018	2019	2020	2021	2022
Cases reported to USSC (number).............................	71,003	67,742	66,873	69,425	76,538	64,565	57,287	64,142
Cases involving a mandatory minimum penalty (number).....	14,138	13,604	13,577	16,228	18,819	15,274	16,439	18,371
Percent subject to mandatory minimum penalties.............	22.2	21.9	21.8	24.7	26.1	25.2	29.9	29.6
Percent receiving relief..	39.2	38.7	37.3	40.6	44.3	44.1	46.5	42.7
Percent not receiving relief......................................	60.8	61.3	62.7	59.4	55.7	55.9	53.5	57.3
Percent remaining subject to mandatory minimum at sentencing..	13.5	13.4	13.7	14.2	14.1	13.7	15.7	16.7
Offenders convicted of an offence carrying a mandatory minimum sentence by race/ethnicity (percent distribution):								
White...	27.2	27.2	26.9	27.3	27.6	29.5	30.1	30.2
Black..	28.9	29.7	29.5	27.4	27.6	26.4	25.0	28.1
Hispanic..	41.5	40.4	41.0	42.7	41.8	41.2	41.7	38.5
Other..	2.4	2.7	2.6	2.6	3.0	2.9	3.2	3.2

Source: U.S. Sentencing Commission, *Quick Facts: Mandatory Minimum Penalties*, August 2023 and earlier reports. See also <www.ussc.gov/research/quick-facts>.

Table 386. Delinquency Cases Disposed by Juvenile Courts by Type of Offense: 1990 to 2021

[In thousands (1,304 represents 1,304,000), except rate. A delinquency offense is an act committed by a juvenile for which an adult could be prosecuted in a criminal court. Disposition of a case involves taking a definite action such as waiving the case to criminal court, dismissing the case, placing the youth on probation, placing the youth in a facility for delinquents, or actions such as fines, restitution, and community service. Data are developed and maintained by the National Center for Juvenile Justice]

Type of offense	1990	1995	2000	2005	2010	2015	2016	2017	2018	2019	2020 [3]	2021
All delinquency offenses	**1,304**	**1,800**	**1,693**	**1,645**	**1,321**	**883**	**829**	**783**	**737**	**712**	**505**	**437**
Case rate [1]	50.8	62.7	55.0	51.2	41.9	28.0	26.2	24.7	23.3	22.3	15.6	13.5
Person offenses [2]	251	405	398	429	335	245	236	231	232	237	173	163
Criminal homicide	2	3	1	1	1	1	1	1	1	1	1	2
Rape	6	9	9	11	9	8	8	8	8	8	6	7
Robbery	25	37	22	26	25	19	19	20	19	19	16	14
Aggravated assault	44	63	48	47	34	25	25	25	26	26	22	20
Simple assault	135	233	256	278	219	160	151	146	146	150	104	95
Property offenses [2]	767	909	703	605	488	301	276	256	222	206	159	132
Burglary	144	147	117	100	85	53	52	50	40	36	31	26
Larceny-theft	344	437	329	272	239	145	125	109	96	87	58	42
Motor vehicle theft	65	53	36	32	16	13	15	17	15	15	14	14
Arson	6	10	8	7	4	3	2	2	2	2	1	1
Drug law violations	68	164	184	182	160	112	106	102	98	94	57	46
Public order offenses [2]	218	322	407	429	338	225	211	194	185	175	116	96
Obstruction of justice	85	131	206	193	161	115	107	98	90	81	55	43
Disorderly conduct	55	90	102	130	99	59	55	49	48	48	28	22
Weapons offenses	29	46	34	42	30	19	18	18	17	17	12	13
Liquor law violations	13	11	16	15	13	6	5	5	4	4	3	2
Nonviolent sex offenses	10	8	13	12	11	11	11	11	11	12	8	8

[1] Number of cases disposed per 1,000 juveniles ages 10 to upper age of juvenile court jurisdiction. The upper age of juvenile court jurisdiction is defined by statute in each state. [2] Total includes other offenses not shown. [3] See footnote 4, Table 387.

Source: U.S. Department of Justice, Office of Juvenile Justice and Delinquency Prevention, Youth in Court: Data Analysis Tools, "Case Rates by Offense, Sex, and Race (1985-2021)," <ojjdp.ojp.gov/statistical-briefing-book/court> and "Easy Access to Juvenile Court Statistics, Detailed Offenses," <www.ojjdp.gov/ojstatbb/ezajcs/>; accessed June 2024.

Table 387. Delinquency Cases Disposed by Juvenile Courts by Type of Offense, Sex, and Race: 2010 to 2021

[See headnote, Table 386. Data are developed and maintained by the National Center for Juvenile Justice]

Item	Number of cases disposed					Case rate [1]				
	2010	2015	2019	2020 [4]	2021	2010	2015	2019	2020 [4]	2021
Male, total	**952,846**	**640,680**	**513,692**	**369,226**	**320,811**	**59.0**	**39.8**	**31.5**	**22.3**	**19.4**
Person	232,540	170,107	163,777	121,017	112,899	14.4	10.6	10.1	7.3	6.8
Property	343,734	220,252	154,007	121,391	102,688	21.3	13.7	9.5	7.3	6.2
Drugs	130,945	87,396	69,151	42,024	34,132	8.1	5.4	4.3	2.5	2.1
Public order	245,627	162,925	126,758	84,793	71,092	15.2	10.1	7.8	5.1	4.3
Female, total	**368,033**	**241,943**	**198,231**	**135,595**	**116,525**	**24.0**	**15.7**	**12.7**	**8.5**	**7.3**
Person	102,507	74,486	73,277	52,354	50,135	6.7	4.8	4.7	3.3	3.2
Property	144,557	80,402	51,916	38,040	29,650	9.4	5.2	3.3	2.4	1.9
Drugs	28,589	24,602	24,380	14,456	12,173	1.9	1.6	1.6	0.9	0.8
Public order	92,381	62,453	48,658	30,745	24,567	6.0	4.0	3.1	1.9	1.6
White, total [2]	**594,778**	**384,381**	**303,281**	**219,191**	**194,266**	**33.1**	**22.1**	**17.9**	**12.8**	**11.4**
Person	140,840	100,071	96,500	72,530	71,590	7.8	5.8	5.7	4.2	4.2
Property	230,724	130,919	85,895	68,666	58,003	12.8	7.5	5.1	4.0	3.4
Drugs	88,383	61,907	49,900	31,009	25,575	4.9	3.6	3.0	1.8	1.5
Public order	134,831	91,484	70,985	46,986	39,098	7.5	5.3	4.2	2.8	2.3
Black, total [2]	**442,494**	**311,273**	**251,727**	**175,075**	**154,184**	**92.5**	**67.0**	**53.2**	**36.0**	**31.7**
Person	134,013	97,302	89,248	62,420	57,888	28.0	20.9	18.9	12.8	11.9
Property	154,486	109,993	79,967	59,549	51,049	32.3	23.7	16.9	12.2	10.5
Drugs	32,560	21,088	17,921	10,573	9,290	6.8	4.5	3.8	2.2	1.9
Public order	121,436	82,889	64,590	42,534	35,957	25.4	17.8	13.7	8.7	7.4
Hispanic, total	**247,158**	**163,043**	**135,215**	**94,030**	**74,927**	**37.5**	**22.8**	**17.5**	**11.9**	**9.5**
Person	52,341	41,641	44,498	32,766	28,496	7.9	5.8	5.8	4.1	3.6
Property	87,724	50,612	33,371	25,673	18,859	13.3	7.1	4.3	3.2	2.4
Drugs	34,109	25,236	22,153	12,697	9,732	5.2	3.5	2.9	1.6	1.2
Public order	72,984	45,554	35,192	22,894	17,839	11.1	6.4	4.5	2.9	2.3
American Indian, total [3]	**19,332**	**14,390**	**13,260**	**10,529**	**9,088**	**33.5**	**24.8**	**22.1**	**17.2**	**14.8**
Person	4,483	3,388	4,075	3,611	3,367	7.8	5.8	6.8	5.9	5.5
Property	7,556	5,441	4,138	3,661	2,881	13.1	9.4	6.9	6.0	4.7
Drugs	2,582	2,366	2,379	1,473	1,216	4.5	4.1	4.0	2.4	2.0
Public order	4,712	3,195	2,668	1,785	1,623	8.2	5.5	4.5	2.9	2.7
Asian/Native Hawaiian/ Pacific Islander, total [2]	**17,117**	**9,536**	**8,440**	**5,995**	**4,870**	**11.0**	**5.4**	**4.4**	**3.1**	**2.5**
Person	3,371	2,190	2,732	2,045	1,693	2.2	1.2	1.4	1.1	0.9
Property	7,801	3,690	2,551	1,881	1,545	5.0	2.1	1.3	1.0	0.8
Drugs	1,901	1,401	1,177	728	491	1.2	0.8	0.6	0.4	0.3
Public order	4,044	2,256	1,980	1,340	1,142	2.6	1.3	1.0	0.7	0.6

[1] Cases per 1,000 juveniles ages 10 to upper age of juvenile court jurisdiction. The upper age of juvenile court jurisdiction is defined by statute in each state. [2] Non-Hispanic. [3] Data do not always allow for identification of Hispanic ethnicity for cases involving American Indian youth. The American Indian group includes an unknown proportion of Hispanic youth. [4] The COVID-19 pandemic may have impacted policies, procedures, and data collection activities regarding referrals to and processing of youth by juvenile courts. Additionally, stay-at-home orders and school closures likely impacted the volume and type of law-violating behavior by youth referred to juvenile court in 2020.

Source: U.S. Department of Justice, Office of Juvenile Justice and Delinquency Prevention, Youth in Court: Data Analysis Tools, "Case Rates by Offense, Sex, and Race (1985-2021)," <ojjdp.ojp.gov/statistical-briefing-book/court> and "Easy Access to Juvenile Court Statistics, Detailed Offenses," <www.ojjdp.gov/ojstatbb/ezajcs/>; accessed June 2024.

Table 388. Child Victims of Abuse and Neglect—Total and First-Time Victims by State: 2022

[For fiscal years ending in year shown. Data are unique counts, which count a child once, regardless of the number of reports concerning that child. Based on available State submissions to National Child Abuse and Neglect Data System (NCANDS) of alleged child abuse and neglect. NCANDS collects case level data on children who received child protective services response in the form of an investigative or alternative response. Each state has its own definition of child abuse and neglect based on standards set by federal law. Child abuse is defined as any recent act or failure to act on the part of a parent or caretaker which results in death, serious physical or emotional harm, sexual abuse or exploitation; or an act or failure to act which presents an imminent risk or serious harm. See source for details]

| State | Total child population | Victims | First-time victims | | State | Total child population | Victims | First-time victims | |
			Number	Rate per 1,000 children				Number	Rate per 1,000 children
Total [1]......	72,969,166	558,899	391,185	5.4	MO..........	1,364,908	3,932	3,420	2.5
AL...........	1,111,562	11,618	9,423	8.5	MT...........	233,753	2,714	2,173	9.3
AK...........	176,523	2,581	1,676	9.5	NE...........	476,677	2,026	1,557	3.3
AZ...........	1,589,010	12,324	7,060	4.4	NV...........	689,778	5,851	3,852	5.6
AR...........	697,119	8,927	7,462	10.7	NH...........	252,924	1,034	847	3.3
CA...........	8,506,027	50,869	40,083	4.7	NJ...........	1,994,109	3,146	2,574	1.3
CO...........	1,215,575	9,777	6,683	5.5	NM...........	459,513	5,817	3,955	8.6
CT...........	731,030	5,032	3,553	4.9	NY...........	3,989,288	50,056	28,845	7.2
DE...........	208,127	1,077	895	4.3	NC...........	2,294,879	23,134	15,590	6.8
DC...........	124,475	1,574	1,088	8.7	ND...........	182,775	1,132	814	4.5
FL...........	4,296,354	24,505	11,046	2.6	OH...........	2,562,550	22,439	16,217	6.3
GA...........	2,510,123	10,524	8,747	3.5	OK...........	953,146	13,546	10,525	11.0
HI...........	297,326	1,228	945	3.2	OR...........	836,988	10,507	6,730	8.0
ID...........	463,404	2,005	1,695	3.7	PA...........	2,624,465	5,005	4,724	1.8
IL...........	2,720,131	32,433	20,623	7.6	RI...........	203,912	2,444	1,647	8.1
IN...........	1,569,923	19,185	13,632	8.7	SC...........	1,117,872	14,572	10,293	9.2
IA...........	724,489	11,150	7,704	10.6	SD...........	219,165	1,451	1,101	5.0
KS...........	690,832	1,861	1,669	2.4	TN...........	1,538,137	6,924	3,523	2.3
KY...........	1,004,575	12,340	7,903	7.9	TX...........	7,456,338	54,207	43,563	5.8
LA...........	1,061,693	7,572	6,063	5.7	UT...........	931,608	8,765	6,001	6.4
ME...........	247,898	3,792	2,044	8.2	VT...........	114,757	672	561	4.9
MD...........	1,346,589	6,564	4,402	3.3	VA...........	1,866,910	4,563	4,285	2.3
MA...........	1,337,434	22,075	12,206	9.1	WA...........	1,646,573	3,389	1,552	0.9
MI...........	2,109,695	23,500	14,840	7.0	WV...........	351,922	5,510	4,480	12.7
MN...........	1,294,162	5,299	5,008	3.9	WI...........	1,245,629	4,082	3,415	2.7
MS...........	678,061	9,028	7,921	11.7	WY...........	130,114	821	629	4.8

[1] Total includes data for Puerto Rico, not shown separately.

Source: U.S. Department of Health and Human Services, Administration for Children and Families, Data & Research, *Child Maltreatment 2022*, January 2024. See also <www.acf.hhs.gov/cb/data-research/child-maltreatment>.

Table 389. Child Abuse and Neglect Victims by Type of Maltreatment and Age and Sex of Victim: 2010 to 2022

[For fiscal years ending in year shown. Data are unique counts, which count a child once, regardless of the number of reports concerning that child. Based on available State submissions to National Child Abuse and Neglect Data System (NCANDS) of alleged child abuse and neglect. NCANDS collects case level data on children who received child protective services response in the form of an investigative or alternative response. Each state has its own definition of child abuse and neglect based on standards set by federal law. Child abuse is defined as any recent act or failure to act on the part of a parent or caretaker which results in death, serious physical or emotional harm, sexual abuse or exploitation; or an act or failure to act which presents an imminent risk or serious harm]

Item	2010	2015	2018	2019	2020	2021	2022
Victims, total [1].........................	688,251	683,487	677,529	656,243	618,399	588,229	558,899
SEX OF VICTIM							
Male..	333,864	332,464	328,281	316,972	297,352	279,501	263,599
Female......................................	352,174	348,087	346,957	337,163	319,230	307,009	293,358
Unknown....................................	2,213	2,936	2,291	2,108	1,817	1,719	1,942
AGE OF VICTIM							
1 year and younger.........................	136,910	144,354	149,828	142,290	136,600	127,499	118,204
2 to 5 years old............................	180,271	172,337	165,016	158,946	150,673	138,128	129,846
6 to 9 years old............................	145,354	153,019	143,389	136,784	125,593	120,243	113,259
10 to 13 years old..........................	119,555	115,153	122,299	122,585	114,410	112,461	106,417
14 to 17 years old..........................	103,764	95,134	94,361	93,049	88,989	88,044	89,384
18 years old and over [2]...................	490	(NA)	(NA)	(NA)	(NA)	(NA)	(NA)
Unknown [3]................................	979	3,490	2,636	2,589	2,134	1,854	1,789
TYPES OF MALTREATMENT [4, 5]							
Neglect.....................................	499,691	514,500	411,969	399,992	470,297	446,838	415,445
Physical abuse.............................	118,502	117,772	72,814	67,678	101,961	93,907	95,026
Sexual abuse...............................	62,057	57,286	47,124	47,205	57,963	59,328	59,044
Psychological or emotional.................	53,426	42,549	15,605	15,672	39,652	37,361	38,030
Medical neglect............................	15,711	15,169	5,720	5,614	12,287	11,303	10,863
Sex trafficking.............................	(NA)	(NA)	339	439	953	1,086	1,084
Multiple maltreatment types................	(NA)	(NA)	105,322	101,973	(NA)	(NA)	(NA)
Other and unknown........................	68,590	47,514	18,636	17,670	36,935	21,336	19,276

NA Not available. [1] Total victims is the sum for states contributing data to the Child File. The number of states not contributing data varies by year. [2] Beginning in 2011, data included in unknown. [3] Includes unborn, unknown age, and, beginning 2011, victims age 18–21. [4] Data for 2010-2017 and 2020-2022 are counts of the number of distinct victims of the specified types of maltreatment. A child may be a victim of more than one type of maltreatment; therefore, the sum of types is greater than the count of victims. For 2018 and 2019, if a victim is reported with two or more maltreatment types, the victim is counted in the multiple maltreatment category once. [5] Not all states use this taxonomy, nor do states define the categories in the same way.

Source: U.S. Department of Health and Human Services, Administration for Children and Families, Data & Research, *Child Maltreatment 2022*, January 2024 and earlier editions, and unpublished data. See also <www.acf.hhs.gov/cb/data-research/child-maltreatment>.

Table 390. Prisoners Under Jurisdiction of Federal or State Correctional Authorities—Summary by State: 2000 to 2022

[For years ending December 31. Jurisdiction refers to the legal authority over a prisoner, regardless of where held. Multiple states reported large changes in prison populations, admissions, and releases between 2019 and 2020 due to criminal justice reforms enacted to address the COVID-19 pandemic. Occasionally, states do not submit data in a given year and estimates are imputed; see source for details]

State	2000	2010	2014	2015	2016	2017	2018	2019	2020	2021	2022
U.S.	1,394,231	1,613,803	1,562,319	1,526,603	1,508,129	1,489,189	1,464,385	1,430,165	1,221,164	1,205,087	1,230,143
Federal [1]	145,416	209,771	210,567	196,455	189,192	183,058	179,898	175,116	152,156	157,314	159,309
State [2]	1,248,815	1,404,032	1,351,752	1,330,148	1,318,937	1,306,131	1,284,487	1,255,049	1,069,008	1,047,773	1,070,834
AL	26,406	31,764	31,771	30,810	28,883	27,608	26,841	28,304	25,328	25,032	26,421
AK [3]	4,173	5,391	5,794	5,338	4,434	4,399	4,380	4,475	4,578	4,639	4,778
AZ	26,510	40,209	42,259	42,719	42,320	42,030	42,005	42,441	37,794	33,914	33,865
AR	11,915	16,204	17,874	17,707	17,537	18,070	17,799	17,759	16,094	17,022	17,625
CA	163,001	165,062	136,085	129,593	130,084	131,039	128,625	122,687	100,396	101,441	97,608
CO	16,833	22,815	20,646	20,041	19,981	19,946	20,372	19,785	16,259	15,865	17,168
CT [3]	18,355	19,321	16,636	15,816	14,957	14,040	13,681	12,823	9,559	9,889	10,506
DE [3]	6,921	6,615	6,955	6,654	6,585	6,443	6,067	5,692	4,710	4,810	4,954
DC [4]	10,352	(NA)	(NA)	(NA)	(NA)	(NA)	(NA)	(NA)	(NA)	(NA)	(NA)
FL	71,319	104,306	102,870	101,424	99,974	98,504	97,538	96,009	81,027	80,417	84,678
GA [3]	44,232	56,432	52,949	52,193	53,627	53,667	53,647	54,816	47,141	47,010	48,439
HI [3]	5,053	5,912	5,866	5,879	5,602	5,630	5,375	5,279	4,171	4,102	4,149
ID [8,9]	5,535	7,431	8,117	8,052	8,252	8,579	8,664	9,437	8,356	8,907	9,110
IL	45,281	48,418	48,278	46,240	43,657	41,427	39,965	38,259	29,729	28,980	29,634
IN	20,125	28,028	29,271	27,355	25,546	26,024	26,877	27,180	26,051	24,972	25,286
IA	7,955	9,455	8,838	8,849	9,031	9,024	9,419	9,282	8,307	8,562	8,473
KS	8,344	9,051	9,877	9,857	9,920	10,015	10,218	10,177	8,779	8,521	8,709
KY	14,919	20,544	21,657	21,701	23,022	23,543	23,431	23,082	18,552	18,560	19,744
LA	35,207	39,445	38,030	36,377	35,682	33,739	32,397	31,609	26,964	26,074	27,296
ME	1,679	2,154	2,242	2,279	2,404	2,404	2,425	2,185	1,714	1,577	1,675
MD	23,538	22,645	21,011	20,764	19,994	19,367	18,856	18,595	15,623	15,134	15,637
MA	10,722	11,313	10,713	9,922	9,403	9,133	8,692	8,205	6,762	6,148	6,001
MI	47,718	44,165	43,390	42,628	41,122	39,666	38,761	38,053	33,617	32,186	32,374
MN	6,238	9,796	10,637	10,798	10,592	10,708	10,101	9,982	8,148	8,003	8,636
MS	20,241	21,067	18,793	18,911	19,192	19,103	19,275	19,417	17,577	17,332	19,802
MO [8]	27,543	30,623	31,942	32,330	32,461	32,601	30,369	26,044	23,062	23,422	23,911
MT [7]	3,105	3,716	3,699	3,685	3,814	3,698	3,765	4,723	3,927	4,313	4,691
NE	3,895	4,587	5,441	5,372	5,302	5,313	5,491	5,682	5,306	5,600	5,649
NV	10,063	12,653	12,537	13,071	13,757	13,721	13,641	12,840	11,249	10,202	10,304
NH	2,257	2,761	2,963	2,897	2,818	2,750	2,722	2,691	2,352	2,127	2,086
NJ	29,784	25,007	21,590	20,489	19,786	19,585	19,362	18,613	12,830	12,506	12,657
NM [2]	5,342	6,763	7,021	7,104	7,055	7,276	7,030	6,723	5,500	5,154	4,970
NY	70,199	56,656	52,518	51,727	50,716	49,461	46,636	43,500	34,128	30,338	31,148
NC	31,266	40,382	37,096	36,617	35,697	36,394	34,899	34,079	29,461	28,995	29,627
ND [2]	1,076	1,487	1,718	1,795	1,791	1,723	1,695	1,794	1,401	1,689	1,817
OH	45,833	51,712	51,519	52,233	52,175	51,478	50,431	50,338	45,036	45,029	45,313
OK [5]	23,181	26,252	27,650	28,547	29,916	28,143	26,956	25,033	22,462	22,391	22,941
OR [2]	10,580	14,876	15,075	15,245	15,166	15,218	15,268	14,961	12,753	13,198	12,518
PA	36,847	51,264	50,694	49,858	49,244	48,333	47,239	45,702	39,357	37,194	37,910
RI [3]	3,286	3,357	3,359	3,248	3,103	2,861	2,767	2,740	2,227	2,238	2,393
SC	21,778	23,578	21,401	20,929	20,858	19,906	19,033	18,608	16,157	15,759	16,318
SD	2,616	3,434	3,608	3,564	3,831	3,970	3,948	3,801	3,250	3,353	3,444
TN	22,166	27,451	28,769	28,172	28,203	28,980	26,321	26,349	22,685	21,995	23,735
TX	166,719	173,649	166,043	163,909	163,703	162,523	163,628	158,429	135,906	133,772	139,631
UT [6]	5,637	6,807	7,031	6,495	6,175	6,219	6,651	6,671	5,448	5,911	6,009
VT [3]	1,697	2,079	1,979	1,750	1,735	1,546	1,659	1,608	1,284	1,287	1,360
VA	30,168	37,638	37,544	38,403	37,813	37,158	36,660	36,091	31,838	30,357	27,162
WA	14,915	18,235	18,120	18,284	19,104	19,656	19,523	19,261	15,724	13,674	13,772
WV	3,856	6,681	6,896	7,118	7,162	7,092	6,775	6,800	6,044	5,847	5,873
WI	20,754	22,729	22,597	22,975	23,377	23,945	24,064	23,956	20,298	20,202	20,873
WY	1,680	2,112	2,383	2,424	2,374	2,473	2,543	2,479	2,087	2,123	2,154

NA Not available. [1] Includes adult prisoners held in nonsecure community corrections facilities and adults and persons age 17 or younger held in privately operated facilities. [2] Total and state estimates for 2018 and 2019 include imputed counts for Oregon and estimates for 2017 include imputed data for New Mexico and North Dakota. Imputed data counts should not be compared to other years' data. [3] Data include both total jail and prison population. Prisons and jails form one integrated system. [4] As of December 31, 2001, sentenced felons from the District of Columbia are the responsibility of the Federal Bureau of Prisons. [5] 2016-2022 counts includes persons who were waiting in county jails to be moved to state prison. [6] Data for 2018 are not comparable to data for previous years. Total counts of the prisoner population from 2018 include an undetermined number of offenders excluded from counts in 2017 due to a change in legal-status requirements for a program for parole violators that was instituted in 2018. [7] Montana implemented a change in prisoner tracking software at the end of 2018, which has rendered counts between 2018 and 2020 incomparable. [8] Idaho and Missouri do not include persons held in federal or other state prisons in its jurisdiction count. [9] Beginning 2021, data not comparable to prior years due to methodology changes.

Source: U.S. Department of Justice, Bureau of Justice Statistics, "Corrections Statistical Analysis Tool," <bjs.gov/index.cfm?ty=nps>, accessed April 2021; and *Prisoners in 2022 - Statistical Tables*, NCJ 307149, November 2023.

Table 391. Jail Inmates by Sex, Age, Race, and Hispanic Origin: 2010 to 2022

[Based on the number of inmates on the last weekday in June, except as noted. Data adjusted for nonresponse and rounded to the nearest 100. Does not include offenders supervised outside of jail facilities. Based on the Annual Survey of Jails and Census of Jails. See source for methodology]

Characteristic	2010	2015 [1]	2017	2018	2019	2020	2021	2022
Total inmates.................	**748,700**	**727,400**	**745,200**	**738,400**	**734,500**	**549,100**	**636,300**	**663,100**
Incarceration rate per 100,000 U.S. residents.........................	242	227	229	226	224	166	192	199
Male, total........................	656,400	623,600	631,500	623,400	623,700	479,400	551,200	570,200
Female, total.....................	92,400	103,800	113,700	115,100	110,700	69,800	85,100	92,900
Juveniles [2]......................	7,600	3,600	3,600	3,400	2,900	2,300	2,000	1,900
Held as adult [3].................	5,600	3,200	3,200	2,700	2,200	2,000	1,700	1,600
Held as juvenile.................	1,900	400	300	700	700	300	200	300
Adults...........................	741,200	723,800	741,600	735,000	731,600	546,900	634,400	661,100
18–24 years old...............	(NA)	(NA)	(NA)	(NA)	(NA)	98,800	105,300	104,600
25–34 years old...............	(NA)	(NA)	(NA)	(NA)	(NA)	193,900	223,500	225,400
35–44 years old...............	(NA)	(NA)	(NA)	(NA)	(NA)	142,200	171,500	184,500
45–54 years old...............	(NA)	(NA)	(NA)	(NA)	(NA)	71,400	84,100	91,300
55–64 years old...............	(NA)	(NA)	(NA)	(NA)	(NA)	33,100	40,700	44,300
65 years or older..............	(NA)	(NA)	(NA)	(NA)	(NA)	7,400	9,400	11,000
White, non-Hispanic............	331,600	351,600	370,100	368,500	362,900	262,100	310,100	317,100
Black, non-Hispanic............	283,200	255,200	250,100	242,300	247,100	192,700	221,200	234,900
American Indian or Alaska Native non-Hispanic...........	9,900	9,000	8,800	9,700	10,200	6,700	7,700	9,500
Asian, non-Hispanic............	4,400	5,200	4,800	4,800	4,700	3,700	3,800	4,800
Native Hawaiian/Other Pacific Islander non-Hispanic.................	700	900	1,000	1,000	800	600	700	1,100
Two or more races....................	800	1,700	2,000	2,800	1,900	1,500	1,900	2,000
Hispanic [4]	118,100	103,900	108,400	109,300	106,900	81,900	90,800	93,700
Rated capacity [5]..................	866,800	901,400	915,100	907,000	907,700	913,700	916,000	915,900

NA Not available. [1] In 2015, the Annual Survey of Jails collected demographic data on the inmate population at year-end instead of midyear. Jails typically hold fewer inmates at year-end than at midyear. The inmate populations were adjusted for seasonal variation and represent estimated midyear counts; see source for Methodology. [2] Juveniles age 17 or younger at midyear. [3] Includes juveniles who were tried or awaiting trial as adults. [4] Persons of Hispanic origin may be of any race. [5] Maximum number of beds or inmates assigned by a rating official to a facility, excluding separate temporary holding areas.

Source: U.S. Department of Justice, Bureau of Justice Statistics, *Jail Inmates in 2022 – Statistical Tables*, NCJ 307086, December 2023, and earlier releases. See also <bjs.ojp.gov/library>.

Table 392. Prisoners Under Federal and State Jurisdiction by Sex, Race, and Hispanic Origin: 1980 to 2022

[As of December 31. Represents prisoners sentenced to more than one year under jurisdiction of federal or state authorities. Jurisdiction refers to the legal authority of state or federal correctional officials over a prisoner, regardless of where the prisoner is held. Federal prisoners includes inmates held in nonsecure privately operated community corrections facilities and juveniles held in contract facilities. From the National Prisoner Statistics Program. See source for methodology]

Year	Total [1]		Sex		Race/ethnicity [3]			Jurisdiction	
	Number [1]	Rate [2]	Male	Female	White [4]	Black [4]	Hispanic	Federal	State
1980..........	315,974	139	303,643	12,331	(NA)	(NA)	(NA)	20,611	295,363
1990..........	739,980	297	699,416	40,564	(NA)	(NA)	(NA)	50,403	689,577
1995..........	1,085,022	411	1,021,059	63,963	(NA)	(NA)	(NA)	83,663	1,001,359
2000..........	1,334,174	470	1,249,130	85,044	(NA)	(NA)	(NA)	125,044	1,209,130
2001..........	1,345,217	470	1,260,033	85,184	(NA)	(NA)	(NA)	136,509	1,208,708
2002..........	1,380,516	477	1,291,450	89,066	(NA)	(NA)	(NA)	143,040	1,237,476
2003..........	1,408,361	483	1,315,790	92,571	(NA)	(NA)	(NA)	151,919	1,256,442
2004..........	1,433,728	487	1,337,730	95,998	(NA)	(NA)	(NA)	159,137	1,274,591
2005..........	1,462,866	492	1,364,178	98,688	(NA)	(NA)	(NA)	166,173	1,296,693
2006..........	1,504,598	501	1,401,261	103,337	507,100	590,300	313,600	173,533	1,331,065
2007..........	1,532,851	506	1,427,088	105,763	499,800	592,900	330,400	179,204	1,353,647
2008..........	1,547,742	506	1,441,384	106,358	499,900	592,800	329,800	182,333	1,365,409
2009..........	1,553,574	504	1,448,239	105,335	490,000	584,800	341,200	187,886	1,365,688
2010..........	1,552,669	500	1,447,766	104,903	490,500	568,500	338,500	190,641	1,362,028
2011..........	1,538,847	492	1,435,141	103,706	480,400	554,400	341,300	197,050	1,341,797
2012..........	1,512,430	480	1,411,076	101,354	470,900	536,600	336,100	196,574	1,315,856
2013..........	1,520,403	479	1,416,102	104,301	469,800	530,100	343,100	195,098	1,325,305
2014..........	1,507,781	472	1,401,685	106,096	463,800	516,800	339,500	191,374	1,316,407
2015..........	1,476,847	459	1,371,879	104,968	450,600	496,400	335,800	178,688	1,298,159
2016 [5].......	1,459,948	450	1,354,109	105,839	440,700	484,600	342,100	171,482	1,288,466
2017 [6].......	1,439,877	442	1,334,828	105,049	436,800	473,000	338,800	166,203	1,273,674
2018 [7].......	1,413,370	431	1,309,194	104,176	430,500	461,500	332,900	163,653	1,249,717
2019 [7].......	1,379,786	419	1,278,484	101,302	422,900	449,900	322,700	158,498	1,221,288
2020..........	1,185,733	357	1,105,750	79,983	360,100	390,700	276,100	142,028	1,043,705
2021..........	1,165,736	350	1,086,337	79,399	356,000	378,000	273,800	144,448	1,021,288
2022..........	1,185,648	355	1,103,170	82,478	367,800	384,600	273,900	146,108	1,039,540

NA Not available. [1] Includes persons of two or more races and other race groups not shown separately. [2] Rate per 100,000 estimated population. Based on U.S. Census Bureau estimated resident population. [3] Rounded to the nearest 100. [4] Excludes persons of Hispanic or Latino origin and persons of two or more races. [5] Total and state estimates include imputed counts for North Dakota, which did not submit data. [6] Total and state estimates include imputed counts for New Mexico and North Dakota, which did not submit 2017 NPS data. [7] Estimates for 2018 and 2019 include imputed counts for Oregon, which did not submit 2018 or 2019 data. 2019 includes imputed counts for Vermont, which provided total jurisdiction counts but could not break down the population by sentence length.

Source: U.S. Department of Justice, Bureau of Justice Statistics, *Prisoners in 2022 – Statistical Tables*, NCJ 307149, November 2023, and earlier reports. See also <bjs.ojp.gov/library>.

Table 393. Prisoners Executed Under Civil Authority by State: 1977 to 2022

[As of December 2021, 30 states and the federal government had death penalty statutes; 20 states and the District of Columbia had no death penalty statute in force. See source for details on status of the death penalty by State]

State	1977 to 2022	2000	2010	2020	2021	2022 (P)
United States [1]...	1,558	85	46	17	11	18
Alabama	70	4	5	1	1	2
Arizona	40	3	1	–	–	3
Arkansas	31	2	–	–	–	–
California	13	1	–	–	–	–
Colorado	1	–	–	–	–	–
Connecticut	1	–	–	–	–	–
Delaware	16	1	–	–	–	–
Florida	99	6	1	–	–	–
Georgia	76	–	2	1	–	–
Idaho	3	–	–	–	–	–
Illinois	12	–	–	–	–	–
Indiana	20	–	–	–	–	–
Kentucky	3	–	–	–	–	–
Louisiana	28	1	1	–	–	–
Maryland	5	–	–	–	–	–
Mississippi	23	–	3	–	1	1
Missouri	93	5	–	1	1	2
Montana	3	–	–	–	–	–
Nebraska	4	–	–	–	–	–
Nevada	12	–	–	–	–	–
New Mexico	1	–	–	–	–	–
North Carolina	43	1	–	–	–	–
Ohio	56	–	8	–	–	–
Oklahoma	119	11	3	–	2	5
Oregon	2	–	–	–	–	–
Pennsylvania	3	–	–	–	–	–
South Carolina	43	1	–	–	–	–
South Dakota	5	–	–	–	–	–
Tennessee	13	1	–	1	–	–
Texas	578	40	17	3	3	5
Utah	7	–	1	–	–	–
Virginia	113	8	3	–	–	–
Washington	5	–	1	–	–	–
Wyoming	1	–	–	–	–	–

P Preliminary – Represents zero. [1] Includes persons executed within the Federal system.

Source: Through 1978, U.S. Law Enforcement Assistance Administration; thereafter, U.S. Department of Justice, Bureau of Justice Statistics, *Capital Punishment, 2021: Statistical Tables*, NCJ 305534, November 2023, and earlier reports. See also <bjs.ojp.gov/library>.

Table 394. Prisoners Executed Under Civil Authority by Sex and Race: 1930 to 2022

[Excludes executions by military authorities. See source for more information]

Period or year	Total [1]	Male	Female	White [2]	Black [2]	His-panic	Period or year	Total [1]	Male	Female	White [2]	Black [2]	His-panic
1930 to 1939....	1,667	1,656	11	827	816	(NA)	1997.......	74	74	–	41	26	5
1940 to 1949....	1,284	1,272	12	490	781	(NA)	1998.......	68	66	2	40	18	8
1950 to 1959....	717	709	8	336	376	(NA)	1999.......	98	98	–	53	33	9
1960 to 1967....	191	190	1	98	93	(NA)	2000.......	85	83	2	43	35	6
1968 to 1976 [3]...	–	–	–	–	–	–	2001.......	66	63	3	45	17	3
1977.............	1	1	–	1	–	–	2002.......	71	69	2	47	18	6
1978.............	–	–	–	–	–	–	2003.......	65	65	–	41	20	3
1979.............	2	2	–	2	–	–	2004.......	59	59	–	36	19	3
1980.............	–	–	–	–	–	–	2005.......	60	59	1	38	19	3
1981.............	1	1	–	1	–	–	2006.......	53	53	–	25	20	8
1982.............	2	2	–	1	1	–	2007.......	42	42	–	22	14	6
1983.............	5	5	–	4	1	–	2008.......	37	37	–	17	17	3
1984.............	21	20	1	13	8	–	2009.......	52	52	–	24	21	7
1985.............	18	18	–	9	7	2	2010.......	46	45	1	28	13	5
1986.............	18	18	–	9	7	2	2011.......	43	43	–	22	16	5
1987.............	25	25	–	11	11	3	2012.......	43	43	–	25	11	7
1988.............	11	11	–	6	5	–	2013.......	39	38	1	23	13	3
1989.............	16	16	–	6	8	2	2014.......	35	33	2	12	18	5
1990.............	23	23	–	16	7	–	2015.......	28	(NA)	(NA)	11	10	7
1991.............	14	14	–	6	7	1	2016.......	20	(NA)	(NA)	16	2	2
1992.............	31	31	–	17	11	2	2017.......	23	(NA)	(NA)	13	8	2
1993.............	38	38	–	19	14	4	2018.......	25	(NA)	(NA)	14	6	5
1994.............	31	31	–	19	11	1	2019.......	22	22	–	14	7	1
1995.............	56	56	–	31	22	2	2020.......	17	17	–	10	5	1
1996.............	45	45	–	29	14	2	2021.......	11	10	1	5	6	–
							2022 (P)...	18	18	–	11	5	(NA)

– Represents zero. NA Not available. P Preliminary. [1] Includes American Indians, Alaska Natives, Asians, Native Hawaiians, and other Pacific Islanders, not shown separately. [2] Excludes persons of Hispanic or Latino origin. In 2017, two of the white prisoners executed in Texas were of Hispanic or Latino origin. [3] In 1972, the U.S. Supreme Court invalidated capital punishment statutes in several states, effecting a moratorium on executions. Executions resumed in 1977 when the Supreme Court found revisions to several state statutes had effectively addressed the issues previously held as unconstitutional.

Source: Through 1978, U.S. Law Enforcement Assistance Administration; thereafter, U.S. Department of Justice, Bureau of Justice Statistics, *Capital Punishment, 2021: Statistical Tables*, NCJ 305534, November 2023. See also <bjs.ojp.gov/library>.

Table 395. Prisoners Under Death Sentence by Race: 1980 to 2021

[As of December 31. Excludes prisoners under sentence of death who remained within local correctional systems pending exhaustion of appellate process or who had not been committed to prison. Data from the National Prisoner Statistics Program]

Year	Total	White [1]	Black [1]	Other [2]	Year	Total	White [1]	Black [1]	Other [2]
1980	692	424	264	4	2002	3,562	1,939	1,551	72
1983	1,209	692	505	12	2003	3,377	1,882	1,417	78
1984	1,420	806	598	16	2004	3,320	1,856	1,390	74
1985	1,575	896	664	15	2005	3,245	1,802	1,366	77
1986	1,800	1,013	762	25	2006	3,233	1,806	1,353	74
1987	1,967	1,128	813	26	2007	3,215	1,806	1,338	71
1988	2,117	1,235	848	34	2008	3,210	1,795	1,343	72
1989	2,243	1,308	898	37	2009	3,173	1,779	1,318	76
1990	2,346	1,368	940	38	2010	3,139	1,743	1,309	87
1991	2,465	1,449	979	37	2011	3,065	1,721	1,274	70
1992	2,580	1,511	1,031	38	2012	3,011	1,684	1,258	69
1993	2,727	1,575	1,111	41	2013	2,983	1,670	1,251	62
1994	2,905	1,653	1,203	49	2014	2,942	1,647	1,233	62
1995	3,064	1,732	1,284	48	2015	2,872	1,606	1,202	64
1996	3,242	1,833	1,358	51	2016	2,797	1,553	1,179	65
1997	3,328	1,864	1,408	56	2017	2,703	1,508	1,129	66
1998	3,465	1,917	1,489	59	2018	2,626	1,470	1,091	65
1999	3,540	1,960	1,515	65	2019	2,563	1,443	1,057	63
2000	3,601	1,989	1,541	71	2020	2,461	1,392	1,009	60
2001	3,577	1,968	1,538	71	2021	2,382	1,353	969	60

[1] Includes persons of Hispanic origin. [2] Includes Asians, Native Hawaiians, Other Pacific Islanders, American Indians, Alaska Natives, and persons for whom only ethnicity was identified.

Source: U.S. Department of Justice, Bureau of Justice Statistics, *Capital Punishment, 2021: Statistical Tables*, NCJ 3005534, November 2023. See also <bjs.ojp.gov/library>.

Table 396. Prisoners—Firearm Possession and Use During Offense That Led to Imprisonment by Type of Controlling Offense: 2016

[For sentenced prisoners and those awaiting sentencing with one offense, that offense is the controlling offense. For sentenced prisoners with multiple offenses and sentences, the controlling offense is the one with the longest sentence. For sentenced prisoners with multiple offenses and one sentence and those awaiting sentencing with multiple offenses, the controlling offense is the most serious offense. Data are from the Survey of Prison Inmates]

Controlling offense	State prisoners			Federal prisoners		
		Percent who—			Percent who—	
	Number [1]	Possessed a firearm [1]	Used a firearm [2]	Number [1]	Possessed a firearm [1]	Used a firearm [2]
Total	**1,211,200**	**20.9**	**13.9**	**170,400**	**20.0**	**5.0**
Violent	667,300	29.1	23.0	20,900	36.2	25.3
Homicide [3]	191,400	43.6	37.2	3,800	35.9	28.4
Rape/sexual assault	144,800	2.0	0.8	2,400	(B)	(B)
Robbery	149,600	43.3	31.5	10,700	46.3	32.1
Assault	149,400	25.0	20.6	2,900	29.0	18.1
Other violent [4]	32,200	17.0	12.6	1,200	34.1	(B)
Property	186,100	[9] 4.9	[9] 2.0	12,000	[9] 2.6	(B)
Burglary	88,100	6.7	3.2	300	(B)	(B)
Other property [5]	98,000	3.3	1.0	11,800	2.4	(B)
Drug	180,800	[9] 8.4	[9] 0.8	80,500	[9] 12.3	[9] 0.6
Trafficking [6]	130,500	9.4	0.9	72,300	12.9	0.7
Possession	45,900	6.1	(B)	3,500	(B)	(B)
Other/unspecified drug	4,300	(B)	(B)	4,700	(B)	(B)
Public order	158,300	[9] 21.5	[9] 5.6	52,900	30.2	[9] 5.3
Weapons [7]	43,800	67.2	15.7	22,200	66.9	11.3
Other public order [8]	114,400	4.0	1.7	30,700	3.6	(B)
Other	3,900	(B)	(B)	1,800	(B)	(B)
Unknown	14,900	[9] 4.3	(B)	2,200	(B)	(B)

B Not calculated. Too few cases to provide a reliable estimate, or coefficient of variation is greater than 50%. [1] Data are estimates. Excludes prisoners who were missing responses on firearm possession; includes prisoners who were missing responses on firearm use. [2] Excludes prisoners who were missing responses on firearm use. [3] Includes murder and negligent and non-negligent manslaughter. [4] Includes kidnapping, blackmail, extortion, hit-and-run driving with bodily injury, child abuse, and criminal endangerment. [5] Includes larceny, theft, motor vehicle theft, arson, fraud, stolen property, destruction of property, vandalism, hit-and-run driving with no bodily injury, criminal tampering, trespassing, entering without breaking, and possession of burglary tools. [6] Includes possession with intent to distribute. [7] Includes being armed while committing a crime; possession of ammunition, concealed weapons, firearms and explosive devices; selling or trafficking weapons; and other weapons offenses. [8] Includes commercialized vice, immigration crimes, DUI, violations of probation/parole, and other public-order offenses. [9] Difference with comparison group (total violent offenders) is significant at the 95% confidence level across main categories, and no testing was done on subcategories (e.g., homicide).

Source: U.S. Department of Justice, Bureau of Justice Statistics, *Source and Use of Firearms Involved in Crimes: Survey of Prison Inmates, 2016*, NCJ 251776, January 2019. See also <bjs.ojp.gov/library>.

Table 397. Adults Under Community Supervision, Probation, and Parole by State: 2022

[As of December 31, 2022. Data are from the Annual Survey of Probation and Parole. Rates computed using the estimated U.S. adult resident population in each jurisdiction on January 1, 2023. Counts may not be actual as reporting agencies may provide estimates on some or all detailed data; see source]

Area	Community supervision [1]		Probation		Parole	
	Number	Rate per 100,000	Number	Rate per 100,000	Number	Rate per 100,000
United States, total	**3,668,820**	**1,401**	**2,990,880**	**1,142**	**698,820**	**267**
Federal	117,760	45	11,940	5	105,820	40
States	3,551,060	1,356	2,978,940	1,137	593,000	226
Alabama	48,690	1,224	42,260	1,116	7,400	186
Alaska [3]	3,620	649	2,880	464	750	134
Arizona	79,740	1,369	73,100	1,191	6,640	114
Arkansas	64,590	2,736	43,090	1,787	22,780	965
California [2,5]	195,440	640	150,470	514	44,980	147
Colorado	81,340	1,750	72,290	1,578	9,050	195
Connecticut	33,550	1,156	31,240	1,048	2,300	79
Delaware	11,150	1,363	10,810	1,210	340	41
District of Columbia	6,050	1,101	4,360	598	1,820	331
Florida	188,410	1,037	184,520	1,038	3,890	21
Georgia	372,470	4,399	359,420	4,169	15,460	183
Hawaii	16,310	1,427	15,080	1,600	1,240	108
Idaho	33,060	2,213	26,430	1,921	6,640	444
Illinois [3]	100,130	1,017	79,900	889	20,230	205
Indiana	107,020	2,026	100,680	1,888	6,340	120
Iowa	32,780	1,320	26,290	1,030	6,880	277
Kansas	19,990	888	14,860	630	5,130	228
Kentucky	64,550	1,836	51,920	1,577	12,630	359
Louisiana	44,480	1,262	26,790	738	18,960	538
Maine	5,390	471	5,390	480	([4])	([4])
Maryland	67,480	1,399	59,320	1,169	8,170	170
Massachusetts	42,790	757	41,550	696	1,660	29
Michigan	121,650	1,533	111,950	1,452	9,700	123
Minnesota	92,770	2,092	86,000	1,927	6,770	153
Mississippi	39,660	1,751	30,380	1,295	9,270	411
Missouri	54,600	1,131	37,460	784	17,140	356
Montana	10,550	1,174	9,330	1,106	1,220	137
Nebraska	12,360	826	11,420	802	940	63
Nevada	17,030	679	11,660	362	5,370	215
New Hampshire	5,430	473	3,780	333	1,650	144
New Jersey [3]	138,910	1,908	123,300	1,687	15,610	215
New Mexico	11,290	680	10,020	648	2,270	137
New York	91,410	584	65,780	453	25,630	164
North Carolina	70,280	829	60,580	726	9,710	115
North Dakota	6,790	1,136	6,080	1,029	720	120
Ohio	206,140	2,239	186,990	2,137	19,150	208
Oklahoma	24,310	788	22,300	567	2,500	81
Oregon	50,730	1,489	29,230	878	21,500	633
Pennsylvania	168,290	1,625	92,660	942	75,630	732
Rhode Island	17,710	1,987	17,320	2,147	380	43
South Carolina	29,480	700	26,130	600	3,510	84
South Dakota	9,110	1,306	5,760	840	3,360	485
Tennessee	71,640	1,289	59,010	1,035	12,630	229
Texas	461,980	2,025	364,180	1,559	100,600	443
Utah	14,480	585	10,670	440	3,820	155
Vermont	3,610	676	2,880	526	730	137
Virginia	62,410	912	60,640	912	1,770	26
Washington	61,500	997	60,280	1,038	10,780	176
West Virginia	10,130	712	6,100	435	4,030	284
Wisconsin [5]	62,260	1,336	39,750	838	22,510	484
Wyoming	5,530	1,219	4,690	1,121	840	185

[1] Community supervision counts are rounded to nearest hundred. December 31, 2022 population excludes 20,880 offenders under community supervision who were on both probation and parole. [2] In California, includes post-release community supervision and mandatory supervision parolees. Parole data not comparable to prior years. [3] Probation counts are estimates of individuals. [4] Maine no longer has a parole program and was removed from the Annual Parole Survey for 2022. [5] Data for parole entries and exits are subject to fluctuation.

Source: U.S. Department of Justice, Bureau of Justice Statistics, *Probation and Parole in the United States, 2022*, NCJ 308575, May 2024. See also <bjs.ojp.gov/library>.

Table 398. Rate of Adults Under Community Supervision, Probation, and Parole: 2000 to 2022

[As of December 31. From the Annual Survey of Probation and Parole. Probation is a court-ordered period of correctional supervision in the community, generally as an alternative to incarceration. Probation can be a combined sentence of incarceration followed by a period of community supervision. Parole is a period of conditional supervised release in the community following a prison term. Parolees include persons released through discretionary or mandatory supervised release from prison]

Year	Rate per 100,000 population			U.S. residents under—		
	Community supervision [1,2]	Probation	Parole	Community supervision [1]	Probation	Parole
2000	2,162	1,818	344	1 in 46	1 in 55	1 in 291
2001	2,184	1,842	342	1 in 46	1 in 54	1 in 292
2002	2,198	1,849	349	1 in 45	1 in 54	1 in 287
2003	2,219	1,865	354	1 in 45	1 in 55	1 in 282
2004	2,226	1,875	351	1 in 45	1 in 53	1 in 285
2005	2,215	1,864	351	1 in 45	1 in 54	1 in 285
2006	2,228	1,875	353	1 in 45	1 in 53	1 in 283
2007	2,237	1,878	361	1 in 45	1 in 53	1 in 277
2008	2,202	1,847	357	1 in 45	1 in 54	1 in 280
2009	2,148	1,797	353	1 in 47	1 in 56	1 in 283
2010	2,067	1,715	356	1 in 48	1 in 58	1 in 281
2011	2,017	1,663	358	1 in 50	1 in 60	1 in 279
2012	1,984	1,634	356	1 in 50	1 in 61	1 in 281
2013	1,949	1,606	349	1 in 51	1 in 62	1 in 287
2014	1,916	1,572	349	1 in 52	1 in 64	1 in 287
2015	1,873	1,527	351	1 in 53	1 in 66	1 in 285
2016	1,811	1,466	349	1 in 55	1 in 68	1 in 287
2017	1,786	1,444	347	1 in 56	1 in 69	1 in 289
2018	1,729	1,391	345	1 in 58	1 in 72	1 in 290
2019	1,701	1,363	343	1 in 59	1 in 73	1 in 291
2020	1,504	1,181	333	1 in 66	1 in 85	1 in 300
2021	1,440	1,140	309	1 in 69	1 in 88	1 in 324
2022	1,401	1,142	267	1 in 71	1 in 88	1 in 375

[1] Adults on probation or parole. [2] Beginning 2008, detail does not sum to total because the community supervision rate was adjusted to exclude parolees who were also on probation.

Source: U.S. Department of Justice, Bureau of Justice Statistics, *Probation and Parole in the United States, 2022*, NCJ 308575, May 2024, and earlier reports. See also <bjs.ojp.gov/library>.

Table 399. Prisoner Recidivism by Selected Characteristics: 2012 to 2017

[Data are shown for state prisoners released in 2012 across 34 states (except as noted) who were arrested for a new crime from 2012 to 2017. See source for details]

Characteristic	Number of released prisoners	Percent		
		Arrested within 5 years of release	Arrested and convicted within 5 years of release [1]	Returned to prison within 5 years of release [2]
Total	**408,300**	**70.8**	**54.4**	**45.8**
SEX				
Male	363,200	71.7	55.4	47.2
Female	45,100	63.1	46.5	34.0
RACE/HISPANIC ORIGIN				
White alone, non-Hispanic	179,000	69.5	53.5	45.5
Black alone, non-Hispanic	147,700	74.0	56.7	48.0
Hispanic	66,500	66.9	51.7	42.3
American Indian/Alaska Native, non-Hispanic	6,200	78.9	63.0	51.2
Asian/Native Hawaiian/Other Pacific Islander, non-Hispanic	2,700	64.8	39.2	28.4
Other [3]	6,100	67.8	56.7	41.0
AGE AT RELEASE				
24 years old and under	66,200	81.0	65.2	56.8
25 to 39 years old	203,600	74.4	58.2	48.8
40 years and older	138,400	60.5	43.8	36.3
40 to 54 years old	116,100	63.8	46.8	38.8
55 to 64 years old	19,100	46.3	30.5	24.5
65 years old and over	3,100	25.6	13.0	14.4
MOST SERIOUS COMMITMENT OFFENSE				
Violent	112,300	65.2	(NA)	(NA)
Property	115,600	78.3	(NA)	(NA)
Drug	103,900	69.8	(NA)	(NA)
Public order	76,500	68.9	(NA)	(NA)
NUMBER OF PRIOR ARRESTS [4]				
4 or fewer	104,500	54.5	(NA)	(NA)
2 or fewer	47,300	47.6	(NA)	(NA)
3 to 4	57,300	60.3	(NA)	(NA)
5 to 9	127,100	70.0	(NA)	(NA)
10 or more	176,600	81.0	(NA)	(NA)

NA Not available. [1] Estimates are based on prisoners released across the 31 states that could provide necessary court data. [2] Estimates are based on prisoners released across the 21 states that could provide necessary data on persons returned to prison for a probation or parole violation or an arrest that led to a new sentence. [3] Includes non-Hispanic persons of two or more races or other unspecified races. [4] Includes arrests in the prisoners' criminal history and the arrest that resulted in the imprisonment.

Source: U.S. Department of Justice, Bureau of Justice Statistics, *Recidivism of Prisoners Released in 34 States in 2012: A 5-Year Follow-Up Period (2012–2017)*, NCJ 255947, July 2021. See also <bjs.ojp.gov/library>.

Table 400. The U.S. Fire Service: Departments, Personnel, and Responses by Type: 2000 to 2020

[In thousands (1,064.2 represents 1,064,200), except where noted. A fire department is a public or private organization that provides fire prevention, fire suppression, and associated emergency and non-emergency services to a jurisdiction such as a county, municipality, or organized fire district]

Item	2000	2005	2010	2015	2016	2017	2018	2019	2020
FIRE DEPARTMENTS (NUMBER)									
Total departments..............................	30,339	30,300	30,125	29,727	29,710	29,819	29,705	29,537	29,452
All career...............................	2,178	2,087	2,495	2,651	2,775	2,785	3,009	2,789	2,785
Mostly career...........................	1,667	1,766	1,860	1,893	2,048	2,316	2,368	2,533	2,459
Mostly volunteer.........................	4,523	4,902	5,290	5,421	5,451	5,405	5,206	5,148	5,335
All volunteer............................	21,971	21,575	20,480	19,762	19,436	19,313	19,122	19,067	18,873
By whether Emergency Medical Service (EMS) provided:									
Provide EMS service only....................	(NA)	12,900	13,440	13,500	(NA)	13,631	(NA)	(NA)	(NA)
Provide EMS service and advance life support..	(NA)	4,260	4,515	4,617	(NA)	4,629	(NA)	(NA)	(NA)
No EMS service.............................	(NA)	13,170	12,170	11,610	(NA)	11,559	(NA)	(NA)	(NA)
FIRE DEPARTMENT PERSONNEL (1,000)									
Total personnel.............................	1,064.2	1,136.7	1,103.3	1,160.5	1,090.1	1,056.2	1,115.0	1,080.8	1,041.2
Career [1]................................	286.8	313.3	335.2	345.6	361.1	373.6	370.0	358.0	364.3
Volunteer [2].............................	777.4	823.7	768.2	814.9	729.0	682.6	745.0	722.8	676.9
RESPONSES BY TYPE (1,000)									
Total responses.............................	20,520	23,252	28,205	33,603	35,320	34,684	36,747	37,272	36,416
Fires......................................	1,708	1,602	1,332	1,346	1,342	1,320	1,319	1,292	1,389
Medical aid................................	12,251	14,374	18,522	21,500	22,751	22,341	23,552	24,481	23,812
False alarms...............................	2,127	2,134	2,187	2,567	2,622	2,547	2,889	2,893	2,760
Malicious mischievous.....................	300	241	163	166	173	141	172	(NA)	(NA)
System malfunctions......................	884	746	709	828	837	752	889	(NA)	(NA)
Unintentional calls.......................	714	838	992	1,200	1,226	1,286	1,379	(NA)	(NA)
Other [3].................................	230	310	324	374	387	369	451	(NA)	(NA)
Mutual aid/assistance......................	864	1,091	1,190	1,493	1,515	1,353	1,513	1,487	1,390
Hazardous material........................	319	375	402	442	425	424	426	440	422
Other hazardous [4].......................	544	667	660	643	685	693	707	744	705
All other [5]..............................	2,708	3,009	3,913	5,646	5,981	6,006	6,343	5,936	5,939

NA Not available. [1] Includes full-time uniform firefighters regardless of assignment (i.e., suppression, administrative, prevention/inspection, etc.). Does not include firefighters who work for the state or federal government or in private fire brigades. [2] Volunteer firefighters include any active part-time (call or volunteer) firefighters. [3] Bomb scares, etc. [4] Arcing wires, bomb removal, power line down, biological hazard, etc. [5] Smoke scares, lock-outs, animal rescue, unauthorized burning, severe weather, etc.

Source: National Fire Protection Association, Quincy, MA, *U.S. Fire Department Profile 2020 Supporting Tables* ©, and *Fire Loss in the United States During 2018* ©, and earlier reports. See also <nfpa.org/education-and-research/research>.

Table 401. Firefighter On-Duty Fatalities and Injuries: 2010 to 2022

[Number, unless otherwise noted. On-duty refers to involvement in operations at the scene of an emergency, whether it is a fire or nonfire incident; responding to or returning from an incident; performing other officially assigned duties including training; and being on call]

Item	2010	2015	2016	2017	2018	2019	2020	2021	2022
Total fatalities [1]......................	89	90	92	93	85	65	[4] 102	[5] 141	[6] 94
Fatalities per 100,000 fires (rate)......	2.33	2.45	2.01	(NA)	(NA)	(NA)	(NA)	(NA)	(NA)
Emergency duty deaths (percent).....	55.6	48.9	41.3	49.5	52.9	61.5	70.6	65.2	66.0
By incident characteristic:									
Wildland related fatalities.............	12	12	15	10	10	7	13	18	19
Incidents with multiple fatalities......	4	3	3	1	2	0	3	2	6
Training fatalities......................	12	7	9	12	9	5	7	9	9
Cause of fatal injury:									
Stress/overexertion [2].................	56	61	44	54	37	37	37	39	37
Vehicle collision......................	12	5	19	12	13	7	15	12	17
Total nonfatal Injuries [3]............	71,875	68,085	62,085	58,835	58,250	60,825	64,875	60,450	65,650
Fireground injuries......................	32,675	29,130	24,325	24,495	22,975	23,825	22,450	19,200	21,325
Injuries at nonfire emergencies........	13,355	14,320	12,780	12,240	11,625	14,150	13,650	13,325	13,200
Nature of injury:									
Burns (fire or chemical)................	2,585	2,020	1,900	1,310	1,550	1,775	1,475	2,000	2,900
Smoke or gas inhalation...............	1,500	1,645	2,355	2,135	3,150	3,075	2,700	1,500	2,175
Other respiratory distress.............	940	1,060	800	850	975	1,075	1,400	1,050	1,450
Burns and smoke inhalation..........	635	535	880	1,525	1,450	1,350	825	750	525
Wound, cut, bleeding, bruise.........	11,110	10,205	9,450	9,470	8,075	9,000	7,675	8,725	8,400
Dislocation, fracture..................	1,820	1,685	1,850	1,330	1,300	1,700	1,675	1,825	1,850
Heart attack or stroke.................	810	920	575	550	825	575	750	975	975
Strain, sprain, muscular pain.........	40,385	37,945	32,650	30,970	29,550	30,500	29,725	27,225	28,450
Thermal stress (frostbite, heat exhaustion)............................	3,195	2,860	2,475	2,095	2,875	3,000	2,375	1,900	2,425
Other.................................	8,895	9,210	9,150	8,600	8,500	8,775	16,275	14,500	16,500
Fire department vehicle collisions.....	14,200	16,600	15,430	15,425	14,425	15,350	15,675	18,775	20,300
Injuries..............................	775	1,150	700	1,005	575	575	550	600	800
Personal vehicle collisions.............	1,000	700	850	795	700	800	725	550	950
Injuries..............................	75	50	175	75	50	10	200	550	250

NA Not available. [1] Includes causes not shown, such as struck by object, caught/trapped, structural collapse, fall, violence, lost/disoriented, and unknown. [2] Stress/overexertion include all firefighter deaths that are cardiac or cerebrovascular in nature such as heart attacks, strokes, and other events such as extreme climatic thermal exposure (heat exhaustion). [3] Includes other types of nonfatal injuries not shown separately. [4] Includes 36 deaths from COVID-19. [5] Includes 63 deaths from COVID-19. [6] Includes 6 deaths from COVID-19.

Source: Fatalities: U.S. Department of Homeland Security, Federal Emergency Management Agency, U.S. Fire Administration, *Firefighter Fatalities in the United States*, annual report, <apps.usfa.fema.gov/firefighter-fatalities>. Nonfatal Injuries: National Fire Protection Association, *United States Firefighter Injuries in 2022* ©, December 2023, and earlier reports. See also <nfpa.org/education-and-research/research>.

Table 402. Fires—Number and Loss by Type and Property Use: 2019 to 2022

[Number of fires in thousands (1,292 represents 1,292,000); property loss in millions of dollars (14,820 represents $14,820,000,000). Based on an annual sample survey of fire departments. No adjustments were made for unreported fires and losses]

Type and property use	Number (1,000)				Direct property loss (mil. dol.) [1]			
	2019	2020	2021	2022	2019	2020 [6]	2021 [7]	2022
Fires, total....................	**1,292**	**1,389**	**1,354**	**1,505**	**14,820**	**21,866**	**15,957**	**18,072**
Structure.............................	482	491	487	523	12,287	12,107	12,751	15,024
Outside of structure [2]...............	71	84	80	95	206	210	156	250
Brush and rubbish...................	422	502	499	574	(X)	(X)	(X)	(X)
Vehicle [3]............................	223	210	209	222	2,229	5,170	2,165	2,649
Other..............................	95	103	80	92	98	179	207	149
Structure fires by property use:								
Residential.........................	362	380	361	383	7,976	8,703	8,949	10,955
1-2 family homes [4]................	265	271	257	280	6,428	6,771	6,972	8,626
Apartments.....................	75	86	82	80	1,339	1,629	1,725	1,911
Other residential [5]...............	22	23	23	23	209	303	252	418
Non-residential.....................	120	111	126	140	4,311	3,404	3,564	4,068

X Not applicable. [1] Direct property damage figures do not include indirect losses (such as business interruption and temporary shelter costs) and adjustments for inflation. [2] Includes outside storage, crops, timber, etc. [3] Includes highway vehicles, and trains, boats, ships, aircraft, farm vehicles, and construction vehicles. [4] Includes manufactured homes. [5] Includes hotels and motels, college dormitories, boarding houses, etc. [6] Includes losses of $4.2 billion from California fires in the wildland-urban interface (WUI) and a blaze that destroyed a naval ship ($3 billion). [7] Includes losses of $678 million from fires in California wildland-urban interface (WUI).

Source: National Fire Protection Association, Quincy, MA, *Fire Loss in the United States During 2022* ©, November 2023, and earlier reports. See also <nfpa.org/education-and-research/research>.

Table 403. Fires and Property Loss and Civilian Fire Deaths and Injuries by Selected Property Type: 2010 to 2022

[In thousands (482 represents 482,000), except as indicated. Based on a sample survey of fire departments]

Item	2010	2015	2016	2017	2018	2019	2020	2021	2022
NUMBER (1,000)									
Structure fires, total........................	**482**	**502**	**476**	**499**	**499**	**482**	**491**	**487**	**523**
Structure fires that were intentionally set.......	28	23	20	23	26	(NA)	(NA)	(NA)	(NA)
PROPERTY LOSS (mil. dol.) [1]									
Structure fires, total........................	**9,716**	**10,280**	**7,898**	**10,700**	**11,066**	**12,287**	**12,107**	**12,751**	**15,024**
Structure fires that were intentionally set.......	585	460	473	582	593	(NA)	(NA)	(NA)	(NA)
CIVILIAN FIRE DEATHS									
Deaths, total [2]................................	**3,120**	**3,280**	**3,390**	**3,390**	**3,655**	**3,704**	**3,500**	**3,800**	**3,790**
Residential property.............................	2,665	2,605	2,800	2,710	2,820	2,870	2,630	2,880	2,760
One- and two-family dwellings................	2,200	2,155	2,410	2,290	2,360	2,390	2,230	2,440	2,240
Apartments....................................	440	405	325	340	360	380	350	400	470
Vehicles [3]......................................	310	500	355	430	560	644	630	680	700
CIVILIAN FIRE INJURIES									
Injuries, total [2]..................................	**17,720**	**15,700**	**14,650**	**14,670**	**15,200**	**16,600**	**15,200**	**14,700**	**13,250**
Residential property.............................	13,800	11,575	11,125	10,910	11,600	12,700	11,900	11,500	10,320
One- and two-family dwellings................	9,400	8,050	7,375	7,470	7,800	8,800	8,600	8,000	7,190
Apartments....................................	3,950	3,025	3,375	3,130	3,400	3,400	2,900	3,100	2,750
Vehicles [3]......................................	1,590	1,875	1,225	1,610	1,500	2,000	1,700	1,500	960

NA Not available. [1] Direct property loss only. [2] Includes deaths or injuries from other types of fires, not shown separately. [3] Includes highway vehicles, and trains, boats, ships, aircraft, farm vehicles, and construction vehicles.

Source: National Fire Protection Association, Quincy, MA, *Fire Loss in the United States During 2022* ©, November 2023, and earlier reports. See also <nfpa.org/education-and-research/research>.

Section 6
Geography and Environment

This section presents a variety of information on the physical environment of the United States, starting with basic area measurement data and ending with climatic data for selected weather stations around the country. The subjects covered between those points are mostly concerned with environmental trends but include related subjects such as land use, water consumption, air pollutant emissions, toxic releases, oil spills, hazardous waste sites, municipal waste and recycling, threatened and endangered wildlife, and the environmental industry.

The information in this section is selected from a wide range of federal agencies that compile the data for various administrative or regulatory purposes, such as the Environmental Protection Agency (EPA), U.S. Geological Survey (USGS), National Oceanic and Atmospheric Administration (NOAA), and the Natural Resources Conservation Service (NRCS).

Area—Land and water area measurements were calculated by computer based on the information contained in a single, consistent geographic database, the Topologically Integrated Geographic Encoding & Referencing system (TIGER®) database, a national geographic and cartographic database prepared by the Census Bureau. The 2023 area measurements may be found in Table 404.

Geography—The USGS conducts investigations, surveys, and research in the fields of geography, geology, topography, geographic information systems, mineralogy, hydrology, and geothermal energy resources as well as natural hazards. The USGS provides United States cartographic data through the Earth Sciences Information Center and water resources data through the *Water Resources of the United States* at <usgs.gov/mission-areas/water-resources>. In a joint project with the U.S. Census Bureau, during the 1980s the USGS provided the basic information on geographic features for input into the TIGER® database. Since then, using a variety of sources, the Census Bureau has updated these features and their related attributes (names, descriptions, etc.) and inserted current information on the boundaries, names, and codes of legal and statistical geographic entities. The measures of land and water area, including their classifications, reflect base feature updates made in the Master Address File (MAF)/TIGER® database showing the names and boundaries of entities and are available on a current basis.

An inventory of the nation's land resources by type of use/cover was conducted by the NRCS every 5 years from 1977 through 1997. Since 2000, data have been gathered annually, though major releases of these data continue to be reported at 5-year intervals. The most recent survey results covered all nonfederal land for the contiguous 48 states. See <nrcs.usda.gov/nri/>.

Environment—The principal federal agency responsible for pollution abatement and control activities is the EPA. It is responsible for establishing and monitoring national air quality standards, water quality activities, solid and hazardous waste disposal, and control of toxic substances. Many of these series now appear in the "Envirofacts" portion of the EPA website at <enviro.epa.gov/>.

The Clean Air Act, which was last amended in 1990, requires the EPA to set National Ambient Air Quality Standards (NAAQS) (40 CFR part 50) for pollutants considered harmful to public health and the environment. The Clean Air Act established two types of national air quality standards. *Primary standards* set limits to protect public health, including the health of "sensitive" populations such as asthmatics, children, and the elderly. *Secondary standards* set limits to protect public welfare, including protection against decreased visibility and damage to animals, crops vegetation, and buildings. See <epa.gov/criteria-air-pollutants/naaqs-table> for more information. The EPA Office of Air Quality Planning and Standards (OAQPS) has set standards for six principal pollutants, which are called "criteria" pollutants. These pollutants are: carbon monoxide, lead, nitrogen dioxide, particulate matter, ozone, and sulfur dioxide. NAAQS are periodically reviewed and revised to include any additional or new health or welfare data. Table 419 gives some of the health-related standards for the six air pollutants having NAAQS. Data gathered from state networks are periodically submitted to EPA. For details, see "Air Trends" on the EPA website at <epa.gov/air-trends/>.

The Toxics Release Inventory (TRI), a database published by the EPA, is a valuable source of information on 794 chemicals that are being used, manufactured, treated, transported, or released into the environment. Sections 313 of the Emergency Planning and Community Right-to-Know Act (EPCRA) and 6607 of the Pollution Prevention Act (PPA) mandate that a publicly-accessible toxic chemical database be developed and maintained by the EPA. The TRI contains information concerning waste management activities and the release of toxic chemicals by facilities that manufacture, process, or otherwise use said materials. Data on the release of these chemicals are collected from about 21,000 facilities that have the equivalent of 10 or more full time employees and meet the established thresholds for manufacturing, processing, or "other use" of listed chemicals. Facilities must report their releases and other waste management quantities. More information can be found at <epa.gov/toxics-release-inventory-tri-program>.

Climate—NOAA, through the National Weather Service and the National Environmental Satellite, Data, and Information Service, is responsible for collecting climate data. NOAA maintains about 8,000 weather stations, of which a portion produce precipitation measurement records, some take hourly readings of a series of weather elements, and the remainder record data once a day. These data are reported using the Storm Events Database (see <ncdc.noaa.gov/stormevents/>, and hourly, daily, and monthly data from nearly 2,400 locations within the U.S., surrounding territories, and other selected areas is viewable at Local Climatological Data <www.ncdc.noaa.gov/cdo-web/datatools> (published by location for major cities). Data can be found in tables 434–438.

Table 404. Land and Water Area of States and Other Entities: 2023

[One square mile = 2.59 square kilometers. The area measurements were derived from the Census Bureau's Master Address File/Topologically Integrated Geographic Encoding and Referencing (MAF/TIGER®) database. The boundaries of the states and equivalent areas are as of January 1, 2023. The land and water areas, including their classifications, reflect base feature updates made in the MAF/TIGER® database through May 2023. For more details, see <www.census.gov/geographies/mapping-files/time-series/geo/tiger-line-file.html>]

State and other area [2]	Total area		Land area [1]		Water area [1]					
					Total		Inland (sq. mi.)	Coastal (sq. mi.)	Great Lakes (sq. mi.)	Territorial (sq. mi.)
	Sq. mi.	Sq. km.	Sq. mi.	Sq. km.	Sq. mi.	Sq. km.				
Total [3]	3,812,025	9,873,098	3,537,326	9,161,631	274,699	711,467	84,415	42,387	60,089	87,808
United States [4]	3,802,840	9,849,309	3,533,298	9,151,201	269,541	698,109	84,300	42,351	60,089	82,800
Alabama	52,420	135,767	50,651	131,185	1,769	4,582	1,052	517	–	200
Alaska	665,781	1,724,364	571,052	1,479,017	94,729	245,347	18,931	26,141	–	49,658
Arizona	113,985	295,220	113,655	294,366	330	854	330	–	–	–
Arkansas	53,198	137,783	51,993	134,660	1,206	3,122	1,206	–	–	–
California	163,694	423,965	155,859	403,673	7,835	20,292	2,752	244	–	4,838
Colorado	104,095	269,605	103,637	268,419	458	1,186	458	–	–	–
Connecticut	5,544	14,358	4,842	12,542	701	1,816	171	530	–	–
Delaware	2,489	6,446	1,949	5,047	540	1,399	91	355	–	94
District of Columbia	68	177	61	158	7	19	7	–	–	–
Florida	71,404	184,934	53,654	138,964	17,749	45,971	4,995	1,349	–	11,405
Georgia	59,423	153,905	57,717	149,485	1,706	4,420	1,210	47	–	450
Hawaii	10,970	28,412	6,423	16,634	4,547	11,777	42	9	–	4,497
Idaho	83,569	216,442	82,645	214,050	923	2,392	923	–	–	–
Illinois	57,913	149,995	55,513	143,778	2,400	6,217	826	–	1,574	–
Indiana	36,421	94,331	35,825	92,787	596	1,544	364	–	232	–
Iowa	56,273	145,746	55,853	144,659	419	1,086	419	–	–	–
Kansas	82,278	213,099	81,759	211,754	520	1,346	520	–	–	–
Kentucky	40,406	104,651	39,485	102,267	921	2,384	921	–	–	–
Louisiana	52,375	135,652	43,217	111,930	9,159	23,721	4,550	2,876	–	1,733
Maine	35,380	91,633	30,845	79,888	4,535	11,745	2,312	590	–	1,633
Maryland	12,406	32,131	9,711	25,152	2,695	6,979	765	1,820	–	110
Massachusetts	10,554	27,335	7,801	20,204	2,753	7,131	483	1,176	–	1,094
Michigan	96,713	250,486	56,610	146,620	40,103	103,866	1,930	–	38,173	–
Minnesota	86,943	225,182	79,631	206,245	7,312	18,937	4,766	–	2,546	–
Mississippi	48,436	125,448	46,924	121,534	1,511	3,915	763	620	–	129
Missouri	69,707	180,540	68,746	178,052	960	2,488	960	–	–	–
Montana	147,043	380,840	145,550	376,973	1,493	3,867	1,493	–	–	–
Nebraska	77,347	200,329	76,815	198,950	533	1,379	533	–	–	–
Nevada	110,571	286,377	109,860	284,537	710	1,840	710	–	–	–
New Hampshire	9,350	24,216	8,954	23,190	396	1,026	327	–	–	69
New Jersey	8,719	22,582	7,355	19,049	1,364	3,533	436	424	–	504
New Mexico	121,593	314,925	121,313	314,199	280	726	280	–	–	–
New York	54,559	141,306	47,123	122,049	7,435	19,257	1,993	976	3,984	482
North Carolina	53,819	139,389	48,624	125,936	5,194	13,454	4,047	–	–	1,148
North Dakota	70,699	183,109	68,994	178,694	1,705	4,415	1,705	–	–	–
Ohio	44,826	116,098	40,859	105,824	3,967	10,275	475	–	3,492	–
Oklahoma	69,899	181,038	68,597	177,664	1,302	3,373	1,302	–	–	–
Oregon	98,379	254,799	95,997	248,630	2,382	6,169	1,061	72	–	1,249
Pennsylvania	46,054	119,280	44,742	115,882	1,312	3,398	564	–	748	–
Rhode Island	1,545	4,001	1,034	2,678	511	1,324	182	64	–	266
South Carolina	32,023	82,940	30,064	77,866	1,959	5,074	1,060	109	–	790
South Dakota	77,116	199,729	75,808	196,342	1,308	3,388	1,308	–	–	–
Tennessee	42,129	109,115	41,233	106,792	897	2,322	897	–	–	–
Texas	268,599	695,668	261,270	676,686	7,329	18,982	5,577	402	–	1,350
Utah	84,898	219,885	82,596	213,922	2,302	5,963	2,302	–	–	–
Vermont	9,615	24,903	9,217	23,873	398	1,031	398	–	–	–
Virginia	42,775	110,786	39,482	102,258	3,293	8,528	1,289	1,565	–	438
Washington	71,301	184,668	66,455	172,119	4,845	12,549	1,713	2,465	–	667
West Virginia	24,230	62,756	24,041	62,266	189	489	189	–	–	–
Wisconsin	65,497	169,636	54,167	140,293	11,329	29,343	1,990	–	9,339	–
Wyoming	97,810	253,326	97,089	251,458	721	1,868	721	–	–	–
Puerto Rico	5,325	13,791	3,424	8,869	1,900	4,922	76	13	–	1,812
Island Areas:	3,860	9,998	603	1,562	3,257	8,436	39	22	–	3,196
American Samoa	581	1,505	76	198	505	1,307	8	–	–	497
Guam	571	1,478	210	544	361	934	8	1	–	352
Northern Mariana Islands	1,976	5,117	182	472	1,793	4,644	6	5	–	1,782
U.S. Virgin Islands	733	1,898	134	348	599	1,550	17	16	–	565

– Represents or rounds to zero. [1] Water area calculations in this table include only perennial water. All other water (intermittent, glacier, and marsh/swamp) is included in this table as part of land area calculations. [2] This table does not include area calculations for the U.S. Minor Outlying Islands. [3] Includes all 50 states, the District of Columbia, Puerto Rico, and the Island Areas. [4] Includes all 50 states and the District of Columbia.

Source: U.S. Census Bureau, unpublished data from the MAF/TIGER® database. See <tigerweb.geo.census.gov>.

Table 405. Great Lakes Profile

[The Great Lakes contain the largest supply of freshwater in the world, holding about 21% of the world's total freshwater and about 84% of the United States' total freshwater. The Lakes are a series of five interconnecting large lakes, one small lake, four connecting channels, and the St. Lawrence Seaway. Combined, the lakes cover an area of over 94,000 square miles (245,000 square kilometers) and contain over 5,400 cubic miles (23,000 cubic kilometers) of water]

Characteristics	Unit	Lake Superior	Lake Michigan	Lake Huron	Lake Erie	Lake Ontario
Volume.....................................	Cubic miles	2,900	1,180	850	116	393
Water surface area [1]...................	Square miles	31,700	22,300	23,000	9,910	7,340
Land drainage area.....................	Square miles	49,300	45,600	[4] 51,700	[5] 30,140	[6] 24,720
Shoreline length [2]......................	Miles	2,726	1,638	3,827	871	712
Depth:						
Average.........................	Feet	483	279	195	62	283
Maximum.........................	Feet	1,332	925	750	210	802
Retention/replacement time [3]........	Years	191	99	22	2.6	6

[1] Includes surface area in both U.S. and Canada. [2] Greater than the sum of the shoreline length for the lakes because it includes the connecting channels (but not the St. Lawrence River). [3] The amount of time it takes for lakes to get rid of pollutants. [4] Includes St. Marys River. [5] Includes the St. Clair-Detroit system. [6] Includes the Niagara River.

Source: U.S. Environmental Protection Agency, The Great Lakes, "Physical Features of the Great Lakes," <www.epa.gov/greatlakes>, accessed August 2024.

Table 406. Great Lakes Length of Shoreline in Separate Basin

[In statute miles]

Shorelines	Total	Canada	U.S.	MI	MN	WI	IL	IN	OH	PA	NY
Total...............	**10,368**	**5,127**	**5,241**	**3,288**	**189**	**820**	**63**	**45**	**312**	**51**	**473**
Lake Superior......	2,980	1,549	1,431	917	189	325	–	–	–	–	–
St. Marys River.....	297	206	91	91	–	–	–	–	–	–	–
Lake Michigan......	1,661	–	1,661	1,058	–	495	63	45	–	–	–
Lake Huron.........	3,350	2,416	934	934	–	–	–	–	–	–	–
St. Clair River......	128	47	81	81	–	–	–	–	–	–	–
Lake St. Clair.......	160	71	89	89	–	–	–	–	–	–	–
Detroit River........	107	43	64	64	–	–	–	–	–	–	–
Lake Erie............	860	366	494	54	–	–	–	–	312	51	77
Niagara River.......	99	34	65	–	–	–	–	–	–	–	65
Lake Ontario........	726	395	331	–	–	–	–	–	–	–	331

– Represents zero.

Source: State of Michigan, Department of Environment, Great Lakes, and Energy, "Great Lakes, Shorelines of the Great Lakes," and U.S. Lake Survey, File no. 3-3284 corrected to 1952, <www.michigan.gov/egle>.

Table 407. Largest Lakes in the United States

[The list of lakes include manmade lakes and those that are only partially within the United States]

Lake	Location	Area in sq. mi.	Lake	Location	Area in sq. mi.
Lake Superior..................	MI-MN-WI-Ontario	31,700	Lake Pontchartrain.......	Louisiana	631
Lake Huron......................	MI-Ontario	23,000	Lake Sakakawea [1].......	North Dakota	520
Lake Michigan..................	IL-IN-MI-WI	22,300	Lake Champlain.........	NY-VT-Quebec	490
Lake Erie.......................	MI-NY-OH-PA-Ontario	9,910	Becharof Lake...........	Alaska	453
Lake Ontario...................	NY-Ontario	7,340	Lake St. Clair.............	MI-Ontario	430
Great Salt Lake................	Utah	2,117	Red Lake.................	Minnesota	427
Lake of the Woods...........	MN-Manitoba-Ontario	1,485	Selawik Lake.............	Alaska	404
Iliamna Lake...................	Alaska	1,014	Fort Peck Lake [1]........	Montana	393
Lake Oahe [1]...................	ND-SD	685	Salton Sea...............	California	347
Lake Okeechobee..............	Florida	662	Rainy Lake...............	MN-Ontario	345

[1] Manmade lakes.

Source: U.S. Geological Survey, 2003, and National Oceanic and Atmospheric Administration, "Great Lakes, 2002" and The National Atlas of the United States of America, *Lakes*, <www.usgs.gov/core-science-systems/national-geospatial-program/small-scale-data>.

Table 408. Coastline Counties Most Frequently Hit by Hurricanes: 1960 to 2008

[Hurricane is a type of tropical cyclone, an intense tropical weather system of strong thunderstorms with a well-defined surface circulation and maximum sustained winds of 74 miles per hour or higher. See <coast.noaa.gov/digitalcoast/> for more info]

County and State	Coastline region	Number of hurricanes	Percent change in population		Percent change in housing units	
			1960 to 2008	2000 to 2008	1960 to 2008	2000 to 2008
Monroe County, FL...................	Gulf of Mexico	15	50.8	-9.2	221.8	4.3
Lafourche Parish, LA................	Gulf of Mexico	14	67.2	2.9	151.5	8.9
Carteret County, NC.................	Atlantic	14	104.3	6.4	366.4	12.4
Dare County, NC....................	Atlantic	13	465.9	12.1	709.6	22.8
Hyde County, NC....................	Atlantic	13	-10.1	-11.1	83.7	5.8
Jefferson Parish, LA.................	Gulf of Mexico	12	108.9	-4.2	201.4	-3.5
Palm Beach County, FL.............	Atlantic	12	454.7	11.9	616.9	15.2
Miami-Dade County, FL.............	Atlantic	11	156.5	6.4	180.6	14.9
St. Bernard Parish, LA..............	Gulf of Mexico	11	17.2	-43.9	-2.6	-67.9
Cameron Parish, LA.................	Gulf of Mexico	11	4.8	-27.6	87.7	-8.1
Terrebonne Parish, LA..............	Gulf of Mexico	11	78.7	3.9	179.4	11.0

Source: U.S. National Oceanic and Atmospheric Administration (NOAA), Coastal Services Center, Historical Hurricane Tracks: 1851 to 2008; U.S. Census Bureau, Current Population Reports, P25-1139, Population Estimates and Projections, "Coastline Population Trends in the United States: 1960 to 2008," May 2010. See also <www.census.gov/topics/preparedness/about/coastal-areas.html>.

Table 409. U.S.–Canada and U.S.–Mexico Border Lengths

[In statute miles. Each statute mile equals one mile]

State	Length of international border	State	Length of international border
United States–Canada total...............	**5,525**	Ohio..	146
Alaska...	1,538	Pennsylvania...................................	42
Idaho..	45	Vermont...	90
Maine..	611	Washington.....................................	427
Michigan..	721		
Minnesota...	547	**United States–Mexico total**...............	**1,933**
Montana...	545	Arizona..	373
New Hampshire..................................	58	California..	140
New York..	445	New Mexico......................................	180
North Dakota.....................................	310	Texas...	1,241

Source: U.S.–Canada lengths: International Boundary Commission, 2003; U.S. Mexico lengths: U.S. Geological Survey; and The National Atlas of the United States, 1976, "Borders," <www.usgs.gov/core-science-systems/national-geospatial-program>.

Table 410. Coastline and Shoreline of the United States by State

[In statute miles. Each statute mile equals one mile. The term coastline is used to describe the general outline of the seacoast. For the table below, United States coastline measurements were made from small-scale maps, and the coastline was generalized. The coastlines of large sounds and bays were included. Measurements were made in 1948. Shoreline is the term used to describe a more detailed measure of the seacoast. The tidal shoreline figures in the table below were obtained in 1939-1940 from the largest-scale charts and maps then available. Shoreline of the outer coast, offshore islands, sounds, and bays was included, as well as the tidal portion of rivers and creeks. Only States with coastline or shoreline are included in the following table]

State	General coastline	Tidal shoreline	State	General coastline	Tidal shoreline
United States.................	**12,383**	**88,633**	Massachusetts...............	192	1,519
			Mississippi.....................	44	359
Alabama.........................	53	607	New Hampshire..............	13	131
Alaska...........................	6,640	33,904	New Jersey....................	130	1,792
California........................	840	3,427	New York.......................	127	1,850
Connecticut.....................	–	618	North Carolina...............	301	3,375
Delaware........................	28	381	Oregon..........................	296	1,410
Florida...........................	1,350	8,426	Pennsylvania..................	–	89
Georgia..........................	100	2,344	Rhode Island..................	40	384
Hawaii............................	750	1,052	South Carolina................	187	2,876
Louisiana........................	397	7,721	Texas............................	367	3,359
Maine.............................	228	3,478	Virginia..........................	112	3,315
Maryland.........................	31	3,190	Washington....................	157	3,026

– Represents zero.

Source: National Oceanic Atmospheric Administration, 1975 and The National Atlas of the United States, "Coastline and Shoreline," <www.usgs.gov/core-science-systems/national-geospatial-program/small-scale-data>. See also <shoreline.noaa.gov/>.

Table 411. Flows of Largest U.S. Rivers—Length, Discharge, and Drainage Area

[A flow of 1,000 cubic ft. per second is equal to 646 million gallons per day, 724,000 acre-feet per year, or 28.3 cubic meters per second. One acre-foot is the volume of water that would cover 1 acre to a depth of 1 foot]

River	Location of mouth	Source stream (name and location)	Length (miles) [1]	Average discharge at mouth (1,000 cubic feet per second)	Drainage area (1,000 sq. miles)
Missouri..................	Missouri	Red Rock Creek, MT	[2] 2,540	76	[3] 529
Mississippi...............	Louisiana	Mississippi River, MN	2,340	[4] 593	[3,5] 1,150
Yukon.....................	Alaska	McNeil River, Canada	1,980	225	[3] 328
St. Lawrence............	Canada	North River, MN	1,900	348	[3] 396
Rio Grande..............	Mexico-Texas	Rio Grande, CO	1,900	([6])	336
Arkansas.................	Arkansas	East Fork Arkansas River, CO	1,460	41	161
Colorado.................	Mexico	Colorado River, CO	1,450	([6])	246
Atchafalaya [7]...........	Louisiana	Tierra Blanca Creek, NM	1,420	58	95
Ohio.......................	Illinois-Kentucky	Allegheny River, PA	1,310	281	203
Red [7]....................	Louisiana	Tierra Blanca Creek, NM	1,290	56	93
Brazos...................	Texas	Blackwater Draw, NM	1,280	([6])	46
Columbia.................	Oregon-Washington	Columbia River, Canada	1,240	265	[3] 258
Snake....................	Washington	Snake River, WY	1,040	57	108
Platte.....................	Nebraska	Grizzly Creek, CO	990	([6])	85
Pecos....................	Texas	Pecos River, NM	926	([6])	44
Canadian...............	Oklahoma	Canadian River, CO	906	([6])	47
Tennessee..............	Kentucky	Courthouse Creek, NC	886	68	41

[1] From source to mouth. [2] The length from the source of the Missouri River to the Mississippi River and thence to the Gulf of Mexico is about 3,710 miles. [3] Drainage area includes both the United States and Canada. [4] Includes about 167,000 cubic feet per second diverted from the Mississippi into the Atchafalaya River but excludes the flow of the Red River. [5] Excludes the drainage areas of the Red and Atchafalaya Rivers. [6] Less than 15,000 cubic feet per second. [7] In east-central Louisiana, the Red River flows into the Atchafalaya River, a distributary of the Mississippi River. Data on average discharge, length, and drainage area include the Red River, but exclude all water diverted into the Atchafalaya from the Mississippi River.

Source: U.S. Geological Survey, *Largest Rivers in the United States*, September 2005, <pubs.usgs.gov/of/1987/ofr87-242/>.

Table 412. Extreme and Mean Elevations by State and Other Areas

[One foot = .305 meter. There are 2,130 square miles of the United States below sea level (Death Valley is the lowest point). There are 20,230 square miles above 10,000 feet (Denali is the highest point in the United States). Minus sign (-) indicates below sea level]

State and other areas	Highest point Name	Elevation Feet	Elevation Meters	Lowest point Name	Elevation Feet	Elevation Meters	Approximate mean elevation Feet	Approximate mean elevation Meters
U.S.	**Denali (AK) [1]**	**20,310**	**6,190**	**Death Valley (CA)**	**-282**	**-86**	**2,500**	**763**
AL	Cheaha Mountain	2,407	734	Gulf of Mexico	([2])	([2])	500	153
AK	Denali [1]	20,310	6,190	Pacific Ocean	([2])	([2])	1,900	580
AZ	Humphreys Peak	12,633	3,853	Colorado River	70	21	4,100	1,251
AR	Magazine Mountain	2,753	840	Ouachita River	55	17	650	198
CA	Mount Whitney	14,494	4,419	Death Valley	-282	-86	2,900	885
CO	Mount Elbert	14,433	4,402	Arikaree River	3,315	1,011	6,800	2,074
CT	Mount Frissell, on south slope	2,380	726	Long Island Sound	([2])	([2])	500	153
DE	Ebright Road [3]	448	137	Atlantic Ocean	([2])	([2])	60	18
DC	Tenleytown at Reno Reservoir	410	125	Potomac River	1	(Z)	150	46
FL	Britton Hill	345	105	Atlantic Ocean	([2])	([2])	100	31
GA	Brasstown Bald	4,784	1,459	Atlantic Ocean	([2])	([2])	600	183
HI	Pu'u Wekiu, Mauna Kea	13,796	4,208	Pacific Ocean	([2])	([2])	3,030	924
ID	Borah Peak	12,662	3,862	Snake River	710	217	5,000	1,525
IL	Charles Mound	1,235	377	Mississippi River	279	85	600	183
IN	Hoosier Hill	1,257	383	Ohio River	320	98	700	214
IA	Hawkeye Point	1,670	509	Mississippi River	480	146	1,100	336
KS	Mount Sunflower	4,039	1,232	Verdigris River	679	207	2,000	610
KY	Black Mountain	4,145	1,264	Mississippi River	257	78	750	229
LA	Driskill Mountain	535	163	New Orleans	-8	-2	100	31
ME	Mount Katahdin	5,268	1,607	Atlantic Ocean	([2])	([2])	600	183
MD	Hoye Crest	3,360	1,025	Atlantic Ocean	([2])	([2])	350	107
MA	Mount Greylock	3,491	1,065	Atlantic Ocean	([2])	([2])	500	153
MI	Mount Arvon	1,979	604	Lake Erie	571	174	900	275
MN	Eagle Mountain	2,301	702	Lake Superior	601	183	1,200	366
MS	Woodall Mountain	806	246	Gulf of Mexico	([2])	([2])	300	92
MO	Taum Sauk Mountain	1,772	540	St. Francis River	230	70	800	244
MT	Granite Peak	12,799	3,904	Kootenai River	1,800	549	3,400	1,037
NE	Panorama Point	5,424	1,654	Missouri River	840	256	2,600	793
NV	Boundary Peak	13,140	4,007	Colorado River	479	146	5,500	1,678
NH	Mount Washington	6,288	1,918	Atlantic Ocean	([2])	([2])	1,000	305
NJ	High Point	1,803	550	Atlantic Ocean	([2])	([2])	250	76
NM	Wheeler Peak	13,161	4,014	Red Bluff Reservoir	2,842	867	5,700	1,739
NY	Mount Marcy	5,344	1,630	Atlantic Ocean	([2])	([2])	1,000	305
NC	Mount Mitchell	6,684	2,039	Atlantic Ocean	([2])	([2])	700	214
ND	White Butte	3,506	1,069	Red River of the North	750	229	1,900	580
OH	Campbell Hill	1,550	473	Ohio River	455	139	850	259
OK	Black Mesa	4,973	1,517	Little River	289	88	1,300	397
OR	Mount Hood	11,239	3,428	Pacific Ocean	([2])	([2])	3,300	1,007
PA	Mount Davis	3,213	980	Delaware River	([2])	([2])	1,100	336
RI	Jerimoth Hill	812	248	Atlantic Ocean	([2])	([2])	200	61
SC	Sassafras Mountain	3,560	1,086	Atlantic Ocean	([2])	([2])	350	107
SD	Harney Peak	7,242	2,209	Big Stone Lake	966	295	2,200	671
TN	Clingmans Dome	6,643	2,026	Mississippi River	178	54	900	275
TX	Guadalupe Peak	8,749	2,668	Gulf of Mexico	([2])	([2])	1,700	519
UT	Kings Peak	13,528	4,126	Beaverdam Wash	2,000	610	6,100	1,861
VT	Mount Mansfield	4,393	1,340	Lake Champlain	95	29	1,000	305
VA	Mount Rogers	5,729	1,747	Atlantic Ocean	([2])	([2])	950	290
WA	Mount Rainier	14,411	4,395	Pacific Ocean	([2])	([2])	1,700	519
WV	Spruce Knob	4,863	1,483	Potomac River	240	73	1,500	458
WI	Timms Hill	1,951	595	Lake Michigan	579	177	1,050	320
WY	Gannett Peak	13,804	4,210	Belle Fourche River	3,099	945	6,700	2,044
Other areas:								
Puerto Rico	Cerro de Punta	4,390	1,339	Atlantic Ocean	([2])	([2])	1,800	549
American Samoa	Lata Mountain	3,160	964	Pacific Ocean	([2])	([2])	1,300	397
Guam	Mount Lamlam	1,332	406	Pacific Ocean	([2])	([2])	330	101
U.S. Virgin Islands	Crown Mountain	1,556	475	Atlantic Ocean	([2])	([2])	750	229

Z Less than .5 meter. [1] Formerly Mount McKinley. The mountain's name was changed on August 28, 2015. [2] Sea level. [3] At DE–PA state line.

Source: For highest and lowest points, see U.S. Geological Survey, "Elevations and Distances in the United States," <pubs.er.usgs.gov/publication/70037974>, released April 2005. For mean elevations, see *Elevations and Distances in the United States*, 1983 edition.

Table 413. Acres of Land Cover by Type and Use: 1997 to 2017

[In millions of acres (1,944 represents 1,944,000,000), except percent. Excludes Alaska and District of Columbia. For inventory-specific glossary of key terms, see <www.nrcs.usda.gov/sites/default/files/2022-10/NRI_glossary.pdf>]

Year	Total surface area [1]	Nonfederal rural land							Devel- oped land	Water areas	Federal land
		Rural land total	Crop- land	CRP land [2]	Pasture- land	Range- land	Forest land	Other rural land			
Land											
1997	1,944	1,395	376	33	120	408	416	41	96	51	403
2002	1,944	1,384	368	31	120	407	416	41	105	51	404
2007	1,944	1,377	359	32	121	407	416	43	111	52	405
2012	1,944	1,373	362	24	123	405	416	43	114	52	405
2017	1,944	1,370	367	16	122	404	417	44	116	52	406
Percent of total land											
1997	100.0	71.7	19.4	1.7	6.2	21.0	21.4	2.1	4.9	2.6	20.7
2002	100.0	71.2	18.9	1.6	6.2	21.0	21.4	2.1	5.4	2.6	20.8
2007	100.0	70.8	18.5	1.7	6.2	20.9	21.4	2.2	5.7	2.7	20.8
2012	100.0	70.6	18.6	1.2	6.3	20.8	21.4	2.2	5.8	2.7	20.8
2017	100.0	70.5	18.9	0.8	6.3	20.8	21.5	2.3	6.0	2.7	20.9

[1] Includes Puerto Rico and Virgin Islands. [2] Conservation Reserve Program (CRP) land. CRP is a federal program established under the Food Security Act of 1985 to assist private landowners to convert highly erodible cropland to vegetative cover for 10 years.

Source: U.S. Department of Agriculture, Natural Resources Conservation Service, *Summary Report: 2017 National Resources Inventory*, September 2020. See also <nrcs.usda.gov/nri>.

Table 414. Wetlands on Nonfederal Land and Water Areas by Land Cover Type for Top 10 States: 2017

[In thousands of acres (111,228 represents 111,228,000). Covers both palustrine (nontidal) and estuarine (tidal) wetlands; see source for details]

Top 10 States	Total	Crop- land [1]	Forest land	Range- land	Other rural land	Developed land	Water area
Wetlands, total [2]	**111,228**	**17,426**	**65,984**	**7,877**	**14,802**	**1,487**	**3,653**
Minnesota	10,636	1,955	6,862	–	1,707	42	70
Louisiana	9,747	1,970	4,996	155	2,385	79	163
Florida	9,010	393	5,133	978	2,156	162	188
Georgia	6,555	217	5,600	–	462	123	153
Michigan	6,023	265	4,647	–	977	74	61
Wisconsin	5,553	933	3,456	–	1,040	48	75
Texas	5,301	983	2,498	762	406	154	498
Maine	5,124	73	4,706	–	287	36	22
North Carolina	4,733	60	4,280	–	265	43	87
Mississippi	4,614	620	3,642	–	92	73	187

– Represents zero. [1] Cultivated and non-cultivated. Includes pastureland and Conservation Reserve Program (CRP) lands. [2] Includes other States and Caribbean areas not shown below.

Source: U.S. Department of Agriculture, Natural Resources Conservation Service, *Summary Report: 2017 National Resources Inventory*, September 2020. See also <nrcs.usda.gov/nri>.

Table 415. Acres of Federal and Non-Federal Land Cover by Type and State: 2017

[In thousands of acres (1,944,146 represents 1,944,146,000), except percent. Excludes Alaska and District of Columbia]

State	Total surface area [1]	Selected nonfederal rural land, percent of total			State	Total surface area [1]	Selected nonfederal rural land, percent of total		
		Crop- land	Range- land	Forest land			Crop- land	Range- land	Forest land
United States [2]	**1,944,146**	**18.9**	**20.8**	**21.5**	Montana	94,110	16.3	39.1	6.3
Alabama	33,424	6.8	0.1	65.3	Nebraska	49,510	41.1	45.9	1.7
Arizona	72,964	1.2	46.0	5.8	Nevada	70,763	0.9	12.4	0.5
Arkansas	34,037	20.9	0.1	44.1	New Hampshire	5,941	1.9	–	63.6
California	101,510	9.2	19.0	13.9	New Jersey	5,216	9.1	–	31.2
Colorado	66,625	12.0	36.9	5.3	New Mexico	77,823	1.9	52.9	7.2
Connecticut	3,195	5.2	–	50.0	New York	31,409	15.8	–	55.9
Delaware	1,534	25.4	–	22.9	North Carolina	33,709	15.0	–	46.5
Florida	37,534	7.1	6.6	35.2	North Dakota	45,251	56.0	23.6	1.0
Georgia	37,741	11.8	–	57.7	Ohio	26,445	42.5	–	27.0
Hawaii	4,123	1.9	27.7	35.6	Oklahoma	44,738	19.5	29.7	18.1
Idaho	53,488	10.1	12.7	7.6	Oregon	62,161	5.8	14.6	19.9
Illinois	36,059	66.4	–	11.3	Pennsylvania	28,995	17.0	–	54.1
Indiana	23,158	57.5	–	17.0	Rhode Island	813	2.2	–	44.2
Iowa	36,017	72.1	–	6.8	South Carolina	19,939	10.5	–	56.2
Kansas	52,661	50.0	29.6	3.6	South Dakota	49,358	36.8	45.3	1.2
Kentucky	25,863	21.5	–	42.4	Tennessee	26,974	17.8	–	44.4
Louisiana	31,377	15.6	0.6	41.7	Texas	171,052	13.8	53.3	9.3
Maine	20,966	1.7	–	83.2	Utah	54,339	2.8	20.4	4.3
Maryland	7,870	18.1	–	29.3	Vermont	6,154	8.4	–	65.7
Massachusetts	5,339	3.9	–	47.7	Virginia	27,087	10.6	–	49.1
Michigan	37,349	21.3	–	44.8	Washington	44,039	14.2	13.6	27.9
Minnesota	54,010	39.9	–	30.3	West Virginia	15,508	4.1	–	67.9
Mississippi	30,527	15.3	–	57.1	Wisconsin	35,920	29.0	–	41.2
Missouri	44,614	34.0	0.2	28.5	Wyoming	62,603	3.1	42.9	1.7

– Represents or rounds to zero. [1] Total surface area includes both Federal and non-Federal land. [2] Includes Puerto Rico and U.S. Virgin Islands, not shown separately.

Source: U.S. Department of Agriculture, Natural Resources Conservation Service, *Summary Report, 2017 National Resources Inventory*, September 2020. See also <nrcs.usda.gov/nri>.

Table 416. U.S. Wetland Resources and Deepwater Habitats by Type: 2009 and 2019

[In thousands of acres (161,148 represents 161,148,000). Covers the conterminous U.S. (excludes Alaska and Hawaii). Wetlands and deepwater habitats are defined separately because the term wetland does not include permanent water bodies. Deepwater habitats are permanently flooded land lying below the deepwater boundary of wetlands. Deepwater habitats include environments where surface water is permanent and often deep, so that water, rather than air, is the principal medium within which the dominant organisms live, whether or not they are attached to the substrate. As in wetlands, the dominant plants are hydrophytes; however, the substrates are considered nonsoil because the water is too deep to support emergent vegetation. In general terms, wetlands are lands where saturation with water is the dominant factor determining the nature of soil development and the types of plant and animal communities living in the soil and on its surface. The single feature that most wetlands share is soil or substrate that is at least periodically saturated with or covered by water. Wetlands are lands transitional between terrestrial and aquatic systems where the water table is usually at or near the surface or the land is covered by shallow water. For more information on wetlands, see the "Classification of Wetlands and Deepwater Habitats of the United States" at <fws.gov/story/2023-04/introduction-wetland-classification>]

Wetland or deepwater category	Estimated area, 2009	Estimated area, 2019	Change, 2009 to 2019
All wetlands and deepwater habitats, total	**161,148**	**161,109**	**-39**
All deepwater habitats, total	44,490	44,672	182
Lacustrine [1] (lakes and reservoirs)	17,068	17,227	159
Riverine [2] (rivers and streams)	7,435	7,402	-33
Estuarine subtidal [3] (open-water, bays)	19,987	20,043	56
All wetlands, total	116,658	116,437	-221
Intertidal wetlands [4]	6,091	6,061	-30
Marine intertidal (near shore)	206	209	3
Estuarine intertidal nonvegetated	1,005	1,035	30
Estuarine intertidal vegetated	4,880	4,817	-63
Freshwater wetlands	110,567	110,376	-191
Palustrine ponds (open-water ponds, aquatic beds)	6,421	6,876	455
All vegetated wetlands	107,014	106,344	-670
Palustrine farmed (farmed wetlands)	2,012	1,973	-40
Freshwater vegetated	102,134	101,527	-607
Freshwater emergent [5] (inland marshes, wet meadows)	30,092	30,008	-84
Freshwater shrub [6] (wetlands with woody plants)	19,187	19,091	-97
Freshwater forested [7] (wetlands with tall woody plants)	52,854	52,428	-426
All non-vegetated wetlands	7,632	8,120	488

[1] The lacustrine system includes deepwater habitats with all of the following characteristics: (1) situated in a topographic depression or a dammed river channel; (2) lacking trees, shrubs, persistent emergents, emergent mosses or lichens with greater than 30 percent coverage; and (3) total area exceeds 20 acres (8 hectares). [2] The riverine system includes deepwater habitats contained within a channel, with the exception of habitats with water containing ocean derived salts in excess of 0.5 parts per thousand. [3] The estuarine system consists of deepwater tidal habitats and adjacent tidal wetlands that are usually semi-enclosed by land but have open, partly obstructed, or sporadic access to the open ocean, and in which ocean water is at least occasionally diluted by freshwater runoff from the land. Subtidal is where the substrate is continuously submerged by marine or estuarine waters. [4] Intertidal is where the substrate is exposed and flooded by tides. Intertidal includes the splash zone of coastal waters. [5] Emergent wetlands are characterized by erect, rooted, herbaceous hydrophytes, excluding mosses and lichens. This vegetation is present for most of the growing season in most years. These wetlands are usually dominated by perennial plants. [6] Shrub wetlands include areas dominated by woody vegetation less than 20 feet tall. The species include true shrubs, young trees, and trees or shrubs that are small or stunted because of environmental conditions. [7] Forested wetlands are characterized by woody vegetation that is 20 feet tall or taller.

Source: U.S. Fish and Wildlife Service, *Status and Trends of Wetlands in the Conterminous United States, 2009 to 2019*, March 2024. See also <www.fws.gov/carp/program/national-wetlands-inventory>.

Table 417. U.S. Water Withdrawals Per Day by End Use: 1950 to 2015

[In billions of gallons of water per day (180 represents 180,000,000,000). Includes the District of Columbia, Puerto Rico and U.S. Virgin Islands, as noted. Withdrawal signifies water physically withdrawn from a source. Includes fresh and saline water; excludes water used for hydroelectric power. For information on changes in data collection and presentation methods, see source report]

Year	Total with-drawals	Public supply	Rural domestic and livestock — Self supplied domestic	Rural domestic and livestock — Live-stock	Irri-gation	Thermo-electric power	Other — Self supplied industrial	Other — Mining	Other — Com-mercial	Other — Aqua-culture
1950 [1]	180	14	2.1	1.5	89	40	37.0	(5)	(5)	(5)
1955 [2]	240	17	2.1	1.5	110	72	39.0	(5)	(5)	(5)
1960 [3]	270	21	2.0	1.6	110	100	38.0	(5)	(5)	(5)
1965 [4]	310	24	2.3	1.7	120	130	46.0	(5)	(5)	(5)
1970 [4]	370	27	2.6	1.9	130	170	47.0	(5)	(5)	(5)
1975 [3]	420	29	2.8	2.1	140	200	45.0	(5)	(5)	(5)
1980 [3]	430	33	3.4	2.2	150	210	45.0	(5)	(5)	(5)
1985 [3]	397	37	3.3	2.2	135	187	25.8	3.4	1.2	2.2
1990 [3]	404	39	3.4	2.3	134	194	22.4	4.9	2.4	2.2
1995 [3]	398	40	3.4	2.3	130	190	21.6	3.6	2.9	3.3
2000 [3]	413	43	3.6	2.4	139	195	19.5	4.1	(NA)	5.8
2005 [3]	410	44	3.7	2.2	127	201	18.1	3.8	(NA)	8.8
2010 [3]	354	42	3.5	2.0	116	162	16.2	4.0	(NA)	9.0
2015 [3]	322	39	3.3	2.0	118	133	14.8	4.0	(NA)	7.6

NA Not available. [1] Population covered: 48 states, District of Columbia (D.C.), and Hawaii. [2] Population covered: 48 states and D.C. [3] Population covered: 50 states, D.C., Puerto Rico, and the Virgin Islands. [4] Population covered: 50 states, D.C., and Puerto Rico. [5] Included in "self-supplied industrial."

Source: U.S. Geological Survey, *Estimated Use of Water in the United States in 2015*, circular 1441, 2018. See also <pubs.er.usgs.gov/publication/cir1441>.

Table 418. Marine Economy Value Added and Gross Output by Activity: 2019 to 2022

[In millions of current dollars (392,190 represents $392,190,000,000). Measures contributions to the U.S. economy of activities related to the nation's oceans, seaports, and the Great Lakes]

Activity	Value added (mil. dol.)				Gross output (mil. dol.)			
	2019	2020	2021	2022	2019	2020	2021	2022
Marine economy, total................................	**392,190**	**357,024**	**424,209**	**476,219**	**660,914**	**579,221**	**684,406**	**776,899**
Living resources, marine..............................	16,612	17,756	21,891	22,744	29,198	30,688	38,572	40,002
Commercial harvest, seafood markets, & processing...	14,526	14,536	16,612	17,976	25,906	25,817	30,150	32,238
Commercial harvest & seafood markets...........	8,552	8,056	9,934	10,595	12,017	11,445	14,961	16,035
Seafood processing..................................	5,974	6,480	6,679	7,382	13,890	14,372	15,188	16,204
Fish-based animal foods............................	47	53	49	45	96	106	106	103
Pharmaceuticals, marine-based....................	2,039	3,167	5,230	4,722	3,195	4,765	8,316	7,662
Construction, coastal & marine.......................	5,509	6,103	5,284	5,973	7,426	8,135	7,335	8,491
Conservation.......................................	3,214	3,491	2,906	3,526	4,187	4,482	3,895	4,829
Dredging...	474	609	618	632	628	794	841	879
Recreation facilities...............................	1,704	1,868	1,640	1,690	2,466	2,691	2,446	2,623
Wind farms..	117	135	121	125	145	169	154	161
Research & education, marine........................	6,770	7,639	8,094	8,655	9,886	11,085	12,122	13,162
Scientific research.................................	4,086	4,990	5,551	5,738	6,535	7,722	8,898	9,370
National defense R&D..............................	146	158	172	182	149	160	175	185
Federal nondefense R&D...........................	1,388	1,906	2,590	2,692	2,132	2,856	3,988	4,251
State and local R&D...............................	1,456	1,543	1,527	1,533	2,237	2,312	2,352	2,421
Nonacademic R&D.................................	1,097	1,383	1,262	1,331	2,016	2,393	2,383	2,513
Educational programs & courses...................	2,556	2,538	2,430	2,797	3,156	3,190	3,045	3,602
Vocational training.................................	78	63	70	73	133	115	124	129
Laboratories.......................................	50	47	44	47	62	59	56	61
Transportation and warehousing, marine.............	29,183	24,383	28,829	33,348	72,220	52,893	57,446	68,166
Freight transportation..............................	19,496	18,735	23,353	25,978	41,324	39,268	46,961	52,793
Passenger transportation..........................	7,564	3,502	2,909	4,295	27,569	10,266	6,537	10,560
Warehousing and storage..........................	2,122	2,146	2,566	3,075	3,327	3,359	3,947	4,813
Professional & technical services, marine...........	5,104	4,973	4,841	5,300	9,443	9,229	9,420	9,485
Minerals, offshore....................................	46,025	32,477	47,927	62,026	78,861	57,446	75,534	96,008
Oil & gas..	44,011	30,551	45,781	59,476	75,392	54,339	72,014	91,731
Sand & gravel.....................................	1,538	1,489	1,704	2,049	2,710	2,392	2,799	3,429
Support services..................................	476	437	443	501	758	715	720	849
Utilities, coastal.....................................	10,454	10,271	13,406	13,756	16,771	15,301	21,755	22,838
Traditional power generation.......................	10,451	10,268	13,402	13,750	16,766	15,296	21,747	22,828
Alternative power generation [1]....................	3	3	5	6	5	5	7	10
Ship & boat building, nonrecreational...............	8,846	9,588	11,104	12,229	16,623	16,650	17,709	20,858
Ship building [2]...................................	7,818	8,762	9,975	10,798	14,653	15,213	15,889	18,433
Barges & other nonpropelled ships................	59	71	72	79	111	123	115	135
Military ships......................................	7,526	8,473	9,661	10,456	14,106	14,712	15,388	17,849
Other ships..	233	218	242	263	436	379	385	449
Boat building [3]..................................	1,027	826	1,129	1,431	1,969	1,438	1,820	2,425
Fishing boats......................................	25	23	25	28	46	40	40	47
Tugboats & towboats..............................	211	196	217	237	395	339	347	404
Outboard motorboats..............................	68	26	50	94	129	43	77	151
Inboard motorboats................................	276	227	342	455	561	406	577	794
Other boats.......................................	448	355	495	618	839	609	779	1,028
Tourism and recreation, coastal & offshore..........	139,357	110,852	140,058	162,743	224,774	169,435	225,376	269,528
Guided tours.......................................	8,675	6,801	8,312	10,945	18,628	15,493	18,485	24,510
Water guided tours................................	5,504	5,201	6,157	7,865	11,855	11,477	13,383	17,379
Other scenic tours................................	3,171	1,600	2,155	3,080	6,773	4,017	5,102	7,131
Recreational fishing, offshore......................	3,015	2,895	3,781	3,735	5,839	5,362	7,303	7,332
Boating & paddling, offshore.......................	20,102	17,829	22,323	24,248	39,320	32,896	42,826	49,732
Sailing...	1,476	1,098	1,408	1,586	2,696	1,941	2,507	2,935
Motorboating......................................	11,791	11,326	13,726	14,210	22,409	20,306	24,381	25,992
Canoeing..	27	38	57	46	45	61	97	78
Kayaking..	115	128	153	130	191	206	267	227
Other boating & paddling [4].......................	6,692	5,239	6,978	8,276	13,978	10,381	15,574	20,500
Other water activities [5]..........................	2,963	4,134	4,732	3,798	4,567	6,379	7,630	6,331
Other coastal recreation...........................	15,527	13,961	16,618	18,291	27,182	23,472	30,200	33,338
Maritime museums & cultural institutions...........	1,467	1,668	1,508	1,703	2,560	2,461	2,633	2,789
Beachgoing..	136	134	162	169	243	244	313	335
Amusement parks.................................	2,232	1,511	2,404	2,835	3,666	2,569	4,045	4,832
Hiking & camping..................................	915	1,298	1,299	1,444	1,630	2,210	2,319	2,593
RVing...	3,299	3,115	3,561	3,932	5,722	5,001	5,798	6,370
Photography.......................................	114	112	126	130	157	156	180	191
Other general expenses............................	7,366	6,123	7,559	8,078	13,205	10,831	14,912	16,227
Trips & travel, coastal.............................	89,076	65,233	84,293	101,726	129,238	85,833	118,931	148,285
Eating & drinking places...........................	11,477	5,757	11,192	13,081	19,188	10,099	19,698	23,017
Hotel & lodging places............................	60,036	53,666	60,694	70,709	75,271	64,085	73,298	85,564
Travel arrangement services.......................	1,651	585	757	1,260	3,951	1,729	2,235	3,728
Transportation services...........................	15,911	5,224	11,651	16,676	30,829	9,920	23,701	35,976
National defense & public administration.............	124,329	132,981	142,774	149,445	195,713	208,358	219,136	228,361
National defense & coast guard.....................	114,290	122,454	131,901	137,765	180,350	191,675	200,728	208,283
Federal public administration.......................	7,246	7,779	8,006	7,960	9,797	11,197	12,355	12,133
State & local public administration.................	2,793	2,748	2,867	3,721	5,566	5,486	6,052	7,944

[1] Consists solely of offshore wind-generated energy. [2] Government and commercial vessels built in shipyards including (but not limited to): naval surface combatants, cargo ships, barges, oil drilling platforms, passenger ships, tugboats, research vessels, submarines, and fishing vessels. [3] Government and commercial vessels not built in shipyards including (but not limited to): commercial fishing boats, motorboats (inboard and outboard), inflatables, tour boats, sailboats, and underwater remote operated vehicles. Activity associated with the manufacture of boats and other water craft used for recreational purposes is included in tourism and recreation sector. [4] Hovercraft, personal watercrafts, pontoon boats, life rafts and associated expenses such as repair services, insurance, fuel, etc. [5] Swimming, snorkeling, SCUBA diving, surfing, and related water activities.

Source: U.S. Bureau of Economic Analysis, *Marine Economy Satellite Account, 2022*, June 2024. See also <www.bea.gov/data/special-topics/marine-economy>.

Table 419. National Ambient Air Pollutant Concentrations by Type of Pollutant: 2010 to 2022

[Data represent composite averages across monitoring stations meeting minimum data completeness requirements for the trend period. Carbon monoxide is based on the second-highest, nonoverlapping, 8-hour average; ozone on the fourth-highest maximum 8-hour value; particulate matter (PM-10) on the second highest daily 24-hour average; fine particulate matter (PM2.5) annual average on the weighted annual mean of daily 24-hour averages; and lead on the maximum rolling three-month average. Based on data from the Air Quality System. $\mu g/m^3$ = micrograms of pollutant per cubic meter of air; ppm = parts per million; ppb = parts per billion]

Pollutant	Unit	Monitoring stations, number	Air quality standard [1]	2010	2015	2017	2018	2019	2020	2021	2022
Carbon monoxide	ppm	158	[2] 9	1.40	1.23	1.19	1.21	1.06	1.26	1.06	1.03
Ozone	ppm	1,070	[3] 0.070	0.069	0.067	0.067	0.068	0.064	0.064	0.066	0.065
Sulfur dioxide	ppb	238	[4] 75	45.0	24.3	14.4	13.9	12.9	11.4	11.5	11.5
Particulates (PM-10)	$\mu g/m^3$	406	[5] 150	82.3	77.1	89.5	83.7	68.9	93.9	80.5	99.8
Fine particulates (PM2.5) annual average	$\mu g/m^3$	578	[6] 12	9.8	8.5	8.1	8.2	7.5	8.1	8.4	7.7
Nitrogen dioxide	ppb	182	[7] 100	41.8	36.9	35.6	35.6	34.7	32.9	32.8	33.3
Lead	$\mu g/m^3$	81	[8] 0.15	0.20	0.04	0.04	0.03	0.03	0.03	0.02	0.02

[1] Refers to the primary National Ambient Air Quality Standard. See <epa.gov/criteria-air-pollutants/naaqs-table>. [2] Based on 8-hour standard of 9 ppm. [3] Based on 8-hour standard of 0.070 ppm. On December 28, 2015, EPA revised the level of the primary and secondary 8-hour ozone standards to 0.070 ppm. [4] Based on a 1-hour daily maximum concentration of 75 ppb. [5] Based on 24-hour (daily) standard of 150 $\mu g/m^3$. The particulates (PM-10) standard replaced the previous standard for total suspended particulates in 1987. In 2006, EPA revoked the annual PM-10 standard. [6] Based on annual standard of 12 $\mu g/m^3$. The PM-2.5 national monitoring network was deployed in 1999. [7] Based on a 1-hour daily maximum concentration of 100 ppb. [8] Based on 3-month rolling average of 0.15 $\mu g/m^3$.

Source: U.S. Environmental Protection Agency, "Air Quality Trends," <www.epa.gov/air-trends>, accessed January 2024.

Table 420. Selected Air Pollutant Emissions: 1990 to 2023

[In thousands of tons (4,320 represents 4,320,000). For documentation regarding the data, see <www.epa.gov/air-emissions-inventories/national-emissions-inventory-nei> and <www.epa.gov/air-emissions-inventories/trends-procedural-documentation>]

Year	Ammonia	Carbon monoxide	Nitrogen oxide	PM-10 [1]	PM-2.5 [1] Total [2]	PM-2.5 [1] Black carbon [3]	PM-2.5 [1] Organic carbon [3]	Sulfur dioxide	VOCs [4]
1990	4,320	154,188	25,527	27,753	7,560	(NA)	(NA)	23,077	24,108
2000	4,907	114,467	22,598	23,747	7,288	(NA)	(NA)	16,347	17,512
2010	4,439	60,247	15,340	16,239	4,616	364	1,186	6,938	13,596
2015	4,546	56,296	11,114	16,146	4,667	278	1,305	3,502	14,148
2016	4,605	54,623	10,037	16,734	4,872	319	1,486	2,696	14,113
2017	4,739	61,422	9,505	17,672	5,524	263	1,574	2,508	15,716
2018	5,218	62,783	9,109	17,130	5,606	262	1,593	2,411	16,156
2019	5,142	48,836	8,602	15,422	4,440	234	1,269	1,965	12,718
2020	5,485	62,437	7,816	16,782	5,822	377	2,106	1,845	16,630
2021	5,142	60,979	7,829	20,014	8,442	556	3,448	2,068	17,920
2022	5,040	49,815	7,339	17,514	6,111	335	2,258	1,853	14,642
2023	5,036	48,840	6,916	17,509	6,101	330	2,254	1,701	14,498

NA Not available. [1] PM = Particulate Matter; PM-10 is equal to or less than ten micrometers in diameter; PM-2.5 is equal to or less than 2.5 microns effective diameter. [2] Includes other types not shown separately. [3] Speciated from PM-2.5. [4] Volatile organic compounds.

Source: U.S. Environmental Protection Agency, "National Emissions Inventory (NEI) Air Pollutant Emissions Trends Data, 1970-2023," <www.epa.gov/air-emissions-inventories/air-pollutant-emissions-trends-data>, accessed February 2024.

Table 421. Air Pollutant Emissions by Selected Pollutant and Source: 2023

[In thousands of tons (5,036 represents 5,036,000). See headnote, Table 420]

Source	Ammonia	Carbon monoxide	Nitrogen oxide	PM-10 [1]	PM-2.5 [1] Total [2]	PM-2.5 [1] Black carbon [3]	PM-2.5 [1] Organic carbon [3]	Sulfur dioxide	VOCs [4]
Total emissions	**5,036**	**48,840**	**6,916**	**17,509**	**6,101**	**330**	**2,254**	**1,701**	**14,498**
Fuel combustion, stationary sources	103	4,764	2,235	930	862	47	370	1,014	629
Electric utilities	16	472	773	124	107	6	19	747	29
Industrial	15	868	950	287	244	12	85	238	113
Other fuel combustion	71	3,424	512	519	512	29	266	29	487
Industrial and other processes	155	3,140	1,204	1,122	662	34	241	482	7,158
Chemical and allied product mfg	22	128	31	17	13	–	1	72	70
Metals processing	1	359	57	40	29	–	2	53	21
Petroleum and related industries	1	703	759	30	25	1	5	194	3,018
Other	36	463	271	742	349	9	146	127	376
Solvent utilization	–	2	1	5	4	–	1	–	2,908
Storage and transport	1	6	3	34	14	–	1	1	570
Waste disposal and recycling	93	1,480	83	254	227	24	85	35	195
Highway vehicles	188	13,006	1,666	191	63	24	16	11	824
Off highway [5]	3	11,632	1,557	100	94	28	36	18	1,000
Miscellaneous [6]	4,588	16,298	254	15,167	4,420	197	1,590	176	4,886

– Rounds to zero. [1] See footnote 1, Table 420. [2] Includes other types not shown separately. [3] Black and organic carbon portions of particulate matter 2.5 (speciated from PM-2.5). [4] Volatile organic compounds. [5] Includes emissions from farm tractors and other farm machinery, construction equipment, industrial machinery, recreational marine vessels, and small general utility engines such as lawn mowers. [6] Includes emissions from forest fires and other kinds of burning, various agricultural activities, fugitive dust from paved and unpaved roads, other construction and mining activities, and natural sources.

Source: U.S. Environmental Protection Agency, "National Emissions Inventory (NEI) Air Pollutant Emissions Trends Data, 1970-2023," <www.epa.gov/air-emissions-inventories/air-pollutant-emissions-trends-data>, accessed February 2024.

Table 422. Greenhouse Gas Emissions by Type and Source: 1990 to 2022

[In millions of metric tons of carbon dioxide equivalent (MMT CO2 Eq.). 6,536.9 represents 6,536,900,000. MMT CO2 Eq. weights each gas by its global warming potential (GWP) value. GWP is a quantified measure of the globally averaged relative radiative forcing impacts of a particular greenhouse gas. The reference gas used is CO2; therefore, GWP-weighted emissions are measured in MMT CO2 Eq. See source for details]

Type and/or source	1990	2000	2010	2018	2019	2020	2021	2022
Total emissions	**6,536.9**	**7,419.9**	**7,066.0**	**6,752.7**	**6,590.1**	**6,001.8**	**6,328.8**	**6,343.2**
BY SOURCE								
Energy	5,381.0	6,242.1	5,919.3	5,570.0	5,422.4	4,862.6	5,173.3	5,199.8
Industrial processes and product use [1]	368.8	411.3	364.7	367.2	371.9	367.9	381.6	383.2
Sulfur hexafluoride (SF6)	37.9	26.5	11.6	7.6	8.4	8.1	8.5	7.6
Hydrofluorocarbons (HFCs)	47.7	114.1	151.9	163.9	168.2	170.3	177.0	182.8
Perfluorocarbons (PFCs)	39.5	28.6	6.8	7.4	7.3	6.6	6.3	6.7
Agriculture	551.1	566.1	599.0	642.4	620.1	599.7	604.8	593.4
Waste	235.9	200.3	183.1	173.2	175.8	171.7	169.2	166.9
Land use, land-use change, and forestry [2]	58.0	63.1	55.2	62.8	58.0	68.4	72.9	67.6
Net flux from land use, land use change, and forestry [3]	-976.7	-983.7	-886.3	-915.5	-863.6	-904.4	-910.6	-854.2
Net emissions (sources and sinks) [4]	5,560.2	6,436.2	6,179.7	5,837.3	5,726.6	5,097.4	5,418.2	5,489.0
BY TYPE AND SOURCE								
Carbon dioxide (CO2), total [5]	**5,131.6**	**6,023.1**	**5,668.7**	**5,362.2**	**5,234.5**	**4,689.0**	**5,017.2**	**5,053.0**
Energy	4,910.9	5,797.0	5,486.6	5,190.6	5,059.1	4,520.2	4,840.7	4,875.5
Fossil fuel combustion	4,752.2	5,620.9	5,339.6	4,988.2	4,852.6	4,341.7	4,654.3	4,699.4
Transportation	1,468.9	1,792.2	1,696.6	1,813.1	1,816.6	1,572.8	1,753.5	1,751.3
Electricity	1,820.0	2,296.2	2,258.6	1,753.4	1,606.7	1,439.6	1,540.9	1,531.7
Industrial	876.5	887.2	791.1	810.5	809.8	762.0	780.5	801.1
Residential	338.6	371.7	334.5	338.9	342.9	314.8	318.0	334.1
Commercial	228.3	236.5	224.3	246.3	251.7	229.3	237.5	258.7
Biomass (wood) [6]	215.2	218.1	215.5	220.0	217.7	190.6	192.5	195.3
Industrial processes and product use	213.7	218.6	173.3	164.4	168.2	160.7	168.8	168.9
Agriculture	7.1	7.6	8.6	7.2	7.2	8.0	7.6	8.6
Land use, land-use change, and forestry (sink)	-1,034.7	-1,046.8	-941.6	-978.3	-921.6	-972.8	-983.4	-921.8
Methane (CH4), total [5]	**871.7**	**815.7**	**807.6**	**771.5**	**754.3**	**735.3**	**720.5**	**702.4**
Energy	409.0	369.9	372.4	336.2	321.7	305.3	293.3	282.4
Industrial processes and product use	0.1	0.1	–	–	–	–	–	–
Agriculture	241.7	264.2	272.1	285.0	280.2	282.4	281.8	276.8
Land use, land-use change, and forestry	53.1	55.7	50.8	55.5	52.5	59.3	62.1	58.4
Waste management	220.9	181.5	163.0	150.2	152.4	147.6	145.3	143.2
Nitrous oxide (N2O), total	**408.2**	**410.9**	**418.3**	**439.5**	**416.4**	**391.2**	**398.2**	**389.7**
Energy	61.2	75.2	60.0	43.2	41.6	37.1	39.2	41.9
Industrial processes and product use	29.6	22.6	19.9	23.1	18.7	20.8	19.7	16.1
Agriculture	302.3	294.2	318.3	350.2	332.6	309.2	315.3	308.0
Land use, land-use change, and forestry	4.8	7.3	4.4	7.3	5.5	9.1	10.7	9.1
Waste management	15.1	18.9	20.0	23.0	23.4	24.1	23.9	23.7

– Represents or rounds to zero. [1] Total includes items not shown separately. [2] Land use, land-use change, and forestry (LULUCF) emissions of CH4 and N2O are reported separately from gross emissions totals. [3] The net LULUCF flux total includes CH4 and N2O emissions plus net LULUCF carbon stock changes. [4] Net emissions total includes emissions and sinks from removals from LULUCF. [5] A methodology refinement for emissions from methanol production was implemented. CH4 emissions from methanol production for every year in the time series are now included in the CO2 emissions estimates to avoid double counting, please see source for more information. [6] Emissions from wood biomass consumption are not included specifically in energy sector totals. Net carbon fluxes from changes in biogenic carbon reservoirs are accounted for in the estimates for land use, land-use change, and forestry.

Source: U.S. Environmental Protection Agency, *Inventory of U.S. Greenhouse Gas Emissions and Sinks, 1990-2022*, April 2024. See also <www.epa.gov/ghgemissions/inventory-us-greenhouse-gas-emissions-and-sinks>.

Table 423. Carbon Dioxide Emissions from Fossil Fuel Combustion by Fuel Type and Sector: 1990 to 2022

[In millions of metric tons of carbon dioxide equivalent (MMT CO2 Eq.); 4,752.2 represents 4,752,200,000. See source for details on methodology]

Fuel and sector	1990	2000	2010	2015	2019	2020	2021	2022
Total [1]	**4,752.2**	**5,620.9**	**5,339.6**	**5,002.9**	**4,852.6**	**4,341.7**	**4,654.3**	**4,699.4**
Coal	**1,719.8**	**2,065.2**	**1,931.2**	**1,427.5**	**1,028.1**	**835.6**	**957.4**	**898.8**
Residential	3.0	1.1	–	–	–	–	–	–
Commercial	12.0	8.8	6.6	3.0	1.6	1.4	1.4	1.4
Industrial	157.8	128.5	94.2	69.8	49.4	43.0	43.0	43.0
Electricity generation	1,546.5	1,926.4	1,827.2	1,351.4	973.5	788.2	910.1	851.5
Natural gas	**998.6**	**1,218.6**	**1,273.1**	**1,455.4**	**1,649.2**	**1,615.7**	**1,622.1**	**1,706.8**
Residential	237.8	270.8	258.9	252.7	275.5	256.4	258.6	272.0
Commercial	142.0	172.5	168.0	175.4	192.9	173.5	180.4	192.3
Industrial	407.4	458.2	407.1	459.6	501.5	489.7	501.2	510.4
Transportation	36.0	35.7	38.2	39.4	58.9	58.7	65.2	70.2
Electricity generation	175.4	280.8	399.5	525.2	616.6	634.8	612.8	659.3
Petroleum	**2,033.3**	**2,336.6**	**2,134.9**	**2,119.7**	**2,174.9**	**1,890.0**	**2,074.4**	**2,093.4**
Residential	97.8	99.8	75.6	64.9	67.4	58.4	59.4	62.1
Commercial	74.3	55.3	49.7	66.4	57.2	54.4	55.7	65.1
Industrial	311.2	300.6	289.8	263.5	258.9	229.3	236.3	247.6
Transportation	1,432.9	1,756.6	1,658.5	1,679.0	1,757.7	1,514.2	1,688.4	1,681.1
Electricity generation	97.5	88.5	31.4	23.7	16.2	16.2	17.7	20.5

– Represents zero. [1] Includes data for geothermal energy-related carbon dioxide emissions and U.S. territories, not shown separately.

Source: U.S. Environmental Protection Agency, *Inventory of U.S. Greenhouse Gas Emissions and Sinks, 1990-2022*, April 2024. See also <www.epa.gov/ghgemissions/inventory-us-greenhouse-gas-emissions-and-sinks>.

Table 424. Air Pollution—Air Quality Index Days at Unhealthy Levels by Selected Metropolitan Statistical Area: 1980 to 2022

[Number of days with AQI (Air Quality Index) values greater than 100 at monitoring sites. AQI integrates information on 6 major pollutants (particulate matter less than 10 microns in diameter, particulate matter less than 2.5 microns in diameter, sulfur dioxide, carbon monoxide, ozone, and nitrogen dioxide) across an entire monitoring network into a single number that represents the worst daily air quality experienced in an urban area. Beginning in 2000, data include particulate matter 2.5 micron in diameter (PM 2.5). An AQI greater than 100 indicates that at least 1 criteria pollutant exceeded air quality standards on a given day; therefore, air quality would be in the unhealthful range on that day. Based on data from the Environmental Protection Agency's Air Quality System database]

Metropolitan statistical area	1980	1990	2000	2010	2016	2017	2018	2019	2020	2021	2022
Akron, OH	55	37	30	18	1	0	1	3	4	3	4
Albany-Schenectady-Troy, NY	32	13	7	9	3	0	3	0	3	2	0
Albuquerque, NM	51	26	35	5	3	4	24	4	10	21	8
Allentown-Bethlehem-Easton, PA	80	30	33	27	11	1	5	4	1	4	0
Atlanta-Sandy Springs-Roswell, GA	85	109	115	47	32	11	10	19	3	8	8
Austin-Round Rock, TX	19	20	35	10	1	4	9	2	2	1	2
Bakersfield, CA	122	176	204	125	116	139	130	95	130	128	23
Baltimore-Columbia-Towson, MD	127	72	59	53	24	15	16	13	3	15	2
Baton Rouge, LA	67	71	87	35	9	8	19	9	6	5	10
Birmingham-Hoover, AL	63	64	108	30	11	3	4	15	3	5	3
Boston-Cambridge-Newton, MA-NH	75	31	18	10	7	5	5	1	0	5	0
Bradenton-Sarasota-Venice, FL	3	13	32	6	0	2	2	2	0	0	0
Bridgeport-Stamford-Norwalk, CT	223	43	31	29	23	16	21	21	13	19	4
Buffalo-Cheektowaga-Niagara Falls, NY	40	23	11	9	6	1	3	0	2	2	2
Charleston-North Charleston, SC	33	17	21	2	5	1	0	1	1	0	2
Charlotte-Concord-Gastonia, NC-SC	119	82	80	38	9	5	10	18	2	3	3
Chicago-Naperville-Joliet, IL-IN-WI	107	89	62	35	28	25	26	13	24	28	13
Cincinnati-Middletown, OH-KY-IN	106	59	44	45	18	9	13	9	7	8	6
Cleveland-Elyria, OH	45	34	55	41	14	6	13	7	11	8	6
Columbia, SC	84	67	58	6	5	2	1	2	1	2	0
Columbus, OH	73	34	41	23	10	3	3	1	3	0	3
Dallas-Fort Worth-Arlington, TX	97	67	75	28	18	24	36	29	24	31	32
Dayton, OH	49	25	31	25	7	3	5	0	4	1	3
Denver-Aurora-Lakewood, CO	144	25	51	38	29	40	57	22	34	67	35
Detroit-Warren-Dearborn, MI	73	32	32	22	18	12	14	12	19	9	10
El Paso, TX	27	40	42	16	6	23	17	13	19	19	15
Fresno, CA	167	138	195	87	105	120	98	66	99	82	32
Grand Rapids-Wyoming, MI	34	32	14	5	10	0	4	0	8	5	4
Hartford-West Hartford-East Hartford, CT	91	29	24	15	16	9	10	8	2	15	1
Hilo, HI	0	0	0	15	5	0	14	0	0	0	0
Houston-Sugarland-Baytown, TX	131	93	88	44	23	25	35	31	24	30	18
Indianapolis-Carmel, IN	101	40	97	23	12	7	13	5	7	7	10
Jacksonville, FL	27	22	32	5	0	1	5	1	3	0	0
Kansas City, MO-KS	81	18	56	23	7	7	13	1	5	13	0
Knoxville, TN	63	63	86	40	14	1	2	3	0	6	1
Las Vegas-Paradise, NV	121	73	56	33	26	29	49	5	25	34	8
Los Angeles-Long Beach-Anaheim, CA	287	234	178	115	108	122	110	91	142	98	33
Louisville/Jefferson County, KY-IN	161	43	51	39	19	6	11	4	7	7	2
Madison, WI	48	6	8	4	3	0	2	0	5	1	0
Memphis, TN-MS-AR	85	64	68	24	8	4	11	5	4	7	9
Miami-Fort Lauderdale-West Palm Beach, FL	90	9	20	5	6	8	4	2	2	3	2
Milwaukee-Waukesha-West Allis, WI	38	28	17	14	9	8	9	3	7	12	5
Minneapolis-St. Paul-Bloomington, MN-WI	50	11	24	12	4	1	5	1	3	8	0
Nashville-Davidson-Murfreesboro-Franklin, TN	31	77	76	28	6	1	7	1	2	5	4
New Haven-Milford, CT	48	40	27	17	14	12	14	14	13	14	1
New Orleans-Metairie, LA	29	36	66	16	4	2	5	1	0	3	3
New York-Newark-Jersey City, NY-NJ-PA	168	89	65	61	30	19	27	16	11	21	11
Oklahoma City, OK	32	21	36	11	3	7	12	2	5	10	8
Omaha-Council Bluffs, NE-IA	78	8	17	11	2	0	5	0	2	5	1
Orlando-Kissimmee-Sanford, FL	12	23	33	8	1	3	3	6	0	0	0
Oxnard-Thousand Oaks-Ventura, CA	161	139	84	18	9	33	17	9	26	10	4
Philadelphia-Camden-Wilmington, PA-NJ-DE-MD	147	83	62	48	18	21	19	16	8	15	4
Phoenix-Mesa-Scottsdale, AZ	105	59	167	59	75	95	85	54	230	237	83
Pittsburgh, PA	94	41	63	61	28	19	15	12	12	9	4
Portland-Vancouver-Hillsboro, OR-WA	21	18	12	3	2	16	10	3	14	1	0
Providence-Warwick, RI-MA	63	32	24	14	6	7	13	2	4	4	3
Richmond, VA	63	45	35	25	4	1	2	0	0	3	1
Riverside-San Bernardino-Ontario, CA	243	250	204	162	161	174	173	145	176	166	93
Sacramento-Arden-Arcade-Roseville, CA	110	124	105	42	59	56	57	20	50	58	17
St. Louis, MO-IL	183	61	52	46	19	12	19	9	11	15	11
Salt Lake City, UT	87	11	52	24	28	48	43	17	21	48	20
San Antonio, TX	34	17	23	11	6	6	11	6	10	12	3
San Diego-Carlsbad, CA	209	191	97	25	42	62	35	25	49	16	7
San Francisco-Oakland-Hayward, CA	49	20	29	14	15	16	19	9	22	10	2
San Jose-Sunnyvale-Santa Clara, CA	56	48	50	13	6	12	18	4	22	7	2
San Juan-Carolina-Caguas, PR	0	0	16	0	13	7	14	19	18	13	2
Scranton-Wilkes-Barre-Hazleton, PA	59	25	15	9	4	0	1	0	0	1	0
Seattle-Tacoma-Bellevue, WA	46	22	28	3	3	24	16	2	14	7	7
Tampa-St. Petersburg-Clearwater, FL	37	33	52	10	3	3	5	5	3	1	1
Toledo, OH	48	26	19	8	5	4	10	1	8	5	5
Tucson, AZ	120	30	23	5	4	7	11	2	13	14	8
Tulsa, OK	78	46	41	8	3	2	11	2	2	10	13
Washington-Arlington-Alexandria, DC-VA-MD-WV	110	87	64	50	16	8	10	11	3	10	4
Wichita, KS	14	12	27	13	1	0	0	0	6	5	2
Youngstown-Warren-Boardman, OH	100	35	26	16	6	4	5	0	4	3	4

Source: U.S. Bureau of Transportation Statistics, "National Transportation Statistics," <www.bts.gov/topics/national-transportation-statistics>, accessed January 2024.

Table 425. Municipal Solid Waste Generation, Materials Recovery, Recycling, Combustion With Energy Recovery, and Discards: 1980 to 2018

[In millions of tons (151.6 represents 151,600,000), except as indicated. Covers post-consumer residential, commercial, and institutional solid wastes that comprise the major portion of typical municipal collections. Excludes mining, agricultural and industrial processing, demolition and construction wastes, sewage sludge, junked autos, and obsolete equipment wastes. Based on material-flows estimating procedure and wet weight as generated]

Item and material	1980	1990	2000	2010	2015	2017	2018
Waste generated	**151.6**	**208.3**	**243.5**	**251.1**	**262.1**	**268.7**	**292.4**
Per person per day (lb.)	3.7	4.6	4.7	4.5	4.5	4.5	4.9
Total materials recovery	**14.5**	**33.2**	**69.5**	**85.4**	**91.0**	**94.0**	**94.0**
Per person per day (lb.)	0.4	0.7	1.4	1.5	1.6	1.6	1.6
Recovery for recycling	14.5	29.0	53.0	65.3	67.6	67.0	69.1
Per person per day (lb.)	0.4	0.6	1.0	1.2	1.2	1.1	1.2
Recovery for composting[1]	(Z)	4.2	16.5	20.2	23.4	27.0	24.9
Per person per day (lb.)	(Z)	0.1	0.3	0.4	0.4	0.5	0.4
Combustion with energy recovery	2.8	29.8	33.7	29.3	33.6	34.2	34.6
Per person per day (lb.)	0.1	0.7	0.7	0.5	0.6	0.6	0.6
Discards to landfill, other disposal	134.4	145.3	140.3	136.3	137.6	140.5	146.1
Per person per day (lb.)	3.2	3.2	2.7	2.4	2.4	2.4	2.4
PERCENT DISTRIBUTION OF GENERATION							
Materials in products	**71.8**	**70.3**	**73.4**	**70.9**	**70.1**	**70.3**	**64.9**
Paper and paperboard	36.4	34.9	36.0	28.4	26.0	24.9	23.1
Glass	10.0	6.3	5.2	4.6	4.4	4.6	4.2
Metals	10.2	7.9	7.8	8.9	9.1	9.4	8.8
Plastics	4.5	8.2	10.5	12.5	13.2	13.2	12.2
Rubber and leather	2.8	2.8	2.7	3.1	3.3	3.4	3.1
Textiles	1.7	2.8	3.9	5.3	6.1	6.3	5.8
Wood	4.6	5.9	5.6	6.3	6.2	6.8	6.2
Other	1.7	1.5	1.6	1.9	1.8	1.7	1.5
Other waste	**28.2**	**29.7**	**26.6**	**29.1**	**29.9**	**29.7**	**35.1**
Food waste	8.6	11.5	12.6	14.2	15.2	15.1	21.6
Yard trimmings	18.1	16.8	12.5	13.3	13.2	13.1	12.1
Miscellaneous inorganic wastes	1.5	1.4	1.4	1.5	1.5	1.5	1.4

Z Less than 5,000 tons or 0.05 percent. [1] Composting of yard trimmings, food scraps, and other municipal solid waste organic material. Does not include backyard composting.

Source: U.S. Environmental Protection Agency, *Advancing Sustainable Materials Management: 2018 Tables and Figures*, December 2020. See also <www.epa.gov/smm>.

Table 426. Environmental Industry—Revenues and Employment by Industry Segment: 2010 to 2023

[327.2 represents $327,200,000,000. Employment data are rounded to the nearest hundred. Covers approximately 30,000 private and public companies engaged in revenue-generating environmental activities. Based on sell-side revenue surveys and models in each segment]

Industry segment	Revenue (billion dollars)				Employment			
	2010	2020	2022	2023	2010	2020	2022	2023
Industry total	**327.2**	**446.2**	**502.7**	**531.5**	**1,671,800**	**1,820,000**	**1,953,900**	**(NA)**
SERVICES								
Analytical services [1]	1.9	2.0	2.2	2.2	17,000	15,800	16,600	(NA)
Wastewater treatment works [2]	47.6	71.0	76.8	80.5	177,800	221,900	237,300	(NA)
Solid waste management [3]	53.4	67.3	74.7	78.9	231,900	228,100	240,700	(NA)
Hazardous waste management [4]	14.3	15.6	17.0	17.3	69,600	67,600	72,200	(NA)
Liquid non-hazardous & specialty waste	9.8	12.1	13.8	14.5	55,700	61,400	68,900	(NA)
Remediation/industrial services	13.9	15.2	16.5	17.1	117,400	105,000	117,000	(NA)
Consulting and engineering	26.8	34.6	39.6	43.2	240,500	240,800	230,600	(NA)
EQUIPMENT								
Water equipment and chemicals	26.9	32.3	35.9	38.1	160,100	162,200	176,800	(NA)
Instrument manufacturing	5.4	8.2	9.1	9.5	37,100	50,100	55,000	(NA)
Air pollution control equipment [5]	14.9	15.8	16.0	16.4	96,400	86,200	86,500	(NA)
Waste management equipment [6]	12.7	15.4	16.3	17.0	86,600	92,100	96,200	(NA)
RESOURCES								
Water utilities [7]	52.8	81.3	87.7	91.9	208,900	273,100	290,700	(NA)
Resource recovery [8]	28.2	21.0	27.3	25.2	101,300	65,800	84,400	(NA)
Clean energy systems and power [9]	18.7	54.3	69.9	79.8	71,500	149,900	181,000	(NA)

NA Not available. [1] Covers environmental laboratory testing and services. [2] Mostly revenues collected by municipal entities for sewage or wastewater plants. [3] Covers public & private sector collection, transportation, transfer stations, disposal, landfill ownership and management for solid waste and recyclables. [4] Transportation and disposal of hazardous, medical, and nuclear waste. [5] Includes stationary and mobile sources. [6] Equipment for handling, storing or transporting solid, liquid or hazardous waste. Includes recycling/remediation equipment. [7] Revenues generated from the sale of water, majority in public sector. [8] Revenues generated from the sale of recovered metals, paper, plastic, etc. [9] Revenues generated from the sale of equipment and systems and electricity.

Source: Environmental Business International, Inc., San Diego, CA, publisher of *Environmental Business Journal*; © 2024 EBI Inc. See also <ebionline.org>.

Table 427. Toxic Chemical Releases and Transfers by Media: 2011 to 2022

[In millions of pounds (4,125.9 represents 4,125,900,000), except as indicated. Based on reports filed to the Toxic Release Inventory (TRI) Program, as required by Section 313 of the Emergency Planning and Community Right-to-Know Act (EPCRA). The Pollution Prevention Act (PPA) of 1990 mandates collection of data on toxic chemicals that are treated on-site, recycled, and combusted for energy recovery. Owners and operators of facilities within specific North American Industry Classification System industries that have 10 or more full-time employees, and that manufacture, process, or otherwise use any listed toxic chemical in quantities greater than the established threshold in the course of a calendar year are covered and required to report. For trend analysis, a 2011 core list of must-be-reported chemicals is used. Includes carcinogens; persistent, bioaccumulative, toxic (PBT) chemicals; and dioxin and dioxin-like compounds. Does not include off-site disposal or other releases transferred to other TRI program facilities that reported the amounts as on-site disposal or other releases]

Media	2011	2015	2017	2018	2019	2020	2021	2022
Total facilities reporting (number).................	**21,924**	**22,382**	**22,082**	**22,273**	**22,121**	**21,623**	**21,498**	**21,721**
Total on- & off-site disposal or other releases.....	**4,125.9**	**3,682.6**	**3,936.7**	**3,680.7**	**3,362.8**	**3,030.2**	**3,205.6**	**3,194.3**
On-site releases............................	3,701.7	3,199.5	3,543.3	3,249.3	2,936.2	2,682.5	2,809.9	2,788.6
Air emissions [1]........................	808.6	677.5	597.9	605.4	584.9	535.6	557.9	553.6
Surface water discharges.................	222.9	199.2	192.9	194.6	200.7	193.8	197.2	195.7
Underground injection class I.............	197.8	209.2	197.5	210.4	177.0	171.3	191.7	176.3
Underground injection class II-V...........	0.2	0.8	1.9	2.0	1.8	1.5	1.5	6.3
RCRA subtitle C landfills [2]...............	69.4	78.4	86.1	89.6	72.1	73.1	84.0	94.6
Other landfills...........................	273.6	283.7	322.1	284.6	233.5	195.5	205.2	209.1
Land treatment/application farming.........	15.0	14.3	14.8	16.1	13.7	13.8	11.7	12.4
Surface impoundments....................	884.9	800.7	883.5	854.4	762.5	733.3	815.7	642.6
Other land disposal......................	1,229.5	935.6	1,246.7	992.3	889.9	764.7	745.2	898.1
Off-site releases.........................	424.2	483.1	393.4	431.4	426.6	347.7	395.7	405.7
Total transfers offsite for further waste management.	**3,724.5**	**3,658.1**	**3,704.7**	**3,875.1**	**3,727.6**	**3,399.1**	**3,614.4**	**3,562.9**
Transfers to recycling.....................	2,370.8	2,203.4	2,351.8	2,444.7	2,343.2	2,051.5	2,185.6	2,169.3
Transfers to energy recovery..............	354.7	412.7	404.5	418.4	434.7	473.8	478.7	435.0
Transfers to treatment...................	550.3	525.2	512.7	543.8	488.7	487.8	518.8	515.8
Transfers to POTWs (treatment) [3]........	242.0	212.9	228.6	207.7	193.4	180.8	196.9	204.5
Transfers to POTWs (other releases) [3]....	0.8	30.4	31.9	53.9	55.7	45.9	38.1	37.3
Transfers off-site for disposal or other releases......	447.8	485.9	403.2	412.3	403.4	337.9	391.2	405.0
Total production-related waste managed...........	**22,714.9**	**28,370.0**	**28,475.4**	**31,110.0**	**29,621.6**	**27,874.3**	**28,756.3**	**27,890.2**
Recycled on-site.........................	6,295.0	11,359.7	11,412.0	14,111.5	13,450.6	12,917.4	12,658.5	12,313.1
Recycled off-site.........................	2,367.8	2,202.6	2,350.1	2,443.2	2,341.7	2,050.9	2,185.1	2,167.6
Energy recovery on-site..................	2,110.7	2,451.8	2,451.4	2,582.7	2,439.2	2,294.6	2,407.0	2,360.7
Energy recovery off-site..................	354.9	411.8	402.9	417.7	434.3	473.2	478.7	434.4
Treated on-site..........................	6,899.7	7,718.1	7,377.5	7,299.5	7,074.8	6,587.7	7,304.9	6,883.3
Treated off-site..........................	524.0	524.4	511.4	542.8	488.7	485.5	517.1	514.9
Quantity disposed or otherwise release of on-/off-site...	4,162.8	3,701.6	3,970.0	3,712.6	3,392.2	3,065.0	3,205.0	3,216.1
Non-production-related waste managed..............	14.6	17.2	13.5	7.8	7.3	7.5	38.6	18.3

[1] Air emissions include both fugitive and point source. [2] RCRA=Resource Conservation and Recovery Act. [3] POTW (Publicly Owned Treatment Work) is a wastewater treatment facility that is owned by a state or municipality.

Source: U.S. Environmental Protection Agency, Toxic Release Inventory (TRI) Program, "TRI Explorer, 2022 National Analysis Dataset (released October 2023)," <enviro.epa.gov/triexplorer/tri_release.chemical>, accessed September 2024.

Table 428. Industrial Pollution—Toxic Chemical Releases by Industry: 2022

[In millions of pounds (3,194.3 represents 3,194,300,000). Based on 21,721 facilities. See headnote, Table 427]

Industry	NAICS [1] code	Total on- and off-site releases	On-site releases			Off-site releases/ transfers to disposal [3]
			Total [2]	Air emissions	Other surface impound- ments	
Total [4].............................	**(X)**	**3,194.3**	**2,788.6**	**553.6**	**633.5**	**405.7**
Natural gas processing.................	211	25.0	11.9	3.7	–	13.0
Coal mining...........................	2121	2.6	2.6	(Z)	0.1	(Z)
Metal mining..........................	2122	1,428.1	1,425.9	1.4	579.3	2.2
Electric utilities.......................	2211	233.6	203.2	63.9	17.2	30.5
Food/beverages/tobacco...............	311/312	150.0	134.3	49.1	0.2	15.7
Textiles..............................	313/314	2.0	1.7	0.8	–	0.2
Leather..............................	316	1.5	0.2	0.2		1.3
Wood products.......................	321	11.5	9.1	9.0	(Z)	2.4
Paper................................	322	137.6	131.9	101.2	1.9	5.8
Printing and publishing................	323/511	1.1	0.8	0.8	–	0.3
Petroleum............................	324	75.8	69.1	32.5	(Z)	6.8
Chemicals............................	325	460.4	385.4	162.6	9.5	75.0
Plastics and rubber...................	326	39.8	32.8	32.4	(Z)	7.0
Nonmetallic mineral products.........	327	24.6	20.8	17.7	0.1	3.7
Primary metals........................	331	293.8	139.2	23.2	24.1	154.6
Fabricated metals.....................	332	42.3	16.3	15.4	(Z)	26.1
Machinery............................	333	5.1	1.2	1.1	(Z)	4.0
Computers/electronic products........	334	5.6	2.9	1.3	–	2.8
Electrical equipment...................	335	10.0	1.7	1.6	(Z)	8.3
Transportation equipment..............	336	32.2	26.2	26.0	(Z)	6.1
Furniture.............................	337	3.5	3.4	3.4	–	0.1
Miscellaneous manufacturing.........	339	6.5	1.8	1.8	–	4.8
Chemical wholesalers.................	4246	3.8	0.8	0.8	–	3.1
Petroleum bulk terminals..............	4247	1.6	1.5	1.5	(Z)	0.1
Hazardous waste......................	562	159.5	138.7	0.3	(Z)	20.8

– Represents zero. X Not applicable. Z less than 50,000 lbs. [1] North American Industry Classification System, see text, Section 12. [2] Includes other on-site releases, not shown separately. [3] Includes off-site disposal to underground injection for Class I wells, Class II to V wells, other surface impoundments, land releases, and other releases, not shown separately. [4] Includes other industries not shown separately, and industries with no specific industry identified, and uses a double counting algorithm.

Source: U.S. Environmental Protection Agency, Toxic Release Inventory (TRI) Program, "TRI Explorer, 2022 National Analysis Dataset (released October 2023)," <enviro.epa.gov/triexplorer/tri_release.chemical>, accessed September 2024.

Geography and Environment 271

Table 429. Pollution—Toxic Chemical Releases by State and Outlying Area: 2022

[In millions of pounds (3,194.3 represents 3,194,300,000). Based on reports filed as required by Section 313 of the EPCRA. See headnote, Table 427]

State and outlying area	Total on- and off-site releases	On-site releases or other disposal Total[2]	Total air emissions	Other surface impoundments	Off-site releases/ transfers to disposal	State and outlying area	Total on- and off-site releases	On-site releases or other disposal Total[2]	Total air emissions	Other surface impoundments	Off-site releases/ transfers to disposal
Total[1]	3,194.3	2,788.6	553.6	633.5	405.7	MO	59.1	45.0	9.8	25.1	14.1
U.S. total	3,187.3	2,782.9	551.4	633.5	404.4	MT	52.5	51.8	2.1	38.5	0.6
AL	83.6	66.3	28.3	(Z)	17.3	NE	16.8	14.1	5.6	(Z)	2.7
AK	777.1	776.4	0.5	296.5	0.7	NV	368.3	361.7	0.7	109.4	6.5
AZ	62.6	61.3	1.7	23.9	1.3	NH	0.4	0.2	0.2	(Z)	0.2
AR	33.3	29.6	13.1	0.6	3.7	NJ	11.0	5.7	1.4	(Z)	5.3
CA	41.8	31.1	7.2	0.1	10.7	NM	11.8	10.7	1.1	0.4	1.1
CO	20.3	17.1	1.9	3.3	3.2	NY	15.9	12.0	3.7	2.6	3.9
CT	1.6	0.5	0.5	(Z)	1.0	NC	51.8	31.6	16.7	1.6	20.1
DE	6.7	6.5	0.5	(Z)	0.2	ND	41.8	36.9	22.5	2.7	4.9
DC	(Z)	(Z)	(Z)	(Z)	(Z)	OH	88.3	60.5	30.3	0.8	27.7
FL	47.3	42.7	17.0	(Z)	4.5	OK	34.5	31.3	18.2	0.2	3.2
GA	43.5	39.3	28.9	0.6	4.2	OR	19.6	16.2	11.6	(Z)	3.4
HI	2.6	2.4	1.7	(Z)	0.2	PA	56.0	32.4	12.0	(Z)	23.5
ID	42.7	41.3	4.9	12.6	1.4	RI	0.4	0.2	0.2	(Z)	0.2
IL	59.3	38.4	21.6	1.3	20.9	SC	39.7	32.7	18.5	4.7	7.0
IN	119.6	69.4	23.6	1.1	50.1	SD	8.6	8.4	2.3	(Z)	0.2
IA	33.1	26.7	18.5	0.5	6.4	TN	74.0	63.9	19.8	18.0	10.1
KS	26.1	19.7	9.0	1.7	6.4	TX	208.0	171.6	52.9	1.4	36.4
KY	56.6	33.8	15.4	0.1	22.8	UT	181.9	177.8	4.7	66.0	4.1
LA	130.7	118.9	46.9	2.1	11.8	VT	0.4	0.2	(Z)	–	0.2
ME	7.2	5.7	2.0	–	1.5	VA	29.9	25.3	13.7	(Z)	4.6
MD	5.6	3.1	1.0	(Z)	2.5	WA	14.8	9.8	5.1	(Z)	5.0
MA	3.8	0.7	0.7	(Z)	3.1	WV	22.1	19.9	11.3	0.8	2.2
MI	53.2	33.9	10.8	6.4	19.4	WI	25.2	14.1	5.8	(Z)	11.1
MN	22.4	17.0	9.4	4.8	5.5	WY	19.0	16.5	2.3	2.5	2.5
MS	54.9	50.5	14.1	3.1	4.5	PR	6.4	5.2	1.9	–	1.3

– Represents zero. Z Less than 50,000 lbs. [1] Total includes all states, Puerto Rico, and other outlying areas not shown separately. [2] Includes other types of release, not shown separately.

Source: U.S. Environmental Protection Agency, Toxic Release Inventory (TRI) Program, "TRI Explorer, 2022 National Analysis Dataset (released October 2023)," <enviro.epa.gov/triexplorer/tri_release.geography>, accessed September 2024.

Table 430. Hazardous Waste Sites on the Superfund National Priority List by State and Outlying Area: 2024

[As of August 16, 2024. Includes final sites listed on the National Priorities List for the Superfund program as authorized by the Comprehensive Environmental Response, Compensation, and Liability Act (CERCLA) of 1980 and the Superfund Amendments and Reauthorization Act (SARA) of 1986. Prior to 2022, data in this table included both final and proposed sites. For information on CERCLA and SARA, see <www.epa.gov/superfund/superfund-amendments-and-reauthorization-act-sara>]

State and outlying area	Total sites	Rank	Percent distribution	Federal	Non-federal	State and outlying area	Total sites	Rank	Percent distribution	Federal	Non-federal
Total[1]	1,339	(X)	(X)	157	1,182	Missouri	33	14	2.5	3	30
United States	1,317	(X)	(X)	155	1,162	Montana	18	23	1.4	–	18
Alabama	12	33	0.9	3	9	Nebraska	18	23	1.4	1	17
Alaska	6	44	0.5	5	1	Nevada	1	48	0.1	–	1
Arizona	10	38	0.8	2	8	New Hampshire	20	20	1.5	1	19
Arkansas	9	41	0.7	–	9	New Jersey	114	1	8.7	6	108
California	96	2	7.3	24	72	New Mexico	15	27	1.1	1	14
Colorado	20	20	1.5	3	17	New York	84	4	6.4	4	80
Connecticut	13	31	1.0	1	12	North Carolina	38	11	2.9	2	36
Delaware	17	25	1.3	1	16	North Dakota	–	51	–	–	–
Dist. of Columbia	1	48	0.1	1	–	Ohio	37	12	2.8	3	34
Florida	52	7	3.9	6	46	Oklahoma	9	41	0.7	1	8
Georgia	17	25	1.3	2	15	Oregon	14	29	1.1	3	11
Hawaii	3	46	0.2	2	1	Pennsylvania	91	3	6.9	6	85
Idaho	6	44	0.5	2	4	Rhode Island	12	33	0.9	2	10
Illinois	46	8	3.5	4	42	South Carolina	28	17	2.1	2	26
Indiana	40	10	3.0	–	40	South Dakota	2	47	0.2	1	1
Iowa	13	31	1.0	1	12	Tennessee	19	22	1.4	3	16
Kansas	14	29	1.1	1	13	Texas	55	6	4.2	4	51
Kentucky	10	38	0.8	1	9	Utah	12	33	0.9	5	7
Louisiana	15	27	1.1	1	14	Vermont	12	33	0.9	–	12
Maine	10	38	0.8	2	8	Virginia	29	16	2.2	11	18
Maryland	21	19	1.6	10	11	Washington	46	8	3.5	13	33
Massachusetts	32	15	2.4	6	26	West Virginia	11	37	0.8	2	9
Michigan	65	5	4.9	–	65	Wisconsin	36	13	2.7	–	36
Minnesota	25	18	1.9	2	23	Wyoming	1	48	0.1	1	–
Mississippi	9	41	0.7	–	9	Puerto Rico	19	(X)	(X)	1	18

– Represents zero. X Not applicable. [1] Total includes areas not shown separately.

Source: U.S. Environmental Protection Agency, "Superfund National Priorities List," <www.epa.gov/superfund>, accessed August 2024.

Table 431. Hazardous Waste Generated, Shipped, and Received by State and Other Area: 2021

[In thousands of tons (35,924.3 represents 35,924,300). Covers hazardous waste regulated under the Resource Conservation and Recovery Act (RCRA) of 1976 as amended. See source for data exclusions]

State and other area	Hazardous waste quantity			State and other area	Hazardous waste quantity		
	Generated	Shipped	Received		Generated	Shipped	Received
Total [1]	**35,924.3**	**8,090.9**	**5,967.5**	Missouri	139.4	89.2	217.0
United States	**35,910.1**	**8,076.5**	**5,967.1**	Montana	6.6	6.7	–
Alabama	888.3	235.0	510.3	Nebraska	27.7	39.9	39.7
Alaska	5.3	5.3	0.2	Nevada	19.2	25.9	104.9
Arizona	72.5	70.7	8.3	New Hampshire	3.2	3.2	–
Arkansas	888.2	265.6	332.8	New Jersey	221.3	226.2	165.7
California	218.9	280.6	116.1	New Mexico	3.8	5.1	2.3
Colorado	63.5	78.2	61.5	New York	266.6	144.9	44.2
Connecticut	35.1	34.9	14.1	North Carolina	137.7	155.4	29.0
Delaware	6.0	5.9	–	North Dakota	351.2	2.2	0.1
District of Columbia	1.0	1.0	–	Ohio	1,486.2	513.2	615.5
Florida	62.9	47.4	14.4	Oklahoma	82.7	75.0	161.7
Georgia	64.0	63.8	0.6	Oregon	64.9	62.8	46.5
Hawaii	541.9	1.0	(Z)	Pennsylvania	213.9	188.7	360.1
Idaho	5.6	7.0	23.4	Rhode Island	7.6	15.1	8.4
Illinois	379.0	186.2	182.9	South Carolina	174.0	179.2	305.7
Indiana	943.0	390.3	511.1	South Dakota	2.2	2.3	0.1
Iowa	53.7	53.0	0.2	Tennessee	212.1	72.9	128.9
Kansas	1,031.8	76.3	139.3	Texas	17,937.4	2,744.1	649.2
Kentucky	813.6	126.2	133.2	Utah	44.9	62.2	99.2
Louisiana	5,274.8	472.3	295.7	Vermont	1.8	3.5	2.2
Maine	2.7	2.8	0.7	Virginia	66.5	65.9	0.6
Maryland	32.3	35.5	43.4	Washington	114.3	94.6	39.2
Massachusetts	50.6	61.5	17.1	West Virginia	45.8	32.8	11.6
Michigan	317.1	317.2	394.1	Wisconsin	211.6	221.8	87.5
Minnesota	80.0	40.4	29.0	Wyoming	9.0	8.4	(Z)
Mississippi	2,227.1	177.1	19.5	Puerto Rico	12.9	13.1	0.2

– Represents zero. Z Less than 50. [1] Includes territories and areas not shown separately.

Source: U.S. Environmental Protection Agency, Office of Resource Conservation and Recovery, RCRAInfo Web, "Biennial Report," <rcrainfo.epa.gov/rcrainfoweb/>, accessed June 2023.

Table 432. Oil Spills in U.S. Waters—Number and Volume: 2000 to 2022

[Based on reported discharges of oil and petroleum based products into U.S. navigable waters, including territorial waters (extending 3 to 12 miles from the coastline), tributaries, the contiguous zone, onto shoreline, or into other waters that threaten the marine environment. Data are from the U.S. Coast Guard; see also *Polluting Incidents In and Around U.S. Waters, A Spill/Release Compendium: 1969–2011*]

Spill source	Number of spills					Spill volume (gallons)				
	2000	2010	2020	2021	2022	2000	2010	2020	2021	2022
Total	**8,354**	**3,008**	**2,194**	**2,220**	**2,118**	**1,431,370**	**207,712,793**	**181,275**	**449,151**	**167,469**
Vessel sources, total	5,560	1,508	1,284	1,274	1,233	1,033,643	894,934	73,010	53,398	80,189
Tankship	111	23	16	15	10	608,176	421,583	636	48	85
Tank barge	229	73	49	39	51	133,540	965	17,592	3,625	11,109
Other vessels [1]	5,220	1,412	1,219	1,220	1,172	291,927	472,386	54,782	49,725	68,995
Nonvessel sources, total	1,645	1,008	910	865	633	373,761	206,809,141	108,265	392,037	39,448
Offshore pipelines	4	34	18	9	9	17	4,627	548	219	45
Onshore pipelines	21	(NA)	(NA)	(NA)	(NA)	17,004	(NA)	(NA)	(NA)	(NA)
Other [2]	1,620	974	767	856	624	356,740	206,804,514	107,211	391,818	39,403
Unknown source	1,149	492	125	81	252	23,966	8,718	506	3,716	47,832

NA Not available. [1] Commercial vessels, fishing boats, freight barges, freight ships, industrial vessels, oil recovery vessels, passenger vessels, unclassified public vessels, recreational boats, research vessels, school ships, tow and tug boats, mobile offshore drilling units, offshore supply vessels, publicly owned tank and freight ships, and vessels not fitting any particular class (unclassified). [2] Deepwater ports, designated waterfront facilities, nonmarine land facilities, fixed offshore and inshore platforms, mobile facility, municipal facility, aircraft, land vehicles, railroad equipment, bridges, factories, fleeting areas, industrial facilities, intakes, locks, marinas, MARPOL reception facilities, nonvessel common carrier facilities, outfalls, sewers, drains, permanently moored facilities, shipyards, and ship repair facilities.

Source: U.S. Bureau of Transportation Statistics, "National Transportation Statistics," <www.bts.gov/topics/national-transportation-statistics>, accessed January 2024.

Table 433. Petroleum and Hazardous Waste Underground Storage Tanks, Releases, and Corrective Actions: 2010 to 2023

[For year ending September 30. EPA collects data from states and territories regarding Underground Storage Tank (UST) systems storing either petroleum or certain hazardous substances. Data shown are for UST systems that store substances identified as being hazardous under the Comprehensive Environmental Response, Compensation, and Liability Act (CERCLA). See <www.epa.gov/ust>]

Year	Active tanks	Closed tanks	Confirmed releases		Cleanups initiated [1]	Cleanups completed		Cleanups remaining
			Current year actions	Cumulative		Current year actions	Cumulative	
2010	597,333	1,748,204	6,328	494,997	470,460	11,591	401,874	93,123
2015	565,956	1,823,543	6,830	528,521	505,468	9,869	456,660	71,861
2019	549,583	1,931,246	5,375	550,897	536,957	8,358	493,589	57,308
2020	543,867	1,946,216	4,944	559,900	545,707	7,211	497,407	62,493
2021	542,333	1,952,817	4,991	564,767	550,956	7,271	502,786	61,981
2022	540,367	1,961,012	4,568	568,981	555,985	6,536	509,091	59,890
2023	538,454	1,975,507	4,354	573,296	560,463	6,596	515,859	57,437

[1] Cleanups initiated are cumulative. Even as a cleanup progresses and is completed, it is still counted in the cleanups initiated category.

Source: Environmental Protection Agency, "Underground Storage Tanks (USTs), UST Performance Measures," <www.epa.gov/ust/ust-performance-measures>, accessed January 2024.

Table 434. Highest and Lowest Temperatures by State Through 2023

[Data have been evaluated by the National Oceanic and Atmospheric Administration National Climatic Data Center, and/or by the State Climate Extremes Committee and determined to be valid. The data may come from sources other than official NOAA-supervised weather stations, but are archived, officially recognized observations]

State	Highest temperatures			Lowest temperatures		
	Station	Temperature (°F)	Date	Station	Temperature (°F)	Date
U.S.	**Greenland Ranch, CA**	**134**	**July 10, 1913**	**Prospect Creek Camp, AK**	**-80**	**Jan. 23, 1971**
AL	Centreville	112	Sept. 6, 1925	New Market	-27	Jan. 30, 1966
AK	Fort Yukon	100	June 27, 1915	Prospect Creek Camp	-80	Jan. 23, 1971
AZ	Lake Havasu City	128	June 29, 1994	Hawley Lake	-40	Jan. 7, 1971
AR	Ozark	120	Aug. 10, 1936	Gravette	-29	Feb. 13, 1905
CA	Greenland Ranch	134	July 10, 1913	Boca	-45	Jan. 20, 1937
CO	John Martin Dam	115	July 20, 2019	Maybell	-61	Feb. 1, 1985
CT	Danbury	106	[1] July 15, 1995	Coventry	-32	[1] Jan. 22, 1961
DE	Millsboro	110	July 21, 1930	Millsboro	-17	Jan. 17, 1893
FL	Monticello	109	June 29, 1931	Tallahassee	-2	Feb. 13, 1899
GA	Greenville	112	[1] Aug. 20, 1983	CCC Camp F-16	-17	Jan. 27, 1940
HI	Pahala	100	Apr. 27, 1931	Mauna Kea Observatory	12	May 17, 1979
ID	Orofino	118	July 28, 1934	Island Park Dam	-60	Jan. 18, 1943
IL	East St. Louis	117	July 14, 1954	Mount Carroll	-38	Jan. 31, 2019
IN	Collegeville	116	July 14, 1936	New Whiteland	-36	Jan. 19, 1994
IA	Keokuk	118	July 20, 1934	Elkader	-47	[1] Feb. 3, 1996
KS	Alton	121	[1] July 24, 1936	Lebanon	-40	Feb. 13, 1905
KY	Greensburg	114	July 28, 1930	Shelbyville	-37	Jan. 19, 1994
LA	Plain Dealing	114	Aug. 10, 1936	Minden	-16	Feb. 13, 1899
ME	North Bridgton	105	[1] July 10, 1911	Big Black River	-50	Jan. 16, 2009
MD	Frederick	109	[1] July 10, 1936	Oakland	-40	Jan. 13, 1912
MA	Chester	107	[1] Aug. 2, 1975	Chester	-35	[1] Jan. 12, 1981
MI	Stanwood	112	July 13, 1936	Vanderbilt	-51	Feb. 9, 1934
MN	Beardsley	115	July 29, 1917	Tower	-60	Feb. 2, 1996
MS	Holly Springs	115	July 29, 1930	Corinth	-19	Jan. 30, 1966
MO	Warsaw	118	July 14, 1954	Warsaw	-40	Feb. 13, 1905
MT	Medicine Lake	117	[1] July 5, 1937	Rogers Pass	-70	Jan. 20, 1954
NE	Minden	118	[1] July 24, 1936	Oshkosh	-47	[1] Dec. 22, 1989
NV	Laughlin	125	June 29, 1994	San Jacinto	-50	Jan. 8, 1937
NH	Nashua	106	July 4, 1911	Mt. Washington	-50	Jan. 22, 1885
NJ	Runyon	110	July 10, 1936	River Vale	-34	Jan. 5, 1904
NM	Waste Isolation Pilot Plant	122	June 27, 1994	Gavilan	-50	Feb. 1, 1951
NY	Troy	108	July 22, 1926	Old Forge	-52	Feb. 18, 1979
NC	Fayetteville	110	Aug. 21, 1983	Mt. Mitchell	-34	Jan. 21, 1985
ND	Steele	121	July 6, 1936	Parshall	-60	Feb. 15, 1936
OH	Gallipolis (near)	113	July 21, 1934	Milligan	-39	Feb. 10, 1899
OK	Altus	120	[1] Aug. 12, 1936	Nowata	-31	Feb. 10, 2011
OR	Pelton Dam	119	[1] June 29, 2021	Seneca	-54	[1] Feb. 10, 1933
PA	Phoenixville	111	[1] July 10, 1936	Smethport	-42	Jan. 5, 1904
RI	Providence	104	Aug. 2, 1975	Wood River Junction	-28	Jan. 11, 1942
SC	Columbia Univ. of SC	113	June 29, 2012	Caesars Head	-19	Jan. 21, 1985
SD	Fort Pierre	120	[1] July 15, 2006	McIntosh	-58	Feb. 17, 1936
TN	Perryville	113	[1] Aug. 9, 1930	Mountain City	-32	Dec. 30, 1917
TX	Monahans	120	[1] June 28, 1994	Seminole	-23	Feb. 8, 1933
UT	Saint George	117	[1] July 10, 2021	Strawberry Tunnel (East)	-50	Jan. 5, 1913
VT	Vernon	107	July 7, 1912	Bloomfield	-50	Dec. 30, 1933
VA	Balcony Falls	110	[1] July 15, 1954	Mountain Lake Bio. Stn.	-30	Jan. 21, 1985
WA	Hanford	120	[1] June 29, 2021	Winthrop	-48	[1] Dec. 30, 1968
WV	Martinsburg	112	[1] July 10, 1936	Lewisburg	-37	Dec. 30, 1917
WI	Wisconsin Dells	114	July 13, 1936	Couderay	-55	[1] Feb. 4, 1996
WY	Diversion Dam	115	[1] July 15, 1988	Riverside Ranger Stn.	-66	Feb. 9, 1933

[1] Also on earlier dates at the same or other places.

Source: U.S. National Oceanic and Atmospheric Administration, National Climatic Data Center, State Climate Extremes Committee, "Maximum and Minimum Temperature Records," <www.ncei.noaa.gov/access/monitoring/scec/records>, accessed April 2024.

Table 435. Highest Temperature of Record—Selected Cities

[In degrees Fahrenheit. Airport data, except as noted. Data for each city are shown for varying periods of record; see source for date ranges for each location]

State	Station	Jan.	Feb.	Mar.	Apr.	May	June	July	Aug.	Sept.	Oct.	Nov.	Dec.	Annual [1]
AL.....	Mobile	84	84	89	94	100	103	104	105	100	98	88	81	105
AK.....	Juneau	60	57	61	74	80	86	90	84	78	63	56	54	90
AZ.....	Phoenix	88	92	100	105	113	122	121	117	118	107	99	88	122
AK.....	Little Rock	83	85	91	95	98	107	112	114	106	98	86	81	114
CA.....	Los Angeles	95	95	98	106	102	112	108	105	113	108	100	92	113
CA. ...	Sacramento	76	78	88	95	105	115	114	112	109	104	87	74	115
CA. ...	San Diego	88	90	93	98	97	101	99	98	111	107	100	88	111
CA. ...	San Francisco	79	81	87	94	97	103	99	98	106	102	86	76	106
CO. ...	Denver	74	83	84	90	96	104	104	102	99	89	81	75	104
CT.....	Hartford	72	77	89	96	99	101	103	102	101	91	83	76	103
DE. ...	Wilmington	75	78	86	94	96	100	103	101	100	98	85	75	103
DC. ...	Washington Nat'l	79	82	89	95	99	104	105	105	101	98	86	79	105
FL. ...	Jacksonville	85	89	94	95	102	103	105	102	100	96	89	85	105
FL. ...	Miami	88	89	93	97	98	98	98	98	97	95	91	89	98
GA. ...	Atlanta	79	80	89	93	97	106	105	104	99	98	84	79	106
HI.	Honolulu	88	88	89	91	93	92	94	95	95	94	93	89	95
ID.	Boise	63	71	81	92	99	110	111	110	102	94	78	65	111
IL.	Chicago	65	72	88	91	97	104	104	101	99	91	78	71	104
IL.	Peoria	70	74	86	92	97	105	104	103	100	93	81	71	105
IN.	Indianapolis	71	77	85	89	95	104	105	102	100	92	81	74	105
IA......	Des Moines	67	75	91	93	99	103	106	108	101	95	81	69	108
KS.....	Wichita	75	87	89	96	102	110	113	111	108	97	86	83	113
KY.....	Louisville	77	82	86	91	95	105	106	105	104	97	85	76	106
LA.	New Orleans	83	85	89	92	97	101	101	102	101	97	88	85	102
ME. ...	Portland	67	68	88	92	94	98	100	103	95	88	74	71	103
MD. ...	Baltimore	75	79	89	94	100	103	106	105	100	99	86	77	106
MA. ...	Boston	74	73	89	94	96	100	103	102	100	90	83	76	103
MI.	Detroit	64	70	86	89	95	104	102	100	98	91	78	69	104
MI.	Sault Ste. Marie	47	49	83	85	90	93	97	98	95	81	75	62	98
MN. ...	Duluth	48	55	75	88	92	94	97	95	95	86	75	55	97
MN. ...	Minneapolis-St. Paul	58	63	83	95	100	103	105	102	98	90	77	68	105
MS. ...	Jackson	83	86	89	94	99	105	106	107	104	99	88	84	107
MO. ...	Kansas City	74	79	87	93	95	105	107	109	106	95	82	74	109
MO. ...	St. Louis	77	85	89	93	98	108	115	107	104	94	85	76	115
MT. ...	Helena	63	69	78	86	93	103	105	105	99	87	76	65	105
NE. ...	Omaha	69	78	91	97	101	105	110	107	103	95	83	69	110
NV. ...	Reno	71	75	83	90	97	104	108	105	102	93	77	71	108
NH. ...	Concord	69	74	89	95	97	98	102	101	98	90	80	73	102
NJ. ...	Atlantic City	78	76	87	94	99	106	105	103	99	96	81	77	106
NM. ...	Albuquerque	69	76	85	89	98	107	105	101	100	91	77	72	107
NY. ...	Albany	71	74	89	93	94	99	100	99	100	91	82	72	100
NY. ...	Buffalo	72	71	82	94	93	96	98	99	98	87	80	74	99
NY. ...	NYC Central Park	72	78	86	96	99	101	106	104	102	94	84	75	106
NC. ...	Charlotte	79	82	90	93	100	104	104	104	104	99	85	80	104
NC. ...	Raleigh	80	84	92	95	97	105	105	105	104	100	88	81	105
ND. ...	Bismarck	63	73	81	93	96	111	112	107	105	95	79	65	112
OH. ...	Cincinnati	74	79	84	89	93	102	104	102	102	95	82	75	104
OH. ...	Cleveland	73	77	83	88	93	104	103	102	101	93	82	77	104
OH. ...	Columbus	74	78	85	89	93	101	104	101	100	94	80	76	104
OK. ...	Oklahoma City	80	92	93	100	104	105	110	113	108	96	87	86	113
OR. ...	Portland	66	71	80	90	100	102	107	107	105	92	73	65	107
PA.....	Philadelphia	74	77	87	95	97	100	104	101	100	96	84	73	104
PA.....	Pittsburgh	75	78	83	89	91	98	103	100	97	89	82	74	103
RI.	Providence	70	72	85	98	96	97	102	104	100	88	81	77	104
SC. ...	Columbia	84	84	91	94	101	109	107	107	101	101	90	83	109
SD. ...	Sioux Falls	66	70	88	94	104	110	110	109	104	94	82	63	110
TN. ...	Memphis	79	81	86	94	99	104	108	107	103	98	86	81	108
TN.	Nashville	78	84	87	91	95	109	107	106	105	99	88	79	109
TX.....	Dallas	88	95	97	100	103	112	112	111	110	100	92	89	112
TX.....	El Paso	80	85	93	98	105	114	112	108	104	96	87	80	114
TX.....	Houston	84	91	91	95	99	107	104	109	109	96	89	85	109
UT.....	Salt Lake City	63	69	80	89	99	105	107	106	100	89	75	69	107
VT.....	Burlington	66	72	84	91	95	100	100	101	98	85	75	68	101
VA.....	Norfolk	80	82	88	97	100	101	105	104	99	95	86	82	105
VA.....	Richmond	81	82	91	96	100	104	105	104	103	99	86	81	105
WA. ...	Seattle	64	70	79	89	93	96	103	99	98	89	74	66	103
WA. ...	Spokane	62	63	72	90	97	105	108	108	98	87	70	60	108
WV. ...	Charleston	80	81	89	94	94	103	104	104	102	94	85	80	104
WI.	Milwaukee	63	71	84	91	95	101	103	103	98	89	77	68	103
WY. ...	Cheyenne	70	71	76	84	91	100	100	98	95	84	75	69	100
PR. ...	San Juan	92	96	96	97	96	97	95	97	97	98	96	94	98

[1] Represents the highest observed temperature in any month.

Source: U.S. National Oceanic and Atmospheric Administration, *Comparative Climatic Data for the United States Through 2020*. See also <www.ncei.noaa.gov/products/land-based-station/comparative-climatic-data>.

Table 436. Lowest Temperature of Record—Selected Cities

[In degrees Fahrenheit. Airport data, except as noted. Data for each city are shown for varying periods of record; see source for date ranges for each location]

State	Station	Jan.	Feb.	Mar.	Apr.	May	June	July	Aug.	Sept.	Oct.	Nov.	Dec.	Annual [1]
AL......	Mobile	3	11	21	32	43	49	62	59	42	30	22	8	3
AK......	Juneau	-22	-22	-15	6	25	31	36	27	23	11	-5	-21	-22
AZ......	Phoenix	17	22	25	34	40	50	61	60	47	34	25	22	17
AR.....	Little Rock	-4	-5	11	28	38	46	54	52	37	28	17	-1	-5
CA.....	Los Angeles	28	29	35	39	43	49	53	51	50	41	38	30	28
CA.....	Sacramento	20	23	26	31	34	41	48	48	42	35	26	18	18
CA.....	San Diego	29	36	39	41	48	50	55	57	51	43	38	34	29
CA.....	San Francisco	30	31	35	40	43	47	47	48	48	43	39	27	27
CO.....	Denver	-25	-25	-10	-2	22	30	43	41	17	3	-10	-25	-25
CT......	Hartford	-26	-21	-8	9	28	37	44	36	27	17	1	-14	-26
DE.....	Wilmington	-14	-6	2	18	30	41	48	43	36	24	14	-7	-14
DC.....	Washington Nat'l	-5	4	14	24	34	47	54	49	39	29	16	3	-5
FL......	Jacksonville	7	19	23	31	45	47	61	63	48	33	21	11	7
FL......	Miami	30	35	32	42	55	60	69	68	68	53	39	30	30
GA.....	Atlanta	-8	5	10	26	37	46	53	55	36	28	3	0	-8
HI.......	Honolulu	52	53	55	56	60	65	66	65	64	61	57	54	52
ID.......	Boise	-17	-15	6	19	22	31	35	34	23	11	-3	-25	-25
IL.......	Chicago	-27	-19	-8	7	24	36	40	41	28	17	1	-25	-27
IL.......	Peoria	-25	-19	-10	14	25	39	47	41	29	19	-2	-23	-25
IN.......	Indianapolis	-27	-21	-7	18	27	37	48	41	32	20	-2	-23	-27
IA.......	Des Moines	-24	-26	-22	9	28	41	47	40	28	14	-4	-22	-26
KS.....	Wichita	-12	-21	-2	15	31	43	51	48	31	18	1	-16	-21
KY.....	Louisville	-22	-19	-1	22	31	42	50	46	33	23	-1	-15	-22
LA......	New Orleans	14	16	25	32	41	50	60	60	42	35	24	11	11
ME.....	Portland	-26	-39	-21	8	23	33	40	33	23	15	3	-21	-39
MD.....	Baltimore	-7	-3	4	20	32	40	50	45	35	25	13	0	-7
MA.....	Boston	-12	-14	1	16	34	41	50	46	37	25	12	-11	-14
MI......	Detroit	-21	-15	-4	10	25	36	41	38	29	17	7	-10	-21
MI......	Sault Ste. Marie	-36	-37	-28	-2	18	26	36	29	25	16	-10	-31	-37
MN.....	Duluth	-39	-39	-29	-5	17	27	35	32	23	8	-23	-34	-39
MN.....	Minneapolis-St. Paul	-34	-32	-32	2	18	34	43	39	26	13	-17	-29	-34
MS.....	Jackson	2	10	15	27	36	47	51	54	35	26	17	4	2
MO.....	Kansas City	-17	-19	-10	12	30	42	51	43	31	17	1	-23	-23
MO.....	St. Louis	-18	-12	-5	22	31	43	51	47	32	22	1	-16	-18
MT.....	Helena	-42	-42	-30	1	17	30	36	28	18	-8	-39	-38	-42
NE.....	Omaha	-23	-21	-16	5	27	38	44	43	25	13	-9	-23	-23
NV.....	Reno	-16	-16	0	13	18	25	33	24	20	8	1	-16	-16
NH.....	Concord	-33	-37	-16	4	21	26	33	29	20	10	-5	-22	-37
NJ.....	Atlantic City	-10	-11	2	12	25	37	42	40	32	20	10	-2	-11
NM.....	Albuquerque	-17	-7	8	18	28	40	52	50	35	19	-7	-7	-17
NY.....	Albany	-28	-22	-21	10	26	35	40	34	24	16	-11	-22	-28
NY.....	Buffalo	-16	-20	-7	12	26	35	43	38	31	20	7	-10	-20
NY.....	NYC Central Park	-6	-15	3	12	32	44	52	50	39	28	5	-13	-15
NC.....	Charlotte	-5	5	4	21	32	45	53	50	39	24	11	2	-5
NC.....	Raleigh	-9	0	11	23	29	38	48	46	37	19	11	4	-9
ND.....	Bismarck	-44	-43	-31	-12	15	30	35	33	11	-10	-30	-43	-44
OH.....	Cincinnati	-25	-15	-11	15	27	39	47	43	31	16	0	-20	-25
OH.....	Cleveland	-20	-17	-5	10	25	31	41	38	32	19	3	-15	-20
OH.....	Columbus	-22	-13	-6	14	25	35	43	39	31	17	-4	-17	-22
OK.....	Oklahoma City	-4	-5	1	20	32	47	53	50	36	16	11	-8	-8
OR.....	Portland	-2	-3	19	29	29	39	43	44	34	26	13	6	-3
PA.....	Philadelphia	-7	-4	7	19	28	44	51	44	35	25	15	1	-7
PA......	Pittsburgh	-22	-12	-5	14	26	34	42	39	31	16	-1	-12	-22
RI.......	Providence	-13	-9	1	14	29	41	48	40	32	20	6	-10	-13
SC.....	Columbia	-1	5	4	26	34	44	54	53	40	23	12	4	-1
SD.....	Sioux Falls	-36	-31	-23	4	17	33	38	34	22	9	-17	-28	-36
TN......	Memphis	-4	-11	12	28	36	48	52	48	36	25	9	-13	-13
TN......	Nashville	-17	-13	2	23	34	42	54	49	36	26	-1	-10	-17
TX......	Dallas	0	7	11	31	39	53	60	56	36	27	17	1	0
TX......	El Paso	-8	1	14	21	31	46	57	56	41	25	1	5	-8
TX......	Houston	12	20	22	31	42	52	62	60	48	29	19	7	7
UT.....	Salt Lake City	-22	-14	2	15	25	35	40	37	27	14	-14	-15	-22
VT......	Burlington	-30	-30	-20	2	24	33	39	35	25	15	-2	-26	-30
VA.....	Norfolk	-3	8	18	28	36	45	54	49	45	27	20	7	-3
VA.....	Richmond	-12	-8	10	23	31	40	51	47	35	21	14	1	-12
WA.....	Seattle	0	1	11	29	28	38	43	44	35	28	6	6	0
WA.....	Spokane	-24	-24	-10	14	24	33	37	35	22	7	-21	-25	-25
WV.....	Charleston	-16	-12	0	19	26	33	46	41	34	17	6	-12	-16
WI......	Milwaukee	-26	-26	-10	12	21	33	40	44	28	18	-5	-20	-26
WY.....	Cheyenne	-30	-34	-21	-8	9	25	33	36	8	-1	-21	-28	-34
PR.....	San Juan	61	62	60	64	66	69	69	70	69	67	66	63	60

[1] Represents the lowest observed temperature in any month.

Source: U.S. National Oceanic and Atmospheric Administration, *Comparative Climatic Data for the United States Through 2020*. See also <www.ncei.noaa.gov/products/land-based-station/comparative-climatic-data>.

Table 437. Average Snow, Hail, Ice Pellets, and Sleet—Selected Cities

[Average in inches. Data for each city are shown for varying periods of record; see source for date ranges for each location. T denotes trace. Stations may show snowfall (hail) during the warm months]

State	Station	Jan.	Feb.	Mar.	Apr.	May	June	July	Aug.	Sept.	Oct.	Nov.	Dec.	Annual
AL.....	Mobile	0.1	0.1	0.1	–	–	–	–	–	–	–	–	0.1	0.4
AK.....	Juneau	25.3	18.2	13.6	2.4	–	–	–	–	–	1.0	12.5	20.6	93.6
AZ.....	Phoenix	–	–	–	–	–	–	–	–	–	–	–	–	–
AR.....	Little Rock	2.0	1.5	0.5	–	–	–	–	–	–	–	0.1	0.6	4.7
CA.....	Los Angeles	–	–	–	–	–	–	–	–	–	–	–	–	–
CA.....	Sacramento	–	–	–	–	–	–	–	–	–	–	–	–	–
CA.....	San Diego	–	–	–	–	–	–	–	–	–	–	–	–	–
CA.....	San Francisco	–	–	–	–	–	–	–	–	–	–	–	–	–
CO.....	Denver	7.4	7.7	11.7	7.9	1.6	–	–	–	1.3	4.0	8.1	7.5	57.2
CT.....	Hartford	13.1	12.7	8.9	1.3	–	–	–	–	–	0.3	1.8	10.0	48.1
DE.....	Wilmington	6.5	6.8	3.2	0.2	–	–	–	–	–	–	0.7	3.2	20.6
DC....	Washington Nat'l	5.3	5.3	2.1	–	–	–	–	–	–	–	0.6	2.7	16.0
FL.....	Jacksonville	–	–	–	–	–	–	–	–	–	–	–	–	–
FL.....	Miami	–	–	–	–	–	–	–	–	–	–	–	–	–
GA....	Atlanta	0.9	0.5	0.4	–	–	–	–	–	–	–	–	0.2	2.0
HI......	Honolulu	–	–	–	–	–	–	–	–	–	–	–	–	–
ID.....	Boise	6.3	3.5	1.6	0.5	0.1	–	–	–	–	0.1	2.1	5.8	20.0
IL.....	Chicago	11.3	9.2	6.1	1.5	–	–	–	–	–	0.3	1.9	8.2	38.5
IL.....	Peoria	6.9	6.0	3.8	0.7	T	–	–	–	–	0.1	1.8	6.0	25.3
IN.....	Indianapolis	7.8	6.2	3.5	0.4	–	–	–	–	–	0.2	1.4	5.7	25.2
IA.....	Des Moines	8.5	8.4	5.6	1.7	0.1	–	–	–	–	0.4	2.7	7.3	34.7
KS.....	Wichita	3.8	4.1	2.4	0.2	–	–	–	–	–	0.1	1.1	3.3	15.0
KY.....	Louisville	5.1	4.3	2.8	0.1	–	–	–	–	–	0.1	0.8	2.2	15.4
LA.....	New Orleans	–	–	–	–	–	–	–	–	–	–	–	0.1	0.1
ME....	Portland	19.1	17.4	12.9	2.8	0.1	–	–	–	–	0.2	2.8	14.7	70.0
MD....	Baltimore	5.9	6.7	3.4	–	–	–	–	–	–	–	0.6	3.1	19.7
MA....	Boston	13.0	12.4	8.0	1.2	–	–	–	–	–	0.1	1.1	8.0	43.8
MI.....	Detroit	11.9	10.7	6.5	1.6	–	–	–	–	–	0.1	2.5	9.7	43.0
MI....	Sault Ste. Marie	30.2	20.3	14.1	6.3	0.4	–	–	–	0.1	2.0	15.5	30.4	119.3
MN....	Duluth	17.1	12.9	13.8	7.6	0.8	–	–	–	0.1	1.9	12.2	17.1	83.5
MN....	Minneapolis-St. Paul	10.3	8.8	10.0	3.1	0.1	–	–	–	–	0.6	6.9	10.1	49.9
MS....	Jackson	0.4	0.3	0.1	–	–	–	–	–	–	–	–	0.2	1.0
MO....	Kansas City	5.3	5.5	2.2	0.5	–	–	–	–	–	0.2	1.2	4.1	19.0
MO....	St. Louis	5.5	4.4	3.7	0.3	–	–	–	–	–	–	1.2	3.6	18.7
MT....	Helena	8.1	6.3	6.7	4.3	1.1	0.1	–	0.1	1.2	2.3	6.1	7.9	44.2
NE.....	Omaha	7.0	7.0	5.5	0.9	0.1	–	–	–	–	0.3	2.3	5.8	28.9
NV.....	Reno	5.3	5.0	3.8	1.0	0.6	–	–	–	–	0.2	1.9	4.5	22.3
NH....	Concord	17.7	15.5	11.7	2.4	0.1	–	–	–	–	0.4	3.4	14.0	65.2
NJ.....	Atlantic City	5.9	6.2	2.3	0.3	–	–	–	–	–	–	0.3	2.8	17.8
NM....	Albuquerque	2.1	1.9	1.4	0.5	–	–	–	–	–	0.2	1.0	2.4	9.5
NY.....	Albany	16.2	13.8	11.2	2.3	0.1	–	–	–	–	0.2	3.7	13.9	61.4
NY.....	Buffalo	24.9	18.2	12.2	2.9	0.2	–	–	–	–	0.5	9.9	23.2	92.0
NY.....	NYC Central Park	7.8	8.8	5.0	0.8	–	–	–	–	–	–	0.8	5.5	28.7
NC....	Charlotte	1.9	1.5	0.9	–	–	–	–	–	–	–	0.1	0.5	4.9
NC....	Raleigh	2.5	2.3	1.0	–	–	–	–	–	–	–	0.1	0.8	6.7
ND....	Bismarck	8.3	7.2	8.4	4.1	0.7	–	–	–	0.1	1.7	6.7	8.5	45.7
OH....	Cincinnati	7.3	5.9	4.0	0.5	–	–	–	–	–	0.2	1.6	4.0	23.5
OH....	Cleveland	14.7	13.0	10.4	2.5	–	–	–	–	–	0.4	4.8	12.0	57.8
OH....	Columbus	8.8	6.8	4.3	0.8	–	–	–	–	–	0.1	1.9	5.5	28.2
OK....	Oklahoma City	2.6	2.3	1.2	–	–	–	–	–	–	–	0.5	1.9	8.5
OR....	Portland	2.9	1.3	0.4	–	–	–	–	–	–	–	0.4	1.3	6.3
PA.....	Philadelphia	6.8	7.2	3.7	0.3	–	–	–	–	–	0.1	0.5	3.6	22.2
PA.....	Pittsburgh	12.0	10.1	7.9	1.5	0.1	–	–	–	–	0.3	3.4	8.4	43.7
RI.....	Providence	10.2	10.1	6.8	0.7	0.1	–	–	–	–	0.1	1.0	7.0	36.0
SC.....	Columbia	0.5	0.7	0.2	–	–	–	–	–	–	–	–	0.2	1.6
SD.....	Sioux Falls	7.0	8.5	8.6	3.2	0.1	–	–	–	–	0.7	5.1	7.8	41.0
TN.....	Memphis	1.8	1.2	0.6	–	–	–	–	–	–	–	0.1	0.4	4.1
TN.....	Nashville	3.5	2.6	1.2	–	–	–	–	–	–	–	0.4	1.0	8.7
TX.....	Dallas	0.9	0.7	0.2	–	–	–	–	–	–	–	0.1	0.2	2.1
TX.....	El Paso	1.1	0.7	0.3	0.3	–	–	–	–	–	–	0.9	1.6	4.9
TX.....	Houston	0.1	0.1	–	–	–	–	–	–	–	–	–	0.1	0.3
UT.....	Salt Lake City	13.0	10.1	9.0	4.8	0.6	–	–	–	0.1	1.3	6.6	12.7	58.2
VT.....	Burlington	19.7	17.4	14.0	3.8	0.1	–	–	–	T	0.3	6.4	18.5	80.2
VA.....	Norfolk	3.0	2.6	0.9	–	–	–	–	–	–	–	–	1.0	7.5
VA.....	Richmond	4.9	3.8	2.1	0.1	–	–	–	–	–	–	0.3	1.9	13.1
WA....	Seattle	4.3	2.0	1.1	–	–	–	–	–	–	–	0.8	2.4	10.6
WA....	Spokane	12.9	7.8	3.6	0.6	0.1	–	–	–	–	0.3	5.5	11.7	42.5
WV....	Charleston	10.5	8.5	5.1	0.7	–	–	–	–	–	0.3	1.9	5.0	32.0
WI.....	Milwaukee	13.8	10.6	8.1	1.9	0.1	–	–	–	–	0.2	2.9	10.3	47.9
WY....	Cheyenne	5.9	7.4	11.1	10.4	3.4	0.2	–	–	0.7	4.4	7.2	7.1	57.8
PR.....	San Juan	–	–	–	–	T	–	–	–	–	–	–	–	–

– Represents zero.

Source: U.S. National Oceanic and Atmospheric Administration, *Comparative Climatic Data for the United States Through 2020.* See also <www.ncei.noaa.gov/products/land-based-station/comparative-climatic-data>.

Table 438. Cloudiness, Average Wind Speed, and Average Relative Humidity—Selected Cities

[Airport data, except as noted. Data shown for varying periods of record; see source for date ranges for each location. M = morning. A = afternoon]

State	Station	Cloudiness-average percent of days annually [1]	Average wind speed (miles per hour, m.p.h.)			Average relative humidity (percent)					
			Annual	January	July	Annual		Jan.		July	
						M	A	M	A	M	A
AL.........	Mobile	72.1	7.4	8.5	5.7	87	57	83	60	90	61
AK.......	Juneau	87.9	7.4	7.3	6.6	84	74	84	80	84	72
AZ.......	Phoenix	42.5	6.1	4.9	7.4	46	23	60	33	42	21
AR.......	Little Rock	67.7	7.0	7.7	6.1	84	57	80	61	87	56
CA........	Los Angeles	49.0	1.9	1.4	2.1	58	54	52	49	65	59
CA........	Sacramento	48.5	6.3	5.0	7.6	78	45	87	69	71	29
CA........	San Diego	60.0	6.3	5.1	7.0	74	63	69	58	80	67
CA........	San Francisco	56.2	10.5	6.8	13.0	87	69	87	66	91	71
CO........	Denver	68.5	8.0	7.8	7.9	50	43	53	54	46	35
CT........	Hartford	77.5	7.8	8.3	6.7	76	53	73	57	78	51
DE........	Wilmington	73.4	8.5	9.2	7.4	78	55	75	59	78	54
DC........	Washington Nat'l (VA)	74.0	8.9	9.5	8.0	74	53	71	55	76	53
FL.........	Jacksonville	74.2	6.7	7.0	5.8	88	56	87	57	89	59
FL.........	Miami	79.5	8.4	8.6	7.2	82	61	84	59	81	63
GA........	Atlanta	70.1	8.3	9.3	7.1	81	55	79	58	86	58
HI.........	Honolulu	75.3	10.3	8.5	11.9	74	56	79	61	70	53
ID.........	Boise	67.1	7.6	6.5	7.4	64	42	79	70	49	20
IL.........	Chicago	77.0	9.9	11.1	8.2	80	60	78	68	81	55
IL.........	Peoria	73.7	8.3	9.4	6.4	83	61	80	70	86	58
IN.........	Indianapolis	76.2	9.5	10.9	7.6	82	60	81	70	83	58
IA.........	Des Moines	71.5	9.8	10.6	8.3	81	60	78	68	84	58
KS........	Wichita	64.9	11.5	11.1	10.7	80	55	79	61	80	50
KY........	Louisville	74.8	7.8	9.0	6.6	79	56	78	64	81	56
LA........	New Orleans	72.3	8.0	9.1	5.9	87	62	84	65	90	65
ME........	Portland	72.3	7.9	8.1	6.9	78	59	75	59	79	60
MD........	Baltimore	71.2	7.2	7.9	6.2	77	53	73	56	78	52
MA........	Boston	73.2	11.5	12.6	10.2	72	57	69	58	72	56
MI.........	Detroit	79.5	9.4	11.0	7.9	80	59	80	69	80	53
MI.........	Sault Ste. Marie	81.9	7.7	7.8	6.7	84	65	80	73	87	61
MN........	Duluth	79.2	10.0	10.6	8.5	82	63	78	70	86	60
MN........	Minneapolis-St. Paul	74.0	9.6	9.6	8.7	79	59	77	68	81	54
MS........	Jackson	69.6	6.1	7.2	4.6	90	57	85	62	93	58
MO........	Kansas City	67.1	10.3	10.9	8.9	81	60	78	64	85	59
MO........	St. Louis	72.6	9.0	10.0	7.6	81	58	79	65	82	55
MT........	Great Falls	78.4	11.5	14.0	9.1	63	46	65	61	60	30
NE........	Omaha	69.6	10.0	10.3	8.6	81	59	79	66	85	57
NV........	Reno	56.7	6.4	4.6	7.2	63	31	75	51	54	18
NH........	Concord	75.3	6.0	6.6	5.1	80	53	76	58	81	51
NJ........	Atlantic City	74.2	8.7	9.5	7.4	80	56	77	58	81	57
NM........	Albuquerque	54.2	8.2	7.3	8.2	53	29	62	40	54	28
NY........	Albany	81.1	7.9	8.7	6.6	79	57	77	63	79	54
NY........	Buffalo	85.2	10.3	12.4	8.9	79	62	79	72	78	55
NY........	Central Park	71.0	6.1	7.6	4.7	70	54	67	56	73	54
NC........	Charlotte	70.4	6.4	6.6	5.7	81	52	78	54	84	55
NC........	Raleigh	69.9	6.5	6.8	6.1	83	53	79	53	86	56
ND........	Bismarck	74.5	9.4	9.2	8.5	81	58	77	71	85	49
OH........	Cincinnati	77.8	8.3	9.7	6.5	81	59	80	68	84	57
OH........	Cleveland	81.9	9.6	11.4	7.8	79	61	79	70	80	56
OH........	Columbus	80.3	7.6	9.2	6.0	80	58	78	68	82	55
OK........	Oklahoma City	61.9	11.3	11.6	9.8	80	55	78	59	82	51
OR........	Portland	81.1	7.4	9.2	7.1	82	59	84	76	77	44
PA........	Philadelphia	74.5	9.2	9.9	8.3	76	54	73	58	77	52
PA........	Pittsburgh	83.8	7.8	9.2	6.2	79	57	77	66	82	54
RI.........	Providence	73.2	9.2	9.7	8.4	75	55	71	57	76	56
SC........	Columbia	68.5	6.1	6.6	5.7	84	50	82	52	86	52
SD........	Sioux Falls	71.2	10.2	10.3	9.1	82	60	77	69	85	55
TN........	Memphis	67.7	8.1	8.9	6.8	80	56	77	62	84	57
TN........	Nashville	71.8	7.0	8.0	5.8	84	56	80	64	87	56
TX........	Dallas	63.0	9.4	8.9	8.9	78	54	76	58	77	49
TX........	El Paso	47.1	8.1	7.4	7.7	50	27	58	34	56	29
TX........	Houston	75.3	7.5	7.9	6.2	89	59	85	62	93	57
UT........	Salt Lake City	65.8	8.4	6.5	9.1	63	43	78	70	47	21
VT........	Burlington	84.1	8.2	9.2	7.0	76	58	74	64	77	53
VA........	Norfolk	71.2	9.5	10.0	8.5	78	57	74	58	80	59
VA........	Richmond	72.9	7.7	8.2	6.9	81	53	78	55	83	55
WA........	Seattle	80.5	7.9	8.4	7.3	82	63	83	76	79	48
WA........	Spokane	76.4	8.7	8.2	8.6	74	52	86	80	59	26
WV........	Charleston	82.2	4.6	5.8	3.5	83	56	78	62	89	58
WI........	Milwaukee	75.3	10.1	11.0	8.9	79	63	76	68	81	60
WY........	Cheyenne	71.2	12.2	14.3	9.9	61	45	55	51	63	38
PR........	San Juan	80.0	7.9	7.7	9.6	78	66	81	65	78	67

[1] Percent of days that are either partly cloudy or cloudy.

Source: U.S. National Oceanic and Atmospheric Administration, *Comparative Climatic Data For the United States Through 2020*. See also <www.ncdc.noaa.gov/ghcn/comparative-climatic-data>.

Table 439. Major U.S. Weather and Climate Disasters: 2023

[1,301.6 represents $1,301,600,000. Cost in CPI-adjusted dollars. Covers only weather and climate related disasters costing $1 billion or more. See source for more information]

Event	Description	Time period	Estimated cost (mil. dol.)	Deaths (number)
East Coast Storm and Flooding	Powerful east coast storm from FL to ME produced widespread impacts from heavy rainfall, flooding, high winds, and coastal erosion. The heavy rainfall and snowmelt were amplified by record-high temperatures in the Northeast.	Dec. 16-18, 2023	$1,301.6	5
Southern Hail Storms	Hail storms impact TX, OK, and MO. The most damaging impacts were in central TX including Austin, Georgetown, Round Rock, and Arlington on September 24.	Sept. 23-24, 2023	$1,694.5	—
Hurricane Idalia	Hurricane Idalia made landfall near Keaton Beach in the Big Bend region of FL as a strong Category 3 hurricane with winds of 125 mph. Idalia was the strongest hurricane to hit the Big Bend region in more than 125 years. Storm surge was about 8 feet above ground at Cedar Key, which caused heavy damage to homes, businesses, vehicles, and other infrastructure. Other Big Bend coastal communities were also inundated by storm surge. Idalia produced 5 to 10 inches of rainfall across the Big Bend region of FL and southeastern portions of GA and the Carolinas. Significant flooding was reported in downtown Charleston, SC and nearby Edisto Beach.	Aug. 29-31, 2023	$3,559.7	5
Minnesota Hail Storms	Numerous hail storms caused extensive damage across south-central MN. Golf ball to baseball-sized hail caused damage to the windows, siding, and roofs of many homes, vehicles, and businesses.	Aug. 11, 2023	$1,828.3	—
Hawaii Firestorm	Devastating wildfires destroyed the historic town of Lahaina on Maui Island of HI. Winds were enhanced from the strength and position of a high-pressure system located northwest of HI, which helped to exacerbate the wildfire as it spread on the island of Maui. This was the deadliest wildfire in the U.S. in over a century. Thousands of homes, vehicles, and businesses were destroyed.	Aug. 8, 2023	$5,665.0	100
Northeastern and Eastern Severe Weather	More than one thousand reports of high wind, severe hail or tornadoes across many Northeastern and Eastern states. August 7 was a prolific day of severe weather with damage reports from GA to NY. These storms caused impacts to many homes, vehicles, businesses, agriculture, and other infrastructure.	Aug. 5-8, 2023	$1,680.2	4
North Central and Eastern Severe Weather	Severe storms caused damage across several North Central and Eastern states. The state most impacted were NE, MO, IL, IN, and WI. High wind, severe hail, and tornadoes caused damage to many homes, vehicles, businesses, and agriculture assets.	July 28-29, 2023	$1,526.6	2
North Central and Southeastern Severe Weather	Severe storms caused damage across several North Central and Southeastern states. The states most impacted were MI, WI, OH, TN, and GA. Ping pong to golf ball-sized hail and high winds damaged many homes, vehicles, businesses, and other infrastructure.	July 19-21, 2023	$1,887.0	1
Northeastern Flooding and North Central Severe Weather	Severe storms brought devastation and flooding to portions of the Northeast, as areas reported up to eight inches of rain within a 24-hour period. Montpelier, Vermont received a record-breaking 5.28 inches of rain, flooding the city and damaging thousands of homes and businesses. Early estimates put the flood damage in West Point, NY at more than $100 ($103.0) million. There was also considerable damage to roads, bridges, and agriculture across the Northeast. Severe storms also caused high wind and hail impacts across WI, MN, and IL.	July 9-15, 2023	$2,230.4	10
Central Severe Weather	Severe storms caused damage across numerous Central states. Most impacted were MO, IL, and IN while there were also damage in many surrounding states. The damage to many homes, vehicles, businesses, and agriculture assets was largely from high wind and damaging hail but there were also scattered tornado impacts.	June 28- July 2, 2023	$1,976.8	3
Rockies Hail Storms and Central and Eastern Severe Weather	Severe hail storms across CO damaged many homes, vehicles. and injured approximately 100 people at a large outdoor concert. This multi-day outbreak of severe weather also produced more than 60 tornadoes across portions of WY, CO, MN, IN, KY, and AR.	June 21-26, 2023	$5,401.4	8
Central and Southern Severe Weather	Severe storms produce over one thousand reports of damaging weather across OK, TX, MS, GA, FL, AR, and OH. Over 70 preliminary tornadoes were reported including an EF-3 tornado in Louin, MS. The damage was most focused in OK.	June 15-18, 2023	$3,881.1	5
Southern Severe Weather	Numerous southern states including TX, LA, MS, AL, GA, TN, AR, SC, and FL were impacted by hail, tornadoes, and high winds.	June 11-14, 2023	$4,153.1	—
Typhoon Mawar	A Category 4 Typhoon struck Guam on May 24 battering the island for 15 hours until the early morning of May 25. Typhoon Mawar's wind speeds of up to 145 mph damaged residential and commercial buildings, vehicles, and infrastructure. Several U.S. military bases including Andersen Air Force Base sustained considerable damage. Guam's international airport also sustained flood damage.	May 24-25, 2023	$4,377.5	2
Texas Hail Storms	TX hail storms impact numerous counties across north central TX. Collin county in particular was impacted by golf ball to tennis ball sized hail causing damage to homes, vehicles, and businesses.	May 18-19, 2023	$1,690.0	—

See footnotes at end of table.

Table 439. Major U.S. Weather and Climate Disasters: 2023-Continued.
See headnote on page 279.

Event	Description	Time period	Estimated cost (mil. dol.)	Deaths (number)
Central and Eastern Tornadoes and Hail Storms	Dozens of tornadoes and severe hail storms from the eastern Rockies and across several central states. The most costly severe hail impacts were focused in CO while numerous tornadoes also impacted western KS, central OK, and eastern NE. TX and ND were also impacted from combination of high winds, hail, and isolated tornadoes.	May 10-12, 2023	$3,563.0	1
Central Severe Weather	Severe weather across numerous central states including MO, IL, IA, and IN. There was additional damage in KY, TN, SC, and TX. Large hail, high winds, and tornadoes caused widespread impact to many homes, businesses, vehicles, farms, and other infrastructure.	May 6-8, 2023	$2,222.5	1
Southern Severe Weather	Southern severe weather across TX, GA, and FL. Considerable hail and wind damage to many homes, businesses, vehicles, and other infrastructure.	Apr. 25-27, 2023	$1,372.8	–
Central Severe Weather	Severe hail, scattered tornadoes, and high winds caused damage across numerous central states. Central OK was impacted by a cluster of tornadoes. TX, MO, NE, KS, IA, IL, and WI were impacted by hail and high wind damage from severe storms.	Apr. 19-20, 2023	$3,078.4	1
Central and Southern Severe Weather	Several central and southern states including MO, AK, IL, TX, LA, and the FL Panhandle were impacted by hail, tornadoes, and high winds.	Apr. 15, 2023	$1,388.3	–
Fort Lauderdale Flash Flood	Historical rainfall and flash flooding inundated Fort Lauderdale and surrounding areas with over 25 inches of rainfall in less than 24 hours. This resulted in many flooded homes, vehicles, and businesses. The Fort Lauderdale Airport also closed on April 13 due to the flooding.	Apr. 12-13, 2023	$1,133.0	–
Central and Eastern Severe Weather	Severe storms produced large hail, high winds, and more than 35 tornadoes across many central and southern states. The states most affected were IL, KY, IA, IN, OH, MO, and MI.	Apr. 4-6, 2023	$2,927.6	5
Southern/Midwestern Drought and Heatwave	Drought conditions impacted numerous Southern and Midwestern states (TX, LA, OK, KS, IL, MO, NE) and surrounding states. Impacts to agriculture include damage to field crops from lack of rainfall and ranchers forced to sell-off livestock early due to high feeding costs. Portions of the Mississippi River have experienced low water levels impacting river commerce. This low flow has also allowed salt water from the Gulf of Mexico to migrate northward, along the bottom of the Mississippi River, impacting water quality in southern LA. Several Northwestern states including WA, OR, and MT have also been impacted by increasing drought effects.	Apr. 1- Sept 30, 2023	$14,786.7	247
Central Tornado Outbreak and Eastern Severe Weather	A historic tornado outbreak across numerous central states caused widespread damage from at least 145 tornadoes. States most impacted were IL, IN, OH, MO, IA, AR, TN, and PA.	Mar. 31- Apr. 1, 2023	$5,853.2	33
Southern and Eastern Severe Weather	Southern and eastern severe storms including more than 40 tornadoes caused damage across MS, AL, GA, TN to many homes, businesses, vehicles, and other infrastructure. Additional high wind damage occurred in parts of OH, WV, and PA.	Mar. 24-26, 2023	$2,927.6	23
Southern and Eastern Severe Weather	Severe storms impact numerous southern and eastern states including TX, AL, MS, TN, KY, IN, and OH. Impacts from high wind and tornadoes cause widespread damage to homes, vehicles, businesses, government buildings, and infrastructure.	Mar. 2-3, 2023	$6,111.1	13
Northeastern Winter Storm/Cold Wave	A strong winter storm produced snow, high winds, and bitter cold across numerous Northeastern states. High winds caused widespread power outages in MA.	Feb. 2-5, 2023	$1,821.1	1
California Flooding	Numerous atmospheric rivers in continuous succession caused severe flooding, record snowfall, and copious rainfall that significantly reduced drought deficits across CA, between late-December and March 2023. Flooding impacted many homes, businesses, levees, agriculture, and other infrastructure particularly across central CA.	Dec. 26, 2022 - Mar. 19, 2023	$4,725.0	22

– Represents zero.

Source: U.S. National Oceanic and Atmospheric Administration, National Centers for Environmental Information, "Billion-Dollar Weather and Climate Disasters, 1980-2024," <www.ncei.noaa.gov/billions/events>; accessed August 2024.

Table 440. Severe Weather Impacts from Tornadoes, Floods, Tropical Storms, Extreme Temperatures, and Lightning: 2000 to 2023

[424 represents $424,000,000]

Weather type	2000	2010	2015	2017	2018	2019	2020	2021	2022	2023
Tornadoes: [1]										
Number..............................	1,072	1,282	1,177	1,429	1,126	1,517	1,082	1,314	1,143	1,321
Lives lost............................	41	45	36	35	10	42	76	104	23	86
Injuries.............................	882	699	924	516	199	537	733	878	314	914
Property loss (mil. dol.)...............	424	1,107	317	632	670	3,102	2,504	233	699	1,371
Floods and flash floods:										
Lives lost............................	38	103	187	136	80	92	57	146	93	70
Injuries.............................	47	310	50	19	21	45	9	60	12	14
Property loss (mil. dol.)...............	1,255	3,927	2,277	60,576	1,188	2,418	914	2,979	2,767	2,090
North Atlantic tropical										
cyclones and hurricanes [2]............	15	21	12	18	15	18	31	21	14	20
Hurricanes..........................	8	12	4	10	8	6	14	7	9	7
Lives lost............................	–	–	14	43	7	–	24	12	116	3
Property loss (mil. dol.)...............	8	15	41	22,383	12,145	24	17,483	8,598	15,443	4,085
Pacific Basin tropical cyclones [2].......	19	12	19	20	22	18	21	19	19	17
Hurricanes..........................	6	3	13	9	12	7	4	8	11	10
Extreme temperature:										
Lives lost............................	184	172	98	134	144	98	363	481	405	218
Injuries.............................	469	593	643	179	506	166	80	68	205	1,870
Property and crop loss (mil. dol.)......	9.2	779.0	2.8	954.1	150.0	1.7	37.2	713.4	5.5	7.3
Cold:										
Lives lost............................	26	34	53	27	36	35	13	106	22	11
Injuries.............................	–	1	3	3	3	1	1	1	–	8
Property and crop loss (mil. dol.).....	9.2	775.2	2.8	954.1	150.0	0.2	31.2	713.4	5.5	7.3
Heat:										
Lives lost............................	158	138	45	107	108	187	350	375	383	207
Injuries.............................	469	592	640	176	503	165	79	67	205	1,862
Property and crop loss (mil. dol.).....	–	4.3	–	(Z)	(Z)	1.5	6.0	0.1	–	–
Lightning:										
Deaths..............................	51	29	27	16	20	20	17	11	19	14
Injuries.............................	364	182	130	86	82	100	53	69	53	56

– Represents zero. Z Less than $500,000. [1] Source: U.S. National Weather Service, <spc.noaa.gov/climo/summary/>. A violent, rotating column of air descending from a cumulonimbus cloud in the form of a tubular- or funnel-shaped cloud, usually characterized by movements along a narrow path and wind speeds from 100 to over 300 miles per hour. Also known as a "twister" or "waterspout." [2] Tropical cyclones include depressions, storms and hurricanes. Fatalities are assumed to be caused by wind-driven debris or structural failure due to winds. For data on individual hurricanes, see National Hurricane Center (NHC) at <www.nhc.noaa.gov/>.

Source: Except as noted, U.S. National Oceanic and Atmospheric Administration (NOAA), National Weather Service (NWS), Office of Climate, Water, and Weather Services, "Weather Related Fatality and Injury Statistics," <www.weather.gov/hazstat/>, accessed August 2024.

Table 441. Top 20 Significant Flood Event Losses Covered by the National Flood Insurance Program, as of June 30, 2022

[In nominal dollars. Covers period beginning in 1978. These events have 500 or more claims closed with payment]

Event	Date	Number of paid losses	Amount paid ($)	Average paid loss ($)
Hurricane Katrina................................	August 24, 2005	208,348	16,213,748,990	77,822
Hurricane Harvey................................	August 24, 2017	92,390	9,045,891,703	98,105
Hurricane Sandy.................................	October 27, 2012	144,846	8,935,331,922	61,693
Hurricane Ike....................................	September 11, 2008	58,126	2,698,055,533	46,417
Mid-summer severe storms in Louisiana......	August 9, 2016	30,016	2,526,665,742	84,205
Hurricane Irene..................................	August 21, 2011	52,493	1,344,050,769	25,607
Hurricane Ivan...................................	September 15, 2004	20,137	1,321,453,781	65,626
Hurricane Ida....................................	August 28, 2021	28,214	1,278,980,429	49,685
Hurricane Irma..................................	September 5, 2017	33,337	1,111,636,521	33,447
Tropical Storm Allison...........................	June 4, 2001	35,561	1,103,995,184	31,045
Tropical Storm Imelda...........................	September 17, 2019	10,939	752,293,443	69,470
Hurricane Florence..............................	September 12, 2018	16,801	741,837,514	44,225
Hurricane Matthew..............................	October 5, 2016	21,817	660,923,619	30,313
Flooding in Louisiana............................	May 8, 1995	35,734	583,739,600	16,336
Hurricane Isaac.................................	August 25, 2012	16,926	563,819,634	33,317
Hurricane Isabel................................	September 17, 2003	23,955	499,598,721	20,858
Early summer storms in Texas.................	May 16, 2015	8,354	487,132,295	58,311
Spring severe storms in Texas.................	April 16, 2016	8,433	471,735,524	55,946
Hurricane Rita...................................	September 23, 2005	14,662	463,881,550	31,638
Tropical Storm Lee..............................	September 5, 2011	11,025	462,307,260	41,933

Source: U.S. Department of Homeland Security, Federal Emergency Management Agency, National Flood Insurance Program, "Significant Flood Events," <nfipservices.floodsmart.gov/reports-flood-insurance-data>, accessed May 2024.

Table 442. Wildland Fires—Number and Acres: 1970 to 2023

[Acres in thousands (3,278.6 represents 3,278,600). As of December 31. Data are for wildland fires only and do not include prescribed fires. Wildland fire is any nonstructural fire that occurs in the wildland including unauthorized human-caused fires and escaped prescribed fire projects]

Year	Total Fires	Total Acres (1,000)	Year	Total Fires	Total Acres (1,000)	State	Top states ranked by wildland acres burned in 2023 Fires	Top states ranked by wildland acres burned in 2023 Acres (1,000)
1970.........	121,736	3,278.6	2013.........	47,579	4,319.5	Total.....	56,580	2,693.9
1975.........	134,872	1,791.3	2014.........	63,612	3,595.6	CA.......	7,364	332.7
1980.........	234,892	5,260.8	2015.........	68,151	10,125.1	AK.......	346	314.3
1985.........	82,591	2,896.1	2016.........	67,743	5,510.0	NM.......	1,019	212.4
1990.........	66,481	4,621.6	2017.........	71,499	10,026.1	TX........	7,102	210.3
1995.........	82,234	1,840.5	2018.........	58,083	8,767.5	OR.......	1,979	202.0
2000.........	92,250	7,393.5	2019.........	50,477	4,664.4	AZ.......	1,837	188.5
2005.........	66,753	8,689.4	2020.........	58,950	10,122.3	NE.......	569	180.7
2010.........	71,971	3,422.7	2021.........	58,985	7,125.6	OK.......	1,580	162.5
2012.........	67,774	9,326.2	2022.........	68,988	7,577.2	WA.......	1,707	151.3

Source: National Interagency Coordination Center, *Wildland Fire Summary and Statistics Annual Report, 2023*, and earlier reports. See also <nifc.gov/nicc/predictive-services/intelligence>.

Table 443. Single Unit Housing Structures at Risk of Wildfire by Census Division: 2021

[In thousands (37,362 represents 37,362,000). Data shown are for single unit housing structures located inside a Wildland-Urban Interface (WUI). WUI is defined by the U.S. Forest Service as an area where homes and other structures are in or adjacent to undeveloped wildland vegetation prone to large scale wildfire, thereby posing a significant threat to human life or property. Based on the American Housing Survey; see Appendix III]

Characteristic	Total	Census division New England	Census division Middle Atlantic	Census division East North Central	Census division West North Central	Census division South Atlantic	Census division East South Central	Census division West South Central	Census division Mountain	Census division Pacific
Total one unit structures [1]	**37,362**	**2,729**	**3,767**	**2,330**	**1,393**	**9,874**	**3,497**	**4,451**	**4,363**	**4,958**
Siding or exterior wall covering:										
Wood....................	7,889	1,050	602	259	356	1,246	448	805	1,122	2,000
Vinyl....................	11,611	1,316	2,009	1,291	545	3,880	1,189	593	522	268
Aluminum................	2,388	95	292	244	136	652	288	278	211	192
Other (brick, asbestos, fiber cement)...	14,448	220	744	441	341	3,854	1,473	2,681	2,338	2,356
Gutters on home:										
Yes.....................	26,669	2,106	3,259	1,816	1,154	7,107	2,368	2,211	2,821	3,826
Frequency of gutter cleaning										
Twice a year or more..................	6,675	498	769	503	299	2,015	615	440	637	900
Once a year............................	10,527	891	1,394	682	453	2,680	868	907	1,004	1,649
Less than once a year................	3,371	322	350	187	129	714	368	297	417	587
Never.................................	5,413	322	697	393	242	1,489	447	526	686	611
No.....................	9,775	591	396	432	225	2,566	1,043	2,141	1,372	1,011
Deck on property:										
Yes.....................	19,062	1,875	2,168	1,505	758	5,134	1,835	1,619	2,013	2,155
No.....................	15,575	633	1,343	680	478	4,133	1,428	2,479	1,964	2,438
Wooden fence on property:										
Yes.....................	11,373	643	665	389	226	2,344	724	2,016	1,553	2,813
No.....................	25,137	2,053	2,982	1,863	1,153	7,329	2,691	2,362	2,651	2,053
Woodpile on property:										
Yes.....................	6,755	821	859	702	314	1,211	495	601	829	922
No.....................	29,750	1,873	2,808	1,541	1,065	8,462	2,908	3,778	3,375	3,940
Shed on property:										
Yes.....................	17,412	1,436	2,065	1,113	685	4,276	1,783	2,051	1,958	2,045
No.....................	19,075	1,259	1,593	1,130	694	5,393	1,625	2,320	2,246	2,815
Vegetation around home:										
Yes.....................	28,634	2,323	3,141	1,894	1,075	7,358	2,492	3,074	3,343	3,934
Within 5 feet of home..................	20,672	1,732	2,362	1,283	688	5,522	1,763	2,301	2,098	2,923
More than 5 feet from home............	7,925	591	779	596	387	1,836	712	774	1,245	1,007
No.....................	7,897	372	528	358	304	2,308	911	1,308	861	946

[1] Includes items not reported, not shown separately.

Source: U.S. Census Bureau, "American Housing Survey: AHS Table Creator," <www.census.gov/programs-surveys/ahs/data.html>, accessed April 2023.

Table 444. Community Resilience Estimates—Population at Risk of Impacts from Disasters by State: 2022

[The Census Bureau's Community Resilience Estimates (CRE) program measures the capacity of individuals and households to absorb, endure, and recover from the health, social, and economic impacts of a disaster such as a hurricane or pandemic. Individual and household risk factors include an income-to-poverty ratio of less than 130 percent; single or zero caregiver household (only one or no individuals living in the household who are aged 18-64); household crowding defined as more than .75 persons per room; communication barriers defined as limited English-speaking households or no one in the household over the age of 16 with a high school diploma; no household member employed full-time, year-round unless all residents of the household are aged 65 years or older; disability posing constraint to significant life activity; no health insurance coverage; being aged 65 years or older; households without a vehicle; and households without broadband internet access. The 2022 CRE are produced using information on individuals and households from the 2022 American Community Survey (ACS) and the Census Bureau's Population Estimates Program (PEP). The ACS universe includes the household population and the population living in institutions, college dormitories, and other group quarters. Based on a sample and subject to sampling variability. For more information, see Methodology and Technical Documentation at <www.census.gov/programs-surveys/community-resilience-estimates.html>, and also <www2.census.gov/programs-surveys/demo/technical-documentation/community-resilience/2022/cre_quickguide_2022.pdf>]

State	Total population	Individuals with zero risk factors		Individuals with 1-2 risk factors		Individuals with 3 or more risk factors	
		Number	Percent	Number	Percent	Number	Percent
United States.......	328,496,586	115,417,153	35.1	145,319,124	44.2	67,760,309	20.6
Alabama..............	4,974,000	1,696,217	34.1	2,070,599	41.6	1,207,184	24.3
Alaska................	726,456	217,967	30.0	358,362	49.3	150,127	20.7
Arizona..............	7,258,726	2,337,773	32.2	3,449,144	47.5	1,471,809	20.3
Arkansas.............	2,989,747	950,459	31.8	1,311,297	43.9	727,991	24.4
California.............	38,627,136	11,176,538	28.9	19,710,485	51.0	7,740,113	20.0
Colorado.............	5,771,236	2,337,002	40.5	2,521,692	43.7	912,542	15.8
Connecticut..........	3,548,322	1,425,529	40.2	1,476,793	41.6	646,000	18.2
Delaware.............	1,002,476	367,592	36.7	435,171	43.4	199,713	19.9
District of Columbia...	647,023	233,016	36.0	274,256	42.4	139,751	21.6
Florida...............	21,964,298	6,841,901	31.2	10,223,404	46.6	4,898,993	22.3
Georgia..............	10,739,778	3,968,876	37.0	4,670,675	43.5	2,100,227	19.6
Hawaii...............	1,430,111	400,971	28.0	743,246	52.0	285,894	20.0
Idaho................	1,904,925	696,457	36.6	878,619	46.1	329,849	17.3
Illinois...............	12,437,174	4,663,409	37.5	5,218,052	42.0	2,555,713	20.6
Indiana..............	6,716,137	2,664,593	39.7	2,740,402	40.8	1,311,142	19.5
Iowa.................	3,139,602	1,331,453	42.4	1,245,497	39.7	562,652	17.9
Kansas...............	2,888,570	1,165,910	40.4	1,190,826	41.2	531,834	18.4
Kentucky.............	4,437,619	1,601,221	36.1	1,849,955	41.7	986,443	22.2
Louisiana.............	4,505,306	1,421,433	31.6	1,962,594	43.6	1,121,279	24.9
Maine................	1,364,943	522,477	38.3	591,162	43.3	251,304	18.4
Maryland.............	6,090,568	2,393,429	39.3	2,583,515	42.4	1,113,624	18.3
Massachusetts........	6,818,948	2,768,436	40.6	2,820,512	41.4	1,230,000	18.0
Michigan.............	9,902,050	3,816,200	38.5	4,085,883	41.3	1,999,967	20.2
Minnesota............	5,655,744	2,443,873	43.2	2,251,256	39.8	960,615	17.0
Mississippi...........	2,876,178	881,617	30.7	1,223,839	42.6	770,722	26.8
Missouri..............	6,087,993	2,385,947	39.2	2,496,334	41.0	1,205,712	19.8
Montana..............	1,108,203	389,587	35.2	507,499	45.8	211,117	19.1
Nebraska.............	1,939,472	809,040	41.7	781,665	40.3	348,767	18.0
Nevada...............	3,155,447	964,148	30.6	1,531,743	48.5	659,556	20.9
New Hampshire.......	1,373,148	599,943	43.7	561,761	40.9	211,444	15.4
New Jersey...........	9,167,760	3,357,732	36.6	3,912,659	42.7	1,897,369	20.7
New Mexico..........	2,088,425	604,822	29.0	970,271	46.5	513,332	24.6
New York.............	19,373,783	5,856,366	30.2	8,564,373	44.2	4,953,044	25.6
North Carolina........	10,527,828	3,838,372	36.5	4,537,428	43.1	2,152,028	20.4
North Dakota.........	762,166	323,973	42.5	303,965	39.9	134,228	17.6
Ohio.................	11,590,793	4,625,108	39.9	4,634,660	40.0	2,331,025	20.1
Oklahoma.............	3,944,885	1,251,433	31.7	1,782,048	45.2	911,404	23.1
Oregon...............	4,192,775	1,431,127	34.1	1,938,737	46.2	822,911	19.6
Pennsylvania.........	12,682,057	4,957,844	39.1	5,088,441	40.1	2,635,772	20.8
Rhode Island.........	1,065,514	412,034	38.7	451,421	42.4	202,059	19.0
South Carolina........	5,197,707	1,850,138	35.6	2,235,417	43.0	1,112,152	21.4
South Dakota.........	893,537	365,525	40.9	352,294	39.4	175,718	19.7
Tennessee............	6,956,049	2,552,343	36.7	2,881,895	41.4	1,521,811	21.9
Texas................	29,620,910	9,465,803	32.0	13,615,263	46.0	6,539,844	22.1
Utah.................	3,345,582	1,447,326	43.3	1,466,289	43.8	431,967	12.9
Vermont..............	629,444	247,303	39.3	274,123	43.6	108,018	17.2
Virginia..............	8,532,298	3,385,837	39.7	3,609,386	42.3	1,537,075	18.0
Washington...........	7,724,756	2,789,213	36.1	3,582,975	46.4	1,352,568	17.5
West Virginia.........	1,737,650	612,565	35.3	716,879	41.3	408,206	23.5
Wisconsin............	5,808,338	2,359,620	40.6	2,378,235	41.0	1,070,483	18.4
Wyoming.............	572,993	209,655	36.6	256,127	44.7	107,211	18.7

Source: U.S. Census Bureau, "Community Resilience Estimates Datasets," <www.census.gov/programs-surveys/community-resilience-estimates/data.html>, accessed April 2024.

Table 445. Drought Conditions—Area and Population Impacted by Level of Drought: 2023

[In percent. For continental United States. Data shown for the last week of each month, as of Tuesday. Dryness and drought conditions are indicated as follows: D0, abnormally dry; D1, moderate drought; D2, severe drought; D3, extreme drought; and D4, exceptional drought. Data are categorical statistics showing percent of the area or population that is in a certain drought category. See source for details. The U.S. Drought Monitor is jointly produced by the National Drought Mitigation Center at the University of Nebraska-Lincoln, the United States Department of Agriculture, and the National Oceanic and Atmospheric Administration]

Week	Area (percent of continental U.S. square miles)						Population (percent of continental U.S. population)					
	None	D0	D1	D2	D3	D4	None	D0	D1	D2	D3	D4
1/31/2023....	38.41	18.94	21.26	13.97	5.68	1.74	54.68	20.48	16.27	6.19	1.85	0.54
2/28/2023....	45.00	16.54	21.15	11.66	4.10	1.55	63.47	19.04	11.37	4.53	1.07	0.51
3/28/2023....	48.18	21.15	16.78	8.63	3.43	1.83	68.66	16.64	6.66	5.89	1.43	0.73
4/25/2023....	53.94	20.51	13.55	6.03	3.72	2.25	62.81	21.20	9.62	3.87	2.01	0.49
5/30/2023....	49.95	31.10	10.81	4.86	2.04	1.24	59.73	28.20	8.56	2.50	0.59	0.41
6/27/2023....	46.52	26.49	17.74	6.67	2.00	0.58	44.36	26.20	20.09	8.22	0.83	0.30
7/25/2023....	49.62	23.25	17.35	7.15	2.36	0.26	54.82	21.44	14.66	7.30	1.65	0.13
8/29/2023....	49.59	16.13	15.24	11.58	5.93	1.53	64.01	11.51	9.19	7.88	5.02	2.39
9/26/2023....	43.65	18.12	15.77	12.32	7.33	2.82	56.13	15.93	9.90	7.32	7.51	3.21
10/31/2023...	45.83	17.64	15.56	13.05	5.74	2.17	52.63	17.64	13.22	9.08	5.80	1.64
11/28/2023...	44.23	19.72	15.71	12.54	5.67	2.13	48.21	21.85	14.36	9.04	4.80	1.74
12/26/2023...	45.71	21.94	15.61	10.30	5.28	1.16	60.16	15.73	13.08	6.41	4.08	0.54

Source: National Drought Mitigation Center, "United States Drought Monitor," <droughtmonitor.unl.edu>, accessed January 2024.

Table 446. Threatened and Endangered Wildlife and Plant Species: 2024

[As of July 2024. Endangered species: one in danger of becoming extinct throughout all or a significant part of its natural range. Threatened species: one likely to become endangered in the foreseeable future]

Item	Total [1]	Mammals	Birds	Reptiles	Amphibians	Fishes	Snails	Clams	Crustaceans	Insects	Arachnids	Plants
Total listings..........	2,379	382	332	144	52	205	54	98	32	98	16	941
Endangered species, total.....................	1,859	329	285	88	33	118	40	77	25	80	16	765
United States [2].........	1,258	66	68	18	25	91	39	75	25	76	11	764
Foreign..................	601	263	217	70	8	27	1	2	–	4	5	1
Threatened species, total.....................	520	53	47	56	19	87	14	21	7	18	–	176
United States [2].........	422	30	25	31	18	78	13	21	7	18	–	174
Foreign..................	98	23	22	25	1	9	1	–	–	–	–	2

– Represents zero. [1] Includes other categories not shown separately. Twenty-four animal species (16 in the U.S. and 8 foreign) are counted more than once, primarily because these animals have distinct population segments (each with its own individual listing status). [2] United States listings include those populations in which the U.S. shares jurisdiction with another nation.

Source: U.S. Fish and Wildlife Service, Environmental Conservation Online System, Threatened & Endangered Species, "Listed Species Summary," <ecos.fws.gov/ecp/>, accessed July 2024.

Elections

This section relates primarily to presidential, congressional, and gubernatorial elections. Also presented are summary tables on congressional legislation; state legislatures; minority and female officeholders; population of voting age; voter participation; and campaign finances.

Official statistics on federal elections, collected by the Clerk of the House, are published biennially in *Statistics of the Presidential and Congressional Election* and *Statistics of the Congressional Election*. Federal elections data also appear in the *Congressional Directory* and in official state documents. Data on reported registration and voting for social and economic groups are obtained by the U.S. Census Bureau as part of the Current Population Survey (CPS) and are published in *Current Population Reports*, Series P20 (see text, Section 1).

Almost all federal, state, and local governmental units in the United States conduct elections for political offices and other purposes. The conduct of elections is regulated by state laws or, in some cities and counties, by local charter. An exception is that the U.S. Constitution prescribes the basis of representation in Congress and the manner of electing the president and grants to Congress the right to regulate the times, places, and manner of electing federal officers. Amendments to the Constitution have prescribed national criteria for voting eligibility. The 15th Amendment, adopted in 1870, gave all male citizens the right to vote regardless of race, color, or previous condition of servitude. The 19th Amendment, adopted in 1920, further extended the right to vote to all citizens regardless of sex. The payment of poll taxes as a prerequisite to voting in federal elections was banned by the 24th Amendment in 1964. In 1971, as a result of the 26th Amendment, eligibility to vote in national elections was extended to all citizens aged 18 years old and over.

Presidential election—The Constitution specifies how the president and vice president are selected. Each state elects, by popular vote, a group of electors equal in number to its total of members of Congress. The 23rd Amendment, adopted in 1961, grants the District of Columbia three presidential electors, a number equal to that of the least populous state. Subsequent to the election, the electors meet in their respective states to vote for president and vice president. Usually, each elector votes for the candidate receiving the most popular votes in his or her state. A majority vote of all electors is necessary to elect the president and vice president. If no candidate receives a majority, the House of Representatives, with each state having one vote, is empowered to elect the president and vice president, again, with a majority of votes required.

The 22nd Amendment to the Constitution, adopted in 1951, limits presidential tenure to two elective terms of 4 years each or to one elective term for any person who, upon succession to the presidency, has held the office or acted as President for more than 2 years.

Congressional election—The Constitution provides that representatives be apportioned among the states according to their population, that a census of population be taken every 10 years as a basis for apportionment, and that each state have at least one representative. At the time of each apportionment, Congress decides what the total number of representatives will be. Since 1912, the total has been 435, except during 1960 to 1962 when it increased to 437, adding one representative each for Alaska and Hawaii. The total reverted to 435 after reapportionment following the 1960 census. Members are elected for 2-year terms, all terms covering the same period. The District of Columbia, American Samoa, Guam, the Northern Mariana Islands, and the U.S. Virgin Islands each elect one nonvoting delegate, and Puerto Rico elects a nonvoting resident commissioner.

The Senate is composed of 100 members, two from each state, who are elected to serve for a term of 6 years. One-third of the Senate is elected every 2 years. Senators were originally chosen by the state legislatures. The 17th Amendment to the Constitution, adopted in 1913, prescribed that senators be elected by popular vote.

Voter eligibility and participation—The Census Bureau publishes estimates of the population of voting age and the percent casting votes in each state for presidential and congressional election years. These voting-age estimates include a number of persons who meet the age requirement but are not eligible to vote, (e.g. aliens and some institutionalized persons). In addition, since 1964, voter participation and voter characteristics data have been collected during November of election years as part of the CPS. Survey data on voting age population estimates includes non-citizens but excludes members of the Armed Forces and institutionalized populations. Data on percent casting votes excludes institutionalized populations, members of the Armed forces and citizens residing outside the U.S. casting absentee ballots.

Statistical reliability—For a discussion of statistical collection and estimation, sampling procedures, and measures of statistical reliability applicable to Census Bureau data, see Appendix III.

Table 447. Participation in Elections for President and U.S. Representatives: 1940 to 2022

[84,728 represents 84,728,000. As of November, except as noted. Estimated resident population 21 years old and over, 1940 to 1970, except as noted, and 18 years old and over thereafter. Includes Armed Forces stationed in the U.S. Prior to 1958, excludes Alaska and prior to 1960, excludes Hawaii. District of Columbia is included in votes cast for President beginning 1964]

Year	Resident population of voting age [1] (1,000)	Votes cast			
		For President (1,000)	Percent of voting-age population	For U.S. Representa-tives (1,000)	Percent of voting-age population
1940................	84,728	49,815	58.8	(NA)	(NA)
1950................	98,134	(X)	(X)	40,430	41.2
1952................	99,929	61,552	61.6	57,571	57.6
1954................	102,075	(X)	(X)	42,583	41.7
1956................	104,515	62,027	59.3	58,886	56.3
1958................	106,447	(X)	(X)	45,719	43.0
1960................	109,672	68,836	62.8	64,124	58.5
1962................	112,952	(X)	(X)	51,242	45.4
1964................	114,090	70,098	61.4	65,879	57.7
1966................	116,638	(X)	(X)	52,902	45.4
1968................	120,285	73,027	60.7	66,109	55.0
1970................	124,498	(X)	(X)	54,259	43.6
1972................	140,777	77,625	55.1	71,188	50.6
1974................	146,338	(X)	(X)	52,313	35.7
1976................	152,308	81,603	53.6	74,259	48.8
1978................	158,369	(X)	(X)	54,584	34.5
1980................	163,945	86,497	52.8	77,874	47.5
1982................	169,643	(X)	(X)	63,881	37.7
1984................	173,995	92,655	53.3	82,422	47.4
1986................	177,922	(X)	(X)	59,758	33.6
1988................	181,956	91,587	50.3	81,682	44.9
1990................	185,812	(X)	(X)	62,355	33.6
1992................	189,493	104,600	55.2	97,198	51.3
1994................	193,010	(X)	(X)	70,494	36.5
1996................	196,789	96,390	49.0	90,233	45.9
1998................	201,270	(X)	(X)	66,605	33.1
2000................	[2] 209,130	105,594	50.5	98,800	47.2
2002................	[2] 214,689	(X)	(X)	74,707	34.8
2004................	[2] 219,508	122,349	55.7	113,192	51.6
2006................	[2] 224,622	(X)	(X)	80,976	36.0
2008................	[2] 229,989	131,407	57.1	122,586	53.3
2010................	[2] 234,576	(X)	(X)	86,785	37.0
2012................	[2] 240,165	129,140	53.8	122,346	50.9
2014................	[2] 244,793	(X)	(X)	78,813	32.2
2016................	[2] 249,372	136,787	54.9	129,833	52.1
2018................	[2] 253,453	(X)	(X)	114,017	45.0
2020................	[2] 257,049	158,482	61.7	153,431	59.7
2022................	[2] 260,046	(X)	(X)	108,443	41.7

X Not applicable. NA Not available. [1] Population age 18 and over in Georgia, 1944-1970, and in Kentucky, 1956–1970; and age 20 and over in Alaska and Hawaii, 1960–1970. Source: Through 1990, U.S. Census Bureau, "Table 4. Participation in Elections for President and U.S. Representatives: 1930 to 1992," May 1994, <www.census.gov/population/socdemo/voting/p25-1117/tab03-04.pdf>. For 1992–1998, "Estimates and Projections of the Voting-Age Population, 1992 to 2000, and Percent Casting Votes for President, by State: November 1992 and 1996," July 2000, <www.census.gov/population/socdemo/voting/proj00/tab03.txt>. For 2000-2009, "Annual Estimates of the Resident Population for Selected Age Groups by Sex for the United States, States, Counties, and Puerto Rico Commonwealth and Municipios: April 1, 2000 to July 1, 2009," <www.census.gov/topics/population.html>, accessed June 2015. For 2010 to 2019, "Annual Estimates of the Resident Population by Single Year of Age and Sex: April 1, 2010 to July 1, 2020," <www2.census.gov/programs-surveys/popest/tables/>. For 2020 on, "Annual Estimates of the Resident Population for Selected Age Groups by Sex for the United States: April 1, 2020 to July 1, 2023 (NC-EST2023-AGESEX)," <www.census.gov/data/tables/time-series/demo/popest/2020s-national-detail.html>, accessed July 2024. [2] 2000 and 2010 as of Apr.1, population estimates base. All other years as of July 1.

Source: Except as noted, U.S. House of Representatives, Office of the Clerk, *Statistics of the Congressional Election of November 8, 2022*, February 2023, and earlier reports. See also <clerk.house.gov/Members#ElectionInformation>.

Table 448. Voters by Whether Voting on Election Day or Utilizing Alternative Early Voting: 2002 to 2022

[Percent distribution of persons voting. As of November. Data are from the November Voting and Registration Supplement to the Current Population Survey (see text, Section 1, and Appendix III)]

Election Year	Total [1]	On election day [2]	Alternative early voting methods		
			Total	Before election day [2]	By mail
2002............................	100.0	85.9	14.1	3.4	10.7
2004 [3].........................	100.0	79.3	20.7	7.8	12.9
2006............................	100.0	80.4	19.6	5.8	13.7
2008 [3].........................	100.0	69.3	30.7	14.3	16.4
2010............................	100.0	73.5	26.5	8.4	18.1
2012 [3].........................	100.0	67.2	32.8	14.3	18.5
2014............................	100.0	68.9	31.2	10.3	20.9
2016 [3].........................	100.0	59.9	40.1	19.1	21.0
2018............................	100.0	59.6	39.7	16.6	23.1
2020 [3].........................	100.0	30.4	69.0	26.0	43.0
2022............................	100.0	49.5	49.8	18.0	31.8

[1] Includes unknown or did not respond to survey question. [2] Voted in person. [3] Presidential election year.

Source: U.S. Census Bureau, "Voting and Registration in the Election of November 2022," <www.census.gov/data/tables/time-series/demo/voting-and-registration/p20-586.html>, accessed May 2023, and earlier reports.

Table 449. Resident Population of Voting-Age, Total Votes Cast, and Percent Casting Votes—States: 2020 and 2022

[256,662 represents 256,662,000. Votes cast as of November. Estimated population, 18 years old and over]

State	Voting-age population (1,000)		Total votes cast (1,000)			Percent casting votes for–		
			Presidential electors	U.S. Representatives		Presidential electors	U.S. Representatives	
	2020 [1]	2022 [2]	2020	2020	2022	2020	2020	2022
U.S.	256,662	260,837	158,482	153,431	108,443	61.7	59.8	41.6
AL.	3,834	3,963	2,323	2,052	1,344	60.6	53.5	33.9
AK.	552	557	360	353	264	65.1	63.9	47.3
AZ.	5,775	5,770	3,387	3,268	2,360	58.7	56.6	40.9
AR.	2,331	2,349	1,219	1,179	895	52.3	50.6	38.1
CA.	30,577	30,523	17,501	16,725	10,656	57.2	54.7	34.9
CO.	4,558	4,624	3,257	3,165	2,472	71.5	69.4	53.5
CT.	2,838	2,895	1,824	1,773	1,261	64.3	62.5	43.6
DE.	782	810	504	488	322	64.5	62.4	39.7
DC.	583	547	343	(X)	(X)	58.8	(X)	(X)
FL.	17,483	17,948	11,067	10,465	7,332	63.3	59.9	40.9
GA.	8,210	8,403	5,001	4,884	3,909	60.9	59.5	46.5
HI.	1,111	1,143	571	580	419	51.4	52.2	36.7
ID.	1,376	1,476	868	850	584	63.1	61.8	39.6
IL.	9,810	9,862	6,034	5,877	4,049	61.5	59.9	41.1
IN.	5,189	5,263	3,033	2,996	1,857	58.5	57.8	35.3
IA.	2,438	2,476	1,700	1,700	1,230	69.7	69.7	49.7
KS.	2,217	2,246	1,372	1,359	1,002	61.9	61.3	44.6
KY.	3,475	3,508	2,137	2,116	1,463	61.5	60.9	41.7
LA.	3,564	3,529	2,148	1,947	1,133	60.3	54.6	32.1
ME.	1,102	1,137	828	828	1,014	75.2	75.2	89.2
MD.	4,722	4,818	3,037	2,954	1,996	64.3	62.6	41.4
MA.	5,552	5,645	3,658	3,658	2,511	65.9	65.9	44.5
MI.	7,840	7,924	5,539	5,423	4,376	70.7	69.2	55.2
MN.	4,356	4,423	3,277	3,194	2,496	75.2	73.3	56.4
MS.	2,274	2,262	1,314	1,228	709	57.8	54.0	31.3
MO.	4,780	4,813	3,026	2,973	2,060	63.3	62.2	42.8
MT.	851	889	604	602	464	70.9	70.7	52.1
NE.	1,463	1,491	956	941	663	65.4	64.4	44.5
NV.	2,441	2,488	1,405	1,356	1,010	57.6	55.5	40.6
NH.	1,113	1,142	806	787	618	72.4	70.7	54.1
NJ.	6,948	7,268	4,549	4,433	2,610	65.5	63.8	35.9
NM.	1,634	1,654	924	904	704	56.6	55.3	42.6
NY.	15,348	15,688	8,662	8,604	5,966	56.4	56.1	38.0
NC.	8,294	8,404	5,525	5,325	3,761	66.6	64.2	44.7
ND.	584	596	362	356	239	62.0	60.9	40.0
OH.	9,125	9,194	5,922	5,762	4,110	64.9	63.1	44.7
OK.	3,027	3,067	1,561	1,551	1,146	51.6	51.2	37.4
OR.	3,381	3,403	2,374	2,308	1,907	70.2	68.3	56.0
PA.	10,162	10,348	6,915	6,779	5,152	68.0	66.7	49.8
RI.	855	890	518	488	358	60.5	57.1	40.2
SC.	4,100	4,165	2,513	2,505	1,602	61.3	61.1	38.5
SD.	674	691	423	398	328	62.7	59.0	47.5
TN.	5,373	5,513	3,054	2,842	1,710	56.8	52.9	31.0
TX.	21,926	22,573	11,315	11,094	7,752	51.6	50.6	34.3
UT.	2,321	2,449	1,488	1,432	1,063	64.1	61.7	43.4
VT.	510	532	371	371	292	72.7	72.7	54.8
VA.	6,724	6,817	4,461	4,335	3,048	66.3	64.5	44.7
WA.	6,028	6,139	4,088	3,944	3,026	67.8	65.4	49.3
WV.	1,429	1,423	781	761	472	54.7	53.3	33.2
WI.	4,574	4,647	3,297	3,238	2,531	72.1	70.8	54.5
WY.	449	451	279	279	198	62.0	62.0	43.9

X Not applicable. [1] As of July 1. Source: U.S. Census Bureau, "Annual Estimates of the Resident Population for Selected Age Groups by Sex for the United States, States, Counties, and Puerto Rico Commonwealth and Municipios: April 1, 2010 to July 1, 2020," <data.census.gov>, accessed July 2021. [2] The estimates are developed from a base that incorporates the 2020 Census, Vintage 2020 estimates, and 2020 Demographic Analysis estimates. Source: U.S. Census Bureau, State Population by Characteristics: 2020-2022, "Annual Estimates of the Resident Population for Selected Age Groups by Sex: April 1, 2020 to July 1, 2022 (SC-EST2022-AGESEX)," <www.census.gov/data/tables/time-series/demo/popest/2020s-state-detail.html>, accessed June 2023.

Source: Except as noted, U.S. House of Representatives, Office of the Clerk, *Statistics of the Congressional Election of November 8, 2022*, February 2023, and earlier reports. See also <clerk.house.gov/Members#ElectionInformation>.

Table 450. Voting-Age Population—Reported Registration and Voting by Selected Characteristics: 2010 to 2022

[229.7 represents 229,700,000. As of November. Covers civilian noninstitutional population 18 years old and over. Voting-age population includes noncitizens. Figures are based on Current Population Survey (see text, Section 1 and Appendix III) and differ from those in Table 447 based on population estimates and official vote counts]

Characteristic	Voting-age population (mil.)							Percent reporting they are registered							Percent reporting they voted						
								Presidential election years			Congressional election years				Presidential election years			Congressional election years			
	2010	2012	2014	2016	2018	2020	2022	2012	2016	2020	2010	2014	2018	2022	2012	2016	2020	2010	2014	2018	2022
Total [1]	229.7	235.2	239.9	245.5	249.7	252.3	255.5	65.1	64.2	66.7	59.8	59.3	61.3	63.2	56.5	56.0	61.3	41.8	38.5	49.0	47.7
AGE																					
18 to 20 years old	12.2	12.3	11.9	11.7	12.0	12.3	11.8	44.2	46.7	52.6	34.4	32.6	40.8	39.1	35.1	36.4	45.5	16.4	14.1	27.2	23.0
21 to 24 years old	16.7	17.6	17.8	13.2	17.0	16.4	17.0	53.1	71.4	58.2	47.2	43.6	49.1	50.1	40.0	55.2	49.9	22.0	17.1	32.1	27.4
25 to 34 years old	41.2	41.1	42.3	43.8	44.8	44.9	44.1	57.0	56.4	61.0	49.8	49.4	52.1	55.3	46.1	46.4	53.7	26.9	24.2	37.0	34.9
35 to 44 years old	39.9	39.6	39.6	39.9	40.8	41.6	43.1	61.7	60.0	62.2	57.3	56.3	57.3	60.2	52.9	51.8	56.4	37.7	32.8	44.2	42.7
45 to 64 years old	80.7	82.1	82.8	83.8	83.3	81.9	82.0	70.4	68.5	69.9	66.3	65.4	66.1	67.1	63.4	61.7	65.5	51.1	46.0	55.0	53.2
65 years old and over	39.0	42.5	45.6	48.7	51.9	55.3	57.4	76.9	75.3	75.8	72.5	73.0	73.3	74.7	69.7	68.4	71.9	58.9	57.5	63.8	64.6
SEX																					
Male	111.1	113.2	115.6	118.5	120.6	121.9	124.3	63.1	62.3	65.1	57.9	57.2	59.5	61.9	54.4	53.8	59.5	40.9	37.2	47.2	46.6
Female	118.6	122.0	124.2	127.0	129.2	130.4	131.1	67.0	66.0	68.2	61.5	61.2	63.0	64.4	58.5	58.1	63.0	42.7	39.6	50.6	48.8
RACE/ETHNICITY																					
White [2]	185.8	187.1	189.3	192.1	194.1	195.2	196.9	66.7	66.3	69.1	61.6	61.3	63.7	65.6	57.6	58.2	63.7	43.4	40.3	51.1	50.6
Black [2]	27.4	28.7	29.7	30.6	31.6	32.2	32.8	68.5	65.3	64.7	58.8	59.7	60.2	60.2	62.0	55.9	58.7	40.7	37.3	48.0	42.3
Asian [2]	11.0	12.5	13.5	14.9	15.7	16.1	16.5	37.2	38.9	45.7	34.1	34.4	37.7	43.9	31.3	33.9	42.8	21.3	19.1	28.9	29.5
Hispanic [3]	32.5	35.2	36.8	39.0	41.0	42.5	44.3	38.9	39.2	44.1	33.8	34.9	37.9	40.7	31.8	32.5	38.8	20.5	18.4	28.5	26.7
REGION [4]																					
Northeast	42.3	42.9	43.5	43.9	44.2	43.6	44.6	65.2	64.0	68.1	59.7	58.3	60.7	63.7	56.6	56.2	62.7	41.6	36.3	48.4	48.9
Midwest	50.1	50.6	51.0	51.6	51.8	52.2	52.7	71.4	70.2	71.7	65.0	65.0	67.5	68.7	62.3	61.4	65.5	45.1	42.3	53.5	51.6
South	84.2	87.1	89.2	92.0	94.5	96.0	97.7	65.3	64.0	65.4	59.4	60.0	60.8	60.9	55.7	54.9	59.4	39.3	38.4	47.3	44.6
West	53.2	54.6	56.1	58.0	59.3	60.4	60.5	58.9	59.3	63.4	55.5	53.7	57.0	61.7	52.3	52.9	59.6	42.7	36.8	48.0	48.6
EDUCATIONAL ATTAINMENT																					
Less than 9th grade	11.1	10.5	9.9	9.8	8.9	8.7	8.5	28.7	24.5	25.3	27.0	24.5	22.9	22.2	21.6	18.3	20.7	15.8	13.2	14.4	13.0
High school:																					
Less than high school graduate	18.8	18.7	18.6	17.7	16.7	15.0	14.5	42.6	39.0	42.8	37.8	37.5	36.6	37.2	32.2	29.3	35.2	20.8	18.2	23.2	22.3
High school graduate or GED [5]	71.0	70.6	70.6	71.3	71.6	73.3	73.5	59.0	57.5	58.4	54.0	53.5	53.1	54.1	48.7	47.4	51.1	35.2	31.5	38.8	37.0
College:																					
Some college or Associate's degree	65.3	67.7	68.8	69.9	69.5	68.8	68.1	71.2	69.8	72.9	65.5	64.0	67.0	69.2	61.5	60.5	66.8	44.4	40.0	52.2	50.1
Bachelor's or advanced degree	63.5	67.8	72.0	76.8	83.1	86.4	90.8	77.2	76.2	77.2	72.5	70.8	72.7	74.0	71.7	71.0	74.2	57.1	52.5	63.9	61.9
EMPLOYMENT STATUS																					
Employed	138.3	142.6	146.2	150.9	156.0	149.2	157.5	67.1	65.9	68.3	61.5	60.4	62.4	64.3	58.6	57.8	63.1	42.5	38.2	49.6	47.4
Unemployed	13.9	11.1	8.4	6.9	5.5	9.9	5.3	56.9	57.0	61.6	52.3	50.7	56.5	53.7	46.1	44.8	52.7	31.6	26.9	40.2	32.4
Not in labor force	77.5	81.6	85.2	87.8	88.2	93.2	92.6	62.8	61.8	64.7	58.0	58.2	59.6	61.8	54.3	53.8	59.4	42.3	40.1	48.4	49.2

[1] Includes other races, not shown separately. [2] Data represent persons who selected this race group only and exclude persons reporting more than one race. [3] Persons of Hispanic origin may be of any race. [4] For composition of regions, see map, inside cover. [5] The General Educational Development (GED) Test measures how well a non-high school graduate has mastered the skills and general knowledge that are acquired in a 4-year high school education. Successfully passing the exam is a credential generally considered to be equivalent to a high school diploma.

Source: U.S. Census Bureau, "Voting and Registration in the Election of November 2022," <www.census.gov/data/tables/time-series/demo/voting-and-registration/p20-586.html>, accessed May 2023, and earlier reports.

Table 451. Persons Reporting Voter Registration and Whether Voted by State: 2022

[255,457 represents 255,457,000. As of November. See headnote, Table 450]

State	Voting-age population (1,000)	Registered	Voted	State	Voting-age population (1,000)	Registered	Voted
United States	**255,457**	**63.2**	**47.7**	Missouri	4,744	74.5	51.9
Alabama	3,857	64.8	43.8	Montana	886	69.1	56.0
Alaska	531	70.2	53.1	Nebraska	1,460	63.9	45.1
Arizona	5,731	62.1	49.6	Nevada	2,451	58.6	45.8
Arkansas	2,277	59.8	42.2	New Hampshire	1,143	70.3	57.2
California	29,870	57.0	43.7	New Jersey	7,163	61.5	44.0
Colorado	4,571	69.2	58.8	New Mexico	1,625	63.1	50.3
Connecticut	2,839	62.6	44.1	New York	15,238	58.4	43.5
Delaware	798	72.4	51.2	North Carolina	8,175	56.1	42.1
District of Columbia	512	76.7	58.6	North Dakota	575	72.8	50.0
Florida	17,520	55.8	43.2	Ohio	9,024	65.3	46.1
Georgia	8,314	63.4	52.0	Oklahoma	2,999	64.6	44.5
Hawaii	1,079	60.3	47.2	Oregon	3,345	77.2	65.3
Idaho	1,489	61.6	46.0	Pennsylvania	10,124	69.2	57.7
Illinois	9,648	63.3	47.7	Rhode Island	880	71.2	52.1
Indiana	5,199	62.7	39.5	South Carolina	4,045	61.6	42.9
Iowa	2,422	71.5	50.2	South Dakota	676	68.1	52.0
Kansas	2,173	73.0	57.0	Tennessee	5,391	64.3	42.5
Kentucky	3,431	67.6	49.3	Texas	22,057	56.3	40.5
Louisiana	3,437	64.4	45.8	Utah	2,455	62.6	49.0
Maine	1,150	74.4	62.7	Vermont	528	74.5	61.4
Maryland	4,716	70.0	53.5	Virginia	6,583	68.2	48.8
Massachusetts	5,518	65.6	50.3	Washington	6,016	68.8	54.7
Michigan	7,777	74.5	61.2	West Virginia	1,406	62.3	38.2
Minnesota	4,380	74.3	61.2	Wisconsin	4,591	70.2	59.1
Mississippi	2,198	71.5	45.7	Wyoming	440	62.3	48.6

Source: U.S. Census Bureau, "Voting and Registration in the Election of November 2022," <www.census.gov/data/tables/time-series/demo/voting-and-registration/p20-586.html>, accessed May 2023.

Table 452. Reported Voting and Registration Among Native and Naturalized Citizens by Race and Hispanic Origin: 2022

[In units indicated (233,546 represents 233,546,000). Data shown for population aged 18 years and over. As of November]

Nativity status, race, and Hispanic origin	Total citizen population (1,000)	Reported registered Number (1,000)	Percent	Not registered Number (1,000)	Percent	Reported voted Number (1,000)	Percent	Did not vote Number (1,000)	Percent
TOTAL									
All races [1]	233,546	161,422	69.1	32,531	13.9	121,916	52.2	73,076	31.3
White alone [2]	182,214	129,133	70.9	24,093	13.2	99,600	54.7	54,515	29.9
White alone, non-Hispanic	154,963	113,427	73.2	17,750	11.5	89,318	57.6	42,600	27.5
Black alone [2]	30,825	19,770	64.1	4,427	14.4	13,899	45.1	10,346	33.6
Asian alone [2]	12,111	7,256	59.9	2,479	20.5	4,869	40.2	4,889	40.4
Hispanic [3]	31,187	18,025	57.8	7,131	22.9	11,807	37.9	13,525	43.4
NATIVE CITIZEN									
All races [1]	209,835	146,950	70.0	27,570	13.1	112,090	53.4	63,307	30.2
White alone [2]	169,498	121,499	71.7	21,361	12.6	94,266	55.6	49,371	29.1
White alone, non-Hispanic	149,747	110,225	73.6	16,820	11.2	86,903	58.0	40,838	27.3
Black alone [2]	27,632	17,858	64.6	3,899	14.1	12,670	45.9	9,109	33.0
Asian alone [2]	4,967	2,743	55.2	885	17.8	1,910	38.4	1,721	34.6
Hispanic [3]	22,889	13,078	57.1	5,175	22.6	8,532	37.3	9,829	42.9
White alone or in combination [4]	173,708	124,338	71.6	22,059	12.7	96,194	55.4	51,014	29.4
Black alone or in combination [4]	29,439	18,957	64.4	4,285	14.6	13,310	45.2	9,956	33.8
Asian alone or in combination [4]	6,341	3,768	59.4	1,056	16.6	2,642	41.7	2,202	34.7
NATURALIZED CITIZEN									
All races [1]	23,711	14,473	61.0	4,961	20.9	9,826	41.4	9,769	41.2
White alone [2]	12,716	7,634	60.0	2,732	21.5	5,334	41.9	5,144	40.5
White alone, non-Hispanic	5,217	3,202	61.4	930	17.8	2,415	46.3	1,763	33.8
Black alone [2]	3,193	1,912	59.9	529	16.6	1,229	38.5	1,237	38.7
Asian alone [2]	7,144	4,513	63.2	1,594	22.3	2,959	41.4	3,168	44.3
Hispanic [3]	8,299	4,947	59.6	1,956	23.6	3,275	39.5	3,696	44.5
White alone or in combination [4]	13,049	7,840	60.1	2,795	21.4	5,489	42.1	5,259	40.3
Black alone or in combination [4]	3,338	2,010	60.2	555	16.6	1,295	38.8	1,296	38.8
Asian alone or in combination [4]	7,290	4,614	63.3	1,613	22.1	3,017	41.4	3,230	44.3

[1] Includes other races, not shown separately. [2] Data shown represent persons who selected this race group only and exclude persons reporting more than one race. [3] Persons of Hispanic origin may be of any race. [4] In combination with one or more races.

Source: U.S. Census Bureau, "Voting and Registration in the Election of November 2022," <www.census.gov/data/tables/time-series/demo/voting-and-registration/p20-586.html>, accessed May 2023.

Table 453. Vote Cast for President by Major Political Party: 1948 to 2020

[In thousands (48,834 represents 48,834,000), except percent and electoral vote. Prior to 1960, excludes Alaska and Hawaii; prior to 1964, excludes DC. Vote cast for major party candidates includes the votes of minor parties cast for those candidates]

Year	Candidates for President		Vote cast for President						
			Total popular vote [1] (1,000)	Democratic			Republican		
				Popular vote		Electoral vote	Popular vote		Electoral vote
	Democratic	Republican		Number (1,000)	Percent		Number (1,000)	Percent	
1948..........	Truman	Dewey	48,834	24,106	49.4	303	21,969	45.0	189
1952..........	Stevenson	Eisenhower	61,552	27,315	44.4	89	33,779	54.9	442
1956..........	Stevenson	Eisenhower	62,027	26,739	43.1	73	35,581	57.4	457
1960..........	Kennedy	Nixon	68,836	34,227	49.7	303	34,108	49.5	219
1964..........	Johnson	Goldwater	70,098	42,825	61.1	486	27,147	38.7	52
1968..........	Humphrey	Nixon	73,027	30,989	42.4	191	31,710	43.4	301
1972..........	McGovern	Nixon	77,625	28,902	37.2	17	46,740	60.2	520
1976..........	Carter	Ford	81,603	40,826	50.0	297	39,148	48.0	240
1980..........	Carter	Reagan	86,497	35,481	41.0	49	43,643	50.5	489
1984..........	Mondale	Reagan	92,655	37,450	40.4	13	54,167	58.5	525
1988..........	Dukakis	Bush	91,587	41,717	45.5	111	48,643	53.1	426
1992..........	Clinton	Bush	104,600	44,858	42.9	370	38,799	37.1	168
1996..........	Clinton	Dole	96,390	47,402	49.2	379	39,198	40.7	159
2000..........	Gore	Bush	105,594	50,996	48.3	266	50,465	47.8	271
2004..........	Kerry	Bush	122,349	58,895	48.1	251	61,873	50.6	286
2008..........	Obama	McCain	131,407	69,498	52.9	365	59,948	45.6	173
2012..........	Obama	Romney	129,140	65,752	50.9	332	60,670	47.0	206
2016..........	Clinton	Trump	136,787	65,677	48.0	227	62,692	45.8	304
2020..........	Biden	Trump	158,482	80,884	51.0	306	73,920	46.6	232

[1] Include votes for minor party candidates, independents, unpledged electors, and scattered write-in votes.

Source: U.S. House of Representatives, Office of the Clerk, *Statistics of the Presidential and Congressional Election*, February 2021, and earlier reports. See also <clerk.house.gov/Members#ElectionInformation>.

Table 454. Vote Cast for Leading Minority Party Candidates for President: 1948 to 2020

[In thousands (1,169 represents 1,169,000). See headnote, Table 453. Data do not include write-ins, scatterings, or votes for candidates who ran on party tickets not shown, unless otherwise noted]

Year	Candidate	Party	Popular vote (1,000)	Candidate	Party	Popular vote (1,000)
1948..........	Strom Thurmond	States' Rights	1,169	Henry Wallace	Progressive	1,156
1952..........	Vincent Hallinan	Progressive	135	Stuart Hamblen	Prohibition	73
1956 [1]........	T. Coleman Andrews	States' Rights	91	Eric Hass	Socialist Labor	41
1960..........	Eric Hass	Socialist Labor	46	Rutherford Decker	Prohibition	46
1964..........	Eric Hass	Socialist Labor	43	Clifton DeBerry	Socialist Workers	22
1968..........	George Wallace	American Independent	9,446	Henning Blomen	Socialist Labor	52
1972 [1]........	John Schmitz	American	993	Benjamin Spock	People's	9
1976..........	Eugene McCarthy	Independent	680	Roger McBride	Libertarian	172
1980..........	John Anderson	Independent	5,251	Ed Clark	Libertarian	920
1984..........	David Bergland	Libertarian	227	Lyndon H. LaRouche	Independent	79
1988..........	Ron Paul	Libertarian	410	Lenora B. Fulani	New Alliance	129
1992..........	H. Ross Perot	Independent	19,722	Andre Marrou	Libertarian	281
1996..........	H. Ross Perot	Reform	7,137	Ralph Nader	Green	527
2000..........	Ralph Nader	Green	2,530	Pat Buchanan	Reform	324
2004..........	Michael Badnarik	Libertarian	369	Ralph Nader	Independent	156
2008..........	Ralph Nader	Independent	739	Bob Barr	Libertarian	515
2012..........	Gary Johnson	Libertarian	1,216	Jill Stein	Green	401
2016..........	Gary Johnson	Libertarian	4,081	Jill Stein	Green	1,351
2020..........	Jo Jorgensen	Libertarian	1,761	Howie Hawkins	Green	372

[1] Data include write-ins, scatterings, and/or votes for candidates who ran on party tickets not shown.

Source: U.S. House of Representatives, Office of the Clerk, *Statistics of the Presidential and Congressional Election*, February 2021, and earlier reports. See also <clerk.house.gov/Members#ElectionInformation>.

Table 455. Electoral Vote Cast for President by Major Political Party—States: 1980 to 2020

[D = Democratic, R = Republican. For composition of regions, see map, inside front cover]

State	1980	1984	1988 [1]	1992	1996	2000 [2]	2004 [3]	2008 [4]	2012	2016 [5]	2020 [6]
Democratic	**49**	**13**	**111**	**370**	**379**	**266**	**251**	**365**	**332**	**227**	**306**
Republican	**489**	**525**	**426**	**168**	**159**	**271**	**286**	**173**	**206**	**304**	**232**
Northeast:											
Democratic	4	–	53	106	106	102	101	101	96	75	95
Republican	118	113	60	–	–	4	–	–	–	21	1
Midwest:											
Democratic	10	10	29	100	100	68	57	97	80	30	57
Republican	135	127	108	29	29	61	66	27	38	88	61
South:											
Democratic	31	3	8	68	80	15	16	71	58	29	45
Republican	138	174	168	116	104	168	173	118	138	165	151
West:											
Democratic	4	–	21	96	93	81	77	96	98	93	109
Republican	98	111	90	23	26	38	47	28	30	30	19
Alabama	R-9	R-9	R-9	R-9	R-9	R-9	R-9	R-9	R-9	R-9	R-9
Alaska	R-3	R-3	R-3	R-3	R-3	R-3	R-3	R-3	R-3	R-3	R-3
Arizona	R-6	R-7	R-7	R-8	D-8	R-8	R-10	R-10	R-11	R-11	D-11
Arkansas	R-6	R-6	R-6	D-6	D-6	R-6	R-6	R-6	R-6	R-6	R-6
California	R-45	R-47	R-47	D-54	D-54	D-54	D-55	D-55	D-55	D-55	D-55
Colorado	R-7	R-8	R-8	D-8	R-8	R-8	R-9	D-9	D-9	D-9	D-9
Connecticut	R-8	R-8	R-8	D-8	D-8	D-8	D-7	D-7	D-7	D-7	D-7
Delaware	R-3	R-3	R-3	D-3	D-3	D-3	D-3	D-3	D-3	D-3	D-3
District of Columbia	D-3	D-3	D-3	D-3	D-3	D-2	D-3	D-3	D-3	D-3	D-3
Florida	R-17	R-21	R-21	R-25	D-25	R-25	R-27	D-27	D-29	R-29	R-29
Georgia	D-12	R-12	R-12	D-13	R-13	R-13	R-15	R-15	R-16	R-16	D-16
Hawaii	D-4	R-4	D-4	D-4	D-4	D-4	D-4	D-4	D-4	D-3	D-4
Idaho	R-4	R-4	R-4	R-4	R-4	R-4	R-4	R-4	R-4	R-4	R-4
Illinois	R-26	R-24	R-24	D-22	D-22	D-22	D-21	D-21	D-20	D-20	D-20
Indiana	R-13	R-12	R-12	R-12	R-12	R-12	R-11	D-11	R-11	R-11	R-11
Iowa	R-8	R-8	D-8	D-7	D-7	D-7	R-7	D-7	D-6	R-6	R-6
Kansas	R-7	R-7	R-7	R-6	R-6	R-6	R-6	R-6	R-6	R-6	R-6
Kentucky	R-9	R-9	R-9	D-8	D-8	R-8	R-8	R-8	R-8	R-8	R-8
Louisiana	R-10	R-10	R-10	D-9	D-9	R-9	R-9	R-9	R-8	R-8	R-8
Maine	R-4	R-4	R-4	D-4	D-4	D-4	D-4	D-4	D-4	D-3	D-3
Maryland	D-10	R-10	R-10	D-10	D-10	D-10	D-10	D-10	D-10	D-10	D-10
Massachusetts	R-14	R-13	D-13	D-12	D-12	D-12	D-12	D-12	D-11	D-11	D-11
Michigan	R-21	R-20	R-20	D-18	D-18	D-18	D-17	D-17	D-16	R-16	D-16
Minnesota	D-10	D-10	D-10	D-10	D-10	D-10	D-9	D-10	D-10	D-10	D-10
Mississippi	R-7	R-7	R-7	R-7	R-7	R-7	R-6	R-6	R-6	R-6	R-6
Missouri	R-12	R-11	R-11	D-11	D-11	R-11	R-11	R-11	R-10	R-10	R-10
Montana	R-4	R-4	R-4	D-3	R-3	R-3	R-3	R-3	R-3	R-3	R-3
Nebraska	R-5	R-5	R-5	R-5	R-5	R-5	R-5	R-4	R-5	R-5	R-4
Nevada	R-3	R-4	R-4	D-4	D-4	R-4	R-5	D-5	D-6	D-6	D-6
New Hampshire	R-4	R-4	R-4	D-4	D-4	R-4	D-4	D-4	D-4	D-4	D-4
New Jersey	R-17	R-16	R-16	D-15	D-15	D-15	D-15	D-15	D-14	D-14	D-14
New Mexico	R-4	R-5	R-5	D-5	D-5	D-5	R-5	D-5	D-5	D-5	D-5
New York	R-41	R-36	D-36	D-33	D-33	D-33	D-31	D-31	D-29	D-29	D-29
North Carolina	R-13	R-13	R-13	R-14	R-14	R-14	R-15	D-15	R-15	R-15	R-15
North Dakota	R-3	R-3	R-3	R-3	R-3	R-3	R-3	R-3	R-3	R-3	R-3
Ohio	R-25	R-23	R-23	D-21	D-21	R-21	R-20	D-20	D-18	R-18	R-18
Oklahoma	R-8	R-8	R-8	R-8	R-8	R-8	R-7	R-7	R-7	R-7	R-7
Oregon	R-6	R-7	D-7	D-7	D-7	D-7	D-7	D-7	D-7	D-7	D-7
Pennsylvania	R-27	R-25	R-25	D-23	D-23	D-23	D-21	D-21	D-20	R-20	D-20
Rhode Island	D-4	R-4	D-4	D-4	D-4	D-4	D-4	D-4	D-4	D-4	D-4
South Carolina	R-8	R-8	R-8	R-8	R-8	R-8	R-8	R-8	R-9	R-9	R-9
South Dakota	R-4	R-3	R-3	R-3	R-3	R-3	R-3	R-3	R-3	R-3	R-3
Tennessee	R-10	R-11	R-11	D-11	D-11	R-11	R-11	R-11	R-11	R-11	R-11
Texas	R-26	R-29	R-29	R-32	R-32	R-32	R-34	R-34	R-38	R-36	R-38
Utah	R-4	R-5	R-5	R-5	R-5	R-5	R-5	R-5	R-6	R-6	R-6
Vermont	R-3	R-3	R-3	D-3	D-3	D-3	D-3	D-3	D-3	D-3	D-3
Virginia	R-12	R-12	R-12	R-13	R-13	R-13	R-13	D-13	D-13	D-13	D-13
Washington	R-9	R-10	D-10	D-11	D-11	D-11	D-11	D-11	D-12	D-8	D-12
West Virginia	D-6	R-6	D-5	D-5	D-5	R-5	R-5	R-5	R-5	R-5	R-5
Wisconsin	R-11	R-11	D-11	D-11	D-11	D-11	D-10	D-10	D-10	R-10	D-10
Wyoming	R-3	R-3	R-3	R-3	R-3	R-3	R-3	R-3	R-3	R-3	R-3

– Represents zero. [1] Excludes one electoral vote cast in West Virginia for Lloyd Bentsen for President. [2] Excludes one electoral vote left blank by a Democratic elector in the District of Columbia. [3] Excludes one electoral vote cast in Minnesota for Democratic vice presidential nominee John Edwards. [4] Excludes one electoral vote cast in Nebraska for Barack Obama. [5] Excludes one electoral vote cast in Hawaii for Bernie Sanders, one electoral vote cast in Maine for Donald J. Trump, one electoral vote each cast in Texas for John Kasich and Ron Paul, and, in Washington, three electoral votes cast for Colin Powell and one electoral vote cast for Faith Spotted Eagle. [6] Excludes one electoral vote cast in Maine for Donald J. Trump and one electoral vote cast in Nebraska for Joe Biden.

Source: U.S. House of Representatives, Office of the Clerk, *Statistics of the Presidential and Congressional Election*, February 2021, and earlier reports. See also <clerk.house.gov/Members#ElectionInformation>.

Table 456. Popular Vote Cast for President by Political Party—States: 2016 and 2020

[In thousands (136,787 represents 136,787,000), except percent]

State	2016					2020				
				Percent of total vote					Percent of total vote	
	Total [1]	Demo-cratic party	Republi-can party	Demo-cratic party	Republi-can party	Total [1]	Demo-cratic party	Republi-can party	Demo-cratic party	Republi-can party
United States.........	136,787	65,677	62,692	48.0	45.8	158,482	80,884	73,920	51.0	46.6
Alabama.................	2,123	730	1,318	34.4	62.1	2,323	850	1,441	36.6	62.0
Alaska....................	319	116	163	36.6	51.3	360	154	190	42.8	52.8
Arizona..................	2,573	1,161	1,252	45.1	48.7	3,387	1,672	1,662	49.4	49.1
Arkansas...............	1,131	380	685	33.7	60.6	1,219	424	761	34.8	62.4
California...............	14,182	8,754	4,484	61.7	31.6	17,501	11,110	6,006	63.5	34.3
Colorado................	2,780	1,339	1,202	48.2	43.3	3,257	1,804	1,365	55.4	41.9
Connecticut............	1,645	898	673	54.6	40.9	1,824	1,081	715	59.3	39.2
Delaware................	442	236	185	53.4	41.9	504	296	201	58.7	39.8
District of Columbia.....	313	283	13	90.5	4.1	343	317	19	92.6	5.4
Florida...................	9,420	4,505	4,618	47.8	49.0	11,067	5,297	5,669	47.9	51.2
Georgia.................	4,115	1,878	2,089	45.6	50.8	5,001	2,475	2,462	49.5	49.2
Hawaii...................	438	267	129	61.0	29.4	571	366	197	64.2	34.5
Idaho....................	690	190	409	27.5	59.3	868	287	554	33.1	63.8
Illinois...................	5,536	3,091	2,146	55.8	38.8	6,034	3,472	2,447	57.5	40.6
Indiana..................	2,735	1,033	1,557	37.8	56.9	3,033	1,242	1,730	41.0	57.0
Iowa.....................	1,566	654	801	41.8	51.2	1,700	759	898	44.6	52.8
Kansas..................	1,184	427	671	36.1	56.7	1,372	570	771	41.6	56.2
Kentucky................	1,924	629	1,203	32.7	62.5	2,137	772	1,327	36.2	62.1
Louisiana...............	2,029	780	1,179	38.4	58.1	2,148	856	1,256	39.9	58.5
Maine....................	772	358	336	46.3	43.5	828	435	361	52.5	43.6
Maryland................	2,781	1,678	943	60.3	33.9	3,037	1,985	976	65.4	32.2
Massachusetts..........	3,379	1,995	1,091	59.1	32.3	3,658	2,382	1,167	65.1	31.9
Michigan................	4,799	2,269	2,280	47.3	47.5	5,539	2,804	2,650	50.6	47.8
Minnesota..............	2,945	1,368	1,323	46.4	44.9	3,277	1,717	1,484	52.4	45.3
Mississippi.............	1,209	485	701	40.1	57.9	1,314	540	757	41.1	57.6
Missouri.................	2,809	1,071	1,595	38.1	56.8	3,026	1,253	1,719	41.4	56.8
Montana................	495	178	279	35.9	56.5	604	245	344	40.6	56.9
Nebraska...............	844	284	496	33.7	58.7	956	375	557	39.2	58.2
Nevada..................	1,125	539	512	47.9	45.5	1,405	703	670	50.1	47.7
New Hampshire.........	744	349	346	46.8	46.5	806	425	366	52.7	45.4
New Jersey.............	3,874	2,148	1,602	55.5	41.4	4,549	2,608	1,883	57.3	41.4
New Mexico.............	798	385	320	48.3	40.0	924	502	402	54.3	43.5
New York................	7,802	4,380	2,527	56.1	32.4	8,662	4,845	2,949	55.9	34.0
North Carolina..........	4,742	2,189	2,363	46.2	49.8	5,525	2,684	2,759	48.6	49.9
North Dakota...........	344	94	217	27.2	63.0	362	115	236	31.8	65.1
Ohio.....................	5,496	2,394	2,841	43.6	51.7	5,922	2,679	3,155	45.2	53.3
Oklahoma...............	1,453	420	949	28.9	65.3	1,561	504	1,020	32.3	65.4
Oregon..................	2,001	1,002	782	50.1	39.1	2,374	1,340	958	56.5	40.4
Pennsylvania............	6,115	2,926	2,971	47.9	48.6	6,915	3,458	3,378	50.0	48.8
Rhode Island...........	464	253	181	54.4	38.9	518	307	200	59.4	38.6
South Carolina..........	2,103	855	1,155	40.7	54.9	2,513	1,092	1,385	43.4	55.1
South Dakota...........	370	117	228	31.7	61.5	423	150	261	35.6	61.8
Tennessee..............	2,508	871	1,523	34.7	60.7	3,054	1,144	1,852	37.5	60.7
Texas...................	8,969	3,878	4,685	43.2	52.2	11,315	5,259	5,890	46.5	52.1
Utah.....................	1,131	311	515	27.5	45.5	1,488	560	865	37.6	58.1
Vermont.................	320	179	95	55.7	29.8	371	243	113	65.5	30.4
Virginia..................	3,983	1,981	1,769	49.8	44.4	4,461	2,414	1,962	54.1	44.0
Washington.............	3,317	1,743	1,222	52.5	36.8	4,088	2,370	1,585	58.0	38.8
West Virginia...........	713	189	489	26.5	68.6	781	236	545	30.2	69.8
Wisconsin...............	2,976	1,383	1,405	46.5	47.2	3,297	1,631	1,610	49.5	48.8
Wyoming................	259	56	174	21.6	67.4	279	73	194	26.4	69.5

[1] Includes other parties.

Source: U.S. House of Representatives, Office of the Clerk, *Statistics of the Presidential and Congressional Election*, February 2021, and earlier reports. See also <clerk.house.gov/Members#ElectionInformation>.

Table 457. Vote Cast for U.S. Senators, 2020 and 2022, and Incumbent Senators as of 2023 by State

[2,316 represents 2,316,000. D = Democrat, R = Republican, I = Independent]

State	2020 Total[2] (1,000)	2020 Percent for leading party	2022 Total[2] (1,000)	2022 Percent for leading party	Incumbent senators and year term expires[1] Name, party, and year	Incumbent senators and year term expires[1] Name, party, and year
Alabama............	2,316	R-60.1	1,414	R-66.6	Katie Britt (R) 2029	Tommy Tuberville (R) 2027
Alaska..............	355	R-53.9	262	R-88.9	Lisa Murkowski (R) 2029	Dan Sullivan (R) 2027
Arizona.............	(X)	(X)	2,572	D-51.4	[3] Mark Kelly (D) 2029	[4] Kyrsten Sinema (I) 2025
Arkansas...........	1,193	R-66.5	901	R-65.7	John Boozman (R) 2029	Tom Cotton (R) 2027
California..........	(X)	(X)	21,615	D-61.0	Dianne Feinstein (D) 2025	Alex Padilla (D) 2029
Colorado...........	3,236	D-53.5	2,500	D-55.9	Michael F. Bennet (D) 2029	John W. Hickenlooper (D) 2027
Connecticut........	(X)	(X)	1,260	D-55.7	Richard Blumenthal (D) 2029	Christopher Murphy (D) 2025
Delaware...........	491	D-59.4	(X)	(X)	Thomas R. Carper (D) 2025	Christopher A. Coons (D) 2027
Florida.............	(X)	(X)	7,758	R-57.7	Marco Rubio (R) 2029	Rick Scott (R) 2025
Georgia............	4,600	D-49.3	3,623	D-50.2	Jon Ossoff (D) 2027	Raphael G. Warnock (D) 2029
Hawaii..............	(X)	(X)	419	D-69.4	Mazie K. Hirono (D) 2025	Brian Schatz (D) 2029
Idaho..............	860	R-62.6	591	R-60.7	Mike Crapo (R) 2029	James E. Risch (R) 2027
Illinois.............	5,969	D- 54.9	4,099	D-56.8	Tammy Duckworth (D) 2029	Richard J. Durbin (D) 2027
Indiana.............	(X)	(X)	1,860	R-58.6	Mike Braun (R) 2025	Todd Young (R) 2029
Iowa...............	1,700	R-50.9	1,230	R-55.4	Joni Ernst (R) 2027	Chuck Grassley (R) 2029
Kansas.............	1,368	R-53.2	1,005	R-60.0	Roger Marshall (R) 2027	Jerry Moran (R) 2029
Kentucky...........	2,135	R-57.8	1,478	R-61.8	Mitch McConnell (R) 2027	Rand Paul (R) 2029
Louisiana..........	2,072	R-61.2	1,383	R-63.4	Bill Cassidy (R) 2027	John Kennedy (R) 2029
Maine.............	828	R-50.4	(X)	(X)	Susan M. Collins (R) 2027	Angus S. King (I) 2025
Maryland...........	(X)	(X)	2,002	D-65.8	Benjamin L. Cardin (D) 2025	Chris Van Hollen (D) 2029
Massachusetts.....	3,658	D-64.5	(X)	(X)	Edward J. Markey (D) 2027	Elizabeth Warren (D) 2025
Michigan...........	5,480	D-49.9	(X)	(X)	Gary C. Peters (D) 2027	Debbie Stabenow (D) 2025
Minnesota.........	3,214	D-48.7	(X)	(X)	Amy Klobuchar (D) 2025	Tina Smith (D) 2027
Mississippi.........	1,311	R-54.1	(X)	(X)	Cindy Hyde-Smith (R) 2027	Roger F. Wicker (R) 2025
Missouri...........	(X)	(X)	2,069	R-55.4	Josh Hawley (R) 2025	Eric Schmitt (R) 2029
Montana...........	606	R-55.0	(X)	(X)	Steve Daines (R) 2027	Jon Tester (D) 2025
Nebraska..........	930	R-62.7	(X)	(X)	Deb Fischer (R) 2025	[5] Pete Ricketts (R) 2027
Nevada.............	(X)	(X)	1,021	D-48.8	Catherine Cortez Masto (D) 2029	Jacky Rosen (D) 2025
New Hampshire....	796	D-56.6	621	D-53.5	Margaret Wood Hassan (D) 2029	Jeanne Shaheen (D) 2027
New Jersey.........	4,440	D-57.2	(X)	(X)	Cory A. Booker (D) 2027	Robert Menendez (D) 2025
New Mexico........	917	D-51.7	(X)	(X)	Martin Heinrich (D) 2025	Ben Ray Luján (D) 2027
New York..........	(X)	(X)	5,966	D-50.7	Kirsten E. Gillibrand (D) 2025	Charles E. Schumer (D) 2029
North Carolina.....	5,475	R-48.7	3,774	R-50.5	Ted Budd (R) 2029	Thom Tillis (R) 2027
North Dakota.......	(X)	(X)	240	R-56.4	Kevin Cramer (R) 2025	John Hoeven (R) 2029
Ohio...............	(X)	(X)	4,133	R-53.0	Sherrod Brown (D) 2025	J. D. Vance (R) 2029
Oklahoma[6]........	1,556	R-62.9	2,301	R-63.0	James Lankford (R) 2029	Markwayne Mullin (R) 2027
Oregon.............	2,321	D-56.9	1,928	D-55.8	Jeff Merkley (D) 2027	Ron Wyden (D) 2029
Pennsylvania.......	(X)	(X)	5,368	D-51.2	Robert P. Casey, Jr. (D) 2025	John Fetterman (D) 2029
Rhode Island.......	494	D-66.5	(X)	(X)	Jack Reed (D) 2027	Sheldon Whitehouse (D) 2025
South Carolina.....	2,513	R-54.5	1,696	R-62.9	Lindsey Graham (R) 2027	Tim Scott (R) 2029
South Dakota......	420	R-65.7	348	R-69.6	Mike Rounds (R) 2027	John Thune (R) 2029
Tennessee.........	2,960	R-62.2	(X)	(X)	Marsha Blackburn (R) 2025	Bill Hagerty (R) 2027
Texas..............	11,144	R-53.5	(X)	(X)	John Cornyn (R) 2027	Ted Cruz (R) 2025
Utah...............	(X)	(X)	1,076	R-53.2	Mike Lee (R) 2029	Mitt Romney (R) 2025
Vermont............	(X)	(X)	292	D-67.3	Bernard Sanders (I) 2025	Peter Welch (D) 2029
Virginia.............	4,405	D-56.0	(X)	(X)	Tim Kaine (D) 2025	Mark R. Warner (D) 2027
Washington.........	(X)	(X)	3,048	D-57.1	Maria Cantwell (D) 2025	Patty Murray (D) 2029
West Virginia.......	779	R-70.3	(X)	(X)	Shelley Moore Capito (R) 2027	Joe Manchin III (D) 2025
Wisconsin..........	(X)	(X)	2,652	R-50.4	Tammy Baldwin (D) 2025	Ron Johnson (R) 2029
Wyoming...........	279	R-71.1	(X)	(X)	John Barrasso (R) 2025	Cynthia M. Lummis (R) 2027

X Not applicable. [1] As of March 24, 2023. [2] Includes vote cast for minor parties. [3] Elected in a special election on November 3, 2020, to complete the term left vacant by the death of John McCain; re-elected in general election on November 8, 2022. [4] Elected in 2018 as a Democrat; changed party affiliation in December 2022. [5] Appointed in January 2023 to complete the term left vacant by the resignation of Ben Sasse. [6] Oklahoma held two senatorial elections in 2022.

Source: U.S. House of Representatives, Office of the Clerk, *Statistics of the Congressional Election of November 8, 2022*, February 2023, and earlier reports; United States Senate, "Senators," <www.senate.gov/senators/index.htm>; and ProQuest research. See also <clerk.house.gov/Members#ElectionInformation>.

Table 458. Vote Cast for U.S. House of Representatives by Major Political Party—States: 2018 to 2022

[In thousands (114,017 represents 114,017,000), except percent. R = Republican and D = Democrat. In each state, totals represent the sum of votes cast in each Congressional District or votes cast for Representative-at-Large in states where only one member is elected. In all years there are numerous districts within the state where either the Republican or Democratic party had no candidate. In some states the Republican and Democratic vote includes votes cast for the party candidate by endorsing parties]

State	2018				2020				2022			
	Total [1]	Demo-cratic	Republi-can	Percent for leading party	Total [1]	Demo-cratic	Republi-can	Percent for leading party	Total [1]	Demo-cratic	Republi-can	Percent for leading party
U.S.........	114,017	60,320	50,467	D-52.9	153,431	77,123	72,467	D-50.3	108,443	51,280	54,228	R-50.0
AL.........	1,660	679	976	R-58.8	2,052	609	1,416	R-69.0	1,344	319	942	R-70.1
AK.........	282	131	150	R-53.1	353	160	192	R-54.4	264	129	129	R-49.1
AZ.........	2,341	1,179	1,139	D-50.4	3,268	1,629	1,639	R-50.1	2,360	1,004	1,325	R-56.1
AR.........	889	313	556	R-62.6	1,179	330	828	R-70.2	895	272	598	R-66.8
CA.........	12,185	8,010	3,973	D-65.7	16,725	11,084	5,641	D-66.3	10,656	6,744	3,860	D-63.3
CO.........	2,514	1,343	1,080	D-53.4	3,165	1,679	1,378	D-53.1	2,472	1,365	1,051	D-55.2
CT.........	1,380	809	512	D-58.6	1,773	1,023	677	D-57.7	1,261	713	521	D-56.5
DE [2].........	354	227	125	D-64.3	488	281	196	D-57.6	322	178	138	D-55.5
FL [2].........	7,021	3,307	3,675	R-52.3	10,465	4,942	5,469	R-52.3	7,332	2,906	4,271	R-58.3
GA.........	3,802	1,814	1,987	R-52.3	4,884	2,393	2,490	R-51.0	3,909	1,864	2,045	R-52.3
HI.........	399	288	87	D-72.2	580	355	155	D-61.2	419	272	124	D-64.8
ID.........	596	207	368	R-61.8	850	256	561	R-66.1	584	181	395	R-67.7
IL.........	4,540	2,758	1,754	D-60.7	5,877	3,355	2,417	D-57.1	4,049	2,271	1,769	D-56.1
IN.........	2,256	1,000	1,248	R-55.3	2,996	1,195	1,739	R-58.0	1,857	716	1,108	R-59.7
IA.........	1,316	665	612	D-50.5	1,700	762	859	R-50.5	1,230	526	678	R-55.1
KS.........	1,050	464	563	R-53.6	1,359	557	776	R-57.1	1,002	425	570	R-56.9
KY.........	1,570	613	935	R-59.6	2,116	735	1,364	R-64.5	1,463	491	953	R-65.1
LA [2].........	1,461	553	836	R-57.2	1,947	727	1,170	R-60.1	1,133	319	774	R-68.3
ME.........	631	344	250	D-54.4	828	469	340	D-56.6	1,014	385	275	D-37.9
MD.........	2,286	1,493	738	D-65.3	2,954	1,913	1,028	D-64.7	1,996	1,291	690	D-64.7
MA.........	2,753	1,944	498	D-70.6	3,658	2,483	699	D-67.9	2,511	1,636	707	D-65.2
MI.........	4,155	2,175	1,853	D-52.4	5,423	2,689	2,618	D-49.6	4,376	2,185	2,083	D-49.9
MN.........	2,577	1,421	1,126	D-55.1	3,194	1,554	1,475	D-48.7	2,496	1,251	1,201	D-50.1
MS.........	939	399	471	R-50.2	1,228	421	807	R-65.7	709	251	454	R-64.1
MO.........	2,418	1,028	1,331	R-55.0	2,973	1,172	1,724	R-58.0	2,060	795	1,224	R-59.4
MT.........	504	233	257	R-50.9	602	262	339	R-56.4	464	159	245	R-52.9
NE.........	697	264	432	R-62.0	941	326	585	R-62.2	663	236	415	R-62.5
NV.........	961	491	440	D-51.1	1,356	666	634	D-49.1	1,010	481	516	R-51.1
NH.........	571	311	249	D-54.5	787	414	354	D-52.6	618	339	278	D-54.9
NJ.........	3,099	1,857	1,199	D-59.9	4,433	2,539	1,843	D-57.3	2,610	1,416	1,160	D-54.3
NM.........	693	404	265	D-58.3	904	496	408	D-54.8	704	388	316	D-55.1
NY.........	6,251	3,761	1,640	D-60.2	8,604	4,717	2,692	D-54.8	5,966	3,028	2,233	D-50.8
NC.........	3,381	1,633	1,707	R-50.5	5,325	2,661	2,631	D-50.0	3,761	1,795	1,957	R-52.0
ND.........	322	114	194	R-60.2	356	98	245	R-69.0	239	(X)	148	R-62.2
OH.........	4,406	2,083	2,291	R-52.0	5,762	2,452	3,253	R-56.5	4,110	1,791	2,319	R-56.4
OK [2].........	1,179	428	731	R-62.0	1,551	476	1,044	R-67.3	1,146	357	761	R-66.4
OR.........	1,848	1,061	703	D-57.4	2,308	1,285	967	D-55.7	1,907	1,013	852	D-53.1
PA.........	4,930	2,713	2,206	D-55.0	6,779	3,347	3,433	R-50.6	5,152	2,437	2,702	R-52.5
RI.........	373	243	130	D-65.0	488	313	110	D-64.0	358	202	150	D-56.4
SC.........	1,709	758	927	R-54.3	2,505	1,077	1,413	R-56.4	1,602	517	1,056	R-65.9
SD.........	336	121	203	R-60.3	398	(X)	322	R-81.0	328	(X)	254	R-77.4
TN.........	2,160	846	1,280	R-59.2	2,842	1,106	1,685	R-59.3	1,710	582	1,099	R-64.3
TX.........	8,203	3,853	4,135	R-50.4	11,094	4,897	5,927	R-53.4	7,752	2,999	4,559	R-58.8
UT.........	1,053	374	617	R-58.7	1,432	506	873	R-61.0	1,063	342	671	R-63.1
VT.........	278	189	71	D-67.8	371	239	96	D-64.4	292	176	78	D-60.5
VA.........	3,313	1,867	1,409	D-56.4	4,335	2,254	2,048	D-52.0	3,048	1,572	1,462	D-51.6
WA.........	3,022	1,889	900	D-62.5	3,944	2,340	1,545	D-59.3	3,026	1,752	1,262	D-57.9
WV.........	578	235	337	R-58.3	761	247	514	R-67.5	472	150	312	R-66.1
WI.........	2,572	1,367	1,173	D-53.2	3,238	1,567	1,661	R-51.3	2,531	1,013	1,403	R-55.4
WY.........	205	60	128	R-62.3	279	67	186	R-66.7	198	47	132	R-66.7

X Not applicable. [1] Includes votes cast for minor parties. [2] State law does not require tabulation of votes for unopposed candidates.

Source: U.S. House of Representatives, Office of the Clerk, *Statistics of the Congressional Election of November 8, 2022*, February 2023. See also <clerk.house.gov/Members#ElectionInformation>.

Table 459. Vote Cast for U.S. House of Representatives by Major Political Party—Congressional Districts: 2022

[As of February 2023. Does not include special elections or votes received from endorsing parties. If multiple candidates from the same party ran in the general election, only the candidate with the leading number of votes is shown]

State and district	Democrat Name	Democrat Percent of total	Republican Name	Republican Percent of total
AL.....	(X)	(X)	(X)	(X)
1st...	[1]	[1]	Carl	83.6
2d....	Harvey-Hall	29.2	Moore	69.1
3d....	Veasey	25.1	Rogers	71.2
4th....	Neighbors	15.2	Aderholt	84.1
5th....	Warner-Stanton	29.6	Strong	67.1
6th....	[1]	[1]	Palmer	83.7
7th....	Sewell	63.5	Nichols	34.8
AK.....	Peltola	48.8	Palin	25.7
AZ.....	(X)	(X)	(X)	(X)
1st...	Hodge	49.6	Schweikert	50.4
2d....	O'Halleran	46.1	Crane	53.9
3d....	Gallego	77.0	Zink	23.0
4th....	Stanton	56.1	Cooper	43.9
5th....	Ramos	37.4	Biggs	56.7
6th....	Engel	49.2	Ciscomani	50.7
7th....	Grijalva	64.5	Pozzolo	35.5
8th....	[1]	[1]	Lesko	96.5
9th....	[1]	[1]	Gosar	97.8
AR.....	(X)	(X)	(X)	(X)
1st...	Hodges	26.2	Crawford	73.8
2d....	Hathaway	35.3	Hill	60.0
3d....	Mallett-Hays	32.9	Womack	63.7
4th....	White	26.2	Westerman	71.0
CA.....	(X)	(X)	(X)	(X)
1st...	Steiner	37.9	LaMalfa	62.1
2d....	Huffman	74.4	Brower	25.6
3d....	Jones	46.4	Kiley	53.6
4th....	Thompson	67.8	Brock	32.2
5th....	Barkley	38.7	McClintock	61.3
6th....	Bera	55.9	Hamilton	44.1
7th....	Matsui	68.3	Semenenko	31.7
8th....	Garamendi	75.7	Recile	24.3
9th....	Harder	54.8	Patti	45.2
10th...	DeSaulnier	78.9	[1]	[1]
11th...	Pelosi	84.0	Dennis	16.0
12th...	Lee	90.5	Slauson	9.5
13th...	Gray	49.8	Duarte	50.2
14th...	Swalwell	69.3	Hayden	30.7
15th...	Mullin	55.5	[1]	[1]
16th...	Eshoo	57.8	[1]	[1]
17th...	Khanna	70.9	Tandon	29.1
18th...	Lofgren	65.9	Hernandez	34.1
19th...	Panetta	68.7	Gorman	31.3
20th...	Wood	32.8	McCarthy	67.2
21st...	Costa	54.2	Maher	45.8
22d...	Salas	48.5	Valadao	51.5
23d...	Marshall	39.0	Obernolte	61.0
24th...	Carbajal	60.6	Allen	39.4
25th...	Ruiz	57.4	Hawkins	42.6
26th...	Brownley	54.5	Jacobs	45.5
27th...	Smith	46.8	Garcia	53.2
28th...	Chu	66.2	Hallman	33.8
29th...	Cárdenas	58.5	[1]	[1]
30th...	Schiff	71.1	[1]	[1]
31st...	Napolitano	59.5	Bocic Martinez	40.5
32d...	Sherman	69.2	Lapointe Volotzky	30.8
33d...	Aguilar	57.7	Porter	42.3
34th...	Gomez	51.2	[1]	[1]
35th...	Torres	57.4	Cargile	42.6
36th...	Lieu	69.8	Collins	30.2
37th...	Kamlager	64.0	[1]	[1]
38th...	Sánchez	58.1	Ching	41.9
39th...	Takano	57.7	Smith	42.3
40th...	Mahmood	43.2	Kim	56.8
41st...	Rollins	47.7	Calvert	52.3
42d...	Garcia	68.4	Briscoe	31.6
43d...	Waters	77.3	Navarro	22.7
44th...	Barragán	72.2	Jones	27.8
45th...	Chen	47.6	Steel	52.4
46th...	Correa	61.8	Gonzales	38.2
47th...	Porter	51.7	Baugh	48.3
48th...	Houlahan	39.6	Issa	60.4
49th...	Levin	52.6	Maryott	47.4
50th...	Peters	62.8	Gustafson	37.2
51st...	Jacobs	61.9	Caplan	38.1
52d...	Vargas	66.7	Geffeney	33.3
CO.....	(X)	(X)	(X)	(X)
1st...	DeGette	80.3	Qualteri	17.5
2d....	Neguse	70.0	Dawson	28.0
3d....	Frisch	49.9	Boebert	50.1
4th....	McCorkle	36.6	Buck	60.9
5th....	Torres	40.3	Lamborn	56.0
6th....	Crow	60.6	Monahan	37.4
7th....	Pettersen	56.4	Aadland	41.4
8th....	Caraveo	48.4	Kirkmeyer	47.7
CT.....	(X)	(X)	(X)	(X)
1st...	Larson	59.4	Lazor	37.5
2d....	Courtney	58.2	France	40.2
3d....	DeLauro	56.8	DeNardis	40.7
4th....	Himes	59.4	Stevenson	39.5
5th....	Hayes	48.8	Logan	48.6
DE.....	Blunt Rochester	55.5	Murphy	43.0
DC.....	Norton	84.7	Rimensnyder	5.7
FL.....	(X)	(X)	(X)	(X)
1st...	Jones	32.1	Gaetz	67.9
2d....	Lawson	40.2	Dunn	59.8
3d....	Hawk	36.3	Cammack	62.5
4th....	Holloway	39.5	Bean	60.5
5th....	[1]	[1]	Rutherford	[2]
6th....	[1]	[1]	Waltz	75.3
7th....	Green	41.5	Mills	58.5
8th....	Terry	35.1	Posey	64.9
9th....	Soto	53.6	Moore	46.4
10th...	Frost	59.0	Wimbish	39.4
11th...	Munns	35.4	Webster	63.1
12th...	Walker	29.6	Bilirakis	70.4
13th...	Lynn	45.1	Luna	53.1
14th...	Castor	56.9	Judge	43.1
15th...	Cohn	41.5	Lee	58.5
16th...	Schneider	37.8	Buchanan	62.1
17th...	Kale	35.5	Steube	63.8
18th...	[1]	[1]	Franklin	74.7
19th...	Banyai	32.0	Donalds	68.0
20th...	Cherfilus-McCormick	72.3	Clark	27.7
21st...	Balderramos Robinson	36.5	Mast	63.5
22d...	Frankel	55.1	Franzese	44.9
23d...	Moskowitz	51.6	Budd	46.8
24th...	Wilson	71.8	Navarro	28.2
25th...	Wasserman Schultz	55.1	Spalding	44.9
26th...	Olivo	29.1	Diaz-Balart	70.9
27th...	Taddeo	42.7	Salazar	57.3
28th...	Asencio	36.3	Gimenez	63.7
GA.....	(X)	(X)	(X)	(X)
1st...	Herring	40.9	Carter	59.1
2d....	Bishop	55.0	West	45.0
3d....	Almonord	31.3	Ferguson	68.7
4th....	Johnson	78.5	Chavez	21.5
5th....	Williams	82.5	Zimm	17.5
6th....	Christian	37.8	McCormick	62.2
7th....	McBath	60.9	Gonsalves	39.1
8th....	Butler	31.4	Scott	68.6
9th....	Ford	27.6	Clyde	72.4
10th...	Johnson-Green	35.5	Collins	64.5
11th...	Daza	37.4	Loudermilk	62.6
12th...	Johnson	40.4	Allen	59.6
13th...	Scott	81.8	Gonzales	18.2
14th...	Flowers	34.1	Greene	65.9
HI......	(X)	(X)	(X)	(X)
1st...	Case	70.9	Kress	25.3
2d....	Tokuda	59.2	Akana	33.6
ID......	(X)	(X)	(X)	(X)
1st...	Peterson	26.3	Fulcher	71.3
2d....	Norman	36.4	Simpson	63.6
IL......	(X)	(X)	(X)	(X)
1st...	Jackson	67.0	Carlson	33.0
2d....	Kelly	67.1	Lynch	32.9
3d....	Ramirez	68.5	Burau	31.5
4th....	García	68.4	Falakos	28.1
5th....	Quigley	69.6	Hanson	28.8
6th....	Casten	54.4	Pekau	45.6
7th....	Davis	99.9	[1]	[1]
8th....	Krishnamoorthi	56.9	Dargis	43.1
9th....	Schakowsky	71.7	Rice	28.3
10th...	Schneider	63.0	Severino	37.0
11th...	Foster	56.5	Lauf	43.5
12th...	Markel	25.0	Bost	75.0
13th...	Budzinski	56.6	Deering	43.4
14th...	Underwood	54.2	Gryder	45.8
15th...	Lange	28.9	Miller	71.1

See footnotes at end of table.

Table 459. Vote Cast for U.S. House of Representatives by Major Political Party—Congressional Districts: 2022-Continued.

See headnote on page 295.

State and district	Democrat Name	Percent of total	Republican Name	Percent of total	State and district	Democrat Name	Percent of total	Republican Name	Percent of total
16th...	Haderlein	33.7	LaHood	66.3	2d.....	Thompson	60.1	Flowers	39.9
17th...	Sorensen	52.0	King	48.0	3d.....	Young	29.3	Guest	70.7
IN......	(X)	(X)	(X)	(X)	4th....	Dupree	24.6	Ezell	73.3
1st...	Mrvan	52.8	Green	47.2	**MO.....**	(X)	(X)	(X)	(X)
2d.....	Steury	32.4	Yakym	64.6	1st....	Bush	72.9	Jones	24.3
3d.....	Snyder	30.1	Banks	65.3	2d.....	Gunby	43.1	Wagner	54.9
4th....	Day	31.8	Baird	68.2	3d.....	Mann	34.9	Luetkemeyer	65.1
5th....	Lee Lake	38.9	Spartz	61.1	4th....	Truman	26.3	Alford	71.3
6th....	Wirth	32.5	Pence	67.5	5th....	Cleaver	61.0	Turk	36.4
7th....	Carson	2.4	Grabovsky	30.6	6th....	Martin	27.5	Graves	70.3
8th....	McCormick	2.7	Bucshon	65.7	7th....	Radaker-Sheafer	26.8	Burlison	70.9
9th....	Fyfe	33.6	Houchin	63.6	8th....	McCallian	21.9	Smith	76.0
IA......	(X)	(X)	(X)	(X)	**MT......**	(X)	(X)	(X)	(X)
1st...	Bohannan	45.9	Miller-Meeks	52.6	1st....	Tranel	46.5	Zinke	49.6
2d.....	Mathis	45.4	Hinson	53.6	2d.....	Ronning	20.2	Rosendale	56.6
3d.....	Axne	48.9	Nunn	49.6	**NE......**	(X)	(X)	(X)	(X)
4th....	Melton	29.6	Feenstra	65.6	1st....	Pansing Brooks	42.1	Flood	57.9
KS......	(X)	(X)	(X)	(X)	2d.....	Vargas	48.7	Bacon	51.3
1st...	Beard	32.3	Mann	67.7	3d.....	Else	15.8	Smith	78.3
2d...	Schmidt	38.5	LaTurner	57.6	**NV......**	(X)	(X)	(X)	(X)
3d.....	Davids	54.9	Adkins	42.8	1st....	Titus	51.6	Robertson	46.0
4th....	Hernandez	36.7	Estes	63.3	2d.....	Krause	37.8	Amodei	59.7
KY......	(X)	(X)	(X)	(X)	3d.....	Lee	52.0	Becker	48.0
1st...	Ausbrooks	25.1	Comer	74.9	4th....	Horsford	52.4	Peters	47.6
2d.....	Linderman	28.1	Guthrie	71.9	**NH......**	(X)	(X)	(X)	(X)
3d.....	McGarvey	62.0	Ray	38.0	1st....	Pappas	54.0	Leavitt	45.9
4th....	Lehman	31.0	Massie	65.0	2d.....	Kuster	55.8	Burns	44.1
5th....	Halbleib	17.8	Rogers	82.2	**NJ......**	(X)	(X)	(X)	(X)
6th....	Young	33.6	Barr	62.7	1st....	Norcross	62.3	Gustafson	35.2
LA......	(X)	(X)	(X)	(X)	2d.....	Alexander	40.0	Van Drew	58.9
1st...	Darling	25.2	Scalise	72.8	3d.....	Kim	55.5	Healey	43.6
2d.....	Carter	77.1	Lux	22.9	4th....	Jenkins	31.4	Smith	66.9
3d.....	LeBlanc	10.5	Higgins	64.3	5th....	Gottheimer	54.7	Pallotta	44.3
4th....	([1])	([1])	Johnson	([2])	6th....	Pallone	57.5	Kiley	41.0
5th....	Dantzler	15.7	Letlow	67.6	7th....	Malinowski	48.6	Kean	51.4
6th....	([1])	([1])	Graves	80.4	8th....	Menendez	73.6	Arroyo	23.4
ME......	(X)	(X)	(X)	(X)	9th....	Pascrell	55.0	Prempeh	43.6
1st...	Pingree	61.4	Thelander	36.1	10th....	Payne	77.6	Pinckney	20.0
2d.....	Golden	[3] 25.2	Poliquin	[3] 22.3	11th....	Sherrill	59.0	DeGroot	40.2
MD......	(X)	(X)	(X)	(X)	12th....	Watson Coleman	63.1	Mayfield	35.9
1st...	Mizeur	43.1	Harris	54.4	**NM......**	(X)	(X)	(X)	(X)
2d.....	Ruppersberger	59.2	Ambrose	40.6	1st....	Stansbury	55.7	Garcia Holmes	44.2
3d.....	Sarbanes	60.2	Morgan	39.7	2d.....	Vasquez	50.3	Herrell	49.6
4th....	Ivey	90.1	Warner	9.7	3d.....	Leger Fernandez	58.2	Martinez Johnson	41.8
5th....	Hoyer	65.9	Palombi	33.9	**NY......**	(X)	(X)	(X)	(X)
6th....	Trone	54.7	Parrott	45.2	1st....	Fleming	41.3	LaLota	47.1
7th....	Mfume	82.1	Collier	17.7	2d.....	Gordon	36.4	Garbarino	51.1
8th....	Raskin	80.2	Coll	18.2	3d.....	Zimmerman	42.9	Santos	47.8
MA......	(X)	(X)	(X)	(X)	4th....	Gillen	47.0	D'Esposito	46.4
1st...	Neal	59.8	Martilli	37.3	5th....	Meeks	72.3	King	21.8
2d.....	McGovern	64.5	Sossa-Paquette	32.8	6th....	Meng	61.8	Zmich	32.1
3d.....	Trahan	61.5	Tran	35.2	7th....	Velázquez	62.3	Pagan	17.2
4th....	Auchincloss	69.2	([1])	([1])	8th....	Jeffries	68.6	Dashevsky	25.5
5th....	Clark	71.6	Colarusso	25.1	9th....	Clarke	59.6	([1])	([1])
6th....	Moulton	61.3	May	34.3	10th....	Goldman	79.4	Hamdan	13.2
7th....	Pressley	80.0	Palmer	14.3	11th....	Rose	37.6	Malliotakis	56.5
8th....	Lynch	66.8	Burke	28.9	12th....	Nadler	73.6	Zumbluskas	16.3
9th....	Keating	57.8	Brown	39.8	13th....	Espaillat	81.6	([1])	([1])
MI......	(X)	(X)	(X)	(X)	14th....	Ocasio-Cortez	60.4	Forte	26.1
1st...	Lorinser	37.4	Bergman	60.0	15th....	Torres	75.1	Sapaskis	15.6
2d.....	Hilliard	34.3	Moolenaar	63.7	16th....	Bowman	57.3	Flisser	33.5
3d.....	Scholten	54.9	Gibbs	42.0	17th....	Maloney	45.8	Lawler	43.2
4th....	Alfonso	42.5	Huizenga	54.4	18th....	Ryan	45.2	Schmitt	42.9
5th....	Goldberg	35.0	Walberg	62.4	19th....	Riley	42.5	Molinaro	44.4
6th....	Dingell	65.9	Williams	34.1	20th....	Tonko	49.3	Joy	37.5
7th....	Slotkin	51.7	Barrett	46.3	21st....	Castelli	38.9	Stefanik	52.0
8th....	Kildee	53.1	Junge	42.8	22d....	Conole	48.5	Williams	42.5
9th....	Jaye	33.2	McClain	63.9	23d...	Della Pia	34.0	Langworthy	53.2
10th...	Marlinga	48.3	James	48.8	24th....	Holden	33.3	Tenney	54.8
11th...	Stevens	61.3	Ambrose	38.7	25th....	Morelle	49.1	Singletary	37.9
12th....	Tlaib	70.8	Elliott	26.3	26th....	Higgins	56.5	Sams	28.1
13th....	Thanedar	71.1	Bivings	24.0	**NC......**	(X)	(X)	(X)	(X)
MN......	(X)	(X)	(X)	(X)	1st....	Davis	52.4	Smith	47.6
1st...	Ettinger	42.3	Finstad	53.8	2d.....	Ross	64.7	Villaverde	35.3
2d.....	Craig	50.9	Kistner	45.6	3d.....	Gaskins	33.1	Murphy	66.9
3d.....	Phillips	59.6	Weiler	40.4	4th....	Foushee	66.9	Geels	33.1
4th....	McCollum	67.6	Xiong	32.3	5th....	Parrish	36.8	Foxx	63.2
5th....	Omar	74.3	Davis	24.5	6th....	Manning	53.9	Castelli	45.0
6th....	Hendricks	37.8	Emmer	62.0	7th....	Graham	42.3	Rouzer	57.7
7th....	Abahsain	27.6	Fischbach	66.9	8th....	Huffman	30.1	Bishop	69.9
8th....	Schultz	42.7	Stauber	57.2	9th....	Clark	43.5	Hudson	56.5
MS......	(X)	(X)	(X)	(X)	10th....	Genant	27.3	McHenry	72.6
1st....	Black	27.0	Kelly	73.0	11th....	Beach-Ferrara	44.5	Edwards	53.8

See footnotes at end of table.

Table 459. Vote Cast for U.S. House of Representatives by Major Political Party—Congressional Districts: 2022-Continued.

See headnote on page 295.

State and district	Democrat Name	Percent of total	Republican Name	Percent of total	State and district	Democrat Name	Percent of total	Republican Name	Percent of total
12th...	Adams	62.7	Lee	37.3	5th....	Hill	33.9	Gooden	64.0
13th...	Nickel	51.6	Hines	48.4	6th....	(¹)	(¹)	Ellzey	100.0
14th...	Jackson	57.7	Harrigan	42.3	7th....	Fletcher	63.8	Teague	36.2
ND.....	(¹)	(¹)	Armstrong	62.2	8th....	Jones	30.5	Luttrell	68.1
OH.....	(X)	(X)	(X)	(X)	9th....	Green	76.7	Leon	23.3
1st....	Landsman	52.8	Chabot	47.2	10th...	Nuno	34.3	McCaul	63.3
2d.....	Meadows	25.5	Wenstrup	74.5	11th...	(¹)	(¹)	Pfluger	100.0
3d.....	Beatty	70.5	Stahley	29.5	12th...	Hunt	35.7	Granger	64.3
4th....	Wilson	30.8	Jordan	69.2	13th...	Brown	24.6	Jackson	75.4
5th....	Swartz	33.1	Latta	66.9	14th...	Williams	29.8	Weber	70.2
6th....	Lyras	32.3	Johnson	67.7	15th...	Vallejo	44.8	De La Cruz	53.3
7th....	Diemer	44.6	Miller	55.3				Armendariz	
8th....	Enoch	35.4	Davidson	64.6	16th...	Escobar	63.5	Jackson	36.5
9th....	Kaptur	56.6	Majewski	43.4	17th...	Woods	33.5	Sessions	66.5
10th...	Esrati	38.3	Turner	61.7	18th...	Jackson Lee	70.7	Montiel	26.2
11th...	Brown	77.8	Brewer	22.2	19th...	(¹)	(¹)	Arrington	80.3
12th...	Rippel-Elton	30.7	Balderson	69.3	20th...	Castro	68.4	Sinclair	31.6
13th...	Sykes	52.7	Gesiotto Gilbert	47.3	21st...	Zapata	37.2	Roy	62.8
14th...	Kilboy	38.3	Joyce	61.7	22d. ..	Jordan	35.5	Nehls	62.2
15th...	Josephson	43.0	Carey	57.0	23d...	Lira	38.8	Gonzales	55.9
OK.....	(X)	(X)	(X)	(X)	24th...	McDowell	40.3	Van Duyne	59.7
1st....	Martin	34.7	Hern	61.2	25th...	(¹)	(¹)	Williams	100.0
2d.....	Andrews	23.4	Brecheen	72.4	26th...	(¹)	(¹)	Burgess	69.3
3d.....	Ross	25.5	Lucas	74.5	27th...	Perez	35.6	Cloud	64.4
4th....	Brannon	33.3	Cole	66.7	28th...	Cuellar	56.7	Garcia	43.3
5th....	Harris-Till	37.4	Bice	59.0	29th...	Garcia	71.4	Schafranek	28.6
OR.....	(X)	(X)	(X)	(X)	30th...	Crockett	74.7	Rodgers	21.7
1st....	Bonamici	67.9	Mann	31.9	31st...	(¹)	(¹)	Carter	100.0
2d.....	Yetter	32.4	Bentz	67.5	32d. ..	Allred	65.4	Swad	34.6
3d.....	Blumenauer	69.9	Harbour	26.3	33d. ..	Veasey	72.0	Gillespie	25.6
4th....	Hoyle	50.5	Skarlatos	43.1	34th...	Gonzalez	52.7	Flores	44.2
5th....	McLeod-Skinner	48.8	Chavez-DeRemer	50.9	35th...	Casar	72.6	McQueen	27.4
6th....	Salinas	50.0	Erickson	47.5	36th...	Haire	30.5	Babin	69.5
PA......	(X)	(X)	(X)	(X)	37th...	Doggett	76.8	Sharon	21.0
1st....	Ehasz	45.1	Fitzpatrick	54.9	38th...	Klussmann	35.5	Hunt	63.0
2d.....	Boyle	75.7	Bashir	24.3	**UT.....**	(X)	(X)	(X)	(X)
3d.....	Evans	95.1	(¹)	(¹)	1st....	Jones	33.0	Moore	67.0
4th....	Dean	61.3	Nascimento	38.7	2d.....	Mitchell	34.0	Stewart	59.7
5th....	Scanlon	65.1	Galluch	34.9	3d.....	Wright	29.5	Curtis	64.4
6th....	Houlahan	58.3	Ciarrocchi	41.7	4th....	McDonald	32.3	Owens	61.1
7th....	Wild	51.0	Scheller	49.0	**VT......**	Balint	60.5	Madden	26.9
8th....	Cartwright	51.2	Bognet	48.8	**VA......**	(X)	(X)	(X)	(X)
9th....	Waldman	30.7	Meuser	69.3	1st....	Jones	43.0	Wittman	56.0
10th...	Daniels	46.2	Perry	53.8	2d.....	Luria	48.2	Kiggans	51.6
11th...	Hollister	38.5	Smucker	61.5	3d.....	Scott	67.2	Namkung	32.6
12th...	Lee	56.2	Doyle	43.8	4th....	McEachin	64.9	Benjamin	34.9
13th...	(¹)	(¹)	Joyce	100.0	5th....	Throneburg	42.2	Good	57.6
14th...	(¹)	(¹)	Reschenthaler	100.0	6th....	Lewis	35.4	Cline	64.4
15th...	Molesevich	30.1	Thompson	69.9	7th....	Spanberger	52.2	Vega	47.6
16th...	Pastore	40.6	Kelly	59.4	8th....	Beyer	73.5	Lipsman	24.8
17th...	Deluzio	53.4	Shaffer	46.6	9th....	DeVaughan	26.5	Griffith	73.2
RI......	(X)	(X)	(X)	(X)	10th...	Wexton	53.2	Cao	46.7
1st....	Cicilline	64.0	Waters	35.8	11th...	Connolly	66.7	Myles	33.0
2d.....	Magaziner	50.4	Fung	46.7	**WA.....**	(X)	(X)	(X)	(Percent)
SC.....	(X)	(X)	(X)	(X)	1st....	DelBene	63.5	Caveleri	36.4
1st....	Andrews	42.5	Mace	56.4	2d.....	Larsen	60.1	Matthews	39.8
2d.....	Larkins	39.8	Wilson	60.0		Gluesenkamp			
3d.....	(¹)	(¹)	Duncan	97.6	3d.....	Perez	50.1	Kent	49.3
4th....	(¹)	(¹)	Timmons	90.8	4th....	White	31.2	Newhouse	66.5
5th....	Hundley	34.5	Norman	64.0	5th....	Hill	40.2	McMorris Rodgers	59.5
6th....	Clyburn	62.0	Buckner	37.9	6th....	Kilmer	60.0	Kreiselmaier	39.9
7th....	Scott	35.1	Fry	64.8	7th....	Jayapal	85.4	Moon	14.2
SD.....	(¹)	(¹)	Johnson	77.4	8th....	Schrier	53.3	Larkin	46.4
TN.....	(X)	(X)	(X)	(X)	9th....	Smith	71.6	Basler	28.2
1st....	Parsons	19.7	Harshbarger	78.3	10th...	Strickland	57.0	Swank	42.9
2d.....	Harmon	32.1	Burchett	67.9	**WV.....**	(X)	(X)	(X)	(X)
3d.....	Gorman	30.2	Fleischmann	68.4	1st....	Watson	28.8	Miller	66.7
4th....	Steele	25.7	DesJarlais	70.6	2d.....	Wendell	34.4	Mooney	65.5
5th....	Campbell	42.3	Ogles	55.8	**WI.....**	(X)	(X)	(X)	(X)
6th....	Cooper	33.7	Rose	66.3	1st....	Roe	45.1	Steil	54.0
7th....	Kelly	38.1	Green	60.0	2d.....	Pocan	71.0	Olsen	26.9
8th....	Williams	24.3	Kustoff	74.0	3d.....	Pfaff	48.1	van Orden	51.8
9th....	Cohen	70.0	Bergmann	26.2	4th....	Moore	75.3	Rogers	22.6
TX......	(X)	(X)	(X)	(X)	5th....	Van Someren	35.6	Fitzgerald	64.4
1st....	Jefferson	21.9	Moran	78.1	6th....	(¹)	(¹)	Grothman	94.9
2d.....	Fulford	34.1	Crenshaw	65.9	7th....	Ausman	38.1	Tiffany	61.9
3d.....	Srivastava	36.9	Self	60.5	8th....	(¹)	(¹)	Gallagher	72.2
4th....	Omere	30.9	Fallon	66.7	**WY.....**	Grey Bull	23.8	Hageman	62.2

X Not applicable. ¹ No candidate on ballot. ² In FL and LA, unopposed candidates are not printed on the ballot. ³ Based on the vote count from round 2 of Maine's ranked-choice general election, which was held because neither candidate received a majority of the vote in round 1.

Source: U.S. House of Representatives, Office of the Clerk, *Statistics of the Congressional Election of November 8, 2022*, February 2023. See also <clerk.house.gov/Members#ElectionInformation>.

Table 460. Apportionment of Membership in House of Representatives by State: 1800 to 2020

[Total membership includes Representatives assigned to newly admitted States after the apportionment acts. Population figures used for apportionment purposes are those determined for States by each decennial census. For more information on apportionment, see <www.census.gov/topics/public-sector/congressional-apportionment/about/historical-perspective.html>]

Membership based on Census of—

State	1800	1830	1840	1850	1860	1870	1880	1890	1900	1910	1920[3]	1930	1940	1950	1960	1970	1980	1990	2000	2010	2020
U.S.	142	242	232	237	243	293	332	357	391	435	435	435	435	437	435	435	435	435	435	435	435
AL	(X)	5	7	7	6	8	8	9	9	10	10	9	9	9	8	7	7	7	7	7	7
AK	(X)	(X)	(X)	(X)	(X)	(X)	(X)	(X)	(X)	(X)	(X)	(X)	(X)	1[1]	1	1	1	1	1	1	1
AZ	(X)	(X)	(X)	(X)	(X)	(X)	(X)	(X)	(X)	1[2]	1	1	2	2	3	4	5	6	8	9	9
AR	(X)	1[1]	1	2	3	4	5	6	7	7	7	7	7	6	4	4	4	4	4	4	4
CA	(X)	(X)	(X)	2	3	4	6	7	8	11	11	20	23	30	38	43	45	52	53	53	52
CO	(X)	(X)	(X)	(X)	(X)	1[1]	1	2	3	4	4	4	4	4	4	5	6	6	7	7	8
CT	7	6	4	4	4	4	4	4	5	5	5	6	6	6	6	6	6	6	5	5	5
DE	1	1	1	1	1	1	1	1	1	1	1	1	1	1	1	1	1	1	1	1	1
FL	(X)	(X)	1[1]	1	1	2	2	2	3	4	4	5	6	8	12	15	19	23	25	27	28
GA	4	9	8	8	7	9	10	11	11	12	12	10	10	10	10	10	10	11	13	14	14
HI	(X)	(X)	(X)	(X)	(X)	(X)	(X)	(X)	(X)	(X)	(X)	(X)	(X)	1[1]	2	2	2	2	2	2	2
ID	(X)	(X)	(X)	(X)	(X)	(X)	(X)	1[1]	1	2	2	2	2	2	2	2	2	2	2	2	2
IL	(X)	3	7	9	14	19	20	22	25	27	27	27	26	25	24	24	22	20	19	18	17
IN	(X)	7	10	11	11	13	13	13	13	13	13	12	11	11	11	11	10	10	9	9	9
IA	(X)	(X)	2[1]	2	6	9	11	11	11	11	11	9	8	8	7	6	6	5	5	4	4
KS	(X)	(X)	(X)	(X)	1[1]	3	7	8	8	8	8	7	6	6	5	5	5	4	4	4	4
KY	6	13	10	10	9	10	11	11	11	11	11	9	9	8	7	7	7	6	6	6	6
LA	(X)	3	4	4	5	6	6	6	7	8	8	8	8	8	8	8	8	7	7	6	6
ME	(X)	8	7	6	5	5	4	4	4	4	4	3	3	3	2	2	2	2	2	2	2
MD	9	8	6	6	5	6	6	6	6	6	6	6	6	7	8	8	8	8	8	8	8
MA	17	12	10	11	10	11	12	13	14	16	16	15	14	14	12	12	11	10	10	9	9
MI	(X)	1[1]	3	4	6	9	11	12	12	13	13	17	17	18	19	19	18	16	15	14	13
MN	(X)	(X)	(X)	2[1]	2	3	5	7	9	10	10	9	9	9	8	8	8	8	8	8	8
MS	(X)	2	4	5	5	6	7	7	8	8	8	7	7	6	5	5	5	5	4	4	4
MO	(X)	2	5	7	9	13	14	15	16	16	16	13	13	11	10	10	9	9	9	8	8
MT	(X)	(X)	(X)	(X)	(X)	(X)	(X)	1[1]	1	2	2	2	2	2	2	2	2	1	1	1	2
NE	(X)	(X)	(X)	(X)	1[1]	1	3	6	6	6	6	5	4	4	3	3	3	3	3	3	3
NV	(X)	(X)	(X)	(X)	1[1]	1	1	1	1	1	1	1	1	1	1	1	2	2	3	4	4
NH	5	5	4	3	3	3	2	2	2	2	2	2	2	2	2	2	2	2	2	2	2
NJ	6	6	5	5	5	7	7	8	10	12	12	14	14	14	15	15	14	13	13	12	12
NM	(X)	(X)	(X)	(X)	(X)	(X)	(X)	(X)	(X)	1[2]	1	1	2	2	2	2	3	3	3	3	3
NY	17	40	34	33	31	33	34	34	37	43	43	45	45	43	41	39	34	31	29	27	26
NC	12	13	9	8	7	8	9	9	10	10	10	11	12	12	11	11	11	12	13	13	14
ND	(X)	(X)	(X)	(X)	(X)	(X)	(X)	1[1]	2	3	3	2	2	2	2	1	1	1	1	1	1
OH	1[1]	19	21	21	19	20	21	21	21	22	22	24	23	23	24	23	21	19	18	16	15
OK	(X)	(X)	(X)	(X)	(X)	(X)	(X)	(X)	5[1]	8	8	9	8	6	6	6	6	6	5	5	5
OR	(X)	(X)	(X)	1[1]	1	1	1	2	2	3	3	3	4	4	4	4	5	5	5	5	6
PA	18	28	24	25	24	27	28	30	32	36	36	34	33	30	27	25	23	21	19	18	17
RI	2	2	2	2	2	2	2	2	2	3	3	2	2	2	2	2	2	2	2	2	2
SC	8	9	7	6	4	5	7	7	7	7	7	6	6	6	6	6	6	6	6	7	7
SD	(X)	(X)	(X)	(X)	(X)	(X)	(X)	2[1]	2	3	3	2	2	2	2	2	1	1	1	1	1
TN	3	13	11	10	8	10	10	10	10	10	10	9	10	9	9	8	9	9	9	9	9
TX	(X)	(X)	2[1]	2	4	6	11	13	16	18	18	21	21	22	23	24	27	30	32	36	38
UT	(X)	(X)	(X)	(X)	(X)	(X)	(X)	1[1]	1	2	2	2	2	2	2	2	3	3	3	4	4
VT	4	5	4	3	3	3	2	2	2	2	2	1	1	1	1	1	1	1	1	1	1
VA	22	21	15	13	11	9	10	10	10	10	10	9	9	10	10	10	10	11	11	11	11
WA	(X)	(X)	(X)	(X)	(X)	(X)	(X)	2[1]	3	5	5	6	6	7	7	7	8	9	9	10	10
WV	(X)	(X)	(X)	(X)	3[1]	3	4	4	5	6	6	6	6	6	5	4	4	3	3	3	2
WI	(X)	(X)	2[1]	3	6	8	9	10	11	11	11	10	10	10	10	9	9	9	8	8	8
WY	(X)	(X)	(X)	(X)	(X)	(X)	(X)	1[1]	1	1	1	1	1	1	1	1	1	1	1	1	1

X Not applicable. [1] Assigned after apportionment. [2] Included in apportionment in anticipation of statehood. [3] No reapportionment occurred based on 1920 population census.

Source: U.S. Census Bureau, "Congressional Apportionment," <www.census.gov/topics/public-sector/congressional-apportionment.html>, accessed May 2021.

Table 461. Composition of Congress by Political Party Affiliation—States: 2017 to 2023

[Figures are for the beginning of the first session, except as noted. Dem. = Democratic; Rep. = Republican]

State	Representatives								Senators							
	115th Cong., 2017		116th Cong.,[1] 2019		117th Cong.,[2] 2021		118th Cong.,[3] 2023		115th Cong.,[4] 2017		116th Cong.,[4] 2019		117th Cong.,[4, 5] 2021		118th Cong.,[4] 2023	
	Dem.	Rep.	Dem.	Rep.	Dem.	Rep.	Dem.	Rep.	Dem.	Rep.	Dem.	Rep.	Dem.	Rep.	Dem.	Rep.
U.S.	194	241	235	197	222	211	212	222	46	52	45	53	48	50	48	49
AL	1	6	1	6	1	6	1	6	–	2	1	1	–	2	–	2
AK	–	1	–	1	–	1	1	–	–	2	–	2	–	2	–	2
AZ	4	5	5	4	5	4	3	6	–	2	1	1	2	–	1	–
AR	–	4	–	4	–	4	–	4	–	2	–	2	–	2	–	2
CA	39	14	46	7	42	11	40	12	2	–	2	–	2	–	2	–
CO	3	4	4	3	4	3	5	3	1	1	1	1	2	–	2	–
CT	5	–	5	–	5	–	5	–	2	–	2	–	2	–	2	–
DE	1	–	1	–	1	–	1	–	2	–	2	–	2	–	2	–
FL	11	16	13	14	11	16	8	20	1	1	–	2	–	2	–	2
GA	4	10	5	9	6	8	5	9	–	2	–	2	2	–	2	–
HI	2	–	2	–	2	–	2	–	2	–	2	–	2	–	2	–
ID	–	2	–	2	–	2	–	2	–	2	–	2	–	2	–	2
IL	11	7	13	5	13	5	14	3	2	–	2	–	2	–	2	–
IN	2	7	2	7	2	7	2	7	1	1	–	2	–	2	–	2
IA	1	3	3	1	1	3	–	4	–	2	–	2	–	2	–	2
KS	–	4	1	3	1	3	1	3	–	2	–	2	–	2	–	2
KY	1	5	1	5	1	5	1	5	–	2	–	2	–	2	–	2
LA	1	5	1	5	1	4	1	5	–	2	–	2	–	2	–	2
ME	1	1	2	–	2	–	2	–	–	1	–	1	–	1	–	1
MD	7	1	7	1	7	1	7	1	2	–	2	–	2	–	2	–
MA	9	–	9	–	9	–	9	–	2	–	2	–	2	–	2	–
MI	5	9	7	7	7	7	7	6	2	–	2	–	2	–	2	–
MN	5	3	5	3	4	4	4	4	2	–	2	–	2	–	2	–
MS	1	3	1	3	1	3	1	3	–	2	–	2	–	2	–	2
MO	2	6	2	6	2	6	2	6	1	1	–	2	–	2	–	2
MT	–	1	–	1	–	1	–	2	1	1	1	1	1	1	1	1
NE	–	3	–	3	–	3	–	3	–	2	–	2	–	2	–	2
NV	3	1	3	1	3	1	3	1	1	1	2	–	2	–	2	–
NH	2	–	2	–	2	–	2	–	2	–	2	–	2	–	2	–
NJ	7	5	11	1	10	2	9	3	2	–	2	–	2	–	2	–
NM	2	1	3	–	2	1	3	–	2	–	2	–	2	–	2	–
NY	18	9	21	6	19	7	15	11	2	–	2	–	2	–	2	–
NC	3	10	3	8	5	8	7	7	–	2	–	2	–	2	–	2
ND	–	1	–	1	–	1	–	1	1	1	–	2	–	2	–	2
OH	4	12	4	12	4	12	5	10	1	1	1	1	1	1	1	1
OK	–	5	1	4	–	5	–	5	–	2	–	2	–	2	–	2
OR	4	1	4	1	4	1	4	2	2	–	2	–	2	–	2	–
PA	5	13	9	8	9	9	9	8	1	1	1	1	1	1	2	–
RI	2	–	2	–	2	–	2	–	2	–	2	–	2	–	2	–
SC	1	6	2	5	1	6	1	6	–	2	–	2	–	2	–	2
SD	–	1	–	1	–	1	–	1	–	2	–	2	–	2	–	2
TN	2	7	2	7	2	7	1	8	–	2	–	2	–	2	–	2
TX	11	25	13	23	13	23	13	25	–	2	–	2	–	2	–	2
UT	–	4	1	3	–	4	–	4	–	2	–	2	–	2	–	2
VT	1	–	1	–	1	–	1	–	1	–	1	–	1	–	1	–
VA	4	7	7	4	7	4	5	5	2	–	2	–	2	–	2	–
WA	6	4	7	3	7	3	8	2	2	–	2	–	2	–	2	–
WV	–	3	–	3	–	3	–	2	1	1	1	1	1	1	1	1
WI	3	5	3	5	3	5	2	6	1	1	1	1	1	1	1	1
WY	–	1	–	1	–	1	–	1	–	2	–	2	–	2	–	2

– Represents zero. [1] Three vacancies—one in Pennsylvania due the resignation of Tom Marino on January 23, 2019; and two in North Carolina, one due to the death of Walter Jones on February 10, 2019, and one due to North Carolina's State Board of Elections and Ethics Reform's refusal to certify the results of the NC-09 election due to irregularities involving absentee ballots. [2] Two vacancies in Louisiana due to the death of Luke Letlow on December 29th, 2020 and the resignation of Cedric L. Richmond on January 15th, 2021. [3] Virginia had one vacancy due to the death of Donald McEachin on November 28, 2022. [4] Vermont and Maine had one Independent senator each. In December 2022, Arizona Senator Sinema switched from the Democratic Party to Independent status. [5] Reflects results of the January 5, 2021 runoff elections in Georgia.

Source: U.S. House of Representatives, Office of the Clerk, *Official List of Members*, January 2023, and earlier editions; and United States Senate, <www.senate.gov/index.htm>, accessed January 2023. See also <clerk.house.gov/member_info/>.

Table 462. Members of Congress—Seniority of Senators and Representatives: 1969 to 2021

[Represents the makeup of Congress on the 1st day of the session]

Congress	Senators Number by length of service — 6 years or less [1]	7-12 years	13-18 years	19+ years	Mean years of service	Representatives Number by terms served — 1-3 terms	4-6 terms	7-9 terms	10+ terms	Mean terms of service
91st (1969)	32 (14)	32	17	19	11.2	171	126	65	73	5.6
92nd (1971)	25 (10)	24	29	22	11.5	162	122	68	83	5.8
93rd (1973)	40 (13)	20	20	20	11.2	162	128	66	76	5.5
94th (1975)	[2] 36 (12)	22	23	19	11.5	196	100	78	61	5.2
95th (1977)	42 (17)	25	13	20	10.6	219	87	70	59	4.9
96th (1979)	48 (20)	24	10	18	9.6	219	95	65	54	4.8
97th (1981)	55 (18)	20	10	15	8.5	209	121	56	49	4.7
98th (1983)	43 (5)	28	16	13	9.6	210	125	45	54	4.7
99th (1985)	32 (7)	38	18	12	10.1	184	138	58	54	5.1
100th (1987)	26 (13)	44	16	14	9.6	163	143	64	65	5.5
101st (1989)	31 (10)	26	29	14	9.8	120	167	86	60	5.8
102nd (1991)	30 (5)	23	28	19	11.1	133	137	91	74	6.1
103rd (1993)	30 (13)	17	32	21	11.3	192	109	69	65	5.2
104th (1995)	29 (11)	26	20	25	12.3	220	78	78	59	4.9
105th (1997)	40 (15)	24	13	23	11.2	243	71	65	56	4.8
106th (1999)	35 (8)	24	16	25	11.2	185	127	58	65	4.8
107th (2001)	37 (11)	21	19	23	11.5	149	155	54	76	5.6
108th (2003)	30 (10)	29	16	25	12.7	149	158	60	68	5.5
109th (2005)	29 (9)	27	15	29	12.5	137	128	97	72	5.9
110th (2007)	29 (10)	26	14	31	13.1	149	116	99	71	6.0
111th (2009)	[3] 32 (11)	19	20	29	14.0	147	102	106	79	6.2
112th (2011)	42 (13)	17	14	27	12.3	170	97	69	97	6.0
113th (2013)	43 (13)	23	15	19	10.2	196	91	72	74	5.7
114th (2015)	45 (13)	24	11	20	9.4	205	91	51	88	5.5
115th (2017)	36 (7)	34	11	19	10.2	177	118	55	85	5.8
116th (2019)	32 (9)	33	17	18	10.1	184	121	56	73	5.4
117th (2021) [4]	26 (8)	37	18	19	12.0	185	121	54	73	5.5

[1] Numbers in parentheses are number of freshman senators. Senators who are currently in their first full term are listed under "6 years or less." [2] Total includes John Durkin (D-NH). After a contested election in 1974, the Senate declared the seat vacant as of August 8, 1975. Durkin was then elected by special election, September 16, 1975, to fill the vacancy. [3] Total includes Al Franken (D-MN), who, on June 30, 2009, was declared elected after a court challenge brought by his Republican opponent; and Roland Burris (D-IL) who was appointed on December 31, 2008 to fill the seat vacated by Barack Obama. Total also includes Joe Biden (D-DE), who resigned his seat on January 15, 2009, but was present on the first day of the session. [4] Includes Jon Ossoff and Raphael Warnock, who were elected on January 5, 2021, and Kamala Harris, who did not resign from office until January 18th, 2021.

Source: The Brookings Institution, "Vital Statistics on Congress" ©, February 2021, <www.brookings.edu/multi-chapter-report/vital-statistics-on-congress>.

Table 463. Women, Black, Asian, and Hispanic Members of Congress by Party Affiliation: 2001 to 2021

[As of beginning of first session of each Congress. Data do not include delegates or commissioners]

Characteristic	107th (2001)	108th (2003)	109th (2005)	110th (2007)	111th (2009) [1]	112th (2011)	113th (2013) [2]	114th (2015)	115th (2017)	116th (2019)	117th (2021) [3]
Women, total	72	73	79	87	91	93	96	104	104	127	143
Representatives	59	59	65	71	74	76	76	84	83	102	118
Democrat	41	38	42	50	57	52	56	62	62	89	89
Republican	18	21	23	21	17	24	20	22	21	13	29
Senators	13	14	14	16	17	17	20	20	21	25	25
Democrat	10	9	9	11	13	12	16	14	16	17	17
Republican	3	5	5	5	4	5	4	6	5	8	8
Black, total	36	37	41	41	39	42	42	46	50	56	62
Representatives	36	37	40	40	39	42	41	44	47	53	58
Democrat	35	37	40	40	39	40	41	42	45	52	56
Republican	1	0	0	0	0	2	0	2	2	1	2
Senators	0	0	1	1	0	0	1	2	3	3	4
Democrat	0	0	1	1	0	0	0	1	2	2	3
Republican	0	0	0	0	0	0	1	1	1	1	1
Asian, total	7	6	7	8	7	10	11	12	16	16	18
Representatives	5	4	5	6	5	8	10	11	13	13	15
Democrat	5	4	4	5	4	7	10	11	13	13	13
Republican	0	0	1	1	1	1	0	0	0	0	2
Senators	2	2	2	2	2	2	1	1	3	3	3
Democrat	2	2	2	2	2	2	1	1	3	3	3
Republican	0	0	0	0	0	0	0	0	0	0	0
Hispanic, total	19	22	25	26	26	29	31	35	42	45	49
Representatives	19	22	23	23	24	27	28	32	38	41	44
Democrat	16	18	19	20	21	19	23	23	28	34	32
Republican	3	4	4	3	3	8	5	9	10	7	12
Senators	0	0	2	3	2	2	3	3	4	4	5
Democrat	0	0	1	2	1	1	1	1	2	2	3
Republican	0	0	1	1	1	1	2	2	2	2	2

[1] Roland Burris was not seated on the first day of the 111th session. [2] Tim Scott, who was appointed on December 17th to replace outgoing Senator Jim DeMint, is included in the Senate totals. [3] Includes both Jon Ossoff and Raphael Warnock, who were elected on January 5, 2021, and Kamala Harris, who did not resign from office until January 18th, 2021.

Source: The Brookings Institution, "Vital Statistics on Congress" ©, February 2021, <www.brookings.edu/multi-chapter-report/vital-statistics-on-congress>.

Table 464. Composition of Congress by Political Party: 1977 to 2023

[D = Democratic, R = Republican. As of beginning of first session of each Congress unless otherwise noted. Data reflect immediate result of elections. Vacancies and third party candidates are noted]

Year	Party and president	Congress	House			Senate		
			Majority party	Minority party	Other	Majority party	Minority party	Other
1977 [1]	D (Carter)	95th	D-292	R-143	–	D-61	R-38	1
1979 [1]	D (Carter)	96th	D-277	R-158	–	D-58	R-41	1
1981 [2]	R (Reagan)	97th	D-242	R-192	1	R-53	D-46	1
1983	R (Reagan)	98th	D-269	R-166	–	R-54	D-46	–
1985	R (Reagan)	99th	D-253	R-182	–	R-53	D-47	–
1987	R (Reagan)	100th	D-258	R-177	–	D-55	R-45	–
1989	R (Bush)	101st	D-260	R-175	–	D-55	R-45	–
1991 [3]	R (Bush)	102nd	D-267	R-167	1	D-56	R-44	–
1993 [3]	D (Clinton)	103rd	D-258	R-176	1	D-57	R-43	–
1995 [3]	D (Clinton)	104th	R-230	D-204	1	R-52	D-48	–
1997 [4]	D (Clinton)	105th	R-226	D-207	2	R-55	D-45	–
1999 [3]	D (Clinton)	106th	R-223	D-211	1	R-55	D-45	–
2001 [4]	R (Bush)	107th	R-221	D-212	2	D-50	R-50	–
2003 [2,5]	R (Bush)	108th	R-229	D-204	1	R-51	D-48	1
2005 [2]	R (Bush)	109th	R-232	D-202	1	R-55	D-44	1
2007 [6]	R (Bush)	110th	D-233	R-202	–	D-49	R-49	2
2009 [5,6,7]	D (Obama)	111th	D-256	R-178	–	D-55	R-41	2
2011 [6]	D (Obama)	112th	R-242	D-193	–	D-51	R-47	2
2013 [5,6]	D (Obama)	113th	R-234	D-200	–	D-53	R-45	2
2015 [6]	D (Obama)	114th	R-247	D-188	–	R-54	D-44	2
2017 [6]	R (Trump)	115th	R-241	D-194	–	R-52	D-46	2
2019 [6,8]	R (Trump)	116th	R-235	D-197	–	R-53	D-45	2
2021 [6,9]	D (Biden)	117th	D-222	R-211	–	R-50	D-48	2
2023 [5,10]	D (Biden)	118th	R-222	D-212	–	D-48	R-49	3

– Represents zero. [1] Senate has one Independent. [2] House and Senate each has one Independent. [3] House has one Independent-Socialist. [4] House has one Independent-Socialist and one Independent. [5] House has one vacancy. [6] Senate has two Independents. [7] Senate has two vacancies. [8] House has three vacancies. [9] House has two vacancies. [10] Senate has three Independents. Kyrsten Sinema of Arizona was elected as a Democrat but changed affiliation to Independent in December 2022.

Source: U.S. House of Representatives, Office of the Clerk, "Member Information," <clerk.house.gov> and *Official List of Members by State*, January 2023 and earlier editions; and U.S. Senate, <www.senate.gov/index.htm>, accessed January 2023.

Table 465. U.S. Congress—Measures Introduced and Enacted and Time in Session: 2007 to 2024

[Excludes simple and concurrent resolutions]

Item	110th Cong., 2007–08	111th Cong., 2009–10	112th Cong., 2011-12	113th Cong., 2013-14	114th Cong., 2015-16	115th Cong., 2017-18	116th Cong., 2019-20	117th Cong., 2021-22	118th Cong., 2023-24 [3]
Measures introduced	11,228	10,778	10,612	9,097	10,223	13,558	16,603	17,820	16,044
Bills	11,081	10,629	10,439	8,919	10,074	11,201	14,150	15,058	13,530
Joint resolutions	147	149	173	178	149	215	192	176	271
Measures enacted	460	385	239	296	329	339	283	334	94
Public [1]	460	383	238	296	329	338	283	332	94
Private [2]	0	2	1	0	0	1	0	2	0
HOUSE OF REPRESENTATIVES									
Number of days	283	286	327	295	288	366	365	330	271
Number of hours	2,138	2,126	1,718	1,471	1,438	1,515	1,352	1,329	1,021
Number of hours per day	7.6	7.4	5.3	5.0	5.0	4.1	3.7	4.0	3.8
SENATE									
Number of days	374	349	323	292	333	386	379	370	273
Number of hours	2,364	2,495	2,032	2,003	1,855	2,181	1,910	2,041	1,337
Number of hours per day	6.3	7.1	6.3	6.9	5.6	5.7	5.1	5.5	4.9

[1] Laws on public matters that apply to all persons. [2] Laws designed to provide legal relief to specified persons or entities adversely affected by laws of general applicability. [3] Current session. Data for January 3, 2023 through June 30, 2024.

Source: U.S. Congress, *Résumé of Congressional Activity*, July 2024, and earlier reports. See also <www.senate.gov/legislative/ResumesofCongressionalActivity1947present.htm>.

Table 466. Congressional Bills Vetoed: 1961 to 2024

Period	President	Total vetoes	Regular vetoes	Pocket vetoes	Vetoes sustained	Bills passed over veto
1961 to 1963	John F. Kennedy	21	12	9	21	0
1963 to 1969	Lyndon B. Johnson	30	16	14	30	0
1969 to 1974	Richard M. Nixon	43	26	17	36	7
1974 to 1977	Gerald R. Ford	66	48	18	54	12
1977 to 1981	Jimmy Carter	31	13	18	29	2
1981 to 1989	Ronald Reagan	78	39	39	69	9
1989 to 1993	George H. W. Bush	44	29	15	43	1
1993 to 2001	William J. Clinton	37	36	1	35	2
2001 to 2009	George W. Bush	12	12	0	8	4
2009 to 2017	Barack Obama	12	12	0	11	1
2017 to 2021	Donald J. Trump	10	10	0	9	1
2021 to 2024 [1]	Joseph R. Biden, Jr.	12	12	0	12	0

[1] For the period January 20, 2021 to August 31, 2024.

Source: U.S. Senate, "Summary of Bills Vetoed," <www.senate.gov/legislative/vetoes/vetoCounts.htm>, accessed August 2024.

Table 467. Number of Governors by Political Party Affiliation: 1975 to 2024

[Reflects figures after inaugurations for each year. State governors only]

Year	Demo-cratic	Republi-can	Inde-pendent or other	Year	Demo-cratic	Republi-can	Inde-pendent or other	Year	Demo-cratic	Republi-can	Inde-pendent or other
1975........	36	13	1	2005........	22	28	–	2019........	23	27	–
1980........	31	19	–	2010........	26	24	–	2020........	24	26	–
1985........	34	16	–	2015........	18	31	1	2021........	23	27	–
1990........	29	21	–	2016........	18	31	1	2022........	22	28	–
1995........	19	30	1	2017........	16	33	1	2023........	24	26	–
2000........	18	30	2	2018........	16	33	1	2024........	23	27	–

– Represents zero.

Source: ProQuest research.

Table 468. Vote Cast for and Governor Elected by State: 2018 to 2021

[D = Democrat, R = Republican, I = Independent]

State	Current governor [1]	Year of election	Total vote [2]	Republican Number of votes	Republican Percent	Democrat Number of votes	Democrat Percent
Alabama...................	Kay Ivey (R)	2018	1,719,589	1,022,457	59.5	694,495	40.4
Alaska.....................	Mike Dunleavy (R)	2018	283,134	145,631	51.4	125,739	44.4
Arizona....................	Doug Ducey (R)	2018	2,376,441	1,330,863	56.0	994,341	41.8
Arkansas..................	Asa Hutchinson (R)	2018	891,509	582,406	65.3	283,218	31.8
California..................	Gavin Newsom (D)	2018	12,464,235	4,742,825	38.1	7,721,410	61.9
Colorado..................	Jared Polis (D)	2018	2,525,062	1,080,801	42.8	1,348,888	53.4
Connecticut [3]............	Ned Lamont (D)	2018	1,406,803	650,138	46.2	694,510	49.4
Delaware..................	John Carney (D)	2020	492,635	190,312	38.6	292,903	59.5
Florida....................	Ron DeSantis (R)	2018	8,220,561	4,076,186	49.6	4,043,723	49.2
Georgia...................	Brian Kemp (R)	2018	3,939,328	1,978,408	50.2	1,923,685	48.8
Hawaii....................	David Ige (D)	2018	390,843	131,719	33.7	244,934	62.7
Idaho.....................	Brad Little (R)	2018	605,131	361,661	59.8	231,081	38.2
Illinois....................	J.B. Pritzker (D)	2018	4,547,657	1,765,751	38.8	2,479,746	54.5
Indiana...................	Eric Holcomb (R)	2020	3,020,388	1,706,727	56.5	968,094	32.1
Iowa......................	Kim Reynolds (R)	2018	1,327,638	667,275	50.3	630,986	47.5
Kansas....................	Laura Kelly (D)	2018	1,055,566	453,645	43.0	506,727	48.0
Kentucky..................	Andy Beshear (D)	2019	1,446,123	707,754	48.9	709,890	49.1
Louisiana.................	John Bel Edwards (D)	2019	1,508,784	734,286	48.7	774,498	51.3
Maine.....................	Janet Mills (D)	2018	630,667	272,311	43.2	320,962	50.9
Maryland..................	Larry Hogan (R)	2018	1,482,029	855,539	57.7	608,810	41.1
Massachusetts............	Charlie Baker (R)	2018	2,674,615	1,781,341	66.6	885,770	33.1
Michigan..................	Gretchen Whitmer (D)	2018	4,250,585	1,859,534	43.7	2,266,193	53.3
Minnesota.................	Tim Walz (D)	2018	2,587,287	1,097,705	42.4	1,393,096	53.8
Mississippi................	Tate Reeves (R)	2019	884,911	459,396	51.9	414,368	46.8
Missouri..................	Mike Parson (R)	2020	3,012,287	1,720,202	57.1	1,225,771	40.7
Montana..................	Greg Gianforte (R)	2020	603,608	328,548	54.4	250,860	41.6
Nebraska.................	Pete Ricketts (R)	2018	697,981	411,812	59.0	286,169	41.0
Nevada...................	Steve Sisolak (D)	2018	971,799	440,320	45.3	480,007	49.4
New Hampshire...........	Chris Sununu (R)	2020	793,260	516,609	65.1	264,639	33.4
New Jersey...............	Phil Murphy (D)	2021	2,614,886	1,255,185	48.0	1,339,471	51.2
New Mexico...............	Michelle Lujan Grisham (D)	2018	696,459	298,091	42.8	398,368	57.2
New York [4]...............	Kathy Hochul (D) [5]	2018	6,097,362	2,207,602	36.2	3,635,340	59.6
North Carolina............	Roy Cooper (D)	2020	5,502,778	2,586,605	47.0	2,834,790	51.5
North Dakota.............	Doug Burgum (R)	2020	357,859	235,629	65.8	90,925	25.4
Ohio......................	Mike DeWine (R)	2018	4,429,582	2,231,917	50.4	2,067,847	46.7
Oklahoma.................	Kevin Stitt (R)	2018	1,186,385	644,579	54.3	500,973	42.2
Oregon....................	Kate Brown (D)	2018	1,866,997	814,988	43.7	934,498	50.1
Pennsylvania..............	Tom Wolf (D)	2018	5,012,555	2,039,882	40.7	2,895,652	57.8
Rhode Island..............	Dan McKee (D)	2018	376,401	139,932	37.2	198,122	52.6
South Carolina............	Henry McMaster (R)	2018	1,707,569	921,342	54.0	784,182	45.9
South Dakota.............	Kristi Noem (R)	2018	338,715	172,706	51.0	161,171	47.6
Tennessee................	Bill Lee (R)	2018	2,243,294	1,336,106	59.6	864,863	38.6
Texas.....................	Greg Abbott (R)	2018	8,343,443	4,656,196	55.8	3,546,615	42.5
Utah......................	Spencer Cox (R)	2020	1,438,711	918,754	63.9	442,754	30.8
Vermont..................	Phil Scott (R)	2020	370,968	248,412	67.0	99,214	26.7
Virginia...................	Glenn Youngkin (R)	2021	3,288,318	1,663,158	50.6	1,599,470	48.6
Washington...............	Jay Inslee (D)	2020	4,056,454	1,749,066	43.1	2,294,243	56.6
West Virginia.............	Jim Justice (R)	2020	768,804	497,944	64.8	237,024	30.8
Wisconsin.................	Tony Evers (D)	2018	2,672,342	1,295,080	48.5	1,324,307	49.6
Wyoming..................	Mark Gordon (R)	2018	203,238	136,412	67.1	55,965	27.5

[1] As of July 2022. [2] Includes minor party and scattered votes. [3] In Connecticut, Republican vote total includes 25,388 votes from the Independent party. Democratic vote total includes 17,861 from the Working Families Party. [4] In New York, Democratic vote includes 68,713 from the Independence Party, 27,733 from the Women's Equality Party, and 114,478 from the Working Families Party. The Republican vote includes 253,624 from the Conservative Party and 27,493 from the Reform Party. [5] New York Lt. Gov. Kathy Hochul was sworn in as governor in Aug. 2021 after Andrew Cuomo resigned.

Source: The Council of State Governments, Lexington, KY, *The Book of the States 2022* ©, and ProQuest research.

Table 469. Political Party Control of State Legislatures by Party: 2000 to 2024

[As of beginning of year. Nebraska has a nonpartisan legislature]

Year	Democratic control	Split control or tie	Republican control	Year	Democratic control	Split control or tie	Republican control	Year	Democratic control	Split control or tie	Republican control
2000	16	15	18	2011	16	8	25	2018	13	4	32
2005	19	10	20	2012	15	7	27	2019	18	1	30
2006	19	10	20	2013	19	4	26	2020	19	1	29
2007	22	12	15	2014	19	3	27	2021	18	1	30
2008	23	14	12	2015	11	8	30	2022	17	2	30
2009	27	8	14	2016	11	8	30	2023	19	1	29
2010	27	8	14	2017	14	3	32	2024	19	2	28

Source: National Conference of State Legislatures, Denver, CO, *State & Legislative Partisan Composition* ©, November 2023 and earlier reports. See also <ncsl.org>.

Table 470. Composition of State Legislatures by Political Party Affiliation: 2021 and 2022

[Figures reflect immediate results of elections, including holdover members in state houses which do not have all of their members running for reelection. Dem. = Democrat, Rep. = Republican, Vac. = Vacancies. In general, the lower house consists of state representatives and the upper house consists of state senators]

State	2021 Lower house				2021 Upper house				2022 Lower house				2022 Upper house			
	Dem.	Rep.	Other	Vac.	Dem.	Rep.	Other	Vac.	Dem.	Rep.	Other	Vac.	Dem.	Rep.	Other	Vac.
U.S. [2,6]	2,450	2,917	30	14	852	1,057	6	8	2,409	2,900	32	70	858	1,060	8	10
AL [2,6]	28	75	–	2	8	26	–	1	28	73	–	4	8	27	–	–
AK [1]	15	21	4	–	7	13	–	–	15	21	4	–	7	13	–	–
AZ [3]	29	31	–	–	14	16	–	–	28	31	–	1	14	16	–	–
AR [1]	22	78	–	–	7	28	–	–	22	78	–	–	7	27	1	–
CA [1]	58	19	1	2	31	9	–	–	60	19	1	–	31	9	–	–
CO [1]	41	24	–	–	20	15	–	–	41	24	–	–	21	14	–	–
CT [3]	96	54	–	1	24	12	–	–	97	54	–	–	23	13	–	–
DE [1]	26	15	–	–	14	7	–	–	26	15	–	–	14	7	–	–
FL [1,6]	42	78	–	–	16	24	–	–	42	76	–	2	16	23	–	1
GA [3]	77	103	–	–	22	34	–	–	76	103	–	1	22	34	–	–
HI [1]	47	4	–	–	24	1	–	–	47	4	–	–	24	1	–	–
ID [3]	12	58	–	–	7	28	–	–	12	58	–	–	7	28	–	–
IL [4]	72	45	–	1	41	18	–	–	73	45	–	–	41	18	–	–
IN [1]	29	71	–	–	11	39	–	–	29	71	–	–	11	39	–	–
IA [1]	41	59	–	–	18	32	–	–	40	60	–	–	18	32	–	–
KS [1]	39	86	–	–	11	29	–	–	38	86	–	1	11	29	–	–
KY [1]	25	75	–	–	8	30	–	–	25	75	–	–	8	30	–	–
LA [2]	35	67	2	1	12	27	–	–	34	68	3	–	11	26	–	2
ME [3]	80	66	5	–	22	13	–	–	77	63	3	8	22	13	–	–
MD [2,6]	99	42	–	–	32	15	–	–	99	42	–	–	32	15	–	–
MA [3,6]	128	30	1	1	37	3	–	–	125	27	1	7	37	3	–	–
MI [1]	52	58	–	–	16	20	–	2	53	56	–	1	16	22	–	–
MN [1]	70	64	–	–	31	34	2	–	69	63	1	1	31	34	1	1
MS [2,6]	46	75	1	–	16	36	–	–	42	76	3	1	16	36	–	–
MO [1]	48	114	–	1	10	24	–	–	48	107	–	8	10	24	–	–
MT [1,6]	33	67	–	–	19	31	–	–	33	67	–	–	19	31	–	–
NE [5]	(5)	(5)	(5)	(5)	(5)	(5)	(5)	(5)	(5)	(5)	(5)	(5)	(5)	(5)	(5)	(5)
NV [1]	26	16	–	–	12	9	–	–	25	16	–	1	11	9	–	1
NH [3]	186	212	–	2	10	14	–	–	179	202	1	18	10	13	–	1
NJ [1]	52	28	–	–	25	15	–	–	46	33	–	1	23	16	–	1
NM [1]	45	24	1	–	27	15	–	–	45	24	1	–	26	15	–	1
NY [3,6]	106	43	1	–	43	20	–	–	106	43	1	–	42	20	–	1
NC [3]	51	69	–	–	22	28	–	–	51	68	–	1	22	28	–	–
ND [2]	14	80	–	–	7	40	–	–	14	80	–	–	7	40	–	–
OH [1]	35	64	–	–	8	25	–	–	35	64	–	–	8	25	–	–
OK [1]	19	82	–	–	9	38	–	1	18	82	–	1	9	39	–	–
OR [1]	37	23	–	–	18	11	1	–	36	23	–	1	18	11	1	–
PA [1]	90	111	–	2	20	27	1	2	89	113	–	1	21	28	1	–
RI [3]	65	10	–	–	33	5	–	–	65	10	–	–	33	5	–	–
SC [1,6]	43	81	–	–	16	30	–	–	43	81	–	–	16	30	–	–
SD [3]	8	62	–	–	3	32	–	–	8	62	–	–	3	32	–	1
TN [1]	26	73	–	–	6	27	–	–	24	72	1	2	6	26	–	1
TX [1]	68	82	–	–	13	18	–	–	65	83	–	2	13	18	–	–
UT [1]	17	58	–	–	6	23	–	–	17	57	–	1	6	23	–	–
VT [3]	92	46	12	–	21	7	2	–	93	46	10	1	21	7	2	–
VA [1]	55	45	–	–	21	18	–	1	51	52	–	1	21	19	–	–
WA [1]	57	41	–	–	29	20	–	–	57	41	–	–	24	25	–	–
WV [1]	23	77	–	–	11	23	–	–	22	78	–	–	11	23	–	–
WI [1]	38	60	–	1	12	20	–	1	38	57	–	4	12	21	–	–
WY [1]	7	51	2	–	2	28	–	–	7	51	2	–	2	28	–	–

– Represents zero. [1] Upper House members serve 4–year terms and Lower House members serve 2–year terms. [2] Members of both houses serve 4–year terms. [3] Members of both houses serve 2–year terms. [4] In Illinois, members serve 4– and 2–year terms depending on district. [5] Nebraska is the only state to have a nonpartisan unicameral legislature and members serve 4–year terms. For 2021 and 2022, the Nebraska legislature has 49 members. [6] Data for 2022 term collected in 2020 and 2021.

Source: The Council of State Governments, Lexington, KY, *The Book of the States 2022*, and earlier reports ©. See also <www.csg.org>.

Table 471. Women Holding State Public Offices by Office and State: 2024

[As of May]

State	Total	Statewide elective executive office[1]	State legislature Total	State legislature Percent
U.S.	**2,530**	**99**	**2,431**	**32.9**
AL	27	2	25	17.9
AK	21	1	20	33.3
AZ	51	5	46	51.1
AR	33	2	31	23.0
CA	54	4	50	41.7
CO	51	2	49	49.0
CT	72	2	70	37.4
DE	27	4	23	37.1
FL	68	2	66	41.3
GA	83	1	82	34.7
HI	30	1	29	38.2
ID	33	2	31	29.5
IL	77	2	75	42.4
IN	42	2	40	26.7
IA	46	2	44	29.3
KS	54	2	52	31.5
KY	45	2	43	31.2
LA	36	2	34	23.6
ME	80	1	79	42.5
MD	81	2	79	42.0
MA	67	5	62	31.0
MI	62	3	59	39.9
MN	78	2	76	37.8
MS	28	1	27	15.5
MO	57	–	57	28.9
MT	51	3	48	32.0
NE	18	–	18	36.7
NV	38	–	38	60.3
NH	161	–	161	38.0
NJ	42	1	41	34.2
NM	53	4	49	43.8
NY	74	2	72	33.8
NC	53	3	50	24.9
ND	41	4	37	26.2
OH	38	–	38	28.8
OK	32	3	29	19.5
OR	41	4	37	41.1
PA	83	2	81	32.0
RI	50	1	49	43.4
SC	29	2	27	15.9
SD	32	3	29	27.6
TN	20	–	20	15.2
TX	58	2	56	30.9
UT	29	1	28	26.9
VT	84	2	82	45.6
VA	50	1	49	35.0
WA	69	2	67	45.6
WV	16	–	16	11.9
WI	43	3	40	30.3
WY	22	2	20	21.5

– Represents zero. [1] Excludes women elected to the judiciary, women appointed to state cabinet-level positions, women elected to executive posts by the legislature, and elected members of university Boards of Trustees or Boards of Education.

Source: Center for American Women and Politics, Eagleton Institute of Politics, Rutgers University, New Brunswick, NJ, "Women in Elective Office," <www.cawp.rutgers.edu/> ©, accessed May 2024.

Table 472. Hispanic Public Elected Officials by Office, 2010 to 2021, and by State, 2021

[As of January or November of year shown]

State	Total[1]	State executives and legislators[2]	County and municipal officials	Judicial and law enforcement	Education and school boards
2010	5,763	275	2,270	874	2,072
2015	6,124	349	2,334	860	2,342
2016	6,176	347	2,388	859	2,344
2017	6,600	377	2,638	879	2,473
2018	6,749	378	2,733	890	2,496
2019	6,832	389	2,775	882	2,535
2020	6,883	384	2,768	903	2,593
2021	**7,087**	**401**	**2,853**	**913**	**2,668**
AL	0	0	0	0	0
AK	1	0	1	0	0
AZ	358	28	128	29	167
AR	5	0	1	2	2
CA	1,833	47	625	128	894
CO	156	14	82	16	38
CT	75	14	43	0	18
DE	4	3	0	0	1
DC	0	0	0	0	0
FL	214	25	109	66	14
GA	13	4	5	3	1
HI	4	4	0	0	0
ID	3	0	3	0	0
IL	134	18	80	8	21
IN	31	3	13	3	12
IA	23	1	13	0	9
KS	13	5	6	1	1
KY	2	1	0	0	1
LA	3	0	1	1	1
ME	2	0	1	0	1
MD	11	3	8	0	0
MA	57	8	28	1	20
MI	18	4	7	4	3
MN	20	6	4	8	2
MS	0	0	0	0	0
MO	3	1	1	0	1
MT	0	0	0	0	0
NE	5	2	1	1	1
NV	33	9	9	7	8
NH	5	3	1	1	0
NJ	169	12	94	1	62
NM	649	52	318	101	138
NY	186	29	66	60	31
NC	6	1	3	1	1
ND	0	0	0	0	0
OH	20	2	11	3	4
OK	4	3	0	0	1
OR	39	5	6	10	17
PA	24	3	16	3	2
RI	35	12	15	0	8
SC	0	0	0	0	0
SD	1	0	1	0	0
TN	3	0	1	1	1
TX	2,808	54	1,094	443	1,164
UT	9	4	2	1	2
VT	2	0	1	0	1
VA	13	5	7	0	1
WA	65	8	40	2	15
WV	4	3	0	1	0
WI	15	2	4	7	2
WY	9	3	4	0	2

[1] Also includes special district officials, not shown separately. [2] Includes U.S. Senators and Representatives, not shown separately.

Source: National Association of Latino Elected and Appointed Officials (NALEO) Educational Fund, Washington, DC, *National Directory of Latino Elected Officials* ©, and earlier reports. See also <www.naleo.org>.

Table 473. Political Action Committees—Financial Activity Summary by Committee Type: 2017 to 2022

[In millions of dollars (4,674.2 represents $4,674,200,000). Covers financial activity during 2-year calendar period indicated]

Committee type	Receipts			Disbursements [1]			Contributions to candidates		
	2017 to 2018	2019 to 2020 [2]	2021 to 2022	2017 to 2018	2019 to 2020 [2]	2021 to 2022	2017 to 2018	2019 to 2020 [2]	2021 to 2022
Total	4,674.2	13,227.9	9,307.7	4,554.1	12,947.1	9,049.1	465.6	448.8	429.7
Corporate	417.2	429.6	383.1	404.8	408.5	362.4	178.1	165.7	145.6
Labor	365.8	384.3	365.3	342.2	385.6	338.2	53.8	51.8	50.7
Trade	174.3	161.7	163.9	164.1	149.8	146.6	87.3	79.0	78.1
Membership	100.4	141.4	116.5	97.6	130.9	108.0	33.0	38.3	26.5
Cooperative	9.1	7.8	7.8	8.4	7.3	7.3	5.1	5.1	5.3
Corporation without stock	14.3	14.3	11.0	14.4	13.2	9.7	7.4	6.7	5.0
Nonconnected	3,593.0	12,088.8	8,260.2	3,522.5	11,851.7	8,076.9	100.8	102.1	118.5

[1] Comprises contributions to candidates, independent expenditures, and other disbursements. [2] See footnote 3, Table 475.

Source: U.S. Federal Election Commission, Campaign Finance Statistics, "Political Action Committee (PAC) Data Summary Tables," <www.fec.gov/campaign-finance-data/campaign-finance-statistics/>, accessed June 2023.

Table 474. Political Action Committees (PACs)—Number and Finances by Committee Type: 2021 and 2022

[In thousands of dollars (9,307,696 represents $9,307,696,000), except number of committees. Covers financial activity during 2-year calendar period indicated]

Committee type	Number of committees	Total receipts	Total disbursements	Debts owed	Cash on hand
Total	9,271	9,307,696	9,049,050	48,238	1,275,856
Separate segregated funds: [1]					
Corporate	1,655	383,136	362,419	34	221,234
Labor	271	365,284	338,170	6,920	162,418
Trade	720	163,864	146,554	42	105,906
Membership	309	116,450	107,994	1,507	45,090
Cooperative	47	7,797	7,323	–	7,502
Corporations without stock	86	10,960	9,737	2	5,284
Nonconnected committees: [2]					
Independent expenditure-only political committees (Super PACs) [3]	2,474	2,737,156	2,496,382	26,149	361,009
Committees with non-contribution accounts (Hybrid PACs) [4]	684	4,712,203	4,751,134	6,946	168,351
Leadership PACs [5]	769	357,557	353,519	525	97,795
Other nonconnected PACs	2,256	453,290	475,818	6,114	101,265

– Represents zero. [1] Committees established and administered by corporations, labor unions, membership organizations or trade associations, which may solicit only from individuals associated with a connected or sponsoring organization. [2] Committees that are not affiliated with corporations, labor unions, membership organizations or trade associations and may solicit contributions from the general public. [3] Committees that may receive unlimited contributions for the purpose of financing independent expenditures and other independent political activity. [4] Committees that may receive unlimited contributions to a segregated bank account for the purpose of financing independent expenditures, other ads that refer to a federal candidate, and generic voter drives in federal elections, while maintaining a separate bank account that is permitted to make contributions to federal candidates. [5] Committees that are directly or indirectly established, financed, maintained or controlled by candidates or individuals holding federal office but are not an authorized committee of the candidate or officeholder and are not affiliated with an authorized committee of a candidate or officeholder.

Source: U.S. Federal Election Commission, Campaign Finance Statistics, "Political action committee data summary tables," <www.fec.gov/campaign-finance-data/political-action-committee-data-summary-tables/>, accessed April 2023. See also <www.fec.gov/press/resources-journalists/political-action-committees-pacs/>.

Table 475. Political Action Committees (PAC) Contributions to Congressional Campaigns by Committee Type: 2019 to 2022

[In millions of dollars (361.6 represents $361,600,000). Covers amounts given to candidates in primary, general, run-off, and special elections during the 2-year calendar period indicated]

Committee type	Total [1]	Democrats	Republicans	Incumbents	Challengers	Open seats [2]
HOUSE OF REPRESENTATIVES						
2019-2020 [3]	361.6	196.0	165.1	318.9	25.8	16.8
2021-2022, total	**356.6**	**183.2**	**172.5**	**303.8**	**32.5**	**19.6**
Corporate	120.4	56.6	63.8	115.5	2.8	2.2
Trade association [4]	87.9	39.6	48.1	79.3	4.9	3.7
Labor	45.4	39.4	6.0	35.7	5.8	3.9
Nonconnected [5]	93.7	43.1	50.0	64.7	18.8	10.3
Cooperative	4.7	2.3	2.3	4.4	0.1	0.2
Corporation without stock	4.5	2.1	2.3	4.2	0.1	0.1
SENATE						
2019-2020 [3]	85.8	28.7	56.7	69.0	10.8	6.0
2021-2022, total	**73.1**	**32.1**	**41.0**	**56.3**	**5.2**	**11.6**
Corporate	25.1	8.8	16.3	22.2	0.4	2.6
Trade association [4]	16.6	6.2	10.5	13.4	0.8	2.5
Labor	5.3	4.8	0.4	3.5	0.7	1.1
Nonconnected [5]	24.8	11.7	13.0	16.1	3.4	5.3
Cooperative	0.7	0.3	0.4	0.6	(Z)	0.1
Corporation without stock	0.6	0.2	0.3	0.5	(Z)	(Z)

Z represents less than $50,000. [1] Includes other parties, not shown separately. [2] Elections in which an incumbent did not seek reelection. [3] Due to COVID-19 related office closures, data excludes some reports filed on paper. [4] Includes membership organizations and health organizations. [5] Represents "ideological" groups as well as other issue groups not necessarily ideological in nature.

Source: U.S. Federal Election Commission, Campaign Finance Statistics, "Political Action Committees (PAC) Data Summary Tables," <www.fec.gov/campaign-finance-data/campaign-finance-statistics>, accessed June 2023.

Table 476. Congressional Campaign Finances—Receipts and Disbursements: 2013 to 2022

[In millions of dollars (1,033.9 represents $1,033,900,000). Covers all campaign finance activity during 2-year calendar period indicated for primary, general, run-off, and special elections. Data have been adjusted to eliminate transfers between all committees within a campaign. For further information on legal limits of contributions, see Federal Election Campaign Act of 1971, as amended]

Item	House of Representatives					Senate				
	2013 to 2014	2015 to 2016	2017 to 2018	2019 to 2020 [3]	2021 to 2022	2013 to 2014	2015 to 2016	2017 to 2018	2019 to 2020 [3]	2021 to 2022
Total receipts [1]	1,033.9	1,049.8	1,740.8	1,959.3	2,092.9	635.4	594.5	1,033.3	2,046.1	1,663.2
Individual contributions	557.0	546.4	1,063.0	1,330.8	1,380.4	439.4	424.2	691.4	1,758.1	1,286.1
Contributions from PAC's	341.9	354.5	406.1	390.2	388.6	98.4	92.8	84.8	86.5	78.1
Candidate contributions & loans	96.4	107.0	165.5	123.4	170.7	51.2	31.6	188.4	69.5	193.2
Democrats	446.4	476.4	1,034.5	1,026.8	1,040.1	299.6	313.4	571.5	1,206.8	940.0
Incumbents	286.1	249.9	299.3	656.8	640.4	204.1	67.0	399.2	273.1	526.2
Challengers	82.9	126.7	446.7	266.7	277.0	41.3	176.2	119.5	889.5	183.7
Open seats [2]	77.3	99.7	288.6	103.3	122.6	54.1	70.1	52.8	44.1	230.0
Republicans	583.7	559.4	693.1	919.6	1,038.4	327.9	278.8	430.8	815.3	711.9
Incumbents	355.5	406.7	494.5	498.7	599.1	90.2	201.3	80.4	656.2	258.4
Challengers	119.7	51.5	61.6	292.1	297.5	144.1	29.1	295.0	107.7	214.8
Open seats [2]	108.5	101.2	137.0	128.7	141.8	93.5	48.5	55.5	51.4	238.6
Others	3.9	14.0	13.1	12.9	14.5	8.0	2.3	30.9	24.0	11.4
Incumbents	0.1	4.4	0.9	2.5	(Z)	–	–	15.6	–	–
Challengers	1.3	5.0	8.0	8.3	5.5	6.4	2.1	15.2	23.9	9.0
Open seats [2]	2.5	4.6	4.2	2.1	9.0	1.5	0.2	0.2	0.1	2.4
Total disbursements	960.8	971.7	1,698.9	1,803.6	2,051.0	654.2	625.3	1,019.5	1,961.6	1,675.6
Democrats	422.5	425.1	983.5	937.2	1,051.5	311.5	316.0	557.8	1,162.2	955.1
Republicans	534.5	533.5	703.0	854.1	985.3	334.8	306.8	436.4	775.6	709.5
Others	3.9	13.1	12.4	12.4	14.2	8.0	2.5	25.3	23.8	11.0

Z represents less than $50,000. – Represents zero. [1] Includes other types of receipts, not shown separately. [2] Elections in which an incumbent did not seek reelection. [3] Due to COVID-19 related office closures, data excludes some reports filed on paper.

Source: U.S. Federal Election Commission, Campaign Finance Statistics, "Congressional Candidate Data Summary Tables," <www.fec.gov/campaign-finance-data/campaign-finance-statistics/>, accessed June 2023.

Table 477. Presidential Campaign Receipts and Disbursements by Political Party: 1995 to 2022

[In millions of dollars (464.0 represents $464,000,000). Covers financial activity during 2-year calendar period indicated]

Item	1995 to 1996	1999 to 2000 [2]	2003 to 2004 [2]	2007 to 2008 [2]	2011 to 2012 [2]	2015 to 2016	2017 to 2018	2019 to 2020 [3]	2021 to 2022
RECEIPTS									
Total	464.0	511.9	850.8	1,550.8	1,379.8	1,540.1	75.3	4,073.9	4.3
Republican	296.4	172.2	362.4	219.6	483.5	673.3	67.6	748.9	3.9
Democrat	123.5	128.4	321.2	747.8	738.5	841.3	7.5	3,298.8	(Z)
Other	44.2	26.7	(NA)	(NA)	4.0	25.5	0.2	26.3	0.4
DISBURSEMENTS [1]									
Total	456.0	527.2	867.5	1,645.0	1,359.8	1,527.5	63.1	4,071.9	1.1
Republican	294.7	186.5	355.0	239.7	483.1	667.5	55.9	757.3	0.9
Democrat	119.4	120.3	332.7	760.4	737.1	834.7	7.0	3,289.8	(Z)
Other	41.9	(NA)	(NA)	(NA)	3.8	25.3	0.2	24.8	0.2

NA Not available. Z Less than $500,000. [1] Comprises operating expenses, transfers to other committees, and other disbursements. [2] Party data reflect only the candidate who stood in the general election. [3] Due to COVID-19 related office closures, data excludes some reports filed on paper.

Source: U.S. Federal Election Commission, Campaign Finance Statistics, "Presidential Candidate Data Summary Tables," <www.fec.gov/campaign-finance-data/campaign-finance-statistics/>, accessed April 2023.

Section 8
State and Local Government Finances and Employment

This section presents data on revenues, expenditures, debt, and employment of state and local governments. Nationwide statistics relating to state and local governments, their numbers, finances, and employment are compiled primarily by the U.S. Census Bureau through a program of censuses and surveys. Every fifth year (for years ending in "2" and "7"), the Census Bureau conducts a Census of Governments involving collection of data for all governmental units in the United States. In addition, the Census Bureau conducts annual surveys which cover all the state governments and a sample of local governments.

Annually, the Census Bureau releases information on financial data for the federal government, nationwide totals for state and local governments, and state-local data by states. A series on state, city, county, and school finances and on state and local public employment is also released annually. Quarterly data releases cover tax revenue and finances of major public employee retirement systems.

Basic information for Census Bureau statistics on governments is obtained by mail canvass from state and local officials; however, financial data for each state government and for many of the large local governments are compiled from their official records and reports by Census Bureau personnel. In over two-thirds of the states, all or part of local government financial data are obtained through central collection arrangements with state governments. Financial data on the federal government's aid to state and local areas are primarily based on the *Budget of the United States Government* published by the Office of Management and Budget.

Governmental units—The governmental structure of the United States includes, in addition to the federal government and the states, thousands of local governments—counties, municipalities, townships, school districts, and many "special districts." In 2017, 90,075 local governments were identified by the Census of Governments (see table 478 and table 479). As defined by the census, governmental units include all agencies or bodies having an organized existence, governmental character, and substantial autonomy. While most of these governments can impose taxes, many of the special districts—such as independent public housing authorities and numerous local irrigation, power, and other types of districts—are financed from rentals, charges for services, benefit assessments, grants from other governments, and other non-tax sources. The count of governments excludes semi-autonomous agencies through which states, cities, and counties sometimes provide for certain functions—for example, "dependent" school systems, state institutions of higher education, and certain other "authorities" and special agencies which are under the administrative or fiscal control of an established governmental unit.

Finances—The financial statistics relate to government fiscal years ending June 30 or at some date within the 12 previous months. The following governments are exceptions and are included as though they were part of the June 30 group: the state

governments of Alabama and Michigan and the city government of The District of Columbia, with fiscal years ending September 30; the state government of Texas ending August 31; and New York State ending March 31. The federal government ended the fiscal year June 30 until 1976 when its fiscal year, by an act of Congress, was revised to extend from October 1 to September 30. A 3-month quarter (July 1 to September 30, 1976) bridged the transition.

Nationwide government finance statistics have been classified and presented in terms of uniform concepts and categories, rather than according to the highly diverse terminology, organization, and fund structure utilized by individual governments.

Statistics on governmental finances distinguish among general government, utilities, liquor stores, and insurance trusts. *General government* comprises all activities except utilities, liquor stores, and insurance trusts. *Utilities* include government water supply, electric light and power, gas supply, and transit systems. *Liquor stores* are operated by 16 states and by local governments in 5 states. *Insurance trusts* relate to employee retirement, unemployment compensation, and other social insurance systems administered by the federal, state, and local governments.

Data for cities or counties relate only to municipal or county and their dependent agencies and do not include amounts for other local governments in the same geographic location. Therefore, expenditure figures for "education" do not include spending by the separate school districts which administer public schools within most municipal or county areas. Variations in the assignment of governmental responsibility for public assistance, health, hospitals, public housing, and other functions to a lesser degree also have an important effect upon reported amounts of city or county expenditure, revenue, and debt.

Employment and payrolls—These data are based mainly on mail canvassing of state and local governments. Payroll includes all salaries, wages, and individual fee payments for the month specified. Employment relates to all persons on governmental payrolls during a pay period of the month covered, including paid officials, temporary help, and (unless otherwise specified) part-time as well as full-time personnel. Effective with the 1997 Census of Governments, the reference period for measuring government employment was changed from October of the calendar year to March of the calendar year. As a result, there was no annual survey of government employment covering the October 1996 period. The prior reference month of October was used from 1958 to 1995. Figures shown for individual governments cover major dependent agencies such as institutions of higher education, as well as the basic central departments and agencies of the government.

Statistical reliability—For a discussion of statistical collection and estimation, sampling procedures, and measures of statistical reliability applicable to Census Bureau data, see Appendix III.

Table 478. Number of Governmental Units by Type: 1977 to 2022

Type of government	1977	1982	1987	1992	1997	2002	2007	2012	2017	2022
Total units	**79,913**	**81,831**	**83,237**	**85,006**	**87,504**	**87,576**	**89,527**	**90,107**	**90,126**	**90,888**
U.S. government	1	1	1	1	1	1	1	1	1	1
State governments	50	50	50	50	50	50	50	50	50	50
Local governments	79,862	81,780	83,186	84,955	87,453	87,525	89,476	90,056	90,075	90,837
County	3,042	3,041	3,042	3,043	3,043	3,034	3,033	3,031	3,031	3,031
Municipal	18,862	19,076	19,200	19,279	19,372	19,429	19,492	19,519	19,495	19,491
Township and town	16,822	16,734	16,691	16,656	16,629	16,504	16,519	16,360	16,253	16,214
School district	15,174	14,851	14,721	14,422	13,726	13,506	13,051	12,880	12,754	12,546
Special district	25,962	28,078	29,532	31,555	34,683	35,052	37,381	38,266	38,542	39,555

Source: U.S. Census Bureau, Census of Governments, "2022 Census of Governments–Organization," <www.census.gov/programs-surveys/cog.html>, accessed August 2023.

Table 479. Number of Local Governments by Type—States: 2022

[Governments in existence in June 2022. See source for details on government classifications <www.census.gov/programs-surveys/gus/technical-documentation/methodology.html>]

State	All govern-mental units [1]	County	Municipal	Township [1]	School district	Special district Total [2]	Natural resources [3]	Fire protection	Housing & community develop-ment
United States	**90,837**	**3,031**	**19,491**	**16,214**	**12,546**	**39,555**	**7,122**	**5,957**	**3,304**
Alabama	1,208	67	462	–	138	541	68	13	147
Alaska	181	15	149	–	–	17	–	–	15
Arizona	674	15	91	–	242	326	105	145	–
Arkansas	1,562	75	500	–	234	753	254	72	117
California	4,494	57	482	–	1,006	2,949	491	354	69
Colorado	3,715	62	272	–	180	3,201	166	259	96
Connecticut	629	–	30	149	17	433	1	64	113
Delaware	334	3	57	–	19	255	233	–	4
District of Columbia	2	–	1	–	–	1	–	–	–
Florida	1,947	66	412	–	95	1,374	117	54	92
Georgia	1,379	152	537	–	180	510	37	–	192
Hawaii	21	3	1	–	–	17	16	–	–
Idaho	1,168	44	199	–	118	807	178	155	11
Illinois	6,930	102	1,295	1,425	890	3,218	1,014	845	113
Indiana	2,648	91	567	1,004	290	696	145	2	61
Iowa	1,826	99	940	–	342	445	124	60	27
Kansas	3,768	103	624	1,267	306	1,468	249	1	169
Kentucky	1,307	118	417	–	171	601	126	144	19
Louisiana	534	60	304	–	69	101	6	1	–
Maine	828	16	23	461	101	227	17	–	30
Maryland	342	23	157	–	–	162	128	–	18
Massachusetts	856	5	56	295	85	415	17	11	250
Michigan	2,860	83	533	1,240	567	437	75	26	–
Minnesota	3,629	87	854	1,779	330	579	143	9	153
Mississippi	967	82	298	–	150	437	232	29	52
Missouri	3,796	114	943	283	529	1,927	321	415	131
Montana	1,228	54	128	–	310	736	132	217	13
Nebraska	2,541	93	528	350	267	1,303	88	412	159
Nevada	187	16	19	–	17	135	34	15	2
New Hampshire	538	10	13	221	166	128	11	14	21
New Jersey	1,328	21	323	241	521	222	14	172	–
New Mexico	1003	33	105	–	96	769	557	–	–
New York	3,447	57	595	930	676	1,189	1	890	–
North Carolina	965	100	552	–	–	313	134	–	93
North Dakota	2,570	53	356	1,305	173	683	72	274	15
Ohio	3,939	88	926	1,308	665	952	103	120	81
Oklahoma	1,840	77	592	–	539	632	103	28	128
Oregon	1,528	36	240	–	223	1,029	189	265	18
Pennsylvania	4,851	66	1,013	1,546	514	1,712	8	–	88
Rhode Island	127	–	8	31	4	84	5	29	26
South Carolina	666	46	271	–	78	271	45	62	42
South Dakota	1,900	66	310	897	149	478	103	78	–
Tennessee	902	92	345	–	14	451	105	1	92
Texas	5,533	254	1,225	–	1,070	2,984	437	264	384
Utah	632	29	254	–	41	308	78	12	20
Vermont	574	14	40	237	121	162	14	14	8
Virginia	522	95	228	–	1	198	47	–	1
Washington	1,890	39	281	–	295	1,275	171	359	42
West Virginia	639	55	231	–	55	298	14	–	33
Wisconsin	3,062	72	605	1,245	437	703	256	1	159
Wyoming	820	23	99	–	55	643	138	71	–

– Represents zero. [1] Includes town governments in the six New England States and in Minnesota, New York, and Wisconsin. [2] Includes other special districts not shown separately. [3] Includes special district governments for soil and water conservation, drainage and flood control, and other natural resources.

Source: U.S. Census Bureau, Census of Governments, "2022 Census of Governments–Organization," <www.census.gov/programs-surveys/cog.html>, accessed August 2023.

Table 480. State and Local Government Current Receipts and Expenditures in the National Income and Product Accounts: 2000 to 2023

[In billions of dollars (1,303.5 represents $1,303,500,000,000). For explanation of national income, see text, Section 13. Minus sign (-) indicates net loss]

Item	2000	2010	2015	2018	2019	2020	2021	2022	2023
Current receipts	**1,303.5**	**1,991.7**	**2,370.2**	**2,643.2**	**2,788.8**	**3,078.0**	**3,577.9**	**3,662.4**	**3,627.1**
Current tax receipts	893.2	1,306.4	1,596.0	1,813.6	1,929.6	1,941.0	2,198.2	2,407.6	2,388.8
Personal current taxes	236.7	294.1	408.3	459.9	497.9	503.0	594.0	632.9	570.2
Income taxes	217.4	265.8	375.3	422.5	459.6	464.0	550.9	588.2	524.6
Other	19.4	28.3	33.0	37.4	38.3	39.0	43.1	44.7	45.6
Taxes on production and imports	621.3	966.3	1,131.6	1,293.6	1,358.2	1,365.2	1,493.3	1,616.0	1,659.3
Sales taxes	221.4	295.1	373.2	426.4	448.0	443.7	514.5	570.8	591.0
Excise taxes	95.5	154.8	179.9	205.6	213.1	204.2	226.1	240.7	246.6
Property taxes	254.7	438.6	489.3	554.6	588.4	607.6	621.7	660.0	686.8
Other	49.8	77.8	89.2	107.0	108.7	109.7	131.0	144.5	134.9
Taxes on corporate income	35.2	46.1	56.1	60.1	73.5	72.9	110.9	158.6	159.4
Contributions for government social insurance	10.8	17.8	19.2	20.4	20.7	20.0	22.2	22.5	21.9
Income receipts on assets	93.6	80.8	80.7	93.2	96.5	94.8	93.8	97.6	100.3
Interest receipts	86.0	66.3	64.1	75.8	78.4	77.7	75.8	78.7	80.7
Dividends	1.4	3.0	5.4	6.0	6.5	6.2	6.3	6.6	6.8
Rents and royalties	6.3	11.4	11.1	11.4	11.6	10.9	11.7	12.4	12.7
Current transfer receipts	299.7	604.4	676.3	723.8	755.4	1,029.3	1,277.0	1,138.0	1,133.6
Federal grants-in-aid	233.1	505.2	533.1	582.6	609.0	878.8	1,110.3	948.9	952.2
From business (net)	28.6	40.3	66.2	54.5	56.0	58.1	64.2	72.1	69.2
From persons	38.0	58.8	76.4	85.2	88.8	92.0	102.0	109.8	111.8
From the rest of the world	–	–	0.6	1.5	1.6	0.5	0.6	7.2	0.4
Current surplus of government enterprises	6.1	-17.7	-1.9	-7.9	-13.3	-7.1	-13.3	-3.2	-17.5
Current expenditures	**1,345.0**	**2,300.6**	**2,586.8**	**2,843.0**	**2,994.7**	**3,129.9**	**3,334.6**	**3,602.1**	**3,777.2**
Consumption expenditures	961.9	1,508.1	1,652.2	1,825.3	1,925.2	2,019.7	2,149.9	2,341.1	2,423.5
Government social benefit payments to persons	271.4	523.9	665.3	731.1	762.7	815.7	900.7	1,012.3	1,061.5
Interest payments	111.1	267.0	268.7	286.0	306.2	293.9	280.9	248.0	291.5
Subsidies	0.5	1.6	0.5	0.6	0.6	0.6	3.1	0.7	0.7
Net state and local government saving	**-41.5**	**-309.0**	**-216.6**	**-199.9**	**-205.9**	**-51.9**	**243.4**	**60.4**	**-150.1**
Social insurance funds	2.0	0.9	3.7	4.9	3.3	1.9	4.1	4.4	3.4
Other	-43.5	-309.9	-220.3	-204.8	-209.2	-53.8	239.2	56.0	-153.5

– Represents zero.

Source: U.S. Bureau of Economic Analysis, National Income and Product Accounts Tables, "Table 3.3. State and Local Government Current Receipts and Expenditures," <www.bea.gov/itable/national-gdp-and-personal-income>, accessed July 2024.

Table 481. Federal Outlays for Grants to State and Local Governments: 1990 to 2024

[135,325 represents $135,325,000,000, except as indicated. For fiscal year ending September 30. Minus sign (-) indicates decrease]

Year	Current dollars						Constant (2017) dollars	
	Total grants (mil. dol.)	Annual percent change [1]	Grants to individuals		Grants as percent of—		Total grants (bil. dol.)	Annual percent change [1]
			Total (mil. dol.)	Percent of total grants	Federal outlays	Gross domestic product		
1990	135,325	11.0	77,431	57.2	10.8	2.3	255.9	5.9
1995	224,991	6.8	145,652	64.7	14.8	3.0	362.2	3.9
2000	285,874	6.7	186,534	65.3	16.0	2.8	415.9	3.8
2001	318,542	11.4	208,008	65.3	17.1	3.0	451.3	8.5
2002	352,895	10.8	231,854	65.7	17.5	3.3	492.2	9.1
2003	388,542	10.1	251,235	64.7	18.0	3.4	530.3	7.7
2004	407,512	4.9	267,046	65.5	17.8	3.4	539.9	1.8
2005	428,018	5.0	278,764	65.1	17.3	3.3	545.7	1.1
2006	434,099	1.4	277,559	63.9	16.3	3.2	533.3	-2.3
2007	443,797	2.2	289,460	65.2	16.3	3.1	526.5	-1.3
2008	461,317	3.9	306,123	66.4	15.5	3.1	525.7	-0.2
2009	537,991	16.6	362,031	67.3	15.3	3.7	610.9	16.2
2010	608,390	13.1	391,427	64.3	17.6	4.1	680.1	11.3
2011	606,770	-0.3	392,713	64.7	16.8	3.9	662.0	-2.7
2012	544,573	-10.3	364,095	66.9	15.4	3.4	580.4	-12.3
2013	546,178	0.3	379,008	69.4	15.8	3.3	571.3	-1.6
2014	576,978	5.6	412,466	71.5	16.5	3.3	593.3	3.9
2015	624,357	8.2	463,392	74.2	16.9	3.4	638.8	7.7
2016	660,836	5.8	495,711	75.0	17.2	3.5	672.1	5.2
2017	674,712	2.1	507,976	75.3	16.9	3.5	674.7	0.4
2018	696,507	3.2	525,813	75.5	17.0	3.4	680.6	0.9
2019	721,140	3.5	549,313	76.2	16.2	3.4	692.3	1.7
2020	829,093	15.0	608,628	73.4	12.7	3.9	784.8	13.4
2021	1,245,280	50.2	689,771	55.4	18.3	5.4	1,129.8	44.0
2022	1,193,343	-4.2	790,692	66.3	19.0	4.7	1,020.8	-9.6
2023	1,083,354	-9.2	816,351	75.4	17.7	4.0	891.4	-12.7
2024, estimate	1,107,586	2.2	770,721	69.6	16.0	3.9	882.8	-1.0

[1] Average annual percent change from previous year.

Source: U.S. Office of Management and Budget, *Budget of the U.S. Government, Fiscal Year 2025: Historical Tables*, March 2024. See also <www.whitehouse.gov/omb/budget>.

Table 482. Federal Outlays for Grants to State and Local Governments—Selected Agencies and Programs: 2000 to 2025

[In millions of dollars (285,874 represents $285,874,000,000). For fiscal year ending September 30. Includes trust funds]

Agency and program	2000	2010	2015	2018	2019	2020	2021	2022	2023	2024, estimate	2025, estimate
Total outlays for grants [1]	**285,874**	**608,390**	**624,357**	**696,507**	**721,140**	**829,093**	**1,245,280**	**1,193,343**	**1,083,354**	**1,107,586**	**1,095,336**
Energy	433	2,656	577	771	819	824	841	601	593	577	762
Natural resources and environment [2]	4,595	9,132	7,043	6,394	6,698	7,211	6,715	7,593	10,945	38,588	18,025
Environmental Protection Agency [2]	3,490	6,883	4,570	3,862	4,103	4,351	4,037	4,609	7,413	33,828	12,915
Agriculture	724	843	707	815	828	804	909	791	888	922	1,145
Broadband Equity, Access, and Deployment Program	–	–	–	–	–	–	–	–	55	1,627	9,194
Universal Service Fund	1,215	1,777	1,739	1,840	2,113	2,141	2,123	2,159	2,471	2,592	2,770
Transportation [3]	32,222	60,981	60,835	64,836	65,637	69,309	86,603	93,914	87,651	97,322	107,978
Grants for airports [3]	1,624	3,156	2,988	3,036	3,303	3,289	8,663	5,627	4,319	4,244	2,943
Federal-aid highways [3]	24,711	30,385	41,205	43,305	43,768	46,327	43,252	43,742	47,688	50,586	53,037
Urban mass transportation [2]	5,262	12,939	11,784	12,608	13,109	13,038	24,220	34,032	23,593	20,474	20,753
Community and regional development	8,665	18,908	14,357	19,089	15,565	52,499	52,287	43,195	38,259	72,822	42,641
Rural Community Advancement Program	479	–	–	–	–	–	–	–	–	–	–
Community Development Fund	4,955	7,043	6,548	5,889	5,178	5,235	6,759	7,515	8,774	13,327	16,212
Homeland Security	2,439	8,483	5,924	12,038	8,988	45,613	43,624	33,600	27,103	54,597	20,539
Federal assistance, FEMA	–	–	–	516	1,350	2,023	2,228	2,397	2,962	3,713	4,229
State and local programs [5]	192	–	–	–	–	–	–	–	–	–	–
Operations and support, FEMA	–	–	–	1,704	903	273	62	22	49	49	49
Disaster relief fund	2,234	5,141	2,919	9,715	6,735	43,317	41,334	31,181	23,819	50,608	15,895
Education, training, employment, social services	36,672	97,586	60,527	60,591	63,106	67,890	89,905	95,807	92,179	87,512	81,404
Education for the disadvantaged [4]	8,511	19,515	15,199	15,277	16,203	15,810	16,084	16,616	17,857	20,635	20,223
School improvement programs	2,394	5,184	4,138	4,060	4,616	4,591	4,622	5,043	5,493	6,427	5,449
Special education	4,696	17,075	12,832	12,753	12,978	12,741	12,533	5,387	15,114	13,854	13,909
Social Services block grant	1,827	2,035	1,832	1,587	1,646	1,727	1,655	1,492	1,599	1,600	1,602
Children and family services programs	5,843	10,473	9,608	10,651	11,240	11,892	13,021	13,687	14,637	15,399	14,538
Training and employment services	2,957	4,592	2,639	2,724	2,684	2,782	2,882	3,003	3,100	3,437	3,491
Health	124,843	290,168	368,026	421,117	442,324	493,400	571,967	647,869	663,717	615,131	637,819
Substance abuse and mental health services [5]	1,931	2,846	2,671	3,258	3,679	4,322	4,892	6,277	7,144	7,942	8,379
Grants to states for Medicaid [5]	117,921	272,771	349,762	389,157	409,421	458,468	520,588	591,949	615,772	567,151	588,913
State children's health insurance fund [5]	1,220	7,887	9,233	17,282	17,689	16,880	16,093	16,670	17,588	17,244	18,136
Income security	68,653	115,156	101,082	110,649	112,566	118,222	177,820	179,251	166,922	167,175	168,719
Supplemental Nutrition Assistance Program (SNAP) (formerly Food Stamp Program) [5]	3,508	5,739	5,100	7,485	7,100	8,006	12,268	10,717	10,848	10,848	10,886
Child nutrition programs [5]	9,060	16,259	20,999	22,803	23,247	22,709	25,744	37,104	29,126	37,492	32,151
Temporary Assistance for Needy Families (TANF) [5]	15,464	17,513	15,940	16,414	15,493	16,551	15,380	15,286	16,459	16,022	16,144
Veterans benefits and services [5]	434	836	1,821	2,061	2,050	2,979	2,896	2,480	2,418	2,651	2,629
Administration of justice	5,263	5,086	3,664	4,195	5,161	9,368	5,467	5,772	6,209	8,555	8,847

– Represents zero. [1] Includes outlays for other functions, agencies, or programs not shown separately. [2] Grants include trust funds. [3] Trust funds. [4] Formerly Accelerating Achievement and Ensuring Equity. [5] Includes grants that are also payments to individuals.

Source: U.S. Office of Management and Budget, *Budget of the U.S. Government, Fiscal Year 2025: Historical Tables*, March 2024. See also <www.whitehouse.gov/omb/budget>.

Table 483. State and Local Governments—Summary of Finances: 2000 to 2021

[In millions of dollars (1,942,328 represents $1,942,328,000,000). For fiscal year ending in year shown; see text, this section. Local government amounts are estimates subject to sampling variation; see Appendix III and source]

Item	2000	2010	2015	2019	2020	2021
Revenue [1]	**1,942,328**	**3,180,023**	**3,416,065**	**4,073,109**	**4,279,544**	**5,731,180**
From federal government	**291,950**	**623,801**	**658,012**	**762,035**	**911,026**	**1,120,201**
From state and local sources	**1,650,379**	**2,556,222**	**2,758,053**	**3,311,075**	**3,368,517**	**4,610,979**
General, net intergovernmental	1,249,373	1,887,045	2,262,308	2,702,376	2,715,831	2,956,199
Taxes	872,351	1,278,847	1,563,701	1,864,241	1,865,325	2,103,241
Property	249,178	443,947	484,251	576,888	601,106	630,208
Sales and gross receipts	309,290	435,571	544,359	644,354	652,466	689,885
Individual income	211,661	261,510	368,862	446,770	424,764	545,142
Corporation net income	36,059	44,108	57,130	67,841	60,791	98,713
Other	66,164	93,710	109,100	128,387	126,198	139,293
Charges and miscellaneous	377,022	608,198	698,607	838,135	850,505	852,958
Utility and liquor stores	89,546	154,758	175,655	193,122	192,883	189,700
Water supply system	30,515	49,327	61,157	73,953	76,354	80,244
Electric power system	42,436	76,492	81,250	84,387	82,119	81,996
Gas supply system	3,954	8,219	7,478	6,922	6,622	6,438
Transit system	8,049	13,003	16,359	17,224	16,464	8,239
Liquor stores	4,592	7,716	9,412	10,637	11,324	12,783
Insurance trust revenue [2]	311,460	514,420	320,090	415,576	459,804	1,465,079
Unemployment compensation	23,366	75,191	49,303	37,202	44,249	87,328
Employee retirement	273,881	416,536	247,486	355,073	390,694	1,353,031
Direct expenditure	**1,742,914**	**3,110,833**	**3,402,229**	**3,986,041**	**4,246,313**	**4,505,661**
By character and object:						
Current operation	1,288,746	2,228,794	2,561,396	3,004,037	3,144,004	3,311,835
Capital outlay	217,063	355,437	336,088	414,033	431,821	433,041
Construction	161,694	284,213	271,190	334,187	349,603	346,179
Equipment, land, and existing structures	55,369	71,224	64,898	79,845	82,218	86,862
Assistance and subsidies	31,375	47,636	57,332	66,483	71,762	76,137
Interest on debt (general and utility)	80,499	119,939	122,305	129,175	130,169	128,086
Insurance benefits and repayments	125,230	359,027	325,109	372,314	468,557	556,562
Expenditure for salaries and wages [3]	548,796	844,650	900,861	1,034,940	1,075,840	1,077,865
By function:						
Direct general expenditure [2]	1,502,768	2,537,892	2,841,079	3,356,637	3,508,285	3,681,234
Education [2]	521,612	860,118	934,353	1,093,843	1,132,137	1,143,137
Higher education	134,352	243,515	273,935	311,498	320,912	311,441
Elementary and secondary	365,181	573,641	609,926	717,415	740,590	755,960
Public welfare	233,350	456,200	613,502	745,661	791,360	862,255
Hospitals	75,976	145,902	170,198	211,872	224,712	236,873
Health	51,366	81,383	91,810	112,838	122,778	140,278
Highways	101,336	155,912	171,084	202,752	205,697	206,436
Police protection	56,798	95,772	104,807	123,057	129,068	134,976
Fire protection	23,102	41,335	45,967	55,631	58,122	61,231
Natural resources	20,235	28,433	28,560	35,722	35,783	36,633
Parks and recreation	25,038	40,247	39,678	48,820	51,308	47,554
Housing and community development	26,590	53,923	49,754	57,808	59,790	65,006
Sanitation and sewerage	45,261	75,620	75,830	90,517	94,103	97,766
Financial administration	29,300	40,241	43,117	50,812	51,928	54,785
Interest on general debt [4]	69,814	105,715	105,613	112,949	113,566	112,695
Utility and liquor stores [4]	114,916	213,914	236,041	257,091	269,472	267,866
Water supply system	35,789	60,655	66,905	78,074	81,108	82,730
Electric power system	39,719	78,478	79,045	80,554	79,635	77,860
Gas supply system	3,724	8,273	7,457	7,829	6,577	6,260
Transit system	31,883	60,149	74,947	81,822	92,845	90,511
Liquor stores	3,801	6,359	7,687	8,811	9,307	10,505
Insurance trust expenditure [2]	125,230	359,027	325,109	372,314	468,557	556,562
Unemployment compensation	18,648	135,367	33,352	27,080	110,620	176,945
Employee retirement	95,679	204,803	275,406	330,848	341,601	362,939
Debt outstanding, year end	**1,451,815**	**2,844,190**	**2,988,463**	**3,198,762**	**3,282,014**	**3,336,669**
Short-term	24,291	45,088	34,621	34,955	40,082	44,537
Long-term	1,427,524	2,799,101	2,953,842	3,163,807	3,241,932	3,292,132
Long-term debt:						
Issued	184,831	398,962	362,594	348,739	441,211	461,309
Retired	121,897	275,810	370,232	291,319	441,160	478,029

[1] Aggregates exclude duplicative transactions between state and local governments; see source. [2] Includes amounts for other items not shown separately. [3] Included in items above. [4] Interest on utility debt included in "utility and liquor stores expenditure." For total interest on debt, see "Interest on debt (general and utility)."

Source: U.S. Census Bureau, Annual Survey of State and Local Government Finances, "Datasets & Tables," <www.census.gov/programs-surveys/gov-finances.html>, accessed August 2023.

Table 484. State and Local Governments—Revenue and Expenditures by Function: 2020 and 2021

[In millions of dollars (4,279,544 represents $4,279,544,000,000). For fiscal year ending in year shown; see text, this section. Local government amounts are estimates subject to sampling variation; see Appendix III and source]

Item	2020			2021		
	Total	State	Local	Total	State	Local
Revenue [1]................	**4,279,544**	**2,725,498**	**2,155,224**	**5,731,180**	**3,975,040**	**2,395,165**
Intergovernmental revenue [1]........	911,026	845,817	666,388	1,120,201	1,006,125	753,102
Total revenue from own sources [1]..........	3,368,517	1,879,681	1,488,836	4,610,979	2,968,916	1,642,063
General revenue from own sources..........	2,715,831	1,461,813	1,254,018	2,956,199	1,684,127	1,272,072
Taxes [2]................	1,865,325	1,059,680	805,645	2,103,241	1,262,528	840,713
Property................	601,106	18,943	582,164	630,208	20,336	609,872
Sales and gross receipts.............	652,466	513,113	139,353	689,885	549,071	140,814
General sales................	443,535	340,816	102,719	477,145	369,706	107,439
Selective sales [2]................	208,931	172,297	36,634	212,739	179,365	33,374
Motor fuel................	52,765	51,123	1,642	53,051	51,453	1,598
Alcoholic beverages.............	7,540	6,829	712	8,248	7,551	697
Tobacco products.............	18,854	18,534	320	19,482	19,120	362
Public utilities.............	27,557	12,204	15,353	27,359	12,011	15,348
Individual income.............	424,764	385,610	39,154	545,142	503,621	41,521
Corporation income.............	60,791	52,345	8,446	98,713	89,316	9,398
Motor vehicle and operators' licenses....	29,578	27,511	2,068	32,463	30,342	2,120
Charges and miscellaneous [2]...........	850,505	402,133	448,373	852,958	421,598	431,360
Current charges [2].............	578,433	242,261	336,172	569,596	243,545	326,051
Education [2].............	135,427	113,971	21,457	123,975	108,122	15,853
Higher education.............	121,592	113,007	8,585	115,204	107,236	7,968
School lunch sales.............	4,253	25	4,228	1,087	8	1,080
Hospitals.............	186,834	81,180	105,654	198,290	88,787	109,503
Highways.............	21,855	12,424	9,430	19,834	11,748	8,086
Airports.............	26,304	1,743	24,561	19,583	1,304	18,280
Sea and inland port facilities.............	6,528	2,075	4,453	6,843	2,339	4,504
Natural resources.............	5,952	3,551	2,401	5,422	3,118	2,305
Parks and recreation.............	11,318	1,656	9,662	9,317	1,521	7,796
Housing and community development....	7,974	968	7,006	8,140	1,122	7,018
Sewerage.............	66,572	1,105	65,467	67,346	1,126	66,220
Solid waste management.............	20,495	240	20,255	21,026	253	20,772
Interest earnings.............	72,714	39,595	33,119	56,697	36,241	20,456
Special assessments.............	11,693	15	11,678	12,341	20	12,320
Sale of property.............	5,482	2,313	3,169	5,126	1,432	3,694
Utility and liquor store revenue.............	192,883	23,118	169,764	189,700	21,830	167,870
Insurance trust revenue.............	459,804	394,750	65,054	1,465,079	1,262,959	202,120
Expenditures [1]................	**4,249,403**	**2,714,083**	**2,157,144**	**4,509,102**	**2,965,009**	**2,219,366**
By character and object:						
Current operation.............	3,144,004	1,447,535	1,696,469	3,311,835	1,557,931	1,753,904
Capital outlay.............	431,821	148,523	283,298	433,041	147,334	285,707
Construction.............	349,603	126,315	223,288	346,179	124,265	221,914
Equipment, land, and existing structures.............	82,218	22,208	60,010	86,862	23,069	63,793
Assistance and subsidies.............	71,762	59,579	12,183	76,137	63,660	12,477
Interest on debt (general and utility).............	130,169	46,629	83,540	128,086	45,226	82,860
Insurance benefits and repayments.............	468,557	404,165	64,391	556,562	489,003	67,559
Expenditure for salaries and wages [3].............	1,075,840	310,990	764,849	1,077,865	310,431	767,434
Intergovernmental expenditure [1].............	3,090	607,652	17,262	3,441	661,855	16,859
Direct expenditure [1].............	4,246,313	2,106,431	2,139,882	4,505,661	2,303,154	2,202,507
General expenditure [2].............	3,508,285	1,660,621	1,847,664	3,681,234	1,768,002	1,913,231
Education [1].............	1,132,137	352,786	779,351	1,143,137	346,228	796,910
Higher education.............	320,912	274,778	46,134	311,441	264,858	46,583
Elementary and secondary education.............	740,590	7,373	733,217	755,960	5,633	750,327
Libraries.............	13,335	441	12,894	13,584	441	13,143
Public welfare.............	791,360	728,286	63,074	862,255	795,862	66,393
Hospitals.............	224,712	101,361	123,351	236,873	106,335	130,537
Health.............	122,778	57,435	65,343	140,278	71,201	69,077
Highways.............	205,697	121,927	83,770	206,436	121,835	84,601
Police protection.............	129,068	17,063	112,005	134,976	18,136	116,840
Fire protection.............	58,122	–	58,122	61,231	–	61,231
Corrections.............	86,037	54,635	31,402	86,906	55,281	31,625
Natural resources.............	35,783	24,426	11,357	36,633	24,540	12,093
Parks and recreation.............	51,308	6,387	44,921	47,554	6,171	41,383
Housing and community development.............	59,790	9,512	50,278	65,006	12,417	52,589
Sewerage.............	64,598	1,412	63,186	67,987	1,477	66,510
Solid waste management.............	29,505	1,688	27,817	29,779	1,220	28,559
Governmental administration.............	159,717	67,698	92,019	168,594	71,230	97,364
Interest on general debt.............	113,566	44,037	69,528	112,695	42,563	70,133
Utility.............	260,164	33,719	226,445	257,360	37,180	220,180
Liquor store expenditure.............	9,307	7,925	1,382	10,505	8,969	1,537
Insurance trust expenditure.............	468,557	404,165	64,391	556,562	489,003	67,559

– Represents or rounds to zero. [1] Aggregates exclude duplicative transactions between levels of government; see source. [2] Includes data for other items not shown separately. [3] Included in items shown above.

Source: U.S. Census Bureau, Annual Survey of State and Local Government Finances, "Datasets & Tables," <www.census.gov/programs-surveys/gov-finances.html>, accessed August 2023.

Table 485. State and Local Governments—Capital Outlays: 2000 to 2021

[In millions of dollars (217,063 represents $217,063,000,000), except percent. For fiscal year ending in year shown; see text, this section. Local government amounts are subject to sampling variation; see Appendix III and source]

Level and function	2000	2010	2015	2016	2017	2018	2019	2020	2021
State & local governments, total	**217,063**	**355,437**	**336,088**	**352,195**	**365,558**	**390,989**	**414,033**	**431,821**	**433,041**
Percent of direct expenditure	12.5	11.4	9.9	10.0	10.0	10.2	10.4	10.2	9.6
By function:[1]									
Education[2]	60,968	93,562	84,148	92,857	98,468	103,963	111,334	119,247	115,679
Elementary and secondary	45,150	60,240	52,892	58,371	63,817	69,594	76,737	84,415	82,897
Higher education	15,257	31,644	30,641	34,024	34,228	33,795	34,016	34,025	32,139
Hospitals[3]	5,502	8,553	8,782	9,074	9,157	9,003	8,992	9,282	9,918
Highways	56,439	89,895	93,810	99,262	101,740	112,088	117,141	116,302	116,386
Natural resources	4,347	5,214	4,697	6,120	5,450	5,278	7,352	6,299	6,610
Parks and recreation	6,916	10,711	8,342	9,261	10,624	10,375	11,563	13,100	12,005
Sewerage	10,093	21,915	17,847	20,042	19,747	22,539	21,892	21,090	22,927
Utilities	24,847	49,258	54,829	50,708	53,479	55,634	57,254	65,997	64,299
State governments, total	**76,233**	**118,011**	**128,925**	**130,229**	**132,026**	**141,986**	**149,379**	**148,523**	**147,334**
Percent of direct expenditure	10.1	8.1	7.9	7.6	7.5	7.7	7.7	7.1	6.4
By function:[1]									
Education[2]	14,077	28,643	28,126	30,915	30,791	30,834	30,726	30,568	27,678
Elementary and secondary	521	1,066	757	923	806	847	819	714	707
Higher education	12,995	25,899	26,753	29,530	29,563	29,413	29,326	29,047	26,328
Hospitals[3]	2,228	2,654	3,562	3,717	3,510	3,761	3,787	4,036	3,693
Highways	41,651	64,755	68,979	72,518	74,641	81,385	87,464	83,753	82,690
Natural resources	2,758	2,337	2,565	3,652	2,696	2,531	3,499	2,949	2,796
Parks and recreation	1,044	910	851	837	931	843	755	1,168	1,195
Sewerage	403	488	60	95	147	133	155	126	143
Utilities	4,232	5,318	12,747	7,211	8,129	10,026	8,625	11,928	14,634
Local governments, total	**140,830**	**237,426**	**207,163**	**221,967**	**233,532**	**249,002**	**264,654**	**283,298**	**285,707**
Percent of direct expenditure	14.3	14.4	11.7	12.2	12.3	12.6	12.9	13.2	13.0
By function:[1]									
Education[2]	46,890	64,919	56,022	61,942	67,677	73,129	80,608	88,679	88,002
Elementary and secondary	44,629	59,174	52,134	57,448	63,011	68,747	75,918	83,701	82,191
Higher education	2,261	5,745	3,888	4,494	4,665	4,382	4,690	4,978	5,811
Hospitals[3]	3,274	5,899	5,219	5,357	5,647	5,242	5,205	5,246	6,225
Highways	14,789	25,140	24,832	26,744	27,100	30,703	29,677	32,549	33,696
Natural resources	1,589	2,878	2,131	2,468	2,754	2,747	3,853	3,350	3,814
Parks and recreation	5,872	9,802	7,490	8,424	9,693	9,532	10,808	11,932	10,810
Sewerage	9,690	21,426	17,788	19,946	19,600	22,405	21,736	20,964	22,784
Utilities	20,615	43,940	42,083	43,496	45,349	45,608	48,629	54,069	49,665

[1] Includes other functions not shown separately. [2] Includes other education, not shown separately. [3] For 2000 only, data include outlays for both health and hospitals.

Source: U.S. Census Bureau, Annual Survey of State and Local Government Finances, "Datasets & Tables," <www.census.gov/programs-surveys/gov-finances.html>, accessed August 2023.

Table 486. State and Local Governments—Expenditures for Public Works: 2000 to 2021

[In millions of dollars (230,569 represents $230,569,000,000), except percent. Represents direct expenditures excluding intergovernmental grants]

Item	Total	Highways	Air trans-portation	Sea and inland port facilities	Sewerage	Solid waste manage-ment	Water supply	Mass transit
2000, total	230,569	101,336	13,160	3,141	28,052	17,208	35,789	31,883
State	74,974	61,942	1,106	863	955	2,347	354	7,407
Local	155,595	39,394	12,054	2,277	27,098	14,861	35,435	24,476
Capital expenditures (percent)	41.9	55.7	51.0	51.5	36.0	8.9	29.5	30.5
2010, total	381,808	155,912	24,209	5,263	51,991	23,629	60,655	60,149
State	111,280	93,127	1,724	1,245	1,118	2,281	378	11,407
Local	270,529	62,786	22,485	4,019	50,873	21,348	60,277	48,742
Capital expenditures (percent)	(NA)	57.7	(NA)	(NA)	42.2	8.9	(NA)	(NA)
2018, total	470,713	194,538	28,624	6,314	60,643	25,997	73,963	80,635
State	144,854	116,681	2,534	2,359	1,245	1,140	438	20,456
Local	325,859	77,856	26,090	3,956	59,397	24,857	73,525	60,179
Capital expenditures (percent)	(NA)	57.6	(NA)	(NA)	37.2	8.9	(NA)	(NA)
2019, total	491,792	202,752	31,616	7,011	62,800	27,717	78,074	81,822
State	152,438	124,267	2,802	2,617	1,317	1,194	483	19,759
Local	339,354	78,485	28,814	4,394	61,483	26,524	77,591	62,063
Capital expenditures (percent)	(NA)	57.8	(NA)	(NA)	34.9	8.3	(NA)	(NA)
2020, total	514,894	205,697	34,258	6,883	64,598	29,505	81,108	92,845
State	154,148	121,927	2,828	2,589	1,412	1,688	522	23,183
Local	360,746	83,770	31,430	4,295	63,186	27,817	80,586	69,662
Capital expenditures (percent)	(NA)	56.5	(NA)	(NA)	32.6	7.6	(NA)	(NA)
2021, total	517,585	206,436	33,356	6,786	67,987	29,779	82,730	90,511
State	157,664	121,835	2,785	2,630	1,477	1,220	533	27,185
Local	359,921	84,601	30,572	4,156	66,510	28,559	82,197	63,326
Capital expenditures (percent)	(NA)	56.4	(NA)	(NA)	33.7	8.0	(NA)	(NA)

NA Not available.

Source: U.S. Census Bureau, Annual Survey of State and Local Government Finances, "Datasets & Tables," <www.census.gov/programs-surveys/gov-finances.html>, accessed August 2023, and unpublished data.

Table 487. State and Local Governments—Indebtedness: 2000 to 2021

[In billions of dollars (1,451.8 represents $1,451,800,000,000). For fiscal year ending in year shown; see text, this section. Local government amounts are estimates subject to sampling variation; see Appendix III and source]

Level and year	Debt outstanding						Long-term	
		Cash and security holdings	Short-term	Long-term			Debt issued	Debt retired
	Total			Total	Public debt for private purposes	All other		
STATE AND LOCAL TOTAL								
2000	1,451.8	3,503.7	24.3	1,427.5	372.6	1,054.9	184.8	121.9
2005	2,085.0	4,439.2	30.8	2,054.3	483.3	1,571.0	323.7	224.6
2010	2,844.2	4,826.0	45.1	2,799.1	625.9	2,173.2	399.0	275.8
2013	2,970.0	5,640.4	31.9	2,938.0	600.5	2,337.6	369.5	355.7
2014	2,980.0	6,095.2	33.7	2,946.3	578.9	2,367.4	303.9	305.8
2015	2,988.5	6,277.8	34.6	2,953.8	566.1	2,387.8	362.6	370.2
2016	3,022.5	6,326.4	34.4	2,988.1	555.2	2,432.9	383.4	370.6
2017	3,065.1	6,931.4	34.9	3,030.2	553.6	2,476.7	409.7	396.7
2018	3,136.5	7,342.6	33.1	3,103.5	551.8	2,551.7	394.6	347.2
2019	3,198.8	7,628.4	35.0	3,163.8	554.1	2,609.7	348.7	291.3
2020	3,282.0	7,864.6	40.1	3,241.9	567.1	2,674.8	441.2	441.2
2021	3,336.7	9,273.0	44.5	3,292.1	568.5	2,723.6	461.3	478.0
STATE GOVERNMENTS								
2000	547.9	2,518.9	6.4	541.5	227.3	314.2	75.0	44.4
2005	810.9	3,153.8	5.6	805.3	297.4	507.9	131.6	93.6
2010	1,115.5	3,323.0	14.7	1,100.8	397.1	703.6	183.7	125.1
2013	1,138.6	3,952.1	5.7	1,133.0	366.2	766.7	148.5	147.0
2014	1,152.3	4,330.8	8.7	1,143.6	355.6	788.0	130.1	123.7
2015	1,155.1	4,415.6	8.6	1,146.5	354.4	792.1	143.3	144.0
2016	1,170.6	4,416.3	9.0	1,161.6	353.9	807.7	142.4	132.1
2017	1,154.2	4,877.9	7.2	1,147.0	348.9	798.1	153.7	159.5
2018	1,170.6	5,173.9	7.5	1,163.0	350.0	813.0	148.8	135.2
2019	1,167.4	5,367.4	8.5	1,158.9	352.4	806.5	119.5	106.0
2020	1,185.0	5,498.9	11.4	1,173.6	359.6	814.0	159.9	212.5
2021	1,208.2	6,585.5	15.4	1,192.8	359.2	833.6	152.1	209.2
LOCAL GOVERNMENTS								
2000	903.9	984.8	17.9	886.0	145.3	740.7	109.8	77.5
2005	1,274.2	1,285.4	25.2	1,249.0	185.9	1,063.0	192.2	131.1
2010	1,728.7	1,503.0	30.4	1,698.3	228.8	1,469.6	215.2	150.7
2013	1,831.3	1,688.4	26.3	1,805.1	234.2	1,570.8	221.0	208.8
2014	1,827.7	1,764.5	25.0	1,802.7	223.3	1,579.4	173.8	182.1
2015	1,833.3	1,862.3	26.1	1,807.3	211.7	1,595.6	219.3	226.2
2016	1,851.9	1,910.0	25.4	1,826.5	201.4	1,625.1	241.1	238.5
2017	1,910.9	2,053.5	27.7	1,883.2	204.7	1,678.5	256.0	237.2
2018	1,966.0	2,168.7	25.5	1,940.4	201.8	1,738.7	245.8	212.0
2019	2,031.4	2,261.0	26.5	2,004.9	201.7	1,803.2	229.2	185.3
2020	2,097.0	2,365.7	28.7	2,068.3	207.5	1,860.8	281.3	228.7
2021	2,128.5	2,687.5	29.2	2,099.3	209.3	1,890.0	309.2	268.8

Source: U.S. Census Bureau, Annual Survey of State and Local Government Finances, "Datasets & Tables," <www.census.gov/programs-surveys/gov-finances.html>, accessed August 2023.

Table 488. New Security Issues—State and Local Governments: 2010 to 2023

[In billions of dollars (460.8 represents $460,800,000,000)]

Type of issue, issuer, or use	2010	2015	2016	2017	2018	2019	2020	2021	2022	2023
All issues, new and refunding [1]	460.8	399.6	431.0	425.6	351.2	434.1	475.0	472.3	378.1	370.5
By type of issue:										
General obligation	137.5	161.1	161.4	152.4	107.6	137.7	168.7	153.0	124.4	131.3
Revenue	323.2	238.7	269.9	273.3	243.6	296.3	306.4	319.3	253.7	239.2
By type of issuer:										
State	55.2	(NA)	(NA)	(NA)	(NA)	(NA)	(NA)	(NA)	(NA)	(NA)
Special district or statutory authority [2]	294.9	(NA)	(NA)	(NA)	(NA)	(NA)	(NA)	(NA)	(NA)	(NA)
Municipality, county, or township	86.6	(NA)	(NA)	(NA)	(NA)	(NA)	(NA)	(NA)	(NA)	(NA)
Issues for new capital	278.5	169.5	168.4	197.5	230.9	233.9	220.1	236.4	261.7	248.7
By use of proceeds:										
Education	60.4	46.5	50.4	57.6	59.1	63.9	57.2	51.7	65.6	67.4
Transportation	32.3	13.9	19.6	20.2	25.7	30.2	29.5	24.6	27.9	21.3
Utilities and conservation	22.3	8.5	3.9	7.4	10.9	15.2	15.7	17.5	14.8	10.0
Industrial aid	35.7	14.7	14.1	17.7	32.6	27.2	21.0	27.2	31.6	39.5
Other purposes	92.4	56.0	56.7	60.5	64.0	55.6	60.9	58.2	82.5	67.0

NA Not available. [1] Par amounts of long-term issues based on date of sale. [2] Includes school districts.

Source: Board of Governors of the Federal Reserve System, Business Finance, "New Security Issues, State and Local Governments," <www.federalreserve.gov/data.htm>, accessed June 2024.

Table 489. State and Local Governments—Total Revenue and Expenditures by State: 2000 to 2021

[In millions of dollars (1,942,328 represents $1,942,328,000,000). For fiscal year ending in year shown; see text, this section. These data cannot be used to compute the deficit or surplus for any single government, as these are estimates for all state and local governments within a state area. For further information, see the *2006 Government Finance and Employment Classification Manual* at <www.census.gov/programs-surveys/gov-finances/technical-documentation/classification-manuals.html>]

State	Revenue				Expenditures			
	2000	2010	2020	2021	2000	2010	2020	2021
United States.........	**1,942,328**	**3,180,023**	**4,279,544**	**5,731,180**	**1,746,943**	**3,115,172**	**4,249,403**	**4,509,102**
Alabama.................	25,726	42,189	55,771	63,621	25,319	42,255	52,770	56,074
Alaska..................	10,525	15,643	14,156	19,274	8,628	14,450	15,166	16,401
Arizona.................	27,778	54,099	73,784	96,255	27,293	53,432	71,817	76,451
Arkansas...............	13,833	24,539	34,398	49,214	12,245	22,798	28,988	31,756
California...............	270,380	453,354	654,299	987,628	236,645	432,363	681,527	743,235
Colorado................	29,603	49,260	79,522	93,706	26,173	48,630	74,096	79,255
Connecticut............	25,828	39,427	51,974	73,407	24,011	39,311	45,068	47,031
Delaware...............	6,224	9,831	14,783	20,240	5,153	9,745	13,281	14,479
District of Columbia....	6,383	11,644	17,429	19,596	6,527	13,682	23,500	22,552
Florida..................	92,402	166,817	208,585	273,982	84,301	163,536	208,608	225,472
Georgia.................	49,310	76,370	102,764	152,072	43,517	78,158	100,522	107,827
Hawaii..................	8,488	14,666	21,260	29,960	8,254	14,340	19,820	21,881
Idaho...................	7,590	12,490	18,075	24,693	6,404	12,054	16,677	17,360
Illinois.................	80,695	126,384	164,345	208,379	74,727	129,518	165,716	177,745
Indiana.................	32,716	54,803	75,111	89,521	31,250	53,247	70,176	73,796
Iowa....................	17,220	31,055	42,963	59,010	17,275	29,537	40,421	42,527
Kansas.................	16,235	26,330	34,317	42,544	14,419	26,536	33,700	36,049
Kentucky...............	25,200	37,560	50,000	64,140	21,473	38,595	51,034	54,704
Louisiana..............	27,109	47,078	53,145	71,741	25,018	48,755	53,609	56,821
Maine..................	8,554	12,557	17,159	21,672	7,652	12,286	15,225	15,949
Maryland...............	33,949	57,493	78,097	101,680	30,598	57,485	81,190	84,783
Massachusetts.........	46,103	76,100	105,554	133,275	44,362	76,679	108,514	116,830
Michigan...............	70,112	93,819	113,133	141,150	61,506	90,935	116,112	118,130
Minnesota..............	38,785	57,410	79,154	121,302	35,424	55,975	78,050	81,882
Mississippi.............	16,672	28,690	32,962	43,545	15,379	27,216	32,421	33,350
Missouri................	31,635	51,592	62,374	86,905	27,953	50,040	62,116	65,403
Montana................	5,643	9,784	12,049	17,364	4,983	9,296	12,088	12,802
Nebraska...............	11,650	20,121	27,101	33,053	10,831	19,315	25,303	27,364
Nevada.................	11,885	22,838	34,046	47,164	11,230	23,856	33,429	33,961
New Hampshire........	6,948	11,581	15,123	18,242	6,222	11,439	14,193	15,055
New Jersey.............	62,331	99,751	120,583	151,618	54,590	102,667	124,406	129,859
New Mexico............	13,073	21,998	28,544	41,041	11,195	22,372	27,687	31,040
New York...............	188,907	313,781	377,520	549,846	171,858	295,467	392,835	407,505
North Carolina.........	50,542	86,699	110,664	146,292	46,135	79,955	108,008	113,125
North Dakota...........	4,495	7,890	13,268	15,013	4,041	6,746	10,968	12,049
Ohio....................	80,074	123,289	155,296	186,963	68,418	113,844	146,111	147,217
Oklahoma..............	18,760	32,939	41,254	53,185	15,962	31,338	38,203	40,991
Oregon.................	28,644	41,031	61,409	88,362	24,086	39,506	65,720	70,030
Pennsylvania...........	80,546	124,379	168,910	209,709	75,624	130,085	174,298	176,925
Rhode Island...........	7,427	11,726	14,587	25,711	6,432	11,303	14,466	15,896
South Carolina.........	23,467	42,509	55,855	68,842	23,436	42,800	56,781	58,442
South Dakota..........	4,277	6,941	9,811	15,365	3,760	6,845	8,864	10,096
Tennessee.............	33,625	54,297	67,581	89,215	32,010	53,554	67,647	69,914
Texas..................	120,666	209,930	332,310	408,425	109,634	218,807	312,364	341,825
Utah...................	14,954	24,149	40,001	47,013	13,044	24,552	38,067	40,643
Vermont................	4,019	7,016	9,773	21,850	3,766	6,781	8,874	11,513
Virginia................	44,175	71,093	100,485	135,481	38,092	67,673	98,135	104,654
Washington............	46,372	71,623	110,693	148,243	41,794	75,167	112,427	116,635
West Virginia...........	10,760	16,993	20,122	26,945	9,990	15,685	20,196	20,919
Wisconsin..............	43,003	66,291	84,936	85,839	34,559	55,839	67,769	71,512
Wyoming...............	7,030	10,176	12,504	11,886	3,743	8,720	10,440	11,387

Source: U.S. Census Bureau, Annual Survey of State and Local Government Finances, "Datasets & Tables," <www.census.gov/programs-surveys/gov-finances.html>, accessed August 2023.

Table 490. State and Local Governments—Revenue by State: 2021

[In millions of dollars (5,731,180 represents $5,731,180,000,000). For fiscal year ending in year shown; see text, this section]

State	Total revenue	General revenue — Total	Intergovernmental from federal government	General revenue from own sources	Select taxes — Total [1]	Property	Sales and gross receipt	Individual income	Corporation income	Current charges and miscellaneous revenue — Total [1]	Current charges — Total [1]	Education	Hospitals	Sewerage	Miscellaneous revenue — Total [1]	Interest earnings	Special assessments	Utility and liquor stores	Insurance trust revenue
U.S.	5,731,180	4,076,400	1,120,201	2,956,199	2,103,241	630,208	689,885	545,142	98,713	852,958	569,596	123,975	198,290	67,346	283,362	56,697	12,341	189,700	1,465,079
AL	63,621	54,523	16,999	37,524	21,397	3,329	10,494	5,037	1,134	16,127	13,051	2,994	8,054	654	3,076	717	36	3,830	5,268
AK	19,274	13,831	5,593	8,238	3,075	1,707	668	—	125	5,163	1,573	168	520	120	3,589	1,030	7	415	5,028
AZ	96,255	72,870	27,433	45,437	33,710	9,106	15,782	6,533	914	11,727	7,174	3,097	688	1,038	4,553	1,032	63	5,655	17,731
AR	49,214	31,836	11,187	20,649	14,707	2,524	7,470	3,467	618	5,942	4,188	1,364	1,517	364	1,754	361	5	1,012	16,366
CA	987,628	630,739	143,666	487,073	360,783	82,076	84,226	146,325	26,097	126,290	93,790	11,796	34,023	10,049	32,500	5,013	3,050	35,219	321,670
CO	93,706	69,275	16,367	52,908	37,215	12,035	12,337	10,247	1,278	15,693	10,832	3,109	3,003	1,271	4,862	1,306	388	3,407	21,024
CT	73,407	52,679	12,902	39,776	34,147	11,871	8,148	10,259	2,607	5,630	3,528	1,281	548	506	2,102	704	20	817	19,912
DE	20,240	15,022	5,328	9,694	6,749	1,111	606	2,148	342	2,945	1,487	611	4	203	1,459	183	36	456	4,762
DC	19,596	16,851	6,311	10,541	8,894	3,008	1,591	2,643	863	1,647	801	34	111	406	846	20	5	391	2,354
FL	273,982	204,951	51,844	153,107	95,628	35,443	46,625	—	3,407	57,479	34,438	3,830	9,890	4,033	23,041	2,694	3,845	10,134	58,897
GA	152,072	99,568	29,074	70,494	49,384	15,082	16,830	14,221	1,751	21,110	15,708	2,878	6,069	2,430	5,402	743	105	4,593	47,911
HI	29,960	21,848	6,159	15,689	11,225	2,321	4,688	3,355	191	4,465	2,233	333	499	529	2,232	340	19	413	7,699
ID	24,693	17,889	5,376	12,513	8,726	2,109	3,255	2,458	351	3,786	2,865	523	815	313	921	183	75	502	6,303
IL	208,379	153,149	36,547	116,602	93,250	31,252	29,205	21,871	5,730	23,352	13,774	3,675	2,271	1,521	9,578	1,989	846	5,320	49,910
IN	89,521	76,988	22,989	53,998	36,528	8,242	14,032	11,784	1,385	17,470	12,988	3,648	5,921	2,043	4,482	1,326	10	2,787	9,746
IA	59,010	39,122	9,167	29,955	18,955	6,193	6,269	4,371	794	11,000	8,535	1,846	4,791	728	2,465	344	20	1,721	18,167
KS	42,544	34,164	7,127	27,037	17,463	5,260	6,195	4,618	727	9,574	7,308	1,420	4,237	543	2,266	365	109	1,686	6,694
KY	64,140	49,828	19,280	30,548	21,066	4,364	7,847	6,887	1,152	9,482	7,431	1,650	3,758	786	2,050	311	35	1,834	12,478
LA	71,741	54,086	21,391	32,696	22,373	4,591	12,266	3,933	588	10,323	6,837	1,824	2,497	561	3,485	513	47	1,188	16,467
ME	21,672	16,658	5,056	11,602	9,353	3,904	2,637	2,075	284	2,250	1,544	321	109	225	706	170	10	395	4,619
MD	101,680	77,615	21,589	56,026	44,717	11,203	11,429	17,229	1,841	11,309	7,441	2,267	192	1,524	3,869	631	121	1,493	22,572
MA	133,275	101,959	30,010	71,949	56,664	19,569	10,714	19,683	3,673	15,285	8,818	2,651	476	1,818	6,467	1,238	11	3,503	27,812
MI	141,150	108,377	32,352	76,025	49,992	16,681	16,166	12,648	1,496	26,033	18,808	5,630	6,144	2,409	7,225	1,478	230	4,933	27,840
MN	121,302	74,288	17,664	56,625	42,590	10,679	11,809	15,171	2,423	14,035	8,784	2,141	2,286	1,310	5,251	967	362	3,103	43,911
MS	43,545	32,069	11,282	20,787	13,100	3,557	5,774	2,516	550	7,687	6,268	1,401	3,803	312	1,419	210	9	1,402	10,074
MO	86,905	58,689	16,248	42,440	28,613	8,227	10,074	8,203	777	13,828	8,433	2,250	3,366	1,260	5,395	1,410	95	2,448	25,767
MT	17,364	13,117	5,524	7,593	5,645	2,036	792	1,889	268	1,948	1,214	472	84	142	734	210	99	336	3,911
NE	33,053	23,402	5,999	17,403	12,475	4,264	3,623	3,131	571	4,928	3,156	979	588	386	1,772	325	92	4,268	5,382
NV	47,164	29,781	7,749	22,032	16,064	3,823	10,135	—	—	5,968	4,058	537	941	611	1,910	504	99	1,506	15,877
NH	18,242	13,763	3,822	9,941	7,504	4,589	985	149	1,010	2,436	1,369	529	7	186	1,068	373	3	921	3,558
NJ	151,618	122,518	26,019	96,499	76,972	32,793	17,965	16,833	5,960	19,527	10,977	3,429	1,209	1,713	8,550	2,125	8	1,900	27,200
NM	41,041	30,669	12,600	18,069	10,955	1,980	5,363	1,199	153	7,115	3,209	638	1,641	234	3,906	975	13	715	9,656
NY	549,846	356,444	97,176	259,268	205,151	66,385	46,153	70,622	12,161	54,118	32,362	3,944	12,452	2,923	21,755	5,715	150	12,581	180,820

See footnotes at end of table.

Table 490. State and Local Governments—Revenue by State: 2021-Continued.
See headnote on page 316.

State	Total revenue	Total	Intergovernmental from federal government	General revenue: General revenue from own sources: Total	Select taxes: Total [1]	Select taxes: Property	Select taxes: Sales and gross receipt	Select taxes: Individual income	Select taxes: Corporation income	Total	Current charges and miscellaneous revenue: Current charges: Total [1]	Current charges: Education	Current charges: Hospitals	Current charges: Sewerage	Miscellaneous revenue: Total [1]	Miscellaneous revenue: Interest earnings	Miscellaneous revenue: Special assessments	Utility and liquor stores	Insurance trust revenue
NC..	146,292	111,838	31,392	80,446	51,658	11,863	19,005	15,908	1,516	28,788	22,267	3,664	13,602	1,693	6,521	804	26	5,390	29,064
ND..	15,013	12,175	3,991	8,184	5,455	1,220	1,728	449	155	2,729	1,287	503	4	84	1,443	745	175	305	2,533
OH..	186,963	131,647	39,354	92,293	62,852	18,256	24,904	16,617	277	29,441	18,004	5,923	5,934	2,490	11,437	2,165	401	5,023	50,293
OK..	53,185	38,796	11,002	27,794	17,823	3,662	7,681	3,768	601	9,971	6,122	2,394	1,435	558	3,849	822	32	2,172	12,217
OR..	88,362	58,059	15,450	42,609	27,604	7,716	3,114	11,257	1,360	15,005	10,345	1,820	3,190	1,338	4,660	730	96	3,106	27,198
PA..	209,709	164,422	50,401	114,021	81,390	21,836	25,802	21,985	4,635	32,631	21,495	6,397	5,675	3,228	11,136	1,450	68	5,280	40,008
RI..	25,711	16,171	6,600	9,571	7,117	2,701	2,156	1,758	258	2,454	1,466	502	3	247	988	384	1	248	9,293
SC..	68,842	53,025	13,418	39,607	22,919	7,166	7,815	5,456	740	16,688	12,931	2,565	7,425	850	3,757	621	78	3,584	12,234
SD..	15,365	8,211	2,308	5,903	4,172	1,488	2,230	–	54	1,732	914	360	105	122	818	292	20	397	6,757
TN..	89,215	61,958	18,683	43,275	29,678	6,456	17,290	179	2,564	13,596	9,181	1,864	3,949	1,198	4,416	1,165	140	8,614	18,643
TX..	408,425	310,103	93,357	216,746	143,675	65,553	68,142	–	–	73,071	44,006	10,678	16,608	5,060	29,065	5,907	663	17,712	80,610
UT..	47,013	39,269	8,771	30,498	18,873	4,104	6,720	6,673	746	11,625	8,896	2,444	3,539	584	2,729	772	71	2,575	5,169
VT..	21,850	8,996	2,786	6,209	4,870	1,936	1,272	1,233	167	1,339	822	522	–	86	517	120	2	335	12,519
VA..	135,481	100,597	24,702	75,895	53,565	16,567	14,785	17,067	1,579	22,330	15,190	4,510	4,800	1,851	7,141	1,283	68	3,115	31,769
WA..	148,243	100,010	24,458	75,552	51,574	14,712	31,163	–	–	23,978	18,224	3,103	5,320	3,201	5,754	1,355	348	7,966	40,266
WV..	26,945	20,272	7,283	12,989	8,386	1,922	3,126	2,254	320	4,603	2,739	838	479	281	1,864	657	13	446	6,227
WI..	85,839	62,440	14,981	47,459	33,549	10,486	9,748	9,036	2,517	13,910	8,786	2,450	2,401	1,250	5,124	945	66	2,156	21,243
WY..	11,886	9,845	3,434	6,411	3,016	1,252	1,049	–	–	3,395	1,940	168	1,311	75	1,455	975	10	390	1,652

– Represents or rounds to zero. [1] Includes items not shown separately.

Source: U.S. Census Bureau, Annual Survey of State and Local Government Finances, "Datasets & Tables," <www.census.gov/programs-surveys/gov-finances.html>, accessed August 2023.

Table 491. State and Local Governments—Expenditures and Debt by State: 2021

[In millions of dollars (4,509,102 represents $4,509,102,000,000). For fiscal year ending in year shown; see text, this section]

State	Total expenditures	General expenditures Total[1]	Direct general expenditures Total[1]	Education	Public welfare	Hospitals	Health	Highways	Police protection	Corrections	Natural resources	Parks and recreation	Housing and community development	Sewerage	Solid waste	Governmental administration	Interest on general debt	Utility and liquor store expenditures	Insurance trust expenditures	Total debt outstanding
U.S.	4,509,102	3,684,674	3,681,234	1,143,137	862,255	236,873	140,278	206,436	134,976	86,906	36,633	47,554	65,006	67,987	29,779	168,594	112,695	267,866	556,562	3,336,669
AL	56,074	47,298	47,298	16,520	8,021	8,142	1,016	2,552	1,451	927	230	497	613	487	384	1,875	1,167	3,705	5,071	34,591
AK	16,401	13,743	13,743	3,251	2,654	513	591	1,303	406	379	364	127	312	140	134	1,042	272	758	1,900	8,662
AZ	76,451	63,319	63,319	20,430	20,931	1,047	1,446	2,940	2,896	1,877	538	787	675	762	508	2,700	1,326	6,167	6,965	39,963
AR	31,756	27,401	27,401	9,274	7,924	1,579	429	2,196	731	538	286	274	255	345	252	1,412	564	994	3,360	20,859
CA	743,235	577,556	574,810	159,873	151,467	36,487	31,690	23,767	24,898	17,995	7,805	7,109	10,545	10,586	4,071	23,192	17,479	54,967	110,712	541,241
CO	79,255	64,482	64,479	20,125	11,896	3,615	1,501	3,602	2,439	1,491	701	1,991	1,588	1,406	179	4,161	2,644	4,551	10,223	69,752
CT	47,031	37,887	37,887	14,639	3,847	1,668	1,297	2,158	1,307	879	173	264	793	574	279	2,111	2,139	1,649	7,496	53,741
DE	14,479	12,699	12,698	4,575	3,150	76	589	804	394	377	83	90	219	159	119	760	318	582	1,198	8,520
DC	22,552	16,761	16,761	3,480	4,711	303	1,335	671	669	276	112	346	636	404	172	1,119	663	3,755	2,037	19,908
FL	225,472	192,443	192,443	50,630	33,266	11,946	8,682	12,130	10,588	5,144	5,021	4,101	2,872	4,999	3,177	8,995	3,643	11,842	21,187	135,832
GA	107,827	85,991	85,991	32,239	14,586	6,150	2,657	5,159	3,223	2,120	600	987	1,111	1,522	889	4,462	1,535	6,678	15,157	62,181
HI	21,881	17,810	17,809	3,617	3,633	504	786	974	579	221	169	314	422	540	281	1,289	403	1,243	2,828	19,704
ID	17,360	15,362	15,362	4,250	3,766	951	354	1,299	535	493	318	219	280	260	212	1,041	256	435	1,564	6,026
IL	177,745	139,435	139,418	42,255	31,599	5,021	2,931	8,986	5,972	2,388	684	2,547	2,567	1,735	528	6,749	7,473	8,883	29,426	165,465
IN	73,796	66,835	66,833	20,242	18,222	6,049	1,501	3,828	1,708	1,246	473	531	1,141	1,569	308	2,596	1,877	2,740	4,221	51,498
IA	42,527	36,698	36,698	11,846	7,678	4,881	514	3,148	947	493	536	418	428	832	364	1,277	639	1,669	4,159	22,303
KS	36,049	31,417	31,417	11,121	5,408	4,284	912	2,013	1,148	572	259	363	240	517	180	1,583	613	1,537	3,094	27,713
KY	54,704	45,983	45,983	12,827	15,934	3,210	1,086	2,260	1,047	903	434	357	457	1,455	239	1,730	1,399	2,119	6,602	54,203
LA	56,821	49,168	48,768	13,937	14,628	3,039	1,079	2,368	1,596	906	1,093	802	584	572	381	2,161	1,141	1,402	6,252	30,581
ME	15,949	14,035	14,035	4,241	4,238	165	328	1,120	353	264	157	94	353	277	123	783	300	351	1,563	9,395
MD	84,783	72,330	72,330	23,448	16,894	444	3,082	3,016	3,149	1,983	790	1,197	2,354	1,649	793	3,656	2,474	4,154	8,300	63,354
MA	116,830	91,292	91,288	26,119	27,157	1,736	2,368	3,408	2,464	1,633	337	506	3,559	1,476	446	3,929	3,215	7,311	18,226	101,552
MI	118,130	97,868	97,864	32,194	21,135	6,253	4,748	5,855	2,919	2,441	446	999	1,292	3,280	562	3,990	2,756	4,694	15,568	80,465
MN	81,882	68,592	68,592	21,027	18,921	2,248	1,852	5,665	2,571	1,167	911	1,376	1,211	1,200	498	3,537	1,581	3,702	9,588	57,045
MS	33,350	28,232	28,232	8,832	6,627	4,263	572	1,867	791	556	321	260	355	278	221	1,263	532	1,395	3,723	14,707
MO	65,403	55,344	55,323	16,528	11,031	5,115	3,159	2,877	2,093	888	398	699	837	1,320	167	2,275	1,774	2,708	7,351	49,648
MT	12,802	11,041	11,041	3,361	2,769	151	458	1,010	374	285	391	105	112	144	105	749	207	360	1,401	5,779
NE	27,364	21,175	21,175	8,171	3,784	795	394	1,884	556	596	305	313	270	372	149	802	379	4,594	1,595	16,054
NV	33,961	26,065	26,048	7,815	4,848	1,283	740	2,104	1,465	865	331	678	385	583	38	1,498	965	1,530	6,366	28,220
NH	15,055	13,150	13,150	4,568	3,054	74	220	796	486	215	49	95	297	221	144	1,110	396	818	1,087	9,798
NJ	129,859	104,423	104,404	39,984	22,207	2,956	2,353	4,339	4,216	2,017	687	645	1,484	1,699	1,068	4,221	3,352	4,959	20,477	99,426
NM	31,040	26,470	26,470	7,311	8,367	1,863	613	1,264	752	807	369	300	215	245	244	1,274	626	780	3,790	15,428
NY	407,505	315,710	315,710	92,005	84,380	20,304	8,399	12,094	10,710	6,097	574	3,137	8,117	4,217	3,896	11,909	14,871	34,510	57,284	383,553

See footnotes at end of table.

Table 491. State and Local Governments—Expenditures and Debt by State: 2021-Continued.

See headnote on page 318.

State	Total expenditures	General expenditures Total¹	Direct general expenditures Total¹	Education	Public welfare	Hospitals	Health	Highways	Police protection	Corrections	Natural resources	Parks and recreation	Housing and community development	Sewerage	Solid waste	Governmental administration	Interest on general debt	Utility and liquor store expenditures	Insurance trust expenditures	Total debt outstanding
NC....	113,125	98,199	98,199	30,109	19,483	13,853	4,612	5,265	3,798	2,234	837	1,268	2,013	1,228	917	4,624	1,977	5,572	9,354	47,113
ND....	12,049	10,649	10,649	3,424	1,766	82	373	1,354	276	226	468	266	98	133	91	578	313	372	1,028	9,386
OH....	147,217	120,882	120,866	37,733	35,010	7,318	3,737	6,016	3,920	2,220	517	1,638	2,271	2,594	623	5,840	3,611	5,194	21,142	94,303
OK....	40,991	34,207	34,161	11,715	7,475	1,613	1,565	3,059	1,180	741	234	545	652	431	330	1,672	515	2,222	4,562	19,241
OR....	70,030	57,447	57,447	16,896	14,356	3,264	2,242	2,683	1,650	1,604	756	748	1,167	1,150	190	3,488	1,383	3,407	9,176	43,386
PA....	176,925	147,632	147,520	47,088	41,079	5,704	6,521	10,676	4,984	3,780	795	1,214	2,514	2,713	984	8,068	4,263	6,971	22,321	128,545
RI....	15,896	13,124	13,106	3,847	3,463	185	697	680	495	226	91	66	266	169	100	842	517	338	2,433	12,207
SC....	58,442	49,787	49,787	16,900	8,945	8,044	1,902	2,208	1,412	802	271	648	567	860	510	2,230	933	3,557	5,099	38,030
SD....	10,096	8,654	8,654	2,694	1,747	137	190	1,213	245	231	169	166	114	124	62	619	197	412	1,030	6,681
TN....	69,914	56,179	56,179	16,092	13,713	4,381	2,323	2,731	2,304	1,236	542	583	1,138	1,030	497	2,955	1,623	8,549	5,185	51,972
TX....	341,825	283,157	283,157	101,148	51,471	24,503	13,087	19,486	9,829	6,299	2,547	3,419	2,958	5,206	1,787	11,308	10,418	21,007	37,661	324,962
UT....	40,643	35,191	35,191	12,645	5,473	3,111	1,346	2,531	891	614	443	646	560	525	237	2,194	535	3,011	2,440	22,120
VT....	11,513	8,850	8,850	3,028	2,067	23	455	736	283	150	141	84	234	100	42	379	145	359	2,304	4,723
VA....	104,654	90,911	90,910	29,530	19,679	5,172	3,062	6,895	2,912	3,018	343	1,159	1,498	1,753	802	4,755	2,313	4,604	9,139	67,667
WA....	116,635	92,608	92,608	30,592	15,752	7,702	5,483	4,935	2,687	2,153	1,367	1,474	1,751	2,406	853	3,258	3,090	11,530	12,497	90,295
WV....	20,919	18,414	18,414	5,677	5,451	588	362	1,748	469	472	213	191	215	281	66	1,153	385	450	2,055	17,039
WI....	71,512	60,803	60,803	20,049	15,675	2,745	2,007	4,020	1,992	1,646	734	760	392	1,376	488	2,783	1,449	2,398	8,311	49,814
WY....	11,387	9,963	9,953	3,235	914	1,337	635	742	222	212	223	150	20	83	89	599	51	369	1,055	2,018

¹ Includes items not shown separately.

Source: U.S. Census Bureau, Annual Survey of State and Local Government Finances, "Datasets & Tables," <www.census.gov/programs-surveys/gov-finances.html>, accessed August 2023.

Table 492. Estimated State and Local Taxes Paid by a Family of Three for Largest City in Selected States: 2021

[Data based on average family of three (two wage earners and one school age child) living in a city where taxes apply. The families in the top four income levels are assumed to own their own home; at the $25,000 income level, the families are assumed to rent and not own their own housing unit. Comprises state and local sales, income, auto, and real estate taxes. Negative number indicates the family would receive a net refund. For definition of median, see Guide to Tabular Presentation]

City	Total taxes paid by gross family income level (dollars)					Total taxes paid as percent of income				
	$25,000	$50,000	$75,000	$100,000	$150,000	$25,000	$50,000	$75,000	$100,000	$150,000
Albuquerque, NM.......	1,923	4,026	6,583	9,023	13,696	7.7	8.1	8.8	9.0	9.1
Atlanta, GA..............	4,493	4,659	7,642	10,578	16,151	18.0	9.3	10.2	10.6	10.8
Baltimore, MD..........	3,876	7,048	10,939	14,745	19,925	15.5	14.1	14.6	14.7	13.3
Boston, MA..............	2,253	3,247	5,105	6,856	12,088	9.0	6.5	6.8	6.9	8.1
Charlotte, NC...........	3,232	4,490	6,979	9,184	13,415	12.9	9.0	9.3	9.2	8.9
Chicago, IL..............	4,699	6,169	9,530	12,372	17,524	18.8	12.3	12.7	12.4	11.7
Columbus, OH..........	3,700	5,123	7,694	10,293	15,216	14.8	10.2	10.3	10.3	10.1
Denver, CO..............	4,314	3,982	6,238	8,132	12,390	17.3	8.0	8.3	8.1	8.3
Detroit, MI...............	3,248	5,845	11,451	15,178	22,546	13.0	11.7	15.3	15.2	15.0
Honolulu, HI.............	5,199	4,045	6,717	9,011	13,269	20.8	8.1	9.0	9.0	8.8
Houston, TX.............	3,592	3,361	4,723	6,006	8,351	14.4	6.7	6.3	6.0	5.6
Indianapolis, IN.........	4,076	5,366	8,334	10,173	14,670	16.3	10.7	11.1	10.2	9.8
Jacksonville, FL........	3,122	3,323	4,934	6,484	9,247	12.5	6.6	6.6	6.5	6.2
Kansas City, MO.......	3,804	5,429	8,885	11,576	17,231	15.2	10.9	11.8	11.6	11.5
Las Vegas, NV..........	3,592	4,290	5,963	7,635	10,600	14.4	8.6	8.0	7.6	7.1
Los Angeles, CA.......	5,367	5,645	8,617	11,465	17,659	21.5	11.3	11.5	11.5	11.8
Louisville, KY...........	3,569	6,537	9,734	12,528	18,085	14.3	13.1	13.0	12.5	12.1
Milwaukee, WI..........	2,595	4,657	8,200	11,326	17,119	10.4	9.3	10.9	11.3	11.4
Minneapolis, MN.......	1,669	3,703	6,205	8,852	15,097	6.7	7.4	8.3	8.9	10.1
Nashville, TN...........	4,484	3,686	4,815	5,892	7,713	17.9	7.4	6.4	5.9	5.1
New Orleans, LA.......	3,509	4,160	6,356	8,537	13,088	14.0	8.3	8.5	8.5	8.7
New York, NY...........	5,020	5,144	8,719	11,887	18,214	20.1	10.3	11.6	11.9	12.1
Oklahoma City, OK.....	3,364	4,462	6,850	9,029	13,212	13.5	8.9	9.1	9.0	8.8
Philadelphia, PA........	5,327	6,102	9,122	12,018	17,354	21.3	12.2	12.2	12.0	11.6
Phoenix, AZ.............	3,813	4,137	6,181	8,143	12,278	15.3	8.3	8.2	8.1	8.2
Portland, OR............	2,500	4,965	7,913	10,822	16,687	10.0	9.9	10.6	10.8	11.1
Seattle, WA.............	5,996	4,301	6,110	7,460	9,877	24.0	8.6	8.1	7.5	6.6
Virginia Beach, VA.....	3,894	4,636	7,671	10,003	14,205	15.6	9.3	10.2	10.0	9.5
Washington, DC........	2,704	3,256	5,833	8,381	13,599	10.8	6.5	7.8	8.4	9.1
Wichita, KS..............	3,268	4,615	6,959	9,248	13,542	13.1	9.2	9.3	9.2	9.0
Average [1]	**3,514**	**4,588**	**7,280**	**9,716**	**14,599**	**14.1**	**9.2**	**9.7**	**9.7**	**9.7**
Median [1]	**3,509**	**4,370**	**6,959**	**9,490**	**14,205**	**14.0**	**8.7**	**9.3**	**9.5**	**9.5**

[1] Based on the largest city in each State and District of Columbia. For complete list of cities, see Table 493.

Source: Government of the District of Columbia, Office of the Chief Financial Officer, *Tax Rates and Tax Burdens in the District of Columbia – A Nationwide Comparison 2021*, May 2023, and earlier reports. See also <ora-cfo.dc.gov/page/tax-burden-studies>.

Table 493. Residential Property Tax Rates for Largest City in Each State: 2021

[The real property tax is a function of housing values, real estate tax rates, assessment levels, and homeowner exemptions and credits. Effective rate is the amount each jurisdiction considers based upon assessment level used. Assessment level is ratio of assessed value to assumed market value. Nominal rates represent the "announced" rates levied by the jurisdiction]

City	Effective tax rate per $100		Assessment level (percent)	Nominal rate per $100	City	Effective tax rate per $100		Assessment level (percent)	Nominal rate per $100
	Rank	Rate				Rank	Rate		
Detroit, MI..............	1	3.48	50.0	6.96	Fargo, ND................	28	1.33	4.5	29.60
Newark, NJ.............	2	3.23	86.4	3.73	Portland, ME............	29	1.30	100.0	1.30
Bridgeport, CT..........	3	3.04	70.0	4.35	Oklahoma City, OK......	30	1.29	11.0	11.77
Indianapolis, IN.........	4	2.95	99.5	2.97	Portland, OR............	31	1.27	47.9	2.64
Milwaukee, WI..........	5	2.55	90.8	[1] 2.81	Los Angeles, CA.........	32	1.18	100.0	1.18
Des Moines, IA.........	6	2.46	54.1	4.55	Sioux Falls, SD..........	33	1.17	79.4	1.47
Houston, TX.............	7	2.28	98.0	2.33	Charleston, SC..........	34	1.15	4.0	28.86
Burlington, VT..........	8	2.24	[3] 105.3	2.12	Minneapolis, MN........	35	1.13	95.7	1.18
Baltimore, MD..........	9	2.14	90.8	2.36	Las Vegas, NV...........	36	1.13	34.5	3.28
Providence, RI..........	10	2.14	87.2	2.46	Boise, ID................	37	1.04	94.0	1.10
Omaha, NE.............	11	2.09	94.0	2.22	Boston, MA..............	38	1.00	92.0	1.09
Chicago, IL.............	12	2.01	[2] 10.0	6.70	Billings, MT..............	39	0.94	1.4	69.94
Jackson, MS............	13	1.92	10.0	19.25	Virginia Beach, VA.......	40	0.91	89.4	1.02
Anchorage, AK..........	14	1.78	95.1	1.80	Charleston, WV.........	41	0.88	55.0	1.61
Manchester, NH........	15	1.70	96.1	1.77	Charlotte, NC...........	42	0.85	88.5	0.97
Jacksonville, FL........	16	1.66	94.4	17.54	Washington, DC.........	43	0.85	97.5	0.85
Wilmington, DE........	17	1.63	27.7	5.89	Nashville, TN...........	44	0.82	25.0	3.29
Atlanta, GA.............	18	1.62	37.4	4.05	Seattle, WA.............	45	0.81	86.8	0.93
Phoenix, AZ.............	19	1.56	10.0	15.61	New York, NY...........	46	0.75	3.6	21.45
Kansas City, MO........	20	1.52	16.1	8.02	Birmingham, AL..........	47	0.72	10.0	7.25
Wichita, KS..............	21	1.52	11.5	14.40	Cheyenne, WY..........	48	0.69	9.5	7.23
Columbus, OH..........	22	1.52	26.1	5.84	Salt Lake City, UT.......	49	0.64	54.7	1.16
Louisville, KY...........	23	1.51	100.0	1.51	Denver, CO..............	50	0.53	7.2	7.46
New Orleans, LA.......	24	1.44	10.0	14.40	Honolulu, HI.............	51	0.35	100.0	0.35
Little Rock, AR.........	25	1.40	19.0	7.00					
Philadelphia, PA........	26	1.36	97.5	1.40	**Unweighted average...**	(X)	**1.51**	**57.1**	**7.32**
Albuquerque, NM.......	27	1.34	33.3	4.23	**Median.................**	(X)	**1.36**	**55.0**	**3.28**

X Not applicable. [1] For Milwaukee, WI, the nominal tax rate takes the assessment sales ratio statistic into account. [2] For Chicago, IL, the state equalizer of 3.2 percent was applied to the assessment level of 10 percent to reflect the equalizer's impact on the final rate. [3] For Vermont, the Common Level of Appraisal value for school funding equalization is used in lieu of a sales ratio statistic.

Source: Government of the District of Columbia, Office of the Chief Financial Officer, *Tax Rates and Tax Burdens in the District of Columbia—A Nationwide Comparison 2021*, May 2023. See also <ora-cfo.dc.gov/page/tax-burden-studies>.

Table 494. Gross Revenue From Parimutuel and Amusement Taxes and Lotteries by State: 2022

[In millions of dollars (108,542.6 represents $108,542,600,000). For fiscal years; see text, this section]

State	Total gross revenue	Amuse-ment taxes [1]	Pari-mutuel taxes [2]	Lottery revenue Total [3]	Apportionment of funds Prizes	Adminis-tration	Proceeds available from ticket sales
United States	**108,542.6**	**10,555.3**	**176.6**	**97,810.6**	**65,227.4**	**4,323.9**	**28,259.3**
Alabama	5.2	–	5.2	(X)	(X)	(X)	(X)
Alaska	6.8	6.8	(X)	(X)	(X)	(X)	(X)
Arizona	1,283.8	8.2	0.2	1,275.4	925.4	69.6	280.4
Arkansas	634.1	85.5	1.9	546.8	402.4	44.3	100.1
California	8,871.5	(X)	18.2	8,853.3	5,825.7	381.8	2,645.7
Colorado	918.7	153.6	0.4	764.7	538.9	47.2	178.6
Connecticut	1,688.5	160.2	5.7	1,522.5	1,041.2	67.7	413.7
Delaware	392.8	(X)	0.1	392.7	223.6	10.6	158.6
Florida	8,999.3	178.2	12.3	8,808.7	6,245.5	198.9	2,364.4
Georgia	5,101.0	(X)	(X)	5,101.0	3,585.3	205.0	1,310.7
Hawaii	–	(X)	(X)	(X)	(X)	(X)	(X)
Idaho	347.8	(X)	1.4	346.3	257.1	15.9	73.3
Illinois	4,660.1	1,258.7	7.7	3,393.8	2,211.4	361.1	821.3
Indiana	2,145.3	556.3	1.7	1,587.3	1,138.5	87.7	361.1
Iowa	781.9	373.5	3.9	404.4	274.2	31.2	99.0
Kansas	296.1	0.3	(X)	295.9	200.2	19.0	76.7
Kentucky	1,637.2	0.1	47.7	1,589.4	1,152.0	77.1	360.3
Louisiana	1,382.6	761.0	5.7	615.9	328.4	28.7	258.7
Maine	430.3	68.1	1.9	360.3	264.8	25.4	70.1
Maryland	3,576.4	1,194.1	1.1	2,381.2	1,689.1	56.5	635.6
Massachusetts	6,157.6	301.5	1.1	5,855.0	4,309.8	111.9	1,433.3
Michigan	4,734.9	285.6	2.9	4,446.4	3,132.4	103.6	1,210.3
Minnesota	894.2	201.8	1.9	690.5	488.8	22.2	179.6
Mississippi	666.3	205.1	0.2	461.0	251.3	10.3	199.5
Missouri	2,066.6	390.9	(X)	1,675.7	1,264.4	55.2	356.2
Montana	200.8	123.3	0.2	77.4	41.2	17.3	18.9
Nebraska	223.2	7.6	0.2	215.4	119.6	20.3	75.6
Nevada	1,356.3	1,356.3	(Z)	(X)	(X)	(X)	(X)
New Hampshire	499.3	24.3	0.5	474.5	321.8	35.1	117.6
New Jersey	3,808.0	387.0	(X)	3,421.0	2,209.1	131.6	1,080.3
New Mexico	207.3	69.3	1.2	136.9	74.1	12.4	50.3
New York	8,881.6	1.5	13.9	8,866.3	4,901.6	388.5	3,576.2
North Carolina	3,887.1	(Z)	(X)	3,887.1	2,544.0	339.1	1,004.0
North Dakota	53.5	23.9	1.6	28.0	15.4	5.3	7.3
Ohio	4,353.8	334.2	4.0	4,015.6	2,791.7	81.7	1,142.2
Oklahoma	359.9	30.9	1.1	328.0	226.7	7.7	93.6
Oregon	1,348.7	12.4	3.2	1,333.1	257.2	105.9	970.0
Pennsylvania	6,394.6	1,758.4	8.7	4,627.5	3,370.0	86.8	1,170.7
Rhode Island	579.0	20.4	0.5	558.1	196.2	16.9	345.0
South Carolina	2,148.9	54.0	(X)	2,095.0	1,486.9	27.6	580.4
South Dakota	246.2	12.3	0.1	233.8	42.9	11.4	179.4
Tennessee	1,761.4	46.1	(X)	1,715.3	1,202.4	31.6	481.4
Texas	8,319.7	17.7	5.1	8,296.9	5,599.7	686.0	2,011.1
Utah	–	(X)	(X)	(X)	(X)	(X)	(X)
Vermont	151.6	(X)	(X)	151.6	100.7	10.5	40.4
Virginia	3,624.4	37.2	1.5	3,585.7	2,676.9	146.6	762.1
Washington	826.3	4.4	1.3	820.6	574.0	30.6	216.0
West Virginia	747.9	39.2	2.9	705.7	152.5	36.2	517.1
Wisconsin	843.5	0.1	–	843.4	557.1	60.1	226.2
Wyoming	40.5	5.4	9.4	25.7	15.7	3.7	6.2

– Represents zero. X Not applicable. Z Less than $50,000. [1] Represents nonlicense taxes. [2] Represents legalized gambling taxes. [3] Excludes commissions.

Source: U.S. Census Bureau, "Annual Survey of State Government Finances," and "Annual Survey of State Government Tax Collections," <www.census.gov/topics/public-sector.html>, accessed June 2024.

Table 495. Lottery Sales—Type of Game and Proceeds: 2000 to 2023

[In millions of dollars (37,201 represents $37,201,000,000). For fiscal years]

Game	2000	2005	2010	2015	2019	2020	2021	2022	2023
Total ticket sales	**37,201**	**47,425**	**54,200**	**66,715**	**82,289**	**82,447**	**98,642**	**99,301**	**104,585**
Instant [1]	15,387	26,006	30,665	41,653	51,109	53,007	64,933	64,580	64,321
Three-digit [2]	5,780	5,858	5,861	5,925	6,282	6,191	7,657	7,275	6,877
Four-digit [2]	2,273	2,869	3,419	3,865	4,376	4,593	5,196	5,202	4,951
Lotto [3]	9,339	9,828	10,894	10,820	14,227	9,740	12,472	12,491	17,290
Other [4]	4,423	2,864	3,362	4,452	6,295	8,916	8,384	9,753	11,146
State proceeds (net income) [5]	11,871	15,792	17,957	21,154	25,330	24,003	27,703	28,722	30,460

[1] Player scratches a latex section on ticket that reveals instantly whether ticket is a winner. [2] Players choose and bet on three or four digits, depending on game, with various payoffs for different straight order or mixed combination bets. [3] Players typically select six digits out of a large field of numbers. Varying prizes are offered for matching three through six numbers drawn by lottery. [4] Includes break-open tickets, spiel, keno, video lottery, etc. [5] Sales minus prizes and expenses equal net government income.

Source: TLF Publications, Inc. © 2024. All Rights Reserved.

Table 496. State Financial Resources, Expenditures, and Balances: 2022 and 2023

[In millions of dollars (2,775,897 represents $2,775,897,000,000). For fiscal year ending in year shown; see text, this section. General funds exclude special funds earmarked for particular purposes, such as highway trust funds and federal funds; they support most on-going broad-based state services, and are available for appropriation to support any governmental activity. Minus sign (-) indicates deficit]

State	Expenditures by fund source				State general fund					
	Total, 2022 actual	2023 estimated			Resources [2,3]		Expenditures [3]		Balance [4]	
		Total [1]	General fund	Federal fund	2022	2023 (P)	2022	2023 (P)	2022	2023 (P)
United States......	**2,775,897**	**2,956,386**	**1,124,754**	**1,044,511**	**1,434,009**	**1,532,002**	**1,061,308**	**1,186,605**	**314,717**	**293,332**
Alabama.............	37,905	37,348	12,874	15,242	15,018	16,969	10,654	14,027	3,423	2,537
Alaska...............	14,446	17,379	8,505	6,005	7,019	6,993	4,591	7,633	1,657	-748
Arizona.............	80,508	(NA)	(NA)	(NA)	17,599	18,127	12,889	15,432	4,710	2,695
Arkansas...........	32,047	34,519	5,848	12,191	7,477	7,059	5,849	6,024	1,628	1,035
California...........	442,237	467,557	234,592	153,230	270,889	260,944	216,785	234,592	55,810	26,352
Colorado...........	35,187	38,101	13,538	12,668	20,951	21,259	17,839	19,032	3,203	2,342
Connecticut.........	41,540	46,034	22,330	12,164	21,991	22,920	20,731	22,327	1,261	594
Delaware............	14,377	15,467	5,861	4,017	7,663	8,900	5,058	5,861	2,605	3,040
Florida.............	103,229	110,977	42,779	43,567	64,050	70,693	38,136	50,893	22,803	19,801
Georgia.............	67,527	62,453	30,996	18,664	40,781	46,735	28,562	30,643	12,219	16,093
Hawaii.............	18,819	19,231	10,757	4,329	11,461	12,811	8,842	10,632	2,619	2,179
Idaho...............	11,077	15,721	4,648	6,284	5,738	5,086	4,418	4,583	1,334	416
Illinois.............	122,624	128,402	45,026	27,936	52,007	55,197	48,332	50,153	2,063	3,852
Indiana.............	48,188	54,712	26,081	22,437	24,064	26,103	18,415	21,611	4,508	831
Iowa...............	28,508	29,143	8,216	10,643	10,037	10,043	8,123	8,212	1,914	1,831
Kansas.............	22,518	24,668	9,240	7,240	10,031	11,137	8,196	8,727	1,835	2,410
Kentucky...........	45,399	50,005	14,350	21,022	17,152	19,297	13,156	14,466	1,878	366
Louisiana...........	39,652	48,224	12,415	24,245	13,812	13,419	12,730	11,871	727	7
Maine.............	12,517	13,010	4,304	4,898	5,744	5,484	4,074	4,447	34	165
Maryland...........	62,833	67,692	28,196	22,296	26,429	30,399	21,199	28,196	5,499	2,584
Massachusetts.......	74,038	79,885	36,740	23,160	82,413	80,405	40,204	51,515	18,200	12,898
Michigan...........	75,633	86,176	17,879	37,311	19,072	20,625	11,428	17,387	7,464	3,138
Minnesota..........	53,812	58,047	27,535	22,825	37,655	43,760	24,686	27,243	11,996	16,305
Mississippi..........	23,090	28,400	6,296	13,154	7,397	6,992	5,766	6,292	4	2
Missouri............	32,143	38,171	12,526	16,233	15,366	18,291	10,467	12,525	4,899	5,766
Montana............	8,728	10,473	2,617	5,118	4,598	5,613	2,753	4,770	1,847	851
Nebraska...........	15,391	17,223	5,154	5,444	7,166	7,008	4,672	5,154	2,494	1,854
Nevada.............	20,101	20,322	4,765	5,773	6,727	7,569	4,537	6,353	1,842	608
New Hampshire......	7,822	8,260	2,045	3,744	1,991	2,288	1,607	2,136	253	–
New Jersey..........	86,999	96,746	53,425	30,298	60,554	61,670	52,234	51,461	8,319	10,209
New Mexico........	22,545	26,188	8,535	11,177	13,216	16,380	8,066	9,868	3,230	4,299
New York............	209,339	220,462	84,474	84,908	121,971	136,250	84,418	90,449	33,053	43,451
North Carolina.......	58,975	59,174	22,565	23,792	39,360	40,712	25,793	26,755	7,166	4,849
North Dakota........	8,088	7,400	2,249	2,588	3,718	4,102	2,323	2,614	1,377	1,488
Ohio...............	90,050	93,639	25,044	39,560	33,490	36,064	26,943	27,074	6,547	8,991
Oklahoma...........	27,147	29,543	7,859	14,528	10,727	12,440	7,442	8,936	2,323	3,050
Oregon.............	67,770	67,869	19,916	19,693	18,946	21,439	13,294	13,837	5,652	7,636
Pennsylvania........	121,277	114,676	41,111	46,856	49,454	51,945	39,351	40,801	5,537	8,983
Rhode Island........	13,203	14,078	5,174	5,826	5,575	5,549	5,240	5,089	210	410
South Carolina.......	32,263	38,752	12,089	15,263	16,705	19,771	9,596	11,765	6,866	6,846
South Dakota.......	1,127	6,023	2,202	2,192	2,254	2,443	2,047	2,231	116	97
Tennessee..........	43,363	54,011	23,528	22,021	25,223	29,430	15,759	20,768	7,432	5,520
Texas...............	138,559	142,474	51,839	58,405	87,708	109,081	61,465	67,324	26,243	39,236
Utah...............	20,893	28,383	11,376	8,873	13,678	14,783	10,254	11,682	3,220	3,101
Vermont.............	7,621	7,893	2,055	3,234	2,459	2,508	2,333	2,098	177	337
Virginia.............	74,922	79,950	27,810	24,762	31,153	33,192	26,420	31,742	4,733	1,450
Washington..........	66,493	71,879	30,744	21,626	33,463	35,109	27,969	31,490	5,494	3,618
West Virginia........	18,830	19,175	3,608	6,035	6,750	8,530	4,740	5,645	1,994	2,885
Wisconsin...........	62,901	64,665	18,864	19,715	23,762	26,705	19,377	20,464	4,299	7,073
Wyoming...........	5,636	4,698	1,470	840	1,543	1,775	1,543	1,775	–	–

P Preliminary. NA Not available. – Represents zero. [1] Includes bonds and other state funds, not shown separately. [2] Includes funds budgeted, adjustments, and balances from previous year. [3] May or may not include budget stabilization fund transfers, depending on state accounting practices. [4] Resources less expenditures, minus adjustments.

Source: National Association of State Budget Officers, Washington, DC, *2023 State Expenditure Report: Fiscal Years 2021-2023* ©, 2023; and *Fiscal Survey of States, Fall 2023* ©, 2023. See also <www.nasbo.org>.

Table 497. State Governments—Summary of Finances: 2000 to 2022

[In millions of dollars (1,260,829 represents $1,260,829,000,000). For fiscal year ending in year shown; see text, this section]

Item	2000	2010	2015	2016	2017	2018	2019	2020	2021	2022
Total revenue	1,260,829	2,039,927	2,164,784	2,141,692	2,297,357	2,455,774	2,534,217	2,677,777	3,123,136	3,075,089
General revenue	984,783	1,567,207	1,860,023	1,917,520	1,973,039	2,103,963	2,195,682	2,320,092	2,704,301	3,051,468
Intergovernmental revenue	274,382	575,372	605,936	641,557	659,496	688,379	708,872	853,472	1,017,029	1,131,664
Total taxes [1]	539,655	705,929	911,430	923,259	949,845	1,033,054	1,084,773	1,059,680	1,262,528	1,473,562
Property taxes [1]	(NA)	(NA)	(NA)	(NA)	(NA)	(NA)	(NA)	(NA)	(NA)	21,597
General sales and gross receipts taxes	174,461	224,314	286,023	291,902	303,553	321,033	335,721	340,816	369,706	431,182
Selective sales and gross receipts taxes	77,685	120,208	144,686	149,255	153,494	165,599	170,170	172,297	179,365	192,260
License taxes	32,598	50,429	52,053	53,909	55,071	57,027	58,914	59,233	64,708	66,978
Individual income taxes	194,573	236,987	336,558	342,376	351,179	393,673	408,935	385,610	503,621	555,887
Corporation net income taxes	32,522	38,006	48,612	45,575	44,617	48,444	59,698	52,345	89,316	148,650
All other taxes	27,815	35,985	43,498	40,241	41,931	47,278	51,335	49,379	55,812	57,009
Current charges	86,467	169,855	201,657	215,373	223,482	234,399	242,752	241,977	243,236	270,261
Miscellaneous general revenue	84,279	116,051	140,999	137,330	140,215	148,130	159,285	164,963	181,508	175,982
Utility revenue	4,513	15,122	14,721	13,828	13,609	14,021	14,360	13,405	10,851	12,215
Liquor stores revenue	3,895	6,495	8,020	7,818	8,338	8,686	9,132	9,714	10,979	11,407
Insurance trust revenue [2]	267,639	451,103	282,020	202,526	302,372	329,104	315,043	334,566	397,004	410,957
Total expenditure	1,084,097	1,943,523	2,161,620	2,244,467	2,322,171	2,414,074	2,515,785	2,751,081	2,986,553	2,784,698
Intergovernmental expenditure	327,070	485,557	525,656	542,753	550,378	562,500	585,295	607,863	662,011	748,952
Direct expenditure	757,027	1,457,965	1,635,964	1,701,714	1,771,793	1,851,574	1,930,491	2,143,218	2,324,543	2,035,746
Current operations	523,114	934,322	1,140,270	1,192,437	1,247,408	1,304,508	1,367,107	1,483,951	1,596,305	1,788,560
Capital outlay	76,233	118,011	128,561	130,532	132,026	141,986	149,379	148,668	147,467	144,124
Insurance benefits and repayments	105,456	320,721	275,454	284,865	297,378	304,980	311,981	404,246	471,716	326,816
Assistance and subsidies	22,136	37,562	45,847	47,966	49,071	51,831	55,012	59,656	63,740	63,185
Interest on debt	30,089	47,351	45,832	45,913	45,910	48,268	47,012	46,697	45,315	39,877
Exhibit: salaries and wages	154,504	244,952	253,951	260,783	272,100	281,093	291,650	304,306	304,163	315,818
General expenditure	964,723	1,593,694	1,847,037	1,926,373	1,989,703	2,070,731	2,166,465	2,305,121	2,468,601	2,745,170
Intergovernmental general expenditure	327,070	485,557	525,656	542,753	550,378	562,500	585,295	607,863	662,011	748,952
Direct general expenditure	637,653	1,108,137	1,321,381	1,383,619	1,439,325	1,508,230	1,581,171	1,697,258	1,806,591	1,996,218
General expenditure, by function:										
Education	346,465	571,147	644,358	669,623	689,588	709,120	736,177	765,393	786,248	881,249
Public welfare	238,890	462,431	613,061	654,770	679,234	706,106	744,141	793,826	866,606	990,507
Hospitals	32,578	64,509	73,645	79,029	85,550	90,324	96,169	104,227	109,320	122,576
Health	42,066	58,245	56,423	58,300	63,181	65,545	69,480	78,587	91,966	100,298
Highways	74,415	111,170	122,417	127,452	129,249	137,339	147,650	149,953	149,750	156,999
Police protection	9,788	13,828	15,267	15,798	16,591	17,264	17,926	20,703	21,793	22,750
Correction	35,129	48,550	51,171	51,481	51,513	53,349	53,594	59,499	60,047	61,396
Natural resources	15,967	21,515	21,572	23,714	24,233	25,018	28,338	28,248	28,483	30,758
Parks and recreation	4,676	5,720	6,060	6,276	6,591	6,614	7,202	7,710	7,617	8,483
Governmental administration	35,527	53,976	60,366	61,591	65,164	67,110	69,797	76,997	82,425	95,421
Interest on general debt	29,187	45,260	43,336	43,404	43,434	45,651	44,431	44,105	42,651	37,487
Other and unallocable	100,034	137,344	91,670	86,940	120,920	133,066	137,470	161,504	206,743	237,246
Utility expenditure	10,723	23,864	44,043	37,737	37,887	40,722	38,928	42,763	46,685	30,254
Liquor store expenditure	3,195	5,244	6,480	6,506	6,925	7,123	7,527	7,930	8,974	9,274
Insurance trust expenditure [2]	105,456	320,721	275,454	284,865	297,378	304,980	311,981	404,246	471,716	326,816
Debt outstanding, long term and short term [3]	547,876	1,115,463	1,155,113	1,170,612	1,154,213	1,170,577	1,167,404	1,185,032	1,208,171	1,113,243
Cash and security holdings	2,518,936	3,323,047	2,996,239	3,009,115	4,877,885	5,173,859	5,367,730	5,484,127	6,562,585	4,630,144

NA Not available. [1] Prior to 2022, property taxes were included in All other taxes. [2] Within insurance trust revenue, net earnings of state-administered pension systems is a calculated statistic, and thus can be positive or negative. Net earnings is the sum of earnings on investments plus gains on investments minus losses on investments. [3] As of fiscal year 2005, the Census Bureau no longer collects government debt information by the character of long-term debt. For further information, see the 2006 Government Finance and Employment Classification Manual at <www.census.gov/programs-surveys/gov-finances/technical-documentation/classification-manuals.html>.

Source: U.S. Census Bureau, "Annual Survey of State Government Finances," <www.census.gov/programs-surveys/state.html>, accessed June 2024.

Table 498. State Governments—Revenue by State: 2021

[In millions of dollars (3,975,040 represents $3,975,040,000,000). For fiscal year ending in year shown; see text, this section. Includes local shares of state imposed taxes]

State	Total revenue [1,2]	General revenue							Utilities and liquor store revenue	Insurance trust revenue
		Total	Intergovernmental revenue		General revenue from own sources					
			Total	Total [1]	From federal government	Total	Total taxes	Current charges	Miscellaneous general revenue		
United States	**3,975,040**	**2,690,251**	**1,006,125**	**987,663**	**1,684,127**	**1,262,528**	**243,545**	**178,053**	**21,830**	**1,262,959**
Alabama	43,770	38,327	15,878	15,729	22,448	14,251	6,255	1,942	477	4,966
Alaska	14,186	9,178	5,260	5,252	3,918	1,053	583	2,281	23	4,985
Arizona	68,592	51,951	25,552	25,217	26,399	20,818	3,237	2,344	39	16,602
Arkansas	42,969	26,645	10,747	10,733	15,898	11,727	2,993	1,178	–	16,324
California	658,433	410,637	116,804	114,089	293,833	248,188	30,990	14,655	335	247,462
Colorado	60,456	40,076	14,385	14,301	25,691	18,818	4,518	2,356	–	20,380
Connecticut	56,023	38,944	12,778	12,193	26,167	22,067	2,408	1,692	39	17,040
Delaware	17,586	13,046	5,315	5,247	7,731	5,396	1,015	1,320	12	4,528
Florida	167,207	114,030	43,680	43,290	70,350	49,314	8,992	12,043	21	53,157
Georgia	105,649	60,940	26,263	26,223	34,677	27,851	4,006	2,820	1	44,708
Hawaii	25,160	17,461	5,974	5,547	11,488	8,047	1,469	1,972	–	7,699
Idaho	19,800	13,265	5,153	5,131	8,112	6,472	1,031	609	234	6,301
Illinois	137,340	97,479	31,263	30,774	66,216	55,532	5,019	5,665	–	39,861
Indiana	65,340	55,820	22,315	22,248	33,504	26,646	3,891	2,968	–	9,520
Iowa	44,704	26,132	8,453	8,409	17,679	11,817	4,274	1,589	416	18,156
Kansas	30,870	24,485	6,617	6,583	17,868	11,616	4,926	1,327	–	6,385
Kentucky	51,217	39,004	18,059	18,011	20,946	14,617	4,820	1,509	–	12,213
Louisiana	53,956	37,908	20,914	20,304	16,994	12,257	2,296	2,440	15	16,034
Maine	16,642	11,784	4,915	4,878	6,869	5,452	887	530	239	4,619
Maryland	68,155	51,031	19,392	19,243	31,639	25,221	3,676	2,743	47	17,078
Massachusetts	98,853	74,529	27,579	26,947	46,950	36,336	5,374	5,240	467	23,858
Michigan	104,860	78,993	29,460	29,265	49,533	34,432	10,377	4,725	1,459	24,408
Minnesota	96,616	53,129	15,733	15,558	37,396	31,793	2,771	2,832	45	43,443
Mississippi	33,941	23,358	10,601	10,567	12,757	9,353	2,485	919	508	10,074
Missouri	61,035	37,442	15,390	15,109	22,052	15,091	3,280	3,681	–	23,593
Montana	14,022	9,977	5,140	5,138	4,837	3,880	533	424	135	3,909
Nebraska	19,296	14,525	5,527	5,483	8,998	6,961	1,003	1,034	–	4,772
Nevada	34,408	18,660	6,589	6,406	12,071	10,416	854	801	40	15,707
New Hampshire	13,389	9,087	4,101	3,660	4,987	3,213	843	931	789	3,513
New Jersey	109,614	82,065	24,884	24,005	57,180	43,683	6,697	6,800	389	27,160
New Mexico	35,055	25,399	12,146	11,874	13,253	7,472	2,165	3,616	–	9,656
New York	330,984	200,233	83,883	82,720	116,349	93,504	11,274	11,571	7,149	123,602
North Carolina	102,738	73,866	28,099	27,929	45,767	34,712	6,854	4,201	1	28,871
North Dakota	11,780	9,332	3,750	3,701	5,582	3,909	828	845	–	2,448
Ohio	139,074	87,271	35,944	35,386	51,327	34,909	9,880	6,537	1,673	50,131
Oklahoma	40,144	27,684	10,355	10,222	17,328	11,299	3,095	2,934	592	11,869
Oregon	69,295	41,602	13,776	13,740	27,827	17,800	6,564	3,463	792	26,901
Pennsylvania	156,317	117,866	46,256	46,167	71,610	49,571	13,524	8,514	2,318	36,134
Rhode Island	21,443	12,681	6,477	6,400	6,205	4,344	1,017	843	18	8,744
South Carolina	48,823	34,997	13,038	12,773	21,959	13,286	6,098	2,575	1,611	12,215
South Dakota	11,849	5,205	2,037	1,995	3,168	2,150	336	683	2	6,642
Tennessee	56,918	41,715	17,341	17,243	24,374	19,978	2,076	2,320	–	15,203
Texas	266,196	193,790	88,753	84,731	105,037	65,377	18,645	21,014	–	72,406
Utah	32,997	27,404	7,403	7,397	20,001	12,632	5,781	1,588	461	5,132
Vermont	20,370	7,838	2,694	2,693	5,144	4,103	598	443	108	12,424
Virginia	97,748	72,188	24,112	22,607	48,076	32,328	10,116	5,632	1,091	24,469
Washington	102,872	63,376	21,113	20,682	42,263	32,614	6,346	3,303	–	39,496
West Virginia	22,371	16,194	6,899	6,781	9,295	6,046	1,608	1,641	132	6,046
Wisconsin	65,795	45,329	14,225	13,992	31,104	22,301	4,988	3,815	–	20,466
Wyoming	8,180	6,375	3,103	3,089	3,272	1,875	249	1,148	153	1,652

– Represents zero. [1] Includes amounts for categories not shown separately. [2] Duplicate intergovernmental transactions are excluded.

Source: U.S. Census Bureau, Annual Survey of State and Local Government Finances, "Datasets & Tables," <www.census.gov/programs-surveys/gov-finances.html>, accessed August 2023.

Table 499. State Government Tax Collections by State: 2023

[In millions of dollars (1,431,860 represents $1,431,860,000,000). Data are for the state fiscal year; see text, this section. Data presented here may differ from data published by state governments; see source for more information]

State	All taxes	Total property taxes	Selective sales and gross receipts		Selective sales tax						License taxes	Selected license taxes			Income taxes			Other taxes	Selected other taxes	
			Total	Total general sales and gross receipts	Total [1]	Alcoholic beverage sales	Insurance premiums	Motor fuels sales	Public utilities	Tobacco products	Total [1]	Corporation	Motor vehicle	Occupation and business n.e.c. [2]	Total	Individual income	Corporation net income	Total [1]	Death and gift	Severance
U.S.	1,431,860	26,043	664,892	460,474	204,418	8,390	32,338	55,264	13,406	17,060	68,847	9,098	33,746	16,309	615,950	472,878	143,072	56,128	8,088	26,666
AL	16,713	554	7,952	4,608	3,345	283	563	965	757	145	625	218	244	71	7,471	5,911	1,560	112	(X)	54
AK	3,271	129	292	(X)	292	42	63	47	5	50	109	(X)	32	16	444	(X)	444	2,296	(X)	2,296
AZ	23,363	1,305	14,863	12,509	2,354	91	811	872	22	256	682	51	341	183	6,323	4,779	1,544	191	–	19
AR	12,759	1,424	6,669	4,980	1,688	79	375	606	(X)	214	434	40	189	135	3,986	3,148	838	246	(X)	98
CA	220,591	3,400	75,400	53,566	21,835	422	3,690	8,653	877	1,634	13,265	83	8,123	4,013	126,316	96,379	29,937	2,210	(Z)	135
CO	18,132	(X)	7,986	4,607	3,379	56	533	708	(X)	351	677	21	385	76	9,123	6,781	2,342	346	–	346
CT	21,895	(X)	8,730	5,548	3,182	73	254	390	255	281	348	37	224	14	12,345	8,845	3,499	472	218	(X)
DE	6,563	(X)	647	(X)	647	32	146	134	52	105	2,651	2,390	64	171	2,997	2,426	571	268	–	(X)
DC	10,338	3,050	2,374	1,919	455	7	161	22	161	9	240	47	40	88	4,175	3,048	1,126	500	95	(X)
FL	61,903	(X)	49,658	39,969	9,689	317	1,993	3,094	1,942	1,015	2,286	279	1,536	208	5,522	(X)	5,522	4,436	(X)	28
GA	33,702	832	11,644	8,980	2,663	223	528	1,120	(X)	231	774	59	433	89	20,257	16,633	3,624	196	–	(X)
HI	10,188	(X)	6,256	4,731	1,525	55	211	82	142	78	333	3	242	56	3,448	3,100	348	150	58	(X)
ID	7,385	(X)	3,742	3,065	676	11	139	405	2	42	458	6	239	64	3,176	2,142	1,034	9	(X)	6
IL	62,987	60	26,756	15,500	11,257	315	547	2,603	1,206	785	3,835	367	2,254	894	31,673	21,811	9,862	662	576	(X)
IN	30,323	15	16,509	11,004	5,505	59	268	1,652	–	372	865	13	368	47	12,932	11,702	1,231	2	(Z)	2
IA	12,967	1	6,243	4,655	1,588	20	173	685	73	184	1,133	82	775	171	5,473	4,635	838	117	87	(X)
KS	13,140	882	5,677	4,359	1,318	169	503	466	(Z)	113	441	16	252	90	6,069	4,507	1,562	71	(X)	71
KY	17,217	791	8,350	5,707	2,642	193	212	745	78	342	601	121	259	150	7,248	6,038	1,210	227	71	147
LA	15,498	98	7,940	4,815	3,125	80	1,229	628	12	239	715	444	84	124	5,903	4,679	1,224	842	–	842
ME	6,440	44	3,061	2,264	798	18	133	247	22	136	319	15	126	126	2,933	2,482	451	82	30	(X)
MD	29,694	1,069	12,642	6,822	5,820	37	857	1,301	149	441	1,029	141	518	316	14,192	12,149	2,043	761	272	(X)
MA	41,603	14	12,422	9,354	3,068	99	614	702	(X)	365	1,328	26	455	417	26,480	21,909	4,571	1,360	974	(X)
MI	37,125	2,717	18,115	12,897	5,218	205	471	1,479	44	735	2,277	36	1,542	269	13,573	11,516	2,057	443	(Z)	36
MN	34,473	775	12,947	8,018	4,929	109	753	884	88	558	1,484	17	934	261	18,639	13,979	4,660	628	267	92
MS	10,330	31	6,589	5,023	1,567	42	437	459	2	128	428	10	206	107	3,231	2,412	818	50	–	50
MO	17,356	42	6,974	4,894	2,079	47	516	896	22	92	731	–	335	212	9,589	8,678	911	21	–	(X)
MT	4,710	389	924	(X)	924	49	164	289	39	67	514	7	199	186	2,595	2,287	308	289	282	(X)
NE	7,327	(Z)	3,400	2,747	653	34	88	374	65	50	199	6	127	35	3,699	3,006	693	29	4	(X)
NV	14,177	1,492	10,904	7,958	2,946	47	547	377	50	170	735	89	228	293	(X)	(X)	(X)	1,046	(X)	80
NH	3,547	306	1,039	(X)	1,039	13	154	180	28	218	575	89	118	267	1,421	149	1,272	206	–	(X)
NJ	51,673	5	20,766	14,742	6,024	181	724	420	1,106	497	2,344	708	667	768	27,202	18,506	8,696	1,356	543	(X)
NM	14,267	117	5,303	4,181	1,122	24	389	322	37	81	337	3	228	54	3,091	2,646	444	5,419	(X)	5,295
NY	125,188	(X)	32,914	19,047	13,867	282	2,457	1,276	770	855	1,902	(Z)	1,420	149	83,092	58,776	24,317	7,280	2,185	(X)

See footnotes at end of table.

Table 499. State Government Tax Collections by State: 2023-Continued.

See headnote on page 325.

State	All taxes	Total property taxes	Sales and gross receipts — Total	Total general sales and gross receipts	Selective sales tax — Total [1]	Alcoholic beverage sales	Insurance premiums	Motor fuels sales	Public utilities	Tobacco products	License taxes — Total [1]	Selected license taxes — Corporation	Motor vehicle	Occupation and business n.e.c. [2]	Income taxes — Total	Individual income	Corporation net income	Other taxes — Total [1]	Death and gift	Severance
NC.....	38,941	(X)	17,629	11,908	5,721	591	1,170	2,377	(Z)	286	2,686	995	1,012	414	18,496	16,856	1,640	130	(Z)	2
ND.....	6,049	5	1,825	1,270	554	11	80	186	34	23	231	(X)	120	84	820	495	324	3,168	(X)	3,168
OH.....	38,747	(X)	25,238	16,455	8,784	119	767	2,727	1,206	809	2,137	268	520	971	11,310	11,310	(Z)	61	(Z)	61
OK.....	13,845	(X)	5,494	3,799	1,696	178	333	595	61	409	1,178	55	867	1	5,169	4,394	775	2,004	–	1,835
OR.....	20,878	21	4,087	1338.53	2,748	19	80	620	22	415	1,560	47	1,001	371	14,893	13,274	1,619	316	298	17
PA.....	55,074	46	27,084	15,401	11,683	477	940	3,374	1,184	1,072	2,892	4	1,308	1,252	22,715	17,007	5,709	2,337	1,470	(X)
RI.....	4,739	5	2,585	1,561	1,024	22	154	139	99	133	185	8	37	86	1,874	1,612	263	89	72	(X)
SC.....	15,649	97	7,459	5,124	2,335	222	338	1,017	30	121	757	170	303	183	7,139	5,782	1,357	197	(X)	(X)
SD.....	2,629	(X)	2,226	1,678	548	21	105	192	4	52	348	9	96	159	48	(X)	48	7	(X)	6
TN.....	23,817	(X)	17,645	13,847	3,798	320	1,274	1,273	7	214	2,596	1,650	316	537	3,159	3	3,156	417	(Z)	1
TX.....	86,776	(X)	73,386	53,676	19,710	1,789	4,065	3,832	828	1,218	3,870	273	2,313	665	(X)	(X)	(X)	9,520	(X)	9,520
UT.....	13,490	(X)	5,582	4,552	1,030	19	203	614	66	106	404	(Z)	271	61	7,364	6,497	867	140	(X)	139
VT.....	4,499	1,211	1,492	585	908	12	72	128	11	75	149	3	76	36	1,510	1,211	300	137	19	(X)
VA.....	37,124	50	14,029	7,427	6,601	282	734	1,815	486	246	1,362	81	522	520	21,015	16,645	4,369	670	–	4
WA.....	38,025	4,484	28,128	22,815	5,313	490	847	1,568	839	329	2,095	56	976	437	847	847	(X)	2,471	854	43
WV.....	7,639	8	3,462	1,813	1,648	24	187	432	126	155	189	1	5	15	3,114	2,694	420	867	–	840
WI.....	23,746	97	10,356	7,456	2,900	78	252	1,178	419	540	1,315	32	715	349	11,859	9,191	2,668	118	(Z)	2
WY.....	3,347	477	1,495	1,296	199	2	33	117	4	20	219	25	103	46	(X)	(X)	(X)	1,155	–	1,146

X Not applicable. Z Less than $500,000. – Represents zero. [1] Includes other items not shown separately. [2] N.e.c. means not elsewhere classified.

Source: U.S. Census Bureau, Annual Survey of State Government Tax Collections, "2023 State Government Tax Tables," <www.census.gov/programs-surveys/stc.html>, accessed May 2024.

Table 500. State Governments—Expenditures and Debt by State: 2021

[In millions of dollars (2,965,009 represents $2,965,009,000,000). For fiscal year ending in year shown; see text, this section]

State	Total expenditures	Intergovern-mental	Direct expenditures: Total	Direct general expenditures: Total [1]	Educa-tion	Public welfare	Hospi-tals	Health	High-ways	Police protec-tion	Correc-tions	Parks and recre-ation	Housing and community devel-opment	Sewer-age	Solid waste man-age-ment	Govern-men-tal admin-istra-tion	Inter-est on gen-eral debt	Utility and liquor store	Insur-ance trust	Cash and security holdings	Total debt out-stand-ing
U.S...	2,965,009	661,855	2,303,154	1,768,002	346,228	795,862	106,335	71,201	121,835	18,136	55,281	6,171	12,417	1,477	1,220	71,230	42,563	46,149	489,003	6,585,515	1,208,171
AL...	39,584	10,182	29,402	24,140	7,641	7,961	3,063	497	1,564	201	722	25	37	–	–	755	363	441	4,821	68,406	9,118
AK...	13,058	2,558	10,500	8,481	1,265	2,644	32	301	1,073	143	372	13	141	–	–	728	181	154	1,866	116,522	5,652
AZ..	52,768	10,709	42,059	35,554	9,075	20,732	–	948	1,284	299	1,200	55	102	–	1	674	380	42	6,463	83,130	8,970
AR...	27,505	7,143	20,361	17,031	3,576	7,913	1,396	332	1,589	108	338	63	19	–	9	894	196	–	3,330	53,549	7,869
CA...	468,989	123,803	345,186	248,221	46,958	129,112	17,644	4,128	11,171	2,290	11,222	916	200	518	354	7,907	5,205	3,149	93,815	1,073,554	144,314
CO...	46,259	9,068	37,191	27,438	7,134	10,887	1,444	986	1,574	291	1,042	104	296	4	8	1,606	876	11	9,743	107,928	22,329
CT..	33,383	7,390	25,993	18,689	4,294	3,762	1,668	1,173	1,466	256	879	39	165	–	79	1,496	1,730	850	6,454	63,835	41,965
DE...	12,755	2,274	10,481	9,196	2,264	3,148	76	546	658	158	377	53	126	13	80	604	249	188	1,096	24,976	5,370
FL....	119,948	21,386	98,562	80,093	14,604	31,672	1,655	6,520	8,147	649	2,895	160	327	–	182	2,624	673	262	18,207	308,723	21,437
GA...	70,472	18,560	51,912	37,883	9,419	14,424	1,350	1,593	3,217	470	1,217	158	293	11	53	1,041	564	77	13,952	150,164	14,628
HI...	16,706	207	16,499	13,671	3,617	3,536	504	744	662	63	221	61	200	–	–	692	135	–	2,828	34,855	11,521
ID....	13,291	3,377	9,914	8,170	1,440	3,737	56	220	739	73	328	42	175	–	–	554	141	182	1,562	37,659	3,423
IL....	114,449	27,561	86,888	64,298	8,796	30,925	1,172	1,738	5,540	534	1,696	92	516	–	9	2,107	3,721	22	22,568	212,854	64,743
IN....	50,906	11,196	39,710	35,597	8,155	18,200	155	1,056	2,630	277	718	63	454	3	5	881	956	–	4,112	79,842	21,782
IA....	28,676	6,388	22,288	17,837	3,314	7,570	2,668	128	1,748	118	314	26	251	1	3	642	192	298	4,153	64,743	6,380
KS...	24,460	6,105	18,355	15,401	2,907	5,375	3,290	547	1,126	120	360	42	133	–	–	562	132	–	2,954	34,386	6,706
KY..	42,541	5,661	36,880	30,331	5,649	15,906	2,524	625	1,664	226	574	90	262	–	27	1,040	586	30	6,519	64,191	15,362
LA...	42,692	8,160	34,532	28,524	5,183	14,552	406	806	1,576	264	564	326	58	–	–	875	803	11	5,996	88,734	16,983
ME...	11,860	1,948	9,912	8,170	1,114	4,182	105	272	706	96	159	8	199	–	–	526	183	179	1,563	28,390	5,628
MD...	57,678	11,212	46,466	37,782	6,812	16,753	389	2,172	1,981	706	1,486	145	999	221	23	2,059	1,344	2,096	6,588	99,715	30,652
MA...	84,962	11,541	73,421	53,510	6,984	27,079	738	2,187	2,267	573	1,633	134	1,545	300	1	2,575	2,589	4,299	15,613	133,309	79,692
MI....	89,051	26,336	62,715	47,900	10,384	19,676	5,363	2,098	2,179	520	1,841	160	875	–	6	1,118	1,247	1,181	13,635	143,547	33,622
MN...	59,821	17,289	42,532	32,553	6,647	17,159	276	1,092	1,971	464	556	222	144	165	15	2,060	373	593	9,386	122,641	16,497
MS...	25,256	6,305	18,951	14,719	2,831	6,600	1,548	484	1,036	143	357	35	34	–	–	528	291	508	3,723	49,566	7,465
MO...	40,620	6,940	33,680	27,211	4,253	10,871	2,706	2,467	1,518	217	659	37	254	–	4	901	868	6	6,463	122,493	19,143
MT...	9,241	1,262	7,979	6,442	1,096	2,715	55	269	750	65	237	17	42	–	–	475	106	137	1,399	26,346	2,623
NE...	13,976	3,217	10,759	9,608	2,336	3,630	198	328	926	83	427	60	1	–	5	341	55	–	1,150	34,231	2,578
NV...	22,147	5,479	16,668	10,291	2,598	4,362	321	340	725	109	357	31	13	–	7	531	153	36	6,341	67,550	3,594
NH....	10,828	2,105	8,723	7,024	1,266	2,743	74	203	445	74	137	23	177	34	34	739	292	639	1,060	20,026	7,226
NJ....	98,743	17,538	81,205	56,881	12,405	21,268	2,659	1,998	2,919	903	1,435	137	739	11	4	2,275	2,363	3,874	20,450	154,020	70,953
NM...	27,429	6,233	21,195	17,402	2,754	8,211	1,607	491	883	141	503	64	87	–	–	726	435	3	3,790	82,063	7,435
NY..	240,386	61,955	178,430	118,893	12,927	70,332	6,636	4,008	5,130	902	3,001	662	716	4	28	6,074	4,345	18,229	41,309	540,410	170,355
NC..	74,822	19,029	55,793	46,422	11,375	17,859	2,905	1,109	4,489	615	1,578	235	265	–	11	2,664	640	75	9,295	167,196	15,074

See footnotes at end of table.

Table 500. State Governments—Expenditures and Debt by State: 2021-Continued.
See headnote on page 327.

State	Total expenditures	Inter-govern-mental	Direct expenditures Total	Direct general expenditures Total[1]	Educa-tion	Public welfare	Hospi-tals	Health	High-ways	Police protec-tion	Correc-tions	Parks and recre-ation	Hous-ing and com-munity devel-opment	Sewer-age	Solid waste man-age-ment	Govern-mental admin-istra-tion	Inter-est on gen-eral debt	Utility and liquor store	Insur-ance trust	Cash and security holdings	Total debt out-stand-ing
ND..	9,218	2,382	6,836	5,830	1,389	1,695	82	282	700	45	123	28	27	–	3	329	114	43	964	41,514	2,683
OH..	103,870	22,420	81,449	59,111	9,686	32,409	5,018	1,661	3,248	485	1,713	128	61	–	23	1,942	1,310	1,367	20,971	307,076	34,850
OK..	29,938	5,676	24,262	19,187	4,689	7,443	279	1,145	2,240	209	611	79	186	–	4	985	217	638	4,437	65,880	8,152
OR..	49,916	8,035	41,882	32,390	5,840	14,056	2,812	1,257	1,453	266	904	83	265	5	11	2,057	338	545	8,947	136,405	14,425
PA..	125,185	25,631	99,555	77,894	12,957	36,595	5,699	2,867	7,809	1,737	2,161	416	158	14	41	3,537	1,640	2,066	19,595	175,059	53,217
RI...	11,882	1,614	10,268	8,315	1,072	3,453	185	676	523	96	226	16	93	58	44	651	422	125	1,828	21,301	9,438
SC..	39,703	7,270	32,434	25,771	6,573	8,912	2,856	1,633	1,680	176	520	130	199	–	–	828	246	1,572	5,090	65,035	12,857
SD..	7,186	1,337	5,849	4,835	820	1,730	40	155	724	57	141	42	59	1	–	412	123	19	995	21,755	3,902
TN..	42,283	10,169	32,115	27,885	5,403	13,427	408	1,814	1,787	251	740	96	378	1	30	1,352	262	1	4,229	91,771	6,919
TX..	200,493	37,204	163,289	128,729	29,616	50,281	9,845	9,299	12,958	1,265	3,669	308	157	101	71	3,077	1,793	99	34,460	555,722	52,664
UT..	27,773	5,145	22,627	19,872	6,234	5,270	2,582	614	1,732	157	374	90	205	–	8	1,322	199	335	2,420	47,800	7,031
VT..	10,193	2,102	8,091	5,779	1,124	2,064	23	444	411	160	149	40	167	2	4	244	106	86	2,227	10,345	3,426
VA..	70,804	14,452	56,352	47,111	10,398	17,811	4,814	1,419	4,584	540	1,596	147	499	1	3	2,170	1,101	1,382	7,859	153,698	31,042
WA..	75,384	20,779	54,604	42,441	10,085	15,313	4,185	3,804	2,410	353	1,273	161	18	–	15	1,012	1,431	38	12,126	189,068	30,207
WV..	17,957	3,484	14,472	12,403	2,298	5,440	194	307	1,650	98	416	53	42	4	10	647	308	114	1,954	29,515	13,369
WI..	50,472	12,535	37,937	30,277	5,904	13,581	2,625	854	2,028	45	1,123	28	45	3	–	1,075	563	19	7,641	174,138	21,978
WY..	7,495	1,505	5,990	4,806	1,065	887	3	563	545	44	138	24	12	–	5	315	25	129	1,055	39,877	924

– Represents or rounds to zero. [1] Includes other direct general expenditures not shown separately.

Source: U.S. Census Bureau, Annual Survey of State and Local Government Finances, "Datasets & Tables," <www.census.gov/programs-surveys/gov-finances.html>, accessed August 2023.

Table 501. Local Governments—Revenue by State: 2021

[In millions of dollars (2,395,165 represents $2,395,165,000,000). For fiscal year ending in year shown; see text, this section. Minus sign (-) indicates decrease]

State	Total revenue	General revenue, total	Inter-govern-mental revenue	General revenue from own sources: Total	Taxes: Total[1]	Taxes: Property	Taxes: Sales and gross receipt	Taxes: Indi-vidual income	Current charges and miscellaneous general revenue: Total	Current charges and miscellaneous general revenue: Total[1]	Current charges: Educa-tion	Current charges: Hospi-tals	Current charges: Sewer-age	Miscellaneous general revenue: Total[1]	Miscellaneous general revenue: Interest earn-ings	Miscellaneous general revenue: Special assess-ment	Utility rev-enue	Liquor store rev-enue	Insur-ance trust rev-enue
U.S...	2,395,165	2,025,175	753,102	1,272,072	840,713	609,872	140,814	41,521	431,360	326,051	15,853	109,503	66,220	105,309	20,456	12,320	166,066	1,804	202,120
AL....	27,851	24,196	9,121	15,076	7,145	2,861	3,479	128	7,931	6,796	199	4,956	654	1,134	397	36	3,353	–	302
AK....	7,246	6,811	2,491	4,321	2,022	1,587	400	–	2,299	990	15	516	120	1,308	130	7	384	9	43
AZ...	38,399	31,655	12,616	19,038	12,893	7,839	4,491	–	6,146	3,937	280	688	1,038	2,209	535	63	5,615	–	1,129
AR...	11,907	10,853	6,102	4,751	2,980	1,216	1,718	–	1,771	1,194	75	160	364	577	195	5	1,012	–	42
CA...	464,050	354,958	161,718	193,240	112,595	78,925	23,034	–	80,645	62,800	1,618	18,384	10,049	17,844	2,529	3,050	34,884	–	74,208
CO...	42,062	38,011	10,795	27,217	18,397	12,035	5,764	–	8,820	6,314	285	1,690	1,271	2,506	516	388	3,407	–	644
CT...	23,681	20,031	6,421	13,609	12,080	11,871	–	–	1,530	1,120	62	–	506	410	65	20	778	–	2,872
DE...	4,439	3,761	1,798	1,964	1,353	1,111	18	–	610	472	8	–	200	138	31	36	444	–	234
DC...	19,736	16,992	6,451	10,541	8,894	3,008	1,591	2,643	1,647	801	34	111	406	846	20	5	391	–	2,354
FL...	131,460	115,607	32,850	82,757	46,313	35,443	8,103	–	36,444	25,446	1,091	8,605	4,033	10,998	1,648	3,845	10,114	–	5,740
GA...	60,951	53,156	17,339	35,816	21,533	14,349	6,572	–	14,284	11,702	317	5,787	2,430	2,582	501	105	4,592	–	3,203
HI...	5,640	5,227	1,026	4,201	3,178	2,321	540	–	1,023	764	–	–	529	260	139	2	413	–	–
ID...	8,058	7,788	3,388	4,400	2,254	2,109	75	–	2,146	1,834	84	804	313	312	75	75	268	–	2
IL.....	96,484	81,115	30,730	50,386	37,718	31,192	5,718	–	12,668	8,755	901	1,332	1,521	3,913	532	846	5,320	–	10,049
IN....	36,687	33,674	13,180	20,494	9,882	8,228	185	1,205	10,612	9,097	191	5,921	2,043	1,515	349	10	2,787	–	226
IA....	20,921	19,605	7,330	12,275	7,138	6,191	747	104	5,137	4,262	403	2,210	728	875	191	20	1,305	–	11
KS....	17,677	15,682	6,513	9,169	5,847	4,444	1,225	1	3,322	2,382	304	890	543	939	146	109	1,686	–	309
KY....	17,958	15,858	6,256	9,602	6,449	3,657	759	1,674	3,153	2,612	92	832	786	542	90	35	1,834	–	265
LA....	24,448	22,841	7,139	15,702	10,116	4,487	5,412	–	5,586	4,541	160	2,489	561	1,045	140	47	1,173	–	434
ME...	7,029	6,873	2,140	4,733	3,900	3,859	8	–	833	657	13	67	225	175	40	10	156	–	–
MD...	43,178	36,237	11,850	24,387	19,497	10,310	841	7,043	4,891	3,765	364	69	1,332	1,126	88	121	1,131	315	5,494
MA...	45,975	38,984	13,985	24,999	20,328	19,559	287	–	4,671	3,444	318	428	1,310	1,227	160	11	3,037	–	3,955
MI....	58,483	51,577	25,085	26,492	15,560	14,284	240	649	10,932	8,431	880	788	2,409	2,500	417	230	3,474	–	3,431
MN...	39,354	35,828	16,599	19,229	10,797	9,869	604	–	8,432	6,013	271	2,077	1,010	2,419	661	362	2,736	322	468
MS...	14,689	13,795	5,765	8,030	3,746	3,527	117	–	4,283	3,783	297	2,624	312	500	136	9	894	–	–
MO...	33,879	29,257	8,868	20,388	13,521	8,189	4,129	487	6,867	5,153	379	2,158	1,260	1,714	475	95	2,448	–	2,174
MT...	5,009	4,807	2,051	2,756	1,765	1,701	23	–	991	681	43	82	142	311	61	99	200	–	2
NE...	16,504	11,626	3,220	8,406	5,514	4,264	582	–	2,892	2,153	172	570	386	738	172	92	4,268	–	611
NV...	20,162	18,527	8,566	9,961	5,648	3,436	1,743	–	4,313	3,204	7	940	611	1,109	221	136	1,466	–	170
NH...	7,149	6,971	2,018	4,954	4,291	4,187	8	–	662	526	11	–	183	137	28	2	133	–	45
NJ...	55,980	54,429	15,110	39,318	33,289	32,788	93	–	6,029	4,279	790	308	1,704	1,750	253	8	1,511	–	40
NM...	10,723	10,008	5,191	4,817	3,483	1,888	1,541	–	1,333	1,043	83	206	234	290	88	13	715	–	–
NY..	268,805	206,154	63,236	142,919	111,647	66,385	18,988	15,625	31,272	21,088	904	6,454	2,923	10,184	1,461	150	5,432	–	57,218

See footnotes at end of table.

State	Total revenue	General revenue, total	Intergovernmental revenue	Taxes Total¹	Property	Sales and gross receipt	Individual income	General revenue from own sources Total	Current charges Total¹	Education	Hospitals	Sewerage	Miscellaneous general revenue Total¹	Interest earnings	Special assessment	Utility revenue	Liquor store revenue	Insurance trust revenue
NC..	60,263	54,681	20,002	34,680	11,863	4,437	–	17,733	15,413	291	11,200	1,693	2,320	270	26	4,246	1,143	193
ND..	5,400	5,010	2,408	2,603	1,215	301	–	1,056	459	37	–	84	597	130	175	305	–	84
OH..	66,259	62,746	21,779	40,966	18,256	2,756	5,954	13,024	8,124	950	1,600	2,490	4,900	1,204	401	3,351	–	162
OK..	17,675	15,747	5,282	10,466	3,662	2,705	–	3,942	3,027	197	1,195	558	915	149	32	1,580	–	348
OR..	28,146	25,535	10,753	14,782	7,695	727	–	4,978	3,782	337	422	1,338	1,197	348	96	2,314	–	297
PA..	79,270	72,434	30,023	42,411	21,796	1,389	6,007	10,592	7,970	531	31	3,228	2,622	959	68	2,962	–	3,874
RI..	5,879	5,100	1,734	3,366	2,697	24	–	594	449	36	–	142	145	29	1	229	–	549
SC..	27,115	25,124	7,476	17,648	7,088	1,695	–	8,015	6,833	85	4,945	850	1,182	166	78	1,972	–	19
SD..	4,628	4,118	1,383	2,735	1,488	446	–	713	578	77	103	122	135	26	20	380	14	115
TN..	40,909	28,855	9,954	18,901	6,456	2,798	–	9,200	7,104	326	3,927	1,198	2,096	883	140	8,614	–	3,439
TX..	185,821	159,906	48,196	111,709	65,553	11,500	–	33,412	25,361	1,593	8,147	5,060	8,051	2,240	663	17,712	–	8,204
UT..	18,566	16,415	5,918	10,497	4,104	1,917	–	4,256	3,115	123	537	584	1,141	122	71	2,114	–	36
VT..	3,571	3,249	2,184	1,065	732	24	–	298	223	9	–	86	74	13	2	227	–	95
VA..	54,851	45,527	17,708	27,819	16,524	3,065	–	6,582	5,073	77	342	1,851	1,509	446	68	2,024	–	7,300
WA..	64,578	55,841	22,552	33,289	10,361	7,150	–	14,329	11,878	81	3,112	3,201	2,451	624	348	7,966	–	771
WV..	6,676	6,181	2,486	3,694	1,914	157	–	1,354	1,131	24	402	272	223	27	13	314	–	181
WI..	33,427	30,494	14,139	16,355	10,390	563	–	5,107	3,799	365	85	1,250	1,309	250	66	2,156	–	777
WY..	5,556	5,319	2,180	3,138	956	122	–	1,998	1,691	63	1,309	75	307	82	10	237	–	–

– Represents or rounds to zero. ¹ Includes corporation income, not shown separately.

Source: U.S. Census Bureau, Annual Survey of State and Local Government Finances, "Datasets & Tables," <www.census.gov/programs-surveys/gov-finances.html>, accessed August 2023.

Table 502. Local Governments—Expenditures and Debt by State: 2021

[In millions of dollars (2,219,366 represents $2,219,366,000,000). For fiscal year ending in year shown; see text, this section]

State	Total expenditures [1]	Total [1]	Direct general expenditures Total [1]	Education	Public welfare	Hospitals	Health	Highways	Police protection	Corrections	Parks and recreation	Housing and community development	Sewerage	Solid waste management	Governmental administration	Interest on general debt	Utility expenditures	Insurance trust expenditures	Debt outstanding
U.S....	2,219,366	2,202,507	1,913,231	796,910	66,393	130,537	69,077	84,601	116,840	31,625	41,383	52,589	66,510	28,559	97,364	70,133	220,180	67,559	2,128,499
AL....	26,692	26,672	23,158	8,879	61	5,079	519	989	1,250	205	472	575	487	384	1,121	803	3,264	250	25,473
AK....	5,902	5,901	5,263	1,986	10	481	290	231	262	7	114	170	140	134	314	91	597	34	3,010
AZ....	34,904	34,392	27,765	11,355	199	1,047	498	1,656	2,597	678	732	573	762	506	2,026	946	6,125	502	30,993
AR....	11,423	11,394	10,370	5,698	11	182	97	607	623	200	210	236	344	243	518	368	994	30	12,990
CA....	395,932	395,303	326,589	112,915	22,355	18,843	27,562	12,596	22,608	6,774	6,193	10,345	10,068	3,717	15,285	12,274	51,818	16,896	396,927
CO....	42,098	42,061	37,041	12,991	1,009	2,171	515	2,029	2,148	449	1,886	1,292	1,402	172	2,555	1,768	4,540	480	47,424
CT....	21,041	21,039	19,198	10,345	85	–	123	692	1,051	–	225	628	574	201	615	409	799	1,042	11,776
DE....	3,998	3,997	3,502	2,311	2	–	42	146	236	–	37	93	145	38	157	69	394	102	3,150
DC....	22,552	22,552	16,761	3,480	4,711	303	1,335	671	669	276	346	636	404	172	1,119	663	3,755	2,037	19,908
FL....	127,214	126,911	112,350	36,026	1,594	10,291	2,162	3,983	9,939	2,249	3,941	2,545	4,999	2,995	6,370	2,970	11,580	2,980	114,395
GA. . .	55,932	55,914	48,108	22,820	162	4,801	1,063	1,942	2,753	903	829	818	1,511	836	3,421	971	6,601	1,205	47,553
HI....	5,381	5,381	4,138	–	98	–	42	312	516	–	253	222	540	281	597	268	1,243	–	8,183
ID....	7,448	7,446	7,192	2,810	29	895	135	560	462	165	177	104	260	212	486	115	253	2	2,603
IL....	90,840	90,840	75,120	33,458	674	3,848	1,193	3,446	5,437	692	2,454	2,051	1,735	520	4,642	3,751	8,862	6,858	100,722
IN....	34,113	34,085	31,236	12,087	23	5,894	446	1,197	1,432	528	468	687	1,566	302	1,716	921	2,740	108	29,716
IA....	20,258	20,239	18,861	8,532	108	2,213	386	1,400	829	179	392	177	831	362	635	448	1,371	7	15,923
KS....	17,697	17,693	16,015	8,214	33	993	365	887	1,027	212	321	107	517	180	1,021	480	1,537	140	21,007
KY....	17,829	17,824	15,651	7,178	28	686	461	596	821	330	267	195	1,455	212	690	813	2,089	83	38,841
LA....	21,949	21,890	20,243	8,753	76	2,632	273	792	1,332	342	476	526	572	381	1,286	337	1,390	256	13,599
ME....	6,039	6,037	5,865	3,127	56	60	55	414	257	105	86	154	277	123	258	116	172	–	3,767
MD....	38,318	38,317	34,548	16,636	141	55	910	1,035	2,442	497	1,051	1,354	1,428	770	1,597	1,129	1,792	1,712	32,702
MA....	43,872	43,405	37,778	19,134	78	998	181	1,140	1,891	–	372	2,014	1,176	445	1,353	626	3,013	2,614	21,860
MI....	55,749	55,410	49,964	21,809	1,459	890	2,650	3,676	2,399	600	839	417	3,280	556	2,872	1,509	3,513	1,933	46,844
MN....	39,450	39,350	36,039	14,380	1,762	1,972	760	3,694	2,107	611	1,154	1,067	1,034	483	1,477	1,207	2,816	202	40,548
MS....	14,399	14,399	13,513	6,001	27	2,714	88	831	648	200	225	321	278	221	735	241	887	–	7,242
MO....	31,702	31,701	28,111	12,275	160	2,409	693	1,359	1,876	229	663	583	1,320	164	1,374	906	2,702	887	30,505
MT. ..	4,823	4,823	4,599	2,265	53	96	189	260	309	48	87	70	144	105	274	101	223	1	3,157
NE....	16,618	16,605	11,567	5,835	154	598	65	958	473	169	254	269	372	143	461	324	4,594	445	13,476
NV....	17,290	17,276	15,757	5,217	485	962	400	1,379	1,356	508	647	372	583	31	967	812	1,494	25	24,626
NH...	6,377	6,332	6,126	3,302	311	–	17	350	412	78	72	119	187	110	371	105	179	27	2,572
NJ....	48,705	48,635	47,523	27,579	939	296	354	1,421	3,313	582	508	745	1,688	1,064	1,946	990	1,086	26	28,473
NM...	9,862	9,845	9,067	4,557	157	256	121	381	611	304	236	128	245	244	547	191	777	–	7,993
NY....	238,946	229,074	196,817	79,079	14,048	13,668	4,391	6,964	9,808	3,096	2,475	7,401	4,213	3,869	5,835	10,526	16,282	15,975	213,198

See footnotes at end of table.

Table 502. Local Governments—Expenditures and Debt by State: 2021-Continued.

See headnote on page 331.

State	Total expenditures [1]	Direct expenditures Total [1]	Direct general expenditures Total [1]	Education	Public welfare	Hospitals	Health	Highways	Police protection	Corrections	Parks and recreation	Housing and community development	Sewerage	Solid waste management	Governmental administration	Interest on general debt	Utility expenditures	Insurance trust expenditures	Debt outstanding
NC. ..	57,428	57,333	51,777	18,734	1,624	10,948	3,504	776	3,182	657	1,033	1,749	1,227	905	1,960	1,336	4,540	59	32,039
ND. ..	5,242	5,213	4,819	2,035	71	–	91	654	230	103	238	71	133	87	249	200	329	64	6,703
OH. ..	66,282	65,752	61,755	28,047	2,602	2,300	2,076	2,768	3,435	507	1,509	2,210	2,594	600	3,898	2,301	3,827	171	59,453
OK. ..	16,385	16,683	14,974	7,026	32	1,333	421	819	970	130	466	466	431	326	687	298	1,584	125	11,090
OR. ..	28,157	28,149	25,057	11,056	300	452	985	1,230	1,384	699	665	902	1,146	179	1,430	1,046	2,862	229	28,962
PA....	77,283	77,258	69,626	34,131	4,484	5	3,654	2,867	3,247	1,619	797	2,357	2,698	944	4,531	2,623	4,905	2,727	75,329
RI.....	5,610	5,610	4,791	2,775	9	–	21	156	398	–	50	173	112	56	191	95	214	605	2,769
SC....	26,061	26,008	24,015	10,327	32	5,188	269	528	1,236	282	517	368	860	510	1,402	687	1,984	9	25,174
SD....	4,249	4,247	3,819	1,874	17	97	34	489	188	90	125	55	124	62	207	74	379	35	2,779
TN....	37,801	37,800	28,295	10,688	286	3,973	509	944	2,053	495	487	760	1,029	467	1,603	1,361	8,549	956	45,052
TX....	181,677	178,536	154,428	71,532	1,190	14,658	3,788	6,528	8,564	2,630	3,111	2,800	5,104	1,716	8,230	8,625	20,908	3,201	272,298
UT....	18,022	18,015	15,319	6,411	202	529	732	799	733	240	556	356	525	229	873	336	2,677	20	15,089
VT....	3,422	3,421	3,071	1,905	3	–	11	325	122	–	44	67	98	38	135	39	274	77	1,297
VA....	48,329	48,301	43,799	19,132	1,869	358	1,643	2,310	2,372	1,422	1,012	999	1,752	799	2,585	1,212	3,222	1,280	36,626
WA. ..	62,288	62,031	50,167	20,506	439	3,518	1,679	2,525	2,335	880	1,313	1,732	2,406	838	2,246	1,659	11,492	371	60,089
WV. ..	6,461	6,447	6,011	3,379	11	394	55	98	371	56	138	172	277	56	505	76	335	100	3,670
WI....	33,631	33,575	30,526	14,145	2,094	120	1,153	1,993	1,947	523	732	347	1,373	488	1,708	886	2,379	670	27,835
WY....	5,386	5,386	5,147	2,170	27	1,334	72	197	178	74	126	8	83	83	284	26	240	–	1,093

– Represents or rounds to zero. [1] Includes other items not shown separately.

Source: U.S. Census Bureau, Annual Survey of State and Local Government Finances, "Datasets & Tables," <www.census.gov/programs-surveys/gov-finances.html>, accessed August 2023.

Table 503. State and Local Government—Employer Costs Per Hour Worked: 2024

[In dollars. As of March. Based on a sample; see source for details]

Occupation and industry	Total compensation	Wages and salaries	Benefits cost					
			Total	Paid leave	Supplemental pay	Insurance	Retirement and savings	Legally required benefits
Total workers	**61.27**	**37.90**	**23.37**	**4.46**	**0.61**	**6.90**	**8.14**	**3.26**
OCCUPATIONAL GROUP								
Management, professional, and related	72.72	46.45	26.27	4.91	0.47	7.51	9.76	3.63
Professional and related	70.54	45.34	25.20	4.35	0.45	7.48	9.42	3.49
Teachers [1]	79.38	52.29	27.09	3.71	0.31	8.01	11.41	3.66
Primary, secondary, and special education school teachers	78.69	51.08	27.61	3.38	0.28	8.45	12.07	3.43
Sales and office	42.83	24.68	18.15	3.73	0.39	6.58	4.95	2.51
Office and administrative support	43.02	24.73	18.29	3.74	0.39	6.66	4.98	2.51
Service	46.18	26.46	19.72	3.84	1.00	5.48	6.64	2.76
INDUSTRY GROUP								
Education and health services	63.56	40.57	22.99	4.00	0.42	7.05	8.36	3.16
Educational services	64.94	41.66	23.29	3.78	0.30	7.14	8.92	3.14
Elementary and secondary schools	62.93	40.41	22.52	3.14	0.26	7.12	9.04	2.97
Junior colleges, colleges, and universities	71.21	45.54	25.67	5.79	0.40	7.19	8.63	3.66
Health care and social assistance	55.22	34.02	21.20	5.29	1.14	6.52	4.98	3.27
Hospitals	57.82	36.38	21.44	5.50	1.28	6.46	4.80	3.40
Public administration	59.90	34.65	25.25	5.51	0.93	6.87	8.44	3.51

[1] Includes postsecondary teachers; primary, secondary, and special education teachers; and other teachers and instructors.

Source: U.S. Bureau of Labor Statistics, National Compensation Survey, *Employer Costs for Employee Compensation–March 2024*, USDL-24-1172, June 2024. See also <www.bls.gov/ecec/home.htm>.

Table 504. State and Local Government—Full-Time Employment and Salary by Sex and Race/Ethnicity: 1980 to 2023

[2,350 represents 2,350,000. As of June 30. Excludes school systems and educational institutions. Based on reports from state governments (42 in 1980; 49 in 1984 through 1987; and 50 from 1989 and thereafter) and a sample of county, municipal, township, and special district jurisdictions. Beginning 1993, only for state and local governments with 100 or more employees. For definition of median, see Guide to Tabular Presentation]

Year and occupation	Employment (1,000)						Median annual salary ($1,000)				
				Minority						Minority	
	Male	Female	White [1]	Total [2]	Black [1]	Hispanic [3]	Male	Female	White [1]	Black [1]	Hispanic [3]
1980	2,350	1,637	3,146	842	619	163	15.2	11.4	13.8	11.5	12.3
1985	2,789	1,952	3,563	1,179	835	248	22.3	17.3	20.6	17.5	19.2
1989	3,030	2,227	3,863	1,394	961	308	26.1	20.6	24.1	20.7	22.7
1990	3,071	2,302	3,918	1,456	994	327	27.3	21.8	25.2	22.0	23.8
1991	3,110	2,349	3,965	1,494	1,011	340	28.4	22.7	26.4	22.7	24.5
1993	2,820	2,204	3,588	1,436	948	341	30.6	24.3	28.5	24.2	26.8
1995	2,960	2,355	3,781	1,534	993	379	33.5	27.0	31.4	26.8	28.6
1997	2,898	2,307	3,676	1,529	973	392	34.6	27.9	32.2	27.4	29.5
1999	2,939	2,393	3,723	1,609	1,012	417	37.0	29.9	34.8	29.6	31.2
2001	3,080	2,554	3,888	1,746	1,077	471	39.8	32.1	37.5	31.5	33.8
2003	3,134	2,610	3,919	1,826	1,097	508	42.2	34.7	40.0	33.6	36.6
2005	3,185	2,644	3,973	1,856	1,100	532	44.1	36.4	41.5	35.3	38.9
2007	3,383	2,823	4,156	2,051	1,138	661	(NA)	(NA)	44.8	38.2	41.0
2009	3,239	2,742	3,976	2,004	1,145	601	50.3	41.5	47.6	40.3	44.8
2011	2,897	2,439	3,525	1,811	1,001	562	51.8	43.1	49.1	41.7	47.0
2013	3,055	2,568	3,671	1,952	1,057	634	52.5	43.8	49.9	42.0	46.8
2015	2,969	2,492	3,536	1,926	1,011	634	54.9	46.5	52.2	44.1	49.8
2017	3,037	2,536	3,512	2,062	1,025	704	(NA)	(NA)	54.0	46.2	52.1
2019	2,976	2,564	3,416	2,124	1,011	738	(NA)	(NA)	57.1	48.8	54.5
2021	2,842	2,487	3,252	2,077	953	719	(NA)	(NA)	60.6	52.2	58.8
2023, total	**3,038**	**2,642**	**3,377**	**2,303**	**1,019**	**819**	**(NA)**	**(NA)**	**66.4**	**56.2**	**64.3**
Officials/administrators	232	226	312	146	57	46	(NA)	(NA)	73.6	73.2	73.6
Professionals	689	1,012	1,043	657	278	191	(NA)	(NA)	71.6	67.6	71.6
Technicians	251	182	262	171	70	66	(NA)	(NA)	62.0	52.3	60.4
Protective service	897	234	712	419	182	178	(NA)	(NA)	69.8	58.6	71.2
Paraprofessionals	94	244	167	170	90	56	(NA)	(NA)	50.1	44.8	50.7
Administrative support	128	606	404	331	136	136	(NA)	(NA)	48.1	46.6	50.0
Skilled craft	367	19	251	136	56	56	(NA)	(NA)	61.0	57.4	64.9
Service/maintenance	379	119	226	273	151	90	(NA)	(NA)	49.8	50.2	51.1

NA Not available. [1] Non-Hispanic. [2] Includes other minority groups, not shown separately. [3] Persons of Hispanic origin may be of any race.

Source: U.S. Equal Employment Opportunity Commission, "Job Patterns for Minorities and Women in State and Local Government," <www.eeoc.gov/data/job-patterns-minorities-and-women-state-and-local-government-eeo-4>, accessed July 2024.

Table 505. State and Local Government Full-Time Equivalent Employment by Selected Function and State: 2023

[In thousands (1,982.0 represents 1,982,000). For March. Data for 2023 are preliminary and subject to sampling error; see Appendix III and source]

State	Total State	Total Local	Elem./sec. State	Elem./sec. Local	Higher ed. State	Higher ed. Local	Public welfare State	Public welfare Local	Health State	Health Local	Hospitals State	Hospitals Local	Highways State	Highways Local	Police State	Police Local	Fire State	Fire Local	Corrections State	Corrections Local	Parks State	Parks Local
U.S.	1,982.0	7,216.4	40.4	6,901.9	1,864.3	314.5	243.6	265.9	200.0	270.6	436.1	609.6	204.2	279.1	104.8	844.2	(X)	391.6	388.0	250.7	34.5	249.3
AL	48.7	100.2	–	100.2	45.7	–	3.9	0.9	6.4	6.4	15.1	23.0	4.2	6.0	1.5	13.2	(X)	6.6	3.9	3.3	0.5	4.2
AK	7.9	16.3	3.1	16.2	4.4	–	1.6	0.1	0.8	0.4	0.3	0.8	2.2	0.6	0.7	1.3	(X)	0.9	2.2	(Z)	0.1	0.7
AZ	41.1	121.7	–	110.7	38.7	0.1	7.0	1.4	2.7	3.0	0.6	3.7	2.5	3.9	2.0	18.0	(X)	10.4	8.1	4.6	0.3	5.2
AR	29.3	68.3	–	68.3	28.2	11.0	3.9	0.1	3.0	3.7	7.1	1.0	3.7	3.7	1.4	8.0	(X)	3.4	4.6	2.4	1.2	1.7
CA	187.6	746.8	–	677.5	183.4	69.4	6.0	80.1	16.2	59.1	69.7	73.7	21.2	22.8	10.5	97.0	(X)	36.7	56.9	31.5	3.9	33.0
CO	62.2	111.8	–	110.4	61.3	1.4	2.8	8.2	2.0	6.0	3.7	8.0	3.0	5.3	1.4	15.3	(X)	8.7	6.8	4.4	1.2	9.0
CT	20.8	93.0	–	93.0	18.6	–	4.2	1.4	4.4	1.1	4.0	–	3.0	3.3	1.6	7.9	(X)	4.3	5.5	–	–	2.0
DE	9.4	20.1	–	18.6	9.0	–	1.6	(Z)	2.0	0.3	0.7	–	1.4	0.4	1.1	1.6	(X)	2.0	2.6	1.4	0.4	0.3
DC	(X)	11.1	(X)	9.0	(X)	0.8	(X)	2.4	(X)	2.2	(X)	–	(X)	2.3	(X)	4.3	(X)	–	(X)	1.4	(X)	1.0
FL	73.0	378.0	–	351.7	70.5	26.3	8.6	4.5	16.6	6.0	3.8	61.5	5.8	12.1	4.2	61.1	(X)	34.2	21.0	16.2	1.3	19.4
GA	70.7	247.3	–	247.3	66.5	–	6.2	1.3	3.8	7.9	7.3	23.6	3.9	7.3	2.9	25.8	(X)	15.1	11.1	9.4	1.3	6.6
HI	37.0	17.0	25.9	–	10.8	–	1.2	0.1	2.2	0.3	2.9	–	0.7	0.9	0.6	4.1	(X)	2.2	2.4	–	0.2	2.1
ID	9.4	37.8	–	35.9	9.0	1.9	1.9	0.1	1.8	1.0	0.6	4.8	1.4	2.2	0.6	4.1	(X)	1.8	2.3	1.7	0.2	1.2
IL	57.5	314.5	–	293.6	55.3	20.8	10.0	3.7	1.8	6.1	11.1	11.9	6.2	11.5	3.1	36.7	(X)	17.6	12.1	10.5	0.6	16.6
IN	57.4	133.8	–	133.3	56.4	–	6.1	0.7	1.8	3.3	1.6	21.3	3.6	5.9	1.7	14.5	(X)	8.5	5.5	6.6	0.1	3.8
IA	24.0	90.9	–	84.0	23.0	6.9	3.0	1.0	0.4	2.0	9.4	13.7	2.3	5.5	0.9	6.5	(X)	2.3	2.7	1.8	0.6	2.3
KS	24.6	92.6	–	85.3	24.0	7.3	2.5	0.6	1.5	3.2	12.3	8.3	2.4	4.4	1.0	8.2	(X)	3.7	2.8	2.5	0.8	2.8
KY	36.4	107.5	(Z)	107.5	34.1	–	6.3	0.3	3.7	4.7	7.8	3.2	4.0	3.0	2.1	8.2	(X)	4.8	3.7	3.8	1.0	2.3
LA	35.0	94.7	0.1	94.7	32.5	–	5.6	0.9	3.8	1.4	10.3	16.7	4.1	4.5	1.7	15.7	(X)	5.2	5.4	6.2	0.8	3.4
ME	7.2	36.3	–	36.3	6.8	–	2.1	0.2	1.0	1.0	0.5	0.5	2.1	1.8	0.3	2.6	(X)	2.0	1.1	0.6	0.3	0.8
MD	43.9	147.1	–	136.4	42.0	10.8	5.7	2.6	7.6	5.5	3.2	0.4	4.2	4.7	2.3	16.3	(X)	7.8	9.8	3.2	0.5	7.3
MA	35.6	168.3	2.4	168.2	32.0	0.2	8.2	2.4	9.3	3.1	3.8	3.8	3.0	5.8	3.6	18.1	(X)	14.1	10.8	–	0.9	2.8
MI	75.5	174.1	–	162.9	74.9	11.1	10.6	3.6	7.9	9.9	19.3	5.7	2.7	7.9	2.9	18.6	(X)	7.7	10.3	–	0.2	3.8
MN	39.2	130.7	–	130.7	37.5	–	3.0	12.4	2.9	3.9	5.2	3.7	5.0	6.8	1.1	12.2	(X)	3.4	4.2	5.0	0.6	4.4
MS	19.2	74.7	–	74.9	17.5	6.5	4.0	0.3	2.6	0.3	11.4	19.3	2.6	4.2	1.1	8.0	(X)	3.6	2.1	5.4	0.4	1.4
MO	29.8	141.4	0.6	136.3	27.6	5.2	6.0	2.5	3.0	4.1	10.7	11.9	4.6	6.2	2.3	15.9	(X)	8.2	9.1	3.2	0.5	4.9
MT	9.1	23.1	0.4	22.9	8.6	0.2	1.4	0.4	0.7	1.3	0.6	0.6	2.0	1.3	0.5	2.3	(X)	0.8	1.1	0.8	0.2	0.6
NE	19.6	55.4	–	51.6	19.0	3.8	2.4	0.9	1.7	1.3	1.5	4.3	2.0	3.1	0.7	4.3	(X)	1.6	3.2	2.7	0.3	1.1
NV	11.0	46.5	–	46.5	10.7	–	3.0	1.7	0.8	0.3	0.8	5.6	2.0	1.0	0.7	8.0	(X)	3.0	2.6	0.7	0.3	3.0
NH	6.9	33.0	–	33.0	6.6	–	2.0	2.0	3.4	0.7	0.6	–	1.4	1.5	0.5	3.4	(X)	2.2	0.9	–	0.3	0.6
NJ	46.9	228.5	–	218.2	40.2	10.2	8.5	7.6	2.0	13.8	12.5	1.1	5.7	8.3	4.7	31.1	(X)	8.0	6.7	5.3	0.9	5.7
NM	18.4	47.7	4.4	44.6	17.4	3.1	1.7	0.5	1.7	17.5	8.2	1.1	2.1	1.5	0.6	5.3	(X)	2.9	3.3	1.8	0.7	2.6
NY	60.8	510.9	–	490.6	56.2	20.3	4.2	38.0	8.7	10.6	43.7	53.3	9.4	25.7	6.0	77.6	(X)	25.8	27.9	21.4	3.2	13.4
NC	66.6	221.2	–	201.0	63.9	20.2	4.2	16.7	1.8	12.5	21.9	49.2	7.7	3.6	6.0	26.0	(X)	10.6	13.0	5.8	1.0	6.6
ND	8.2	19.7	–	19.7	7.9	–	0.9	0.9	1.7	1.5	0.6	–	0.9	1.3	0.4	1.8	(X)	0.6	0.9	0.7	0.2	1.2
OH	75.2	254.1	–	249.8	73.0	4.3	2.7	19.7	4.4	5.3	18.8	11.2	5.8	11.6	2.4	29.6	(X)	18.5	12.1	8.7	0.6	9.6
OK	29.5	97.9	–	97.9	27.8	–	6.4	0.3	5.3	5.5	1.0	12.1	2.8	5.1	1.7	9.5	(X)	4.9	4.1	1.8	0.8	1.7
OR	29.5	78.6	–	71.1	28.7	7.5	11.1	1.8	2.3	5.5	9.8	2.9	3.6	3.5	1.3	7.4	(X)	4.7	4.9	3.5	0.4	3.9
PA	60.9	237.2	–	229.2	58.2	8.0	10.8	12.7	4.2	10.7	7.8	(Z)	11.5	10.7	6.5	25.5	(X)	6.6	16.2	12.4	1.2	3.3
RI	9.0	16.6	3.1	16.6	5.4	–	1.5	0.1	1.1	0.8	0.5	–	0.8	0.8	0.3	2.8	(X)	2.5	1.4	–	0.1	0.4
SC	39.6	107.1	–	107.1	36.5	–	6.0	0.3	5.2	2.9	7.2	19.6	3.6	2.5	2.1	12.8	(X)	7.0	6.3	3.0	0.8	4.1
SD	5.7	21.7	–	21.7	5.3	–	1.5	0.3	0.6	1.5	0.5	0.5	1.0	1.5	0.4	1.9	(X)	0.6	0.6	0.9	1.2	0.8
TN	36.7	143.1	–	143.1	34.8	–	7.3	1.3	4.2	6.8	2.7	24.0	3.7	6.8	2.1	19.6	(X)	8.6	5.7	6.5	1.2	4.4
TX	148.6	805.8	0.3	761.3	145.6	44.5	23.8	3.9	18.0	33.0	28.6	68.1	13.5	21.6	7.5	75.4	(X)	33.0	33.2	26.1	1.3	19.6
UT	35.6	59.6	–	59.6	33.3	–	3.1	0.9	2.9	4.2	12.5	0.5	1.6	2.0	0.9	6.1	(X)	3.3	3.1	2.2	0.3	4.5
VT	4.8	19.0	–	19.0	4.5	1.3	1.4	(Z)	0.6	0.1	0.2	–	1.0	1.2	0.5	1.8	(X)	0.4	0.9	–	0.1	0.3
VA	61.7	210.2	–	208.9	59.5	–	3.1	10.3	6.8	6.3	12.2	2.3	7.6	4.2	3.2	18.6	(X)	12.6	12.3	10.0	1.1	8.0
WA	58.8	129.4	–	119.4	57.3	–	12.3	1.8	10.0	4.6	16.1	21.6	7.0	6.9	2.1	12.0	(X)	11.6	8.9	4.2	0.8	6.2
WV	14.9	42.2	–	42.2	13.7	–	3.1	(Z)	0.9	1.4	1.0	2.0	5.3	0.9	1.0	3.0	(X)	1.0	2.8	–	0.7	3.0
WI	37.7	128.8	–	119.4	36.6	9.4	1.9	11.9	1.7	4.9	3.6	1.4	1.3	8.7	1.0	14.7	(X)	5.0	8.0	3.4	0.2	3.0
WY	4.0	20.3	–	18.3	3.8	2.0	0.6	0.1	0.8	0.4	0.6	7.6	1.6	0.7	0.2	1.7	(X)	0.6	0.9	0.7	0.2	0.9

– Represents zero. X Not applicable. Z Less than 50. [1] Includes other categories, not shown separately.

Source: U.S. Census Bureau, "Survey of Public Employment and Payroll Datasets and Tables," <www.census.gov/programs-surveys/apes.html>, accessed July 2024.

Table 506. State and Local Government Employment and Average Monthly Earnings by State: 2010 to 2023

[4,378 represents 4,378,000. As of March. Employment numbers are for full -time equivalent (FTE) employees; average monthly earnings data are for full time employees. Full-time equivalent is a computed statistic representing the number of full-time employees that could have been employed if the reported number of hours worked by part-time employees had been worked by full-time employees. Beginning 2019, this data is calculated using a linear model based on historical data; prior to 2019, data was calculated separately for each function of a government by dividing the "part-time hours paid" by the standard number of hours for full-time employees in the particular government and then adding the resulting quotient to the number of full-time employees. See source for more information]

| State | Full-time equivalent employment (1,000) | | | | | | Average monthly earnings (dol.) | | | | | |
| | State | | | Local [1] | | | State | | | Local [1] | | |
	2010	2020	2023 (P)	2010	2020	2023 (P)	2010	2020	2023 (P)	2010	2020	2023 (P)
United States......	**4,378**	**4,513**	**4,441**	**12,171**	**12,372**	**12,432**	**4,620**	**5,978**	**6,708**	**4,310**	**5,332**	**5,917**
Alabama.............	90	97	96	198	191	193	4,099	5,120	5,719	3,240	4,054	4,634
Alaska................	27	24	24	28	27	27	5,176	6,360	7,070	4,935	5,896	6,175
Arizona..............	67	75	77	225	212	213	4,365	5,537	6,448	4,163	5,023	5,692
Arkansas............	63	63	63	106	107	106	3,795	4,684	4,907	3,208	3,576	3,972
California.............	411	452	466	1,381	1,457	1,450	5,740	8,302	9,034	5,787	7,431	8,288
Colorado.............	71	97	98	199	223	221	5,033	6,599	7,339	4,230	5,327	6,060
Connecticut.........	63	58	57	123	123	127	5,632	7,341	8,381	5,063	6,325	6,665
Delaware.............	26	27	26	23	25	26	4,113	5,323	5,951	4,484	5,314	5,634
Dist. of Columbia....	(X)	(X)	(X)	44	50	52	(X)	(X)	(X)	5,900	7,580	8,454
Florida................	184	183	177	727	723	725	3,861	4,804	5,532	3,986	4,653	5,310
Georgia..............	124	129	125	392	398	407	3,795	4,708	5,441	3,439	4,372	4,940
Hawaii...............	58	59	56	15	17	17	3,943	5,236	5,700	5,040	6,493	7,384
Idaho................	22	25	25	55	62	65	4,280	5,869	6,084	3,341	4,134	4,684
Illinois...............	131	125	124	513	497	509	5,324	6,581	7,043	4,716	5,779	6,212
Indiana..............	90	90	89	254	239	238	4,023	5,205	5,925	3,547	4,301	4,863
Iowa.................	51	51	50	124	139	143	5,326	7,078	7,394	3,831	4,714	5,107
Kansas..............	44	56	55	156	147	145	4,178	5,159	5,671	3,361	4,181	4,546
Kentucky.............	81	81	78	161	162	160	3,940	4,961	5,653	3,101	3,799	4,311
Louisiana............	89	83	80	187	182	177	4,282	4,671	5,195	3,397	3,832	4,144
Maine................	21	21	21	51	50	52	4,063	5,133	5,886	3,545	4,308	4,891
Maryland.............	88	96	97	215	224	226	4,650	6,608	6,961	5,190	6,214	6,838
Massachusetts.......	95	106	105	233	240	251	4,973	6,721	7,393	4,800	6,117	6,750
Michigan.............	146	151	147	329	292	289	5,208	6,398	7,233	4,618	5,042	5,533
Minnesota...........	80	83	83	201	218	215	5,338	6,348	7,030	4,447	5,498	6,117
Mississippi...........	57	54	52	136	130	129	3,537	4,547	5,105	2,985	3,577	4,078
Missouri..............	89	84	80	234	234	231	3,518	4,399	5,211	3,502	4,134	4,683
Montana..............	20	21	21	38	36	38	4,016	5,061	5,740	3,476	4,352	4,878
Nebraska.............	33	36	37	88	91	91	4,013	5,142	5,630	3,785	5,010	5,547
Nevada..............	28	30	29	86	89	88	4,891	5,522	6,168	5,149	5,825	6,308
New Hampshire......	19	19	18	53	51	50	4,584	5,788	6,380	3,813	4,762	5,361
New Jersey..........	152	145	129	356	335	345	5,767	6,495	6,957	5,449	6,553	7,132
New Mexico..........	48	46	46	80	77	77	3,978	5,192	5,998	3,440	4,156	4,813
New York.............	251	256	240	975	978	953	5,484	6,634	7,545	5,315	6,669	7,193
North Carolina.......	146	151	142	402	409	414	3,886	5,480	6,377	3,690	4,471	5,124
North Dakota.........	18	18	18	26	29	31	4,103	5,325	5,768	3,550	4,680	5,062
Ohio.................	140	134	139	466	447	458	4,995	5,971	6,901	4,101	4,893	5,401
Oklahoma............	71	64	63	146	146	155	3,864	4,798	5,249	3,119	3,992	4,250
Oregon..............	65	76	78	133	136	139	4,452	5,987	6,907	4,348	5,717	6,505
Pennsylvania........	168	157	149	429	402	394	4,564	6,037	6,687	4,290	5,316	5,832
Rhode Island.........	19	21	20	31	29	27	5,298	6,430	7,026	4,953	6,097	6,404
South Carolina.......	77	85	83	171	195	188	3,810	4,583	5,486	3,557	4,324	4,696
South Dakota........	14	14	14	31	33	34	3,938	4,959	5,786	3,149	4,079	4,421
Tennessee...........	83	80	79	247	259	265	3,822	5,041	5,767	3,358	4,185	4,625
Texas................	318	323	315	1,134	1,230	1,252	4,280	5,718	6,602	3,604	4,504	5,093
Utah.................	51	65	69	90	98	103	4,409	5,751	6,764	3,706	4,950	5,601
Vermont.............	14	14	14	26	23	25	4,645	6,004	6,790	3,589	5,188	5,517
Virginia..............	125	131	129	319	328	337	4,384	5,747	6,368	3,905	4,907	5,426
Washington..........	123	137	139	226	263	266	4,913	6,389	7,179	5,416	7,277	8,278
West Virginia........	39	39	38	62	61	62	3,554	4,579	5,097	3,219	3,695	3,983
Wisconsin............	72	66	69	211	214	209	4,901	5,980	6,795	4,239	5,054	5,489
Wyoming.............	14	13	12	37	38	38	4,240	4,908	5,740	4,068	4,982	5,442

P Preliminary. X Not applicable. [1] Estimates subject to sampling variation; see Appendix III and source. Data from Census years ending in '2' or '7' are not subject to sampling error.

Source: U.S. Census Bureau, Census of Governments, "Survey of Public Employment & Payroll Datasets & Tables," and "Annual Survey of Public Employment and Payroll Datasets and Tables," <www.census.gov/programs-surveys/apes.html>, accessed July 2024.

Table 507. State and Local Government Employment and Payrolls by Function: 2010 to 2023

[Employees in thousands (19,527 represents 19,527,000); payroll in millions of dollars (70,318.9 represents $70,318,900,000). Data are for the month of March. Covers both full-time and part-time employees]

Function	Employees (1,000)			Payrolls (mil. dol.)		
	Total	State	Local [1]	Total	State	Local [1]
2010..	19,527	5,326	14,201	70,318.9	19,579.2	50,739.7
2011..	19,302	5,314	13,988	70,483.5	19,971.9	50,511.6
2012..	19,247	5,286	13,961	70,994.7	20,172.8	50,821.9
2013..	19,086	5,282	13,804	71,437.4	20,501.6	50,935.7
2014..	19,229	5,330	13,900	73,157.0	21,120.2	52,036.8
2015..	19,293	5,344	13,949	75,071.7	21,568.4	53,503.3
2016..	19,406	5,368	14,038	77,324.7	22,148.7	55,176.0
2017..	19,574	5,462	14,113	80,755.8	23,109.8	57,645.9
2018..	19,639	5,472	14,167	83,155.2	23,873.7	59,281.5
2019..	19,685	5,497	14,188	86,245.0	24,770.2	61,474.7
2020..	19,760	5,493	14,267	89,653.3	25,915.9	63,737.4
2021..	18,812	5,245	13,567	89,927.6	25,933.5	63,994.0
2022..	19,220	5,255	13,965	94,595.5	26,941.5	67,654.0
2023, total [2]............................	**19,584**	**5,364**	**14,220**	**100,310.8**	**28,745.4**	**71,565.4**
Financial administration........................	461	172	289	2,658.9	1,060.1	1,598.8
Other government administration...............	441	58	383	1,788.5	342.8	1,445.7
Judicial and legal..............................	441	182	259	2,781.1	1,256.7	1,524.4
Police protection...............................	1,003	107	896	7,133.8	812.1	6,321.7
Fire protection..................................	473	–	473	3,126.9	–	3,126.9
Corrections......................................	650	393	257	4,002.0	2,449.9	1,552.1
Streets and highways..........................	500	207	293	2,813.2	1,256.1	1,557.0
Air transportation...............................	54	4	50	363.3	27.0	336.3
Sea and inland port facilities..................	15	5	10	116.3	41.2	75.0
Public welfare...................................	527	247	280	2,734.3	1,259.7	1,474.6
Health...	501	206	295	2,806.3	1,186.9	1,619.3
Hospitals..	1,130	469	662	7,365.8	3,045.2	4,320.6
Social insurance administration................	68	68	1	386.7	381.0	5.7
Solid waste management.......................	112	2	110	537.8	15.4	522.4
Sewerage..	134	2	132	797.1	14.2	782.9
Parks and recreation...........................	428	39	389	1,279.0	155.3	1,123.7
Housing and community development.........	114	3	112	651.5	17.7	633.8
Natural resources..............................	192	143	48	989.6	762.2	227.4
Water supply....................................	191	1	190	1,151.0	5.1	1,145.9
Electric power...................................	79	4	74	742.3	42.4	699.8
Gas supply......................................	12	–	12	73.3	–	73.3
Transit...	260	39	221	1,825.0	322.9	1,502.1
Elementary and secondary education.........	7,822	49	7,773	35,872.6	224.5	35,648.1
Higher education................................	3,197	2,684	513	14,449.6	12,429.3	2,020.3
Other education.................................	82	82	–	466.2	466.2	–
Libraries...	176	1	175	580.7	5.2	575.5
State liquor stores..............................	14	14	–	42.1	42.1	–
All other and unallocable.......................	506	182	324	2,776.0	1,124.0	1,652.1

– Represents or rounds to zero. [1] Data for local governments are subject to sampling error, except for data collected during census years ending in '2' and '7.' Data collected during census years are not subject to sampling and do not contain sampling error. See Appendix III and source. [2] Data for 2023 are preliminary.

Source: U.S. Census Bureau, "Annual Survey of Public Employment and Payroll, Datasets and Tables," <www.census.gov/programs-surveys/apes.html>, accessed June 2024.

Section 9
Federal Government Finances and Employment

This section presents statistics relating to the financial structure and civilian employment of the federal government. The fiscal data cover taxes, other receipts, outlays, and debt. The principal sources of fiscal data are the *Budget of the United States Government* and related documents, published annually by the Office of Management and Budget (OMB), and the U.S. Department of the Treasury's *Combined Statement of Receipts, Outlays, and Balances of the United States Government*. Detailed data on tax returns and collections are published annually by the Internal Revenue Service. Data on staffing, payrolls, and retirements are published by the Office of Personnel Management (OPM). Data on federally owned land and real property are collected by the General Services Administration and presented online at <www.gsa.gov/reference/reports/real-property-reports>.

Budget concept—Under the unified budget concept, all federal monies are included in one comprehensive budget. These monies comprise both federal funds and trust funds. Federal funds are derived mainly from taxes and borrowing and are not restricted by law to any specific government purpose. Trust funds, such as the Unemployment Trust Fund, collect certain taxes and other receipts for use in carrying out specific purposes or programs in accordance with the terms of the trust agreement or statute. Fund balances include both cash balances with the Treasury and investments in U.S. securities. Part of the balance is obligated, part unobligated. Prior to 1985, the budget totals, under provisions of law, excluded some federal activities—including the Federal Financing Bank, the Postal Service, the Synthetic Fuels Corporation, and the lending activities of the Rural Electrification Administration. The Balanced Budget and Emergency Deficit Control Act of 1985 (P.L.99-177) repealed the off-budget status of these entities and placed Social Security (Federal Old-Age and Survivors Insurance and the Federal Disability Insurance Trust Funds) off-budget. Though Social Security is now off-budget and by law excluded from coverage of the congressional budget resolutions, it continues to be a federal program.

Receipts arising from the government's sovereign powers are reported as governmental receipts and all other receipts, i.e., from business or market-oriented activities, and are offset against outlays. Outlays are reported on a checks-issued (net) basis (i.e., outlays are recorded at the time the checks to pay bills are issued).

Debt concept—For most of U.S. history, the total debt consisted of debt borrowed by the Treasury (i.e., public debt). The present debt series includes both public debt and agency debt. The *gross federal debt* includes money borrowed by the Treasury and by various federal agencies; it is the broadest generally used measure of the federal debt. *Total public debt* is covered by a statutory debt limitation and includes only borrowing by the Treasury.

Treasury receipts and outlays—All receipts of the government, with a few exceptions, are deposited to the credit of the U.S. Treasury regardless of ultimate disposition. Under the Constitution, no money may be withdrawn from the Treasury unless appropriated by the Congress.

The day-to-day cash operations of the federal government clearing through the accounts of the U.S. Treasury are reported in the *Daily Treasury Statement*. Extensive detail on the public debt is published in the *Monthly Statement of the Public Debt of the United States*.

Budget receipts such as taxes, customs duties, and miscellaneous receipts, which are collected by government agencies, and outlays represented by checks issued and cash payments made by disbursing officers as well as government agencies, are reported in the *Monthly Treasury Statement of Receipts and Outlays of the United States Government* and in the Treasury's *Combined Statement of Receipts, Outlays, and Balances of the United States Government*. These deposits in and payments from accounts maintained by government agencies are on the same basis as the unified budget.

The quarterly *Treasury Bulletin* contains data on fiscal operations and related Treasury activities, including financial statements of government corporations and other business-type activities.

Income tax returns and tax collections—Tax data are compiled by the Internal Revenue Service of the Treasury Department. The annual *Internal Revenue Service Data Book* gives a detailed account of tax collections by kind of tax. The agency's annual *Statistics of Income* reports present detailed data from individual income tax returns and corporation income tax returns as well as historical tax data. The quarterly *Statistics of Income Bulletin* presents data on such diverse subjects as tax-exempt organizations, unincorporated businesses, fiduciary income tax and estate tax returns, sales of capital assets by individuals, international income and taxes reported by corporations and individuals, and estate tax wealth.

Employment and payrolls—The Office of Personnel Management collects employment, payroll, and retirement data from all departments and agencies of the federal government, except the Central Intelligence Agency, the National Security Agency, the National Geospatial-Intelligence Agency, and the Defense Intelligence Agency. Employment figures represent the number of persons who occupied civilian positions at the end of the report month shown and who are paid for services rendered to the federal government, regardless of the nature of appointment or method of payment. Federal payrolls include all payments for personnel services rendered during the report month and payments for accumulated annual leave of employees who separate from the service. Since most federal employees are paid on a biweekly basis, the calendar month earnings are partially estimated on the basis of the number of work days in each month where payroll periods overlap.

Federal employment and payroll figures are published by the Office of Personnel Management in the FedScope database system. The OPM also publishes employment data on minority groups, white- and blue-collar workers, employment by geographic area, and salary and wage distribution of federal employees. General schedule is primarily white-collar; wage system primarily blue-collar. Data on federal employment are also issued by the Bureau of Labor Statistics in its *Monthly Labor Review* and *Employment and Earnings Online*.

Table 508. Federal Budget—Receipts and Outlays: 1960 to 2024

[92.5 represents $92,500,000,000. For fiscal years ending in year shown; see text, Section 8. See also headnote, Table 510]

Fiscal year	In current dollars (billion dollars)			In constant (2017) dollars (billion dollars)			As percent of GDP [1]		
	Receipts	Outlays	Surplus or deficit (-)	Receipts	Outlays	Surplus or deficit (-)	Receipts	Outlays	Surplus or deficit (-)
1960...............	92.5	92.2	0.3	735.8	733.4	2.4	17.3	17.3	0.1
1970...............	192.8	195.6	-2.8	1,144.3	1,161.1	-16.9	18.4	18.7	-0.3
1980...............	517.1	590.9	-73.8	1,483.0	1,694.7	-211.7	18.5	21.2	-2.6
1990...............	1,032.0	1,253.0	-221.0	1,865.4	2,265.0	-399.6	17.5	21.2	-3.7
2000...............	2,025.2	1,789.0	236.2	2,858.4	2,525.0	333.4	20.0	17.7	2.3
2001...............	1,991.1	1,862.8	128.2	2,736.1	2,559.9	176.2	18.9	17.7	1.2
2002...............	1,853.1	2,010.9	-157.8	2,506.6	2,720.0	-213.4	17.1	18.6	-1.5
2003...............	1,782.3	2,159.9	-377.6	2,341.1	2,837.1	-496.0	15.8	19.2	-3.3
2004...............	1,880.1	2,292.8	-412.7	2,406.1	2,934.3	-528.2	15.6	19.1	-3.4
2005...............	2,153.6	2,472.0	-318.3	2,665.0	3,059.0	-393.9	16.8	19.3	-2.5
2006...............	2,406.9	2,655.0	-248.2	2,877.7	3,174.4	-296.7	17.6	19.5	-1.8
2007...............	2,568.0	2,728.7	-160.7	2,983.6	3,170.3	-186.7	18.0	19.1	-1.1
2008...............	2,524.0	2,982.5	-458.6	2,834.4	3,349.3	-514.9	17.1	20.2	-3.1
2009...............	2,105.0	3,517.7	-1,412.7	2,372.6	3,964.9	-1,592.3	14.5	24.3	-9.8
2010...............	2,162.7	3,457.1	-1,294.4	2,386.3	3,814.5	-1,428.2	14.5	23.2	-8.7
2011...............	2,303.5	3,603.1	-1,299.6	2,484.1	3,885.5	-1,401.5	14.9	23.3	-8.4
2012...............	2,450.0	3,526.6	-1,076.6	2,592.3	3,731.4	-1,139.1	15.2	21.9	-6.7
2013...............	2,775.1	3,454.9	-679.8	2,892.8	3,601.5	-708.6	16.6	20.7	-4.1
2014...............	3,021.5	3,506.3	-484.8	3,103.1	3,601.0	-497.9	17.3	20.1	-2.8
2015...............	3,249.9	3,691.8	-442.0	3,324.4	3,776.4	-452.1	17.9	20.3	-2.4
2016...............	3,268.0	3,852.6	-584.6	3,322.1	3,916.5	-594.3	17.5	20.7	-3.1
2017...............	3,316.2	3,981.6	-665.4	3,316.2	3,981.6	-665.4	17.1	20.6	-3.4
2018...............	3,329.9	4,109.0	-779.1	3,259.5	4,022.1	-762.6	16.3	20.1	-3.8
2019...............	3,463.4	4,447.0	-983.6	3,333.0	4,279.6	-946.6	16.3	20.9	-4.6
2020...............	3,421.2	6,553.6	-3,132.5	3,246.5	6,219.0	-2,972.5	16.1	30.8	-14.7
2021...............	4,047.1	6,822.5	-2,775.4	3,725.9	6,281.0	-2,555.1	17.6	29.7	-12.1
2022...............	4,897.3	6,273.3	-1,375.9	4,242.0	5,433.7	-1,191.8	19.4	24.8	-5.4
2023...............	4,440.9	6,134.7	-1,693.7	3,683.3	5,088.1	-1,404.8	16.5	22.7	-6.3
2024, estimate......	5,081.5	6,940.9	-1,859.4	4,090.8	5,587.6	-1,496.8	18.0	24.6	-6.6

[1] Gross domestic product; see text, Section 13.

Source: U.S. Office of Management and Budget, *Budget of the U.S. Government, Fiscal Year 2025: Historical Tables*, March 2024. See also <www.whitehouse.gov/omb/budget>.

Table 509. Federal Budget Debt: 1960 to 2024

[290.5 represents $290,500,000,000. As of the end of the fiscal year. See text, Section 8]

Fiscal year	Total (billion dollars)					As percent of GDP [1]				
	Gross federal debt	Federal govern-ment accounts	Held by the public			Gross federal debt	Federal govern-ment accounts	Held by the public		
			Total	Federal Reserve System	Other			Total	Federal Reserve System	Other
1960.............	290.5	53.7	236.8	26.5	210.3	54.4	10.0	44.3	5.0	39.4
1970.............	380.9	97.7	283.2	57.7	225.5	36.4	9.3	27.1	5.5	21.5
1980.............	909.0	197.1	711.9	120.8	591.1	32.6	7.1	25.5	4.3	21.2
1990.............	3,206.3	794.7	2,411.6	234.4	2,177.1	54.4	13.5	40.9	4.0	36.9
2000.............	5,628.7	2,218.9	3,409.8	511.4	2,898.4	55.6	21.9	33.7	5.1	28.6
2001.............	5,769.9	2,450.3	3,319.6	534.1	2,785.5	54.8	23.3	31.5	5.1	26.5
2002.............	6,198.4	2,658.0	3,540.4	604.2	2,936.2	57.2	24.5	32.7	5.6	27.1
2003.............	6,760.0	2,846.6	3,913.4	656.1	3,257.3	59.9	25.2	34.7	5.8	28.9
2004.............	7,354.7	3,059.1	4,295.5	700.3	3,595.2	61.1	25.4	35.7	5.8	29.9
2005.............	7,905.3	3,313.1	4,592.2	736.4	3,855.9	61.6	25.8	35.8	5.7	30.0
2006.............	8,451.4	3,622.4	4,829.0	768.9	4,060.0	62.0	26.6	35.4	5.6	29.8
2007.............	8,950.7	3,915.6	5,035.1	779.6	4,255.5	62.6	27.4	35.2	5.4	29.7
2008.............	9,986.1	4,183.0	5,803.1	491.1	5,311.9	67.5	28.3	39.2	3.3	35.9
2009.............	11,875.9	4,331.1	7,544.7	769.2	6,775.5	82.1	29.9	52.2	5.3	46.8
2010.............	13,528.8	4,509.9	9,018.9	811.7	8,207.2	90.9	30.3	60.6	5.5	55.1
2011.............	14,764.2	4,636.0	10,128.2	1,664.7	8,463.5	95.5	30.0	65.5	10.8	54.7
2012.............	16,050.9	4,769.8	11,281.1	1,645.3	9,635.8	99.6	29.6	70.0	10.2	59.8
2013.............	16,719.4	4,736.7	11,982.7	2,072.3	9,910.4	100.2	28.4	71.8	12.4	59.4
2014.............	17,794.5	5,014.6	12,779.9	2,451.7	10,328.2	102.1	28.8	73.3	14.1	59.3
2015.............	18,120.1	5,003.4	13,116.7	2,461.9	10,654.7	99.8	27.5	72.2	13.6	58.7
2016.............	19,539.5	5,371.8	14,167.6	2,463.5	11,704.2	104.8	28.8	76.0	13.2	62.8
2017.............	20,205.7	5,540.3	14,665.4	2,465.4	12,200.0	104.3	28.6	75.7	12.7	63.0
2018.............	21,462.3	5,712.7	15,749.6	2,313.2	13,436.4	105.0	28.0	77.1	11.3	65.7
2019.............	22,669.5	5,868.8	16,800.7	2,113.3	14,687.4	106.6	27.6	79.0	9.9	69.0
2020.............	26,902.5	5,885.8	21,016.7	4,445.5	16,571.2	126.3	27.6	98.7	20.9	77.8
2021.............	28,385.6	6,101.5	22,284.0	5,433.2	16,850.9	123.8	26.6	97.2	23.7	73.5
2022.............	30,838.6	6,585.1	24,253.4	5,634.9	18,618.5	121.9	26.0	95.8	22.3	73.6
2023.............	32,989.0	6,753.4	26,235.6	4,952.9	21,282.7	122.3	25.0	97.2	18.4	78.9
2024, estimate. ..	35,107.9	6,951.7	28,156.2	(NA)	(NA)	124.3	24.6	99.6	(NA)	(NA)

NA Not available. [1] Gross domestic product; see text, Section 13.

Source: U.S. Office of Management and Budget, *Budget of the U.S. Government, Fiscal Year 2025: Historical Tables*, March 2024. See also <www.whitehouse.gov/omb/budget>.

Table 510. Federal Budget Outlays by Type: 2000 to 2024

[1,789.0 represents $1,789,000,000,000. For fiscal years ending September 30. Given the inherent imprecision in adjusting outlays for inflation, the data shown in constant dollars present a reasonable perspective, not precision. The deflators and the categories that are deflated are as comparable over time as feasible. Minus sign (-) indicates offset]

Type	Unit	2000	2010	2020	2021	2022	2023	2024, estimate
Current dollar outlays............	**Bil. dol.**	**1,789.0**	**3,457.1**	**6,553.6**	**6,822.5**	**6,273.3**	**6,134.7**	**6,940.9**
National defense [1]................	Bil. dol.	294.4	693.5	724.6	753.9	765.6	820.3	907.7
Nondefense, total.................	Bil. dol.	1,494.6	2,763.6	5,829.0	6,068.6	5,507.6	5,314.4	6,033.2
Payments for individuals..........	Bil. dol.	1,067.4	2,305.9	4,216.7	4,628.9	4,525.1	4,337.6	4,438.4
Direct payments [2]............	Bil. dol.	876.6	1,906.7	3,604.2	3,934.9	3,729.8	3,515.8	3,660.8
Grants to state and local governments......	Bil. dol.	190.7	399.2	612.5	694.0	795.3	821.8	777.6
All other grants................	Bil. dol.	95.1	209.2	216.6	551.3	398.0	261.5	330.0
Net interest [2]................	Bil. dol.	222.9	196.2	345.5	352.3	475.9	658.3	888.6
All other [2]................	Bil. dol.	151.7	134.4	1,156.6	659.9	343.6	188.9	521.1
Undistributed offsetting receipts [2]...........	Bil. dol.	-42.6	-82.1	-106.4	-123.9	-235.0	-131.9	-144.9
Constant (2017) dollar outlays..........	**Bil. dol.**	**2,525.0**	**3,814.5**	**6,219.0**	**6,281.0**	**5,433.7**	**5,088.1**	**5,587.6**
National defense [1]................	Bil. dol.	452.2	757.0	684.6	693.3	663.2	680.4	733.1
Nondefense, total.................	Bil. dol.	2,072.6	3,057.4	5,534.6	5,587.5	4,770.6	4,407.7	4,854.5
Payments for individuals..........	Bil. dol.	1,449.3	2,545.4	4,024.6	4,288.7	3,938.7	3,612.1	3,583.5
Direct payments [2]............	Bil. dol.	1,189.5	2,104.5	3,440.1	3,645.8	3,246.7	2,928.1	2,956.1
Grants to state and local governments......	Bil. dol.	259.8	440.9	584.5	642.9	692.0	684.0	627.4
All other grants................	Bil. dol.	155.0	238.9	200.4	487.1	329.0	207.6	255.6
Net interest [2]................	Bil. dol.	307.0	218.8	327.6	322.9	407.7	539.3	709.0
All other [2]................	Bil. dol.	232.3	148.7	1,081.0	601.0	297.6	158.3	423.5
Undistributed offsetting receipts [2]...........	Bil. dol.	-71.0	-94.3	-99.2	-112.4	-202.3	-109.3	-116.9
Outlays as percent of GDP [3]...............	**Percent**	**17.7**	**23.2**	**30.8**	**29.7**	**24.8**	**22.7**	**24.6**
National defense [1]................	Percent	2.9	4.7	3.4	3.3	3.0	3.0	3.2
Nondefense, total.................	Percent	14.8	18.6	27.4	26.5	21.8	19.7	21.4
Payments for individuals..........	Percent	10.6	15.5	19.8	20.2	17.9	16.1	15.7
Direct payments [2]............	Percent	8.7	12.8	16.9	17.2	14.7	13.0	13.0
Grants to state and local governments......	Percent	1.9	2.7	2.9	3.0	3.1	3.0	2.8
All other grants................	Percent	0.9	1.4	1.0	2.4	1.6	1.0	1.2
Net interest [2]................	Percent	2.2	1.3	1.6	1.5	1.9	2.4	3.1
All other [2]................	Percent	1.5	0.9	5.4	2.9	1.4	0.7	1.8
Undistributed offsetting receipts [2]...........	Percent	-0.4	-0.6	-0.5	-0.5	-0.9	-0.5	-0.5

[1] Includes a small amount of grants to state and local governments and direct payments for individuals. [2] Includes some off-budget amounts; most of the off-budget amounts are direct payments for individuals (social security benefits). [3] Gross domestic product; see text, Section 13.

Source: U.S. Office of Management and Budget, *Budget of the U.S. Government, Fiscal Year 2025: Historical Tables*, March 2024. See also <www.whitehouse.gov/omb/budget>.

Table 511. Federal Budget Outlays by Agency: 2000 to 2024

[In billions of dollars (1,789.0 represents $1,789,000,000,000). For fiscal years ending September 30]

Department or other unit	2000	2010	2015	2020	2021	2022	2023	2024, estimated
Outlays, total.........	**1,789.0**	**3,457.1**	**3,691.9**	**6,553.6**	**6,822.5**	**6,273.3**	**6,134.7**	**[2] 6,940.9**
Legislative branch...........	2.9	5.8	4.3	5.4	5.3	5.8	6.5	7.6
Judicial branch............	4.1	7.2	7.1	8.3	8.3	8.7	9.0	9.6
Agriculture............	75.1	129.5	139.1	184.2	235.2	245.2	228.9	254.8
Commerce............	7.8	13.2	9.0	15.9	13.1	11.7	12.0	20.5
Defense—Military...........	281.0	666.7	562.5	690.4	717.6	726.5	775.9	844.9
Education............	33.5	93.7	90.0	204.4	260.4	639.4	-41.1	250.7
Energy............	15.0	30.8	25.4	32.0	33.7	22.4	34.4	58.3
Health and Human Services...........	382.3	854.1	1,027.5	1,504.0	1,466.7	1,642.9	1,708.5	1,669.4
Homeland Security...........	13.2	44.5	42.6	92.0	91.1	80.9	89.0	134.2
Housing and Urban Development...........	30.8	60.1	35.5	33.2	35.1	29.3	55.2	56.3
Interior............	8.0	13.2	12.3	16.4	15.8	13.9	15.9	23.1
Justice............	16.8	29.6	26.9	39.6	39.3	39.6	44.3	51.6
Labor............	31.9	173.1	45.2	477.5	404.8	51.7	87.5	84.4
State............	6.7	23.8	26.5	32.9	35.8	33.2	33.0	37.3
Transportation............	41.6	77.8	75.4	100.3	104.9	113.7	109.5	121.1
Treasury............	390.5	444.3	485.6	1,151.7	1,633.8	1,162.2	1,106.9	1,345.6
Veterans Affairs...........	47.0	108.3	159.2	218.4	233.8	273.9	301.0	346.0
Corps of Engineers—Civil Works............	4.2	9.9	6.7	7.6	7.9	8.2	7.8	8.2
Other Defense—Civil Programs............	32.8	54.0	63.0	65.2	58.1	56.9	68.9	67.0
Environmental Protection Agency............	7.2	11.0	7.0	8.7	8.3	9.3	12.6	41.1
Executive Office of the President............	0.3	0.6	0.4	0.4	0.4	0.5	0.5	0.7
General Services Administration............	0.1	0.9	-0.9	-0.3	-1.3	-1.2	-0.7	0.1
International Assistance Programs............	12.1	20.0	24.4	21.7	20.1	36.0	36.1	46.5
National Aeronautics and Space Administration...	13.4	18.9	18.3	21.5	22.2	23.1	25.3	24.9
National Science Foundation............	3.4	6.7	6.8	7.3	7.4	8.1	9.0	10.4
Office of Personnel Management............	48.7	69.9	91.7	105.6	108.6	113.6	122.5	127.9
Small Business Administration............	-0.4	6.1	-0.7	577.4	322.7	23.2	26.1	33.2
Social Security Administration (on-budget)........	45.1	70.8	87.4	98.0	92.7	111.9	112.8	115.1
Social Security Administration (off-budget)........	396.2	683.4	856.8	1,055.9	1,099.7	1,170.1	1,303.5	1,402.1
Other independent agencies (on-budget).........	8.8	-7.5	16.0	21.8	17.2	31.9	129.0	103.9
Other independent agencies (off-budget).........	2.0	4.7	-1.7	-2.4	-2.7	-0.4	5.8	1.1
Undistributed offsetting receipts [1]............	-173.0	-267.9	-257.6	-241.6	-273.4	-418.9	-301.1	-329.0

[1] Includes some off-budget amounts; most of the off-budget amounts are direct payments to individuals (social security benefits). [2] Total for FY2024 includes amount for allowances, not shown separately.

Source: U.S. Office of Management and Budget, *Budget of the U.S. Government, Fiscal Year 2025: Historical Tables*, March 2024. See also <www.whitehouse.gov/omb/budget>.

Table 512. Federal Budget Outlays by Detailed Function: 1990 to 2024

[In billions of dollars (1,253.0 represents $1,253,000,000,000). For fiscal years ending September 30. Minus sign (-) indicates decrease]

Superfunction and function	1990	2000	2010	2015	2020	2021	2022	2023	2024, estimate
Total outlays [1]	**1,253.0**	**1,789.0**	**3,457.1**	**3,691.9**	**6,553.6**	**6,822.5**	**6,273.3**	**6,134.7**	**6,940.9**
National defense [1]	299.3	294.4	693.5	589.7	724.6	753.9	765.6	820.3	907.7
Department of Defense—Military	289.7	281.0	666.7	562.5	690.4	717.6	726.5	775.9	859.5
Military personnel	75.6	76.0	155.7	145.2	161.4	172.6	180.8	183.9	189.8
Operation and maintenance	88.3	105.8	276.0	247.2	278.9	286.2	291.3	317.6	323.4
Procurement	81.0	51.7	133.6	101.3	139.1	141.4	136.2	141.7	147.9
Research, development, test, and evaluation	37.5	37.6	77.0	64.1	99.9	105.7	107.1	122.0	137.3
Military construction	5.1	5.1	21.2	8.1	8.9	9.1	9.7	10.3	14.0
Atomic energy defense activities	9.0	12.1	19.3	18.7	24.5	25.8	28.3	32.6	35.9
International affairs [1]	13.8	17.2	45.2	52.0	67.7	47.0	71.9	69.3	69.8
International development and humanitarian assistance	5.5	6.5	19.0	24.1	28.2	33.4	34.2	37.6	36.3
International security assistance	8.7	6.4	11.4	12.9	12.1	9.2	26.1	29.3	19.7
Conduct of foreign affairs	3.0	4.7	13.6	13.2	16.6	15.3	14.4	14.6	15.3
General science, space, and technology	14.4	18.6	30.1	29.4	34.0	35.5	37.4	41.3	43.8
General science and basic research	2.8	6.2	11.7	11.7	13.3	14.0	15.2	16.8	19.8
Space flight, research, and supporting activities	11.6	12.4	18.4	17.7	20.7	21.5	22.2	24.5	24.0
Energy [1]	3.3	-0.8	11.6	6.8	7.1	6.0	-9.1	-0.4	27.1
Energy supply	2.0	-1.8	5.8	4.7	5.5	4.8	4.1	4.6	18.9
Natural resources and environment [1]	17.1	25.0	43.7	36.0	42.5	44.2	41.4	47.4	94.0
Water resources	4.4	5.1	11.7	7.8	8.9	9.6	10.4	10.5	16.6
Conservation and land management	4.0	6.8	10.8	10.5	13.5	14.8	10.1	11.9	21.7
Recreational resources	1.4	2.5	3.9	3.5	4.2	4.2	4.5	4.9	5.7
Pollution control and abatement	5.2	7.4	10.8	7.2	8.7	8.4	9.2	12.5	40.8
Agriculture	11.6	36.5	21.4	18.5	47.3	47.4	33.1	33.7	39.5
Farm income stabilization	9.6	33.4	16.5	13.4	26.4	16.7	16.4	24.6	24.4
Agricultural research and services	2.1	3.0	4.9	5.1	20.9	30.7	16.6	9.0	15.1
Commerce and housing credit [1]	67.6	3.2	-82.3	-37.9	572.1	307.8	-19.1	100.8	58.0
Mortgage credit	3.8	-3.3	35.8	-35.7	-26.5	-31.8	-43.4	-22.2	-32.0
Postal service	2.1	2.1	-0.7	-1.6	-2.3	-2.7	2.6	5.8	1.2
Deposit insurance	57.9	-3.1	-32.0	-12.8	-7.2	-9.0	-11.5	91.2	48.2
Transportation [1]	29.5	46.9	92.0	89.5	145.6	154.3	131.0	126.4	144.7
Ground transportation	19.0	31.7	60.8	59.1	78.9	81.6	89.9	84.2	93.5
Air transportation	7.2	10.6	21.4	20.0	55.1	59.9	28.4	29.2	32.0
Water transportation	3.2	4.4	9.4	10.0	11.2	12.3	12.3	12.5	18.3
Community and regional development [1]	8.5	10.6	23.9	20.7	81.9	44.7	70.0	86.6	124.8
Community development	3.5	5.5	9.9	7.8	6.4	9.0	17.0	11.7	15.8
Disaster relief and insurance	2.1	2.6	10.7	9.0	71.3	32.3	46.9	68.5	100.2
Education, training, employment, and social services [1]	37.2	53.8	128.6	122.0	237.8	298.4	677.3	-2.2	292.2
Elementary, secondary, and vocational education	9.9	20.6	73.3	40.0	51.4	90.5	122.7	111.4	116.6
Higher education	11.1	10.1	20.9	51.3	153.0	172.7	518.1	-152.6	131.6
Research and general education aids	1.6	2.5	3.6	3.5	3.9	4.1	4.3	4.7	5.0
Training and employment	5.6	6.8	9.9	7.1	6.6	7.3	7.6	7.4	8.1
Social services	8.1	12.6	19.2	18.3	21.0	21.9	22.7	24.8	28.5
Health	57.7	154.5	369.1	482.3	747.6	796.5	914.1	888.6	858.0
Health care services	47.6	136.2	330.7	446.4	703.8	750.0	864.6	835.2	801.1
Health research and training	8.6	16.0	34.2	31.4	38.8	41.0	42.6	48.1	49.9
Consumer and occupational health and safety	1.5	2.3	4.1	4.5	5.0	5.4	6.9	5.3	7.0
Medicare	98.1	197.1	451.6	546.2	776.2	696.5	755.1	847.5	847.4
Income security [1]	148.8	253.7	622.1	508.8	1,263.6	1,647.7	866.1	774.7	760.5
General retirement and disability insurance (excluding social security)	5.1	5.2	6.6	7.8	2.1	6.2	12.1	50.4	25.1
Federal employee retirement and disability	52.0	77.1	119.8	139.1	153.8	156.1	168.7	179.4	181.5
Unemployment compensation	18.9	23.0	160.1	35.0	475.1	396.2	36.8	33.9	56.4
Housing assistance	15.9	28.9	58.7	47.8	53.0	89.8	76.5	67.1	69.6
Food and nutrition assistance	24.1	32.5	95.1	104.8	115.4	168.4	193.9	173.0	183.9
Social security	248.6	409.4	706.7	887.8	1,095.8	1,134.6	1,218.7	1,354.3	1,458.0
Veterans' benefits and services [1]	29.1	47.0	108.5	159.8	218.7	234.3	274.4	301.6	346.3
Income security for veterans	15.3	25.0	49.3	76.4	110.1	115.8	139.9	151.1	164.7
Veterans education, training, and rehabilitation	0.2	1.3	8.1	13.4	12.8	12.0	11.9	12.6	13.3
Hospital and medical care for veterans	12.1	19.5	45.7	61.9	90.6	99.9	110.7	125.5	147.2
Veterans housing	0.5	0.4	0.5	0.7	-3.4	-3.4	1.6	0.4	2.6
Administration of justice	10.2	28.5	54.4	51.9	72.0	71.4	71.3	80.4	89.9
Federal law enforcement activities	4.8	12.1	28.7	26.9	37.8	38.3	38.2	42.5	46.4
Federal litigative and judicial activities	3.6	7.8	14.5	14.7	17.9	18.4	18.5	19.1	19.2
Federal correctional activities	1.3	3.7	6.3	7.0	7.8	7.7	7.5	8.4	8.9
Criminal justice assistance	0.5	4.9	4.8	3.2	8.5	7.1	7.1	10.5	15.4
General government	10.5	13.0	23.0	21.0	180.1	273.9	133.2	38.2	42.7
Net interest [1]	184.3	222.9	196.2	223.2	345.5	352.3	475.9	658.3	888.6
Interest on Treasury debt securities (gross)	264.7	361.9	413.9	402.4	522.6	562.4	717.6	879.2	1,143.6
Interest received by on-budget trust funds	-46.3	-69.3	-67.3	-45.8	-56.4	-76.3	-116.2	-102.6	-115.9
Interest received by off-budget trust funds	-16.0	-59.8	-118.5	-96.0	-78.8	-73.3	-67.7	-66.5	-68.2
Undistributed offsetting receipts [2]	-36.6	-42.6	-82.1	-115.8	-106.4	-123.9	-235.0	-131.9	-144.9

[1] Includes functions not shown separately. [2] Includes some off-budget amounts; most of the off-budget amounts are direct payments for individuals (social security benefits).

Source: U.S. Office of Management and Budget, *Budget of the U.S. Government, Fiscal Year 2025: Historical Tables*, March 2024. See also <www.whitehouse.gov/omb/budget>.

Table 513. Federal Budget Outlays for Payments for Individuals by Category and Major Program: 1990 to 2024

[In billions of dollars (592.4 represents $592,400,000,000). For fiscal years ending September 30]

Category and program	1990	2000	2010	2015	2020	2021	2022	2023	2024, estimate
Total, payments for individuals	**592.4**	**1,067.4**	**2,307.0**	**2,654.9**	**4,218.4**	**4,630.7**	**4,527.0**	**4,339.8**	**4,440.9**
Social security and railroad retirement	253.3	410.7	706.6	890.2	1,100.1	1,139.5	1,221.9	1,357.3	1,462.0
Social security:									
Old age and survivors insurance	221.9	351.4	576.6	738.0	945.1	987.4	1,069.2	1,197.7	1,297.1
Disability insurance	24.4	54.4	123.5	143.4	144.3	140.9	142.6	149.7	153.7
Railroad retirement (excl. social security)	7.0	4.8	6.5	8.9	10.7	11.3	10.1	9.9	11.2
Federal employees' retirement and insurance	64.1	100.4	166.7	211.9	263.1	272.0	308.8	331.5	347.9
Military retirement	21.5	32.8	50.6	56.7	62.3	63.1	71.5	74.7	71.8
Civil service retirement	31.0	45.1	69.5	81.8	91.0	92.5	96.7	104.1	110.3
Veterans service-connected compensation	10.7	20.8	43.5	69.7	105.6	112.1	135.7	148.4	161.2
Other	0.8	1.7	3.2	3.7	4.1	4.3	4.9	4.4	4.5
Unemployment assistance	17.5	21.1	158.3	32.7	472.1	387.7	48.0	31.0	52.1
Medical care [1]	167.4	368.6	876.8	1,111.0	1,564.0	1,582.3	1,755.2	1,898.5	1,907.6
Medicare:									
Hospital insurance	65.9	127.9	245.6	273.5	395.8	326.8	339.6	390.7	391.3
Supplementary medical insurance	41.5	87.2	264.9	348.6	500.1	495.3	556.9	604.2	617.0
State children's health insurance	–	1.2	7.9	9.2	16.9	16.1	16.7	17.9	17.2
Medicaid	41.1	117.9	272.8	349.8	458.5	520.6	591.9	615.8	567.2
Indian health	1.1	2.4	4.4	4.6	5.3	8.7	5.4	5.9	6.9
Hospital and medical care for veterans	12.3	20.1	48.5	63.7	90.3	101.0	112.4	126.8	147.8
Health resources and services	1.4	3.9	7.1	7.7	10.5	12.1	14.1	13.7	13.3
Substance abuse and mental health services	1.2	2.5	3.3	3.1	5.2	5.9	7.4	8.3	9.2
Uniformed Services retiree health care fund	–	–	8.4	10.0	10.6	11.2	11.2	11.6	12.8
Refundable premium tax credit and cost sharing reductions	–	–	–	27.2	51.5	64.6	79.5	82.6	101.5
Assistance to students	11.2	10.9	55.5	74.7	175.7	185.4	553.3	202.4	144.8
Veterans' education benefits	0.8	1.6	8.8	13.6	13.1	12.2	12.1	12.7	13.4
Student assistance, Department of Education and other	10.4	9.2	46.8	61.1	162.6	173.2	541.2	189.7	131.4
Housing assistance	15.9	28.6	57.6	46.7	51.8	54.3	57.0	62.1	67.7
Food and nutrition assistance	24.0	32.4	95.0	104.6	115.0	167.9	193.3	172.5	183.5
SNAP (including Puerto Rico) [2]	15.9	18.3	70.5	76.1	85.6	134.5	148.5	134.6	138.7
Child nutrition and special milk programs	5.0	9.2	16.4	21.0	22.7	25.8	37.2	29.2	37.6
Supplemental feeding programs (WIC and CSFP [3])	2.1	4.0	6.5	6.3	5.0	5.0	5.6	6.8	5.2
Commodity donations and other	1.0	0.9	1.6	1.1	1.6	2.6	2.0	1.8	2.0
Public assistance and related programs	34.9	88.5	183.2	175.3	464.1	826.9	371.8	263.6	235.8
Supplemental security income program	11.5	29.7	44.0	52.3	53.8	53.4	58.9	57.7	54.5
Family support payments to states and TANF [4]	12.2	18.4	24.8	20.7	21.6	20.1	20.1	21.7	21.4
Low income home energy assistance	1.3	1.5	4.6	3.4	3.8	4.4	7.2	5.9	5.2
Earned income tax credit	4.4	26.1	54.7	60.1	57.6	60.8	64.3	55.5	56.4
Child care assistance for low income families	–	3.3	5.9	5.1	10.0	15.3	26.0	26.5	20.8
Veterans' non-service-connected pensions	3.6	3.0	4.4	5.3	4.8	4.2	4.1	3.5	3.0
Payments to states for foster care/adoption assistance	1.6	5.5	7.0	7.3	8.8	9.7	9.2	9.8	9.9
Child tax credit and child and dependent care tax credit	–	0.8	22.7	20.6	27.8	79.0	138.9	29.0	28.8
U.S. coronavirus payments and credits	–	–	–	–	275.4	579.7	42.6	53.5	35.2
Other public assistance	0.3	0.3	15.2	0.4	0.6	0.5	0.5	0.6	0.6
All other payments for individuals [1]	4.0	6.3	7.3	7.8	12.5	14.5	17.7	20.9	39.6
Coal miners and black lung benefits	1.5	1.5	0.5	0.4	0.4	0.3	0.3	0.4	0.5
Veterans' insurance and burial benefits	1.4	1.4	1.3	1.2	0.4	0.5	0.4	-0.4	0.6
Aging services programs	–	0.9	1.5	1.7	2.4	2.7	2.7	3.0	3.5
Energy employees compensation fund	–	–	1.1	1.0	1.6	1.7	1.8	2.2	2.5
September 11th victim compensation	–	–	–	0.1	1.5	1.8	1.5	1.8	2.0
Refugee assistance and other	1.1	2.5	2.9	3.3	6.2	7.5	10.9	13.3	27.5

– Represents zero. [1] Includes other items not shown separately. [2] Supplemental Nutrition Assistance Program, formerly known as food stamps. [3] WIC is Women, Infants, and Children. CSFP is Commodity Supplemental Food Program. [4] TANF is Temporary Assistance for Needy Families.

Source: U.S. Office of Management and Budget, *Budget of the U.S. Government, Fiscal Year 2025: Historical Tables*, March 2024. See also <www.whitehouse.gov/omb/budget>.

Table 514. Federal Budget Receipts by Source: 1990 to 2024

[In billions of dollars (1,032.0 represents $1,032,000,000,000). For fiscal years ending September 30. Receipts reflect collections. Covers both federal funds and trust funds; see text, this section]

Source	1990	2000	2010	2015	2020	2021	2022	2023	2024, estimate
Total federal receipts	**1,032.0**	**2,025.2**	**2,162.7**	**3,249.9**	**3,421.2**	**4,047.1**	**4,897.3**	**4,440.9**	**5,081.5**
(On-budget)	750.3	1,544.6	1,531.0	2,479.5	2,455.7	3,094.8	3,831.4	3,247.2	3,841.5
(Off-budget)	281.7	480.6	631.7	770.4	965.4	952.3	1,066.0	1,193.8	1,240.0
Individual income taxes	466.9	1,004.5	898.5	1,540.8	1,608.7	2,044.4	2,632.1	2,176.5	2,503.4
Corporation income taxes	93.5	207.3	191.4	343.8	211.8	371.8	424.9	419.6	612.8
Social insurance and retirement receipts	380.0	652.9	864.8	1,065.3	1,310.0	1,314.1	1,483.5	1,614.5	1,720.5
Excise taxes	35.3	68.9	66.9	98.3	86.8	75.3	87.7	75.8	99.7
Other	56.2	91.7	141.0	201.8	203.9	241.5	269.1	154.6	145.1
Social insurance and retirement receipts	**380.0**	**652.9**	**864.8**	**1,065.3**	**1,310.0**	**1,314.1**	**1,483.5**	**1,614.5**	**1,720.5**
Employment and general retirement, total	353.9	620.5	815.9	1,010.4	1,261.7	1,251.9	1,410.7	1,558.1	1,658.8
Old–age and survivors insurance (off–budget)	255.0	411.7	540.0	658.5	825.3	814.0	911.2	1,020.4	1,060.0
Disability insurance (off–budget)	26.6	68.9	91.7	111.8	140.1	138.3	154.8	173.3	180.0
Hospital insurance	68.6	135.5	180.1	234.2	291.8	294.8	339.1	357.8	412.6
Railroad retirement/pension fund	2.3	2.7	2.3	3.3	2.7	2.9	3.2	3.7	3.6
Unemployment insurance funds	21.6	27.6	44.8	51.2	43.1	56.6	66.5	49.4	54.1
Other retirement	4.5	4.8	4.1	3.7	5.2	5.6	6.3	6.9	7.6
Federal employees retirement, employee share	4.4	4.7	4.1	3.6	5.2	5.6	6.3	6.9	7.6
Excise taxes, total	**35.3**	**68.9**	**66.9**	**98.3**	**86.8**	**75.3**	**87.7**	**75.8**	**99.7**
Federal funds [1]	15.6	22.7	18.3	37.8	29.6	18.4	24.1	5.2	26.9
Alcohol	5.7	8.1	9.2	9.6	9.5	10.3	10.2	9.5	9.6
Tobacco	4.1	7.2	17.2	14.5	12.4	12.1	11.3	10.3	9.7
Telephone	3.0	5.7	1.0	0.6	0.4	0.3	0.3	0.3	0.3
Ozone–depleting chemicals/products	0.4	0.1	–	–	–	–	–	–	–
Transportation fuels	–	0.8	-11.0	-3.4	-6.5	-6.0	-5.1	-15.2	-5.8
Health insurance providers	–	–	–	11.3	15.3	0.2	–	–	–
Indoor tanning services	–	–	–	0.1	0.1	0.1	0.1	0.1	0.1
Trust funds [1]	19.8	46.2	48.7	60.5	57.2	56.9	63.7	70.6	72.8
Transportation	13.9	35.0	35.0	40.8	42.8	43.5	46.6	42.2	44.0
Airport and airway	3.7	9.7	10.6	14.3	9.0	8.2	11.4	22.3	19.9
Black lung disability	0.7	0.5	0.6	0.6	0.3	0.3	0.2	0.3	0.3
Inland waterway	0.1	0.1	0.1	0.1	0.1	0.1	0.1	0.1	0.1
Hazardous substance superfund	0.8	(Z)	–	–	–	–	0.4	1.2	2.2
Oil spill liability	0.1	0.2	0.5	0.5	0.4	0.6	0.6	0.3	0.5
Aquatic resources	0.2	0.3	0.6	0.6	0.6	0.6	0.6	0.6	0.6
Leaking underground storage tank	0.1	0.2	0.2	0.2	0.2	0.2	0.2	0.2	0.2
Tobacco assessments	–	–	0.9	(Z)	–	(Z)	(Z)	(Z)	–
Vaccine injury compensation	0.2	0.1	0.2	0.3	0.3	0.3	0.3	0.2	0.3
Supplementary medical insurance	–	–	–	3.0	3.2	2.8	2.8	2.8	4.3

– Represents zero. Z Represents less than $50,000,000. [1] Includes other funds, not shown separately.

Source: U.S. Office of Management and Budget, *Budget of the U.S. Government, Fiscal Year 2025: Historical Tables*, March 2024. See also <www.whitehouse.gov/omb/budget>.

Table 515. Federal Trust Fund Income, Outlays, and Balances: 2023 to 2025

[In billions of dollars (22.7 represents $22,700,000,000). For fiscal years ending September 30. Income reflects receipts deposited. Outlays are on a checks-issued basis less refunds collected. Balances reflect funds that have not been spent. See text, this section, for discussion of the budget concept and trust funds]

Fund type	Income			Outlays			Balances [1]		
	2023	2024, estimate	2025, estimate	2023	2024, estimate	2025, estimate	2023	2024, estimate	2025, estimate
Airport and airway trust fund	22.7	20.6	21.1	-16.9	-17.8	-19.1	18.2	21.0	23.0
Civil service retirement and disability fund	130.2	135.4	140.1	-104.2	-110.5	-114.9	1,037.8	1,062.7	1,087.9
Federal employees' health benefits fund	63.4	68.2	72.2	-65.1	-69.7	-72.1	25.5	24.0	24.1
Employee life insurance fund	5.3	6.8	7.0	-3.8	-3.8	-3.9	52.3	55.2	58.3
Foreign military sales trust fund	52.7	41.4	42.6	-39.7	-38.9	-40.1	51.5	54.0	56.5
Foreign service retirement and disability fund	1.5	1.5	1.4	-1.1	-1.2	-1.2	21.1	21.4	21.7
Highway trust fund	48.4	50.0	47.8	-60.3	-64.9	-68.9	121.6	106.7	85.6
Medicare:									
Hospital insurance (HI) trust fund	424.3	481.2	617.9	-410.5	-406.8	-438.9	192.0	266.4	445.4
Supplementary insurance trust fund	610.3	655.9	715.9	-615.3	-628.1	-710.3	158.4	186.2	191.8
Military retirement fund	218.1	265.0	256.7	-74.7	-71.8	-80.3	1,321.4	1,514.6	1,691.0
Railroad retirement trust funds	17.4	14.8	16.9	-15.7	-17.0	-16.9	21.9	19.7	19.6
Social security:									
Disability insurance trust fund	180.8	189.5	197.9	-152.5	-156.3	-163.6	142.9	176.2	210.5
Old-age and survivors trust fund	1,152.2	1,197.8	1,240.7	-1,202.1	-1,301.4	-1,386.2	2,673.8	2,570.2	2,424.8
Unemployment trust funds	51.6	58.0	60.6	-36.1	-55.4	-52.5	53.0	55.5	63.6
Other trust funds	31.9	33.6	34.7	-29.2	-33.5	-31.8	21.3	23.7	27.1

[1] Balances available on a cash basis (rather than an authorization basis) at the end of the year. Balances are primarily invested in federal debt securities.

Source: U.S. Office of Management and Budget, *Budget of the U.S. Government, Fiscal Year 2025: Analytical Perspectives*, March 2024. See also <www.whitehouse.gov/omb/budget>.

Table 516. Tax Expenditure Estimates Relating to Individual and Corporate Income Taxes by Selected Function: 2023 to 2026

[In millions of dollars (15,990 represents $15,990,000,000). For fiscal years ending September 30. Tax expenditures are defined as revenue losses attributable to provisions of the federal tax laws that allow a special exclusion, exemption, or deduction from gross income or that provide a special credit, a preferential rate of tax, or a deferral of liability. Data are based upon current tax law enacted as of July 31, 2022; see source for more information. Minus sign (-) indicates decrease]

Function and provision	2023	2024	2025	2026
National defense:				
Exclusion of benefits and allowances to armed forces personnel.........................	15,990	16,600	17,250	17,940
International affairs:				
Exclusion of income earned abroad by U.S. citizens..............................	5,420	5,600	5,730	5,870
Reduced tax rate on active income of controlled foreign corporations...........................	45,190	46,540	47,940	41,940
General science, space, and technology:				
Expensing of research and experimentation expenditures (normal tax method)................	-38,660	-28,850	-17,940	-5,610
Credit for increasing research activities.....................................	28,220	30,040	31,880	33,800
Energy:				
Energy production credit..	7,450	7,570	9,530	13,540
Energy investment credit..	25,970	27,510	18,670	13,760
Tax credits for clean vehicles.....................................	10,560	15,570	23,580	28,930
Credit for residential energy efficient property...........................	7,090	9,250	6,150	4850
Commerce and housing:				
Financial institutions and insurance:				
Exclusion of life insurance death benefits...............................	15,320	16,260	16,670	17,360
Housing:				
Deductibility of mortgage interest on owner–occupied homes.........................	31,820	30,770	30,920	67,280
Deductibility of state and local property tax on owner–occupied homes.......................	6,910	6,410	6,090	34,180
Capital gains exclusion on home sales.................................	54,410	58,230	60,400	66,830
Exclusion of net imputed rental income.................................	147,240	151,950	156,250	174,960
Exception from passive loss rules for $25,000 of rental loss.....................................	5,470	5,460	5,600	5,840
Credit for low–income housing investments...............................	12,800	13,630	14,400	15,130
Commerce:				
Capital gains (except agriculture, timber, iron ore, and coal)...........................	115,630	114,130	118,590	132,180
Step–up basis of capital gains at death................................	49,240	33,560	35,940	38,960
Accelerated depreciation of machinery and equipment (normal tax method)....................	10,430	-3,730	-11,580	-18,420
Allow 20-percent deduction to certain pass-through income..............	37,240	61850	65180	27000
Transportation:				
Exclusion of reimbursed employee parking expenses............................	1,827	1,890	1,957	2,025
Education, training, employment, and social services:				
Education:				
Exclusion of scholarship and fellowship income (normal tax method).........................	4,430	4,670	4,920	5,440
Tax credits and deductions for postsecondary education expenses........................	13,940	13,860	13,660	13,390
Exclusion of interest on bonds for private nonprofit educational facilities......................	2,280	1,850	1,900	2,070
Deductibility of charitable contributions to educational institutions.........................	6,230	6,290	6,300	7,360
Training, employment, and social services:				
Exclusion of employee meals and lodging (other than military)...............................	7,530	6,960	6,900	8,140
Credit for child and dependent care expenses.............................	3,480	3,690	3,850	3,920
Deductibility of charitable contributions, other than education and health..............	47,410	47,940	48,030	56,740
Health:				
Exclusion of employer contributions for medical insurance premiums and medical care.................	215,860	231,010	246,510	289,890
Self–employed medical insurance premiums...............................	8,150	8,520	9,030	11,210
Medical Savings Accounts/Health Savings Accounts...........................	12,830	13,610	14,180	16,270
Deductibility of medical expenses...................................	12,260	12,900	13,550	18,620
Exclusion of interest on hospital construction bonds........................	3,120	2,530	2,600	2,830
Refundable Premium Assistance Tax Credit.............................	15,047	14,935	15,413	12,440
Deductibility of charitable contributions (health).......................	9,000	9,060	9,050	10,110
Income security:				
Child tax credit [1]..	67,520	63,740	65,370	45,890
Exclusion of workers' compensation benefits...........................	8,870	8,870	8,870	8,860
Net exclusion of pension contributions and earnings:				
Defined benefit employer plans....................................	70,100	68,860	68,880	77,890
Defined contribution employer plans................................	133,860	136,290	141,780	170,240
Individual Retirement Accounts (IRAs)...............................	32,690	33,210	34,470	41,470
Self-employed plans..	43,180	43,960	45,730	54,910
Exclusion of other employee benefits:				
Premiums on group term life insurance................................	3,440	3,500	3,610	4,100
Earned income tax credit.......................................	2,700	3,030	3,180	3,290
Recovery rebate credits...	3,460	990	220	–
Social security:				
Exclusion of social security benefits:				
Social security benefits for retired and disabled workers, spouses, dependents, and survivors...........	30,700	30,810	30,440	34,430
Veterans' benefits and services:				
Exclusion of veterans' death benefits and disability compensation............................	11,640	13,120	14,040	15,200
General purpose fiscal assistance:				
Exclusion of interest on public purpose state and local bonds............................	29,810	24,120	24,880	27,000
Deductibility of nonbusiness state and local tax, other than owner-occupied homes.............	7,030	6,580	6,090	65,920
Interest:				
Deferral of interest on U.S. savings bonds................................	820	810	800	800
Addendum: Aid to state and local governments:				
Deductibility of:				
Property taxes on owner–occupied homes.............................	6,910	6,410	6,090	34,180
Nonbusiness state and local taxes other than on owner–occupied homes....................	7,030	6,580	6,090	65,920
Exclusion of interest on state and local bonds for:				
Public purposes...	29,810	24,120	24,880	27,000
Private nonprofit educational facilities...............................	2,280	1,850	1,900	2,070
Hospital construction...	3,120	2,530	2,600	2,830

– Represents or rounds to zero. [1] Child tax credit includes the credit for other dependents.

Source: U.S. Department of the Treasury, "Tax Expenditures," <home.treasury.gov/policy-issues/tax-policy/tax-expenditures>, accessed March 2024.

Table 517. Gross Government Fixed Investment by Type: 2000 to 2022

[In millions of dollars (388,850 represents $388,850,000,000)]

Type	2000	2010	2015	2018	2019	2020	2021	2022
Gross government fixed investment [1]	**388,850**	**644,504**	**629,431**	**730,649**	**774,969**	**816,469**	**826,783**	**876,759**
Federal	157,388	297,249	271,030	311,878	332,452	364,801	377,956	406,513
National defense	83,415	176,205	145,944	161,447	174,428	187,103	189,485	202,440
Nondefense	73,973	121,045	125,086	150,431	158,024	177,699	188,471	204,073
State and local	231,461	347,254	358,401	418,771	442,517	451,668	448,827	470,246
Structures [2]	**188,318**	**312,419**	**301,199**	**345,698**	**371,645**	**379,508**	**367,978**	**387,380**
Federal	13,760	32,625	19,760	20,768	24,648	28,307	25,118	28,431
National defense	5,396	16,654	7,100	8,433	9,388	11,515	11,644	12,775
New	5,400	16,658	7,104	8,437	9,392	11,519	11,648	12,779
Residential	1,079	1,578	581	538	543	629	684	670
Industrial	279	686	696	995	1,280	1,471	1,899	2,142
Military facilities [3]	4,042	14,394	5,827	6,904	7,569	9,419	9,065	9,967
Net purchases of used structures	-4	-4	-4	-4	-4	-4	-4	-4
Nondefense	8,364	15,971	12,659	12,335	15,260	16,791	13,474	15,656
New	9,506	14,466	13,310	13,244	15,813	18,556	13,920	15,693
Residential	(NA)	(NA)	(NA)	(NA)	(NA)	(NA)	(NA)	(NA)
Office	1,578	1,592	1,098	1,539	1,661	1,234	1,475	1,560
Commercial	753	650	674	1,418	1,341	948	1,004	1,270
Health care	774	2,127	2,242	2,216	2,114	2,026	2,043	2,565
Educational	366	379	426	317	210	103	106	116
Public safety	1,661	448	129	433	1,953	6,359	1,874	452
Amusement and recreation	610	640	332	386	365	441	513	565
Transportation	383	288	333	280	276	348	311	741
Power	71	949	1,626	507	278	220	342	440
Highways and streets	575	875	440	696	997	675	847	1,468
Conservation and development	2,046	5,323	4,637	4,614	5,961	5,586	4,792	5,593
Other [4]	689	1,195	1,274	750	606	558	587	882
Net purchases of used structures	-1,142	1,505	-651	-909	-553	-1,765	-446	-38
State and local	174,558	279,794	281,440	324,930	346,997	351,201	342,860	358,949
New	170,552	275,140	278,150	320,764	342,460	346,065	337,337	353,143
Residential	4,340	6,939	4,720	6,275	6,743	6,324	6,001	5,929
Office	15,039	22,445	20,788	23,077	23,122	24,406	24,214	24,918
Commercial	240	450	441	334	335	381	339	300
Health care	2,904	6,554	5,856	6,255	6,296	6,857	7,335	7,646
Educational	45,636	72,767	71,584	88,321	95,365	94,897	87,504	85,714
Public safety	4,499	4,920	3,968	4,007	4,364	5,224	5,203	5,342
Amusement and recreation	6,155	7,549	6,829	8,363	9,620	9,359	8,433	8,602
Transportation	14,826	23,923	29,051	32,068	37,906	40,735	37,705	36,390
Power	4,073	9,918	8,879	9,840	10,165	9,411	9,788	11,811
Highways and streets	52,149	80,412	88,147	101,207	106,280	105,868	106,474	116,340
Sewer systems	9,032	20,829	17,917	19,931	20,235	21,092	22,856	25,806
Water systems	8,649	14,578	15,216	15,869	16,472	16,439	16,532	18,828
Conservation and development	2,700	3,428	4,144	4,441	4,736	4,302	4,204	4,728
Other [5]	311	427	609	776	823	770	750	788
Net purchases of used structures	4,006	4,654	3,290	4,166	4,537	5,136	5,523	5,806
Equipment	**87,382**	**148,068**	**131,137**	**149,612**	**160,968**	**168,305**	**169,510**	**168,320**
Federal	48,602	108,478	91,430	104,234	115,286	119,918	119,767	117,804
National defense	37,777	89,313	72,605	84,106	94,955	95,401	96,062	92,381
Aircraft	7,755	16,669	17,618	19,660	24,908	19,448	20,157	20,936
Missiles	2,667	5,578	6,566	4,700	5,068	6,730	6,528	6,461
Ships	6,582	11,776	13,548	15,526	17,162	18,564	18,333	18,180
Vehicles	1,863	9,382	2,400	3,188	3,975	4,801	5,207	5,187
Electronics	4,030	12,316	6,059	7,421	8,012	8,524	8,602	8,699
Other equipment	14,880	33,593	26,414	33,611	35,830	37,333	37,235	32,918
Nondefense	10,825	19,165	18,826	20,128	20,331	24,518	23,706	25,423
State and local	38,780	39,590	39,706	45,379	45,682	48,387	49,743	50,516
Intellectual property products [2]	**113,150**	**184,016**	**197,095**	**235,338**	**242,356**	**268,656**	**289,295**	**321,059**
Federal	95,026	156,146	159,840	186,875	192,518	216,577	233,070	260,278
National defense	40,242	70,237	66,239	68,908	70,085	80,187	81,779	97,284
Software	6,045	8,094	10,429	15,689	16,602	17,776	19,917	21,936
Research and development	34,197	62,143	55,810	53,220	53,483	62,410	61,862	75,348
Nondefense	54,784	85,909	93,601	117,967	122,433	136,390	151,292	162,994
Software	11,565	17,637	22,983	32,915	34,413	36,524	40,786	44,758
Research and development	43,219	68,272	70,617	85,053	88,020	99,866	110,505	118,237
State and local	18,124	27,870	37,255	48,463	49,838	52,080	56,225	60,781
Software	9,503	12,752	18,212	26,718	27,899	30,046	33,663	37,650
Research and development	8,621	15,118	19,043	21,745	21,939	22,033	22,562	23,132
Addenda:								
Government enterprise gross fixed investment	58,885	104,630	105,812	123,886	130,794	129,680	130,164	138,951
Federal	5,923	9,847	9,216	10,126	10,560	10,244	11,049	12,761
State and local	52,962	94,784	96,596	113,760	120,234	119,436	119,115	126,190

NA Not available. [1] Consists of general government and government enterprise expenditures for fixed assets. [2] Structures, software, and research and development include compensation of government employees engaged in new own-account investment and related expenditures for goods and services. [3] Consists of Department of Defense new structures, except family housing. [4] Consists of lodging, religious, communication, sewage and waste disposal, water supply structures, and manufacturing. [5] Consists of lodging, communication, and manufacturing.

Source: U.S. Bureau of Economic Analysis, National Income and Product Accounts Tables, "Table 5.9.5. Gross Government Fixed Investment by Type," <www.bea.gov/itable/national-gdp-and-personal-income>, accessed June 2024.

Table 518. Internal Revenue Gross Collections by Type of Tax: 2010 to 2023

[2,345 represents $2,345,000,000,000, except percent. For fiscal years ending September 30. See text, this section, for information on taxes]

Type of tax	Gross collections (bil. dol.)						Percent of total					
	2010	2015	2020	2021	2022	2023	2010	2015	2020	2021	2022	2023
United States, total............	**2,345**	**3,303**	**3,493**	**4,112**	**4,902**	**4,694**	**100.0**	**100.0**	**100.0**	**100.0**	**100.0**	**100.0**
Individual income taxes...........	1,164	1,760	1,837	2,294	2,819	2,509	49.6	53.3	52.6	55.8	57.5	54.6
Withheld by employers...........	900	1,241	1,269	1,532	1,763	1,726	38.4	37.6	36.3	37.3	36.0	36.8
Tax payments [1]....................	264	519	568	762	1,056	784	11.3	15.7	16.3	18.5	21.5	16.7
Estate and trust income tax.......	12	33	34	54	85	52	0.5	1.0	1.0	1.3	1.7	1.1
Employment taxes...................	824	1,022	1,268	1,258	1,418	1,566	35.1	31.0	36.3	30.6	28.9	33.4
Old-age and disability insurance........................	813	1,007	1,257	1,247	1,405	1,551	34.7	30.5	36.0	30.3	28.7	33.0
Unemployment insurance........	7	9	6	6	7	8	0.3	0.3	0.2	0.2	0.1	0.2
Railroad retirement................	5	6	5	5	6	7	0.2	0.2	0.1	0.1	0.1	0.2
Business income taxes [2].........	278	390	264	419	476	457	11.9	11.8	7.5	10.2	9.7	9.7
Estate and gift taxes...............	20	20	18	28	33	35	0.8	0.6	0.5	0.7	0.7	0.8
Excise taxes.......................	47	77	72	58	71	74	2.0	2.3	2.1	1.4	1.4	1.6

[1] Includes collections of estimated income tax and payments made in conjunction with individual income tax return filings. [2] Includes corporate income tax and tax-exempt organization unrelated business income tax.

Source: U.S. Internal Revenue Service, *IRS Data Book 2023*, April 2024, and earlier editions. See also <www.irs.gov/statistics/soi-tax-stats-irs-data-book>.

Table 519. Individual Income Tax Summary: 1986 to 2021

[In units as indicated (103,045 represents 103,045,000). Based on a sample of returns; see Appendix III]

Year	Total returns filed (1,000)	Taxable returns		Adjusted gross income (less deficit) (bil. dol.)	Total income tax (bil. dol.)	Average tax rate (percent)	Average adjusted gross income (less deficit) per return		Average total income tax per return	
		Number (1,000)	Percent of total returns				Current dollars	Constant dollars [1]	Current dollars	Constant dollars [1]
1986.........	103,045	83,967	81.5	2,440	367	15.1	29,062	26,516	4,374	3,991
1987.........	106,996	86,724	81.1	2,701	369	13.7	31,142	27,414	4,257	3,747
1988.........	109,708	87,135	79.4	2,990	413	13.8	34,313	29,005	4,738	4,005
1989.........	112,136	89,178	79.5	3,158	433	13.7	35,415	28,560	4,855	3,915
1990.........	113,717	89,862	79.0	3,299	447	13.6	36,711	28,088	4,976	3,807
1991.........	114,730	88,734	77.3	3,337	448	13.4	37,603	27,609	5,054	3,711
1992.........	113,605	86,732	76.3	3,484	476	13.7	40,168	28,630	5,491	3,914
1993.........	114,602	86,435	75.4	3,564	503	14.1	41,233	28,535	5,817	4,026
1994.........	115,943	87,619	75.6	3,737	535	14.3	42,646	28,776	6,104	4,119
1995.........	118,218	89,253	75.5	4,008	588	14.7	44,901	29,463	6,593	4,326
1996.........	120,351	90,929	75.6	4,342	658	15.2	47,750	30,433	7,239	4,614
1997.........	122,422	93,471	76.4	4,765	731	15.3	50,980	31,763	7,824	4,875
1998.........	124,771	93,048	74.6	5,160	789	15.3	55,458	33,836	8,475	5,171
1999.........	127,075	94,546	74.4	5,581	877	15.7	59,028	35,431	9,280	5,570
2000.........	129,374	96,818	74.8	6,083	981	16.1	62,832	36,488	10,129	5,882
2001.........	130,255	94,764	72.8	5,847	888	15.2	61,702	34,840	9,370	5,291
2002.........	130,076	90,964	69.9	5,641	797	14.1	62,015	34,472	8,762	4,870
2003.........	130,424	88,922	68.2	5,747	748	13.0	64,625	35,122	8,412	4,572
2004.........	132,226	89,102	67.4	6,266	832	13.3	70,318	37,225	9,337	4,943
2005.........	134,373	90,593	67.4	6,857	935	13.6	75,687	38,754	10,319	5,284
2006.........	138,395	92,741	67.0	7,439	1,024	13.8	80,218	39,791	11,041	5,477
2007 [2]........	142,979	96,273	67.3	8,072	1,116	13.8	83,851	40,449	11,588	5,590
2008.........	142,451	90,660	63.6	7,583	1,032	13.6	83,647	38,851	11,379	5,285
2009.........	140,494	81,890	58.3	6,778	866	12.8	82,765	38,579	10,575	4,929
2010.........	142,892	84,476	59.1	7,246	952	13.1	85,778	39,338	11,266	5,166
2011.........	145,370	91,694	63.1	7,693	1,046	13.6	83,901	37,299	11,402	5,069
2012.........	144,928	93,110	64.2	8,442	1,188	14.1	90,669	39,491	12,759	5,557
2013.........	147,351	94,532	64.2	8,426	1,235	14.7	89,133	38,261	13,065	5,608
2014.........	148,607	96,544	65.0	9,103	1,378	15.1	94,285	39,827	14,271	6,028
2015.........	150,493	99,041	65.8	9,551	1,458	15.3	96,433	40,686	14,720	6,211
2016.........	150,272	100,052	66.6	10,226	1,446	14.1	102,206	42,584	14,453	6,022
2017.........	152,903	103,747	67.9	10,395	1,605	15.4	100,197	40,877	15,473	6,312
2018.........	153,774	100,424	65.3	10,850	1,539	14.2	108,042	43,026	15,322	6,102
2019.........	157,797	104,006	65.9	11,210	1,581	14.1	107,783	42,159	15,204	5,947
2020.........	164,359	102,960	62.6	12,592	1,711	13.6	122,297	47,254	16,615	6,420
2021.........	160,824	104,574	65.0	13,880	2,196	15.8	132,729	48,983	21,003	7,751

[1] Constant dollars are calculated using the U.S. Bureau of Labor Statistics' Consumer Price Index, chained to 1982-84 dollars. [2] Total number of returns does not include returns filed by individuals only to receive economic stimulus payment with no other reason to file.

Source: U.S. Internal Revenue Service, *Individual Income Tax Returns Complete Report 2021*, April 2024. See also <www.irs.gov/statistics/soi-tax-stats-individual-income-tax-return-form-1040-statistics>.

Table 520. Federal Individual Income Tax Returns—Adjusted Gross Income (AGI) by Selected Source of Income and Income Class: 2021

[In millions of dollars ($13,879,929 represents $13,879,929,000,000), except as indicated. For the tax year. Minus sign (-) indicates net loss was greater than net income. Based on a sample of returns; see source and Appendix III]

Item	Total [1]	Adjusted gross income class						
		Under $10,000 [1]	$10,000 to $19,999	$20,000 to $29,999	$30,000 to $39,999	$40,000 to $49,999	$50,000 to $99,999	$100,000 and over
Number of taxable returns (1,000)....	**104,574**	**332**	**4,281**	**9,664**	**10,942**	**10,179**	**33,980**	**35,197**
Adjusted gross income (AGI) [2]........	**13,879,929**	**-11,026**	**72,005**	**243,662**	**382,385**	**457,336**	**2,444,793**	**10,290,773**
Salaries and wages......................	8,193,036	1,211	44,123	182,830	298,847	360,699	1,823,690	5,481,585
Percent of AGI.......................	59.0	-11.0	61.3	75.1	78.2	78.9	74.6	53.3
Interest received.........................	147,516	[5] 543	275	936	1,239	1,675	11,054	131,793
Dividends in AGI........................	653,901	1,309	612	1,690	2,688	4,319	37,926	605,358
Business or profession, net profit less loss.....................	332,858	[5] -216	2,051	7,073	8,552	8,540	50,864	255,992
Sales of property, net gain less loss [3].....................	2,047,282	[5] 4,213	[5] 474	[5] 829	1,808	3,066	37,080	1,999,813
Pensions and annuities in AGI..........	804,862	156	9,278	19,857	32,685	37,939	235,840	469,105
Rents and royalties, net income less loss [4]..................	72,424	[5] 3	97	567	461	547	5,354	65,394
Number of all returns (1,000)..........	**160,824**	**21,530**	**19,843**	**17,651**	**16,123**	**12,782**	**37,312**	**35,583**
Adjusted gross income [2]...............	**14,795,614**	**-84,198**	**296,748**	**440,856**	**561,386**	**573,155**	**2,664,095**	**10,343,571**
Salaries and wages......................	9,022,353	92,648	196,009	321,184	445,172	456,243	1,996,403	5,514,694
Interest received.........................	159,054	5,689	1,676	1,855	1,836	2,198	12,305	133,495
Dividends in AGI........................	682,868	8,630	4,487	4,847	5,503	6,345	44,113	608,942
Business or profession, net profit less loss.....................	411,501	-4,027	27,874	23,057	18,808	16,389	67,981	261,420
Sales of property, net gain less loss [3].....................	2,083,240	13,462	2,738	3,481	5,260	5,724	46,276	2,006,300
Pensions and annuities in AGI..........	858,038	10,967	25,618	31,944	36,743	40,462	241,447	470,857
Rents and royalties, net income less loss [4]..................	68,402	-4,516	1,130	718	188	352	5,008	65,522

[1] Includes a small number of returns with no adjusted gross income. [2] Includes other sources, not shown separately. [3] Includes sales of capital assets. [4] Excludes rental passive losses disallowed in the computation of AGI. [5] Use caution because underlying data are based on a small number of returns.

Source: U.S. Internal Revenue Service, "SOI Tax Stats - Individual Statistical Tables by Size of Adjusted Gross Income," <www.irs.gov/statistics/soi-tax-stats-individual-income-tax-return-form-1040-statistics>, accessed February 2024.

Table 521. Federal Individual Income Tax Returns—Total and Selected Sources of Adjusted Gross Income: 2020 and 2021

[In units as indicated (164,359 represents 164,359,000). For tax years. Based on a sample of returns; see source and Appendix III. Use caution comparing trends because of changes in tax law. Minus sign (-) indicates decrease]

Item	2020		2021		Change in amount, 2020-2021	
	Number of returns (1,000)	Amount (mil. dol.)	Number of returns (1,000)	Amount (mil. dol.)	Net change (mil. dol.)	Percent change
Adjusted gross income (less deficit) [1].................	**164,359**	**12,591,789**	**160,824**	**14,795,614**	**2,203,825**	**17.5**
Salaries and wages..........................	130,099	8,416,496	126,082	9,022,353	605,857	7.2
Taxable interest.............................	48,346	127,376	48,990	103,535	-23,841	-18.7
Ordinary dividends..........................	31,087	327,877	32,247	386,961	59,085	18.0
Qualified dividends.........................	29,013	260,244	30,525	295,906	35,662	13.7
Business or profession net income (less loss).............	27,727	337,175	28,652	411,501	74,326	22.0
Net capital gain (less loss)....................	25,084	1,117,710	28,571	2,032,553	914,844	81.8
Capital gain distributions [2].................	14,863	66,544	16,967	156,121	89,576	134.6
Sales of property other than capital assets, net gain (less loss)...............	1,949	33,789	1,996	50,686	16,898	50.0
Sales of property other than capital assets, net gain. ..	992	53,559	1,106	71,725	18,166	33.9
Taxable social security benefits................	23,057	374,167	23,798	412,830	38,663	10.3
Total rental and royalty net income (less net loss) [3]......	9,913	54,964	9,802	68,402	13,438	24.4
Partnership and S corporation net income (less loss).....	9,002	707,432	10,525	975,656	268,225	37.9
Estate and trust net income (less loss).....................	651	31,483	674	43,489	12,006	38.1
Farm net income (less loss)...................	1,738	-21,864	1,724	-26,142	-4,278	19.6
Farm net income.........................	471	12,887	449	13,337	450	3.5
Unemployment compensation................	29,901	405,284	15,809	208,872	-196,411	-48.5
Taxable pensions and annuities..............	30,412	827,598	29,357	858,038	30,441	3.7
Taxable Individual Retirement Account (IRA) distributions...........................	13,101	284,005	15,584	408,382	124,377	43.8
Other net income (less loss) [4]..............	6,956	37,254	6,385	50,539	13,286	35.7
Gambling earnings...........................	1,687	28,438	2,249	46,631	18,193	64.0

[1] Includes other sources of income not shown separately. [2] Includes both Schedule D and Form 1040 or 1040A capital gain distributions. [3] Includes farm rental net income (less loss). [4] Other net income (less loss) represents data reported on Form 1040, except net operating losses, foreign-earned income exclusions, cancellation of debt, taxable health savings account distributions, and gambling earnings.

Source: U.S. Internal Revenue Service, *Statistics of Income—Individual Income Tax Returns 2021*, Publication 1304, April 2024. See also <www.irs.gov/statistics/soi-tax-stats-individual-income-tax-return-form-1040-statistics>.

Table 522. Federal Individual Income Tax Returns—Net Capital Gains and Capital Gain Distributions: 1990 to 2021

[12,122 represents 12,122,000. For tax years. Based on a sample of returns; see source and Appendix III. Minus sign (-) indicates decrease]

Tax year	Net capital gain (less loss)				Capital gain distributions [2]			
	Number of returns (1,000)	Current dollars (mil. dol.)	Constant (1982-1984) dollars [1]		Number of returns (1,000)	Current dollars (mil. dol.)	Constant (1982-1984) dollars [1]	
			Amount (mil. dol.)	Percent change			Amount (mil. dol.)	Percent change
1990	12,122	113,159	86,579	(NA)	5,069	3,905	2,988	(NA)
1991	12,682	101,559	74,566	-13.9	5,796	4,665	3,425	14.6
1992	13,353	116,394	82,961	11.3	5,917	7,426	5,293	54.5
1993	14,466	141,577	97,977	18.1	9,998	11,995	8,301	56.8
1994	14,809	139,545	94,160	-3.9	9,803	11,322	7,640	-8.0
1995	15,285	166,758	109,421	16.2	10,744	14,391	9,443	23.6
1996	16,636	245,961	156,763	43.3	12,778	24,722	15,757	66.9
1997	24,240	356,083	221,859	41.5	14,969	45,132	28,120	78.5
1998	25,690	446,084	273,671	23.4	16,070	46,147	28,311	0.7
1999	21,494	530,796	318,605	16.4	17,012	59,473	35,698	26.1
2000	22,875	614,740	356,992	12.0	17,546	79,079	45,923	28.6
2001	23,470	325,169	183,608	-48.6	12,216	13,609	7,684	-83.3
2002	23,250	238,368	132,501	-27.8	7,567	5,343	2,970	-61.4
2003	21,890	294,022	159,794	20.6	7,265	4,695	2,552	-14.1
2004	22,389	471,736	249,728	56.3	10,733	15,336	8,119	218.2
2005	22,040	663,057	339,507	36.0	13,393	35,581	18,219	124.4
2006	22,069	771,046	382,463	12.7	14,511	59,417	29,473	61.8
2007	22,144	895,674	431,979	12.9	15,714	86,397	41,669	41.4
2008	20,409	466,579	216,708	-49.8	11,544	21,954	10,197	-75.5
2009	19,540	231,187	107,761	-50.3	4,191	2,411	1,124	-89.0
2010	20,160	363,809	166,842	54.8	6,567	6,270	2,875	155.9
2011	20,272	375,260	166,827	0.0	8,859	14,171	6,300	119.1
2012	20,241	620,670	270,334	62.0	10,412	17,829	7,766	23.3
2013	20,539	483,414	207,512	-23.2	12,845	44,774	19,220	147.5
2014	20,190	687,388	290,360	39.9	13,665	79,059	33,396	73.8
2015	19,955	694,952	293,208	1.0	14,056	74,060	31,247	-6.4
2016	20,124	614,215	255,916	-12.7	13,233	42,534	17,722	-43.3
2017	21,170	843,116	343,960	34.4	14,173	73,274	29,893	68.7
2018	21,241	911,823	363,121	5.6	14,200	101,059	40,245	34.6
2019	21,705	853,487	333,840	-8.1	13,912	70,119	27,427	-31.9
2020	25,084	1,117,710	431,863	29.4	14,863	66,544	25,712	-6.3
2021	28,571	2,032,553	750,103	73.7	16,967	156,121	57,616	124.1

NA Not available. [1] Constant dollars were calculated using the U.S. Bureau of Labor Statistics consumer price index for urban consumers (CPI-U, 1982-84=100). See Table 764. [2] For 1989-1996, and 1999 and later years, capital gain distributions are the sum of the amounts reported on Form 1040 and Schedule D. For 1997 and 1998, capital gain distributions were reported entirely on the Schedule D.

Source: U.S. Internal Revenue Service, *Statistics of Income—Individual Income Tax Returns 2021*, Publication 1304, April 2024. See also <www.irs.gov/statistics/soi-tax-stats-individual-income-tax-return-form-1040-statistics>.

Table 523. Alternative Minimum Tax: 1988 to 2021

[114 represents 114,000. For tax years. Based on a sample of returns; see source and Appendix III]

Tax year	Highest statutory alternative minimum tax rate (percent) [1]	Alternative minimum tax		Tax year	Highest statutory alternative minimum tax rate (percent) [1]	Alternative minimum tax	
		Number of returns (1,000)	Amount (mil. dol.)			Number of returns (1,000)	Amount (mil. dol.)
1988	21	114	1,028	2005	28	4,005	17,421
1989	21	117	831	2006	28	3,967	21,565
1990	21	132	830	2007	28	4,109	24,110
1991	24	244	1,213	2008	28	3,935	25,649
1992	24	287	1,357	2009	28	3,828	22,580
1993	28	335	2,053	2010	28	4,020	27,461
1994	28	369	2,212	2011	28	4,248	30,479
1995	28	414	2,291	2012	28	4,225	32,770
1996	28	478	2,813	2013	28	3,940	27,426
1997	28	618	4,005	2014	28	4,278	28,646
1998	28	853	5,015	2015	28	4,468	31,166
1999	28	1,018	6,478	2016	28	4,634	31,016
2000	28	1,304	9,601	2017	28	5,075	36,404
2001	28	1,120	6,757	2018	28	244	4,023
2002	28	1,911	6,854	2019	28	170	2,793
2003	28	2,358	9,470	2020	28	157	2,937
2004	28	3,096	13,029	2021	28	244	5,599

[1] Beginning 1997, the top rate on most long-term capital gains was 20 percent; beginning 2003, the rate was 15 percent; beginning 2018, the rate returned to 20 percent.

Source: U.S. Internal Revenue Service, *Statistics of Income—Individual Income Tax Returns 2021*, Publication 1304, April 2024. See also <www.irs.gov/statistics/soi-tax-stats-individual-income-tax-return-form-1040-statistics>.

Table 524. Federal Individual Income Tax Returns—Sources of Net Losses Included in Adjusted Gross Income: 2020 and 2021

[27,880 represents 27,880,000. For tax years. Based on a sample of returns; see source and Appendix III]

Item	2020 Number of returns (1,000)	2020 Amount (mil. dol.)	2021 Number of returns (1,000)	2021 Amount (mil. dol.)	Percent change in amount, 2020-2021
Total net losses	**27,880**	**691,702**	**26,386**	**703,271**	**1.7**
Business or profession net loss	7,750	99,203	7,547	105,580	6.4
Net capital loss [1]	9,165	19,311	8,074	16,242	-15.9
Net loss, sales of property other than capital assets	957	19,770	890	21,039	6.4
Total rental and royalty net loss [2]	3,716	51,916	3,497	56,766	9.3
Partnership and S corporation net loss	3,100	224,177	3,444	260,841	16.4
Estate and trust net loss	45	4,658	49	5,899	26.7
Farm net loss	1,267	34,751	1,275	39,479	13.6
Net operating loss [3]	1,323	224,130	1,156	185,261	-17.3
Other net loss [4]	556	13,786	454	12,163	-11.8

[1] As reported on Form 1040, Schedule D. Includes only the portion of capital losses allowable in the calculation of adjusted gross income. Only $3,000 of net capital loss per return ($1,500 for married filing separately) are allowed to be included in negative total income. Any excess is carried forward to future years. [2] Includes farm rental net loss. [3] Net operating loss is the excess loss of a business when taxable income for a prior year was less than zero. [4] Other net loss represents losses reported on Form 1040, Schedule 1, line 8, except net operating loss and the foreign-earned income exclusion.

Source: U.S. Internal Revenue Service, Statistics of Income, "SOI Tax Stats - Individual Statistical Tables by Size of Adjusted Gross Income," <www.irs.gov/statistics/soi-tax-stats-individual-statistical-tables-by-size-of-adjusted-gross-income>, accessed February 2024.

Table 525. Federal Individual Income Tax Returns—Adjusted Gross Income, Taxable Income, and Total Income Tax: 2010 to 2021

[142,892 represents 142,892,000. For tax years. Based on a sample of returns; see source and Appendix III]

Year	2010 Number of returns (1,000)	2010 Amount (mil. dol.)	2020 Number of returns (1,000)	2020 Amount (mil. dol.)	2021 Number of returns (1,000)	2021 Amount (mil. dol.)	Percent change in amount, 2020-2021
Adjusted gross income (less deficit)	142,892	8,089,142	164,359	12,591,789	160,824	14,795,614	17.5
Exemptions [1]	287,679	1,049,272	(NA)	(NA)	(NA)	(NA)	(NA)
Taxable income	107,304	5,502,001	127,425	9,812,731	128,520	11,767,185	19.9
Total income tax	84,476	951,674	102,960	1,710,686	104,574	2,196,348	28.4
Alternative minimum tax	4,020	27,461	157	2,937	244	5,599	90.6

NA Not available. [1] The number of returns represent the number of exemptions. Personal and dependent exemptions were suspended for tax years 2018-2021.

Source: U.S. Internal Revenue Service, Statistics of Income, *Individual Income Tax Returns Complete Report 2021,* April 2024, and earlier editions. See also <www.irs.gov/statistics/soi-tax-stats-individual-income-tax-return-form-1040-statistics>.

Table 526. Federal Individual Income Tax Returns—Number, Adjusted Gross Income (AGI), and Income Tax by Size of AGI: 2020 and 2021

[164,359 represents 164,359,000. Based on a sample of returns; see Appendix III]

Size of AGI	Number of returns (1,000) 2020	Number of returns (1,000) 2021	AGI (bil. dol.) 2020	AGI (bil. dol.) 2021	Total income tax (bil. dol.) 2020	Total income tax (bil. dol.) 2021	Income tax as a percent of AGI 2020	Income tax as a percent of AGI 2021
Total	164,359	160,824	12,592	14,796	1,710.7	2,196.3	13.6	14.8
Under $1	5,260	4,099	-275	-172	0.1	0.2	(NA)	-0.1
$1 to 9,999	20,464	17,432	100	88	0.2	0.2	0.2	0.2
$10,000 to $19,999	20,604	19,843	307	297	2.3	1.5	0.7	0.5
$20,000 to $29,999	19,242	17,651	480	441	10.9	10.9	2.3	2.5
$30,000 to $49,999	29,930	28,905	1,173	1,135	50.3	50.4	4.3	4.4
$50,000 to $99,999	36,983	37,312	2,635	2,664	192.2	198.8	7.3	7.5
$100,000 to $199,999	22,415	24,044	3,060	3,297	334.6	365.2	10.9	11.1
$200,000 to $499,999	7,615	9,046	2,187	2,619	366.8	443.4	16.8	16.9
$500,000 to $999,999	1,238	1,617	833	1,093	194.9	252.6	23.4	23.1
$1,000,000 to $1,499,999	273	377	329	455	86.8	119.1	26.4	26.2
$1,500,000 to $1,999,999	109	156	188	268	51.7	72.7	27.5	27.1
$2,000,000 to $4,999,999	158	234	471	699	131.8	192.5	28.0	27.5
$5,000,000 to $9,999,999	41	63	278	435	77.9	118.7	28.0	27.3
$10,000,000 or more	27	45	824	1,478	210.2	370.2	25.5	25.1

NA Not available.

Source: U.S. Internal Revenue Service, Statistics of Income, *Individual Income Tax Returns Complete Report 2021,* April 2024. See also <www.irs.gov/statistics/soi-tax-stats-individual-income-tax-return-form-1040-statistics>.

Table 527. Federal Individual Income Tax Returns—Selected Itemized Deductions and the Standard Deduction: 2020 and 2021

[15,535 represents 15,535,000. For tax years. Based on a sample of returns; see source and Appendix III. Minus sign (-) indicates decrease]

Item	2020		2021		Percent change, 2020–2021	
	Number of returns [1] (1,000)	Amount (mil. dol.)	Number of returns [1] (1,000)	Amount (mil. dol.)	Number of returns [1]	Amount
Total itemized deductions	**15,535**	**607,515**	**14,843**	**659,681**	**-4.5**	**8.6**
Medical and dental expenses after adjusted gross income (AGI) limitation	3,942	77,248	3,693	75,886	-6.3	-1.8
Taxes paid [2]	15,401	124,226	14,688	119,542	-4.6	-3.8
State and local income taxes	11,257	207,853	10,770	250,997	-4.3	20.8
State and local general sales taxes	3,733	8,064	3,541	7,643	-5.1	-5.2
Interest paid [3]	12,531	178,555	11,754	163,274	-6.2	-8.6
Home mortgage interest	12,290	157,788	11,510	138,865	-6.3	-12.0
Charitable contributions	12,637	204,663	12,118	263,251	-4.1	28.6
Other than cash contributions	7,047	85,720	6,519	121,375	-7.5	41.6
Casualty and theft losses	7	275	10	726	53.2	163.6
Total unlimited miscellaneous deductions [4]	723	22,408	934	36,913	29.2	64.7
Basic standard deduction	**143,551**	**2,445,087**	**141,873**	**2,452,790**	**-1.2**	**0.3**
Additional standard deduction	**25,304**	**49,592**	**26,009**	**52,824**	**2.8**	**6.5**

[1] Returns with no adjusted gross income are excluded from the deduction counts. For this reason, the sum of the number of returns with total itemized deductions and the number of returns with total standard deduction is less than the total number of returns for all filers. [2] Includes real estate taxes, personal property taxes, and other taxes, not shown separately. [3] Includes investment interest, deductible mortgage "points," and qualified mortgage interest premiums, not shown separately. [4] Includes casualty or theft loss of income producing property deduction, and gambling loss deduction.

Source: U.S. Internal Revenue Service, Statistics of Income Tax Stats, "Individual Statistical Tables by Size of Adjusted Gross Income," and "Individual Income Tax Returns Complete Report, Basic Tables," <www.irs.gov/statistics/soi-tax-stats-individual-income-tax-return-form-1040-statistics>, accessed May 2024.

Table 528. Federal Individual Income Tax Returns—Statutory Adjustments: 2020 and 2021

[36,918 represents 36,918,000. For tax years. Use caution comparing trends because of changes in tax law. Based on a sample of returns; see source and Appendix III. Minus sign (-) indicates decrease]

Item	2020		2021		Percent change in amount, 2020-2021
	Number of returns (1,000)	Amount (mil. dol.)	Number of returns (1,000)	Amount (mil. dol.)	
Total statutory adjustments	**36,918**	**137,167**	**32,836**	**141,161**	**2.9**
Educator expenses deduction	3,437	904	3,115	826	-8.6
Certain business expenses of reservists, performing artists, etc.	316	2,533	273	2,083	-17.8
Health savings account deduction	2,009	5,949	1,934	5,889	-1.0
Moving expenses adjustment	81	208	94	269	29.2
Self-employment tax deduction	20,353	33,293	21,622	38,596	15.9
Payments to a self-employed retirement (Keogh) plan	947	26,091	999	28,919	10.8
Self-employment health insurance deduction	3,640	30,149	3,667	30,805	2.2
Penalty on early withdrawal of savings	379	209	307	124	-40.6
Alimony paid	420	10,697	378	9,744	-8.9
Payments to an Individual Retirement Account (IRA)	2,465	13,575	2,416	13,683	0.8
Student loan interest deduction	10,104	7,753	4,942	4,289	-44.7
Tuition and fees deduction	1,295	3,176	(NA)	(NA)	(NA)
Other adjustments [1]	294	2,514	154	4,503	79.1

NA Not available. [1] Includes domestic production activities deduction, foreign housing adjustment, medical savings accounts deduction, and other adjustments.

Source: U.S. Internal Revenue Service, Statistics of Income, "SOI Tax Stats - Individual Statistical Tables by Size of Adjusted Gross Income," <www.irs.gov/statistics/soi-tax-stats-individual-statistical-tables-by-size-of-adjusted-gross-income>, accessed May 2024.

Table 529. IRS Audits—Individual Income Tax Returns Examined: 2015 to 2021

[In units as indicated (150,675 represents 150,675,000). An IRS audit is a review/examination of an organization's or individual's tax return to determine if income, expenses, and credits are being reported accurately. Includes tax returns selected for examination based on an earned income tax credit claim, and the resulting recommended additional taxes]

Year	Returns filed [1] (1,000)	Returns examined				Number of returns examined with no change (1,000)	Recommended additional tax (mil. dol.)
		Total (1,000)	Closed [2] (1,000)	In process [3] (1,000)	Percent examined		
2015	150,675	877	871	6	0.6	81	8,446
2016	150,447	798	787	11	0.5	80	7,974
2017	153,063	728	717	12	0.5	85	8,077
2018	153,928	536	523	12	0.3	62	6,304
2019	157,952	487	474	13	0.3	57	4,491
2020 [4]	164,511	467	433	35	0.3	66	3,263
2021 [4]	161,207	341	269	73	0.2	51	1,622

[1] Includes all returns filed for the specified tax year as of December 31, 2023. [2] Includes examinations that were closed as of September 30, 2023. Represents a distinct count of taxpayers by tax year and form type. During the course of an examination, additional related returns within the statute of limitations may require examination; these related return closures are counted by the appropriate tax year and form type. [3] Includes examinations that are in an open examination status. [4] Within the 3-year statute of limitations; therefore, the percentage covered and recommended additional tax will increase in future years as additional examinations are opened.

Source: U.S. Internal Revenue Service, *IRS Data Book 2023*, April 2024. See also <www.irs.gov/statistics/soi-tax-stats-irs-data-book>.

Table 530. Federal Individual Income Tax Returns—Itemized Deductions and Statutory Adjustments by Size of Adjusted Gross Income: 2021

[14,843 represents 14,843,000. Based on a sample of returns; see Appendix III]

Item	Unit	Total [1]	Adjusted gross income class						
			Under $10,000 [1]	$10,000 to $19,999	$20,000 to $29,999	$30,000 to $39,999	$40,000 to $49,999	$50,000 to $99,999	$100,000 and over
RETURNS WITH ITEMIZED DEDUCTIONS									
Number of returns	1,000	14,843	174	270	361	467	614	3,826	9,130
Amount of deductions [2]	Mil. dol.	659,681	4,164	7,580	9,050	12,607	15,707	102,174	508,399
Medical and dental expenses: [3]									
Returns	1,000	3,693	131	201	249	269	317	1,302	1,225
Amount	Mil. dol.	75,886	2,473	4,252	4,199	5,065	5,668	24,690	29,539
Taxes paid:									
Returns	1,000	14,688	161	253	341	457	604	3,779	9,093
Amount	Mil. dol.	119,542	647	1,207	1,535	2,244	3,286	26,251	84,371
State and local taxes: [4]									
Returns	1,000	14,645	159	251	340	455	599	3,760	9,082
Amount	Mil. dol.	362,508	717	1,402	1,646	2,582	3,503	29,400	323,257
Real estate taxes:									
Returns	1,000	12,779	107	173	223	311	424	3,222	8,319
Amount	Mil. dol.	99,984	551	980	1,091	1,514	2,144	15,908	77,795
Interest paid:									
Returns	1,000	11,754	77	137	191	280	375	2,974	7,720
Amount	Mil. dol.	163,274	857	1,457	1,941	2,773	3,983	29,524	122,740
Home mortgage interest:									
Returns	1,000	11,510	76	132	186	274	374	2,949	7,519
Amount	Mil. dol.	138,865	814	1,335	1,821	2,508	3,589	26,841	101,957
Charitable contributions:									
Returns	1,000	12,118	87	162	253	338	445	2,917	7,915
Amount	Mil. dol.	263,251	124	434	1,127	1,808	2,216	17,332	240,210
RETURNS WITH STATUTORY ADJUSTMENTS									
Number of returns [1]	1,000	32,836	3,210	4,009	2,991	2,471	2,291	7,728	10,135
Amount of adjustments [2]	Mil. dol.	141,161	4,097	4,492	4,941	5,110	5,285	21,594	95,641
Payments to IRAs: [5]									
Returns	1,000	2,416	48	88	155	230	200	761	934
Amount	Mil. dol.	13,683	185	355	601	922	868	4,119	6,632
Deduction for self-employment tax:									
Returns	1,000	21,622	2,900	3,583	2,305	1,596	1,267	4,114	5,859
Amount	Mil. dol.	38,596	1,330	2,795	2,353	2,008	1,779	6,847	21,484
Self-employment health insurance:									
Returns	1,000	3,667	206	183	202	188	191	737	1,960
Amount	Mil. dol.	30,805	978	554	765	827	875	3,892	22,915
Payments to Keogh plans:									
Returns	1,000	999	[6] 6	11	[6] 12	12	19	102	835
Amount	Mil. dol.	28,919	[6] 166	87	[6] 93	66	290	1,146	27,071

[1] For returns with statutory adjustments, includes a small number of taxable returns with no adjusted gross income. [2] Includes other deductions and adjustments, not shown separately. [3] After AGI limitation. [4] State and local taxes include income taxes and sales taxes. [5] Individual Retirement Accounts. [6] Includes estimates that should be used with caution because of the small number of sample returns on which they are based.

Source: U.S. Internal Revenue Service, Statistics of Income, "SOI Tax Stats - Individual Statistical Tables by Size of Adjusted Gross Income," <www.irs.gov/statistics/soi-tax-stats-individual-statistical-tables-by-size-of-adjusted-gross-income>, accessed February 2024.

Table 531. Federal Individual Income Tax Returns—Selected Tax Credits: 2020 and 2021

[69,357 represents 69,357,000. For tax years. Based on a sample of returns; see source and Appendix III. Use caution comparing trends because of changes in tax law]

Item	2020		2021		Percent change, 2020-2021	
	Number of returns (1,000)	Amount (mil. dol.)	Number of returns (1,000)	Amount (mil. dol.)	Number of returns (1,000)	Amount (mil. dol.)
Total tax credits [1]	**69,357**	**150,785**	**67,228**	**150,057**	**-3.1**	**-0.5**
Child care credit	5,050	2,827	602	1,078	-88.1	-61.9
Earned income credit [2]	2,746	684	15,303	9,374	457.3	1,270.3
Foreign tax credit	9,201	21,625	10,827	29,483	17.7	36.3
General business credit	433	4,932	523	7,067	20.7	43.3
Prior-year minimum tax credit	148	1,363	124	1,493	-16.2	9.6
Child tax credit	39,330	84,415	11,779	8,725	-70.1	-89.7
Education credit [3]	7,419	7,881	8,123	8,280	9.5	5.1
Retirement savings contribution credit	9,401	1,750	9,199	1,759	-2.1	0.5
Residential energy credit	2,291	3,901	2,607	5,333	13.8	36.7
Recovery rebate credit [2, 4]	15,971	17,062	5,071	7,093	-68.3	-58.4

[1] Includes credits not shown separately. [2] Represents portion of credit used to offset income tax before credits. [3] Excludes refundable portion. [4] Most eligible taxpayers received this credit as an advance payment, referred to as Economic Impact Payments. This credit expired at the end of the 2021 tax year.

Source: U.S. Internal Revenue Service, Statistics of Income, "SOI Tax Stats - Individual Statistical Tables by Size of Adjusted Gross Income," <www.irs.gov/statistics/soi-tax-stats-individual-statistical-tables-by-size-of-adjusted-gross-income>, accessed February 2024.

Table 532. Federal Individual Income Tax Returns by State: 2021

[In units as indicated (159,515 represents 159,515,000). For tax year. Data may not agree with data in other tables due to differing survey methodology used to derive state data]

State	Total number of returns (1,000)	Adjusted gross income (mil. dol.)			Itemized deductions (mil. dol.)				Income tax after credits (mil. dol.)
		Total [1]	Salaries and wages	Net capital gain [2]	Total [1]	State and local income tax	Real estate taxes	Home mortgage interest paid	
United States......	159,515	14,775,706	9,012,497	2,050,444	658,123	253,189	100,643	136,146	2,224,647
Alabama.............	2,163	155,245	98,408	14,993	6,555	1,375	337	1,034	19,567
Alaska...............	350	29,234	18,540	2,533	734	20	124	186	3,949
Arizona..............	3,374	281,728	170,654	36,323	12,034	2,959	1,073	2,580	39,226
Arkansas............	1,307	99,907	57,202	15,477	7,079	1,257	203	455	12,407
California............	18,827	2,118,835	1,309,298	327,228	125,799	82,950	23,443	34,695	358,590
Colorado............	2,953	304,224	181,365	51,230	13,895	4,193	1,372	3,649	45,938
Connecticut..........	1,821	224,339	129,845	39,304	9,802	5,742	1,996	1,911	39,340
Delaware............	498	41,590	25,238	3,306	1,625	624	169	401	5,659
District of Columbia..	346	45,606	28,291	6,788	2,727	1,766	372	788	8,439
Florida...............	10,838	1,040,525	525,609	211,491	41,110	5,774	5,772	6,858	165,218
Georgia.............	4,935	403,700	256,222	54,070	20,690	5,778	2,262	4,059	57,441
Hawaii...............	694	55,815	33,562	6,245	2,830	1,143	242	1,085	7,304
Idaho................	866	73,687	41,378	11,560	3,040	1,061	268	600	9,824
Illinois...............	6,139	592,320	360,183	83,412	23,265	7,992	4,598	4,012	90,703
Indiana..............	3,262	239,435	157,364	22,245	7,347	2,198	593	1,009	30,385
Iowa.................	1,490	115,646	74,391	8,875	3,595	1,049	455	469	14,326
Kansas..............	1,368	112,495	69,601	12,563	4,145	1,394	449	530	15,198
Kentucky............	1,998	134,293	88,714	10,925	3,823	1,366	394	686	16,375
Louisiana...........	2,014	138,629	88,672	13,517	6,516	1,195	369	859	18,576
Maine...............	717	54,231	33,328	5,716	1,550	648	239	308	6,829
Maryland............	3,050	296,871	193,381	30,081	20,716	8,535	3,035	5,491	43,990
Massachusetts.......	3,552	451,765	263,457	81,692	20,140	8,942	3,416	4,470	77,369
Michigan............	4,879	379,392	233,735	36,725	12,701	3,434	1,692	1,876	50,453
Minnesota...........	2,848	264,717	168,141	27,862	9,693	5,102	1,313	2,016	37,289
Mississippi..........	1,271	73,855	49,730	4,604	2,950	572	199	421	8,387
Missouri.............	2,888	223,783	139,060	22,499	7,761	2,008	789	1,131	29,983
Montana.............	547	45,433	24,156	7,740	1,775	659	187	341	6,078
Nebraska...........	937	78,157	48,338	8,490	2,969	410	330	317	10,329
Nevada.............	1,561	148,091	76,444	31,139	7,407	1,043	591	1,209	23,072
New Hampshire......	729	77,744	48,228	11,593	2,365	423	513	481	12,026
New Jersey..........	4,576	501,275	323,980	55,913	24,071	11,511	6,589	5,552	81,709
New Mexico..........	983	62,780	38,494	5,823	2,127	459	199	417	7,456
New York............	9,813	1,068,753	615,576	185,290	52,274	40,192	10,607	9,726	185,454
North Carolina.......	4,899	394,936	253,368	43,030	14,898	4,999	1,543	3,049	53,982
North Dakota........	368	33,399	19,119	4,441	1,165	145	80	113	4,532
Ohio.................	5,772	434,524	278,160	40,420	11,657	3,721	1,763	1,829	57,286
Oklahoma...........	1,723	118,785	76,339	10,833	5,384	965	390	649	14,762
Oregon..............	2,048	177,923	107,776	19,677	9,424	3,982	1,358	2,193	24,246
Pennsylvania........	6,412	552,509	341,745	60,779	18,692	5,417	2,828	3,259	78,676
Rhode Island........	561	46,774	30,055	4,877	1,552	556	296	390	6,467
South Carolina.......	2,448	183,220	111,541	20,753	7,389	2,200	612	1,447	23,976
South Dakota........	442	37,896	20,941	4,825	1,453	67	101	120	5,098
Tennessee...........	3,246	261,681	161,463	35,343	8,692	601	770	1,491	36,422
Texas...............	13,490	1,183,079	748,325	161,868	49,998	2,032	8,446	8,044	176,645
Utah.................	1,487	141,489	87,381	22,597	9,287	2,569	709	1,753	20,011
Vermont.............	336	26,811	16,016	3,179	849	342	154	139	3,423
Virginia..............	4,121	403,444	258,571	45,556	20,969	7,345	3,077	5,707	59,894
Washington..........	3,760	437,734	269,506	68,563	19,720	840	2,957	4,778	69,699
West Virginia........	788	47,518	32,424	2,338	955	353	61	176	5,317
Wisconsin...........	2,938	239,583	151,106	23,333	7,135	2,581	1,109	1,130	31,673
Wyoming............	282	32,240	14,025	9,292	1,907	200	94	120	4,988
Puerto Rico [3]........	77	3,802	2,154	707	67	33	4	9	405
Other [4].............	720	84,259	61,900	20,785	1,822	467	103	129	8,256

[1] Includes other items, not shown separately. [2] Less loss. [3] Returns from Puerto Rico represent individuals who are employees of the U.S government or earned income outside of Puerto Rico, but within the U.S., and the amount is above the filing threshold. For more information on Puerto Rican returns, see <www.irs.gov/taxtopics/tc901>. [4] Includes returns filed from Army Post Office and Fleet Post Office addresses by members of the armed forces stationed overseas and returns filed by other U.S. citizens abroad.

Source: U.S. Internal Revenue Service, Statistics of Income Bulletin, "Historical Data Tables," <www.irs.gov/statistics/soi-tax-stats-historical-data-tables>, accessed May 2024.

Table 533. Federal Tax Refunds Issued by State and Type of Refund: 2023

[In millions of dollars (659,052 represents $659,052,000,000). Collection and refund data may not be comparable for a given fiscal year because payments made in prior years may be refunded in the current fiscal year. Adjustments made in FY2023 to prior-year returns may result in negative amounts when such adjustments exceed current-year refunds. Classification by state is based on an individual's address or a corporation's principal place of business]

State	Total federal tax refunds [2]	Business income tax refunds [3]	Individual income tax refunds	Estate and trust income tax refunds	Employment tax refunds [4]	Estate tax refunds	Gift tax refunds	Excise tax refunds [5]
United States [1]............	**659,052**	**43,855**	**461,212**	**5,236**	**144,724**	**1,749**	**102**	**2,175**
Alabama....................	6,809	86	4,996	47	1,658	12	(Z)	10
Alaska.....................	968	19	738	8	198	(D)	–	(D)
Arizona....................	10,524	320	7,234	55	2,864	22	(Z)	28
Arkansas..................	4,246	333	2,918	17	966	3	(Z)	8
California.................	70,131	4,452	41,507	433	23,270	297	10	162
Colorado..................	9,295	397	6,093	78	2,700	14	1	12
Connecticut...............	7,281	1,119	4,284	84	1,724	30	1	38
Delaware..................	2,319	506	1,071	199	522	(D)	(D)	18
District of Columbia.......	1,846	326	1,003	12	472	(D)	(D)	6
Florida....................	39,484	866	28,213	397	9,703	168	7	130
Georgia...................	16,674	761	11,534	66	4,246	30	1	36
Hawaii....................	2,158	159	1,425	16	544	(D)	(D)	4
Idaho.....................	2,690	104	1,831	9	736	(D)	(D)	8
Illinois...................	23,406	2,663	14,260	407	5,806	88	21	162
Indiana...................	9,796	416	7,122	54	2,159	6	(Z)	38
Iowa......................	4,523	513	3,051	20	903	4	1	31
Kansas....................	4,433	316	2,817	43	1,244	(D)	(D)	8
Kentucky..................	5,954	243	4,243	32	1,411	11	1	14
Louisiana.................	7,375	250	5,039	28	2,030	(D)	(D)	15
Maine.....................	1,919	89	1,302	25	489	(D)	(D)	11
Maryland..................	10,057	530	6,814	124	2,566	16	(Z)	7
Massachusetts.............	12,732	832	8,055	188	3,570	54	1	32
Michigan..................	15,389	831	10,325	216	3,928	66	(Z)	22
Minnesota.................	10,535	2,356	5,524	66	2,535	14	(Z)	40
Mississippi................	4,634	123	3,018	11	1,465	(D)	(D)	10
Missouri..................	9,457	553	6,098	81	2,705	(D)	(D)	9
Montana..................	1,396	37	1,042	7	306	(D)	(D)	4
Nebraska.................	2,754	257	1,887	14	579	7	(Z)	9
Nevada...................	5,744	117	3,931	232	1,419	37	1	7
New Hampshire............	2,259	42	1,592	50	568	2	(Z)	5
New Jersey................	18,069	2,678	10,483	189	4,490	88	2	139
New Mexico...............	2,807	14	2,008	14	763	(D)	(D)	2
New York..................	36,211	3,146	22,232	392	10,128	188	19	106
North Carolina............	14,802	999	10,341	85	3,332	19	(Z)	26
North Dakota.............	1,153	20	760	6	360	(D)	(D)	5
Ohio......................	22,215	5,307	11,727	80	4,950	25	3	123
Oklahoma.................	5,944	276	4,095	57	1,413	15	1	88
Oregon...................	5,975	163	3,814	36	1,935	20	(Z)	7
Pennsylvania..............	21,074	1,717	13,755	223	5,316	37	(Z)	26
Rhode Island.............	1,730	78	1,161	18	456	(D)	(D)	2
South Carolina............	6,627	185	4,964	34	1,427	6	1	9
South Dakota.............	1,370	38	937	114	277	(D)	(D)	2
Tennessee.................	10,557	424	7,590	81	2,389	10	1	63
Texas.....................	57,057	6,134	37,342	510	12,417	117	11	526
Utah......................	5,740	144	3,418	28	2,096	(D)	(D)	29
Vermont..................	913	16	646	8	241	(D)	(D)	1
Virginia...................	12,889	869	9,079	86	2,815	19	1	20
Washington...............	12,416	338	8,647	88	3,274	47	10	12
West Virginia.............	2,084	13	1,663	6	397	(D)	(D)	2
Wisconsin.................	8,463	978	5,600	101	1,712	18	-2	55
Wyoming..................	962	13	672	56	189	(D)	(D)	2

– Represents zero. D Data withheld to avoid disclosure regarding specific taxpayers; data are included in U.S. totals. Z Less than $500,000. [1] Includes refunds not shown separately, including to Armed Services members overseas and for U.S. territories. [2] Includes overpayment refunds, refunds resulting from examination activity, refundable tax credits, and other refunds required by law. Also includes $10.2 billion in interest, of which $1.1 billion was paid to corporations and $9.1 billion was paid to all others (related to individual, employment, estate, gift, and excise tax returns). Excludes refunds credited to taxpayer accounts for tax liability in a subsequent year. [3] Includes refunds of taxes on corporation income (Form 1120 series) and on unrelated business income from tax-exempt organizations (Form 990–T). [4] Includes refunds of self-employment income taxes under the Self-Employment Insurance Contributions Act; railroad retirement taxes under the Railroad Retirement Tax Act; unemployment insurance taxes under the Federal Unemployment Tax Act; and Old-age, Survivors, Disability, and Hospital Insurance (OASDHI) taxes on salaries and wages under the Federal Insurance Contributions Act. [5] Excludes refunds of excise taxes collected by U.S. Customs and Border Protection and the Alcohol and Tobacco Tax and Trade Bureau. Beginning with FY2015, some refunds which had been classified as excise tax refunds in prior years, were reclassified as corporate tax refunds.

Source: U.S. Internal Revenue Service, *IRS Data Book 2023*, April 2024. See also <www.irs.gov/statistics/soi-tax-stats-irs-data-book>.

Table 534. Individuals Due an Unclaimed Income Tax Refund by State: 2020

[1,037,161 represents $1,037,161,000. Data are estimates, and are for unclaimed income tax refunds for taxpayers who did not file a 2020 Form 1040 federal income tax return. Taxpayers have a 3-year window in which to claim a tax refund, after which the money becomes the property of the U.S. Treasury]

State	Total persons (number)	Value of potential refunds ($1,000) [1]	Median potential refund (dol.)	State	Total persons (number)	Value of potential refunds ($1,000) [1]	Median potential refund (dol.)
Total U.S.	**938,800**	**1,037,161**	**932**	Missouri	19,500	20,803	893
Alabama	15,200	16,840	926	Montana	3,400	3,632	851
Alaska	3,700	4,335	931	Nebraska	4,700	5,007	901
Arizona	25,400	26,940	871	Nevada	10,200	11,144	890
Arkansas	8,700	9,393	923	New Hampshire	4,200	4,923	982
California	88,200	94,226	835	New Jersey	24,400	27,408	920
Colorado	18,500	20,110	894	New Mexico	6,500	7,033	868
Connecticut	9,800	11,344	978	New York	51,400	60,837	1,029
Delaware	3,600	4,157	945	North Carolina	27,500	29,304	895
District of Columbia	2,900	3,504	968	North Dakota	2,200	2,483	953
Florida	53,200	58,211	891	Ohio	31,400	32,940	909
Georgia	36,400	39,176	900	Oklahoma	14,300	15,567	902
Hawaii	5,200	5,973	979	Oregon	15,300	15,858	847
Idaho	4,500	4,370	761	Pennsylvania	38,600	43,413	1,031
Illinois	36,200	40,608	956	Rhode Island	2,600	2,981	986
Indiana	19,200	20,893	922	South Carolina	11,900	12,565	840
Iowa	9,600	10,602	953	South Dakota	2,200	2,346	892
Kansas	8,700	9,286	900	Tennessee	16,800	18,007	909
Kentucky	10,600	11,236	920	Texas	93,400	107,130	960
Louisiana	15,100	17,357	957	Utah	7,800	8,192	836
Maine	3,800	4,030	923	Vermont	1,700	1,819	911
Maryland	22,200	26,365	991	Virginia	25,900	28,945	914
Massachusetts	21,800	25,072	975	Washington	26,200	31,110	976
Michigan	34,900	38,275	976	West Virginia	3,800	4,130	950
Minnesota	13,500	14,044	818	Wisconsin	11,800	12,139	837
Mississippi	8,100	8,685	861	Wyoming	2,100	2,416	961

[1] Excluding credits.

Source: U.S. Internal Revenue Service, News Release, "Time running out to claim $1 billion in refunds for tax year 2020, taxpayers face May 17 deadline," IR-2024-80, March 25, 2024. See also <www.irs.gov/newsroom>.

Table 535. Federal Employees—Summary Characteristics: 1990 to 2023

[In percent, except as indicated. As of September 30. For civilian employees of executive branch agencies participating in Office of Personnel Management's Central Personnel Data File (CPDF)]

Characteristic	1990	2000	2005	2010	2015	2020	2021	2022	2023
Average age (years) [1]	42.3	46.3	46.9	46.8	47.4	47.3	47.3	47.3	47.1
Average length of service (years)	13.4	17.1	16.4	14.3	13.7	13.0	12.9	12.8	12.4
Civil Service Retirement System eligible [2]	8.0	17.0	33.0	57.0	81.1	96.5	97.3	97.8	98.5
Bachelor's degree or higher	35.0	41.0	43.0	46.0	51.0	52.3	52.8	53.2	53.3
Sex:									
Male	57.0	55.0	56.0	55.9	56.8	55.9	55.6	55.0	54.2
Female	43.0	45.0	44.0	44.1	43.2	44.1	44.4	45.0	45.8
Race and Hispanic origin:									
Total minorities	27.4	30.4	31.7	33.3	35.3	37.6	38.4	39.0	39.7
Black	16.7	17.1	17.0	17.5	17.7	18.1	18.2	18.3	18.4
Hispanic	5.4	6.6	7.4	7.7	8.4	9.3	9.5	9.8	10.1
Asian	(NA)	(NA)	(NA)	(NA)	5.7	6.2	6.5	6.7	6.8
American Indian/Alaska Native	1.8	2.2	2.1	2.1	1.7	1.6	1.6	1.6	1.6
Disabled	7.0	7.0	7.0	7.0	12.5	10.9	11.0	11.3	11.6
Veterans preference	30.0	24.0	22.0	23.1	25.9	25.9	25.6	25.1	24.4
Vietnam era veterans	17.0	14.0	11.0	8.0	3.2	1.2	0.9	0.7	0.6
Retired military	4.9	3.9	5.4	7.0	8.3	8.1	7.9	7.6	7.3
Retired officers	0.5	0.5	1.0	1.6	1.9	1.9	1.8	1.8	1.7
Average base salary (dollars) [1]	32,026	51,618	64,175	76,231	81,249	91,525	93,075	96,253	101,619

NA Not available. [1] For full-time permanent employees. [2] Represents full-time permanent employees under the Civil Service Retirement System (excludes hires since January 1984).

Source: U.S. Office of Personnel Management, Office of Workforce Information, *The Fact Book, Federal Civilian Workforce Statistics*, annual. 2008 to 2015, Central Personnel Data File, "Profile of Federal Civilian Non-Seasonal Full-Time Employees," <www.opm.gov/policy-data-oversight/data-analysis-documentation/federal-employment-reports/>. As of 2020, unpublished data.

Table 536. Full-Time Federal Civilian Employment—Employees and Average Pay by Pay System: 2010 to 2023

[1,950 represents 1,950,000. As of September 30. Data are shown for all full-time nonseasonal employees. Includes employees in U.S., U.S. territories, foreign countries, and unspecified locations. Excludes postal employees and other selected agencies; see <www.fedscope.opm.gov /datadefn/aboutehri_sdm.asp> for details. See text, this section, for explanation of general schedule and wage system]

Pay system	Employees (1,000)				Average annual pay (dol.)			
	2010	2015	2020	2023	2010	2015	2020	2023
Total, excluding postal	**1,950**	**1,940**	**2,054**	**2,139**	**75,707**	**70,548**	**90,956**	**101,451**
General schedule and equivalently graded	1,410	1,430	1,473	1,533	73,656	67,078	87,964	96,989
Prevailing rate pay plans (blue collar)	195	185	185	174	52,056	53,049	59,959	67,052
Other white collar pay plans	344	325	396	433	97,480	95,893	116,628	131,277

Source: U.S. Office of Personnel Management, "FedScope," <www.fedscope.opm.gov>, accessed March 2024.

Table 537. Federal Government Civilian Employment by State: 2010 to 2023

[As of September 30. For agencies excluded from total, see <www.fedscope.opm.gov/datadefn/aboutehri_sdm.asp>]

State	2010	2015	2018	2019	2020	2021	2022	2023
U.S. [1]	2,061,320	2,029,293	2,056,092	2,087,269	2,134,575	2,144,744	2,132,723	2,207,442
AL	42,267	38,006	38,017	38,678	39,474	39,301	38,671	40,434
AK	14,072	11,606	10,962	10,923	11,268	11,299	11,246	11,448
AZ	42,409	31,421	31,195	32,082	33,410	32,707	32,464	33,918
AR	14,741	13,207	13,003	13,110	13,180	13,306	13,384	14,164
CA	172,547	140,618	140,882	143,597	148,734	146,552	143,388	148,052
CO	40,744	37,208	37,058	37,497	38,575	38,744	38,334	40,275
CT	8,671	8,035	7,837	7,969	8,198	8,125	8,304	7,695
DE	3,425	3,085	3,047	3,075	3,278	3,237	3,366	3,680
DC	167,893	147,050	168,518	168,499	171,292	171,148	162,511	160,491
FL	88,933	76,472	79,000	81,610	84,916	85,919	86,806	92,157
GA	80,229	70,294	71,789	73,203	75,788	76,513	75,949	78,930
HI	25,354	21,919	22,490	23,218	23,465	23,723	23,784	24,322
ID	10,496	9,698	9,776	9,703	9,959	9,967	9,741	10,430
IL	51,136	41,266	40,223	40,610	41,828	42,068	41,959	44,174
IN	24,734	22,156	22,939	23,907	24,861	23,764	23,562	24,443
IA	9,245	8,647	8,691	8,538	8,821	8,893	8,898	9,603
KS	17,792	15,998	16,091	16,319	16,561	16,599	17,074	17,812
KY	26,523	22,500	22,054	21,160	21,423	21,609	21,653	23,031
LA	21,075	17,886	18,539	18,789	18,922	18,683	18,455	19,245
ME	11,132	10,277	10,993	11,177	11,568	11,662	11,824	12,201
MD	128,281	129,005	128,746	128,356	132,361	135,385	138,429	142,390
MA	29,223	25,118	24,104	24,596	24,756	24,986	24,531	25,384
MI	30,023	25,439	25,219	25,688	26,005	26,581	27,028	29,077
MN	18,561	16,097	16,323	16,556	16,823	16,936	16,833	17,727
MS	19,353	17,998	17,717	18,101	18,277	18,329	18,279	19,046
MO	38,351	33,828	34,644	35,209	37,220	37,427	35,848	36,951
MT	12,010	10,350	10,158	10,268	10,380	10,749	10,630	11,030
NE	10,686	9,644	9,685	9,718	9,924	9,846	9,738	10,214
NV	11,475	10,980	11,419	11,750	12,246	12,610	12,824	13,778
NH	4,436	4,354	4,373	4,463	4,444	4,412	4,572	4,876
NJ	30,101	20,511	19,970	20,244	20,812	20,975	21,230	22,390
NM	27,682	22,069	21,297	21,746	22,097	22,039	21,906	22,568
NY	68,202	51,541	50,377	50,719	51,125	51,336	50,622	53,418
NC	43,678	43,007	44,279	45,302	46,290	47,239	47,240	49,913
ND	6,723	5,425	5,418	5,453	5,517	5,557	5,465	5,617
OH	53,014	48,213	49,589	50,397	50,916	51,239	51,603	54,805
OK	39,463	36,863	38,788	39,020	39,988	40,441	39,920	41,460
OR	22,470	20,125	20,072	20,144	20,525	20,249	19,704	20,443
PA	69,792	59,111	60,156	61,500	62,386	62,836	63,200	65,505
RI	7,135	7,228	7,422	7,714	7,729	7,867	8,041	8,278
SC	21,675	20,603	21,172	21,967	22,590	22,760	22,688	23,957
SD	8,849	8,231	8,315	8,252	8,482	8,513	8,398	8,747
TN	28,822	26,186	25,867	26,363	27,160	27,696	28,332	31,602
TX	140,292	110,270	112,247	114,377	120,024	121,283	120,473	126,791
UT	31,051	27,575	28,634	30,144	31,372	32,074	31,904	33,113
VT	4,495	3,194	3,162	3,246	3,235	3,120	3,154	3,292
VA	145,449	133,300	134,523	136,486	139,058	139,807	140,724	143,527
WA	57,894	54,139	54,403	54,979	55,607	55,670	55,003	56,977
WV	16,287	15,034	14,857	15,349	16,043	16,161	16,300	16,970
WI	15,809	15,274	15,604	15,738	16,242	16,538	16,638	17,585
WY	6,640	6,328	6,310	6,325	6,479	6,476	6,432	6,687

[1] Total does not include employees based in U.S. Territories or foreign countries and includes data that have been suppressed for security purposes; see source for details.

Source: U.S. Office of Personnel Management, "FedScope," <www.fedscope.opm.gov>, accessed March 2024.

Table 538. Federal Executive Branch Retirements: 2015 to 2019

[For fiscal years ending September 30. Covers non-seasonal, full-time permanent employees. Data are from the Enterprise Human Resources Integration database, which primarily covers Executive Branch employees excluding the Postal Service and intelligence agencies; for more information, see source]

Characteristic	2015	2016	2017	2018	2019
Total retirements	**61,958**	**59,712**	**59,183**	**62,883**	**63,059**
Sex:					
Male	34,525	33,517	33,450	35,489	36,026
Female	27,433	26,195	25,732	27,393	27,032
Race:					
White	43,618	42,180	41,445	43,506	42,989
Black	9,958	9,422	9,670	10,477	11,002
Hispanic	4,031	3,921	3,975	4,376	4,557
Other	4,333	4,181	4,078	4,509	4,500
Retirement type:					
Disability	4,015	2,756	1,686	2,992	3,314
Early out	1,235	900	741	1,129	771
Other	1,441	1,398	1,607	1,456	1,406
Voluntary	55,267	54,658	55,149	57,306	57,568
Average retirement age (years)	61.3	61.7	61.8	61.8	61.8
Average length of service (years)	26.7	26.1	25.7	25.2	24.9

Source: U.S. Office of Personnel Management, *Retirement Statistics and Trend Analysis: Fiscal Year 2015 to Fiscal Year 2019*. See also <www.opm.gov/policy-data-oversight/data-analysis-documentation/federal-employment-reports>.

Table 539. Federal Government Civilian Employees by Agency: 2000 to 2025

[In thousands, except percent (1,814 represents 1,814,000). Shown for fiscal years ending September 30 in the year shown. Data shown for full-time equivalent (FTE) executive branch employees, excluding the U.S. Postal Service]

Fiscal year	Total Executive branch	Department of Defense	Civilian agencies									
			Total	Agriculture	HHS, ED, SSA[1]	Homeland Security	Interior	Justice	Transportation	Treasury	Veterans Affairs	Other
NUMBER (1,000)												
2000......	1,814	660	1,153	95	128	67	67	95	57	113	203	328
2005......	1,830	653	1,177	100	128	143	70	103	56	110	222	244
2010......	2,128	741	1,386	96	137	173	71	113	57	112	285	342
2015......	2,042	725	1,317	86	139	179	64	114	54	95	335	251
2016......	2,057	725	1,332	87	140	184	64	115	54	93	345	249
2017......	2,062	726	1,336	87	140	182	65	118	55	92	352	245
2018......	2,061	730	1,331	84	138	186	63	113	54	89	363	241
2019......	2,085	742	1,344	81	138	192	62	112	53	88	376	242
2020......	2,180	777	1,403	79	139	198	61	114	53	91	389	279
2021......	2,183	783	1,400	84	142	202	62	116	54	94	403	244
2022......	2,186	772	1,413	85	142	203	62	115	53	94	412	248
2023......	2,238	775	1,463	88	144	212	63	115	54	99	434	255
2024 [2]...	2,306	796	1,510	92	148	206	65	120	56	99	458	265
2025 [2]...	2,328	795	1,532	94	152	218	66	123	58	107	448	267
PERCENT												
2000......	100.0	36.4	63.6	5.2	7.0	3.7	3.7	5.3	3.1	6.3	11.2	18.1
2005......	100.0	35.7	64.3	5.4	7.0	7.8	3.8	5.6	3.0	6.0	12.1	13.4
2010......	100.0	34.8	65.2	4.5	6.5	8.1	3.3	5.3	2.7	5.3	13.4	16.1
2015......	100.0	35.5	64.5	4.2	6.8	8.8	3.1	5.6	2.7	4.7	16.4	12.3
2016......	100.0	35.3	64.7	4.2	6.8	8.9	3.1	5.6	2.6	4.5	16.8	12.1
2017......	100.0	35.2	64.8	4.2	6.8	8.8	3.1	5.7	2.7	4.5	17.0	11.9
2018......	100.0	35.4	64.6	4.1	6.7	9.0	3.1	5.5	2.6	4.3	17.6	11.7
2019......	100.0	35.6	64.4	3.9	6.6	9.2	3.0	5.4	2.5	4.2	18.0	11.6
2020......	100.0	35.6	64.4	3.6	6.4	9.1	2.8	5.2	2.5	4.2	17.9	12.8
2021......	100.0	35.9	64.1	3.8	6.5	9.2	2.8	5.3	2.5	4.3	18.5	11.2
2022......	100.0	35.3	64.7	3.9	6.5	9.3	2.8	5.3	2.4	4.3	18.8	11.4
2023......	100.0	34.6	65.4	3.9	6.4	9.5	2.8	5.1	2.4	4.4	19.4	11.4
2024 [2]...	100.0	34.5	65.5	4.0	6.4	9.0	2.8	5.2	2.4	4.3	19.9	11.5
2025 [2]...	100.0	34.2	65.8	4.0	6.5	9.3	2.8	5.3	2.5	4.6	19.3	11.5

[1] Department of Health and Human Services, Department of Education, and Social Security Administration. [2] Estimate.

Source: U.S. Office of Management and Budget, *Budget of the U.S. Government, Fiscal Year 2025: Historical Tables*, March 2024, <www.whitehouse.gov/omb/historical-tables/>.

Table 540. Area of Federally Owned Buildings by State: 2022

[2,814.5 represents 2,814,500,000. As of September 30. For executive branch departments and agencies subject to the Chief Financial Officers Act of 1990]

State	Total building area (mil. sq. ft.) [1]	Owned building area (mil. sq. ft.)	Leased building area (mil. sq. ft.)	State	Total building area (mil. sq. ft.) [1]	Owned building area (mil. sq. ft.)	Leased building area (mil. sq. ft.)
Total..............	**2,814.5**	**2,413.8**	**277.1**	Missouri...........	52.2	37.6	11.8
Alabama............	60.6	52.6	4.6	Montana..........	16.5	13.5	2.3
Alaska.............	40.5	38.4	1.4	Nebraska..........	15.9	13.2	1.7
Arizona............	59.0	53.4	4.1	Nevada...........	34.1	31.2	2.1
Arkansas...........	24.1	19.4	1.5	New Hampshire...	5.0	3.4	0.6
California...........	272.4	249.1	19.7	New Jersey.......	40.7	34.9	3.5
Colorado...........	63.8	55.5	7.4	New Mexico.......	58.9	54.5	3.2
Connecticut........	12.2	9.8	1.0	New York..........	86.8	74.5	8.5
Delaware...........	6.6	5.4	0.5	North Carolina....	96.8	87.9	6.2
Dist. of Columbia...	87.0	67.7	19.3	North Dakota......	17.0	14.0	1.0
Florida.............	117.2	100.4	12.4	Ohio..............	63.7	55.8	5.4
Georgia............	117.8	105.0	9.3	Oklahoma.........	62.2	54.1	5.9
Hawaii.............	50.5	48.3	1.0	Oregon............	24.8	18.9	3.0
Idaho..............	17.8	15.1	1.6	Pennsylvania......	77.9	65.2	9.8
Illinois.............	66.1	56.6	5.5	Rhode Island......	9.7	8.7	0.6
Indiana.............	33.5	27.2	3.0	South Carolina....	53.7	49.1	2.4
Iowa...............	16.1	11.0	1.9	South Dakota.....	17.2	14.8	0.9
Kansas............	34.1	28.0	3.2	Tennessee.........	52.7	46.4	3.4
Kentucky...........	49.8	44.4	2.9	Texas.............	197.1	171.7	21.6
Louisiana...........	41.2	29.7	3.6	Utah..............	33.8	28.2	3.3
Maine..............	10.9	9.2	0.8	Vermont...........	4.5	3.0	1.0
Maryland...........	136.9	115.0	19.0	Virginia...........	183.0	152.1	29.3
Massachusetts......	33.4	28.6	2.9	Washington........	85.8	78.2	5.5
Michigan...........	26.9	19.2	4.4	West Virginia......	22.4	17.5	2.5
Minnesota..........	19.4	12.0	2.3	Wisconsin.........	22.7	17.1	2.5
Mississippi.........	38.3	30.0	2.1	Wyoming..........	14.5	12.3	0.9

[1] Includes museum trust and state government owned. Non-federal government entities hold title to the real property asset but rights for use have been granted to the Federal Government in a method other than a leasehold arrangement; in the case of a museum trust, the trust holds title but Federal funds may be received to cover operational and maintenance costs.

Source: U.S. General Services Administration, "Federal Real Property Profile (FRPP) Summary Report Library," <www.gsa.gov/policy-regulations/policy/real-property-policy/data-collection-and-reports/frpp-summary-report-library>, accessed December 2023.

National Security and Veterans Affairs

This section displays data for national security (national defense and homeland security) and benefits for veterans. Data are presented on national defense and its human and financial costs; active and reserve military personnel; federally sponsored programs and benefits for veterans; and funding, budget and selected agencies for homeland security. The principal sources of these data are the *Veterans Benefits Administration Annual Benefits Report*, U.S. Department of Veterans Affairs; *Budget-in-Brief*, U.S. Department of Homeland Security; and *The Budget of the United States Government*, Office of Management and Budget.

Department of Defense (DoD)—The U.S. Department of Defense is responsible for providing the military forces of the United States. It includes the Office of the Secretary of Defense, the Joint Chiefs of Staff, the Army, the Navy, the Air Force, and the defense agencies. The U.S. Space Force was established on December 20, 2019, when the National Defense Authorization Act was signed into law. The President serves as Commander-in-Chief of the Armed Forces; from him, the authority flows to the Secretary of Defense and through the Joint Chiefs of Staff to the commanders of unified and specified commands (e.g., U.S. Strategic Command).

Reserve components—The Reserve components of the Armed Forces consist of the Army National Guard of the United States, Army Reserve, Naval Reserve, Marine Corps Reserve, Air National Guard, Air Force Reserve, and Coast Guard Reserve. They provide trained personnel and units available for active duty in the Armed Forces during times of war or national emergency, and at such other times as national security may require. The National Guard has dual federal/state responsibilities and uses jointly provided equipment, facilities, and budget support. The President is empowered to mobilize the National Guard and to use the Armed Forces as he considers necessary to enforce federal authority in any state. There is in each Armed Force a ready reserve, a standby reserve, and a retired reserve. The Ready Reserve includes the Selected Reserve, which provides trained and ready units and individuals to augment the active forces during times of war or national emergency, or at other times when required; and the Individual Ready Reserve, which is a manpower pool that can be called to active duty during times of war or national emergency and would normally be used as individual fillers for active, guard, and reserve units, and as a source of combat replacements. Most of the Ready Reserve serves in an active status.

Department of Veterans Affairs (VA)—A veteran is someone 18 years and older (there are a few 17-year-old veterans) who is not currently on active duty, but who once served on active duty in the United States Army, Navy, Air Force, Marine Corps, or Coast Guard, or who served in the Merchant Marine during World War II. There are many groups whose active service makes them veterans including: those who incurred a service-connected disability during active duty for training in the Reserves or National Guard even though that service would not otherwise have counted for veteran status, and members of a national guard or reserve component who have been ordered to active duty by order of the President or those who have a full-time military job. The latter are called AGRs (Active Guard and Reserve). No one who has received a dishonorable discharge is a veteran.

The VA administers laws authorizing benefits for eligible former and present members of the Armed Forces and for the beneficiaries of deceased members. Veterans' benefits available under various acts of Congress include compensation for service-connected disability or death; pensions for non-service-connected disability or death; vocational rehabilitation, education and training; home loan insurance; life insurance; health care; special housing and automobiles or other conveyances for certain disabled veterans; burial and plot allowances; and educational assistance to families of deceased or totally disabled veterans, servicemen missing in action, or prisoners of war. Since these benefits are legislated by Congress, the dates they were enacted and the dates they apply to veterans may be different from the actual dates the conflicts occurred. VA estimates of veterans cover all persons discharged from active U.S. military service under conditions other than dishonorable.

Department of Homeland Security (DHS)—The creation of DHS, which began operations in March 2003, represents a fusion of 22 federal agencies from different legacy agencies (the Coast Guard and Secret Service remained intact) to coordinate and centralize the leadership of many homeland security activities under a single department. The largest organizations under DHS include: Customs and Border Protection (CBP), Immigration and Customs Enforcement (ICE), Transportation Security Administration (TSA), Federal Emergency Management Agency (FEMA), and the Coast Guard.

Coast Guard—The Coast Guard is a military, multi-mission, maritime organization that promotes safety and safeguards U.S. economic and security interests throughout the maritime environment. Of the five Armed Services of the United States, it is the only military organization within the DHS. Unlike its sister services in the Department of Defense (DoD), the Coast Guard is also a law enforcement and regulatory agency with broad domestic authorities.

Federal Emergency Management Agency (FEMA)—FEMA manages and coordinates the federal response to and recovery from major domestic disasters and emergencies of all types in accordance with the Robert T. Stafford Disaster Relief and Emergency Assistance Act. The agency ensures the effectiveness of emergency response providers at all levels of government in responding to terrorist attacks, major disasters, and other emergencies. Through the Disaster Relief Fund, FEMA provides individual and public assistance to help families and communities impacted by declared disasters rebuild and recover. FEMA is also the principal component for preparing state and local governments to prevent or respond to threats or incidents of terrorism and other catastrophic events, through their state and local programs.

The Customs and Border Protection (CBP)—CBP is responsible for managing, securing, and controlling

U.S. borders. This includes carrying out traditional border-related responsibilities, such as stemming the tide of illegal drugs and illegal aliens; securing and facilitating legitimate global trade and travel; and protecting the food supply and agriculture industry from pests and disease. CBP is composed of the Border Patrol and Inspections (both moved from Immigration and Naturalization Service) along with Customs (absorbed from the U.S. Department of Treasury) and Animal and Plant Health Inspections Services (absorbed from the U.S. Department of Agriculture).

The Immigration and Customs Enforcement (ICE)

—ICE's mission is to protect America and uphold public safety by targeting the people, money, and materials crossing the nation's borders that support terrorist and criminal activities. ICE is the largest investigation arm of DHS. ICE is composed of five law enforcement divisions: Investigations, Intelligence, Federal Protective Service, International Affairs, and Detention and Removal Operations. ICE investigates a wide range of national security, financial, and smuggling violations including drug smuggling, human trafficking, illegal arms exports, financial crimes, commercial fraud, human smuggling, document fraud, money laundering, child pornography/exploitation, and immigration fraud.

The Transportation Security Administration (TSA)

—TSA was created as part of the Aviation and Transportation Security Act in 2001. TSA was originally part of the U.S. Department of Transportation, but was moved to DHS. TSA's mission is to provide security to our nation's transportation systems with a primary focus on aviation security.

Table 541. National Defense Outlays and Veterans' Benefits: 1965 to 2029

[In billions of dollars (56.3 represents $56,300,000,000), except percent. For fiscal year ending in year shown; see text, Section 8. Includes outlays of Department of Defense, Department of Veterans Affairs, and other agencies for activities primarily related to national defense and veterans programs. For explanation of average annual percent change, see Guide to Tabular Presentation. Minus sign (-) indicates decrease]

| Year | National defense and veterans' outlays | | | | Annual percent change [1] | | | Defense outlays, percent of— | |
| | Total outlays | Defense outlays | | Veterans' outlays | Total outlays | Defense outlays | Veterans' outlays | Federal outlays | Gross domestic product [2] |
		Current dollars	Constant (2012) dollars						
1965	56.3	50.6	406.9	5.7	-6.8	-7.6	0.7	42.8	7.1
1970	90.4	81.7	521.7	8.7	0.3	-1.0	13.6	41.8	7.8
1975	103.1	86.5	381.6	16.6	11.2	9.0	24.0	26.0	5.4
1980	155.2	134.0	402.6	21.2	13.9	15.2	6.3	22.7	4.8
1985	279.0	252.7	547.9	26.3	10.3	11.1	2.7	26.7	5.9
1990	328.4	299.3	567.7	29.1	-1.6	-1.4	-3.2	23.9	5.1
1995	310.0	272.1	466.4	37.9	-2.9	-3.4	0.8	17.9	3.6
2000	341.4	294.4	452.3	47.0	7.4	7.1	8.8	16.5	2.9
2001	349.8	304.7	452.7	45.0	2.4	3.5	-4.3	16.4	2.9
2002	399.4	348.5	501.2	51.0	14.2	14.3	13.2	17.3	3.2
2003	461.6	404.7	546.8	56.8	15.6	16.2	11.5	18.7	3.6
2004	515.5	455.8	593.4	59.7	11.7	12.6	5.1	19.9	3.8
2005	565.4	495.3	615.5	70.1	9.7	8.7	17.4	20.0	3.9
2006	591.7	521.8	621.6	69.8	4.6	5.4	-0.4	19.7	3.8
2007	624.1	551.3	635.5	72.8	5.5	5.6	4.3	20.2	3.9
2008	700.8	616.1	683.6	84.7	12.3	11.8	16.3	20.7	4.2
2009	756.6	661.0	735.0	95.5	8.0	7.3	12.8	18.8	4.6
2010	802.0	693.5	757.0	108.5	6.0	4.9	13.5	20.1	4.7
2011	832.8	705.6	748.3	127.3	3.8	1.7	17.3	19.6	4.6
2012	802.5	677.9	709.2	124.7	-3.6	-3.9	-2.0	19.2	4.2
2013	772.5	633.4	658.3	139.0	-3.7	-6.6	11.5	18.3	3.8
2014	753.1	603.5	617.4	149.6	-2.5	-4.7	7.6	17.2	3.5
2015	749.4	589.7	601.0	159.8	-0.5	-2.3	6.8	16.0	3.2
2016	767.9	593.4	602.7	174.6	2.5	0.6	9.2	15.4	3.2
2017	775.3	598.7	598.7	176.6	1.0	0.9	1.2	15.0	3.1
2018	810.1	631.3	615.4	178.9	4.5	5.4	1.3	15.4	3.1
2019	885.6	685.7	655.0	199.8	9.3	8.6	11.7	15.4	3.2
2020	943.2	724.6	684.6	218.7	6.5	5.7	9.4	11.1	3.4
2021	988.2	753.9	693.3	234.3	4.8	4.0	7.1	11.1	3.3
2022	1,040.1	765.6	663.2	274.4	5.2	1.6	17.1	12.2	3.0
2023	**1,121.9**	**820.3**	**680.4**	**301.6**	**7.9**	**7.1**	**9.9**	**13.4**	**3.0**
2024, estimate	1,254.1	907.7	733.1	346.3	11.8	10.7	14.8	13.1	3.2
2025, estimate	1,296.9	926.8	733.6	370.1	3.4	2.1	6.9	12.8	3.2
2026, estimate	1,325.2	933.0	723.4	392.2	2.2	0.7	6.0	12.6	3.1
2027, estimate	1,359.1	947.2	719.4	411.9	2.6	1.5	5.0	12.3	3.0
2028, estimate	1,418.9	967.1	719.5	451.8	4.4	2.1	9.7	12.0	2.9
2029, estimate	1,424.0	988.7	720.5	435.3	0.4	2.2	-3.6	11.9	2.9

[1] Change from immediate prior year. [2] Represents fiscal year GDP; for definition, see text, Section 13.

Source: U.S. Office of Management and Budget, *Budget of the U.S. Government, Fiscal Year 2025: Historical Tables*, March 2024. See also <www.whitehouse.gov/omb/budget/>.

Table 542. Department of Defense Property—Sites, Land, and Assets: 2024

[In units, as indicated (2,232.3 represents $2,232,300,000,000). Department of Defense (DoD) real property inventory as of September 30, 2023, baseline for FY2024. A site is a physical location owned by, leased to, or otherwise under the jurisdiction of a DoD component. Data shown for DoD sites located in the U.S. must be larger than 10 acres and have a plant replacement value (PRV) greater than $10 million. Sites located in a foreign country must be larger than 10 acres or have a PRV greater than $10 million]

Asset type	Unit	Total	Army	Navy	Air Force	Marine Corps	WHS [1]
DoD sites, total	Number	4,806	(NA)	(NA)	(NA)	(NA)	(NA)
Acres of land, total	**Number**	**26,754,058**	**13,345,177**	**2,527,618**	**8,280,785**	**2,599,245**	**1,233**
United States	Number	25,792,203	13,133,053	2,178,430	7,953,894	2,525,593	1,233
Territories	Number	203,675	14,379	185,797	3,499	–	–
Overseas	Number	758,180	197,745	163,391	323,392	73,652	–
Facility assets, total [2]	**Number**	**712,258**	**374,011**	**118,684**	**168,231**	**50,387**	**945**
Buildings	Number	292,823	140,048	59,075	67,687	25,835	178
Structures	Number	217,837	100,832	36,655	62,121	17,736	493
Linear structures	Number	201,598	133,131	22,954	38,423	6,816	274
Plant replacement value of assets, total [3]	**Bil. dol.**	**2,232.3**	**827.3**	**520.9**	**680.3**	**192.5**	**11.3**
Buildings	Bil. dol.	1,375.5	532.4	299.3	401.5	131.4	10.9
Structures	Bil. dol.	380.8	115.5	138.6	100.7	25.8	0.2
Linear structures	Bil. dol.	476.0	179.4	83.0	178.2	35.3	0.1

NA Not available. – Represents zero. [1] Washington Headquarters Service. [2] Buildings (roofed and floored facilities enclosed by exterior walls); structures (facilities other than buildings or linear structures, constructed on or in the land, such as towers, storage tanks, wharfs, and piers); and linear structures (facilities that traverse land such as runways, roads, rail lines, pipelines, fences, pavements, and electrical distribution lines and are reported by a linear unit of measure). [3] PRV calculated cost to replace the current physical plant (facilities and supporting infrastructure) using today's construction costs (labor and materials) and standards (methodologies and codes).

Source: U.S. Department of Defense, Office of the Deputy Assistant Secretary of Defense (OASD) for Sustainment, "Base Structure Report (BSR) – FY2024 BSR," <www.acq.osd.mil/eie/BSI/BEI_Library.html>, accessed July 2024.

Table 543. National Defense Budget Authority and Outlays for Defense Functions: 2000 to 2025

[In billions of dollars (304.0 represents $304,000,000,000). For year ending September 30. Data include defense budget authority and outlays by other departments. Minus sign (-) indicates decrease]

Function	2000	2010	2015	2018	2019	2020	2021	2022	2023	2024 est.	2025 est.
Total budget authority	**304.0**	**721.2**	**598.4**	**726.9**	**745.4**	**774.5**	**759.6**	**838.6**	**919.8**	**968.0**	**921.0**
Department of Defense—Military	290.3	695.6	570.8	694.6	712.3	738.7	719.5	795.6	874.4	920.6	872.2
Military personnel	73.8	157.1	145.9	150.9	157.3	163.3	172.9	178.1	184.8	192.9	204.4
Operation and maintenance	108.7	293.6	246.6	274.1	283.1	301.5	285.6	320.2	340.5	320.8	338.0
Procurement	55.0	135.8	102.1	147.5	146.8	141.0	140.9	153.6	177.0	164.0	167.7
Research, development, test, and evaluation	38.7	80.2	63.9	92.0	95.5	105.2	106.1	119.3	140.6	140.4	143.9
Military construction	5.1	22.6	5.7	10.4	11.3	16.7	7.1	13.4	16.7	16.7	15.6
Family housing	3.5	2.3	1.1	1.4	1.6	1.5	1.5	1.5	2.4	2.3	2.0
Other	5.4	4.0	5.6	18.4	16.6	9.5	5.4	9.3	12.5	83.4	-0.1
Atomic energy defense activities	12.4	18.2	19.0	23.3	24.0	26.0	29.4	32.0	33.9	35.3	36.9
Defense-related activities	1.3	7.3	8.5	9.0	9.1	9.7	10.8	11.1	11.5	12.1	12.0
Total outlays	**294.4**	**693.5**	**589.7**	**631.3**	**685.7**	**724.6**	**753.9**	**765.6**	**820.3**	**907.7**	**926.8**
Department of Defense—Military	281.0	666.7	562.5	600.8	653.7	690.4	717.6	726.5	775.9	859.5	878.5
Military personnel	76.0	155.7	145.2	145.8	156.3	161.4	172.6	180.8	183.9	189.8	202.8
Operation and maintenance	105.8	276.0	247.2	256.7	271.7	278.9	286.2	291.3	317.6	323.4	330.2
Procurement	51.7	133.6	101.3	112.7	124.7	139.1	141.4	136.2	141.7	147.9	166.5
Research, development, test, and evaluation	37.6	77.0	64.1	77.0	89.3	99.9	105.7	107.1	122.0	137.3	138.8
Military construction	5.1	21.2	8.1	6.7	7.4	8.9	9.1	9.7	10.3	14.0	17.4
Family housing	3.4	3.2	1.2	1.2	1.2	1.3	1.5	1.4	1.5	1.7	2.0
Other	1.4	0.1	-4.7	0.8	3.2	1.0	1.1	0.0	-1.1	45.4	20.6
Atomic energy defense activities	12.1	19.3	18.7	20.9	22.8	24.5	25.8	28.3	32.6	35.9	35.6
Defense-related activities	1.2	7.5	8.5	9.5	9.3	9.7	10.5	10.9	11.8	12.3	12.7

Source: U.S. Office of Management and Budget, *Budget of the U.S. Government, Fiscal Year 2025: Historical Tables*, March 2024. See also <www.whitehouse.gov/omb/budget/>.

Table 544. Military Personnel and Families by Selected Characteristics: 2010 to 2022

[In units, as indicated. Reserve and National Guard includes Selected Reserve only, unless otherwise noted. Personnel data are primarily from Defense Manpower Data Center (DMDC). Family member data are from the Defense Enrollment and Eligibility Reporting System]

Characteristic	2010 Active Duty	2010 Reserve and Guard	2020 Active Duty	2020 Reserve and Guard	2021 Active Duty	2021 Reserve and Guard	2022 Active Duty	2022 Reserve and Guard
MILITARY PERSONNEL								
Total (number)	**1,417,370**	**857,261**	**1,333,822**	**802,248**	**1,335,848**	**800,064**	**1,304,720**	**772,910**
Ratio of officers to enlisted members	1 to 5.0	1 to 5.7	1 to 4.7	1 to 4.9	1 to 4.7	1 to 4.8	1 to 4.5	1 to 4.7
Separations from duty (number)	176,248	133,223	157,548	121,671	156,689	114,088	174,813	120,858
Retired personnel (number) [1]	1,540,830	716,228	1,584,665	786,399	1,576,053	785,285	1,577,424	790,412
PERCENT								
Male	85.6	82.1	82.8	78.9	82.7	78.6	82.5	78.4
Female	14.4	17.9	17.2	21.1	17.3	21.4	17.5	21.6
Minority race/ethnicity [2]	30.0	24.1	31.1	27.5	31.1	26.9	31.2	27.1
Duty location in the U.S. & territories	86.4	99.1	87.9	99.6	87.5	99.3	87.5	99.1
25 years old and under	44.2	33.3	45.0	38.5	44.4	32.8	43.5	32.2
With bachelor's degree or higher	17.7	19.4	22.5	25.4	22.8	26.1	23.5	27.4
Married	56.4	48.2	49.9	43.9	50.0	43.8	49.9	43.8
In dual-military marriages	6.7	2.6	6.8	2.6	7.0	2.6	7.2	2.6
MILITARY FAMILIES								
Family members (number)	**1,983,236**	**1,161,631**	**1,569,841**	**1,023,295**	**1,551,972**	**1,015,386**	**1,507,987**	**985,581**
Spouses (number)	725,877	413,295	597,737	357,220	594,110	354,255	578,952	344,716
Adult dependents (number)	9,485	1,961	7,619	1,473	6,909	2,193	6,350	1,281
PERCENT								
With children	44.1	43.2	35.9	40.5	35.4	40.2	35.1	40.3
With children age 5 & under	42.3	27.9	41.4	31.1	41.0	30.7	40.7	30.5
Single parents	5.4	9.3	3.9	8.6	3.9	8.5	3.9	8.5
Average age at birth of first child (years)	24.9	26.6	25.9	28.6	26.1	28.7	26.3	28.7

[1] Retired Reserve and Guard includes ready reserve. [2] Black or African American, Asian, American Indian or Alaska Native, Native Hawaiian or Other Pacific Islander, multi-racial, or other/unknown.

Source: U.S. Department of Defense, Office of the Deputy Assistant Secretary of Defense, Military Community and Family Policy, *2022 Demographics Profile of the Military Community*, and earlier reports. See also <www.militaryonesource.mil/data-research-and-statistics/>.

Table 545. Department of Defense Personnel by Service Branch and Sex: 1960 to 2023

[In thousands (2,475 represents 2,475,000). As of end of fiscal year; see text, Section 8. Includes National Guard, Reserve, and retired regular personnel on extended or continuous active duty. Excludes Space Force, except as noted. Excludes Coast Guard. Other officer candidates are included under enlisted personnel]

Year	Total 1,2,3	Army Total 1	Army Male Officers	Army Male Enlisted	Army Female Officers	Army Female Enlisted	Navy 2 Total 1	Navy Male Officers	Navy Male Enlisted	Navy Female Officers	Navy Female Enlisted	Marine Corps Total 1	MC Male Officers	MC Male Enlisted	MC Female Officers	MC Female Enlisted	Air Force Total 1	AF Male Officers	AF Male Enlisted	AF Female Officers	AF Female Enlisted
1960	2,475	873	96.7	761.7	4.3	8.3	617	67.3	539.6	2.7	5.4	171	15.9	152.5	0.1	1.5	815	126.3	677.3	3.7	5.7
1965	2,654	969	108.2	846.5	3.8	8.5	670	75.4	582.7	2.6	5.3	190	16.9	171.6	0.1	1.4	825	127.9	685.3	4.1	4.7
1970	3,065	1,323	161.8	1,141.5	5.2	11.5	691	78.1	600.2	2.9	5.8	260	24.7	232.9	0.3	2.1	791	125.3	648.0	4.7	9.0
1975	2,128	784	98.4	640.3	4.6	37.7	535	62.3	448.5	3.7	17.5	196	18.7	174.2	0.3	2.8	613	100.0	477.8	5.0	25.2
1980	2,051	777	91.4	612.3	7.6	61.7	527	58.1	429.9	4.9	30.1	189	17.5	163.8	0.5	6.2	558	89.5	404.1	8.5	51.9
1985	2,151	781	99.2	598.6	10.8	68.4	571	64.1	449.3	6.9	45.7	198	19.3	169.0	0.7	9.0	602	96.1	430.9	11.9	58.1
1986	2,169	781	98.7	597.3	11.3	69.7	581	64.7	456.8	7.3	47.2	200	19.4	169.8	0.6	9.2	608	96.6	433.8	12.4	61.2
1987	2,174	781	96.4	596.4	11.6	71.6	587	64.8	462.3	7.2	47.7	200	19.4	169.9	0.6	9.1	607	94.4	431.8	12.6	63.2
1988	2,138	772	95.3	588.0	11.8	72.0	593	64.7	466.3	7.3	49.7	197	19.3	168.0	0.7	9.0	576	92.1	405.5	12.9	61.5
1989	2,130	770	94.8	583.7	12.2	74.3	593	64.5	463.9	7.5	52.1	197	19.3	168.0	0.7	9.0	571	90.6	399.3	13.4	63.7
1990	2,044	732	91.6	552.8	12.4	71.2	579	64.2	450.9	7.8	52.1	197	19.3	168.3	0.7	8.7	535	86.7	370.2	13.3	60.8
1991	1,986	711	91.5	535.2	12.5	67.8	570	63.0	443.6	8.0	51.4	194	19.3	165.7	0.7	8.3	510	83.7	349.9	13.3	59.1
1992	1,807	610	83.3	449.3	11.7	61.7	542	60.7	417.0	8.3	51.0	185	18.4	157.1	0.6	7.9	470	77.3	319.9	12.7	56.1
1993	1,705	572	76.9	419.8	11.1	60.2	510	57.7	389.7	8.3	49.3	178	17.4	152.8	0.6	7.2	444	71.7	301.5	12.3	54.5
1994	1,610	541	74.1	393.5	10.9	59.0	469	54.0	355.1	8.0	47.9	174	17.4	149.0	0.6	7.0	426	68.7	287.0	12.3	54.0
1995	1,518	509	72.2	364.7	10.8	57.3	435	51.1	324.1	7.9	47.9	175	17.3	149.6	0.7	7.4	400	65.9	265.9	12.1	52.1
1996	1,472	491	70.0	347.5	10.6	59.0	417	49.7	308.2	7.8	46.9	175	17.2	149.1	0.8	7.8	389	64.3	255.8	12.0	52.8
1997	1,439	492	68.9	345.9	10.4	62.4	396	48.4	290.5	7.8	44.8	174	17.0	147.6	0.8	8.5	377	62.0	245.5	12.0	53.8
1998	1,407	484	68.1	339.8	10.4	61.4	382	47.2	280.2	7.8	42.9	173	17.0	146.3	0.9	8.9	368	59.9	237.4	12.0	54.2
1999	1,386	479	66.6	336.6	10.5	61.5	373	45.8	271.3	7.7	43.9	173	17.0	145.5	0.9	9.3	361	58.5	231.5	11.8	54.6
2000	1,384	482	65.9	338.5	10.8	62.9	373	45.7	271.7	7.8	43.8	173	17.0	145.9	0.9	9.5	356	57.2	227.3	11.8	55.0
2001	1,385	481	65.0	336.6	11.0	63.4	378	46.0	273.4	8.0	46.6	173	17.0	145.4	1.0	9.6	354	57.0	224.4	11.8	55.6
2002	1,414	487	66.5	340.8	11.5	63.2	385	46.8	278.7	8.2	47.3	174	17.0	145.5	1.0	9.5	368	59.1	233.4	12.9	58.6
2003	1,434	499	68.0	351.5	12.0	63.5	382	46.8	275.7	8.2	47.3	178	17.9	149.4	1.1	9.6	375	60.5	237.0	13.5	60.0
2004	1,427	500	68.6	357.5	12.3	61.0	373	46.1	272.8	8.1	46.1	178	17.7	149.0	1.1	9.7	377	60.5	242.3	13.6	60.2
2005	1,389	493	69.1	353.1	12.4	57.9	363	45.0	265.5	7.8	44.5	180	17.7	151.2	1.0	9.8	354	59.7	224.7	13.4	55.6
2006	1,385	505	69.0	365.0	12.5	58.5	350	44.0	255.0	7.6	43.2	180	18.0	151.0	1.1	10.0	349	58.0	223.0	12.8	55.8
2007	1,380	522	71.0	379.0	13.0	58.8	338	44.0	244.0	7.6	42.2	186	18.0	156.0	1.1	10.5	333	54.0	214.0	11.8	53.4
2008	1,402	544	74.0	392.0	13.5	59.7	332	44.0	235.0	7.7	41.4	199	19.0	167.0	1.2	11.1	327	53.0	207.0	11.9	51.4
2009	1,419	553	76.0	399.0	14.3	59.4	329	44.0	231.0	7.9	42.2	203	19.0	170.0	1.2	11.7	333	53.0	211.0	12.1	52.0
2010	1,431	566	79.0	407.0	15.1	60.3	328	44.0	228.0	8.2	43.4	202	18.0	169.0	1.3	12.2	334	54.0	212.0	12.4	50.9
2011	1,425	565	82.0	403.0	15.7	60.2	325	44.6	224.0	8.5	44.0	201	21.0	167.0	1.3	12.4	333	53.0	213.0	12.3	50.3
2012	1,400	550	82.4	389.6	16.0	57.4	318	44.2	216.8	8.6	44.3	198	20.4	163.8	1.3	12.6	333	52.5	214.2	12.5	49.8
2013	1,383	532	82.4	373.3	16.2	55.7	324	44.9	219.0	9.0	47.0	196	19.9	161.8	1.4	12.8	330	52.1	212.7	12.7	49.1
2014	1,338	508	81.1	352.7	16.2	53.8	326	45.2	219.1	9.2	48.1	188	19.5	154.2	1.4	12.8	316	49.9	203.4	12.4	46.7
2015	1,314	491	78.7	338.9	15.9	53.4	328	44.8	219.3	9.4	49.9	183	19.2	150.1	1.5	12.6	311	48.6	200.0	12.4	46.3
2016	1,301	475	76.4	325.5	15.7	53.2	325	44.6	215.5	9.8	50.2	184	19.2	149.5	1.5	13.3	318	48.4	204.5	12.6	48.3
2017	1,307	476	75.9	325.0	15.9	54.4	324	44.4	213.6	10.1	51.4	184	19.5	149.4	1.6	13.9	323	48.7	206.9	12.9	50.1
2018	1,317	476	75.9	325.0	16.1	54.6	330	44.4	217.0	10.4	53.6	185	19.7	149.7	1.7	14.3	326	49.3	207.2	13.3	51.8
2019	1,339	484	75.9	330.2	16.5	56.8	337	44.4	221.5	10.7	55.9	186	19.7	149.7	1.8	14.9	332	50.0	209.8	13.9	54.2
2020	1,347	485	76.0	330.3	17.0	57.6	347	44.6	227.8	11.1	58.6	181	19.6	145.2	1.8	14.3	334	49.9	210.1	14.3	55.2
2021	1,348	486	76.2	331.0	17.2	57.6	348	44.6	228.4	11.4	58.8	180	19.7	143.7	2.0	14.3	335	50.2	210.0	14.7	55.6
2022 4	1,317	466	76.1	313.4	17.6	54.2	344	44.7	225.0	11.8	58.5	175	19.4	138.7	2.1	14.3	332	49.9	208.2	15.0	55.3
2023	1,286	454	74.9	303.7	17.7	52.8	332	43.5	216.1	11.8	56.6	173	19.1	136.7	2.2	14.6	319	46.1	200.8	14.6	53.1

1 Includes cadets, midshipmen, and others, not shown separately. 2 Beginning 1980, excludes Navy Reserve personnel on active duty for Training and Administration of Reserves (TARS). 3 Beginning 2022, total includes data for Space Force, not shown separately. 4 For 2022 only, Air Force data includes personnel for Space Force.

Source: U.S. Department of Defense, Statistical Information Analysis Division, Selected Manpower Statistics, discontinued; and Defense Manpower Data Center, "Active Duty Military Personnel by Service by Rank/Grade," <dwp.dmdc.osd.mil/>, accessed January 2024.

Table 546. Military Personnel on Active Duty by Rank or Grade: 2000 to 2023

[As of September 30]

Rank/grade	2000	2010	2019	2020	2021	2022	2023
Total	1,384,338	1,430,985	1,339,036	1,346,651	1,348,479	1,317,067	1,286,027
Total officers	217,178	234,000	232,889	234,336	236,061	236,642	234,252
General – Admiral	34	39	37	45	41	41	37
Lieutenant General – Vice Admiral	119	150	142	153	157	152	132
Major General – Rear Admiral (U)	282	310	295	281	294	286	252
Brigadier General – Rear Admiral (L)	436	482	409	417	409	384	388
Colonel – Captain	11,304	12,160	11,080	11,246	11,197	11,110	10,894
Lieutenant Colonel – Commander	27,461	28,773	27,152	27,569	27,800	27,529	27,008
Major – LT Commander	43,229	45,295	43,908	45,066	45,402	45,664	45,076
Captain – Lieutenant	68,106	74,997	73,820	72,602	73,507	73,780	73,564
1st Lieutenant – Lieutenant (JG)	24,713	25,523	29,228	31,411	32,136	31,399	31,007
2nd Lieutenant – Ensign	26,405	27,128	28,590	27,145	26,222	27,028	26,232
Chief Warrant Officer W-5	473	746	774	749	736	766	743
Chief Warrant Officer W-4	2,029	3,233	2,647	2,657	2,748	2,628	2,516
Chief Warrant Officer W-3	3,824	4,795	5,153	4,975	4,802	4,738	4,570
Chief Warrant Officer W-2	6,674	7,489	6,768	7,078	7,463	7,570	7,482
Warrant Officer W-1	2,089	2,880	2,886	2,942	3,122	3,567	4,351
Total enlisted	1,154,624	1,183,200	1,092,937	1,099,125	1,099,378	1,067,667	1,038,827
E-9	10,240	10,192	10,472	10,414	10,438	10,477	10,552
E-8	26,035	27,331	27,477	27,271	26,916	26,677	26,165
E-7	97,717	97,070	92,617	93,945	92,584	93,868	91,877
E-6	164,857	170,856	160,725	167,362	168,739	167,132	162,811
E-5	229,492	249,981	226,193	225,035	227,526	223,038	219,803
E-4	250,999	279,315	253,718	265,002	267,687	261,814	254,344
E-3	196,276	228,152	189,579	192,764	196,229	186,958	169,136
E-2	98,983	75,177	71,703	66,465	66,472	54,891	57,451
E-1	80,025	45,126	60,453	50,867	42,787	42,812	46,688
Cadets and Midshipmen	12,536	13,785	13,210	13,190	13,040	12,758	12,948

Source: U.S. Department of Defense, Statistical Information Analysis Division, *Atlas/Data Abstract for the United States and Selected Areas*, annual, discontinued; and "Active Duty Military Personnel by Rank/Grade," <dwp.dmdc.osd.mil/dwp/app/dod-data-reports/workforce-reports>, accessed January 2024.

Table 547. Military Retirement System—Disabled and Non-Disabled Personnel and Payments: 2022

[Payment in thousands of dollars (5,224,890 represents $5,224,890,000). As of September 30. The data published in the source report are produced from files maintained by the Defense Manpower Data Center; data are compiled primarily from the "Retiree and Survivor Pay" files. Data are shown by state of mailing address, which may not necessarily match the state of residence. Only those members in plans administered by the Department of Defense (DoD) are included in this table. Data are preliminary due to reporting delays for members who retired or died within one month of the September 30 reporting date; these data were not processed in time to be included. For more information, see Introduction and Overview, source]

State	Retired military personnel [1]			Monthly payment ($1,000)	State	Retired military personnel [1]			Monthly payment ($1,000)
	Total	Disabled [2]	Non-disabled			Total	Disabled [2]	Non-disabled	
Total [3]	2,190,448	313,776	1,876,672	5,224,890	MS	28,181	3,616	24,565	58,072
					MO	39,608	6,410	33,198	82,444
U.S.	1,995,314	294,608	1,700,706	4,641,026	MT	10,170	1,444	8,726	22,983
AL	63,268	8,082	55,186	152,334	NE	14,538	1,682	12,856	35,223
AK	10,877	1,719	9,158	25,902	NV	30,184	3,318	26,866	72,618
AZ	58,782	7,383	51,399	141,360	NH	9,576	1,242	8,334	22,900
AR	25,147	3,659	21,488	52,160	NJ	18,453	3,362	15,091	34,502
CA	141,264	19,549	121,715	333,705	NM	20,257	2,519	17,738	49,346
CO	53,489	8,301	45,188	146,498	NY	39,613	8,182	31,431	69,681
CT	9,970	1,621	8,349	21,013	NC	104,290	16,255	88,035	257,187
DE	9,479	984	8,495	20,748	ND	5,611	613	4,998	11,325
DC	2,196	360	1,836	6,574	OH	48,997	8,568	40,429	103,976
FL	214,569	25,998	188,571	556,546	OK	36,351	5,435	30,916	78,697
GA	102,519	16,384	86,135	235,580	OR	20,232	3,518	16,714	42,484
HI	18,051	1,977	16,074	48,227	PA	51,836	7,682	44,154	108,160
ID	15,789	2,193	13,596	35,958	RI	5,082	706	4,376	12,070
IL	35,845	6,303	29,542	77,206	SC	64,042	8,036	56,006	150,737
IN	27,444	5,314	22,130	50,874	SD	9,192	912	8,280	20,631
IA	13,815	2,257	11,558	26,474	TN	59,976	9,072	50,904	136,334
KS	22,406	3,426	18,980	52,554	TX	226,814	38,464	188,350	555,861
KY	28,936	5,000	23,936	62,003	UT	18,278	2,300	15,978	42,372
LA	26,000	4,527	21,473	55,527	VT	3,921	609	3,312	7,566
ME	12,020	1,611	10,409	25,644	VA	155,832	13,727	142,105	499,564
MD	55,508	6,114	49,394	148,866	WA	72,916	9,382	63,534	178,896
MA	17,721	3,026	14,695	34,858	WV	11,095	1,699	9,396	22,423
MI	31,516	6,415	25,101	58,184	WI	23,047	3,631	19,416	44,177
MN	19,963	2,962	17,001	36,952	WY	5,969	730	5,239	13,595

[1] Represents military personnel (officers and enlisted) receiving and not receiving pay from DoD. [2] A disabled military member is entitled to disability retired pay if the disability is permanent and stable, is not the result of the member's intentional misconduct or willful neglect, was not incurred during a period of unauthorized absence, and either: (1) the member has at least 20 years of service; or (2) at the time of determination, the disability is at least 30 percent (under a standard schedule of rating disabilities by the Veterans Administration) and one of four additional conditions are met. For details on these conditions and additional information, see Overview, source. [3] Includes states, U.S. territories, and retirees living in foreign countries.

Source: U.S. Department of Defense, Office of the Actuary, *Statistical Report on the Military Retirement System, Fiscal Year Ended September 30, 2022*, October 2023. See also <actuary.defense.gov>.

Table 548. U.S. Active Duty Military Deaths and Personnel Wounded in Action by Conflict and Manner of Death: 2001 to 2024

[As of August 20, 2024. See source for details. Data include deaths where wounding occurred in theater and death occurred elsewhere]

Item	Operation Enduring Freedom (OEF) [1]	Operation Iraqi Freedom (OIF) [2]	Operation New Dawn (OND) [3]	Operation Inherent Resolve (OIR) [4]	Operation Freedom's Sentinel (OFS) [5]
Deaths, total	**2,350**	**4,418**	**74**	**116**	**109**
Total hostile deaths	[6] **1,845**	**3,481**	**38**	**23**	**77**
Killed in action	1,370	2,676	22	12	51
Died of wounds	472	798	16	11	26
Died while missing in action	(NA)	1	–	–	–
Died while captured	(NA)	5	–	–	–
Died while detained	(NA)	1	–	–	–
Died of terrorist activities	2	–	–	–	–
Total non-hostile deaths	**505**	**937**	**36**	**93**	**32**
Accident	306	570	7	32	19
Illness or injury	62	97	10	21	2
Homicide	14	37	3	3	1
Self-inflicted	112	222	13	32	8
Undetermined	10	11	3	1	2
Pending	1	–	–	4	–
Wounded in action	**20,149**	**31,994**	**298**	**488**	**620**

– Represents zero. NA Not available. [1] OEF October 2001-December 2014 combat operations in Afghanistan and against al Qaeda. [2] OIF March 2003-September 2010 combat operations in Iraq. [3] OND September 2010-December 2011, to advise and train Iraqi security forces in Iraq. [4] OIR August 2014-present, to support Iraqi Security Force operations against the Islamic State of Iraq and the Levant (ISIL). [5] OFS began in 2015 to train, advise, and assist Afghan National Defense and Security Forces in Afghanistan and conduct counterterrorism operations against the remnants of al Qaeda. [6] Includes 1 death not attributed to a manner of death.

Source: U.S. Department of Defense, Defense Manpower Data Center, "Defense Casualty Analysis System, Conflict Casualties," <dcas.dmdc.osd.mil/dcas/app>, accessed August 2024.

Table 549. U.S. Military Personnel on Active Duty Overseas by Selected Country: 2010 to 2023

[As of September 30. Data from Defense Manpower Data Center (DMDC)]

Country	2010	2015	2016	2017	2018 [1]	2019 [1]	2020 [1]	2021 [1]	2022 [1]	2023 [1]
Total overseas [2]	**339,360**	**213,067**	**198,557**	**215,249**	[3] **172,370**	[3] **174,253**	[3] **168,766**	[3] **174,711**	[3] **171,736**	[3] **168,571**
Afghanistan	81,875	9,392	9,027	13,329	([3])	([3])	([3])	([3])	([3])	([3])
Australia	163	1,201	187	1,239	1,496	2,858	1,085	1,768	1,580	2,243
Bahrain	4,626	5,160	5,370	8,610	4,214	4,202	4,004	4,031	3,698	3,474
Belgium	1,157	1,202	852	867	1,049	1,046	1,147	1,143	1,143	1,105
British Indian Ocean Territory	484	486	294	264	299	325	230	223	222	220
Canada	131	146	139	129	144	144	132	143	155	162
Cuba (Guantanamo)	870	782	797	753	831	776	738	629	596	566
Djibouti	990	1,970	1,702	3,132	954	88	176	68	509	409
Egypt	262	350	356	375	280	276	269	292	199	253
Germany	43,911	35,216	34,612	34,516	35,116	35,275	33,959	35,468	35,781	35,188
Greece	380	371	360	433	410	389	380	429	387	368
Honduras	391	660	397	505	467	474	370	372	342	391
Hungary	50	70	207	215	202	194	77	77	78	81
Iraq	38,591	4,231	4,626	7,402	([3])	([3])	([3])	([3])	149	0
Israel	21	56	32	41	47	69	94	106	113	112
Italy	8,836	11,614	12,090	11,756	12,703	12,902	12,249	12,436	12,432	12,405
Japan	46,313	55,744	38,834	44,562	54,281	55,245	53,732	56,010	53,973	53,246
Jordan	42	1,861	1,556	1,862	59	95	254	88	112	110
Kenya	23	96	40	208	46	44	52	97	49	49
Korea, South	27,869	24,934	24,190	23,635	25,813	26,525	26,416	25,593	25,372	24,159
Kosovo	52	87	366	384	(NA)	(NA)	17	14	30	14
Kuwait	17,584	8,809	5,818	9,241	1,863	1,798	2,169	2,614	714	595
Kyrgyzstan	5,483	83	67	65	5	2	8	9	12	11
Netherlands	433	399	382	407	404	393	415	422	434	425
Niger	2	139	8	510	8	13	16	30	19	16
Norway	68	83	77	344	474	556	733	81	90	105
Pakistan	268	116	121	111	35	27	66	67	66	66
Philippines	546	234	36	101	145	170	185	126	211	257
Poland	18	61	53	173	150	163	165	167	264	216
Portugal	699	464	197	192	233	232	252	259	251	244
Qatar	12,036	5,219	3,216	4,666	783	545	490	487	397	335
Romania	7	611	682	451	294	108	124	132	138	133
Saudi Arabia	325	515	371	402	323	314	382	1,396	320	287
Singapore	216	252	176	206	205	200	206	187	218	239
Somalia	2	232	106	285	60	85	73	50	7	18
Spain	1,396	3,393	3,272	3,940	3,602	3,658	3,169	3,234	3,164	3,212
Syria	3	(NA)	(NA)	1,547	([3])	([3])	([3])	([3])	([3])	([3])
Thailand	201	108	296	309	316	303	100	99	110	113
Turkey	1,721	2,081	2,139	1,950	1,695	1,659	1,685	1,753	1,735	1,778
United Arab Emirates	1,427	2,620	1,510	3,455	414	352	195	200	362	174
United Kingdom	8,764	8,062	8,404	8,341	9,137	9,254	9,287	9,576	9,840	9,949
Yemen	104	8	7	14	4	7	4	5	([3])	4
Guam	5,423	6,531	3,977	4,590	6,199	5,560	6,140	6,273	6,667	6,363
Puerto Rico	654	725	142	176	158	161	163	161	176	644

NA Not available. [1] As of December 2017, excludes personnel on temporary duty, or deployed in support of contingency operations. [2] Includes items not shown separately, and also personnel in unknown and classified locations. [3] Questions concerning DoD personnel strength numbers are deferred to OSD Public Affairs/Joint Chiefs of Staff.

Source: U.S. Department of Defense, DoD Personnel, Workforce Reports & Publications, "Military and Civilian Personnel by Service/Agency by State/Country," <dwp.dmdc.osd.mil/>, accessed April 2024.

Table 550. Suicides of Military Personnel by Component and Service: 2019 to 2022

[Includes confirmed and suspected suicides reported as of March 31, 2023 for calendar years shown. Rates are unadjusted per 100,000 service members. Data are from the Armed Forces Medical Examiner System (AFMES)]

Component and service	Number				Rate			
	2019	2020	2021	2022	2019	2020	2021	2022
Active Component....................	**349**	**383**	**328**	**331**	**26.3**	**28.6**	**24.3**	**25.1**
Army..........................	145	174	175	135	30.5	36.2	36.1	28.9
Marine Corps.........................	47	63	43	61	25.3	34.5	23.9	34.9
Navy................................	74	65	59	71	22.1	19.0	17.0	20.6
Air Force............................	83	81	51	64	25.1	24.3	15.3	19.7
Space Force.........................	–	–	–	–	–	–	–	–
Reserve......................	**66**	**77**	**76**	**64**	**18.5**	**21.7**	**21.8**	**19.1**
Army..........................	37	42	46	37	19.4	22.2	24.8	20.8
Marine Corps.........................	9	10	14	6	(S)	(S)	(S)	(S)
Navy................................	7	13	10	7	(S)	(S)	(S)	(S)
Air Force............................	13	12	6	14	(S)	(S)	(S)	(S)
National Guard......................	**90**	**121**	**120**	**97**	**20.5**	**27.5**	**27.0**	**22.2**
Army..........................	76	105	105	82	22.9	31.5	31.2	24.8
Air Force............................	14	16	15	15	(S)	(S)	(S)	(S)

– Represents zero. S Rates are considered unreliable when the number of suicide deaths is less than 20.

Source: U.S. Department of Defense, Defense Suicide Prevention Office, *Department of Defense Annual Report on Suicide in the Military, Calendar Year 2022*, 2023. See also <www.dspo.mil/>.

Table 551. Sexual Assault in the Military—Incident Reports and Victims by Type of Report and Selected Characteristics: 2020 to 2023

[Data are for fiscal years. Reports of sexual assault (rape, aggravated sexual assault, sexual assault, aggravated sexual contact, abusive sexual contact, wrongful sexual contact, non-consensual sodomy, and attempts to commit these offenses) by or against Service Members. Restricted Reporting allows victim confidential access to medical care and advocacy services. When a victim makes an unrestricted report, the report is also referred to a Military Criminal Investigation Organization for investigation and command is notified]

Item	Unrestricted				Restricted			
	2020	2021	2022	2023	2020	2021	2022	2023
REPORTS [1]								
Total...................	**5,519**	**6,220**	**5,809**	**5,366**	**2,176**	**2,510**	**3,001**	**2,979**
Service member on service member....................	2,947	3,323	2,856	2,777	1,293	1,456	1,823	1,783
Service member on non-service member..............	833	907	747	606	53	27	49	49
Non-service member on service member..............	157	185	257	226	416	483	484	495
Unidentified subject on service member................	625	780	581	777	412	496	455	384
Unknown....................	957	1,025	1,368	980	2	48	190	268
VICTIMS IN COMPLETED INVESTIGATIONS [2]								
Total...................	**5,165**	**5,533**	**4,952**	**4,641**	**(X)**	**(X)**	**(X)**	**(X)**
Service member victims................	4,208	4,608	4,137	3,981	(X)	(X)	(X)	(X)
Non-service member victims..............	957	925	812	660	(X)	(X)	(X)	(X)
VICTIMS [3]								
By sex:								
Male...........................	960	1,060	983	1,098	451	559	680	756
Female.........................	4,201	4,470	3,893	3,497	1,725	1,942	2,314	2,215
By age:								
0-15 years old...................	29	44	35	35	153	201	141	135
16-19 years old..................	1,454	1,608	1,353	1,187	606	670	740	692
20-24 years old..................	2,173	2,371	2,052	1,837	924	1,080	1,351	1,310
25-34 years old..................	883	884	770	801	384	465	639	689
35-49 years old..................	154	169	162	158	82	88	98	121
50-64 years old..................	12	13	13	13	1	6	5	4
65 years and older................	130	99	2	–	–	–	–	–
SERVICE MEMBER VICTIMS								
By service branch:								
Army...........................	1,934	2,240	1,614	1,676	675	(NA)	976	933
Navy...........................	1,008	1,101	1,208	1,079	544	(NA)	706	746
Marines.........................	473	482	574	550	366	(NA)	435	452
Air Force........................	791	784	738	669	535	(NA)	817	777
Space Force.....................	–	–	2	5	–	–	7	5
Coast Guard....................	1	–	–	–	–	(NA)	–	3

– Represents zero. X Not applicable. NA Not available. [1] Reports of sexual assault during the fiscal year. [2] Victims in investigations completed during the fiscal year. Includes victims of unknown sex, age, and service branch, not shown separately. [3] For unrestricted reports, data shown for victims in investigations completed during the fiscal year.

Source: U.S. Department of Defense, *Annual Report on Sexual Assault in the Military, Fiscal Year 2023*, May 2024, and earlier reports. See also <sapr.mil/reports>.

Table 552. U.S. Foreign Military Sales by Selected Country: 1950 to 2022

[In thousands of dollars (788,618,466 represents $788,618,466,000). For fiscal year ending September 30. Foreign Military Sales (FMS) is a security assistance program authorized by the Arms Export Control Act (AECA) and conducted on the basis of formal contracts and agreements between the U.S. Government and authorized recipient governments or international organizations. Sales numbers include new sales implemented in a given fiscal year and any adjustments (increases or decreases) to existing programs via amendments or modifications implemented that fiscal year. Minus (-) sign indicates negative sales numbers, an indication that the amount of program decreases were more than combined new sales and positive adjustments]

Country	1950 to 2017	2018	2019	2020	2021	2022
Total [1]	**788,618,466**	**55,657,932**	**55,385,850**	**50,781,535**	**34,809,699**	**51,924,768**
Afghanistan	13,071,166	-1,859	1,576,712	1,071,477	1,263,903	-553,208
Armenia	47,082	2,698,501	103	2	-1	1,292
Australia	34,826,998	5,331	1,638,806	1,718,362	937,503	6,668,630
Bahrain	3,249,924	24,789	1,946,173	66,971	452,024	170,183
Barbados	7,856	1,462,956	330	270	–	470
Belgium	4,792,013	32,999	5,456,525	41,778	109,225	61,650
Benin	6,120	2,425,463	–	200	–	–
Brazil	2,554,893	747	41,767	19,274	101,744	21,452
Bulgaria	183,930	–	1,261,030	16,905	28,043	38,110
Canada	10,182,817	–	1,074,081	517,415	2,555,819	381,440
Chile	1,330,866	948	23,143	39,635	585,584	41,502
China	259,714	193,479	–	–	–	–
Colombia	2,960,207	–	35,326	62,880	71,639	24,102
Croatia	85,377	37,287	3,425	85,068	-419	206,911
Czechia	220,688	–	72,715	663,996	9,550	56,343
Denmark	4,139,119	–	261,842	154,374	35,164	41,804
Egypt	38,813,558	212	509,143	783,017	2,027,882	1,492,083
Estonia	148,644	66,184	35,559	610	37,267	49,601
Finland	5,182,748	600	114,043	24,830	90,560	11,830,599
France	6,144,304	–	304,993	246,337	1,516,440	665,079
Georgia	356,871	20,807	40,575	62,880	51,949	33,610
Germany	17,411,151	153,118	1,160,998	501,525	1,097,410	440,019
Greece	14,250,570	–	39,872	408,137	314,601	728,590
Guatemala	61,476	127,818	-147	–	500	28,330
Guinea-Bissau	3,104	1,349,336	–	–	–	–
Hungary	191,473	–	13,062	13,570	515,135	13,536
India	9,958,074	800	6,203	3,363,691	320,196	-254,035
Iraq	23,470,538	282,197	1,362,267	367,847	386,405	449,926
Israel	46,946,645	81,818	1,489,743	1,058,778	1,478,486	2,428,277
Italy	4,600,782	–	53,016	151,648	935,623	114,836
Ivory Coast	5,626	735,887	–	225	155	–
Japan	36,789,067	598,754	6,880,409	1,982,589	3,903,518	2,803,481
Jordan	6,941,125	91,369	269,595	197,837	153,551	1,731,564
Kosovo	21,987	3,498,907	2,708	11,116	22,425	16,181
Kuwait	17,691,267	280,671	386,229	908,479	1,256,741	240,167
Latvia	147,965	–	204,264	38,193	23,076	21,365
Lebanon	1,925,170	7,456,131	157,286	109,436	67,119	144,061
Lithuania	203,234	94,384	22,107	136,545	319,585	49,698
Malaysia	1,686,200	–	24,573	38,957	63,229	106,302
Morocco	5,244,821	48,828	12,401	4,538,590	53,481	-9,509
Netherlands	13,877,095	523	324,402	450,998	522,238	83,349
New Zealand	660,206	241,444	11,468	991,810	58,576	39,048
Niger	103,063	1,689,914	7,386	6,245	12	2,051
Nigeria	203,629	1,130,964	3,451	2,851	-510	20
Norway	8,816,798	–	202,082	242,354	36,781	162,499
Pakistan	10,401,371	496,414	-10,827	146,151	73,161	35,137
Panama	165,057	154,624	298	19,445	2,216	13,573
Philippines	2,031,591	–	90,669	140,047	90,326	134,717
Poland	6,505,780	–	673,495	4,709,501	126,642	4,825,772
Qatar	38,101,408	96,769	661,679	604,415	-68,443	5,424
Romania	854,546	–	1,099,099	768,211	986,416	103,811
Saint Lucia	9,969	1,187,680	–	–	–	–
Saudi Arabia	145,005,292	–	14,971,804	1,175,239	1,564,781	1,512,311
Seychelles	2,869	14,274,963	–	1,020	8	250
Singapore	9,595,158	4,177	137,499	1,291,281	24,773	800,649
Slovakia	368,003	475	1,881,342	11,854	119,900	43,438
Somalia	151,783	443,227	–	–	–	–
South Korea	36,752,266	4,709	2,688,444	2,124,078	1,901,969	947,262
Spain	9,940,090	–	1,788,391	140,088	186,487	199,111
Sudan	311,521	560,886	–	–	–	–
Sweden	1,152,169	–	17,298	96,721	11,154	39,149
Switzerland	4,194,855	890	41,665	88,956	36,912	5,698,627
Taiwan	31,146,119	1,148,715	875,552	11,777,426	2,678,026	2,057,122
Tajikistan	21,358	176,151	124	–	–	3,903
Thailand	6,555,911	1,677,158	16,710	247,699	297,798	83,271
Tunisia	1,496,515	–	67,118	58,740	175,458	31,105
Turkey	20,910,524	11	134,780	82,195	256,859	196,621
Ukraine	821,239	37,032	272,465	510,599	333,050	2,119,402
United Arab Emirates	24,415,256	584	1,087,905	3,567,997	359,734	203,254
United Kingdom	29,905,322	250,782	572,223	440,842	2,861,109	869,004
Uruguay	739,015	398,873	–	–	–	4,986
NATO North Atlantic Treaty Organization	347,135	11,041	143,954	218,877	170,328	227,516

– Represents zero. [1] Includes countries, programs, and classified totals not shown separately.

Source: U.S. Department of Defense, Defense Security Cooperation Agency, *Historical Sales Book, Fiscal Years 1950-2022*. See also <www.dsca.mil/resources/dsca-historical-sales-book>.

Table 553. Veterans by Selected Period of Service, State, and Island Area: 2023

[In thousands (18,250 represents 18,250,000). As of September 30. The Veteran Population Projection Model 2020 (VetPop2020) is the Department of Veterans Affairs (VA) latest official estimate and projection of the veteran population. It is based on tabulations prepared for the VA Office of the Actuary; recent American Community Survey, Internal Revenue Service, and Social Security Administration data; administrative data and projections of service member separations from active duty provided by the Department of Defense, Defense Manpower Data Center and the Office of the Actuary; and VA data on veterans benefits. Data may not sum due to rounding]

State and Island Area	Total [1,2]	Gulf War era [3]	Vietnam era [4]	State and Island Area	Total [1,2]	Gulf War era [3]	Vietnam era [4]
United States [5]	**18,250**	**8,193**	**5,638**	Montana	85	39	27
Alabama	348	171	107	Nebraska	117	55	35
Alaska	69	44	17	Nevada	216	100	63
Arizona	495	209	168	New Hampshire	94	36	32
Arkansas	201	90	68	New Jersey	299	109	96
California	1,487	656	464	New Mexico	142	63	49
Colorado	369	194	104	New York	663	247	208
Connecticut	153	56	48	North Carolina	681	331	197
Delaware	68	27	24	North Dakota	50	24	15
District of Columbia	27	15	6	Ohio	681	261	217
Florida	1,433	600	462	Oklahoma	278	137	85
Georgia	673	351	180	Oregon	267	102	91
Hawaii	105	55	29	Pennsylvania	698	252	232
Idaho	126	56	42	Rhode Island	56	23	18
Illinois	553	231	174	South Carolina	386	186	122
Indiana	380	157	122	South Dakota	62	29	20
Iowa	178	70	59	Tennessee	441	200	141
Kansas	182	84	54	Texas	1,534	825	424
Kentucky	268	120	84	Utah	127	66	37
Louisiana	262	127	77	Vermont	39	15	14
Maine	106	42	37	Virginia	684	403	179
Maryland	348	177	94	Washington	525	248	167
Massachusetts	276	101	89	West Virginia	125	48	42
Michigan	517	186	177	Wisconsin	324	121	107
Minnesota	286	105	95	Wyoming	45	19	15
Mississippi	180	88	52	Puerto Rico	70	25	24
Missouri	392	168	128	Island Areas & Foreign	80	49	21

[1] Veterans serving in more than one period of service are counted only once in the total. [2] Current civilians discharged from active duty, other than for training only without service-connected disability. [3] Service from August 2, 1990 to the present. [4] Service from August 5, 1964 to May 7, 1975. [5] U.S. total includes Puerto Rico and Island Areas & Foreign.

Source: U.S. Department of Veterans Affairs, National Center for Veterans Analysis and Statistics, "The Veteran Population Projection Model 2020 (VetPop2020)," <www.va.gov/vetdata/veteran_population.asp>, accessed July 2024.

Table 554. Veterans Living by Period of Service, Age, and Sex: 2023

[In thousands (18,250 represents 18,250,000). As of September 30. Includes veterans living outside the United States. Based on the Department of Veterans Affairs' (VA) latest official estimate and projection of the veteran population, the Veteran Population Projection Model 2020 (VetPop2020)]

Period of service and age	Total	Male	Female	Period of service and age	Total	Male	Female
Total	**18,250**	**16,183**	**2,067**	30 to 34 years old	881	714	166
PERIOD OF SERVICE				35 to 39 years old	1,029	837	192
Wartime vets [1]	14,271	12,626	1,644	40 to 44 years old	1,151	930	220
Gulf War Era [2]	8,193	6,804	1,389	45 to 49 years old	1,085	892	193
Vietnam Era [3]	5,638	5,382	256	50 to 54 years old	1,385	1,180	204
Korean conflict [4]	783	756	27	55 to 59 years old	1,617	1,405	213
World War II	120	113	6	60 to 64 years old	1,805	1,567	238
Peacetime	3,979	3,557	422	65 to 69 years old	1,718	1,527	191
AGE				70 to 74 years old	1,772	1,657	115
Under 20 years old	10	7	3	75 to 79 years old	2,327	2,254	73
20 to 24 years old	251	200	51	80 to 84 years old	1,262	1,222	40
25 to 29 years old	634	512	122	85 years old and over	1,324	1,279	45

[1] Veterans who served in more than one wartime period are counted only once in the total. [2] Service from August 2, 1990 to the present. [3] Service from August 5, 1964 to May 7, 1975. [4] Service during period June 27, 1950 to January 31, 1955.

Source: U.S. Department of Veterans Affairs, National Center for Veterans Analysis and Statistics, "The Veteran Population Projection Model 2020 (VetPop2020)," <www.va.gov/vetdata/Veteran_Population.asp>, accessed July 2024.

Table 555. Veterans Benefits—Expenditures by Program and Compensation for Service-Connected Disabilities: 2000 to 2023

[In millions of dollars (47,086 represents $47,086,000,000). For years ending September 30]

Program	2000	2010	2015	2017	2018	2019	2020	2021	2022	2023
Total expenditures...............	47,086	108,635	167,210	180,591	180,604	202,405	217,954	224,122	266,753	284,673
Medical care......................	19,637	42,372	65,561	69,710	71,303	77,803	86,808	88,218	103,704	109,011
Construction.....................	466	1,618	1,828	1,467	1,177	1,238	1,531	1,677	1,730	4,247
General operating expenses......................	1,016	6,101	8,056	9,223	9,513	10,117	10,798	8,751	12,967	12,730
Compensation and pension.....................	22,012	47,785	75,787	84,138	82,776	97,638	104,566	111,805	134,608	145,586
Vocational rehabilitation and education..................	1,610	8,260	13,408	13,182	13,178	13,811	12,688	11,583	10,750	12,435
All other [1]........................	2,345	2,499	2,570	2,871	2,656	1,798	1,563	2,088	2,994	663
Compensation for service-connected disabilities............	15,511	36,486	60,213	69,991	76,709	84,915	91,426	98,543	112,058	133,089

[1] Includes insurance, indemnities, and miscellaneous funds and expenditures and offsets from public receipts. Excludes expenditures from personal funds of patients.

Source: U.S. Department of Veterans Affairs, "Geographic Distribution of VA Expenditures (GDX): Summary Expenditures by State," <va.gov/vetdata/Expenditures.asp>, accessed June 2024; and *Annual Benefits Report, Fiscal Year 2023*, February 2024, and earlier reports. See also <benefits.va.gov/REPORTS/abr>.

Table 556. Veterans Compensation and Pension Benefits—Number on Rolls by Period of Service and Status: 1990 to 2023

[In thousands (3,584 represents 3,584,000). As of September 30. Living veterans refers to veterans receiving compensation for disability incurred or aggravated while on active duty, and war veterans receiving pension benefits for non-service connected disabilities and/or who are age 65 and older. Survivors include veterans' spouses, dependent children, and (based on need) dependent parents of veterans]

Period of service and veteran status	1990	2000	2010	2015	2016	2017	2018	2019	2020	2021	2022	2023
Total........................	3,584	3,236	4,070	5,061	5,247	5,442	5,619	5,787	5,906	5,686	6,194	6,422
Living veterans................	2,746	2,672	3,524	4,464	4,645	4,829	5,003	5,183	5,301	5,420	5,591	5,816
Compensation [1]..............	2,184	2,308	3,210	4,169	4,356	4,553	4,743	4,944	5,082	5,225	5,417	5,662
Pension [2]....................	562	364	314	295	289	277	260	239	220	195	174	154
Survivors of veterans.........	838	564	546	597	602	613	616	604	605	600	603	607
Compensation [1]..............	320	307	347	390	399	411	423	434	446	461	478	497
Pension [2]....................	518	257	199	206	203	201	193	170	159	140	126	109
World War I and earlier.......	198	34	6	3	3	2	2	2	2	1	1	1
Living veterans..............	18	(Z)	(Z)	(Z)	(Z)	(Z)	(Z)	(Z)	(Z)	(Z)	(Z)	(Z)
World War II...................	1,723	968	529	357	320	286	249	205	171	135	108	86
Living veterans..............	1,294	676	298	160	135	112	89	69	52	36	25	17
Korean conflict [3].............	390	323	275	262	256	249	238	221	204	180	160	142
Living veterans..............	305	255	209	186	178	169	158	145	130	110	94	81
Vietnam era [4]..................	774	969	1,447	1,765	1,803	1,840	1,868	1,890	1,889	1,870	1,863	1,869
Living veterans..............	685	848	1,261	1,514	1,538	1,560	1,572	1,581	1,566	1,531	1,507	1,496
Gulf War era [5]................	(X)	334	1,140	1,915	2,090	2,267	2,441	2,622	2,784	2,976	3,194	3,445
Living veterans..............	(X)	326	1,117	1,883	2,057	2,231	2,403	2,581	2,741	2,929	3,143	3,390
Peacetime......................	495	607	673	759	775	797	821	848	856	859	868	879
Living veterans..............	444	567	638	720	737	758	781	806	813	814	822	832

X Not applicable. Z Fewer than 500. [1] Compensation is based on military service-connected disability and death. [2] Pension is based on need and includes coverage for veterans with disabilities not connected to military service. [3] Service during period June 27, 1950 to January 31, 1955. [4] Service from August 5, 1964 to May 7, 1975. [5] Service from August 2, 1990 to the present.

Source: U.S. Department of Veterans Affairs, 1990 to 1995, *Annual Report of the Secretary of Veterans Affairs*; 1996 to 2010, *Annual Accountability Report* and unpublished data; and beginning 2011, *Annual Benefits Report, Fiscal Year 2023*, February 2024 and earlier reports. See also <benefits.va.gov/REPORTS/abr>.

Table 557. Veteran Income, Education, Poverty, and Disability Status Compared to Nonveteran Population: 2021 and 2022

[257,084 represents 257,084,000. Data are based on American Community Survey (ACS). The ACS universe includes the civilian household and group quarters population. Based on a sample and subject to sampling variability]

Characteristic	2021			2022		
	Total	Veterans	Nonveterans	Total	Veterans	Nonveterans
Population 18 years old and over (1,000).......	**257,084**	**16,502**	**240,582**	**259,616**	**16,200**	**243,415**
INCOME						
Median income in past 12 months (dollars) [1].......	36,107	46,775	35,411	39,185	50,476	38,254
Male..	(NA)	47,467	42,314	(NA)	51,091	46,366
Female......................................	(NA)	40,761	29,886	(NA)	44,237	31,706
EDUCATIONAL ATTAINMENT						
Population 25 years old and over...................	227,349	16,292	211,057	228,832	15,987	212,844
Less than high school graduate (percent)........	10.7	4.7	11.1	10.4	4.5	10.9
High school graduate or equivalency (percent)...	26.3	27.1	26.3	26.1	26.9	26.1
Some college or associate's degree (percent)....	28.0	36.9	27.3	27.8	37.0	27.1
Bachelor's degree or higher (percent)............	35.0	31.3	35.3	35.6	31.6	35.9
POVERTY AND DISABILITY STATUS						
Population for whom poverty status is determined...	250,877	16,283	234,594	253,241	15,927	237,314
Below poverty in the past 12 months (percent)...	11.6	7.4	11.9	11.6	7.5	11.9
With any disability (percent)......................	15.5	30.1	14.5	16.0	30.6	15.0

NA Not available. [1] For population with income.

Source: U.S. Census Bureau, American Community Survey, S2101, "Veteran Status," <data.census.gov>, accessed November 2023.

Table 558. Veterans by Sex, Race, and Hispanic Origin: 2021 and 2022

[See headnote, Table 557]

Characteristic	2021			2022		
	Total veterans	18 to 64 years	65 years and over	Total veterans	18 to 64 years	65 years and over
Total...................................	**16,501,502**	**8,385,977**	**8,115,525**	**16,200,322**	**8,217,339**	**7,982,983**
Male..	14,843,173	7,088,101	7,755,072	14,529,085	6,945,208	7,583,877
Female......................................	1,658,329	1,297,876	360,453	1,671,237	1,272,131	399,106
White alone...............................	12,330,235	5,613,020	6,717,215	12,025,853	5,467,573	6,558,280
Male..	11,287,142	4,844,523	6,442,619	10,981,989	4,721,134	6,260,855
Female......................................	1,043,093	768,497	274,596	1,043,864	746,439	297,425
Black or African American alone........	2,034,818	1,331,923	702,895	2,014,035	1,299,298	714,737
Male..	1,705,986	1,049,853	656,133	1,667,595	1,012,748	654,847
Female......................................	328,832	282,070	46,762	346,440	286,550	59,890
American Indian/Alaska Native alone..	120,944	79,421	41,523	122,579	76,939	45,640
Male..	104,163	64,997	39,166	105,689	63,224	42,465
Female......................................	16,781	14,424	2,357	16,890	13,715	3,175
Asian alone...............................	312,697	191,142	121,555	333,249	213,126	120,123
Male..	269,647	154,105	115,542	287,329	175,606	111,723
Female......................................	43,050	37,037	6,013	45,920	37,520	8,400
Native Hawaiian and other Pacific Islander alone............................	33,796	24,116	9,680	35,601	24,594	11,007
Male..	28,529	19,677	8,852	30,230	20,057	10,173
Female......................................	5,267	4,439	828	5,371	4,537	834
Some other race alone..................	443,293	311,155	132,138	450,865	319,512	131,353
Male..	387,966	262,387	125,579	394,348	269,550	124,798
Female......................................	55,327	48,768	6,559	56,517	49,962	6,555
Two or more races........................	1,225,719	835,200	390,519	1,218,140	816,297	401,843
Male..	1,059,740	692,559	367,181	1,061,905	682,889	379,016
Female......................................	165,979	142,641	23,338	156,235	133,408	22,827
Hispanic or Latino origin [1]...............	1,359,383	945,020	414,363	1,400,832	973,758	427,074
Male..	1,188,233	797,165	391,068	1,231,959	826,767	405,192
Female......................................	171,150	147,855	23,295	168,873	146,991	21,882

[1] Persons of Hispanic or Latino origin may be of any race.

Source: U.S. Census Bureau, American Community Survey, Tables B21001, C21001A, C21001B, C21001C, C21001D, C21001E, C21001F, C21001G, and C21001I, <data.census.gov>, accessed November 2023.

Table 559. Deferred Action for Childhood Arrivals (DACA) Recipients by Selected Characteristics and Top Country of Birth: 2024

[The active DACA population are individuals who have an approved I-821D Consideration of DACA form with expiration on or after March 31, 2024. Data are estimates. Individuals who have obtained Lawful Permanent Resident Status or U.S. Citizenship are excluded]

Characteristic	Number	Top 20 countries of birth	Number
Total..........	**528,300**	Mexico..........................	428,340
SEX		El Salvador....................	20,770
Female...........	288,840	Guatemala.....................	13,970
Male.............	238,830	Honduras......................	12,680
Not available....	620	Peru...........................	4,850
AGE [1]		South Korea...................	4,730
16 to 20 years old...........	1,650	Brazil.........................	3,900
21 to 25 years old...........	105,980	Ecuador.......................	3,630
26 to 30 years old...........	193,900	Colombia......................	3,080
31 to 35 years old...........	140,730	Argentina.....................	2,560
36 to 40 years old...........	74,370	Philippines....................	2,540
41 to 42 years old...........	11,660	Jamaica.......................	1,730
Not available................	10	India..........................	1,660
Median age...................	29	Venezuela.....................	1,610
MARITAL STATUS		Dominican Republic............	1,440
Single.........................	358,640	Uruguay.......................	1,320
Married........................	154,550	Bolivia........................	1,110
Divorced.......................	13,970	Trinidad and Tobago..........	1,110
Widowed.......................	620	Nicaragua.....................	1,030
Not available..................	510	Costa Rica....................	1,010

[1] Age as of March 31, 2024.

Source: Department of Homeland Security, U.S. Citizenship and Immigration Services, "Immigration and Citizenship Data," <www.uscis.gov/tools/reports-and-studies/immigration-and-citizenship-data>, accessed July 2024.

Table 560. Customs and Border Patrol Drug Seizures: 2019 to 2023

[In units, as indicated. For fiscal years ending September 30. Data are from U.S. Border Patrol (USBP) and Office of Field Operations (OFO)]

Year	Total	Mari-juana	Metham-phetamine	Cocaine	Heroin	Fentanyl	Ecstasy	LSD	Ket-amine	Khat	Other drugs
SEIZURE EVENTS (number)											
2019....................	60,031	20,366	4,576	2,812	1,532	814	6,902	2,683	1,355	217	25,676
2020....................	70,923	18,067	5,907	3,225	2,563	1,174	6,847	3,744	597	181	28,616
2021....................	82,946	13,860	5,786	3,873	2,276	1,515	4,834	2,221	1,378	537	46,666
2022....................	62,465	15,020	4,224	2,838	620	1,496	2,041	1,223	1,259	504	33,240
2023....................	53,538	18,595	3,450	2,402	380	1,351	1,469	546	1,321	187	23,837
SEIZED WEIGHT (pounds)											
2019....................	902,573	556,401	141,970	101,140	6,227	2,804	2,223	560	953	36,257	54,038
2020....................	1,059,249	582,393	177,684	58,002	5,763	4,791	2,120	725	1,134	111,959	114,679
2021....................	913,326	319,447	191,834	97,638	5,400	11,201	1,201	38	10,848	202,820	72,899
2022....................	655,780	154,797	175,410	70,293	1,871	14,700	1,248	36	13,756	174,550	49,119
2023....................	549,238	149,582	140,408	81,085	1,511	27,023	649	11	7,831	70,044	71,094

Source: Department of Homeland Security, U.S. Customs and Border Protection, "Drug Seizure Statistics," <www.cbp.gov/newsroom/stats/drug-seizure-statistics>, accessed January 2024.

Table 561. Department of Homeland Security Total Budget Authority and Personnel by Organization: 2023 and 2024

[101,798,063 represents $101,798,063,000. For the fiscal year ending September 30. Data for 2023 are revised enacted data. Not all activities carried out by the Department of Homeland Security (DHS) constitute homeland security funding (e.g., Coast Guard search and rescue activities)]

Organization or activity	Budget authority (thousand dollars)		Full-time employees (number)	
	2023	2024	2023	2024
Total..	**101,798,063**	**103,609,636**	**247,512**	**248,615**
Departmental management and operations [1]..........................	5,098,197	5,189,105	6,557	6,575
Analysis and operations...............................	316,640	316,640	946	946
Office of the Inspector General.......................	214,879	214,879	778	778
U.S. Customs & Border Protection....................	20,968,070	21,233,998	63,054	63,610
U.S. Immigration & Customs Enforcement...............	9,138,570	9,138,570	20,917	20,917
Transportation Security Administration................	9,541,290	9,541,290	56,193	56,193
U.S. Coast Guard....................................	13,915,211	13,934,081	51,252	51,252
U.S. Secret Service..................................	3,092,103	3,090,180	8,163	8,163
Cybersecurity and Infrastructure Security Agency [2]...	2,907,138	2,907,138	3,222	3,222
Federal Emergency Management Agency (FEMA)........	30,139,177	30,546,146	14,607	14,702
FEMA Grants [2].....................................	3,571,895	3,571,895	([3])	([3])
U.S. Citizenship & Immigration Services...............	5,260,247	6,291,068	21,666	22,100
Federal Law Enforcement Training Center..............	406,547	406,547	1,085	1,085
Science & Technology Directorate (S&T)..............	900,541	900,541	544	544
Countering Weapons of Mass Destruction..............	430,972	430,972	252	252

[1] Comprised of the Office of the Secretary & Executive Management, and the Management Directorate, which includes the Under Secretary for Management and its team of chief officers. [2] Includes appropriations for various state and local programs, Emergency Management Performance Grants, and Assistance to Firefighters Grants. [3] Employee data are included with FEMA full-time employees.

Source: U.S. Department of Homeland Security, *Budget-in-Brief, Fiscal Year 2025*, March 2024. See also <www.dhs.gov/dhs-budget>.

Table 562. Homeland Security Grants by State and Outlying Area: 2023 and 2024

[In thousands of dollars (1,120,000 represents $1,120,000,000). For years ending September 30. The Homeland Security Grant Program consists of the following: State Homeland Security Program (SHSP), Urban Areas Security Initiative (UASI), and Operation Stonegarden. These programs support activities to prevent, protect against, prepare for and respond to acts of terrorism, and to secure U.S. borders]

State/territory	2023	2024	State/territory	2023	2024	State/territory	2023	2024
Total........	1,120,000	1,008,000	KS..............	4,848	4,363	OK..............	4,848	4,363
			KY..............	4,848	4,363	OR..............	8,648	7,773
U.S.............	1,108,963	998,524	LA..............	7,253	6,325	PA..............	26,608	23,901
			ME..............	6,088	5,423	RI..............	4,848	4,363
AL..............	4,948	4,427	MD..............	10,875	9,778	SC..............	4,848	4,363
AK..............	4,848	4,363	MA..............	22,837	20,513	SD..............	4,848	4,363
AZ..............	25,998	23,885	MI..............	12,222	10,975	TN..............	6,348	5,709
AR..............	4,848	16,565	MN..............	11,160	10,047	TX..............	102,001	92,872
CA..............	202,199	169,867	MS..............	5,153	4,558	UT..............	4,848	4,363
CO..............	8,748	7,863	MO..............	10,293	9,250	VT..............	5,648	5,123
CT..............	4,848	4,363	MT..............	6,378	5,693	VA..............	11,936	10,733
DE..............	4,848	4,363	NE..............	4,848	4,363	WA..............	14,010	12,382
DC..............	55,445	49,778	NV..............	10,098	9,075	WV..............	4,848	4,363
FL..............	36,309	31,751	NH..............	5,048	4,553	WI..............	4,848	4,363
GA..............	13,064	11,719	NJ..............	25,706	23,090	WY..............	4,848	4,363
HI..............	6,348	5,709	NM..............	7,803	7,115	AS [1]..........	1,108	997
ID..............	5,022	4,523	NY..............	244,828	219,962	GU [1]..........	1,108	997
IL..............	80,069	71,901	NC..............	8,885	7,988	MP [1]..........	1,108	997
IN..............	6,493	5,840	ND..............	6,388	5,714	PR [1]..........	6,521	5,432
IA..............	4,848	4,363	OH..............	10,552	10,705	VI [1]..........	1,193	1,052

[1] AS—American Samoa, GU—Guam, MP—Northern Mariana Islands, PR—Puerto Rico, VI—Virgin Islands.

Source: U.S. Department of Homeland Security, Federal Emergency Management Agency, *Grant Programs Directorate Information Bulletin*, No. 517, August 2024, and earlier reports. See also <www.fema.gov/grants/preparedness>.

Table 563. Urban Areas Security Initiative (UASI) Grant Program: 2024

[In thousands of dollars (553,500 represents $553,500,000). For year ending September 30. The UASI Program provides financial assistance to address the unique planning, organization, equipment, training, and exercise needs of high-risk urban areas to build capacity to prevent, protect against, prepare for and respond to acts of terrorism]

State	Urban area	Amount	State	Urban area	Amount
Total........	(X)	553,500	MI............	Detroit	4,712
AZ............	Phoenix	4,712	MN............	Minneapolis-Saint Paul (Twin Cities)	4,712
CA............	Anaheim/Santa Ana Area	4,712	MO............	Kansas City	1,477
CA............	San Francisco Bay Area	32,755	MO............	St. Louis	3,411
CA............	Los Angeles/Long Beach	59,395	NV............	Las Vegas	4,712
CA............	Riverside	3,500	NJ............	Jersey City/Newark	16,723
CA............	Sacramento	3,411	NY............	New York City	156,131
CA............	San Diego	14,761	NC............	Charlotte	3,411
CO............	Denver	3,500	OH............	Cincinnati	1,477
DC............	National Capital Region	45,201	OH............	Cleveland	1,477
FL............	Jacksonville	1,346	OH............	Columbus	1,500
FL............	Miami/Fort Lauderdale	13,040	OR............	Portland	3,411
FL............	Orlando	3,411	PA............	Philadelphia	14,941
FL............	Tampa	3,411	PA............	Pittsburgh	1,477
GA............	Atlanta	6,911	TN............	Nashville	1,346
HI............	Honolulu	1,346	TX............	Austin	1,346
IL............	Chicago	59,395	TX............	Dallas/Fort Worth/Arlington	14,941
IN............	Indianapolis	1,477	TX............	Houston	21,749
LA............	New Orleans	1,477	TX............	San Antonio	3,411
MD............	Baltimore	3,411	VA............	Hampton Roads Area	3,411
MA............	Boston	14,941	WA............	Seattle	5,610

X Not applicable.

Source: U.S. Department of Homeland Security, Federal Emergency Management Agency, *Grant Programs Directorate Information Bulletin*, No. 517, August 2024. See also <www.fema.gov/grants/preparedness>.

Table 564. Preparedness Grant Programs: 2010 to 2024

[In millions of dollars (2,968 represents $2,968,000,000). For years ending September 30. Preparedness grants help develop and sustain capabilities at state, local, tribal and territorial levels and in high-risk transit systems, ports and along U.S. borders to prevent, protect against, respond to, recover from and mitigate terrorism and other high-consequence disasters and emergencies]

Program	2010	2015	2016	2017	2018	2019	2020	2021	2022	2023	2024
Total [1]......................	2,968	1,617	1,617	1,622	1,687	1,715	1,780	1,970	1,639	2,000	1,979
Homeland Security Grant Program [1]....	1,786	1,044	1,037	1,037	1,067	1,095	1,120	1,120	1,120	1,120	1,008
State Homeland Security Program.....	842	402	402	402	402	415	415	415	415	415	374
Urban Areas Security Initiative........	833	587	580	580	580	590	615	615	615	615	554
Operation Stonegarden.................	60	55	55	55	85	90	90	90	90	90	81
Emergency Management Performance Grants Program..........	330	350	350	350	350	350	355	[2] 455	(NA)	355	320
Tribal Homeland Security Grant Program..................................	10	10	10	10	10	10	15	15	15	15	14
Nonprofit Security Grant Program........	19	13	20	25	60	60	90	180	250	305	455
Emergency Operations Center Grant Program..................................	58	(NA)	(NA)	(NA)	(NA)	(NA)	(NA)	(NA)	49	(NA)	(NA)
Transit Security Grant Program..........	253	87	87	88	88	88	88	88	93	93	84
Intercity Passenger Rail Program (AMTRAK).................................	20	10	10	10	10	10	10	10	10	10	9
Port Security Grant Program..............	288	100	100	100	100	100	100	100	100	100	90
Intercity Bus Security Grant Program....	12	3	3	2	2	2	2	2	2	2	1

NA Not available. [1] Includes grant programs not listed separately. [2] American Rescue Plan Act (ARPA) of 2021 provides $100 million in additional funding.

Source: U.S. Department of Homeland Security, Federal Emergency Management Agency, *Grant Programs Directorate Information Bulletin*, No. 517, August 2024, and earlier reports. See also <www.fema.gov/grants/preparedness>.

Table 565. Foreign Visitor Overstays by Country of Citizenship: 2022

[For fiscal year ending Sept. 30. Data shown for foreign nationals entering the U.S. as nonimmigrant visitors for business or pleasure (except as noted) through an air or sea point of entry. An overstay is a nonimmigrant who was lawfully admitted to the U.S. for an authorized period but stayed or remains in the U.S. beyond the lawful admission period. Data cover overstays of people who remained in the U.S. beyond their authorized period of admission with no evidence of an extension to their period of admission nor adjustment to another immigration status. The Visa Waiver Program (VWP) allows citizens of specific countries to travel to the U.S. for tourism, business, or while in transit for up to 90 days without obtaining a visa. Data are generated from Department of Homeland Security's Arrival and Departure Information System (ADIS)]

Country of citizenship	Expected departures	Overstays (number)			Overstays (percent)	
		Total	Out-of-country [1]	Suspected in-country [2]	Total	Suspected in-country [2]
Total [3, 4]	**23,243,127**	**853,955**	**58,788**	**795,167**	**3.67**	**3.42**
North American, total [4]	**6,552,082**	**151,247**	**10,672**	**140,575**	**2.31**	**2.15**
Canada	2,919,709	20,127	5,210	14,917	0.69	0.51
Mexico	3,632,373	131,120	5,462	125,658	3.61	3.46
VISA WAIVER PROGRAM						
Total [3, 5]	**7,413,023**	**97,632**	**12,706**	**84,926**	**1.32**	**1.15**
United Kingdom	1,823,632	10,210	1,707	8,503	0.56	0.47
France	850,449	6,906	681	6,225	0.81	0.73
Germany	785,270	4,693	666	4,027	0.60	0.51
Spain	508,188	28,356	1,914	26,442	5.58	5.20
Italy	441,569	9,920	970	8,950	2.25	2.03
Chile	390,806	11,589	1,280	10,309	2.97	2.64
Korea, South	343,829	3,120	982	2,138	0.91	0.62
Netherlands	306,374	1,902	342	1,560	0.62	0.51
Australia	263,249	2,422	886	1,536	0.92	0.58
Ireland	240,762	1,253	191	1,062	0.52	0.44
Japan	160,637	1,024	235	789	0.64	0.49
Sweden	148,831	832	164	668	0.56	0.45
Switzerland	135,399	868	161	707	0.64	0.52
Belgium	115,854	749	102	647	0.65	0.56
Denmark	114,877	455	84	371	0.40	0.32
Poland	113,463	1,762	309	1,453	1.55	1.28
Portugal	86,743	4,117	366	3,751	4.75	4.32
Austria	78,825	477	59	418	0.61	0.53
Norway	75,283	386	87	299	0.51	0.40
Taiwan	51,296	1,826	467	1,359	3.56	2.65
Czechia	50,390	445	90	355	0.88	0.70
New Zealand	47,459	675	279	396	1.42	0.83
Finland	46,230	177	38	139	0.38	0.30
Singapore	43,746	327	129	198	0.75	0.45
Greece	42,416	1,112	202	910	2.62	2.15
Hungary	37,350	755	120	635	2.02	1.70
NON-VISA WAIVER PROGRAM						
Total [3, 6]	**7,031,887**	**504,636**	**16,827**	**487,809**	**7.18**	**6.94**
Colombia	1,138,810	60,484	1,338	59,146	5.31	5.19
Brazil	417,886	16,157	911	15,246	3.87	3.65
Peru	416,751	9,187	476	8,711	2.20	2.09
Ecuador	408,547	14,277	371	13,906	3.49	3.40
Dominican Republic	408,418	25,389	447	24,942	6.22	6.11
Venezuela [7]	389,944	172,640	1,013	171,627	44.27	44.01
India	364,912	17,650	2,384	15,266	4.84	4.18
Argentina	354,225	4,875	315	4,560	1.38	1.29
Guatemala	289,236	7,229	220	7,009	2.50	2.42
Costa Rica	277,468	5,402	176	5,226	1.95	1.88
Honduras	251,151	9,193	273	8,920	3.66	3.55
Israel	231,885	2,056	248	1,808	0.89	0.78
El Salvador	221,159	5,288	246	5,042	2.39	2.28
Jamaica	175,010	16,532	471	16,061	9.45	9.18
Bahamas, The	164,220	7,655	399	7,256	4.66	4.42
Panama	108,956	1,702	88	1,614	1.56	1.48
China	86,934	21,285	1,319	19,966	24.48	22.97
Philippines	86,391	6,684	604	6,080	7.74	7.04
Russia	80,363	7,207	248	6,959	8.97	8.66
Turkey	75,677	2,726	177	2,549	3.60	3.37
Haiti	64,022	8,144	191	7,953	12.72	12.42
Bolivia	57,258	1,881	82	1,799	3.29	3.14
Nicaragua	52,064	3,474	113	3,361	6.67	6.46
Trinidad and Tobago	49,268	1,197	141	1,056	2.43	2.14
Pakistan	47,540	3,500	153	3,347	7.36	7.04
Ukraine	44,326	4,098	154	3,944	9.25	8.90
Guyana	43,333	4,115	150	3,965	9.50	9.15
Nigeria	43,173	9,207	158	9,049	21.33	20.96
Egypt	41,123	3,264	155	3,109	7.94	7.56
Uruguay	35,465	975	46	929	2.75	2.62
Indonesia	32,846	1,870	100	1,770	5.69	5.39
Paraguay	30,748	672	32	640	2.19	2.08
Romania	29,392	904	104	800	3.08	2.72

[1] Individuals whose departure was recorded after their lawful admission period expired. [2] Individuals for whom no departure has been recorded. [3] Includes data from countries not shown separately. [4] Includes all nonimmigrant visa classes, including students and exchange visitors and other in-scope visitors. [5] Includes only business and pleasure visitors. Excludes students, exchange visitors, and other in-scope visitors. [6] Includes travelers identified by CBP having Temporary Protected Status (TPS) eligibility: 222 out of country and 136,913 suspected in country overstays. [7] Includes TPS travelers: 222 out of country and 127,330 suspected in country overstays.

Source: Department of Homeland Security, *Fiscal Year 2022 Entry/Exit Overstay Report*, June 2023. See also <www.dhs.gov/publication/entryexit-overstay-report>.

Table 566. Noncitizens Returned or Removed by Leading Crime Category and Country of Nationality: 2015 to 2022

[For year ending September 30. For definitions of immigration enforcement terms, see source. Ranked by data for most recent year]

Crime category and country of nationality	2015	2016	2017	2018	2019	2020	2021	2022
Noncitizens returned, removed, expelled...	**454,064**	**438,809**	**384,817**	**487,566**	**518,210**	**611,586**	**1,334,860**	**1,474,086**
Returns [1]	129,636	106,478	100,452	159,958	171,120	167,452	178,003	261,387
Administrative [2]	43,237	30,341	15,072	72,756	89,719	113,857	128,339	180,266
Enforcement [2]	86,399	76,137	85,380	87,202	81,401	53,595	49,664	81,121
Removals [3]	324,428	332,331	284,365	327,608	347,090	237,364	85,783	108,733
Noncriminal	201,613	215,597	175,846	179,405	177,192	118,222	24,666	45,507
Criminal [4]	122,815	116,734	108,519	148,203	169,898	119,142	61,117	63,226
Expulsions [5]	(X)	(X)	(X)	(X)	(X)	206,770	1,071,074	1,103,966
Criminal removals by crime category:								
Immigration	37,621	37,128	28,533	41,834	63,066	39,961	6,899	9,628
Dangerous drugs	22,445	21,687	19,635	18,087	16,718	13,243	8,611	8,583
Assault	13,359	12,168	12,334	12,286	12,464	9,479	5,717	5,575
Traffic offenses	16,090	15,111	15,668	17,439	18,449	12,373	4,125	3,466
Sexual assault	2,505	2,495	2,439	2,429	2,362	2,070	1,944	1,802
Weapon offenses	3,524	3,477	3,222	3,200	3,002	2,501	1,710	1,625
Sex offenses	1,959	1,978	2,113	2,084	1,897	1,679	1,454	1,441
Burglary	3,463	3,126	3,033	2,781	2,591	1,975	1,101	1,199
Robbery	2,034	1,917	2,014	1,857	1,634	1,315	1,066	954
Invasion of privacy	373	329	378	461	456	305	98	931
All other including unknown	19,442	17,318	19,150	45,745	47,259	34,241	28,392	28,022
Criminal removals by country of nationality:								
Mexico	88,863	83,087	73,328	90,180	98,329	78,438	37,978	40,781
Honduras	8,519	8,629	9,229	12,693	17,995	9,605	3,197	3,714
Guatemala	10,483	10,599	11,034	19,812	23,125	10,290	4,406	3,511
Colombia	792	766	616	2,306	2,564	1,601	2,721	2,702
El Salvador	7,186	6,754	6,418	7,054	8,798	5,041	2,035	2,012
Dominican Republic	1,519	1,487	1,509	1,504	1,619	1,490	1,368	1,100
Brazil	283	335	405	1,184	1,484	1,330	448	972
Jamaica	638	623	666	992	1,241	1,171	1,221	914
Ecuador	487	466	499	898	1,479	1,507	784	674
Peru	210	207	177	499	523	328	497	547
India	134	103	158	463	629	549	534	544
Canada	264	257	205	561	756	572	416	524

X Not applicable. [1] Returns are the confirmed movement of an inadmissible or deportable noncitizen out of the U.S., not based on an order of removal. [2] Administrative returns include foreign vessel crew members from 2005 to 2017, and both crew members and administrative withdrawals since 2018. Administrative withdrawals are withdrawals of application for admission that are terminated without prejudice. Enforcement returns are all returns with the exception of crew members and administrative withdrawals. [3] Removals are the compulsory and confirmed movement of an inadmissible or deportable noncitizen out of the U.S., based on an order of removal. A noncitizen who is removed has administrative or criminal consequences placed on subsequent reentry. [4] Persons removed based on a prior criminal conviction. [5] Expulsions on public health grounds under U.S. Code Title 42 in response to the COVID-19 pandemic. Includes persons who were expelled more than once during the 12 month period.

Source: U.S. Department of Homeland Security, Office of Homeland Security Statistics, *Immigration Enforcement Actions: 2022*, and "Yearbook of Immigration Statistics, 2022," <www.dhs.gov/ohss/topics/immigration>, accessed December 2023.

Table 567. Noncitizens Apprehended or Arrested by Program and Border Patrol Sector: 2000 to 2022

[As of the end of September. Border Patrol apprehensions and Immigration and Customs Enforcement (ICE) administrative arrests]

Program and sector	2000	2010	2015	2019	2020 [3]	2021 [3]	2022 [3]
Total	**1,814,729**	**796,587**	**462,388**	**1,013,539**	**518,597**	**1,743,802**	**2,362,769**
Investigations	138,291	18,290	7,288	10,939	9,974	7,553	5,366
Enforcement and Removal Operations [1]	(X)	314,915	117,983	143,099	103,603	74,082	142,750
Border Patrol (apprehensions)	1,676,438	463,382	337,117	859,501	405,020	1,662,167	2,214,653
APPREHENSIONS BY SECTOR							
All southwest sectors	**1,643,679**	**447,731**	**331,333**	**851,508**	**400,635**	**1,659,206**	**2,206,437**
Del Rio, Texas	157,178	14,694	19,013	57,269	40,342	259,294	480,932
Rio Grande Valley, Texas	133,243	59,766	147,257	339,135	90,203	549,077	468,124
Yuma, Arizona	108,747	7,116	7,142	68,269	8,804	114,488	310,094
El Paso, Texas	115,696	12,251	14,495	182,143	54,396	193,918	307,844
Tucson, Arizona	616,346	212,202	63,397	63,490	66,074	191,232	251,984
San Diego, California	151,681	68,565	26,290	58,049	53,277	142,459	176,290
Laredo, Texas	108,973	35,287	35,888	38,378	51,425	112,241	106,843
El Centro, California	238,126	32,562	12,820	35,138	27,487	59,231	72,378
Big Bend, Texas (formerly Marfa)	13,689	5,288	5,031	9,637	8,627	37,266	31,948
All other sectors	**32,759**	**15,651**	**5,784**	**7,993**	**4,385**	**2,961**	**8,216**
Miami, Florida	6,237	4,651	1,752	1,891	1,302	1,031	4,009
Ramey, Puerto Rico	1,731	398	557	562	356	670	1,640
Swanton, Vermont	1,957	1,422	341	1,056	574	365	1,065
Blaine, Washington	2,581	673	282	524	227	112	407
New Orleans, Louisiana	6,478	3,171	849	1,132	572	344	329
Houlton, Maine	489	56	32	52	104	57	303
Detroit, Michigan	2,057	1,669	637	1,322	455	32	125
Buffalo, New York	1,570	2,422	291	537	302	143	90
Spokane, Washington	1,324	356	190	428	236	54	87
Grand Forks, North Dakota	562	543	789	412	227	90	81
Havre, Montana	1,568	290	64	77	30	63	80
Livermore, California [2]	6,205	(X)	(X)	(X)	(X)	(X)	(X)

X Not applicable. [1] Includes arrests of fugitive and nonfugitive noncitizens under the Office of Detention and Removal Operations, National Fugitive Operations Program. Beginning in 2008, includes all administrative arrests conducted by ICE ERO. [2] Livermore sector closed August 31, 2004. [3] Includes encounters resulting in expulsions, see footnote 5 in Table 566.

Source: U.S. Department of Homeland Security, Office of Homeland Security Statistics, "2022 Yearbook of Immigration Statistics," and earlier reports, <www.dhs.gov/ohss/topics/immigration/yearbook>, accessed December 2023.

Table 568. Noncitizens Apprehended or Arrested: 1925 to 2022

[As of the end of September; prior to 1976, the fiscal year ended June 30. Prior to 1952, data refer to Border Patrol Apprehensions. Detention and Removal Operations data are included beginning in 2006. Beginning in 2008, includes all administrative arrests conducted by U.S. Immigration and Customs Enforcement (ICE), Office of Enforcement and Removal Operations (ERO). Beginning in 2009, data also include administrative arrests conducted under the 287(g) program (Delegation of Immigration Authority). Beginning in 2012, data also include enforcement encounters by CBP Office of Field Operations (OFO), reflecting attempted unlawful entries into the United States]

Year	Number	Year	Number	Year	Number	Year	Number
1925...........	22,199	1975...........	766,600	2003...........	1,046,422	2013...........	786,223
1930...........	20,880	1980...........	910,361	2004...........	1,264,232	2014...........	805,334
1935...........	11,016	1985...........	1,348,749	2005...........	1,291,065	2015...........	596,560
1940...........	10,492	1990...........	1,169,939	2006...........	1,206,408	2016 [1]........	683,782
1945...........	69,164	1995...........	1,394,554	2007...........	960,673	2017...........	607,677
1950...........	468,339	1998...........	1,679,439	2008...........	1,043,759	2018...........	739,486
1955...........	254,096	1999...........	1,714,035	2009...........	889,212	2019...........	1,175,841
1960...........	70,684	2000...........	1,814,729	2010...........	796,587	2020 [2]........	609,265
1965...........	110,371	2001...........	1,387,486	2011...........	678,606	2021...........	1,865,379
1970...........	345,353	2002...........	1,062,270	2012...........	795,735	2022...........	2,584,220

[1] Prior to 2016, only one administrative arrest could be counted for the same person on the same day; beginning 2016, the reporting methodology was revised to align with ICE ERO reporting, which may include multiple arrests on a single day. [2] Includes USBP encounters resulting in expulsions on public health grounds under U.S. Code Title 42 in response to the COVID-19 pandemic.

Source: U.S. Department of Homeland Security, Office of Homeland Security Statistics, "2022 Yearbook of Immigration Statistics," <www.dhs.gov/ohss/topics/immigration/yearbook>, accessed December 2023.

Table 569. Value of Counterfeit Goods Seized for Intellectual Property Rights Violations by Commodity and Country of Origin: 2014 to 2022

[In thousands of dollars (1,226,348 represents $1,226,348,000), except as indicated. Customs and Border Protection enforces Intellectual Property Rights (IPR), most visibly by seizing products that infringe IPR such as trademarks, copyrights, and patents. Value of goods seized represent Manufacturer's Suggested Retail Price (MSRP), which is the price at which merchandise is sold at retail to the consumer or what the value of the counterfeit goods would have been at retail had they been genuine. Updates to the CBP seizure database may result in a slight difference in multi-year comparisons]

Commodity and country	2014	2015	2016	2017	2018	2019	2020	2021	2022
Number of IPR seizures [1]...........	23,140	28,865	31,560	34,143	33,810	27,599	72,537	102,490	102,297
Total MSRP value of IPR seizures...........	1,226,348	1,352,495	1,382,903	1,206,382	1,399,874	1,555,269	1,309,157	3,330,037	2,981,748
VALUE BY COMMODITY									
Jewelry, watches, and parts...........	375,397	580,792	653,590	460,162	618,167	687,167	435,249	1,186,747	1,147,592
Handbags/wallets/backpacks.........	342,032	208,379	234,079	234,452	226,506	212,782	282,702	972,495	993,341
Wearing apparel/accessories.........	113,686	157,196	110,806	74,881	115,164	343,732	157,227	487,371	375,851
Consumer electronics/parts...........	162,209	132,479	122,892	85,116	89,593	105,957	173,830	171,011	121,868
Footwear...........	49,523	64,967	51,231	41,490	77,501	37,994	63,146	96,691	92,568
Pharmaceuticals/personal care.......	72,939	75,062	73,716	69,759	131,458	48,772	56,190	185,043	88,038
Consumer products...................	(NA)	(NA)	(NA)	46,265	40,846	27,908	49,696	72,075	51,510
Optical media [2]...................	18,781	32,504	8,166	27,574	(NA)	(NA)	(NA)	(NA)	17,338
Computers/technology components..	26,652	38,393	19,319	(NA)	29,940	13,217	(NA)	24,553	14,383
Automotive/aerospace................	(NA)	(NA)	(NA)	(NA)	14,862	12,143	11,064	(NA)	13,805
Toys..............................	8,178	9,757	(NA)	12,128	10,590	(NA)	(NA)	25,421	(NA)
Labels/tags........................	17,675	33,336	17,053	80,951	(NA)	(NA)	19,824	(NA)	(NA)
Batteries.........................	(NA)	(NA)	(NA)	(NA)	(NA)	(NA)	(NA)	(NA)	(NA)
Transportation/parts................	(NA)	(NA)	55,199	(NA)	(NA)	(NA)	(NA)	(NA)	(NA)
All other commodities [3]...............	39,273	19,630	36,851	73,604	45,248	65,598	60,229	108,630	65,455
VALUE BY COUNTRY OF ORIGIN [4]									
China............................	772,629	697,084	616,881	554,632	761,115	1,030,182	660,767	1,888,299	1,766,567
Hong Kong........................	310,437	472,331	599,785	386,242	440,345	397,277	428,962	613,463	680,857
Philippines........................	(NA)	(NA)	(NA)	(NA)	(NA)	(NA)	(NA)	45,692	81,619
Turkey............................	(NA)	(NA)	(NA)	4,983	5,759	14,241	31,237	60,347	73,759
Thailand..........................	(NA)	(NA)	(NA)	1,857	(NA)	(NA)	12,602	(NA)	35,254
Colombia..........................	(NA)	(NA)	4,221	(NA)	(NA)	(NA)	(NA)	23,981	(NA)
Vietnam...........................	2,422	(NA)	(NA)	4,392	5,192	13,556	25,804	(NA)	(NA)
Korea, South.......................	2,515	3,789	3,585	4,235	10,136	5,633	25,283	(NA)	(NA)
India..............................	5,541	6,409	14,668	8,342	19,952	9,540	12,862	(NA)	(NA)
Taiwan............................	3,082	(NA)	(NA)	4,902	5,008	(NA)	12,144	(NA)	(NA)
Netherlands.......................	(NA)	(NA)	(NA)	(NA)	(NA)	(NA)	11,797	(NA)	(NA)
Pakistan..........................	(NA)	(NA)	4,776	(NA)	2,779	12,157	(NA)	(NA)	(NA)
Singapore.........................	2,538	10,267	7,706	4,997	(NA)	10,453	(NA)	(NA)	(NA)
Dominican Republic.................	(NA)	(NA)	(NA)	(NA)	(NA)	9,542	(NA)	(NA)	(NA)
Cambodia.........................	(NA)	(NA)	7,015	(NA)	(NA)	(NA)	(NA)	(NA)	(NA)
Bangladesh........................	(NA)	(NA)	4,592	(NA)	(NA)	(NA)	(NA)	(NA)	(NA)
Mexico............................	(NA)	(NA)	3,539	(NA)	(NA)	(NA)	(NA)	(NA)	(NA)
United Kingdom / Great Britain.......	(NA)	4,358	(NA)	(NA)	(NA)	(NA)	(NA)	(NA)	(NA)
United Arab Emirates................	3,791	3,433	(NA)	(NA)	(NA)	(NA)	(NA)	(NA)	(NA)
Italy..............................	(NA)	2,849	(NA)	(NA)	(NA)	(NA)	(NA)	(NA)	(NA)
Malaysia..........................	(NA)	2,345	(NA)	(NA)	4,674	(NA)	(NA)	(NA)	(NA)
Canada...........................	12,460	1,974	(NA)	3,037	7,799	(NA)	(NA)	(NA)	(NA)
Switzerland.......................	(NA)	(NA)	(NA)	(NA)	(NA)	(NA)	(NA)	(NA)	(NA)
Kenya............................	2,293	(NA)	(NA)	(NA)	(NA)	(NA)	(NA)	(NA)	(NA)
All other countries....................	108,639	147,656	116,135	228,763	137,114	52,689	87,699	698,256	343,692

NA Not available. [1] As of 2021, data are reported by seizure lines (product lines within a unique seizure). [2] Includes motion pictures on tape, laser disc, and DVD; interactive and computer software on CD-ROM, and floppy discs; and music on CD or tape. [3] Shipments with multiple products are categorized as "All other commodities." [4] Aggregate seizure data reflect the reported country of origin, not necessarily where the seized goods were produced.

Source: U.S. Department of Homeland Security, Customs and Border Protection, *Intellectual Property Rights Seizure Statistics FY2022*, May 2024, and earlier reports. See also <www.cbp.gov/trade/priority-issues/ipr/statistics>.

Table 570. Airline Passengers Screened and Firearms Discovered at TSA Airport Checkpoints: 2018 to 2023

[In units indicated (813.8 represents 813,800,000). Firearms are those found in carry-on bags]

Item	2018	2019	2020	2021	2022	2023	Top 5 airports for firearm discoveries	Firearms found in 2023 (number)
Passengers & crew screened (millions)...	813.8	848.1	324.0	585.3	761.0	858.0	Atlanta (ATL)................	451
							Dallas Fort Worth (DFW)...	378
Firearms found (number).................	4,244	4,432	3,257	5,972	6,542	6,737	Houston (IAH)..............	311
Percent loaded..........................	86	87	83	86	88	93	Phoenix (PHX).............	235
Airports with firearms discovered (number).................................	249	278	234	268	262	265	Nashville (BNA).............	188

Source: U.S. Department of Homeland Security, Transportation Security Administration, "TSA detects 6,737 firearms at airport security checkpoints in 2023," <www.tsa.gov/news/press/releases>, and earlier releases.

Social Insurance and Human Services

This section presents data related to government expenditures for social insurance and human services; the population receiving government assistance; government programs for Old-Age, Survivors, and Disability Insurance (OASDI), commonly known as Social Security; state and local government employee retirement; private retirement savings plans; government unemployment and disability insurance; federal supplemental security income payments and aid to the needy; child and other welfare services; and federal food programs. Also included here are selected data on workers' compensation, child support, child care, homelessness, social assistance organizations, and the nonprofit sector.

A principal source for these data is the Social Security Administration's *Annual Statistical Supplement to the Social Security Bulletin*, which presents current and historical data on social security benefits and beneficiaries. Additional sources of data include the Census Bureau's Annual Social and Economic Supplement of the Current Population Survey, and the Survey of Income and Program Participation (conducted as a series of surveys over a period of time spanning several years); and the Department of Health and Human Services' Administration for Children and Families.

Social insurance under the Social Security Act—Programs established by the Social Security Act provide protection against wage loss resulting from retirement, prolonged disability, death, or unemployment, and protection against the cost of medical care during old age and disability. The federal OASDI program provides monthly benefits to retired or disabled insured workers and their dependents, and to survivors of insured workers. To be eligible, a worker must have had a specified period of employment in which OASDI taxes were paid. The age of eligibility for full retirement benefits had been 65 for many years. For persons born in 1938 or later, that age gradually increases until it reaches age 67 for those born in 1960 and later. Reduced benefits may be obtained as early as age 62. The worker's spouse is under the same limitations. Survivor benefits are payable to dependents of deceased insured workers. Disability benefits are payable to an insured worker under full retirement age with a prolonged disability, and to the disabled worker's dependents on the same basis as dependents of retired workers. Disability benefits are provided at age 50 to the disabled widow or widower of a deceased worker who was fully insured at the time of death. Disabled children, age 18 or older, of retired, disabled, or deceased workers are also eligible for benefits. A special lump sum benefit may be payable on the death of an insured worker to a spouse or minor children. For information on the Medicare program, see Section 3, Health and Nutrition.

Retirement, survivors, and disability insurance benefits are funded by a payroll tax on annual earnings (up to a maximum share of earnings set by law) of workers, employers, and the self-employed. The maximum taxable earnings are adjusted annually to reflect increasing wage levels (see Table 577). The Old Age and Survivors Insurance trust fund pays retirement and survivors benefits; the Disability Insurance trust fund pays disability benefits. These two funds are separate entities by law. Also administered by the Social Security Administration is the Supplemental Security Income (SSI) program, funding for which does not come from the social security trust funds but the General Fund of the U.S. Treasury.

Retirement—Social security benefits are a component of retirement income. This section also includes data on the use of individual retirement savings plans and accounts, including benefits sponsored by employers. The Bureau of Labor Statistics collects detailed data for the National Compensation Survey on the availability of and participation in employer-sponsored defined benefit and defined contribution retirement savings plans. Defined benefit plans are funded by the employer; defined contribution plans require the employee to save for retirement. Additional data on individual retirement savings also come from surveys conducted by the Investment Company Institute.

Unemployment insurance—Unemployment insurance is administered by the U.S. Employment and Training Administration and each state's employment security agency. By agreement with the U.S. Secretary of Labor, state agencies also administer unemployment compensation for eligible former military personnel and federal employees. Under state unemployment insurance laws, benefits related to an individual's past earnings are paid to eligible unemployed workers. State laws vary concerning the length of time benefits are paid and their amount. In most states, benefits are payable for 26 weeks and, during periods of high unemployment, extended benefits are payable under a federal-state program to those who have exhausted their regular state benefits. Some states also supplement the basic benefit with allowances for dependents. Unemployment insurance is financed through Federal and state employer payroll taxes. Generally, employers pay both Federal and state unemployment taxes for workers paid $1,500 or more during any quarter of a calendar year, or if they had at least 1 employee during any day of the week during 20 weeks in a calendar year (weeks need not be consecutive).

Workers' compensation—All states provide protection against work-connected injuries, illnesses, and deaths, although some states exclude certain workers (e.g., domestic workers). Workers' compensation is the only social insurance system run almost entirely by states, with no federal guidelines. Federal laws cover federal employees and longshoremen and harbor workers. In addition, the Department of Labor administers "black lung" benefit programs for coal miners disabled by pneumoconiosis and for specified dependents and survivors. Specified occupational diseases are compensable to some extent. In most states, benefits are related to the worker's salary. The benefits may or may not be augmented by dependents' allowances or automatically adjusted to prevailing wage levels.

Income support—Income support programs are designed to provide benefits that assist persons with limited income and resources. The Supplemental Security Income (SSI) program and Temporary

Assistance for Needy Families (TANF) program are the major programs providing monthly payments. In addition, a number of programs provide money payments or in-kind benefits for special needs or purposes. Several programs offer food and nutritional services. Also, various federal-state programs provide energy assistance, public housing, and subsidized housing to individuals and families with low incomes. General assistance may also be available at the state or local level.

The SSI program, administered by the Social Security Administration, provides income support to persons with low income and few resources who are age 65 and older, or blind or disabled, and children with disabilities who have limited income and resources. Unlike social security, SSI benefits are not based on a person's work history, and the program is financed by general tax revenues. Eligibility requirements and federal payment standards are nationally uniform. Most states supplement the basic SSI payment for all or selected categories of persons.

The Personal Responsibility and Work Opportunity Reconciliation Act of 1996 contains provisions that replaced the Aid to Families With Dependent Children (AFDC), Job Opportunities and Basic Skills (JOBS), and Emergency Assistance programs with the TANF block grant program. The federal government provides grants to states, the District of Columbia, and U.S. territories that use the money to fund monthly cash assistance payments to low-income families with children and numerous additional services to encourage economic self-sufficiency. The law creating TANF contains strong work requirements, comprehensive child support enforcement, support for families moving from welfare to work, and other features. States design and operate their own TANF programs, including setting income eligibility thresholds and benefits levels, and may use funds for various purposes to encourage self-sufficiency in addition to providing basic assistance. The TANF program became effective as soon as each state submitted a complete implementation plan, but no later than July 1, 1997.

Federal nutrition assistance—The U.S. Department of Agriculture's Food and Nutrition Service administers the Supplemental Nutrition Assistance Program (SNAP), formerly knows as food stamps. The program provides assistance in purchasing food to individuals and households meeting limits on income and assets.

SNAP also includes work requirements, with some exceptions. Programs are managed locally by states and territories. Benefits come on an electronic benefits transfer card that recipients use much like a bank debit card for purchasing eligible food items in retail food stores. The monthly amount of benefits, also known as allotments, is determined by household size and income. Households without income receive the determined monthly cost of a nutritionally adequate diet for their household size. This amount is regularly updated to account for food price increases. Households are expected to spend about 30 percent of their own resources on food, thus for households with income, the program provides a benefit that equals the maximum monthly allotment according to household size minus 30 percent of the household's net monthly income.

The USDA website has detailed information regarding eligibility for SNAP, including income limits and maximum monthly SNAP allotments by household size, at <www.fns.usda.gov/snap/recipient/eligibility>. All households in which all members receive TANF or SSI are categorically eligible for SNAP without meeting these income or resource criteria. Households are certified for varying lengths of time, depending on their income sources and individual circumstances.

Health services—For information about the Medicaid program, see Section 3, Health and Nutrition.

Noncash benefits—The U.S. Census Bureau annually collects data on the characteristics of recipients of noncash (in-kind) benefits to supplement the collection of annual money income data in the Current Population Survey (see text, Section 1, Population, and Section 13, Income, Expenditures, Poverty, and Wealth). Noncash benefits are those benefits received in a form other than money which serve to enhance or improve the economic well-being of the recipient. As for money income, the data for noncash benefits are for the calendar year prior to the date of the interview. The major categories of noncash benefits covered are public transfers (e.g., SNAP, school lunch, public housing, and Medicaid) and employer or union-provided benefits to employees.

Statistical reliability—For discussion of statistical collection, estimation, and sampling procedures and measures of statistical reliability applicable to Census Bureau data, see Appendix III.

Table 571. Government Transfer Payments to Individuals—Summary: 1990 to 2022

[In billions of current dollars (568.1 represents $568,100,000,000)]

Year	Government transfer payments to individuals, total	Retirement and disability insurance benefits	Medical payments	Income maintenance benefits	Unemploy-ment insurance benefits	Veterans benefits	Education and training assistance payments [1]	Other [2]
1990	568.1	263.9	188.8	65.4	18.2	17.7	12.3	1.7
2000	1,032.4	424.5	427.2	110.6	21.0	25.0	21.9	2.3
2005	1,473.5	545.5	655.6	165.9	32.3	36.4	33.0	4.9
2010	2,260.4	724.9	938.4	256.0	139.7	58.0	64.5	78.8
2011	2,288.7	747.4	970.1	264.1	107.9	63.3	65.0	70.9
2012	2,300.2	796.2	1,001.6	267.6	84.4	70.1	63.7	16.5
2013	2,363.2	832.8	1,040.5	271.2	63.1	79.1	63.8	12.8
2014	2,475.6	870.3	1,117.7	271.0	35.8	84.2	64.7	31.9
2015	2,612.3	908.0	1,197.7	273.7	32.9	92.6	63.4	44.1
2016	2,694.1	930.4	1,250.5	270.7	32.3	96.8	64.1	49.4
2017	2,784.3	958.9	1,291.5	269.8	30.6	111.4	65.7	56.3
2018	2,901.9	1,005.9	1,349.7	262.8	28.0	119.7	69.8	66.0
2019	3,062.7	1,065.6	1,428.9	271.9	27.8	130.9	73.9	63.7
2020	4,062.6	1,114.4	1,503.0	318.5	529.8	145.4	76.6	374.8
2021	4,483.7	1,152.2	1,640.4	468.2	324.2	154.1	78.1	666.5
2022	3,846.7	1,249.3	1,771.1	449.9	22.4	170.5	82.9	100.4

[1] See footnote 9, Table 572. [2] See footnote 10, Table 572.

Source: U.S. Bureau of Economic Analysis, Regional Economic Accounts, Annual Personal Income and Employment by State, "Personal Current Transfer Receipts (SAINC35)," <www.bea.gov/data/economic-accounts/regional>, accessed December 2023.

Table 572. Government Transfer Payments to Individuals by Payment Type: 1990 to 2022

[In millions of current dollars (568,060 represents $568,060,000,000)]

Payment type	1990	2000	2010	2015	2020	2021	2022
Total	**568,060**	**1,032,404**	**2,260,351**	**2,612,314**	**4,062,567**	**4,483,663**	**3,846,653**
Retirement & disability insurance benefits	263,888	424,461	724,895	907,978	1,114,448	1,152,161	1,249,338
Social security	244,135	401,393	690,174	871,793	1,077,928	1,114,600	1,211,508
Railroad retirement & disability	7,221	8,267	10,779	12,228	13,126	13,169	13,597
Workers' compensation (federal & state)	8,618	10,898	15,505	13,721	12,807	12,422	12,469
Other government retirement & disability insurance [1]	3,914	3,903	8,437	10,236	10,587	11,970	11,764
Medical payments	188,808	427,194	938,402	1,197,744	1,503,012	1,640,430	1,771,132
Medicare	107,638	219,117	513,390	634,938	816,782	874,460	926,088
Public assistance medical care [2]	78,176	205,021	410,957	547,528	671,054	749,686	827,323
Military medical insurance [3]	2,994	3,056	14,055	15,278	15,176	16,284	17,721
Income maintenance benefits	65,441	110,582	256,034	273,685	318,495	468,166	449,854
Supplemental Security Income (SSI)	16,670	31,675	49,158	56,661	57,932	56,920	58,946
Earned income tax credit	6,313	30,423	59,778	69,620	67,435	67,872	71,947
Supplemental Nutrition Assistance Program	14,741	14,565	66,515	68,737	98,703	149,034	127,687
Family assistance [4]	19,187	18,440	22,421	20,953	20,540	20,491	20,500
Other, excluding family assistance [5]	8,530	15,479	58,162	57,714	73,885	173,849	170,774
Unemployment insurance compensation	18,208	20,989	139,715	32,861	529,825	324,193	22,437
State unemployment insurance compensation	17,644	20,223	137,016	31,827	528,817	323,452	21,974
Unemployment compensation for federal civilian employees	215	226	535	203	220	228	146
Unemployment compensation for railroad employees	89	81	116	90	210	135	82
Unemployment compensation for veterans	144	181	1,155	389	239	166	102
Other unemployment compensation [6]	116	278	893	352	339	212	133
Veterans benefits	17,687	25,004	57,962	92,568	145,416	154,064	170,510
Veterans pension & disability	15,550	21,966	48,455	76,515	111,917	118,674	134,252
Veterans readjustment [7]	257	1,322	7,976	12,699	10,541	10,065	9,689
Veterans life insurance benefits	1,868	1,706	1,442	1,185	821	770	626
Other assistance to veterans [8]	12	10	89	2,169	22,137	24,555	25,943
Federal education & training assistance payments [9]	12,286	21,851	64,511	63,410	76,621	78,148	82,937
Other payments to individuals [10]	1,742	2,323	78,832	44,068	374,750	666,501	100,445

[1] Mostly temporary disability, pension benefit guaranty, black lung, and Panama Canal construction annuity payments. [2] Medicaid and other medical vendor payments. [3] Payments made under TRICARE Program for medical care of dependents of active duty and retired military personnel. [4] Through 1995, Emergency Assistance and Aid to Families with Dependent Children. Beginning 1998, Temporary Assistance for Needy Families benefits. [5] Mostly general assistance; food expenditures under Special Supplemental Nutrition Program for Women, Infants, and Children (WIC); other needs assistance; refugee assistance; foster home care and adoption assistance; Additional Child Tax Credits; and energy assistance. [6] Trade adjustment allowance, Redwood Park benefit, public service employment benefit, and transitional benefit. [7] Mostly veterans' readjustment benefit payments, educational assistance to spouses and children of disabled or deceased veterans, and payments to paraplegics and for autos and conveyances for disabled veterans. [8] Mostly state and local government payments to veterans and Veterans Choice and VA Community Care benefits. [9] Mostly federal fellowship payments (including National Science Foundation fellowships and traineeships, and subsistence payments to state maritime academy cadets), interest subsidy on higher education loans, Pell Grants, Job Corps payments, education exchange payments, and state education assistance payments. [10] Mostly other refundable tax credits; Bureau of Indian Affairs payments; Alaska Permanent Fund dividend payments; compensation of survivors of public safety officers; compensation of victims of crime; disaster relief payments; supplemental payments to United Mine Workers health benefits; compensation for Japanese internment; the American Recovery and Reinvestment Act of 2009 funded Federal Additional Compensation for unemployment, COBRA premium reduction; Economic Recovery lump sum payment; Affordable Care Act cost sharing reduction; lost wages assistance during COVID-19 pandemic; and other special payments to individuals.

Source: U.S. Bureau of Economic Analysis, Regional Economic Accounts, Annual Personal Income and Employment by State, "Personal Current Transfer Receipts (SAINC35)," <www.bea.gov/data/economic-accounts/regional>, accessed December 2023.

Table 573. Government Transfer Payments to Individuals by State: 2020 to 2022

[In millions of current dollars not adjusted for inflation (4,062,567 represents $4,062,567,000,000)]

State	2020, total	2021, total	2022							
			Total	Retire-ment and disability insurance benefits	Medical payments	Income mainte-nance benefits	Unem-ployment insurance benefits	Veterans benefits	Educa-tion and training assis-tance [1]	Other [2]
United States.........	**4,062,567**	**4,483,663**	**3,846,653**	**1,249,338**	**1,771,132**	**449,854**	**22,437**	**170,510**	**82,937**	**100,445**
Alabama.................	59,768	68,019	60,504	21,572	23,574	7,490	81	4,079	1,721	1,987
Alaska...................	8,986	10,054	10,382	2,040	4,042	1,153	48	773	75	2,250
Arizona.................	90,277	99,435	88,992	28,554	41,799	7,920	193	4,266	4,767	1,494
Arkansas...............	37,580	42,037	38,048	12,779	18,033	3,651	79	2,089	867	550
California...............	533,869	568,088	465,496	126,296	230,254	67,954	4,536	14,321	11,473	10,662
Colorado...............	58,830	66,227	58,471	18,742	25,593	7,755	377	3,583	1,465	956
Connecticut............	45,254	48,862	42,891	14,757	21,294	3,850	370	930	773	918
Delaware...............	13,073	14,589	14,121	4,874	6,637	1,304	42	505	489	270
District of Columbia....	9,518	10,343	8,921	1,562	5,411	1,407	49	196	235	59
Florida.................	266,458	304,831	272,927	94,209	114,436	25,635	389	14,259	5,511	18,489
Georgia.................	115,408	127,633	108,740	36,180	42,297	15,816	159	7,600	2,675	4,012
Hawaii..................	18,615	19,687	16,181	5,518	6,832	2,201	153	1,079	197	201
Idaho...................	18,555	21,634	19,753	7,389	8,061	2,273	74	1,155	341	460
Illinois.................	149,321	165,368	136,490	44,884	61,037	20,366	1,348	3,806	2,525	2,523
Indiana.................	78,758	90,125	78,885	27,574	36,839	8,610	193	2,671	1,887	1,109
Iowa....................	35,605	39,170	34,480	13,035	15,606	2,903	228	1,319	690	700
Kansas.................	30,335	33,881	29,720	11,599	12,639	2,702	116	1,433	446	785
Kentucky...............	60,059	67,089	58,166	18,539	29,027	5,867	195	2,417	1,492	628
Louisiana...............	61,501	68,503	59,761	16,570	30,348	7,650	132	2,620	1,466	975
Maine...................	18,527	20,404	19,089	6,507	8,475	2,268	88	1,061	283	408
Maryland...............	70,250	77,683	66,110	21,523	32,090	7,087	353	3,105	916	1,035
Massachusetts..........	99,748	104,206	88,173	25,539	43,400	13,587	1,101	2,067	1,213	1,267
Michigan...............	139,203	143,442	118,744	44,950	52,175	12,683	663	3,909	2,504	1,859
Minnesota..............	67,724	75,360	65,055	21,926	31,554	6,305	775	2,416	1,419	660
Mississippi.............	37,391	41,014	35,232	12,026	15,301	4,269	40	1,846	794	956
Missouri................	70,965	78,824	70,753	25,204	32,843	6,099	176	3,435	1,187	1,810
Montana................	12,811	14,173	12,535	4,836	5,327	872	70	892	196	342
Nebraska...............	19,844	22,927	20,195	7,365	8,740	1,669	58	1,147	414	802
Nevada.................	38,202	41,893	32,618	10,823	13,720	3,996	219	2,282	935	643
New Hampshire........	16,202	17,372	15,524	6,614	6,506	868	37	760	505	235
New Jersey.............	114,118	126,238	102,934	35,803	47,890	10,616	1,787	2,077	2,184	2,575
New Mexico............	27,956	32,036	29,252	8,254	13,935	4,591	127	1,500	429	417
New York...............	302,436	321,325	264,906	73,354	144,085	33,854	1,884	4,397	4,169	3,163
North Carolina.........	120,788	139,709	122,942	42,121	50,203	14,417	148	8,298	2,821	4,934
North Dakota...........	7,987	8,768	7,725	2,791	3,468	600	60	438	124	243
Ohio....................	145,718	159,290	137,316	45,726	66,606	14,797	563	4,880	2,939	1,805
Oklahoma..............	45,044	51,699	46,845	15,232	19,753	5,793	162	3,579	971	1,354
Oregon.................	54,928	60,877	53,060	17,922	25,268	5,210	431	2,660	687	882
Pennsylvania...........	187,639	198,717	168,459	57,363	84,307	15,685	1,150	4,800	2,339	2,816
Rhode Island...........	15,053	16,273	13,614	4,703	6,489	1,389	126	402	300	205
South Carolina.........	62,546	70,460	63,537	23,656	24,721	6,958	112	4,331	1,780	1,980
South Dakota..........	8,962	10,668	9,747	3,551	3,764	1,208	24	603	141	455
Tennessee.............	80,626	90,559	79,038	28,401	33,115	9,063	139	4,619	1,644	2,057
Texas..................	294,637	342,201	291,891	84,938	130,972	38,844	1,758	18,807	5,503	11,070
Utah...................	24,840	29,857	25,529	8,790	10,232	2,953	131	1,114	1,036	1,271
Vermont................	8,686	9,013	8,168	3,033	3,682	714	44	284	237	174
Virginia.................	91,653	103,546	93,877	31,880	41,283	9,354	126	6,871	2,096	2,267
Washington............	88,628	99,219	83,281	30,798	35,698	8,158	918	4,489	2,006	1,213
West Virginia...........	25,649	28,722	25,652	8,980	11,290	2,806	93	1,442	549	491
Wisconsin..............	65,810	74,655	65,627	25,399	28,222	6,223	274	2,451	1,400	1,656
Wyoming...............	6,226	6,958	6,297	2,654	2,255	412	40	446	119	371

[1] Mostly federal fellowship payments (National Science Foundation fellowships and traineeships, subsistence payments to state maritime academy cadets, and other federal fellowships), interest subsidy on higher education loans, Pell Grants, Job Corps payments, education exchange payments, and state education assistance payments. [2] Mostly other refundable tax credits; Bureau of Indian Affairs payments; Alaska Permanent Fund dividend payments; compensation of survivors of public safety officers; compensation of victims of crime; disaster relief payments; supplemental payments to United Mine Workers health benefits; compensation for Japanese internment; the American Recovery and Reinvestment Act of 2009 funded Federal Additional Compensation for unemployment, COBRA premium reduction; Economic Recovery lump sum payment; Affordable Care Act cost sharing reductions; lost wages assistance during the COVID-19 pandemic; and other special payments to individuals.

Source: U.S. Bureau of Economic Analysis, Regional Economic Accounts, Annual Personal Income and Employment by State, "Personal Current Transfer Receipts (SAINC35)," <www.bea.gov/data/economic-accounts/regional>, accessed December 2023.

Table 574. Number of Persons With Income by Source of Income: 2022

[In thousands (239,100 represents 239,100,000). Persons age 15 and over as of March of following year. Based on Current Population Survey, Annual Social and Economic Supplement (CPS ASEC); see text, Sections 1 and 13, and Appendix III]

Source of income	Total persons with income	Age 65 and over	Men	Women	White[1]	Black[1]	Asian[1]	Hispanic origin[2]
Total[3]	**239,100**	**55,700**	**119,400**	**119,700**	**185,300**	**30,090**	**15,340**	**39,180**
Earnings	170,900	12,930	90,380	80,490	130,900	21,880	11,650	31,630
Wages and salary	161,800	11,270	84,920	76,890	123,500	21,080	11,120	29,740
Nonfarm self-employment	12,510	1,737	7,204	5,310	10,020	1,298	746	2,352
Farm self-employment	2,102	336	1,310	791	1,765	215	72	200
Social Security	56,330	46,230	25,430	30,900	46,300	6,231	2,493	5,062
SSI (supplemental security income)	5,711	1,440	2,778	2,933	3,733	1,480	274	983
Public assistance	1,747	261	494	1,253	1,114	467	65	439
Veterans' benefits	4,710	2,199	3,881	829	3,726	657	157	403
Survivor benefits	3,249	2,129	848	2,401	2,824	234	103	231
Disability benefits	2,598	489	1,322	1,276	1,983	417	85	371
Unemployment compensation	3,073	297	1,762	1,311	2,296	451	145	621
Workers' compensation	1,192	191	625	567	895	208	31	170
Property income	150,500	38,250	74,580	75,870	121,100	14,320	10,420	17,210
Interest	147,900	37,420	73,180	74,760	119,200	14,100	10,200	16,830
Dividends	36,600	10,640	20,460	16,130	30,240	2,145	3,350	2,280
Rents, royalties, estates or trusts	12,380	4,551	6,505	5,878	10,260	756	1,103	1,014
Retirement income[3]	30,190	23,360	14,780	15,400	25,930	2,572	1,065	1,779
Company or union retirement	11,540	9,616	6,251	5,284	9,900	1,047	371	693
Federal government retirement	1,867	1,435	946	921	1,502	220	78	149
Military retirement	1,109	624	772	337	865	163	38	60
State or local government retirement	6,589	4,876	2,759	3,830	5,718	580	178	440
Annuities	4,153	3,436	1,737	2,416	3,716	230	138	154
Retirement accounts[4]	11,120	9,856	5,644	5,477	10,040	487	450	421
Pension income[3]	20,510	16,900	10,550	9,962	17,690	1,790	665	1,105
Company or union retirement	10,200	8,826	5,892	4,309	8,769	933	329	577
Federal government retirement	1,457	1,212	842	614	1,169	179	62	90
Military retirement	637	365	555	82	515	75	28	27
State or local government retirement	5,822	4,600	2,437	3,385	5,117	471	145	321
Annuities	3,942	3,328	1,665	2,277	3,536	216	132	130
Alimony	210	49	5	205	191	11	7	16
Child support	3,210	49	233	2,977	2,363	601	93	591
Educational assistance	6,634	49	2,732	3,901	4,693	1,039	537	1,240
Financial assistance from outside the household	2,547	300	963	1,584	1,774	322	313	422

[1] Refers to people who reported specified race only and no other race category. [2] Persons of Hispanic origin may be of any race. [3] Includes other income sources not shown. [4] Includes 401k, 403b, and individual retirement accounts, Keogh plans (tax-deferred retirement plans for self-employed persons and unincorporated businesses), simplified employee pensions, and other plan types.

Source: U.S. Census Bureau, "Current Population Survey Tables for Personal Income: Table PINC-08," <www.census.gov/topics/income-poverty/income/data/tables.html>, accessed November 2023.

Table 575. Median Income by Source and Age, Sex, and Race/Ethnicity: 2022

[In dollars. See headnote in Table 574]

Source of income	All persons	Age 65 and over	Men	Women	White[1]	Black[1]	Asian[1]	Hispanic origin[2]
Total[3]	**40,480**	**29,740**	**48,450**	**32,790**	**41,010**	**35,220**	**50,570**	**31,980**
Earnings	47,960	39,690	52,770	41,320	49,120	41,830	61,940	36,470
Wages and salary	49,160	41,090	55,090	41,670	50,160	42,010	63,400	36,820
Nonfarm self-employment	21,540	20,450	25,760	16,630	21,510	19,400	30,460	21,740
Farm self-employment	1,935	12,570	2,104	1,708	2,064	1,401	(B)	1,441
Social Security	17,690	18,520	20,170	15,930	18,280	15,470	15,230	14,610
SSI (supplemental security income)	9,545	6,715	9,898	9,085	9,745	9,331	9,021	9,037
Public assistance	3,129	2,663	2,485	3,396	3,025	3,069	(B)	2,934
Veterans' benefits	17,050	15,630	16,560	17,850	16,560	18,860	18,200	16,970
Survivor benefits	10,960	10,060	12,140	10,690	10,690	11,080	18,840	10,990
Disability benefits	10,610	10,620	11,360	9,805	10,690	10,610	7,420	10,520
Unemployment compensation	3,735	4,182	3,644	3,853	3,720	3,955	2,362	3,599
Workers' compensation	8,414	9,835	8,586	8,270	8,145	9,156	(B)	10,810
Property income[3]	1,577	1,730	1,623	1,535	1,595	1,436	1,639	1,423
Dividends	1,627	1,934	1,632	1,621	1,658	1,450	1,530	1,451
Rents, royalties, estates or trusts	5,258	6,134	5,289	5,226	5,203	4,293	6,902	5,791
Retirement income[3]	16,000	15,940	19,060	13,120	16,040	15,590	16,600	14,250
Company or union retirement	11,270	11,030	13,430	8,896	11,250	11,520	10,770	11,930
Federal government retirement	24,370	24,490	26,640	19,990	23,880	26,680	26,990	16,140
Military retirement	23,320	21,520	26,530	15,840	23,220	22,700	(B)	(B)
State or local government retirement	23,330	24,270	28,270	19,840	23,510	21,320	25,910	19,940
Annuities	7,001	6,848	7,495	6,680	6,899	9,002	7,134	7,142
Retirement accounts[4]	9,037	8,294	10,800	7,112	9,161	6,664	10,210	9,898
Pension income[3]	16,480	15,730	19,680	13,310	16,310	17,160	16,480	16,270
Company or union retirement	11,330	11,040	13,550	8,279	11,270	11,690	10,840	11,250
Federal government retirement	27,850	26,380	30,770	25,950	27,180	29,490	(B)	25,500
Military retirement	27,310	24,130	28,630	23,290	27,500	24,580	(B)	(B)
State or local government retirement	25,630	24,980	31,730	21,930	25,560	24,790	29,160	26,990
Annuities	6,828	6,780	7,322	6,495	6,786	7,907	6,888	7,003
Alimony	10,070	(B)	(B)	9,802	9,261	(B)	(B)	(B)
Child support	4,299	(B)	2,948	4,435	4,357	4,079	5,700	4,475
Educational assistance	5,762	(B)	5,827	5,718	5,693	5,729	7,152	4,884
Financial assistance from outside the household	4,611	2,920	4,221	4,834	4,498	3,017	6,836	3,145

B Base less than 75,000. [1] See footnote 1, Table 574. [2] See footnote 2, Table 574. [3] See footnote 3, Table 574. [4] See footnote 4, Table 574.

Source: U.S. Census Bureau, "Current Population Survey Tables for Personal Income: Table PINC-08," <www.census.gov/topics/income-poverty/income/data/tables.html>, accessed November 2023.

Table 576. Persons Living in Households Receiving Selected Benefits by Selected Characteristics: 2022

[330,100 represents 330,100,000, except percent. Based on Current Population Survey, Annual Social and Economic Supplement (CPS ASEC); see text of Section 1 and Appendix III. Persons who live in a household in which someone (a nonrelative or a relative) receives aid. Not every person tallied here receive the aid themselves. Excludes members of the Armed Forces except those living off post or with their families on post. Population controls are based on 2020 Census. SNAP = Supplemental Nutrition Assistance Program]

Characteristic	Total pop- ulation (1,000)	In household receiving means-tested assistance [1]		In household receiving means-tested cash assistance		In household receiving SNAP (food stamps)		In household in which one or more persons are covered by Medicaid		Living in public or subsidized housing	
		(1,000)	Percent	(1,000)	Percent	(1,000)	Percent	(1,000)	Percent	(1,000)	Percent
Total.................	330,100	129,000	39.1	17,850	5.4	40,700	12.3	86,740	26.3	13,080	4.0
Under 18 years.................	71,950	42,630	59.2	3,825	5.3	13,360	18.6	27,530	38.3	3,553	4.9
18 to 24 years....................	30,460	13,030	42.8	1,529	5.0	3,776	12.4	8,975	29.5	1,372	4.5
25 to 34 years....................	44,910	16,610	37.0	2,044	4.6	5,247	11.7	12,500	27.8	1,661	3.7
35 to 44 years....................	43,490	18,570	42.7	2,042	4.7	5,086	11.7	11,620	26.7	1,364	3.1
45 to 54 years....................	40,000	14,110	35.3	2,250	5.6	3,894	9.7	8,937	22.3	1,129	2.8
55 to 59 years....................	20,380	5,990	29.4	1,474	7.2	2,035	10.0	4,590	22.5	650	3.2
60 to 64 years....................	21,010	6,315	30.1	1,689	8.0	2,448	11.7	4,926	23.4	801	3.8
65 years and over................	57,880	11,790	20.4	2,994	5.2	4,845	8.4	7,658	13.2	2,551	4.4
Male...........................	163,100	62,510	38.3	8,704	5.3	18,810	11.5	41,820	25.6	5,690	3.5
Female........................	167,000	66,530	39.8	9,144	5.5	21,880	13.1	44,920	26.9	7,391	4.4
White alone [2]..................	248,800	89,340	35.9	11,680	4.7	25,740	10.3	59,480	23.9	7,014	2.8
Black alone [2]..................	44,520	23,680	53.2	4,169	9.4	10,280	23.1	16,410	36.8	4,417	9.9
Asian alone [2].................	21,590	7,829	36.3	862	4.0	1,771	8.2	4,977	23.1	568	2.6
Hispanic [3]...................	63,800	37,570	58.9	4,103	6.4	11,730	18.4	27,610	43.3	3,272	5.1
In married couple families.......	197,200	66,050	33.5	6,917	3.5	13,870	7.0	40,030	20.3	2,602	1.3
In families with male house-holder, no spouse present.....	20,870	11,880	56.9	1,647	7.9	3,720	17.8	8,801	42.2	983	4.7
In families with female house-holder, no spouse present....	47,420	33,030	69.7	5,579	11.8	15,280	32.2	25,520	53.8	4,775	10.1

[1] Means-tested assistance includes means-tested cash assistance, supplemental nutrition assistance program benefits, Medicaid, and public or subsidized housing. [2] Refers to people who reported specific race and did not report any other race category. [3] People of Hispanic origin may be of any race.

Source: U.S. Census Bureau, *Poverty in the United States: 2022*, Current Population Reports, P60-280, September 2023; and "Current Population Survey Detailed Tables for Poverty: Table POV-08," <www.census.gov/topics/income-poverty/poverty/data/tables.html>, accessed November 2023.

Table 577. Social Security—Covered Employment, Earnings, and Contribution Rates: 1990 to 2023

[164.3 represents 164,300,000. Includes the Island Areas of the U.S. Represents all reported employment. Data are estimated. OASDI is Old-age, Survivors, and Disability Insurance; SMI is Supplementary Medical Insurance. All data are subject to revision by source]

Item	Unit	1990	2000	2010	2015	2019	2020	2021	2022	2023
Workers with insured status [1]......	**Million**	**164.3**	**185.4**	**204.2**	**214.6**	**225.1**	**226.8**	**228.9**	**230.7**	**232.6**
Male..............................	Million	86.8	95.5	103.4	108.2	112.9	113.7	114.4	115.2	116.0
Female............................	Million	77.5	89.9	100.7	106.4	112.2	113.2	114.4	115.5	116.6
Under 20 years old.................	Million	4.8	4.9	2.5	2.3	3.1	3.1	3.3	3.3	3.2
Age 20 to 24......................	Million	16.6	16.0	16.0	15.8	16.4	16.4	16.6	16.9	17.1
Age 25 to 29......................	Million	20.7	17.5	19.3	20.3	21.0	20.8	20.6	20.5	20.4
Age 30 to 34......................	Million	21.3	19.3	18.7	19.8	20.8	21.1	21.5	21.7	21.8
Age 35 to 39......................	Million	19.4	21.3	18.2	18.8	20.0	20.1	20.3	20.4	20.7
Age 40 to 44......................	Million	17.0	21.4	19.6	18.3	18.4	18.9	19.3	19.6	19.9
Age 45 to 49......................	Million	12.8	19.2	21.2	19.5	18.7	18.2	17.9	17.8	18.0
Age 50 to 54......................	Million	10.1	16.5	20.9	20.8	19.1	19.1	19.1	19.0	18.7
Age 55 to 59......................	Million	8.8	12.2	18.3	20.3	20.5	20.1	19.7	19.2	18.8
Age 60 to 64......................	Million	8.6	9.3	15.4	17.5	19.1	19.4	19.5	19.6	19.6
Age 65 to 69......................	Million	8.0	7.9	11.1	14.7	16.1	16.6	17.0	17.4	17.8
Age 70 to 74......................	Million	6.4	7.1	8.1	10.2	12.9	13.6	13.9	14.1	14.4
Age 75 and older..................	Million	9.9	12.8	14.9	16.4	18.9	19.3	20.1	21.2	22.3
Workers reported with—										
Taxable earnings [2]..............	Million	133.0	154.7	157.0	168.1	177.0	175.2	176.9	180.7	182.8
Maximum earnings [2]..............	Million	7.6	9.6	9.0	10.5	10.9	10.8	11.4	12.7	11.6
Earnings in covered employment [2]....	Bil. dol.	2,716	4,832	6,294	7,806	9,222	9,387	10,379	11,145	11,710
Reported taxable [2]..............	Bil. dol.	2,359	4,008	5,307	6,473	7,696	7,747	8,391	9,202	9,670
Percent of total..................	Percent	86.9	82.9	84.3	82.9	83.5	82.5	80.8	82.6	82.6
Average per worker:										
Total earnings [2]................	Dollars	20,423	31,237	40,079	46,433	52,103	53,590	58,683	61,685	64,064
Taxable earnings [2]..............	Dollars	17,737	25,908	33,792	38,503	43,481	44,226	47,442	50,928	52,900
Annual maximum taxable earnings [3]........................	Dollars	51,300	76,200	106,800	118,500	132,900	137,700	142,800	147,000	160,200
Contribution rates for OASDI: [4]										
Each employer and employee........	Percent	7.65	7.65	7.65	7.65	7.65	7.65	7.65	7.65	7.65
Self-employed [5].................	Percent	15.30	15.30	15.30	15.30	15.30	15.30	15.30	15.30	15.30
SMI, monthly premium (as of Jan. 1)...	Dollars	28.60	45.50	110.50	104.90	135.50	144.60	148.50	170.10	164.90

[1] Estimated number fully insured for retirement and/or survivor benefits as of end of year. [2] Includes self-employment. Averages per worker computed with unrounded earnings and worker amounts, and may not agree with rounded table amounts. [3] Beginning in 1994, the upper limit on earnings subject to HI taxes was removed. [4] OASDI tax rates for employees and self-employed workers were reduced by 2 percent for 2011 and 2012. This reduction is being made up by transfers from the General Fund of the Treasury to the OASI and DI trust funds. [5] Half of self-employment tax is deductible for income tax purposes and for computing self-employment income subject to social security tax.

Source: U.S. Social Security Administration, *Annual Statistical Supplement to the Social Security Bulletin, 2024* and unpublished data. See also <www.ssa.gov/policy/docs/statcomps/supplement/index.html>.

Table 578. Social Security (OASDI)—Benefits by Type of Beneficiary: 1990 to 2023

[39,832 represents 39,832,000. A person eligible to receive more than one type of benefit is generally classified or counted only once as a retired-worker beneficiary. OASDI = Old-age, Survivors, and Disability Insurance. See also headnote, Table 579]

Type of beneficiary	1990	2000	2010	2015	2019	2020	2021	2022	2023
Number of benefits [1] (1,000).............	**39,832**	**45,415**	**54,032**	**59,963**	**64,064**	**64,851**	**65,228**	**65,994**	**67,077**
Retired workers [2].................	24,838	28,499	34,593	40,089	45,094	46,330	47,293	48,588	50,148
Disabled workers [3]...............	3,011	5,042	8,204	8,909	8,378	8,151	7,877	7,604	7,366
Wives and husbands [2,4]..............	3,367	2,963	2,477	2,478	2,544	2,428	2,262	2,114	1,984
Children.................	3,187	3,803	4,313	4,297	4,051	4,004	3,908	3,848	3,782
Under age 18.............	2,497	2,976	3,209	3,096	2,798	2,755	2,672	2,614	2,548
Disabled children [5].............	600	729	949	1,068	1,141	1,150	1,143	1,140	1,142
Students [6].............	89	98	155	133	113	99	94	94	92
Of retired workers.............	422	459	580	649	702	704	687	682	686
Of deceased workers.............	1,776	1,878	1,913	1,893	1,916	1,936	1,976	2,020	2,037
Of disabled workers.............	989	1,466	1,820	1,755	1,434	1,363	1,245	1,146	1,060
Widowed mothers and fathers [7].......	304	203	158	140	117	115	114	112	108
Widows and widowers [2,8]........	5,111	4,901	4,286	4,050	3,878	3,823	3,774	3,728	3,796
Parents [2].............	6	3	2	1	1	1	1	1	1
Special benefits [9].............	7	(Z)	(Z)	(NA)	(NA)	(NA)	(NA)	(NA)	(NA)
AVERAGE MONTHLY BENEFIT, CURRENT DOLLARS									
Retired workers [2].............	603	844	1,176	1,342	1,503	1,544	1,658	1,825	1,905
Retired worker and wife [2]..............	1,027	1,420	1,930	2,249	2,583	2,635	2,793	3,021	3,090
Disabled workers [3].............	587	786	1,068	1,166	1,258	1,277	1,358	1,483	1,537
Wives and husbands [2,4].............	298	416	561	669	767	778	820	880	890
Children of retired workers.............	259	395	577	651	713	730	782	857	890
Children of deceased workers.............	406	550	752	832	902	918	978	1,067	1,103
Children of disabled workers.............	164	228	318	351	391	399	428	471	492
Widowed mothers and fathers [7].............	409	595	849	940	1,034	1,054	1,126	1,232	1,278
Widows and widowers, nondisabled [2].........	556	810	1,134	1,286	1,423	1,455	1,555	1,705	1,774
Parents [2].............	482	704	998	1,133	1,271	1,299	1,393	1,538	1,590
Special benefits [9].............	167	217	276	(NA)	(NA)	(NA)	(NA)	(NA)	(NA)
AVERAGE MONTHLY BENEFIT, CONSTANT (2023) DOLLARS [10]									
Retired workers [2].............	1,382	1,489	1,645	1,740	1,794	1,818	1,824	1,886	1,905
Retired worker and wife [2].............	2,354	2,503	2,701	2,917	3,083	3,103	3,073	3,123	3,090
Disabled workers [3].............	1,346	1,386	1,494	1,512	1,502	1,504	1,494	1,533	1,537
Wives and husbands [2,4].............	683	734	785	868	916	916	902	909	890
Children of deceased workers.............	931	970	1,052	1,079	1,077	1,081	1,077	1,103	1,103
Widowed mothers and fathers [7].............	938	1,049	1,188	1,219	1,234	1,241	1,239	1,273	1,278
Widows and widowers, nondisabled [2].........	1,275	1,428	1,587	1,668	1,699	1,714	1,711	1,762	1,774
Number of benefits awarded (1,000)........	**3,717**	**4,290**	**5,697**	**5,440**	**5,700**	**5,761**	**5,400**	**5,609**	**5,794**
Retired workers [2].............	1,665	1,961	2,634	2,839	3,175	3,368	3,186	3,413	3,614
Disabled workers [3].............	468	622	1,027	741	679	620	540	509	524
Wives and husbands [2,4].............	379	385	409	463	523	435	368	391	409
Children.............	695	777	1,045	798	721	695	636	635	617
Widowed mothers and fathers [7].............	58	40	32	25	21	22	25	23	19
Widows and widowers [2,8].............	452	505	550	573	581	621	644	636	611
Parents [2].............	(Z)	(Z)	(Z)	(Z)	(Z)	(Z)	(Z)	(Z)	(Z)
Special benefits [9].............	(Z)	(Z)	(Z)	(NA)	(NA)	(NA)	(NA)	(NA)	(NA)
BENEFIT PAYMENTS DURING YEAR (bil. dol.)									
Total [11].........	**247.8**	**407.6**	**701.6**	**886.2**	**1,047.9**	**1,095.9**	**1,133.2**	**1,232.0**	**1,379.0**
Monthly benefits [12].............	247.6	407.4	701.4	886.0	1,047.7	1,095.6	1,132.9	1,231.0	1,379.0
Retired workers [2].............	156.8	253.5	443.4	592.4	738.0	783.5	822.4	907.0	1,030.0
Disabled workers [3].............	22.1	49.8	115.1	133.9	137.0	135.2	132.4	136.0	144.0
Wives and husbands [2,4].............	14.5	19.4	24.6	29.3	34.0	34.5	33.5	34.0	35.0
Children.............	12.0	19.3	30.7	33.5	35.4	35.9	36.0	38.5	42.0
Under age 18.............	9.0	14.1	21.4	22.3	22.6	22.8	22.7	24.3	26.4
Disabled children [5].............	2.5	4.6	8.0	10.0	11.6	12.0	12.2	13.1	14.4
Students [6].............	0.5	0.7	1.3	1.2	1.2	1.1	1.0	1.1	1.2
Of retired workers.............	1.3	2.1	4.1	5.2	6.1	6.3	6.4	6.8	7.4
Of deceased workers.............	8.6	12.5	18.0	19.6	21.3	21.8	22.4	24.7	27.3
Of disabled workers.............	2.2	4.7	8.5	8.7	8.0	7.8	7.1	7.0	7.3
Widowed mothers and fathers [7].............	1.4	1.4	1.6	1.6	1.5	1.5	1.5	1.6	1.7
Widows and widowers [2,8].............	40.7	63.9	86.0	95.1	102.6	105.0	107.1	114.6	125.5
Parents [2].............	(Z)	(Z)	(Z)	(Z)	(Z)	(Z)	(Z)	(Z)	(Z)
Special benefits [9].............	(Z)	(Z)	(Z)	(NA)	(NA)	(NA)	(NA)	(NA)	(NA)
Lump sum.............	0.2	0.2	0.2	0.2	0.2	0.2	0.2	0.2	0.2

NA Not available. Z Fewer than 500 or less than $50 million. [1] Number of benefit payments in current-payment status, i.e., actually being made at a specified time with no deductions or with deductions amounting to less than a month's benefit. [2] Age 62 and over. [3] Disabled workers under full retirement age. [4] Includes spouse beneficiaries with entitled children in their care and entitled divorced spouses. [5] Age 18 and over. Disability began before age 22. [6] Full-time students age 18 and 19. [7] Includes surviving divorced mothers and fathers with entitled children in their care. [8] Includes widows and widowers and surviving divorced widows and widowers age 60 and over, and disabled widows and widowers age 50 and over. [9] Benefits for persons age 72 and over not insured under regular or transitional provisions of Social Security Act. [10] Constant dollar figures are based on the consumer price index (CPI-U) for December as published by the U.S. Bureau of Labor Statistics. [11] Represents total disbursements of benefit checks by the U.S. Department of the Treasury during the years specified. [12] Distribution by type estimated.

Source: U.S. Social Security Administration, *Annual Statistical Supplement to the Social Security Bulletin, 2024*, and earlier editions. See also <www.ssa.gov/policy/index.html>.

Table 579. Social Security—Beneficiaries, Annual Payments, and Average Monthly Benefit, 2010 to 2023, and by State and Other Area, 2023

[54,032 represents 54,032,000. Number of beneficiaries in current-payment status, and annual and average monthly benefit as of December. Data for 2000 are based on 10-percent sample of administrative records. All other years are 100 percent data. See also headnote, Table 578]

Year, state, and other area	Number of beneficiaries (1,000)				Annual payments [2] (mil. dol.)				Average monthly benefit (dol.)		
	Total	Retired workers and dependents [1]	Survivors	Disabled workers and dependents	Total	Retired workers and dependents [1]	Survivors	Disabled workers and dependents	Retired workers [3]	Disabled workers	Widows and widowers [4]
2010................	54,032	37,489	6,358	10,184	701,436	471,505	105,740	124,191	1,176	1,068	1,134
2015................	59,963	43,073	6,084	10,806	886,012	626,378	116,352	143,282	1,342	1,166	1,286
2016................	60,907	44,266	6,031	10,610	911,132	651,280	117,149	142,703	1,360	1,171	1,301
2017................	61,903	45,498	5,994	10,411	941,252	680,233	118,279	142,740	1,404	1,197	1,338
2018................	62,906	46,803	5,940	10,162	988,373	723,542	121,175	143,656	1,461	1,234	1,388
2019................	64,064	48,227	5,912	9,925	1,047,677	777,259	125,369	145,049	1,503	1,258	1,423
2020................	64,851	49,358	5,875	9,618	1,095,649	823,868	128,294	143,487	1,544	1,277	1,455
2021................	65,228	50,146	5,864	9,218	1,132,927	861,874	131,057	139,996	1,658	1,358	1,555
2022................	65,994	51,293	5,861	8,841	1,231,416	947,071	140,870	143,475	1,825	1,483	1,705
Total, 2023 [5,6].....	67,077	52,730	5,833	8,514	1,379,019	1,072,644	154,530	151,845	1,905	1,537	1,774
United States.........	65,492	51,524	5,620	8,348	1,358,890	1,058,949	150,689	149,252	(NA)	(NA)	(NA)
Alabama.............	1,179	838	119	222	23,559	16,717	2,967	3,875	1,856	1,507	1,750
Alaska..............	115	93	10	12	2,282	1,810	261	211	1,837	1,523	1,775
Arizona.............	1,499	1,228	120	151	31,668	25,612	3,253	2,803	1,949	1,597	1,831
Arkansas............	718	509	69	140	13,853	9,839	1,668	2,346	1,790	1,470	1,696
California...........	6,376	5,273	515	588	128,741	103,945	13,825	10,971	1,866	1,579	1,722
Colorado............	959	795	74	91	20,369	16,636	2,071	1,662	1,958	1,550	1,859
Connecticut..........	722	587	53	82	16,423	13,317	1,577	1,529	2,114	1,608	2,001
Delaware............	241	197	18	27	5,434	4,403	505	526	2,090	1,663	1,969
District of Columbia.....	84	65	7	12	1,705	1,347	156	202	1,917	1,378	1,657
Florida.............	5,070	4,132	387	551	104,439	83,824	10,465	10,150	1,894	1,579	1,796
Georgia.............	1,982	1,513	184	285	39,828	30,155	4,606	5,067	1,859	1,539	1,763
Hawaii..............	297	255	20	22	6,151	5,208	551	392	1,908	1,586	1,752
Idaho...............	395	319	31	46	8,028	6,394	837	797	1,880	1,512	1,850
Illinois.............	2,315	1,847	203	265	48,814	38,327	5,678	4,809	1,934	1,546	1,872
Indiana.............	1,422	1,082	132	208	30,211	22,914	3,615	3,682	1,966	1,530	1,921
Iowa................	688	550	56	82	14,327	11,400	1,536	1,391	1,921	1,464	1,857
Kansas..............	589	465	50	73	12,566	9,934	1,382	1,250	1,982	1,489	1,902
Kentucky............	1,023	715	111	197	19,950	13,824	2,707	3,419	1,803	1,500	1,701
Louisiana...........	941	662	121	158	18,073	12,398	3,005	2,670	1,759	1,472	1,672
Maine...............	369	286	28	56	7,222	5,575	711	936	1,816	1,451	1,741
Maryland............	1,068	860	86	122	23,628	18,921	2,406	2,301	2,054	1,599	1,901
Massachusetts..........	1,324	1,043	96	185	28,376	22,337	2,695	3,344	2,003	1,549	1,872
Michigan............	2,300	1,763	199	337	49,576	37,864	5,656	6,056	1,997	1,564	1,944
Minnesota...........	1,124	918	78	127	24,342	19,885	2,225	2,232	2,016	1,530	1,913
Mississippi..........	692	491	76	125	13,134	9,273	1,750	2,111	1,756	1,465	1,660
Missouri............	1,358	1,023	124	212	27,468	20,637	3,166	3,665	1,869	1,493	1,815
Montana.............	259	212	21	26	5,122	4,123	547	452	1,817	1,463	1,796
Nebraska............	371	297	30	44	7,737	6,188	830	719	1,937	1,442	1,851
Nevada..............	593	484	45	64	11,995	9,573	1,217	1,205	1,843	1,623	1,797
New Hampshire.........	334	263	22	49	7,434	5,918	642	874	2,094	1,586	1,998
New Jersey...........	1,699	1,379	131	188	38,769	31,106	3,917	3,746	2,110	1,711	1,967
New Mexico...........	468	363	43	62	9,076	6,989	1,036	1,051	1,799	1,450	1,660
New York............	3,765	2,987	290	488	79,266	62,139	8,074	9,053	1,951	1,600	1,823
North Carolina........	2,276	1,770	185	321	46,864	36,425	4,706	5,733	1,909	1,540	1,793
North Dakota.........	147	118	13	15	2,957	2,344	358	255	1,856	1,440	1,767
Ohio................	2,463	1,867	247	349	49,763	37,227	6,550	5,986	1,858	1,475	1,816
Oklahoma............	838	620	85	133	16,796	12,370	2,176	2,250	1,856	1,475	1,781
Oregon..............	928	759	67	102	19,400	15,693	1,891	1,816	1,918	1,510	1,858
Pennsylvania.........	2,932	2,286	248	398	62,818	48,678	6,964	7,176	1,979	1,549	1,886
Rhode Island.........	237	184	16	37	4,992	3,899	449	644	1,972	1,520	1,881
South Carolina........	1,267	984	108	175	26,290	20,368	2,748	3,174	1,926	1,568	1,786
South Dakota.........	197	161	16	20	3,943	3,211	403	329	1,848	1,444	1,742
Tennessee............	1,538	1,149	148	241	31,252	23,357	3,709	4,186	1,890	1,502	1,782
Texas...............	4,677	3,633	480	563	93,853	71,571	12,490	9,792	1,865	1,516	1,718
Utah................	458	367	42	50	9,751	7,733	1,159	859	1,988	1,526	1,972
Vermont.............	162	128	11	22	3,385	2,711	302	372	1,961	1,449	1,833
Virginia.............	1,647	1,302	136	209	35,162	27,689	3,697	3,776	1,985	1,551	1,839
Washington..........	1,453	1,189	105	158	31,682	25,733	3,070	2,879	2,022	1,549	1,928
West Virginia.........	477	336	56	85	9,529	6,585	1,460	1,484	1,839	1,516	1,760
Wisconsin...........	1,333	1,075	98	160	28,208	22,684	2,728	2,796	1,957	1,513	1,905
Wyoming.............	126	102	10	14	2,679	2,139	292	248	1,950	1,536	1,913
American Samoa.......	6.1	3.2	1.3	1.6	73	37	18	18	1,117	1,070	1,010
Guam...............	20	16	2.8	1.8	288	210	51	27	1,302	1,428	1,178
Northern Mariana Islands................	3.9	2.9	0.7	0.4	42	28	10	4.0	977	1,117	933
Puerto Rico...........	828	583	95	150	11,431	7,395	1,685	2,351	1,225	1,351	1,092
U.S. Virgin Islands......	22	19	1.8	1.4	392	327	40	25	1,608	1,561	1,439
Abroad..............	704	582	112	10	7,894	5,693	2,033	168	1,016	1,552	1,020

NA Not available. [1] Data for 1990-2006 include special benefits for persons age 72 years and over not insured under regular or transitional provisions of Social Security Act. [2] Unnegotiated checks not deducted. [3] Excludes persons with special benefits. [4] Nondisabled only. [5] Includes those with state or area unknown. [6] 2023 data are preliminary.

Source: U.S. Social Security Administration, *Annual Statistical Supplement to the Social Security Bulletin, 2024*, and earlier reports. See also <www.ssa.gov/policy/index.html>.

Table 580. Social Security Trust Funds: 1990 to 2023

[In billions of dollars (286.7 represents $286,700,000,000). Trust fund operations and asset reserves reflect the 12 months of benefits scheduled for payment in each year]

Type of trust fund	1990	2000	2010	2018	2019	2020	2021	2022	2023
OLD-AGE AND SURVIVORS INSURANCE (OASI)									
Total income [1]	286.7	490.5	677.1	831.0	917.9	968.3	942.9	1,056.7	1,166.9
Net payroll tax contributions	266.1	421.4	544.8	715.9	805.1	856.0	838.2	945.9	1,054.1
Taxation of benefits	4.8	11.6	22.1	34.5	34.9	39.0	37.2	47.1	49.8
Interest received [2]	16.4	57.5	108.2	80.7	77.9	73.3	67.5	63.5	63.0
Total expenditures [1]	227.5	358.3	584.9	853.5	911.4	961.0	1,001.9	1,097.5	1,237.3
Benefit payments [3]	223.0	352.7	577.4	844.9	902.8	952.4	993.1	1,088.1	1,227.4
Asset reserves, end of year	214.2	931.0	2,429.0	2,797.9	2,804.3	2,811.7	2,752.6	2,711.9	2,641.5
DISABILITY INSURANCE (DI)									
Total income [1]	28.8	77.9	104.0	172.3	143.9	149.7	145.5	165.1	183.8
Net payroll tax contributions	28.4	71.1	92.5	169.2	139.4	145.3	142.4	160.7	179.0
Taxation of benefits	0.1	0.7	1.9	0.5	1.6	1.7	0.5	1.6	1.0
Interest received [2]	0.9	6.9	9.3	2.6	2.9	2.8	2.6	2.8	3.8
Total expenditures [1]	25.6	56.8	127.7	146.8	147.9	146.3	142.6	146.5	154.8
Benefit payments [3]	24.8	55.0	124.2	143.7	145.1	143.6	140.1	143.6	151.9
Asset reserves, end of year	11.1	118.5	179.9	97.1	93.1	96.6	99.4	118.0	147.0

[1] Includes other income or expenses not shown separately. [2] Includes relatively small amounts of gifts to the fund. [3] Includes payments for vocational rehabilitation services furnished to disabled persons receiving benefits because of their disabilities. Amounts reflect deductions for unnegotiated benefit checks.

Source: U.S. Social Security Administration, Office of the Chief Actuary, "Statistical Tables," <www.ssa.gov/oact/STATS/index.html>, accessed March 2024.

Table 581. Retirement Employee Benefit Participation by Worker Characteristics: 2010 to 2023

[In percent. Based on National Compensation Survey (NCS). The March 2023 NCS obtained data from 6,990 private industry establishments of all sizes, representing approximately 126.23 million workers; see Appendix III. Defined benefit plans provide retirement benefits based on employer benefit formulas that may take into account salary, years of service, and age. Defined contribution plans provide benefits based on employer and employee contributions to individual employee accounts and the rate of return on money invested; the retirement benefit depends on the account balance at retirement. See source for more information]

Characteristic	Total [1]				Defined benefit				Defined contribution			
	2010	2020	2022	2023	2010	2020	2022	2023	2010	2020	2022	2023
All workers	**50**	**51**	**52**	**53**	**19**	**11**	**11**	**11**	**41**	**47**	**48**	**49**
Management, professional, and related	68	71	73	74	25	16	15	14	60	68	70	72
Service	23	25	24	25	7	5	5	4	18	22	21	23
Sales and office	53	52	50	51	16	9	8	7	46	49	47	50
Natural resources, construction, and maintenance	51	48	50	54	26	17	18	18	40	41	43	46
Production, transportation, and material moving	51	54	55	55	24	14	16	16	38	47	47	46
Full-time	59	61	62	63	22	14	14	13	50	57	58	59
Part-time	21	20	20	22	8	5	5	5	15	17	17	19
Union	82	82	84	84	67	54	56	58	44	51	53	53
Nonunion	46	48	49	50	13	8	7	7	41	47	47	49

[1] Total is less than the sum of the individual retirement items because many employees participate in both types of plans.

Source: U.S. Bureau of Labor Statistics, Annual Summary on Benefit Coverage, *National Compensation Survey: Employee Benefits in the United States, March 2023*, September 2023, and previous editions. See also <bls.gov/ebs/home.htm>.

Table 582. Households Owning Individual Retirement Accounts (IRAs): 2000 to 2023

[In percent. Based on the source's Annual Mutual Fund Shareholder Tracking Survey. Prior to 2014, the survey was based on a sample of landline telephone numbers only. In 2014, the survey implemented a revised sampling and weighting methodology, including a sample of landline and cellular telephone numbers. Beginning 2022, the survey switched to a self-administered online survey, and includes a revised sampling and weighting methodology and an increased sample size. The 2023 survey is based on a sample of 6,073 households. See source indicated in footnote 4 for details]

Year and characteristic	Any type of IRA [1]	Traditional IRA	Roth IRA	Employer-sponsored IRA [2]	Year and characteristic	Any type of IRA [1]	Traditional IRA	Roth IRA	Employer-sponsored IRA [2]
2000	35.7	28.7	9.2	6.8	2021 [3]	36.7	28.2	21.0	6.6
2005	37.9	30.0	12.8	7.4	2022 [3, 4]	41.9	31.2	24.6	3.7
2010	41.4	32.8	16.6	8.0	**2023, total [4, 5]**	**42.2**	**31.3**	**24.3**	**3.8**
2015 [3]	32.3	24.4	16.3	5.4	Under 35 years	34.0	17.0	26.0	3.0
2017 [3]	34.8	27.8	19.7	6.0	35 to 44 years	36.0	21.0	24.0	4.0
2018 [3]	33.4	26.0	17.6	5.9	45 to 54 years	39.0	28.0	27.0	4.0
2019 [3]	36.1	28.1	19.4	6.1	55 to 64 years	44.0	35.0	25.0	4.0
2020 [3]	37.3	28.6	20.5	6.7	65 years and over	53.0	48.0	21.0	4.0

[1] Excludes ownership of Coverdell Education Savings Accounts, which were referred to as Education IRAs before July 2001. [2] Employer-sponsored IRAs include SEP IRAs, SAR-SEP IRAs, and SIMPLE IRAs. [3] Beginning 2014, fluctuating incidence likely results in part from a revised sampling methodology. See source for details. [4] Beginning 2022, data are not directly comparable to data from earlier surveys due to changes in survey sampling and weighting methodology. For details, see "The Role in IRAs in US Households' Saving for Retirement, 2022," *ICI Research Perspective* 29, No. 1, February 2023, <www.ici.org/system/files/2023-02/per29-01_0.pdf>; and "Ownership of Mutual Funds and Shareholder Sentiment, 2023," *ICI Research Perspective* 29, No. 10, October 2023, <www.ici.org/files/2023/per29-10.pdf>. [5] Age is based on the age of the sole or co-decision maker for household saving and investing.

Source: Investment Company Institute, Washington, DC, Holden, Sarah, and Daniel Schrass, "Supplemental Tables: The Role of IRAs in US Households' Saving for Retirement, 2023," ICI Research Perspective 30, No. 1, February 2024 ©. See also <www.ici.org/research/retirement>.

Table 583. State and Local Government Retirement Systems—Beneficiaries and Finances: 2020 to 2023

[In billions of dollars (238.8 represents $238,800,000,000), except as indicated. For fiscal years closed during the 12 months ending June 30. Covers public employee pension systems classified as defined benefit plans. Based on the Annual Survey of Public Pensions. For state-administered pension plans, each pension fund is treated as a separate unit of analysis rather than as part of a larger system]

Year and level of government	Number of bene-ficiaries (1,000)	Receipts			Earnings on invest-ments	Benefits and withdrawals			Cash and investment holdings
		Contributions				Total benefits paid	Admin-istrative costs	With-drawals	
		Total	Employee	Govern-ment					
2020: All systems.........	11,494	238.8	57.8	181.0	94.4	334.5	21.1	7.1	4,598.0
State-administered......	9,841	190.6	48.4	142.2	76.2	273.3	16.5	5.5	3,746.0
Locally administered....	1,653	48.2	9.4	38.8	18.3	61.2	4.6	1.6	852.1
2021: All systems.........	11,694	244.5	58.3	186.2	113.4	355.9	25.3	7.1	5,605.9
State-administered......	10,024	194.8	48.7	146.2	91.6	291.6	19.5	5.3	4,584.4
Locally administered....	1,670	49.6	9.6	40.1	21.8	64.3	5.8	1.8	1,021.5
2022: All systems.........	11,952	278.3	61.6	216.7	106.9	366.8	28.1	8.3	5,410.6
State-administered......	10,167	217.5	51.5	166.1	86.6	301.3	21.6	6.4	4,436.4
Locally administered....	1,786	60.7	10.1	50.7	20.3	65.5	6.5	1.9	974.2
2023: All systems......	**12,220**	**286.1**	**68.9**	**217.1**	**105.5**	**392.9**	**28.2**	**8.8**	**5,515.8**
State-administered......	10,492	234.4	58.1	176.3	85.6	321.5	21.5	7.1	4,550.5
Locally administered....	1,728	51.7	10.8	40.9	19.9	71.4	6.7	1.7	965.4

Source: U.S. Census Bureau, Annual Survey of Public Pensions, "Annual Survey of Public Pensions: State & Local Tables," <www.census.gov/programs-surveys/aspp.html>, accessed June 2024.

Table 584. Defined Benefit Retirement Plan Participation Among Workers by Plan Status: 2023

[In percent. All workers participating in defined benefit plans = 100 percent. Based on the March 2023 National Compensation Survey; survey drew responses from 6,990 private industry establishments of all sizes, representing about 126.23 million workers. Excludes farm and private households, the self-employed, Federal government, and establishments with no workers in the survey scope. For more information, see Appendix III, and source]

Characteristic	Open plans [1]	Frozen plans [2]				
		All participants accrue benefits	Some participants accrue benefits	No participants accrue benefits [3]	Workers in plans frozen 11 to 15 years	Workers in plans frozen over 15 years
All workers.................	**60**	**22**	**3**	**14**	**41**	**33**
OCCUPATION						
Management, professional, and related.........................	50	22	5	22	48	28
Management, business, and financial.........................	49	21	5	25	46	25
Professional and related.................................	51	23	6	20	50	30
Service...	77	(NA)	(NA)	8	39	(NA)
Sales and office...	46	25	3	26	40	33
Sales and related.......................................	49	20	1	30	46	47
Office and administrative support........................	45	27	4	24	38	29
Natural resources, construction, and maintenance............	78	18	1	3	26	50
Construction, extraction, farming, fishing, and forestry.......	87	11	(NA)	(NA)	(NA)	67
Installation, maintenance, and repair.......................	65	28	3	4	35	42
Production, transportation, and material moving...............	65	26	2	7	33	39
Production..	40	39	6	15	27	43
Transportation and material moving........................	74	21	1	4	39	35
WORK STATUS						
Full time...	58	23	4	16	40	34
Part time..	76	21	1	3	55	26
UNION STATUS						
Union...	80	15	1	4	37	36
Nonunion...	45	28	6	22	42	32
AVERAGE WAGE PERCENTILE [4]						
Lowest 25 percent.......................................	71	25	(NA)	(NA)	64	17
Lowest 10 percent.......................................	87	13	(NA)	(NA)	80	(NA)
Second 25 percent.......................................	63	22	1	13	40	25
Third 25 percent...	59	22	4	14	34	41
Highest 25 percent.......................................	57	22	4	17	43	32
Highest 10 percent.......................................	45	26	5	24	47	35
INDUSTRY						
Goods-producing industries...............................	53	29	7	12	41	38
Manufacturing...	31	42	10	17	44	36
Service-providing industries..............................	62	20	2	15	41	31
Trade, transportation, and utilities.........................	69	25	2	4	35	37
Information..	43	30	(NA)	28	38	59
Financial activities.......................................	39	22	1	38	43	16
Professional and business services.........................	62	(NA)	(NA)	18	44	43
Education and health services.............................	67	15	4	14	43	24

NA Not available. [1] Plans open to new participants. [2] New employees are not allowed in the plan. Benefit accruals may continue for existing participants. [3] Participants in these plans stopped accruing benefits on the date the plan was frozen. The benefit the employee receives is calculated as of the day the plan was frozen. [4] Based on the average wage for the occupation, which may include workers with earnings both above and below the threshold. For values, see "Technical Note" in source.

Source: U.S. Bureau of Labor Statistics, Annual Summary on Benefit Coverage, *National Compensation Survey: Employee Benefits in the United States, March 2023*, September 2023. See also <www.bls.gov/ebs/>.

Table 585. Private Pension Plans—Summary by Type of Plan: 2000 to 2021

[In units as indicated (735.7 represents 735,700). Excludes "one-participant plans." Pension plans include defined benefit plans and defined contribution plans. A defined benefit plan, funded by the employer, promises a specific monthly benefit at retirement, often determined by a formula that includes factors such as salary, age, and job tenure. A defined contribution plan requires the employee to make contributions to an individual account; employers may add contributions to accounts for each employee. The retirement benefit is dependent upon the account balance at retirement, which will reflect contributions, investment gains or losses, and fees charged to the account. Employee Stock Ownership Plans (ESOP) and 401(k) plans are included among defined contribution plans. Data are based on Form 5500 series reports filed with the Department of Labor and exclude (1) selected pension plans qualified under sections 403(b), 457(b) and 457(f) of the Internal Revenue Code, (2) most SARSEP, SEP and SIMPLE IRA plans, (3) unfunded excess benefit plans, (4) selected church plans, (5) unfunded pension plan for select group of management or highly compensated employees, (6) individual retirement accounts (IRAs), and (7) governmental plans. See source for changes in methodology over time]

Item	Unit	Total				Defined benefit plan				Defined contribution plan			
		2000	2010	2020	2021	2000	2010	2020	2021	2000	2010	2020	2021
Number of plans	1,000	735.7	701.0	746.6	765.1	48.8	46.5	46.6	46.4	686.9	654.5	700.0	718.7
Total participants [1]	Million	103.3	129.7	142.3	146.2	41.6	41.4	31.9	31.2	61.7	88.3	110.4	114.9
Active participants [2]	Million	73.1	90.6	97.3	99.5	22.2	17.2	12.0	11.6	50.9	73.4	85.3	87.9
Assets [3]	Bil. dol.	4,203	6,282	11,909	13,170	1,986	2,448	3,544	3,670	2,216	3,833	8,365	9,499
Contributions [4]	Bil. dol.	232	445	694	733	33	131	108	76	199	314	586	657
Benefits [5]	Bil. dol.	341	457	960	1,055	128	170	257	278	214	287	704	777

[1] Includes active, retired, and separated vested participants not yet in pay status. Also includes double counting of workers in more than one plan. [2] Active participants includes individuals who are eligible to elect to have the employer make payments to a 401(k) type plan (even if individuals are not contributing) and nonvested individuals who are earning or retaining credited service under the plan. [3] Asset amounts shown exclude funds held by life insurance companies under allocated group insurance contracts for payment of retirement benefits. [4] Includes both employer and employee contributions. [5] Includes benefits paid directly from trust funds and premium payments made from plans to insurance carriers. Excludes benefits paid directly by insurance carriers.

Source: U.S. Department of Labor, Employee Benefits Security Administration, Retirement Bulletins, *Private Pension Plan Bulletin Historical Tables and Graphs, 1975-2021,* September 2023.

Table 586. Characteristics of U.S. Households Owning Individual Retirement Accounts (IRAs): 2023

[Data are based on a 2023 mutual fund shareholder tracking survey of 6,073 households, and a 2023 IRA owners survey of 3,255 U.S. households owning traditional or Roth IRAs; both surveys were conducted via a self-administered survey online]

Characteristic	Unit	Households owning IRAs				House-holds not own-ing IRAs
		Total	Tradi-tional IRA	Roth IRA	Employer-spon-sored [1]	
MEDIAN PER HOUSEHOLD						
Age of household sole or co-decision maker for saving & investing	Years	57	62	52	55	49
Household income [2]	Dollars	110,000	112,500	112,500	120,000	55,000
Household financial assets [3]	Dollars	375,000	500,000	400,000	375,000	20,000
Household financial assets in traditional or Roth IRAs	Dollars	100,000	175,000	100,000	(NA)	(X)
Share of household financial assets in type of IRA indicated	Percent	36	33	17	(NA)	(X)
PERCENT OF HOUSEHOLDS						
Household has defined contribution account or defined benefit plan coverage (total) [4]	Percent	85	81	86	78	55
Defined contribution retirement plan account	Percent	75	69	78	70	47
Defined benefit plan coverage	Percent	42	41	40	35	23
Types of IRAs owned: [4]						
Traditional IRA	Percent	74	100	60	52	(X)
Roth IRA	Percent	57	46	100	47	(X)
Employer-sponsored IRA [1]	Percent	9	6	7	100	(X)

X Not applicable. NA Not available. [1] Employer-sponsored IRAs include SEP IRAs, SAR-SEP IRAs, and SIMPLE IRAs. [2] Total reported is household income before taxes in 2022. [3] Household financial assets include assets in employer-sponsored retirement plans but exclude the household's primary residence. [4] Multiple responses are included.

Source: Investment Company Institute, Washington, DC. Holden, Sarah, and Daniel Schrass, "Supplemental Tables: The Role of IRAs in US Households' Saving for Retirement, 2023," ICI Research Perspective 30, No. 1, February 2024 ©. See also <www.ici.org/research/retirement>.

Table 587. Households with Assets in Individual Retirement Accounts (IRAs) by Type of IRA: 2022 and 2023

[Shown as percent of households with assets in IRAs, by household asset size group. Data are based on an annual survey of approximately 3,200 U.S. households owning traditional IRAs and Roth IRAs, conducted via a self-administered survey online. The IRA Owners Survey excludes households owning only employer-sponsored IRAs (SEP, SAR-SEP, and SIMPLE IRAs) or Coverdell Education Savings Accounts]

Size of assets	Unit	2022			2023		
		Total assets in IRAs	Type of IRA owned		Total assets in IRAs	Type of IRA owned	
			Traditional IRAs	Roth IRAs		Traditional IRAs	Roth IRAs
ASSETS IN TYPE OF IRA							
Less than $10,000	Percent	15	13	22	13	11	21
$10,000 to $24,999	Percent	11	11	20	11	11	18
$25,000 to $49,999	Percent	10	11	14	10	11	14
$50,000 to $99,999	Percent	14	15	18	14	14	18
$100,000 to $249,999	Percent	19	20	16	19	21	17
$250,000 or more	Percent	31	30	10	33	32	12
TOTAL ASSETS IN IRAs							
Mean	Dollars	235,700	227,200	95,900	252,480	238,060	106,250
Median	Dollars	100,000	90,000	40,000	100,000	100,000	42,500

Source: Investment Company Institute, Washington, DC. Holden, Sarah, and Daniel Schrass, "Supplemental Tables: The Role of IRAs in US Households' Saving for Retirement, 2023," ICI Research Perspective 30, No. 1, February 2024, and previous edition ©. See also <www.ici.org/research/retirement>.

Table 588. Defined Contribution 401(k) Type Plans, Active Participants, Assets, Contributions, Benefits, and Return Rates: 1990 to 2021

[Participants in thousands (19,466 represents 19,466,000); values in millions of dollars (384,854 represents $384,854,000,000). Excludes "one-participant plans." Based on Form 5500 filings with Department of Labor. See source for changes in methodology over time]

Year	Number of 401(k) type plans	Active participants [1] (1,000)	Total assets [2] (mil. dol.)	Total contributions [3] (mil. dol.)	Total benefits [4] (mil. dol.)	Investment rates of return [5]
1990	97,614	19,466	384,854	48,998	32,028	(NA)
1995	200,813	27,759	863,918	87,416	62,163	(NA)
2000	348,053	39,847	1,724,549	169,238	172,211	-3.8
2005	436,207	54,623	2,395,792	223,533	189,822	6.3
2010	518,675	60,510	3,142,141	267,584	245,474	12.0
2011	513,496	61,371	3,146,851	285,679	252,692	0.1
2012	516,293	63,088	3,530,122	306,092	284,677	11.2
2013	527,047	64,495	4,179,351	327,886	328,680	18.3
2014	533,769	62,651	4,399,891	349,216	365,657	6.7
2015	546,896	65,307	4,382,033	377,743	385,907	0.1
2016	560,373	67,121	4,738,481	398,920	391,540	7.6
2017	571,841	68,187	5,476,365	429,440	425,013	15.8
2018	588,499	70,335	5,229,194	464,578	473,790	-4.5
2019	604,424	72,202	6,242,230	499,522	519,038	20.1
2020	621,509	72,214	7,068,770	517,108	614,814	14.1
2021	644,671	74,905	8,020,485	582,681	680,261	14.9

NA Not available. [1] Since 2005, includes individuals who are eligible to elect to have the employer make payments to a 401(k) type plan (even if individuals are not contributing), and nonvested individuals who are earning or retaining credited service under the plan. Prior to 2005, active participants were adjusted to exclude individuals who were not contributing to the retirement plan and not entitled to receive benefits. Between 2009 and 2013, all participants reported on the Form 5500-SF were assumed to be active. Since 2014, active participants are separately reported on the Form 5500-SF. [2] Excludes funds held by life insurance companies under allocated group insurance contracts for payment of retirement benefits. [3] Includes both employer and employee contributions. [4] Includes both benefits paid directly from trust funds and premium payments made by plans to insurance carriers. Amounts exclude benefits paid directly by insurance carriers. [5] For plans with 100 or more participants.

Source: U.S. Department of Labor, Employee Benefits Security Administration, Retirement Bulletins, *Private Pension Plan Bulletin Historical Tables and Graphs, 1975-2021*, September 2023. See also <www.dol.gov/agencies/ebsa/researchers/statistics/retirement-bulletins/private-pension-plan>.

Table 589. Individual Retirement Arrangement (IRA) Contributions and Fair Market Value for Taxpayers by Adjusted Gross Income: 2020

[22,134 represents $22,134,000,000; average contributions and values in whole dollars. Based on information reported on matched samples of IRS Forms 1040, 1099-R, and 5498. Data are based on a sample. Totals may not add due to rounding]

Adjusted gross income class [1]	Contributions			End-of-year fair market value		
	Number of taxpayers	Total contributions (mil. dol.)	Average contribution (dol.)	Number of taxpayers	Total value (mil. dol.)	Average value (dol.)
TRADITIONAL IRA PLANS						
All taxpayers	**4,961,960**	**22,134**	**4,461**	**50,723,742**	**10,721,942**	**211,379**
No adjusted gross income [2]	51,544	199	3,862	755,502	114,783	151,929
$1 to $4,999	25,109	49	1,966	1,032,200	100,067	96,946
$5,000 to $9,999	47,513	106	2,237	1,183,959	119,571	100,993
$10,000 to $14,999	70,853	198	2,797	1,427,630	149,015	104,380
$15,000 to $19,999	77,343	238	3,075	1,284,779	131,014	101,974
$20,000 to $24,999	98,412	341	3,460	1,442,250	149,541	103,686
$25,000 to $29,999	121,447	413	3,401	1,509,840	176,321	116,781
$30,000 to $39,999	250,833	772	3,080	2,966,811	335,684	113,146
$40,000 to $49,999	268,928	910	3,385	2,962,636	394,726	133,235
$50,000 to $74,999	574,546	2,247	3,911	6,899,071	1,050,330	152,242
$75,000 to $99,999	506,996	1,945	3,837	6,189,951	1,118,754	180,737
$100,000 to $199,999	1,325,385	5,985	4,515	14,219,665	3,463,145	243,546
$200,000 to $499,999	1,080,454	5,872	5,435	6,861,376	2,435,567	354,968
$500,000 to $999,999	313,541	1,918	6,119	1,320,127	602,801	456,624
$1,000,000 or more	149,054	939	6,303	667,946	380,622	569,839
ROTH IRA PLANS						
All taxpayers	**9,210,723**	**32,982**	**3,581**	**23,604,965**	**1,233,130**	**52,240**
No adjusted gross income [2]	91,605	337	3,683	332,820	20,548	61,740
$1 to $4,999	178,229	349	1,958	392,775	10,664	27,149
$5,000 to $9,999	232,873	652	2,799	447,065	11,902	26,622
$10,000 to $14,999	224,114	671	2,996	458,547	11,901	25,953
$15,000 to $19,999	257,984	721	2,795	527,741	18,538	35,127
$20,000 to $24,999	236,023	511	2,165	520,457	13,336	25,623
$25,000 to $29,999	297,596	798	2,683	586,599	16,143	27,520
$30,000 to $39,999	567,849	1,507	2,654	1,152,080	33,059	28,695
$40,000 to $49,999	614,375	1,812	2,950	1,248,923	44,114	35,322
$50,000 to $74,999	1,453,755	4,954	3,408	3,058,274	111,288	36,389
$75,000 to $99,999	1,273,706	4,751	3,730	2,906,052	125,563	43,208
$100,000 to $199,999	3,246,708	13,741	4,232	7,481,062	393,355	52,580
$200,000 to $499,999	495,578	1,986	4,007	3,572,045	265,868	74,430
$500,000 to $999,999	30,624	141	4,612	632,164	72,247	114,285
$1,000,000 or more	9,705	51	5,220	288,362	84,605	293,400

[1] For joint returns, both taxpayers are placed into the same adjusted gross income class, as determined by the total amount on the return. [2] Includes deficits.

Source: U.S. Internal Revenue Service, Statistics of Income, "SOI Tax Stats – Accumulation and Distribution of Individual Retirement Arrangements (IRA)," <www.irs.gov/statistics/soi-tax-stats-accumulation-and-distribution-of-individual-retirement-arrangements>, accessed June 2023.

Table 590. State Unemployment Insurance—Summary: 2000 to 2022

[In units as indicated (2,110 represents 2,110,000). Includes unemployment compensation for state and local government employees where covered by state law]

Item	Unit	2000	2010	2016	2017	2018	2019	2020	2021	2022
Insured unemployment, average weekly.........	1,000	2,110	4,487	2,099	1,948	1,755	1,684	10,093	3,191	1,503
Percent of covered employment [1]...............	Percent	1.7	3.6	1.5	1.4	1.2	1.2	7.4	2.3	1.0
Insured unemployment as percent of total unemployment, annual...................	Percent	18.5	15.1	13.5	14.0	13.9	14.0	39.0	18.5	12.5
Unemployment benefits, average weekly........	Dollars	221	299	344	351	356	369	319	350	401
Percent of weekly wage.........................	Percent	32.9	33.7	33.7	33.3	32.7	32.7	26	26.9	29.9
Weeks compensated..............................	Million	96.0	203.1	94.8	87.6	79.3	76.0	470.8	135.8	62.0
Beneficiaries, first payments.....................	1,000	7,033	10,727	6,097	5,696	5,167	5,125	30,829	7,631	4,363
Average duration of benefits [2]....................	Weeks	13.7	18.9	15.5	15.4	15.3	14.8	15.3	17.8	14.2
Claimants exhausting benefits....................	1,000	2,144	6,365	2,324	2,120	1,928	1,760	11,436	4,742	1,518
Exhaustion rate (percent of first payments) [3]...	Percent	31.8	53.4	36.3	35.4	35.5	34.7	43.2	40.3	31.2
Contributions collected [4].........................	Bil. dol.	19.9	35.9	38.9	36.8	34.9	33.6	31.6	38.6	42.6
Benefits paid...................................	Bil. dol.	19.4	53.9	29.5	27.8	25.6	25.5	129.8	38.4	21.9
Unemployment trust fund reserves [5].............	Bil. dol.	54.1	9.5	47.0	55.2	66.6	75.7	24.7	39.1	55.9
Average employer tax rate as percent of taxable wages...................	Percent	1.8	3.0	2.4	2.2	2.0	1.9	1.7	1.9	1.7

[1] Insured unemployment as percent of average covered employment. [2] Weeks compensated during the year divided by the number of first payments. May include more than one period of continuous unemployment. [3] Percent of claimants who started receiving unemployment insurance benefits who also received the maximum benefits they were entitled to before the end of their benefit year. Based on first payments for 12-month period ending June 30. [4] Contributions collected through unemployment taxes paid by employers and by employees in states that tax workers. [5] Reserves as of December 31 are the funds on deposit in a State's account, as reported by the U.S. Treasury. Trust fund balances are the major portion of reserves. The reserves for all States have been adjusted to contain amounts loaned or advanced from the Federal Unemployment Account. These advances, which can be used only for the payment of unemployment benefits, must be repaid.

Source: U.S. Department of Labor, Employment and Training Administration, Unemployment Insurance Data, "Benefits and Claims: Annual Program and Financial Data (Handbook 394)," <oui.doleta.gov/unemploy/DataDashboard.asp>, accessed December 2023.

Table 591. State Unemployment Insurance by State and Island Area: 2022

[In units as indicated (4,362.7 represents 4,362,700). See headnote, Table 590. For state data on insured unemployment, see Table 662. Please note that temporary provisions made during the coronavirus disease 2019 (COVID-19) pandemic may have affected usual unemployment insurance procedures and reporting]

State and Island Area	Bene-ficiaries, first payments (1,000)	Benefits paid (mil. dol.)	Avg. weekly unemploy-ment benefits (dol.)	Average duration of benefits (weeks)	State and Island Area	Bene-ficiaries, first payments (1,000)	Benefits paid (mil. dol.)	Avg. weekly unemploy-ment benefits (dol.)	Average duration of benefits (weeks)
Total [1].....	4,362.7	21,852.3	401	14.2	MT..........	16.5	81.0	463	10.9
AL..........	30.9	59.7	249	7.7	NE..........	12.6	53.0	385	11.5
AK..........	12.7	55.7	286	16.6	NV..........	46.4	208.0	401	13.2
AZ..........	52.3	158.1	257	13.1	NH..........	8.2	25.3	335	9.4
AR..........	25.6	55.5	280	9.2	NJ..........	207.0	1,689.3	535	16.8
CA..........	889.9	4,559.2	342	16.3	NM..........	23.0	119.4	385	15.0
CO..........	68.2	374.8	483	12.5	NY..........	352.8	1,878.0	395	17.5
CT..........	80.5	369.4	431	12.7	NC..........	57.1	133.7	279	9.0
DE..........	9.3	34.9	303	15.3	ND..........	10.5	57.3	498	12.2
DC..........	9.2	46.8	395	16.1	OH..........	117.6	562.1	427	12.2
FL..........	140.4	311.0	252	9.8	OK..........	34.7	149.3	364	13.4
GA..........	92.2	123.9	323	9.7	OR..........	63.6	451.6	473	15.0
HI..........	19.7	141.6	541	15.5	PA..........	210.2	1,142.0	433	14.4
ID..........	23.8	69.4	392	8.8	RI..........	24.2	121.9	419	13.6
IL..........	227.9	1,379.9	441	15.0	SC..........	38.9	100.1	283	10.0
IN..........	62.5	177.3	296	11.1	SD..........	4.1	21.9	409	13.1
IA..........	51.6	234.1	476	10.7	TN..........	44.1	125.8	243	11.0
KS..........	23.5	80.5	435	10.3	TX..........	299.3	1,653.1	448	13.9
KY..........	27.0	179.7	398	18.5	UT..........	27.5	130.1	491	10.7
LA..........	27.3	109.6	222	15.9	VT..........	10.5	42.6	441	11.5
ME..........	15.6	82.3	406	13.5	VA..........	20.0	120.1	338	22.9
MD..........	52.0	334.8	360	16.4	WA..........	123.3	873.1	603	13.2
MA..........	156.8	1,136.8	603	16.1	WV..........	25.0	87.7	316	12.5
MI..........	172.0	629.3	354	10.5	WI..........	83.2	273.7	330	11.7
MN..........	106.6	793.9	521	15.7	WY..........	7.6	39.4	436	12.1
MS..........	17.0	23.6	217	10.4	PR..........	46.2	24.3	202	14.2
MO..........	53.2	157.8	276	11.9	VI..........	0.8	9.1	475	(NA)

NA Not available. [1] Includes all States, District of Columbia, Puerto Rico, and Virgin Islands.

Source: U.S. Department of Labor, Employment and Training Administration, Unemployment Insurance Data, "Benefits and Claims: Annual Program and Financial Data (Handbook 394)," <oui.doleta.gov/unemploy/DataDashboard.asp>, accessed December 2023.

Table 592. Workers' Compensation Costs and Payments: 2000 to 2021

[In units as indicated (127.1 represents 127,100,000). See headnote, Table 593]

Item	2000	2010	2013	2014	2015	2016	2017	2018	2019	2020	2021
Workers covered (mil.).........................	127.1	124.6	130.1	132.8	139.5	138.5	140.4	142.6	144.4	135.6	140.2
Covered wages (bil. dol.)......................	4,495	5,834	6,491	6,821	7,207	7,432	7,787	8,178	8,560	8,694	9,497
Employer costs [1] (bil. dol.)................	**62.4**	**74.9**	**91.8**	**96.6**	**99.2**	**100.2**	**101.8**	**102.1**	**100.7**	**92.0**	**96.0**
Private carriers..................................	36.9	43.8	56.4	58.8	60.8	61.7	62.5	62.2	61.2	56.7	57.1
State funds......................................	12.7	17.0	18.4	19.1	19.2	19.3	20.3	20.3	20.0	16.9	19.3
Self-insured employers........................	9.2	9.9	12.5	13.8	13.7	13.5	12.7	12.6	12.0	10.8	11.5
Federal programs [2]...........................	3.6	4.2	4.6	4.9	5.4	5.7	6.3	7.0	7.5	7.5	8.1
Benefits paid [2] (bil. dol.)..................	**47.7**	**58.5**	**63.8**	**63.6**	**63.1**	**62.7**	**62.8**	**63.0**	**63.1**	**59.4**	**60.0**
By private carriers..............................	26.9	31.1	35.4	35.3	34.7	34.8	34.9	35.0	35.4	32.9	32.9
From state funds................................	7.4	9.8	9.5	9.3	9.1	9.0	8.9	8.8	8.7	8.5	8.5
Self-insured employers........................	10.5	13.9	15.2	15.4	15.6	15.4	15.6	15.7	15.6	14.8	15.4
Federal programs [3]...........................	3.0	3.7	3.7	3.7	3.7	3.6	3.5	3.5	3.4	3.3	3.2
Type of benefit:											
Medical..	20.9	28.7	32.3	32.4	31.8	31.5	31.5	31.5	31.5	28.2	28.5
Cash...	26.8	29.8	31.5	31.2	31.3	31.2	31.3	31.5	31.6	31.2	31.5
Per $100 of covered wages: (dol.)											
Employer costs.................................	1.39	1.28	1.41	1.42	1.38	1.35	1.31	1.25	1.18	1.06	1.01
Benefits paid...................................	1.06	1.00	0.98	0.93	0.87	0.84	0.81	0.77	0.74	0.68	0.63

[1] Estimates of employer costs are equal to the sum of: premiums and deductibles paid to private insurers and state funds; benefits and administrative costs paid by self-insured employers; and assessments paid to special funds (e.g., second-injury funds). [2] Benefits are calendar-year payments to injured workers and to providers of their medical care, including benefits paid by employers through deductible policies. [3] Includes benefits paid plus administrative costs. Also includes costs to the Federal government under the Federal Employees' Compensation Act and employer costs associated with the Federal Black Lung Disability Trust fund, and employer costs associated with the Longshore and Harbor Workers' Compensation Act.

Source: National Academy of Social Insurance, Washington, DC, *Workers' Compensation: Benefits, Costs, and Coverage, 2021,* February 2024 ©. See also <www.nasi.org/research/workers-compensation-2/>.

Table 593. Workers' Compensation Payments by State: 2017 to 2021

[In millions of dollars (62,753 represents $62,753,000,000). Calendar-year data. Workers' compensation provides funding for medical care, rehabilitation, and wage replacement (cash benefits) for workers who are injured on the job or who contract work-related illnesses. It also pays benefits to families of workers who die of work-related causes. Workers' compensation benefits are paid by private insurance carriers, by state or federal workers' compensation funds, or by self-insured employers. See source for data estimation methodology]

State	2017	2018	2019	2020	2021	State	2017	2018	2019	2020	2021
Total....................	**62,753**	**63,007**	**63,095**	**59,402**	**60,039**	Missouri...................	977	990	1,013	1,011	968
						Montana..................	242	230	226	228	216
Alabama..................	601	643	670	615	608	Nebraska.................	311	319	318	305	312
Alaska....................	213	208	209	190	172	Nevada...................	358	392	401	394	409
Arizona...................	745	748	756	667	727	New Hampshire.........	210	210	210	208	199
Arkansas.................	278	248	237	220	224	New Jersey..............	2,438	2,451	2,499	2,272	2,374
California.................	12,206	12,322	12,462	11,874	12,428	New Mexico.............	298	302	321	288	268
Colorado..................	813	776	833	787	763	New York................	6,225	6,275	6,171	5,892	5,514
Connecticut..............	911	871	889	849	901	North Carolina..........	1,106	1,069	1,080	978	1,036
Delaware.................	217	241	192	187	188	North Dakota...........	157	149	107	107	107
District of Columbia.....	114	114	124	102	83	Ohio......................	1,801	1,770	1,729	1,563	1,609
Florida....................	3,921	3,843	3,844	3,589	3,540	Oklahoma................	577	512	479	476	474
Georgia...................	1,474	1,496	1,513	1,436	1,436	Oregon...................	679	666	699	689	732
Hawaii....................	325	358	384	363	379	Pennsylvania............	2,817	2,902	2,882	2,715	2,704
Idaho.....................	283	291	316	289	305	Rhode Island............	149	148	158	144	128
Illinois...................	2,350	2,259	2,197	1,966	1,968	South Carolina..........	932	975	1,027	1,073	1,011
Indiana...................	596	578	606	581	569	South Dakota...........	130	119	121	124	115
Iowa......................	659	655	603	577	582	Tennessee...............	662	624	659	623	658
Kansas...................	407	400	418	410	402	Texas.....................	1,426	1,536	1,519	1,349	1,345
Kentucky.................	538	572	551	511	515	Utah......................	267	265	284	261	268
Louisiana.................	871	902	880	762	800	Vermont..................	144	139	144	122	131
Maine.....................	256	262	253	237	230	Virginia...................	982	933	885	761	789
Maryland.................	958	977	923	811	807	Washington.............	2,463	2,536	2,614	2,619	2,782
Massachusetts..........	1,169	1,216	1,241	1,176	1,294	West Virginia............	412	431	405	376	359
Michigan..................	917	909	894	790	801	Wisconsin................	1,168	1,195	1,223	1,061	1,073
Minnesota................	1,018	1,055	1,067	1,039	1,044	Wyoming.................	176	165	180	168	165
Mississippi...............	318	304	305	299	311	**Federal, total [1]**........	**3,483**	**3,455**	**3,375**	**3,265**	**3,218**

[1] Federal benefits include: those paid under the Federal Employees' Compensation Act for civilian employees; the portion of the black lung benefit program that is financed by employers; and a portion of benefits under the Longshore and Harbor Workers' Compensation Act (LHWCA) that are not reflected in state data, namely, benefits paid by self-insured employers and by special funds under the LHWCA. See Appendix B in source for more information about federal programs.

Source: National Academy of Social Insurance, Washington, DC, *Workers' Compensation: Benefits, Costs, and Coverage, 2021,* February 2024 ©. See also <www.nasi.org/research/workers-compensation-2/>.

Table 594. Supplemental Security Income (SSI)—Recipients and Payments: 1990 to 2022

[In units as indicated (4,817 represents 4,817,000). Recipients and monthly payment as of December; total payments for the calendar year. Recipients include persons with a federal SSI payment and/or state supplementation. Payments are federally administered, including both federal SSI and federally administered state supplementation]

Program	Unit	1990	2000	2010	2015	2018	2019	2020	2021	2022
Recipients, total	**1,000**	**4,817**	**6,602**	**7,912**	**8,310**	**8,129**	**8,077**	**7,960**	**7,696**	**7,542**
Aged	1,000	1,454	1,289	1,184	1,157	1,169	1,167	1,136	1,116	1,138
Blind	1,000	84	79	69	68	69	69	68	66	64
Disabled	1,000	3,279	5,234	6,659	7,084	6,891	6,841	6,756	6,515	6,340
Payments, total[1]	**Mil. dol.**	**16,133**	**30,672**	**48,195**	**54,966**	**54,847**	**55,852**	**56,285**	**55,538**	**55,772**
Aged	Mil. dol.	3,559	4,540	5,454	5,729	5,924	6,070	6,139	6,099	6,358
Blind	Mil. dol.	329	386	423	448	463	476	482	480	494
Disabled	Mil. dol.	12,245	25,746	42,317	48,788	48,460	49,307	49,664	48,960	48,921
Average monthly payment	**Dollars**	**276**	**379**	**501**	**541**	**551**	**566**	**576**	**584**	**622**
Aged	Dollars	208	300	400	428	437	449	458	464	496
Blind	Dollars	319	413	522	558	569	583	592	600	645
Disabled	Dollars	303	398	518	560	570	585	595	605	645

[1] Totals for Aged, Blind, and Disabled are derived. The derivation creates slight discrepancies summing to total.

Source: U.S. Social Security Administration, *Annual Statistical Supplement to the Social Security Bulletin, 2023*, November 2023; and *SSI Annual Statistical Report, 2022,* December 2023. See also <www.ssa.gov/policy/docs/statcomps/supplement/index.html> and <www.ssa.gov/policy/docs/statcomps/ssi_asr/index.html>.

Table 595. Supplemental Security Income (SSI)—Recipients and Payments by State and Other Area: 2010 to 2022

[In units as indicated (7,912 represents 7,912,000). Recipients as of December; payments for calendar year. Data cover federally administered payments, which includes federal SSI payments and federally administered state supplementation]

State and other area	Recipients (1,000)			Payments (mil. dol.)			State and other area	Recipients (1,000)			Payments (mil. dol.)		
	2010	2020	2022	2010	2020	2022		2010	2020	2022	2010	2020	2022
Total[1]	**7,912**	**7,960**	**7,542**	**48,195**	**56,285**	**55,772**	MO	134	135	129	785	914	928
U.S.	**7,911**	**7,959**	**7,541**	**48,189**	**56,278**	**55,764**	MT	18	17	16	98	115	115
AL	172	157	147	996	1,067	1,052	NE	26	29	28	144	194	204
AK	12	12	11	70	82	82	NV	41	56	54	241	401	400
AZ	110	119	112	644	834	826	NH	18	18	17	103	119	117
AR	107	103	96	603	712	709	NJ	169	174	165	1,001	1,195	94
CA	1,269	1,194	1,133	8,870	9,417	9,875	NM	60	61	56	340	407	398
CO	66	72	68	377	491	494	NY	681	602	573	4,445	4,208	4,180
CT	58	67	65	340	465	480	NC	219	228	217	1,243	1,559	1,555
DE	16	17	16	91	122	123	ND	8	8	8	43	54	54
DC	24	25	24	153	187	189	OH	286	306	292	1,784	2,182	2,200
FL	484	575	548	2,760	3,922	3,945	OK	94	96	92	541	667	681
GA	228	258	249	1,317	1,780	1,812	OR	75	88	84	439	621	627
HI	25	22	21	157	161	161	PA	358	348	329	2,229	2,521	2,533
ID	27	31	28	155	208	207	RI	33	32	31	201	220	219
IL	273	260	245	1,662	1,838	1,844	SC	112	114	107	635	778	769
IN	118	127	122	716	908	926	SD	14	15	14	75	96	99
IA	48	52	49	266	345	344	TN	175	173	163	1,023	1,195	1,196
KS	46	47	46	269	325	337	TX	617	633	594	3,316	4,182	4,165
KY	192	168	156	1,116	1,148	1,143	UT	28	31	30	160	219	225
LA	175	170	161	989	1,182	1,188	VT	15	15	14	87	103	102
ME	35	36	34	196	239	241	VA	148	155	148	832	1,062	1,081
MD	107	120	115	658	876	882	WA	137	147	138	881	1,062	1,057
MA	193	179	168	1,211	1,219	1,214	WV	80	69	65	472	480	477
MI	254	266	251	1,581	1,913	1,923	WI	107	116	109	625	810	808
MN	86	93	88	516	665	667	WY	6	7	7	35	46	48
MS	126	114	108	699	760	766	MP[2]	1	1	1	6	8	8

[1] Includes Northern Marianas and recipients whose residence was "unknown." Total may not equal sum due to rounding. [2] Northern Marianas.

Source: U.S. Social Security Administration, *Annual Statistical Supplement to the Social Security Bulletin, 2023*, November 2023, and previous editions. See also <www.ssa.gov/policy/docs/statcomps/supplement/index.html>.

Table 596. Temporary Assistance for Needy Families (TANF)—Families and Recipients: 1980 to 2023

[In thousands (3,712 represents 3,712,000). Average monthly families and recipients for the calendar year through 2018; beginning with 2019, data are shown for the fiscal year ending in September. Prior to TANF, the cash assistance program to families was called Aid to Families with Dependent Children (1980–1996). Under the Personal Responsibility and Work Opportunity Reconciliation Act of 1996, the program became TANF. See text, this section. Includes Puerto Rico, Guam, and Virgin Islands]

Year	Families	Recipients	Year	Families	Recipients	Year	Families	Recipients
1980	3,712	10,774	2008	1,633	3,795	2016	1,174	2,678
1990	4,057	11,695	2009	1,769	4,154	2017	1,075	2,486
2000	2,215	5,778	2010	1,858	4,403	2018	984	2,197
2003	2,024	4,929	2011	1,846	4,363	2019[1]	917	2,045
2004	1,979	4,748	2012	1,723	4,017	2020[1]	894	2,037
2005	1,894	4,469	2013	1,612	3,713	2021[1]	804	1,848
2006	1,777	4,148	2014	1,476	3,407	2022[1]	793	1,863
2007	1,674	3,897	2015	1,300	3,010	2023[1]	826	1,987

[1] Data are for the fiscal year ending in September of the year shown.

Source: U.S. Department of Health and Human Services, Administration for Children and Families, State TANF Data and Reports, "Caseload Data," <www.acf.hhs.gov/ofa/programs/tanf/data-reports>, accessed March 2024.

Table 597. Temporary Assistance for Needy Families (TANF)—Recipients by State and Island Area: 2020 to 2023

[In thousands (894.1 represents 894,100). Data are shown for the fiscal year ending in September. See headnote, Table 596]

State and Island Area	Families 2020	Families 2022	Families 2023	Recipients 2020	Recipients 2022	Recipients 2023	State and Island Area	Families 2020	Families 2022	Families 2023	Recipients 2020	Recipients 2022	Recipients 2023
Total [1]	894.1	793.2	825.9	2,036.5	1,862.8	1,986.6	MT	3.0	1.9	1.7	7.2	4.3	4.0
U.S.	889.4	789.1	822.9	2,023.6	1,851.8	1,978.3	NE	4.1	2.8	2.6	9.7	6.3	5.9
AL	7.2	5.7	5.6	16.2	12.7	13.0	NV	7.8	6.1	5.9	20.2	15.8	15.1
AK	2.3	1.6	1.1	6.0	4.1	3.0	NH	3.5	2.6	2.5	7.2	5.2	5.0
AZ	7.8	5.8	5.2	16.2	11.9	10.7	NJ	9.3	9.1	9.2	22.1	22.7	22.6
AR	2.3	1.2	0.9	5.2	2.6	2.2	NM	10.6	10.9	7.7	26.6	28.0	18.7
CA	277.8	269.5	306.9	688.4	712.6	824.6	NY	81.3	77.2	80.3	182.9	173.1	181.5
CO	13.9	11.8	12.1	34.2	28.5	29.4	NC	13.9	12.4	8.6	24.3	22.5	16.6
CT	7.3	4.7	5.1	15.3	10.1	11.7	ND	1.0	0.7	0.5	2.4	1.7	1.3
DE	3.0	2.8	3.0	8.3	7.8	8.4	OH	52.0	42.4	40.8	96.8	74.7	72.5
DC	7.4	5.5	3.5	21.6	16.6	9.1	OK	5.6	3.8	3.6	12.6	8.2	7.7
FL	40.5	27.5	36.1	68.7	44.6	72.7	OR	14.6	16.8	18.2	32.6	37.4	38.9
GA	8.5	6.4	5.0	15.5	12.4	8.8	PA	36.1	28.7	27.4	87.7	70.5	68.4
HI	5.0	4.5	3.1	14.4	13.3	8.6	RI	3.5	2.8	3.1	8.6	7.3	8.2
ID	1.9	1.5	1.5	2.8	2.2	2.1	SC	7.8	6.5	5.7	17.5	14.9	12.9
IL	10.7	10.2	10.1	21.2	20.3	20.6	SD	2.8	2.3	2.4	5.6	4.6	4.7
IN	6.3	4.4	4.6	13.7	9.4	10.3	TN	17.3	13.6	13.8	36.5	28.0	29.5
IA	7.2	4.8	4.4	16.9	11.6	10.6	TX	20.8	11.8	9.7	45.5	22.2	18.5
KS	4.1	3.1	2.8	4.1	3.1	2.8	UT	2.8	2.0	1.9	6.4	4.4	4.4
KY	15.6	11.7	11.6	31.3	23.5	24.1	VT	2.1	1.8	1.7	4.2	3.7	3.5
LA	3.6	3.3	4.5	8.6	7.8	11.4	VA	15.6	18.8	17.5	33.0	37.7	36.6
ME	3.4	3.4	3.6	8.1	8.4	9.1	WA	27.4	29.6	31.8	61.6	71.4	79.4
MD	20.4	15.5	15.2	50.3	41.3	44.9	WV	6.1	5.3	5.1	11.8	10.3	9.9
MA	29.4	32.0	34.6	67.2	75.7	82.5	WI	14.4	11.8	11.4	30.6	24.7	23.7
MI	13.6	8.5	8.7	34.9	22.0	23.1	WY	0.5	0.5	0.5	1.2	1.0	1.1
MN	15.1	14.4	13.7	35.2	33.8	30.5	GU	0.4	0.3	0.2	1.0	0.9	0.5
MS	2.6	1.6	1.6	4.8	2.5	2.7	PR	4.3	3.6	2.8	11.6	9.8	7.6
MO	8.6	5.6	4.9	19.7	12.5	11.2	VI	0.1	0.1	0.1	0.3	0.2	0.2

[1] Includes Guam (GU), Puerto Rico (PR), and the Virgin Islands (VI).

Source: U.S. Department of Health and Human Services, Administration for Children and Families, State TANF Data and Reports, "Caseload Data," <www.acf.hhs.gov/ofa/programs/tanf/data-reports>, accessed March 2024.

Table 598. Household Use of Community Food and Nutrition Assistance—Receipt of Free Groceries and Free Meals by Household Characteristics: 2022

[In thousands (132,073 represents 132,073,000), except percent. Based on the 2022 Current Population Survey Food Security Supplement that asked questions about the receipt of free groceries (from food pantry, food bank, church, or other place) and the receipt of free meals (from church, shelter, home-delivered meal service such as Meals on Wheels, or other place), among households with incomes below 185 percent of the Federal poverty level, and households above this level that indicated difficulty in meeting food needs. Data cover the receipt of free groceries or meals at least once during the 12-month period ended December 2022, for persons occupying housing units. The CPS excludes persons who are homeless, and may also miss persons in tenuous housing arrangements (such as temporarily living with another family). See source for more information]

Category	Free groceries Total households [1] (1,000)	Free groceries Number receiving (1,000)	Free groceries Percent receiving	Free meals Total households [1] (1,000)	Free meals Number receiving (1,000)	Free meals Percent receiving
All households	132,073	8,317	6.3	131,932	2,896	2.2
All persons in households	326,167	21,497	6.6	325,807	6,320	1.9
Adults in households	254,130	15,168	6.0	253,909	4,907	1.9
Children in households	72,038	6,328	8.8	71,899	1,413	2.0
Households by food security status: [2]						
Food-secure households	115,288	3,460	3.0	115,188	1,279	1.1
Food-insecure households	16,735	4,850	29.0	16,697	1,613	9.7
Households with low food security	10,068	2,453	24.4	10,052	719	7.2
Households with very low food security	6,667	2,396	35.9	6,645	894	13.5

[1] Totals exclude households that did not answer questions about the receipt of community food and nutrition assistance, and also households that did not answer questions about food security. [2] Food secure households report zero or 1-2 indications, typically anxiety over food sufficiency or supply, with little or no indication of changes in diets or food intake. Households with low food security report reduced quality, variety, or desirability of diet, with little or no indication of reduced food intake. Households with very low food security report multiple indications of disrupted eating patterns and reduced food intake.

Source: U.S. Department of Agriculture, Economic Research Service, *Statistical Supplement to Household Food Security in the United States in 2022*, October 2023. See also <www.ers.usda.gov/topics/food-nutrition-assistance/food-security-in-the-u-s/>.

Table 599. Temporary Assistance for Needy Families (TANF)—Expenditures by State: Fiscal Years 2020 to 2022

[In millions of dollars (28,984.0 represents $28,984,000,000). Represents federal and state funds expended in fiscal year. Negative values occur when contracted obligations are fulfilled or terminated and the actual cost for the service is less than the obligated amount. Expenditures on basic assistance include cash, payments, vouchers, and other forms of benefits designed to meet a family's ongoing basic needs (food, clothing, shelter, utilities, household goods, personal care items, and general incidental expenses)]

State	2020, Total	2021, Total	2022 Total [1]	2022 Expenditures on basic assistance	State	2020, Total	2021, Total	2022 Total [1]	2022 Expenditures on basic assistance
U.S.	28,984.0	28,037.9	29,230.4	7,223.0	MO	349.6	351.6	369.5	21.6
AL	176.4	177.1	168.7	12.8	MT	37.8	31.3	26.0	8.1
AK	78.5	67.0	60.0	31.8	NE	86.9	78.2	83.0	19.2
AZ	335.6	318.1	363.0	35.9	NV	110.9	115.4	118.6	31.1
AR	84.1	88.1	116.0	3.3	NH	79.6	68.4	60.3	26.6
CA	6,345.2	5,747.6	6,400.0	2,877.8	NJ	1,402.3	1,347.1	1,353.6	82.2
CO	446.4	422.3	396.5	61.4	NM	272.3	298.2	412.3	52.3
CT	479.1	449.2	525.7	24.5	NY	4,585.8	4,826.1	4,824.5	1,576.5
DE	126.3	98.0	149.3	7.2	NC	543.8	531.3	514.3	26.1
DC	312.4	425.3	297.7	172.8	ND	39.2	30.7	28.7	2.7
FL	783.5	770.5	672.7	117.0	OH	1,123.3	1,080.6	1,078.8	205.9
GA	482.5	450.2	459.7	85.1	OK	107.7	84.3	119.1	11.3
HI	211.0	198.4	169.4	33.0	OR	245.7	173.0	217.8	76.9
ID	35.9	33.0	35.4	6.3	PA	919.9	782.8	889.5	101.4
IL	1,156.3	1,148.9	1,186.9	42.9	RI	150.3	124.6	128.8	20.3
IN	271.5	225.8	207.2	13.7	SC	166.1	156.3	163.0	30.7
IA	152.0	143.5	147.4	24.3	SD	26.8	27.1	26.4	12.3
KS	166.9	151.4	149.3	10.3	TN	164.8	270.5	270.3	68.4
KY	263.7	220.5	218.1	162.6	TX	952.5	927.0	996.0	19.4
LA	197.5	206.9	240.0	20.8	UT	74.1	60.8	63.1	13.7
ME	110.5	115.4	135.1	37.4	VT	80.8	71.4	77.8	13.3
MD	522.6	579.9	614.6	74.4	VA	267.6	297.7	309.5	98.2
MA	1,014.4	965.7	1,040.7	296.8	WA	943.1	1,002.0	1,038.6	211.3
MI	1,255.8	1,160.2	1,245.1	99.0	WV	133.5	124.5	126.3	45.7
MN	515.9	441.6	404.7	109.0	WI	489.0	484.9	443.9	69.8
MS	76.8	57.3	60.1	4.3	WY	29.5	29.9	27.4	13.2

[1] In addition to basic assistance, TANF provides funding for numerous additional activities covering work, education and training, work supports (including assistance for transportation, and work-related supplies and fees), financial education, supportive counseling services, child care and early education, child welfare services, prevention of out-of-wedlock pregnancies, and other services, as well as funding for program management.

Source: U.S. Department of Health and Human Services, Administration for Children and Families, State TANF Data and Reports, "Expenditure Data," <www.acf.hhs.gov/ofa/programs/tanf/data-reports>, accessed March 2024.

Table 600. Federal Food Programs: Fiscal Years 1990 to 2023

[20.0 represents 20,000,000, except as noted. For fiscal years ending September 30. Program data include Puerto Rico, Virgin Islands, Guam, American Samoa, Northern Marianas, and the former Trust Territory when a federal food program was operated in these areas. Participation data are average monthly figures except as noted]

Program	Unit	1990	2000	2010	2015	2020	2021	2022	2023 (P)
Supplemental nutrition assistance program: [1]									
Participants	Million	20.0	17.2	40.3	45.8	39.9	41.6	41.2	42.2
Value of benefits	Mil. dol.	14,143	14,983	64,702	69,645	74,157	107,932	113,973	107,062
Average monthly benefit value per recipient	Dollars	59	73	134	127	155	216	230	212
Nutrition assistance program for Puerto Rico: [2]									
Federal grant	Mil. dol.	937	1,268	2,001	1,951	1,938	2,038	2,502	2,816
National school lunch program (NSLP):									
Children participating [3]	Million	24.1	27.3	31.8	30.5	22.4	11.0	30.1	28.6
Total lunches served	Million	4,009	4,575	5,278	5,005	3,210	2,155	4,952	4,659
Free lunches served	Percent	41.5	48.2	55.9	65.4	72.0	98.8	94.7	67.0
Reduced-price lunches served	Percent	6.8	8.9	9.4	7.2	4.9	0.2	0.6	3.8
Federal cost (cash payments)	Mil. dol.	3,214	5,493	9,752	11,696	9,021	8,359	21,462	15,793
School breakfast (SB):									
Children participating [3]	Million	4.1	7.6	11.7	14.0	12.3	7.0	15.7	14.7
Federal cash payments	Mil. dol.	599	1,393	2,859	3,892	3,548	3,130	6,503	5,265
Special supplemental food program for Women, Infants, and Children (WIC): [4]									
Participants	Million	4.5	7.2	9.2	8.0	6.2	6.2	6.3	6.6
Federal cost for food	Mil. dol.	1,637	2,853	4,562	4,176	2,884	2,666	3,587	4,422
Child and adult care (CACFP): [5]									
Participants [6]	Million	1.5	2.7	3.4	4.2	4.3	4.8	4.8	4.7
Federal cash payments	Mil. dol.	719	1,500	2,398	3,009	2,765	3,497	3,626	3,576
Federal cost of food commodities for: [7]									
School food programs [8]	Mil. dol.	617	655	1,128	1,307	1,296	964	1,515	1,512
The Emergency Food Assistance Program (TEFAP) [9]	Mil. dol.	282	182	566	451	654	1,115	915	1,163

P Preliminary. [1] The program name was changed from Food Stamp to Supplemental Nutrition Assistance (SNAP) in October 2008. [2] Puerto Rico receives a grant in lieu of SNAP benefits. [3] Average participation per day are 9-month averages (excludes summer months). Includes children in public and nonprofit private elementary and secondary schools and in residential child care institutions. [4] WIC serves pregnant, postpartum and breastfeeding women, infants, and children up to age 5. [5] CACFP provides year-round subsidies to feed preschool children and elderly and disabled adults in day care centers, and children and youth in emergency shelters for the homeless and eligible afterschool care programs. [6] Average quarterly daily attendance at participating institutions. [7] Includes the federal cost of commodity entitlements, cash-in-lieu of commodities, and bonus foods. [8] National school lunch and breakfast programs, and special milk program. [9] Emergency food assistance is food made available to hunger relief organizations such as food banks and soup kitchens. It is not disaster relief. Participants are not reported.

Source: U.S. Department of Agriculture, Food and Nutrition Service, "Program Data, Overview," <www.fns.usda.gov/pd/overview>, accessed March 2024.

Table 601. Supplemental Nutrition Assistance Program (SNAP) Beneficiaries and Benefits by State: 2010 to 2023

[40,302 represents 40,302,000; 64,702 represents $64,702,000,000. Participation data are average monthly number participating in fiscal year ending September 30. The Food Stamp Program was renamed the Supplemental Nutrition Assistance Program (SNAP) in October 2008]

State	Persons (1,000) 2010	2020	2023	Benefits (mil. dol.) 2010	2020	2023
Total [1]	40,302	39,853	42,153	64,702	74,157	107,062
U.S.	40,245	39,786	42,084	64,562	73,989	106,808
AL	805	731	776	1,226	1,359	2,049
AK	76	83	55	159	198	246
AZ	1,018	833	898	1,588	1,469	1,882
AR	467	371	250	686	661	545
CA	3,239	4,312	5,217	5,692	7,819	14,387
CO	405	483	564	688	913	1,448
CT	336	372	393	570	722	1,045
DE	113	120	121	171	215	296
DC	118	116	139	196	225	379
FL	2,603	3,177	3,090	4,417	6,065	6,757
GA	1,591	1,566	1,543	2,565	2,906	3,242
HI	138	165	158	358	564	842
ID	194	146	124	300	241	249
IL	1,646	1,866	2,031	2,784	3,382	5,440
IN	813	601	599	1,291	1,091	1,302
IA	340	311	263	526	546	509
KS	270	200	187	403	337	499
KY	778	555	554	1,186	998	1,121
LA	826	831	897	1,286	1,576	2,355
ME	230	160	168	356	277	422
MD	561	701	671	878	1,271	1,692
MA	749	821	1,084	1,166	1,472	3,091
MI	1,776	1,254	1,430	2,809	2,297	3,610
MN	430	409	461	625	959	1,441
MS	576	430	399	847	772	849
MO	901	715	665	1,361	1,325	1,519
MT	114	104	85	177	193	168
NE	163	157	156	238	254	314
NV	278	449	493	415	807	1,156
NH	104	73	75	152	117	187
NJ	622	701	771	1,030	1,289	1,975
NM	357	469	488	542	904	1,295
NY	2,758	2,658	2,886	4,985	5,119	8,296
NC	1,346	1,318	1,594	2,072	2,392	4,041
ND	60	46	45	95	84	98
OH	1,607	1,397	1,418	2,734	3,100	3,548
OK	582	597	682	900	1,056	1,721
OR	705	635	732	1,067	1,171	1,830
PA	1,575	1,795	1,927	2,333	3,249	4,705
RI	139	146	143	238	279	396
SC	797	596	619	1,256	1,102	1,544
SD	95	78	71	153	144	165
TN	1,224	869	752	1,966	1,774	1,800
TX	3,552	3,551	3,396	5,447	6,300	8,779
UT	247	164	158	367	280	390
VT	86	69	71	124	117	196
VA	786	730	843	1,213	1,331	2,178
WA	956	871	896	1,387	1,598	2,283
WV	341	306	307	487	518	756
WI	715	647	707	1,000	1,104	1,703
WY	35	27	30	52	46	67

[1] Includes Guam and the Virgin Islands. Does not include Puerto Rico, American Samoa, and the Northern Marianas, which receive nutrition assistance grants in lieu of SNAP.

Source: U.S. Department of Agriculture, Food and Nutrition Service, Supplemental Nutrition Assistance Program (SNAP), "National and/or State Level Monthly and/or Annual Data," <www.fns.usda.gov/pd/supplemental-nutrition-assistance-program-snap>, accessed March 2024.

Table 602. Supplemental Nutrition Assistance Program (SNAP) Households and Participants by Type: 1990 to 2022

[7,811 represents 7,811,000. For fiscal years ending September 30, except as noted. Covers the 50 states, DC, Guam, and the Virgin Islands; data for 1990 exclude Guam and the Virgin Islands. The Food Stamp Program was renamed Supplemental Nutrition Assistance Program (SNAP) in October 2008. Based on a sample of households from the SNAP Quality Control (QC) System. Beginning 2000, estimates are adjusted to exclude receipt of benefits by ineligible households and those receiving disaster assistance (including emergency allotments issued during the coronavirus disease 2019 (COVID-19) pandemic)]

Fiscal year	Households Total (1,000)	Percent of total with: Children	Elderly [1]	Disabled [2]	Participants Total (1,000)	Percent of total Children	Elderly [1]
1990	7,811	60.3	18.1	8.9	20,440	49.6	7.7
1995	10,883	59.7	16.0	18.9	26,955	51.5	7.1
2000	7,252	54.6	20.4	26.7	16,916	51.6	9.6
2001	7,276	54.2	19.7	26.6	16,850	51.3	9.3
2002	8,010	55.1	17.9	25.7	18,608	51.4	8.5
2003	8,971	55.1	17.1	22.1	20,764	50.8	8.1
2004	10,069	54.3	17.3	22.7	23,279	50.0	8.2
2005	10,852	53.7	17.1	23.0	24,794	49.9	8.3
2006	11,313	52.0	17.9	23.1	25,472	49.1	8.7
2007	11,561	51.0	17.8	23.8	25,775	48.9	8.8
2008	12,464	50.6	18.5	22.6	27,607	48.4	9.1
2009	14,981	49.9	16.6	21.2	32,889	47.5	8.3
2010	18,369	48.7	15.5	19.8	39,759	46.6	7.9
2011	20,803	47.1	16.5	20.2	44,148	45.1	8.5
2012	22,046	45.3	17.2	20.0	46,022	44.5	9.0
2013	22,802	44.8	17.4	20.3	47,098	44.4	9.3
2014	22,445	43.6	19.0	20.4	45,874	44.2	10.1
2015	22,293	42.7	19.6	20.2	45,184	44.0	10.6
2016	21,511	42.9	21.8	20.3	43,539	44.1	11.8
2017	20,597	41.7	24.1	20.8	41,491	43.5	13.1
2018	19,727	41.2	26.0	20.7	39,519	43.7	14.1
2019	18,802	39.5	28.1	21.1	37,202	42.7	15.6
2020 [3]	18,657	38.1	28.6	21.8	36,363	42.0	16.2
2020 [4]	16,686	37.0	27.7	21.5	32,170	40.9	15.5
2021 [5]	(NA)	(NA)	(NA)	(NA)	(NA)	(NA)	(NA)
2022	20,717	35.5	31.4	18.8	39,246	39.5	18.3

NA Not available. [1] Persons age 60 and over. [2] Non-elderly individuals with disabilities. Fluctuations in 1995, 2003, 2016 and 2017 are in part due to changes in the definition of a household with an individual with a disability. Changes involve primarily raising and lowering the age to be considered "nonelderly," and the inclusion of households receiving supplemental security income and/or other government benefits due to a disability. See source, appendix A, for details. [3] Data cover October 2019 to February 2020 period. Due to the COVID-19 pandemic, the Food and Nutrition Service (FNS) waived quality control reviews starting in March 2020. Most states did not collect data March-May 2020. See source for more information. [4] Data are from 47 states and territories, for June-September 2020 period. California, Delaware, Maine, Maryland, New York, and DC did not provide data. Due to the COVID-19 pandemic, the FNS waived quality control reviews starting in March 2020. See source for more information. [5] No report was issued for FY2021 because data were incomplete due to COVID-19 pandemic-related administrative waivers in place through most of the year.

Source: U.S. Department of Agriculture, Food and Nutrition Service, Characteristics of Supplemental Nutrition Assistance Program Households: Fiscal Year 2022, Report No. SNAP-22-CHAR, June 2024. See also <www.fns.usda.gov/research-analysis>.

Table 603. Supplemental Nutrition Assistance Program (SNAP) Households and Participants—Summary: 2022

[20,717 represents 20,717,000. For fiscal year ending September 30. Based on a sample of households from the Supplemental Nutrition Assistance Program Quality Control (QC) System. SNAP QC data adjust Food and Nutrition Service data to exclude ineligible participants and those receiving disaster assistance (including emergency allotments issued during the coronavirus disease 2019 (COVID-19) pandemic)]

Characteristic	Households Number (1,000)	Households Percent	Characteristic	Participants Number (1,000)	Participants Percent
Total households............	20,717	100.0	Total participants..............	39,246	100.0
With children [1]............	7,346	35.5	Children............	15,516	39.5
Single-adult households..........	4,634	22.4	Under age 5............	4,538	11.6
Married-couple households..........	1,148	5.5	Age 5 to 17............	10,978	28.0
With elderly persons............	6,500	31.4	Nonelderly adults............	16,549	42.2
Living alone............	5,333	25.7	Age 18 to 35............	7,735	19.7
Not living alone............	1,167	5.6	Age 36 to 59............	8,814	22.5
With disabled nonelderly persons..........	3,897	18.8	Elderly, age 60 and over............	7,181	18.3
Living alone............	2,556	12.3	Male............	16,749	42.7
Not living alone............	1,341	6.5	Female............	22,497	57.3
With earned income............	5,331	25.7	White, non-Hispanic............	13,844	35.3
Wages and salaries............	4,445	21.5	Black, non-Hispanic............	10,211	26.0
With unearned income............	12,799	61.8	Hispanic............	5,916	15.1
TANF [2]............	566	2.7	Asian, non-Hispanic............	1,454	3.7
Supplemental security income............	4,788	23.1	Native American, non-Hispanic..........	568	1.4
Social security............	6,685	32.3	Multiracial, non-Hispanic..........	333	0.8
With no gross income............	4,248	20.5	Race unknown............	6,920	17.6

[1] Includes other multiple-adult households and children-only households, not shown separately. [2] Temporary Assistance for Needy Families (TANF) program.

Source: U.S. Department of Agriculture, Food and Nutrition Service, *Characteristics of Supplemental Nutrition Assistance Program Households: Fiscal Year 2022*, Report No. SNAP-22-CHAR, June 2024. See also <www.fns.usda.gov/research-analysis>.

Table 604. Children Under Age 6 in Child Care by Type of Child Care Arrangement by Child and Family Characteristics: 2019

[In percent, except as indicated (21,195 represents 21,195,000). Covers children under age 6 (from birth through age 5) not enrolled in kindergarten who are in a nonparental care arrangement on a weekly basis. Children may have multiple weekly care arrangements, thus a single child may be represented in multiple columns. Based on the Early Childhood Program Participation Survey, a component of the National Household Education Surveys (NHES) Program. The NHES methodology changes over time and users should use caution when comparing results here to previous surveys. Detail may not sum to totals because of rounding]

Selected child or family characteristic	Number of children (1,000)	Children in weekly nonparental care arrangement [1] At least one nonparental care arrangement	Relative	Nonrelative care	Center-based care [2]	Children with no weekly nonparental care
Total children under age 6..............	21,195	59	38	20	62	41
Age of child:						
Under 1 year old............	4,621	42	58	26	32	58
1 to 2 years old............	8,425	55	44	25	47	45
3 to 5 years old............	8,149	74	26	14	83	26
Non-Hispanic race of child:						
White............	10,420	61	34	23	65	39
Black............	2,706	63	45	13	59	37
Asian or Pacific Islander............	1,181	55	35	12	67	45
Other [3]............	1,463	59	32	23	62	41
Hispanic, any race............	5,424	56	44	16	57	44
Number of parents in household:						
Two parents............	17,105	58	35	20	63	42
One parent............	4,089	65	50	17	60	35
Highest education of parents/guardians:						
Less than high school............	1,884	43	49	[6] 18	55	57
High school/GED [4]............	4,001	49	49	17	56	51
Vocational/technical/some college............	5,061	56	43	17	58	44
Bachelor's degree............	5,988	64	34	21	64	36
Graduate/professional degree............	4,261	75	29	23	70	25
Household income:						
$20,000 or less............	2,401	51	43	17	64	49
$20,001 to $50,000............	5,063	46	45	14	59	54
$50,001 to $75,000............	3,659	55	46	22	50	45
$75,001 to $100,000............	2,849	58	42	18	59	42
Over $100,000............	7,223	74	29	22	69	26
Assistance to pay for primary child care arrangement: [5]						
Parents received assistance............	1,577	100	28	26	81	(X)
Parents did not receive assistance............	7,013	100	25	27	71	(X)
No fee for care............	4,004	100	64	5	40	(X)

[1] Estimates represent about 12,594,000 children who have at least one weekly nonparental care arrangement. Eleven percent of children's parents reported having more than one type of regularly scheduled weekly nonparental care arrangement. [2] Includes day care centers, Head Start programs, preschools, prekindergartens, and other early childhood programs. [3] Includes children of all other races or multiple races, non-Hispanic. [4] GED, General Educational Development diploma. [5] Assistance could be from a state welfare or family assistance program, a relative, an employer, another social service, or someone else. [6] Interpret data with caution. The coefficient of variation (CV) for this estimate is between 30 and 50 percent.

Source: U.S. National Center for Education Statistics, National Household Education Surveys Program, *Early Childhood Program Participation: 2019, First Look,* May 2021, NCES 2020-075REV. See also <nces.ed.gov/nhes/>.

Table 605. Parents and Guardians Who Receive Child Support by Selected Characteristics: 2022

[In thousands (165,800 represents 165,800,000). Covers parents and guardians age 15 and over. Questions on child support are asked of parents and guardians about whether they received child support payments for their children under age 21 from the children's parent who lived outside of their household. Data are from the Survey of Income and Program Participation (SIPP)]

Characteristic of parent or guardian	Parents and guardians							
	Total		Lived with children under age of 21		Received any child support		Received child support payments irregularly [1]	
	Number	Percent	Number	Percent	Number	Percent	Number	Percent
Total	**165,800**	**100.0**	**70,980**	**100.0**	**4,085**	**100.0**	**815**	**100.0**
Has child support agreement (formal or informal) with other parent	6,305	3.8	6,305	8.9	3,698	90.5	670	82.2
Received child support payments during year	4,085	2.5	4,085	5.8	4,085	100.0	815	100.0
Received the same amount in all 12 months	3,269	2.0	3,269	4.6	3,269	80.0	–	–
Did not receive child support payments during year	161,800	97.5	66,890	94.2	–	–	–	–
Sex:								
Male	76,090	45.9	31,750	44.7	353	8.7	136	16.7
Female	89,750	54.1	39,230	55.3	3,731	91.3	679	83.3
Age:								
Under 20 years	582	0.4	131	0.2	(D)	(D)	–	–
20 to 29 years	8,196	4.9	6,477	9.1	387	9.5	56	6.9
30 to 39 years	26,050	15.7	22,960	32.4	1,603	39.2	344	42.3
40 to 49 years	31,700	19.1	25,420	35.8	1,378	33.7	250	30.7
50 to 59 years	32,990	19.9	12,950	18.3	624	15.3	134	16.4
60 years and older	66,330	40.0	3,030	4.3	(D)	(D)	30	3.7
Race and Hispanic origin:								
White alone	129,700	78.2	54,580	76.9	3,162	77.4	547	67.1
Black alone	20,620	12.4	8,283	11.7	608	14.9	118	14.5
Asian alone	9,959	6.0	5,480	7.7	101	2.5	49	6.0
Multiple or other race	5,552	3.3	2,631	3.7	214	5.2	101	12.3
Hispanic, any race	28,760	17.3	16,100	22.7	956	23.4	208	25.6
Educational attainment: [2]								
No high school diploma	17,350	10.6	6,818	9.8	383	9.5	106	13.3
High school diploma or GED [3]	44,030	27.0	15,280	22.0	1,088	26.9	164	20.7
Some college, no degree	26,540	16.3	10,570	15.2	990	24.5	151	19.0
Associate's degree	15,760	9.7	6,937	10.0	667	16.5	131	16.4
Bachelor's degree or higher	59,580	36.5	29,810	42.9	916	22.6	242	30.5
Poverty status: [4]								
Household income below poverty	13,910	8.4	6,242	8.8	662	16.2	187	23.0
Household income at or above poverty	151,900	91.6	64,730	91.2	3,422	83.8	628	77.0

– Represents or rounds to zero. D Data suppressed to avoid individual disclosure. [1] Varying or no payment amounts. [2] For persons age 25 and over. [3] General Education Development credential. [4] Includes every individual in the household.

Source: U.S. Census Bureau, Survey of Income and Program Participation Tables: SIPP Detailed Program Receipt Tables: 2022, "Table 15. Parents and Guardians Receiving Child Support in 2022," <www.census.gov/programs-surveys/sipp/data.html>, accessed July 2024.

Table 606. Child Support Enforcement Program—Caseload and Finances: 2010 to 2023

[(15,859 represents 15,859,000). For fiscal years ending September 30. Includes Puerto Rico, Guam, and the Virgin Islands. The Child Support Program is a federal/state/tribal/local partnership that operates under Title IV-D of the Social Security Act. Includes IV-A cases in which children are eligible for Temporary Assistance for Needy Families (TANF); and IV-E cases in which children are entitled to foster care maintenance; case types reflect Social Security Act Titles IV-A and IV-E. Child support collected for families not receiving TANF goes to the family to help it remain self-sufficient. Most child support collected on behalf of TANF and foster care families goes to Federal and State governments to offset program payments. Data are reported by state and tribal agencies]

Item	Unit	2010	2015	2020	2021 (P)	2022 (P)	2023 (P)
Total cases	1,000	**15,859**	**14,745**	**13,204**	**12,666**	**12,300**	**12,054**
Number of children	1,000	17,509	15,899	13,821	13,202	12,824	12,661
Paternities established or acknowledged, total	1,000	1,734	1,484	1,224	1,473	1,276	1,275
Support orders established, total	1,000	1,297	1,016	620	611	627	595
FINANCES							
Total distributed collections	Mil. dol.	**26,556**	**28,559**	**31,423**	**29,522**	**27,404**	**26,677**
Total payments to families or foster care	Mil. dol.	24,474	26,592	28,660	27,250	25,514	24,961
Total medical support	Mil. dol.	303	511	804	716	648	635
Total passed through	Mil. dol.	135	112	98	97	100	114
Total fees withheld by state	Mil. dol.	37	53	77	77	73	70
Total assistance reimbursement [1]	Mil. dol.	1,607	1,292	1,784	1,382	1,070	896
Current Assistance Collections [2]	Mil. dol.	1,015	808	795	709	616	610
Former Assistance Collections [3]	Mil. dol.	8,971	8,959	9,591	8,776	7,574	7,063
Medicaid Never Assistance Collections [4]	Mil. dol.	4,729	7,368	9,950	9,654	9,415	9,334
Never Assistance Collections [5]	Mil. dol.	11,840	11,425	11,087	10,383	9,800	9,670
Estimated incentive payments [6]	Mil. dol.	463	481	523	509	527	(NA)
Total administrative expenditures	Mil. dol.	5,776	5,749	6,004	5,908	6,109	6,443
Cost effectiveness ratio [7]	Dol.	4.88	5.26	5.51	5.27	4.73	4.37

P Preliminary. NA Not available. [1] Equals collections that will be divided between State and Federal governments to reimburse either Title IV-A (TANF) payments or Title IV-E (foster care) maintenance payments. [2] Made on behalf of families currently receiving Title IV-A or Title IV-E assistance. [3] For families formerly receiving Title IV-A or Title IV-E assistance. [4] Collections received and distributed on behalf of children who are receiving Child Support Enforcement services under Title IV-D of the Social Security Act, and who either currently receive or formerly received Medicaid payments, but who do not and never did receive assistance under either Title IV-A (TANF) or Title IV-E of the Social Security Act. [5] For families never receiving public assistance under Medicaid, TANF, or Foster Care. [6] Money states earn for operating an efficient child support program. [7] Ratio of dollars collected to dollars expended.

Source: U.S. Department of Health and Human Services, Administration for Children & Families, Office of Child Support Enforcement, *Preliminary Report FY2023*, June 2024, and earlier editions. See also <www.acf.hhs.gov/css/data>.

Table 607. Children in Foster Care and Awaiting Adoption: 2022

[Data cover fiscal year ending September 30 of year shown, and are current as of May 9, 2023. Data are preliminary. States may resubmit data, and therefore estimates may change. Due to missing data for some characteristics, data may not sum to totals. Foster care means 24-hour substitute care for children placed away from their parents or guardians and for whom the title IV-E agency has placement and care responsibility. See source for more information]

Characteristics of children	In foster care [1]	Entered foster care	Exited foster care	Waiting to be adopted [1,2]	Adopted [3]
Total	**368,530**	**186,602**	**201,372**	**108,877**	**53,665**
SEX					
Male	188,190	(NA)	(NA)	56,934	27,292
Female	180,253	(NA)	(NA)	51,931	26,363
AGE					
Under 1 year	25,338	37,065	7,590	3,470	851
1 to 5 years	123,883	52,778	73,155	42,926	28,553
6 to 10 years	81,728	37,938	46,448	27,146	14,002
11 to 15 years	82,571	41,020	38,434	26,547	8,153
16 to 17 years	40,264	14,981	15,236	8,788	1,968
18 to 20 years	14,404	2,789	17,545	(NA)	134
Mean age, years	8.2	6.9	8.3	7.6	6.1
Median age, years	7.0	6.0	7.0	7.0	5.0
RACE/ETHNICITY [4]					
American Indian/Alaska Native	8,987	4,276	4,411	2,250	927
Asian	1,979	1,237	1,221	439	207
Black	83,085	38,720	40,515	23,050	8,466
White	156,570	84,004	91,411	46,474	27,179
Hispanic origin [5]	79,090	37,008	42,449	25,213	10,889
Two or more races	29,466	14,580	16,396	9,434	5,032
TIME IN CARE					
Mean months	22.5	(X)	22.6	34.9	[6] 12.4
Median months	15.5	(X)	17.5	29.3	[6] 9.0

NA Not available. X Not applicable. [1] As of September 30. [2] Includes children whose goal is adoption and/or whose parents' parental rights have been terminated. Excludes children age 16 and older whose parents' parental rights have been terminated and whose goal is emancipation. [3] Children adopted with public agency involvement. Data are from the Adoption and Foster Care Analysis and Reporting System (AFCARS) Adoption file; the number of adoptions reported here may not equal the number reported as discharges to adoption from foster care. [4] Race groups exclude children of Hispanic origin. [5] Children of Hispanic origin may be of any race. [6] Time elapsed from termination of parental rights to adoption.

Source: U.S. Department of Health and Human Services, Administration for Children and Families, *The Adoption and Foster Care Analysis and Reporting System Report, Preliminary FY2022 Estimates as of May 9, 2023,* No. 30. See also <www.acf.hhs.gov/cb/data-research>.

Table 608. Child Care Mean Hourly Cost by Type of Child Care Arrangement and Child and Family Characteristics: 2019

[In dollars. Covers children from birth through age 5. Estimates represent 8,101,000 children who are not in kindergarten, and who have at least one regularly scheduled weekly nonparental care arrangement with an out-of-pocket expense. Excludes children for whom no fee was charged, or for whom another source paid the entire fee. Data cover the primary care arrangement where the child spends the most time. Data are for the primary provider for each type of child care arrangement a child may have. Some children may have multiple types of weekly child care arrangements. Based on the Early Childhood Program Participation Survey, a component of the National Household Education Surveys (NHES) Program. The NHES methodology changes over time and users should use caution when comparing results here to previous surveys. Detail may not sum to totals because of rounding]

Selected child and family characteristics	Hourly cost by type of primary care			Selected child and family characteristics	Hourly cost by type of primary care		
	Relative care	Non-relative care	Center-based care [1]		Relative care	Non-relative care	Center-based care [1]
Total children under 6 years old	**6.05**	**7.75**	**8.22**	Region:			
Age of child:				Northeast	7.90	10.55	10.20
Under 1 year old	6.63	8.85	7.91	South	5.80	7.35	6.71
1 to 2 years old	5.43	8.03	8.92	Midwest	4.09	5.29	7.05
3 to 5 years old	6.64	6.72	7.88	West	6.54	8.80	10.16
Non-Hispanic race of child:							
White	6.76	6.48	7.51	Household income:			
Black	4.29	6.66	6.97	$20,000 or less	7.85	(B)	[6] 8.26
Asian or Pacific Islander	6.45	[6] 16.45	11.87	$20,001 to $50,000	3.91	6.02	6.73
Other or multiple races	[6] 7.95	9.58	9.54	$50,001 to $75,000	5.87	5.27	5.60
Hispanic, any race	6.34	10.04	9.59	$75,001 to $100,000	7.10	5.40	7.85
Family type:				Over $100,000	6.85	9.07	9.16
Two parents or guardians	6.49	7.78	8.35				
One parent or guardian	5.10	7.60	7.55	Poverty status of household: [4]			
Parents' highest education: [2]				At or above poverty	6.07	7.50	8.26
Less than high school	6.79	[6] 7.91	3.47	Below poverty	5.97	[6] 10.00	7.71
High school/GED [3]	5.40	[6] 8.96	7.20				
Vocational/technical or some college	5.53	5.51	6.23	Assistance to pay for primary child care arrangement: [5]			
Bachelor's degree	6.38	6.83	8.37	Received assistance	6.16	[6] 8.88	6.82
Graduate/professional degree	7.20	9.50	9.53	Did not receive assistance	6.02	7.58	8.43

B Reporting standards not met. There are too few cases for a reliable estimate. [1] Includes day care centers, Head Start programs, preschools, and prekindergartens. [2] Parents or guardians. [3] GED, General Educational Development diploma. [4] Children are considered poor if living in households with incomes below the poverty threshold, which is a dollar amount determined by the federal government, given household size and composition. Income is reported in categories rather than in exact amounts, and therefore the poverty measures are approximations. [5] Assistance to parents could be from a state welfare or family assistance program, a relative, an employer, another social service, or someone else. Parents were asked about assistance only for the primary arrangement within each type of care. [6] Interpret data with caution. The coefficient of variation for this estimate is 30 percent or greater.

Source: U.S. National Center for Education Statistics, *Early Childhood Program Participation: 2019, First Look,* May 2021, NCES 2020-075REV. See also <nces.ed.gov/nhes/>.

Table 609. Head Start—Summary: 2010 to 2023

[Funding data in millions of dollars (7,233.7 represents $7,233,700,000); all other data in thousands (904.1 represents 904,100). For fiscal years. The Head Start program serves children, families, and pregnant women in all 50 states, DC, and six territories. Data on cumulative enrollment, staff, and volunteers are submitted by Head Start grantees and delegates. Federal funding covers all Head Start programs, including Early Head Start, American Indian and Alaska Native programs, and Migrant and Seasonal Head Start Programs]

Item	2010	2015	2018	2019	2020 [4]	2021	2022	2023
Federal funding (million dollars)......	7,233.7	8,598.1	9,838.7	[5] 10,028.5	[5] 10,613.1	[5] 10,748.1	11,036.6	(NA)
Funded enrollment slots [1].............	904.1	944.6	887.1	873.0	852.5	839.1	833.1	(NA)
Cumulative enrollment [2]..........	**1,117.7**	**1,100.4**	**1,054.5**	**1,046.9**	**(NA)**	**756.1**	**801.0**	**799.9**
Children age 2 and under............	146.3	193.2	257.9	265.9	(NA)	231.4	247.2	245.4
Children age 3.........................	386.7	399.4	364.0	363.5	(NA)	224.6	266.6	266.3
Children age 4.........................	548.0	480.1	404.7	391.4	(NA)	280.2	266.3	269.2
Children age 5 and older.............	23.2	12.2	12.4	10.3	(NA)	8.3	8.0	6.2
Hispanic/Latino........................	405.4	414.0	385.7	387.7	(NA)	280.1	298.3	289.6
Non-Hispanic/non-Latino.............	712.3	686.3	668.7	659.1	(NA)	476.0	502.7	493.2
American Indian/Alaska Native.......	41.7	45.4	41.1	40.1	(NA)	26.5	27.7	27.9
Asian..................................	19.0	21.8	22.8	22.5	(NA)	17.1	16.6	16.6
Black/African American...............	326.5	318.3	312.7	310.7	(NA)	215.8	236.4	235.2
Native Hawaiian/Pacific Islander.....	6.9	9.8	7.1	7.1	(NA)	5.0	5.7	5.8
White..................................	450.3	473.5	461.2	462.1	(NA)	348.1	366.1	364.4
Biracial/multiracial....................	83.9	107.2	103.3	102.2	(NA)	78.7	83.3	85.4
Other/unspecified race or ethnicity [6].........................	189.4	124.3	106.2	102.2	(NA)	64.9	65.1	64.8
Total staff [3].............................	228.3	230.0	246.0	254.2	(NA)	243.7	240.7	230.3
Total volunteers........................	1,335.9	1,141.5	1,046.3	1,060.9	(NA)	378.5	464.6	542.0
Parent volunteers....................	881.1	782.2	738.7	749.5	(NA)	294.9	356.7	400.5

NA Not available. [1] Funded enrollment is the number of children and pregnant women supported by federal Head Start funds at any one time during the year. Data are derived from the annual Administration for Children and Families budget and congressional documents, and do not reflect changes made during the year. [2] Cumulative enrollment refers to actual number of children and pregnant women served, including enrollees who left during the year and enrollees who filled those vacancies. More children and families may receive Head Start services cumulatively throughout the year than indicated by funded enrollment numbers. [3] Excludes contracted staff. [4] Due to the coronavirus disease 2019 (COVID-19) pandemic, the Office of Head Start did not require program information reporting for FY2020. [5] Not included is supplemental funding for FY2019 to FY2021 for expenses related to several natural disasters, including the COVID-2019 pandemic in FY2021. Amounts are: FY2019, $55 million; FY2020, $750 million; FY2021, $1,250 million. [6] Prior to 2023, data cover persons with other and unspecified race. Beginning 2023, data also include persons with unspecified Hispanic ethnicity.

Source: U.S. Department of Health and Human Services, Administration for Children and Families, Early Childhood Learning & Knowledge Center, "Head Start Program Facts Sheets," and *Head Start Federal Funding and Funded Enrollment History*, <eclkc.ohs.acf.hhs.gov/about-us /article/office-head-start-ohs>; *Justification of Estimates for Appropriations Committees, Fiscal Year 2023*; and "Program Information Report, Head Start Enterprise System," <eclkc.ohs.acf.hhs.gov/data-ongoing-monitoring/article/program-information-report-pir>, accessed June 2024.

Table 610. Social Assistance Services—Nonemployer Establishments and Receipts: 2010 to 2021

[Receipts in millions of dollars (12,753 represents $12,753,000,000). Includes only firms subject to federal income tax. Nonemployers are businesses with no paid employees. Nonemployer firm receipts may include commissions or earnings]

Kind of business	NAICS code [1]	2010	2015	2017	2018	2019	2020	2021
ESTABLISHMENTS								
Social assistance, total.............................	624	**912,247**	**822,350**	**729,150**	**784,922**	**756,780**	**707,009**	**745,880**
Individual and family services.......................	6241	141,971	163,337	170,672	176,958	174,068	170,787	179,256
Community food and housing, and emergency and other relief services.................	6242	6,080	6,355	6,512	6,296	6,123	7,038	8,250
Vocational rehabilitation services.....................	6243	11,984	12,916	12,510	12,355	11,889	11,201	10,909
Child day care services.............................	6244	752,212	639,742	539,456	589,313	564,700	517,983	547,465
RECEIPTS (mil. dol)								
Social assistance, total.............................	624	**12,753**	**13,238**	**12,992**	**14,100**	**14,328**	**13,491**	**15,220**
Individual and family services.......................	6241	2,599	3,492	3,881	4,176	4,403	4,567	5,141
Community food and housing, and emergency and other relief services.................	6242	96	111	114	122	122	136	161
Vocational rehabilitation services.....................	6243	287	341	343	351	353	327	351
Child day care services.............................	6244	9,772	9,294	8,653	9,451	9,449	8,462	9,566

[1] North American Industry Classification System; see text, Section 15. Data for 2010 based on NAICS 2007; data for 2013 to 2016 based on NAICS 2012; and beginning 2017, data based on 2017 NAICS.

Source: U.S. Census Bureau, Nonemployer Statistics, "All Sectors: Nonemployer Statistics by Legal Form of Organization and Receipts Size Class for the U.S., States, and Selected Geographies: 2021," <data.census.gov/>, accessed March 2024, and earlier releases.

Table 611. Social Assistance Services—Revenue for Employer Firms: 2021 and 2022

[In millions of dollars (253,226 represents $253,226,000,000). Based on Census Bureau's Service Annual Survey and administrative data. Estimates have been adjusted using results of the 2017 Economic Census where applicable. In some instances, results from the 2017 Economic Census may reflect revisions based on additional analytical review following the release of the 2017 Geographic Area Statistics. See Appendix III]

Kind of business	NAICS code [1]	2021 Total	2021 Taxable firms	2021 Tax-exempt firms	2022 Total	2022 Taxable firms	2022 Tax-exempt firms
Social assistance, total.............................	624	253,226	72,882	180,344	273,292	82,592	190,700
Child and youth services.............................	62411	23,585	2,627	20,958	24,751	3,094	21,657
Services for elderly and disabled persons.........	62412	60,568	29,958	30,610	65,462	32,758	32,704
Other individual and family services................	62419	51,508	6,359	45,149	59,230	7,622	51,608
Community food services............................	62421	22,068	76	21,992	18,158	82	18,076
Community housing services.........................	62422	17,679	186	17,493	19,770	284	19,486
Emergency and other relief services...............	62423	12,448	143	12,305	12,756	185	12,571
Vocational rehabilitation services...................	6243	15,163	2,084	13,079	16,284	2,268	14,016
Child day care services.............................	6244	50,207	31,449	18,758	56,881	36,299	20,582

[1] 2012 North American Industry Classification System.

Source: U.S. Census Bureau, Service Annual Survey, "Service Annual Survey Latest Data (NAICS-basis): 2022," <www.census.gov/programs-surveys/sas/data/tables.html>, accessed February 2024.

Table 612. Homeless Population by Type and Shelter Status: 2010 to 2023

[Data are point-in-time (PIT) counts made on a single night in January by Continuums of Care (CoCs) in all States, DC, and U.S. territories. Data are not independently verified by the Department of Housing and Urban Development (HUD). CoCs are required to provide an unduplicated count of homeless persons according to HUD standards. Sheltered homeless people may be staying in emergency shelters, hotels/motels paid for by charities or government programs, transitional housing programs, or safe havens (temporary shelter for hard-to-serve individuals). People staying in places not designed for use as regular accommodations, including cars, abandoned buildings, transit stations, and campgrounds, are considered unsheltered]

Homeless population by type	2010	2018	2019	2020	2021 [3]	2022 [4]	2023
Total...	637,077	552,830	567,715	580,466	(NA)	582,462	653,104
Male..	(NA)	332,925	343,187	352,211	182,673	352,836	395,160
Female..	(NA)	216,211	219,911	223,578	141,497	222,970	250,009
Transgender & gender nonconforming.......	(NA)	3,694	4,617	4,621	1,956	6,678	7,935
Sheltered.................................	403,543	358,363	356,422	354,386	326,126	348,630	396,494
Unsheltered..............................	233,534	194,467	211,293	226,080	(NA)	233,832	256,610
Individuals [1]................................	395,140	372,417	396,045	408,891	(NA)	421,392	467,020
Sheltered.................................	212,218	194,340	199,531	199,478	194,749	204,897	227,795
Unsheltered..............................	182,922	178,077	196,514	209,413	(NA)	216,495	239,225
Persons in families with children..............	241,937	180,413	171,670	171,575	(NA)	161,070	186,084
Sheltered.................................	191,325	164,023	156,891	154,908	131,377	143,733	168,699
Unsheltered..............................	50,612	16,390	14,779	16,667	(NA)	17,337	17,385
Children under age 18, total..................	(NA)	111,592	107,069	106,364	(NA)	98,244	111,620
Sheltered.................................	(NA)	101,086	97,153	95,713	80,656	87,960	101,072
Unsheltered..............................	(NA)	10,506	9,916	10,651	(NA)	10,284	10,548
Children under age 18, unaccompanied......	8,153	4,093	3,976	3,389	(NA)	2,695	3,240
Sheltered.................................	4,349	2,014	1,874	1,682	1,345	1,510	1,732
Unsheltered..............................	3,804	2,079	2,102	1,707	(NA)	1,185	1,508
Chronically homeless individuals [2]..........	106,062	88,640	96,141	110,528	(NA)	127,768	143,105
Sheltered.................................	43,329	30,754	35,200	37,111	44,346	49,153	50,137
Unsheltered..............................	62,733	57,886	60,941	73,417	(NA)	78,615	92,968
Chronically homeless people in families [2]...	(NA)	8,273	9,442	9,795	(NA)	10,593	11,208
Sheltered.................................	(NA)	5,821	7,407	6,760	7,233	7,625	7,850
Unsheltered..............................	(NA)	2,452	2,035	3,035	(NA)	2,968	3,358
Veterans......................................	74,087	37,878	37,085	37,252	(NA)	33,129	35,574
Sheltered.................................	43,437	23,312	22,740	22,048	19,750	19,565	20,067
Unsheltered..............................	30,650	14,566	14,345	15,204	(NA)	13,564	15,507
Severely mentally ill...........................	107,539	111,122	116,179	120,642	(NA)	122,888	137,076
Sheltered.................................	71,989	58,942	63,936	62,023	64,131	65,543	69,548
Unsheltered..............................	35,550	52,180	52,243	58,619	(NA)	57,345	67,528
Chronic substance abuse.....................	139,853	86,647	88,873	98,646	(NA)	95,001	108,035
Sheltered.................................	95,049	45,372	45,804	43,216	39,428	40,563	42,207
Unsheltered..............................	44,804	41,275	43,069	55,430	(NA)	54,438	65,828
Persons with HIV/AIDS........................	14,498	10,064	10,945	10,632	(NA)	9,910	10,882
Sheltered.................................	10,590	7,244	7,733	7,287	6,820	6,237	6,861
Unsheltered..............................	3,908	2,820	3,212	3,345	(NA)	3,673	4,021
Domestic violence victims....................	66,878	48,666	44,752	48,532	(NA)	48,373	74,436
Sheltered.................................	49,709	30,607	31,509	32,695	30,545	32,226	36,958
Unsheltered..............................	17,169	18,059	13,243	15,837	(NA)	16,147	37,478

NA Not available. [1] People who are not part of a family with children. Includes homeless single adults, unaccompanied youth, or individuals in multiple-adult or multiple-child households. [2] Continuously homeless for a year or more, or with at least four episodes of homelessness in the last 3 years. [3] Due to the COVID-19 pandemic, communities had the option to cancel or modify the unsheltered survey portion of their counts. [4] The count was conducted during the last 10 days in January through early March. A number of CoCs conducted a sheltered-only count in 2022 and a partial unsheltered count in 2021. Unsheltered totals are carried over from 2021; demographic subtotals may not sum to reported population total.

Source: U.S. Department of Housing and Urban Development, HUD Exchange, "PIT and HIC Data Since 2007: 2007-2023 Point-in-Time Estimates by State," <www.hudexchange.info/resource/3031/pit-and-hic-data-since-2007/>, accessed January 2023; and 2023 CoC (Continuum of Care) Homeless Populations and Subpopulations Report, November 2023 and earlier reports. See also <www.hudexchange.info/programs/coc/coc-homeless-populations-and-subpopulations-reports/>.

Table 613. Emergency and Transitional Beds in Homeless Assistance Systems: 2023

[Data cover all States, DC, and selected U.S. territories as available. Data were reported by approximately 380 Continuums of Care, and were collected during the last week in January 2023. Data represent inventory available during the entire year except as noted. Data are not independently verified by Department of Housing and Urban Development (HUD)]

Homeless program	Dedicated units/beds [1]					Other beds	
	Total year-round beds	Family units	Family beds	Adult-only beds	Child-only beds	Seasonal beds [2]	Overflow/ voucher [3]
Total	**1,112,545**	**162,035**	**480,824**	**628,251**	**3,470**	**16,860**	**25,217**
Shelter for homeless people	449,567	64,259	200,714	245,662	3,191	16,860	25,217
Emergency shelters	358,435	50,877	161,204	194,539	2,692	16,860	25,217
Safe haven [4]	2,506	0	0	2,506	0	(X)	(X)
Transitional housing [5]	88,626	13,382	39,510	48,617	499	(X)	(X)
Permanent housing	662,978	97,776	280,110	382,589	279	(X)	(X)
Permanent supportive housing [6]	395,986	42,300	122,124	273,818	44	(X)	(X)
Rapid re-housing	144,765	31,820	93,132	51,500	133	(X)	(X)
Other permanent housing [7]	122,227	23,656	64,854	57,271	102	(X)	(X)

X Not applicable. [1] Dedicated beds are available for use throughout the year and are considered part of the stable inventory of beds for homeless persons. [2] Seasonal beds are typically available during particularly high-demand seasons of the year (e.g. winter months in the North or summer months in the South). [3] Overflow beds are typically used during unanticipated emergencies (e.g., precipitous temperature drops or a natural disaster that displaces residents). Voucher beds are made available in a hotel or motel, and often function like overflow beds. [4] A safe haven provides private or semiprivate temporary shelter and services to people with severe mental illness and are limited to serving no more than 25 people within a facility. [5] Provides a place to stay with supportive services for up to 24 months. [6] Provides long-term housing with supportive services for formerly homeless people with disabilities, and often also those with chronic homelessness. [7] May or may not include services, and does not require people to have a disability.

Source: U.S. Department of Housing and Urban Development, HUD Exchange, *2023 Continuum of Care Homeless Assistance Programs: Housing Inventory Count Report,* December 2023. See also <www.hudexchange.info/programs/coc/coc-housing-inventory-count-reports/>.

Table 614. Domestic Private Foundations—Financial Information: 2000 to 2020

[409.5 represents $409,500,000,000. Data are based on IRS Form 990–PF]

Item	2000	2005	2010	2014	2015	2016	2017	2018	2019	2020
Number of tax returns	66,738	79,535	93,436	97,484	99,683	100,488	101,194	102,078	103,299	103,968
Nonoperating foundations [1]	61,501	72,800	86,254	88,878	90,699	91,396	92,897	93,106	93,908	94,888
Operating foundations [2]	5,238	6,734	7,181	8,606	8,984	9,092	8,297	8,972	9,390	9,081
FINANCES (billions of dollars)										
Total assets, book value [3]	409.5	481.8	584.2	738.4	754.3	796.5	883.3	895.0	965.8	1,080.0
Total assets, fair market value [3]	471.6	545.9	641.0	830.3	829.4	889.4	1,005.7	987.8	1,106.7	1,274.3
Investments in securities	361.4	373.1	353.3	459.3	451.7	476.7	551.2	525.8	599.4	682.6
Total revenue	72.8	76.4	72.5	119.5	107.0	114.1	139.0	144.7	141.7	172.3
Total expenses	37.4	42.8	60.1	79.2	81.0	88.1	93.4	98.1	111.2	117.6
Contributions, gifts, and grants paid	27.6	31.9	44.7	57.6	58.7	65.8	70.2	74.9	86.4	92.3
Excess of revenue over expenses (net)	35.3	33.5	12.3	40.3	26.0	26.0	45.7	46.6	30.6	54.6
Net investment income [4]	48.8	44.3	29.8	59.9	48.8	44.2	64.9	72.4	66.0	83.7

[1] Generally provide charitable support through grants and other financial means to charitable organizations; the majority of foundations are nonoperating. [2] Generally conduct their own charitable activities, e.g., museums. [3] Data for book and fair market value of assets were reduced to avoid overstating the joint assets of the Bill and Melinda Gates Foundation and the Bill and Melinda Gates Foundation Trust, by tax year as follows: 2010, $36.7 billion; 2014, $43.4 billion; 2015, $39.3 billion; 2016, $40.3 billion; 2017, $50.7 billion; 2018, $46.8 billion; 2019, $49.8 billion; and 2020, $49.9 billion. [4] Equals gross investment income less allowable deductions. Represents income not considered related to a foundation's charitable purpose, e.g., interest, dividends, and capital gains. Foundations could be subject to an excise tax on such income.

Source: Internal Revenue Service, Statistics of Income, "SOI Tax Stats – Domestic Private Foundation and Charitable Trust Statistics," <www.irs.gov/statistics>, accessed June 2024.

Table 615. Volunteering and Charitable Giving Rates by Selected Characteristics: 2017 to 2021

[As percent of residents. Data are based on a household survey of the noninstitutionalized population age 16 and over, and cover volunteering or charitable giving in the past year ending in September of the year shown. Survey is conducted by the Census Bureau for AmeriCorps]

Characteristic	Volunteering [1]			Charitable giving [2]		
	2017	2019	2021	2017	2019	2021
Total	**30.3**	**30.0**	**23.2**	**52.2**	**50.5**	**48.1**
SEX AND AGE						
Male	26.5	26.4	21.0	49.4	47.9	45.7
Female	33.8	33.4	25.3	54.7	52.9	50.2
16 to 54 years	31.0	30.6	23.5	46.5	44.7	42.7
55 years and over	29.0	29.1	22.7	62.3	60.3	56.9
RACE AND HISPANIC ETHNICITY						
American Indian or Alaskan Native	22.0	20.2	18.7	32.8	36.7	32.4
Asian	22.1	23.7	16.5	46.1	44.7	43.3
Black or African American	25.2	23.2	17.7	41.4	38.4	36.3
Native Hawaiian or Pacific Islander	30.5	25.0	21.5	49.0	39.7	41.3
White	31.9	31.8	24.7	54.8	53.2	50.8
Two or more races	29.1	30.0	24.8	45.6	47.0	40.6
Hispanic	19.0	18.6	12.6	37.3	34.2	30.5

[1] Formally for an organization or association. [2] Money, assets, or property worth $25 or more to charitable or religious organizations.

Source: AmeriCorps, "2017-2021 CEV Findings: National Rates of All Measures by Demographics from the Current Population Survey Civic Engagement and Volunteering Supplement," and "2017-2021 CEV Findings: National Rates of All Measures from the Current Population Survey Civic Engagement and Volunteering Supplement," <data.americorps.gov/>, accessed June 2023.

Table 616. Volunteering and Charitable Giving by State: 2019 and 2021

[As a percent of residents nationally and in each state or DC. Data are based on a household survey of the noninstitutionalized population age 16 and over. Data cover volunteering through an organization or association, and donations (money or possessions) worth over $25 to a non-political organization (including charities, schools, and religious organizations), during the past year ending September of the year shown. Survey is conducted by the Census Bureau for AmeriCorps]

State	Volunteering 2019	Volunteering 2021	Charitable giving 2019	Charitable giving 2021	State	Volunteering 2019	Volunteering 2021	Charitable giving 2019	Charitable giving 2021
Total U.S.	**30.0**	**23.2**	**50.5**	**48.1**	Missouri	36.5	30.5	53.9	55.0
Alabama	25.8	19.5	51.0	40.1	Montana	37.4	31.1	54.6	56.7
Alaska	35.5	27.3	50.2	47.7	Nebraska	43.5	33.9	61.2	61.1
Arizona	26.2	23.5	46.6	48.5	Nevada	21.8	16.8	37.4	41.3
Arkansas	29.7	20.9	54.3	52.4	New Hampshire	32.2	27.9	59.6	59.4
California	24.9	18.3	44.1	39.0	New Jersey	26.1	19.9	54.4	51.1
Colorado	42.2	26.2	65.0	55.5	New Mexico	27.7	19.7	42.7	44.3
Connecticut	31.4	28.8	54.6	61.5	New York	22.7	21.7	45.4	47.7
Delaware	30.7	29.8	55.6	49.3	North Carolina	30.4	22.8	49.9	47.6
District of Columbia	39.2	34.2	52.3	61.4	North Dakota	32.9	26.9	58.1	56.7
Florida	24.2	15.9	41.4	36.8	Ohio	37.1	24.3	55.0	47.1
Georgia	28.2	19.9	48.1	46.0	Oklahoma	27.6	23.6	45.8	46.5
Hawaii	32.1	19.7	49.2	45.0	Oregon	37.0	28.0	61.1	57.4
Idaho	34.5	28.2	53.0	57.0	Pennsylvania	35.8	25.6	59.5	51.9
Illinois	33.0	28.3	56.6	56.1	Rhode Island	25.6	20.1	60.2	54.4
Indiana	34.0	27.6	50.6	52.2	South Carolina	31.3	21.8	54.0	51.5
Iowa	33.1	29.9	53.5	58.2	South Dakota	46.9	34.2	66.3	55.8
Kansas	34.0	31.5	59.9	54.0	Tennessee	31.7	23.8	53.6	47.0
Kentucky	26.2	22.6	45.0	44.7	Texas	26.4	21.3	45.3	45.5
Louisiana	27.8	21.9	50.0	41.8	Utah	49.5	40.7	65.7	53.0
Maine	35.7	34.9	54.2	53.0	Vermont	37.4	29.1	54.0	50.0
Maryland	34.0	23.7	59.3	47.4	Virginia	35.4	27.2	55.9	54.8
Massachusetts	30.7	23.1	52.6	53.9	Washington	33.8	25.0	54.8	55.1
Michigan	30.2	24.4	46.9	51.6	West Virginia	30.6	22.4	48.0	46.2
Minnesota	40.1	35.5	60.2	61.8	Wisconsin	37.5	24.9	58.8	52.5
Mississippi	26.0	21.2	41.4	40.9	Wyoming	31.0	39.2	49.2	52.2

Source: AmeriCorps, Open Data, "Civic Engagement and Volunteering (CEV) Supplement," <data.americorps.gov/>, accessed April 2023.

Table 617. Individual Noncash Charitable Contributions by Type of Donation and Recipient: 2021

[42,503,262 represents $42,503,262,000. Covers individual noncash charitable contributions worth more than $500 reported on IRS Form 1040, Individual Income Tax Return; Schedule A, Itemized Deductions; and IRS Form 8283, Noncash Charitable Contributions]

Type of donation or recipient	Number of returns [1]	Number of donations	Donor's cost [2] ($1,000)	Fair market value ($1,000)	Amount carried to Schedule A [3] ($1,000)
Total returns with noncash donations	**2,967,551**	**9,522,629**	**42,503,262**	**132,932,175**	**116,652,516**
TYPE OF DONATION					
Corporate stock, mutual funds, and other investments	216,263	594,824	14,055,304	91,076,255	89,700,614
Real estate, land, and easements	11,213	14,815	4,775,616	24,664,776	10,593,383
Art and collectibles	41,492	68,331	581,682	1,908,640	1,402,501
Food	84,160	190,142	113,904	164,396	150,663
Clothing and accessories	1,945,949	4,567,590	10,595,817	5,734,717	5,698,046
Electronics	141,273	193,581	598,531	398,502	351,245
Household items	1,321,069	3,176,071	8,999,153	4,351,766	4,328,599
Cars, planes, boats, and other vehicles	51,277	52,817	989,311	340,423	317,037
Other types of donations [4]	340,591	664,459	1,793,943	4,292,700	4,110,428
TYPE OF RECIPIENT					
Arts, culture, and humanities	68,984	300,730	924,153	5,367,876	3,253,103
Educational institutions	108,495	174,506	1,708,720	6,503,287	6,118,993
Environment and animal-related organizations	60,482	110,779	3,272,334	18,301,470	7,919,765
Health and medical research	221,784	402,957	1,875,887	3,324,018	3,297,608
Large organizations	2,283,190	6,264,274	16,860,038	10,989,724	10,543,273
Public and societal benefit	506,362	1,024,500	3,033,458	4,453,369	4,001,550
Religious organizations	337,935	696,622	2,457,110	4,516,187	4,349,951
Donor-advised funds	99,324	232,506	3,972,200	37,491,106	36,988,861
Foundations	50,780	117,385	7,262,619	36,987,529	35,469,932
Other recipients	148,059	198,371	1,136,742	4,997,608	4,709,480

[1] Does not equal the sum of returns by type of donation and recipient because a return could have more than one type of donation and recipient. [2] Not every donation has a donor cost reported. [3] Form 8283 has two sections. Filers complete either Section A or Section B depending on the type of property donated and the amount claimed as a deduction. Amount carried to Schedule A (Form 1040, for itemized deductions) is the fair market value from Section A (items with a deduction of $5,000 or less, and all publicly traded securities) plus the lesser of the fair market value, the amount claimed, or the appraised value on Section B (items with a deduction of more than $5,000). [4] Includes intellectual property, services, airline tickets and miles, and other donations.

Source: U.S. Internal Revenue Service, Individual Income Tax Statistics, "SOI Tax Stats - Individual Noncash Charitable Contributions," <www.irs.gov/statistics/soi-tax-stats-individual-noncash-charitable-contributions>, accessed April 2024.

Table 618. Nonprofit Charitable Organizations—Financial Information: 2000 to 2020

[In billions of dollars (1,562.5 represents $1,562,500,000,000), except as indicated. Includes data reported by organizations described in Internal Revenue Code, Section 501(c)(3), excluding private foundations and most religious organizations. Prior to 2010, organizations with receipts under $25,000 were not required to file. Beginning with 2010, organizations with receipts under $50,000 were not required to file]

Year	Number of tax returns (1,000)	Total assets	Net assets	Revenue Total[1]	Contributions, gifts, and grants	Program service revenue[2]	Total expenses	Excess of revenue over expenses (net)
2000	230.2	1,562.5	1,023.2	866.2	199.1	579.1	796.4	69.8
2005	286.6	2,241.9	1,411.3	1,252.9	276.3	852.6	1,137.9	115.0
2006	301.2	2,549.7	1,617.7	1,370.9	303.2	920.2	1,230.4	140.5
2007	313.1	2,683.4	1,674.4	1,445.9	324.5	980.3	1,317.2	128.7
2008	315.2	2,521.2	1,434.7	1,378.3	322.0	1,038.0	1,396.4	-18.1
2009	320.8	2,697.1	1,564.2	1,481.1	327.4	1,085.9	1,433.9	47.2
2010	269.5	2,946.5	1,772.4	1,593.0	344.9	1,147.3	1,497.2	95.8
2011	274.3	3,030.1	1,781.9	1,647.9	357.4	1,194.2	1,558.4	89.5
2012	279.4	3,274.0	1,970.4	1,734.2	371.1	1,248.2	1,624.1	110.1
2013	285.9	3,507.6	2,184.0	1,828.2	394.1	1,296.1	1,700.4	127.8
2014	293.0	3,711.1	2,288.0	1,949.9	422.5	1,384.1	1,801.3	148.6
2015	298.4	3,801.4	2,303.6	2,013.0	430.6	1,468.0	1,908.2	104.8
2016	302.1	4,027.9	2,519.0	2,124.4	465.3	1,530.5	2,013.3	111.2
2017	307.6	4,355.0	2,771.4	2,284.0	500.0	1,623.4	2,121.2	162.8
2018	300.4	4,239.8	2,664.4	2,299.0	485.9	1,664.9	2,186.3	112.7
2019	304.2	4,752.7	2,920.6	2,425.0	556.2	1,713.1	2,283.3	141.7
2020	286.1	5,515.1	3,544.1	2,686.3	700.8	1,778.3	2,420.9	265.5

[1] Includes other sources of revenue not shown separately. [2] Represents fees collected by organizations in support of their tax-exempt purposes, such as tuition and fees at educational institutions, hospital patient charges, and admission and activity fees collected by museums and other nonprofit organizations or institutions.

Source: U.S. Internal Revenue Service, Statistics of Income, "SOI Tax Stats – Charities & Other Tax-Exempt Organizations Statistics," November 2023, <www.irs.gov/statistics>, accessed March 2024.

Table 619. Individual Charitable Contributions by State: 2021

[In units as indicated (12,074 represents 12,074; 261,590 represents $261,590,000,000). Covers returns primarily for 2021 tax year that were filed during 2022, but may also include a limited number of returns for earlier tax years that were also received during 2022. Data reflect tax returns as initially processed and do not reflect amended returns or errors that were corrected after initial processing. Data will not agree with data in other tables due to differing survey methodology used to derive state data. Data may not sum due to rounding]

State	Charitable contributions, itemized — Number of returns (1,000)	Amount (mil. dol.)	Charitable contributions, standard deduction[1] — Number of returns (1,000)	Amount (mil. dol.)	State	Charitable contributions, itemized — Number of returns (1,000)	Amount (mil. dol.)	Charitable contributions, standard deduction[1] — Number of returns (1,000)	Amount (mil. dol.)
Total[2]	12,074	261,590	47,994	17,950	MO	144	3,453	861	334
AL	133	3,267	740	291	MT	33	746	174	63
AK	15	258	92	34	NE	48	1,554	310	122
AZ	237	4,134	973	351	NV	102	2,449	423	150
AR	63	5,292	358	147	NH	42	911	238	86
CA	2,297	43,544	5,287	1,903	NJ	513	6,402	1,629	632
CO	255	5,178	853	300	NM	44	709	262	95
CT	171	3,284	640	238	NY	831	25,114	3,094	1,140
DE	38	496	158	60	NC	325	6,109	1,551	594
DC	57	986	97	28	ND	13	668	111	44
FL	640	17,573	3,199	1,184	OH	238	4,709	1,737	643
GA	462	8,888	1,425	531	OK	91	2,239	477	188
HI	60	589	220	76	OR	183	3,399	552	198
ID	58	1,401	276	110	PA	354	6,417	2,171	829
IL	430	9,690	1,983	745	RI	37	430	192	71
IN	134	3,535	972	372	SC	154	3,192	762	295
IA	73	1,266	492	194	SD	16	893	141	57
KS	74	1,926	410	160	TN	157	4,432	981	385
KY	86	1,539	627	248	TX	825	22,052	3,603	1,345
LA	107	1,854	582	222	UT	175	5,046	473	195
ME	30	532	210	75	VT	14	355	100	35
MD	509	6,745	843	302	VA	463	7,030	1,193	441
MA	336	8,407	1,234	445	WA	315	7,983	1,062	387
MI	234	4,521	1,558	592	WV	20	337	181	71
MN	203	3,573	956	366	WI	140	2,758	984	371
MS	69	1,233	371	146	WY	12	1,287	78	31

[1] A temporary change in tax law allows taxpayers who take the standard deduction to claim a deduction for qualifying charitable cash contributions on Form 1040. For 2021 tax year, individuals and married individuals filing separate returns can claim up to $300 for cash contributions; the maximum deduction for married individuals filing joint returns is $600. [2] Includes returns from Puerto Rico and Other areas, not shown separately. Other areas include returns filed from Army Post Office and Fleet Post Office addresses by members of the armed forces stationed overseas, and returns filed by other U.S. citizens abroad.

Source: U.S. Internal Revenue Service, Statistics of Income, Individual Income Tax Return (Form 1040) Statistics: State Data, "Statistics of Income Historic Table 2," <www.irs.gov/statistics/soi-tax-stats-individual-income-tax-return-form-1040-statistics>, accessed March 2024.

Labor Force, Employment, and Earnings

This section presents statistics on the labor force; its distribution by occupation and industry affiliation; and the supply of, demand for, and conditions of labor. Chief sources of labor force data are the Current Population Survey (CPS) conducted by the U.S. Census Bureau for the Bureau of Labor Statistics (BLS), and the BLS's Current Employment Statistics (CES) program. Data from these statistical programs are available on the BLS website. Detailed data on the labor force are also available from the Local Area Unemployment Statistics (LAUS) program, also available on the BLS website.

Types of data—Most statistics in this section are obtained by two methods: household interviews or questionnaires; and reports of establishment payroll records. Each method provides data that the other cannot suitably supply. Population characteristics, for example, are readily obtainable only from the household survey, while detailed industrial classifications can be readily derived only from establishment records.

CPS data are obtained from a monthly sample survey of the population. The CPS is used to gather data for the calendar week, generally the week including the 12th of the month, and provides current comprehensive data on the labor force (see text, Section 1, Population). The CPS provides information on the work status of the population without duplication since each person is classified as employed, unemployed, or not in the labor force. Employed persons holding more than one job are counted only once, according to the job at which they worked the most hours during the survey week.

CES "Employment and Earnings Tables" present data including national totals of the number of persons in the civilian labor force by sex, disability status, race, Hispanic origin, and age; the number employed; hours of work; industry and occupational groups; usual weekly earnings; and the number unemployed, as well as reasons for and duration of unemployment. Annual data shown in this section are averages of monthly figures for each calendar year, unless otherwise specified.

The CPS also produces annual estimates of employment and unemployment for each state, 50 large metropolitan statistical areas, and selected cities. These estimates are published annually in *Geographic Profile of Employment and Unemployment* available at <www.bls.gov/opub/geographic-profile>.

Data based on establishment records are compiled by the BLS and cooperating state agencies as part of an ongoing Current Employment Statistics (CES) program. The BLS collects survey data monthly from a probability-based sample of nonfarm business establishments. Data collection centers perform initial enrollment of each firm via telephone, collect the data for several months via Computer Assisted Telephone Interviewing (CATI), and where possible transfer respondents to a self-reporting mode such as touch-tone data entry, fax, or web collection. Very large, multi-establishment firms' ongoing reporting is established via Electronic Data Interchange (EDI). CES data are adjusted annually to data from government unemployment insurance administrative records, which are supplemented by data from other government agencies. The estimates exclude self-employed persons, private household workers, unpaid family workers, agricultural workers, and members of the Armed Forces.

The CES counts workers each time they appear on a payroll during the reference period (the payroll period that includes the 12th of the month). Thus, unlike the CPS, a person with two jobs is counted twice. The establishment survey is designed to provide estimates of nonfarm wage and salary employment, average weekly hours, and average hourly and weekly earnings by detailed industry for the nation, states, and selected metropolitan areas. Establishment survey data also are published in "Employment and Earnings Tables." Historical national data are available at <www.bls.gov/ces/>. Historical data for states and metropolitan areas are available at <www.bls.gov/sae/>. CES estimates are currently classified by the 2022 North American Industry Classification System (NAICS). All published series for the nation have a NAICS-based history extending back to at least 1990. Employment series for total nonfarm and other high-level aggregates start in 1939.

For more information on data concepts, sample design, and estimating methods for the CES Survey, see the BLS Handbook of Methods, Chapter 2 <www.bls.gov/opub/hom/>. For information regarding revisions and collection rates, see <www.bls.gov/web/empsit/cesbmart.htm>.

Labor force—According to the CPS definitions, the civilian labor force comprises all civilians in the noninstitutionalized population aged 16 years and over classified as "employed" or "unemployed" according to specific criteria. *Employed* civilians comprise (a) all civilians, who, during the reference week, did any work for pay or profit (minimum of an hour's work) or worked 15 hours or more as unpaid workers in a family enterprise and (b) all civilians who were not working but who had jobs or businesses from which they were temporarily absent for noneconomic reasons (illness, weather conditions, vacation, labor-management dispute, etc.) whether they were paid for the time off or were seeking other jobs. *Unemployed* persons comprise all civilians who had no employment during the reference week, who made specific efforts to find a job within the previous 4 weeks (such as applying directly to an employer or to a public employment service or checking with friends) and who were available for work during that week, except for temporary illness. Persons on layoff from a job and expecting recall also are classified as unemployed. All other civilian persons, 16 years old and over, are classified as "not in the labor force."

Various breaks in the CPS data series have occurred over time due to the introduction of population adjustments and other changes. For details on these breaks in series and the effect that they had on the CPS data, see the BLS website at <www.bls.gov/cps/documentation.htm#concepts>.

Beginning in January of each year, the CPS data reflect the introduction of revised population controls. For additional information on the effects of revised population controls on estimates from the CPS, see <www.bls.gov/cps/documentation.htm#pop>.

Hours and earnings—Average hourly earnings, based on establishment data from the CES, are gross earnings (i.e., earnings before payroll deductions) and include overtime premiums; they exclude irregular bonuses and value of payments in kind. Hours are those for which pay was received. Annual wages and salaries, as presented by the CPS, consist of total monies received for work performed by an employee during the income year. It includes wages, salaries, commissions, tips, piece-rate payments, and cash bonuses earned before deductions were made for taxes, bonds, union dues, etc. Persons who worked 35 hours or more per week are classified as working full-time.

Industry and occupational groups—Industry data derived from the CPS for 1983 to 1991 utilize the 1980 census industrial classification developed from the 1972 Standard Industrial Classification (SIC). CPS data from 1971 to 1982 were based on the 1970 census classification system, which was developed from the 1967 SIC. Most of the industry categories were not affected by the change in classification.

The occupational classification system used in the 1980 census and in the CPS for 1983 to 1991, evolved from the 1980 Standard Occupational Classification (SOC) system, first introduced in 1977. Occupational categories used in the 1980 census classification system are so radically different from the 1970 census system used in the CPS through 1982 that their implementation represented a break in historical data series.

Beginning in January 1992, the occupational and industrial classification systems used in the 1990 census were introduced into the CPS. (These systems were largely based on the 1980 SOC and the 1987 SIC systems, respectively.)

Beginning in 2003, the 2002 occupational and industrial classification systems were introduced into the CPS. These systems were derived from the 2000 SOC and the 2002 NAICS. The composition of detailed occupational and industrial classifications in the new classification systems was substantially changed from the previous systems in use, as was the structure for aggregating them into broad groups. Consequently, the use of the new classification systems created breaks in existing data series at all levels of aggregation. CPS data using the new classification systems are available for data from 2000. Additional information on the occupational and industrial classifications systems used in the CPS, including changes over time, appear on the BLS website at <www.bls.gov/cps/documentation.htm#oi>. Establishments responding to the establishment survey are classified according to the most recent classifications, the 2022 NAICS. Previously they were classified according to the SIC manual. See text, Section 15, Business Enterprise, for information about the SIC manual and NAICS.

Productivity—BLS publishes data on output per hour (labor productivity), output per combined unit of labor and capital input (multifactor productivity), and for industry groups and industries, output per combined unit of capital, labor, energy, materials, and purchased service inputs. Labor productivity and related indexes are published for the business sector as a whole and its major subsectors: nonfarm business, manufacturing, and nonfinancial corporations, and for over 200 detailed industries. Productivity indexes that take into account capital, labor, energy, materials, and service inputs are published for 18 major manufacturing industry groups, 86 detailed manufacturing industries, utility services, and air and railroad transportation. The major sector data are published in the BLS quarterly *Productivity and Costs* and in the annual *Total Factor Productivity* release. Industry productivity measures are updated and published annually in the *Productivity and Costs by Industry* and *Total Factor Productivity Trends for Detailed Industries*. The latest data are available at the Productivity website at <www.bls.gov/productivity/>. Detailed information on methods, limitations, and data sources appears in the BLS *Handbook of Methods*, Chapters 10 and 11 at <www.bls.gov/opub/hom/home.htm> and <www.bls.gov/productivity/handbook-of-methods.htm>.

Unions—As defined here, unions include traditional labor unions and employee associations similar to labor unions. Data on union membership status provided by BLS are for employed wage and salary workers and relate to their principal job. Earnings by union membership status are usual weekly earnings of full-time wage and salary workers. The information is collected through the Current Population Survey.

Work stoppages—Work stoppages include all strikes and lockouts known to BLS that last for at least 1 full day or shift and involve 1,000 or more workers. All stoppages, whether or not authorized by a union, legal or illegal, are counted. Excluded are work slowdowns and instances where employees report to work late or leave early to attend meetings or rallies.

Seasonal adjustment—Many economic statistics reflect a regularly recurring seasonal movement that can be estimated on the basis of past experience. By eliminating that part of the change, which can be ascribed to usual seasonal variation (e.g., climate or school openings and closings), it is possible to observe the cyclical and other nonseasonal movements in the series. However, in evaluating deviations from the seasonal pattern—that is, changes in a seasonally adjusted series—it is important to note that seasonal adjustment is merely an approximation based on past experience. Seasonally adjusted estimates have a broader margin of possible error than the original data on which they are based, since they are subject not only to sampling and other errors, but also are affected by the uncertainties of the adjustment process itself. Consistent with BLS practices, annual estimates will be published only for not seasonally-adjusted data.

Statistical reliability—For discussion of statistical collection, estimation, sampling procedures, and measures of statistical reliability applicable to Census Bureau and BLS data, see Appendix III.

Table 620. Civilian Population—Employment Status: 1970 to 2023

[In thousands (137,085 represents 137,085,000), except as indicated. Annual averages of monthly figures. Civilian noninstitutionalized population 16 years old and over. Revisions to population controls and other changes can affect the comparability of data over time; see BLS Handbook of Methods, <www.bls.gov/opub/hom>. Based on Current Population Survey; see text, Section 1 and Appendix III]

Year	Civilian noninsti-tutional population	Civilian labor force				Unemployed		Not in labor force	
		Total	Percent of population	Employed	Employ-ment/population ratio [1]	Number	Percent of labor force	Number	Percent of population
1970	137,085	82,771	60.4	78,678	57.4	4,093	4.9	54,315	39.6
1980	167,745	106,940	63.8	99,303	59.2	7,637	7.1	60,806	36.2
1990	189,164	125,840	66.5	118,793	62.8	7,047	5.6	63,324	33.5
2000	212,577	142,583	67.1	136,891	64.4	5,692	4.0	69,994	32.9
2005	226,082	149,320	66.0	141,730	62.7	7,591	5.1	76,762	34.0
2007	231,867	153,124	66.0	146,047	63.0	7,078	4.6	78,743	34.0
2008	233,788	154,287	66.0	145,362	62.2	8,924	5.8	79,501	34.0
2009	235,801	154,142	65.4	139,877	59.3	14,265	9.3	81,659	34.6
2010	237,830	153,889	64.7	139,064	58.5	14,825	9.6	83,941	35.3
2011	239,618	153,617	64.1	139,869	58.4	13,747	8.9	86,001	35.9
2012	243,284	154,975	63.7	142,469	58.6	12,506	8.1	88,310	36.3
2013	245,679	155,389	63.2	143,929	58.6	11,460	7.4	90,290	36.8
2014	247,947	155,922	62.9	146,305	59.0	9,617	6.2	92,025	37.1
2015	250,801	157,130	62.7	148,834	59.3	8,296	5.3	93,671	37.3
2016	253,538	159,187	62.8	151,436	59.7	7,751	4.9	94,351	37.2
2017	255,079	160,320	62.9	153,337	60.1	6,982	4.4	94,759	37.1
2018	257,791	162,075	62.9	155,761	60.4	6,314	3.9	95,716	37.1
2019	259,175	163,539	63.1	157,538	60.8	6,001	3.7	95,636	36.9
2020	260,329	160,742	61.7	147,795	56.8	12,947	8.1	99,587	38.3
2021	261,445	161,204	61.7	152,581	58.4	8,623	5.3	100,241	38.3
2022	263,973	164,287	62.2	158,291	60.0	5,996	3.6	99,686	37.8
2023	266,942	167,116	62.6	161,037	60.3	6,080	3.6	99,826	37.4

[1] Civilian employed as a percent of the civilian noninstitutional population.

Source: U.S. Bureau of Labor Statistics, CPS Tables, "Employment status of the civilian noninstitutional population, 1953 to Date," January 2024, <www.bls.gov/cps/tables.htm>.

Table 621. Civilian Labor Force and Participation Rate Projections: 2023 to 2033

[167.1 represents 167,100,000. Civilian noninstitutionalized population 16 years old and over. Based on Current Population Survey; see text, Section 1 and Appendix III]

Race, Hispanic origin, sex, and age	Civilian labor force (mil.)						Participation rate (percent) [1]					
	2023 [2]	2029	2030	2031	2032	2033	2023 [2]	2029	2030	2031	2032	2033
Total [3]	167.1	170.9	171.5	172.1	172.7	173.3	62.6	61.6	61.4	61.3	61.2	61.2
Male	88.9	90.1	90.3	90.5	90.7	90.9	68.1	66.5	66.2	66.0	65.8	65.6
16 and 17 years	1.2	1.0	1.0	1.0	1.0	1.0	25.3	23.9	23.7	23.5	23.3	23.0
18 and 19 years	2.0	1.9	1.8	1.8	1.8	1.8	49.3	47.1	46.7	46.4	46.0	45.7
20 to 24 years	8.0	7.7	7.6	7.5	7.4	7.2	72.5	70.1	69.7	69.3	68.9	68.5
25 to 29 years	9.5	9.8	9.7	9.6	9.6	9.6	88.1	86.5	86.3	86.0	85.7	85.3
30 to 34 years	10.4	10.1	10.2	10.4	10.5	10.4	90.5	89.4	89.2	89.0	88.8	88.6
35 to 39 years	10.0	10.4	10.4	10.2	10.2	10.1	90.4	89.4	89.3	89.1	89.0	88.8
40 to 44 years	9.7	10.0	10.1	10.2	10.3	10.4	90.1	89.2	89.0	88.8	88.7	88.5
45 to 49 years	8.7	9.6	9.6	9.7	9.7	9.7	89.8	89.0	88.8	88.7	88.5	88.4
50 to 54 years	8.7	8.3	8.4	8.6	8.7	8.9	85.8	85.0	84.8	84.7	84.6	84.4
55 to 59 years	7.9	7.7	7.5	7.3	7.3	7.3	79.2	79.1	79.1	79.0	79.0	79.0
60 to 64 years	6.6	6.3	6.3	6.4	6.4	6.4	64.2	66.0	66.3	66.6	66.8	67.1
65 to 69 years	3.4	3.8	3.9	3.9	3.8	3.8	38.1	41.2	41.7	42.3	42.8	43.3
70 to 74 years	1.6	2.0	2.0	2.1	2.1	2.2	22.4	23.7	23.9	24.2	24.4	24.6
75 and over years	1.1	1.6	1.7	1.8	1.9	2.0	10.9	12.0	12.2	12.4	12.6	12.8
Female	78.2	80.8	81.2	81.6	82.0	82.5	57.3	56.9	56.9	56.9	56.9	56.9
16 and 17 years	1.3	1.1	1.1	1.1	1.1	1.1	27.7	26.2	25.9	25.7	25.4	25.2
18 and 19 years	1.9	1.8	1.7	1.7	1.7	1.7	48.8	46.9	46.6	46.3	46.0	45.7
20 to 24 years	7.7	7.6	7.6	7.5	7.4	7.3	70.1	69.9	69.9	69.9	69.9	69.8
25 to 29 years	8.4	8.9	8.9	8.8	8.8	8.9	77.9	78.4	78.4	78.5	78.6	78.6
30 to 34 years	9.0	8.8	8.9	9.2	9.3	9.3	78.4	78.7	78.7	78.8	78.8	78.9
35 to 39 years	8.5	9.0	8.9	8.8	8.8	8.8	77.6	77.5	77.5	77.4	77.4	77.4
40 to 44 years	8.3	8.6	8.7	8.8	8.9	9.0	77.3	76.8	76.7	76.7	76.6	76.5
45 to 49 years	7.6	8.4	8.5	8.5	8.6	8.6	77.9	78.0	78.0	78.0	78.0	78.1
50 to 54 years	7.7	7.5	7.7	7.9	8.0	8.2	75.2	76.3	76.5	76.6	76.8	77.0
55 to 59 years	7.0	7.0	6.9	6.8	6.8	6.9	68.4	70.7	71.1	71.4	71.8	72.2
60 to 64 years	5.7	5.6	5.6	5.7	5.8	5.8	52.5	56.3	56.9	57.6	58.2	58.8
65 to 69 years	2.9	3.4	3.4	3.4	3.4	3.4	29.1	32.8	33.4	34.1	34.7	35.4
70 to 74 years	1.4	1.7	1.8	1.8	1.8	1.9	16.4	18.0	18.3	18.6	18.9	19.2
75 and over years	0.9	1.3	1.3	1.4	1.5	1.6	6.3	7.3	7.5	7.7	7.9	8.1
White male	68.9	68.6	68.5	68.4	68.3	68.3	68.2	66.3	66.0	65.8	65.6	65.4
White female	58.4	59.2	59.3	59.4	59.5	59.6	56.5	55.9	55.8	55.8	55.7	55.8
Black male	10.5	10.9	11.0	11.0	11.1	11.2	65.6	64.1	63.8	63.6	63.4	63.2
Black female	11.3	11.9	12.0	12.1	12.2	12.3	61.0	60.8	60.8	60.7	60.8	60.8
All others male [4]	9.4	10.6	10.8	11.0	11.2	11.4	70.7	70.2	70.1	70.0	70.0	70.0
All others female [4]	8.5	9.7	9.9	10.1	10.3	10.5	58.7	59.0	59.0	59.1	59.2	59.3
Hispanic male [5]	17.9	19.8	20.1	20.3	20.6	20.9	75.1	73.9	73.6	73.4	73.2	73.0
Hispanic female [5]	13.9	15.9	16.2	16.5	16.8	17.2	58.7	59.4	59.5	59.6	59.7	59.8

[1] Civilian labor force as a percent of the civilian noninstitutional population projections. [2] Data for 2023 are actual. [3] Includes other races, not shown separately. [4] Includes those classified as being of multiple racial origin and categories of Asian, American Indian and Alaska Native, and Native Hawaiian and Other Pacific Islander. [5] Persons of Hispanic origin may be of any race.

Source: U.S. Bureau of Labor Statistics, "Employment Projections Program," <www.bls.gov/emp/data/labor-force.htm>, accessed August 2024.

Table 622. Civilian Population—Employment Status by Sex, Race, and Ethnicity: 1990 to 2023

[In thousands (90,377 represents 90,377,000), except as indicated. Annual averages of monthly figures. Revisions to population controls and other changes affect the comparability of data over time; see BLS Handbook of Methods, <www.bls.gov/opub/hom/>. For totals see Table 620]

Year, sex, race, and Hispanic origin	Civilian noninstitutionalized population	Civilian labor force				Unemployed		Not in labor force	
		Total	Percent of population	Employed	Employment/ population ratio [1]	Number	Percent of labor force	Number	Percent of population
Male:									
1990	90,377	69,011	76.4	65,104	72.0	3,906	5.7	21,367	23.6
2000	101,964	76,280	74.8	73,305	71.9	2,975	3.9	25,684	25.2
2010	115,174	81,985	71.2	73,359	63.7	8,626	10.5	33,189	28.8
2020	125,922	85,204	67.7	78,560	62.4	6,644	7.8	40,718	32.3
2021	126,487	85,505	67.6	80,829	63.9	4,676	5.5	40,983	32.4
2022	128,617	87,421	68.0	84,203	65.5	3,218	3.7	41,197	32.0
2023	130,476	88,877	68.1	85,500	65.5	3,377	3.8	41,599	31.9
Female:									
1990	98,787	56,829	57.5	53,689	54.3	3,140	5.5	41,957	42.5
2000	110,613	66,303	59.9	63,586	57.5	2,717	4.1	44,310	40.1
2010	122,656	71,904	58.6	65,705	53.6	6,199	8.6	50,752	41.4
2020	134,407	75,538	56.2	69,234	51.5	6,304	8.3	58,869	43.8
2021	134,958	75,699	56.1	71,752	53.2	3,948	5.2	59,259	43.9
2022	135,356	76,866	56.8	74,089	54.7	2,778	3.6	58,490	43.2
2023	136,466	78,239	57.3	75,537	55.4	2,702	3.5	58,227	42.7
White: [2]									
1990	160,625	107,447	66.9	102,261	63.7	5,186	4.8	53,178	33.1
2000	176,220	118,545	67.3	114,424	64.9	4,121	3.5	57,675	32.7
2010	192,075	125,084	65.1	114,168	59.4	10,916	8.7	66,991	34.9
2020	201,306	124,431	61.8	115,341	57.3	9,090	7.3	76,875	38.2
2021	201,881	124,145	61.5	118,291	58.6	5,854	4.7	77,737	38.5
2022	203,214	125,957	62.0	121,908	60.0	4,049	3.2	77,257	38.0
2023	204,515	127,327	62.3	123,165	60.2	4,162	3.3	77,188	37.7
Black: [2]									
1990	21,477	13,740	64.0	12,175	56.7	1,565	11.4	7,737	36.0
2000	24,902	16,397	65.8	15,156	60.9	1,241	7.6	8,505	34.2
2010	28,708	17,862	62.2	15,010	52.3	2,852	16.0	10,846	37.8
2020	33,344	20,177	60.5	17,873	53.6	2,304	11.4	13,167	39.5
2021	33,613	20,482	60.9	18,726	55.7	1,756	8.6	13,131	39.1
2022	34,131	21,236	62.2	19,937	58.4	1,300	6.1	12,895	37.8
2023	34,667	21,886	63.1	20,674	59.6	1,212	5.5	12,781	36.9
Asian: [2, 3]									
2000	9,330	6,270	67.2	6,043	64.8	227	3.6	3,060	32.8
2010	11,199	7,248	64.7	6,705	59.9	543	7.5	3,951	35.3
2020	16,467	10,331	62.7	9,437	57.3	894	8.7	6,136	37.3
2021	16,521	10,545	63.8	10,016	60.6	529	5.0	5,976	36.2
2022	16,933	10,921	64.5	10,615	62.7	306	2.8	6,012	35.5
2023	17,591	11,439	65.0	11,096	63.1	344	3.0	6,152	35.0
Hispanic: [4]									
1990	15,904	10,720	67.4	9,845	61.9	876	8.2	5,184	32.6
2000	23,938	16,689	69.7	15,735	65.7	954	5.7	7,249	30.3
2010	33,713	22,748	67.5	19,906	59.0	2,843	12.5	10,964	32.5
2020	44,182	28,970	65.6	25,952	58.7	3,018	10.4	15,213	34.4
2021	44,902	29,424	65.5	27,429	61.1	1,995	6.8	15,479	34.5
2022	46,171	30,601	66.3	29,299	63.5	1,302	4.3	15,570	33.7
2023	47,532	31,818	66.9	30,343	63.8	1,475	4.6	15,714	33.1
Mexican:									
1990	9,752	6,707	68.8	6,146	63.0	561	8.4	3,045	31.2
2000	15,333	10,783	70.3	10,144	66.2	639	5.9	4,550	29.7
2010	21,267	14,403	67.7	12,622	59.4	1,781	12.4	6,864	32.3
2020	26,393	17,278	65.5	15,568	59.0	1,710	9.9	9,116	34.5
2021	27,000	17,713	65.6	16,532	61.2	1,181	6.7	9,287	34.4
2022	27,692	18,422	66.5	17,626	63.6	796	4.3	9,271	33.5
2023	28,167	18,890	67.1	18,014	64.0	876	4.6	9,277	32.9
Puerto Rican:									
1990	1,718	960	55.9	870	50.6	91	9.5	758	44.1
2000	2,193	1,411	64.3	1,318	60.1	92	6.6	783	35.7
2010	3,110	1,906	61.3	1,612	51.8	293	15.4	1,204	38.7
2020	4,019	2,491	62.0	2,200	54.7	291	11.7	1,527	38.0
2021	4,065	2,435	59.9	2,236	55.0	199	8.2	1,630	40.1
2022	4,175	2,449	58.7	2,310	55.3	139	5.7	1,725	41.3
2023	4,223	2,553	60.5	2,421	57.3	133	5.2	1,670	39.5
Cuban:									
1990	918	603	65.7	559	60.9	44	7.2	315	34.3
2000	1,174	740	63.1	707	60.3	33	4.5	434	37.0
2010	1,549	970	62.6	850	54.9	120	12.4	579	37.4
2020	2,086	1,303	62.5	1,181	56.6	122	9.4	783	37.5
2021	2,115	1,289	60.9	1,217	57.6	72	5.6	826	39.1
2022	2,188	1,394	63.7	1,352	61.8	42	3.0	793	36.2
2023	2,230	1,427	64.0	1,379	61.8	48	3.4	803	36.0

[1] Civilian employed as a percent of the civilian noninstitutional population. [2] Beginning with the 2003 CPS, respondents could choose more than one race. Beginning in 2003, data represent persons who selected this race group only and exclude persons reporting more than one race. The CPS in prior years allowed respondents to report only one race group. [3] Prior to 2003, Asian includes Pacific Islanders. [4] Persons of Hispanic origin may be of any race. Includes persons of other Hispanic or Latino ethnicity, not shown separately.

Source: U.S. Bureau of Labor Statistics, CPS Tables, "Employment status of the civilian noninstitutional population by age, sex, and race" and "Employment status of the Hispanic or Latino population by sex, age, and detailed ethnic group," January 2024, and earlier releases, <www.bls.gov/cps/tables.htm>.

Table 623. Foreign-Born and Native-Born Populations—Employment Status by Selected Characteristics: 2023

[266,942 represents 266,942,000. For civilian noninstitutional population 16 years old and over, except as indicated. The foreign born are persons who reside in the United States but who were born outside the country or in one of its outlying areas to parents who were not U.S. citizens. The foreign born include legally admitted immigrants, refugees, temporary residents such as students and temporary workers, and undocumented immigrants. Annual averages of monthly figures. Based on Current Population Survey; see text, Section 1 and Appendix III]

Characteristic	Civilian noninstitu-tionalized population (1,000)	Civilian labor force					Not in the labor force (1,000)
		Total (1,000)	Participa-tion rate [1]	Employed (1,000)	Unemployed		
					Number (1,000)	Unemploy-ment rate	
Total.........	266,942	167,116	62.6	161,037	6,080	3.6	99,826
Male.........	130,476	88,877	68.1	85,500	3,377	3.8	41,599
Female.........	136,466	78,239	57.3	75,537	2,702	3.5	58,227
FOREIGN BORN							
Total [2].........	46,651	31,051	66.6	29,932	1,119	3.6	15,600
Male.........	22,840	17,704	77.5	17,091	613	3.5	5,136
Female.........	23,811	13,347	56.1	12,841	506	3.8	10,464
Age:							
16 to 24 years old.........	3,698	2,037	55.1	1,880	157	7.7	1,661
25 to 34 years old.........	7,432	5,905	79.5	5,655	250	4.2	1,527
35 to 44 years old.........	10,014	8,097	80.9	7,841	257	3.2	1,917
45 to 54 years old.........	9,545	7,817	81.9	7,589	228	2.9	1,728
55 to 64 years old.........	7,678	5,412	70.5	5,245	167	3.1	2,266
65 years old and over.........	8,283	1,783	21.5	1,722	61	3.4	6,500
Race and Hispanic ethnicity:							
White, non-Hispanic.........	7,850	4,766	60.7	4,612	155	3.2	3,084
Black, non-Hispanic.........	4,562	3,324	72.9	3,197	126	3.8	1,238
Asian, non-Hispanic.........	11,930	7,789	65.3	7,575	214	2.8	4,141
Hispanic [3].........	21,696	14,790	68.2	14,180	610	4.1	6,906
Educational attainment:							
Total, 25 years old and over.........	42,953	29,015	67.5	28,052	962	3.3	13,938
Less than a high school diploma.........	9,315	5,371	57.7	5,129	241	4.5	3,944
High school graduates, no college [4].........	11,299	7,338	64.9	7,067	271	3.7	3,961
Some college or associate's degree.........	6,441	4,378	68.0	4,250	127	2.9	2,063
Bachelor's degree and higher [5].........	15,897	11,928	75.0	11,606	322	2.7	3,969
NATIVE BORN							
Total [2].........	220,291	136,065	61.8	131,104	4,961	3.6	84,226
Male.........	107,636	71,173	66.1	68,409	2,764	3.9	36,463
Female.........	112,655	64,892	57.6	62,695	2,197	3.4	47,763
Age:							
16 to 24 years old.........	35,641	20,092	56.4	18,492	1,600	8.0	15,549
25 to 34 years old.........	37,095	31,398	84.6	30,182	1,216	3.9	5,697
35 to 44 years old.........	33,440	28,333	84.7	27,559	775	2.7	5,107
45 to 54 years old.........	30,414	24,990	82.2	24,397	593	2.4	5,424
55 to 64 years old.........	33,724	21,839	64.8	21,317	522	2.4	11,885
65 years old and over.........	49,977	9,412	18.8	9,157	255	2.7	40,565
Race and Hispanic ethnicity:							
White, non-Hispanic.........	154,634	94,343	61.0	91,617	2,726	2.9	60,291
Black, non-Hispanic.........	27,814	17,045	61.3	16,039	1,006	5.9	10,769
Asian, non-Hispanic.........	5,181	3,343	64.5	3,232	111	3.3	1,838
Hispanic [3].........	25,836	17,027	65.9	16,162	865	5.1	8,809
Educational attainment:							
Total, 25 years and over.........	184,650	115,973	62.8	112,612	3,361	2.9	68,677
Less than a high school diploma.........	10,166	3,810	37.5	3,540	270	7.1	6,356
High school graduates, no college [4].........	52,120	28,590	54.9	27,462	1,127	3.9	23,530
Some college or associate's degree.........	50,485	31,425	62.2	30,463	962	3.1	19,060
Bachelor's degree and higher [5].........	71,880	52,149	72.5	51,147	1,002	1.9	19,731

[1] Civilian labor force as a percent of the civilian noninstitutionalized population. [2] Includes other races, not shown separately. [3] Persons of Hispanic origin may be of any race. [4] Includes persons with a high school diploma or equivalent. [5] Includes persons with bachelor's, master's, professional, and doctoral degrees.

Source: U.S. Bureau of Labor Statistics, *Foreign-Born Workers: Labor Force Characteristics—2023*, USDL 24-1008, May 2024. See also <www.bls.gov/news.release/forbrn.toc.htm>.

Table 624. Employment Status of Veterans by Period of Service and Sex: 2023

[In thousands (257,687 represents 257,687,000). For civilian noninstitutional population 18 years old and over. Veterans are defined as men and women who have previously served on active duty in the U.S. Armed Forces and who were civilians at the time of the survey. Veterans are counted in only one period of service, their most recent wartime period; veterans who served in both a wartime period and any other service period are classified in the wartime period. See text, Section 10. Annual averages of monthly figures. Based on Current Population Survey; see text, Section 1 and Appendix III]

Veteran status, period of service, and sex	Civilian non-institutional population	Civilian labor force						Not in labor force
		Total	Percent of population	Employed		Unemployed		
				Total	Percent of population	Total	Percent of labor force	
Total, 18 years and over.............	257,687	164,666	63.9	158,863	61.6	5,803	3.5	93,021
Veterans.........................	**17,898**	**8,632**	**48.2**	**8,391**	**46.9**	**241**	**2.8**	**9,267**
Gulf War era, total.................	7,995	6,136	76.7	5,955	74.5	181	2.9	1,859
Gulf War era II [1]................	5,039	4,008	79.5	3,877	76.9	131	3.3	1,031
Gulf War era I [2].................	2,956	2,128	72.0	2,079	70.3	50	2.3	828
WWII, Korean War, and Vietnam era [3]......	5,968	808	13.5	787	13.2	21	2.5	5,160
Other service periods [4]............	3,935	1,688	42.9	1,648	41.9	40	2.4	2,247
Nonveterans [5]...................	239,789	156,034	65.1	150,472	62.8	5,562	3.6	83,755
Male, 18 years and over.............	125,793	87,694	69.7	84,468	67.1	3,226	3.7	38,099
Veterans.........................	**15,858**	**7,480**	**47.2**	**7,276**	**45.9**	**204**	**2.7**	**8,378**
Gulf War era, total.................	6,627	5,164	77.9	5,012	75.6	152	2.9	1,463
Gulf War era II [1]................	4,118	3,342	81.2	3,234	78.5	109	3.2	776
Gulf War era I [2].................	2,509	1,822	72.6	1,779	70.9	43	2.4	687
WWII, Korean War, and Vietnam era [3]......	5,715	786	13.8	768	13.4	19	2.4	4,929
Other service periods [4]............	3,516	1,530	43.5	1,496	42.5	34	2.2	1,986
Nonveterans [5]...................	109,935	80,214	73.0	77,192	70.2	3,022	3.8	29,721
Female, 18 years and over.............	131,894	76,972	58.4	74,394	56.4	2,578	3.3	54,922
Veterans.........................	**2,040**	**1,152**	**56.5**	**1,115**	**54.6**	**37**	**3.2**	**888**
Gulf War era, total.................	1,368	972	71.0	943	68.9	29	3.0	396
Gulf War era II [1]................	920	665	72.3	643	69.8	22	3.4	255
Gulf War era I [2].................	447	306	68.5	300	67.0	6	2.1	141
WWII, Korean War, and Vietnam era [3]......	253	22	8.6	20	7.9	2	(S)	231
Other service periods [4]............	419	158	37.7	152	36.2	6	3.9	261
Nonveterans [5]...................	129,854	75,820	58.4	73,280	56.4	2,541	3.4	54,034

S No data or data that do not meet publication criteria (values not shown where base is less than 35,000.) [1] Gulf War era II: September 2001–present. [2] Gulf War era I: August 1990–August 2001. [3] World War II: December 1941–December 1946. Korean War: July 1950–January 1955. Vietnam era: August 1964–April 1975. [4] Other service periods: all other time periods. [5] Nonveterans are men and women who never served on active duty in the U.S. Armed Forces.

Source: U.S. Bureau of Labor Statistics, *Employment Situation of Veterans—2023*, USDL 24-0544, March 2024. See also <www.bls.gov/news.release/vet.nr0.htm>.

Table 625. Labor Force Status of Persons With and Without a Disability: 2023

[33,501 represents 33,501,000. For civilian noninstitutional population 16 years old and over. Persons with a disability are those who have a physical, mental, or emotional condition that causes serious difficulty with their daily activities. Annual averages of monthly figures. Based on the Current Population Survey; see text, Section 1 and Appendix III]

Characteristic	Civilian non-institutional population (1,000)	Civilian labor force					Not in the labor force (1,000)
		Total (1,000)	Participation rate [1]	Employed (1,000)	Unemployed		
					Number (1,000)	Unemployment rate	
WITH DISABILITY							
Total..........................	**33,501**	**8,112**	**24.2**	**7,528**	**585**	**7.2**	**25,389**
Sex:							
Male............................	15,687	4,186	26.7	3,884	302	7.2	11,501
Female..........................	17,814	3,926	22.0	3,644	282	7.2	13,888
Age:							
16 to 64 years....................	16,685	6,715	40.2	6,196	519	7.7	9,970
16 to 19 years....................	876	237	27.0	194	43	18.0	639
20 to 24 years....................	1,240	643	51.8	567	76	11.8	597
25 to 34 years....................	2,591	1,477	57.0	1,341	135	9.2	1,115
35 to 44 years....................	2,600	1,247	48.0	1,157	90	7.2	1,353
45 to 54 years....................	3,344	1,357	40.6	1,269	89	6.5	1,987
55 to 64 years....................	6,032	1,754	29.1	1,668	86	4.9	4,278
65 years and over.................	16,816	1,397	8.3	1,331	66	4.7	15,419
WITHOUT DISABILITY							
Total..........................	**233,441**	**159,004**	**68.1**	**153,509**	**5,495**	**3.5**	**74,437**
Sex:							
Male............................	114,789	84,691	73.8	81,616	3,075	3.6	30,098
Female..........................	118,652	74,313	62.6	71,893	2,420	3.3	44,339
Age:							
16 to 64 years....................	191,998	149,206	77.7	143,961	5,245	3.5	42,792
16 to 19 years....................	16,347	6,123	37.5	5,453	671	11.0	10,224
20 to 24 years....................	20,876	15,126	72.5	14,158	967	6.4	5,750
25 to 34 years....................	41,936	35,826	85.4	34,496	1,330	3.7	6,110
35 to 44 years....................	40,854	35,183	86.1	34,242	941	2.7	5,670
45 to 54 years....................	36,615	31,450	85.9	30,717	733	2.3	5,166
55 to 64 years....................	35,370	25,497	72.1	24,894	603	2.4	9,873
65 years and over.................	41,443	9,798	23.6	9,548	250	2.6	31,645

[1] Civilian labor force as a percent of the civilian noninstitutional population.

Source: U.S. Bureau of Labor Statistics, *Persons with A Disability: Labor Force Characteristics—2023*, USDL 24-0349, February 2024. See also <www.bls.gov/cps/demographics.htm#disability>.

Table 626. Civilian Labor Force—Percent Distribution by Sex and Age: 2000 to 2023

[142,583 represents 142,583,000. Civilian noninstitutionalized population 16 years old and over. Annual averages of monthly figures. Revisions to population controls and other changes can affect the comparability of data over time; see BLS Handbook of Methods, <www.bls.gov/opub/hom/>. Based on Current Population Survey; see text, Section 1 and Appendix III]

Year and sex	Civilian labor force (1,000)	Percent distribution						
		16 to 19 years	20 to 24 years	25 to 34 years	35 to 44 years	45 to 54 years	55 to 64 years	65 years and over
Total:								
2000.....................	142,583	5.8	10.0	23.0	26.3	21.8	10.1	3.0
2010.....................	153,889	3.8	9.8	21.8	21.7	23.4	15.1	4.4
2015.....................	157,130	3.6	9.9	22.0	20.7	21.6	16.5	5.6
2020.....................	160,742	3.6	9.0	22.7	21.1	20.0	17.0	6.6
2023.....................	167,116	3.8	9.4	22.3	21.8	19.6	16.3	6.7
Male:								
2000.....................	76,280	5.6	9.9	23.4	26.3	21.3	10.2	3.3
2010.....................	81,985	3.6	9.6	22.4	22.1	23.0	14.8	4.5
2015.....................	83,620	3.5	9.6	22.5	21.0	21.4	16.3	5.8
2020.....................	85,204	3.4	8.7	22.9	21.4	19.9	16.9	6.9
2023.....................	88,877	3.6	9.0	22.4	22.1	19.6	16.4	6.9
Female:								
2000.....................	66,303	6.0	10.2	22.5	26.4	22.3	9.9	2.7
2010.....................	71,904	4.1	10.0	21.2	21.2	23.8	15.6	4.2
2015.....................	73,510	3.8	10.2	21.6	20.5	21.8	16.8	5.4
2020.....................	75,538	3.8	9.4	22.5	20.8	20.1	17.1	6.3
2023.....................	78,239	4.0	9.9	22.2	21.5	19.6	16.2	6.5

Source: U.S. Bureau of Labor Statistics, CPS Tables, "Employment status of the civilian noninstitutional population by age, sex, and race," January 2024, and earlier releases, <www.bls.gov/cps/tables.htm>.

Table 627. Civilian Labor Force and Participation Rates by Educational Attainment, Sex, Race, and Hispanic Origin: 2010 to 2023

[132,955 represents 132,955,000. Civilian noninstitutional population 25 years old and over. Annual averages of monthly figures. Revisions to population controls and other changes can affect the comparability of data over time; see BLS Handbook of Methods, <www.bls.gov/opub/hom/>. See Table 660 for unemployment data. Rates are based on annual average civilian noninstitutional population of each specified group and represent the proportion of each specified group in the civilian labor force]

Year, sex, and race/ethnicity	Civilian labor force					Participation rate [1] (percent)				
		Percent distribution								
	Total (1,000)	Less than a high school diploma	High school graduate, no college	Some college or associate degree	College graduate	Total	Less than a high school diploma	High school graduate, no college	Some college or associate degree	College graduate
Total: [2]										
2010...............	132,955	8.9	28.8	27.7	34.6	66.5	46.3	61.6	70.5	76.7
2015...............	135,907	8.1	26.0	27.6	38.4	64.0	45.4	57.2	66.6	74.4
2020...............	140,535	6.4	24.7	25.9	43.0	63.1	44.9	55.9	63.5	72.4
2023...............	144,988	6.3	24.8	24.7	44.2	63.7	47.1	56.7	62.9	73.0
Male:										
2010...............	71,129	10.6	30.4	25.6	33.4	74.1	59.1	71.4	76.7	81.3
2015...............	72,698	9.7	28.1	25.8	36.4	71.5	58.3	67.2	73.1	79.0
2020...............	74,929	7.7	27.6	24.9	39.9	70.0	56.7	65.9	70.0	76.7
2023...............	77,652	7.6	27.6	23.8	41.0	70.2	59.4	66.0	69.0	76.9
Female:										
2010...............	61,825	7.0	26.9	30.1	36.0	59.5	33.5	52.4	65.4	72.4
2015...............	63,209	6.2	23.6	29.6	40.7	57.2	32.3	47.6	61.1	70.2
2020...............	65,608	4.9	21.4	27.1	46.6	56.7	32.6	45.7	57.9	68.7
2023...............	67,336	4.8	21.6	25.7	47.9	57.6	34.3	46.9	57.5	69.6
White: [3]										
2010...............	108,274	8.9	28.7	27.5	34.9	66.5	47.7	61.2	70.1	76.5
2015...............	107,366	8.1	25.9	27.5	38.5	63.8	46.7	56.7	65.9	74.0
2020...............	109,013	6.5	24.7	26.0	42.8	62.7	46.8	55.7	62.8	71.6
2023...............	110,601	6.6	24.7	24.8	43.9	62.9	49.2	55.9	61.7	71.7
Black: [3]										
2010...............	15,114	9.4	33.3	32.8	24.5	65.8	38.8	63.8	73.5	79.5
2015...............	16,279	7.5	30.9	33.3	28.3	63.9	37.5	58.8	70.2	77.7
2020...............	17,453	6.0	29.4	30.5	34.1	62.7	35.7	56.3	66.4	76.6
2023...............	18,910	5.5	29.7	29.3	35.6	65.4	39.5	59.3	67.4	78.2
Asian: [3]										
2010...............	6,601	7.3	18.8	17.1	56.7	68.7	44.1	62.8	70.6	75.9
2015...............	8,200	6.1	17.1	16.0	60.9	66.7	40.8	58.8	68.1	73.7
2020...............	9,428	4.8	14.6	13.2	67.4	66.4	41.4	54.9	63.5	73.5
2023...............	10,394	4.3	14.5	13.3	67.8	68.4	39.1	56.2	66.1	76.1
Hispanic: [4]										
2010...............	18,987	31.4	30.8	21.7	16.0	71.4	61.9	73.9	77.8	81.7
2015...............	21,618	27.7	29.8	23.6	18.9	69.3	59.3	69.6	75.5	80.1
2020...............	24,249	21.1	30.8	24.2	24.0	68.5	57.0	67.9	73.3	78.5
2023...............	26,427	20.3	32.2	22.6	24.9	69.8	58.3	69.1	73.8	80.0

[1] Civilian labor force as a percent of the civilian noninstitutional population. [2] Includes other races, not shown separately. [3] For persons in this race group only. See footnote 2, Table 622. [4] Persons of Hispanic origin may be of any race.

Source: U.S. Bureau of Labor Statistics, CPS Tables, "Employment status of the civilian noninstitutional population 25 years and over by educational attainment, sex, race, and Hispanic or Latino ethnicity," January 2024, and earlier releases, <www.bls.gov/cps/tables.htm>.

Table 628. Civilian Labor Force by Employment Status and Sex by State: 2023

[In thousands (167,116 represents 167,116,000), except ratio and rate. Civilian noninstitutionalized population 16 years old and over. Annual averages of monthly figures. Data for states may not sum to national totals due to rounding]

State	Labor force		Employed		Employ- ment/ population ratio [1]	Unemployed					Participation rate [3]	
						Number		Rate [2]				
	Total	Female	Total	Female		Total	Female	Total	Male	Female	Male	Female
United States.....	**167,116**	**78,239**	**161,037**	**75,537**	**60.3**	**6,080**	**2,702**	**3.6**	**3.8**	**3.5**	**68.1**	**57.3**
Alabama............	2,308	1,088	2,254	1,061	55.9	55	26	2.4	2.3	2.4	63.5	51.5
Alaska.............	354	165	337	158	61.5	17	7	4.7	5.0	4.4	66.8	62.1
Arizona............	3,695	1,686	3,551	1,629	59.7	144	57	3.9	4.4	3.4	68.6	55.9
Arkansas..........	1,376	645	1,328	620	55.4	48	26	3.5	3.1	4.0	62.9	52.4
California...........	19,287	8,749	18,382	8,369	59.1	905	380	4.7	5.0	4.3	68.5	55.6
Colorado...........	3,221	1,500	3,117	1,458	66.0	104	43	3.2	3.5	2.8	72.5	63.8
Connecticut........	1,881	907	1,811	880	61.4	70	27	3.7	4.4	3.0	68.3	59.6
Delaware..........	501	244	483	236	58.1	18	8	3.6	3.8	3.3	64.9	56.0
District of Columbia.........	394	200	375	191	67.6	19	9	4.8	4.8	4.7	75.2	67.4
Florida...............	10,961	5,176	10,661	5,028	57.8	300	148	2.7	2.6	2.9	64.6	54.6
Georgia.............	5,310	2,515	5,131	2,440	59.6	179	75	3.4	3.7	3.0	68.2	55.7
Hawaii.............	675	326	654	317	58.2	20	9	3.0	3.2	2.8	63.7	56.6
Idaho..............	963	442	931	427	60.8	32	15	3.3	3.2	3.4	68.2	57.6
Illinois..............	6,405	2,994	6,126	2,872	61.1	279	122	4.4	4.6	4.1	69.7	58.4
Indiana.............	3,397	1,586	3,277	1,532	61.0	120	54	3.5	3.6	3.4	68.5	58.1
Iowa...............	1,706	783	1,655	762	65.6	50	21	2.9	3.2	2.7	73.0	62.1
Kansas............	1,523	706	1,480	686	65.2	43	20	2.8	2.9	2.8	72.7	61.6
Kentucky..........	2,008	934	1,923	894	54.2	86	40	4.3	4.2	4.3	62.2	51.4
Louisiana..........	2,064	998	1,987	963	56.1	77	35	3.7	3.9	3.5	63.2	53.8
Maine..............	692	332	671	321	57.8	21	10	3.0	2.9	3.2	63.5	55.9
Maryland...........	3,213	1,551	3,125	1,515	63.9	87	37	2.7	3.1	2.4	71.1	60.7
Massachusetts......	3,756	1,838	3,629	1,788	62.9	127	51	3.4	4.0	2.8	68.6	61.9
Michigan...........	5,024	2,360	4,830	2,268	59.7	194	92	3.9	3.8	3.9	67.2	57.3
Minnesota..........	3,097	1,479	3,007	1,438	66.3	90	41	2.9	3.0	2.8	71.4	65.2
Mississippi..........	1,229	583	1,191	562	52.2	38	21	3.1	2.6	3.6	59.9	48.5
Missouri...........	3,077	1,451	2,985	1,410	61.0	93	41	3.0	3.2	2.9	68.1	57.9
Montana...........	582	273	565	266	62.0	17	7	2.9	3.3	2.5	67.4	60.4
Nebraska..........	1,055	498	1,031	489	67.5	23	9	2.2	2.5	1.9	73.0	65.2
Nevada............	1,600	728	1,521	697	59.5	79	32	5.0	5.5	4.3	68.5	56.8
New Hampshire.....	752	349	734	341	62.9	18	9	2.4	2.4	2.4	69.3	59.6
New Jersey.........	4,824	2,247	4,598	2,152	61.8	226	96	4.7	5.1	4.3	71.1	58.9
New Mexico........	945	442	908	426	53.9	37	16	3.9	4.2	3.7	60.9	51.4
New York..........	9,708	4,610	9,293	4,446	58.5	415	164	4.3	4.9	3.6	66.5	56.1
North Carolina.......	5,226	2,510	5,058	2,420	59.0	168	90	3.2	2.9	3.6	66.3	56.1
North Dakota.......	418	187	409	184	67.9	8	3	2.0	2.2	1.8	74.8	63.6
Ohio...............	5,794	2,742	5,596	2,656	59.8	198	86	3.4	3.6	3.2	66.8	57.2
Oklahoma..........	1,975	906	1,906	872	61.1	69	33	3.5	3.3	3.6	70.0	56.9
Oregon.............	2,136	1,005	2,057	967	59.3	79	38	3.7	3.6	3.8	66.0	57.3
Pennsylvania.......	6,516	3,102	6,313	3,005	60.2	203	97	3.1	3.1	3.1	66.7	57.9
Rhode Island.......	579	277	559	270	62.0	19	8	3.3	3.9	2.7	68.7	59.8
South Carolina......	2,475	1,206	2,397	1,168	56.1	78	38	3.1	3.1	3.2	62.4	53.8
South Dakota.......	489	226	479	222	68.1	9	4	1.9	2.2	1.6	73.9	64.8
Tennessee..........	3,390	1,591	3,276	1,540	58.0	114	51	3.4	3.5	3.2	65.9	54.5
Texas...............	15,159	6,943	14,556	6,661	62.3	604	282	4.0	3.9	4.1	71.4	58.5
Utah................	1,794	793	1,746	771	67.8	48	23	2.7	2.5	2.8	76.9	62.2
Vermont............	352	169	346	166	63.7	6	3	1.8	2.0	1.7	68.1	61.8
Virginia.............	4,569	2,190	4,443	2,128	64.7	126	62	2.8	2.7	2.8	71.5	61.9
Washington.........	4,026	1,830	3,859	1,761	61.7	167	69	4.1	4.5	3.8	70.2	58.4
West Virginia.......	769	360	741	348	51.8	28	11	3.7	4.2	3.2	58.0	49.6
Wisconsin...........	3,144	1478	3,044	1,433	64.0	100	44	3.2	3.4	3.0	70.4	61.8
Wyoming...........	298	134	289	129	62.6	9	4	3.0	2.7	3.3	69.7	59.2

[1] Civilian employment as a percent of civilian noninstitutionalized population. [2] The unemployed as a percent of the civilian labor force. [3] Percent of civilian noninstitutionalized population of each specified group in the civilian labor force.

Source: U.S. Bureau of Labor Statistics, Labor Force Statistics from the Current Population Survey, "Employment status of the civilian noninstitutional population by sex, age, and race," <www.bls.gov/cps/tables.htm>; and Local Area Unemployment Statistics, "Expanded State Employment Status Demographic Data," <www.bls.gov/lau/>; accessed July 2024.

Table 629. Civilian Labor Force Status by Selected Metropolitan Statistical Area: 2023

[167,116 represents 167,116,000. Civilian noninstitutional population 16 years old and over. Annual averages of monthly figures. Data are derived from the Local Area Unemployment Statistics program, a Federal-State cooperative effort in which monthly estimates of total employment and unemployment are prepared for approximately 7,500 areas. For definitions of metropolitan statistical areas, see Appendix II]

Metropolitan statistical area ranked by 2020 population	Civilian labor force (1,000)	Unemployment rate [1]	Metropolitan statistical area ranked by 2020 population	Civilian labor force (1,000)	Unemployment rate [1]
United States, total	167,116	3.6	Sacramento-Roseville-Arden-Arcade, CA	1,129	4.3
New York-Newark-Jersey City, NY-NJ-PA	10,368	4.4	Pittsburgh, PA	1,179	3.5
Los Angeles-Long Beach-Anaheim, CA	6,605	4.7	Austin-Round Rock, TX	1,455	3.3
Chicago-Naperville-Elgin, IL-IN-WI	4,925	4.3	Las Vegas-Henderson-Paradise, NV	1,186	5.4
Dallas-Fort Worth-Arlington, TX	4,377	3.7	Cincinnati, OH-KY-IN	1,142	3.3
Houston-The Woodlands-Sugar Land, TX	3,622	4.2	Kansas City, MO-KS	1,164	2.9
Washington-Arlington-Alexandria, DC-VA-MD-WV	3,482	2.6	Columbus, OH	1,129	3.1
Philadelphia-Camden-Wilmington, PA-NJ-DE-MD	3,256	3.6	Indianapolis-Carmel-Anderson, IN	1,123	3.0
Miami-Fort Lauderdale-West Palm Beach, FL	3,242	2.5	Cleveland-Elyria, OH	1,034	3.7
Atlanta-Sandy Springs-Roswell, GA	3,233	3.1	San Jose-Sunnyvale-Santa Clara, CA	1,071	3.6
Boston-Cambridge-Nashua, MA-NH [2]	2,797	3.1	Nashville-Davidson-Murfreesboro-Franklin, TN	1,145	2.6
Phoenix-Mesa-Scottsdale, AZ	2,645	3.5	Virginia Beach-Norfolk-Newport News, VA-NC	880	3.1
San Francisco-Oakland-Hayward, CA	2,517	3.7	Providence-Warwick, RI-MA [2]	708	3.2
Riverside-San Bernardino-Ontario, CA	2,172	4.7	Jacksonville, FL	845	3.0
Detroit-Warren-Dearborn, MI	2,183	3.6	Milwaukee-Waukesha-West Allis, WI	820	3.3
Seattle-Tacoma-Bellevue, WA	2,262	3.7	Oklahoma City, OK	749	3.0
Minneapolis-St. Paul-Bloomington, MN-WI	2,024	2.7	Raleigh, NC	795	3.0
San Diego-Carlsbad, CA	1,596	3.9	Memphis, TN-MS-AR	623	4.0
Tampa-St. Petersburg-Clearwater, FL	1,692	3.0	Richmond, VA	721	3.0
Denver-Aurora-Lakewood, CO	1,742	3.2	Louisville-Jefferson County, KY-IN	663	3.7
Baltimore-Columbia-Towson, MD	1,488	2.1	New Orleans-Metairie, LA	586	3.8
St. Louis, MO-IL	1,475	3.2	Salt Lake City, UT	733	2.7
Orlando-Kissimmee-Sanford, FL	1,476	2.9	Hartford-West Hartford-East Hartford, CT [2]	617	3.7
Charlotte-Concord-Gastonia, NC-SC	1,458	3.2	Buffalo-Cheektowaga-Niagara Falls, NY	549	3.8
San Antonio-New Braunfels, TX	1,284	3.7	Birmingham-Hoover, AL	571	2.3
Portland-Vancouver-Hillsboro, OR-WA	1,358	3.6	Rochester, NY	526	3.6

[1] Percent of the civilian labor force unemployed. [2] New England City and Town Areas (NECTA). See Appendix II.

Source: U.S. Bureau of Labor Statistics, "Local Area Unemployment Statistics," <www.bls.gov/lau/>, accessed May 2024.

Table 630. School Enrollment and Labor Force Status of Teenagers and Young Adults: 2023

[In thousands (39,392 represents 39,392,000), except rate. As of October. Covers civilian noninstitutional population age 16 to 24. Based on Current Population Survey; see text, Section 1 and Appendix III]

Characteristic	Population	Civilian labor force	Employed	Unemployed Total	Unemployed Rate [1]	Not in labor force
Total persons age 16 to 24 [2]	39,392	22,255	20,358	1,897	8.5	17,138
Enrolled in school [2]	21,439	8,003	7,413	590	7.4	13,436
Enrolled in high school	9,533	2,447	2,144	303	12.4	7,085
Male	4,995	1,231	1,051	180	14.6	3,764
Female	4,538	1,217	1,093	124	10.2	3,321
Enrolled in college	11,906	5,556	5,269	287	5.2	6,350
Male	5,356	2,188	2,072	116	5.3	3,168
Female	6,551	3,368	3,197	171	5.1	3,183
Enrolled in two-year college	2,563	1,477	1,404	72	4.9	1,086
Enrolled in four-year college	9,343	4,079	3,865	214	5.3	5,264
White:						
Enrolled in high school	6,851	1,943	1,720	223	11.5	4,907
Enrolled in college	8,507	4,164	3,982	182	4.4	4,343
Black or African American:						
Enrolled in high school	1,493	261	221	40	15.5	1,232
Enrolled in college	1,594	700	646	54	7.7	895
Asian:						
Enrolled in high school	458	29	28	1	(NA)	429
Enrolled in college	1,176	386	357	29	7.6	789
Hispanic: [3]						
Enrolled in high school	2,421	496	399	97	19.6	1,925
Enrolled in college	2,340	1,184	1,143	40	3.4	1,156
Not enrolled in school [2]	17,953	14,251	12,945	1,307	9.2	3,702
White	13,315	10,595	9,758	837	7.9	2,720
Black	2,691	2,188	1,881	307	14.0	503
Asian	698	515	480	34	6.7	184
Hispanic [3]	5,002	3,981	3,578	403	10.1	1,021

NA Not available. [1] Percent unemployed of civilian labor force in each category. [2] Includes other races, not shown separately. [3] Persons of Hispanic origin may be of any race.

Source: U.S. Bureau of Labor Statistics, *College Enrollment and Work Activity of Recent High School and College Graduates—2023*, USDL 24-0742, April 2024. See also <www.bls.gov/news.release/hsgec.toc.htm>.

Table 631. Labor Force Participation Rates by Marital Status, Sex, and Age: 1970 to 2023

[In percent. For the civilian noninstitutional population 16 years old and over. Annual averages of monthly figures. Participation rate is the civilian labor force as a percent of the civilian noninstitutional population. Based on Current Population Survey; see text, Section 1 and Appendix III]

Marital status and year	Male participation rate							Female participation rate						
	Total	16–19 years	20–24 years	25–34 years	35–44 years	45–64 years	65 years and over	Total	16–19 years	20–24 years	25–34 years	35–44 years	45–64 years	65 years and over
Single: [1]														
1970	65.5	54.6	73.8	87.9	86.2	75.7	25.2	56.8	44.7	73.0	81.4	78.6	73.0	19.7
1980	72.6	59.9	81.3	89.2	82.2	66.9	16.8	64.4	53.6	75.2	83.3	76.9	65.6	13.9
1990	74.8	55.1	81.6	89.9	84.5	67.3	15.7	66.7	51.7	74.5	80.9	80.8	66.2	12.1
2000	73.6	52.5	80.5	89.4	82.9	69.7	17.3	68.9	51.1	76.1	83.9	80.9	69.9	10.8
2010	67.3	34.6	73.1	85.8	83.7	67.6	25.0	63.3	34.9	69.8	81.3	78.2	69.4	20.1
2015	66.8	33.9	71.7	85.6	81.2	64.6	26.6	62.9	34.1	69.3	79.7	77.6	65.8	20.9
2017	67.4	34.4	72.9	85.6	82.8	64.2	26.3	64.3	35.7	69.8	81.7	78.9	66.0	23.7
2018	67.7	34.0	72.1	85.9	83.4	66.4	25.9	64.5	35.9	70.2	81.4	78.4	66.3	25.2
2019	68.1	34.7	72.9	86.0	82.6	67.0	26.5	65.0	35.7	71.5	81.9	77.9	67.0	24.4
2020	66.3	33.9	69.8	83.3	81.0	66.3	26.4	63.5	34.9	68.3	80.2	77.7	66.6	23.6
2021	67.6	35.7	71.9	84.2	81.6	65.8	26.7	64.3	36.5	69.2	80.7	77.3	66.7	21.7
2022	68.0	36.1	72.2	85.8	81.6	66.7	25.0	64.7	37.1	69.3	82.0	79.4	65.5	23.1
2023	68.5	36.3	71.6	86.6	82.3	67.7	26.1	65.2	37.4	70.9	82.0	79.1	67.0	23.3
Married: [2]														
1970	86.1	92.3	94.7	98.0	98.1	91.2	29.9	40.5	37.8	47.9	38.8	46.8	44.0	7.3
1980	80.9	91.3	96.9	97.5	97.2	84.3	20.5	49.8	49.3	61.4	58.8	61.8	46.9	7.3
1990	78.6	92.1	95.6	96.9	96.7	82.6	17.5	58.4	49.5	66.1	69.6	74.0	56.5	8.5
2000	77.3	79.5	94.1	96.7	95.8	83.0	19.2	61.1	53.2	63.8	70.3	74.8	65.4	10.1
2010	75.8	78.2	89.3	94.3	94.5	83.6	23.5	61.0	40.2	60.9	68.8	72.8	68.8	15.2
2015	73.4	75.9	89.7	93.5	94.2	83.1	25.2	58.1	47.1	61.6	67.1	71.9	66.0	16.8
2017	72.9	80.1	89.1	93.4	94.1	83.5	25.4	58.2	50.6	61.0	68.4	72.3	67.0	17.0
2018	73.1	89.5	88.9	94.4	94.4	83.9	25.7	58.2	48.7	61.7	69.4	72.4	67.2	17.1
2019	73.0	89.9	90.6	94.4	94.6	84.3	26.4	58.6	48.4	62.4	70.5	73.5	67.6	17.9
2020	71.4	77.3	89.0	93.5	93.7	83.2	25.3	57.4	36.6	61.4	70.4	72.7	66.6	17.0
2021	70.9	86.3	89.5	93.7	93.8	83.3	24.7	56.9	43.8	63.5	70.6	72.3	66.8	16.3
2022	71.3	80.7	90.0	94.2	93.8	83.9	25.1	57.9	61.8	63.5	72.1	74.0	67.4	16.8
2023	71.4	73.5	89.6	94.5	94.3	84.6	24.3	58.6	49.0	63.8	73.3	76.2	68.1	17.0
Other: [3]														
1970	60.7	(B)	90.4	93.7	91.1	78.5	19.3	40.3	48.6	60.3	64.6	68.8	61.9	10.0
1980	67.5	(B)	92.6	94.1	91.9	73.3	13.7	43.6	50.0	68.4	76.5	77.1	60.2	8.2
1990	68.9	(B)	93.1	93.0	90.7	74.9	12.0	47.2	53.9	65.4	77.0	82.1	65.0	8.4
2000	66.8	60.5	88.1	93.2	89.9	73.9	12.9	49.0	46.0	74.0	83.1	82.9	69.8	8.7
2010	63.0	37.6	78.8	89.0	88.5	71.8	17.2	48.8	35.2	66.3	77.7	80.7	68.8	12.1
2015	58.8	36.6	73.0	87.0	86.8	70.3	17.7	46.7	42.9	67.0	75.4	79.0	66.4	13.4
2017	59.0	34.7	77.5	88.7	87.9	71.1	19.0	46.0	31.8	63.5	79.0	79.7	66.0	13.5
2018	58.3	33.3	75.3	87.0	87.6	71.7	19.1	45.9	31.9	64.3	79.8	80.6	66.4	13.8
2019	58.2	39.0	71.3	86.9	88.0	72.0	19.6	45.9	31.7	66.9	79.3	81.0	67.2	14.2
2020	57.1	41.0	74.8	87.6	86.6	71.7	19.3	44.3	38.5	65.0	77.7	80.5	66.5	13.5
2021	56.0	40.4	76.6	88.7	86.5	71.0	18.7	43.9	34.8	66.9	76.8	79.7	67.0	13.2
2022	56.0	37.4	73.2	87.0	87.8	71.1	19.6	43.9	31.3	67.5	80.0	80.6	67.3	13.0
2023	55.5	39.6	67.9	87.4	87.6	71.5	19.4	44.0	36.1	66.8	79.6	80.0	68.9	13.9

B Percentage not shown where base is less than 50,000. [1] Never married. [2] Spouse present. [3] Widowed, divorced, and separated (married, spouse absent).

Source: U.S. Bureau of Labor Statistics, Current Population Survey, unpublished data. See also <www.bls.gov/cps/home.htm>.

Table 632. Marital Status of Women in the Civilian Labor Force: 1970 to 2023

[31,543 represents 31,543,000. For civilian noninstitutional population 16 years and over. Annual averages of monthly figures. Based on the Current Population Survey; see text, Section 1 and Appendix III]

Year	Female civilian labor force (1,000)				Female participation rate (percent) [3]			
	Total	Never married	Married [1]	Other [2]	Total	Never married	Married [1]	Other [2]
1970	31,543	7,265	18,475	5,804	43.3	56.8	40.5	40.3
1980	45,487	11,865	24,980	8,643	51.5	64.4	49.8	43.6
1990	56,829	14,612	30,901	11,315	57.5	66.7	58.4	47.2
2000	66,303	17,849	35,146	13,308	59.9	68.9	61.1	49.0
2010	71,904	20,592	36,742	14,570	58.6	63.3	61.0	48.8
2012	72,648	21,506	36,436	14,706	57.7	62.8	59.5	48.3
2013	72,722	22,070	36,137	14,515	57.2	63.0	58.9	47.3
2014	73,039	22,320	36,082	14,637	57.0	62.9	58.4	47.3
2015	73,510	22,738	36,135	14,637	56.7	62.9	58.1	46.7
2016	74,433	23,321	36,387	14,725	56.8	63.4	57.9	46.9
2017	75,174	23,993	36,776	14,405	57.0	64.3	58.2	46.0
2018	75,979	24,556	36,885	14,538	57.1	64.5	58.2	45.9
2019	76,852	25,023	37,214	14,615	57.4	65.0	58.6	45.9
2020	75,539	24,749	37,157	13,633	56.2	63.5	57.4	44.3
2021	75,699	25,766	36,260	13,673	56.1	64.3	56.9	43.9
2022	76,867	26,232	37,142	13,493	56.8	64.7	57.9	43.9
2023	78,240	26,917	37,779	13,544	57.3	65.2	58.6	44.0

[1] Spouse present. [2] Widowed, divorced, and separated (married, spouse absent). [3] Civilian labor force as a percent of the civilian noninstitutional population.

Source: U.S. Bureau of Labor Statistics, Current Population Survey, unpublished data. See also <www.bls.gov/cps/home.htm>.

Table 633. Married Couples by Labor Force Status of Spouses: 1990 to 2023

[52,317 represents 52,317,000. As of March. For opposite-sex married family groups only. Based on the Annual Social and Economic Supplement (ASEC) to the Current Population Survey; for details see source and Appendix III]

| Year | Number (1,000) | | | | | Percent distribution | | | | |
| | All married couples | In labor force | | | Husband & wife not in labor force | All married couples | In labor force | | | Husband & wife not in labor force |
		Husband & wife	Husband only	Wife only			Husband & wife	Husband only	Wife only	
TOTAL										
1990...........	52,317	28,056	13,013	2,453	8,794	100.0	53.6	24.9	4.7	16.8
2000...........	55,311	31,095	11,815	3,301	9,098	100.0	56.2	21.4	6.0	16.4
2010...........	60,384	32,731	13,074	4,526	10,053	100.0	54.2	21.7	7.5	16.6
2015...........	62,230	31,688	14,164	4,757	11,622	100.0	50.9	22.8	7.6	18.7
2018...........	63,739	32,373	14,202	4,826	12,339	100.0	50.8	22.3	7.6	19.4
2019...........	63,882	32,773	13,614	4,976	12,519	100.0	51.3	21.3	7.8	19.6
2020...........	64,248	32,598	13,626	4,804	13,222	100.0	50.7	21.2	7.5	20.6
2021...........	62,963	31,581	13,166	4,813	13,404	100.0	50.2	20.9	7.6	21.3
2022...........	63,191	32,144	13,169	4,715	13,163	100.0	50.9	20.8	7.5	20.8
2023...........	63,869	32,785	12,676	4,756	13,652	100.0	51.3	19.8	7.4	21.4
WITH CHILDREN UNDER AGE 18										
1990...........	24,537	15,768	7,667	558	544	100.0	64.3	31.2	2.3	2.2
2000...........	25,248	17,116	6,950	795	387	100.0	67.8	27.5	3.1	1.5
2010...........	25,317	16,710	7,220	962	425	100.0	66.0	28.5	3.8	1.7
2015...........	24,857	15,828	7,454	987	589	100.0	63.7	30.0	4.0	2.4
2018...........	24,555	15,903	7,132	1,043	476	100.0	64.8	29.0	4.2	1.9
2019...........	24,421	16,175	6,868	921	458	100.0	66.2	28.1	3.8	1.9
2020...........	24,378	16,196	6,720	957	506	100.0	66.4	27.6	3.9	2.1
2021...........	23,879	15,666	6,665	992	555	100.0	65.6	27.9	4.2	2.3
2022...........	23,908	16,193	6,368	896	452	100.0	67.7	26.6	3.7	1.9
2023...........	24,040	16,607	6,052	942	440	100.0	69.1	25.2	3.9	1.8
WITH CHILDREN UNDER AGE 6										
1990...........	12,051	6,932	4,692	192	235	100.0	57.5	38.9	1.6	2.0
2000...........	11,393	6,984	4,077	211	121	100.0	61.3	35.8	1.9	1.1
2010...........	11,599	6,924	4,181	335	159	100.0	59.7	36.0	2.9	1.4
2015...........	10,862	6,351	3,969	320	222	100.0	58.5	36.5	2.9	2.0
2018...........	11,001	6,464	4,025	356	157	100.0	58.8	36.6	3.2	1.4
2019...........	10,903	6,697	3,770	290	147	100.0	61.4	34.6	2.7	1.3
2020...........	10,979	6,846	3,605	326	202	100.0	62.4	32.8	3.0	1.8
2021...........	10,458	6,447	3,439	363	209	100.0	61.6	32.9	3.5	2.0
2022...........	10,695	6,843	3,366	319	167	100.0	64.0	31.5	3.0	1.6
2023...........	10,449	6,823	3,175	314	136	100.0	65.3	30.4	3.0	1.3

Source: U.S. Census Bureau, Families and Living Arrangements, Historical Families Tables, "Table MC-1. Opposite-Sex Married Couples by Labor Force Status of Spouses: 1986 to Present," <www.census.gov/data/tables/time-series/demo/families/families.html>, accessed May 2024.

Table 634. Employed Civilians and Weekly Hours: 2000 to 2023

[In thousands (136,891 represents 136,891,000), except as indicated. Annual averages of monthly figures. Civilian noninstitutionalized population 16 years old and over. Based on Current Population Survey; see text, Section 1 and Appendix III]

Item	2000	2010	2015	2019	2020	2021	2022	2023
Total employed...............	**136,891**	**139,064**	**148,834**	**157,538**	**147,795**	**152,581**	**158,291**	**161,037**
Age:								
16 to 19 years old..................	7,189	4,378	4,734	5,150	4,695	5,266	5,600	5,647
20 to 24 years old..................	13,229	12,699	14,022	14,172	12,497	13,409	13,778	14,725
25 to 34 years old..................	31,549	30,229	32,742	35,807	33,426	34,578	35,300	35,838
35 to 44 years old..................	36,433	30,663	31,252	33,127	31,807	32,734	34,624	35,399
45 to 54 years old..................	30,310	33,191	32,643	32,042	30,099	30,554	31,654	31,986
55 to 64 years old..................	14,002	21,636	24,975	26,893	25,454	25,912	26,761	26,562
65 years old and over..............	4,179	6,268	8,465	10,347	9,818	10,127	10,574	10,879
Sex:								
Male..............................	73,305	73,359	79,131	83,460	78,560	80,829	84,203	85,500
Female...........................	63,586	65,705	69,703	74,078	69,234	71,752	74,089	75,537
Marital status:								
Single (never married).............	36,967	38,800	45,148	50,855	47,137	51,272	53,516	54,976
Married, spouse present............	78,287	77,874	79,935	82,315	78,925	78,867	81,905	83,088
Widowed, divorced, separated.......	21,636	22,390	23,751	24,369	21,733	22,443	22,869	22,973
Class of worker:								
Nonagricultural industries.........	134,427	136,858	146,411	155,113	145,446	150,290	156,001	158,772
Wage and salary worker [1]........	125,114	127,914	137,678	146,262	136,881	140,993	146,814	149,692
Self-employed....................	9,205	8,860	8,665	8,799	8,511	9,230	9,129	9,030
Unpaid family workers............	108	84	68	53	55	67	58	50
Agriculture and related industries...	2,464	2,206	2,422	2,425	2,349	2,291	2,290	2,264
Wage and salary worker [1]........	1,421	1,353	1,547	1,658	1,578	1,524	1,514	1,531
Self-employed....................	1,010	821	844	741	742	727	745	698
Unpaid family workers............	33	33	32	26	29	40	32	35
Weekly hours:								
Nonagricultural industries:								
Wage and salary workers [1].......	39.6	38.3	38.7	39.1	38.4	38.9	38.8	38.7
Self-employed....................	39.7	35.6	36.1	36.1	34.3	35.0	35.3	34.9
Unpaid family workers............	32.5	33.3	28.9	32.3	30.9	31.3	30.6	30.2

[1] Includes the incorporated self-employed.

Source: U.S. Bureau of Labor Statistics, "Labor Force Statistics from the Current Population Survey," <www.bls.gov/cps>, accessed May 2024.

Table 635. Labor Force Participation Rates of Married Women by Race/Ethnicity and Presence and Age of Own Children: 2019 to 2023

[In percent. For the civilian noninstitutional population 16 years old and over. Annual averages of monthly figures. Participation rate is the civilian labor force as a percent of the civilian noninstitutional population for each group specified. Data are shown for married women with spouse present. Prior to 2020, estimates of married persons included only persons in opposite-sex couples. Beginning 2020, estimates of married persons include persons in opposite-sex and same-sex couples; therefore data by marital status are not strictly comparable with data from earlier years. Children are biological, step-, or adopted children living in the household who are under age 18. Not included are nieces, nephews, grandchildren, other related and unrelated children, and children not living in the household. Based on Current Population Survey; see text, Section 1, and Appendix III]

Presence and age of children	2019	2020	2021	2022	2023				
					Total	White	Black	Asian	His-panic [1]
Married women, total............................	**58.6**	**57.4**	**56.9**	**57.9**	**58.6**	**57.6**	**66.1**	**60.7**	**57.3**
No children under 18 years..........................	51.7	50.4	49.6	50.1	50.4	49.4	57.1	53.7	53.6
With children under 18 years........................	69.9	69.2	69.3	71.1	72.7	72.5	80.2	69.8	61.3
With own children under 6 years...................	64.0	64.3	64.3	66.5	68.0	68.0	75.8	66.0	55.0
With own children under age 3...................	62.2	62.9	62.6	65.4	66.4	66.7	73.1	63.7	50.8
With own child under 1 year old...............	60.5	60.6	62.2	63.5	63.2	64.2	63.8	60.7	49.4
With own child 1 year old......................	63.2	63.1	62.4	66.2	67.3	67.6	77.3	62.1	51.6
With own child 2 years old....................	62.9	65.0	63.2	66.6	68.6	68.5	77.3	68.0	51.4
With own children 6 to 17 years, none younger..	74.5	73.1	73.3	74.7	76.1	75.8	83.6	72.8	65.9

[1] Persons of Hispanic origin may be of any race.

Source: U.S. Bureau of Labor Statistics, Current Population Survey, "Marital and family labor force statistics," <www.bls.gov/cps/data.htm>, accessed July 2024.

Table 636. Persons at Work by Hours Worked Per Week: 2023

[In thousands (155,167 represents 155,167,000), except as indicated. Civilian noninstitutionalized population 16 years old and over. Annual averages of monthly figures. Persons "at work" are a subgroup of employed persons. This subgroup excludes those absent from their jobs during the survey reference period for reasons such as vacation, illness, or industrial dispute. Based on Current Population Survey; see text, Section 1, and Appendix III]

Hours of work per week	Persons at work (1,000)			Percent distribution		
	Total	Agriculture and related industries	Non-agricultural industries	Total	Agriculture and related industries	Non-agricultural industries
Total..	**155,167**	**2,179**	**152,987**	**100.0**	**100.0**	**100.0**
1 to 34 hours...................................	34,869	587	34,282	22.5	26.9	22.4
1 to 4 hours..................................	1,613	42	1,571	1.0	1.9	1.0
5 to 14 hours.................................	5,475	134	5,341	3.5	6.2	3.5
15 to 29 hours...............................	17,082	269	16,813	11.0	12.4	11.0
30 to 34 hours...............................	10,699	142	10,557	6.9	6.5	6.9
35 hours and over.............................	120,298	1,592	118,705	77.5	73.1	77.6
35 to 39 hours...............................	9,390	97	9,293	6.1	4.4	6.1
40 hours.....................................	76,549	737	75,812	49.3	33.8	49.6
41 hours and over............................	34,359	758	33,600	22.1	34.8	22.0
41 to 48 hours.............................	12,184	141	12,043	7.9	6.5	7.9
49 to 59 hours.............................	13,453	247	13,205	8.7	11.3	8.6
60 hours and over..........................	8,722	370	8,352	5.6	17.0	5.5
Average weekly hours of:						
Total persons at work.........................	38.5	41.0	38.5	(X)	(X)	(X)
Persons usually working full-time [1].............	41.9	46.7	41.9	(X)	(X)	(X)

X Not applicable. [1] Full-time workers are those who usually worked 35 hours or more per week (at all jobs).

Source: U.S. Bureau of Labor Statistics, CPS Tables, "Persons at work in agriculture and nonagricultural industries by hours of work," January 2024, <www.bls.gov/cps/tables.htm>.

Table 637. Persons With a Job, But Not at Work by Reason: 1990 to 2023

[In thousands (6,160 represents 6,160,000), except percent. For civilian noninstitutionalized population 16 years old and over. Annual averages of monthly figures. Based on Current Population Survey; see text, Section 1 and Appendix III]

Reason for not working	1990	2000	2010	2015	2017	2018	2019	2020	2021	2022	2023
Total not at work....................	**6,160**	**5,681**	**5,060**	**5,066**	**5,607**	**5,367**	**5,298**	**6,734**	**5,822**	**6,234**	**5,870**
Percent of employed................	5.2	4.2	3.6	3.4	3.7	3.4	3.4	4.6	3.9	3.9	3.6
Reason for not working:											
Vacation............................	3,529	3,109	2,487	2,563	2,893	2,724	2,702	1,903	2,201	2,692	2,866
Illness..............................	1,341	1,156	942	907	951	981	960	1,463	1,436	1,583	1,099
Child care problems.................	(NA)	(NA)	(NA)	32	30	33	33	66	56	59	47
Other family/personal obligations..	(NA)	(NA)	(NA)	259	266	269	271	266	318	326	305
Labor/industrial dispute............	24	14	8	5	5	6	11	5	9	7	29
Bad weather........................	90	89	172	119	241	179	125	92	149	90	93
Maternity or paternity leave........	(NA)	(NA)	(NA)	322	315	331	344	355	364	396	430
School/training.....................	(NA)	(NA)	(NA)	134	135	131	140	99	125	141	140
Civic/military duty..................	(NA)	(NA)	(NA)	8	9	6	7	7	6	7	7
All other...........................	1,177	1,313	1,451	718	762	707	706	2,479	1,158	932	854

NA Not available.

Source: U.S. Bureau of Labor Statistics, Current Population Survey, unpublished data. See also <www.bls.gov/cps/>.

Table 638. Self-Employed Workers by Industry and Occupation: 2000 to 2023

[In thousands (10,214 represents 10,214,000). Civilian noninstitutionalized population 16 years old and over. Annual averages of monthly figures. Data represent the unincorporated self-employed. Excludes the incorporated self-employed who are considered wage and salary workers. Based on the occupational and industrial classification derived from those used in the 2000 census. Beginning with data for 2020, based on the 2018 Census occupational classification and the 2017 Census industry classification. See text, this section. Based on the Current Population Survey (CPS); see text, Section 1 and Appendix III]

Industry and occupation	2000	2010	2015	2018	2019	2020	2021	2022	2023
Total self-employed....................	10,214	9,681	9,509	9,707	9,539	9,253	9,956	9,874	9,728
INDUSTRY									
Agriculture and related industries.....................	1,010	821	844	766	741	742	727	745	698
Mining.................................	12	20	21	10	14	10	13	14	11
Construction.........................	1,728	1,699	1,603	1,650	1,671	1,558	1,704	1,696	1,562
Manufacturing.......................	334	304	288	258	264	273	272	323	308
Wholesale and retail trade..........	1,221	962	870	812	762	772	853	734	759
Transportation and utilities..........	348	360	397	443	550	531	601	696	684
Information...........................	139	139	161	144	139	143	154	150	140
Financial activities..................	735	641	625	724	678	744	808	788	765
Professional and business services..................	1,927	1,999	1,944	2,054	1,982	1,922	2,065	1,927	1,923
Education and health services.......	1,107	1,100	1,069	1,072	1,034	1,000	1,057	966	990
Leisure and hospitality...............	660	610	698	701	683	604	652	724	753
Other services.......................	993	1,028	988	1,075	1,022	954	1,052	1,112	1,136
OCCUPATION									
Management, professional, and related occupations........................	4,169	3,928	3,958	4,109	4,051	3,964	4,187	4,132	4,138
Service occupations.................	1,775	1,885	1,948	2,023	1,904	1,772	1,993	1,842	1,894
Sales and office occupations.........	1,982	1,586	1,470	1,432	1,432	1,441	1,584	1,514	1,484
Natural resources, construction, and maintenance occupations........................	1,591	1,635	1,482	1,463	1,405	1,384	1,459	1,551	1,393
Production, transportation, and material moving occupations........................	698	647	650	679	748	692	732	835	820

Source: U.S. Bureau of Labor Statistics, "Labor Force Statistics from the Current Population Survey," <www.bls.gov/cps/tables.htm>, accessed July 2024; and unpublished CPS data.

Table 639. Multiple Jobholders: 2023

[8,087 represents 8,087,000. Annual average of monthly figures. Civilian noninstitutionalized population 16 years old and over. Multiple jobholders are employed persons who either had jobs as wage or salary workers with two or more different employers; were self-employed and also held a wage and salary job; or were unpaid family workers and also held a wage and salary job. Based on the Current Population Survey; see text, Section 1 and Appendix III]

Characteristic	Total		Male		Female	
	Number (1,000)	Percent of employed	Number (1,000)	Percent of employed	Number (1,000)	Percent of employed
Total [1,2]......................	8,087	5.0	3,904	4.6	4,183	5.5
Age:						
16 to 19 years old...............	202	3.6	77	2.7	125	4.4
20 to 24 years old...............	700	4.8	261	3.5	439	6.0
25 to 54 years old...............	5,441	5.3	2,687	4.9	2,754	5.7
55 to 64 years old...............	1,303	4.9	637	4.5	666	5.4
65 years old and over............	441	4.1	243	4.1	198	4.0
Race and ethnicity:						
White.............................	6,098	5.0	3,005	4.5	3,093	5.5
Black.............................	1,231	6.0	545	5.5	686	6.4
Asian.............................	410	3.7	212	3.6	199	3.8
Hispanic [3]......................	1,034	3.4	527	3.1	507	3.8
Marital status:						
Married, spouse present [4]........	4,058	4.9	2,265	4.9	1,793	4.8
Widowed, divorced, or separated...	1,330	5.8	462	4.7	868	6.6
Single, never married............	2,699	4.9	1,176	4.0	1,522	6.0
Full- or part-time status: [5]						
Primary job full-time, secondary job part-time.............	4,663	(S)	2,440	(S)	2,222	(S)
Both jobs part-time..............	1,935	(S)	689	(S)	1,245	(S)
Both jobs full-time..............	392	(S)	217	(S)	175	(S)
Hours vary on primary or secondary job..................	1,032	(S)	530	(S)	502	(S)

S No data or data do not meet publication criteria. [1] Includes a small number of persons who work part-time on their primary job and full-time on their secondary job(s), not shown separately. [2] Includes other races, not shown separately. [3] Persons of Hispanic origin may be of any race. [4] Refers to persons in both opposite-sex and same-sex married couples. [5] Full-time work is 35 or more hours per week; part-time work is less than 35 hours per week.

Source: U.S. Bureau of Labor Statistics, CPS Tables, "Multiple jobholders by selected characteristics," January 2024, <www.bls.gov/cps/tables.htm>.

Table 640. Working Poor and People and Families in the Labor Force by Poverty Status: 2010 to 2022

[In thousands (146,859 represents 146,859,000), except rate. The labor force includes people working or looking for work for at least 27 weeks during the year. The working poor rate is the number of individuals in the labor force (working or looking for work) whose incomes are below the official poverty level, as a percent of all people in the labor force. Based on the Current Population Survey, Annual Social and Economic Supplement]

Characteristic	2010	2014	2015	2016	2017	2018	2019	2020	2021	2022
Total in the labor force [1] ...	**146,859**	**150,319**	**152,230**	**153,364**	**154,762**	**156,454**	**157,769**	**153,201**	**156,347**	**158,965**
In poverty.................	10,512	9,487	8,560	7,572	6,946	6,964	6,318	6,306	6,352	6,425
Working poor rate.............	7.2	6.3	5.6	4.9	4.5	4.5	4.0	4.1	4.1	4.0
Unrelated individuals..........	34,099	35,018	35,953	35,789	36,959	37,082	36,805	37,080	37,856	38,170
In poverty.................	3,947	3,395	3,137	2,792	2,524	2,684	2,445	2,424	2,496	2,435
Working poor rate.............	11.6	9.7	8.7	7.8	6.8	7.2	6.6	6.5	6.6	6.4
Primary families [2].............	64,931	66,732	67,193	67,628	67,588	68,099	68,318	66,781	67,860	67,780
In poverty.................	5,269	5,108	4,607	4,082	3,854	3,628	3,232	3,260	3,257	3,315
Working poor rate.............	8.1	7.7	6.9	6.0	5.7	5.3	4.7	4.9	4.8	4.9

[1] Includes individuals in families, not shown separately. [2] Primary families with at least one member in the labor force for more than half the year.

Source: U.S. Bureau of Labor Statistics, "A Profile of the Working Poor, 2022," <www.bls.gov/opub/reports/working-poor/2022/home.htm>, accessed August 2024.

Table 641. Average Number of Jobs Held From Ages 18 to 56 During 1978 to 2020

[For persons ages 55 to 64 in 2020-2021 (and who were ages 14 to 22 when first interviewed in 1979). A job is an uninterrupted period of work with a particular employer. Educational attainment as of 2020-2021 survey. Based on the National Longitudinal Survey of Youth 1979; see source for details]

Sex, race, ethnicity and educational attainment	Average jobs held [1]	Average number of jobs held by age			
		18 to 24 years	25 to 34 years	35 to 44 years	45 to 56 years
Total [2]........................	**12.7**	**5.6**	**4.5**	**2.9**	**2.3**
Less than a high school diploma..........................	12.6	5.1	4.7	2.9	1.9
High school graduate, no college...........................	12.3	5.2	4.4	2.9	2.2
Some college or associate's degree........................	13.2	5.7	4.7	3.1	2.6
Bachelor's degree or more..............................	12.8	6.2	4.4	2.8	2.5
Male.................................	12.8	5.8	4.7	2.9	2.3
Less than a high school diploma..........................	14.1	6.2	5.6	3.1	1.9
High school graduate, no college...........................	12.7	5.7	4.7	2.8	2.2
Some college or associate's degree........................	13.4	5.9	4.9	3.0	2.5
Bachelor's degree or more..............................	12.1	5.9	4.2	2.8	2.4
Female.................................	12.5	5.4	4.3	2.9	2.4
Less than a high school diploma..........................	10.4	3.7	3.4	2.5	1.8
High school graduate, no college...........................	11.7	4.7	4.0	2.9	2.1
Some college or associate's degree........................	13.1	5.6	4.5	3.1	2.6
Bachelor's degree or more..............................	13.4	6.5	4.5	2.8	2.5
White, non-Hispanic.................................	12.7	5.8	4.5	2.8	2.4
Less than a high school diploma..........................	13.3	5.6	4.9	3.0	1.9
High school graduate, no college...........................	12.3	5.4	4.3	2.8	2.2
Some college or associate's degree........................	13.5	6.0	4.7	3.0	2.6
Bachelor's degree or more..............................	12.7	6.3	4.4	2.8	2.4
Black, non-Hispanic.................................	12.3	4.8	4.7	3.2	2.3
Less than a high school diploma..........................	10.8	3.8	4.4	2.6	1.5
High school graduate, no college...........................	12.3	4.6	4.8	3.2	2.2
Some college or associate's degree........................	12.2	4.8	4.6	3.4	2.5
Bachelor's degree or more..............................	13.4	5.6	4.6	3.2	2.8
Hispanic [3].................................	12.2	5.1	4.3	3.0	2.4
Less than a high school diploma..........................	11.6	4.5	4.3	2.8	2.1
High school graduate, no college...........................	11.9	5.0	4.1	2.9	2.2
Some college or associate's degree........................	13.1	5.4	4.5	3.2	2.7
Bachelor's degree or more..............................	12.5	5.4	4.4	2.8	2.4

[1] Jobs held in more than one age category were counted in each category, but only once in the total. [2] Includes other races, not shown separately. [3] Persons of Hispanic origin may be of any race.

Source: U.S. Bureau of Labor Statistics, *Number of Jobs, Labor Market Experience, Marital Status and Health for those Born 1957-1964,* USDL 23-1854, August 2023. See also <www.bls.gov/news.release/nlsoy.nr0.htm>.

Table 642. Distribution of Workers by Tenure With Current Employer by Selected Characteristics: 2022

[139,890 represents 139,890,000. As of January. From a supplement to the January Current Population Survey. For employed wage and salary workers 16 years old and over. Data exclude the incorporated and unincorporated self-employed; see source and Appendix III]

Characteristic	Number employed (1,000)	Percent distribution by tenure with current employer								Median years [1]
		12 months or less	13-23 months	2 years	3-4 years	5-9 years	10-14 years	15-19 years	20 years or more	
Total [2]	**139,890**	**24.3**	**5.7**	**5.2**	**17.9**	**19.9**	**9.7**	**6.4**	**10.8**	**4.1**
AGE AND SEX										
16 to 19 years old	4,983	78.5	8.8	6.0	6.4	0.3	(B)	(B)	(B)	(NA)
20 years old and over	134,907	22.3	5.6	5.1	18.4	20.6	10.1	6.7	11.2	(NA)
20 to 24 years old	12,934	54.2	12.4	9.9	19.1	4.3	(B)	(B)	(B)	1.2
25 to 34 years old	32,546	30.6	7.6	7.2	25.9	23.2	5.0	0.6	(B)	2.8
35 to 44 years old	30,927	19.2	5.3	4.7	18.8	25.4	14.0	9.2	3.4	4.7
45 to 54 years old	27,665	12.9	4.0	3.9	15.4	21.2	13.2	10.4	18.9	6.9
55 to 64 years old	23,090	11.6	2.5	2.5	12.6	19.3	12.6	10.1	28.9	9.8
65 years old and over	7,745	11.2	2.2	3.0	11.7	19.5	13.9	9.9	28.5	9.9
Male	**72,383**	**22.9**	**5.5**	**5.1**	**18.1**	**20.1**	**10.3**	**6.6**	**11.4**	**4.3**
16 to 19 years old	2,416	78.4	8.2	6.1	6.6	0.5	(B)	(B)	(B)	(NA)
20 years old and over	69,967	21.0	5.4	5.0	18.5	20.8	10.7	6.8	11.8	(NA)
20 to 24 years old	6,477	51.9	11.7	10.2	21.1	5.1	0.1	(B)	(B)	1.3
25 to 34 years old	16,999	28.9	7.5	7.3	25.6	24.3	5.7	0.6	(B)	2.9
35 to 44 years old	16,300	17.7	5.1	4.5	18.8	25.4	14.8	9.8	3.9	5.0
45 to 54 years old	14,209	12.0	3.8	3.7	14.9	21.0	13.3	11.0	20.3	7.5
55 to 64 years old	11,864	11.3	2.6	2.1	12.6	18.7	13.7	9.0	30.2	10.0
65 years old and over	4,117	11.4	1.9	2.9	13.5	18.8	14.1	9.9	27.5	9.7
Female	**67,507**	**25.7**	**6.0**	**5.3**	**17.7**	**19.6**	**9.1**	**6.3**	**10.3**	**3.8**
16 to 19 years old	2,567	78.6	9.4	5.8	6.1	0.1	(B)	(B)	(B)	(NA)
20 years old and over	64,940	23.7	5.9	5.3	18.2	20.3	9.4	6.6	10.7	(NA)
20 to 24 years old	6,457	56.6	13.1	9.6	17.2	3.5	(B)	(B)	(B)	1.1
25 to 34 years old	15,546	32.5	7.7	7.1	26.1	21.9	4.3	0.5	(B)	2.7
35 to 44 years old	14,627	20.9	5.6	4.9	18.8	25.3	13.1	8.5	2.8	4.5
45 to 54 years old	13,456	13.9	4.3	4.1	15.9	21.5	13.1	9.8	17.5	6.3
55 to 64 years old	11,226	11.9	2.4	2.9	12.7	20.0	11.4	11.4	27.4	9.5
65 years old and over	3,628	11.0	2.7	3.1	9.6	20.2	13.7	10.0	29.7	10.0
RACE AND HISPANIC ORIGIN										
White [3]	107,284	23.4	5.8	5.1	17.5	19.9	9.9	6.7	11.6	(NA)
Male	56,560	22.0	5.7	4.9	17.5	20.2	10.6	6.9	12.2	(NA)
Female	50,724	24.9	6.0	5.3	17.6	19.6	9.2	6.5	11.0	(NA)
Black [3]	17,214	28.6	5.0	5.0	18.8	18.7	9.0	5.8	9.1	(NA)
Male	8,048	28.7	4.5	5.4	19.3	18.2	8.8	5.5	9.6	(NA)
Female	9,166	28.5	5.3	4.7	18.3	19.1	9.2	6.1	8.7	(NA)
Asian [3]	9,889	22.5	5.9	5.9	21.3	22.1	10.0	4.9	7.5	(NA)
Male	5,053	19.9	5.6	6.0	23.2	23.5	10.1	4.4	7.3	(NA)
Female	4,835	25.1	6.2	5.7	19.4	20.6	9.9	5.4	7.7	(NA)
Hispanic [4]	26,167	27.5	5.4	6.5	19.1	20.7	8.7	5.0	7.1	(NA)
Male	14,596	25.5	4.9	6.3	19.0	21.5	10.2	5.2	7.4	(NA)
Female	11,572	29.9	6.0	6.8	19.3	19.7	6.9	4.7	6.8	(NA)

B No data or base less than 75,000. NA Not available. [1] Median definition, see Guide to Tabular Presentation. [2] Includes other races, not shown separately. [3] For persons in this race group only. See footnote 2, Table 622. [4] Persons of Hispanic origin may be of any race.

Source: U.S. Bureau of Labor Statistics, "Employee Tenure in 2022," USDL 22-1894, September 2022, <www.bls.gov/news.release/tenure.toc.htm>.

Table 643. Part-Time Workers by Reason: 2023

[34,869 represents 34,869,000, except hours. For persons working 1 to 34 hours during the reference week of the survey. For civilian noninstitutionalized population 16 years old and over. Annual average of monthly figures. Based on the Current Population Survey; see text, Section 1 and Appendix III]

Reason	All industries			Nonagricultural industries		
		Usually work—			Usually work—	
	Total	Full-time	Part-time	Total	Full-time	Part-time
Total working fewer than 35 hours	**34,869**	**10,377**	**24,492**	**34,282**	**10,220**	**24,062**
Economic reasons	4,069	1,431	2,638	3,996	1,388	2,609
Slack work or business conditions	2,812	1,195	1,617	2,765	1,165	1,600
Could find only part time work	939	(S)	939	931	(S)	931
Seasonal work	207	126	81	191	113	77
Job started or ended during the week	110	110	(S)	109	109	(S)
Non-economic reasons	30,800	8,945	21,855	30,286	8,832	21,453
Child-care problems	1,230	92	1,139	1,217	90	1,127
Other family or personal obligations	4,792	663	4,129	4,706	653	4,053
Health or medical limitations	1,159	(S)	1,159	1,143	(S)	1,143
In school or training	6,029	71	5,959	5,975	70	5,905
Retired or social security limit on earnings	2,886	(S)	2,886	2,761	(S)	2,761
Vacation or personal day	4,231	4,231	(S)	4,193	4,193	(S)
Holiday, legal, or religious	978	978	(S)	974	974	(S)
Weather-related curtailment	258	258	(S)	232	232	(S)
Other	9,236	2,653	6,583	9,084	2,619	6,465
Average hours per week:						
Economic reasons	23.1	23.6	22.8	23.1	23.6	22.8
Noneconomic reasons	21.3	24.7	19.9	21.3	24.7	20.0

S No data or data do not meet publication standards.

Source: U.S. Bureau of Labor Statistics, CPS Tables, "Persons at work 1 to 34 hours in all and in nonagricultural industries by reason for working less than 35 hours and usual full- or part-time status," January 2024, <www.bls.gov/cps/tables.htm>.

Table 644. Displaced Workers by Selected Characteristics: 2024

[In percent, except total (2,578 represents 2,578,000). As of January 2024. For persons 20 years old and over with job tenure of 3 years or more who lost or left a job between January 2021 and December 2023 because of plant closings or moves, insufficient work for workers to do, or the abolishment of their positions. Based on Current Population Survey; see source and Appendix III]

Characteristic	Total (1,000)	Employment status in January 2024			Reason for job loss, 2021-2023		
		Employed	Unemployed	Not in the labor force	Plant or company closed down or moved	Insufficient work	Position or shift abolished
Total [1]............................	**2,578**	**65.7**	**16.1**	**18.2**	**36.5**	**26.0**	**37.5**
20 to 24 years old.....................	92	85.1	14.9	(3)	35.9	31.1	32.9
25 to 54 years old.....................	1,524	74.5	16.7	8.8	38.4	25.8	35.9
55 to 64 years old.....................	710	55.3	16.1	28.6	30.6	27.6	41.8
65 years old and over...............	253	34.4	13.1	52.5	41.6	21.0	37.3
Males.................................	1,428	65.2	14.9	19.9	35.8	29.0	35.1
20 to 24 years old.....................	60	(3)	(3)	(3)	(3)	(3)	(3)
25 to 54 years old.....................	860	75.8	15.4	8.8	36.6	30.4	33.0
55 to 64 years old.....................	390	46.0	17.3	36.6	33.3	27.0	39.8
65 years old and over...............	118	40.7	3.9	55.4	32.9	28.5	38.6
Females..............................	1,151	66.2	17.6	16.2	37.3	22.2	40.5
20 to 24 years old.....................	32	(3)	(3)	(3)	(3)	(3)	(3)
25 to 54 years old.....................	664	72.9	18.3	8.8	40.7	19.7	39.6
55 to 64 years old.....................	319	66.5	14.6	18.8	27.4	28.4	44.2
65 years old and over...............	135	29.0	21.1	50.0	49.3	14.5	36.2
White only............................	2,052	64.1	16.2	19.7	36.5	25.1	38.4
Male..............................	1,131	59.9	17.2	22.9	35.6	27.8	36.6
Female............................	921	69.3	14.9	15.8	37.6	21.7	40.6
Black only............................	298	72.7	15.6	11.7	29.6	33.4	37.0
Male..............................	175	92.5	0.7	6.8	30.5	31.0	38.5
Female............................	123	44.6	36.7	18.7	28.3	36.7	35.0
Asian only............................	155	63.5	17.9	18.6	43.9	25.5	30.6
Male..............................	83	76.7	10.1	13.3	42.2	42.1	15.7
Female............................	72	(3)	(3)	(3)	(3)	(3)	(3)
Hispanic [2]...........................	454	67.0	21.6	11.5	42.0	25.3	32.7
Male..............................	239	73.6	21.2	5.2	45.4	27.6	27.0
Female............................	216	59.7	21.9	18.4	38.3	22.8	38.9

[1] Includes other races not shown separately. [2] Persons of Hispanic or Latino origin may be of any race. [3] No data or data do not meet publication criteria (base is less than 75,000).

Source: U.S. Bureau of Labor Statistics, *Worker Displacement: 2021-2023*, USDL 24-1777, August 2024. See also <www.bls.gov/news.release/disp.toc.htm>.

Table 645. Persons Not in the Labor Force By Age, Sex, and Reason: 2023

[In thousands (99,826 represents 99,826,000). For civilian noninstitutional population 16 years old and over. Persons who are neither employed nor unemployed are not in the labor force. This includes retired persons, students, those taking care of children or other family members, and others who are neither working nor seeking work. Annual average of monthly figures. Based on the Current Population Survey; see text, Section 1, and Appendix III]

Status and reason	Total	Age			Sex	
		16 to 24 years old	25 to 54 years old	55 years old and over	Male	Female
Total not in the labor force..	**99,826**	**17,210**	**21,400**	**61,215**	**41,599**	**58,227**
Do not want a job now [1]...	94,496	15,574	19,172	59,749	39,072	55,424
Want a job now [1]...	5,330	1,636	2,228	1,466	2,527	2,803
In the previous year:						
Did not search for a job..	3,277	943	1,280	1,054	1,514	1,763
Did search for a job, but not in past 4 weeks [2].....................	2,053	693	948	412	1,013	1,040
Not available for work now.......................................	595	253	252	90	261	333
Available for work now, but not looking for work [3]..............	1,458	440	696	322	752	706
Reason for not currently looking for work:						
Discouraged over job prospects [4]...........................	370	101	186	83	226	144
Family responsibilities..	151	17	102	31	56	95
In school or training..	146	115	28	3	71	75
Ill health or disability...	124	16	52	56	55	69
Other [5]...	667	191	327	149	344	323

[1] Includes some persons who are not asked if they want a job. [2] Persons who had a job in previous 12 months must have searched since the end of that job. [3] Persons who want a job, have searched for work during the previous 12 months, and were available to take a job during the reference week, but had not looked for work in the past 4 weeks; persons are referred to as "marginally attached to the labor force." [4] Includes reasons such as believes no work available, could not find work, lacks necessary schooling or training, employer thinks too young or old, and other types of discrimination. [5] Includes reasons such as child care and transportation problems.

Source: U.S. Bureau of Labor Statistics, CPS Tables, "Persons not in the labor force by desire and availability for work, age, and sex," January 2024, <www.bls.gov/cps/tables.htm>.

Table 646. Employment Status of Parents by Age of Youngest Child and Family Type: 2019 to 2023

[In thousands (33,460 represents 33,460,000), except percent distribution. Annual average of monthly figures. For families with own children under age 18 living in the household (biological children, step-children, and adopted children). Based on the Current Population Survey, see text, Section 1, and Appendix III]

Characteristic	Number					Percent distribution				
	2019	2020	2021	2022	2023	2019	2020	2021	2022	2023
WITH OWN CHILDREN UNDER 18 YEARS OLD										
Total families	**33,460**	**33,047**	**32,756**	**33,253**	**32,610**	**100.0**	**100.0**	**100.0**	**100.0**	**100.0**
Parent(s) employed	30,584	29,259	29,198	30,318	29,958	91.4	88.5	89.1	91.2	91.9
No parent employed	2,876	3,788	3,558	2,934	2,652	8.6	11.5	10.9	8.8	8.1
Total married-couple families [1]	23,005	22,921	22,156	22,672	22,605	100.0	100.0	100.0	100.0	100.0
Parent(s) employed	22,421	21,846	21,372	22,088	22,059	97.5	95.3	96.5	97.4	97.6
Both parents employed	14,810	13,705	13,794	14,746	15,156	64.4	59.8	62.3	65.0	67.0
Only one parent employed	7,611	8,141	7,577	7,342	6,903	33.1	35.5	34.2	32.4	30.5
Neither parent employed	583	1,075	784	584	546	2.5	4.7	3.5	2.6	2.4
Opposite-sex married couple families	22,923	22,826	22,050	22,528	22,469	100.0	100.0	100.0	100.0	100.0
Parent(s) employed	22,342	21,755	21,269	21,946	21,926	97.5	95.3	96.5	97.4	97.6
Mother employed	15,841	15,044	14,955	15,808	16,173	69.1	65.9	67.8	70.2	72.0
Both parents employed	14,754	13,642	13,720	14,648	15,059	64.4	59.8	62.2	65.0	67.0
Mother employed, not father	1,088	1,402	1,234	1,160	1,114	4.7	6.1	5.6	5.1	5.0
Father employed, not mother	6,501	6,711	6,315	6,139	5,753	28.4	29.4	28.6	27.2	25.6
Neither parent employed	581	1,071	780	581	543	2.5	4.7	3.5	2.6	2.4
Families maintained by mother [2]	7,850	7,526	7,904	7,852	7,364	100.0	100.0	100.0	100.0	100.0
Mother employed	5,934	5,344	5,624	5,892	5,614	75.6	71.0	71.2	75.0	76.2
Mother not employed	1,916	2,181	2,280	1,960	1,750	24.4	29.0	28.8	25.0	23.8
Families maintained by father [2]	2,605	2,601	2,696	2,729	2,641	100.0	100.0	100.0	100.0	100.0
Father employed	2,228	2,069	2,202	2,338	2,285	85.5	79.6	81.7	85.7	86.5
Father not employed	377	531	494	391	356	14.5	20.4	18.3	14.3	13.5
WITH OWN CHILDREN 6 to 17 YEARS OLD										
Total families	**19,351**	**19,246**	**19,029**	**19,379**	**19,126**	**100.0**	**100.0**	**100.0**	**100.0**	**100.0**
Parent(s) employed	17,700	17,109	17,058	17,722	17,615	91.5	88.9	89.6	91.5	92.1
No parent employed	1,651	2,137	1,971	1,657	1,511	8.5	11.1	10.4	8.5	7.9
Total married-couple families [1]	12,943	12,939	12,553	12,848	12,911	100.0	100.0	100.0	100.0	100.0
Parent(s) employed	12,555	12,315	12,085	12,472	12,563	97.0	95.2	96.3	97.1	97.3
Both parents employed	8,766	8,090	8,140	8,679	8,975	67.7	62.5	64.9	67.6	69.5
Only one parent employed	3,790	4,224	3,945	3,793	3,588	29.3	32.6	31.4	29.5	27.8
Neither parent employed	388	624	467	376	348	3.0	4.8	3.7	2.9	2.7
Opposite-sex married couple families	12,898	12,887	12,491	12,763	12,823	100.0	100.0	100.0	100.0	100.0
Parent(s) employed	12,512	12,266	12,026	12,389	12,477	97.0	95.2	96.3	97.1	97.3
Mother employed	9,469	8,944	8,908	9,377	9,637	73.4	69.4	71.3	73.5	75.2
Both parents employed	8,736	8,058	8,098	8,622	8,910	67.7	62.5	64.8	67.6	69.5
Mother employed, not father	733	886	810	755	728	5.7	6.9	6.5	5.9	5.7
Father employed, not mother	3,043	3,322	3,118	3,011	2,840	23.6	25.8	25.0	23.6	22.1
Neither parent employed	387	621	464	374	346	3.0	4.8	3.7	2.9	2.7
Families maintained by mother [2]	4,842	4,731	4,881	4,846	4,581	100.0	100.0	100.0	100.0	100.0
Mother employed	3,835	3,538	3,687	3,818	3,656	79.2	74.8	75.5	78.8	79.8
Mother not employed	1,007	1,193	1,194	1,028	925	20.8	25.2	24.5	21.2	20.2
Families maintained by father [2]	1,566	1,576	1,595	1,684	1,634	100.0	100.0	100.0	100.0	100.0
Father employed	1,311	1,256	1,286	1,432	1,396	83.7	79.7	80.6	85.0	85.4
Father not employed	255	320	309	253	238	16.3	20.3	19.4	15.0	14.6
WITH OWN CHILDREN UNDER 6 YEARS OLD										
Total families	**14,109**	**13,801**	**13,727**	**13,874**	**13,484**	**100.0**	**100.0**	**100.0**	**100.0**	**100.0**
Parent(s) employed	12,884	12,150	12,140	12,596	12,344	91.3	88.0	88.4	90.8	91.5
No parent employed	1,225	1,651	1,587	1,278	1,141	8.7	12.0	11.6	9.2	8.5
Total married-couple families [1]	10,061	9,983	9,603	9,824	9,694	100.0	100.0	100.0	100.0	100.0
Parent(s) employed	9,866	9,531	9,286	9,616	9,496	98.1	95.5	96.7	97.9	98.0
Both parents employed	6,045	5,614	5,654	6,066	6,181	60.1	56.2	58.9	61.8	63.8
Only one parent employed	3,821	3,917	3,632	3,549	3,315	38.0	39.2	37.8	36.1	34.2
Neither parent employed	195	451	317	208	198	1.9	4.5	3.3	2.1	2.0
Opposite-sex married couple families	10,025	9,939	9,559	9,765	9,646	100.0	100.0	100.0	100.0	100.0
Parent(s) employed	9,830	9,490	9,243	9,558	9,449	98.1	95.5	96.7	97.9	98.0
Mother employed	6,372	6,100	6,046	6,430	6,536	63.6	61.4	63.3	65.9	67.8
Both parents employed	6,017	5,584	5,622	6,026	6,149	60.0	56.2	58.8	61.7	63.8
Mother employed, not father	355	516	424	404	386	3.5	5.2	4.4	4.1	4.0
Father employed, not mother	3,458	3,390	3,197	3,127	2,913	34.5	34.1	33.4	32.0	30.2
Neither parent employed	194	450	316	207	197	1.9	4.5	3.3	2.1	2.0
Families maintained by mother [2]	3,008	2,795	3,023	3,005	2,783	100.0	100.0	100.0	100.0	100.0
Mother employed	2,099	1,807	1,937	2,074	1,958	69.8	64.6	64.1	69.0	70.4
Mother not employed	909	988	1,086	931	825	30.2	35.4	35.9	31.0	29.6
Families maintained by father [2]	1,040	1,024	1,101	1,045	1,007	100.0	100.0	100.0	100.0	100.0
Father employed	918	813	916	906	890	88.3	79.4	83.2	86.7	88.3
Father not employed	122	211	185	139	118	11.7	20.6	16.8	13.3	11.7

[1] Includes both opposite-sex and same-sex married-couple families. [2] Includes families with no spouse of either sex present.

Source: U.S. Bureau of Labor Statistics, *Employment Characteristics of Families—2023,* USDL 24-0743, April 2024, and earlier releases. See also <www.bls.gov/news.release/famee.toc.htm>.

Table 647. Employed Civilians by Occupation, Sex, Race, and Hispanic Origin: 2023

[161,037 represents 161,037,000. Civilian noninstitutionalized population 16 years old and over. Annual average of monthly figures. Based on Current Population Survey; see text, Section 1 and Appendix III. Occupations reflect the 2018 Standard Occupational Classification]

Occupation	Total employed	Percent of total			
		Female	Black [1]	Asian [1]	Hispanic [2]
Total, 16 years and over...	**161,037**	**46.9**	**12.8**	**6.9**	**18.8**
Management, professional, and related occupations..................	**70,275**	**51.8**	**10.6**	**9.3**	**11.2**
Management, business, and financial operations occupations.........	30,544	45.7	9.8	7.5	11.8
Management occupations [3]..	20,906	41.9	9.2	7.0	12.1
Chief executives...	1,780	30.6	5.2	7.3	6.3
General and operations managers..................................	1,359	37.1	8.4	5.8	13.0
Marketing managers...	567	62.4	7.1	7.1	10.6
Sales managers..	569	33.1	4.8	2.9	11.7
Public relations and fundraising managers........................	110	66.4	12.2	3.0	9.2
Facilities managers..	149	23.4	11.1	1.5	9.4
Computer and information systems managers......................	793	27.7	7.9	17.7	9.6
Financial managers..	1,411	56.2	10.1	9.9	11.9
Human resources managers..	335	76.5	14.7	5.4	12.8
Industrial production managers....................................	279	19.1	6.3	8.4	14.3
Purchasing managers..	241	47.7	16.1	8.0	7.3
Transportation, storage, and distribution managers...............	382	21.4	13.1	5.1	13.5
Farmers, ranchers, and other agricultural managers..............	876	27.4	1.4	0.8	6.4
Construction managers..	1,136	10.6	4.8	2.0	16.1
Education and childcare administrators...........................	1,108	68.6	15.5	5.7	12.0
Architectural and engineering managers..........................	206	12.8	5.4	18.4	9.5
Food service managers..	1,198	46.7	11.5	12.2	19.3
Lodging managers...	141	61.6	10.2	13.3	9.8
Medical and health services managers............................	838	71.8	14.2	5.7	10.7
Property, real estate, and community association managers.......	880	51.7	10.4	5.5	12.6
Social and community service managers...........................	486	71.7	17.5	3.5	11.2
Managers, all other..	5,666	37.5	9.2	7.1	13.1
Business and financial operations occupations [3]...................	9,638	54.0	11.0	8.6	11.2
Wholesale and retail buyers, except farm products..............	225	57.6	8.0	6.8	23.3
Purchasing agents, except wholesale, retail, and farm products..	319	51.9	11.7	6.4	9.1
Claims adjusters, appraisers, examiners, and investigators.......	362	55.2	18.1	2.3	10.4
Compliance officers...	333	51.8	12.5	4.2	14.5
Cost estimators..	148	17.7	0.3	1.9	7.6
Human resources workers..	980	76.5	14.7	6.0	16.7
Training and development specialists..............................	138	56.7	14.1	3.5	12.5
Logisticians...	197	38.7	22.2	6.6	16.1
Project management specialists....................................	935	47.3	9.6	10.1	7.8
Management analysts..	1,060	46.6	6.9	11.7	6.9
Meeting, convention, and event planners..........................	169	69.2	11.8	7.1	17.5
Market research analysts and marketing specialists..............	511	61.7	7.3	10.3	10.8
Business operations specialists, all other.........................	531	57.7	12.7	7.7	14.1
Accountants and auditors..	1,624	57.0	11.9	12.7	8.5
Financial and investment analysts.................................	395	43.9	13.8	11.7	8.3
Personal financial advisors..	506	32.6	6.4	6.3	8.6
Credit counselors and loan officers...............................	343	51.6	10.6	5.6	16.4
Tax preparers...	116	66.3	11.8	9.3	17.2
Other financial specialists...	135	57.8	14.0	12.6	10.6
Professional and related occupations.................................	39,731	56.5	11.3	10.7	10.8
Computer and mathematical occupations [3]......................	6,502	26.9	9.2	24.0	8.8
Computer systems analysts.......................................	513	37.8	12.0	18.3	9.4
Information security analysts.....................................	231	19.3	11.1	7.9	12.6
Computer programmers...	402	21.5	6.5	24.2	9.9
Software developers..	2,134	20.2	6.5	36.2	6.0
Computer support specialists.....................................	687	26.2	13.2	15.0	9.7
Database administrators and architects..........................	122	30.8	10.6	29.3	2.1
Network and computer systems administrators...................	202	16.7	8.6	14.7	11.6
Computer occupations, all other.................................	1,197	26.0	12.4	18.5	11.8
Operations research analysts.....................................	138	55.0	16.1	13.0	8.7
Other mathematical science occupations.........................	402	50.7	7.4	24.4	8.8
Architecture and engineering occupations [3].....................	3,602	16.7	6.1	13.1	10.1
Architects, except landscape and naval..........................	203	31.0	3.5	10.1	11.3
Aerospace engineers...	166	15.2	8.6	12.7	3.6
Civil engineers...	517	16.9	7.2	12.7	11.4
Electrical and electronics engineers..............................	250	11.6	7.7	17.4	10.1
Industrial engineers, including health and safety.................	298	24.6	6.1	12.6	10.3
Mechanical engineers...	433	10.1	6.2	12.8	9.5
Engineers, all other..	669	15.4	5.9	18.2	9.9
Other engineering technologists and technicians, except drafters..	366	17.3	8.5	7.8	13.5
Life, physical, and social science occupations [3].................	1,870	49.8	8.2	16.5	9.9
Biological scientists..	118	55.0	3.1	9.8	5.4
Medical scientists..	130	51.8	8.3	41.1	9.4
Physical scientists, all other.....................................	441	43.1	9.2	29.7	7.5
Other psychologists..	153	78.4	7.4	4.1	10.7
Other life, physical, and social science technicians..............	304	58.6	12.3	13.0	8.0
Community and social service occupations [3].....................	2,879	69.6	19.6	3.9	14.5
Substance abuse and behavioral disorder counselors............	133	78.1	15.6	6.2	13.8
Educational, guidance, and career counselors and advisors......	384	79.2	17.2	2.5	14.1
Mental health counselors...	219	74.6	18.4	2.8	16.8
Counselors, all other...	255	72.3	23.1	3.5	11.3
Social workers, all other..	704	84.2	23.2	3.2	17.1
Social and human service assistants..............................	245	75.3	24.4	5.0	19.8
Clergy..	403	21.4	9.5	7.4	7.5
Legal occupations..	1,897	52.1	10.0	4.4	9.7

See footnotes at end of table.

Table 647. Employed Civilians by Occupation, Sex, Race, and Hispanic Origin: 2023-Continued.

See headnote on page 418.

Occupation	Total employed	Percent of total			
		Female	Black [1]	Asian [1]	His-panic [2]
Lawyers	1,189	39.5	6.8	4.4	5.7
Paralegals and legal assistants	434	83.0	15.3	5.0	16.8
Education, training, and library occupations [3]	9,403	72.8	11.2	5.7	12.1
Postsecondary teachers	1,013	46.6	8.4	10.9	7.9
Preschool and kindergarten teachers	669	96.7	18.7	3.2	16.5
Elementary and middle school teachers	3,436	78.6	11.2	3.8	11.1
Secondary school teachers	944	56.9	6.1	2.7	9.6
Special education teachers	341	86.6	9.8	2.8	7.2
Tutors	141	70.4	6.7	8.1	24.3
Other teachers and instructors	973	62.5	14.2	6.4	13.0
Librarians and media collections specialists	146	82.5	7.0	5.5	11.1
Teaching assistants	1,426	79.5	12.3	9.7	16.9
Other educational instruction and library workers	204	78.8	14.4	4.6	11.1
Arts, design, entertainment, sports, and media occupations [3]	3,478	48.0	9.6	6.7	13.0
Artists and related workers	334	51.6	6.7	8.1	11.3
Graphic designers	312	54.7	6.8	8.5	13.4
Other designers	384	43.1	8.3	10.7	13.8
Producers and directors	167	43.6	12.1	5.3	11.0
Coaches and scouts	288	40.9	14.6	5.6	14.4
Musicians and singers	170	27.1	15.9	5.0	10.9
Public relations specialists	140	76.2	11.2	3.4	7.8
Editors	125	56.6	3.5	4.6	6.5
Writers and authors	271	53.8	5.5	4.9	9.0
Broadcast, sound, and lighting technicians	124	12.2	4.5	3.0	11.1
Photographers	228	48.5	9.2	6.3	10.4
Television, video, and film camera operators and editors	148	18.8	12.5	6.3	16.8
Healthcare practitioners and technical occupations [3]	10,099	75.9	13.5	9.5	9.5
Dentists	164	39.5	4.3	14.5	8.0
Dietitians and nutritionists	114	86.3	13.0	8.2	14.5
Pharmacists	354	57.8	10.0	20.8	5.8
Other physicians	903	45.5	9.0	20.2	6.7
Physician assistants	178	68.8	4.8	6.4	7.5
Occupational therapists	155	88.6	8.0	4.8	4.8
Physical therapists	312	67.5	5.0	5.2	6.0
Speech-language pathologists	185	94.3	6.4	2.6	6.9
Therapists, all other	303	83.9	16.2	3.7	14.1
Registered nurses	3,472	87.4	15.6	8.9	8.9
Nurse practitioners	276	89.8	13.5	7.3	5.5
Clinical laboratory technologists and technicians	302	76.3	14.3	15.0	11.8
Dental hygienists	206	95.7	4.0	5.6	11.8
Radiologic technologists and technicians	259	70.3	8.0	6.8	12.6
Emergency medical technicians	156	39.4	9.2	4.0	16.6
Pharmacy technicians	330	79.3	14.8	9.3	17.6
Psychiatric technicians	113	69.5	33.0	4.2	22.6
Surgical technologists	110	76.9	22.0	2.8	12.1
Veterinary technologists and technicians	142	89.9	5.7	2.5	10.2
Licensed practical and licensed vocational nurses	584	88.7	31.8	5.8	12.6
Medical records specialists	211	88.9	14.4	6.2	12.2
Miscellaneous health technologists and technicians	146	72.7	18.9	7.9	10.0
Other healthcare practitioners and technical occupations	130	66.7	13.8	9.0	10.6
Service occupations	**26,171**	**57.2**	**17.0**	**6.3**	**27.3**
Healthcare support occupations [3]	5,123	84.3	25.0	7.6	21.2
Home health aides	585	87.2	29.8	14.0	24.9
Personal care aides	1,521	79.8	25.3	7.9	21.7
Nursing assistants	1,261	90.1	38.1	6.5	15.0
Massage therapists	145	83.7	8.0	6.5	12.4
Dental assistants	288	92.8	8.4	4.9	32.1
Medical assistants	593	88.8	15.0	5.2	31.8
Phlebotomists	139	90.3	20.2	9.7	19.9
Other healthcare support workers	237	72.1	22.3	7.1	17.8
Protective service occupations [3]	3,105	24.1	22.3	3.2	16.1
Firefighters	296	3.9	8.0	1.3	16.7
Correctional officers and jailers	300	33.9	27.1	3.5	12.8
Detectives and criminal investigators	145	26.3	16.7	2.3	9.7
Police officers	702	14.4	14.2	2.8	16.7
Private detectives and investigators	123	43.0	19.2	3.1	10.4
Security guards and gambling surveillance officers	925	24.9	36.1	4.4	20.2
Other protective service workers	137	45.7	8.7	3.9	13.1
Food preparation and serving related occupations	8,189	53.9	13.5	6.9	29.6
Chefs and head cooks	476	23.3	18.9	18.5	20.7
First-line supervisors of food preparation and serving workers	542	53.5	17.0	3.3	22.8
Cooks	2,016	39.8	17.2	7.0	39.6
Food preparation workers	933	58.7	15.5	4.9	29.8
Bartenders	408	50.8	7.3	3.1	22.3
Fast food and counter workers	885	66.3	10.0	5.2	24.6
Waiters and waitresses	1,805	68.8	9.9	8.5	26.4
Food servers, nonrestaurant	215	69.2	18.9	6.9	24.9
Dining room and cafeteria attendants and bartender helpers	303	43.3	9.7	4.6	32.6
Dishwashers	268	23.1	14.5	4.0	37.9
Hosts and hostesses, restaurant, lounge, and coffee shop	327	86.5	8.2	5.1	25.9
Building and grounds cleaning and maintenance occupations	5,534	42.1	14.3	2.7	41.6
First-line supervisors of housekeeping and janitorial workers	321	44.1	17.3	2.1	31.8
First-line supervisors of landscaping, lawn service, and groundskeeping workers	283	8.0	12.0	1.4	30.4
Janitors and building cleaners	2,204	38.7	16.7	2.6	35.1

See footnotes at end of table.

Occupation	Total employed	Percent of total			
		Female	Black [1]	Asian [1]	His-panic [2]
Maids and housekeeping cleaners.............................	1,380	88.4	16.1	4.3	51.9
Landscaping and groundskeeping workers..................	1,119	7.3	8.6	1.7	49.6
Tree trimmers and pruners.....................................	118	3.0	5.5	1.6	36.7
Personal care and service occupations [3].................	4,220	74.8	13.5	10.5	19.8
Supervisors of personal care and service workers.......	253	65.8	10.6	20.5	11.2
Animal caretakers...	361	76.0	6.0	1.3	16.5
Other entertainment attendants and related workers....	231	42.9	14.0	6.4	14.8
Barbers...	149	28.4	31.1	4.6	39.3
Hairdressers, hairstylists, and cosmetologists............	717	92.1	13.2	6.8	18.0
Manicurists and pedicurists...................................	324	83.5	6.4	64.8	13.7
Childcare workers...	1,036	93.8	15.8	3.8	25.9
Exercise trainers and group fitness instructors...........	257	56.7	10.9	6.2	16.8
Recreation workers..	182	58.9	17.7	2.5	12.9
Personal care and service workers, all other..............	143	60.7	8.3	7.8	20.9
Sales and office occupations.............................	**30,279**	**60.6**	**13.5**	**5.5**	**17.6**
Sales and related occupations [3]...........................	14,325	48.7	11.7	6.1	16.6
First-line supervisors of retail sales workers.............	3,157	44.6	11.1	6.8	14.2
First-line supervisors of non-retail sales workers........	1,268	35.9	8.3	6.2	16.4
Cashiers..	2,576	69.8	16.3	8.1	22.7
Parts salespersons..	117	22.9	5.4	1.2	16.2
Retail salespersons...	2,721	49.2	13.4	5.2	19.6
Advertising sales agents.......................................	111	52.7	7.3	2.7	8.4
Insurance sales agents...	632	54.9	13.3	4.1	18.2
Securities, commodities, and financial services sales agents.........................	249	24.6	8.6	9.0	11.8
Sales representatives of services, except advertising, insurance, financial services, and travel...............	638	31.6	10.7	4.1	10.1
Sales representatives, wholesale and manufacturing....	1,152	27.9	6.0	4.1	11.0
Real estate brokers and sales agents.......................	1,031	57.0	8.8	6.6	11.2
Sales and related workers, all other.........................	339	56.1	12.0	5.1	17.4
Office and administrative support occupations [3]........	15,954	71.2	15.1	5.0	18.5
First-line supervisors of office and administrative support workers......	1,154	65.8	12.5	3.5	16.6
Billing and posting clerks......................................	436	91.4	14.8	3.8	16.5
Bookkeeping, accounting, and auditing clerks.............	1,210	86.2	7.2	5.8	15.9
Payroll and timekeeping clerks...............................	132	88.2	12.3	8.2	19.4
Tellers..	204	78.9	15.4	4.3	16.2
Financial clerks, all other......................................	128	57.7	14.7	11.2	11.9
Customer service representatives............................	2,822	65.3	18.2	5.3	19.8
File clerks..	130	76.0	15.4	4.5	17.0
Interviewers, except eligibility and loan....................	205	79.6	25.2	3.0	24.9
Loan interviewers and clerks..................................	125	76.9	13.6	2.4	17.4
Receptionists and information clerks........................	1,196	89.1	12.8	3.5	22.5
Reservation and transportation ticket agents and travel clerks....................	123	45.9	19.9	7.8	19.1
Couriers and messengers.....................................	929	27.8	23.7	5.1	21.7
Dispatchers, except police, fire, and ambulance.........	184	54.4	14.3	4.5	19.2
Postal service mail carriers...................................	302	34.7	21.9	5.7	13.3
Production, planning, and expediting clerks................	212	43.6	6.5	7.2	16.1
Shipping, receiving, and inventory clerks...................	621	36.8	12.5	5.5	29.1
Executive secretaries and executive administrative assistants................	210	90.0	18.5	4.1	15.0
Secretaries and administrative assistants, except legal, medical, and executive............	1,841	91.9	11.1	3.1	14.8
Data entry keyers..	224	72.7	16.1	7.6	17.6
Insurance claims and policy processing clerks...........	308	80.1	19.2	6.1	17.9
Office clerks, general...	1,274	81.3	13.6	6.4	20.5
Office and administrative support workers, all other.....	447	68.8	12.0	5.2	18.6
Natural resources, construction, and maintenance occupations.............	**14,326**	**5.8**	**7.8**	**1.8**	**34.5**
Farming, fishing, and forestry occupations [3]............	987	27.1	5.1	0.9	44.6
Miscellaneous agricultural workers.........................	731	28.7	3.9	0.8	49.2
Construction and extraction occupations [3]..............	8,457	4.3	7.2	1.3	40.8
First-line supervisors of construction trades and extraction workers........	702	5.1	4.8	1.4	26.6
Brickmasons, blockmasons, and stonemasons...........	117	1.5	1.1	–	50.5
Carpenters...	1,275	3.1	5.2	1.3	44.2
Carpet, floor, and tile installers and finishers.............	114	5.8	1.5	1.5	61.1
Construction laborers...	2,223	4.5	9.1	1.3	51.9
Construction equipment operators...........................	395	1.0	5.7	0.7	20.7
Drywall installers, ceiling tile installers, and tapers.....	162	4.1	7.9	0.9	74.3
Electricians..	959	2.9	6.7	1.6	24.6
Painters and paperhangers....................................	561	10.4	5.5	0.4	60.6
Plumbers, pipefitters, and steamfitters.....................	635	2.2	10.1	2.2	28.3
Roofers...	235	4.4	5.5	0.5	63.1
Sheet metal workers..	127	6.5	9.9	1.5	16.9
Construction and building inspectors.......................	115	10.5	9.4	5.4	20.6
Installation, maintenance, and repair occupations [3]...	4,881	4.1	9.4	2.9	21.6
First-line supervisors of mechanics, installers, and repairers........	239	7.1	5.6	1.8	15.2
Computer, automated teller, and office machine repairers...........	134	13.8	14.7	10.8	9.3
Radio and telecommunications equipment installers and repairers.........	116	5.9	11.5	3.0	18.2
Aircraft mechanics and service technicians...............	124	4.3	9.5	5.0	21.1
Automotive body and related repairers.....................	127	6.8	9.6	1.8	21.6
Automotive service technicians and mechanics..........	933	2.5	8.1	3.5	28.7
Bus and truck mechanics and diesel engine specialists........	334	1.6	6.9	1.8	20.6
Heavy vehicle and mobile equipment service technicians and mechanics........	201	2.3	3.7	0.2	19.3
Heating, air conditioning, and refrigeration mechanics and installers.........	546	2.3	9.5	0.7	23.1
Industrial and refractory machinery mechanics...........	416	3.9	9.9	5.5	18.9
Maintenance and repair workers, general..................	672	4.7	12.2	3.6	24.0
Electrical power-line installers and repairers..............	130	2.3	4.1	–	13.6
Telecommunications line installers and repairers........	160	5.3	19.2	0.6	12.9

See footnotes at end of table.

Table 647. Employed Civilians by Occupation, Sex, Race, and Hispanic Origin: 2023-Continued.

See headnote on page 418.

Occupation	Total employed	Percent of total			
		Female	Black [1]	Asian [1]	His-panic [2]
Other installation, maintenance, and repair workers............	190	4.1	6.9	3.6	33.5
Production, transportation, and material moving occupations............	**19,986**	**24.9**	**17.8**	**4.8**	**25.1**
Production occupations [3]............	8,280	29.9	14.7	5.4	25.6
First-line supervisors of production and operating workers............	776	23.5	14.0	6.4	18.5
Electrical, electronics, and electromechanical assemblers............	114	45.9	24.8	14.9	24.9
Other assemblers and fabricators............	1,048	37.1	21.3	7.3	25.5
Bakers............	233	65.5	7.4	5.6	37.1
Butchers and other meat, poultry, and fish processing workers............	243	27.6	16.3	7.3	36.6
Food processing workers, all other............	140	27.3	22.1	3.1	39.9
Machinists............	307	6.3	6.0	7.5	13.3
Welding, soldering, and brazing workers............	559	5.8	11.1	2.3	26.4
Other metal workers and plastic workers............	361	20.8	16.0	7.5	21.1
Printing press operators............	148	24.7	14.7	3.8	22.0
Laundry and dry-cleaning workers............	121	74.5	13.0	5.3	44.4
Sewing machine operators............	129	70.7	10.9	4.4	41.1
Inspectors, testers, sorters, samplers, and weighers............	793	39.0	13.5	6.9	17.8
Packaging and filling machine operators and tenders............	301	57.3	24.5	4.6	48.4
Painting workers............	142	11.3	13.8	2.7	36.2
Other production workers............	1,280	28.8	16.8	4.1	28.1
Transportation and material moving occupations [3]............	11,706	21.4	20.1	4.4	24.8
Supervisors of transportation and material moving workers............	349	25.5	19.6	8.6	19.3
Aircraft pilots and flight engineers............	211	8.3	3.6	2.7	10.7
Flight attendants............	115	78.0	16.3	3.7	20.0
Bus drivers, school............	218	56.1	23.7	1.1	14.8
Bus drivers, transit and intercity............	284	37.2	32.5	3.1	19.4
Driver/sales workers and truck drivers............	3,551	6.9	20.5	3.5	24.1
Taxi drivers............	456	15.3	24.9	19.5	23.9
Motor vehicle operators, all other............	212	18.2	27.4	4.9	19.1
Industrial truck and tractor operators............	629	9.5	24.6	1.9	31.1
Cleaners of vehicles and equipment............	401	20.4	19.7	3.3	33.5
Laborers and freight, stock, and material movers, hand............	2,090	24.2	19.3	2.7	27.1
Packers and packagers, hand............	690	51.7	25.8	6.3	35.3
Stockers and order fillers............	1,640	36.5	15.5	4.8	23.6
Refuse and recyclable material collectors............	112	12.8	17.1	0.3	33.7

– Represents or rounds to zero. [1] Data represent persons who selected this race group only and exclude persons reporting more than one race. See also comments on race in the text for Section 1. [2] Persons of Hispanic origin may be of any race. [3] Includes other occupations, not shown separately.

Source: U.S. Bureau of Labor Statistics, CPS Tables, "Employed persons by detailed occupation, sex, race, and Hispanic or Latino ethnicity," January 2024, <www.bls.gov/cps/tables.htm>.

Table 648. Employed Workers With Contract, On-Call, Temporary, and Traditional Work Arrangements: 2017

[In thousands (153,331 represents 153,331,000). As of February. For employed workers 16 years old and over. Based on the Current Population Survey; see text, Section 1 and Appendix III]

Characteristic	Total employed [1]	Workers with alternative arrangements				Workers with traditional arrangements
		Independent contractors	On-call workers	Temporary help agency workers	Workers provided by contract firms	
Total employed............	**153,331**	**10,614**	**2,579**	**1,356**	**933**	**137,853**
16 to 19 years old............	4,842	43	107	25	14	4,647
20 to 24 years old............	14,212	330	263	195	53	13,370
25 to 34 years old............	33,991	1,593	516	303	224	31,361
35 to 44 years old............	32,065	2,160	565	283	207	28,849
45 to 54 years old............	32,745	2,562	446	276	206	29,263
55 to 64 years old............	26,236	2,426	399	170	124	23,110
65 years old and over............	9,240	1,500	283	105	106	7,253
Male............	81,545	6,820	1,355	709	625	72,035
16 to 19 years old............	2,365	42	53	20	9	2,235
20 to 24 years old............	7,412	187	169	100	28	6,931
25 to 34 years old............	18,169	1,016	271	170	157	16,554
35 to 44 years old............	17,585	1,430	329	122	144	15,557
45 to 54 years old............	17,099	1,611	208	166	146	14,971
55 to 64 years old............	13,840	1,547	209	81	81	11,914
65 years old and over............	5,076	986	117	50	60	3,873
Female............	71,785	3,794	1,224	647	308	65,818
16 to 19 years old............	2,477	1	55	5	5	2,412
20 to 24 years old............	6,800	143	94	95	25	6,439
25 to 34 years old............	15,823	577	245	133	67	14,807
35 to 44 years old............	14,480	730	237	161	63	13,292
45 to 54 years old............	15,646	951	238	110	60	14,292
55 to 64 years old............	12,396	878	190	88	44	11,196
65 years old and over............	4,164	514	166	55	45	3,380
Full-time workers............	125,240	7,485	1,428	1,042	785	114,496
Part-time workers............	28,091	3,129	1,151	314	148	23,357

[1] Includes day laborers (an alternative arrangement) and a small number of workers who were both "on call" and "provided by contract firms," not shown separately.

Source: U.S. Bureau of Labor Statistics, *Contingent and Alternative Employment Arrangements, May 2017*, USDL 18–0942, June 2018. See also <www.bls.gov/cps/lfcharacteristics.htm#contingent>.

Table 649. Employment and Annual and Hourly Wages by Occupation: 2023

[In dollars, except employment. As of May. Data from the Occupational Employment Statistics survey. For definition of mean and median, see Guide to Tabular Presentation]

Occupation	Employment (number)	Mean hourly wage	Annual wages [1]	Median hourly wage
All occupations [2]	**151,853,870**	**31.48**	**65,470**	**23.11**
Management occupations	10,495,770	66.23	137,750	56.19
Top executives	3,751,510	65.43	136,100	49.74
General and operations managers	3,507,810	62.18	129,330	48.69
Operations specialties managers	2,513,900	74.59	155,150	65.47
Business and financial operations occupations	10,087,830	43.55	90,580	38.00
Business operations specialists	7,048,350	42.33	88,040	37.74
Financial specialists	3,039,480	46.37	96,460	38.50
Computer and mathematical occupations	5,177,400	54.39	113,140	50.10
Computer occupations	4,804,840	54.46	113,270	50.20
Software and web developers, programmers, and testers	2,176,710	62.74	130,500	61.11
Software developers	1,656,880	66.40	138,110	63.59
Architecture and engineering occupations	2,539,660	47.64	99,090	43.95
Engineers	1,703,700	53.79	111,890	49.36
Life, physical, and social science occupations	1,389,430	42.24	87,870	37.63
Community and social service occupations	2,418,130	28.36	58,980	25.00
Legal occupations	1,240,630	64.34	133,820	47.70
Educational instruction and library occupations	8,744,560	31.92	66,400	28.82
Preschool, elementary, middle, secondary, and special education teachers	4,261,430	([3])	68,890	([3])
Elementary and middle school teachers	2,048,970	([3])	70,950	([3])
Arts, design, entertainment, sports, and media occupations	2,106,490	36.31	75,520	28.33
Healthcare practitioners and technical occupations	9,284,210	49.07	102,060	38.86
Healthcare diagnosing or treating practitioners	6,151,910	60.00	124,800	47.48
Registered nurses	3,175,390	45.42	94,480	41.38
Health technologists and technicians	3,010,670	27.38	56,950	24.64
Healthcare support occupations	7,063,530	18.37	38,220	17.38
Nursing, psychiatric, and home health aides	5,122,130	16.89	35,120	16.62
Home health and personal care aides	3,689,350	16.05	33,380	16.12
Protective service occupations	3,504,330	27.74	57,710	22.96
Food preparation and serving related occupations	13,247,870	16.58	34,490	15.50
Cooks and food preparation workers	3,546,860	16.35	34,010	16.36
Cooks	2,667,250	16.52	34,360	16.50
Food and beverage serving workers	6,893,410	15.89	33,060	14.50
Fast food and counter workers	3,676,580	14.48	30,110	14.20
Waiters and waitresses	2,237,850	17.56	36,530	15.36
Building and grounds cleaning and maintenance occupations	4,429,070	18.43	38,320	17.30
Building cleaning and pest control workers	3,116,220	17.36	36,100	16.72
Building cleaning workers	3,022,470	17.23	35,840	16.63
Janitors and cleaners, except maids and housekeeping cleaners	2,172,500	17.43	36,250	16.84
Personal care and service occupations	3,040,630	18.48	38,430	16.47
Sales and related occupations	13,380,660	25.62	53,280	17.67
Retail sales workers	7,655,030	16.59	34,520	15.36
Cashiers	3,319,210	14.78	30,750	14.30
Retail salespersons	3,684,740	17.64	36,690	16.19
Sales representatives, services	2,245,510	41.28	85,860	30.36
Sales representatives, wholesale and manufacturing	1,600,700	41.79	86,920	35.13
Office and administrative support occupations	18,533,450	23.05	47,940	21.39
Supervisors of office and administrative support workers	1,504,570	32.99	68,620	30.50
Financial clerks	2,739,760	23.01	47,860	22.02
Bookkeeping, accounting, and auditing clerks	1,501,910	23.84	49,580	22.81
Information and record clerks	5,537,420	20.49	42,610	18.77
Customer service representatives	2,858,710	20.92	43,520	19.08
Material recording, scheduling, dispatching, and distributing workers	2,316,650	24.25	50,430	22.40
Secretaries and administrative assistants	3,171,290	23.95	49,810	22.12
Secretaries and administrative assistants, except legal, medical, and executive	1,785,430	21.87	45,490	21.29
Farming, fishing, and forestry occupations	432,200	19.22	39,970	17.08
Construction and extraction occupations	6,225,630	29.57	61,500	26.77
Construction trades workers	4,588,620	28.53	59,350	25.00
Installation, maintenance, and repair occupations	5,989,460	28.13	58,500	25.92
Vehicle and mobile equipment mechanics, installers, and repairers	1,708,100	26.81	55,760	24.42
Maintenance and repair workers, general	1,503,150	23.87	49,650	22.45
Production occupations	8,770,170	22.90	47,620	20.98
Assemblers and fabricators	1,924,970	20.90	43,470	19.10
Metal workers and plastic workers	1,605,180	23.73	49,350	22.53
Transportation and material moving occupations	13,752,760	22.45	46,690	19.26
Motor vehicle operators	4,353,340	23.96	49,830	22.83
Driver/sales workers and truck drivers	3,511,470	24.43	50,810	23.14
Heavy and tractor-trailer truck drivers	2,044,400	26.92	55,990	26.12
Material moving workers	7,989,980	19.05	39,620	17.93
Laborers and material movers	6,935,980	18.46	38,400	17.65
Laborers and freight, stock, and material movers, hand	3,008,300	19.12	39,760	18.10
Stockers and order fillers	2,872,680	18.27	37,990	17.50

[1] Annual wages have been calculated by multiplying the hourly mean wage by a "year-round, full-time" hours figure of 2,080 hours; for those occupations where there is not an hourly mean wage published, the annual wage has been directly calculated from the reported survey data. [2] Includes occupations not shown separately. [3] Wages for some occupations that do not generally work year-round full-time are reported as either hourly wages or as annual salaries, depending on how they are typically paid.

Source: U.S. Bureau of Labor Statistics, Occupational Employment Statistics, *Occupational Employment and Wages—May 2023*, USDL 24 0628, April 2024. See also <www.bls.gov/oes/>.

Table 650. Employed Civilians by Occupation and State: 2023

[In thousands (161,037 represents 161,037,000). Civilian noninstitutionalized population 16 years old and over. Excludes persons with no previous work experience. Based on the Current Population Survey see text, Section 1 and Appendix III]

State	Total employed	Management, business, and financial	Professional and related	Service occupations	Sales and related	Office and administrative	Farming, fishing, and forestry	Construction and extraction occupations	Installation, maintenance, and repair	Production	Transportation and material-moving
Total U.S....	161,037	30,544	39,731	26,171	14,325	15,954	987	8,457	4,881	8,280	11,706
AL............	2,254	323	496	339	234	231	(S)	123	102	199	193
AK............	337	63	80	55	26	39	(S)	20	(S)	(S)	27
AZ............	3,551	589	864	631	400	383	(S)	209	111	124	220
AR............	1,328	195	287	238	116	141	(S)	74	57	110	99
CA............	18,382	3,417	4,755	3,210	1,585	1,695	205	963	473	732	1,347
CO............	3,117	716	866	442	267	298	(S)	152	(S)	(S)	157
CT............	1,811	373	491	273	178	186	(S)	74	(S)	91	98
DE............	483	93	117	87	37	48	(S)	23	(S)	22	37
DC............	375	129	151	39	16	24	(S)	(S)	(S)	(S)	(S)
FL............	10,661	1,971	2,327	1,891	1,191	1,130	(S)	618	322	364	814
GA............	5,131	950	1,243	762	467	513	(S)	269	216	266	410
HI............	654	114	145	142	60	74	(S)	35	(S)	(S)	40
ID............	931	160	222	149	91	91	(S)	51	(S)	46	67
IL............	6,126	1,222	1,528	958	470	623	(S)	259	164	371	511
IN............	3,277	552	734	461	258	366	(S)	169	122	305	287
IA............	1,655	312	353	250	138	162	(S)	90	(S)	100	147
KS............	1,480	281	371	219	111	159	(S)	(S)	(S)	108	98
KY............	1,923	312	412	300	170	195	(S)	113	(S)	154	189
LA............	1,987	310	470	364	183	175	(S)	139	73	98	163
ME............	671	130	166	107	63	59	(S)	(S)	(S)	(S)	(S)
MD............	3,125	654	997	484	215	266	(S)	(S)	(S)	(S)	180
MA............	3,629	805	1,149	565	275	272	(S)	189	(S)	110	180
MI............	4,830	829	1,158	757	434	538	(S)	204	140	397	341
MN............	3,007	638	772	391	240	287	(S)	124	(S)	226	206
MS............	1,191	159	238	207	102	110	(S)	76	(S)	113	121
MO............	2,985	572	608	505	269	341	(S)	168	(S)	202	208
MT............	565	122	129	91	49	56	(S)	38	(S)	(S)	35
NE............	1,031	209	226	140	89	112	(S)	(S)	(S)	83	78
NV............	1,521	242	275	351	140	171	(S)	104	(S)	70	130
NH............	734	149	196	96	71	78	(S)	39	(S)	(S)	41
NJ............	4,598	976	1,275	668	397	456	(S)	218	106	157	340
NM............	908	148	226	166	84	94	(S)	58	(S)	36	60
NY............	9,293	1,707	2,605	1,844	742	889	(S)	429	220	266	573
NC............	5,058	907	1,142	794	500	488	(S)	306	143	353	389
ND............	409	81	94	57	36	38	(S)	24	(S)	25	32
OH............	5,596	1,120	1,379	843	460	556	(S)	208	155	405	456
OK............	1,906	337	428	300	190	194	(S)	114	101	110	113
OR............	2,057	436	489	333	177	205	(S)	115	57	87	142
PA............	6,313	1,238	1,629	938	552	615	(S)	288	184	287	546
RI............	559	97	143	102	54	57	(S)	(S)	(S)	34	39
SC............	2,397	399	542	363	240	255	(S)	131	95	184	177
SD............	479	89	101	65	(S)	(S)	(S)	(S)	(S)	(S)	(S)
TN............	3,276	582	770	489	296	342	(S)	173	115	247	256
TX............	14,556	2,728	3,288	2,455	1,374	1,417	(S)	1,018	452	689	1,097
UT............	1,746	347	447	258	146	192	(S)	94	(S)	91	118
VT............	346	70	102	49	29	30	(S)	(S)	(S)	(S)	(S)
VA............	4,443	1,070	1,207	668	368	408	(S)	199	(S)	(S)	251
WA............	3,859	835	1,021	583	323	350	(S)	174	105	168	243
WV............	741	110	169	128	58	76	(S)	53	32	39	72
WI............	3,044	554	690	450	243	342	(S)	143	(S)	286	228
WY............	289	47	62	47	23	31	(S)	24	16	14	22

S Data are not shown when the labor force base does not meet publication standard of reliability for the particular area, as determined by the sample size.

Source: U.S. Bureau of Labor Statistics, "Geographic Profile of Employment and Unemployment, 2023," <www.bls.gov/opub/geographic-profile>, accessed July 2024.

Table 651. Fastest Growing and Largest Growth Occupations—Projections by Occupation: 2022 to 2032

[In thousands (11.2 represents 11,200), except as noted. Estimates based on the Current Employment Statistics survey, the Occupational Employment and Wage Statistics survey, and the Current Population Survey. See source(s) for methodological assumptions. Occupations based on the 2018 Standard Occupational Classification system. Additional information is available in the Occupational Outlook Handbook <www.bls.gov/ooh>]

Occupation	Employment (1,000)		Change, 2022–2032		Median annual wage (dollars), 2022	Typical education needed for entry [1]
	2022	2032	Number (1,000)	Percent		
FASTEST GROWING						
Wind turbine service technicians	11.2	16.2	5.0	44.9	57,320	Postsecondary nondegree award
Nurse practitioners	266.3	384.9	118.6	44.5	121,610	Master's degree
Data scientists	168.9	228.2	59.4	35.2	103,500	Bachelor's degree
Statisticians	33.3	43.9	10.5	31.6	98,920	Master's degree
Information security analysts	168.9	222.2	53.2	31.5	112,000	Bachelor's degree
Medical and health services managers	509.5	654.2	144.7	28.4	104,830	Bachelor's degree
Epidemiologists	10.0	12.7	2.7	26.7	78,520	Master's degree
Physician assistants	148.0	187.3	39.3	26.5	126,010	Master's degree
Physical therapist assistants	100.7	126.9	26.3	26.1	62,770	Associate's degree
Software developers	1,594.5	2,004.9	410.4	25.7	127,260	Bachelor's degree
Occupational therapy assistants	45.1	56.0	10.8	24.0	64,250	Associate's degree
Actuaries	30.0	36.9	7.0	23.2	113,990	Bachelor's degree
Computer and information research scientists	36.5	44.8	8.3	22.7	136,620	Master's degree
Operations research analysts	109.9	134.7	24.7	22.5	85,720	Bachelor's degree
Solar photovoltaic installers	29.4	35.9	6.6	22.3	45,230	High school diploma or equivalent
Home health and personal care aides	3,715.5	4,520.1	804.6	21.7	30,180	High school diploma or equivalent
Taxi drivers	177.3	213.7	36.4	20.6	30,670	No formal educational credential
Veterinary technologists and technicians	122.9	148.1	25.2	20.5	38,240	Associate's degree
Veterinary assistants and laboratory animal caretakers	114.8	138.3	23.5	20.5	34,740	High school diploma or equivalent
Personal care and service workers, all other	87.0	104.9	17.9	20.5	34,670	High school diploma or equivalent
Cooks, restaurant	1,361.2	1,638.9	277.6	20.4	34,110	No formal educational credential
Software quality assurance analysts and testers	200.8	241.6	40.8	20.3	99,620	Bachelor's degree
Veterinarians	89.5	107.2	17.7	19.7	103,260	Doctoral or professional degree
Financial examiners	65.6	78.5	12.8	19.5	82,210	Bachelor's degree
Speech-language pathologists	171.4	204.5	33.1	19.3	84,140	Master's degree
Health specialties teachers, postsecondary	262.8	313.0	50.2	19.1	100,300	Doctoral or professional degree
Substance abuse, behavioral disorder, and mental health counselors	388.2	459.6	71.5	18.4	49,710	Bachelor's degree
Logisticians	208.7	246.9	38.3	18.3	77,520	Bachelor's degree
Massage therapists	134.3	158.9	24.6	18.3	49,860	Postsecondary nondegree award
Nursing instructors and teachers, postsecondary	85.9	101.5	15.6	18.2	78,580	Doctoral or professional degree
LARGEST JOB GROWTH						
Home health and personal care aides	3,715.5	4,520.1	804.6	21.7	30,180	High school diploma or equivalent
Software developers	1,594.5	2,004.9	410.4	25.7	127,260	Bachelor's degree
Cooks, restaurant	1,361.2	1,638.9	277.6	20.4	34,110	No formal educational credential
Stockers and order fillers	2,851.6	3,030.3	178.6	6.3	34,220	High school diploma or equivalent
Registered nurses	3,172.5	3,349.9	177.4	5.6	81,220	Bachelor's degree
Laborers and freight, stock, and material movers, hand	2,988.5	3,147.3	158.8	5.3	36,110	No formal educational credential
General and operations managers	3,507.8	3,655.1	147.3	4.2	98,100	Bachelor's degree
Medical and health services managers	509.5	654.2	144.7	28.4	104,830	Bachelor's degree
Light truck drivers	1,164.6	1,298.4	133.8	11.5	40,410	High school diploma or equivalent
Financial managers	792.6	919.2	126.6	16.0	139,790	Bachelor's degree
Nurse practitioners	266.3	384.9	118.6	44.5	121,610	Master's degree
Market research analysts and marketing specialists	868.6	985.2	116.6	13.4	68,230	Bachelor's degree
Medical assistants	764.4	870.2	105.9	13.9	38,270	Postsecondary nondegree award
Management analysts	987.6	1,083.3	95.7	9.7	95,290	Bachelor's degree
Heavy and tractor-trailer truck drivers	2,192.3	2,281.5	89.3	4.1	49,920	Postsecondary nondegree award
Computer and information systems managers	557.4	643.3	86.0	15.4	164,070	Bachelor's degree
Substance abuse, behavioral disorder, and mental health counselors	388.2	459.6	71.5	18.4	49,710	Bachelor's degree
Accountants and auditors	1,538.4	1,605.8	67.4	4.4	78,000	Bachelor's degree
Lawyers	826.3	888.7	62.4	7.5	135,740	Doctoral or professional degree
Construction laborers	1,418.6	1,480.5	61.9	4.4	40,750	No formal educational credential
First-line supervisors of food preparation and serving workers	1,221.7	1,281.8	60.0	4.9	37,050	High school diploma or equivalent
Industrial machinery mechanics	402.2	462.1	59.9	14.9	59,830	High school diploma or equivalent
Data scientists	168.9	228.2	59.4	35.2	103,500	Bachelor's degree
Maintenance and repair workers, general	1,607.2	1,664.4	57.2	3.6	44,980	High school diploma or equivalent
Nursing assistants	1,361.3	1,417.8	56.5	4.1	35,760	Postsecondary nondegree award
Project management specialists	881.3	936.0	54.7	6.2	95,370	Bachelor's degree
Information security analysts	168.9	222.2	53.2	31.5	112,000	Bachelor's degree
Animal caretakers	339.0	391.5	52.5	15.5	29,530	High school diploma or equivalent
Human resources specialists	874.5	925.9	51.4	5.9	64,240	Bachelor's degree
Computer systems analysts	531.4	582.6	51.1	9.6	102,240	Bachelor's degree

[1] An occupation is placed into 1 of 8 categories that best describes the typical education needed by most workers to enter that occupation. For more information, see "Measures of Education and Training" at <www.bls.gov/emp/documentation/education/tech.htm>.

Source: U.S. Bureau of Labor Statistics, Employment Projections, "EP Data Tables—Occupations," <www.bls.gov/emp/tables.htm>, accessed November 2023.

Table 652. Employment Projections by Industry: 2022 to 2032

[2,826.3 represents 2,826,300. Estimates based on the Current Employment Statistics program. See source for methodological assumptions. Minus sign (-) indicates decline]

Industry	2022 NAICS code [1]	Employment (1,000)		Change, 2022–2032 (1,000)	Compound annual rate of change 2022–2032
		2022	2032		
LARGEST GROWTH					
Individual and family services........................	6241	2,826.3	3,518.4	692.1	2.2
Computer systems design and related services........................	5415	2,456.8	2,931.6	474.8	1.8
Home health care services........................	6216	1,533.6	1,843.8	310.2	1.9
Hospitals........................	622	5,165.0	5,429.0	264.0	0.5
Warehousing and storage........................	493	1,936.8	2,191.1	254.3	1.2
Management of companies and enterprises........................	55	2,490.4	2,731.6	241.2	0.9
Outpatient care centers........................	6214	1,034.1	1,253.6	219.5	1.9
Offices of other health practitioners........................	6213	1,084.7	1,292.6	207.9	1.8
Couriers and messengers........................	492	1,129.0	1,331.6	202.6	1.7
Offices of physicians........................	6211	2,808.8	3,009.8	201.0	0.7
FASTEST GROWTH					
Other electrical equipment and component manufacturing........................	3359	152.2	204.9	52.7	3.0
Individual and family services........................	6241	2,826.3	3,518.4	692.1	2.2
Outpatient care centers........................	6214	1,034.1	1,253.6	219.5	1.9
Commercial and industrial machinery and equipment rental and leasing........................	5324	172.1	208.2	36.1	1.9
Home health care services........................	6216	1,533.6	1,843.8	310.2	1.9
Offices of other health practitioners........................	6213	1,084.7	1,292.6	207.9	1.8
Web search portals, libraries, archives, and other information services........................	519	189.2	225.8	36.6	1.8
Computer systems design and related services........................	5415	2,456.8	2,931.6	474.8	1.8
Couriers and messengers........................	492	1,129.0	1,331.6	202.6	1.7
Office administrative services........................	5611	593.2	703.6	110.4	1.7
LARGEST DECLINES					
All other retail........................	444, 449, 456, 457, 458, 459	7,137.1	6,770.6	-366.5	-0.5
General Merchandise retailers........................	455	3,136.5	3,038.9	-97.6	-0.3
Motor vehicle parts manufacturing........................	3363	553.0	456.1	-96.9	-1.9
Wholesale trade........................	42	5,962.6	5,877.8	-84.8	-0.1
Food and beverage retailers........................	445	3,193.4	3,112.5	-80.9	-0.3
Printing and related support activities........................	323	380.4	317.0	-63.4	-1.8
Religious organizations........................	8131	1,615.5	1,568.2	-47.3	-0.3
Postal Service........................	491	602.5	556.1	-46.4	-0.8
Consumer goods rental and general rental centers........................	5322, 5323	162.0	128.8	-33.2	-2.3
Child day care services........................	6244	956.7	926.6	-30.1	-0.3
MOST RAPIDLY DECLINING					
Coal mining........................	2121	40.4	22.9	-17.5	-5.5
Manufacturing and reproducing magnetic and optical media........................	3346	11.9	7.5	-4.5	-4.6
Pulp, paper, and paperboard mills........................	3221	88.6	68.2	-20.4	-2.6
Apparel, leather and allied product manufacturing........................	315, 316	120.3	92.7	-27.7	-2.6
Lessors of nonfinancial intangible assets (except copyrighted works)........................	533	22.4	17.6	-4.8	-2.4
Hardware manufacturing........................	3325	24.6	19.6	-5.0	-2.3
Consumer goods rental and general rental centers........................	5322, 5323	162.0	128.8	-33.2	-2.3
Other transportation equipment manufacturing........................	3369	40.9	32.6	-8.2	-2.2
Other federal government enterprises........................	(X)	87.1	70.1	-17.0	-2.1
Other furniture related product manufacturing........................	3379	36.0	29.0	-7.0	-2.1

X Not applicable. [1] Based on the North American Industry Classification System, 2022; see text, Section 15.

Source: U.S. Bureau of Labor Statistics, Employment Projections, "EP Data Tables—Industries," <www.bls.gov/emp/tables.htm>, accessed November 2023.

Table 653. Occupations of the Employed by Race/Ethnicity and Educational Attainment: 2023

[In thousands (140,664 represents 140,664,000). Annual averages of monthly figures. Civilian noninstitutional population 25 years old and over. Based on Current Population Survey; see text, Section 1 and Appendix III]

Race/ethnicity and educational attainment	Total employed	Managerial, professional, and related	Service	Sales and office	Natural resources, construction, and maintenance	Production, transportation, and material-moving
Total [1]	**140,664**	**65,944**	**19,982**	**25,386**	**12,406**	**16,946**
Less than a high school diploma	8,669	723	2,721	863	2,319	2,043
High school graduate, no college	34,529	6,460	7,416	7,325	5,376	7,953
Some college or associate degree	34,714	12,125	6,082	8,482	3,405	4,619
Bachelor's degree or higher	62,752	46,637	3,762	8,716	1,305	2,332
White	**107,626**	**50,805**	**14,049**	**19,779**	**10,629**	**12,363**
Less than a high school diploma	6,896	606	1,987	665	2,036	1,603
High school graduate, no college	26,430	5,230	5,021	5,765	4,617	5,797
Some college or associate degree	26,638	9,611	4,318	6,537	2,873	3,299
Bachelor's degree or higher	47,661	35,358	2,724	6,812	1,102	1,664
Black	**18,061**	**6,985**	**3,645**	**3,342**	**1,018**	**3,071**
Less than a high school diploma	936	62	403	113	123	234
High school graduate, no college	5,269	759	1,523	976	447	1,563
Some college or associate degree	5,287	1,602	1,159	1,296	322	908
Bachelor's degree or higher	6,568	4,561	559	957	125	366
Asian	**10,115**	**6,171**	**1,387**	**1,442**	**234**	**881**
Less than a high school diploma	436	36	191	56	29	124
High school graduate, no college	1,464	236	512	321	83	310
Some college or associate degree	1,339	421	312	321	76	208
Bachelor's degree or higher	6,877	5,478	372	743	46	239
Hispanic [2]	**25,433**	**7,187**	**5,660**	**4,110**	**4,310**	**4,167**
Less than a high school diploma	5,098	267	1,694	324	1,673	1,141
High school graduate, no college	8,152	1,077	2,102	1,465	1,657	1,852
Some college or associate degree	5,764	1,776	1,189	1,374	676	749
Bachelor's degree or higher	6,419	4,068	674	947	305	426

[1] Includes other races, not shown separately. [2] Persons of Hispanic origin may be of any race.

Source: U.S. Bureau of Labor Statistics, Current Population Survey, unpublished data. See also <www.bls.gov/cps/>.

Table 654. Employment by Industry, Sex, Race, and Hispanic Origin: 2000 to 2023

[In thousands (136,891 represents 136,891,000), except percent. Civilian noninstitutional population 16 years old and over. Annual average of monthly figures. Based on Current Population Survey; see text, Section 1, Population, and Appendix III]

Industry	Total				2023, percent of total			
	2000	2010	2020	2023	Female	Black [1]	Asian [1]	Hispanic [2]
Total employed	**136,891**	**139,064**	**147,795**	**161,037**	**46.9**	**12.8**	**6.9**	**18.8**
Agriculture and related industries	2,464	2,206	2,349	2,264	29.3	3.3	0.8	25.4
Mining and related industries	475	731	684	590	15.3	6.3	2.8	22.5
Construction	9,931	9,077	10,786	11,896	10.8	6.7	1.7	34.0
Manufacturing	19,644	14,081	14,550	15,570	29.5	10.8	7.6	18.1
Durable goods	12,519	8,789	9,129	10,065	25.8	9.6	8.0	16.0
Nondurable goods	7,125	5,293	5,421	5,506	36.4	13.0	6.7	22.0
Wholesale trade	4,216	3,805	3,380	3,259	31.7	8.7	5.8	19.2
Retail trade	15,763	15,934	15,609	16,528	47.7	12.7	6.5	18.8
Transportation and utilities	7,380	7,134	8,552	9,949	24.3	20.7	5.6	21.1
Transportation and warehousing	6,096	5,880	7,170	8,452	24.9	22.7	5.8	22.2
Utilities	1,284	1,253	1,382	1,497	21.0	9.5	4.1	14.6
Information	4,059	3,149	2,594	2,971	38.3	11.0	10.5	12.8
Financial activities	9,374	9,350	10,646	11,018	51.1	12.0	8.7	12.8
Finance and insurance	6,641	6,605	7,605	7,746	52.8	12.6	9.6	11.7
Real estate and rental and leasing	2,734	2,745	3,040	3,272	47.3	10.8	6.5	15.3
Professional and business services	13,649	15,253	18,816	20,735	42.2	10.9	10.0	17.6
Professional and technical services	8,266	9,115	12,643	13,726	42.7	8.5	13.3	10.3
Management, administrative, and waste services	5,383	6,138	6,173	7,009	41.4	15.7	3.5	31.8
Education and health services	26,188	32,062	34,105	36,378	74.4	15.5	6.8	14.0
Educational services	11,255	13,155	13,369	14,029	68.9	11.9	6.1	12.9
Health care and social assistance	14,933	18,907	20,736	22,348	77.8	17.8	7.3	14.7
Hospitals	5,202	6,249	7,305	7,467	74.6	16.9	9.4	11.9
Health services, except hospitals	7,009	9,406	10,284	11,201	78.1	17.5	6.8	15.1
Social assistance	2,722	3,252	3,147	3,680	83.5	20.2	4.5	19.3
Leisure and hospitality	11,186	12,530	11,480	14,288	50.8	12.5	7.2	25.9
Arts, entertainment, and recreation	2,539	2,966	2,601	3,529	44.1	11.6	4.8	16.6
Accommodation and food services	8,647	9,564	8,879	10,759	53.0	12.8	8.0	29.0
Other services	6,450	6,769	6,742	7,605	53.3	10.9	7.8	21.7
Other services, except private households	5,731	6,102	6,088	6,932	49.6	10.8	8.2	19.5
Private households	718	667	654	673	92.0	11.9	3.9	44.8
Public administration	6,113	6,983	7,501	7,984	46.0	18.4	5.1	13.2

[1] Persons in this race group only. See footnote 2, Table 622. [2] Persons of Hispanic origin may be of any race.

Source: U.S. Bureau of Labor Statistics, CPS Tables, "Employed persons by detailed industry, sex, race, and Hispanic or Latino ethnicity," January 2024, and earlier releases, <www.bls.gov/cps/tables.htm>.

Table 655. Unemployed Workers—Summary: 1990 to 2023

[In thousands (7,047 represents 7,047,000), except as indicated. For civilian noninstitutionalized population 16 years old and over. Annual averages of monthly figures. Revisions to population controls and other changes can affect the comparability of data over time. Based on the Current Population Survey; see text, Section 1 and Appendix III]

Item	1990	2000	2010	2015	2018	2019	2020	2021	2022	2023
UNEMPLOYED										
Total [1]	**7,047**	**5,692**	**14,825**	**8,296**	**6,314**	**6,001**	**12,947**	**8,623**	**5,996**	**6,080**
16 to 19 years old	1,212	1,081	1,528	966	759	746	1,025	696	675	713
20 to 24 years old	1,299	1,022	2,329	1,501	1,048	1,024	1,990	1,317	1,039	1,044
25 to 34 years old	1,995	1,207	3,386	1,905	1,450	1,384	3,080	2,092	1,425	1,465
35 to 44 years old	1,328	1,133	2,703	1,351	1,003	930	2,177	1,586	1,046	1,031
45 to 54 years old	723	762	2,769	1,259	938	890	2,042	1,323	788	821
55 to 64 years old	386	355	1,660	978	789	710	1,839	1,138	699	689
65 years and over	105	132	449	337	327	317	795	472	323	316
Male	3,906	2,975	8,626	4,490	3,398	3,227	6,644	4,676	3,218	3,377
16 to 19 years old	667	599	863	531	422	408	526	373	351	392
20 to 24 years old	715	547	1,398	865	596	602	1,016	739	593	591
25 to 34 years old	1,092	602	1,993	1,030	763	741	1,664	1,167	760	829
35 to 44 years old	711	557	1,534	695	515	475	1,126	852	548	558
45 to 54 years old	413	398	1,614	649	490	471	995	685	404	450
55 to 64 years old	249	189	962	536	435	361	916	603	376	388
65 years and over	59	83	262	184	177	170	401	257	187	169
Female	3,140	2,717	6,199	3,807	2,916	2,774	6,304	3,948	2,778	2,702
16 to 19 years old	544	483	665	435	338	339	500	323	324	321
20 to 24 years old	584	475	931	636	452	421	974	578	446	453
25 to 34 years old	902	604	1,392	874	687	643	1,416	925	666	637
35 to 44 years old	617	577	1,169	656	488	455	1,050	733	498	473
45 to 54 years old	310	364	1,156	610	448	419	1,047	638	384	371
55 to 64 years old	137	165	698	442	354	350	924	535	323	301
65 years and over	46	50	187	153	150	147	394	216	136	147
White [2]	5,186	4,121	10,916	5,662	4,354	4,159	9,090	5,854	4,049	4,162
Black [2]	1,565	1,241	2,852	1,846	1,322	1,251	2,304	1,756	1,300	1,212
Asian [2,3]	(NA)	227	543	347	304	280	894	529	306	344
Hispanic [4]	876	954	2,843	1,726	1,323	1,248	3,018	1,995	1,302	1,475
UNEMPLOYMENT RATE [5] (percent)										
Total [1]	**5.6**	**4.0**	**9.6**	**5.3**	**3.9**	**3.7**	**8.1**	**5.3**	**3.6**	**3.6**
16 to 19 years old	15.5	13.1	25.9	16.9	12.9	12.7	17.9	11.7	10.8	11.2
20 to 24 years old	8.8	7.2	15.5	9.7	6.9	6.7	13.7	8.9	7.0	6.6
25 to 34 years old	5.6	3.7	10.1	5.5	3.9	3.7	8.4	5.7	3.9	3.9
35 to 44 years old	4.1	3.0	8.1	4.1	3.0	2.7	6.4	4.6	2.9	2.8
45 to 54 years old	3.6	2.5	7.7	3.7	2.8	2.7	6.4	4.2	2.4	2.5
55 to 64 years old	3.3	2.5	7.1	3.8	2.9	2.6	6.7	4.2	2.5	2.5
65 years and over	3.0	3.1	6.7	3.8	3.3	3.0	7.5	4.5	3.0	2.8
Male	5.7	3.9	10.5	5.4	3.9	3.7	7.8	5.5	3.7	3.8
16 to 19 years old	16.3	14.0	28.8	18.4	14.5	13.8	18.4	12.5	11.2	12.3
20 to 24 years old	9.1	7.3	17.8	10.8	7.7	7.7	13.7	9.7	7.8	7.4
25 to 34 years old	5.5	3.4	10.9	5.5	3.9	3.7	8.5	5.9	3.9	4.2
35 to 44 years old	4.1	2.8	8.5	4.0	2.8	2.6	6.2	4.6	2.9	2.8
45 to 54 years old	3.7	2.4	8.6	3.6	2.8	2.7	5.9	4.1	2.3	2.6
55 to 64 years old	3.8	2.4	8.0	3.9	3.0	2.5	6.4	4.2	2.6	2.7
65 years and over	3.0	3.3	7.1	3.8	3.2	2.9	6.8	4.3	3.1	2.8
Female	5.5	4.1	8.6	5.2	3.8	3.6	8.3	5.2	3.6	3.5
16 to 19 years old	14.7	12.1	22.8	15.5	11.3	11.5	17.5	10.8	10.4	10.1
20 to 24 years old	8.5	7.1	13.0	8.5	6.2	5.7	13.8	8.1	6.2	5.9
25 to 34 years old	5.6	4.1	9.1	5.5	4.0	3.7	8.3	5.4	3.9	3.7
35 to 44 years old	4.2	3.3	7.7	4.4	3.2	2.9	6.7	4.6	3.0	2.8
45 to 54 years old	3.4	2.5	6.8	3.8	2.8	2.7	6.9	4.2	2.5	2.4
55 to 64 years old	2.8	2.5	6.2	3.6	2.7	2.7	7.2	4.2	2.5	2.4
65 years and over	3.1	2.7	6.2	3.9	3.3	3.1	8.3	4.6	2.9	2.9
White [2]	4.8	3.5	8.7	4.6	3.5	3.3	7.3	4.7	3.2	3.3
Black [2]	11.4	7.6	16.0	9.6	6.5	6.1	11.4	8.6	6.1	5.5
Asian [2,3]	(NA)	3.6	7.5	3.8	3.0	2.7	8.7	5.0	2.8	3.0
Hispanic [4]	8.2	5.7	12.5	6.6	4.7	4.3	10.4	6.8	4.3	4.6
PERCENT WITHOUT WORK FOR—										
Fewer than 5 weeks	46.3	44.9	18.7	28.9	34.4	34.8	28.6	24.8	37.0	34.7
5 to 14 weeks	32.0	31.9	22.0	27.7	29.7	29.8	36.5	23.0	28.5	30.7
15 weeks and over	21.6	23.2	59.3	43.3	35.9	35.4	34.8	52.2	34.5	34.6
15 to 26 weeks	11.7	11.8	16.0	15.3	14.5	14.3	19.4	13.5	12.6	15.2
27 weeks and over	10.0	11.4	43.3	28.1	21.4	21.1	15.4	38.7	21.9	19.4
Unemployment duration, average (weeks) [6]	12.0	12.6	33.0	29.2	22.7	21.6	16.5	28.7	22.6	20.6

NA Not available. [1] Includes other races not shown separately. [2] For persons reporting this race group only. [3] Prior to 2003, includes Pacific Islanders. [4] Persons of Hispanic or Latino origin may be of any race. [5] Unemployed as percent of civilian labor force in specified group. [6] Beginning 2011, the CPS increased the maximum duration of unemployment that respondents could report from 2 years to 5 years. For more information, see <www.bls.gov/cps/duration.htm>.

Source: U.S. Bureau of Labor Statistics, "Labor Force Statistics from the Current Population Survey," <www.bls.gov/cps>, accessed February 2024.

Table 656. Unemployed Jobseekers' Job Search Methods: 2023

[6,080 represents 6,080,000. For the civilian noninstitutionalized population 16 years old and over. Annual averages of monthly data. Jobseekers may use more than one job search method. Based on the Current Population Survey; see text, Section 1 and Appendix III]

| Characteristic | Population (1,000) | | Jobseekers' job search methods (percent) | | | | | | | Average number of methods used |
	Total unemployed	Total jobseekers[1]	Contact employer directly	Sent out a resume or filled out applications	Placed or answered ads	Friends or relatives	Public employment agency	Private employment agency	Other activities	
Total, 16 years and over[2]...	**6,080**	**5,269**	**51.5**	**53.7**	**12.3**	**24.2**	**12.7**	**8.7**	**15.5**	**1.8**
AGE										
16 to 19 years old..............	713	664	49.3	58.8	10.1	17.3	6.6	2.7	11.2	1.6
20 to 24 years old..............	1,044	963	52.1	54.2	11.5	20.7	11.1	6.7	14.3	1.7
25 to 34 years old..............	1,465	1,298	52.8	54.6	12.2	24.4	13.7	9.4	16.0	1.8
35 to 44 years old..............	1,031	882	50.5	55.6	13.7	27.0	14.7	10.7	16.3	1.9
45 to 54 years old..............	821	675	54.3	51.9	14.2	28.4	15.0	10.9	16.7	1.9
55 to 64 years old..............	689	554	50.6	49.0	13.3	28.2	15.2	11.8	18.2	1.9
65 years old and over..........	316	234	46.0	41.2	10.1	24.4	11.2	8.2	18.0	1.6
SEX AND AGE										
Male, total......................	3,377	2,886	53.2	51.5	12.3	25.8	13.2	9.2	15.6	1.8
16 to 19 years old..............	392	364	48.7	58.9	9.9	19.7	7.6	3.4	10.6	1.6
20 to 24 years old..............	591	539	51.5	52.3	11.4	22.0	12.3	6.9	13.6	1.7
25 to 34 years old..............	829	720	55.1	51.7	11.9	26.7	13.5	10.1	15.7	1.9
35 to 44 years old..............	558	466	54.2	54.6	13.7	28.0	15.0	11.0	16.6	1.9
45 to 54 years old..............	450	363	55.5	47.3	16.1	28.9	14.6	10.5	18.5	1.9
55 to 64 years old..............	388	307	54.2	46.5	12.8	29.9	15.8	13.8	19.4	1.9
65 years old and over........	169	127	50.4	38.7	8.6	26.9	13.4	8.1	18.0	1.7
Female, total....................	2,702	2,383	49.4	56.4	12.3	22.3	12.1	8.1	15.4	1.8
16 to 19 years old..............	321	300	50.0	58.7	10.3	14.5	5.4	1.9	11.8	1.5
20 to 24 years old..............	453	424	52.8	56.7	11.5	19.0	9.5	6.5	15.3	1.7
25 to 34 years old..............	637	578	50.0	58.2	12.7	21.5	13.9	8.7	16.4	1.8
35 to 44 years old..............	473	415	46.3	56.8	13.7	25.9	14.4	10.4	16.0	1.8
45 to 54 years old..............	371	312	52.9	57.3	11.9	27.9	15.4	11.4	14.7	1.9
55 to 64 years old..............	301	247	46.1	52.1	13.9	26.1	14.4	9.3	16.6	1.8
65 years old and over........	147	107	40.8	44.2	11.8	21.6	8.6	8.4	18.1	1.6
RACE/ETHNICITY										
White[3]...........................	4,162	3,510	51.6	53.2	12.6	24.2	12.3	8.4	15.8	1.8
Male...........................	2,368	1,967	53.4	51.7	12.7	25.5	13.0	8.9	15.4	1.8
Female.........................	1,794	1,543	49.3	55.1	12.6	22.6	11.4	7.8	16.3	1.8
Black[3]...........................	1,212	1,115	51.2	53.3	10.8	22.8	14.4	8.8	13.7	1.8
Male...........................	599	546	53.1	48.4	9.9	24.9	14.6	9.0	13.4	1.7
Female.........................	612	568	49.4	57.9	11.7	20.8	14.3	8.6	13.9	1.8
Asian[3]...........................	344	318	52.6	59.7	16.5	29.5	12.0	13.0	19.7	2.0
Male...........................	204	189	55.5	58.4	18.0	31.5	12.3	13.7	22.7	2.1
Female.........................	139	129	48.5	61.6	14.3	26.6	11.5	12.0	15.2	1.9
Hispanic[4].......................	1,475	1,233	49.9	47.9	9.5	29.3	13.6	8.1	12.7	1.7
Male...........................	839	680	52.9	44.3	9.1	30.5	14.8	8.6	12.5	1.7
Female.........................	635	554	46.2	52.3	10.1	27.8	12.2	7.6	13.0	1.7

[1] Excludes persons on temporary layoff. [2] Includes other races not shown separately. [3] Data for this race group only. [4] Persons of Hispanic or Latino origin may be of any race.

Source: U.S. Bureau of Labor Statistics, CPS Tables, "Unemployed jobseekers by sex, age, race, Hispanic or Latino ethnicity, and active jobsearch methods used," January 2024, <www.bls.gov/cps/tables.htm>.

Table 657. Unemployed Persons by Sex and Reason: 2010 to 2023

[In thousands (8,626 represents 8,626,000). For civilian noninstitutionalized population 16 years old and over. Annual averages of monthly figures. Revisions to population controls and other changes affect comparability of data over time. Based on Current Population Survey; see text, Section 1 and Appendix III]

Sex and reason	2010	2013	2014	2015	2016	2017	2018	2019	2020	2021	2022	2023
Male, total..............	**8,626**	**6,314**	**5,190**	**4,490**	**4,187**	**3,743**	**3,398**	**3,227**	**6,644**	**4,676**	**3,218**	**3,377**
Job losers[1]..............	5,919	3,690	2,926	2,441	2,232	2,038	1,772	1,611	5,045	2,901	1,623	1,744
Job leavers...............	457	465	416	397	414	382	413	444	367	407	444	425
Reentrants...............	1,608	1,491	1,279	1,178	1,108	961	896	851	952	1,079	884	892
New entrants.............	641	668	569	474	433	362	317	321	280	288	267	317
Female, total..........	**6,199**	**5,146**	**4,426**	**3,807**	**3,564**	**3,239**	**2,916**	**2,774**	**6,304**	**3,948**	**2,778**	**2,702**
Job losers[1]..............	3,331	2,383	1,952	1,622	1,508	1,397	1,218	1,175	4,725	2,198	1,143	1,126
Job leavers...............	432	467	408	423	444	396	381	370	316	396	413	398
Reentrants...............	1,858	1,716	1,550	1,357	1,222	1,118	1,032	959	1,017	1,124	1,007	939
New entrants.............	579	579	517	405	390	328	285	270	246	229	215	239

[1] Includes persons who completed temporary jobs.

Source: U.S. Bureau of Labor Statistics, CPS Tables, "Unemployed jobseekers by sex, reason for unemployment, and active jobsearch methods used," January 2024, and earlier releases, <www.bls.gov/cps/tables.htm>.

Table 658. Unemployment Rates by Industry and by Sex: 2010 to 2023

[In percent. Civilian noninstitutionalized population 16 years old and over. Annual averages of monthly figures. Rate represents unemployment as a percent of labor force in each specified group. Based on Current Population Survey; see text, Section 1 and Appendix III]

Industry	Total				Male		Female	
	2010	2020	2022	2023	2022	2023	2022	2023
Total [1]	**9.6**	**8.1**	**3.6**	**3.6**	**3.7**	**3.8**	**3.6**	**3.5**
Wage and salary workers:								
Agriculture and related industries...........................	13.9	8.1	5.6	5.6	5.3	5.0	6.2	7.0
Mining, quarrying, and oil and gas extraction..............	9.4	11.3	3.0	2.7	3.3	2.7	1.4	2.9
Construction...	20.6	8.7	4.6	4.6	4.7	4.7	3.4	3.7
Manufacturing..	10.6	6.8	3.0	2.8	2.8	2.8	3.4	3.0
Wholesale trade..	7.3	5.6	2.4	2.6	2.0	2.3	3.3	3.1
Retail trade...	10.0	8.9	4.4	4.5	4.4	4.6	4.6	4.5
Transportation and utilities...............................	8.4	9.3	4.1	4.1	3.9	3.9	4.7	4.7
Transportation and warehousing........................	9.4	10.4	4.4	4.5	4.2	4.3	5.0	5.0
Utilities...	3.4	2.4	1.9	2.0	1.8	1.8	2.3	2.8
Information...	9.7	7.5	2.9	3.2	2.5	3.0	3.8	3.6
Telecommunications....................................	9.2	4.4	1.9	2.1	1.5	1.8	3.1	3.1
Financial activities..	6.9	3.8	1.9	2.2	1.7	2.2	2.2	2.2
Finance and insurance.................................	6.6	2.9	1.7	2.2	1.6	2.0	1.9	2.3
Real estate and rental and leasing....................	7.6	6.4	2.6	2.2	2.1	2.5	3.1	2.0
Professional and business services.......................	10.8	6.7	3.5	3.7	3.2	3.7	3.9	3.7
Professional and technical services....................	6.5	4.5	2.2	2.6	1.9	2.5	2.6	2.9
Management, administrative, and waste services.......	16.8	11.0	6.1	5.9	5.8	6.1	6.5	5.6
Education and health services.............................	5.8	5.7	2.7	2.4	2.7	2.6	2.7	2.4
Educational services....................................	6.4	8.1	3.5	3.0	3.6	3.5	3.4	2.7
Health care and social assistance.....................	5.6	5.1	2.5	2.3	2.3	2.2	2.5	2.3
Leisure and hospitality....................................	12.2	19.4	5.8	5.3	5.4	5.2	6.1	5.4
Arts, entertainment, and recreation....................	11.6	23.1	5.6	4.6	5.7	4.8	5.4	4.3
Accommodation and food services.....................	12.3	18.5	5.8	5.5	5.3	5.4	6.3	5.7
Other services...	8.5	9.8	3.1	3.1	3.2	2.9	2.9	3.2
Government workers.......................................	4.4	4.8	2.1	2.0	2.1	2.0	2.0	1.9

[1] Includes a small number of persons whose last job was in the Armed Forces.

Source: U.S. Bureau of Labor Statistics, CPS Tables, "Unemployed persons by industry, class of worker, and sex," January 2024, and earlier releases, <www.bls.gov/cps/tables.htm>.

Table 659. Unemployment by Occupation: 2010 to 2023

[14,825 represents 14,825,000. Civilian noninstitutionalized population 16 years old and over. Annual averages of monthly data. Rate represents unemployment as a percent of the labor force for each specified group. Based on Current Population Survey; see text, Section 1 and Appendix III]

Occupation	Number unemployed (1,000)				Unemployment rate				
							2023		
	2010	2020	2022	2023	2010	2020	Total	Male	Female
Total [1]	**14,825**	**12,947**	**5,996**	**6,080**	**9.6**	**8.1**	**3.6**	**3.8**	**3.5**
Management, professional, and related occupations.............................	2,566	3,029	1,355	1,432	4.7	4.5	2.0	2.0	2.0
Management, business, and financial operations..	1,117	1,149	530	604	5.1	4.1	1.9	1.9	2.0
Management..	762	752	330	361	4.8	3.9	1.7	1.7	1.7
Business and financial operations..................	355	397	200	243	5.6	4.4	2.5	2.5	2.4
Professional and related occupations...............	1,449	1,880	825	828	4.5	4.9	2.0	2.1	2.0
Computer and mathematical.........................	195	199	118	138	5.2	3.4	2.1	2.0	2.1
Architecture and engineering........................	173	117	52	64	6.2	3.6	1.8	1.5	3.1
Life, physical, and social science...................	69	72	26	32	4.6	4.3	1.7	1.8	1.5
Community and social services......................	114	87	54	66	4.6	3.1	2.3	2.7	2.1
Legal...	48	53	26	19	2.7	2.7	1.0	0.5	1.4
Education, training, and library.....................	379	678	254	243	4.2	7.1	2.5	3.0	2.3
Arts, design, entertainment, sports, and media..................................	269	372	144	130	8.9	10.9	3.6	3.6	3.6
Healthcare practitioner and technical..............	203	303	152	137	2.5	3.1	1.3	1.2	1.4
Service occupations...................................	2,819	3,407	1,281	1,240	10.3	13.0	4.5	4.7	4.4
Healthcare support..................................	276	380	203	187	7.6	7.3	3.5	3.4	3.5
Protective service...................................	207	162	108	93	5.9	5.1	2.9	2.6	4.0
Food preparation and serving-related..............	1,079	1,595	480	493	12.4	19.6	5.7	5.8	5.6
Building and grounds cleaning and maintenance..	780	623	319	306	12.8	10.9	5.2	5.4	5.1
Personal care and service...........................	477	648	170	161	8.7	16.0	3.7	3.9	3.6
Sales and office.......................................	3,315	2,591	1,176	1,146	9.0	8.0	3.6	3.7	3.6
Sales and related....................................	1,596	1,367	579	581	9.4	8.8	3.9	3.4	4.4
Office and administrative support..................	1,719	1,224	598	565	8.7	7.3	3.4	4.3	3.1
Natural resources, construction, and maintenance......................................	2,504	1,298	658	659	16.1	8.9	4.4	4.3	6.1
Farming, fishing, and forestry.......................	193	120	71	74	16.3	10.3	7.0	6.8	7.4
Construction and extraction.........................	1,809	862	477	480	20.1	10.1	5.4	5.3	7.1
Installation, maintenance, and repair..............	503	316	110	105	9.3	6.4	2.1	2.1	2.5
Production, transportation, and material moving....	2,365	2,076	1,027	1,030	12.8	10.2	4.9	4.7	5.4
Production...	1,206	747	332	328	13.1	9.0	3.8	3.5	4.6
Transportation and material moving................	1,159	1,329	695	702	12.4	11.1	5.7	5.5	6.2

[1] Includes a small number of persons whose last job was in the Armed Forces.

Source: U.S. Bureau of Labor Statistics, CPS Tables, "Unemployed persons by occupation and sex," January 2024, and earlier releases, <www.bls.gov/cps/tables.htm>.

Table 660. Unemployed and Unemployment Rates by Educational Attainment, Sex, Race, and Hispanic Origin: 2020 to 2023

[9,932 represents 9,932,000. Annual averages of monthly figures. Civilian noninstitutionalized population 25 years old and over. See Table 627 for civilian labor force and participation rate data. Revisions to population controls and other changes can affect the comparability of data over time. Based on Current Population Survey; see text, Section 1 and Appendix III]

Year, sex, and race/ethnicity	Unemployed (1,000)					Unemployment rate [1]				
	Total	Less than a high school diploma	High school graduate, no college	Some college or associate's degree	Bachelor's degree or higher	Total	Less than a high school diploma	High school graduate, no college	Some college or associate's degree	Bachelor's degree or higher
Total: [2]										
2020.....................	9,932	1,041	3,135	2,831	2,925	7.1	11.7	9.0	7.8	4.8
2022.....................	4,282	490	1,422	1,120	1,250	3.0	5.5	4.0	3.1	2.0
2023.....................	4,323	511	1,399	1,089	1,324	3.0	5.6	3.9	3.0	2.1
Male:										
2020.....................	5,101	606	1,776	1,362	1,357	6.8	10.6	8.6	7.3	4.5
2022.....................	2,275	302	808	556	609	3.0	5.1	3.8	3.0	2.0
2023.....................	2,395	302	852	573	668	3.1	5.1	4.0	3.1	2.1
Female:										
2020.....................	4,831	435	1,359	1,469	1,568	7.4	13.6	9.7	8.3	5.1
2022.....................	2,007	188	614	564	641	3.0	6.0	4.2	3.3	2.0
2023.....................	1,929	209	547	516	657	2.9	6.4	3.8	3.0	2.0
White only:										
2020.....................	7,028	743	2,148	2,007	2,130	6.4	10.5	8.0	7.1	4.6
2022.....................	2,921	342	931	754	894	2.7	4.8	3.4	2.8	1.9
2023.....................	2,975	369	928	737	941	2.7	5.1	3.4	2.7	1.9
Black only:										
2020.....................	1,726	169	666	540	351	9.9	16.1	13.0	10.2	5.9
2022.....................	918	102	368	270	178	5.0	9.8	6.6	4.9	2.8
2023.....................	849	96	341	248	164	4.5	9.3	6.1	4.5	2.4
Asian only:										
2020.....................	746	75	189	129	353	7.9	16.6	13.7	10.3	5.6
2022.....................	226	11	40	35	140	2.3	2.9	2.7	2.6	2.1
2023.....................	278	16	46	41	175	2.7	3.6	3.0	3.0	2.5
Hispanic: [3]										
2020.....................	2,229	572	753	523	381	9.2	11.2	10.1	8.9	6.6
2022.....................	886	250	312	186	138	3.5	4.8	3.7	3.2	2.2
2023.....................	994	265	361	205	163	3.8	4.9	4.2	3.4	2.5

[1] Unemployed as percent of the civilian labor force. [2] Includes other races, not shown separately. [3] Persons of Hispanic origin may be of any race.

Source: U.S. Bureau of Labor Statistics, CPS Tables, "Employment status of the civilian noninstitutional population 25 years and over by educational attainment, sex, race, and Hispanic or Latino ethnicity," January 2024 and earlier releases, <www.bls.gov/cps/tables.htm>.

Table 661. Unemployed Persons by Reason for Unemployment and Duration: 2023

[6,080 represents 6,080,000. Annual averages of monthly data. Based on Current Population Survey; see text, Section 1 and Appendix III]

Age, sex, and reason	Total unemployed (1,000)	Percent distribution by duration				
		Less than 5 weeks	5 to 14 weeks	15 weeks and over		
				Total	15 to 26 weeks	27 weeks or longer
Total 16 years old and over..................................	**6,080**	**34.7**	**30.7**	**34.6**	**15.2**	**19.4**
16 to 19 years old..............................	713	47.2	31.6	21.2	10.8	10.4
Males, 20 years old and over............................	**2,985**	**32.3**	**30.0**	**37.7**	**16.4**	**21.3**
Job losers and persons who completed temporary jobs.....	1,676	35.8	30.9	33.3	15.8	17.5
On temporary layoff.................................	463	54.0	30.9	15.1	11.6	3.6
Not on temporary layoff.............................	1,213	28.9	30.9	40.2	17.4	22.8
Permanent job losers.............................	872	27.4	31.6	41.0	18.2	22.9
Persons who completed temporary jobs..................	341	32.7	29.1	38.2	15.5	22.6
Job leavers...	401	35.1	29.3	35.6	16.4	19.2
Reentrants...	767	24.5	27.8	47.6	17.3	30.4
New entrants.......................................	141	25.0	32.8	42.2	18.8	23.4
Females, 20 years old and over..........................	**2,382**	**34.0**	**31.3**	**34.7**	**15.1**	**19.6**
Job losers and persons who completed temporary jobs.....	1,086	37.2	31.5	31.3	15.6	15.6
On temporary layoff.................................	299	57.1	32.4	10.5	6.4	4.2
Not on temporary layoff.............................	787	29.7	31.2	39.1	19.2	20.0
Permanent job losers.............................	579	28.2	31.0	40.8	20.7	20.1
Persons who completed temporary jobs..................	209	33.8	31.7	34.5	14.9	19.6
Job leavers...	365	38.3	33.7	28.0	13.1	14.8
Reentrants...	809	29.1	30.1	40.8	14.9	25.9
New entrants.......................................	121	25.4	29.9	44.7	16.7	28.0

Source: U.S. Bureau of Labor Statistics, CPS Tables, "Unemployed persons by reason for unemployment, sex, age, and duration of unemployment," January 2024, <www.bls.gov/cps/tables.htm>.

Table 662. Total Unemployed and Insured Unemployed by State: 2000 to 2022

[5,692 represents 5,692,000. Civilian noninstitutionalized population 16 years old and over. Annual averages of monthly figures, except as noted. State total unemployment estimates come from the Local Area Unemployment Statistics program, while U.S. totals come from the Current Population Survey; see text, Section 1 and Appendix III. U.S. totals derived by independent population controls; therefore, state data may not add to U.S. totals. Unemployment data are based on population controls updated annually]

State	Total unemployed								Insured unemployed [2,4]			
	Number (1,000)				Percent [1]				Number (1,000)		Percent [3]	
	2000	2010	2020	2022	2000	2010	2020	2022	2020	2022	2020	2022
United States.........	**5,692**	**14,825**	**12,947**	**5,996**	**4.0**	**9.6**	**8.1**	**3.6**	**10,093**	**1,503**	**7.4**	**1.0**
Alabama.................	99	228	145	58	4.6	10.4	6.4	2.5	74	5	4.0	0.3
Alaska..................	20	30	29	15	6.3	8.2	8.3	4.2	24	4	8.4	1.4
Arizona.................	100	319	271	137	4.0	10.3	7.8	3.8	133	17	4.8	0.6
Arkansas...............	53	107	83	44	4.2	7.9	6.2	3.2	52	8	4.5	0.6
California..............	826	2,292	1,922	820	4.9	12.5	10.1	4.3	1,825	345	11.3	2.0
Colorado...............	64	249	208	98	2.7	9.2	6.8	3.1	136	22	5.3	0.8
Connecticut............	37	183	149	78	2.1	9.6	8.0	4.1	146	21	9.6	1.3
Delaware...............	15	38	36	21	3.6	8.7	7.5	4.3	26	4	6.3	0.8
District of Columbia....	18	35	31	18	5.7	10.0	7.9	4.7	40	3	7.5	0.6
Florida.................	297	992	819	321	3.8	10.8	8.1	3.0	351	37	4.2	0.4
Georgia................	147	503	329	164	3.5	10.7	6.5	3.1	400	38	9.5	0.8
Hawaii.................	26	44	78	22	4.2	6.8	11.7	3.3	72	6	13.8	1.1
Idaho..................	31	67	50	27	4.7	8.8	5.5	2.8	23	5	3.1	0.6
Illinois.................	288	694	586	294	4.4	10.5	9.3	4.6	393	74	7.2	1.3
Indiana................	94	321	242	103	3.0	10.1	7.3	3.1	150	21	5.2	0.7
Iowa...................	43	102	86	48	2.7	6.1	5.2	2.8	80	11	5.5	0.7
Kansas................	53	104	87	40	3.8	7.0	5.8	2.6	59	7	4.5	0.5
Kentucky..............	81	213	130	82	4.1	10.3	6.5	4.0	105	10	6.0	0.5
Louisiana..............	104	157	177	76	5.2	7.5	8.6	3.7	162	11	9.3	0.6
Maine..................	23	59	34	19	3.3	8.4	5.1	2.8	39	5	6.9	0.8
Maryland..............	99	241	208	95	3.5	7.8	6.4	3.0	135	18	5.7	0.7
Massachusetts.........	94	281	348	137	2.8	8.1	9.3	3.7	312	52	9.5	1.5
Michigan...............	188	581	486	202	3.6	12.2	10.0	4.1	381	43	9.7	1.0
Minnesota.............	85	218	195	79	3.0	7.4	6.3	2.6	206	40	7.7	1.4
Mississippi............	70	132	99	48	5.3	10.1	8.0	3.8	81	6	7.6	0.5
Missouri...............	101	289	186	79	3.4	9.5	6.2	2.6	109	15	4.2	0.6
Montana...............	23	36	32	15	4.8	7.2	5.8	2.7	26	5	5.8	1.0
Nebraska..............	26	47	44	23	2.8	4.7	4.3	2.2	27	4	2.9	0.4
Nevada................	44	187	203	81	4.1	13.8	13.5	5.2	173	16	13.9	1.1
New Hampshire........	18	45	51	17	2.7	6.1	6.7	2.3	34	2	5.5	0.3
New Jersey............	157	441	437	184	3.7	9.7	9.4	3.9	315	90	8.5	2.2
New Mexico............	42	72	73	39	5.0	7.8	7.9	4.1	57	8	7.6	1.0
New York..............	413	840	936	417	4.5	8.7	9.8	4.3	960	145	11.3	1.6
North Carolina.........	155	498	348	190	3.7	10.7	7.2	3.7	160	16	3.8	0.3
North Dakota...........	10	14	20	8	3.0	3.7	4.9	2.0	16	3	4.1	0.7
Ohio...................	237	604	470	230	4.1	10.3	8.2	4.0	286	37	5.7	0.7
Oklahoma..............	50	115	116	58	3.0	6.5	6.3	3.1	82	11	5.5	0.7
Oregon................	94	214	160	85	5.2	10.7	7.6	3.9	134	23	7.4	1.2
Pennsylvania..........	258	522	577	263	4.2	8.2	8.9	4.1	502	73	9.3	1.3
Rhode Island..........	22	67	52	18	4.0	11.6	9.2	3.2	40	7	9.3	1.6
South Carolina.........	73	246	139	77	3.7	11.3	6.0	3.2	108	11	5.4	0.5
South Dakota..........	10	22	19	10	2.5	4.9	4.2	2.0	9	1	2.3	0.3
Tennessee.............	110	304	246	114	3.9	9.8	7.4	3.4	139	12	4.9	0.4
Texas.................	455	1,005	1,069	578	4.4	8.2	7.7	3.9	711	101	6.0	0.8
Utah..................	38	107	79	41	3.3	7.9	4.8	2.4	43	8	2.9	0.5
Vermont...............	9	23	19	8	2.8	6.3	5.6	2.3	25	2	9.0	0.8
Virginia................	82	305	279	123	2.3	7.3	6.4	2.8	190	12	5.3	0.3
Washington............	158	316	331	163	5.1	9.1	8.5	4.1	244	38	7.7	1.1
West Virginia...........	45	70	64	30	5.6	8.7	8.2	3.9	45	7	7.4	1.0
Wisconsin..............	101	262	200	90	3.4	8.5	6.4	2.9	148	24	5.5	0.9
Wyoming...............	10	21	17	10	3.8	6.9	5.9	3.4	9	2	3.4	0.6

[1] Total unemployment as percent of civilian labor force. [2] Number of average weekly jobless workers who are receiving state unemployment benefits. Source: U.S. Employment and Training Administration, "Unemployment Insurance, Financial Data Handbook 394," <oui.doleta.gov/unemploy/hb394.asp>, accessed May 2024. [3] Those currently collecting unemployment insurance as a percent of the total number of eligible workers. [4] U.S. totals include Puerto Rico and the Virgin Islands.

Source: Except as noted, U.S. Bureau of Labor Statistics, "Local Area Unemployment Statistics," <www.bls.gov/lau/>, accessed May 2024.

Table 663. Nonfarm Establishments—Employees, Hours, and Earnings by Industry: 2010 to 2023

[130,345 represents 130,345,000. Annual averages of monthly data. Based on data from establishment reports. Includes all full- and part-time employees who worked during, or received pay for, any part of the pay period including the 12th of the month. Excludes proprietors, the self-employed, farm workers, unpaid family workers, private household workers, and Armed Forces. Establishment data shown here conform to industry definitions in the 2022 North American Industry Classification System (NAICS) and are adjusted to March employment benchmarks. Based on the Current Employment Statistics Program; see source and Appendix III]

Item and year	Total nonfarm	Private industry																Government
		Total [1]	Construction	Manufacturing	Wholesale trade	Retail trade	Transportation and warehousing	Utilities	Information	Finance and insurance	Real estate and rental and leasing	Professional and technical services	Administrative and waste services	Educational services	Health care and social assistance	Arts entertainment and recreation	Accommodations and food services	
EMPLOYEES (1,000)																		
2010	130,345	107,854	5,518	11,528	5,387	14,404	4,179	553	2,707	5,761	1,934	7,486	7,419	3,155	16,820	1,913	11,135	22,490
2016	144,335	122,111	6,728	12,354	5,787	15,777	5,004	556	2,794	6,148	2,139	8,881	8,981	3,570	19,069	2,252	13,408	22,224
2017	146,607	124,257	6,969	12,439	5,814	15,789	5,178	555	2,814	6,262	2,189	9,058	9,142	3,668	19,520	2,333	13,718	22,350
2018	148,908	126,454	7,288	12,688	5,841	15,728	5,426	553	2,839	6,337	2,253	9,282	9,294	3,715	19,923	2,383	13,913	22,455
2019	150,904	128,291	7,493	12,817	5,889	15,560	5,665	549	2,864	6,433	2,321	9,536	9,319	3,741	20,421	2,437	14,149	22,613
2020	142,186	120,200	7,257	12,167	5,633	14,809	5,640	543	2,721	6,489	2,215	9,435	8,529	3,478	19,796	1,773	11,375	21,986
2021	146,285	124,311	7,436	12,354	5,710	15,253	6,145	545	2,856	6,544	2,262	9,902	9,067	3,587	20,065	1,980	12,171	21,973
2022	152,520	130,329	7,763	12,812	5,978	15,489	6,606	559	3,063	6,678	2,384	10,499	9,536	3,757	20,579	2,315	13,512	22,191
2023	156,051	133,269	8,018	12,940	6,116	15,590	6,565	575	3,027	6,731	2,466	10,825	9,457	3,818	21,525	2,518	14,075	22,782
WEEKLY EARNINGS [2] (dollars)																		
2010	(NA)	635.86	891.83	764.99	813.98	399.72	707.93	1,262.89	939.67	(NA)	(NA)	1,073.43	536.08	(NA)	652.07	363.91	266.78	(NA)
2016	(NA)	723.20	1,031.88	855.77	929.03	446.47	807.25	1,502.09	1,068.22	(NA)	(NA)	1,223.94	585.46	(NA)	737.17	380.57	310.02	(NA)
2017	(NA)	742.42	1,061.98	876.10	958.33	462.08	813.69	1,540.27	1,100.00	(NA)	(NA)	1,254.18	605.86	(NA)	755.48	387.40	323.66	(NA)
2018	(NA)	767.01	1,108.59	908.01	979.76	482.25	835.39	1,569.38	1,139.25	(NA)	(NA)	1,294.63	622.68	(NA)	776.46	389.91	338.00	(NA)
2019	(NA)	790.64	1,135.73	921.68	1,007.42	502.16	847.97	1,566.91	1,198.97	(NA)	(NA)	1,321.57	655.82	(NA)	798.79	395.68	351.58	(NA)
2020	(NA)	837.39	1,145.52	928.94	1,023.97	541.29	870.19	1,639.19	1,287.99	(NA)	(NA)	1,367.24	707.62	(NA)	842.18	432.47	343.29	(NA)
2021	(NA)	886.54	1,203.43	986.27	1,078.69	570.57	918.63	1,701.21	1,346.21	(NA)	(NA)	1,430.22	772.33	(NA)	903.92	445.28	396.45	(NA)
2022	(NA)	937.44	1,278.43	1,028.10	1,140.02	598.03	981.55	1,798.67	1,380.56	(NA)	(NA)	1,522.13	845.14	(NA)	967.64	476.72	432.22	(NA)
2023	(NA)	979.95	1,367.03	1,073.49	1,179.70	623.35	1,055.01	1,878.39	1,428.29	(NA)	(NA)	1,596.19	887.11	(NA)	1,004.90	486.06	450.44	(NA)
WEEKLY HOURS [2]																		
2010	(NA)	33.4	38.4	41.1	37.9	30.2	37.1	42.0	36.3	(NA)	(NA)	35.9	33.9	(NA)	32.2	23.8	25	(NA)
2016	(NA)	33.6	39.7	41.9	38.6	29.7	38.8	42.5	35.5	(NA)	(NA)	36.3	33.9	(NA)	32.3	23.2	25.2	(NA)
2017	(NA)	33.7	39.7	41.9	39.0	30.2	38.4	42.5	35.8	(NA)	(NA)	36.5	34.0	(NA)	32.4	22.9	25.2	(NA)
2018	(NA)	33.8	40.0	42.2	38.9	30.3	38.4	42.7	35.6	(NA)	(NA)	36.6	34.0	(NA)	32.4	22.5	25.3	(NA)
2019	(NA)	33.6	39.8	41.6	38.7	30.3	37.9	42.4	35.3	(NA)	(NA)	36.4	34.1	(NA)	32.4	21.6	25.2	(NA)
2020	(NA)	33.9	39.2	40.7	38.2	30.8	38.3	42.6	36.0	(NA)	(NA)	36.5	34.7	(NA)	32.7	22.2	24.4	(NA)
2021	(NA)	34.2	39.5	41.4	38.8	30.8	38.5	42.5	36.5	(NA)	(NA)	36.6	35.4	(NA)	32.8	22.5	25.3	(NA)
2022	(NA)	34.0	39.5	41.0	39.0	30.4	37.8	42.6	36.4	(NA)	(NA)	36.8	35.6	(NA)	32.7	22.3	25.0	(NA)
2023	(NA)	33.9	39.9	40.7	38.8	30.4	37.8	42.4	36.0	(NA)	(NA)	37.0	35.4	(NA)	32.7	22.0	24.7	(NA)
HOURLY EARNINGS [2] (dollars)																		
2010	(NA)	19.04	23.22	18.61	21.46	13.24	19.10	30.04	25.87	(NA)	(NA)	29.93	15.81	(NA)	20.23	15.27	10.68	(NA)
2016	(NA)	21.53	25.97	20.44	24.07	15.02	20.83	35.33	30.05	(NA)	(NA)	33.72	17.26	(NA)	22.83	16.38	12.32	(NA)
2017	(NA)	22.05	26.74	20.90	24.58	15.31	21.22	36.22	30.74	(NA)	(NA)	34.41	17.82	(NA)	23.35	16.94	12.85	(NA)
2018	(NA)	22.71	27.75	21.54	25.16	15.90	21.75	36.76	31.97	(NA)	(NA)	35.42	18.32	(NA)	23.96	17.31	13.37	(NA)
2019	(NA)	23.51	28.52	22.15	26.06	16.60	22.36	36.91	33.93	(NA)	(NA)	36.27	19.24	(NA)	24.67	18.30	13.95	(NA)
2020	(NA)	24.68	29.21	22.80	26.81	17.58	22.71	38.46	35.74	(NA)	(NA)	37.41	20.39	(NA)	25.76	19.52	14.07	(NA)
2021	(NA)	25.90	30.48	23.81	27.77	18.53	23.83	40.00	36.90	(NA)	(NA)	39.02	21.81	(NA)	27.54	19.78	15.68	(NA)
2022	(NA)	27.56	32.35	25.07	29.21	19.66	25.99	42.26	37.91	(NA)	(NA)	41.38	23.72	(NA)	29.55	21.34	17.31	(NA)
2023	(NA)	28.94	34.26	26.38	30.40	20.50	27.93	44.30	39.66	(NA)	(NA)	43.18	25.06	(NA)	30.74	22.05	18.26	(NA)

NA Not available. [1] Includes other industries not shown separately. [2] Average hours and earnings of production and nonsupervisory employees.

Source: U.S. Bureau of Labor Statistics, Current Employment Statistics, "Employment, Hours, and Earnings—National," <www.bls.gov/ces/data/>, accessed April 2024.

Table 664. Employees in Nonfarm Establishments by State and Industry: 2023

[In thousands (155,777.7 represents 155,777,700). Includes all full- and part-time employees who worked during, or received pay for, any part of the pay period reported. Excludes proprietors, the self-employed, farm workers, unpaid family workers, private household workers, and Armed Forces. Compiled from data supplied by cooperating state agencies. Based on North American Industry Classification System, 2017; see text, section 15]

State	Total [1]	Con-struction	Manu-facturing	Trade, transpor-tation and utilities	Infor-mation	Fin-ancial activi-ties [2]	Profes-sional and business ser-vices [3]	Educa-tion and health ser-vices [4]	Leisure and hospi-tality [5]	Other ser-vices [6]	Govern-ment
U.S........	155,777.7	7,965.0	12,903.5	28,863.8	2,984.3	9,044.6	22,667.0	25,392.6	16,482.2	5,891.9	22,953.8
AL.........	2,164.2	101.2	281.8	408.1	23.4	104.4	267.2	259.4	204.5	103.4	401.7
AK.........	328.6	17.2	12.9	65.8	4.6	10.9	27.9	51.6	35.7	11.8	78.6
AZ.........	3,194.8	211.9	194.5	617.0	51.1	242.1	467.4	518.2	351.5	101.9	425.1
AR.........	1,350.4	63.4	162.5	267.4	12.8	70.2	156.5	207.4	126.9	67.4	210.6
CA.........	17,825.0	913.5	1,334.2	3,107.1	559.0	814.3	2,775.4	3,100.0	2,010.6	587.9	2,603.7
CO.........	2,942.0	183.8	151.1	506.5	77.7	180.5	498.5	369.9	351.8	127.1	473.3
CT. [7]......	1,694.2	62.3	158.5	298.9	31.0	118.4	221.2	355.2	153.1	62.8	232.3
DE [7].......	483.7	23.9	27.3	89.9	3.6	50.5	64.9	83.0	52.2	18.9	69.4
DC [7].......	766.0	15.0	1.0	30.4	19.8	26.3	175.5	121.5	76.0	67.2	233.3
FL.........	9,754.9	629.4	422.2	1,970.3	158.7	682.7	1,623.1	1,475.4	1,296.2	366.5	1,124.7
GA.........	4,904.7	220.6	429.0	1,040.6	118.7	278.7	774.6	660.0	511.3	166.7	694.9
HI [7]........	632.2	38.1	12.7	117.2	8.1	27.7	71.7	88.7	118.5	26.3	123.2
ID.........	846.4	68.3	75.1	161.3	9.4	41.5	109.7	126.3	93.1	27.5	130.0
IL.........	6,113.4	234.9	577.6	1,226.7	93.3	401.5	950.1	967.2	592.1	250.5	812.4
IN.........	3,238.6	161.9	534.3	634.9	26.6	148.7	363.7	499.0	312.2	130.6	421.1
IA.........	1,589.3	83.2	226.6	311.8	18.6	108.1	146.2	233.2	140.6	56.0	262.9
KS.........	1,443.0	68.1	173.2	275.8	18.3	76.5	177.8	207.0	133.0	53.2	253.9
KY.........	2,016.4	89.6	256.2	426.9	23.0	96.7	229.1	302.9	203.8	71.7	307.8
LA.........	1,953.6	130.5	138.4	372.6	19.3	97.4	219.2	334.3	220.5	73.5	316.8
ME.........	649.3	33.6	53.9	120.5	8.2	33.7	76.5	130.2	68.3	22.1	100.2
MD.........	2,746.6	160.1	111.3	469.0	34.8	139.4	477.8	461.3	261.4	105.4	524.7
MA.........	3,713.1	173.1	237.4	562.4	95.7	230.2	631.6	826.6	357.3	137.7	460.0
MI.........	4,451.0	188.9	614.7	813.5	57.9	231.2	654.3	688.6	422.5	169.9	602.1
MN.........	2,984.8	135.0	325.8	532.3	44.4	189.9	385.8	565.1	267.3	113.7	419.3
MS.........	1,179.8	48.1	144.6	247.5	9.9	45.3	117.1	150.8	134.0	39.6	236.7
MO.........	2,976.7	143.6	286.6	562.0	49.0	184.4	380.6	508.0	310.4	115.2	432.5
MT.........	520.0	37.1	21.7	100.8	5.6	28.0	51.7	83.6	72.9	19.4	92.1
NE.........	1,048.9	60.9	104.9	198.5	17.2	70.4	126.1	161.8	96.9	37.0	174.3
NV.........	1,538.9	113.1	67.3	297.0	19.2	76.9	215.5	164.6	349.7	44.8	175.9
NH.........	698.9	31.3	70.7	140.2	11.8	34.5	98.4	126.1	73.8	24.6	86.7
NJ.........	4,320.7	165.5	254.9	910.7	77.9	269.0	720.4	751.9	398.9	171.1	598.9
NM.........	872.9	52.7	28.7	145.5	10.0	35.4	120.1	144.7	99.3	28.0	185.2
NY.........	9,710.7	391.1	422.6	1,486.5	283.5	746.8	1,393.4	2,221.3	915.4	387.0	1,457.7
NC.........	4,939.2	259.4	469.8	931.5	85.2	306.8	743.1	667.3	529.6	197.7	743.1
ND.........	437.4	27.7	28.4	92.2	5.6	25.1	34.9	67.7	39.9	15.3	82.6
OH.........	5,618.6	238.3	688.1	1,056.7	67.9	324.9	741.7	938.1	564.4	209.0	780.0
OK.........	1,754.4	82.8	139.1	321.6	17.9	83.9	209.2	258.3	180.5	70.5	358.8
OR.........	1,978.5	116.8	190.4	364.4	36.1	103.2	264.5	319.6	206.5	64.5	306.4
PA.........	6,086.3	259.7	566.2	1,142.8	93.3	339.7	840.1	1,315.0	561.9	257.3	687.4
RI.........	504.1	21.4	40.4	77.2	5.8	35.2	69.7	108.5	59.1	22.1	64.5
SC.........	2,305.8	112.5	263.8	441.8	29.1	122.3	311.6	282.5	279.9	86.8	371.1
SD.........	462.3	28.4	45.3	91.6	5.1	27.9	37.3	76.7	49.4	18.3	81.0
TN.........	3,308.1	153.7	363.9	681.6	55.5	185.5	457.5	473.6	360.6	127.6	444.1
TX.........	13,912.7	823.7	955.9	2,760.8	234.7	904.0	2,122.6	1,893.5	1,482.9	472.8	2,048.3
UT.........	1,722.4	134.6	152.9	315.6	43.1	98.1	249.6	235.2	171.8	45.7	265.0
VT.........	309.6	15.8	28.5	52.5	4.6	12.0	33.2	62.7	34.5	10.0	55.0
VA.........	4,170.1	215.2	246.4	672.6	70.4	221.7	808.6	582.6	412.1	199.2	734.0
WA.........	3,599.6	232.2	274.5	616.6	169.3	165.2	548.6	533.6	344.3	123.4	586.5
WV.........	711.1	33.1	46.1	122.7	7.9	25.8	72.9	133.2	71.9	24.0	152.3
WI.........	3,012.6	136.6	479.2	553.5	47.5	159.6	331.2	470.4	282.7	145.2	402.8
WY.........	291.2	22.2	10.4	52.5	3.2	11.5	21.7	29.3	38.5	16.1	68.9

[1] Includes mining and logging, not shown separately. [2] Finance and insurance; and real estate and rental and leasing. [3] Professional, scientific, and technical services; management of companies and enterprises; and administrative and support, and waste management and remediation services. [4] Education services; and health care and social assistance. [5] Arts, entertainment, and recreation; and accommodations and food services. [6] Includes repair and maintenance; personal and laundry services; and membership associations and organizations. [7] Mining and logging is combined with construction.

Source: U.S. Bureau of Labor Statistics, State and Metro Area Employment, Hours, and Earnings, Annual Average Tables, "Employees on nonfarm payrolls in States and selected areas by major industry," <www.bls.gov/sae/tables/>, accessed May 2024.

Table 665. Nonfarm Industries—Employees and Earnings: 2000 to 2023

[Annual averages of monthly figures (132,011 represents 132,011,000). Covers all full- and part-time employees who worked during, or received pay for, any part of the pay period including the 12th of the month. See also headnote, Table 663]

Industry	2022 NAICS code [1]	All employees (1,000)				Average hourly earnings [2] (dol.)			
		2000	2010	2020	2023	2000	2010	2020	2023
Total nonfarm	(X)	**132,011**	**130,345**	**142,186**	**156,051**	**(NA)**	**(NA)**	**(NA)**	**(NA)**
Goods-producing [3]	(X)	24,649	17,751	20,023	21,598	15.27	20.28	25.41	29.63
Service-providing [4]	(X)	107,362	112,594	122,163	134,453	(NA)	(NA)	(NA)	(NA)
Total private	(X)	**111,222**	**107,854**	**120,200**	**133,269**	**14.01**	**19.04**	**24.68**	**28.94**
Mining and logging	(X)	**599**	**705**	**600**	**640**	**16.55**	**23.82**	**30.42**	**34.41**
Logging	1133	79	50	46	45	13.70	18.85	22.74	27.74
Mining, quarrying, and oil and gas extraction	21	**520**	**655**	**553**	**595**	**16.94**	**24.24**	**31.09**	**34.90**
Oil and gas extraction	211	125	159	130	117	19.43	27.36	38.50	43.32
Mining, except oil and gas	212	225	204	176	187	18.07	24.63	28.33	34.37
Support activities for mining	213	171	292	247	291	14.55	22.95	30.29	32.97
Construction	23	**6,787**	**5,518**	**7,257**	**8,018**	**17.48**	**23.22**	**29.21**	**34.26**
Construction of buildings	236	1,633	1,230	1,606	1,811	16.74	22.73	28.99	33.78
Residential building	2361	823	572	809	927	15.18	19.80	26.38	30.09
Nonresidential building	2362	809	658	798	884	18.18	25.13	31.44	37.08
Heavy and civil engineering construction	237	937	825	1,046	1,116	16.80	23.76	30.74	36.06
Highway, street, and bridge construction	2373	340	287	346	370	18.17	23.76	29.92	35.50
Specialty trade contractors	238	4,217	3,463	4,605	5,091	17.91	23.22	28.88	33.95
Foundation, structure, and building exterior contractors	2381	919	680	905	995	16.93	21.20	27.38	31.54
Building equipment contractors	2382	1,897	1,634	2,209	2,483	19.52	24.89	31.00	36.48
Building finishing contractors	2383	857	634	799	833	16.44	22.06	26.62	30.95
Manufacturing	31-33	**17,263**	**11,528**	**12,167**	**12,940**	**14.32**	**18.61**	**22.80**	**26.38**
Durable goods	(X)	**10,877**	**7,064**	**7,573**	**8,102**	**14.93**	**19.81**	**23.76**	**27.53**
Wood products	321	615	342	396	418	11.63	14.85	19.18	23.19
Nonmetallic mineral products	327	554	371	399	421	14.53	17.48	22.67	25.61
Cement and concrete products	3273	234	170	194	206	14.64	17.84	24.15	26.30
Primary metals	331	622	362	354	374	16.64	20.13	23.96	28.15
Iron and steel mills and ferroalloy production	3311	135	87	82	83	(NA)	(NA)	(NA)	(NA)
Foundries	3315	217	112	103	108	14.72	18.22	22.63	27.00
Fabricated metal products	332	1,753	1,282	1,386	1,454	13.77	17.94	22.16	25.13
Architectural and structural metals	3323	428	321	383	412	13.43	17.47	22.20	24.78
Machine shops and threaded products	3327	365	313	335	343	14.53	18.68	23.38	26.51
Machinery	333	1,457	996	1,055	1,135	15.21	18.96	24.62	27.14
Agricultural, construction, and mining machinery	3331	222	208	201	221	14.21	18.95	23.69	28.56
HVAC and commercial refrigeration equip	3334	194	125	133	148	(NA)	(NA)	(NA)	(NA)
Metalworking machinery	3335	274	155	164	162	16.66	20.00	24.49	26.55
Computer and electronic products	334	1,820	1,095	1,063	1,108	14.73	22.78	25.59	30.57
Computer and peripheral equipment	3341	302	158	160	163	(NA)	(NA)	(NA)	(NA)
Communications equipment	3342	239	117	86	86	14.39	23.88	21.92	30.32
Semiconductors and electronic components	3344	676	369	369	395	13.46	20.35	22.61	24.87
Electronic instruments	3345	488	406	418	433	15.80	24.82	30.39	36.78
Electrical equipment and appliances	335	591	360	384	415	13.23	16.87	20.59	25.20
Household appliances	3352	106	60	62	65	(NA)	(NA)	(NA)	(NA)
Electrical equipment	3353	210	136	136	147	13.28	16.51	21.15	26.78
Transportation equipment	336	2,057	1,333	1,591	1,791	18.89	25.23	28.03	31.91
Motor vehicles	3361	291	153	206	296	24.45	29.05	30.08	33.05
Motor vehicle parts	3363	840	419	530	573	17.95	20.66	22.08	26.51
Aerospace products and parts	3364	517	478	507	534	20.52	33.65	39.69	45.09
Ship and boat building	3366	154	125	140	155	(NA)	(NA)	(NA)	(NA)
Furniture and related products	337	680	357	359	358	11.73	15.06	19.02	22.75
Household and institutional furniture	3371	441	223	226	228	11.40	14.75	18.72	22.46
Miscellaneous durable goods manufacturing	339	728	567	586	628	11.93	16.56	20.77	23.98
Medical equipment and supplies	3391	305	303	317	334	12.70	17.56	22.10	25.07
Nondurable goods	(X)	**6,386**	**4,464**	**4,594**	**4,838**	**13.31**	**16.80**	**21.28**	**24.50**
Food manufacturing	311	1,553	1,451	1,615	1,725	11.77	14.41	18.90	22.40
Fruit and vegetable preserving	3114	197	173	170	169	11.90	14.56	19.01	22.09
Dairy products	3115	136	130	153	165	14.85	18.92	23.30	25.87
Animal slaughtering and processing	3116	507	489	537	548	10.27	12.69	16.64	21.08
Bakeries and tortilla manufacturing	3118	306	277	294	337	11.45	14.44	18.45	21.30
Textile mills	313	378	119	96	91	11.23	13.56	17.46	20.61
Textile product mills	314	230	119	103	99	10.31	11.79	16.03	19.87
Apparel	315	484	157	90	90	8.61	11.43	16.90	19.62
Paper and paper products	322	605	395	355	357	15.91	20.04	23.32	24.86
Pulp, paper, and paperboard mills	3221	191	112	92	88	(NA)	(NA)	(NA)	(NA)
Converted paper products	3222	413	282	263	269	(NA)	(NA)	(NA)	(NA)
Printing and related support activities	323	807	488	375	370	14.09	16.91	20.06	21.91
Petroleum and coal products	324	123	114	108	108	(NA)	(NA)	(NA)	(NA)
Chemicals	325	980	787	845	900	17.09	21.07	26.03	29.77
Basic chemicals	3251	188	142	149	156	21.06	24.93	30.66	35.83
Resin, rubber, and artificial fibers	3252	136	89	90	97	(NA)	(NA)	(NA)	(NA)
Pharmaceuticals and medicines	3254	274	277	315	346	17.27	21.95	24.86	27.45
Plastics and rubber products	326	951	625	707	738	12.70	15.71	20.20	23.98
Plastics products	3261	737	502	576	603	12.04	15.47	20.14	23.72
Trade, transportation, and utilities	(X)	**26,153**	**24,523**	**26,624**	**28,847**	**13.28**	**16.78**	**21.40**	**25.25**
Wholesale trade	42	**5,888**	**5,387**	**5,633**	**6,116**	**16.24**	**21.46**	**26.81**	**30.40**
Durable goods, merchant wholesalers	423	3,342	2,848	3,081	3,395	16.83	21.30	27.02	31.13
Motor vehicles and parts	4231	361	317	345	379	14.37	17.86	22.89	28.30
Lumber and construction supplies	4233	233	196	242	262	13.79	18.87	24.69	26.87
Commercial equipment	4234	758	657	678	748	20.35	25.29	32.27	36.49
Household appliances and electrical and electronic goods	4236	438	328	342	375	19.51	23.42	29.51	33.04

See footnotes at end of table.

Industry	2022 NAICS code [1]	All employees (1,000)				Average hourly earnings [2] (dol.)			
		2000	2010	2020	2023	2000	2010	2020	2023
Hardware, and plumbing and heating equipment and supplies............	4237	253	227	278	310	15.21	20.14	25.31	27.70
Machinery and supplies........................	4238	739	629	687	757	16.57	21.27	27.60	32.46
Nondurable goods, merchant wholesalers....	424	2,131	2,026	2,065	2,207	14.54	20.03	24.74	27.63
Paper and paper products....................	4241	184	135	121	116	15.87	22.96	24.93	26.75
Drugs and druggists' goods...................	4242	212	219	235	259	(NA)	(NA)	(NA)	(NA)
Apparel and piece goods......................	4243	166	141	131	149	14.70	21.54	23.91	26.15
Grocery and related products.................	4244	704	726	751	817	13.73	19.33	22.75	26.81
Alcoholic beverages..........................	4248	130	166	200	217	15.80	20.14	25.37	25.76
Wholesale trade agents and brokers..........	425	415	513	487	514	20.37	28.21	34.53	37.85
Retail trade............	**44, 45**	**15,262**	**14,404**	**14,809**	**15,590**	**10.86**	**13.24**	**17.58**	**20.50**
Motor vehicle and parts dealers..............	441	1,852	1,634	1,905	2,045	14.93	17.06	22.52	26.42
Automobile dealers.........................	4411	1,217	1,012	1,203	1,276	16.95	18.22	24.52	28.45
Auto parts, accessories, and tire retailers....	4413	503	493	550	591	11.05	14.56	18.01	21.83
Furniture, home furnishings, electronics, and appliance retailers....................	449	1,215	981	863	848	12.80	16.18	21.94	22.97
Furniture and home furnishings retailers.....	4491	557	449	423	433	12.36	15.34	19.98	23.40
Furniture retailers.........................	44911	292	219	203	212	13.38	16.21	21.29	24.91
Electronics and appliance retailers..........	4492	658	532	441	416	13.17	16.87	23.75	22.57
Building material & garden supply retailers....	444	1,150	1,139	1,368	1,406	11.27	14.14	19.68	24.71
Building material and supplies dealers.......	4441	988	1,010	1,202	1,217	11.32	14.16	19.97	25.23
Food and beverage retailers.................	445	3,081	2,866	3,162	3,239	9.82	12.15	14.58	17.13
Beer, wine, and liquor retailers.............	4453	141	137	159	178	10.43	11.95	15.09	17.49
Health and personal care retailers..........	456	959	1,008	1,010	1,097	11.75	17.04	20.67	23.13
Gasoline stations and fuel dealers............	457	1,042	901	999	1,060	8.71	11.01	13.76	17.64
Clothing, clothing accessories, shoe, and jewelry retailers.........................	458	1,357	1,384	1,002	1,147	10.10	11.81	17.23	20.94
Clothing and clothing accessories retailers...	4581	986	1,068	747	852	10.06	11.21	16.49	19.78
Shoe retailers.............................	4582	194	182	152	172	8.99	11.83	16.96	23.93
Jewelry, luggage, and leather goods..........	4583	177	133	104	123	11.51	15.61	22.01	24.03
Sporting goods, hobby, musical instrument, book, and miscellaneous retailers..........	459	1,734	1,450	1,396	1,530	10.25	12.80	16.48	19.88
Sporting goods, hobby, and musical instrument retailers......................	4591	452	473	441	497	9.73	12.09	15.95	21.24
Book retailers and news dealers.............	4592	171	124	62	72	9.10	11.48	16.03	18.49
General merchandise retailers.................	455	2,872	3,042	3,104	3,218	9.30	11.08	15.78	17.37
Department retailers.......................	4551	1,743	1,488	936	960	(NA)	(NA)	(NA)	(NA)
Florists....................................	4593	132	71	54	62	9.06	11.38	15.06	17.95
Office supplies and stationery retailers.......	45941	206	146	85	71	12.66	14.88	17.46	16.76
Gift, novelty, and souvenir retailers..........	45942	269	161	115	136	8.36	11.05	13.34	17.44
Used merchandise retailers..................	4595	113	130	160	205	8.43	11.04	14.00	15.88
Transportation and warehousing............	**48, 49**	**4,401**	**4,179**	**5,640**	**6,565**	**15.00**	**19.10**	**22.71**	**27.93**
Air transportation...........................	481	614	458	441	552	13.57	24.56	35.62	45.59
Scheduled air transportation..................	4811	570	417	396	494	(NA)	(NA)	(NA)	(NA)
Rail transportation...........................	482	206	183	150	153	(NA)	(NA)	(NA)	(NA)
Water transportation.........................	483	56	62	60	70	(NA)	(NA)	(NA)	(NA)
Truck transportation.........................	484	1,406	1,251	1,471	1,567	15.86	18.62	24.40	29.01
General freight trucking.....................	4841	1,013	868	1,022	1,103	16.37	18.51	24.35	29.16
Specialized freight trucking.................	4842	393	383	449	463	14.52	18.89	24.50	28.66
Transit and ground passenger transport.......	485	376	436	370	428	11.88	14.98	19.33	25.04
Taxi and limousine service..................	4853	72	68	49	59	(NA)	(NA)	(NA)	(NA)
School and employee bus transportation. . .	4854	152	186	150	184	11.42	14.90	20.20	24.20
Urban transit systems and interurban, rural, and charter bus transportation........	4851, 2, 5	101	100	80	82	(NA)	(NA)	(NA)	(NA)
Pipeline transportation.......................	486	46	42	51	52	(NA)	(NA)	(NA)	(NA)
Scenic and sightseeing transportation.........	487	28	27	21	30	(NA)	(NA)	(NA)	(NA)
Support activities for transportation............	488	546	553	701	823	14.54	21.01	24.32	29.01
Couriers and messengers...................	492	605	528	967	1,083	13.51	17.67	18.62	22.72
Couriers and express delivery services......	4921	546	480	815	894	(NA)	(NA)	(NA)	(NA)
Warehousing and storage....................	493	518	638	1,405	1,808	14.49	15.57	18.47	22.90
Utilities........................	**22**	**601**	**553**	**543**	**575**	**22.75**	**30.04**	**38.46**	**44.30**
Power generation and supply.................	2211	434	398	381	401	23.13	31.25	38.97	45.60
Natural gas distribution......................	2212	121	108	110	114	23.41	28.36	41.95	46.31
Water, sewage and other systems...........	2213	46	47	52	60	16.93	23.73	25.69	29.11
Information..........................	**51**	**3,630**	**2,707**	**2,721**	**3,027**	**19.07**	**25.87**	**35.74**	**39.66**
Publishing industries........................	513	1,059	779	830	945	20.22	26.80	39.40	44.95
Newspaper, periodical, book, and directory publishers.......................	5131	798	518	326	289	15.37	21.27	28.97	35.48
Software publishers........................	5132	261	261	504	656	28.48	36.41	45.41	48.66
Motion picture and sound recording............	512	383	370	301	419	21.25	22.11	30.25	27.38
Broadcasting and content providers............	516	392	333	366	347	17.40	24.45	33.00	39.84
Radio and television broadcasting...........	5161	166	137	126	121	16.74	24.01	30.22	33.24
Media streaming services, social networks, & other media networks & content providers. . .	5162	226	196	240	227	17.91	24.79	34.41	43.20
Telecommunications.........................	517	1,397	903	688	646	18.59	26.24	32.13	33.90
Wired telecommunications carriers...........	517111	922	603	498	466	18.62	25.99	32.79	32.61
Wireless telecommunications carriers (except satellite).........................	517112	186	170	99	86	14.40	25.35	27.26	30.81
Web search portals, libraries, archives, and other information services......................	519	85	80	174	180	21.84	27.31	38.64	34.66
Financial activities.........................	**(X)**	**7,783**	**7,695**	**8,704**	**9,197**	**15.04**	**21.55**	**29.09**	**33.84**
Finance and insurance........................	**52**	**5,773**	**5,761**	**6,489**	**6,731**	**(NA)**	**(NA)**	**(NA)**	**(NA)**
Credit intermediation and related activities....	522	2,548	2,550	2,668	2,631	13.14	18.25	26.19	29.97
Depository credit intermediation..............	5221	1,723	1,763	1,772	1,799	12.01	17.65	24.76	29.01
Commercial banking....................	52211	1,325	1,366	1,388	1,393	11.92	17.70	25.24	29.55

See footnotes at end of table.

Table 665. Nonfarm Industries—Employees and Earnings: 2000 to 2023-Continued.

See headnote on page 434.

Industry	2022 NAICS code [1]	All employees (1,000)				Average hourly earnings [2] (dol.)			
		2000	2010	2020	2023	2000	2010	2020	2023
Nondepository credit intermediation.........	5222	606	532	589	538	15.41	20.00	30.77	32.41
Activities related to credit intermediation.....	5223	219	255	308	295	15.42	18.27	24.94	31.28
Securities, commodity contracts, and investments, and funds and trusts........	523, 5	851	850	965	1,102	20.04	31.21	42.99	50.45
Securities and commodity contracts brokerage and exchanges...................	5231, 2	569	471	447	483	20.05	31.72	42.68	50.59
Funds, trusts, and other financial vehicles and investment activities............	5239, 50	282	379	518	619	20.03	30.49	43.27	50.35
Insurance carriers and related activities.......	524	2,351	2,341	2,836	2,975	17.47	24.58	31.25	36.07
Insurance carriers........................	5241	1,544	1,445	1,627	1,624	18.03	25.95	32.65	38.36
Insurance agencies, brokerages, and related services.................	5242	807	896	1,209	1,352	16.32	22.18	29.23	33.08
Real estate and rental and leasing...........	**53**	**2,011**	**1,934**	**2,215**	**2,466**	**(NA)**	**(NA)**	**(NA)**	**(NA)**
Real estate................................	531	1,316	1,396	1,696	1,858	12.26	17.37	23.49	28.14
Lessors of real estate......................	5311	610	565	599	630	11.19	16.52	22.34	26.13
Offices of real estate agents and brokers....	5312	281	286	360	406	12.57	17.10	22.98	29.27
Activities related to real estate.............	5313	424	544	738	822	13.60	18.37	24.71	29.14
Rental and leasing services....................	532	667	514	496	586	11.69	15.96	22.07	25.31
Automotive equipment rental and leasing....	5321	208	161	189	228	(NA)	(NA)	(NA)	(NA)
Consumer goods rental......................	5322	292	198	122	132	(NA)	(NA)	(NA)	(NA)
Machinery/equipment rental and leasing.....	5324	103	114	157	193	14.95	19.83	27.59	30.39
Professional and business services...........	**(X)**	**16,725**	**16,824**	**20,376**	**22,840**	**15.53**	**22.79**	**29.23**	**34.21**
Professional, scientific, and technical services..........................	**54**	**6,732**	**7,486**	**9,435**	**10,825**	**20.62**	**29.93**	**37.41**	**43.18**
Legal services................................	5411	1,066	1,114	1,129	1,184	21.38	31.04	37.28	46.00
Accounting, tax preparation, bookkeeping, and payroll services......................	5412	867	887	994	1,149	14.42	21.03	27.77	31.56
Architectural and engineering services........	5413	1,239	1,276	1,504	1,660	20.49	30.22	35.69	40.45
Specialized design services....................	5414	132	113	133	153	15.32	22.36	30.09	32.29
Computer systems design and related.........	5415	1,259	1,456	2,197	2,500	27.11	37.12	44.44	50.76
Management and technical consulting.........	5416	694	1,031	1,528	1,867	20.87	28.54	37.40	41.60
Scientific research and development..........	5417	517	623	764	936	21.39	35.63	45.13	54.82
Advertising and related services.............	5418	498	410	450	508	17.01	24.64	31.20	36.36
Management of companies and enterprises..	**55**	**1,821**	**1,919**	**2,412**	**2,558**	**15.28**	**23.67**	**31.41**	**33.37**
Administrative and support & waste management and remediation services.....	**56**	**8,172**	**7,419**	**8,529**	**9,457**	**11.70**	**15.81**	**20.39**	**25.06**
Administrative and support services...........	561	7,859	7,062	8,082	8,956	11.53	15.60	20.11	24.75
Office administrative services..................	5611	264	407	521	620	14.68	23.56	30.06	34.01
Employment services.........................	5613	3,850	2,724	3,117	3,640	11.90	16.19	20.70	25.83
Temporary help services......................	56132	2,636	2,094	2,522	2,870	11.79	14.23	19.73	24.57
Business support services.....................	5614	788	811	815	744	11.10	14.53	18.87	23.27
Travel arrangement and reservation...........	5615	299	186	165	191	12.72	17.10	24.46	29.84
Investigation and security services............	5616	690	782	907	1,004	9.79	14.15	18.47	22.90
Services to buildings and dwellings............	5617	1,571	1,745	2,101	2,251	10.02	12.97	17.41	20.99
Waste management & remediation services.....	562	313	357	447	500	15.29	19.32	24.80	29.93
Waste collection.............................	5621	100	141	191	215	12.97	17.50	21.83	26.36
Waste treatment and disposal.................	5622	119	96	100	105	(NA)	(NA)	(NA)	(NA)
Private education and health services........	**(X)**	**15,252**	**19,975**	**23,275**	**25,342**	**13.91**	**19.95**	**25.40**	**30.29**
Educational services, private.................	**61**	**2,390**	**3,155**	**3,478**	**3,818**	**(NA)**	**(NA)**	**(NA)**	**(NA)**
Elementary and secondary schools............	6111	716	849	1,037	1,154	(NA)	(NA)	(NA)	(NA)
Junior colleges, colleges, universities, and professional schools.........................	6112,3	1,275	1,690	1,724	1,745	(NA)	(NA)	(NA)	(NA)
Business, computer, and management training.........................	6114	86	78	71	89	(NA)	(NA)	(NA)	(NA)
Technical and trade schools....................	6115	91	126	106	121	(NA)	(NA)	(NA)	(NA)
Other schools and instruction.................	6116	184	309	386	514	(NA)	(NA)	(NA)	(NA)
Educational support services..................	6117	39	103	154	195	(NA)	(NA)	(NA)	(NA)
Health care and social assistance.............	**62**	**12,861**	**16,820**	**19,796**	**21,525**	**13.93**	**20.23**	**25.76**	**30.74**
Health care.................................	621,2,3	10,858	13,777	15,850	16,953	14.63	21.71	27.87	33.37
Ambulatory health care services..............	621	4,320	5,975	7,498	8,461	15.00	21.68	27.89	32.95
Offices of physicians........................	6211	1,801	2,264	2,632	2,921	15.65	24.03	33.51	39.80
Offices of dentists..........................	6212	688	828	889	1,027	15.96	22.65	27.63	31.22
Offices of other health practitioners..........	6213	438	671	926	1,155	14.24	20.48	24.73	28.88
Outpatient care centers.....................	6214	425	649	970	1,061	15.36	22.81	27.90	33.05
Medical and diagnostic laboratories..........	6215	162	228	282	321	15.74	23.48	26.82	33.95
Home health care services...................	6216	633	1,085	1,495	1,627	12.86	16.64	20.10	23.71
Hospitals...................................	622	3,954	4,679	5,137	5,338	16.71	26.11	33.25	39.66
General medical and surgical hospitals......	6221	3,745	4,357	4,715	4,886	16.75	26.33	33.56	40.10
Psychiatric and substance abuse hospitals..	6222	86	109	153	158	(NA)	(NA)	(NA)	(NA)
Nursing and residential care facilities..........	623	2,583	3,124	3,214	3,154	10.67	14.21	18.05	22.01
Skilled nursing care facilities..................	6231	1,514	1,657	1,499	1,417	11.08	15.26	19.21	23.47
Residential intellectual and developmental disability, mental health & substance abuse facilities.....................	6232	437	565	623	637	9.96	13.06	17.30	21.20
Continuing care retirement communities and assisted living facilities for the elderly........	6233	478	741	932	944	9.83	12.89	16.63	20.53
Social assistance.............................	624	2,003	3,043	3,947	4,571	9.72	12.75	16.24	19.66
Individual and family services.................	6241	821	1,664	2,617	3,034	10.30	13.07	16.46	19.96
Community food and housing, and emergency and other relief services........	6242	117	143	186	220	10.95	14.41	19.47	22.72
Vocational rehabilitation services.............	6243	370	388	282	281	9.57	12.47	16.07	19.10
Child day care services.......................	6244	696	848	861	1,036	8.88	11.99	14.97	18.38
Leisure and hospitality.......................	**(X)**	**11,862**	**13,049**	**13,148**	**16,593**	**8.32**	**11.31**	**14.71**	**18.76**
Arts, entertainment, and recreation...........	**71**	**1,788**	**1,913**	**1,773**	**2,518**	**10.68**	**15.27**	**19.52**	**22.05**
Performing arts, spectator sports, and									

See footnotes at end of table.

Table 665. Nonfarm Industries—Employees and Earnings: 2000 to 2023-Continued.

See headnote on page 434.

Industry	2022 NAICS code [1]	All employees (1,000) 2000	2010	2020	2023	Average hourly earnings [2] (dol.) 2000	2010	2020	2023
related industries	711	382	406	336	577	13.11	21.01	29.56	29.16
Museums, historical sites, and similar institutions	712	110	128	138	172	12.20	15.60	20.09	22.41
Amusements, gambling, and recreation	713	1,296	1,379	1,299	1,770	9.86	13.38	16.33	19.45
Accommodation and food services	**72**	**10,074**	**11,135**	**11,375**	**14,075**	**7.92**	**10.68**	**14.07**	**18.26**
Accommodation	721	1,884	1,760	1,471	1,891	9.48	13.02	15.53	20.38
Traveler accommodation	7211	1,837	1,703	1,416	1,806	9.49	13.07	15.53	20.51
Food services and drinking places	722	8,189	9,376	9,904	12,184	7.49	10.15	13.83	17.87
Full-service restaurants	722511	3,845	4,482	4,212	5,355	7.78	10.93	15.18	19.34
Limited-service restaurants	722513	3,042	3,418	4,178	4,645	6.80	8.86	12.13	15.48
Special food services	7223	491	543	497	744	9.45	11.83	16.02	20.95
Drinking places, alcoholic beverages	7224	391	341	268	433	7.24	10.15	15.68	21.32
Other services	**81**	**5,168**	**5,330**	**5,329**	**5,826**	**12.73**	**17.06**	**22.58**	**26.19**
Repair and maintenance	811	1,242	1,139	1,281	1,453	13.28	16.82	22.22	25.92
Automotive repair and maintenance	8111	888	801	898	1,019	12.45	15.55	20.51	24.48
Electronic and precision equipment repair and maintenance	8112	107	98	100	106	16.30	19.40	26.88	30.25
Commercial and industrial machinery repair and maintenance	8113	161	172	208	242	15.53	21.03	27.07	30.45
Personal and laundry services	812	1,243	1,265	1,239	1,536	10.18	13.42	16.99	21.17
Personal care services	8121	490	601	583	733	10.18	13.97	16.82	23.90
Death care services	8122	136	131	132	138	13.04	17.46	21.19	21.61
Dry-cleaning and laundry services	8123	388	302	239	261	9.17	11.80	15.26	18.45
Other personal services	8129	229	232	286	404	10.52	12.43	17.28	18.79
Pet care services, except veterinary	81291	31	63	122	183	12.12	12.83	15.88	19.39
Parking lots and garages	81293	93	111	95	125	8.81	11.18	15.14	16.38
Religious, grantmaking, civic, professional, and similar organizations	813	2,683	2,926	2,808	2,837	13.66	18.76	24.97	28.91
Grantmaking and giving services	8132	116	178	177	196	14.65	23.51	34.56	38.85
Social advocacy organizations	8133	143	202	232	275	12.08	17.36	24.16	26.68
Civic and social organizations	8134	404	392	271	346	9.85	12.16	18.43	20.22
Business, professional, labor, political, and similar organizations	8139	473	477	457	471	15.98	22.67	31.26	34.94
Government	(X)	**20,790**	**22,490**	**21,986**	**22,782**	**(NA)**	**(NA)**	**(NA)**	**(NA)**
Federal	(X)	2,865	2,977	2,930	2,925	(NA)	(NA)	(NA)	(NA)
Federal, except U.S. Postal Service	(X)	1,985	2,318	2,328	2,321	(NA)	(NA)	(NA)	(NA)
U.S. Postal Service	(X)	880	659	602	604	(NA)	(NA)	(NA)	(NA)
State	(X)	4,786	5,137	5,135	5,304	(NA)	(NA)	(NA)	(NA)
Local	(X)	13,139	14,376	13,921	14,552	(NA)	(NA)	(NA)	(NA)

NA Not available. X Not applicable. [1] Based on the North American Industry Classification System, 2022. See text, Section 15. [2] Production employees in the goods-producing industries and nonsupervisory employees in service-providing industries. [3] Mining and logging, construction, and manufacturing. [4] Trade, transportation and utilities, information, financial activities, professional and business services, education and health services, leisure and hospitality, other services, and government.

Source: U.S. Bureau of Labor Statistics, Current Employment Statistics, "Employment, Hours, and Earnings—National," <www.bls.gov/ces/>, accessed August 2024.

Table 666. Women Employed by Nonfarm Industry: 2000 to 2023

[63,398 represents 63,398,000. Annual averages of monthly data. For coverage, see headnote, Table 663]

Industry	Women employees (1,000) 2000	2010	2020	2023	Percent of total employees 2000	2010	2020	2023
Total nonfarm	**63,398**	**65,089**	**70,687**	**77,733**	**48.0**	**49.9**	**49.7**	**49.8**
Total private	**51,627**	**52,260**	**58,033**	**64,447**	**46.4**	**48.5**	**48.3**	**48.4**
Construction	846	723	961	1,136	12.5	13.1	13.2	14.2
Manufacturing	5,359	3,268	3,472	3,762	31.0	28.3	28.5	29.1
Trade, transportation, and utilities	10,834	9,969	10,439	11,314	41.4	40.7	39.2	39.2
Wholesale trade	1,812	1,619	1,685	1,872	30.8	30.1	29.9	30.6
Retail trade	7,669	7,206	7,205	7,526	50.3	50.0	48.7	48.3
Transportation and warehousing	1,202	1,006	1,416	1,765	27.3	24.1	25.1	26.9
Utilities	151	139	133	151	25.1	25.1	24.6	26.3
Information	1,697	1,104	1,085	1,225	46.7	40.8	39.9	40.5
Financial activities	4,697	4,530	4,925	5,114	60.3	58.9	56.6	55.6
Professional and business services	7,704	7,494	9,326	10,511	46.1	44.5	45.8	46.0
Professional, scientific, and technical services	3,156	3,537	4,432	5,156	46.9	47.2	47.0	47.6
Management of companies and enterprises	937	963	1,204	1,291	51.4	50.2	49.9	50.5
Administrative and support & waste management and remediation services	3,612	2,995	3,690	4,063	44.2	40.4	43.3	43.0
Private education and health services	11,703	15,435	17,962	19,491	76.7	77.3	77.2	76.9
Private educational services	1,417	1,929	2,173	2,429	59.3	61.2	62.5	63.6
Health care and social assistance	10,286	13,505	15,788	17,062	80.0	80.3	79.8	79.3
Leisure and hospitality	6,082	6,819	6,975	8,704	51.3	52.3	53.0	52.5
Arts, entertainment, and recreation	815	886	841	1,201	45.6	46.3	47.4	47.7
Accommodation and food services	5,267	5,933	6,135	7,503	52.3	53.3	53.9	53.3
Other services	2,614	2,821	2,805	3,107	50.6	52.9	52.6	53.3
Government	**11,771**	**12,829**	**12,654**	**13,286**	**56.6**	**57.0**	**57.6**	**58.3**
Federal	1,231	1,326	1,324	1,348	43.0	44.5	45.2	46.1
State government	2,464	2,639	2,781	2,910	51.5	51.4	54.2	54.9
Local government	8,076	8,864	8,549	9,027	61.5	61.7	61.4	62.0

Source: U.S. Bureau of Labor Statistics, Current Employment Statistics, "Employment, Hours, and Earnings—National," <www.bls.gov/ces/data>, accessed June 2024.

Table 667. Job Gains and Job Losses of Private Sector Establishments by Industry Sector: 2000 to 2023

[In thousands (16,145 represents 16,145,000). For year ending in March. Based on the Quarterly Census of Employment and Wages (QCEW). Excludes self-employed and certain nonprofit organizations. Minus sign (-) indicates a decrease in employment and comes from either closing establishments or contracting establishments. For more information, see source]

Year and industry	Gross job gains			Gross job losses			Net change [1]
	Total	Expanding establishments	Opening establishments	Total	Contracting establishments	Closing establishments	
2000	16,145	10,620	5,525	13,160	8,291	4,869	2,985
2009	10,149	6,668	3,481	15,969	11,706	4,263	-5,820
2010	10,075	6,839	3,236	12,760	9,142	3,618	-2,685
2011	11,629	8,295	3,334	9,721	6,623	3,098	1,908
2012	12,216	8,662	3,554	9,546	6,508	3,038	2,670
2013	12,045	8,553	3,492	9,924	6,829	3,095	2,121
2014	12,282	8,700	3,582	10,008	6,945	3,063	2,274
2015	12,834	9,143	3,691	10,115	6,940	3,175	2,719
2016	13,168	9,394	3,774	10,656	7,426	3,230	2,512
2017	12,953	9,156	3,797	10,921	7,638	3,283	2,032
2018	13,116	9,359	3,757	10,948	7,635	3,313	2,168
2019	13,134	9,377	3,757	11,289	7,855	3,434	1,845
2020	12,746	8,972	3,774	12,379	8,671	3,708	367
2021	12,522	8,648	3,874	18,001	14,059	3,942	-5,479
2022	17,911	13,247	4,664	10,982	7,675	3,307	6,929
2023, Total private	**15,970**	**11,374**	**4,596**	**12,687**	**8,727**	**3,960**	**3,283**
Goods producing	2,477	1,942	535	2,076	1,531	545	401
Natural resources and mining	226	172	54	217	161	56	9
Construction	1,230	896	334	1,021	704	317	209
Manufacturing	1,021	874	147	838	666	172	183
Service providing	13,494	9,432	4,062	10,611	7,198	3,413	2,883
Wholesale trade	685	528	157	501	330	171	184
Retail trade	1,342	966	376	1,324	994	330	18
Transportation and warehousing	662	494	168	712	562	150	-50
Utilities	43	35	8	25	20	5	18
Information	388	281	107	390	289	101	-2
Financial activities	1,055	776	279	962	670	292	93
Professional and business services	3,271	2,341	930	2,878	2,062	816	393
Education and health services	2,648	1,975	673	1,716	1,045	671	932
Leisure and hospitality	2,436	1,577	859	1,558	935	623	878
Other services	654	436	218	483	277	206	171

[1] Net change is the difference between total gross job gains and total gross job losses.

Source: U.S. Bureau of Labor Statistics, Business Employment Dynamics, "Annual Business Employment Dynamics Data," <www.bls.gov/bdm/bdmann.htm>, accessed May 2024.

Table 668. Private Sector Gross Job Gains and Job Losses by State: 2023

[In thousands (15,970 represents 15,970,000). For year ending in March. Based on the Quarterly Census of Employment and Wages (QCEW). Excludes self-employed and certain nonprofit organizations. Minus sign (-) indicates a decrease in employment and comes from either closing establishments or contracting establishments. For more information, see source]

State	Gross job gains			Gross job losses			Net change [1]
	Total	Expanding establishments	Opening establishments	Total	Contracting establishments	Closing establishments	
U.S.	15,970	11,374	4,596	12,687	8,727	3,960	3,283
AL	221	149	72	169	119	49	52
AK	27	21	6	21	15	6	7
AZ	371	260	111	287	192	95	84
AR	128	88	40	92	66	26	35
CA	1,907	1,296	611	1,825	1,251	574	82
CO	325	226	99	270	175	95	55
CT	154	107	46	133	92	42	20
DE	51	34	17	37	24	13	14
DC	69	48	20	53	37	15	16
FL	1,253	831	422	891	539	353	362
GA	561	387	175	441	295	146	120
HI	61	44	17	43	31	12	18
ID	91	61	30	83	49	34	8
IL	546	425	121	438	313	125	108
IN	292	223	68	244	181	63	48
IA	130	99	31	119	87	33	11
KS	142	98	43	110	77	34	31
KY	198	141	57	147	113	34	51
LA	193	139	54	158	111	47	35
ME	57	40	17	47	32	16	10
MD	273	183	90	229	152	77	44
MA	327	250	77	271	191	79	56
MI	387	292	96	318	230	88	69
MN	258	189	69	208	147	62	50
MS	117	81	36	100	71	29	17
MO	287	204	83	227	156	71	60
MT	56	37	19	44	28	16	12
NE	96	68	28	75	51	24	21
NV	182	132	50	133	91	43	49
NH	68	47	21	55	39	16	13
NJ	439	318	121	359	255	104	81
NM	88	61	27	68	44	24	20
NY	1,000	716	284	739	482	257	261
NC	528	376	152	392	261	131	135
ND	40	29	11	29	21	8	11
OH	496	383	113	421	316	105	75
OK	181	118	63	127	83	44	54
OR	198	141	57	177	119	57	22
PA	531	415	116	423	315	108	109
RI	50	34	16	41	28	13	9
SC	259	173	86	190	130	60	69
SD	39	28	11	31	22	9	8
TN	342	245	97	266	195	71	76
TX	1,588	1,155	433	1,068	740	328	521
UT	191	130	61	158	110	47	34
VT	29	19	10	23	14	8	6
VA	413	288	125	321	214	107	92
WA	383	295	88	307	227	80	77
WV	68	46	22	57	39	18	12
WI	252	183	69	203	146	58	49
WY	27	18	8	21	14	7	6

[1] Net change is the difference between total gross job gains and total gross job losses.

Source: U.S. Bureau of Labor Statistics, Business Employment Dynamics, "Annual Business Employment Dynamics Data," <www.bls.gov/bdm/bdmann.htm>, accessed May 2024.

Table 669. Hires and Separations Affecting Establishment Payrolls By Industry: 2020 to 2023

[72,555 represents 72,555,000. Hires represent any additions to payrolls, including new and rehired employees, full- and part-time workers, short-term and seasonal workers, and other hires. Separations represent terminations of employment, including quits, layoffs, and discharges, and other separations. Based on a monthly survey of private nonfarm establishments and governmental entities]

Industry	Annual hires (1,000)				Annual separations (1,000)			
	2020	2021	2022	2023	2020	2021	2022	2023
Total..............	**72,555**	**76,170**	**76,816**	**71,024**	**80,898**	**68,886**	**72,231**	**68,062**
Total private industry..........................	68,372	71,765	71,986	66,353	75,760	64,901	67,737	64,038
Mining and logging........................	198	229	275	290	334	209	228	276
Construction..............................	4,970	4,361	4,422	4,459	4,988	4,162	4,133	4,207
Manufacturing..........................	4,815	5,351	5,508	4,770	5,373	4,979	5,144	4,740
Durable goods........................	2,750	2,959	3,024	2,574	3,157	2,724	2,765	2,502
Nondurable goods.....................	2,064	2,394	2,484	2,197	2,215	2,253	2,377	2,239
Trade, transportation, and utilities..........	15,445	16,187	15,576	14,234	16,126	15,045	15,101	14,120
Wholesale trade.......................	1,812	2,130	2,200	1,952	2,109	1,901	1,959	1,860
Retail trade............................	9,825	10,223	9,304	8,550	10,357	9,900	9,250	8,439
Transportation, warehousing, and utilities................................	3,809	3,834	4,072	3,731	3,658	3,243	3,891	3,821
Information..............................	983	1,337	1,273	905	1,166	1,075	1,151	992
Financial activities.....................	2,656	2,744	2,904	2,462	2,731	2,518	2,713	2,379
Finance and insurance....................	1,667	1,822	1,908	1,522	1,635	1,719	1,812	1,494
Real estate and rental and leasing........	988	920	997	941	1,095	799	903	889
Professional and business services........	13,434	15,097	14,946	12,906	13,923	13,743	14,261	12,727
Education and health services..............	9,347	9,344	10,275	10,693	10,384	8,824	9,402	9,625
Educational services.....................	1,128	1,244	1,177	1,153	1,473	906	1,123	1,064
Health care and social assistance........	8,219	8,101	9,099	9,541	8,909	7,920	8,279	8,563
Leisure and hospitality....................	13,483	14,350	14,123	13,091	17,150	11,919	13,067	12,523
Arts, entertainment, and recreation.......	1,634	1,979	2,011	2,072	2,265	1,561	1,764	1,888
Accommodation and food services.......	11,849	12,370	12,111	11,017	14,887	10,356	11,304	10,634
Other services...........................	3,042	2,763	2,690	2,547	3,582	2,429	2,538	2,445
Government workers.......................	4,183	4,405	4,828	4,671	5,140	3,988	4,489	4,024
Federal.................................	886	524	501	533	826	542	511	451
State and local.........................	3,297	3,883	4,330	4,139	4,310	3,445	3,982	3,572

Source: U.S. Bureau of Labor Statistics, *Job Openings and Labor Turnover—January 2024*, USDL 24-0449, March 2024. See also <www.bls.gov/jlt/news.htm>.

Table 670. Job Separations Affecting Establishment Payrolls by Type and Industry: 2023

[44,379 represents 44,379,000. Covers all private nonfarm establishments. Separations are the total number of terminations of employment occurring at any time during the year, and are reported by type of separation—quits, layoffs and discharges, and other separations]

Industry	Number (1,000)			Rate (percent) [1]		
	Annual quits [2]	Annual layoffs and discharges [3]	Annual other separations [4]	Annual quits [2]	Annual layoffs and discharges [3]	Annual other separations [4]
Total..............	**44,379**	**19,759**	**3,927**	**2.4**	**1.1**	**0.2**
Total private industry..........................	42,015	18,743	3,280	2.6	1.2	0.2
Mining and logging........................	175	82	19	2.3	1.1	0.2
Construction..............................	1,979	2,075	154	2.1	2.2	0.2
Manufacturing..........................	3,006	1,480	252	1.9	1.0	0.2
Durable goods........................	1,560	786	155	1.6	0.8	0.2
Nondurable goods.....................	1,446	696	96	2.5	1.2	0.2
Trade, transportation, and utilities............	9,592	3,826	702	2.8	1.1	0.2
Wholesale trade.......................	1,178	575	105	1.6	0.8	0.1
Retail trade............................	6,179	1,874	387	3.3	1.0	0.2
Transportation, warehousing, and utilities................................	2,235	1,375	207	2.6	1.6	0.2
Information..............................	476	390	126	1.3	1.1	0.3
Financial activities.....................	1,554	599	225	1.4	0.5	0.2
Finance and insurance....................	998	333	167	1.2	0.4	0.2
Real estate and rental and leasing..........	559	266	62	1.9	0.9	0.2
Professional and business services..........	7,266	4,662	799	2.7	1.7	0.3
Education and health services...............	7,018	2,065	543	2.3	0.7	0.2
Educational services.....................	672	331	60	1.5	0.7	0.1
Health care and social assistance...........	6,348	1,731	481	2.5	0.7	0.2
Leisure and hospitality....................	9,444	2,799	278	4.7	1.4	0.1
Arts, entertainment, and recreation.........	997	844	48	3.3	2.8	0.2
Accommodation and food services..........	8,447	1,954	233	5.0	1.2	0.1
Other services...........................	1,503	764	178	2.1	1.1	0.3
Government workers...........................	2,364	1,012	648	0.9	0.4	0.2
Federal.................................	212	86	153	0.6	0.2	0.4
State and local.........................	2,151	925	493	0.9	0.4	0.2

[1] Annual average rates, equal to the sum of the 12 monthly separation levels as a percent of the sum of the 12 monthly CES employment levels. [2] Quits are voluntary separations by employees (except for retirements, which are reported as other separations). [3] Layoffs and discharges are involuntary separations initiated by the employer and include layoffs with no intent to rehire; formal layoffs lasting or expected to last more than seven days; discharges resulting from mergers, downsizing, or closings, firings or other discharges for cause; terminations of permanent or short term employees; and terminations of seasonal employees. [4] Other separations include retirements, transfers to other locations, deaths, and separations due to disability.

Source: U.S. Bureau of Labor Statistics, *Job Openings and Labor Turnover— January 2024*, USDL 24-0499, March 2024. See also <www.bls.gov/jlt/news.htm>.

Table 671. Private Nonprofit Establishments, Employees, and Average Annual Wages by Selected Industry: 2017

[In units, as indicated. 122,387 represents 122,387,000. Data from Bureau of Labor Statistics' Quarterly Census of Employment and Wages and IRS Exempt Organization Business Master File]

Industry	NAICS code	All establishments			501(c)(3) nonprofit establishments			501(c)(3) percent of total employ-ment
		Establish-ments (number)	Annual average employ-ment (1,000s)	Annual wages per employee (dollars)	Establish-ments (number)	Annual average employ-ment (1,000s)	Annual wages per employee (dollars)	
Total private	(X)	9,536,831	122,387	55,338	299,457	12,489	53,667	10.2
Agriculture, forestry, fishing and hunting	11	104,445	1,261	34,464	338	3	34,981	0.2
Construction	23	784,852	6,919	60,735	930	9	46,364	0.1
Manufacturing	31-33	346,723	12,407	66,840	267	7	38,240	0.1
Wholesale trade	42	612,359	5,899	75,904	732	4	57,227	0.1
Retail trade	44-45	1,042,096	15,854	31,217	5,750	93	22,467	0.6
Transportation and warehousing	48-49	242,932	4,947	51,726	893	21	34,523	0.4
Information	51	162,702	2,793	105,722	4,705	68	52,650	2.4
Finance and insurance	52	484,801	5,909	106,185	1,301	44	95,789	0.7
Real estate and rental and leasing	53	385,826	2,180	56,970	3,916	36	38,779	1.7
Professional, scientific, and technical services	54	1,183,104	8,996	93,687	11,944	270	80,686	3.0
Management of companies and enterprises	55	64,772	2,278	119,885	4,633	281	69,142	12.3
Administrative and support and waste management and remediation services	56	534,038	9,065	39,621	5,098	101	53,689	1.1
Educational services	61	117,479	2,824	50,053	32,832	2,004	55,389	70.9
Elementary and secondary schools	6111	17,969	811	41,234	12,879	684	41,766	84.3
Colleges, universities, and professional schools	6113	8,934	1,242	64,605	5,331	1,138	66,097	91.6
Health care and social assistance	62	1,532,134	19,322	49,076	138,319	8,307	54,742	43.0
Hospitals	622	10,024	5,018	62,595	5,171	4,207	63,923	83.8
Other residential care facilities	6239	6,585	165	31,853	3,680	112	33,615	67.8
Community food and housing, and emergency and other relief services	6242	11,389	169	37,870	9,871	154	37,301	91.2
Vocational rehabilitation services	6243	9,574	335	26,599	6,940	289	25,542	86.1
Arts, entertainment, and recreation	71	141,502	2,294	37,759	15,261	356	29,810	15.5
Performing arts companies	7111	10,026	123	49,541	3,498	70	38,353	57.0
Museums, historical sites, and similar institutions	712	6,475	163	34,795	4,960	141	35,759	86.5
Accommodation and food services	72	697,728	13,607	20,731	1,909	38	20,838	0.3
Other services (except public administration)	81	839,795	4,435	37,320	66,719	838	39,198	18.9
Religious, grantmaking, civic, professional, and similar organizations	813	146,264	1,370	43,941	64,730	819	39,353	59.8
Religious organizations	8131	23,174	192	28,976	18,324	163	29,495	84.9
Grantmaking and giving services	8132	16,042	143	66,667	14,118	131	66,139	91.5
Social advocacy organizations	8133	22,277	212	48,115	18,070	185	47,191	87.6
Civic and social organizations	8134	25,771	392	19,976	8,992	280	18,957	71.3

Source: U.S. Bureau of Labor Statistics, Business Employment Dynamics, "Research Data on the Nonprofit Sector," <www.bls.gov/bdm/nonprofits/nonprofits.htm>, accessed May 2019.

Table 672. Indexes of Total Factor Productivity and Related Measures: 2000 to 2023

[2017=100. Data shown for private nonfarm business. Total Factor Productivity is a measure of economic performance comparing the amount of goods and services produced (output) to the amount of combined inputs used to produce those goods and services. Measured using output and compensation data published by the Bureau of Economic Analysis (BEA), hours data published by other BLS programs, and capital data supplied by BEA and U.S. Department of Agriculture. See source for details]

Year	Productivity				Combined inputs			
	Total factor produc-tivity [1]	Labor productivity	Output per unit of capital input	Value added output [2]	Combined units of labor and capital input	Labor input [3]	Capital input [4]	Capital intensity [5]
2000	87.3	71.8	109.1	68.3	78.2	88.1	62.6	65.8
2005	94.9	84.0	105.6	78.3	82.5	87.8	74.1	79.6
2010	97.3	94.5	97.8	81.8	84.1	84.3	83.7	96.7
2015	99.5	98.0	101.0	95.2	95.7	96.6	94.2	97.0
2020	101.8	110.0	95.1	103.7	101.9	97.7	109.0	115.7
2021	105.1	111.5	99.8	111.2	105.8	102.5	111.4	111.7
2022	103.3	109.2	99.0	113.4	109.7	106.9	114.5	110.2
2023	104.1	110.5	98.8	116.3	111.8	108.2	117.7	111.9
ANNUAL PERCENT CHANGE								
2000	1.2	3.0	-1.8	4.3	3.1	1.7	6.2	4.8
2005	1.5	2.2	0.5	4.0	2.4	1.9	3.5	1.7
2010	2.6	3.3	2.2	3.3	0.7	0.4	1.1	1.1
2015	0.8	1.3	0.7	3.8	3.0	2.9	3.0	0.6
2020	-0.2	5.9	-5.2	-2.8	-2.5	-5.6	2.6	11.7
2021	3.2	1.3	4.9	7.3	3.9	5.0	2.3	-3.4
2022	-1.6	-2.1	-0.7	2.0	3.7	4.3	2.8	-1.3
2023	0.7	1.3	-0.2	2.6	1.9	1.2	2.8	1.5

[1] Derived by dividing an index of real output by an index of combined inputs of labor and capital. [2] Gross domestic product originating in the private nonfarm business sector. [3] Index of hours worked of all persons including employees, proprietors, and unpaid family workers, classified by age, education, and gender. [4] Services derived from the stock of physical assets and intellectual property assets. [5] Ratio of capital input growth to labor hours growth.

Source: U.S. Bureau of Labor Statistics, "Total Factor Productivity - 2023," March 2024. See also <www.bls.gov/productivity/home>.

Table 673. Productivity and Related Measures for Selected NAICS Industries: 1987 to 2023

[For a discussion of productivity measures and methodology, see text, this section and BLS Handbook of Methods, Chapter 11, <www.bls.gov/opub/hom/>. Minus sign (-) indicates decrease]

Industry	2017 NAICS code [1]	Average annual percent change [2]							
		1987 to 2023 [3]				2022 to 2023			
		Labor produc-tivity	Unit labor costs	Output	Hours	Labor produc-tivity	Unit labor costs	Output	Hours
Mining...................................	21	1.8	1.9	1.6	-0.2	1.0	4.3	5.8	4.8
Oil and gas extraction........................	211	3.4	1.4	2.0	-1.3	5.8	-0.9	7.4	1.5
Mining, except oil and gas.................	212	0.9	2.1	-0.2	-1.1	-2.8	10.1	-1.4	1.4
Coal mining.................................	2121	1.2	1.6	-1.9	-3.1	-4.9	16.8	-2.0	3.1
Utilities...............................	22	1.8	1.7	1.3	-0.6	1.2	5.6	2.3	1.1
Power generation and supply.................	2211	2.6	0.9	1.8	-0.8	-4.9	11.9	-3.1	1.9
Natural gas distribution....................	2212	0.5	3.4	–	-0.5	22.9	-12.5	22.2	-0.5
Water, sewage and other systems.............	2213	-1.6	4.8	0.7	2.3	6.4	3.7	5.0	-1.3
Manufacturing:									
Food......................................	311	0.5	2.4	1.0	0.5	-1.3	7.3	-1.9	-0.6
Fruit and vegetable preserving and specialty. . .	3114	0.9	2.2	0.7	-0.2	5.7	3.3	-1.5	-6.8
Dairy products.............................	3115	0.8	2.4	1.1	0.3	-6.6	9.0	-2.1	4.9
Animal slaughtering and processing..........	3116	0.3	2.6	1.3	1.0	-4.0	5.2	-2.3	1.7
Bakeries and tortilla manufacturing........	3118	–	2.3	0.2	0.3	-2.9	7.8	-1.8	1.1
Beverages and tobacco products.............	312	-1.0	3.4	-0.4	0.6	-5.9	9.8	-4.0	2.0
Textile mills.............................	313	2.1	0.6	-2.7	-4.7	9.6	–	-2.6	-11.1
Apparel...................................	315	0.1	1.8	-5.9	-6.0	7.7	2.0	-2.9	-9.8
Leather and allied products................	316	1.2	2.3	-3.4	-4.5	-2.3	3.7	-0.6	1.7
Paper and paper products...................	322	1.0	2.1	-0.6	-1.7	-1.1	8.8	-6.2	-5.2
Converted paper products...................	3222	0.5	2.7	-0.6	-1.1	-2.7	8.4	-7.2	-4.6
Printing and related support activities....	323	1.0	1.6	-1.1	-2.0	-2.7	7.3	-5.6	-3.0
Petroleum and coal products................	324	2.0	2.6	0.9	-1.0	4.7	6.4	0.4	-4.0
Chemicals.................................	325	0.7	2.4	0.6	-0.2	-2.3	3.8	-1.5	0.8
Pharmaceuticals and medicines..............	3254	-0.7	3.8	1.1	1.9	2.9	-0.2	2.8	-0.2
Plastics and rubber products...............	326	1.1	1.9	0.9	-0.2	-2.4	7.3	-4.7	-2.4
Plastics products..........................	3261	1.0	2.0	1.1	0.1	-2.8	7.7	-5.3	-2.6
Wood products.............................	321	0.7	2.6	-0.2	-0.8	-5.6	6.4	-5.8	-0.3
Nonmetallic mineral products...............	327	0.7	2.0	0.3	-0.5	-3.6	6.9	-1.8	1.9
Primary metals.............................	331	1.2	1.6	-0.5	-1.6	-3.5	7.7	-1.3	2.3
Fabricated metal products..................	332	0.7	2.1	0.5	-0.3	-3.5	8.6	-2.3	1.2
Forging and stamping.......................	3321	1.5	1.5	–	-1.4	-2.6	10.3	-7.1	-4.5
Cutlery and hand tools.....................	3322	0.9	1.5	-1.0	-1.8	-3.2	0.9	-2.0	1.3
Architectural and structural metals........	3323	0.3	2.7	0.7	0.4	-4.6	7.4	-0.3	4.5
Machine shops and threaded products........	3327	1.5	1.6	1.8	0.3	-0.7	6.8	-1.5	-0.8
Other fabricated metal products............	3329	0.4	2.1	–	-0.4	-4.0	10.4	-1.9	2.2
Machinery.................................	333	1.3	1.6	0.8	-0.5	-3.4	10.1	-3.3	0.1
Agriculture, construction, and mining machinery.............................	3331	1.7	1.3	1.8	0.1	-3.9	13.0	-2.5	1.5
Industrial machinery.......................	3332	0.7	1.8	0.6	-0.1	-5.4	8.5	-4.7	0.8
Computer and electronic products..........	334	7.2	-3.9	5.3	-1.7	-0.5	6.3	-1.1	-0.6
Semiconductors and electronic components....	3344	10.5	-6.8	9.3	-1.1	0.8	6.0	0.5	-0.3
Electronic instruments.....................	3345	2.3	0.9	1.0	-1.3	-3.1	8.4	-2.7	0.4
Electrical equipment and appliances........	335	1.3	1.8	–	-1.4	-5.3	8.9	-2.1	3.4
Transportation equipment...................	336	1.8	0.6	1.4	-0.4	-1.0	3.9	3.4	4.5
Motor vehicles.............................	3361	1.8	0.7	1.8	–	2.2	1.2	6.1	3.8
Motor vehicle parts........................	3363	2.4	-0.6	2.3	-0.2	4.0	-1.0	8.4	4.3
Aerospace products and parts...............	3364	0.9	2.0	-0.4	-1.2	-3.6	8.2	2.5	6.4
Ship and boat building.....................	3366	1.4	1.9	0.9	-0.5	-6.5	9.1	-3.0	3.8
Furniture and related products.............	337	0.8	2.1	-0.6	-1.5	-3.8	10.1	-10.0	-6.5
Household and institutional furniture......	3371	0.7	2.2	-0.9	-1.6	-3.3	8.6	-10.8	-7.7
Miscellaneous manufacturing................	339	1.4	1.6	1.3	-0.1	-2.8	4.0	-1.1	1.7
Medical equipment and supplies.............	3391	1.9	1.3	2.7	0.8	-0.4	1.8	–	0.3
Wholesale trade...........................	42	2.4	1.5	2.7	0.3	-1.6	6.4	0.4	2.1
Durable goods..............................	423	3.7	0.3	4.0	0.3	-3.2	9.2	-1.2	2.0
Nondurable goods...........................	424	1.0	3.0	1.2	0.2	-0.6	4.5	1.6	2.2
Electronic markets and agents and brokers.......	425	1.3	1.4	2.5	1.2	1.5	-0.9	3.5	1.9
Retail trade.............................	44-45	3.1	0.2	3.3	0.1	1.6	0.5	1.6	-0.1
Motor vehicle and parts dealers............	441	2.0	1.2	2.7	0.6	3.1	-4.9	4.0	0.9
Automobile dealers.........................	4411	2.1	1.3	2.7	0.6	3.6	-6.7	4.5	0.9
Other motor vehicle dealers................	4412	2.1	1.3	3.4	1.3	-4.0	-0.4	-2.1	2.0
Auto parts, accessories, and tire stores..........	4413	1.4	1.3	1.9	0.6	3.6	1.8	4.4	0.7
Furniture and home furnishings stores..........	442	3.6	-0.4	3.1	-0.5	0.3	3.4	-7.2	-7.4
Furniture stores...........................	4421	3.3	-0.3	2.8	-0.5	2.3	1.4	-4.4	-6.5
Home furnishings stores....................	4422	4.1	-0.5	3.5	-0.5	-2.4	6.3	-10.6	-8.4
Electronics and appliance stores..........	443	10.3	-6.3	9.7	-0.5	10.2	-5.4	5.1	-4.7
Building material and garden supply stores.......	444	2.3	0.6	2.8	0.5	-1.4	5.2	-3.9	-2.6
Building material and supplies dealers..........	4441	2.2	0.7	2.8	0.6	-3.1	6.6	-4.9	-1.9
Lawn and garden equipment and supplies stores..............................	4442	3.0	-0.2	3.0	–	9.5	-3.4	2.5	-6.4
Food and beverage stores...................	445	0.8	2.4	0.7	-0.1	-0.4	7.2	-1.3	-0.9
Grocery stores.............................	4451	0.7	2.6	0.7	–	0.2	6.7	-1.3	-1.4
Specialty food stores......................	4452	0.4	2.2	-0.2	-0.6	-8.1	15.0	-3.4	5.1
Beer, wine and liquor stores...............	4453	2.0	1.0	1.6	-0.4	-1.0	8.0	-0.6	0.3
Health and personal care stores...........	446	2.2	1.2	2.8	0.6	4.7	1.9	3.9	-0.8
Gasoline stations..........................	447	1.0	2.3	0.9	-0.1	-7.5	11.9	-4.6	3.2
Clothing and clothing accessories stores..........	448	4.4	-1.0	3.5	-0.9	2.1	3.7	0.2	-1.8
Clothing stores............................	4481	4.7	-1.2	3.9	-0.8	6.3	2.1	4.1	-2.1
Shoe stores................................	4482	3.0	-0.2	2.1	-0.8	-5.1	7.4	-3.5	1.7
Jewelry, luggage, and leather goods stores.....	4483	4.3	-0.6	2.8	-1.5	-8.4	9.6	-12.4	-4.3
Sporting goods, hobby, book, and music stores..	451	3.9	-0.4	3.6	-0.2	1.4	5.3	-1.0	-2.4

See footnotes at end of table.

Table 673. Productivity and Related Measures for Selected NAICS Industries: 1987 to 2023-Continued.

See headnote on page 441.

Industry	2017 NAICS code [1]	Average annual percent change [2]							
		1987 to 2023 [3]				2022 to 2023			
		Labor produc-tivity	Unit labor costs	Output	Hours	Labor produc-tivity	Unit labor costs	Output	Hours
Sporting goods and musical instrument stores..	4511	4.6	-0.9	4.6	–	1.6	7.1	-1.0	-2.5
Book, periodical, and music stores............	4512	0.7	1.8	-0.6	-1.3	0.5	-7.1	-1.0	-1.5
General merchandise stores.....................	452	3.3	-0.4	3.8	0.6	-5.9	4.4	-2.0	4.1
Department stores...........................	4522	1.2	1.0	–	-1.1	-7.5	6.7	-5.2	2.5
Other general merchandise stores............	4523	4.8	-1.2	6.7	1.8	-6.0	4.2	-1.4	4.9
Miscellaneous store retailers...................	453	3.6	-0.6	3.2	-0.3	3.0	-0.6	4.0	1.0
Florists...................................	4531	2.8	0.2	0.3	-2.4	-2.4	0.4	8.4	11.0
Office supplies, stationery and gift stores.......	4532	5.0	-1.9	3.0	-2.0	-3.7	6.0	-4.8	-1.1
Used merchandise stores....................	4533	4.4	-1.7	5.8	1.3	3.3	2.3	3.7	0.3
Other miscellaneous store retailers...........	4539	1.9	0.6	2.8	0.9	5.6	-3.2	6.2	0.6
Nonstore retailers............................	454	9.1	-3.9	9.5	0.4	12.3	-8.6	9.3	-2.7
Electronic shopping and mail-order houses.....	4541	10.5	-4.7	14.1	3.2	14.2	-10.2	10.2	-3.5
Vending machine operators.....................	4542	0.2	3.4	-2.1	-2.3	-16.4	23.6	-10.3	7.3
Direct selling establishments....................	4543	3.5	-0.1	1.4	-2.0	5.0	0.9	2.2	-2.7
Transportation and warehousing:									
Air transportation............................	481	2.1	1.4	2.3	0.2	-2.4	7.1	12.4	15.2
Line-haul railroads...........................	482111	3.3	-0.2	1.3	-1.9	-3.5	14.7	1.0	4.7
Truck transportation..........................	484	0.8	1.8	2.1	1.3	-0.2	4.7	-3.6	-3.4
General freight trucking.....................	4841	1.1	1.4	2.4	1.3	-0.3	5.5	-5.2	-5.0
Used household and office goods moving.......	48421	-0.4	2.9	–	0.4	(NA)	(NA)	(NA)	(NA)
Postal service [4]............................	491	-0.2	3.1	-0.8	-0.6	-5.7	17.1	-7.9	-2.3
Couriers and messengers......................	492	-2.4	5.3	1.1	3.6	-7.1	17.9	-10.4	-3.6
Warehousing and storage......................	493	0.2	2.0	5.4	5.1	-4.0	12.3	-8.0	-4.1
General warehousing and storage.............	49311	1.3	1.2	6.8	5.4	(NA)	(NA)	(NA)	(NA)
Refrigerated warehousing and storage.........	49312	0.1	1.8	3.2	3.0	(NA)	(NA)	(NA)	(NA)
Information:									
Publishing....................................	511	4.1	1.2	4.3	0.2	3.0	3.0	3.8	0.8
Newspaper, book, and directory publishers.....	5111	0.5	3.0	-2.7	-3.2	8.7	-0.8	-1.8	-9.6
Software publishers..........................	5112	9.9	-4.6	16.9	6.4	0.3	3.3	5.0	4.7
Motion picture and video exhibition............	51213	0.4	2.8	0.5	0.1	(NA)	(NA)	(NA)	(NA)
Broadcasting, except internet...................	515	3.2	0.4	2.8	-0.4	7.3	-3.1	6.2	-1.0
Radio and television broadcasting...............	5151	2.7	0.7	2.1	-0.6	1.6	2.9	1.1	-0.5
Cable and other subscription programming......	5152	4.8	-0.8	5.5	0.7	12.4	-8.2	8.9	-3.1
Wired telecommunications carriers..............	517311	3.5	–	2.0	-1.5	-4.3	9.7	-7.6	-3.5
Wireless telecommunications carriers............	517312	11.3	-8.6	16.2	4.4	2.1	9.1	-2.0	-3.9
Finance and insurance:									
Commercial banking..........................	52211	2.5	2.6	2.4	-0.1	5.8	-0.9	6.6	0.8
Real estate and rental and leasing:									
Passenger car rental..........................	532111	2.0	2.2	2.1	–	(NA)	(NA)	(NA)	(NA)
Truck, trailer and RV rental and leasing..........	53212	2.5	1.2	3.1	0.7	0.2	9.8	-0.2	-0.4
Video tape and disc rental......................	532282	4.7	3.9	-5.7	-9.9	(NA)	(NA)	(NA)	(NA)
Professional and technical services:									
Accounting and bookkeeping services............	5412	2.0	1.8	2.7	0.8	-0.1	3.8	1.5	1.6
Architectural services.........................	54131	1.8	1.5	2.8	1.0	(NA)	(NA)	(NA)	(NA)
Engineering services..........................	54133	1.0	2.8	2.6	1.6	0.3	4.7	4.1	3.8
Advertising agencies..........................	54181	2.0	1.8	2.9	0.8	(NA)	(NA)	(NA)	(NA)
Photography studios, portrait...................	541921	1.9	1.3	1.4	-0.5	(NA)	(NA)	(NA)	(NA)
Administrative and waste services:									
Employment placement agencies.................	56131	4.9	0.1	6.2	1.2	(NA)	(NA)	(NA)	(NA)
Travel arrangement and reservation services....	5615	7.4	-1.8	4.8	-2.4	-4.8	13.7	13.6	19.3
Janitorial services............................	56172	2.7	1.0	4.1	1.4	(NA)	(NA)	(NA)	(NA)
Health care and social assistance:									
Medical and diagnostic laboratories.............	6215	2.3	0.5	5.4	3.1	1.2	1.8	-0.2	-1.4
Arts, entertainment, and recreation:									
Amusement parks and arcades...................	7131	0.7	3.4	1.4	0.6	-7.2	10.4	0.4	8.2
Fitness and recreational sports centers..........	71394	10.2	-6.2	10.2	-0.1	(NA)	(NA)	(NA)	(NA)
Accommodation and food services:									
Food services and drinking places...............	722	0.8	2.9	2.3	1.5	0.7	4.7	4.3	3.6
Special food services..........................	7223	0.8	1.9	2.0	1.2	(NA)	(NA)	(NA)	(NA)
Drinking places, alcoholic beverages............	7224	-0.1	3.3	0.1	0.2	(NA)	(NA)	(NA)	(NA)
Restaurants and other eating places............	72251	0.8	3.0	2.4	1.6	0.4	4.8	3.5	3.1
Other services:									
Automotive repair and maintenance..............	8111	1.0	2.4	1.6	0.7	-4.0	10.4	-5.2	-1.3
Reupholstery and furniture repair................	81142	-0.5	3.4	-2.8	-2.3	(NA)	(NA)	(NA)	(NA)
Personal care services.........................	8121	0.8	3.3	1.9	1.1	(NA)	(NA)	(NA)	(NA)
Funeral homes and funeral services..............	81221	-0.2	3.6	-0.1	0.1	(NA)	(NA)	(NA)	(NA)
Dry cleaning and laundry services................	8123	0.3	3.2	-0.8	-1.1	-1.6	7.2	2.5	4.2
Coin-operated laundries and drycleaners.........	81231	1.9	2.3	0.4	-1.5	(NA)	(NA)	(NA)	(NA)
Dry cleaning and laundry services..............	81232	0.9	2.3	-1.7	-2.6	(NA)	(NA)	(NA)	(NA)
Photofinishing................................	81292	1.5	2.4	-5.3	-6.7	(NA)	(NA)	(NA)	(NA)

NA Not available. – Represents zero or rounds to less than half the unit of measurement shown. [1] North American Industry Classification System, 2017 (NAICS); see text, Section 15. [2] Average annual percent change based on compound rate formula. Rates of change are calculated using index numbers to three decimal places. [3] For NAICS 484, 4841, 493, 49311, and 49312, annual percent changes are for 1992-2022. For NAICS 71394, average annual percent change is for 2002-2022. For NAICS 5412 and 5615, average annual percent changes are for 1997-2022. For NAICS 56131 and 6215, average annual percent changes are for 1994-2022. For NAICS 7131, average annual percent change is for 2007-2022. [4] For NAICS 491, average annual percent change is for the fiscal year ending in September.

Source: U.S. Bureau of Labor Statistics, Labor Productivity and Costs, "Productivity and Costs by Industry," <www.bls.gov/lpc/data>, accessed September 2024.

Table 674. Labor Productivity and Related Measures: 1980 to 2023

[See text, this section. Minus sign (-) indicates decrease]

Item	1980	1990	2000	2010	2019	2020	2021	2022	2023
INDEXES (2012=100)									
Output per hour, business sector.............	48.2	57.7	72.2	94.5	103.6	108.9	110.9	108.7	110.3
Nonfarm business.............................	49.4	58.1	72.3	94.4	103.6	109.0	110.8	108.7	110.2
Manufacturing..............................	(NA)	48.6	71.1	103.1	97.9	98.5	100.1	98.9	98.3
Output, business sector.........................	32.9	46.6	68.9	82.1	106.4	103.4	110.9	113.1	116.0
Nonfarm business [1].........................	33.0	46.6	68.9	82.0	106.5	103.5	111.0	113.3	116.2
Manufacturing [2]...........................	(NA)	67.1	97.5	94.8	99.9	93.0	97.5	100.3	99.8
Hours [3], business sector....................	68.3	80.9	95.5	86.8	102.7	95.0	100.1	104.0	105.2
Nonfarm business.............................	66.9	80.3	95.3	86.8	102.8	95.0	100.2	104.2	105.5
Manufacturing..............................	(NA)	137.9	137.2	91.9	102.0	94.4	97.5	101.4	101.6
Compensation per hour [4], business sector......	24.4	41.5	61.7	85.4	107.4	116.0	121.8	126.5	132.1
Nonfarm business.............................	24.6	41.6	61.7	85.3	107.4	116.1	121.8	126.3	131.8
Manufacturing..............................	(NA)	43.8	63.4	87.7	104.8	111.9	114.5	118.5	124.7
Real hourly compensation [4], business sector....	69.2	75.6	88.0	96.2	103.0	109.8	110.0	105.6	105.9
Nonfarm business.............................	69.7	75.8	88.0	96.1	103.0	109.9	110.0	105.5	105.7
Manufacturing..............................	(NA)	79.8	90.5	98.8	100.5	105.9	103.3	99.0	100.0
Unit labor costs [5], business sector..............	50.6	71.9	85.4	90.4	103.7	106.6	109.9	116.3	119.7
Nonfarm business.............................	49.8	71.6	85.3	90.3	103.7	106.6	109.9	116.2	119.7
Manufacturing..............................	(NA)	90.0	89.2	85.1	107.1	113.6	114.4	119.9	126.9
ANNUAL PERCENT CHANGE [6]									
Output per hour, business sector.............	–	2.0	3.1	3.2	2.1	5.1	1.8	-1.9	1.4
Nonfarm business.............................	–	1.7	3.0	3.3	2.2	5.2	1.7	-1.9	1.4
Manufacturing..............................	(NA)	3.3	3.5	6.3	-2.2	0.6	1.6	-1.2	-0.6
Output, business sector.........................	-0.9	1.6	4.5	3.2	2.8	-2.8	7.2	1.9	2.6
Nonfarm business [1].........................	-0.8	1.5	4.4	3.3	3.0	-2.8	7.2	2.1	2.6
Manufacturing [2]...........................	(NA)	0.1	2.7	7.0	-2.0	-6.9	4.9	2.8	-0.5
Hours [3], business sector....................	-0.9	-0.4	1.3	–	0.8	-7.5	5.3	3.9	1.2
Nonfarm business.............................	-0.8	-0.2	1.3	–	0.8	-7.6	5.5	4.0	1.2
Manufacturing..............................	(NA)	-3.1	-0.8	0.6	0.1	-7.4	3.2	4.0	0.1
Compensation per hour [4], business sector......	10.7	6.2	7.0	1.8	3.9	8.0	5.0	3.8	4.4
Nonfarm business.............................	10.7	6.0	7.0	1.8	3.9	8.2	4.9	3.7	4.4
Manufacturing..............................	(NA)	5.5	6.5	0.6	2.5	6.8	2.3	3.6	5.2
Real hourly compensation [4], business sector....	-0.5	1.2	3.4	0.1	2.0	6.6	0.2	-4.0	0.3
Nonfarm business.............................	-0.4	1.0	3.5	0.2	2.0	6.7	0.1	-4.1	0.2
Manufacturing..............................	(NA)	0.5	3.0	-1.0	0.7	5.4	-2.4	-4.2	1.0
Unit labor costs [5], business sector..............	10.7	4.2	3.7	-1.4	1.8	2.8	3.1	5.8	2.9
Nonfarm business.............................	10.8	4.2	3.9	-1.4	1.7	2.8	3.2	5.7	3.0
Manufacturing..............................	(NA)	2.1	2.9	-5.4	4.8	6.2	0.7	4.8	5.9

– Represents or rounds to zero. NA Not available. [1] Real value-added output, the output produced that has been adjusted for changes in inventory (gross output) and the removal of intermediate inputs (energy, material, and services). [2] Refers to real sectoral output, amount of goods and services produced by an industry for delivery to consumers outside that industry. [3] Hours at work of all persons engaged in the business and nonfarm business sectors (employees, proprietors, and unpaid family workers), and employees' and proprietors' hours in manufacturing. [4] Wages and salaries of employees plus employers' contributions for social insurance and private benefit plans. Also includes an estimate of same for self-employed. Real compensation deflated by the Consumer Price Index research series; see text, Section 14. [5] Hourly compensation divided by output per hour. [6] All changes are from the immediate prior year.

Source: U.S. Bureau of Labor Statistics, Labor Productivity and Costs, "Major Sector Productivity and Costs," <www.bls.gov/data/#productivity>, accessed April 2024.

Table 675. Employed Persons and Average Hours Worked Per Day at Workplace and at Home: 2023

[175,956 represents 175,956,000. Civilian noninstitutionalized population 15 years old and over, except as indicated. Includes work at main job and any other jobs. Excludes travel related to work. Based on the American Time Use Survey]

Characteristic	Total employed (1,000)	Employed persons who worked on an average day [1]					
		Total		Worked at workplace		Worked at home [2]	
		Percent of employed	Hours of work	Percent of those who worked	Hours of work	Percent of those who worked	Hours of work
Total...........................	**175,956**	**64.7**	**7.75**	**72.6**	**7.86**	**34.6**	**5.12**
Work status: [3]							
Full-time workers [4]............	141,092	69.7	8.15	73.0	8.19	35.0	5.37
Part-time workers [4]............	34,864	44.7	5.28	69.5	5.66	32.3	3.45
Male [3].............................	94,673	66.7	8.02	73.6	8.15	33.5	5.07
Full-time workers [4]............	80,988	71.6	8.26	74.9	8.30	33.0	5.23
Part-time workers [4]............	13,685	37.7	5.29	(S)	6.04	(S)	3.59
Female [3]...........................	81,283	62.5	7.42	71.3	7.48	35.9	5.19
Full-time workers [4]............	60,104	67.1	7.98	70.3	8.02	37.8	5.55
Part-time workers [4]............	21,179	49.3	5.28	75.1	5.51	28.6	3.35
Jobholding status:							
Single jobholders..............	160,147	63.8	7.77	73.5	7.91	33.1	5.14
Multiple jobholders............	15,809	73.9	7.62	64.6	7.33	47.5	5.05
Educational attainment: [5]							
Less than high school........	9,203	62.3	8.06	85.0	8.03	11.0	4.67
High school diploma [6]........	36,328	67.1	8.16	85.1	8.02	22.0	4.89
Some college..................	33,066	66.9	8.18	79.6	8.18	26.5	5.47
Bachelor's degree or higher..	71,394	67.8	7.47	57.1	7.83	52.4	5.20

S Data do not meet publication standards. [1] Individuals may have worked at more than one location. [2] "Working at home" includes any time persons did work at home and is not restricted to persons whose usual workplace is their home. [3] Includes workers whose hours vary. [4] Full-time workers usually worked 35 or more hours per week at all jobs combined; part-time workers worked fewer than 35 hours per week. [5] For persons 25 years old and over. [6] Includes persons with a high school diploma or equivalent.

Source: U.S. Bureau of Labor Statistics, American Time Use Survey—2023 Results, USDL 24-1208, June 2024. See also <www.bls.gov/tus>.

Table 676. Annual Total Compensation and Wages and Salary Accruals Per Full-Time Equivalent Employee by Industry: 2010 to 2022

[In dollars. Compensation averages are equal to the sum of wages and salaries and of supplements to wages and salaries; supplements are made on behalf of employees but are not included in regular wage payments to employees, such as contributions for employee pension and insurance funds, and employer contributions for government social insurance. Wages and salaries consist of cash remuneration of labor, including sick or vacation pay, severance pay, commissions, tips, and bonuses. Based on the 2017 North American Industry Classification System (NAICS); see text, Section 15]

Industry	Total annual compensation (average)				Annual salary and wages			
	2010	2020	2021	2022	2010	2020	2021	2022
Compensation of employees..................	**66,212**	**87,566**	**92,124**	**94,864**	**53,239**	**71,479**	**75,726**	**78,465**
Domestic industries................................	65,823	86,981	91,308	93,835	52,939	71,013	75,069	77,634
Private industries................................	62,441	83,670	88,281	91,021	51,913	70,550	74,846	77,383
Agriculture, forestry, fishing, and hunting........	37,634	50,814	50,589	52,638	30,610	40,668	41,216	41,936
Mining..	107,738	132,385	132,731	141,916	91,837	113,323	112,315	120,889
Utilities..	123,905	172,871	174,175	174,726	89,603	120,900	124,180	128,605
Construction....................................	63,648	83,807	86,598	90,679	52,757	70,450	72,704	76,394
Manufacturing..................................	75,485	94,157	97,469	101,032	59,997	76,457	79,555	82,629
Wholesale trade................................	78,065	102,690	110,356	114,607	67,167	88,242	95,524	99,541
Retail trade....................................	38,464	51,309	55,036	56,051	32,028	42,934	46,288	47,137
Transportation and warehousing.................	62,458	75,348	79,048	81,715	49,744	61,505	64,658	67,214
Information....................................	98,952	167,854	191,776	179,192	81,295	147,403	165,364	155,667
Finance and insurance..........................	104,130	143,754	154,932	156,297	88,165	124,074	134,082	134,951
Real estate and rental and leasing..............	58,043	82,134	88,223	92,896	49,209	71,550	76,453	81,358
Professional, scientific, and technical services..	95,391	129,340	137,102	140,548	82,570	113,152	120,396	122,960
Management of companies and enterprises [1]...	126,701	158,322	171,940	171,689	103,873	137,756	147,854	148,316
Administrative and waste management services...	44,896	60,733	64,472	68,846	37,374	51,321	55,455	60,063
Educational services............................	50,711	65,927	69,788	69,663	41,367	53,380	56,094	56,517
Health care and social assistance...............	59,618	74,930	77,482	81,606	48,977	61,038	64,229	67,741
Arts, entertainment, and recreation..............	49,745	70,403	71,771	75,790	42,672	60,834	61,674	65,732
Accommodation and food services..............	27,965	37,657	42,971	45,218	24,138	32,756	37,700	40,085
Other services, except government.............	41,739	59,082	60,692	64,576	35,876	51,112	52,966	55,839
Government...................................	82,264	105,421	108,837	110,704	57,925	73,587	76,358	79,137
Federal.......................................	104,416	128,454	132,527	136,335	74,664	89,002	90,920	92,990
State and local................................	76,234	99,252	102,409	103,804	53,369	69,457	72,407	75,407

[1] Consists of offices of bank and other holding companies and of corporate, subsidiary, and regional managing offices.

Source: U.S. Bureau of Economic Analysis, National Income and Product Accounts Tables, "Table 6.2D. Compensation of Employees by Industry," "Table 6.5D. Full-Time Equivalent Employees by Industry," and "Table 6.6D. Wages and Salaries Per Full-Time Equivalent Employee by Industry," <www.bea.gov/itable/>, accessed November 2023.

Table 677. Average Hourly and Weekly Earnings of Employees by Private Industry Group: 2000 to 2023

[In dollars. Average earnings include overtime. Data are for production and nonsupervisory employees. See headnote, Table 663]

Private industry group	Current dollars					Constant (1982–84) dollars [1]				
	2000	2010	2020	2022	2023	2000	2010	2020	2022	2023
AVERAGE HOURLY EARNINGS										
Total private...........................	**14.01**	**19.04**	**24.68**	**27.56**	**28.94**	**8.29**	**8.90**	**9.78**	**9.57**	**9.68**
Mining and logging..........................	16.55	23.82	30.42	32.64	34.41	9.80	11.13	12.06	11.33	11.51
Construction................................	17.48	23.22	29.21	32.35	34.26	10.35	10.85	11.58	11.23	11.46
Manufacturing..............................	14.32	18.61	22.80	25.07	26.38	8.48	8.70	9.04	8.71	8.82
Trade, transportation, and utilities [2]........	13.28	16.78	21.40	24.00	25.25	7.86	7.84	8.48	8.33	8.45
Wholesale trade..........................	16.24	21.46	26.81	29.21	30.40	9.62	10.03	10.63	10.14	10.17
Retail trade..............................	10.86	13.24	17.58	19.66	20.50	6.43	6.19	6.97	6.83	6.86
Transportation and warehousing.........	15.00	19.10	22.71	25.99	27.93	8.88	8.93	9.00	9.02	9.34
Utilities..................................	22.75	30.04	38.46	42.26	44.30	13.47	14.04	15.25	14.67	14.82
Information.................................	19.07	25.87	35.74	37.91	39.66	11.29	12.09	14.17	13.16	13.26
Financial activities [2]......................	15.04	21.55	29.09	32.15	33.84	8.90	10.07	11.53	11.16	11.32
Professional and business services [2]......	15.53	22.79	29.23	32.55	34.21	9.19	10.65	11.59	11.30	11.44
Private education and health services [2]...	13.91	19.95	25.40	29.02	30.29	8.24	9.32	10.07	10.08	10.13
Health care and social assistance........	13.93	20.23	25.76	29.55	30.74	8.25	9.45	10.21	10.26	10.28
Leisure and hospitality [2]....................	8.32	11.31	14.71	17.82	18.76	4.93	5.29	5.83	6.19	6.27
Other services.............................	12.73	17.06	22.58	24.89	26.19	7.54	7.97	8.95	8.64	8.76
AVERAGE WEEKLY EARNINGS										
Total private...........................	**481**	**636**	**837**	**937**	**980**	**285**	**297**	**332**	**326**	**328**
Mining and logging..........................	735	1,063	1,365	1,549	1,646	435	497	541	538	551
Construction................................	686	892	1,146	1,278	1,367	406	417	454	444	457
Manufacturing..............................	591	765	929	1,028	1,073	350	358	368	357	359
Trade, transportation, and utilities [2]........	449	558	730	818	859	266	261	290	284	287
Wholesale trade..........................	630	814	1,024	1,140	1,180	373	380	406	396	395
Retail trade..............................	333	400	541	598	623	197	187	215	208	208
Transportation and warehousing.........	560	708	870	982	1,055	331	331	345	341	353
Utilities..................................	955	1,263	1,639	1,799	1,878	565	590	650	625	628
Information.................................	701	940	1,288	1,381	1,428	415	439	511	479	478
Financial activities [2]......................	540	780	1,079	1,197	1,252	320	365	428	416	419
Professional and business services [2]......	535	799	1,047	1,182	1,243	317	373	415	410	416
Private education and health services [2]...	448	639	825	946	985	265	299	327	329	330
Health care and social assistance........	447	652	842	968	1,005	265	305	334	336	336
Leisure and hospitality [2]....................	217	281	355	439	456	129	131	141	152	152
Other services.............................	413	524	706	777	818	245	245	280	270	274

[1] Earnings in current dollars divided by the Consumer Price Index (CPI-W) on a 1982–84 base; see text, Section 14. [2] For composition of industries, see Table 665.

Source: U.S. Bureau of Labor Statistics, Current Employment Statistics, "Employment, Hours, and Earnings—National," <www.bls.gov/ces/data>, accessed April 2024.

Table 678. Employment and Wages of Private Sector and Government Employees: 2000 to 2023

[7,879 represents 7,879,000. Based on federal-state cooperative program, The Quarterly Census of Employment and Wages (QCEW), also referenced as ES-202. Includes workers covered by state unemployment insurance laws and federal civilian workers covered by unemployment compensation for federal employees. Excludes most agricultural workers on small farms, all Armed Forces, elected officials in most states, railroad employees, most domestic workers, most student workers at school, value of meals and lodging, and tips and other gratuities]

Employment and wages	Unit	2000	2010	2015	2020	2021	2022	2023
Establishments:								
Total	**1,000**	**7,879**	**8,993**	**9,523**	**10,488**	**10,909**	**11,519**	**11,866**
Excluding federal	1,000	7,829	8,926	9,462	10,426	10,848	11,458	11,805
Private	1,000	7,622	8,696	9,224	10,185	10,606	11,216	11,561
Federal government	1,000	50	67	61	61	61	61	61
State government	1,000	65	67	69	70	70	71	72
Local governments	1,000	141	164	169	171	171	172	172
Average annual employment:								
Total	**1,000**	**129,877**	**127,820**	**139,492**	**139,104**	**143,780**	**150,026**	**153,141**
Excluding federal	1,000	127,006	124,840	136,735	136,176	140,897	147,162	150,211
Private	1,000	110,015	106,201	118,308	117,940	122,717	128,718	131,290
Federal government	1,000	2,871	2,981	2,756	2,928	2,883	2,864	2,930
State government	1,000	4,370	4,606	4,567	4,593	4,540	4,541	4,658
Local governments	1,000	12,620	14,032	13,861	13,643	13,640	13,903	14,263
Annual wages:								
Total	**Bil. dol.**	**4,588**	**5,976**	**7,385**	**8,906**	**9,721**	**10,500**	**11,081**
Excluding federal	Bil. dol.	4,455	5,769	7,170	8,655	9,464	10,234	10,795
Private	Bil. dol.	3,888	4,934	6,256	7,577	8,348	9,055	9,533
Federal government	Bil. dol.	133	206	215	250	257	266	287
State government	Bil. dol.	159	226	255	302	312	331	356
Local governments	Bil. dol.	409	610	659	776	803	849	905
Average annual wage per employee:								
Total	**Dol.**	**35,323**	**46,751**	**52,942**	**64,021**	**67,610**	**69,986**	**72,360**
Excluding federal	Dol.	35,077	46,215	52,439	63,560	67,168	69,543	71,862
Private	Dol.	35,337	46,455	52,876	64,247	68,029	70,346	72,608
Federal government	Dol.	46,228	69,198	77,900	85,467	89,205	92,771	97,874
State government	Dol.	36,296	48,960	55,878	65,762	68,835	72,813	76,493
Local governments	Dol.	32,387	43,493	47,573	56,884	58,870	61,036	63,485
Average weekly wage per employee:								
Total	**Dol.**	**679**	**899**	**1,018**	**1,231**	**1,300**	**1,346**	**1,392**
Excluding federal	Dol.	675	889	1,008	1,222	1,292	1,337	1,382
Private	Dol.	680	893	1,017	1,236	1,308	1,353	1,396
Federal government	Dol.	889	1,331	1,498	1,644	1,715	1,784	1,882
State government	Dol.	698	942	1,075	1,265	1,324	1,400	1,471
Local governments	Dol.	623	836	915	1,094	1,132	1,174	1,221

Source: U.S. Bureau of Labor Statistics, Quarterly Census of Employment and Wages, "Employment and Wages Data Viewer," and earlier releases, <www.bls.gov/cew/>, accessed August 2024.

Table 679. Average Annual Wage by State and Island Area: 2022 and 2023

[In dollars, except percent change. See headnote, Table 678]

State/area	Average wage per employee 2022	2023	Percent change, 2022 to 2023	State/area	Average wage per employee 2022	2023	Percent change, 2022 to 2023
United States	**69,986**	**72,360**	**3.4**	Montana	54,514	57,236	5.0
Alabama	57,309	59,784	4.3	Nebraska	57,276	59,175	3.3
Alaska	65,316	68,776	5.3	Nevada	61,970	63,793	2.9
Arizona	64,733	67,172	3.8	New Hampshire	72,249	74,445	3.0
Arkansas	54,034	55,692	3.1	New Jersey	78,567	80,570	2.5
California	84,436	87,490	3.6	New Mexico	55,262	58,110	5.2
Colorado	74,432	77,114	3.6	New York	89,552	91,428	2.1
Connecticut	81,237	83,769	3.1	North Carolina	63,218	65,624	3.8
Delaware	67,816	69,364	2.3	North Dakota	60,215	63,321	5.2
District of Columbia	113,915	117,888	3.5	Ohio	60,994	63,083	3.4
Florida	63,771	66,435	4.2	Oklahoma	53,992	56,340	4.3
Georgia	65,646	67,557	2.9	Oregon	66,312	68,283	3.0
Hawaii	61,483	64,207	4.4	Pennsylvania	67,281	69,250	2.9
Idaho	54,236	56,300	3.8	Rhode Island	64,499	66,126	2.5
Illinois	72,756	74,632	2.6	South Carolina	55,551	57,932	4.3
Indiana	58,052	59,666	2.8	South Dakota	54,055	56,067	3.7
Iowa	57,377	59,363	3.5	Tennessee	62,103	64,718	4.2
Kansas	56,178	58,400	4.0	Texas	69,614	72,318	3.9
Kentucky	55,802	58,204	4.3	Utah	61,173	63,854	4.4
Louisiana	56,576	59,065	4.4	Vermont	59,603	61,813	3.7
Maine	58,134	60,328	3.8	Virginia	71,134	74,253	4.4
Maryland	73,667	76,052	3.2	Washington	84,010	88,559	5.4
Massachusetts	89,800	91,512	1.9	West Virginia	53,159	55,964	5.3
Michigan	63,881	65,901	3.2	Wisconsin	59,203	61,073	3.2
Minnesota	69,724	71,522	2.6	Wyoming	56,320	59,080	4.9
Mississippi	47,427	49,128	3.6	Puerto Rico	32,015	33,673	5.2
Missouri	59,224	61,708	4.2	Virgin Islands	51,070	51,530	0.9

Source: U.S. Bureau of Labor Statistics, Quarterly Census of Employment and Wages, "Employment and Wages, Annual Averages, 2023," and earlier editions, <www.bls.gov/cew>, accessed August 2024.

Table 680. Full-Time Wage and Salary Workers—Number and Earnings: 2010 to 2023

[99,531 represents 99,531,000. Earnings shown in current dollars; data represent annual averages of usual weekly earnings. Full-time workers are those who usually worked 35 hours or more per week at all jobs combined. Based on the Current Population Survey; see text, Section 1 and Appendix III. For definition of median, see Guide to Tabular Presentation]

Sex, race/ethnicity, and occupation	Number of workers (1,000)			Median weekly earnings (dollars)		
	2010	2020	2023	2010	2020	2023
All workers [1]	**99,531**	**110,387**	**120,907**	**747**	**984**	**1,117**
Male	55,059	60,911	66,700	824	1,082	1,202
Female	44,472	49,476	54,207	669	891	1,005
White [2]	80,656	85,142	91,336	765	1,003	1,138
Black [2]	11,658	14,044	16,452	611	794	920
Asian [2]	4,946	7,353	8,597	855	1,310	1,474
Hispanic [3]	14,837	19,558	22,834	535	758	874
OCCUPATION [4]						
Management, professional and related occupations	39,145	50,023	56,077	1,063	1,356	1,527
Management, business, and financial operations	15,648	20,811	23,989	1,155	1,461	1,630
Professional and related occupations	23,497	29,213	32,088	1,008	1,270	1,458
Computer and mathematical	3,202	5,083	6,129	1,289	1,633	1,890
Architecture and engineering	2,366	2,933	3,374	1,255	1,575	1,785
Life, physical, and social science	1,127	1,401	1,583	1,062	1,336	1,541
Community and social services	1,909	2,187	2,334	802	1,003	1,147
Legal occupations	1,248	1,410	1,490	1,213	1,540	1,880
Education, training, and library	6,535	7,012	7,524	913	1,096	1,180
Arts, design, entertainment, sports, and media	1,431	1,681	1,858	920	1,179	1,343
Healthcare practitioner and technical	5,678	7,504	7,795	986	1,227	1,404
Service occupations	14,424	13,771	15,818	479	621	721
Healthcare support	2,219	3,210	3,467	471	606	713
Protective service	2,872	2,690	2,706	747	982	1,113
Food preparation and serving-related	3,823	3,353	4,325	406	530	660
Building and grounds cleaning and maintenance	3,310	3,138	3,520	446	603	692
Personal care and service	2,199	1,380	1,799	455	616	725
Sales and office occupations	23,060	21,165	21,667	631	809	923
Sales and related	9,121	8,958	9,148	666	880	1,001
Office and administrative support	13,939	12,207	12,519	619	781	891
Natural resources, construction, and maintenance	9,869	10,690	11,368	719	905	1,001
Farming, fishing, and forestry	729	787	731	416	589	689
Construction and extraction	5,020	5,826	6,517	709	906	985
Installation, maintenance, and repair	4,120	4,077	4,120	794	984	1,092
Production, transportation, and material-moving	13,034	14,738	15,977	599	746	869
Production	6,861	6,820	7,313	599	775	895
Transportation and material-moving	6,172	7,917	8,664	599	719	841

[1] Includes other races, not shown separately. [2] For persons in this race group only. [3] Persons of Hispanic origin may be of any race. [4] As of January 2020, occupations reflect the introduction of the 2018 Census occupational classification system, derived from the 2018 Standard Occupational Classification (SOC). No historical data have been revised. Data for 2020 and thereafter are not strictly comparable with earlier years.

Source: U.S. Bureau of Labor Statistics, CPS Tables, "Median weekly earnings of full-time wage and salary workers by selected characteristics," and "Median weekly earnings of full-time wage and salary workers by detailed occupation and sex," January 2024 and earlier releases, <www.bls.gov/cps/tables.htm>.

Table 681. Median Usual Weekly Earnings of Full-Time Wage and Salary Workers by Sex and Education: 1990 to 2023

[In current dollars. For wage and salary workers 25 years old and over. Wages and salaries are collected before taxes and other deductions and include overtime pay, commissions, or tips usually received at principal job. Earnings reported on basis other than weekly are converted to a weekly equivalent. Excludes all incorporated and unincorporated self-employed. Revisions to population controls and other changes can affect the comparability of data over time; see text this section and <www.bls.gov/cps/eetech_methods.pdf>. Based on Current Population Survey; see text, Section 1 and Appendix III]

Year and sex	Total	Less than a high school diploma	High school, no college [1]	Some college or associate's degree	Bachelor's degree and higher [2]
CURRENT DOLLARS					
Male:					
1990	512	349	459	542	741
2000	693	406	591	691	1,020
2010	874	486	710	845	1,330
2020	1,144	674	881	1,027	1,644
2022	1,219	745	945	1,111	1,765
2023	1,273	768	991	1,165	1,870
Female:					
1990	369	240	315	395	535
2000	516	304	420	505	756
2010	704	388	543	638	986
2020	929	525	671	779	1,239
2022	1,002	594	735	847	1,372
2023	1,060	619	770	895	1,437
WOMEN'S EARNINGS AS PERCENT OF MEN'S					
1990	72.1	68.8	68.6	72.9	72.2
2000	74.5	74.9	71.1	73.1	74.1
2010	80.5	79.8	76.5	75.5	74.1
2020	81.2	77.9	76.2	75.9	75.4
2022	82.2	79.7	77.8	76.2	77.7
2023	83.3	80.6	77.7	76.8	76.8

[1] Includes persons with a high school diploma or equivalent. [2] Includes bachelor's, master's, professional, or doctoral degree.

Source: U.S. Bureau of Labor Statistics, "Weekly & Hourly Earnings from the Current Population Survey," <www.bls.gov/cps/data.htm>, accessed February 2024.

Table 682. Workers With Earnings by Occupation of Longest Held Job and Sex: 2022

[80,490 represents 80,490,000. As of March. For definition of median, see Guide to Tabular Presentation. Based on the Current Population Survey, Annual Social and Economic Supplement (CPS ASEC); includes civilian noninstitutional population 15 years old and over, and military personnel who live in households with at least one other civilian adult. See text, Section 1, and Appendix III]

Major occupation group of longest job held in 2022	All workers				Full-time, year-round			
	Female		Male		Female		Male	
	Number (1,000)	Median earnings (dol.)	Number (1,000)	Median earnings (dol.)	Number (1,000)	Median earnings (dol.)	Number (1,000)	Median earnings (dol.)
Total...........	80,490	41,320	90,380	52,770	52,790	52,360	68,570	62,350
Management, business, and financial occupations...........	14,230	67,310	16,840	88,410	11,660	73,220	14,580	95,400
Professional and related occupations...........	23,790	57,000	17,830	81,630	16,380	66,720	14,240	92,170
Service occupations...........	16,050	23,930	12,370	31,630	8,101	34,120	7,461	43,490
Sales and office occupations...........	19,840	35,740	12,310	47,370	12,590	46,030	8,842	57,960
Natural resources, construction, and maintenance...........	821	26,970	14,250	46,620	486	37,340	10,850	51,660
Production, transportation, and material-moving occupations...........	5,712	30,800	16,240	41,450	3,533	36,490	12,090	50,170
Armed Forces...........	51	(B)	546	60,590	40	(B)	500	61,170

B Base less than 75,000.

Source: U.S. Census Bureau, "Current Population Survey Tables for Personal Income: Table PINC-06," <www.census.gov/data/tables/time-series/demo/income-poverty/cps-pinc.html>, accessed November 2023.

Table 683. Employment Cost Index (ECI) for Total Compensation by Occupation and Industry: 2010 to 2023

[As of December (2005 = 100). The ECI is a measure of the rate of change in compensation (wages, salaries, and employer costs for employee benefits). Data are not seasonally adjusted. Industry classifications based on North American Industry Classification System (NAICS); occupation classifications based on the 2018 Standard Occupational Classification (SOC)]

Occupational group and industry	Indexes (December 2005 = 100)				Annual percent change from immediate prior year			
	2010	2020	2022	2023	2010	2020	2022	2023
Civilian workers [1]...........	**113.2**	**142.2**	**155.4**	**161.9**	**2.0**	**2.5**	**5.1**	**4.2**
State and local government...........	**116.2**	**144.9**	**155.8**	**163.0**	**1.8**	**2.3**	**4.8**	**4.6**
Workers, by occupational group:								
Management, professional and related occupations...	115.5	143.2	153.3	160.2	1.5	2.1	4.6	4.5
Sales and office occupations...........	116.6	148.0	159.0	167.0	1.9	2.8	5.0	5.0
Service occupations...........	118.0	149.1	163.3	171.4	2.3	2.8	6.0	5.0
Workers, by industry division:								
Service-providing industries: [2]								
Education and health services [2]...........	115.6	143.4	154.0	160.8	1.5	2.2	4.8	4.4
Schools...........	115.3	142.9	153.2	159.9	1.4	2.2	4.7	4.4
Health care and social assistance [2]...........	117.9	146.7	160.4	167.4	2.2	2.2	5.5	4.4
Hospitals...........	117.0	143.9	156.9	163.6	2.4	2.2	5.2	4.3
Public administration...........	116.8	146.8	158.6	166.7	1.9	2.4	5.3	5.1
Private industry workers [3]...........	**112.5**	**141.6**	**155.3**	**161.6**	**2.1**	**2.6**	**5.1**	**4.1**
Workers, by occupational group:								
Management, professional, and related occupations...	113.0	139.5	150.8	156.8	2.1	2.0	4.4	4.0
Sales and office occupations...........	111.6	143.2	159.1	165.2	2.2	3.2	6.1	3.8
Natural resources, construction, and maintenance occupations...........	113.3	141.3	152.9	159.7	1.9	2.5	4.2	4.4
Production, transportation, and material moving occupations...........	111.5	143.8	158.2	165.5	2.4	3.3	4.8	4.6
Service occupations...........	113.5	145.6	166.6	173.2	1.5	3.6	6.9	4.0
Workers, by industry division:								
Goods-producing industries [2]...........	111.1	138.9	150.6	156.3	2.3	2.3	4.6	3.8
Construction...........	112.7	140.3	151.4	157.7	0.9	2.4	4.3	4.2
Manufacturing...........	110.0	138.5	150.3	155.8	2.8	2.4	4.7	3.7
Service-providing industries [2]...........	113.0	142.4	156.6	163.1	2.0	2.7	5.2	4.2
Trade, transportation, and utilities...........	111.4	145.1	160.1	167.5	2.4	3.1	4.9	4.6
Information...........	110.0	139.9	152.3	157.5	1.6	3.1	5.3	3.4
Financial activities...........	111.4	141.4	153.8	159.0	2.6	2.3	5.3	3.4
Professional and business services...........	114.6	142.4	155.2	161.0	2.0	2.7	4.9	3.7
Education and health services...........	114.7	140.2	154.1	161.1	1.7	2.2	5.5	4.5
Leisure and hospitality...........	114.1	144.7	166.3	173.0	1.2	3.4	6.4	4.0
Bargaining status:								
Union...........	114.8	146.3	156.6	163.7	3.3	2.8	3.6	4.5
Nonunion...........	112.1	140.9	155.0	161.2	1.8	2.6	5.3	4.0

[1] Includes workers in the private nonfarm economy except those in private households, and workers in the public sector except those in the federal government. [2] Includes all other items not shown separately. [3] Excludes farm and household workers.

Source: U.S. Bureau of Labor Statistics, Employment Cost Trends, "Employment Cost Index," <www.bls.gov/eci>, accessed June 2024.

Table 684. Federal and State Minimum Wage Rates: 1940 to 2024

[In current dollars. Wage rates are as of January 1, except as noted. Where an employee is subject to both the state and federal minimum wage laws, the employee is entitled to the higher minimum wage rate]

Year	Federal minimum wage rates per hour	State	2024 minimum wage rates per hour	State	2024 minimum wage rates per hour	State	2024 minimum wage rates per hour
1940	0.30	AL	(X)	KY	7.25	ND	7.25
1945 (as of Oct. 24)	0.40	AK	11.73	LA	(X)	OH	[7] 7.25-10.45
1950 (as of Jan. 25)	0.75	AZ	14.35	ME	14.15	OK	[8] 2.00-7.25
1960	1.00	AR	[2] 11.00	MD	15.00	OR	[11] 14.20
1965 (as of Sept. 3)	1.25	CA	16.00	MA	15.00	PA	7.25
1970 (as of Feb. 1)	1.45	CO	14.42	MI	[1] 10.33	RI	14.00
1975	2.10	CT	15.69	MN	[4] 8.85-10.85	SC	(X)
1980	3.10	DE	13.25	MS	(X)	SD	11.20
1985	3.35	DC	17.00	MO	12.30	TN	(X)
1990 (as of Apr. 1)	3.80	FL	[9] 12.00	MT	[5] 4.00-10.30	TX	7.25
1995	4.25	GA	[3] 5.15	NE	[2] 12.00	UT	7.25
2000	5.15	HI	14.00	NV	[6] 10.25-11.25	VT	[1] 13.67
2005	5.15	ID	7.25	NH	7.25	VA	[2] 12.00
2007 (as of Jul. 24)	5.85	IL	[2] 14.00	NJ	15.13	WA	16.28
2008 (as of Jul. 24)	6.55	IN	[1] 7.25	NM	12.00	WV	[3] 8.75
2009 (as of Jul. 24)	7.25	IA	7.25	NY	[10] 15.00	WI	7.25
2024	**7.25**	KS	7.25	NC	7.25	WY	5.15

X Not applicable. [1] Employers of 2 or more. [2] Employers of 4 or more. [3] Employers of 6 or more. [4] Minnesota: $8.85 for small employer (annual revenues less than $500,000); $10.85 for large employer (annual revenues $500,000 or more). [5] Lower rate for businesses with gross annual sales of $110,000 or less. [6] Nevada: $11.25 with no qualifying health insurance offered by employer; $10.25 with qualifying health insurance offered by employer. On July 1, 2024, Nevada minimum wage will increase to $12.00 for all employees. [7] Ohio: $7.25 for those employers grossing $385,000 or less. [8] Oklahoma: $7.25 for employers of 10 or more full time employees at any one location, and employers with gross sales over $100,000 regardless of number of full-time employees. All other employers, $2.00. [9] Florida minimum wage is adjusted annually based on a set formula. The Florida minimum wage is scheduled to increase by $1.00 every September 30th until reaching $15.00 on September 30, 2026. [10] Basic minimum rate: $15.00; $16.00 (Nassau, Suffolk, Westchester Counties, & NYC). [11] Oregon minimum wage is adjusted annually on July 1 based on a set formula. The minimum wage is $15.45 in the Portland metro area and $13.20 in non-urban counties.

Source: U.S. Department of Labor, Wage and Hour Division, "Changes in Basic Minimum Wages in Non-Farm Employment Under State Law: Selected Years 1968 to 2022," and "State Minimum Wage Laws," <www.dol.gov/agencies/whd/minimum-wage/state>, accessed May 2024.

Table 685. Workers Paid Hourly Rates At or Below Federal Minimum Wage by Selected Characteristics: 2023

[80,538 represents 80,538,000. Data are annual averages. For employed wage and salary workers, excluding all self-employed. Based on the Current Population Survey; see text, Section 1 and Appendix III]

Characteristic	Number of workers paid hourly rates (1,000)				Percent of workers paid hourly rates at or below federal minimum wage		
		At or below federal minimum wage					
	Total	Total	At prevailing federal minimum wage	Below prevailing federal minimum wage	Total	At prevailing federal minimum wage	Below prevailing federal minimum wage
Total, 16 years and over [1]	**80,538**	**869**	**81**	**789**	**1.1**	**0.1**	**1.0**
16 to 24 years	16,591	386	47	339	2.3	0.3	2.0
25 years and over	63,947	483	34	449	0.8	0.1	0.7
Male, 16 years old and over	40,314	270	29	241	0.7	0.1	0.6
16 to 24 years	8,205	96	23	72	1.2	0.3	0.9
25 years and over	32,110	174	6	169	0.5	–	0.5
Female, 16 years old and over	40,224	599	51	548	1.5	0.1	1.4
16 to 24 years	8,386	290	23	267	3.5	0.3	3.2
25 years and over	31,837	309	28	281	1.0	0.1	0.9
White [2]	60,299	666	56	610	1.1	0.1	1.0
Men	30,758	211	18	194	0.7	0.1	0.6
Women	29,541	455	38	416	1.5	0.1	1.4
Black [2]	12,353	130	16	114	1.1	0.1	0.9
Men	5,741	34	8	26	0.6	0.1	0.5
Women	6,612	96	8	88	1.4	0.1	1.3
Asian [2]	4,083	27	3	25	0.7	0.1	0.6
Men	1,888	9	–	9	0.5	–	0.5
Women	2,195	18	3	15	0.8	0.1	0.7
Hispanic [3]	18,841	168	20	148	0.9	0.1	0.8
Men	10,211	63	11	52	0.6	0.1	0.5
Women	8,630	104	9	96	1.2	0.1	1.1
Full-time workers	61,220	443	31	412	0.7	0.1	0.7
Men	33,552	153	11	142	0.5	–	0.4
Women	27,668	290	20	270	1.0	0.1	1.0
Part-time workers [4]	19,233	423	49	374	2.2	0.3	1.9
Men	6,727	115	18	97	1.7	0.3	1.4
Women	12,506	308	31	277	2.5	0.2	2.2
Private sector industries	70,935	839	77	761	1.2	0.1	1.1
Public sector industries	9,603	31	3	27	0.3		0.3

– Represents or rounds to zero. [1] Includes other races, not shown separately. Also includes a small number of multiple jobholders whose full- or part-time status cannot be determined for their principal job. [2] For persons in this race group only. [3] Persons of Hispanic or Latino origin may be of any race. [4] Working fewer than 35 hours per week.

Source: U.S. Bureau of Labor Statistics, CPS Tables, "Wage and salary workers paid hourly rates with earnings at or below the prevailing Federal minimum wage by selected characteristics and by occupation and industry," January 2024, <www.bls.gov/cps/tables.htm>.

Table 686. Earnings by Sex and Women's Earnings as a Percent of Men's Earnings by Occupation: 2019 to 2022

[Median earnings in inflation-adjusted dollars for the full-time, year round civilian employed population age 16 years and over. Estimates subject to sampling variability. Based on the American Community Survey]

Occupation	2019 Median earnings 2019 inflation-adjusted — Female	Male	Women's earnings as a percent of men's earnings	2021 Median earnings 2021 inflation-adjusted — Female	Male	Women's earnings as a percent of men's earnings	2022 Median earnings 2022 inflation-adjusted — Female	Male	Women's earnings as a percent of men's earnings
Total:	43,394	53,544	81.0	49,532	60,775	81.5	51,400	62,668	82.0
Management, business, science, and arts	60,523	81,524	74.2	65,070	88,377	73.6	68,211	92,092	74.1
Management, business, and financial	65,379	85,162	76.8	71,013	92,261	77.0	74,230	95,730	77.5
Management	66,767	87,792	76.1	73,091	94,833	77.1	76,066	99,144	76.7
Business and financial operations	62,437	80,061	78.0	67,890	85,910	79.0	71,856	90,069	79.8
Computer, engineering, and science	75,030	88,755	84.5	80,406	94,701	84.9	83,152	99,692	83.4
Computer and mathematical	77,356	91,377	84.7	83,834	99,619	84.2	87,509	103,298	84.7
Architecture and engineering	76,547	87,639	87.3	81,303	93,381	87.1	85,163	96,938	87.9
Life, physical, and social science	66,846	75,732	88.3	72,227	80,169	90.1	73,766	82,726	89.2
Education, legal, community service, arts, and media	50,476	61,996	81.4	54,006	67,526	80.0	56,064	70,370	79.7
Community and social service	47,043	49,699	94.7	51,294	52,184	98.3	53,745	54,946	97.8
Legal	71,530	130,503	54.8	77,844	143,425	54.3	80,673	150,658	53.5
Educational instruction, and library	48,833	60,576	80.6	51,984	63,859	81.4	53,519	66,043	81.0
Arts, design, entertainment, sports, and media	52,040	60,198	86.4	59,452	65,256	91.1	60,840	67,623	90.0
Healthcare practitioners and technical	62,299	85,126	73.2	68,247	91,134	74.9	72,119	95,762	75.3
Health diagnosing and treating practitioners and other technical	72,382	111,696	64.8	78,417	113,729	69.0	82,243	120,174	68.4
Health technologists and technicians	42,088	50,138	83.9	45,513	55,908	81.4	48,512	58,076	83.5
Service	27,100	35,657	76.0	30,400	39,859	76.3	31,960	41,475	77.1
Healthcare support	30,163	32,452	92.9	32,091	35,982	89.2	34,691	39,160	88.6
Protective service	42,869	57,824	74.1	46,812	63,543	73.7	50,411	64,749	77.9
Fire fighting and prevention, and other protective service workers including supervisors	35,729	46,567	76.7	40,149	51,943	77.3	41,572	53,592	77.6
Law enforcement workers including supervisors	52,376	66,716	78.5	55,453	71,593	77.5	61,104	75,273	81.2
Food preparation and serving related	23,440	27,441	85.4	25,231	29,956	84.2	27,393	32,097	85.3
Building and grounds cleaning and maintenance	24,196	31,831	76.0	26,624	35,078	75.9	29,141	37,239	78.3
Personal care and service	27,066	33,951	79.7	29,446	37,026	79.5	31,713	40,014	79.3
Sales and office	37,229	50,536	73.7	40,877	53,083	77.0	42,390	56,483	75.0
Sales and related	36,458	54,461	66.9	41,002	61,244	66.9	42,808	63,240	67.7
Office and administrative support	37,457	43,475	86.2	40,842	47,069	86.8	42,303	50,124	84.4
Natural resources, construction, and maintenance	32,398	45,682	70.9	36,158	50,056	72.2	37,784	51,568	73.3
Farming, fishing, and forestry	23,252	31,640	73.5	27,443	35,735	76.8	29,304	37,396	78.4
Construction and extraction	35,282	43,525	81.1	39,846	47,149	84.5	40,164	50,558	79.4
Installation, maintenance, and repair	41,472	50,347	82.4	43,061	52,346	82.3	46,973	54,928	85.5
Production, transportation, and material moving	30,303	41,468	73.1	32,332	43,975	73.5	35,409	46,944	75.4
Production	30,856	43,346	71.2	34,003	46,794	72.7	36,546	49,667	73.6
Transportation	32,462	46,894	69.2	36,219	50,848	71.2	38,252	53,242	71.8
Material moving	26,999	32,305	83.6	30,257	35,459	85.3	32,174	37,573	85.6

Source: U.S. Census Bureau, American Community Survey, B24022, "Sex by Occupation and Median Earnings in the Past 12 Months (in Inflation-Adjusted Dollars) for the Full-time, Year-Round Civilian Employed Population 16 Years and Over," <data.census.gov>, accessed November 2023.

Table 687. Median Earnings of College Graduates by Age, Sex, and Occupation: 2019

[In dollars. Estimated annual earnings of the full-time, year-round civilian employed population aged 25 to 64 with a bachelor's degree or higher level of education. Data are from the 2019 American Community Survey. Based on a sample and subject to sampling variability; see text, Section 1 and Appendix III]

Occupation	Total	Sex		Age			
		Male	Female	25 to 34 years old	35 to 44 years old	45 to 54 years old	55 to 64 years old
Total	**74,010**	**86,370**	**63,860**	**58,330**	**78,740**	**86,240**	**87,060**
Management, business, science, and arts	80,670	95,950	69,630	62,100	83,500	92,470	96,920
Management, business, and financial	90,930	102,200	77,960	66,540	93,650	104,800	106,800
Management	100,200	112,300	82,400	68,330	100,600	113,700	117,400
Business and financial operations	80,290	90,160	72,140	65,440	84,430	92,320	94,060
Computer, engineering, and science	95,290	100,300	82,410	76,430	100,500	110,100	111,000
Computer and mathematical	99,010	101,400	87,150	81,320	101,700	110,900	107,000
Architecture and engineering	98,620	100,500	87,540	78,930	101,400	112,700	120,300
Life, physical, and social science	76,670	81,810	71,710	55,830	82,420	96,270	101,200
Education, legal, community service, arts, and media	59,000	66,900	55,350	48,130	61,070	66,160	69,430
Community and social service	51,490	52,670	51,000	44,540	53,410	57,000	57,360
Legal	114,700	137,200	93,460	79,020	117,100	134,800	145,400
Educational instruction and library	55,780	61,690	53,620	45,600	57,170	62,410	66,140
Arts, design, entertainment, sports, and media	62,890	66,800	60,790	52,350	71,170	76,110	71,170
Healthcare practitioners and technical	81,940	111,300	76,640	65,690	90,270	95,130	99,250
Service	45,350	55,300	36,430	39,730	51,350	52,460	42,490
Healthcare support	36,070	38,760	35,550	32,910	37,850	39,070	37,070
Protective service	72,970	76,720	60,790	56,410	80,590	91,100	76,030
Food preparation and serving related	31,920	35,870	30,420	31,090	35,700	31,450	33,550
Building and grounds cleaning and maintenance	36,400	41,250	28,300	32,300	37,280	37,230	37,400
Personal care and service	37,080	41,820	35,180	35,600	39,710	38,460	39,770
Sales and office	57,400	71,780	49,750	47,190	62,150	67,260	62,800
Sales and related	75,290	82,660	61,330	57,540	82,090	90,120	81,620
Office and administrative support	47,200	53,170	45,120	41,410	50,280	52,010	51,640
Natural resources, construction, and maintenance	52,200	52,440	47,930	46,060	55,950	60,400	57,030
Farming, fishing, and forestry	40,480	41,710	33,340	33,010	42,390	50,510	40,960
Construction and extraction	51,470	51,630	47,140	46,890	53,920	56,210	52,330
Installation, maintenance, and repair	57,590	58,490	55,490	47,070	60,690	65,060	65,600
Production, transportation, and material moving	48,720	51,430	39,380	41,740	51,000	50,960	51,450
Production	50,570	53,700	40,690	45,590	52,630	51,860	51,290
Transportation and material moving	46,630	50,240	36,900	38,720	49,490	50,120	51,610
Transportation	53,620	56,470	42,470	47,350	53,380	57,180	60,980
Material moving	35,350	36,800	31,460	31,040	37,260	38,480	37,540

Source: U.S. Census Bureau, Industry and Occupation, "Detailed Occupation by Sex Education Age Earnings: ACS 2019," <www.census.gov/data/tables/2022/demo/acs-2019.html>, accessed August 2022.

Table 688. Workers' Earnings by Certification and License Status and Selected Characteristics: 2023

[In dollars, unless otherwise noted (120,907 represents 120,907,000). Data shown for wage and salary workers aged 16 years old and over, unless otherwise noted. Excludes self-employed workers. Certifications are issued by a non-governmental certification body and convey that an individual has the knowledge or skill to perform a specific job. A license is awarded by a government agency and conveys a legal authority to work in an occupation. For definition of median, see Guide to Tabular Presentation]

Characteristic	Full-time wage and salary workers (1,000)	Median weekly earnings				
			With a certification or license [1]			Without a certification or license
		Total	Total	Certification only	With a license [2]	
Total workers, 16 years old and over	**120,907**	**1,117**	**1,364**	**1,463**	**1,355**	**1,024**
AGE						
16 to 24 years old	11,426	714	824	775	831	705
25 to 54 years old	84,062	1,166	1,385	1,503	1,373	1,095
55 years old and over	25,420	1,186	1,456	1,519	1,448	1,117
SEX						
Men	66,700	1,202	1,483	1,583	1,466	1,136
Women	54,207	1,005	1,260	1,270	1,259	922
RACE/ETHNICITY						
White	91,336	1,138	1,392	1,465	1,384	1,046
Black or African American	16,452	920	1,125	1,161	1,114	878
Asian	8,597	1,474	1,678	1,912	1,593	1,426
Hispanic or Latino	22,834	874	1,154	1,184	1,151	827
EDUCATIONAL ATTAINMENT						
Workers, 25 years old and over	109,482	1,170	1,399	1,506	1,388	1,100
Less than a high school diploma	6,047	708	817	(S)	809	703
High school graduates, no college [3]	26,327	899	1,029	1,120	1,017	885
Some college or associate degree	26,526	1,016	1,128	1,252	1,107	989
Bachelor's degree and higher	50,582	1,609	1,634	1,815	1,615	1,591

S Indicates no data or data that do not meet publication standards. [1] A person may have more than one certification or license. [2] Persons with a license may also have a certification. [3] Includes persons with a high school diploma or equivalent.

Source: U.S. Bureau of Labor Statistics, "Labor Force Statistics from the Current Population Survey," <www.bls.gov/cps/certifications-and-licenses.htm>, accessed February 2024.

Table 689. Median Annual Earnings by Field of Bachelor's Degree and Sex: 2022

[In units as indicated (64,090 represents 64,090,000). Field of bachelor's degree for first major. Data are shown for population age 25 to 64 with a bachelor's or higher degree and with earnings. Data are from the 2022 American Community Survey and based on a sample and subject to sampling variability]

Field of degree	Total population (1,000s)	Percent of degrees by sex		Annual earnings (dollars)			Women's earnings as a percent of men's earnings
		Male	Female	Total	Men	Women	
Total............	**64,090**	**46.3**	**53.7**	**74,150**	**89,300**	**63,230**	**70.8**
SCIENCE & ENGINEERING							
Computer science........................	1,665	75.1	24.9	108,500	115,500	91,990	79.6
Engineering.............................	695	81.3	18.7	100,600	103,300	76,160	73.7
Civil engineering........................	556	77.7	22.3	99,660	101,900	86,590	85.0
Electrical engineering....................	1,197	84.5	15.5	121,600	123,800	105,200	85.0
Mechanical engineering..................	1,033	88.1	11.9	106,200	108,000	92,380	85.5
Mathematics............................	700	57.0	43.0	86,560	99,050	73,500	74.2
Biology.................................	2,201	44.2	55.8	81,550	96,620	72,200	74.7
Chemistry..............................	613	56.9	43.1	94,680	103,000	80,180	77.8
Psychology.............................	3,075	26.3	73.7	62,270	76,090	58,490	76.9
Economics..............................	1,267	64.9	35.1	101,400	107,300	84,750	79.0
Political science........................	1,440	56.8	43.2	86,380	94,950	77,090	81.2
Sociology...............................	879	31.4	68.6	63,660	75,030	59,470	79.3
Nursing................................	2,842	12.1	87.9	79,600	90,890	77,640	85.4
Other science & engineering degrees [1]....	11,870	51.0	49.0	77,910	92,050	65,150	70.8
BUSINESS							
General business........................	2,844	57.2	42.8	80,120	90,080	66,690	74.0
Accounting.............................	2,290	45.3	54.7	84,880	100,000	75,010	75.0
Business management & administration...	3,839	51.3	48.7	75,600	87,090	63,640	73.1
Marketing..............................	1,516	42.8	57.2	75,930	89,420	66,090	73.9
Finance................................	1,429	65.5	34.5	99,900	106,400	79,940	75.1
Other business degrees..................	1,615	49.1	50.9	77,160	91,000	64,900	71.3
EDUCATION							
General education.......................	1,876	22.4	77.6	58,000	68,420	55,030	80.4
Elementary education....................	1,491	9.6	90.4	54,900	64,380	54,070	84.0
Other education degrees.................	2,032	29.3	70.7	58,120	66,560	54,600	82.0
ARTS, HUMANITIES & OTHER							
Communications........................	1,658	38.2	61.8	67,840	75,400	64,130	85.1
English language & literature.............	1,670	33.6	66.4	65,060	75,850	61,150	80.6
Liberal arts.............................	745	38.1	61.9	61,380	70,850	55,790	78.7
History.................................	1,166	60.8	39.2	73,560	81,270	62,980	77.5
Fine arts...............................	685	38.3	61.7	53,450	60,900	49,530	81.3
Commercial art & graphic design..........	723	34.2	65.8	59,770	69,930	54,350	77.7
Family & consumer sciences..............	493	9.5	90.5	52,850	70,440	51,590	73.2
Physical fitness, parks, recreation, & leisure...............................	856	54.7	45.3	61,580	65,120	55,600	85.4
Criminal justice & fire protection..........	1,385	58.2	41.8	64,690	74,250	54,150	72.9
Social work.............................	638	13.0	87.0	55,060	60,090	54,380	90.5
Other degrees..........................	5,103	47.2	52.8	62,100	69,830	55,740	79.8

[1] Science and engineering related fields are included within the "other science and engineering degrees" category.

Source: U.S. Census Bureau, American Community Survey, "2022 American Community Survey Detailed Field of Degree and Median Annual Earnings Table Package," <www.census.gov/data/tables/2022/demo/educational-attainment/acs-detailed-tables.html>, accessed March 2024.

Table 690. Labor Law Compliance Actions and Employees Receiving Payment of Back Wages by Industry: 2021 to 2023

[In units as indicated. For fiscal year ending September 30. Data are shown for low wage industries with a high number of Fair Labor Standards Act (FLSA) violations. The FLSA establishes minimum wage, overtime pay, recordkeeping, and child labor standards affecting full-time and part-time workers in the private sector and in federal, state, and local governments. For more information see, <www.dol.gov/sites/dolgov/files/WHD/legacy/files/Digital_Reference_Guide_FLSA.pdf>]

Industry	Compliance actions (number)			Back wages (dollars)			Employees receiving back wages (number)		
	2021	2022	2023	2021	2022	2023	2021	2022	2023
Agriculture.........................	1,000	879	831	8,432,451	5,815,943	6,892,220	10,379	8,260	7,341
Amusement........................	287	182	173	1,208,259	420,904	267,238	1,063	665	573
Animal processing..................	51	45	38	439,674	621,436	887,866	527	846	759
Apparel manufacturing.............	76	114	53	1,305,534	989,237	594,618	588	359	178
Auto repair........................	546	308	250	4,350,665	1,334,622	1,777,967	3,564	1,249	1,202
Child care services.................	435	347	372	832,770	545,157	618,719	1,523	1,190	1,411
Construction.......................	3,034	2,268	2,134	36,068,080	32,913,795	35,558,598	21,341	17,127	17,944
Food services......................	4,237	3,840	4,095	34,741,032	27,142,447	29,648,592	29,209	22,531	25,908
Guard services.....................	497	607	638	6,252,652	3,900,935	5,250,544	5,343	4,606	4,913
Hair, nail & skin care services. ..	107	76	92	309,585	275,896	55,105	317	207	112
Health care........................	2,555	2,431	2,492	38,773,832	32,530,676	31,799,787	31,707	33,756	24,330
Hotels and motels..................	602	595	544	2,445,609	4,636,891	2,494,921	3,099	3,018	3,256
Janitorial services..................	456	339	408	2,426,106	3,397,300	3,755,640	2,861	1,295	5,066
Landscaping services.............	293	252	207	3,218,093	2,670,300	3,063,867	5,317	1,947	1,894
Logistics...........................	82	42	41	485,803	604,674	169,620	204	531	128
Retail..............................	2,705	1,813	1,655	13,470,209	7,448,019	8,391,802	14,734	6,715	9,643
Temporary help....................	471	400	266	2,602,223	8,192,262	9,251,121	4,883	6,764	4,478
Trucking...........................	696	692	813	5,055,844	2,927,974	1,931,426	1,880	1,214	3,886
Utilities............................	37	28	58	252,334	60,932	128,981	214	50	219
Warehousing.......................	75	93	90	2,362,567	245,024	1,532,150	1,654	159	1,415

Source: U.S. Department of Labor, Wage and Hour Division, "Fiscal Year Data for WHD," <www.dol.gov/agencies/whd/data/charts> accessed February 2024.

Table 691. Average Hours Spent Per Day on Primary Activities by Married Mothers and Fathers by Employment Status: 2015 to 2019

[Data are shown for households with own children under age 18. Data are averages for the 2015-2019 period and cover an individual's main activity. Does not include secondary activities done simultaneously]

Activity	Both spouses work full time		Mother employed part time and father employed full time		Mother not employed and father employed full time	
	Mothers	Fathers	Mothers	Fathers	Mothers	Fathers
Total, all activities................................	24.00	24.00	24.00	24.00	24.00	24.00
Personal care activities............................	9.20	8.63	9.21	8.60	9.59	8.90
Sleeping..	8.37	8.04	8.49	7.99	8.93	8.27
Household activities................................	1.88	1.37	2.71	1.30	3.82	1.00
Housework..	0.73	0.27	1.05	0.22	1.60	0.16
Food preparation and cleanup....................	0.83	0.42	1.22	0.41	1.75	0.30
Lawn and garden care..........................	0.05	0.24	0.08	0.23	0.11	0.19
Purchasing goods and services....................	0.49	0.34	0.56	0.29	0.64	0.35
Grocery shopping................................	0.14	0.07	0.17	0.05	0.22	0.07
Consumer goods purchases, except grocery shopping........	0.27	0.21	0.30	0.20	0.34	0.22
Caring for and helping household members....................	1.43	0.94	1.97	0.89	2.73	0.88
Caring for and helping household children.....................	1.41	0.91	1.95	0.88	2.71	0.86
Physical care..	0.61	0.31	0.71	0.29	1.01	0.23
Education-related activities........................	0.10	0.07	0.23	0.04	0.28	0.06
Reading to/with children..........................	0.05	0.03	0.08	0.04	0.09	0.03
Playing/doing hobbies with children........................	0.28	0.27	0.39	0.28	0.63	0.33
Working and work-related activities [1]........................	5.10	6.14	2.92	6.33	0.05	6.37
Working [1]..	5.08	6.11	2.88	6.31	0.02	6.35
Leisure and sports....................................	2.86	3.60	3.19	3.45	3.71	3.31
Socializing and communicating........................	0.57	0.57	0.65	0.61	0.81	0.71
Watching television................................	1.45	1.98	1.45	1.81	1.84	1.68
Participating in sports, exercise, and recreation...............	0.19	0.28	0.25	0.33	0.25	0.25
Travel..	1.40	1.41	1.40	1.45	1.17	1.45
Travel related to caring for/helping household children........	0.26	0.16	0.33	0.14	0.32	0.09
Other activities, not elsewhere classified.........................	1.63	1.57	2.04	1.70	2.28	1.74

[1] Estimates include a small amount of work time done by persons who do not meet the American Time Use Survey definition of employed.

Source: U.S. Bureau of Labor Statistics, "American Time Use Survey," <www.bls.gov/tus/#tables>, accessed August 2020.

Table 692. Workers With Access to Unmarried Domestic Partner Benefits for Partners of Same and Opposite Sex by Selected Characteristics: 2015 to 2023

[In percent. All workers = 100 percent. As of March. For employees in private industry. Based on National Compensation Survey (NCS). See headnote, Table 695, and Appendix III]

Characteristic	Defined benefit retirement survivor benefits for partners						Healthcare benefits for partners					
	Same sex			Opposite sex			Same sex			Opposite sex		
	2015	2020	2023	2015	2020	2023	2015	2020	2023	2015	2020	2023
Total....................................	**10**	**10**	**8**	**10**	**9**	**8**	**37**	**43**	**46**	**32**	**40**	**43**
WORKER CHARACTERISTICS												
Management, professional, and related..............................	16	16	13	17	16	13	53	61	64	45	56	62
Service....................................	4	4	2	4	3	2	20	24	26	17	24	27
Sales and office............................	10	9	7	11	9	7	40	44	44	35	42	42
Natural resources, construction, and maintenance.............................	10	9	9	10	8	7	28	38	39	24	36	36
Production, transportation, and material moving............................	10	10	10	9	9	9	32	39	45	28	35	41
Full-time [1].................................	12	11	9	12	11	9	44	51	55	38	47	52
Part-time [1].................................	5	5	5	5	5	5	17	18	18	15	18	18
Union [2]...................................	31	37	33	28	31	31	54	65	72	41	57	61
Nonunion [2]...............................	8	7	6	9	7	6	35	41	43	31	39	42
AVERAGE HOURLY WAGE [3]												
Lowest 25 percent..........................	3	2	2	4	3	2	17	20	23	15	20	23
Lowest 10 percent..........................	2	1	1	2	1	1	9	14	15	7	14	14
Second 25 percent..........................	8	7	5	8	7	5	35	41	44	32	39	43
Third 25 percent...........................	12	11	10	11	10	10	44	49	54	38	46	51
Highest 25 percent.........................	21	21	17	21	20	16	57	67	68	47	60	64
Highest 10 percent..........................	22	24	19	22	22	18	66	75	75	56	67	70
ESTABLISHMENT CHARACTERISTICS												
1 to 99 workers............................	5	4	3	5	4	3	23	29	34	22	29	33
100 or more workers........................	17	16	15	17	15	14	53	58	60	44	53	57
Goods producing [4].........................	9	9	8	9	8	7	33	42	45	30	40	43
Service producing [4]........................	11	10	8	11	10	8	37	43	46	32	40	44

[1] Employees are classified as working either a full-time or part-time schedule based on the definition used by each establishment. [2] See footnote 6, Table 695. [3] The National Compensation Survey—Benefits program presents wage data in percentiles rather than dollar amounts; for calculation detail, see "Technical Note" in source. [4] See Table 665 for composition of goods- and service-producing industries.

Source: U.S. Bureau of Labor Statistics, National Compensation Survey, Annual Summaries on Benefit Coverage, "Employee Benefits in the United States, March 2023," <www.bls.gov/ebs/>, accessed January 2024.

Table 693. Employer Costs for Employee Compensation Per Hour Worked: 2023

[In dollars. As of December. Based on the National Compensation Survey (NCS). See Appendix III]

Compensation component	Total civilian workers	State and local government workers	Private industry workers						
			Total	Goods producing [1]	Service providing [2]	Union workers	Non-union workers	1–99 workers	100 workers or more
Total compensation.........	**45.42**	**60.56**	**43.11**	**44.75**	**42.78**	**56.80**	**41.86**	**34.71**	**52.95**
Wages and salaries.........	31.29	37.53	30.33	30.31	30.34	34.41	29.96	25.80	35.64
Total benefits.........	14.13	23.03	12.77	14.44	12.44	22.39	11.90	8.90	17.30
Paid leave [3].........	3.41	4.43	3.26	2.82	3.34	4.06	3.18	2.17	4.53
Vacation.........	1.67	1.65	1.67	1.40	1.72	2.06	1.63	1.09	2.35
Holiday.........	1.00	1.28	0.96	0.98	0.95	1.18	0.94	0.67	1.30
Sick.........	0.52	1.14	0.43	0.31	0.45	0.61	0.41	0.28	0.60
Supplemental pay [3].........	1.56	0.59	1.71	2.37	1.58	2.37	1.65	1.01	2.53
Overtime [4].........	0.40	0.26	0.43	0.90	0.33	1.18	0.36	0.29	0.58
Insurance [3].........	3.61	6.72	3.14	3.88	2.99	7.00	2.79	2.12	4.34
Health insurance.........	3.42	6.55	2.94	3.63	2.81	6.54	2.62	2.00	4.05
Retirement and savings.........	2.37	8.07	1.50	1.82	1.43	4.79	1.20	0.84	2.26
Defined benefit.........	1.36	7.51	0.42	0.68	0.37	3.01	0.19	0.22	0.66
Defined contributions.........	1.00	0.55	1.07	1.14	1.06	1.78	1.01	0.62	1.60
Legally required.........	3.18	3.23	3.17	3.55	3.09	4.16	3.08	2.76	3.64
Social Security and Medicare.........	2.57	2.58	2.57	2.64	2.56	3.02	2.53	2.17	3.03
Social Security [5].........	2.05	1.97	2.06	2.13	2.05	2.43	2.03	1.75	2.42
Medicare.........	0.52	0.62	0.51	0.51	0.51	0.59	0.50	0.42	0.61
Federal unemployment.........	0.02	([6])	0.03	0.02	0.03	0.03	0.03	0.03	0.03
State unemployment.........	0.13	0.07	0.14	0.16	0.14	0.18	0.14	0.14	0.14
Workers' compensation.........	0.45	0.58	0.43	0.72	0.37	0.93	0.39	0.42	0.44

[1] Based on the 2012 North American Industry Classification System (NAICS). See text, this section. Includes mining, construction, and manufacturing. Excludes the agriculture, forestry, farming, and hunting sector. [2] Based on the 2012 NAICS. Includes utilities; wholesale and retail trade; transportation and warehousing; information; finance and insurance; real estate and rental and leasing; professional and technical services; management of companies and enterprises, administrative and waste services; education services; health care and social assistance; arts, entertainment, and recreation; accommodations and food services; and other services, except public administration. [3] Includes costs for other items not shown separately. [4] Includes premium pay for work in addition to regular work schedule, such as, overtime, weekends, and holidays. [5] Comprises the Old-Age, Survivors, and Disability Insurance Program (OASDI). [6] Cost per hour worked is $0.01 or less.

Source: U.S. Bureau of Labor Statistics, *Employer Costs for Employee Compensation—December 2023*, USDL 24-0485, March 2024. See also <www.bls.gov/eci>.

Table 694. Workers With Access to Retirement and Health Care Benefits by Selected Characteristics: 2023

[In percent. All workers = 100 percent. As of March. For employees in private industry. Based on National Compensation Survey (NCS). See headnote, Table 695, and Appendix III]

Characteristic	Retirement benefits			Healthcare benefits			
	All plans [1]	Defined benefit [2]	Defined contribution [2]	Medical care	Dental care	Vision care	Outpatient prescription drug coverage
Total.........	**70**	**15**	**67**	**72**	**41**	**27**	**71**
WORKER CHARACTERISTICS							
Management, professional, and related.........	86	20	85	89	60	36	88
Service.........	43	5	41	44	19	13	43
Sales and office.........	73	11	72	68	37	26	67
Natural resources, construction, and maintenance.........	70	20	64	78	41	29	77
Production, transportation, and material moving.........	75	20	67	79	45	33	78
Full-time [3].........	79	17	76	87	51	34	86
Part-time [3].........	44	7	40	25	11	9	24
Union [4].........	94	66	63	96	70	55	94
Nonunion [4].........	68	10	68	69	39	25	69
AVERAGE HOURLY WAGE [5]							
Lowest 25 percent.........	48	4	46	41	17	12	41
Lowest 10 percent.........	37	2	36	28	11	7	28
Second 25 percent.........	69	11	66	73	38	27	72
Third 25 percent.........	81	18	77	87	53	35	85
Highest 25 percent.........	90	29	86	94	65	41	93
Highest 10 percent.........	92	29	91	95	71	46	95
ESTABLISHMENT CHARACTERISTICS							
1 to 99 workers.........	57	6	56	59	29	19	58
100 or more workers.........	86	25	81	87	57	38	86
Goods producing [6].........	78	18	75	85	50	35	84
Service producing [6].........	69	14	66	69	40	26	68

[1] Employees may have access to defined benefit and/or defined contribution plans. Total excludes duplication. [2] A defined benefit plan is a retirement plan that uses a specific, predetermined formula to calculate the amount of an employee's guaranteed future benefit. A defined contribution plan provides benefits based on employer and employee contributions to individual employee accounts and the rate of return on money invested; the retirement benefit depends on the account balance at retirement. [3] Employees are classified as working either a full-time or part-time schedule based on the definition used by each establishment. [4] See footnote 6, Table 695. [5] The National Compensation Survey—Benefits program presents wage data in percentiles rather than dollar amounts; for calculation detail, see "Technical Note" in source. [6] See Table 665 for composition of goods- and service-producing industries.

Source: U.S. Bureau of Labor Statistics, National Compensation Survey, Annual Summaries on Benefit Coverage, "Employee Benefits in the United States, March 2023," <www.bls.gov/ebs/>, accessed January 2024.

Table 695. Workers With Access to Selected Employee Benefits: 2023

[In percent. All workers = 100 percent. As of March. For employees in private industry establishments of all sizes, representing approximately 126.2 million workers. Excludes agricultural establishments, private households, and the self-employed. An employee has access to a benefit plan if the plan is made available by the employer, regardless of whether the employee participates in the plan. See Appendix III. For definitions of items, see glossary at <www.bls.gov/ebs/publications/national-compensation-survey-glossary-of-employee-benefit-terms.htm>]

Characteristic	Leave benefits						Quality of life benefits				Nonproduction bonuses	
	Paid holidays	Paid sick leave	Paid vacation	Paid jury duty leave	Family leave [1] Paid	Family leave [1] Unpaid	Employer assistance for child care [2]	Flexible workplace [3]	Flexible work schedule	Subsidized commuting	All nonproduction bonuses [4]	End of year bonus
Total	**80**	**78**	**79**	**57**	**27**	**89**	**11**	**9**	**16**	**9**	**44**	**12**
WORKER CHARACTERISTIC												
Management, professional, and related occupations	92	93	92	76	42	93	20	22	30	18	54	19
Service occupations	54	61	55	37	14	82	9	1	12	6	30	6
Sales and office occupations	84	80	79	55	29	90	9	11	16	7	44	12
Natural resources, construction, and maintenance occupations	86	73	85	51	18	87	5	3	4	4	46	15
Production, transportation, and material moving occupations	88	76	86	58	20	91	6	2	6	4	46	9
Full-time [5]	91	87	92	66	31	91	13	12	17	11	51	15
Part-time [5]	49	51	40	32	14	82	6	2	13	4	25	5
Union [6]	92	86	92	73	23	95	(NA)	1	4	10	39	4
Nonunion [6]	79	77	78	56	27	88	11	10	17	9	45	13
AVERAGE HOURLY WAGE [7]												
Lowest 25 percent	60	56	55	36	13	82	6	1	10	3	30	6
Lowest 10 percent	47	39	43	27	5	79	4	1	11	2	24	5
Second 25 percent	83	82	83	55	26	90	9	5	11	7	42	11
Third 25 percent	91	86	92	65	29	91	11	10	15	8	51	15
Highest 25 percent	94	94	94	78	44	94	21	24	30	20	59	19
Highest 10 percent	95	96	95	81	51	95	25	31	38	25	65	22
ESTABLISHMENT CHARACTERISTICS												
1 to 99 workers	74	72	72	46	20	84	6	8	14	5	40	15
100 or more workers	89	86	88	70	36	95	17	11	18	13	49	10
Goods producing [8]	91	75	90	57	25	90	8	5	9	4	54	17
Service producing [8]	78	78	77	57	27	89	12	10	18	10	42	12
CENSUS DIVISION [9]												
New England	80	87	77	79	32	81	15	9	19	12	43	12
Middle Atlantic	79	83	78	73	40	89	14	11	21	12	43	13
South Atlantic	82	74	82	57	24	87	11	9	15	8	49	15
East South Central	85	65	82	76	24	85	8	7	10	6	50	13
West South Central	75	64	75	55	26	91	9	10	17	9	48	17
East North Central	82	74	80	55	22	93	11	10	17	9	44	11
West North Central	78	70	79	49	21	90	11	10	15	6	40	11
Mountain	82	82	82	50	26	87	13	7	13	3	43	8
Pacific	80	94	79	42	27	91	10	10	16	13	40	11

NA Not available. [1] Some workers may have access to both types of plans. [2] A workplace program that provides for either the full or partial cost of caring for an employee's children in a nursery, day care center, or a babysitter in facilities either on or off the employer's premises. [3] Permits employees to work an agreed-upon portion of their work schedule at home or at some other approved location. [4] Includes cash profit-sharing, employee recognition, end-of-year, holiday, payment in lieu of benefits, longevity, referral, and all other bonuses. [5] Employees are classified as working either a full-time or part-time schedule based on the definition used by each establishment. [6] Union workers are those whose wages are determined through collective bargaining. [7] The National Compensation Survey—Benefits program presents wage data in percentiles rather than dollar amounts; see "Technical Note" in source. [8] See Table 665, for composition of goods- and service-producing industries. [9] For composition of census divisions, see inside front cover.

Source: U.S. Bureau of Labor Statistics, National Compensation Survey, Annual Summaries on Benefit Coverage, "Employee Benefits in the United States, March 2023," <www.bls.gov/ebs/home.htm>, accessed August 2024.

Table 696. Industries With the Highest Total Case Incidence Rates for Nonfatal Injuries and Illnesses: 2022

[Rates per 100 full-time employees. Private industry unless otherwise noted. Incidence rates refer to any Occupational Safety & Health Administration (OSHA)-recordable occupational injury or illness, whether or not it resulted in days away from work, job transfer, or restriction. Incidence rates were calculated as: number of injuries and illnesses divided by total hours worked by all employees during the year multiplied by 200,000 as base for 100 full-time equivalent workers (working 40 hours per week, 50 weeks per year)]

Industry	NAICS code [1]	Incidence rate	Industry	NAICS code [1]	Incidence rate
All industries, including state and local government [2]	(X)	**3.0**	Psychiatric and substance abuse hospitals	6222	7.7
Nursing care facilities (skilled nursing)	6231	13.1	Cotton ginning	115111	7.4
Skiing facilities	71392	12.1	Performing arts companies	7111	7.4
Nursing and residential care facilities [3]	623	11.8	Scheduled passenger air transportation	481111	7.2
Veterinary services	54194	11.3	Framing contractors	23813	7.1
Correctional institutions [3]	92214	11.3	Aluminum foundries (except die-casting)	331524	7.1
Hospitals [3]	622	10.2	Hog and pig farming [2]	1122	6.9
Couriers and express delivery services	4921	9.8	Steel foundries (except investment)	331513	6.9
Other animal production [2]	1129	9.3	Nursing and residential care facilities [4]	623	6.9
Continuing care retirement communities and assisted living facilities for the elderly	6233	8.1	Motor home manufacturing	336213	6.8
Amusement and theme parks	71311	7.9	Cut stock, resawing lumber, and planing	321912	6.7
Ambulance services	62191	7.8	Wood container and pallet manufacturing	32192	6.7
Manufactured (mobile) home manufacturing	321991	7.7	Light truck and utility vehicle manufacturing	336112	6.7
			Truck trailer manufacturing	336212	6.7

X Not applicable. [1] Based on the North American Industry Classification System, 2017 (NAICS). See text, this section. [2] Excludes farms with fewer than 11 employees. [3] State government. [4] Local government.

Source: U.S. Bureau of Labor Statistics, Injuries, Illnesses, and Fatalities, Survey of Occupational Injuries and Illnesses Data, "Supplemental News Release Tables," <www.bls.gov/iif/>, accessed June 2024.

Table 697. Nonfatal Occupational Injuries and Illnesses by Industry: 2020 to 2022

[3,229.2 represents 3,229,200. Rates per 100 full-time employees. Except as noted, data refer to any Occupational Safety and Health Administration (OSHA) recordable occupational injury or illness, whether or not it resulted in days away from work, job transfer, or restriction. Incidence rates were calculated as: number of injuries and illnesses divided by total hours worked by all employees during the year multiplied by 200,000 as base for 100 full-time equivalent workers (working 40 hours per week, 50 weeks per year)]

Industry	2017 NAICS code [1]	Number of cases (1,000)			Incidence rate of cases		
		2020	2021	2022	2020	2021	2022
Total	(X)	**3,229.2**	**3,250.7**	**3,504.6**	**2.9**	**2.9**	**3.0**
Private industry [2]	(X)	**2,654.7**	**2,607.9**	**2,804.2**	**2.7**	**2.7**	**2.7**
Agriculture, forestry, fishing, hunting [2]	11	45.9	43.5	39.5	4.6	4.6	4.1
Mining [3]	21	7.5	6.7	8.5	1.2	1.3	1.4
Construction	23	174.1	169.2	169.6	2.5	2.5	2.4
Manufacturing	31–33	373.3	385.1	396.8	3.1	3.3	3.2
Wholesale trade	42	132.2	130.9	147.6	2.4	2.5	2.6
Retail trade	44–45	341.1	404.7	422.7	3.1	3.6	3.7
Transportation and warehousing [4]	48–49	206.9	253.1	276.3	4.0	4.6	4.8
Utilities	22	8.4	9.0	9.5	1.5	1.7	1.7
Information	51	19.6	18.8	27.2	0.8	0.7	1.0
Finance and insurance	52	17.4	21.9	15.9	0.3	0.4	0.3
Real estate and rental and leasing	53	41.8	38.8	44.4	2.1	2.0	2.2
Professional, scientific, and technical services	54	59.5	77.2	81.1	0.7	0.9	0.9
Management of companies and enterprises	55	14.9	13.1	18.6	0.6	0.6	0.8
Administrative and support & waste management and remediation services	56	103.4	97.1	106.3	2.0	1.9	1.9
Educational services	61	22.5	32.5	40.2	1.1	1.7	2.0
Health care and social assistance	62	806.2	623.0	665.3	5.5	4.3	4.5
Arts, entertainment, and recreation	71	34.3	39.0	55.0	3.0	3.7	4.2
Accommodation and food services	72	191.0	196.3	221.1	2.6	2.7	2.7
Other services, except public administration	81	54.7	48.3	58.6	1.8	1.6	1.8
State and local government [2]	(X)	**574.5**	**642.8**	**700.4**	**3.9**	**4.5**	**4.9**
State government	(X)	131.1	127.0	144.7	3.3	3.2	3.8
Local government	(X)	443.4	515.8	555.7	4.2	5.0	5.2

X Not applicable. [1] North American Industry Classification System, 2017; see text, this section. [2] Excludes farms with fewer than 11 employees. [3] Data for Mining (2017 NAICS Sector 21) include establishments not governed by the Mine Safety and Health Administration rules and reporting, such as those in Oil and Gas Extraction and related support activities. Data for mining operators in coal, metal, and nonmetal mining are provided to BLS by the Mine Safety and Health Administration, U.S. Department of Labor. Independent mining contractors are excluded from the coal, metal, and nonmetal mining industries. These data do not reflect the changes the Occupational Safety and Health Administration made to its recordkeeping requirements effective January 1, 2002; therefore, estimates for these industries are not comparable to estimates in other industries. [4] Data for employers in railroad transportation are provided to BLS by the Federal Railroad Administration, U.S. Department of Transportation.

Source: U.S. Bureau of Labor Statistics, "Employer-Reported Workplace Injuries and Illnesses – 2022, Supplemental Files, Summary Tables," <www.bls.gov/news.release/osh.toc.htm>, accessed November 2023.

Table 698. Fatal Work Injuries by Event or Exposure: 2022

[For the 50 states and the District of Columbia. Based on the Census of Fatal Occupational Injuries. For details, see source]

Event or exposure	Number of fatalities	Percent distribu-tion	Event or exposure	Number of fatalities	Percent distribu-tion
Total [1]	**5,486**	**100.0**	Fires and explosions	107	2.0
Violence & other injuries [1]	849	15.5	Falls, slips, trips	865	15.8
Homicides [1]	524	9.6	Exposure to harmful substances or		
Shooting	435	7.9	environments [1]	839	15.3
Stabbing, cutting, slashing, piercing	44	0.8	Exposure to electricity	145	2.6
Self-inflicted injury, intentional (suicide)	267	4.9	Exposure to caustic, noxious or allergenic		
Transportation incidents [1]	2,066	37.7	substances	586	10.7
Aircraft incidents	101	1.8	Oxygen deficiency	56	1.0
Railway incidents	43	0.8	Contacts with objects and equipment [1]	738	13.5
Pedestrians struck by vehicle [2]	325	5.9	Struck by object or equipment [1]	484	8.8
Water vehicle incidents	31	0.6	Struck by falling object or equipment	238	4.3
Roadway incident with motor vehicle [1]	1,369	25.0	Struck by flying object	19	0.3
Collision between vehicles	763	13.9	Caught in or compressed by equipment		
Noncollision accidents	249	4.5	or objects	142	2.6
Nonroadway accident involving motor vehicle	185	3.4	Caught or crushed in collapsing materials	95	1.7

[1] Includes other causes not shown separately. [2] Including mobile equipment.

Source: U.S. Bureau of Labor Statistics, "Census of Fatal Occupational Injuries—Current Data," <www.bls.gov/iif>, accessed January 2024.

Table 699. Worker Fatalities on the Job by Industry and Occupation: 2022

[Based on the Census of Fatal Occupational Injuries. For details, see source]

Industry group	Deaths Number	Deaths Rate [1]	Occupations with highest fatal work injury rates	Deaths Number	Deaths Rate [1]
Total	**5,486**	**3.7**	Logging workers	54	100.7
			Roofers	105	57.5
			Fishing & hunting workers	16	50.9
Agriculture [2]	417	18.6	Helpers, construction trades	20	38.5
Mining [3]	113	16.6	Aircraft pilots & flight engineers	72	35.9
Construction	1,069	9.6	Driver/sales workers & truck drivers	1,115	30.4
Manufacturing	404	2.6	Refuse & recyclable material collectors	22	22.6
Wholesale trade	171	5.4	Structural iron & steel workers	14	21.3
Retail trade	301	2.1	Underground mining machine operators	8	20.1
Transportation & warehousing	1,053	14.1	Miscellaneous agricultural workers	146	20.0
Utilities	36	3.4	Grounds maintenance workers	222	18.9
Information	48	1.9	First-line supervisors of landscaping,		
Financial activities [4]	100	0.9	lawn service, & groundskeeping workers	47	17.3
Professional & technical svcs [4]	76	0.6	First-line supervisors of construction trades & extraction workers	113	16.4
Educational & health services	178	0.8	Construction laborers	320	15.6
Leisure & hospitality [4]	306	2.8	Farmers, ranchers, & other agricultural managers	148	14.9
Other services [5]	200	2.9	Electrical power-line installers & repairers	20	14.9
Government	481	2.1	Maintenance & repair workers, general	95	14.9

[1] The rate represents the number of fatal occupational injuries per 100,000 full-time equivalent workers. [2] Includes forestry, fishing, and hunting. [3] Includes oil and gas extraction. [4] For composition of industry, see Table 665. [5] Excludes public service administration.

Source: U.S. Bureau of Labor Statistics, Census of Fatal Occupational Injuries, "Fatal Injury Rates," <www.bls.gov/iif/>, accessed January 2024.

Table 700. Nonfatal Occupational Injury and Illness Cases in Private Industry by Type of Injury or Illness and Days Away from Work: 2021 to 2022

[2,246.9 represents 2,246,900. Data are for the 2021 to 2022 period. Covers work-related injuries and illnesses involving one or more days of missed work]

Type of work-related injury or illness	Number of injury or illness cases (1,000)								Median number of days away from work
	All cases	1 day	2 days	3-5 days	6-10 days	11-20 days	21-30 days	31 days or more	
Total [1]	**2,246.9**	**229.1**	**174.8**	**412.7**	**461.1**	**331.1**	**115.3**	**522.9**	**10**
Traumatic injuries and disorders	1,638.7	215.2	161.6	283.0	201.3	175.7	102.4	499.6	9
Traumatic injuries to bones, nerves, spinal cord	153.4	6.5	6.6	15.0	13.0	17.2	13.4	81.7	36
Fractures	149.1	6.3	6.3	14.1	12.6	16.9	13.2	79.6	36
Traumatic injuries to muscles, tendons, ligaments, joints, etc.	589.7	52.3	47.2	93.9	72.6	68.6	42.5	212.7	14
Sprains, strains, tears	548.0	50.6	45.1	90.3	69.3	62.5	37.6	192.5	13
Open wounds	195.9	48.9	25.7	37.5	25.6	20.1	9.6	28.6	4
Surface wounds and bruises	172.8	29.2	22.9	37.2	22.7	17.0	8.5	35.3	5
Burns and corrosions	35.5	6.3	4.7	7.4	4.4	5.6	2.8	4.2	5
Concussions	30.9	3.1	4.1	7.1	4.5	3.4	1.6	7.1	7
Other traumatic injuries and disorders	414.1	62.5	46.4	76.1	53.2	39.9	21.4	114.6	7
Soreness, pain, hurt–nonspecified injury	327.3	43.4	35.1	58.3	39.3	33.4	18.0	99.8	8
Diseases and disorders of body systems	22.7	1.7	1.2	2.7	3.3	3.0	1.8	9.3	19
Infectious and parasitic diseases	562.9	7.8	10.5	123.4	253.5	150.3	9.9	7.6	10
Mental disorders and syndromes	4.1	0.2	0.1	0.4	–	0.5	0.2	2.0	30

– Represents zero. [1] Total includes unclassified and ill-defined conditions.

Source: U.S. Bureau of Labor Statistics, Survey of Occupational Injuries and Illnesses, 2021-2022 Cases, "R.67. Detailed nature by number of days away from work," <www.bls.gov/iif/>, accessed January 2024.

Table 701. Labor Union Membership by Sector: 1990 to 2023

[16,776 represents 16,776,000. Annual averages of monthly figures. For wage and salary workers in agriculture and nonagricultural industries. Based on the Current Population Survey and subject to sampling error. For methodological details, see source]

Sector	1990	2000	2010	2015	2018	2019	2020	2021	2022	2023
TOTAL (1,000)										
Union members..................	16,776	16,258	14,715	14,786	14,740	14,567	14,250	14,004	14,280	14,415
Covered by unions...............	19,105	17,944	16,290	16,433	16,374	16,375	15,936	15,795	15,996	16,186
Public sector workers:										
Union members.................	6,477	7,110	7,623	7,234	7,162	7,059	7,168	6,978	7,061	7,007
Covered by unions..............	7,680	7,976	8,406	8,023	7,862	7,813	7,915	7,745	7,832	7,763
Private sector workers:										
Union members.................	10,299	9,148	7,092	7,552	7,578	7,508	7,082	7,026	7,219	7,408
Covered by unions..............	11,425	9,969	7,884	8,410	8,512	8,562	8,021	8,050	8,164	8,424
PERCENT										
Union members..................	16.0	13.5	11.9	11.1	10.5	10.3	10.8	10.3	10.1	10.0
Covered by unions...............	18.2	14.9	13.1	12.3	11.7	11.6	12.1	11.6	11.3	11.2
Public sector workers:										
Union members.................	36.4	37.5	36.2	35.2	33.9	33.6	34.8	33.9	33.2	32.5
Covered by unions..............	43.1	42.0	40.0	39.0	37.2	37.2	38.4	37.6	36.8	36.0
Private sector workers:										
Union members.................	11.8	9.0	6.9	6.7	6.4	6.2	6.3	6.1	6.0	6.0
Covered by unions..............	13.1	9.8	7.7	7.4	7.2	7.1	7.2	7.0	6.8	6.8

Source: *Union Membership and Coverage Database from the Current Population Survey*, accessed at <unionstats.com>, authored by Barry Hirsch of Georgia State University, David Macpherson of Trinity University, and William Even of Miami University. Copyright 2024.

Table 702. Labor Union Members by Selected Characteristics: 2023

[In units as indicated (144,541 represents 141,541,000). Annual averages of monthly data. Covers employed wage and salary workers 16 years old and over. Excludes self-employed workers whose businesses are incorporated and not incorporated. Based on Current Population Survey; see text, Section 1 and Appendix III]

Characteristic	Employed wage and salary workers			Median usual weekly earnings [3] (dollars)			
		Percent					
	Total (1,000)	Union members [1]	Repre-sented by union [2]	Total	Union members [1]	Repre-sented by union [2]	Not repre-sented by union
Total [4].........................	**144,541**	**10.0**	**11.2**	**1,117**	**1,263**	**1,253**	**1,090**
SEX							
Men.............................	75,079	10.5	11.6	1,202	1,341	1,333	1,180
Women...........................	69,462	9.5	10.7	1,005	1,174	1,165	983
AGE							
16 to 24 years old............................	19,759	4.4	5.2	714	809	810	709
25 to 34 years old............................	33,584	9.0	10.2	1,045	1,160	1,150	1,027
35 to 44 years old............................	31,731	11.1	12.4	1,250	1,375	1,374	1,232
45 to 54 years old............................	28,177	12.6	14.0	1,255	1,390	1,381	1,232
55 to 64 years old............................	22,980	12.0	13.3	1,217	1,289	1,280	1,205
65 years and over............................	8,310	8.6	9.7	1,080	1,152	1,150	1,064
RACE/ETHNICITY							
White [5].........................	109,689	9.8	11.1	1,138	1,294	1,277	1,115
Men..............................	57,949	10.3	11.4	1,225	1,367	1,353	1,204
Women...........................	51,740	9.3	10.6	1,021	1,204	1,188	997
Black [5].........................	19,182	11.8	13.1	920	1,102	1,099	901
Men..............................	9,017	13.2	14.5	970	1,156	1,159	937
Women...........................	10,165	10.5	11.8	889	1,048	1,037	872
Asian [5].........................	10,044	7.8	9.0	1,474	1,422	1,437	1,482
Men..............................	5,261	7.9	9.2	1,635	1,444	1,472	1,680
Women...........................	4,783	7.8	8.8	1,299	1,378	1,369	1,289
Hispanic [6]......................	27,361	9.0	10.0	874	1,112	1,098	841
Men..............................	15,027	9.2	10.1	915	1,162	1,147	893
Women...........................	12,334	8.8	9.9	800	1,041	1,028	776
INDUSTRY [7]							
Private sector.....................	122,963	6.0	6.9	1,087	1,184	1,168	1,077
Mining...........................	577	4.3	4.9	1,424	(B)	(B)	1,438
Construction.......................	8,920	10.7	11.4	1,044	1,424	1,411	1,007
Manufacturing.....................	14,922	7.9	9.1	1,148	1,135	1,107	1,153
Wholesale and retail trade.................	18,012	3.9	4.6	900	896	900	900
Transportation and utilities.................	7,624	16.5	17.5	1,063	1,321	1,293	1,018
Information.......................	2,582	7.4	7.8	1,572	1,689	1,702	1,562
Financial activities..................	9,284	1.7	2.4	1,385	1,154	1,170	1,393
Professional and business services.......	16,820	2.3	3.0	1,407	987	1,052	1,417
Education and health services............	24,344	8.1	9.3	1,097	1,199	1,193	1,078
Leisure and hospitality.....................	12,660	2.9	3.4	747	900	891	740
Other services...........................	5,970	3.0	3.6	923	1,151	1,136	915
Public sector.....................	21,577	32.5	36.0	1,229	1,346	1,341	1,161

B Base is less than 50,000. [1] Members of a labor union or an employee association similar to a labor union. [2] Members of a labor union or an employee association similar to a union as well as workers who report no union affiliation but whose jobs are covered by a union or an employee association contract. [3] For full-time employed wage and salary workers. [4] Includes other races not shown separately. Also includes a small number of multiple jobholders whose full- and part-time status cannot be determined for their principal job. [5] For persons in this race group only. [6] Persons of Hispanic origin may be of any race. [7] For composition of industries, see Table 665.

Source: U.S. Bureau of Labor Statistics, *Union Members—2023*, USDL 24-0096, January 2024. See also <www.bls.gov/news.release/union2.toc.htm>.

Table 703. Labor Union Membership by State: 2010 and 2023

[Annual averages of monthly figures (14,715.1 represents 14,715,100). For wage and salary workers in agriculture and nonagricultural industries. Data represent union members by place of residence. Based on the Current Population Survey and subject to sampling error. For methodological details, see source]

State	Union members (1,000)		Workers covered by unions (1,000)		Percent of workers					
					Union members		Covered by unions		Private sector union members	
	2010	2023	2010	2023	2010	2023	2010	2023	2010	2023
United States......	**14,715.1**	**14,415.2**	**16,289.5**	**16,186.3**	**11.9**	**10.0**	**13.1**	**11.2**	**6.9**	**6.0**
Alabama [1]............	183.3	154.9	202.8	179.6	10.1	7.4	11.2	8.6	5.7	4.6
Alaska.................	67.6	45.3	73.0	46.7	22.9	14.8	24.8	15.3	11.2	7.2
Arizona [1].............	161.0	132.5	203.0	152.4	6.4	4.2	8.1	4.8	3.6	2.4
Arkansas [1]...........	43.6	62.0	58.6	70.6	4.0	5.1	5.4	5.8	2.7	4.3
California..............	2,431.3	2,513.7	2,577.8	2,768.4	17.5	15.4	18.6	16.9	9.3	8.8
Colorado..............	140.4	189.4	170.9	236.3	6.6	6.9	8.0	8.6	3.8	4.3
Connecticut...........	258.3	255.3	269.7	272.1	16.7	15.8	17.4	16.9	8.3	6.7
Delaware..............	40.2	38.7	43.9	44.2	11.4	8.9	12.5	10.1	5.8	4.6
District of Columbia..	25.9	31.6	30.0	36.1	9.0	9.1	10.5	10.4	5.9	4.6
Florida [1].............	391.7	441.5	488.0	577.0	5.6	4.7	6.9	6.1	2.3	2.5
Georgia [1]............	153.3	211.9	191.3	251.2	4.0	4.6	5.0	5.4	2.5	2.9
Hawaii................	111.3	138.1	120.3	146.5	21.8	24.1	23.5	25.5	14.6	15.2
Idaho [1]..............	41.5	36.3	50.1	43.9	7.1	4.5	8.6	5.4	3.6	2.8
Illinois................	843.8	707.8	891.2	755.9	15.5	12.8	16.4	13.7	9.5	8.0
Indiana [3]............	278.6	243.8	312.8	276.8	10.9	8.0	12.2	9.1	8.2	6.3
Iowa [1]...............	158.2	106.3	191.8	129.9	11.4	7.1	13.8	8.7	7.1	4.8
Kansas [1]............	83.7	120.0	111.0	143.6	6.8	8.8	9.1	10.5	4.5	6.5
Kentucky [6]..........	146.5	151.8	166.1	193.8	8.9	8.8	10.1	11.2	7.2	6.1
Louisiana [1]..........	75.6	76.0	96.0	90.8	4.3	4.3	5.5	5.1	3.2	2.8
Maine.................	62.9	51.8	70.7	61.3	11.6	9.1	13.0	10.8	5.1	4.3
Maryland..............	296.1	302.6	328.8	361.5	11.6	10.7	12.9	12.8	6.1	5.1
Massachusetts.......	414.8	410.7	446.4	442.1	14.5	12.6	15.6	13.5	7.0	7.1
Michigan [3]...........	627.3	565.9	658.7	624.7	16.5	12.8	17.3	14.1	11.1	9.7
Minnesota............	384.6	354.2	397.3	376.4	15.6	13.2	16.1	14.1	8.4	7.6
Mississippi [1]........	46.3	75.9	58.3	106.3	4.5	7.0	5.6	9.8	3.7	5.7
Missouri [7]...........	244.3	254.4	274.4	284.7	9.9	9.3	11.1	10.4	8.5	7.2
Montana..............	46.1	55.6	52.2	60.9	12.7	11.8	14.4	13.0	5.6	6.8
Nebraska [1]..........	75.3	68.0	95.6	87.9	9.3	7.2	11.8	9.4	4.8	3.8
Nevada [1]............	151.3	170.9	169.9	200.7	15.0	12.4	16.8	14.5	10.8	9.4
New Hampshire.......	63.2	62.0	72.6	72.7	10.2	9.3	11.7	10.9	4.4	3.7
New Jersey...........	636.9	677.6	660.0	727.6	17.1	16.1	17.7	17.3	9.0	10.0
New Mexico...........	54.8	60.2	72.4	72.8	7.3	7.5	9.7	9.1	2.6	3.6
New York.............	1,958.7	1,710.1	2,098.6	1,785.2	24.2	20.6	26.0	21.5	13.7	12.2
North Carolina [1].....	116.7	124.2	179.6	151.5	3.2	2.7	4.9	3.3	1.8	1.9
North Dakota [1]......	23.0	22.4	28.4	26.9	7.4	6.2	9.1	7.5	4.6	4.0
Ohio..................	654.9	640.2	701.9	690.3	13.7	12.5	14.7	13.5	8.4	7.0
Oklahoma [2]..........	77.4	116.4	98.5	133.0	5.5	6.8	6.9	7.8	3.5	3.0
Oregon................	245.1	254.9	267.9	270.0	16.2	14.1	17.7	15.0	9.1	7.2
Pennsylvania.........	770.2	749.3	831.4	821.8	14.7	13.0	15.9	14.2	9.3	7.8
Rhode Island.........	74.9	62.6	79.4	67.4	16.4	12.4	17.4	13.3	8.4	7.8
South Carolina [1].....	79.6	49.0	106.8	62.8	4.6	2.3	6.2	3.0	2.7	1.6
South Dakota [1]......	20.0	15.3	23.5	17.8	5.6	3.6	6.6	4.2	3.0	1.8
Tennessee [1].........	115.5	178.2	142.5	204.9	4.7	6.0	5.8	6.9	2.2	3.8
Texas [1]..............	545.4	588.5	676.7	703.9	5.4	4.5	6.7	5.4	3.2	2.6
Utah [1]...............	74.6	65.1	95.6	133.8	6.5	4.1	8.4	8.4	3.9	1.9
Vermont..............	34.2	43.0	39.5	46.4	11.8	14.3	13.6	15.4	5.3	8.2
Virginia [1]............	160.6	175.3	196.4	226.0	4.6	4.3	5.7	5.6	2.9	2.4
Washington...........	551.8	574.5	605.2	630.2	19.4	16.5	21.3	18.1	10.7	10.0
West Virginia [5]......	99.9	60.4	111.4	69.6	14.8	8.7	16.5	10.1	11.2	6.7
Wisconsin [4]..........	354.9	205.0	379.8	232.2	14.2	7.4	15.1	8.4	8.4	5.6
Wyoming [1]...........	18.1	14.3	20.7	17.0	7.4	5.6	8.4	6.6	4.9	3.0

[1] Right to work state as of 2000. [2] Passed right to work law in 2001. [3] Passed right to work law in 2012. [4] Passed right to work law in 2015. [5] Passed right to work law in 2016. [6] Passed right to work law in 2017. [7] Passed right to work law in 2017; rejected by voters in 2018.

Source: *Union Membership and Coverage Database from the Current Population Survey*, accessed at <unionstats.com>, authored by Barry Hirsch of Georgia State University, David Macpherson of Trinity University, and William Even of Miami University. Copyright 2024.

Table 704. Work Stoppages: 1960 to 2023

[896 represents 896,000. Excludes work stoppages involving fewer than 1,000 workers and lasting less than 1 day. The term "major work stoppage" includes both worker-initiated strikes and employer-initiated lockouts that involve 1,000 or more workers. Information is based on reports of labor disputes appearing in daily newspapers, trade journals, and other public sources]

| Year | Number of work stop-pages [1] | Workers involved [2] (1,000) | Days idle total | | Year | Number of work stop-pages [1] | Workers involved [2] (1,000) | Days idle total | |
			Number [3] (1,000)	Percent estimated working time [4]				Number [3] (1,000)	Percent estimated working time [4]
1960........	222	896	13,260	0.09	2003.......	14	129	4,091	0.01
1970........	381	2,468	52,761	0.29	2004.......	17	171	3,344	0.01
1980........	187	795	20,844	0.09	2005.......	22	100	1,736	0.01
1985........	54	324	7,079	0.03	2006.......	20	70	2,688	0.01
1986........	69	533	11,861	0.05	2007.......	21	189	1,265	(Z)
1987........	46	174	4,481	0.02	2008.......	15	72	1,954	0.01
1988........	40	118	4,381	0.02	2009.......	5	13	124	(Z)
1989........	51	452	16,996	0.07	2010......	11	45	302	(Z)
1990........	44	185	5,926	0.02	2011.......	19	113	1,020	(Z)
1991........	40	392	4,584	0.02	2012.......	19	148	1,131	(Z)
1992........	35	364	3,989	0.01	2013.......	15	55	290	(Z)
1993........	35	182	3,981	0.01	2014.......	11	34	200	(Z)
1994........	45	322	5,021	0.02	2015.......	12	47	740	(Z)
1995........	31	192	5,771	0.02	2016.......	15	99	1,543	(Z)
1996........	37	273	4,889	0.02	2017.......	7	25	440	(Z)
1997........	29	339	4,497	0.01	2018.......	20	485	2,815	0.01
1998........	34	387	5,116	0.02	2019.......	25	426	3,244	0.01
1999........	17	73	1,996	0.01	2020.......	8	27	966	(Z)
2000........	39	394	20,419	0.06	2021.......	16	81	1,552	(Z)
2001........	29	99	1,151	(Z)	2022.......	23	121	2,313	0.01
2002........	19	46	660	(Z)	2023.......	33	459	16,673	0.04

Z Less than 0.005 percent. [1] Beginning in year indicated. [2] Workers counted more than once if involved in more than one stoppage during the year. [3] Resulting from all stoppages in effect in a year, including those that began in an earlier year. The number of total days of idleness is computed by multiplying the number of workers idled by the number of lost workdays during the reference period. [4] Agricultural and government employees are included in the total working time; private household and forestry and fishery employees are excluded.

Source: U.S. Bureau of Labor Statistics, *Major Work Stoppages in 2023*, USDL 24-0348, February 2024. See also <www.bls.gov/wsp>.

Section 13
Income, Expenditures, Poverty, and Wealth

This section presents data on gross domestic product (GDP), gross national product (GNP), national and personal income, savings and investment, money income, poverty, and national and personal wealth. The data on income and expenditures measure two aspects of the U.S. economy. One aspect relates to the National Income and Product Accounts (NIPA), a summation reflecting the entire complex of the nation's economic income and output and the interaction of its major components; the other relates to personal and household income and wealth, and consumer expenditures.

The primary source for data on GDP, GNP, national and personal income, gross saving and investment, fixed assets, and consumer durables come from the Bureau of Economic Analysis (BEA), issued monthly in the *Survey of Current Business*, and available through an interactive tool on the BEA's website, <www.bea.gov/itable/>. Revisions occur annually. The BEA conducts a comprehensive revision about every 5 years using data from the Census Bureau's Economic Census. The most recent comprehensive revisions occurred in 2023. The 2023 update includes the National Income and Product Accounts, the Industry Economic Accounts, and the Regional Economic Accounts. Discussions are available on the BEA's website.

Sources of income distribution data are the Annual Social and Economic Supplement of the Current Population Survey (CPS), and the American Community Survey, both products of the U.S. Census Bureau (see text, Section 1). Annual data on income of families, individuals, and households are presented in Current Population Reports, *Income in the United States,* and *Poverty in the United States.* These reports, with additional detailed statistics and historical data, are available on the Census Bureau's website at <www.census.gov/topics/income-poverty.html>.

Data on the household sector's savings and assets are published by the Board of Governors of the Federal Reserve System in the quarterly statistical release, *Financial Accounts of the United States.* Data from this report are available online in several different formats for downloading at <www.federalreserve.gov/releases/z1/>. The Federal Reserve Board also periodically conducts the *Survey of Consumer Finances,* which presents financial information on family assets and net worth. The most recent survey is available online at <www.federalreserve.gov/econres/scfindex.htm>. Detailed information on personal wealth is published periodically by the Internal Revenue Service (IRS) in the *SOI (Statistics of Income) Bulletin.*

National income and product—*GDP,* or value added, is the value of the goods and services produced by the nation's economy less the value of the goods and services used up in production. GDP is equal to the sum of personal consumption expenditures, gross private domestic investment, net exports of goods and services, and government consumption expenditures and gross investment. The goods and services included are largely those bought for final use (excluding illegal transactions) in the market economy. A number of inclusions, however, represent imputed values, the most important of which is the

rental value of owner-occupied housing. GDP, in this broad context, measures the output attributable to the factors of production located in the United States. GDP by state is the gross market value of the goods and services attributable to labor and property located in a state. It is the state counterpart of the nation's GDP.

The BEA releases GDP and related data in current dollar estimates, which reflect the value when transactions occurred, and in real values that are inflation-adjusted estimates that exclude the effects of price changes. Quantities, or "real" volume measures, and prices are expressed as index numbers with a specified reference year equal to 100 (currently 2017). Quantity and price indexes are calculated using a Fisher-chained weighted formula that incorporates weights from two adjacent periods (years for annual data). Chained-dollar values are calculated by multiplying the quantity index by the current dollar value in the reference year (2017) and then dividing by 100. Percent changes calculated from real quantity indexes and chained-dollar levels are conceptually the same; any differences are due to rounding. Chained-dollar values are not additive because the relative weights for a given period differ from those of the reference year. In tables that display chained-dollar values, a "residual" line shows the difference between the sum of detailed chained-dollar series and its corresponding aggregate.

Gross national product measures the market value of the goods, services, and structures produced by labor and property supplied by U.S. residents regardless of where they are located. GNP is equal to GDP plus income receipts from the rest of the world less income payments to the rest of the world.

National income includes all net incomes, net of consumption of fixed capital (CFC), earned in production. National income is also the sum of compensation of employees, proprietors' income with inventory valuation adjustment (IVA) and capital consumption adjustment (CCAdj), rental income with CCAdj, corporate profits with IVA and CCAdj, net interest and miscellaneous payments, taxes on production and imports less subsidies, business current transfer payments (net), and current surplus of government enterprises, less subsidies.

Capital consumption adjustment is used to convert measures of depreciation that are based on historical-cost accounting—such as the capital consumption allowances reported on tax returns—to NIPA measures of private consumption of fixed capital that are based on current cost with consistent service lives and with empirically based depreciation schedules. Inventory valuation adjustment represents the difference between the book value of inventories used up in production and the cost of replacing them.

Personal income is the current income that persons receive in return for their provision of labor, land, and capital used in current production, plus current transfer receipts less contributions for government social insurance (domestic). Classified as "persons" are households, nonprofit institutions that primarily serve households, private trust funds, and private noninsured welfare funds. Personal current transfer receipts from government and business include items such as social security benefits, public assistance, and payments for personal injury, and exclude transfers among persons. Also included are certain nonmonetary types of income—chiefly, estimated net rental value to owner-occupants of their homes and the value of services furnished without payment by financial intermediaries. Capital gains (and losses) are excluded.

Disposable personal income is personal income less personal current taxes. It is the income available to persons for spending or saving. Personal taxes are primarily income taxes and personal property taxes.

Gross domestic product by industry—The BEA also prepares estimates of value added by industry. *Value added* is a measure of the contribution of each private industry and of government to the nation's GDP. It is defined as an industry's gross output (which consists of sales or receipts and other operating income, commodity taxes, and inventory change) minus its intermediate inputs (which consist of energy, raw materials, semi-finished goods, and purchased services). The three primary components of value added are an industry group's return to domestic labor (compensation of employees), its net return to government (taxes on production and imports less subsidies), and its return to domestic capital (gross operating surplus). Data are available by industry and for Federal and state and local government. Industries are classified according to the North American Industry Classification System.

Regional Economic Accounts—These accounts consist of estimates of state and local area personal income and of gross domestic product by state, and are consistent with estimates of personal income and gross domestic product in the BEA's national economic accounts. BEA's estimates of state and local area personal income provide a framework for analyzing individual state and local economies, and they show how the economies compare with each other. The *personal income* of a state and/or local area is the income received by, or on behalf of, the residents of that state or area. Estimates of labor and proprietors' earnings by place of work indicate the economic activity of business and government within that area, and estimates of personal income by place of residence indicate the income within the area that is available for spending. BEA prepares estimates for states, counties, and metropolitan statistical areas.

Gross domestic product by state estimates measure the value added to the nation's production by the labor and property in each state. GDP by state data include breakdowns of each industry's contribution to each state economy. GDP estimates are available in current dollars and in real (chained dollars) by industry.

Consumer Expenditure Survey—The Consumer Expenditure Survey program began in 1980. The principal objective of the survey is to collect current consumer expenditure data, which provide a continuous flow of data on consumer spending habits. The data are necessary for revisions of the Consumer Price Index. The survey is conducted by the Census Bureau for the Bureau of Labor Statistics. See Appendix III for more information.

Money income of households, families, and individuals—Money income statistics are based on data collected in various field surveys of income conducted since 1936. Since 1947, the Census Bureau

collects data annually and publishes results in *Current Population Reports*, P60 Series. See Appendix III for more information on Census Bureau surveys. *Money income* as defined by the Census Bureau differs from the BEA concept of "personal income." Data on consumer income collected in the CPS cover money income received (exclusive of certain money receipts such as capital gains) before payments for personal income taxes, social security, union dues, Medicare deductions, etc. Money income excludes tax credits and noncash benefits (see Section 11) such as nutritional assistance (food stamps), health benefits, and subsidized housing; for farm families, noncash benefits from goods produced and consumed on the farm; and for some nonfarm residents, noncash benefits such as the use of business transportation and facilities, and full or partial payments by business for retirement programs, medical and educational expenses, etc. These elements should be considered when comparing income levels. None of the aggregate income concepts (GDP, national income, or personal income) is exactly comparable with money income, although personal income is the closest. For a definition of families and households, see text, Section 1.

Poverty—Families and unrelated individuals are classified as being above or below poverty following the Office of Management and Budget's Statistical Policy Directive 14. The Census Bureau uses a set of thresholds that vary by family size and composition. Official poverty thresholds do not vary geographically, but they are updated every year to reflect changes in the consumer price index (CPI-U). The official poverty definition uses money income before taxes and does not include capital gains nor noncash benefits (such as public housing, Medicaid, and Supplemental Nutrition Assistance Program benefits). More information is available on the Census Bureau website at <www.census.gov/topics/income-poverty/poverty.html>, and on the U.S. Department of Health and Human Services website at <aspe.hhs.gov/topics/poverty-economic-mobility/poverty-guidelines>.

Supplemental Measure of Poverty—The official poverty measure, in use since the 1960s, estimates poverty rates by looking at a family's or an individual's cash income. The Census Bureau's supplemental poverty measure (SPM), developed after years of research and analysis, is a more complex statistic that starts with a household's cash income, then adds tax credits and noncash government benefits (such as nutritional assistance and housing subsidies) and subtracts necessary expenses (including taxes, health care, child care, and work expenses such as commuting costs). Thresholds for the SPM are derived from Consumer Expenditure Survey data on expenditures for basic necessities (food, shelter, clothing and utilities) and are adjusted for geographic differences in the cost of housing. Unlike the official poverty thresholds, the SPM thresholds are not intended to assess eligibility for government programs. Instead, this new measure serves as an additional indicator of economic well-being and provides a deeper understanding of economic conditions and policy effects. More detailed information, including the history and methodology for developing the SPM, can be found online at <www2.census.gov/programs-surveys/supplemental-poverty-measure/datasets/spm/spm_techdoc.pdf>

Statistical reliability—For discussions of statistical collections performed by the Census Bureau, see Appendix III.

Table 705. Gross Domestic Product in Current and Chained (2017) Dollars: 1990 to 2023

[In billions of dollars (5,963 represents $5,963,000,000,000). For explanation of gross domestic product and chained dollars, see text, this section. Minus sign (-) indicates decrease]

Item	1990	2000	2005	2010	2012	2013	2014	2015	2016	2017	2018	2019	2020	2021	2022	2023
CURRENT DOLLARS																
Gross domestic product	5,963	10,251	13,039	15,049	16,254	16,881	17,608	18,295	18,805	19,612	20,657	21,521	21,323	23,594	25,744	27,361
Personal consumption expenditures	3,809	6,767	8,769	10,260	11,047	11,388	11,874	12,297	12,727	13,291	13,934	14,418	14,206	16,043	17,512	18,571
Durable goods	497	913	1,129	1,049	1,144	1,192	1,247	1,316	1,356	1,416	1,489	1,523	1,629	2,006	2,129	2,199
Nondurable goods	994	1,541	1,954	2,269	2,494	2,550	2,639	2,639	2,677	2,796	2,925	3,006	3,084	3,500	3,868	3,993
Services	2,318	4,314	5,686	6,942	7,410	7,646	7,988	8,342	8,694	9,078	9,520	9,888	9,493	10,536	11,515	12,379
Gross private domestic investment	993	2,038	2,535	2,165	2,622	2,838	3,074	3,288	3,278	3,468	3,725	3,892	3,748	4,216	4,757	4,844
Fixed investment	979	1,984	2,477	2,112	2,551	2,733	2,989	3,148	3,239	3,435	3,668	3,820	3,786	4,205	4,599	4,790
Nonresidential	739	1,498	1,621	1,735	2,119	2,221	2,425	2,508	2,529	2,661	2,856	2,993	2,869	3,078	3,433	3,716
Residential	240	485	856	377	432	512	564	641	710	774	812	827	916	1,126	1,166	1,074
Change in private inventories	15	55	58	54	71	105	85	140	39	33	56	72	-38	12	157	54
Net exports of goods and services	-78	-381	-740	-532	-552	-478	-509	-524	-503	-543	-593	-579	-626	-858	-971	-799
Exports	552	1,096	1,302	1,857	2,218	2,288	2,379	2,271	2,236	2,388	2,538	2,538	2,150	2,550	2,995	3,027
Imports	630	1,477	2,041	2,390	2,769	2,766	2,887	2,795	2,739	2,932	3,131	3,117	2,777	3,408	3,966	3,826
Government consumption expenditures and gross investment	1,239	1,826	2,475	3,156	3,136	3,133	3,169	3,233	3,303	3,397	3,590	3,790	3,995	4,193	4,447	4,745
Federal	562	633	948	1,300	1,287	1,227	1,217	1,223	1,237	1,266	1,346	1,422	1,523	1,594	1,636	1,772
National defense	405	393	609	828	814	764	744	730	729	748	795	851	885	899	928	995
Nondefense	157	240	338	472	473	463	473	492	508	518	551	571	639	696	707	777
State and local	676	1,193	1,528	1,855	1,849	1,905	1,952	2,011	2,066	2,131	2,244	2,368	2,471	2,599	2,811	2,973
CHAINED (2017) DOLLARS [1]																
Gross domestic product	10,055	14,096	15,988	16,790	17,443	17,812	18,262	18,800	19,142	19,612	20,194	20,692	20,234	21,408	21,822	22,377
Personal consumption expenditures	6,372	9,167	10,677	11,336	11,686	11,890	12,226	12,639	12,949	13,291	13,655	13,928	13,577	14,718	15,091	15,426
Durable goods	(NA)	(NA)	(NA)	921	1,025	1,088	1,168	1,258	1,326	1,416	1,509	1,559	1,683	1,965	1,960	2,042
Nondurable goods	(NA)	(NA)	(NA)	2,394	2,425	2,479	2,552	2,646	2,720	2,796	2,870	2,952	3,050	3,308	3,328	3,355
Services	(NA)	(NA)	(NA)	8,065	8,265	8,342	8,516	8,739	8,905	9,078	9,277	9,420	8,868	9,483	9,836	10,066
Gross private domestic investment	1,274	2,445	2,782	2,309	2,735	2,939	3,129	3,323	3,320	3,468	3,668	3,780	3,602	3,914	4,103	4,052
Fixed investment	(NA)	(NA)	(NA)	2,270	2,678	2,842	3,053	3,194	3,287	3,435	3,612	3,708	3,630	3,887	3,939	3,965
Nonresidential	(NA)	(NA)	(NA)	1,794	2,137	2,239	2,421	2,499	2,545	2,661	2,844	2,950	2,811	2,975	3,132	3,272
Residential	(NA)	(NA)	(NA)	473	533	601	627	693	742	774	769	761	816	904	823	735
Change in private inventories	(NA)	(NA)	(NA)	54	69	104	85	134	33	33	54	71	-30	13	128	44
Net exports of goods and services	(NA)	(NA)	(NA)	-388	-338	-304	-348	-476	-506	-543	-594	-617	-663	-934	-1,051	-928
Exports	665	1,323	1,466	1,907	2,126	2,190	2,276	2,283	2,294	2,388	2,456	2,469	2,145	2,281	2,440	2,504
Imports	711	1,733	2,177	2,295	2,465	2,495	2,623	2,760	2,800	2,932	3,050	3,086	2,808	3,215	3,491	3,432
Government consumption expenditures and gross investment	2,544	2,851	3,226	3,540	3,356	3,276	3,247	3,314	3,379	3,397	3,465	3,601	3,716	3,705	3,670	3,820
Federal	(NA)	(NA)	(NA)	1,423	1,358	1,284	1,252	1,253	1,260	1,266	1,310	1,360	1,443	1,462	1,421	1,481
National defense	(NA)	(NA)	(NA)	897	848	792	760	745	741	748	775	816	839	823	800	828
Nondefense	(NA)	(NA)	(NA)	524	509	491	491	508	519	518	535	544	604	639	621	653
State and local	(NA)	(NA)	(NA)	2,117	1,998	1,992	1,995	2,061	2,119	2,131	2,155	2,241	2,274	2,244	2,250	2,339
Residual	-89	43	13	-59	-26	-9	-7	-7	-2	—	-1	-5	-15	-15	-14	-28

- Represents zero. NA Not available. [1] Chained (2017) dollar series are calculated as the product of the chain-type quantity index and the 2017 current-dollar value of the corresponding series, divided by 100. Because the formula for the chain-type quantity indexes uses weights of more than one period, the corresponding chained-dollar estimates are usually not additive. The residual line is the difference between the first line and the sum of the most detailed lines.

Source: U.S. Bureau of Economic Analysis, National Income and Product Accounts, "Table 1.1.5. Gross Domestic Product," and "Table 1.1.6. Real Gross Domestic Product, Chained Dollars," <www.bea.gov/itable/national-gdp-and-personal-income>, accessed June 2024.

Table 706. Real Gross Domestic Product, Chained (2017) Dollars—Annual Percent Change: 2000 to 2023

[Percent change from immediate previous year; for example, 2000, change from 1999. For explanation of chained dollars, see text, this section. Minus sign (-) indicates decrease]

Component	2000	2010	2015	2017	2018	2019	2020	2021	2022	2023
Gross domestic product (GDP)	**4.1**	**2.7**	**2.9**	**2.5**	**3.0**	**2.5**	**-2.2**	**5.8**	**1.9**	**2.5**
Personal consumption expenditures	5.0	1.9	3.4	2.6	2.7	2.0	-2.5	8.4	2.5	2.2
Durable goods	8.6	5.6	7.7	6.8	6.6	3.3	8.0	16.7	-0.3	4.2
Nondurable goods	3.2	1.6	3.7	2.8	2.6	2.9	3.3	8.5	0.6	0.8
Services	5.0	1.5	2.6	1.9	2.2	1.5	-5.9	6.9	3.7	2.3
Gross private domestic investment	6.7	14.0	6.2	4.4	5.8	3.1	-4.7	8.7	4.8	-1.2
Fixed investment	7.1	3.1	4.6	4.5	5.1	2.7	-2.1	7.1	1.3	0.6
Nonresidential	9.3	4.5	3.2	4.6	6.9	3.7	-4.7	5.9	5.2	4.5
Structures	8.1	-16.0	0.2	2.6	5.8	2.5	-9.5	-3.2	-2.1	13.2
Equipment	9.7	20.2	3.8	3.8	5.9	1.1	-10.1	6.4	5.2	-0.3
Intellectual property products	9.5	2.7	4.7	6.9	8.9	7.8	4.5	10.4	9.1	4.5
Residential	0.7	-3.1	10.6	4.3	-0.7	-0.9	7.2	10.7	-9.0	-10.6
Exports	8.3	12.6	0.3	4.1	2.9	0.5	-13.1	6.3	7.0	2.6
Goods	9.8	15.2	-0.3	4.1	4.2	0.2	-10.0	7.6	5.8	2.6
Services	4.5	7.5	1.7	4.1	0.3	1.2	-18.7	3.8	9.6	2.5
Imports	13.0	13.0	5.2	4.7	4.0	1.2	-9.0	14.5	8.6	-1.7
Goods	13.1	15.4	5.8	4.5	5.1	0.6	-5.9	14.6	6.8	-1.6
Services	12.7	3.6	2.5	5.7	-0.6	4.0	-21.9	13.9	17.5	-1.7
Government consumption expenditures and gross investment	1.8	-0.1	2.0	0.6	2.0	3.9	3.2	-0.3	-0.9	4.1
Federal	0.3	4.0	0.1	0.5	3.5	3.8	6.1	1.4	-2.8	4.2
National defense	-0.9	2.9	-2.0	1.0	3.5	5.3	2.8	-1.9	-2.8	3.4
Nondefense	2.3	6.0	3.4	-0.2	3.4	1.7	10.9	5.9	-2.9	5.2
State and local	2.7	-2.8	3.3	0.6	1.1	4.0	1.4	-1.3	0.2	4.0

Source: U.S. Bureau of Economic Analysis, National Income and Product Accounts, "Table 1.1.1. Percent Change From Preceding Period in Real Gross Domestic Product," and "Table 1.1.6. Real Gross Domestic Product, Chained Dollars," <www.bea.gov/itable/national-gdp-and-personal-income>, accessed June 2024.

Table 707. Gross Domestic Product in Current and Chained (2017) Dollars by Type of Product and Sector: 2000 to 2023

[In billions of dollars (10,251 represents $10,251,000,000,000). For explanation of chained dollars, see text, this section]

Type of product and sector	2000	2010	2017	2018	2019	2020	2021	2022	2023
CURRENT DOLLARS									
Gross domestic product	**10,251**	**15,049**	**19,612**	**20,657**	**21,521**	**21,323**	**23,594**	**25,744**	**27,361**
Product:									
Goods	3,437	4,394	5,861	6,201	6,463	6,492	7,355	8,198	8,594
Durable goods	2,083	2,477	3,286	3,524	3,661	3,609	4,058	4,505	4,772
Nondurable goods	1,354	1,917	2,576	2,677	2,802	2,884	3,298	3,693	3,822
Services [1]	5,827	9,595	12,074	12,677	13,197	12,928	14,141	15,313	16,414
Structures	987	1,060	1,677	1,779	1,862	1,902	2,098	2,233	2,353
Sector:									
Business [2]	7,876	11,138	14,942	15,777	16,450	16,048	18,089	19,875	21,053
Nonfarm [3]	7,799	11,021	14,803	15,640	16,330	15,931	17,908	19,652	20,850
Farm	77	117	139	137	120	117	181	224	203
Households and institutions	1,191	1,965	2,423	2,539	2,656	2,778	2,916	3,166	3,448
General government [4]	1,184	1,946	2,247	2,341	2,415	2,497	2,589	2,703	2,860
Federal	360	640	702	730	753	787	823	865	915
State and local	824	1,306	1,545	1,611	1,662	1,710	1,766	1,839	1,946
CHAINED (2017) DOLLARS									
Gross domestic product	**14,096**	**16,790**	**19,612**	**20,194**	**20,692**	**20,234**	**21,408**	**21,822**	**22,377**
Product:									
Goods	3,414	4,448	5,861	6,166	6,407	6,463	7,026	7,272	7,476
Durable goods	(NA)	2,444	3,286	3,528	3,638	3,584	3,936	4,138	4,279
Nondurable goods	(NA)	2,007	2,576	2,639	2,769	2,880	3,091	3,138	3,203
Services [1]	9,024	11,092	12,074	12,316	12,556	12,054	12,642	12,946	13,286
Structures	1,788	1,300	1,677	1,713	1,734	1,731	1,769	1,655	1,671
Sector:									
Business [2]	10,302	12,264	14,942	15,457	15,896	15,455	16,575	16,895	17,338
Nonfarm [3]	10,199	12,139	14,803	15,312	15,765	15,324	16,433	16,770	17,203
Farm	103	123	139	144	130	130	141	129	137
Households and institutions	1,848	2,302	2,423	2,472	2,505	2,507	2,562	2,629	2,693
General government [4]	1,971	2,245	2,247	2,266	2,293	2,270	2,280	2,306	2,355
Federal	573	710	702	707	715	736	745	743	753
State and local	1,402	1,536	1,545	1,559	1,577	1,534	1,536	1,563	1,602

NA Not available. [1] Includes government consumption expenditures, which are for services (such as education and national defense) produced by government. In current dollars, these services are valued at their cost of production. [2] Equals gross domestic product excluding gross value added of households and institutions and of general government. [3] Equals gross domestic business value added excluding gross farm value added. [4] Equals compensation of general government employees plus general government consumption of fixed capital.

Source: U.S. Bureau of Economic Analysis, National Income and Product Accounts Tables, <www.bea.gov/itable/national-gdp-and-personal-income>, accessed June 2024.

Table 708. Gross Domestic Product in Current and Chained (2017) Dollars by Industry: 2010 to 2023

[In billions of dollars (15,049 represents $15,049,000,000,000). Based on 2017 North American Industry Classification System (NAICS); see text, Section 15. GDP by industry is the contribution of each private industry and of government to the nation's output, or GDP. An industry's GDP, or its "value added," is equal to its gross output (sales or receipts and other operating income, commodity taxes, and inventory change) minus its intermediate inputs (energy, raw materials, semifinished goods, and services that are purchased from domestic industries or from foreign sources). Detail may not add to total due to rounding]

Industry	Current dollars				Chained (2017) dollars [1]			
	2010	2020	2022	2023	2010	2020	2022	2023
Gross domestic product	**15,049**	**21,323**	**25,744**	**27,361**	**16,790**	**20,234**	**21,822**	**22,377**
Private industries	12,939	18,612	22,807	24,254	14,367	17,762	19,283	19,804
Agriculture, forestry, fishing, and hunting	146	161	271	252	156	174	170	180
Farms	117	117	224	203	123	130	129	137
Forestry, fishing, and related activities	29	44	47	48	33	43	42	44
Mining	306	202	457	381	199	306	245	293
Oil and gas extraction	189	103	325	237	89	211	136	180
Mining, except oil and gas	70	57	78	83	64	55	55	57
Mining support activities	48	41	55	61	53	47	61	59
Utilities	279	345	438	434	291	332	318	344
Construction	526	952	1,090	1,204	657	856	828	836
Manufacturing	1,788	2,148	2,650	2,805	1,951	2,127	2,278	2,291
Durable goods	954	1,200	1,407	1,527	990	1,172	1,297	1,319
Wood products	23	43	62	60	30	37	34	37
Nonmetallic mineral products	38	64	73	77	48	59	60	54
Primary metals	51	56	92	92	41	72	80	93
Fabricated metal products	120	148	165	182	134	135	126	122
Machinery	127	150	182	199	149	139	162	152
Computer and electronic products	229	273	302	312	193	279	303	299
Electrical equipment, appliances, and components	51	58	63	70	53	53	50	51
Motor vehicles, bodies & trailers, & parts	89	143	156	184	97	148	201	223
Other transportation equipment	121	144	173	204	137	138	168	187
Furniture and related products	22	29	31	31	24	27	27	23
Miscellaneous manufacturing	83	92	107	116	88	88	103	103
Nondurable goods	834	948	1,243	1,278	964	956	985	978
Food & beverage & tobacco	224	290	312	340	250	267	307	301
Textile mills and textile product mills	16	16	17	17	16	15	15	14
Apparel and leather and allied products	10	9	10	11	11	10	10	10
Paper products	56	65	69	70	61	68	60	56
Printing and related support activities	39	36	42	44	38	35	35	32
Petroleum and coal products	124	60	200	188	127	88	82	84
Chemical products	303	392	501	513	390	387	413	424
Plastics and rubber products	62	80	90	94	68	77	66	61
Wholesale trade	888	1,300	1,547	1,614	1,000	1,200	1,147	1,125
Retail trade	864	1,336	1,621	1,738	922	1,235	1,182	1,294
Transportation and warehousing	434	637	921	971	514	604	699	730
Air transportation	84	64	152	183	102	71	156	173
Rail transportation	34	42	51	51	41	37	43	39
Water transportation	15	13	21	20	16	13	13	12
Truck transportation	114	196	263	265	136	174	170	176
Transit & ground passenger transport	31	40	57	65	38	42	60	67
Pipeline transportation	20	38	50	53	25	33	37	38
Other transportation & support	91	163	211	211	118	149	148	165
Warehousing and storage	45	82	115	121	40	80	92	84
Information	755	1,178	1,393	1,475	671	1,221	1,506	1,598
Publishing industries, except internet (includes software)	179	302	358	389	158	312	391	420
Motion picture and sound recording	91	76	100	103	91	79	101	105
Broadcasting and telecommunications	376	485	512	520	319	499	549	558
Data processing, internet publishing, & related services	109	315	422	463	103	334	469	521
Finance and insurance	993	1,709	1,933	1,988	1,344	1,542	1,592	1,547
Real estate and rental and leasing	1,997	2,898	3,397	3,668	2,301	2,676	2,962	2,999
Professional, scientific, and technical services	1,065	1,672	2,013	2,182	1,138	1,651	1,973	2,071
Legal services	205	288	329	339	268	254	263	256
Computer systems design, related services	203	393	458	486	175	435	547	608
Miscellaneous services	657	991	1,226	1,357	712	969	1,181	1,238
Management of companies & enterprises	265	405	480	506	262	431	524	538
Administrative and waste management services	438	649	821	856	494	615	732	721
Educational services	199	256	293	316	242	237	259	266
Health care and social assistance	1,112	1,619	1,856	2,036	1,217	1,531	1,665	1,752
Ambulatory health care services	532	765	896	981	556	743	836	901
Hospitals	370	538	600	656	417	506	527	542
Nursing and residential care facilities	121	165	178	195	138	146	149	152
Social assistance	90	151	182	204	107	136	154	160
Arts, entertainment, and recreation	152	170	271	317	178	156	240	259
Performing arts, spectator sports, museums, & related	88	100	160	193	103	95	150	168
Amusements, gambling, & recreation	65	70	111	124	76	61	91	93
Accommodation and food services	404	524	810	914	500	480	645	658
Accommodation	112	127	216	240	135	133	180	191
Food services and drinking places	292	397	595	674	365	347	465	468
Other services, except government	328	453	544	597	392	407	434	428
Government	2,110	2,711	2,937	3,107	2,461	2,465	2,526	2,560
Federal	699	859	939	994	772	802	802	813
State and local	1,411	1,852	1,997	2,113	1,689	1,663	1,724	1,748

[1] Chained (2017) dollar series are calculated as the product of the chain-type quantity index and the 2017 current-dollar value of the corresponding series, divided by 100. Because the formula for the chain-type quantity indexes uses weights of more than one period, the corresponding chained-dollar estimates are usually not additive.

Source: U.S. Bureau of Economic Analysis, Industry Economic Accounts, "GDP by Industry," <www.bea.gov/itable/gdp-by-industry>, accessed June 2024.

Income, Expenditures, Poverty, and Wealth   465

Table 709. Relation of GDP, GNP, Net National Product, National Income, Personal Income, Disposable Personal Income, and Personal Saving: 2000 to 2023

[In billions of dollars (10,251 represents $10,251,000,000,000). For definitions, see text, this section. Minus sign (-) indicates deficit or net disbursement]

Item	2000	2010	2015	2019	2020	2021	2022	2023
Gross domestic product (GDP)	**10,251**	**15,049**	**18,295**	**21,521**	**21,323**	**23,594**	**25,744**	**27,361**
Plus: Income receipts from the rest of the world. . . .	391	760	861	1,175	993	1,112	1,253	1,457
Less: Income payments to the rest of the world. . . .	352	554	640	893	778	929	1,071	1,293
Equals: Gross national product (GNP)	**10,289**	**15,255**	**18,515**	**21,803**	**21,538**	**23,778**	**25,926**	**27,525**
Less: Consumption of fixed capital	1,511	2,390	2,923	3,480	3,626	3,873	4,300	4,586
Equals: Net national product	**8,778**	**12,864**	**15,592**	**18,323**	**17,912**	**19,904**	**21,626**	**22,939**
Less: Statistical discrepancy	-96	69	-93	42	58	-5	-52	510
Equals: National income	**8,874**	**12,795**	**15,685**	**18,281**	**17,854**	**19,910**	**21,678**	**22,430**
Less:								
Corporate profits [1]	826	1,774	2,173	2,470	2,383	2,923	3,209	3,258
Taxes on production and imports less subsidies...	663	1,007	1,216	1,460	864	1,189	1,683	1,732
Contributions for government social insurance....	706	984	1,205	1,425	1,449	1,558	1,702	1,803
Net interest and miscellaneous payments on assets	504	438	496	515	529	505	457	185
Business current transfer payments (net)	85	126	154	161	145	189	217	214
Current surplus of government enterprises	11	-19	-3	-12	-2	-5	4	-10
Plus: Personal income receipts on assets	1,456	1,748	2,345	2,950	2,914	3,215	3,432	3,613
Personal current transfer receipts	1,087	2,325	2,685	3,144	4,230	4,642	4,002	4,101
Equals: Personal income	**8,621**	**12,557**	**15,474**	**18,356**	**19,629**	**21,408**	**21,841**	**22,961**
Less: Personal current taxes	1,236	1,238	1,941	2,199	2,256	2,743	3,138	2,756
Equals: Disposable personal income	**7,385**	**11,319**	**13,533**	**16,157**	**17,373**	**18,664**	**18,702**	**20,205**
Less: Personal outlays	7,068	10,648	12,742	14,966	14,694	16,544	18,080	19,305
Equals: Personal saving	**317**	**671**	**791**	**1,191**	**2,679**	**2,121**	**623**	**900**

[1] Corporate profits with inventory valuation and capital consumption adjustments.

Source: U.S. Bureau of Economic Analysis, National Income and Product Accounts, "Table 1.7.5. Relation of Gross Domestic Product, Gross National Product, Net National Product, National Income, and Personal Income," and "Table 2.1. Personal Income and Its Disposition," <www.bea.gov/itable/national-gdp-and-personal-income>, accessed June 2024

Table 710. Gross Saving and Investment: 2000 to 2023

[In billions of dollars (2,126 represents $2,126,000,000,000), except as noted. Minus (-) sign indicates deficit]

Item	2000	2010	2015	2019	2020	2021	2022	2023
Gross saving	**2,126**	**2,301**	**3,588**	**4,177**	**3,937**	**4,201**	**4,700**	**4,495**
Net saving	615	-90	665	697	311	327	400	-90
Net private saving	497	1,538	1,439	1,947	3,258	2,824	1,402	1,724
Domestic business	180	866	648	756	579	703	779	824
Undistributed corporate profits	140	970	713	661	691	1,030	1,093	1,126
Inventory valuation adjustment, corporate	-17	-48	58	2	-17	-257	-96	40
Capital consumption adjustment, corporate	57	-57	-122	94	-95	-69	-218	-341
Households and institutions	317	671	791	1,191	2,679	2,121	623	900
Personal saving	317	671	791	1,191	2,679	2,121	623	900
Net government saving	118	-1,627	-774	-1,250	-2,946	-2,497	-1,002	-1,814
Federal	160	-1,318	-557	-1,044	-2,894	-2,740	-1,062	-1,664
State and local	-41	-309	-217	-206	-52	243	60	-150
Consumption of fixed capital	1,511	2,390	2,923	3,480	3,626	3,873	4,300	4,586
Private	1,232	1,933	2,398	2,882	3,008	3,214	3,578	3,822
Domestic business	1,005	1,537	1,906	2,267	2,360	2,492	2,757	2,966
Households and institutions	227	397	492	615	647	722	821	856
Government	280	457	525	598	618	659	722	764
Federal	163	244	272	299	309	326	351	371
State and local	117	213	253	299	308	333	372	393
Gross domestic investment, capital account transactions, and net lending	**2,030**	**2,370**	**3,495**	**4,219**	**3,995**	**4,195**	**4,648**	**5,005**
Gross domestic investment	2,427	2,810	3,918	4,667	4,565	5,043	5,633	5,836
Gross private domestic investment	2,038	2,165	3,288	3,892	3,748	4,216	4,757	4,844
Gross government investment	389	645	629	775	816	827	877	993
Capital account transactions (net) [1]	5	7	8	7	6	4	5	14
Net lending or net borrowing	-401	-447	-431	-455	-576	-851	-991	-845
Statistical discrepancy	-96	69	-93	42	58	-5	-52	510
Addenda:								
Gross private saving	1,728	3,471	3,837	4,829	6,265	6,038	4,979	5,546
Gross government saving	398	-1,170	-249	-652	-2,328	-1,838	-280	-1,051
Federal	323	-1,075	-285	-745	-2,585	-2,414	-711	-1,294
State and local	75	-96	36	93	257	576	432	243
Net domestic investment	916	420	995	1,188	939	1,170	1,334	1,251
Gross saving as a percent of gross national income	20.5	15.2	19.3	19.2	18.3	17.7	18.1	16.6
Net saving as a percent of gross national income	5.9	-0.6	3.6	3.2	1.4	1.4	1.5	-0.3
Disaster losses [2]	—	—	—	—	—	62	60	—

– Represents zero. [1] Consists of capital transfers and the acquisition and disposal of nonproduced nonfinancial assets. [2] Consists of damages to fixed assets.

Source: U.S. Bureau of Economic Analysis, National Income and Product Accounts, "Table 5.1 Saving and Investment by Sector," <www.bea.gov/itable/national-gdp-and-personal-income>, accessed June 2024.

Table 711. Gross Domestic Product by State in Current and Chained (2017) Dollars: 2010 to 2023

[In billions of dollars (15,049.0 represents $15,049,000,000,000). For definition of gross domestic product by state or chained dollars, see text, this section]

State	Current dollars					Chained (2017) dollars [2]				
	2010	2020	2021	2022	2023	2010	2020	2021	2022	2023
United States [1]	**15,049.0**	**21,323.0**	**23,594.0**	**25,744.1**	**27,360.9**	**16,789.8**	**20,234.1**	**21,407.7**	**21,822.0**	**22,376.9**
Alabama	177.5	235.1	258.0	281.6	300.2	199.5	222.1	231.9	235.8	241.8
Alaska	53.7	51.3	58.6	65.7	67.3	53.7	50.3	51.0	50.3	53.0
Arizona	250.5	386.4	432.3	475.7	508.3	282.3	362.6	390.8	403.5	414.3
Arkansas	101.7	135.9	151.9	166.0	176.2	113.0	128.1	135.6	137.4	140.8
California	1,938.6	3,068.8	3,416.9	3,641.6	3,862.2	2,153.9	2,925.1	3,146.2	3,167.5	3,233.2
Colorado	256.8	397.6	447.1	491.3	520.4	279.4	380.9	407.0	416.1	428.0
Connecticut	234.0	275.8	295.9	319.3	340.2	266.8	258.6	268.8	276.7	282.5
Delaware	58.1	77.6	83.0	90.2	93.6	68.3	72.6	74.4	75.2	74.3
District of Columbia	106.1	146.9	156.1	165.1	174.8	120.4	137.8	142.7	144.0	145.5
Florida	753.0	1,140.1	1,292.4	1,439.1	1,579.5	852.0	1,068.4	1,164.8	1,218.4	1,279.1
Georgia	419.0	637.9	701.6	767.4	805.4	471.6	602.3	639.2	655.8	661.1
Hawaii	66.7	84.6	93.1	101.1	108.0	76.1	79.6	84.1	85.2	86.9
Idaho	56.1	88.2	98.8	110.9	118.8	62.6	82.8	88.0	91.7	94.9
Illinois	663.9	860.7	944.0	1,025.7	1,083.0	755.4	810.2	852.7	864.2	875.6
Indiana	284.7	377.9	423.0	470.3	497.0	320.7	359.2	384.1	396.0	401.5
Iowa	142.5	199.4	220.8	238.3	248.9	161.6	187.1	198.5	197.8	200.4
Kansas	129.2	177.7	191.8	209.3	226.0	143.9	168.5	172.8	174.8	182.3
Kentucky	166.7	218.8	237.9	259.0	277.7	186.7	206.3	214.6	217.6	225.2
Louisiana	226.6	236.1	263.2	292.0	309.6	253.5	228.8	234.0	231.3	238.2
Maine	52.8	72.1	78.9	85.8	91.1	60.0	67.4	70.9	72.4	73.8
Maryland	313.9	413.4	446.9	480.1	512.3	352.6	388.5	405.9	412.3	421.0
Massachusetts	409.3	589.0	645.4	691.5	733.9	462.3	556.2	591.9	604.4	615.1
Michigan	393.2	530.2	576.5	622.6	659.0	441.3	502.5	531.5	539.9	547.8
Minnesota	274.6	379.4	413.1	448.0	471.8	308.1	358.1	374.7	379.1	383.6
Mississippi	94.8	116.2	128.4	140.0	146.4	106.7	109.9	114.2	114.2	114.9
Missouri	262.0	335.3	365.1	396.9	422.3	296.0	315.3	330.1	336.6	344.1
Montana	38.1	53.1	60.0	67.1	70.6	42.5	50.2	53.0	54.0	55.2
Nebraska	91.9	135.3	149.4	164.9	178.4	103.9	126.9	133.5	137.1	144.2
Nevada	125.1	176.0	200.1	222.9	239.4	142.6	165.8	181.1	187.2	192.2
New Hampshire	65.3	88.6	99.1	105.0	111.1	73.0	83.2	89.9	90.2	91.3
New Jersey	491.2	630.2	692.2	754.9	799.3	554.8	596.0	629.0	646.7	656.5
New Mexico	84.9	100.4	111.7	125.5	130.2	90.7	97.5	99.6	101.3	105.5
New York	1,217.7	1,766.9	1,911.3	2,048.4	2,152.3	1,431.6	1,650.6	1,724.5	1,763.5	1,775.7
North Carolina	422.3	601.1	659.5	716.0	766.9	482.0	564.8	597.3	609.1	625.7
North Dakota	35.7	55.3	63.2	72.7	74.1	38.7	55.7	55.4	54.8	58.0
Ohio	500.3	692.1	759.6	826.0	872.7	563.8	654.6	686.2	689.7	698.2
Oklahoma	155.3	191.7	217.7	242.7	254.1	158.1	190.8	193.5	191.6	201.7
Oregon	163.2	251.9	275.4	297.3	316.5	180.7	237.7	250.1	254.7	260.1
Pennsylvania	604.6	777.4	844.4	911.8	965.1	666.8	736.5	764.6	772.3	789.5
Rhode Island	49.4	62.1	67.2	72.8	77.3	56.1	58.2	60.8	62.2	63.2
South Carolina	166.8	249.5	271.5	297.5	322.3	188.8	233.7	244.9	250.9	259.9
South Dakota	38.2	56.2	62.6	68.8	72.4	44.8	52.7	55.1	55.0	56.3
Tennessee	258.7	390.2	438.2	485.7	523.2	292.7	366.6	396.6	412.1	425.4
Texas	1,255.7	1,798.6	2,087.5	2,402.1	2,563.5	1,323.1	1,772.2	1,873.5	1,924.0	2,032.9
Utah	118.3	205.7	232.1	256.4	272.6	133.7	194.8	210.0	213.9	219.2
Vermont	27.5	34.5	37.6	40.8	43.1	30.9	32.3	33.9	34.6	35.1
Virginia	425.5	565.1	613.9	663.1	707.1	475.7	533.8	562.9	577.0	590.8
Washington	363.5	621.5	688.6	738.1	801.5	403.5	590.4	630.8	641.1	672.1
West Virginia	66.2	77.0	86.5	97.4	99.5	71.8	74.0	75.5	76.5	80.1
Wisconsin	256.2	343.8	369.0	396.2	414.0	287.7	323.0	334.5	335.7	336.5
Wyoming	37.6	36.7	42.2	49.1	50.2	39.1	36.2	36.9	37.3	39.3

[1] The difference between the United States and sum-of-states reflects overseas activity, economic activity taking place outside the borders of the United States by the military and associated federal civilian support staff. [2] Real GDP is in millions of chained 2017 dollars. Calculations are performed on unrounded data. Chained (2017) dollar series are calculated as the product of the chain-type quantity index and the 2017 current-dollar value of the corresponding series, divided by 100. Because the formula for the chain-type quantity indexes uses weights of more than one period, the corresponding chained-dollar estimates are usually not additive. The difference between the United States and sum-of-states reflects federal military and civilian activity located overseas.

Source: U.S. Bureau of Economic Analysis, Regional Economic Accounts, GDP by State, Interactive Data, "Annual Gross Domestic Product (GDP) by State," <www.bea.gov/data/economic-accounts/regional>, accessed June 2024.

Table 712. Gross Domestic Product by Selected Industry and State: 2023

[In billions of current dollars (27,360.9 represents $27,360,900,000,000). For definition of gross domestic product by state, see text, this section. Industries based on 2017 North American Industry Classification System; see text, Section 15]

State	Total [1]	Manu-facturing	Whole-sale trade	Retail trade	Infor-mation	Finance and insur-ance	Real estate, rental, and leasing	Profes-sional and technical services	Health care and social assis-tance	Govern-ment [2]
United States [3]	27,360.9	2,804.7	1,613.7	1,738.5	1,475.1	1,988.2	3,668.2	2,182.0	2,036.0	3,107.4
Alabama	300.2	48.1	17.6	22.7	6.1	15.7	34.7	19.1	21.8	48.1
Alaska	67.3	1.9	1.7	3.4	1.6	1.4	6.9	2.2	5.5	12.4
Arizona	508.3	40.8	28.1	37.9	16.2	34.1	86.6	29.4	42.5	56.4
Arkansas	176.2	25.9	14.1	14.1	3.6	7.8	19.3	6.9	15.1	19.9
California	3,862.2	417.0	205.8	232.1	411.6	191.5	530.3	371.6	252.7	407.6
Colorado	520.4	29.1	28.0	31.1	31.1	26.2	81.8	58.0	30.7	58.3
Connecticut	340.2	40.7	18.5	20.0	18.7	44.2	45.7	24.1	28.9	29.9
Delaware	93.6	6.7	2.7	4.2	1.3	20.8	18.0	5.9	7.4	8.7
District of Columbia	174.8	(D)	1.9	2.0	11.8	6.7	16.2	35.5	8.2	55.1
Florida	1,579.5	77.7	110.2	127.4	53.9	90.4	293.5	129.1	125.2	143.4
Georgia	805.4	77.2	58.3	52.3	48.9	58.0	110.4	57.8	53.4	84.7
Hawaii	108.0	1.8	3.3	8.3	2.6	4.3	18.6	4.9	7.8	20.7
Idaho	118.8	11.7	8.2	10.0	2.7	5.3	16.9	7.3	9.9	13.3
Illinois	1,083.0	133.4	85.3	65.5	39.5	88.5	136.4	91.9	79.4	95.5
Indiana	497.0	127.4	29.4	31.1	7.9	25.2	51.8	23.7	40.3	42.7
Iowa	248.9	41.2	15.0	14.8	6.0	32.3	22.2	8.7	15.5	25.3
Kansas	226.0	32.9	13.8	14.5	10.2	11.2	28.8	12.3	16.6	26.5
Kentucky	277.7	45.1	20.4	18.9	6.8	14.3	29.4	12.1	26.0	33.5
Louisiana	309.6	57.5	16.6	22.6	5.0	14.0	34.3	14.5	25.8	33.2
Maine	91.1	8.1	4.4	8.5	1.7	5.9	14.4	5.3	9.8	10.7
Maryland	512.3	26.9	21.9	29.3	20.3	22.4	78.2	54.2	38.7	105.3
Massachusetts	733.9	56.6	34.1	35.0	42.8	60.8	101.3	107.5	67.5	66.2
Michigan	659.0	107.7	44.6	47.4	17.3	32.1	89.5	51.9	55.2	65.3
Minnesota	471.8	57.2	33.6	28.8	15.9	37.6	58.0	32.6	44.8	42.6
Mississippi	146.4	22.0	7.6	13.1	3.1	6.9	16.7	5.0	11.2	23.9
Missouri	422.3	48.3	28.0	29.3	14.8	28.9	52.7	30.7	38.3	43.7
Montana	70.6	4.3	4.0	5.3	1.8	3.4	9.8	4.4	6.9	9.1
Nebraska	178.4	19.9	10.8	9.0	4.6	22.0	16.0	7.5	12.6	19.2
Nevada	239.4	10.7	9.8	17.4	6.2	13.4	35.4	12.3	14.6	23.1
New Hampshire	111.1	10.7	7.9	8.9	4.1	7.0	15.7	10.3	9.8	10.5
New Jersey	799.3	65.4	66.9	50.1	36.2	50.7	128.5	77.4	66.9	74.3
New Mexico	130.2	4.4	4.0	7.8	2.9	4.5	15.3	10.9	9.3	30.1
New York	2,152.3	83.8	88.2	105.5	173.4	416.9	302.0	186.3	165.4	210.2
North Carolina	766.9	103.5	47.2	49.6	28.9	66.6	92.6	57.4	52.6	90.6
North Dakota	74.1	5.7	5.5	4.2	1.6	3.1	7.0	2.3	5.9	7.2
Ohio	872.7	131.0	53.8	58.4	20.4	94.8	100.1	48.4	75.7	87.0
Oklahoma	254.1	20.2	12.2	17.4	6.3	10.2	27.9	10.7	19.1	40.2
Oregon	316.5	36.4	17.6	19.7	13.4	13.5	43.3	19.9	27.6	42.3
Pennsylvania	965.1	109.7	54.4	61.1	47.2	62.2	122.0	76.8	98.8	85.2
Rhode Island	77.3	6.1	4.1	5.1	1.9	6.3	11.6	5.1	7.8	10.3
South Carolina	322.3	42.5	20.6	25.6	8.4	14.9	47.5	19.3	21.5	44.2
South Dakota	72.4	5.5	4.8	5.4	1.6	10.5	6.7	2.6	6.5	7.3
Tennessee	523.2	69.8	34.5	41.9	17.1	29.4	61.6	31.5	47.3	52.2
Texas	2,563.5	296.4	195.1	159.1	102.7	145.9	331.9	190.1	147.8	236.8
Utah	272.6	30.8	12.5	22.1	13.7	22.9	33.0	20.5	14.7	28.7
Vermont	43.1	3.6	2.0	3.7	1.2	2.1	5.8	3.4	4.5	5.9
Virginia	707.1	51.7	31.5	42.5	31.0	37.7	96.8	91.3	46.2	115.9
Washington	801.5	68.6	39.5	55.2	132.0	27.9	102.7	63.9	47.3	89.2
West Virginia	99.5	9.1	4.5	7.4	1.8	3.5	10.3	3.9	10.2	15.6
Wisconsin	414.0	68.0	27.4	28.7	14.4	31.0	46.9	21.5	36.7	42.2
Wyoming	50.2	(D)	1.6	3.1	0.8	1.6	5.4	1.9	2.1	7.4

D Not shown to avoid disclosure of confidential information; estimates are included in higher-level totals. [1] Includes industries not shown separately. [2] Includes federal civilian and military, and state and local government. [3] The difference between the United States and sum-of-states reflects overseas activity, economic activity taking place outside the borders of the United States by the military and associated federal civilian support staff.

Source: U.S. Bureau of Economic Analysis, Regional Economic Accounts, GDP by State, Interactive Data, "Annual Gross Domestic Product (GDP) by State," <www.bea.gov/data/economic-accounts/regional>, accessed June 2024.

Table 713. Household Production Value: 1965 to 2020

[In billions of dollars (277.4 represents $277,400,000,000). Measures the value of time spent on the unpaid work of household production tasks. Household production hours are aggregated across seven categories: housework, cooking, odd jobs, gardening, shopping, child care, and domestic travel related to these tasks. The value of these nonmarket services is the product of the wage rate of general purpose domestic workers and the number of hours worked]

Year	Household production value (bil. dol.)	Year	Household production value (bil. dol.)	Year	Household production value (bil. dol.)	Year	Household production value (bil. dol.)
1965	277.4	2000	2,921.6	2007	3,631.5	2014	4,212.3
1970	428.0	2001	2,800.3	2008	3,828.5	2015	4,405.7
1975	707.4	2002	2,780.7	2009	3,691.9	2016	4,571.0
1980	1,106.9	2003	3,045.1	2010	3,643.5	2017	4,506.0
1985	1,467.0	2004	3,185.0	2011	3,704.6	2018	4,668.6
1990	1,902.6	2005	3,210.2	2012	3,780.4	2019	4,638.8
1995	2,395.9	2006	3,407.9	2013	4,096.5	2020	5,316.8

Source: U.S. Bureau of Economic Analysis, Special Topics, "Household Production Satellite Account," <www.bea.gov/data/special-topics/household-production>, accessed March 2022.

Table 714. Financial Accounts of the United States—Composition of Individuals' Savings: 1990 to 2023

[In billions of dollars (676.4 represents $676,400,000,000). Combined statement for households, nonprofit organizations, and nonfinancial noncorporate business. Minus sign (-) indicates decrease. All data are subject to revision]

Composition of savings	1990	2000	2010	2019	2020	2021	2022	2023
Net acquisition of financial assets	**676.4**	**925.7**	**1,099.9**	**2,502.4**	**4,475.3**	**3,644.1**	**2,228.6**	**1,760.6**
Foreign deposits	1.4	7.6	4.5	-1.2	7.8	-0.2	3.4	-5.2
Checkable deposits and currency	13.1	-91.5	-39.2	38.2	2,042.5	1,049.6	431.9	-186.2
Time and savings deposits	43.8	340.9	183.2	610.5	628.0	875.0	-721.9	-397.4
Money market fund shares	43.1	184.1	-319.8	449.0	438.1	115.6	283.5	727.1
Debt securities	144.1	-72.7	197.0	145.5	-602.2	-1,000.5	1,523.1	1,089.1
Treasury securities	32.9	-188.5	267.8	127.1	-331.6	-649.9	1,123.9	817.5
Agency and GSE-backed securities [1]	35.9	31.0	42.0	34.3	-297.8	-21.0	672.2	174.7
Municipal securities	35.8	17.6	79.1	-64.0	-26.8	-112.2	30.6	93.2
Corporate and foreign bonds	39.5	67.1	-191.9	48.1	54.0	-217.4	-303.6	3.8
Loans	81.6	115.3	42.2	39.8	114.7	88.6	-46.7	-69.5
Corporate equities [2]	-66.2	-323.7	-55.0	345.8	624.6	1,103.4	590.2	-57.2
Mutual fund shares	29.8	81.9	260.5	303.8	-159.5	542.2	-724.1	-164.2
Trade receivables	5.9	10.1	6.1	-1.2	22.5	11.8	13.2	14.3
Life insurance reserves	28.2	44.3	16.6	20.0	93.4	30.9	58.9	55.2
Pension entitlements	333.9	446.6	668.1	431.9	427.7	230.1	504.7	551.1
Miscellaneous and other assets	17.7	182.7	131.8	120.2	837.7	597.6	312.4	203.7
Gross investment in nonfinancial assets	**827.6**	**1,587.1**	**1,669.4**	**2,776.2**	**2,936.7**	**3,513.3**	**3,735.1**	**3,759.4**
Minus: Consumption of fixed capital	618.4	1,012.4	1,568.3	2,135.4	2,238.7	2,486.2	2,825.6	2,970.0
Equals: Net investment in nonfinancial assets	**209.2**	**574.8**	**101.1**	**640.8**	**698.1**	**1,027.1**	**909.5**	**789.4**
Net increase in liabilities	**240.5**	**923.8**	**-194.4**	**770.3**	**1,676.6**	**2,198.4**	**1,723.9**	**808.2**
Home mortgages	207.0	423.0	-129.2	299.5	479.9	890.7	896.1	381.7
Other mortgages	-4.4	106.3	-33.3	125.7	276.2	291.8	279.4	193.3
Consumer credit	15.1	176.5	-28.2	185.2	-12.0	237.8	345.5	125.6
Other loans and advances	6.2	16.4	37.8	26.8	238.5	171.3	-82.2	25.6
Other liabilities	16.6	201.5	-41.6	133.1	694.1	606.7	285.0	82.0
Personal saving, FOF concept (FOF) [3]	660.8	612.3	1,367.2	2,388.0	3,499.8	2,425.2	1,406.7	1,637.7
Personal saving, NIPA concept (FOF) [3]	584.0	369.0	1,311.2	2,160.7	3,217.5	1,952.7	1,016.6	1,267.1
Personal saving, NIPA concept (NIPA) [4]	360.6	316.8	671.4	1,190.9	2,678.6	2,120.5	622.8	912.2

[1] GSE = government-sponsored enterprises. [2] Only directly held and those in closed-end and exchange-traded funds. Other equities are included in mutual funds, life insurance reserves, and pension entitlements. [3] Flow of Funds measure. [4] National Income and Product Accounts measure.

Source: Board of Governors of the Federal Reserve System, "Z.1 Financial Accounts of the United States: Summary Table F.6 Derivation of Measures of Personal Saving," March 2024, <www.federalreserve.gov/releases/Z1/current/default.htm>, accessed March 2024.

Table 715. Government Consumption Expenditures and Gross Investment by Level of Government and Type: 2010 to 2023

[In billions of dollars (3,156 represents $3,156,000,000,000). Government consumption expenditures are services (such as education and national defense) produced by government that are valued at their cost of production; excludes government sales to other sectors and government own-account investment (construction, software, and research and development). Gross government investment consists of general government and government enterprise expenditures for fixed assets; inventory investment is included in government consumption expenditures. For explanation of national income and chained dollars, see text, Section 13]

Level of government and type	Current dollars				Chained (2017) dollars			
	2010	2020	2022	2023	2010	2020	2022	2023
Government consumption expenditures and gross investment, total	**3,156**	**3,995**	**4,447**	**4,745**	**3,540**	**3,716**	**3,670**	**3,820**
Consumption expenditures	2,511	3,178	3,570	3,753	2,826	2,945	2,929	3,009
Gross investment	645	816	877	993	713	771	741	811
Structures	312	380	387	460	370	345	293	333
Equipment	148	168	168	180	151	167	152	158
Intellectual property products	184	269	321	353	195	260	302	324
Federal	**1,300**	**1,523**	**1,636**	**1,772**	**1,423**	**1,443**	**1,421**	**1,481**
Consumption expenditures	1,003	1,159	1,229	1,329	1,107	1,091	1,053	1,092
Gross investment	297	365	407	443	315	352	369	391
Structures	33	28	28	33	39	26	22	24
Equipment	108	120	118	122	111	118	106	107
Intellectual property products	156	217	260	287	167	208	241	260
National defense	**828**	**885**	**928**	**995**	**897**	**839**	**800**	**828**
Consumption expenditures	652	698	726	777	711	658	618	637
Gross investment	176	187	202	218	186	181	183	191
Structures	17	12	13	14	20	11	10	11
Equipment	89	95	92	96	91	94	85	86
Intellectual property products	70	80	97	107	76	76	89	94
Nondefense	**472**	**639**	**707**	**777**	**524**	**604**	**621**	**653**
Consumption expenditures	351	461	503	552	395	433	435	455
Gross investment	121	178	204	225	129	171	186	200
Structures	16	17	16	19	19	15	12	13
Equipment	19	25	25	26	20	24	22	22
Intellectual property products	86	136	163	180	91	132	153	165
State and local	**1,855**	**2,471**	**2,811**	**2,973**	**2,117**	**2,274**	**2,250**	**2,339**
Consumption expenditures	1,508	2,020	2,341	2,423	1,719	1,855	1,874	1,916
Gross investment	347	452	470	550	398	419	375	422
Structures	280	351	359	427	331	319	272	309
Equipment	40	48	51	58	40	48	46	51
Intellectual property products	28	52	61	65	28	52	60	64

Source: U.S. Bureau of Economic Analysis, National Income and Product Accounts Tables, "Table 3.9.5 Government Consumption Expenditures and Gross Investment" and "Table 3.9.6 Real Government Consumption Expenditures and Gross Investment, Chained Dollars," <www.bea.gov/itable/national-gdp-and-personal-income>, accessed June 2024.

Table 716. Personal Consumption Expenditures by Function: 2010 to 2022

[In billions of dollars (10,260 represents $10,260,000,000,000). For definition of chained dollars, see text, this section. Minus sign (-) indicates decrease]

Function	Current dollars				Chained (2017) dollars			
	2010	2015	2020	2022	2010	2015	2020	2022
Personal consumption expenditures [1]	**10,260**	**12,297**	**14,206**	**17,512**	**11,336**	**12,639**	**13,577**	**15,091**
Food and nonalcoholic beverages purchased for off-premises consumption	679	809	1,007	1,179	748	796	959	973
Alcoholic beverages purchased for off-premises consumption	108	132	189	214	113	134	181	195
Clothing, footwear, and related services	332	397	381	518	348	395	404	510
Clothing (garments, cleaning, repair, and rental)	269	316	299	408	281	314	320	406
Footwear [2]	62	81	82	110	66	81	84	104
Housing [1]	1,648	1,879	2,324	2,618	1,977	2,009	2,114	2,196
Rental of tenant-occupied nonfarm housing [3]	361	446	530	593	446	480	478	494
Imputed rental of owner-occupied nonfarm housing [4]	1,268	1,411	1,771	1,999	1,507	1,506	1,613	1,679
Household utilities and fuels	324	338	372	467	359	348	361	369
Water supply and sanitation	78	91	110	121	105	98	100	101
Electricity, gas, and other fuels	246	247	262	347	255	250	262	268
Furnishings, household equipment, and routine household maintenance [1]	411	495	621	756	378	480	603	647
Furniture, furnishings, and floor coverings [5]	128	153	193	247	110	145	194	211
Household appliances [6]	50	64	77	95	44	59	70	74
Tools and equipment for house and garden	20	32	49	60	20	32	48	51
Medical products, appliances, and equipment [1]	379	477	589	658	452	506	579	639
Pharmaceutical and other medical products [7]	326	418	523	575	397	446	514	559
Outpatient services	775	935	1,080	1,288	823	953	1,041	1,183
Physician services [8]	411	496	570	662	423	499	554	617
Dental services	104	117	119	161	124	123	110	140
Paramedical services [9]	260	322	391	465	279	331	377	426
Hospital and nursing home services	925	1,125	1,274	1,489	1,042	1,161	1,175	1,298
Transportation	962	1,182	1,144	1,770	984	1,180	1,137	1,331
Motor vehicles	288	416	458	617	298	406	449	479
New motor vehicles	182	277	293	375	196	277	291	319
Net purchases of used motor vehicles	106	139	166	242	101	130	158	162
Motor vehicle operation [1]	570	624	602	927	565	632	599	662
Motor vehicle fuels, lubricants, and fluids	312	297	238	478	280	298	256	294
Motor vehicle maintenance and repair	137	159	178	226	155	165	164	185
Public transportation (ground, air, water)	104	142	84	227	117	142	87	201
Telephone and related communication equipment	18	28	25	32	6	20	37	65
Postal and delivery services	15	14	16	18	18	14	14	14
Telecommunication services	148	157	169	183	113	137	187	215
Internet access	40	70	84	100	40	69	85	97
Recreation [1]	884	1,059	1,284	1,707	828	1,045	1,310	1,645
Video and audio equipment	83	69	67	86	42	57	88	117
Information processing equipment	95	120	225	295	61	107	273	368
Services related to video/audio goods and computers	97	123	138	154	118	133	129	135
Sports and recreational goods and related services	177	234	334	433	149	221	355	425
Magazines, newspapers, books, and stationery	75	75	106	134	80	75	97	112
Gambling	109	130	125	172	123	134	119	144
Pets, pet products, and related services	76	99	135	172	84	101	128	146
Education [1]	240	270	294	327	307	284	276	296
Higher education	155	173	188	196	200	181	176	179
Food services	537	696	735	1,060	639	730	674	859
Accommodations [10]	99	138	89	177	117	143	92	156
Financial services	479	622	724	807	691	698	655	630
Insurance [1]	289	355	425	445	337	376	395	402
Life insurance	78	88	92	99	90	92	86	86
Net health insurance	143	187	238	236	162	196	221	215
Net motor vehicle and other transportation insurance	60	68	81	96	78	76	74	88
Personal care [11]	207	248	252	336	221	251	240	298
Personal items [12]	85	98	98	142	89	102	102	134
Social services and religious activities [13]	139	176	224	272	163	185	205	227
Professional and other services [1]	159	180	212	248	192	192	198	214
Legal services	87	96	109	123	105	102	103	106
Accounting and other business services	28	36	50	64	36	39	46	53
Funeral and burial services	24	26	28	34	27	27	27	31
Tobacco	98	104	121	122	124	114	105	93
Net foreign travel and expenditures abroad by:								
U.S. residents [1]	-12	-51	-14	42	-27	-57	-13	54
Foreign travel by U.S. residents	112	137	49	170	115	134	49	167
Less: Expenditures in the United States by nonresidents	132	195	74	139	150	200	72	122
Final consumption expenditures of nonprofit institutions serving households (NPISHs) [14]	294	364	485	532	335	384	462	424

[1] Includes other expenditures not shown separately. [2] Also includes repair and hire of footwear. [3] Rent for space (see footnote 4), and for appliances, furnishings, and furniture. [4] Rent for space and for heating and plumbing facilities, water heaters, lighting fixtures, kitchen cabinets, linoleum, storm windows and doors, window screens, and screen doors; excludes rent for appliances and furniture and purchases of fuel and electricity. [5] Includes clocks, lamps, lighting fixtures, other household decorative items, and repair of furniture, furnishings, and floor coverings. [6] Includes appliance repair. [7] Excludes drug preparations and related products dispensed by physicians, hospitals, and other medical services. [8] Offices of physicians, HMO medical centers, and freestanding ambulatory surgical and emergency centers. [9] Includes home health care, medical laboratories, and other health professionals (except physicians) and services. [10] Hotels, motels, other traveler accommodations, clubs, and housing at schools. [11] Cosmetics, toiletries, and personal care appliances and services. [12] Jewelry, watches, luggage, and similar items. [13] Household purchases from business, government, and nonprofit institutions providing social services and religious activities. Purchases from nonprofit establishments exclude unrelated sales, secondary sales, and sales to businesses, government, and the rest of the world, but include membership dues and fees. [14] Net expenses of NPISHs, defined as their gross operating expenses less primary sales to households.

Source: U.S. Bureau of Economic Analysis, National Income and Product Accounts, "Table 2.5.5. Personal Consumption Expenditures by Function," and "Table 2.5.6. Real Personal Consumption Expenditures by Function, Chained Dollars," <www.bea.gov/itable/national-gdp-and-personal-income>, accessed November 2023.

Table 717. Personal Income By Source and Disposition: 2000 to 2023

[In billions of dollars (8,621 represents $8,621,000,000,000), except as indicated. For definition of personal income and chained dollars, see text, this section]

Item	2000	2010	2015	2019	2020	2021	2022	2023
Personal income...............................	**8,621**	**12,557**	**15,474**	**18,356**	**19,629**	**21,408**	**21,841**	**22,961**
Compensation of employees, received..................	5,847	7,925	9,699	11,448	11,595	12,546	13,439	14,234
Wages and salaries...............................	4,825	6,373	7,859	9,325	9,465	10,313	11,116	11,798
Supplements to wages and salaries.............	1,022	1,553	1,840	2,123	2,130	2,233	2,323	2,436
Proprietors' income [1].............................	754	1,109	1,348	1,554	1,584	1,749	1,791	1,848
Farm..	31	39	55	32	44	72	82	54
Nonfarm...	722	1,070	1,292	1,522	1,539	1,677	1,709	1,794
Rental income of persons [2].....................	183	434	601	684	756	814	878	967
Personal income receipts on assets............	1,456	1,748	2,345	2,950	2,914	3,215	3,432	3,613
Personal interest income........................	1,069	1,211	1,348	1,603	1,510	1,515	1,627	1,773
Personal dividend income.......................	386	537	997	1,346	1,403	1,699	1,805	1,841
Personal current transfer receipts...........	1,087	2,325	2,685	3,144	4,230	4,642	4,002	4,101
Government social benefits to persons [3]	1,045	2,281	2,635	3,089	4,183	4,554	3,903	3,996
Social security [4].............................	401	690	872	1,031	1,078	1,115	1,212	1,357
Unemployment insurance....................	21	139	33	27	530	324	22	22
Veterans' benefits............................	25	58	93	131	145	154	171	173
Other current transfer receipts, from business (net).......	42	44	50	56	47	88	99	104
Less: Contributions for government social insurance.......	706	984	1,205	1,425	1,449	1,558	1,702	1,803
Less: Personal current taxes...................	1,236	1,238	1,941	2,199	2,256	2,743	3,138	2,756
Equals: Disposable personal income..............	**7,385**	**11,319**	**13,533**	**16,157**	**17,373**	**18,664**	**18,702**	**20,205**
Less: Personal outlays............................	7,068	10,648	12,742	14,966	14,694	16,544	18,080	19,305
Personal consumption expenditures............	6,767	10,260	12,297	14,418	14,206	16,043	17,512	18,571
Personal interest payments [5].................	218	242	263	341	286	274	326	489
Personal current transfer payments...........	83	145	181	208	202	227	242	245
Equals: Personal saving........................	**317**	**671**	**791**	**1,191**	**2,679**	**2,121**	**623**	**900**
Personal saving as a percentage of disposable personal income..................	4.3	5.9	5.8	7.4	15.4	11.4	3.3	4.5
Addenda:								
Disposable personal income:								
Total, billions of chained (2017) dollars [6].....................	10,004	12,505	13,908	15,609	16,603	17,123	16,117	16,784
Per capita:								
Current dollars.................................	26,151	36,532	42,013	48,885	52,359	56,156	56,068	60,276
Chained (2017) dollars........................	35,424	40,361	43,179	47,225	50,039	51,519	48,317	50,069

[1] With inventory valuation and capital consumption adjustments. [2] With capital consumption adjustment. [3] Includes other benefits not shown separately. [4] Social security benefits include benefits distributed from the Old-Age and Survivors Insurance Trust Fund and the Disability Insurance Trust Fund. [5] Consists of nonmortgage interest paid by households. [6] The current-dollar measure is deflated by the implicit price deflator for personal consumption expenditures.

Source: U.S. Bureau of Economic Analysis, National Income and Product Accounts, "Table 2.1. Personal Income and Its Disposition," <www.bea.gov/itable/national-gdp-and-personal-income>, accessed June 2024.

Table 718. Selected Per Capita Income and Product Measures in Current and Chained (2017) Dollars: 1980 to 2023

[In dollars. Based on U.S. Census Bureau estimated population including Armed Forces abroad, and institutionalized population; based on monthly averages. For explanation of chained dollars, see text, this section]

Year	Current dollars					Chained (2017) dollars				
	Gross domestic product	Gross national product	Personal income	Disposable personal income	Personal consumption expenditures	Gross domestic product	Gross national product	Personal income	Disposable personal income	Personal consumption expenditures
1980............	12,547	12,697	10,207	8,892	7,688	31,869	32,299		22,842	19,748
1990............	23,835	23,974	19,639	17,262	15,225	40,191	40,451		28,878	25,470
2000............	36,300	36,436	30,529	26,151	23,963	49,915	50,089		35,424	32,461
2001............	37,100	37,277	31,530	27,186	24,801	49,893	50,117		36,102	32,935
2002............	37,954	38,113	31,776	28,122	25,521	50,260	50,458		36,861	33,452
2003............	39,420	39,621	32,625	29,172	26,635	51,191	51,438		37,451	34,194
2004............	41,660	41,921	34,153	30,577	28,070	52,682	52,999		38,304	35,164
2005............	44,052	44,305	35,630	31,533	29,626	54,015	54,309		38,396	36,073
2006............	46,234	46,390	37,822	33,281	31,046	54,994	55,163		39,414	36,767
2007............	47,976	48,293	39,550	34,603	32,306	55,561	55,910		39,954	37,302
2008............	48,498	48,975	40,801	35,851	33,001	55,104	55,625		40,205	37,009
2009............	47,123	47,612	39,271	35,520	32,194	53,213	53,750		39,946	36,205
2010............	48,570	49,234	40,526	36,532	33,115	54,189	54,912		40,361	36,586
2011............	49,952	50,714	42,619	37,964	34,259	54,604	55,416		40,908	36,915
2012............	51,645	52,384	44,222	39,426	35,102	55,422	56,196		41,705	37,131
2013............	53,235	53,961	44,367	39,077	35,914	56,172	56,920		40,798	37,496
2014............	55,094	55,830	46,258	40,671	37,154	57,139	57,884		41,876	38,255
2015............	56,797	57,480	48,038	42,013	38,177	58,364	59,051		43,179	39,237
2016............	57,931	58,644	48,944	42,910	39,207	58,968	59,681		43,659	39,891
2017............	60,002	60,898	50,978	44,710	40,662	60,002	60,898		44,710	40,662
2018............	62,825	63,708	53,310	47,002	42,380	61,418	62,321		46,059	41,530
2019............	65,115	65,968	55,539	48,885	43,622	62,606	63,469		47,225	42,141
2020............	64,265	64,912	59,159	52,359	42,816	60,983	61,639		50,039	40,919
2021............	70,988	71,540	64,410	56,156	48,269	64,410	64,959		51,519	44,283
2022............	77,178	77,723	65,476	56,068	52,498	65,420	65,932		48,317	45,240
2023............	81,624	82,114	68,499	60,276	55,400	66,755	67,207		50,069	46,019

Source: U.S. Bureau of Economic Analysis, National Income and Product Accounts, "Table 7.1. Selected Per Capita Product and Income Series in Current and Chained Dollars," <www.bea.gov/itable/national-gdp-and-personal-income>, accessed June 2024.

Table 719. Total and Per Capita Real Personal Income in Constant (2017) Dollars By State: 2010 to 2022

[13,862,568 represents $13,862,568,000,000. Estimates of real personal income are current-dollar estimates adjusted by the corresponding regional price parities (RPPs) and the national personal consumption expenditures (PCE) price index. The result is a constant dollar (using 2017 as the base year) estimate of real personal income. Regional price parities measure the difference in prices across states for a given year and are expressed as a percentage of the overall national price level; the national PCE price index measures national price changes over time. Using the RPPs in combination with the PCE price index allows for comparisons of the purchasing power of personal income across states and over time. For more information, see <www.bea.gov/system/files/methodologies/Methodology-for-Regional-Price-Parities_0.pdf>]

State	Real personal income, total (millions of constant 2017 dollars)					Real per capita personal income [1] (constant 2017 dollars)				
	2010	2015	2020	2021	2022	2010	2015	2020	2021	2022
United States......	13,862,568	15,896,448	18,741,359	19,626,221	18,803,662	44,808	49,394	56,533	59,110	56,419
Alabama..............	199,934	215,148	252,612	264,054	253,984	41,757	43,835	50,207	52,290	50,053
Alaska................	37,929	41,763	42,899	42,306	42,599	53,121	56,504	58,532	57,623	58,069
Arizona..............	237,914	281,348	361,548	390,082	371,495	37,162	41,903	50,355	53,694	50,480
Arkansas.............	117,680	134,941	154,353	161,672	159,684	40,280	45,429	51,209	53,390	52,430
California.............	1,624,235	1,951,177	2,370,532	2,476,630	2,306,734	43,519	50,074	60,011	63,271	59,103
Colorado.............	226,621	279,327	346,298	373,562	373,024	44,902	51,326	59,863	64,282	63,875
Connecticut..........	227,261	228,819	253,773	261,629	243,876	63,476	63,350	70,544	72,206	67,254
Delaware............	40,291	46,905	54,798	55,820	56,734	44,779	49,657	55,233	55,553	55,709
District of Columbia..	37,023	45,163	52,002	53,695	49,299	61,216	67,849	77,515	80,287	73,383
Florida................	805,720	920,580	1,163,424	1,248,415	1,217,815	42,760	45,696	53,888	57,193	54,746
Georgia..............	395,188	460,267	560,065	582,055	556,053	40,688	45,162	52,197	53,954	50,954
Hawaii................	57,292	62,962	70,086	72,682	69,266	41,970	43,527	48,300	50,224	48,095
Idaho.................	59,590	70,479	96,755	103,498	103,154	37,925	42,395	52,322	54,349	53,199
Illinois................	588,137	683,753	752,460	775,012	725,404	45,785	52,739	58,848	61,090	57,654
Indiana...............	274,617	314,400	366,691	385,618	374,525	42,305	47,431	54,014	56,596	54,811
Iowa..................	141,341	163,695	177,134	190,106	188,091	46,319	52,197	55,518	59,451	58,769
Kansas...............	135,440	150,963	167,796	173,330	170,230	47,376	51,652	57,114	58,997	57,958
Kentucky.............	176,725	195,536	227,986	239,443	226,240	40,634	44,004	50,580	53,132	50,138
Louisiana.............	207,754	220,101	245,610	253,842	238,347	45,712	47,125	52,801	54,860	51,925
Maine.................	57,178	61,518	72,475	76,408	71,837	43,057	46,058	53,151	55,479	51,855
Maryland.............	293,197	317,546	360,432	369,248	355,923	50,625	52,493	58,386	59,801	57,736
Massachusetts.......	365,866	414,493	475,931	503,053	465,702	55,691	60,375	68,032	71,971	66,701
Michigan.............	404,923	471,529	539,498	554,585	528,588	40,984	47,214	53,577	55,251	52,679
Minnesota............	256,175	298,148	342,486	356,783	347,519	48,225	54,113	59,982	62,468	60,785
Mississippi...........	116,273	122,246	140,774	146,528	134,708	39,144	40,954	47,589	49,677	45,818
Missouri..............	263,458	289,283	333,183	345,789	338,259	43,938	47,602	54,141	56,045	54,753
Montana..............	42,684	48,308	60,683	64,939	65,459	43,077	46,701	55,822	58,704	58,297
Nebraska.............	90,297	106,813	114,875	123,076	121,519	49,338	56,086	58,531	62,680	61,750
Nevada...............	110,621	130,621	167,893	185,039	176,628	40,941	45,719	53,887	58,810	55,582
New Hampshire......	65,788	72,074	85,177	89,864	82,663	49,950	53,641	61,785	64,766	59,247
New Jersey..........	456,219	500,906	569,453	593,573	567,278	51,790	55,187	61,418	64,046	61,250
New Mexico..........	81,362	85,379	103,129	110,822	104,614	39,402	40,734	48,683	52,357	49,501
New York............	947,703	1,067,426	1,222,601	1,264,254	1,189,919	48,800	53,135	60,801	63,666	60,472
North Carolina........	408,988	456,418	567,555	587,520	569,464	42,730	45,797	54,314	55,605	53,226
North Dakota.........	36,920	45,624	49,631	51,826	53,364	54,692	59,820	63,669	66,621	68,481
Ohio..................	501,428	570,521	650,326	669,428	640,897	43,444	48,871	55,124	56,903	54,516
Oklahoma............	170,858	194,705	212,940	225,187	219,978	45,446	49,911	53,706	56,420	54,724
Oregon...............	153,692	180,643	222,777	233,996	213,907	40,049	44,953	52,482	54,976	50,448
Pennsylvania.........	597,832	666,523	768,876	796,770	750,418	47,012	51,674	59,170	61,233	57,849
Rhode Island.........	48,728	52,167	60,962	62,903	57,290	46,190	48,421	55,605	57,342	52,380
South Carolina.......	181,307	211,939	263,889	269,398	261,255	39,126	43,675	51,422	51,875	49,456
South Dakota.........	41,935	48,212	55,355	59,850	60,828	51,386	56,578	62,351	66,784	66,857
Tennessee............	272,918	307,763	380,539	402,904	386,370	42,936	46,540	54,946	57,819	54,794
Texas.................	1,113,309	1,342,796	1,562,645	1,672,001	1,663,095	44,111	49,009	53,456	56,565	55,382
Utah..................	101,139	126,146	170,963	185,146	183,600	36,432	42,061	52,063	55,448	54,307
Vermont..............	28,864	31,450	34,975	36,928	34,816	46,082	49,460	54,402	57,077	53,806
Virginia...............	389,492	430,400	503,603	519,935	506,086	48,535	51,300	58,311	60,057	58,281
Washington...........	307,766	371,324	464,746	485,192	460,723	45,638	51,713	60,169	62,680	59,175
West Virginia.........	75,391	77,821	88,592	88,552	85,805	40,655	42,149	49,453	49,594	48,337
Wisconsin............	259,228	293,608	338,059	350,201	338,615	45,543	50,674	57,334	59,557	57,465
Wyoming.............	30,338	34,774	39,517	41,071	39,983	53,752	59,581	68,414	70,876	68,772

[1] Real per capita personal income for states is real personal income divided by total midyear population. BEA produced intercensal population statistics for 2010 to 2019 that are tied to the Census Bureau decennial counts for 2010 and 2020 to create consistent time series that are used to prepare per capita personal income statistics.

Source: U.S. Bureau of Economic Analysis, Regional Economic Accounts, Real Personal Income by State and Metro Area, "SARPI Real personal income and real personal consumption expenditures (PCE) by state," <www.bea.gov/data/income-saving/real-personal-income-states-and-metropolitan-areas>, accessed February 2024.

Table 720. Total and Per Capita Personal Income in Current Dollars by State: 2000 to 2023

[In millions of current dollars (8,620,234 represents $8,620,234,000,000). Represents income that all persons who are residents receive from all sources, except for capital gains/losses. Persons include individuals, nonprofit institutions that primarily serve individuals, private noninsured welfare funds, and private trust funds. State estimates of personal income are conceptually and statistically consistent with the national estimates of personal income in the National Income and Product Accounts (NIPAs). State estimates together with the estimate for the District of Columbia sum to a national total that equals the NIPA estimate except for some small differences in the treatment of U.S. residents working abroad, the income of foreign residents working in the U.S., and the use of more current source data. For more information, see <www.bea.gov/system/files/methodologies/SPI-Methodology.pdf>]

State	Personal income, total (millions of dollars)					Per capita personal income (dollars) [1]				
	2000	2010	2020	2022	2023	2000	2010	2020	2022	2023
United States......	**8,620,234**	**12,547,501**	**19,609,985**	**21,820,248**	**22,952,028**	**30,551**	**40,557**	**59,151**	**65,473**	**68,531**
Alabama...............	108,003	162,069	230,873	258,362	271,640	24,258	33,849	45,882	50,920	53,175
Alaska................	20,092	35,374	45,366	50,350	52,524	31,996	49,543	61,894	68,664	71,616
Arizona...............	135,574	216,224	374,312	430,084	458,154	26,271	33,774	52,084	58,390	61,652
Arkansas.............	60,886	94,127	142,112	160,254	166,722	22,731	32,218	47,145	52,604	54,347
California.............	1,127,550	1,609,998	2,767,521	3,006,647	3,133,679	33,175	43,138	70,058	77,013	80,423
Colorado.............	146,561	206,053	375,158	442,213	463,852	33,872	40,827	64,848	75,708	78,918
Connecticut..........	146,217	219,801	278,374	300,751	316,311	42,857	61,392	77,810	83,340	87,447
Delaware.............	26,587	36,981	55,338	64,407	67,478	33,810	41,101	55,792	63,177	65,392
District of Columbia..	24,828	38,212	60,179	64,473	68,515	43,401	63,182	89,707	96,092	100,909
Florida................	471,588	730,690	1,221,122	1,441,599	1,543,132	29,387	38,778	56,556	64,804	68,248
Georgia..............	236,617	337,421	552,249	617,553	646,108	28,760	34,741	51,456	56,588	58,581
Hawaii...............	35,403	56,649	82,761	88,973	93,501	29,174	41,499	57,030	61,813	65,151
Idaho................	32,667	50,202	91,889	109,776	115,988	25,139	31,950	49,687	56,615	59,035
Illinois................	411,221	540,881	787,488	851,243	890,438	33,072	42,107	61,569	67,653	70,953
Indiana..............	171,032	231,026	351,107	398,523	411,993	28,075	35,590	51,716	58,329	60,038
Iowa.................	80,083	116,536	167,779	192,742	199,960	27,341	38,190	52,580	60,238	62,351
Kansas..............	75,871	113,843	161,705	177,475	187,406	28,166	39,822	55,037	60,433	63,732
Kentucky............	100,475	144,336	211,967	234,282	245,889	24,815	33,187	47,019	51,929	54,326
Louisiana............	106,908	173,007	233,715	250,171	261,159	23,907	38,067	50,239	54,527	57,100
Maine................	35,091	50,487	74,042	83,951	88,094	27,478	38,018	54,263	60,425	63,117
Maryland.............	188,437	287,359	400,176	432,933	456,408	35,480	49,617	64,820	70,236	73,849
Massachusetts.......	244,147	346,270	541,421	590,400	614,807	38,381	52,708	77,371	84,551	87,812
Michigan.............	301,060	352,074	531,530	572,325	599,366	30,250	35,635	52,780	57,043	59,714
Minnesota............	159,595	225,972	349,887	393,569	412,364	32,348	42,539	61,270	68,874	71,866
Mississippi...........	61,605	92,714	125,761	136,330	141,428	21,628	31,213	42,510	46,388	48,110
Missouri..............	156,202	221,760	320,593	357,195	379,838	27,857	36,984	52,091	57,825	61,302
Montana.............	20,771	35,671	58,209	68,477	72,407	22,982	36,000	53,540	60,984	63,918
Nebraska............	49,570	75,194	111,348	126,474	134,135	28,924	41,086	56,715	64,263	67,800
Nevada..............	64,313	100,750	170,269	197,291	208,159	31,858	37,288	54,646	62,092	65,168
New Hampshire......	43,796	61,881	93,582	103,122	108,323	35,323	46,983	67,877	73,711	77,260
New Jersey..........	329,592	448,931	657,894	714,990	749,993	39,095	50,962	70,952	77,206	80,724
New Mexico..........	41,922	69,500	98,782	110,303	115,082	23,019	33,658	46,629	52,190	54,428
New York............	683,214	943,393	1,405,029	1,483,802	1,557,496	35,955	48,579	69,886	75,423	79,581
North Carolina.......	221,516	343,104	541,078	621,706	655,369	27,410	35,847	51,759	58,125	60,484
North Dakota........	16,591	29,759	47,621	54,829	57,494	25,842	44,084	61,087	70,391	73,341
Ohio.................	323,813	422,204	623,836	679,233	711,895	28,496	36,580	52,875	57,759	60,402
Oklahoma............	83,332	139,695	199,233	226,308	237,145	24,124	37,157	50,245	56,306	58,499
Oregon..............	96,914	137,926	239,863	264,174	276,973	28,257	35,941	56,504	62,314	65,426
Pennsylvania........	372,691	535,336	783,826	836,778	879,310	30,339	42,098	60,315	64,506	67,839
Rhode Island........	31,875	44,974	64,757	69,514	72,859	30,350	42,631	59,061	63,551	66,480
South Carolina.......	100,705	151,746	250,288	283,246	301,581	25,025	32,747	48,769	53,615	56,123
South Dakota........	20,201	33,683	52,793	62,028	64,676	26,727	41,274	59,462	68,171	70,353
Tennessee...........	153,990	227,613	359,634	411,035	435,067	26,998	35,809	51,924	58,311	61,049
Texas................	591,738	982,053	1,611,228	1,879,420	1,995,594	28,253	38,910	55,114	62,585	65,422
Utah.................	54,231	88,941	169,940	201,012	214,713	24,162	32,038	51,748	59,449	62,823
Vermont..............	17,680	25,989	37,274	40,790	43,032	29,002	41,492	57,974	63,035	66,463
Virginia..............	231,870	364,678	530,920	599,042	634,985	32,631	45,443	61,469	69,021	72,855
Washington..........	192,318	285,437	522,714	586,520	622,365	32,538	42,327	67,669	75,345	79,659
West Virginia........	40,252	60,532	80,741	88,745	93,080	22,275	32,642	45,067	50,024	52,585
Wisconsin............	158,494	222,261	326,837	362,245	378,080	29,493	39,048	55,427	61,496	63,963
Wyoming.............	14,545	26,185	37,866	42,585	45,461	29,426	46,395	65,551	73,216	77,837

[1] Per capita personal income is total personal income divided by total midyear population. BEA produced intercensal population statistics for 2010 to 2019 that are tied to the Census Bureau decennial counts for 2010 and 2020 to create consistent time series that are used to prepare per capita personal income statistics.

Source: U.S. Bureau of Economic Analysis, Regional Economic Accounts, Personal Income by State, Interactive Data, "SAINC1 State annual personal income summary: personal income, population, per capita personal income," <www.bea.gov/data/income-saving/personal-income-by-state>, accessed March 2024.

Table 721. Disposable Personal Income Per Capita in Current Dollars by State: 2000 to 2023

[In dollars, except as indicated. Per capita disposable personal income is total disposable personal income divided by total midyear population. Disposable personal income is total personal income minus personal current taxes. It is the portion of personal income that is available for saving and spending. The estimate of personal income in the United States is derived as the sum of the state estimates and the estimate for the District of Columbia; it differs from the estimate of personal income in the national income and product accounts (NIPAs) because of differences in coverage, in the methodologies used to prepare the estimates, and in the timing of the availability of source data. See text, Section 13]

State	2000	2010	2015	2020	2021	2022	2023	Index, compared to U.S. average		
								2020	2022	2023
United States...........	**26,173**	**36,562**	**42,034**	**52,350**	**56,172**	**56,065**	**60,299**	**100.0**	**100.0**	**100.0**
Alabama..................	21,527	31,091	34,538	41,836	45,186	45,251	48,163	79.9	80.7	79.9
Alaska...................	28,557	45,803	51,514	57,337	60,065	62,303	65,899	109.5	111.1	109.3
Arizona..................	22,931	31,055	35,676	46,930	50,097	51,203	55,333	89.6	91.3	91.8
Arkansas.................	20,168	29,569	35,422	42,991	46,639	46,910	49,360	82.1	83.7	81.9
California................	27,424	38,364	45,854	59,964	64,382	63,115	68,267	114.5	112.6	113.2
Colorado.................	28,739	36,521	44,766	57,094	62,483	64,803	69,353	109.1	115.6	115.0
Connecticut..............	34,766	53,613	55,282	66,202	67,378	67,787	73,888	126.5	120.9	122.5
Delaware.................	29,217	37,146	41,776	49,250	51,075	54,362	57,800	94.1	97.0	95.9
District of Columbia......	36,365	55,437	62,894	75,310	80,246	76,700	84,161	143.9	136.8	139.6
Florida...................	25,680	35,672	39,849	50,311	55,476	55,857	60,397	96.1	99.6	100.2
Georgia..................	24,815	31,536	36,840	46,065	49,587	48,919	51,921	88.0	87.3	86.1
Hawaii...................	25,593	38,005	41,904	50,869	53,877	53,114	57,427	97.2	94.7	95.2
Idaho....................	22,016	29,405	34,930	44,520	48,070	49,693	52,950	85.0	88.6	87.8
Illinois...................	28,299	37,816	44,014	54,421	58,602	57,721	62,317	104.0	103.0	103.3
Indiana..................	24,587	32,427	37,717	46,607	50,801	51,319	53,943	89.0	91.5	89.5
Iowa.....................	24,173	34,811	40,547	47,433	51,918	53,238	56,247	90.6	95.0	93.3
Kansas...................	24,519	36,135	41,720	49,426	51,785	52,742	56,940	94.4	94.1	94.4
Kentucky.................	21,739	30,208	34,605	42,597	46,296	45,890	48,937	81.4	81.9	81.2
Louisiana................	21,391	35,121	38,554	46,488	50,057	49,364	52,557	88.8	88.0	87.2
Maine....................	23,993	34,735	38,407	48,782	52,045	52,858	56,489	93.2	94.3	93.7
Maryland.................	30,019	43,934	47,369	56,137	58,801	58,648	63,688	107.2	104.6	105.6
Massachusetts...........	30,947	46,213	51,670	66,091	69,720	68,866	74,342	126.2	122.8	123.3
Michigan.................	26,131	32,498	38,078	47,545	50,175	49,696	53,246	90.8	88.6	88.3
Minnesota...............	27,520	37,886	44,169	53,609	57,585	58,638	62,963	102.4	104.6	104.4
Mississippi...............	19,541	28,902	32,164	39,421	42,852	42,186	44,436	75.3	75.2	73.7
Missouri.................	24,288	33,719	37,867	46,946	49,827	50,695	54,995	89.7	90.4	91.2
Montana.................	20,277	32,947	38,335	47,769	51,266	52,822	56,691	91.2	94.2	94.0
Nebraska................	25,384	37,521	44,548	51,096	55,923	56,647	61,114	97.6	101.0	101.4
Nevada..................	27,743	34,193	39,224	49,061	54,219	53,876	57,934	93.7	96.1	96.1
New Hampshire..........	30,496	43,139	48,393	61,072	63,940	64,491	69,245	116.7	115.0	114.8
New Jersey..............	32,751	45,094	50,093	62,032	65,282	64,689	69,883	118.5	115.4	115.9
New Mexico..............	20,534	31,133	34,305	43,092	46,912	47,271	50,029	82.3	84.3	83.0
New York................	29,930	41,863	46,705	59,243	62,900	60,463	66,393	113.2	107.8	110.1
North Carolina...........	23,734	32,609	36,820	46,280	50,144	50,654	53,929	88.4	90.3	89.4
North Dakota.............	23,329	40,263	47,201	56,029	59,804	63,367	67,093	107.0	113.0	111.3
Ohio.....................	24,546	33,042	38,877	47,638	50,730	50,619	54,146	91.0	90.3	89.8
Oklahoma................	21,224	34,211	40,009	46,276	50,456	50,965	53,761	88.4	90.9	89.2
Oregon..................	24,061	32,252	38,284	49,658	53,447	53,089	57,306	94.9	94.7	95.0
Pennsylvania.............	26,217	37,915	43,308	53,885	56,282	55,624	60,071	102.9	99.2	99.6
Rhode Island.............	26,192	38,651	42,430	52,707	55,913	54,687	58,735	100.7	97.5	97.4
South Carolina...........	22,092	30,130	35,575	43,988	47,125	47,056	50,345	84.0	83.9	83.5
South Dakota............	24,167	38,533	43,893	54,796	59,725	61,638	64,656	104.7	109.9	107.2
Tennessee...............	24,299	33,456	38,283	47,843	52,047	52,540	56,041	91.4	93.7	92.9
Texas....................	24,894	35,830	41,976	50,296	54,722	55,733	59,422	96.1	99.4	98.5
Utah.....................	21,088	29,220	35,392	45,643	49,587	50,999	55,371	87.2	91.0	91.8
Vermont..................	25,326	38,043	43,064	52,111	54,066	54,918	59,330	99.5	98.0	98.4
Virginia..................	27,760	40,560	44,896	53,854	57,713	58,609	63,625	102.9	104.5	105.5
Washington..............	28,072	38,886	46,604	60,420	65,310	65,098	70,589	115.4	116.1	117.1
West Virginia.............	19,902	29,891	33,458	41,413	44,722	45,087	48,184	79.1	80.4	79.9
Wisconsin................	25,421	35,286	40,515	49,583	53,514	53,759	57,210	94.7	95.9	94.9
Wyoming.................	25,465	42,254	50,085	58,622	62,015	63,301	69,039	112.0	112.9	114.5

Source: U.S. Bureau of Economic Analysis, Regional Economic Accounts, Personal Income by State, Interactive Data, "SAINC51 State annual disposable personal income summary: disposable personal income, population, and per capita disposable personal income," <www.bea.gov/data/income-saving/personal-income-by-state>, accessed June 2024.

Table 722. Personal Income by Selected Large Metropolitan Area: 2010 to 2022

[11,074,668 represents $11,074,668,000,000. MSA=Metropolitan Statistical Area. The MSAs used by the Bureau of Economic Analysis are defined in the Office of Management and Budget Bulletin No. 20-01 issued March 6, 2020. Per capita personal income was computed using Census Bureau midyear population estimates]

Metropolitan statistical area	Personal income			Personal income per capita			Index (U.S.= 100), 2022
	2010 (mil. dol.)	2020 (mil. dol.)	2022 (mil. dol.)	2010 (dollars)	2020 (dollars)	2022 (dollars)	
United States (metropolitan portion)............	**11,074,668**	**17,514,916**	**19,506,222**	**41,994**	**61,202**	**67,767**	**100.0**
New York-Newark-Jersey City, NY-NJ-PA MSA.....	1,024,295	1,541,128	1,649,540	54,062	76,868	84,084	124.1
Los Angeles-Long Beach-Anaheim, CA MSA........	567,109	914,040	984,031	44,169	69,362	76,445	112.8
Chicago-Naperville-Elgin, IL-IN-WI MSA.............	419,944	632,332	684,652	44,319	65,862	72,512	107.0
Dallas-Fort Worth-Arlington, TX MSA................	266,251	472,842	559,971	41,657	61,681	70,493	104.0
Houston-The Woodlands-Sugar Land, TX MSA.....	271,341	426,115	501,653	45,627	59,674	68,344	100.9
Washington-Arlington-Alexandria, DC-VA-MD-WV MSA...............................	331,552	478,396	529,084	58,370	75,141	83,010	122.5
Philadelphia-Camden-Wilmington, PA-NJ-DE-MD MSA..............................	287,820	422,834	457,424	48,175	67,745	73,291	108.2
Atlanta-Sandy Springs-Alpharetta, GA MSA.........	205,049	354,846	398,881	38,666	58,140	64,107	94.6
Miami-Fort Lauderdale-Pompano Beach, FL MSA............................	240,570	398,326	477,224	43,094	64,949	77,732	114.7
Phoenix-Mesa-Chandler, AZ MSA...................	147,394	266,602	310,170	35,092	54,747	61,840	91.3
Boston-Cambridge-Newton, MA-NH MSA...........	263,769	417,539	461,055	57,744	84,684	94,082	138.8
Riverside-San Bernardino-Ontario, CA MSA........	128,204	217,300	235,278	30,231	47,177	50,407	74.4
San Francisco-Oakland-Berkeley, CA MSA..........	262,865	511,105	566,659	60,501	107,815	123,736	182.6
Detroit-Warren-Dearborn, MI MSA..................	164,173	249,492	266,492	38,240	56,901	61,322	90.5
Seattle-Tacoma-Bellevue, WA MSA.................	167,149	329,387	371,608	48,456	81,785	92,113	135.9
Minneapolis-St. Paul-Bloomington, MN-WI MSA....	154,434	245,388	277,635	46,226	66,431	75,164	110.9
Tampa-St. Petersburg-Clearwater, FL MSA........	108,031	170,937	197,743	38,760	53,629	60,091	88.7
San Diego-Chula Vista-Carlsbad, CA MSA..........	136,162	222,600	243,507	43,889	67,536	74,326	109.7
Denver-Aurora-Lakewood, CO MSA.................	112,249	212,395	253,166	43,948	71,515	84,788	125.1
Baltimore-Columbia-Towson, MD MSA..............	130,958	186,681	202,523	48,203	65,676	71,420	105.4
St. Louis, MO-IL MSA............................	118,793	172,495	195,248	42,571	61,190	69,698	102.8
Orlando-Kissimmee-Sanford, FL MSA...............	71,903	127,863	149,152	33,600	47,705	53,959	79.6
Charlotte-Concord-Gastonia, NC-SC MSA..........	87,282	155,196	179,575	38,793	58,149	65,156	96.1
San Antonio-New Braunfels, TX MSA...............	78,690	128,843	146,522	36,557	50,165	55,180	81.4
Portland-Vancouver-Hillsboro, OR-WA MSA.........	88,505	157,503	174,246	39,646	62,550	69,435	102.5
Austin-Round Rock-Georgetown, TX MSA..........	71,526	148,240	181,871	41,402	64,453	75,119	110.8
Sacramento-Roseville-Folsom, CA MSA.............	87,892	148,100	161,774	40,802	61,712	66,940	98.8
Pittsburgh, PA MSA...............................	100,859	145,501	154,556	42,763	61,414	65,792	97.1
Las Vegas-Henderson-Paradise, NV MSA..........	69,690	119,564	137,404	35,707	52,562	59,150	87.3
Cincinnati, OH-KY-IN MSA.........................	85,411	132,831	147,802	39,883	58,803	65,253	96.3
Kansas City, MO-KS MSA..........................	83,318	126,055	140,120	41,371	57,427	63,417	93.6
Columbus, OH MSA...............................	73,745	119,728	132,344	38,682	55,902	61,228	90.4
Indianapolis-Carmel-Anderson, IN MSA..............	78,743	127,710	147,181	41,593	60,412	68,719	101.4
Cleveland-Elyria, OH MSA.........................	82,442	118,688	129,815	39,702	56,884	62,921	92.8
Nashville-Davidson--Murfreesboro--Franklin, TN MSA.................................	69,486	127,569	151,538	42,071	63,891	74,035	109.2
San Jose-Sunnyvale-Santa Clara, CA MSA........	110,730	244,542	274,331	60,111	122,544	141,516	208.8
Virginia Beach-Norfolk-Newport News, VA-NC MSA.....................................	69,421	94,167	104,567	40,417	52,283	57,873	85.4
Jacksonville, FL MSA..............................	52,611	88,459	105,113	38,986	54,849	62,729	92.6
Providence-Warwick, RI-MA MSA...................	67,264	99,548	106,698	41,924	59,500	63,746	94.1
Milwaukee-Waukesha, WI MSA.....................	67,942	95,297	106,308	43,647	60,530	68,155	100.6
Raleigh-Cary, NC MSA............................	49,384	86,983	104,836	43,418	61,360	70,628	104.2
Oklahoma City, OK MSA...........................	49,574	76,701	88,565	39,411	53,642	60,687	89.6
Richmond, VA MSA...............................	50,800	80,711	91,393	42,736	61,305	68,205	100.6
Memphis, TN-MS-AR MSA.........................	48,755	68,693	75,195	37,012	51,325	56,440	83.3
Louisville/Jefferson County, KY-IN MSA.............	45,582	70,258	78,988	37,825	54,631	61,490	90.7
Salt Lake City, UT MSA...........................	38,977	71,070	82,410	35,696	56,393	65,085	96.0
New Orleans-Metairie, LA MSA.....................	51,311	71,446	77,015	42,926	56,248	61,801	91.2
Hartford-East Hartford-Middletown, CT MSA........	60,827	80,130	85,260	50,090	66,219	69,787	103.0
Buffalo-Cheektowaga, NY MSA.....................	43,640	63,137	65,507	38,394	54,208	56,414	83.2
Birmingham-Hoover, AL MSA.......................	41,878	61,205	69,538	39,422	54,817	62,262	91.9
Grand Rapids-Kentwood, MI MSA...................	36,175	59,953	67,984	36,377	55,061	62,131	91.7
Rochester, NY MSA...............................	42,787	60,524	62,601	39,598	55,630	57,902	85.4
Tucson, AZ MSA..................................	33,461	51,842	57,601	34,099	49,601	54,464	80.4
Tulsa, OK MSA...................................	39,375	56,847	64,755	41,883	55,882	62,618	92.4
Fresno, CA MSA..................................	29,067	48,553	51,316	31,181	48,095	50,549	74.6
Urban Honolulu, HI MSA...........................	43,034	61,015	64,653	44,945	60,273	64,936	95.8
Worcester, MA-CT MSA............................	39,303	58,554	62,214	42,734	59,994	63,475	93.7
Omaha-Council Bluffs, NE-IA MSA..................	39,223	58,045	66,986	45,186	59,897	68,586	101.2
Bridgeport-Stamford-Norwalk, CT MSA..............	94,335	110,675	120,546	102,572	115,859	125,185	184.7
Greenville-Anderson, SC MSA.....................	27,261	44,463	50,060	33,020	47,775	52,202	77.0
Albuquerque, NM MSA............................	30,704	44,640	49,613	34,521	48,654	53,954	79.6
Bakersfield, CA MSA..............................	25,810	40,301	41,099	30,669	44,490	44,862	66.2
Knoxville, TN MSA................................	28,474	45,680	52,879	34,890	51,776	58,239	85.9
Albany-Schenectady-Troy, NY MSA.................	38,478	56,503	60,595	44,146	62,798	66,984	98.8
North Port-Sarasota-Bradenton, FL MSA............	29,652	53,947	64,463	42,177	64,391	72,316	106.7

Source: U.S. Bureau of Economic Analysis, Regional Economic Accounts, Personal Income by County, Metro, and Other Areas, "CAINC1 County and MSA personal income summary: personal income, population, per capita personal income," <www.bea.gov/itable/regional-gdp-and-personal-income>, accessed December 2023.

Table 723. Households by Income Level and Median Income by State: 2022

[In thousands (129,871 represents 129,871,000), except as indicated. The American Community Survey universe includes the household population and the population living in institutions, college dormitories, and other group quarters. Based on a sample and subject to sampling variability; see text, Section 1 and Appendix III. For definition of median, see Guide to Tabular Presentation]

State	Number of households (1,000)								Median income (dollars)
	Total	Under $25,000	$25,000 to $49,999	$50,000 to $74,999	$75,000 to $99,999	$100,000 to $149,999	$150,000 to $199,999	$200,000 and over	
United States........	129,871	20,768	23,259	21,096	16,651	21,945	11,273	14,879	74,755
Alabama...............	2,016	446	415	337	253	300	130	134	59,674
Alaska.................	275	34	39	43	36	60	31	31	88,121
Arizona................	2,850	415	522	495	392	506	245	275	74,568
Arkansas..............	1,216	275	275	220	154	163	63	67	55,432
California.............	13,551	1,840	1,947	1,865	1,628	2,386	1,440	2,445	91,551
Colorado..............	2,385	286	359	361	320	453	256	351	89,302
Connecticut...........	1,434	203	211	197	180	254	155	233	88,429
Delaware..............	402	50	70	64	56	81	38	44	82,174
District of Columbia. ..	327	48	38	40	35	54	34	78	101,027
Florida................	8,826	1,445	1,741	1,533	1,182	1,412	677	836	69,303
Georgia...............	4,092	658	758	687	546	691	336	417	72,837
Hawaii.................	495	64	68	73	59	99	55	76	92,458
Idaho.................	717	99	137	136	111	129	50	55	72,785
Illinois................	5,056	802	866	805	651	889	455	587	76,708
Indiana...............	2,726	450	568	490	383	452	198	185	66,785
Iowa..................	1,331	206	261	244	189	231	103	97	69,588
Kansas................	1,175	192	233	209	158	198	89	95	68,925
Kentucky..............	1,829	392	390	321	230	273	113	110	59,341
Louisiana.............	1,817	438	389	297	209	258	113	112	55,416
Maine.................	605	99	118	106	83	105	47	48	69,543
Maryland..............	2,376	294	329	321	298	444	275	416	94,991
Massachusetts.........	2,798	403	388	355	317	494	309	532	94,488
Michigan..............	4,090	705	821	720	538	669	305	331	66,986
Minnesota.............	2,322	302	377	377	320	442	236	268	82,338
Mississippi............	1,148	289	258	199	140	151	55	56	52,719
Missouri..............	2,522	450	524	452	337	407	175	177	64,811
Montana..............	464	78	94	83	70	74	31	35	67,631
Nebraska.............	803	126	161	140	108	140	65	64	69,597
Nevada...............	1,198	182	228	211	163	215	95	106	72,333
New Hampshire.......	557	63	81	89	73	103	64	83	89,992
New Jersey............	3,517	432	488	482	408	636	405	666	96,346
New Mexico...........	848	184	180	139	106	132	54	53	59,726
New York..............	7,774	1,370	1,227	1,112	900	1,276	727	1,162	79,557
North Carolina........	4,299	724	872	762	559	688	319	376	67,481
North Dakota..........	331	52	61	58	47	59	27	27	71,970
Ohio..................	4,878	865	987	866	644	782	360	374	65,720
Oklahoma.............	1,573	318	346	285	195	233	99	98	59,673
Oregon................	1,726	265	303	287	229	309	149	183	75,657
Pennsylvania..........	5,294	877	979	897	666	889	441	545	71,798
Rhode Island..........	447	71	65	69	58	85	45	53	81,854
South Carolina........	2,136	387	456	371	288	332	141	160	64,115
South Dakota.........	368	59	70	68	53	67	26	25	69,728
Tennessee.............	2,847	498	594	513	377	447	204	214	65,254
Texas.................	11,088	1,747	2,087	1,895	1,419	1,796	962	1,182	72,284
Utah..................	1,130	107	169	192	163	237	127	134	89,168
Vermont...............	277	40	53	47	38	47	27	24	73,991
Virginia................	3,381	468	520	503	412	610	347	520	85,873
Washington............	3,080	378	437	454	405	583	324	500	91,306
West Virginia..........	736	176	166	128	90	104	37	35	54,329
Wisconsin.............	2,491	376	484	452	340	450	199	190	70,996
Wyoming..............	243	39	47	43	34	45	19	16	70,042
Puerto Rico...........	1,289	662	327	139	72	50	20	20	24,112

Source: U.S. Census Bureau, 2022 American Community Survey, B19001, "Household Income in the Past 12 Months (In 2022 Inflation-Adjusted Dollars)"; and B19013, "Median Household Income in the Past 12 Months (In 2022 Inflation-Adjusted Dollars)"; <data.census.gov/>, accessed November 2023.

Table 724. Families by Income Level and Median Income by State: 2022

[In thousands (83,304 represents 83,304,000), except as indicated. The American Community Survey universe includes the household population and the population living in institutions, college dormitories, and other group quarters. Based on a sample and subject to sampling variability; see text, Section 1 and Appendix III. For definition of median, see Guide to Tabular Presentation]

State	Number of families (1,000)								Median income (dollars)
	Total	Under $25,000	$25,000 to $49,999	$50,000 to $74,999	$75,000 to $99,999	$100,000 to $149,999	$150,000 to $199,999	$200,000 and over	
United States...	**83,304**	**7,978**	**12,353**	**13,089**	**11,596**	**16,703**	**9,138**	**12,448**	**92,148**
Alabama...	1,309	175	230	226	189	255	114	121	77,668
Alaska...	176	14	19	26	22	45	25	25	105,329
Arizona...	1,844	168	286	311	279	383	191	227	88,679
Arkansas...	778	101	160	148	120	136	55	58	70,708
California...	9,151	821	1,205	1,230	1,116	1,728	1,087	1,964	104,823
Colorado...	1,464	95	163	199	199	321	199	288	109,592
Connecticut...	903	67	99	110	116	182	126	203	115,183
Delaware...	264	18	32	42	39	62	33	37	100,128
District of Columbia..	124	12	10	12	9	19	15	47	146,477
Florida...	5,684	577	972	995	830	1,083	536	691	83,410
Georgia...	2,733	276	441	453	392	530	276	365	86,642
Hawaii...	335	24	42	45	41	78	44	62	108,285
Idaho...	491	37	79	90	89	106	42	48	85,193
Illinois...	3,138	283	422	475	433	653	372	500	96,948
Indiana...	1,740	164	280	314	280	364	172	165	84,508
Iowa...	822	64	119	139	136	188	91	85	90,851
Kansas...	740	61	109	130	117	165	76	83	89,712
Kentucky...	1,172	153	216	207	173	228	99	96	76,119
Louisiana...	1,131	176	213	192	152	206	94	99	72,866
Maine...	371	28	58	68	57	81	38	42	88,063
Maryland...	1,546	107	172	188	185	317	219	359	117,294
Massachusetts...	1,724	134	189	198	192	342	231	438	120,263
Michigan...	2,549	253	400	444	383	522	259	287	85,865
Minnesota...	1,456	93	166	211	214	340	197	234	105,324
Mississippi...	754	119	156	139	112	129	50	49	66,973
Missouri...	1,570	150	263	281	243	326	153	153	83,420
Montana...	282	23	45	53	48	59	26	27	83,580
Nebraska...	502	41	72	84	77	115	57	56	92,676
Nevada...	774	76	124	132	118	163	75	85	85,593
New Hampshire...	358	18	37	50	50	80	53	70	112,950
New Jersey...	2,378	168	260	294	274	475	329	578	117,988
New Mexico...	516	70	103	88	73	96	44	43	74,341
New York...	4,738	525	637	644	583	901	552	896	99,066
North Carolina...	2,785	284	470	488	410	537	268	328	83,448
North Dakota...	194	13	25	32	30	47	23	24	97,853
Ohio...	2,983	298	470	515	449	616	309	326	86,001
Oklahoma...	1,018	127	191	188	149	191	86	87	75,476
Oregon...	1,041	87	151	167	149	221	117	150	93,384
Pennsylvania...	3,295	295	482	529	461	689	368	471	93,029
Rhode Island...	267	20	28	41	36	61	37	44	105,989
South Carolina...	1,398	156	254	237	215	272	124	141	79,886
South Dakota...	225	19	30	40	38	54	23	21	89,573
Tennessee...	1,847	198	323	330	279	360	172	184	80,910
Texas...	7,483	820	1,226	1,202	1,015	1,401	804	1,014	86,267
Utah...	831	48	96	135	125	201	109	117	102,177
Vermont...	164	12	23	25	26	37	22	20	96,345
Virginia...	2,192	177	266	301	277	446	278	446	107,101
Washington...	1,935	135	208	260	268	420	251	394	109,192
West Virginia...	463	69	91	87	68	85	33	30	70,318
Wisconsin...	1,511	115	212	266	235	350	171	161	91,700
Wyoming...	153	14	24	28	24	36	16	13	86,552
Puerto Rico...	821	359	229	108	55	40	15	15	29,544

Source: U.S. Census Bureau, 2022 American Community Survey, B19101, "Family Income in the Past 12 Months (In 2022 Inflation-Adjusted Dollars)"; and B19113, "Median Family Income in the Past 12 Months (In 2022 Inflation-Adjusted Dollars)"; <data.census.gov/>, accessed November 2023.

Table 725. Consumer Unit Expenditures—Annual Averages by Major Type of Expenditure: 1990 to 2022

[Consumer units in thousands (96,968 represents 96,968,000); expenditures in dollars. Based on Consumer Expenditure Survey. Data are averages for the noninstitutional population. Expenditures are direct out-of-pocket expenditures. Consumers units may be all members in a housing unit (families), a person living alone or sharing a household with others and financially independent, or 2 or more unrelated persons living together who share expenses]

Type of expenditure	1990	2000	2010	2018	2019	2020 [4]	2021	2022
Number of consumer units (1,000)	96,968	109,367	121,107	131,439	132,242	131,234	133,595	134,090
Expenditures [1] (average dollars)	**28,381**	**38,045**	**48,109**	**61,224**	**63,036**	**61,334**	**66,928**	**72,967**
Food	4,296	5,158	6,129	7,923	8,169	7,316	8,289	9,343
Food at home [1]	2,485	3,021	3,624	4,464	4,643	4,942	5,259	5,703
Cereals and bakery products	368	453	502	569	583	640	672	712
Meats, poultry, fish, and eggs	668	795	784	961	980	1,075	1,115	1,216
Dairy products	295	325	380	449	455	474	492	532
Fruits and vegetables	408	521	679	858	876	977	1,033	1,099
Other food at home	746	927	1,278	1,627	1,749	1,776	1,947	2,144
Food away from home	1,811	2,137	2,505	3,459	3,526	2,375	3,030	3,639
Alcoholic beverages	293	372	412	583	579	478	554	583
Housing [1]	8,703	12,319	16,557	20,091	20,679	21,409	22,624	24,298
Shelter	4,836	7,114	9,812	11,747	12,190	12,604	13,258	14,507
Utilities, fuels, and public services	1,890	2,489	3,660	4,049	4,055	4,158	4,223	4,549
Apparel and services	1,618	1,856	1,700	1,866	1,883	1,434	1,754	1,945
Transportation [1]	5,120	7,417	7,677	9,761	10,742	9,826	10,961	12,295
Vehicle purchases	2,129	3,418	2,588	3,975	4,394	4,523	4,828	4,496
Gasoline, other fuels, motor oil	1,047	1,291	2,132	2,109	2,094	1,568	2,148	3,120
Other vehicle expenses [3]	1,642	2,281	2,464	2,859	3,474	3,471	3,534	3,834
Public transportation	302	427	493	818	781	263	452	845
Health care [2]	1,480	2,066	3,157	4,968	5,193	5,177	5,452	5,850
Entertainment	1,422	1,863	2,504	3,226	3,090	2,912	3,568	3,458
Personal care products and services	364	564	582	768	786	646	771	866
Reading	153	146	100	108	92	114	114	117
Education	406	632	1,074	1,407	1,443	1,271	1,226	1,335
Tobacco products, smoking supplies	274	319	362	347	320	315	341	371
Personal insurance and pensions	2,592	3,365	5,373	7,296	7,165	7,246	7,873	8,742
Life and other personal insurance	345	399	318	465	520	486	473	519
Pensions and Social Security	2,248	2,966	5,054	6,831	6,645	6,760	7,400	8,223

[1] Includes expenditures not shown separately. [2] Due to changes implemented with the 2014 questionnaire on health insurance, 2014 and subsequent data are not directly comparable to data from previous years. [3] In 2019, the data source used to estimate spending on vehicle insurance was switched from the Diary Survey to the Interview Survey. For more information, see <www.bls.gov/cex/2019-vehicle-insurance.htm>. [4] Regarding the impact of the coronavirus disease 2019 (COVID-19) pandemic on the Consumer Expenditure Survey, see <www.bls.gov/covid19/effects-of-covid-19-pandemic-and-response-on-the-consumer-expenditure-surveys.htm>

Source: U.S. Bureau of Labor Statistics, Consumer Expenditure Surveys, CE Tables, "Top line means tables, Multiyear means, 2021-2022," <www.bls.gov/cex/tables.htm>, accessed November 2023; and previous releases.

Table 726. Consumer Expenditures—Annual Averages by Metropolitan Statistical Area: 2021 to 2022

[In dollars. Annual averages for all consumer units, for 2-year period 2021 to 2022. See headnote, Table 725]

Metropolitan statistical area	Total expenditures [1]	Food	Housing Total [1]	Shelter	Utility, fuels [2]	Transportation Total [1]	Vehicle purchases	Gasoline and motor oil	Health care
Anchorage, Alaska	82,799	12,172	25,141	14,716	5,007	13,745	5,797	3,191	5,635
Atlanta, Georgia	72,537	9,075	24,914	15,220	4,669	12,354	4,682	2,851	5,450
Baltimore, Maryland	82,095	10,661	26,047	15,839	4,341	14,457	7,297	2,692	6,310
Boston, Massachusetts	89,795	10,873	31,679	20,863	4,860	11,697	4,334	2,309	6,923
Chicago, Illinois	74,266	9,371	27,212	16,856	4,565	9,569	2,858	2,432	5,946
Dallas-Fort Worth, Texas	71,932	8,755	25,975	16,149	4,713	12,568	5,593	2,525	5,204
Denver, Colorado	84,293	9,876	30,893	18,756	4,564	12,994	4,437	2,531	6,458
Detroit, Michigan	68,866	8,464	21,746	12,788	4,471	12,566	4,022	2,752	5,567
Honolulu, Hawaii	74,965	12,941	27,799	18,941	4,913	10,103	3,700	2,571	5,133
Houston, Texas	73,772	6,849	24,773	14,874	4,601	13,658	5,631	3,190	5,256
Los Angeles, California	77,024	10,174	28,300	18,632	4,252	13,112	5,054	3,154	4,768
Miami, Florida	64,943	7,992	24,248	16,218	3,656	11,970	4,822	2,535	3,862
Minneapolis-St. Paul, Minnesota	82,883	9,416	27,591	16,523	4,489	10,018	2,556	2,346	6,688
New York City	83,064	10,643	31,213	21,479	4,633	10,326	3,115	1,731	5,154
Philadelphia, Pennsylvania	85,897	10,492	28,453	16,916	5,060	11,247	[3] 3,877	2,368	6,958
Phoenix, Arizona	71,750	8,330	24,843	15,233	4,316	11,736	4,248	2,640	6,445
San Diego, California	86,299	10,449	31,853	21,884	3,812	12,619	4,662	3,140	5,134
San Francisco, California	101,880	13,137	41,367	29,662	4,650	12,991	4,649	2,694	6,222
Seattle, Washington	93,905	10,497	33,090	22,062	4,188	14,481	6,193	2,677	5,373
St. Louis, Missouri	71,182	9,519	22,255	11,725	4,546	12,262	5,357	2,564	6,071
Tampa, Florida	67,636	8,022	23,686	13,949	4,188	11,940	5,152	2,268	6,067
Washington, DC	94,171	11,326	33,285	22,102	4,778	12,162	4,521	2,395	7,001

[1] Includes expenditures not shown separately. [2] Includes public services. [3] Data are likely to have large sampling errors.

Source: U.S. Bureau of Labor Statistics, Consumer Expenditure Surveys, CE Tables, "Geographic means tables: Calendar two year means tables by geographic areas," <www.bls.gov/cex/tables.htm>, accessed November 2023.

Table 727. Personal Consumption Expenditures—Total and Per Capita by State: 2000 to 2022

[Total in millions of current dollars (6,767,179 represents $6,767,179,000,000); per capita amounts in current dollars. Per capita values are computed from unrounded data. The Bureau of Economic Analysis produced intercensal population figures for 2010 to 2019 that are tied to the Census Bureau decennial counts for 2010 and 2020 to create consistent time series that are used to prepare per capita statistics]

State	Total personal consumption expenditures (million dollars)					Per capita personal consumption expenditures (dollars)				
	2000	2010	2020	2021	2022	2000	2010	2020	2021	2022
United States	6,767,179	10,260,256	14,206,231	16,042,964	17,511,745	23,983	33,164	42,853	48,318	52,542
Alabama	89,749	132,314	175,482	197,820	215,105	20,158	27,635	34,878	39,174	42,391
Alaska	17,108	28,538	35,006	39,633	43,413	27,243	39,968	47,762	53,982	59,179
Arizona	121,419	196,474	291,543	334,350	368,867	23,528	30,689	40,605	46,023	50,123
Arkansas	50,566	77,458	105,434	118,796	128,662	18,878	26,513	34,979	39,231	42,245
California	844,374	1,297,976	1,885,029	2,146,539	2,352,362	24,843	34,777	47,720	54,838	60,272
Colorado	117,038	175,993	273,942	314,542	346,723	27,049	34,871	47,355	54,126	59,371
Connecticut	100,902	146,714	184,319	204,252	219,068	29,575	40,978	51,237	56,371	60,413
Delaware	21,313	33,744	44,677	50,944	55,535	27,103	37,503	45,032	50,700	54,532
Dist. of Columbia	22,598	34,550	46,913	52,905	57,595	39,504	57,127	69,929	79,105	85,732
Florida	412,230	643,276	964,080	1,114,052	1,234,951	25,688	34,139	44,655	51,038	55,516
Georgia	188,710	283,318	412,232	471,228	517,335	22,937	29,170	38,419	43,681	47,406
Hawaii	30,345	48,013	63,901	71,696	78,714	25,006	35,173	44,038	49,543	54,655
Idaho	26,127	41,810	64,147	75,485	84,364	20,106	26,609	34,689	39,639	43,508
Illinois	311,532	438,820	561,360	627,074	683,721	25,055	34,161	43,902	49,429	54,341
Indiana	133,147	190,661	259,287	290,017	318,274	21,856	29,371	38,193	42,565	46,579
Iowa	63,280	92,936	120,917	135,091	145,481	21,604	30,456	37,898	42,247	45,455
Kansas	61,303	89,031	113,232	124,678	135,312	22,758	31,143	38,541	42,438	46,069
Kentucky	83,592	123,482	164,459	184,891	199,412	20,645	28,392	36,486	41,027	44,193
Louisiana	87,153	134,427	173,941	194,871	207,377	19,489	29,578	37,393	42,115	45,178
Maine	30,892	47,265	62,955	71,245	77,287	24,190	35,592	46,170	51,730	55,789
Maryland	139,848	216,639	269,585	299,768	324,575	26,332	37,406	43,670	48,549	52,651
Massachusetts	188,310	276,971	368,685	414,258	448,337	29,603	42,160	52,701	59,267	64,214
Michigan	229,632	307,993	414,400	461,919	496,511	23,073	31,173	41,154	46,019	49,482
Minnesota	133,056	191,367	249,336	278,984	302,148	26,969	36,025	43,668	48,846	52,849
Mississippi	50,272	77,187	96,883	108,194	116,654	17,649	25,986	32,751	36,681	39,678
Missouri	132,088	191,636	247,702	276,572	300,328	23,557	31,960	40,251	44,827	48,613
Montana	19,352	32,821	45,730	53,116	58,291	21,413	33,123	42,067	48,015	51,913
Nebraska	38,737	59,014	79,234	89,281	97,455	22,603	32,246	40,371	45,469	49,522
Nevada	50,853	85,450	126,437	145,289	161,819	25,190	31,625	40,581	46,176	50,922
New Hampshire	34,576	53,357	70,801	78,403	84,869	27,887	40,511	51,357	56,507	60,828
New Jersey	237,684	352,741	453,152	514,108	556,465	28,193	40,043	48,875	55,472	60,082
New Mexico	36,371	58,777	74,209	84,561	91,584	19,971	28,465	35,031	39,950	43,336
New York	466,230	713,168	961,434	1,059,484	1,152,505	24,536	36,723	47,813	53,354	58,571
North Carolina	181,526	280,868	408,184	467,930	511,778	22,462	29,345	39,063	44,287	47,834
North Dakota	13,769	23,211	35,084	38,282	41,013	21,446	34,383	45,008	49,209	52,631
Ohio	260,381	355,280	468,366	520,162	561,568	22,914	30,782	39,700	44,215	47,768
Oklahoma	67,414	105,036	137,768	155,214	169,016	19,516	27,938	34,747	38,889	42,046
Oregon	80,982	121,721	179,459	202,810	221,162	23,612	31,718	42,277	47,649	52,159
Pennsylvania	304,665	453,398	574,142	635,949	696,634	24,801	35,654	44,184	48,874	53,703
Rhode Island	25,334	36,597	47,361	53,435	57,771	24,122	34,690	43,199	48,711	52,820
South Carolina	85,735	137,523	195,696	222,947	244,163	21,305	29,678	38,134	42,930	46,220
South Dakota	15,478	25,961	36,652	41,174	44,579	20,478	31,811	41,284	45,944	48,997
Tennessee	126,062	186,470	261,449	297,834	326,338	22,102	29,336	37,751	42,741	46,280
Texas	471,789	771,625	1,176,164	1,343,753	1,473,924	22,526	30,573	40,235	45,460	49,082
Utah	44,950	74,729	125,533	146,419	162,917	20,027	26,919	38,228	43,850	48,189
Vermont	15,571	23,877	30,324	33,123	36,069	25,541	38,121	47,168	51,197	55,743
Virginia	176,025	287,570	370,614	415,582	452,040	24,772	35,834	42,913	48,003	52,057
Washington	152,295	236,857	356,914	403,721	440,420	25,767	35,123	46,208	52,155	56,567
West Virginia	35,057	53,259	66,990	73,693	78,923	19,401	28,720	37,395	41,273	44,460
Wisconsin	124,866	184,794	238,385	267,490	290,411	23,235	32,465	40,430	45,491	49,284
Wyoming	11,358	19,193	25,580	28,313	30,466	22,979	34,006	44,286	48,858	52,403

Source: U.S. Bureau of Economic Analysis, Regional Economic Accounts, "Personal Consumption Expenditures by State," <www.bea.gov/data/consumer-spending/state>, accessed November 2023.

Table 728. Consumer Unit Expenditures—Averages by Income Level: 2022

[In dollars. See headnote, Table 725. See source for definitions, standard errors, and other information]

Income level	Total expenditures [1]	Food	Housing			Transportation			Health care	Pensions & social security
			Total [1]	Shelter	Utilities, fuels [2]	Total [1]	Vehicle purchases	Gasoline & motor oil		
All consumer units	72,967	9,343	24,298	14,507	4,549	12,295	4,496	3,120	5,850	8,223
BY INCOME										
Less than $15,000	31,066	5,337	12,816	8,067	2,605	4,556	([3])	1,514	2,722	244
$15,000 to $29,999	37,534	5,040	14,429	8,648	3,199	5,949	1,974	1,733	4,035	749
$30,000 to $39,999	45,424	6,038	17,442	10,031	3,820	8,093	2,533	2,314	4,544	1,867
$40,000 to $49,999	49,951	7,154	19,487	11,886	4,062	8,535	2,659	2,520	4,477	2,680
$50,000 to $69,999	57,942	8,170	20,553	12,359	4,292	9,705	2,686	3,063	5,748	4,285
$70,000 to $99,999	70,871	9,336	23,523	13,796	4,735	12,888	4,677	3,524	6,152	7,369
$100,000 to $149,999	89,354	11,732	28,337	16,688	5,420	16,215	6,133	4,103	7,099	11,683
$150,000 to $199,999	116,773	14,021	35,588	20,614	6,102	21,190	9,697	4,485	7,764	17,560
$200,000 and over	167,088	17,678	49,709	30,471	6,860	24,764	9,857	4,701	9,885	29,802

[1] Includes expenditures not shown separately. [2] Includes public services. [3] Data are suppressed due to the relative standard error being equal to or greater than 25 percent.

Source: U.S. Bureau of Labor Statistics, Consumer Expenditure Surveys, CE Tables, "Calendar year means, shares across all items, and variances by demographic characteristics, 2022," <www.bls.gov/cex/tables.htm>, accessed November 2023.

Table 729. Consumer Expenditures—Average for All Consumer Units by Race, Hispanic Origin, and Age of Householder: 2022

[In dollars. See headnote, Table 725. See source for definitions, standard errors, and other information]

Expenditure type	All consumer units [1]	White and other races [2]	Asian	Black or African American	Hispanic [3]	Age of householder — Under 25 years	Age of householder — 65 years old and over
Expenditures, total	**72,967**	**74,333**	**87,950**	**57,996**	**64,330**	**46,359**	**57,818**
Food	9,343	9,527	11,507	7,180	9,302	5,898	7,306
Food at home	5,703	5,786	6,945	4,598	5,684	3,347	4,797
Cereals and bakery products	712	717	933	578	657	394	605
Cereals and cereal products	215	213	337	173	213	137	157
Bakery products	497	504	595	405	444	257	448
Meats, poultry, fish, and eggs [4]	1,216	1,193	1,675	1,141	1,393	817	1,019
Beef	317	325	361	251	394	167	273
Pork	246	244	310	232	267	([5])	212
Poultry	215	205	291	242	276	146	160
Fish and seafood	183	162	408	206	184	99	173
Eggs	87	85	138	74	113	65	67
Dairy products [4]	532	560	522	360	521	309	481
Fresh milk and cream	168	173	212	120	186	110	141
Fruits and vegetables [4]	1,099	1,097	1,584	884	1,168	640	944
Fresh fruits	406	404	611	322	458	224	354
Fresh vegetables	352	352	594	239	362	214	305
Processed vegetables	197	198	227	175	192	118	161
Other food at home [4]	2,144	2,219	2,232	1,636	1,945	1,186	1,748
Sugar and other sweets	197	203	204	160	159	81	181
Nonalcoholic beverages	584	604	549	476	597	317	465
Food away from home	3,639	3,741	4,562	2,582	3,618	2,551	2,509
Alcoholic beverages	583	634	390	354	417	394	469
Housing	24,298	24,404	29,560	21,395	22,964	16,837	20,362
Shelter	14,507	14,389	19,818	12,975	14,086	11,737	11,692
Owned dwellings	8,230	8,438	11,030	5,738	5,847	1,614	7,526
Mortgage interest and charges	3,101	3,113	4,902	2,258	2,530	680	1,618
Property taxes	2,570	2,624	4,063	1,591	1,757	492	2,643
Maintenance, repairs, insurance, other expenses	2,559	2,701	2,065	1,890	1,560	([5])	3,266
Rented dwellings	4,990	4,584	7,164	6,596	7,609	9,358	3,021
Other lodging	1,287	1,368	1,623	640	630	([5])	1,145
Utilities, fuels, and public services [4]	4,549	4,583	4,262	4,459	4,433	2,574	4,236
Natural gas	535	525	611	566	438	244	534
Electricity	1,683	1,703	1,457	1,655	1,664	1,029	1,586
Telephone (includes mobile service)	1,431	1,431	1,339	1,475	1,572	903	1,156
Water and other public services	739	751	813	636	707	365	750
Household operations	1,849	1,900	2,204	1,384	1,371	835	1,578
Personal services	488	489	802	347	380	([5])	([5])
Other household expenses	1,361	1,410	1,402	1,037	990	660	1,456
Housekeeping supplies [4]	787	809	692	691	679	314	787
Laundry and cleaning supplies	170	173	136	164	226	50	159
Postage and stationery	128	138	106	73	102	([5])	141
Household furnishings and equipment [4]	2,606	2,723	2,584	1,886	2,396	1,377	2,070
Household textiles	138	146	([5])	100	169	([5])	106
Furniture	746	757	697	701	639	421	547
Major appliances	408	422	372	335	447	183	346
Miscellaneous household equipment	1,138	1,216	1,184	637	981	594	907
Apparel and services [4]	1,945	1,859	2,337	2,310	2,197	1,184	1,130
Men and boys	454	438	590	487	577	([5])	217
Women and girls	735	715	758	([5])	749	321	522
Footwear	399	368	318	631	485	([5])	231
Transportation	12,295	12,434	15,299	10,151	12,586	9,583	8,172
Vehicle purchases (net outlay) [4]	4,496	4,510	7,175	3,263	4,374	4,170	2,649
Cars and trucks, new	2,195	2,165	5,299	([5])	1,827	([5])	1,517
Cars and trucks, used	2,239	2,284	1,705	2,188	2,516	2,458	1,128
Gasoline, other fuels, and motor oil	3,120	3,230	2,771	2,581	3,663	2,495	2,004
Other vehicle expenses	3,834	3,866	3,716	3,685	3,878	2,373	2,939
Vehicle finance charges	295	300	239	288	342	224	132
Maintenance and repairs	1,160	1,191	1,011	1,033	1,148	519	968
Vehicle rental, leases, licenses, other charges	787	792	916	704	607	420	607
Vehicle insurance	1,592	1,584	1,550	1,660	1,781	1,210	1,232
Public transportation	845	827	1,636	622	671	546	579
Health care	5,850	6,183	5,643	3,869	3,964	1,353	7,540
Entertainment	3,458	3,772	2,599	1,880	2,329	2,075	2,672
Personal care products and services	866	862	943	854	840	540	706
Reading	117	124	108	74	67	([5])	152
Education	1,335	1,330	2,880	712	895	2,960	373
Tobacco products and smoking supplies	371	386	162	371	213	226	261
Miscellaneous	1,009	1,061	940	710	695	([5])	943
Cash contributions	2,755	2,953	([5])	1,726	1,046	([5])	4,443
Personal insurance and pensions	8,742	8,804	13,311	6,410	6,815	4,244	3,289
Life and other personal insurance	519	517	577	506	256	([5])	533
Pensions and social security	8,223	8,286	12,734	5,904	6,558	4,172	2,756
Personal taxes	**10,809**	**11,150**	**18,762**	**5,297**	**3,735**	**1,794**	**3,466**

[1] Includes other races not shown separately. [2] Other races includes Native Hawaiian or other Pacific Islander, American Indian or Alaska Native, and respondents reporting more than one race. [3] People of Hispanic origin may be of any race. [4] Includes other types, not shown separately. [5] Data are suppressed due to the relative standard error being equal to or greater than 25 percent.

Source: U.S. Bureau of Labor Statistics, Consumer Expenditure Surveys, CE Tables, "Calendar year means, shares across all items, and variances by demographic characteristics, 2022," <www.bls.gov/cex/tables.htm>, accessed November 2023.

Table 730. Consumer Expenditures—Averages for All Consumer Units by Region and Size of Unit: 2022

[In dollars. For composition of regions, see map, inside front cover. See headnote, Table 725. See source for definitions, standard errors, and other information]

Expenditure type	Region				Size of consumer unit				
	North-east	Mid-west	South	West	One person	Two persons	Three persons	Four persons	Five or more
Expenditures, total	**79,741**	**69,870**	**65,576**	**83,317**	**44,312**	**76,468**	**86,265**	**101,514**	**96,814**
Food	10,199	8,827	8,443	10,699	5,235	9,363	11,158	13,055	14,790
Food at home	6,303	5,559	5,135	6,342	3,224	5,635	6,862	8,012	9,066
Cereals and bakery products	825	703	622	786	392	682	865	1,026	1,191
Cereals and cereal products	251	206	184	248	109	198	267	324	389
Bakery products	574	496	438	537	283	484	599	703	802
Meats, poultry, fish, and eggs [1]	1,325	1,148	1,149	1,308	666	1,196	1,521	1,640	2,020
Beef	279	311	323	344	164	323	409	414	525
Pork	241	261	233	260	125	234	333	349	408
Poultry	240	191	204	236	125	198	265	308	359
Fish and seafood	264	138	160	200	([2])	181	210	228	314
Eggs	91	73	81	107	52	85	108	115	136
Dairy products [1]	615	523	460	599	305	530	644	740	819
Fresh milk and cream	193	160	143	200	96	159	206	247	270
Fruits and vegetables [1]	1,294	1,040	916	1,317	622	1,085	1,272	1,607	1,744
Fresh fruits	486	379	329	502	221	398	476	580	694
Fresh vegetables	427	311	283	451	210	352	402	529	500
Processed vegetables	222	206	179	199	110	196	230	294	301
Other food at home [1]	2,244	2,146	1,988	2,333	1,239	2,143	2,559	2,999	3,292
Sugar and other sweets	197	204	186	211	109	205	233	271	301
Nonalcoholic beverages	607	573	566	607	348	580	681	774	954
Food away from home	3,896	3,268	3,309	4,357	2,011	3,728	4,297	5,042	5,724
Alcoholic beverages	679	591	506	634	446	717	608	660	435
Housing	27,433	21,907	21,494	28,938	17,477	24,528	27,433	32,048	30,893
Shelter	17,197	12,314	12,240	18,378	11,553	14,533	15,884	18,004	17,425
Owned dwellings	9,791	7,952	6,961	9,471	4,882	8,531	9,726	11,953	11,022
Mortgage interest and charges	3,042	2,672	2,614	4,372	1,424	2,817	4,025	5,477	5,062
Property taxes	4,056	2,736	1,857	2,508	1,598	2,735	3,074	3,589	3,096
Maintenance, repair, insurance, other expenses	2,692	2,544	2,491	2,591	1,861	2,979	2,627	2,887	2,863
Rented dwellings	5,697	3,154	4,249	7,429	5,949	4,452	4,576	4,313	5,188
Other lodging	1,710	1,208	1,030	1,478	721	1,550	1,582	1,739	1,215
Utilities, fuels, and public services [1]	4,829	4,534	4,481	4,468	2,865	4,679	5,455	5,872	6,471
Natural gas	753	854	314	451	369	543	627	650	755
Electricity	1,571	1,480	1,922	1,550	1,131	1,752	1,971	2,087	2,279
Telephone services (includes mobile)	1,448	1,378	1,425	1,478	820	1,444	1,785	1,993	2,107
Water and other public services	568	686	734	927	461	752	861	986	1,090
Household operations	2,052	1,721	1,662	2,135	1,053	1,645	2,398	3,282	2,483
Personal services	617	502	355	605	([2])	124	844	1,616	1,063
Other household expenses	1,435	1,219	1,307	1,531	966	1,521	1,554	1,666	1,420
Housekeeping supplies [1]	810	810	740	828	503	862	951	932	1,000
Laundry and cleaning supplies	157	175	166	181	102	178	219	188	262
Postage and stationery	109	111	107	195	90	149	119	172	134
Household furnishings and equipment [1]	2,544	2,528	2,371	3,127	1,503	2,809	2,745	3,958	3,515
Household textiles	118	165	117	165	85	142	174	152	([2])
Furniture	741	721	721	816	354	871	700	1,248	1,015
Major appliances	407	418	362	477	205	433	449	677	572
Miscellaneous household equipment	1,087	1,059	1,017	1,459	734	1,169	1,236	1,681	1,470
Apparel and services [1]	2,312	1,765	1,785	2,104	945	1,798	2,107	3,422	3,468
Men and boys	557	435	427	439	164	379	492	867	1,037
Women and girls	851	669	687	790	395	752	762	1,178	1,139
Footwear	439	336	366	483	237	341	406	648	773
Transportation	12,093	11,912	11,932	13,420	6,479	12,452	15,919	18,714	16,945
Vehicle purchases (net outlay)	4,259	4,423	4,565	4,624	2,103	4,282	6,372	7,837	5,928
Cars and trucks, new	2,123	2,246	2,031	2,481	1,064	2,253	3,056	3,935	([2])
Cars and trucks, used	2,093	2,094	2,470	2,092	998	1,970	3,226	3,820	3,664
Gasoline, other fuels, and motor oil	2,631	3,012	3,187	3,472	1,590	3,141	3,936	4,467	5,015
Other vehicle expenses	4,005	3,764	3,579	4,206	2,233	4,116	4,678	5,189	5,049
Vehicle finance charges	248	297	308	305	122	287	411	466	486
Maintenance and repair	1,080	1,208	1,065	1,338	713	1,310	1,360	1,341	1,555
Vehicle rental, leases, licenses, other charges	1,156	865	529	876	464	846	963	1,218	829
Vehicle insurance	1,520	1,394	1,676	1,688	934	1,674	1,944	2,164	2,179
Public transportation	1,198	712	601	1,119	553	913	933	1,221	952
Health care	6,069	6,569	5,376	5,828	3,770	6,878	6,660	7,288	6,045
Entertainment	3,509	3,701	2,831	4,262	1,918	3,839	4,068	4,752	4,541
Personal care products and services	979	842	768	971	547	916	993	1,109	1,219
Reading	152	109	80	160	101	134	110	130	101
Education	2,166	1,483	893	1,326	712	1,136	1,871	2,123	2,211
Tobacco products/smoking supplies	327	463	391	287	274	400	469	369	444
Miscellaneous	1,097	979	906	1,143	710	1,148	1,181	1,076	1,146
Cash contributions	2,732	1,910	2,750	([2])	1,742	4,165	2,093	2,463	2,572
Personal insurance and pensions	9,995	8,812	7,422	9,979	3,956	8,996	11,594	14,305	12,005
Life and other personal insurance	606	524	439	586	221	649	636	738	590
Pensions and social security	9,390	8,288	6,983	9,393	3,735	8,347	10,958	13,567	11,415
Personal taxes	**14,898**	**10,257**	**7,976**	**13,064**	**5,828**	**12,584**	**14,493**	**16,877**	**7,876**

[1] Includes other types not shown separately. [2] Data are suppressed due to the relative standard error being equal to or greater than 25 percent.

Source: U.S. Bureau of Labor Statistics, Consumer Expenditure Surveys, CE Tables, "Calendar year means, shares across all items, and variances by demographic characteristics, 2022," <www.bls.gov/cex/tables.htm>, accessed November 2023.

Table 731. Money Income of Households—Percent Distribution by Income Level, Race, and Hispanic Origin in Constant (2022) Dollars: 2000 to 2022

[In percent except as noted (108,200 represents 108,200,000). Households as of March of following year. Income in 2022 Chained Consumer Price Index for all Urban Consumers (C-CPI-U) adjusted dollars. Based on Current Population Survey, Annual Social and Economic Supplement (CPS ASEC); see text, this section and Section 1, and Appendix III. For definition of median, see Guide to Tabular Presentation. A household consists of all the persons who occupy a housing unit. Household count excludes persons living in group quarters and institutions. For 2001 data and earlier, the CPS allowed respondents to report only one race group. Beginning with the 2003 CPS covering data for 2002, refers to respondents reporting only one race. Two basic ways of defining a race group are possible: a group such as Asian may be defined as 1) those who reported Asian and no other race (the race-alone concept), or 2) those who reported Asian regardless of whether they also reported another race (the race-alone-or-in-combination concept). Data users should exercise caution when comparing trends over time due to changes in CPS ASEC methodology and data processing. Changes are noted below as appropriate. See source for more information]

Year and race/ethnicity	Number of house-holds (1,000)	Percent distribution							Median income (dollars)
		Under $15,000	$15,000 to $24,999	$25,000 to $34,999	$35,000 to $49,999	$50,000 to $74,999	$75,000 to $99,999	$100,000 and over	
ALL HOUSEHOLDS [1]									
2000 [4]	108,200	8.2	8.8	8.2	12.6	17.0	13.3	31.9	67,470
2010 [5]	119,900	9.6	9.5	9.1	12.1	16.5	12.6	30.6	64,300
2020 [6,7,8]	129,200	8.1	7.7	7.5	10.3	15.6	12.1	38.7	76,660
2022	131,400	8.3	7.4	7.6	10.6	16.2	12.3	37.5	74,580
WHITE [2]									
2000 [4]	90,030	7.0	8.5	7.9	12.4	17.0	13.6	33.5	70,570
2010 [5]	96,310	8.0	9.2	8.8	12.0	16.6	13.0	32.5	67,480
2020 [6,7,8]	100,900	6.9	7.2	7.3	10.1	15.6	12.4	40.5	80,750
2022	101,400	7.4	7.2	7.4	10.4	16.2	12.6	38.9	77,250
BLACK [2]									
2000 [4]	13,170	16.1	11.2	10.9	14.6	17.5	11.8	18.0	47,670
2010 [5]	15,270	19.7	12.4	11.4	13.4	16.4	10.4	16.2	41,920
2020 [6,7,8]	17,320	15.5	11.0	10.0	12.2	16.7	10.9	23.8	51,880
2022	18,080	13.7	9.9	10.3	12.6	18.0	11.4	23.9	52,860
ASIAN AND PACIFIC ISLANDER [2]									
2000 [4]	3,963	6.8	6.0	5.2	9.9	15.1	12.2	44.8	89,590
2010 [5]	5,212	8.4	6.3	7.4	8.5	14.2	12.9	42.2	83,850
2020 [6,7,8]	7,002	6.3	5.7	4.6	7.2	13.1	10.1	53.0	107,300
2022	7,609	7.5	4.7	4.5	6.9	12.0	10.4	54.1	108,700
HISPANIC [3]									
2000 [4]	10,030	10.0	10.8	10.9	15.5	19.8	13.0	20.0	53,300
2010 [5]	14,440	12.6	11.2	12.1	15.1	17.6	11.7	19.8	49,110
2020 [6,7,8]	18,340	9.2	8.7	9.0	13.5	17.8	13.1	28.6	62,480
2022	19,320	9.8	8.1	8.9	12.7	18.5	13.5	28.4	62,800

[1] Includes other races not shown separately. [2] Beginning 2002, data represent White alone, Black alone, or Asian alone. [3] People of Hispanic origin may be of any race. [4] Data reflect implementation of Census 2000-based population controls and a 28,000 household sample expansion. [5] Beginning with 2009 income data, the Census Bureau expanded the upper income intervals used to calculate medians to $250,000 or more. Medians falling in the upper open-ended interval are plugged with "$250,000." Before 2009, the upper open-ended interval was $100,000 and a plug of "$100,000" was used. Data reflect implementation of Census 2010-based population controls. [6] Beginning 2013, data are based on redesigned income questions. Beginning 2017, data reflect use of an updated processing system. [7] See source for information on the impact of the coronavirus 2019 (COVID-19) pandemic on the CPS ASEC. [8] Implementation of 2020 Census-based population controls.

Source: U.S. Census Bureau, *Income in the United States: 2022,* Current Population Reports, P60-279, September 2023; and "Historical Income Tables: Households, Table H-17," <www.census.gov/topics/income-poverty/income/data/tables.html>, accessed October 2023.

Table 732. Money Income of Households—Median Income by Race and Hispanic Origin in Current and Constant (2022) Dollars: 2000 to 2022

[In dollars. Constant 2022 dollars adjusted using the Chained Consumer Price Index for all Urban Consumers (C-CPI-U) for 2000 to 2022 income. See headnote, Table 731. Beginning 2013, data are based on redesigned questions on income]

Year	Median income in current dollars					Median income in constant (2022) dollars				
	All house-holds [1]	White [2]	Black [2]	Asian, Pacific Islander [2]	His-panic [3]	All house-holds [1]	White [2]	Black [2]	Asian, Pacific Islander [2]	His-panic [3]
2000 [4,5]	41,990	43,920	29,670	55,760	33,170	67,470	70,570	47,670	89,590	53,300
2010 [6,7]	49,280	51,710	32,120	64,260	37,630	64,300	67,480	41,920	83,850	49,110
2015 [8]	56,520	60,110	36,900	77,170	45,150	68,410	72,760	44,670	93,410	54,650
2016	59,040	61,860	39,490	81,430	47,680	70,840	74,220	47,380	97,710	57,200
2017 [9]	61,140	64,830	39,370	81,390	50,170	72,090	76,450	46,420	95,970	59,150
2018	63,180	66,940	41,360	87,190	51,450	73,030	77,380	47,810	100,800	59,470
2019 [10]	68,700	72,200	45,440	98,170	56,110	78,250	82,240	51,750	111,800	63,910
2020 [10,11]	68,010	71,630	46,030	95,180	55,430	76,660	80,750	51,880	107,300	62,480
2021 [10]	70,780	74,260	48,300	101,400	57,980	76,330	80,080	52,080	109,400	62,520
2022	74,580	77,250	52,860	108,700	62,800	74,580	77,250	52,860	108,700	62,800

[1] Includes other races not shown separately. [2] Beginning 2002, data represent White alone, Black alone, or Asian alone. [3] People of Hispanic origin may be of any race. [4] Use of Census 2000-based population controls. [5] Implementation of 28,000 household sample expansion. [6] Beginning with 2009 data, Census Bureau expanded upper income intervals used to calculate medians to $250,000 or more. Before 2009, upper open-ended interval was $100,000 and a plug of "$100,000" was used. [7] Implementation of Census 2010-based population controls. [8] Beginning 2014, data are based on redesigned income questions. [9] Implementation of an updated processing system. [10] See source for information on the impact of the coronavirus 2019 (COVID-19) pandemic on the CPS ASEC. [11] Implementation of 2020 Census-based population controls.

Source: U.S. Census Bureau, *Income in the United States: 2022,* Current Population Reports, P60-279, September 2023; and "Historical Income Tables: Households, Table H-5," <www.census.gov/topics/income-poverty/income/data/tables.html>, accessed October 2023.

Table 733. Money Income of Households—Households by Income Level and Selected Characteristics: 2022

[131,400 represents 131,400,000. Households as of March of the following year. Based on Current Population Survey, Annual Social and Economic Supplement (CPS ASEC); see text, this section and Section 1, and Appendix III. For definition of median, see Guide to Tabular Presentation]

Characteristic	Total house-holds	Under $15,000	$15,000 to $24,999	$25,000 to $34,999	$35,000 to $49,999	$50,000 to $74,999	$75,000 to $99,999	$100,000 and over	Median house-hold income [1] (dollars)
Total.............................	**131,400**	**10,972**	**9,772**	**10,013**	**13,888**	**21,324**	**16,205**	**49,260**	**74,580**
Region: [2]									
Northeast........................	22,630	1,856	1,694	1,627	2,118	3,405	2,647	9,285	80,360
Midwest.........................	28,280	2,195	2,147	2,204	3,125	4,745	3,591	10,272	73,070
South............................	51,080	4,763	4,023	4,273	5,830	8,612	6,263	17,311	68,230
West.............................	29,440	2,157	1,907	1,910	2,816	4,564	3,702	12,386	82,890
Type of household:									
Family household..............	84,330	3,816	3,256	4,763	7,538	13,339	11,385	40,239	95,450
Married-couple................	62,180	1,713	1,583	2,626	4,649	8,751	8,280	34,572	110,800
Male householder, spouse absent..............	7,128	389	379	620	774	1,462	1,131	2,375	73,630
Female householder, spouse absent..............	15,030	1,716	1,295	1,519	2,115	3,126	1,976	3,288	56,030
Nonfamily household...........	47,100	7,157	6,516	5,249	6,350	7,988	4,817	9,023	45,440
Male householder..............	22,740	3,037	2,562	2,274	2,984	4,008	2,530	5,345	51,930
Female householder...........	24,360	4,118	3,956	2,975	3,367	3,978	2,286	3,681	40,200
Age of householder:									
15 to 24 years...................	6,136	772	528	641	939	1,265	817	1,172	52,460
25 to 34 years...................	20,720	1,109	938	1,421	2,229	3,909	3,096	8,021	80,240
35 to 44 years...................	22,530	1,225	971	1,184	1,870	3,428	2,902	10,950	96,630
45 to 54 years...................	21,500	1,220	881	980	1,684	3,060	2,655	11,018	101,500
55 to 64 years...................	23,410	2,361	1,667	1,438	2,116	3,395	2,796	9,638	81,240
65 years and over..............	37,130	4,285	4,787	4,349	5,048	6,267	3,938	8,455	50,290
Size of household:									
One person......................	38,100	6,713	6,143	4,802	5,445	6,494	3,496	5,005	38,350
Two people......................	45,960	2,568	2,196	3,113	4,935	8,166	6,384	18,595	81,990
Three people....................	19,770	865	642	951	1,581	3,062	2,781	9,893	100,000
Four people.....................	16,040	488	467	616	1,081	1,964	1,979	9,443	117,900
Five people......................	7,192	215	210	315	503	1,010	986	3,952	108,900
Six people.......................	2,721	66	76	159	195	375	364	1,484	107,600
Seven or more people...........	1,656	58	40	59	148	251	214	883	109,100
Number of earners:									
No earners.......................	32,740	8,611	6,056	4,414	4,314	4,171	2,073	3,103	28,410
One earner.......................	46,490	2,153	3,280	4,764	7,339	10,881	6,437	11,629	61,300
Two earners and more...........	52,200	209	436	835	2,234	6,271	7,695	34,531	127,900
Two earners.....................	41,770	179	396	720	2,019	5,562	6,543	26,347	121,300
Three earners...................	7,764	25	39	111	174	604	967	5,842	146,300
Four earners or more...........	2,675	5	–	4	43	103	184	2,336	181,400
Work experience of householder:									
Total.............................	131,400	10,972	9,772	10,013	13,888	21,324	16,205	49,260	74,580
Worked..........................	86,000	2,054	3,158	4,744	7,943	14,263	12,121	41,721	96,730
Worked at full-time jobs........	73,310	927	1,922	3,494	6,489	12,097	10,574	37,806	101,800
50 weeks or more.............	64,440	368	1,192	2,716	5,436	10,561	9,332	34,837	106,200
27 to 49 weeks...............	5,796	132	377	480	690	1,050	876	2,193	78,630
26 weeks or less..............	3,074	427	354	299	361	484	366	782	53,890
Worked at part-time jobs.......	12,690	1,128	1,236	1,249	1,454	2,166	1,546	3,906	63,610
50 weeks or more.............	7,277	430	677	698	838	1,336	883	2,414	67,780
27 to 49 weeks...............	2,585	225	214	266	299	396	349	836	67,740
26 weeks or less..............	2,826	473	345	285	318	434	315	658	49,700
Did not work.....................	45,430	8,919	6,615	5,269	5,944	7,062	4,083	7,542	39,520
Educational attainment of householder: [3]									
Total.............................	125,300	10,201	9,245	9,371	12,948	20,059	15,385	48,084	75,980
Less than 9th grade.............	3,672	761	627	491	515	553	322	404	33,830
9th to 12th grade (no diploma)...................	5,960	1,273	940	736	810	960	478	763	35,470
High school graduate...........	31,830	3,767	3,549	3,503	4,589	5,865	3,817	6,740	51,470
Some college, no degree.......	20,090	1,720	1,785	1,761	2,531	3,629	2,647	6,017	64,150
Associate's degree.............	13,560	907	872	992	1,483	2,533	1,959	4,818	74,920
Bachelor's degree or more......	50,180	1,771	1,471	1,888	3,021	6,518	6,163	29,351	118,300
Bachelor's degree.............	30,070	1,172	1,018	1,261	1,995	4,206	3,912	16,506	108,800
Master's degree..............	15,050	439	323	500	775	1,846	1,828	9,346	128,000
Professional degree...........	2,135	66	68	64	127	212	173	1,426	157,800
Doctoral degree...............	2,919	94	61	63	124	256	248	2,072	151,400
Housing tenure:									
Owner occupied..................	86,780	4,847	4,815	5,404	7,982	13,177	11,051	39,510	90,630
Renter occupied.................	43,260	5,835	4,735	4,431	5,753	7,963	5,037	9,509	51,730
Occupier paid no cash rent.......	1,387	290	222	178	153	186	116	243	35,480

– Represents zero. [1] Median income calculated using $2,500 income intervals. Medians falling in the upper open-ended interval are plugged with "$250,000." [2] For composition of regions, see map, inside front cover. [3] Data shown for householders age 25 and over.

Source: U.S. Census Bureau, *Income in the United States: 2022*, Current Population Reports, P60-279, September 2023; and "Current Population Survey Tables for Household Income: Table HINC-01," <www.census.gov/topics/income-poverty/income/data/tables.html>, accessed October 2023.

Table 734. Money Income of Households—Households by Income Level, Race, and Hispanic Origin: 2022

[131,400 represents 131,400,000. Households as of March of the following year. Based on Current Population Survey, Annual Social and Economic Supplement (ASEC); see text, this section and Section 1, and Appendix III]

Income level	Number of households (1,000)					Percent distribution				
	All races [1]	White alone	Black alone	Asian alone	His-panic [2]	All races [1]	White alone	Black alone	Asian alone	His-panic [2]
All households..............	**131,400**	**101,400**	**18,080**	**7,609**	**19,320**	**100.0**	**100.0**	**100.0**	**100.0**	**100.0**
Under $10,000...............	6,436	4,371	1,439	383	1,126	4.9	4.3	8.0	5.0	5.8
$10,000 to $14,999...........	4,536	3,097	1,046	187	775	3.5	3.1	5.8	2.5	4.0
$15,000 to $19,999...........	4,725	3,461	912	191	715	3.6	3.4	5.0	2.5	3.7
$20,000 to $24,999...........	5,047	3,817	879	165	850	3.8	3.8	4.9	2.2	4.4
$25,000 to $29,999...........	4,728	3,610	818	137	826	3.6	3.6	4.5	1.8	4.3
$30,000 to $34,999...........	5,285	3,862	1,047	204	885	4.0	3.8	5.8	2.7	4.6
$35,000 to $39,999...........	4,674	3,542	789	177	857	3.6	3.5	4.4	2.3	4.4
$40,000 to $44,999...........	4,761	3,628	784	156	761	3.6	3.6	4.3	2.1	3.9
$45,000 to $49,999...........	4,453	3,357	712	192	839	3.4	3.3	3.9	2.5	4.3
$50,000 to $59,999...........	9,090	6,931	1,513	374	1,436	6.9	6.8	8.4	4.9	7.4
$60,000 to $74,999...........	12,234	9,455	1,749	539	2,144	9.3	9.3	9.7	7.1	11.1
$75,000 to $84,999...........	7,174	5,600	976	340	1,188	5.5	5.5	5.4	4.5	6.1
$85,000 to $99,999...........	9,031	7,149	1,084	449	1,417	6.9	7.1	6.0	5.9	7.3
$100,000 to $149,999........	21,571	17,390	2,155	1,416	2,848	16.4	17.1	11.9	18.6	14.7
$150,000 to $199,999........	12,029	9,682	1,084	946	1,341	9.2	9.5	6.0	12.4	6.9
$200,000 to $249,999........	6,024	4,790	533	557	595	4.6	4.7	2.9	7.3	3.1
$250,000 and over............	9,636	7,680	558	1,197	716	7.3	7.6	3.1	15.7	3.7

[1] Includes other races, not shown separately. [2] Persons of Hispanic origin may be of any race.

Source: U.S. Census Bureau, *Income in the United States: 2022*, Current Population Reports, P60-279, September 2023; and "Current Population Survey Tables for Household Income: Table HINC-06," <www.census.gov/topics/income-poverty/income/data/tables.html>, accessed October 2023.

Table 735. Share of Aggregate Income Received by Each Fifth and Top 5 Percent of Households: 1990 to 2022

[In units as indicated (94,310 represents 94,310,000). Households as of March of the following year. Income in constant 2022 dollars adjusted using the Chained Consumer Price Index for all Urban Consumers (C-CPI-U) for 2000 to 2022 income, and for income prior to 2000 adjusted using the Consumer Price Index for all Urban Consumers Retroactive Series (R-CPI-U-RS). The shares method ranks households from highest to lowest on the basis of income and then divides them into groups of equal population size, typically quintiles. The aggregate income of each group is then divided by the overall aggregate income to derive shares. Based on the Current Population Survey, Annual Social and Economic Supplement (CPS ASEC); see text, this section and Section 1, and Appendix III. For data collection changes over time, see source. See also headnote, Table 731]

Year	Number of house-holds (1,000)	Income at selected positions in constant (2022) dollars					Percent distribution of aggregate income					
		Upper limit of each fifth				Top 5 percent, lower limit	Lowest 5th	Second 5th	Third 5th	Fourth 5th	Highest 5th	Top 5 percent
		Lowest	Second	Third	Fourth							
1990...................	94,310	25,670	48,600	74,350	113,400	194,600	3.8	9.6	15.9	24.0	46.6	18.5
1995 [1].................	99,630	25,960	48,530	75,730	117,400	203,700	3.7	9.1	15.2	23.3	48.7	21.0
2000 [2, 3]...............	108,200	28,800	53,030	83,840	131,400	233,300	3.6	8.9	14.8	23.0	49.8	22.1
2005...................	114,400	27,650	51,890	83,120	132,200	239,300	3.4	8.6	14.6	23.0	50.4	22.2
2006...................	116,000	28,070	52,920	84,050	135,900	243,800	3.4	8.6	14.5	22.9	50.5	22.3
2007...................	116,800	27,710	53,400	84,680	136,600	241,800	3.4	8.7	14.8	23.4	49.7	21.2
2008...................	117,200	27,290	51,380	82,640	132,100	237,200	3.4	8.6	14.7	23.3	50.0	21.5
2009 [4].................	117,500	27,060	51,000	81,750	132,300	238,100	3.4	8.6	14.6	23.2	50.3	21.7
2010 [5].................	119,900	26,100	49,590	80,250	130,500	235,500	3.3	8.5	14.6	23.4	50.3	21.3
2011...................	121,100	25,640	48,750	79,020	128,600	235,400	3.2	8.4	14.3	23.0	51.1	22.3
2012...................	122,500	25,580	49,370	80,190	129,300	237,400	3.2	8.3	14.4	23.0	51.0	22.3
2013 [6].................	123,900	25,760	50,340	82,440	135,200	251,700	3.1	8.2	14.3	23.0	51.4	22.2
2014...................	124,600	25,920	49,820	82,510	135,800	249,900	3.1	8.2	14.3	23.2	51.2	21.9
2015...................	125,800	27,600	52,670	87,160	141,600	259,600	3.1	8.2	14.3	23.2	51.1	22.1
2016...................	126,200	28,800	54,710	89,830	145,200	270,300	3.1	8.3	14.2	22.9	51.5	22.6
2017 [7].................	127,700	29,270	55,680	90,970	149,300	287,800	3.0	8.1	14.0	22.6	52.3	23.2
2018...................	128,600	29,590	57,790	91,940	150,300	287,500	3.1	8.3	14.1	22.6	52.0	23.1
2019 [8].................	128,500	31,990	60,940	98,510	162,300	307,500	3.1	8.3	14.1	22.7	51.9	23.0
2020 [8, 9]...............	129,200	30,740	59,280	96,420	160,100	310,000	3.0	8.2	14.0	22.6	52.2	23.0
2021 [8].................	131,200	30,200	59,310	96,770	160,800	308,700	2.9	8.0	13.9	22.6	52.7	23.5
2022...................	131,400	30,000	58,020	94,000	153,000	295,000	3.0	8.2	14.0	22.5	52.1	23.5

[1] Data reflect full implementation of the 1990 Census-based sample design and metropolitan definitions, 7,000 household sample reduction, and revised race edits. [2] Implementation of Census 2000-based population controls. [3] Implementation of a 28,000 household sample expansion. [4] Beginning with 2009 income data, the Census Bureau expanded the upper income interval used to calculate medians to $250,000 or more. Medians falling in the upper open-ended interval are plugged with "$250,000." [5] Implementation of Census 2010-based population controls. [6] Beginning 2013, data are based on redesigned income questions. [7] Implementation of an updated processing system. [8] See source for information on the impact of the coronavirus 2019 (COVID-19) pandemic on the CPS ASEC. [9] Implementation of 2020 Census-based population controls.

Source: U.S. Census Bureau, *Income in the United States: 2022,* Current Population Reports, P60-279, September 2023; and "Historical Income Tables: Households, Tables H1 and H2," <www.census.gov/topics/income-poverty/income/data/tables.html>, accessed October 2023.

Table 736. Money Income of Families—Families by Income Level, Race, and Hispanic Origin: 2022

[84,350 represents 84,350,000. Families as of March of the following year. Based on Current Population Survey Annual Social and Economic Supplement (CPS ASEC); see text, this section, Section 1, and Appendix III. A family is a group of persons residing together and related by birth, marriage, or adoption. See also headnote in Table 731 regarding changes in the CPS ASEC]

Income level	Number of families (1,000)					Percent distribution				
	All races	White alone	Black alone	Asian alone	His-panic [1]	All races	White alone	Black alone	Asian alone	His-panic [1]
All families	**84,350**	**65,670**	**10,440**	**5,508**	**14,240**	**100.0**	**100.0**	**100.0**	**100.0**	**100.0**
Under $10,000	3,033	2,087	638	160	758	3.6	3.2	6.1	2.9	5.3
$10,000 to $14,999	1,348	928	257	64	354	1.6	1.4	2.5	1.2	2.5
$15,000 to $19,999	1,548	1,080	304	94	418	1.8	1.6	2.9	1.7	2.9
$20,000 to $24,999	1,978	1,427	380	76	579	2.3	2.2	3.6	1.4	4.1
$25,000 to $29,999	2,312	1,650	499	69	587	2.7	2.5	4.8	1.3	4.1
$30,000 to $34,999	2,609	1,843	530	129	594	3.1	2.8	5.1	2.3	4.2
$35,000 to $39,999	2,521	1,923	387	113	601	3.0	2.9	3.7	2.1	4.2
$40,000 to $44,999	2,632	1,946	441	116	577	3.1	3.0	4.2	2.1	4.1
$45,000 to $49,999	2,577	1,958	383	123	596	3.1	3.0	3.7	2.2	4.2
$50,000 to $59,999	5,495	4,249	825	242	1,129	6.5	6.5	7.9	4.4	7.9
$60,000 to $74,999	7,838	6,079	1,109	348	1,612	9.3	9.3	10.6	6.3	11.3
$75,000 to $84,999	4,653	3,665	600	249	871	5.5	5.6	5.7	4.5	6.1
$85,000 to $99,999	6,489	5,142	811	315	1,138	7.7	7.8	7.8	5.7	8.0
$100,000 to $149,999	16,250	13,160	1,566	1,103	2,269	19.3	20.0	15.0	20.0	15.9
$150,000 to $199,999	9,738	7,902	843	761	1,059	11.5	12.0	8.1	13.8	7.4
$200,000 to $249,999	5,004	3,998	430	469	492	5.9	6.1	4.1	8.5	3.5
$250,000 and over	8,316	6,634	439	1,077	608	9.9	10.1	4.2	19.6	4.3

[1] Persons of Hispanic origin may be of any race.

Source: U.S. Census Bureau, *Income in the United States: 2022,* Current Population Reports, P60-279, September 2023; and "Current Population Survey Tables for Family Income: Table FINC-07," <www.census.gov/topics/income-poverty/income/data/tables.html>, accessed October 2023.

Table 737. Money Income of Families—Percent Distribution of Families by Income Level in Constant (2022) Dollars: 2000 to 2022

[73,780 represents 73,780,000. Income in 2022 Chained Consumer Price Index for all Urban Consumers (C-CPI-U) adjusted dollars. Families as of March of the following year. Based on Current Population Survey Annual Social and Economic Supplement (CPS ASEC); see text, this section and Section 1, and Appendix III. For definition of median, see Guide to Tabular Presentation. For comments on race, see headnote Table 731. Data users should exercise caution when comparing trends over time due to changes in CPS ASEC methodology and data processing. See source for more information]

Year and race/ethnicity	Number of families (1,000)	Percent distribution							Median income (dollars)
		Under $15,000	$15,000 to $24,999	$25,000 to $34,999	$35,000 to $49,999	$50,000 to $74,999	$75,000 to $99,999	$100,000 and over	
ALL FAMILIES [1]									
2000 [4]	73,780	4.8	5.7	7.0	11.5	17.2	14.6	39.2	81,520
2010 [5]	79,560	6.5	6.1	7.6	11.3	16.7	13.7	38.2	78,600
2020 [6]	83,720	5.1	4.5	5.7	9.0	15.0	12.9	47.7	95,080
2022	84,350	5.2	4.2	5.8	9.2	15.8	13.2	46.6	92,750
WHITE [2]									
2000 [4]	61,330	3.8	5.0	6.5	11.1	17.3	15.0	41.3	85,210
2010 [5]	63,980	5.2	5.5	7.1	11.1	16.7	14.1	40.4	82,100
2020 [6]	65,710	4.2	3.9	5.3	8.6	14.8	13.1	49.9	99,820
2022	65,670	4.6	3.8	5.3	8.9	15.7	13.4	48.2	96,340
BLACK [2]									
2000 [4]	8,731	11.4	10.1	10.7	15.0	18.0	13.0	21.8	54,110
2010 [5]	9,571	14.7	10.1	11.6	13.4	17.6	11.7	20.9	50,360
2020 [6]	10,230	10.6	8.0	8.8	11.9	17.8	12.3	30.6	64,900
2022	10,440	8.6	6.6	9.9	11.6	18.5	13.5	31.4	66,760
ASIAN AND PACIFIC ISLANDER [2]									
2000 [4]	2,982	3.8	4.9	4.7	8.9	14.7	12.7	50.2	100,600
2010 [5]	3,879	5.3	4.8	5.7	8.4	13.8	13.2	48.8	98,150
2020 [6]	5,179	3.6	4.2	3.7	6.6	12.8	9.9	59.3	123,600
2022	5,508	4.1	3.1	3.6	6.4	10.7	10.2	61.9	126,200
HISPANIC ORIGIN [3]									
2000 [4]	8,017	8.1	10.5	11.1	15.9	20.1	13.5	20.8	55,340
2010 [5]	11,280	11.5	10.5	12.1	15.4	17.9	12.0	20.7	51,280
2020 [6]	13,700	7.1	7.1	8.7	13.8	18.2	13.7	31.4	67,700
2022	14,240	7.8	7.0	8.3	12.5	19.2	14.1	31.0	67,880

[1] Includes other races not shown separately. [2] Beginning 2002, represents White alone, Black alone, or Asian alone. [3] People of Hispanic origin may be of any race. [4] Data reflect implementation of Census 2000-based population controls and a 28,000 household sample expansion. [5] Implementation of Census 2010-based population controls. Beginning with 2009 income data, the Census Bureau expanded the upper income intervals used to calculate medians to $250,000 or more. Medians falling in the upper open-ended interval are plugged with "$250,000." [6] Data are based on redesigned income questions, and reflect an updated CPS ASEC processing system. See source for information on the impact of the coronavirus 2019 (COVID-19) pandemic on CPS ASEC data collection and response. Beginning 2020, data reflect implementation of 2020 Census-based population controls.

Source: U.S. Census Bureau, *Income in the United States: 2022,* Current Population Reports, P60-279, September 2023; and "Historical Income Tables: Families, Table F-23," <www.census.gov/topics/income-poverty/income/data/tables.html>, accessed November 2023.

Table 738. Money Income of Families—Median Income by Race and Hispanic Origin in Current and Constant (2022) Dollars: 2000 to 2022

[In dollars. For 2001 and earlier data, respondents could report only one race group. Beginning with the 2003 CPS covering data for 2002, respondents could choose a single race (the "race alone" concept) or more than one race (includes the "race-alone-or-in-combination" concept). See also comments on race in the text for Section 1, Population. See also headnote, Table 737]

Year	Median income in current dollars					Median income in constant (2022) dollars				
	All races [1]	White [2]	Black [2]	Asian, Pacific Islander [2]	His-panic [3]	All races [1]	White [2]	Black [2]	Asian, Pacific Islander [2]	His-panic [3]
2000 [4].............	50,730	53,030	33,680	62,620	34,440	81,520	85,210	54,110	100,600	55,340
2010 [5].............	60,240	62,910	38,590	75,220	39,300	78,600	82,100	50,360	98,150	51,280
2015 [6].............	70,700	74,290	45,780	90,850	47,330	85,580	89,930	55,420	110,000	57,290
2016.............	72,710	76,260	49,370	93,500	51,110	87,240	91,510	59,230	112,200	61,320
2017 [7].............	76,140	80,140	50,650	94,710	53,600	89,770	94,500	59,720	111,700	63,200
2018.............	78,650	81,980	53,110	101,200	55,090	90,900	94,750	61,380	117,000	63,680
2019 [8].............	86,010	89,660	58,520	112,200	60,930	97,970	102,100	66,650	127,800	69,400
2020 [8, 9].............	84,350	88,550	57,570	109,600	60,060	95,080	99,820	64,900	123,600	67,700
2021 [8].............	88,590	92,430	59,540	118,400	62,300	95,530	99,660	64,200	127,700	67,180
2022.............	92,750	96,340	66,760	126,200	67,880	92,750	96,340	66,760	126,200	67,880

[1] Includes other races not shown separately. [2] Beginning 2002, data represent White alone, Black alone, or Asian alone. [3] Persons of Hispanic origin may be of any race. [4] Implementation of Census 2000-based population controls and 28,000 household sample expansion. [5] Beginning 2009, Census Bureau expanded upper income intervals used to calculate medians to $250,000 or more. Medians falling in the upper open-ended interval are plugged with "$250,000." Before 2009, the upper open-ended interval was $100,000 and a plug of "$100,000" was used. Implementation of Census 2010-based population controls. [6] Beginning 2013, data are based on redesigned income questions. [7] Implementation of an updated processing system. [8] See source for information on the impact of the coronavirus disease 2019 (COVID-19) pandemic on the CPS ASEC. [9] Implementation of 2020 Census-based population controls.

Source: U.S. Census Bureau, *Income in the United States: 2022*, Current Population Reports, P60-279, September 2023; and "Historical Income Tables: Families, Table F-05," <www.census.gov/topics/income-poverty/income/data/tables.html>, accessed November 2023.

Table 739. Money Income of Families—Distribution of Families by Income Level and Selected Characteristics: 2022

[84,350 represents 84,350,000. See headnote, Table 737. Median income is calculated using $2,500 income intervals. Medians falling in the upper open-ended interval are plugged with "$250,000." For composition of regions, see map inside front cover]

Characteristic	Number of families (1,000)								Median income (dollars)
	Total	Under $15,000	$15,000 to $24,999	$25,000 to $34,999	$35,000 to $49,999	$50,000 to $74,999	$75,000 to $99,999	$100,000 and over	
All families.....................	**84,350**	**4,381**	**3,527**	**4,921**	**7,730**	**13,336**	**11,144**	**39,314**	**92,750**
Region:									
Northeast.........................	14,190	652	565	774	1,125	1,979	1,668	7,422	104,600
Midwest...........................	17,610	765	604	881	1,540	2,883	2,503	8,435	96,650
South..............................	33,360	2,030	1,601	2,372	3,471	5,531	4,465	13,889	83,030
West..............................	19,200	934	756	894	1,595	2,943	2,509	9,567	99,580
Type of family:									
Married-couple families..........	62,180	1,720	1,603	2,631	4,666	8,801	8,294	34,472	110,500
Male householder, no spouse present..............	7,130	501	448	664	927	1,519	1,048	2,024	65,740
Female householder, no spouse present..............	15,040	2,159	1,475	1,626	2,139	3,016	1,803	2,820	50,680
Unrelated subfamilies............	392	94	43	56	80	51	23	43	35,250
Age of householder:									
15 to 24 years old...............	2,842	377	207	317	339	603	381	616	57,210
25 to 34 years old...............	12,560	826	563	854	1,309	2,152	1,746	5,112	81,830
35 to 44 years old...............	17,480	898	693	844	1,357	2,499	2,090	9,099	103,400
45 to 54 years old...............	16,470	595	453	609	1,043	2,059	2,022	9,687	117,800
55 to 64 years old...............	15,200	713	618	669	1,029	2,088	2,074	8,006	105,700
65 years old and over...........	19,800	972	995	1,629	2,654	3,932	2,830	6,793	73,100
Number of earners:									
No earners........................	14,590	2,996	1,420	1,728	2,252	2,481	1,400	2,314	42,220
One earner........................	25,880	1,212	1,762	2,517	3,736	5,876	3,548	7,232	64,050
Two earners or more.............	43,880	172	346	677	1,743	4,977	6,197	29,765	132,000
Educational attainment of householder:									
All persons age 25 and over....	81,510	4,004	3,320	4,604	7,392	12,731	10,762	38,699	94,910
Less than 9th grade..............	2,442	325	321	313	413	455	272	343	43,630
9th to 12th grade (no diploma)...	3,552	408	412	432	545	707	396	649	49,160
High school graduate (includes equivalency)......................	20,030	1,463	1,204	1,850	2,887	4,128	2,887	5,609	65,050
Some college, no degree.........	12,620	737	587	794	1,352	2,407	1,904	4,837	81,120
Associate's degree...............	9,079	364	325	444	874	1,633	1,446	3,993	89,830
Bachelor's degree or more........	33,790	705	471	771	1,321	3,403	3,857	23,262	142,200
Bachelor's degree................	20,020	464	333	517	875	2,231	2,542	13,055	130,200
Master's degree.................	10,330	166	99	193	354	958	1,052	7,506	154,900
Professional degree..............	1,418	30	20	32	47	109	88	1,092	196,500
Doctoral degree..................	2,026	45	19	28	46	106	174	1,609	185,300

Source: U.S. Census Bureau, *Income in the United States: 2022*, Current Population Reports, P60-279, September 2023; and "Current Population Survey Tables for Family Income: Table FINC-01," <www.census.gov/topics/income-poverty/income/data/tables.html>, accessed November 2023.

Table 740. Median Income of Families by Type of Family in Current and Constant (2022) Dollars: 1990 to 2022

[In dollars. See headnote, Table 737. For definition of median, see Guide to Tabular Presentation]

| Year | Current dollars | | | | | | Constant (2022) dollars | | | |
| | All families | Married-couple families | | | Male householder, no spouse present | Female householder, no spouse present | All families | Married-couple families | Male householder, no spouse present | Female householder, no spouse present |
		Total	Wife in paid labor force	Wife not in paid labor force						
1990...............	35,350	39,900	46,777	30,265	29,050	16,930	72,610	81,940	59,660	34,780
1995 [1]...........	40,610	47,060	55,823	32,375	30,360	19,690	73,230	84,860	54,740	35,500
1996...............	42,300	49,710	58,381	33,748	31,600	19,910	74,310	87,320	55,510	34,980
1997...............	44,570	51,590	60,669	36,027	32,960	21,020	76,650	88,730	56,690	36,160
1998...............	46,740	54,180	63,751	37,161	35,680	22,160	79,300	91,930	60,540	37,600
1999 [2]..........	48,830	56,500	66,478	38,480	37,340	23,760	81,170	93,920	62,070	39,500
2000 [3]..........	50,730	59,100	69,235	39,982	37,730	25,720	81,520	94,960	60,620	41,320
2001...............	51,410	60,340	70,834	40,782	36,590	25,750	80,780	94,810	57,500	40,460
2002...............	51,680	61,130	72,806	40,102	37,740	26,420	80,210	94,880	58,570	41,010
2003...............	52,680	62,280	75,170	41,122	38,030	26,550	80,100	94,690	57,820	40,370
2004...............	54,060	63,630	76,854	42,215	40,360	26,970	80,190	94,370	59,870	40,000
2005...............	56,190	65,910	78,755	44,457	41,110	27,240	81,000	95,000	59,260	39,270
2006...............	58,410	69,400	82,788	45,757	41,840	28,830	81,820	97,230	58,620	40,390
2007...............	61,360	72,590	86,435	47,329	44,360	30,300	83,800	99,140	60,590	41,380
2008...............	61,520	72,740	86,621	48,502	43,570	30,130	81,060	95,840	57,410	39,700
2009 [4]..........	60,090	71,630	85,948	47,649	41,500	29,770	79,490	94,750	54,900	39,380
2010 [5]..........	60,240	72,240	87,397	48,733	43,210	29,160	78,600	94,270	56,380	38,050
2011...............	60,970	73,790	89,017	50,414	43,070	30,260	77,170	93,390	54,510	38,300
2012 [6]..........	62,240	75,540	91,779	50,881	42,360	30,690	77,280	93,790	52,600	38,100
2013 [6]..........	63,820	76,340	94,299	51,839	44,480	31,410	78,290	93,650	54,560	38,530
2013 [7]..........	65,470	78,610	96,062	54,231	47,190	31,130	80,320	96,440	57,890	38,190
2014 [8]..........	66,630	80,810	99,983	54,779	47,600	31,770	80,600	97,750	57,570	38,430
2015...............	70,700	84,320	103,699	56,010	49,770	34,130	85,580	102,100	60,250	41,310
2016...............	72,710	86,810	106,082	58,694	51,570	36,660	87,240	104,200	61,870	43,980
2017...............	75,940	90,150	110,893	61,901	52,950	37,100	89,540	106,300	62,440	43,740
2017 [9]..........	76,140	91,110	(NA)	(NA)	51,700	36,820	89,770	107,400	60,960	43,410
2018...............	78,650	93,330	(NA)	(NA)	54,340	40,230	90,900	107,900	62,800	46,500
2019 [10].........	86,010	102,000	(NA)	(NA)	61,710	43,360	97,970	116,200	70,280	49,390
2020 [10,11].....	84,350	101,600	(NA)	(NA)	60,220	43,880	95,080	114,500	67,890	49,470
2021 [10].........	88,590	106,700	(NA)	(NA)	61,980	45,440	95,530	115,000	66,830	49,000
2022...............	92,750	110,500	(NA)	(NA)	65,740	50,680	92,750	110,500	65,740	50,680

NA Not available. [1] Implementation of 1990 Census-based sample design and metropolitan definitions, 7,000 household sample reduction, and revised race edits. [2] Implementation of Census 2000-based population controls. [3] Implementation of 28,000 household sample expansion. [4] Median income is calculated using $2,500 income intervals. Beginning with 2009 data, the Census Bureau expanded the upper income intervals used to calculate medians to $250,000 or more. Medians falling in the upper open-ended interval are plugged with "$250,000." Before 2009, the upper open-ended interval was $100,000 and a plug of "$100,000" was used. [5] Implementation of 2010 Census-based population controls. [6] The 2014 CPS ASEC included redesigned questions for income. The redesigned income questions were implemented to a subsample of the 98,000 addresses using a probability split panel design. Approximately 68,000 addresses received a set of income questions similar to those used in the 2013 CPS ASEC and the remaining 30,000 addresses received the redesigned income questions. The source of these 2013 estimates is the portion of the CPS ASEC sample that received the income questions consistent with the 2013 CPS ASEC, approximately 68,000 addresses. [7] The source of these 2013 estimates is the portion of the CPS ASEC sample which received the redesigned income questions, approximately 30,000 addresses. [8] Implementation of redesigned questionnaire for the full CPS ASEC survey sample. [9] Implementation of an updated CPS ASEC processing system. [10] See source for information on the impact of the coronavirus disease 2019 (COVID-19) pandemic on the CPS ASEC. [11] Implementation of 2020 Census-based population controls.

Source: U.S. Census Bureau, *Income in the United States: 2022*, Current Population Reports, P60-279, September 2023; and "Historical Income Tables: Families, Table F-7," <www.census.gov/topics/income-poverty/income/data/tables.html>, accessed November 2023.

Table 741. Median Income of People in Constant (2022) Dollars by Sex, Race, and Hispanic Origin: 2010 to 2022

[In dollars. People age 15 and over as of March of the following year. Constant dollars adjusted with the Chained Consumer Price Index for all Urban Consumers (C-CPI-U). Based on the Current Population Survey, Annual Social and Economic Supplement (CPS ASEC); see text, this section and Section 1 and Appendix III. See also headnote, Table 737]

| Race and Hispanic origin | Male | | | | | Female | | | | |
	2010 [1]	2015 [2]	2020 [3,4]	2021	2022	2010 [1]	2015 [2]	2020 [3,4]	2021	2022
All races [5].................	**42,030**	**44,960**	**48,130**	**49,520**	**48,450**	**27,110**	**28,770**	**33,150**	**33,360**	**32,790**
White alone..................	44,860	47,800	51,310	51,430	50,240	27,270	29,390	33,740	33,670	32,600
Black alone..................	30,400	33,170	35,250	36,550	37,300	25,640	26,160	30,130	30,710	32,370
Asian alone..................	46,750	52,900	58,410	61,120	61,120	30,750	32,120	36,350	36,950	40,640
Hispanic [6]..................	29,260	34,030	36,160	39,180	37,260	21,260	22,880	25,820	27,310	26,800
White alone, non-Hispanic...	48,480	51,090	56,570	55,470	52,720	28,340	31,020	35,500	35,200	35,180

[1] See footnote 5, Table 740. [2] Beginning 2013, data are based on redesigned income questions. [3] Beginning 2017, data reflect use of an updated processing system. [4] Implementation of 2020 Census-based population controls. [5] Includes other races not shown separately. [6] Persons of Hispanic origin may be of any race.

Source: U.S. Census Bureau, *Income in the United States: 2022*, Current Population Reports, P60-279, September 2023; and "Historical Income Tables: People, Tables P-2 and P-5," <www.census.gov/topics/income-poverty/income/data/tables.html>, accessed November 2023.

Table 742. Money Income of People—People by Income Level and by Sex and Selected Characteristics: 2022

[133,100 represents 133,100,000. People age 15 and over as of March of following year. Based on the Current Population Survey, Annual Social and Economic Supplement (CPS ASEC); see text, this section and Section 1, and Appendix III. Median income is calculated using $2,500 income intervals. Medians falling in the upper open-ended interval are plugged with "$250,000." For definition of median, see Guide to Tabular Presentation]

Characteristic	All persons (1,000)	People with income (1,000)									Median income (current dollars)
		Total	Under $5,000 or loss	$5,000 to $9,999	$10,000 to $14,999	$15,000 to $24,999	$25,000 to $34,999	$35,000 to $49,999	$50,000 to $74,999	$75,000 and over	
MALE											
Total..........................	**133,100**	**119,400**	**6,787**	**4,350**	**6,183**	**13,296**	**13,164**	**17,134**	**22,763**	**35,753**	**48,450**
Age:											
15 to 24 years................	22,210	13,970	3,100	1,647	1,456	2,171	2,033	1,808	1,125	631	18,510
25 to 34 years................	22,680	21,190	706	553	676	1,804	2,514	3,892	5,319	5,726	51,020
35 to 44 years................	21,830	20,720	535	364	597	1,508	1,825	2,822	4,877	8,192	61,460
45 to 54 years................	19,910	18,910	571	362	531	1,363	1,431	2,529	3,893	8,233	65,230
55 to 64 years................	20,230	19,130	818	530	1,069	1,941	1,617	2,366	3,523	7,267	56,740
65 years and over...........	26,300	25,510	1,058	895	1,854	4,510	3,743	3,716	4,025	5,707	37,430
Educational attainment:											
Total [1].....................	110,900	105,500	3,687	2,704	4,727	11,126	11,130	15,325	21,635	35,127	52,300
Less than 9th grade..........	4,013	3,601	190	227	436	813	694	627	441	173	26,620
9th to 12th grade [2]...........	6,083	5,393	282	322	614	1,086	903	913	843	427	29,430
High school graduate [3].......	33,080	30,910	1,243	1,072	2,073	4,608	4,466	5,631	6,810	5,006	39,960
Some college, no degree.....	16,340	15,480	614	414	553	1,695	1,811	2,711	3,593	4,094	49,550
Associate's degree...........	10,450	10,130	383	193	291	830	1,078	1,688	2,559	3,108	53,730
Bachelor's degree or more. ..	40,980	39,950	974	477	760	2,094	2,177	3,754	7,393	22,320	83,380
Bachelor's degree............	25,510	24,770	609	314	533	1,417	1,531	2,620	4,993	12,749	76,520
Master's degree.............	10,870	10,650	226	123	162	513	475	834	1,781	6,539	94,280
Professional degree.........	1,859	1,823	62	18	34	81	69	130	237	1,189	113,400
Doctoral degree..............	2,739	2,706	78	20	31	81	101	172	382	1,840	107,700
Housing tenure:											
Owner-occupied...............	93,290	84,310	4,979	2,723	3,785	8,476	8,173	11,017	16,023	29,139	52,390
Renter-occupied...............	38,600	33,990	1,718	1,526	2,319	4,624	4,841	5,978	6,540	6,448	38,920
Occupier paid no cash rent..................	1,259	1,128	89	102	79	197	150	142	199	172	31,680
Region:											
Northeast.....................	22,890	20,670	1,424	732	989	2,187	2,043	2,779	3,818	6,695	50,570
Midwest......................	27,420	25,280	1,399	907	1,204	2,648	2,752	3,661	5,265	7,446	50,170
South.........................	50,860	44,860	2,331	1,731	2,534	5,516	5,380	6,539	8,323	12,507	45,550
West..........................	31,990	28,620	1,633	981	1,456	2,945	2,988	4,156	5,353	9,107	50,380
FEMALE											
Total.......................	**138,400**	**119,700**	**11,737**	**6,550**	**10,488**	**17,917**	**15,360**	**16,960**	**19,092**	**21,577**	**32,790**
Age:											
15 to 24 years................	21,650	13,680	3,342	1,857	1,575	2,360	1,891	1,236	967	447	15,200
25 to 34 years................	22,240	19,590	1,575	717	944	2,107	2,702	3,724	4,056	3,761	41,250
35 to 44 years................	21,660	19,220	1,683	607	846	2,024	2,087	2,917	3,857	5,198	46,470
45 to 54 years................	20,100	18,030	1,448	514	947	1,819	1,913	2,763	3,566	5,061	47,130
55 to 64 years................	21,160	18,970	1,928	849	1,622	2,626	2,201	2,693	3,104	3,950	36,140
65 years and over...........	31,580	30,200	1,761	2,009	4,555	6,980	4,566	3,628	3,542	3,156	24,630
Educational attainment:											
Total [1].....................	116,700	106,000	8,394	4,694	8,913	15,557	13,469	15,725	18,125	21,131	36,450
Less than 9th grade..........	4,027	2,885	312	392	665	716	371	223	142	63	15,710
9th to 12th grade [2]...........	5,404	4,232	507	425	880	1,094	610	408	203	105	17,220
High school graduate [3].......	31,030	27,180	2,269	1,781	3,565	5,785	4,515	4,501	3,223	1,542	25,360
Some college, no degree.....	16,920	15,490	1,350	675	1,426	2,785	2,499	2,689	2,547	1,520	31,000
Associate's degree...........	13,030	12,150	941	464	877	1,691	1,962	2,234	2,408	1,574	35,770
Bachelor's degree or more. ..	46,340	44,060	3,015	958	1,499	3,485	3,513	5,670	9,599	16,320	59,090
Bachelor's degree............	28,100	26,480	2,085	648	1,093	2,417	2,462	3,912	5,842	8,022	51,430
Master's degree.............	14,390	13,840	758	238	331	886	893	1,503	3,117	6,114	67,130
Professional degree.........	1,699	1,650	65	40	38	107	92	117	265	927	82,890
Doctoral degree..............	2,143	2,093	107	30	37	77	68	139	372	1,262	90,420
Housing tenure:											
Owner-occupied...............	96,310	84,460	8,657	4,249	6,727	12,043	10,086	11,527	13,908	17,269	35,470
Renter-occupied...............	40,940	34,230	2,977	2,194	3,665	5,703	5,097	5,313	5,063	4,218	30,340
Occupier paid no cash rent..................	1,133	991	102	106	97	174	178	122	123	90	25,780
Region:											
Northeast.....................	24,160	21,380	1,923	1,132	1,877	3,037	2,638	2,823	3,367	4,580	35,340
Midwest......................	28,230	25,430	2,498	1,415	2,103	3,838	3,435	3,801	4,245	4,099	32,660
South.........................	53,790	45,570	4,558	2,510	4,284	7,197	5,816	6,599	7,234	7,370	31,780
West..........................	32,210	27,300	2,758	1,493	2,225	3,845	3,471	3,738	4,247	5,525	34,330

[1] Population age 25 and over. [2] No diploma attained. [3] Includes high school equivalency.

Source: U.S. Census Bureau, *Income in the United States: 2022*, Current Population Reports, P60-279, September 2023; and "Current Population Survey Tables for Personal Income: Table PINC-01," <www.census.gov/topics/income-poverty/income/data/tables.html>, accessed November 2023.

Table 743. Average Earnings of Year-Round, Full-Time Workers by Educational Attainment: 2022

[In dollars. For people 18 years old and over as of March of the following year. Based on the Current Population Survey, Annual Social and Economic Supplement (ASEC); see text, this section and Section 1, and Appendix III. See source for information on the impact of the coronavirus disease 2019 (COVID-19) pandemic on the CPS ASEC data collection]

| Sex and age | All workers | Less than 9th grade | High school | | College | | |
			9th to 12th grade (no diploma)	High school graduate [1]	Some college, no degree	Associate degree	Bachelor's degree or more
Male, total	**88,380**	**48,760**	**51,650**	**59,590**	**70,920**	**73,580**	**125,700**
18 to 24 years old	42,520	27,740	31,390	38,680	42,470	44,210	64,930
25 to 34 years old	73,280	38,460	52,840	52,640	60,300	63,400	98,440
35 to 44 years old	92,970	40,250	52,470	63,080	70,560	73,510	128,400
45 to 54 years old	102,600	54,810	54,610	68,420	81,760	79,950	143,800
55 to 64 years old	101,000	58,530	55,500	68,220	81,610	84,060	145,900
65 years old and over	94,670	79,650	60,670	64,650	90,700	86,940	119,300
Female, total	**70,050**	**37,760**	**42,140**	**45,650**	**53,400**	**59,420**	**90,790**
18 to 24 years old	39,850	(B)	35,350	31,900	35,850	39,770	56,320
25 to 34 years old	64,530	(B)	33,130	43,000	47,620	59,400	77,940
35 to 44 years old	77,300	32,210	45,400	48,340	52,880	61,480	98,730
45 to 54 years old	77,800	46,590	53,950	46,790	64,620	61,270	100,300
55 to 64 years old	71,590	33,360	34,480	51,930	60,010	61,930	95,940
65 years old and over	66,320	(B)	43,000	48,650	53,410	56,250	87,570

B Base figure too small to meet statistical standards for reliability of derived figure. [1] Includes general educational development credential.

Source: U.S. Census Bureau, *Income in the United States: 2022,* Current Population Reports, P60-279, September 2023; and "Current Population Survey Tables for Personal Income: Table PINC-04," <www.census.gov/topics/income-poverty/income/data/tables.html>, accessed November 2023.

Table 744. Per Capita Money Income in Current and Constant (2022) Dollars by Race and Hispanic Origin: 2000 to 2022

[In dollars. Constant dollars based on the Chained Consumer Price Index for all Urban Consumers (C-CPI-U). People as of March of following year. Based on the Current Population Survey, Annual Social and Economic Supplement (ASEC); see text, this section, Section 1, and Appendix III. See headnote, Table 741]

| Year | Current dollars | | | | | Constant (2022) dollars | | | | |
	All races [1]	White [2]	Black [2]	Asian [2]	Hispanic [3]	All races [1]	White [2]	Black [2]	Asian [2]	Hispanic [3]
2000 [4]	22,350	23,580	14,800	23,350	12,650	35,910	37,890	23,780	37,520	20,330
2010 [5]	26,560	28,360	18,020	28,670	15,040	34,660	37,000	23,510	37,420	19,630
2015 [6]	31,650	33,560	22,450	36,280	19,460	38,320	40,630	27,180	43,920	23,550
2016	33,210	35,170	23,620	38,160	20,430	39,840	42,200	28,340	45,780	24,510
2017 [7]	35,050	37,300	24,150	40,520	20,750	41,330	43,990	28,470	47,780	24,460
2018	36,080	38,320	24,730	43,190	21,980	41,700	44,300	28,590	49,930	25,400
2019 [8]	39,160	41,370	27,590	47,530	23,290	44,600	47,120	31,430	54,130	26,530
2020 [8,9]	38,930	41,110	28,020	46,280	23,230	43,890	46,340	31,590	52,170	26,180
2021 [8]	41,290	43,670	29,650	49,740	25,400	44,520	47,090	31,970	53,630	27,390
2022	42,980	44,930	32,300	54,140	26,870	42,980	44,930	32,300	54,140	26,870

[1] Includes other races, not shown separately. [2] As of 2002, data refer to people reporting specified race alone. Data for Asian in 2000 include Pacific Islander. [3] People of Hispanic origin may be of any race. [4] Implementation of Census 2000-based population controls, and of a 28,000 household sample expansion. [5] Implementation of Census 2010-based population controls. [6] Beginning 2013, data are based on redesigned income questions. [7] Implementation of an updated processing system. [8] See source for information on the impact of the coronavirus disease 2019 (COVID-19) pandemic on the CPS ASEC. [9] Implementation of 2020 Census-based population controls.

Source: U.S. Census Bureau, *Income in the United States: 2022*, Current Population Reports, P60-279, September 2023; and "Historical Income Tables: People, Table P-1," <www.census.gov/topics/income-poverty/income/data/tables.html>, accessed November 2023.

Table 745. Money Income of People—People by Income Level and by Sex, Race, and Hispanic Origin: 2022

[In thousands (133,100 represents 133,100,000). People age 15 years and over as of March of the following year. Based on Current Population Survey, Annual Social and Economic Supplement (ASEC); see text, this section, Section 1, and Appendix III]

| Income level | Male | | | | | Female | | | | |
	All races [1]	White alone	Black alone	Asian alone	Hispanic [2]	All races [1]	White alone	Black alone	Asian alone	Hispanic [2]
Total	**133,100**	**103,000**	**16,440**	**8,692**	**24,380**	**138,400**	**104,900**	**18,900**	**9,309**	**24,120**
Under $10,000 [3]	24,854	17,480	4,171	1,836	5,553	36,992	27,430	4,739	2,950	9,227
$10,000 to $19,999	12,447	9,216	2,089	646	2,677	19,572	14,878	2,910	1,065	3,433
$20,000 to $29,999	13,200	10,302	1,735	585	3,074	16,238	12,673	2,267	734	2,962
$30,000 to $39,999	13,071	10,141	1,801	615	3,190	13,953	10,510	2,271	669	2,571
$40,000 to $49,999	11,059	8,673	1,393	567	2,380	10,962	8,343	1,645	558	1,631
$50,000 to $59,999	10,582	8,415	1,252	539	2,055	9,199	6,917	1,442	555	1,248
$60,000 to $74,999	12,181	9,745	1,407	611	2,008	9,893	7,652	1,259	667	1,217
$75,000 to $84,999	6,080	5,040	508	384	796	4,831	3,767	590	330	544
$85,000 to $99,999	5,913	4,883	453	423	721	4,496	3,456	535	382	356
$100,000 to $149,999	12,380	9,907	1,009	1,161	1,129	7,294	5,507	845	731	582
$150,000 to $199,999	5,274	4,244	338	605	421	2,491	1,886	200	344	192
$200,000 to $249,999	2,403	1,948	122	279	159	933	717	79	118	73
$250,000 and above	3,709	3,028	164	441	213	1,529	1,166	120	208	86

[1] Includes other races not shown separately. [2] Persons of Hispanic origin may be of any race. [3] Includes persons without income.

Source: U.S. Census Bureau, *Income in the United States: 2022,* Current Population Reports, P60-279, September 2023; and "Current Population Survey Tables for Personal Income: Table PINC-11," <www.census.gov/topics/income-poverty/income/data/tables.html>, accessed November 2023.

Table 746. Household, Family, and Per Capita Income, and Individuals and Families Below Poverty Level by City: 2022

[The American Community Survey universe includes the household population and the population living in institutions, college dormitories, and other group quarters. Based on a sample and subject to sampling variability; see text, Section 1 and Appendix III. For definition of median, see Guide to Tabular Presentation. CDP is Census designated place]

City	Median household income (dol.)	Median family income (dol.)	Per capita income (dol.)	Number below poverty level [1]		Percent below poverty level	
				Individuals [1]	Families	Individuals [1]	Families
Albuquerque, NM.	64,757	81,968	38,150	78,694	12,849	14.2	9.7
Anaheim, CA.	85,133	87,324	33,963	47,982	8,524	14.1	11.0
Arlington, TX.	70,433	86,261	32,995	45,119	7,791	11.7	8.6
Atlanta, GA.	83,251	108,457	61,617	81,337	12,710	17.3	13.4
Aurora, CO.	81,395	95,151	39,083	43,113	7,533	11.0	8.3
Austin, TX.	89,415	124,627	60,120	106,566	13,847	11.1	6.5
Bakersfield, CA.	72,017	80,777	32,161	66,351	12,464	16.3	12.9
Baltimore, MD.	55,198	69,089	36,760	102,322	16,356	18.5	13.4
Boston, MA.	86,331	104,898	58,125	103,901	16,747	17.1	12.7
Charlotte, NC.	74,401	93,815	49,498	103,905	17,928	11.8	8.8
Chicago, IL.	70,386	84,694	45,449	450,869	77,425	17.2	13.3
Cincinnati, OH.	48,130	73,519	37,429	78,983	11,965	26.6	19.4
Cleveland, OH.	37,351	46,389	26,784	111,738	20,365	31.8	26.7
Colorado Springs, CO.	78,568	96,549	42,456	45,296	7,017	9.5	5.6
Columbus, OH.	61,727	76,383	36,434	160,285	24,754	18.1	12.4
Corpus Christi, TX.	60,958	70,683	33,277	51,983	10,829	16.8	13.1
Dallas, TX.	65,400	72,989	44,729	228,878	41,210	17.8	14.3
Denver, CO.	88,213	113,051	59,271	82,743	11,134	11.8	7.4
Detroit, MI.	36,453	44,030	22,097	205,986	37,980	33.8	29.7
El Paso, TX.	52,645	59,931	28,229	145,773	31,417	21.7	18.8
Fort Worth, TX.	71,527	87,954	34,972	113,005	20,524	12.0	9.0
Fresno, CA.	64,196	74,085	30,533	110,260	18,077	20.6	15.1
Greensboro, NC.	55,120	72,834	33,383	62,208	10,962	21.9	15.4
Henderson, NV.	81,695	99,477	45,896	33,243	6,710	10.1	7.8
Honolulu CDP, HI.	82,006	102,416	47,565	41,298	6,235	12.4	8.1
Houston, TX.	60,426	67,753	39,521	471,670	97,869	20.7	18.0
Indianapolis, IN.	61,501	79,999	35,856	136,637	25,325	15.9	12.2
Irvine, CA.	123,003	159,100	60,089	33,255	5,758	11.2	7.8
Jacksonville, FL.	69,309	80,631	36,958	133,541	26,151	14.1	10.6
Kansas City, MO.	62,175	83,808	38,681	72,972	11,196	14.6	9.5
Las Vegas, NV.	68,905	81,748	36,962	91,817	16,767	14.1	10.8
Lexington-Fayette, KY.	62,908	91,666	41,855	45,248	6,849	14.7	8.8
Lincoln, NE.	62,391	93,029	37,508	39,138	5,565	14.0	8.4
Long Beach, CA.	80,493	96,970	41,896	61,270	9,535	13.8	9.6
Los Angeles, CA.	76,135	86,380	45,270	627,915	100,720	16.8	12.2
Louisville/Jefferson Co., KY [2]	63,049	84,846	38,692	99,807	18,173	16.3	11.8
Memphis, TN.	50,622	60,687	31,620	130,166	24,515	21.4	17.4
Mesa, AZ.	79,496	91,691	38,873	48,541	8,336	9.5	6.5
Miami, FL.	60,989	70,518	45,596	82,957	14,070	18.7	14.2
Milwaukee, WI.	49,270	61,554	29,250	121,692	20,532	22.1	18.0
Minneapolis, MN.	74,473	114,719	49,617	70,368	8,456	17.2	10.3
Nashville-Davidson, TN [2]	71,767	94,648	47,049	93,510	15,714	14.1	9.9
New Orleans, LA.	52,322	72,477	37,635	79,455	13,158	22.2	17.2
New York, NY.	74,694	85,338	48,448	1,497,382	276,284	18.3	14.4
Newark, NJ.	49,688	61,238	25,171	70,767	12,872	24.0	18.6
Oakland, CA.	93,146	109,528	62,020	59,357	9,045	13.9	9.9
Oklahoma City, OK.	63,713	80,833	35,902	106,100	19,027	15.5	11.2
Omaha, NE.	67,450	93,389	39,602	65,482	11,021	13.8	9.6
Orlando, FL.	65,354	69,657	41,392	44,338	7,769	14.2	10.3
Philadelphia, PA.	56,517	68,701	36,077	329,385	56,951	21.7	16.0
Phoenix, AZ.	75,969	87,764	39,089	224,868	41,805	13.9	10.8
Pittsburgh, PA.	63,380	86,800	41,745	52,929	5,695	19.0	10.4
Portland, OR.	81,119	116,384	51,761	79,125	10,245	12.7	7.8
Raleigh, NC.	75,424	102,382	47,035	50,533	7,077	11.0	6.7
Riverside, CA.	81,228	92,562	32,762	39,772	6,356	12.8	8.6
Sacramento, CA.	80,254	95,483	40,502	71,169	11,974	13.7	10.1
San Antonio, TX.	58,829	70,532	30,790	269,701	49,726	18.7	14.6
San Diego, CA.	100,010	117,105	52,701	150,973	22,113	11.3	7.1
San Francisco, CA.	136,692	167,861	89,736	82,817	9,221	10.4	5.4
San Jose, CA.	133,835	151,689	62,552	86,223	13,162	9.0	5.7
San Juan, PR.	25,928	36,520	25,695	118,111	23,990	37.4	32.8
Santa Ana, CA.	79,351	81,900	26,991	34,364	5,394	11.3	8.6
Seattle, WA.	115,409	177,781	82,716	73,706	7,832	10.1	5.2
St. Paul, MN.	67,725	87,494	41,137	46,772	7,185	16.0	11.0
Stockton, CA.	76,231	88,891	31,510	47,277	8,729	14.8	12.4
Tampa, FL.	71,089	90,174	49,506	62,219	11,158	16.3	12.7
Tucson, AZ.	51,281	70,019	30,456	100,563	14,552	19.2	12.3
Tulsa, OK.	54,040	69,784	35,447	80,530	14,086	20.0	14.6
Virginia Beach, VA.	83,245	103,451	44,287	44,673	8,969	10.0	7.7
Washington, DC.	101,027	146,477	71,699	85,676	10,725	13.3	8.7
Wichita, KS.	59,277	78,568	34,134	71,126	11,765	18.3	12.6

[1] Poverty status was determined for all people except institutionalized people, people in military group quarters, people in college dormitories, and unrelated individuals under 15 years old. [2] Represents metropolitan government (balance) of locality.

Source: U.S. Census Bureau, 2022 American Community Survey, Tables DP03, B01003, B17001, and B17019, <data.census.gov>, accessed November 2023. See also <www.census.gov/topics/income-poverty/poverty.html>.

Table 747. Persons and Families Below Poverty Level—Number and Rate by State: 2022

[Represents number and percent below poverty in the past 12 months. Poverty status was determined for all people except institutionalized people, people in military group quarters, people in college dormitories, and unrelated individuals under 15 years old. These groups were excluded from the numerator and denominator when calculating poverty rates. Based on a sample and subject to sampling variability; see Appendix III]

State	Persons			Families		
	Population for whom poverty status is determined	Number in poverty	Percent in poverty	Population for whom poverty status is determined	Number in poverty	Percent in poverty
United States.................	325,521,470	40,951,625	12.6	83,304,153	7,397,060	8.9
Alabama.......................	4,929,195	800,395	16.2	1,308,988	156,434	12.0
Alaska.........................	715,594	78,608	11.0	175,789	12,783	7.3
Arizona........................	7,210,801	897,852	12.5	1,843,530	163,520	8.9
Arkansas......................	2,958,098	496,311	16.8	777,933	92,156	11.8
California......................	38,307,718	4,670,324	12.2	9,150,804	791,385	8.6
Colorado......................	5,727,379	540,517	9.4	1,464,182	84,877	5.8
Connecticut...................	3,514,107	345,695	9.8	902,539	58,372	6.5
Delaware......................	995,107	93,285	9.4	263,885	17,172	6.5
District of Columbia...........	642,853	85,676	13.3	123,868	10,725	8.7
Florida........................	21,764,366	2,762,679	12.7	5,684,399	513,201	9.0
Georgia.......................	10,655,140	1,348,344	12.7	2,733,234	255,593	9.4
Hawaii.........................	1,402,729	142,378	10.2	335,052	22,120	6.6
Idaho..........................	1,889,431	202,517	10.7	491,073	33,282	6.8
Illinois.........................	12,306,019	1,469,643	11.9	3,137,923	261,687	8.3
Indiana........................	6,645,013	834,550	12.6	1,740,106	153,401	8.8
Iowa...........................	3,103,543	339,867	11.0	821,960	55,554	6.8
Kansas........................	2,852,901	342,670	12.0	740,407	56,739	7.7
Kentucky......................	4,389,492	722,865	16.5	1,172,125	139,365	11.9
Louisiana......................	4,467,616	829,565	18.6	1,131,137	158,362	14.0
Maine.........................	1,347,498	145,161	10.8	370,935	23,080	6.2
Maryland......................	6,042,925	581,748	9.6	1,546,282	101,399	6.6
Massachusetts.................	6,763,338	700,156	10.4	1,724,355	118,421	6.9
Michigan......................	9,828,430	1,315,899	13.4	2,548,560	232,144	9.1
Minnesota.....................	5,599,770	540,079	9.6	1,456,312	87,319	6.0
Mississippi....................	2,841,445	544,104	19.1	754,264	106,894	14.2
Missouri.......................	6,005,542	791,030	13.2	1,569,735	136,115	8.7
Montana.......................	1,098,173	133,233	12.1	282,216	20,540	7.3
Nebraska......................	1,920,017	215,838	11.2	501,595	38,520	7.7
Nevada........................	3,139,138	390,848	12.5	773,666	70,549	9.1
New Hampshire.................	1,359,894	98,057	7.2	358,120	14,859	4.1
New Jersey....................	9,103,154	882,045	9.7	2,378,459	162,630	6.8
New Mexico....................	2,072,033	364,725	17.6	516,464	65,202	12.6
New York......................	19,185,089	2,734,819	14.3	4,738,232	489,664	10.3
North Carolina.................	10,417,219	1,329,157	12.8	2,785,497	259,795	9.3
North Dakota..................	751,246	86,192	11.5	193,761	12,611	6.5
Ohio...........................	11,468,520	1,540,922	13.4	2,983,145	277,374	9.3
Oklahoma.....................	3,897,556	610,254	15.7	1,017,586	115,881	11.4
Oregon........................	4,161,550	503,935	12.1	1,041,083	79,737	7.7
Pennsylvania..................	12,553,587	1,483,365	11.8	3,294,814	260,588	7.9
Rhode Island..................	1,052,644	113,878	10.8	266,935	17,929	6.7
South Carolina.................	5,140,248	717,348	14.0	1,398,412	139,855	10.0
South Dakota..................	879,804	109,889	12.5	224,853	17,217	7.7
Tennessee.....................	6,897,298	915,683	13.3	1,846,572	178,104	9.6
Texas..........................	29,416,679	4,113,641	14.0	7,483,376	813,294	10.9
Utah...........................	3,329,192	273,052	8.2	830,599	46,433	5.6
Vermont.......................	624,770	65,162	10.4	164,496	10,853	6.6
Virginia........................	8,442,437	891,390	10.6	2,191,916	161,178	7.4
Washington....................	7,651,971	763,469	10.0	1,935,445	125,249	6.5
West Virginia..................	1,721,567	308,825	17.9	463,064	60,433	13.1
Wisconsin.....................	5,763,986	617,037	10.7	1,511,105	103,335	6.8
Wyoming......................	567,648	66,943	11.8	153,365	13,130	8.6
Puerto Rico....................	3,195,054	1,333,111	41.7	820,788	318,268	38.8

Source: U.S. Census Bureau, 2022 American Community Survey: B17001, "Poverty Status in the Past 12 Months by Sex by Age"; and B17019, "Poverty Status in the Past 12 Months of Families by Household Type by Tenure"; <data.census.gov/>, accessed November 2023.

Table 748. Poverty Thresholds by Size of Family Unit: 1980 to 2022

[In dollars per year. The official poverty definition uses money income before taxes and does not include capital gains and noncash benefits (such as public housing and food stamps). For information on the official poverty thresholds, see text, this section. For more on poverty, see <www.census.gov/topics/income-poverty/poverty.html>. See also headnote, Table 749]

Size of family unit	1980	1990	2000 [2]	2005	2010 [3]	2015 [4]	2020 [5, 6]	2021	2022
One person (unrelated individual) [1] ..	4,190	6,652	8,791	9,973	11,140	12,080	13,180	13,790	14,880
Under age 65.........................	4,290	6,800	8,959	10,160	11,340	12,330	13,470	14,100	15,230
Age 65 and over.....................	3,949	6,268	8,259	9,367	10,460	11,370	12,410	13,000	14,040
Two persons..........................	5,363	8,509	11,240	12,760	14,220	15,390	16,750	17,530	18,900
Householder under age 65.........	5,537	8,794	11,590	13,150	14,680	15,950	17,410	18,230	19,690
Householder age 65 and over......	4,983	7,905	10,420	11,820	13,190	14,340	15,660	16,400	17,710
Three persons........................	6,565	10,420	13,740	15,580	17,370	18,870	20,590	21,560	23,280
Four persons.........................	8,414	13,360	17,600	19,970	22,320	24,260	26,500	27,740	29,950
Five persons.........................	9,966	15,790	20,820	23,610	26,440	28,740	31,420	32,870	35,510
Six persons..........................	11,270	17,840	23,530	26,680	29,900	32,540	35,500	37,160	40,160
Seven persons.......................	12,760	20,240	26,750	30,250	34,020	37,000	40,410	42,160	45,690
Eight persons........................	14,200	22,580	29,700	33,610	37,950	41,030	44,760	47,090	51,010
Nine or more persons................	16,900	26,850	35,150	40,290	45,220	49,180	53,900	56,330	60,300

[1] A person living alone or with non-relatives. [2] Implementation of 2000 Census-based population controls and sample expanded by 28,000 households. [3] Implementation of 2010 Census-based population controls. [4] Beginning 2013, data are based on redesigned income questions. [5] Beginning 2017, data reflect an updated processing system. [6] Implementation of 2020 Census-based population controls.

Source: U.S. Census Bureau, *Poverty in the United States: 2022,* Current Population Reports, P60-280, September 2023; and "Poverty Thresholds," <www.census.gov/topics/income-poverty/poverty/data/tables.html>, accessed November 2023.

Table 749. People Below Poverty Level by Race and Hispanic Origin, and Below 125 Percent of Poverty Level: 1990 to 2022

[33,590 represents 33,590,000. People as of March of the following year. Based on Current Population Survey, Annual Social and Economic Supplement (ASEC); see text, this section, Section 1, and Appendix III. Beginning with 2003 CPS ASEC covering data for 2002, refers to persons of specified race only and who did not report any other race category; "Asian" replaced "Asian Pacific Islander." For information on measuring poverty, see <www.census.gov/topics/income-poverty/poverty/guidance/poverty-measures.html>. Data users should exercise caution when comparing trends over time due to changes in CPS ASEC methodology and data processing. Changes are noted below for the years as appropriate. See source for more information]

Year	Number of persons below poverty (1,000)					Percent of persons below poverty					Below 125 percent of poverty level [1]	
	All races [2]	White	Black	Asian	His-panic [3]	All races [2]	White	Black	Asian	His-panic [3]	Number (1,000)	Percent of total pop-ulation
1990..........	33,590	22,330	9,837	858	6,006	13.5	10.7	31.9	12.2	28.1	44,840	18.0
1995 [4].....	36,430	24,420	9,872	1,411	8,574	13.8	11.2	29.3	14.6	30.3	48,760	18.5
1996..........	36,530	24,650	9,694	1,454	8,697	13.7	11.2	28.4	14.5	29.4	49,310	18.5
1997..........	35,570	24,400	9,116	1,468	8,308	13.3	11.0	26.5	14.0	27.1	47,850	17.8
1998..........	34,480	23,450	9,091	1,360	8,070	12.7	10.5	26.1	12.5	25.6	46,040	17.0
1999 [5].....	32,790	22,170	8,441	1,285	7,876	11.9	9.8	23.6	10.7	22.7	45,030	16.3
2000 [6].....	31,580	21,650	7,982	1,258	7,747	11.3	9.5	22.5	9.9	21.5	43,610	15.6
2001..........	32,910	22,740	8,136	1,275	7,997	11.7	9.9	22.7	10.2	21.4	45,320	16.1
2002..........	34,570	23,470	8,602	1,161	8,555	12.1	10.2	24.1	10.1	21.8	47,080	16.5
2003..........	35,860	24,270	8,781	1,401	9,051	12.5	10.5	24.4	11.8	22.5	48,690	16.9
2004 [7].....	37,040	25,330	9,014	1,201	9,122	12.7	10.8	24.7	9.8	21.9	49,690	17.1
2005..........	36,950	24,870	9,168	1,402	9,368	12.6	10.6	24.9	11.1	21.8	49,330	16.8
2006..........	36,460	24,420	9,048	1,353	9,243	12.3	10.3	24.3	10.3	20.6	49,690	16.8
2007..........	37,280	25,120	9,237	1,349	9,890	12.5	10.5	24.5	10.2	21.5	50,880	17.0
2008..........	39,830	26,990	9,379	1,576	10,990	13.2	11.2	24.7	11.8	23.2	53,810	17.9
2009..........	43,570	29,830	9,944	1,746	12,350	14.3	12.3	25.8	12.5	25.3	56,840	18.7
2010 [8].....	46,340	31,080	10,750	1,899	13,520	15.1	13.0	27.4	12.2	26.5	60,670	19.8
2011..........	46,250	30,850	10,930	1,973	13,240	15.0	12.8	27.6	12.3	25.3	60,950	19.8
2012..........	46,500	30,820	10,910	1,921	13,620	15.0	12.7	27.2	11.7	25.6	61,200	19.7
2013 [9].....	46,270	31,290	10,190	2,255	13,360	14.8	12.9	25.2	13.1	24.7	60,400	19.3
2014..........	46,660	31,090	10,760	2,137	13,100	14.8	12.7	26.2	12.0	23.6	61,340	19.4
2015..........	43,120	28,570	10,020	2,078	12,130	13.5	11.6	24.1	11.4	21.4	56,910	17.9
2016..........	40,620	27,110	9,234	1,908	11,140	12.7	11.0	22.0	10.1	19.4	54,430	17.0
2017 [10]....	39,560	26,030	9,224	1,891	10,820	12.3	10.5	21.7	9.7	18.3	53,510	16.6
2018..........	38,150	24,950	8,884	1,996	10,530	11.8	10.1	20.8	10.1	17.6	51,710	16.0
2019 [11]....	33,980	22,510	8,073	1,464	9,545	10.5	9.1	18.8	7.3	15.7	46,540	14.3
2020 [11, 12]...	37,550	25,180	8,556	1,645	10,520	11.5	10.1	19.6	8.1	17.0	50,240	15.3
2021 [11]....	37,930	24,920	8,583	1,922	10,690	11.6	10.0	19.5	9.3	17.1	50,450	15.4
2022..........	37,920	26,050	7,626	1,866	10,780	11.5	10.5	17.1	8.6	16.9	50,150	15.2

[1] People with incomes below 125 percent of poverty level. [2] Includes races not shown separately. [3] People of Hispanic origin may be of any race. [4] The 1994 CPS ASEC was revised to allow for coding of different income amounts on selected questionnaire items. Child support and alimony limits decreased to $49,999. Limits increased in the following categories: earnings to $999,999; social security to $49,999; supplemental security income and public assistance income to $24,999; and veterans' benefits to $99,999. [5] Implementation of 2000 Census-based population controls. [6] Implementation of a 28,000 household expansion. [7] Data revised to reflect a correction to the weights in the 2005 CPS ASEC. [8] Implementation of 2010 Census-based population controls. [9] Beginning 2013, data from redesigned income questions. [10] Implementation of an updated processing system. [11] See source for information on the impact of the coronavirus disease 2019 (COVID-19) pandemic on the CPS ASEC. [12] Implementation of 2020 Census-based population controls.

Source: U.S. Census Bureau, *Poverty in the United States: 2022,* Current Population Reports, P60-280, September 2023; and "Historical Poverty Tables: People and Families, Tables 2 and 6," <www.census.gov/topics/income-poverty/poverty/data/tables.html>, accessed November 2023.

Table 750. Children Below Poverty Level by Race and Hispanic Origin: 1990 to 2022

[12,720 represents 12,720,000. Persons as of March of the following year. Covers only children under age 18 related in families. Based on Current Population Survey, Annual Social and Economic Supplement (CPS ASEC); see text, this section, Section 1, and Appendix III. See headnote, Table 749]

Year	Number of children below poverty level (1,000)					Percent of children below poverty level				
	All races [1]	White	Black	Asian	His-panic [2]	All races [1]	White	Black	Asian	His-panic [2]
1990............	12,720	7,696	4,412	356	2,750	19.9	15.1	44.2	17.0	37.7
1995 [3].........	14,000	8,474	4,644	532	3,938	20.2	15.5	41.5	18.6	39.3
2000 [4, 5]........	11,010	6,834	3,495	407	3,342	15.6	12.4	30.9	12.5	27.6
2001............	11,180	7,086	3,423	353	3,433	15.8	12.8	30.0	11.1	27.4
2002............	11,650	7,203	3,570	302	3,653	16.3	13.1	32.1	11.4	28.2
2003............	12,340	7,624	3,750	331	3,982	17.2	13.9	33.6	12.1	29.5
2004 [6].........	12,470	7,876	3,702	265	3,985	17.3	14.3	33.4	9.4	28.6
2005............	12,340	7,652	3,743	312	3,977	17.1	13.9	34.2	11.0	27.7
2006............	12,300	7,522	3,690	351	3,959	16.9	13.6	33.0	12.0	26.6
2007............	12,800	8,002	3,838	345	4,348	17.6	14.4	34.3	11.8	28.3
2008............	13,510	8,441	3,781	430	4,888	18.5	15.3	34.4	14.2	30.3
2009............	14,770	9,440	3,919	444	5,419	20.1	17.0	35.3	13.6	32.5
2010 [7].........	15,600	9,590	4,271	477	5,815	21.5	17.9	39.0	14.0	34.3
2011............	15,540	9,643	4,247	466	5,820	21.4	18.1	38.6	13.0	33.7
2012............	15,440	9,547	4,097	470	5,773	21.3	17.9	37.5	13.3	33.3
2013 [8].........	15,120	9,702	3,678	538	5,638	20.9	18.4	33.8	14.4	32.2
2014............	14,990	9,172	4,036	492	5,522	20.7	17.4	37.1	13.4	31.3
2015............	13,960	8,838	3,571	420	5,139	19.2	16.7	32.7	11.4	28.6
2016............	12,800	7,963	3,382	412	4,764	17.6	15.1	30.6	10.7	26.3
2017 [9].........	12,360	7,520	3,280	405	4,525	17.0	14.3	30.2	10.1	24.7
2018............	11,490	6,783	3,212	426	4,316	15.9	13.0	29.4	10.8	23.4
2019 [10]........	10,170	6,209	2,831	272	3,796	14.1	12.0	26.3	7.0	20.6
2020 [10, 11].....	11,440	7,053	3,033	347	4,195	15.7	13.6	27.4	8.2	22.7
2021 [10]........	10,800	6,392	2,990	365	4,033	15.0	12.5	27.0	8.7	21.9
2022............	10,530	6,666	2,434	371	3,980	14.8	13.3	22.1	8.7	21.5

[1] Includes other races, not shown separately. [2] People of Hispanic origin may be of any race. [3] See Table 749, footnote 4. [4] Data reflect Census 2000-based population controls. [5] Sample expanded by 28,000 households. [6] Data have been revised to reflect a correction to the weights in the 2005 ASEC. [7] Implementation of 2010 Census-based population controls. [8] Beginning 2013, data are based on redesigned income questions. [9] Implementation of an updated processing system. [10] See Table 749, footnote 11. [11] See Table 749, footnote 12.

Source: U.S. Census Bureau, *Poverty in the United States: 2022*, Current Population Reports, P60-280, September 2023; and "Historical Poverty Tables: People and Families, Table 3," <www.census.gov/topics/income-poverty/poverty/data/tables.html>, accessed November 2023.

Table 751. People Below Poverty Level by Selected Characteristics: 2022

[37,920 represents 37,920,000. People as of March of the following year. Based on the Current Population Survey, Annual Social and Economic and Supplement (CPS ASEC). Data by education cover people age 25 and over, based on the highest grade completed]

Characteristic	Number below poverty level (1,000)					Percent below poverty level				
	All races [1]	White alone	Black alone	Asian alone	His-panic [2]	All races [1]	White alone	Black alone	Asian alone	His-panic [2]
Total..................	**37,920**	**26,050**	**7,626**	**1,866**	**10,780**	**11.5**	**10.5**	**17.1**	**8.6**	**16.9**
Male......................	17,100	11,750	3,369	878	5,057	10.5	9.5	16.0	8.3	15.7
Female....................	20,820	14,300	4,257	988	5,719	12.5	11.5	18.2	8.9	18.1
AGE										
Under 18 years old..........	10,780	6,849	2,491	377	4,057	15.0	13.5	22.3	8.8	21.7
Age 18 to 64 years old.......	21,240	14,880	4,097	1,097	5,804	10.6	9.9	14.9	7.7	14.6
18 to 24 years old........	4,663	3,110	883	360	1,216	15.3	14.0	19.8	18.3	16.4
25 to 34 years old........	4,563	3,040	961	220	1,408	10.2	9.4	14.0	6.4	14.5
35 to 44 years old........	3,992	2,797	783	190	1,380	9.2	8.6	13.2	5.6	15.2
45 to 54 years old........	3,287	2,346	623	177	956	8.2	7.7	12.1	5.8	12.4
55 to 59 years old........	2,017	1,488	374	81	413	9.9	9.3	15.1	6.3	13.3
60 to 64 years old........	2,719	2,099	474	68	431	12.9	12.5	18.4	6.1	16.2
65 years old and over.......	5,897	4,320	1,038	392	915	10.2	9.0	17.6	12.9	16.9
65 to 74 years old........	3,189	2,269	631	198	493	9.4	8.2	17.0	11.1	14.6
75 years old and over......	2,708	2,050	406	195	422	11.3	10.2	18.6	15.5	20.6
EDUCATION [3]										
No high school diploma.......	7,636	5,398	1,452	293	3,255	20.6	19.6	27.2	14.4	23.3
High school, no college.......	10,150	7,029	2,172	363	2,317	13.6	12.2	19.1	12.1	15.2
Some college, less than 4-year degree................	6,870	4,902	1,296	362	1,174	10.1	9.3	13.1	12.4	11.1
College, 4-year degree or higher................	4,305	3,058	608	525	639	4.7	4.3	7.0	5.2	7.4
NATIVITY [4]										
Native.....................	31,000	21,250	6,982	708	6,518	11.0	9.7	17.9	8.0	15.8
Foreign born...............	6,928	4,794	643	1,158	4,258	14.2	16.7	11.8	9.1	18.8
Naturalized citizen..........	2,257	1,364	269	520	1,051	9.4	10.9	8.5	6.9	12.9
Not a citizen.............	4,671	3,430	375	638	3,207	18.8	21.2	16.2	12.2	22.1

[1] Includes other races, not shown separately. [2] Persons of Hispanic origin may be of any race. [3] Highest education level for persons age 25 and over. [4] For persons age 15 and over.

Source: U.S. Census Bureau, *Poverty in the United States: 2022*, Current Population Reports, P60-280, September 2023; and "Current Population Survey Detailed Tables for Poverty: Tables POV01, and POV09," <www.census.gov/topics/income-poverty/poverty/data/tables.html>, accessed November 2023.

Table 752. Families Below Poverty Level by Presence of Working Family Members and Family Type: 2022

[7,400 represents 7,400,000. Population as of March of the following year. A primary family is a group of two or more people, one of whom is the householder, related by birth, marriage, or adoption and residing together. All such people (including related subfamily members) are considered as members of one family. Based on the 2023 Current Population Survey, Annual Social and Economic Supplement (CPS ASEC); see text, this section and Section 1, and Appendix III]

Family by presence of workers	Families below poverty level							
	All families		Married-couple families		Families with male householder, no spouse present		Families with female householder, no spouse present	
	Number (1,000)	Percent	Number (1,000)	Percent	Number (1,000)	Percent	Number (1,000)	Percent
TOTAL FAMILIES								
Primary families, total	**7,400**	**8.8**	**3,117**	**5.0**	**821**	**11.5**	**3,462**	**23.0**
Primary families with no workers	3,651	25.0	1,613	14.5	365	42.0	1,673	64.0
Primary families with at least one worker	3,749	5.4	1,504	2.9	456	7.3	1,789	14.4
One working family member	3,030	11.7	1,063	7.2	399	11.9	1,568	20.4
Two or more working family members	719	1.6	441	1.2	57	2.0	220	4.6
Primary families with no members working full-time year-round [1]	5,931	23.4	2,365	13.5	678	33.8	2,888	49.8
With at least one part-time or part-year worker [2]	2,280	21.1	753	11.6	313	27.5	1,215	38.2
Primary families with at least one member who worked full-time year-round [1]	1,469	2.5	751	1.7	143	2.8	574	6.2
One full-time year-round worker	1,377	4.3	681	3.1	138	3.9	557	7.9
Two or more full-time year-round workers	92	0.3	70	0.3	5	0.3	17	0.8
FAMILIES WITH CHILDREN UNDER AGE 18								
Primary families, total	**4,604**	**12.7**	**1,339**	**5.4**	**508**	**16.3**	**2,758**	**32.0**
Primary families with no workers	1,659	80.5	261	64.9	175	66.5	1,223	87.6
Primary families with at least one worker	2,946	8.6	1,078	4.4	333	11.6	1,535	21.3
One working family member	2,423	18.2	745	12.9	309	14.4	1,369	25.6
Two or more working family members	523	2.5	333	1.8	24	3.3	166	8.9
Primary families with no members working full-time year-round [1]	3,358	51.7	708	31.6	402	51.6	2,249	64.8
With at least one part-time or part-year worker [2]	1,699	38.4	447	24.3	227	43.9	1,026	49.4
Primary families with at least one member who worked full-time year-round [1]	1,246	4.2	631	2.8	106	4.5	509	9.9
One full-time year-round worker	1,180	6.8	580	5.3	105	5.2	495	11.2
Two or more full-time year-round workers	66	0.5	51	0.4	1	0.3	15	2.0

[1] A year-round full-time worker is someone who usually works 35 hours or more per week for 50 weeks or more during the calendar year. [2] A part-time worker is someone who works less than 35 hours per week in a majority of weeks worked during the year. Part-year work is classified as working less than 50 weeks in a year.

Source: U.S. Census Bureau, *Poverty in the United States: 2022*, Current Population Reports, P60-280, September 2023; and "Current Population Survey Detailed Tables for Poverty: Tables POV-05 and POV-06," <www.census.gov/topics/income-poverty/poverty/data/tables.html>, accessed November 2023.

Table 753. Families Below Poverty Level by Race and Hispanic Origin, and Below 125 Percent of Poverty Level: 2000 to 2022

[6,400 represents 6,400,000. Families with and without children under age 18, as of March of the following year. Based on Current Population Survey, Annual Social and Economic Supplement (ASEC); see text, this section and Section 1, and Appendix III. For data collection changes over time, see <www.census.gov/topics/income-poverty/income/guidance/cps-methodology-changes.html>. See Table 752 for definition of family. Beginning with the 2003 CPS covering data for 2002, respondents could choose more than one race. For 2001 data and earlier, the CPS allowed respondents to report only one race group]

Year	Number of families below poverty (1,000)					Percent of families below poverty					Below 125 percent of poverty level	
	All races [1]	White [2]	Black [2]	Asian [2]	His-panic [3]	All races [1]	White [2]	Black [2]	Asian [2]	His-panic [3]	Number (1,000)	Percent
2000 [4]	6,400	4,333	1,686	233	1,540	8.7	7.1	19.3	7.8	19.2	9,032	12.2
2005	7,657	5,068	1,997	289	1,948	9.9	8.0	22.1	9.0	19.7	10,442	13.5
2010 [5]	9,400	6,305	2,311	362	2,739	11.8	9.9	24.1	9.3	24.3	12,448	15.6
2011	9,497	6,334	2,334	401	2,651	11.8	9.8	24.2	9.7	22.9	12,500	15.5
2012	9,520	6,299	2,327	387	2,807	11.8	9.7	23.7	9.4	23.5	12,669	15.7
2013 [6]	9,645	6,526	2,204	448	2,865	11.7	9.9	22.4	10.2	23.1	12,605	15.3
2014	9,467	6,310	2,265	401	2,684	11.6	9.7	22.9	8.9	21.5	12,635	15.5
2015	8,589	5,743	2,082	374	2,502	10.4	8.8	21.1	8.0	19.6	11,603	14.1
2016	8,081	5,433	1,893	340	2,253	9.8	8.3	19.0	7.2	17.3	11,083	13.4
2017 [7]	7,790	5,135	1,898	367	2,178	9.3	7.8	18.9	7.4	16.4	10,696	12.8
2018	7,504	5,004	1,730	387	2,057	9.0	7.6	17.7	7.6	15.5	10,241	12.3
2019 [8]	6,554	4,323	1,618	291	1,833	7.8	6.5	16.3	5.7	13.9	9,104	10.9
2020 [8,9]	7,284	4,910	1,721	330	2,028	8.7	7.5	16.8	6.4	14.8	9,981	11.9
2021 [8]	7,415	4,846	1,790	381	2,115	8.8	7.3	17.4	7.1	15.0	9,943	11.8
2022	7,400	5,136	1,493	346	2,169	8.8	7.8	14.3	6.3	15.2	9,976	11.8

[1] Includes other races, not shown separately. [2] Beginning 2002, data refer to persons who reported specified race only and no other race; prior to 2002, Asian included Pacific Islander. [3] People of Hispanic origin may be of any race. [4] Implementation of Census 2000 based population controls and sample expanded by 28,000 households. [5] Implementation of Census 2010-based population controls. [6] Beginning 2013, data are based on redesigned income questions. [7] Implementation of an updated processing system. [8] See source for information on the impact of the coronavirus disease 2019 (COVID-19) pandemic on the CPS ASEC. [9] Implementation of 2020 Census-based population controls.

Source: U.S. Census Bureau, *Poverty in the United States: 2022*, Current Population Reports, P60-280, September 2023; and "Historical Poverty Tables: People and Families, Table 4," and "Current Population Survey Detailed Tables for Poverty: Table POV04," <www.census.gov/topics/income-poverty/poverty/data/tables.html>, accessed November 2023.

Table 754. Families Below Poverty Level by Selected Characteristics: 2022

[In thousands (7,400 represents 7,400,000), except as noted. All families as of March of the following year. Based on the 2023 Current Population Survey, Annual Social and Economic Supplement (CPS ASEC); see text, this section and Section 1, and Appendix III. Data below represent persons who selected each race group only and exclude persons reporting more than one race. See also comments on race in the text for Section 1]

Characteristic	Number below poverty level (1,000)					Percent below poverty level				
	All races [1]	White alone	Black alone	Asian alone	His-panic [2]	All races [1]	White alone	Black alone	Asian alone	His-panic [2]
Total families	**7,400**	**5,136**	**1,493**	**346**	**2,169**	**8.8**	**7.8**	**14.3**	**6.3**	**15.2**
Age of householder:										
18 to 24 years old	557	344	146	21	166	20.5	18.1	33.7	12.3	17.8
25 to 34 years old	1,504	962	356	47	498	12.0	10.5	18.5	5.4	17.6
35 to 44 years old	1,797	1,218	381	81	653	10.3	9.3	16.5	5.9	18.5
45 to 54 years old	1,115	780	232	53	353	6.8	6.2	10.8	4.3	11.6
55 to 64 years old	1,102	851	172	42	265	7.3	7.0	10.1	4.8	12.2
65 years old and over	1,306	963	206	103	222	6.6	5.8	10.9	10.6	13.3
Type of family:										
Married couple	3,117	2,480	287	227	900	5.0	4.9	5.6	5.1	10.0
Male householder, no spouse present	821	542	188	29	266	11.5	10.6	15.6	6.5	14.0
Female householder, no spouse present	3,462	2,114	1,018	91	1,002	23.0	22.2	24.5	15.0	29.6
Families with children [3]	4,604	3,094	1,038	163	1,557	12.7	11.4	19.6	6.4	19.8
Married couple	1,339	1,066	95	99	560	5.4	5.5	4.4	4.6	11.7
Male householder, no spouse present	508	347	114	5	166	16.3	15.1	20.7	4.9	19.4
Female householder, no spouse present	2,758	1,681	829	58	831	32.0	31.9	32.3	22.9	37.7

[1] Includes other races not shown separately. [2] Hispanic persons may be of any race. [3] Children under age 18 related to the householder.

Source: U.S. Census Bureau, *Poverty in the United States: 2022*, Current Population Reports, P60-280, September 2023; and "Current Population Survey Detailed Tables for Poverty: Table POV04," <www.census.gov/topics/income-poverty/poverty/data/tables.html>, accessed November 2023.

Table 755. People Below Poverty Level Under Official and Supplemental Poverty Measures by Selected Characteristics: 2022

[In units as indicated (330,600 represents 330,600,000). People as of March the following year. The official poverty measure counts gross income before taxes, and the threshold is the same across all states. The supplemental poverty measure (SPM) was developed for research purposes, and counts cash income, noncash government benefits, and tax credits, and deducts selected expenses such as taxes, health care and work-related expenses, and child support paid; the SPM poverty threshold varies across states and accounts for recent expenditures for food, clothing, shelter and utilities. Both poverty thresholds are adjusted for families by composition and size. For more information, see <www.census.gov/topics/income-poverty/poverty/guidance/poverty-measures.html> and <www.census.gov/topics/income-poverty/supplemental-poverty-measure.html>. While the official poverty measure excludes unrelated individuals under the age 15, for the purposes of comparison to the SPM, estimates presented here under the official poverty measure include unrelated individuals under age 15. Estimates may not sum to totals due to rounding. Based on the Current Population Survey, Annual Social and Economic and Supplement (CPS ASEC)]

Characteristic	Total persons (1,000)	Persons in poverty under official poverty measure [1]		Persons in poverty under supplemental poverty measure (SPM)		Difference in persons in poverty, SPM minus official poverty measure	
		Number (1,000s)	Percent	Number (1,000s)	Percent	Number (1,000s)	Percent
Total [2]	**330,600**	**37,980**	**11.5**	**40,900**	**12.4**	**2,929**	**0.9**
Sex:							
Male	163,400	17,140	10.5	19,460	11.9	2,320	1.4
Female	167,200	20,840	12.5	21,450	12.8	609	0.4
Age:							
Under 18 years old	72,500	10,840	14.9	8,983	12.4	-1,854	-2.6
18 to 64 years old	200,200	21,240	10.6	23,730	11.9	2,493	1.2
65 years old and over	57,880	5,897	10.2	8,187	14.1	2,290	4.0
Family unit type:							
Married couple	196,700	10,710	5.4	14,910	7.6	4,200	2.1
Cohabiting partners	28,290	6,708	23.7	3,480	12.3	-3,228	-11.4
Female reference person	41,640	9,389	22.5	9,419	22.6	30	0.1
Male reference person	16,370	1,631	10.0	2,405	14.7	774	4.7
Unrelated individuals	47,640	9,540	20.0	10,690	22.4	1,153	2.4
Race and Hispanic origin:							
White alone	249,200	26,090	10.5	28,520	11.4	2,438	1.0
White alone, non-Hispanic	193,500	16,710	8.6	17,680	9.1	967	0.5
Black alone	44,620	7,637	17.1	7,671	17.2	34	0.1
Asian alone	21,600	1,866	8.6	2,502	11.6	636	2.9
American Indian and Alaska Native alone	4,003	998	24.9	930	23.2	-67	-1.7
Two or more races	9,711	1,180	12.2	1,106	11.4	-74	-0.8
Hispanic [3]	63,960	10,790	16.9	12,360	19.3	1,564	2.4
Education:							
Persons age 25 and over	227,700	22,480	9.9	26,530	11.7	4,051	1.8
No high school diploma	19,530	4,929	25.2	5,446	27.9	517	2.6
High school, no college	64,110	8,519	13.3	10,000	15.6	1,485	2.3
Some college	56,730	5,286	9.3	6,053	10.7	768	1.4
Bachelor's degree or higher	87,310	3,742	4.3	5,024	5.8	1,282	1.5

[1] Includes unrelated individuals under age 15. [2] Includes data for other races not shown separately. [3] Persons of Hispanic origin may be of any race.

Source: U.S. Census Bureau, *Poverty in the United States: 2022*, Current Population Report P60-280, September 2023, <www.census.gov/library/publications/2023/demo/p60-280.html>.

Table 756. Nonfinancial Assets Held by Families by Type of Asset: 2022

[Value of assets in thousands of constant (2022) dollars (333 represents $333,000). Families include one-person units and, as used in this table, are comparable to the U.S. Census Bureau's household concept. Based on internal data from the Survey of Consumer Finances; see Appendix III. All dollar amounts are adjusted to 2022 dollars using the "current methods" version of the consumer price index (CPI) for all urban consumers. For definition of median, see Guide to Tabular Presentation. For data on financial assets, see Table 1202]

Family characteristic	Any financial or non-financial asset	Any non-financial asset	Vehicles	Primary residence	Other resi-dential property	Equity in nonresi-dential property	Bus-iness equity	Other asset
PERCENT OF FAMILIES HOLDING ASSET								
All families, total	**99.7**	**92.3**	**86.6**	**66.1**	**12.9**	**5.9**	**14.6**	**7.4**
Age of reference person:								
Under 35 years old	99.2	86.5	80.7	38.5	4.7	(B)	11.3	6.5
35 to 44 years old	99.5	92.1	87.0	61.1	9.4	3.9	15.7	4.1
45 to 54 years old	99.9	93.8	90.9	70.7	12.2	6.2	17.8	5.4
55 to 64 years old	99.9	94.6	89.6	77.8	18.6	7.5	18.7	7.5
65 to 74 years old	99.9	93.8	87.9	76.1	19.0	11.0	14.1	11.3
75 years old and over	99.9	94.1	84.2	81.0	15.5	7.7	8.6	10.7
Race or ethnicity of respondent:								
White, non-Hispanic	99.9	95.5	90.8	73.1	14.3	7.1	16.0	9.1
Black/African-American, non-Hispanic	99.1	80.8	72.1	46.3	9.5	3.7	11.0	(B)
Hispanic or Latino	99.2	87.9	78.2	51.1	6.9	2.1	9.8	(B)
Other or multiple race	99.2	88.6	84.2	57.3	13.0	4.6	14.1	8.5
Tenure:								
Owner occupied	100.0	100.0	93.1	100.0	16.9	8.0	17.6	8.0
Renter occupied or other	99.1	77.2	74.0	(B)	5.0	1.8	8.6	6.1
MEDIAN VALUE [1] ($1,000)								
All families, total	**333**	**282**	**28**	**323**	**225**	**125**	**90**	**20**
Age of family head:								
Under 35 years old	71	54	24	250	120	(B)	10	11
35 to 44 years old	311	283	30	350	280	55	50	20
45 to 54 years old	427	356	33	380	270	160	83	20
55 to 64 years old	474	366	32	350	250	100	152	27
65 to 74 years old	475	327	27	320	183	160	200	20
75 years old and over	382	286	19	287	140	125	250	30
Race or ethnicity of respondent:								
White, non-Hispanic	417	316	29	330	260	150	105	20
Black/African-American, non-Hispanic	107	134	23	250	100	25	42	(B)
Hispanic or Latino	103	172	25	275	160	300	40	(B)
Other or multiple race	261	267	28	400	214	100	50	15
Tenure:								
Owner occupied	534	398	33	323	250	133	120	23
Renter occupied or other	25	19	16	(B)	150	95	16	12

B Base too small to meet statistical standards for reliability of derived figure. [1] Median value of asset for families holding such assets.

Source: Board of Governors of the Federal Reserve System, 2022 Survey of Consumer Finances, *Changes in U.S. Family Finances From 2019 to 2022: Evidence from the Survey of Consumer Finances,* October 2023; and "Historic Tables." See also <www.federalreserve.gov/econres/scfindex.htm>.

Table 757. Family Net Worth—Median and Mean Net Worth in Constant (2022) Dollars by Selected Family Characteristics: 2010 to 2022

[Net worth in thousands of constant (2022) dollars (105.5 represents $105,500). Constant dollar figures are based on Consumer Price Index for all urban consumers published by U.S. Bureau of Labor Statistics. Families include one-person units and, as used in this table, are comparable to the U.S. Census Bureau's household concept. Based on internal data from the Survey of Consumer Finances; see Appendix III. For definition of mean and median, see Guide to Tabular Presentation]

Family characteristic	2010 Median	2010 Mean	2013 Median	2013 Mean	2016 Median	2016 Mean	2019 Median	2019 Mean	2022 Median	2022 Mean
All families	**105.5**	**681.2**	**103.4**	**680.5**	**120.0**	**853.5**	**141.1**	**868.0**	**192.9**	**1,063.7**
Age of family head:										
Under 35 years old	12.7	89.2	13.2	96.1	13.5	93.9	16.1	88.5	39.0	183.5
35 to 44 years old	57.5	297.0	59.4	442.0	73.8	356.0	105.9	505.6	135.6	549.6
45 to 54 years old	161.0	782.7	134.0	674.8	153.2	897.2	195.4	965.9	247.2	975.8
55 to 64 years old	245.0	1,202.6	211.2	1,016.3	231.0	1,439.8	246.3	1,363.1	364.5	1,566.9
65 to 74 years old	282.3	1,158.7	295.5	1,345.3	275.5	1,314.7	308.8	1,411.6	409.9	1,794.6
75 years old and over	296.1	925.8	247.9	821.2	326.6	1,315.9	295.4	1,133.2	335.6	1,624.1
Race or ethnicity of respondent:										
White, non-Hispanic	178.3	893.9	180.7	898.5	210.9	1,151.6	218.1	1,140.0	285.0	1,367.2
Black or African-American, non-Hispanic	21.8	135.7	16.8	126.0	21.1	170.3	28.0	165.1	44.9	211.5
Hispanic or Latino	22.1	157.9	17.5	137.1	25.4	235.8	41.9	191.8	61.6	227.5
Other or multiple race	58.2	458.1	52.5	473.6	79.8	564.5	86.4	761.8	132.9	849.8
Tenure:										
Owner occupied	238.3	974.4	248.7	996.6	285.5	1,275.5	295.5	1,277.5	396.2	1,530.9
Renter occupied or other	6.9	78.2	6.8	89.5	6.2	112.2	7.3	110.8	10.4	154.9

Source: Board of Governors of the Federal Reserve System, 2022 Survey of Consumer Finances, *Changes in U.S. Family Finances From 2019 to 2022: Evidence from the Survey of Consumer Finances,* October 2023; and "Historic Tables." See also <www.federalreserve.gov/econres/scfindex.htm>.

Table 758. Household and Nonprofit Organization Sector Balance Sheet: 1990 to 2023

[In billions of dollars (26,370 represents $26,370,000,000,000), unless otherwise noted. As of December 31. Sector includes domestic hedge funds, private equity funds, and personal trusts. For details of financial assets and liabilities, see Table 1201 and Table 1203]

Item	1990	2000	2010	2019	2020	2021	2022	2023
Assets	**26,370**	**52,006**	**80,162**	**133,504**	**148,604**	**169,084**	**164,597**	**176,743**
Nonfinancial assets [1]	10,084	17,550	25,648	39,876	43,605	51,219	55,644	57,911
Real estate [2]	7,941	14,161	20,717	33,486	36,813	43,403	47,118	49,093
Households [3]	7,146	12,834	18,821	29,888	32,984	38,902	42,595	44,844
Consumer durable goods [4]	2,039	3,202	4,536	5,670	6,026	6,998	7,646	7,878
Financial assets [1]	16,286	34,456	54,514	93,628	104,999	117,865	108,953	118,832
Time and savings deposits	2,682	3,032	6,136	9,845	10,300	11,064	10,271	9,838
Money market fund shares	421	1,296	1,790	2,273	2,691	2,804	3,082	3,806
Debt securities [1]	1,310	1,663	4,046	4,308	3,825	2,986	4,434	5,671
Treasury securities	308	257	679	1,401	1,148	436	1,462	2,321
Municipal securities	660	475	1,901	1,916	1,941	1,808	1,621	1,766
Corporate and foreign bonds	228	397	1,121	212	250	290	281	311
Corporate equities [2]	1,705	7,107	8,683	21,140	26,006	31,656	26,419	31,996
Miscellaneous other equity	3,094	5,048	6,539	12,137	13,200	15,574	16,239	15,768
Mutual fund shares	471	2,557	4,730	10,010	10,996	12,830	9,759	11,005
Life insurance reserves	399	858	1,308	1,786	1,922	2,000	1,987	2,090
Pension entitlements [5]	4,982	11,055	18,339	28,063	29,789	31,560	28,921	30,964
Liabilities [1]	**3,736**	**7,430**	**14,104**	**16,613**	**17,206**	**18,851**	**19,969**	**20,529**
Loans [1]	3,561	7,125	13,536	15,952	16,527	18,140	19,228	19,751
Home mortgages [6]	2,490	4,817	9,993	10,479	10,865	11,927	12,697	13,053
Consumer credit	824	1,741	2,647	4,192	4,185	4,549	4,894	5,020
Net worth	**22,634**	**44,576**	**66,057**	**116,891**	**131,398**	**150,233**	**144,628**	**156,214**
Replacement cost value of structures:								
Residential [1]	4,287	7,732	12,732	18,912	20,347	24,042	26,981	27,652
Households	4,184	7,596	12,529	18,607	20,023	23,675	26,573	27,238
Nonresidential (nonprofits)	469	808	1,415	2,088	2,157	2,439	2,833	2,921
Disposable personal income	4,319	7,385	11,319	16,157	17,373	18,664	18,702	20,222
Owners' equity in real estate	4,657	8,017	8,828	19,409	22,119	26,975	29,898	31,791
Owners' equity as percent of real estate	65.2	62.5	46.9	64.9	67.1	69.3	70.2	70.9

[1] Includes other types of assets and/or liabilities not shown separately. [2] At market value. [3] Includes all types of owner-occupied housing, including farm houses, mobile homes, second homes that are not rented, vacant homes for sale, and vacant land. [4] At replacement (current) cost. [5] Includes public and private defined benefit and defined contribution pension plans and annuities, including those in IRAs (individual retirement accounts) and at life insurance companies. Excludes social security. [6] Includes loans made under home equity lines of credit and home equity loans secured by junior liens.

Source: Board of Governors of the Federal Reserve System, "Z.1 Financial Accounts of the United States: B.101 Balance Sheet of Households and Nonprofit Organizations," March 2024, <www.federalreserve.gov/releases/z1/default.htm>, accessed March 2024.

Table 759. Net Stock of Fixed Assets and Consumer Durable Goods in Current and Chained (2017) Dollars: 1990 to 2022

[In billions of dollars (18,894 represents $18,894,000,000,000)]

Item	1990	2000	2010	2018	2019	2020	2021	2022
CURRENT DOLLARS								
Net stock, total	**18,894**	**30,959**	**50,514**	**68,252**	**70,998**	**74,285**	**84,439**	**93,589**
Fixed assets	16,855	27,757	45,979	62,780	65,328	68,259	77,441	85,943
Private	12,774	21,418	34,465	47,622	49,640	51,933	59,280	66,103
Nonresidential	7,071	11,608	18,682	25,227	26,442	27,049	30,074	33,417
Equipment	2,424	3,805	5,226	7,086	7,321	7,447	8,021	8,629
Structures	4,055	6,468	11,284	14,774	15,524	15,653	17,775	20,078
Intellectual property products	592	1,335	2,172	3,367	3,597	3,949	4,278	4,710
Residential	5,702	9,810	15,783	22,394	23,198	24,883	29,206	32,686
Government	4,081	6,339	11,514	15,159	15,688	16,326	18,161	19,840
Nonresidential	3,939	6,110	11,182	14,710	15,226	15,835	17,589	19,198
Equipment	534	655	923	1,045	1,074	1,109	1,185	1,254
Structures	2,907	4,798	9,246	12,419	12,877	13,378	14,982	16,422
Intellectual property products	498	656	1,012	1,245	1,275	1,347	1,422	1,522
Residential	142	229	332	449	462	491	572	641
Consumer durable goods	**2,039**	**3,202**	**4,536**	**5,472**	**5,670**	**6,026**	**6,998**	**7,646**
Motor vehicles and parts	649	1,051	1,288	1,662	1,706	1,769	2,092	2,297
Furnishings and durable household equipment	649	977	1,396	1,677	1,751	1,906	2,235	2,434
Recreational goods and vehicles	419	724	1,061	1,222	1,275	1,413	1,635	1,785
Other	322	449	791	911	938	938	1,037	1,130
CHAINED (2017) DOLLARS								
Net stock, total	**(NA)**	**(NA)**	**57,870**	**65,374**	**66,595**	**67,710**	**69,039**	**70,165**
Fixed assets	(NA)	(NA)	53,757	59,816	60,807	61,644	62,548	63,351
Private	(NA)	(NA)	40,439	45,502	46,332	46,995	47,764	48,461
Nonresidential	(NA)	(NA)	20,727	24,467	25,044	25,402	25,801	26,236
Equipment	(NA)	(NA)	5,191	7,002	7,217	7,285	7,386	7,514
Structures	(NA)	(NA)	13,286	14,189	14,365	14,477	14,557	14,637
Intellectual property products	(NA)	(NA)	2,322	3,278	3,468	3,648	3,873	4,125
Residential	(NA)	(NA)	19,795	21,038	21,296	21,600	21,968	22,238
Government	(NA)	(NA)	13,314	14,315	14,476	14,651	14,786	14,891
Nonresidential	(NA)	(NA)	12,898	13,893	14,053	14,228	14,364	14,471
Equipment	(NA)	(NA)	970	1,024	1,046	1,071	1,089	1,098
Structures	(NA)	(NA)	10,847	11,669	11,789	11,909	11,993	12,058
Intellectual property products	(NA)	(NA)	1,081	1,200	1,219	1,251	1,287	1,324
Residential	(NA)	(NA)	417	422	423	423	422	421
Consumer durable goods	**(NA)**	**(NA)**	**4,175**	**5,565**	**5,805**	**6,103**	**6,573**	**6,939**

NA Not available.

Source: U.S. Bureau of Economic Analysis, National Data, "Fixed Assets Accounts Tables," <www.bea.gov/itable/fixed-assets>, accessed December 2023.

Table 760. Top Wealth Holders With Gross Assets of $11.4 Million or More by Type of Property, Sex, and Size of Net Worth: 2019

[7,570,717 represents $7,570,717,000,000. Figures are estimates from the Personal Wealth Study, based on a sample of Federal estate tax returns (Form 706). Covers the segment of the population for whom personal wealth is at least equal to the estate tax filing threshold in effect for the estimation period; for 2019, the Federal estate tax filing threshold was $11.4 million or more in gross estate. Based on the estate multiplier technique to estimate the wealth of living individuals; for more information on this methodology, see source]

Sex and net worth	Number of top wealth holders	Assets (mil. dol.)					
		Total [1]	Personal residences	Other real estate	Closely held stock	Publicly traded stock	Retirement assets
Both sexes, total....................	**249,364**	**7,570,717**	**287,205**	**563,460**	**883,777**	**1,646,005**	**397,407**
Size of net worth:							
Under $11.4 million [2]...................	43,894	468,474	34,698	49,857	39,525	84,652	42,953
$11.4 million to under $20 million.....	113,249	1,751,344	107,193	171,091	144,578	397,507	186,040
$20 million to under $50 million........	72,012	2,219,669	89,872	193,314	230,958	472,111	128,485
$50 million to or more..................	20,209	3,131,230	55,442	149,198	468,716	691,735	39,928
Males, total.........................	**147,582**	**4,923,058**	**169,125**	**335,265**	**681,108**	**987,604**	**265,548**
Size of net worth:							
Under $11.4 million [2]...................	27,346	309,548	18,656	33,020	35,530	42,598	31,905
$11.4 million to under $20 million.....	62,241	976,757	61,335	112,190	101,879	190,062	90,845
$20 million to under $50 million........	44,395	1,371,095	49,932	116,843	149,359	282,953	110,936
$50 million to or more..................	13,599	2,265,659	39,201	73,212	394,340	471,991	31,863
Females, total.......................	**101,782**	**2,647,659**	**118,080**	**228,194**	**202,669**	**658,401**	**131,859**
Size of net worth:							
Under $11.4 million [2]...................	16,548	158,926	16,042	16,837	3,995	42,055	11,049
$11.4 million to under $20 million.....	51,008	774,587	45,858	58,900	42,699	207,445	95,195
$20 million to under $50 million........	27,617	848,574	39,940	76,472	81,600	189,158	17,549
$50 million to or more..................	6,609	865,571	16,241	75,985	74,376	219,744	8,065

[1] Total assets is the sum of all assets owned by the individual before subtracting debts, mortgages, and liens owed to others. Includes other types of assets, not shown separately. [2] Includes individuals with zero or negative net worth.

Source: U.S. Internal Revenue Service, Statistics of Income Division, "SOI Tax Stats - Personal Wealth Statistics," May 2023, <www.irs.gov/statistics/soi-tax-stats-personal-wealth-statistics>.

Table 761. Top Wealth Holders With Net Worth of $11.4 Million or More—Number, Net Worth, and Assets by State: 2019

[6,838,150 represents $6,838,150,000,000. Estimates from the Personal Wealth Study, based on a sample of federal estate tax returns (Form 706). Covers the segment of the population for whom personal wealth is at least equal to the estate tax filing threshold in effect for the estimation period; for 2019, estates with combined gross assets and prior taxable gifts exceeding $11.4 million were required to file. Estimates of wealth by State can be subject to significant year-to-year fluctuations. This is especially true for individuals at the extreme tail of the net worth distribution and for States with relatively small decedent populations. Based on the estate multiplier technique to estimate the wealth of living individuals; for more information on this methodology, see source. Please note that data by state are for top wealth holders with net worth, not total assets, of at least $11.4 million, to maintain consistency with previous data releases; totals here will not match totals in Table 762 and Table 760. Detail may not sum to totals due to rounding]

State	Number of top wealth holders	Net worth (mil. dol.)	Total assets [1] (mil. dol.)	State	Number of top wealth holders	Net worth (mil. dol.)	Total assets [1] (mil. dol.)
Total [2]....................	**205,470**	**6,838,150**	**7,102,243**	Missouri....................	2,075	84,937	93,153
				Montana....................	721	13,593	13,651
Alabama....................	1,329	43,299	44,551	Nebraska....................	583	26,198	26,538
Alaska.....................	(D)	(D)	(D)	Nevada.....................	1,528	28,248	28,840
Arizona....................	3,637	93,649	95,484	New Hampshire..........	761	14,497	14,761
Arkansas...................	2,374	48,532	48,645	New Jersey...............	4,988	134,980	141,977
California..................	38,202	1,509,854	1,575,494	New Mexico...............	311	6,977	7,073
Colorado...................	2,474	115,124	117,496	New York..................	18,816	880,917	912,105
Connecticut................	2,839	84,746	86,200	North Carolina............	3,370	77,846	79,255
Delaware...................	297	8,685	8,819	North Dakota..............	914	21,838	22,056
District of Columbia.......	542	17,691	19,705	Ohio.......................	5,112	128,492	129,642
Florida.....................	20,697	628,901	687,113	Oklahoma..................	1,022	29,034	31,953
Georgia....................	2,019	55,166	56,730	Oregon.....................	1,506	46,511	49,061
Hawaii.....................	272	11,892	12,128	Pennsylvania..............	9,868	278,155	282,548
Idaho......................	1,462	58,559	62,667	Rhode Island..............	(D)	(D)	(D)
Illinois.....................	7,205	223,395	232,440	South Carolina............	1,420	32,392	33,368
Indiana....................	4,633	90,593	91,407	South Dakota.............	153	3,721	3,802
Iowa.......................	952	20,486	23,084	Tennessee.................	2,100	49,223	51,053
Kansas.....................	1,399	34,007	37,909	Texas.....................	20,117	581,066	600,809
Kentucky...................	3,675	64,868	65,638	Utah.......................	632	13,453	14,650
Louisiana..................	2,663	69,627	71,359	Vermont...................	467	41,215	41,301
Maine......................	787	14,176	14,337	Virginia....................	3,055	89,863	92,292
Maryland...................	2,997	54,129	57,496	Washington................	5,465	214,433	216,860
Massachusetts.............	4,449	112,184	114,561	West Virginia.............	137	2,185	2,199
Michigan...................	4,979	94,756	95,722	Wisconsin.................	2,456	86,014	86,240
Minnesota.................	2,931	56,449	57,538	Wyoming...................	616	150,529	152,097
Mississippi.................	1,115	17,913	19,612	Other areas [2]............	2,713	256,492	261,951

D Data not shown to avoid disclosure of information about specific taxpayers; however, data are included in appropriate totals. [1] Total assets (or gross estate) is a Federal estate tax concept of wealth, in that it includes the sum of all assets owned and the cash value (not full face value) of life insurance minus indebtedness. [2] Includes U.S. territories and possessions.

Source: U.S. Internal Revenue Service, Statistics of Income Division, "SOI Tax Stats - Personal Wealth Statistics," May 2023, <www.irs.gov/statistics/soi-tax-stats-personal-wealth-statistics>.

Table 762. Top Wealth Holders With Gross Assets of $11.4 Million or More—Debts, Mortgages, and Net Worth: 2019

[7,570,717 represents $7,570,717,000,000. Figures are estimates from the Personal Wealth Study, based on a sample of Federal estate tax returns (Form 706). Covers the segment of the population for whom personal wealth is at least equal to the estate tax filing threshold in effect for the estimation period; for 2019, the Federal estate tax filing threshold was $11.4 million or more in gross estate. Based on the estate multiplier technique to estimate the wealth of living individuals from Federal estate tax return data; for more information on this methodology, see source]

Sex and net worth	Total assets [1]		Debts and mortgages		Net worth [2]	
	Number of top wealth holders	Amount (mil. dol.)	Number of top wealth holders	Amount (mil. dol.)	Number of top wealth holders	Amount (mil. dol.)
Both sexes, total........................	**249,364**	**7,570,717**	**174,542**	**352,431**	**249,364**	**7,218,286**
Size of net worth:						
Under $11.4 million [3].......................	43,894	468,474	34,919	88,338	43,894	380,136
$11.4 million to under $20 million.........	113,249	1,751,344	77,354	67,228	113,249	1,684,116
$20 million to under $50 million...........	72,012	2,219,669	46,663	123,903	72,012	2,095,767
$50 million or more........................	20,209	3,131,230	15,606	72,963	20,209	3,058,267
Males, total.............................	**147,582**	**4,923,058**	**102,607**	**257,966**	**147,582**	**4,665,093**
Size of net worth:						
Under $11.4 million [3].......................	27,346	309,548	21,814	56,663	27,346	252,885
$11.4 million to under $20 million.........	62,241	976,757	42,994	50,412	62,241	926,344
$20 million to under $50 million...........	44,395	1,371,095	27,741	97,731	44,395	1,273,364
$50 million or more........................	13,599	2,265,659	10,059	53,159	13,599	2,212,500
Females, total...........................	**101,782**	**2,647,659**	**71,935**	**94,466**	**101,782**	**2,553,193**
Size of net worth:						
Under $11.4 million [3].......................	16,548	158,926	13,105	31,675	16,548	127,251
$11.4 million to under $20 million.........	51,008	774,587	34,360	16,816	51,008	757,772
$20 million to under $50 million...........	27,617	848,574	18,923	26,172	27,617	822,403
$50 million or more........................	6,609	865,571	5,547	19,803	6,609	845,767

[1] Total assets (or gross estate) is a Federal estate tax concept of wealth, in that it includes the sum of all assets owned and the cash value of life insurance instead of the full face value of life insurance minus indebtedness. [2] Net worth is defined as total assets minus debts and mortgages. [3] Includes individuals with zero or negative net worth.

Source: U.S. Internal Revenue Service, Statistics of Income Division, "SOI Tax Stats - Personal Wealth Statistics," May 2023, <www.irs.gov/statistics/soi-tax-stats-personal-wealth-statistics>.

Prices

The Prices section contains producer and consumer price indexes and actual prices for selected commodities. The primary sources of the data are monthly publications of the U.S. Department of Labor, Bureau of Labor Statistics (BLS), which include *Consumer Price Index, Producer Price Index,* and *U.S. Import and Export Price Indexes.* These reports are available in various formats including comprehensive databases for the respective price indexes at <www.bls.gov/data/>. The Bureau of Economic Analysis (BEA) is the source for gross domestic product measures. Table 767 on housing price indexes contains data from the Federal Housing Finance Agency's Housing Price Index. Other commodity, housing, and energy prices may be found in the Energy and Utilities; Forestry, Fishing and Mining; and Construction and Housing sections.

Most price data is measured by an index. An index is a tool that simplifies the measurement of movements in a numerical series. An index allows you to properly compare two or more values in different time periods or places by comparing both to a base year. An index of 110, for example, means there has been a 10-percent increase in price since the reference period; similarly, an index of 90 means a 10-percent decrease. Movements of the index from one date to another can be expressed as changes in index points (simply, the difference between index levels), but it is more useful to express the movements as percent changes. This is because index points are affected by the level of the index in relation to its reference period, while percent changes are not.

Consumer price indexes (CPI)—The CPI is a measure of the average change in prices over time in a "market basket" of goods and services purchased either by urban wage earners and clerical workers or by all urban consumers. The all urban consumer group represents over 90 percent of the total U.S. population and is based on the expenditures of residents of urban or metropolitan areas, including wage earners and clerical workers; professional, managerial, and technical workers; the self-employed; short-term workers; the unemployed; and retirees and others not in the labor force. Not included in the CPI are the spending patterns of people living in rural nonmetropolitan areas, farm households, people in the Armed Forces, and those in institutions, such as prisons and mental hospitals. Consumer inflation for all urban consumers is measured by two indexes, the Consumer Price Index for All Urban Consumers (CPI-U) and the Chained Consumer Price Index for All Urban Consumers (C-CPI-U). The broadest and most comprehensive CPI is called the All Items Consumer Price Index for All Urban Consumers (CPI-U) for the U.S. City Average. CPIs in this section generally have a base of 1982–84 = 100.

The CPI represents all goods and services purchased for consumption by the reference population. BLS has classified all expenditure items into more than 200 categories, arranged into eight major groups which are food and beverages, housing, apparel, transportation, medical care, recreation, education and communication, and other goods and services. The CPI does not include investment items, such as stocks, bonds, real estate, and life insurance, as these items relate to savings and not to day-to-day consumption expenses.

The CPI is a product of a series of interrelated samples. Data from the 2010 Decennial Census determines the urban areas from which data on prices are collected and the housing units within each area that are eligible for use in the shelter component of the CPI. The Census of Population also provides data on the number of consumers represented by each area selected as a CPI price collection area. The CPI collects prices for approximately 80,000 goods and services. Prices are collected each month in 75 urban areas across the country from about 6,000 housing units and approximately 23,000 retail establishments. The CPI also uses data from the Consumer Expenditure (CE) survey which collects data on the out-of-pocket expenses spent to acquire all consumer products and services. There is a time lag between the expenditure survey and its use in the CPI. For example, CPI data in 2023 was based on data collected from the Consumer Expenditure Survey for 2021. That year, over 20,000 consumers from around the country provided information each quarter on their spending habits in the interview survey. To collect information on frequently purchased items, such as food and personal care products, another 12,000 consumers kept diaries listing everything they bought during a 2-week period. Expenditure information from those diaries and quarterly interviews determines the relative importance, or weight, of the item categories in the CPI index structure.

Producer price index (PPI)—Dating from 1890, the PPI is the oldest continuous statistical series published by BLS. The PPI is a family of indexes that measures the average change over time in the selling prices received by domestic producers of goods and services. Imports are excluded. The target set of goods and services included in the PPI is the entire marketed output of U.S. producers. The set includes both goods and services purchased by other producers as inputs to their operations or as capital investment, as well as goods and services purchased by consumers either directly from the service producer or indirectly from a retailer. About 10,000 PPIs for individual products and groups of products are released each month.

PPIs are published for the output of almost all industries in the goods-producing sectors of the U.S. economy, and, while more indexes are gradually being introduced, are currently available for approximately 69 percent of the service sector. For any given industry, producers are usually selected for the PPI survey using a systematic sampling from a listing of all firms that file with the Unemployment Insurance System. Establishments are asked to report their prices as of Tuesday of the week containing the 13th of the month. The PPI sample includes over 16,000 establishments providing approximately 64,000 price quotations per month supplemented with data from other sources for some areas. Currently, some PPIs have an index base set at 1982 = 100, while the remainder have an index base that corresponds with the month prior to the month that the index was introduced. For further detail regarding the PPI, see the BLS *Handbook of Methods*, Chapter 14, <www.bls.gov/opub/hom/pdf/ppi-20111028.pdf>.

In January 2014, PPI transitioned from the Stage of Processing (SOP) system to the Final Demand–Intermediate Demand (FD-ID) system as its primary index aggregation structure. The transition to the FD-ID system is the culmination of a long-standing PPI objective to improve the SOP system (domestically produced goods for domestic, nongovernment consumption) by incorporating PPIs for services, construction, government purchases, and exports. The FD portion of the FD-ID system expands coverage relative to the finished goods stage of the SOP system by including indexes that examine inflation from the producer perspective for goods, services, and construction sold as personal consumption, capital investment, government purchase, and export. The ID portion of the system allows data users to examine inflation from the producer perspective for goods, services, and construction sold to businesses as inputs to production, excluding capital investment.

BEA price indexes—BEA chain-weighted price indexes are weighted averages of the detailed price indexes used in the deflation of the goods and services that make up the gross domestic product (GDP) and its major components. Growth rates are constructed for years and quarters using quantity weights for the current and preceding year or quarter; these growth rates are used to move the index for the preceding period forward a year or quarter at a time. All chain-weighted price indexes are expressed in terms of the reference year value 2017 = 100.

Personal consumption expenditures (PCE) price and quantity indexes are based on market transactions for which there are corresponding price measures. The price index provides a measure of the prices paid by persons for domestic purchases of goods and services. PCEs are defined as market value of spending by individuals and not-for-profit institutions on all goods and services. Personal consumption expenditures also include the value of certain imputed goods and services—such as the rental value of owner-occupied homes and compensation paid in kind—such as employer-paid health and life insurance premiums. The PCE price index is known for capturing inflation (or deflation) across a wide range of consumer expenses and for reflecting changes in consumer behavior. More information on this index may be found at <www.bea.gov/data/personal-consumption-expenditures-price-index>.

Measures of inflation—Inflation is a period of rising price levels for goods and factors of production. Inflation results in a decline in the purchasing power

of the dollar. It is suggested that changes in price levels be compared from the same month of the prior year and not as a change from the prior month. The BLS offers several indexes that measure different aspects of inflation, three of which are included in this section. The CPI measures inflation as experienced by consumers in their day-to-day living expenses. The PPI measures prices at the producer level only. The International Price Program measures change in the prices of imports and exports of nonmilitary goods and services between the United States and other countries.

Whereas the CPI and PPI measure a benchmark approach to price levels, the BEA's Personal Consumption Expenditures uses a chain-weight approach which links weighted averages from adjoining years.

Other measures of inflation include spot market price indexes from Barchart and the employment cost, hourly compensation, and unit labor cost indexes from the BLS. Found in Section 12, Labor Force, Employment, and Earnings, these BLS indexes are used as a measure of the change in cost of the labor factor of production and the capital factor of production.

International price indexes—The BLS International Price Program produces Import/Export Price Indexes (MXP) for nonmilitary goods and services traded between the United States and the rest of the world.

The U.S. Import and U.S. Export Price Indexes measure the change over time in the prices of goods or services purchased from abroad by U.S. residents (imports) or sold to foreign buyers by U.S. residents (exports). The reference period for the indexes is 2000 = 100, unless otherwise indicated. The product universe for both the import and export indexes includes raw materials, agricultural products, semifinished manufactures, and finished manufactures, including both capital and consumer goods. Price data for these items are collected primarily via a secure internet address.

To the extent possible, the data gathered refer to prices at the U.S. border for exports and at either the foreign border or the U.S. border for imports. Survey respondents provide prices for items based on actual transactions that occur as close as possible to the first day of the month for which the data are to be published. The recorded price is the actual transaction price for which an item is purchased or sold. The transaction price ideally accounts for discounts and surcharges paid or charged; duties on imports are not counted as part of the price.

Table 763. Purchasing Power of the Dollar: 1950 to 2023

[Indexes: PPI, 1982=$1.00; CPI, 1982-84=$1.00. Producer prices prior to 1961 and consumer prices prior to 1964 exclude Alaska and Hawaii. Producer prices based on final demand, finished goods index. Data is obtained by dividing the average price index for the 1982=100, PPI and the 1982-84=100, CPI base periods (100.0) by the price index for a given period and expressing the result in dollars and cents. Annual figures are based on average of monthly data]

Year	Annual average as measured by—		Year	Annual average as measured by—	
	Producer prices	Consumer prices		Producer prices	Consumer prices
1950	3.546	4.149	1993	0.802	0.692
1955	3.279	3.731	1994	0.797	0.675
1960	2.994	3.378	1995	0.782	0.656
1965	2.933	3.175	1996	0.762	0.637
1966	2.841	3.086	1997	0.759	0.623
1967	2.809	2.994	1998	0.765	0.613
1968	2.732	2.874	1999	0.752	0.600
1969	2.632	2.725	2000	0.725	0.581
1970	2.545	2.577	2001	0.711	0.565
1971	2.469	2.469	2002	0.720	0.556
1972	2.392	2.392	2003	0.698	0.543
1973	2.193	2.252	2004	0.673	0.529
1974	1.901	2.028	2005	0.642	0.512
1975	1.718	1.859	2006	0.623	0.496
1976	1.645	1.757	2007	0.600	0.482
1977	1.546	1.650	2008	0.565	0.464
1978	1.433	1.534	2009	0.580	0.466
1979	1.289	1.377	2010	0.556	0.459
1980	1.136	1.214	2011	0.524	0.445
1981	1.041	1.100	2012	0.515	0.436
1982	1.000	1.036	2013	0.508	0.429
1983	0.984	1.004	2014	0.499	0.422
1984	0.964	0.962	2015	0.516	0.422
1985	0.955	0.929	2016	0.521	0.417
1986	0.969	0.912	2017	0.505	0.408
1987	0.949	0.880	2018	0.490	0.398
1988	0.926	0.845	2019	0.486	0.391
1989	0.880	0.806	2020	0.493	0.386
1990	0.839	0.765	2021	0.452	0.369
1991	0.822	0.734	2022	0.398	0.342
1992	0.812	0.713	2023	0.393	0.328

Source: U.S. Bureau of Labor Statistics, "CPI Databases," <www.bls.gov/cpi/#data>; and "PPI Databases," <www.bls.gov/ppi/#data>; accessed June 2024.

Table 764. Consumer Price Indexes (CPI-U) by Major Group: 1990 to 2023

[1982-84=100, except as indicated. Represents annual averages of monthly figures. Reflects buying patterns of all urban consumers. Minus sign (-) indicates decrease. See text, this section]

Year	All items	Com-mod-ities	Ser-vices	Food	Food and bever-ages	Energy	All items less food and energy	Hous-ing	Apparel	Trans-porta-tion	Medical care	Educa-tion and com-munica-tion [1]
1990	130.7	122.8	139.2	132.4	132.1	102.1	135.5	128.5	124.1	120.5	162.8	(NA)
2000	172.2	149.2	195.3	167.8	168.4	124.6	181.3	169.6	129.6	153.3	260.8	102.5
2005	195.3	160.2	230.1	190.7	191.2	177.1	200.9	195.7	119.5	173.9	323.2	113.7
2010	218.1	174.6	261.3	219.6	220.0	211.4	221.3	216.3	119.5	193.4	388.4	129.9
2011	224.9	183.9	265.8	227.8	227.9	243.9	225.0	219.1	122.1	212.4	400.3	131.5
2012	229.6	187.6	271.4	233.8	233.7	246.1	229.8	222.7	126.3	217.3	414.9	133.8
2013	233.0	187.7	277.9	237.0	237.0	244.4	233.8	227.4	127.4	217.4	425.1	135.9
2014	236.7	187.9	285.1	242.7	242.4	243.6	237.9	233.2	127.5	215.9	435.3	137.5
2015	237.0	181.7	291.7	247.2	246.8	202.9	242.2	238.1	125.9	199.1	446.8	138.2
2016	240.0	179.2	299.9	247.9	247.7	189.5	247.6	244.0	126.0	194.9	463.7	139.1
2017	245.1	181.2	308.1	250.1	249.8	204.5	252.2	251.2	125.6	201.6	475.3	136.5
2018	251.1	184.6	316.6	253.6	253.3	219.9	257.6	258.5	125.7	210.7	484.7	136.8
2019	255.7	185.3	325.1	258.3	258.0	215.3	263.2	266.0	124.1	210.1	498.4	137.8
2020	258.8	184.8	332.0	267.2	266.6	196.9	267.7	271.8	118.1	201.3	518.9	140.3
2021	271.0	199.2	341.4	277.8	276.8	238.3	277.3	280.7	121.0	230.7	525.3	142.6
2022	292.7	220.9	362.6	305.4	303.3	298.3	294.3	300.8	127.1	266.3	546.6	143.8
2023	304.7	223.5	384.5	323.0	320.5	283.3	308.4	320.2	130.6	267.0	549.1	145.2
PERCENT CHANGE [2]												
1990	5.4	5.2	5.5	5.8	5.8	8.3	5.0	4.5	4.6	5.6	9.0	(NA)
2000	3.4	3.3	3.4	2.3	2.3	16.9	2.4	3.5	-1.3	6.2	4.1	1.3
2005	3.4	3.6	3.3	2.4	2.5	17.0	2.2	3.3	-0.7	6.6	4.2	1.9
2010	1.6	2.9	0.8	0.8	0.8	9.5	1.0	-0.4	-0.5	7.9	3.4	2.0
2011	3.2	5.3	1.7	3.7	3.6	15.4	1.7	1.3	2.2	9.8	3.0	1.2
2012	2.1	2.0	2.1	2.6	2.5	0.9	2.1	1.6	3.4	2.3	3.7	1.8
2013	1.5	–	2.4	1.4	1.4	-0.7	1.8	2.1	0.9	–	2.5	1.5
2014	1.6	0.1	2.6	2.4	2.3	-0.3	1.7	2.6	0.1	-0.7	2.4	1.2
2015	0.1	-3.3	2.3	1.9	1.8	-16.7	1.8	2.1	-1.3	-7.8	2.6	0.5
2016	1.3	-1.4	2.8	0.3	0.3	-6.6	2.2	2.5	0.1	-2.1	3.8	0.7
2017	2.1	1.1	2.7	0.9	0.9	7.9	1.8	3.0	-0.3	3.4	2.5	-1.9
2018	2.4	1.9	2.8	1.4	1.4	7.5	2.1	2.9	–	4.5	2.0	0.2
2019	1.8	0.4	2.7	1.9	1.8	-2.1	2.2	2.9	-1.3	-0.3	2.8	0.7
2020	1.2	-0.3	2.1	3.4	3.3	-8.5	1.7	2.2	-4.8	-4.2	4.1	1.8
2021	4.7	7.8	2.8	3.9	3.8	21.0	3.6	3.3	2.5	14.6	1.2	1.6
2022	8.0	10.9	6.2	9.9	9.6	25.2	6.2	7.2	5.0	15.5	4.1	0.8
2023	4.1	1.2	6.0	5.8	5.7	-5.0	4.8	6.4	2.8	0.2	0.5	1.0

– Represents or rounds to zero. NA Not available. [1] Dec. 1997=100. [2] Change from immediate prior year. 1990 change from 1989.

Source: U.S. Bureau of Labor Statistics, "CPI Databases," <www.bls.gov/cpi/data.htm>, accessed May 2024.

Table 765. Consumer Price Indexes (CPI-U) and Annual Percent Change for Selected Urban Areas: 2023

[1982-84=100. Percent changes computed from annual averages of monthly figures published by source. In January 2018, BLS introduced a new geographic area sample for the Consumer Price Index (CPI) that utilizes the 2010 Decennial Census and incorporates an updated area sample design; see source for more information. Local area CPI indexes are by-products of the national CPI program. Each local index has a smaller sample size than the national index and is therefore subject to substantially more sampling and other measurement error. As a result, local area indexes show greater volatility than the national index, although their long-term trends are similar. Minus sign (-) indicates decrease. See also text, this section and Appendix III]

Urban area	Consumer Price Index						Medical care	Fuels and utilities
	All items	Food and beverage	Food	Housing	Apparel	Transportation		
U.S. city average	**304.7**	**320.5**	**323.0**	**320.2**	**130.6**	**267.0**	**549.1**	**305.5**
Atlanta-Sandy Springs-Roswell, GA	303.9	317.1	334.5	325.5	158.9	275.0	(NA)	368.1
Baltimore-Columbia-Towson, MD	306.0	326.1	326.3	306.3	131.7	272.9	507.0	302.1
Boston-Cambridge-Newton, MA-NH	326.0	338.2	342.8	349.1	137.7	232.8	734.5	411.7
Chicago-Naperville-Elgin, IL-IN-WI	282.5	315.0	315.4	298.6	90.0	236.2	542.5	250.9
Dallas-Fort Worth-Arlington, TX	288.0	325.3	320.8	289.7	118.7	263.9	503.2	308.9
Denver-Aurora-Lakewood, CO	320.3	296.6	304.0	326.1	116.2	327.9	707.0	294.5
Detroit-Warren-Dearborn, MI	283.7	284.6	286.0	276.4	107.3	315.9	(NA)	314.6
Houston-The Woodlands-Sugar Land, TX	267.6	292.9	295.6	262.7	177.9	232.1	542.1	188.2
Los Angeles-Long Beach-Anaheim, CA	321.6	328.8	330.5	366.9	119.6	264.3	553.5	475.2
Miami-Fort Lauderdale-West Palm Beach, FL	335.5	318.8	327.0	375.7	157.1	275.8	606.4	230.4
Minneapolis-St. Paul-Bloomington, MN-WI	292.7	355.4	344.5	277.8	149.8	250.8	625.0	274.0
New York-Newark-Jersey City, NY-NJ-PA	322.0	331.9	333.4	344.8	133.0	275.0	563.8	241.4
Philadelphia-Camden-Wilmington, PA-NJ-DE-MD	303.3	293.7	296.1	320.9	110.6	265.8	593.3	270.3
Phoenix-Mesa-Scottsdale, AZ	179.5	184.7	187.6	202.1	145.8	156.1	222.7	194.0
San Diego-Carlsbad, CA	362.0	313.9	312.2	437.4	178.5	291.0	560.4	496.7
San Francisco-Oakland-Hayward, CA	339.1	361.2	364.3	392.2	115.2	251.9	588.8	568.5
Seattle-Tacoma-Bellevue, WA	340.8	355.8	359.3	406.9	132.4	295.7	440.8	325.0
St. Louis, MO-IL	275.1	326.1	325.8	268.0	143.9	242.2	503.8	274.1
Tampa-St. Petersburg-Clearwater, FL	292.3	291.2	293.5	317.4	146.3	261.1	490.9	269.5
Urban Alaska	260.4	256.7	266.4	231.1	156.8	288.7	723.9	358.4
Urban Hawaii	326.0	353.1	356.9	347.6	126.2	270.8	508.8	458.7
Washington-Arlington-Alexandria, DC-VA-MD-WV	305.3	300.7	309.6	318.0	164.1	267.1	513.2	286.2
PERCENT CHANGE, 2022-2023								
U.S. city average	**4.1**	**5.7**	**5.8**	**6.4**	**2.8**	**0.2**	**0.5**	**2.4**
Atlanta-Sandy Springs-Roswell, GA	4.9	6.7	6.9	8.1	1.1	-0.5	(NA)	(NA)
Baltimore-Columbia-Towson, MD	3.8	5.1	5.0	5.7	3.3	-0.5	3.7	10.5
Boston-Cambridge-Newton, MA-NH	3.7	6.9	6.9	6.2	1.6	-1.0	–	3.1
Chicago-Naperville-Elgin, IL-IN-WI	3.3	4.7	4.4	4.1	1.9	0.4	0.4	-8.0
Dallas-Fort Worth-Arlington, TX	5.2	7.2	7.4	7.1	2.8	2.0	1.3	-3.4
Denver-Aurora-Lakewood, CO	5.2	5.9	6.0	7.8	3.6	2.2	0.4	10.5
Detroit-Warren-Dearborn, MI	5.8	5.9	5.6	8.8	2.9	4.9	(NA)	1.2
Houston-The Woodlands-Sugar Land, TX	3.5	7.3	7.5	4.9	-0.2	0.6	-0.5	-15.4
Los Angeles-Long Beach-Anaheim, CA	3.5	4.7	4.9	4.9	1.9	-1.5	1.3	8.1
Miami-Fort Lauderdale-West Palm Beach, FL	7.7	6.2	6.5	12.8	7.8	-0.1	0.1	9.5
Minneapolis-St. Paul-Bloomington, MN-WI	2.7	5.7	5.9	3.4	4.1	2.8	-0.3	-1.7
New York-Newark-Jersey City, NY-NJ-PA	3.8	5.0	5.0	4.8	3.1	-0.1	-0.8	-1.7
Philadelphia-Camden-Wilmington, PA-NJ-DE-MD	4.4	6.0	6.2	6.7	0.8	-0.6	0.2	1.8
Phoenix-Mesa-Scottsdale, AZ	5.2	6.1	6.3	9.0	0.9	-1.8	6.1	4.7
San Diego-Carlsbad, CA	5.1	2.4	2.3	9.0	3.1	-0.9	3.7	10.9
San Francisco-Oakland-Hayward, CA	3.7	4.9	5.1	4.5	3.5	-1.2	1.5	4.8
Seattle-Tacoma-Bellevue, WA	5.8	5.8	5.8	7.7	1.7	2.6	1.8	6.7
St. Louis, MO-IL	3.8	5.4	5.5	5.5	6.3	1.1	-0.4	5.4
Tampa-St. Petersburg-Clearwater, FL	6.8	5.9	6.0	10.7	3.1	0.9	5.9	8.9
Urban Alaska	1.5	-2.2	-2.6	3.4	2.5	–	4.5	3.5
Urban Hawaii	3.1	4.4	4.8	2.7	14.3	-0.5	(NA)	-0.3
Washington-Arlington-Alexandria, DC-VA-MD-WV	3.1	3.9	4.0	4.7	5.0	1.8	-3.6	3.2

NA Not available. – Represents or rounds to zero.

Source: U.S. Bureau of Labor Statistics, CPI Databases, "All Urban Consumers (Current Series)," <www.bls.gov/cpi/data.htm>, accessed May 2024.

Table 766. Consumer Price Indexes for All Urban Consumers (CPI-U) for Selected Items and Groups: 2000 to 2023

[1982-1984=100, unless otherwise noted. Annual averages of monthly figures. Reflects buying patterns of all urban consumers. For information about the CPI methodology, see the U.S. Bureau of Labor Statistics Handbook of Methods, Consumer Price Index at <www.bls.gov/opub/hom/cpi/home.htm>]

Item	2000	2010	2015	2019	2020	2021	2022	2023
All items..	**172.2**	**218.1**	**237.0**	**255.7**	**258.8**	**271.0**	**292.7**	**304.7**
Food and beverages..............................	**168.4**	**220.0**	**246.8**	**258.0**	**266.6**	**276.8**	**303.3**	**320.5**
Food...	167.8	219.6	247.2	258.3	267.2	277.8	305.4	323.0
Food at home..................................	167.9	215.8	242.3	241.8	250.2	258.9	288.5	302.9
Cereals and bakery products......................	188.3	250.4	274.1	276.6	282.6	289.1	326.7	354.3
Cereals and cereal products.......................	175.9	217.6	234.1	227.6	231.8	235.8	268.2	287.6
Rice, pasta, and cornmeal.......................	150.7	224.4	241.6	238.0	243.9	245.5	277.0	294.2
Rice [1,2]...	99.3	156.9	167.2	162.6	164.9	166.5	184.9	196.1
Bakery products [2].............................	194.1	268.0	296.6	304.8	312.1	319.9	360.5	393.0
Bread [2]......................................	107.4	159.8	178.7	184.1	190.7	194.5	217.2	237.9
Cakes, cupcakes, and cookies....................	187.9	251.7	278.8	291.2	294.9	302.7	340.1	370.3
Other bakery products...........................	191.5	247.1	266.4	269.9	275.9	282.8	322.9	350.9
Meats, poultry, fish and eggs......................	154.5	207.7	260.3	249.8	265.2	282.8	313.7	319.4
Meats, poultry, and fish.........................	155.5	208.6	258.5	253.3	269.3	287.5	315.0	321.2
Meats......................................	150.7	206.2	264.2	255.3	274.2	295.2	319.4	326.0
Beef and veal.............................	148.1	224.5	322.5	307.4	337.0	368.4	387.8	401.8
Uncooked ground beef..................	125.2	203.6	295.3	269.3	296.2	310.4	335.5	345.0
Uncooked beef steaks [2]...............	109.1	153.3	214.6	207.4	224.7	251.7	258.2	271.4
Pork......................................	156.5	190.0	218.7	212.7	226.0	245.5	266.8	263.7
Poultry....................................	159.8	204.0	237.3	231.5	244.4	256.9	294.4	303.5
Chicken [2]..............................	102.5	131.8	152.1	149.9	157.3	165.7	190.2	193.7
Fish and seafood...........................	190.4	243.2	286.3	298.5	308.2	324.9	354.6	355.7
Eggs..	131.9	192.8	286.2	203.9	212.5	222.1	293.7	297.7
Dairy products [2].............................	160.7	199.2	222.4	218.7	228.3	231.4	259.2	269.5
Milk [2]......................................	107.8	133.6	147.5	140.7	148.5	153.6	175.1	176.1
Cheese and related products....................	162.8	204.8	233.6	228.7	240.7	241.1	262.6	268.0
Ice cream and related products.................	164.4	195.0	219.2	221.8	230.4	232.2	255.3	274.3
Fruits and vegetables............................	204.6	273.5	293.8	300.9	304.9	314.8	341.7	350.2
Fresh fruits and vegetables......................	238.8	314.8	337.7	349.5	352.3	364.1	391.3	394.3
Fresh fruits.................................	258.3	322.3	352.0	360.1	357.1	376.5	406.3	409.1
Fresh vegetables...........................	219.4	305.5	321.4	337.1	345.8	349.7	374.2	377.4
Processed fruits and vegetables [2]..............	105.6	146.6	158.5	156.2	161.6	166.2	186.2	201.0
Nonalcoholic beverages and beverage materials...	137.8	161.6	167.9	170.8	176.9	181.8	201.9	216.0
Juices and nonalcoholic drinks [2]................	105.6	124.5	128.5	133.4	139.5	143.6	158.9	171.2
Carbonated drinks..........................	123.4	154.7	159.6	169.5	178.9	185.9	205.6	221.6
Nonfrozen noncarbonated juices and drinks [2]....	104.2	114.8	117.9	120.4	125.3	128.2	142.0	152.7
Beverage materials including coffee and tea [2].....	97.9	114.0	120.4	116.6	117.8	120.5	134.8	141.8
Coffee......................................	154.0	186.4	205.5	193.2	194.2	199.3	227.9	237.2
Other food at home..............................	155.6	191.1	209.3	211.1	217.3	222.9	251.8	269.7
Sugar and sweets.............................	154.0	201.2	216.1	220.2	227.6	234.4	258.8	281.2
Candy and chewing gum [2].......................	103.8	132.5	145.4	150.0	154.9	159.2	174.1	190.5
Fats and oils..................................	147.4	200.6	227.3	226.4	229.5	240.1	284.5	310.1
Frozen and freeze dried prepared food.............	148.5	165.3	170.9	166.7	172.2	176.3	202.7	213.5
Snacks.......................................	166.3	216.6	250.6	251.8	259.3	263.6	295.9	312.7
Spices, seasonings, condiments, sauces...........	175.6	214.4	235.6	242.9	249.4	254.5	282.1	304.3
Other miscellaneous food [2].....................	107.5	121.7	131.8	132.1	136.7	140.4	158.0	169.0
Food away from home.............................	169.0	226.1	256.1	284.4	293.9	307.3	330.8	354.3
Full service meals and snacks [2].................	106.8	141.1	159.4	176.4	181.5	189.7	205.8	218.4
Limited service meals and snacks [2]..............	106.3	143.9	163.3	182.1	189.9	202.7	217.4	232.6
At employee sites and schools [2].................	104.4	141.0	161.7	181.2	176.9	113.8	125.3	195.2
From vending machines and mobile vendors [2].......	102.4	133.1	146.3	165.5	170.2	178.0	192.7	221.2
Other food away from home [2]....................	109.0	159.3	179.6	196.4	200.6	206.4	218.2	233.4
Alcoholic beverages.............................	174.7	223.3	239.5	252.5	257.2	262.8	274.0	285.4
Alcoholic beverages at home......................	158.1	191.0	197.3	205.5	209.0	212.5	219.2	226.0
Beer, ale, and other malt beverages at home........	156.8	201.0	215.0	230.1	238.1	242.3	254.4	267.4
Distilled spirits at home...........................	162.3	188.8	192.6	194.8	196.2	202.1	205.1	209.1
Wine at home.................................	151.6	169.7	168.5	171.8	172.2	174.0	178.1	181.4
Alcoholic beverages away from home................	207.1	291.9	330.5	355.2	363.1	373.4	394.6	418.4
Housing..	**169.6**	**216.3**	**238.1**	**266.0**	**271.8**	**280.7**	**300.8**	**320.2**
Shelter...	193.4	248.4	278.8	318.1	325.9	334.6	354.2	380.6
Rent of primary residence.........................	183.9	249.4	286.0	331.1	341.5	349.1	370.2	399.6
Lodging away from home [2].......................	117.5	133.7	153.0	165.9	148.9	163.4	181.3	189.1
Other lodging away from home including hotels and motels..............................	252.4	280.4	317.4	339.5	299.2	331.7	372.8	389.7
Owners' equivalent rent of primary residence [3]........	198.7	256.6	285.9	325.7	334.8	343.4	363.1	390.3
Tenants' and household insurance [2]................	103.7	125.7	146.4	151.8	151.1	150.7	150.5	153.3
Fuels and utilities.................................	137.9	214.2	230.1	242.6	243.9	260.5	298.2	305.5
Household energy..............................	122.8	189.3	194.7	200.0	199.5	215.2	253.3	257.2
Fuel oil and other fuels........................	129.7	275.1	256.2	280.8	237.6	302.6	447.9	388.0
Fuel oil....................................	130.3	282.9	254.3	282.4	218.0	286.4	482.5	400.2
Propane, kerosene, and firewood [4]...............	155.5	320.6	305.9	329.1	319.8	390.0	456.8	435.5
Energy services.............................	128.0	192.9	198.7	203.5	204.5	218.9	254.1	260.6
Electricity.................................	128.5	193.1	209.2	213.4	214.6	223.9	253.1	267.8
Utility (piped) gas service.....................	132.0	189.7	164.6	171.0	171.4	200.1	251.8	233.7
Water and sewer and trash collection services [2].......	106.5	170.9	214.0	244.7	252.5	261.5	273.2	288.1
Water and sewerage maintenance..................	227.5	380.7	492.9	568.1	585.6	604.0	629.6	659.2
Garbage and trash collection [5]...................	269.8	384.4	432.0	481.9	498.7	522.3	549.3	589.3
Household furnishings and operations...............	**128.2**	**125.5**	**122.6**	**123.8**	**125.9**	**131.6**	**143.5**	**148.4**
Furniture and bedding............................	134.4	119.7	114.7	113.6	113.7	123.0	138.0	135.8
Living room, kitchen, and dining room furniture [2]......	102.4	88.9	86.8	88.0	88.1	96.7	111.0	108.7
Appliances [2].................................	96.3	86.9	79.3	77.5	79.6	84.5	88.5	87.9
Other household equipment and furnishings [2]..........	98.0	70.8	59.1	50.7	50.3	51.7	55.3	55.2
Clocks, lamps, and decorator items..................	111.7	62.9	47.1	37.1	36.8	37.8	40.9	40.7

See footnotes at end of table.

Table 766. Consumer Price Indexes for All Urban Consumers (CPI-U) for Selected Items and Groups: 2000 to 2023-Continued.

See headnote on page 505.

Item	2000	2010	2015	2019	2020	2021	2022	2023
Nonelectric cookware and tableware [2]	98.4	96.6	90.4	81.2	78.6	81.0	85.1	83.2
Tools, hardware, outdoor equipment and supplies [2]	97.0	91.6	91.1	90.9	92.6	95.8	106.2	114.1
Tools, hardware, and supplies [2]	97.3	96.5	100.1	99.7	100.4	104.4	115.6	123.0
Outdoor equipment and supplies [2]	96.8	88.9	86.8	86.7	89.0	91.8	101.9	110.5
Housekeeping supplies	153.4	183.3	186.8	189.9	196.1	199.2	218.6	233.6
Household cleaning products [2]	105.1	120.6	118.9	120.8	124.4	127.6	139.7	147.8
Household paper products [2]	113.8	158.0	169.2	175.5	185.8	194.0	213.5	231.4
Miscellaneous household products [2]	104.3	116.9	119.0	119.2	121.0	119.3	131.0	139.9
Household operations [2]	110.5	150.3	166.9	194.5	200.6	213.5	(NA)	240.2
Domestic services [2]	109.7	144.4	155.6	169.6	174.5	190.5	203.1	214.1
Gardening and lawncare services [2]	111.4	155.3	171.8	205.3	215.4	222.2	(NA)	247.8
Apparel	**129.6**	**119.5**	**125.9**	**124.1**	**118.1**	**121.0**	**127.1**	**130.6**
Men's and boy's apparel	129.7	111.9	119.6	118.5	113.1	116.0	122.4	126.6
Men's apparel	133.1	117.5	124.0	120.2	115.7	118.2	125.2	129.8
Men's shirts and sweaters [2]	98.3	78.6	79.5	76.3	70.6	71.1	76.1	78.5
Boys' apparel	116.2	91.5	103.0	110.0	101.2	105.8	110.3	113.5
Women's and girl's apparel	121.5	107.1	111.2	106.7	99.7	100.9	106.0	109.3
Women's apparel	121.9	109.5	114.4	109.2	100.6	101.6	107.1	110.4
Women's suits and separates [2]	98.2	83.9	81.8	75.5	69.5	69.6	73.4	75.3
Women's underwear, nightwear, swimwear, and accessories [2]	101.8	96.0	105.2	104.2	100.5	101.6	107.3	112.0
Girls' apparel	119.7	95.4	96.0	94.3	95.0	97.3	100.5	103.6
Footwear	123.8	128.0	136.8	136.7	133.2	138.1	144.5	144.8
Men's footwear	129.5	127.6	137.9	140.2	137.7	144.2	149.4	148.6
Women's footwear	119.6	125.3	128.9	124.2	120.6	124.5	130.6	131.9
Jewelry and watches [4]	137.0	152.4	160.0	171.5	170.4	183.2	188.0	197.6
Jewelry [4]	141.2	161.2	165.5	172.5	167.0	181.2	185.7	196.8
Transportation	**153.3**	**193.4**	**199.1**	**210.1**	**201.3**	**230.7**	**266.3**	**267.0**
Private transportation	149.1	188.7	193.7	205.8	198.7	229.7	265.2	266.4
New and used motor vehicles [2]	100.8	97.1	100.8	99.5	100.7	114.5	128.2	127.7
New vehicles	142.8	138.0	147.1	146.8	147.6	156.2	172.5	178.9
Used cars and trucks	155.8	143.1	147.1	139.8	144.2	182.6	205.9	191.2
Leased cars and trucks [6]	(NA)	97.0	84.2	86.9	(NA)	(NA)	(NA)	115.8
Motor fuel	129.3	239.2	213.1	233.2	195.2	265.1	350.3	313.3
Gasoline (all types)	128.6	238.6	212.0	232.0	194.1	264.0	347.7	311.6
Motor vehicle parts and equipment	101.5	137.0	144.2	146.4	148.1	155.1	175.8	180.8
Motor vehicle maintenance and repair	177.3	248.0	270.7	296.0	306.0	317.9	344.1	383.8
Motor vehicle insurance	256.7	375.2	460.6	571.0	544.6	565.3	609.8	716.0
Motor vehicle fees [2]	107.3	165.5	178.9	192.9	195.6	198.0	201.4	206.8
Public transportation	209.6	251.4	268.7	259.5	227.5	231.2	277.3	267.6
Airline fare	239.4	278.2	292.2	265.4	217.5	217.5	283.1	267.2
Medical care	**260.8**	**388.4**	**446.8**	**498.4**	**518.9**	**525.3**	**546.6**	**549.1**
Medical care commodities	238.1	314.7	354.6	381.3	383.2	377.1	388.1	404.3
Prescription drugs	285.4	407.8	479.3	526.8	532.1	522.4	533.9	549.5
Nonprescription drugs [10]	(NA)	100.0	97.8	97.3	96.4	95.9	100.1	106.6
Medical care services	266.0	411.2	476.2	536.1	562.7	573.1	597.7	595.6
Professional medical services	237.7	328.2	361.5	382.6	389.9	401.9	411.8	419.1
Physicians' services	244.7	331.3	366.1	383.2	389.9	406.5	411.9	412.6
Dental services	258.5	398.8	452.2	496.2	511.1	522.5	543.7	574.3
Eyeglasses and eye care [4]	149.7	176.7	184.0	191.4	192.9	194.0	198.7	202.2
Services by other medical professionals [4]	161.9	214.4	228.2	239.2	242.1	247.9	258.1	258.7
Hospital and related services	317.3	607.7	761.9	885.2	921.1	950.0	985.5	1,028.0
Hospital services [7]	115.9	227.2	290.1	338.8	353.0	363.5	376.8	392.1
Nursing homes and adult day services [7]	117.0	177.0	206.4	235.3	241.7	249.6	260.1	273.8
Health insurance [9]	(NA)	106.6	123.6	155.2	179.8	172.0	196.0	151.3
Recreation [2]	**103.3**	**113.3**	**115.9**	**120.6**	**122.2**	**125.2**	**130.8**	**136.1**
Video and audio [2]	101.0	99.1	99.6	104.7	107.1	110.4	112.7	115.9
Cable, satellite, and live streaming tv service [5]	266.8	372.4	422.8	479.4	500.1	520.6	541.3	569.6
Pets, pet products and services [2]	106.1	154.4	167.3	178.0	180.1	184.9	201.5	217.6
Sporting goods	119.0	118.8	114.6	112.3	113.7	121.2	127.5	126.9
Other recreational goods [2]	87.8	57.8	47.0	35.2	33.5	33.5	34.5	34.5
Other recreation services [2]	111.7	145.1	156.2	171.8	174.7	176.2	183.1	193.4
Club membership for shopping clubs, fraternal or other organizations & participant sports fees [2]	108.9	123.5	130.1	142.9	145.0	146.1	151.5	157.6
Admissions	230.5	322.8	354.1	389.2	396.6	395.6	412.1	440.1
Recreational reading materials	188.3	220.7	240.7	255.6	267.0	273.7	284.7	285.6
Education and communication [2]	**102.5**	**129.9**	**138.2**	**137.8**	**140.3**	**142.6**	**143.8**	**145.2**
Education [2]	112.5	199.3	240.5	265.8	270.7	274.6	282.1	290.7
Educational books and supplies	279.9	505.6	648.2	685.4	677.7	687.1	712.5	701.2
Tuition, other school fees, and childcare	324.0	573.2	688.8	762.7	777.7	788.7	810.1	836.5
College tuition and fees	331.9	638.2	785.9	865.4	877.3	884.9	904.0	921.4
Day care and preschool [11]	156.3	240.4	275.4	303.3	311.9	317.7	330.3	348.9
Communication	93.6	84.7	80.2	73.2	74.5	75.9	75.4	75.1
Postage and delivery services [2]	103.2	145.9	174.6	194.8	202.7	211.2	220.0	230.6
Information and information processing [2]	92.8	81.5	76.4	69.2	70.4	71.6	71.1	70.7
Telephone services [2]	98.5	102.4	99.3	89.4	92.2	94.4	94.8	95.3
Wireless telephone services [2]	76.0	62.4	55.2	46.4	47.3	48.2	47.9	47.8
Residential telephone services [10]	(NA)	101.6	113.4	120.8	128.9	136.2	142.3	150.6
Information technology, hardware, and services [8]	25.9	9.4	8.1	7.4	7.3	7.4	7.2	7.1
Other goods and services	**271.1**	**381.3**	**414.9**	**451.3**	**462.4**	**476.8**	**506.4**	**537.3**
Tobacco and smoking products	394.9	807.3	930.8	1,115.9	1,171.6	1,256.4	1,347.5	1,435.7
Cigarettes [2]	159.9	329.0	380.0	457.0	481.6	518.1	556.6	594.2
Personal care	165.6	206.6	220.8	234.0	238.3	243.5	257.9	273.4
Personal care products	153.7	161.1	163.3	160.7	160.1	159.7	166.5	176.3
Hair, dental, shaving, and misc. products [2]	103.3	104.3	103.7	103.0	103.8	103.8	110.1	118.5
Cosmetics, perfume, bath, nail preparations								

See footnotes at end of table.

Table 766. Consumer Price Indexes for All Urban Consumers (CPI-U) for Selected Items and Groups: 2000 to 2023-Continued.

See headnote on page 505.

Item	2000	2010	2015	2019	2020	2021	2022	2023
and implements....................	166.8	182.2	188.2	182.8	179.5	178.5	182.5	189.8
Personal care services...................	178.1	229.6	247.2	271.4	283.2	297.5	313.7	328.9
Haircuts and other personal care services [2]...........	108.7	140.1	150.8	165.6	172.8	181.5	191.4	200.7
Miscellaneous personal services........................	252.3	354.1	399.3	448.9	456.7	465.4	495.2	530.4
Legal services [4]......................	189.3	288.1	323.6	364.8	368.7	374.4	399.4	432.9
Funeral expenses [4]....................	187.8	282.0	313.7	337.9	343.3	348.8	360.2	379.3
SPECIAL AGGREGATE INDEXES								
Commodities...................	149.2	174.6	181.7	185.3	184.8	199.2	220.9	223.5
Commodities less food and beverages..................	137.7	150.4	149.2	149.5	145.7	161.0	179.9	177.3
Nondurables less food and beverages..................	147.4	189.9	189.4	196.5	185.5	204.9	234.3	230.7
Nondurables less food, beverages, and apparel......	162.5	238.1	233.3	245.9	231.5	261.5	306.0	298.1
Durables.............................	125.4	111.3	109.1	104.8	105.7	116.9	128.1	126.4
Services...............................	195.3	261.3	291.7	325.1	332.0	341.4	362.6	384.5
Rent of shelter [3].....................	201.3	258.8	290.4	331.6	339.9	349.1	369.8	397.6
Transportation services.................	196.1	259.8	291.0	325.0	312.8	324.2	357.8	396.2
Other services........................	229.9	309.6	339.4	358.9	367.8	375.8	388.1	404.2
All items less food........................	173.0	217.8	235.4	255.2	257.5	269.9	290.7	301.9
All items less shelter......................	165.7	208.6	223.3	234.2	235.7	249.1	271.7	278.4
All items less medical care...............	167.3	209.7	226.9	244.0	246.4	258.8	280.4	292.9
Commodities less food.................	139.2	153.0	152.2	152.9	149.3	164.4	183.3	181.0
Nondurables less food.................	149.1	191.9	192.3	199.7	189.7	208.2	236.6	233.9
Nondurables less food and apparel..........	162.9	235.6	232.7	245.3	232.8	260.3	301.6	295.4
Nondurables.................................	158.2	205.3	217.6	226.6	225.0	240.0	268.1	274.5
Apparel less footwear..................	126.2	113.3	118.8	116.6	110.2	112.5	118.4	122.4
Services less rent of shelter [3]............	202.9	284.4	315.8	342.8	348.6	359.1	382.4	398.8
Services less medical care services...........	188.9	249.6	277.7	309.1	314.5	323.9	344.8	368.4
Energy....................................	124.6	211.4	202.9	215.3	196.9	238.3	298.3	283.3
All items less energy......................	178.6	220.5	242.3	261.8	266.9	276.6	295.1	309.7
All items less food and energy..............	181.3	221.3	242.2	263.2	267.7	277.3	294.3	308.4
Commodities less food and energy commodities.......	144.9	143.6	146.1	144.4	144.6	153.8	165.5	166.9
Energy commodities....................	129.5	242.6	216.7	237.4	198.8	269.1	357.5	319.2
Services less energy services...............	202.1	268.3	301.1	337.3	344.8	353.8	373.8	397.1
Domestically produced farm food..................	170.1	221.6	251.0	249.5	258.4	267.4	298.6	313.4
Utilities and public transportation..................	152.6	203.1	214.8	218.0	218.5	227.9	249.2	254.5

NA Not available. [1] Special indexes based on a substantially smaller sample. [2] December 1997=100. [3] December 1982=100. [4] December 1986=100. [5] December 1983=100. [6] December 2001=100. [7] December 1996=100. [8] December 1988=100. [9] December 2005=100. [10] December 2009=100. [11] December 1990=100.

Source: U.S. Bureau of Labor Statistics, CPI Databases, "All Urban Consumers (Current Series)," <www.bls.gov/cpi/data.htm>, accessed May 2024.

Table 767. Single-Family Housing Price Indexes by State: 2005 to 2023

[Data are for the fourth quarter of the year shown. Index 1991, 1st quarter = 100. Purchase only indexes. Data are seasonally adjusted. The index reflects average price changes in repeat sales or refinancings on the same properties. The information is obtained by reviewing repeat mortgage transactions on single-family properties whose mortgages have been purchased or securitized by either Fannie Mae or Freddie Mac; for more information on methodology, see source]

State	2005	2010	2015	2020	2022	2023	State	2005	2010	2015	2020	2022	2023
U.S....	**215.7**	**181.3**	**218.0**	**303.4**	**386.8**	**411.9**	MO......	196.3	177.1	200.8	277.6	348.7	376.6
AL.......	182.6	175.2	190.0	259.2	335.6	350.5	MT......	273.0	277.1	335.2	480.0	669.3	694.4
AK.......	207.6	219.9	245.0	288.3	339.1	358.6	NE.......	193.2	187.1	222.6	306.7	385.1	403.8
AZ.......	302.9	172.8	254.0	394.8	535.3	570.7	NV.......	268.6	124.6	193.5	303.0	387.7	400.8
AR.......	185.1	175.4	195.4	250.4	328.4	347.6	NH.......	237.6	193.5	212.2	304.7	396.5	432.8
CA.......	283.5	159.3	230.4	326.1	398.0	417.6	NJ.......	252.4	211.4	212.1	274.9	345.4	384.7
CO.......	267.6	253.7	351.4	533.9	668.6	690.8	NM.......	213.9	209.0	213.6	285.9	364.4	382.8
CT.......	193.6	164.4	161.7	199.4	249.0	279.4	NY.......	212.2	201.5	208.2	280.2	345.9	379.2
DE.......	208.3	185.5	187.5	236.0	303.0	317.4	NC.......	181.8	179.8	199.1	286.6	395.2	422.8
DC.......	313.9	311.2	444.0	580.0	622.4	615.1	ND.......	191.2	222.5	297.6	338.7	395.5	414.8
FL.......	298.8	171.7	240.9	362.4	522.2	558.0	OH.......	173.6	149.6	168.5	238.7	296.0	323.3
GA.......	190.2	152.0	193.9	283.5	382.2	409.6	OK.......	177.2	190.7	217.6	272.7	348.2	366.1
HI.......	206.4	177.8	221.2	280.7	383.6	370.4	OR.......	295.1	251.6	337.3	497.5	607.5	617.3
ID.......	228.3	188.9	249.0	456.2	602.0	605.2	PA.......	188.7	183.2	196.1	260.4	319.2	341.2
IL.......	202.6	171.7	180.5	221.5	267.4	289.8	RI.......	235.3	180.5	192.7	279.3	342.8	394.6
IN.......	164.7	155.0	174.9	251.7	316.6	342.0	SC......	185.6	179.0	203.9	283.1	386.0	423.3
IA.......	190.1	193.0	217.4	273.3	332.2	350.7	SD......	208.6	216.3	255.9	343.0	446.5	476.8
KS.......	188.2	188.5	208.8	284.8	349.2	380.0	TN......	184.4	179.7	212.3	315.8	436.0	463.2
KY.......	184.2	186.2	205.7	276.8	348.7	371.0	TX......	171.0	183.0	237.9	327.2	429.0	440.7
LA.......	213.8	225.5	254.7	302.6	353.8	361.3	UT......	254.4	248.4	317.5	515.9	682.3	696.0
ME.......	220.6	200.1	211.6	307.6	418.5	449.5	VT......	208.4	203.5	210.3	275.6	357.2	404.5
MD.......	253.4	204.3	220.4	280.1	331.8	351.2	VA......	233.1	204.6	225.2	296.9	369.2	396.2
MA.......	251.1	211.3	240.4	334.3	405.8	442.8	WA......	241.2	218.0	273.2	444.4	552.7	570.4
MI.......	198.9	141.9	184.0	265.2	326.8	358.3	WV......	181.5	187.2	205.7	236.4	284.4	319.6
MN.......	250.6	203.2	239.7	329.9	390.6	406.5	WI......	221.6	202.6	217.2	305.9	381.9	417.4
MS.......	178.9	174.1	190.5	230.1	286.7	314.5	WY......	257.4	277.6	316.5	389.9	491.8	510.0

Source: Federal Housing Finance Agency, "House Price Index Datasets, Quarterly Data, Purchase-Only Indexes," <www.fhfa.gov/DataTools /Downloads/Pages/House-Price-Index-Datasets.aspx#qpo>, accessed March 2024.

Table 768. Average Prices of Selected Fuels and Electricity: 1990 to 2023

[Fuels in dollars per unit; electricity in cents per kWh. Represents price to end-users, except as noted]

Item	Unit	1990	2000	2010	2015	2019	2020	2021	2022	2023
Crude oil, composite [1]	Barrel	22.22	28.26	76.69	48.39	59.38	39.75	67.83	95.29	77.67
Motor gasoline: [2]										
Unleaded regular	Gallon	1.16	1.51	2.79	2.45	2.64	2.17	3.05	4.09	3.66
Unleaded premium	Gallon	1.35	1.69	3.05	2.87	3.21	2.79	3.69	4.86	4.47
No. 2 fuel oil (heating oil)	Gallon	0.73	0.93	2.46	2.02	2.27	1.66	2.41	(NA)	(NA)
No. 2 diesel fuel	Gallon	0.73	0.94	2.31	1.82	2.11	1.49	2.20	(NA)	(NA)
Propane, consumer grade	Gallon	0.75	0.60	1.48	0.48	0.60	0.50	1.09	(NA)	(NA)
Residual fuel oil	Gallon	0.44	0.60	1.71	1.29	1.58	1.25	1.86	(NA)	(NA)
Natural gas, residential	1,000 cu/ft	5.80	7.76	11.39	10.38	10.51	10.78	12.18	14.75	15.23
Electricity, residential	kWh	7.83	8.24	11.54	12.65	13.01	13.15	13.66	15.04	15.98

NA Not available. [1] Refiner acquisition cost. [2] Average, all service.

Source: U.S. Energy Information Administration, *Monthly Energy Review*, June 2024. See also <www.eia.gov/totalenergy/data/monthly/>.

Table 769. Retail Gasoline Prices—U.S. Total and Selected Cities: 2020 to 2023

[In dollars per gallon. Prices are annual averages. Gasoline is classified by octane rating: regular, 85 or less; midgrade, 88-90; and premium, greater than 90. Octane requirements may vary by altitude]

Area	Regular				Midgrade				Premium			
	2020	2021	2022	2023	2020	2021	2022	2023	2020	2021	2022	2023
U.S. total	**2.17**	**3.01**	**3.95**	**3.52**	**2.58**	**3.43**	**4.44**	**4.04**	**2.83**	**3.69**	**4.74**	**4.37**
Boston, MA	2.14	2.92	4.01	3.47	2.50	3.26	4.42	3.94	2.70	3.45	4.70	4.30
Chicago, IL	2.31	3.20	4.39	3.83	2.69	3.57	4.81	4.34	3.11	3.98	5.24	4.80
Cleveland, OH	2.07	2.90	3.79	3.36	2.42	3.22	4.15	3.82	2.78	3.59	4.53	4.27
Denver, CO	2.18	3.12	3.71	3.49	2.55	3.51	4.11	3.92	2.81	3.77	4.41	4.24
Houston, TX	1.82	2.62	3.45	3.01	2.24	3.03	3.90	3.51	2.47	3.27	4.17	3.81
Los Angeles, CA	3.04	3.99	5.28	4.78	3.30	4.27	5.61	5.12	3.34	4.31	5.65	5.17
Miami, FL	2.10	2.90	3.77	3.42	2.46	3.25	4.18	3.84	2.75	3.52	4.49	4.12
New York, NY	2.18	3.01	3.94	3.45	2.55	3.34	4.36	3.96	2.71	3.53	4.63	4.30
San Francisco, CA	3.14	4.13	5.41	4.77	3.38	4.36	5.65	5.01	3.53	4.53	5.82	5.23
Seattle, WA	2.84	3.61	4.74	4.63	3.19	3.93	5.17	5.07	3.24	4.01	5.17	5.08

Source: U.S. Energy Information Administration, "Weekly Retail Gasoline and Diesel Prices," <www.eia.gov/dnav/pet/pet_pri_gnd_dcus_nus_w.htm>, accessed March 2024.

Table 770. Weekly Food Cost of a Nutritious Diet by Type of Family and Individual: 2010 to 2023

[In dollars. As of December. Suggested plans assume that food for all meals and snacks is purchased at the store and prepared at home. Food Plans are based on 2001-02 data and updated to current dollars by using the Consumer Price Index for specific food items. See source for details]

Family and individual type	2010			2020			2023		
	Low cost plan	Moderate cost plan	Liberal plan	Low cost plan	Moderate cost plan	Liberal plan	Low cost plan	Moderate cost plan	Liberal plan
FAMILIES									
Family of two (male & female):									
19 to 50 years old	103.40	128.40	160.80	118.50	147.10	183.90	(NA)	(NA)	(NA)
51 to 70 years old	99.20	122.60	148.00	113.70	141.70	171.30	(NA)	(NA)	(NA)
Family of four:									
Couple (male & female),									
19 to 50 years old and children aged—									
2 to 3 and 4 to 5 years old	150.20	185.50	229.90	172.80	213.40	263.70	(NA)	(NA)	(NA)
6 to 8 and 9 to 11 years old	176.60	221.00	268.50	203.90	255.00	308.70	(NA)	(NA)	(NA)
INDIVIDUALS [1]									
Child:									
1 year old	26.80	30.60	37.10	30.60	34.80	42.10	35.70	40.50	49.10
2 to 3 years old	27.50	33.30	40.50	32.10	38.50	46.90	37.60	45.20	54.80
4 to 5 years old	28.70	35.50	43.30	32.90	41.20	49.60	38.90	48.00	58.20
6 to 8 years old	39.20	48.20	56.90	46.50	56.10	66.00	55.40	66.00	77.30
9 to 11 years old	43.40	56.10	65.50	49.70	65.10	75.60	58.90	75.80	88.30
Male:									
12 to 13 years old	49.50	61.70	72.70	57.40	71.80	84.40	68.70	85.30	99.80
14 to 18 years old	50.80	63.80	73.40	58.10	73.60	85.10	69.70	87.20	101.50
19 to 50 years old	50.30	62.90	77.10	57.70	72.30	88.60	68.90	86.40	104.90
51 to 70 years old	47.60	58.60	71.10	54.50	68.10	82.30	64.80	81.20	97.20
71 years old and over	47.00	58.50	71.90	53.50	66.70	82.30	64.10	79.10	96.60
Female:									
12 to 13 years old	42.90	51.90	63.00	49.20	59.90	73.10	58.40	69.70	86.50
14 to 18 years old	43.10	52.00	63.90	49.20	58.90	72.90	58.60	69.60	86.30
19 to 50 years old	43.70	53.80	69.00	50.00	61.40	78.60	59.70	72.80	93.00
51 to 70 years old	42.50	52.90	63.50	48.80	60.70	73.50	58.20	72.00	86.40
71 years old and over	42.10	52.50	63.40	48.10	60.10	72.40	58.10	71.40	85.40

NA Not available. [1] The costs given are for individuals in 4-person families. For individuals in other size families, the following adjustments are suggested: 1-person, add 20 percent; 2-person, add 10 percent; 3-person, add 5 percent; 5- or 6-person, subtract 5 percent; and 7-or-more person, subtract 10 percent.

Source: U.S. Department of Agriculture, Center for Nutrition Policy and Promotion, "USDA Food Plans: Monthly Cost of Food Reports," <www.fns.usda.gov/cnpp/usda-food-plans-cost-food-monthly-reports>, accessed March 2024.

Table 771. Food—Retail Prices of Selected Items: 1990 to 2023

[In dollars per pound, except as indicated. As of December. See Appendix III]

Food	1990	2000	2005	2010	2015	2020	2021	2022	2023
Cereals and bakery products:									
Flour, white, all purpose....................	0.24	0.28	0.30	0.44	0.50	0.45	0.39	0.52	0.54
Rice, white, long grain, raw...................	0.49	(NA)	0.52	0.73	0.71	0.79	0.82	0.97	0.99
Spaghetti and macaroni......................	0.85	0.88	0.87	1.19	1.29	1.31	1.09	1.43	1.38
Bread, white, pan............................	0.70	0.99	1.05	1.39	1.43	1.54	1.53	1.87	2.02
Bread, whole wheat..........................	(NA)	1.36	1.29	1.88	1.95	2.20	2.10	2.42	2.65
Beef:									
Ground beef, 100% beef.....................	1.63	1.63	2.30	2.38	4.06	3.95	4.60	4.80	5.21
Ground chuck, 100% beef....................	2.02	1.98	2.61	2.93	4.03	4.20	4.79	4.76	5.12
Ground beef, lean and extra lean............	(NA)	2.33	2.91	3.49	5.89	5.72	6.32	6.39	6.67
Beef roasts (all, uncooked).................	(NA)	2.93	3.73	4.15	5.48	5.87	6.95	6.72	7.35
Beef steaks (all, uncooked).................	(NA)	4.09	5.03	5.60	7.51	8.09	9.93	9.46	10.65
Round steak, USDA Choice...................	3.42	3.28	4.12	4.30	5.93	6.34	7.34	7.06	7.99
Sirloin steak, boneless......................	4.24	4.81	5.93	6.07	8.29	8.98	11.06	10.17	11.69
Pork:									
Bacon, sliced...............................	2.28	3.03	3.33	4.16	5.73	5.83	7.21	6.96	6.77
Chops, center cut, bone-in..................	3.32	3.46	3.28	3.58	4.09	4.25	4.36	4.67	4.33
Ham, boneless, excluding canned............	(NA)	2.75	3.09	3.47	4.03	4.47	4.83	5.37	5.50
Poultry, fish, and eggs:									
Chicken, fresh, whole.......................	0.86	1.08	1.06	1.28	1.44	1.62	1.61	1.83	1.96
Chicken breast, boneless....................	(NA)	(NA)	(NA)	3.32	3.28	3.29	3.73	4.35	4.08
Chicken legs, bone-in.......................	1.17	1.26	1.33	1.48	1.57	1.54	1.73	1.95	1.86
Turkey, frozen, whole.......................	0.96	0.99	1.07	1.38	1.45	(NA)	(NA)	(NA)	(NA)
Tuna, light, chunk, canned..................	2.11	1.92	(NA)	(NA)	3.26	(NA)	(NA)	(NA)	(NA)
Eggs, grade A large (dozen)................	1.00	0.96	1.35	1.79	2.75	1.48	1.79	4.25	2.51
Dairy products:									
Milk, fresh, whole, fortified (per gal.)..........	(NA)	2.79	3.24	3.32	3.31	3.54	3.74	4.21	4.01
Milk, low-fat, reduced fat, skim, per gallon...	(NA)	(NA)	(NA)	(NA)	(NA)	3.12	3.36	3.85	3.68
Yogurt, per 8 ounce.........................	(NA)	(NA)	(NA)	(NA)	(NA)	1.25	1.27	1.47	1.63
Butter, in sticks............................	(NA)	(NA)	(NA)	(NA)	(NA)	3.53	3.47	4.81	4.51
American processed cheese..................	(NA)	3.69	3.92	3.80	4.35	4.20	3.89	4.66	4.96
Cheddar cheese, natural.....................	(NA)	3.76	4.43	4.93	5.33	5.54	5.26	6.00	5.55
Ice cream, prepack., bulk, reg. (1/2 gal.).....	2.54	3.66	3.69	4.58	4.73	4.93	4.77	5.56	6.02
Fresh fruits and vegetables:									
Apples, Red Delicious.......................	0.77	0.82	0.97	1.20	1.40	(NA)	(NA)	(NA)	(NA)
Bananas....................................	0.43	0.49	0.48	0.59	0.58	0.57	0.62	0.63	0.63
Oranges, navel..............................	0.56	0.62	0.89	1.02	1.23	1.33	1.45	1.49	1.60
Grapefruit..................................	0.56	0.58	1.10	0.99	1.09	(NA)	(NA)	(NA)	1.78
Grapes, Thompson seedless.................	(NA)	2.36	2.76	2.87	2.83	2.20	(NA)	(NA)	(NA)
Lemons.....................................	0.97	1.11	1.51	1.60	1.98	1.90	2.01	2.09	2.07
Pears, Anjou................................	0.79	(NA)	1.00	1.42	(NA)	(NA)	(NA)	(NA)	(NA)
Strawberries, dry pint, per 12 ounces........	(NA)	(NA)	2.67	3.07	3.50	3.29	(NA)	3.86	3.57
Lettuce, iceberg............................	0.58	0.85	0.85	0.99	1.48	(NA)	(NA)	(NA)	1.53
Lettuce, romaine............................	(NA)	(NA)	(NA)	1.83	2.21	(NA)	3.27	3.57	2.68
Tomatoes, field grown.......................	0.86	1.57	1.85	1.59	1.93	1.89	1.91	2.23	2.00
Peppers, sweet.............................	(NA)	(NA)	(NA)	2.40	(NA)	(NA)	(NA)	(NA)	(NA)
Potatoes, white.............................	0.32	0.35	0.50	0.58	0.64	0.75	0.78	0.95	0.96
Sugar and fats and oils:									
Sugar, white, all sizes.......................	0.43	0.41	0.45	0.64	0.64	0.67	0.69	0.84	0.96
Margarine, tubs, soft........................	(NA)	0.84	0.91	1.62	1.86	(NA)	(NA)	(NA)	(NA)
Peanut butter, creamy, all sizes..............	2.07	1.96	1.70	1.99	2.68	(NA)	(NA)	(NA)	(NA)
Nonalcoholic beverages:									
All soft drinks, 2 liter........................	(NA)	(NA)	(NA)	(NA)	(NA)	1.61	1.71	2.13	2.11
All soft drinks, per 12 oz can in 12-pack.....	(NA)	(NA)	(NA)	(NA)	(NA)	0.39	0.44	0.54	0.57
Coffee, 100% ground roast, all sizes.........	2.94	3.21	3.24	4.15	4.49	4.52	4.97	6.47	6.09
Prepared foods:									
Potato chips, per 16 ounces.................	2.97	3.44	3.46	4.74	4.41	5.08	5.15	6.28	6.41

NA Not available.

Source: U.S. Bureau of Labor Statistics, CPI Databases, "Average Price Data," <www.bls.gov/cpi/data.htm>, accessed May 2024.

Table 772. Employment Cost Index for Total Compensation, Wages and Salaries, and Benefits: 2013 to 2023

[As of December (2005=100). Data are not seasonally adjusted. For data by industry, see Table 683]

Compensation type and occupation	2013	2014	2015	2016	2017	2018	2019	2020	2021	2022	2023
Total compensation:											
All civilian workers [1].....................	120.0	122.7	125.1	127.9	131.2	135.0	138.7	142.2	147.9	155.4	161.9
Private industry workers...............	119.4	122.2	124.5	127.2	130.5	134.4	138.0	141.6	147.8	155.3	161.6
State and local government workers..	122.2	124.7	127.8	130.9	134.2	137.7	141.7	144.9	148.6	155.8	163.0
Wages and salaries:											
All civilian workers [1].....................	118.7	121.2	123.7	126.6	129.8	133.8	137.7	141.3	147.7	155.2	161.9
Private industry workers...............	119.0	121.6	124.2	127.1	130.6	134.7	138.7	142.6	149.7	157.4	164.1
State and local government workers..	117.5	119.4	121.6	124.1	126.7	129.7	133.0	135.4	139.0	145.6	152.4
Benefits:											
All civilian workers [1].....................	123.0	126.2	128.4	131.1	134.4	138.1	141.2	144.5	148.6	155.9	161.9
Private industry workers...............	120.5	123.5	125.1	127.3	130.2	133.6	136.2	139.1	143.2	150.1	155.5
State and local government workers..	132.0	135.8	140.6	145.0	149.7	154.4	159.5	164.4	168.5	176.9	185.1

[1] Includes workers in the private nonfarm economy except those in private households and workers in the public sector except the federal government.

Source: U.S. Bureau of Labor Statistics, Employment Cost Trends, "Employment Cost Index," <www.bls.gov/eci/data.htm>, accessed March 2024.

Table 773. Indexes of Spot Primary Market Prices: 1990 to 2023

[1967=100. Represents unweighted geometric average of price quotations of 23 commodities. The indexes are computed daily and therefore are much more sensitive to changes in market conditions than a monthly producer price index]

Items and number	1990	2000	2005	2010	2015	2017	2018	2019	2020	2021	2022	2023
All commodities (23).....	**258.1**	**224.0**	**303.3**	**520.3**	**374.8**	**432.5**	**409.2**	**401.6**	**443.8**	**578.3**	**554.8**	**510.3**
Foodstuffs (10)................	206.4	184.7	241.7	440.3	335.0	336.0	324.2	338.5	362.1	490.6	533.4	465.5
Raw industrials (13).........	301.2	255.8	354.7	583.8	404.9	514.7	480.4	451.8	510.7	647.7	569.8	543.6
Livestock and products (5)..	292.7	265.5	326.6	528.0	392.2	437.3	396.4	386.8	429.5	605.4	656.5	484.6
Metals (5)......................	283.2	214.0	440.9	1,006.2	556.0	911.6	829.9	752.1	903.5	1,277.6	1,011.6	1,032.2
Textiles and fibers (4).......	257.6	245.7	252.5	342.1	271.9	304.5	286.9	280.9	304.8	357.4	323.1	317.9
Fats and oils (4).............	188.7	163.6	223.4	478.3	315.2	380.8	357.4	366.5	423.6	691.4	755.4	571.2

Source: cmdty by Barchart, Chicago, IL, *Commodity Index Report*, weekly ©. See also <www.barchart.com/cmdty>.

Table 774. Producer Price Indexes—Final and Intermediate Demand: 2010 to 2023

[November 2009=100, except as noted. Minus sign (-) indicates decrease. For information on producer prices, see Bureau of Labor Statistics, <www.bls.gov/ppi/>]

Commodity type	2010	2015	2019	2020	2021	2022	2023
FINAL DEMAND PRICE INDEX							
Total..	**101.8**	**109.9**	**118.2**	**118.4**	**126.7**	**138.8**	**141.5**
Final demand goods.............................	102.8	109.1	115.5	113.8	125.8	142.6	143.0
Final demand foods............................	103.7	118.4	118.9	120.4	131.0	149.3	150.5
Final demand energy..........................	107.2	98.6	105.0	91.5	119.5	156.2	143.8
Final demand goods less foods and energy...	101.4	109.9	117.6	118.5	126.2	136.8	140.7
Final demand services...........................	101.3	110.0	119.1	120.2	126.7	135.9	139.7
Final demand trade services.................	101.7	111.6	119.7	121.7	130.7	148.8	151.5
Final demand transportation and warehousing services...........	103.2	115.3	125.5	121.2	130.9	154.3	150.6
Final demand services less trade, transportation, and warehousing...................................	100.9	108.7	118.2	119.5	124.5	128.3	133.2
INTERMEDIATE DEMAND PRICE INDEX							
Processed goods for intermediate demand [1]......................	183.4	188.0	198.1	192.5	230.0	267.9	258.1
Processed foods and feeds [1].................	171.7	197.7	192.5	196.0	219.9	250.7	245.8
Processed energy goods [1].....................	187.8	168.9	179.2	157.9	211.0	285.0	253.2
Processed materials less foods and energy [1].......................	180.8	189.4	201.1	198.9	233.0	261.1	257.1
Unprocessed goods for intermediate demand [1]......................	212.2	189.1	185.9	167.6	242.3	316.8	255.5
Unprocessed foodstuffs and feedstuffs [1]...................	152.4	181.4	165.3	159.4	199.8	253.2	227.1
Unprocessed energy materials [1]...............	216.7	141.1	143.4	106.7	191.3	289.8	202.3
Unprocessed nonfood materials less energy [1].....................	329.1	296.0	323.4	346.0	462.6	490.7	445.7
Services for intermediate demand...............	101.1	110.2	121.4	121.9	130.7	139.8	146.0
Trade services for intermediate demand.........................	100.8	113.1	125.0	131.0	150.6	168.4	172.2
Transportation and warehousing services for intermediate demand........................	103.3	119.1	129.0	128.3	139.5	156.4	155.8
Services less trade, transportation, and warehousing for intermediate demand.................	100.7	107.8	119.1	118.3	123.7	129.1	137.1
FINAL DEMAND PERCENT CHANGE [2]							
Total..	**(NA)**	**-0.9**	**1.7**	**0.2**	**7.0**	**9.5**	**2.0**
Final demand goods.............................	(NA)	-4.3	0.4	-1.5	10.6	13.3	0.3
Final demand foods............................	(NA)	-2.6	1.9	1.3	8.8	14.0	0.8
Final demand energy..........................	(NA)	-20.6	-4.5	-12.9	30.6	30.7	-7.9
Final demand goods less foods and energy...	(NA)	0.4	1.4	0.8	6.5	8.4	2.9
Final demand services...........................	(NA)	0.9	2.2	0.9	5.4	7.3	2.8
Final demand trade services.................	(NA)	1.3	2.4	1.7	7.4	13.8	1.8
Final demand transportation and warehousing services...........	(NA)	-2.0	2.9	-3.4	8.0	17.9	-2.4
Final demand services less trade, transportation, and warehousing...................................	(NA)	1.1	2.1	1.1	4.2	3.1	3.8
INTERMEDIATE DEMAND PERCENT CHANGE [2]							
Processed goods for intermediate demand........................	6.3	-6.9	-1.4	-2.8	19.5	16.5	-3.7
Processed foods and feeds....................	3.4	-6.2	0.5	1.8	12.2	14.0	-2.0
Processed energy goods.......................	15.6	-20.1	-6.1	-11.9	33.6	35.0	-11.2
Processed materials less foods and energy...	4.3	-3.0	-0.3	-1.1	17.1	12.1	-1.5
Unprocessed goods for intermediate demand........................	21.1	-24.1	-7.1	-9.8	44.5	30.8	-19.4
Unprocessed foodstuffs and feedstuffs..............	13.3	-13.7	0.9	-3.6	25.4	26.7	-10.3
Unprocessed energy materials.................	22.6	-39.5	-15.0	-25.6	79.3	51.5	-30.2
Unprocessed nonfood materials less energy...	32.5	-14.4	-5.1	7.0	33.7	6.1	-9.2
Services for intermediate demand...............	(NA)	1.2	2.4	0.4	7.2	7.0	4.4
Trade services for intermediate demand.........................	(NA)	2.4	4.2	4.8	15.0	11.8	2.3
Transportation and warehousing services for intermediate demand........................	(NA)	-0.3	2.9	-0.5	8.8	12.1	-0.4
Services less trade, transportation, and warehousing for intermediate demand.................	(NA)	1.2	1.8	-0.7	4.6	4.3	6.2

NA Not available. [1] 1982=100. [2] Change from immediate prior year. 2010, change from 2009.

Source: U.S. Bureau of Labor Statistics, PPI Databases, "Commodity Data including "headline" FD-ID Indexes," <www.bls.gov/ppi/data.htm>, accessed June 2024.

Table 775. Producer Price Indexes—Final and Intermediate Demand by Commodity: 2010 to 2023

[1982=100, unless otherwise noted. For information on producer prices, see Bureau of Labor Statistics, <www.bls.gov/ppi/>]

Commodity type	2010	2015	2019	2020	2021	2022	2023
Final demand (Nov. 2009=100)	**101.8**	**109.9**	**118.2**	**118.4**	**126.7**	**138.8**	**141.5**
Final demand goods (Nov. 2009=100)	**102.8**	**109.1**	**115.5**	**113.8**	**125.8**	**142.6**	**143.0**
Final demand foods (Nov. 2009=100)	**103.7**	**118.4**	**118.9**	**120.4**	**131.0**	**149.3**	**150.5**
Fresh fruits & melons	123.8	124.2	136.3	139.1	146.4	172.9	171.9
Fresh & dry vegetables	178.5	200.2	239.2	243.9	228.0	345.2	303.4
Grains	160.2	151.9	149.6	147.3	235.8	287.3	232.8
Eggs for fresh use (Dec. 1991=100)	123.4	219.3	116.1	132.6	144.4	322.6	243.5
Oilseeds	191.0	176.6	160.1	175.7	256.1	285.9	260.5
Bakery products	244.8	275.0	291.9	292.2	295.5	330.5	354.1
Milled rice	183.6	199.0	205.9	220.9	227.9	267.2	296.3
Dry macaroni, spaghetti, and egg noodle products (June 1985=100)	170.7	216.2	202.5	205.1	208.4	267.4	291.4
Beef & veal	157.1	243.6	209.0	213.4	268.5	254.5	288.8
Pork, except sausage	142.6	145.6	144.1	147.2	170.7	166.9	160.8
Processed young chickens	149.0	174.0	162.6	158.9	198.1	224.6	192.9
Processed turkeys	132.1	164.3	146.0	145.9	183.6	264.2	208.6
Unprocessed and prepared seafood	272.4	322.0	349.9	350.8	413.0	440.7	423.0
Dairy products	174.0	193.6	201.3	202.2	206.1	243.7	228.8
Processed fruits & vegetables	176.6	197.7	208.9	212.4	219.1	246.4	280.7
Confectionery end products	236.4	282.8	283.1	280.6	275.4	294.8	304.1
Soft drinks	183.9	196.7	213.5	218.1	227.8	256.0	282.8
Coffee (whole bean, ground, & instant)	190.2	204.7	194.2	194.9	198.0	227.5	247.2
Shortening, cooking oil, and margarine	233.6	243.3	239.0	243.0	325.9	412.8	370.8
Frozen specialty food	176.4	189.5	185.6	186.0	188.6	214.7	230.7
Final demand energy (Nov. 2009=100)	**107.2**	**98.6**	**105.0**	**91.5**	**119.5**	**156.2**	**143.8**
Liquefied petroleum gas	301.8	109.8	123.8	89.3	204.5	265.6	156.7
Residential electric power (Dec. 1990=100)	154.7	172.2	181.9	181.7	188.3	209.2	224.9
Residential natural gas (Dec. 1990=100)	201.7	184.4	200.8	202.3	236.1	292.7	281.8
Gasoline	225.3	177.2	183.3	129.2	218.8	304.5	260.0
Home heating oil & distillates	207.5	160.9	186.4	120.9	194.7	343.0	267.2
No. 2 diesel fuel	232.9	181.4	221.3	175.7	315.9	524.2	393.8
Other final demand goods (Nov. 2009=100)	**101.4**	**109.9**	**117.6**	**118.5**	**126.2**	**136.8**	**140.7**
Alcoholic beverages	175.1	192.6	199.8	202.4	201.3	211.2	218.6
Women's, girls', and infants' apparel (Dec. 2003=100)	101.6	105.2	108.3	107.7	106.6	108.4	107.0
Men's and boys' apparel (Dec. 2003=100)	101.5	113.0	117.4	118.4	120.2	132.1	137.5
Textile house furnishings	131.7	162.8	169.2	169.0	169.4	178.5	182.4
Footwear	162.4	196.0	208.8	210.0	216.2	235.6	250.6
Industrial chemicals	269.2	242.2	252.6	226.3	309.3	353.6	318.3
Pharmaceutical preparations (June 2001=100)	155.1	212.8	268.4	273.9	277.0	281.8	289.2
Soaps and detergents	161.2	175.7	182.1	183.6	189.5	212.3	236.4
Cosmetics and other toilet preparations	149.9	161.4	167.0	167.9	168.8	178.4	188.8
Tires, tubes, tread, & repair materials	138.1	149.3	152.1	152.6	159.3	181.9	195.3
Agricultural machinery and equipment	203.5	222.2	237.3	242.8	258.0	300.9	316.6
Construction machinery and equipment	191.4	217.0	232.6	236.6	248.1	274.4	298.5
Industrial material handling equipment	183.1	207.0	225.4	228.8	244.4	278.3	296.5
Electronic computers (Feb. 2023 =100)	170.7	115.2	93.6	87.1	88.1	97.9	98.7
Textile machinery and equipment	165.9	176.1	172.2	173.8	174.6	185.5	185.6
Paper industries machinery (June 1982=100)	197.2	216.2	227.8	229.2	235.1	257.0	275.7
Printing trades machinery and equipment	155.4	162.3	164.6	165.3	167.9	177.0	180.9
Transformers and power regulators	223.1	212.8	232.0	234.7	277.2	363.5	381.7
Oil field and gas field machinery	200.7	216.5	219.6	217.9	221.4	236.1	251.2
Mining machinery and equipment	221.5	260.6	298.0	307.4	326.0	377.5	418.3
Household furniture	187.4	203.9	219.9	222.8	239.1	266.5	273.5
Household appliances	110.5	116.8	123.6	125.6	129.7	144.9	149.5
Home electronic equipment	52.9	51.3	52.0	53.0	55.0	60.4	62.3
Lawn and garden equipment	141.7	143.7	149.7	151.4	155.7	171.4	180.2
Passenger cars	129.0	133.4	134.9	134.6	137.8	141.6	141.1
Light motor trucks	153.3	171.4	177.8	176.8	182.8	191.9	199.2
Heavy motor trucks	195.7	218.1	232.3	234.6	236.5	241.5	246.9
Truck trailers	181.5	201.0	225.2	225.6	251.4	329.8	329.4
Aircraft	263.0	290.8	307.0	310.6	314.1	327.3	343.1
Ships (Dec. 1985=100)	215.1	225.2	227.7	230.6	234.0	245.6	250.2
Railroad equipment	184.4	201.9	203.7	204.4	206.5	211.5	214.9
Final demand services (Nov. 2009=100)	**101.3**	**110.0**	**119.1**	**120.2**	**126.7**	**135.9**	**139.7**
Final demand trade services (Nov. 2009=100)	**101.7**	**111.6**	**119.7**	**121.7**	**130.7**	**148.8**	**151.5**
Furnishings wholesaling (Mar. 2009=100)	78.5	89.1	98.5	101.8	113.3	138.3	137.8
Apparel wholesaling (Mar. 2009=100)	97.3	117.9	121.6	122.1	116.9	120.5	131.5
Food & alcohol wholesaling (June 2009=100)	105.7	105.2	114.6	116.2	119.6	133.7	139.5
Food & alcohol retailing (Mar. 2009=100)	98.9	126.4	134.7	136.7	139.0	161.1	176.7
Health, beauty, & optical goods retailing (Mar. 2009=100)	107.8	118.9	123.6	126.0	130.3	137.2	143.8
Apparel, jewelry, footwear, & accessories retailing (June 2009=100)	104.2	113.9	112.8	107.7	118.4	125.1	127.7
Automobiles & automobile parts retailing (June 2009=100)	105.9	101.2	95.4	105.2	158.1	204.2	169.0
Sporting goods, including boats, retailing (Mar. 2009=100)	96.6	108.9	114.2	116.5	124.4	125.2	121.9
Furniture retailing (Mar. 2009=100)	99.7	102.2	104.9	109.4	127.8	144.8	146.4
Major household appliances retailing (Mar. 2009=100)	97.3	80.5	96.8	105.6	117.3	126.6	130.1
Book retailing (Mar. 2009=100)	104.8	110.3	120.2	127.0	131.1	136.4	136.1
Final demand transportation & warehousing services (Nov. 2009=100)	**103.2**	**115.3**	**125.5**	**121.2**	**130.9**	**154.3**	**150.6**
Rail transportation of freight & mail (Dec. 2008=100)	101.6	116.5	128.4	128.3	134.7	147.6	150.8
Truck transportation of freight (June 2009=100)	102.0	113.4	125.4	124.7	140.3	166.3	153.1
Air transportation of freight (Dec. 2008=100)	100.1	112.5	111.8	113.3	117.7	127.8	121.2
Courier, messenger, & U.S. postal services (June 2009=100)	105.5	131.5	145.8	150.6	159.0	174.1	185.0
Rail transportation of passengers (Dec. 2008=100)	100.7	115.2	125.4	127.6	130.2	132.6	133.6

See footnotes at end of table.

Table 775. Producer Price Indexes—Final and Intermediate Demand by Commodity: 2010 to 2023-Continued.

See headnote on page 511.

Commodity type	2010	2015	2019	2020	2021	2022	2023
Airline passenger services (Dec. 2008=100).............................	102.8	112.3	117.7	103.6	104.2	127.4	134.1
Other final demand services (Nov. 2009=100).....................	**100.9**	**108.7**	**118.2**	**119.5**	**124.5**	**128.3**	**133.2**
Sales of books..	317.1	363.9	392.6	402.0	418.9	445.8	478.1
Cellphone & other wireless telecom services (Mar. 2009=100)........	94.4	77.6	63.7	63.3	63.3	64.0	64.9
Cable & satellite subscriber services (Dec. 2008=100)................	103.7	112.7	135.3	137.9	144.1	151.5	166.9
Internet access services (Mar. 2009=100).............................	98.3	98.2	93.4	92.5	91.9	91.1	91.2
Processed goods for intermediate demand................	**183.4**	**188.0**	**198.1**	**192.5**	**230.0**	**267.9**	**258.1**
Processed materials less foods & feeds...................	**184.4**	**187.2**	**198.8**	**192.1**	**231.0**	**269.6**	**259.4**
Synthetic fibers...	111.6	121.3	131.9	127.2	145.0	159.3	163.5
Processed yarns & threads..	130.0	135.6	141.2	136.9	158.5	195.8	177.5
Finished fabrics...	137.1	154.0	161.4	162.5	177.6	200.6	202.7
Commercial electric power...	182.5	195.8	199.6	200.4	210.3	235.4	252.1
Industrial electric power..	193.1	223.7	243.3	240.2	251.1	279.5	301.4
Commercial natural gas (Dec. 1990=100).............................	208.0	176.6	191.5	187.3	230.3	299.8	270.8
Industrial natural gas (Dec. 1990=100)...............................	202.0	158.6	149.2	138.3	187.4	252.6	220.3
Natural gas to electric power (Dec. 1990=100).......................	174.8	159.6	152.2	149.8	208.4	272.2	236.6
Jet fuels...	225.5	171.3	202.4	124.6	197.7	359.4	294.6
Prepared paint...	237.1	273.0	299.1	305.2	329.9	406.3	420.3
Medicinal and botanical chemicals, drugs, and other products........	175.2	177.1	181.3	181.4	181.3	184.4	185.9
Biological products, including diagnostics...............................	223.7	256.4	275.6	281.1	296.6	311.1	326.2
Fats & oils, inedible...	244.3	204.9	193.4	201.8	339.2	395.8	340.6
Plastic resins & materials..	210.1	228.0	225.5	215.0	299.8	306.7	275.1
Synthetic rubber...	215.5	197.6	207.0	192.2	225.0	252.8	229.3
Plastic construction products...	190.9	213.1	229.4	233.5	285.5	351.9	346.5
Softwood lumber..	160.8	192.7	215.4	280.3	397.7	384.9	264.4
Hardwood lumber...	187.3	221.1	215.1	207.0	279.2	289.7	258.5
Millwork...	207.0	237.2	263.5	274.5	318.6	367.2	355.2
Plywood...	176.7	198.9	202.9	229.3	335.2	337.6	281.4
Paper...	182.1	189.8	200.6	195.4	214.3	241.7	248.7
Paperboard..	224.9	243.1	268.1	256.6	296.7	347.4	338.3
Paper boxes & containers...	219.4	247.3	269.5	268.1	289.6	341.1	349.0
Foundry & forge shop products...	191.2	209.2	211.9	214.0	230.7	269.8	280.3
Steel mill products..	191.7	177.1	204.0	184.4	350.9	381.5	319.6
Primary nonferrous metals..	210.3	170.7	184.3	191.4	245.2	256.6	243.0
Aluminum mill shapes..	171.9	172.4	197.5	180.6	225.7	254.6	233.2
Copper & brass mill shapes...	421.3	356.9	392.8	404.0	573.0	589.7	580.0
Nonferrous wire & cable..	258.1	238.2	247.4	247.8	314.6	355.6	354.2
Hardware..	194.0	209.7	223.8	227.6	245.9	276.9	286.0
Plumbing fixtures & fittings...	231.4	257.1	281.6	287.9	296.0	326.6	334.5
Heating equipment..	221.5	248.2	279.2	284.0	312.4	367.0	388.7
Fabricated structural metal products....................................	201.1	215.6	239.8	238.7	298.7	365.5	365.0
Air conditioning & refrigeration equipment.............................	163.8	179.2	200.2	204.0	221.9	272.8	291.3
Motors, generators, motor generator sets..............................	190.6	211.6	221.3	222.5	231.8	267.9	287.2
Electronic components & accessories....................................	73.5	68.2	65.3	64.7	64.7	67.4	68.0
Internal combustion engines..	161.7	168.4	169.5	171.1	172.9	183.9	196.7
Machine shop products...	174.7	184.0	194.3	195.6	198.7	211.4	221.2
Cement, hydraulic...	193.5	223.4	258.1	260.7	271.0	296.9	333.1
Concrete products...	210.6	239.4	271.7	279.1	292.9	329.9	366.1
Motor vehicle parts...	121.8	125.9	127.1	127.8	131.8	138.1	141.0
Aircraft engines & engine parts (Dec. 1985=100)....................	197.4	221.2	229.7	231.8	235.2	242.8	251.4
Aircraft parts & auxiliary equipment (June 1985=100)...............	167.7	183.3	188.5	191.8	193.8	198.2	208.1
Medical/surgical/personal aid devices..................................	169.0	176.2	182.8	185.4	187.2	193.8	199.7
Unprocessed goods for intermediate demand................	**212.2**	**189.1**	**185.9**	**167.6**	**242.3**	**316.8**	**255.5**
Unprocessed foodstuffs & feedstuffs........................	**152.4**	**181.4**	**165.3**	**159.4**	**199.8**	**253.2**	**227.1**
Wheat..	157.2	153.3	138.3	148.7	214.8	281.3	216.4
Corn..	160.8	149.6	151.4	143.5	242.5	289.6	235.2
Slaughter cattle..	139.8	225.6	171.1	162.7	181.0	213.9	261.0
Slaughter hogs...	92.6	80.6	83.8	75.7	118.2	126.4	99.8
Broilers and other meat type chickens..................................	221.3	246.8	242.3	190.9	279.8	411.6	357.2
Slaughter turkeys...	173.0	234.3	186.3	220.0	253.8	318.7	299.3
Raw milk...	121.9	127.7	141.9	139.7	142.6	195.0	156.2
Hay and hayseeds...	214.3	309.2	338.2	322.9	377.9	506.7	439.1
Raw cane sugar & byproducts..	179.9	149.4	155.5	172.0	177.8	204.4	235.6
Unprocessed nonfood materials..............................	**249.3**	**183.7**	**192.0**	**165.3**	**261.3**	**347.9**	**265.0**
Raw cotton..	117.9	101.6	100.5	97.3	143.4	181.1	129.0
Hides & skins...	224.9	258.8	128.7	107.5	151.9	120.2	108.2
Coal...	189.5	194.0	199.9	189.0	189.5	279.5	282.6
Natural gas..	185.8	105.4	85.5	67.5	150.0	245.3	93.1
Crude petroleum...	218.6	129.5	157.7	102.1	185.0	261.5	213.2
Logs, bolts, timber, pulpwood and wood chips.........................	213.4	241.9	239.9	239.0	262.3	275.5	268.9
Recyclable paper...	421.5	291.8	181.2	244.6	430.1	400.0	230.0
Iron ores...	147.1	132.0	145.5	148.7	175.5	203.7	210.1
Iron & steel scrap..	541.1	342.8	413.3	406.6	689.7	643.3	583.1
Nonferrous metal ores (Dec. 1983=100)...............................	298.6	272.6	360.1	439.9	514.2	544.2	537.6
Copper base scrap..	548.2	427.6	410.3	420.7	622.6	613.6	606.1
Aluminum base scrap...	241.6	208.7	178.0	155.9	261.1	282.9	251.6
Construction sand, gravel, & crushed stone...........................	262.2	299.9	348.7	364.3	378.8	416.9	458.1

Source: U.S. Bureau of Labor Statistics, PPI Databases, "Commodity Data including "headline" FD-ID Indexes," <www.bls.gov/ppi/data.htm>, accessed June 2024.

Table 776. Chain-Type Price Indexes for Personal Consumption Expenditures by Type of Expenditure: 2000 to 2022

[2017=100. For explanation of "chain-type," see text, Section 13. See also Table 716]

Type of expenditure	2000	2005	2010	2015	2019	2020	2021	2022
Personal consumption expenditures..........................	**73.8**	**82.1**	**90.5**	**97.3**	**103.5**	**104.6**	**109.0**	**116.0**
Household consumption expenditures [1]............................	73.5	81.9	90.6	97.4	103.5	104.6	108.9	115.8
Food and beverages purchased for off-premises consumption.......	71.9	80.2	91.3	101.1	101.5	104.9	108.2	119.3
Food and nonalcoholic beverages purchased for off-premises consumption..........	70.8	79.4	90.7	101.6	101.4	105.0	108.5	121.2
Alcoholic beverages purchased for off-premises consumption......	78.8	86.1	95.3	98.5	102.4	104.3	106.2	109.7
Food produced and consumed on farms...........................	69.0	81.3	87.8	109.7	96.9	95.1	111.2	143.4
Clothing, footwear, and related services..............	103.4	96.2	95.3	100.7	99.1	94.4	96.5	101.6
Clothing...	106.4	97.9	95.8	100.8	98.9	93.6	95.3	100.5
Garments..	110.2	99.6	96.3	101.1	98.4	92.7	94.2	99.3
Women's and girls' clothing...................	109.4	99.7	96.4	100.2	96.2	89.8	91.0	95.5
Men's and boys' clothing.....................	110.6	99.0	95.4	102.1	101.1	96.5	99.0	104.5
Children's and infants' clothing...............	113.5	101.5	99.3	104.2	103.8	97.9	98.0	105.9
Footwear [2].......................................	90.3	89.6	93.6	100.1	100.0	97.6	101.1	105.8
Housing, utilities, and fuels.......................	62.7	74.4	84.4	94.1	106.3	108.9	112.3	120.3
Housing...	63.9	74.4	83.4	93.5	106.9	109.9	112.7	119.2
Rental of tenant-occupied nonfarm housing [3]........	59.8	70.5	80.9	92.8	107.5	110.8	113.3	120.1
Imputed rental of owner-occupied nonfarm housing [4]..............	65.1	75.4	84.1	93.7	106.7	109.7	112.6	119.0
Household utilities and fuels......................	57.9	75.3	90.4	97.2	103.0	102.9	110.2	126.8
Water supply and sanitation..................	46.6	57.2	75.0	93.5	106.8	110.2	114.2	119.3
Electricity, gas, and other fuels..............	62.5	82.8	96.6	98.6	101.5	100.1	108.7	129.5
Electricity..................................	60.8	71.4	91.3	98.9	100.9	101.5	105.8	119.7
Natural gas................................	76.8	123.6	109.2	95.2	99.6	98.7	114.9	144.7
Fuel oil and other fuels....................	52.5	86.0	113.5	104.0	113.8	90.8	118.5	185.2
Furnishings, household equipment, & routine household maintenance........................	113.9	110.6	108.5	103.2	101.4	103.1	108.0	117.0
Furniture, furnishings, and floor coverings [5]......	138.3	128.3	116.5	105.4	99.8	99.5	105.6	117.4
Household textiles...............................	193.4	160.7	127.1	106.8	95.6	97.8	96.9	100.6
Household appliances [6]..........................	111.4	109.3	115.1	107.8	106.5	110.9	121.2	128.1
Glassware, tableware, and household utensils [7]........	143.4	128.1	120.3	105.2	92.5	90.6	90.8	96.3
Health...	66.2	77.9	89.7	96.8	103.2	105.4	107.5	110.2
Medical products, appliances, and equipment..........	63.0	73.7	83.8	94.2	101.3	101.7	100.2	103.0
Pharmaceutical and other medical products [8].........	59.8	71.2	82.1	93.6	101.2	101.8	100.2	102.8
Pharmaceutical products....................	59.5	71.0	81.9	93.5	101.1	101.8	100.2	102.8
Other medical products.....................	96.2	97.6	99.5	100.2	102.6	99.5	96.6	101.8
Therapeutic appliances and equipment...........	86.6	91.7	96.5	99.1	102.4	101.3	100.2	104.0
Outpatient services................................	74.4	83.4	94.1	98.1	102.2	103.8	106.9	108.8
Physician services [9].............................	80.6	87.2	97.1	99.3	101.7	102.9	106.7	107.2
Dental services.................................	54.7	68.6	84.4	95.7	105.0	108.1	110.6	115.0
Paramedical services...........................	74.2	84.0	93.2	97.2	102.0	103.7	105.8	109.1
Hospital and nursing home services.................	61.1	75.2	88.8	96.8	104.9	108.4	111.6	114.8
Hospitals [10].................................	61.3	75.4	88.9	97.2	104.5	107.9	111.2	114.4
Nursing homes...............................	60.4	74.4	87.9	95.0	107.2	111.5	113.5	116.9
Transportation...	78.0	87.0	97.7	100.1	104.0	100.7	114.5	133.0
Motor vehicles.....................................	101.5	98.0	96.8	102.3	100.4	102.1	115.3	128.7
New motor vehicles.............................	96.8	93.2	93.0	99.8	99.9	100.5	106.1	117.4
Net purchases of used motor vehicles...........	112.1	108.5	104.6	106.9	101.4	104.7	131.6	149.2
Motor vehicle operation...........................	64.7	83.7	100.9	98.8	106.4	100.5	117.2	140.0
Motor vehicle parts and accessories...........	72.5	78.6	94.3	100.1	103.0	104.9	108.8	121.7
Motor vehicle fuels, lubricants, and fluids......	59.8	90.3	111.4	99.7	109.3	93.3	124.4	162.7
Public transportation..............................	76.2	74.8	88.8	99.6	103.8	96.0	97.2	112.7
Ground transportation [11].......................	58.1	70.8	86.0	96.3	101.6	99.1	102.8	104.4
Air transportation..............................	84.6	76.0	90.2	101.6	105.3	94.1	93.9	115.0
Water transportation...........................	138.4	109.9	98.3	95.7	99.6	95.7	101.7	100.7
Communication..	141.1	132.8	129.5	112.3	94.0	91.4	89.3	87.3
Telecommunication services.......................	131.7	125.2	130.4	114.9	92.4	90.4	88.2	85.2
Internet access.................................	125.8	125.1	100.6	101.3	100.7	99.9	101.1	102.9
Recreation...	121.8	114.1	106.9	101.3	99.0	98.0	100.2	103.8
Video and audio equipment, computers, and related services......	254.5	183.5	130.1	105.5	93.2	88.9	89.1	88.8
Video and audio equipment......................	542.8	381.3	199.2	121.4	82.5	76.4	76.5	73.2
Sports and recreational goods and related services.............	137.8	126.0	118.7	106.1	95.3	94.1	98.0	102.0
Sports and recreational vehicles...............	89.2	91.2	95.1	99.0	104.5	106.7	112.5	115.9
Other sporting and recreational goods...........	159.9	140.4	127.6	108.8	91.8	89.5	92.8	96.8
Magazines, newspapers, books, and stationery...........	83.7	87.5	93.9	99.7	104.8	109.4	112.9	120.1
Education..	42.4	59.5	78.3	95.1	104.9	106.7	108.0	110.4
Higher education.................................	40.3	57.7	77.5	95.5	105.1	106.6	107.5	109.8
Net foreign travel and expenditures abroad by U.S. residents:								
Foreign travel by U.S. residents...................	61.8	80.5	97.5	102.0	101.2	99.9	98.6	102.0
Less: Expenditures in the United States by nonresidents.............	67.6	76.8	88.1	97.6	104.5	103.3	106.0	114.2

[1] Consists of household purchases of goods and services from business, government, nonprofit institutions, and the rest of the world. [2] Consists of shoes and other footwear, and of repair and hire of footwear. [3] Consists of rent for space (see footnote 4) and rent for appliances, furnishings, and furniture. [4] Consists of rent for space and for heating and plumbing facilities, water heaters, lighting fixtures, kitchen cabinets, linoleum, storm windows and doors, window screens, and screen doors, but excludes rent for appliances and furniture and purchases of fuel and electricity. [5] Includes clocks, lamps, lighting fixtures, and other household decorative items; also includes repair of furniture, furnishings, and floor coverings. [6] Consists of major household appliances, small electric household appliances, and repair of household appliances. [7] Consists of dishes, flatware, and non-electric cookware and tableware. [8] Excludes drug preparations and related products dispensed by physicians, hospitals, and other medical services. [9] Consists of offices of physicians, health maintenance organization medical centers, and freestanding ambulatory surgical and emergency centers. [10] Consists of nonprofit hospitals, proprietary hospitals, and government hospitals. Consists of primary sales of these hospitals for personal consumption. [11] Includes railway transportation, taxicab services, school and employee services, limousine services, and airport bus fares.

Source: U.S. Bureau of Economic Analysis, National Income and Product Accounts Tables, "Table 2.5.4. Price Indexes for Personal Consumption Expenditures by Function," <www.bea.gov/itable>, accessed November 2023.

Table 777. Chain-Type Price Indexes for Gross Domestic Product: 2000 to 2022

[2017=100. For explanation of "chain-type," see text, Section 13]

Component	2000	2005	2010	2015	2017	2018	2019	2020	2021	2022
Gross domestic product...........	**72.7**	**81.5**	**89.6**	**97.3**	**100.0**	**102.3**	**104.0**	**105.4**	**110.2**	**118.0**
Personal consumption expenditures...	**73.8**	**82.1**	**90.5**	**97.3**	**100.0**	**102.0**	**103.5**	**104.6**	**109.0**	**116.0**
Goods............................	94.1	96.2	100.5	101.4	100.0	100.8	100.4	99.6	104.6	113.5
Durable goods....................	140.3	125.3	113.9	104.6	100.0	98.6	97.7	96.8	102.1	108.6
Nondurable goods.................	76.1	84.3	94.8	99.7	100.0	101.9	101.9	101.1	105.8	116.2
Services.........................	65.2	76.0	86.1	95.5	100.0	102.6	105.0	107.1	111.1	117.1
Gross private domestic investment.....	**83.3**	**91.0**	**93.7**	**98.7**	**100.0**	**101.5**	**103.0**	**104.2**	**107.8**	**116.1**
Fixed investment..................	82.5	90.2	93.0	98.6	100.0	101.6	103.0	104.3	108.2	116.8
Nonresidential...................	92.1	93.8	96.7	100.3	100.0	100.4	101.5	102.1	103.5	109.6
Structures......................	50.3	68.8	83.5	97.7	100.0	101.2	105.3	106.8	110.5	126.7
Equipment......................	117.8	107.8	102.5	101.5	100.0	99.9	100.0	99.5	100.1	106.2
Intellectual property products...........	98.1	96.2	98.6	100.6	100.0	100.6	100.9	102.2	103.2	105.0
Residential......................	60.8	78.3	79.6	92.5	100.0	105.6	108.7	112.3	124.6	141.8
Net exports of goods and services:										
Exports..........................	82.9	88.8	97.4	99.5	100.0	103.3	102.8	100.2	111.8	122.8
Goods..........................	89.0	94.4	103.3	101.4	100.0	103.5	101.9	97.9	111.7	124.8
Services........................	71.5	78.5	86.5	95.8	100.0	102.9	104.6	104.9	111.6	117.9
Imports..........................	85.2	93.8	104.1	101.3	100.0	102.7	101.0	98.9	106.0	113.6
Goods..........................	88.9	96.6	107.1	102.1	100.0	102.7	100.5	97.8	105.2	113.0
Services........................	70.0	81.9	91.2	98.0	100.0	102.5	103.3	104.0	109.5	115.9
Government consumption expenditures and gross investment...	**64.1**	**76.7**	**89.1**	**97.6**	**100.0**	**103.6**	**105.2**	**107.5**	**113.2**	**121.2**
Federal..........................	69.1	81.7	91.4	97.6	100.0	102.8	104.6	105.6	109.0	115.1
National defense..................	69.1	82.6	92.3	98.1	100.0	102.6	104.3	105.5	109.2	116.0
Nondefense......................	69.3	80.5	90.1	97.0	100.0	103.0	104.9	105.8	108.8	113.9
State and local....................	61.0	73.7	87.6	97.6	100.0	104.1	105.6	108.7	115.8	125.0

Source: U.S. Bureau of Economic Analysis, National Income and Product Accounts Tables, "Table 1.1.4 Price Indexes for Gross Domestic Product," <www.bea.gov/itable>, accessed November 2023.

Table 778. Import and Export Price Indexes by End-Use Category: 1990 to 2024

[As of June. Import indexes are weighted by the 2000 Tariff Schedule of the United States Annotated, a scheme for describing and reporting product composition and value of U.S. imports. Import prices are based on U.S. dollar prices paid by importer. Export indexes are weighted by 2000 export values according to the Schedule B classification system of the U.S. Census Bureau. Prices used in these indexes were collected from a sample of U.S. manufacturers of exports and are factory transaction prices, except as noted. Minus sign (-) indicates decrease]

Year	Index (2000 = 100)						Percent change [1]					
	Imports			Exports			Imports			Exports		
	Total	Petro-leum imports	Non-petro-leum imports	Total	Agri-cultural exports	Non-agri-cultural exports	Total	Petro-leum imports	Non-petro-leum imports	Total	Agri-cultural exports	Non-agri-cultural exports
1990..........	90.8	55.4	96.4	95.1	107.7	93.5	-0.8	-13.4	0.5	-0.1	-4.0	0.5
1991..........	93.4	63.2	98.3	96.1	104.3	95.3	2.9	14.1	2.0	1.1	-3.2	1.9
1992..........	94.8	66.0	99.5	96.5	104.0	95.8	1.5	4.4	1.2	0.4	-0.3	0.5
1993..........	95.0	60.4	100.5	96.9	100.3	96.7	0.2	-8.5	1.0	0.4	-3.6	0.9
1994..........	96.3	57.6	102.6	98.5	109.3	97.5	1.4	-4.6	2.1	1.7	9.0	0.8
1995..........	101.4	62.9	107.6	104.5	117.0	103.3	5.3	9.2	4.9	6.1	7.0	5.9
1996..........	100.7	66.4	106.2	105.4	140.8	101.7	-0.7	5.6	-1.3	0.9	20.3	-1.5
1997..........	98.8	62.5	104.3	103.2	120.5	101.5	-1.9	-5.9	-1.8	-2.1	-14.4	-0.2
1998..........	93.1	44.3	100.5	99.9	110.8	98.8	-5.8	-29.1	-3.6	-3.2	-8.0	-2.7
1999..........	92.9	54.5	98.8	98.2	101.1	97.9	-0.2	23.0	-1.7	-1.7	-8.8	-0.9
2000 [2]........	100.2	101.9	99.9	100.1	100.5	100.0	7.9	87.0	1.1	1.9	-0.6	2.1
2001..........	97.6	89.4	98.9	99.4	100.9	99.3	-2.6	-12.3	-1.0	-0.7	0.4	-0.7
2002..........	94.1	85.3	96.2	98.0	100.7	97.8	-3.6	-4.6	-2.7	-1.4	-0.2	-1.5
2003..........	96.2	96.4	97.3	99.5	110.0	98.7	2.2	13.0	1.1	1.5	9.2	0.9
2004..........	101.7	129.7	99.7	103.4	127.4	101.5	5.7	34.5	2.5	3.9	15.8	2.8
2005..........	109.2	181.5	102.0	106.7	123.9	105.4	7.4	39.9	2.3	3.2	-2.7	3.8
2006..........	117.3	242.6	104.2	111.2	124.1	110.3	7.4	33.7	2.2	4.2	0.2	4.6
2007..........	120.0	245.6	107.1	116.0	146.7	113.8	2.3	1.2	2.8	4.3	18.2	3.2
2008..........	145.5	450.3	114.9	126.1	195.2	121.2	21.3	83.3	7.3	8.7	33.1	6.5
2009..........	120.0	241.5	107.4	117.8	169.7	114.1	-17.5	-46.4	-6.5	-6.6	-13.1	-5.9
2010..........	125.2	267.4	110.7	122.2	165.3	119.1	4.3	10.7	3.1	3.7	-2.6	4.4
2011..........	142.2	397.8	116.4	134.5	217.2	128.6	13.6	48.8	5.1	10.1	31.4	8.0
2012..........	138.7	357.2	116.3	131.7	204.5	126.5	-2.5	-10.2	-0.1	-2.1	-5.8	-1.6
2013..........	138.8	364.9	115.7	132.8	224.2	126.2	0.1	2.2	-0.5	0.8	9.6	-0.2
2014..........	140.5	387.9	115.8	133.0	221.4	126.6	1.2	6.3	0.1	0.2	-1.2	0.3
2015..........	126.6	229.7	112.8	125.3	184.3	120.9	-9.9	-40.8	-2.6	-5.8	-16.8	-4.5
2016..........	120.7	173.1	110.5	120.9	181.9	116.3	-4.7	-24.6	-2.0	-3.5	-1.3	-3.8
2017..........	122.4	178.7	112.0	121.6	174.9	117.5	1.4	3.2	1.4	0.6	-3.8	1.0
2018..........	128.2	255.4	113.5	128.0	184.2	123.7	4.7	42.9	1.3	5.3	5.3	5.3
2019..........	125.6	236.6	112.0	126.0	180.5	121.8	-2.0	-7.4	-1.3	-1.6	-2.0	-1.5
2020..........	120.6	142.6	111.9	120.3	172.4	116.3	-4.0	-39.7	-0.1	-4.5	-4.5	-4.5
2021..........	134.2	267.6	119.6	140.6	230.0	133.9	11.3	87.7	6.9	16.9	33.4	15.1
2022..........	148.5	456.5	126.0	166.7	265.3	159.3	10.7	70.6	5.4	18.6	15.3	19.0
2023..........	139.4	294.6	123.5	147.0	239.8	139.8	-6.1	-35.5	-2.0	-11.8	-9.6	-12.2
2024..........	141.6	323.0	124.7	148.0	228.2	141.8	1.6	9.6	1.0	0.7	-4.8	1.4

[1] Change from immediate prior year. [2] June 2000 may not equal 100 because indexes were reweighted to an "average" trade value in 2000.

Source: U.S. Bureau of Labor Statistics, Import/Export Price Indexes, "History Tables: Complete Historical Index Information," <www.bls.gov/mxp/>, accessed July 2024.

Table 779. Export Price Indexes—Selected Commodities: 2010 to 2024

[2000=100, except as noted. As of June. Indexes are weighted by 2000 export values according to the Schedule B commodity classification system of the U.S. Census Bureau. Prices used in these indexes were collected from a sample of U.S. manufacturers of exports and are factory transaction prices; see source]

Commodity	2010	2015	2019	2020	2021	2022	2023	2024
All commodities	**122.2**	**125.3**	**126.0**	**120.3**	**140.6**	**166.7**	**147.0**	**148.0**
Live animals and animal products	172.2	193.5	217.8	208.9	258.9	290.3	261.3	276.8
Vegetable products	177.5	206.1	199.1	184.6	269.2	319.9	269.5	239.6
Fruit and nuts	131.0	175.1	139.9	122.9	140.6	146.7	137.6	157.1
Cereals	171.4	194.4	205.7	182.4	296.2	373.7	301.5	237.1
Wheat and meslin	151.6	198.3	197.0	196.6	250.7	391.4	259.4	243.8
Corn (maize)	174.3	181.1	204.7	164.3	326.0	355.7	302.8	220.0
Oilseeds	196.2	204.7	186.9	185.0	304.3	347.0	279.4	241.6
Prepared foodstuffs, beverages, and tobacco	139.3	153.2	153.5	151.2	174.5	181.2	188.0	180.7
Mineral products	247.9	211.3	217.0	147.5	251.6	461.0	268.1	272.6
Fuels	239.2	205.0	208.5	139.1	240.8	448.1	255.8	259.7
Petroleum oils, excluding crude	231.5	228.8	217.2	142.7	245.4	476.5	279.5	(NA)
Chemicals and related products	144.5	143.9	138.6	134.2	153.1	166.3	163.6	156.8
Plastics and rubber products	136.8	143.0	143.9	136.1	176.3	177.0	(NA)	(NA)
Woodpulp and paper products	117.6	123.7	124.5	122.8	142.0	156.6	(NA)	(NA)
Textiles	115.7	122.2	121.4	116.6	128.4	(NA)	(NA)	(NA)
Stone and glass products	115.9	122.4	127.5	126.3	133.4	147.2	146.9	152.8
Gems and precious metals	211.0	233.8	245.3	276.3	334.0	329.7	318.6	337.6
Base metals	160.4	153.1	158.5	151.1	196.9	219.7	210.2	214.6
Iron and steel (Dec. 2020=100)	(NA)	(NA)	(NA)	(NA)	143.5	(NA)	(NA)	(NA)
Copper	217.0	191.3	178.6	165.7	284.8	290.8	257.7	310.9
Aluminum	117.8	115.5	104.1	91.1	137.7	154.5	146.1	158.5
Machinery	95.5	97.1	98.0	98.0	99.3	104.1	106.6	108.7
Nonelectrical machinery	106.8	113.5	116.3	115.7	118.4	124.9	130.5	133.4
Computer equipment	53.1	43.8	35.5	33.5	33.0	34.2	33.7	31.6
Electrical machinery	83.2	79.3	78.3	79.0	78.9	82.0	81.7	83.0
Transportation equipment	121.4	130.8	137.2	137.6	140.1	146.8	150.1	155.3
Motor vehicles and their parts	108.5	115.0	116.7	116.1	118.2	123.4	124.9	129.7
Instruments	106.2	107.8	110.0	110.3	111.3	114.0	117.4	120.3
Miscellaneous manufactured articles	108.1	111.3	112.9	114.1	118.3	129.1	136.7	137.6

NA Not available.

Source: U.S. Bureau of Labor Statistics, Import/Export Price Indexes, "History Tables: Complete Historical Index Information," <www.bls.gov/mxp/>, accessed July 2024.

Table 780. Import Price Indexes—Selected Commodities: 2010 to 2024

[2000=100, unless otherwise noted. As of June. Indexes are weighted by the 2000 Tariff Schedule of the United States Annotated, a scheme for describing and reporting product composition and value of U.S. imports. Import prices are based on U.S. dollar prices paid by importer]

Commodity	2010	2015	2019	2020	2021	2022	2023	2024
All commodities	**125.2**	**126.6**	**125.6**	**120.6**	**134.2**	**148.5**	**139.4**	**141.6**
Live animals and animal products	143.0	185.2	195.7	193.0	229.0	237.8	234.0	240.6
Meat	183.2	234.5	265.8	293.2	368.2	342.6	326.1	352.2
Fish	107.1	127.3	139.6	128.8	153.9	165.1	151.5	149.4
Vegetable products	169.5	201.8	215.1	213.5	216.7	250.8	245.8	249.1
Vegetables	326.2	459.9	506.8	482.7	383.2	418.6	477.0	600.4
Fruit and nuts	106.8	95.5	124.5	114.2	114.1	127.9	116.1	103.4
Prepared foodstuffs, beverages and tobacco	141.2	160.7	165.3	168.0	174.8	187.2	195.6	211.9
Mineral products	248.5	210.9	215.4	138.0	250.9	438.9	280.8	301.6
Fuels	244.9	208.1	212.7	133.3	246.5	434.3	272.5	295.2
Chemicals and related products	139.3	148.3	156.1	153.6	166.4	179.6	172.4	173.4
Organic chemicals	133.8	123.7	127.5	120.1	140.3	154.0	144.6	136.3
Pharmaceutical products	117.9	136.7	152.3	154.4	152.5	148.7	148.4	156.8
Plastics and rubber products	136.7	142.1	140.9	138.2	153.1	162.3	158.4	154.1
Hides, skins, and leather products	114.5	128.1	124.6	(NA)	(NA)	(NA)	(NA)	(NA)
Wood products	134.3	138.6	143.5	152.3	376.7	(NA)	(NA)	(NA)
Woodpulp and paper products	112.5	111.9	120.2	113.0	119.6	130.2	(NA)	(NA)
Textiles	103.1	114.5	114.2	114.4	115.7	120.1	120.8	121.0
Footwear	106.1	122.3	121.3	122.7	123.2	123.3	123.6	123.6
Stone and glass products	123.8	132.8	132.1	131.9	132.0	134.7	138.6	137.7
Gems and precious metals	161.5	170.8	177.6	200.0	248.8	235.2	232.1	242.3
Gold	430.5	424.4	476.6	613.4	677.0	660.9	702.9	836.4
Platinum (Dec. 2019=100)	(NA)	(NA)	(NA)	110.0	210.2	145.1	88.4	69.7
Base metals	180.2	168.1	174.3	164.3	213.2	254.2	234.1	234.5
Iron and steel	238.8	181.6	216.9	188.0	282.5	(NA)	(NA)	(NA)
Articles of iron and steel	149.9	148.2	149.8	146.0	170.8	207.0	203.1	190.7
Copper	313.8	299.8	271.5	266.8	432.1	417.5	371.5	455.8
Aluminum	132.8	131.5	130.6	120.3	174.6	210.6	190.2	207.3
Machinery	86.5	82.5	79.3	79.1	80.1	82.7	82.6	82.1
Nonelectrical machinery	87.9	87.7	85.5	84.9	86.3	89.1	89.7	89.9
Electrical machinery	85.2	77.6	73.5	73.5	74.2	76.6	76.0	75.0
Transportation equipment	109.7	114.6	113.5	114.5	116.2	119.4	121.5	123.9
Motor vehicles and their parts	108.8	113.2	112.6	113.7	115.4	118.7	120.6	123.1
Instruments	100.8	103.7	101.6	102.0	102.5	105.3	108.1	110.9
Miscellaneous manufactured articles	106.5	112.8	112.2	110.9	112.6	118.1	120.3	120.7
Furniture	109.4	117.3	118.3	116.6	119.4	125.6	127.7	127.5

NA Not available.

Source: U.S. Bureau of Labor Statistics, Import/Export Price Indexes, "History Tables: Complete Historical Index Information," <www.bls.gov/mxp/>, accessed July 2024.

Section 15
Business Enterprise

This section relates to the place and behavior of the business firm and to business initiative in the American economy. It includes data on the number, type, and size of businesses; financial data of domestic and multinational U.S. corporations; business investments, expenditures, and profits; and sales and inventories.

The principal sources of these data are the *Survey of Current Business*, published online by the Bureau of Economic Analysis (BEA); the web site of the Board of Governors of the Federal Reserve System at <www.federalreserve.gov/data.htm>; the annual *Statistics of Income (SOI)* reports of the Internal Revenue Service (IRS); and the U.S. Census Bureau's Economic Census, *County Business Patterns* annual series, *Quarterly Financial Report for Manufacturing, Mining, Trade, and Selected Service Industries (QFR)*, the Annual Business Survey, and, through 2021, the Annual Capital Expenditures Survey. See also BEA Interactive Tables <apps.bea.gov/itable/>.

Business firms—A firm is generally defined as a business organization or entity consisting of one or more domestic establishment locations under common ownership or control. The terms firm, business, company, and enterprise are used interchangeably throughout this section. A firm doing business in more than one industry is classified by industry according to the major activity of the firm as a whole.

The IRS concept of a business firm relates primarily to the legal entity used for tax reporting purposes. A sole proprietorship is an unincorporated business owned by one person and may include large enterprises with many employees and hired managers and part-time operators. A partnership is an unincorporated business owned by two or more persons, each of whom has a financial interest in the business. A corporation is a business that is legally incorporated under state laws. While many corporations file consolidated tax returns, most corporate tax returns represent individual corporations, some of which are affiliated through common ownership or control with other corporations filing separate returns.

Economic Census—The Economic Census is the major source of facts about the structure and functioning of the nation's economy. It provides essential information for government, business, industry, and the general public. It establishes benchmarks for economic indicators such as the gross domestic product estimates, production and price indexes, business sales, and other statistical series that measure short-term changes in economic conditions. The Census Bureau takes the Economic Census every 5 years, covering years ending in "2" and "7." Data from the 2022 Economic Census are being released on a flow basis between January 2024 and March 2026.

The Economic Census is collected on an establishment basis. A company operating at more than one location is required to file a separate report for each store, factory, shop, or other location. Companies engaged in distinctly different lines of activity at one location are requested to submit separate reports, if the business records permit such a separation, and if the activities are substantial in size. Each establishment is assigned a separate industry classification based on its primary activity and not that of its parent company. Establishments responding to the establishment survey are classified into industries on the basis of their principal product or activity (determined by self-reporting, annual sales volume, or products manufactured by a plant). The statistics issued by industry in the Economic Census are classified primarily on the North American Industry Classification System (NAICS).

Data from the Economic Census is released via the Census Bureau's dissemination platform at <data.census.gov>. The American FactFinder® service was discontinued in 2020. More detailed information about the scope, coverage, methodology, classification system, data items, and publications for the Economic Censuses and related surveys is available at <www.census.gov/programs-surveys/economic-census.html>.

Annual Business Survey—The Annual Business Survey replaces the five-year Survey of Business Owners (SBO) for employer businesses, the Annual Survey of Entrepreneurs (ASE), the Business R&D and Innovation for Microbusinesses survey (BRDI-M), and the innovation section of the Business R&D and Innovation Survey (BRDI-S). It is collected on an company or firm basis, not an establishment basis, and provides information on selected economic and demographic characteristics for businesses and business owners by sex, ethnicity, race, and veteran status. Data are published in a series of releases: *Characteristics of Businesses*, *Characteristics of Business Owners*, *Company Summary*, and a variable module designed to capture information on relevant business components.

North American Industry Classification System (NAICS)—NAICS is the standard used by federal statistical agencies in classifying business establishments for the purpose of collecting, analyzing, and publishing statistical data related to the U.S. business economy. NAICS was developed under the auspices of the Office of Management and Budget (OMB), and adopted in 1997 to replace the Standard Industrial Classification (SIC) system. The official *2022 NAICS Manual* includes definitions for each industry, background information, tables showing changes between the 2017 and 2022 revisions, and a comprehensive index. Noticeable changes were made to 7 of the 20 NAICS sectors during the 2022 revision of NAICS. Those sectors were 21 (mining), 31-33 (manufacturing), 42 (wholesale trade), 44-45 (retail trade), 51 (information), 52 (finance and insurance), and 81 (other services). The 2017 revision impacted 28 of the 2012 NAICS 6-digit industries, and the 2012 revision impacted 6 of the 2007 NAICS 6-digit industries. For more information, see <www.census.gov/naics/>.

Quarterly Financial Report—The Quarterly Financial Report (QFR) program publishes quarterly aggregate statistics on the financial conditions of U.S. corporations. The QFR requests companies to report estimates from their statements of income and retained earnings, balance sheets, and financial and operating ratios. The statistical data are classified and aggregated by type of industry and asset size. The QFR sample includes corporations that have a plurality of business activity in manufacturing industries with domestic assets of $250,000 and above, and mining, wholesale, retail, and selected service industries with assets of $50 million and above. The data are available in the *Quarterly Financial Report for Manufacturing, Mining, Trade, and Selected Service Industries* at <www.census.gov/econ/qfr/index.html>.

Multinational enterprises—BEA collects financial and operating data on U.S. multinational enterprises. These data provide a picture of the overall activities of foreign affiliates and U.S. parent enterprises, using a variety of indicators of their financial structure and operations. The data on foreign affiliates cover the entire operations of the affiliate, irrespective of the percentage of U.S. ownership. These data cover items such as sales, value added, employment and compensation of employees, capital expenditures, exports and imports, and research and development expenditures. Separate tabulations are available for all affiliates and for affiliates that are majority-owned by their U.S. parent(s). More information is available at <www.bea.gov/data/economic-accounts/international#omc>.

Statistical reliability—For a discussion of statistical collection, estimation, and sampling procedures and measures of reliability applicable to data from the Census Bureau and the Internal Revenue Service, see Appendix III.

Table 781. Number of Tax Returns, Receipts, and Net Income by Type of Business: 1990 to 2021

[14,783 represents 14,783,000. Covers active enterprises only. Nonfarm sole proprietorship and partnership data are for tax year shown, which covers returns processed by the IRS during the following calendar year. Corporation data are for tax year shown, which covers (a) corporate returns with accounting periods for the calendar year ending December of year shown and (b) those returns with accounting periods for the noncalendar year ending between July of year shown and June of the following year. Figures are estimates based on sample of unaudited tax returns; see Appendix III]

Year	Number of returns (1,000)			Business receipts [2] (bil. dol.)			Net income (less loss) [3] (bil. dol.)		
	Nonfarm proprietor-ships [1]	Partner-ships	Corpora-tions	Nonfarm proprietor-ships [1]	Partner-ships	Corpora-tions	Nonfarm proprietor-ships [1]	Partner-ships	Corpora-tions
1990...........	14,783	1,554	3,717	731	483	9,860	141	17	383
1995...........	16,424	1,581	4,474	807	761	12,786	169	107	736
2000...........	17,903	2,058	5,045	1,021	2,062	17,637	215	269	987
2001...........	18,338	2,132	5,136	1,017	2,278	17,504	217	276	649
2002...........	18,926	2,242	5,267	1,030	2,414	17,297	221	271	597
2003...........	19,710	2,375	5,401	1,050	2,546	18,264	230	301	822
2004...........	20,591	2,547	5,558	1,140	2,819	19,976	248	385	1,170
2005...........	21,468	2,764	5,671	1,223	3,280	21,800	270	546	2,027
2006...........	22,075	2,947	5,841	1,278	3,571	23,310	278	667	2,024
2007...........	23,123	3,096	5,869	1,324	3,847	24,217	281	683	1,950
2008...........	22,614	3,146	5,847	1,317	4,344	24,718	265	458	1,061
2009...........	22,660	3,169	5,825	1,178	3,562	21,585	245	410	971
2010...........	23,004	3,248	5,814	1,196	3,946	23,058	268	594	1,422
2011...........	23,427	3,285	5,823	1,266	4,455	25,198	283	581	1,406
2012...........	23,554	3,389	5,841	1,302	4,690	26,029	305	778	1,872
2013...........	24,075	3,461	5,888	1,342	5,069	26,850	302	769	1,994
2014...........	24,632	3,611	6,001	1,394	5,186	28,075	317	837	2,145
2015...........	25,226	3,715	6,120	1,444	4,877	27,492	332	781	2,034
2016...........	25,526	3,763	6,189	1,422	4,919	27,575	328	792	1,913
2017...........	26,426	3,905	6,325	1,531	5,460	29,180	346	810	1,656
2018...........	27,117	4,010	6,442	1,590	5,904	30,837	349	885	3,391
2019...........	27,817	3,821	6,474	1,640	5,397	31,367	355	761	2,869
2020...........	28,353	4,281	6,402	1,605	5,902	33,404	337	760	3,568
2021...........	29,310	4,468	(NA)	1,868	7,016	(NA)	411	1,195	(NA)

NA Not available. [1] Covers nonfarm businesses with and without net income. [2] Excludes investment income for S corporations; for definition, see footnote 1, Table 789. [3] Net income (less loss) is defined differently by form of organization, basically as follows: (a) Proprietorships: Total taxable receipts less total business deductions, including cost of sales and operations, depletion, and certain capital expensing, excluding charitable contributions and owners' salaries; (b) Partnerships: Total taxable receipts (including investment income except capital gains) less deductions, including cost of sales and operations and certain payments to partners, excluding charitable contributions, oil and gas depletion, and certain capital expensing; and (c) Corporations: Includes "Total net income (less deficit)" from S Corporations; net income is before income tax.

Source: U.S. Internal Revenue Service, "Tax Statistics," <www.irs.gov/statistics>, accessed July 2024.

Table 782. Number of Business Tax Returns by Size of Receipts: 2000 to 2020

[In thousands (5,045 represents 5,045,000). Covers active enterprises only. Figures are estimates based on a sample of unaudited tax returns; see Appendix III]

Size-class of receipts	2000	2005	2010	2014	2015	2016	2017	2018	2019	2020
Corporations, total...............	**5,045**	**5,671**	**5,814**	**6,001**	**6,120**	**6,189**	**6,325**	**6,442**	**6,474**	**(NA)**
Under $25,000 [1].....................	1,220	1,300	1,484	1,419	1,442	1,437	1,499	1,508	1,497	(NA)
$25,000 to $99,999.................	783	884	977	953	974	969	968	992	996	(NA)
$25,000 to $49,999.................	305	340	385	(NA)	(NA)	(NA)	(NA)	(NA)	(NA)	(NA)
$50,000 to $99,999.................	477	544	592	(NA)	(NA)	(NA)	(NA)	(NA)	(NA)	(NA)
$100,000 to $499,999...............	1,515	1,755	1,731	1,810	1,821	1,856	1,894	1,930	1,943	(NA)
$500,000 to $999,999...............	582	644	618	670	707	719	713	730	748	(NA)
$1,000,000 or more.................	946	1,088	1,005	1,151	1,176	1,207	1,251	1,282	1,290	(NA)
Partnerships, total...............	**2,058**	**2,764**	**3,249**	**3,611**	**3,715**	**3,763**	**3,905**	**4,010**	**3,822**	**4,281**
Under $25,000 [1].....................	1,105	1,465	1,788	1,951	2,031	1,993	2,055	2,166	2,020	2,332
$25,000 to $49,999.................	183	218	238	267	275	345	347	306	302	342
$50,000 to $99,999.................	187	233	289	316	293	278	297	312	298	336
$100,000 to $499,999...............	353	489	531	590	621	645	670	661	645	681
$500,000 to $999,999...............	92	131	151	175	171	171	184	198	196	216
$1,000,000 or more.................	137	227	252	312	325	331	353	368	360	375
Nonfarm proprietorships, total...............	**17,903**	**21,468**	**23,004**	**24,632**	**25,226**	**25,526**	**26,426**	**27,117**	**27,817**	**28,353**
Under $25,000 [1].....................	11,997	14,456	16,258	17,181	17,528	17,718	18,066	18,372	18,764	19,738
$25,000 to $49,999.................	2,247	2,587	2,652	2,886	2,991	3,080	3,306	3,515	3,572	3,418
$50,000 to $99,999.................	1,645	1,981	1,892	2,034	2,107	2,215	2,333	2,424	2,562	2,404
$100,000 to $499,999...............	1,733	2,091	1,869	2,130	2,181	2,087	2,273	2,355	2,452	2,324
$500,000 to $999,999...............	190	235	219	251	265	271	279	278	289	297
$1,000,000 or more.................	92	117	114	150	154	155	170	172	178	173

NA Not available. [1] Includes firms with no receipts.

Source: U.S. Internal Revenue Service, Tax Statistics, "Corporation Complete Report, Table 3.1," <www.irs.gov/statistics/soi-tax-stats-corporation-tax-statistics>; "Partnerships, Historical and Projected Data, Historical Table 12," <www.irs.gov/statistics/soi-tax-stats-partnership-statistics>; and "SOI Tax Stats - Nonfarm Sole Proprietorship Statistics," <www.irs.gov/statistics/soi-tax-stats-nonfarm-sole-proprietorship-statistics>; accessed May 2023.

Table 783. Nonfarm Sole Proprietorships—Selected Income and Deduction Items: 2000 to 2021

[In billions of dollars (1,021 represents $1,021,000,000,000), except as indicated. Data are for tax year shown, which covers returns processed by the IRS during the following calendar year. All figures are estimates based on samples. Tax law changes have affected the comparability of the data over time; see Statistics of Income reports for a description]

Item	2000	2010	2015	2016	2017	2018	2019	2020	2021
Number of returns (1,000)	17,905	23,004	25,226	25,526	26,426	27,117	27,817	28,353	29,310
Returns with net income (1,000)	13,308	17,007	18,785	18,959	19,434	19,635	20,069	19,977	21,102
Business receipts	1,021	1,196	1,444	1,422	1,531	1,590	1,640	1,605	1,868
Income from sales and operations	1,008	1,176	1,423	1,404	1,511	1,570	1,616	1,580	1,840
Business deductions [1]	806	929	1,113	1,095	1,187	1,242	1,283	1,269	1,458
Cost of sales and operations [1]	387	367	432	411	432	442	439	452	518
Labor costs	29	27	37	36	42	41	43	42	45
Purchases	269	240	265	239	255	254	250	255	299
Materials and supplies	43	45	61	64	65	70	70	72	81
Advertising	10	13	16	16	17	18	19	18	21
Car and truck expenses	46	73	90	89	97	106	116	104	117
Commissions	12	12	17	16	19	19	21	19	24
Contract labor	(NA)	34	54	57	65	69	77	77	92
Depreciation	32	35	38	38	42	51	52	55	66
Insurance	14	16	20	20	21	22	23	24	25
Interest paid [2]	12	11	9	9	10	11	12	10	11
Legal and professional services	7	10	13	13	15	15	16	16	18
Office expenses	10	12	13	13	15	15	16	17	19
Rent paid [3]	33	42	48	48	51	54	56	52	58
Repairs	12	15	19	18	21	22	23	24	28
Salaries and wages (net)	63	74	89	91	97	98	101	100	109
Supplies	22	30	38	39	44	47	51	55	65
Taxes paid	14	18	20	20	21	21	22	20	23
Travel	8	12	17	17	18	19	20	13	17
Utilities	19	24	31	32	33	34	37	36	38
Net income (less loss) [4]	215	268	332	328	346	349	355	337	411
Net income [4]	245	323	392	389	416	430	443	436	517
Constant (2017) Dollars [5]									
Business receipts	1,404	1,334	1,483	1,448	1,531	1,554	1,577	1,523	1,695
Business deductions	1,109	1,036	1,144	1,115	1,187	1,215	1,234	1,204	1,323
Net income (less loss)	295	299	341	334	346	341	342	320	373

NA Not available. [1] Includes other amounts not shown separately. [2] Interest paid includes "mortgage interest" and "other interest paid on business indebtedness." [3] Rent paid includes "Rent on machinery and equipment" and "Rent on other business property." [4] After adjustment for the passive loss carryover from prior years; therefore, "business receipts" minus "total deductions" do not equal "net income." [5] Based on the overall implicit price deflator for gross domestic product.

Source: U.S. Internal Revenue Service, "SOI Tax Stats - Nonfarm Sole Proprietorship Statistics," <www.irs.gov/uac/SOI-Tax-Stats-Nonfarm-Sole-Proprietorship-Statistics>, accessed August 2024.

Table 784. Partnerships—Selected Income and Balance Sheet Items: 2000 to 2020

[In billions of dollars (6,694 represents $6,694,000,000,000), except as indicated. Covers active partnerships only. Data are for tax year shown, which covers returns processed by the IRS during the following calendar year. All figures are estimates based on samples]

Item	2000	2005	2010	2015	2016	2017	2018	2019	2020
Number of returns (1,000)	2,058	2,764	3,248	3,715	3,763	3,905	4,010	3,821	4,281
Returns with net income (1,000)	1,261	1,580	1,635	2,152	2,196	2,200	2,205	2,111	2,285
Number of partners (1,000)	13,660	16,212	22,428	27,093	28,164	27,501	27,448	25,269	28,247
Assets [1,2]	6,694	13,734	19,820	27,366	28,950	32,404	34,348	36,048	43,183
Depreciable assets (net)	1,487	2,176	3,263	4,423	4,751	5,185	5,380	5,315	6,088
Inventories, end of year	150	315	277	343	367	378	411	391	438
Land	359	607	913	1,143	1,200	1,307	1,359	1,339	1,529
Liabilities [1,2]	3,696	7,483	8,994	11,019	12,022	13,125	14,346	14,942	17,099
Accounts payable	230	400	492	529	583	618	621	566	741
Short-term debt [3]	252	373	481	351	407	433	452	450	484
Long-term debt [4]	1,132	1,772	2,693	3,222	3,477	3,844	4,064	4,136	4,780
Nonrecourse loans	639	914	1,225	1,270	1,318	1,378	1,462	1,489	1,627
Partners' capital accounts [2]	2,999	6,251	10,826	16,347	16,928	19,279	20,002	21,107	26,084
Total receipts [1]	2,405	3,863	4,721	5,798	5,886	6,536	7,097	6,563	7,211
Business receipts	2,062	3,280	3,946	4,877	4,919	5,460	5,904	5,397	5,902
Deductions from a trade or business [1]	2,136	3,317	4,128	5,018	5,094	5,726	6,213	5,803	6,451
Cost of goods sold/operations	1,226	1,976	2,336	2,696	2,660	3,012	3,343	2,878	3,256
Salaries and wages	201	293	405	578	607	657	700	712	775
Taxes paid	31	47	63	87	89	95	99	92	105
Interest paid	93	103	86	85	97	111	107	114	128
Depreciation [5]	116	140	247	325	352	416	482	505	545
Net income (less loss)	269	546	594	781	792	810	885	761	760
Net income	410	724	904	1,137	1,173	1,278	1,382	1,342	1,476

[1] Includes items not shown separately. [2] Assets, liabilities, and partners' capital accounts are understated because not all partnerships file complete balance sheets. [3] Mortgages, notes, and bonds payable in less than 1 year. [4] Mortgages, notes, and bonds payable in 1 year or more. [5] Represents the more complete amounts reported in depreciation computation schedules, rather than the amounts reported as the depreciation deduction.

Source: U.S. Internal Revenue Service, "SOI Tax Stats - Partnership Statistics," <www.irs.gov/uac/SOI-Tax-Stats-Partnership-Statistics>, accessed December 2022.

Table 785. Partnerships—Selected Items by Industry: 2021

[In billions of dollars (50,832 represents $50,832,000,000,000), except as indicated. Covers active partnerships only. Data are for tax year shown, which covers returns processed by the IRS during 2022. Figures are estimates based on samples. Based on the North American Industry Classification System (NAICS), 2012; see text, this section. Minus sign (-) indicates net loss]

Industry	NAICS code	Partnerships (1,000)			Total assets [3]	Business receipts	Total deductions	Net income (less loss) minus deductions [4]	Net income	Net loss
		Total	With net income	With net loss						
Total [1]	(X)	4,468	2,567	1,901	50,832	7,016	7,111	3,893	4,837	943
Agriculture, forestry, fishing, and hunting	11	148	76	72	304	48	64	10	22	13
Mining	21	45	27	17	801	213	171	61	84	23
Utilities	22	9	4	5	643	250	268	-12	29	41
Construction	23	177	128	49	366	484	466	32	46	13
Manufacturing	31–33	65	37	28	1,005	1,068	1,045	54	85	31
Wholesale trade	42	98	38	61	526	953	932	39	50	12
Retail trade	44–45	184	98	86	331	826	816	48	58	10
Transportation and warehousing	48–49	76	45	31	783	372	374	20	42	22
Information	51	45	21	25	1,105	394	400	14	58	44
Finance and insurance	52	460	273	187	31,303	358	551	2,598	2,920	322
Real estate and rental and leasing	53	2,218	1,290	927	10,110	266	304	566	837	271
Professional, scientific, and technical services	54	279	171	108	708	721	600	192	221	28
Management of companies (holding companies)	55	49	28	21	1,545	46	83	178	211	33
Administrative and support & waste management and remediation services	56	102	58	45	185	166	175	14	24	10
Health care and social assistance	62	101	68	33	343	395	379	60	78	18
Arts, entertainment, and recreation	71	69	30	39	217	99	114	5	22	17
Accommodation and food services	72	180	85	94	472	284	295	8	38	30
Educational and other services [2]	61/81	162	89	73	87	74	74	6	12	7

X Not applicable. [1] Includes businesses not allocable to individual industries. [2] The educational and other services sectors were combined due to disclosure concerns. [3] Total assets are understated because not all partnerships file complete balance sheets. [4] Total income (less loss) minus total deductions is the sum of ordinary business income (less loss), partners distributive share income and deductions, net rental real estate income (less loss) and other net rental income (less loss). This is considered a more complete measure of partnership income and represents the entire amount passed through to partners. Not comparable with previously published measures of income and loss.

Source: U.S. Internal Revenue Service, "SOI Tax Stats - Partnership Statistics," <www.irs.gov/statistics/soi-tax-stats-partnership-statistics>, accessed March 2024.

Table 786. Nonfinancial Noncorporate Business Balance Sheet: 2000 to 2023

[In billions of dollars (7,859 represents $7,859,000,000,000), except as noted. Represents year-end (4th quarter) outstandings]

Item	2000	2005	2010	2015	2019	2020	2021	2022	2023
Assets	7,859	11,956	12,213	16,480	20,715	22,857	26,180	27,348	27,108
Nonfinancial assets	6,387	9,725	9,006	11,939	14,743	15,847	18,471	19,300	18,922
Real estate [1]	5,641	8,790	7,887	10,623	13,271	14,338	16,810	17,506	17,159
Residential	3,327	5,394	4,513	5,926	7,655	8,440	10,056	10,546	10,293
Nonresidential	2,315	3,397	3,374	4,696	5,616	5,898	6,755	6,961	6,866
Equipment [2]	447	562	683	811	895	922	1,000	1,071	967
Residential [3]	35	42	43	50	65	76	88	91	87
Nonresidential	412	521	639	761	831	846	912	980	880
Intellectual property products [2]	114	154	191	243	319	348	375	413	478
Inventories [2]	185	218	244	262	258	240	285	309	319
Financial assets	1,473	2,231	3,207	4,541	5,972	7,010	7,709	8,048	8,186
Checkable deposits and currency	181	224	182	254	331	391	470	512	519
Time and savings deposits	248	474	706	861	1,083	1,286	1,382	1,453	1,497
Money market fund shares	49	69	77	88	108	128	131	137	139
Debt securities	43	61	54	66	76	78	76	77	78
U.S. Treasury securities	40	56	48	62	72	73	71	72	73
Municipal securities	2	4	6	4	4	5	5	5	5
Loans	23	36	42	42	51	53	52	55	56
Mortgages	23	36	42	42	51	53	52	55	56
Equity in Farm Credit System	3	4	7	9	13	13	14	15	18
Trade receivables	342	431	533	671	763	940	1,020	1,071	1,088
Miscellaneous assets	583	931	1,606	2,550	3,547	4,120	4,566	4,728	4,789
Liabilities and equity, total	7,859	11,956	12,213	16,480	20,715	22,857	26,180	27,348	27,108
Liabilities	2,820	4,207	5,702	6,730	8,553	9,631	10,568	11,105	11,350
Loans [4]	1,939	2,927	3,987	4,725	5,978	6,504	6,889	7,322	7,489
Depository institution loans n.e.c. [5]	402	671	928	1,145	1,485	1,586	1,556	1,634	1,623
Mortgages	1,381	2,093	2,853	3,348	4,237	4,564	4,904	5,216	5,398
Foreign direct investment, intercompany debt	1	1	1	2	7	6	5	6	5
Trade payables	267	335	426	520	542	673	742	785	789
Taxes payable	65	87	99	123	162	170	202	214	220
Miscellaneous liabilities	549	858	1,189	1,360	1,863	2,278	2,729	2,779	2,847
Equity	5,039	7,749	6,511	9,750	12,162	13,226	15,612	16,242	15,758
Net worth	5,039	7,749	6,511	9,750	12,162	13,226	15,612	16,242	15,758
Debt as percent of net worth	38.5	37.8	61.2	48.5	49.2	49.2	44.1	45.1	47.5

[1] At market value. [2] At replacement (current) cost. [3] Durable goods in rental properties. [4] Includes data for other loans and advances, not shown separately. [5] Not elsewhere classified.

Source: Board of Governors of the Federal Reserve System, "Financial Accounts of the United States - Z.1," March 2024, <www.federalreserve.gov/releases/z1/>.

Table 787. Nonfinancial Corporate Business Sector Balance Sheet: 2000 to 2023

[In billions of dollars (21,986 represents $21,986,000,000,000), except percent. Represents year-end outstandings]

Item	2000	2005	2010	2015	2019	2020	2021	2022	2023
Assets	**21,986**	**27,910**	**28,274**	**37,104**	**48,887**	**51,066**	**57,648**	**57,551**	**59,751**
Nonfinancial assets	10,890	14,606	15,068	20,368	24,837	25,857	29,412	30,550	30,220
Real estate [1]	5,571	8,359	7,623	11,297	14,044	14,673	17,065	17,089	16,166
Equipment [2]	2,894	3,263	3,844	4,616	5,323	5,404	5,827	6,283	6,541
Intellectual property products [2]	1,085	1,365	1,741	2,184	2,827	3,107	3,359	3,687	4,042
Inventories [2]	1,340	1,619	1,860	2,270	2,643	2,673	3,161	3,492	3,471
Financial assets [3]	11,096	13,305	13,205	16,736	24,049	25,209	28,235	27,001	29,532
Checkable deposits and currency	228	336	490	838	1,341	1,785	2,050	2,010	1,998
Money market fund shares	214	359	555	576	590	712	813	740	916
Debt securities	125	215	217	216	338	377	410	369	446
Corporate equities	1,718	1,059	917	1,500	2,318	2,543	3,145	2,398	2,831
U.S. direct investment abroad: equity	2,250	2,905	3,704	4,970	6,215	6,763	7,980	6,694	7,780
Mutual fund shares	118	134	186	248	326	376	444	358	407
Trade receivables	1,939	2,108	2,203	2,754	4,053	3,916	4,414	4,595	4,797
Liabilities and equity, total [3]	**25,295**	**27,991**	**32,230**	**47,846**	**67,047**	**76,735**	**89,773**	**77,478**	**90,402**
Liabilities	**9,888**	**11,703**	**14,271**	**19,268**	**24,383**	**24,167**	**25,012**	**26,731**	**27,320**
Debt securities	2,751	3,092	4,088	5,819	6,988	7,684	7,933	8,012	8,249
Commercial paper	278	90	83	179	195	132	138	198	218
Municipal securities [4]	154	250	511	549	601	607	618	619	618
Corporate bonds	2,319	2,752	3,495	5,091	6,193	6,945	7,176	7,195	7,413
Loans [3]	2,065	2,435	2,303	2,935	3,880	4,220	4,703	5,427	5,388
Depository institution loans n.e.c. [5]	919	613	499	988	1,059	1,208	1,123	1,475	1,484
Mortgages	445	918	858	816	983	987	1,089	1,259	1,317
Foreign direct investment in U.S.: intercompany debt	281	276	406	508	392	321	312	382	376
Trade payables	1,541	1,699	1,739	2,104	2,920	2,765	3,194	3,443	3,555
Taxes payable	78	86	78	74	268	275	250	277	271
Total equity (market value)	**15,407**	**16,288**	**17,958**	**28,578**	**42,664**	**52,568**	**64,761**	**50,748**	**63,082**
Net worth	**12,098**	**16,207**	**14,002**	**17,836**	**24,504**	**26,899**	**32,635**	**30,820**	**32,431**
Debt as percent of net worth	39.8	34.1	45.6	49.1	44.4	44.3	38.7	43.6	42.0

[1] At market value. [2] At replacement (current) cost. [3] Includes items not shown separately. [4] Industrial revenue bonds. Issued by state and local governments to finance private investment and secured in interest and principal by the industrial user of the funds. [5] Not elsewhere classified.

Source: Board of Governors of the Federal Reserve System, "Financial Accounts of the United States - Z.1," March 2024, <www.federalreserve.gov/releases/z1/>.

Table 788. Corporate Funds—Sources and Uses: 2000 to 2023

[In billions of dollars (451 represents $451,000,000,000)]

Item	2000	2005	2010	2015	2019	2020	2021	2022	2023
Profits before tax	451	1,044	1,055	1,330	1,267	1,511	2,234	2,452	2,468
- Taxes on corporate income	165	263	204	284	197	209	298	417	431
- Net dividends	251	176	382	684	668	833	1,110	1,233	1,064
+ Inventory valuation adjustment (IVA)	-17	-36	-48	58	2	-17	-257	-96	19
+ Capital consumption allowance [1]	788	808	1,099	1,335	1,796	1,703	1,811	1,867	1,918
+ Foreign earnings retained abroad	103	-29	212	197	45	102	81	114	66
- Net capital transfers	–	-16	21	-3	-12	14	-10	30	-1
=Gross saving less net capital transfers paid	908	1,364	1,711	1,956	2,257	2,244	2,472	2,656	2,977
Gross investment	1,155	1,375	1,524	1,751	2,384	2,153	2,343	3,062	3,155
Capital expenditures [2]	1,156	1,218	1,310	1,951	2,197	2,022	2,232	2,732	2,720
Fixed investment [3]	1,107	1,166	1,257	1,802	2,126	2,048	2,215	2,483	2,674
Inventory change + IVA	50	51	54	120	72	-26	11	144	49
Net lending (+) or net borrowing (-) [2]	-1	157	213	-200	187	131	112	331	435
Net acquisition of financial assets [2]	1,484	935	554	1,143	2,405	433	1,335	1,169	1,037
Foreign deposits	-7	10	13	-19	25	4	31	24	22
Checkable deposits and currency	35	101	126	47	141	444	265	-40	-12
Time and savings deposits	35	10	6	11	14	77	6	13	99
Money market fund shares	17	53	-170	19	108	122	101	-74	176
Debt securities	19	42	-5	4	69	37	38	-18	72
Loans	6	3	-4	23	5	14	14	21	21
Mortgages	1	2	-1	24	6	14	14	21	21
Mutual fund shares	(Z)	1	7	12	5	10	22	-4	-4
Trade receivables	282	278	142	33	541	-137	498	181	202
Miscellaneous assets	1,121	601	191	782	1,480	-244	231	868	325
Net increase in liabilities and equity [2]	1,485	778	340	1,344	2,218	302	1,223	839	602
Debt securities [2]	192	7	247	444	316	696	253	79	237
Commercial paper	48	-8	25	-3	-2	-62	6	59	20
Corporate bonds	143	-29.568	189	434	302	753	235	19	218
Loans	157	287	-301	201	319	340	289	623	49
Depository institution loans n.e.c. [4]	51	-22	-87	111	24	148	-83	266	9
Other loans and advances [5]	78	110	-109	-7	128	188	298	202	-18
Mortgages	29	199	-105	97	166	4	74	155	58
Foreign direct investment: intercompany debt	56	(Z)	-8	40	-7	-65	-1	70	2
Trade payables	313	199	157	24	230	-156	430	248	112
Taxes payable	7	-2	43	-21	-8	8	-26	28	-6
Miscellaneous liabilities [2]	602	424	159	730	1,461	-578	107	63	529
Claims of pension fund on sponsor	118	93	-21	59	73	-6	150	59	66
Corporate equities	-36	-241	-127	-450	-325	-107	-215	-536	-612

– Represents zero. Z Less than $500 million. [1] Consumption of fixed capital plus capital consumption adjustment. [2] Includes other items not shown separately. [3] Nonresidential fixed investment plus residential fixed investment. [4] Not elsewhere classified. [5] Loans from rest of the world, U.S. government, and nonbank financial institutions.

Source: Board of Governors of the Federal Reserve System, "Financial Accounts of the United States - Z.1," March 2024, <www.federalreserve.gov/releases/z1/>.

Table 789. Corporations—Selected Financial Items: 2000 to 2020

[In billions of dollars (47,027 represents $47,027,000,000,000), except as noted. Covers active corporations only. Corporation data are for tax year shown, which covers (a) corporate returns with accounting periods for the calendar year ending December of year shown and (b) those returns with accounting periods for the noncalendar year ending between July of year shown and June of the following year. All corporations are required to file returns except those specifically exempt. See source for changes in law affecting comparability of historical data]

Item	2000	2010	2015	2016	2017	2018	2019	2020
Number of returns (1,000)	5,045	5,814	6,120	6,189	6,325	6,442	6,474	6,402
Number with net income (1,000)	2,819	3,265	3,801	3,881	3,936	4,018	4,007	3,648
S Corporation returns [1] (1,000)	2,860	4,128	4,487	4,592	4,726	4,875	4,940	4,893
Assets [2]	47,027	79,905	97,048	101,991	107,889	108,505	114,840	124,513
Cash	1,820	3,893	5,305	5,374	5,611	5,284	5,896	8,170
Notes and accounts receivable	8,754	12,718	13,753	15,102	16,359	15,738	14,980	14,781
Inventories	1,272	1,544	1,991	2,000	2,080	2,225	2,257	2,136
Investments in government obligations	1,236	2,730	3,450	4,107	4,328	4,519	4,537	6,332
Mortgage and real estate	2,822	7,914	8,151	8,192	8,447	8,767	11,134	11,560
Depreciable assets	7,292	9,875	12,350	12,680	13,121	13,790	14,591	14,557
Depletable assets	191	661	1,038	923	917	945	923	825
Land	303	548	669	691	715	747	808	762
Liabilities [2]	47,027	79,905	97,048	101,991	107,889	108,505	114,840	124,513
Accounts payable	3,758	5,768	6,111	6,433	7,000	6,295	6,691	7,185
Short-term debt [3]	4,020	3,752	3,643	3,404	3,568	3,621	4,108	3,550
Long-term debt [4]	6,184	14,680	14,998	15,753	16,436	16,732	17,830	18,627
Net worth [2, 5]	17,349	28,938	38,072	40,834	44,753	45,133	46,453	52,838
Capital stock	3,966	3,064	3,472	3,588	3,619	3,758	3,784	3,698
Paid-in or capital surplus	12,265	24,283	31,327	33,175	34,692	35,055	35,411	39,717
Retained earnings [6]	3,627	3,534	6,341	7,364	9,981	10,142	11,366	13,514
Receipts [2, 7]	20,606	26,199	31,030	31,208	32,962	35,180	35,910	33,404
Business receipts [7, 8]	17,637	23,058	27,492	27,575	29,180	30,837	31,367	29,179
Interest [9]	1,628	1,366	1,107	1,190	1,344	1,587	1,710	1,293
Rents and royalties	254	307	376	402	397	423	453	488
Deductions [2, 7]	19,692	24,944	29,102	29,395	31,384	32,850	33,608	31,218
Cost of goods sold [8]	11,135	14,502	17,044	16,948	18,117	19,193	19,245	17,593
Compensation of officers	401	435	501	498	513	493	500	508
Rent paid on business property	380	467	529	540	549	566	593	551
Taxes paid	390	493	580	590	602	632	650	593
Interest paid	1,272	888	728	793	910	982	1,120	845
Depreciation	614	728	822	857	976	1,138	1,177	1,031
Advertising	234	256	316	325	336	354	379	336
Net income (less loss) [7, 10]	928	1,356	2,034	1,913	1,656	3,391	2,869	2,673
Net income	1,337	1,836	2,531	2,458	2,281	3,954	3,527	3,568
Deficit	409	480	498	545	625	563	659	895
Income subject to tax	760	1,022	1,375	1,271	1,002	1,957	1,733	1,780
Income tax before credits [11]	266	358	481	446	359	404	383	394
Income tax after credits [12]	204	223	330	316	265	245	257	277

[1] Represents certain small corporations with a limit on the number of shareholders, mostly individuals, electing to be taxed at the shareholder level. [2] Includes items not shown separately. [3] Payable in less than 1 year. [4] Payable in 1 year or more. [5] Net worth is the sum of capital stock, additional paid-in capital, retained earnings appropriated, retained earnings unappropriated, and adjustments to shareholders' equity, minus cost of treasury stock. [6] Appropriated and unappropriated and adjustments to shareholders' equity. [7] Receipts, deductions, and net income of S corporations are limited to those from trade or business. Those from investments are excluded. [8] Includes gross sales and cost of sales of securities, commodities, and real estate by exchanges, brokers, or dealers selling on their own accounts. Excludes investment income. [9] Includes tax-exempt interest in state and local government obligations. [10] Excludes regulated investment companies. [11] Consists of regular (and alternative tax) only. [12] Includes minimum tax, alternative minimum tax, adjustments for prior year credits, and other income-related taxes.

Source: U.S. Internal Revenue Service, "SOI Tax Stats - Corporation Complete Report," <www.irs.gov/statistics/soi-tax-stats-corporation-complete-report>, accessed June 2024.

Table 790. IRS Audits—Corporate and Partnership Income Tax Returns Filed and Examined: 2013 to 2021

[In units as indicated (13,763,924 represents $13,763,924,000). An IRS audit is a review/examination of an organization's or individual's tax return to determine if income, expenses, and credits are being reported accurately. Includes tax returns selected for examination based on an earned income tax credit claim, and the resulting recommended additional taxes]

Year	Returns filed [1] (number)	Returns examined				Returns examined with no change (number)	Recommended additional tax ($1,000)
		Total (number)	Closed [2] (number)	In process [3] (number)	Percent coverage		
CORPORATIONS							
2013	1,625,306	19,315	19,083	232	1.2	6,426	13,763,924
2015	1,626,264	15,624	15,084	540	1.0	4,952	14,042,491
2020 [4]	1,499,042	9,619	5,158	4,461	0.6	2,383	352,032
2021 [4]	1,556,982	4,168	1,481	2,687	0.3	599	42,358
PARTNERSHIPS							
2013	3,460,699	10,463	10,291	172	0.3	4,708	(NA)
2015	3,715,187	8,414	7,903	511	0.2	3,240	(NA)
2020 [4]	4,645,903	3,014	420	2,594	0.1	343	(NA)
2021 [4]	4,467,584	4,434	405	4,029	0.1	361	(NA)
S CORPORATIONS							
2013	4,257,909	14,837	14,718	119	0.3	[5] 4,834	(NA)
2015	4,487,336	9,949	9,649	300	0.2	2,702	(NA)
2020 [4]	4,892,722	3,275	1,212	2,063	0.1	395	(NA)
2021 [4]	5,120,552	4,819	896	3,923	0.1	505	(NA)

NA Not available. [1] Includes all returns filed for the specified tax year as of December 31, 2023. [2] Includes examinations closed as of September 30, 2023. Represents a distinct count of taxpayers by tax year and form type. During the course of an examination, additional related returns within the statute of limitations may require examination; these related return closures are counted by the appropriate tax year and form type. [3] Includes examinations that are in an open examination status. [4] Data for years within the normal 3-year statute of limitations will change; use data with caution. [5] Data subject to revision; however, revisions are not shown here in order to prevent disclosure of specific taxpayers.

Source: U.S. Internal Revenue Service, *IRS Data Book 2023*, April 2024. See also <www.irs.gov/statistics/soi-tax-stats-irs-data-book>.

Table 791. Economic Census Summary (NAICS 2022 Basis): 2022

[22 represents 22,000. Covers establishments with payroll. Data are based on the 2022 Economic Census, which are subject to nonsampling error. Data for the construction sector are also subject to sampling errors. For details on survey methodology and nonsampling and sampling errors, see Appendix III]

Kind of business	2022 NAICS code [1]	Establish- ments (1,000)	Sales, receipts, or shipments (bil. dol.)	Annual payroll (bil. dol.)	Paid employees [2] (1,000)
Mining, quarrying, and oil and gas extraction..........	21	22	597	52	565
Oil & gas extraction.................................	211	5	413	12	105
Mining (except oil & gas).............................	212	6	98	14	173
Support activities for mining.........................	213	12	86	25	287
Utilities..	22	21	745	76	676
Construction...	23	802	2,924	530	7,606
Construction of buildings.............................	236	250	1,223	124	1,631
Heavy and civil engineering construction.............	237	37	397	83	1,037
Specialty trade contractors..........................	238	515	1,304	322	4,938
Manufacturing...	31-33	286	7,061	815	12,261
Wholesale trade...	42	377	11,644	514	6,247
Merchant wholesalers, durable goods................	423	220	4,861	312	3,634
Merchant wholesalers, nondurable goods............	424	122	6,054	186	2,362
Wholesale electronic markets and agents and brokers.................................	425	35	728	16	250
Retail trade...	44-45	1,042	6,969	615	17,140
Motor vehicle & parts dealers........................	441	122	1,590	129	2,068
Building material & garden equipment & supplies dealers.................................	444	78	550	55	1,458
Food & beverage retailers...........................	445	161	975	99	3,476
Furniture, home furnishings, electronics, and appliance retailers..............	449	77	352	33	773
General merchandise retailers.......................	455	62	1,303	129	3,998
Health and personal care retailers...................	456	99	648	47	1,147
Gasoline stations and fuel dealers...................	457	121	762	31	1,102
Clothing, clothing accessories, shoe, and jewelry retailers...........................	458	131	394	42	1,581
Sporting goods, hobby, musical instrument, and book stores................................	459	191	395	49	1,536
Transportation & warehousing [3].....................	48-49	294	1,367	352	6,311
Air transportation...................................	481	4	285	51	557
Water transportation................................	483	2	49	6	71
Truck transportation................................	484	172	442	98	1,708
Transit & ground passenger transportation..........	485	20	59	24	689
Pipeline transportation..............................	486	4	70	6	50
Scenic & sightseeing transportation.................	487	3	5	1	26
Support activities for transportation.................	488	51	244	53	841
Couriers & messengers..............................	492	18	152	45	1,034
Warehousing & storage..............................	493	21	63	66	1,334
Information..	51	164	2,220	521	4,542
Motion picture and sound recording industries.......	512	31	135	23	383
Publishing industries.................................	513	38	595	203	1,446
Broadcasting and content providers..................	516	13	351	77	597
Telecommunications.................................	517	59	660	81	991
Data processing, hosting, and related services......	518	19	333	83	686
Other information services...........................	519	4	146	56	438
Finance & insurance [4]................................	52	479	5,677	825	7,478
Real estate & rental & leasing [5].....................	53	469	960	161	2,630
Professional, scientific, & technical services..........	54	976	2,807	1,054	11,570
Management of companies & enterprises..............	55	54	(S)	487	4,492
Admin & support and waste management & remediation services.............................	56	456	1,471	672	14,349
Administrative & support services....................	561	427	1,333	641	13,817
Waste management & remediation services..........	562	29	138	32	532
Educational services [6]................................	61	89	95	31	868
Health care & social assistance........................	62	975	3,377	1,285	22,136
Ambulatory health care services.....................	621	676	1,459	571	8,734
Hospitals...	622	7	1,343	472	6,347
Nursing & residential care facilities..................	623	94	285	123	3,215
Social assistance.....................................	624	199	(S)	(S)	(S)
Arts, entertainment, & recreation......................	71	160	343	106	2,697
Performing arts, spectator sports, & related industries.................................	711	67	151	52	578
Museums, historical sites, & similar institutions......	712	8	22	6	157
Amusement, gambling, & recreation industries......	713	86	170	47	1,963
Accommodation & food services......................	72	771	1,227	340	14,091
Accommodation.......................................	721	70	301	66	1,824
Food services & drinking places.....................	722	701	926	274	12,267
Other services (except public administration)..........	81	596	716	174	3,997
Repair & maintenance...............................	811	225	248	69	1,454
Personal and laundry services........................	812	265	146	47	1,579
Religious, grantmaking, civic, professional, and similar organizations.............................	813	105	322	58	964

S Data do not meet publication standards. [1] Based on North American Industry Classification System, 2022; see text, this section. [2] For pay period including March 12. [3] Railroad transportation and U.S. Postal Service are out of scope. For detailed industries, see Table 1097. [4] Funds, trusts, and other financial vehicles are out of scope. [5] For detailed industries, see Table 1194. [6] Elementary and secondary schools, junior colleges, and colleges, universities, and professional schools are out of scope.

Source: U.S. Census Bureau, 2022 Economic Census of the United States, Table EC2200BASIC, "All Sectors: Summary Statistics for the U.S.: 2022," <data.census.gov>, accessed June 2024.

Table 792. Nonemployer Establishments and Receipts by Industry: 2015 to 2021

[24,331 represents 24,331,000. Includes only firms subject to federal income tax. Nonemployers are businesses with no paid employees. Data originate chiefly from administrative records of the Internal Revenue Service; see Appendix III. Data for 2015 based on NAICS 2012 and data for 2020 onwards based on NAICS 2017]

Industry	NAICS code	Establishments (1,000)			Receipts (mil. dol.)		
		2015	2020	2021	2015	2020	2021
All industries...	(X)	**24,331**	**27,152**	**28,478**	**1,148,716**	**1,330,804**	**1,501,874**
Agriculture, forestry, fishing and hunting................	11	236	256	256	11,014	12,063	13,328
Mining, quarrying, and oil and gas extraction............	21	98	68	73	6,111	4,042	5,099
Utilities..	22	20	15	15	981	1,015	1,076
Construction..	23	2,430	2,879	2,787	146,341	187,130	197,648
Manufacturing..	31–33	355	357	368	17,473	18,921	20,435
Wholesale trade...	42	417	394	387	37,946	38,746	40,778
Retail trade...	44–45	1,986	2,257	2,370	87,352	98,440	109,294
Transportation & warehousing...............................	48–49	1,528	3,189	3,600	83,890	121,301	155,338
Information...	51	329	335	388	12,762	13,404	16,004
Finance & insurance...	52	718	758	761	55,329	69,235	78,099
Real estate & rental & leasing..............................	53	2,636	2,988	3,074	259,768	309,053	336,213
Professional, scientific, & technical services............	54	3,411	3,690	3,832	157,584	178,993	201,674
Administrative and support & waste management and remediation services...............	56	2,069	2,555	2,608	46,393	60,882	68,089
Educational services...	61	710	761	815	9,893	11,714	13,635
Health care & social assistance...........................	62	1,979	2,008	2,124	64,702	71,922	80,321
Arts, entertainment, & recreation..........................	71	1,342	1,339	1,514	34,549	35,411	45,131
Accommodation & food services...........................	72	371	492	571	17,658	17,343	21,294
Other services (except public administration)...........	81	3,695	2,812	2,936	98,971	81,192	98,420

X Not applicable.

Source: U.S. Census Bureau, Nonemployer Statistics, "All Sectors: Nonemployer Statistics by Legal Form of Organization and Receipts Size Class for the U.S., States, and Selected Geographies: 2021," <data.census.gov>, accessed March 2024. See also <www.census.gov/programs-surveys/nonemployer-statistics.html>.

Table 793. Establishments, Employees, and Payroll by Employment-Size Class: 1990 to 2022

[In units as noted (6,176 represents 6,176,000). Excludes self-employed individuals, employees of private households, railroad employees, agricultural production employees, and most government employees. Employees are for the pay period including March 12. Covers establishments with payroll. An establishment is a single physical location where business is conducted or where services or industrial operations are performed. For statement on methodology, see Appendix III]

Employment-size class	Unit	1990	2000	2010	2015	2019	2020	2021	2022
Establishments, total............	1,000	**6,176**	**7,070**	**7,397**	**7,664**	**7,959**	**8,000**	**8,149**	**8,299**
Under 20 employees................	1,000	5,354	6,069	6,408	6,559	6,781	6,819	7,037	7,120
20 to 99 employees.................	1,000	684	826	824	919	979	981	926	984
100 to 499 employees..............	1,000	122	157	148	166	177	177	164	172
500 to 999 employees..............	1,000	10	12	11	13	14	14	13	14
1,000 or more employees..........	1,000	6	7	7	7	7	8	9	8	9
Employees, total.................	1,000	**93,476**	**114,065**	**111,970**	**124,086**	**132,989**	**134,163**	**128,346**	**135,748**
Under 20 employees................	1,000	24,373	27,569	28,958	29,406	30,309	30,143	30,278	31,199
20 to 99 employees.................	1,000	27,414	33,147	32,730	36,640	38,928	38,981	36,463	38,832
100 to 499 employees..............	1,000	22,926	29,736	27,718	31,416	33,553	33,758	31,414	33,040
500 to 999 employees..............	1,000	6,551	8,291	7,331	8,550	9,369	9,448	8,977	9,440
1,000 or more employees..........	1,000	12,212	15,322	15,233	18,074	20,831	21,834	21,214	23,238
Annual payroll, total..............	Bil. dol.	**2,104**	**3,879**	**4,941**	**6,253**	**7,429**	**7,565**	**8,279**	**8,965**
Under 20 employees................	Bil. dol.	485	818	1,057	1,235	1,388	1,384	1,571	1,654
20 to 99 employees.................	Bil. dol.	547	1,006	1,281	1,584	1,834	1,822	1,986	2,156
100 to 499 employees..............	Bil. dol.	518	1,031	1,280	1,651	1,960	1,979	2,119	2,295
500 to 999 employees..............	Bil. dol.	174	336	410	550	672	683	729	785
1,000 or more employees..........	Bil. dol.	381	690	913	1,235	1,574	1,696	1,874	2,075

Source: U.S. Census Bureau, County Business Patterns, "All Sectors: County Business Patterns, including ZIP Code Business Patterns, by Legal Form of Organization and Employment Size Class for the U.S., States, and Selected Geographies: 2022," <data.census.gov>, accessed June 2024. See also <www.census.gov/programs-surveys/cbp.html>.

Table 794. Establishments, Employees, and Payroll by Employment-Size Class and Industry: 2010 to 2022

[Establishments and employees in thousands (7,396.6 represents 7,396,600); payroll in billions of dollars (4,941.0 represents $4,941,000,000,000). See headnote, Table 793. Data for 2010 data based on NAICS 2007 and data for 2020 and 2022 based on NAICS 2017. See text, this section]

Industry	NAICS code	2010, total	2020, total	2022 Total	2022 Under 20 employ-ees	2022 20 to 99 employ-ees	2022 100 to 499 employ-ees	2022 500 to 999 employ-ees	2022 1,000 or more employ-ees
ESTABLISHMENTS (1,000s)									
Total....................................	(X)	7,396.6	8,000.2	8,298.6	7,119.9	983.7	172.2	13.9	9.0
Agriculture, forestry, fishing & hunting.........	11	21.7	22.7	23.3	21.9	1.3	0.2	(Z)	(Z)
Mining, quarrying, & oil and gas extraction....	21	27.1	23.9	23.2	18.5	3.8	0.7	0.1	(Z)
Utilities.................................	22	17.6	19.5	20.4	14.9	4.3	1.1	0.1	(Z)
Construction............................	23	682.7	753.3	800.7	728.7	62.7	8.6	0.5	0.2
Manufacturing...........................	31–33	300.0	283.5	285.5	196.3	63.4	22.5	2.3	1.0
Wholesale trade.........................	42	414.6	391.1	388.7	327.2	52.0	8.6	0.6	0.2
Retail trade.............................	44–45	1,068.0	1,036.8	1,045.9	882.1	134.4	28.8	0.4	0.1
Transportation and warehousing...............	48–49	208.5	257.8	294.4	248.9	35.0	8.9	1.0	0.6
Information.............................	51	135.4	160.9	160.9	136.6	18.3	5.0	0.7	0.3
Finance and insurance....................	52	473.5	476.8	480.5	441.0	30.4	7.3	1.1	0.7
Real estate and rental and leasing.............	53	347.3	437.7	466.7	448.7	15.9	1.9	0.1	(Z)
Professional, scientific, & technical services..	54	851.5	943.2	974.3	894.0	66.0	12.5	1.1	0.6
Management of companies and enterprises...	55	50.9	52.4	51.2	33.2	11.6	5.1	0.8	0.6
Administrative & support and waste management & remediation services.........	56	381.8	431.1	450.5	382.3	49.8	15.2	1.8	1.4
Educational services......................	61	90.1	110.1	114.8	90.9	19.0	4.0	0.4	0.4
Health care and social assistance.............	62	812.9	928.2	976.4	812.3	134.5	25.2	2.1	2.2
Arts, entertainment, and recreation...........	71	123.2	151.9	163.0	139.8	19.5	3.4	0.2	0.1
Accommodation and food services.............	72	644.0	733.9	771.9	544.6	217.1	9.6	0.4	0.2
Other services [1]........................	81	725.5	771.3	797.8	749.6	44.4	3.6	0.2	0.1
Unclassified establishments..................	99	20.5	14.0	8.5	8.5	(NA)	(NA)	(NA)	(NA)
EMPLOYEES (1,000s)									
Total....................................	(X)	111,970	134,163	135,748	31,199	38,832	33,040	9,440	23,238
Agriculture, forestry, fishing & hunting.........	11	156	167	169	74	50	31	7	8
Mining, quarrying, & oil and gas extraction....	21	582	578	508	89	159	151	50	60
Utilities.................................	22	638	637	645	74	187	212	97	75
Construction............................	23	5,389	7,182	7,362	2,661	2,453	1,567	329	351
Manufacturing...........................	31–33	10,863	12,000	12,188	1,118	2,817	4,576	1,525	2,152
Wholesale trade.........................	42	5,599	6,145	6,143	1,574	2,071	1,651	422	426
Retail trade.............................	44–45	14,497	15,808	15,922	4,827	5,140	5,396	258	301
Transportation and warehousing...............	48–49	4,012	5,712	6,108	868	1,491	1,731	666	1,353
Information.............................	51	3,124	3,577	3,634	560	775	1,019	457	823
Finance and insurance....................	52	5,929	6,682	6,832	1,764	1,214	1,499	728	1,627
Real estate and rental and leasing.............	53	1,946	2,281	2,333	1,223	604	360	90	56
Professional, scientific, & technical services..	54	7,822	9,554	10,152	2,848	2,629	2,449	770	1,456
Management of companies and enterprises...	55	2,833	3,571	3,662	170	523	1,086	548	1,335
Administrative & support and waste management & remediation services.........	56	8,977	12,718	13,579	1,444	2,128	3,111	1,233	5,664
Educational services......................	61	3,274	3,832	3,744	434	801	777	313	1,420
Health care and social assistance.............	62	17,788	21,217	21,171	4,217	5,394	4,686	1,461	5,414
Arts, entertainment, and recreation...........	71	2,004	2,505	2,318	511	808	616	136	246
Accommodation and food services.............	72	11,312	14,377	13,793	3,718	7,999	1,501	246	330
Other services [1]........................	81	5,204	5,602	5,472	3,015	1,589	621	105	141
Unclassified establishments..................	99	([2])	17	12	11	(NA)	(NA)	(NA)	(NA)
ANNUAL PAYROLL (BIL. DOLLARS)									
Total....................................	(X)	4,941.0	7,564.8	8,965.0	1,654.0	2,156.3	2,294.7	784.7	2,075.3
Agriculture, forestry, fishing & hunting.........	11	5.3	8.0	8.9	3.9	2.9	1.6	0.3	0.2
Mining, quarrying, & oil and gas extraction....	21	46.1	49.3	55.6	7.6	15.9	18.1	5.9	8.0
Utilities.................................	22	55.4	73.6	78.7	7.5	20.8	26.2	13.0	11.2
Construction............................	23	261.0	458.9	534.4	155.2	185.8	135.3	29.0	29.1
Manufacturing...........................	31–33	550.4	738.2	851.3	59.8	174.1	311.8	111.4	194.2
Wholesale trade.........................	42	339.1	464.6	535.2	115.2	165.6	146.0	44.4	64.0
Retail trade.............................	44–45	359.4	484.9	584.1	164.0	196.2	195.1	11.8	17.1
Transportation and warehousing...............	48–49	166.8	292.4	345.5	49.6	84.3	95.0	34.5	82.1
Information.............................	51	224.0	439.8	515.7	44.3	72.7	146.5	75.4	176.7
Finance and insurance....................	52	472.4	753.5	845.1	158.1	166.7	210.7	93.6	216.1
Real estate and rental and leasing.............	53	80.5	131.7	162.1	76.2	44.3	28.8	7.6	5.3
Professional, scientific, & technical services..	54	543.1	893.8	1,067.8	222.0	265.2	297.5	99.4	183.7
Management of companies and enterprises...	55	281.8	410.0	464.5	24.0	61.8	131.6	70.1	177.0
Administrative & support and waste management & remediation services.........	56	304.1	571.0	764.3	77.8	112.3	143.2	54.3	376.6
Educational services......................	61	110.4	159.2	180.4	14.5	31.8	39.2	12.8	82.3
Health care and social assistance.............	62	752.9	1,116.5	1,279.5	240.5	277.4	252.0	90.0	419.6
Arts, entertainment, and recreation...........	71	62.3	78.6	110.0	26.6	24.7	33.6	15.0	10.1
Accommodation and food services.............	72	185.6	249.5	353.1	95.8	186.6	46.9	9.4	14.4
Other services [1]........................	81	140.3	190.7	228.2	110.8	67.5	35.5	6.8	7.5
Unclassified establishments..................	99	0.3	0.6	0.6	0.5	(NA)	(NA)	(NA)	(NA)

NA Not available. X Not applicable. Z Less than 50 establishments, 500 employees, or $500 million. [1] Except public administration. [2] 10,000 to 24,999 employees.

Source: U.S. Census Bureau, County Business Patterns, "All Sectors: County Business Patterns, including ZIP Code Business Patterns, by Legal Form of Organization and Employment Size Class for the U.S., States, and Selected Geographies: 2022," <data.census.gov>, accessed June 2024. See also <www.census.gov/programs-surveys/cbp.html>.

Table 795. Employer Firms by Industry and Owner's Education and Age: 2021

[In thousands (4,355 represents 4,355,000). Includes all U.S. firms with paid employees operating during the survey reference year with receipts of $1,000 or more and classified in the 2017 North American Industry Classification System (NAICS). Based on the 2022 Annual Business Survey that collected data for 2021; see <www.census.gov/programs-surveys/abs/technical-documentation/methodology.html>]

Industry	NAICS code	Highest education level of owner						Age of owner			
		Total [1]	High school or less	Some college, no degree	Associate's or technical degree	Bachelor's degree	Advanced degree [2]	Total [1]	Under 35	35 to 64	65 or over
All industries [3]	(X)	4,355	902	590	476	1,361	1,025	4,355	233	3,131	992
Forestry, fishing & hunting, and agricultural support services	113-115	19	7	3	2	5	2	19	2	13	4
Mining, quarrying, and oil & gas extraction	21	15	4	3	1	5	1	15	1	9	5
Utilities	22	2	(Z)	(Z)	(Z)	1	(Z)	2	(Z)	2	1
Construction	23	555	200	98	106	123	28	555	29	421	105
Manufacturing	31-33	230	57	36	30	77	29	230	10	152	69
Wholesale trade	42	236	47	37	24	101	28	236	9	157	70
Retail trade	44-45	485	135	83	54	159	53	485	29	333	123
Transportation & warehousing [4]	48-49	129	51	23	18	29	9	129	9	93	27
Information	51	63	6	8	4	31	14	63	6	44	13
Finance & insurance [5]	52	182	16	26	12	94	35	182	7	127	48
Real estate & rental & leasing	53	266	38	40	24	117	46	266	11	173	82
Professional, scientific, & technical services	54	717	33	54	37	267	325	716	30	519	167
Management of companies & enterprises	55	17	2	2	1	9	3	17	(Z)	10	6
Administrative & support and waste management & remediation	56	253	68	47	32	78	28	253	16	187	51
Educational services	61	50	4	6	3	20	16	49	4	36	9
Health care & social assistance	62	446	14	15	17	53	346	446	22	338	86
Arts, entertainment, & recreation	71	86	13	12	7	39	15	86	7	62	17
Accommodation & food services	72	370	121	59	38	115	36	370	27	276	67
Other services (except public administration) [6]	81	274	89	41	68	57	19	274	18	202	55

X Not applicable. Z Less than 500. [1] Total firms that reported either education or age of owner in survey response. [2] Master's, doctorate, or professional degree. [3] Firms with more than one domestic establishment are counted in each industry in which they operate, but only once in the total. Includes unclassified industries, not shown separately. [4] Excludes rail transportation (NAICS 482) and the postal service (NAICS 491). [5] Excludes monetary authorities-central banks (NAICS 521) and funds, trusts, and other financial vehicles (NAICS 525). [6] Excludes religious, grantmaking, civic, professional, and similar organizations (NAICS 813) and private households (NAICS 814).

Source: U.S. Census Bureau, Annual Business Survey, Table AB2100CSCBO, "Owner Characteristics of Respondent Employer Firms by Sector, Sex, Ethnicity, Race, and Veteran Status for the U.S., States, and Metro Areas: 2021," <data.census.gov>, accessed November 2023.

Table 796. Telework Arrangements of Establishments and Employees by Frequency and Industry: 2022

[Estimates based on the 2022 Business Response Survey conducted in August and September 2022. Numbers in parenthesis are North American Industry Classification codes. Percentages may not sum due to rounding]

Item	Establishments		Employment in establishments	
	Number	Percent	Number	Percent
Any employees teleworking before the COVID-19 pandemic [1]	1,976,740	23.3	31,700,691	26.1
No employees teleworking before the COVID-19 pandemic [1]	6,594,584	76.7	89,388,647	73.9
2022				
Establishments with:				
All employees teleworking all of the time	996,374	11.1	4,082,025	3.3
Employees teleworking some of the time	1,464,501	16.4	39,206,590	31.9
All employees teleworking rarely or never	6,487,976	72.5	79,611,896	64.8
Establishments that expect the amount of time employees are permitted to telework will:				
Increase	163,114	1.8	2,945,910	2.4
Decrease	272,936	3.0	5,614,456	4.6
Stay about the same	8,512,801	95.1	114,340,145	93.0
EMPLOYEES TELEWORKING SOME OF THE TIME				
Total, private sector	**1,464,501**	**16.4**	**39,206,590**	**31.9**
Natural resources and mining (11-21)	7,937	5.9	257,526	14.5
Utilities (22)	4,226	21.0	192,338	35.2
Construction (23)	68,268	8.4	1,432,143	19.1
Manufacturing (31-33)	64,508	18.3	5,167,607	41.7
Wholesale trade (42)	125,979	21.8	2,024,453	35.2
Retail trade (44-45)	90,855	8.9	2,707,339	17.4
Transportation and warehousing (48-49)	25,200	9.2	1,624,894	26.9
Information (51)	54,898	25.2	1,522,058	53.0
Financial activities (52-53)	209,296	22.0	4,411,709	52.3
Professional and business services (54-56)	479,600	24.0	9,132,046	42.4
Educational services (61)	35,216	26.3	1,419,291	49.6
Health care and social assistance (62)	178,700	18.5	7,191,221	37.2
Arts, entertainment, and recreation (71)	23,345	15.2	514,776	25.8
Accommodation and food services (72)	12,895	1.8	546,756	4.4
Other services, except public administration (81)	83,631	13.7	1,062,432	26.8

[1] Pre-pandemic statistics reflect data for establishments open in February 2020.

Source: U.S. Bureau of Labor Statistics, "Business Response Survey on Telework, Hiring, and Vacancies, 2022," <www.bls.gov/brs/data/tables/2022/>, accessed April 2023.

Table 797. Franchised Businesses by Type of Business: 2017

[172,396 represents $172,396,000,000. Data shown for franchisor- and franchisee-owned establishments with paid employees]

Kind of business	NAICS code [1]	Establishments (number)	Revenue (mil. dol.)	Annual payroll (mil. dol.)	Paid employees (number)
Limited-service restaurants..............................	722513	144,941	172,396	44,141	3,214,717
Full-service restaurants...................................	722511	31,418	45,542	15,664	975,055
Hotels (except casino hotels) and motels..............	721110	31,244	125,148	28,340	1,039,949
New car dealers...	441110	21,637	906,487	62,676	1,166,388
Offices of real estate agents and brokers..............	531210	21,529	33,180	3,181	63,132
Beauty salons...	812112	21,462	6,586	2,759	134,598
Snack and nonalcoholic beverage bars.................	722515	21,011	13,388	3,437	252,050
Gasoline stations with convenience stores.............	447110	17,782	65,570	2,813	139,236
Electronics stores...	443142	10,992	32,564	2,421	125,385
Fitness and recreational sports centers................	713940	9,757	6,021	1,626	127,609
Tax preparation services.................................	541213	8,022	2,226	597	80,086
Janitorial services..	561720	7,484	6,092	2,184	103,885
Convenience stores.......................................	445120	5,282	9,052	792	40,781

[1] Based on the 2017 North American Industry Classification System (NAICS); see text, this section.

Source: U.S. Census Bureau, 2017 Economic Census, Table "EC1700FRAN: Selected Sectors: Franchise Status for the U.S. and States: 2017," <data.census.gov>, accessed November 2021.

Table 798. Employer Firms, Employment, and Payroll by Employment Size of Firm and State: 2020 and 2021

[6,141 represents 6,141,000. A firm is an aggregation of all establishments owned by a parent company (within a state) with some annual payroll. A firm may have an establishment in a single location or multiple establishments in more than one location]

State	Employer firms (1,000)						Employment (1,000), 2021			Annual payroll (bil. dol.), 2021		
	2020			2021								
	Total	Less than 20 employ-ees	Less than 500 employ-ees	Total	Less than 20 employ-ees	Less than 500 employ-ees	Total	Less than 20 employ-ees	Less than 500 employ-ees	Total	Less than 20 employ-ees	Less than 500 employ-ees
U.S.......	6,141	5,472	6,120	6,295	5,668	6,275	128,346	21,464	58,951	8,279	1,047	3,229
AL.........	75	62	72	77	65	75	1,719	277	803	87	11	37
AK.........	17	15	16	18	15	17	251	59	134	17	3	8
AZ.........	116	99	113	121	104	118	2,601	381	1,113	148	18	56
AR.........	51	44	49	52	45	50	1,030	178	489	51	7	21
CA.........	805	717	799	825	744	819	14,835	2,685	6,985	1,296	158	470
CO.........	146	127	142	150	132	146	2,417	458	1,147	161	24	66
CT.........	70	58	67	70	60	68	1,442	246	678	106	13	42
DE.........	22	18	21	24	19	22	409	72	201	27	4	12
DC.........	19	14	17	19	14	18	483	59	233	49	5	21
FL.........	485	441	480	511	466	505	8,877	1,491	3,627	492	68	178
GA.........	191	166	187	201	175	196	4,034	628	1,738	239	29	87
HI.........	25	21	24	25	22	24	469	83	238	26	4	12
ID.........	44	38	42	47	41	45	645	147	365	33	6	16
IL.........	255	221	250	258	226	253	5,271	806	2,298	354	42	138
IN.........	110	92	107	113	94	109	2,755	397	1,211	145	16	56
IA.........	63	53	61	64	55	62	1,352	216	617	70	9	29
KS.........	57	48	55	58	49	56	1,188	198	583	63	8	27
KY.........	67	56	64	68	57	65	1,617	238	685	81	9	30
LA.........	81	68	79	83	70	81	1,593	296	868	83	12	41
ME.........	34	30	33	35	31	34	505	112	275	27	5	13
MD.........	111	93	107	112	96	109	2,283	381	1,108	150	20	67
MA.........	144	123	140	145	126	142	3,176	489	1,396	264	29	101
MI.........	173	147	169	175	151	172	3,768	614	1,787	217	29	92
MN.........	119	101	116	121	104	118	2,627	395	1,192	167	19	64
MS.........	44	37	42	45	38	43	931	160	430	41	6	17
MO.........	116	98	112	117	100	114	2,478	389	1,112	138	16	52
MT.........	34	30	33	35	31	34	380	113	251	18	5	11
NE.........	44	37	42	45	38	43	852	149	414	45	6	19
NV.........	57	47	54	59	50	57	1,158	186	524	62	10	26
NH.........	31	26	29	31	26	30	587	110	294	37	6	17
NJ.........	193	168	190	195	172	192	3,571	653	1,729	256	34	105
NM.........	34	28	32	35	29	33	606	118	322	30	5	14
NY.........	457	408	452	456	414	452	7,887	1,422	3,651	664	78	244
NC.........	185	160	181	192	167	188	3,904	642	1,725	220	28	80
ND.........	20	16	19	20	17	19	333	68	190	19	3	10
OH.........	183	153	179	186	157	182	4,822	682	2,090	265	29	101
OK.........	73	62	71	74	64	72	1,347	252	696	67	10	31
OR.........	97	84	94	99	86	96	1,576	340	843	95	15	43
PA.........	230	196	225	233	201	228	5,280	824	2,396	317	37	124
RI.........	24	20	23	25	21	23	413	81	211	24	4	11
SC.........	87	74	84	90	77	88	1,936	306	823	94	13	36
SD.........	22	19	21	23	20	22	364	77	208	18	3	9
TN.........	102	84	98	105	88	102	2,704	381	1,127	147	17	55
TX.........	467	404	461	486	425	480	10,798	1,675	4,851	660	81	255
UT.........	73	64	71	77	67	74	1,434	233	655	80	10	33
VT.........	17	15	17	18	15	17	240	59	147	13	3	7
VA.........	156	133	152	160	138	156	3,341	543	1,536	218	26	88
WA.........	159	139	156	163	144	160	2,821	546	1,364	224	28	83
WV.........	26	21	24	26	21	24	519	92	248	24	3	10
WI.........	108	90	105	109	92	106	2,519	395	1,212	142	17	59
WY.........	19	16	18	19	17	19	199	62	129	10	3	6

Source: U.S. Census Bureau, Statistics of U.S. Businesses (SUSB), "2021 SUSB Annual Data Tables by Establishment Industry," and earlier releases, <www.census.gov/programs-surveys/susb/data/tables.html>, accessed February 2024.

Table 799. Employer Firms, Employment, and Annual Payroll by Employment Size of Firm and Industry: 2021

[6,295 represents 6,295,000. A firm is an aggregation of all establishments owned by a parent company (within a geographic location and/or industry) with some annual payroll. A firm may have an establishment in a single location or multiple establishments in more than one location. Employment is measured in March and payroll is annual; some firms may have zero employment in March but with paid employees at some time during the year. Numbers in parentheses represent 2017 North American Industry Classification System codes; see text, this section]

Industry and data type	Unit	Total	All industries—employment size of firm						
			0 to 4	5 to 9	10 to 19	20 to 99	100 to 499	Less than 500	500 or more
Total, all industries [1]:									
Firms..................................	1,000	6,295	4,010	1,022	637	519	88	6,275	20
Employment..........................	1,000	128,346	6,178	6,726	8,559	20,219	17,269	58,951	69,395
Annual payroll.......................	Bil. dol.	8,279	345	302	401	1,078	1,104	3,229	5,050
Construction (23):									
Firms..................................	1,000	765	512	122	69	53	7	763	1
Employment..........................	1,000	7,062	792	795	925	2,035	1,214	5,761	1,301
Annual payroll.......................	Bil. dol.	490	42	41	55	141	96	376	114
Manufacturing (31–33):									
Firms..................................	1,000	239	100	44	36	43	12	235	4
Employment..........................	1,000	11,710	178	292	487	1,763	2,086	4,807	6,904
Annual payroll.......................	Bil. dol.	785	10	13	24	100	130	277	508
Wholesale trade (42):									
Firms..................................	1,000	281	164	45	31	30	7	277	3
Employment..........................	1,000	5,926	267	297	412	1,147	1,057	3,180	2,746
Annual payroll.......................	Bil. dol.	498	18	19	28	82	83	229	268
Retail trade (44–45):									
Firms..................................	1,000	646	395	127	68	47	8	644	2
Employment..........................	1,000	15,531	695	832	895	1,770	1,115	5,306	10,225
Annual payroll.......................	Bil. dol.	541	26	27	32	83	61	228	313
Transportation & warehousing (48–49):									
Firms..................................	1,000	225	159	24	17	18	4	223	2
Employment..........................	1,000	5,694	202	159	228	714	603	1,907	3,787
Annual payroll.......................	Bil. dol.	317	10	8	11	35	31	95	222
Information (51):									
Firms..................................	1,000	88	59	11	7	7	2	87	1
Employment..........................	1,000	3,415	81	72	96	290	393	931	2,483
Annual payroll.......................	Bil. dol.	506	8	5	7	26	47	93	413
Finance & insurance (52):									
Firms..................................	1,000	245	180	35	13	11	4	244	2
Employment..........................	1,000	6,738	301	222	174	464	715	1,875	4,864
Annual payroll.......................	Bil. dol.	825	20	16	17	53	91	197	628
Professional, scientific and technical services (54):									
Firms..................................	1,000	860	644	104	58	43	8	857	3
Employment..........................	1,000	9,531	902	676	767	1,643	1,418	5,407	4,125
Annual payroll.......................	Bil. dol.	981	65	46	59	153	156	479	502
Management of companies and enterprises (55):									
Firms..................................	1,000	26	4	1	1	5	8	19	7
Employment..........................	1,000	3,484	4	3	7	66	284	365	3,120
Annual payroll.......................	Bil. dol.	435	1	(Z)	1	6	27	36	399
Administrative & support and waste management & remediation services (56):									
Firms..................................	1,000	370	242	54	32	30	8	366	4
Employment..........................	1,000	12,510	345	352	433	1,163	1,417	3,710	8,799
Annual payroll.......................	Bil. dol.	673	19	16	20	56	65	176	497
Educational services (61):									
Firms..................................	1,000	100	52	16	13	14	4	99	1
Employment..........................	1,000	3,488	77	109	170	598	679	1,632	1,856
Annual payroll.......................	Bil. dol.	167	3	3	5	23	33	67	101
Health care and social assistance (62):									
Firms..................................	1,000	683	363	135	89	73	18	678	4
Employment..........................	1,000	20,682	593	906	1,194	2,928	3,417	9,038	11,644
Annual payroll.......................	Bil. dol.	1,189	38	43	57	135	158	431	758
Accommodation and food services (72):									
Firms..................................	1,000	557	225	114	112	96	8	555	2
Employment..........................	1,000	12,142	351	762	1,529	3,391	1,458	7,491	4,651
Annual payroll.......................	Bil. dol.	299	16	18	36	83	35	188	110
Other services (except public administration) (81):									
Firms..................................	1,000	717	478	135	62	36	4	716	1
Employment..........................	1,000	5,105	834	876	819	1,278	549	4,357	748
Annual payroll.......................	Bil. dol.	206	29	29	30	51	28	166	40

Z Less than $500 million. [1] Includes other industries, not shown separately.

Source: U.S. Census Bureau, Statistics of U.S. Businesses (SUSB), "2021 SUSB Annual Data Tables by Establishment Industry," <www.census.gov/programs-surveys/susb/data/tables.html>, accessed February 2024.

Table 800. Employer Firms, Establishments, Employment, and Annual Payroll by Firm Size: 1990 to 2021

[5,074 represents 5,074,000. Firms are an aggregation of all establishments owned by a parent company with some annual payroll. Establishments are locations with active payroll in any quarter. This table illustrates the importance of changes in employment size over time, not job growth, as enterprises can grow or decline and change employment size cells over time]

Item	Total	Employment size of firm						
		0 to 4 [1]	5 to 9	10 to 19	20 to 99	100 to 499	Less than 500	500 or more
Firms (1,000):								
1990	5,074	3,021	952	563	454	70	5,060	14
2000	5,653	3,397	1,021	617	516	84	5,635	17
2010	5,735	3,575	968	617	475	82	5,717	17
2015	5,901	3,644	1,005	617	526	89	5,881	19
2020	6,141	3,828	1,005	639	553	95	6,120	21
2021	6,295	4,010	1,022	637	519	88	6,275	20
Establishments (1,000):								
1990	6,176	3,032	971	600	590	255	5,448	728
2000	7,070	3,406	1,035	652	674	312	6,080	990
2010	7,397	3,583	982	653	648	354	6,220	1,176
2015	7,664	3,650	1,016	649	698	367	6,380	1,284
2020	8,000	3,836	1,018	672	721	372	6,618	1,382
2021	8,149	4,019	1,037	672	690	365	6,783	1,366
Employment (1,000):								
1990	93,469	5,117	6,252	7,543	17,710	13,545	50,167	43,302
2000	114,065	5,593	6,709	8,286	20,277	16,260	57,124	56,941
2010	111,970	5,926	6,359	8,288	18,554	15,869	54,997	56,973
2015	124,086	5,877	6,614	8,298	20,645	17,503	58,938	65,148
2020	134,163	6,018	6,620	8,604	21,707	18,660	61,609	72,554
2021	128,346	6,178	6,726	8,559	20,219	17,269	58,951	69,395
Annual payroll (bil. dol.):								
1990	2,104	117	114	144	352	279	1,007	1,097
2000	3,879	186	174	231	608	528	1,727	2,152
2010	4,941	227	212	283	719	666	2,107	2,834
2015	6,253	263	244	322	876	846	2,551	3,702
2020	7,565	295	265	353	979	1,016	2,908	4,657
2021	8,279	345	302	401	1,078	1,104	3,229	5,050

[1] Employment is measured in March; therefore, some firms (start-ups after March, closures before March, and seasonal firms) will have zero employment and some annual payroll.

Source; U.S. Census Bureau, Statistics of U.S. Businesses (SUSB), "SUSB Historical Data," <www.census.gov/programs-surveys/susb/data/tables.html>, accessed February 2024.

Table 801. Firms with Employees Who Worked from Home by Industry: 2019

[2,686.0 represents 2,686,000. Based on the 2020 Annual Business Survey, see headnote Table 795]

Industry	2017 NAICS Code	Total reporting firms [1] (1,000)	Firms with employees who worked from home		Firms with no employees who worked from home	
			Number (1,000)	Percent	Number (1,000)	Percent
Total	(X)	**2,686.0**	**754.0**	**28.1**	**1,932.0**	**71.9**
Forestry, fishing & hunting, and agricultural support services	113-115	12.2	1.6	13.3	10.6	86.7
Mining, quarrying, and oil and gas extraction	21	7.9	2.0	25.8	5.9	74.2
Utilities	22	1.1	0.4	35.6	0.7	64.4
Construction	23	356.8	60.4	16.9	296.4	83.1
Manufacturing	31-33	104.5	20.4	19.6	84.0	80.4
Wholesale trade	42	144.8	56.8	39.2	88.0	60.8
Retail trade	44-45	276.4	36.0	13.0	240.4	87.0
Transportation and warehousing [2]	48-49	78.7	16.4	20.8	62.4	79.2
Information	51	30.6	20.7	67.6	9.9	32.4
Finance and insurance [3]	52	129.1	53.5	41.4	75.7	58.6
Real estate and rental and leasing	53	155.0	73.7	47.5	81.3	52.5
Professional, scientific, and technical services	54	448.6	257.4	57.4	191.2	42.6
Management of companies and enterprises	55	10.5	4.1	39.0	6.4	61.0
Administrative & support and waste management & remediation services	56	163.6	40.4	24.7	123.2	75.3
Educational services	61	31.6	11.6	36.7	20.0	63.3
Healthcare and social assistance	62	312.2	63.4	20.3	248.8	79.7
Arts, entertainment, and recreation	71	51.4	18.3	35.6	33.1	64.4
Accommodation and food services	72	209.2	9.6	4.6	199.7	95.4
Other services, except public administration [4]	81	182.5	17.1	9.4	165.4	90.6

X Not applicable. [1] Firms reporting whether they had employees who worked from home. [2] Excludes rail transportation (NAICS 482) and the postal service (NAICS 491). [3] Excludes central banks (NAICS 521) and funds, trusts, and other financial vehicles (NAICS 525). [4] Excludes religious, grantmaking, civic, professional, and similar organizations (NAICS 813) and private households (NAICS 814).

Source: U.S. Census Bureau, Annual Business Survey, "Business Characteristics of Respondent Employer Firms by Sector, Sex, Ethnicity, Race, and Veteran Status for the U.S., States, and Metro Areas: 2019," <data.census.gov>, accessed May 2022.

Table 802. Job Creation and Job Destruction of Active Establishments by Firm Age: 2021

[7,193 represents 7,193,000. An establishment is a single physical location where business is conducted or where services or industrial operations are performed. A firm is a business organization consisting of one or more domestic establishments that are under common ownership or control. Firms may have one or more establishments. The firm and the establishment are the same for single-establishment firms. Data cover nonfarm private establishments with paid employees; exclusions include self-employed individuals, employees of private households, and railroad, agricultural production, and most government employees. Data are from the Business Dynamics Statistics (BDS) program and compiled from the Longitudinal Business Database. The BDS program is based on the same basic source data as the Census Bureau's County Business Patterns and Statistics of U.S. Business programs, but differences in how the source data are processed lead to differences in published statistics. For more information, see <www.census.gov/programs-surveys/bds/documentation/methodology.html>]

Firm age [1]	Establish-ments (1,000)	Employees (1,000)	Percent of employ-ment	Job creation [2]		Job destruction [3]		Net job creation		
				Total (1,000)	Rate	Total (1,000)	Rate	Total (1,000)	Rate	Percent of net job creation
Total..........................	7,193	126,865	100.0	14,641	11.3	20,563	15.8	-5,922	-4.6	100.0
Startups.......................	479	2,183	1.7	2,183	200.0	(X)	(X)	2,183	200.0	-36.9
1 year.........................	357	2,342	1.8	622	26.3	655	27.7	-33	-1.4	0.6
2 years........................	318	2,275	1.8	454	19.5	567	24.3	-113	-4.8	1.9
3 years........................	279	2,249	1.8	408	17.7	529	22.9	-121	-5.2	2.0
4 years........................	256	2,181	1.7	376	16.7	507	22.6	-131	-5.8	2.2
5 years........................	237	2,103	1.7	326	15.0	473	21.8	-147	-6.8	2.5
6 to 10 years..................	898	9,592	7.6	1,272	12.8	2,005	20.1	-733	-7.4	12.4
11 to 15 years.................	705	8,602	6.8	1,012	11.3	1,680	18.8	-669	-7.5	11.3
16 to 20 years.................	579	8,402	6.6	896	10.3	1,456	16.8	-561	-6.5	9.5
21 to 25 years.................	478	7,950	6.3	760	9.2	1,455	17.5	-695	-8.4	11.7
26 years and older............	1,268	28,635	22.6	2,346	7.9	4,492	15.1	-2,146	-7.2	36.2
Unknown\left censored [4]....	1,339	50,350	39.7	4,006	7.7	6,748	13.0	-2,742	-5.3	46.3

X Not applicable. [1] Establishment age is computed by taking the difference between the current year of operation and the birth year. Firm age is computed from the age of the establishments belonging to that particular firm. [2] Job creation is employment gains from either establishments opening or establishments expanding. [3] Job destruction is all employment losses from either establishments contracting or establishments closing (shutting down). [4] Within the BDS, all firms/establishments born prior to 1976 have an unknown birth year and are therefore of an unknown age and are grouped into the age category "left censored."

Source: U.S. Census Bureau, Center for Economic Studies, "Business Dynamics Statistics (BDS)," <www.census.gov/programs-surveys/bds.html>, accessed November 2023.

Table 803. Establishments Born, Exited, and Jobs Created and Lost, 2000 to 2021, and by Employment Size of Establishment, 2021

[In thousands (6,301 represents 6,301,000), except rate. An establishment is a single physical location at which business is conducted or where services or industrial operations are performed]

Item	Establish-ments	Employees	Establishments born			Establishments exited		
			Number	Rate	Jobs created	Number	Rate	Jobs lost
2000..............................	6,301	113,581	681	10.8	6,159	629	10.0	5,366
2010..............................	6,672	111,312	637	9.5	4,769	707	10.5	4,730
2015..............................	6,910	123,231	689	10.0	5,378	605	8.8	4,301
2020..............................	7,177	132,734	680	9.5	5,166	667	9.3	4,752
2021, total.......................	7,193	126,865	754	10.5	4,980	737	10.3	5,153
Establishment size:								
1 to 4 employees...............	3,780	8,366	667	17.7	1,563	638	16.9	1,521
5 to 9 employees...............	1,355	9,415	46	3.4	617	53	3.9	707
10 to 19 employees............	946	13,011	23	2.4	621	27	2.8	725
20 to 99 employees............	925	36,145	16	1.8	1,244	18	1.9	1,310
100 to 499 employees.........	167	31,449	2	1.1	687	2	1.1	659
500 to 999 employees.........	13	8,875	(Z)	0.8	141	(Z)	0.7	121
1,000 employees or more.....	8	19,604	(Z)	0.4	108	(Z)	0.4	110

Z Less than 500 establishments.

Source: U.S. Census Bureau, "Business Dynamics Statistics (BDS)," <www.census.gov/programs-surveys/bds.html>, accessed November 2023.

Table 804. Small Business Administration Loans to Minority-Owned Small Businesses: 2000 to 2023

[3,675 represents $3,675,000,000. For year ending September 30. A small business must be independently owned and operated, must not be dominant in its particular industry, and must meet standards set by the Small Business Administration as to its annual receipts or number of employees. Includes 7(a) loans, 504 loans, and, beginning 2015, Community Advantage loans]

Year	Number of loans					Amount (mil. dol.)				
	Total minority loans [1]	Black	Asian or Pacific Islander	Hispanic	Amer-ican Indian	Total minority loans [1]	Black	Asian or Pacific Islander	Hispanic	Amer-ican Indian
2000...........	12,041	2,183	5,827	3,491	540	3,675	415	2,390	767	102
2010...........	11,235	1,707	5,942	3,192	387	3,982	345	2,743	806	86
2015...........	17,240	2,409	8,752	5,617	462	7,953	652	5,527	1,625	149
2019...........	15,091	2,464	6,972	5,249	406	8,188	779	5,387	1,845	177
2020...........	11,128	1,719	5,219	3,878	312	7,116	593	4,739	1,644	141
2021...........	16,163	2,742	7,792	5,192	437	12,911	1,068	8,753	2,812	278
2022...........	16,477	3,631	6,694	5,712	440	10,815	1,148	6,837	2,592	239
2023...........	20,556	4,779	7,500	7,747	529	11,171	1,454	6,433	3,005	278

[1] Beginning 2009, includes loans to business owners of other minority groups not shown separately.

Source: U.S. Small Business Administration; through 2016, "Weekly Lending Reports;" thereafter, "7(a) and 504 Summary Report," <data.sba.gov/dataset/office-of-capital-access>, accessed November 2023.

Table 805. Employer Firm Ownership by Industry and Sex, Race/Ethnicity, and Veteran Status: 2021

[In thousands (3,595.7 represents 3,595,700). Includes all U.S. firms with paid employees operating during the survey reference year with receipts of $1,000 or more and classified in the 2017 North American Industry Classification System (NAICS). Each owner had the option of selecting more than one race and is therefore included in each race selected. Race groups include persons of Hispanic and non-Hispanic ethnicity. Based on the 2022 Annual Business Survey that collected data for 2021]

Industry	NAICS code	Sex		Race/ethnicity						Veteran owned
		Male	Fe-male	White	Black	American Indian and Alaska Native	Asian	Native Hawaiian & other Pacific Islander	His-panic [1]	
All industries [2]	(X)	3,595.7	1,275.5	4,835.0	161.0	48.6	643.0	8.3	406.1	304.8
Agriculture, forestry, fishing and hunting [3]	11	17.0	3.4	24.7	0.1	(S)	0.3	(Z)	1.8	1.2
Mining, quarrying, and oil & gas extraction	21	11.9	(S)	15.7	(Z)	0.3	0.1	(Z)	0.8	1.0
Utilities	22	2.6	0.3	3.3	0.1	(Z)	0.1	(Z)	0.1	0.3
Construction	23	578.3	71.7	712.8	10.0	10.1	16.1	(S)	70.6	47.3
Manufacturing	31-33	160.3	35.5	213.5	2.1	1.3	11.6	0.2	11.5	15.2
Wholesale trade	42	191.7	45.3	232.0	2.8	1.5	35.7	(S)	16.3	16.4
Retail trade	44-45	377.6	136.7	498.0	10.3	3.9	114.9	(S)	33.9	26.3
Transportation & warehousing [4]	48-49	152.7	31.7	184.6	12.2	2.5	15.5	0.5	28.4	12.9
Information	51	55.9	13.1	68.9	1.9	0.6	7.3	0.1	3.8	3.1
Finance & insurance [5]	52	165.1	40.5	211.9	5.1	1.5	10.4	0.3	13.9	15.9
Real estate & rental & leasing	53	189.5	94.3	314.3	6.2	(S)	23.2	(S)	19.9	19.4
Professional, scientific, & technical services	54	539.5	209.4	731.6	22.4	5.9	73.9	1.1	44.7	52.2
Management of companies and enterprises	55	13.6	(S)	16.4	0.2	(Z)	1.0	(Z)	0.4	(S)
Administrative & support and waste management & remediation services	56	226.0	76.5	324.9	12.5	3.4	13.7	(S)	39.0	20.8
Educational services	61	26.6	32.3	57.7	3.4	0.6	8.1	(S)	3.9	3.4
Health care & social assistance	62	315.6	222.3	463.8	45.0	5.6	87.8	0.6	37.3	33.7
Arts, entertainment, & recreation	71	64.5	28.7	102.1	5.2	0.8	4.1	(S)	4.3	5.1
Accommodation & food services	72	311.6	118.2	364.3	8.7	4.8	151.9	0.9	46.8	14.4
Other services (except public administration) [6]	81	216.9	113.8	317.3	12.5	3.4	68.0	0.8	28.8	17.7
Industries not classified	99	6.8	2.8	11.3	0.7	0.2	0.8	(Z)	0.7	0.6

X Not applicable. S Data does not meet publication standards. Z Less than 50. [1] A Hispanic firm owner may be of any race and therefore may be included in more than one race group. [2] Firms with more than one domestic establishment are counted in each industry in which they operate but only once in the total. [3] Excludes crop production (NAICS 111) and animal production and aquaculture (NAICS 112). [4] Excludes rail transportation (NAICS 482) and the postal service (NAICS 491). [5] Excludes monetary authorities-central banks (NAICS 521) and funds, trusts, and other financial vehicles (NAICS 525). [6] Excludes religious, grantmaking, civic, professional, and similar organizations (NAICS 813) and private households (NAICS 814).

Source: U.S. Census Bureau, Annual Business Survey, Table AB2100CSA01, "Statistics for Employer Firms by Industry, Sex, Ethnicity, Race, and Veteran Status for the U.S., States, and Metro Areas: 2021," <data.census.gov>, accessed November 2023.

Table 806. Women-Owned Employer Firms by Kind of Business: 2021

[2,141,620,033 represents $2,141,620,033,000. Data are shown for U.S. firms with paid employees, operating during the survey reference year, and with receipts of $1,000 or more. Based on the 2022 Annual Business Survey that collected data for 2021; see <www.census.gov/programs-surveys/abs/technical-documentation/methodology.html>]

Kind of business	NAICS code [1]	Firms (number)	Sales, value of shipments, or revenue ($1,000)	Employees [2] (number)	Annual payroll ($1,000)
Total [3]	(X)	1,275,523	2,141,620,033	10,547,062	499,390,485
Forestry, fishing & hunting, and agricultural support services	113–115	3,399	([7])	34,332	1,297,258
Mining, quarrying, and oil & gas extraction	21	(S)	(S)	([10])	(S)
Utilities	22	326	([7])	3,123	254,516
Construction	23	71,652	([8])	638,691	42,553,574
Manufacturing	31–33	35,519	([8])	630,794	34,132,079
Wholesale trade	42	45,282	([8])	413,910	26,987,391
Retail trade	44–45	136,689	([8])	859,694	29,775,918
Transportation and warehousing [4]	48–49	31,700	([8])	285,997	13,050,158
Information	51	13,050	([8])	103,591	11,174,292
Finance and insurance [5]	52	40,542	([8])	243,305	18,501,569
Real estate and rental and leasing	53	94,295	([8])	299,165	17,264,980
Professional, scientific, and technical services	54	209,381	([8])	1,074,195	77,385,018
Management of companies and enterprises	55	(S)	(S)	([11])	(S)
Administrative & support and waste management & remediation services	56	76,457	([8])	1,389,880	70,928,183
Educational services	61	32,280	([8])	282,109	9,311,458
Health care and social assistance	62	222,341	([8])	2,143,909	81,745,446
Arts, entertainment, and recreation	71	28,665	([8])	155,404	7,310,676
Accommodation and food services	72	118,164	([8])	1,417,652	34,891,300
Other services (except public administration) [6]	81	113,807	([8])	489,531	15,419,518
Industries not classified	99	2,761	([9])	4,785	159,929

X Not applicable. S Estimate does not meet publication standards. [1] Based on the 2017 North American Industry Classification System (NAICS); see text, this section. [2] Paid employees for pay period including March 12. [3] Firms with more than one domestic establishment are counted in each industry in which they operate, but only once in the total. [4] Excludes rail transportation (NAICS 482) and the postal service (NAICS 491). [5] Excludes monetary authorities-central banks (NAICS 521) and funds, trusts, and other financial vehicles (NAICS 525). [6] Excludes religious, grantmaking, civic, professional, and similar organizations (NAICS 813) and private households (NAICS 814). [7] $1 billion to less than $5 billion dollars. [8] $5 billion dollars or more. [9] $500 million to less than $1 billion dollars. [10] 10,000 to 24,999 employees. [11] 50,000 to 99,999 employees.

Source: U.S. Census Bureau, Annual Business Survey, Table AB2100CSA01, "Statistics for Employer Firms by Industry, Sex, Ethnicity, Race, and Veteran Status for the U.S., States, and Metro Areas: 2021," <data.census.gov>, accessed November 2023.

Table 807. Minority-Owned Employer Firms by Kind of Business: 2021

[1,847,924,133 represents $1,847,924,133,000. Data are shown for U.S. firms with paid employees, operating during the survey reference year, and with receipts of $1,000 or more. Based on the 2022 Annual Business Survey that collected data for 2021; see <www.census.gov/programs-surveys/abs/technical-documentation/methodology.html>]

Kind of business	NAICS code [1]	Firms (number)	Sales, value of shipments, or revenue ($1,000)	Employees [2] (number)	Annual payroll ($1,000)
Total [3]	(X)	1,230,751	1,847,924,133	9,549,207	411,537,164
Forestry, fishing & hunting, and agricultural support services	113–115	2,418	([7])	78,416	2,613,854
Mining, quarrying, and oil & gas extraction	21	1,205	([8])	10,862	737,758
Utilities	22	308	([8])	1,843	170,128
Construction	23	100,674	([7])	558,802	30,182,325
Manufacturing	31–33	26,117	([7])	390,310	20,003,067
Wholesale trade	42	55,439	([7])	368,670	22,957,936
Retail trade	44–45	161,726	([7])	849,822	27,270,911
Transportation and warehousing [4]	48–49	56,770	([7])	345,518	14,626,079
Information	51	13,282	([7])	116,666	14,834,788
Finance and insurance [5]	52	30,058	([7])	158,245	11,620,215
Real estate and rental and leasing	53	50,280	([7])	151,713	7,937,752
Professional, scientific, and technical services	54	144,264	([7])	841,565	71,313,283
Management of companies and enterprises	55	1,615	(S)	28,542	2,782,126
Administrative & support and waste management & remediation services	56	66,398	([7])	1,046,059	40,654,531
Educational services	61	15,544	([7])	82,448	2,344,194
Health care and social assistance	62	171,862	([7])	1,654,049	65,811,014
Arts, entertainment, and recreation	71	14,180	([7])	59,986	4,294,964
Accommodation and food services	72	209,233	([7])	2,374,316	57,942,577
Other services (except public administration) [6]	81	109,760	([7])	427,834	13,296,647
Industries not classified	99	2,234	([9])	3,543	143,012

X Not applicable. S Data does not meet publishing standards. [1] Based on the 2017 North American Industry Classification System (NAICS); see text, this section. [2] Paid employees for pay period including March 12. [3] Firms with more than one domestic establishment are counted in each industry in which they operate, but only once in the total. [4] Excludes rail transportation (NAICS 482) and the postal service (NAICS 491). [5] Excludes monetary authorities-central banks (NAICS 521) and funds, trusts, and other financial vehicles (NAICS 525). [6] Excludes religious, grantmaking, civic, professional, and similar organizations (NAICS 813) and private households (NAICS 814). [7] $5 billion or more. [8] $1 billion to less than $5 billion. [9] $500 million to less than $1 billion.

Source: U.S. Census Bureau, Annual Business Survey (ABS), Table AB2100CSA01, "Statistics for Employer Firms by Industry, Sex, Ethnicity, Race, and Veteran Status for the U.S., States, and Metro Areas: 2021," <data.census.gov>, accessed November 2023.

Table 808. Hispanic-Owned Employer Firms by Kind of Business: 2021

[572,911,936 represents $572,911,936,000. Data are shown for U.S. firms with paid employees, operating during the survey reference year, and with receipts of $1,000 or more. Based on the 2022 Annual Business Survey that collected data for 2021; see <www.census.gov/programs-surveys/abs/technical-documentation/methodology.html>]

Kind of business	NAICS code [1]	Firms (number)	Sales, value of shipments, or revenue ($1,000)	Employees [2] (number)	Annual payroll ($1,000)
Total [3]	(X)	406,086	572,911,936	2,985,954	124,404,221
Forestry, fishing & hunting, and agricultural support services	113–115	1,771	([10])	72,922	2,428,363
Mining, quarrying, and oil & gas extraction	21	755	([9])	7,048	435,453
Utilities	22	136	([8])	617	50,544
Construction	23	70,571	([10])	391,742	20,397,810
Manufacturing	31–33	11,547	([10])	152,807	7,401,079
Wholesale trade	42	16,298	([10])	108,359	6,172,366
Retail trade	44–45	33,923	([10])	205,066	7,044,594
Transportation and warehousing [4]	48–49	28,354	([10])	139,855	6,308,762
Information	51	3,816	([10])	17,389	1,554,188
Finance and insurance [5]	52	13,880	([10])	76,955	5,098,754
Real estate and rental and leasing	53	19,883	([10])	62,866	3,223,989
Professional, scientific, and technical services	54	44,684	([10])	194,104	13,124,234
Management of companies and enterprises	55	447	(S)	9,145	704,110
Administrative & support and waste management & remediation services	56	38,963	([10])	464,493	17,515,316
Educational services	61	3,874	([9])	18,218	572,534
Health care and social assistance	62	37,269	([10])	326,066	12,016,853
Arts, entertainment, and recreation	71	4,323	([9])	16,958	730,120
Accommodation and food services	72	46,795	([10])	610,429	15,652,064
Other services (except public administration) [6]	81	28,767	([10])	109,470	3,932,034
Industries not classified	99	742	([7])	1,444	41,056

X Not applicable. S Data does not meet publication standards. [1] Based on the 2017 North American Industry Classification System (NAICS); see text, this section. [2] Paid employees for pay period including March 12. [3] Firms with more than one domestic establishment are counted in each industry in which they operate, but only once in the total. [4] Excludes rail transportation (NAICS 482) and the postal service (NAICS 491). [5] Excludes monetary authorities-central banks (NAICS 521) and funds, trusts, and other financial vehicles (NAICS 525). [6] Excludes religious, grantmaking, civic, professional, and similar organizations (NAICS 813) and private households (NAICS 814). [7] $150 million to less than $500 million. [8] $500 million to less than $1 billion. [9] $1 billion to less than $5 billion. [10] $5 billion or more.

Source: U.S. Census Bureau, Annual Business Survey, Table AB2100CSA01, "Statistics for Employer Firms by Industry, Sex, Ethnicity, Race, and Veteran Status for the U.S., States, and Metro Areas: 2021," <data.census.gov>, accessed November 2023.

Table 809. Black-Owned Employer Firms by Kind of Business: 2021

[183,299,174 represents $183,299,174,000. Data are shown for U.S. firms with paid employees, operating during the survey reference year, and with receipts of $1,000 or more. Based on the 2022 Annual Business Survey that collected data for 2021; see <www.census.gov/programs-surveys/abs/technical-documentation/methodology.html>]

Kind of business	NAICS code [1]	Firms (number)	Sales, value of shipments, or revenue ($1,000)	Employees [2] (number)	Annual payroll ($1,000)
Total [3]	(X)	161,031	183,299,174	1,407,659	53,632,835
Forestry, fishing & hunting, and agricultural support services	113–115	70	[8]	1,202	21,486
Mining, quarrying, and oil & gas extraction	21	31	[7]	81	5,540
Utilities	22	74	[10]	285	15,311
Construction	23	10,044	[12]	52,025	2,795,097
Manufacturing	31–33	2,065	[12]	30,888	1,494,349
Wholesale trade	42	2,818	[12]	16,786	935,557
Retail trade	44–45	10,312	[12]	53,948	1,907,151
Transportation and warehousing [4]	48–49	12,154	[12]	96,537	2,953,753
Information	51	1,893	[11]	15,110	1,416,347
Finance and insurance [5]	52	5,080	[11]	15,678	960,768
Real estate and rental and leasing	53	6,210	[11]	21,176	823,199
Professional, scientific, and technical services	54	22,411	[12]	123,963	8,991,131
Management of companies and enterprises	55	155	(S)	3,116	203,916
Administrative & support and waste management & remediation services	56	12,470	[12]	248,339	8,908,172
Educational services	61	3,385	[11]	17,677	600,063
Health care and social assistance	62	45,015	[12]	502,202	14,829,497
Arts, entertainment, and recreation	71	5,196	[12]	13,943	2,097,128
Accommodation and food services	72	8,742	[12]	144,380	2,999,864
Other services (except public administration) [6]	81	12,468	[12]	49,398	1,646,009
Industries not classified	99	677	[9]	926	28,498

X Not applicable. S Data does not meet publication standards. [1] Based on the 2017 North American Industry Classification System (NAICS); see text, this section. [2] Paid employees for pay period including March 12. [3] Firms with more than one domestic establishment are counted in each industry in which they operate, but only once in the total. [4] Excludes rail transportation (NAICS 482) and the postal service (NAICS 491). [5] Excludes monetary authorities-central banks (NAICS 521) and funds, trusts, and other financial vehicles (NAICS 525). [6] Excludes religious, grantmaking, civic, professional, and similar organizations (NAICS 813) and private households (NAICS 814). [7] $15 million to less than $50 million. [8] $50 million to less than $75 million. [9] $150 million to less than $500 million. [10] $500 million to less than $1 billion. [11] $1 billion to less than $5 billion. [12] $5 billion or more.

Source: U.S. Census Bureau, Annual Business Survey, Table AB2100CSA01, "Statistics for Employer Firms by Industry, Sex, Ethnicity, Race, and Veteran Status for the U.S., States, and Metro Area: 2021," <data.census.gov>, accessed November 2023.

Table 810. Asian-Owned Employer Firms by Kind of Business: 2021

[1,049,841,988 represents $1,049,841,988,000. Data are shown for U.S. firms with paid employees, operating during the survey reference year, and with receipts of $1,000 or more. Based on the 2022 Annual Business Survey that collected data for 2021; see <www.census.gov/programs-surveys/abs/technical-documentation/methodology.html>]

Kind of business	NAICS code [1]	Firms (number)	Sales, value of shipments, or revenue ($1,000)	Employees [2] (number)	Annual payroll ($1,000)
Total [3]	(X)	642,950	1,049,841,988	4,963,171	222,536,174
Forestry, fishing & hunting, and agricultural support services	113–115	315	[7]	3,871	114,961
Mining, quarrying, and oil & gas extraction	21	120	[8]	948	84,793
Utilities	22	77	[8]	859	94,897
Construction	23	16,144	[10]	82,317	5,096,666
Manufacturing	31–33	11,616	[10]	193,997	10,457,986
Wholesale trade	42	35,707	[10]	238,300	15,567,880
Retail trade	44–45	114,886	[10]	578,719	17,856,136
Transportation and warehousing [4]	48–49	15,512	[10]	100,410	4,910,317
Information	51	7,270	[10]	80,962	11,609,743
Finance and insurance [5]	52	10,418	[10]	64,190	5,308,308
Real estate and rental and leasing	53	23,166	[10]	64,318	3,696,967
Professional, scientific, and technical services	54	73,938	[10]	496,529	47,025,813
Management of companies and enterprises	55	978	(S)	15,721	1,808,811
Administrative & support and waste management & remediation services	56	13,692	[10]	308,716	13,199,283
Educational services	61	8,092	[9]	44,486	1,112,591
Health care and social assistance	62	87,824	[10]	806,069	37,390,762
Arts, entertainment, and recreation	71	4,112	[9]	25,658	1,084,761
Accommodation and food services	72	151,933	[10]	1,593,051	38,667,887
Other services (except public administration) [6]	81	68,007	[10]	262,879	7,373,494
Industries not classified	99	768	[7]	1,172	74,119

X Not applicable. S Data does not meet publication standards. [1] Based on the 2017 North American Industry Classification System (NAICS); see text, this section. [2] Paid employees for pay period including March 12. [3] Firms with more than one domestic establishment are counted in each industry in which they operate, but only once in the total. [4] Excludes rail transportation (NAICS 482) and the postal service (NAICS 491). [5] Excludes monetary authorities-central banks (NAICS 521) and funds, trusts, and other financial vehicles (NAICS 525). [6] Excludes religious, grantmaking, civic, professional, and similar organizations (NAICS 813) and private households (NAICS 814). [7] $150 million to less than $500 million. [8] $500 million to less than $1 billion. [9] $1 billion to less than $5 billion. [10] $5 billion or more.

Source: U.S. Census Bureau, Annual Business Survey, Table AB2100CSA01, "Statistics for Employer Firms by Industry, Sex, Ethnicity, Race, and Veteran Status for the U.S., States, and Metro Areas: 2021," <data.census.gov/>, accessed November 2023.

Table 811. American Indian and Alaska Native-Owned Employer Firms by Kind of Business: 2021

[54,372,040 represents $54,372,040,000. Data are shown for U.S. firms with paid employees, operating during the survey reference year, and with receipts of $1,000 or more. Based on the 2022 Annual Business Survey that collected data for 2021; see <www.census.gov/programs-surveys/abs/technical-documentation/methodology.html>]

Kind of business	NAICS code [1]	Firms (number)	Sales, value of shipments, or revenue ($1,000)	Employees [2] (number)	Annual payroll ($1,000)
Total [3]	(X)	**48,582**	**54,372,040**	**307,933**	**12,948,023**
Forestry, fishing & hunting, and agricultural support services	113–115	(S)	(S)	([12])	(S)
Mining, quarrying, and oil & gas extraction	21	305	([9])	2,784	213,163
Utilities	22	21	([8])	78	9,154
Construction	23	10,065	([11])	57,019	2,994,100
Manufacturing	31–33	1,344	([10])	13,945	645,676
Wholesale trade	42	1,455	([11])	8,754	444,058
Retail trade	44–45	3,881	([11])	17,455	567,657
Transportation and warehousing [4]	48–49	2,525	([10])	14,893	630,237
Information	51	635	([9])	2,353	162,486
Finance and insurance [5]	52	1,467	([9])	4,410	212,331
Real estate and rental and leasing	53	(S)	(S)	([12])	(S)
Professional, scientific, and technical services	54	5,931	([10])	25,820	1,736,222
Management of companies and enterprises	55	17	(S)	252	24,874
Administrative & support and waste management & remediation services	56	3,404	([10])	36,298	1,293,128
Educational services	61	585	([8])	1,748	52,195
Health care and social assistance	62	5,625	([10])	44,247	1,413,084
Arts, entertainment, and recreation	71	842	([9])	3,882	415,688
Accommodation and food services	72	4,816	([10])	47,686	1,109,929
Other services (except public administration) [6]	81	3,380	([10])	14,299	593,488
Industries not classified	99	179	([7])	267	5,536

X Not applicable. S Data does not meet publication standards. [1] Based on the 2017 North American Industry Classification System (NAICS); see text, this section. [2] Paid employees for pay period including March 12. [3] Firms with more than one domestic establishment are counted in each industry in which they operate, but only once in the total. [4] Excludes rail transportation (NAICS 482) and the postal service (NAICS 491). [5] Excludes monetary authorities-central banks (NAICS 521) and funds, trusts, and other financial vehicles (NAICS 525). [6] Excludes religious, grantmaking, civic, professional, and similar organizations (NAICS 813) and private households (NAICS 814). [7] $15 million to less than $50 million. [8] $150 million to less than $500 million. [9] $500 million to less than $1 billion. [10] $1 billion to less than $5 billion. [11] $5 billion or more. [12] 5,000 to 9,999 employees.

Source: U.S. Census Bureau, Annual Business Survey, Table AB2100CSA01, "Statistics for Employer Firms by Industry, Sex, Ethnicity, Race, and Veteran Status for the U.S., States, and Metro Areas: 2021," <data.census.gov>, accessed November 2023.

Table 812. Bankruptcy Petitions by Type and Chapter: 2000 to 2023

[For years ending June 30. Covers only bankruptcy cases filed under the Bankruptcy Reform Act of 1978. Bankruptcy: legal recognition that a company or individual is insolvent and must restructure or liquidate assets. Section 101 of the U.S. Bankruptcy Code defines consumer (nonbusiness) debt as that incurred by an individual primarily for a personal, family, or household purpose. If the debtor is a corporation or partnership, or if debt related to operation of a business predominates, the nature of the debt is business]

Item	2000	2005	2010	2015	2019	2020	2021	2022	2023
Total filed	**1,276,922**	**1,637,254**	**1,572,597**	**879,736**	**773,361**	**682,363**	**462,309**	**380,634**	**418,724**
Chapter 7 [1]	885,447	1,196,212	1,133,320	568,679	479,043	440,593	335,886	239,750	239,125
Chapter 9 [2]	8	6	12	7	3	6	4	1	5
Chapter 11 [3]	9,947	6,703	14,272	6,672	7,007	7,355	6,871	4,429	5,986
Chapter 12 [4]	732	290	660	357	535	580	438	201	147
Chapter 13 [5]	380,770	433,945	424,242	303,945	286,635	233,644	118,864	136,169	173,362
Section 304 [6]	18	98	(X)	(X)	(X)	(X)	(X)	(X)	(X)
Chapter 15 [7]	(X)	(X)	91	76	138	185	246	84	99
Business [8]	**36,910**	**32,406**	**59,608**	**25,046**	**22,483**	**22,482**	**18,511**	**12,748**	**15,724**
Nonbusiness [9]	**1,240,012**	**1,604,848**	**1,512,989**	**854,690**	**750,878**	**659,881**	**443,798**	**367,886**	**403,000**
Chapter 7 [1]	864,183	1,174,681	1,091,322	551,808	464,978	426,876	325,420	232,115	230,406
Chapter 11 [3]	722	847	1,827	1,078	1,039	777	496	464	409
Chapter 13 [5]	375,107	429,315	419,836	301,802	284,861	232,228	117,882	135,307	172,185
Total pending	**1,400,416**	**1,750,562**	**1,659,399**	**1,316,672**	**1,032,572**	**954,786**	**807,243**	**694,287**	**660,128**

X Not applicable. [1] Chapter 7, liquidation of nonexempt assets of businesses or individuals. [2] Chapter 9, adjustment of debts of a municipality. [3] Chapter 11, individual or business reorganization. [4] Chapter 12, adjustment of debts of a family farmer with regular income, effective November 26, 1986. [5] Chapter 13, adjustment of debts of an individual with regular income. [6] Chapter 11, U.S.C., Section 304, cases ancillary to foreign proceedings. [7] Chapter 15 was added and Section 304 was terminated by changes in Bankruptcy Laws effective October 2005. [8] Business bankruptcies include those filed under Chapters 7, 9, 11, 12, 13, or 15. [9] Includes other petitions, not shown separately.

Source: Administrative Office of the United States Courts, "Caseload Statistics Data Tables," <www.uscourts.gov/statistics-reports/caseload-statistics-data-tables>, accessed February 2024.

Table 813. Bankruptcy Cases Filed by State: 2000 to 2023

[In thousands (1,276.9 represents 1,276,900). For years ending June 30. Covers only bankruptcy cases filed under the Bankruptcy Reform Act of 1978. Bankruptcy: legal recognition that a company or individual is insolvent and must restructure or liquidate. Petitions "filed" means the commencement of a proceeding through the presentation of a petition to the clerk of the court]

State	2000	2005	2010	2015	2017	2018	2019	2020	2021	2022	2023
Total [1]	**1,276.9**	**1,637.3**	**1,572.6**	**879.7**	**796.0**	**775.6**	**773.4**	**682.4**	**462.3**	**380.6**	**418.7**
Alabama	31.4	42.6	34.9	25.2	27.2	26.7	26.6	24.2	15.3	15.3	17.5
Alaska	1.4	1.6	1.1	0.4	0.5	0.4	0.5	0.4	0.3	0.2	0.2
Arizona	21.7	32.4	40.7	18.0	15.4	16.1	16.7	15.6	11.7	9.0	9.0
Arkansas	16.3	25.5	16.9	10.4	10.7	10.5	10.6	9.7	5.9	5.2	5.9
California	160.6	122.6	242.0	91.9	73.4	69.5	69.0	61.7	46.5	33.5	33.8
Colorado	15.6	30.2	31.9	16.0	12.5	11.8	11.4	10.1	7.5	5.3	5.7
Connecticut	11.4	11.8	11.3	6.6	5.7	5.9	6.2	5.4	3.4	2.6	2.8
Delaware	4.9	3.6	4.5	2.7	2.8	3.2	2.9	3.1	2.5	1.3	1.7
District of Columbia	2.6	1.9	1.3	0.8	0.7	0.8	0.8	0.7	0.4	0.2	0.3
Florida	74.0	85.8	107.4	62.4	44.7	41.3	45.8	42.7	34.5	28.0	26.7
Georgia	57.9	77.3	77.8	51.1	48.1	45.7	44.5	38.4	22.4	21.6	26.2
Hawaii	5.0	3.2	3.7	1.6	1.4	1.5	1.6	1.6	1.5	1.0	1.0
Idaho	7.3	9.7	8.3	4.4	3.8	3.7	3.7	3.3	2.4	1.6	1.6
Illinois	62.3	83.6	80.8	58.8	52.3	49.7	47.9	42.1	24.3	19.6	22.4
Indiana	37.5	55.9	49.3	28.0	24.0	23.0	23.0	20.7	15.8	13.3	13.9
Iowa	8.2	14.3	10.4	4.7	4.2	4.6	4.7	4.6	3.2	2.4	2.6
Kansas	11.4	17.3	11.4	7.2	6.8	6.8	6.8	5.7	3.9	3.2	3.4
Kentucky	20.8	29.2	26.0	15.8	15.5	15.4	15.1	13.9	9.9	8.4	9.6
Louisiana	23.1	31.1	19.5	14.3	13.4	13.5	13.3	10.7	6.5	6.4	7.9
Maine	4.1	4.7	4.1	2.0	1.4	1.5	1.4	1.3	0.8	0.6	0.6
Maryland	31.1	28.5	29.1	19.0	17.5	17.5	17.4	15.0	9.2	7.5	8.5
Massachusetts	16.7	19.6	22.9	9.6	8.6	8.5	8.1	6.2	3.6	3.4	3.6
Michigan	36.4	68.5	71.0	33.6	30.6	30.2	30.0	26.8	18.7	16.0	18.0
Minnesota	15.4	19.4	22.6	11.3	9.6	9.9	9.8	9.1	5.8	5.5	6.1
Mississippi	17.9	21.8	14.8	10.9	11.9	12.6	12.6	11.5	6.6	6.5	8.6
Missouri	26.3	39.2	32.9	19.9	18.4	17.8	17.0	15.3	10.7	8.8	9.2
Montana	3.3	4.4	3.1	1.4	1.3	1.3	1.3	1.1	0.7	0.6	0.6
Nebraska	5.6	9.6	7.9	4.3	4.0	4.0	4.1	3.8	3.0	2.3	2.2
Nevada	14.3	16.3	31.0	10.2	8.9	9.0	9.8	8.8	8.0	5.8	6.0
New Hampshire	3.9	4.9	5.7	2.3	1.8	1.8	1.8	1.5	0.8	0.7	0.7
New Jersey	38.7	40.7	39.7	26.1	26.5	26.7	25.9	20.0	11.9	10.3	11.0
New Mexico	7.1	10.1	6.6	3.6	3.4	3.3	3.2	2.8	1.9	1.2	1.0
New York	61.7	81.7	58.2	30.9	31.6	34.2	35.5	28.4	17.3	14.1	17.5
North Carolina	25.8	37.5	27.7	16.2	14.7	14.3	13.4	11.9	7.1	6.1	6.8
North Dakota	2.0	2.5	1.6	0.6	0.8	0.8	0.8	0.7	0.6	0.4	0.4
Ohio	53.6	95.8	72.9	39.9	37.4	37.9	37.2	33.3	22.7	18.5	19.6
Oklahoma	19.3	28.2	15.1	9.4	9.5	9.6	9.5	8.7	6.5	5.3	5.7
Oregon	18.1	25.3	20.1	11.5	9.1	9.0	8.9	8.2	5.5	4.0	4.9
Pennsylvania	43.8	62.3	38.8	22.7	22.4	21.7	21.4	17.9	12.0	9.6	10.5
Rhode Island	4.8	4.4	5.4	2.7	2.2	2.3	2.0	1.7	1.2	0.9	0.8
South Carolina	11.7	15.2	9.7	7.1	6.6	6.6	6.8	6.1	3.7	3.4	3.8
South Dakota	2.1	2.9	2.0	1.2	1.0	1.1	1.0	0.9	0.7	0.5	0.6
Tennessee	47.1	60.8	52.5	37.3	35.8	34.5	34.0	29.0	17.4	16.0	19.2
Texas	62.9	97.5	57.8	34.7	35.6	33.5	35.2	32.3	22.1	18.9	22.9
Utah	14.4	20.5	17.0	13.0	11.7	10.3	9.6	8.8	6.6	5.2	5.4
Vermont	1.6	1.7	1.7	0.7	0.5	0.6	0.6	0.5	0.3	0.2	0.2
Virginia	37.1	38.8	37.8	23.2	22.8	22.8	22.9	20.6	14.1	11.1	12.5
Washington	31.2	37.7	33.5	19.7	15.5	13.9	13.0	10.9	7.1	5.2	5.7
West Virginia	8.2	12.6	6.6	3.3	3.4	3.1	2.9	2.7	1.9	1.5	1.4
Wisconsin	18.0	29.0	30.0	19.9	17.1	16.9	16.4	14.2	10.5	8.0	8.0
Wyoming	2.0	2.5	1.5	0.9	1.0	1.0	0.9	0.7	0.7	0.5	0.4

[1] Includes Island Areas, not shown separately.

Source: Administrative Office of the United States Courts, "Caseload Statistics Data Tables," <www.uscourts.gov/statistics-reports/caseload-statistics-data-tables>, accessed February 2024.

Table 814. Patent and Trademark Applications and Issuances: 2010 to 2023

[For the fiscal year ending September 30. Covers U.S. patents issued to citizens of the United States and residents of foreign countries]

Type	2010	2015	2017	2018	2019	2020	2021	2022	2023 (P)
Patent applications filed..................	510,060	618,062	650,350	647,572	666,843	653,311	650,654	647,320	650,519
Utility [1]...................................	479,332	578,121	604,298	599,174	619,017	603,669	593,294	589,572	594,143
Reissue...................................	1,138	1,087	1,049	989	1,096	1,153	1,140	1,247	931
Plant (botanical)...........................	1,013	1,119	1,071	1,049	1,159	1,050	964	933	813
Design....................................	28,577	37,735	43,932	46,360	45,571	46,105	54,201	54,476	53,665
Patents issued.............................	233,127	322,448	347,372	339,512	370,423	399,055	374,590	353,107	346,152
Utility [1]...................................	207,915	295,459	315,367	306,912	336,846	360,784	338,334	318,496	310,245
Reissue...................................	861	531	392	500	554	608	513	458	446
Plant (botanical)...........................	978	1,020	1,246	1,251	1,193	1,350	1,269	1,081	788
Design....................................	23,373	25,438	30,367	30,849	31,830	36,313	34,474	33,072	34,673
Trademarks:									
Applications including additional classes [2]...........................	368,939	503,889	594,107	638,847	673,233	738,112	943,928	787,795	737,018
Applications filed [2]........................	280,649	369,877	435,384	468,926	494,513	553,505	732,007	570,077	537,182
Trademarks registered.....................	164,330	208,660	242,709	273,808	297,774	295,728	337,814	362,597	316,322
Trademarks renewed.......................	46,734	58,284	84,727	90,192	72,270	71,575	65,063	74,662	93,328

P Preliminary. [1] Utility patents include chemical, electrical, and mechanical applications. [2] "Applications filed" refers to the number of individual trademark applications received by the USPTO. There are, however, 47 different classes of items in which a trademark may be registered. An application must request registration in at least one class, but may request registration in multiple classes. Each class application must be individually researched for registerability. "Applications filed, including additional classes" reflects this fact.

Source: U.S. Patent and Trademark Office, "FY2023 Workload Tables," <www.uspto.gov/about-us/performance-and-planning/uspto-annual-reports>, accessed March 2024.

Table 815. Patents Issued and Trademarks Registered by State: 2022 and 2023

[For the fiscal year ending September 30. Includes only U.S. patents and trademarks granted to residents of the United States and territories]

State	Patents issued		Trademarks registered		State	Patents issued		Trademarks registered	
	2022	2023 (P)	2022	2023 (P)		2022	2023 (P)	2022	2023 (P)
Total [1]....................	155,598	156,197	174,759	176,214	Missouri................	1,212	1,187	2,246	2,200
Alabama..................	550	497	962	1,095	Montana................	218	185	490	441
Alaska....................	56	45	131	110	Nebraska...............	336	345	600	614
Arizona...................	2,938	2,830	3,369	3,486	Nevada.................	895	1,023	2,708	2,862
Arkansas.................	313	346	696	703	New Hampshire........	883	842	583	589
California.................	43,865	45,512	34,202	33,494	New Jersey.............	4,338	4,304	6,079	5,922
Colorado..................	3,321	3,461	4,053	4,202	New Mexico............	412	428	454	523
Connecticut..............	2,627	2,357	2,013	2,027	New York...............	8,176	7,584	15,653	15,480
Delaware.................	291	317	1,858	2,031	North Carolina..........	3,457	3,437	4,317	4,382
Dist. of Columbia........	311	308	1,347	1,365	North Dakota...........	132	172	170	173
Florida....................	4,919	5,081	14,428	15,288	Ohio....................	4,445	4,143	4,146	4,275
Georgia...................	2,710	2,648	6,424	6,356	Oklahoma..............	617	565	844	851
Hawaii....................	170	146	498	495	Oregon.................	3,540	3,670	2,093	1,947
Idaho.....................	1,220	1,269	608	680	Pennsylvania...........	4,325	4,229	4,836	4,780
Illinois....................	5,019	5,024	6,517	6,305	Rhode Island...........	396	414	484	513
Indiana...................	2,195	1,986	1,891	1,898	South Carolina.........	1,042	1,046	1,719	1,791
Iowa......................	1,103	1,058	786	880	South Dakota...........	133	135	209	262
Kansas...................	831	842	790	768	Tennessee.............	1,386	1,343	2,770	2,915
Kentucky.................	754	751	1,163	1,158	Texas..................	11,448	11,557	13,176	13,748
Louisiana.................	363	445	1,016	963	Utah....................	1,605	1,713	2,246	2,383
Maine.....................	188	177	395	411	Vermont................	300	332	280	267
Maryland..................	1,983	1,941	3,280	3,290	Virginia.................	2,683	3,017	3,832	3,812
Massachusetts...........	7,684	7,786	4,186	4,148	Washington............	7,297	6,908	3,757	3,516
Michigan..................	5,966	6,032	3,561	3,649	West Virginia...........	90	95	194	229
Minnesota................	3,851	3,669	3,006	2,868	Wisconsin..............	2,624	2,632	2,051	1,946
Mississippi...............	186	161	435	410	Wyoming...............	133	138	732	1,003

P Preliminary. [1] Includes data for unspecified states or areas, and U.S. territories, not shown separately.

Source: U.S. Patent and Trademark Office, "FY2023 Workload Tables," <www.uspto.gov/about-us/performance-and-planning/uspto-annual-reports>, accessed March 2024.

Table 816. Copyright Registration by Subject Matter: 2000 to 2022

[In thousands (497.6 represents 497,600). For years ending September 30. Comprises claims to copyrights registered for both U.S. and foreign works. Semiconductor chips and renewals are not considered copyright registration claims]

Subject matter	2000	2010	2015	2016	2017	2018	2019	2020	2021	2022
Total copyright basic registrations.......	497.6	636.0	443.0	414.1	451.7	559.5	547.7	443.9	403.3	484.6
Monographs [1]............................	169.7	245.8	175.5	168.8	153.0	197.3	185.9	152.0	128.9	189.0
Serials...................................	69.0	90.5	55.1	41.9	49.5	54.9	41.9	26.1	23.6	29.9
Performing arts [2]........................	138.9	124.5	80.1	75.3	103.5	136.4	147.5	183.1	100.8	106.4
Works of the visual arts [3]................	85.8	97.2	89.2	85.6	86.5	93.7	88.8	82.7	80.4	88.9
Sound recordings.........................	34.2	77.9	43.0	42.4	59.2	77.2	83.7	([4])	69.5	70.1
Renewals.................................	16.8	0.1	0.8	0.2	0.4	0.4	0.1	–	0.2	0.2
Mask work (semiconductor chip products)................................	0.7	0.3	0.1	(Z)	(Z)	0.2	(Z)	–	(Z)	(Z)

Z Less than 50. – Represents zero. [1] Includes computer software and machine readable works. [2] Includes musical works, dramatic works, choreography, pantomimes, motion pictures, and filmstrips. [3] Two-dimensional works of fine and graphic art, including prints and art reproductions; sculptural works; technical drawings and models; photographs; commercial prints and labels; and works of applied arts, cartographic works, and multimedia works. [4] Data for 2020 included with performing arts.

Source: The Library of Congress, *Annual Report of the Librarian of Congress, For the Fiscal Year Ending September 30, 2022,* 2023, and earlier reports. See also <www.loc.gov/about/reports-and-budgets/annual-reports/>.

Table 817. Net Stock of Private Fixed Assets by Industry: 2010 to 2022

[In billions of dollars (34,465 represents $34,465,000,000,000). Estimates as of Dec. 31. Fixed assets are assets that are used repeatedly, or continuously, for a year or more in the production of goods or services. Net stock estimates are presented in terms of current-cost, and cover equipment, structures, and intellectual property products. (pt) = part]

Industry	NAICS code [1]	2010	2015	2019	2020	2021	2022
Private fixed assets............................	(X)	**34,465**	**41,462**	**49,640**	**51,933**	**59,280**	**66,103**
Agriculture, forestry, fishing, and hunting.........................	11	487	636	705	720	804	881
Farms [2]...	111, 112	438	576	631	646	721	790
Forestry, fishing, and related activities.........................	113-115	49	61	74	75	83	91
Mining..	21	1,574	2,169	2,054	1,797	1,766	1,782
Oil and gas extraction................................	211	1,327	1,813	1,673	1,415	1,351	1,324
Mining, except oil and gas...........................	212	137	196	224	231	259	292
Support activities for mining.........................	213	109	161	157	151	157	166
Utilities...	22	1,857	2,285	2,774	2,902	3,280	3,531
Construction..	23	264	303	354	365	405	452
Manufacturing..	31-33	3,137	3,686	4,327	4,532	4,944	5,479
Durable goods......................................	(X)	1,630	1,880	2,133	2,206	2,400	2,662
Wood products...................................	321	38	42	49	50	58	68
Nonmetallic mineral products.....................	327	89	95	110	114	126	141
Primary metals...................................	331	161	174	200	204	224	249
Fabricated metal products.........................	332	161	189	217	225	252	284
Machinery..	333	199	233	261	271	295	328
Computer and electronic products.................	334	467	534	575	599	640	701
Electrical equipment, appliances, and components.........	335	66	74	85	87	96	106
Motor vehicles, bodies and trailers, and parts.................	3361-3363	186	244	291	297	323	357
Other transportation equipment...................	3364, 3365, 3369	153	166	192	197	209	230
Furniture and related products....................	337	21	23	27	29	32	37
Miscellaneous manufacturing.....................	339	89	105	126	132	145	161
Nondurable goods..................................	(X)	1,507	1,806	2,194	2,326	2,544	2,817
Food and beverage and tobacco products..............	311, 312	285	335	405	419	467	529
Textile mills and textile product mills........................	313, 314	42	41	42	42	46	52
Apparel and leather and allied products..........	315, 316	18	18	19	19	21	23
Paper products...................................	322	110	120	130	135	146	162
Printing and related support activities............	323	49	47	49	48	52	57
Petroleum and coal products......................	324	195	243	288	293	314	342
Chemical products................................	325	717	900	1,136	1,239	1,352	1,488
Plastics and rubber products......................	326	91	103	125	131	145	165
Wholesale trade.......................................	42	490	586	707	720	832	952
Retail trade...	44-45	1,131	1,304	1,543	1,580	1,915	2,229
Transportation and warehousing [3]...................	48-49	1,095	1,326	1,596	1,628	1,794	1,935
Air transportation..................................	481	219	250	297	302	316	341
Railroad transportation............................	482	359	419	454	462	485	510
Water transportation...............................	483	44	56	64	65	70	75
Truck transportation...............................	484	106	140	172	169	185	201
Transit and ground passenger transportation..............	485	42	47	60	61	66	69
Pipeline transportation............................	486	161	231	317	326	384	404
Warehousing and storage..........................	493	40	49	65	70	86	103
Information...	51	1,816	2,119	2,625	2,744	3,031	3,350
Publishing industries (includes software).............	511	249	313	356	370	396	431
Motion picture and sound recording industries..............	512	258	277	316	325	347	376
Broadcasting and telecommunications.............	515, 517	1,211	1,333	1,552	1,577	1,704	1,836
Information and data processing services.............	516 (pt), 518, 519	97	196	401	473	583	707
Finance and insurance................................	52	1,152	1,339	1,610	1,662	1,871	2,109
Federal Reserve banks............................	521	10	10	11	11	13	15
Credit intermediation and related activities....................	522	716	857	1,030	1,046	1,158	1,281
Securities, commodity contracts, and investments............	523	152	164	207	222	257	298
Insurance carriers and related activities.............	524	235	268	321	342	393	455
Funds, trusts, and other financial vehicles............	525	40	40	41	41	50	60
Real estate and rental and leasing....................	53	17,228	20,704	25,293	27,009	31,626	35,438
Real estate..	531	16,880	20,223	24,722	26,455	31,049	34,831
Rental and leasing services and lessors of intangible assets [4]...............	532, 533	348	480	571	554	577	606
Professional, scientific, and technical services [3].................	54	562	648	828	894	1,014	1,162
Legal services....................................	5411	42	45	50	51	56	62
Computer systems design and related services.............	5415	93	98	128	139	159	182
Management of companies and enterprises [5]..................	55	355	381	414	416	470	536
Administrative and waste management services................	56	245	296	352	364	402	447
Administrative and support services................	561	153	195	236	245	268	297
Waste management and remediation services................	562	92	101	116	119	134	150
Educational services..................................	61	469	568	688	704	781	904
Health care and social assistance....................	62	1,219	1,465	1,758	1,826	2,036	2,343
Ambulatory health care services...................	621	317	365	431	451	506	584
Hospitals..	622	773	937	1,125	1,164	1,288	1,478
Nursing and residential care facilities.............	623	76	97	119	125	145	170
Social assistance..................................	624	53	66	83	86	97	112
Arts, entertainment, and recreation...................	71	289	359	476	494	549	615
Performing arts, spectator sports, museums, and related activities...............	711, 712	142	173	213	220	243	274
Amusements, gambling, and recreation industries............	713	147	185	263	274	306	342
Accommodation and food services....................	72	542	647	785	800	899	998
Accommodation....................................	721	327	395	485	494	536	582
Food services and drinking places.................	722	215	252	301	306	363	416
Other services, except government...................	81	556	640	751	774	862	959

X Not applicable. [1] Based on North American Industry Classification System; see text this section. [2] NAICS crop and animal production. [3] Includes other activities, not shown separately. [4] Intangible assets include patents, trademarks, and franchise agreements, but not copyrights. [5] Consists of bank and other holding companies.

Source: U.S. Bureau of Economic Analysis, National Economic Accounts, "Table 3.1ESI. Current-Cost Net Stock of Private Fixed Assets by Industry," <www.bea.gov/itable/>, accessed February 2024.

Table 818. Capital Expenditures: 2010 to 2022

[In billions of dollars (1,106 represents $1,106,000,000,000). Based on the Annual Capital Expenditure Survey, which is a sample survey and subject to sampling error; see source for details]

Item	All companies				Companies with employees				Companies without employees			
	2010	2020	2021	2022	2010	2020	2021	2022	2010	2020	2021 [1]	2022
Capital expenditures, total	**1,106**	**1,708**	**1,682**	**2,197**	**1,036**	**1,599**	**1,682**	**1,900**	**70**	**109**	**(NA)**	**297**
Structures	430	680	632	912	396	620	632	723	33	59	(NA)	189
New	395	628	583	815	368	582	583	671	28	46	(NA)	143
Used	34	51	49	97	29	38	49	52	6	13	(NA)	45
Equipment	676	1,028	1,050	1,285	640	979	1,050	1,177	36	50	(NA)	108
New	638	966	995	1,200	612	924	995	1,115	27	41	(NA)	85
Used	38	62	55	85	28	54	55	62	10	8	(NA)	23
Capitalized computer software [2]	(NA)	(NA)	(NA)	(NA)	(NA)	118	132	135	(NA)	(NA)	(NA)	(NA)
Capital leases [2]	16	51	43	54	15	51	43	49	1	1	(NA)	5

NA Not available. [1] Data for companies without employees was not collected in 2021. [2] Included in structures and equipment data shown above.

Source: U.S. Census Bureau, "2022 Annual Capital Expenditures Survey Tables," and earlier reports, <www.census.gov/programs-surveys/aces.html>, accessed September 2024.

Table 819. Capital Expenditures by Industry: 2000 to 2022

[In billions of dollars (1,090 represents $1,090,000,000,000). Covers only companies with employees. Data from 2000 based on the North American Industry Classification System (NAICS), 1997; 2005 data based on NAICS 2002; 2010 data based on NAICS 2007; 2015 data based on NAICS 2012; and, beginning 2018, data based on NAICS 2017. Based on the Annual Capital Expenditure Survey, which is a sample survey and subject to sampling error; see source for details]

Industry	NAICS code	2000	2005	2010	2015	2019	2020	2021	2022
Total expenditures	(X)	**1,090**	**1,063**	**1,036**	**1,548**	**1,806**	**1,599**	**1,682**	**1,900**
Forestry, fishing, and agricultural services	113–115	1	3	3	3	4	3	3	4
Mining	21	43	67	116	174	161	98	84	113
Utilities	22	61	58	94	131	173	182	178	188
Construction	23	25	30	18	33	51	52	45	54
Manufacturing	31–33	215	166	161	245	273	257	284	314
Durable goods	321, 327, 33	134	92	87	128	142	128	155	179
Nondurable goods	31, 322–326	81	73	74	117	131	128	129	135
Wholesale trade	42	34	41	31	42	40	36	40	49
Retail trade	44–45	70	74	65	86	99	105	120	135
Transportation and warehousing	48–49	60	57	59	117	131	98	94	118
Information	51	160	91	97	133	177	170	195	254
Finance and insurance	52	134	161	103	165	195	175	174	179
Real estate and rental and leasing	53	92	103	81	152	180	136	160	165
Professional, scientific, & technical services	54	34	33	28	33	44	40	46	45
Management of companies and enterprises	55	5	3	5	5	7	7	8	10
Administrative & support and waste management & remediation services	56	18	18	17	26	31	29	28	38
Educational services	61	18	17	23	33	32	33	29	31
Health care and social assistance	62	52	74	78	94	114	105	115	109
Arts, entertainment, and recreation	71	19	14	12	16	25	18	19	27
Accommodation and food services	72	26	31	20	33	41	31	31	40
Other services (except public administration)	81	21	20	21	23	25	23	26	25
Structure and equipment expenditures serving multiple industry categories	(X)	2	2	2	4	3	2	2	2

X Not applicable.

Source: U.S. Census Bureau, "2022 Annual Capital Expenditures Survey Tables," and earlier reports, <www.census.gov/programs-surveys/aces.html>, accessed September 2024.

Table 820. Private Domestic Investment in Current and Chained (2017) Dollars: 2000 to 2022

[In billions of dollars (2,038 represents $2,038,000,000,000). Covers equipment, structures, and intellectual property products. For explanation of chained dollars; see text, Section 13]

Item	2000	2005	2010	2015	2019	2020	2021	2022
CURRENT DOLLARS								
Gross private domestic investment	**2,038**	**2,535**	**2,165**	**3,288**	**3,892**	**3,748**	**4,216**	**4,757**
Less: Consumption of fixed capital	1,232	1,623	1,933	2,398	2,882	3,008	3,214	3,578
Equals: Net private domestic investment	807	912	232	891	1,011	741	1,002	1,179
Fixed investment	1,984	2,477	2,112	3,148	3,820	3,786	4,205	4,599
Less: Consumption of fixed capital	1,232	1,623	1,933	2,398	2,882	3,008	3,214	3,578
Equals: Net fixed investment	752	855	178	750	938	778	990	1,022
Nonresidential	1,498	1,621	1,735	2,508	2,993	2,869	3,078	3,433
Residential	485	856	377	641	827	916	1,126	1,166
Change in private inventories	55	58	54	140	72	-38	12	157
CHAINED (2017) DOLLARS								
Gross private domestic investment	**2,445**	**2,782**	**2,309**	**3,323**	**3,780**	**3,602**	**3,914**	**4,103**
Less: Consumption of fixed capital	1,492	1,828	2,096	2,431	2,795	2,881	2,967	3,067
Equals: Net private domestic investment	953	954	214	892	985	721	947	1,036
Fixed investment	2,405	2,746	2,270	3,194	3,708	3,630	3,887	3,939
Nonresidential	1,628	1,728	1,794	2,499	2,950	2,811	2,975	3,132
Residential	799	1,093	473	693	761	816	904	823
Change in private inventories	75	67	54	134	71	-30	13	128

Source: U.S. Bureau of Economic Analysis, National Economic Accounts, "Table 5.2.5. Gross and Net Domestic Investment by Major Type" and "Table 5.2.6. Real Gross and Net Domestic Investment by Major Type, Chained Dollars," <www.bea.gov/itable/>, accessed November 2023.

Table 821. Private Fixed Investment in Intellectual Property Products by Type: 2010 to 2022

[In millions of dollars (411,339 represents $411,339,000,000). Private fixed investment measures spending by private businesses, nonprofit institutions, and households on fixed assets including intellectual property products, which are defined as research and development, software, and entertainment, literary, and artistic originals]

Type	2010	2015	2019	2020	2021	2022
Total	**578,170**	**778,879**	**1,072,893**	**1,135,518**	**1,266,300**	**1,405,351**
Software	**226,384**	**316,260**	**447,751**	**479,211**	**533,818**	**598,083**
Prepackaged [1]	80,262	127,011	196,555	215,477	247,718	284,501
Custom	100,366	130,372	179,973	188,468	209,617	229,320
Own account	45,755	58,877	71,223	75,266	76,483	84,261
Research and development (R&D) [2]	**282,427**	**385,339**	**533,217**	**567,023**	**642,138**	**703,131**
Business	263,670	362,716	503,589	535,332	608,661	668,860
Manufacturing	184,165	238,593	297,907	314,426	340,524	361,207
Pharmaceutical and medicine	57,313	70,309	102,055	108,399	119,156	120,270
Chemical, excluding pharmaceutical and medicine	10,367	11,971	11,038	10,821	10,644	11,042
Semiconductor and other electronic component	23,418	33,042	37,921	44,522	50,652	57,614
Other computer and electronic product	31,826	38,984	45,858	47,684	49,305	52,729
Motor vehicles, bodies and trailers, and parts	11,954	20,022	26,245	25,698	29,453	32,087
Aerospace products and parts	11,004	13,607	10,835	11,348	11,707	12,727
Other manufacturing	38,283	50,658	63,956	65,955	69,606	74,738
Nonmanufacturing	79,505	124,123	205,681	220,906	268,137	307,654
Scientific research and development services	8,414	9,218	12,512	14,479	18,883	20,722
All other nonmanufacturing	71,091	114,904	193,170	206,427	249,254	286,932
Software publishers	27,573	37,917	35,777	37,838	43,183	46,633
Financial and real estate services	2,573	5,760	12,535	15,899	23,548	27,693
Computer systems design and related services	13,002	14,988	22,759	21,094	21,924	23,112
Other nonmanufacturing	27,944	56,240	122,098	131,597	160,600	189,494
Nonprofit institutions serving households	18,756	22,623	29,629	31,691	33,477	34,270
Universities and colleges [3]	2,680	4,987	6,744	7,131	7,254	7,422
Other nonprofit institutions	16,076	17,637	22,884	24,560	26,222	26,848
Entertainment, literary, and artistic originals	**69,359**	**77,281**	**91,925**	**89,284**	**90,344**	**104,138**
Theatrical movies	18,128	16,725	19,052	18,812	19,146	22,583
Long-lived television programs	31,754	42,027	51,050	49,156	49,347	54,740
Books	9,823	9,366	9,539	9,134	9,104	9,603
Music	6,982	6,101	8,306	8,438	9,001	12,014
Other	2,672	3,061	3,979	3,743	3,746	5,199

[1] Excludes software embedded, or bundled, in computers and other equipment. [2] R&D asset types are defined by the type of funder. Includes R&D expenditures for software. [3] Includes R&D investment by private universities and colleges. R&D investment by public universities and colleges is included in state and local government investment.

Source: U.S. Bureau of Economic Analysis, National Income and Product Accounts Tables, "Table 5.6.5. Private Fixed Investment in Intellectual Property Products by Type," <www.bea.gov/itable/national-gdp-and-personal-income>, accessed June 2024. See also <www.bea.gov/data/special-topics/intellectual-property>.

Table 822. Paycheck Protection Program Loans by Industry: 2020 and 2021

[In units as indicated (525.0 represents $525,000,000,000). The Coronavirus Aid, Relief, and Economic Security Act (CARES) temporarily added the Paycheck Protection Program (PPP) to the U.S. Small Business Administration's (SBA's) 7(a) Loan Program to assist small businesses and nonprofit institutions in covering payroll and other operational expenses during the COVID-19 pandemic. Lending was available in three rounds from April 3 to April 16, 2020, April 27 to August 8, 2020, and December 27, 2020 to May 31, 2021. Data for 2020 are for Round 1 and 2 of PPP approved lending through August 8, 2020; data for 2021 are for Round 3 approvals through May 31, 2021]

Industry	2020 Number of loans	2020 Net loans (bil. dol.)	2020 Percent of total value	2021 Number of loans	2021 Net loans (bil. dol.)	2021 Percent of total value
Total	**5,212,128**	**525.0**	**100**	**6,681,929**	**277.70**	**100**
Accommodation and food services	383,561	42.5	8	462,478	41.51	15
Construction	496,551	65.1	12	558,180	33.44	12
Health care and social assistance	532,775	67.8	13	485,698	28.82	10
Professional, scientific, and technical services	681,111	66.8	13	657,326	28.56	10
Other services, except public administration	583,385	31.7	6	1,107,768	27.35	10
Manufacturing	238,494	54.1	10	221,216	22.15	8
Transportation and warehousing	229,565	17.5	3	763,810	15.77	6
Retail trade	472,418	40.6	8	468,043	15.26	5
Administrative and support & waste management and remediation services	258,907	26.6	5	393,563	12.96	5
Wholesale trade	174,707	27.7	5	187,490	10.38	4
Agriculture, forestry, fishing, and hunting	149,535	8.1	2	532,884	10.02	4
Arts, entertainment, and recreation	130,760	8.2	2	223,882	7.45	3
Real estate and rental and leasing	262,921	15.7	3	262,928	7.34	3
Educational services	88,022	12.1	2	101,773	5.12	2
Information	73,824	9.3	2	75,128	4.12	1
Finance and insurance	181,493	12.2	2	127,088	3.42	1
Mining	22,503	4.5	1	21,676	2.84	1
Public administration	14291	1.8	(Z)	18,359	0.78	(Z)
Management of companies and enterprises	9,472	1.6	(Z)	6,812	0.46	(Z)
Utilities	8,331	1.5	(Z)	5,827	0.39	(Z)
Unclassified establishments	219,502	9.7	2	(X)	(X)	(X)

X Not applicable. Z Less than 0.5%.

Source: U.S. Small Business Administration, "Paycheck Protection Program (PPP) Report Approvals through 05/31/2021" and earlier reports, <www.sba.gov/funding-programs/loans/covid-19-relief-options/paycheck-protection-program/ppp-data>, accessed April 2022.

Table 823. Business Cycle Expansions and Contractions—Months of Duration: 1945 to 2020

[A trough is the low point of a business cycle; a peak is the high point. Contraction, or recession, is the period from peak to subsequent trough; expansion is the period from trough to subsequent peak. Business cycle reference dates are determined by the National Bureau of Economic Research, Inc]

Business cycle reference date				Contraction (Peak to trough)	Expansion (Previous trough to peak)	Length of cycle	
Peak		Trough				Trough from previous trough	Peak from previous peak
Month	Year	Month	Year				
February........................	1945	October	1945	8	[1] 80	[1] 88	[2] 93
November.....................	1948	October	1949	11	37	48	45
July............................	1953	May	1954	10	45	55	56
August.........................	1957	April	1958	8	39	47	49
April...........................	1960	February	1961	10	24	34	32
December.....................	1969	November	1970	11	106	117	116
November.....................	1973	March	1975	16	36	52	47
January........................	1980	July	1980	6	58	64	74
July............................	1981	November	1982	16	12	28	18
July............................	1990	March	1991	8	92	100	108
March..........................	2001	November	2001	8	120	128	128
December.....................	2007	June	2009	18	73	91	81
February........................	2020	April	2020	2	128	130	146
Average, all cycles: 1945 to 2020...............	(X)	(X)	(X)	10.3	64.2	74.5	75.0

X Not applicable. [1] Previous trough: June 1938. [2] Previous peak: May 1937.

Source: National Bureau of Economic Research, Inc., Cambridge, MA, "US Business Cycle Expansions and Contractions," <www.nber.org/research/data/us-business-cycle-expansions-and-contractions>, accessed July 2021 ©.

Table 824. The Conference Board Leading, Coincident, and Lagging Economic Indexes®: 2010 to 2023

[458.5 represents 458,500]

Item	Unit	2010	2015	2020	2022	2023
The Conference Board Leading Economic Index® (LEI) for the U.S., composite......................	2016=100	81.8	99.4	107.2	115.1	106.3
Average weekly hours, manufacturing...........................	Hours	41.1	41.8	40.7	41.1	40.7
Average weekly initial claims for unemployment insurance.........................	1,000	458.5	277.1	1,289.0	213.7	221.8
Manufacturers' new orders, consumer goods and materials (1982 dollars).....................................	Mil. dol.	122,219	134,686	120,048	121,299	123,998
Building permits, new private housing units....................	1,000	604	1,177	1,478	1,682	1,518
Manufacturers' new orders, nondefense capital goods excluding aircraft (1982 dollars).....................	Mil. dol.	36,339	37,582	33,550	35,782	34,680
Leading Credit Index™ (standard deviation from the mean)..	Std. dev.	-0.8	-0.1	0.8	1.2	0.7
Interest rate spread, 10-year Treasury bonds less federal funds..	Percent	3.04	2.00	0.52	1.27	-1.07
The Conference Board Coincident Economic Index® (CEI) for the U.S., composite..................................	2016=100	88.1	99.1	102.4	109.1	110.9
Employees on nonagricultural payrolls.........................	1,000	130,335	141,801	142,165	152,531	156,066
Index of industrial production....................................	2012=100	91.6	100.9	95.1	102.7	102.9
Personal income less transfer payments (2012 dollars).......	Bil. dol.	11,303	13,143	14,715	15,372	15,667
Manufacturing and trade sales (2012 dollars).................	Mil. dol.	1,134,770	1,315,580	1,382,771	1,482,543	1,497,538
Composite index of 7 lagging indicators	2016=100	82.4	97.1	110.2	114.4	117.9
Inventories to sales ratio, manufacturing and trade...........	Ratio	1.4	1.5	1.6	1.5	1.6
Average duration of unemployment.............................	Weeks	33.1	29.1	18.2	22.6	20.6
Consumer installment credit to personal income ratio........	Percent	20.2	22.1	21.3	21.7	21.7
Commercial and industrial loans outstanding (2012 dollars).....................................	Mil. dol.	940,879	1,415,333	1,648,815	1,509,819	1,516,498
Change in labor cost per unit of output, manufacturing........	Percent	-2.4	4.1	4.5	5.8	5.5
Change in consumer price index for services.................	Percent	0.9	2.4	1.9	7.1	5.2
Average prime rate...	Percent	3.3	3.3	3.5	4.9	8.2

Source: The Conference Board, New York, NY 10022-6601, *Business Cycle Indicators* (BCI), monthly. Reproduced with permission from The Conference Board, Inc. © 2024, The Conference Board, Inc. For more information, see <www.conference-board.org/data>.

Table 825. Manufacturing and Trade—Sales and Inventories: 2000 to 2023

[In billions of dollars (834 represents $834,000,000,000), except ratios. Based on North American Industry Classification System (NAICS); see text, this section]

Year	Sales, average monthly [1]				Inventories [2]				Inventory-sales ratio [3]			
	Total	Manufac-turing	Retail trade	Mer-chant whole-salers	Total	Manufac-turing	Retail trade	Mer-chant whole-salers	Total	Manufac-turing	Retail trade	Mer-chant whole-salers
2000......	834	351	249	235	1,196	481	406	309	1.41	1.35	1.59	1.29
2001......	818	331	255	232	1,119	427	394	298	1.42	1.38	1.58	1.32
2002......	823	326	261	236	1,140	423	415	301	1.36	1.29	1.55	1.26
2003......	855	335	272	248	1,148	408	431	308	1.34	1.25	1.56	1.22
2004......	926	359	289	278	1,242	441	460	340	1.30	1.19	1.56	1.17
2005......	1,006	395	307	303	1,314	475	472	368	1.27	1.17	1.51	1.17
2006......	1,069	418	323	328	1,409	523	486	399	1.28	1.20	1.49	1.17
2007......	1,128	443	333	352	1,488	563	501	425	1.28	1.22	1.49	1.17
2008......	1,161	456	328	377	1,466	543	477	446	1.31	1.26	1.52	1.20
2009......	989	369	301	319	1,331	505	428	398	1.38	1.39	1.47	1.29
2010......	1,089	409	318	362	1,450	554	453	443	1.27	1.28	1.39	1.15
2011......	1,207	458	342	407	1,567	607	471	489	1.26	1.29	1.35	1.15
2012......	1,268	475	359	434	1,658	625	507	526	1.28	1.30	1.38	1.18
2013......	1,306	485	372	450	1,727	632	545	550	1.29	1.30	1.41	1.19
2014......	1,346	491	387	469	1,790	643	561	585	1.32	1.31	1.43	1.22
2015......	1,303	461	394	448	1,823	638	588	597	1.39	1.40	1.46	1.33
2016......	1,296	447	404	445	1,857	636	610	611	1.42	1.42	1.50	1.35
2017......	1,357	462	420	475	1,917	659	626	633	1.39	1.39	1.47	1.31
2018......	1,437	491	438	509	2,002	678	653	671	1.36	1.37	1.46	1.28
2019......	1,435	478	450	507	2,043	708	655	680	1.42	1.46	1.47	1.35
2020......	1,382	434	464	484	1,992	702	623	666	1.44	1.62	1.34	1.37
2021......	1,633	507	543	583	2,258	808	664	785	1.28	1.49	1.15	1.24
2022......	1,835	577	587	671	2,529	859	747	923	1.34	1.47	1.24	1.31
2023......	1,838	578	600	660	2,534	856	780	899	1.37	1.48	1.27	1.37

[1] Averages of monthly not-seasonally-adjusted figures. [2] Seasonally adjusted end-of-year data. [3] Averages of seasonally adjusted monthly ratios.

Source: U.S. Census Bureau, "Manufacturing & Trade Inventories & Sales," <www.census.gov/mtis/index.html>, accessed July 2024.

Table 826. Industrial Production Indexes by Industry: 2000 to 2023

[2017 = 100. Indexes are not seasonally adjusted]

Industry	NAICS code [1]	2000	2005	2010	2015	2020	2021	2022	2023
Total index..............................	([2])	**92.5**	**96.7**	**91.6**	**100.9**	**95.1**	**99.3**	**102.7**	**102.9**
Manufacturing (SIC) [3]........................	([4])	**96.7**	**101.9**	**93.5**	**100.2**	**92.8**	**97.4**	**100.0**	**99.5**
Manufacturing (NAICS).......................	31–33	93.2	99.2	92.4	100.1	93.0	97.7	100.3	100.0
Durable goods.............................	([5])	81.8	89.9	86.2	100.4	91.3	96.8	100.7	100.9
Wood products..........................	321	116.9	124.8	79.6	95.3	95.8	99.1	99.9	94.2
Nonmetallic mineral products............	327	119.9	125.2	86.6	99.2	97.3	100.5	107.3	105.7
Primary metals.........................	331	114.6	108.2	103.8	105.7	86.6	96.1	94.6	94.8
Fabricated metal products................	332	113.4	107.0	92.9	102.6	93.1	96.7	100.4	99.6
Machinery..............................	333	110.5	103.6	95.7	103.7	90.6	97.6	102.9	100.9
Computers and electronic products......	334	31.1	49.3	71.7	90.9	105.7	110.2	112.8	114.3
Electrical equipment, appliances, and components.......................	335	134.3	112.5	92.7	100.9	96.3	101.0	105.0	104.5
Motor vehicles and parts.................	3361–3363	83.6	88.0	66.9	99.7	88.1	94.4	101.2	106.4
Aerospace and other misc. transportation equipment.................	3364–3369	70.2	74.0	86.8	102.3	75.6	80.5	84.1	88.3
Furniture and related products............	337	139.2	141.7	86.9	100.6	87.6	88.7	90.7	81.2
Miscellaneous products..................	339	96.0	110.3	108.3	105.2	92.0	102.0	107.9	107.7
Nondurable goods.........................	([6])	107.9	110.6	99.8	99.7	94.9	98.5	100.0	99.1
Food, beverage, and tobacco products..	311–312	93.2	97.5	94.8	98.6	100.1	101.6	102.4	100.8
Textile and product mills................	313–314	220.4	190.7	113.8	109.0	88.0	92.2	88.9	81.3
Apparel and leather.....................	315–316	516.8	285.8	136.5	107.3	82.2	92.1	90.6	89.2
Paper..................................	322	124.1	116.2	100.6	101.9	95.1	95.1	93.4	85.7
Printing and related support.............	323	146.3	132.9	105.0	99.0	84.8	85.8	89.3	83.3
Petroleum and coal products.............	324	82.5	92.6	90.6	90.7	78.6	88.7	89.7	90.7
Chemical...............................	325	103.0	117.0	108.5	101.9	95.3	99.7	102.2	103.7
Plastics and rubber products.............	326	110.3	110.2	89.0	99.9	95.0	101.0	103.7	102.7
Other manufacturing (non-NAICS) [7]........	1133, 5111	223.8	196.7	129.4	105.2	85.3	87.7	88.3	82.4
Mining...............................	**21**	**83.9**	**79.3**	**82.5**	**104.6**	**103.1**	**106.4**	**114.4**	**119.9**
Electric and gas utilities....................	**2211–2212**	**90.7**	**98.0**	**101.2**	**101.2**	**101.0**	**103.0**	**106.2**	**104.1**
Electric power generation, transmission, and distribution.............	2211	89.6	98.3	101.5	101.0	100.0	102.1	104.8	103.5
Natural gas distribution.................	2212	97.0	95.6	99.5	102.7	106.9	108.2	114.1	107.7

[1] Except as noted, based on North American Industry Classification System, 2012; see text, this section. [2] Includes NAICS codes 31–33, 1133, 5111, 21, 2211, and 2212. [3] Standard Industrial Classification (SIC); see text, this section. [4] Includes NAICS codes 31–33, 1133, and 5111. [5] Includes NAICS codes 321, 327, and 331–339. [6] Includes NAICS codes 311–316, and 322–326. [7] Industries that have traditionally been considered to be manufacturing (logging and newspaper, periodical, book, and directory publishing).

Source: Board of Governors of the Federal Reserve System, "Industrial Production and Capacity Utilization, G.17," <www.federalreserve.gov/data.htm>, accessed July 2024.

Table 827. Index of Industrial Capacity and Utilization Rate: 1990 to 2023

[2017 output = 100. Seasonally adjusted. Annual figures are averages of monthly data. The capacity index is an indicator of the maximum sustainable output a plant can maintain under realistic circumstances; capacity here is expressed as a proportion of 2017 actual output. Capacity utilization rate is a measure of output as a proportion of capacity; this is the output index divided by the capacity index]

| Year | Index of capacity | | Utilization rate | | | | |
| | Total industry | Manufacturing [1] | Total industry | Stage of process | | | Manufacturing [1] |
				Crude [2]	Primary and semifinished [3]	Finished [4]	
1990	75.7	76.4	82.3	88.0	82.3	80.5	81.4
2000	113.4	121.2	81.5	88.6	84.0	76.9	79.8
2005	120.5	129.5	80.3	86.8	82.2	75.6	78.7
2010	124.8	132.8	73.4	83.7	71.6	70.9	70.4
2015	130.5	131.2	77.3	79.6	77.5	76.0	76.4
2016	130.6	131.4	75.6	74.0	76.8	74.8	75.7
2017	130.2	130.6	76.8	78.4	77.5	75.4	76.6
2018	129.2	129.1	79.8	85.9	80.1	76.8	78.4
2019	130.3	128.7	78.6	85.4	78.7	75.8	77.2
2020	130.5	127.7	72.9	73.1	73.5	72.2	72.7
2021	127.8	126.1	77.7	82.1	77.6	75.9	77.2
2022	127.3	125.9	80.7	87.9	79.7	77.8	79.4
2023	130.3	127.2	79.0	87.7	77.4	77.1	78.2

[1] Manufacturing consists of those industries included in the North American Industry Classification System (NAICS) definition of manufacturing plus those industries—logging and newspaper, periodical, book, and directory publishing—that have traditionally been considered to be a part of manufacturing and are included in the industrial sector under the Standard Industrial Classification (SIC) system. [2] Crude processing covers a relatively small portion of total industrial capacity and consists of logging (NAICS 1133), much of mining (excluding stone, sand, and gravel mining, and oil and gas drilling, NAICS 21231, 21221–2, and 213111) and some basic manufacturing industries, including basic chemicals (NAICS 3251); fertilizers, pesticides, and other agricultural chemicals (NAICS 32531, 2); pulp, paper, and paperboard mills (NAICS 3221); and alumina, aluminum, and other nonferrous production and processing mills (NAICS 3313, 4). [3] Primary and semifinished processing loosely corresponds to the previously published aggregate, primary processing. Includes utilities and portions of several 2-digit SIC industries included in the former advanced processing group. These include printing and related support activities (NAICS 3231); paints and adhesives (NAICS 3255); and newspaper, periodical, book, and directory publishers (NAICS 5111). [4] Finished processing generally corresponds to the previously published aggregate, advanced processing. Includes oil and gas well drilling and carpet and rug mills.

Source: Board of Governors of the Federal Reserve System, "Industrial Production and Capacity Utilization, G.17," <www.federalreserve.gov/data.htm>, accessed July 2024.

Table 828. Corporate Profits, Taxes, and Dividends: 2000 to 2023

[In billions of dollars (826.4 represents $826,400,000,000). Covers corporations organized for profit and other entities treated as corporations. Represents profits to U.S. residents, without deduction of depletion charges and exclusive of capital gains and losses; intercorporate dividends from profits of domestic corporations are eliminated; and net receipts of dividends, reinvested earnings of incorporated foreign affiliates, and earnings of unincorporated foreign affiliates are added. Minus (-) sign indicates loss]

Item	2000	2010	2015	2018	2019	2020	2021	2022	2023
Corporate profits with IVA and CCAdj [1]	826.4	1,774.5	2,173.1	2,365.2	2,470.3	2,383.3	2,922.8	3,208.7	3,258.0
Taxes on corporate income	233.4	272.3	396.1	297.4	297.4	307.5	404.6	542.4	585.2
Profits after tax with IVA and CCAdj [1]	593.0	1,502.2	1,777.0	2,067.7	2,172.9	2,075.8	2,518.1	2,666.3	2,672.9
Net dividends	413.1	636.0	1,128.7	1,319.9	1,416.8	1,496.7	1,814.7	1,887.3	1,848.8
Undistributed profits with IVA and CCAdj [1]	179.9	866.2	648.3	747.8	756.1	579.1	703.4	779.0	824.1
Addenda for corporate cash flow:									
Net cash flow with IVA and CCAdj [1]	1,018.5	2,157.5	2,238.8	2,530.7	2,661.9	2,536.1	2,764.9	3,009.5	3,296.5
Undistributed profits with IVA and CCAdj [1]	179.9	866.2	648.3	747.8	756.1	579.1	703.4	779.0	824.1
Consumption of fixed capital	838.6	1,270.7	1,587.2	1,793.6	1,893.4	1,970.6	2,074.3	2,288.9	2,471.8
Less: Capital transfers paid (net)	–	-20.6	-3.2	10.7	-12.4	13.6	12.8	58.5	-0.6

– Represents or rounds to zero. [1] Inventory valuation adjustment (IVA) and capital consumption adjustment (CCAdj).

Source: U.S. Bureau of Economic Analysis, National Income and Product Accounts Tables, "Table 1.12. National Income by Type of Income," <www.bea.gov/itable/>, accessed July 2024.

Table 829. Corporate Profits With Inventory Valuation and Capital Consumption Adjustments—Financial and Nonfinancial Industries: 2000 to 2023

[In billions of dollars (826 represents $826,000,000,000). Based on the North American Industry Classification System; see text, this section. Minus sign (-) indicates loss. See headnote, Table 828]

Industry group	2000	2010	2015	2018	2019	2020	2021	2022	2023
Corporate profits with IVA/CCAdj [1]	**826**	**1,774**	**2,173**	**2,365**	**2,470**	**2,383**	**2,923**	**3,209**	**3,258**
Domestic industries	681	1,389	1,778	1,845	1,937	1,935	2,489	2,736	2,747
Rest of the world	146	386	395	521	533	448	434	473	511
Corporate profits with IVA [1]	**770**	**1,831**	**2,295**	**2,267**	**2,377**	**2,478**	**2,992**	**3,427**	**3,599**
Domestic industries	624	1,445	1,900	1,746	1,844	2,030	2,558	2,954	3,089
Financial [2]	190	438	512	479	575	536	581	599	557
Nonfinancial	434	1,008	1,388	1,267	1,269	1,494	1,977	2,355	2,532
Utilities	24	31	20	17	12	27	34	43	45
Manufacturing	175	282	421	362	353	328	464	709	744
Wholesale trade	59	99	154	108	126	158	172	226	237
Retail trade	51	116	170	146	150	243	276	285	359
Transportation and warehousing	9	45	61	45	35	38	95	103	120
Information	-12	102	135	115	134	120	156	168	188
Other nonfinancial [3]	126	333	426	475	458	579	780	822	839
Rest of the world	146	386	395	521	533	448	434	473	511

[1] Inventory valuation adjustment (IVA) and capital consumption adjustment (CCAdj). [2] Consists of finance and insurance and bank and other holding companies. [3] Consists of agriculture, forestry, fishing, and hunting; mining; construction; real estate and rental and leasing; professional, scientific, and technical services; administrative and waste management services; educational services; health care and social assistance; arts, entertainment, and recreation; accommodation and food services; and other services, except government.

Source: U.S. Bureau of Economic Analysis, National Income and Product Accounts Tables, "Table 6.16D. Corporate Profits by Industry," <www.bea.gov/itable/national-gdp-and-personal-income>, accessed July 2024.

Table 830. Corporate Profits Before Taxes by Industry: 2000 to 2022

[In billions of dollars (786 represents $786,000,000,000). Profits are without inventory valuation and capital consumption adjustments. Covers corporations organized for profit and other entities treated as corporations. Represents profits to U.S. residents, without deduction of depletion charges and exclusive of capital gains and losses; intercorporate dividends from profits of domestic corporations are eliminated; net receipts of dividends, reinvested earnings of incorporated foreign affiliates, and earnings of unincorporated foreign affiliates are added]

Industry	NAICS code [1]	2000	2010	2015	2019	2020	2021	2022
Corporate profits before tax..........................	(X)	**786**	**1,879**	**2,238**	**2,375**	**2,495**	**3,249**	**3,523**
Domestic industries..............................	(X)	641	1,493	1,842	1,842	2,047	2,816	3,050
Agriculture, forestry, fishing, and hunting.............	11	1	8	12	4	9	14	16
Mining......................................	21	15	33	-10	-18	-48	45	118
Utilities....................................	221	25	31	19	11	27	35	44
Construction...............................	23	36	27	77	104	171	164	150
Manufacturing.............................	31-33	185	299	386	345	330	598	727
Wholesale trade...........................	42	63	117	137	127	164	244	266
Retail trade................................	44-45	54	126	168	155	250	308	308
Transportation and warehousing.............	48-49	10	45	60	34	38	97	104
Information................................	51	-12	102	135	135	121	157	168
Finance and insurance.....................	52	95	250	354	396	406	443	417
Real estate and rental and leasing..........	53	9	27	65	41	60	88	84
Professional, scientific, and technical services.........	54	9	82	79	95	114	113	122
Management of companies and enterprises [2].........	551111, 2	94	187	158	179	130	139	181
Administrative and waste management services.......	56	9	28	34	43	52	60	64
Educational services.......................	61	2	11	5	5	6	6	8
Health care and social assistance..........	62	23	78	86	103	149	166	151
Arts, entertainment, and recreation.........	71	3	8	11	16	7	23	21
Accommodation and food services.........	72	14	18	44	42	34	79	69
Other services, except public administration............	81	6	15	21	24	28	39	33
Rest of the world [3]...........................	(X)	146	386	395	533	448	434	473

X Not applicable. [1] Based on North American Industry Classification System, 2017; see text, this section. [2] Consists of bank and other holding companies. [3] Consists of receipts by all U.S. residents, including both corporations and persons, of dividends from foreign corporations, and, for U.S. corporations, their share of reinvested earnings of their incorporated foreign affiliates, and earnings of unincorporated foreign affiliates, net of corresponding payments.

Source: U.S. Bureau of Economic Analysis, National Income and Product Accounts Tables, "Table 6.17D. Corporate Profits Before Tax by Industry," <www.bea.gov/itable/national-gdp-and-personal-income>, accessed July 2024.

Table 831. U.S. Majority-Owned Foreign Affiliates—Value Added by Industry of Affiliate and Country: 2021

[In millions of dollars (1,576,435 represents $1,576,435,000,000). Data are preliminary. A foreign affiliate is a foreign business enterprise owned or controlled by a U.S. parent enterprise. A majority-owned foreign affiliate (MOFA) is a foreign business enterprise in which a U.S. parent enterprise owns or controls more than 50% of the voting securities. Numbers in parentheses represent North American Industry Classification System codes; see text, this section]

Country	All industries [1]	Mining (21)	Manufacturing (31-33) Total [1]	Manufacturing (31-33) Chemicals (325)	Wholesale trade (42)	Information (51)	Finance and insurance (52)	Professional, scientific, and technical services (54)
All countries [2]..........	**1,576,435**	**104,174**	**624,363**	**131,578**	**197,149**	**123,483**	**136,385**	**158,223**
United Kingdom..........	193,304	2,329	55,234	9,018	12,656	21,221	50,180	24,395
Canada....................	141,272	11,848	52,853	6,682	14,976	5,300	7,275	8,344
Ireland....................	129,969	(D)	50,768	24,358	11,108	28,068	1,246	20,060
China.....................	93,426	995	57,750	10,686	12,686	2,424	2,051	5,307
Germany.................	88,088	608	44,236	8,772	14,131	3,699	2,337	9,707
Singapore................	72,923	383	34,134	7,416	11,465	5,718	14,502	2,195
Mexico....................	59,898	4,423	29,169	3,404	5,658	952	923	2,409
Australia..................	56,141	10,077	15,083	1,562	7,784	6,497	3,705	6,048
France....................	55,249	(D)	23,183	5,497	7,320	3,610	3,377	5,599
Netherlands..............	53,187	754	21,582	8,232	6,621	2,212	8,423	4,400
Switzerland...............	53,060	283	17,720	5,635	19,860	3,620	358	3,157
Japan.....................	51,448	–	19,113	4,222	8,702	4,032	2,962	7,942
India......................	44,420	107	7,407	2,235	2,988	6,869	5,126	19,259
Italy.......................	33,218	141	11,693	2,894	3,503	1,279	989	3,163
Belgium...................	30,463	(D)	15,038	8,213	5,559	1,853	4,750	1,195
Brazil......................	28,935	767	17,570	4,966	3,088	2,562	2,668	2,900
Hong Kong...............	25,000	1	4,620	846	5,361	673	7,079	4,131
Korea, South............	20,338	(D)	11,694	1,350	2,560	678	2,688	804
Israel.....................	18,606	(D)	9,967	395	1,850	1,418	299	4,025
Indonesia................	17,393	8,312	7,700	(D)	624	98	379	90
Spain.....................	17,294	23	8,583	2,789	2,511	756	-5	2,458
Russia....................	14,829	2,120	8,519	580	1,402	281	241	983
Thailand..................	14,182	(D)	8,493	873	1,999	111	521	288
Taiwan....................	13,378	3	8,331	591	1,506	1,108	752	587
Poland....................	12,741	29	6,158	347	3,151	443	240	1,232

– Represents or rounds to zero. D Data withheld to avoid disclosure. [1] Includes other industries, not shown separately. [2] Includes other countries, not shown separately.

Source: U.S. Bureau of Economic Analysis, International Economic Accounts, "Activities of U.S. Multinational Enterprises, Majority-owned Foreign Affiliates, Value Added by Country and Industry 2009-2021," <www.bea.gov/international/di1usdop.htm>, accessed December 2023.

Table 832. U.S. Multinational Enterprises—Value Added, Employment, and Capital Expenditures: 2010 to 2021

[Value added and capital expenditures in billions of dollars (4,191 represents $4,191,000,000,000); employees in thousands. Consists of U.S. parent enterprises and their foreign affiliates. U.S. parent comprises the domestic operations of a multinational enterprise and is a U.S. person that owns or controls, directly or indirectly, 10 percent or more of the voting securities of an incorporated foreign business enterprise, or an equivalent interest in an unincorporated foreign business enterprise. A U.S. person can be an incorporated business enterprise. A foreign affiliate is a foreign business enterprise owned or controlled by a U.S. parent enterprise. A majority-owned foreign affiliate (MOFA) is a foreign business enterprise in which a U.S. parent enterprise owns or controls more than 50% of the voting securities]

Item	2010	2013	2014	2015	2016	2017	2018	2019	2020	2021 (P)
VALUE ADDED (bil. dol.)										
Parents and MOFAs	4,191	4,882	5,380	5,308	5,218	5,318	5,670	5,648	5,296	6,643
Parents	2,949	3,487	3,889	3,949	3,916	3,902	4,212	4,232	3,966	5,066
MOFAs	1,242	1,395	1,490	1,359	1,302	1,416	1,458	1,416	1,330	1,576
EMPLOYEES (1,000s)										
Parents and MOFAs	34,105	35,768	41,640	42,127	42,288	42,363	42,884	43,230	42,869	43,328
Parents	22,791	23,349	27,587	28,046	28,023	27,982	28,532	29,076	28,893	29,521
MOFAs	11,313	12,419	14,052	14,081	14,265	14,382	14,352	14,154	13,976	13,807
CAPITAL EXPENDITURES (bil. dol.)										
Parents and MOFAs	607	817	968	927	837	856	913	923	856	917
Parents	441	594	722	713	641	666	723	731	676	729
MOFAs	166	223	245	215	195	190	190	192	180	189

P Preliminary.

Source: U.S. Bureau of Economic Analysis, International Economic Accounts, "Activities of U.S. Multinational Enterprises in 2021," <www.bea.gov/data/intl-trade-investment/activities-us-multinational-enterprises-mnes>, accessed December 2023, and earlier reports.

Table 833. U.S. Multinational Enterprises—Selected Characteristics: 2021

[In billions of dollars (54,531 represents $54,531,000,000,000), except employment. Data are preliminary. Consists of U.S. parent enterprises and their foreign affiliates. U.S. parent comprises the domestic operations of a multinational and is a U.S. person that owns or controls, directly or indirectly, 10 percent or more of the voting securities of an incorporated foreign business enterprise, or an equivalent interest in an unincorporated foreign business enterprise. A U.S. person can be an incorporated business enterprise. A majority-owned foreign affiliate (MOFA) is a foreign business enterprise in which a U.S. parent enterprise owns or controls more than 50 percent of the voting securities]

Industry	NAICS code [1]	U.S. parents [2]				Majority-owned foreign affiliates [3]		
		Total assets	Capital expenditures	Value added	Employment (1,000)	Capital expenditures	Value added	Employment (1,000)
All industries	(X)	54,531	729	5,066	29,521	189	1,576	13,807
Mining [4]	21	542	21	98	197	28	104	201
Oil and gas extraction	211	276	16	56	44	21	62	35
Manufacturing [4]	31-33	9,961	209	1,696	7,398	76	624	5,292
Food	311	818	17	147	946	6	35	492
Beverages and tobacco products	312	437	4	43	101	3	58	215
Petroleum and coal products	324	1,136	21	164	199	2	(D)	12
Chemicals [4]	325	2,594	37	331	1,006	14	132	602
Pharmaceuticals and medicines	3254	1,784	18	198	492	5	71	266
Machinery	333	575	10	116	639	4	49	539
Computers and electronic products [4]	334	1,381	31	318	881	22	130	879
Computers and peripheral equipment	3341	420	9	142	221	1	52	233
Transportation equipment [4]	336	1,571	53	285	1,502	10	62	1,062
Motor vehicles, bodies and trailers, & parts	3361-3363	881	42	143	678	9	52	965
Wholesale trade	42	2,368	62	303	1,771	9	197	969
Retail trade [4]	44, 45	1,505	90	518	6,806	7	78	1,343
General merchandise stores	452	341	17	186	2,680	2	(D)	([5])
Information [4]	51	3,652	118	641	1,975	20	123	701
Publishing industries	511	731	16	137	482	(D)	60	259
Broadcasting (except internet)	515	430	5	37	241	(Z)	4	23
Telecommunications	517	1,558	59	230	657	4	13	101
Finance and insurance [4]	52	31,798	74	745	3,061	7	136	766
Insurance carriers and related activities	524	8,873	18	213	1,279	1	27	238
Professional, scientific, & technical services [4]	54	1,093	12	315	1,770	9	158	1,597
Computer systems design & related services	5415	519	5	93	528	6	65	752
Other industries [4]	(X)	3,611	142	750	6,543	32	155	2,939
Utilities	22	874	49	92	164	3	8	26
Transportation and warehousing	48-49	688	28	195	1,400	8	36	462
Real estate & rental and leasing	53	581	32	92	376	13	50	214
Administration, support, and waste management	56	267	5	87	1,221	2	45	1,153

X Not applicable. D Data withheld to avoid disclosure. Z Less than $500 million. [1] Based on North American Industry Classification System; see text, this section. [2] Data are by industry of U.S. parent. [3] Data are by industry of foreign affiliate. [4] Includes other industries, not shown separately. [5] 100,000 or more employees.

Source: U.S. Bureau of Economic Analysis, International Economic Accounts, "Direct Investment and Multinational Enterprises," <www.bea.gov/itable/direct-investment-multinational-enterprises>, accessed December 2023.

Table 834. U.S. Multinational Enterprises—Value Added: 2020 and 2021

[In billions of dollars (5,296 represents $5,296,000,000,000). A U.S. parent comprises the domestic operations of a multinational and is a U.S. person that owns or controls 10 percent or more of the voting securities, or the equivalent, of a foreign business enterprise. A U.S. person can be an incorporated business enterprise. A majority-owned foreign affiliate is a foreign business enterprise in which a U.S. parent enterprise owns or controls more than 50% of the voting securities. Data are by industry of U.S. parent. Based on the North American Industry Classification System (NAICS). See text this section]

Industry	NAICS [1] code	U.S. multinationals		U.S. parents		Majority-owned foreign affiliates	
		2020	2021 (P)	2020	2021 (P)	2020	2021 (P)
All industries..	**(X)**	**5,296**	**6,643**	**3,966**	**5,066**	**1,330**	**1,576**
Mining [2]..	21	84	128	64	98	20	29
Oil and gas extraction......................................	211	38	66	33	56	5	10
Manufacturing [2]..	31-33	1,914	2,482	1,266	1,696	648	786
Food..	311	166	190	130	147	37	43
Beverages and tobacco products.........................	312	65	60	50	43	15	16
Petroleum and coal products.............................	324	151	288	72	164	80	125
Chemicals [2]..	325	368	507	230	331	138	176
Pharmaceuticals and medicines.........................	3254	219	308	133	198	86	110
Machinery...	333	144	177	90	116	54	61
Computers and electronic products [2]...................	334	404	503	238	318	166	185
Computers and peripheral equipment.................	3341	177	234	95	142	82	92
Semiconductors and other electronic components.....	3344	113	142	65	87	48	55
Transportation equipment [2]...............................	336	285	362	212	285	74	77
Motor vehicles, bodies and trailers, and parts.........	3361-3363	145	197	99	143	46	53
Wholesale trade..	42	287	370	233	303	54	66
Retail trade [2]..	44, 45	511	587	442	518	69	69
General merchandise stores..............................	452	(NA)	(NA)	161	186	(D)	(D)
Information [2]..	51	639	769	516	641	123	128
Publishing industries......................................	511	174	199	110	137	64	63
Broadcasting (except internet)...........................	515	38	43	30	37	8	7
Telecommunications..	517	217	240	207	230	10	10
Finance and insurance [2]....................................	52	742	975	560	745	181	230
Depository credit intermediation (banking)............	5221	231	292	214	267	17	25
Insurance carriers and related activities................	524	173	250	143	213	30	37
Professional, scientific, and technical services [2]......	54	380	420	283	315	97	106
Computer systems design and related services.........	5415	125	148	72	93	52	55
Other industries [2]..	(X)	740	912	603	750	138	162
Utilities..	22	88	97	81	92	7	5
Transportation and warehousing.........................	48-49	160	224	137	195	23	29
Real estate and rental and leasing.......................	53	92	118	72	92	20	26
Administration, support, and waste management........	56	99	116	74	87	25	29
Accommodation and food services......................	72	61	74	47	59	15	16

P Preliminary. X Not applicable. NA Not available. D Data withheld to avoid disclosure. [1] Based on North American Industry Classification System; see text, this section. [2] Includes other industries, not shown separately.

Source: U.S. Bureau of Economic Analysis, International Economic Accounts, "Direct Investment and Multinational Enterprises," <www.bea.gov/itable/direct-investment-multinational-enterprises>, accessed December 2023.

Section 16
Science and Technology

This section presents statistics on scientific, engineering, and technological resources, with emphasis on patterns of research and development (R&D) funding and education and employment in science and engineering fields.

The National Science Foundation (NSF) gathers data chiefly through recurring surveys and reports the data via detailed statistical tables, information briefs, and annual, biennial, and special reports; see <nsf.gov/statistics>. Areas of coverage include R&D expenditures; Federal R&D funding; scientific employment; graduate enrollment and support in academic science and engineering; and characteristics of doctoral scientists and engineers and of recent graduates in the United States. Major surveys include: The Survey of Federal Funds for Research and Development; Higher Education R&D Survey; Survey of Graduate Students and Postdoctorates in Science and Engineering; and Business R&D Survey. Other important reports and data collections include: *Science and Engineering Indicators; National Patterns of R&D Resources; Federal R&D Funding by Budget Function;* and *Doctorate Recipients from U.S. Universities.* Statistical surveys in these areas pose problems of concept and definition and the data should therefore be regarded as broad estimates rather than precise, quantitative statements. See sources for methodological and technical details.

The National Science Board's biennial *Science and Engineering Indicators* at <nsf.gov/statistics/seind/> contains data and analysis of international and domestic science and technology, including education and workforce statistics.

Research and development outlays—NSF defines *research* as "systematic study directed toward fuller scientific knowledge of the subject studied" and *development* as "the systematic use of scientific knowledge directed toward the production of useful materials, devices, systems, or methods, including design and development of prototypes and

processes." *Basic research* is generally defined as research activities aimed at acquiring new knowledge or understanding without specific immediate commercial applications or uses. *Applied research* is generally defined as activities aimed at solving a specific problem or meeting a specific commercial objective.

National coverage of R&D expenditures is developed primarily from periodic surveys in four principal economic sectors: (1) *government*, made up primarily of federal executive agencies; (2) *industry*, consisting of manufacturing and nonmanufacturing firms and the federally funded research and development centers (FFRDCs) they administer; (3) *universities and colleges*, composed of universities, colleges, and their affiliated institutions, agricultural experiment stations, and associated schools of agriculture and of medicine, and FFRDCs administered by educational institutions; and (4) *other nonprofit institutions*, consisting of organizations such as private philanthropic foundations, nonprofit research institutes, voluntary health agencies, and FFRDCs administered by nonprofit organizations.

The R&D funds reported consist of current operating costs, including planning and administration costs, except as otherwise noted. They exclude funds for routine testing, mapping and surveying, collection of general purpose data, dissemination of scientific information, and training of scientific personnel.

Scientists, engineers, and technicians—*Scientists and engineers* are defined as persons engaged in scientific and engineering work at a level requiring a knowledge of sciences equivalent at least to that acquired through completion of a 4-year college course. *Technicians* are defined as persons engaged in technical work at a level requiring knowledge acquired through a technical institute, junior college, or other type of training less extensive than 4-year college training. Craftsmen and skilled workers are excluded.

Table 835. Research and Development (R&D) Expenditures by Source of Funding: 1960 to 2022

[In millions of dollars (13,711 represents $13,711,000,000), except percent]

Year	Total	Sources of funds					Percent of total				
		Federal government	Industry	Universities & colleges [1]	Non-profit	Non-federal government	Federal government	Industry	Universities & colleges [1]	Non-profit	Non-federal government
1960......	13,711	8,915	4,516	67	123	90	65.0	32.9	0.5	0.9	0.7
1970......	26,271	14,984	10,449	259	343	237	57.0	39.8	1.0	1.3	0.9
1980......	63,224	29,986	30,929	920	871	519	47.4	48.9	1.5	1.4	0.8
1985......	114,671	52,641	57,962	1,743	1,491	834	45.9	50.5	1.5	1.3	0.7
1990......	151,993	61,610	83,208	3,187	2,589	1,399	40.5	54.7	2.1	1.7	0.9
1991......	160,876	60,783	92,300	3,458	2,852	1,483	37.8	57.4	2.1	1.8	0.9
1992......	165,350	60,915	96,229	3,569	3,113	1,525	36.8	58.2	2.2	1.9	0.9
1993......	165,730	60,528	96,549	3,709	3,388	1,557	36.5	58.3	2.2	2.0	0.9
1994......	169,207	60,777	99,204	3,938	3,665	1,623	35.9	58.6	2.3	2.2	1.0
1995......	183,625	62,969	110,871	4,110	3,925	1,751	34.3	60.4	2.2	2.1	1.0
1996......	197,346	63,394	123,417	4,436	4,239	1,861	32.1	62.5	2.2	2.1	0.9
1997......	211,894	64,362	136,208	4,852	4,571	1,902	30.4	64.3	2.3	2.2	0.9
1998......	225,759	65,908	147,774	5,193	4,963	1,920	29.2	65.5	2.3	2.2	0.9
1999......	244,451	66,817	164,545	5,654	5,399	2,036	27.3	67.3	2.3	2.2	0.8
2000......	267,950	67,238	185,975	6,270	6,285	2,182	25.1	69.4	2.3	2.3	0.8
2001......	278,539	73,793	188,408	6,874	7,122	2,341	26.5	67.6	2.5	2.6	0.8
2002......	277,911	78,873	180,704	7,673	8,109	2,553	28.4	65.0	2.8	2.9	0.9
2003......	291,365	85,133	186,171	8,286	8,988	2,788	29.2	63.9	2.8	3.1	1.0
2004......	302,731	90,795	191,346	8,637	9,028	2,926	30.0	63.2	2.9	3.0	1.0
2005......	325,288	95,413	207,775	9,353	9,771	2,977	29.3	63.9	2.9	3.0	0.9
2006......	350,908	99,938	227,182	10,176	10,320	3,293	28.5	64.7	2.9	2.9	0.9
2007......	377,890	105,128	246,815	10,933	11,420	3,594	27.8	65.3	2.9	3.0	1.0
2008......	404,777	117,615	258,020	11,738	13,184	4,221	29.1	63.7	2.9	3.3	1.0
2009......	402,931	125,765	246,609	12,057	14,205	4,296	31.2	61.2	3.0	3.5	1.1
2010......	406,599	126,617	248,126	12,262	15,292	4,303	31.1	61.0	3.0	3.8	1.1
2011......	426,214	127,014	266,426	13,103	15,284	4,386	29.8	62.5	3.1	3.6	1.0
2012......	433,698	123,837	275,728	14,282	15,694	4,158	28.6	63.6	3.3	3.6	1.0
2013......	454,232	120,131	297,188	15,341	17,327	4,244	26.4	65.4	3.4	3.8	0.9
2014......	475,938	118,367	318,410	16,176	18,771	4,214	24.9	66.9	3.4	3.9	0.9
2015......	494,470	119,532	333,242	17,260	20,160	4,277	24.2	67.4	3.5	4.1	0.9
2016......	521,686	118,174	360,290	18,729	19,497	4,995	22.7	69.1	3.6	3.7	1.0
2017......	553,612	122,470	386,538	19,880	19,648	5,076	22.1	69.8	3.6	3.5	0.9
2018......	604,028	131,098	426,488	20,989	20,201	5,252	21.7	70.6	3.5	3.3	0.9
2019......	665,557	135,779	482,227	21,885	20,193	5,474	20.4	72.5	3.3	3.0	0.8
2020......	716,870	148,169	520,364	22,560	20,102	5,676	20.7	72.6	3.1	2.8	0.8
2021......	789,072	147,531	591,009	23,783	21,017	5,733	18.7	74.9	3.0	2.7	0.7
2022 [2]....	885,563	159,833	672,868	25,514	21,447	5,902	18.0	76.0	2.9	2.4	0.7

[1] Figures for university and college R&D prior to 2003 cover only science and engineering (S&E) fields; in 2003 and later years, R&D in non-S&E fields is also included. Also, adjustments have been made to university and college R&D for 1998 and later years to eliminate double counting of funds passed through from one academic institution to another. [2] Estimated.

Source: U.S. National Science Foundation, National Center for Science and Engineering Statistics, *National Patterns of R&D Resources, 2021-22 Data Update*, NSF 24-318, January 2024. See also <ncses.nsf.gov/data-collections/national-patterns>.

Table 836. National Research and Development (R&D) Expenditures as a Percent of Gross Domestic Product by Country: 1990 to 2022

Year	United States [1, 5]	Japan [2]	Germany [3]	France	United Kingdom	Italy [9]	Canada	South Korea	OECD total [4]	Russia	China
1990....	2.56	[6] 2.66	[6] 2.61	2.27	1.95	[6] 1.20	1.48	(NA)	(NA)	1.89	(NA)
2000....	2.62	2.86	2.41	[7] 2.09	1.61	1.00	1.86	[10] 2.13	2.12	0.98	[7] 0.89
2005....	2.50	3.13	2.44	2.05	1.55	1.04	1.97	[10] 2.52	2.13	0.99	1.31
2010....	2.71	3.10	2.73	[7] 2.18	[6] 1.64	1.22	1.83	3.32	2.28	1.05	1.71
2011....	2.74	3.21	2.81	2.19	1.65	1.20	1.79	3.59	2.31	1.02	1.78
2012....	2.67	3.17	2.88	2.23	[6] 1.58	1.26	[7] 1.77	3.85	2.30	1.03	1.91
2013....	2.70	[7] 3.28	2.84	2.24	1.62	1.30	1.71	3.95	2.33	1.03	2.00
2014....	2.71	3.37	2.88	[7] 2.28	[6, 7, 8] 2.26	[6] 1.34	[7] 1.71	4.08	2.35	1.07	2.02
2015....	[7] 2.77	3.24	2.93	2.23	[6, 8] 2.28	1.34	1.69	3.98	2.37	1.10	2.06
2016....	2.84	3.11	2.94	2.22	[6, 8] 2.32	[7] 1.37	1.73	3.99	2.37	1.10	2.10
2017....	2.88	3.17	3.05	2.20	[6, 8] 2.33	1.37	1.69	4.29	2.41	1.11	2.12
2018....	2.99	[7] 3.22	3.11	2.20	[6, 7, 8] 2.71	1.42	1.74	4.52	2.49	0.99	2.14
2019....	3.15	3.22	[8] 3.17	2.19	[8] 2.67	1.46	1.76	4.63	2.56	1.04	2.24
2020....	3.42	3.26	[8] 3.13	2.27	[8] 2.94	1.51	1.93	4.80	2.72	1.10	2.41
2021....	[7] 3.48	3.28	[8] 3.13	[8] 2.22	[8] 2.90	1.43	1.86	4.91	2.72	(NA)	2.43
2022....	[8] 3.59	3.41	[8] 3.13	[8] 2.18	(NA)	[8] 1.32	[8] 1.71	[8] 5.21	2.73	(NA)	2.56

NA Not available. [1] Excludes most or all capital expenditure. [2] Data on Japanese research and development after 1996 may not be consistent with data in earlier years because of changes in methodology. [3] Data for 1990 are for West Germany only. [4] Organisation for Economic Cooperation and Development. Values for the OECD are estimated for all years. [5] Excludes R&D expenditures by state and local governments. [6] Estimated value. [7] Time series break. [8] Provisional. [9] Except for 1990, data for Italy excludes extramural R&D expenditures. [10] Excluding R&D in the social sciences and humanities.

Source: Organisation for Economic Co-operation and Development (OECD), 2024, OECD Data Explorer, Science, technology, and innovation: Research and development (R&D), "Main Science and Technology Indicators (MSTI database)" ©, <data-explorer.oecd.org>, accessed July 2024.

Table 837. Research and Development (R&D) Expenditures By Performing Sector and Source of Funds: 1990 to 2022

[In millions of dollars (151,993 represents $151,993,000,000). For calendar year. FFRDCs are federally funded research and development centers]

Year	Total	All federal research	Federal intramural [1]	FFRDCs [2]	Non-federal government	Industry Total [3]	Industry Funded by Industry [4]	Industry Funded by Federal government	Universities & colleges Total	Univ Funded by Federal government	Univ Funded by Non-federal government	Univ Funded by Industry	Univ Funded by Universities & colleges	Univ Funded by Nonprofits	Other nonprofit institutions Total	Other nonprofit Funded by Federal government	Other nonprofit Funded by Industry	Other nonprofit Funded by Nonprofits
R&D TOTAL																		
1990	151,993	23,524	15,671	7,853	(NA)	107,404	81,602	25,802	16,939	9,939	1,399	1,166	3,187	1,249	4,126	2,346	440	1,340
2000	267,950	28,516	19,247	9,269	(NA)	199,961	182,844	17,117	29,916	17,095	2,182	2,112	6,270	2,258	9,557	4,510	1,020	4,027
2010	406,599	50,798	31,970	18,828	691	278,977	218,187	34,199	58,083	34,681	3,674	2,953	12,262	4,515	18,050	7,093	1,266	9,691
2015	494,470	52,847	34,199	18,649	595	355,821	289,892	26,990	64,604	33,563	3,782	3,844	17,260	6,156	20,604	6,247	1,605	12,751
2018	604,028	58,356	36,793	21,563	643	445,563	357,862	25,192	74,890	37,745	4,224	4,584	20,667	7,670	24,576	9,937	2,486	11,312
2019	665,557	62,802	39,870	22,932	675	498,175	405,960	22,653	78,157	39,528	4,363	4,806	21,568	7,893	25,749	10,901	2,778	11,212
2020	716,072	65,093	41,227	23,866	683	543,220	443,398	29,772	80,823	41,436	4,470	4,838	22,250	7,830	27,053	11,959	3,103	11,112
2021 [5]	789,072	66,786	41,464	25,322	685	608,625	500,300	24,587	85,787	44,683	4,621	5,080	23,506	7,897	27,190	11,620	3,010	11,958
2022 [5]	885,563	73,338	46,960	26,378	697	692,748	573,667	27,325	91,451	47,738	4,766	5,493	25,236	8,219	27,329	11,679	3,026	12,019
BASIC RESEARCH																		
1990	23,029	5,352	2,319	3,033	(NA)	4,629	3,760	869	11,126	6,889	847	705	1,929	756	1,922	947	245	730
2000	42,033	7,801	3,765	4,037	(NA)	7,040	6,115	925	22,290	13,469	1,501	1,453	4,314	1,553	4,902	2,099	566	2,236
2010	76,475	11,747	5,111	6,637	103	16,371	13,239	1,406	38,756	23,690	2,277	1,785	8,016	2,989	9,498	3,414	703	5,381
2015	84,428	10,017	5,890	4,127	100	21,792	15,933	2,038	41,514	22,193	2,299	2,211	10,985	3,826	11,005	3,034	891	7,080
2018	97,885	11,096	6,827	4,269	107	29,204	21,100	2,535	47,321	24,502	2,454	2,606	13,001	4,760	10,157	4,301	995	4,525
2019	105,011	11,932	7,352	4,580	120	32,582	24,558	2,349	49,335	25,489	2,535	2,733	13,626	4,953	11,041	4,805	1,167	4,709
2020	111,802	12,105	7,316	4,789	125	36,371	27,909	2,200	50,837	26,518	2,619	2,747	14,055	4,898	12,364	5,217	1,469	5,262
2021 [5]	118,626	11,688	6,604	5,084	120	40,845	31,364	2,404	54,047	28,693	2,726	2,885	14,841	4,902	11,926	4,646	1,408	5,591
2022 [5]	129,435	13,202	7,959	5,244	121	46,287	35,918	2,676	57,838	30,768	2,833	3,128	16,004	5,105	11,987	4,670	1,415	5,620
APPLIED RESEARCH																		
1990	34,897	4,808	3,652	1,156	(NA)	24,399	18,432	5,967	4,406	2,140	453	377	1,031	404	1,284	780	120	384
2000	56,503	7,856	6,105	1,750	(NA)	39,176	36,494	2,682	6,361	3,081	558	540	1,604	578	3,110	1,831	258	1,021
2010	78,885	13,203	8,016	5,187	572	44,906	34,912	4,705	14,387	8,539	1,000	760	3,060	1,028	5,818	3,041	321	2,456
2015	97,059	16,698	9,347	7,351	481	56,472	43,330	6,102	16,980	8,838	1,083	1,079	4,425	1,557	6,429	2,791	407	3,231
2018	118,316	19,704	11,111	8,593	514	66,587	50,898	5,355	20,563	10,448	1,286	1,353	5,476	2,001	10,947	4,652	1,069	4,864
2019	130,225	20,523	11,264	9,258	523	76,176	57,549	5,246	21,540	10,965	1,338	1,439	5,732	2,066	11,463	5,375	1,139	4,597
2020	132,524	21,117	11,554	9,563	514	78,371	58,766	5,906	22,297	11,527	1,360	1,433	5,928	2,050	10,226	4,902	1,094	3,919
2021 [5]	144,037	21,305	11,132	10,173	521	88,707	66,451	3,491	23,528	12,341	1,391	1,476	6,236	2,085	9,977	5,080	947	3,761
2022 [5]	159,927	24,078	13,299	10,779	536	100,334	76,060	3,869	24,951	13,103	1,427	1,583	6,656	2,182	10,028	5,106	952	3,780
DEVELOPMENT																		
1990	94,067	13,363	9,700	3,663	(NA)	78,376	59,410	18,966	1,407	910	99	83	226	89	920	619	75	226
2000	169,414	12,859	9,377	3,482	(NA)	153,745	140,235	13,510	1,265	545	123	119	352	127	1,545	580	195	771
2010	251,239	25,848	18,844	7,004	16	217,700	170,036	28,089	4,941	2,452	397	408	1,186	498	2,734	638	242	1,854
2015	312,982	26,132	18,961	7,171	14	277,557	230,629	18,850	6,111	2,533	401	554	1,850	774	3,169	422	307	2,440
2018	387,827	27,556	18,856	8,701	23	349,771	285,863	17,301	7,006	2,796	485	625	2,191	910	3,472	983	423	1,923
2019	430,323	30,347	21,253	9,094	31	389,418	323,854	15,058	7,282	3,074	491	634	2,211	874	3,245	721	472	1,906
2020	472,545	31,870	22,356	9,514	44	428,479	356,724	21,666	7,690	3,391	492	658	2,267	882	4,463	1,840	539	1,931
2021 [5]	526,408	33,793	23,728	10,065	44	479,072	402,485	18,690	8,213	3,650	505	719	2,429	911	5,287	1,894	656	2,606
2022 [5]	596,199	36,058	25,703	10,355	40	546,125	461,689	20,779	8,663	3,867	505	782	2,576	932	5,314	1,904	659	2,619

NA Not available. [1] Federal intramural performers are agencies of the federal government, with work carried on directly by agency personnel. Intramural expenditures include those for federal intramural R&D as well as cost associated with administering extramural R&D. Extramural R&D is performed outside the federal sector with federal funds under contract, grant, or cooperative agreement. [2] R&D expenditures of FFRDCs are chiefly federally funded; the remainder reflects funding from state or local government, businesses, other nonprofit organizations, and other sources. [3] Beginning 2008, total funding for industry R&D includes other sources of funding, including funding from other nonfederal U.S. sources and sources outside the U.S. [4] Through 2007, includes all other nonfederal sources. Beginning 2008, excludes other sources of funding not shown separately, including funding from parent or unaffiliated businesses outside the U.S. and foreign subsidiaries of U.S. businesses. [5] Estimates.

Source: U.S. National Science Foundation, National Center for Science and Engineering Statistics, *National Patterns of R&D Resources: 2021-22 Data Update*, NSF 24-318, January 2024. See also <ncses.nsf.gov/data-collections/national-patterns>.

Table 838. Federal Obligations for Research by Field of Science: 2010 to 2022

[In millions of dollars (63,728 represents $63,728,000,000). For years ending September 30. Excludes development, and research and development (R&D) plant (facilities and fixed equipment)]

Field of science	2010	2015	2017	2018	2019	2020	2021	2022 (P)
Research, total.................	**63,728**	**63,825**	**69,871**	**74,588**	**81,118**	**85,305**	**86,244**	**88,464**
Basic.................................	31,795	31,527	33,271	36,195	40,017	41,547	42,494	43,790
Applied..............................	31,933	32,298	36,600	38,392	41,101	43,758	43,750	44,674
Computer sciences and mathematics.......	3,412	3,863	3,894	4,207	4,330	5,912	(NA)	(NA)
Engineering..........................	11,081	11,984	13,207	13,759	15,279	13,222	13,374	13,861
Geosciences, atmospheric sciences, and ocean sciences..................	3,339	4,414	4,470	4,568	5,075	5,039	3,569	6,052
Life sciences........................	33,909	30,625	34,090	36,994	38,304	42,525	38,178	38,511
Physical sciences....................	5,871	6,510	6,581	7,881	9,816	8,420	8,044	11,112
Psychology..........................	2,156	1,995	2,081	2,327	2,754	3,276	3,770	3,776
Social sciences......................	1,197	1,136	1,027	1,039	1,156	1,137	1,370	1,449
Other sciences, n.e.c. [1]............	2,763	3,299	4,521	3,812	4,405	5,773	(NA)	(NA)

P Data are preliminary. NA Not available. [1] Not elsewhere classified.

Source: U.S. National Science Foundation, *Federal Funds for Research and Development, Fiscal Years 2021-22; Data Tables*, NSF 24-309, December 2023. See also <www.nsf.gov/statistics/fedfunds/>.

Table 839. Federal Budget Authority for Research and Development (R&D) by Selected Budget Function: 2010 to 2023

[In millions of current dollars (146,596 represents $146,596,000,000). For year ending September 30. Excludes R&D plant]

Function	2010	2015	2018	2019	2020 [2]	2021 [2]	2022 [2]	2023 (P)
Total [1]..........................	**146,596**	**136,090**	**140,701**	**145,615**	**163,875**	**158,550**	**180,196**	**195,135**
National defense......................	86,517	72,560	68,325	71,396	79,389	77,219	83,857	97,765
Health................................	31,488	30,331	37,151	38,755	43,936	40,877	44,943	47,572
General science and basic research.....	9,280	10,068	10,692	10,961	11,620	12,118	13,246	13,819
Space flight, research, and supporting activities..................	8,232	10,875	10,455	10,016	14,158	11,512	14,453	15,132
Energy...............................	2,455	3,153	4,212	4,433	4,391	4,381	6,340	6,696
Natural resources and environment......	2,237	2,161	2,383	2,486	2,653	3,395	2,848	2,996
Agriculture...........................	2,043	1,989	2,074	2,205	2,332	2,514	3,000	2,893
Transportation........................	1,496	1,363	1,551	1,582	1,674	1,685	2,274	1,940
Veterans benefits and services...........	1,034	1,178	1,286	1,370	1,366	1,436	1,588	1,622

P Preliminary. [1] Includes other functions, not shown separately. [2] Agencies in several functions received emergency COVID-19 pandemic-related funding for R&D or R&D plant in FYs 2020-22. This funding may be included in this table's data; agency reporting is not clear in all cases.

Source: U.S. National Science Foundation, "Federal R&D Funding by Budget Function: Fiscal Years 2022-24, Data Tables," <ncses.nsf.gov/data-collections/federal-budget-function>, accessed April 2024, and earlier releases.

Table 840. Federal Research and Development (R&D) Budget by Federal Agency: 2023 to 2025

[In millions of dollars (199,955 represents $199,955,000,000). Table shows funding levels for departments or independent agencies with more than $200 million in R&D activities in 2025. For fiscal years ending September 30. R&D refers to actual research and development activities as well as R&D equipment and facilities. R&D facilities (also known as R&D plants) includes construction, repair, or alteration of physical plant used in the conduct of R&D]

Federal agency	2023	2024, estimated	2025, proposed
Total research and development [1, 2].............	**199,955**	**194,564**	**201,949**
Defense.................................	95,541	90,632	92,757
Health and Human Services................	48,393	47,591	51,364
Energy.................................	20,790	22,237	23,440
National Aeronautics and Space Administration..........	11,691	11,797	11,715
National Science Foundation..............	7,988	7,800	8,122
Agriculture.............................	3,380	3,379	3,283
Commerce..............................	5,141	3,930	3,926
Veterans Affairs........................	1,684	1,799	1,709
Transportation..........................	1,411	1,462	1,513
Interior................................	1,296	1,258	1,330
Basic research [2].....................	**47,023**	**46,105**	**47,684**
Defense.................................	2,847	2,519	2,493
Health and Human Services................	23,097	22,748	23,602
Energy.................................	6,775	6,324	6,923
National Aeronautics and Space Administration..........	5,115	5,417	5,302
National Science Foundation..............	6,290	6,134	6,267
Agriculture.............................	1,392	1,386	1,383
Applied research [2]...................	**49,725**	**47,930**	**51,221**
Defense.................................	8,013	6,237	6,024
Health and Human Services................	24,819	24,363	27,262
Energy.................................	6,643	7,086	7,351
National Aeronautics and Space Administration..........	1,843	1,948	2,228
National Science Foundation..............	1,178	1,155	1,215
Agriculture.............................	1,371	1,372	1,358
Commerce..............................	1,637	1,495	1,412

[1] Total includes experimental development and facilities and equipment, not shown separately. [2] Incudes other agencies not shown separately.

Source: U.S. Office of Management and Budget, *Budget of the U.S. Government, Fiscal Year 2025: Analytical Perspectives*, March 2024. See also <www.whitehouse.gov/omb/budget>.

Table 841. Funds for Domestic Business Research and Development (R&D) Performed by Companies by Industry: 2021

[In millions of dollars (602,499 represents $602,499,000,000), except percent. For the calendar year. The data represent for-profit nonfarm companies that have ten or more paid employees in the United States, have at least one establishment that is in business during the survey year, and is located in the United States. Beginning in survey year 2018, statistics represent companies that performed or funded $50,000 or more of R&D. This change affects the comparability of these estimates with estimates published for years prior to 2018. Covers basic research, applied research, and development performed by the company and others. Based on the Business Enterprise R&D Survey]

Industry	NAICS [1] code	Domestic R&D paid for by the company and others		Domestic R&D paid for by the company	
		Value (million dollars)	As a percent of domestic sales [2]	Value (million dollars)	As a percent of domestic sales [2]
All industries, total [3]	(X)	602,499	4.6	527,804	4.0
All manufacturing industries, total [3]	31–33	326,060	5.0	287,666	4.4
Chemicals	325	109,490	8.4	97,097	7.4
Pharmaceuticals and medicines	3254	100,220	16.1	88,524	14.2
Machinery	333	17,730	4.2	16,726	3.9
Semiconductor machinery	333242	5,349	17.9	5,182	17.4
Computer and electronic products	334	101,063	13.0	94,211	12.1
Electrical equipment, appliances, and components	335	5,494	3.5	5,007	3.2
Transportation equipment	336	50,760	5.0	34,405	3.4
Aerospace products and parts	3364	[4] 21,468	6.9	9,900	3.2
All nonmanufacturing industries, total [3]	(X)	276,439	4.2	240,138	3.7
Information	51	147,855	8.7	146,488	8.6
Software publishers	5112	39,049	12.9	38,441	12.7
Professional, scientific, and technical services	54	66,496	13.7	32,083	6.6
Computer systems design and related services	5415	20,409	10.2	17,188	8.6
Scientific research and development services	5417	[4] 34,142	41.2	6,123	7.4

X Not applicable. [1] 2012 North American Industry Classification System (NAICS); see text, Section 15. [2] Includes companies located in the United States that performed or funded R&D. [3] Includes industries not shown separately. [4] More than 50% of the estimate is a combination of imputation and reweighting to account for nonresponse.

Source: U.S. National Science Foundation, Business Enterprise Research and Development Survey: 2021, "Data Tables," <ncses.nsf.gov/surveys/business-enterprise-research-development/2021#data>, accessed November 2023.

Table 842. Academic and Industrial Research and Development (R&D) Expenditures by State: 2021

[In millions of dollars (85,787 represents $85,787,000,000). Industry R&D data refer to calendar years; other R&D data refer to fiscal years but are used here as approximations to calendar year data]

State	Academic R&D [2] (mil. dol.)	Academic R&D per $1,000 of state GDP	Industry-performed R&D (mil. dol.)	Industry R&D per $1,000 of state GDP	State	Academic R&D [2] (mil. dol.)	Academic R&D per $1,000 of state GDP	Industry-performed R&D (mil. dol.)	Industry R&D per $1,000 of state GDP
U.S. [1]	85,787	3.64	608,625	25.80	MO	1,583	4.34	7,060	19.33
AL	1,272	5.51	2,910	12.60	MT	330	5.50	261	4.35
AK	197	3.36	207	3.53	NE	576	3.86	1,067	7.14
AZ	1,516	3.51	9,386	21.71	NV	309	1.54	1,033	5.16
AR	388	2.55	497	3.27	NH	499	5.04	3,183	32.12
CA	11,230	3.29	211,615	61.93	NJ	1,353	1.95	25,049	36.19
CO	1,747	3.91	8,098	18.11	NM	473	4.23	1,693	15.15
CT	1,494	5.05	8,429	28.49	NY	7,577	3.96	26,319	13.77
DE	255	3.07	3,592	43.30	NC	3,504	5.31	15,490	23.49
DC	718	4.60	744	4.76	ND	308	4.87	343	5.43
FL	2,769	2.14	9,688	7.50	OH	2,788	3.67	11,545	15.20
GA	2,950	4.20	6,448	9.19	OK	623	2.86	1,056	4.85
HI	295	3.17	409	4.39	OR	929	3.37	11,292	41.00
ID	166	1.68	2,258	22.86	PA	4,935	5.84	17,555	20.79
IL	2,914	3.09	16,485	17.46	RI	426	6.34	837	12.45
IN	1,699	4.02	9,514	22.49	SC	753	2.77	1,857	6.84
IA	931	4.22	3,045	13.79	SD	101	1.61	221	3.53
KS	785	4.09	2,748	14.33	TN	1,630	3.72	2,776	6.34
KY	655	2.75	1,486	6.25	TX	6,850	3.28	28,264	13.54
LA	831	3.16	530	2.01	UT	994	4.28	3,962	17.07
ME	165	2.09	499	6.32	VT	198	5.27	456	12.13
MD	4,914	10.99	6,432	14.39	VA	1,942	3.16	8,179	13.32
MA	4,569	7.08	39,749	61.58	WA	1,881	2.73	49,083	71.28
MI	2,842	4.93	22,381	38.82	WV	231	2.67	522	6.03
MN	1,115	2.70	8,248	19.97	WI	1,771	4.80	6,781	18.38
MS	491	3.83	343	2.67	WY	93	2.21	93	2.21

[1] States will not sum to U.S. totals because the U.S. totals include data for outlying areas (Puerto Rico, Guam, American Samoa, and Virgin Islands), R&D expenditures that cannot be allocated to specific states, and double counting of universities and colleges data. [2] State level university R&D data have not been adjusted to eliminate double counting of funds passed through from one academic institution to another. See source for more information.

Source: U.S. National Science Foundation, National Center for Science and Engineering Statistics, *National Patterns of R&D Resources: 2021-22 Data Update*, NSF 24-318, January 2024. See also <ncses.nsf.gov/data-collections/national-patterns>.

Table 843. Higher Education Research and Development (R&D) Expenditures, Total and in Science and Engineering: 2010 to 2022

[In millions of dollars (61,287 represents $61,287,000,000). Data include R&D expenditures for both science and engineering (S&E) as well as non S&E fields, except for data by field. Beginning with FY2012, includes institutions reporting $1 million or more in total R&D expenditures; prior to FY2012 includes all institutions. Totals may not add due to rounding. Reference period is the fiscal year of the surveyed institutions. Data are based on the Higher Education R&D (HERD) Survey, which in 2010 succeeded the Survey of Research and Development Expenditures at Colleges and Universities; see source for details]

Characteristic	2010	2015	2018	2019	2020	2021	2022
Expenditures, total	**61,287**	**68,520**	**79,024**	**83,488**	**86,302**	**89,695**	**97,681**
Basic research	40,949	44,386	49,888	52,720	54,372	56,197	61,698
Applied & experimental R&D	20,337	24,134	29,136	30,768	31,930	33,498	35,982
SOURCE OF FUNDS							
Federal government	37,478	37,847	41,860	44,460	46,107	49,116	53,971
State and local government	3,887	3,855	4,313	4,511	4,594	4,742	4,907
Institutions' own funds	11,943	16,562	20,178	21,071	21,989	22,443	24,493
Business or industry	3,202	4,003	4,720	5,059	5,183	5,116	5,702
Nonprofit organizations	3,730	4,220	5,445	5,691	5,744	5,594	5,974
Other	1,048	2,033	2,507	2,696	2,685	2,684	2,633
FIELD							
Science and engineering, total	**58,388**	**64,906**	**74,382**	**78,633**	**81,266**	**84,581**	**91,823**
Computer and information sciences	1,638	1,962	2,398	2,637	2,925	2,953	3,225
Geosciences	2,992	3,246	3,160	3,186	3,281	3,295	3,690
Life sciences	34,984	38,769	45,606	48,227	49,615	52,350	56,498
Mathematics and statistics	592	641	750	769	801	773	880
Physical sciences	4,622	4,649	5,232	5,551	5,672	5,737	6,168
Psychology	1,078	1,184	1,261	1,328	1,365	1,330	1,444
Social sciences	2,000	2,315	2,722	2,806	2,951	2,828	3,165
Other sciences	1,156	1,078	890	916	954	1,025	1,156
Engineering	9,326	11,063	12,363	13,214	13,702	14,292	15,597

Source: U.S. National Science Foundation, "Higher Education Research and Development: Fiscal Year 2022, Data Tables," and earlier reports, <ncses.nsf.gov/surveys/higher-education-research-development/2022>, accessed January 2024.

Table 844. Federal Research and Development (R&D) Obligations to Selected Universities and Colleges: 2000 to 2021

[In millions of dollars (17,271.7 represents $17,271,700,000). Year ending September 30. Top 40 institutions receiving Federal Research & Development (R&D) funds in FY2021. From the Survey of Federal Science and Engineering Support to Universities, Colleges, and Nonprofit Institutions. Included are colleges of liberal arts; schools of arts and sciences; professional schools, as in engineering and medicine, including affiliate hospitals and associated research institutes; and agricultural experiment stations. Does not cover academic Federally Funded Research and Development Centers (FFRDC) administered by higher education institutions. Includes administrative expenses for R&D and excludes investments in physical assets, routine testing, quality control, and monitoring, and training of scientific and technical personnel]

Top 40 institutions ranked by 2021 obligations	2000	2010 [2]	2015	2019	2020	2021
Total, all institutions [1]	**17,271.7**	**30,749.4**	**26,772.3**	**34,825.4**	**36,202.5**	**39,283.1**
Johns Hopkins University	795.5	1,515.8	1,340.7	1,856.1	1,915.2	1,817.7
New York University	130.0	257.1	263.8	430.2	436.8	893.8
Duke University	232.2	496.8	428.5	629.1	639.3	810.5
University of California—San Diego	314.4	613.2	536.6	679.6	652.4	792.9
University of Washington, all campuses	396.1	736.6	611.9	726.6	728.4	787.2
University of Michigan, all campuses	346.7	686.6	606.1	745.8	755.6	774.6
Columbia University in the City of New York	284.6	497.6	476.1	653.4	699.9	761.4
University of California—San Francisco	289.2	531.3	528.5	675.4	644.4	714.9
Stanford University	355.0	516.8	504.0	612.5	630.6	696.5
University of California—Los Angeles	372.4	548.8	481.8	555.1	750.6	686.6
University of Pennsylvania	348.5	609.0	494.6	625.5	593.6	681.7
University of Pittsburgh, all campuses	246.2	497.1	450.0	581.8	600.2	679.3
University of Colorado—Boulder	272.3	427.0	416.7	511.5	538.9	657.8
Washington University, Saint Louis	287.3	445.5	391.6	535.1	543.5	639.5
Yale University	260.0	470.5	370.8	530.7	552.6	596.1
University of North Carolina at Chapel Hill	232.7	429.7	416.8	535.6	523.3	541.6
Northwestern University	151.5	282.0	337.0	470.8	478.0	509.0
Pennsylvania State University, all campuses	230.1	413.1	362.9	520.0	462.7	508.2
Vanderbilt University	138.4	399.1	329.3	422.5	518.4	507.8
Cornell University, all campuses	240.1	359.8	296.4	423.7	427.2	497.6
Emory University	145.6	303.1	324.2	398.0	510.4	486.6
University of Southern California	203.9	378.9	289.2	408.7	416.9	484.7
Harvard University	299.9	548.7	425.5	486.2	439.8	484.7
University of Minnesota, all campuses	276.8	420.3	359.5	426.9	440.0	473.6
Massachusetts Institute of Technology	248.9	340.2	350.5	320.6	289.9	443.4
Mount Sinai School of Medicine	119.5	216.5	262.4	395.7	416.3	436.1
University of Wisconsin—Madison	263.4	461.9	386.6	435.6	448.2	429.1
Baylor College of Medicine	172.3	251.6	227.5	302.9	349.6	394.9
University of California—Davis	148.5	313.2	315.4	328.5	341.6	385.6
The Ohio State University, all campuses	140.8	313.6	232.5	311.6	318.0	353.3
Georgia Institute of Technology—Atlanta	58.4	234.9	295.2	620.1	683.9	345.5
University of Alabama at Birmingham	182.9	236.0	254.2	348.8	336.1	336.5
University of Texas at Austin	135.0	192.9	203.4	301.6	350.4	330.1
University of Florida	129.2	228.2	239.0	314.9	287.6	319.9
University of Chicago	144.5	252.8	224.2	274.1	304.8	317.2
Boston University	139.4	226.0	188.2	292.7	261.0	316.0
University of Maryland at College Park	120.7	179.9	206.3	232.8	239.3	310.8
University of California—Berkeley	196.2	306.0	295.0	239.8	230.6	304.6
University of Utah	125.0	230.2	201.4	376.0	314.9	301.1
Rutgers, The State University of New Jersey	178.1	292.1	201.7	258.7	260.8	300.5

[1] Includes other institutions, not shown separately. [2] Includes American Recovery and Reinvestment Act of 2009 obligations.

Source: U.S. National Science Foundation, National Center for Science and Engineering Statistics, "NCES Survey Data," <ncsesdata.nsf.gov/home>, accessed January 2024. See also <www.nsf.gov/statistics/fedsupport/>.

Table 845. Research and Development (R&D) Spending and Employment by Company Size: 2021

[Expenditures in millions of dollars (602,499 represents $602,499,000,000); employment in thousands (23,654 represents 23,654,000). Data are from the Business Enterprise Research and Development Survey. Data represent all for-profit, nonfarm companies that are publicly or privately held, have ten or more employees in the United States, and that performed or funded $50,000 or more in R&D]

Company size	Domestic R&D expenditures [1] (mil. dollars)	R&D as a percent of domestic sales of R&D performers or funders	R&D as a percent of domestic sales of R&D performers	Domestic employment of R&D performing companies		
				Total employment (1,000s)	R&D employment [2] (1,000s)	R&D employment as a percent of total employment
All companies	**602,499**	**4.6**	**4.7**	**23,654**	**2,132**	**9.0**
Small companies:						
10–19 employees	5,477	15.3	16.3	85	36	42.4
20–49 employees	15,061	14.4	14.9	298	99	33.2
Medium companies:						
50–99 employees	14,540	9.9	10.1	418	92	22.0
100–249 employees	24,023	6.3	6.4	886	157	17.7
Large companies:						
250–499 employees	23,932	6.4	6.6	741	110	14.8
500–999 employees	27,432	5.5	5.7	926	110	11.9
1,000–4,999 employees	94,615	4.7	4.8	3,148	340	10.8
5,000–9,999 employees	62,817	4.1	4.2	1,933	211	10.9
10,000–24,999 employees	104,607	4.7	4.7	3,260	309	9.5
25,000 or more employees	229,995	4.0	4.1	11,959	668	5.6

[1] Domestic R&D paid for by the company and others and performed by the company. [2] Includes researchers, R&D technicians, and other supporting staff.

Source: U.S. National Science Foundation, Business Enterprise Research and Development Survey: 2021, "Data Tables," <ncses.nsf.gov/surveys/business-enterprise-research-development/2021#data>, accessed November 2023.

Table 846. Temporary Visa Holders Awarded Doctorates in Science and Engineering For Top 10 Countries of Origin: 2010 to 2022

[Based on the Survey of Earned Doctorates; for information, see <ncses.nsf.gov/surveys/earned-doctorates>]

Country of origin	2010	2013	2014	2015	2016	2017	2018	2019	2020	2021	2022
All temporary visa holders [1]	**13,636**	**15,674**	**15,839**	**16,129**	**16,477**	**16,288**	**17,582**	**18,324**	**18,473**	**17,771**	**19,633**
Science	7,809	8,676	8,764	8,902	9,471	9,085	9,629	10,097	10,047	9,662	10,838
Engineering	3,866	4,759	4,961	5,108	4,842	5,037	5,575	5,680	5,950	5,673	6,253
COUNTRY											
China [2]	3,457	4,443	4,650	4,970	5,141	5,147	5,692	5,755	5,730	5,607	6,031
India	1,994	2,074	2,208	2,119	2,085	1,884	1,922	1,910	2,111	2,138	2,510
Iran	(D)	380	463	608	664	728	869	882	896	741	791
South Korea	1,076	1,012	928	920	891	815	729	824	756	733	761
Bangladesh	(NA)	96	127	146	178	224	271	271	369	381	522
Saudi Arabia	26	53	76	98	175	232	294	431	471	368	386
Taiwan	501	571	558	514	499	435	445	426	417	375	374
Canada	339	332	321	318	272	288	307	313	281	267	356
Nepal	(NA)	(D)	163	162	208	209	219	230	(D)	242	305
Turkey	405	391	360	386	380	392	364	324	305	272	289

NA Not available. D Data is suppressed to avoid disclosure of confidential information. [1] Total includes doctorates awarded in fields other than science and engineering and to temporary visa holders from other countries, not shown separately. [2] Includes Hong Kong.

Source: U.S. National Science Foundation, National Center for Science and Engineering Statistics, "Doctorate Recipients from U.S. Universities: 2022, Data Tables," <ncses.nsf.gov/surveys/earned-doctorates/>, accessed January 2024, and earlier reports.

Table 847. Science and Engineering (S&E) Degrees Awarded by Degree Level and Sex of Recipient: 2012 to 2021

[Aggregated for degrees in the following: agricultural sciences and natural resources, biological and biomedical sciences, computer and information sciences, engineering, mathematics and statistics, multidisciplinary/interdisciplinary sciences, physical sciences, psychology, social sciences, and geosciences, atmospheric sciences, and ocean sciences. Data are from the Integrated Postsecondary Education Data System (IPEDS) and classified according to the National Center for Science and Engineering Statistics (NCSES) Taxonomy of Disciplines (TOD). The NCSES TOD differs from the taxonomy covered in earlier editions of this table; therefore, data are not comparable]

Academic year ending	Bachelor's degree				Master's degree				Doctoral degree [1]			
	Total S&E	Men	Women	Percent women	Total S&E	Men	Women	Percent women	Total S&E	Men	Women	Percent women
2012	628,836	309,035	319,801	50.9	154,402	83,314	71,088	46.0	40,878	22,312	18,566	45.4
2013	657,959	325,012	332,947	50.6	158,787	85,299	73,488	46.3	42,513	23,241	19,272	45.3
2014	680,302	338,235	342,067	50.3	163,584	87,838	75,746	46.3	44,830	24,251	20,579	45.9
2015	694,701	347,669	347,032	50.0	173,854	94,841	79,013	45.4	45,343	24,527	20,816	45.9
2016	711,624	355,250	356,374	50.1	191,012	105,823	85,189	44.6	45,936	24,976	20,960	45.6
2017	730,573	365,934	364,639	49.9	201,311	111,928	89,383	44.4	46,596	25,232	21,364	45.8
2018	754,094	376,830	377,264	50.0	203,441	111,161	92,280	45.4	47,782	25,604	22,178	46.4
2019	773,662	384,634	389,028	50.3	205,067	110,032	95,035	46.3	48,712	26,119	22,593	46.4
2020	795,235	389,786	405,449	51.0	210,637	111,839	98,798	46.9	48,984	25,889	23,095	47.1
2021	811,706	390,393	421,313	51.9	217,146	113,565	103,581	47.7	47,763	24,887	22,876	47.9

[1] Doctoral degrees include health sciences degrees.

Source: U.S. National Science Foundation, Science and Engineering Indicators 2024, *Higher Education in Science and Engineering, Supplemental Tables*, NSB-2023-32, November 2023. See also <www.nsf.gov/statistics/seind/>.

Table 848. Graduate Science and Engineering Students in Doctorate-Granting Colleges by Characteristic and Field: 2018 to 2022

[In thousands (602.3 represents 602,300). As of Fall. Includes outlying areas. Based on the Survey of Graduate Students and Postdoctorates in Science and Engineering (GSS). In 2017, the GSS underwent a redesign that included a reorganization of the taxonomy of academic disciplines to align with the National Center for Science and Engineering Statistics Taxonomy of Disciplines (TOD); additional changes were made for the GSS 2020. Therefore, data from 2017 and after are not fully comparable to earlier data. For more information on the methodology, see National Science Foundation (NSF) website at <nsf.gov/statistics/srvygradpostdoc/>]

Field of science or engineering	Number (1,000s)					Percent of number				
	2018	2019	2020	2021	2022	2018	2019	2020	2021	2022
Total, all surveyed fields	**602.3**	**627.1**	**628.2**	**689.9**	**724.4**	**(X)**	**(X)**	**(X)**	**(X)**	**(X)**
Science/engineering	541.4	565.0	564.8	618.9	650.9	(X)	(X)	(X)	(X)	(X)
Engineering, total	156.5	157.9	151.1	162.3	170.1	(X)	(X)	(X)	(X)	(X)
Sciences, total	384.9	407.1	413.7	456.6	480.8	(X)	(X)	(X)	(X)	(X)
Agricultural & veterinary sciences	9.1	9.1	10.3	10.8	11.1	(X)	(X)	(X)	(X)	(X)
Biological sciences	81.6	85.4	87.7	94.2	96.5	(X)	(X)	(X)	(X)	(X)
Computer & information	80.3	89.1	87.2	106.5	131.3	(X)	(X)	(X)	(X)	(X)
Geosciences [2]	11.6	11.2	11.0	11.6	11.3	(X)	(X)	(X)	(X)	(X)
Math & statistics	29.0	30.9	29.6	32.3	32.7	(X)	(X)	(X)	(X)	(X)
Multidisciplinary & interdisciplinary studies	9.0	9.8	12.8	14.2	17.9	(X)	(X)	(X)	(X)	(X)
Natural resources & conservation	10.1	10.5	11.2	12.7	12.6	(X)	(X)	(X)	(X)	(X)
Physical sciences	41.1	42.0	41.6	43.2	43.2	(X)	(X)	(X)	(X)	(X)
Psychology	41.7	46.0	50.6	55.4	51.0	(X)	(X)	(X)	(X)	(X)
Social sciences	71.3	73.2	71.6	75.7	73.2	(X)	(X)	(X)	(X)	(X)
Health fields, total	60.9	62.1	63.4	71.0	73.5	(X)	(X)	(X)	(X)	(X)
FEMALE STUDENTS										
Total, all surveyed fields	**270.9**	**287.7**	**295.6**	**330.6**	**343.1**	**45.0**	**45.9**	**47.1**	**47.9**	**47.4**
Science/engineering	225.5	240.8	247.6	276.4	287.0	41.7	42.6	43.8	44.7	44.1
Engineering, total	39.6	41.5	40.8	45.0	47.5	25.3	26.3	27.0	27.7	27.9
Sciences, total	185.9	199.3	206.9	231.4	239.5	48.3	49.0	50.0	50.7	49.8
Agricultural & veterinary sciences	4.9	5.0	6.1	6.5	6.6	54.3	55.4	59.1	60.1	59.2
Biological sciences	46.9	50.0	52.3	57.3	59.5	57.5	58.5	59.6	60.9	61.7
Computer & information	24.0	27.1	26.5	33.4	42.2	29.8	30.4	30.4	31.3	32.2
Geosciences [2]	5.2	5.3	5.4	5.9	5.8	45.0	47.0	48.7	50.7	51.6
Math & statistics	10.7	11.3	10.5	11.7	11.7	36.7	36.7	35.5	36.3	35.9
Multidisciplinary & interdisciplinary studies	4.8	5.2	6.8	7.9	9.3	53.0	52.8	52.9	55.5	51.7
Natural resources & conservation	5.5	6.0	6.6	7.7	7.6	54.7	57.1	58.7	60.5	60.1
Physical sciences	13.8	14.5	14.6	15.7	15.9	33.7	34.5	35.0	36.3	36.8
Psychology	31.6	35.6	39.8	44.2	40.8	75.8	77.2	78.6	79.8	79.9
Social sciences	38.4	39.4	38.4	41.1	40.1	53.9	53.9	53.6	54.3	54.8
Health fields, total	45.4	46.9	48.0	54.1	56.1	74.5	75.4	75.7	76.3	76.4
FOREIGN STUDENTS [1]										
Total, all surveyed fields	**219.7**	**224.6**	**202.5**	**233.4**	**280.3**	**36.5**	**35.8**	**32.2**	**33.8**	**38.7**
Science/engineering	211.9	216.8	195.1	225.0	270.6	39.1	38.4	34.5	36.4	41.6
Engineering, total	83.5	81.6	71.1	77.6	88.1	53.4	51.7	47.1	47.8	51.8
Sciences, total	128.3	135.2	124.0	147.5	182.5	33.3	33.2	30.0	32.3	38.0
Agricultural & veterinary sciences	2.9	2.8	2.9	3.2	3.6	31.8	31.2	28.4	29.6	32.4
Biological sciences	17.6	18.6	17.7	20.3	23.0	21.5	21.8	20.2	21.6	23.8
Computer & information	46.5	50.0	43.4	58.0	83.0	57.8	56.1	49.8	54.4	63.2
Geosciences [2]	2.7	2.5	2.3	2.5	2.6	22.9	22.6	21.2	21.9	23.4
Math & statistics	15.6	16.5	14.5	16.6	17.7	53.7	53.3	48.7	51.5	54.3
Multidisciplinary & interdisciplinary studies	2.5	2.9	3.8	4.2	7.3	28.1	29.8	29.5	29.6	40.7
Natural resources & conservation	1.6	1.6	1.5	1.9	2.0	16.1	15.4	13.6	14.6	15.7
Physical sciences	16.3	16.6	15.7	16.6	17.2	39.7	39.5	37.7	38.3	39.9
Psychology	3.0	3.3	3.4	3.8	4.5	7.3	7.1	6.7	6.9	8.9
Social sciences	19.7	20.4	18.7	20.4	21.5	27.6	27.8	26.1	27.0	29.4
Health fields, total	7.8	7.9	7.3	8.4	9.7	12.8	12.6	11.5	11.8	13.2
PART-TIME STUDENTS										
Total, all surveyed fields	**144.8**	**157.4**	**171.8**	**182.7**	**186.0**	**24.0**	**25.1**	**27.3**	**26.5**	**25.7**
Science/engineering	126.1	137.5	149.9	158.6	161.4	23.3	24.3	26.5	25.6	24.8
Engineering, total	39.4	39.8	42.9	42.1	42.8	25.2	25.2	28.4	26.0	25.2
Sciences, total	86.7	97.7	107.0	116.5	118.6	22.5	24.0	25.9	25.5	24.7
Agricultural & veterinary sciences	2.4	2.5	3.2	3.2	3.4	26.3	27.7	31.4	29.9	30.3
Biological sciences	11.1	12.7	14.0	15.5	16.1	13.6	14.9	16.0	16.4	16.7
Computer & information	27.8	32.1	36.1	38.2	40.8	34.6	36.0	41.4	35.8	31.1
Geosciences [2]	2.2	2.0	1.9	2.0	1.9	18.7	17.8	17.7	17.6	16.4
Math & statistics	5.0	6.0	6.4	6.4	6.7	17.2	19.4	21.7	20.0	20.5
Multidisciplinary & interdisciplinary studies	2.9	3.4	4.4	5.2	6.0	32.5	34.7	34.6	36.8	33.4
Natural resources & conservation	2.8	3.0	3.4	3.9	4.1	27.5	29.1	30.4	30.4	32.3
Physical sciences	3.9	4.3	4.5	4.8	4.6	9.4	10.2	10.8	11.2	10.7
Psychology	11.3	13.2	14.5	17.8	16.3	27.2	28.7	28.7	32.1	32.0
Social sciences	17.3	18.5	18.5	19.5	18.7	24.2	25.3	25.8	25.7	25.6
Health fields, total	18.7	19.9	21.9	24.1	24.6	30.7	32.0	34.5	34.0	33.5

X Not applicable. [1] Temporary residents. [2] Earth or geosciences, atmospheric, and ocean sciences.

Source: U.S. National Science Foundation, National Center for Science and Engineering Statistics, Data Explorer, "Survey of Graduate Students and Postdoctorates in Science and Engineering," <ncsesdata.nsf.gov/explorer>, accessed September 2024. See also <www.nsf.gov/statistics/srvygradpostdoc>.

Table 849. Science and Engineering (S&E) Degrees as Percent of Higher Education Degrees Conferred by State: 2022

[Represents degrees conferred in the academic year ending in 2022. Includes bachelor's, master's, and doctoral degrees; associate's degrees and professional degrees are not included. At the doctoral level only, health sciences are also included in S&E fields of study. S&E fields include agricultural sciences and natural resources; biological and biomedical sciences; computer and information sciences; engineering; geosciences, atmospheric sciences, and ocean sciences; mathematics and statistics; multidisciplinary and interdisciplinary sciences; physical sciences; psychology; and social sciences. Based on data from the National Center for Education Statistics, Integrated Postsecondary Education Data System]

State	S&E degrees conferred	All higher education degrees	S&E higher education degrees (percent)	State	S&E degrees conferred	All higher education degrees	S&E higher education degrees (percent)	State	S&E degrees conferred	All higher education degrees	S&E higher education degrees (percent)
U.S. [1]	1,071,629	2,999,194	35.7	KS	7,974	27,256	29.3	ND	2,611	8,347	31.3
				KY	12,475	42,279	29.5	OH	31,815	94,293	33.7
AL	13,567	49,161	27.6	LA	10,462	35,363	29.6	OK	9,259	29,079	31.8
AK	711	2,064	34.4	ME	3,830	10,164	37.7	OR	13,011	29,846	43.6
AZ	25,337	105,665	24.0	MD	27,604	59,121	46.7	PA	48,967	128,935	38.0
AR	5,924	22,854	25.9	MA	45,397	109,072	41.6	RI	5,589	15,338	36.4
CA	144,133	319,551	45.1	MI	30,110	78,978	38.1	SC	11,480	35,578	32.3
CO	22,793	54,389	41.9	MN	20,052	68,672	29.2	SD	2,740	7,853	34.9
CT	13,358	35,914	37.2	MS	6,482	23,610	27.5	TN	13,933	49,384	28.2
DE	3,728	10,702	34.8	MO	16,767	56,937	29.4	TX	72,104	207,856	34.7
DC	9,467	23,581	40.1	MT	2,881	7,024	41.0	UT	18,626	77,444	24.1
FL	53,359	154,699	34.5	NE	6,629	21,277	31.2	VT	3,632	8,163	44.5
GA	30,478	81,428	37.4	NV	4,424	12,962	34.1	VA	32,719	90,070	36.3
HI	2,693	7,644	35.2	NH	10,293	35,904	28.7	WA	21,444	47,944	44.7
ID	5,649	16,519	34.2	NJ	24,786	63,950	38.8	WV	7,089	23,430	30.3
IL	36,798	114,883	32.0	NM	4,007	11,428	35.1	WI	17,933	46,932	38.2
IN	23,685	72,726	32.6	NY	82,921	224,411	37.0	WY	1,249	2,727	45.8
IA	10,442	29,565	35.3	NC	29,833	81,628	36.5	PR	8,117	23,672	34.3

[1] Total higher education degrees and S&E degrees include U.S. territories.

Source: National Science Foundation, Science and Engineering Indicators 2024, "Science and Engineering State Indicators," <ncses.nsf.gov/indicators/states>, accessed August 2024.

Table 850. Doctorates Conferred in Science and Engineering by Field, Sex, Citizenship Status, Race, and Hispanic Origin: 2022

[In percent, except as indicated. Covers 12-month period ended June 30, 2022. Beginning in 2021, a modified version of the 2020 Classification of Instruction Programs codes was used in the survey data collection using the new broad and major fields; therefore, the data are not comparable to previously presented data. For more information, see source. For methodology, see <www.nsf.gov/statistics/srvydoctorates/>]

Characteristic	Total [1]	Biological and biomedical sciences	Computer and information sciences	Engineering	Health sciences	Mathematics and statistics	Physical sciences Total [1]	Chemistry	Physics	Psychology	Social sciences
Total conferred (number) [2]	**45,924**	**9,386**	**2,188**	**10,763**	**2,808**	**2,144**	**5,428**	**2,782**	**1,972**	**3,900**	**5,049**
SEX											
Male	55.9	46.6	75.6	72.8	31.1	71.0	67.3	59.1	79.5	25.2	47.7
Female	44.1	53.4	24.4	27.2	68.9	29.0	32.7	40.9	20.5	74.8	52.3
CITIZENSHIP											
U.S. citizen or permanent resident	58.4	71.9	35.4	41.2	70.3	45.1	57.3	59.8	53.0	84.5	63.2
Temporary visa holders	37.3	25.0	60.2	54.1	23.3	50.7	39.1	36.3	43.1	8.4	33.0
RACE/ETHNICITY [3]											
Total conferred (number)	**26,801**	**6,745**	**774**	**4,436**	**1,973**	**966**	**3,108**	**1,665**	**1,046**	**3,295**	**3,191**
Non-Hispanic:											
American Indian/ Alaska Native	0.2	0.1	0.1	0.1	0.2	0.2	0.2	0.1	0.2	0.3	0.5
Asian	11.3	12.3	19.8	15.3	9.7	12.5	10.2	10.3	10.5	7.1	9.1
Black or African American	6.0	4.8	5.4	4.2	13.8	2.7	2.6	2.9	1.6	8.7	9.2
White	66.4	65.9	61.1	64.8	63.4	68.4	72.1	72.1	73.6	65.3	64.6
Two or more races	3.6	4.1	3.2	3.8	2.5	5.2	3.4	3.4	3.4	3.6	3.5
Hispanic or Latino [4]	9.4	10.8	5.6	8.2	7.9	6.1	8.3	7.7	7.6	11.4	10.5
Other/unknown [5]	3.0	2.0	4.8	3.7	2.5	4.9	3.2	3.5	3.0	3.5	2.5

[1] Includes other fields not shown separately. [2] Includes respondents who did not report sex or citizenship status. [3] Covers U.S. citizens and permanent residents only. [4] Persons reporting Hispanic or Latino ethnicity may be of any race or combination of races. [5] Includes Native Hawaiians or Other Pacific Islanders and other non-Hispanic race, and individuals who did not report race nor ethnicity.

Source: U.S. National Science Foundation, National Center for Science and Engineering Statistics, "Doctorate Recipients from U.S. Universities: 2022, Data Tables," <ncses.nsf.gov/surveys/earned-doctorates/>, accessed January 2024.

Table 851. Doctorates Awarded by Field of Study: 2010 to 2022

[Based on the Survey of Earned Doctorates. For description of methodology, see <www.nsf.gov/statistics/srvydoctorates/>]

Field of study	2010	2015	2017	2018	2019	2020	2021 [1]	2022 [1]
Total, all fields........................	**48,028**	**54,886**	**54,552**	**55,078**	**55,609**	**55,208**	**52,194**	**57,596**
Science and engineering, total...................	**34,997**	**41,175**	**41,288**	**42,144**	**42,898**	**42,565**	**40,834**	**45,479**
Science, total........................	27,419	31,300	31,512	31,980	32,600	32,097	30,601	33,949
Life sciences........................	11,319	12,493	12,554	12,754	12,748	12,541	11,800	13,211
Agricultural sciences and natural resources.......	1,100	1,434	1,493	1,442	1,488	1,469	1,334	1,434
Biological/biomedical sciences..................	8,046	8,783	8,566	8,782	8,678	8,403	8,138	9,218
Health sciences........................	2,173	2,276	2,495	2,530	2,582	2,669	2,328	2,559
Physical and earth sciences.................	4,995	5,916	6,082	6,329	6,579	6,241	5,776	6,649
Chemistry........................	2,304	2,666	2,699	2,807	2,939	2,761	2,552	3,060
Geosciences, atmospheric and ocean sciences..	862	1,057	1,169	1,185	1,272	1,241	1,064	1,181
Physics and astronomy.................	1,829	2,193	2,214	2,337	2,368	2,239	2,160	2,408
Mathematics and computer sciences............	3,223	3,818	3,842	4,022	4,230	4,387	4,370	4,854
Computer and information sciences..............	1,633	2,003	1,998	2,000	2,220	2,363	2,360	2,606
Mathematics and statistics.................	1,590	1,815	1,844	2,022	2,010	2,024	2,010	2,248
Psychology and social sciences..............	7,882	9,073	9,034	8,875	9,043	8,928	8,655	9,235
Psychology........................	3,420	3,776	3,925	3,821	3,909	3,868	3,779	3,990
Anthropology........................	507	492	446	424	445	447	400	415
Economics........................	1,073	1,255	1,239	1,244	1,247	1,212	1,229	1,287
Political science and government.............	728	859	743	734	707	636	581	678
Sociology........................	639	741	683	668	632	605	560	611
Other social sciences..................	1,515	1,950	1,998	1,984	2,103	2,160	2,106	2,254
Engineering, total........................	7,578	9,875	9,776	10,164	10,298	10,468	10,233	11,530
Aerospace, aeronautical and astronautical.........	252	361	379	383	379	399	372	374
Bioengineering and biomedical.................	824	1,125	1,032	1,133	1,163	1,082	1,064	1228
Chemical........................	822	1,002	931	981	980	994	1,022	1142
Civil........................	643	632	713	675	700	795	621	898
Electrical, electronics and communications........	1,778	1,997	1,879	1,943	1,799	1,971	2,081	2,193
Industrial and manufacturing...................	215	243	249	272	234	304	361	381
Materials science........................	670	871	937	992	992	879	934	1136
Mechanical........................	983	1,466	1,398	1,503	1,532	1,633	1,444	1,676
Other........................	1,391	2,178	2,258	2,282	2,519	2,411	2,334	2,502
Non-science and engineering, total..............	**13,031**	**13,711**	**13,264**	**12,934**	**12,711**	**12,643**	**11,360**	**12,117**
Education........................	5,287	5,098	4,826	4,818	4,633	4,714	4,252	4,509
Humanities........................	5,015	5,594	5,286	5,139	5,051	4,924	4,134	4,464
Professional/other/unknown...............	2,729	3,019	3,152	2,977	3,027	3,005	2,974	3,144

[1] Beginning in 2021, a modified version of the 2020 Classification of Instructional Programs (CIP) codes was used in the survey data collection. To facilitate trend data comparisons, the data collected for 2021 using the new codes were mapped to historical codes; therefore, trend data for 2021 should be treated as estimates and not actual counts. See "Survey of Earned Doctorates Field of Study Taxonomy Changes in 2021 and Impact on Trend Data" for more information, <ncses.nsf.gov/pubs/ncses23200>.

Source: U.S. National Science Foundation, National Center for Science and Engineering Statistics, "Doctorate Recipients from U.S. Universities: 2022, Data Tables," <ncses.nsf.gov/surveys/earned-doctorates/>, accessed January 2024; and earlier reports.

Table 852. Employed Scientists and Engineers by Sex, Race/Ethnicity, and Selected Characteristics: 2021

[In thousands (30,255 represents 30,255,000). Scientists and engineers are individuals who have a bachelor's or higher degree, and have an S&E (Science and Engineering) or S&E-related degree or occupation. Data are based on various NSF (National Science Foundation) and non-NSF surveys; see <ncses.nsf.gov/pubs/nsf23315/technical-notes> for details]

Characteristic	Total [1]	Female	Male	Hispanic or Latino [2]	Asian [3]	Black or African American [3]	White [3]	More than one race [3]
All employed scientists and engineers....	**30,255**	**14,387**	**15,868**	**2,953**	**4,240**	**2,241**	**20,007**	**673**
Age:								
Under 30 years........................	4,790	2,524	2,265	639	723	301	2,942	162
30-39 years........................	8,549	4,225	4,323	931	1,320	605	5,446	220
40-49 years........................	6,974	3,442	3,532	708	1,112	587	4,341	167
50-75 years........................	9,942	4,196	5,746	675	1,085	748	7,278	123
Employment status:								
Employed, full-time........................	25,917	11,668	14,249	2,554	3,713	1,983	16,961	581
Employed, part-time........................	4,338	2,720	1,619	399	527	258	3,046	92
Highest degree attained:								
Bachelor's........................	16,827	7,755	9,072	1,824	2,035	1,184	11,296	401
Master's........................	9,187	4,788	4,399	781	1,479	800	5,886	203
Doctorate........................	1,827	744	1,083	128	426	95	1,148	25
Professional........................	2,414	1,100	1,314	220	300	162	1,677	44
By occupation:								
S&E occupations........................	7,894	2,300	5,594	692	1,665	399	4,943	169
Science occupations....................	5,945	1,988	3,957	514	1,348	333	3,598	133
Engineering occupations....................	1,949	312	1,636	178	316	65	1,345	36
S&E related occupations.................	9,522	5,494	4,028	843	1,264	756	6,412	189
Non-S&E related occupations...............	12,840	6,593	6,246	1,418	1,312	1,087	8,652	315
By employment sector:								
Business or industry........................	16,656	6,488	10,168	1,541	2,765	1,015	10,910	362
Federal government........................	1,408	594	814	154	148	180	879	41
Nonprofit........................	3,571	2,360	1,211	358	382	352	2,368	84
Self-employed........................	1,664	809	855	134	187	86	1,213	38
State or local government.................	1,828	967	861	245	192	226	1,110	41
Universities and 4-year colleges..............	2,408	1,291	1,117	217	433	142	1,562	44
Other educational institutions................	2,721	1,879	842	305	133	241	1,965	64

[1] Total includes other races, not shown separately. [2] Persons of Hispanic origin may be of any race. [3] Non-Hispanic.

Source: U.S. National Science Foundation, National Center for Science and Engineering Statistics, "Diversity and STEM: Women, Minorities, and Persons with Disabilities - Data Tables," <ncses.nsf.gov/pubs/nsf23315/data-tables>, accessed August 2024.

Table 853. Science and Engineering (S&E) Degree Holders by Occupation: 2019

[In thousands (22,791 represents 22,791,000). Data represents all workers who attained their highest degree (bachelor's or higher) in an S&E or S&E-related field. Detail may not add to total due to rounding]

Occupation	Total S&E and S&E-related degree holders	Employees by field of highest degree [1]						S&E related fields [5]
		Total S&E fields	Computer and mathematical sciences	Biological, agricultural, and environmental life sciences [2]	Physical and related sciences [3]	Social and related sciences [4]	Engineering	
All occupations........................	22,791	15,362	2,837	2,437	889	5,474	3,725	7,429
S&E occupations....................	**6,137**	**5,709**	**1,670**	**705**	**422**	**754**	**2,159**	**428**
Computer & mathematical scientists...........	2,828	2,642	1,584	94	79	258	628	186
Computer & information scientists [6].........	2,546	2,393	1,429	80	66	218	600	153
Computer support specialists...............	183	168	95	(S)	(S)	22	31	15
Computer system analysts.................	268	246	155	13	5	26	47	22
Network/computer systems administrators........................	129	125	80	2	4	17	21	4
Software developers......................	568	536	345	15	16	23	137	32
Computer engineers—software..............	816	776	441	3	18	39	276	40
Mathematical scientists...................	184	164	76	13	12	39	24	20
Biological, agricultural, & environmental life scientists [6]........................	656	579	4	488	47	18	22	77
Biological & medical scientists [6]..............	471	404	4	328	42	11	19	67
Biological scientists [7].....................	134	128	(S)	118	3	3	1	6
Medical scientists (excluding practitioners)........................	151	107	(S)	89	8	3	6	44
Physical & related scientists [6].............	(NA)	374	4	87	246	8	28	(S)
Chemists, except biochemists............	(NA)	117	(S)	31	78	(S)	7	(S)
Physicists & astronomers.................	46	45	(S)	(S)	38	(S)	6	1
Social & related scientists [6]...............	521	477	6	17	1	448	5	44
Psychologists, including clinical...........	196	188	(S)	(S)	(S)	182	(S)	8
Postsecondary teachers—social sciences...	142	139	1	4	(S)	134	(S)	3
Engineers [6].............................	1,740	1,637	71	19	49	22	1,477	103
Aerospace, aeronautical, or astronautical engineers...............	116	112	3	(S)	5	(S)	104	4
Civil, architectural, or sanitary engineers....	280	271	1	2	(S)	1	262	9
Electrical or computer hardware engineers..	389	371	33	(S)	9	(S)	327	18
Mechanical engineers....................	350	325	4	2	1	1	316	25
S&E-related occupations................	**7,440**	**2,131**	**366**	**660**	**176**	**367**	**562**	**5,309**
Health-related occupations [6]...............	5,175	696	27	389	52	211	17	4,479
Diagnosing/treating practitioners [8]...........	1,252	98	(S)	60	(S)	11	2	1,154
Registered nurses, pharmacists, dieticians, therapists, physician assistants, & nurse practitioners...........	2,732	148	(S)	88	2	51	(S)	2,584
S&E managers..........................	777	517	106	68	37	57	249	260
Computer & information systems managers....................	150	140	82	(S)	(S)	11	32	10
Engineering managers....................	289	258	23	3	12	(S)	213	31
Medical & health services managers.........	273	60	(S)	20	(S)	32	(S)	213
S&E precollege teachers [9]...............	477	237	74	72	30	48	13	240
S&E technicians & technologists [6]...........	768	635	132	129	54	48	272	133
Computer programmers..................	96	88	49	2	(S)	10	22	8
Electrical, electronic, industrial, & mechanical technicians................	240	200	29	19	7	15	130	40
Other S&E-related occupations [6]............	242	46	27	2	3	4	10	196
Architects.............................	203	22	(S)	2	(S)	(S)	10	181
Non-S&E occupations....................	**9,214**	**7,522**	**801**	**1,072**	**291**	**4,352**	**1,004**	**1,692**
Non-S&E managers......................	1,476	1,205	161	162	56	509	317	271
Management-related occupations [6]...........	1,997	1,717	265	236	64	916	236	280
Accountants, auditors, & other financial specialists...................	578	516	93	31	7	344	41	62
Personnel, training, & labor relations specialists...................	231	187	16	13	(S)	128	20	44
Non-S&E precollege teachers [6]..............	563	405	22	67	11	289	14	158
Prekindergarten and kindergarten...........	105	84	(S)	12	(S)	68	(S)	21
Elementary............................	215	169	13	18	(S)	127	6	46
Secondary—other subjects.................	108	69	(S)	16	(S)	43	6	39
Special education—primary & secondary....	90	50	2	9	(S)	37	(S)	40
Non-S&E postsecondary teachers...........	108	78	4	(S)	5	61	2	30
Social services & related occupations [6].......	724	605	(S)	29	9	541	7	119
Counselors [10]............................	340	280	(S)	6	(S)	270	(S)	60
Social workers.........................	319	264	(S)	16	(S)	239	(S)	55
Sales & marketing occupations.............	1,229	996	87	131	41	602	134	233
Arts, humanities, & related occupations.......	222	183	9	(S)	(S)	123	8	39
Other non-S&E occupations [6]................	2,892	2,332	234	404	99	1,309	285	560

NA Not available. S Data suppressed for reasons of confidentiality and/or reliability. [1] Includes bachelor's, master's, and doctorate degrees. [2] Biological sciences include biology, ecology, nutritional sciences, pharmacology, zoology, and related fields. [3] Physical sciences include chemistry; earth, atmospheric, and ocean sciences; physics and astronomy; and related fields. [4] Social sciences include economics, political science, psychology, sociology and anthropology, linguistics, geography, history and philosophy of science, and related fields. [5] S&E-related fields include health fields, science and math teacher education, technology and technical fields, architecture, and actuarial science. [6] Includes other occupations not shown separately. [7] Includes botanists, ecologists, zoologists, etc. [8] Includes dentists, optometrists, physicians, psychiatrists, podiatrists, surgeons, and veterinarians. [9] Secondary teachers in computer, mathematics, sciences, and social sciences. [10] Includes educational, vocational, mental health, substance abuse, etc.

Source: U.S. National Science Foundation, Science & Engineering Indicators, *The STEM Labor Force of Today: Scientists, Engineers, and Skilled Technical Workers, Supplemental Tables,* NSB-2021-2, August 2021. See also <www.nsf.gov/statistics/seind/>.

Table 854. Civilian Employment of Scientists, Engineers, and Related Occupations by Occupation and Industry: 2022

[In thousands (557.4 represents 557,400). As of 2018, the Standard Occupational Classification (SOC) system classifies workers into over 860 detailed occupations. Industry classifications correspond to 2022 North American Industry Classification (NAICS) industrial groups]

Occupation	Total employ-ment, all workers [1]	Wage and salary workers						Self em-ployed [3]
		Mining (NAICS 21) [2]	Con-struction (NAICS 23)	Manu-facturing (NAICS 31–33)	Informa-tion (NAICS 51)	Profes-sional, scientific, technical services (NAICS 54)	Govern-ment	
Computer and information systems.............	557.4	1.0	2.7	36.5	78.6	181.1	28.4	6.4
Architectural and engineering managers.......	201.5	1.8	3.5	73.0	3.1	75.2	16.8	0.5
Natural science managers.....................	86.3	0.2	(NA)	7.2	0.1	40.3	18.1	(NA)
Computer and mathematical scientists [4].......	5,277.6	5.4	22.0	312.7	732.8	1,851.2	297.1	108.5
Computer occupations........................	4,929.1	4.8	21.5	299.8	705.0	1,751.5	271.2	106.0
Mathematical science occupations...........	348.5	0.6	0.5	12.9	27.8	99.7	25.8	2.5
Surveyors, cartographers, and photogrammetrists...........................	64.8	0.9	3.7	0.1	0.4	43.0	10.1	2.7
Engineers [4].................................	1,736.1	19.8	59.2	589.3	33.1	546.8	209.7	35.4
Aerospace engineers.........................	63.8	(NA)	(NA)	26.5	0.2	21.5	10.5	(NA)
Civil engineers...............................	326.3	0.7	38.1	4.5	0.4	171.1	82.6	11.5
Computer hardware engineers................	78.1	(NA)	0.1	23.0	5.0	35.3	5.4	1.5
Electrical and electronics engineers..........	299.7	0.7	8.7	94.6	24.2	81.6	27.3	5.1
Industrial engineers [5]........................	349.3	2.5	4.4	232.4	1.3	48.7	5.2	0.1
Mechanical engineers........................	286.1	1.1	4.4	134.3	(NA)	87.6	16.6	2.9
Drafters, engineering, and mapping technicians [4]...............................	663.6	6.2	29.4	188.0	3.9	264.6	76.9	14.9
Engineering technicians, except drafters.....	402.1	5.1	5.2	143.1	2.3	121.2	67.4	5.5
Surveying and mapping technicians...........	64.2	0.8	1.8	0.1	(NA)	39.4	7.2	6.5
Life, physical, and social science occupations................................	1,473.7	12.6	20.3	150.5	3.8	379.8	353.9	76.9
Life scientists...............................	344.4	(NA)	0.1	31.0	(NA)	118.8	76.4	3.6
Physical scientists...........................	267.8	4.5	0.6	39.0	2.0	98.1	75.9	5.2
Social scientists and related occupations.....	326.1	0.2	0.2	0.1	0.3	34.7	94.0	59.9
Life, physical, & social science technicians...	397.0	3.1	1.5	55.3	0.4	110.6	83.0	7.1

NA Not available. [1] Includes other industries not shown separately. [2] Includes oil and gas extraction. [3] Includes unpaid family workers. [4] Includes other occupations not shown separately. [5] Includes health and safety engineers.

Source: U.S. Bureau of Labor Statistics, Employment Projections, Tables, "Industry-occupation matrix data, by industry," <www.bls.gov/emp/tables.htm>, accessed July 2024.

Table 855. Top Metropolitan Areas with the Largest Number of Workers in Science and Engineering Occupations: 2019

[In thousands, except as indicated (146,875 represents 146,875,000). As of May. Ranked for top 19 metro areas with highest number of S&E (science and engineering) workers. Data are from U.S. Bureau of Labor Statistics' Occupational Employment Statistics Survey. Excludes metropolitan statistical areas where S&E proportions were suppressed. Differences among employment estimates may not be statistically significant; see source for details]

Metropolitan area	Workers employed		Metropolitan workers in S&E occupations as percentage of national total in S&E occupations
	All occupations	S&E occupations	
U.S. total...	**146,875**	**7,317**	**100.0**
Top 19 total..	**56,041**	**3,668**	**50.1**
New York-Newark-Jersey City, NY-NJ-PA.....................	9,655	440	6.0
Washington-Arlington-Alexandria, DC-VA-MD-WV...............	3,179	345	4.7
Los Angeles-Long Beach-Anaheim, CA........................	6,240	291	4.0
Boston-Cambridge-Nashua, MA-NH............................	2,798	233	3.2
San Francisco-Oakland-Hayward, CA.........................	2,472	229	3.1
Chicago-Naperville-Elgin, IL-IN-WI........................	4,676	214	2.9
Dallas-Fort Worth-Arlington, TX...........................	3,657	210	2.9
Seattle-Tacoma-Bellevue, WA...............................	2,021	202	2.8
San Jose-Sunnyvale-Santa Clara, CA........................	1,141	194	2.6
Atlanta-Sandy Springs-Roswell, GA.........................	2,744	171	2.3
Houston-The Woodlands-Sugar Land, TX......................	3,052	162	2.2
Philadelphia-Camden-Wilmington, PA-NJ-DE-MD...............	2,876	160	2.2
Detroit-Warren-Dearborn, MI...............................	1,981	153	2.1
Minneapolis-St. Paul-Bloomington, MN-WI...................	1,971	130	1.8
Denver-Aurora-Lakewood, CO................................	1,513	119	1.6
Phoenix-Mesa-Scottsdale, AZ...............................	2,121	111	1.5
San Diego-Carlsbad, CA....................................	1,495	109	1.5
Baltimore-Columbia-Towson, MD.............................	1,376	100	1.4
Austin-Round Rock, TX.....................................	1,073	95	1.3

Source: U.S. National Science Foundation, Science & Engineering Indicators, *The STEM Labor Force of Today: Scientists, Engineers, and Skilled Technical Workers, Supplemental Tables*, NSB-2021-2, August 2021. See also <www.nsf.gov/statistics/seind/>.

Table 856. Employment and Median Salary of Worker With Highest Degree in Science and Engineering (S&E) Field by Sex and Occupation: 2019

[Rounded to the nearest 1,000. Data are for full-time workers who typically work 35 or more hours weekly in their principal job. Data are from National Science Foundation, National Survey of College Graduates]

Occupation	Total		Female			Male		
	Number	Median salary (dollars)	Number	Percent	Median salary (dollars)	Number	Percent	Median salary (dollars)
All occupations............................	13,130,000	80,000	4,822,000	36.7	63,000	8,308,000	63.3	94,000
S&E...................................	5,211,000	96,000	1,357,000	26.0	82,000	3,854,000	74.0	100,000
Engineers................................	1,550,000	100,000	234,000	15.1	90,000	1,316,000	84.9	100,000
Computer and mathematical scientists..	2,465,000	105,000	557,000	22.6	94,000	1,908,000	77.4	108,000
Biological, agricultural, and environmental life scientists............	510,000	64,000	234,000	45.9	65,000	277,000	54.3	64,000
Physical scientists......................	330,000	72,000	110,000	33.3	59,000	220,000	66.7	80,000
Social scientists.........................	356,000	75,000	223,000	62.6	70,000	133,000	37.4	84,000
S&E related occupations....................	1,864,000	76,000	648,000	34.8	62,000	1,216,000	65.2	89,000
Health-related occupations................	537,000	52,000	328,000	61.1	55,000	210,000	39.1	48,000
Non-S&E related occupations..............	6,055,000	67,000	2,817,000	46.5	55,000	3,238,000	53.5	80,000

Source: U.S. National Science Foundation, Science & Engineering Indicators, *The STEM Labor Force of Today: Scientists, Engineers, and Skilled Technical Workers, Supplemental Tables*, NSB-2021-2, August 2021. See also <www.nsf.gov/statistics/seind/>.

Table 857. Federal Discretionary Outlays for General Science and Space and Other Technology: 1990 to 2025

[In billions of dollars (14.4 represents $14,400,000,000). For fiscal years ending in year shown; see text, Section 8]

Year	Current dollars			Constant (2017) dollars		
	Total	General science and research	Space/other technologies	Total	General science and research	Space/other technologies
1990 [1]..................	14.4	2.8	11.6	32.5	6.3	26.2
2000....................	18.6	6.2	12.4	28.5	9.4	19.0
2010....................	30.0	11.6	18.4	33.2	12.9	20.3
2020....................	33.9	13.2	20.7	31.7	12.3	19.4
2021....................	35.4	13.9	21.5	32.2	12.6	19.6
2022....................	37.2	15.0	22.2	32.2	13.0	19.2
2023....................	40.3	15.8	24.5	33.8	13.3	20.5
2024, estimate........	43.0	19.0	24.0	34.9	15.4	19.5
2025, estimate........	43.3	19.2	24.0	34.5	15.3	19.2

[1] Due to the effects of the Credit Reform Act of 1990 on the measurement and classification of Federal credit activities, the discretionary outlays for years prior to 1992 are not strictly comparable to those for 1992 and beyond.

Source: U.S. Office of Management and Budget, *Budget of the U.S. Government, Fiscal Year 2025: Historical Tables*, March 2024. See also <www.whitehouse.gov/omb/budget>.

Table 858. Space-Related Industries Gross Output and Value Added by Industry: 2019 to 2022

[In millions of current dollars (216,724 represents $216,724,000,000). The space economy consists of space-related goods and services, both public and private. This includes goods and services that are used in space, or directly support those used in space (space vehicles, launch pads, weapons systems, insurance); require direct input from space to function or directly support those that do (satellite telecommunications and broadcasting, GPS and positioning, navigation, and timing equipment); and are associated with studying space (including research and development, educational services, and planetariums)]

Industry	Gross output (mil. dol.)				Value added (mil. dol.)			
	2019	2020	2021	2022	2019	2020	2021	2022
Space-related industries, total [1]................	216,724	210,576	216,061	232,061	127,376	124,249	124,346	131,776
Private industries....................................	178,901	172,182	175,809	187,311	99,856	97,010	96,633	100,649
Construction..	1,804	1,725	999	1,340	1,180	1,152	650	840
Manufacturing [1]..................................	55,263	52,670	53,212	56,351	34,530	32,738	33,955	33,253
Computer and electronic products [2].............	30,081	28,501	28,590	30,344	20,024	18,543	19,559	19,206
Other transportation equipment [3]................	22,708	21,942	21,974	23,232	12,744	12,551	12,527	12,086
Wholesale trade...................................	44,481	44,975	50,315	54,486	21,753	23,443	23,495	25,584
Retail trade...	627	461	671	764	495	346	499	547
Transportation and warehousing....................	1,373	1,262	1,305	2,437	751	682	694	1,232
Information [1]......................................	59,634	56,334	52,914	52,632	32,044	29,643	27,923	28,141
Broadcasting and telecommunications [4]...........	57,821	54,568	51,039	50,357	30,740	28,360	26,576	26,504
Professional and business services................	12,474	11,381	12,894	14,842	6,960	6,705	7,080	8,153
Educational services, health care, and social assistance [5].....................................	2,809	3,037	3,133	3,894	1,871	2,068	2,096	2,534
Government [5].......................................	37,822	38,394	40,252	44,751	27,520	27,240	27,713	31,127
Federal..	34,789	35,069	36,881	40,943	25,482	24,980	25,481	28,666
State and local....................................	3,033	3,324	3,371	3,808	2,038	2,260	2,232	2,461
Addenda: Space Economy excluding satellite television, satellite radio, and educational services [6].........	169,641	166,669	176,066	193,177	102,457	101,599	103,881	111,633

[1] Includes other industries, not shown separately. [2] Includes manufacturing of satellites; ground equipment; search, detection, navigation, and guidance systems (GPS/PNT equipment). [3] Includes manufacturing of space vehicles and space weapons systems (intercontinental ballistic missiles). [4] Includes direct-to-home satellite television services. [5] Includes spending on personnel, operations, and maintenance. Government spending on private sector investment (structures, equipment, intellectual property) is included within the individual industries. [6] Represents a narrower interpretation of the "Space Economy" definition. These commodities are primarily produced by the information and educational services industries.

Source: U.S. Bureau of Economic Analysis, Special Topics: Space Economy, "Space Economy Data, 2017-2022," <www.bea.gov/data/special-topics/space-economy>, accessed July 2024.

Table 859. Space-Related Industries Employment and Compensation by Industry: 2019 to 2022

[Employment in thousands (367 represents 367,000); compensation in millions of current dollars (52,632 represents $52,632,000,000). Excludes government employees. The space economy consists of space-related goods and services, both public and private. This includes goods and services that are used in space, or directly support those used in space (space vehicles, launch pads, weapons systems, insurance); require direct input from space to function or directly support those that do (satellite telecommunications and broadcasting, GPS and positioning, navigation, and timing equipment); and are associated with studying space (including research and development, educational services, and planetariums)]

Industry	Employment [1] (1,000)				Compensation [2] (mil. dol.)			
	2019	2020	2021	2022	2019	2020	2021	2022
Space-related industries, private, total........	**367**	**350**	**341**	**347**	**52,632**	**52,358**	**52,968**	**54,453**
Manufacturing..	117	114	117	108	23,919	23,808	24,528	23,468
Wholesale trade......................................	79	76	73	75	9,190	9,297	9,582	10,450
Information..	96	87	77	76	10,665	10,252	9,748	9,788
Professional and business services................	41	38	39	47	5,804	5,703	6,041	6,922
Educational services, health care, and social assistance...	20	23	23	26	1,603	1,942	1,972	2,348
All other private industries...........................	14	12	12	15	1,451	1,356	1,097	1,477

[1] Includes full time and part time employees. [2] Compensation consists of wages and salaries and employer contributions to pensions and insurance.

Source: U.S. Bureau of Economic Analysis, Special Topics: Space Economy, "Space Economy Data, 2017-2022," <www.bea.gov/data/special-topics/space-economy>, accessed July 2024.

This section presents statistics on farms and farm operators; farm income, expenditures, and debt; farm output, productivity, and marketings; foreign trade in agricultural products; specific crops; livestock, poultry, and their products; and direct marketing to consumers.

The principal sources are the data collected by the National Agricultural Statistics Service (NASS), the Economic Research Service (ERS), and the Foreign Agricultural Service (FAS) of the U.S. Department of Agriculture (USDA) and published in reports or databases. The ERS publishes data on farm assets, debt, and income on the internet at <ers.usda.gov/data-products/farm-income-and-wealth-statistics>. The ERS also provides data on commodity supply and disappearance via commodity outlook reports, yearbooks, and databases, available on the ERS site at <ers.usda.gov/data-products>. Sources of current data on agricultural exports and imports include the Global Agricultural Trade System database provided by the FAS at <apps.fas.usda.gov/gats/> and the "Foreign Agricultural Trade of the United States (FATUS)" data, published by the ERS, available on the ERS site at <ers.usda.gov/data-products/foreign-agricultural-trade-of-the-united-states-fatus>.

The field offices of the NASS collect data on crops, livestock and products, agricultural prices, farm employment, and other related subjects mainly through sample surveys. Information is obtained on crops, livestock, and products pertaining to agricultural production and marketing. State estimates and supporting information are sent to the Agricultural Statistics Board of NASS, which reviews the estimates and issues reports containing state and national data. Among these reports are annual summaries such as *Crop Production, Crop Values, Agricultural Prices,* and *Meat Animals Production, Disposition, and Income.* The NASS also provides data through the QuickStats database at <quickstats.nass.usda.gov>.

With the release of the January 2021 data, the USDA adopted the World Trade Organization (WTO) definitions of agricultural products and revised historical data to reflect the new definitions, both adding and removing some products from the definitions. The change was made in order to harmonize U.S. trade reporting practices with those of the international community and ensure that USDA numbers are aligned with those of the Office of the U.S. Trade Representative, which already uses the WTO definition when negotiating WTO binding trade agreements. For additional information, please see <www.fas.usda.gov/updated-agricultural-products-definition-trade-reporting>. For general information on foreign trade, see text, Section 28, Foreign Commerce and Aid.

The USDA conducts the Census of Agriculture every 5 years for years ending in "2" and "7" and collects information concerning all areas of farming and ranching operations, including production expenses, market value of products, and operator characteristics. The information from the 2022 Census of Agriculture is available in print form and on the internet at <nass.usda.gov/Publications/AgCensus/

2022/>. An evaluation of coverage has been conducted for each census of agriculture since 1945 to provide estimates of the completeness of census farm counts. Beginning with the 1997 Census of Agriculture, census farm counts and totals were statistically adjusted for coverage and reported at the county level. The size of the adjustments varies considerably by state. In general, farms not on the census mail list tended to be small in acreage, production, and sales of farm products.

For more explanation about census mail list compilation, collection methods, coverage measurement, and adjustments, see Appendix A, *2022 Census of Agriculture,* Volume 1, <nass.usda.gov/Publications/AgCensus/2022/>.

Farms and farmland—The definitions of a farm have varied through time. Since 1850, when minimum criteria defining a farm for census purposes first were established, the farm definition has changed nine times. The current definition, first used for the 1974 census, is any place from which $1,000 or more of agricultural products were produced and sold, or normally would have been sold, during the census year.

Acreage designated as "land in farms" consists primarily of agricultural land used for crops, pasture, or grazing. It also includes woodland and wasteland not actually under cultivation or used for pasture or grazing, provided it was part of the farm operator's total operation. Land in farms includes acres set aside under annual commodity acreage programs as well as acres idled by federal conservation programs for places meeting the farm definition. Land in farms is an operating unit concept and includes land owned and operated as well as land rented from others. All grazing land, except land used under government permits on a per-head basis, was included as "land in farms," provided it was part of a farm or ranch.

Farm income and expenses—The final agricultural sector output comprises cash receipts from farm marketings of crops and livestock, federal government payments made directly to farmers for farm-related activities, rental value of farm homes, value of farm products consumed in farm homes, and other farm-related income such as machine hire and custom work. Farm marketings represent quantities of agricultural products sold by farmers multiplied by prices received per unit of production at the local market. Information on prices received for farm products is generally obtained by the NASS Agricultural Statistics Board from surveys of firms (such as grain elevators, packers, and processors) purchasing agricultural commodities directly from producers. In some cases, the price information is obtained directly from the producers. Farm expense data cover farm debt and source of loans. Also presented are price indices for expenses such as wages, production inputs such as livestock and feed, and other items such as machinery and repairs.

Crops—Estimates of crop acreage and production by the NASS are based on current sample survey data obtained from individual producers and objective yield counts, reports of carlot shipments, market records, personal field observations by field statisticians, and reports from other sources.

Prices received by farmers are marketing year average prices and do not include allowances for outstanding loans, government purchases, deficiency payments or disaster payments. These averages are based on monthly prices weighted by monthly sales during specific periods. All state marketing year average prices are based on individual state marketing years, while U.S. marketing year average prices are based on standard U.S. marketing years for each crop. For a description of how U.S. prices are computed as well as a listing of the crop marketing years, see *Crop Values Annual Summary.*

Value of production is computed by multiplying state prices by each state's production. The U.S. value of production is the sum of state values for all states. Value of production figures should not be confused with cash receipts from farm marketings, which relate to sales during a calendar year, irrespective of the year of production.

Livestock—Annual inventory numbers of livestock and estimates of livestock, dairy, and poultry production prepared by the Department of Agriculture are based on information from farmers and ranchers obtained by probability survey sampling methods.

Statistical reliability—For a discussion of statistical collection and estimation, sampling procedures, and measures of statistical reliability pertaining to Department of Agriculture data, see Appendix III.

Table 860. Selected Characteristics of Farms by North American Industry Classification System (NAICS): 2022

[543,087,166 represents $543,087,166,000. See text this section and Appendix III]

Industry	NAICS code [1]	Farms	Land in farms (acres)	Harvested cropland (acres)	Market value of agricultural products sold ($1,000) Total	Crops	Livestock [2]
Total................................	**(X)**	**1,900,487**	**880,100,848**	**301,327,737**	**543,087,166**	**280,628,093**	**262,459,072**
Crop production..............	111	964,777	431,119,301	254,250,439	276,067,625	266,567,647	9,499,978
Oilseed and grain farming...............	1111	330,930	279,532,622	207,147,035	163,840,219	156,330,851	7,509,367
Soybean farming....................	11111	85,688	38,777,315	30,844,945	21,103,254	20,805,337	297,917
Oilseed (except soybean) farming......	11112	1,105	1,856,208	1,222,179	556,449	547,438	9,011
Dry pea and bean farming..........	11113	735	770,854	482,261	271,173	269,831	1,342
Wheat farming.....................	11114	23,550	39,135,092	21,116,666	7,398,594	7,129,863	268,731
Corn farming......................	11115	167,911	118,456,830	97,388,523	93,122,557	91,180,491	1,942,066
Rice farming........................	11116	2,138	3,254,210	2,324,985	2,768,910	2,691,214	77,696
Other grain farming..................	11119	49,803	77,282,113	53,767,476	38,619,282	33,706,677	4,912,605
Vegetable and melon farming..............	11121	41,793	9,557,499	5,867,514	28,792,987	28,658,050	134,936
Potato farming.................	111211	2,610	3,021,808	2,298,543	6,500,168	6,481,079	19,089
Other vegetable (except potato) and melon farming.....................	111219	39,183	6,535,691	3,568,971	22,292,819	22,176,972	115,847
Fruit and tree nut farming................	1113	97,343	14,468,554	6,420,942	33,585,214	33,464,344	120,870
Orange groves....................	11131	3,712	758,177	454,355	1,553,446	1,542,130	11,316
Citrus (except orange) groves...........	11132	3,402	509,749	266,437	1,690,092	1,682,987	7,105
Noncitrus fruit and tree nut farming......	11133	90,229	13,200,628	5,700,150	30,341,676	30,239,228	102,448
Apple orchards....................	111331	10,812	2,710,799	486,911	4,042,370	4,033,871	8,499
Grape vineyards..................	111332	18,024	2,230,495	1,102,023	6,700,625	6,685,568	15,056
Strawberry farming.................	111333	3,039	227,541	104,347	4,125,682	4,121,921	3,761
Berry (except strawberry) farming......	111334	12,070	1,220,535	298,501	2,121,252	2,114,849	6,404
Tree nut farming....................	111335	23,819	4,937,480	2,894,657	8,572,636	8,540,686	31,949
Fruit and tree nut combination farming..............	111336	1,641	284,252	132,179	556,196	535,757	20,439
Other noncitrus fruit farming...........	111339	20,824	1,589,526	681,532	4,222,916	4,206,576	16,340
Greenhouse, nursery, and floriculture production..........................	1114	50,785	3,486,935	1,375,423	21,791,011	21,740,466	50,545
Food crops grown under cover.......	11141	4,199	174,637	17,951	2,361,878	2,356,741	5,137
Nursery and floriculture production......	11142	46,586	3,312,298	1,357,472	19,429,133	19,383,725	45,407
Nursery and tree production............	111421	29,528	2,794,239	1,225,552	11,982,956	11,948,813	34,143
Floriculture production.................	111422	17,058	518,059	131,920	7,446,177	7,434,912	11,265
Other crop farming.....................	1119	443,926	124,073,691	33,439,525	28,058,195	26,373,935	1,684,260
Tobacco farming......................	11191	1,399	755,963	402,159	731,207	710,846	20,361
Cotton farming.......................	11192	7,724	13,244,022	6,500,499	5,164,960	5,104,694	60,265
Sugarcane farming....................	11193	592	1,497,054	1,026,429	2,130,304	2,122,332	7,972
Hay farming.........................	11194	235,498	51,319,967	17,097,360	9,481,324	8,915,788	565,536
All other crop farming.................	11199	198,713	57,256,685	8,413,078	10,550,401	9,520,275	1,030,126
Animal production......................	112	935,710	448,981,547	47,077,298	267,019,540	14,060,446	252,959,094
Cattle ranching and farming............	1121	568,972	362,228,361	38,793,276	142,202,010	8,622,486	133,579,524
Beef cattle ranching and farming.......	11211	545,819	348,169,551	29,076,114	81,837,545	5,403,879	76,433,666
Beef cattle ranching and farming......	112111	534,633	335,905,281	25,860,643	35,972,756	3,275,635	32,697,121
Cattle feedlots....................	112112	11,186	12,264,270	3,215,471	45,864,789	2,128,244	43,736,544
Dairy cattle and milk production........	11212	23,153	14,058,810	9,717,162	60,364,465	3,218,607	57,145,859
Hog and pig farming....................	1122	21,865	5,105,245	3,592,095	37,682,205	3,337,759	34,344,447
Poultry and egg production..............	1123	75,597	7,090,663	2,127,892	77,896,667	1,288,860	76,607,807
Chicken egg production...............	11231	50,090	2,503,961	475,125	14,931,542	264,069	14,667,473
Broilers and other meat-type chicken production...................	11232	14,971	3,319,512	1,180,266	49,378,451	666,176	48,712,275
Turkey production.....................	11233	2,291	742,213	396,170	8,707,655	316,300	8,391,355
Poultry hatcheries....................	11234	295	14,994	3,018	4,034,083	3,127	4,030,956
Other poultry production................	11239	7,950	509,983	73,313	844,937	39,188	805,748
Sheep and goat farming.................	1124	79,398	10,569,032	317,959	955,651	51,314	904,337
Sheep farming.......................	11241	39,814	7,259,144	213,808	607,952	37,184	570,769
Goat farming........................	11242	39,584	3,309,888	104,151	347,699	14,130	333,569
Animal aquaculture......................	1125	4,637	1,165,127	38,180	2,222,585	20,860	2,201,724
Other animal production.................	1129	185,241	62,823,119	2,207,896	6,060,422	739,167	5,321,255
Apiculture..........................	11291	15,622	753,921	19,698	530,290	7,967	522,323
Horse and other equine production....	11292	119,101	24,316,943	767,954	2,208,714	35,747	2,172,967
Fur-bearing animal and rabbit production............................	11293	556	23,414	3,012	56,752	1,564	55,188
All other animal production..............	11299	49,962	37,728,841	1,417,232	3,264,666	693,889	2,570,777

X Not applicable. [1] Based on the North American Industry Classification System (NAICS); see text, Section 15. [2] Includes poultry and poultry products sold.

Source: U.S. Department of Agriculture, National Agricultural Statistics Service, *2022 Census of Agriculture*, Vol. 1, February 2024. See also <www.nass.usda.gov/AgCensus/>.

Table 861. Farms—Number and Acreage: 2000 to 2023

[2,167 represents 2,167,000. As of June. Based on 1974 census definition; for definition of farms and farmland, see text, this section. Data for census years have been adjusted for underenumeration]

Item	Unit	2000	2005	2010	2015	2019	2020	2021	2022	2023
Number of farms..........	1,000	2,167	2,099	2,150	2,064	2,008	1,992	1,960	1,901	1,895
Land in farms.............	Million acres	945	928	916	906	895	893	889	880	879
Average per farm........	Acres	436	442	426	439	446	448	454	463	464

Source: U.S. Department of Agriculture, National Agricultural Statistics Service, *Farm Numbers and Land in Farms, Final Estimates, 2013–2017* and earlier reports; and *Farms and Land in Farms 2023 Summary*, February 2024. See also <www.nass.usda.gov/Publications/>.

Table 862. Farms—Number and Acreage by State: 2020 and 2023

[1,992 represents 1,992,000. See headnote, Table 861]

State	Farms (1,000)		Land in farms (mil. acres)		Acreage per farm		State	Farms (1,000)		Land in farms (mil. acres)		Acreage per farm	
	2020	2023	2020	2023	2020	2023		2020	2023	2020	2023	2020	2023
United States.....	**1,992**	**1,895**	**893.1**	**878.6**	**448**	**464**	Missouri.............	93	88	27.4	27.0	294	308
							Montana............	26	24	57.9	57.6	2,218	2,370
Alabama...........	39	37	8.4	8.6	217	232	Nebraska...........	46	44	44.7	44.0	982	991
Alaska..............	1	1	0.9	0.9	773	725	Nevada.............	3	3	6.1	5.9	1,906	1,903
Arizona............	18	16	26.0	25.0	1,413	1,524	New Hampshire....	4	4	0.4	0.4	98	106
Arkansas...........	41	37	13.9	13.7	338	366	New Jersey.........	10	10	0.7	0.7	72	70
California...........	68	63	24.3	23.8	356	378	New Mexico.........	24	21	39.8	39.1	1,665	1,871
Colorado...........	38	36	31.4	30.0	824	836	New York...........	33	31	6.8	6.5	208	212
Connecticut........	5	5	0.4	0.4	69	73	North Carolina......	45	43	8.4	8.1	185	191
Delaware...........	2	2	0.5	0.5	226	242	North Dakota.......	26	25	39.1	38.5	1,516	1,552
Florida..............	47	44	9.7	9.7	207	218	Ohio................	78	76	13.7	13.7	176	181
Georgia............	41	39	10.1	10.0	247	256	Oklahoma..........	76	70	34.0	32.9	450	468
Hawaii..............	7	7	1.1	1.1	155	159	Oregon.............	37	36	15.7	15.3	428	431
Idaho..............	24	23	11.5	11.5	475	509	Pennsylvania.......	52	49	7.2	7.1	139	145
Illinois..............	71	71	26.8	26.3	376	372	Rhode Island.......	1	1	0.1	0.1	55	57
Indiana.............	55	53	14.8	14.6	268	274	South Carolina......	24	23	4.7	4.6	195	204
Iowa...............	86	87	30.5	30.0	353	346	South Dakota.......	29	28	43.0	42.3	1,468	1,495
Kansas.............	58	56	45.5	44.8	787	807	Tennessee.........	68	63	10.8	10.7	159	170
Kentucky...........	73	69	12.8	12.4	174	179	Texas...............	243	231	126.0	125.0	519	541
Louisiana...........	27	25	8.0	8.0	299	323	Utah................	18	17	10.6	10.5	599	603
Maine..............	7	7	1.3	1.2	176	171	Vermont............	7	7	1.2	1.2	179	185
Maryland...........	12	13	2.0	2.0	161	159	Virginia.............	42	39	7.7	7.3	185	187
Massachusetts.....	7	7	0.5	0.5	69	66	Washington.........	35	32	14.4	13.9	415	434
Michigan...........	47	45	9.8	9.5	209	210	West Virginia.......	23	23	3.5	3.5	153	154
Minnesota..........	67	65	25.4	25.4	379	389	Wisconsin..........	63	59	14.2	13.8	226	236
Mississippi.........	34	31	10.4	10.3	310	331	Wyoming............	12	11	29.1	28.8	2,509	2,743

Source: U.S. Department of Agriculture, National Agricultural Statistics Service, "Quick Stats," <quickstats.nass.usda.gov/>, accessed February 2024. See also <www.nass.usda.gov/Publications/>.

Table 863. Farms by Size and Type of Organization: 1987 to 2022

[2,088 represents 2,088,000. For comments on adjustment, see text, this section]

Size and type of organization	Unit	Not adjusted for coverage		Adjusted for coverage [1]					
		1987	1992	1997	2002	2007	2012	2017	2022
Farms...........................	1,000	2,088	1,925	2,216	2,129	2,205	2,109	2,042	1,900
Land in farms..................	Mil. acres	964	946	955	938	922	915	900	880
Average size of farm............	Acres	462	491	431	441	418	434	441	463
Farms by size:									
1 to 9 acres................	1,000	183	166	205	179	233	224	273	235
10 to 49 acres.............	1,000	412	388	531	564	620	590	583	567
50 to 179 acres............	1,000	645	584	694	659	661	634	565	531
180 to 499 acres...........	1,000	478	428	428	389	368	346	315	288
500 to 999 acres...........	1,000	200	186	179	162	150	143	133	120
1,000 to 1,999 acres........	1,000	102	102	103	99	93	91	88	76
2,000 acres or more........	1,000	67	71	74	78	80	82	85	83
Farms by type of organization:									
Family or individual...........	1,000	1,809	1,653	1,923	1,910	1,906	1,829	1,751	1,610
Partnership..................	1,000	200	187	186	130	174	138	130	125
Corporation..................	1,000	67	73	90	74	96	107	117	128
Other [2].....................	1,000	12	12	17	16	28	36	44	37

[1] Data have been adjusted for coverage; see text, this section. [2] Cooperative, estate or trust, institutional, etc.

Source: U.S. Department of Agriculture, National Agricultural Statistics Service, *2022 Census of Agriculture*, Vol. 1, February 2024, and earlier reports. See also <www.nass.usda.gov/AgCensus/>.

Table 864. Farms—Number and Acreage by Size of Farm: 2017 and 2022

[2,042 represents 2,042,000. Data have been adjusted for coverage; see text, this section]

Size of farm	Number of farms (1,000)		Land in farms (mil. acres)		Cropland harvested (mil. acres)		Percent distribution, 2022		
	2017	2022	2017	2022	2017	2022	Number of farms	All land in farms	Cropland harvested
Total....................	2,042	1,900	900.2	880.1	320.0	301.3	100.0	100.0	100.0
Under 10 acres................	273	235	1.3	1.1	0.4	0.3	12.3	0.1	0.1
10 to 49 acres.................	583	567	14.8	14.2	4.1	3.9	29.8	1.6	1.3
50 to 69 acres.................	135	130	7.8	7.6	2.2	2.1	6.8	0.9	0.7
70 to 99 acres.................	163	153	13.4	12.6	3.9	3.8	8.1	1.4	1.2
100 to 139 acres..............	149	138	13.6	16.0	5.2	4.8	7.3	1.8	1.6
140 to 179 acres..............	117	109	14.6	17.1	5.8	5.4	5.7	1.9	1.8
180 to 219 acres..............	74	70	17.3	13.7	5.0	4.6	3.7	1.6	1.5
220 to 259 acres..............	57	52	18.4	12.4	5.0	4.5	2.7	1.4	1.5
260 to 499 acres..............	184	167	65.8	59.5	27.0	24.2	8.8	6.8	8.0
500 to 999 acres..............	133	120	92.9	83.7	45.9	40.6	6.3	9.5	13.5
1,000 to 1,999 acres..........	88	76	120.7	105.2	66.2	55.5	4.0	12.0	18.4
2,000 acres or more...........	85	83	519.6	536.9	149.4	151.6	4.4	61.0	50.3

Source: U.S. Department of Agriculture, National Agricultural Statistics Service, *2022 Census of Agriculture*, Vol. 1, February 2024. See also <www.nass.usda.gov/AgCensus/>.

Table 865. Farms—Number, Acreage, and Value by Tenure of Principal Operator and Type of Organization: 2017 and 2022

[2,042 represents 2,042,000. Full owners own all the land they operate. Part owners own a part and rent from others the rest of the land they operate. A principal operator is the person primarily responsible for the on-site, day-to-day operation of the farm or ranch business. Data have been adjusted for coverage; see text, this section]

Item and year	Unit	Total [1]	Tenure of operator			Type of organization		
			Full owner	Part owner	Tenant	Family or individual	Partner-ship	Corpora-tion
NUMBER OF FARMS								
2017...............................	1,000	2,042	1,409	493	140	1,751	130	117
2022...............................	1,000	1,900	1,357	424	120	1,610	125	128
Under 50 acres.................	1,000	802	706	50	45	722	29	38
50 to 179 acres................	1,000	531	407	95	29	464	29	26
180 to 499 acres...............	1,000	288	162	107	20	236	25	21
500 to 999 acres...............	1,000	120	45	65	10	90	14	14
1,000 acres or more...........	1,000	160	37	107	16	99	29	28
LAND IN FARMS								
2017...............................	Mil. acres	900	310	503	87	541	158	140
2022...............................	Mil. acres	880	312	490	78	509	158	151
VALUE								
Value of land and buildings, 2022..............	Bil. dol.	3,385	1,203	1,894	288	2,155	572	575
Value of farm products sold, 2022..............	Bil. dol.	543	196	292	55	255	128	155

[1] Includes other types, not shown separately.

Source: U.S. Department of Agriculture, National Agricultural Statistics Service, *2022 Census of Agriculture*, Vol. 1, February 2024, and earlier reports. See also <www.nass.usda.gov/AgCensus/>.

Table 866. Corporate Farms—Characteristics by Type: 2002 to 2022

[150.9 represents 150,900,000. Data have been adjusted for coverage; see text, this section and Appendix III]

Item	Unit	All corpora-tions	Family held corporations			Other corporations		
			Total	1 to 10 stock-holders	11 or more stock-holders	Total	1 to 10 stock-holders	11 or more stock-holders
Farms:								
2002..................................	Number	73,752	66,667	65,017	1,650	7,085	6,010	1,075
2007..................................	Number	96,074	85,837	83,796	2,041	10,237	9,330	907
2012..................................	Number	106,716	95,142	92,834	2,308	11,574	10,438	1,136
2017..................................	Number	116,840	104,155	101,851	2,304	12,685	11,541	1,144
2022								
Farms..................................	Number	127,648	108,693	106,658	2,035	18,955	17,340	1,615
Percent distribution......................	Percent	100.0	85.2	83.6	1.6	14.8	13.6	1.3
Land in farms............................	Mil. acres	150.9	134.3	126.5	7.8	16.6	13.8	2.7
Average per farm........................	Acres	1,182	1,235	1,186	3,829	875	798	1,698
Value of—								
Land and buildings....................	Bil. dol.	575.2	506.5	484.5	22.0	68.7	54.6	14.1
Average per farm.....................	$1,000	4,506	4,660	4,543	10,820	3,625	3,146	8,761
Farm products sold...................	Bil. dol.	155.5	124.8	117.4	7.5	30.6	20.4	10.2
Average per farm.....................	$1,000	1,218	1,149	1,100	3,668	1,616	1,179	6,305

Source: U.S. Department of Agriculture, National Agricultural Statistics Service, *2022 Census of Agriculture*, Vol. 1, February 2024, and earlier reports. See also <www.nass.usda.gov/AgCensus/>.

Table 867. Farms—Number, Acreage, and Value by State: 2017 and 2022

[2,042 represents 2,042,000. Data have been adjusted for coverage; see text, this section and Appendix III]

State	Number of farms (1,000)		Land in farms (mil. acres)		Average size of farm (acres)		Total value of land and buildings [1] (bil. dol.)		Market value of agricultural products sold and government payments (mil. dol.)	
	2017	2022	2017	2022	2017	2022	2017	2022	2017	2022
U.S.............	2,042	1,900	900.2	880.1	441	463	2,679.0	3,385.3	397,466	553,524
AL...............	41	37	8.6	8.6	211	231	25.6	31.6	6,115	9,099
AK...............	1	1	0.8	0.9	858	742	0.6	0.9	73	93
AZ...............	19	17	26.1	25.5	1,369	1,528	21.2	22.5	3,874	5,255
AR...............	43	38	13.9	13.7	326	363	43.9	53.8	9,973	14,098
CA...............	71	63	24.5	24.2	348	383	229.4	317.7	45,282	59,482
CO...............	39	36	31.8	30.2	818	838	51.2	72.5	7,690	9,512
CT...............	6	5	0.4	0.4	69	74	4.8	5.2	582	718
DE...............	2	2	0.5	0.5	228	242	4.4	5.0	1,481	2,101
FL...............	48	45	9.7	9.7	204	217	57.4	71.0	7,416	10,326
GA...............	42	39	10.0	9.9	235	253	34.9	42.4	9,821	13,436
HI...............	7	7	1.1	1.1	155	160	10.6	12.0	572	689
ID...............	25	23	11.7	11.5	468	505	33.5	48.6	7,697	11,025
IL...............	73	71	27.0	26.3	372	370	196.5	221.4	17,531	26,745
IN...............	57	54	15.0	14.6	264	272	98.4	120.6	11,450	18,142
IA...............	86	87	30.6	30.0	355	345	215.8	277.4	29,639	44,720
KS...............	59	56	45.8	44.8	781	804	84.6	104.1	19,292	24,427
KY...............	76	69	13.0	12.4	171	179	48.8	61.3	5,865	8,095
LA...............	27	25	8.0	8.0	292	319	24.4	28.7	3,350	4,940
ME...............	8	7	1.3	1.2	172	174	3.4	4.6	676	879
MD...............	12	13	2.0	2.0	160	158	15.6	18.3	2,517	3,399
MA...............	7	7	0.5	0.5	68	66	5.4	6.4	479	621
MI...............	48	46	9.8	9.5	205	208	48.4	55.7	8,388	12,356
MN...............	69	66	25.5	25.4	371	388	123.8	155.4	18,790	29,066
MS...............	35	31	10.4	10.3	298	328	28.6	34.5	6,410	8,373
MO...............	95	88	27.8	27.0	291	308	94.0	124.7	10,850	15,059
MT...............	27	24	58.1	57.6	2,149	2,374	53.2	74.7	3,805	5,022
NE...............	46	44	45.0	44.0	971	989	123.9	151.1	22,623	29,835
NV...............	3	3	6.1	5.9	1,790	1,889	5.6	6.6	671	984
NH...............	4	4	0.4	0.4	103	106	2.2	3.0	191	255
NJ...............	10	10	0.7	0.7	74	71	9.9	11.4	1,105	1,500
NM...............	25	21	40.7	39.1	1,624	1,865	21.2	32.8	2,646	3,079
NY...............	33	31	6.9	6.5	205	212	22.2	26.7	5,428	8,104
NC...............	46	43	8.4	8.1	182	190	39.1	44.6	13,008	18,857
ND...............	26	25	39.3	38.5	1,492	1,537	67.1	82.4	8,701	13,173
OH...............	78	76	14.0	13.7	179	180	86.6	109.8	9,692	15,549
OK...............	79	70	34.2	32.9	435	467	59.2	72.1	7,698	8,970
OR...............	38	36	16.0	15.3	424	430	38.8	56.5	5,099	6,907
PA...............	53	49	7.3	7.1	137	144	47.7	56.6	7,833	10,365
RI...............	1	1	0.1	0.1	55	56	0.9	1.4	59	96
SC...............	25	23	4.7	4.6	191	201	17.0	19.8	3,064	4,481
SD...............	30	28	43.2	42.3	1,443	1,495	89.4	109.7	10,141	13,679
TN...............	70	63	10.9	10.7	155	170	42.6	55.3	3,915	5,217
TX...............	248	231	127.0	125.5	511	544	243.5	313.6	25,673	33,265
UT...............	18	17	10.8	10.5	587	604	19.6	31.9	1,866	2,405
VT...............	7	7	1.2	1.2	175	180	4.2	4.8	787	1,042
VA...............	43	39	7.8	7.3	180	187	36.1	38.8	4,021	5,563
WA...............	36	32	14.7	13.9	410	432	40.9	53.0	9,803	12,998
WV...............	24	23	3.7	3.5	155	156	9.7	11.7	763	958
WI...............	65	59	14.3	13.8	221	236	70.2	84.3	11,554	16,846
WY...............	12	11	29.0	28.8	2,430	2,729	22.6	36.3	1,502	1,719

[1] As of December 31.

Source: U.S. Department of Agriculture, National Agricultural Statistics Service, *2022 Census of Agriculture*, Vol. 1, February 2024.

Table 868. Farms—Number, Value of Sales, and Government Payments by Economic Class of Farm: 2022

[1,900 represents 1,900,000. Economic class of farm is a combination of market value of agricultural products sold and federal farm program payments. Data have been adjusted for coverage; see text, this section and Appendix III]

Economic class	Number of farms (1,000)		Market value of agricultural products sold and government payments (mil. dol.)		
	Total	Receiving government payments	Total	Agricultural products sold	Government payments
Total.........................	**1,900**	**483**	**553,524**	**543,087**	**10,437**
Less than $1,000.........................	375	12	60	54	6
$1,000 to $2,499.........................	211	41	346	282	64
$2,500 to $4,999.........................	193	39	690	572	118
$5,000 to $9,999.........................	215	43	1,523	1,311	212
$10,000 to $24,999.........................	242	58	3,885	3,434	450
$25,000 to $49,999.........................	153	46	5,419	4,913	506
$50,000 to $99,999.........................	121	44	8,571	7,982	589
$100,000 to $249,999...................	126	55	20,245	19,130	1,115
$250,000 to $499,999...................	87	44	31,100	29,775	1,326
$500,000 to $999,999...................	70	40	49,649	47,893	1,756
$1,000,000 to $2,499,999..............	61	36	98,033	95,843	2,190
$2,500,000 to $4,999,999..............	30	16	103,471	102,255	1,216
$5 million or more.........................	16	8	230,532	229,644	888

Source: U.S. Department of Agriculture, National Agricultural Statistics Service, *2022 Census of Agriculture*, Vol. 1, February 2024.

Table 869. Farms—Number, Acreage, and Value of Sales by Size of Sales: 2017 and 2022

[2,042 represents 2,042,000. Data have been adjusted for coverage; see text, this section and Appendix III]

Market value of agricultural products sold	Farms (1,000)	Acreage Total (mil.)	Acreage Average per farm	Value of sales Total (mil. dol.)	Value of sales Average per farm (dol.)	Percent distribution Farms	Percent distribution Acreage	Percent distribution Value of sales
2017								
Total.................................	**2,042**	**900.2**	**441**	**388,523**	**190,245**	**100.0**	**100.0**	**100.0**
Less than $2,500.......................	792	103.6	131	404	510	38.8	11.5	0.1
$2,500 to $4,999......................	185	16.1	87	663	3,577	9.1	1.8	0.2
$5,000 to $9,999......................	208	24.7	119	1,478	7,101	10.2	2.7	0.4
$10,000 to $24,999....................	228	50.0	219	3,650	15,994	11.2	5.6	0.9
$25,000 to $49,999....................	144	50.0	347	5,100	35,389	7.1	5.6	1.3
$50,000 to $99,999....................	119	66.3	555	8,478	70,982	5.8	7.4	2.2
$100,000 to $249,999..................	131	119.6	914	21,171	161,697	6.4	13.3	5.4
$250,000 to $499,999..................	88	126.6	1,441	31,319	356,545	4.3	14.1	8.1
$500,000 to $999,999..................	70	131.7	1,889	49,339	707,846	3.4	14.6	12.7
$1,000,000 or more....................	77	211.6	2,752	266,922	3,472,604	3.8	23.5	68.7
2022								
Total.................................	**1,900**	**880.1**	**463**	**543,087**	**190,245**	**100.0**	**100.0**	**100.0**
Less than $2,500.......................	679	106.0	156	349	514	35.7	12.0	0.1
$2,500 to $4,999......................	166	11.5	69	594	3,573	8.7	1.3	0.1
$5,000 to $9,999......................	192	20.2	105	1,360	7,095	10.1	2.3	0.3
$10,000 to $24,999....................	222	41.8	188	3,567	16,049	11.7	4.7	0.7
$25,000 to $49,999....................	144	40.3	280	5,100	35,408	7.6	4.6	0.9
$50,000 to $99,999....................	116	54.8	472	8,237	70,876	6.1	6.2	1.5
$100,000 to $249,999..................	123	98.3	799	19,716	160,334	6.5	11.2	3.6
$250,000 to $499,999..................	85	113.0	1,326	30,549	358,284	4.5	12.8	5.6
$500,000 to $999,999..................	68	119.0	1,760	48,249	713,310	3.6	13.5	8.9
$1,000,000 or more....................	105	275.1	2,610	425,365	4,036,337	5.5	31.3	78.3

Source: U.S. Department of Agriculture, National Agricultural Statistics Service, *2022 Census of Agriculture*, Vol. 1, February 2024, and earlier reports. See also <www.nass.usda.gov/AgCensus/>.

Table 870. Farmers by Selected Producer Characteristic: 2017 and 2022

[A producer is a person who is involved in making decisions for the farm operation, including decisions about planting, harvesting, livestock management, and marketing. A producer may be the owner, a household member of the owner, hired manager, tenant, renter, or sharecropper. Data were collected for a maximum of 4 producers per farm. See source for more details]

Characteristic	2017	2022	Characteristic	2017	2022
Total producers..................	**3,399,834**	**3,374,044**	Primary occupation:		
By sex:			Farming...............................	1,416,848	1,415,315
Male.................................	2,172,373	2,149,318	Other................................	1,982,986	1,958,729
Female...............................	1,227,461	1,224,726	By place of residence:		
			On farm operated...................	2,530,442	2,377,305
By age:			Not on farm operated...............	869,392	996,739
Under 25 years......................	50,943	57,000	Days of work off farm:		
25 to 34 years......................	234,496	239,480	None.................................	1,311,334	1,297,470
35 to 44 years......................	390,345	426,616	Any..................................	2,088,500	2,076,574
45 to 54 years......................	614,654	519,430	1 to 49 days.....................	285,477	305,643
55 to 64 years......................	955,354	837,525	50 to 99 days....................	151,972	158,388
65 to 74 years......................	757,936	826,931	100 to 199 days..................	282,056	274,730
75 years and older..................	396,106	467,062	200 days or more.................	1,368,995	1,337,813
Average age.........................	57.5	58.1	Years on present farm:		
			2 years or less.....................	201,061	175,441
By race/ethnicity:			3 or 4 years........................	268,316	275,254
American Indian/Alaska Native....	58,199	56,203	5 to 9 years........................	495,022	640,008
Asian................................	22,016	22,788	10 years or more....................	2,435,435	2,283,341
Black or African American..........	45,508	41,807	Years operating any farm:		
Native Hawaiian or other			5 years or less.....................	474,198	481,821
Pacific Islander.....................	3,018	3,419	6 to 10 years.......................	434,076	529,894
White................................	3,244,344	3,219,263	11 years or more....................	2,491,560	2,362,329
More than one race reported.......	26,749	30,564	Military service:		
			Never served........................	3,029,215	3,068,291
Hispanic or Latino [1].................	112,451	112,379	Served [2]............................	370,619	305,753

[1] Persons of Hispanic origin may be of any race. [2] Includes producers who currently or previously served on active duty in the U.S. Armed Forces.

Source: U.S. Department of Agriculture, National Agricultural Statistics Service, *2022 Census of Agriculture*, Vol. 1, February 2024. See also <www.nass.usda.gov/AgCensus/>.

Table 871. Family Farm Household Income and Wealth: 2015 to 2022, and by Farm Type, 2022

[In dollars, except for number of farms. Based on Agricultural Resource Management Survey (ARMS) Phase III. A family farm is defined as one in which the majority of the ownership of the farm business is held by related individuals. Nearly all farms (97 percent in 2022) are family farms. The farm operator is the person who runs the farm, making the day-to-day management decisions. The operator could be an owner, hired manager, cash tenant, share tenant, and/or a partner. If land is rented or worked on shares, the tenant or renter is the operator. For multiple-operator farms, a principal operator is identified as the individual making most of the day-to-day decisions about the operation. If secondary operators are the spouses of principal operators, both operators are considered part of the principal operator household]

| Item | | | | | 2022 | | | |
| | | | | | | ERS farm typology | | |
	2015	2019	2020	2021	Total	Rural residence farms [1]	Intermedi-ate farms [2]	Commer-cial farms [3]
Number of family farms	**2,032,300**	**1,967,617**	**1,963,389**	**1,960,695**	**1,939,972**	**1,036,334**	**720,107**	**183,531**
INCOME PER FAMILY FARM HOUSEHOLD								
Net earnings from farming activities	24,740	21,701	25,566	30,821	32,852	-929	4,081	336,492
Off-farm income of the household	95,140	101,638	96,688	104,460	123,223	151,385	89,074	98,198
Earned income	65,814	73,320	63,530	67,838	86,643	116,226	49,230	66,399
Unearned income	29,326	28,318	33,158	36,622	36,580	35,159	39,844	31,799
Total household income, mean [4]	119,880	123,339	122,255	135,281	156,076	150,456	93,154	434,690
WEALTH PER FAMILY FARM HOUSEHOLD								
Assets, mean [4]	1,599,151	1,946,066	1,915,447	2,305,069	2,553,996	2,070,105	2,144,357	6,893,631
Farm assets	1,012,486	1,178,070	1,227,474	1,430,624	1,582,335	929,347	1,429,135	5,870,630
Non-farm assets	586,666	767,996	687,974	874,444	971,661	1,140,758	715,222	1,023,001
Debt, mean [4]	190,885	214,832	200,889	204,190	220,105	149,511	150,453	892,007
Farm debt	101,430	99,248	97,252	95,565	103,578	27,889	59,057	705,655
Non-farm debt	89,454	115,584	103,637	108,625	116,526	121,622	91,397	186,352
Net worth, mean [4]	1,408,267	1,731,234	1,714,559	2,100,879	2,333,891	1,920,594	1,993,904	6,001,624
Farm net worth	911,055	1,078,822	1,130,222	1,335,059	1,478,757	901,458	1,370,078	5,164,975
Non-farm net worth	497,211	652,412	584,337	765,819	855,135	1,019,136	623,825	836,649

[1] Farms in which the principal operator is retired or has a major occupation other than farming. [2] Farms with farming as the operator's major occupation, but with less than $350,000 in gross sales. [3] Farms with more than $350,000 in gross sales. [4] For definition of mean see Guide to Tabular Presentation.

Source: U.S. Department of Agriculture, Economic Research Service, "Farm Household Income and Characteristics," <www.ers.usda.gov/data-products/farm-household-income-and-characteristics.aspx>, accessed January 2024.

Table 872. Farm Type, Acreage, and Production: 2000 to 2022

[2,166 represents 2,166,000. Based on Agricultural Resource Management Survey (ARMS). The farm typology used by the Economic Research Service was revised in 2013, and has been applied to data beginning in 2011. For more information, see <www.ers.usda.gov/publications/pub-details/?pubid=43744>]

Type of farm	Unit	2000	2010	2015	2017	2018	2019	2020	2021	2022
Total farms:										
Number of farms	1,000	2,166	2,193	2,059	2,034	2,021	2,015	2,011	2,004	1,994
Total value of production	Mil. dol.	177,286	286,758	368,144	361,648	347,884	338,972	368,890	407,546	449,600
Total acres operated	Mil.	995	912	850	844	812	797	832	876	847
Acres operated per farm	Acres	459	416	413	415	402	395	414	437	425
Commercial farms: [1]										
Number of farms	1,000	178	264	212	214	208	209	217	219	238
Total value of production	Mil. dol.	121,202	240,769	279,081	275,649	273,770	266,034	293,784	334,952	365,423
Total acres operated	Mil.	392	482	439	407	424	408	430	481	454
Acres operated per farm	Acres	2,205	1,829	2,066	1,899	2,036	1,952	1,981	2,192	1,907
Intermediate farms: [2]										
Number of farms	1,000	668	618	632	752	743	757	794	797	720
Total value of production	Mil. dol.	41,813	30,270	61,283	64,433	54,652	51,342	55,331	49,351	61,281
Total acres operated	Mil.	392	242	232	255	248	233	269	235	239
Acres operated per farm	Acres	587	392	367	339	333	307	338	295	332
Residence farms: [3]										
Number of farms	1,000	1,320	1,311	1,215	1,067	1,069	1,049	999	988	1,036
Total value of production	Mil. dol.	14,272	15,719	27,780	21,565	19,462	21,597	19,775	23,243	22,896
Total acres operated	Mil.	211	187	179	181	140	156	133	160	154
Acres operated per farm	Acres	160	143	147	170	131	149	133	162	149

[1] Data for 2010 and earlier include farms with sales of $250,000 or more. Beginning in 2011, data are for farms with $350,000 or more gross cash farm income and nonfamily farms. [2] Data for 2010 and earlier include small family farms whose operators report farming as their major occupation. Beginning in 2011, data are for farms with less than $350,000 in gross cash farm income and a principal operator whose primary occupation is farming. [3] Data for 2010 and earlier include retirement and residential farms. Beginning in 2011, data are for farms with less than $350,000 in gross cash farm income and where the principal operator is either retired or has a primary occupation other than farming.

Source: U.S. Department of Agriculture, Economic Research Service, "ARMS Farm Financial and Crop Production Practices," <www.ers.usda.gov/data-products/arms-farm-financial-and-crop-production-practices.aspx>, accessed March 2024.

Table 873. Farms with Renewable Energy Systems by Type of Farm: 2017

[Farms reporting renewable energy systems on their operation. Based on the 1974 definition of farms and farmland, see text, this section. Farm types are based on the USDA's Economic Research Service typology. Family farms, farms in which the majority of the business is owned by the operator and individuals related to the operator, are classified based on the gross cash farm income (GCFI). GCFI includes sales of crops and livestock, fees for delivering commodities under production contracts, government payments, and farm-related income]

Energy system	All farms	Family farms							Non-family farms [1]
		Small			Mid-sized	Large-scale			
		Total	GCFI less than $150,000	GCFI $150,000 to $349,999	GCFI $350,000 to $999,999	Total	GCFI $1,000,000 to $4,999,999	GCFI $5,000,000 and more	
Number of farms, total............	2,042,220	1,798,439	1,668,776	129,663	108,304	52,592	47,056	5,536	82,885
Number of farms with any renewable energy system....	**133,176**	**111,486**	**100,653**	**10,833**	**9,934**	**5,543**	**4,767**	**776**	**6,213**
Percent of all farms..............	6.5	6.2	6.0	8.4	9.2	10.5	10.1	14.0	7.5
By type of system:									
Solar panels......................	90,142	77,944	71,347	6,597	4,994	2,984	2,450	534	4,220
Wind turbines.....................	14,136	9,950	8,138	1,812	2,120	1,113	1,017	96	953
Methane digesters...............	686	406	357	49	62	142	66	76	76
Geothermal/geoexchange systems...................	30,343	24,803	22,351	2,452	3,026	1,466	1,380	86	1,048
Small hydro systems.............	1,710	1,465	1,331	134	81	47	42	5	117
Biodiesel..........................	2,034	1,580	1,345	235	206	116	107	9	132
Ethanol...........................	1,759	1,340	1,141	199	195	118	113	5	106
Other.............................	3171	2855	2637	218	119	60	47	13	137
Wind rights leased to others.......	20,072	14,426	11,634	2,792	3,093	1,364	1,255	109	1,189

[1] Any farm where the operator and persons related to the operator do not own a majority of the business.

Source: U.S. Department of Agriculture, National Agricultural Statistics Service, *2017 Census of Agriculture, Farm Typology*, Volume 2, January 2021. See also <www.nass.usda.gov/AgCensus/>.

Table 874. Sales of Agricultural Products Direct to Consumers: 2012 to 2022

[1,309,827 represents $1,309,827,000. Data cover farms that sell products for human consumption directly to consumers at roadside stands, farmers' markets, pick-your-own, on-farm stores, and community support agricultural arrangements. Excludes non-edible products such as nursery crops, cut flowers, and wool, but includes livestock sales. Sales of agricultural products by vertically integrated operations through their own processing and marketing operations are also excluded. Beginning with 2017 data, includes value added sales and is not directly comparable to prior value of direct sales data]

Item	Number of farms with direct sales	Number of farms with direct and value added sales		Value of direct sales ($1,000)	Value of direct and value added sales ($1,000)	
	2012	2017	2022	2012	2017	2022
Total, all farms with direct sales...............	**144,530**	**130,056**	**116,617**	**1,309,827**	**2,805,310**	**3,263,074**
Percent of all farms.............................	6.9	6.4	6.1	0.3	0.7	0.6
BY VALUE OF SALES						
$1 to $499..	37,398	30,695	26,158	7,770	6,559	5,539
$500 to $999.......................................	20,170	17,318	14,466	13,685	11,615	9,519
$1,000 to $4,999..................................	52,750	43,934	38,706	121,750	101,770	86,928
$5,000 to $9,999..................................	14,452	13,707	12,465	97,308	92,663	83,333
$10,000 to $24,999...............................	11,045	11,669	11,272	164,774	176,745	171,370
$25,000 to $49,999...............................	4,244	5,068	5,081	143,722	172,716	173,397
$50,000 or more...................................	4,471	7,665	8,469	760,819	2,243,242	2,732,990
BY PRIMARY ACTIVITY OF FARM [1,2]						
Oilseed and grains.................................	8,715	5,143	4,361	63,321	64,610	67,536
Vegetables and melons............................	23,218	20,013	15,949	420,466	632,095	475,969
Fruit and tree nuts.................................	18,399	19,724	19,571	319,523	1,267,029	1,880,064
Greenhouse and nursery [3].......................	6,031	6,105	6,038	59,845	107,661	98,910
Beef cattle ranching and farming..................	35,980	28,156	19,741	147,315	179,653	201,272
Dairy cattle and milk production...................	2,982	2,264	1,244	43,546	152,584	71,470
Hog and pig farming...............................	3,897	3,552	2,724	15,970	20,662	34,025
Poultry and egg production........................	9,999	8,107	14,344	36,782	88,818	84,510
Sheep and goat farming............................	10,198	9,538	6,733	19,647	32,240	34,196

[1] Based on the farms' North American Industry Classification (NAICS) codes indicating main commodity type produced. [2] Includes other types, not shown separately. [3] Includes floriculture.

Source: U.S. Department of Agriculture, National Agricultural Statistics Service, *2022 Census of Agriculture*, Vol. 1, February 2024, and earlier reports. See also <www.nass.usda.gov/AgCensus/>.

Table 875. Farm to School Program Participation by State: 2019

[Percent, except total. For school year ending in 2019. Farm to School programs support a range of farm to school activities in which schools serve locally produced foods in their cafeteria and expose students to food and agricultural education experiences. The 2019 Farm to School Census collected data on farm to school activities from School Food Authorities (SFA) that participated in the National School Lunch Program (NSLP) in the 2018-2019 school year. The SFA is the entity responsible for school food service operations. Respondents included public, private and charter school SFAs, as well as residential child care institutions participating in NSLP]

State	Total SFAs (number)	Percent of SFAs	Served local foods [1]	Had an edible school garden	Served products from school based gardens or farms [2]	Organized field trips to farms	Had farmers visit cafeteria or classroom	Promoted local foods at school in general [3]	Spending on local food costs as a percent of total food costs [4]
United States....	18,832	65.4	76.8	34.3	48.4	30.7	15.3	42.3	19.9
Alabama............	140	65.7	73.9	46.7	41.9	32.6	19.6	55.4	12.2
Alaska..............	48	60.4	62.1	51.7	53.3	13.8	10.3	41.4	12.7
Arizona............	341	52.2	74.7	25.3	24.4	26.4	9.6	33.1	26.8
Arkansas..........	259	68.0	68.8	34.1	58.3	25.6	16.5	30.7	22.8
California..........	843	70.7	76.7	47.8	34.4	29.9	18.1	40.1	27.5
Colorado..........	127	59.1	68.0	49.3	56.8	32.0	21.3	50.7	18.1
Connecticut.......	129	80.6	85.6	36.5	47.4	17.3	13.5	60.6	19.5
Delaware..........	38	86.8	90.9	42.4	64.3	27.3	9.1	66.7	18.9
District of Columbia........	41	82.9	91.2	55.9	21.1	38.2	8.8	38.2	23.9
Florida.............	201	63.7	77.3	39.8	27.5	30.5	21.1	46.1	18.2
Georgia............	215	84.7	89.6	62.1	50.4	49.5	46.7	65.9	23.3
Hawaii.............	23	87.0	85.0	70.0	28.6	70.0	35.0	55.0	28.8
Idaho..............	140	67.9	68.4	35.8	44.1	21.1	11.6	34.7	20.8
Illinois.............	516	54.7	63.1	22.7	43.8	38.7	15.6	26.2	20.3
Indiana............	299	56.9	80.6	28.2	37.5	43.5	13.5	28.8	17.1
Iowa...............	268	60.4	66.0	36.4	54.2	30.9	11.1	31.5	16.8
Kansas............	276	59.8	77.6	27.9	63.0	44.2	22.4	31.5	16.7
Kentucky..........	170	69.4	67.8	35.6	42.9	35.6	29.7	37.3	12.1
Louisiana..........	153	55.6	69.4	36.5	22.6	20.0	8.2	29.4	14.9
Maine..............	143	83.2	80.7	58.0	69.6	31.9	24.4	57.1	17.1
Maryland...........	50	82.0	80.5	41.5	23.5	24.4	17.1	58.5	15.5
Massachusetts.....	317	72.2	81.2	48.5	65.8	23.1	15.7	63.3	16.3
Michigan..........	576	77.1	84.5	25.9	42.6	25.9	11.7	48.0	20.8
Minnesota.........	398	65.8	79.0	38.5	69.3	29.0	14.5	44.3	15.8
Mississippi.........	153	71.9	66.4	32.7	27.8	20.0	14.5	46.4	20.0
Missouri...........	507	51.5	69.7	25.7	50.7	28.4	12.6	30.3	22.8
Montana...........	153	68.6	83.8	37.1	53.8	30.5	14.3	50.5	21.8
Nebraska..........	251	66.1	75.3	31.9	67.9	25.3	15.1	39.8	15.8
Nevada............	28	46.4	38.5	46.2	16.7	46.2	23.1	7.7	37.8
New Hampshire....	41	82.9	76.5	55.9	68.4	47.1	11.8	55.9	11.2
New Jersey........	421	72.7	78.4	32.0	27.6	34.6	8.8	57.2	17.4
New Mexico.......	180	52.8	80.0	27.4	42.3	24.2	18.9	40.0	20.7
New York..........	661	77.3	83.6	36.8	58.0	28.6	13.7	54.4	20.4
North Carolina.....	174	62.6	81.7	25.7	10.7	42.2	27.5	56.9	17.7
North Dakota.......	143	65.7	73.4	24.5	78.3	34.0	24.5	35.1	12.7
Ohio...............	674	58.3	76.3	25.2	54.5	30.5	8.7	34.1	18.7
Oklahoma..........	315	45.1	55.6	21.1	50.0	23.2	11.3	22.5	19.2
Oregon............	182	85.2	89.0	45.8	57.7	40.0	13.5	58.7	20.9
Pennsylvania.......	522	75.3	80.9	27.7	45.9	34.4	11.2	38.2	21.5
Rhode Island.......	57	78.9	88.9	28.9	46.2	37.8	20.0	66.7	16.5
South Carolina.....	119	60.5	76.4	44.4	21.9	36.1	26.4	37.5	17.7
South Dakota......	133	44.4	72.9	28.8	41.2	28.8	13.6	30.5	14.6
Tennessee.........	177	72.9	80.6	41.1	37.7	34.9	20.9	41.1	13.0
Texas..............	850	62.9	75.7	19.8	30.2	12.3	8.6	41.9	22.7
Utah...............	130	59.2	84.4	35.1	40.7	32.5	14.3	28.6	18.9
Vermont...........	44	88.6	82.1	84.6	63.6	51.3	33.3	59.0	17.5
Virginia............	151	82.8	84.0	41.6	46.2	33.6	32.8	51.2	9.5
Washington........	224	67.9	76.3	36.8	39.3	21.1	14.5	46.7	24.8
West Virginia.......	64	78.1	80.0	50.0	60.0	40.0	22.0	48.0	16.3
Wisconsin..........	477	70.2	75.2	41.2	68.1	41.8	18.5	46.0	18.2
Wyoming...........	59	67.8	72.5	40.0	68.8	35.0	20.0	32.5	9.5
American Samoa...	1	100.0	–	–	(NA)	(NA)	(NA)	(NA)	8.5
Guam..............	3	33.3	100.0	100.0	(NA)	100.0	(NA)	100.0	4.8
Northern Mariana Islands...........	1	100.0	100.0	–	(NA)	(NA)	(NA)	(NA)	1.3
Puerto Rico.........	27	92.6	88.0	24.0	16.7	12.0	12.0	48.0	58.3
Virgin Islands.......	1	100.0	100.0	–	(NA)	(NA)	(NA)	100.0	10.0

– Represents or rounds to zero. NA Not available. [1] The definition of "local" is determined by individual respondents. The Census questionnaire asked respondents how they defined "local" as it relates to their food procurement. Respondents could choose from one of seven options or specify a different definition: (a) produced within a 20 mile radius, (b) produced within a 50 mile radius, (c) produced within a 100 mile radius, (d) produced within a 200 mile radius, (e) produced within the county, (f) produced within the state, and (g) produced within the region. [2] Responses only include SFAs that had edible school gardens during the 2018-2019 school year. [3] Promotion activities include promoting local foods via cafeteria signs, posters, and newsletters, and through themed or branded events such as "Harvest of the Month"; and implementing strategies to encourage student selection and consumption of local foods. [4] For SFAs participating in farm to school programs. Costs include milk.

Source: U.S. Department of Agriculture, Food and Nutrition Service, "2019 Farm to School Census Data Explorer," <farmtoschoolcensus. fns.usda.gov/census-results/census-data-explorer>, accessed June 2022. See also <www.fns.usda.gov/f2s/farm-to-school>.

Table 876. Certified Organic Farms—Value of Sales and Marketing Practices by State: 2021

[In units, as indicated (309,625 represents $309,625,000). Includes certified organic producers who have been certified by state or private agencies accredited by the U.S. Department of Agriculture (USDA). Excludes operations transitioning to certified organic operations. Organic food must be produced without the use of conventional pesticides, petroleum-based or sewage sludge-based fertilizers, herbicides, pesticides, genetic engineering (biotechnology), antibiotics, growth hormones, or irradiation. Land must have no prohibited substances applied to it for at least 3 years before the harvest of an organic crop. Data are from the USDA's Certified Organic Survey]

State	Certified organic farms (number)	Farms by percent of total value of sales from organic production (number)					Farms by marketing practices (number)		Value of sales by marketing practices ($1,000)	
		Less than 25 percent	25 to 49 percent	50 to 74 percent	75 to 99 percent	100 percent	Consumer direct sales [1]	Retail markets, institutions or food hubs [2]	Consumer direct sales [1]	Retail markets, institutions or food hubs [2]
United States....	**17,445**	**1,444**	**879**	**2,031**	**2,786**	**10,305**	**3,261**	**3,309**	**309,625**	**2,020,715**
Alabama...........	18	–	–	–	5	13	8	6	460	700
Alaska..............	9	4	–	–	–	5	3	3	(D)	(D)
Arizona.............	62	10	8	8	5	31	13	25	655	80,605
Arkansas...........	82	4	3	20	5	50	5	20	38	5,910
California..........	3,061	349	152	196	238	2,126	610	803	126,438	1,116,500
Colorado...........	265	27	19	21	44	154	29	56	2,615	7,350
Connecticut........	54	–	3	5	7	39	30	26	1,650	2,014
Delaware..........	8	–	–	2	1	5	2	–	(D)	–
Florida.............	134	3	3	14	27	87	47	35	3,699	21,157
Georgia............	121	14	8	12	11	76	23	33	1,807	19,624
Hawaii..............	144	10	4	17	6	107	52	63	3,151	15,996
Idaho...............	245	35	15	39	29	127	32	25	1,985	18,226
Illinois.............	354	30	28	62	70	164	45	24	6,062	2,902
Indiana.............	697	33	36	112	141	375	42	29	1,973	2,673
Iowa...............	799	62	56	137	183	361	49	51	1,554	3,152
Kansas.............	129	13	9	18	33	56	13	15	380	608
Kentucky...........	207	13	13	42	47	92	43	21	924	482
Louisiana..........	19	–	–	–	1	18	3	2	120	(D)
Maine..............	496	33	17	47	65	334	208	181	9,342	11,970
Maryland...........	112	10	3	11	17	71	36	30	5,216	5,906
Massachusetts.....	89	2	1	11	12	63	49	38	3,933	21,259
Michigan...........	572	42	29	41	75	385	115	83	7,497	8,428
Minnesota.........	650	75	38	98	123	316	91	76	3,620	4,089
Mississippi........	15	–	–	2	2	11	–	7	–	13,616
Missouri...........	397	12	31	50	88	216	10	63	4,304	32,309
Montana...........	206	43	7	30	28	98	45	46	1,263	9,075
Nebraska..........	220	24	28	34	48	86	7	5	594	454
Nevada............	43	5	4	6	4	24	11	12	332	100
New Hampshire....	93	1	3	12	13	64	40	31	1,620	1,321
New Jersey........	70	9	3	5	10	43	22	14	2,044	(D)
New Mexico.......	93	–	5	14	15	59	33	23	2,127	1,323
New York..........	1,407	61	41	135	230	940	362	290	18,453	39,473
North Carolina.....	335	61	19	50	46	159	54	37	2,031	2,566
North Dakota.......	113	11	9	31	18	44	7	4	112	(D)
Ohio...............	800	46	16	63	173	502	77	83	3,258	5,558
Oklahoma..........	48	9	2	8	3	26	5	12	223	1,407
Oregon.............	491	47	38	64	46	296	127	121	13,527	30,750
Pennsylvania.......	1,125	52	51	145	265	612	148	159	13,416	85,780
Rhode Island.......	28	3	–	–	8	17	26	14	918	785
South Carolina.....	40	7	4	4	5	20	16	–	128	–
South Dakota......	106	17	11	17	19	42	16	10	312	91
Tennessee.........	46	6	5	8	1	26	7	13	270	1,563
Texas..............	258	30	19	52	25	132	20	66	6,145	30,296
Utah...............	53	8	3	4	14	24	4	7	87	(D)
Vermont............	693	18	7	47	80	541	214	200	21,638	28,170
Virginia............	166	9	3	20	35	99	27	25	669	9,354
Washington........	730	101	67	111	113	338	185	217	19,603	350,321
West Virginia.......	27	–	–	–	4	23	7	4	6	81
Wisconsin..........	1,455	89	58	195	334	779	243	201	12,862	8,033
Wyoming...........	60	6	–	11	14	29	(NA)	(NA)	(NA)	(NA)

– Represents zero. D Withheld to avoid disclosing data for individual farms. NA Not available. [1] Sales may be through farmers markets, on-farm stores or stands, roadside stands or stores, u-pick, community supported agriculture (CSAs), or online marketplaces operated by the farming operation. [2] Sales to outlets that sell to consumers. Sales outlets include supermarkets, supercenters, restaurants, caterers, grocery stores, food cooperatives, K-12 schools, colleges and universities, hospitals, workplace cafeterias, prisons, and foodbanks.

Source: U.S. Department of Agriculture, National Agricultural Statistics Service, *Certified Organic Survey, 2021 Summary*, December 2022. See also <www.nass.usda.gov/Surveys/Guide_to_NASS_Surveys/Organic_Production/index.php>.

Table 877. Organic Agriculture—Number of Farms, Acreage, and Value of Sales, 2014 to 2021, and for Leading States, 2021

[5,454,979 represents $5,454,979,000. Includes all known organic producers that are certified organic; certified producers are those who have been certified by state or private agencies accredited by the USDA. Organic food must be produced without the use of conventional pesticides, petroleum-based or sewage sludge-based fertilizers, herbicides, pesticides, genetic engineering (biotechnology), antibiotics, growth hormones, or irradiation. Animals raised on an organic operation must not be fed antibiotics or growth hormones, be fed 100 percent organic feed, and given access to the outdoors. Land must have no prohibited substances applied to it for at least 3 years before the harvest of an organic crop]

| Year and leading states | Organic farms (number) | Organic land (acres) | Value of sales ($1,000) [1] | | | |
			Total product sales	Crops [2]	Livestock and poultry	Livestock and poultry products
2014...................	14,093	3,670,560	5,454,979	3,290,188	660,340	1,504,452
2015...................	12,818	4,361,849	6,163,472	3,509,632	743,227	1,910,613
2019...................	16,585	5,495,274	9,925,911	5,786,759	1,663,077	2,476,075
2021, U.S. total [3]....	**17,445**	**4,895,279**	**11,205,222**	**6,149,608**	**2,197,171**	**2,858,443**
California..............	3,061	813,710	3,550,489	2,702,502	490,715	357,272
Washington............	730	134,911	1,139,532	938,344	72,379	128,809
Pennsylvania.........	1,125	104,805	1,094,356	150,002	730,185	214,169
Texas.................	258	240,806	572,212	179,324	45,736	347,152
Oregon................	491	228,152	386,245	249,076	21,571	115,598
New York..............	1,407	331,438	327,910	115,514	31,154	181,242
Wisconsin.............	1,455	245,333	312,592	102,846	35,360	174,386
North Carolina........	335	38,888	308,063	55,448	214,185	38,430
Michigan..............	572	117,424	271,925	103,712	(D)	(D)
Colorado..............	265	190,809	252,696	106,401	23,028	123,267

[1] Value of sales of commodities; excludes value-added organic products. [2] Includes nursery and greenhouse. [3] Includes other states not shown separately.

Source: U.S. Department of Agriculture, National Agricultural Statistics Service, *Certified Organic Survey, 2021 Summary*, December 2022. See also <www.nass.usda.gov/Surveys/Guide_to_NASS_Surveys/Organic_Production/>.

Table 878. Adoption of Genetically Engineered Crops: 2000 to 2024

[As percent of all crops planted. As of June. Based on June Agricultural Survey conducted by National Agricultural Statistical Services (NASS). Excludes conventionally bred herbicide tolerant varieties. Insect resistant varieties include only those containing bacillus thuringiensis (Bt). The Bt varieties include those that contain more than one gene that can resist different types of insects. Stacked gene varieties include only those varieties containing biotechnology traits for both herbicide tolerance and insect resistance. May not add to total due to rounding]

Genetically engineered crop	2000	2010	2015	2017	2018	2019	2020	2021	2022	2023	2024
Corn.................................	**25**	**86**	**92**	**92**	**92**	**92**	**92**	**93**	**93**	**93**	**94**
Insect resistant..................	18	16	4	3	2	3	3	3	3	3	3
Herbicide tolerant...............	6	23	12	12	10	9	10	9	9	9	7
Stacked gene....................	1	47	77	77	80	80	79	81	81	82	83
Cotton...............................	**61**	**93**	**94**	**96**	**94**	**98**	**96**	**97**	**95**	**97**	**96**
Insect resistant..................	15	15	5	5	3	3	5	3	3	3	3
Herbicide tolerant...............	26	20	10	11	9	6	8	6	6	8	6
Stacked gene....................	20	58	79	80	82	89	83	88	86	86	87
Soybean............................	**54**	**93**	**94**	**94**	**94**	**94**	**94**	**95**	**95**	**95**	**96**
Insect resistant..................	(X)	(X)	(X)	(X)	(X)	(X)	(X)	(X)	(X)	(X)	(X)
Herbicide tolerant...............	54	93	94	94	94	94	94	95	95	95	96
Stacked gene....................	(X)	(X)	(X)	(X)	(X)	(X)	(X)	(X)	(X)	(X)	(X)

X Not applicable.

Source: U.S. Department of Agriculture, Economic Research Service, "Adoption of Genetically Engineered Crops in the U.S.," <www.ers.usda.gov/data-products/adoption-of-genetically-engineered-crops-in-the-u-s/>, accessed August 2024.

Table 879. Farm Production Expenses: 2017 and 2022

[2,042 represents 2,042,000. Data have been adjusted for coverage; see text, this section and Appendix III]

| Production expenses | 2017 | | | 2022 | | |
	Farms (1,000)	Expenses (mil. dol.)	Percent of total	Farms (1,000)	Expenses (mil. dol.)	Percent of total
Total..........................	**2,042**	**326,391**	**100.0**	**1,900**	**424,142**	**100.0**
Fertilizer.........................	1,025	23,543	7.2	890	36,144	8.5
Chemicals........................	894	17,585	5.4	864	23,606	5.6
Seeds, plants, vines, and trees............	703	20,970	6.4	734	25,581	6.0
Livestock and poultry..............	556	44,934	13.8	469	51,377	12.1
Feed.............................	1,262	62,625	19.2	1,091	88,374	20.8
Gasoline and fuel.................	1,922	13,474	4.1	1,800	18,385	4.3
Utilities..........................	1,339	9,009	2.8	1,273	11,145	2.6
Supplies, repairs, and maintenance........	1,665	19,671	6.0	1,569	25,895	6.1
Farm labor [1]....................	709	39,231	12.0	631	51,936	12.2
Customwork and custom hauling........	428	7,555	2.3	391	10,051	2.4
Cash rent for land, buildings and grazing fees..............	482	21,060	6.5	440	27,311	6.4
Rent and lease for machinery, equipment, and farm share..	138	2,424	0.7	132	3,216	0.8
Interest expense..................	669	12,396	3.8	611	13,442	3.2
Property taxes....................	1,920	9,415	2.9	1,786	11,036	2.6
Medical supplies, veterinary, custom services for livestock..	944	4,446	1.4	716	5,211	1.2
Other production expenses............	849	18,052	5.5	1,073	21,431	5.1

[1] Includes hired and contract labor.

Source: U.S. Department of Agriculture, National Agricultural Statistics Service, *2022 Census of Agriculture*, Vol. 1, February 2024. See also <www.nass.usda.gov/AgCensus/>.

Table 880. Balance Sheet of the Farming Sector: 2000 to 2023

[In billions of dollars, except as indicated (1,203 represents $1,203,000,000,000). As of December 31. Balance sheet estimates exclude the personal portion of farm households' assets and debts]

Item	2000	2010	2015	2016	2017	2018	2019	2020	2021	2022	2023
Assets	**1,203**	**2,171**	**2,880**	**2,914**	**3,006**	**3,019**	**3,049**	**3,131**	**3,424**	**3,788**	**4,014**
Investments and other financial assets	57	135	88	78	81	73	87	92	113	118	122
Investment in cooperatives	(NA)	6	7	7	8	7	6	5	7	6	6
Financial assets and net accounts receivable	(NA)	130	80	71	73	65	81	87	106	112	116
Inventories	110	168	187	180	180	173	163	163	181	202	214
Crops	28	57	53	56	57	60	50	51	58	72	66
Livestock and poultry	77	91	118	109	107	97	99	98	104	109	128
Purchased inputs [1]	5	20	16	15	16	16	14	14	18	21	20
Real estate [2]	946	1,660	2,366	2,401	2,473	2,503	2,520	2,597	2,822	3,156	3,339
Value of machinery and motor vehicles [3]	90	208	240	255	272	271	279	279	308	312	339
Debt [4]	**164**	**279**	**357**	**374**	**390**	**403**	**420**	**441**	**474**	**496**	**519**
Real estate	85	154	209	226	236	246	268	289	324	334	345
Commercial banks [5]	30	51	79	84	88	93	98	97	101	107	109
Farm Credit System	30	72	97	104	107	113	125	141	158	165	168
Farm Service Agency	3	3	5	6	6	7	8	9	11	11	12
Farmer Mac [6]	(NA)	4	5	5	6	7	8	9	10	10	10
Individuals and others [5]	11	10	10	12	13	10	11	13	23	18	21
Storage facility loans	(NA)	1	1	1	1	1	1	1	1	1	1
Life insurance companies	11	12	13	13	15	16	18	19	21	23	23
Nonreal estate	79	125	148	148	154	157	153	153	150	162	174
Commercial banks [5]	45	56	73	73	73	75	71	63	65	69	72
Farm Credit System	17	39	48	49	51	53	53	55	57	62	70
Farm Service Agency	4	4	4	4	4	4	4	4	3	3	3
Individuals and others [5]	13	26	23	22	26	24	25	31	25	29	30
Equity	**1,039**	**1,892**	**2,523**	**2,540**	**2,616**	**2,617**	**2,629**	**2,689**	**2,950**	**3,292**	**3,495**
FINANCIAL RATIOS (percent)											
Farm debt/asset ratio	13.62	12.85	12.39	12.84	12.99	13.34	13.79	14.10	13.85	13.10	12.93
Farm debt/equity ratio	15.77	14.74	14.14	14.73	14.93	15.39	16.00	16.41	16.08	15.07	14.85

NA Not available. [1] Purchased inputs represent value of prepaid expenses on supplies such as fertilizer and lime applied, seed, feed, and other inputs purchased for next year's production. It also includes the seed, fertilizer, fuel, and other expenses already invested in crops. [2] Includes farmland, buildings, and other service structures. Includes farm real estate assets leased from non-operator landlords. [3] Includes automobiles, trucks, and farm machinery leased to farm operators. [4] Reflects outstanding agricultural sector debt where it is held rather than where it originated. Excludes debt on operator dwellings and for nonfarm purposes. Sector-level estimates of farm debt report aggregate data by lender type and therefore do not identify who owes the debt. [5] Beginning with 2012, farm sector debt held by savings associations is reported with the commercial bank lender group instead of the individuals and others grouping. [6] The Federal Agricultural Mortgage Corporation (known as Farmer Mac) operates as a federally sponsored enterprise providing a secondary market for agricultural real estate mortgage loans, rural housing mortgage loans, and rural utility cooperative loans.

Source: U.S. Department of Agriculture, Economic Research Service, "U.S. and State Farm Income and Wealth Statistics," <www.ers.usda.gov/data-products/farm-income-and-wealth-statistics.aspx>, accessed September 2024.

Table 881. Farm Sector Output and Value Added: 2000 to 2022

[In millions of dollars (204,316 represents $204,316,000,000). For definition of value added and explanation of chained dollars, see text, Section 13. Minus sign (-) indicates decrease]

Item	2000	2005	2010	2015	2017	2018	2019	2020	2021	2022
CURRENT DOLLARS										
Farm output	204,316	253,551	320,921	403,163	395,529	395,074	387,522	389,321	472,080	564,709
Cash receipts from farm marketings	197,589	241,431	321,651	380,926	380,920	385,329	384,776	381,870	456,730	564,577
Farm products consumed on farms	318	384	386	622	433	436	487	571	650	675
Other farm income	8,426	11,840	12,139	21,195	20,236	17,543	17,495	18,130	17,188	19,957
Change in farm finished goods inventories	-2,016	-104	-13,255	420	-6,061	-8,235	-15,236	-11,250	-2,488	-20,501
Less: Intermediate goods and services consumed	127,660	147,235	203,878	256,904	256,798	258,248	267,061	272,331	291,132	341,192
Equals: Gross farm value added	76,656	106,316	117,043	146,259	138,731	136,825	120,461	116,990	180,947	223,517
Less: Consumption of fixed capital	22,807	27,484	33,063	46,489	46,598	46,899	47,545	48,138	50,734	56,861
Equals: Net farm value added	53,850	78,832	83,980	99,771	92,133	89,926	72,916	68,852	130,213	166,656
Compensation of employees	19,645	22,033	24,281	27,205	30,857	28,423	28,627	30,592	30,590	32,831
Taxes on production and imports	4,626	5,345	7,516	9,345	9,408	9,342	9,771	10,339	10,777	11,974
Less: Subsidies to operators	19,960	20,914	10,516	9,195	10,115	12,446	21,108	44,515	25,154	13,251
Net operating surplus	49,449	72,369	62,715	72,416	61,983	64,607	55,627	72,436	114,001	135,102
CHAINED (2017) DOLLARS										
Farm output, total	(NA)	(NA)	346,715	367,926	395,529	395,055	389,640	401,515	396,657	377,288
Cash receipts from farm marketings	(NA)	(NA)	351,654	347,347	380,920	385,082	386,990	394,588	383,735	376,550
Farm products consumed on farms	(NA)	(NA)	439	568	433	441	503	600	585	471
Other farm income	(NA)	(NA)	12,351	20,404	20,236	17,216	17,002	17,441	13,895	13,625
Change in farm finished goods inventories	(NA)	(NA)	-16,731	180	-6,061	-8,076	-15,120	-12,384	-2,884	-15,044
Less: Intermediate goods and services consumed	(NA)	(NA)	223,865	233,402	256,798	251,156	258,825	270,055	254,386	248,515
Equals: Gross farm value added	(NA)	(NA)	123,315	134,828	138,731	144,141	129,973	130,193	141,052	128,634
Less: Consumption of fixed capital	(NA)	(NA)	36,736	47,632	46,598	46,030	45,728	45,689	46,027	46,493
Equals: Net farm value added	(NA)	(NA)	84,030	87,226	92,133	98,259	83,741	84,032	94,765	83,197

NA Not available.

Source: U.S. Bureau of Economic Analysis, National Income and Product Accounts, "Table 7.3.5. Farm Sector Output, Gross Value Added, and Net Value Added," and "Table 7.3.6. Real Farm Sector Output, Real Gross Value Added, and Real Net Value Added, Chained Dollars," <www.bea.gov/itable/>, accessed August 2024.

Table 882. Value Added to Economy by Agricultural Sector: 2000 to 2023

[In billions of dollars (218.4 represents $218,400,000,000). Value of agricultural sector production is the gross value of the commodities and services produced within a year. Net value-added is the sector's contribution to the national economy and is the value of farm sector production minus the value of intermediate goods used. Net farm income is the farm operators' share of income from the sector's production activities. Minus sign (-) indicates decrease]

Item	2000	2010	2015	2016	2017	2018	2019	2020	2021	2022	2023
Value of agricultural production	**218.4**	**344.1**	**430.0**	**399.3**	**413.9**	**411.8**	**407.4**	**410.5**	**492.3**	**602.1**	**596.1**
Value of crop production	95.0	168.1	184.3	189.3	187.9	187.0	179.6	193.1	245.3	271.8	272.8
Crop cash receipts	92.5	180.3	187.9	195.8	194.9	196.0	193.8	202.5	246.0	282.8	276.7
Cotton	2.9	7.5	4.8	5.5	7.6	7.5	6.8	6.8	7.2	8.2	7.2
Feed crops	20.5	55.1	56.9	55.4	53.9	57.3	58.4	57.5	83.4	99.7	92.8
Food grains	6.5	14.3	12.3	11.3	11.2	12.1	11.5	11.8	15.3	16.6	16.6
Fruits and tree nuts	12.3	21.6	28.4	29.7	30.6	29.4	29.2	27.8	30.6	26.9	28.8
Oil crops	13.5	36.5	35.5	44.0	41.1	39.5	36.2	43.8	52.0	64.8	62.4
Tobacco	2.3	1.3	1.6	1.3	1.4	1.2	1.0	0.8	0.9	1.0	1.0
Vegetables and melons	15.8	17.4	20.4	19.5	20.5	18.7	19.1	21.1	19.5	25.2	26.1
All other crops	18.6	26.5	28.0	28.9	28.6	30.3	31.5	32.8	37.1	40.4	41.8
Home consumption	0.2	0.1	0.3	0.2	0.2	0.1	0.2	0.2	0.2	0.3	0.3
Value of inventory adjustment [1]	2.2	-12.3	-3.8	-6.6	-7.1	-9.2	-14.3	-9.6	-1.0	-11.3	-4.2
Value of livestock production	99.1	140.2	194.1	165.4	176.9	177.0	175.2	165.2	194.6	256.8	247.9
Animals and products cash receipts	99.6	140.9	189.5	162.7	175.6	176.1	175.6	165.0	196.4	259.8	249.6
Milk and dairy products	20.6	31.4	35.7	34.5	37.9	35.2	40.5	40.4	41.8	57.2	45.9
Meat animals	53.0	69.1	98.8	82.7	88.0	88.0	88.0	82.5	100.7	116.9	128.3
Miscellaneous livestock	4.1	5.7	6.7	6.7	6.9	6.9	7.1	7.0	7.7	8.5	8.3
Poultry and eggs	21.9	34.7	48.3	38.8	42.8	46.0	40.0	35.2	46.2	77.2	67.1
Home consumption	0.1	0.3	0.4	0.3	0.3	0.3	0.3	0.4	0.5	0.5	0.5
Value of inventory adjustment [1]	-0.6	-0.9	4.3	2.4	1.1	0.7	-0.7	-0.2	-2.2	-3.6	-2.2
Farm-related income	24.4	35.8	51.5	44.5	49.0	47.8	52.6	52.2	52.4	73.5	75.4
Forest products sold	0.8	0.5	0.7	0.7	0.7	0.7	0.6	0.6	0.7	0.7	0.7
Gross imputed rental value of farm dwellings	12.7	15.8	17.1	16.6	17.9	18.7	17.9	18.0	20.1	21.7	21.7
Machine hire and custom work	2.2	3.8	4.7	3.6	4.6	3.9	4.1	3.8	4.6	5.3	5.7
Other farm income	8.7	15.7	29.0	23.6	25.8	24.6	30.0	29.8	27.0	45.8	47.2
Less: Intermediate product expenses [2]	119.1	189.1	235.7	221.6	228.0	230.1	233.1	239.2	257.3	306.8	319.3
Farm origin	47.9	82.2	110.1	99.5	104.5	104.9	109.2	108.9	118.2	143.6	150.3
Feed purchased	24.5	45.4	58.5	55.6	54.5	53.8	59.4	56.8	65.2	83.6	80.0
Livestock and poultry purchased	15.9	20.4	30.3	22.1	27.4	29.2	28.5	29.0	30.7	34.9	43.0
Seed purchased	7.5	16.3	21.3	21.8	22.5	21.9	21.2	23.0	22.3	25.0	27.3
Manufactured inputs	28.7	50.1	59.1	56.5	56.3	57.9	56.8	58.9	67.7	82.9	82.1
Electricity	3.0	4.6	5.7	5.6	5.8	6.1	5.7	6.0	6.4	6.4	7.1
Fertilizers, lime, and soil conditioners	10.0	21.0	25.5	23.5	22.0	23.2	22.3	24.4	29.5	36.6	35.8
Pesticides	8.5	10.7	14.6	15.2	15.7	15.4	15.5	16.5	17.8	21.4	21.6
Petroleum fuel and oils	7.2	13.8	13.2	12.2	12.8	13.2	13.2	12.0	13.9	18.5	17.6
Other intermediate expenses [2]	42.5	56.8	66.5	65.6	67.2	67.3	67.1	71.4	71.4	80.3	86.8
Machine hire and custom work	4.1	4.3	4.8	4.4	4.6	4.3	5.2	5.1	4.9	5.4	6.3
Marketing, storage, and transportation	7.5	9.0	9.2	9.7	9.8	11.9	10.1	11.1	10.5	11.2	12.7
Repair and maintenance of capital items [2]	10.9	14.6	16.6	15.9	16.6	15.3	15.7	17.4	18.2	20.1	21.2
Miscellaneous expenses [2]	19.9	29.0	35.9	35.5	36.3	35.7	36.2	37.8	37.9	43.7	46.7
Total insurance premiums [3]	4.8	7.5	10.0	9.6	10.3	9.9	9.9	10.2	12.3	15.1	15.4
Irrigation	(NA)	0.8	1.4	1.3	1.6	1.5	1.7	1.6	1.6	1.6	1.9
Less: Contract labor	2.7	3.9	5.7	6.0	5.9	6.0	6.6	6.5	6.7	6.5	7.2
Plus: Net government transactions [4]	15.8	0.9	-2.7	0.3	-1.9	0.1	8.3	30.7	10.4	-1.0	-4.6
Direct government payments [5]	23.2	12.4	10.8	13.0	11.5	13.7	22.4	45.6	26.0	15.6	12.3
Property taxes [2]	7.4	11.5	13.5	12.6	13.5	13.6	14.1	14.9	15.5	16.6	16.9
Motor vehicle registration and licensing fees	0.5	0.6	0.7	0.7	0.7	0.7	0.7	0.8	0.8	0.8	0.9
Equals: Gross value added	**112.5**	**152.1**	**185.8**	**171.9**	**178.0**	**175.8**	**176.0**	**195.5**	**238.8**	**287.8**	**265.0**
Less: Capital consumption [2]	20.1	17.6	41.3	44.4	35.7	29.2	28.1	28.9	24.2	32.7	33.2
Equals: Net value added	**92.4**	**134.5**	**144.5**	**127.5**	**142.4**	**146.6**	**148.0**	**166.6**	**214.6**	**255.1**	**231.7**
Less: Factor payments to stakeholders [6]	41.7	57.4	62.8	65.2	66.6	64.2	66.0	67.8	68.3	73.1	85.3
Employee compensation [7]	17.9	23.6	26.4	28.4	30.4	28.1	28.5	30.5	30.4	35.9	41.6
Net rent paid to operator landlords	(NA)	2.1	4.7	4.5	4.1	3.7	3.9	4.1	4.3	3.1	3.6
Net rent paid to nonoperator landlords	9.2	14.8	15.4	14.9	13.5	11.7	12.8	13.8	14.2	9.8	11.6
Total interest expenses	14.6	16.9	16.4	17.3	18.7	20.7	20.7	19.4	19.5	24.3	28.5
Equals: Net farm income	**50.7**	**77.1**	**81.7**	**62.3**	**75.7**	**82.4**	**82.0**	**98.8**	**146.3**	**182.0**	**146.5**

NA Not available. [1] A positive value of inventory change represents current-year production not sold by December 31. A negative value is an offset to production from prior years included in current-year sales. [2] Including expenses associated with operator dwellings. [3] Includes federal and private crop and livestock insurance premiums as well as casualty, hail, motor vehicle and all other insurance premiums. [4] Direct government payments minus motor vehicle registration and licensing fees and property taxes. [5] Government payments reflect payments made directly to all recipients in the farm sector, including landlords. The nonoperator landlords share is offset by its inclusion in rental expenses paid to these landlords and thus is not reflected in net farm income or net cash income. [6] Prior to 2008, factor payments to stakeholders only includes net rent paid to nonoperator landlords. [7] Includes hired labor and non-cash employee compensation.

Source: U.S. Department of Agriculture, Economic Research Service, "U.S. and State Farm Income and Wealth Statistics," <www.ers.usda.gov/data-products/farm-income-and-wealth-statistics.aspx>, accessed September 2024.

Table 883. Value of Agricultural Production, Income, and Government Payments by State: 2020 and 2022

[In millions of dollars (406,319 represents $406,319,000,000). See headnote, Table 882. Minus sign (-) indicates loss]

State	Value of agricultural production 2020	Value of agricultural production 2022	Net farm income 2020	Net farm income 2022	Government payments, 2022
U.S.........	406,319	595,752	94,624	182,834	15,561
AL...........	5,417	9,251	700	2,646	131
AK...........	49	72	-11	2	15
AZ...........	4,386	5,975	569	1,428	68
AR...........	8,926	14,506	1,120	4,176	460
CA...........	52,146	62,089	14,016	18,012	637
CO...........	8,376	10,679	1,178	2,173	454
CT...........	674	1,054	176	345	18
DE...........	1,292	2,220	266	1,217	23
FL...........	8,712	10,439	1,733	3,342	196
GA...........	8,776	14,259	1,889	4,837	362
HI...........	684	854	134	172	22
ID...........	8,981	12,268	2,578	4,221	197
IL...........	18,336	30,115	4,550	11,312	400
IN...........	12,132	18,997	3,234	6,748	167
IA...........	27,002	47,325	3,440	15,329	1,023
KS...........	17,951	25,218	4,469	3,981	562
KY...........	6,521	9,924	1,669	3,876	156
LA...........	3,670	4,679	1,338	1,400	286
ME...........	751	1,135	229	379	21
MD...........	2,467	3,912	379	1,539	43
MA...........	589	863	164	243	23
MI...........	8,864	13,019	2,111	3,603	174
MN...........	18,614	28,764	4,420	9,699	858
MS...........	5,310	8,341	1,033	2,382	276
MO...........	11,216	16,395	3,040	4,933	470
MT...........	4,618	6,221	1,477	2,604	649
NE...........	21,861	31,711	5,276	6,575	559
NV...........	824	1,245	205	490	41
NH...........	252	421	50	152	7
NJ...........	1,463	1,990	560	654	20
NM...........	3,366	4,325	990	1,208	189
NY...........	5,774	8,901	1,823	3,319	93
NC...........	11,845	18,761	1,508	5,206	292
ND...........	9,251	14,935	2,984	6,838	1,459
OH...........	10,574	16,411	2,773	5,804	192
OK...........	6,891	10,014	1,442	2,313	633
OR...........	5,712	7,360	981	1,852	247
PA...........	7,677	11,626	1,569	4,329	134
RI...........	74	118	22	43	5
SC...........	2,604	3,951	288	694	103
SD...........	10,778	16,172	3,691	6,415	1,090
TN...........	4,145	5,997	619	1,459	113
TX...........	23,293	36,842	5,820	12,760	1,632
UT...........	2,099	3,088	615	1,279	145
VT...........	820	1,241	232	435	21
VA...........	4,124	6,466	568	2,352	119
WA...........	11,049	13,846	2,560	2,296	369
WV...........	841	1,211	48	389	25
WI...........	12,666	18,117	3,661	4,549	223
WY...........	1,878	2,429	442	826	158

Source: U.S. Department of Agriculture, Economic Research Service, "U.S. and State Farm Income and Wealth Statistics," <www.ers.usda.gov/data-products/farm-income-and-wealth-statistics.aspx>, accessed January 2024.

Table 884. Farm Income—Cash Receipts From Farm Marketings: 2010 to 2023

[In millions of dollars (321,196 represents $321,196,000,000). Represents gross receipts from commercial market sales as well as net Commodity Credit Corporation loans. The source estimates and publishes individual cash receipt values only for major commodities and major producing states. The U.S. receipts for individual commodities, computed as the sum of the reported states, may understate the value of sales for some commodities, with the balance included in the appropriate category labeled "other" or "miscellaneous." The degree of underestimation in some of the minor commodities can be substantial]

Commodity	2010	2020	2022	2023	Commodity	2010	2020	2022	2023
Total [1]	321,196	367,499	542,608	526,284	Broccoli..................	727	997	1,133	1,070
Animals and products...........	140,871	165,008	259,834	249,593	Carrots..................	647	747	1,295	1,823
Meat animals................	69,144	82,478	116,923	128,297	Corn, sweet.............	952	798	900	1,000
Cattle and calves...............	51,246	63,321	86,288	101,114	Lettuce..................	2,213	5,066	5,565	4,826
Hogs........................	17,898	19,157	30,634	27,183	Lettuce, head..........	1,058	1,613	1,801	1,545
Dairy products, milk..............	31,372	40,357	57,241	45,928	Onions..................	1,050	995	1,843	1,510
Poultry/eggs [1]...................	34,690	35,171	77,210	67,054	Peppers, bell...........	592	622	697	613
Broilers...................	23,692	21,267	50,584	42,566	Tomatoes................	2,281	1,587	1,813	2,758
Chicken eggs..............	6,553	8,692	19,434	17,860	Tomatoes, fresh.......	1,355	727	648	716
Turkeys...................	4,372	5,193	7,117	6,567	Cantaloupes............	305	322	385	321
Miscellaneous animals [1]..........	5,664	7,002	8,461	8,314	Watermelons............	499	599	821	787
Aquaculture....................	474	473	553	538	Fruits/nuts [1].............	21,613	27,832	26,914	28,828
Honey.......................	282	308	382	344	Grapefruit.............	291	199	158	170
Crops............................	180,325	202,491	282,774	276,691	Lemons.................	395	665	586	615
Food grains [1]...................	14,314	11,776	16,619	16,590	Oranges.................	1,997	1,712	1,529	985
Rice.........................	3,263	2,869	3,328	3,517	Apples..................	2,311	2,939	3,107	3,044
Wheat.......................	11,021	8,818	13,182	12,968	Cherries................	756	910	743	675
Feed crops [1]...................	55,143	57,522	99,719	92,836	Grapes..................	4,024	4,791	5,996	6,834
Corn.........................	47,540	47,515	86,951	80,097	Peaches.................	617	591	675	656
Hay..........................	5,217	7,291	9,831	9,785	Pears...................	387	343	354	365
Sorghum grain.................	1,487	1,775	1,650	1,555	Blueberries.............	644	974	1,165	1,074
Cotton........................	7,465	6,808	8,194	7,157	Cranberries.............	299	288	304	301
Tobacco......................	1,336	823	985	996	Raspberries.............	259	389	441	372
Oil crops [1].....................	36,544	43,840	64,789	62,374	Strawberries............	2,261	2,592	3,259	3,399
Peanuts......................	824	1,211	1,548	1,550	Almonds................	2,903	5,251	3,536	3,880
Soybeans.....................	34,665	41,479	61,345	58,998	Pistachios..............	1,159	2,623	1,861	2,980
Sunflower....................	507	497	685	653	Walnuts.................	1,028	947	454	692
Vegetables and melons [1]........	17,405	21,061	25,180	26,064	All other crops [1]..........	26,506	32,829	40,376	41,847
Beans, dry....................	780	1,138	1,082	1,251	Sugarcane..............	1,075	1,265	1,587	2,248
Potatoes......................	3,336	3,712	4,294	4,859	Sugar beets.............	1,734	1,300	2,009	2,991
Sweet potatoes..................	472	687	656	676	Floriculture..............	4,149	4,796	6,688	6,691
Beans, snap.....................	434	282	396	362	Mushrooms.............	884	940	866	881

[1] Includes other commodities not shown separately.

Source: U.S. Department of Agriculture, Economic Research Service, "U.S. and State Farm Income and Wealth Statistics," <www.ers.usda.gov/data-products/farm-income-and-wealth-statistics.aspx>, accessed September 2024.

Table 885. Cash Receipts for Cattle, Corn, Milk, and Soybeans—Total and for Leading States: 2023

[In millions of dollars (101,114 represents $101,114,000,000). See headnote Table 884]

State	Value	State	Value	State	Value	State	Value
Cattle and calves...	**101,114**	**Corn...**	**80,097**	**Milk...**	**45,928**	**Soybeans...**	**58,998**
Nebraska...	16,119	Iowa...	14,072	California...	8,134	Illinois...	9,610
Kansas...	13,718	Illinois...	13,106	Wisconsin...	6,151	Iowa...	8,141
Texas...	13,374	Nebraska...	8,970	New York...	3,490	Minnesota...	5,014
Iowa...	5,158	Minnesota...	7,912	Idaho...	3,460	Indiana...	4,776
Colorado...	4,988	Indiana...	5,621	Texas...	3,357	Missouri...	3,886

Source: U.S. Department of Agriculture, Economic Research Service, "U.S. and State Farm Income and Wealth Statistics," <www.ers.usda.gov/data-products/farm-income-and-wealth-statistics.aspx>, accessed September 2024.

Table 886. Farm Marketings: 2022 and 2023; and Principal Commodities, 2023, by State

[In millions of dollars (542,608 represents 542,608,000,000). See headnote Table 884]

State	2022			2023			State rank for total farm marketings and three principal commodities in order of marketing receipts
	Total	Animals and products	Crops	Total	Animals and products	Crops	
U.S........	542,608	259,834	282,774	526,284	249,593	276,691	**Cattle and calves, corn, soybeans**
AL...........	8,730	7,014	1,716	7,953	6,262	1,691	25—Broilers, cattle and calves, chicken eggs
AK...........	49	10	39	51	11	40	50—Floriculture, hay, cattle and calves
AZ...........	5,241	2,227	3,014	5,293	2,398	2,895	29—Cattle and calves, milk/dairy, lettuce
AR...........	13,985	8,571	5,414	13,175	7,617	5,558	14—Broilers, soybeans, rice
CA...........	58,629	17,367	41,262	59,444	15,780	43,664	1—Milk/dairy, grapes, cattle and calves
CO...........	9,040	6,321	2,719	9,531	6,504	3,027	20—Cattle and calves, milk/dairy, corn
CT...........	726	257	469	719	237	482	45—Floriculture, milk/dairy, chicken eggs
DE...........	2,073	1,621	452	1,856	1,427	429	39—Broilers, corn, soybeans
FL...........	9,067	2,079	6,989	9,466	2,163	7,303	21—Floriculture, sugarcane, cattle and calves
GA...........	13,236	8,893	4,344	12,572	8,064	4,508	15—Broilers, cotton lint, chicken eggs
HI...........	689	194	495	672	197	475	46—Cattle and calves, coffee, floriculture
ID...........	11,283	6,843	4,440	11,036	6,350	4,686	19—Milk/dairy, cattle and calves, potatoes
IL...........	28,096	3,622	24,475	27,544	3,522	24,022	5—Corn, soybeans, hogs
IN...........	18,371	6,312	12,059	17,101	5,864	11,237	8—Corn, soybeans, chicken eggs
IA...........	44,816	20,327	24,489	40,753	18,127	22,626	2—Corn, hogs, soybeans
KS...........	23,678	13,722	9,956	23,666	15,317	8,349	7—Cattle and calves, corn, wheat
KY...........	8,280	4,503	3,777	8,073	4,359	3,715	24—Soybeans, broilers, cattle and calves
LA...........	4,130	1,293	2,837	4,435	1,224	3,211	33— Sugarcane, soybeans, corn
ME...........	908	384	524	902	366	536	44—Potatoes, milk/dairy, chicken eggs
MD...........	3,331	1,988	1,343	2,978	1,726	1,251	36—Broilers, corn, soybeans
MA...........	550	165	385	515	151	364	47—Floriculture, cranberries, milk/dairy
MI...........	12,246	5,224	7,022	11,554	4,751	6,803	18—Milk/dairy, corn, soybeans
MN...........	26,093	10,209	15,883	25,449	9,385	16,064	6—Corn, soybeans, hogs
MS...........	7,866	4,647	3,220	7,438	4,133	3,305	26—Broilers, soybeans, corn
MO...........	14,951	6,145	8,806	15,550	7,053	8,497	10—Soybeans, cattle and calves, corn
MT...........	4,639	1,988	2,651	5,095	2,297	2,798	31—Cattle and calves, wheat, hay
NE...........	32,015	15,973	16,041	32,129	18,073	14,055	3—Cattle and calves, corn, soybeans
NV...........	1,024	623	401	987	671	316	41—Cattle and calves, hay, milk/dairy
NH...........	279	165	114	259	152	107	48—Chicken eggs, milk/dairy, floriculture
NJ...........	1,662	246	1,416	1,613	237	1,376	40—Floriculture, chicken eggs, blueberries
NM...........	3,844	2,987	857	3,995	3,090	905	34—Cattle and calves, milk/dairy, pecans
NY...........	7,800	4,958	2,841	7,151	4,370	2,780	27—Milk/dairy, corn, cattle and calves
NC...........	17,300	12,707	4,592	15,653	10,918	4,735	9—Broilers, hogs, turkeys
ND...........	11,344	1,563	9,781	12,165	1,730	10,434	16—Soybeans, wheat, corn
OH...........	15,634	6,240	9,394	14,114	5,576	8,538	12—Soybeans, corn, chicken eggs
OK...........	9,672	7,865	1,807	8,770	7,159	1,610	22—Cattle and calves, hogs, broilers
OR...........	6,646	2,135	4,511	6,667	2,268	4,400	28—Cattle and calves, milk/dairy, hay
PA...........	9,846	6,602	3,244	8,634	5,825	2,809	23—Milk/dairy, chicken eggs, broilers
RI...........	107	34	73	105	32	73	49—Chicken eggs, turkeys, floriculture
SC...........	3,650	2,100	1,550	3,416	1,860	1,556	35—Broilers, corn, cotton lint
SD...........	14,195	5,899	8,296	13,990	5,900	8,089	13—Corn, cattle and calves, soybeans
TN...........	5,325	2,099	3,226	5,249	2,098	3,150	30—Soybeans, cattle and calves, broilers
TX...........	30,637	22,237	8,400	29,724	22,262	7,462	4—Cattle and calves, broilers, milk/dairy
UT...........	2,818	2,056	762	2,460	1,769	691	37—Cattle and calves, chicken eggs, milk/dairy
VT...........	1,055	805	250	931	712	219	43—Milk/dairy, cattle and calves, maple products
VA...........	5,178	3,387	1,791	4,803	3,021	1,782	32—Broilers, cattle and calves, turkeys
WA...........	12,361	4,122	8,238	12,047	4,295	7,752	17—Cattle and calves, apples, milk/dairy
WV...........	939	714	226	977	748	229	42—Cattle and calves, broilers, turkeys
WI...........	16,711	11,003	5,708	15,503	9,960	5,543	11—Milk/dairy, cattle and calves, corn
WY...........	1,862	1,388	475	2,122	1,579	543	38—Cattle and calves, hay, hogs

Source: U.S. Department of Agriculture, Economic Research Service, "U.S. and State Farm Income and Wealth Statistics," <www.ers.usda.gov/data-products/farm-income-and-wealth-statistics.aspx>, accessed September 2024.

Table 887. Indexes of Prices Received and Paid by Farmers: 2010 to 2023

[2011=100]

Item	2010	2020	2022	2023	Item	2010	2020	2022	2023
Prices received, all products....	**87**	**95**	**130**	**119**	Seed and plants.................	93	113	132	139
Crops...........................	87	101	124	107	Fertilizer [2]........................	77	68	148	111
Food grains.....................	74	80	124	104	Agricultural chemicals..........	100	95	156	137
Feed grains.....................	42	40	40	42	Fuels.............................	78	58	111	96
Oil-bearing crops..............	81	98	115	104	Supplies and repairs............	96	117	139	144
Fruits and nuts.................	89	137	154	152	Trucks and autos................	97	107	125	129
Commercial vegetables.........	104	127	175	156	Farm machinery.................	94	125	153	163
Animals and products...........	86	89	139	134	Building materials...............	97	121	164	165
Livestock.......................	82	90	121	136	Agricultural services............	98	117	136	143
Dairy products..................	81	90	126	101	Rent.............................	93	118	124	127
Poultry and eggs................	102	85	196	158					
					Interest..........................	92	110	132	158
Prices paid, total [1]...............	**90**	**110**	**137**	**140**	Taxes............................	96	127	146	153
Production.......................	88	106	137	138	Wage rates......................	99	138	157	166
Feed...........................	80	106	138	134					
Livestock and poultry...........	86	98	123	152	Parity ratio [3].....................	96	80	94	88

[1] Includes production items, interest, taxes, wage rates, and a family living component. The family living component is the Consumer Price Index for all urban consumers from the Bureau of Labor Statistics. See text, Section 14 and Table 763. [2] Includes lime and soil conditioners. [3] Ratio of prices received by farmers to prices paid.

Source: U.S. Department of Agriculture, National Agricultural Statistics Service, "Quick Stats," <quickstats.nass.usda.gov/>, accessed August 2024.

Table 888. Farm and Marketing Bill Share of the U.S. Food Dollar (Nominal) by Selected Characteristics: 2000 to 2022

[In percent. The food dollar series measures annual expenditures by U.S. consumers on domestically produced food; a food dollar represents the average $1 expenditure. Farm share is measured as the average payment from each food dollar expenditure that farmers receive for their raw food dollar commodities. The food marketing bill is measured as the average value added to the raw food dollar from each consumer food dollar expenditure. Based on input-output data from the Bureau of Labor Statistics and Bureau of Economic Analysis]

Item	2000	2010	2015	2017	2018	2019	2020	2021	2022
SHARE OF FOOD DOLLAR									
Food dollar, total:									
Farm share........................	15.8	16.9	16.6	15.5	15.3	15.0	15.2	15.2	14.9
Marketing bill share...............	84.2	83.1	83.4	84.5	84.7	85.0	84.8	84.8	85.1
Food at home dollar:									
Farm share........................	22.5	25.0	25.2	24.0	24.0	23.6	22.9	24.0	24.1
Marketing bill share...............	77.5	75.0	74.8	76.0	76.0	76.4	77.1	76.0	75.9
Food away from home dollar:									
Farm share........................	6.2	5.0	4.2	4.0	3.8	3.7	3.3	3.5	3.6
Marketing bill share...............	93.8	95.0	95.8	96.0	96.2	96.3	96.7	96.5	96.4
Food and beverage dollar: [1]									
Farm share........................	13.1	14.0	13.5	12.6	12.4	12.2	12.5	12.6	12.4
Marketing bill share...............	86.9	86.0	86.5	87.4	87.6	87.8	87.5	87.4	87.6
Home food and beverage dollar: [1]									
Farm share........................	18.0	20.4	20.7	19.6	19.4	19.2	18.4	19.4	19.5
Marketing bill share...............	82.0	79.6	79.3	80.4	80.6	80.8	81.6	80.6	80.5
Away food and beverage dollar: [1]									
Farm share........................	5.4	4.1	3.4	3.2	3.1	3.0	2.9	3.0	3.0
Marketing bill share...............	94.6	95.9	96.6	96.8	96.9	97.0	97.1	97.0	97.0
MARKETING BILL COST COMPONENTS									
Primary factors:									
Salary and benefits [2]...............	52.9	49.0	50.1	51.2	51.2	51.5	53.7	50.2	49.3
Output taxes [3].....................	7.3	9.3	9.2	9.2	9.2	9.0	3.9	5.8	8.8
Property income [4]..................	34.6	36.1	35.7	34.5	34.3	34.7	37.6	39.1	36.8
Imports [5]..........................	5.1	5.6	5.1	5.2	5.2	4.9	4.8	4.9	5.0
Industry groups: [6]									
Farm and agribusiness [7]............	10.6	11.2	10.9	10.1	9.9	9.7	9.7	10.3	10.0
Food processing...................	18.2	16.2	15.6	15.8	15.2	15.2	16.4	14.8	14.4
Packaging.........................	4.2	3.1	2.7	2.8	2.9	2.9	3.0	2.7	2.7
Transportation.....................	3.8	3.5	3.7	3.6	3.8	3.9	3.9	3.6	3.5
Wholesale trade...................	9.4	10.3	11.3	11.2	10.9	10.9	11.3	11.1	10.7
Retail trade........................	13.0	14.2	13.4	13.2	12.9	12.9	13.9	12.8	12.4
Food services......................	28.4	29.0	30.7	32.0	32.5	33.1	30.0	32.5	34.1
Energy............................	4.7	5.6	4.0	3.8	4.0	3.6	3.3	3.9	3.8
Finance and insurance.............	3.8	2.9	3.4	3.2	3.3	3.2	3.5	3.2	3.2
Advertising........................	2.5	2.4	2.5	2.6	2.8	2.9	3.1	3.4	3.4
Legal and accounting..............	1.5	1.6	1.8	1.7	1.8	1.8	1.9	1.8	1.8

[1] Includes alcoholic beverages and soft drinks. [2] Pre-tax employee wages plus employer and employee costs for employee benefits. [3] Value of excise, sales, property, and severance taxes (less subsidies), customs duties, and other non-tax government fees levied on establishments. [4] Allocated compensation to various owners for services on behalf of a domestic establishment that directs sales to the U.S. food supply. Includes machinery, equipment, structures, natural resources, product inventory, and other tangible or intangible assets. [5] Food and non-food commodities imported from international sources and used by U.S. food supply chain industries producing for the U.S. market. [6] For each industry group, the amount shown excludes value-added contributions to the food dollar that trace back to other supply chain industry groups. For example, the value of energy used by the transportation and packaging industries is deducted from those groups and included with the energy group. [7] Farm and agribusiness value-added contributions from non-farm supply chain industry groups, such as energy, transportation, and financial services, are deducted from the farm share and therefore the industry group series value for farms and agribusiness is smaller than the farm share value of the marketing bill series.

Source: U.S. Department of Agriculture, Economic Research Service, "Food Dollar Series," <www.ers.usda.gov/data-products/food-dollar-series.aspx>, accessed November 2023.

Table 889. Federal Government Subsidies for Agriculture by Farm and Payment Characteristics: 2000 to 2022

[932 represents 932,000. Based on Agricultural Resource Management Survey (ARMS)]

Payment and farm characteristic	Unit	2000	2010	2015	2018	2019	2020	2021	2022
Farms receiving government payments.............................	**1,000**	**932**	**772**	**574**	**583**	**628**	**809**	**687**	**495**
Farms not receiving government payments...........................	1,000	1,234	1,421	1,485	1,438	1,387	1,202	1,317	1,500
All government payments...................	**Mil. dol.**	**16,093**	**9,205**	**8,577**	**10,396**	**16,003**	**28,833**	**15,616**	**8,071**
Countercyclical-type payments [1]...........	Mil. dol.	–	659	4,319	1,977	1,928	3,716	1,863	799
Direct payments [2]................................	Mil. dol.	4,720	4,102	(X)	(X)	(X)	(X)	(X)	(X)
Conservation payments [3].....................	Mil. dol.	1,287	2,530	2,688	2,841	3,090	3,155	2,443	2,648
Marketing loan benefits payments [4]........	Mil. dol.	5,519	158	112	519	874	1,491	744	392
Other government program payments [5]. . .	Mil. dol.	4,567	1,756	1,458	5,058	10,111	20,472	10,567	3,219
Average payments per participating farm. . .	Dollars	17,260	11,924	14,946	17,822	25,481	35,646	22,741	16,308
Commercial farms [6]...........................	Dollars	61,997	32,054	41,092	51,374	78,050	135,352	65,240	47,236
Intermediate farms [7].........................	Dollars	16,411	7,210	9,092	9,924	11,731	14,180	12,794	9,474
Residence farms [8]...........................	Dollars	4,870	4,713	6,749	6,288	8,147	7,474	8,354	6,746
Average payment by select production specialty: [9]									
Corn.......................................	Dollars	33,182	15,690	24,941	28,118	39,730	52,777	33,403	18,867
General cash grains [10]......................	Dollars	36,300	21,959	30,432	39,385	64,810	70,214	43,817	40,175
Soybeans.................................	Dollars	17,046	12,810	12,913	22,098	31,907	35,064	22,893	16,537
Wheat....................................	Dollars	34,973	38,163	30,315	30,196	38,152	70,077	50,435	62,997
Cattle....................................	Dollars	7,197	8,244	12,970	9,206	12,105	19,267	13,409	15,597
Dairy.....................................	Dollars	16,705	10,190	15,609	19,269	33,233	141,675	84,045	27,851
Hogs.....................................	Dollars	25,594	19,547	21,410	40,753	61,083	107,995	39,267	41,480
Poultry...................................	Dollars	8,279	9,749	7,013	13,795	14,255	35,052	30,032	11,397

– Represents or rounds to zero. X Not applicable. [1] Countercyclical-type program payments are made to producers of eligible crops based on historical production of program crops, but the payment rates depend on market prices. [2] Direct payments are payments made to producers based on historical acreage of program crops and historical yields. [3] Conservation program payments are payments made to producers that include land-retirement programs as well as working-land programs that provide payments for maintaining or adopting resource conservation practices on land in production. [4] Marketing loan benefits are payments made to farmers based on market prices for eligible commodities falling below program target prices. Marketing assistance loan programs are based on current production and tend to provide payments when market prices fall below target levels. [5] Other government program payments include payments from disaster relief programs and emergency payments that tend to be temporary, as-needed government responses to natural disasters. Also includes milk income support programs, the tobacco transition program, peanut quota buyouts, and/or all other programs not specified in ARMS questionnaires. [6] Data for 2010 and earlier include farms with sales of $250,000 or more. Beginning in 2011, data are for farms with $350,000 or more gross cash farm income and nonfamily farms. [7] Data for 2010 and earlier include small family farms whose operators report farming as their major occupation. Beginning in 2011, data are for farms with less than $350,000 in gross cash farm income and a principal operator whose primary occupation is farming. [8] Data for 2010 and earlier include retirement and residential farms. Beginning in 2011, data are for farms with less than $350,000 in gross cash farm income and where the principal operator is either retired or has a primary occupation other than farming. [9] Production specialty is where that commodity is the majority of value of production for the farm. [10] Sorghum and rice.

Source: U.S. Department of Agriculture, Economic Research Service, "ARMS Farm Financial and Crop Production Practices," <www.ers.usda.gov/data-products/arms-farm-financial-and-crop-production-practices.aspx>, accessed March 2024.

Table 890. Percent of U.S. Agricultural Consumption Imported: 2010 to 2022

[In percent. Import value share of consumption. The import share of food available for consumption based on value is the ratio of imported food value to domestic consumption value. Value of food consumption is estimated as production value excluding stocks, plus imports, then minus exports. See source for more information]

Commodity group	2010	2015	2016	2017	2018	2019	2020	2021	2022
Total food and beverages...............	**12.3**	**14.8**	**15.1**	**15.8**	**16.5**	**16.8**	**17.3**	**17.3**	**(NA)**
Animal foods [1]..............................	4.7	6.3	6.1	5.9	6.0	6.3	6.6	7.0	(NA)
Plant foods [2]...............................	18.6	23.1	23.5	25.2	25.8	25.7	27.0	26.5	(NA)
Non-manufactured products...........	**10.8**	**12.4**	**13.6**	**14.0**	**14.4**	**14.9**	**16.0**	**14.3**	**13.6**
Crops....................................	15.8	20.3	21.0	22.2	22.7	23.5	24.6	22.0	20.8
Food grains...........................	18.4	24.1	22.1	29.3	25.9	30.8	32.1	18.2	22.9
Feed grains...........................	1.1	1.9	1.7	1.7	1.4	1.3	1.4	1.2	1.3
Oilseeds..............................	3.4	6.4	4.2	4.7	4.0	4.5	4.8	4.2	4.6
Vegetables and melons................	29.2	31.6	35.8	34.4	38.1	40.1	41.1	44.7	40.4
Fruits and tree nuts....................	37.1	44.4	44.0	46.5	49.6	51.3	51.5	52.6	59.3
Sweeteners...........................	45.0	46.9	44.8	47.1	45.0	45.3	48.3	43.1	45.0
Livestock................................	3.1	3.0	3.0	2.9	2.8	3.1	3.2	3.0	2.8
Manufactured products.................	**18.4**	**22.9**	**22.0**	**23.7**	**24.4**	**24.2**	**24.6**	**26.2**	**(NA)**
Grain & oilseed milling products........	30.9	46.7	44.5	57.0	56.0	49.2	56.8	57.4	(NA)
Sugar & confections....................	33.4	35.5	35.7	36.2	36.3	35.9	38.1	37.4	(NA)
Preserved fruit & vegetables............	22.1	25.6	26.3	27.2	27.9	27.9	27.9	31.0	(NA)
Dairy products..........................	6.7	9.9	9.0	8.4	8.3	8.4	8.1	10.0	(NA)
Meat products..........................	13.8	21.8	17.9	18.6	18.5	19.1	18.3	18.7	(NA)
Bakery products........................	8.5	10.7	11.4	12.6	13.7	13.8	14.2	15.4	(NA)
Other foods.............................	13.6	17.2	15.9	16.0	20.1	20.2	20.8	23.0	(NA)
Beverages..............................	25.6	27.9	27.9	33.2	31.8	32.2	33.8	34.2	(NA)

NA Not available. [1] Animal products include red meats, poultry meat and eggs, and dairy products. [2] Plant or crop food products include food grains, vegetable oils, fruits, nuts, vegetables, sweeteners (sugarcane, sugar beets, honey), tropical products (coffee, cocoa, spices), grain and oilseed milling products, sugar and confections, and bakery products.

Source: U.S. Department of Agriculture, Economic Research Service, "U.S. Agricultural Trade," <www.ers.usda.gov/topics/international-markets-trade/us-agricultural-trade/>, accessed August 2024.

Table 891. Agricultural Exports and Imports by Selected Commodity: 2010 to 2023

[In thousands (3,355 represents 3,355,000). 1 kiloliter equals 264.17 gallons. Includes Puerto Rico, U.S. territories, and shipments under foreign aid programs. Imports are imports for consumption; see text, Section 28 for definition. Commodity and commodity grouping definitions used are Foreign Agricultural Trade of the United States (FATUS) groupings. In January 2021, the U.S. Department of Agriculture adopted the World Trade Organization (WTO) definitions of agricultural products and revised historical data to reflect the new definitions. Therefore, data here may not be comparable to data presented in previous editions. See source for details]

Commodity	Unit	2010	2015	2019	2020	2021	2022	2023
EXPORTS								
Red meat and products [1]	Metric tons	3,355	3,577	4,973	5,289	5,438	5,191	5,259
Poultry meat	Metric tons	3,401	3,271	3,574	3,654	3,619	3,520	3,553
Wheat, unmilled	Metric tons	27,608	21,258	26,949	26,114	23,911	20,534	17,833
Wheat flour	Metric tons	332	309	279	278	244	219	194
Rice, paddy, milled	Metric tons	4,464	3,880	3,631	3,280	3,399	2,475	2,742
Feed grains	Metric tons	54,504	54,604	44,473	58,598	75,950	64,198	50,017
Feed grain products	Metric tons	1,081	851	922	918	973	905	877
Feeds and fodders [2]	Metric tons	19,024	22,725	21,193	21,173	22,281	21,115	19,694
Fruits and preparations	Metric tons	3,750	3,740	3,240	3,110	3,028	2,673	2,707
Fruit juices	Kiloliters	1,112	869	548	515	510	508	478
Vegetables, fresh	Metric tons	2,140	2,236	2,437	2,336	2,496	2,276	2,320
Oilcake and meal	Metric tons	10,004	11,689	12,348	13,025	12,430	12,033	14,229
Oilseeds	Metric tons	43,282	48,914	53,248	64,747	53,757	57,630	49,117
Vegetable oils	Metric tons	3,644	2,759	2,434	2,812	2,495	2,220	1,382
Tobacco, unmanufactured	Metric tons	179	156	101	94	103	102	111
Cotton, excluding linters	Metric tons	2,956	2,396	3,560	3,814	2,960	3,391	2,780
IMPORTS								
Red meat and products [1]	Metric tons	1,291	1,817	1,683	1,764	1,939	2,036	2,014
Wheat, excluding seed	Metric tons	2,490	2,448	1,822	1,878	1,468	1,703	2,459
Oats, unmilled	Metric tons	1,567	1,672	1,477	1,577	1,423	1,308	1,402
Biscuits and wafers	Metric tons	796	1,066	1,624	1,699	1,913	2,114	2,152
Feeds and fodders [2]	Metric tons	1,423	2,221	1,839	1,951	2,159	2,269	2,082
Fruits and preparations	Metric tons	10,580	13,362	14,482	14,769	15,335	15,827	15,950
Fruit juices	Kiloliters	4,274	4,477	4,640	4,030	4,728	5,786	5,273
Vegetables, fresh	Metric tons	5,472	6,568	8,069	8,324	8,933	9,240	9,211
Sugar, cane and beet	Metric tons	2,982	3,254	2,891	3,575	2,950	3,171	3,112
Coffee, including products	Metric tons	1,390	1,584	1,753	1,593	1,643	1,707	1,460
Wine	Kiloliters	959	1,157	1,269	1,298	1,493	1,498	1,281
Malt beverages	Kiloliters	3,161	3,675	4,259	4,312	4,667	4,807	4,762
Oilseeds and oilnuts	Metric tons	1,223	1,643	1,169	1,273	1,313	1,526	1,357
Vegetable oils and waxes	Metric tons	3,925	5,174	6,044	5,983	6,495	7,264	8,956
Oilcake and meal	Metric tons	1,504	4,020	3,989	4,170	4,108	3,608	4,205
Tobacco, unmanufactured	Metric tons	164	155	131	108	133	125	116

[1] Includes variety meats. [2] Excluding oilcake and meal.

Source: U.S. Department of Agriculture, Foreign Agricultural Service, "Global Agricultural Trade System," <apps.fas.usda.gov/gats/>, accessed August 2024.

Table 892. Agricultural Chemical and Fertilizer Exports and General Imports by Type: 2010 to 2023

[In thousands of metric tons (43,657 represents 43,657,000). Metric ton = 1.102 short tons or .984 long tons. Includes Puerto Rico, U.S. territories, and shipments under foreign aid programs. Commodity and commodity grouping definitions used are Foreign Agricultural Trade of the United States (FATUS) commodity code groupings. See source for details]

Commodity	2010	2015	2017	2018	2019	2020	2021	2022	2023
GENERAL IMPORTS [1]									
Fertilizers, total	**43,657**	**35,676**	**33,437**	**34,477**	**31,852**	**31,616**	**36,210**	**28,695**	**31,111**
Potassium	10,230	10,275	12,288	12,903	11,632	11,975	13,585	11,083	11,929
Nitrogen	17,171	18,304	14,004	12,779	12,048	11,291	13,518	10,662	11,392
Phosphate	16,200	6,975	7,028	8,694	8,099	8,264	9,004	6,886	7,722
Mixed/organic fertilizer	56	122	117	101	73	85	104	63	68
Agricultural chemicals, total	**90**	**115**	**141**	**142**	**114**	**138**	**175**	**216**	**133**
Fungicides	25	33	38	40	35	38	42	38	31
Herbicides	15	19	34	33	20	18	24	50	32
Insecticides	1	1	2	2	1	1	2	3	1
Other pesticides	49	61	68	68	58	80	106	125	68
EXPORTS									
Fertilizers, total	**10,310**	**9,916**	**11,835**	**10,565**	**10,165**	**9,604**	**8,284**	**12,443**	**11,589**
Potassium	333	54	83	61	103	103	69	299	157
Nitrogen	1,741	2,346	4,001	3,557	3,055	2,934	2,155	4,977	5,206
Phosphate	7,820	6,467	6,619	6,180	6,389	6,124	5,123	5,583	4,926
Mixed/organic fertilizer	416	1,048	1,133	767	618	443	937	1,584	1,299
Agricultural chemicals, total	**146**	**150**	**1,172**	**1,154**	**1,166**	**1,211**	**1,251**	**315**	**254**
Fungicides	15	19	19	20	19	20	23	23	20
Herbicides	83	81	117	94	86	88	86	94	74
Insecticides	27	24	–	–	–	–	–	–	–
Other pesticides	22	26	1,036	1,041	1,061	1,103	1,142	198	160

– Represents or rounds to zero. [1] Total shipments arriving in the U.S., including both merchandise that enters consumption channels immediately and merchandise entered into bonded warehouses or Foreign Trade Zones under Customs custody.

Source: U.S. Department of Agriculture, Foreign Agricultural Service, "Global Agricultural Trade System," <apps.fas.usda.gov/gats/>, accessed August 2024.

Table 893. Agricultural Exports and Imports—Value: 2005 to 2023

[In billions of dollars, except percent (2.3 represents $2,300,000,000). Includes Puerto Rico, U.S. territories, and shipments under foreign aid programs. Excludes fish, forest products, distilled liquors, manufactured tobacco, and products made from cotton; includes raw tobacco, raw cotton, rubber, beer and wine, and processed agricultural products]

Year	Trade balance	Exports, domestic products	Percent of all exports	Imports for consumption	Percent of all imports	Year	Trade balance	Exports, domestic products	Percent of all exports	Imports for consumption	Percent of all imports
2005	2.3	65.6	8.2	63.3	3.8	2017	13.7	142.9	10.9	129.2	5.6
2010	33.1	118.7	10.6	85.6	4.5	2018	6.7	144.7	10.2	138.0	5.4
2012	37.2	145.9	10.8	108.8	4.8	2019	-0.5	141.1	10.1	141.6	5.7
2013	37.5	148.5	10.8	111.0	5.0	2020	3.4	149.7	12.4	146.3	6.3
2014	35.8	154.5	11.0	118.7	5.1	2021	6.0	176.6	11.9	170.6	6.1
2015	16.1	137.2	10.7	121.1	5.4	2022	-2.4	195.9	11.2	198.3	6.1
2016	16.3	138.9	11.3	122.6	5.6	2023	-20.1	174.9	10.3	194.9	6.3

Source: U.S. Department of Agriculture, Economic Research Service, "Foreign Agricultural Trade of the United States (FATUS)," <www.ers.usda.gov/data-products/foreign-agricultural-trade-of-the-united-states-fatus/>, accessed August 2024.

Table 894. Agricultural Imports—Value by Selected Commodity: 2010 to 2023

[In millions of dollars (85,582 represents $85,582,000,000). For calendar year. Data are imports for consumption; for definition, see text, Section 28. Includes Puerto Rico, U.S. territories, and shipments under foreign aid programs. In January 2021, the U.S. Department of Agriculture adopted the World Trade Organization (WTO) definitions of agricultural products and revised historical data to reflect the new definitions. Therefore, data here may not be comparable to data presented in previous editions. See source for details]

Commodity [1]	Value (mil. dol.)							Percent distribution		
	2010	2015	2019	2020	2021	2022	2023	2010	2020	2023
Total [2]	85,582	121,122	141,562	146,282	170,617	198,270	194,941	100.0	100.0	100.0
Cattle, live	1,575	2,195	1,799	1,756	1,564	1,722	2,371	1.8	1.2	1.2
Beef and veal	2,830	6,655	5,997	6,818	8,181	8,408	9,009	3.3	4.7	4.6
Pork	1,185	1,622	1,478	1,464	2,104	2,420	1,962	1.4	1.0	1.0
Dairy products	2,619	3,493	3,111	3,216	3,927	5,260	5,347	3.1	2.2	2.7
Grains and feeds	7,788	11,085	14,094	15,112	16,865	21,429	22,223	9.1	10.3	11.4
Fruits and preparations	9,168	14,047	18,131	18,573	21,300	23,857	24,327	10.7	12.7	12.5
Vegetables and preparations [3]	9,318	12,063	15,081	16,843	18,218	20,290	21,620	10.9	11.5	11.1
Sugar and related products	4,047	4,600	4,651	5,157	5,678	6,852	7,169	4.7	3.5	3.7
Cocoa and products	4,295	4,860	4,977	5,052	5,634	6,050	6,152	5.0	3.5	3.2
Coffee and products	4,943	6,303	6,100	6,019	7,237	10,223	8,766	5.8	4.1	4.5
Wine	4,279	5,478	6,335	5,823	7,399	7,545	6,868	5.0	4.0	3.5
Malt beverages	3,506	4,547	5,633	5,816	6,435	6,793	6,868	4.1	4.0	3.6
Oilseeds and products	5,681	8,706	9,123	9,707	13,587	18,576	18,631	6.6	6.6	9.6

[1] Commodity and commodity grouping definitions used are the Foreign Agricultural Trade of the United States (FATUS) commodity code groupings. See source for more details. [2] Includes other commodities not shown separately. [3] Includes pulses.

Source: U.S. Department of Agriculture, Foreign Agricultural Service, "Global Agricultural Trade System," <apps.fas.usda.gov/gats/>, accessed May 2024.

Table 895. Agricultural Imports—Value by Selected Country of Origin: 2010 to 2023

[In millions of dollars (85,582 represents $85,582,000,000). Data are imports for consumption; for definition, see text, Section 28. In January 2021, the U.S. Department of Agriculture adopted the World Trade Organization (WTO) definitions of agricultural products and revised historical data to reflect the new definitions. Therefore, data here may not be comparable to data presented in previous editions. See source for details]

Country	Value (mil. dol.)							Percent distribution		
	2010	2015	2019	2020	2021	2022	2023	2010	2020	2023
Total	85,582	121,122	141,562	146,282	170,617	198,270	194,941	100.0	100.0	100.0
Australia [1]	2,314	4,277	3,522	3,382	3,548	4,324	4,410	2.7	2.3	2.3
Brazil	3,141	3,974	4,061	4,049	4,748	6,253	6,181	3.7	2.8	3.2
Canada	16,773	22,443	24,363	25,324	31,248	37,521	40,146	19.6	17.3	20.6
Chile	2,298	2,863	2,806	2,766	3,132	3,430	3,091	2.7	1.9	1.6
China	3,309	4,302	3,730	3,823	4,081	4,737	4,724	3.9	2.6	2.4
Colombia	1,983	2,434	2,672	2,722	3,352	4,246	3,920	2.3	1.9	2.0
European Union-27 [2, 3]	16,615	22,776	28,378	27,449	32,017	35,820	32,900	19.4	18.8	16.9
France [1]	3,372	4,797	6,521	5,907	7,601	8,156	6,617	3.9	4.0	3.4
Ireland	2,415	3,559	4,441	4,186	4,422	5,462	4,957	2.8	2.9	2.5
Italy [1]	3,181	4,376	5,393	5,541	6,547	7,369	7,402	3.7	3.8	3.8
Netherlands	2,270	2,346	2,568	2,723	2,963	3,225	2,962	2.7	1.9	1.5
Spain	1,225	1,765	2,223	1,943	2,482	3,177	2,942	1.4	1.3	1.5
Guatemala	1,361	1,951	2,148	2,196	2,491	2,787	2,897	1.6	1.5	1.5
India	1,599	2,679	2,655	2,725	3,045	3,407	3,089	1.9	1.9	1.6
Indonesia	1,260	2,009	2,355	2,371	3,647	5,101	3,807	1.5	1.6	2.0
Mexico	14,291	22,188	30,216	32,920	37,954	43,295	45,391	16.7	22.5	23.3
New Zealand [1]	1,686	2,899	2,374	2,624	3,054	3,411	3,403	2.0	1.8	1.7
Peru	976	1,681	2,582	2,848	3,054	3,939	3,806	1.1	1.9	2.0
Singapore	105	96	3,056	3,262	3,537	4,186	3,174	0.1	2.2	1.6
Thailand	1,435	2,035	2,532	2,754	2,839	3,550	3,042	1.7	1.9	1.6
Rest of world	16,438	22,514	24,113	25,066	28,872	32,265	30,958	19.2	17.1	15.9

[1] Data is a summarization of component countries. [2] For consistency, data for all years are shown on the basis of 27 countries in the European Union; see footnote 3, Table 1387. [3] Includes countries not shown separately.

Source: U.S. Department of Agriculture, Foreign Agricultural Service, "Global Agricultural Trade System," <apps.fas.usda.gov/gats/>, accessed May 2024.

Table 896. Selected Farm Products—U.S. and World Production and Exports: 2010 to 2023

[315.6 represents 315,600,000. Metric ton = 1.102 short tons or .984 long tons]

Commodity	Unit	Quantity						United States as percent of world		
		United States			World					
		2010	2020	2023	2010	2020	2023	2010	2020	2023
PRODUCTION [1]										
Corn for grain..............	Mil. metric tons	315.6	357.8	389.7	849.3	1,131.9	1,223.8	37.2	31.6	31.8
Cotton.....................	Million bales [2]	18.1	14.6	12.1	113.6	113.7	113.6	15.9	12.8	10.6
Soybeans..................	Mil. metric tons	90.7	114.7	113.3	265.1	369.2	395.1	34.2	31.1	28.7
Rice, milled...............	Mil. metric tons	7.6	7.2	6.9	451.4	509.3	520.4	1.7	1.4	1.3
Wheat.....................	Mil. metric tons	58.9	49.5	49.3	650.3	772.7	789.7	9.1	6.4	6.2
EXPORTS [3]										
Corn......................	Mil. metric tons	46.5	69.8	57.2	91.6	182.9	200.6	50.8	38.2	28.5
Cotton.....................	Million bales [2]	14.4	16.4	11.8	34.9	49.0	44.7	41.2	33.4	26.3
Soybeans..................	Mil. metric tons	41.0	61.7	46.3	91.4	165.2	177.3	44.8	37.3	26.1
Rice, milled basis..........	Mil. metric tons	3.5	3.0	3.1	35.2	51.7	54.5	10.0	5.7	5.7
Wheat [4]...................	Mil. metric tons	35.1	27.0	19.2	133.0	203.5	220.8	26.4	13.3	8.7

[1] Production years vary by commodity. In most cases, includes harvests from July 1 of the year shown through June 30 of the following year. [2] Bales of 480 lb. net weight. [3] Data are for local marketing year beginning in year shown. See source for more information. [4] Includes wheat flour on a grain equivalent.

Source: U.S. Department of Agriculture, Foreign Agricultural Service, "Production, Supply and Distribution Online," <apps.fas.usda.gov/psdonline>, accessed August 2024.

Table 897. Percent of U.S. Agricultural Commodity Output Exported: 2010 to 2022

[In percent. All export shares are estimated from export and production values]

Commodity group	2010	2015	2016	2017	2018	2019	2020	2021	2022
Total agriculture......................	**18.3**	**18.7**	**19.0**	**19.5**	**19.3**	**18.6**	**19.6**	**20.0**	**(NA)**
Total food and beverages............	**18.2**	**18.5**	**18.9**	**19.1**	**18.7**	**18.2**	**19.5**	**20.0**	**(NA)**
Animal foods [1].........................	9.5	9.1	9.6	10.1	10.2	10.3	10.6	11.1	(NA)
Plant foods [2].........................	28.1	29.5	29.4	30.0	29.2	28.1	30.5	31.0	(NA)
Non-manufactured products........	**23.3**	**21.5**	**23.8**	**23.3**	**22.4**	**21.9**	**25.3**	**25.1**	**23.8**
Crops..........................	34.5	35.5	36.5	36.5	35.2	34.7	38.6	37.8	35.9
Food grains...........................	63.6	62.1	63.3	69.5	58.4	70.4	69.2	60.1	60.3
Feed grains...........................	20.8	20.9	22.7	21.6	25.6	16.7	21.2	26.8	22.5
Oilseeds...........................	52.5	55.2	54.0	54.0	45.1	53.7	60.1	54.1	54.1
Vegetables and melons.............	16.6	16.0	17.6	17.3	17.7	18.8	18.2	19.9	16.4
Fruits and tree nuts.................	38.2	45.1	41.4	42.7	44.6	45.9	45.1	44.0	48.5
Sweeteners...........................	6.5	5.2	3.9	4.6	4.8	3.7	4.4	3.3	3.2
Livestock...........................	0.8	0.5	0.6	0.7	0.8	0.7	0.8	0.9	0.7
Manufactured products..............	**18.5**	**21.1**	**19.3**	**20.7**	**20.5**	**19.7**	**19.5**	**20.6**	**(NA)**
Grain & oilseed milling products.....	44.7	53.7	48.6	58.7	58.4	50.9	58.1	55.1	(NA)
Sugar & confections...................	12.8	17.3	16.5	16.9	17.0	15.8	14.8	15.5	(NA)
Preserved fruit & vegetables.......	16.1	18.2	17.9	17.7	16.4	16.6	14.8	15.5	(NA)
Dairy products.......................	12.2	16.9	14.2	15.4	14.8	15.0	15.4	18.0	(NA)
Meat products.......................	31.8	32.9	30.6	33.1	32.4	32.5	30.4	30.1	(NA)
Bakery products.......................	4.3	5.3	4.9	5.1	5.3	5.3	5.1	5.2	(NA)
Other foods...........................	14.5	18.2	17.7	16.5	17.2	16.9	16.1	17.6	(NA)
Beverages...........................	10.2	13.4	11.4	13.4	13.0	11.7	12.3	12.5	(NA)

NA Not available. [1] Animal products include red meats, poultry meat and eggs, and dairy products. [2] Plant or crop food products include food grains, vegetable oils, fruits, nuts, vegetables, sweeteners (sugarcane, sugar beets, honey), tropical products (coffee, cocoa, spices), grain and oilseed milling products, sugar and confections, and bakery products.

Source: U.S. Department of Agriculture, Economic Research Service, "U.S. Agricultural Trade," <www.ers.usda.gov/topics/international-markets-u-s-trade/u-s-agricultural-trade/>, accessed August 2024.

Table 898. Top 10 U.S. Export Markets for Soybeans, Corn, Wheat, and Poultry: 2023

[In thousands of metric tons (48,248 represents 48,248,000). Commodity and commodity grouping definitions used are the Foreign Agricultural Trade of the United States (FATUS) commodity code groupings. In January 2021, the U.S. Department of Agriculture adopted the World Trade Organization (WTO) definitions of agricultural products; data reflect the new definitions. See source for details]

Soybeans		Corn		Wheat [1]		Poultry meat	
Country	Amount	Country	Amount	Country	Amount	Country	Amount
World, total.......	**48,248**	**World, total**.......	**45,563**	**World, total**.......	**17,833**	**World, total**.......	**3,553**
China..............	26,390	Mexico..............	18,619	Mexico..............	3,103	Mexico..............	877
Mexico..............	4,772	Japan..............	7,213	Philippines...........	2,278	Taiwan..............	273
Germany............	2,967	China..............	5,607	Japan..............	2,060	Cuba..............	262
Japan..............	2,296	Colombia...........	4,037	Korea, South........	1,203	Philippines...........	173
Indonesia...........	2,095	Canada..............	2,592	China..............	1,156	Canada..............	164
Italy.................	1,187	Guatemala...........	921	Taiwan..............	1,037	Guatemala...........	148
Taiwan..............	1,070	Korea, South........	897	Thailand..............	657	China..............	135
Spain...............	995	Taiwan..............	866	Colombia..............	461	Angola..............	104
Egypt...............	830	Honduras...........	780	Vietnam..............	419	Vietnam..............	102
Netherlands........	720	Saudi Arabia.........	607	Nigeria..............	407	Congo, Rep. of......	94
Rest of world........	4,926	Rest of world........	3,424	Rest of world........	5,052	Rest of world........	1,220

[1] Unmilled.

Source: U.S. Department of Agriculture, Foreign Agricultural Service, "Global Agricultural Trade System," <apps.fas.usda.gov/gats>, accessed August 2024.

Table 899. Agricultural Exports—Value by Principal Commodity: 2000 to 2023

[In millions of dollars (55,916 represents $55,916,000,000). Includes Puerto Rico, U.S. territories, and shipments under foreign aid programs. Commodity and commodity grouping definitions used are the Foreign Agricultural Trade of the United States (FATUS) commodity code groupings. In January 2021, the U.S. Department of Agriculture adopted the World Trade Organization (WTO) definitions of agricultural products and revised historical data to reflect the new definitions. See source for details]

Commodity	Value (mil. dol.)							Percent distribution		
	2000	2010	2015	2020	2021	2022	2023	2020	2022	2023
Total agricultural exports......	**55,916**	**118,719**	**137,216**	**149,672**	**176,631**	**195,680**	**174,172**	**100.0**	**100.0**	**100.0**
Animals and animal products [1]....	11,679	22,501	26,901	30,947	37,615	40,832	37,328	20.7	20.9	21.4
Red meat and meat products.....	5,276	9,336	12,407	16,098	19,599	20,531	19,420	10.8	10.5	11.1
Poultry and poultry products......	2,235	4,806	4,915	5,109	6,283	7,019	6,613	3.4	3.6	3.8
Grains and feeds [1].................	13,616	29,219	31,271	31,729	44,394	47,248	38,516	21.2	24.1	22.1
Wheat and products..............	3,578	7,061	5,977	6,612	7,560	8,698	6,435	4.4	4.4	3.7
Corn............................	4,469	9,792	8,271	9,246	18,629	18,571	13,111	6.2	9.5	7.5
Fruits and preparations............	2,743	5,262	6,285	5,832	6,132	5,764	5,814	3.9	2.9	3.3
Nuts and preparations.............	1,322	4,795	9,058	8,982	9,450	9,612	9,579	6.0	4.9	5.5
Vegetables and preparations [2].....	3,112	5,375	6,995	6,853	7,302	7,673	8,118	4.6	3.9	4.7
Oilseeds and products [1]...........	8,675	27,511	28,694	35,496	39,083	46,770	39,811	23.7	23.9	22.9
Soybeans.......................	5,258	18,611	18,862	25,516	27,418	34,359	27,723	17.0	17.6	15.9
Vegetable oils and waxes........	1,324	4,039	3,341	3,281	3,998	4,303	2,839	2.2	2.2	1.6
Tobacco, unmanufactured..........	1,204	1,168	1,109	666	827	845	981	0.4	0.4	0.6
Cotton, excluding linters...........	1,873	5,734	3,889	5,949	5,675	8,908	5,949	4.0	4.6	3.4
Other................................	11,692	17,155	23,015	23,218	26,152	28,026	28,076	15.5	14.3	16.1

[1] Includes commodities not shown separately. [2] Includes pulses (legumes).

Source: U.S. Department of Agriculture, Foreign Agricultural Service, "Global Agricultural Trade System," <apps.fas.usda.gov/gats/>, accessed August 2024.

Table 900. Agricultural Exports—Value by World Region and Selected Country of Destination: 2000 to 2023

[55,916 represents $55,916,000,000. Includes Puerto Rico, U.S. territories, and shipments under foreign aid programs. In January 2021, the U.S. Department of Agriculture adopted the World Trade Organization (WTO) definitions of agricultural products and revised historical data to reflect the new definitions. Therefore, data here may not be comparable to data presented in previous editions. See source for details]

Country	Value (mil. dol.)							Percent distribution		
	2000	2010	2015	2020	2021	2022	2023	2020	2022	2023
Total agricultural exports [1]....	**55,916**	**118,719**	**137,216**	**149,672**	**176,631**	**195,680**	**174,172**	**100.0**	**100.0**	**100.0**
Canada.............................	7,822	17,687	22,153	22,278	25,304	28,669	28,383	14.9	14.7	16.3
Mexico.............................	6,468	14,700	17,899	18,343	25,466	28,457	28,381	12.3	14.5	16.3
Caribbean..........................	1,442	3,248	3,451	3,644	4,406	5,270	5,204	2.4	2.7	3.0
Central America.....................	1,133	2,949	3,805	4,334	5,911	6,745	6,211	2.9	3.4	3.6
South America......................	1,747	4,292	6,672	7,104	7,981	8,687	8,229	4.7	4.4	4.7
Asia, excluding Middle East [2]......	22,398	50,383	57,474	68,918	80,446	87,661	70,477	46.0	44.8	40.5
China [3]...........................	1,726	17,555	20,362	26,405	32,769	38,104	28,844	17.6	19.5	16.6
Indonesia.........................	667	2,243	2,190	2,821	2,904	3,270	3,030	1.9	1.7	1.7
Japan.............................	11,471	12,238	11,553	11,729	14,186	14,679	11,889	7.8	7.5	6.8
Korea, South......................	2,661	5,333	6,185	7,593	9,309	9,505	7,496	5.1	4.9	4.3
Taiwan............................	2,067	3,211	3,169	3,260	3,826	4,299	3,687	2.2	2.2	2.1
Europe [2].........................	8,620	12,250	15,008	13,825	14,712	16,470	16,526	9.2	8.4	9.5
European Union [4].................	6,221	8,208	10,999	10,383	10,972	12,325	12,616	6.9	6.3	7.2
Russia............................	633	1,141	433	208	241	143	99	0.1	0.1	0.1
Middle East.........................	3,060	6,124	5,714	5,150	5,715	6,834	6,203	3.4	3.5	3.6
Africa [2]...........................	2,374	5,766	3,604	4,592	5,490	6,158	3,740	3.1	3.1	2.1
Egypt.............................	1,066	2,097	1,052	1,936	2,080	2,332	792	1.3	1.2	0.5
Oceania............................	580	1,563	2,162	2,201	2,089	2,191	2,072	1.5	1.1	1.2

[1] Totals include transshipments through Canada, but transshipments are not distributed by country after 2000. [2] Includes areas not shown separately. [3] China includes Macao; however, Hong Kong remains separate economically until 2050 and is not included. [4] For consistency, data for all years are shown on the basis of the 27 countries currently in the European Union.

Source: U.S. Department of Agriculture, Foreign Agricultural Service, "Global Agricultural Trade System," <apps.fas.usda.gov/gats/>, accessed August 2024.

Table 901. Cropland Used for Crops and Acres Harvested: 2010 to 2023

[In millions of acres (335 represents 335,000,000)]

Item	2010	2015	2017	2018	2019	2020	2021	2022	2023 (P)
Cropland used for crops..................	**335**	**336**	**338**	**337**	**322**	**329**	**335**	**328**	**334**
Cropland harvested [1]...........................	315	315	314	310	296	303	310	296	305
Crop failure.....................................	5	7	9	12	11	11	10	16	12
Cultivated summer fallow......................	14	13	15	16	15	15	15	15	17
Cropland idled by all federal programs [2, 3]................................	31	24	23	23	22	22	21	22	(NA)
Acres of crops harvested [4]...............	**322**	**322**	**320**	**316**	**302**	**309**	**316**	**302**	**313**

P Preliminary. NA Not available. [1] Land supporting one or more harvested crops. [2] Includes only the Conservation Reserve Program; all other federal acreage reduction programs were eliminated by the Federal Agricultural Improvement Act of 1996. [3] Data are for fiscal years. [4] Area in principal crops harvested plus acreages in fruits, vegetables for sale, tree nuts, and other minor crops. Acres are counted twice for land that is double cropped.

Source: U.S. Department of Agriculture, Economic Research Service, "Major Land Uses," <ers.usda.gov/data-products/major-land-uses.aspx>, accessed August 2024; and Farm Service Agency, "CRP Enrollment and Rental Payments by State, 1986-2022," <fsa.usda.gov/programs-and-services/conservation-programs/reports-and-statistics/index>, accessed August 2024.

Table 902. Cotton, Hay, and Potatoes—Acreage and Production: 2000 to 2023

[13.1 represents 13,100,000. Calendar year except as indicated. Marketing year begins January 1 for potatoes, May 1 for hay, and August 1 for cotton. Acreage, production, and yield of all crops are periodically revised on basis of census data]

Item	Unit	2000	2010	2015	2020	2021	2022	2023
COTTON								
Acreage harvested	Million	13.1	10.7	8.1	8.2	10.3	7.3	6.4
Yield per acre	Pounds	632	812	766	854	820	953	899
Production	Mil. bales [2]	17.2	18.1	12.9	14.6	17.5	14.5	12.1
Price per unit [1]	Cents/lb.	51.6	84.6	64.5	68.9	94.7	89.1	77.7
Value of production	Mil. dol.	4,260	7,347	3,989	4,829	7,963	6,186	4,635
HAY								
Acreage harvested	Million	60.4	59.6	54.5	51.7	50.4	48.7	52.8
Yield per acre	Tons	2.5	2.4	2.5	2.4	2.4	2.3	2.3
Production	Mil. tons	153.6	145.0	134.7	125.8	119.8	111.7	118.8
Price per unit [3, 4]	Dol./ton	84.60	114.00	145.00	156.00	193.00	239.00	208.00
Value of production	Mil. dol.	11,557	14,607	16,568	17,446	19,649	21,523	21,313
POTATOES								
Acreage harvested	Million	1.3	1.0	1.1	0.9	0.9	0.9	1.0
Yield per acre	Cwt. [5]	381	401	419	460	444	438	459
Production	Mil. cwt. [5]	513.5	404.5	448.6	419.8	412.6	402.1	440.8
Price per unit [1]	Dol./cwt. [5]	5.08	9.20	8.79	9.30	10.20	12.90	12.80
Value of production	Mil. dol.	2,590	3,725	3,942	3,902	4,204	5,166	5,647

[1] Marketing year average price. U.S. prices are computed by weighting U.S. monthly prices by estimated monthly marketings and do not include an allowance for outstanding loans and government purchases and payments. [2] Bales of 480 pounds, net weight. [3] Prices are for hay sold baled. [4] Season average prices received by farmers. U.S. prices are computed by weighting state prices by estimated sales. [5] Cwt = hundredweight (100 pounds).

Source: U.S. Department of Agriculture, National Agricultural Statistics Service, "Quick Stats," <quickstats.nass.usda.gov>, accessed August 2024.

Table 903. Horticultural Specialty Crop Operations, Value of Sales, and Total Land Area Used to Grow Horticultural Crops: 2019

[In units as indicated (13,778,944 represents $13,778,944,000). Horticultural specialty operation is defined as any place that produced and sold $10,000 or more of horticultural specialty products. Excludes mushrooms as well as grass seeds, vegetables, and fruits grown in the open. See source for more information]

Item	Operations	Value of sales ($1,000)	Total land area [1] Green-houses (1,000 square feet)	Shade structures (1,000 square feet)	Natural shade (acres)	Area in open (acres) [2]
Horticultural specialty crops, total	**20,655**	**13,778,944**	**884,816**	**391,987**	**6,729**	**549,063**
Annual bedding/garden plants	6,687	2,244,460	251,202	18,304	425	13,822
Herbaceous perennial plants, potted	5,108	922,616	33,699	6,461	255	5,177
Potted flowering plants for indoor or patio use	3,977	1,200,387	65,746	23,107	148	2,102
Foliage plants for indoor or patio use	2,336	691,472	43,171	85,422	67	2,261
Cut flowers	2,035	385,668	37,529	8,414	178	20,798
Cut cultivated greens	644	99,984	3,411	151,479	1,564	4,008
Nursery stock sold	6,458	4,545,276	247,458	82,982	3,552	367,290
Propagative material	1,038	720,448	29,307	3,760	135	20,858
Sod, sprigs, or plugs	1,068	1,271,561	(D)	(D)	(D)	(D)
Dried bulbs, corms, rhizomes, and tubers	263	60,072	791	(D)	9	6,446
Food crops grown under protection	2,994	703,469	79,046	2,997	56	10,247
Transplants for commercial vegetable production [3]	491	369,864	26,117	(D)	0	5,011
Vegetable seeds	335	127,198	1,461	(D)	(D)	42,523
Flower seeds	166	43,927	(D)	21	0	6,409
Aquatic plants	238	25,034	976	94	12	(D)
Cultivated Christmas trees	2,857	357,190	414	163	(D)	13,141
Short rotation woody crops	18	5,090	(NA)	(NA)	(NA)	(NA)
Tobacco transplants [4]	99	5,228	(NA)	(NA)	(NA)	(NA)

D Withheld to avoid disclosure. NA Not available. [1] Total land area represents the land utilized on the operation for horticultural production. [2] Excludes acres in production for Christmas trees or sod, sprigs, or plugs. [3] Includes strawberries. [4] Includes transplants grown for sale; excludes transplants for the farmer's own use.

Source: U.S. Department of Agriculture, National Agricultural Statistics Service, *2019 Census of Horticultural Specialties,* Vol. 3, December 2020. See also <www.agcensus.usda.gov/Publications/Census_of_Horticulture_Specialties/>.

Table 904. Corn—Acreage, Production, and Value by Leading State: 2021 to 2023

[84,988 represents 84,988,000. One bushel of corn (bu.) = 56 pounds. State value of production is computed by multiplying the state price by its production; acreage harvested and production value for the United States is the sum of state values]

State	Acreage harvested (1,000 acres) 2021	2022	2023	Yield per acre (bu.) 2021	2022	2023	Production (mil. bu.) 2021	2022	2023	Price per unit ($/bu.) 2021	2022	2023	Value of production (mil. dol.) 2021	2022	2023
U.S. [1]....	84,988	78,705	86,513	177	173	177	15,018	13,651	15,342	6.00	6.54	4.80	90,264	89,453	73,887
IA.........	12,450	12,350	12,550	204	200	201	2,540	2,470	2,523	6.10	6.62	4.85	15,493	16,351	12,234
IL......	10,850	10,600	11,050	202	214	206	2,192	2,268	2,276	5.96	6.40	4.75	13,063	14,518	10,812
NE.......	9,560	8,820	9,500	194	165	182	1,855	1,455	1,729	5.96	6.77	4.95	11,054	9,852	8,559
MN.......	7,790	7,490	8,180	177	195	185	1,379	1,461	1,513	5.91	6.27	4.75	8,149	9,158	7,188
IN.........	5,270	5,130	5,310	195	190	203	1,028	975	1,078	6.07	6.48	4.70	6,238	6,316	5,066
SD........	5,480	5,010	5,620	134	132	152	734	661	854	6.11	6.50	4.50	4,487	4,299	3,844
OH........	3,340	3,180	3,400	193	187	198	645	595	673	5.92	6.28	4.60	3,816	3,734	3,097
KS........	5,400	4,440	5,150	139	115	119	751	511	613	6.02	7.04	4.90	4,519	3,595	3,003
MO........	3,430	3,110	3,670	159	161	153	545	501	562	6.15	6.71	4.80	3,354	3,360	2,695
WI........	3,000	2,990	3,140	180	180	176	540	538	553	6.00	6.11	4.40	3,240	3,288	2,432
ND........	3,630	2,650	3,800	105	130	143	381	345	543	5.86	6.16	4.45	2,234	2,122	2,418
MI........	1,990	1,940	2,060	174	168	168	346	326	346	5.86	6.16	4.30	2,029	2,008	1,488
TX........	1,850	1,610	2,100	128	95	122	237	153	256	6.18	7.57	5.60	1,463	1,158	1,435
KY........	1,420	1,330	1,500	192	156	187	273	207	281	5.79	6.72	4.90	1,579	1,394	1,374
AR........	830	695	830	184	173	183	153	120	152	5.95	6.78	5.20	909	815	790
NC........	905	775	900	149	126	147	135	98	132	6.30	7.34	5.75	850	717	761
MS........	700	565	770	181	165	181	127	93	139	5.59	6.87	5.35	708	640	746
TN........	930	785	890	170	130	173	158	102	154	5.67	6.72	4.80	896	686	739
LA........	565	435	680	183	170	175	103	74	119	5.29	6.66	5.55	547	493	660
CO........	1,140	970	1,015	129	121	122	147	117	124	6.08	7.36	5.30	894	864	656

[1] Includes other states, not shown separately.

Source: U.S. Department of Agriculture, National Agricultural Statistics Service, "Quick Stats," <quickstats.nass.usda.gov/>, accessed March 2024.

Table 905. Soybeans—Acreage, Production, and Value by Leading State: 2021 to 2023

[86,292 represents 86,292,000. One bushel of soybeans (bu.) = 60 pounds. State value of production is computed by multiplying the state price by its production; value for the United States is the sum of state values]

State	Acreage harvested (1,000 acres) 2021	2022	2023	Yield per acre (bu.) 2021	2022	2023	Production (mil. bu.) 2021	2022	2023	Price per unit ($/bu.) 2021	2022	2023	Value of production (mil. dol.) 2021	2022	2023
U.S. [1]...	86,292	86,174	82,356	52	50	51	4,464	4,270	4,165	13.30	14.20	12.70	59,140	60,696	52,815
IL........	10,510	10,750	10,300	65	63	63	683	677	649	13.50	14.30	12.70	9,223	9,685	8,241
IA........	10,030	10,030	9,880	63	59	58	632	587	573	13.40	14.20	12.60	8,467	8,332	7,220
MN.......	7,580	7,390	7,280	47	50	48	356	370	349	13.40	14.10	12.50	4,774	5,210	4,368
IN........	5,640	5,830	5,480	60	58	61	338	335	334	13.30	14.40	12.80	4,501	4,827	4,279
OH.......	4,880	5,080	4,730	57	56	58	278	282	274	13.60	14.40	12.60	3,783	4,060	3,457
MO.......	5,640	6,040	5,520	49	46	48	276	275	265	13.80	14.40	12.70	3,814	3,957	3,365
NE.......	5,570	5,650	5,180	63	49	52	351	277	267	12.70	14.20	12.60	4,457	3,931	3,361
SD.......	5,390	5,070	5,070	40	38	44	216	193	223	13.10	14.10	12.40	2,824	2,717	2,766
ND.......	7,120	5,670	6,160	26	35	36	182	198	219	12.60	13.70	12.30	2,288	2,719	2,690
AR.......	3,000	3,140	2,950	52	52	54	156	163	159	12.90	14.20	13.10	2,012	2,319	2,087
MS.......	2,170	2,290	2,130	54	54	56	117	124	119	12.40	13.90	13.40	1,453	1,719	1,598
KS.......	4,800	4,720	4,030	40	28	26	192	130	105	12.90	14.30	12.60	2,477	1,856	1,320
WI.......	2,070	2,150	2,060	55	54	51	114	116	105	12.70	13.80	12.40	1,446	1,602	1,303
KY.......	1,840	1,940	1,820	56	51	55	103	99	100	13.10	14.40	12.90	1,350	1,425	1,291
MI.......	2,140	2,240	2,030	51	47	46	109	105	93	14.00	14.70	13.00	1,528	1,548	1,214

[1] Includes other states, not shown separately.

Source: U.S. Department of Agriculture, National Agricultural Statistics Service, "Quick Stats," <quickstats.nass.usda.gov/>, accessed March 2024.

Table 906. Wheat—Acreage, Production, and Value by Leading State: 2021 to 2023

[37,145 represents 37,145,000. One bushel of wheat (bu.) = 60 pounds. State value of production is computed by multiplying the price per unit by total production, for each state; value for the United States is the sum of production values for all states]

State	Acreage harvested (1,000 acres) 2021	2022	2023	Yield per acre (bu.) 2021	2022	2023	Production (mil. bu.) 2021	2022	2023	Price per unit ($/bu.) 2021	2022	2023	Value of production (mil. dol.) 2021	2022	2023
U.S. [1].....	37,145	35,485	37,272	44	47	49	1,646	1,650	1,812	7.63	8.83	7.20	12,232	14,205	12,762
ND.........	6,090	6,135	6,530	32	49	47	196	300	308	9.35	8.83	7.45	1,834	2,648	2,293
KS.........	7,000	6,600	5,750	52	37	35	364	244	201	6.74	8.71	7.50	2,453	2,127	1,509
MT.........	4,530	4,915	5,025	22	28	37	101	139	187	8.84	9.24	7.35	889	1,287	1,372
WA.........	2,230	2,270	2,240	39	63	51	87	144	113	8.67	8.13	6.30	756	1,171	713
ID..........	1,132	1,077	1,035	68	87	86	77	94	89	6.88	8.03	7.15	527	751	637
MN.........	1,160	1,210	1,260	48	61	62	56	74	78	8.92	9.15	7.40	497	675	578
TX.........	2,000	1,300	2,100	37	30	37	74	39	78	6.51	9.15	7.20	482	357	559
CO.........	1,880	1,430	1,820	37	25	41	70	36	75	6.84	8.33	7.00	476	298	522
OK.........	2,950	2,450	2,450	39	28	28	115	69	69	6.64	8.92	7.35	764	612	504
SD.........	1,290	1,440	1,350	34	50	45	44	72	61	8.35	8.68	7.35	366	625	447

[1] Includes other states, not shown separately.

Source: U.S. Department of Agriculture, National Agricultural Statistics Service, "Quick Stats," <quickstats.nass.usda.gov/>, accessed March 2024.

Table 907. Commercial Vegetable and Other Specified Crops—Area, Production, and Value: 2021 to 2023

[4.8 represents 4,800. Except as noted, relates to commercial production for fresh market and processing combined. Includes market garden areas but excludes minor producing acreage in minor producing states. Value is for season or crop year and should not be confused with calendar-year income. Hundredweight (cwt.) is the unit used for fresh market yield and production and is equal to one hundred pounds]

Crop	Area harvested (1,000 acres)			Utilized production [1] (1,000 cwt.)			Value of production [2] (mil. dol.)		
	2021	2022	2023	2021	2022	2023	2021	2022	2023
Artichokes....................	4.8	4.9	4.3	792	760	774	55	46	64
Asparagus....................	16.4	16.2	15.7	588	553	595	68	68	72
Beans, snap..................	175.8	170.3	154.1	14,773	15,129	14,122	290	396	362
Broccoli......................	116.6	127.7	109.0	15,084	16,951	15,010	786	1,133	1,070
Cabbage.....................	54.1	52.6	51.7	20,373	21,974	21,175	491	633	598
Cantaloupes..................	43.6	45.6	43.4	11,574	12,772	10,801	302	385	321
Carrots......................	63.7	74.5	65.8	28,385	32,064	29,353	977	1,295	1,823
Cauliflower...................	48.7	47.4	45.7	8,766	9,693	8,280	404	666	579
Celery.......................	27.8	27.5	26.9	15,275	14,713	13,854	375	450	363
Corn, sweet..................	382.0	367.6	359.5	60,747	60,251	62,065	767	900	1,000
Fresh market..............	(NA)	(NA)	(NA)	16,168	14,998	15,794	567	621	707
Processed................	(NA)	(NA)	(NA)	44,579	45,252	46,271	200	278	292
Cucumbers...................	88.1	84.5	81.9	13,838	13,306	14,188	270	299	290
Lettuce, head................	136.0	133.5	123.8	45,703	44,277	44,387	1,275	1,801	1,545
Lettuce, leaf.................	78.5	78.8	76.9	15,902	17,758	17,769	835	1,593	1,276
Lettuce, Romaine............	129.5	127.0	131.3	36,908	36,041	41,733	1,430	2,170	2,005
Onions.......................	143.7	135.0	133.7	71,815	69,268	72,423	1,325	1,843	1,510
Peas, green..................	127.9	124.6	116.0	4,466	5,674	5,229	70	101	103
Peppers, bell.................	32.0	34.2	34.3	10,652	11,169	10,623	475	697	613
Pumpkins....................	70.0	71.2	64.3	16,457	17,253	15,768	234	286	235
Spinach......................	62.1	68.0	73.0	8,002	9,439	9,324	567	633	731
Squash......................	43.4	42.6	40.1	6,956	6,487	5,926	220	222	215
Tomatoes....................	277.2	272.0	301.8	228,671	223,799	270,585	1,515	1,813	2,758
Fresh market..............	(NA)	(NA)	(NA)	13,369	13,881	14,249	611	648	716
Processed................	(NA)	(NA)	(NA)	215,301	209,918	256,337	904	1,165	2,043
Watermelons.................	104.7	103.4	101.2	35,027	35,472	36,852	620	821	787

NA Not available. [1] Utilized production is the amount of a crop sold plus the quantities used at home or held in storage. It is equal to the difference between the total production and what was harvested but not sold. [2] Fresh market vegetables valued at f.o.b. (free on board) shipping point. Processing vegetables are equivalent returns at packinghouse door.

Source: U.S. Department of Agriculture, National Agricultural Statistics Service, "Quick Stats," <quickstats.nass.usda.gov/>, accessed March 2024.

Table 908. Fruits and Nuts: Utilized Production and Value, 2010 to 2023; and Leading Producing States, 2023

[4,603 represents 4,603,000]

Fruits and nuts	Utilized production [1] (1,000 tons)				Value of utilized production (mil. dol.)				Leading states in order of production, 2023
	2010	2020	2022	2023	2010	2020	2022	2023	
NONCITRUS FRUITS									
Apples [2]......................	4,603	4,972	4,844	5,545	2,311	2,939	3,107	3,044	WA, MI, NY
Apricots......................	66	31	29	36	48	32	28	49	CA, WA
Avocados....................	174	150	128	128	479	428	503	250	CA, FL, HI
Blueberries..................	247	363	384	364	644	974	1,165	1,074	WA, OR, GA
Cherries, sweet..............	308	294	220	343	716	859	690	636	WA, CA, OR
Cranberries..................	340	390	399	404	299	288	304	301	WI, MA, NJ
Dates........................	29	52	64	49	37	165	209	181	CA, AZ
Grapes.......................	7,429	6,040	5,962	5,909	4,024	4,791	5,996	6,834	CA, WA
Kiwifruit (CA)................	33	39	36	27	25	76	85	78	CA
Nectarines...................	233	142	132	143	129	143	169	242	CA
Olives (CA)...................	206	75	86	121	137	64	76	95	CA
Peaches......................	1,130	646	633	578	617	591	675	656	CA, SC, PA
Pears........................	813	673	647	664	387	343	354	365	WA, OR, CA
Plums (CA)..................	142	81	66	85	79	96	96	140	CA
Raspberries..................	75	101	80	69	200	389	441	372	CA, WA
Strawberries.................	1,426	1,334	1,425	1,376	2,261	2,592	3,259	3,399	CA, FL
CITRUS FRUITS									
Grapefruit....................	1,238	570	374	347	291	199	158	173	CA, TX, FL
Lemons.......................	882	1,084	1,058	1,088	395	665	586	571	CA, AZ
Oranges......................	8,243	5,254	3,426	2,544	1,997	1,712	1,529	1,046	CA, FL, TX
Tangerines and mandarins......	596	944	736	963	275	821	705	772	CA, FL
NUTS [3]									
Almonds (CA)....................	1,414	2,585	2,060	1,975	2,903	5,251	3,536	3,880	CA
Hazelnuts (OR).................	28	63	78	94	67	133	101	127	OR
Macadamia nuts (HI).............	20	20	19	18	30	49	33	31	HI
Pecans.......................	147	157	144	153	675	448	520	515	GA, NM, AZ
Pistachios (CA).................	261	523	441	745	1,159	2,623	1,861	2,980	CA
Walnuts (CA)..................	504	789	756	824	1,028	947	454	692	CA

[1] Excludes quantities not harvested or not marketed. Utilized production is the amount sold plus the quantities used at home or held in storage. [2] Production in commercial orchards with 100 or more bearing-age trees. [3] In-shell equivalent.

Source: U.S. Department of Agriculture, National Agricultural Statistics Service, *Noncitrus Fruits and Nuts Final Estimates 2007-2012*, October 2014; *Citrus Fruits Final Estimates, 2008-2012*, August 2014; *Citrus Fruits 2024 Summary*, August 2024; *Noncitrus Fruits and Nuts 2023 Summary*, May 2024; and "Quick Stats" <quickstats.nass.usda.gov/>. See also <www.nass.usda.gov/Publications/>.

Table 909. Tree Nuts—Supply and Use: 2010 to 2022

[In thousands of pounds (shelled) (422,055 represents 422,055,000). Season begins in July for hazelnuts, August for almonds, September for pistachios and walnuts, and October for pecans]

Year	Beginning stocks	Marketable production [1]	Imports	Supply, total	Domestic availability	Exports	Ending stocks
Total nuts:							
2010..........................	422,055	2,482,242	485,098	3,389,395	1,195,946	1,786,058	407,391
2015..........................	585,250	2,665,812	668,081	3,919,144	1,308,364	2,035,232	575,549
2020..........................	683,490	4,505,379	705,699	5,894,568	1,904,480	3,057,362	932,726
2021..........................	932,726	4,301,194	785,441	6,019,361	1,753,088	3,030,736	1,235,538
2022, total [2, 3]......	**1,235,538**	**3,837,399**	**657,721**	**5,730,658**	**1,852,933**	**2,808,137**	**1,069,588**
Almonds.....................	836,806	2,528,099	20,268	3,385,173	709,285	1,875,595	800,292
Pecans......................	71,294	(NA)	127,252	325,733	204,783	57,767	63,182
Pistachios..................	200,486	442,917	973	644,377	230,500	326,994	86,883
Hazelnuts..................	5,816	61,707	6,621	74,144	32,400	36,173	5,571
Walnuts.....................	121,135	660,362	1,205	782,702	282,497	386,545	113,660

NA Not available. [1] Utilized production minus inedibles and noncommercial usage. [2] Includes macadamia nuts, Brazil nuts, cashew nuts, pine nuts, chestnuts, and mixed nuts, not shown separately. [3] Data are preliminary.

Source: U.S. Department of Agriculture, Economic Research Service, "Fruit and Tree Nut Yearbook Tables," <www.ers.usda.gov/data-products/fruit-and-tree-nut-data/fruit-and-tree-nut-yearbook-tables/>, accessed November 2023.

Table 910. Honey—Bee Colonies, Yield, and Production: 2000 to 2023

[2,622 represents 2,622,000. Includes only beekeepers with five or more colonies. Colonies were not included if honey was not harvested]

Year	Honey-producing colonies [1] (1,000)	Yield per colony (pounds)	Production (1,000 pounds)	Average price per pound (cents)	Value of production (1,000 dollars)
2000....................	2,622	84.0	220,286	60	132,865
2005....................	2,409	72.5	174,614	92	160,994
2010....................	2,692	65.6	176,462	162	285,692
2015....................	2,661	58.9	156,705	208	325,946
2018....................	2,828	54.5	154,008	221	340,358
2019....................	2,812	55.8	156,922	199	312,275
2020....................	2,706	54.5	147,594	210	309,947
2021....................	2,697	47.0	126,744	265	335,872
2022....................	2,667	47.0	125,331	301	377,246
2023....................	2,509	55.2	138,571	252	349,199

[1] Honey producing colonies are the maximum number of colonies from which honey was taken during the year. It is possible to take honey from colonies that did not survive the entire year.

Source: U.S. Department of Agriculture, National Agricultural Statistics Service, *Honey–Final Estimates 2013-2017*, June 2019, and earlier editions; and *Honey*, March 2024. See also <www.nass.usda.gov/Surveys/Guide_to_NASS_Surveys/Bee_and_Honey>.

Table 911. Vegetables and Dry Edible Beans—Supply and Utilization: 2000 to 2023

[40,556 represents 40,556,000,000. Data for calendar year except where noted. Food availability is a proxy for food consumption. Vegetable data excludes melons]

Item	Unit	2000	2010	2015	2020	2021	2022	2023 (P)
VEGETABLES, FRESH MARKET								
Production...........................	Mil. lbs.	40,556	37,894	35,976	36,943	35,465	36,292	35,969
Imports.............................	Mil. lbs.	5,499	10,931	13,183	16,313	17,551	18,016	17,710
Total supply........................	Mil. lbs.	47,400	50,394	50,906	54,883	54,544	55,608	55,001
Exports.............................	Mil. lbs.	3,750	3,421	3,107	3,142	3,258	2,992	2,999
Ending stocks [1]...................	Mil. lbs.	1,266	1,488	1,685	1,527	1,300	1,323	1,279
Domestic availability...............	Mil. lbs.	41,427	44,652	45,462	49,770	49,615	50,902	50,371
Per capita availability..............	Lbs.	146.7	144.2	141.7	150.8	149.3	152.6	150.3
VEGETABLES, PROCESSED MARKET [2]								
Production...........................	Mil. lbs.	36,427	37,511	41,136	33,014	31,546	31,281	35,911
Imports.............................	Mil. lbs.	5,254	9,439	12,510	16,320	17,315	18,447	16,502
Total supply........................	Mil. lbs.	63,558	72,988	75,943	69,149	64,701	63,555	66,302
Exports [3]..........................	Mil. lbs.	5,357	7,429	11,118	8,474	8,559	8,412	8,218
Ending stocks......................	Mil. lbs.	23,322	28,036	30,683	20,864	19,073	18,430	19,628
Domestic availability...............	Mil. lbs.	34,865	37,511	34,132	39,807	37,067	36,711	38,454
Per capita availability..............	Lbs.	123.5	121.1	106.4	120.6	111.5	110.1	114.7
POTATOES, FRESH MARKET								
Utilized production [4]...............	Mil. lbs.	13,185	11,342	10,982	9,953	9,768	9,314	9,832
Imports.............................	Mil. lbs.	805	916	882	1,105	1,031	1,337	1,395
Total supply........................	Mil. lbs.	13,990	12,258	11,864	11,059	10,799	10,651	11,226
Exports.............................	Mil. lbs.	677	856	905	1,108	1,316	1,214	1,278
Domestic availability...............	Mil. lbs.	13,314	11,402	10,960	9,951	9,483	9,437	9,948
Per capita availability..............	Lbs.	47.1	36.9	34.2	30.1	28.5	28.3	29.7
DRY EDIBLE BEANS								
Production...........................	Mil. lbs.	2,654	3,180	3,006	3,647	2,526	2,942	2,863
Imports.............................	Mil. lbs.	129	289	350	438	420	441	532
Total supply........................	Mil. lbs.	4,546	4,471	4,571	5,666	4,714	4,624	4,981
Exports.............................	Mil. lbs.	788	1,001	947	1,144	1,028	743	1,120
Domestic availability...............	Mil. lbs.	2,170	2,222	2,287	2,658	2,354	2,210	2,337
Per capita availability..............	Lbs.	7.7	7.2	7.1	8.1	7.1	6.6	7.0

P Preliminary. [1] Applies only to brussel sprouts, onions, and okra. [2] Includes vegetables for canning and freezing. Excludes potatoes. [3] Includes canned, frozen, and dehydrated vegetables converted to a fresh-weight basis. [4] Crop year utilization for the past season and the current season distributed on a calendar year basis using National Agricultural Statistics Service potato marketing distributions.

Source: U.S. Department of Agriculture, Economic Research Service, "Vegetable and Pulses Yearbook Datasets," accessed August 2024. See also <www.ers.usda.gov/data-products/vegetables-and-pulses-data.aspx>.

Table 912. Organic Vegetable, Fruit, and Field Crops—Farms, Production, and Value of Sales: 2021

[Unit column indicates quantity harvested and sales. Includes certified organic producers who have been certified by state or private agencies accredited by the USDA. Organic food must be produced without the use of conventional pesticides, petroleum-based or sewage sludge-based fertilizers, herbicides, pesticides, genetic engineering (biotechnology), antibiotics, growth hormones, or irradiation. Land must have no prohibited substances applied to it for at least 3 years before the harvest of an organic crop. Cwt = hundredweight (100 pounds)]

Commodity	Unit	Farms (number)	Acres harvested (number)	Quantity harvested	Sales Quantity	Sales Value of sales (1,000 dollars)
Vegetables, potatoes, and melons [1,2]..	(X)	3,347	237,096	(X)	(X)	1,913,727
Beans, snap.............................	Cwt	866	4,546	226,755	226,755	17,388
Broccoli.................................	Cwt	827	14,799	2,407,791	2,407,791	134,920
Cabbage, all............................	Cwt	998	3,187	440,779	440,746	24,275
Cantaloupes and muskmelons.........	Cwt	426	1,073	271,311	271,310	12,538
Carrots..................................	Cwt	919	12,210	3,648,562	3,643,038	122,627
Cauliflower..............................	Cwt	480	7,845	830,891	830,891	56,928
Celery...................................	Cwt	397	4,525	1,717,424	1,717,424	61,862
Garlic....................................	Cwt	1,052	1,853	160,522	160,522	16,363
Herbs....................................	Pounds	888	2,186	10,856,044	10,856,039	21,724
Lettuce..................................	Cwt	1,140	45,964	3,925,855	3,925,855	275,586
Onions, all..............................	Cwt	1,005	7,895	3,627,899	3,627,898	140,457
Peas, green.............................	Tons	552	8,936	253,301	253,301	16,677
Peppers, bell............................	Cwt	994	1,595	249,175	249,175	21,354
Potatoes................................	Cwt	898	24,526	5,246,466	5,246,441	182,858
Spinach..................................	Cwt	609	26,165	2,135,951	2,135,946	215,430
Squash...................................	Cwt	1,465	8,068	986,541	986,541	60,188
Sweet corn..............................	Cwt	514	11,887	1,389,765	1,389,765	34,347
Sweet potatoes.........................	Cwt	403	8,252	1,098,106	1,098,106	46,290
Tomatoes................................	Cwt	1,211	11,334	5,565,869	5,565,869	112,420
Watermelon.............................	Cwt	445	1,828	328,394	328,394	15,578
Apples, all...............................	Pounds	756	31,002	983,905,883	983,896,097	628,773
Grapes, all...............................	Tons	774	42,283	211,477	211,315	309,221
Citrus fruits, all [1]......................	Tons	641	13,533	135,771	135,771	108,311
Lemons..................................	Tons	319	5,092	56,483	56,483	40,497
Oranges, all.............................	Tons	288	4,780	45,539	45,538	33,262
Other fruits and berries [1]...............	(X)	2,566	52,888	(X)	(X)	1,027,069
Avocado.................................	Tons	339	4,463	7,736	7,736	26,262
Peaches.................................	Tons	231	3,206	26,409	26,409	51,666
Pears....................................	Tons	281	3,635	31,328	31,327	26,211
Plums....................................	Tons	192	671	3,861	3,861	9,328
Blueberries, cultivated, all..............	Pounds	611	12,372	95,787,052	95,776,556	220,529
Strawberries............................	Cwt	546	5,301	1,495,299	1,494,673	335,964
Tree nuts [1]..............................	(X)	417	34,330	(X)	(X)	125,951
Almonds.................................	Pounds	110	13,372	17,813,092	17,813,092	65,499
Walnuts, English........................	Tons	206	8,853	8,381	8,381	18,470
Field crops [1]............................	(X)	8,819	2,343,998	(X)	(X)	1,498,321
Barley for grain or seed................	Bushels	429	70,204	3,986,655	3,122,548	23,692
Corn for grain or seed.................	Bushels	3,962	374,977	49,467,464	45,053,009	423,875
Corn for silage or greenchop...........	Tons	1,222	62,916	1,161,889	422,493	30,122
Hay, all dry..............................	Tons	4,554	591,671	1,758,890	1,191,013	222,172
Oats for grain or seed..................	Bushels	1,012	53,477	3,932,406	3,366,672	19,548
Soybeans for beans.....................	Bushels	2,591	250,495	9,505,846	9,071,060	241,968
Wheat, all...............................	Bushels	1,426	376,682	12,497,632	12,236,895	139,327

X Not applicable. [1] Includes commodities not shown separately. [2] Vegetables grown in the open.

Source: U.S. Department of Agriculture, National Agricultural Statistics Service, *Certified Organic Survey 2021 Summary*, December 2022. See also <www.nass.usda.gov/Surveys/Guide_to_NASS_Surveys/Organic_Production/index.php>.

Table 913. Organic Livestock and Poultry—Farms, Inventory, and Value of Sales: 2019 and 2021

[Includes all known organic producers that are certified organic. Certified producers are those who have been certified by state or private agencies accredited by the USDA. Animals raised on an organic operation must meet animal health and welfare standards, not be fed antibiotics or growth hormones, be fed 100 percent organic feed, and must be provided access to the outdoors]

Type of livestock and poultry	2019 Farms (number)	2019 Inventory [1] (number)	2019 Value of sales (dollars)	2021 Farms (number)	2021 Inventory [1] (number)	2021 Value of sales (dollars)
Milk cows................................	3,134	337,540	71,731,366	2,528	334,315	66,061,000
Beef cows...............................	533	39,412	9,111,635	442	32,924	10,273,570
Other cattle [2]..........................	3,667	280,797	211,796,720	2,957	255,968	239,350,229
Hogs and pigs...........................	166	15,041	8,105,916	103	15,424	7,773,487
Sheep and lambs........................	109	8,281	1,175,158	88	9,145	1,548,515
Goats and kids..........................	59	4,075	113,131	67	3,918	201,054
Other livestock [3].......................	52	(X)	192,060	36	(X)	540,917
Chickens, layers.........................	1,057	18,450,112	11,316,343	1,167	25,415,572	9,682,150
Chickens, broilers.......................	369	23,020,265	1,115,102,146	433	36,534,985	1,508,820,309
Turkeys..................................	129	903,160	139,301,405	152	1,170,620	195,872,486
Other poultry [4].........................	162	(X)	95,131,213	164	(X)	157,047,461

X Not applicable. [1] As of December 31. [2] Includes organic bulls, beef calves, replacement milk heifers, etc. [3] Includes organic livestock not listed separately on the report form, such as farm raised bison, deer, rabbits, and fish. [4] Includes organic poultry not listed separately on the report form, including ducks, quail, etc.

Source: U.S. Department of Agriculture, National Agricultural Statistics Service, *2021 Organic Survey*, December 2022, and earlier reports. See also <www.nass.usda.gov/Surveys/Guide_to_NASS_Surveys/Organic_Production/index.php>.

Table 914. Meat Supply and Consumption: 2000 to 2023

[In millions of pounds, carcass weight equivalent (82,372 represents 82,372,000,000). Carcass weight equivalent is the weight of the animal minus entrails, head, hide, and internal organs; includes fat and bone. Covers federal and state inspected, and farm slaughtered]

Year and type of meat	Production	Imports	Supply [1]	Exports	Consump-tion [2]	Ending stocks
RED MEAT AND POULTRY [3]						
2000	82,372	4,144	88,460	9,343	77,073	2,044
2010	91,744	3,459	97,196	13,960	81,123	2,114
2015	94,289	4,875	101,230	14,275	84,593	2,361
2020	106,172	4,713	113,389	18,248	92,866	2,274
2021	106,420	5,069	113,764	18,389	93,353	2,021
2022	107,068	5,360	114,449	17,609	94,498	2,343
2023 (P)	106,474	5,329	114,147	17,637	94,294	2,215
RED MEATS, TOTAL						
2000	46,299	4,127	51,313	3,760	46,556	996
2010	49,155	3,323	53,591	6,538	45,908	1,145
2015	48,520	4,698	54,408	7,282	45,806	1,320
2020	55,774	4,545	61,648	10,233	50,198	1,217
2021	55,906	4,889	62,012	10,455	50,410	1,147
2022	55,564	5,092	61,803	9,896	50,652	1,256
2023 (P)	54,540	5,152	60,948	9,867	49,950	1,130
Beef: [4]						
2000	26,888	3,032	30,332	2,468	27,338	525
2010	26,389	2,298	29,251	2,300	26,366	585
2015	23,760	3,368	27,719	2,267	24,769	683
2020	27,244	3,339	31,225	2,951	27,559	716
2021	28,016	3,345	32,076	3,428	27,973	676
2022	28,358	3,390	32,424	3,544	28,156	723
2023 (P)	27,034	3,725	31,482	3,038	27,807	638
Pork:						
2000	18,952	965	20,378	1,287	18,639	453
2010	22,456	859	23,840	4,223	19,077	541
2015	24,517	1,116	26,191	5,010	20,592	590
2020	28,318	904	29,869	7,280	22,122	467
2021	27,690	1,180	29,337	7,024	21,868	446
2022	27,011	1,344	28,801	6,346	21,950	504
2023 (P)	27,318	1,142	28,965	6,824	21,670	471
Veal:						
2000	225	(⁴)	230	(⁴)	225	5
2010	143	(⁴)	152	(⁴)	148	4
2015	88	(⁴)	94	(⁴)	88	6
2020	69	(⁴)	75	(⁴)	66	9
2021	58	(⁴)	68	(⁴)	64	4
2022	59	(⁴)	62	(⁴)	61	1
2023 (P)	53	(⁴)	54	(⁴)	53	1
Lamb and mutton:						
2000	234	130	372	5	354	13
2010	168	166	348	16	317	15
2015	155	214	403	4	357	41
2020	143	302	479	3	451	25
2021	143	364	532	3	506	22
2022	136	358	517	6	484	27
2023 (P)	135	284	446	5	421	20
POULTRY, TOTAL [3]						
2000	36,073	16	37,147	5,583	30,516	1,048
2010	42,589	136	43,605	7,422	35,215	968
2015	45,768	177	46,822	6,994	38,787	1,041
2020	50,398	167	51,740	8,015	42,669	1,057
2021	50,514	180	51,751	7,934	42,943	874
2022	51,504	268	52,646	7,713	43,846	1,087
2023 (P)	51,934	177	53,199	7,770	44,344	1,085
Broiler chickens:						
2000	30,209	13	31,017	4,918	25,302	798
2010	36,515	107	37,238	6,762	29,703	773
2015	39,620	131	40,430	6,321	33,278	832
2020	44,106	145	45,188	7,368	36,989	830
2021	44,419	155	45,403	7,342	37,356	705
2022	45,713	176	46,594	7,287	38,415	892
2023 (P)	45,890	131	46,914	7,260	38,819	835
Other chicken:						
2000	531	2	541	220	312	9
2010	504	4	510	78	428	4
2015	522	2	527	144	375	8
2020	549	2	556	75	477	4
2021	537	3	544	44	497	3
2022	569	7	579	20	554	5
2023 (P)	587	4	597	21	569	7
Turkeys:						
2000	5,333	1	5,589	445	4,902	241
2010	5,570	25	5,857	581	5,084	192
2015	5,627	45	5,865	529	5,135	201
2020	5,743	21	5,997	571	5,203	223
2021	5,558	22	5,804	548	5,090	166
2022	5,222	85	5,473	407	4,877	190
2023 (P)	5,457	42	5,689	490	4,956	243

P Preliminary. [1] Total supply equals production plus imports plus ending stocks of previous year. [2] Includes shipments to territories. [3] Poultry production is ready-to-cook production; prior to 2001, includes other production (not federally inspected). [4] Veal exports and imports included with beef.

Source: U.S. Department of Agriculture, Economic Research Service, "Livestock and Meat Domestic Data," <ers.usda.gov/data-products/livestock-meat-domestic-data.aspx>, accessed August 2024.

Table 915. Livestock Inventory and Production: 2010 to 2023

[94.1 represents 94,100,000. Production in live weight; includes animals-for-slaughter market, younger animals shipped to other states for feeding or breeding purposes, farm slaughter and custom slaughter consumed on farms where produced, minus livestock shipped into states for feeding or breeding with an adjustment for changes in inventory. Prices are for the marketing year, which for cattle and sheep and lambs starts January 1; for hogs the marketing year starts December 1]

Type of livestock	Unit	2010	2015	2016	2017	2018	2019	2020	2021	2022	2023
ALL CATTLE [1]											
Inventory (number on farms): [2]	Mil.	94.1	89.2	91.9	93.6	94.3	94.7	93.8	93.6	91.8	88.8
Total value	Bil. dol.	78.3	141.3	129.6	103.8	108.1	97.6	96.1	97.2	102.1	109.7
Value per head	Dol.	833	1,584	1,410	1,109	1,146	1,032	1,026	1,039	1,112	1,235
Production: Quantity	Bil. lb.	41.4	41.5	42.7	44.2	45.7	44.6	51.2	40.4	45.7	44.1
Cattle, price per 100 pounds [3]	Dol.	92.2	147	119	120	115	116	109	121	142	173
Calves, price per 100 pounds	Dol.	117.0	247	158	168	170	159	161	171	195	261
Value of production	Bil. dol.	36.9	60.1	48.6	50.4	49.2	48.2	55.0	42.2	61.9	73.7
HOGS AND PIGS											
Inventory (number on farms): [4]	Mil.	64.7	67.6	69.0	71.3	73.1	75.1	77.3	77.0	74.6	75.0
Total value	Bil. dol.	5.4	9.7	6.6	6.6	7.2	7.4	7.9	7.7	8.8	9.4
Value per head	Dol.	83	144	96	92	99	98	102	100	117	125
Production: Quantity	Bil. lb.	30.3	34.7	35.9	37.0	40.3	41.9	40.4	40.0	40.7	42.6
Price per 100 pounds	Dol.	54.1	55.3	49.3	53.1	50.2	51.4	46.9	67.3	72.2	62.7
Value of production	Bil. dol.	16.0	18.8	17.4	19.2	19.9	21.2	18.0	28.9	30.1	25.3
SHEEP AND LAMBS											
Inventory (number on farms): [2]	Mil.	5.6	5.3	5.3	5.3	5.3	5.2	5.2	5.2	5.2	5.1
Total value	Mil. dol.	761.1	1,127.2	1,071.5	1,067.9	1,071.4	1,062.7	1,068.8	1,076.6	1,134.2	1,206.9
Value per head	Dol.	135	214	202	203	204	203	205	207	220	235
Production: Quantity	Mil. lb.	405	(NA)	(NA)	(NA)	(NA)	(NA)	(NA)	(NA)	(NA)	(NA)
Value of production	Mil. dol.	442.9	(NA)	(NA)	(NA)	(NA)	(NA)	(NA)	(NA)	(NA)	(NA)

NA Not available. [1] Includes milk cows. [2] As of January 1. [3] Cattle weighing 500 pounds or more. [4] As of December 1 of preceding year.

Source: U.S. Department of Agriculture, National Agricultural Statistics Service, "Quick Stats," <quickstats.nass.usda.gov/>, accessed June 2024. See also *Meat Animals Production, Disposition, and Income Annual Summary*, <www.nass.usda.gov/Publications>.

Table 916. Livestock Operations by Size of Herd: 2010 to 2022

[In thousands (935 represents 935,000). Operations are any place having one or more head on hand on December 31]

Size of herd	2010	2012	2017	2022	Size of herd	2010	2012	2017	2022
CATTLE [1]					MILK COWS [2]				
Total operations	935	913	883	732	**Total operations**	63	64	55	36
1 to 49 head	635	637	599	503	1 to 49 head	31	34	28	19
50 to 99 head	129	118	119	93	50 to 99 head	16	15	12	6
100 to 499 head	142	130	136	107	100 head or more	16	14	14	11
500 to 999 head	19	17	18	17					
1,000 head or more	11	11	11	12	HOGS AND PIGS				
					Total operations	69	63	66	61
BEEF COWS [2]					1 to 99 head	49	47	52	48
Total operations	742	728	729	622	100 to 499 head	5	4	3	2
1 to 49 head	588	594	577	494	500 to 999 head	3	2	1	1
50 to 99 head	82	71	80	63	1,000 to 1,999 head	4	3	2	2
100 to 499 head	66	57	66	58	2,000 to 4,999 head	5	5	5	5
500 head or more	6	5	6	7	5,000 head or more	3	3	4	4

[1] Includes calves. [2] Included in operations with cattle.

Source: U.S. Department of Agriculture, National Agricultural Statistics Service, *Farms, Land in Farms, and Livestock Operations 2010 Summary*, February 2011. Beginning with 2012 data, *Census of Agriculture*, Vol. 1, February 2024, and earlier reports. See also <www.nass.usda.gov/Publications/>.

Table 917. Hogs and Pigs—Number, Production, and Slaughter by Leading State: 2021 to 2023

[74,606 represents 74,606,000. Production in live weight. See headnote, Table 915]

State	Number on farms [1] (1,000)			Quantity produced (mil. lb.)			Value of production (mil. dol.)			Commercial slaughter [2] (mil. lb.)	
	2021	2022	2023	2021	2022	2023	2021	2022	2023	2022	2023
U.S. [3]	**74,606**	**74,956**	**75,461**	**39,992**	**40,674**	**42,581**	**28,875**	**30,050**	**25,345**	**36,254**	**36,730**
IA	23,900	24,100	25,000	13,236	14,377	14,271	9,510	10,536	8,674	10,935	11,466
MN	8,900	9,000	9,300	4,608	4,653	4,762	3,320	3,415	2,889	3,495	3,402
NC	8,000	8,300	7,900	4,244	4,185	4,469	3,085	3,151	2,470	(D)	(D)
IL	5,400	5,500	5,500	2,776	2,851	3,091	2,007	2,096	1,869	3,170	3,330
IN	4,350	4,450	4,500	2,078	2,063	2,261	1,515	1,520	1,363	2,434	2,472
NE	3,700	3,600	3,800	1,685	1,464	1,499	1,233	1,083	895	2,141	2,172
MO	3,500	3,350	3,100	1,357	1,238	2,323	1,016	942	1,297	2,468	2,526

D Withheld to avoid disclosing data for individual operations. Data included in U.S. total. [1] As of December 1. [2] Includes slaughter in federally inspected and other plants, but excludes animals slaughtered on farms. [3] Includes other states, not shown separately.

Source: U.S. Department of Agriculture, National Agricultural Statistics Service, "Quick Stats," <quickstats.nass.usda.gov/>, accessed July 2024. See also *Meat Animals Production, Disposition, and Income Annual Summary* and *Livestock Slaughter Annual Summary*, <www.nass.usda.gov/Publications/>.

Table 918. Cattle and Calves—Number, Production, and Value by Leading State: 2021 to 2023

[93,587 represents 93,587,000. Includes milk cows. See headnote, Table 915]

State	Number on farms [1] (1,000)			Production (mil. lb.)			Value of production (mil. dol.)			Commercial slaughter [2] (mil. lb.)	
	2021	2022	2023	2021	2022	2023	2021	2022	2023	2022	2023
U.S. [3]	**93,587**	**91,789**	**88,841**	**40,358**	**45,696**	**44,062**	**42,213**	**61,937**	**73,737**	**46,893**	**44,731**
TX	13,100	12,700	12,500	3,000	6,649	6,183	1,734	9,780	11,350	7,993	7,428
NE	6,850	6,800	6,500	5,812	5,865	5,610	6,079	7,422	8,776	10,330	9,737
KS	6,550	6,500	6,200	4,713	4,928	4,724	4,909	6,327	7,429	9,432	9,006
CA	5,150	5,200	5,200	1,557	2,307	2,371	1,265	3,144	3,965	2,184	2,037
OK	5,300	5,200	4,600	1,642	2,140	1,987	1,862	3,263	3,891	95	82
MO	4,300	4,050	4,100	630	1,380	1,348	577	2,162	2,655	366	386
IA	3,600	3,750	3,500	2,128	2,244	1,882	2,685	3,356	3,466	762	794
SD	4,000	3,800	3,500	1,736	1,663	1,588	2,243	2,497	2,986	704	630
WI	3,400	3,450	3,350	1,258	1,534	1,519	1,325	2,061	2,518	1,914	1,823
CO	2,700	2,670	2,650	2,046	1,875	1,729	2,392	2,599	2,782	3,208	3,127
ID	2,500	2,550	2,500	1,266	1,277	1,268	1,432	1,751	2,123	745	774

[1] As of January 1. [2] Data cover cattle only. Includes slaughter in federally inspected and other slaughter plants; excludes animals slaughtered on farms. [3] Includes other states, not shown separately.

Source: U.S. Department of Agriculture, National Agricultural Statistics Service, "Quick Stats," <quickstats.nass.usda.gov>, accessed July 2024. See also *Meat Animals Production, Disposition, and Income Annual Summary* and *Livestock Slaughter Annual Summary*, <www.nass.usda.gov/Publications>.

Table 919. Milk Cows—Number, Production, and Value by Leading State: 2021 to 2023

[9,449 represents 9,449,000]

State	Number on farms [1] (1,000)			Milk produced on farms [2] (mil. lb.)			Milk produced per milk cow [2] (pounds)			Value of production [3] (mil. dol.)		
	2021	2022	2023	2021	2022	2023	2021	2022	2023	2021	2022	2023
U.S. [4]	**9,449**	**9,400**	**9,386**	**226,238**	**226,416**	**226,364**	**23,943**	**24,087**	**24,117**	**41,948**	**57,494**	**46,130**
CA	1,720	1,719	1,714	41,861	41,800	40,902	24,338	24,316	23,863	7,577	10,408	8,139
WI	1,274	1,272	1,270	31,708	31,882	32,123	24,889	25,064	25,294	5,961	7,843	6,200
ID	652	656	667	16,412	16,628	16,827	25,172	25,348	25,228	3,069	4,290	3,466
TX	622	646	642	15,599	16,531	16,565	25,079	25,590	25,802	2,839	4,232	3,363
NY	627	624	630	15,540	15,646	16,079	24,785	25,074	25,522	2,937	4,099	3,505
PA	474	468	466	10,114	9,949	9,859	21,338	21,259	21,157	1,932	2,636	2,110
MN	461	453	452	10,537	10,472	10,500	22,857	23,117	23,230	2,002	2,628	2,027
MI	440	429	438	11,911	11,737	12,073	27,070	27,359	27,564	2,096	2,887	2,415
NM	317	288	271	7,781	7,145	6,663	24,546	24,809	24,587	1,268	1,679	1,239

[1] Average number during year. Represents cows and heifers that have calved, kept for milk; excluding heifers not yet fresh. [2] Excludes milk sucked by calves. [3] Valued at average returns per 100 pounds of milk in combined marketings of milk and cream. Includes value of milk fed to calves. [4] Includes other states, not shown separately.

Source: U.S. Department of Agriculture, National Agricultural Statistics Service, "Quick Stats," <quickstats.nass.usda.gov/>, accessed July 2024. See also *Milk: Production, Disposition, and Income Annual Summary*, <www.nass.usda.gov/Publications>.

Table 920. Milk Production and Manufactured Dairy Products: 2010 to 2023

[63 represents 63,000]

Item	Unit	2010	2015	2017	2018	2019	2020	2021	2022	2023
Number of farms with milk cows	**1,000**	**63**	**(NA)**	**55**	**(NA)**	**(NA)**	**(NA)**	**(NA)**	**36**	**(NA)**
Cows and heifers that have calved, kept for milk [1]	Mil. head	9.1	9.3	9.4	9.4	9.3	9.4	9.4	9.4	9.4
Milk produced on farms	Bil. lb.	193	209	216	218	218	223	226	226	226
Production per cow	1,000 lb.	21.1	22.4	22.9	23.2	23.4	23.8	23.9	24.1	24.1
Milk marketed by producers [2]	Bil. lb.	192	208	215	217	217	222	225	225	225
Value of milk produced	Bil. dol.	31.5	35.9	38.1	35.4	40.7	40.6	41.9	57.5	46.1
Cash receipts from marketing of milk and cream [2]	Bil. dol.	31.4	35.7	37.9	35.2	40.5	40.4	41.8	57.2	45.9
Number of dairy manufacturing plants	**Number**	**1,250**	**1,273**	**1,305**	**1,275**	**1,270**	**1,231**	**1,201**	**1,204**	**1,183**
Manufactured dairy products:										
Butter (including whey butter)	Mil. lb.	1,564	1,850	1,847	1,968	1,994	2,146	2,063	2,059	2,115
Cheese, total [3]	Mil. lb.	10,443	11,831	12,640	13,037	13,137	13,240	13,761	14,084	14,211
American (excl. full-skim American)	Mil. lb.	4,289	4,694	5,072	5,254	5,232	5,338	5,615	5,672	5,845
Cream and Neufchatel	Mil. lb.	745	876	918	915	935	1,012	1,026	1,118	1,092
All Italian varieties	Mil. lb.	4,416	5,082	5,395	5,570	5,671	5,612	5,769	5,904	5,854
Cottage cheese—creamed and lowfat	Mil. lb.	719	681	675	695	686	671	642	638	713
Nonfat dry milk [4]	Mil. lb.	1,563	1,822	1,835	1,778	1,851	1,952	2,047	1,955	1,868
Dry whey [5]	Mil. lb.	1,013	978	1,035	999	978	959	892	915	938
Yogurt, plain and flavored	Mil. lb.	4,181	4,646	4,478	4,453	4,378	4,510	4,744	4,466	4,590
Ice cream, regular	Mil. gal.	929	897	871	852	879	916	880	925	849
Ice cream, lowfat [6]	Mil. gal.	415	439	461	460	474	463	478	446	451

NA Not available. [1] Average number during year, excluding heifers not yet fresh. [2] Comprises sales to plants and dealers, and retail sales by farmers direct to consumers. [3] Includes varieties not shown separately. [4] Data for 2000 includes dry skim milk for animal feed. [5] Includes animal but excludes modified whey production. [6] Includes freezer-made milkshake in most states.

Source: U.S. Department of Agriculture, National Agricultural Statistics Service, "Quick Stats," <quickstats.nass.usda.gov/>, accessed August 2024. See also *Dairy Products Annual Summary*; *Milk Production, Disposition, and Income Annual*; and *Farms, Land in Farms, And Livestock Operations, Summary*; <www.nass.usda.gov/Publications/index>.

Table 921. Milk Production and Commercial Use in All Products: 2013 to 2023

[In billions of pounds milkfat basis (11.4 represents 11,400,000,000) except as noted. Beginning in 2011, commercial uses and stocks from government uses and stocks are not separated, and there are no longer government-subsidized exports. Therefore the data in this table are not comparable to data previously presented. See <www.ers.usda.gov/data-products/dairy-data/documentation/>]

| Year | Begin- ning stocks | Farm milk supply use | | | Imports | Total supply | Utilization | | | Apparent domestic human use [2] | Milk price per 100 pounds (dollars) |
		Produc- tion	Farm use	Farm market- ings			Exports	Ending stocks	Disap- pear- ance [1]		
2013.....	11.4	201.3	1.0	200.3	3.8	215.4	12.1	10.3	193.0	191.8	20.10
2014.....	10.3	206.0	1.0	205.1	4.4	219.8	12.2	10.4	197.1	195.8	24.00
2015.....	10.4	208.5	1.0	207.5	5.8	223.7	8.5	12.3	203.0	201.5	17.10
2016.....	12.3	212.5	1.0	211.5	6.9	230.7	8.4	12.7	209.6	208.2	16.30
2017.....	12.7	215.5	1.0	214.5	6.0	233.2	9.2	13.4	210.6	209.2	17.70
2018.....	13.4	217.6	1.0	216.6	6.3	236.3	10.4	13.8	212.1	210.6	16.30
2019.....	13.8	218.4	1.0	217.4	6.9	238.2	9.1	13.6	215.4	214.0	18.70
2020.....	13.6	223.3	1.1	222.2	6.8	242.6	9.3	15.6	217.7	215.8	18.10
2021.....	15.6	226.2	1.0	225.2	6.5	247.4	11.5	14.3	221.5	219.7	18.50
2022.....	14.3	226.4	1.0	225.4	7.1	246.8	12.8	14.4	219.6	218.2	25.30
2023.....	14.4	226.4	1.0	225.4	7.4	247.1	10.5	13.8	222.9	(NA)	20.50

NA Not available. [1] Domestic disappearance equals total commercial supply minus exports and ending stocks. [2] Apparent human use is domestic disappearance and household farm use minus net shipments to U.S. territories; use as animal food; and milk and products pooled on Federal Milk Marketing Orders (FMMOs) that is dumped, used for animal feed, destroyed, or lost by a handler in a vehicular accident, flood, fire, or similar occurrence beyond the handler's control.

Source: U.S. Department of Agriculture, Economic Research Service, "Dairy Data," <www.ers.usda.gov/data-products/dairy-data.aspx>, accessed August 2024.

Table 922. Chicken, Turkey, and Egg Production: 2010 to 2023

[457 represents 457,000,000. For years ending November 30, except as noted]

Item	Unit	2010	2015	2016	2017	2018	2019	2020	2021	2022	2023
Chickens: [1]											
Number [2]..............	Million	457	484	501	515	534	533	522	527	517	523
Value per head [2]........	Dollars	3.58	4.38	4.23	4.20	4.33	4.47	5.20	5.69	6.56	7.20
Value, total [2]............	Mil. dol.	1,637	2,116	2,115	2,163	2,312	2,380	2,714	2,996	3,395	3,761
Number sold...........	Million	173	199	208	190	191	185	188	185	171	178
Value of sales...........	Mil. dol.	73	105	88	47	50	38	19	15	75	62
PRODUCTION											
Broiler chickens: [3]											
Number.................	Million	8,624	8,689	8,777	8,914	9,038	9,177	9,222	9,131	9,191	9,155
Weight.................	Bil. lb.	49.2	53.4	54.3	55.6	56.8	58.3	59.4	59.2	59.5	59.7
Production value........	Mil. dol.	23,692	28,716	25,936	30,232	31,750	28,314	21,267	31,520	50,584	42,566
Turkeys: [4]											
Number.................	Million	244	233	244	245	238	229	224	217	210	218
Weight.................	Bil. lb.	7.1	7.0	7.5	7.5	7.4	7.4	7.3	7.2	6.7	7.0
Production value........	Mil. dol.	4,372	5,708	6,184	4,874	3,789	4,310	5,193	5,912	7,117	6,567
Eggs:											
Average number of layers.................	Thousand	341,505	356,370	369,949	381,175	378,160	399,689	392,804	391,050	379,900	382,338
Eggs per layer..........	Number	269	276	279	281	273	283	286	288	289	286
Total production........	Billion	91.8	98.3	103.2	107.2	103.1	113.3	112.3	112.7	109.9	109.5
Production value........	Mil. dol.	6,553	13,763	6,591	7,635	10,369	7,337	8,692	8,775	19,434	17,860

[1] Excludes commercial broilers. [2] As of December 1. [3] Young chickens of the heavy breeds and other meat-type birds, to be marketed at 2-5 lbs. live weight and from which no pullets are kept for egg production. Not included in sales of chickens. [4] Data for turkeys are for year ending August 31.

Source: U.S. Department of Agriculture, National Agricultural Statistics Service, "Quick Stats," <quickstats.nass.usda.gov/>, accessed June 2024. See also *Poultry—Production and Value* and *Chickens and Eggs*, <www.nass.usda.gov/Publications>.

Table 923. Broiler Chicken and Turkey Production by Leading State: 2020 to 2023

[In millions of pounds, live weight production (59,406 represents 59,406,000,000)]

| State | Broiler chickens | | | Turkeys | | | State | Broiler chickens | | | Turkeys | | |
	2020	2022	2023	2020	2022	2023		2020	2022	2023	2020	2022	2023
U.S. [1].....	59,406	59,510	59,700	7,324	6,670	6,986	MS......	4,613	4,293	4,422	(NA)	(NA)	(NA)
AL.........	6,605	6,746	6,600	(NA)	(NA)	(NA)	MO......	1,490	1,751	1,731	581	351	366
AR.........	7,348	7,360	7,442	566	546	543	NC......	7,883	8,103	7,905	1,096	1,033	1,070
CA.........	(NA)	(NA)	(NA)	232	193	198	OH......	552	572	573	285	279	291
DE.........	1,929	1,802	1,889	(NA)	(NA)	(NA)	OK......	1,494	1,507	1,508	(NA)	(NA)	(NA)
FL.........	391	391	396	(NA)	(NA)	(NA)	PA.......	1,260	1,279	1,339	222	215	222
GA.........	8,083	7,850	8,154	(NA)	(NA)	(NA)	SC......	1,875	1,814	1,776	(NA)	(NA)	(NA)
IN..........	(NA)	(NA)	(NA)	806	772	834	SD......	(NA)	(NA)	(NA)	206	112	142
IA..........	(NA)	(NA)	(NA)	505	487	508	TN......	1,031	1,144	1,114	(NA)	(NA)	(NA)
KY.........	1,944	1,679	1,805	(NA)	(NA)	(NA)	TX.......	4,637	4,918	4,819	(NA)	(NA)	(NA)
MD.........	1,868	1,750	1,751	(NA)	(NA)	(NA)	VA.......	1,712	1,885	1,812	446	414	429
MI.........	(NA)	(NA)	(NA)	232	219	220	WV......	274	298	326	126	116	127
MN........	358	260	393	1,092	979	1,055	WI.......	226	228	238	(NA)	(NA)	(NA)

NA Not available. [1] Includes other states, not shown separately.

Source: U.S. Department of Agriculture, National Agricultural Statistics Service, "Quick Stats," <quickstats.nass.usda.gov/>, accessed July 2024. See also *Poultry—Production and Value*, <www.nass.usda.gov/Publications>.

Forestry, Fishing, and Mining

This section presents data on the area, ownership, production, trade, reserves, and disposition of natural resources, defined here as including forestry, fisheries, and mining and mineral products.

Forestry—This section presents data on the area, ownership, and timber resource of commercial timberland; forestry statistics covering the National Forests and Forest Service cooperative programs; product data for lumber, pulpwood, woodpulp, paper and paperboard; and similar data.

The principal sources of data relating to forests and forest products are *Forest Resources of the United States, 2017; U.S. Timber Production, Trade, Consumption, and Price Statistics, 1965 to 2017; Land Areas of the National Forest System*, issued annually by the Forest Service of the U.S. Department of Agriculture; *Agricultural Statistics*, issued by the Department of Agriculture; and through 2021, reports of the Annual Survey of Manufactures issued by the U.S. Census Bureau, see <www.census.gov/programs-surveys/asm.html>. Further sources used in this section and issued by the U.S. Census Bureau include the annual *County Business Patterns* reports and the Economic Census. Additional information is published in the *Paper Industry Annual Statistical Summary* of the American Forest and Paper Association, Washington, DC.

The completeness and reliability of statistics on forests and forest products vary considerably. The data for forest land area and stand volumes are much more reliable for areas that have been recently surveyed than for those for which only estimates are available. In general, more data are available for lumber and other manufactured products such as particle board and softwood panels, etc., than for the primary forest products such as poles and piling and fuelwood.

Fisheries—The principal source of data relating to fisheries is data issued annually by the National Marine Fisheries Service (NMFS), National Oceanic and Atmospheric Administration (NOAA). The NMFS collects and disseminates data on commercial landings of fish and shellfish. Annual reports include quantity and value of commercial landings of fish and shellfish, disposition of landings, and number and kinds of fishing vessels and fishing gear. Reports for the fish-processing industry include annual output for wholesaling, and fish processing establishments and annual and seasonal employment. The principal source for these data is the annual *Fisheries of the United States*. Additional government sources include *Agricultural Statistics*, *Trout Production*, and *Catfish Production*, issued by the National Agricultural Statistics service of the U.S. Department of Agriculture.

Mining and mineral products—This section presents data relating to mineral industries and their products, summary measures of production and employment, and more detailed data on production, prices, imports and exports, consumption, and distribution for specific industries and products. Data on mining and mineral products may also be found in Sections 19, 21, 28, and 30 of this *Abstract*; data on mining employment may be found in Section 12.

Mining comprises the extraction of minerals occurring naturally (coal, ores, crude petroleum, natural gas) and quarrying, well operation, milling, refining and processing, and other preparation customarily done at the mine or well site or as a part of extraction activity. (Mineral preparation plants are usually operated together with mines or quarries.) Exploration for minerals is included as is the development of mineral properties.

The principal governmental sources of these data are the *Minerals Yearbook* and *Mineral Commodity Summaries*, published by the U.S. Geological Survey, U.S. Department of the Interior, and various monthly and annual publications of the Energy Information Administration, U.S. Department of Energy. See text, Section 19, for a list of Department of Energy publications.

Mineral statistics, with principal emphasis on commodity detail, have been collected by the U.S. Geological Survey and the former Bureau of Mines since 1880. Current data in U.S. Geological Survey publications cover quantity and value of nonfuel minerals produced, sold, or used by producers, or shipped; quantity of minerals stocked; crude materials treated and prepared minerals recovered; and consumption of mineral raw materials.

The Economic Census, conducted by the Census Bureau at various intervals since 1840, collects data on mineral industries. Beginning with the 1967 census, legislation provides for a census to be conducted every 5 years for years ending in "2" and "7." Data from the 2022 Economic Census are being released on a flow basis between January 2024 and March 2026. Economic Census data are based on the North American Industry Classification System (NAICS). The Census provides information on operating costs, capital expenditures, labor, equipment, and energy requirements in relation to their value of shipments and other receipts for mineral industry establishments.

Table 924. Natural Resource–Related Industries—Establishments, Employees, and Annual Payroll by Industry: 2020 and 2022

[In units as indicated (1,499.5 represents 1,499,500; 99,131 represents $99,131,000,000). Excludes most government employees, railroad employees, and self-employed persons. See source for definitions and statement on reliability of data. An establishment is a single physical location where business is conducted or where services or industrial operations are performed. See Appendix III]

Industry	NAICS code [1]	Establishments (number)		Number of employees [2] (1,000)		Annual payroll (mil. dol.)	
		2020	2022	2020	2022	2020	2022
Natural resource–related industries, total.........	(X)	**64,272**	**64,327**	**1,499.5**	**1,478.0**	**99,131**	**114,517**
Percent of all industries....................................	(X)	0.8	0.8	1.1	1.1	1.3	1.3
Forestry, fishing, hunting, and agriculture support...	**11**	**22,747**	**23,332**	**167.2**	**168.6**	**8,003**	**8,922**
Forestry and logging...............................	113	8,212	8,126	50.7	49.7	2,611	2,773
Timber tract operations..................................	1131	465	477	3.6	3.8	230	248
Forest nurseries and gathering forest products........	1132	188	184	1.0	1.0	42	52
Logging...	1133	7,559	7,465	46.1	45.0	2,340	2,473
Fishing, hunting and trapping...........................	114	2,927	3,071	7.1	7.2	465	533
Fishing..	1141	2,559	2,637	5.3	5.3	394	447
Hunting and trapping..............................	1142	368	434	1.8	1.9	70	86
Agriculture and forestry support activities................	115	11,608	12,135	109.4	111.7	4,927	5,616
Crop production support activities......................	1151	5,086	5,263	74.0	73.0	3,341	3,680
Animal production support activities....................	1152	4,675	4,893	21.7	23.0	852	999
Forestry support activities...........................	1153	1,847	1,979	13.7	15.6	734	937
Mining, quarrying and oil, and gas extraction.........	**21**	**23,908**	**23,180**	**577.9**	**508.0**	**49,312**	**55,559**
Oil and gas extraction...................................	211	5,779	5,276	100.2	84.8	14,281	14,716
Mining (except oil and gas).............................	212	5,812	6,057	170.8	167.7	13,331	14,873
Coal mining..	2121	576	501	43.3	39.8	3,349	4,000
Metal ore mining......................................	2122	303	329	39.3	40.1	3,600	4,177
Nonmetallic mineral mining and quarrying..............	2123	4,933	5,227	88.2	87.8	6,382	6,697
Mining support activities.................................	213	12,317	11,847	306.9	255.5	21,700	25,971
Timber–related manufacturing............................	(X)	**17,617**	**17,815**	**754.4**	**801.4**	**41,816**	**50,036**
Wood product manufacturing.............................	321	13,747	13,993	412.7	446.1	18,904	24,478
Sawmills and wood preservation........................	3211	3,038	3,067	87.7	89.7	4,389	5,402
Veneer, plywood and engineered wood product manufacturing..	3212	1,427	1,445	79.0	85.1	3,990	5,014
Other wood product manufacturing.....................	3219	9,282	9,481	246.0	271.2	10,525	14,062
Paper manufacturing....................................	322	3,870	3,822	341.7	355.3	22,912	25,558
Pulp, paper and paperboard mills........................	3221	430	416	92.5	91.7	7,969	8,261
Converted paper product manufacturing................	3222	3,440	3,406	249.2	263.6	14,943	17,297

X Not applicable. [1] Data based on North American Industry Classification System (NAICS), 2017. [2] Covers full- and part-time employees who are on the payroll in the pay period including March 12.

Source: U.S. Census Bureau, County Business Patterns, "All Sectors: County Business Patterns, including ZIP Code Business Patterns, by Legal Form of Organization and Employment Size Class for the U.S., States, and Selected Geographies: 2022," <data.census.gov>, accessed June 2024. See also <census.gov/programs-surveys/cbp.html>.

Table 925. Natural Resource–Related Industries—Establishments, Sales, Payroll, and Employees by Industry: 2022

[597 represents $597,000,000,000. Includes only establishments with payroll. Data are based on the 2022 Economic Census, which is subject to nonsampling error. For details on methodology and nonsampling and sampling errors, see Appendix III]

Industry	2022 NAICS code [1]	Establishments (number)	Value of shipments (bil. dol.)	Annual payroll (bil. dol.)	Paid employees [2] (1,000)
Mining..	21	22,472	597	52	565
Oil & gas extraction...............................	211	5,039	413	12	105
Mining (except oil & gas)..........................	212	5,819	98	14	173
Mining support activities...........................	213	11,614	86	25	287
Manufacturing [3]......................................	31–33	286,493	7,061	815	12,261
Wood product manufacturing......................	321	14,183	171	23	435
Paper manufacturing...............................	322	3,876	220	25	348
Petroleum & coal products manufacturing........	324	2,089	882	12	101

[1] Data based on North American Industry Classification System (NAICS), 2022. [2] For pay period including March 12. [3] Includes other industries, not shown separately.

Source: U.S. Census Bureau, 2022 Economic Census of the United States, Table EC2221BASIC, "Mining: Summary Statistics for the U.S.: 2022," and Table EC2231BASIC, "Manufacturing: Summary Statistics for the U.S.: 2022," <data.census.gov>, accessed June 2024.

Table 926. Gross Domestic Product of Natural Resource-Related Industries in Current and Chained (2017) Dollars by Industry: 2020 to 2023

[In billions of dollars (21,323.0 represents $21,323,000,000,000). Data are based on the North American Industry Classification System (NAICS); see text, Section 15. Data include nonfactor charges (capital consumption allowances, indirect business taxes, etc.) as well as factor charges against gross product; corporate profits and capital consumption allowances have been shifted from a company to an establishment basis]

Industry	Current dollars				Chained (2017) dollars			
	2020	2021	2022	2023	2020	2021	2022	2023
All industries, total [1]	**21,323.0**	**23,594.0**	**25,744.1**	**27,360.9**	**20,234.1**	**21,407.7**	**21,822.0**	**22,376.9**
Private industries	18,612.2	20,784.8	22,807.5	24,253.5	17,761.9	18,909.5	19,283.1	19,804.2
Natural resource-related industries [2]	**470.1**	**682.3**	**859.5**	**763.0**	**583.7**	**553.4**	**509.8**	**566.6**
Percent of all industries	2.2	2.9	3.3	2.8	2.9	2.6	2.3	2.5
Agriculture, forestry, fishing, and hunting	160.8	225.7	270.8	251.7	173.7	183.7	170.1	180.1
Farms	117.0	180.9	223.5	203.5	130.2	141.1	128.6	136.6
Forestry, fishing, and related activities	43.8	44.7	47.3	48.3	43.0	42.1	41.6	43.6
Mining	201.6	332.0	457.4	380.9	305.6	269.5	245.3	293.4
Oil and gas extraction	103.2	222.0	324.5	236.7	210.9	161.0	135.8	180.0
Mining, except oil and gas	57.1	67.4	78.3	83.2	55.1	54.8	54.9	56.7
Support activities for mining	41.3	42.7	54.6	60.9	47.4	52.6	61.4	59.1
Timber-related manufacturing	107.8	124.6	131.2	130.4	104.5	100.2	94.4	93.1
Wood products	42.9	60.0	62.1	60.0	36.9	35.8	34.3	36.9
Paper products	64.9	64.6	69.2	70.4	67.5	64.4	60.2	56.3

[1] Includes industries not shown separately. [2] Sum of agriculture, forestry, fishing, and hunting; mining; and timber-related manufacturing.

Source: U.S. Bureau of Economic Analysis, Industry Economic Data, GDP-by-Industry, "Value Added by Industry" and "Real Value Added by Industry," <www.bea.gov/itable/gdp-by-industry>, accessed May 2024.

Table 927. Timber–Based Manufacturing Industries—Establishments, Shipments, Payroll, and Employees: 2017

[107,214,630 represents $107,214,630,000. Includes only establishments or firms with payroll. See Appendix III]

Industry	NAICS code [1]	Establish-ments (number)	Value of shipments ($1,000)	Annual payroll ($1,000)	Paid employees [2]
Wood product manufacturing	**321**	**14,645**	**107,214,630**	**16,814,046**	**393,459**
Saw mills	321113	2,891	26,076,004	3,491,826	72,958
Wood preservation	321114	415	6,598,491	508,251	10,268
Hardwood veneer and plywood manufacturing	321211	236	3,129,223	508,967	12,069
Softwood veneer and plywood manufacturing	321212	86	4,240,227	709,411	13,965
Engineered wood member (except truss) manufacturing	321213	112	2,067,452	251,214	4,982
Truss manufacturing	321214	800	6,492,236	1,264,406	30,994
Reconstituted wood product manufacturing	321219	203	8,615,109	819,591	13,719
Wood window and door manufacturing	321911	1,117	12,212,352	2,338,538	52,071
Cut stock, resawing lumber, and planing	321912	833	5,878,591	841,300	21,555
Other millwork (including flooring)	321918	1,568	7,282,366	1,256,121	32,983
Wood container and pallet manufacturing	321920	2,729	9,551,288	1,956,953	55,389
Manufactured home (mobile home) manufacturing	321991	236	4,271,307	845,405	21,182
Prefabricated wood building manufacturing	321992	644	4,207,937	765,697	17,777
All other miscellaneous wood product manufacturing	321999	2,775	6,592,047	1,256,366	33,547
Paper manufacturing	**322**	**4,046**	**186,385,471**	**21,277,301**	**333,712**
Pulp mills	322110	35	6,862,408	823,592	9,349
Paper (except newsprint) mills	322121	167	36,968,156	3,522,358	48,615
Newsprint mills	322122	9	880,301	103,890	1,248
Paperboard mills	322130	156	32,734,398	3,215,993	36,586
Corrugated and solid fiber box manufacturing	322211	1,236	44,943,191	5,255,689	84,975
Folding paperboard box manufacturing	322212	448	12,486,722	1,946,488	35,462
Other paperboard container manufacturing	322219	289	8,401,957	1,042,956	21,698
Paper bag and coated and treated paper manufacturing	322220	751	21,521,926	2,841,491	47,945
Stationery product manufacturing	322230	378	5,769,014	763,851	16,048
Sanitary paper product manufacturing	322291	132	11,449,543	1,047,846	17,566
All other converted paper product manufacturing	322299	445	4,367,855	713,147	14,220

[1] North American Industry Classification System, 2017. [2] For pay period including March 12.

Source: U.S. Census Bureau, 2017 Economic Census, "EC1700BASIC: All sectors: Summary Statistics for the U.S., States, and Selected Geographies: 2017," <data.census.gov>, accessed November 2021.

Table 928. Timber-Based Manufacturing Industries—Employees, Payroll, and Shipments: 2021

[In units, as indicated (11,206 represents 11,206,000). Based on the Annual Survey of Manufactures, see Appendix III]

Selected industry	NAICS code [1]	All employees			Produc-tion workers, total (1,000)	Value added by manufactures		Value of ship-ments (mil. dol.)
		Number (1,000)	Payroll			Total (mil. dol.)	Per produc-tion worker (dol.)	
			Total (mil. dol.)	Per employee (dol.)				
Manufacturing, all industries [2]	31–33	11,206	727,734	64,942	7,966	2,789,460	350,179	6,079,602
Timber-based manufacturing, total	321–322	729	43,583	59,761	579	169,286	292,152	353,013
Percent of total manufacturing	(X)	6.5	6.0	(X)	7.3	6.1	(X)	5.8
Wood product manufacturing	321	399	20,466	51,310	327	78,536	240,376	154,756
Sawmills and wood preservation	3211	82	4,645	56,880	71	26,152	370,450	47,776
Veneer, plywood, and engineered wood product	3212	74	4,234	57,035	59	19,168	327,238	37,155
Other wood product	3219	243	11,587	47,689	198	33,216	168,138	69,825
Millwork	32191	108	5,497	50,914	86	16,998	197,861	34,527
Wood container and pallet	32192	57	2,489	43,732	49	6,270	128,366	13,744
All other wood products	32199	78	3,600	46,115	63	9,947	158,410	21,554
Manufactured (mobile) home	321991	23	994	43,319	19	2,732	144,203	5,714
Prefabricated wood building	321992	19	932	47,829	15	2,527	172,477	6,461
All other misc. wood product	321999	36	1,673	46,979	29	4,688	160,572	9,379
Paper manufacturing	322	330	23,117	69,962	253	90,750	359,088	198,258
Pulp, paper, and paperboard mills	3221	91	7,810	85,997	69	41,444	599,395	75,347
Pulp mills	32211	9	971	102,768	7	3,663	501,681	7,446
Paper mills	32212	44	3,384	76,122	33	18,341	561,827	32,836
Paperboard mills	32213	37	3,455	93,600	29	19,440	665,833	35,065
Converted paper product	3222	240	15,307	63,884	184	49,306	268,582	122,910
Paperboard container	32221	140	9,073	65,012	109	25,853	236,310	73,517
Paper bag and coated and treated paper	32222	51	3,435	67,313	37	9,896	264,144	23,973
Stationery product	32223	14	741	52,113	11	1,793	156,555	5,141
Other converted paper products	32229	35	2,059	59,137	25	11,766	465,638	20,280

X Not applicable. [1] North American Industry Classification System, 2017; see text, Section 15. [2] Includes other industries, not shown separately.

Source: U.S. Census Bureau, Annual Survey of Manufactures, "Summary Statistics for Industry Groups and Industries in the U.S.: 2018-2021," <data.census.gov>, accessed February 2023.

Table 929. Forest Land and Timberland by Type of Owner and Region: 2017

[In thousands of acres (765,493 represents 765,493,000). As of January 1. Data are from the U.S. Forest Service's Forest Inventory and Analysis National Program. Forest land is land at least 10 percent stocked by forest trees of any size, including land that formerly had such tree cover and that will be naturally or artificially regenerated. The minimum area for classification of forest land is 1 acre and a crown width of at least 120 feet wide. Timberland is forest land that is producing or is capable of producing crops of industrial wood and that is not withdrawn from timber utilization by statute or administrative regulation]

Region	Forest land, total	Timberland						
		Total	Federal				State, county, and municipal	Private [1]
			Total	National forest	Bureau of Land Manage-ment lands	Other		
Total	**765,493**	**514,425**	**108,178**	**96,138**	**6,109**	**5,931**	**47,095**	**359,152**
North	175,789	164,894	11,348	10,146	12	1,190	25,650	127,896
Northeast	84,727	78,539	2,852	2,355	–	498	10,102	65,586
North Central	91,062	86,355	8,495	7,792	12	692	15,549	62,310
South	245,513	208,092	16,397	12,258	–	4,138	9,561	182,135
Southeast	89,692	85,754	7,016	5,061	–	1,955	5,618	73,119
South Central	155,821	122,338	9,380	7,197	–	2,183	3,942	109,016
Rocky Mountains	130,641	69,654	47,111	44,206	2,688	217	3,193	19,350
Great Plains	6,797	6,084	1,217	1,051	18	148	265	4,602
Intermountain	123,844	63,569	45,894	43,154	2,670	70	2,927	14,748
Pacific Coast	213,549	71,784	33,323	29,527	3,409	386	8,691	29,771
Alaska	128,735	12,996	4,874	3,848	812	213	4,810	3,313
Pacific Northwest	51,827	41,462	19,200	16,802	2,299	98	3,637	18,625
Pacific Southwest [2]	32,986	17,326	9,249	8,877	297	75	245	7,833

– Represents or rounds to zero. [1] Includes Indian lands. [2] Includes Hawaii.

Source: U.S. Forest Service, National Assessment - Resources Planning Act (RPA), *Forest Resources of the United States, 2017: A Technical Document Supporting the Forest Service 2020 Update of the RPA Assessment,* May 2018. See also <doi.org/10.2737/WO-GTR-97>.

Table 930. National Forest System Lands by State: 2023

[In thousands of acres (233,296 represents 233,296,000). As of September 30, 2023. Data do not include Delaware, District of Columbia, Hawaii, Iowa, Maryland, Massachusetts, New Jersey, and Rhode Island]

State	Total lands	National Forest System lands[1]	Other lands[2]	State	Total lands	National Forest System lands[1]	Other lands[2]
United States....	**233,296**	**193,130**	**40,166**	Nevada...........	6,188	5,760	428
Alabama...........	1,290	673	617	New Hampshire.......	851	754	97
Alaska...........	23,944	22,141	1,803	New Mexico.........	10,249	9,230	1,019
Arizona...........	11,813	11,180	633	New York...........	17	16	(Z)
Arkansas...........	3,600	2,594	1,007	North Carolina.......	3,140	1,258	1,882
California...........	24,290	20,833	3,457	North Dakota.........	1,106	1,103	3
Colorado...........	15,960	14,490	1,470	Ohio...........	856	244	612
Connecticut..........	(Z)	(Z)	–	Oklahoma...........	883	400	483
Florida...........	1,750	1,217	533	Oregon...........	17,655	15,700	1,954
Georgia...........	1,856	868	988	Pennsylvania........	741	514	227
Idaho...........	21,714	20,449	1,264	South Carolina.......	1,538	639	899
Illinois...........	958	305	653	South Dakota........	2,436	2,007	429
Indiana...........	647	204	443	Tennessee...........	1,368	725	643
Kansas...........	109	109	(Z)	Texas...........	2,013	757	1,256
Kentucky...........	2,232	819	1,414	Utah...........	9,205	8,193	1,012
Louisiana...........	1,032	608	424	Vermont...........	837	414	423
Maine...........	94	54	41	Virginia...........	3,258	1,674	1,584
Michigan...........	4,888	2,879	2,009	Washington.........	11,985	9,338	2,647
Minnesota...........	5,488	2,845	2,642	West Virginia.........	1,893	1,047	846
Mississippi...........	2,382	1,191	1,191	Wisconsin...........	2,003	1,526	476
Missouri...........	3,093	1,510	1,583	Wyoming...........	9,725	9,226	499
Montana...........	19,195	17,254	1,942	Puerto Rico.........	56	29	27
Nebraska...........	562	351	211	Virgin Islands........	(Z)	(Z)	–

– Represents zero. Z Less than 500 acres. [1] National Forest System is a nationally significant system of federally owned units of forest, range, and related land consisting of national forests, purchase units, national grasslands, land utilization project areas, experimental forest areas, experimental range areas, designated experimental areas, and other land areas; water areas; and interests in lands that are administered by USDA Forest Service or designated for administration through the Forest Service. [2] Other lands are lands within the unit boundaries in private, state, county, and municipal ownership and the federal lands over which the Forest Service has no jurisdiction. Also includes lands offered to the United States and approved for acquisition and subsequent Forest Service administration, but to which title has not yet been accepted by the United States.

Source: U.S. Forest Service, *Land Areas of the National Forest System as of September 30, 2023*, October 2023. See also <www.fs.usda.gov/land/staff/lar/LAR2023/lar2023index.html>.

Table 931. Timber Volume, Growth, and Removal on Timberland by Species Group and Region: 2016 and 2017

[In millions of cubic feet (1,116,012 represents 1,116,012,000,000). Data are from the U.S. Forest Service's Forest Inventory and Analysis National Program]

Region	2017 Net volume[1]						2016 Net growth and removals of growing stock					
	All timber[2]			Growing stock[3]			Timber growth[4]			Timber removals[5]		
	All species	Soft-woods	Hard-woods	All species	Soft-woods	Hard-woods	All species	Soft-woods	Hard-woods	All species	Soft-woods	Hard-woods
Total....	**1,116,012**	**598,873**	**517,139**	**985,238**	**560,526**	**424,712**	**25,009**	**15,468**	**9,542**	**13,041**	**8,901**	**4,140**
North...........	314,204	68,278	245,926	270,041	60,601	209,440	5,932	1,546	4,386	2,491	654	1,837
Northeast...........	172,556	41,465	131,091	152,780	37,108	115,672	3,264	917	2,347	1,176	377	799
North Central........	141,647	26,813	114,834	117,261	23,494	93,768	2,668	629	2,039	1,315	277	1,038
South...........	377,781	149,800	227,981	319,088	141,307	177,781	13,764	9,268	4,496	7,859	5,647	2,212
Southeast...........	167,894	71,539	96,355	142,603	67,540	75,063	6,393	4,285	2,108	3,527	2,736	790
South Central........	209,887	78,261	131,626	176,485	73,767	102,717	7,371	4,983	2,388	4,333	2,911	1,422
Rocky Mountains...	144,222	128,750	15,472	130,005	119,102	10,903	299	189	109	405	396	8,626
Great Plains.........	8,476	2,537	5,938	4,487	1,885	2,601	57	-2	59	34	29	6
Intermountain........	135,747	126,213	9,534	125,518	117,217	8,301	242	192	50	370	367	3
Pacific Coast........	279,805	252,044	27,760	266,104	239,515	26,589	5,015	4,465	550	2,286	2,204	82
Alaska...........	39,229	35,639	3,590	37,140	33,761	3,379	254	133	121	39	39	(Z)
Pacific Northwest....	166,844	153,680	13,163	159,238	146,480	12,758	3,707	3,423	284	1,892	1,811	81
Pacific Southwest[6]..	73,732	62,725	11,007	69,726	59,273	10,452	1,054	909	145	355	355	(Z)

Z Less than 500,000. [1] As of January 1. [2] Includes growing stock, live cull and sound dead. [3] Live trees of commercial species meeting specified standards of quality or vigor. Cull trees are excluded. Includes only trees 5.0-inches in diameter or larger at 4 1/2 feet above ground. [4] The net increase in the volume of trees during a specified year. Components include the increment in net volume of trees at the beginning of the specific year surviving to its end, plus the net volume of trees reaching the minimum size class during the year, minus the volume of trees that died during the year, and minus the net volume of trees that became cull trees during the year. [5] The net volume of trees removed from the inventory during a specified year by harvesting, cultural operations such as timber stand improvement, or land clearing. [6] Includes Hawaii.

Source: U.S. Forest Service, National Assessment - Resources Planning Act (RPA), *Forest Resources of the United States, 2017: A Technical Document Supporting the Forest Service 2020 Update of the RPA Assessment,* May 2018. See also <doi.org/10.2737/WO-GTR-97>.

Table 932. Timber Removals—Roundwood Product Output by Source and Species Group: 2016

[In millions of cubic feet (13,972 represents 13,972,000,000). Data are from U.S. Forest Service's Forest Inventory and Analysis National Program]

Source and species group	Total	Sawlogs	Pulpwood	Veneer logs	Other products [1]	Fuelwood [2]
Total............................	**13,972**	**5,521**	**5,368**	**660**	**728**	**1,695**
Softwoods............................	9,480	4,075	3,640	590	576	599
Hardwoods............................	4,493	1,446	1,728	69	153	1,096
Growing stock [3].....................	11,650	5,334	4,773	648	563	332
Softwoods............................	8,393	3,959	3,280	582	423	149
Hardwoods............................	3,257	1,374	1,493	65	141	183
Other sources [4].....................	2,323	187	596	12	165	1,363
Softwoods............................	1,086	115	360	8	153	450
Hardwoods............................	1,236	72	235	4	12	913

[1] Includes poles, pilings, posts, cooperage and miscellaneous products. [2] Downed and dead wood volume left on the ground after trees have been cut on timberland and used for conversion to some form of energy, primarily in residential use. [3] Includes live trees of commercial species meeting specified standards of quality or vigor. Cull trees are excluded. Includes only trees 5.0 inches in diameter or larger at 4.5 feet above the ground. [4] Includes salvable dead trees, rough and rotten trees, trees of noncommercial species, trees less than 5.0 inches in diameter at 4.5 feet above the ground, tops, and roundwood harvested from nonforest land (for example, fence rows).

Source: U.S. Forest Service, National Assessment - Resources Planning Act (RPA), *Forest Resources of the United States, 2017: A Technical Document Supporting the Forest Service 2020 Update of the RPA Assessment,* May 2018. See also <doi.org/10.2737/WO-GTR-97>.

Table 933. Timber Products—Production, Foreign Trade, and Consumption by Type of Product: 1990 to 2017

[In millions of cubic feet, roundwood equivalent (15,577 represents 15,577,000,000)]

Type of product	1990	2000	2010	2011	2012	2013	2014	2015	2016	2017
Industrial roundwood:										
Domestic production.............	15,577	15,528	11,006	11,587	12,046	12,547	12,954	13,124	13,329	13,643
Softwoods........................	10,968	10,327	8,235	8,672	9,079	9,399	9,630	9,715	9,925	10,181
Hardwoods........................	4,609	5,201	2,771	2,914	2,967	3,148	3,324	3,409	3,403	3,463
Imports............................	3,044	4,626	2,488	2,469	2,564	2,838	3,119	3,257	3,615	3,522
Exports............................	2,413	2,039	1,888	2,118	2,073	2,320	2,304	2,214	2,216	2,315
Consumption.....................	16,208	18,115	11,607	11,938	12,537	13,065	13,769	14,167	14,727	14,851
Softwoods........................	11,620	12,830	8,912	9,120	9,681	10,073	10,585	10,931	11,495	11,624
Hardwoods........................	4,588	5,285	2,695	2,818	2,856	2,992	3,184	3,235	3,233	3,227
Lumber:										
Domestic production.............	7,317	7,384	4,569	5,005	5,219	5,607	5,995	6,065	6,143	6,338
Imports............................	1,905	2,943	1,422	1,403	1,480	1,703	1,915	2,097	2,426	2,328
Exports............................	697	435	389	454	464	519	545	492	527	580
Consumption.....................	8,526	9,892	5,602	5,955	6,234	6,791	7,366	7,670	8,042	8,086
Plywood and veneer:										
Domestic production.............	1,423	1,187	655	651	679	703	693	688	703	729
Imports............................	97	154	161	166	176	205	209	244	263	285
Exports............................	109	51	55	52	57	55	46	39	43	47
Consumption.....................	1,410	1,290	760	765	798	853	856	893	923	967
Pulp products:										
Domestic production.............	5,313	5,881	4,863	4,922	5,088	5,068	5,016	5,056	5,099	5,081
Imports............................	1,038	1,448	880	875	874	902	969	882	896	875
Exports............................	645	776	802	887	864	1,040	1,016	1,009	995	1,013
Consumption.....................	5,705	6,553	4,941	4,911	5,099	4,929	4,969	4,929	5,000	4,943
Logs: [1]										
Imports............................	4	72	20	19	28	26	22	29	24	32
Exports............................	674	422	407	485	432	463	444	363	390	393
Pulpwood chips, exports..........	288	355	235	241	256	242	253	311	262	280
Other industrial timber products: [2]										
Production and consumption....	562	300	277	283	373	463	552	642	732	822
Fuelwood:										
Production and consumption....	2,900	1,622	1,725	1,804	1,882	1,960	2,039	2,117	2,195	2,273

[1] Prior to 2010, pulpwood logs are not included in logs. [2] Includes cooperage logs, poles and piling, fence posts, hewn ties, round mine timbers, box bolts, etc.

Source: U.S. Forest Service, *U.S. Timber Production, Trade, Consumption, and Price Statistics, 1965-2017,* July 2019. See also <www.fs.usda.gov/treesearch/pubs/58506>.

Table 934. Selected Timber Products—Imports and Exports: 1990 to 2017

[In million board feet (13,107 represents 13,107,000,000), except as indicated]

Product	Unit	1990	2000	2010	2012	2013	2014	2015	2016	2017
IMPORTS										
Lumber, total.................	Mil. bd. ft.	13,107	20,243	9,769	10,172	11,713	13,170	14,429	16,730	16,058
Softwood.....................	Mil. bd. ft.	12,875	19,449	9,468	9,864	11,358	12,729	13,947	16,323	15,704
Hardwood...................	Mil. bd. ft.	232	795	301	308	355	441	482	407	354
From Canada...............	Mil. bd. ft.	11,918	18,616	9,151	9,633	11,044	12,311	13,413	15,555	14,479
Logs, total [1]...................	Mil. bd. ft. [2]	23	450	126	176	164	139	139	116	153
Softwood.....................	Mil. bd. ft.	13	390	99	136	120	99	97	79	69
Hardwood...................	Mil. bd. ft.	10	59	28	41	44	40	42	37	83
From Canada...............	Mil. bd. ft.	19	426	120	133	161	137	136	114	147
Paper and board [3]............	1,000 tons	12,195	17,356	11,144	10,441	10,967	11,301	10,746	10,512	10,454
Woodpulp....................	1,000 tons	4,893	7,227	6,163	5,599	6,112	6,126	5,872	6,161	6,026
Plywood......................	Mil. sq. ft. [4]	1,687	2,902	3,046	3,339	3,873	3,955	4,609	4,926	5,314
EXPORTS										
Lumber, total.................	Mil. bd. ft.	4,566	2,700	2,425	2,900	3,250	3,387	3,056	3,261	3,585
To: Canada...................	Mil. bd. ft.	658	701	621	634	636	600	533	553	549
Japan......................	Mil. bd. ft.	1,270	325	179	189	207	162	153	130	122
European Union...........	Mil. bd. ft.	686	507	209	166	164	196	174	189	173
Softwood....................	Mil. bd. ft.	3,753	1,400	1,347	1,582	1,788	1,734	1,563	1,602	1,700
Hardwood...................	Mil. bd. ft.	813	1,300	1,078	1,318	1,462	1,653	1,493	1,659	1,885
Logs, total [1]...................	Mil. bd. ft. [2]	4,213	2,638	2,542	2,698	2,897	2,778	1,742	1,872	1,888
To: Canada...................	Mil. bd. ft. [2]	396	1,350	835	754	641	593	507	464	386
Japan......................	Mil. bd. ft. [2]	2,626	934	425	469	531	478	324	314	303
China......................	Mil. bd. ft. [2]	362	22	780	1,052	1,399	1,385	741	942	1,028
Softwood....................	Mil. bd. ft.	3,994	2,066	2,074	2,280	2,550	2,336	1,411	1,515	1,522
Hardwood...................	Mil. bd. ft.	220	573	468	418	348	442	330	357	366
Paper and board [3]............	1,000 tons	5,163	8,701	8,781	9,036	12,842	12,743	12,326	11,679	12,274
Woodpulp....................	1,000 tons	5,905	6,409	8,265	8,125	8,147	7,901	8,096	8,315	8,367
Plywood......................	Mil. sq. ft. [4]	1,766	916	1,004	1,039	990	832	710	774	859

[1] Prior to 2000, pulpwood logs are not included. [2] Log scale. [3] Includes paper and board products. Excludes hardboard. [4] 3/8 inch basis.

Source: U.S. Forest Service. *U.S. Timber Production, Trade, Consumption, and Price Statistics, 1965-2017*, July 2019. See also <www.fs.usda.gov/treesearch/pubs/58506>.

Table 935. Lumber Production and Consumption by Species Group: 1990 to 2017

[In billion board feet (48.1 represents 48,100,000,000), except per capita in board feet. Per capita consumption based on estimated resident population as of July 1]

Item	1990	1995	2000	2005	2010	2011	2012	2013	2014	2015	2016	2017
Production, total.................	**48.1**	**44.9**	**48.6**	**50.9**	**30.5**	**33.3**	**34.8**	**37.3**	**39.8**	**40.3**	**40.8**	**42.2**
By species:												
Softwoods......................	35.8	32.2	36.0	39.8	24.8	26.8	28.3	30.0	31.5	32.0	32.5	33.9
Hardwoods.....................	12.3	12.6	12.6	11.2	5.7	6.6	6.5	7.3	8.3	8.3	8.3	8.3
Consumption, total..............	**55.3**	**60.3**	**66.6**	**72.3**	**37.7**	**40.6**	**43.6**	**47.2**	**50.9**	**54.0**	**53.6**	**38.6**
Per capita.......................	221	229	236	244	122	130	139	149	159	168	166	118
By species:												
Softwoods......................	43.6	48.4	54.6	61.6	32.7	35.0	38.0	40.9	43.7	46.8	46.6	32.2
Hardwoods.....................	11.7	12.0	11.9	10.6	4.9	5.7	5.6	6.3	7.1	7.2	7.0	6.4

Source: U.S. Forest Service, *U.S. Timber Production, Trade, Consumption, and Price Statistics, 1965-2017*, July 2019. See also <www.fs.usda.gov/treesearch/pubs/58506>.

Table 936. Pulpwood Consumption, Woodpulp Production, and Paper and Board Production and Consumption: 1990 to 2017

[In thousands (99,361 represents 99,361,000) except where otherwise indicated]

Item	Unit	1990	2000	2010	2012	2013	2014	2015	2016	2017
Pulpwood consumption.......	1,000 cords [1]	99,361	95,904	89,306	90,744	87,319	86,714	84,979	85,798	84,152
Woodpulp production [2].......	1,000 tons	63,048	62,758	55,343	55,475	54,466	53,367	52,646	52,701	52,701
Paper and board: [3]										
Production.....................	1,000 tons	78,679	94,491	82,968	80,916	80,478	79,488	79,024	78,342	78,445
Consumption [4]................	1,000 tons	85,711	103,147	85,331	82,321	78,603	78,046	77,444	77,175	76,625
Per capita..................	Pounds	686	731	551	524	497	489	482	477	470

[1] One cord equals 128 cubic feet. [2] Includes dissolving and special alpha pulps; excludes defibrated/exploded pulps and screenings. [3] Excludes wet machine board and construction grades. [4] Production plus imports, minus exports.

Source: U.S. Forest Service, *U.S. Timber Production, Trade, Consumption, and Price Statistics, 1965-2017*, July 2019. See also <www.fs.usda.gov/treesearch/pubs/58506>.

Table 937. Selected Timber Products—Producer Price Indexes: 1990 to 2023

[1982=100, unless otherwise noted. For information about producer prices, see text, Section 14]

Product	1990	2000	2010	2015	2019	2020	2021	2022	2023
Lumber and wood products	**129.7**	**178.2**	**192.7**	**221.9**	**236.7**	**254.5**	**315.5**	**337.8**	**301.1**
Lumber	124.6	178.8	167.3	199.3	210.4	248.2	347.0	342.6	257.5
Softwood lumber	123.8	178.6	160.8	192.7	215.4	280.3	397.7	384.9	264.4
Softwood cut stock and dimension	129.7	195.3	206.0	199.7	204.1	235.6	363.9	347.4	254.7
Softwood lumber, not edge worked [1]	(NA)	(NA)	85.8	104.9	114.4	154.1	217.7	206.0	135.4
Softwood lumber, MFPL [1, 2]	(NA)	(NA)	111.5	128.3	169.2	188.3	267.0	295.1	255.3
Hardwood lumber	131.0	185.9	187.3	221.1	215.1	207.0	279.2	289.7	258.5
Millwork	130.4	176.4	207.0	237.2	263.5	274.5	318.6	367.2	355.2
General millwork	132.0	178.0	211.2	238.0	256.9	261.7	283.6	325.5	332.9
Prefabricated structural members	122.3	175.1	185.6	232.6	295.6	338.4	498.3	582.0	476.6
Plywood	114.2	157.6	176.7	198.9	202.9	229.3	335.2	337.6	281.4
Softwood veneer and plywood	119.6	173.3	197.1	234.5	222.8	270.6	449.6	429.5	324.0
Hardwood veneer and plywood [3]	(NA)	(NA)	103.6	108.6	123.9	125.2	140.4	159.9	160.3
Other wood products	114.7	130.5	142.5	161.4	176.6	177.8	206.6	231.6	217.3
Wood pallets and pallet containers	127.6	178.5	206.6	242.1	281.1	283.0	361.3	421.2	376.2
Wood boxes	119.1	155.2	183.0	199.4	211.5	220.2	242.9	258.8	233.9
Pulp, paper, and allied products	**141.2**	**183.7**	**236.9**	**248.8**	**259.4**	**259.9**	**288.6**	**328.7**	**332.7**
Pulp, paper, and products, excl. building paper	132.9	161.4	206.8	218.4	227.3	224.7	250.7	285.8	286.8
Woodpulp	151.3	145.3	186.0	181.6	174.0	141.7	193.1	236.9	220.0
Recyclable paper	138.9	282.5	421.5	291.8	181.2	244.6	430.1	400.0	230.0
Paper	128.8	149.8	182.1	189.8	200.6	195.4	214.3	241.7	248.7
Writing and printing papers	129.1	146.6	179.5	183.6	197.2	191.0	200.7	232.0	244.5
Newsprint	119.6	127.5	125.6	113.6	138.8	115.6	127.1	164.7	160.3
Paperboard	135.7	176.7	224.9	243.1	268.1	256.6	296.7	347.4	338.3
Converted paper and paperboard products	135.2	162.7	209.0	228.2	241.4	241.3	256.5	294.4	306.5
Sanitary paper products, including stock	135.3	146.7	181.8	182.2	182.7	184.1	187.0	206.3	222.0
Paper, plastic, and foil bags	156.6	173.7	246.0	280.5	285.7	285.3	318.4	348.8	354.0
Paper boxes and containers	129.9	172.6	219.4	247.3	269.5	268.1	289.6	341.1	349.0
Paperboard fiber drums	130.6	180.6	293.4	354.7	433.5	447.4	506.3	555.4	540.4
Office supplies and accessories	121.4	133.8	159.9	174.0	193.7	192.0	199.0	246.4	267.7
Die-cut paper & paperboard office supplies [1]	(NA)	(NA)	125.2	143.8	174.0	176.1	184.4	242.1	283.7
Fiber cans, tubes, and similar fiber products	147.8	205.5	268.6	283.0	331.6	340.8	370.5	466.6	492.4
Building paper & building board mill products	112.2	138.8	168.4	186.3	200.1	260.5	411.3	414.3	322.4
Hardboard, particleboard & fiberboard products	107.5	132.8	158.5	175.2	188.8	245.8	388.0	390.8	304.2

NA Not available. [1] December 2003=100. [2] Made from purchased lumber. [3] December 2005=100.

Source: U.S. Bureau of Labor Statistics, "Producer Price Indexes," <www.bls.gov/ppi>, accessed July 2024.

Table 938. Paper and Paperboard—Production and New Supply: 1990 to 2022

[In millions of short tons (80.55 represents 80,550,000). 1 short ton = 2,000 lbs]

Item	1990	2000	2010	2015	2018	2019	2020	2021	2022
Production, total	**80.55**	**96.05**	**83.70**	**79.80**	**78.87**	**75.38**	**73.60**	**75.15**	**72.71**
Paper, total	39.36	45.52	35.51	29.60	26.25	24.35	21.60	21.02	20.71
Paperboard, total	39.42	48.97	47.46	49.40	51.86	50.28	51.23	53.36	51.22
Recycled & unbleached Kraft board	29.39	37.59	36.41	39.30	41.86	40.44	41.58	43.61	41.95
Recycled	9.03	15.79	15.05	16.89	(NA)	(NA)	(NA)	(NA)	(NA)
Unbleached kraft	20.36	21.80	21.36	22.41	(NA)	(NA)	(NA)	(NA)	(NA)
Semichemical	5.64	5.95	5.44	4.75	4.61	4.48	4.53	4.62	4.18
Bleached kraft	4.26	5.30	5.62	5.35	5.40	5.36	5.12	5.13	5.10
Wet machine board and construction grades	1.82	1.56	0.73	0.80	0.76	0.76	0.77	0.77	0.77
New supply, all grades, excluding products	**87.68**	**105.02**	**84.16**	**79.99**	**79.41**	**76.13**	**73.25**	**75.78**	**74.64**
Paper, total	49.49	57.13	40.34	34.43	31.38	28.98	25.44	25.10	25.57
Newsprint	13.41	12.92	5.00	3.51	2.54	2.11	1.57	1.46	1.41
Printing/writing papers	25.46	32.99	23.73	19.08	16.53	14.56	11.29	11.36	11.95
Packaging and industrial converting papers	4.72	4.27	4.18	4.17	4.41	4.42	4.34	4.52	4.40
Tissue	5.90	6.95	7.43	7.68	7.90	7.88	8.23	7.76	7.82
Paperboard, total	36.30	46.02	43.06	44.77	47.29	46.42	47.07	49.93	48.34

NA Not available.

Source: American Forest and Paper Association, Washington, DC, *Paper Industry Annual Statistical Summary* ©.

Table 939. Per Capita Consumption of Fishery Products: 1910 to 2021

[In units, as indicated. 92.2 represents 92,200,000. Annual per capita consumption of seafood products represents the pounds of edible meat consumed from domestically-caught and imported fish and shellfish adjusted for exports, divided by the civilian resident population of the United States as of July 1 of each year; see source for details]

Year	Civilian resident population (millions)	Pounds per capita			Year	Civilian resident population (millions)	Pounds per capita		
		Total	Fresh and frozen	Canned	Cured			Total	Fresh and frozen	Canned	Cured

Year	Civilian resident population (millions)	Total	Fresh and frozen	Canned	Cured	Year	Civilian resident population (millions)	Total	Fresh and frozen	Canned	Cured
1910 [1]....	92.2	11.2	4.5	2.8	3.9	2008......	302.9	17.6	13.1	4.1	0.3
1920 [1]....	106.5	11.8	6.3	3.2	2.3	2009......	305.8	17.4	13.2	3.9	0.3
1930.....	122.9	10.2	5.8	3.4	1.0	2010......	308.4	17.7	13.1	4.1	0.3
1940.....	132.1	11.0	5.7	4.6	0.7	2011......	310.4	17.8	13.4	4.0	0.3
1950.....	150.8	11.8	6.3	4.9	0.6	2012......	312.7	16.8	12.9	3.6	0.3
1960.....	178.1	10.3	5.7	4.0	0.6	2013......	314.9	17.9	13.8	3.8	0.3
1970.....	201.9	11.8	6.9	4.5	0.4	2014......	317.6	17.3	13.5	3.5	0.3
1980.....	225.6	12.4	7.4	4.7	0.3	2015......	320.2	18.8	14.6	4.0	0.3
1990.....	247.8	15.1	9.5	5.3	0.3	2016......	321.9	18.3	14.4	3.6	0.3
2000.....	280.9	16.8	11.6	4.9	0.3	2017......	324.5	19.1	15.1	3.9	0.3
2004.....	292.4	17.6	12.9	4.4	0.3	2018......	326.0	19.0	15.0	3.6	0.3
2005.....	295.3	18.2	13.4	4.5	0.3	2019......	327.1	19.3	15.1	3.8	0.3
2006.....	298.2	18.4	14.0	4.2	0.3	2020......	331.5	19.0	14.6	4.3	0.3
2007.....	300.5	18.4	14	4.1	0.3	2021......	333.1	20.5	16.4	3.7	0.3

[1] Resident population is used.

Source: U.S. National Oceanic and Atmospheric Administration, National Marine Fisheries Service, "Fisheries One Stop Shop," <www.fisheries.noaa.gov/foss/>, accessed May 2024. See also <www.fisheries.noaa.gov/national/sustainable-fisheries/fisheries-united-states>.

Table 940. Fishery Products—Domestic Catch, Imports, and Disposition: 2010 to 2022

[Live weight, in millions of pounds (13,644 represents 13,644,000,000)]

Item	2010	2015	2016	2017	2018	2019	2020	2021	2022
Total supply....................	**13,644**	**13,219**	**13,437**	**13,630**	**13,889**	**13,362**	**14,230**	**15,712**	**16,649**
Edible, for human food.............	12,407	12,457	12,562	13,093	13,050	13,045	13,559	14,804	15,093
Finfish........................	7,860	7,926	7,866	8,017	7,803	7,934	8,272	8,172	8,802
Shellfish [1]......................	4,547	4,531	4,696	5,076	5,246	5,111	5,287	6,631	6,291
For industrial use [2]...............	1,237	762	875	538	839	317	672	909	1,556
Domestic catch....................	**8,275**	**9,749**	**9,650**	**9,954**	**9,423**	**9,366**	**8,397**	**8,573**	**8,347**
Edible, for human food..........	6,562	7,770	7,546	8,251	7,529	7,586	6,718	7,107	6,770
Finfish........................	5,247	6,639	6,446	7,137	6,436	6,622	5,794	5,769	5,392
Shellfish [1]......................	1,316	1,131	1,100	1,115	1,093	965	924	1,337	1,377
For industrial use [2]...............	1,713	1,979	2,104	1,702	1,894	1,780	1,679	1,466	1,578
Imports [3]........................	**11,493**	**12,077**	**12,298**	**12,653**	**12,990**	**12,433**	**13,049**	**14,383**	**14,863**
Edible, for human food..........	11,010	11,460	11,624	11,880	12,251	11,793	12,298	13,460	13,800
Finfish........................	7,094	7,408	7,465	7,396	7,587	7,203	7,553	7,677	8,398
Shellfish [1]......................	3,916	4,052	4,159	4,484	4,663	4,589	4,745	5,784	5,403
For industrial use [2]...............	483	617	675	773	739	641	751	923	1,063
Exports...........................	**6,124**	**8,607**	**8,512**	**8,976**	**8,523**	**8,438**	**7,215**	**7,244**	**6,562**
Edible, for human food..........	5,165	6,773	6,608	7,039	6,730	6,334	5,457	5,763	5,477
Finfish........................	4,480	6,121	6,045	6,516	6,220	5,892	5,075	5,274	4,988
Shellfish [1]......................	685	652	563	523	510	442	382	490	489
For industrial use [1]...............	959	1,834	1,903	1,938	1,794	2,104	1,758	1,480	1,085
Disposition of domestic catch.................	**8,275**	**9,749**	**9,650**	**9,954**	**9,423**	**9,366**	**8,397**	**8,573**	**8,347**
Fresh and frozen [4]..................	6,554	7,643	7,575	8,122	7,472	7,455	6,600	6,841	6,536
Canned [4]...........................	372	361	183	289	179	169	185	309	217
Cured................................	99	68	58	139	141	150	118	129	142
Reduced to meal, oil, etc...........	1,250	1,677	1,834	1,403	1,630	1,592	1,495	1,294	1,452

[1] For univalve and bivalve mollusks (conchs, clams, oysters, scallops, etc.), the weight of meats, excluding the shell, is reported. [2] Processed into meal, oil, solubles, and shell products, or used as bait and animal food. [3] Includes landings of tuna caught by foreign vessels in American Samoa. [4] Includes for human food and for bait and animal food.

Source: U.S. National Oceanic and Atmospheric Administration, National Marine Fisheries Service, "Fisheries One Stop Shop," <www.fisheries.noaa.gov/foss/>, accessed May 2024.

Table 941. Supply of Selected Shellfish and Fish Products: 2010 to 2022

[In millions of pounds (1,750 represents 1,750,000,000). Totals available for U.S. consumption are supply minus exports plus imports. Round weight is the complete or full weight as caught]

Species	Unit	2010	2015	2016	2017	2018	2019	2020	2021	2022
Shrimp..................	Heads-off weight	1,750	1,764	1,835	2,049	2,154	2,112	2,318	2,722	2,585
Tuna, canned...........	Canned weight	833	704	671	641	689	731	846	694	725
Snow crab..............	Round weight	197	216	205	194	174	187	218	236	148
Clams..................	Meat weight	103	97	87	76	78	82	51	89	119
Salmon, canned [1]......	Canned weight	73	101	-11	92	33	96	61	98	85
American lobster........	Round weight	188	222	231	201	196	205	187	244	200
Spiny lobster...........	Round weight	58	13	27	46	46	43	43	47	39
Scallops................	Meat weight	85	62	68	71	87	80	73	85	72
Oysters................	Meat weight	58	64	62	67	72	56	59	66	79
King crab...............	Round weight	44	52	50	46	49	55	54	58	47
Crab meat, canned....	Canned weight	66	64	61	64	71	64	58	69	64

[1] The method of calculating canned salmon supply does not incorporate annual beginning and ending warehouse stock. Due to the biennial nature of the pink salmon fishery, some salmon canned in one year may be exported in the following year.

Source: U.S. National Oceanic and Atmospheric Administration, National Marine Fisheries Service, "Fisheries One Stop Shop," <www.fisheries.noaa.gov/foss/>, accessed May 2024.

Table 942. Fishery Landings—Quantity and Value of Domestic Catch by Species: 2022

[In thousands (8,347,472 represents 8,347,472,000). Displays data for species with landings over 10 million pounds]

Species	Quantity (1,000)		Value ($1,000)	Species	Quantity (1,000)		Value ($1,000)
	Pounds	Metric tons			Pounds	Metric tons	
Total [1]	**8,347,472**	**3,786**	**5,887,275**	Salmon, Chinook	11,223	5	51,874
Catfish, Blue	10,698	5	6,644	Salmon, Chum	91,251	41	97,208
Clam, Quahog, Ocean	30,235	14	26,258	Salmon, Coho	12,970	6	20,510
Clam, Surf, Atlantic	51,583	23	50,721	Salmon, Pink	216,250	98	108,573
Cod, Pacific	402,998	183	183,113	Salmon, Sockeye	383,247	174	548,903
Crab, Blue	115,462	52	220,352	Scallop, Sea	31,806	14	480,374
Crab, Dungeness	36,413	17	181,200	Scup	12,109	5	10,047
Crab, Jonah	13,230	6	22,008	Seaweed, Rockweed	12,843	6	523
Flounder, Arrowtooth	38,087	17	4,773	Shark, Dogfish, Spiny	10,252	5	2,274
Flounder, Summer	10,217	5	26,151	Shrimp, Brown	53,580	24	95,707
Goosefish	14,683	7	12,944	Shrimp, Northern Pink	15,105	7	38,582
Haddock	11,054	5	17,960	Shrimp, Northern White	116,429	53	235,310
Hake, Pacific (Whiting)	576,960	262	64,060	Shrimp, Ocean	65,539	30	30,444
Halibut, Pacific	25,038	11	136,950	Skate, Winter	12,447	6	3,258
Herring, Pacific	95,129	43	14,789	Sole, Dover	10,198	5	4,094
Lobster, American	120,586	55	519,846	Sole, Flathead	31,188	14	5,762
Mackerel, Atka	128,425	58	31,525	Sole, Rock	40,324	18	7,771
Mullet, Striped	10,664	5	9,315	Sole, Yellowfin	333,986	151	61,941
Oyster, Eastern	18,232	8	212,579	Squid, California Market	146,715	67	87,739
Pollock, Walleye	2,703,995	1,227	512,995	Squid, Longfin Loligo	40,607	18	60,638
Rockfish, Pacific Ocean Perch	137,661	62	25,473	Squid, Shortfin Illex	12,586	6	6,874
Rockfish, Widow	26,688	12	7,442	Tuna, Albacore	16,452	7	35,650
Sablefish	69,228	31	169,457	Tuna, Bigeye	16,408	7	84,125

[1] Total for all fishery landings, including those species not shown separately and species withheld or not reported.

Source: U.S. National Oceanic and Atmospheric Administration, National Marine Fisheries Service, "Fisheries One Stop Shop," <www.fisheries.noaa.gov/foss/>, accessed May 2024. See also <www.fisheries.noaa.gov/national/sustainable-fisheries/fisheries-united-states>.

Table 943. Fishery Landings—Quantity and Value of Catch by Selected Port: 2010 to 2022

[In millions (101 represents 101,000,000. Data shown for top 25 ports by volume for most recent year]

Landing port	Quantity (millions of pounds)					Value (millions of dollars)				
	2010	2015	2020	2021	2022	2010	2015	2020	2021	2022
Astoria, OR	101	92	182	155	150	31	38	43	53	42
Atlantic City, NJ	24	26	18	18	27	17	20	12	12	23
Bayou La Batre, AL	3	20	28	29	28	5	37	62	77	60
Cape May-Wildwood, NJ	43	77	104	114	65	81	72	93	148	40
Cordova, AK	148	162	42	123	65	84	65	26	70	76
Dulac-Chauvin, LA	33	31	27	31	36	45	45	39	54	59
Dutch Harbor, AK	515	787	800	745	614	163	218	187	249	160
Egegik, AK	(NA)	(NA)	20	16	35	(NA)	(NA)	30	26	47
Empire-Venice, LA	354	379	210	303	498	59	111	68	102	163
Gloucester, MA	89	68	49	47	34	57	44	50	80	59
Honolulu, HI	24	32	25	27	26	72	97	76	119	122
Intracoastal City, LA	335	428	137	296	295	31	33	16	34	25
Ketchikan, AK	76	84	21	60	54	41	40	16	44	46
Kodiak, AK	325	514	364	299	285	128	138	88	121	139
Los Angeles, CA	187	15	15	20	37	38	8	13	17	27
Naknek, AK	124	176	154	161	235	101	69	242	245	299
New Bedford, MA	133	124	115	104	88	306	322	377	570	443
Newport, OR	57	65	117	113	100	31	33	60	74	48
Petersburg, AK	50	70	18	44	37	36	39	21	38	37
Point Judith, RI	36	46	43	44	39	32	46	47	72	71
Port Hueneme-Oxnard-Ventura, CA	131	44	7	38	105	37	21	13	32	74
Reedville, VA	426	350	302	301	325	34	33	64	467	52
Seward, AK	75	94	26	31	18	69	59	23	37	41
Sitka, AK	75	87	30	79	69	62	59	33	73	78
Westport, WA	101	84	113	133	112	39	65	51	72	87

NA Not available.

Source: U.S. National Oceanic and Atmospheric Administration, National Marine Fisheries Service, "Fisheries One Stop Shop," <www.fisheries.noaa.gov/foss/>, accessed May 2024. See also <www.fisheries.noaa.gov/national/sustainable-fisheries/fisheries-united-states>.

Table 944. Fisheries—Quantity and Value of Domestic Catch: 1960 to 2022

[In millions of pounds (5,014 represents 5,014,000,000), except as noted. Data shown for commercial landings]

Year	Quantity [1] (mil. lbs.) Total	For human food	For industrial products [2]	Value (mil. dol.)	Average price per lb. (cents)	Year	Quantity [1] (mil. lbs.) Total	For human food	For industrial products [2]	Value (mil. dol.)	Average price per lb. (cents)
1960......	5,014	(NA)	(NA)	339	6.8	1996......	9,337	(NA)	(NA)	3,476	37.2
1970......	4,938	(NA)	(NA)	595	12.0	1997......	9,575	(NA)	(NA)	3,501	36.6
1971......	5,239	(NA)	(NA)	639	12.2	1998......	8,950	(NA)	(NA)	3,142	35.1
1972......	5,046	(NA)	(NA)	737	14.6	1999......	9,048	(NA)	(NA)	3,503	38.7
1973......	5,068	(NA)	(NA)	923	18.2	2000......	8,820	(NA)	(NA)	3,587	40.7
1974......	5,220	(NA)	(NA)	916	17.5	2001......	9,247	(NA)	(NA)	3,178	34.4
1975......	5,139	(NA)	(NA)	961	18.7	2002......	9,203	7,058	2,144	3,040	33.0
1976......	5,652	(NA)	(NA)	1,333	23.6	2003......	9,285	7,344	1,941	3,265	35.2
1977......	5,444	(NA)	(NA)	1,531	28.1	2004......	9,583	7,714	1,869	3,664	38.2
1978......	6,228	(NA)	(NA)	1,892	30.4	2005......	9,557	7,932	1,625	3,880	40.6
1979......	6,524	(NA)	(NA)	2,289	35.1	2006......	9,603	7,942	1,661	4,142	43.1
1980......	6,607	(NA)	(NA)	2,248	34.0	2007......	9,328	7,537	1,791	4,187	44.9
1981......	6,056	(NA)	(NA)	2,380	39.3	2008......	8,380	6,679	1,701	4,419	52.7
1982......	6,472	(NA)	(NA)	2,375	36.7	2009......	8,079	6,197	1,882	3,854	47.7
1983......	6,427	(NA)	(NA)	2,320	36.1	2010......	8,275	6,562	1,713	4,552	55.0
1984......	6,428	(NA)	(NA)	2,326	36.2	2011......	9,907	7,956	1,952	5,508	55.6
1985......	6,365	(NA)	(NA)	2,338	36.7	2012......	9,717	7,550	2,167	5,528	56.9
1986......	6,120	(NA)	(NA)	2,819	46.1	2013......	9,785	7,975	1,810	5,521	56.4
1987......	6,997	(NA)	(NA)	3,209	45.9	2014......	9,551	7,880	1,672	5,565	58.3
1988......	7,363	(NA)	(NA)	3,549	48.2	2015......	9,749	7,770	1,979	5,345	54.8
1989......	8,725	(NA)	(NA)	3,370	38.6	2016......	9,650	7,546	2,104	5,474	56.7
1990......	9,778	(NA)	(NA)	3,592	36.7	2017......	9,954	8,251	1,702	5,792	58.2
1991......	9,602	(NA)	(NA)	3,356	35.0	2018......	9,423	7,529	1,894	5,586	59.3
1992......	9,919	(NA)	(NA)	3,705	37.4	2019......	9,366	7,586	1,780	5,557	59.3
1993......	9,931	(NA)	(NA)	3,273	33.0	2020......	8,397	6,718	1,679	4,828	57.5
1994......	10,060	(NA)	(NA)	3,634	36.1	2021......	8,573	7,107	1,466	6,516	76.0
1995......	9,629	(NA)	(NA)	3,742	38.9	2022......	8,347	6,770	1,578	5,887	70.5

NA Not available. [1] Live weight. [2] Processed into meal, oil, solubles, and shell products, or used as bait and animal food.

Source: U.S. National Oceanic and Atmospheric Administration, National Marine Fisheries Service, "Fisheries One Stop Shop," <www.fisheries.noaa.gov/foss/>, accessed May 2024. See also <www.fisheries.noaa.gov/national/sustainable-fisheries/fisheries-united-states>.

Table 945. U.S. Private Aquaculture—Trout and Catfish Production and Value: 1990 to 2023

[67.8 represents 67,800,000. Data are for calendar year and foodsize fish (trout at least 12 inches long; catfish weighing at least three quarters of a pound). Data are based on surveys of trout and catfish farms. For descriptions of surveys, see under "Catfish Production" and "Trout Production" at <www.nass.usda.gov/Surveys/Guide_to_NASS_Surveys/index.php>]

Item	Unit	1990	1995	2000	2005	2010	2015	2020	2021	2022	2023
TROUT FOODSIZE											
Number sold.......................	Mil.	67.8	60.2	58.4	55.6	38.7	45.4	25.9	26.5	27.0	27.2
Total weight.......................	Mil. lb.	56.8	55.6	59.0	59.9	45.3	57.9	44.5	44.9	43.5	43.0
Total value of sales................	Mil. dol.	64.6	60.8	63.3	63.5	63.2	96.4	88.6	91.6	97.8	93.1
Avg. price received by processors....................	Dol./lb.	1.14	1.09	1.07	1.06	1.40	1.66	1.99	2.04	2.25	2.16
Percent sold to processors........	Percent	58.0	68.0	69.7	66.0	63.4	57.6	66.3	66.9	67.9	66.4
CATFISH FOODSIZE											
Number sold.......................	Mil.	272.9	321.8	420.1	395.6	263.4	195.5	204.4	191.3	206.0	204.6
Total weight.......................	Mil. lb.	392.4	481.5	633.8	605.5	478.9	317.4	324.1	325.4	328.9	327.8
Total value of sales................	Mil. dol.	305.1	378.1	468.8	427.8	375.1	346.4	352.1	402.4	421.6	405.0
Avg. price received by processors....................	Dol./lb.	0.78	0.79	0.74	0.71	0.78	1.09	1.09	1.24	1.28	1.24

Source: U.S. Department of Agriculture, National Agricultural Statistics Service, *Trout Production*, February 2024, and *Catfish Production*, February 2024. See also <www.nass.usda.gov/Publications/Reports_by_Release_Day/index.php>.

Table 946. Mineral and Mining Industries—Employment, Hours, and Earnings: 2010 to 2023

[In units as indicated. 654.7 represents 654,700. Industries based on North American Classification System (NAICS) 2022. Based on the Current Employment Statistics Program, see Appendix III]

Industry and item	Unit	2010	2015	2018	2019	2020	2021	2022	2023
All mining: [1]									
All employees..................	1,000	654.7	760.3	677.8	678.1	553.0	514.1	560.5	595.3
Avg. weekly hours............	Number	43.6	44.2	46.4	46.5	44.8	45.6	46.2	45.5
Avg. weekly earnings.........	Dollars	1,222	1,407	1,541	1,599	1,588	1,620	1,689	1,757
Production workers............	1,000	482.6	550.1	499.4	492.8	385.4	374.7	417.4	453.2
Oil and gas extraction:									
All employees..................	1,000	158.7	193.4	142.3	143.6	129.8	112.2	116.3	117.2
Avg. weekly hours............	Number	40.6	41.2	42.4	42.8	41.8	41.2	42.8	42.1
Avg. weekly earnings.........	Dollars	1,461	1,744	1,952	2,030	2,017	1,915	1,977	2,106
Production workers............	1,000	89.0	107.6	78.5	81.0	74.2	68.4	72.3	75.9
Coal mining:									
All employees..................	1,000	80.7	64.1	51.6	50.5	39.8	37.5	40.9	42.7
Avg. weekly hours............	Number	47.5	45.6	47.0	48.3	44.6	45.3	46.9	47.4
Avg. weekly earnings.........	Dollars	1,335	1,487	1,545	1,617	1,520	1,614	1,763	1,831
Metal ore mining:									
All employees..................	1,000	36.7	41.8	41.7	42.2	41.4	41.2	42.8	43.6
Avg. weekly hours............	Number	38.9	43.3	43.5	44.1	43.8	41.6	42.5	41.6
Avg. weekly earnings.........	Dollars	1,123	1,370	1,406	1,469	1,504	1,572	1,757	1,784
Nonmetallic minerals mining, and quarrying:									
All employees..................	1,000	87.0	91.8	98.0	97.8	95.1	97.3	99.4	100.8
Avg. weekly hours............	Number	42.4	45.2	45.0	46.7	46.0	45.3	44.3	43.9
Avg. weekly earnings.........	Dollars	935	1,139	1,239	1,352	1,346	1,334	1,335	1,375

[1] Includes other industries not shown separately.

Source: U.S. Bureau of Labor Statistics, Current Employment Statistics, "Employment, Hours, and Earnings—National," <www.bls.gov/ces/data>, accessed March 2024.

Table 947. Mine Safety: 2010 to 2023

[In units, as indicated. 162.3 represents $162,300,000. Calendar year data]

Item	Total			Coal			Metal and non-metal		
	2010	2020	2023	2010	2020	2023	2010	2020	2023
Number of mines.........................	14,283	12,756	12,614	1,938	1,015	994	12,345	11,741	11,620
Number of miners.......................	362,028	297,459	324,180	136,055	63,766	68,607	225,973	233,693	255,573
Fatalities (number)......................	72	29	40	48	5	9	24	24	31
Fatal injury rate [1].......................	0.024	0.012	0.014	0.038	0.009	0.014	0.013	0.012	0.014
All injury rate [1].........................	2.83	1.85	1.83	3.47	2.73	2.73	2.38	1.60	1.56
Mining area inspection hours per mine [2]................................	63	43	43	259	200	223	23	21	22
Citations and orders [3].................	170,020	77,829	95,652	96,315	28,662	39,145	73,705	49,167	56,507
S&S citations and orders [4] (percent)...	32	18	19	32	17	19	31	18	19
Amount assessed [5] (mil. dol.)..........	162.3	40.5	70.6	110.2	17.9	31.5	52.1	22.7	39
Coal production (mil. tons)...............	1,086	535	578	1,086	535	578	(X)	(X)	(X)

X Not applicable. [1] Reported injury rates per 200,000 hours worked. [2] Includes on-site Inspection Time (metal/non-metal), MMU Pit Time (Coal), Outby Area Time (Coal), Surface Area Time (Coal), and Citation/Order writing On-Site. On-site inspection hours represent hours entered by Authorized Representatives of the Secretary (AR) for certain inspection activities and task codes. [3] Citations and orders are those not vacated. [4] A violation that "significantly and substantially" contributes to the cause and effect of a coal or other mine safety or health hazard. [5] Government penalties or fines.

Source: U.S. Mine Safety and Health Administration, Office of Program Education and Outreach Services, "Mine Safety and Health At a Glance," <www.msha.gov/msha-glance>, accessed May 2024.

Table 948. Mining and Primary Metal Production Indexes: 1990 to 2023

[Index 2017=100]

Industry group	2017 NAICS code	1990	2000	2010	2015	2019	2020	2021	2022	2023
Mining [1].............................	**21**	**87.1**	**83.9**	**82.5**	**104.6**	**120.8**	**103.1**	**106.4**	**114.4**	**119.9**
Oil and gas extraction [1]..............	211	64.4	60.9	62.8	99.2	130.1	122.6	123.1	130.7	141.0
Crude oil............................	21112	78.6	62.2	58.6	100.9	131.5	121.0	120.3	127.3	138.1
Natural gas.........................	211130	63.6	68.9	76.6	98.4	124.7	124.6	127.7	134.9	141.3
Coal mining............................	2121	144.7	146.0	142.6	115.9	92.3	68.7	74.9	77.4	75.6
Metal ore mining......................	2122	112.7	119.8	99.3	102.2	95.9	94.9	92.1	85.6	79.6
Iron ore.............................	21221	121.9	135.6	106.9	96.2	97.9	79.5	99.2	81.4	80.7
Gold ore and silver ore.............	21222	126.8	151.4	99.0	91.2	85.3	82.6	79.9	74.3	74.0
Copper, nickel, lead, and zinc.......	21223	114.7	114.8	89.9	109.4	99.4	95.1	96.9	97.5	89.0
Oil and gas drilling....................	213111	106.3	98.5	114.9	121.9	128.4	75.5	89.9	112.6	116.7
Primary metal manufacturing [1]......	**331**	**99.6**	**114.6**	**103.8**	**105.7**	**97.3**	**86.6**	**96.1**	**94.6**	**94.8**
Iron and steel.........................	3311, 3312	95.2	110.5	101.7	101.5	95.2	87.1	102.1	95.7	96.8
Aluminum.............................	3313	100.0	102.2	89.8	108.1	101.5	91.8	96.8	95.9	91.2
Nonferrous metals [1]..................	3314	102.8	105.0	125.6	113.9	101.6	92.3	95.3	105.0	108.4

[1] Includes other industries not shown separately.

Source: Board of Governors of the Federal Reserve System, "Industrial Production and Capacity Utilization, G.17," <www.federalreserve.gov/data.htm>, accessed July 2024.

Table 949. Mineral Production: 2010 to 2023

[In units as indicated (1,084.4 represents 1,084,400,000). Data represent production as measured by mine shipments, mine sales, or marketable production. See Appendix IV for information on weights and measures]

Minerals and metals	Unit	2010	2015	2020	2022	2023 [6]
FUEL MINERALS						
Coal, total............................	Mil. short tons	1,084.4	896.9	535.4	594.2	(NA)
Bituminous...........................	Mil. short tons	489.5	404.4	237.9	270.5	(NA)
Subbituminous.......................	Mil. short tons	514.8	419.5	245.8	273.6	(NA)
Lignite...............................	Mil. short tons	78.2	70.9	49.4	47.5	(NA)
Anthracite...........................	Mil. short tons	1.8	2.1	2.4	2.5	(NA)
Natural gas (marketed production)...............	Tril. cu. ft.	22.4	28.8	36.5	39.4	41.3
Petroleum (crude)........................	Mil. barrels [1]	2,002	3,445	4,143	4,377	4,721
Uranium concentrate (recoverable content)........	Mil. lb.	4.2	3.3	(D)	0.2	0.1
NONFUEL MINERALS						
Barite, primary, sold/used by producers............	1,000 metric tons	662	433	(D)	(D)	(D)
Boron minerals, sold or used by producers........	1,000 metric tons	(D)	(D)	(D)	(D)	(D)
Bromine, sold or used by producers...............	1,000 metric tons	(D)	(D)	(D)	(D)	(D)
Cement [2]...........................	Mil. metric tons	66	84	89	[7] 93	91
Clays...............................	1,000 metric tons	25,600	25,500	25,400	25,500	26,000
Diatomite...........................	1,000 metric tons	595	832	822	827	830
Feldspar............................	1,000 metric tons	500	520	420	[7] 540	590
Fluorspar, finished shipments................	1,000 metric tons	(NA)	(NA)	(NA)	(NA)	(NA)
Garnet (industrial).....................	1,000 metric tons	34	77	101	76	68
Gypsum, crude........................	Mil. metric tons	10	19	21	22	22
Helium [3]...........................	Mil. cu. meters	75	71	72	65	60
Lime, sold or used by producers [4]...........	Mil. metric tons	18	18	16	17	17
Mica, scrap/flake, sold or used by producers.......	1,000 metric tons	56	33	35	42	38
Peat, sales by producers.....................	1,000 metric tons	628	455	388	[7] 510	510
Perlite, processed, sold or used................	1,000 metric tons	414	444	501	458	450
Phosphate rock, marketable................	Mil. metric tons	26	27	24	[7] 20	20
Potash (K2O equivalent), marketable............	1,000 metric tons	930	740	460	430	400
Pumice & pumicite, sold and used.............	1,000 metric tons	241	310	578	295	310
Salt [2].............................	Mil. metric tons	43	45	43	[7] 41	42
Sand & gravel:						
Construction.............................	Mil. metric tons	807	880	925	953	920
Industrial.............................	Mil. metric tons	32	102	76	114	130
Soda ash (sodium carbonate)......................	1,000 metric tons	10,600	11,600	9,990	11,300	11,000
Stone:						
Crushed and broken.......................	Mil. metric tons	1,160	1,340	1,460	1,550	1,500
Dimension.............................	1,000 metric tons	1,670	2,700	2,120	2,380	2,300
Sulfur: total shipments......................	1,000 metric tons	9,170	9,560	7,900	8,620	8,600
Talc................................	1,000 metric tons	604	615	491	511	450
Vermiculite concentrate, sold or used..............	1,000 metric tons	100	100	100	100	100
METALS						
Aluminum.............................	1,000 metric tons	1,726	1,587	1,010	861	750
Copper (recoverable content)........................	1,000 metric tons	1,110	1,380	1,200	1,230	1,100
Gold, mine production......................	Metric tons	231	214	193	173	170
Iron ore, usable (gross weight)......................	Mil. metric tons	50	46	38	39	44
Lead (recoverable content).........................	1,000 metric tons	369	370	297	264	260
Magnesium metal.......................	1,000 metric tons	(D)	(D)	(D)	(D)	(D)
Molybdenum, mine.......................	1,000 metric tons	59	47	51	35	34
Nickel ore, refinery byproduct......................	1,000 metric tons	(D)	(D)	(D)	(D)	(D)
Palladium metal.............................	Kilograms	11,600	12,500	14,600	10,100	9,800
Platinum metal...........................	Kilograms	3,450	3,670	4,200	3,000	2,900
Silicon (Si content) [5]......................	1,000 metric tons	176	411	(D)	265	(D)
Silver, mine production......................	Metric tons	1,280	1,090	1,080	1,010	1,000
Titanium concentrate, (TiO2 content)...............	1,000 metric tons	200	200	100	200	200
Vanadium (recoverable content)......................	Metric tons	1,060	–	17	–	–
Zinc, ore and concentrate.....................	1,000 metric tons	748	825	723	761	750

NA Not available. D Withheld to avoid disclosing individual company data. – Represents or rounds to zero. [1] 42-gallon barrels. [2] Excludes Puerto Rico. [3] Extracted from natural gas. Both grade A and crude helium. [4] Includes Puerto Rico. [5] For 2006-2010, ferrosilicon only; silicon metal withheld to avoid disclosing proprietary data. Beginning 2012, covers ferrosilicon and miscellaneous silicon alloys, and metallurgical-grade silicon metal. [6] Nonfuel minerals and metals estimated. [7] Estimated.

Source: Nonfuels, through 1994, U.S. Bureau of Mines; thereafter, U.S. Geological Survey, *Mineral Commodity Summaries 2023*, January 2023, and earlier reports; see also <www.usgs.gov/centers/nmic/publications>. Fuels, U.S. Energy Information Administration, *Annual Energy Review 2011*, September 2012, and earlier reports; *Annual Coal Report, 2022*, October 2023; *2023 Domestic Uranium Production Report,* and earlier reports, <www.eia.gov/nuclear/data.php>; and "Natural Gas Gross Withdrawals and Production," <www.eia.gov/naturalgas/data.php>, and "Crude Oil Production," <www.eia.gov/petroleum/data.php>, accessed August 2024.

Table 950. Nonfuel Mineral Commodities—Summary: 2022

[920 represents 920,000. Except as noted, data are for mine or crude production, and average price or value are in dollars per metric ton]

Mineral	Unit	Mineral disposition		Net import reliance [1,2] (percent)	Con-sumption, apparent	Average price per unit (dollars)	Employ-ment (number)
		Produc-tion	Exports				
Alumina (metal equivalent)	1,000 metric tons	920	174	65	2,620	[3] 518	[21] 30,200
Aluminum	1,000 metric tons	861	3,040	52	4,760	[4] 1.53	[21] 30,200
Antimony (contained)	Metric tons	–	[5] 4,266	84	25,100	[4] 6.18	(NA)
Asbestos	Metric tons	–	–	100	290	[7] 2,630	–
Barite	1,000 metric tons	(D)	86	>75	(D)	[6] 145	380
Bauxite (metal equiv.)	1,000 metric tons	(D)	10	>75	(D)	32	(NA)
Beryllium (contained)	Metric tons	175	61	6	187	[8] 660	(NA)
Bismuth (contained)	Metric tons	–	502	97	2,610	[4] 3.90	(NA)
Boron (B2O3 content)	1,000 metric tons	(D)	[9] 240	([10])	(D)	[11] 485	1,400
Bromine (contained)	Metric tons	(D)	[12] 19,400	<25	(D)	[27] 3.29	1,050
Cadmium (contained)	Metric tons	(D)	[13] 68	<25	(D)	[8,14] 3.42	(NA)
Cement	1,000 metric tons	[15] 93,000	902	22	120,000	140	12,800
Chromium	1,000 metric tons	[16] 91	133	84	573	[17] 274	(NA)
Clays	1,000 metric tons	[18] 25,500	[18] 3,620	([10])	22,200	(NA)	5,300
Cobalt (contained)	Metric tons	[19] 1,900	5,360	73	7,090	[4] 30.78	(NA)
Copper (mine, recoverable)	1,000 metric tons	1,230	353	41	1,800	[4] 4.11	12,000
Diamond, stones (industrial)	Million carats	–	(Z)	91	0.9	[20] 8.40	(NA)
Diatomite	1,000 metric tons	827	63	([10])	778	416	370
Feldspar	1,000 metric tons	540	3	34	810	104	220
Fluorspar	1,000 metric tons	(NA)	24	100	502	[11] 223	15
Garnet (industrial)	Metric tons	76,400	23,300	76	321,000	194	90
Gemstones	Million dollars	[22] 97.05	[23] 1,890	99	26,200	(NA)	1,100
Germanium (contained)	Kilograms	(D)	6,600	>50	(NA)	[8] 1,294	(NA)
Gold (contained)	Metric tons	173	420	([10])	257	[24] 1,802	12,300
Graphite (natural)	Metric tons	–	9,500	100	79,700	[25] 1,200	(NA)
Gypsum (crude)	1,000 metric tons	22,300	39	16	43,700	11.0	4,500
Iodine	Metric tons	(D)	1,140	>50	(D)	[27] 45.81	60
Iron ore (usable)	1,000 metric tons	39,000	11,400	([10])	30,600	156.42	4,790
Iron and steel scrap (metal)	Million metric tons	[28] 63.7	20	([10])	48	[43] 379	26,600
Iron and steel slag (metal)	Million metric tons	16	(Z)	10	16	53	1,500
Lead (contained)	1,000 metric tons	273	255	38	1,630	[4] 1.17	1,870
Lime [30]	1,000 metric tons	17,000	303	<1	17,000	151	(NA)
Lithium	Metric tons	(D)	2,440	>25	(D)	68,100	70
Magnesium compounds	1,000 metric tons	[26] 412	104	55	906	(NA)	280
Magnesium metal	1,000 metric tons	(D)	9	>50	(D)	[4] 7.59	400
Manganese (gross weight)	1,000 metric tons	–	1	100	804	[31] 5.97	(NA)
Mercury [32]	Metric tons	(NA)	–	(NA)	(NA)	[8] 33	(NA)
Mica, scrap and flake	Metric tons	42,000	4,450	30	60,200	100	(NA)
Molybdenum (contained)	Metric tons	34,600	51,100	([10])	12,400	[8] 41.35	940
Nickel (contained) [34]	Metric tons	17,500	70,600	54	210,000	25,815	(NA)
Niobium (columbium)	Metric tons	–	687	100	8,420	[8] 25	(NA)
Nitrogen (fixed)-ammonia	1,000 metric tons	13,800	720	7	14,800	[35] 1,070	1,600
Peat	1,000 metric tons	350	43	80	1,750	27.49	510
Perlite	1,000 metric tons	672	22	32	680	68	150
Phosphate rock	1,000 metric tons	19,800	(NA)	12	22,300	98.00	1,900
Platinum-group metals	Kilograms	[36] 13,100	[36] 65,300	[37] 77	[37] 53,100	[24,37] 967	1,555
Potash (K2O equivalent)	1,000 metric tons	[44] 430	267	92	[44] 5,100	[38] 1,790	900
Pumice and pumicite	1,000 metric tons	295	14	23	383	65	140
Salt	1,000 metric tons	41,000	890	30	57,000	[39] 210	4,100
Silicon, metal	1,000 metric tons	[40] 265	47	<50	[40] 495	[4] 3.62	(NA)
Silver (contained)	Metric tons	1,010	275	67	6,320	[24] 21.88	1,400
Soda ash (sodium carbonate)	1,000 metric tons	11,300	6,490	([10])	4,740	178.52	2,400
Stone (crushed)	Million metric tons	1,550	(Z)	1	1,600	14.23	70,400
Sulfur (all forms)	1,000 metric tons	8,640	1,863	9	9,480	[41] 178.50	2,400
Talc	1,000 metric tons	511	196	21	698	303	316
Thallium (contained)	Kilograms	–	2,150	(NA)	13	[8] 9,400	(NA)
Tin (contained)	Metric tons	[19] 13,330	32,240	77	41,400	[4] 15.46	(NA)
Titanium dioxide	Metric tons	1,150,000	378,000	([10])	1,040,000	3,450	3,200
Tungsten (contained)	Metric tons	(D)	4,294	>50	(D)	[42] 275	(NA)
Vermiculite	1,000 metric tons	100	8	10	120	(NA)	70
Zinc (contained)	1,000 metric tons	761	644	([10])	[33] 975	[4] 1.90	2,720
Zirconium (ZrO2)	Metric tons	<100,000	13,095	<50	<100,000	[29] 1,940	(NA)

– Represents or rounds to zero. < Less than. > Greater than. D Withheld to avoid disclosing company proprietary data. NA Not available. Z Less than .05 million metric tons or less than half a unit shown. [1] Net imports calculated as imports minus exports and may include adjustments for industry stock changes. [2] Calculated as percent of apparent consumption. [3] Alumina, average value, U.S. imports (f.a.s.). [4] Dollars per pound. [5] Ore and concentrates not included. [6] Average unit value, ground, ex-works, dollars per metric ton. [7] Dollars per American ton. [8] Dollars per kilogram. [9] Boric acid, gross weight. [10] Net exporter. [11] Average value of imports (cost, insurance, and freight, c.i.f.). [12] Elemental bromine and compounds. [13] Unwrought cadmium and powders. [14] Average free market price for 99.95% purity in 10-ton lots; cost, insurance, and freight; global ports. Source: Fastmarkets MB. [15] Production for Portland and masonry cement includes cement made from imported clinker; excludes Puerto Rico. [16] Recycling production. [17] Unit value of imported chromite ore. Dollars per metric ton gross weight. [18] Excludes attapulgite. [19] Secondary production. [20] Value of imports, dollars per carat. [21] Alumina and aluminum production workers. Source: U.S. Department of Labor, Bureau of Labor Statistics. [22] Natural gemstone production, 9.95 million dollars; laboratory-created (synthetic) gemstone production, 87.1 million dollars. [23] Includes reexports. [24] Dollars per troy ounce. [25] Average dollars per metric ton at foreign ports. Price of flake imports. Graphite lump/chip (Sri Lankan) price, $2,590 per ton. [26] Magnesium compound shipments. [27] Average value of imports (c.i.f.), dollars per kilogram. [28] Iron and steel scrap production includes receipts for purchased scrap. Exports excludes rails for rerolling and other uses, and ships, boats, and other vessels for scrapping. [29] Unit value based on annual imports for consumption from Australia, Senegal, and South Africa. [30] Lime production data are sold or used by producers. Price data are for quicklime only. [31] 44% Mn metallurgical ore, per metric ton unit, contained Mn; cost, insurance, and freight (c.i.f.) value, U.S. ports. [32] Mercury not produced as principal commodity in U.S. since 1992; secondary production (recycled) not reported. [33] Value for refined zinc. [34] Primary and secondary materials. [35] Dollars per short ton, average, f.o.b. Gulf Coast. [36] Platinum and palladium. [37] Platinum. [38] Dollars per ton of K2O, all products. [39] Vacuum and open pan, bulk, pellets and packaged, f.o.b. mine and plant. [40] Combined for ferrosilicon and silicon metal. [41] Elemental sulfur, f.o.b., mine or plant. [42] A metric ton unit of tungsten trioxide (WO3) contains 7.93 kilograms of tungsten. Platts Metals Week. [43] No 1. Heavy Melting composite price. [44] Data are rounded to avoid disclosing company proprietary data.

Source: U.S. Geological Survey, *Mineral Commodity Summaries 2024*, January 2024. See also <www.usgs.gov/centers/national-minerals-information-center/mineral-commodity-summaries>.

Table 951. Selected Fuel and Nonfuel Mineral Products—Average Prices: 1990 to 2023

Year	Copper, cathode (cents/lb.)	Platinum[1] (dol./troy oz.)	Gold[2] (dol./troy oz.)	Silver[2] (dol./troy oz.)	Lead[3] (cents/lb.)	Nickel[4] (cents/lb.)	Tin (New York)[4] (cents/lb.)	Zinc[5] (cents/lb.)	Sulfur crude[6] (dol./metric ton)	Bituminous coal[7] (dol./short ton)	Crude oil[7] (dol./bbl.)	Natural gas[8] (dol./1,000 cu. ft.)
1990.........	123	467	385	4.82	46	402	386	75	80	27.43	20.03	3.03
1995.........	138	425	386	5.15	42	373	416	56	44	25.56	14.62	2.78
2000.........	88	549	280	5.00	44	392	370	56	25	24.15	26.72	4.62
2001.........	77	533	272	4.39	44	270	315	44	10	25.36	21.84	5.72
2002.........	76	543	311	4.62	44	307	292	39	12	26.57	22.51	4.12
2003.........	85	694	365	4.91	44	437	340	41	29	26.57	27.56	5.85
2004.........	134	849	411	6.69	55	627	547	52	33	30.56	36.77	6.65
2005.........	174	900	446	7.34	61	669	483	67	31	36.80	50.28	8.67
2006.........	315	1,144	606	11.61	77	1,100	565	159	33	39.32	59.69	8.61
2007.........	328	1,308	699	13.43	124	1,688	899	154	36	40.80	66.52	8.16
2008.........	319	1,578	874	15.00	120	957	1,129	89	264	51.39	94.04	9.18
2009.........	241	1,208	975	14.69	87	665	837	78	2	55.44	56.35	6.48
2010.........	348	1,616	1,228	20.20	109	989	1,240	102	70	60.88	74.71	6.18
2011.........	406	1,725	1,572	35.28	122	1,038	1,575	106	160	68.50	95.73	5.63
2012.........	367	1,555	1,673	31.22	114	795	1,283	96	124	66.04	94.52	4.73
2013.........	340	1,490	1,415	23.89	110	681	1,352	96	69	60.61	95.99	4.88
2014.........	318	1,388	1,269	19.09	106	765	1,023	107	80	55.99	87.39	5.71
2015.........	256	1,056	1,163	15.72	91	537	756	96	88	51.57	44.39	4.26
2016.........	225	990	1,252	17.20	94	435	839	101	38	48.40	38.29	3.71
2017.........	285	951	1,261	17.08	115	472	937	139	46	55.6	48.05	4.16
2018.........	299	883	1,272	15.73	111	595	936	141	81	59.43	61.40	4.23
2019.........	280	867	1,395	16.24	100	631	868	124	51	58.93	55.59	3.81
2020.........	287	886	1,774	20.58	91	625	799	111	25	50.05	36.86	3.43
2021.........	432	1,094	1,801	25.23	113	838	1,580	146	91	61.68	65.84	6.02
2022.........	411	967	1,802	21.88	117	1,171	1,546	190	179	97.96	93.97	6.89
2023[9].......	400	1,000	1,900	23.40	115	980	1,300	152	100	(NA)	76.10	5.29

NA Not available. [1] Annual average dealer prices. [2] 99.95 percent purity. [3] North American delivered basis. 1990-2012, North American producer price. Beginning 2013, North American market price. [4] Nickel: London Metal Exchange. Tin: S&P Global Platts Metals Week composite. [5] S&P Global Platts Metals Week price for North American special high grade zinc. Average prices for 1990 are for U.S. high grade zinc. [6] F.o.b. (Free on Board). [7] Average value at the point of production or domestic first purchase price. [8] Citygate price. Citygate is a point or measuring station at which a distributing gas utility receives gas from a natural gas pipeline company or transmission system. [9] Estimated.

Source: Nonfuels, through 1994, U.S. Bureau of Mines; thereafter, U.S. Geological Survey, *Mineral Commodity Summaries 2024*, January 2024 and earlier reports. Fuels, U.S. Energy Information Administration, *Monthly Energy Review*, March 2024 and earlier reports; and *Annual Coal Report, 2022*, October 2023 and earlier reports. See also <www.usgs.gov/centers/nmic/mineral-commodity-summaries>, <www.eia.gov/coal/annual/>, and <www.eia.gov/totalenergy/data/monthly>.

Table 952. Value of Domestic Nonfuel Mineral Production by State: 2000 to 2023

[In millions of dollars (39,400 represents $39,400,000,000)]

State	2000	2010	2020[1]	2023[1]	State	2000	2010	2020[1]	2023[1]
United States[2]........	**39,400**	**66,400**	**82,300**	**105,000**	Missouri..............	1,370	2,010	3,030	3,160
					Montana.............	596	1,140	1,680	1,290
Alabama..................	930	969	1,580	2,010	Nebraska.............	[3] 84	234	[3] 215	[3] 260
Alaska...................	1,140	3,400	3,160	4,100	Nevada...............	2,980	7,700	9,140	8,880
Arizona..................	2,510	6,790	7,030	9,500	New Hampshire.....	[3] 57	[3] 94	110	[3] 203
Arkansas................	484	709	869	1,180	New Jersey..........	[3] 291	[3] 258	345	515
California................	3,270	2,890	4,680	[3] 5,080	New Mexico.........	786	1,020	864	1,450
Colorado................	592	1,850	1,620	2,220	New York............	1,020	1,310	1,690	[3] 1,750
Connecticut.............	[3] 112	[3] 148	[3] 190	264	North Carolina......	744	880	[3] 1,150	2,500
Delaware................	[3] 14	[3] 12	[3] 23	[3] 17	North Dakota........	35	[3] 70	[3] 74	[3] 78
Florida....................	1,820	2,680	3,520	[3] 2,900	Ohio.................	999	1,170	[3] 1,340	[3] 1,580
Georgia..................	1,620	1,430	2,020	[3] 2,620	Oklahoma............	473	702	1,040	1,210
Hawaii...................	[3] 92	106	128	154	Oregon..............	299	312	513	[3] 527
Idaho....................	358	1,180	[3] 247	[3] 482	Pennsylvania........	[3] 1,250	[3] 1,670	[3] 1,750	[3] 2,220
Illinois...................	913	924	[3] 1,100	1,770	Rhode Island........	[3] 20	[3] 33	[3] 48	[3] 109
Indiana..................	695	782	[3] 695	1,440	South Carolina......	[3] 551	[3] 468	[3] 895	1,680
Iowa.....................	503	583	[3] 727	879	South Dakota.......	233	258	449	549
Kansas..................	629	1,090	[3] 1,250	[3] 915	Tennessee..........	737	831	1,330	1,950
Kentucky................	501	762	[3] 566	[3] 919	Texas...............	1,950	2,780	6,090	9,750
Louisiana................	325	549	[3] 656	[3] 1,070	Utah.................	1,430	4,380	3,150	3,140
Maine....................	96	110	[3] 148	[3] 116	Vermont.............	[3] 67	[3] 121	[3] 119	[3] 160
Maryland................	[3] 358	[3] 305	[3] 429	[3] 431	Virginia..............	710	1,040	1,370	1,590
Massachusetts..........	[3] 200	[3] 233	[3] 267	[3] 329	Washington..........	607	712	630	796
Michigan.................	1,640	2,190	2,630	4,060	West Virginia........	172	272	[3] 164	[3] 231
Minnesota...............	1,460	[3] 4,180	[3] 4,090	[3] 6,820	Wisconsin............	[3] 372	509	[3] 1,020	[3] 1,510
Mississippi..............	149	198	[3] 286	338	Wyoming.............	978	1,860	2,440	3,170

[1] Preliminary. [2] Includes data not distributed to States, not shown separately. [3] Partial data only; excludes values withheld to avoid disclosing individual company data.

Source: U.S. Geological Survey, "Minerals Yearbook," <www.usgs.gov/centers/national-minerals-information-center/minerals-yearbook-metals-and-minerals>, accessed June 2024; and *Mineral Commodities Summaries 2024*, January 2024, and earlier reports. See also <www.usgs.gov/centers/national-minerals-information-center/commodity-statistics-and-information>.

Table 953. Net U.S. Imports of Selected Minerals and Metals as Percent of Apparent Consumption: 1980 to 2023

[In percent. Net imports are the difference between imports and exports plus or minus government stockpile and industry stock changes]

Rank order of net imports	1980	1990	2000	2010	2015	2020	2021	2022	2023 [1]
Fluorspar	87	91	100	100	100	100	100	100	100
Manganese	98	100	100	100	100	100	100	100	100
Mica (sheet)	100	100	100	100	100	100	100	100	100
Niobium	100	100	100	100	100	100	100	100	100
Strontium	100	100	100	100	100	100	100	100	100
Tantalum	90	86	80	100	100	100	100	100	100
Potash	65	68	80	83	89	92	93	92	91
Platinum	(NA)	(NA)	78	91	66	76	75	77	83
Zinc (refined)	60	64	72	73	81	79	76	77	77
Barite	44	71	84	75	78	>75	>75	>75	>75
Bauxite	(NA)	98	100	100	>75	>75	>75	>75	>75
Titanium	(NA)	(NA)	79	65	85	89	90	81	75
Chromium	67	80	77	63	64	73	80	84	74
Tin	79	71	88	73	76	76	81	77	74
Silver	7	(NA)	43	65	67	80	76	67	69
Cobalt	93	84	78	81	73	76	73	73	67
Vanadium	35	(D)	100	82	100	59	61	60	58
Nickel	76	64	54	41	50	46	49	54	57
Tungsten	53	81	66	63	>25	>50	>50	>50	>50
Copper	16	15	37	32	32	38	45	41	46
Aluminum	([2])	([2])	33	14	41	38	40	52	44
Palladium	(NA)	(NA)	84	49	53	34	35	31	37
Gypsum	21	27	27	12	10	15	16	16	18
Iron and steel	13	13	18	6	29	12	13	17	13
Sulfur	14	15	18	19	14	21	15	9	8

NA Not available. > Greater than. [1] Preliminary. [2] Net exporter.

Source: Through 1990, U.S. Bureau of Mines; thereafter, U.S. Geological Survey, *Mineral Commodity Summaries 2024*, January 2024, and earlier reports. See also <www.usgs.gov/centers/nmic>.

Table 954. Crude Petroleum and Natural Gas Extraction Industry—Establishments, Employees, and Payroll by State: 2022

[10,449,305 represents $10,449,305,000. Based on the North American Classification System (NAICS) 2017. Excludes self-employed individuals, employees of private households, railroad employees, agricultural production employees, and most government employees. See source for definitions and statement on reliability of data. An establishment is a single physical location where business is conducted or where services or industrial operations are performed. See Appendix III]

State	Crude petroleum extraction (NAICS 211120)			Natural gas extraction (NAICS 211130)		
	Establish-ments	Number of employees [1]	Annual payroll ($1,000)	Establish-ments	Number of employees [1]	Annual payroll ($1,000)
United States	**3,973**	**58,551**	**10,449,305**	**1,303**	**26,219**	**4,266,223**
Alabama	13	90	10,331	5	33	2,775
Alaska	15	1,527	303,814	9	233	53,325
Arizona	8	64	1,771	5	9	1,098
Arkansas	52	281	36,837	19	257	21,887
California	106	3,870	649,119	18	128	19,777
Colorado	199	3,380	846,898	63	1,687	296,267
Florida	13	29	2,172	6	41	5,882
Georgia	6	5	221	(NA)	(NA)	(NA)
Illinois	121	471	26,058	4	56	5,867
Indiana	22	142	9,234	3	6	180
Kansas	262	1,036	70,156	27	235	19,826
Kentucky	39	214	13,677	21	434	32,127
Louisiana	204	3,146	435,039	95	1,813	271,432
Massachusetts	3	4	457	3	22	1,748
Michigan	35	330	30,202	22	289	23,798
Minnesota	3	4	225	(NA)	(NA)	(NA)
Mississippi	46	388	38,117	9	58	5,369
Missouri	3	5	404	(NA)	(NA)	(NA)
Montana	62	491	63,030	7	144	16,014
Nebraska	12	52	3,367	(NA)	(NA)	(NA)
Nevada	9	40	4,430	(NA)	(NA)	(NA)
New Jersey	3	11	2,649	(NA)	(NA)	(NA)
New Mexico	91	1,994	275,073	44	1,324	169,884
New York	14	49	2,811	8	39	3,634
North Carolina	(NA)	(NA)	(NA)	3	5	1,505
North Dakota	58	2,277	475,272	11	761	124,143
Ohio	97	487	27,672	60	1,034	82,530
Oklahoma	660	5,769	735,445	142	2,433	314,247
Pennsylvania	78	839	107,679	93	2,678	552,345
South Dakota	3	38	4,907	(NA)	(NA)	(NA)
Texas	1,536	29,643	6,060,138	503	10,198	1,942,231
Utah	26	431	57,166	10	192	25,392
Virginia	(NA)	(NA)	(NA)	11	189	25,380
Washington	5	16	2,341	(NA)	(NA)	(NA)
West Virginia	70	656	49,892	67	1,248	152,842
Wyoming	82	741	99,580	25	655	93,031

NA Not available. [1] Covers full- and part-time employees who are on the payroll in the pay period including March 12.

Source: U.S. Census Bureau, County Business Patterns, "All Sectors: County Business Patterns, including ZIP Code Business Patterns, by Legal Form of Organization and Employment Size Class for the U.S., States, and Selected Geographies: 2022," <data.census.gov>, accessed June 2024.

Table 955. Petroleum Industry—Production, Foreign Trade, Reserves, and Refineries: 1990 to 2023

[In units as indicated (2,685 represents 2,685,000,000); mil. bbl. = millions of barrels. For definitions, see source below]

Item	Unit	1990	2000	2010	2015	2020	2021	2022	2023
Crude oil production, total [1]	Mil. bbl.	2,685	2,125	2,002	3,445	4,131	4,113	4,347	4,718
Average price per barrel	Dollars	20	27	75	44	37	66	94	76
Lower 48 states [2]	Mil. bbl.	2,037	1,771	1,783	3,269	3,968	3,953	4,188	4,563
Alaska	Mil. bbl.	647	354	219	176	163	160	160	155
Imports: Crude oil [1, 3]	Mil. bbl.	2,151	3,320	3,363	2,687	2,150	2,232	2,293	2,364
Refined petroleum products	Mil. bbl.	775	874	942	761	728	861	747	743
Exports: Crude oil [1]	Mil. bbl.	40	18	15	170	1,173	1,081	1,305	1,481
Proved reserves	Bil. bbl.	26	22	23	32	36	41	(NA)	(NA)
Operable refineries	Number	205	158	148	140	135	129	130	129
Daily capacity (Jan. 1)	1,000 bbl.	15,572	16,512	17,584	17,967	18,976	18,128	17,944	18,060
Refinery input, total	Mil. bbl.	5,325	5,964	6,345	6,871	6,063	6,463	6,703	6,721
Crude oil [1]	Mil. bbl.	4,894	5,514	5,374	5,909	5,202	5,528	5,832	5,826
Hydrocarbon gas liquids	Mil. bbl.	171	139	161	189	186	200	207	227
Other liquids [4]	Mil. bbl.	260	311	810	773	676	734	664	667
Refinery output, total [5]	Mil. bbl.	5,574	6,311	6,735	7,258	6,401	6,812	7,080	7,095
Hydrocarbon gas liquids	Mil. bbl.	182	258	240	224	200	225	223	220
Motor gasoline [6]	Mil. bbl.	2,540	2,910	3,306	3,560	3,200	3,478	3,493	3,520
Jet fuel (kerosene type)	Mil. bbl.	478	588	517	580	373	478	590	625
Distillate fuel oil	Mil. bbl.	1,067	1,310	1,542	1,819	1,734	1,704	1,829	1,791
Residual fuel oil	Mil. bbl.	347	255	213	152	69	78	92	99
Petroleum coke	Mil. bbl.	202	266	296	319	281	279	295	294
Asphalt and road oil	Mil. bbl.	164	192	138	124	117	124	124	120
Still gas	Mil. bbl.	246	241	245	249	223	235	241	239
Utilization rate	Percent	87	93	86	91	79	87	92	91

NA Not available. [1] Includes lease condensate. [2] Excluding Alaska and Hawaii. [3] Includes imports for the Strategic Petroleum Reserve. [4] Unfinished oils (net), other hydrocarbons, hydrogen, aviation and motor gasoline blending components (net). Beginning 1995, also includes oxygenates (net). [5] Includes other products not shown separately. [6] Finished motor gasoline. Beginning 1995, also includes ethanol blended into motor gasoline.

Source: U.S. Energy Information Administration, "Petroleum & Other Liquids Data," <www.eia.gov/petroleum/data.php>, and "Monthly Energy Review," <www.eia.gov/totalenergy/data/monthly/>; accessed July 2024.

Table 956. Crude Oil and Petroleum Products Supply, Disposition, and Ending Stocks: 2023

[In millions of barrels (4,721.1 represents 4,721,100,000). Minus sign (-) indicates decrease]

Commodity	Supply				Disposition				
	Field production [1]	Refinery and blender net production	Imports	Adjustments [2]	Stock change	Refinery and blender net inputs	Exports	Products supplied [3]	Ending stocks [4]
Crude oil	4,721.1	(X)	2,364.5	2.0	-20.5	5,826.4	1,481.0	–	781.1
Hydrocarbon gas liquids	2,347.3	220.3	61.4	(X)	12.2	226.9	960.7	1,261.5	223.3
Natural gasoline	271.4	(NA)	–	(X)	1.7	72.3	37.2	–	26.8
Ethane	956.7	2.6	(NA)	(X)	12.3	(NA)	171.8	775.3	65.8
Propane	733.2	101.6	39.1	(X)	3.2	(NA)	582.3	288.2	79.7
Normal butane	221.4	30.8	13.0	(X)	-2.8	71.2	168.2	23.6	38.9
Isobutane	164.5	-5.5	2.7	(X)	-1.5	83.4	1.2	76.6	10.7
Finished motor gasoline	(X)	3,519.6	42.8	-0.7	0.7	(X)	298.9	3,264.4	18.1
Kerosene-type jet fuel	(X)	624.9	46.4	(X)	4.7	(X)	63.7	602.9	39.8
Distillate fuel oil [4]	(X)	1,791.0	61.3	(NA)	11.9	(X)	404.8	1,435.5	130.7

– Represents or rounds to zero. NA Not available. X Not applicable. [1] Represents crude oil production on leases, natural gas liquids production at natural gas processing plants, new supply of other hydrocarbons/oxygenates and motor gasoline blending components, and fuel ethanol blended into finished motor gasoline. [2] Includes an adjustment for crude oil, previously referred to as "Unaccounted For Crude Oil." Also included is an adjustment for motor gasoline blending components, fuel ethanol, and for 2011-2020 an adjustment for distillate fuel oil. [3] Products supplied is equal to field production, plus refinery and blender net production, plus import, plus adjustments, minus stock change, minus refinery and blender net inputs, minus exports. [4] Total stocks do not include distillate fuel oil stocks located in the Northeast Heating Oil Reserve.

Source: U.S. Energy Information Administration, "Petroleum Supply and Disposition," <www.eia.gov/petroleum/data.php#summary>, accessed August 2024.

Table 957. Natural Gas Plant Liquids Production: 1990 to 2023

[In units as indicated (569 represents 569,000,000). Barrels of 42 gallons]

Item	Unit	1990	2000	2005	2010	2015	2020	2021	2022	2023
Field production	Mil. bbl.	569	699	627	757	1,220	1,894	1,980	2,166	2,347
Ethane	Mil. bbl.	174	263	237	317	412	738	784	878	957
Propane	Mil. bbl.	173	197	182	214	418	616	637	683	733
Normal butane	Mil. bbl.	54	58	49	57	122	169	185	204	221
Isobutane	Mil. bbl.	55	69	62	68	110	158	152	156	165
Natural gasoline	Mil. bbl.	113	112	97	101	158	214	222	244	271
Natural gas processed	Tril. cu. ft.	14.6	17.0	14.9	16.3	20.7	24.7	24.7	25.6	(NA)

NA Not available.

Source: U.S. Energy Information Administration, "Natural Gas Plant Processing," <www.eia.gov/naturalgas/data.php> and "Natural Gas Plant Field Production," <www.eia.gov/petroleum/data.php>; accessed August 2024.

Table 958. Crude Petroleum and Natural Gas—Production and Value for Major Producing States: 2010 to 2023

[In units as indicated (2,002 represents 2,002,000,000 barrels)]

State	Crude petroleum Quantity (mil. bbl.)				Value (mil. dol.) [2]				Natural gas marketed production [1] Quantity (bil. cu. ft.)			
	2010	2015	2020	2023	2010	2015	2020	2023	2010	2015	2020	2023
Total [3]	**2,002**	**3,445**	**4,143**	**4,721**	**149,555**	**152,941**	**152,693**	**359,275**	**22,382**	**28,772**	**36,521**	**41,296**
Alabama	7	10	4	4	540	432	155	265	223	168	117	(NA)
Alaska [4]	215	170	159	152	15,561	6,970	5,418	11,264	374	344	339	368
Arkansas	6	6	4	4	407	268	146	320	927	1,010	481	393
California	200	201	142	118	14,930	9,185	5,719	9,233	287	237	156	130
Colorado	33	122	172	167	2,406	4,950	5,389	12,484	1,578	1,689	1,997	1,824
Florida	2	2	1	1	(NA)	(NA)	(NA)	(NA)	12	1	1	(NA)
Illinois	9	10	7	7	664	419	272	513	2	2	2	(NA)
Indiana	2	2	1	2	134	99	54	114	7	7	4	(NA)
Kansas	40	45	28	28	2,931	1,963	1,026	2,040	325	284	163	134
Kentucky	3	3	2	2	178	130	84	135	135	96	90	(NA)
Louisiana	68	64	36	34	5,289	3,087	1,417	2,640	2,210	1,805	3,206	4,306
Michigan	7	7	4	5	523	298	165	351	131	108	76	(NA)
Mississippi	24	25	14	13	1,832	1,167	535	952	74	58	29	(NA)
Montana	25	29	19	23	1,779	1,153	634	1,649	88	51	38	42
Nebraska	2	2	2	2	162	96	58	118	2	(Z)	(Z)	(NA)
New Mexico	66	148	375	666	4,960	6,575	13,838	51,048	1,292	1,245	1,966	3,164
New York	(Z)	(Z)	(Z)	(Z)	(NA)	(NA)	(NA)	(NA)	36	17	10	(NA)
North Dakota	113	430	434	432	7,908	17,795	15,448	31,576	82	471	887	1,120
Ohio	5	27	24	30	352	1,031	796	2,106	78	1,007	2,390	2,263
Oklahoma	70	166	173	157	5,277	7,443	6,402	11,855	1,827	2,500	2,673	2,817
Pennsylvania	3	7	6	5	226	276	179	331	573	4,813	7,169	7,620
South Dakota	2	2	1	1	111	71	34	66	2	1	(Z)	(NA)
Texas	427	1,262	1,773	2,012	32,532	56,717	65,905	154,444	6,715	7,890	9,813	11,540
Utah	25	37	31	56	1,679	1,511	1,082	3,751	432	417	242	287
West Virginia	2	12	19	19	130	390	581	1,257	265	1,315	2,568	3,239
Wyoming	54	86	89	97	3,670	3,514	3,059	7,159	2,306	1,809	1,206	951
Federal offshore	588	564	615	684	(NA)	(NA)	(NA)	(NA)	2,275	1,307	794	728
Lower 48 states [5]	1,783	3,269	3,979	4,566	133,789	145,739	147,409	347,992	22,008	28,428	36,181	40,928

Z Less than 500,000. NA Not available. [1] Excludes nonhydrocarbon gases. [2] Crude petroleum production value calculated using production quantity and domestic crude oil first purchase price. [3] Includes other states, not shown separately. State production includes state offshore production, as well as extractions from the Gulf of Mexico not distributed to states. U.S. level totals shown in Table 955 and Table 960 may contain revisions not carried to state level. [4] Alaska crude oil production and value for North Slope only. [5] Value of crude petroleum calculated using production for lower 48 states and first purchase price for U.S. less Alaskan North slope crude oil.

Source: U.S. Energy Information Administration, "Petroleum & Other Liquids Data," <www.eia.gov/petroleum/data.cfm> and "Natural Gas Data," <www.eia.gov/naturalgas/data.cfm>; accessed August 2024.

Table 959. Crude Oil and Natural Gas Proved Reserves by State: 2019 to 2022

[47,172 represents 47,172,000,000. As of December 31. Proved reserves are estimated volumes of hydrocarbon resources that analysis of geologic and engineering data demonstrates with reasonable certainty are recoverable under existing economic and operating conditions. Data are from Energy Information Administration (EIA) Form EIA-23L, which collects data from a sample of U.S. operators of oil and natural gas fields. Form EIA-23L was redesigned for the 2022 reporting year, see source for details]

Area	Crude oil and lease condensate proved reserves (million barrels)				Natural gas, wet after lease separation, proved reserves (billion cubic feet)			
	2019	2020	2021	2022	2019	2020	2021	2022
United States [1]	**47,172**	**38,212**	**44,418**	**48,321**	**495,380**	**473,285**	**625,373**	**691,025**
Alabama	48	39	32	27	1,423	1,530	1,333	1,307
Alaska	2,680	2,425	3,179	3,357	9,380	36,529	99,801	125,238
Arkansas	34	30	36	39	5836	4,983	6087	6,455
California	2,213	1,497	1,717	1,492	1,369	1,122	1,228	1,070
Colorado	1,557	1,169	1,488	1,442	24,115	20,412	22,071	22,586
Kansas	327	290	304	335	2,303	2,114	2,406	3,151
Kentucky	8	4	(NA)	(NA)	1,369	1,249	1,345	(NA)
Louisiana	449	375	414	446	36,779	37,570	40,008	40,296
Michigan	49	40	54	46	1,261	891	1,165	1302
Mississippi	117	93	122	113	227	167	246	250
Montana	323	262	324	388	631	570	736	624
Nebraska	12	12	14	13	2	2	3	(NA)
New Mexico	3,738	3,539	4,909	6,192	24,305	26,129	36,134	46,017
New York	(NA)	(NA)	(NA)	(NA)	81	115	92	86
North Dakota	5,899	3,672	4,361	4,965	13,083	8,563	11,359	12,982
Ohio	316	279	326	348	34,748	28,100	32,247	32,825
Oklahoma	2,342	1,758	1,739	1830	35,823	30091	39,488	41771
Pennsylvania	130	97	90	68	107,392	97,802	106,963	106,311
South Dakota	9	7	10	9	(NA)	(NA)	(NA)	(NA)
Texas	19,797	16,689	18,620	20,309	126,150	114,732	149,062	170,262
Utah	298	389	550	634	2,362	2,381	3,772	3,668
Virginia	–	–	(NA)	(NA)	2,298	1,951	2,094	(NA)
West Virginia	233	169	206	174	40,130	38,462	46,938	50,932
Wyoming	1,151	795	1,083	1,072	18,325	13,126	15,778	15,261
Lower 48 states	44,492	35,787	41,239	44,963	486,000	436,756	525,572	565,787
Federal offshore	5,350	4,505	4,764	4,939	5,939	4,654	4,946	5,127

NA Not available. – Represents or rounds to zero. [1] Includes other states not shown separately.

Source: U.S. Energy Information Administration, "U.S. Crude Oil and Natural Gas Proved Reserves," <www.eia.gov/naturalgas/crudeoilreserves/>, acessed July 2024.

ProQuest Statistical Abstract of the United States: 2025

Table 960. Dry Natural Gas—Supply, Consumption, Reserves, and Marketed Production: 1990 to 2023

[270 represents 270,000. Data are for dry natural gas, plus a small amount of supplemental gaseous fuels. Minus sign (-) indicates debit]

Item	Unit	1990	2000	2010	2015	2020	2021	2022	2023 (P)
Producing wells (year-end)............	1,000	270	342	488	575	483	(NA)	(NA)	(NA)
Proved reserves [1]......................	Bil. cu. ft.	169,346	177,427	304,625	307,730	445,299	589,236	(NA)	(NA)
Gross withdrawals.....................	Bil. cu. ft.	21,523	24,174	26,816	32,915	40,730	41,677	43,802	45,633
Marketed production [2]................	Bil. cu. ft.	18,593.8	20,197.5	22,381.9	28,772.0	36,520.8	37,337.9	39,428.4	41,296.1
Minus: Natural gas plant liquids production [3].........................	Bil. cu. ft.	784.1	1,015.5	1,066.4	1,706.6	2,709.7	2,808.6	3,075.3	3,427.2
Equals: Dry production................	Bil. cu. ft.	17,809.7	19,182.0	21,315.5	27,065.5	33,811.1	34,529.3	36,353.0	37,868.9
Plus: Supplemental gas supplies.....	Bil. cu. ft.	122.8	90.2	64.6	58.6	63.1	66.0	73.1	63.4
Equals: Dry production with supplemental gas.....................	Bil. cu. ft.	17,932.5	19,272.2	21,380.1	27,124.1	33,874.3	34,595.3	36,426.1	37,932.2
Plus: Withdrawals from storage [4].....	Bil. cu. ft.	1,933.8	3,498.2	3,274.4	3,099.7	3,411.9	3,761.1	4,174.6	3,292.4
Plus: Imports........................	Bil. cu. ft.	1,532.3	3,781.6	3,740.8	2,718.1	2,551.2	2,808.0	3,024.2	2,929.3
Plus: Balancing item [5]................	Bil. cu. ft.	307.3	-305.7	115.5	-267.9	-386.8	-188.0	-565.1	-197.2
Equals: Total supply..................	Bil. cu. ft.	21,705.8	26,246.3	28,510.7	32,674.0	39,450.6	40,976.4	43,059.8	43,956.8
Minus: Exports.......................	Bil. cu. ft.	85.6	243.7	1,136.8	1,783.5	5,284.7	6,652.6	6,903.9	7,610.7
Minus: Additions to storage [4].........	Bil. cu. ft.	2,433.5	2,684.3	3,291.4	3,638.3	3,589.8	3,677.9	3,897.8	3,840.0
Equals: Consumption, total...........	Bil. cu. ft.	19,173.6	23,333.1	24,086.8	27,243.9	30,602.6	30,645.7	32,288.2	32,506.1
Lease and plant fuel.................	Bil. cu. ft.	1,236.4	1,150.9	1,285.6	1,576.4	1,851.2	1,850.7	1,882.8	1,972.0
Pipeline fuel [6].......................	Bil. cu. ft.	(NA)	642.2	674.1	678.2	1,020.4	1,131.5	1,212.3	1,220.5
Residential........................	Bil. cu. ft.	4,391.3	4,996.2	4,782.4	4,612.9	4,674.5	4,716.7	4,964.2	4,483.1
Commercial [7].......................	Bil. cu. ft.	2,622.7	3,182.5	3,102.6	3,201.7	3,162.7	3,289.1	3,509.1	3,310.1
Industrial..........................	Bil. cu. ft.	(NA)	8,142.2	6,826.2	7,521.9	8,213.0	8,374.7	8,536.9	8,537.0
Vehicle fuel........................	Bil. cu. ft.	(NA)	12.8	28.7	39.4	49.1	54.5	65.0	53.1
Electric power sector................	Bil. cu. ft.	(NA)	5,206.3	7,387.2	9,613.4	11,631.7	11,228.6	12,118.0	12,930.3
World production (dry).................	Tril. cu. ft.	73.4	86.8	113.8	125.6	138.3	144.2	145.1	(NA)
U.S. production (dry).................	Tril. cu. ft.	17.8	19.2	21.3	27.1	33.8	34.5	36.4	(NA)
U.S. percent of world...............	Percent	24.3	22.1	18.7	21.5	24.4	23.9	25.1	(NA)

P Preliminary. NA Not available. [1] Estimated, end of year. [2] Gross withdrawals less gas used for repressuring, quantities vented and flared, and nonhydrocarbon gases removed in treating or processing operations. Includes all quantities of gas used in field and processing plant operations. [3] Volumetric reduction in natural gas resulting from the removal of natural gas plant liquids, which are transferred to petroleum supply. [4] Underground storage. [5] Quantities lost and imbalances in data due to differences among data sources. Since 1980, excludes in-transit shipments that cross U.S.-Canada border (i.e., natural gas delivered to its destination via the other country). [6] Natural gas consumed in the operation of pipelines, primarily in compressors. [7] Includes gas used by local, State, and Federal agencies engaged in nonmanufacturing activities.

Source: U.S. Energy Information Administration, "Natural Gas Data," <www.eia.gov/naturalgas/data.php>; "Monthly Energy Review, Natural Gas," <www.eia.gov/totalenergy/data/monthly/#naturalgas>; and "International Energy Statistics," <www.eia.gov/international/overview/world>; accessed August 2024.

Table 961. Shale Natural Gas Production and Proved Reserves: 2010 to 2021

[In billions of cubic feet (5,336 represents 5,336,000,000,000). For states not listed, no production or reserves were reported. Natural gas produced from organic (black) shale formations]

State	Production					Proved reserves [1]				
	2010	2015	2019	2020	2021	2010	2015	2019	2020	2021
United States.......	**5,336**	**15,213**	**25,556**	**26,139**	**27,985**	**97,449**	**175,601**	**353,086**	**317,756**	**393,779**
Alabama..............	–	(NA)	–	–	–	–	(NA)	–	–	–
Alaska...............	–	–	–	–	–	–	–	–	–	–
Arkansas.............	794	923	471	419	387	12,526	7,164	5,093	4,210	5,127
California.............	(NA)	2	(NA)	(NA)	(NA)	(NA)	31	(NA)	(NA)	(NA)
Colorado.............	1	325	149	116	301	4	3,115	2,500	1,331	4,149
Kansas..............	(NA)	1	–	–	–	(NA)	5	–	–	–
Kentucky.............	4	1	–	–	–	10	13	–	–	–
Louisiana.............	1,232	1,153	2,518	2,555	2,942	20,070	9,154	29,553	28,533	35,630
Michigan.............	120	65	72	57	53	2,306	1,006	1,138	823	1,092
Mississippi...........	(NA)	3	–	–	–	(NA)	11	–	–	–
Montana.............	13	39	21	16	15	186	360	268	227	254
New Mexico..........	6	46	1,101	1,337	1,642	123	1,044	13,827	14,667	22,245
North Dakota.........	64	545	1,043	970	1,052	1,185	6,904	12,542	8,376	11,146
Ohio.................	–	959	2,558	2,320	2,207	–	12,430	34,376	27,775	31,790
Oklahoma............	403	993	1,490	1,195	1,239	9,670	18,672	20,897	15,483	20,750
Pennsylvania.........	396	4,597	6,782	7,040	7,546	10,708	53,484	105,394	96,699	105,586
Texas...............	2,218	4,353	7,440	7,844	8,262	38,048	42,626	93,477	87,296	116,848
Virginia..............	(NA)	3	–	–	–	(NA)	76	–	–	–
West Virginia.........	80	1,163	1,911	2,270	2,339	2,491	19,226	34,020	32,335	39,160
Wyoming.............	–	36	–	–	–	1	204	–	–	–

– Represents or rounds to zero. NA Not available. [1] Proved reserves of natural gas as of December 31 of the report year are the estimated quantities which analysis of geological and engineering data demonstrate with reasonable certainty to be recoverable in future years from known reservoirs under existing economic and operating conditions.

Source: U.S. Energy Information Administration, "Natural Gas Data," <www.eia.gov/naturalgas/data.cfm>, accessed June 2023.

Table 962. Coal Production, Supply, Disposition, and Prices: 2000 to 2023

[In millions of short tons (1,073.6 represents 1,073,600,000). 1 short ton = 2,000 lbs]

Item	2000	2010	2015	2020	2021	2022	2023
Production, total	**1,073.6**	**1,084.4**	**896.9**	**535.4**	**577.4**	**594.2**	**(NA)**
Consumption by sector:							
Total	1,084.1	1,048.5	798.1	476.7	545.7	515.5	426.5
Commercial	3.7	3.1	1.5	0.8	0.8	0.8	0.7
Industrial	94.1	70.4	58.2	40.1	43.4	41.9	38.6
Coke plants	28.9	21.1	19.7	14.4	17.6	16.0	15.8
Other industrial plants	65.2	49.3	38.5	25.7	25.8	25.9	22.9
Combined heat and power (CHP)	28.0	24.6	17.0	9.5	9.7	9.6	8.6
Noncombined heat and power	37.2	24.7	21.5	16.2	16.1	16.3	14.2
Electric power	985.8	975.1	738.4	435.8	501.4	472.8	387.2
Year-end coal stocks:							
Total	140.3	231.7	238.8	159.8	115.4	114.0	154.7
Residential and commercial	(NA)	0.6	0.4	0.3	0.2	0.2	0.2
Industrial	6.1	6.5	6.6	4.5	4.3	4.1	4.6
Coke plants	1.5	1.9	2.2	1.7	1.7	1.6	1.7
Other industrial plants	4.6	4.5	4.4	2.8	2.6	2.5	3.0
Electric power	102.3	174.9	195.9	131.4	91.9	88.9	131.4
Producers/distributors	31.9	49.8	35.9	23.6	19.0	20.8	18.4
U.S. coal trade:							
Net exports [1]	46.0	62.4	62.6	63.9	79.7	79.6	95.8
Exports	58.5	81.7	74.0	69.1	85.1	86.0	99.8
Steam coal	25.7	25.6	28.0	27.1	40.1	39.5	48.5
Metallurgical coal	32.8	56.1	46.0	42.0	45.0	46.5	51.3
Coke	1.3	1.5	0.9	0.7	2.1	2.3	1.5
Imports	12.5	19.4	11.3	5.1	5.4	6.3	4.0
Average delivered price (dollars per short ton) to:							
Electric power sector	24.28	44.27	42.60	36.36	37.51	44.92	47.39

NA Not available. [1] Exports minus imports.

Source: U.S. Energy Information Administration, *Annual Coal Report 2022*, October 2023, and earlier reports, <www.eia.gov/coal/annual/>; "Monthly Energy Review," <www.eia.gov/totalenergy/data/monthly/>, March 2024; and "Coal Data," <www.eia.gov/coal/data.cfm>, accessed April 2024.

Table 963. Coal and Coke—Summary: 1990 to 2022

[In millions of short tons (1,029 represents 1,029,000,000), except as indicated. Includes coal consumed at mines. Recoverability varies between 40 and 90 percent for individual deposits; 50 percent or more of overall U.S. coal reserve base is believed to be recoverable]

Item	Unit	1990	2000	2010	2015	2019	2020	2021	2022
COAL									
Production, total [1, 2]	Mil. sh. tons	**1,029**	**1,074**	**1,084**	**897**	**706**	**535**	**577**	**594**
Average price per short ton	Dollars	21.76	16.78	35.61	31.81	36.07	31.41	36.45	54.46
Anthracite production [2]	Mil. sh. tons	3.5	4.6	1.8	2.1	2.6	2.4	2.1	2.5
Bituminous coal and lignite [3]	Mil. sh. tons	1,026	1,069	1,083	895	704	533	575	592
Underground	Mil. sh. tons	425	374	337	307	267	196	221	222
Surface [2]	Mil. sh. tons	605	700	747	590	439	340	357	372
Exports	Mil. sh. tons	106	58	82	74	94	69	85	86
Imports	Mil. sh. tons	3	13	17	11	7	5	5	6
Consumption [4]	Mil. sh. tons	904	1,084	1,049	798	587	477	546	516
Electric power sector [5]	Mil. sh. tons	783	986	975	738	539	436	501	473
Industrial	Mil. sh. tons	115	94	70	58	47	40	43	42
Number of mines	Number	3,243	1,453	1,285	853	669	552	512	548
Daily employment	1,000	135	85	86	66	53	42	40	44
Production, by state:									
Alabama	Mil. sh. tons	29	19	20	13	14	12	9	10
Illinois	Mil. sh. tons	60	33	33	56	46	32	37	37
Indiana	Mil. sh. tons	36	28	35	34	32	20	19	24
Kentucky	Mil. sh. tons	173	131	105	61	36	24	26	29
Montana	Mil. sh. tons	38	38	45	42	34	26	29	28
Ohio	Mil. sh. tons	35	22	27	17	8	4	3	2
Pennsylvania	Mil. sh. tons	71	75	59	50	50	36	42	40
Virginia	Mil. sh. tons	47	33	22	14	12	10	11	11
West Virginia	Mil. sh. tons	169	158	135	96	93	67	79	83
Wyoming	Mil. sh. tons	184	339	443	376	277	219	239	245
Other states	Mil. sh. tons	187	197	161	138	104	86	84	85
World production	Mil. sh. tons	5,187	5,134	8,208	8,707	8,902	8,486	8,900	9,436
U.S. percent of world	Percent	19.8	20.9	13.2	10.3	7.9	6.3	6.5	6.3
COKE									
Production	Mil. sh. tons	27.6	20.8	15.0	13.8	12.9	10.4	12.5	11.4
Imports	Mil. sh. tons	0.8	4.0	1.2	0.1	0.1	0.2	0.1	0.1
Exports	Mil. sh. tons	0.6	1.3	1.5	0.9	1.0	0.7	2.1	2.3
Consumption [6]	Mil. sh. tons	27.8	23.2	14.8	13.1	11.9	9.8	10.7	9.2

[1] Includes bituminous coal, subbituminous coal, lignite, and anthracite. [2] Beginning 2005, includes a small amount of refuse recovery. [3] Includes subbituminous. [4] Includes other categories not shown separately. [5] Electricity-only and combined-heat-and-power (CHP) plants whose primary business is to sell electricity and/or heat to the public. [6] Consumption is calculated as the sum of production and imports minus exports and stock change.

Source: U.S. Energy Information Administration, *Annual Energy Review 2011*, September 2012; *Annual Coal Report 2022*, October 2023; *Quarterly Coal Report*, April 2024; *Monthly Energy Review*, March 2024; and "International Energy Statistics," <www.eia.gov/international/data /world>, accessed March 2024. See also <www.eia.gov/totalenergy> and <www.eia.gov/coal/annual>.

Table 964. Demonstrated Coal Reserves by Major Producing State: 2020 and 2022

[Reserves in millions of short tons (471,811 represents 471,811,000,000). As of January 1 the following year. The demonstrated reserve base represents the sum of coal in both measured and indicated resource categories of reliability. Measured resources of coal are estimates that have a high degree of geologic assurance from sample analyses and measurements from closely spaced and geologically well-known sample sites. Indicated resources are estimates based partly from sample and analyses and measurements and partly from reasonable geologic projections]

State	2020				2022			
		Reserves (mil. short tons)				Reserves (mil. short tons)		
			Method of mining				Method of mining	
	Number of mines	Total reserves	Under-ground	Surface	Number of mines	Total reserves	Under-ground	Surface
United States [1]	**552**	**471,811**	**325,241**	**146,570**	**548**	**470,024**	**324,344**	**145,680**
Alabama	26	3,768	667	3,101	22	3,730	632	3,098
Alaska	1	6,083	5,423	660	1	6,081	5,423	658
Arkansas	(NA)	415	271	144	(NA)	415	271	144
Colorado	7	15,595	10,840	4,754	10	15,552	10,798	4,754
Illinois	14	103,247	86,782	16,466	14	103,100	86,636	16,464
Indiana	18	8,686	8,315	371	14	8,614	8,267	347
Iowa	(NA)	2,189	1,732	457	(NA)	2,189	1,732	457
Kansas	(NA)	970	(NA)	970	(NA)	970	(NA)	970
Kentucky	97	27,987	15,541	12,446	111	27,886	15,453	12,433
Kentucky, Eastern	90	9,359	459	8,900	108	9,323	436	8,887
Kentucky, Western	7	18,628	15,082	3,546	3	18,563	15,017	3,546
Louisiana	(NA)	(NA)	(NA)	(NA)	1	366	(NA)	366
Maryland	11	592	554	38	14	588	552	35
Missouri	1	5,983	1,479	4,504	1	5,983	1,479	4,504
Montana	6	118,440	70,814	47,626	5	118,358	70,785	47,573
New Mexico	3	11,705	5,997	5,708	3	11,678	5,991	5,687
North Dakota	5	8,515	(NA)	8,515	5	8,449	(NA)	8,449
Ohio	10	22,794	17,153	5,641	10	22,785	17,146	5,638
Oklahoma	2	1,533	1,221	312	1	1,533	1,221	312
Pennsylvania	134	25,921	21,826	4,095	108	25,764	21,679	4,084
Anthracite [2]	46	7,162	3,840	3,322	36	7,157	3,840	3,317
Bituminous	88	18,759	17,986	773	72	18,607	17,840	767
Tennessee	2	744	494	251	1	744	494	251
Texas	7	11,695	(NA)	11,695	4	11,652	(NA)	11,652
Utah	7	4,857	4,596	261	6	4,811	4,551	260
Virginia	41	1,217	766	451	40	1,178	735	444
Washington	(NA)	1,340	1,332	8	(NA)	1,340	1,332	8
West Virginia	135	29,917	26,869	3,048	151	29,614	26,602	3,012
Wyoming	16	56,720	42,415	14,304	16	56,113	42,409	13,704

NA Not available. [1] Includes other states not shown separately. [2] All of the anthracite mines in the United States are located in northeastern Pennsylvania.

Source: U.S. Energy Information Administration, *Annual Coal Report 2022*, October 2023, and earlier reports. See also <www.eia.gov/coal/annual/>.

Table 965. Uranium Concentrate Industry—Summary: 1990 to 2023

[In units as indicated (1.7 represents 1,700,000). See also Section 19, Table 985]

Item	Unit	1990	2000	2010	2015	2019	2020	2021	2022	2023
Exploration and development, surface drilling	Mil. ft.	1.7	1.0	4.9	0.9	(D)	(D)	0.1	0.5	1.1
Expenditures	Mil. dol.	(NA)	5.6	44.6	28.7	(D)	(D)	(D)	9.40	28.5
Mines operated	Number	39	10	9	9	6	6	3	5	5
Underground	Number	27	1	4	1	1	1	–	–	–
Open pit	Number	2	–	–	–	–	–	–	–	–
In situ leaching	Number	7	4	4	7	5	5	3	4	5
Other sources [1]	Number	3	5	1	1	–	–	–	1	–
Mine production	1,000 pounds	5,876	3,123	4,237	3,711	174	(D)	21	194	50
Underground	1,000 pounds	(D)	(D)	(D)	(D)	(D)	(D)	(D)	(D)	(D)
Open pit	1,000 pounds	1,881	–	–	–	–	–	–	–	–
In situ leaching	1,000 pounds	(D)	2,995	(D)	(D)	(D)	(D)	(D)	(D)	(D)
Other sources [1]	1,000 pounds	3,995	128	(D)	(D)	(D)	(D)	(D)	(D)	(D)
Uranium concentrate production	1,000 pounds	8,886	3,958	4,228	3,343	174	(D)	21	194	50
Concentrate shipments from mills and plants	1,000 pounds	12,957	3,187	5,137	4,023	190	(D)	(D)	162	560
Employment	Person-years [2]	1,335	627	1,073	625	265	225	207	196	340

– Represents zero. D Data withheld to avoid disclosing figures for individual companies. NA Not available. [1] Includes mine water, mill site cleanup and mill tailings, and well field restoration as sources of uranium. [2] A person-year is defined as one whole year, or fraction thereof, worked by an employee, including contracted man power. 12 months worked is 1 person year.

Source: U.S. Energy Information Administration, through 2002, *Uranium Industry*, annual. Thereafter, *Domestic Uranium Production Report*, May 2024, and earlier reports. See also <www.eia.gov/uranium/production/annual>.

This section presents statistics on fuel resources, energy production and consumption, electric energy, renewable energy, and the electric and gas utility industries. The principal sources are the U.S. Department of Energy's Energy Information Administration (EIA) and the American Gas Association, Arlington, VA. The Department of Energy was created in October 1977 and assumed and centralized the responsibilities of all or part of several agencies including the Federal Power Commission (FPC), the U.S. Bureau of Mines, the Federal Energy Administration, and the U.S. Energy Research and Development Administration. For additional data on transportation, see Section 23; on fuels, see Section 18; and on energy-related housing characteristics, see Section 20.

The EIA, in its *Annual Energy Review*, provided statistics and trend data on energy supply, demand, and prices. Information was included on petroleum and natural gas, coal, electricity, hydroelectric power, nuclear power, solar, wind, wood, and geothermal energy. Due to budget constraints the EIA suspended publication of the *Annual Energy Review* in 2013. Data previously found in the *Annual Energy Review* can now be found in the *Monthly Energy Review*, which presents data on current supply, disposition, and price data for energy resources and monthly publications on petroleum, coal, natural gas, and electric power. Additional EIA reports include the *Electric Power Annual*; *Natural Gas Annual*; *Petroleum Supply Annual*; *U.S. Crude Oil and Natural Gas*; *Electric Sales, Revenue, and Price*; *State Energy Data System (SEDS)*; *Annual Energy Outlook*; *Uranium Marketing Annual Report*; *Domestic Uranium Production Report—Quarterly*; and *International Energy Statistics*. These various reports contain state, national, and international data on the production of electricity, net summer capability of generating plants, fuels used in energy production, energy sales and consumption, and hydroelectric power. The EIA also provides access to regular data updates through its Open Data program. For more information, please refer to the EIA's Open Data program's web site <www.eia.gov/opendata/>.

Data on residential energy consumption, expenditures, and conservation activities are available from EIA's Residential Energy Consumption Survey (RECS) and are published every 4 years. The Commercial Buildings Energy Consumption Survey (CBECS), collects information on the stock of U.S. commercial buildings, their energy-related characteristics, and their energy consumption and expenditures. Data on manufacturing energy consumption, use, and expenditures are also collected every 4 years from EIA's Manufacturing Energy Consumption Survey (MECS). Due to the long gaps between the RECS, CBECS, and MECS, tables are rotated in and out of Section 19 in an effort to keep the data as current as possible. The results from these surveys are published at <www.eia.gov/consumption>.

The American Gas Association, in its annual yearbook,

Gas Facts, presents data on gas utilities and financial and operating statistics.

Btu conversion factors—Various energy sources are converted from original units to the thermal equivalent using British thermal units (Btu). A Btu is the amount of energy required to raise the temperature of 1 pound of water 1 degree Fahrenheit (F) at or near 39.2 degrees F. Factors are calculated annually from the latest final annual data available; some are revised as a result.

Electric power industry—In recent years, EIA has restructured the industry categories it once used to gather and report electricity statistics. The electric power industry, previously divided into electric utilities and non-utilities, now consists of the Electric Power Sector, the Commercial Sector, and the Industrial Sector.

The Electric Power Sector is composed of electricity-only and combined-heat-and-power plants (CHPs) whose primary business is to sell electricity, or electricity and heat, to the public.

Electricity-only plants are composed of traditional electric utilities, and nontraditional participants, including energy service providers, power marketers, independent power producers (IPPs), and the portion of CHPs that produce only electricity.

A utility is defined as a corporation, person, agency, authority, or other legal entity or instrumentality aligned with distribution facilities for delivery of electric energy for use primarily by the public. Electric utilities include investor-owned electric utilities, municipal and state utilities, federal electric utilities, and rural electric cooperatives.

An independent power producer is an entity defined as a corporation, person, agency, authority, or other legal entity or instrumentality that owns or operates facilities whose primary business is to produce electricity for use by the public. They are not generally aligned with distribution facilities and are not considered electric utilities.

Combined-heat-and-power producers are plants designed to produce both heat and electricity from a single heat source. These types of electricity producers can be independent power producers or industrial or commercial establishments. As some independent power producers are CHPs, their information is included in the data for the combined-heat-and-power sector.

The Commercial Sector consists of commercial CHPs and commercial electricity-only plants. Industrial CHPs and industrial electricity-only plants make up the Industrial Sector. For more information, please refer to the *Electric Power Annual* web site at <www.eia.gov/electricity/annual/>.

Table 966. Utilities—Establishments, Revenue, Payroll, and Employees by Kind of Business: 2017

[577,100 represents $577,100,000,000. Includes only establishments or firms with payroll. Data based on the 2017 Economic Census. See Appendix III]

Kind of business	NAICS code [1]	Establish-ments (number)	Revenue Total (mil. dol.)	Revenue Per paid employee (dol.)	Annual payroll Total (mil. dol.)	Annual payroll Per paid employee (dol.)	Paid employees for pay period including March 12 (number)
Utilities................................	22	18,913	577,100	876,541	67,667	102,777	658,384
Electric power generation, transmission, & distribution...............................	2211	11,496	461,919	888,903	56,541	108,806	519,651
Electric power generation.............................	22111	3,280	119,266	860,216	15,610	112,590	138,647
Hydroelectric power generation........................	221111	523	3,334	915,503	328	90,185	3,642
Fossil fuel electric power generation.............	221112	1,711	75,455	992,072	8,193	107,715	76,058
Nuclear electric power generation................	221113	176	29,014	597,959	6,063	124,959	48,521
Solar electric power generation....................	221114	205	1,801	832,698	222	102,581	2,163
Wind electric power generation....................	221115	454	7,762	1,556,811	511	102,400	4,986
Geothermal electric power generation...........	221116	34	974	801,967	121	99,859	1,214
Biomass electric power generation...............	221117	141	906	460,174	163	82,940	1,968
Other electric power generation...................	221118	36	21	219,832	9	96,179	95
Electric power transmission, control & distribution...............................	22112	8,216	342,653	899,342	40,931	107,429	381,004
Electric bulk power transmission & control.................................	221121	273	13,772	893,328	1,828	118,571	15,416
Electric power distribution.........................	221122	7,943	328,881	899,596	39,103	106,960	365,588
Natural gas distribution.............................	2212	2,550	100,586	1,096,344	8,155	88,890	91,747
Water, sewage, & other systems....................	2213	4,867	14,595	310,623	2,970	63,215	46,986
Water supply & irrigation systems...................	22131	4,108	11,759	307,997	2,411	63,152	38,180
Sewage treatment facilities.........................	22132	634	1,524	239,375	337	52,977	6,367
Steam & air-conditioning supply....................	22133	125	1,312	537,732	222	90,919	2,439

[1] North American Industry Classification System, 2017; see text, Section 15.

Source: U.S. Census Bureau, 2017 Economic Census, EC1700BASIC, "All Sectors: Summary Statistics for the U.S., States, and Selected Geographies: 2017," <data.census.gov>, accessed November 2021.

Table 967. Utilities—Employees, Annual Payroll, and Establishments by Industry: 2021 and 2022

[74,801 represents $74,801,000,000. Excludes most government employees, railroad employees, and self-employed persons. An establishment is a single physical location where business is conducted or where services or industrial operations are performed. See Appendix III]

Industry	NAICS code [1]	2021 Estab-lish-ments	2021 Number of employ-ees [2]	2021 Annual payroll (mil. dol.)	2021 Average payroll per em-ployee (dol.)	2022 Estab-lish-ments	2022 Number of employ-ees [2]	2022 Annual payroll (mil. dol.)	2022 Average payroll per em-ployee (dol.)
Utilities, total.............................	22	19,896	633,738	74,801	118,031	20,425	645,214	78,715	121,998
Electric power generation, transmission and distribution...........	2211	12,481	497,375	61,889	124,431	12,902	505,132	64,829	128,341
Electric power generation................	22111	3,856	124,532	15,943	128,021	4,082	130,954	17,231	131,580
Hydroelectric power......................	221111	555	4,582	484	105,621	552	4,633	508	109,652
Fossil fuel electric power...............	221112	1,783	63,653	8,076	126,876	1,799	66,913	8,826	131,904
Nuclear electric power..................	221113	175	40,144	5,352	133,324	164	38,376	5,133	133,757
Solar electric power.....................	221114	460	4,811	620	128,819	621	7,822	1,054	134,801
Wind electric power.....................	221115	611	7,644	1,014	132,698	629	8,410	1,139	135,474
Geothermal electric power.............	221116	36	1,310	155	118,145	44	1,335	167	125,025
Biomass electric power.................	221117	110	1,942	189	97,505	113	2,513	274	108,968
Other electric power generation.......	221118	126	[3] 446	52	117,372	160	[3] 952	129	135,716
Electric power transmission, control & distribution....................	22112	8,625	372,843	45,946	123,231	8,820	374,178	47,598	127,208
Electric bulk power transmission & control.............................	221121	335	16,205	2,220	137,007	364	19,570	2,960	151,231
Electric power distribution.............	221122	8,290	356,638	43,726	122,605	8,456	354,608	44,639	125,882
Natural gas distribution....................	2212	2,441	89,775	9,682	107,850	2,420	91,556	10,270	112,167
Water, sewage, & other systems.........	2213	4,974	46,588	3,230	69,334	5,103	48,526	3,616	74,513
Water supply & irrigation systems......	22131	4,338	39,514	2,745	69,477	4,430	40,710	3,003	73,765
Sewage treatment facilities..............	22132	545	5,775	353	61,113	562	6,096	415	68,055
Steam & air-conditioning supply........	22133	91	1,299	132	101,535	111	1,720	198	115,109

[1] North American Industry Classification System, 2017; see text, Section 15. [2] Covers full- and part-time employees who are on the payroll in the pay period including March 12. [3] Data is flagged for high noise; the value was changed by 5 percent or more to avoid disclosure of data for individual businesses.

Source: U.S. Census Bureau, County Business Patterns, "All Sectors: County Business Patterns, including ZIP Code Business Patterns, by Legal Form of Organization and Employment Size Class for the U.S., States, and Selected Geographies: 2022," <data.census.gov>, accessed June 2024. See also <www.census.gov/programs-surveys/cbp.html>.

Table 968. Energy Supply and Disposition by Type of Fuel: 1973 to 2023

[In quadrillion British thermal units (Btu) (61.59 represents 61,590,000,000,000). For definition of Btu, see source and text, this section]

Year	Production					Renewable energy[4]					Net imports, total[7]	Consumption					
	Total[1]	Crude oil[2]	Dry natural gas	Coal[3]	Nuclear electric power	Total[1]	Hydro-electric power[5]	Bio-mass[6]	Solar/photo-voltaic	Wind		Total[1,8]	Petro-leum[9]	Natural gas[10]	Coal	Nuclear electric power	Renew-able energy, total[4]
1973	61.59	19.49	22.19	13.99	0.91	2.48	0.94	1.53	(NA)	(NA)	12.58	73.72	34.81	22.51	12.97	0.91	2.48
1975	59.14	17.73	19.64	14.99	1.90	2.54	1.03	1.50	(NA)	(NA)	11.71	69.79	32.70	19.95	12.66	1.90	2.54
1980	65.16	18.25	19.91	18.60	2.74	3.45	0.95	2.48	(NA)	(NA)	12.10	76.04	34.16	20.24	15.42	2.74	3.45
1985	65.60	18.99	16.98	19.33	4.08	4.02	0.97	3.02	(Z)	(Z)	7.58	74.27	30.87	17.70	17.48	4.08	4.02
1990	68.49	15.57	18.33	22.49	6.10	3.86	1.00	2.74	0.06	0.01	14.06	82.26	33.50	19.60	19.17	6.10	3.86
1995	68.87	13.89	19.08	22.13	7.08	4.29	1.06	3.10	0.06	0.01	17.68	88.67	34.34	22.67	20.09	7.08	4.30
1996	69.90	13.72	19.34	22.79	7.09	4.48	1.18	3.16	0.07	0.01	19.02	91.40	35.59	23.08	21.00	7.09	4.48
1997	69.87	13.66	19.39	23.31	6.60	4.47	1.22	3.11	0.06	0.01	20.63	91.96	36.07	23.22	21.45	6.60	4.46
1998	70.51	13.24	19.61	24.05	7.07	4.17	1.10	2.93	0.06	0.01	22.24	92.60	36.72	22.83	21.66	7.07	4.17
1999	69.37	12.45	19.34	23.30	7.61	4.20	1.09	2.97	0.06	0.02	23.48	94.23	37.73	22.91	21.62	7.61	4.20
2000	69.26	12.36	19.66	22.74	7.86	4.09	0.94	3.01	0.06	0.02	24.90	96.69	38.15	23.82	22.58	7.86	4.10
2001	70.03	12.28	20.17	23.55	8.03	3.51	0.74	2.62	0.06	0.02	26.32	94.42	38.08	22.77	21.91	8.03	3.51
2002	68.69	12.16	19.38	22.73	8.15	3.77	0.90	2.71	0.06	0.04	25.72	95.58	38.12	23.51	21.90	8.15	3.77
2003	67.86	11.96	19.63	22.09	7.96	3.91	0.94	2.80	0.05	0.04	26.99	95.81	38.71	22.83	22.32	7.96	3.92
2004	68.20	11.55	19.07	22.85	8.22	4.09	0.92	3.00	0.05	0.05	29.14	98.03	40.14	22.92	22.47	8.22	4.11
2005	67.38	10.97	18.56	23.19	8.16	4.22	0.92	3.10	0.05	0.06	30.20	98.10	40.22	22.57	22.80	8.16	4.23
2006	68.52	10.77	19.02	23.79	8.21	4.43	0.99	3.21	0.05	0.09	29.92	97.23	39.73	22.24	22.45	8.21	4.48
2007	69.41	10.74	19.79	23.49	8.46	4.58	0.84	3.47	0.06	0.12	29.34	98.97	39.37	23.66	22.75	8.46	4.59
2008	71.04	10.61	20.70	23.85	8.43	5.08	0.87	3.87	0.06	0.19	26.02	96.65	36.77	23.84	22.39	8.43	5.07
2009	70.28	11.34	21.14	21.62	8.36	5.31	0.93	3.96	0.06	0.25	22.77	91.63	34.78	23.42	19.69	8.36	5.29
2010	72.54	11.61	21.81	22.04	8.43	5.94	0.89	4.55	0.07	0.32	21.69	95.14	35.32	24.57	20.83	8.43	5.90
2011	75.20	12.01	23.41	22.22	8.27	6.40	1.09	4.71	0.08	0.41	18.38	93.97	34.64	24.95	19.66	8.27	6.31
2012	76.55	13.85	24.61	20.68	8.06	6.19	0.94	4.55	0.09	0.48	15.80	91.68	33.83	26.09	17.38	8.06	6.15
2013	78.98	15.87	24.86	20.00	8.24	6.56	0.92	4.83	0.12	0.57	12.84	94.25	34.40	26.81	18.04	8.24	6.59
2014	84.79	18.61	26.72	20.29	8.34	6.84	0.88	5.05	0.16	0.62	10.97	95.33	34.66	27.38	18.00	8.34	6.80
2015	85.37	19.70	28.07	17.95	8.34	6.85	0.85	5.03	0.20	0.65	10.89	94.48	35.37	28.19	15.55	8.34	6.83
2016	81.05	18.53	27.58	14.67	8.43	7.19	0.91	5.13	0.25	0.77	11.26	94.09	35.71	28.40	14.23	8.43	7.12
2017	84.37	19.55	28.29	15.63	8.42	7.50	1.02	5.17	0.33	0.87	7.51	93.90	36.04	28.06	13.84	8.42	7.38
2018	91.96	22.81	31.88	15.36	8.44	7.74	1.00	5.31	0.38	0.93	3.61	97.40	36.89	31.16	13.25	8.44	7.53
2019	97.60	25.60	35.19	14.26	8.45	7.75	0.98	5.22	0.43	1.01	-0.61	96.60	36.87	32.26	11.32	8.45	7.59
2020	91.86	23.57	35.06	10.70	8.25	7.47	0.97	4.71	0.51	1.15	-3.48	88.85	32.33	31.64	9.18	8.25	7.30
2021	93.84	23.40	35.81	11.60	8.13	7.81	0.86	4.91	0.63	1.29	-3.62	93.36	35.24	31.71	10.55	8.13	7.64
2022	98.53	24.71	37.66	12.04	8.06	8.31	0.87	5.07	0.76	1.48	-5.83	94.79	35.32	33.35	9.89	8.06	8.09
2023	102.77	26.86	39.25	11.76	8.10	8.42	0.82	5.16	0.88	1.45	-7.82	93.69	35.52	33.61	8.18	8.10	8.24

NA Not available. Z Less than 5 trillion. [1] Includes other types of fuel not shown separately. [2] Includes lease condensate. [3] Beginning 1989, includes waste coal supplied. Beginning 2001, also includes a small amount of refuse recovery. [4] Electricity net generation from conventional hydroelectric power, geothermal, solar, and wind. Consumption of electricity from wood, biomass waste, and alcohol fuels; geothermal heat pump and direct use energy; and solar thermal direct use energy. [5] Conventional hydroelectricity net generation. [6] Organic nonfossil material of biological origin constituting a renewable energy source. [7] Imports minus exports. [8] Includes coal coke net imports and electricity net imports, not shown separately. [9] Petroleum products supplied, including natural gas plant liquids and crude oil burned as fuel. Does not include biofuels that have been blended with petroleum. [10] Excludes supplemental gaseous fuels.

Source: U.S. Energy Information Administration, *Monthly Energy Review*, March 2024. See also <www.eia.gov/totalenergy/data/monthly>.

Table 969. Energy Supply and Disposition by Type of Fuel—Estimates, 2022, and Projections, 2025 to 2050

[Quadrillion Btu (104.76 represents 104,760,000,000,000,000) per year. Btu = British thermal unit. For definition of Btu, see source and text, this section. Projections are "reference" or mid-level forecasts. See report for methodology and assumptions used in generating projections]

Type of fuel	2022, estimate	Projections					
		2025	2030	2035	2040	2045	2050
Production, total............................	**104.76**	**108.03**	**112.32**	**117.36**	**118.69**	**121.32**	**124.25**
Crude oil and lease condensate......................	24.59	26.69	27.66	27.45	26.86	27.11	27.39
Natural gas plant liquids............................	7.77	8.31	8.06	8.34	8.63	9.08	9.31
Natural gas, dry......................................	37.81	37.05	38.41	40.96	42.38	43.04	43.62
Coal [1]...	11.79	11.33	7.09	7.07	6.44	6.19	5.95
Nuclear power..	8.06	8.17	7.92	7.31	6.53	6.54	6.53
Renewable energy [2]................................	12.92	15.67	22.35	25.51	27.14	28.66	30.78
Other [3]..	1.83	0.80	0.84	0.71	0.70	0.70	0.68
Imports, total..............................	**21.82**	**21.82**	**21.64**	**21.82**	**22.15**	**22.15**	**21.36**
Crude oil...	13.82	15.31	15.59	15.85	16.05	15.77	14.81
Petroleum and other liquids [4].....................	4.76	4.03	3.80	3.68	3.70	3.75	3.77
Natural gas..	2.98	2.35	2.07	2.13	2.23	2.48	2.63
Other imports [5].....................................	0.25	0.13	0.18	0.17	0.17	0.16	0.16
Exports, total..............................	**27.85**	**31.63**	**35.68**	**39.52**	**40.14**	**40.23**	**38.96**
Petroleum and other liquids [6].....................	18.54	20.58	22.20	22.98	23.05	23.14	21.93
Natural gas..	7.16	8.34	10.67	13.72	14.36	14.39	14.30
Coal..	2.15	2.72	2.81	2.82	2.72	2.70	2.72
Consumption, total.........................	**99.19**	**97.75**	**97.96**	**99.13**	**100.25**	**102.69**	**105.94**
Petroleum and other liquids [7].....................	36.82	36.38	35.46	34.77	34.64	35.05	36.00
Natural gas..	33.18	30.45	29.29	28.71	29.63	30.43	31.13
Coal [8]...	9.69	8.65	4.40	4.30	3.81	3.55	3.21
Nuclear power..	8.06	8.17	7.92	7.31	6.53	6.54	6.53
Renewable energy [9]................................	11.16	13.84	20.61	23.75	25.36	26.85	28.81
Other [10]...	0.27	0.26	0.28	0.28	0.28	0.27	0.27
Prices (2022 dollars per unit):							
Crude oil spot prices (dol. per barrel):							
Brent spot price......................................	102.13	87.05	90.16	93.55	96.39	98.60	101.34
West Texas Intermediate spot price..................	95.88	85.23	87.19	90.03	92.76	94.86	97.68
Natural gas at Henry Hub (dol. per mil. Btu)..........	6.52	3.49	2.91	3.68	3.94	3.91	3.77
Coal minemouth price (dol. per ton) [11]................	37.85	40.78	52.80	53.33	59.12	62.54	65.41
Electricity price (cents per kWh)....................	12.2	11.0	10.4	10.7	11.2	11.3	11.0

[1] Includes waste coal. [2] Includes grid-connected electricity from conventional hydroelectric power; biomass (including wood and wood waste, and other biomass); landfill gas; biogenic municipal waste; wind; photovoltaic and solar thermal sources; and nonelectric energy from renewable sources, such as active and passive solar systems, and wood. Excludes electricity imports using renewable sources and nonmarketed renewable energy. [3] Includes nonbiogenic municipal waste, hydrogen, methanol, and some domestic inputs to refineries. [4] Includes imports of finished petroleum products, unfinished oils, alcohols, ethers, blending components, and renewable fuels such as ethanol. [5] Includes coal, coal coke (net), and electricity (net). Excludes imports of fuel used in nuclear power plants. [6] Includes crude oil, petroleum products, ethanol, and biodiesel. [7] Includes petroleum-derived fuels and non-petroleum-derived fuels, such as ethanol, biodiesel, and coal-based synthetic liquids. Petroleum coke, which is a solid, is included. Also included are hydrocarbon gas liquids and crude oil consumed as a fuel. [8] Excludes coal converted to coal-based synthetic liquids and natural gas. [9] Includes grid-connected electricity from wood and wood waste, non-electric energy from wood, and biofuels heat and coproducts used in the production of liquid fuels, but excludes the energy content of the liquid fuels. See also footnote 2. [10] Includes non-biogenic municipal waste, hydrogen, and net electricity imports. [11] Includes reported prices for both open market and captive mines.

Source: U.S. Energy Information Administration, *Annual Energy Outlook 2023*, March 2023. See also <www.eia.gov/outlooks/aeo>.

Table 970. Energy Consumption by End-Use Sector: 1980 to 2023

[Trillion Btu (15,082.0 represents 15,082,000,000,000,000). Btu=British thermal unit. Represents consumption of fossil fuels and renewable energy, plus electricity retail sales and electrical system energy losses. For definition of Btu, see source and text, this section]

Year	Residential	Commercial [1]	Industrial [1]	Transportation	Year	Residential	Commercial [1]	Industrial [1]	Transportation
1980.........	15,082.0	10,055.3	31,208.7	19,693.7	2002.........	20,080.4	16,673.4	32,011.8	26,804.7
1981.........	14,631.0	10,095.5	29,919.3	19,511.3	2003.........	20,389.9	16,659.5	31,881.1	26,877.1
1982.........	14,758.0	10,215.2	26,749.4	19,085.9	2004.........	20,373.0	16,979.3	32,863.9	27,822.5
1983.........	14,586.2	10,245.2	26,482.4	19,172.5	2005.........	20,878.6	17,163.3	31,802.5	28,256.6
1984.........	15,171.1	10,772.8	28,639.7	19,651.4	2006.........	19,884.0	16,949.3	31,709.6	28,692.5
1985.........	15,343.6	10,845.4	27,999.7	20,084.3	2007.........	20,810.6	17,571.1	31,773.2	28,810.9
1986.........	15,243.0	10,967.0	27,460.6	20,784.9	2008.........	20,893.6	17,650.8	30,684.7	27,417.1
1987.........	15,632.0	11,393.5	28,673.3	21,465.5	2009.........	20,208.4	17,048.6	27,782.2	26,587.2
1988.........	16,574.7	12,087.9	30,045.1	22,314.8	2010.........	20,986.6	17,219.5	29,958.4	26,970.5
1989.........	17,102.9	12,580.5	30,560.9	22,475.0	2011.........	20,285.7	16,952.1	30,123.5	26,597.7
1990.........	16,206.2	12,650.3	30,978.1	22,415.2	2012.........	18,871.2	16,446.4	30,230.4	26,127.1
1991.........	16,677.7	12,834.8	30,587.7	22,114.3	2013.........	19,982.5	16,896.7	30,761.7	26,613.5
1992.........	16,722.7	12,865.9	31,836.5	22,411.9	2014.........	20,337.9	17,194.8	30,921.2	26,875.4
1993.........	17,498.0	13,181.1	31,839.3	22,667.3	2015.........	19,520.3	17,096.6	30,613.1	27,252.8
1994.........	17,461.8	13,509.1	32,773.2	23,315.5	2016.........	18,928.7	16,838.1	30,520.2	27,810.0
1995.........	17,747.3	13,985.2	33,125.4	23,808.2	2017.........	18,471.1	16,540.2	30,842.7	28,047.3
1996.........	18,633.5	14,384.4	33,967.4	24,415.3	2018.........	20,023.1	17,072.0	31,812.9	28,503.7
1997.........	18,103.9	14,860.8	34,268.0	24,718.6	2019.........	19,574.9	16,637.9	31,715.6	28,669.2
1998.........	18,162.6	15,213.2	34,009.2	25,221.0	2020.........	18,795.1	15,322.4	30,288.4	24,450.2
1999.........	18,766.1	15,615.7	33,932.4	25,912.5	2021.........	18,990.7	15,913.7	31,394.1	27,069.6
2000.........	19,731.7	16,503.8	33,944.7	26,512.4	2022.........	19,478.4	16,591.1	31,094.8	27,629.2
2001.........	19,462.8	16,566.1	32,153.6	26,239.4	2023.........	18,431.7	16,116.9	31,106.5	28,057.4

[1] Includes energy consumed at combined-heat-and-power (CHP) and electricity-only plants within the sector.

Source: U.S. Energy Information Administration, *Monthly Energy Review*, March 2024. See also <www.eia.gov/totalenergy/data/monthly>.

Table 971. Energy Consumption by Mode of Transportation: 2010 to 2022

[27 represents 27,000,000,000,000. Btu = British thermal unit. For conversion rates for each fuel type, see source]

Mode	Trillion Btu				Physical units		
	2010	2020	2022	Unit	2010	2020	2022
AIR [1]							
Aviation gasoline..........................	27	24	27	Mil. gal.	221	204	224
Jet fuel..	1,686	1,158	1,806	Mil. gal.	12,492	8,575	13,377
HIGHWAY							
Light duty vehicle, short wheel base & motorcycle [2]...	10,491	9,254	(NA)	Mil. gal.	87,215	76,936	(NA)
Light duty vehicle, long wheel base [2]..................	4,360	4,263	(NA)	Mil. gal.	36,251	35,438	(NA)
Single-unit 2-axle 6-tire or more truck...................	1,816	1,874	(NA)	Mil. gal.	15,097	15,577	(NA)
Combination truck [3].......................	3,600	3,511	(NA)	Mil. gal.	29,927	29,186	(NA)
Bus..	231	246	(NA)	Mil. gal.	1,921	2,047	(NA)
TRANSIT [4]							
Electricity.......................................	22	21	20	Mil. kWh	6,414	6,198	5,938
Diesel (includes bio-diesel)................	87	67	67	Mil. gal.	633	491	486
Gasoline and other nondiesel fuels [5]..................	12	11	11	Mil. gal.	98	94	91
Compressed natural gas..................	18	24	24	Mil. gal.	126	172	172
RAIL [6]							
Distillate/diesel fuel.........................	489	415	(NA)	Mil. gal.	3,557	3,022	(NA)
Electricity.......................................	2	1	1	Mil. kWh	559	349	432
WATER							
Residual fuel oil..............................	770	218	(NA)	Mil. gal.	5,143	1,457	(NA)
Distillate/diesel fuel oil.....................	275	250	(NA)	Mil. gal.	2,003	1,817	(NA)
Gasoline...	140	280	(NA)	Mil. gal.	1,167	2,326	(NA)
PIPELINE							
Natural gas....................................	699	1,058	1,257	Mil. cu. ft.	674,124	1,020,360	1,212,338

NA Not available. [1] Includes general aviation and certified carriers, domestic operations only; and fuel used in air taxi operations, but not commuter operations. [2] "Light duty vehicle, short wheel base" includes passenger cars, light trucks, vans and sport utility vehicles with a wheelbase (WB) equal to or less than 121 inches. "Light duty vehicle, long wheel base" includes large passenger cars, vans, pickup trucks, and sport/utility vehicles with wheelbases (WB) larger than 121 inches. [3] A power unit (truck tractor) and one or more trailing units (a semitrailer or trailer). [4] Includes light, heavy, and commuter rail; motor bus; trolley bus; van pools; automated guideway; and demand-responsive vehicles. [5] Includes gasoline, liquefied petroleum gas, liquefied natural gas, methane, ethanol, bunker fuel, kerosene, grain additive, and other fuel. [6] Includes Amtrak and freight service carriers that have an annual operating revenue of $250 million or more.

Source: U.S. Department of Transportation, Bureau of Transportation Statistics, "National Transportation Statistics," <www.bts.gov/topics/national-transportation-statistics>, accessed March 2024.

Table 972. Renewable Energy Consumption by Source and Sector: 2000 to 2023

[In trillion Btu (4,095.6 represents 4,095,600,000,000,000). For definition of Btu, see source and text, this section. Renewable energy is obtained from sources that are essentially inexhaustible, unlike fossil fuels of which there is a finite supply]

Source and sector	2000	2010	2015	2020	2021	2022	2023
Consumption, total..................	**4,095.6**	**5,895.7**	**6,829.5**	**7,300.6**	**7,644.2**	**8,090.8**	**8,244.6**
Conventional hydroelectric power [1].........	940.3	887.8	849.9	973.4	858.4	869.3	818.4
Geothermal energy [2].........................	68.7	111.4	117.8	117.7	118.0	118.4	119.7
Biomass energy [3]..........................	3,008.2	4,505.6	5,014.9	4,545.1	4,750.6	4,856.7	4,978.1
Solar energy [4].............................	59.3	67.9	196.2	511.3	626.9	764.6	877.5
Wind energy [5].............................	19.1	323.0	650.7	1,153.0	1,290.4	1,481.8	1,450.9
Residential [6].............................	**486.0**	**636.3**	**639.2**	**535.9**	**552.6**	**661.7**	**724.7**
Wood [7].......................................	420.0	540.5	512.7	345.1	344.1	422.5	450.3
Geothermal [2]................................	8.6	36.8	39.6	39.6	39.6	39.6	39.6
Solar [4]..	57.4	59.0	86.9	151.2	168.8	199.7	234.8
Commercial [8]............................	**127.2**	**133.6**	**193.0**	**215.4**	**225.1**	**273.6**	**274.7**
Biomass [3]....................................	119.1	110.9	151.9	147.0	148.6	189.6	184.9
Hydroelectric [1]..............................	0.3	0.3	0.1	0.7	0.9	0.9	0.8
Geothermal [2]................................	7.6	18.5	19.7	21.2	21.4	19.7	19.7
Solar energy [4]..............................	0.2	3.9	20.8	45.9	53.6	62.8	68.8
Wind energy [5]..............................	(NA)	0.1	0.4	0.6	0.6	0.6	0.5
Industrial [9]................................	**1,900.0**	**2,331.1**	**2,488.5**	**2,291.9**	**2,357.0**	**2,319.8**	**2,249.3**
Biomass [3]....................................	1,881.5	2,320.3	2,474.3	2,270.0	2,335.6	2,297.3	2,225.5
Hydroelectric [1]..............................	14.1	5.7	4.8	3.4	3.2	3.1	3.1
Geothermal [2]................................	4.4	4.2	4.2	4.2	4.2	4.2	4.2
Solar energy [4]..............................	(Z)	0.9	5.0	12.2	13.6	14.8	16.2
Wind energy [5]..............................	(NA)	(NA)	0.2	2.1	0.4	0.4	0.4
Transportation [10].........................	**134.9**	**1,074.5**	**1,351.0**	**1,355.5**	**1,496.0**	**1,573.1**	**1,788.4**
Fuel ethanol...................................	134.9	1,041.4	1,109.9	1,004.4	1,109.5	1,111.4	1,128.4
Biodiesel [11]..................................	(NA)	33.2	190.6	239.4	218.2	211.6	247.4
Electric power [12].........................	**1,447.4**	**1,720.2**	**2,157.7**	**2,901.8**	**3,013.5**	**3,262.6**	**3,207.5**
Biomass [3]....................................	452.8	459.4	524.9	427.6	426.2	374.2	329.0
Hydroelectric [1]..............................	925.8	881.8	844.9	969.2	854.3	865.4	814.5
Geothermal [2]................................	48.1	51.9	54.3	52.7	52.8	54.9	56.2
Solar [4]..	1.7	4.1	83.4	302.0	390.8	487.4	557.8
Wind [5]..	19.1	322.9	650.1	1,150.4	1,289.5	1,480.8	1,450.0

NA Not available. Z Less than 50 billion. [1] Power produced from the kinetic energy of falling water. [2] As used at electric power plants, hot water or steam extracted from geothermal reservoirs supplied to steam turbines at electric power plants that drive generators to produce electricity. [3] Wood and wood-derived fuels, municipal solid waste, fuel ethanol, and biodiesel. [4] The radiant energy of the sun, which can be converted into other forms of energy. Solar thermal and photovoltaic electricity net generation and solar thermal direct use energy. [5] Energy present in wind motion that can be converted to mechanical energy for driving pumps, mills, and electric power generators. [6] Living quarters for private households; excludes institutional living quarters. [7] Wood and wood-derived fuels. [8] Service-providing facilities and equipment of businesses, governments, and other private and public organizations. Includes commercial combined-heat-and-power and commercial electricity-only plants. [9] All facilities and equipment used for producing, processing, or assembling goods. Includes industrial combined-heat-and-power and industrial electricity-only plants. [10] Beginning 2009, includes other renewable diesel fuel and other renewable fuels consumption, not shown separately. [11] Any liquid biofuel suitable as a diesel fuel substitute, additive, or extender. [12] Electricity-only and combined-heat-and-power plants whose primary business is to sell electricity and/or heat to the public. Includes sources not shown separately.

Source: U.S. Energy Information Administration, *Monthly Energy Review*, March 2024. See also <www.eia.gov/totalenergy/data/monthly>.

Table 973. Energy Consumption—End-Use Sector and Selected Source by State: 2022

[In trillions of British thermal units (94,774 represents 94,774,000,000,000,000 Btu), except as indicated. For definition of Btu, see source and text, this section. U.S. totals may not equal sum of states due to independent rounding and/or interstate flows of electricity that are not allocated to the states. For technical notes and documentation, see source <www.eia.gov/state/seds/seds-technical-notes-complete.php?sid=US>]

State	Total [1,2]	Per capita [3] (mil. Btu)	End-use sector [4]				Source				
			Resi-dential	Com-mercial	Indus-trial [2]	Trans-portation	Petro-leum [5]	Natural gas (dry) [6]	Coal	Hydro-electric power [7]	Nuclear electric power
U.S.	94,774	284	19,534	16,545	31,050	27,632	36,944	33,411	9,886	869	8,046
AL	1,902	375	333	244	774	552	609	787	298	35	441
AK	724	987	50	55	430	189	254	438	19	6	–
AZ	1,527	207	404	337	219	567	639	468	154	18	333
AR	1,053	346	218	173	379	283	342	398	212	12	149
CA	6,882	176	1,204	1,193	1,539	2,916	3,385	2,131	30	60	183
CO	1,464	251	339	253	372	501	591	530	233	5	–
CT	708	196	235	178	69	226	317	307	–	1	172
DE	275	270	65	52	81	77	116	90	2	–	–
DC	141	210	36	83	5	18	19	30	–	–	–
FL	4,325	194	1,183	930	477	1,739	1,893	1,660	172	1	321
GA	2,836	260	697	527	739	875	981	813	181	11	355
HI	270	188	30	37	48	156	246	3	8	(Z)	–
ID	519	268	123	79	148	170	197	142	2	29	–
IL	3,676	292	925	744	1,109	893	1,192	1,150	497	(Z)	1,031
IN	2,619	383	514	357	1,180	569	728	917	719	1	–
IA	1,423	445	193	159	771	298	447	467	228	3	–
KS	1,001	341	189	175	370	267	358	319	227	(Z)	94
KY	1,673	371	338	249	589	497	601	403	523	15	–
LA	4,246	925	302	239	2,951	756	1,679	2,074	97	3	169
ME	335	241	87	58	83	108	172	63	1	10	–
MD	1,203	195	371	351	87	395	432	311	62	6	154
MA	1,315	188	394	367	135	420	550	432	–	3	–
MI	2,707	270	754	579	664	711	862	1,088	424	5	271
MN	1,760	308	402	338	568	447	610	534	185	3	153
MS	1,100	374	192	151	405	353	400	622	66	–	90
MO	1,733	281	513	384	294	544	635	323	567	5	93
MT	395	352	91	72	118	116	181	94	131	34	–
NE	846	430	143	123	381	200	246	199	224	4	59
NV	706	222	157	130	143	276	315	302	36	6	–
NH	297	213	94	65	38	100	155	60	4	4	114
NJ	2,014	218	567	546	258	645	802	755	6	(Z)	295
NM	688	325	108	103	248	230	265	302	138	(Z)	–
NY	3,453	176	1,025	970	329	1,128	1,374	1,403	6	94	280
NC	2,569	240	673	558	534	807	948	747	163	16	445
ND	671	861	64	90	381	136	175	199	369	6	–
OH	3,503	298	844	651	1,137	872	1,078	1,424	540	2	175
OK	1,526	380	245	209	617	456	539	783	107	6	–
OR	857	202	181	134	233	306	346	298	1	107	–
PA	3,737	288	881	559	1,445	852	1,150	1,938	436	9	794
RI	187	171	61	47	22	57	82	94	–	(Z)	–
SC	1,623	307	374	289	498	464	519	361	151	7	567
SD	358	394	49	42	166	102	124	103	25	15	–
TN	2,102	298	505	420	514	664	740	440	205	31	372
TX	13,781	459	1,633	1,546	7,338	3,269	6,730	4,982	933	2	434
UT	849	251	192	176	201	281	331	287	238	2	–
VT	125	193	41	25	16	42	74	14	–	4	–
VA	2,428	280	544	734	417	734	833	666	68	4	294
WA	1,571	202	335	241	376	621	750	382	42	269	103
WV	835	471	154	107	384	192	210	285	537	6	–
WI	1,769	300	431	363	535	440	560	622	233	7	105
WY	496	853	50	54	288	105	148	173	390	3	–

– Represents zero. Z Less than 500 billion Btu. [1] Includes other sources, not shown separately. [2] U.S. total energy and U.S. industrial sector include net imports of coal coke that are not allocated to the states. [3] Based on estimated resident population as of July 1. [4] End-use sector data include electricity sales and associated electrical system energy losses. [5] Includes fuel ethanol blended into motor gasoline. [6] Includes supplemental gaseous fuels. [7] Conventional hydroelectric power. Does not include pumped-storage hydroelectricity.

Source: U.S. Energy Information Administration, "State Energy Data System," <www.eia.gov/state/seds>, accessed July 2024.

Table 974. Energy-related Carbon Dioxide Emissions by Sector and State: 2021

[4,911.2 represents 4,911,200,000. Total state CO2 emissions include those from direct fuel use across all sectors as well as primary fuels consumed for electricity generation. Covers emissions released at the location where fossil fuels are consumed. Regarding fuels that are used in one state to generate electricity consumed in another state, emissions are attributed to the state in which the electricity is generated and fuels are combusted. Data are derived from EIA's State Energy Data System]

State	Total carbon dioxide emissions (mil. metric tons)	Percent of carbon dioxide emissions by sector					Metric tons per capita
		Commercial	Electric Power	Residential	Industrial	Transpor- tation	
Total [1]	**4,911.2**	**5.0**	**31.4**	**6.6**	**20.0**	**37.0**	**14.8**
Alabama	108.4	2.2	43.5	1.9	18.1	34.3	21.5
Alaska	38.9	5.9	7.2	4.5	47.3	35.1	53.0
Arizona	83.0	3.8	41.3	3.0	5.6	46.3	11.4
Arkansas	62.0	5.8	46.0	3.3	13.4	31.5	20.5
California	324.0	6.0	10.9	8.1	19.7	55.3	8.3
Colorado	85.4	5.2	35.8	9.7	15.4	33.8	14.7
Connecticut	36.6	11.7	25.2	19.6	4.4	39.0	10.1
Delaware	13.0	8.2	13.6	7.5	29.4	41.3	12.9
District of Columbia	2.5	34.9	–	26.8	1.0	37.4	3.8
Florida	226.3	3.0	40.3	0.6	5.4	50.6	10.4
Georgia	124.1	3.7	32.9	5.9	10.2	47.2	11.5
Hawaii	17.3	3.1	33.3	0.4	5.6	57.6	12.0
Idaho	20.5	7.2	9.8	9.9	16.5	56.7	10.8
Illinois	184.2	7.7	28.5	12.5	18.8	32.6	14.5
Indiana	166.4	3.7	41.4	4.9	26.1	23.9	24.4
Iowa	73.1	5.2	33.0	6.6	28.1	27.1	22.9
Kansas	59.8	4.5	37.2	6.3	22.6	29.3	20.3
Kentucky	111.3	2.4	51.1	2.8	13.4	30.3	24.7
Louisiana	188.6	1.3	16.1	1.1	57.7	23.8	40.8
Maine	14.4	12.2	8.8	18.5	11.2	49.3	10.5
Maryland	52.6	9.9	21.4	10.8	5.4	52.5	8.5
Massachusetts	56.1	13.2	10.9	22.3	5.9	47.6	8.0
Michigan	147.8	7.3	35.8	12.8	11.9	32.2	14.7
Minnesota	83.2	8.2	25.5	11.2	20.1	35.0	14.6
Mississippi	63.1	2.5	40.0	2.4	18.0	37.2	21.4
Missouri	117.0	4.0	51.5	5.4	7.3	31.8	19.0
Montana	28.5	5.7	43.7	6.0	15.9	28.7	25.8
Nebraska	47.2	4.5	41.9	5.2	19.3	29.1	24.0
Nevada	39.4	5.8	34.7	6.6	7.8	45.1	12.5
New Hampshire	13.3	10.6	15.8	18.5	5.5	49.6	9.6
New Jersey	89.1	11.1	15.0	16.6	9.4	47.9	9.6
New Mexico	45.9	4.0	37.3	4.9	18.3	35.5	21.7
New York	156.0	13.9	16.0	21.6	5.3	43.1	7.9
North Carolina	115.6	4.5	34.7	4.7	8.7	47.4	10.9
North Dakota	56.5	2.2	48.5	1.9	31.7	15.7	72.7
Ohio	194.0	6.2	35.3	8.9	19.3	30.3	16.5
Oklahoma	87.8	3.6	30.5	4.5	26.3	35.1	22.0
Oregon	38.5	6.4	21.4	7.6	12.1	52.5	9.1
Pennsylvania	213.5	5.4	36.3	9.0	23.1	26.2	16.4
Rhode Island	10.6	8.8	31.7	20.0	5.6	33.9	9.7
South Carolina	69.3	3.3	36.1	3.1	10.5	47.0	13.4
South Dakota	15.2	5.4	15.8	6.7	26.2	45.9	16.9
Tennessee	92.7	4.6	25.9	4.7	15.4	49.3	13.3
Texas	663.5	2.1	27.2	1.8	36.4	32.4	22.4
Utah	62.1	4.8	48.2	6.6	11.0	29.3	18.6
Vermont	5.6	16.6	0.1	24.3	7.4	51.6	8.6
Virginia	98.0	6.1	24.9	6.4	11.8	50.8	11.3
Washington	73.8	6.4	13.3	8.2	15.8	56.3	9.5
West Virginia	88.4	1.9	66.7	1.9	15.0	14.6	49.5
Wisconsin	92.5	7.2	37.9	10.3	12.9	31.7	15.7
Wyoming	54.6	1.7	62.4	1.7	20.4	13.7	94.3

– Represents zero. [1] For the United States as a whole, see, EIA's *Monthly Energy Review,* Section 11: Environment. The total for all states is different from the national-level estimate because of differing methodologies. These values are unadjusted. See source for details on the data series differences.

Source: U.S. Energy Information Agency, "Energy-Related CO2 Emission Data Tables," <www.eia.gov/environment/emissions/state/>, accessed November 2023.

Table 975. Energy Expenditures and Average Fuel Prices by Source and Sector: 1990 to 2022

[In millions of dollars (474,652 represents $474,652,000,000), except as indicated. Btu = British thermal units. For definition of Btu, see text, this section. End-use sector and electric utilities exclude expenditures and prices on energy sources such as hydropower, solar, wind, and geothermal. Also excludes expenditures for reported amounts of energy consumed by the energy industry for production, transportation, and processing operations]

Source and sector	1990	2000	2010	2015	2018	2019	2020	2021	2022
EXPENDITURES (mil. dol.)									
Total [1, 2, 3]	**474,652**	**687,711**	**1,214,278**	**1,128,449**	**1,271,998**	**1,223,875**	**1,007,680**	**1,316,978**	**1,719,438**
Natural gas [3]	65,278	119,094	161,303	140,294	157,762	150,288	134,958	194,617	269,473
Petroleum products	237,677	359,403	717,098	623,513	742,677	700,359	504,707	758,652	1,052,199
Motor gasoline [4]	126,558	192,153	376,492	342,578	387,586	370,930	268,098	403,022	526,258
Coal	28,419	27,959	50,235	36,559	29,203	25,363	19,523	23,271	26,788
Retail electricity	176,691	231,578	365,913	388,344	403,349	398,774	390,934	419,304	481,757
Residential sector [5]	110,910	155,299	249,772	248,045	267,013	264,333	260,959	281,896	332,089
Commercial sector [2, 3]	79,602	113,421	177,662	185,970	193,165	189,335	173,852	198,929	242,917
Industrial sector [2, 3]	103,351	140,963	221,657	186,825	213,584	197,712	167,346	231,510	285,241
Transportation sector [2]	180,790	278,028	565,187	507,609	598,236	572,494	405,523	604,642	859,191
Motor gasoline [4]	123,845	189,836	369,433	329,609	373,095	356,962	256,276	386,884	502,702
Electric utilities [2]	40,627	60,053	94,782	76,333	75,615	64,852	53,959	92,203	126,113
AVERAGE FUEL PRICES (dol. per mil. Btu)									
All sectors	**8.29**	**10.33**	**18.92**	**17.31**	**18.61**	**17.96**	**16.24**	**19.98**	**25.66**
Residential sector [5]	11.87	14.21	22.37	22.93	23.29	23.13	23.86	25.51	28.88
Commercial sector [2]	11.87	13.90	20.92	20.72	20.67	20.40	20.14	22.17	25.55
Industrial sector [2]	5.30	6.50	12.14	9.88	10.66	9.90	8.71	11.56	14.50
Transportation sector	8.33	10.77	21.54	19.16	21.74	20.83	17.43	23.38	32.63
Electric utilities [2]	1.48	1.71	2.63	2.28	2.33	2.08	1.84	3.07	4.17

[1] Includes other sources not shown separately. [2] There are no direct fuel costs for hydroelectric, geothermal, wind, photovoltaic, or solar thermal energy. [3] Natural gas as it is consumed; includes supplemental gaseous fuels that are commingled with natural gas. [4] Beginning 1993, includes fuel ethanol blended into motor gasoline. [5] There are no direct fuel costs for geothermal, photovoltaic, or solar thermal energy.

Source: U.S. Energy Information Administration, "State Energy Data System (SEDS)," <www.eia.gov/state/seds>, accessed July 2024.

Table 976. Fuel Ethanol and Biodiesel—Summary: 2000 to 2023

[233.1 represents 233,100,000,000,000. Btu=British thermal units. For definition of Btu, see source and text, this section. Minus sign (-) indicates an excess of exports over imports, except where noted]

Fuel	2000	2010	2015	2018	2019	2020	2021	2022	2023
FUEL ETHANOL									
Feedstock [1] (tril. Btu)	233.1	1,823.5	2,012.5	2,187.3	2,139.9	1,885.8	2,030.2	2,078.9	2,112.4
Production:									
1,000 barrels	38,627	316,617	352,553	383,127	375,678	331,928	357,517	365,731	371,895
Tril. Btu	137.7	1,127.8	1,254.4	1,361.3	1,335.5	1,180.7	1,271.0	1,299.4	1,321.7
Net imports [2] (1,000 barrels)	116	-9,115	-17,632	-39,410	-30,276	-27,692	-28,135	-29,631	-33,481
Stocks [3] (1,000 barrels)	3,400	17,941	21,596	23,418	22,352	24,663	22,036	24,245	23,589
Stock change [4] (1,000 barrels)	-624	1,347	2,857	375	-1,066	2,311	-2,627	2,209	-837
Consumption:									
1,000 barrels	39,367	306,155	332,064	343,342	346,468	301,925	332,010	333,891	339,251
Tril. Btu	140.3	1,090.5	1,181.5	1,219.9	1,231.7	1,073.9	1,180.3	1,186.3	1,205.7
BIODIESEL									
Feedstock [5] (tril. Btu)	(NA)	44.4	163.4	240.3	223.1	234.7	221.0	209.8	219.8
Production:									
1,000 barrels	(NA)	8,177	30,080	44,222	41,060	43,207	40,686	38,620	40,447
Tril. Btu	(NA)	43.8	161.2	236.99	220.04	231.55	218.04	206.96	216.76
Net imports (1,000 barrels)	(NA)	-2,024	6,308	1,499	1,348	1,226	553	279	5,949
Stocks [6] (1,000 barrels)	(NA)	672	3,943	4,662	3,907	3,665	4,187	3,608	3,827
Stock change [4] (1,000 barrels)	(NA)	-39.0	813	394	-756	-241	522	-580	228
Consumption:									
1,000 barrels	(NA)	6,192	35,575	45,326	43,163	44,675	40,717	39,478	46,168
Tril. Btu	(NA)	33.2	190.6	242.9	231.3	239.4	218.2	211.6	247.4

NA Not available. [1] Total corn and other biomass inputs to the production of undenatured ethanol used for fuel ethanol. [2] Through 2009, data are for fuel ethanol imports only; data for fuel ethanol exports are not available. Beginning 2010, data are for fuel ethanol imports minus fuel ethanol exports. [3] Stocks are at end of year. [4] A negative number indicates a decrease in stocks. [5] Total vegetable oil and other biomass inputs to the production of biodiesel. [6] Stocks are at end of period. Includes biodiesel stocks at (or in) refineries, pipelines, and bulk terminals. Beginning in 2011, also includes stocks at biodiesel production plants.

Source: U.S. Energy Information Administration, *Monthly Energy Review*, March 2024. See also <www.eia.gov/totalenergy/data/monthly>.

Table 977. Energy Expenditures—End-Use Sector and Selected Source by State: 2022

[In millions of dollars (1,719,438 represents $1,719,438,000,000). End-use sector and electric utilities exclude expenditures on energy sources such as hydroelectric, geothermal, wind, or solar energy. Also excludes expenditures for reported amounts of energy consumed by the energy industry for production, transportation, and processing operations. For technical notes and documentation, see source, <www.eia.gov/state/seds/seds-technical-notes-complete.php>]

State	Total [1,2]	End-use sector				Source			
		Resi-dential	Com-mercial	Indus-trial [2]	Transpor-tation	Petroleum products [3]	Natural gas [4]	Coal	Electricity sales
U.S.	1,719,438	332,089	242,917	285,241	859,191	1,052,199	269,473	26,788	481,757
AL.	31,000	5,369	3,757	6,044	15,829	17,868	6,054	929	10,056
AK.	9,570	972	1,028	1,404	6,166	7,628	905	86	1,230
AZ.	32,961	5,942	4,408	3,149	19,462	22,079	4,246	442	9,525
AR.	17,392	2,999	2,132	3,592	8,669	10,147	3,614	501	4,837
CA.	200,008	32,779	32,185	21,493	113,551	123,820	26,496	121	55,918
CO.	28,371	5,144	3,631	3,853	15,743	18,231	4,358	449	6,634
CT.	18,124	5,979	3,406	1,123	7,616	10,446	3,368	–	5,852
DE.	4,817	1,069	701	544	2,503	2,966	758	6	1,332
DC.	2,574	576	1,404	89	505	608	436	–	1,530
FL.	89,282	19,425	13,141	5,986	50,731	55,441	14,502	643	31,129
GA.	50,946	11,124	7,314	7,077	25,431	28,563	8,013	728	17,406
HI.	9,294	1,248	1,431	1,500	5,115	7,201	139	30	3,575
ID.	9,809	1,614	924	1,533	5,739	6,750	983	14	2,230
IL.	60,710	13,752	9,140	9,380	28,438	33,454	11,911	1,196	15,937
IN.	39,628	7,046	4,414	9,932	18,235	21,393	7,228	2,560	11,540
IA.	22,165	3,531	2,628	6,497	9,510	13,189	4,031	418	5,187
KS.	17,246	3,181	2,572	3,229	8,264	10,022	2,734	429	4,714
KY.	27,349	4,494	3,083	4,827	14,945	17,204	3,045	1,301	7,852
LA.	44,877	4,690	3,480	23,075	13,632	27,494	10,675	279	9,237
ME.	8,347	2,401	1,322	933	3,692	5,650	715	6	2,072
MD.	24,773	6,185	5,159	1,353	12,076	14,167	3,479	191	7,950
MA.	33,811	10,320	7,174	2,636	13,680	17,842	6,244	–	10,843
MI.	46,032	11,064	7,148	6,267	21,553	25,280	9,195	1,231	13,250
MN.	29,964	6,129	4,634	5,163	14,038	17,648	4,767	439	7,896
MS.	17,590	2,850	2,123	2,949	9,668	10,910	4,026	262	5,007
MO.	30,586	6,422	4,018	3,254	16,892	19,410	3,612	1,104	8,237
MT.	7,162	1,257	922	975	4,008	4,934	700	283	1,480
NE.	12,714	1,826	1,330	2,963	6,595	8,060	1,749	291	2,989
NV.	16,152	2,671	1,857	2,162	9,462	10,748	2,613	122	4,302
NH.	7,646	2,393	1,291	611	3,351	4,944	718	18	2,279
NJ.	40,015	8,932	7,900	3,107	20,076	23,512	7,368	32	10,921
NM.	11,755	1,693	1,451	1,466	7,145	8,158	1,405	406	2,703
NY.	80,625	22,909	18,646	4,503	34,567	42,943	15,122	22	26,246
NC.	46,021	9,321	6,427	5,254	25,019	29,314	6,640	603	13,363
ND.	8,184	896	1,028	2,786	3,474	5,371	690	605	2,123
OH.	56,787	12,129	7,328	10,687	26,643	31,854	11,546	1,916	15,773
OK.	24,645	4,299	3,159	4,287	12,901	14,871	5,055	288	6,868
OR.	19,474	3,273	2,270	2,696	11,235	12,683	2,121	5	5,217
PA.	62,889	15,889	7,348	12,124	27,530	36,211	13,889	1,856	17,162
RI.	4,720	1,519	917	415	1,869	2,666	1,053	–	1,462
SC.	26,170	5,092	3,299	3,962	13,818	15,389	3,111	539	8,885
SD.	6,060	932	689	1,236	3,204	3,979	749	53	1,406
TN.	36,357	6,495	5,418	4,280	20,164	22,319	3,499	740	11,090
TX.	202,632	27,940	18,373	66,554	89,764	138,675	28,154	2,157	47,454
UT.	14,881	2,142	1,741	1,747	9,251	10,437	2,191	516	2,904
VT.	3,580	1,092	627	389	1,472	2,416	140	–	930
VA.	42,435	8,443	8,277	3,982	21,734	24,893	5,591	306	14,215
WA.	34,113	5,823	4,158	3,123	21,008	23,360	2,955	140	8,124
WV.	10,873	1,973	1,149	2,407	5,345	6,803	894	1,273	3,210
WI.	30,556	6,204	4,332	5,278	14,741	17,918	5,132	585	8,351
WY.	6,526	641	626	2,126	3,133	4,332	853	671	1,326

– Represents zero. [1] Total expenditures are the sum of purchases for each source (including electricity sales) less electric power sector purchases of fuel. There are no direct fuel costs for hydroelectric, geothermal, wind, or solar energy. [2] Includes sources not shown separately, such as electricity imports and exports and coal coke net imports, which are not allocated to the states. [3] Includes fuel ethanol blended into motor gasoline. [4] Includes supplemental gaseous fuels.

Source: U.S. Energy Information Administration, "State Energy Data System," <www.eia.gov/state/seds>, accessed July 2024.

Table 978. Energy Imports and Exports by Type of Fuel: 1980 to 2023

[In quadrillion Btu (12.10 represents 12,100,000,000,000,000 Btu). Btu=British thermal units; for definition, see text, this section]

Type of fuel	1980	1990	2000	2010	2015	2018	2019	2020	2021	2022	2023
Net imports, total [1]	**12.10**	**14.06**	**24.90**	**21.69**	**10.89**	**3.61**	**-0.61**	**-3.48**	**-3.62**	**-5.83**	**-7.82**
Coal	-2.39	-2.70	-1.21	-1.62	-1.60	-2.70	-2.17	-1.62	-1.95	-1.96	-2.34
Natural gas (dry)	0.96	1.46	3.62	2.69	0.99	-0.68	-1.89	-2.72	-3.83	-3.87	-4.68
Petroleum [2]	13.50	15.29	22.31	20.58	11.29	7.07	3.50	0.87	2.25	0.12	-0.67
Other [3]	0.04	0.01	0.18	0.04	0.21	-0.07	-0.06	-0.01	-0.08	-0.12	-0.13
Imports, total	15.80	18.82	28.87	29.87	23.79	24.83	22.87	19.99	21.46	21.51	21.70
Coal	0.03	0.07	0.31	0.48	0.26	0.12	0.14	0.10	0.11	0.14	0.09
Natural gas (dry)	1.01	1.55	3.87	3.83	2.79	2.96	2.81	2.61	2.88	3.10	3.00
Petroleum [2]	14.66	17.12	24.42	25.36	20.41	21.50	19.64	16.98	18.20	18.00	18.36
Other [3]	0.10	0.08	0.26	0.19	0.34	0.25	0.28	0.29	0.27	0.27	0.25
Exports, total	3.69	4.75	3.96	8.18	12.90	21.22	23.48	23.46	25.07	27.33	29.52
Coal	2.42	2.77	1.53	2.10	1.85	2.82	2.31	1.72	2.06	2.09	2.43
Natural gas (dry)	0.05	0.09	0.25	1.15	1.80	3.64	4.70	5.33	6.71	6.97	7.68
Petroleum	1.16	1.82	2.11	4.78	9.12	14.43	16.14	16.11	15.95	17.88	19.02
Other [3]	0.07	0.07	0.08	0.15	0.13	0.32	0.33	0.30	0.35	0.39	0.39

[1] Imports minus exports. Minus sign (-) indicates exports are greater than imports. [2] Includes imports into the Strategic Petroleum Reserve. [3] Coal coke, electricity, and biomass fuel.

Source: U.S. Energy Information Administration, *Monthly Energy Review*, March 2024. See also <www.eia.gov/totalenergy/data/monthly/>.

Table 979. U.S. Foreign Trade in Natural Gas, Crude Oil, Petroleum Products, and Coal: 1980 to 2023

[985 represents 985,000,000,000 cubic feet. Minus sign (-) indicates trade deficit]

Mineral fuel	Unit	1980	1990	2000	2010	2015	2020	2021	2022	2023 (P)
Natural gas:										
Imports	Bil. cu. ft.	985	1,532	3,782	3,741	2,718	2,551	2,808	3,024	2,929
Exports	Bil. cu. ft.	49	86	244	1,137	1,784	5,285	6,653	6,904	7,611
Net trade [1]	Bil. cu. ft.	-936	-1,447	-3,538	-2,604	-935	2,734	3,845	3,880	4,682
Crude oil: [2]										
Imports [3]	Mil. barrels	1,926	2,151	3,320	3,363	2,687	2,150	2,232	2,293	2,364
Exports	Mil. barrels	105	40	18	15	170	1,173	1,081	1,305	1,481
Net trade [1]	Mil. barrels	-1,821	-2,112	-3,301	-3,348	-2,518	-977	-1,150	-987	-883
Petroleum products:										
Imports	Mil. barrels	(NA)	775	874	942	761	728	861	747	743
Exports	Mil. barrels	(NA)	273	362	843	1,560	1,937	2,034	2,169	2,224
Net trade [1]	Mil. barrels	(NA)	-502	-512	-98	798	1,209	1,173	1,422	1,481
Coal:										
Imports	Mil. sh. tons	1	3	13	19	11	5	5	6	4
Exports	Mil. sh. tons	92	106	58	82	74	69	85	86	100
Net trade [1]	Mil. sh. tons	91	103	46	62	63	64	80	80	96

P Preliminary. NA Not available. [1] Exports minus imports. [2] Includes lease condensate. [3] Includes Strategic Petroleum Reserve imports.

Source: U.S. Energy Information Administration, *Monthly Energy Review*, March 2024; and "Petroleum and Other Liquids, Imports/Exports," <www.eia.gov/petroleum/data.cfm>, accessed April 2024.

Table 980. Crude Oil Imports Into the U.S. by Country of Origin: 2000 to 2023

[In millions of barrels (3,320 represents 3,320,000,000). A barrel contains 42 gallons. Crude oil imports are reported by the Petroleum Administration for Defense (PAD) District in which they are to be processed. A PAD District is a geographic aggregation of the 50 states and D.C. into 5 districts. Includes crude oil imported for storage in the Strategic Petroleum Reserve (SPR). Total Organization of Petroleum Exporting Countries (OPEC) excludes, and non-OPEC includes, petroleum imported into the United States indirectly from members of OPEC, primarily from Caribbean and West European areas, as petroleum products that were refined from crude oil produced by OPEC]

Country of origin	2000	2010	2015	2016	2017	2018	2019	2020	2021	2022	2023
Total imports	**3,320**	**3,363**	**2,687**	**2,873**	**2,909**	**2,835**	**2,482**	**2,150**	**2,232**	**2,293**	**2,364**
OPEC, total [1,2]	**1,663**	**1,662**	**976**	**1,164**	**1,138**	**943**	**541**	**298**	**291**	**357**	**377**
Iraq	227	152	84	154	219	189	121	64	55	89	78
Kuwait	96	71	74	76	53	28	16	8	8	10	8
Libya	(NA)	16	1	4	21	20	22	3	33	29	29
Nigeria	320	359	20	76	113	64	68	24	39	34	56
Saudi Arabia	558	395	384	402	347	318	182	182	130	166	127
Venezuela	448	333	283	271	226	185	29	(NA)	(NA)	(NA)	49
Non-OPEC, total [2]	**1,657**	**1,701**	**1,712**	**1,709**	**1,771**	**1,893**	**1,942**	**1,852**	**1,940**	**1,935**	**1,987**
Angola	108	140	45	58	47	33	12	10	12	16	12
Argentina	19	11	7	4	(NA)	8	11	12	10	23	19
Brazil	2	93	69	53	72	46	44	28	38	53	68
Canada	493	719	1,157	1,181	1,258	1,353	1,392	1,316	1,372	1,386	1,414
Colombia	116	124	136	162	121	108	116	91	66	81	74
Ecuador	46	76	82	87	75	64	73	62	54	52	47
Ghana	(NA)	(NA)	(NA)	(NA)	6	4	9	9	19	21	14
Guyana	(NA)	(NA)	(NA)	(NA)	(NA)	(NA)	(NA)	10	28	28	36
Kazakhstan	(NA)	7	(NA)	(NA)	(NA)	8	12	6	7	8	12
Mexico	480	421	251	213	222	243	219	240	213	232	267
Trinidad and Tobago	20	16	3	3	3	3	17	14	14	16	13
United Kingdom	106	44	4	7	9	21	23	10	15	14	14

NA Not available. [1] Countries listed under OPEC and non-OPEC are based on current affiliations. OPEC and non-OPEC totals are based on affiliations for the stated period of time, which may differ from current affiliations. Indonesia withdrew from OPEC in January 2009, rejoined in 2016 and withdrew again in December 2016; Angola joined OPEC in January 2007 and withdrew in January 2024; Ecuador withdrew from OPEC in January 1993, rejoined in November 2007 and withdrew again in January 2020, Gabon terminated its membership in 1995 and rejoined in July 2016; Equatorial Guinea joined OPEC in May 2017; Congo (Republic of) joined OPEC in June 2018; and Qatar withdrew from OPEC in January 2019. [2] Includes countries not shown separately.

Source: U.S. Energy Information Administration, Petroleum & Other Liquids, "U.S. Imports by Country of Origin," <www.eia.gov/petroleum/data.php#imports>, accessed April 2024.

Table 981. Crude Oil and Refined Products—Summary: 1980 to 2023

[13,481 represents 13,481,000 bbl. One barrel (bbl.) contains 42 gallons. Data are averages]

Year	Crude oil [1] (1,000 bbl. per day)					Refined oil products (1,000 bbl. per day)			Total oil imports [5] (1,000 bbl. per day)	Crude oil stocks [1,2] (mil. bbl.)	
	Refinery and blender input	Domestic production	Imports Total [3]	Imports Strategic reserve [4]	Exports	Domestic demand	Imports	Exports		Total [6]	Strategic reserve [7]
1980....	13,481	8,597	5,263	44	287	17,056	1,646	258	6,909	466	108
1981....	12,470	8,572	4,396	256	228	16,058	1,599	367	5,996	594	230
1982....	11,774	8,649	3,488	165	236	15,296	1,625	579	5,113	644	294
1983....	11,685	8,688	3,329	234	164	15,231	1,722	575	5,051	723	379
1984....	12,044	8,879	3,426	197	181	15,726	2,011	541	5,437	796	451
1985....	12,002	8,971	3,201	118	204	15,726	1,866	577	5,067	814	493
1986....	12,716	8,680	4,178	48	154	16,281	2,045	631	6,224	843	512
1987....	12,854	8,349	4,674	73	151	16,665	2,004	613	6,678	890	541
1988....	13,246	8,140	5,107	51	155	17,283	2,295	661	7,402	890	560
1989....	13,401	7,613	5,843	56	142	17,325	2,217	717	8,061	921	580
1990....	13,409	7,355	5,894	27	109	16,988	2,123	748	8,018	908	586
1991....	13,301	7,417	5,782	(NA)	116	16,714	1,844	885	7,627	893	569
1992....	13,411	7,171	6,083	10	89	17,033	1,805	861	7,888	893	575
1993....	13,613	6,847	6,787	15	98	17,237	1,833	904	8,620	922	587
1994....	13,866	6,662	7,063	12	99	17,718	1,933	843	8,996	929	592
1995....	13,973	6,560	7,230	(NA)	95	17,725	1,605	855	8,835	895	592
1996....	14,195	6,465	7,508	(NA)	110	18,309	1,971	871	9,478	850	566
1997....	14,662	6,452	8,225	(NA)	108	18,620	1,936	896	10,162	868	563
1998....	14,889	6,252	8,706	(NA)	110	18,917	2,002	835	10,708	895	571
1999....	14,804	5,881	8,731	8	118	19,519	2,122	822	10,852	852	567
2000....	15,067	5,822	9,071	8	50	19,701	2,389	990	11,459	826	541
2001....	15,128	5,801	9,328	11	20	19,649	2,543	951	11,871	862	550
2002....	14,947	5,744	9,140	16	9	19,761	2,390	975	11,530	877	599
2003....	15,304	5,649	9,665	(NA)	12	20,034	2,599	1,014	12,264	907	638
2004....	15,475	5,441	10,088	77	27	20,731	3,057	1,021	13,145	961	676
2005....	15,220	5,184	10,126	52	32	20,802	3,588	1,133	13,714	992	685
2006....	15,242	5,086	10,118	8	25	20,687	3,589	1,292	13,707	984	689
2007....	15,156	5,074	10,031	7	27	20,680	3,437	1,405	13,468	965	697
2008....	14,648	5,000	9,783	19	29	19,498	3,132	1,773	12,915	1,010	702
2009....	14,336	5,357	9,013	56	44	18,771	2,678	1,980	11,691	1,034	727
2010....	14,724	5,484	9,213	(NA)	42	19,178	2,580	2,311	11,793	1,039	727
2011....	14,806	5,674	8,935	(NA)	47	18,896	2,501	2,939	11,436	1,004	696
2012....	14,999	6,524	8,527	(NA)	67	18,482	2,071	3,137	10,598	1,033	695
2013....	15,312	7,495	7,730	(NA)	134	18,967	2,129	3,487	9,859	1,023	696
2014....	15,848	8,791	7,344	(NA)	351	19,100	1,897	3,824	9,241	1,052	691
2015....	16,188	9,439	7,363	(NA)	465	19,532	2,086	4,273	9,449	1,144	695
2016....	16,187	8,846	7,850	(NA)	591	19,692	2,205	4,670	10,055	1,180	695
2017....	16,590	9,357	7,969	(NA)	1,158	19,952	2,175	5,218	10,144	1,084	663
2018....	16,969	10,951	7,768	(NA)	2,048	20,512	2,174	5,553	9,943	1,092	649
2019....	16,563	12,311	6,801	(NA)	2,982	20,543	2,340	5,490	9,141	1,068	635
2020....	14,212	11,318	5,875	(NA)	3,206	18,186	1,988	5,292	7,863	1,124	638
2021....	15,147	11,268	6,114	(NA)	2,963	19,890	2,360	5,573	8,474	1,015	594
2022....	15,977	11,911	6,281	(NA)	3,576	20,010	2,048	5,944	8,329	802	372
2023....	15,963	12,933	6,478	(NA)	4,058	20,246	2,036	6,092	8,514	781	355

NA Not available. [1] Includes lease condensate. [2] Crude oil at end of period. Includes commercial and Strategic Petroleum Reserve (SPR) stocks. [3] Includes Strategic Petroleum Reserve. [4] Through 2000, includes imports by SPR only; beginning in 2004, includes imports by SPR, and imports into SPR by others. [5] Crude oil (including Strategic Petroleum Reserve imports) plus refined products. [6] Beginning in 1981, includes stocks of Alaskan crude oil in transit. [7] Crude oil stocks in the Strategic Petroleum Reserve include non-U.S. stocks held under foreign or commercial storage agreements.

Source: U.S. Energy Information Administration, *Monthly Energy Review*, March 2024. See also <www.eia.gov/totalenergy/data/monthly>.

Table 982. Petroleum and Coal Products Corporations—Sales, Net Profit, and Profit Per Dollar of Sales: 2010 to 2023

[1,077.1 represents $1,077,100,000,000. Covers North American Industry Classification System (NAICS) 324. Profit rates are averages of quarterly figures at annual rates]

Item	Unit	2010	2015	2016	2017	2018	2019	2020	2021	2022	2023
Sales....................	Bil. dol.	1,077.1	834.3	681.9	850.1	1,029.3	985.3	636.5	971.2	1,440.4	1,205.4
Net profit:											
Before income taxes..............	Bil. dol.	56.0	21.0	1.2	34.0	70.9	30.9	-68.2	84.7	193.5	119.1
After income taxes................	Bil. dol.	54.2	24.0	11.2	48.0	63.3	29.7	-52.1	72.2	166.1	104.3
Depreciation [1]......................	Bil. dol.	30.8	33.6	34.6	35.2	34.7	38.4	39.2	38.3	36.9	40.8
Profits per dollar of sales:											
Before income taxes..............	Cents	5.2	2.5	0.2	4.0	6.9	3.1	-10.7	8.7	13.4	9.9
After income taxes................	Cents	5.0	2.9	1.6	5.7	6.2	3.0	-8.2	7.4	11.5	8.6
Stockholders' equity [2]..............	Bil. dol.	456.6	540.0	525.7	545.9	582.2	606.9	541.3	532.2	599.2	644.4

[1] Includes depletion, and amortization of property, plant, and equipment. [2] Averages of quarterly figures.

Source: U.S. Census Bureau, Quarterly Financial Report (QFR), Manufacturing, Mining, Wholesale Trade, and Selected Service Industries, "Time Series/Trend Charts," <www.census.gov/econ/qfr>, accessed April 2024.

Table 983. Nuclear Power Plants—Number, Capacity, and Generation: 1980 to 2023

[51.8 represents 51,800,000 kilowatts (kW)]

Item	1980	1990	2000	2010	2015	2019	2020	2021	2022	2023
Operable generating units [1,2]	71	112	104	104	99	96	94	93	92	93
Net summer capacity [2,3] (mil. kW)	51.8	99.6	97.9	101.2	98.7	98.1	96.5	95.5	94.7	95.7
Net generation (bil. kWh)	251.1	576.9	753.9	807.0	797.2	809.4	789.9	779.6	771.5	775.3
Percent of total electricity net generation	11.0	19.0	19.8	19.6	19.5	19.6	19.7	19.0	18.2	18.6
Capacity factor [4] (percent)	56.3	66.0	88.1	91.1	92.3	93.5	92.5	92.8	92.7	93.1

[1] Total of nuclear generating units holding full-power licenses, or equivalent permission to operate, at the end of the year. Includes units retaining full-power licenses during long, non-routine shutdowns that for a time rendered them unable to generate electricity. [2] As of year-end. [3] Net summer capacity is the peak steady hourly output that generating equipment is expected to supply to system load, exclusive of auxiliary and other power plant, as demonstrated by a test at the time of summer peak demand. [4] Through 2007, annual capacity factors are calculated as the annual nuclear electricity net generation divided by the annual maximum possible nuclear electricity net generation (the sum of the monthly values for maximum possible nuclear electricity net generation). Please note that as of 2008, the methodology changed; see U.S. Energy Information Administration, *Electric Power Monthly*, Appendix C, under "Average Capacity Factors."

Source: U.S. Energy Information Administration, *Monthly Energy Review*, March 2024. See also <www.eia.gov/totalenergy/data/monthly>.

Table 984. Nuclear Power Plants—Number of Reactors, Net Generation, and Net Summer Capacity by State: 2022

[771,537 represents 771,537,000,000 kilowatt hours (kWh)]

State	Number of reactors	Nuclear net generation Total (mil. kWh)	Nuclear net generation Percent of total [1]	Nuclear net summer capacity Total (mil. kWh)	Nuclear net summer capacity Percent of total [2]	State	Number of reactors	Nuclear net generation Total (mil. kWh)	Nuclear net generation Percent of total [1]	Nuclear net summer capacity Total (mil. kWh)	Nuclear net summer capacity Percent of total [2]
U.S.	**92**	**771,537**	**18.2**	**94.7**	**8.2**	MS	1	8,600	12.7	1.4	9.5
						MO	1	8,875	11.2	1.2	5.6
AL	5	42,314	29.2	5.5	18.9	NE	1	5,619	13.8	0.8	7.1
AZ	3	31,943	30.5	3.9	14.0	NH	1	10,922	58.2	1.2	28.0
AR	2	14,324	21.7	1.8	12.2	NJ	3	28,319	43.5	3.5	20.7
CA	2	17,593	8.7	2.2	2.6	NY	4	26,812	21.4	3.3	8.3
CT	2	16,464	38.2	2.1	20.9	NC	5	42,644	31.8	5.1	14.6
FL	4	30,768	11.9	3.7	5.5	OH	2	16,827	12.4	2.1	7.8
GA	4	34,074	26.9	4.1	11.2	PA	8	76,166	31.8	9.1	18.5
IL	11	98,870	53.4	11.6	26.2	SC	7	54,370	55.1	6.6	27.2
KS	1	8,982	14.4	1.2	6.6	TN	4	35,635	45.7	4.5	21.0
LA	2	16,165	15.3	2.1	8.6	TX	4	41,607	7.9	5.0	3.3
MD	2	14,811	39.9	1.7	14.3	VA	4	28,197	31.5	3.6	12.2
MI [3]	3	26,013	22.1	3.3	10.9	WA	1	9,852	8.4	1.2	3.7
MN	3	14,696	24.9	1.7	9.0	WI	2	10,077	16.5	1.2	7.2

[1] Percent of total electric power generation. See also Table 992. [2] Percent of total net summer capacity. See also Table 992. [3] Michigan had four operating nuclear reactors at the beginning of 2022. The Palisades nuclear plant ceased operations in May 2022.

Source: U.S. Energy Information Administration, *Electric Power Annual 2022*, October 2023; "Nuclear & Uranium: Capacity and Generation by State and Reactor," and "Electricity: Detailed and historical electricity data by survey," <www.eia.gov/electricity/data/state/>, accessed March 2024.

Table 985. Uranium Concentrate—Supply, Inventories, and Average Prices: 1990 to 2023

[8.89 represents 8,890,000 pounds (lbs.). For years ending December 31. For additional data on uranium, see Table 949 and Table 965]

Item	Unit	1990	2000	2010	2015	2019	2020	2021	2022	2023
Production [1]	Mil. lbs.	8.89	3.98	4.23	3.34	0.17	(D)	0.02	0.19	0.05
Imports [2]	Mil. lbs.	23.7	44.9	55.3	64.2	42.9	39.6	41.3	32.1	32.0
Exports [2]	Mil. lbs.	2.0	13.6	23.1	25.7	11.7	9.9	7.5	2.5	1.4
Electric plant purchases from domestic suppliers	Mil. lbs.	20.5	24.3	16.2	19.6	(D)	10.5	8.2	4.4	5.9
Loaded into U.S. nuclear reactors [3]	Mil. lbs.	(NA)	51.5	44.3	47.4	43.2	48.6	44.4	44.4	[5] 43.9
Inventories, total	Mil. lbs.	129.1	111.3	111.3	135.5	130.7	131.0	141.7	143.1	[5] 152.1
At domestic suppliers	Mil. lbs.	26.4	56.5	24.7	14.3	17.5	24.2	33.2	40.7	[5] 42.1
At electric plants	Mil. lbs.	102.7	54.8	86.5	121.1	113.1	106.9	108.5	102.4	[5] 110.0
Average price per pound: Purchased imports [4]	Dollars	12.55	9.84	47.01	42.95	34.77	33.79	33.26	40.31	41.88
Domestic purchases	Dollars	15.70	11.45	44.88	43.03	(D)	35.92	35.18	43.15	45.09

D Data withheld. NA Not available. [1] Data are for uranium concentrate, a yellow or brown powder obtained by the milling of uranium ore, processing of in situ leach mining solutions, or as a by-product of phosphoric acid production. [2] Includes transactions by uranium buyers (consumers). Buyer imports and exports prior to 1990 are believed to be small. [3] Does not include any fuel rods removed from reactors and later reloaded into the reactor. [4] For purchases made by U.S. suppliers and by U.S. owners and operators of civilian nuclear power plants. [5] Preliminary.

Source: U.S. Energy Information Administration, *Monthly Energy Review*, <www.eia.gov/totalenergy/data/monthly/>, August 2024. See also <www.eia.gov/nuclear/data.php>.

Table 986. Renewable Energy Generating Capacity and Generation Projections: Estimates, 2022, and Projections, 2025 to 2050

[In gigawatts, unless otherwise noted. Reference case projections are business-as-usual trend estimates, given known technology, as well as market, demographic, and technological trends. Based on results from EIA's National Energy Modeling System]

Net summer capacity and generation	2022, estimate	Projections						Annual growth 2022-2050 (percent)
		2025	2030	2035	2040	2045	2050	
ELECTRIC POWER SECTOR [1]								
Total net summer capacity	**308.57**	**442.58**	**728.89**	**870.15**	**957.29**	**1,053.59**	**1,163.06**	**4.9**
Conventional hydroelectric power	79.22	79.25	79.33	79.33	79.35	79.35	79.38	(Z)
Geothermal [2]	2.54	2.57	3.07	3.46	3.91	4.34	5.06	2.5
Municipal waste [3]	3.24	3.56	4.08	4.70	5.39	6.01	6.45	2.5
Wood and other biomass [4]	2.68	2.68	2.53	2.54	2.54	2.54	2.61	-0.1
Solar thermal	1.48	1.48	1.48	1.48	1.48	1.48	1.48	–
Solar photovoltaic [5]	74.98	182.28	338.26	434.82	515.31	602.75	694.69	8.3
Wind	143.97	167.88	290.15	320.42	325.91	333.73	350.00	3.2
Offshore wind	0.46	2.89	9.99	23.39	23.39	23.39	23.39	15.0
Total generation (bil. kWh)	**888.45**	**1,222.67**	**2,085.85**	**2,446.24**	**2,656.50**	**2,839.99**	**3,080.39**	**4.5**
Conventional hydroelectric power	275.05	298.41	294.96	290.48	288.01	286.81	283.60	0.1
Geothermal [2]	15.60	16.90	20.95	24.10	27.79	31.49	37.21	3.2
Biogenic municipal waste [6]	13.81	16.23	20.22	25.08	30.68	35.70	39.31	3.8
Wood and other biomass	11.06	11.16	9.87	10.06	10.16	10.09	11.02	-(Z)
Dedicated plants	10.88	11.04	9.77	9.93	10.04	9.96	10.89	(Z)
Co-firing	0.17	0.11	0.09	0.13	0.12	0.12	0.12	-1.2
Solar thermal	2.94	2.97	2.90	2.48	2.42	2.12	2.06	-1.3
Solar photovoltaic [5]	131.16	365.27	770.42	968.16	1,148.39	1,292.88	1,490.42	9.1
Wind	437.40	505.67	934.94	1,047.66	1,063.20	1,094.39	1,131.80	3.5
Offshore wind	1.45	6.07	31.58	78.22	85.84	86.52	84.99	15.7
END-USE SECTORS [7]								
Total net summer capacity	**55.09**	**73.92**	**99.11**	**127.59**	**158.83**	**192.87**	**231.53**	**5.3**
Conventional hydropower	0.23	0.23	0.23	0.23	0.23	0.23	0.23	–
Geothermal	–	–	–	–	–	–	–	(X)
Municipal waste [3]	0.09	0.09	0.09	0.09	0.09	0.09	0.09	–
Biomass	5.56	5.40	5.60	5.78	5.91	6.05	6.24	0.4
Solar photovoltaic [5]	48.59	67.56	92.51	120.79	151.89	185.80	224.26	5.6
Wind	0.62	0.64	0.68	0.70	0.71	0.71	0.71	0.5
Total generation (bil. kWh)	**101.92**	**129.70**	**169.09**	**212.73**	**259.81**	**311.52**	**370.10**	**4.7**
Conventional hydropower	1.11	1.11	1.11	1.11	1.11	1.11	1.11	–
Geothermal	–	–	–	–	–	–	–	(X)
Municipal waste [3]	0.54	0.53	0.53	0.53	0.53	0.53	0.53	-(Z)
Biomass	28.51	27.69	28.72	29.61	30.31	31.01	32.00	0.4
Solar photovoltaic [5]	70.94	99.51	137.83	180.56	226.93	277.94	335.53	5.7
Wind	0.82	0.85	0.89	0.92	0.92	0.93	0.93	0.4
ALL SECTORS								
Total net summer capacity	**363.66**	**516.51**	**827.99**	**997.74**	**1,116.12**	**1,246.47**	**1,394.59**	**4.9**
Conventional hydropower	79.45	79.48	79.56	79.57	79.58	79.58	79.61	(Z)
Geothermal	2.54	2.57	3.07	3.46	3.91	4.34	5.06	2.5
Municipal waste [3]	3.33	3.65	4.17	4.79	5.47	6.10	6.54	2.4
Wood and other biomass [4]	8.24	8.09	8.13	8.32	8.45	8.59	8.85	0.3
Solar [5]	125.05	251.31	432.25	557.09	668.69	790.03	920.43	7.4
Wind	145.05	171.41	300.82	344.51	350.01	357.83	374.10	3.4
Total generation (bil. kWh)	**990.37**	**1,352.37**	**2,254.94**	**2,658.96**	**2,916.31**	**3,151.51**	**3,450.50**	**4.6**
Conventional hydropower	276.16	299.52	296.07	291.60	289.13	287.92	284.71	0.1
Geothermal	15.60	16.90	20.95	24.10	27.79	31.49	37.21	3.2
Municipal waste [8]	14.34	16.76	20.75	25.61	31.21	36.23	39.85	3.7
Wood and other biomass	39.57	38.85	38.59	39.67	40.47	41.10	43.02	0.3
Solar [5]	205.04	467.75	911.16	1,151.19	1,377.75	1,572.94	1,828.00	8.1
Wind	439.67	512.59	967.41	1,126.80	1,149.96	1,181.84	1,217.71	3.7

– Represents zero. Z Less than .05%. X Not applicable. [1] Includes electricity-only and combined heat and power plants that have a regulatory status. [2] Includes both hydrothermal resources and near-field enhanced geothermal systems (EGS). [3] Includes municipal waste, landfill gas, and municipal sewage sludge. Incremental growth is assumed to be for landfill gas facilities. All municipal waste is included, although a portion of the municipal waste stream contains petroleum-derived plastics and other non-renewable sources. [4] Facilities co-firing biomass and coal are classified as coal. [5] Does not include off-grid photovoltaics (PV). [6] Includes biogenic municipal waste, landfill gas, and municipal sludge. Incremental growth is assumed to be for landfill gas facilities. [7] Includes combined heat and power plants and electricity-only plants in the commercial and industrial sectors with nonregulatory status. Also includes small on-site generating systems in the residential, commercial, and industrial sectors used primarily for own-use generation, but which may also sell some power to the grid. [8] Includes biogenic municipal waste from the power sector and all municipal waste from the end-use sectors, landfill gas, and municipal sewage sludge. Incremental growth in the power sector is assumed to be for landfill gas facilities.

Source: U.S. Energy Information Administration, *Annual Energy Outlook 2023*, March 2023. See also <www.eia.gov/forecasts/aeo>.

Table 987. Solar Energy Generation—Total and Small-Scale by State: 2015 to 2023

[In thousands of megawatt hours (39,032 represents 39,032,000), except percent. All solar generation includes utility- and small-scale generation. Small-scale solar is defined as having a generating capacity of less than one megawatt. Small-scale solar residential systems are typically installed on rooftops; commercial and industrial systems may be installed on rooftops or on the ground. For more information, see source]

States	All solar generation			Small-scale solar generation			Small-scale generation as a percent of all solar		
	2015	2020	2023	2015	2020	2023	2015	2020	2023
United States..........	**39,032**	**130,721**	**238,120**	**14,139**	**41,522**	**73,619**	**36**	**32**	**31**
Alabama.................	3	384	1,200	3	15	22	100	4	2
Alaska....................	(NA)	7	24	(NA)	7	18	(NA)	100	75
Arizona..................	4,827	8,749	11,779	1,370	2,912	4,431	28	33	38
Arkansas...............	6	358	1,199	5	86	403	83	24	34
California...............	20,829	47,680	68,816	6,014	17,407	28,102	29	37	41
Colorado................	643	2,204	5,310	391	701	1,703	61	32	32
Connecticut...........	216	949	1,659	199	735	1,243	92	77	75
Delaware..............	128	183	346	79	128	190	62	70	55
District of Columbia......	32	131	231	32	119	205	100	91	89
Florida....................	380	7,627	17,808	156	1,117	3,749	41	15	21
Georgia.................	229	4,109	8,103	100	329	520	44	8	6
Hawaii...................	687	1,695	2,053	632	1,211	1,409	92	71	69
Idaho....................	6	653	1,090	6	87	238	100	13	22
Illinois...................	76	506	3,478	27	427	1,536	36	84	44
Indiana..................	168	526	2,241	12	167	361	7	32	16
Iowa......................	41	232	911	41	210	390	100	91	43
Kansas..................	6	106	210	5	48	129	83	45	61
Kentucky...............	14	94	287	14	51	131	100	54	46
Louisiana..............	153	296	598	153	257	307	100	87	51
Maine....................	19	117	1,189	19	89	607	100	76	51
Maryland...............	457	1,522	2,372	339	994	1,404	74	65	59
Massachusetts..........	1,314	3,726	5,652	862	2,322	3,668	66	62	65
Michigan...............	39	310	1,610	38	155	298	97	50	19
Minnesota..............	28	1,773	2,320	26	140	324	93	8	14
Mississippi............	2	445	656	2	15	23	100	3	4
Missouri................	162	461	895	145	360	721	90	78	81
Montana................	8	67	316	8	34	76	100	51	24
Nebraska..............	1	74	132	1	20	49	100	27	37
Nevada..................	1,844	6,407	11,423	186	872	1,690	10	14	15
New Hampshire..........	24	161	303	24	157	299	100	98	99
New Jersey.............	2,062	3,809	5,033	1,435	2,504	3,413	70	66	68
New Mexico.............	757	2,114	3,223	142	365	702	19	17	22
New York................	689	3,130	6,447	589	2,290	3,973	85	73	62
North Carolina...........	1,460	8,633	12,085	86	360	757	6	4	6
North Dakota.............	–	1	2	–	1	2	–	100	100
Ohio......................	151	400	1,734	95	237	418	63	59	24
Oklahoma..............	5	93	239	3	30	166	60	32	69
Oregon..................	116	1,335	2,401	92	257	515	79	19	21
Pennsylvania...........	325	729	1,480	261	590	1,070	80	81	72
Rhode Island...........	28	494	1,068	13	299	607	46	61	57
South Carolina..........	11	2,092	3,368	7	371	593	64	18	18
South Dakota...........	1	4	51	1	2	4	100	50	8
Tennessee.............	136	413	1,045	60	89	72	44	22	7
Texas....................	624	10,151	31,739	223	1,614	4,337	36	16	14
Utah......................	99	3,117	4,823	67	546	906	68	18	19
Vermont.................	102	357	439	54	174	239	53	49	54
Virginia..................	30	1,585	6,072	30	214	717	100	14	12
Washington.............	56	296	882	55	250	518	98	84	59
West Virginia...........	4	15	47	4	15	47	100	100	100
Wisconsin..............	29	223	1,530	27	129	287	93	58	19
Wyoming................	3	178	203	3	13	29	100	7	14

NA Not available. – Represents or rounds to zero.

Source: Energy Information Administration, "Electricity Data Browser," <www.eia.gov/electricity/data/browser>, accessed May 2024.

Table 988. Energy Distribution System Reliability—Number and Duration of Electric Interruption Events: 2013 to 2022

[The average number and length in minutes of non-momentary electric interruptions the average customer in the United States experienced annually. Data include only utilities that use the IEEE 1366-2003 or the IEEE 1366-2012 standard set by the Institute of Electrical and Electronics Engineers (IEEE)]

Year	All events (with major event days) [1]			Without major event days			Loss of supply removed [2]		
	Minutes per year (SAIDI) [3]	Interruptions per year (SAIFI) [4]	Average minutes per interruption (CAIDI) [5]	Minutes per year (SAIDI) [3]	Interruptions per year (SAIFI) [4]	Average minutes per interruption (CAIDI) [5]	Minutes per year (SAIDI) [3]	Interruptions per year (SAIFI) [4]	Average minutes per interruption (CAIDI) [5]
2013............	227.2	1.2	191.5	111.9	1.0	112.6	225.5	1.1	202.6
2014............	236.2	1.3	188.0	114.2	1.0	110.0	244.8	1.2	203.7
2015............	209.0	1.3	163.9	117.0	1.1	109.1	198.2	1.2	170.4
2016............	268.4	1.3	202.2	119.8	1.1	110.7	257.0	1.2	209.0
2017............	505.9	1.4	356.2	117.0	1.0	114.3	489.6	1.3	390.6
2018............	349.2	1.3	260.5	121.4	1.1	115.5	338.5	1.2	283.8
2019............	295.5	1.3	221.8	122.2	1.0	117.5	289.1	1.2	243.0
2020............	456.1	1.4	329.3	116.0	1.0	114.5	460.5	1.2	371.9
2021............	475.8	1.4	331.2	125.7	1.0	120.9	404.5	1.3	312.6
2022............	333.0	1.4	233.5	131.1	1.1	120.2	324.7	1.3	246.9

[1] A major event day is any day that exceeds a daily threshold called Tmed, a duration statistic calculated from daily interruption values from the past five years. [2] Excludes outages due to loss of supply from the high-voltage/bulk power system. [3] SAIDI = System Average Interruption Duration Index, the minutes of non-momentary electric interruptions the average customer experienced per year. [4] SAIFI = System Average Interruption Frequency Index, the number of non-momentary electric interruptions the average customer experienced per year. [5] CAIDI = Customer Average Interruption Duration Index, the average number of minutes it took to restore non-momentary electric interruptions.

Source: U.S. Energy Information Administration, *Electric Power Annual 2022*, October 2023. See also <www.eia.gov/electricity/annual/>.

Table 989. Electricity Net Generation by Sector and Source: 2000 to 2023

[3,802.1 represents 3,802,100,000,000 kilowatt hours (kWh). Data are for fuels consumed to produce electricity. Also includes fuels consumed to produce useful thermal output at a small number of electric utility combined-heat-and-power (CHP) plants]

Sector and source	Unit	2000	2010	2015	2020	2021	2022	2023
Net generation, total............	Bil. kWh.	**3,802.1**	**4,125.1**	**4,078.7**	**4,009.8**	**4,109.7**	**4,230.7**	**4,178.2**
Electric power sector, total..................	Bil. kWh.	3,637.5	3,972.4	3,920.4	3,853.7	3,957.2	4,073.9	4,022.3
Commercial sector [1]........................	Bil. kWh.	7.9	8.6	12.6	13.0	12.8	16.7	16.7
Industrial sector [2]............................	Bil. kWh.	156.7	144.1	145.7	143.1	139.8	140.0	139.2
Net generation by source, all sectors:								
Fossil fuels, total...........................	Bil. kWh.	2,692.5	2,883.4	2,728.4	2,429.3	2,507.8	2,553.2	2,505.2
Coal [3]....................................	Bil. kWh.	1,966.3	1,847.3	1,352.4	773.4	898.0	831.5	675.3
Petroleum [4]..............................	Bil. kWh.	111.2	37.1	28.2	17.3	19.2	22.9	16.5
Natural gas [5]............................	Bil. kWh.	601.0	987.7	1,334.7	1,626.8	1,579.2	1,687.1	1,802.1
Other gases [6]...........................	Bil. kWh.	14.0	11.3	13.1	11.8	11.4	11.7	11.5
Nuclear electric power....................	Bil. kWh.	753.9	807.0	797.2	789.9	779.6	771.5	775.3
Hydroelectric pumped storage [7]..........	Bil. kWh.	-5.5	-5.5	-5.1	-5.3	-5.1	-6.0	-5.9
Renewable energy, total....................	Bil. kWh.	356.5	427.4	544.2	783.0	815.3	900.8	893.5
Conventional hydroelectric power..........	Bil. kWh.	275.6	260.2	249.1	285.3	251.6	254.8	239.9
Biomass, total.............................	Bil. kWh.	60.7	56.1	63.6	54.7	54.3	51.8	47.5
Wood [8]...............................	Bil. kWh.	37.6	37.2	41.9	36.2	36.5	35.5	31.4
Waste [9]..............................	Bil. kWh.	23.1	18.9	21.7	18.5	17.8	16.4	16.0
Geothermal...............................	Bil. kWh.	14.1	15.2	15.9	15.9	16.0	16.1	16.5
Solar [10].................................	Bil. kWh.	0.5	1.2	24.9	89.2	115.3	143.8	164.5
Wind.......................................	Bil. kWh.	5.6	94.7	190.7	337.9	378.2	434.3	425.2
Other [11].....................................	Bil. kWh.	4.8	12.9	14.0	12.9	12.1	11.1	10.0
Consumption of fuels for electricity generation:								
Coal [3]....................................	Mil. short tons	994.9	979.7	739.6	435.4	500.4	471.6	386.6
Petroleum, total............................	Mil. bbl.	195.2	65.1	49.1	33.4	37.0	43.7	30.0
Distillate fuel oil [12]......................	Mil. bbl.	31.7	14.1	12.4	8.0	10.6	14.7	8.6
Residual fuel oil [13]......................	Mil. bbl.	143.4	24.0	14.1	8.3	9.0	11.9	10.3
Other liquids [14]........................	Mil. bbl.	1.4	2.1	2.4	1.7	2.0	2.1	1.8
Petroleum coke............................	Mil. short tons	3.7	5.0	4.0	3.1	3.1	3.0	1.8
Natural gas [5]............................	Bil. cu. ft.	5,691.5	7,680.2	10,016.6	11,928.1	11,502.6	12,384.1	13,223.1
Other gases [6]............................	Tril. Btu.	126.0	90.1	106.0	69.6	65.1	64.3	63.6
Biomass....................................	Tril. Btu.	825.9	630.3	719.6	580.1	577.9	555.8	493.5
Wood [8].................................	Tril. Btu.	495.8	349.5	406.7	318.4	328.3	323.8	274.4
Waste [9]................................	Tril. Btu.	330.1	280.8	313.0	261.7	249.6	232.0	219.1
Other [11]....................................	Tril. Btu.	46.2	184.4	203.6	192.8	186.7	156.9	142.8

[1] Commercial combined-heat-and-power (CHP) and commercial electricity-only plants. [2] Industrial CHP and industrial electricity-only plants. [3] Anthracite, bituminous coal, subbituminous coal, lignite, waste coal, and coal synfuel. [4] Distillate fuel oil, residual fuel oil, petroleum coke, jet fuel, kerosene, other petroleum, waste oil, and beginning in 2011, propane. [5] Includes a small amount of supplemental gaseous fuels. [6] Blast furnace gas and other manufactured and waste gases derived from fossil fuels. Through 2010, also includes propane. [7] Pumped storage facility production minus energy used for pumping. [8] Wood and wood-derived fuels. [9] Municipal solid waste from biogenic sources, landfill gas, sludge waste, agricultural byproducts, and other biomass. Through 2000, also includes nonrenewable waste (municipal solid waste from non-biogenic sources and tire-derived fuels). [10] Solar thermal and photovoltaic energy. Does not include small-scale solar photovoltaic generation. [11] Batteries, chemicals, hydrogen, pitch, purchased steam, sulfur, miscellaneous technologies, and beginning 2001, nonrenewable waste (municipal solid waste from nonbiogenic sources and tire-derived fuels). [12] Fuel oil numbers 1, 2, and 4. For 1990 through 2000, electric utility data also include small amounts of kerosene and jet fuel. [13] Fuel oil numbers 5 and 6. For 1990 through 2000, electric utility data also include a small amount of fuel oil number 4. [14] Jet fuel, kerosene, other petroleum liquids, waste oil, and beginning in 2011, propane.

Source: U.S. Energy Information Administration, *Monthly Energy Review*, March 2024. See also <www.eia.gov/totalenergy/data/monthly>.

Table 990. Total Electric Net Summer Capacity for All Sectors by Energy Source: 2000 to 2022

[In million kilowatts (811.7 represents 811,700,000). Data are shown for utility scale capacity at year end. For plants that use multiple sources of energy, capacity is assigned to the predominant energy source]

Source	2000	2010	2015	2017	2018	2019	2020	2021	2022
Net summer capacity, total	**811.7**	**1,039.1**	**1,064.1**	**1,084.4**	**1,094.7**	**1,099.1**	**1,115.7**	**1,145.9**	**1,161.4**
Fossil fuels, total	598.9	782.2	758.5	748.2	747.8	739.1	731.2	731.8	724.2
Coal [1]	315.1	316.8	279.7	256.5	242.8	228.7	215.6	209.8	189.3
Petroleum [2]	61.8	55.6	36.8	33.3	32.2	31.4	27.6	28.2	30.8
Natural gas [3]	219.6	407.0	439.4	456.0	470.2	476.6	485.8	491.9	502.4
Other gases [4]	2.3	2.7	2.5	2.4	2.5	2.5	2.3	1.9	1.7
Nuclear electric power	97.9	101.2	98.7	99.6	99.4	98.1	96.5	95.5	94.7
Hydroelectric pumped storage	19.5	22.2	22.6	22.8	22.8	22.8	23.0	23.0	23.0
Renewable energy, total	94.9	132.6	182.5	210.8	222.3	236.5	261.9	289.2	309.1
Conventional hydroelectric power	79.4	78.8	79.7	79.8	79.9	79.8	79.9	79.9	80.1
Biomass, total	10.0	11.4	14.1	14.0	13.7	13.1	12.9	12.4	12.1
Wood [5]	6.1	7.0	9.0	8.8	8.7	8.4	8.3	7.9	7.8
Other biomass [6]	3.9	4.4	5.1	5.1	5.0	4.7	4.6	4.5	4.3
Geothermal	2.8	2.4	2.5	2.5	2.4	2.6	2.6	2.6	2.6
Solar [7]	0.4	0.9	13.7	27.0	31.9	37.5	48.1	61.6	72.9
Wind	2.4	39.1	72.6	87.6	94.4	103.6	118.4	132.8	141.4
Other [8]	0.5	0.9	1.8	2.9	2.3	2.6	3.1	6.3	10.4

[1] Coal includes anthracite, bituminous, subbituminous, lignite, and waste coal; coal synfuel and refined coal; and, beginning in 2011, coal-derived synthesis gas. Prior to 2011, coal-derived synthesis gas was included in other gases. [2] Distillate fuel oil, residual fuel oil, petroleum coke, jet fuel, kerosene, other petroleum, waste oil, and, beginning in 2011, synthetic gas and propane. Prior to 2011, synthetic gas and propane were included in other gases. [3] Includes a small amount of supplemental gaseous fuels that cannot be identified separately. [4] Blast furnace gas, propane gas, and other manufactured and waste gases derived from fossil fuels. [5] Wood and wood-derived fuels. [6] Municipal solid waste, landfill gas, sludge waste, agricultural byproducts, other biomass solids, other biomass liquids, and other biomass gases (including digester gases, methane, and other biomass gases). [7] Solar thermal and photovoltaic energy. [8] Batteries, hydrogen, purchased steam, sulfur, tire-derived fuels and other miscellaneous energy sources.

Source: U.S. Energy Information Administration, *Electric Power Annual 2022*, October 2023, and earlier reports. See also <www.eia.gov/electricity/annual/>.

Table 991. Electricity—End Use and Average Retail Prices: 2000 to 2022

[3,592.4 represents 3,592,400,000,000. Beginning 2003, the category "other" has been replaced by "transportation," and the categories "commercial" and "industrial" have been redefined. Data represent revenue from electricity retail sales divided by the amount of retail electricity sold (in kilowatt-hours). Prices include state and local taxes, energy or demand charges, customer service charges, environmental surcharges, franchise fees, fuel adjustments, and other miscellaneous charges applied to end-use customers during normal billing operations. Prices do not include deferred charges, credits, or other adjustments, such as fuel or revenue from purchased power, from previous reporting periods. Data are from a census of electric utilities. Data also include energy service providers selling to retail customers]

Item	2000	2010	2015	2017	2018	2019	2020	2021	2022
END USE (Billion kilowatt-hours)									
Total end use [1]	**3,592.4**	**3,886.8**	**3,900.2**	**3,864.3**	**4,003.1**	**3,954.4**	**3,856.4**	**3,944.8**	**4,066.9**
Direct use [2]	170.9	131.9	141.2	141.0	143.9	143.3	138.7	138.9	139.7
Retail sales, total [3]	3,421.4	3,754.8	3,759.0	3,723.4	3,859.2	3,811.2	3,717.7	3,805.9	3,927.2
Residential	1,192.4	1,445.7	1,404.1	1,378.6	1,469.1	1,440.3	1,464.6	1,470.5	1,509.2
Commercial [4]	1,159.3	1,330.2	1,360.8	1,352.9	1,381.8	1,360.9	1,287.4	1,328.4	1,390.9
Industrial [5]	1,064.2	971.2	986.5	984.3	1,000.7	1,002.4	959.1	1,000.6	1,020.5
Transportation [6]	5.4	7.7	7.6	7.5	7.7	7.6	6.5	6.3	6.6
AVERAGE RETAIL PRICES (Cents per kilowatt-hour)									
Total	**6.81**	**9.83**	**10.41**	**10.48**	**10.53**	**10.54**	**10.59**	**11.1**	**12.36**
Residential	8.24	11.54	12.65	12.89	12.87	13.01	13.15	13.66	15.04
Commercial [7]	7.43	10.19	10.64	10.66	10.67	10.68	10.59	11.22	12.41
Industrial [5]	4.64	6.77	6.91	6.88	6.92	6.81	6.67	7.18	8.32
Transportation [6]	(NA)	10.56	10.09	9.68	9.70	9.66	9.90	10.20	11.59
Other [8]	6.56	(NA)	(NA)	(NA)	(NA)	(NA)	(NA)	(NA)	(NA)

NA Not available. [1] The sum of "total retail sales" and "direct use." [2] Use of electricity that is 1) self-generated, 2) produced by either the same entity that consumes the power or an affiliate, and 3) used in direct support of a service or industrial process located within the same facility or group of facilities that house the generating equipment. Direct use is exclusive of station use. [3] Electricity retail sales to ultimate customers reported by electric utilities and, beginning in 2000, other energy service providers. [4] Includes public street and highway lighting, interdepartmental sales, and other sales to public authorities. [5] Beginning 2003, includes agriculture and irrigation. [6] Includes sales to railroads and railways. [7] Beginning 2003, includes public street and highway lighting, interdepartmental sales, and other sales to public authorities. [8] Public street and highway lighting, interdepartmental sales, other sales to public authorities, agriculture and irrigation, and transportation including railroads and railways.

Source: U.S. Energy Information Administration, *Electric Power Annual 2022*, October 2023, and earlier reports. See also <www.eia.gov/electricity/>.

Table 992. Electric Power Industry—Net Generation and Net Summer Capacity by State: 2010 to 2022

[4,125.1 represents 4,125,100,000,000. Capacity as of December 31. Covers utilities for public use]

State	Net generation (billion kilowatt-hours)								Net summer capacity (million kilowatts)	
	2010	2020	2022 Total [1] (bil. kWh)	Percent from— Petro-leum	Natural gas	Hydro-electric	Nuclear	Coal	2020	2022
United States..........	4,125.1	4,009.8	4,230.7	0.5	39.9	6.0	18.2	19.7	1,115.7	1,161.4
Alabama.................	152.2	137.5	144.8	(Z)	43.0	7.0	29.2	17.9	28.7	28.9
Alaska.................	6.8	6.3	6.7	12.7	48.2	25.6	–	10.9	2.8	2.8
Arizona.................	111.8	109.3	104.7	(Z)	43.0	5.1	30.5	12.8	27.1	28.2
Arkansas.................	61.0	54.6	65.9	0.1	39.5	5.3	21.7	30.9	14.8	15.0
California.................	204.1	193.1	203.4	0.1	47.4	8.7	8.7	0.1	78.1	86.0
Colorado.................	50.7	54.1	58.0	(Z)	26.6	2.3	–	37.4	17.6	18.1
Connecticut.............	33.3	41.2	43.1	0.7	57.0	0.7	38.2	–	10.3	10.1
Delaware.................	5.6	5.2	5.3	2.0	89.5	–	–	2.0	3.4	3.3
District of Columbia.....	0.2	0.2	0.2	(Z)	50.1	–	–	–	(Z)	0.1
Florida.................	229.1	250.8	258.9	0.5	74.7	0.1	11.9	6.0	61.8	66.9
Georgia.................	137.6	120.1	126.5	0.4	47.3	2.5	26.9	13.3	37.3	36.2
Hawaii.................	10.8	9.1	9.3	71.3	–	1.2	–	6.9	3.0	2.9
Idaho.................	12.0	17.7	16.3	(Z)	26.6	51.4	–	(Z)	5.2	5.4
Illinois.................	201.4	173.4	185.2	(Z)	10.7	0.1	53.4	21.9	44.4	44.2
Indiana.................	125.2	90.1	98.1	0.1	32.8	0.4	–	52.4	27.3	26.9
Iowa.................	57.5	59.6	73.0	0.1	10.1	1.4	–	24.9	21.3	22.5
Kansas.................	47.9	54.5	62.2	-0.4	5.4	(Z)	14.4	32.5	17.0	18.4
Kentucky.................	98.2	63.5	69.1	0.1	24.5	6.6	–	68.0	17.6	17.6
Louisiana.................	102.9	100.8	105.5	2.9	68.5	0.9	15.3	7.7	25.6	24.7
Maine.................	17.0	10.0	12.8	2.1	32.5	24.0	–	0.3	4.9	5.1
Maryland.................	43.6	36.0	37.1	0.4	37.6	4.8	39.9	12.5	13.8	11.9
Massachusetts..........	42.8	18.2	21.0	3.6	75.0	4.2	–	–	13.0	12.8
Michigan.................	111.6	106.6	117.5	1.3	35.1	1.2	22.1	29.3	29.6	30.5
Minnesota.................	53.7	56.5	59.0	-0.1	14.8	1.6	24.9	27.4	17.9	18.5
Mississippi.................	54.5	66.6	67.8	(Z)	76.3	–	12.7	8.3	14.6	14.7
Missouri.................	92.3	72.6	79.4	0.2	10.3	1.7	11.2	66.6	22.0	21.1
Montana.................	29.8	23.4	27.1	1.7	2.7	36.5	–	43.0	5.9	6.4
Nebraska.................	36.6	36.8	40.7	0.1	3.1	2.6	13.8	49.0	9.8	10.8
Nevada.................	35.1	40.4	42.6	(Z)	58.3	4.0	–	6.4	12.1	13.5
New Hampshire..........	22.2	16.4	18.8	2.4	24.0	6.4	58.2	1.6	4.5	4.5
New Jersey.................	65.7	61.1	65.1	0.2	51.3	(Z)	43.5	0.8	17.4	16.7
New Mexico.................	36.3	34.1	40.9	(Z)	26.8	0.3	–	32.5	9.1	10.2
New York.................	137.0	129.4	125.2	1.5	48.2	21.9	21.4	–	40.2	39.7
North Carolina.................	128.7	124.4	134.3	0.2	43.3	3.5	31.8	10.9	35.1	35.4
North Dakota.................	34.7	42.2	44.4	0.1	3.3	4.0	–	55.9	9.2	9.4
Ohio.................	143.6	122.5	135.8	0.9	50.7	0.4	12.4	31.7	27.0	27.4
Oklahoma.................	72.3	83.4	84.6	(Z)	42.6	2.1	–	10.6	28.7	32.6
Oregon.................	55.1	63.6	61.3	(Z)	31.1	51.1	–	–	16.7	17.2
Pennsylvania.................	229.8	230.1	239.3	0.1	54.4	1.1	31.8	10.0	48.9	49.1
Rhode Island.................	7.7	8.9	7.8	0.8	89.1	0.1	–	–	2.1	2.2
South Carolina..........	104.2	98.5	98.7	0.2	24.5	2.2	55.1	14.4	24.1	24.3
South Dakota.................	10.0	14.1	17.9	0.1	8.0	23.8	–	10.5	5.4	6.3
Tennessee.................	82.3	80.6	78.0	0.2	21.2	11.8	45.7	20.4	21.4	21.6
Texas.................	411.7	473.5	525.6	0.1	48.7	0.1	7.9	16.2	128.9	148.9
Utah.................	42.2	37.1	39.4	0.1	28.2	1.5	–	56.8	9.3	9.6
Vermont.................	6.6	2.2	2.2	0.2	0.1	52.2	–	–	0.8	0.8
Virginia.................	73.0	103.1	89.5	0.7	54.5	1.3	31.5	3.7	27.9	29.2
Washington.................	103.5	116.1	116.7	(Z)	12.5	67.6	8.4	3.1	30.7	30.9
West Virginia.................	80.8	56.7	56.7	0.3	3.7	2.9	–	89.5	14.9	15.0
Wisconsin.................	64.3	61.4	61.2	0.3	38.0	3.3	16.5	35.8	16.5	16.7
Wyoming.................	48.1	42.0	46.3	0.1	3.6	1.6	–	72.3	9.6	10.1

– Represents zero. Z Represents less than .05 percent of net electricity generation, or less than .05 million kilowatts summer capacity. [1] Includes other sources not shown separately.

Source: U.S. Energy Information Administration, Electric Power Annual, "Data Tables," <www.eia.gov/electricity/annual/>; and "Detailed and historical electricity data by survey, State-level," <www.eia.gov/electricity/data.php>; accessed March 2024.

Table 993. Electricity Generation Existing Summer and Winter Capacity by Energy Source and Producer Type: 2022

[Capacity in megawatts. Data shown are for utility scale power plants that have at least 1 megawatt of generation capacity. For plants that use multiple sources of energy, capacity is assigned to the predominant energy source]

Source and producer type	Number of generators	Generator nameplate capacity	Net summer capacity	Net winter capacity
Total	**25,378**	**1,253,744**	**1,161,432**	**1,201,699**
ENERGY SOURCE				
Fossil fuels, total	11,101	808,815	724,217	762,823
Coal [1]	510	205,446	189,316	190,502
Petroleum [2]	3,978	35,527	30,775	33,885
Natural gas	6,542	565,951	502,397	536,698
Other gases [3]	71	1,892	1,728	1,738
Nuclear electric power	92	99,435	94,659	97,026
Hydroelectric pumped storage	152	22,008	23,044	22,949
Renewable energy, total	13,497	312,847	309,107	308,439
Conventional hydroelectric power	4,005	79,960	80,068	79,497
Wind	1,509	141,952	141,402	141,426
Solar [4]	5,790	73,196	72,862	72,123
Biomass, total	2,028	13,774	12,127	12,300
Wood [5]	313	8,874	7,805	7,924
Other biomass [6]	1,715	4,899	4,322	4,376
Geothermal	165	3,965	2,649	3,093
Other energy sources [7]	536	10,639	10,406	10,463
PRODUCER TYPE				
Electric power sector, total	21,944	1,216,764	1,129,201	1,167,507
Electric utilities	9,649	664,893	612,812	633,531
Independent power producers				
Non-combined heat and power plants	11,854	521,243	488,925	504,487
Combined heat and power plants	441	30,628	27,463	29,488
Commercial and industrial sectors, total	3,434	36,980	32,231	34,193
Commercial	1,904	5,974	5,450	5,551
Industrial	1,530	31,006	26,781	28,641

[1] Coal includes anthracite, bituminous, subbituminous, lignite, and waste coal; coal synfuel and refined coal; and coal-derived synthesis gas. [2] Petroleum includes distillate fuel oil, residual fuel oil, jet fuel, kerosene, petroleum coke, waste oil, and synthetic gas and propane. [3] Includes blast furnace gas. [4] Solar thermal and photovoltaic energy. [5] Wood and wood-derived fuels. [6] Other biomass includes municipal solid waste, landfill gas, sludge waste, agricultural byproducts, and other biomass solids, liquids, and gases (including digester gases, methane, and other biomass gases). [7] Includes batteries, hydrogen, purchased steam, sulfur, tire-derived fuels and other miscellaneous energy sources.

Source: U.S. Energy Information Administration, *Electric Power Annual 2022*, October 2023. See also <www.eia.gov/electricity/annual>.

Table 994. Electric Energy Retail Sales by Class of Service and State: 2022

[In billions of kilowatt-hours (3,927.2 represents 3,927,200,000,000). Data include both bundled and unbundled consumers]

State	Total [1]	Residential	Commercial	Industrial	State	Total [1]	Residential	Commercial	Industrial
United States	**3,927.2**	**1,509.2**	**1,390.9**	**1,020.5**	Missouri	80.3	37.2	29.8	13.2
Alabama	87.0	32.9	22.4	31.7	Montana	15.6	5.9	5.0	4.7
Alaska	6.0	2.1	2.6	1.4	Nebraska	33.8	11.0	9.6	13.2
Arizona	84.2	38.4	31.5	14.3	Nevada	39.3	14.3	12.4	12.6
Arkansas	49.0	19.3	11.8	18.0	New Hampshire	10.8	4.8	4.1	1.9
California	251.9	89.5	114.1	47.5	New Jersey	74.4	30.1	37.4	6.8
Colorado	56.8	20.6	21.1	15.0	New Mexico	27.2	7.3	9.1	10.8
Connecticut	27.8	13.2	11.6	2.8	New York	143.2	52.2	72.2	16.2
Delaware	11.5	5.2	4.3	2.0	North Carolina	139.2	62.4	49.2	27.5
District of Columbia	10.2	2.5	7.3	0.2	North Dakota	25.4	5.3	8.4	11.7
Florida	248.8	134.2	96.9	17.6	Ohio	149.5	53.3	46.1	50.1
Georgia	145.0	61.1	49.5	34.2	Oklahoma	69.5	25.5	22.2	21.8
Hawaii	9.0	2.7	2.8	3.5	Oregon	56.3	20.7	16.7	18.9
Idaho	26.2	10.0	6.8	9.4	Pennsylvania	145.0	56.4	37.2	50.9
Illinois	135.9	46.5	47.1	41.8	Rhode Island	7.6	3.2	3.7	0.6
Indiana	100.0	34.1	23.5	42.5	South Carolina	82.8	32.3	24.1	26.3
Iowa	54.2	15.2	12.5	26.5	South Dakota	13.5	5.3	4.9	3.2
Kansas	42.0	14.4	15.8	11.7	Tennessee	102.1	43.6	35.7	22.8
Kentucky	75.3	26.8	19.7	28.8	Texas	475.4	170.6	160.7	143.9
Louisiana	95.1	31.4	23.5	40.1	Utah	33.4	11.3	12.9	9.1
Maine	11.9	5.1	4.1	2.7	Vermont	5.5	2.2	1.9	1.4
Maryland	59.7	28.1	27.6	3.6	Virginia	132.3	46.7	68.6	16.9
Massachusetts	51.0	20.0	24.4	6.2	Washington	90.9	39.8	29.8	21.2
Michigan	100.6	35.0	37.1	28.5	West Virginia	33.0	11.1	7.3	14.6
Minnesota	66.6	23.4	22.5	20.6	Wisconsin	69.9	22.9	23.4	23.6
Mississippi	49.0	18.9	14.1	16.0	Wyoming	16.5	3.0	3.6	9.9

[1] Includes transportation, not shown separately.

Source: U.S. Energy Information Administration, "Historical State Data," <www.eia.gov/electricity/data/state/>, accessed November 2023.

Table 995. Electric Energy Average Retail Price by Class of Service and State: 2022

[In cents per kilowatt-hour (kWh). Data include both bundled and unbundled consumers]

State	Total [1]	Residential	Commercial	Industrial	State	Total [1]	Residential	Commercial	Industrial
United States	**12.36**	**15.04**	**12.41**	**8.32**	Missouri	10.26	11.74	9.55	7.67
Alabama	11.59	14.25	13.16	7.72	Montana	9.97	11.33	10.68	7.49
Alaska	20.73	23.10	20.06	18.43	Nebraska	8.83	10.79	8.82	7.21
Arizona	11.31	13.02	10.80	7.86	Nevada	10.94	13.78	10.14	8.50
Arkansas	9.91	12.05	10.26	7.38	New Hampshire	21.07	25.46	18.69	15.15
California	22.33	25.84	21.81	17.09	New Jersey	14.80	16.74	13.75	12.12
Colorado	11.75	14.19	11.58	8.63	New Mexico	10.02	13.84	11.07	6.56
Connecticut	21.08	24.61	18.54	15.07	New York	18.33	22.08	18.19	7.55
Delaware	11.83	13.71	10.98	8.79	North Carolina	9.60	11.62	8.75	6.54
District of Columbia	14.94	14.18	15.60	7.74	North Dakota	8.42	10.92	8.45	7.28
Florida	12.51	13.90	11.19	9.16	Ohio	10.64	13.85	10.39	7.45
Georgia	12.00	13.80	12.10	8.65	Oklahoma	10.05	12.44	10.34	6.96
Hawaii	39.72	43.03	40.18	36.71	Oregon	9.26	11.42	9.35	6.81
Idaho	8.51	10.37	8.27	6.71	Pennsylvania	11.86	15.94	10.73	8.21
Illinois	11.94	15.65	11.32	8.57	Rhode Island	19.30	23.21	16.23	17.96
Indiana	11.66	14.59	12.86	8.65	South Carolina	10.74	13.59	10.86	7.13
Iowa	9.57	13.15	10.55	7.06	South Dakota	10.44	12.09	10.21	8.04
Kansas	11.47	13.99	11.51	8.30	Tennessee	10.89	12.25	12.02	6.55
Kentucky	10.51	12.91	11.78	7.41	Texas	10.16	13.76	9.05	7.13
Louisiana	10.41	12.93	11.93	7.54	Utah	8.80	10.84	8.39	6.84
Maine	17.44	22.44	15.40	11.03	Vermont	16.99	19.93	17.29	11.88
Maryland	13.32	14.46	12.65	10.01	Virginia	10.75	13.34	9.66	7.99
Massachusetts	21.27	25.97	18.67	17.06	Washington	9.05	10.26	9.49	6.17
Michigan	13.20	17.86	12.55	8.33	West Virginia	9.74	13.23	10.42	6.74
Minnesota	12.04	14.25	12.30	9.25	Wisconsin	11.95	15.62	11.85	8.49
Mississippi	10.36	12.41	11.76	6.71	Wyoming	8.24	11.09	9.55	6.89

[1] Includes transportation, not shown separately.

Source: U.S. Energy Information Administration, "Historical State Data," <www.eia.gov/electricity/data/state/>, accessed November 2023.

Table 996. Electric Power Industry—Generation, Sales, Revenue, and Customers: 2010 to 2023

[4,125 represents 4,125,000,000,000 kilowatt-hours (kWh). Sales and revenue are to and from ultimate customers]

Item	Unit	2010	2015	2016	2017	2018	2019	2020	2021	2022	2023
Generation [1]	Bil. kWh	4,125	4,079	4,078	4,035	4,181	4,131	4,010	4,110	4,231	4,178
Sales	Bil. kWh	3,755	3,759	3,762	3,723	3,859	3,811	3,718	3,806	3,927	3,861
Residential	Bil. kWh	1,446	1,404	1,411	1,379	1,469	1,440	1,465	1,470	1,509	1,455
Percent of total	Percent	38.5	37.4	37.5	37.0	38.1	37.8	39.4	38.6	38.4	37.7
Commercial	Bil. kWh	1,330	1,361	1,367	1,353	1,382	1,361	1,287	1,328	1,391	1,375
Industrial	Bil. kWh	971	987	977	984	1,001	1,002	959	1,001	1,020	1,025
Transportation	Bil. kWh	8	8	7	8	8	8	7	6	7	7
Revenue	Mil. dol.	368,918	391,341	386,509	390,322	406,420	401,738	393,639	422,323	485,249	491,124
Residential	Mil. dol.	166,778	177,624	177,077	177,661	189,033	187,436	192,663	200,834	226,990	232,463
Percent of total	Percent	45.2	45.4	45.8	45.5	46.5	46.7	48.9	47.6	46.8	47.3
Commercial	Mil. dol.	135,554	144,781	142,643	144,242	147,425	145,280	136,372	149,008	172,600	175,231
Industrial	Mil. dol.	65,772	68,166	66,068	67,691	69,218	68,285	63,956	71,835	84,895	82,566
Transportation	Mil. dol.	814	771	722	728	744	737	648	646	765	864
Ultimate customers	1,000	144,140	148,633	150,055	151,780	153,339	154,898	156,523	158,433	160,162	(NA)
Residential	1,000	125,718	129,812	131,069	132,580	133,893	135,250	136,682	138,309	139,854	(NA)
Commercial	1,000	17,674	17,986	18,148	18,359	18,605	18,694	18,849	19,102	19,258	(NA)
Industrial	1,000	748	836	838	840	840	954	992	1,022	1,050	(NA)
Transportation	1,000	(Z)	(Z)	(Z)	(Z)	(Z)	(Z)	(Z)	(Z)	(Z)	(NA)
Average retail price of electricity	Cents/kWh	9.8	10.4	10.3	10.5	10.5	10.5	10.6	11.1	12.4	12.7
Residential	Cents/kWh	11.5	12.7	12.6	12.9	12.9	13.0	13.2	13.7	15.0	16.0
Commercial	Cents/kWh	10.2	10.6	10.4	10.7	10.7	10.7	10.6	11.2	12.4	12.7
Industrial	Cents/kWh	6.8	6.9	6.8	6.9	6.9	6.8	6.7	7.2	8.3	8.1
Transportation	Cents/kWh	10.6	10.1	9.6	9.7	9.7	9.7	9.9	10.2	11.6	12.7

NA Data not available. Z less than 500. [1] Generation at utility scale facilities.

Source: Energy Information Administration, *Electric Power Annual 2022*, October 2023; and "Electricity Data Browser," <www.eia.gov/electricity/data/browser>, accessed March 2024.

Table 997. Revenue and Expense Statistics for Major U.S. Investor-Owned Electric Utilities: 2000 to 2022

[In millions of dollars (233,915 represents $233,915,000,000). Covers investor-owned electric utilities that met any one or more of the following conditions, during each of the last 3 years: 1 million megawatt-hours of total sales, 100 megawatt-hours of annual sales for resale, 500 megawatt-hours of annual power exchange delivered, or 500 megawatt-hours of annual wheeling (deliveries plus losses) for others. Missing or erroneous respondent data may result in slight imbalances in some of the expense account subtotals]

Item	2000	2010	2015	2018	2019	2020	2021	2022
Utility operating revenues.........	**233,915**	**285,512**	**282,695**	**293,868**	**293,000**	**294,756**	**329,138**	**381,129**
Electric utility............................	213,634	260,119	260,121	268,421	266,876	269,869	299,956	344,355
Other utility...............................	20,281	25,393	22,574	25,447	26,124	24,888	29,181	36,774
Utility operating expenses..........	**210,250**	**253,022**	**242,728**	**253,944**	**250,136**	**240,802**	**271,078**	**315,491**
Electric utility............................	191,564	234,173	228,366	238,526	234,892	227,084	253,979	292,247
Operation.............................	132,607	166,922	149,939	163,479	157,265	144,335	163,952	196,589
Production.........................	107,554	128,831	107,201	104,185	99,518	93,505	110,775	140,287
Cost of fuel.....................	32,407	44,138	34,711	33,592	29,614	25,856	34,771	49,486
Purchased power.................	62,608	67,284	52,970	53,060	50,378	50,407	61,627	80,032
Other.............................	12,561	17,409	19,521	17,533	19,526	17,242	14,377	10,768
Transmission......................	2,713	6,948	9,624	11,387	11,941	12,949	15,310	15,872
Distribution........................	3,092	4,007	4,406	4,806	5,218	5,480	5,659	5,973
Customer accounts................	4,239	5,091	5,184	4,969	4,978	5,775	5,249	5,658
Customer service..................	1,826	4,741	6,445	6,019	6,156	5,868	6,192	6,659
Sales................................	405	185	201	203	204	211	215	255
Administrative and general........	12,768	17,120	16,878	31,911	29,248	20,546	20,553	21,886
Maintenance..........................	12,064	14,957	16,392	17,786	19,898	20,030	20,875	21,834
Depreciation..........................	20,636	20,951	26,847	32,125	34,883	38,208	39,666	42,104
Taxes and other.....................	24,479	31,343	35,188	25,136	22,846	24,510	29,485	31,720
Other utility............................	18,686	18,849	14,362	15,418	15,245	13,718	17,100	23,244
Net utility operating income.......	**23,665**	**32,490**	**39,968**	**39,924**	**42,864**	**53,954**	**58,060**	**65,638**

Source: U.S. Energy Information Administration, *Electric Power Annual 2022*, October 2023, and earlier reports. See also <www.eia.gov/electricity/annual/>.

Table 998. Renewable Energy Net Generation of Electricity by Source and State: 2023

[In millions of kilowatt-hours (239,855 represents 239,855,000,000). Data based on results from the Energy Information Agency's annual survey form EIA-923. For more on net generation, see Table 992]

State	Hydro-electric	Other renewable				State	Hydro-electric	Other renewable			
		Total [1]	Wind	Bio-mass [2]	Solar [3]			Total [1]	Wind	Bio-mass [2]	Solar [3]
U.S......	**239,855**	**727,281**	**425,235**	**47,464**	**238,120**	MO.......	1,377	7,815	6,811	109	895
AL........	9,979	4,248	(NA)	3,048	1,200	MT........	7,677	4,905	4,561	28	316
AK........	1,355	194	131	39	24	NE........	850	12,172	11,951	89	132
AZ........	5,805	13,700	1,733	188	11,779	NV........	1,303	16,066	291	56	11,423
AR........	3,595	1,963	(NA)	764	1,199	NH........	1,262	1,465	411	751	303
CA........	31,887	99,553	14,897	4,878	68,816	NJ........	12	5,723	18	672	5,033
CO........	1,324	21,456	16,009	137	5,310	NM.......	119	18,186	14,899	28	3,223
CT........	341	2,090	10	421	1,659	NY........	27,700	12,990	4,903	1,640	6,447
DE........	(NA)	427	4	77	346	NC........	4,871	14,294	519	1,690	12,085
DC........	(NA)	289	(NA)	58	231	ND........	1,446	14,688	14,686	–	2
FL........	229	21,313	(NA)	3,505	17,808	OH........	506	4,868	2,828	306	1,734
GA........	3,376	13,238	(NA)	5,135	8,103	OK........	1,858	38,235	37,731	265	239
HI........	89	3,327	643	283	2,053	OR........	24,829	12,214	8,668	933	2,401
ID........	6,748	3,937	2,324	437	1,090	PA........	2,731	6,358	3,268	1,610	1,480
IL........	96	25,815	22,054	283	3,478	RI........	(S)	1,478	175	235	1,068
IN........	382	12,103	9,487	375	2,241	SC........	2,445	5,281	(NA)	1,913	3,368
IA........	751	42,988	41,869	208	911	SD........	3,563	9,465	9,389	25	51
KS........	13	27,734	27,462	62	210	TN........	9,300	1,519	23	451	1,045
KY........	4,677	708	(NA)	421	287	TX........	854	152,720	119,836	1,145	31,739
LA........	939	2,572	(NA)	1,974	598	UT........	541	6,105	684	77	4,823
ME........	3,061	5,193	2,451	1,553	1,189	VT........	1,179	1,140	340	361	439
MD.......	1,858	3,184	482	330	2,372	VA........	1,521	9,300	47	3,181	6,072
MA.......	908	6,784	197	935	5,652	WA.......	60,840	9,729	7,601	1,246	882
MI........	1,075	12,073	8,447	2,016	1,610	WV.......	1,647	2,143	2,087	9	47
MN.......	717	18,159	14,665	1,174	2,320	WI........	1,577	4,342	1,759	1,053	1,530
MS........	(NA)	1,949	(NA)	1,293	656	WY.......	634	9,086	8,883	(NA)	203

NA Not available. – Represents or rounds down to zero. S Figure does not meet standards for reliability due to a large relative standard error. [1] Includes generation from geothermal energy, not shown separately. [2] Includes wood and wood derived fuels, landfill gas, biogenic municipal solid waste, and other biomass waste. [3] Includes generation from all utility-scale solar and small-scale solar photovoltaic sources.

Source: Energy Information Administration, "Electricity Data Browser," <www.eia.gov/electricity/data/browser>, accessed April 2024.

Table 999. Major Power Outages by Type of Disturbance and Duration: 2023

[Data shown for power outages lasting 20 hours or longer]

Type of disturbance	Month	Counties and/or states affected	Duration	Number of customers affected [1]
Severe Weather.........	July	Tennessee: Shelby County	164 Hours, 10 Minutes	216,000
Severe Weather.........	January	Texas	152 Hours, 45 Minutes	360,000
Severe Weather.........	February	Texas: Travis County	89 Hours, 39 Minutes	173,879
Severe Weather.........	February	Michigan: Van Buren, Kalamazoo, St. Joseph, Calhoun, Branch, Hillsdale, Jackson, Washtenaw, Monroe, Lenawee, Ingham, Barry, Allegan, Ottawa, Eaton, Shiawassee, and Clinton Counties	69 Hours, 31 Minutes	261,043
Severe Weather.........	July	Maryland	63 Hours, 0 Minutes	53,630
Severe Weather.........	January	Texas: Harris County	52 Hours, 55 Minutes	100,731
Severe Weather.........	March	Texas	52 Hours, 0 Minutes	470,000
Severe Weather.........	March	Michigan	50 Hours, 17 Minutes	67,893
Severe Weather.........	March	Connecticut, Massachusetts, Vermont, Rhode Island, New Hampshire, Maine	48 Hours, 20 Minutes	83,000
Severe Weather.........	September	Texas: Dallas, Tarrant, McLennan, Angelina, Bell, Williamson, and Smith Counties	45 Hours, 1 Minutes	130,000
Severe Weather.........	April	Ohio, West Virginia, Virginia	44 Hours, 47 Minutes	118,000
Severe Weather.........	July	Georgia	43 Hours, 47 Minutes	35,257
Severe Weather.........	September	Texas: Tarrant and Dallas Counties	43 Hours, 16 Minutes	190,000
Severe Weather.........	March	Michigan	42 Hours, 11 Minutes	200,000
Severe Weather.........	February	California: Los Angeles County	42 Hours, 0 Minutes	153,555
Severe Weather.........	July	West Virginia, Virginia	37 Hours, 45 Minutes	52,098
Severe Weather.........	July	Illinois: Winnebago, Cook, Will, DeKalb, and Kendall Counties	37 Hours, 0 Minutes	122,921
Suspicious Activity......	October	Nevada	36 Hours, 0 Minutes	0
Severe Weather.........	January	Connecticut, Rhode Island, Massachusetts, Vermont, New Hampshire, Maine	34 Hours, 12 Minutes	41,000
Severe Weather.........	September	Connecticut, Massachusetts, Maine, Rhode Island, Vermont, New Hampshire	30 Hours, 50 Minutes	114,000
Severe Weather.........	October	Texas	30 Hours, 14 Minutes	153,000
Severe Weather.........	March	New York	29 Hours, 35 Minutes	(NA)
Severe Weather.........	March	Wisconsin: Walworth, Waukesha, Milwaukee, Racine, Ozaukee, and Kenosha Counties	24 Hours, 0 Minutes	100,000
Severe Weather.........	January	California: Sacramento County	23 Hours, 0 Minutes	185,434
Severe Weather.........	June	Arkansas, Mississippi	22 Hours, 15 Minutes	64,732
Severe Weather.........	June	Georgia, Alabama	22 Hours, 1 Minutes	(NA)
Severe Weather.........	July	Michigan	20 Hours, 30 Minutes	90,354
Severe Weather.........	April	Texas: Hidalgo, Cameron, Willacy, and Starr Counties	20 Hours, 0 Minutes	168,419

NA Not available. [1] Number of customers affected are preliminary estimates.

Source: U.S. Energy Information Administration, *Electric Power Monthly*, March 2024. See also <www.eia.gov/electricity/monthly>.

Table 1000. Gas Utility Industry—Summary: 1990 to 2022

[54,261 represents 54,261,000. Covers natural, manufactured, mixed, and liquid petroleum gas. Based on a questionnaire mailed to all privately and municipally owned gas utilities in the United States, except those with annual revenues less than $25,000]

Item	Unit	1990	2000	2005	2010	2015	2020	2021	2022
End users [1]	**1,000**	**54,261**	**61,262**	**64,395**	**64,960**	**65,612**	**69,349**	**70,296**	**71,150**
Residential	1,000	49,802	56,494	59,569	60,246	60,922	64,500	65,407	66,222
Commercial	1,000	4,246	4,610	4,678	4,582	4,559	4,721	4,759	4,800
Industrial	1,000	166	157	145	129	120	118	118	118
Other	1,000	48	2	2	3	10	10	11	10
Sales [2]	**Tril. Btu** [3]	**9,842**	**9,232**	**8,848**	**7,980**	**7,602**	**7,357**	**7,845**	**8,342**
Residential	Tril. Btu	4,468	4,741	4,516	4,371	4,080	3,971	4,250	4,497
Percent of total	Percent	45.4	51.4	51.0	54.8	53.7	54.0	54.2	53.9
Commercial	Tril. Btu	2,192	2,077	2,056	1,842	1,766	1,616	1,831	1,991
Industrial	Tril. Btu	3,010	1,698	1,654	1,209	1,172	1,062	1,150	1,186
Other	Tril. Btu	171	715	622	558	584	713	614	668
Revenues [2]	**Mil. dol.**	**45,153**	**59,243**	**96,909**	**72,886**	**60,923**	**61,972**	**77,666**	**100,256**
Residential	Mil. dol.	25,000	35,828	55,680	47,231	40,451	43,239	49,761	63,853
Percent of total	Percent	55.4	60.5	57.5	64.8	66.4	69.8	64.1	63.7
Commercial	Mil. dol.	10,604	13,339	22,653	16,578	14,057	13,170	16,329	22,687
Industrial	Mil. dol.	8,996	7,432	13,751	6,437	4,434	3,561	6,127	8,761
Other	Mil. dol.	553	2,645	4,825	2,640	1,982	2,002	5,450	4,955
Prices per mil. Btu [3]	**Dollars**	**4.59**	**6.42**	**10.95**	**9.13**	**7.99**	**7.96**	**9.90**	**12.02**
Residential	Dollars	5.60	7.56	12.33	10.81	9.91	10.25	11.71	14.20
Commercial	Dollars	4.84	6.42	11.02	9.00	7.96	7.54	9.20	11.40
Industrial	Dollars	2.99	4.38	8.31	5.32	3.78	3.20	5.50	7.39
Gas mains mileage	**1,000**	**1,189**	**1,369**	**1,438**	**1,531**	**1,594**	**1,648**	**1,659**	**1,785**
Field and gathering	1,000	32	27	23	19	18	17	17	111
Transmission	1,000	292	297	297	308	301	302	302	301
Distribution	1,000	865	1,046	1,118	1,204	1,276	1,329	1,341	1,372
Construction expenditures	**Mil. dol.**	**7,899**	**8,624**	**10,089**	**11,042**	**21,074**	**29,854**	**35,448**	**32,989**
Transmission	Mil. dol.	2,886	1,590	3,368	3,524	6,578	7,268	9,102	7,551
Distribution	Mil. dol.	3,714	5,437	5,129	5,674	11,614	18,765	22,404	20,873
Production and storage	Mil. dol.	309	138	179	151	135	614	377	532
General	Mil. dol.	770	1,273	1,070	1,185	1,928	2,494	2,635	2,870
Underground storage	Mil. dol.	219	185	343	509	819	714	931	1,163

[1] Annual average. [2] Excludes sales for resale. [3] For definition of Btu (British thermal unit), see text, this section.

Source: American Gas Association, Washington, DC, *Annual Statistics* ©. See also <www.aga.org>.

Table 1001. Gas Utility Industry—Customers, Sales, and Revenues by State: 2022

[70,815 represents 70,815,000. Covers natural, manufactured, mixed, and liquid petroleum gas. Based on questionnaire mailed to all privately and municipally owned gas utilities in U.S., except those with annual revenues less than $25,000. For definition of Btu, see text, this section]

State	Customers [1] (1,000) Total	Resi-dential	Sales [2] (tril. Btu) Total	Resi-dential	Revenues [2] (mil. dol.) Total	Resi-dential	State	Customers [1] (1,000) Total	Resi-dential	Sales [2] (tril. Btu) Total	Resi-dential	Revenues [2] (mil. dol.) Total	Resi-dential
U.S.	70,815	65,887	8,342	4,497	100,256	63,853	MO	1,567	1,450	170	107	2,129	1,481
AL	864	789	110	32	1,242	528	MT	328	289	38	24	384	242
AK	154	140	105	21	835	224	NE	532	487	64	36	710	445
AZ	1,417	1,358	81	44	1,135	751	NV	984	937	75	49	830	599
AR	635	566	56	32	814	526	NH	131	114	14	8	255	152
CA	11,328	10,890	623	429	11,231	8,353	NJ	3,066	2,853	319	241	3,886	2,915
CO	2,048	1,892	239	147	2,693	1,811	NM	625	575	58	38	660	458
CT	430	367	110	51	1,604	899	NY	4,621	4,290	509	371	7,451	5,839
DE	211	197	20	12	258	179	NC	1,526	1,390	146	75	2,029	1,238
DC	145	138	13	9	200	148	ND	179	154	47	14	408	152
FL	901	860	58	18	904	457	OH	665	629	77	55	1,007	732
GA	370	336	66	17	744	265	OK	1,074	978	98	63	1,267	903
HI	32	29	3	1	139	34	OR	881	796	95	51	1,021	629
ID	500	455	58	37	425	287	PA	2,745	2,558	286	217	3,978	3,126
IL	4,008	3,756	502	392	6,449	5,225	RI	269	248	25	19	427	331
IN	1,925	1,772	223	144	2,332	1,607	SC	778	715	114	35	1,271	524
IA	1,059	958	151	73	1,491	924	SD	232	205	28	15	272	160
KS	972	887	109	68	1,369	939	TN	1,365	1,223	170	75	1,840	908
KY	864	777	103	51	1,250	713	TX	5,436	5,098	1,384	240	12,057	3,833
LA	979	919	92	37	1,069	562	UT	1,129	1,057	115	82	1,119	826
ME	47	36	12	3	190	63	VT	55	49	14	4	140	61
MD	1,066	1,009	89	68	1,403	1,111	VA	1,306	1,211	136	78	1,799	1,217
MA	1,702	1,571	193	123	3,613	2,453	WA	1,382	1,271	160	97	1,843	1,205
MI	3,517	3,267	455	325	4,784	3,547	WV	371	337	41	26	436	303
MN	1,770	1,624	293	156	3,167	1,827	WI	2,019	1,840	324	155	2,868	1,692
MS	479	431	51	23	616	327	WY	124	110	18	9	210	123

[1] Averages for the year. [2] Excludes sales for resale.

Source: American Gas Association, Washington, DC, *Annual Statistics* ©. See also <www.aga.org>.

Table 1002. Privately Owned Gas Utility Industry—Balance Sheet and Income Account: 1990 to 2022

[In millions of dollars (121,686 represents $121,686,000,000). The gas utility industry consists of pipeline and distribution companies. Excludes operations of companies distributing gas in bottles or tanks]

Item	1990	1995	2000	2005	2010	2015	2020	2021	2022
COMPOSITE BALANCE SHEET									
Assets, total	**121,686**	**141,965**	**165,709**	**196,215**	**220,860**	**262,805**	**367,210**	**378,993**	**478,419**
Total utility plant	112,863	143,636	162,206	207,976	239,718	292,252	402,887	408,086	494,773
Depreciation and amortization	49,483	62,723	69,366	91,794	92,012	104,615	122,185	123,627	157,362
Utility plant (net)	63,380	80,912	92,839	116,183	147,707	187,637	280,703	284,459	337,412
Investment and fund accounts	23,872	26,489	10,846	16,331	7,132	12,202	8,647	10,367	17,235
Current and accrued assets	23,268	18,564	35,691	32,325	27,288	21,309	25,136	27,517	38,889
Deferred debits [1]	9,576	13,923	24,279	29,574	37,307	40,253	51,178	55,151	82,811
Liabilities, total	**121,686**	**141,965**	**165,709**	**196,215**	**220,860**	**262,805**	**367,210**	**378,993**	**478,419**
Capitalization, total	74,958	90,581	96,079	120,949	133,414	157,916	249,821	261,839	330,002
Capital stock	43,810	54,402	47,051	62,470	74,157	87,760	137,434	144,398	175,259
Long-term debts	31,148	35,548	48,267	58,264	59,223	70,194	112,387	117,441	154,290
Current and accrued liabilities	29,550	28,272	42,312	34,936	28,564	26,408	36,997	43,731	52,300
Deferred income taxes [2]	11,360	14,393	17,157	24,937	34,401	43,688	48,721	50,331	61,510
Other liabilities and credits	5,818	8,715	10,161	15,393	24,515	34,793	31,671	23,092	34,607
COMPOSITE INCOME ACCOUNT									
Operating revenues, total	**66,027**	**58,390**	**72,042**	**102,018**	**82,315**	**72,298**	**76,793**	**82,211**	**113,392**
Minus: Operating expenses [3]	60,137	50,760	64,988	89,385	71,761	61,229	38,730	46,709	66,075
Operation and maintenance	51,627	37,966	54,602	77,673	57,758	45,746	41,865	49,811	70,113
Federal, state, and local taxes	4,957	6,182	6,163	7,513	7,569	7,872	8,200	7,353	9,805
Equals: Operating income	5,890	7,630	7,053	12,632	10,554	11,069	16,660	14,843	21,128
Utility operating income	6,077	7,848	7,166	12,812	11,045	11,620	16,895	15,411	21,779
Income before interest charges	8,081	9,484	7,589	13,972	12,368	12,049	17,484	15,533	22,911
Net income	4,410	5,139	4,245	9,777	8,619	8,719	13,041	11,349	16,977
Dividends	3,191	4,037	3,239	2,419	2,080	1,487	1,879	1,504	1,154

[1] Includes capital stock discount and expense and reacquired securities. [2] Includes reserves for deferred income taxes. [3] Includes expenses not shown separately.

Source: American Gas Association, Washington, DC, *Annual Statistics* ©. See also <www.aga.org>.

Table 1003. Sewage Treatment Facilities and Employees: 2021 and 2022

[Due to disclosure avoidance guidelines, data are not presented for States with fewer than 3 contributing establishments. Data for paid employees is subject to moderate and high noise and most values have been changed by 2 to 5 percent or 5 or more percent to avoid disclosure of data for individual businesses. Data are based on the North American Industry Classification System (NAICS) 2017; see text, Section 15]

| State | Sewage treatment facilities (NAICS 22132) | | | | State | Sewage treatment facilities (NAICS 22132) | | | |
| | 2021 | | 2022 | | | 2021 | | 2022 | |
	Number of establish-ments	Paid employees	Number of establish-ments	Paid employees		Number of establish-ments	Paid employees	Number of establish-ments	Paid employees
U.S..............	**545**	**5,775**	**562**	**6,096**	MO..............	16	78	16	77
AL..............	12	361	14	391	MT..............	5	9	5	37
AK..............	(NA)	(NA)	(NA)	(NA)	NE..............	3	32	(NA)	(NA)
AZ..............	17	165	16	192	NV..............	(NA)	(NA)	(NA)	(NA)
AR..............	6	81	7	86	NH..............	4	23	4	20
CA..............	35	286	35	298	NJ..............	10	149	10	152
CO..............	6	114	6	119	NM..............	7	199	7	203
CT..............	6	83	6	85	NY..............	24	438	53	472
DE..............	4	67	4	64	NC..............	20	115	18	106
DC..............	(NA)	(NA)	(NA)	(NA)	ND..............	(NA)	(NA)	(NA)	(NA)
FL..............	35	586	33	646	OH..............	7	56	6	52
GA..............	12	259	10	261	OK..............	16	128	15	123
HI..............	16	91	15	91	OR..............	3	7	3	7
ID..............	6	47	6	46	PA..............	49	405	45	543
IL..............	18	209	20	172	RI..............	(NA)	(NA)	(NA)	(NA)
IN..............	21	102	20	121	SC..............	10	62	9	52
IA..............	3	103	3	104	SD..............	(NA)	(NA)	(NA)	(NA)
KS..............	(NA)	(NA)	(NA)	(NA)	TN..............	8	31	8	33
KY..............	4	35	4	33	TX..............	60	489	62	495
LA..............	22	199	21	200	UT..............	(NA)	(NA)	(NA)	(NA)
ME..............	(NA)	(NA)	(NA)	(NA)	VT..............	(NA)	(NA)	(NA)	(NA)
MD..............	4	20	3	19	VA..............	7	36	8	49
MA..............	7	96	7	91	WA..............	5	54	5	54
MI..............	16	184	13	182	WV..............	4	33	5	38
MN..............	14	101	13	89	WI..............	4	13	5	18
MS..............	12	166	12	185	WY..............	(NA)	(NA)	(NA)	(NA)

NA Not available.

Source: U.S. Census Bureau, County Business Patterns, "All Sectors: County Business Patterns, including ZIP Code Business Patterns, by Legal Form of Organization and Employment Size Class for the U.S., States, and Selected Geographies: 2022," <data.census.gov>, accessed June 2024.

Energy and Utilities   637

Section 20
Construction and Housing

This section presents data on the construction industry and on various indicators of its activity and costs; on housing units and their characteristics and occupants; and on the characteristics of commercial buildings.

The principal source of these data is the U.S. Census Bureau, which issues a variety of current publications, as well as data from the decennial census. *Construction Spending*, available at <census.gov/construction/c30/c30index.html>, presents data on all types of construction. Reports of the censuses of construction industries (see below) are also issued on various topics. Current residential construction statistics compiled by the Census Bureau appear in its *New Residential Construction*, <census.gov/construction/nrc/>; *New Residential Sales*, <census.gov/construction/nrs/>; and *Characteristics of New Housing*, <www.census.gov/construction/chars/>.

Other Census Bureau publications include the quarterly *Housing Vacancies and Homeownership*, <www.census.gov/housing/hvs>; the quarterly *Survey of Market Absorption*, <www.census.gov/programs-surveys/soma.html>; the biennial *American Housing Survey* (formerly *Annual Housing Survey*), <www.census.gov/programs-surveys/ahs/data.html>; and other reports of the censuses of housing and of construction industries.

Other sources include the Bureau of Economic Analysis, which presents data on residential fixed assets; the U.S. Energy Information Administration, which provides data on commercial and residential buildings through its periodic sample surveys; and the Federal Financial Institutions Examination Council, which provides data on home purchase loans. Additional data on mortgage activity are covered in Section 25, Banking and Finance.

Censuses and surveys—Censuses of the construction industry were first conducted by the Census Bureau for 1929, 1935, and 1939; beginning in 1967, a census has been taken every 5 years for years ending in "2" and "7". The construction sector of the Economic Census covers all employer establishments primarily engaged in (1) building construction by general contractors or operative builders; (2) heavy (nonbuilding) construction by general contractors; and (3) construction by special trade contractors. This sector includes construction management and land subdividers and developers. The census is conducted in accordance with the North American Industrial Classification System (NAICS). See text, Section 15, Business Enterprise.

The *American Housing Survey* (*Current Housing Reports* Series H-150 and H-170), which began in 1973, provided an annual and ongoing series of data on selected housing and demographic characteristics until 1983. In 1984, the name of the survey was changed from the *Annual Housing Survey*. Currently, national data are collected every other year, and data for selected metropolitan areas are collected on a rotating basis. The supplemental sample of housing units is selected for no more than 30 metropolitan units and combined with the national sample in order to produce metropolitan estimates using the national survey. More information about the survey can be found at <census.gov/programs-surveys/ahs.html>

Housing units—In general, a housing unit is a house, an apartment, a group of rooms or a single room occupied or intended for occupancy as separate living quarters; that is, the occupants live separately from any other individual in the building, and there is direct access from the outside or through a common hall. Transient accommodations, barracks for workers, and institutional-type quarters are not counted as housing units.

Statistical reliability—For a discussion of statistical collection and estimation, sampling procedures, and measures of statistical reliability applicable to Census Bureau data, see Appendix III.

Table 1004. Construction—Establishments, Employees, and Payroll by Kind of Business (NAICS Basis): 2021 and 2022

[7,062 represents 7,062,000. Covers establishments with payroll. Excludes most government employees, railroad employees, and self-employed persons. For statement on methodology, see Appendix III]

Kind of business	NAICS code [1]	Establishments		Paid employees [2] (1,000)		Annual payroll (mil. dol.)	
		2021	2022	2021	2022	2021	2022
Construction......................................	**23**	**780,257**	**800,651**	**7,062**	**7,362**	**489,515**	**534,390**
Construction of buildings.............................	236	244,227	251,634	1,487	1,576	111,184	124,104
Residential building construction...................	2361	202,052	209,456	815	883	53,247	60,610
New single-family housing construction (except for-sale builders).........................	236115	58,031	59,568	221	238	13,276	15,139
New multifamily housing construction (except for-sale builders).........................	236116	3,662	3,931	48	51	4,582	5,221
New housing for-sale builders....................	236117	12,535	12,612	122	131	13,167	14,780
Residential remodelers...........................	236118	127,824	133,345	425	463	22,222	25,470
Nonresidential building construction..............	2362	42,175	42,178	671	694	57,938	63,493
Industrial building construction...................	23621	3,172	3,173	69	75	5,750	6,471
Commercial and institutional building construction..	23622	39,003	39,005	602	619	52,188	57,023
Heavy and civil engineering construction..........	237	38,155	38,214	986	1,012	82,562	87,804
Utility system construction........................	2371	19,522	19,721	583	600	47,329	49,791
Water and sewer line and related structures....	23711	10,742	10,818	157	164	11,674	12,686
Oil and gas pipeline and related structures......	23712	2,172	2,166	174	176	14,139	14,580
Power and communication line and related structures................................	23713	6,608	6,737	252	260	21,516	22,524
Land subdivision..................................	2372	4,655	4,618	22	23	2,005	2,184
Highway, street, and bridge construction..........	2373	9,465	9,202	303	307	26,648	28,345
Other heavy and civil engineering construction...	2379	4,513	4,673	79	82	6,580	7,484
Specialty trade contractors.........................	238	497,875	510,803	4,589	4,773	295,769	322,483
Foundation, structure, and building exterior contractors......................................	2381	102,137	104,432	905	923	54,619	59,135
Poured concrete foundation and structures contractors....................................	23811	22,237	22,699	246	255	15,669	17,341
Structural steel and precast concrete contractors....................................	23812	3,839	3,972	78	79	5,301	5,722
Framing contractors.............................	23813	12,224	12,524	87	89	4,393	4,722
Masonry contractors.............................	23814	18,457	18,481	139	137	7,819	8,134
Glass and glazing contractors...................	23815	6,630	6,756	66	65	4,165	4,311
Roofing contractors.............................	23816	23,690	24,532	202	205	12,086	13,301
Siding contractors..............................	23817	8,954	9,191	40	42	2,162	2,275
Other foundation, structure, and building exterior contractors...........................	23819	6,106	6,277	49	51	3,024	3,330
Building equipment contractors....................	2382	193,994	199,350	2,173	2,272	149,570	163,110
Electrical contractors............................	23821	79,292	81,842	909	952	62,736	68,413
Plumbing, heating, and air-conditioning contractors....................................	23822	106,854	109,601	1,124	1,177	75,282	82,235
Other building equipment contractors...........	23829	7,848	7,907	139	143	11,552	12,462
Building finishing contractors......................	2383	124,953	127,033	822	847	45,609	49,080
Drywall and insulation contractors...............	23831	19,986	20,162	257	257	15,175	15,951
Painting and wall covering contractors..........	23832	37,210	37,963	191	198	9,607	10,453
Flooring contractors.............................	23833	17,640	18,069	83	86	4,581	4,912
Tile and terrazzo contractors.....................	23834	10,502	10,710	58	59	3,148	3,283
Finish carpentry contractors.....................	23835	31,866	32,169	162	168	8,869	9,698
Other building finishing contractors..............	23839	7,749	7,960	71	79	4,230	4,783
Other specialty trade contractors..................	2389	76,791	79,988	689	731	45,971	51,158
Site preparation contractors......................	23891	38,839	39,686	413	436	28,519	31,540
All other specialty trade contractors.............	23899	37,952	40,302	276	295	17,452	19,618

[1] Data are based on the North American Industry Classification System (NAICS) 2017; see text, Section 15. [2] Employees on the payroll for the pay period including March 12.

Source: U.S. Census Bureau, County Business Patterns, "All Sectors: County Business Patterns, including ZIP Code Business Patterns, by Legal Form of Organization and Employment Size Class for the U.S., States, and Selected Geographies: 2022," <data.census.gov>, accessed June 2024. See also <www.census.gov/programs-surveys/cbp.html>.

Table 1005. Construction Industries—Establishments, Shipments, Payroll, and Employees: 2017

[1,994,166,047 represents $1,994,166,047,000. Includes only establishments with payroll]

Industry	2017 NAICS code [1]	Establish-ments (number)	Value of shipments ($1,000)	Annual payroll ($1,000)	Paid employees [2] Total	Construction workers
Construction............................	**23**	**715,364**	**1,994,166,047**	**398,815,537**	**6,647,047**	**4,989,303**
Construction of buildings..........................	236	214,085	800,474,908	85,499,623	1,345,938	857,765
Residential buildings..............................	2361	171,814	342,010,528	37,276,291	694,023	453,287
New single-family housing (except for-sale builders).........................	236115	48,673	68,574,751	8,530,682	176,059	119,553
New multifamily housing (except for-sale builders). ..	236116	3,200	46,910,655	3,595,548	44,444	24,062
New housing for-sale builders......................	236117	17,123	148,898,346	10,298,600	132,191	50,793
Residential remodelers...........................	236118	102,818	77,626,776	14,851,461	341,329	258,879
Nonresidential buildings.........................	2362	42,271	458,464,380	48,223,332	651,915	404,478
Industrial buildings..............................	23621	3,164	25,454,943	4,479,129	71,562	49,219
Commercial and institutional buildings................	23622	39,107	433,009,437	43,744,203	580,353	355,259
Heavy and civil engineering construction............	237	38,016	318,079,667	72,037,723	1,007,942	785,314
Utility system....................................	2371	19,142	158,659,104	42,300,448	594,859	480,820
Water and sewer line and related structures..........	23711	10,838	44,333,746	9,613,699	150,664	116,563
Oil and gas pipeline and related structures..........	23712	2,226	49,691,899	15,491,081	211,334	178,222
Power and communication line and related structures.....	23713	6,078	64,633,459	17,195,668	232,861	186,035
Land subdivision.................................	2372	4,893	9,376,544	1,586,225	23,692	9,862
Highway, street, and bridge.......................	2373	9,721	126,575,188	23,248,153	322,243	245,658
Other heavy and civil engineering..................	2379	4,260	23,468,831	4,902,897	67,148	48,974
Specialty trade contractors.......................	238	463,263	875,611,472	241,278,191	4,293,167	3,346,224
Foundation, structure, and building exterior..........	2381	92,711	178,670,037	45,019,907	866,527	695,994
Poured concrete foundation and structure.............	23811	20,707	52,694,411	13,122,241	239,062	205,652
Structural steel and precast concrete...............	23812	3,577	15,476,984	4,663,204	77,366	64,447
Framing...	23813	11,516	16,165,452	3,630,233	85,674	72,421
Masonry...	23814	18,329	23,560,290	6,852,561	141,977	121,823
Glass and glazing................................	23815	5,816	14,124,308	3,498,088	61,758	39,977
Roofing...	23816	19,366	40,770,160	9,145,104	178,559	130,909
Siding..	23817	7,812	6,574,724	1,466,580	35,070	24,079
Other foundation, structure, and building exterior.....	23819	5,588	9,303,708	2,641,896	47,061	36,686
Building equipment...............................	2382	184,566	411,178,579	121,531,110	1,999,953	1,532,225
Electrical and other wiring installation................	23821	73,907	171,416,144	51,456,683	845,813	677,055
Plumbing, heating, and air-conditioning................	23822	103,275	206,208,216	60,218,491	1,020,861	754,717
Other building equipment..........................	23829	7,384	33,554,219	9,855,936	133,279	100,453
Building finishing................................	2383	116,026	136,104,427	38,592,728	800,677	635,737
Drywall and insulation............................	23831	18,359	45,083,613	13,522,558	258,608	224,797
Painting and wall covering.........................	23832	35,484	25,388,981	8,438,133	190,200	161,916
Flooring...	23833	15,925	18,039,180	3,800,490	78,494	52,036
Tile and terrazzo.................................	23834	9,787	9,264,998	2,687,228	57,235	45,376
Finish carpentry..................................	23835	29,697	27,561,178	6,807,059	145,852	102,006
Other building finishing...........................	23839	6,774	10,766,477	3,337,260	70,288	49,606
Other specialty trade.............................	2389	69,960	149,658,429	36,134,446	626,010	482,268
Site preparation..................................	23891	35,417	97,460,244	22,894,974	385,177	307,808
All other specialty trade..........................	23899	34,543	52,198,185	13,239,472	240,833	174,460

[1] North American Industry Classification System, 2017. [2] For pay period including March 12.

Source: U.S. Census Bureau, 2017 Economic Census, "EC1723BASIC: Construction: Summary Statistics for the U.S., States, and Selected Geographies: 2017," <data.census.gov>, accessed November 2021.

Table 1006. Value of New Construction Put in Place: 1990 to 2023

[In millions of dollars (476,778 represents $476,778,000,000). Represents value of construction put in place during year; differs from building permit and construction contract data in timing and coverage. Includes installed cost of normal building service equipment and selected types of industrial production equipment (largely site fabricated). Excludes cost of shipbuilding, land, and most types of machinery and equipment. For methodology, see <www.census.gov/construction/c30/meth.html>]

Year	Total	Private Total	Residential buildings	Non-residential	Public Total	Federal	State and local
1990.................	476,778	369,300	191,103	178,197	107,478	12,099	95,379
1995.................	548,666	408,655	228,121	180,534	140,011	15,751	124,260
2000.................	802,756	621,431	346,138	275,293	181,325	14,168	167,157
2005.................	1,116,811	882,651	624,574	258,077	234,160	17,300	216,860
2009.................	911,767	596,872	252,751	344,121	314,895	28,439	286,456
2010.................	812,964	508,998	245,743	263,255	303,966	31,133	272,833
2011.................	791,237	504,830	247,028	257,803	286,407	31,654	254,753
2012.................	854,401	575,091	273,730	301,360	279,311	26,933	252,378
2013.................	914,582	643,900	329,640	314,260	270,682	23,727	246,955
2014.................	1,015,292	739,164	377,461	361,704	276,128	22,416	253,712
2015.................	1,132,116	838,348	431,769	406,579	293,768	22,548	271,220
2016.................	1,213,144	916,171	479,415	436,756	296,972	22,242	274,731
2017.................	1,279,841	983,302	539,013	444,289	296,539	21,267	275,272
2018.................	1,333,183	1,023,016	557,558	465,457	310,167	21,979	288,188
2019.................	1,391,039	1,046,693	546,554	500,139	344,346	26,277	318,069
2020.................	1,499,570	1,130,370	634,726	495,644	369,200	28,958	340,241
2021.................	1,653,375	1,295,753	799,201	496,553	357,622	25,037	332,585
2022.................	1,902,703	1,519,223	922,756	596,467	383,480	28,315	355,165
2023.................	2,023,662	1,573,005	866,900	706,105	450,658	33,594	417,063

Source: U.S. Census Bureau, "Construction Spending - Data, Historical Value Put in Place," <www.census.gov/construction/c30/historical_data.html>, accessed July 2024.

Table 1007. New Privately Owned Housing Units Authorized by State: 2022 and 2023

[1,680.4 represents 1,680,400. Data for 2022 is based on the 2014 Universe, which includes approximately 20,100 places in the United States that have building permit systems in 2014. Beginning January 2023, the universe for the data is now based on an annually updated universe. For 2023, data includes approximately 19,900 places in the United States that have building permit systems in 2023]

State	Housing units (1,000)			Valuation (mil. dol.)			State	Housing units (1,000)			Valuation (mil. dol.)		
	2022	2023 Total	2023 1-unit [1]	2022	2023 Total	2023 1-unit [1]		2022	2023 Total	2023 1-unit [1]	2022	2023 Total	2023 1-unit [1]
U.S.....	1,680.4	1,511.1	920.0	384,447	365,373	274,471	MO.......	20.9	16.8	11.0	4,836	4,267	3,496
AL........	19.5	20.3	16.3	4,704	5,084	4,460	MT........	6.5	4.3	2.3	1,278	1,035	753
AK........	0.6	0.9	0.6	185	262	214	NE........	11.1	8.9	4.7	1,871	1,700	1,224
AZ.......	61.5	58.4	34.4	14,522	13,564	9,959	NV........	20.0	18.5	13.0	4,413	4,687	3,879
AR........	14.4	12.8	9.4	3,011	2,837	2,384	NH........	4.8	4.6	3.0	1,378	1,380	1,073
CA.......	120.8	111.8	58.5	29,021	27,863	17,917	NJ........	36.9	32.8	13.2	6,133	5,161	2,900
CO.......	48.3	39.4	19.6	12,722	11,044	7,459	NM.......	8.6	8.5	6.8	1,781	2,503	2,293
CT........	5.9	6.3	2.1	1,602	1,467	911	NY........	53.4	48.8	9.7	11,123	10,193	3,882
DE........	6.4	5.8	4.7	913	828	706	NC........	94.1	98.9	65.9	21,997	22,742	18,309
DC........	7.7	3.0	0.2	1,031	428	46	ND........	3.4	2.6	1.5	840	689	501
FL........	210.0	193.8	125.8	51,250	50,736	38,626	OH........	30.8	27.3	16.0	7,585	6,965	5,562
GA.......	77.5	63.6	44.4	16,036	14,675	11,955	OK........	13.9	13.4	10.3	3,399	3,216	2,854
HI........	4.3	3.8	2.4	1,788	1,606	1,152	OR........	20.3	17.7	9.8	4,573	4,646	3,346
ID........	18.7	17.9	12.1	4,699	4,424	3,498	PA........	28.1	25.3	15.9	6,617	6,023	4,805
IL........	20.5	16.9	9.6	4,750	4,521	3,239	RI........	1.4	1.2	0.7	388	282	230
IN........	28.2	27.1	17.0	7,196	7,695	5,961	SC........	46.0	42.5	37.2	11,915	11,282	10,665
IA........	12.7	11.2	7.4	3,164	3,111	2,480	SD........	9.4	7.1	3.3	1,827	1,456	958
KS........	9.6	9.5	4.9	2,494	2,457	1,721	TN........	52.6	47.5	31.3	11,786	11,508	9,182
KY........	15.1	15.4	7.8	3,324	3,013	2,100	TX........	263.0	232.4	149.9	52,816	50,827	40,692
LA........	15.5	14.2	11.2	3,631	3,238	2,790	UT........	31.7	25.4	14.9	7,993	6,987	5,033
ME.......	7.1	6.2	4.5	1,668	1,610	1,381	VT........	2.4	2.5	1.3	549	573	416
MD.......	22.9	18.5	10.5	4,612	4,284	2,932	VA........	39.7	36.1	21.3	7,994	7,434	5,806
MA.......	16.8	13.2	5.1	5,228	4,417	2,380	WA.......	49.0	37.1	18.1	11,225	9,518	6,551
MI........	21.8	20.6	14.4	5,873	5,651	4,484	WV.......	3.4	4.0	3.3	761	761	713
MN.......	31.1	25.7	12.8	7,550	6,694	4,321	WI........	21.1	21.5	11.5	5,856	5,973	4,311
MS.......	7.6	7.7	7.1	1,419	1,479	1,421	WY.......	3.0	1.7	1.4	1,124	575	540

[1] The 1-unit structure category is a single-family home. It includes fully detached, semi-detached (semi-attached, side-by-side), row houses, and townhouses.

Source: U.S. Census Bureau, Construction Reports, "Building Permits Survey," <www.census.gov/construction/bps/>, accessed May 2024.

Table 1008. New Residential Building Permits—Total and for Single-Family Homes by Region: 2014 to 2023

[1,052.1 represents 1,052,100. Data through 2022 based on the 2014 Universe, which includes approximately 20,100 places in the United States that have building permit systems in 2014. Beginning January 2023, the universe for the data is now based on an annually updated universe. For 2023, data includes approximately 19,900 places in the United States that have building permit systems in 2023]

Year	Total	1-unit [1]	Northeast Total	Northeast 1-unit [1]	Midwest Total	Midwest 1-unit [1]	South Total	South 1-unit [1]	West Total	West 1-unit [1]
HOUSING UNITS (1,000)										
2014..................	1,052.1	640.3	118.5	54.6	165.2	101.0	524.1	347.7	244.3	137.1
2015..................	1,182.6	696.0	162.0	52.4	170.6	104.7	572.8	378.2	277.2	160.7
2016..................	1,206.6	750.8	116.4	54.3	186.1	112.4	594.5	406.0	309.6	178.1
2017..................	1,282.0	820.0	123.6	54.2	195.1	121.5	626.9	447.6	336.4	196.7
2018..................	1,328.8	855.3	123.4	53.9	185.5	117.9	677.1	474.9	342.8	208.7
2019..................	1,386.0	862.1	141.2	52.7	184.8	114.2	710.3	486.2	349.8	209.0
2020..................	1,471.1	979.4	134.8	56.3	202.1	128.0	776.3	568.5	358.0	226.7
2021..................	1,737.0	1,115.4	164.8	65.0	227.6	142.9	917.5	655.2	427.1	252.2
2022..................	1,680.4	973.9	156.8	61.5	220.8	121.5	909.3	577.2	393.5	213.6
2023..................	1,511.1	920.0	140.8	55.5	195.1	114.0	829.9	556.5	345.3	194.0
VALUATION (mil. dol.)										
2014..................	194,350	149,633	20,568	13,369	30,467	23,588	92,009	75,576	51,306	37,100
2015..................	223,611	166,277	26,513	13,131	32,968	25,148	102,723	83,584	61,408	44,414
2016..................	237,102	182,207	21,821	13,921	36,069	27,684	111,212	91,251	68,000	49,352
2017..................	258,505	200,600	22,969	13,954	38,525	30,102	122,214	102,896	74,798	53,647
2018..................	271,120	210,850	23,328	13,916	38,481	30,313	131,120	108,674	78,192	57,948
2019..................	280,534	213,271	24,608	13,854	39,104	30,383	137,328	110,864	79,494	58,169
2020..................	307,210	243,424	25,052	14,549	43,681	34,735	155,607	131,373	82,869	62,767
2021..................	380,036	295,965	32,047	18,730	53,561	42,526	193,675	161,693	100,753	73,016
2022..................	384,447	281,955	34,686	19,338	53,841	39,466	200,597	157,544	95,323	65,608
2023..................	365,373	274,471	31,107	17,979	51,179	38,257	194,372	155,641	88,715	62,595

[1] The 1-unit structure category is a single-family home. It includes fully detached, semi-detached (semi-attached, side-by-side), row houses, and townhouses.

Source: U.S. Census Bureau, Construction Reports, "Building Permits Survey," <www.census.gov/construction/bps/>, accessed May 2024.

Table 1009. Value of Private Construction Put in Place: 2010 to 2023

[In millions of dollars (508,998 represents $508,998,000,000). Represents value of construction put in place during year; differs from building permit and construction contract data in timing and coverage. For methodology, see <www.census.gov/construction/c30/meth.html>]

Type of construction	2010	2015	2017	2018	2019	2020	2021	2022	2023
Total private construction [1]	**508,998**	**838,348**	**983,302**	**1,023,016**	**1,046,693**	**1,130,370**	**1,295,753**	**1,519,223**	**1,573,005**
Residential	245,743	431,769	539,013	557,558	546,554	634,726	799,201	922,756	866,900
New single family	112,569	221,128	270,163	289,582	279,962	309,388	423,869	453,217	400,423
New multifamily	18,395	62,157	74,011	77,544	82,215	91,737	106,175	114,756	135,778
Improvements [2]	114,780	148,484	194,840	190,432	184,377	233,601	269,156	354,784	330,699
Nonresidential	263,255	406,579	444,289	465,457	500,139	495,644	496,553	596,467	706,105
Lodging	11,201	21,436	28,065	30,453	32,318	27,418	18,561	19,650	24,303
Office [1]	24,368	47,864	59,918	66,835	77,536	80,523	77,545	82,372	84,268
General	22,203	43,307	52,593	57,694	66,751	68,719	65,576	67,662	63,399
Data center [3]	(X)	2,744	4,666	6,934	8,481	9,231	9,947	12,583	18,201
Financial	2,122	1,669	2,392	2,049	2,137	2,482	1,956	2,057	2,615
Commercial [1]	37,154	64,493	84,479	82,808	80,269	85,573	93,659	127,205	137,078
Automotive [1]	3,546	5,830	8,127	7,638	6,191	7,323	6,756	8,959	11,234
Sales	1,355	2,164	3,128	3,202	2,072	1,965	1,652	2,384	3,317
Service/parts	1,679	2,885	3,928	3,289	2,867	4,025	3,833	4,886	5,982
Parking	511	780	1,071	1,148	1,253	1,333	1,271	1,690	1,935
Food/beverage	4,605	7,273	8,155	8,678	9,310	8,756	8,318	11,767	13,884
Food	2,027	3,109	3,231	2,748	3,667	4,082	3,445	4,290	4,992
Dining/drinking	1,911	2,589	3,416	4,027	4,226	3,519	3,831	6,025	7,462
Fast food	667	1,575	1,508	1,904	1,416	1,155	1,042	1,452	1,429
Multi-retail [1]	12,486	20,036	24,048	20,818	14,615	10,922	10,378	14,660	17,168
General merchandise	3,794	2,362	1,864	2,581	2,361	2,237	2,795	3,819	3,054
Shopping center	6,725	13,752	17,558	14,676	9,355	6,865	6,215	8,544	11,263
Shopping mall	1,332	3,035	3,921	2,861	2,072	975	545	779	1,460
Other commercial [1]	4,220	5,225	5,219	5,494	7,374	7,775	7,673	8,349	8,460
Drug store	1,077	535	358	255	325	389	459	395	324
Building supply store	772	586	650	593	742	804	998	1,155	1,318
Other stores	1,741	2,881	3,129	2,777	4,197	4,402	4,452	5,033	4,561
Warehouse [1]	5,661	16,850	29,053	33,056	34,758	42,376	52,046	71,960	74,687
General commercial	5,229	15,699	24,745	27,921	29,852	37,512	47,732	66,130	67,124
Ministorage	401	963	3,932	4,893	4,646	4,642	4,197	5,745	7,430
Farm	6,637	9,280	9,877	7,123	8,023	8,421	8,489	11,511	11,646
Health care	29,552	30,939	33,517	33,962	36,751	39,051	40,246	46,328	52,188
Hospital	21,528	19,665	20,210	20,747	20,996	20,246	19,993	22,133	24,166
Medical building	5,276	7,056	9,229	9,653	11,170	13,348	15,030	19,797	24,247
Special care	2,748	4,219	4,078	3,562	4,585	5,457	5,224	4,397	3,775
Educational [1]	13,418	17,688	21,232	22,346	21,627	18,801	16,666	20,000	23,257
Preschool	492	355	554	598	708	667	623	861	1,477
Primary/secondary	2,585	3,676	4,574	5,111	5,068	5,249	4,506	5,315	6,336
Higher education [1]	8,322	11,932	12,934	13,657	13,083	10,325	9,002	10,744	12,125
Instructional	4,993	5,472	5,775	5,759	5,628	4,184	4,585	5,424	6,170
Dormitory	1,654	3,931	4,528	4,532	4,559	4,254	3,127	3,695	3,903
Sports/recreation	790	1,055	1,300	1,487	1,363	861	740	927	912
Other educational [1]	1,687	1,471	2,393	2,116	1,915	1,937	1,986	2,451	2,753
Gallery/museum	1,522	1,038	1,628	1,573	1,422	1,520	1,635	1,854	2,191
Religious	5,237	3,589	3,586	3,499	3,730	3,469	3,090	3,187	3,801
House of worship	4,214	3,029	3,028	2,956	3,100	2,781	2,429	2,390	3,281
Other religious	1,023	561	558	543	631	689	661	797	520
Auxiliary building	795	491	508	434	413	431	321	286	326
Public safety	241	225	107	204	240	92	101	136	205
Amusement and recreation [1]	6,483	10,032	14,518	15,712	15,785	13,548	13,684	17,092	18,791
Theme/amusement park	353	1,213	2,125	2,054	1,810	1,417	926	1,606	2,257
Sports	1,596	3,452	6,071	5,652	4,492	4,674	4,859	4,371	4,096
Fitness	1,150	1,192	1,289	1,835	2,073	1,843	1,271	1,642	2,043
Performance/meeting center	565	724	1,204	1,950	2,541	1,730	1,661	2,482	2,183
Social center	914	869	899	1,249	1,588	1,529	2,027	2,581	2,862
Movie theater/studio	426	832	835	976	985	678	533	878	1,420
Transportation [1]	9,894	13,563	14,796	17,880	17,183	16,311	16,366	18,054	20,594
Air	259	886	3,458	4,144	4,421	4,232	4,496	5,050	5,040
Land	9,503	12,412	11,041	13,154	12,075	11,468	11,196	12,699	15,296
Railroad	8,973	11,653	10,089	11,204	10,621	10,423	9,803	10,804	12,880
Communication	17,689	21,505	23,571	24,320	22,111	23,770	22,853	24,209	27,593
Power	66,117	91,503	89,774	94,390	110,427	110,593	110,473	111,073	116,965
Electricity	48,972	67,123	65,136	70,422	78,741	88,478	89,126	91,000	96,848
Gas	8,297	12,546	15,745	18,787	19,316	15,787	18,977	18,480	18,733
Oil	8,848	11,834	8,893	5,181	12,370	6,328	2,370	1,590	1,384
Sewage and waste disposal	439	375	240	408	683	419	478	944	1,638
Water supply	717	542	277	287	409	574	658	828	1,215
Manufacturing	40,607	82,382	69,970	72,005	80,537	75,069	81,634	124,458	193,135
Food/beverage/tobacco	4,000	7,216	8,447	9,661	7,050	7,444	10,984	14,976	16,036
Textile/apparel/leather/furniture	591	639	865	528	161	260	378	1,035	627
Wood	438	347	1,320	1,759	2,197	1,055	988	1,635	2,042
Paper/printing/publishing	634	1,035	1,522	2,444	2,298	1,792	1,512	2,255	2,907
Petroleum/coal	11,612	4,428	3,938	3,557	3,933	3,017	2,634	2,752	1,928
Chemical	7,580	37,818	32,245	30,698	34,717	30,118	29,939	30,340	34,153
Plastic/rubber	728	3,317	3,157	4,257	3,026	1,334	1,444	1,869	2,341
Nonmetallic mineral	1,150	1,153	1,038	660	790	979	1,456	2,193	2,166
Primary metal	4,738	6,142	2,823	2,088	3,670	3,772	4,476	6,430	8,853
Fabricated metal	1,104	1,212	1,972	1,653	1,547	1,302	1,972	2,482	1,685
Machinery	1,030	1,938	903	1,252	2,175	2,179	1,668	1,494	2,316
Computer/electronic/electrical	4,614	3,510	2,141	5,487	8,308	9,167	12,093	42,658	101,602
Transportation equipment	1,962	12,639	8,818	6,765	8,196	9,630	8,872	9,483	11,191

X Not applicable. [1] Includes other types of construction not shown separately. [2] Private residential improvement does not include expenditures on rental, vacant, or seasonal properties. [3] Prior to 2014, expenditures for data center were included as part of general office.

Source: U.S. Census Bureau, "Construction Spending - Data, Historical Value Put in Place," <www.census.gov/construction/c30/c30index.html>, accessed July 2024.

Table 1010. Value of State and Local Government Construction Put in Place: 2010 to 2023

[In millions of dollars (272,833 represents $272,833,000,000)]

Type of construction	2010	2015	2017	2018	2019	2020	2021	2022	2023
Total construction [1]	**272,833**	**271,220**	**275,272**	**288,188**	**318,069**	**340,241**	**332,585**	**355,165**	**417,063**
Residential	7,576	6,032	6,233	5,782	6,143	8,437	8,644	8,696	9,379
Multifamily	6,536	5,224	5,911	5,368	5,517	7,393	7,745	7,862	8,602
Nonresidential	265,256	265,188	269,039	282,406	311,925	331,804	323,941	346,469	407,684
Office	8,317	5,924	6,049	6,905	8,052	9,761	9,213	10,127	11,510
Commercial [1]	1,456	1,396	1,505	1,936	2,334	2,738	2,113	2,205	2,343
Automotive	769	852	618	982	1,485	1,790	1,206	983	710
Parking	675	807	602	899	1,051	1,199	879	911	682
Warehouse	286	245	403	324	290	287	335	428	684
Health care	6,193	5,537	6,372	6,508	6,498	6,912	7,476	8,521	9,550
Hospital	4,789	4,276	4,409	4,726	4,019	4,210	4,851	5,193	5,115
Medical building	747	816	1,167	1,095	1,703	1,529	1,452	1,943	2,309
Special care	657	446	795	687	777	1,174	1,174	1,384	2,125
Educational [1]	71,948	65,782	73,992	77,168	85,154	90,359	82,976	82,381	94,895
Primary/secondary [1]	44,559	38,221	46,488	50,226	56,212	62,696	58,403	57,932	66,045
Elementary	13,171	10,538	14,362	15,850	16,126	18,164	17,747	17,367	20,437
Middle/junior high	7,029	7,520	9,557	10,138	10,706	11,813	10,275	11,014	12,709
High	24,055	19,765	21,429	22,772	27,828	31,396	29,187	28,460	31,045
Higher education [1]	24,384	25,116	24,882	24,375	25,971	24,483	21,141	20,800	24,649
Instructional	14,138	13,390	13,815	14,499	14,582	14,476	12,954	13,771	15,032
Parking	593	552	414	406	773	491	379	359	679
Administration	357	590	540	436	331	344	295	263	261
Dormitory	3,371	4,130	3,219	2,779	3,900	3,454	2,560	2,112	2,873
Library	662	684	511	562	469	401	359	222	325
Student union/cafeteria	1147	1306	1,590	1,505	1,619	1,247	959	557	515
Sports/recreation	2398	2,885	3,325	2,750	2,625	2,405	2,421	2,557	3,037
Infrastructure	1381	1,570	1,296	1,407	1,624	1,458	1,136	907	1,793
Other educational [1]	2,223	1,902	1,643	1,616	2,049	2,171	2,366	2,345	2,819
Library/archive	1386	1,144	990	1,004	1,392	1,596	1,841	1,454	1,667
Public safety [1]	7,586	5,859	6,216	7,090	8,065	9,366	8,990	8,966	11,381
Correctional	4,624	3,619	3,698	4,222	5,034	5,732	5,235	5,091	6,157
Detention	2,789	1,981	2,071	2,493	2,932	3,462	3,482	3,042	3,499
Police/sheriff	1836	1,638	1,626	1,730	2,102	2,270	1,754	2,049	2,659
Other public safety	2,962	2,240	2,518	2,868	3,031	3,634	3,754	3,875	5,223
Fire/rescue	1747	1,561	2,092	2,358	2,450	2,942	3,199	3,137	4,375
Amusement and recreation [1]	9,668	10,048	11,570	11,909	14,201	14,202	12,783	13,711	16,466
Sports	1,819	1,759	1,614	2,242	3,335	3,499	3,048	2,961	3,897
Performance/meeting center	1,841	1,587	1,926	2,580	3,489	3,203	2,277	1,770	1,875
Convention center	1,119	850	1,032	1,562	2,358	2,255	1,509	1,012	905
Social center	1,561	1,120	1,568	1,509	1,767	1,745	1,794	1,882	2,246
Neighborhood center	1395	1055	1,338	1,219	1,516	1,478	1,473	1,433	1,822
Park/camp	4,259	5,441	6,348	5,412	5,115	5,453	5,481	6,774	8,027
Transportation	26,493	29,365	29,286	32,811	37,598	41,398	39,254	38,433	39,233
Air [1]	11,897	10,762	12,297	16,094	18,140	21,386	19,902	17,703	18,647
Passenger terminal	6,503	4,969	7,751	11,172	12,256	14,034	12,582	10,886	10,350
Runway	4,710	5,213	3,819	4,336	4,795	6,388	6,294	5,473	6,828
Land [1]	12,954	16,940	15,444	14,920	16,690	17,255	16,989	17,940	17,989
Passenger terminal	3,380	4584	3,744	3,154	2,180	1,216	1,116	1,996	2,350
Mass transit	6,447	7,842	7,726	7,824	10,399	11,435	11,415	10,801	9,215
Railroad	751	1666	1,169	1,486	1,844	2,576	2,482	2,752	3,537
Water	1,642	1,663	1,545	1,796	2,769	2,756	2,363	2,790	2,597
Dock/marina	1115	1233	1,215	1,405	2,498	2,572	2,215	2,569	2,454
Dry dock/marine terminal	527	430	331	392	271	184	149	222	143
Power [1]	10,770	10,307	5,401	4,612	7,115	7,121	8,176	9,684	15,958
Electrical	9,972	9,019	4,599	3,684	5,933	6,017	6,141	7,801	12,436
Distribution	3,253	2,623	2,586	2,253	4,382	4,700	5,215	5,680	6,610
Highway and street	81,309	90,810	88,290	90,405	97,520	100,809	101,652	112,855	135,029
Pavement	51,433	54,073	54,404	57,224	66,245	73,317	73,720	85,718	103,170
Lighting	1975	1,520	1,936	2,301	2,463	2,529	2,814	3,530	5,350
Retaining wall	1,250	1071	819	1,451	1,273	1,515	1,490	1,650	1,629
Tunnel	810	830	1,119	674	550	486	1,106	1,426	1,760
Bridge	24,222	31,765	28,935	27,412	25,794	21,253	21,225	18,764	21,282
Toll/weigh	214	210	292	312	273	246	220	133	158
Maintenance building	275	429	344	333	318	637	493	814	925
Rest facility/streetscape	1130	910	441	698	603	826	585	820	756
Sewage and waste disposal	24,555	23,403	22,415	23,219	25,044	26,437	27,968	31,789	39,527
Sewage/dry waste [1]	13,234	14,009	13,277	12,994	13,331	12,537	12,739	13,833	17,039
Plant	3,755	2,839	2,660	2,612	2,629	1,908	1,398	920	1,244
Line/pump station	9,375	10,986	10,427	10,220	10,551	10,475	11,047	12,719	15,524
Waste water	11,321	9,394	9,138	10,226	11,713	13,901	15,229	17,956	22,488
Plant	9,428	7,001	6,984	7,027	8,461	9,780	10,363	11,945	15,141
Line/drain	1,893	2,393	2,154	3,199	3,252	4,120	4,866	6,011	7,346
Water supply	14,420	12,760	13,701	14,855	15,613	18,010	19,294	22,815	26,169
Plant	5,683	4,432	5,077	5,105	5,206	5,665	5,938	6,863	7,470
Well	383	295	415	501	752	715	923	822	930
Line	6,246	6,098	5,865	6,654	7,189	8,096	9,362	11,125	12,919
Pump station	970	642	1,015	1,150	1,071	1,688	1,610	2,280	2,580
Reservoir	393	401	883	857	720	879	654	747	933
Tank/tower	744	892	446	587	676	968	807	979	1,336
Conservation and development [1]	2035	3,133	3,393	3,719	3,256	3,426	3,238	4,077	4,611
Dam/levee	783	958	1,105	1,250	1,136	1,364	1,289	1,181	1,229
Breakwater/jetty	675	1405	1,171	1,255	1,181	1,249	1,283	1,819	2,149
Dredging	173	301	300	272	238	244	328	441	571

[1] Includes other types of construction, not shown separately.

Source: U.S. Census Bureau, "Construction Spending - Data, Historical Value Put in Place," <www.census.gov/construction/c30/c30index.html>, accessed July 2024.

Table 1011. Construction of New Privately Owned Housing Units Started: 1960 to 2023

[In thousands of units (1,252 represents 1,252,000). For composition of regions, see map inside front cover]

Year	Total	1 unit structures	Northeast	Midwest	South	West
1960	1,252	995	221	292	429	309
1970	1,434	813	218	294	612	311
1980	1,292	852	125	218	643	306
1990	1,193	895	131	253	479	329
1995	1,354	1,076	118	290	615	331
1996	1,477	1,161	132	322	662	361
1997	1,474	1,134	137	304	670	363
1998	1,617	1,271	149	331	743	395
1999	1,641	1,302	156	347	746	392
2000	1,569	1,231	155	318	714	383
2001	1,603	1,273	149	330	732	391
2002	1,705	1,359	158	350	782	416
2003	1,848	1,499	163	374	839	472
2004	1,956	1,611	175	356	909	516
2005	2,068	1,716	190	357	996	525
2006	1,801	1,465	167	280	910	444
2007	1,355	1,046	143	210	681	321
2008	906	622	121	135	453	196
2009	554	445	62	97	278	117
2010	587	471	72	98	298	120
2011	609	431	68	101	308	133
2012	781	535	80	128	398	175
2013	925	618	97	150	464	215
2014	1,003	648	110	163	496	235
2015	1,112	715	138	153	556	266
2016	1,174	782	116	182	585	291
2017	1,203	849	111	180	599	313
2018	1,250	876	111	173	630	336
2019	1,290	888	115	169	685	321
2020	1,380	991	112	192	736	341
2021	1,601	1,127	137	216	848	401
2022	1,553	1,005	142	206	834	371
2023	1,420	948	115	185	792	328

Source: U.S. Census Bureau, New Residential Construction, "Historical Time Series," <www.census.gov/construction/nrc/data.html>, accessed June 2024.

Table 1012. Characteristics of New Privately Owned Single-Family Houses Completed: 2010 to 2023

[Percent distribution, except as noted (496 represents 496,000). Data are shown as percent distribution of houses by each set of characteristics, for all houses completed (includes new houses completed, houses built for sale completed, contractor-built and owner-built houses completed, and houses completed for rent). Excludes houses for which the type of characteristic was not reported. Percents are computed using unrounded data]

Characteristic	2010	2020	2022	2023	Characteristic	2010	2020	2022	2023
Total houses (1,000)	496	912	1,022	999	Bedrooms	100	100	100	100
Construction type	100	100	100	100	2 or less	13	10	9	11
Site built	95	97	98	97	3	52	46	43	44
Modular	2	1	1	1	4 or more	35	44	48	45
Other	2	2	1	2	Bathrooms	100	100	100	100
Exterior wall material	100	100	100	100	1-1/2 or less	8	3	3	4
Brick	23	19	19	20	2	36	35	33	34
Wood	8	5	4	5	2-1/2 or more	32	28	29	28
Stucco	17	27	27	27	3 baths or more	25	34	35	34
Vinyl siding	36	25	24	24	Heating fuel	100	100	100	100
Fiber cement	13	22	23	22	Gas	54	55	51	47
Other	2	2	2	2	Electricity	43	45	48	52
Floor area	100	100	100	100	Oil [3]	1	(NA)	(NA)	(NA)
Under 1,400 sq. ft.	13	7	7	9	Other or none [3]	2	1	1	1
1,400 to 1,799 sq. ft.	19	18	16	18	Heating system	100	100	100	100
1,800 to 2,399 sq. ft.	27	32	32	30	Forced air furnace	56	59	55	53
2,400 to 2,999 sq. ft.	18	21	22	20	Electric heat pump	38	39	43	45
3,000 to 3,999 sq. ft.	15	15	16	15	Other or none	5	2	2	3
4,000 or more	7	8	8	8	Central air-conditioning	100	100	100	100
Average (sq. ft.)	2,392	2,480	2,509	2,485	With	88	95	97	98
Median (sq. ft.)	2,169	2,261	2,299	2,233	Without	12	5	3	2
Number of stories	100	100	100	100	Fireplaces	100	100	100	100
1	47	50	48	49	No fireplace	51	63	65	68
2 or more [1]	53	50	51	51	1 or more	49	36	34	32
Foundation	100	100	100	100	Parking facilities	100	100	100	100
Full or partial basement	30	22	21	18	Garage	85	91	92	91
Slab and other [2]	52	65	68	72	Carport	1	1	1	2
Crawl space	18	12	11	10	No garage or carport	13	7	8	8

NA Not available. [1] Includes houses with 1-1/2 and 2-1/2 stories and split-level houses. [2] Includes raised supports such as pilings and piers, and other types. [3] Beginning in 2014, heating oil and kerosene are included in "Other or none" category.

Source: U.S. Census Bureau, "Characteristics of New Housing, Annual Data," <www.census.gov/construction/chars/index.html>, accessed June 2024.

Table 1013. Construction Materials—Producer Price Indexes: 2010 to 2023

[1982=100, except as noted. This index, more formally known as the special commodity grouping index for construction materials, covers materials incorporated as integral parts of a building or normally installed during construction and not readily removable. Excludes consumer durables such as kitchen ranges, refrigerators, etc. For discussion of producer price indexes, see text, Section 14]

Commodity	2010	2015	2018	2019	2020	2021	2022	2023
Construction materials	**194.5**	**213.6**	**235.7**	**235.7**	**239.2**	**303.4**	**341.5**	**331.8**
Architectural coatings	264.1	302.3	320.7	343.5	352.6	382.0	484.4	508.9
Plastic construction products	190.9	213.1	226.1	229.4	233.5	285.5	351.9	346.5
Softwood cut stock and dimension	206.0	199.7	228.1	204.1	235.6	363.9	347.4	254.7
Softwood lumber, not edge worked [1]	85.8	104.9	131.0	114.4	154.1	217.7	206.0	135.4
Softwood lumber, made from purchased lumber [1]	111.5	128.3	171.4	169.2	188.3	267.0	295.1	255.3
Hardwood cut stock and dimension	186.2	246.6	262.9	256.0	255.6	342.2	342.7	295.9
Hardwood flooring [2]	161.2	195.8	184.7	193.8	188.7	218.7	260.0	263.4
Millwork	207.0	237.2	259.5	263.5	274.5	318.6	367.2	355.2
Softwood veneer and plywood	197.1	234.5	274.5	222.8	270.6	449.6	429.5	324.0
Hardwood veneer and plywood [3]	103.6	108.6	123.5	123.9	125.2	140.4	159.9	160.3
Prefabricated wood buildings and components [4]	215.6	240.4	263.7	270.2	277.7	328.5	392.4	380.9
Building paper and building board mill products	168.4	186.3	222.9	200.1	260.5	411.3	414.3	322.4
Pressure and soil pipe and fittings, cast iron	348.4	392.9	398.5	403.5	410.8	466.4	562.7	587.5
Hot rolled steel sheet and strip, incl. tin mill products [5]	150.7	115.9	149.6	136.0	113.8	287.4	(NA)	(NA)
Hot rolled steel bars, plates, and structural shapes [5]	192.9	185.2	205.9	205.2	187.0	257.8	322.9	293.9
Extruded aluminum shapes, including rod, bar, and wire [6]	105.6	104.6	121.5	118.6	111.6	145.6	171.7	162.3
Builders' hardware [7]	219.4	244.5	256.7	264.0	269.3	291.6	328.0	336.5
Plumbing fixtures and fittings	231.4	257.1	270.2	281.6	287.9	296.0	326.6	334.5
Heating equipment	221.5	248.2	266.5	279.2	284.0	312.4	367.0	388.7
Metal doors, sash, and trim	208.1	233.6	260.1	269.8	276.4	322.2	419.7	431.2
Sheet metal products	191.0	199.3	212.7	218.2	217.0	259.5	313.6	316.9
Fabricated structural metal bar joists and concrete reinforcing bars	176.1	190.5	216.4	214.9	215.4	289.1	360.4	362.2
Fabricated metal pipe, tube, and fittings [8]	(NA)	101.5	104.9	106.0	105.9	125.4	140.4	144.4
Residential electric lighting fixtures, except portable [9]	121.1	130.4	133.9	145.2	149.8	157.7	174.8	177.4
Elevators, escalators, and other lifts	133.8	145.4	155.0	161.7	164.2	171.5	198.6	209.6
Air purification equipment/industrial and commercial fans and blowers	192.2	217.3	228.6	238.4	241.3	254.1	286.9	299.4
Plumbing and heating valves (low pressure) [10]	249.5	292.6	(NA)	(NA)	(NA)	(NA)	374.9	(NA)
Electric switches [11]	124.4	153.4	149.9	150.4	152.9	162.1	171.2	182.6
Wire connectors for electrical circuitry [11]	132.1	138.8	137.7	139.4	141.0	151.6	169.3	178.7
Current-carrying wiring devices not elsewhere classified [12]	105.2	111.3	111.3	112.7	111.8	117.6	131.2	189.7
Noncurrent-carrying electrical conduit and fittings [6, 13]	119.2	134.1	141.8	141.5	148.5	236.0	321.2	281.5
Other noncurrent-carrying wiring devices [6, 14]	126.4	135.6	141.7	147.9	151.1	167.0	198.6	207.5
Carpets and rugs	167.5	184.1	193.1	196.0	194.8	201.9	206.0	210.0
Resilient (hard surface) floor coverings	203.2	(NA)	236.8	242.5	243.4	248.6	256.7	262.3
Flat glass (float, sheet, and plate process) [15]	(NA)	(NA)	(NA)	(NA)	(NA)	(NA)	(NA)	93.7
Construction sand, gravel, and crushed stone	262.2	299.9	334.7	348.7	364.3	378.8	416.9	458.1
Cement, hydraulic	193.5	223.4	252.1	258.1	260.7	271.0	296.9	333.1
Concrete products	210.6	239.4	263.7	271.7	279.1	292.9	329.9	366.1
Clay construction products excluding refractories	179.4	182.4	187.7	189.6	192.7	199.4	213.9	228.9
Prepared asphalt and tar roofing and siding products	218.9	223.2	233.8	243.9	249.2	277.7	326.9	339.3
Roofing asphalts, pitches, coatings, and cement	227.5	234.3	221.4	224.7	222.8	230.7	255.1	264.8
Gypsum products	206.6	293.1	342.6	320.9	322.0	374.3	444.2	460.3
Insulation materials	146.6	182.6	194.7	193.3	195.4	217.3	253.6	267.4
Paving mixtures and blocks	279.4	313.0	313.4	322.6	312.9	324.2	378.3	395.4
Cut stone and stone products [4]	147.8	156.8	168.1	174.9	179.8	191.7	223.4	235.3

NA Not available. [1] December 2003=100. [2] June 1984=100. [3] December 2005=100. [4] June 1984=100. [5] June 1982=100. [6] December 2004=100. [7] Includes lock units, key blanks, door and window hardware, cabinet hardware, etc. [8] December 2011=100. [9] June 1998=100. [10] December 1982=100. [11] December 1999=100. [12] June 2006=100. [13] Includes plastic conduit and fittings. [14] Includes boxes, covers, bar hangers, etc. [15] December 2022=100.

Source: U.S. Bureau of Labor Statistics, "Producer Price Indexes," <www.bls.gov/ppi/data.htm>, accessed June 2024.

Table 1014. Subsidized Apartments Completed by Type of Subsidy: 2015 to 2022

[Data shown for rental apartments in buildings with five units or more. Detail may not sum to totals because of rounding and because more than one subsidy could be selected per unit. Based on a sample and subject to sampling variability; see source for details]

Completions and type of subsidy	2015	2017	2018	2019	2020	2021	2022
Total apartments completed	310,000	346,800	335,600	342,900	364,700	363,700	359,100
Subsidized apartments completed	**29,160**	**35,200**	**31,910**	**36,840**	**40,990**	**39,760**	**42,550**
Percent subsidized	9.4	10.1	9.5	10.7	11.2	10.9	11.8
Subsidized by type: [1]							
Section 8	10,680	12,080	16,570	10,090	17,260	16,300	19,050
Housing for Elderly Direct Loan Program	1,163	(S)	1,790	1,536	(S)	(S)	3,445
Low Income Housing Tax Credit (LIHTC)	19,190	21,630	15,020	24,930	22,680	24,280	27,590
Federal tax exempt multifamily bond financing	(S)	2,223	(S)	2,870	(S)	4,388	1,414
Other subsidized programs	6,881	10,080	9,871	10,500	11,420	9,258	17,990

S Data estimates do not meet publication standards. [1] Respondents were instructed to select all subsidies that applied to the building.

Source: U.S. Census Bureau, "Survey of Market Absorption of New Multifamily Units, Table Creator," <www.census.gov/programs-surveys/soma/data/tools.html>, accessed April 2024.

Table 1015. Housing Starts and Average Length of Time to Completion of New Privately Owned Single-Family Homes: 1990 to 2023

[895 represents 895,000. For buildings started in permit-issuing places]

Year	Total [1]	Built for sale	Contractor built	Owner built	North-east	Mid-west	South	West
STARTS (1,000)								
1990	895	529	196	147	104	193	371	226
1995	1,076	712	199	133	102	234	485	256
2000	1,231	871	195	128	118	260	556	297
2002	1,359	999	198	125	118	277	628	336
2003	1,499	1,120	205	127	116	309	686	388
2004	1,611	1,240	198	130	128	306	743	433
2005	1,716	1,358	197	129	138	306	831	441
2006	1,465	1,121	189	119	118	235	757	356
2007	1,046	760	151	104	93	171	540	242
2008	622	408	107	74	63	102	324	133
2009	445	297	83	51	44	76	232	93
2010	471	306	83	55	52	79	247	93
2011	431	287	74	47	41	74	229	86
2012	535	373	82	47	46	92	283	114
2013	618	457	91	45	55	102	326	134
2014	648	460	110	50	51	106	346	145
2015	715	526	109	50	55	107	387	165
2016	782	579	116	49	60	121	421	179
2017	849	635	116	55	62	130	453	204
2018	876	660	119	51	64	123	466	222
2019	888	669	124	55	57	120	497	214
2020	990	764	123	53	60	136	553	241
2021	1,127	868	140	59	68	148	644	268
2022	1,005	720	146	58	63	130	581	231
2023	948	680	123	55	61	118	564	205
COMPLETION (months)								
1990	6.4	5.9	5.3	10.3	9.3	5.6	5.7	6.9
1995	5.9	5.2	5.8	9.5	7.4	6.0	5.4	6.0
2000	6.2	5.6	6.5	9.2	7.5	6.4	5.9	6.0
2002	6.1	5.5	6.6	9.6	7.3	6.4	5.6	6.2
2003	6.2	5.5	6.8	9.9	7.5	6.7	5.7	6.2
2004	6.2	5.7	7.0	9.1	7.3	6.7	5.8	6.3
2005	6.4	5.9	7.6	9.8	7.7	6.6	6.0	6.8
2006	6.9	6.3	7.8	10.7	8.3	7.1	6.3	7.4
2007	7.1	6.5	7.9	10.2	8.5	7.4	6.5	8.0
2008	7.7	6.8	8.5	11.1	8.9	8.2	6.7	9.0
2009	7.9	6.6	8.7	11.9	10.7	8.2	6.7	9.0
2010	6.9	5.8	7.6	11.0	10.1	7.3	5.9	7.3
2011	6.6	5.4	7.7	10.8	8.9	6.9	5.9	6.8
2012	6.0	4.9	7.3	10.5	8.5	6.5	5.2	6.1
2013	6.0	5.0	7.5	11.0	8.4	6.7	5.5	5.6
2014	6.2	5.4	7.5	10.8	8.6	6.9	5.7	6.2
2015	6.3	5.5	7.6	11.1	8.9	7.0	5.8	6.1
2016	6.6	5.8	7.8	11.5	9.6	6.9	6.0	6.7
2017	6.5	5.7	8.1	11.2	9.5	7.2	5.9	6.7
2018	6.7	5.9	8.4	11.4	9.3	7.5	6.0	7.1
2019	7.0	6.1	8.9	12.3	11.1	7.7	6.1	7.7
2020	6.8	5.9	8.8	11.8	10.7	7.4	5.9	7.5
2021	7.2	6.5	9.4	12.1	10.7	8.0	6.5	7.6
2022	8.3	7.6	10.1	12.2	10.7	8.7	7.6	9.2
2023	8.6	7.5	10.7	13.7	11.9	9.2	7.6	9.9

[1] Includes units built for rent not shown separately. [2] For composition of regions, see map, inside front cover.

Source: U.S. Census Bureau, "New Residential Construction," <www.census.gov/construction/nrc/index.html>, accessed August 2024.

Table 1016. Price Indexes of New Single-Family Houses Sold by Region: 1980 to 2023

[2005=100. Based on kinds of homes sold in 2005. Includes value of the lot. Excludes contractor-built and owner-built houses, and houses built for rent. For composition of regions, see map, inside front cover]

Year	Total	North-east	Midwest	South	West	Year	Total	North-east	Midwest	South	West
1980	38.9	30.2	41.2	44.4	31.9	2009	95.1	97.1	96.0	101.1	84.8
1990	55.7	58.0	58.6	60.6	46.2	2010	95.0	101.1	96.9	99.5	85.4
1996	66.0	63.2	72.5	71.2	55.3	2011	94.4	100.0	97.8	99.6	83.2
1997	67.5	65.9	74.3	72.7	56.5	2012	97.6	102.1	101.6	102.7	86.3
1998	69.2	66.1	76.0	74.4	58.4	2013	104.7	108.2	105.3	110.2	94.7
1999	72.8	69.1	79.5	78.1	62.0	2014	110.2	115.2	112.6	115.4	99.5
2000	75.6	73.0	83.5	80.7	64.4	2015	112.9	115.7	116.4	118.3	101.9
2001	77.9	76.7	84.4	82.8	67.1	2016	120.4	121.1	118.7	125.1	113.3
2002	81.4	80.2	86.1	86.3	71.5	2017	126.8	130.5	126.5	131.9	117.9
2003	86.0	84.3	90.6	89.4	78.2	2018	132.4	127.6	128.9	136.2	128.9
2004	92.8	91.6	96.7	94.4	88.2	2019	135.5	127.7	134.1	141.9	127.5
2005	100.0	100.0	100.0	100.0	100.0	2020	140.7	136.0	141.3	145.8	133.0
2006	104.8	102.6	102.9	105.4	105.2	2021	161.8	152.0	159.9	166.4	157.3
2007	104.9	101.5	102.8	107.5	102.6	2022	185.6	168.9	182.6	194.3	176.4
2008	99.5	100.8	98.9	103.7	92.7	2023	186.6	192.1	188.2	198.9	165.1

Source: U.S. Census Bureau, "Construction Price Indexes," <www.census.gov/construction/cpi/index.html>, accessed July 2024.

Table 1017. New Privately Owned Single-Family Houses Sold by Region and Type of Financing, 2010 to 2023, and by Sales-Price Group, 2023

[In thousands (323 represents 323,000). Based on a national probability sample of monthly interviews with builders or owners of single-family houses for which building permits have been issued or, for nonpermit areas, on which construction has started. Components may not add to total due to rounding. For details, see source and Appendix III. For composition of regions, see map inside front cover]

Year and sales-price group	Total sold	Region				Financing type			
		Northeast	Midwest	South	West	Conventional [1]	FHA insured [2]	VA guaranteed [3]	Cash
2010..........................	323	31	45	173	74	189	81	35	19
2015..........................	501	24	61	286	130	348	81	42	30
2017..........................	613	40	72	339	163	442	86	49	36
2018..........................	617	32	76	348	160	461	74	43	39
2019..........................	683	30	72	399	182	469	119	52	42
2020..........................	822	37	93	474	218	570	153	63	37
2021..........................	771	36	86	453	196	571	106	45	48
2022..........................	641	33	66	392	150	489	55	35	62
2023..........................	**666**	**33**	**68**	**412**	**153**	**490**	**89**	**33**	**55**
Under $300,000.........	92	1	11	78	3	48	29	6	9
$300,000 to $399,999. ..	192	3	24	143	22	127	38	11	16
$400,000 to $499,999. ..	134	3	14	78	40	102	16	7	9
$500,000 to $599,999. ..	97	4	10	50	33	81	4	4	7
$600,000 to $699,999. ..	54	4	4	26	19	47	1	2	3
$700,000 to $799,999. ..	30	3	2	13	13	27	(Z)	1	2
$800,000 to $899,999. ..	20	2	1	8	9	17	(Z)	1	2
$900,000 to $999,999. ..	12	4	(Z)	4	4	11	–	(Z)	1
$1,000,000 and over.....	35	10	1	12	11	29	(Z)	1	5

– Represents zero. Z Less than 500 units. [1] Includes houses reporting other types of financing, not shown separately. [2] Federal Housing Administration. [3] U.S. Department of Veterans Affairs.

Source: U.S. Census Bureau, "Characteristics of New Housing, Annual Data" <www.census.gov/construction/chars/index.html>, accessed June 2024.

Table 1018. Median Sales Price of New Privately Owned Single-Family Houses Sold by Region: 1990 to 2023

[In dollars. For definition of median, see Guide to Tabular Presentation. For composition of regions, see map inside front cover. Based on a national probability sample of monthly interviews with builders or owners of single-family houses selected from building permits and a canvassing of areas not requiring permits. For more details, see source]

Year	U.S.	Northeast	Midwest	South	West	Year	U.S.	Northeast	Midwest	South	West
1990........	122,900	159,000	107,900	99,000	147,500	2017........	323,100	490,400	284,400	291,200	390,000
2000........	169,000	227,400	169,700	148,000	196,400	2018........	326,400	484,600	290,900	294,600	410,600
2005........	240,900	343,800	216,900	197,300	332,600	2019........	321,500	482,500	289,200	289,000	408,000
2010........	221,800	329,900	197,700	196,800	259,300	2020........	330,900	505,900	297,200	293,600	414,400
2014........	288,500	398,000	273,800	264,000	339,000	2021........	383,500	572,200	334,100	336,200	509,400
2015........	294,200	442,800	276,700	271,500	348,500	2022........	434,500	624,500	396,200	387,800	568,200
2016........	307,800	428,300	277,100	281,400	367,700	2023........	428,600	760,700	396,300	388,800	536,200

Source: U.S. Census Bureau, "Characteristics of New Housing, Annual Data," <www.census.gov/construction/chars/index.html>, accessed June 2024.

Table 1019. New Manufactured (Mobile) Homes Placed for Residential Use and Average Sales Price by Region: 2000 to 2023

[280.9 represents 280,900. A mobile home is a moveable dwelling, 8 feet or more wide and 40 feet or more long, designed to be towed on its own chassis, with transportation gear integral to the unit when it leaves the factory, and without need of permanent foundation. Excluded are travel trailers, motor homes, and modular housing. Data are based on a probability sample and subject to sampling variability; see source. For composition of regions, see map inside front cover]

Year	Units placed (1,000)					Average sales price (dollars)				
	Total	Northeast	Midwest	South	West	U.S.	Northeast	Midwest	South	West
2000............	280.9	14.9	48.7	178.7	38.6	46,400	47,000	47,900	44,300	54,100
2005............	122.9	9.2	17.1	68.1	28.5	62,600	67,000	60,600	55,700	79,900
2010............	50.7	3.8	5.8	34.6	6.6	62,800	65,200	60,700	60,000	79,000
2011............	47.6	3.3	6.3	31.5	6.5	60,500	62,700	60,800	58,400	70,600
2012............	52.8	3.9	7.9	34.4	6.6	62,200	63,400	60,900	60,100	75,300
2013............	56.3	4.0	7.5	37.4	7.5	64,000	66,500	62,900	61,200	79,100
2014 [1]........	44.1	3.0	6.8	27.5	6.8	65,300	67,900	60,600	63,000	80,700
2015 [1]........	45.6	3.1	6.6	28.5	7.5	68,000	72,100	60,800	65,100	88,200
2016 [1]........	51.5	3.1	8.2	32.3	7.8	70,600	77,600	61,500	68,500	88,500
2017 [1]........	53.9	3.6	7.7	34.9	7.8	71,900	78,400	65,400	68,200	97,600
2018 [1]........	55.1	4.0	8.6	33.8	8.7	78,500	80,100	72,100	75,700	99,000
2019 [1]........	62.2	4.0	9.0	40.1	9.0	81,900	81,300	72,100	80,600	99,400
2020 [1]........	60.5	3.5	8.1	41.0	7.9	87,000	85,200	76,700	85,800	106,000
2021 [1,2]......	66.8	4.4	11.4	41.4	9.5	108,100	100,300	96,400	108,100	123,700
2022 [1,2]......	60.6	4.6	10.8	35.3	10.0	127,300	123,400	112,400	126,900	148,500
2023 [1,2]......	62.1	4.2	9.7	40.3	7.9	124,300	125,900	112,200	123,300	143,600

[1] Beginning 2014, data not comparable to prior years due to a change in methodology. See source for details. [2] Beginning in 2021, placements include homes that are leased or sold, and homes placed on site but not yet sold or leased. Prior to 2021, placements represented units that were sold and placed.

Source: U.S. Census Bureau, Manufactured Housing Survey, "MHS Annual Data," <www.census.gov/programs-surveys/mhs.html>, accessed July 2024.

Table 1020. Existing Single-Family Homes Sold and Price by Region: 1990 to 2023

[2,914 represents 2,914,000. Includes existing detached single-family homes and townhomes. Based on a representative sample of data (adjusted and aggregated to regional and national totals) reported by participating real estate multiple listing services. Sales are based on closings and may differ from other estimates. For definition of median, see Guide to Tabular Presentation. See Table 1022 for data on condominiums and cooperatives. For composition of regions, see map inside front cover]

Year	Homes sold (1,000)					Median sales price (dollars)				
	U.S.	Northeast	Midwest	South	West	U.S.	Northeast	Midwest	South	West
1990	2,914	513	804	1,008	589	97,300	146,200	76,700	86,300	141,200
1995	3,519	615	940	1,212	752	117,000	146,500	96,500	99,200	153,600
1996	3,797	656	986	1,283	872	122,600	147,800	102,800	105,000	160,200
1997	3,964	683	1,004	1,356	921	129,000	152,400	108,900	111,300	169,000
1998	4,495	745	1,129	1,592	1,029	136,000	157,100	116,300	118,000	179,500
1999	4,649	728	1,145	1,704	1,072	141,200	160,700	121,600	122,100	189,400
2000	4,603	715	1,116	1,707	1,065	147,300	161,200	125,600	130,300	199,200
2001	4,735	710	1,154	1,795	1,076	156,600	169,400	132,300	139,600	211,700
2002	4,974	730	1,217	1,872	1,155	167,600	190,100	138,300	149,700	234,300
2003	5,446	770	1,323	2,073	1,280	180,200	220,300	143,700	159,700	254,700
2004	5,958	821	1,389	2,310	1,438	195,200	254,400	151,500	171,800	289,100
2005	6,180	838	1,411	2,457	1,474	219,000	281,600	168,300	181,100	340,300
2006	5,677	787	1,314	2,352	1,224	221,900	280,300	164,800	183,700	350,500
2007	4,398	587	1,091	1,819	901	217,900	288,100	161,400	178,800	342,500
2008	3,665	471	882	1,439	873	196,600	271,500	150,500	169,400	276,100
2009	3,870	480	918	1,460	1,012	172,100	243,200	142,900	155,000	215,400
2010	3,708	465	859	1,426	958	173,100	243,900	140,800	153,700	220,700
2011	3,787	449	863	1,471	1,004	166,200	237,500	135,800	149,300	204,500
2012	4,128	492	1,002	1,605	1,029	177,200	237,200	143,700	158,400	234,300
2013	4,484	540	1,122	1,775	1,047	197,400	248,900	155,700	174,200	276,400
2014	4,344	533	1,060	1,789	962	208,900	252,200	164,200	182,900	294,400
2015	4,646	576	1,162	1,885	1,023	223,900	262,500	175,500	196,400	319,100
2016	4,838	617	1,222	1,955	1,044	235,500	265,400	184,400	209,200	342,900
2017	4,892	615	1,222	1,989	1,066	248,800	275,700	196,200	222,700	369,400
2018	4,742	581	1,192	1,972	997	261,600	289,200	201,700	231,600	388,600
2019	4,765	581	1,183	2,016	985	274,600	301,900	214,500	241,900	405,200
2020	5,066	604	1,264	2,175	1,023	300,200	341,700	235,400	265,100	451,500
2021	5,413	633	1,313	2,358	1,109	357,100	394,100	263,300	317,500	558,800
2022	4,480	521	1,119	1,997	843	392,800	426,000	281,900	359,500	617,100
2023	3,659	409	917	1,680	653	394,100	444,400	290,800	362,000	602,600

Source: NATIONAL ASSOCIATION OF REALTORS ®. See also <www.nar.realtor/research-and-statistics>.

Table 1021. Median Sales Price of Existing Single-Family Homes by Selected Metropolitan Area: 2020 and 2023

[In thousands of dollars (300.2 represents $300,200). Covers existing detached single-family homes and townhouses. Based on a representative sample of data reported by participating real estate multiple listing services. Sales are based on closings and may differ from other estimates. Areas are metropolitan statistical areas defined by Office of Management and Budget, though in some areas an exact match is not possible from available data]

Metropolitan area	2020	2023	Metropolitan area	2020	2023
United States, total	300.2	394.1	New Orleans-Metairie, LA	240.5	275.9
Allentown-Bethlehem-Easton, PA-NJ	234.9	326.6	New York-Jersey City-White Plains, NY-NJ	442.4	623.9
Anaheim-Santa Ana-Irvine, CA	900.0	1,260.0	New York-Newark-Jersey City, NY-NJ-PA	469.1	636.9
Atlanta-Sandy Springs-Marietta, GA	260.8	370.0	Oklahoma City, OK	174.9	243.8
Atlantic City-Hammonton, NJ	247.2	318.5	Omaha-Council Bluffs, NE-IA	220.6	290.0
Baltimore-Columbia-Towson, MD	328.5	388.6	Orlando-Kissimmee-Sanford, FL	301.6	434.0
Boston-Cambridge-Newton, MA-NH	563.7	714.0	Philadelphia-Camden-Wilmington, PA-NJ-DE-MD	272.9	349.8
Boulder, CO	645.9	857.2	Phoenix-Mesa-Scottsdale, AZ	333.0	459.6
Bridgeport-Stamford-Norwalk, CT	544.0	694.1	Portland-South Portland, ME	356.2	505.1
Charleston-North Charleston, SC	324.4	423.2	Portland-Vancouver-Hillsboro, OR-WA	451.0	584.8
Chicago-Naperville-Elgin, IL-IN-WI	287.6	351.2	Providence-Warwick, RI-MA	347.3	460.9
Cincinnati, OH-KY-IN	208.9	282.0	Raleigh, NC	325.2	459.9
Cleveland-Elyria, OH	179.5	214.3	Reno, NV	440.8	585.8
Colorado Springs, CO	361.7	460.4	Richmond, VA	303.4	393.0
Dallas-Fort Worth-Arlington, TX	287.2	381.9	Riverside-San Bernardino-Ontario, CA	422.6	565.0
Deltona-Daytona Beach-Ormond Beach, FL	244.9	355.0	Sacramento-Roseville-Arden-Arcade, CA	421.0	527.1
Denver-Aurora-Lakewood, CO	492.7	661.0	St. Louis, MO-IL	205.8	254.4
Des Moines-West Des Moines, IA	229.6	288.0	Salem, OR	353.6	452.7
Eugene, OR	354.9	465.4	Salt Lake City, UT	391.0	542.2
Hartford-West Hartford-East Hartford, CT	264.5	355.9	San Diego-Carlsbad, CA	710.0	931.2
Houston-The Woodlands-Sugar Land, TX	263.8	340.3	San Francisco-Oakland-Hayward, CA	1,100.0	1,272.5
Indianapolis-Carmel-Anderson, IN	227.6	305.2	San Jose-Sunnyvale-Santa Clara, CA	1,385.0	1,765.0
Las Vegas-Henderson-Paradise, NV	331.0	450.4	Seattle-Tacoma-Bellevue, WA	596.9	735.0
Little Rock-North Little Rock-Conway, AR	166.9	208.9	Tampa-St. Petersburg-Clearwater, FL	272.0	405.0
Los Angeles-Long Beach-Glendale, CA	673.1	833.4	Trenton, NJ	300.0	398.8
Louisville/Jefferson County, KY-IN	212.1	263.8	Tucson, AZ	265.1	377.1
Madison, WI	326.4	417.9	Urban Honolulu, HI	851.5	1,055.9
Memphis, TN-MS-AR	221.2	274.5	Virginia Beach-Norfolk-Newport News, VA-NC	275.0	334.4
Miami-Fort Lauderdale-West Palm Beach, FL	398.0	593.0	Washington-Arlington-Alexandria, DC-VA-MD-WV	475.4	602.7
Milwaukee-Waukesha-West Allis, WI	291.3	372.4			
Minneapolis-St. Paul-Bloomington, MN-WI	315.2	379.9			
New Haven-Milford, CT	265.9	356.9			

Source: NATIONAL ASSOCIATION OF REALTORS ®. See also <www.nar.realtor/research-and-statistics>.

Table 1022. Existing Apartment Condominiums and Cooperatives—Units Sold and Median Sales Price by Region: 1990 to 2023

[272 represents 272,000. Based on data (adjusted and aggregated to regional and national totals) reported by participating real estate multiple listing services. Sales are based on closings and may differ from other estimates. Data shown here reflect revisions from prior estimates. For definition of median, see Guide to Tabular Presentation. For composition of regions, see map inside front cover]

Year	Units sold (1,000)					Median sales price (dollars)				
	U.S.	Northeast	Midwest	South	West	U.S.	Northeast	Midwest	South	West
1990	272	73	55	80	64	86,900	107,500	70,200	64,200	114,600
1995	333	108	66	96	63	89,000	92,500	90,700	67,800	114,800
2000	571	197	106	160	108	114,000	108,500	121,700	84,200	149,100
2005	896	331	177	245	143	223,900	245,100	189,100	187,300	283,800
2010	474	95	53	202	124	171,700	242,200	150,500	118,500	154,700
2015	608	115	78	266	149	210,700	249,300	157,900	162,900	294,500
2016	614	116	82	263	153	220,700	256,600	166,200	172,600	321,300
2017	619	116	80	271	152	234,300	271,700	175,200	183,800	345,600
2018	601	110	77	273	141	241,000	284,600	177,600	184,500	361,500
2019	579	106	72	270	131	249,500	294,900	184,400	193,500	369,900
2020	578	103	74	275	126	266,300	313,700	192,300	210,900	390,200
2021	707	124	86	347	150	302,200	344,900	216,700	253,400	448,000
2022	546	104	74	253	115	334,500	372,500	231,000	288,000	491,200
2023	428	82	58	198	90	348,300	396,200	243,900	298,000	486,100

Source: NATIONAL ASSOCIATION OF REALTORS ®. See also <www.nar.realtor/research-and-statistics>.

Table 1023. New Unfurnished Apartments Completed and Rented in 3 Months by Region: 2015 to 2022

[268.3 represents 268,300. Structures with five or more units, privately financed, nonsubsidized, unfurnished rental apartments. Based on sample and subject to sampling variability; see source for details. For composition of regions, see map, inside front cover]

Year and rent	Number (1,000)					Percent rented in 3 months				
	U.S.	North-east	Midwest	South	West	U.S.	North-east	Midwest	South	West
2015	268.3	32.0	47.4	117.8	71.1	60	63	67	53	66
2016	266.3	30.5	41.0	128.1	66.7	55	49	56	51	64
2017	294.8	42.2	43.9	138.9	69.9	54	55	56	51	61
2018	277.8	36.3	39.0	125.5	77.1	54	49	55	53	59
2019	279.8	35.6	39.7	120.4	84.1	56	65	55	53	56
2020	301.4	23.0	48.5	149.1	80.8	51	78	47	50	49
2021	305.2	39.3	49.2	157.4	59.3	69	78	68	70	59
2022	**294.4**	**37.6**	**55.4**	**124.8**	**76.6**	**62**	**68**	**60**	**65**	**57**
Less than $850	3.1	0.6	0.8	(S)	0.3	75	96	60	71	91
$850 to $1,049	10.1	(S)	4.5	4.6	0.8	71	(S)	57	83	81
$1,050 to $1,249	22.3	(S)	9.8	5.7	(S)	68	84	65	57	82
$1,250 to $1,449	31.8	(S)	12.3	13.1	5.5	69	79	65	71	71
$1,450 to $1,649	43.1	(S)	9.9	25.5	6.1	66	59	60	67	71
$1,650 to $1,849	40.9	3.0	7.1	22.7	8.2	66	84	48	72	56
$1,850 to $2,409	34.4	4.0	5.1	16.1	9.2	65	84	57	66	61
$2,050 to $2,249	21.6	2.5	2.1	10.3	6.8	63	87	60	63	54
$2,250 to $2,449	18.8	4.7	1.2	7.2	5.7	57	67	67	57	45
$2,450 to $2,699	16.4	6.0	0.9	5.2	4.2	55	54	60	56	54
$2,700 to $2,999	15.0	3.3	0.7	5.4	5.5	59	75	52	58	53
$3,000 or more	36.9	10.4	(S)	7.7	17.8	47	57	42	42	43
Median asking rent (dol.)	$1,829	$2,492	$1,455	$1,757	$2,100	(X)	(X)	(X)	(X)	(X)

X Not applicable. S Data withheld because they did not meet publication standards.

Source: U.S. Census Bureau, "Survey of Market Absorption of New Multifamily Units, Table Creator," <www.census.gov/programs-surveys/soma/data/tools.html>, accessed April 2024.

Table 1024. Aging-Ready Housing Units by Census Division and Aging-Accessible Feature: 2019

[In percent, except as noted (124.1 represents 124,100,000). For occupied units only. Aging-ready households have a minimum of three basic design elements: a step-free entryway and a bedroom and full bathroom on the entry level. Based on the American Housing Survey (AHS)]

Aging-accessible feature	Total units		Census division								
	Mil-lions	Per-cent	New England	Middle Atlantic	East North Central	West North Central	South Atlantic	East South Central	West South Central	Moun-tain	Pacific
Total housing units	**124.1**	**100.0**	**4.8**	**13.0**	**15.0**	**7.0**	**19.7**	**6.2**	**11.7**	**7.6**	**15.0**
Aging ready homes	**50.2**	**40.4**	**19.6**	**26.6**	**27.0**	**34.6**	**43.5**	**48.0**	**61.6**	**47.6**	**47.2**
HOME LAYOUT											
Step-free entryway	66.5	53.6	33.6	47.6	39.9	49.3	58.0	56.0	69.1	57.7	59.8
Single-floor home	63.8	51.4	29.2	28.8	33.4	31.3	60.6	65.8	76.4	58.8	64.0
Multiple-floor unit with bedroom on entry level	27.6	45.8	43.0	37.3	49.5	52.3	41.1	62.4	55.9	48.0	43.1
Multiple-floor unit with full bath on entry level	34.6	57.4	59.3	49.0	60.7	63.8	52.0	71.4	67.2	59.2	54.5
Multiple-floor unit with both bedroom and full bath on entry level	26.0	43.2	40.6	34.1	47.7	49.8	39.0	59.2	53.9	45.3	39.2
MOBILITY FEATURES											
Ramps in home	6.3	5.1	4.8	5.8	4.1	5.1	5.1	7.2	5.7	3.8	4.8
Chair lift, stair lift, or platform lift	1.2	1.0	1.4	1.4	1.0	1.1	1.1	0.3	0.5	0.5	0.9

Source: U.S. Census Bureau, Current Population Reports, *Aging-Ready Homes in the United States—Perception Versus Reality of Aging-Accessibility Needs: 2019*, P23-219, October 2023.

Table 1025. Total Housing Inventory for the United States: 2000 to 2023

[In thousands (116,264 represents 116,264,000), except percent. Based on the Current Population Survey/Housing Vacancy Survey and subject to sampling error; see source and Appendix III for details]

Item	2000	2010	2015	2017	2018	2019	2020	2021	2022	2023
All housing units...............	**116,264**	**131,810**	**135,201**	**137,221**	**138,347**	**139,511**	**140,758**	**142,125**	**143,719**	**145,353**
Vacant................................	13,680	18,908	17,420	17,381	16,980	16,749	14,885	15,369	15,107	15,021
Year-round vacant..................	10,315	14,422	13,025	13,209	12,989	12,895	11,301	11,644	11,433	11,458
For rent............................	2,980	4,322	3,292	3,398	3,231	3,181	2,855	2,869	2,746	3,118
For sale only.......................	1,088	2,000	1,421	1,257	1,191	1,114	838	727	714	701
Rented or sold......................	935	915	1,083	1,163	1,107	1,091	922	1,057	954	925
Held off market....................	5,313	7,182	7,228	7,393	7,459	7,508	6,685	6,991	7,019	6,714
Occasional use....................	1,901	2,264	2,019	2,182	2,114	2,158	1,985	2,009	2,126	2,017
Usual residence elsewhere......	1,050	1,266	1,355	1,354	1,365	1,344	1,117	1,200	1,191	1,132
Other..............................	2,363	3,654	3,853	3,856	3,979	4,006	3,583	3,782	3,701	3,565
Seasonal [1]........................	3,364	4,485	4,396	4,170	3,990	3,854	3,583	3,726	3,674	3,563
Total occupied.......................	102,584	112,902	117,781	119,842	121,367	122,762	125,874	126,756	128,611	130,333
Owner...............................	69,223	75,462	74,983	76,533	78,157	79,252	83,852	82,965	84,588	85,880
Renter..............................	33,362	37,441	42,797	43,309	43,210	43,510	42,022	43,791	44,023	44,452
PERCENT DISTRIBUTION										
All housing units...................	100.0	100.0	100.0	100.0	100.0	100.0	100.0	100.0	100.0	100.0
Vacant................................	11.8	14.3	12.9	12.7	12.3	12.0	10.6	10.8	10.5	10.3
Total occupied.......................	88.2	85.7	87.1	87.3	87.7	88.0	89.4	89.2	89.5	89.7
Owner...............................	59.5	57.3	55.5	55.8	56.5	56.8	59.6	58.4	58.9	59.1
Renter..............................	28.7	28.4	31.7	31.6	31.2	31.2	29.9	30.8	30.6	30.6

[1] Includes vacant seasonal mobile homes.

Source: U.S. Census Bureau, "Housing Vacancies and Home Ownership, Historical Tables," <www.census.gov/housing/hvs/index.html>, accessed March 2024.

Table 1026. Occupied Housing Inventory by Age of Householder: 2000 to 2023

[In thousands (102,584 represents 102,584,000). Based on the Current Population Survey/Housing Vacancy Survey; see source for details]

Age of householder	2000	2010	2015	2017	2018	2019	2020	2021	2022	2023
Total...................	**102,584**	**112,902**	**117,782**	**119,842**	**121,367**	**122,762**	**125,874**	**126,756**	**128,611**	**130,333**
Under 25 years old.....	5,966	6,116	6,144	5,959	6,023	5,970	5,282	5,740	5,904	6,146
25 to 29 years old......	8,199	9,125	9,041	9,303	9,531	9,570	9,448	9,333	9,212	9,264
30 to 34 years old.......	9,941	9,569	10,127	10,187	10,232	10,476	10,766	11,005	11,305	11,389
35 to 39 years old.......	11,576	9,888	9,858	10,384	10,573	10,593	11,050	10,990	11,210	11,341
40 to 44 years old......	12,016	10,624	10,123	9,762	9,667	9,975	10,462	10,700	11,088	11,212
45 to 49 years old......	10,837	11,798	10,603	10,569	10,490	10,228	10,404	10,182	10,223	10,244
50 to 54 years old......	9,416	11,829	11,490	10,921	10,841	10,708	10,803	10,889	11,141	11,066
55 to 59 years old......	7,457	10,534	11,608	11,637	11,533	11,592	11,870	11,484	11,325	11,150
60 to 64 years old......	6,013	9,432	10,533	11,023	11,305	11,446	11,919	12,046	12,173	12,006
65 to 69 years old......	5,680	7,104	9,333	9,799	10,001	10,136	10,543	10,798	11,146	11,358
70 to 74 years old.......	5,421	5,499	6,715	7,587	8,017	8,375	8,999	9,091	9,390	9,624
75 years old and over...	10,061	11,388	12,205	12,712	13,154	13,692	14,329	14,498	14,493	15,535

Source: U.S. Census Bureau, "Housing Vacancies and Home Ownership, Historical Tables," <www.census.gov/housing/hvs/index.html>, accessed March 2024.

Table 1027. Vacancy Rates for Housing Units—Characteristics: 2010 to 2023

[In percent. Rate is the proportion of vacant housing for rent or for sale to the total rental and homeowner supply, which comprises occupied units, units rented or sold and awaiting occupancy, and vacant units available for rent or sale. Based on the Current Population Survey/Housing Vacancy Survey; see source for details. For composition of regions, see map inside front cover]

Characteristic	Rental units					Homeowner units				
	2010	2015	2020	2022	2023	2010	2015	2020	2022	2023
Total units............	**10.2**	**7.1**	**6.3**	**5.8**	**6.5**	**2.6**	**1.8**	**1.0**	**0.8**	**0.8**
Northeast..................	7.6	5.5	5.2	4.2	4.3	1.7	1.9	1.0	0.9	0.7
Midwest....................	10.8	7.6	7.1	6.6	7.1	2.6	1.7	0.9	0.8	0.7
South......................	12.7	8.9	7.8	7.2	8.2	2.8	2.1	1.1	0.9	0.9
West.......................	8.2	5.1	4.4	4.4	5.1	2.7	1.4	0.8	0.7	0.8
Units in structure:										
1 unit.....................	9.2	7.1	5.5	5.2	5.6	2.2	1.7	0.9	0.7	0.7
2 units or more..........	11.1	7.2	6.8	6.3	7.2	9.2	5.1	2.9	3.5	3.2
5 units or more..........	11.7	7.4	7.5	6.6	7.6	9.2	4.5	2.9	3.4	3.2
Units with:										
3 rooms or fewer........	13.8	9.9	10.0	9.6	10.8	14.8	13.6	6.9	7.6	8.7
4 rooms..................	10.5	7.0	5.8	5.1	5.9	5.7	4.4	2.1	2.0	1.7
5 rooms..................	8.9	6.1	4.7	4.1	4.4	3.0	2.2	1.1	1.0	0.8
6 rooms or more........	7.1	5.6	4.9	4.8	5.1	1.7	1.2	0.7	0.5	0.5

Source: U.S. Census Bureau, "Housing Vacancies and Home Ownership: Annual Statistics: 2023," <www.census.gov/housing/hvs/index.html>, accessed March 2024.

Table 1028. Housing Units and Tenure—States: 2022

[143,773 represents 143,773,000. The American Community Survey universe includes the household population and the population living in institutions, college dormitories, and other group quarters. Based on a sample and subject to sampling variability; see Appendix III]

State	Housing units (1,000) Total	Occu-pied	Vacant Total [1]	For rent only	For sale only	For sea-sonal use [2]	Owner-occupied units Total (1,000)	Owner-occupied Average household size (persons)	Renter-occupied units Total (1,000)	Renter-occupied Average household size (persons)
United States.............	143,773	129,871	13,902	2,440	724	4,547	84,649	2.63	45,222	2.27
Alabama....................	2,340	2,016	323	41	13	76	1,416	2.54	600	2.22
Alaska.....................	329	275	55	6	1	27	182	2.69	93	2.31
Arizona....................	3,187	2,850	336	56	17	163	1,922	2.59	929	2.39
Arkansas..................	1,396	1,216	180	30	8	42	809	2.56	408	2.20
California.................	14,627	13,551	1,076	244	59	347	7,566	2.94	5,985	2.66
Colorado..................	2,590	2,385	206	44	10	91	1,584	2.54	800	2.12
Connecticut...............	1,540	1,434	107	17	9	26	950	2.62	484	2.10
Delaware..................	466	402	63	3	2	43	298	2.51	104	2.37
District of Columbia........	361	327	34	13	2	2	134	2.10	193	1.82
Florida....................	10,258	8,826	1,431	226	64	778	5,930	2.51	2,897	2.39
Georgia...................	4,539	4,092	447	92	29	78	2,696	2.71	1,397	2.41
Hawaii....................	568	495	73	12	3	36	310	2.92	185	2.67
Idaho.....................	797	717	80	9	5	45	519	2.70	198	2.46
Illinois....................	5,452	5,056	396	83	29	45	3,392	2.60	1,664	2.09
Indiana...................	2,977	2,726	251	43	13	38	1,930	2.56	797	2.14
Iowa......................	1,438	1,331	107	20	6	22	959	2.47	372	1.96
Kansas...................	1,293	1,175	117	26	7	12	796	2.57	379	2.12
Kentucky..................	2,024	1,829	195	26	9	30	1,258	2.50	571	2.18
Louisiana.................	2,113	1,817	296	46	14	45	1,229	2.55	588	2.26
Maine.....................	752	605	146	7	4	111	449	2.33	157	1.92
Maryland..................	2,559	2,376	183	32	13	47	1,610	2.67	766	2.26
Massachusetts.............	3,036	2,798	239	38	9	103	1,742	2.61	1,056	2.08
Michigan..................	4,605	4,090	516	56	25	234	2,992	2.52	1,098	2.08
Minnesota.................	2,548	2,322	226	30	10	126	1,674	2.57	648	1.98
Mississippi................	1,343	1,148	194	30	5	24	803	2.52	345	2.38
Missouri..................	2,826	2,522	304	45	15	81	1,705	2.54	817	2.06
Montana..................	529	464	65	7	2	36	319	2.48	145	2.07
Nebraska.................	864	803	61	10	3	14	530	2.58	273	2.03
Nevada...................	1,329	1,198	130	35	8	36	723	2.69	476	2.53
New Hampshire............	649	557	91	5	1	66	403	2.58	155	2.08
New Jersey................	3,785	3,517	268	39	16	127	2,273	2.73	1,244	2.33
New Mexico...............	957	848	109	13	7	33	602	2.55	247	2.17
New York.................	8,586	7,774	811	130	42	282	4,204	2.64	3,570	2.23
North Carolina.............	4,893	4,299	593	117	36	181	2,868	2.53	1,431	2.20
North Dakota..............	378	331	46	12	3	12	216	2.42	116	1.96
Ohio......................	5,293	4,878	415	63	23	55	3,285	2.49	1,593	2.06
Oklahoma.................	1,777	1,573	204	35	10	28	1,029	2.58	544	2.30
Oregon...................	1,859	1,726	133	25	7	53	1,085	2.52	642	2.19
Pennsylvania..............	5,815	5,294	521	83	29	139	3,658	2.52	1,636	2.03
Rhode Island..............	486	447	39	6	1	18	283	2.54	164	2.01
South Carolina............	2,447	2,136	311	50	13	108	1,539	2.48	598	2.22
South Dakota.............	408	368	40	7	1	13	256	2.53	112	2.05
Tennessee................	3,145	2,847	298	54	17	48	1,914	2.51	933	2.26
Texas....................	12,135	11,088	1,048	298	68	180	6,927	2.85	4,161	2.33
Utah.....................	1,229	1,130	99	18	5	43	804	3.12	325	2.52
Vermont..................	339	277	62	3	2	47	204	2.41	73	1.78
Virginia...................	3,685	3,381	305	48	18	76	2,278	2.60	1,103	2.28
Washington...............	3,313	3,080	234	49	14	77	1,976	2.64	1,104	2.19
West Virginia.............	862	736	125	14	6	30	548	2.40	188	2.16
Wisconsin.................	2,770	2,491	279	35	6	164	1,696	2.47	795	1.97
Wyoming.................	277	243	34	5	1	13	177	2.45	66	2.03

[1] Includes other reasons not shown separately. [2] For seasonal, recreational, or occasional use.

Source: U.S. Census Bureau, 2022 American Community Survey, B25002, "Occupancy Status"; B25003, "Tenure"; B25004, "Vacancy Status"; and B25010, "Average Household Size of Units by Tenure"; <data.census.gov/>, accessed November 2023.

Table 1029. Net Stock of Residential Fixed Assets: 2000 to 2022

[In billions of dollars (10,040 represents $10,040,000,000,000). End of year estimates]

Item	2000	2010	2015	2016	2017	2018	2019	2020	2021	2022
Total residential fixed assets........	**10,040**	**16,115**	**19,360**	**20,648**	**21,617**	**22,843**	**23,660**	**25,374**	**29,778**	**33,328**
By type of owner and legal form of organization:										
Private.....................................	9,810	15,783	18,968	20,233	21,188	22,394	23,198	24,883	29,206	32,686
Corporate................................	100	169	207	219	235	250	256	271	307	340
Noncorporate............................	9,710	15,614	18,761	20,014	20,954	22,145	22,942	24,612	28,899	32,346
Government..............................	229	332	392	416	428	449	462	491	572	641
Federal.................................	75	98	108	114	117	121	123	130	150	168
State and local.........................	154	234	284	302	312	328	339	362	423	474
By tenure group: [1]										
Owner-occupied.........................	7,596	12,529	15,121	16,177	16,929	17,912	18,607	20,023	23,675	26,573
Tenant-occupied.........................	2,408	3,531	4,163	4,388	4,599	4,836	4,953	5,243	5,976	6,612

[1] Excludes stocks of other nonfarm residential assets, which consists primarily of dormitories and of fraternity and sorority houses.

Source: U.S. Bureau of Economic Analysis, Fixed Assets Accounts Tables, "Table 5.1 Current-Cost Net Stock of Residential Fixed Assets by Type of Owner, Legal Form of Organization, and Tenure Group," <www.bea.gov/itable/fixed-assets>, accessed November 2023.

Table 1030. Homeowner and Rental Vacancy Rates by State: 2023

[In percent. From the Current Population Survey/Housing Vacancy Survey, and includes the civilian noninstitutionalized population, people in noninstitutional group quarters, and military households off post or with families on post (must include 1 household member who is a civilian adult). Based on a sample and subject to sampling variability; see Appendix III]

State	Home-owner vacancy rate	Rental vacancy rate	State	Home-owner vacancy rate	Rental vacancy rate	State	Home-owner vacancy rate	Rental vacancy rate
United States......	**0.8**	**6.5**	Iowa.............	0.8	8.2	North Carolina....	0.5	7.6
			Kansas..........	1.1	8.3	North Dakota.....	0.7	8.5
			Kentucky.........	0.5	3.5	Ohio..............	0.6	5.5
Alabama..............	0.9	9.3	Louisiana.........	1.5	8.4	Oklahoma.........	1.3	8.5
Alaska...............	0.7	4.9	Maine.............	0.7	2.9	Oregon............	0.8	6.0
Arizona..............	0.9	7.7	Maryland..........	0.5	7.3	Pennsylvania.....	0.7	6.1
Arkansas............	1.2	11.1	Massachusetts. ..	0.4	2.5	Rhode Island.....	0.3	3.7
California............	0.7	4.4	Michigan..........	0.7	7.3	South Carolina. ..	0.6	10.3
Colorado.............	0.9	5.1	Minnesota.........	0.6	6.9	South Dakota.....	0.9	6.5
Connecticut.........	0.7	3.8	Mississippi.......	0.8	8.6	Tennessee........	0.9	7.8
Delaware............	0.4	3.6	Missouri..........	0.8	7.4	Texas.............	1.3	9.2
Dist. of Columbia. ...	1.1	7.4	Montana..........	0.8	4.5	Utah..............	0.7	5.3
Florida..............	1.0	8.5	Nebraska.........	0.6	4.9	Vermont...........	0.3	3.5
Georgia.............	1.1	8.3	Nevada...........	1.0	7.0	Virginia...........	0.6	4.9
Hawaii...............	0.7	8.9	New Hampshire..	0.3	4.7	Washington.......	0.7	4.2
Idaho................	0.7	5.2	New Jersey.......	0.6	3.1	West Virginia.....	0.9	7.1
Illinois...............	0.6	7.5	New Mexico......	0.9	5.8	Wisconsin........	0.5	5.1
Indiana..............	0.8	10.5	New York.........	1.0	4.7	Wyoming..........	0.9	4.4

Source: U.S. Census Bureau, "Housing Vacancies and Home Ownership: Annual Statistics: 2023," <www.census.gov/housing/hvs/index.html>, accessed March 2024.

Table 1031. Homeowner and Rental Vacancy Rates by Metropolitan Statistical Area: 2023

[In percent. From the Current Population Survey/Housing Vacancy Survey, and includes the civilian noninstitutionalized population, people in noninstitutional group quarters, and military households off post or with families on post (must include 1 household member who is a civilian adult). Data are based on 2010 metropolitan/nonmetropolitan definitions. Subject to sampling error; see source and Appendix III for details]

Metropolitan statistical area	Home-owner vacancy rate	Rental vacancy rate	Metropolitan statistical area	Home-owner vacancy rate	Rental vacancy rate
Inside metropolitan areas...................	**0.8**	**6.5**	Memphis, TN-AR-MS..........................	0.4	11.4
Akron, OH..	1.1	4.9	Miami-Fort Lauderdale-West Palm Beach, FL...........	0.9	8.4
Albany-Schenectady-Troy, NY..................	0.1	4.1	Milwaukee-Waukesha-West Allis, WI..........	0.8	4.1
Albuquerque, NM................................	0.7	6.1	Minneapolis-St. Paul-Bloomington, MN-WI............	0.5	8.1
Allentown-Bethlehem-Easton, PA-NJ..........	0.4	7.9	Nashville-Davidson-Murfreesboro-Franklin, TN........	0.9	9.3
Atlanta-Sandy Springs-Roswell, GA...........	1.2	8.7	New Haven-Milford, CT.......................	0.8	3.3
Austin-Round Rock, TX..........................	1.3	9.0	New Orleans-Metairie, LA.....................	1.6	9.2
Baltimore-Columbia-Towson, MD...............	0.6	9.4	New York-Newark-Jersey City, NY-NJ-PA.........	0.9	3.9
Baton Rouge, LA.................................	0.9	6.6	North Port-Bradenton-Sarasota, FL............	0.7	5.4
Birmingham-Hoover, AL.........................	1.3	12.2	Oklahoma City, OK...........................	1.6	10.6
Boston-Cambridge-Newton, MA-NH...........	0.6	2.5	Omaha-Council Bluffs, NE-IA.................	0.9	4.3
Bridgeport-Stamford-Norwalk, CT.............	0.9	3.0	Orlando-Kissimmee-Sanford, FL..............	1.1	7.0
Buffalo-Cheektowaga-Niagara Falls, NY......	0.2	9.7	Philadelphia-Camden-Wilmington, PA-NJ-DE-MD.....	0.9	5.2
Cape Coral-Fort Myers, FL......................	2.3	15.3	Phoenix-Mesa-Scottsdale, AZ.................	0.7	8.0
Charleston-N. Charleston-Summerville, SC...	0.5	12.0	Pittsburgh, PA...............................	0.9	6.3
Charlotte-Concord-Gastonia, NC-SC..........	0.4	6.6	Portland-Vancouver-Hillsboro, OR-WA........	0.8	6.8
Chicago-Naperville-Elgin, IL....................	0.5	5.6	Providence-Warwick, RI-MA..................	0.3	3.7
Cincinnati, OH-KY-IN............................	0.2	7.2	Raleigh, NC..................................	0.5	8.8
Cleveland-Elyria, OH............................	0.5	4.7	Richmond, VA................................	0.2	5.2
Columbia, SC.....................................	1.0	8.5	Riverside-San Bernardino-Ontario, CA........	0.9	3.7
Columbus, OH....................................	0.8	5.8	Rochester, NY................................	0.8	2.0
Dallas-Ft. Worth-Arlington, TX.................	0.8	8.4	Sacramento-Roseville-Arden-Arcade, CA.....	0.6	4.2
Dayton, OH.......................................	0.4	5.3	St. Louis, MO-IL..............................	0.6	7.8
Denver-Aurora-Lakewood, CO..................	0.7	5.3	Salt Lake City, UT............................	0.6	6.2
Detroit-Warren-Dearborn, MI...................	1.0	9.3	San Antonio-New Braunfels, TX...............	1.3	8.8
Fresno, CA..	1.1	3.4	San Diego-Carlsbad, CA......................	0.2	4.1
Grand Rapids-Wyoming, MI.....................	0.1	3.2	San Francisco-Oakland-Hayward, CA.........	0.5	6.6
Greensboro-High Point, NC.....................	0.1	5.7	San Jose-Sunnyvale-Santa Clara, CA.........	0.3	3.3
Hartford-West Hartford-East Hartford, CT....	0.7	4.9	Seattle-Tacoma-Bellevue, WA................	0.6	4.0
Houston-The Woodlands-Sugar Land, TX....	1.4	10.9	Syracuse, NY.................................	0.7	6.4
Indianapolis-Carmel-Anderson, IN.............	0.8	8.8	Tampa-St. Petersburg-Clearwater, FL.........	1.0	8.5
Jacksonville, FL..................................	0.7	9.4	Toledo, OH...................................	0.9	7.2
Kansas City, MO-KS.............................	1.2	7.6	Tucson, AZ...................................	1.3	10.2
Knoxville, TN.....................................	0.8	4.2	Tulsa, OK....................................	0.8	6.7
Las Vegas-Henderson-Paradise, NV..........	1.1	7.2	Urban Honolulu, HI...........................	0.5	6.8
Little Rock-North Little Rock-Conway, AR.....	0.9	10.8	Virginia Beach-Norfolk-Newport News, VA.....	0.5	5.1
Los Angeles-Long Beach-Anaheim, CA.......	0.6	4.0	Washington-Arlington-Alexandria, DC-VA-MD-WV. ...	0.3	5.5
Louisville/Jefferson County, KY-IN.............	0.4	3.6	Worcester, MA................................	0.1	1.9

Source: U.S. Census Bureau, "Housing Vacancies and Home Ownership: Annual Statistics: 2023," <www.census.gov/housing/hvs/index.html>, accessed March 2024.

Table 1032. Housing Units—Characteristics by Occupancy and Tenure: 2019 and 2021

[In thousands of units (139,684 represents 139,684,000), except as indicated. As of Fall. Based on the American Housing Survey; see Appendix III]

Characteristic	2019 Total housing units [1]	2019 Occupied Total	2019 Owner	2019 Renter	2019 Vacant	2021 Total housing units [1]	2021 Occupied Total	2021 Owner	2021 Renter	2021 Vacant
Total units	**139,684**	**124,135**	**79,475**	**44,660**	**12,968**	**142,153**	**128,504**	**82,513**	**45,991**	**11,338**
Percent distribution	100.0	88.9	56.9	32.0	9.3	100.0	90.4	64.2	35.8	8.0
Units in structure:										
Single family detached	87,379	79,335	66,781	12,554	6,407	88,650	81,744	69,508	12,236	5,525
Single family attached	7,179	6,482	3,962	2,520	589	8,925	8,155	4,486	3,669	639
2 to 4 units	10,659	9,118	1,304	7,814	1,431	9,720	8,519	1,285	7,234	1,092
5 to 9 units	6,825	6,008	543	5,465	772	6,247	5,574	504	5,070	626
10 to 19 units	6,080	5,164	434	4,730	830	7,654	6,899	416	6,482	717
20 to 49 units	5,537	4,706	474	4,231	769	5,241	4,510	479	4,031	657
50 or more units	7,667	6,472	839	5,632	1,073	7,642	6,311	821	5,489	1,184
Manufactured/mobile home [2]	8,262	6,756	5,061	1,694	1,097	8,013	6,731	4,977	1,754	897
Year structure built:										
Median year (est.)	1977	1978	1979	1975	1975	1978	1979	1980	1977	1975
2020 to 2021	(X)	(X)	(X)	(X)	(X)	1,183	1,017	767	249	140
2015 to 2019	(NA)	(NA)	(NA)	(NA)	(NA)	6,526	5,949	4,091	1,858	498
2010 to 2014	(NA)	(NA)	(NA)	(NA)	(NA)	5,518	5,075	2,631	2,444	368
2005 to 2009	8,871	7,939	5,680	2,259	751	8,488	7,729	5,673	2,056	648
2000 to 2004	10,392	9,409	6,365	3,044	778	10,993	10,222	6,703	3,519	633
1995 to 1999	10,372	9,429	6,651	2,778	799	9,818	9,088	6,353	2,735	596
1990 to 1994	7,236	6,550	4,707	1,843	536	7,443	6,825	4,892	1,932	475
1985 to 1989	10,031	8,906	5,653	3,254	916	9,711	8,778	5,710	3,068	755
1980 to 1984	8,600	7,529	4,624	2,905	853	9,156	8,109	4,860	3,249	820
1970 to 1979	20,391	17,967	11,244	6,723	2,022	20,636	18,472	11,505	6,967	1,768
1960 to 1969	14,777	13,190	8,106	5,084	1,308	14,644	13,200	8,311	4,889	1,222
1950 to 1959	14,252	12,835	8,640	4,195	1,197	13,616	12,368	8,339	4,029	1,086
1940 to 1949	6,511	5,566	3,326	2,240	761	6,436	5,747	3,623	2,124	557
1930 to 1939	3,989	3,437	1,920	1,517	464	3,711	3,239	1,866	1,373	375
1920 to 1929	5,444	4,770	2,566	2,203	614	5,539	4,922	2,670	2,253	539
1919 or earlier	8,875	7,690	4,490	3,200	1,061	8,734	7,765	4,520	3,245	856
Stories in structure: [3]										
1 story	43,219	38,293	26,739	11,554	3,891	43,702	39,274	28,091	11,183	3,585
2 stories	47,788	42,749	27,232	15,517	4,368	48,141	43,923	27,718	16,205	3,612
3 stories	29,533	26,819	17,022	9,797	2,412	30,685	28,410	18,108	10,302	1,974
4 to 6 stories	7,567	6,798	2,767	4,031	706	8,078	7,288	3,028	4,260	713
7 or more stories	3,219	2,626	578	2,048	494	3,472	2,816	555	2,262	558
Foundation: [4]										
Full basement	28,934	26,832	23,332	3,500	1,784	29,324	27,484	24,008	3,477	1,549
Partial building	9,666	8,934	7,896	1,038	623	10,022	9,519	8,399	1,120	406
Crawlspace	20,373	18,080	14,517	3,563	1,744	21,112	19,101	15,513	3,588	1,579
Concrete slab	33,575	30,359	23,804	6,555	2,583	35,950	32,983	25,470	7,513	2,408
Equipment:										
With complete kitchen facilities [5]	135,293	122,697	79,127	43,570	10,365	137,979	126,758	82,064	44,694	9,165
Kitchen sink	139,008	123,891	79,420	44,471	12,605	141,490	128,208	82,420	45,788	11,035
Refrigerator	136,503	123,550	79,230	44,320	10,686	139,424	127,842	82,191	45,651	9,495
Cooking stove or range	135,713	122,432	78,719	43,713	10,997	138,407	126,722	81,710	45,012	9,594
Microwave oven only	905	773	349	424	99	970	808	323	485	142
Dishwasher	100,337	91,727	65,011	26,716	7,227	103,277	95,807	67,872	27,934	6,191
Washing machine	114,171	106,448	77,313	29,134	6,163	117,364	110,370	80,375	29,995	5,607
Clothes dryer	112,503	104,891	76,585	28,306	6,078	115,909	108,991	79,699	29,292	5,532
Main heating equipment:										
Warm-air furnace	91,470	82,186	55,309	26,877	7,943	94,495	86,064	57,843	28,221	7,190
Steam or hot water system	11,909	10,912	6,323	4,589	903	11,807	10,946	6,482	4,464	779
Electric heat pump	16,404	14,294	9,887	4,407	1,699	16,368	14,660	10,235	4,425	1,353
Built-in electric units	5,825	4,995	1,870	3,125	662	5,932	5,262	1,984	3,279	541
Floor, wall, or pipeless furnace	6,474	5,624	2,384	3,239	731	6,016	5,375	2,234	3,141	555
Room heaters with flue	938	821	454	367	100	938	791	434	357	95
Room heaters without flue	813	711	449	262	85	735	681	432	249	44
Portable electric heaters	2,364	2,103	1,118	986	168	2,469	2,223	1,122	1,101	170
Stoves	1,418	1,195	938	257	142	1,329	1,149	927	222	96
Fireplaces with inserts	226	204	158	46	(S)	208	198	163	(S)	(S)
Fireplaces without inserts	85	74	68	S	(S)	122	99	89	(S)	(S)
Cooking stove	75	72	36	36	(S)	97	75	(S)	44	(S)
None	1,129	594	316	279	372	1,062	579	344	236	345
Main cooling equipment:										
Central air conditioning	97,947	88,632	61,297	27,335	7,871	101,481	93,098	64,505	28,593	7,080
Room air conditioning	26,332	24,628	12,441	12,188	1,422	27,342	25,704	12,920	12,784	1,373
None	15,406	10,875	5,738	5,137	3,675	13,331	9,703	5,088	4,614	2,884
Source of water:										
Public system or private company	(NA)	110,171	67,391	42,780	(NA)	(NA)	114,454	70,286	44,168	(NA)
Individual well	(NA)	13,755	11,927	1,828	(NA)	(NA)	13,688	11,979	1,709	(NA)
Means of sewage disposal:										
Public sewer	(NA)	103,565	61,395	42,170	(NA)	(NA)	108,574	64,892	43,682	(NA)
Septic tank or cesspool	(NA)	20,293	17,931	2,362	(NA)	(NA)	19,489	17,387	2,102	(NA)

X Not applicable. NA Not available. S Estimate did not meet publication standards or withheld to avoid disclosure. [1] Includes seasonal units, not shown separately. [2] Includes trailers. [3] Excludes mobile homes; includes basements and finished attics. [4] Includes only single family homes (1 unit, attached or detached). [5] A complete kitchen includes sink, refrigerator, and oven or burners.

Source: U.S. Census Bureau, "American Housing Survey: AHS Table Creator," <www.census.gov/programs-surveys/ahs/data.html>, accessed October 2022.

Table 1033. Housing Units by Number of Units in Structure and State: 2022

[In percent, except total units. The American Community Survey universe includes the household population and the population living in institutions, college dormitories, and other group quarters. Based on a sample and subject to sampling variability; see Appendix III]

State	Total housing units	Percent of units by units in structures—					
		1-unit, detached and attached	2 units	3 or 4 units	5 or 9 units	10 or more units	Mobile home, boat, RV, van, etc.
United States.......	**143,772,895**	**67.5**	**3.3**	**4.3**	**4.5**	**14.6**	**5.7**
Alabama..............	2,339,582	71.2	1.9	2.9	3.9	7.6	12.5
Alaska...............	329,160	70.4	5.4	7.4	5.3	7.6	3.8
Arizona..............	3,186,554	69.8	1.4	3.0	3.4	12.9	9.4
Arkansas.............	1,395,735	70.9	3.2	3.4	3.6	7.2	11.7
California.............	14,627,041	64.6	2.4	5.5	5.5	18.4	3.6
Colorado.............	2,590,205	69.5	1.6	3.1	4.2	18.0	3.7
Connecticut..........	1,540,292	64.9	6.8	8.5	4.8	14.3	0.8
Delaware.............	465,804	76.7	1.0	2.1	3.6	10.0	6.6
District of Columbia...	360,862	32.2	4.4	7.6	6.4	49.4	–
Florida................	10,257,553	60.9	2.1	3.8	4.8	19.9	8.4
Georgia..............	4,539,156	71.0	2.2	3.1	4.3	11.4	8.1
Hawaii...............	568,058	63.2	1.9	4.1	6.3	23.9	0.5
Idaho................	796,968	78.1	1.9	4.6	2.2	6.1	7.1
Illinois................	5,452,461	64.4	5.0	6.2	6.5	15.7	2.2
Indiana..............	2,977,176	76.6	2.4	3.6	4.7	8.3	4.4
Iowa.................	1,438,456	76.8	2.0	3.4	3.9	10.9	3.1
Kansas..............	1,292,571	76.7	2.6	3.8	3.6	9.3	4.0
Kentucky............	2,023,679	70.1	2.7	4.3	4.7	7.1	11.1
Louisiana............	2,113,178	68.1	3.7	4.3	3.4	7.6	12.8
Maine................	751,697	72.3	4.8	5.5	4.0	5.5	8.0
Maryland.............	2,559,057	72.2	1.5	2.1	5.0	17.9	1.3
Massachusetts........	3,036,303	56.4	9.5	10.8	5.8	16.6	0.9
Michigan.............	4,605,363	76.7	2.3	2.6	4.1	9.1	5.2
Minnesota............	2,547,867	73.4	2.2	2.1	2.2	17.2	2.9
Mississippi...........	1,342,764	70.5	2.3	3.3	3.4	5.3	15.2
Missouri..............	2,826,295	73.7	3.2	4.7	3.6	9.4	5.5
Montana.............	529,167	73.9	2.7	4.7	2.7	6.9	9.1
Nebraska............	863,831	75.3	1.9	2.6	4.4	13.2	2.6
Nevada..............	1,328,788	65.5	1.4	5.7	6.3	15.6	5.5
New Hampshire.......	648,571	69.3	4.9	4.9	5.2	10.9	4.9
New Jersey...........	3,785,097	63.3	8.3	5.9	4.6	16.9	1.0
New Mexico..........	956,743	68.8	1.6	3.9	2.6	7.3	15.8
New York.............	8,585,784	46.5	9.6	6.9	5.2	29.7	2.2
North Carolina.......	4,892,627	70.0	2.0	2.8	3.7	10.6	10.9
North Dakota.........	377,722	63.9	1.3	2.7	3.9	20.7	7.5
Ohio.................	5,293,227	73.8	3.7	4.2	4.5	10.4	3.5
Oklahoma............	1,776,732	74.2	2.0	2.9	4.0	8.1	8.8
Oregon..............	1,859,349	67.6	2.6	4.4	4.3	13.9	7.3
Pennsylvania.........	5,815,191	75.2	4.3	4.0	3.1	9.8	3.6
Rhode Island.........	486,017	60.8	9.5	10.6	4.6	13.5	0.9
South Carolina.......	2,446,680	68.4	1.7	3.0	3.8	8.7	14.4
South Dakota........	408,009	72.1	1.4	3.3	3.7	12.4	7.1
Tennessee...........	3,144,583	72.3	2.4	3.1	4.2	9.6	8.4
Texas................	12,135,376	67.4	1.8	3.4	4.5	16.2	6.6
Utah.................	1,228,707	74.8	2.6	3.9	3.1	12.7	3.0
Vermont..............	338,998	71.9	5.4	5.7	4.4	7.0	5.6
Virginia..............	3,685,233	72.7	1.6	2.7	4.5	14.2	4.4
Washington...........	3,313,479	66.6	2.1	3.2	4.5	17.9	5.7
West Virginia.........	861,686	73.4	2.0	3.0	2.6	5.1	13.9
Wisconsin............	2,770,355	70.7	5.8	3.4	4.9	12.0	3.1
Wyoming.............	277,106	72.7	1.9	4.6	3.3	6.1	11.6

– Represents or rounds to zero.

Source: U.S. Census Bureau, 2022 American Community Survey, B25024 "Units in Structure," <data.census.gov/>, accessed November 2023.

Table 1034. Housing Units—Size of Units and Lot: 2019 and 2021

[In thousands (139,684 represents 139,684,000), except as indicated. As of Fall. Based on the American Housing Survey; see Appendix III]

Characteristic	2019					2021				
	Total housing units [1]	Occupied			Vacant	Total housing units [1]	Occupied			Vacant
		Total	Owner	Renter			Total	Owner	Renter	
Total units	**139,684**	**124,135**	**79,475**	**44,660**	**12,968**	**142,153**	**128,504**	**82,513**	**45,991**	**11,338**
Rooms:										
1 room	633	505	(S)	476	100	654	480	(S)	464	150
2 rooms	1,686	1,333	117	1,216	250	1,703	1,299	100	1,200	311
3 rooms	11,841	9,850	1,151	8,699	1,718	12,020	10,135	1,138	8,998	1,593
4 rooms	23,631	19,541	6,253	13,288	3,336	24,146	20,661	6,315	14,346	2,894
5 rooms	32,034	28,018	16,751	11,267	3,336	32,285	28,903	17,550	11,353	2,823
6 rooms	29,407	26,736	20,816	5,920	2,283	30,443	28,001	21,845	6,156	2,014
7 rooms	19,289	17,955	15,678	2,276	1,128	19,648	18,598	16,441	2,157	893
8 rooms	11,577	11,067	10,073	994	408	11,566	11,125	10,286	840	362
9 rooms	5,299	5,071	4,761	310	211	5,236	5,066	4,777	289	133
10 rooms or more	4,287	4,060	3,847	214	198	4,451	4,235	4,046	189	166
Bathrooms:										
No complete bathroom	291	127	35	92	93	335	136	(S)	113	103
1 bathroom	46,181	39,218	13,298	25,920	5,950	45,879	39,819	13,221	26,598	5,191
1 and one-half bathrooms	16,072	14,212	9,658	4,554	1,515	15,383	14,067	9,651	4,416	1,102
2 bathrooms	42,636	38,501	27,897	10,604	3,441	44,300	40,438	29,084	11,354	3,161
2 and one-half bathrooms	17,898	16,704	14,408	2,296	1,007	18,414	17,405	15,093	2,312	852
3 bathrooms	13,483	12,594	11,606	988	708	14,578	13,705	12,695	1,010	693
4 or more bathrooms	3,125	2,779	2,574	205	252	3,264	2,933	2,746	188	235
Square footage of unit:										
Less than 500	3,675	2,954	530	2,425	570	3,733	3,002	556	2,446	588
500 to 749	9,759	8,080	1,213	6,867	1,389	9,831	8,280	1,311	6,969	1,290
750 to 999	17,427	14,695	4,482	10,213	2,332	17,452	15,173	4,542	10,631	1,979
1,000 to 1,499	33,086	29,272	17,898	11,374	3,179	33,761	30,271	18,540	11,731	2,872
1,500 to 1,999	25,227	23,016	18,881	4,135	1,851	25,789	23,926	19,895	4,031	1,515
2,000 to 2,499	16,480	15,293	13,484	1,809	959	16,768	15,756	13,966	1,789	832
2,500 to 2,999	8,779	8,237	7,654	583	467	8,870	8,417	7,912	506	367
3,000 to 3,999	8,275	7,684	7,209	475	466	8,503	8,030	7,590	440	380
4,000 or more	4,285	3,932	3,607	325	278	4,298	3,967	3,655	312	251
Not reported	12,691	10,972	4,518	6,453	1,478	13,149	11,682	4,546	7,135	1,264
Median square footage	1,473	1,500	1,800	980	1,200	1,480	1,500	1,800	969	1,139
Lot size:										
Single detached and attached units and mobile homes [2]	99,671	89,786	73,742	16,045	7,842	102,001	93,411	76,480	16,931	6,830
Less than one-eighth acre	14,239	12,516	8,988	3,528	1,426	14,861	13,457	9,525	3,932	1,148
One-eighth to one-quarter acre	32,124	29,588	23,377	6,211	2,134	33,565	31,335	24,944	6,391	1,854
One-quarter to one-half acre	19,134	17,430	15,152	2,279	1,390	19,638	18,191	15,660	2,531	1,169
One-half up to one acre	9,621	8,624	7,540	1,084	743	9,623	8,688	7,516	1,172	692
1 up to 5 acres	15,752	14,043	12,202	1,841	1,259	15,564	14,138	12,401	1,738	1,152
5 up to 10 acres	3,312	2,942	2,556	386	285	3,362	3,035	2,609	426	237
10 or more acres	5,488	4,642	3,927	715	604	5,386	4,566	3,824	742	579

S Estimate did not meet publication standards or withheld to avoid disclosure. [1] Includes seasonal units, not shown separately. [2] Does not include cooperatives or condominiums.

Source: U.S. Census Bureau, "American Housing Survey: AHS Table Creator," <www.census.gov/programs-surveys/ahs/data.html>, accessed October 2022.

Table 1035. Occupied Housing Units—Tenure by Race of Householder: 2005 to 2021

[In thousands (108,871 represents 108,871,000), except percent. As of Fall. Based on the American Housing Survey; see Appendix III]

Race of householder and tenure	2005	2009	2011	2013	2015	2017	2019	2021
ALL RACES [1]								
Occupied units, total	**108,871**	**111,806**	**114,907**	**115,852**	**118,290**	**121,560**	**124,135**	**128,504**
Owner-occupied	74,931	76,428	76,091	75,650	74,299	77,567	79,475	82,513
Percent of occupied	68.8	68.4	66.2	65.3	62.8	63.8	64.0	64.2
Renter-occupied	33,940	35,378	38,816	40,201	43,991	43,993	44,660	45,991
WHITE [2]								
Occupied units, total	**89,449**	**91,137**	**92,820**	**93,284**	**93,748**	**95,324**	**96,999**	**99,310**
Owner-occupied	65,023	65,935	65,357	65,088	63,049	65,234	66,433	68,362
Percent of occupied	72.7	72.3	70.4	69.8	67.3	68.4	68.5	68.8
Renter-occupied	24,426	25,202	27,463	28,196	30,699	30,089	30,566	30,948
BLACK [2]								
Occupied units, total	**13,447**	**13,993**	**14,694**	**15,015**	**16,002**	**16,552**	**17,114**	**18,128**
Owner-occupied	6,471	6,547	6,662	6,480	6,665	7,131	7,397	7,877
Percent of occupied	48.1	46.8	45.3	43.2	41.7	43.1	43.2	43.5
Renter-occupied	6,975	7,446	8,033	8,535	9,337	9,421	9,717	10,250
HISPANIC ORIGIN [3]								
Occupied units, total	**11,651**	**12,739**	**13,841**	**14,675**	**15,620**	**16,496**	**17,299**	**18,428**
Owner-occupied	5,752	6,439	6,530	6,897	7,109	7,763	8,355	8,988
Percent of occupied	49.4	50.5	47.2	47.0	45.5	47.1	48.3	48.8
Renter-occupied	5,899	6,300	7,311	7,778	8,511	8,733	8,945	9,440

[1] Includes other races not shown separately. [2] The 2003 American Housing Survey (AHS) allowed respondents to choose more than one race. Beginning in 2003, data represent householders who selected this race group only and exclude householders reporting more than one race. See also comments on race in the text for Section 1 and the below cited source. [3] Persons of Hispanic origin may be of any race.

Source: U.S. Census Bureau, "American Housing Survey: AHS Table Creator," <www.census.gov/programs-surveys/ahs/data.html>, accessed October 2022.

Table 1036. Homeownership Rates by Age of Householder and Household Type: 2000 to 2023

[In percent. Represents the proportion of owner households to the total number of occupied households. Based on the Current Population Survey/Housing Vacancy Survey, and includes the civilian noninstitutionalized population, people in noninstitutional group quarters, and military in households off post or with their families on post (must have 1 household member who is a civilian adult). See source and Appendix III for details]

Age of householder and household type	2000	2005	2010	2015	2018	2019	2020	2021	2022	2023
Total..............................	**67.4**	**68.9**	**66.9**	**63.7**	**64.4**	**64.6**	**66.6**	**65.5**	**65.8**	**65.9**
AGE OF HOUSEHOLDER										
Less than 25 years old......................	21.7	25.7	22.8	21.8	22.7	23.2	25.7	24.3	25.4	23.6
25 to 29 years old............................	38.1	40.9	36.8	31.7	32.5	32.9	35.3	34.6	35.6	35.2
30 to 34 years old............................	54.6	56.8	51.6	45.9	47.7	48.0	49.1	48.4	48.8	49.4
35 to 39 years old............................	65.0	66.6	61.9	55.3	57.6	57.2	60.0	58.5	59.2	59.2
40 to 44 years old............................	70.6	71.7	67.9	61.6	62.9	63.2	65.5	64.6	65.2	66.2
45 to 49 years old............................	74.7	75.0	72.0	68.0	68.4	68.2	68.8	67.3	68.6	68.8
50 to 54 years old............................	78.5	78.3	75.0	71.8	71.7	71.9	73.2	72.0	72.2	72.1
55 to 59 years old............................	80.4	80.6	77.7	74.7	74.0	73.9	74.9	73.2	74.0	75.1
60 to 64 years old............................	80.3	81.9	80.4	76.2	76.8	76.6	78.2	76.8	76.2	76.4
65 to 69 years old............................	83.0	82.8	81.6	79.3	79.3	78.8	79.6	78.9	78.8	78.4
70 to 74 years old............................	82.6	82.9	82.4	81.3	80.6	80.6	82.1	81.4	80.2	80.5
75 years old and over........................	77.7	78.4	78.9	77.2	76.6	77.3	79.0	78.7	78.6	78.5
Less than 35 years old.......................	40.8	43.0	39.1	35.0	36.2	36.7	39.1	38.2	39.0	38.6
35 to 44 years old............................	67.9	69.3	65.0	58.5	60.1	60.1	62.7	61.5	62.2	62.6
45 to 54 years old............................	76.5	76.6	73.5	70.0	70.1	70.1	71.1	69.7	70.5	70.5
55 to 64 years old............................	80.3	81.2	79.0	75.4	75.4	75.2	76.6	75.1	75.1	75.7
65 years and over............................	80.4	80.6	80.5	78.9	78.5	78.6	80.0	79.5	79.1	79.0
TYPE OF HOUSEHOLD										
Family households:										
Married-couple families.................	82.4	84.2	82.1	79.6	80.8	81.0	82.2	82.1	82.3	82.7
Male householder, no spouse present......	57.5	59.1	56.9	53.8	56.3	56.1	57.5	56.7	58.7	57.3
Female householder, no spouse present...	49.1	51.0	48.6	45.9	47.9	48.6	50.8	49.3	49.8	50.7
Nonfamily households:										
One-person.....................................	53.6	55.6	55.3	52.2	51.8	51.8	54.1	53.0	52.8	52.7
Male householder.............................	47.4	50.3	51.3	48.5	47.4	48.5	50.7	49.3	49.2	49.5
Female householder..........................	58.1	59.6	58.6	55.3	55.4	54.6	57.0	56.1	55.9	55.4
Two-or-more-persons:.......................	39.1	43.0	41.9	38.3	39.8	40.2	42.0	40.9	41.8	40.6
Male householder.............................	38.0	41.7	40.7	36.6	38.6	39.7	41.6	40.0	41.8	40.5
Female householder..........................	40.6	44.7	41.9	40.7	41.5	40.8	42.6	42.1	41.8	40.7

Source: U.S. Census Bureau, "Housing Vacancies and Home Ownership: Annual Statistics: 2023," <www.census.gov/housing/hvs/index.html>, accessed March 2024.

Table 1037. Homeownership Rates by State: 2000 to 2023

[In percent. Represents the proportion of owner households to the total number of occupied households. Based on the Current Population Survey/Housing Vacancy Survey, and includes the civilian noninstitutionalized population, people in noninstitutional group quarters, and military in households off post or with their families on post (must have 1 household member who is a civilian adult). See source and Appendix III for details]

State	2000	2010	2020	2021	2022	2023	State	2000	2010	2020	2021	2022	2023
United States.....	**67.4**	**66.9**	**66.6**	**65.5**	**65.8**	**65.9**	Missouri.............	74.2	71.2	71.1	72.8	70.6	68.7
Alabama.............	73.2	73.2	74.8	73.4	72.1	73.8	Montana.............	70.2	68.1	68.4	68.1	68.3	71.0
Alaska...............	66.4	65.7	64.1	64.0	65.1	64.3	Nebraska............	70.2	70.4	69.8	68.4	69.0	68.4
Arizona..............	68.0	66.6	68.7	65.2	68.1	69.7	Nevada..............	64.0	59.7	61.2	60.5	60.3	61.2
Arkansas............	68.9	67.9	68.8	66.1	66.8	65.9	New Hampshire....	69.2	74.9	74.5	74.0	74.6	74.3
California............	57.1	56.1	55.9	54.2	55.3	55.8	New Jersey.........	66.2	66.5	64.3	62.7	64.2	62.7
Colorado............	68.3	68.5	64.9	65.9	67.4	67.2	New Mexico........	73.7	68.6	70.3	69.0	71.1	70.3
Connecticut.........	70.0	70.8	66.9	66.1	64.8	68.2	New York...........	53.4	54.5	53.6	53.6	53.9	53.3
Delaware............	72.0	74.7	77.9	73.5	74.9	75.7	North Carolina......	71.1	69.5	68.7	65.8	65.9	66.9
Dist. of Columbia...	41.9	45.6	42.5	42.3	42.3	40.2	North Dakota........	70.7	67.1	64.2	63.5	65.4	65.7
Florida...............	68.4	69.3	68.7	67.2	67.3	67.3	Ohio.................	71.3	69.7	69.4	67.4	66.0	66.6
Georgia..............	69.8	67.1	67.3	64.0	64.7	65.5	Oklahoma...........	72.7	69.2	71.0	67.0	68.5	68.0
Hawaii...............	55.2	56.1	58.8	58.1	59.2	61.8	Oregon..............	65.3	66.3	65.2	65.8	64.9	64.1
Idaho................	70.5	72.4	71.5	71.0	71.3	71.0	Pennsylvania.......	74.7	72.2	69.9	70.2	70.7	71.0
Illinois...............	67.9	68.8	67.3	68.3	66.7	67.8	Rhode Island.......	61.5	62.8	64.5	62.8	65.8	64.4
Indiana..............	74.9	71.2	72.7	73.0	72.6	73.3	South Carolina......	76.5	74.8	73.6	73.2	74.7	73.0
Iowa.................	75.2	71.1	72.1	72.1	73.8	71.8	South Dakota.......	71.2	70.6	71.4	71.1	70.8	69.3
Kansas..............	69.3	67.4	69.5	69.3	69.0	68.5	Tennessee..........	70.9	71.0	70.0	67.7	67.3	68.9
Kentucky............	73.4	70.3	72.5	72.1	71.4	69.4	Texas...............	63.8	65.3	66.5	64.1	63.6	63.6
Louisiana............	68.1	70.4	69.1	68.9	69.6	67.3	Utah.................	72.7	72.5	71.7	68.8	71.2	70.3
Maine................	76.5	73.8	77.1	75.9	74.9	75.5	Vermont.............	68.7	73.6	73.1	72.3	72.7	73.7
Maryland............	69.9	68.9	72.0	69.7	71.8	71.6	Virginia.............	73.9	68.7	70.4	68.0	67.4	69.1
Massachusetts......	59.9	65.3	62.7	62.0	61.2	61.9	Washington.........	63.6	64.4	64.1	63.4	66.6	66.3
Michigan............	77.2	74.5	74.3	73.0	74.0	74.1	West Virginia........	75.9	79.0	78.2	79.0	78.6	77.0
Minnesota...........	76.1	72.6	74.5	75.6	75.1	74.0	Wisconsin...........	71.8	71.0	67.9	68.3	70.0	69.2
Mississippi..........	75.2	74.8	74.2	71.3	73.1	75.5	Wyoming............	71.0	73.4	73.9	72.1	75.3	74.5

Source: U.S. Census Bureau, "Housing Vacancies and Home Ownership: Annual Statistics: 2023," <www.census.gov/housing/hvs/index.html>, accessed March 2024.

Table 1038. Occupied Housing Units—Costs by Census Division: 2021

[In thousands of units (82,513 represents 82,513,000), except as indicated. As of Fall. See headnote, Table 1039, for an explanation of housing costs. Based on the American Housing Survey; see Appendix III. For composition of census divisions, see map inside front cover]

Category	Total units	New England Division	Middle Atlantic Division	East North Central Division	West North Central Division	South Atlantic Division	East South Central Division	West South Central Division	Mountain Division	Pacific Division
OWNER-OCCUPIED UNITS										
Total	82,513	4,013	10,121	13,158	6,064	17,079	5,294	9,752	6,218	10,814
Monthly housing costs:										
Less than $100	151	(S)	(S)	(S)	(S)	36	(S)	(S)	(S)	(S)
$100 to $199	933	(NA)	48	61	(S)	335	149	174	49	(S)
$200 to $249	1,081	(S)	33	119	84	336	171	219	(S)	(S)
$250 to $299	1,527	(S)	74	144	110	476	243	278	148	51
$300 to $349	1,832	(S)	87	341	103	503	293	283	143	68
$350 to $399	2,329	(S)	142	424	175	546	301	369	198	152
$400 to $449	2,258	24	174	393	149	596	242	319	197	166
$450 to $499	2,447	(S)	210	453	204	625	245	366	171	151
$500 to $599	5,117	80	497	1,023	480	1,159	406	723	342	407
$600 to $699	4,579	146	416	888	434	964	355	608	310	456
$700 to $799	4,226	179	458	836	386	843	293	466	284	481
$800 to $999	7,872	337	973	1,667	663	1,465	547	846	537	837
$1,000 to $1,249	8,416	412	1,040	1,593	579	1,773	538	928	517	1,036
$1,250 to $1,499	7,862	463	1,107	1,437	590	1,546	443	838	643	794
$1,500 to $1,999	11,562	662	1,526	1,683	1,040	2,177	539	1,349	1,098	1,487
$2,000 to $2,499	7,262	480	1,027	892	542	1,444	246	718	636	1,275
$2,500 to $2,999	4,749	458	745	466	176	854	130	500	418	1,002
$3,000 or more	8,310	710	1,552	733	267	1,401	136	746	412	2,353
Median amount (dollars)	1,200	1,703	1,462	1,030	1,063	1,086	773	1,056	1,284	1,724
RENTER-OCCUPIED UNITS										
Total	45,991	2,093	6,513	6,060	2,758	8,561	2,562	5,583	3,483	8,380
Monthly housing costs:										
Less than $100	147	(S)	43	(S)	(S)	22	(S)	12	(S)	(S)
$100 to $199	500	13	81	62	(S)	96	39	71	52	62
$200 to $249	730	37	120	135	52	128	71	73	46	68
$250 to $299	708	36	137	115	49	119	44	68	38	103
$300 to $349	533	44	105	84	(S)	81	48	48	(S)	77
$350 to $399	531	45	81	89	45	65	49	43	32	82
$400 to $449	534	24	70	86	52	96	63	46	25	71
$450 to $499	612	42	63	97	38	102	69	80	(S)	104
$500 to $599	1,698	68	137	252	194	323	200	293	93	139
$600 to $699	2,160	69	259	415	187	341	213	303	176	196
$700 to $799	2,622	57	273	572	234	477	277	420	138	174
$800 to $999	5,912	215	650	1,196	592	969	444	907	383	555
$1,000 to $1,249	7,076	334	936	1,169	408	1,389	315	1,100	572	853
$1,250 to $1,499	5,859	235	776	663	304	1,430	240	641	564	1,006
$1,500 to $1,999	7,206	393	1,223	482	249	1,509	141	756	717	1,736
$2,000 to $2,499	3,360	207	548	180	60	584	47	297	232	1,204
$2,500 to $2,999	1,609	112	288	62	38	243	(S)	55	73	719
$3,000 or more	2,266	99	512	129	63	277	(S)	122	61	957
No cash rent	1,928	(S)	209	239	132	311	227	247	241	259
Median amount (dollars) [1]	1,184	1,274	1,305	961	923	1,238	831	1,060	1,264	1,657

NA Not available. S Estimate does not meet publication standards or has been withheld to avoid disclosure. [1] Excludes no cash rent.

Source: U.S. Census Bureau, "American Housing Survey; AHS Table Creator," <www.census.gov/programs-surveys/ahs/data.html>, accessed October 2022.

Table 1039. Occupied Housing Units—Financial Summary by Selected Characteristics of the Householder: 2021

[In thousands of units (128,504 represents 128,504,000), except as indicated. As of Fall. Housing costs include real estate taxes, property insurance, utilities, fuel, water, garbage collection, homeowner association fees, cooperative or condominium fees, mobile home fees, routine maintenance, mortgages, other charges in mortgages, and mortgage insurance. Based on the American Housing Survey; see Appendix III]

Characteristic	Total occupied units	Tenure		Black [1]		Hispanic origin [2]		Elderly			
								65 to 74 years old		75 years old and over	
		Owner	Renter	Owner	Renter	Owner	Renter	Owner	Renter	Owner	Renter
Total units [3]	**128,504**	**82,513**	**45,991**	**7,877**	**10,250**	**8,988**	**9,440**	**15,551**	**4,362**	**11,485**	**3,324**
Monthly housing costs:											
Less than $100	298	151	147	(S)	57	(S)	20	40	(S)	41	16
$100 to $199	1,433	933	500	193	180	95	105	219	89	183	57
$200 to $249	1,811	1,081	730	179	238	105	117	275	141	302	124
$250 to $299	2,236	1,527	708	216	224	143	106	385	158	377	126
$300 to $349	2,365	1,832	533	234	178	195	102	483	115	499	114
$350 to $399	2,861	2,329	531	320	168	196	95	640	101	735	84
$400 to $449	2,792	2,258	534	287	142	212	85	636	101	601	87
$450 to $499	3,059	2,447	612	297	164	228	85	665	98	624	60
$500 to $599	6,815	5,117	1,698	438	452	524	241	1,356	222	1,300	169
$600 to $699	6,739	4,579	2,160	446	595	556	367	1,276	285	1,050	155
$700 to $799	6,848	4,226	2,622	383	717	414	429	1,178	286	878	161
$800 to $999	13,783	7,872	5,912	715	1,596	769	1,151	1,799	568	1,424	310
$1,000 to $1,249	15,492	8,416	7,076	712	1,713	985	1,592	1,787	619	1,133	381
$1,250 to $1,499	13,720	7,862	5,859	747	1,406	761	1,365	1,328	350	851	283
$1,500 to $1,999	18,767	11,562	7,206	985	1,333	1,397	1,933	1,534	418	689	276
$2,000 to $2,499	10,622	7,262	3,360	698	480	960	781	719	221	338	168
$2,500 to $2,999	6,358	4,749	1,609	404	190	597	326	455	69	153	88
$3,000 or more	10,576	8,310	2,266	588	210	839	341	775	182	307	355
Median amount (dol.) [4]	1,193	1,200	1,184	1,060	1,041	1,279	1,275	864	942	701	1,014
Monthly housing costs as percent of income: [5]											
Less than 5 percent	3,198	2,861	337	265	73	275	53	515	(S)	298	(S)
5 to 9 percent	12,885	11,607	1,278	916	256	1,083	233	2,521	85	1,482	35
10 to 14 percent	17,757	14,445	3,311	1,401	622	1,338	481	2,587	164	1,765	97
15 to 19 percent	18,188	13,416	4,772	1,064	870	1,212	929	2,141	260	1,482	102
20 to 24 percent	15,538	10,287	5,251	771	1,006	1,098	1,089	1,608	343	1,229	202
25 to 29 percent	11,562	6,712	4,849	615	1,117	835	1,000	1,195	404	892	272
30 to 34 percent	8,763	4,694	4,069	528	968	634	871	882	360	658	261
35 to 39 percent	6,179	3,177	3,002	296	726	414	649	605	324	586	175
40 to 49 percent	8,246	4,070	4,177	476	1,010	584	928	793	435	743	342
50 to 59 percent	4,699	2,304	2,396	232	523	296	685	552	320	408	192
60 to 69 percent	3,100	1,383	1,717	178	454	172	377	331	199	255	143
70 to 99 percent	4,678	2,121	2,556	234	617	294	556	517	326	449	253
100 percent or more [4,6]	9,322	4,345	4,977	705	1,348	563	1,104	1,179	733	1,084	836
Median amount (percent) [4,6]	23	19	31	21	34	22	33	19	40	22	48
Median monthly costs (dol.): [4,7]											
Electricity	108	122	83	123	80	130	87	108	74	107	73
Piped gas	46	53	29	49	28	44	25	51	28	50	26
Fuel oil	125	125	100	125	83	125	83	125	100	125	(S)

S Estimate did not meet publication standards or was withheld to avoid disclosure. [1] For persons who selected this race group only. [2] Persons of Hispanic origin may be of any race. [3] Include units with no cash rents, not shown separately. [4] For explanation of median, see Guide to Tabular Presentation. [5] Money income before taxes. [6] Excludes households with zero or negative income and those with no cash rent. [7] Includes only units where costs were paid separately.

Source: U.S. Census Bureau, "American Housing Survey: AHS Table Creator," <www.census.gov/programs-surveys/ahs/data.html>, accessed October 2022.

Table 1040. Owner-Occupied Housing Units—Value and Costs by State: 2022

[In percent, except as indicated (84,649 represents 84,649,000). Data are from the American Community Survey. Based on a sample and subject to sampling variability; see Appendix III. For definition of median, see Guide to Tabular Presentation]

State	Total (1,000)	Percent of units with value of— $99,999 or less	Percent of units with value of— $100,000 to $199,999	Percent of units with value of— $200,000 or more	Median value (dol.)	Median selected monthly owner costs [1] (dol.)	Selected monthly owner costs as a percent income in the past 12 months [1] Less than 15.0 percent	Selected monthly owner costs as a percent income in the past 12 months [1] 15.0 to 24.9 percent	Selected monthly owner costs as a percent income in the past 12 months [1] 25.0 to 29.9 percent	Selected monthly owner costs as a percent income in the past 12 months [1] 30.0 percent or more
U.S............	84,649	12.1	16.6	71.2	320,900	1,775	27.4	34.4	9.9	27.8
AL.............	1,416	23.6	26.3	50.2	200,900	1,293	34.7	33.5	8.2	22.8
AK.............	182	8.9	10.5	80.6	336,900	2,019	24.6	35.6	10.4	29.0
AZ.............	1,922	9.5	7.2	83.3	402,800	1,616	29.6	33.6	9.9	26.1
AR.............	809	25.5	29.7	44.9	179,800	1,216	33.6	34.9	8.3	22.5
CA.............	7,566	4.4	2.8	92.8	715,900	2,673	19.6	31.1	11.1	37.6
CO.............	1,584	5.2	3.7	91.1	531,100	2,098	24.7	34.7	10.8	29.3
CT.............	950	4.2	11.6	84.1	347,200	2,215	24.0	35.2	10.8	29.6
DE.............	298	8.0	10.4	81.6	337,200	1,629	31.7	33.8	9.9	24.1
DC.............	134	1.4	2.1	96.5	711,100	2,893	28.1	33.2	11.7	26.5
FL.............	5,930	9.7	11.5	78.8	354,100	1,746	23.0	31.8	10.5	33.9
GA.............	2,696	12.9	16.5	70.6	297,400	1,599	30.9	34.7	9.0	24.9
HI.............	310	3.6	2.3	94.1	820,100	2,683	19.4	27.3	10.8	41.3
ID.............	519	7.1	6.8	86.1	432,500	1,512	28.7	34.5	9.1	27.4
IL.............	3,392	14.7	23.2	62.1	251,600	1,804	27.1	35.7	10.0	26.8
IN.............	1,930	17.5	30.1	52.4	208,700	1,281	36.5	34.8	8.1	20.2
IA.............	959	19.3	32.2	48.5	194,600	1,411	32.4	37.7	9.3	20.2
KS.............	796	22.7	25.7	51.5	206,600	1,542	29.1	38.9	8.9	22.6
KY.............	1,258	21.9	29.1	49.0	196,300	1,316	33.5	34.8	8.3	22.8
LA.............	1,229	21.1	26.4	52.5	209,200	1,472	29.2	32.8	9.2	28.2
ME.............	449	12.6	18.7	68.7	290,600	1,573	26.1	34.1	10.0	29.4
MD.............	1,610	5.5	8.6	85.9	398,100	2,097	28.7	34.8	9.7	26.2
MA.............	1,742	3.3	3.6	93.2	534,700	2,489	23.9	34.7	10.8	30.2
MI.............	2,992	17.5	26.3	56.2	224,400	1,435	31.6	34.9	9.1	23.9
MN.............	1,674	8.1	14.7	77.3	314,600	1,784	28.3	37.6	10.0	23.6
MS.............	803	31.8	28.6	39.6	162,500	1,267	29.9	32.9	9.8	26.6
MO.............	1,705	17.1	27.6	55.3	221,200	1,377	33.1	35.7	9.0	21.6
MT.............	319	10.6	11.5	77.9	366,400	1,611	25.5	34.6	10.9	28.8
NE.............	530	15.0	25.2	59.8	232,400	1,586	29.2	38.6	9.4	22.3
NV.............	723	5.9	4.2	89.9	434,700	1,730	24.5	33.6	10.3	30.8
NH.............	403	6.0	8.5	85.4	384,700	2,157	21.6	37.8	11.8	28.6
NJ.............	2,273	4.7	7.4	87.9	428,900	2,553	22.1	35.1	11.0	31.5
NM.............	602	18.2	20.3	61.5	243,100	1,408	29.4	31.1	9.6	29.2
NY.............	4,204	10.4	15.7	73.9	400,400	2,355	24.6	31.9	9.9	33.1
NC.............	2,868	13.3	19.6	67.1	280,600	1,444	33.4	33.6	8.8	23.6
ND.............	216	17.4	20.7	62.0	243,100	1,638	28.1	40.5	8.9	22.3
OH.............	3,285	17.8	31.1	51.0	204,100	1,381	34.0	36.2	8.8	20.6
OK.............	1,029	22.2	29.9	47.9	191,700	1,409	29.9	35.3	9.7	24.6
OR.............	1,085	6.2	4.3	89.5	475,600	1,946	23.0	34.4	10.4	31.8
PA.............	3,658	15.0	23.8	61.2	245,500	1,601	31.4	34.8	9.3	24.1
RI.............	283	3.5	4.4	92.0	383,900	2,021	24.1	36.0	11.3	28.4
SC.............	1,539	17.2	20.6	62.2	254,600	1,378	32.4	32.4	9.5	25.1
SD.............	256	16.9	21.1	62.0	245,000	1,526	27.1	40.5	9.9	22.0
TN.............	1,914	13.1	18.7	68.2	284,800	1,442	30.4	34.8	9.4	25.0
TX.............	6,927	14.2	19.0	66.9	275,400	1,904	24.5	35.6	10.5	28.9
UT.............	804	4.6	2.8	92.6	499,500	1,822	28.0	37.6	10.4	23.8
VT.............	204	8.7	16.6	74.7	304,700	1,750	20.4	38.3	11.2	29.8
VA.............	2,278	8.1	12.6	79.3	365,700	1,919	28.6	36.2	9.9	24.8
WA.............	1,976	5.1	3.8	91.1	569,500	2,227	23.4	35.5	11.4	29.3
WV.............	548	32.6	31.2	36.2	155,100	1,161	39.0	34.0	7.8	18.6
WI.............	1,696	10.1	25.9	64.1	252,800	1,545	28.5	38.2	9.5	23.4
WY.............	177	12.0	14.8	73.2	292,300	1,564	26.1	36.9	10.8	26.2

[1] For homes with a mortgage. Selected monthly owner costs are the sum of payments for mortgages, deeds of trust, contracts to purchase, or similar debts on the property (including payments for the first mortgage, second mortgages, home equity loans, and other junior mortgages); real estate taxes; fire, hazard, and flood insurance on the property; utilities; and fuels. It also includes, where appropriate, the monthly condominium fee for condominiums and mobile home costs.

Source: U.S. Census Bureau, 2022 American Community Survey, B25075, "Value"; B25077, "Median Value"; B25088, "Median Selected Monthly Owner Costs by Mortgage Status"; and B25091, "Mortgage Status by Selected Monthly Owner Cost as a Percentage of Household Income in the Past 12 Months"; <data.census.gov/>, accessed November 2023. See also <census.gov/programs-surveys/acs/>.

Table 1041. Renter-Occupied Housing Units—Gross Rent by State: 2022

[In percent, except as indicated (45,222 represents 45,222,000). Data are from the American Community Survey. For definition of median, see Guide to Tabular Presentation. Based on a sample and subject to sampling variability; see Appendix III]

State	Total [1] (1,000)	Percent of units with gross rent of—					Median gross rent (dol.)	Gross rent as a percent of household income in the past 12 months [3]			
		$299 or less [2]	$300 to $499	$500 to $749	$750 to $999	$1,000 or more		Less than 15.0 percent	15.0 to 24.9 percent	25.0 to 29.9 percent	30.0 percent or more
U.S...........	45,222	3.0	4.0	9.4	15.2	68.3	1,300	11.6	22.6	10.6	48.2
AL.............	600	4.7	7.7	20.9	25.4	41.3	913	12.7	22.3	8.6	42.7
AK.............	93	1.3	3.0	5.3	17.0	73.5	1,329	15.4	26.8	9.8	39.3
AZ.............	929	2.1	2.1	6.3	12 3	77.1	1,450	10.5	22.5	11.0	49.4
AR.............	408	4.9	7.6	24.7	30.3	32.5	846	13.7	24.3	9.8	40.4
CA.............	5,985	1.5	2.4	3.2	5.8	87.1	1,870	9.9	21.4	10.4	53.1
CO.............	800	2.4	1.9	3.6	7.5	84.6	1,646	9.5	22.9	12.3	50.9
CT.............	484	4.0	4.0	6.4	10.9	74.7	1,360	10.4	22.0	10.8	49.5
DE.............	104	3.7	3.5	5.2	11.1	76.4	1,274	11.7	25.2	11.1	44.8
DC.............	193	3.0	2.8	3.0	5.0	86.2	1,843	12.5	25.5	12.3	45.3
FL.............	2,897	1.8	2.1	4.5	9.7	81.9	1,525	8.1	18.7	10.2	56.3
GA.............	1,397	2.5	3.8	10.5	15.9	67.3	1,269	11.4	22.2	10.8	47.6
HI.............	185	2.6	2.9	3.9	6.0	84.6	1,813	9.8	19.5	9.2	52.9
ID.............	198	2.6	5.2	11.9	21.0	59.3	1,138	12.5	24.9	11.2	43.5
IL.............	1,664	3.4	4.6	10.5	18.9	62.6	1,170	12.3	24.1	10.4	45.9
IN.............	797	3.5	4.1	16.0	29.9	46.6	972	12.2	24.3	10.4	44.9
IA.............	372	3.5	6.0	22.5	29.8	38.1	891	15.7	24.2	10.9	41.7
KS.............	379	2.5	6.3	18.0	25.8	47.4	975	14.4	26.1	9.3	43.5
KY.............	571	4.9	8.0	21.7	26.7	38.7	891	14.6	22.1	9.6	42.5
LA.............	588	4.5	7.1	16.5	23.3	48.6	984	10.7	19.0	8.7	48.5
ME.............	157	5.5	7.5	12.4	22.2	52.5	1,033	11.9	24.2	11.8	42.8
MD.............	766	3.1	3.1	4.1	7.9	81.8	1,550	11.3	23.5	10.3	48.8
MA.............	1,056	5.2	6.1	5.4	7.7	75.6	1,634	11.3	21.4	11.3	50.5
MI.............	1,098	4.3	5.0	13.5	22.4	54.7	1,052	12.8	22.1	10.3	46.6
MN.............	648	3.3	5.2	10.3	16.5	64.7	1,200	11.4	24.6	11.3	47.2
MS.............	345	6.1	7.9	22.2	26.5	37.3	873	12.2	19.6	9.4	42.4
MO.............	817	3.5	6.4	18.8	25.7	45.6	954	13.8	24.7	11.0	42.2
MT.............	145	4.2	7.7	17.4	20.3	50.4	1,005	14.2	24.9	11.0	40.3
NE.............	273	3.1	5.8	17.2	25.6	48.3	983	13.9	26.0	9.6	43.3
NV.............	476	1.3	1.3	4.1	10.9	82.5	1,461	8.4	21.5	10.5	54.3
NH.............	155	2.5	3.8	4.8	12.2	76.8	1,396	10.0	25.9	12.9	46.3
NJ.............	1,244	3.4	3.2	3.7	7.3	82.3	1,555	11.7	23.0	10.9	49.7
NM.............	247	4.3	5.3	18.7	25.9	45.8	955	11.3	20.6	9.9	47.6
NY.............	3,570	4.2	4.6	7.0	10.6	73.7	1,499	13.3	21.4	10.2	49.4
NC.............	1,431	2.9	4.7	13.5	19.8	59.0	1,131	12.8	23.5	10.6	44.0
ND.............	116	3.4	6.1	24.9	30.7	34.9	863	19.9	26.1	9.6	38.0
OH.............	1,593	4.6	5.1	19.0	26.8	44.5	949	14.4	23.9	10.8	43.2
OK.............	544	3.7	5.9	18.7	29.0	42.8	937	13.7	23.6	10.2	42.9
OR.............	642	2.3	2.5	6.5	12.3	76.4	1,370	9.1	23.3	11.5	49.9
PA.............	1,636	4.3	5.3	12.9	19.1	58.4	1,116	12.9	23.9	10.5	44.7
RI.............	164	9.3	6.3	6.6	11.3	66.5	1,254	13.8	23.5	11.5	44.8
SC.............	598	2.9	4.5	14.6	21.8	56.2	1,084	10.1	22.4	10.2	46.5
SD.............	112	6.5	8.8	23.5	23.9	37.3	866	16.8	24.3	14.0	35.8
TN.............	933	3.4	5.6	13.7	20.4	57.0	1,096	12.5	22.7	11.1	44.1
TX.............	4,161	1.9	2.6	7.1	16.0	72.5	1,290	10.0	23.2	10.7	49.6
UT.............	325	1.9	3.1	6.2	12.9	75.8	1,372	11.3	26.6	11.6	45.0
VT.............	73	4.2	5.2	8.8	21.4	60.4	1,141	11.6	23.3	10.3	47.0
VA.............	1,103	2.8	3.1	7.4	12.4	74.2	1,441	12.2	23.1	11.5	46.3
WA.............	1,104	2.5	2.2	4.4	8.1	82.8	1,630	11.3	23.5	11.5	48.6
WV.............	188	7.5	10.3	26.0	28.4	27.8	795	12.8	19.4	8.8	41.8
WI.............	795	2.6	4.7	15.8	27.8	49.1	992	15.0	26.0	10.4	42.8
WY.............	66	3.7	8.9	18.0	29.5	39.9	895	15.5	25.0	8.4	38.6

[1] Includes units with no cash rent. [2] Includes only units with cash rent. [3] Percent distribution of rental units by gross rent as a percent of household income. Percentage calculated from totals which include units "not computed"; therefore, rows will not total 100 percent.

Source: U.S. Census Bureau, 2022 American Community Survey, B25063, "Gross Rent"; B25064, "Median Gross Rent"; and B25070, "Gross Rent as a Percentage of Household Income in Past 12 Months"; <data.census.gov/>, accessed November 2023.

Table 1042. Occupied Housing Units—Characteristics by Poverty Status: 2021

[128,504 represents 128,504,000. As of Fall. Based on the American Housing Survey (AHS); see Appendix III. The AHS uses a poverty definition based on household income received during the 12 months just before the survey. This differs from other poverty estimates so data will not be comparable to data in other tables. The poverty thresholds consider only money income, not assets of benefits in kind, and are updated every year to reflect changes in the Consumer Price Index; see <www2.census.gov/programs-surveys/ahs/2021/ 2021%20AHS%20Definitions.pdf> for details]

Characteristic	Total (1,000)	Poverty level (percent)				
		Less than 50 percent	50 to 99 percent	100 to 149 percent	150 to 199 percent	200 percent or more
Total units	**128,504**	**100.0**	**100.0**	**100.0**	**100.0**	**100.0**
Tenure:						
Owner	82,513	44.3	39.1	48.7	54.0	71.7
Renter	45,991	55.7	60.9	51.3	46.0	28.3
Units in structure:						
1, detached	81,744	45.6	43.6	52.1	55.4	69.7
1, attached	8,155	6.7	5.7	6.2	6.0	6.4
2 to 4	8,519	9.8	11.5	9.1	8.8	5.3
5 to 9	5,574	6.9	8.0	5.8	5.7	3.4
10 to 19	6,899	8.1	7.4	7.6	6.7	4.5
20 to 49	4,510	5.4	5.0	4.3	4.0	3.0
50 or more	6,311	9.1	8.4	6.4	4.6	4.0
Manufactured/mobile home or trailer	6,731	8.2	10.2	8.5	8.7	3.7
Square footage of unit:						
Less than 500	3,002	6.0	4.7	4.5	3.0	1.4
500 to 749	8,280	11.4	11.5	9.6	8.6	4.8
750 to 999	15,173	15.7	18.0	16.0	15.8	9.9
1,000 to 1,499	30,271	22.5	22.2	25.6	27.9	23.0
1,500 to 1,999	23,926	13.2	12.4	14.1	16.5	20.6
2,000 to 2,499	15,756	7.3	5.6	6.9	9.5	14.4
2,500 to 2,999	8,417	2.7	2.7	3.2	3.9	8.0
3,000 to 3,999	8,030	2.7	1.9	2.6	3.0	7.8
4,000 or more	3,967	1.6	1.0	1.5	1.3	3.8
Not reported	11,682	16.9	19.9	16.2	10.7	6.2
Monthly total housing costs as a percent of household income:						
Less than 5 percent	3,198	(NA)	(NA)	(NA)	(NA)	3.5
5 to 9 percent	12,885	(Z)	0.3	1.6	2.7	13.8
10 to 14 percent	17,757	(NA)	1.7	4.5	7.3	18.2
15 to 19 percent	18,188	0.2	2.1	5.1	8.1	18.5
20 to 24 percent	15,538	0.3	4.2	7.3	11.4	14.7
25 to 29 percent	11,562	0.5	7.7	8.2	11.2	9.8
30 to 34 percent	8,763	0.7	8.0	8.7	10.0	6.7
35 to 39 percent	6,179	0.4	5.9	8.7	9.3	4.2
40 to 49 percent	8,246	1.3	10.4	14.0	14.8	4.7
50 to 59 percent	4,699	1.2	9.0	10.5	8.1	2.1
60 to 69 percent	3,100	1.5	8.5	8.3	4.6	1.0
70 to 99 percent	4,678	5.1	16.5	11.8	6.1	1.0
100 percent or more [1]	9,322	57.1	23.1	8.7	4.4	0.9
Description of area within 1/2 block: [2]						
Single-family detached houses	94,280	62.9	64.9	68.0	70.6	76.2
Single-family attached houses	18,406	15.3	13.4	14.5	14.1	14.3
Multiunit residential buildings	33,515	37.2	37.1	31.6	30.4	22.7
Manufactured/mobile homes	9,205	9.7	12.4	10.7	10.5	5.6
Commercial or institutional [3]	38,158	40.0	38.0	35.0	32.3	26.9
Industrial structures or factories	6,709	7.8	7.5	6.7	6.4	4.4
Primary air conditioning:						
With primary air conditioning	118,801	90.0	90.2	91.2	91.8	93.1
Central air conditioning	93,098	64.2	59.8	64.5	66.4	76.2
Room air conditioning	25,704	25.8	30.4	26.8	25.4	17.0
Unit does not have air conditioning	9,703	10.0	9.8	8.8	8.2	6.9
Equipment:						
With complete kitchen [4]	126,758	96.9	97.7	98.5	98.6	98.9
Lacking complete kitchen facilities	1,746	3.1	2.3	1.5	1.4	1.1
Kitchen sink	128,208	99.0	99.6	99.6	99.8	99.9
Refrigerator	127,842	98.6	99.2	99.5	99.6	99.6
Cooking stove or range	126,722	97.0	97.7	97.6	98.1	99.0
Dishwasher	95,807	56.0	48.3	55.4	64.0	82.5
Washing machine	110,370	71.9	69.1	76.8	80.8	90.6
Clothes dryer	108,991	69.6	66.6	74.9	79.3	89.9
Selected deficiencies: [2]						
Signs of mice or rats inside home in last 12 months	15,289	13.4	15.6	13.5	12.4	11.1
Signs of cockroaches in last 12 months	14,482	16.2	16.1	14.5	13.8	9.6
Holes in floors	1,852	3.5	3.0	1.7	1.8	1.0
Open cracks or holes (interior)	7,155	8.6	8.0	8.0	6.2	4.7
Broken plaster or peeling paint (interior)	2,788	4.0	3.7	3.4	2.7	1.6
Exposed wiring	3,013	3.8	3.4	2.8	2.4	2.0
Rooms without electric outlets	2,443	3.3	2.3	2.7	1.8	1.6

NA Not available. Z Less than 0.05%. [1] May reflect a temporary situation, living off savings, or response error. [2] More than one category may apply to a unit. [3] Examples include stores, restaurants, schools, or hospitals. [4] Includes a sink, refrigerator, and oven or burners.

Source: U.S. Census Bureau, "American Housing Survey: AHS Table Creator," <www.census.gov/programs-surveys/ahs/data.html>, accessed November 2022.

Table 1043. Occupied Housing Units—Characteristics by Census Division: 2021

[In thousands (128,504 represents 128,504,000), except as indicated. As of Fall. Based on the American Housing Survey; see Appendix III]

Characteristic	Total units	New England	Middle Atlantic	East North Central	West North Central	South Atlantic	East South Central	West South Central	Moun- tain	Pacific
Total units....................	**128,504**	**6,106**	**16,633**	**19,217**	**8,822**	**25,641**	**7,856**	**15,335**	**9,701**	**19,194**
Units in structure:										
Single family detached.........	81,744	3,736	8,822	13,387	6,181	15,957	5,612	10,461	6,227	11,361
Single family attached..........	8,155	221	1,672	982	444	2,153	289	448	661	1,284
2 to 4 units......................	8,519	913	1,811	1,332	455	1,125	381	671	456	1,375
5 to 9 units......................	5,574	308	660	960	229	1,041	383	636	365	992
10 to 19 units...................	6,899	300	861	776	442	1,491	194	1,070	566	1,198
20 to 49 units...................	4,510	209	766	473	372	800	134	497	311	948
50 or more units..............	6,311	314	1,658	735	305	1,114	116	479	366	1,224
Manufactured/mobile home [1]...	6,731	105	382	573	392	1,945	748	1,063	743	781
Year structure built:										
Median year (estimated date)..	1979	1966	1960	1971	1976	1987	1983	1988	1989	1977
2020 to 2021.....................	1,017	(S)	55	80	(S)	231	66	235	139	143
2015 to 2019.....................	5,949	190	376	535	385	1,454	422	1,204	672	711
2010 to 2014.....................	5,075	107	390	557	407	1,108	341	1,078	533	554
2005 to 2009.....................	7,729	180	599	727	441	2,114	594	1,264	778	1,034
2000 to 2004.....................	10,222	310	726	1,273	638	2,670	725	1,560	1,032	1,286
1995 to 1999.....................	9,088	215	618	1,295	614	2,296	589	1,296	1,044	1,121
1990 to 1994.....................	6,825	259	555	1,005	487	1,728	440	679	541	1,130
1985 to 1989.....................	8,778	410	681	1,145	511	2,271	551	1,013	760	1,436
1980 to 1984.....................	8,109	344	710	855	509	1,906	538	1,234	736	1,276
1970 to 1979.....................	18,472	793	1,868	2,638	1,227	3,548	1,334	2,298	1,523	3,244
1960 to 1969.....................	13,200	581	1,858	2,121	929	2,319	880	1,382	761	2,369
1950 to 1959.....................	12,368	715	2,160	2,397	938	1,877	567	1,074	553	2,088
1940 to 1949.....................	5,747	302	1,086	1,161	307	840	337	462	220	1,033
1930 to 1939.....................	3,239	232	920	602	228	350	165	196	100	446
1920 to 1929.....................	4,922	386	1,458	1,071	405	475	123	193	114	698
1919 or earlier..................	7,765	1,062	2,572	1,757	746	455	185	169	194	625
Stories in structure: [2]										
1 story..........................	39,274	269	903	3,319	1,456	9,851	3,840	8,555	3,650	7,431
2 stories.........................	43,923	1,996	5,049	7,350	3,783	7,677	2,470	4,389	3,507	7,702
3 stories.........................	28,410	2,896	6,441	6,688	2,646	4,439	667	948	1,464	2,221
4 to 6 stories....................	7,288	691	2,624	958	460	1,157	95	277	266	759
7 or more stories...............	2,816	148	1,235	329	84	557	36	93	65	269
Foundation: [3]										
Full basement...................	27,484	2,890	6,462	8,127	3,937	3,020	793	41	1,545	670
Partial building.................	9,519	650	2,158	2,430	1,239	1,190	532	117	647	556
Crawlspace......................	19,101	165	708	2,065	765	5,117	2,456	2,084	1,244	4,497
Concrete slab...................	32,983	222	1,116	1,714	654	8,636	2,093	8,422	3,427	6,699
Equipment:										
With complete kitchen facilities [4]......................	126,758	6,035	16,298	19,040	8,740	25,325	7,741	15,152	9,546	18,881
Lacking complete kitchen facilities [4]......................	1,746	70	335	177	82	316	115	183	155	313
Kitchen sink.....................	128,208	6,091	16,578	19,188	8,816	25,568	7,842	15,315	9,651	19,159
Refrigerator.....................	127,842	6,089	16,531	19,139	8,801	25,496	7,825	15,252	9,651	19,058
Cooking stove or range.........	126,722	6,045	16,385	18,992	8,701	25,258	7,751	15,132	9,567	18,890
Microwave oven only...........	808	26	85	152	75	135	57	74	54	150
Dishwasher......................	95,807	4,565	10,817	13,243	6,735	20,592	5,691	11,618	7,902	14,642
Washing machine................	110,370	4,952	12,453	16,532	7,779	23,302	7,272	13,688	8,701	15,692
Clothes dryer....................	108,991	4,905	12,077	16,451	7,773	22,932	7,205	13,577	8,621	15,449
Main heating equipment:										
Warm-air furnace................	86,064	2,534	8,536	16,072	7,336	14,684	4,924	12,250	7,276	12,453
Steam or hot water system.....	10,946	2,628	5,616	1,188	516	413	(S)	(S)	259	306
Electric heat pump..............	14,660	112	454	432	388	8,358	1,909	1,299	931	777
Built-in electric units............	5,262	419	1,059	827	288	528	215	130	298	1,498
Floor, wall, or pipeless furnace..........................	5,375	186	571	389	145	632	229	464	390	2,368
Room heaters with flue.........	791	82	75	90	(S)	96	93	99	84	159
Room heaters without flue.....	681	(S)	(S)	(S)	(S)	173	151	224	(S)	37
Portable electric heaters.......	2,223	(S)	72	57	36	439	207	696	82	616
Stoves...........................	1,149	(S)	168	91	(S)	138	(S)	(S)	309	233
Fireplaces with inserts.........	198	–	(S)	(S)	(S)	(S)	(S)	(S)	(S)	56
Fireplaces without inserts......	99	(S)	(S)	(S)	(S)	(S)	(S)	(S)	(S)	37
Cooking stove...................	75	–	(S)	–	–	(S)	(S)	(S)	–	(S)
None............................	579	(S)	(S)	–	–	37	–	(S)	(S)	523
Main cooling equipment:										
Central air conditioning.........	93,098	2,097	7,834	14,274	7,379	23,196	6,795	13,670	7,494	10,358
Room air conditioning...........	25,704	3,438	7,671	4,072	1,221	1,995	936	1,483	1,080	3,808
None............................	9,703	571	1,129	871	221	450	124	181	1,127	5,028
Source of water:										
Public system or private company....................	114,454	4,860	14,349	16,118	7,743	22,377	7,494	14,526	8,890	18,096
Individual well..................	13,688	1,235	2,259	3,079	1,068	3,207	350	778	732	981
Means of sewage disposal:										
Public sewer.....................	108,574	4,486	14,180	15,953	7,482	21,113	5,867	13,443	8,525	17,525
Septic tank or cesspool.........	19,489	1,601	2,393	3,178	1,323	4,465	1,956	1,829	1,116	1,628

– Represents or rounds to zero. S Estimate did not meet publication standards or withheld to avoid disclosure. [1] Includes trailers. [2] Excludes mobile homes; includes basements and finished attics. [3] Covers only single family homes (1 unit, attached or detached). [4] A complete kitchen includes sink, refrigerator, and oven or burners.

Source: U.S. Census Bureau, "American Housing Survey: AHS Table Creator," <www.census.gov/programs-surveys/ahs/data.html>, accessed November 2022.

Table 1044. Occupied Housing Units—Heating Equipment and Fuels: 2013 to 2021

[115,852 represents 115,852,000. As of Fall. Data beginning 2011-2019 based on Census 2010 controls; data for 2021 based on Census 2020 controls. Based on American Housing Survey]

Type of equipment or fuel	Number (1,000)					Percent distribution				
	2013	2015	2017	2019	2021	2013	2015	2017	2019	2021
Occupied units, total	**115,852**	**118,290**	**121,560**	**124,135**	**128,504**	**100.0**	**100.0**	**100.0**	**100.0**	**100.0**
MAIN HEATING EQUIPMENT										
Warm air furnace	74,712	76,207	79,382	82,186	86,064	64.5	64.4	65.3	66.2	67.0
Steam or hot water	12,448	10,919	11,095	10,912	10,946	10.7	9.2	9.1	8.8	8.5
Electric heat pumps	13,526	13,980	14,128	14,294	14,660	11.7	11.8	11.6	11.5	11.4
Built-in electric units	5,064	4,616	4,925	4,995	5,262	4.4	3.9	4.1	4.0	4.1
Floor, wall, or pipeless furnace	4,571	5,963	5,616	5,624	5,375	3.9	5.0	4.6	4.5	4.2
Room heaters with flue	851	776	740	821	791	0.7	0.7	0.6	0.7	0.6
Room heaters without flue	1,034	647	749	711	681	0.9	0.5	0.6	0.6	0.5
Portable electric heaters	1,589	1,879	2,018	2,103	2,223	1.4	1.6	1.7	1.7	1.7
Stoves	1,050	1,197	1,348	1,195	1,149	0.9	1.0	1.1	1.0	0.9
Fireplaces with inserts	183	212	212	204	198	0.2	0.2	0.2	0.2	0.2
Fireplaces without inserts	61	87	83	74	99	0.1	0.1	0.1	0.1	0.1
Cooking stove	68	68	58	72	75	0.1	0.1	(Z)	0.1	0.1
Other	309	919	357	349	402	0.3	0.8	0.3	0.3	0.3
None	386	818	848	594	579	0.3	0.7	0.7	0.5	0.5
MAIN HEATING FUEL										
Housing units with heating fuel	115,465	117,472	120,712	123,541	127,925	100.0	100.0	100.0	100.0	100.0
Electricity	42,041	48,323	52,329	53,605	56,273	36.4	41.1	43.4	43.4	44.0
Utility gas	58,225	54,791	54,091	56,025	57,736	50.4	46.6	44.8	45.3	45.1
Bottled, tank, or liquid propane gas	5,198	4,703	5,074	5,279	5,482	4.5	4.0	4.2	4.3	4.3
Fuel oil	7,173	6,111	5,865	5,722	5,733	6.2	5.2	4.9	4.6	4.5
Kerosene or other liquid fuel	450	543	556	431	382	0.4	0.5	0.5	0.3	0.3
Coal or coke	98	80	89	84	71	0.1	0.1	0.1	0.1	0.1
Wood	1,992	2,197	2,305	2,118	1,980	1.7	1.9	1.9	1.7	1.5
Solar energy	31	40	(S)	(S)	(S)	(Z)	(Z)	(S)	(S)	(S)
Other	257	684	372	247	223	0.2	0.6	0.3	0.2	0.2
COOKING FUEL										
Housing units with cooking fuel	115,694	117,849	121,183	123,672	128,115	100.0	100.0	100.0	100.0	100.0
Electricity	69,330	71,262	72,874	74,452	76,061	59.9	60.5	60.1	60.2	59.4
Piped gas	41,503	41,400	42,609	43,469	46,075	35.9	35.1	35.2	35.1	36.0
Bottled gas	4,791	4,986	5,607	5,648	5,887	4.1	4.2	4.6	4.6	4.6
Other	71	200	92	103	93	0.1	0.2	0.1	0.1	0.1

S Estimate does not meet publication standards or has been withheld to avoid disclosure. Z represents less than 0.05%.

Source: U.S. Census Bureau, "American Housing Survey: AHS Table Creator," <www.census.gov/programs-surveys/ahs/data.html>, accessed November 2022.

Table 1045. Occupied Housing Units—Housing Amenities and Deficiencies by Selected Characteristics of the Householder: 2021

[In thousands of units (82,513 represents 82,513,000). As of Fall. Based on the American Housing Survey; see Appendix III]

Characteristic	Total occupied units		Black [1]		Hispanic origin [2]		Elderly			
							65 to 74 years old		75 years old and over	
	Owner	Renter	Owner	Renter	Owner	Renter	Owner	Renter	Owner	Renter
Total units	**82,513**	**45,991**	**7,877**	**10,250**	**8,988**	**9,440**	**15,551**	**4,362**	**11,485**	**3,324**
Selected amenities:										
Porch, deck, balcony or patio	77,293	33,037	7,082	6,997	8,102	6,342	14,641	2,776	10,795	2,101
Usable fireplace	39,268	6,364	3,068	1,095	3,106	1,154	7,379	467	5,207	325
Separate dining room	47,867	15,463	4,964	3,998	5,216	3,396	9,077	1,363	6,784	786
With 2 or more living rooms or recreation rooms	36,174	4,003	2,890	590	2,751	541	7,035	362	5,159	318
Garage or carport with home	67,272	18,091	5,603	2,820	6,983	3,866	12,604	1,588	9,694	1,199
Selected deficiencies:										
Signs of mice or rats in last 12 months	10,229	5,059	856	1,416	709	1,112	2,041	505	1,347	188
Signs of cockroaches in last 12 months	7,002	7,479	1,039	2,189	1,200	2,167	1,427	751	906	351
Holes in floors	938	914	117	257	145	224	169	61	117	(S)
Open cracks or holes (interior)	3,917	3,238	522	877	489	646	692	271	394	84
Broken/peeling paint or plaster (interior)	1,250	1,538	173	426	167	380	283	105	123	57
Exposed wiring	1,712	1,301	204	251	203	290	319	131	243	92
Rooms without electric outlet	1,251	1,193	165	293	133	267	205	97	202	52
Water leakage from inside structure [3]	5,790	4,681	675	1,237	618	891	974	329	518	177
Water leakage from outside structure [3]	7,573	3,871	846	1,004	730	774	1,378	306	888	132
Sagging roof [4]	1,434	517	156	99	231	103	254	42	151	(S)
Missing roof material [4]	2,500	830	409	153	338	142	500	89	245	(S)
Hole in roof [4]	1,052	435	147	114	214	87	239	(S)	116	(S)
Missing bricks, siding, or other outside wall material [4]	2,009	748	236	138	243	130	289	50	166	(S)
Boarded up windows [4]	824	451	70	79	194	72	136	(S)	69	(S)
Broken windows [4]	3,161	1,203	354	198	500	222	578	96	278	25
Foundation crumbling or has open crack or hole [4]	3,822	1,227	478	265	509	209	793	95	451	51
Units with mold in the last 12 months	1,624	2,204	286	580	245	518	333	150	188	58

S Does not meet publication standards. [1] For persons who selected this race group only. [2] Persons of Hispanic origin may be of any race. [3] During the 12 months prior to the survey. [4] Excludes multiunit structures.

Source: U.S. Census Bureau, "American Housing Survey: AHS Table Creator," <www.census.gov/programs-surveys/ahs/data.html>, accessed November 2022.

Table 1046. Household Energy Consumption and Expenditures by Selected Characteristics: 2020

[123.5 represents 123,500,000. Btu=British thermal units; for definition, see text, Section 19. Includes all primary occupied housing units in the 50 states and the District of Columbia. Vacant housing units, second homes, military houses, and common areas in apartment buildings are excluded. Consumption and expenditures for biomass (wood), coal, district steam, and solar thermal are excluded. Electricity consumption from on-site solar photovoltaic generation (i.e., solar panels) is included. Data from the Residential Energy Consumption Survey (RECS). Data were collected between March 2019 and February 2021]

Characteristic	Total housing units (millions)	Energy consumption				Energy expenditures			
		Total (trillion Btu)	Per household (million Btu)	Per household member (million Btu)	Per square foot (thousand Btu)	Total (billion dollars)	Per household (dollars)	Per household member (dollars)	Per square foot (dollars)
All homes.....................	**123.5**	**9,481**	**76.8**	**31.3**	**42.2**	**232.8**	**1,884**	**768**	**1.04**
Region:									
Northeast.........................	21.9	1,956	89.2	36.8	48.8	49.6	2,263	932	1.24
Midwest...........................	27.0	2,619	96.9	40.9	48.3	51.2	1,892	798	0.94
South..............................	46.8	3,116	66.5	27.2	36.8	86.1	1,839	753	1.02
West...............................	27.7	1,790	64.6	25.0	39.1	45.8	1,653	641	1.00
Housing unit type:									
Single-family detached..........	77.1	7,293	94.6	35.9	41.8	169.9	2,205	836	0.97
Single-family attached..........	7.5	500	67.1	27.6	41.6	12.3	1,653	681	1.02
Apartment buildings with 2-4 units.....................	9.3	500	53.5	22.2	54.7	13.1	1,406	585	1.44
Apartment buildings with 5 or more units.....................	22.8	769	33.7	17.9	37.2	25.3	1,107	589	1.22
Mobile homes.....................	6.8	419	61.3	25.3	50.5	12.1	1,773	731	1.46
Housing tenure:									
Owned.............................	82.9	7,501	90.5	35.9	41.6	177.0	2,135	847	0.98
Single-family..................	73.2	6,950	94.9	37.0	41.2	161.1	2,200	857	0.96
Apartments....................	4.3	218	50.6	25.8	42.5	6.4	1,474	754	1.24
Mobile homes..................	5.4	333	61.8	26.5	49.4	9.6	1,779	764	1.42
Rented [1]........................	40.6	1,980	48.8	21.0	44.8	55.7	1,372	591	1.26
Single-family..................	11.3	843	74.6	25.4	46.8	21.1	1,869	636	1.17
Apartments....................	27.9	1,051	37.7	18.5	42.6	32.1	1,151	563	1.30
Mobile homes..................	1.5	86	59.5	21.3	55.1	2.5	1,752	627	1.62
Year of construction:									
Before 1950......................	20.3	1,836	90.6	39.3	51.3	40.6	2,006	869	1.14
1950 to 1959.....................	12.5	1,058	84.8	35.5	50.1	24.3	1,948	816	1.15
1960 to 1969.....................	12.8	980	76.8	32.3	47.0	23.6	1,854	779	1.13
1970 to 1979.....................	18.3	1,306	71.2	29.7	43.2	33.3	1,814	756	1.10
1980 to 1989.....................	16.3	1,086	66.6	27.7	39.2	29.4	1,802	749	1.06
1990 to 1999.....................	17.2	1,336	77.8	30.3	38.9	33.4	1,946	757	0.97
2000 to 2009.....................	16.2	1,236	76.5	29.0	35.9	31.2	1,927	732	0.90
2010 to 2015.....................	5.5	360	65.1	24.5	32.5	9.6	1,730	652	0.86
2016 to 2020.....................	4.6	284	62.3	24.1	31.2	7.4	1,633	633	0.82
Total square footage: [2]									
Fewer than 1,000................	30.0	1,265	42.1	21.2	57.0	36.9	1,231	620	1.66
1,000 to 1,499...................	28.1	1,733	61.7	25.6	51.1	45.6	1,624	674	1.34
1,500 to 1,999...................	22.2	1,778	80.0	30.9	46.8	43.5	1,957	757	1.14
2,000 to 2,499...................	15.6	1,430	91.5	35.2	41.3	33.9	2,172	836	0.98
2,500 to 2,999...................	10.3	1,072	104.0	37.7	38.6	24.2	2,349	851	0.87
3,000 or greater.................	17.3	2,203	127.4	44.5	32.3	48.6	2,809	982	0.71
Number of household members:									
1 member.........................	33.6	1,845	54.9	54.9	39.4	45.6	1,357	1,357	0.97
2 members........................	45.3	3,554	78.4	39.2	40.9	86.2	1,901	951	0.99
3 members........................	18.3	1,581	86.6	28.9	44.4	39.5	2,160	720	1.11
4 members........................	15.6	1,443	92.8	23.2	44.3	35.2	2,265	566	1.08
5 members........................	6.4	611	94.9	19.0	45.1	15.3	2,368	474	1.13
6 or more members..............	4.4	446	102.2	15.0	49.1	11.1	2,535	372	1.22
Annual household income:									
Less than $5,000.................	4.5	253	56.5	21.7	49.5	6.8	1,512	580	1.33
$5,000 to $9,999.................	4.0	208	51.9	23.9	48.2	5.5	1,379	636	1.28
$10,000 to $19,999..............	10.3	588	57.4	28.9	44.5	15.0	1,462	735	1.13
$20,000 to $39,999..............	24.1	1,568	65.1	29.7	44.7	38.8	1,614	735	1.11
$40,000 to $59,999..............	19.6	1,372	70.0	30.3	42.0	33.8	1,724	747	1.03
$60,000 to $99,999..............	27.7	2,178	78.6	31.1	42.1	53.3	1,925	763	1.03
$100,000 to $149,999...........	16.5	1,462	88.4	32.4	40.3	35.5	2,147	786	0.98
$150,000 or more................	16.9	1,852	109.8	37.6	40.1	44.0	2,608	893	0.95
Main heating fuel [3]									
Natural gas.......................	62.7	5,996	95.6	38.1	48.2	122.4	1,952	777	0.98
Electricity.........................	42.6	2,081	48.9	20.7	31.6	70.1	1,647	697	1.06
Fuel oil/kerosene................	4.9	547	110.8	46.1	51.5	14.5	2,941	1,222	1.37
Propane...........................	5.2	512	98.2	41.3	43.7	13.9	2,675	1,123	1.19
Wood..............................	2.3	115	50.9	20.3	25.6	3.8	1,676	669	0.84

[1] Rented includes households that occupy their primary housing units without paying rent. [2] Total square footage includes all basements, finished or conditioned (heated or cooled) areas of attics, and conditioned garage space that is attached to the home. Unconditioned and unfinished areas in attics and attached garages are excluded. [3] Includes other types of fuel not shown separately. Also includes households that do not use heating equipment.

Source: U.S. Energy Information Administration, 2020 RECS Survey Data, "Consumption & Energy Expenditures (C&E) Tables," <eia.gov/consumption/residential/index.php>, accessed April 2023.

Table 1047. Average Energy Consumption and Expenditures Per Household by End Use and State: 2020

[76.8 represents 76,800,000. Btu=British thermal units; for definition, see text, Section 19. Includes all primary occupied housing units in the 50 states and the District of Columbia. Excludes vacant housing units, second homes, military houses, and common areas in apartment buildings. Also excludes consumption and expenditures for biomass (wood), coal, district steam, and solar thermal energy. Electricity consumption from on-site solar photovoltaic generation (i.e., solar panels) is included. Data are from the Residential Energy Consumption Survey (RECS)]

State	Average energy consumption (million Btu per household)				Average energy expenditures (dollars per household)			
	Total [1]	Space heating [2]	Water heating	Air conditioning	Total [1]	Space heating [2]	Water heating	Air conditioning
U.S. total	76.8	34.4	14.1	7.9	1,884	519	287	299
Alabama	64.4	19.2	11.2	10.5	2,082	479	340	401
Alaska	125.1	81.1	24.8	0.8	3,018	1,254	486	55
Arizona	62.1	10.2	10.9	17.6	1,994	230	278	658
Arkansas	75.7	30.5	13.2	9.8	1,926	564	306	332
California	53.7	14.8	16.3	5.6	1,656	270	292	290
Colorado	87.5	46.2	16.7	4.5	1,342	406	175	142
Connecticut	91.9	51.5	15.6	4.1	2,808	963	385	267
Delaware	72.0	30.2	13.1	6.1	1,910	593	330	221
District of Columbia	50.7	19.7	11.1	5.0	1,197	320	229	176
Florida	50.6	5.7	8.6	14.9	1,654	186	272	492
Georgia	73.9	24.7	13.8	10.3	2,180	512	369	390
Hawaii	30.3	1.3	8.7	9.7	2,058	99	569	638
Idaho	89.2	42.7	18.3	4.5	1,520	476	268	133
Illinois	99.3	59.0	14.6	5.1	1,720	606	190	195
Indiana	96.2	51.5	15.0	6.0	2,111	705	291	240
Iowa	99.0	56.5	13.9	5.0	1,854	598	197	191
Kansas	90.4	43.4	15.2	8.8	1,984	536	244	344
Kentucky	74.6	31.3	12.6	7.8	1,848	570	289	258
Louisiana	67.8	12.8	13.1	15.4	1,704	244	275	452
Maine	88.8	51.8	14.9	2.6	2,304	948	342	126
Maryland	75.0	33.4	13.3	6.5	1,924	630	304	239
Massachusetts	87.7	47.7	15.8	4.2	2,453	859	337	249
Michigan	108.3	67.1	14.7	4.2	2,192	717	225	221
Minnesota	100.3	59.3	15.2	3.5	1,833	647	243	137
Mississippi	70.9	22.0	12.8	12.6	1,887	446	296	407
Missouri	88.8	45.1	13.4	7.8	1,909	627	250	276
Montana	87.6	46.9	18.2	2.8	1,511	518	247	99
Nebraska	88.4	45.3	15.1	5.7	1,586	528	197	180
Nevada	76.7	21.3	15.9	12.6	1,690	292	241	415
New Hampshire	91.1	53.0	14.9	3.4	2,530	981	386	183
New Jersey	102.9	52.6	19.1	6.0	2,034	575	257	282
New Mexico	76.9	35.2	16.2	6.2	1,492	380	202	226
New York	82.3	43.0	16.1	4.4	2,319	761	392	266
North Carolina	62.7	22.3	11.7	8.4	1,731	464	311	283
North Dakota	94.3	56.2	14.3	2.9	1,648	665	242	89
Ohio	93.6	52.4	14.2	5.2	1,847	698	236	181
Oklahoma	84.6	33.4	15.6	10.8	1,803	485	251	333
Oregon	67.4	28.8	16.1	3.5	1,642	480	366	123
Pennsylvania	89.5	47.3	14.5	5.3	2,015	743	296	201
Rhode Island	98.0	58.2	17.2	3.9	2,617	953	348	244
South Carolina	61.7	17.3	11.4	10.4	1,918	405	333	381
South Dakota	87.1	47.9	14.2	4.5	1,709	567	245	159
Tennessee	73.0	27.0	12.7	8.9	1,759	466	297	275
Texas	66.2	16.3	12.1	13.6	1,800	310	262	460
Utah	93.0	42.3	18.9	6.3	1,647	461	221	208
Vermont	88.6	52.3	15.6	2.4	2,407	953	400	135
Virginia	75.2	28.0	14.0	7.6	2,023	537	349	272
Washington	67.1	30.0	15.9	3.0	1,461	518	310	87
West Virginia	82.1	42.3	13.4	5.9	1,976	748	333	204
Wisconsin	91.5	55.0	12.4	3.3	1,779	567	216	143
Wyoming	98.6	60.3	15.7	3.4	1,802	748	238	126

[1] Includes end uses not shown separately. [2] Includes main (primary) and secondary space heating equipment.

Source: U.S. Energy Information Administration, 2020 RECS Survey Data, "State Data," <eia.gov/consumption/residential/index.php>, accessed August 2024.

Table 1048. Household Energy Insecurity By Selected Characteristics: 2020

[In percent, except total units (123.5 represents 123,500,000). Data are from the Residential Energy Consumption Survey (RECS). Energy insecurity defined in this table includes only those issues collected as part of the RECS questionnaire. Other factors, such as energy costs as a percentage of household income, could be considered as household energy insecurity, but are not included here. Respondents may report more than one energy insecurity issue. Data were collected in late 2020 and early 2021. Includes all primary occupied housing units in the 50 states and the District of Columbia. Vacant housing units, seasonal units, and group quarters are excluded. Housing units located on military installations are included]

| Characteristic | Total housing units (millions) | Percent of households reporting: | | | | | |
		Any household energy insecurity	Reducing or forgoing food or medicine to pay energy costs	Leaving home at unhealthy temperature	Receiving disconnect or delivery stop notice	Unable to use heating equipment [1]	Unable to use cooling equipment [1]
All homes........................	**123.5**	**27.2**	**19.9**	**9.9**	**10.0**	**4.0**	**5.1**
Region:							
Northeast............................	21.9	25.3	17.4	10.9	8.4	3.6	3.8
Midwest.............................	27.0	24.3	18.0	7.4	10.4	3.5	3.8
South................................	46.8	29.9	22.8	9.9	12.1	4.5	6.6
West.................................	27.7	26.9	18.9	11.4	7.3	4.0	4.9
Housing unit type:							
Single-family detached...............	77.1	22.2	15.5	7.6	8.2	3.6	4.9
Single-family attached...............	7.5	28.2	21.1	10.7	10.2	3.4	4.6
Apartment buildings with 2-4 units...	9.3	44.9	35.5	17.2	16.6	5.6	6.3
Apartment buildings with 5 or more units...	22.8	30.6	23.1	12.0	9.9	2.7	3.9
Mobile homes........................	6.8	47.0	36.7	16.8	21.2	11.4	11.6
Number of household members:							
1 member............................	33.6	25.4	18.1	10.9	7.8	3.2	3.6
2 members...........................	45.3	21.1	14.8	8.0	7.0	2.8	4.1
3 members...........................	18.3	32.1	24.2	10.1	11.9	5.2	5.6
4 members...........................	15.6	32.6	25.1	10.3	13.5	4.4	7.0
5 members...........................	6.4	38.0	30.0	11.6	18.9	8.1	9.6
6 or more members...................	4.4	47.6	36.4	15.6	24.9	10.3	12.8
Annual household income:							
Less than $5,000....................	4.5	58.0	46.9	24.8	26.6	11.2	12.1
$5,000 to $9,999....................	4.0	56.1	46.6	21.2	19.5	9.5	8.0
$10,000 to $19,999..................	10.3	46.8	37.7	20.7	18.1	8.0	8.6
$20,000 to $39,999..................	24.1	39.7	31.3	15.0	14.4	6.3	8.2
$40,000 to $59,999..................	19.6	29.3	21.5	8.9	11.5	4.2	5.8
$60,000 to $99,999..................	27.7	20.1	12.8	5.7	7.0	2.0	3.3
$100,000 to $149,999...............	16.5	11.1	6.1	4.1	3.7	1.2	2.1
$150,000 or more...................	16.9	7.2	2.6	3.1	1.5	0.8	1.4
Householder age 60 or older: [2]							
Yes.................................	52.1	19.2	13.3	8.4	5.3	2.7	3.6
No..................................	71.4	33.0	24.7	10.9	13.4	4.9	6.2
Children under age 18 in household:							
Yes.................................	34.6	37.2	29.0	11.5	17.1	6.5	8.1
No..................................	89.0	23.3	16.4	9.2	7.3	3.0	4.0
Ethnicity of householder: [2]							
Hispanic or Latino..................	14.0	47.0	36.7	17.2	16.0	6.6	8.5
Not Hispanic or Latino..............	109.5	24.7	17.8	8.9	9.2	3.7	4.7
Race of householder: [2, 3]							
White...............................	100.0	23.2	16.8	8.5	8.0	3.2	4.3
Hispanic or Latino..................	12.0	45.8	36.8	16.8	15.5	6.3	8.3
Not Hispanic or Latino..............	87.9	20.1	14.0	7.3	7.0	2.8	3.7
Black or African American...........	13.0	52.0	40.2	17.5	26.0	9.5	11.0
Hispanic or Latino..................	0.6	55.6	41.3	17.5	22.2	(S)	(S)
Not Hispanic or Latino..............	12.3	51.9	40.2	17.5	26.2	9.4	10.9
Asian...............................	6.1	25.2	17.0	12.4	3.5	3.0	4.3
American Indian or Alaska Native....	1.1	51.9	38.0	15.7	17.6	10.2	6.5
Native Hawaiian or Other Pacific Islander.............................	0.4	42.9	34.3	(S)	(S)	(S)	(S)
More than one race..................	3.1	46.1	34.2	16.5	17.1	5.8	10.0
Housing tenure: [4]							
Owned...............................	82.9	20.4	14.2	7.2	6.6	3.4	4.6
Rented..............................	40.6	41.0	31.6	15.3	16.9	5.1	6.2

S Data withheld because either the relative standard error was greater than 50% or fewer than 10 cases responded. [1] Includes inability to use equipment at any time during the previous 12 months because equipment was broken and household could not have it repaired, or because of an electricity, natural gas, or bulk fuel disruption due to lack of payment. [2] A householder is a person in whose name the home is owned or rented. These characteristics refer to the householder that completed the RECS questionnaire. [3] Householders were permitted to select more than one racial category to describe themselves. These householders are only included as "more than one race." [4] Rented includes households that occupy their primary housing units without paying rent.

Source: U.S. Energy Information Administration, 2020 RECS Survey Data, "Housing Characteristics Tables," <www.eia.gov/consumption/residential/>, accessed May 2023.

Table 1049. Home Remodeling—Number of Households With Work Done by Amount Spent: 2024

[In thousands (3,277 represents 3,277,000), except percent. As of Spring 2024. For work done in the prior 12 months. Based on a household survey and subject to sampling error; see source]

Remodeling project	Total households with work done [1]		Households with work done by outside contractor	Number of households by amount spent		
	Number	Percent of households		Under $1,000	$1,000 to $2,999	Over $3,000
Conversion of garage/attic/basement into living space..........	3,277	1.3	780	502	528	1,468
Remodel bathroom...................	16,518	6.4	7,387	4,204	3,421	6,907
Remodel kitchen....................	9,425	3.7	3,898	1,492	1,716	4,692
Remodel bedroom..................	6,345	2.5	1,402	2,971	1,326	938
Convert room to home office..........	3,954	1.5	327	2,146	451	335
Remodel other rooms...............	5,931	2.3	1,350	2,117	1,021	1,565
Add bathroom......................	1,531	0.6	579	158	410	505
Add other rooms - exterior addition....	1,177	0.5	615	83	118	635
Add deck/porch/patio..............	5,106	2.0	2,411	1,120	980	2,417
Roofing...........................	10,102	3.9	8,169	1,157	1,565	6,271
Siding - vinyl/metal................	2,548	1.0	1,622	382	272	1,364
Aluminum windows.................	1,164	0.5	674	197	286	354
Clad-wood/wood windows..........	927	0.4	533	98	157	427
Vinyl windows.....................	3,930	1.5	2,591	597	606	2,028
Ceramic tile floors.................	2,879	1.1	1,331	1,154	724	574
Hardwood floors...................	4,564	1.8	2,103	1,113	902	1,589
Laminate flooring..................	6,897	2.7	2,717	2,721	1,646	1,353
Vinyl flooring.....................	5,065	2.0	1,763	1,735	1,163	1,399
Carpeting.........................	4,466	1.7	3,114	1,119	1,084	1,663
Kitchen cabinets...................	5,221	2.0	2,171	1,176	909	1,957
Kitchen counter tops...............	5,326	2.1	3,057	1,264	998	2,133
Skylights.........................	1,060	0.4	581	419	303	78
Exterior doors.....................	5,684	2.2	2,742	2,590	1,294	919
Interior doors.....................	3,520	1.4	1,340	1,797	434	441
Garage doors.....................	3,148	1.2	1,958	984	1,014	615
Concrete or masonry work..........	6,023	2.3	3,725	1,588	1,218	2,311
Landscaping......................	17,992	7.0	4,551	9,831	2,786	2,172
Swimming pool - in ground..........	964	0.4	517	41	58	558
Ceramic wall tile..................	2,443	1.0	840	1,199	470	301

[1] Includes no response and amount unknown.

Source: © MRI-Simmons Spring 2024 USA Study. Courtesy of MRI-Simmons. See also <www.mrisimmons.com/>.

Table 1050. Residential Mortgage Home Purchase Loans by Borrower Race/Ethnicity and Income Level: 2010 to 2022

[In percent, except as noted. Includes conventional and nonconventional first-lien home-purchase loans for 1- to 4-family owner-occupied, site-built homes. Based on data collected under the Home Mortgage Disclosure Act (HDMA). In 2018 significant changes were made to HMDA data collection. Therefore, beginning in 2018, data are not strictly comparable to prior years. See source for more information]

Race/ethnicity and income	2010	2015	2016	2017	2018	2019	2020	2021	2022
Home purchase loans (1,000)............	**2,157**	**3,134**	**3,463**	**3,606**	**3,594**	**3,736**	**4,101**	**4,378**	**3,533**
PERCENT DISTRIBUTION OF HOME PURCHASE LOANS									
Borrower race and ethnicity: [1]									
All borrowers.............................	100.0	100.0	100.0	100.0	100.0	100.0	100.0	100.0	100.0
Asian....................................	5.5	5.3	5.5	5.8	5.9	5.7	5.5	7.1	7.6
Black or African American................	6.0	5.5	6.0	6.4	6.8	7.0	7.3	7.9	8.1
Hispanic White..........................	8.1	8.3	8.8	8.8	8.9	9.2	9.1	9.2	9.1
Non-Hispanic White......................	67.6	68.1	66.4	64.9	62.0	60.3	59.1	55.6	54.4
Other minority [2]........................	0.9	0.8	0.8	0.9	0.8	0.8	0.9	1.0	1.0
Joint.....................................	2.7	3.5	3.6	3.7	3.6	3.7	3.9	4.1	4.4
Missing..................................	9.1	8.5	8.9	9.6	12.0	13.3	14.1	15.1	15.4
Borrower income: [3]									
Low or moderate.........................	35.4	27.9	26.2	26.3	28.0	28.6	30.4	28.7	27.8
Middle...................................	25.6	26.1	26.4	26.7	26.7	27.2	27.4	27.0	27.3
High.....................................	37.3	44.9	46.4	46.0	43.9	43.1	41.2	43.2	43.8
DENIAL RATES FOR HOME PURCHASE LOANS									
Applicant race and ethnicity: [1]									
All applicants [4].........................	15.6	12.1	11.5	10.7	9.8	8.9	9.3	8.3	9.1
Asian....................................	15.9	12.7	11.6	10.6	10.2	9.1	9.7	7.9	9.6
Black or African American................	24.9	20.8	19.8	18.4	17.4	15.9	18.1	15.3	16.8
Hispanic white...........................	21.8	16.2	15.0	13.4	13.1	11.6	12.5	10.6	12.0
Non-Hispanic white......................	13.0	10.0	9.5	8.8	7.9	7.0	6.9	6.3	6.7
Other minority [2]........................	22.0	17.2	16.6	14.7	14.3	13.0	13.7	12.4	13.8

[1] Applications are placed in one category for race and ethnicity. The application is designated as "joint" if one applicant was reported as White and the other was reported as one or more minority races or if the application is designated as White with one Hispanic applicant and one non-Hispanic applicant. If there are two applicants and each reports a different minority race, the application is designated as two or more minority races. If an applicant reports two races and one is White, that applicant is categorized under the minority race. Otherwise, the applicant is categorized under the first race reported. [2] Consists of applications by American Indians or Alaska Natives, Native Hawaiians or other Pacific Islanders, and borrowers reporting two or more minority races. [3] Not shown are borrowers whose income was not used or not applicable. The categories for the borrower-income group are as follows: low- or moderate-income is less than 80 percent of estimated current area median family income (AMFI), middle-income is at least 80 percent and less than 120 percent of AMFI, and high-income is at least 120 percent of AMFI. [4] Includes other race/ethnic groups not shown separately.

Source: Consumer Financial Protection Bureau, Federal Financial Institutions Examination Council, *Data Point: 2022 Mortgage Market Activity and Trends*, September 2023. See also <www.consumerfinance.gov/data-research/research-reports/>.

Table 1051. Median Loan Amount for Home Purchase and Refinance Loans by Borrower Race/Ethnicity and Income Level: 2019 to 2022

[In thousands of dollars (237 represents $237,000). Includes conventional and nonconventional first-lien home-purchase loans for 1- to 4-family owner-occupied, site-built homes. Based on data collected under the Home Mortgage Disclosure Act (HDMA); see source for more information]

Race/ethnicity and income	Home purchase loans				Refinance loans			
	2019	2020	2021	2022	2019	2020	2021	2022
HOME PURCHASE LOANS								
All home purchase loans.....................	**237**	**256**	**289**	**315**	**250**	**259**	**245**	**232**
Borrower race and ethnicity: [1]								
Asian..................................	340	362	414	449	387	359	355	370
Black or African American.................	217	236	264	297	222	235	221	216
Hispanic White...........................	221	241	272	300	244	250	243	238
Non-Hispanic White.......................	227	247	274	295	239	246	232	220
Other minority [2].........................	234	254	278	299	250	261	245	237
Joint....................................	291	315	353	381	304	303	294	288
Borrower income: [3]								
Low or moderate.........................	161	180	195	202	170	180	174	168
Middle..................................	225	248	276	300	224	235	229	236
High....................................	321	350	394	429	328	319	319	336

[1] Applications are placed in one category for race and ethnicity. The application is designated as "joint" if one applicant was reported as White and the other was reported as one or more minority races or if the application is designated as White with one Hispanic applicant and one non-Hispanic applicant. If there are two applicants and each reports a different minority race, the application is designated as two or more minority races. If an applicant reports two races and one is White, that applicant is categorized under the minority race. Otherwise, the applicant is categorized under the first race reported. [2] Consists of applications by American Indians or Alaska Natives, Native Hawaiians or other Pacific Islanders, and borrowers reporting two or more minority races. [3] The categories for the borrower-income group are as follows: low- or moderate-income is less than 80 percent of estimated current area median family income (AMFI), middle-income is at least 80 percent and less than 120 percent of AMFI, and high-income is at least 120 percent of AMFI.

Source: Bureau of Consumer Financial Protection, Federal Financial Institutions Examination Council, *Data Point: 2022 Mortgage Market Activity and Trends*, September 2023. See also <www.consumerfinance.gov/data-research/research-reports/>.

Table 1052. Commercial Buildings—Summary: 2018

[5,918 represents 5,918,000. Covers roofed and walled structures whose principal activities are nonresidential, nonagricultural, and nonindustrial and that are larger than 1,000 square feet. Building type based on predominant activity in which the occupants were engaged. Based on the Commercial Buildings Energy Consumption Survey (CBECS), a sample survey of building representatives conducted in 2018; subject to sampling variability]

Characteristic	All buildings (1,000)	Total floor-space (mil. sq. ft.)	Total workers in all buildings (1,000)	Mean square foot per building [1] (1,000)	Mean square foot per worker [1]	Mean operating hours per week [1]
All buildings................................	**5,918**	**96,423**	**85,796**	**16.3**	**1,072**	**62**
Building floorspace (sq. ft.):						
1,001 to 5,000...........................	2,833	8,025	9,717	2.8	676	57
5,001 to 10,000..........................	1,359	10,204	9,085	7.5	982	61
10,001 to 25,000.........................	981	15,838	12,244	16.1	1,225	65
25,001 to 50,000.........................	386	13,957	10,744	36.2	1,279	78
50,001 to 100,000........................	218	15,302	12,846	70.3	1,165	79
100,001 to 200,000.......................	93	13,003	11,428	140.2	1,123	84
200,001 to 500,000.......................	40	11,776	10,508	293.9	1,109	96
Over 500,000............................	9	8,317	9,224	947.6	897	115
Principal activity within building:						
Education................................	437	13,623	10,370	31.1	1,314	51
Food sales..............................	163	1,006	917	6.2	1,097	110
Food service............................	286	1,385	2,884	4.8	480	81
Health care.............................	137	4,018	6,656	29.3	604	60
Inpatient.............................	9	2,259	3,597	264.8	628	168
Outpatient............................	129	1,760	3,059	13.7	575	52
Lodging.................................	207	6,976	2,764	33.7	2,431	165
Mercantile..............................	517	10,781	8,882	20.9	1,214	64
Retail (other than mall)....................	350	5,193	3,251	14.8	1,597	66
Enclosed and strip malls..................	167	5,588	5,631	33.5	992	61
Office..................................	970	16,662	32,843	17.2	507	54
Public assembly.........................	488	7,192	3,338	14.7	2,082	51
Public order and safety...................	81	1,538	1,587	18.9	954	131
Religious worship........................	439	5,471	1,948	12.5	2,656	28
Service.................................	867	6,240	4,736	7.2	1,243	53
Warehouse and storage...................	1,004	17,483	7,081	17.4	2,222	71
Other..................................	113	2,435	1,598	21.5	1,360	82
Vacant.................................	208	1,612	(S)	7.8	(S)	5

S Data withheld because either the relative standard error was greater than 50 percent or fewer than 20 buildings were sampled. [1] For explanation of mean, see Guide to Tabular Presentation.

Source: U.S. Energy Information Administration, Commercial Buildings Energy Consumption Survey (CBECS), "2018 CBECS Survey Data," <www.eia.gov/consumption/commercial/>, accessed November 2022.

This section presents summary data for manufacturing as a whole and more detailed information for major industry groups and selected products. The types of measures shown at the different levels include data for establishments, employment and payroll, value and quantity of production and shipments, value added by manufacture, inventories, and various indicators of financial status.

The principal source of these data was the U.S. Census Bureau's Annual Survey of Manufactures. The Annual Survey of Manufactures (ASM) was discontinued after the 2021 survey year and data collection ended in late 2022. The data formerly collected for the ASM will now be collected as part of the Annual Integrated Economic Survey (AIES) for survey year 2023, which began data collection in early 2024. Reports on current activities of industries or current movements of individual commodities are also compiled by such government agencies as the Bureau of Economic Analysis; Bureau of Labor Statistics; the Department of Commerce, International Trade Administration; and by private research or trade associations.

The Census Bureau's *Quarterly Financial Report* publishes up-to-date aggregate statistics on the financial results and position of U.S. corporations. Based upon a sample survey, the QFR presents estimated statements of income and retained earnings, balance sheets, and related financial and operating ratios for manufacturing corporations with assets of $5 million or over, and mining, wholesale trade and retail trade corporations with assets of $50 million and over or above industry-specific receipt cut-off values. These statistical data are classified by industry and by asset size.

Several private trade associations provide industry coverage for certain sections of the economy.

Censuses and annual surveys—The first census of manufactures covered the year 1809. Between 1809 and 1963, a census was conducted at periodic intervals. Since 1967, it has been conducted every 5 years for years ending in "2" and "7". Results from the census are presented in this section utilizing the North American Industry Classification System (NAICS). Census data, either directly reported or estimated from administrative records, are obtained for every manufacturing plant with one or more paid employees. For additional information see text, Section 15, Business Enterprise, and the Census Bureau website at <census.gov/programs-surveys/economic-census.html>.

The Annual Survey of Manufactures (ASM), conducted for the first time in 1949, collected data for the years between censuses for the more general measure of manufacturing activity covered in detail by the censuses. The annual survey data was estimates derived from a scientifically selected sample of establishments. The ASM was a sample survey of approximately 50,000 establishments conducted annually, except for years ending in 2 and 7, at which time ASM statistics are included in the manufacturing sector of the Economic Census. In 2017, there were approximately 291,000 active manufacturing establishments. For sample efficiency and cost considerations, the manufacturing population was partitioned into two groups: (1) establishments eligible to be mailed a questionnaire, defined as the mail stratum, which was comprised of larger single-location manufacturing companies and all manufacturing establishments of multi-location companies, supplemented annually with new large single-location companies from IRS data and new multi-location companies from The Report of Organization; and (2) establishments not eligible to be mailed a questionnaire, defined as the nonmail stratum, which includes small- and medium-sized single establishment companies.

Establishments and classification—Each of the establishments covered in the 2017 Economic Census—Manufacturing was classified in accordance with the industry definitions in the 2017 NAICS manual. In the NAICS, an industry is generally defined as a group of establishments that have similar production processes. To the extent practical, the system uses supply-based or production-oriented concepts in defining industries. The resulting group of establishments must be significant in terms of number, value added by manufacture, value of shipments, and number of employees. Establishments frequently make products classified both in their industry (primary products) and other industries (secondary products). Industry statistics (employment, payroll, value added by manufacture, value of shipments, etc.) reflect the activities of the establishments, which may make both primary and secondary products. Product statistics, however, represent the output of all establishments without regard for the classification of the producing establishment. For this reason, when relating the industry statistics, especially the value of shipments, to the product statistics, the composition of the industry's output should be considered.

Establishment—An establishment is a single physical location where business is conducted or where services or industrial operations are performed. Data in this sector includes those establishments where manufacturing is performed. A separate report is required for each manufacturing establishment (plant) with one employee or more that is in operation at any time during the year. An establishment not in operation for any portion of the year is requested to return the report form with the proper notation in the "Operational Status" section of the form. In addition, the establishment is requested to report data on any employees, capital expenditures, inventories, or shipment from inventories during the year.

Durable goods—Items with a normal life expectancy of 3 years or more. Automobiles, furniture, household appliances, and mobile homes are common examples.

Nondurable goods—Items which generally last for only a short time (3 years or less). Food, beverages, clothing, shoes, and gasoline are common examples.

Statistical reliability—For a discussion of statistical collection and estimation, sampling procedures, and measures of statistical reliability applicable to Census Bureau data, see Appendix III.

Table 1053. Manufacturing—Contribution to Gross Domestic Product in Current and Chained (2017) Dollars by Industry: 2000 to 2023

[In billions of dollars (10,251.0 represents $10,251,000,000,000). Value added GDP is the contribution of each industry's labor and capital to its gross output and to the overall gross domestic product (GDP) of the United States. Value added is equal to an industry's gross output (sales or receipts and other operating income, commodity taxes, and inventory change) minus its intermediate inputs (consumption of goods and services purchased from other industries or imported). Current-dollar value added is calculated as the sum of distributions by an industry to its labor and capital which are derived from the components of gross domestic income]

Industry	NAICS [1]	2000	2010	2020	2021	2022	2023
CURRENT DOLLARS							
Gross domestic product, total [2]	(X)	**10,251.0**	**15,049.0**	**21,323.0**	**23,594.0**	**25,744.1**	**27,360.9**
Private industries	(X)	8,927.9	12,939.5	18,612.2	20,784.8	22,807.5	24,253.5
Manufacturing	31–33	**1,549.8**	**1,788.3**	**2,148.1**	**2,366.5**	**2,649.7**	**2,804.7**
Durable goods	33, 321, 327	924.6	954.1	1,199.7	1,270.3	1,406.9	1,526.8
Wood products	321	28.3	23.3	42.9	60.0	62.1	60.0
Nonmetallic mineral products	327	42.6	38.4	63.7	67.7	73.1	77.4
Primary metals	331	47.0	50.9	56.1	74.0	91.8	91.7
Fabricated metal products	332	121.3	120.0	148.1	144.7	164.9	181.9
Machinery	333	113.1	127.3	149.9	155.8	182.1	199.1
Computer & electronic products	334	225.3	228.7	273.3	292.3	301.8	311.7
Electrical equipment, appliances, & components	335	45.7	50.8	57.6	57.0	63.2	69.8
Motor vehicles, bodies & trailers, & parts	3361–63	137.5	88.8	142.7	138.7	156.4	184.3
Other transportation equipment	3364–66, 69	71.1	120.8	143.9	151.8	173.0	203.7
Furniture & related products	337	33.5	21.8	29.5	29.3	31.2	31.0
Nondurable goods	31, 32 [3]	625.2	834.3	948.5	1,096.2	1,242.8	1,277.9
Food & beverage & tobacco products	311, 312	163.2	223.5	289.6	306.0	311.9	340.3
Textile mills & textile product mills	313, 314	28.0	15.6	15.9	16.5	17.5	17.3
Apparel & leather & allied products	315, 316	22.2	10.4	9.5	10.0	10.4	10.7
Paper products	322	62.2	56.4	64.9	64.6	69.2	70.4
Printing & related support activities	323	43.7	39.5	36.4	38.8	42.3	44.1
Petroleum & coal products	324	52.7	123.8	60.3	133.5	199.9	188.2
Chemical products	325	187.8	303.3	391.7	447.5	501.4	513.2
Plastics & rubber products	326	65.5	61.8	80.2	79.1	90.4	93.6
CHAINED (2017) DOLLARS							
Gross domestic product, total [2]	(X)	**14,096.0**	**16,789.8**	**20,234.1**	**21,407.7**	**21,822.0**	**22,376.9**
Private industries	(X)	11,928.9	14,366.6	17,761.9	18,909.5	19,283.1	19,804.2
Manufacturing	31–33	**1,641.1**	**1,950.8**	**2,127.1**	**2,248.1**	**2,277.8**	**2,290.6**
Durable goods	33, 321, 327	754.8	990.2	1,171.7	1,249.5	1,297.0	1,319.3
Wood products	321	31.7	29.6	36.9	35.8	34.3	36.9
Nonmetallic mineral products	327	59.6	48.1	59.0	61.2	59.8	54.4
Primary metals	331	47.9	40.8	71.8	66.4	80.5	92.5
Fabricated metal products	332	164.9	133.9	135.3	136.5	125.5	121.5
Machinery	333	142.0	148.7	138.5	153.9	161.8	151.7
Computer & electronic products	334	55.6	193.2	279.1	303.0	303.0	298.5
Electrical equipment, appliances, & components	335	54.5	52.5	52.8	52.9	50.1	50.8
Motor vehicles, bodies & trailers, & parts	3361–63	105.0	96.9	148.0	169.8	200.8	223.0
Other transportation equipment	3364–66, 69	105.8	136.6	137.9	149.9	167.6	187.1
Furniture & related products	337	42.3	24.0	27.3	28.1	26.6	22.5
Nondurable goods	31, 32 [3]	916.8	964.2	955.7	999.6	985.4	978.3
Food & beverage & tobacco products	311, 312	231.2	250.1	267.5	285.5	307.1	300.9
Textile mills & textile product mills	313, 314	28.6	16.4	15.0	15.6	15.1	14.1
Apparel & leather & allied products	315, 316	20.0	11.1	9.8	10.3	10.5	10.5
Paper products	322	76.5	61.4	67.5	64.4	60.2	56.3
Printing & related support activities	323	38.3	38.4	35.1	37.4	35.0	32.3
Petroleum & coal products	324	102.8	127.2	88.1	105.9	82.3	83.9
Chemical products	325	313.0	390.4	387.0	399.0	413.0	424.2
Plastics & rubber products	326	75.3	68.3	76.9	74.8	65.8	61.0

X Not applicable. [1] North American Industry Classification System (NAICS) code; see text, Section 15. [2] Includes other industries not shown separately. For additional industries, see Table 708. [3] Except NAICS 321 and 327.

Source: U.S. Bureau of Economic Analysis, Industry Data, Gross Domestic Product by Industry, "Value Added by Industry," <www.bea.gov/itable/>, accessed June 2024.

Table 1054. Manufacturing Plants Using Industrial Robotic Equipment and Employees Exposed to Robots by Industry: 2019

[In percent. Industrial robotic equipment (or industrial robots) are automatically controlled, reprogrammable, and multipurpose machines used in industrial automated operations. Data shown for establishments that have either active robots at the plant, capital expenditures on robotic equipment, or purchases of robots. Data are experimental and based on the 2018 and 2019 Annual Survey of Manufactures]

Industry	2017 NAICS code [1]	Plants with robots	Employees exposed to robots	Industry	2017 NAICS code [1]	Plants with robots	Employees exposed to robots
Manufacturing	**31-33**	**11.1**	**25.7**	Chemical	325	6.7	14.3
Food	311	13.7	25.4	Plastics & rubber products	326	23.2	34.6
Beverage & tobacco products	312	4.7	11.3	Nonmetallic mineral products	327	6.3	18.5
Textile mills	313	6.2	11.1	Primary metal	331	18.9	31.2
Textile product mills	314	2.9	7.7	Fabricated metal products	332	13.4	23.7
Apparel	315	0.8	1.4	Machinery	333	14.7	29.4
Leather & allied products	316	4.6	17.0	Computer & electronic products	334	9.9	18.2
Wood products	321	4.1	6.2	Electrical equipment & appliances [2]	335	18.9	34.1
Paper	322	9.9	16.9	Transportation equipment	336	28.6	47.6
Printing & related activities	323	3.1	[3] 8.7	Furniture & related products	337	7.4	18.6
Petroleum & coal products	324	4.1	8.7	Miscellaneous	339	7.5	20.2

[1] Based on the North American Industry Classification System, 2017 (NAICS). [2] Includes component manufacturing. [3] Standard error exceeds 40% of the estimate.

Source: U.S. Census Bureau, "Annual Survey of Manufactures Industrial Robotic Equipment: 2018 and 2019," <www.census.gov/library/publications/2022/econ/2019-asm-robotic-equipment.html>, accessed August 2022.

Table 1055. Manufacturing—Establishments, Employees, and Annual Payroll by Industry: 2021 and 2022

[128,346 represents 128,346,000. Excludes most government employees, railroad employees, and self-employed persons. See Appendix III]

Industry	NAICS code [1]	Establishments		Employees (1,000) [2]		Payroll (mil. dol.)	
		2021	2022	2021	2022	2021	2022
All industries, total........................	**(X)**	**8,148,606**	**8,298,562**	**128,346**	**135,748**	**8,278,574**	**8,965,035**
Manufacturing, total....................	**31–33**	**283,015**	**285,500**	**11,710**	**12,188**	**785,196**	**851,308**
Percent of all industries.................	(X)	3.47	3.44	9.12	8.98	9.48	9.50
Food..	311	29,512	30,503	1,605	1,652	82,787	89,111
Beverage and tobacco products............	312	11,704	12,373	250	281	14,489	15,871
Textile mills.......................................	313	1,816	1,786	83	84	4,093	4,237
Textile product mills..........................	314	5,219	5,206	103	106	4,597	4,754
Apparel manufacturing.......................	315	4,872	4,733	65	70	2,452	2,785
Leather and allied products.................	316	1,086	1,076	24	25	1,032	1,132
Wood products..................................	321	13,887	13,993	420	446	21,721	24,478
Paper...	322	3,842	3,822	340	355	23,729	25,558
Printing and related support activities......	323	22,580	22,651	370	389	19,531	21,675
Petroleum and coal products...............	324	2,097	2,111	100	101	11,481	12,495
Chemical...	325	14,186	14,601	854	896	78,234	84,134
Plastics and rubber products...............	326	11,518	11,487	787	813	44,286	47,311
Nonmetallic mineral products..............	327	14,958	14,951	399	408	24,507	26,765
Primary metal...................................	331	3,717	3,579	339	352	24,709	27,861
Fabricated metal products..................	332	53,743	54,040	1,360	1,413	82,824	89,650
Machinery...	333	21,858	21,759	1,012	1,065	72,087	79,858
Computer and electronic products..........	334	11,435	11,285	784	797	76,367	80,268
Electrical equipment, appliance, and components...................................	335	5,254	5,369	337	354	24,158	25,371
Transportation equipment....................	336	11,332	11,565	1,594	1,655	118,007	130,078
Furniture and related products..............	337	14,394	14,606	349	371	16,879	18,477
Miscellaneous...................................	339	24,005	24,004	535	557	37,225	39,440

X Not applicable. [1] Data based on North American Industry Classification System (NAICS) 2017. See text, Section 15. [2] Covers full- and part-time employees who are on the payroll in the pay period including March 12.

Source: U.S. Census Bureau, County Business Patterns, CB2200CBP, "All Sectors: County Business Patterns, including ZIP Code Business Patterns, by Legal Form of Organization and Employment Size Class for the U.S., States, and Selected Geographies: 2022," <data.census.gov>, accessed June 2024. See also <www.census.gov/programs-surveys/cbp.html>.

Table 1056. Manufacturing—Establishments, Employees, and Annual Payroll by State: 2022

[12,188 represents 12,188,000. Excludes most government employees, railroad employees, and self-employed persons. Data are for North American Industry Classification System (NAICS) 2017, codes 31–33. See Appendix III]

State	Establish-ments	Employees (1,000) [1]	Payroll (mil. dol.)	State	Establish-ments	Employees (1,000) [1]	Payroll (mil. dol.)
United States.......	**285,500**	**12,188**	**851,308**	Missouri..............	5,490	278	17,790
Alabama...............	4,145	268	16,784	Montana..............	1,415	22	1,363
Alaska.................	564	11	796	Nebraska.............	1,769	102	6,276
Arizona................	4,456	171	13,274	Nevada...............	2,027	61	4,450
Arkansas..............	2,529	161	9,091	New Hampshire.....	1,755	68	4,979
California.............	35,936	1,161	103,372	New Jersey..........	7,075	220	16,274
Colorado..............	5,105	135	10,034	New Mexico..........	1,311	30	1,725
Connecticut..........	3,772	152	13,021	New York.............	13,931	412	28,842
Delaware.............	608	30	2,114	North Carolina.......	8,704	467	28,237
District of Columbia...	106	1	56	North Dakota........	691	28	1,800
Florida.................	13,942	353	22,928	Ohio...................	13,390	686	44,919
Georgia...............	7,860	403	24,169	Oklahoma............	3,245	125	7,899
Hawaii.................	743	10	509	Oregon...............	5,309	175	13,226
Idaho..................	2,102	68	4,502	Pennsylvania........	13,245	561	37,417
Illinois.................	12,530	535	37,810	Rhode Island........	1,206	41	2,707
Indiana................	7,964	527	34,102	South Carolina.......	3,990	254	16,346
Iowa...................	3,418	222	14,605	South Dakota........	1,039	47	2,686
Kansas................	2,699	167	11,528	Tennessee...........	5,800	348	21,987
Kentucky..............	3,659	255	15,847	Texas.................	20,781	848	62,853
Louisiana.............	3,050	117	9,827	Utah...................	3,655	146	9,810
Maine..................	1,690	56	3,511	Vermont..............	1,020	30	1,929
Maryland..............	2,859	105	8,068	Virginia...............	4,963	246	15,917
Massachusetts.......	6,008	233	20,427	Washington..........	6,745	257	20,372
Michigan..............	12,196	595	39,166	West Virginia.........	1,075	47	3,030
Minnesota............	6,800	320	22,773	Wisconsin............	8,505	477	31,070
Mississippi............	2,019	148	8,292	Wyoming.............	604	10	802

[1] Covers full- and part-time employees who are on the payroll in the pay period including March 12.

Source: U.S. Census Bureau, County Business Patterns, CB2200CBP, "All Sectors: County Business Patterns, including ZIP Code Business Patterns, by Legal Form of Organization and Employment Size Class for the U.S., States, and Selected Geographies: 2022," <data.census.gov>, accessed June 2024. See also <www.census.gov/programs-surveys/cbp.html>.

Table 1057. Manufactures—Summary by Selected Industry: 2021

[Employee data in thousands (11,206.0 represents 11,206,000); financial data in millions of dollars (727,734 represents $727,734,000,000), except as noted. Based on data from the Annual Survey of Manufactures]

Industry based on shipments	2017 NAICS code [1]	All employees			Production workers [2] (1,000)	Value added by manufactures [3] (mil. dol.)	Value of shipments [4] (mil. dol.)
		Number [2] (1,000)	Payroll				
			Total (mil. dol.)	Per employee (dol.)			
Manufacturing, total [5]................................	31–33	11,206.0	727,734	64,942	7,965.8	2,789,460	6,079,602
Food [5]...	311	1,509.3	79,700	52,805	1,215.4	355,968	904,148
Animal food...............................	3111	57.3	3,544	61,822	43.0	25,044	65,898
Grain and oil seed milling...............	3112	52.9	3,769	71,278	40.0	25,756	105,595
Sugar and confectionery products...........	3113	78.2	4,340	55,502	60.3	18,010	40,174
Fruit and vegetable preserving and specialty food........	3114	152.9	8,550	55,934	124.1	35,945	77,746
Dairy products.............................	3115	151.6	9,358	61,717	111.9	43,037	130,297
Animal slaughtering and processing...........	3116	526.8	25,027	47,504	458.9	92,947	266,997
Seafood product preparation and packaging............	3117	32.0	1,540	48,166	26.1	5,324	14,343
Bakeries and tortilla.........................	3118	253.3	12,026	47,478	194.9	45,401	76,513
Beverage and tobacco products.............	312	224.1	13,594	60,649	132.1	107,192	165,963
Beverage...................................	3121	212.9	12,644	59,395	123.5	63,238	114,937
Textile mills...................................	313	77.9	3,888	49,939	63.3	11,530	26,521
Textile product mills...........................	314	97.0	4,267	44,005	75.4	11,864	23,699
Apparel [5]....................................	315	62.5	2,242	35,875	48.5	5,228	9,411
Cut and sew apparel.......................	3152	47.6	1,736	36,482	37.1	4,148	7,389
Leather and allied products...................	316	25.1	1,041	41,555	19.4	2,462	4,746
Wood products [5]..............................	321	398.9	20,466	51,310	326.7	78,536	154,756
Sawmills and wood preservation...............	3211	81.7	4,645	56,880	70.6	26,152	47,776
Paper..	322	330.4	23,117	69,962	252.7	90,750	198,258
Pulp, paper, and paperboard mills.............	3221	90.8	7,810	85,997	69.1	41,444	75,347
Converted paper products..................	3222	239.6	15,307	63,884	183.6	49,306	122,910
Printing and related support activities...........	323	351.8	19,172	54,490	255.0	46,347	78,051
Petroleum and coal products.................	324	100.4	11,388	113,393	66.8	144,384	610,355
Chemical [5]..................................	325	778.1	66,824	85,876	490.2	472,584	832,277
Basic chemical.............................	3251	145.6	13,870	95,265	92.8	122,857	252,756
Pharmaceutical and medicine...............	3254	266.1	26,042	97,882	153.0	186,130	248,438
Soap, cleaning compound, and toilet preparation........	3256	100.9	6,355	62,991	68.6	48,271	81,118
Plastics and rubber products.................	326	773.4	42,281	54,667	608.2	139,989	273,327
Plastics products...........................	3261	638.1	34,329	53,796	499.9	115,029	228,428
Rubber product.............................	3262	135.3	7,952	58,774	108.3	24,960	44,899
Nonmetallic mineral products.................	327	384.7	23,047	59,905	298.7	80,096	144,233
Glass and glass product....................	3272	81.9	4,620	56,436	63.6	14,730	26,419
Cement and concrete products..............	3273	176.9	10,728	60,626	141.5	37,175	69,520
Primary metal [5]..............................	331	317.9	22,643	71,218	249.2	126,132	280,821
Iron and steel mills and ferroalloy.............	3311	72.6	6,748	92,897	59.3	57,933	118,821
Foundries..................................	3315	96.1	5,834	60,694	76.2	15,200	27,531
Fabricated metal products [5].................	332	1,296.4	78,663	60,677	968.9	217,542	393,280
Forging and stamping.......................	3321	90.4	5,348	59,168	68.2	15,301	31,627
Cutlery and hand tool manufacturing............	3322	31.8	1,880	59,044	23.5	6,560	10,423
Architectural and structural metals............	3323	350.8	20,963	59,754	256.4	58,817	113,646
Boiler, tank, and shipping container............	3324	80.2	5,560	69,330	59.8	17,383	38,281
Machine shops, turned product and screw, nut, and bolt................................	3327	335.9	20,013	59,585	259.7	43,444	68,813
Coating, engraving, heat treating, and allied activities.................................	3328	110.2	6,186	56,124	87.8	17,636	29,556
Machinery [5].................................	333	996.7	68,439	68,666	643.8	197,236	396,517
Agriculture, construction, and mining machinery.....	3331	174.0	11,356	65,265	121.2	41,983	96,197
Industrial machinery.......................	3332	105.8	9,249	87,430	58.6	20,351	38,310
HVAC and commercial refrigeration equipment..........	3334	143.0	7,591	53,104	102.1	26,161	48,853
Metalworking machinery....................	3335	128.5	8,577	66,776	91.9	20,109	32,485
Engine, turbine, and power transmission equipment.....	3336	87.1	6,094	69,967	56.8	18,257	41,449
Computer and electronic products [5]...........	334	758.8	68,311	90,021	353.0	183,550	324,311
Computer and peripheral equipment...........	3341	38.6	3,365	87,057	13.9	9,047	18,602
Communications equipment..................	3342	83.0	7,860	94,737	30.8	16,740	33,536
Semiconductor and other electronic component..........	3344	252.9	21,362	84,481	150.5	55,201	108,001
Navigational, measuring, medical, and control instruments................................	3345	369.3	34,774	94,164	148.8	99,458	158,052
Electrical equipment, appliance, and component [5]........	335	341.2	22,814	66,856	228.8	73,796	143,285
Electrical equipment.......................	3353	114.6	7,723	67,377	74.3	22,021	44,195
Other electrical equipment and component............	3359	134.7	9,688	71,944	85.8	29,621	57,435
Transportation equipment [5].................	336	1,534.2	107,675	70,185	1,081.9	302,448	878,695
Motor vehicle..............................	3361	230.8	17,532	75,952	183.9	76,026	320,054
Motor vehicle parts........................	3363	549.7	30,209	54,955	418.0	82,419	240,786
Aerospace product and parts................	3364	398.0	38,009	95,491	220.4	87,289	185,283
Ship and boat building......................	3366	138.6	9,021	65,090	94.1	22,571	41,716
Furniture and related products [5]..............	337	333.1	16,070	48,248	253.5	41,245	75,707
Miscellaneous [5].............................	339	513.9	32,092	62,445	334.2	100,580	161,242
Medical equipment and supplies..............	3391	270.2	18,849	69,748	171.4	62,293	94,889

[1] North American Industrial Classification System, 2017; see text, Section 15. [2] Includes all full-time and part-time employees on payrolls of operating manufacturing establishments. All employees represents the average of production workers plus all other employees for the payroll period ended nearest the 12th of March. [3] Adjusted value added; takes into account (a) value added by merchandising operations (difference between sales value and cost of merchandise sold without further manufacture, processing, or assembly), plus (b) net change in finished goods and work-in-process inventories between beginning and end of year. [4] Received or receivable net selling values, "free on board" (FOB) plant (exclusive of freight and taxes), of all products shipped as well as all miscellaneous receipts. In the case of multiunit companies, the manufacturer was requested to report the value of products transferred to other establishments of the same company at full economic or commercial value. [5] Includes industries not shown separately.

Source: U.S. Census Bureau, Annual Survey of Manufactures, "Annual Survey of Manufactures: Summary Statistics for Industry Groups and Industries in the U.S.: 2018-2021," December 2022, <data.census.gov/>, accessed June 2023. See also <www.census.gov/programs-surveys/asm.html>.

Table 1058. Manufactures—Summary by State: 2021

[Employment data in thousands (11,206.0 represents 11,206,000); financial data in millions of dollars (727,734 represents $727,734,000,000). Based on data from the Annual Survey of Manufactures. Data are for North American Industry Classification System (NAICS) 2017 codes 31–33. Sum of state totals may not add to U.S. total due to independent rounding. See Appendix III]

State	All employees [1] Number (1,000)	Payroll Total (mil. dol.)	Payroll Per employee (dol.)	Production workers [1] Number (1,000)	Production workers [1] Wages (mil. dol.)	Value added by manufactures [2] Total (mil. dol.)	Value added by manufactures [2] Per production worker (dol.)	Value of shipments [3] (mil. dol.)
United States.............	11,206.0	727,734	64,942	7,965.8	420,636	2,789,460	350,179	6,079,602
Alabama.....................	252.7	14,757	58,403	189.9	9,527	61,511	323,903	153,946
Alaska.......................	11.1	615	55,515	9.4	443	1,889	200,480	6,368
Arizona......................	146.8	10,208	69,526	94.0	4,775	35,149	373,860	67,600
Arkansas....................	149.2	7,940	53,218	119.7	5,566	33,486	279,665	72,751
California...................	1,081.5	83,272	76,997	688.2	38,372	290,205	421,707	565,938
Colorado....................	122.1	8,473	69,395	84.7	4,826	25,969	306,578	55,283
Connecticut................	144.2	11,536	80,022	81.8	4,955	36,663	447,951	60,075
Delaware...................	25.3	1,591	62,989	18.9	988	9,801	517,253	19,276
District of Columbia........	1.2	61	50,509	0.9	45	190	202,787	344
Florida......................	305.2	19,044	62,405	208.0	10,243	64,319	309,258	123,239
Georgia.....................	359.2	20,967	58,375	272.6	13,283	85,810	314,829	189,889
Hawaii......................	10.5	514	48,945	7.1	309	2,351	329,187	5,799
Idaho.......................	60.8	4,022	66,109	46.0	2,616	12,445	270,299	27,250
Illinois......................	496.1	31,745	63,985	359.5	19,002	118,929	330,824	279,567
Indiana.....................	486.4	29,839	61,343	374.5	19,983	128,322	342,612	289,518
Iowa........................	210.5	13,050	62,002	155.2	8,012	56,396	363,448	133,228
Kansas......................	152.9	9,804	64,111	112.2	6,086	35,164	313,457	90,877
Kentucky...................	231.7	13,733	59,260	181.3	9,413	53,918	297,441	142,666
Louisiana...................	109.2	8,555	78,351	78.1	5,299	65,133	833,490	200,768
Maine.......................	48.6	2,958	60,889	36.4	1,961	9,584	263,103	17,271
Maryland....................	93.5	6,769	72,430	61.2	3,426	24,840	405,958	45,222
Massachusetts..............	228.7	17,854	78,061	133.3	7,529	52,568	394,457	94,249
Michigan....................	557.1	34,146	61,294	403.1	21,140	107,640	267,017	258,114
Minnesota..................	297.9	19,945	66,957	204.2	10,957	62,834	307,778	137,450
Mississippi.................	139.1	7,350	52,837	110.4	5,031	35,342	320,235	74,095
Missouri.....................	263.5	16,405	62,264	193.3	10,194	58,071	300,346	127,491
Montana....................	18.0	1,065	59,137	12.9	662	4,589	354,482	14,211
Nebraska...................	94.2	5,429	57,620	73.9	3,763	27,636	374,097	67,550
Nevada.....................	47.2	3,044	64,537	33.5	1,908	10,693	319,586	20,016
New Hampshire.............	63.4	4,366	68,906	42.2	2,255	11,803	279,681	22,421
New Jersey.................	203.3	13,903	68,391	139.8	7,486	51,204	366,339	101,687
New Mexico................	23.4	1,397	59,799	17.0	859	6,085	357,372	15,603
New York...................	373.2	25,101	67,253	253.9	13,699	97,665	384,725	172,573
North Carolina..............	418.6	24,273	57,992	314.6	14,941	109,600	348,423	211,847
North Dakota...............	25.6	1,542	60,236	19.4	1,001	7,384	380,242	18,572
Ohio........................	637.7	39,347	61,698	465.9	24,296	143,808	308,640	321,905
Oklahoma..................	114.8	6,973	60,731	85.9	4,496	28,426	331,090	67,439
Oregon.....................	166.0	11,578	69,736	115.5	6,351	37,295	322,867	72,716
Pennsylvania...............	512.1	31,516	61,545	363.3	18,839	117,147	322,427	234,355
Rhode Island...............	37.2	2,493	66,955	25.8	1,377	7,110	275,649	13,408
South Carolina..............	221.0	13,749	62,221	163.8	8,618	64,113	391,310	127,590
South Dakota...............	43.9	2,426	55,205	32.4	1,560	8,233	254,280	21,110
Tennessee..................	318.0	18,626	58,578	238.5	11,864	76,581	321,110	164,491
Texas.......................	759.6	52,205	68,731	530.1	29,151	272,140	513,348	652,399
Utah........................	131.6	8,172	62,105	91.8	4,622	30,415	331,366	63,995
Vermont....................	28.9	1,876	64,897	19.6	1,003	4,905	250,717	9,585
Virginia.....................	229.0	13,991	61,092	166.0	8,692	61,647	371,448	108,796
Washington.................	249.5	17,966	72,000	169.1	9,794	37,004	218,833	113,611
West Virginia...............	43.8	2,818	64,349	32.7	1,918	12,161	371,698	25,430
Wisconsin...................	451.6	27,963	61,924	327.1	16,995	89,227	272,754	191,431
Wyoming....................	9.5	761	79,663	7.1	503	4,064	572,108	8,585

[1] Includes all full-time and part-time employees on the payrolls of operating manufacturing establishments during the pay period that included March 12. Included are employees on paid sick leave, paid holidays, and paid vacations; not included are proprietors and partners of unincorporated businesses. [2] Value added is derived by subtracting the cost of materials, supplies, containers, fuel, purchased electricity, and contract work from the value of shipments (products manufactured plus receipts for services rendered). The result of this calculation is adjusted by the addition of value added by merchandising operations (i.e., the difference between the sales value and the cost of merchandise sold without further manufacture, processing, or assembly) plus the net change in finished goods and work-in-process between the beginning and end of year inventories. [3] Includes extensive and unmeasurable duplication from shipments between establishments in the same industry classification.

Source: U.S. Census Bureau, Annual Survey of Manufactures, "Annual Survey of Manufactures: Summary Statistics for Industry Groups and Industries in the U.S.: 2018-2021," December 2022, <data.census.gov/>, accessed June 2023. See also <www.census.gov/programs-surveys/asm.html>

Table 1059. Manufacturing Industries—Employees by Industry: 2000 to 2023

[Annual averages of monthly figures (132,011 represents 132,011,000). Minus sign (-) indicates decrease. Covers all full- and part-time employees who worked during, or received pay for, any part of the pay period including the 12th of the month. Based on data from establishment reports. Excludes proprietors, the self-employed, farm workers, unpaid family and volunteer workers, private household workers, and Armed Forces]

Industry	2017 NAICS code [1]	All employees (1,000)					Percent change		
		2000	2010	2020	2022	2023	2000-2010	2010-2020	2020-2023
All industries.....................................	(X)	**132,011**	**130,345**	**142,186**	**152,520**	**156,051**	**-1.3**	**9.1**	**9.8**
Manufacturing...............................	**31–33**	**17,263**	**11,528**	**12,167**	**12,812**	**12,940**	**-33.2**	**5.5**	**6.4**
Percent of all industries......................	(X)	13.1	8.8	8.6	8.4	8.3	(X)	(X)	(X)
Durable goods....	(X)	10,877	7,064	7,573	7,968	8,102	-35.1	7.2	7.0
Wood products [2]	321	615	342	396	428	418	-44.4	15.8	5.6
Sawmills & wood preservation....................	3211	134	82	88	93	92	-38.5	6.6	4.4
Nonmetallic mineral products [2]....................	327	554	371	399	418	421	-33.1	7.7	5.5
Cement & concrete products....................	3273	234	170	194	201	206	-27.4	14.4	5.8
Primary metals [2].....................	331	622	362	354	364	374	-41.7	-2.4	5.7
Iron & steel mills & ferroalloy production.......	3311	135	87	82	82	83	-35.9	-5.5	1.6
Steel products from purchased steel.............	3312	73	52	54	56	60	-28.7	4.0	9.6
Alumina, aluminum & other nonferrous metal production and processing........................	3313,4	197	112	114	119	123	-43.1	2.2	7.9
Foundries...	3315	217	112	103	107	108	-48.4	-7.8	4.5
Fabricated metal products [2]....................	332	1,753	1,282	1,386	1,432	1,454	-26.9	8.1	4.9
Architectural & structural metals.................	3323	428	321	383	401	412	-25.0	19.2	7.7
Machine shops; turned product; screw, nut & bolt............................	3327	365	313	335	339	343	-14.4	7.0	2.5
Coating, engraving, & heat treating metals......	3328	175	122	129	129	130	-30.0	5.4	1.0
Machinery [2]..	333	1,457	996	1,055	1,106	1,135	-31.6	5.9	7.6
Agricultural, construction, & mining machinery..........................	3331	222	208	201	212	221	-6.4	-3.2	9.7
HVAC & commercial refrigeration equipment. ..	3334	194	125	133	142	148	-35.9	6.7	11.5
Metalworking machinery............................	3335	274	155	164	162	162	-43.3	5.5	-0.7
Engine, turbine & power transmission equipment........................	3336	111	92	91	89	93	-17.6	-1.3	2.4
Other general purpose machinery..............	3339	344	226	262	280	286	-34.4	16.0	9.1
Computer & electronic products [2]....................	334	1,820	1,095	1,063	1,090	1,108	-39.9	-2.9	4.2
Computer & peripheral equipment..............	3341	302	158	160	162	163	-47.8	1.3	2.2
Communications equipment....................	3342	239	117	86	86	86	-50.8	-27.1	0.7
Semiconductors & electronic components......	3344	676	369	369	389	395	-45.4	-0.2	7.0
Navigational, measuring, electromedical, and control instruments........	3345	488	406	418	423	433	-16.7	2.8	3.6
Electrical equipment & appliances [2]...............	335	591	360	384	406	415	-39.2	6.9	8.0
Household appliances..........................	3352	106	60	62	69	65	-43.3	2.7	6.2
Electrical equipment.............................	3353	210	136	136	143	147	-35.1	0.3	7.8
Transportation equipment [2].....................	336	2,057	1,333	1,591	1,718	1,791	-35.2	19.3	12.6
Motor vehicles.................................	3361	291	153	206	282	296	-47.6	35.2	43.3
Motor vehicle bodies & trailers.................	3362	183	107	151	172	172	-41.4	40.9	13.7
Motor vehicle parts..............................	3363	840	419	530	552	573	-50.1	26.6	8.1
Aerospace products & parts....................	3364	517	478	507	501	534	-7.5	6.1	5.3
Ship & boat building............................	3366	154	125	140	151	155	-19.1	12.2	10.6
Furniture & related products [2].....................	337	680	357	359	379	358	-47.5	0.6	-0.4
Household & institutional furniture & kitchen cabinets....................	3371	441	223	226	242	228	-49.3	1.3	0.5
Miscellaneous manufacturing....................	339	728	567	586	628	628	-22.1	3.4	7.2
Medical equipment & supplies....................	3391	305	303	317	335	334	-0.7	4.8	5.4
Other miscellaneous manufacturing..............	3399	423	264	269	293	294	-37.6	1.7	9.3
Nondurable goods......................	(X)	6,386	4,464	4,594	4,844	4,838	-30.1	2.9	5.3
Food manufacturing [2].....................	311	1,553	1,451	1,615	1,697	1,725	-6.6	11.3	6.8
Fruit & vegetable preserving & specialty food...	3114	197	173	170	177	169	-12.6	-1.7	-0.3
Dairy products..................................	3115	136	130	153	161	165	-4.2	17.2	8.2
Animal slaughtering & processing................	3116	507	489	537	532	548	-3.5	9.7	2.0
Bakeries & tortilla manufacturing................	3118	306	277	294	328	337	-9.7	6.3	14.6
Textile mills [2].....................................	313	378	119	96	97	91	-68.5	-19.6	-4.9
Fabric mills.....................................	3132	192	53	45	46	43	-72.2	-15.2	-4.9
Textile product mills [2]............................	314	230	119	103	104	99	-48.2	-13.9	-3.5
Textile furnishings mills........................	3141	129	57	45	44	40	-55.7	-21.8	-9.2
Apparel [2]...	315	484	157	90	92	90	-67.6	-42.5	-0.3
Paper & paper products........................	322	605	395	355	363	357	-34.7	-10.1	0.6
Pulp, paper, & paperboard mills...............	3221	191	112	92	89	88	-41.3	-17.7	-5.2
Converted paper products....................	3222	413	282	263	274	269	-31.7	-7.0	2.6
Printing & related support activities..............	323	807	488	375	379	370	-39.6	-23.0	-1.5
Petroleum & coal products......................	324	123	114	108	106	108	-7.5	-5.5	0.3
Chemicals [2].....................................	325	980	787	845	901	900	-19.8	7.5	6.5
Basic chemicals................................	3251	188	142	149	152	156	-24.5	4.8	4.5
Pharmaceuticals & medicines.................	3254	274	277	315	347	346	0.9	13.8	10.0
Soaps, cleaning compounds, & toiletries........	3256	129	102	112	118	116	-20.6	9.3	4.2
Plastics & rubber products [2]........................	326	951	625	707	754	738	-34.3	13.1	4.4
Plastics products..............................	3261	737	502	576	617	603	-31.9	14.8	4.7
Rubber products...............................	3262	214	123	131	137	135	-42.5	6.6	3.0
Beverage, tobacco, and leather and allied products [2].....................	312,6	276	211	300	352	361	-23.5	42.2	20.4
Beverages....................................	3121	175	167	264	314	324	-4.5	58.1	22.9

X Not applicable. [1] Based on the North American Industry Classification System, 2017 (NAICS); see text, this section and Section 15. [2] Includes other industries, not shown separately.

Source: U.S. Bureau of Labor Statistics, Current Employment Statistics, "Employment, Hours, and Earnings—National," <www.bls.gov/ces/data>, accessed March 2024.

Table 1060. Manufacturing Industries—Average Weekly Hours and Average Weekly Overtime Hours of Production Workers: 2000 to 2023

[Covers all full- and part-time employees who worked during, or received pay for, any part of the pay period including the 12th of the month]

Industry	2022 NAICS code [1]	Average weekly hours of production workers					Average weekly overtime hours of production workers				
		2000	2010	2020	2022	2023	2000	2010	2020	2022	2023
Total...............................	31–33	41.3	41.1	40.7	41.0	40.7	4.7	3.8	3.7	4.0	3.6
Durable goods....................	(X)	41.8	41.4	40.9	41.3	41.0	4.8	3.8	3.7	4.1	3.7
Wood products......................	321	41.0	39.1	41.7	41.3	40.6	4.1	3.0	4.3	4.7	3.7
Nonmetallic mineral products.....	327	41.6	41.7	43.4	43.8	44.1	6.1	4.7	5.5	5.6	5.3
Primary metals.....................	331	44.2	43.7	42.1	44.0	43.0	6.5	5.7	4.9	5.9	5.6
Fabricated metal products........	332	41.9	41.4	40.7	41.1	40.9	4.9	3.9	3.5	3.7	3.5
Machinery..........................	333	42.3	42.1	41.0	41.2	40.1	5.1	3.9	3.1	3.9	3.0
Computer and electronic products...........................	334	41.4	40.9	40.0	39.8	39.7	4.6	2.9	2.7	3.0	2.8
Electrical equipment and appliances.......................	335	41.6	41.1	40.7	41.3	40.4	3.7	3.6	3.4	3.5	3.0
Transportation equipment........	336	43.3	42.9	41.6	42.2	42.3	5.6	4.7	4.6	5.1	5.0
Furniture and related products....	337	39.2	38.5	39.6	39.5	39.2	3.5	2.3	2.9	2.9	2.4
Miscellaneous manufacturing.....	339	39.0	38.7	38.4	39.5	38.6	3.1	2.7	2.0	2.9	2.2
Nondurable goods.................	(X)	40.3	40.8	40.5	40.5	40.3	4.5	3.8	3.8	3.7	3.5
Food manufacturing................	311	40.1	40.7	41.3	40.5	40.0	4.9	4.6	4.2	4.1	4.1
Textile mills........................	313	41.4	41.2	43.7	43.2	41.4	4.8	3.3	4.6	(NA)	(NA)
Textile product mills...............	314	38.7	39.0	38.5	37.7	36.8	3.4	2.4	3.0	2.3	1.2
Apparel.............................	315	35.7	36.6	36.6	38.0	38.8	2.1	1.1	2.0	1.9	(NA)
Paper and paper products........	322	42.8	42.9	42.4	42.2	40.3	5.7	4.9	4.8	4.3	3.0
Printing and related support activities.........................	323	39.2	38.2	38.1	38.6	38.2	3.7	2.2	2.4	3.0	2.0
Petroleum and coal products......	324	42.7	43.0	43.8	(NA)	(NA)	6.5	6.4	8.8	(NA)	(NA)
Chemicals..........................	325	42.2	42.2	40.9	40.9	41.4	5.0	3.6	3.8	3.7	3.3
Plastics and rubber products......	326	40.8	41.9	39.5	40.9	41.3	3.9	4.0	3.1	3.6	3.2
Misc. nondurable manufacturing..	329	40.5	37.8	37.1	(NA)	(NA)	5.4	2.3	2.5	(NA)	(NA)

X Not applicable. NA Not available. [1] Based on the North American Industry Classification System (NAICS), 2022; see text, this section and Section 15.

Source: U.S. Bureau of Labor Statistics, Current Employment Statistics, "Employment, Hours, and Earnings — National," <www.bls.gov/ces/data/home.htm>, accessed May 2024.

Table 1061. Indexes of Employment and Hours Worked of All Persons in Manufacturing: 2010 to 2023

[2017=100. Based on Current Employment Statistics and supplemented with Current Population Survey. Employment and hours of all persons include those of paid employees, the self employed (partners and proprietors), and unpaid family workers. See text, Section 12]

Industry	NAICS code [1]	Employment					Hours worked				
		2010	2020	2021	2022	2023	2010	2020	2021	2022	2023
Food manufacturing..............	311	89.9	100.9	102.3	106.2	108.2	89.2	101.4	104.3	105.5	104.9
Beverage and tobacco products..........................	312	68.8	103.0	112.0	125.1	126.3	74.4	97.9	109.5	121.6	124.0
Textile mills........................	313	111.2	86.5	86.8	86.6	79.9	110.7	91.7	93.8	92.7	82.4
Textile product mills..............	314	98.2	87.0	86.3	90.5	81.7	93.3	81.7	83.0	85.2	76.3
Apparel manufacturing...........	315	132.1	75.9	73.6	86.8	79.3	135.3	74.6	74.3	83.5	75.3
Leather and allied products.....	316	96.4	88.6	88.6	93.4	90.1	110.0	93.7	91.6	92.3	93.9
Wood product manufacturing. ..	321	86.4	97.4	102.6	105.9	106.4	84.2	96.3	103.1	104.9	104.6
Paper and paper products.......	322	107.7	96.5	95.0	98.7	97.3	106.6	94.4	96.1	97.9	92.9
Printing and related support activities.........................	323	114.1	85.0	84.7	86.3	84.8	113.0	82.2	85.2	86.1	83.5
Petroleum and coal products....	324	99.7	94.0	91.9	93.1	95.1	98.2	95.7	98.4	99.6	95.5
Chemical manufacturing.........	325	95.0	102.8	105.5	109.3	109.5	96.2	101.4	103.4	108.2	109.1
Plastics and rubber products....	326	87.1	98.9	102.2	105.4	103.1	87.7	95.8	99.7	103.5	101.0
Nonmetallic mineral products. ..	327	90.6	96.4	97.8	100.7	102.3	86.3	95.4	94.9	99.9	101.8
Primary metal products..........	331	98.1	95.6	94.5	99.0	102.1	98.2	93.2	93.5	98.5	100.7
Fabricated metal products.......	332	90.8	97.3	97.1	100.4	102.1	88.7	92.3	93.5	97.0	98.2
Machinery manufacturing........	333	92.5	97.6	97.5	103.0	105.1	91.4	93.6	95.2	101.9	102.0
Computer and electronic products...........................	334	105.7	102.9	102.4	105.0	106.3	106.1	99.5	99.1	102.3	101.8
Electrical equipment and appliances.......................	335	91.9	98.4	101.0	104.0	107.0	88.6	92.5	96.5	99.3	102.6
Transportation equipment.......	336	81.1	96.4	99.9	104.4	108.7	80.6	91.7	96.5	102.7	107.3
Furniture and related products..	337	91.2	91.0	93.9	96.2	91.6	87.5	91.1	95.1	97.0	90.7
Miscellaneous manufacturing. ..	339	95.7	98.1	99.9	105.2	106.2	94.8	94.3	98.5	102.4	104.1

[1] North American Industry Classification System; see text, Section 15.

Source: U.S. Bureau of Labor Statistics, Productivity, OPT Data - Tables, "Labor Productivity and Cost Measures," <bls.gov/productivity/tables/>, accessed August 2024.

Table 1062. Average Hourly Earnings of Production Workers in Manufacturing Industries by State: 2020 to 2023

[In dollars. Data are based on the North American Industry Classification System (NAICS). Based on the Current Employment Statistics Program. Covers full- and part-time employees who received pay for any part of the pay period including the 12th of the month. Excludes proprietors, self-employed, unpaid family or volunteer workers, farm workers, and domestic workers. See source, and Appendix III]

State	2020	2021	2022	2023	State	2020	2021	2022	2023
United States........	**22.80**	**23.81**	**25.07**	**26.38**	Montana.................	20.55	21.04	21.65	23.36
Alabama.................	20.37	21.41	23.22	23.87	Nebraska..............	20.68	21.59	23.49	24.75
Alaska.................	25.64	26.87	26.31	25.21	Nevada.................	20.10	20.53	21.96	22.73
Arizona.................	20.77	21.99	23.66	24.51	New Hampshire.......	22.98	23.77	24.71	25.70
Arkansas................	18.77	19.74	20.35	21.50	New Jersey..........	24.16	24.85	25.65	25.36
California..............	24.06	25.27	26.32	28.28	New Mexico...........	20.28	19.46	21.89	24.07
Colorado...............	26.53	25.41	27.45	30.72	New York.............	23.06	24.29	24.99	25.43
Connecticut............	29.00	28.07	28.09	29.11	North Carolina.........	19.02	19.91	21.18	22.06
Delaware...............	21.24	22.22	24.27	26.59	North Dakota..........	21.33	23.19	25.46	26.42
Florida.................	24.02	24.82	26.61	28.34	Ohio...................	21.67	22.65	24.24	25.57
Georgia.................	21.00	22.28	23.53	23.75	Oklahoma.............	20.08	21.49	21.72	23.78
Hawaii.................	23.48	22.93	24.91	27.15	Oregon................	23.04	23.63	25.27	26.86
Idaho..................	19.60	20.41	22.31	22.86	Pennsylvania..........	22.56	23.57	24.85	25.99
Illinois.................	22.11	22.54	23.96	24.49	Rhode Island..........	20.29	22.01	23.78	24.94
Indiana.................	20.98	21.40	23.31	24.57	South Carolina........	21.87	23.63	24.14	24.95
Iowa...................	20.94	22.51	24.16	24.94	South Dakota..........	19.58	20.31	22.16	23.74
Kansas.................	20.76	20.96	21.92	23.31	Tennessee.............	20.33	21.57	22.49	23.68
Kentucky...............	22.48	23.88	24.35	24.54	Texas..................	23.40	25.80	27.25	28.71
Louisiana...............	22.41	21.62	23.37	26.84	Utah...................	20.92	22.32	25.09	26.38
Maine..................	22.43	22.76	24.10	26.15	Vermont...............	20.65	21.62	23.73	26.00
Maryland...............	22.15	21.97	22.22	25.68	Virginia...............	20.19	21.07	22.20	24.61
Massachusetts........	24.96	25.33	27.00	27.35	Washington............	28.32	28.03	29.89	29.71
Michigan...............	22.51	23.41	25.02	26.27	West Virginia..........	21.79	21.20	22.78	24.36
Minnesota..............	23.69	24.75	26.06	27.50	Wisconsin.............	21.90	22.15	23.62	24.95
Mississippi.............	21.27	20.46	21.02	20.78	Wyoming...............	26.82	27.60	29.46	33.10
Missouri................	22.04	22.93	24.16	25.47	Puerto Rico...........	12.13	12.04	12.79	13.39

Source: U.S. Bureau of Labor Statistics, Current Employment Statistics, "Employment, Hours, and Earnings – National," <www.bls.gov/ces/data>, and "Employment, Hours, and Earnings – State and Metro Area," <www.bls.gov/sae/data>; accessed March 2024.

Table 1063. Manufacturing Full–Time Equivalent (FTE) Employees and Wages by Industry: 2010 to 2022

[120,519 represents 120,519,000. Based on National Income and Product Account tables. Full-time equivalent employees equals the number of employees on full-time schedules plus the number of employees for part-time schedules converted to full-time basis]

Industry	2012 NAICS code [1]	Full-time equivalent (FTE) employees (1,000)				Wage and salary accruals per FTE worker (dol.)			
		2010	2020	2021	2022	2010	2020	2021	2022
Domestic industries, total........	(X)	**120,519**	**133,388**	**137,519**	**143,393**	**52,939**	**71,013**	**75,069**	**77,634**
Manufacturing.........................	**31–33**	**11,223**	**11,844**	**12,087**	**12,523**	**59,997**	**76,457**	**79,555**	**82,629**
Percent of all industries.................	(X)	9.3	8.9	8.8	8.7	113.3	107.7	106.0	106.4
Durable goods...........................	(X)	6,900	7,413	7,539	7,826	63,311	80,463	84,290	87,329
Wood products........................	321	333	389	400	420	38,149	52,593	57,753	61,732
Nonmetallic mineral products..........	327	357	388	395	410	50,628	65,894	68,971	71,979
Primary metals........................	331	353	345	342	359	61,058	74,007	81,059	86,519
Fabricated metal products.............	332	1,249	1,348	1,357	1,404	51,445	62,987	66,295	69,533
Machinery.............................	333	975	1,030	1,044	1,092	62,656	76,704	79,749	83,392
Computer and electronic products......	334	1,079	1,047	1,043	1,071	96,001	139,032	150,852	150,370
Electrical equipment, appliances, and components..........................	335	351	375	385	400	59,438	75,126	78,315	80,234
Motor vehicles, bodies and trailers, and parts..............................	3361–3363	666	881	948	989	57,922	67,152	67,990	72,900
Other transportation equipment........	3364–3365	645	689	672	699	79,421	99,349	100,768	105,741
Furniture and related products.........	337	345	351	365	369	39,980	52,083	54,279	56,936
Miscellaneous manufacturing..........	339	547	570	588	613	56,903	72,576	76,053	78,521
Nondurable goods........................	(X)	4,322	4,431	4,548	4,698	54,706	69,755	71,704	74,799
Food and beverage and tobacco products..........................	311–312	1,561	1,794	1,862	1,940	44,711	58,049	59,563	62,003
Textile mills and textile product mills. ..	313–314	230	191	194	195	39,110	50,805	53,729	55,999
Apparel and leather and allied products.............................	315	179	110	112	114	38,244	50,214	53,309	57,378
Paper products.........................	322	382	347	347	357	61,586	75,587	77,679	81,002
Printing and related support activities..	323	472	367	363	368	45,783	54,921	57,129	60,310
Petroleum and coal products...........	324	109	108	104	104	97,162	124,045	124,162	134,759
Chemical products......................	325	775	832	858	882	84,813	106,707	108,418	112,920
Plastics and rubber products...........	326	615	682	709	738	47,778	60,342	63,817	66,310

X Not applicable. [1] North American Industry Classification System, 2012; see text, Section 15.

Source: U.S. Bureau of Economic Analysis, National Income and Product Accounts, "Table 6.5D. Full-Time Equivalent Employees by Industry," and "Table 6.6D. Wages and Salaries Per Full-Time Equivalent Employee by Industry," <www.bea.gov/itable/>, accessed November 2023.

Table 1064. Manufacturers' Shipments, Inventories, and New Orders: 1995 to 2023

[In billions of dollars (3,480 represents $3,480,000,000,000), except ratio. Data are not seasonally adjusted, except ratios as noted. Based on the Manufacturers' Shipments, Inventories, and Orders (M3) survey. See source for details]

Year	Shipments	Inventories (December 31) [1]	Ratio of inventories to shipments [2]	New orders	Unfilled orders (December 31)
1995	3,480	415	1.41	3,427	443
1996	3,597	421	1.40	3,567	485
1997	3,835	433	1.36	3,780	508
1998	3,900	439	1.37	3,808	492
1999	4,032	453	1.34	3,957	501
2000	4,209	470	1.37	4,161	545
2001	3,970	417	1.33	3,869	506
2002	3,915	412	1.30	3,823	476
2003	4,015	398	1.20	3,976	503
2004	4,309	429	1.17	4,289	555
2005	4,742	461	1.14	4,764	652
2006	5,016	509	1.22	5,090	796
2007	5,319	547	1.22	5,397	946
2008	5,469	529	1.42	5,452	995
2009	4,424	491	1.29	4,206	825
2010	4,911	538	1.28	4,896	870
2011	5,492	589	1.30	5,512	953
2012	5,697	607	1.30	5,710	1,015
2013	5,814	614	1.29	5,899	1,146
2014	5,889	626	1.35	5,953	1,256
2015	5,533	622	1.44	5,433	1,206
2016	5,364	620	1.39	5,296	1,188
2017	5,549	643	1.38	5,492	1,184
2018	5,891	662	1.39	5,822	1,168
2019	5,734	691	1.53	5,561	1,046
2020	5,204	686	1.51	5,151	1,046
2021	6,080	790	1.49	6,164	1,189
2022	6,922	838	1.49	6,941	1,270
2023	6,932	836	1.48	6,994	1,393

[1] Inventories are stated at current cost. [2] Ratio based on December seasonally adjusted inventory data.

Source: U.S. Census Bureau, Manufacturers' Shipments, Inventories, and Orders, "Time Series/Trend Charts," <www.census.gov/manufacturing/m3/index.html>, accessed June 2024.

Table 1065. Ratios of Manufacturers' Inventories to Shipments and Unfilled Orders to Shipments by Industry Group: 2000 to 2023

[Based on the Manufacturers' Shipments, Inventories, and Orders (M3) survey. Ratio based on December seasonally adjusted inventory and unfilled orders data. See source for details]

Industry	2017 NAICS code [1]	2000	2010	2019	2020	2021	2022	2023
INVENTORIES-TO-SHIPMENTS RATIO								
All manufacturing industries	(X)	**1.37**	**1.28**	**1.53**	**1.51**	**1.49**	**1.49**	**1.48**
Durable goods	(X)	1.56	1.63	1.88	1.82	1.89	1.86	1.87
Wood products	321	1.41	1.39	1.38	1.15	1.19	1.22	1.18
Nonmetallic mineral products	327	1.26	1.52	1.36	1.19	1.20	1.27	1.31
Primary metals	331	1.77	1.56	2.04	1.64	1.69	1.79	1.71
Fabricated metals	332	1.56	1.57	1.75	1.69	1.79	1.84	1.77
Machinery	333	2.05	1.86	2.28	2.27	2.30	2.49	2.54
Computers and electronic products	334	1.47	1.58	1.83	1.83	1.93	1.90	1.88
Electrical equipment, appliances, and components	335	1.41	1.47	1.77	1.71	1.84	1.90	1.86
Transportation equipment	336	1.42	1.68	1.92	1.97	2.09	1.83	1.89
Furniture and related products	337	1.36	1.17	1.26	1.27	1.52	1.53	1.50
Miscellaneous products	339	1.83	1.72	2.03	1.87	1.91	1.89	1.92
Nondurable goods	(X)	1.13	0.98	1.18	1.19	1.12	1.14	1.11
Food products	311	0.86	0.79	0.86	0.84	0.87	0.90	0.88
Beverages and tobacco products	312	1.50	1.65	2.07	2.00	2.01	1.84	1.68
Textile mills	313	1.54	1.25	1.43	1.40	1.48	1.70	1.70
Textile product mills	314	1.87	1.67	1.83	1.72	1.86	1.90	1.87
Apparel	315	1.91	1.62	2.18	2.52	2.26	2.62	2.68
Leather and allied products	316	1.88	1.78	2.73	2.45	2.41	2.66	2.35
Paper products	322	1.11	0.98	1.01	0.99	1.03	1.06	1.04
Printing	323	0.78	0.77	0.89	0.92	1.01	0.97	0.92
Petroleum and coal products	324	0.68	0.73	0.83	0.86	0.67	0.73	0.73
Chemical products	325	1.35	1.23	1.61	1.59	1.47	1.49	1.44
Plastics and rubber products	326	1.24	1.20	1.35	1.29	1.35	1.40	1.32
UNFILLED ORDERS-TO-SHIPMENTS RATIO								
All manufacturing industries	(X)	**4.02**	**6.14**	**6.50**	**6.59**	**6.61**	**6.60**	**7.09**
Durable goods	(X)	4.02	6.14	6.50	6.59	6.61	6.60	7.09
Primary metals	331	1.52	1.87	1.52	1.34	1.43	1.45	1.45
Fabricated metals	332	2.13	2.79	3.14	3.47	3.76	3.76	3.65
Machinery	333	2.66	3.82	3.56	4.04	4.33	4.19	3.99
Computers and electronic products	334	4.24	5.92	5.93	6.41	6.26	6.08	5.89
Electrical equipment, appliances, and components	335	1.83	1.96	2.57	3.03	3.44	3.49	3.43
Transportation equipment	336	8.06	14.33	14.09	13.99	14.49	13.70	15.73
Furniture and related products	337	1.29	1.39	1.56	1.87	2.27	1.88	1.83

X Not applicable. [1] Based on the North American Industry Classification System, 2017; see text, this section and Section 15.

Source: U.S. Census Bureau, Manufacturers' Shipments, Inventories, and Orders, "Historical Data," <www.census.gov/manufacturing/m3/historical/timeseries.html>, accessed June 2024.

Table 1066. Value of Manufacturers' Shipments, Inventories, and New Orders by Industry: 2000 to 2023

[In billions of dollars (4,209 represents $4,209,000,000,000). Data are not seasonally adjusted. Based on the Manufacturers' Shipments, Inventories, and Orders (M3) survey. See source for details]

Industry	2017 NAICS code [1]	2000	2010	2015	2020	2021	2022	2023
SHIPMENTS								
All manufacturing industries	**(X)**	**4,209**	**4,911**	**5,533**	**5,204**	**6,080**	**6,922**	**6,932**
Durable goods	(X)	2,374	2,281	2,782	2,623	2,953	3,271	3,373
Wood products	321	94	69	97	118	155	164	160
Nonmetallic mineral products	327	97	90	118	133	144	156	159
Primary metals	331	157	231	229	202	281	324	320
Fabricated metals	332	268	295	349	346	393	427	428
Machinery	333	292	316	381	355	397	440	452
Computers and electronic products	334	511	328	302	308	324	346	353
Electrical equipment, appliances, and components	335	125	110	127	129	143	157	169
Transportation equipment	336	640	636	952	817	879	1,004	1,077
Furniture and related products	337	75	60	74	71	76	82	82
Miscellaneous products	339	115	145	154	144	161	172	173
Nondurable goods	(X)	1,835	2,631	2,751	2,580	3,127	3,651	3,559
Food products	311	435	654	778	827	904	954	956
Beverages and tobacco products	312	112	130	155	156	166	190	211
Textile mills	313	52	30	29	24	27	27	25
Textile product mills	314	34	21	24	21	24	25	24
Apparel	315	60	13	11	8	9	10	10
Leather and allied products	316	10	5	5	4	5	6	6
Paper products	322	165	172	185	182	198	206	208
Printing	323	104	83	82	74	78	87	87
Petroleum and coal products	324	235	628	510	358	610	931	806
Chemical products	325	449	705	737	692	832	915	930
Plastics and rubber products	326	178	189	234	234	273	301	296
INVENTORIES (as of December 31)								
All manufacturing industries	**(X)**	**470**	**538**	**622**	**686**	**790**	**838**	**836**
Durable goods	(X)	298	313	383	419	481	508	514
Wood products	321	10	8	11	13	16	16	16
Nonmetallic mineral products	327	10	11	13	14	15	17	17
Primary metals	331	22	31	32	32	45	46	45
Fabricated metals	332	34	40	47	50	62	64	64
Machinery	333	49	52	65	68	80	91	93
Computers and electronic products	334	63	42	42	47	52	54	54
Electrical equipment, appliances, and components	335	15	14	16	18	22	25	25
Transportation equipment	336	69	90	129	146	154	157	162
Furniture and related products	337	8	6	7	8	9	10	10
Miscellaneous products	339	18	20	21	24	26	27	27
Nondurable goods	(X)	172	225	239	267	308	330	322
Food products	311	32	44	53	60	67	72	70
Beverages and tobacco products	312	14	18	23	27	29	31	30
Textile mills	313	6	3	3	3	3	4	3
Textile product mills	314	5	3	4	3	4	4	4
Apparel	315	9	2	2	2	2	2	2
Leather and allied products	316	2	1	1	1	1	1	1
Paper products	322	15	14	16	15	17	18	18
Printing	323	6	5	5	6	7	7	6
Petroleum and coal products	324	13	43	28	28	38	47	44
Chemical products	325	52	73	81	96	108	111	110
Plastics and rubber products	326	18	19	24	26	33	34	33
NEW ORDERS								
All manufacturing industries	**(X)**	**4,161**	**4,896**	**5,433**	**5,151**	**6,164**	**6,941**	**6,994**
Durable goods	(X)	2,327	2,265	2,682	2,571	3,037	3,290	3,435
Wood products	321	94	(NA)	(NA)	(NA)	(NA)	(NA)	(NA)
Nonmetallic mineral products	327	97	(NA)	(NA)	(NA)	(NA)	(NA)	(NA)
Primary metals	331	154	244	225	202	293	324	320
Fabricated metals	332	270	304	338	354	420	427	429
Machinery	333	295	334	372	363	420	447	448
Computers and electronic products	334	436	270	245	265	267	286	293
Electrical equipment, appliances, and components	335	126	110	127	133	152	160	170
Transportation equipment	336	663	638	932	787	947	1,074	1,203
Furniture and related products	337	75	60	75	72	78	81	81
Miscellaneous products	339	117	(NA)	(NA)	(NA)	(NA)	(NA)	(NA)
Nondurable goods	(X)	1,835	2,631	2,751	2,580	3,127	3,651	3,559

NA Not available. X Not applicable. [1] Based on the North American Industry Classification System, 2017; see text, this section and Section 15.

Source: U.S. Census Bureau, Manufacturers' Shipments, Inventories, and Orders, "Annual Benchmark Data and Benchmark Procedures," <www.census.gov/manufacturing/m3/index.html>, and "Historical Data," <www.census.gov/manufacturing/m3/historical/timeseries.html>; accessed June 2024.

Table 1067. Value of Manufacturers' Shipments, Inventories, and New Orders by Market Grouping: 2000 to 2023

[In billions of dollars (4,209 represents $4,209,000,000,000). Data are not seasonally adjusted. Based on the Manufacturers' Shipments, Inventories, and Orders (M3) survey. See source for details]

Market grouping	2000	2010	2015	2019	2020	2021	2022	2023
SHIPMENTS								
All manufacturing industries	**4,209**	**4,911**	**5,533**	**5,734**	**5,204**	**6,080**	**6,922**	**6,932**
Consumer goods	1,501	2,059	2,257	2,384	2,126	2,535	3,016	2,952
Consumer durable goods	391	323	458	470	436	472	526	540
Consumer nondurable goods	1,109	1,735	1,799	1,914	1,690	2,062	2,491	2,412
Aircraft and parts	112	147	210	180	148	152	173	211
Defense aircraft and parts	25	63	55	53	60	55	55	57
Nondefense aircraft and parts	87	84	155	127	88	97	118	154
Construction materials and supplies	445	444	554	606	593	686	747	747
Motor vehicles and parts	471	401	639	656	570	620	709	738
Computers and related products	110	42	27	20	17	19	21	24
Information technology industries	400	270	258	266	258	271	289	296
Nondefense capital goods	808	728	884	859	765	839	932	986
Excluding aircraft	758	675	779	786	713	780	860	886
Defense capital goods	67	130	112	131	146	144	150	162
INVENTORIES								
(as of December 31)								
All manufacturing industries	**470**	**538**	**622**	**691**	**686**	**790**	**838**	**836**
Consumer goods	128	169	179	206	204	233	251	246
Consumer durable goods	26	21	27	32	30	38	40	39
Consumer nondurable goods	102	148	151	174	173	195	210	207
Aircraft and parts	36	55	79	84	93	90	89	92
Defense aircraft and parts	9	12	11	12	13	13	14	14
Nondefense aircraft and parts	27	43	68	72	80	76	76	78
Construction materials and supplies	49	52	63	73	71	87	91	91
Motor vehicles and parts	22	22	34	40	38	48	50	51
Computers and related products	8	4	4	3	3	3	4	3
Information technology industries	51	36	36	38	37	42	45	45
Nondefense capital goods	127	135	173	185	189	204	218	224
Excluding aircraft	107	100	116	125	123	141	156	160
Defense capital goods	17	21	22	20	21	23	23	24
NEW ORDERS								
All manufacturing industries	**4,161**	**4,896**	**5,433**	**5,561**	**5,151**	**6,164**	**6,941**	**6,994**
Consumer goods	1,502	2,059	2,257	2,385	2,131	2,536	3,016	2,953
Consumer durable goods	393	323	458	471	441	474	525	541
Consumer nondurable goods	1,109	1,735	1,799	1,914	1,690	2,062	2,491	2,412
Aircraft and parts	131	155	184	43	103	202	239	337
Defense aircraft and parts	31	63	50	48	59	58	56	63
Nondefense aircraft and parts	99	91	134	-5	44	145	183	275
Construction materials and supplies	447	451	555	611	603	711	749	747
Motor vehicles and parts	468	403	641	655	574	632	708	738
Computers and related products	108	40	27	20	18	19	21	24
Information technology industries	410	273	251	270	269	272	291	297
Nondefense capital goods	831	748	845	727	733	915	1,005	1,102
Excluding aircraft	768	685	761	788	723	815	868	882
Defense capital goods	80	137	106	134	169	146	151	165

Source: U.S. Census Bureau, Manufacturers' Shipments, Inventories, and Orders, "Historical Data," <www.census.gov/manufacturing/m3/historical/timeseries.html>, accessed June 2024.

Table 1068. Finances and Profits of Manufacturing Corporations: 2005 to 2023

[In billions of dollars (5,411 represents $5,411,000,000,000). Data exclude estimates for corporations with less than $250,000 in assets at time of sample selection; beginning in the 4th quarter 2020, the asset level for inclusion was raised to $5 million]

Item	2005 [1]	2010 [2]	2015 [3]	2016 [3]	2017 [4]	2018 [4]	2019 [4]	2020 [4]	2021 [4]	2022 [4]	2023 [4]
Net sales	5,411	5,756	6,433	6,249	6,552	6,971	6,836	6,068	7,212	8,320	7,990
Net operating profit	359	420	516	502	530	572	528	434	723	835	726
Net profit:											
Before taxes	524	584	612	649	681	720	645	456	1,108	1,143	948
After taxes	401	478	506	541	549	636	584	419	984	1,009	850
Cash dividends	179	180	275	276	290	312	313	310	329	365	380
Net income retained in business	222	298	231	265	259	324	271	109	655	643	469

[1] Based on the North American Industry Classification System (NAICS), 2002. [2] Based on NAICS 2007. [3] Based on NAICS 2012. [4] Based on NAICS 2017.

Source: U.S. Census Bureau, Quarterly Financial Report (QFR) Manufacturing, Mining, Wholesale Trade, and Selected Service Industries, "Time Series/Trend Charts," <www.census.gov/econ/qfr>, accessed April 2024.

Table 1069. Manufacturing Corporations—Selected Finances: 2000 to 2023

[In billions of dollars (4,548 represents $4,548,000,000,000). Data are not necessarily comparable from year to year due to changes in accounting procedures, industry classifications, and other changes in methodology; for details, see source. Through 2000, based on Standard Industrial Classification code; beginning 2001, based on North American Industry Classification System; see text, Section 15. Minus sign (-) indicates loss]

Year	All manufacturing corporations			Durable goods			Nondurable goods		
		Profits [1]			Profits [1]			Profits [1]	
	Sales	Before taxes	After taxes	Sales	Before taxes	After taxes	Sales	Before taxes	After taxes
2000..............	4,548	381	275	2,457	191	132	2,091	190	144
2001 [2].............	4,295	83	36	2,321	-69	-76	1,974	152	112
2002..............	4,216	195	135	2,261	46	22	1,956	150	113
2003..............	4,397	306	237	2,283	118	88	2,114	188	149
2004..............	4,934	447	348	2,537	200	157	2,397	248	192
2005..............	5,411	524	401	2,731	211	161	2,681	313	240
2006..............	5,783	605	470	2,910	249	193	2,873	356	278
2007..............	6,060	603	443	3,016	247	159	3,044	356	283
2008..............	6,374	388	266	2,970	98	43	3,405	290	223
2009..............	5,110	361	286	2,427	84	55	2,683	276	232
2010..............	5,756	584	478	2,708	287	232	3,048	297	245
2011..............	6,486	722	594	2,927	335	284	3,558	387	310
2012..............	6,668	676	564	3,102	303	260	3,567	373	304
2013..............	6,743	722	601	3,178	358	294	3,566	365	308
2014..............	6,903	745	609	3,342	378	308	3,561	367	301
2015..............	6,433	612	506	3,367	324	265	3,065	289	241
2016..............	6,249	649	541	3,320	333	273	2,929	316	268
2017..............	6,552	681	549	3,403	373	273	3,149	308	276
2018..............	6,971	720	636	3,611	399	356	3,359	321	280
2019..............	6,836	645	584	3,556	359	330	3,280	286	255
2020..............	6,068	456	419	3,219	322	296	2,849	134	123
2021..............	7,212	1,108	984	3,659	625	561	3,553	482	423
2022..............	8,320	1,143	1,009	3,984	552	488	4,336	591	521
2023..............	7,990	948	850	4,009	539	487	3,980	409	363

[1] Beginning 1998, profits before and after income taxes reflect inclusion of minority stockholders' interest in net income before and after income taxes. [2] Beginning 2001, data reported based on the North American Industry Classification System.

Source: U.S. Census Bureau, Quarterly Financial Report (QFR) Manufacturing, Mining, Wholesale Trade, and Selected Service Industries, "Time Series/Trend Charts," <www.census.gov/econ/qfr/index.html>, accessed April 2024.

Table 1070. Motor Vehicle Manufactures—Summary by Selected Industry: 2021

[56,643 represents $56,643,000,000. Based on the Annual Survey of Manufactures; see Appendix III]

Industry	2017 NAICS code [1]	All employees [2]			Production workers [2]	Value of product shipments [3] (mil. dol.)
			Payroll			
		Number	Total (mil. dol.)	Payroll per employee (dol.)		
Motor vehicle manufacturing, total.....................	**3361-3363**	**937,900**	**56,643**	**60,394**	**729,083**	**620,402**
Motor vehicle, total...........................	3361	230,830	17,532	75,952	183,880	320,054
Automobile and light duty motor vehicle...................	33611	199,581	15,631	78,318	159,044	296,049
Automobile...............................	336111	71,870	5,776	80,361	50,335	85,557
Light truck and utility vehicle.............................	336112	127,711	9,855	77,169	108,709	210,492
Heavy duty truck...........................	33612	31,249	1,901	60,838	24,836	24,006
Motor vehicle body and trailer.......................	3362	157,372	8,903	56,570	127,213	59,561
Motor vehicle body...........................	336211	47,446	2,619	55,208	36,761	15,766
Truck trailer................................	336212	38,333	1,947	50,803	31,632	12,857
Motor home................................	336213	11,373	718	63,150	8,670	5,927
Travel trailer and camper...................	336214	60,220	3,617	60,071	50,150	25,010
Motor vehicle parts............................	3363	549,698	30,209	54,955	417,990	240,786
Motor vehicle gasoline engine and engine parts..........	33631	57,697	3,578	62,017	43,699	34,321
Motor vehicle electrical and electronic equipment........	33632	56,614	3,135	55,376	41,191	23,874
Motor vehicle steering and suspension....................	33633	33,813	1,935	57,216	23,296	14,217
Motor vehicle brake system........................	33634	19,447	1,004	51,649	14,462	9,172
Motor vehicle transmission and power train parts........	33635	77,309	4,748	61,410	60,089	41,094
Motor vehicle seating and interior trim.....................	33636	65,638	3,090	47,075	50,941	24,943
Motor vehicle metal stamping...........................	33637	99,139	5,437	54,846	78,257	33,945
Other motor vehicle parts......................	33639	140,040	7,281	51,995	106,056	59,220

[1] North American Industry Classification System, 2017; see text, Section 15. [2] Includes all full-time and part-time employees on the payrolls of operating manufacturing establishments during any part of the pay period that included the 12th of the month specified on the report form. Included are employees on paid sick leave, paid holidays, and paid vacations; not included are proprietors and partners of unincorporated businesses. [3] Includes extensive and unmeasurable duplication from shipments between establishments in the same industry classification.

Source: U.S. Census Bureau, Annual Survey of Manufactures, "Annual Survey of Manufactures: Summary Statistics for Industry Groups and Industries in the U.S.: 2018-2021," <data.census.gov/>, accessed June 2023.

Table 1071. Motor Vehicle Manufactures—Employees, Payroll, and Shipments by Major Producing State: 2021

[17,531,974 represents $17,531,974,000. Industry based on the 2017 North American Industry Classification System (NAICS); see text, Section 15. See footnote 3, Table 1070 for information regarding shipments. Based on the Annual Survey of Manufactures; see Appendix III]

State	Motor vehicle manufacturing (NAICS 3361)			Motor vehicle parts manufacturing (NAICS 3363)		
	Employees	Payroll ($1,000)	Value of shipments ($1,000)	Employees	Payroll ($1,000)	Value of shipments ($1,000)
United States [1]	230,830	17,531,974	320,054,428	549,698	30,208,642	240,786,351
Alabama	12,789	1,013,925	27,003,775	28,259	1,393,371	15,639,832
Alaska	([2])	(D)	(D)	([2])	(D)	(D)
Arizona	27	2,218	34,612	1,905	100,950	807,143
Arkansas	([2])	692	(D)	4,871	233,288	1,615,798
California	22,477	(D)	(D)	13,404	807,655	5,179,745
Colorado	([2])	(D)	(D)	1,185	74,456	495,996
Connecticut	([2])	(D)	(D)	([8])	(D)	(D)
Delaware	([2])	(D)	(D)	([4])	(D)	28,104
Florida	1,365	83,297	384,676	2,721	135,680	1,018,310
Georgia	([8])	(D)	(D)	14,637	764,263	8,698,619
Hawaii	(NA)	(NA)	(NA)	([2])	(D)	(D)
Idaho	([4])	(D)	(D)	305	(D)	(D)
Illinois	12,738	849,565	12,736,918	25,950	1,321,971	8,852,869
Indiana	19,512	1,365,390	36,405,604	58,768	3,316,287	24,665,247
Iowa	([3])	(D)	(D)	4,934	199,152	1,333,806
Kansas	([7])	(D)	(D)	2,185	120,671	831,274
Kentucky	23,047	1,701,108	31,994,654	36,123	1,810,948	15,242,123
Louisiana	(NA)	(NA)	(NA)	310	(D)	(D)
Maine	([3])	(D)	(D)	([4])	(D)	(D)
Maryland	([2])	(D)	(D)	687	36,228	(D)
Massachusetts	([3])	(D)	(D)	647	35,083	(D)
Michigan	37,501	2,856,647	54,799,882	116,262	6,708,789	49,146,681
Minnesota	1,548	84,219	770,680	2,463	134,206	804,192
Mississippi	([9])	(D)	(D)	5,179	266,559	2,036,642
Missouri	12,712	(D)	(D)	11,809	633,693	4,738,574
Montana	([3])	(D)	(D)	([3])	(D)	26,451
Nebraska	([3])	(D)	(D)	4,288	213,978	1,572,540
Nevada	80	(D)	(D)	264	(D)	(D)
New Hampshire	([2])	(D)	(D)	1,427	89,543	391,019
New Jersey	([2])	(D)	(D)	988	61,810	320,558
New Mexico	(NA)	(NA)	(NA)	([3])	(D)	(D)
New York	40	2,792	(D)	10,116	619,334	4,058,609
North Carolina	([8])	(D)	(D)	18,543	990,610	9,372,632
North Dakota	([5])	(D)	(D)	687	29,245	138,568
Ohio	23,463	1,736,780	26,851,717	70,477	4,042,938	30,027,471
Oklahoma	([7])	(D)	(D)	984	53,718	233,057
Oregon	([6])	(D)	(D)	796	53,386	282,977
Pennsylvania	([8])	(D)	(D)	7,131	332,804	2,576,091
Rhode Island	(NA)	(NA)	(NA)	([4])	(D)	(D)
South Carolina	12,934	971,357	21,329,590	18,973	1,074,120	10,300,493
South Dakota	([5])	(D)	(D)	762	40,094	197,181
Tennessee	10,738	889,712	13,472,451	39,253	2,127,062	20,573,738
Texas	9,859	810,713	(D)	16,173	859,648	6,628,444
Utah	([3])	(D)	(D)	3,472	177,310	1,906,750
Vermont	([2])	(D)	(D)	([5])	(D)	(D)
Virginia	([8])	(D)	(D)	3,875	176,663	(D)
Washington	([6])	(D)	(D)	2,209	121,575	496,815
West Virginia	([5])	(D)	(D)	3,241	203,125	2,790,172
Wisconsin	([7])	(D)	(D)	9,876	561,829	5,120,427
Wyoming	([2])	(D)	(D)	([3])	1,933	8,449

D Withheld to avoid disclosing data on individual companies; data are included in higher level totals. NA Not available. [1] Includes states not shown separately. [2] 0 to 19 employees. [3] 20 to 99 employees. [4] 100 to 249 employees. [5] 250 to 499 employees. [6] 500 to 999 employees. [7] 1,000 to 2,499 employees. [8] 2,500 to 4,999 employees. [9] 5,000 to 9,999 employees.

Source: U.S. Census Bureau, Annual Survey of Manufactures, "Annual Survey of Manufactures: Summary Statistics for Industry Groups and Industries in the U.S.: 2018-2021," <data.census.gov/>, accessed July 2023.

Table 1072. General Aviation Airplane Shipments and Billings: 1990 to 2023

[2,008 represents $2,008,000,000. Data are for U.S. manufactured airplanes. Totals may not add up due to rounding]

Type of airplane	1990	2000	2010	2018	2019	2020	2021	2022	2023
Companies reporting	**14**	**15**	**12**	**18**	**18**	**18**	**17**	**16**	**16**
Airplane units shipped (number)	**1,144**	**2,816**	**1,334**	**1,746**	**1,771**	**1,555**	**1,686**	**1,954**	**2,104**
Total piston	695	1,913	746	829	883	885	905	1,026	1,136
Single-engine	608	1,810	679	771	825	854	890	1,005	1,113
Multi-engine	87	103	67	58	58	31	15	21	23
Total turbine	449	903	588	917	888	670	781	928	968
Turboprop	281	315	224	444	385	317	376	440	475
Business jet	168	588	364	473	503	353	405	488	493
Factory net billings (mil. dol.)	**2,008**	**8,558**	**7,875**	**11,598**	**13,972**	**13,972**	**10,793**	**11,385**	**11,284**
Total piston	92	446	368	466	513	(NA)	(NA)	(NA)	(NA)
Single-engine	68	(NA)	(NA)	(NA)	(NA)	(NA)	(NA)	(NA)	(NA)
Multi-engine	24	(NA)	(NA)	(NA)	(NA)	(NA)	(NA)	(NA)	(NA)
Total turbine	1,916	8,112	7,506	11,132	13,459	(NA)	(NA)	(NA)	(NA)
Turboprop	644	934	724	1,151	1,006	(NA)	(NA)	(NA)	(NA)
Business jet	1,272	7,178	6,782	9,981	12,453	(NA)	(NA)	(NA)	(NA)

NA Not available.

Source: General Aviation Manufacturers Association, *2019 Databook* ©, 2020, and earlier reports; and "2023 Market Overview and Historical Data ©," <gama.aero/facts-and-statistics/statistical-databook-and-industry-outlook/annual-data/>, accessed August 2024.

Table 1073. Beverage Manufacturing Industry—Brewery, Distillery, and Winery Establishments and Employment: 2010 to 2022

[Beverage manufacturer data are from the Quarterly Census of Employment and Wages (QCEW). Covers North American Industry Classification System (NAICS) 31212, 31213, 31214, and 31211]

Industry characteristic	2010	2014	2015	2016	2017	2018	2019	2020	2021	2022
Establishments (number):										
Breweries	527	1,616	2,190	2,843	3,509	4,156	4,733	5,093	5,452	5,772
Wineries	2,616	3,560	3,848	4,083	4,343	4,643	4,845	5,014	5,257	5,526
Distilleries	145	424	558	675	805	964	1,115	1,248	1,424	1,606
Soft drink and ice manufacturing	1,845	1,864	1,858	1,969	2,053	2,065	2,079	2,119	2,230	2,416
Employment (number):										
Breweries	24,864	40,101	48,401	58,580	68,148	77,911	86,668	79,457	94,107	105,352
Wineries	40,830	52,879	57,003	60,436	64,212	67,832	70,596	63,817	70,228	75,836
Distilleries	7,252	10,579	11,075	12,207	13,759	15,839	17,699	18,148	21,701	25,182
Soft drink and ice manufacturing	94,225	93,333	94,334	102,793	104,743	103,124	101,550	101,533	104,604	106,307
Average weekly wages (in dollars):										
Breweries	1,321	1,129	1,163	969	906	866	857	924	906	906
Wineries	773	803	833	846	861	871	889	981	1,005	1,020
Distilleries	1,352	1,415	1,462	1,362	1,300	1,279	1,230	1,298	1,266	1,321
Soft drink and ice manufacturing	938	980	1,020	1,028	1,044	1,079	1,101	1,168	1,211	1,262

Source: U.S. Bureau of Labor Statistics, Quarterly Census of Employment and Wages, "Employment and Wages Data Viewer," <www.bls.gov/cew/home.htm>, accessed March 2024.

Section 22
Wholesale and Retail Trade

This section presents statistics relating to the distributive trades, specifically wholesale trade and retail trade. Data shown for the trades are classified by kind of business and cover sales, establishments, employees, payrolls, and other items. The principal sources of these data are from the U.S. Census Bureau and include the Economic Census, annual and monthly surveys, and the County Business Patterns program. These data are supplemented by several tables from trade associations, such as the National Automobile Dealers Association.

Data on wholesale and retail trade are also covered in several other sections. For instance, employment and earnings data appear in Section 12, Labor Force, Employment, and Earnings; gross domestic product of the industry (Table 708) appears in Section 13, Income, Expenditures, Poverty, and Wealth; and financial data from the quarterly *Statistics of Income Bulletin*, published by the Internal Revenue Service, appear in Section 15, Business Enterprise.

Censuses—Censuses of wholesale trade and retail trade have been taken at various intervals since 1929. Beginning with the 1967 Economic Census, legislation provides for a census to be conducted every 5 years (for years ending in "2" and "7"). The industries covered in the censuses and surveys of business are defined in the North American Industry Classification System (NAICS). Retail trade refers to places of business primarily engaged in retailing merchandise to the general public; and wholesale trade, to establishments primarily engaged in selling goods to other businesses and normally operating from a warehouse or office that have little or no display of merchandise. Census Bureau tables in this section primarily utilize the 2012 or 2017 NAICS codes. NAICS codes are reviewed every 5 years to identify areas for revision, so that the classification system can keep pace with the changing economy. For information on this system and how it affects the comparability of wholesale and retail statistics historically, see text, Section 15, Business Enterprise, and especially the Census Bureau Web site at <www.census.gov/naics/>.

The 2012 and 2017 Economic Censuses have three series of publications for these two sectors: 1) subject series with reports such as product lines and establishment and firm sizes, 2) geographic reports with individual reports for each state, and 3) industry series with individual reports for industry groups. Data from the 2022 Economic Census are being released on a flow basis between January 2024 and March 2026. For information on these series, see the Census Bureau Web site at <www.census.gov/programs-surveys/economic-census.html>.

Current surveys—Current sample surveys conducted by the Census Bureau cover various aspects of wholesale and retail trade. Its *Monthly Retail Trade* release at <www.census.gov/retail/index.html> contains monthly estimates of sales, inventories, and inventory/sales ratios for the United States, by kind of business. Annual figures on retail sales, year-end inventories, purchases, accounts receivable, and gross margins by kind of business are located on the Census Bureau Web site at <www.census.gov/programs-surveys/arts.html>.

Statistics from the Census Bureau's monthly wholesale trade survey include national estimates of sales, inventories, and inventory/sales ratios for merchant wholesalers excluding manufacturers' sales branches and offices. Data are presented by major summary groups "durable and nondurable," and 4-digit NAICS industry groups. Merchant wholesalers excluding manufacturers' sales branches and offices are those wholesalers who take title to the goods they sell (e.g., jobbers, exporters, importers, industrial distributors). These data, based on reports submitted by a sample of firms, appear in the *Monthly Wholesale Trade Report*. This report includes monthly sales, inventories, and inventories/sales ratios and data on annual sales, inventories, and year-end inventories/sales ratios. The *Annual Wholesale Trade Report* provides data on merchant wholesalers excluding manufacturers' sales branches and offices as well as summary data for all merchant wholesalers. This report also provides separate data for manufacturers' sales branches and offices, and electronic markets, agents, brokers, and commission merchants. Included in the *Annual Wholesale Trade Report* are data on annual sales, year-end inventories, inventories/sales ratios, operating expenses, purchases, and gross margins. These reports are available on the Census Bureau Web site at <www.census.gov/wholesale/index.html>.

E-commerce—Electronic commerce (or e-commerce) is the sale of goods and services over the internet and extranet, electronic data interchange (EDI) network, electronic mail, or other online systems. Payment may or may not be made online. E-commerce data are collected in four separate Census Bureau surveys. These surveys use different measures of economic activity such as shipments for manufacturing, sales for wholesale and retail trade, and revenues for service industries. Data can be found at <www.census.gov/programs-surveys/e-stats.html>. Consequently, measures of total economic and e-commerce activity vary by economic sector, are conceptually and definitionally different, and therefore, are not additive. This edition has several tables on e-commerce sales, such as Tables 1077, 1087, and 1088 in this section; and Table 1298 in Section 27, Accommodation, Food Services, and Other Services.

Statistical reliability—For a discussion of statistical collection and estimation, sampling procedures, and measures of statistical reliability applicable to Census Bureau data, see Appendix III.

Table 1074. Wholesale and Retail Trade—Establishments, Sales, Payroll, and Employees: 2022

[In units as indicated (11,644 represents $11,644,000,000,000). Covers establishments with payroll. Based on data from the Economic Census; see Appendix III]

Kind of business	2022 NAICS code [1]	Establishments (number)	Sales (bil. dollars)	Annual payroll (bil. dollars)	Paid employees (1,000)
Wholesale trade	**42**	**376,526**	**11,644**	**514**	**6,247**
Wholesale trade, durable goods	423	219,992	4,861	312	3,634
Wholesale trade, nondurable goods	424	121,528	6,054	186	2,362
Wholesale electronic markets and agents and brokers	425	35,006	728	16	250
Retail trade	**44-45**	**1,041,555**	**6,969**	**615**	**17,140**
Motor vehicle and parts dealers	441	121,964	1,590	129	2,068
Building material and garden equipment and supplies dealers	444	78,123	550	55	1,458
Food and beverage retailers	445	160,962	975	99	3,476
Furniture, home furnishings, electronics, and appliance retailers	449	77,242	352	33	773
General merchandise retailers	455	62,313	1,303	129	3,998
Health and personal care retailers	456	99,085	648	47	1,147
Gasoline stations and fuel dealers	457	120,805	762	31	1,102
Clothing, clothing accessories, shoe, and jewelry retailers	458	130,550	394	42	1,581
Sporting goods, hobby, musical instrument, book and miscellaneous retailers	459	190,511	395	49	1,536

[1] North American Industrial Classification System, 2022; see text, Section 15.

Source: U.S. Census Bureau, "EC2200BASIC: All Sectors: Summary Statistics for the U.S.: 2022," <data.census.gov>, accessed July 2024.

Table 1075. Wholesale Trade—Nonemployer Firms and Receipts by Industry Type: 2021

[40,777,769 represents $40,777,769,000. Includes only firms subject to federal income tax. Nonemployers are businesses with no paid employees. Each distinct business income tax return filed by a nonemployer business is counted as a firm]

Industry type	2017 NAICS code [1]	Firms				Receipts ($1,000)
		Total	Corporations [2]	Individual proprietorships [3]	Partnerships [4]	
Wholesale trade, total	**42**	**387,165**	**66,640**	**291,581**	**28,944**	**40,777,769**
Durable goods merchant wholesalers	**423**	**184,103**	**35,292**	**134,048**	**14,763**	**20,711,240**
Motor vehicle and motor vehicle parts and supplies merchant wholesalers	4231	15,775	3,073	11,645	1,057	2,417,496
Furniture and home furnishing merchant wholesalers	4232	10,874	1,727	8,424	723	1,119,762
Lumber and other construction materials merchant wholesalers	4233	6,804	1,302	4,860	642	911,903
Professional and commercial equipment and supplies merchant wholesalers	4234	10,853	2,222	7,521	1,110	1,277,092
Metal and mineral (except petroleum) merchant wholesalers	4235	2,244	510	1,561	173	355,834
Household appliance and electrical and electronic goods merchant wholesalers	4236	8,222	2,416	5,023	783	1,084,662
Hardware and plumbing and heating equipment and supplies merchant wholesalers	4237	3,763	892	2,536	335	452,005
Machinery, equipment, and supplies merchant wholesalers	4238	16,185	4,320	10,171	1,694	2,347,252
Miscellaneous durable goods merchant wholesalers	4239	109,383	18,830	82,307	8,246	10,745,234
Nondurable goods merchant wholesalers	**424**	**138,643**	**23,289**	**104,252**	**11,102**	**14,411,768**
Paper and paper product merchant wholesalers	4241	3,906	768	2,877	261	423,113
Drugs and druggists' sundries merchant wholesalers	4242	2,353	554	1,506	293	242,269
Apparel, piece goods, and notions merchant wholesalers	4243	26,158	3,446	21,149	1,563	1,793,138
Grocery and related products merchant wholesalers	4244	26,212	5,244	18,684	2,284	4,127,106
Farm product raw material merchant wholesalers	4245	5,572	574	4,587	411	620,283
Chemical and allied products merchant wholesalers	4246	2,894	837	1,707	350	429,952
Petroleum and petroleum products merchant wholesalers	4247	1,957	413	1,325	219	265,206
Beer, wine, and distilled alcoholic beverage merchant wholesalers	4248	6,331	863	4,404	1,064	651,345
Miscellaneous nondurable goods merchant wholesalers	4249	63,260	10,590	48,013	4,657	5,859,356
Wholesale electronic markets and agents and brokers	**425**	**64,419**	**8,059**	**53,281**	**3,079**	**5,654,761**
Business to business electronics markets	42511	9,376	1,260	7,559	557	900,413
Wholesale trade agents and brokers	42512	55,043	6,799	45,722	2,522	4,754,348

[1] North American Industry Classification System, 2017; see text, Section 15. [2] A legally incorporated business under state laws. [3] Also referred to as "sole proprietorship," an unincorporated business with a sole owner. Includes self-employed persons. [4] An unincorporated business where two or more persons join to carry on a trade or business with each having a shared financial interest in the business.

Source: U.S. Census Bureau, Nonemployer Statistics, "All Sectors: Nonemployer Statistics by Legal Form of Organization and Receipts Size Class for the U.S., States, and Selected Geographies: 2021," <data.census.gov>, accessed March 2024.

Table 1076. Wholesale Trade—Establishments, Employees, and Payroll: 2021 and 2022

[390.8 represents 390,800. Covers establishments with payroll. Excludes self-employed individuals, employees of private households, railroad employees, agricultural production employees, and most government employees. For statement on methodology, see Appendix III]

Kind of business	NAICS code [1]	Establishments (1,000) 2021	2022	Employees [2] (1,000) 2021	2022	Payroll (bil. dol.) 2021	2022
Wholesale trade, total..........................	**42**	**390.8**	**388.7**	**5,926**	**6,143**	**497.7**	**535.2**
Merchant wholesalers, durable goods.........................	423	230.2	228.8	3,458	3,559	303.2	326.4
Motor vehicle and motor vehicle parts and supply merchant wholesalers...	4231	22.7	22.7	405	417	26.9	29.2
Furniture and home furnishing merchant wholesalers......	4232	12.2	12.0	156	166	11.2	12.2
Lumber and other construction materials merchant wholesalers...	4233	18.2	17.9	266	266	19.5	20.7
Professional and commercial equipment and supplies merchant wholesalers...	4234	34.3	33.7	653	668	71.6	75.5
Metal and mineral (except petroleum) merchant wholesalers...	4235	9.1	8.9	141	144	11.2	12.3
Household appliances and electrical and electronic goods merchant wholesalers...................	4236	27.0	26.4	503	517	61.7	64.8
Hardware, plumbing and heating equipment and supplies merchant wholesalers...........................	4237	19.9	20.3	268	277	20.4	22.9
Machinery, equipment, and supplies merchant wholesalers...	4238	55.3	54.9	750	767	58.3	64.4
Miscellaneous durable goods merchant wholesalers.......	4239	31.6	32.1	315	337	22.5	24.5
Merchant wholesalers, nondurable goods.....................	424	123.9	123.7	2,228	2,334	178.5	191.3
Paper and paper product merchant wholesalers............	4241	8.2	7.8	133	131	9.0	9.7
Drugs and druggists' sundries merchant wholesalers......	4242	10.3	10.0	307	312	44.5	45.6
Apparel, piece goods and notions merchant wholesalers..	4243	13.8	13.7	164	173	12.2	13.0
Grocery and related product merchant wholesalers.........	4244	34.7	34.9	784	847	50.4	55.6
Farm product raw material merchant wholesalers..........	4245	6.1	6.2	62	66	4.2	4.5
Chemical and allied products merchant wholesalers.......	4246	11.9	11.7	158	163	14.1	15.2
Petroleum and petroleum products merchant wholesalers...	4247	6.3	6.3	97	100	8.8	9.8
Beer, wine, and distilled alcoholic beverages................	4248	4.7	4.8	201	211	14.6	15.9
Miscellaneous nondurable goods merchant wholesalers...	4249	27.8	28.3	322	333	20.6	22.1
Wholesale electronic markets and agents and brokers......	425	36.7	36.2	240	250	16.1	17.5

[1] Data based on North American Industry Classification System (NAICS) 2017. See text, Section 15. [2] Covers full- and part-time employees who are on the payroll in the pay period including March 12.

Source: U.S. Census Bureau, County Business Patterns, CB2200CBP, "County Business Patterns, including ZIP Code Business Patterns, by Legal Form of Organization and Employment Size Class for the U.S., States, and Selected Geographies: 2022," <data.census.gov>, accessed June 2024. See also <www.census.gov/programs-surveys/cbp.html>.

Table 1077. Merchant Wholesale Trade Sales—Total and E-Commerce: 2022

[8,056,099 represents $8,056,099,000,000. Covers only businesses with paid employees. Excludes manufacturers' sales branches and offices. Based on the Annual Wholesale Trade Survey; see Appendix III]

Kind of business	NAICS code [1]	Value of sales (mil. dol.) Total	E-commerce [2]	E-commerce as percent of total sales	Percent distribution of e-commerce sales
Total merchant wholesale trade...............................	**42**	**8,056,099**	**2,300,642**	**28.6**	**100.0**
Durable goods...	**423**	**3,771,544**	**967,872**	**25.7**	**42.1**
Motor vehicles, parts and supplies.........................	4231	554,818	226,758	40.9	9.9
Furniture and home furnishings.............................	4232	113,138	32,254	28.5	1.4
Lumber and other construction materials.................	4233	252,420	(S)	(S)	(S)
Professional and commercial equipment and supplies..........	4234	606,303	181,791	30.0	7.9
Computers and peripheral equipment and software............	42343	309,262	96,164	31.1	4.2
Medical, dental, and hospital equipment and supplies.........	42345	181,460	(S)	(S)	(S)
Metals and minerals (except petroleum)...................	4235	265,775	(S)	(S)	(S)
Household appliances and electrical and electronic goods.....	4236	800,383	274,785	34.3	11.9
Hardware, plumbing and heating equipment...................	4237	230,962	47,728	20.7	2.1
Machinery, equipment and supplies...........................	4238	590,933	84,597	14.3	3.7
Miscellaneous durable goods.................................	4239	356,812	64,912	18.2	2.8
Nondurable goods...	**424**	**4,284,555**	**(S)**	**(S)**	**(S)**
Paper and paper products...................................	4241	103,493	(S)	(S)	(S)
Drugs and druggists' sundries..............................	4242	911,700	(S)	(S)	(S)
Apparel, piece goods and notions...........................	4243	170,090	47,227	27.8	2.1
Groceries and related products.............................	4244	862,035	(S)	(S)	(S)
Farm product raw materials.................................	4245	324,671	21,770	6.7	0.9
Chemical and allied products...............................	4246	169,352	(S)	(S)	(S)
Petroleum and petroleum products.........................	4247	1,147,008	(S)	(S)	(S)
Beer, wine, and distilled alcoholic beverages....................	4248	191,095	34,877	18.3	1.5
Miscellaneous nondurable goods...........................	4249	405,111	(S)	(S)	(S)

S Figure does not meet publication standards. [1] North American Industry Classification System, 2012. See text, Section 15. [2] The total quantity response rate for NAICS code 42 e-commerce sales at the "merchant wholesalers, except manufacturers' sales branches and offices" level was 37.3 percent. Data users should use caution when drawing conclusions from these estimates.

Source: U.S. Census Bureau, "Annual Report for Wholesale Trade: 2022," <www.census.gov/programs-surveys/awts/data/tables.html>, accessed March 2024.

Table 1078. Merchant Wholesalers' Sales and Inventories by Kind of Business: 2010 to 2022

[In billions of dollars (4,339.2 represents $4,339,200,000,000), except ratios. Inventories and inventories/sales ratios as of December, not seasonally adjusted. Excludes manufacturers' sales branches and offices. Data adjusted using final results of the 2017 Economic Census. Based on data from the Annual Wholesale Trade Survey and the Monthly Wholesale Trade Survey; see Appendix III]

Kind of business	NAICS code [1]	2010	2015	2018	2019	2020	2021	2022
SALES								
Merchant wholesalers	**42**	**4,339.2**	**5,379.3**	**6,105.2**	**6,083.7**	**5,811.2**	**7,001.7**	**8,056.1**
Durable goods	**423**	**2,001.1**	**2,554.0**	**2,925.6**	**2,912.3**	**2,853.0**	**3,384.6**	**3,771.5**
Motor vehicles, parts, and supplies	4231	304.8	433.1	469.1	483.2	441.1	489.4	554.8
Furniture and home furnishings	4232	57.4	81.2	94.5	96.4	95.0	110.0	113.1
Lumber and other construction materials	4233	86.5	122.9	162.3	163.0	171.5	222.2	252.4
Professional, commercial equipment and supplies	4234	397.8	446.3	505.4	521.2	517.0	576.1	606.3
Computer, peripheral equipment and software	42343	220.1	232.7	264.3	265.9	269.0	295.1	309.3
Medical, dental, and hospital equipment and supplies	42345	(NA)	121.1	136.9	148.5	157.8	177.0	181.5
Metals and minerals (except petroleum)	4235	138.4	162.3	193.3	181.8	146.5	224.5	265.8
Household appliances and electrical and electronic goods	4236	391.2	546.2	615.7	591.1	597.6	709.4	800.4
Hardware, plumbing, heating equipment and supplies	4237	96.1	134.1	160.6	168.2	172.5	204.6	231.0
Machinery, equipment, and supplies	4238	305.3	409.4	463.7	464.2	449.5	503.9	590.9
Miscellaneous durable goods	4239	223.7	218.7	261.0	243.1	262.4	344.6	356.8
Nondurable goods	**424**	**2,338.1**	**2,825.3**	**3,179.6**	**3,171.4**	**2,958.2**	**3,617.1**	**4,284.6**
Paper and paper products	4241	86.0	92.8	92.3	90.1	84.0	91.9	103.5
Drugs and druggists' sundries	4242	415.9	605.3	693.6	722.0	765.5	826.2	911.7
Apparel, piece goods, and notions	4243	137.0	168.5	165.6	164.0	127.5	159.4	170.1
Grocery and related products	4244	491.3	633.3	675.6	682.9	672.7	760.5	862.0
Farm product raw materials	4245	188.3	230.0	212.2	199.9	205.7	265.5	324.7
Chemical and allied products	4246	102.7	117.4	131.4	126.1	115.4	145.4	169.4
Petroleum and petroleum products	4247	591.0	576.8	763.2	727.7	510.7	826.4	1,147.0
Beer, wine, and distilled alcoholic beverages	4248	111.3	134.8	150.8	158.8	170.8	186.8	191.1
Miscellaneous nondurable goods	4249	214.5	266.6	294.9	299.9	306.0	354.9	405.1
INVENTORIES								
Merchant wholesalers	**42**	**445.5**	**598.9**	**673.9**	**682.6**	**672.1**	**791.8**	**930.4**
Durable goods	**423**	**255.8**	**351.1**	**402.0**	**404.5**	**390.6**	**462.0**	**552.1**
Motor vehicles, parts, and supplies	4231	40.7	61.5	64.6	66.1	60.2	66.3	82.0
Furniture and home furnishings	4232	8.6	12.0	13.7	13.3	13.0	16.1	19.6
Lumber and other construction materials	4233	10.2	14.5	20.3	20.6	21.6	29.1	32.5
Professional, commercial equipment and supplies	4234	32.9	41.3	48.7	50.1	49.3	57.6	62.3
Computer, peripheral equipment and software	42343	13.2	15.4	18.8	18.4	18.0	22.0	21.3
Medical, dental, and hospital equipment and supplies	42345	(NA)	15.5	17.9	19.3	20.9	22.6	25.6
Metals and minerals (except petroleum)	4235	22.7	27.4	35.5	32.6	29.0	42.4	45.7
Household appliances and electrical and electronic goods	4236	35.8	51.2	56.3	55.8	55.7	69.1	88.5
Hardware, plumbing, heating equipment and supplies	4237	16.8	23.1	28.2	29.0	30.2	38.2	46.2
Machinery, equipment, and supplies	4238	63.5	92.1	102.2	104.9	99.6	102.1	128.3
Miscellaneous durable goods	4239	24.8	28.1	32.6	32.1	31.9	41.1	46.9
Nondurable goods	**424**	**189.7**	**247.8**	**271.8**	**278.1**	**281.5**	**329.8**	**378.3**
Paper and paper products	4241	7.6	8.6	8.8	8.2	8.3	9.1	9.9
Drugs and druggists' sundries	4242	38.9	64.5	67.4	68.6	75.4	80.7	89.8
Apparel, piece goods, and notions	4243	20.2	28.4	28.2	28.7	23.3	28.3	39.1
Grocery and related products	4244	27.3	37.2	40.4	41.4	41.0	49.3	55.5
Farm product raw materials	4245	28.6	26.5	31.9	32.4	39.5	46.8	48.0
Chemical and allied products	4246	9.4	11.9	13.1	12.4	11.6	15.0	17.0
Petroleum and petroleum products	4247	23.2	19.6	21.9	23.5	21.1	27.3	32.0
Beer, wine, and distilled alcoholic beverages	4248	10.7	14.2	15.8	17.1	17.0	19.4	23.1
Miscellaneous nondurable goods	4249	23.8	36.8	44.2	45.6	44.2	54.0	63.9
INVENTORIES/SALES RATIO								
Merchant wholesalers	**42**	**1.03**	**1.11**	**1.10**	**1.12**	**1.16**	**1.13**	**1.15**
Durable goods	**423**	**1.28**	**1.37**	**1.37**	**1.39**	**1.37**	**1.36**	**1.46**
Motor vehicles, parts, and supplies	4231	1.33	1.42	1.38	1.37	1.37	1.35	1.48
Furniture and home furnishings	4232	1.49	1.47	1.45	1.38	1.37	1.46	1.74
Lumber and other construction materials	4233	1.18	1.18	1.25	1.27	1.26	1.31	1.29
Professional, commercial equipment and supplies	4234	0.83	0.92	0.96	0.96	0.95	1.00	1.03
Computer, peripheral equipment and software	42343	0.60	0.66	0.71	0.69	0.67	0.75	0.69
Medical, dental, and hospital equipment and supplies	42345	(NA)	1.28	1.31	1.30	1.32	1.28	1.41
Metals and minerals (except petroleum)	4235	1.64	1.69	1.83	1.79	1.98	1.89	1.72
Household appliances and electrical and electronic goods	4236	0.91	0.94	0.91	0.94	0.93	0.97	1.11
Hardware, plumbing, heating equipment and supplies	4237	1.75	1.72	1.75	1.72	1.75	1.87	2.00
Machinery, equipment, and supplies	4238	2.08	2.25	2.20	2.26	2.22	2.03	2.17
Miscellaneous durable goods	4239	1.11	1.29	1.25	1.32	1.22	1.19	1.31
Nondurable goods	**424**	**0.81**	**0.88**	**0.85**	**0.88**	**0.95**	**0.91**	**0.88**
Paper and paper products	4241	0.88	0.93	0.95	0.91	0.99	0.99	0.96
Drugs and druggists' sundries	4242	0.94	1.07	0.97	0.95	0.99	0.98	0.98
Apparel, piece goods, and notions	4243	1.47	1.68	1.70	1.75	1.82	1.77	2.30
Grocery and related products	4244	0.56	0.59	0.60	0.61	0.61	0.65	0.64
Farm product raw materials	4245	1.52	1.15	1.51	1.62	1.92	1.76	1.48
Chemical and allied products	4246	0.91	1.01	1.00	0.99	1.01	1.03	1.01
Petroleum and petroleum products	4247	0.39	0.34	0.29	0.32	0.41	0.33	0.28
Beer, wine, and distilled alcoholic beverages	4248	0.97	1.06	1.05	1.08	1.00	1.04	1.21
Miscellaneous nondurable goods	4249	1.11	1.38	1.50	1.52	1.44	1.52	1.58

NA Not available. [1] North American Industry Classification System, 2012. See text, Section 15.

Source: U.S. Census Bureau, "Annual Report for Wholesale Trade: 2022," <www.census.gov/programs-surveys/awts.html>, accessed March 2024.

Table 1079. Wholesale and Retail Trade—Establishments, Employees, and Payroll by State: 2021 and 2022

[5,926 represents 5,926,000. Covers establishments with payroll. Excludes self-employed individuals, employees of private households, railroad employees, agricultural production employees, and most government employees. Data based on North American Industry Classification System (NAICS), 2017. See text, Section 15. For statement on methodology, see Appendix III]

State	Wholesale trade (NAICS 42)						Retail trade (NAICS 44, 45)					
	Establishments		Employees [1] (1,000)		Annual payroll (mil. dol.)		Establishments		Employees [1] (1,000)		Annual payroll (mil. dol.)	
	2021	2022	2021	2022	2021	2022	2021	2022	2021	2022	2021	2022
U.S.........	390,842	388,706	5,926	6,143	497,750	535,196	1,036,879	1,045,890	15,531	15,922	541,354	584,116
AL............	5,003	4,979	74	76	4,910	5,330	17,661	17,855	229	233	7,204	7,713
AK............	722	706	8	8	549	570	2,397	2,426	33	34	1,242	1,334
AZ............	6,487	6,650	98	104	7,817	8,631	17,541	17,832	343	350	12,950	13,960
AR............	3,247	3,271	47	52	2,935	3,369	10,469	10,696	139	143	4,550	4,863
CA............	56,523	56,104	781	806	79,901	84,024	105,805	107,053	1,634	1,688	66,977	71,895
CO............	7,064	6,960	102	106	9,979	10,570	18,590	18,698	285	289	10,375	11,324
CT............	3,829	3,739	65	66	6,222	6,623	11,612	11,649	173	179	6,389	6,838
DE............	1,263	1,255	18	20	2,077	2,380	3,732	3,735	53	55	1,770	1,936
DC............	393	387	3	3	335	368	1,664	1,649	20	22	731	806
FL............	30,850	30,998	334	356	23,697	26,790	75,295	75,743	1,091	1,136	37,705	41,649
GA............	12,636	12,603	207	218	15,907	17,481	35,518	35,823	485	504	15,816	17,392
HI............	1,460	1,421	16	16	1,000	1,095	4,384	4,426	61	65	2,272	2,543
ID............	2,183	2,269	32	33	2,474	2,593	6,176	6,335	90	94	3,191	3,507
IL............	16,671	16,366	310	319	27,902	29,378	36,105	35,947	572	571	19,049	20,516
IN............	7,298	7,254	120	124	8,811	9,284	20,821	21,110	330	331	10,535	11,339
IA............	4,781	4,762	67	68	4,374	4,638	11,062	11,150	186	181	5,338	5,620
KS............	4,196	4,193	61	63	4,378	4,654	9,547	9,580	144	144	4,365	4,715
KY............	3,974	3,947	69	74	4,646	5,050	14,773	15,021	214	215	6,685	7,208
LA............	5,158	5,086	69	71	4,545	4,963	15,835	15,929	219	222	6,881	7,277
ME............	1,459	1,452	17	18	1,230	1,323	6,006	6,096	82	84	2,857	3,156
MD............	5,098	4,990	85	89	7,032	7,530	16,885	16,707	283	293	9,858	10,534
MA............	6,913	6,802	142	150	16,002	17,544	22,474	22,637	345	363	14,160	15,350
MI............	10,231	10,191	177	186	13,501	15,121	32,865	32,936	454	463	15,251	16,488
MN............	7,354	7,225	137	141	12,440	13,495	17,768	17,816	297	300	9,482	10,189
MS............	2,566	2,546	39	42	2,439	2,885	11,160	11,334	135	137	3,954	4,166
MO............	7,028	6,885	126	131	8,329	9,226	19,815	20,006	309	306	9,762	10,382
MT............	1,562	1,587	15	15	960	1,010	4,576	4,696	59	62	2,064	2,264
NE............	3,067	3,065	41	41	2,780	2,963	6,878	6,931	108	108	3,371	3,697
NV............	3,205	3,261	39	44	2,772	3,365	8,839	9,012	152	158	5,607	6,191
NH............	1,758	1,730	24	24	2,266	2,148	5,718	5,754	91	94	3,415	3,603
NJ............	13,119	13,064	263	269	28,233	29,700	29,885	30,031	440	459	16,423	17,812
NM............	1,641	1,631	20	20	1,356	1,286	6,012	6,282	90	93	2,975	3,181
NY............	27,463	27,012	307	315	27,537	28,821	72,828	72,674	849	871	33,130	34,479
NC............	11,266	11,333	191	201	15,828	17,573	34,963	35,465	513	522	15,624	17,001
ND............	1,702	1,707	21	22	1,476	1,628	3,123	3,130	46	46	1,560	1,659
OH............	12,842	12,586	226	229	16,428	17,409	34,090	34,367	552	555	17,974	19,260
OK............	4,389	4,328	54	57	3,489	3,832	13,277	13,319	184	187	5,929	6,310
OR............	4,994	4,913	75	76	6,003	6,185	13,914	13,998	214	216	7,671	8,381
PA............	13,422	13,162	246	247	20,996	21,651	40,439	40,488	634	660	20,844	22,283
RI............	1,267	1,266	19	19	1,513	1,655	3,566	3,593	47	51	1,672	1,805
SC............	4,854	4,928	76	78	5,305	5,629	18,025	18,490	257	265	7,832	8,502
SD............	1,539	1,568	19	20	1,198	1,371	3,742	3,868	53	54	1,675	1,818
TN............	6,588	6,526	119	120	8,778	9,301	22,874	23,204	332	338	10,970	11,919
TX............	33,091	33,635	512	541	41,632	46,901	82,077	83,788	1,319	1,374	45,886	50,182
UT............	3,693	3,676	64	64	4,575	4,802	10,332	10,315	168	175	5,945	6,520
VT............	708	679	11	10	808	790	3,014	2,927	36	37	1,275	1,352
VA............	6,643	6,593	102	106	8,458	8,910	25,776	26,037	420	430	13,448	14,424
WA............	8,828	8,687	132	135	11,375	12,134	20,755	20,787	343	344	13,637	14,421
WV............	1,327	1,311	17	17	982	1,007	5,616	5,721	78	80	2,322	2,559
WI............	6,649	6,582	122	124	9,128	9,728	17,988	18,178	305	308	9,709	10,644
WY............	838	835	7	7	444	480	2,612	2,646	31	32	1,046	1,150

[1] Covers full- and part-time employees who are on the payroll in the pay period including March 12.

Source: U.S. Census Bureau, County Business Patterns, CB2200CBP, "County Business Patterns, including ZIP Code Business Patterns, by Legal Form of Organization and Employment Size Class for the U.S., States, and Selected Geographies: 2022," <data.census.gov>, accessed June 2024.

Table 1080. Retail Trade—Establishments, Employees, and Payroll: 2021 and 2022

[1,036.9 represents 1,036,900. Covers establishments with payroll. Excludes self-employed individuals, employees of private households, railroad employees, agricultural production employees, and most government employees. For statement on methodology, see Appendix III]

Kind of business	NAICS code [1]	Establishments (1,000)		Employees (1,000) [2]		Payroll (bil. dol.)	
		2021	2022	2021	2022	2021	2022
Retail trade, total........................	**44–45**	**1,036.9**	**1,045.9**	**15,531**	**15,922**	**541.4**	**584.1**
Motor vehicle and parts dealers........................	441	119.9	120.7	1,958	2,030	123.1	132.6
Automobile dealers........................	4411	47.3	47.4	1,258	1,299	93.8	101.0
New car dealers........................	44111	21.6	21.8	1,095	1,111	84.6	91.3
Used car dealers........................	44112	25.6	25.6	163	188	9.1	9.7
Other motor vehicle dealers........................	4412	13.8	14.1	163	172	10.0	10.8
Recreational vehicle dealers........................	44121	2.9	3.0	55	60	4.1	4.3
Motorcycle and boat and other motor vehicle dealers [3]......	44122	10.9	11.1	108	112	5.9	6.5
Motorcycle, ATV, and all other motor vehicle dealers........	441228	6.6	6.8	71	74	3.7	4.1
Automotive parts, accessories, and tire stores........................	4413	58.9	59.2	537	560	19.4	20.8
Automotive parts and accessories stores........................	44131	38.3	38.8	360	388	11.6	12.5
Tire dealers........................	44132	20.6	20.5	177	171	7.8	8.3
Furniture and home furnishing stores........................	442	45.4	45.6	428	444	17.3	17.9
Furniture stores........................	4421	22.0	22.3	197	197	9.8	9.9
Home furnishings stores........................	4422	23.4	23.3	232	247	7.5	8.0
Floor covering stores........................	44221	10.1	9.9	70	73	3.7	4.0
Other home furnishings stores [3]........................	44229	13.3	13.4	162	174	3.8	4.1
Window treatment stores........................	442291	2.1	2.2	8	9	0.4	0.4
Electronics and appliance stores........................	443	22.8	21.3	223	220	9.3	9.3
Household appliance stores........................	443141	6.0	5.6	50	50	2.5	2.6
Electronics stores........................	443142	16.8	15.8	172	170	6.8	6.7
Building material & garden equipment & supplies dealers.......	444	72.4	73.2	1,378	1,446	49.0	54.4
Building material & supplies dealers [3]........................	4441	55.2	55.3	1,208	1,267	42.8	47.7
Home centers........................	44411	6.0	6.0	[5] 749	[5] 804	[5] 20.4	[5] 23.6
Hardware stores........................	44413	15.1	15.0	149	148	4.8	4.9
Lawn & garden equipment & supplies stores [3]........................	4442	17.2	17.8	170	179	6.3	6.7
Nursery, garden center, and farm supply stores........................	44422	13.4	13.4	140	147	4.9	5.2
Food & beverage stores........................	445	154.2	159.0	3,331	3,328	86.8	92.4
Grocery stores........................	4451	96.5	99.1	2,987	2,970	77.6	82.6
Supermarkets & grocery (except convenience) stores........	44511	62.3	62.6	2,834	2,797	74.3	78.8
Convenience stores........................	44512	34.2	36.4	153	173	3.4	3.9
Specialty food stores........................	4452	22.1	23.8	160	164	4.2	4.5
Beer, wine, & liquor stores [4]........................	4453	35.5	36.2	184	194	5.0	5.3
Health & personal care stores [3]........................	446	92.3	90.9	990	1,036	36.9	41.0
Pharmacies & drug stores........................	44611	43.9	42.7	663	673	25.9	28.9
Cosmetics, beauty supplies, & perfume stores........................	44612	17.8	17.5	144	176	3.9	4.3
Optical goods stores........................	44613	11.5	11.7	76	78	2.5	3.0
Gasoline stations........................	447	110.9	109.2	977	988	24.3	27.0
Gasoline stations with convenience stores........................	44711	98.1	96.5	830	832	20.0	22.0
Other gasoline stations........................	44719	12.9	12.8	147	156	4.4	5.0
Clothing & clothing accessories stores........................	448	123.6	120.9	1,359	1,450	32.5	36.6
Clothing stores [3]........................	4481	84.6	82.5	1,055	1,139	23.4	26.4
Men's clothing stores........................	44811	6.4	6.0	36	45	1.3	1.5
Women's clothing stores........................	44812	26.9	25.9	194	203	4.3	4.8
Children's & infants' clothing stores........................	44813	4.1	3.8	[5] 34	29	0.6	0.6
Family clothing stores........................	44814	27.5	26.9	637	690	12.9	14.7
Shoe stores........................	4482	18.9	18.3	202	202	4.1	4.5
Jewelry, luggage, & leather goods stores [3]........................	4483	20.2	20.1	102	108	5.0	5.8
Jewelry stores........................	44831	19.3	19.3	96	101	4.6	5.3
Sporting goods, hobby, musical instrument, & book stores......	451	41.2	42.5	450	473	11.3	13.0
Sporting goods, hobby, and musical instrument stores [3]......	4511	34.8	36.0	403	423	10.2	11.9
Sporting goods stores........................	45111	20.0	20.6	239	252	6.6	7.9
Hobby, toy, and game stores........................	45112	8.0	8.5	102	107	2.3	2.6
Book stores and news dealers [3]........................	4512	6.4	6.4	[5] 46	[5] 51	1.0	1.1
Book stores........................	451211	5.6	5.7	[5] 44	[5] 48	0.9	1.1
General merchandise stores........................	452	56.7	58.7	2,767	2,696	75.7	77.1
Department stores........................	4522	3.6	3.0	330	248	7.1	6.5
General merchandise stores........................	4523	53.1	55.7	2,437	2,449	68.6	70.6
Warehouse clubs and supercenters........................	452311	8.1	8.1	1,898	1,954	59.2	60.8
All other general merchandise stores........................	452319	45.0	47.6	539	495	9.4	9.8
Miscellaneous store retailers [3]........................	453	107.1	112.8	726	795	21.5	24.5
Florists........................	4531	11.8	12.0	50	57	1.2	1.4
Office supplies, stationery, and gift stores........................	4532	23.1	23.5	160	169	4.0	4.4
Office supplies and stationery stores........................	45321	4.5	4.3	49	47	1.2	1.3
Gift, novelty, and souvenir stores........................	45322	18.6	19.2	112	123	2.8	3.1
Used merchandise stores........................	4533	18.6	19.2	190	209	4.4	5.0
Other miscellaneous store retailers [3]........................	4539	53.6	58.2	326	360	11.9	13.7
Pet and pet supplies stores........................	45391	9.7	10.0	115	121	3.3	3.7
Nonstore retailers [3]........................	454	90.3	91.0	944	1,014	53.7	58.2
Electronic shopping & mail-order houses........................	4541	55.1	55.6	734	781	43.3	46.5
Direct selling establishments........................	4543	31.8	32.1	175	194	8.9	10.1
Fuel dealers........................	45431	7.9	7.8	72	74	4.0	4.3

[1] Data based on North American Industry Classification System (NAICS), 2017. See text, Section 15. [2] Covers full- and part-time employees who are on the payroll in the pay period including March 12. [3] Includes other kinds of business, not shown separately. [4] Includes government employees. [5] Data flagged for noise; the value was changed to avoid disclosure of data for individual businesses.

Source: U.S. Census Bureau, County Business Patterns, CB2200CBP, "County Business Patterns, including ZIP Code Business Patterns, by Legal Form of Organization and Employment Size Class for the U.S., States, and Selected Geographies: 2022," <data.census.gov>, accessed June 2024.

Table 1081. Retail Trade—Nonemployer Firms and Receipts by Industry: 2021

[109,294,174 represents $109,294,174,000. Nonemployers are businesses with no paid employees. See headnote, Table 1075]

Industry type	2017 NAICS code [1]	Firms				Receipts ($1,000)
		Total	Corpora-tions [2]	Individual proprietor-ships [3]	Partner-ships [4]	
Retail trade, total..	**44–45**	**2,369,980**	**119,696**	**2,165,180**	**85,104**	**109,294,174**
Motor vehicle & parts dealers.....................................	441	163,875	14,328	142,753	6,794	19,773,831
Furniture & home furnishings stores.............................	442	36,252	4,270	29,449	2,533	2,587,573
Electronics and appliance stores.................................	443	21,506	2,771	17,701	1,034	1,363,496
Building material & garden equipment & supplies dealers......	444	36,712	3,338	31,543	1,831	2,532,439
Building material & supplies dealers..........................	4441	21,366	2,644	17,370	1,352	1,858,093
Food & beverage stores...	445	99,142	10,236	81,764	7,142	7,187,569
Grocery stores..	4451	38,100	4,385	31,766	1,949	3,040,516
Specialty food stores...	4452	52,469	4,463	43,800	4,206	2,904,220
Health & personal care stores....................................	446	177,664	8,122	164,184	5,358	5,098,521
Gasoline stations..	447	6,674	1,390	4,710	574	879,270
Clothing & clothing accessories stores...........................	448	218,118	10,443	197,925	9,750	8,218,214
Clothing stores...	4481	168,542	7,622	152,707	8,213	5,893,504
Jewelry, luggage, and leather goods stores...................	4483	42,240	2,385	38,629	1,226	1,912,423
Sporting goods, hobby, musical instrument, & book stores.....	451	80,912	4,522	71,759	4,631	3,819,771
Book stores and news dealer..................................	4512	10,620	560	9,552	508	409,329
General merchandise stores......................................	452	39,500	2,125	35,680	1,695	1,941,712
Miscellaneous store retailers....................................	453	305,898	19,785	269,399	16,714	15,768,459
Office supplies, stationery, and gift stores....................	4532	49,015	3,060	43,201	2,754	1,989,732
Nonstore retailers...	454	1,183,727	38,366	1,118,313	27,048	40,123,319
Electronic shopping & mail-order houses.......................	4541	308,210	16,199	279,709	12,302	14,838,590
Direct selling establishments.................................	4543	860,325	20,787	826,121	13,417	24,658,575

[1] North American Industry Classification System, 2017; see text, Section 15. [2] A legally incorporated business under state laws. [3] Also referred to as "sole proprietorship," an unincorporated business with a sole owner. Includes self-employed persons. [4] An unincorporated business where two or more persons join to carry on a trade or business with each having a shared financial interest in the business.

Source: U.S. Census Bureau, Nonemployer Statistics, "All Sectors: Nonemployer Statistics by Legal Form of Organization and Receipts Size Class for the U.S., States, and Selected Geographies: 2021," <data.census.gov>, accessed March 2024.

Table 1082. Retail Industries—Employees, Average Weekly Hours, and Average Hourly Earnings: 2010 to 2023

[14,404 represents 14,404,000. Annual averages of monthly figures. Covers all full- and part-time employees who worked during, or received pay for, any part of the pay period including the 12th of the month]

Industry	NAICS code [1]	Employees (1,000)			Average weekly hours [2]			Average hourly earnings [2] (dol.)		
		2010	2020	2023	2010	2020	2023	2010	2020	2023
Retail trade, total....................	**44–45**	**14,404**	**14,809**	**15,590**	**30.2**	**30.8**	**30.4**	**13.24**	**17.58**	**20.50**
Motor vehicle and parts dealers.....................	441	1,634	1,905	2,045	36.5	36.5	36.8	17.06	22.52	26.42
Automobile dealers................................	4411	1,012	1,203	1,276	36.7	36.4	37.0	18.22	24.52	28.45
Other motor vehicle dealers.......................	4412	130	152	178	33.6	35.0	36.0	17.24	22.36	26.10
Automotive parts, accessories, and tire............	4413	493	550	591	36.9	37.1	36.4	14.56	18.01	21.83
Building material and garden equipment and supplies dealers................................	444	1,139	1,368	1,406	33.9	34.9	36.0	14.14	19.68	24.71
Building material and supplies dealers............	4441	1,010	1,202	1,217	34.2	35.2	36.8	14.16	19.97	25.23
Lawn and garden equipment and supplies........	4442	129	166	189	31.7	33.3	30.3	14.05	17.46	20.63
Food and beverage retailers.......................	445	2,866	3,162	3,239	29.1	28.6	28.4	12.15	14.58	17.13
Grocery and convenience retailers................	4451	2,504	2,783	2,823	29.1	28.6	28.7	12.21	14.46	17.06
Supermarkets and other grocery retailers........	44511	2,323	2,589	2,612	28.9	28.6	28.4	12.27	14.55	17.07
Convenience retailers and vending machine operators.....................	44513	182	194	212	32.5	29.6	32.8	11.45	13.26	16.94
Specialty food retailers..........................	4452	224	220	237	29.9	27.6	26.6	11.55	15.83	17.89
Beer, wine, and liquor retailers..................	4453	137	159	178	27.2	28.8	25.5	11.95	15.09	17.49
Furniture, home furnishings, electronics, and appliance retailers................................	449	981	863	848	30.5	33.2	32.3	16.18	21.94	22.97
Furniture and home furnishings retailers..........	4491	449	423	433	29.3	32.0	30.0	15.34	19.98	23.40
Electronics and appliance retailers...............	4492	532	441	416	31.6	34.4	34.6	16.87	23.75	22.57
General merchandise retailers.....................	455	3,042	3,104	3,218	31.7	30.4	30.4	11.08	15.78	17.37
Health and personal care retailers [3].............	456	1,008	1,010	1,097	29.6	29.5	29.0	17.04	20.67	23.13
Pharmacies and drug retailers....................	45611	731	697	725	29.4	29.4	29.1	17.62	21.51	24.44
Gasoline stations and fuel dealers.................	457	901	999	1,060	31.4	31.2	31.1	11.01	13.76	17.64
Gasoline stations................................	4571	819	927	988	30.7	30.6	30.8	10.25	12.82	16.86
Fuel dealers.....................................	4572	81	72	72	38.6	39.5	36.7	17.14	22.80	27.21
Clothing, clothing accessories, shoe, and jewelry..	458	1,384	1,002	1,147	21.5	23.9	21.8	11.81	17.23	20.94
Clothing and clothing accessories retailers.......	4581	1,068	747	852	20.5	23.0	20.8	11.21	16.49	19.78
Shoe retailers...................................	4582	182	152	172	23.4	25.2	23.0	11.83	16.96	23.93
Jewelry, luggage, and leather goods retailers.....	4583	133	104	123	28.2	29.7	27.4	15.61	22.01	24.03
Sporting goods, hobby, musical instrument, book, and miscellaneous retailers.................	459	1,450	1,396	1,530	26.7	28.7	26.9	12.80	16.48	19.88
Sporting goods, hobby, and musical instrument...	4591	473	441	497	24.1	27.7	24.8	12.09	15.95	21.24
Book retailers and news dealers..................	4592	124	62	72	22.5	24.0	24.5	11.48	16.03	18.49
Florists...	4593	71	54	62	22.8	26.6	24.6	11.38	15.06	17.95
Office supplies, stationery, and gift retailers.......	4594	308	199	208	27.2	25.6	23.0	13.16	15.21	17.20
Used merchandise retailers.......................	4595	130	160	205	29.7	29.3	27.9	11.04	14.00	15.88
Other miscellaneous retailers [3]..................	4599	345	480	487	31.3	31.5	30.9	14.53	18.28	21.60
Pet and pet supplies retailers....................	45991	108	131	138	28.1	28.9	26.7	13.40	16.31	19.85

[1] Based on the North American Industry Classification System (NAICS), 2022; see text, this section and Section 15. [2] Data shown for production and nonsupervisory employees. [3] Includes other kind of businesses, not shown separately.

Source: U.S. Bureau of Labor Statistics, Current Employment Statistics, "Employment, Hours, and Earnings—National," <www.bls.gov/ces/data>, accessed March 2024.

Table 1083. Retail Trade—Sales by Kind of Business: 2000 to 2022

[In billions of dollars (2,983.3 represents $2,983,300,000,000). Data have been adjusted using final results of the 2017 Economic Census]

Kind of business	NAICS code [1]	2000	2010	2015	2019	2020	2021	2022
Retail sales, total............................	**44, 45**	**2,983.3**	**3,818.0**	**4,725.7**	**5,401.5**	**5,565.7**	**6,519.8**	**7,041.0**
GAFO, total [2]................................	(X)	862.7	1,114.4	1,262.5	1,303.8	1,226.6	1,457.4	1,536.1
Motor vehicle and parts dealers...................	441	796.2	742.9	1,105.0	1,235.2	1,206.6	1,478.4	1,521.0
Automobile dealers................................	4411	687.8	621.2	950.7	1,063.2	1,022.3	1,261.7	1,293.1
New car dealers............................	44111	630.1	549.5	849.7	940.9	903.3	1,094.4	1,126.9
Used car dealers...........................	44112	57.7	71.7	101.0	122.3	119.0	167.3	166.2
Other motor vehicle dealers...................	4412	45.0	43.8	63.3	75.3	86.3	103.5	104.1
Auto parts, accessories, and tire stores........	4413	63.4	77.9	90.9	96.8	98.0	113.2	123.8
Furniture and home furnishings stores............	442	91.2	85.2	107.8	120.5	113.5	141.1	143.6
Furniture stores................................	4421	50.6	46.7	58.3	64.3	62.6	79.4	79.9
Home furnishings stores........................	4422	40.6	38.5	49.6	56.2	50.9	61.7	63.8
Electronics and appliance stores [3].................	443	90.4	99.6	100.1	90.8	74.8	94.1	92.8
Electronics stores............................	443142	77.8	84.1	82.9	73.9	56.5	72.8	70.5
Building materials, garden equipment, and supplies dealers................................	444	229.0	260.6	324.3	372.5	421.0	481.2	511.7
Food and beverage stores [3].....................	445	444.8	580.5	687.3	774.4	849.6	890.7	957.2
Grocery stores................................	4451	402.5	520.8	616.1	693.9	759.4	793.4	858.3
Supermarkets and other grocery (except convenience) stores........................	44511	381.4	498.0	590.7	661.8	728.8	756.6	814.3
Beer, wine and liquor stores..................	4453	28.5	41.4	49.1	56.8	66.0	70.2	70.4
Health and personal care stores [3].................	446	155.2	260.4	306.2	347.0	354.7	386.7	402.9
Pharmacies and drug stores...................	44611	130.9	222.2	255.6	288.3	302.4	323.0	336.3
Gasoline stations...............................	447	249.8	448.3	455.6	513.7	429.4	572.7	736.1
Clothing and clothing accessory stores [3]..........	448	167.7	213.3	256.6	268.0	201.5	292.4	303.4
Clothing stores [3]............................	4481	118.1	158.3	187.3	195.5	138.8	201.8	210.5
Shoe stores................................	4482	22.9	27.2	35.3	37.3	29.4	39.4	40.1
Jewelry, luggage, and leather goods stores......	4483	26.7	27.8	33.9	35.3	33.3	51.2	52.9
Sporting goods, hobby, musical instrument, and book stores [3]............................	451	67.6	78.2	85.5	79.4	83.8	102.6	103.0
Sporting goods stores.........................	45111	25.3	37.4	47.0	44.8	52.3	63.9	63.4
Hobby, toy, and game stores...................	45112	16.9	15.8	18.1	16.3	17.0	21.5	21.9
Book stores and news dealers..................	4512	16.1	16.3	11.6	9.5	6.6	8.7	9.0
General merchandise stores [3].....................	452	404.2	603.8	680.5	715.5	728.7	797.5	862.1
Department stores............................	4521	232.5	184.8	165.1	134.7	112.3	133.5	136.0
Discount department stores....................	452112	136.2	119.9	107.8	95.1	91.0	102.3	104.1
Other general merchandise stores...............	4529	171.8	419.0	515.4	580.9	616.4	664.0	726.1
Warehouse clubs and supercenters............	45291	139.6	368.0	447.4	500.1	525.3	569.6	626.2
Miscellaneous store retailers [3]...................	453	106.7	104.2	118.5	131.8	128.8	160.0	171.3
Office supplies, stationery, and gift stores........	4532	41.7	34.3	32.0	29.6	24.2	29.7	31.1
Office supplies and stationery stores............	45321	22.7	18.8	14.5	10.7	10.2	10.1	10.0
Gift, novelty, and souvenir stores.............	45322	18.9	15.5	17.5	18.9	14.0	19.6	21.2
Used merchandise stores..........................	4533	9.8	11.8	16.2	18.4	16.6	22.5	24.3
Nonstore retailers [3]............................	454	180.5	341.0	498.4	752.5	973.4	1,122.5	1,235.9
Electronic shopping and mail-order houses......	4541	113.8	263.5	419.0	659.3	884.4	1,019.9	1,117.0
Direct selling establishments......................	4543	58.1	71.0	72.2	84.3	82.0	95.3	110.0
Fuel dealers...............................	45431	26.7	35.5	32.9	35.0	29.3	35.6	47.4

X Not applicable. [1] North American Industry Classification System, 2012; see text, Section 15. [2] GAFO (General Merchandise, Apparel, Furniture, and Office Supplies) represents stores classified in the following NAICS codes: 442, 443, 448, 451, 452, and 4532. [3] Includes other kinds of businesses, not shown separately.

Source: U.S. Census Bureau, "Annual Retail Trade Survey (ARTS) Tables," <www.census.gov/programs-surveys/arts/data/tables.html>, accessed March 2024.

Table 1084. Retail Trade Corporations—Sales, Net Profit, and Profit Per Dollar of Sales: 2022 and 2023

[3,995.8 represents $3,995,800,000,000. Represents North American Industry Classification System (NAICS) groups 44 and 45. Covers corporations with assets of $50,000,000 or more]

Item	Unit	Total retail trade		Food and beverage stores (NAICS 445)		Clothing & general merchandise stores (NAICS 448, 452)		All other retail stores	
		2022	2023	2022	2023	2022	2023	2022	2023
Sales.................................	Bil. dol.	3,995.8	4,073.0	557.9	582.2	1,206.0	1,221.7	2,231.9	2,269.1
Net profit:									
Before income taxes..................	Bil. dol.	161.4	211.8	20.8	22.8	55.3	56.4	85.3	132.5
After income taxes....................	Bil. dol.	128.3	173.6	16.7	18.9	43.8	44.7	67.8	109.9
Profits per dollar of sales:									
Before income taxes..................	Cents	4.0	5.2	3.7	3.9	4.6	4.6	3.8	5.8
After income taxes....................	Cents	3.2	4.3	3.0	3.3	3.6	3.7	3.0	4.8
Stockholders' equity [1].................	Bil. dol.	766.2	814.2	81.3	81.3	188.4	192.8	496.5	540.1

[1] Averages of quarterly figures.

Source: U.S. Census Bureau, Quarterly Financial Report (QFR) Manufacturing, Mining, Trade, and Selected Service Industries, "Time Series/Trend Charts," <www.census.gov/econ/qfr/>, accessed August 2024.

Table 1085. Retail Trade—Estimated Per Capita Sales by Selected Kind of Business: 2000 to 2022

[Estimates are shown in dollars and are based on data from the Annual Retail Trade Survey and the Census Bureau's Population Estimates Program. Based on estimated resident population estimates as of July 1. Data have been adjusted using final results of the 2017 Economic Census. For additional information, see source and Appendix III]

Kind of business	NAICS code [1]	2000	2010	2015	2019	2020	2021	2022
Retail, total.	**44–45**	**10,573**	**12,343**	**14,738**	**16,456**	**16,788**	**19,635**	**21,127**
Total excluding motor vehicle and parts dealers	*44–45, ex 441*	7,751	9,942	11,292	12,693	13,149	15,183	16,563
Motor vehicle and parts dealers.	441	2,822	2,402	3,446	3,763	3,639	4,452	4,564
Furniture and home furnishings stores.	442	323	275	336	367	342	425	431
Electronics and appliance stores.	443	320	322	312	277	226	283	278
Building material and garden equipment and supplies dealers.	444	812	842	1,011	1,135	1,270	1,449	1,535
Food and beverage stores.	445	1,576	1,877	2,144	2,359	2,563	2,682	2,872
Health and personal care stores.	446	550	842	955	1,057	1,070	1,165	1,209
Gasoline stations.	447	885	1,449	1,421	1,565	1,295	1,725	2,209
Clothing and clothing accessories stores.	448	594	690	800	817	608	881	910
Sporting goods, hobby, musical instrument, and book stores.	451	240	253	267	242	253	309	309
General merchandise stores.	452	1,433	1,952	2,122	2,180	2,198	2,402	2,587
Miscellaneous store retailers.	453	378	337	369	402	388	482	514
Nonstore retailers.	454	640	1,102	1,554	2,293	2,936	3,381	3,709

[1] North American Industry Classification System, 2012; see text, Section 15.

Source: U.S. Census Bureau, "Annual Retail Trade Survey (ARTS) Tables," <www.census.gov/programs-surveys/arts/data/tables.html>, accessed March 2024.

Table 1086. Retail Trade—Merchandise Inventories and Inventory/Sales Ratios by Kind of Business: 2020 to 2023

[Inventories in billions of dollars (623.5 represents $623,500,000,000). As of Dec. 31. Estimates exclude food services. Includes warehouses. Adjusted for seasonal variations. Sales data also adjusted for holiday and trading-day differences. Based on data from the Monthly Retail Trade Survey, Annual Retail Trade Survey, and administrative records; see Appendix III]

Kind of business	NAICS code [1]	Inventories				Inventory/sales ratio			
		2020	2021	2022	2023	2020	2021	2022	2023
Retail inventories, total [2]	**44–45**	**623.5**	**663.7**	**747.3**	**779.6**	**1.26**	**1.19**	**1.28**	**1.28**
Total excluding motor vehicle and parts dealers	44–45, ex 441	431.3	501.7	552.9	538.9	1.12	1.15	1.20	1.13
Motor vehicle and parts dealers.	441	192.2	162.0	194.3	240.7	1.73	1.33	1.59	1.80
Furniture, home furnishings, electronics, and appliance stores.	442, 443	24.1	30.2	34.1	29.9	1.41	1.60	1.83	1.61
Building material and garden equipment and supplies dealers.	444	62.0	74.8	85.4	78.6	1.70	1.81	2.02	1.92
Food and beverage stores.	445	53.2	54.6	60.3	61.2	0.76	0.71	0.74	0.74
Clothing and clothing accessories stores.	448	45.2	52.3	59.2	59.2	2.25	2.12	2.38	2.26
General merchandise stores.	452	78.2	91.7	98.7	96.3	1.28	1.35	1.35	1.29
Department stores.	4521	18.2	22.3	22.8	21.3	1.88	2.00	2.03	1.94

[1] North American Industry Classification System; see text, Section 15. [2] Includes other kind of businesses, not shown separately.

Source: U.S. Census Bureau, Monthly Retail Trade Report, "Retail Inventories and Inventories/Sales Ratios," <www.census.gov/retail/index.html>, accessed June 2024.

Table 1087. Retail Trade Sales, Total and E–Commerce, by Kind of Business: 2022

[7,040,995 represents $7,040,995,000,000. Covers retailers with and without payroll. Based on the Annual Retail Trade Survey; see Appendix III]

Kind of business	NAICS code [1]	Value of sales (mil. dol.)		E-commerce as percent of total sales	Percent distribution of e-commerce sales
		Total	E-commerce		
Retail trade, total.	**44-45**	**7,040,995**	**1,012,636**	**14.4**	**100.0**
Motor vehicle and parts dealers.	441	1,521,010	(D)	(D)	(D)
Furniture and home furnishings stores.	442	143,646	4,779	3.3	0.5
Electronics and appliance stores.	443	92,760	2,788	3.0	0.3
Building material and garden equipment and supplies stores.	444	511,690	3,878	0.8	0.4
Food and beverage stores.	445	957,185	27,445	2.9	2.7
Health and personal care stores.	446	402,880	(D)	(D)	(D)
Gasoline stations.	447	736,082	(D)	(D)	(D)
Clothing and clothing accessories stores.	448	303,413	20,968	6.9	2.1
Sporting goods, hobby, book, and music stores.	451	102,993	6,128	5.9	0.6
General merchandise stores.	452	862,133	(D)	(D)	(D)
Miscellaneous store retailers.	453	171,265	(S)	(S)	(S)
Nonstore retailers.	454	1,235,938	873,421	70.7	86.3
Electronic shopping and mail-order houses.	4541	1,117,046	870,459	77.9	86.0

S Data do not meet publication standards because of high sampling variability or poor response quality. D Withheld to avoid disclosing individual company data. [1] North American Industry Classification System, 2012; see text, Section 15.

Source: U.S. Census Bureau, "Annual Retail Trade Survey (ARTS) Tables," <www.census.gov/programs-surveys/arts/data/tables.html>, accessed March 2024.

Table 1088. Electronic Shopping and Mail-Order Houses, Total and E–Commerce Sales, by Merchandise Line: 2021 and 2022

[1,019,866 represents $1,019,866,000,000. Represents 2012 North American Industry Classification System code 4541, which comprises establishments primarily engaged in retailing all types of merchandise using nonstore means, including catalogs, toll-free telephone numbers, and electronic media, such as interactive television or computer. Covers businesses with and without paid employees. Based on the Annual Retail Trade Survey; see Appendix III]

Merchandise line	2021			2022		
	Value of sales (million dollars)		E-commerce as percent of total sales	Value of sales (million dollars)		E-commerce as percent of total sales
	Total	E-commerce		Total	E-commerce	
Total...	1,019,866	815,430	80.0	1,117,046	870,459	77.9
Books (includes audio books and e-books)...........	22,524	20,966	93.1	22,846	21,238	93.0
Clothing and clothing accessories (includes footwear)................................	133,146	124,365	93.4	(S)	(S)	(S)
Computer and peripheral & communications equipment and related products.................	(S)	(S)	(S)	(S)	(S)	(S)
Computer software (including video game)..........	(S)	(S)	(S)	(S)	(S)	(S)
Drugs, health aids, beauty aids......................	214,603	76,883	35.8	258,144	84,354	32.7
Electronics and appliances............................	88,930	82,274	92.5	92,252	85,507	92.7
Food, beer, and wine................................	40,663	37,856	93.1	41,505	38,287	92.2
Furniture and home furnishings......................	131,773	124,311	94.3	137,588	131,165	95.3
Jewelry..	14,183	12,015	84.7	(S)	(S)	(S)
Audio and video recordings [1].......................	18,392	17,286	94.0	20,602	19,410	94.2
Office equipment and supplies.......................	(S)	(S)	(S)	(S)	(S)	(S)
Sporting goods.....................................	40,515	37,040	91.4	39,083	33,642	86.1
Toys, hobby goods, and games.......................	30,041	28,042	93.3	30,902	28,682	92.8
Other merchandise [2]................................	150,805	132,399	87.8	153,080	132,182	86.3
Nonmerchandise receipts [3]..........................	(S)	(S)	(S)	74,545	68,610	92.0

S Figure does not meet publication standards. [1] Includes purchased downloads. [2] Includes other merchandise such as collectibles, souvenirs, auto parts and accessories, hardware, and lawn and garden equipment and supplies. [3] Includes auction commissions, shipping and handling, customer training, customer support, and advertising.

Source: U.S. Census Bureau, "Annual Retail Trade Survey (ARTS) Tables," <www.census.gov/programs-surveys/arts/data/tables.html>, accessed March 2024.

Table 1089. Franchised New Car Dealerships—Summary: 2000 to 2023

[In units as indicated (8.8 represents 8,800,000)]

Item	Unit	2000	2005	2010	2015	2018	2019	2020	2021	2022	2023
Dealerships [1]........................	Number	20,490	19,898	16,181	16,545	16,753	16,682	16,623	16,676	16,773	16,835
Sales.............................	Bil. dol.	(NA)	(NA)	(NA)	938	1,026	1,027	980	1,184	1,205	1,207
New light duty vehicle sales.......	Millions	(NA)	16.9	11.6	17.4	17.2	17.1	14.5	14.9	13.7	15.5
New cars sold....................	Millions	8.8	7.7	5.6	7.5	5.3	4.8	3.4	3.3	2.9	3.1
New light trucks sold..............	Millions	(NA)	9.3	5.9	9.9	11.9	12.3	11.1	11.6	10.9	12.4
Average retail new vehicle selling price......................	Dollars	(NA)	(NA)	30,079	33,456	35,608	36,824	38,961	42,379	46,287	47,014
Used vehicles sold.................	Millions	20.5	19.7	15.3	14.1	14.4	14.9	13.7	14.7	12.9	12.7
Employment.......................	1,000	1,114	1,138	892	1,085	1,132	1,134	1,078	1,055	1,070	1,101
Annual payroll.....................	Bil. dol.	46.1	51.5	42.4	61.8	66.5	68.8	68.1	83.2	95.0	92.5
Average dealer pretax profits as percent of sales..................	Percent	(NA)	(NA)	(NA)	2.7	2.2	2.3	(NA)	(NA)	(NA)	(NA)
Inventory: [2]											
Domestic: [3]											
Total.........................	Millions	3.2	3.0	1.7	1.9	2.1	1.9	2.1	0.9	1.4	1.9
Days' supply....................	Days	68	70	60	72	76	67	47	26	38	44
Imported: [3]											
Total.........................	Millions	0.5	0.6	0.5	1.7	1.8	1.7	0.7	0.2	0.3	0.4
Days' supply....................	Days	50	52	55	53	54	50	52	22	27	35

NA Not available. [1] Light-duty new vehicle dealerships, as of December 31. [2] Annual average. [3] Classification based on location of automobile production.

Source: National Automobile Dealers Association, <www.nada.org>. *NADA Data 2023: Annual Financial Profile of America's Franchised New-Car Dealerships*, annual ©.

Table 1090. New Motor Vehicle Sales and Car Production: 1990 to 2023

[In thousands of vehicles (14,137 represents 14,137,000). Data are primarily from Wards Intelligence, Southfield, MI]

Type of vehicle	1990	2000	2010	2015	2018	2019	2020	2021	2022	2023
New motor vehicle sales..	**14,137**	**17,812**	**11,773**	**17,857**	**17,713**	**17,488**	**14,881**	**15,409**	**14,230**	**16,009**
New car sales...................	9,300	8,778	5,636	7,529	5,310	4,720	3,402	3,350	2,859	3,117
Domestic.....................	6,897	6,762	3,791	5,595	4,087	3,544	2,560	2,376	2,043	2,252
Import........................	2,403	2,016	1,844	1,933	1,223	1,176	842	974	815	864
New truck sales................	4,837	9,034	6,137	10,329	12,403	12,768	11,480	12,058	11,372	12,893
Light.........................	4,560	8,572	5,919	9,879	11,915	12,241	11,070	11,597	10,896	12,386
Domestic....................	3,957	7,720	5,020	8,097	9,153	9,622	8,615	9,006	8,816	9,911
Import......................	603	852	899	1,782	2,761	2,620	2,455	2,590	2,080	2,475
Heavy........................	278	462	218	449	488	527	410	462	476	507
Domestic car production....	**6,231**	**5,471**	**2,731**	**4,163**	**2,790**	**2,512**	**1,898**	**1,565**	**1,704**	**1,741**

Source: U.S. Bureau of Economic Analysis, National Economic Accounts, "Supplemental Information & Additional Data: Motor Vehicles," <www.bea.gov/data/gdp/gross-domestic-product#supp>, accessed August 2024.

Table 1091. Retail Sales and Leases of New and Used Vehicles: 2010 to 2022

[In thousands, except as noted (48,500 represents 48,500,000). Data are primarily from Edmunds, except as noted]

Item	2010	2014	2015	2016	2017	2018	2019	2020	2021	2022
Vehicle sales and leases, total	**48,500**	**52,758**	**54,727**	**56,162**	**56,435**	**57,545**	**57,865**	**(NA)**	**(NA)**	**(NA)**
New vehicle sales and leases	11,589	16,516	17,472	17,559	17,231	17,312	17,059	14,555	15,016	13,782
Passenger cars	5,724	7,695	7,532	6,882	6,104	5,326	4,733	3,426	3,326	2,895
Light trucks	5,865	8,821	9,940	10,677	11,127	11,986	12,326	11,129	11,690	10,887
New vehicle sales	9,610	12,944	13,473	13,251	13,048	13,077	12,817	11,014	11,741	11,522
Passenger cars	4,515	5,751	5,559	4,981	4,479	4,005	3,506	2,511	2,533	2,453
Light trucks	5,095	7,193	7,914	8,270	8,568	9,072	9,311	8,502	9,208	9,069
New vehicle leases	1,979	3,572	3,999	4,308	4,183	4,234	4,242	3,541	3,275	2,260
Passenger cars	1,209	1,944	1,973	1,901	1,624	1,320	1,227	915	793	442
Light trucks	770	1,628	2,026	2,407	2,559	2,914	3,015	2,626	2,482	1,817
Used vehicle sales [1]	36,911	36,242	37,255	38,602	39,204	40,233	40,807	(NA)	(NA)	(NA)
Electric vehicle sales: [2]										
Hybrid electric	275	452	384	347	363	338	399	455	799	(NA)
Plug-in hybrid electric	(Z)	55	43	73	91	124	86	69	173	(NA)
Electric	–	64	71	87	104	207	234	239	459	(NA)
New and used vehicle sales, total value [3] (billion dollars)	**945**	**1,176**	**1,273**	**1,340**	**1,371**	**1,435**	**1,477**	**(NA)**	**(NA)**	**(NA)**
New vehicle sales	347	535	580	599	606	626	636	571	683	644
Used vehicle sales	598	641	693	741	764	809	841	(NA)	(NA)	(NA)
Average price [3] (current dollars):										
New and used vehicle sales	25,809	26,600	27,506	28,044	28,329	28,757	29,302	(NA)	(NA)	(NA)
New vehicle sales	35,417	35,500	36,412	36,888	37,158	37,414	38,003	39,251	45,458	46,724
Used vehicle sales	16,200	17,700	18,600	19,200	19,500	20,100	20,600	(NA)	(NA)	(NA)

– Represents zero or value too small to report. Z Less than 500. NA Not available. [1] Used car sales include sales from franchised dealers, independent dealers, and casual sales. [2] Data from U.S. Department of Energy, Energy Vehicle Technologies Office. Includes new sales of light duty vehicles certified for highway use. [3] Includes leased vehicles.

Source: U.S. Bureau of Transportation Statistics, "National Transportation Statistics," <www.bts.gov/topics/national-transportation-statistics>, accessed August 2023.

Table 1092. Food and Alcoholic Beverage Expenditures by Sales Outlet: 2000 to 2023

[In millions of dollars (294,292 represents $294,292,000,000). In constant dollars (1988=100). Includes taxes and tips. Data are shown for final purchasers, including individuals and households, government (food assistance programs, Medicare/Medicaid inpatient meals, expensed meals), and businesses (expensed meals) for final use by individuals and households (including food assistance programs)]

Sales outlet	2000	2010	2015	2019	2020	2021	2022	2023
Food at home	294,292	329,764	352,917	397,798	413,257	430,329	422,086	411,194
Grocery stores	199,081	195,127	198,563	219,675	233,839	234,835	226,760	221,831
Convenience stores	7,167	5,588	5,496	6,421	5,899	6,884	7,384	6,725
Other food stores	7,825	8,016	8,337	8,643	8,556	9,245	8,724	8,650
Warehouse clubs and supercenters	35,858	74,881	87,595	92,889	93,198	98,195	95,944	93,655
Other stores and foodservice	30,758	33,873	33,401	37,926	34,464	39,927	42,336	38,873
Mail order and home delivery	10,648	9,355	15,253	27,706	32,839	36,425	36,250	36,950
Direct selling by farmers, manufacturers, and wholesalers	2,187	1,905	3,228	3,509	3,430	3,573	3,515	3,282
Home production and donations	767	1,019	1,042	1,029	1,032	1,245	1,174	1,228
Food away from home (FAFH)	287,324	331,167	405,442	455,373	386,050	460,210	491,775	516,924
Full-service restaurants	100,586	114,118	140,630	153,455	113,000	156,147	170,505	176,495
Limited-service restaurants	93,964	114,508	134,709	154,140	145,170	165,548	173,395	179,131
Drinking places	1,461	1,999	2,099	2,697	1,584	2,508	2,780	2,954
Hotels and motels	15,568	12,172	15,652	16,450	9,444	13,094	15,647	17,760
Retail stores and vending	13,396	16,151	37,723	52,262	52,465	54,800	56,804	53,249
Recreational places	12,245	11,224	13,038	14,080	8,725	11,290	13,516	14,970
Schools and colleges	23,019	32,221	30,963	29,771	27,128	25,293	28,615	41,199
Other FAFH sales, not elsewhere classified	9,117	9,670	9,890	10,528	7,818	7,482	9,013	9,682
Food furnished and donated	17,968	19,104	20,738	21,990	20,718	24,049	21,500	21,484
Alcohol at home	41,684	49,608	62,608	74,353	80,390	87,340	91,305	89,880
Liquor stores	18,093	22,743	26,018	28,855	32,962	34,499	33,544	33,294
Food stores	11,546	13,396	17,076	19,316	20,545	21,374	22,625	22,330
All other	12,044	13,469	19,514	26,182	26,882	31,467	35,136	34,257
Alcohol away from home	32,755	32,889	38,974	44,466	31,261	44,365	49,871	52,927
Eating and drinking places	26,059	26,834	31,833	36,647	26,138	37,589	41,777	43,886
Hotels and motels	3,500	2,917	3,732	4,016	2,329	3,277	3,985	4,569
All other	3,195	3,138	3,410	3,803	2,794	3,499	4,109	4,472

Source: U.S. Department of Agriculture, Economic Research Service, "Food Expenditure Series," <www.ers.usda.gov/data-products/food-expenditure-series/>, accessed June 2024.

Transportation

This section presents data on civil air transportation, both passenger and cargo, and on water transportation, including inland waterways, oceanborne commerce, the merchant marine, cargo, and vessel tonnages.

This section also presents statistics on revenues, passenger and freight traffic volume, and employment in various revenue-producing modes of the transportation industry, including motor vehicles, trains, and pipelines. Data are also presented on highway mileage and finances, motor vehicle travel, accidents, and registrations; and characteristics of public transit, railroads, and pipelines.

The principal source of transportation data is the annual *National Transportation Statistics* publication of the U.S. Bureau of Transportation Statistics. Principal sources of water transportation data is provided by the Corps of Engineers of the Department of Army. In addition, the U.S. Census Bureau in its Commodity Flow Survey (part of the Economic Census, taken every 5 years, for years ending in "2" and "7") provides data on the type, weight, and value of commodities shipped by manufacturing establishments in the United States, by means of transportation, origin, and destination. This census is conducted in accordance with the North American Industry Classification System (NAICS). See text, Section 15, Business Enterprise, for a discussion of the Economic Census and NAICS.

The Bureau of Transportation Statistics (BTS) was established within the U.S. Department of Transportation (DOT) in 1992 to collect, report, and analyze transportation data. BTS products include reports to Congress, the Secretary of Transportation, and stakeholders in the nation's transportation community. These stakeholders include: federal agencies, state and local governments, metropolitan planning organizations, universities, the private sector, and the general public. Congress requires, by congressional mandate laid out in 49 U.S.C. 111 (1), the BTS to report on transportation statistics to the President and Congress. *The Transportation Statistics Annual Report* (TSAR) provides a data overview of U.S. transportation issues; it can be found online at <www.bts.gov/tsar>. The BTS publication *National Transportation Statistics* (NTS), a companion report to the TSAR, has more comprehensive and longer time-series data. NTS presents information on the U.S. transportation system, including its physical components, safety record, economic performance, energy use, and environmental impacts. The BTS publication *State Transportation Statistics* presents a statistical profile of transportation in the 50 states and the District of Columbia. This profile includes infrastructure, freight movement and passenger travel, system safety, vehicles, transportation-related economy and finance, energy usage, and the environment.

The principal compiler of data on public roads and on operation of motor vehicles is the U.S. Department of Transportation's (DOT) Federal Highway Administration (FHWA). These data appear in FHWA's annual *Highway Statistics* and other publications.

The U.S. National Highway Traffic Safety Administration (NHTSA), through its *Traffic Safety Facts Annual Report Tables*, <cdan.dot.gov/tsftables/tsfar.htm>, and Fatality and Injury Reporting System Tool (FIRST), <cdan.dot.gov/query>, presents descriptive statistics about traffic crashes of all severities, from those that result in property damage to those that result in the loss of life. The tool compiles motor vehicle crash data from the Fatality Analysis Reporting System (FARS), the General Estimates System (GES), and Crash Report Sampling System (CRSS). Other publications and reports can be found at the National Center for Statistics and Analysis (NCSA), NCSA Tools, Publications, and Data, located on the internet at <cdan.nhtsa.gov>. DOT's Federal Railroad Administration (FRA), Office of Safety Analysis presents railroad safety information, including accidents and incidents, inspections, and highway-rail crossing data at its "Safety Data," located at <safetydata.fra.dot.gov/officeofsafety>.

Civil aviation—Federal promotion and regulation of civil aviation have been carried out by the Federal Aviation Administration (FAA) and the Civil Aeronautics Board (CAB). The CAB promoted and regulated the civil air transportation industry within the United States and between the United States and foreign countries. The Board granted licenses to provide air transportation service, approved or disapproved proposed rates and fares, and approved or disapproved proposed agreements and corporate relationships involving air carriers. In December 1984, the CAB ceased to exist as an agency. Some of its functions were transferred to the DOT, as outlined below. The responsibility for investigation of aviation accidents resides with the National Transportation Safety Board.

The Office of the Secretary, DOT aviation activities include: negotiation of international air transportation rights, selection of U.S. air carriers to serve capacity controlled international markets, oversight of international rates and fares, maintenance of essential air service to small communities, and consumer affairs. DOT's Bureau of Transportation Statistics (BTS) handles aviation information functions formerly assigned to CAB. Prior to BTS, the Research and Special Programs Administration handled these functions.

The principal activities of the FAA include: the promotion of air safety; controlling the use of navigable airspace; prescribing regulations dealing with the competency of airmen, airworthiness of aircraft, and air traffic control; operation of air route traffic control centers, airport traffic control towers, and flight service stations; the design, construction, maintenance, and inspection of navigation, traffic control, and communications equipment; and the development of general aviation.

The CAB published monthly and quarterly financial and traffic statistical data for the certificated route air carriers. BTS continues these publications, including both certificated and noncertificated (commuter) air carriers. The FAA annually publishes data on the use of airway facilities; data related to the location of airmen, aircraft, and airports; the volume of activity in the field of nonair carrier (general aviation) flying; and aircraft production and registration.

General aviation comprises all civil flying (including such commercial operations as small demand air taxis, agriculture application, powerline patrol, etc.) but excludes certificated route air carriers, supplemental operators, large-aircraft commercial operators, and commuter airlines.

Air carriers and service—The CAB previously issued "certificates of public convenience and necessity" under Section 401 of the Federal Aviation Act of 1958 for scheduled and nonscheduled (charter) passenger services and cargo services. It also issued certificates under Section 418 of the Act to cargo air carriers for domestic all-cargo service only. The DOT Office of the Secretary now issues the certificates under a "fit, willing, and able" test of air carrier operations. Carriers operating only a 60-seat-or-less aircraft are given exemption authority to carry passengers, cargo, and mail in scheduled and nonscheduled service under Part 298 of the DOT (formerly CAB) regulations. Exemption authority carriers who offer scheduled passenger service to an essential air service point must meet the "fit, willing, and able" test.

Vessel shipments, entrances, and clearances—Shipments by dry cargo vessels comprise shipments on all types of watercraft, except tanker vessels; shipments by tanker vessels comprise all types of cargo, liquid and dry, carried by tanker vessels. A vessel is reported as entered only at the first port which it enters in the United States, whether or not cargo is unloaded at that port.

A vessel is reported as cleared only at the last port at which clearance is made to a foreign port, whether or not it takes on cargo. Army and Navy vessels entering or clearing without commercial cargo are not included in the figures.

Units of measurement—Cargo (or freight) tonnage and shipping weight both represent the gross weight of the cargo including the weight of containers, wrappings, crates, etc.; however, shipping weight excludes lift and cargo vans and similar substantial outer containers. Other tonnage figures generally refer to stowing capacity of vessels, 100 cubic feet being called 1 ton. *Gross tonnage* comprises the space within the frames and the ceiling of the hull, together with those closed-in spaces above deck available for cargo, stores, passengers, or crew, with certain minor exceptions. Net or registered tonnage is the gross tonnage less the spaces occupied by the propelling machinery, fuel, crew quarters, master's cabin, and navigation spaces. Net tonnage represents space available for cargo and passengers. The net tonnage capacity of a ship may bear little relation to weight of cargo. Deadweight tonnage is the weight in long tons required to depress a vessel from light water line (that is, with only the machinery and equipment on board) to load line. It is, therefore, the weight of the cargo, fuel, etc., which a vessel is designed to carry with safety.

Functional systems—Roads and streets are assigned to groups according to the character of service intended. The functional systems are (1) arterial highways that generally handle the long trips, (2) collector facilities that collect and disperse traffic between the arterials and the lower systems, and (3) local roads and streets that primarily serve direct access to residential areas, farms, and other local areas.

Regulatory bodies—The Federal Energy Regulatory Commission (FERC) is an independent agency that regulates the interstate transmission of electricity, natural gas, and oil. FERC also reviews proposals to build liquefied natural gas (LNG) terminals and interstate natural gas pipelines, and licenses hydropower projects. The Energy Policy Act of 2005 gave FERC additional responsibilities such as regulating the transmission and wholesale sales of electricity in interstate commerce.

The Surface Transportation Board (STB) was created in the Interstate Commerce Commission Termination Act of 1995, Pub. L. No.104-88, 109 Stat. 803 (1995) (ICCTA), and is the successor agency to the Interstate Commerce Commission. The STB is an economic regulatory agency that Congress charged with the fundamental missions of resolving railroad rate and service disputes and reviewing proposed railroad mergers. The STB makes decisions independently, although it is administratively affiliated with the Department of Transportation.

The STB serves as both an adjudicatory and a regulatory body. The agency has jurisdiction over railroad rate and service issues and rail restructuring transactions (mergers, line sales, line construction, and line abandonment); certain trucking company, moving van, and noncontiguous ocean shipping company rate matters; certain intercity passenger bus company structure, financial, and operational matters; and rates and services of certain pipelines not regulated by the Federal Energy Regulatory Commission. Other ICC regulatory functions were either eliminated or transferred to the Federal Highway Administration or the Bureau of Transportation Statistics within DOT.

Rail carriers are regulated by the STB and subject to the Uniform System of Accounts and required to file annual and periodic reports. Railroads are classified based on their annual operating revenues. The class to which a carrier belongs is determined by comparing its adjusted operating revenues for 3 consecutive years to the following scale: Class I, $1.05 billion or more; Class II, $47.3 million to $1.05 billion; and Class III, $0 to $47.3 million. Operating revenue dollar ranges are indexed for inflation.

Postal Service—The U.S. Postal Service provides mail processing and delivery services within the United States. The Postal Accountability and Enhancement Act of 2006 was the most significant legislative change to the Postal Service since 1971 when the Postal Reorganization Act of 1970 created the Postal Service as an independent establishment of the Federal Executive Branch.

The Postal Service Reform Act of 2022 (PSRA), was signed into law on April 6, 2022. The financial provisions will eliminate large unpaid obligations and reduce the size of the Postal Service's annual budget deficit. At the same time, operational provisions will increase transparency and improve the quality of service provided to customers. The PSRA removes the Postal Service's obligation to prefund retiree health benefits and eliminates all previously imposed prefunding requirements that remain unpaid. The Act also requires new retirees and their dependents who wish to retain their Postal Service health benefits to participate in Medicare if they are eligible starting in 2025. The Postal Service will be subject to additional procedural requirements regarding the establishment of performance targets and will continue reporting on its success in meeting those targets. The Postal Service must make service performance information more accessible through the creation of a publicly available dashboard,

Revenue and cost analysis describes the Postal Service's system of attributing revenues and costs to classes of mail and service. This system draws primarily upon probability sampling techniques to develop estimates of revenues, volumes, and weights, as well as costs by class of mail and special service. The costs attributed to classes of mail and special services are primarily incremental costs that vary in response to changes in volume. The remaining cost balance represents "institutional costs." Statistics on revenues, volume of mail, and distribution of expenditures are presented in the Postal Service's annual reports *Public Cost and Revenue Analysis* and *Annual Report to Congress*.

Statistical reliability—For a discussion of statistical collection and estimation, sampling procedures, and measures of statistical reliability applicable to Census Bureau data, see Appendix III.

Table 1093. Transportation-Related Components of U.S. Gross Domestic Product: 2010 to 2022

[In billions of dollars (1,395.7 represents $1,395,700,000,000), except percent. For explanation of chained dollars, see text, Section 13]

Item	2010	2015	2019	2020	2021	2022
CURRENT DOLLARS						
Total transportation-related final demand [1]	**1,395.7**	**1,758.6**	**1,968.7**	**1,650.2**	**2,002.9**	**(NA)**
Total gross domestic product (GDP)	15,049.0	18,295.0	21,521.4	21,323.0	23,594.0	25,744.1
Transportation as a percent of GDP	9.3	9.6	9.1	7.7	8.5	(NA)
Personal consumption of transportation	1,022.0	1,249.9	1,437.5	1,225.3	1,615.9	1,866.1
Motor vehicles and parts	344.5	490.7	545.1	547.0	700.8	730.8
Motor vehicle fuels, lubricants, and fluids	312.1	297.4	328.7	238.4	361.1	477.5
Transportation services	305.2	393.5	480.7	358.7	459.6	562.2
Motor vehicle and other transportation insurance	60.3	68.2	83.0	81.2	94.4	95.6
Gross private domestic investment	145.7	323.3	324.9	236.9	231.0	249.0
Transportation structures	9.9	13.5	16.8	15.9	16.0	17.0
Transportation equipment	135.8	309.8	308.1	221.0	215.1	232.0
Net exports of transportation-related goods and service [2]	-85.0	-149.0	-170.8	-168.8	-202.4	-260.3
Exports (+)	260.3	355.8	380.2	258.9	292.4	345.0
Civilian aircraft, engines, and parts	71.9	119.5	126.0	72.0	79.9	94.4
Automotive vehicles, engines, and parts	112.0	151.9	163.1	129.4	146.4	159.7
Transport	76.4	84.4	91.1	57.5	66.1	91.0
Imports (-)	345.3	504.9	550.9	427.7	494.7	605.3
Civilian aircraft, engines, and parts	31.3	55.2	62.8	44.9	41.5	47.7
Automotive vehicles, engines, and parts	225.6	350.0	375.3	309.9	346.5	399.9
Transport	88.4	99.6	112.8	73.0	106.7	157.6
Government transportation-related purchases	301.2	322.7	372.7	372.0	400.2	(NA)
Federal purchases [3]	38.5	40.4	44.3	43.0	50.2	(NA)
State and local purchases [3]	238.1	268.6	312.2	316.4	335.5	(NA)
Defense-related purchases [4]	24.6	13.6	16.1	12.5	14.5	16.8
CHAINED (2017) DOLLARS						
Total transportation-related final demand [1]	**1,475.7**	**1,776.9**	**1,862.4**	**1,591.3**	**1,755.2**	**(NA)**
Total gross domestic product (GDP)	16,789.8	18,799.6	20,692.1	20,234.1	21,407.7	21,822.0
Transportation as a percent of GDP	8.8	9.5	9.0	7.9	8.2	(NA)
Personal consumption of transportation	1,051.5	1,257.2	1,380.1	1,212.0	1,420.1	1,422.5
Motor vehicles and parts	357.5	481.3	540.6	533.5	613.4	572.6
Motor vehicle fuels, lubricants, and fluids	280.3	298.2	300.8	255.5	290.2	293.5
Transportation services	335.8	401.6	461.6	348.6	426.8	468.6
Motor vehicle and other transportation insurance	78.0	76.1	77.2	74.4	89.7	87.8
Gross private domestic investment	163.8	332.9	320.5	234.7	239.8	241.9
Transportation structures	11.4	14.1	15.9	14.7	14.0	13.7
Transportation equipment	152.4	318.7	304.6	220.0	225.7	228.2
Net exports of transportation-related goods and service [2]	-78.7	-138.5	-174.1	-169.4	-193.6	-133.4
Exports (+)	284.0	360.5	370.9	253.1	277.3	407.3
Civilian aircraft, engines, and parts	87.3	126.0	119.6	67.4	72.5	180.7
Automotive vehicles, engines, and parts	116.4	151.0	161.2	128.2	143.5	150.5
Transport	80.3	83.4	90.1	57.5	61.3	76.1
Imports (-)	362.7	499.0	545.0	422.5	470.9	540.6
Civilian aircraft, engines, and parts	38.5	56.3	59.8	42.6	38.1	42.0
Automotive vehicles, engines, and parts	227.3	345.9	377.9	309.6	340.7	380.3
Transport	96.9	96.8	107.4	70.3	92.2	118.4
Government transportation-related purchases	327.0	313.9	331.5	329.5	326.9	(NA)
Federal purchases [3]	39.9	38.7	39.1	37.6	42.5	(NA)
State and local purchases [3]	260.3	261.7	277.5	279.6	270.5	(NA)
Defense-related purchases [4]	26.8	13.5	15.0	12.3	13.9	13.8

NA Not available. [1] Sum of total personal consumption of transportation, total gross private domestic investment, net exports of transportation-related goods and services, and total government transportation-related purchases. [2] Exports minus imports. [3] Federal purchases and state and local purchases are the sum of consumption expenditures and gross investment. [4] Defense-related purchases are the sum of transportation of material and travel.

Source: U.S. Bureau of Transportation Statistics, "National Transportation Statistics," <www.bts.gov/product/national-transportation-statistics>, accessed March 2024.

Table 1094. Employment in Transportation and Warehousing: 2010 to 2023

[In thousands (4,179 represents 4,179,000). Annual average of monthly figures. Based on Current Employment Statistics program; see Appendix III]

Industry	NAICS code [1]	2010	2015	2017	2018	2019	2020	2021	2022	2023
Transportation and warehousing	**48–49**	**4,179**	**4,859**	**5,178**	**5,426**	**5,665**	**5,640**	**6,145**	**6,606**	**6,565**
Air transportation	481	458	459	492	497	505	441	460	506	552
Rail transportation	482	183	204	182	182	174	150	146	147	153
Water transportation	483	62	66	65	65	67	60	58	65	70
Truck transportation	484	1,251	1,453	1,457	1,496	1,529	1,471	1,515	1,577	1,567
Transit and ground passenger	485	436	485	495	495	494	370	377	411	428
Pipeline transportation	486	42	50	49	50	52	51	50	51	52
Scenic and sightseeing	487	27	33	35	35	36	21	23	30	30
Support activities	488	553	663	701	729	754	701	726	793	823
Couriers and messengers	492	528	613	676	740	827	967	1,089	1,118	1,083
Warehousing and storage	493	638	834	1,027	1,139	1,229	1,405	1,701	1,908	1,808

[1] North American Industry Classification System 2022, see text, Sections 12 and 15.

Source: U.S. Bureau of Labor Statistics, Current Employment Statistics, "Employment, Hours, and Earnings—National," <www.bls.gov/ces/data>, accessed March 2024.

Table 1095. Transportation and Warehousing—Establishments, Employees, and Payroll by Industry: 2021 and 2022

[Employment in thousands (5,693.6 represents 5,693,600); payroll in millions of dollars (316,774.1 represents $316,774,100,000). Covers establishments with payroll. Excludes self-employed individuals, railroad employees, and most government employees. For statement on methodology, see Appendix III. County Business Patterns excludes rail transportation (NAICS 482) and the Postal Service (NAICS 491)]

Industry	NAICS code [1]	Establishments		Paid employees (1,000) [2]		Annual payroll (mil. dol.)	
		2021	2022	2021	2022	2021	2022
Transportation & warehousing...................	**48–49**	**279,148**	**294,354**	**5,693.6**	**6,108.1**	**316,774.1**	**345,454.9**
Air transportation..........................	481	4,543	4,645	465.4	493.9	42,208.5	47,077.8
Scheduled air transportation................	4811	2,174	2,172	417.0	441.0	36,871.9	40,848.6
Scheduled passenger air transportation.............	481111	1,797	1,787	407.4	432.8	35,988.6	40,064.0
Scheduled freight air transportation.............	481112	377	385	9.7	8.2	883.3	784.6
Nonscheduled air transportation....................	4812	2,369	2,473	48.4	52.9	5,336.6	6,229.2
Water transportation.........................	483	1,792	1,780	56.4	60.6	5,286.9	6,071.2
Deep sea, coastal, & Great Lakes water transportation........................	4831	1,112	1,095	37.7	41.2	3,763.3	4,384.5
Inland water transportation...................	4832	680	685	18.7	19.5	1,523.6	1,686.6
Inland water freight transportation................	483211	371	382	15.9	16.2	1,346.2	1,488.4
Inland water passenger transportation..............	483212	309	303	2.8	3.2	177.4	198.2
Truck transportation.........................	484	163,565	174,556	1,659.2	1,731.7	92,120.4	101,455.8
General freight trucking....................	4841	110,003	119,948	1,164.9	1,224.2	64,664.9	71,439.8
General freight trucking, local..............	48411	41,896	45,436	294.8	317.3	13,864.1	15,469.4
General freight trucking, long distance..............	48412	68,107	74,512	870.0	906.9	50,800.7	55,970.4
Specialized freight trucking...................	4842	53,562	54,608	494.3	507.5	27,455.5	30,016.0
Used household & office goods moving...........	48421	9,547	9,803	102.3	105.9	4,346.4	4,706.5
Specialized freight (except used goods) trucking, local..............	48422	32,217	32,829	225.1	228.0	13,071.3	14,260.7
Specialized freight (except used goods) trucking, long-distance..............	48423	11,798	11,976	166.9	173.6	10,037.8	11,048.9
Transit & ground passenger transportation.............	485	19,226	19,713	393.0	428.2	16,848.3	16,370.3
Urban transit systems....................	4851	637	652	44.7	45.3	2,605.7	2,764.0
Mixed mode systems...................	485111	33	38	0.7	0.8	30.3	42.1
Commuter rail.......................	485112	19	17	4.1	4.0	407.1	412.9
Bus and other motor vehicle mode systems.........	485113	525	537	38.6	39.1	2,081.9	2,209.6
Other........................	485119	60	60	1.3	1.4	[3] 86.4	99.4
Interurban & rural bus transportation..................	4852	554	549	[3] 13.3	13.5	553.1	560.4
Taxi & limousine service..................	4853	7,022	7,387	43.9	47.4	[3] 4,990.5	2,597.0
Taxi service......................	48531	3,108	3,162	26.8	21.6	[3] 4,292.1	1,577.2
Limousine service....................	48532	3,914	4,225	17.1	25.8	698.4	1,019.9
School & employee bus transportation...............	4854	4,002	4,000	194.5	210.6	5,301.5	6,177.3
Charter bus industry....................	4855	1,137	1,129	17.3	24.4	742.1	1,081.2
Other transit & ground passenger transportation......	4859	5,874	5,996	79.2	86.9	2,655.4	3,190.4
Special needs transportation...................	485991	3,812	3,825	61.2	63.9	2,020.4	2,339.3
Pipeline transportation.......................	486	3,446	3,392	[3] 45.3	44.5	5,714.5	6,026.4
Pipeline transportation of crude oil....................	4861	658	649	10.0	9.7	1,327.2	1,346.6
Pipeline transportation of natural gas.................	4862	2,068	2,021	[3] 26.3	25.9	3,274.4	3,515.7
Other pipeline transportation......................	4869	720	722	9.0	9.0	1,112.9	1,164.1
Scenic & sightseeing transportation...................	487	3,068	3,211	17.8	24.1	969.4	1,242.3
Scenic & sightseeing transportation, land.............	4871	682	709	5.9	8.4	262.9	361.3
Scenic & sightseeing transportation, water.........	4872	2,119	2,243	9.8	12.9	582.0	708.6
Scenic & sightseeing transportation, other............	4879	267	259	2.1	2.8	124.5	172.4
Support activities for transportation....................	488	48,609	50,045	766.8	832.0	47,082.4	54,525.3
Support activities for air transportation................	4881	6,286	6,506	189.2	209.3	9,663.6	11,247.7
Airport operations....................	48811	2,300	2,410	103.2	117.6	3,916.0	4,756.8
Air traffic control.......................	488111	217	221	[3] 1.7	1.8	128.9	138.4
Other support activities for air transportation.........	48819	3,986	4,096	86.0	91.8	5,747.6	6,491.0
Support activities for rail transportation..................	4882	1,658	1,761	42.0	45.0	2,364.2	2,981.8
Support activities for water transportation..............	4883	2,632	2,617	95.8	103.4	8,055.0	8,847.4
Port and harbor operations...........................	48831	349	346	12.7	13.3	911.8	994.2
Marine cargo handling...........................	48832	481	475	61.8	69.2	5,432.1	6,047.2
Navigational services to shipping...................	48833	1,047	1,044	14.2	13.7	1,205.5	1,237.7
Other support activities for water transportation.....	48839	755	752	7.2	7.3	505.6	568.4
Support activities for road transportation................	4884	14,090	14,488	114.3	123.8	4,883.4	5,588.0
Motor vehicle towing....................	48841	10,119	10,554	64.5	69.8	3,003.7	3,452.2
Freight transportation arrangement....................	4885	21,832	22,383	301.8	323.3	20,717.1	24,269.4
Other support activities for transportation..............	4889	2,111	2,290	23.6	27.0	1,398.9	1,590.9
Couriers & messengers...........................	492	16,647	17,033	1,090.9	1,198.0	48,077.8	47,750.3
Couriers.........................	4921	11,285	11,667	954.1	1,048.1	40,915.0	40,746.6
Local messengers & local delivery....................	4922	5,362	5,366	136.8	149.9	7,162.9	7,003.7
Warehousing & storage.............................	493	18,252	19,979	1,198.9	1,295.1	58,465.9	64,935.5

[1] Data based on 2017 North American Industry Classification System (NAICS). See text, Section 15. [2] Covers full- and part-time employees who are on the payroll in the pay period including March 12. [3] Data flagged for high noise; the value was changed by 5 percent or more to avoid disclosure of data for individual businesses.

Source: U.S. Census Bureau, County Business Patterns, "All Sectors: County Business Patterns, including ZIP Code Business Patterns, by Legal Form of Organization and Employment Size Class for the U.S., States, and Selected Geographies: 2022," <data.census.gov>, accessed June 2024. See also <www.census.gov/programs-surveys/cbp.html>.

Table 1096. Transportation Sector—Estimated Revenue by Kind of Business: 2018 to 2022

[In millions of dollars (1,041,262 represents $1,041,262,000,000). For taxable employer firms. Based on the Service Annual Survey; see Appendix III]

Kind of business	NAICS code [1]	2018	2019	2020	2021	2022
Transportation and warehousing (excl. 482 and 491).......	**4849y**	**1,041,262**	**1,080,621**	**943,941**	**1,167,343**	**1,429,998**
Air transportation [2].......	481	224,702	236,787	111,727	167,354	254,631
Scheduled passenger air transportation.........	481111	195,170	206,768	82,765	133,488	209,247
Scheduled freight air transportation.........	481112	6,079	6,519	6,651	7,643	11,895
Nonscheduled chartered passenger air transportation.........	481211	15,378	16,376	15,015	19,022	24,499
Nonscheduled chartered freight air transportation.........	481212	5,981	4,846	4,857	4,987	6,045
Water transportation [2]........	483	46,114	48,825	29,803	27,527	50,732
Deep sea freight transportation.........	483111	6,032	6,365	6,315	7,134	9,343
Deep sea passenger transportation.........	483112	24,746	26,502	9,497	5,476	21,890
Coastal and great lakes freight transportation.........	483113	7,901	8,089	7,091	7,623	9,896
Coastal and great lakes passenger transportation.........	483114	641	703	611	799	1,017
Inland water freight transportation.........	483211	6,245	6,588	5,834	6,004	7,700
Inland water passenger transportation.........	483212	549	578	455	491	886
Truck transportation.........	484	313,809	320,817	318,602	376,903	445,509
General freight trucking, local.........	48411	35,887	37,915	39,427	49,553	59,261
General freight trucking, long-distance, truckload.........	484121	124,337	124,566	126,768	152,753	183,482
General freight trucking, long-distance, less than truckload.....	484122	49,982	51,897	50,515	60,003	68,411
Used household and office goods moving.........	48421	16,389	16,492	16,762	19,593	21,968
Specialized freight (except used goods) trucking, local.........	48422	44,685	46,794	44,650	48,134	56,574
Specialized freight (except used goods) trucking, long-distance.........	48423	42,529	43,153	40,480	46,867	55,813
Transit and ground passenger transportation [2].........	485	50,248	55,888	39,360	45,771	61,192
Urban transit systems.........	4851	6,268	6,509	6,123	6,484	6,708
Interurban and rural bus transportation.........	4852	1,718	1,708	995	(S)	1,234
Taxi service.........	48531	14,030	17,287	10,410	12,169	20,721
Limousine service.........	48532	4,407	4,543	2,277	2,950	4,767
School and employee bus transportation.........	4854	11,723	12,641	9,706	11,340	12,262
Charter bus industry.........	4855	3,843	4,101	1,934	2,628	4,226
Pipeline transportation [2].........	486	54,527	60,325	58,338	62,906	68,450
Pipeline transportation of crude oil.........	4861	13,397	14,958	13,761	13,961	15,588
Pipeline transportation of natural gas.........	4862	30,722	33,999	32,638	35,953	38,259
Pipeline transportation of refined petroleum products.........	48691	10,039	10,989	11,597	12,667	14,250
Scenic and sightseeing transportation [2].........	487	4,318	4,426	2,062	3,489	4,474
Scenic and sightseeing transportation, land.........	4871	1,364	1,417	514	823	1,170
Scenic and sightseeing transportation, water.........	4872	2,292	2,463	1,320	2,308	2,806
Support activities for transportation [2].........	488	210,573	210,620	224,754	295,919	346,520
Airport operations.........	48811	9,130	9,552	10,303	11,616	15,375
Other support activities for air transportation.........	48819	18,053	19,680	19,317	19,954	22,148
Support activities for rail transportation.........	4882	6,178	6,532	6,477	6,157	6,725
Port and harbor operations.........	48831	3,419	3,646	3,832	4,258	5,092
Marine cargo handling.........	48832	10,679	10,588	10,331	12,317	14,313
Navigational services to shipping.........	48833	4,407	4,009	3,731	3,874	4,383
Other support activities for water transportation.........	48839	1,698	1,792	1,839	2,211	2,744
Motor vehicle towing.........	48841	7,606	8,338	8,893	10,793	12,694
Freight transportation arrangement.........	4885	143,040	139,631	152,785	215,590	252,417
Couriers and messengers.........	492	97,111	101,664	117,144	138,738	143,781
Couriers and express delivery services.........	4921	90,784	94,941	108,614	128,093	131,931
Local messengers and local delivery.........	4922	6,327	6,723	8,530	10,645	11,850
Warehousing and storage.........	493	39,860	41,269	42,151	48,736	54,709
General warehousing and storage.........	49311	25,383	26,192	27,376	32,549	37,750
Refrigerated warehousing and storage.........	49312	6,123	6,523	6,271	7,081	(S)
Farm product warehousing and storage.........	49313	832	876	825	859	990

S Estimate does not meet publication standards. [1] Data are based on the 2012 North American Industry Classification System NAICS; see text, this section and Section 15. [2] Includes other kinds of business not shown separately.

Source: U.S. Census Bureau, Service Annual Survey, "Service Annual Survey Latest Data (NAICS-basis): 2022," <www.census.gov/programs-surveys/sas/data.html>, accessed February 2024.

Table 1097. Transportation and Warehousing—Establishments, Revenue, Payroll, and Employees by Industry: 2022

[1,366,618 represents $1,366,618,000,000. For establishments with payroll. Based on the 2022 Economic Census. Paid employees for pay period including March 12. See Appendix III]

Industry	NAICS code [1]	Number of establish-ments	Revenue (mil. dol.)	Annual payroll (mil. dol.)	Paid employees (1,000)
Transportation and warehousing total..................	**48–49**	**294,054**	**1,366,618**	**351,922**	**6,311.2**
Air transportation..........	481	4,448	284,689	51,433	557.2
Water transportation..........	483	1,644	49,111	5,928	71.1
Truck transportation..........	484	171,824	441,509	98,378	1,707.9
Transit and ground passenger transportation..........	485	19,553	58,637	24,042	689.4
Pipeline transportation..........	486	3,593	69,519	6,220	49.8
Scenic and sightseeing transportation..........	487	3,155	4,812	1,293	26.3
Support activities for transportation..........	488	50,852	243,861	53,293	841.0
Couriers and messengers..........	492	17,736	151,596	45,355	1,034.2
Warehousing and storage..........	493	21,249	62,883	65,980	1,334.4

[1] Data based on the 2022 North American Industry Classification System (NAICS); see text, Section 15.

Source: U.S. Census Bureau, 2022 Economic Census, EC2248BASIC, "Transportation and Warehousing: Summary Statistics for the U.S., States, and Selected Geographies: 2022," <data.census.gov/>, accessed May 2024.

Table 1098. Transportation and Warehousing—Nonemployer Establishments and Receipts by Kind of Business: 2010 to 2021

[1,021.2 represents 1,021,200. Includes only firms subject to federal income tax. Nonemployers are businesses with no paid employees. Data originate chiefly from administrative records of the Internal Revenue Service; see Appendix III]

Kind of business	NAICS code [1]	Establishments (1,000)			Receipts (mil. dol.)		
		2010	2020	2021	2010	2020	2021
Transportation and warehousing.............	**48–49**	**1,021.2**	**3,189.1**	**3,599.7**	**60,746**	**121,301**	**155,338**
Air transportation....................................	481	19.1	22.9	25.0	1,219	1,481	1,695
Water transportation.................................	483	6.6	7.4	7.7	490	558	641
Truck transportation................................	484	490.3	791.9	848.7	42,485	78,497	96,777
General freight trucking..........................	4841	445.1	727.7	782.0	39,277	73,872	91,581
General freight trucking, local...................	48411	168.7	238.0	253.0	12,144	21,190	25,099
General freight trucking, long-distance........	48412	276.4	489.7	529.0	27,133	52,682	66,482
Specialized freight trucking......................	4842	45.2	64.1	66.7	3,207	4,625	5,196
Transit and ground passenger transportation....	485	218.4	1,239.3	1,237.2	7,463	21,973	32,316
Urban transit system..............................	4851	1.1	2.0	2.1	39	58	80
Interurban and rural bus transportation..........	4852	1.5	2.4	2.3	67	71	81
Taxi and limousine service.......................	4853	176.4	1,133.9	1,131.7	6,107	19,362	29,020
School and employee bus transportation........	4854	6.9	6.2	6.1	191	183	205
Charter bus industry..............................	4855	3.8	3.4	3.3	172	133	152
Other transit and ground passenger transportation....................................	4859	28.7	91.5	91.9	887	2,167	2,778
Pipeline transportation.............................	486	0.9	1.4	1.4	76	87	94
Scenic and sightseeing transportation...........	487	4.9	6.1	6.7	163	205	271
Support activities for transportation...............	488	105.2	132.1	136.2	4,624	7,080	8,122
Couriers and messengers.........................	492	166.6	967.2	1,313.7	3,772	10,661	14,570
Warehousing and storage.........................	493	9.2	20.8	23.0	455	757	850

[1] 2010 data based on the 2007 North American Industry Classification System (NAICS); and beginning 2017, data based on 2017 NAICS.

Source: U.S. Census Bureau, Nonemployer Statistics, "All Sectors: Nonemployer Statistics by Legal Form of Organization and Receipts Size Class for the U.S., States, and Selected Geographies: 2021," <data.census.gov>, accessed March 2024.

Table 1099. Transportation System Mileage Within the United States: 1985 to 2022

[3,864 represents 3,864,000. Numbers, except where indicated]

System	Unit	1985	1990	1995	2000	2005	2010	2015	2020	2022
Highway [1]......................	1,000	3,864	3,867	3,912	3,936	3,996	4,067	4,155	4,173	4,197
Class 1 rail [2]....................	Number	145,764	119,758	108,264	99,250	95,830	95,700	93,628	91,773	91,285
Amtrak [2]........................	Number	24,000	24,000	24,000	23,000	22,007	21,178	21,358	20,787	21,220
Transit: [3]										
Commuter rail [4]..............	Number	3,574	4,132	4,160	5,209	7,118	7,630	7,697	7,930	7,934
Heavy rail [5]....................	Number	1,293	1,351	1,458	1,558	1,622	1,617	1,643	1,663	1,681
Light rail [6].....................	Number	384	483	568	834	1,188	1,497	1,893	2,096	2,127
Navigable channels [7]..........	Number	25,000	25,000	25,000	25,000	25,000	25,000	25,000	25,000	25,000
Oil pipeline [8]..................	Number	(NA)	(NA)	(NA)	(NA)	166,760	181,836	208,812	229,395	229,443
Gas pipeline [9].................	1,000	1,641	1,871	2,028	2,115	2,287	2,427	2,509	2,604	2,733

NA Not available. [1] All public road and street mileage in the 50 states and the District of Columbia. Beginning in 1998, approximately 43,000 miles of Bureau of Land Management Roads are excluded. [2] Data represent miles of road owned (aggregate length of road, excluding yard tracks, sidings, and parallel lines). Portions of class I freight railroads, Amtrak, and commuter rail networks share common trackage. Amtrak data represent miles of road operated. [3] Transit system length is measured in directional route-miles; see source. [4] Urban passenger train service for short-distance travel between a central city and adjacent suburb. Does not include rapid rail transit or light rail service. [5] Also known as subway, elevated (railway), or metropolitan railway (metro). [6] A streetcar-type vehicle operated on city streets. Beginning in 2011, "Light rail" includes light rail, street car rail, and hybrid rail. [7] Estimated sums of domestic waterways which include rivers, bays, channels, and the inner route of the Southeast Alaskan Islands, but does not include the Great Lakes or deep ocean traffic. Beginning in 2007, includes waterways connecting the Great Lakes and the St. Lawrence Seaway inside the U.S. [8] Includes trunk and gathering lines for crude-oil pipeline and highly volatile liquid (HVL), carbon dioxide, and other hazardous liquid systems. Oil pipeline data has been discontinued for years prior to 2001. [9] Data includes gathering, transmission, service, and distribution mains.

Source: U.S. Bureau of Transportation Statistics, "National Transportation Statistics," <www.bts.gov/content/system-mileage-within-united-states>, accessed May 2024.

Table 1100. U.S. Aircraft, Vehicles, and Other Conveyances: 2000 to 2022

[Number except as noted (225,821 represents 225,821,000)]

Mode	2000	2010	2015	2017	2018	2019	2020	2021	2022
AIR									
Air carrier [1]	7,826	7,185	6,876	7,196	7,475	7,628	5,884	5,815	6,852
General aviation [2] (active fleet)	217,533	223,370	210,031	211,757	211,749	210,981	204,140	209,194	209,140
HIGHWAY, REGISTERED VEHICLES (1,000s)									
Total registered vehicles	225,821	250,070	263,610	272,481	273,602	276,491	275,936	282,355	(NA)
Light duty vehicle, short wheel base [3]	133,621	190,203	189,618	193,672	192,856	194,349	194,883	197,236	(NA)
Motorcycle	4,346	8,010	8,601	8,715	8,666	8,596	8,347	9,881	(NA)
Light duty vehicle, long wheel base [4]	79,085	40,242	53,299	56,881	57,854	59,465	58,796	60,439	(NA)
Trucks [5]	5,926	8,217	8,456	9,337	10,328	10,160	9,908	10,716	(NA)
Truck, combination	2,097	2,553	2,747	2,892	2,906	2,925	2,991	3,143	(NA)
Bus	746	846	889	983	992	995	1,010	939	(NA)
TRANSIT									
Motor bus	58,578	63,108	63,573	63,759	63,284	64,000	63,903	62,836	62,766
Light rail cars [6]	1,306	2,096	2,478	2,557	2,729	2,811	2,799	2,859	2,892
Heavy rail cars [7]	10,311	11,510	10,737	10,705	10,763	11,198	11,064	10,942	10,880
Trolley bus	652	571	611	539	571	572	633	563	563
Commuter rail cars and locomotives	5,497	6,768	7,151	7,129	7,023	7,144	7,524	7,545	7,645
Demand responsive	22,087	32,696	32,490	33,012	33,253	34,613	34,633	31,553	31,777
Other [8]	7,705	18,066	18,601	18,104	17,803	17,491	17,511	13,748	13,451
RAIL									
Class I, freight cars	560,154	397,730	330,996	306,268	293,742	270,378	252,400	243,087	(NA)
Class I, locomotive	20,028	23,893	26,574	26,547	26,086	24,597	23,544	23,264	(NA)
Nonclass I freight cars	132,448	101,755	(NA)	(NA)	(NA)	(NA)	(NA)	(NA)	(NA)
Car companies' and shippers' freight cars	688,194	809,544	(NA)	(NA)	(NA)	(NA)	(NA)	(NA)	(NA)
Amtrak, passenger train car	1,894	1,274	1,428	1,405	1,403	1,415	1,313	1,529	(NA)
Amtrak, locomotive	378	282	423	419	431	403	384	395	(NA)
WATER									
Non-self-propelled vessels [9]	35,008	31,906	32,819	32,808	33,266	33,600	34,209	34,364	(NA)
Self-propelled vessels [10]	10,410	10,775	10,108	9,344	9,904	10,152	10,339	10,392	(NA)
Ocean-going self-propelled vessels (1,000 gross tons and over) [11]	282	221	170	176	182	182	185	183	178
Recreational boats (1,000s)	12,782	12,439	11,867	11,962	11,853	11,879	11,838	11,958	11,770

NA Not available. [1] Air carrier aircraft are those carrying passengers or cargo for hire under 14 CFR 121 and 14 CFR 135. Number of aircraft is the monthly average number of aircraft reported in use for the last three months of the year. [2] Includes air taxi aircraft. [3] Data for 2000-06 are for passenger cars. Beginning 2007, data are for Light Duty Vehicles Short Wheel Base—passenger cars, light trucks, vans and sport utility vehicles with a wheelbase of 121 inches or less. [4] Data for 2000-06 are for 2-axle, 4-tire vehicles other than passenger cars, motorcycles, and buses. Beginning 2007, data are for Light Duty Vehicles Long Wheel Base—large passenger cars, vans, pickup trucks, and sport/utility vehicles with wheelbases larger than 121 inches. [5] Includes trucks on a single frame with at least 2 axles and 6 tires. [6] Fixed rail streetcar or trolley, for example. [7] Metro, subway, or rapid transit, for example. [8] Includes Alaska railroad, automated guideway transit, cable car, ferry boat, inclined plane, monorail, and vanpool. [9] Includes dry-cargo barges, tank barges, and railroad-car floats. [10] Includes dry-cargo and/or passenger, offshore supply vessels, railroad-car ferries, tankers, and towboats. [11] 2000-06 data include private and government owned vessels of 1,000 gross tons or more. Beginning 2007, data are reported only for privately owned vessels of 1,000 gross tons or more.

Source: U.S. Bureau of Transportation Statistics, "National Transportation Statistics," <www.bts.gov/topics/national-transportation-statistics>, accessed April 2024.

Table 1101. Transportation Shipments by Mode: 2019 and 2022

[19,932 represents 19,932,000,000. All truck, rail, water, and pipeline movements that involve more than one mode, including exports and imports that change mode at international gateways, are included in multiple modes & mail to avoid double counting. Data do not include imports and exports that pass through the United States from a foreign origin to a foreign destination by any mode]

Mode	2019				2022			
	Total	Domestic	Exports	Imports	Total	Domestic	Exports	Imports
WEIGHT (millions of tons)								
Total	**19,932**	**17,825**	**1,139**	**968**	**19,611**	**17,414**	**1,208**	**989**
Truck	12,852	11,941	468	443	12,641	11,747	448	446
Rail	1,599	1,160	267	172	1,567	1,081	319	167
Water	821	657	113	51	784	626	118	40
Air, air and truck	7	2	3	2	8	2	4	2
Multiple modes and mail	653	538	63	52	624	514	57	53
Pipeline	3,905	3,437	221	247	3,901	3,364	258	280
Other and unknown	96	89	5	2	86	80	5	2
VALUE (billions of 2017 dollars)								
Total	**18,945**	**15,126**	**1,575**	**2,243**	**18,761**	**14,838**	**1,522**	**2,401**
Truck	13,809	11,294	985	1,530	13,611	11,032	933	1,646
Rail	584	226	138	220	563	215	133	214
Water	268	182	47	39	253	174	44	36
Air, air and truck	611	150	237	223	655	154	242	259
Multiple modes and mail	2,582	2,343	78	161	2,596	2,361	65	170
Pipeline	1,061	929	73	59	1,058	901	89	68
Other and unknown	30	2	17	11	26	2	16	8

Source: U.S. Department of Transportation, Bureau of Transportation Statistics, *Transportation Statistics Annual Report 2023*, December 2023. See also <www.bts.gov/TSAR>.

Table 1102. Shipment Characteristics by Mode of Transportation: 2012 and 2017

[13,852,143 represents $13,852,143,000,000. For business establishments in mining, manufacturing, wholesale trade, and selected retail and services industries. 2017 industries classified by the 2012 North American Industry Classification System (NAICS). 2012 industries classified by 2007 NAICS. Selected auxiliary establishments are also included. Based on the Commodity Flow Survey, conducted as part of the Economic Census; see Appendix III]

Mode of transportation	Value (mil. dol.)		Tons (1,000)		Ton-miles (mil.)		Average miles per shipment	
	2012	2017	2012	2017	2012	2017	2012	2017
All modes.................	13,852,143	14,517,812	11,299,409	12,468,902	2,969,506	3,116,876	630	679
Single modes.................	11,900,364	11,737,969	10,905,518	11,604,764	2,697,418	2,479,593	262	243
Truck [1]...............	10,132,229	10,398,910	8,060,166	8,843,334	1,247,717	1,327,094	227	206
For-hire truck...............	6,504,636	6,968,184	4,298,693	5,232,034	1,050,942	1,162,179	508	369
Private truck..............	3,627,592	3,430,726	3,761,472	3,611,300	196,775	164,915	58	45
Rail.......................	473,070	254,209	1,628,537	1,251,240	1,211,481	824,763	805	579
Water......................	301,554	243,855	575,996	804,392	192,866	259,610	908	259
Inland water..............	218,927	117,321	424,542	471,854	118,742	177,494	275	188
Great Lakes..............	424	614	31,403	41,947	10,959	15,638	347	304
Deep sea................	59,878	120,651	72,987	268,634	22,130	50,866	1,157	359
Multiple waterways.........	22,325	5,268	47,064	21,958	41,035	15,612	1,034	525
Air (includes truck and air).....	450,575	496,637	4,845	8,019	5,810	9,822	1,295	1,403
Pipeline [2]..............	542,936	344,357	635,975	697,778	(S)	(S)	(S)	(S)
Multiple modes..............	1,950,753	2,777,749	357,047	770,504	271,832	637,155	922	953
Parcel, U.S. Postal Service or courier....................	1,688,242	2,117,135	28,490	38,008	22,716	29,838	922	953
Truck and rail.................	224,833	348,047	213,814	471,398	169,524	443,188	988	1,177
Truck and water..............	29,035	251,439	56,720	109,861	48,568	51,853	1,562	784
Rail and water.............	7,976	43,638	55,570	143,013	29,170	102,715	1,073	1,075
Other multiple modes...........	668	17,490	2,452	8,224	1,853	9,562	(S)	1,425
Other and unknown modes..	1,026	2,095	36,844	93,634	256	128	(S)	1

S Data do not meet publication standards due to high sampling variability or other reasons. [1] Truck as a single mode includes shipments that went by private truck only, for-hire truck only, or a combination of private truck and for-hire truck. [2] Commodity Flow Survey data exclude shipments of crude oil.

Source: U.S. Department of Transportation, Bureau of Transportation Statistics, and U.S. Census Bureau, Commodity Flow Survey, "Geographic Area Series: Shipment Characteristics by Origin Geography by Mode: 2017 and 2012," <data.census.gov>, accessed July 2021. See also <www.census.gov/programs-surveys/cfs.html>.

Table 1103. Hazardous Shipments—Value, Tons, and Ton-Miles: 2012 and 2017

[2,334,425 represents $2,334,425,000,000. For business establishments in mining, manufacturing, wholesale trade, and selected retail industries. Data cover industries classified by the 2012 North American Industry Classification System (NAICS). Also includes auxiliary establishments of multi-establishment companies. Due to definitional and processing changes made each survey year, any data comparisons between one CFS survey and another should be made with caution, see Methodology. Based on the Commodity Flow Survey, conducted as part of the Economic Census; see Appendix III]

Mode of transportation and class of material	Value (mil. dol.)		Tons (1,000)		Ton-miles (mil.)		Average miles per shipment	
	2012	2017	2012	2017	2012	2017	2012	2017
All modes................................	2,334,425	1,680,231	2,580,153	2,967,965	307,524	382,472	114	189
Single modes............................	2,304,743	1,612,129	2,552,868	2,889,521	275,628	307,204	68	72
Truck [1].............................	1,466,021	1,091,250	1,531,405	1,814,848	96,559	126,800	56	63
For-hire truck..........................	870,893	567,599	882,288	932,658	62,018	92,146	150	153
Private truck, company-owned............	595,128	523,651	649,117	882,190	34,541	34,655	33	28
Rail...................................	79,222	39,040	110,988	90,387	84,850	61,669	808	640
Water................................	217,816	137,109	283,561	304,189	54,902	60,934	212	72
Air (includes truck and air)................	4,380	4,817	261	251	271	201	1,120	1,333
Pipeline [2]............................	537,304	339,912	626,652	679,846	(S)	(S)	(S)	(S)
Multiple modes [3]......................	29,682	68,101	27,285	78,444	31,896	75,268	654	947
Parcel, U.S. Postal Service or courier.......	10,294	13,475	305	345	178	236	650	949
Class of Material....................	2,334,425	1,680,231	2,580,153	2,967,965	307,524	382,472	114	189
Class 1, Explosives..........................	18,397	14,936	4,045	3,290	1,012	1,011	840	1,046
Class 2, Gases.............................	125,054	114,845	164,794	227,616	33,157	28,880	57	210
Class 3, Flammable and combustible liquid..............................	2,016,681	1,373,803	2,203,490	2,466,634	204,573	269,803	93	100
Class 4, Flammable solid; spontaneously combustible material; dangerous when wet material........................	5,415	5,308	11,321	28,210	5,804	7,614	565	478
Class 5, Oxidizers and organic peroxides...	7,562	9,753	12,025	14,978	5,479	5,827	437	204
Class 6, Toxic materials and infectious substances..........................	15,196	13,298	7,612	6,358	3,607	3,838	513	828
Class 7, Radioactive materials..............	12,288	6,945	(S)	427	39	42	34	63
Class 8, Corrosive materials................	75,850	79,322	125,287	151,007	37,784	45,704	264	273
Class 9, Miscellaneous hazardous material..........................	57,981	62,020	51,006	69,444	16,068	19,753	530	944

S Data do not meet publication standards. [1] Truck as a single mode includes shipments that went by private truck only, for-hire truck only, or a combination of private truck and for-hire truck. [2] Commodity Flow Survey Data exclude shipments of crude oil. [3] Includes other modes not shown.

Source: U.S. Department of Transportation, Bureau of Transportation Statistics, and U.S. Census Bureau, 2017 Commodity Flow Survey, CF1700H01, "Hazardous Materials Series: HazMat Shipment Characteristics by Mode for the United States: 2017 and 2012," and CF1700H02, "Hazardous Materials Series: HazMat Shipment Characteristics by Hazardous Class or Division for the United States: 2017 and 2012," <data.census.gov>, accessed July 2020. See also <census.gov/programs-surveys/cfs.html>.

Table 1104. Transportation Accidents, Deaths, and Injuries: 2010 to 2021
[5,419 represents 5,419,000]

Mode	Unit	Accidents			Deaths			Injuries		
		2010	2020	2021	2010	2020	2021	2010	2020	2021
Air, total..............................	Number	1,507	1,145	1,220	477	358	371	278	205	244
Air carrier.............................	Number	30	15	23	2	–	–	17	8	13
Commuter............................	Number	6	5	9	–	5	2	2	–	7
On-demand..........................	Number	30	39	34	17	21	25	3	11	5
General aviation.....................	Number	1,441	1,086	1,154	458	332	344	256	188	219
Land:										
Highway crashes [1]...................	1,000	5,419	5,251	6,103	33.0	39.0	42.9	2,248	2,282	2,498
Passenger car occupants...........	1,000	5,350	4,746	4,543	12.5	12.6	13.5	1,256	1,023	1,109
Motorcyclists......................	1,000	96	106	105	4.5	5.5	5.9	82	79	83
Light truck occupants..............	1,000	3,775	3,803	4,749	9.8	11.3	12.8	737	884	984
Large truck occupants..............	1,000	276	439	524	0.5	0.8	1.0	20	42	42
Bus occupants.....................	1,000	54	31	49	(Z)	(Z)	(Z)	18	8	12
Pedestrians........................	1,000	(NA)	(NA)	(NA)	4.3	6.6	7.4	70	55	61
Pedalcyclists......................	1,000	(NA)	(NA)	(NA)	0.6	0.9	1.0	52	39	42
Other...............................	1,000	15	19	874	0.7	1.2	1.3	13	153	166
Railroad [2].............................	Number	10,032	7,424	7,806	735	726	852	8,379	5,566	5,950
Highway-rail grade crossing [3]......	Number	453	523	511	261	194	232	888	702	687
Transit [4].............................	Number	3,492	5,490	6,307	224	289	321	23,107	15,421	16,566
Waterborne [5]........................	Number	9,889	7,818	6,992	821	853	715	3,770	3,546	3,054
Recreational boating [6].............	Number	4,604	5,265	4,439	672	767	658	3,153	3,191	2,641
Pipeline...............................	Number	586	574	633	22	15	13	108	37	33
Hazard liquid........................	Number	350	332	347	1	5	–	3	10	1
Gas..................................	Number	236	242	286	21	10	13	105	27	32

– Represents zero. NA Not available. Z Less than 50. [1] Highway crashes often involve more than one motor vehicle, and hence "total highway crashes" is smaller than the sum of the components. Data on deaths are from U.S. National Highway Traffic Safety Administration and are based on deaths within 30 days of the accident. Includes only police reported crashes. [2] Accidents and incidents resulting from freight and passenger rail operations including commuter rail. Grade crossing accidents are also included when classified as a train accident. Deaths and injuries exclude those in highway-rail grade crossing accidents involving motor vehicles. Incidents also include occupational illness. [3] Accidents and incidents occurring at highway-rail crossings resulting from freight and passenger rail operations including commuter rail. Public highway-rail grade crossing incidents, fatalities, and injuries involving motor vehicles are excluded and counted under Highway. [4] Includes light, heavy, and commuter rail; motor bus; trolley bus; van pools; automated guideway; and demand-responsive vehicle. Includes deaths confirmed within 30 days of a transit incident. Excludes suicides and suicide attempts. [5] Total waterborne includes incidents involving other types of vessels, not shown separately. [6] Covers occurrences involving a vessel or its equipment that results in 1) a death; 2) an injury that requires medical treatment beyond first aid; 3) damage to a vessel and other property, totaling to more than $500 or complete loss of a vessel; or 4) the disappearance of the vessel under circumstances that indicate death or injury.

Source: U.S. Bureau of Transportation Statistics, "National Transportation Statistics," <www.bts.gov/topics/national-transportation-statistics>, accessed April 2024.

Table 1105. On-Time Flight Arrivals and Departures at Major U.S. Airports: 2023
[In percent. All U.S. airlines with 1 percent or more of total U.S. domestic scheduled airline passenger revenues are required to report on-time data. Based on gate arrival and departure times for operations of U.S. major airlines. A flight is considered on time if it operated within 15 minutes of the scheduled time shown in the carrier's computerized reservation system. See source for data on individual airlines]

Airport	Code	On-time destination arrivals				On-time origin departures			
		1st quarter	2nd quarter	3rd quarter	4th quarter	1st quarter	2nd quarter	3rd quarter	4th quarter
Total, all airports [1]............................	**(X)**	**76.8**	**76.0**	**75.4**	**84.6**	**77.9**	**76.3**	**75.5**	**84.3**
Atlanta, Hartsfield-Jackson Intl...............	ATL	81.5	79.6	79.7	89.0	78.3	74.2	75.0	87.3
Baltimore/Washington Intl......................	BWI	82.1	75.5	74.3	84.3	75.7	66.2	63.7	74.3
Boston, Logan Intl.............................	BOS	76.2	74.9	65.2	82.3	77.1	76.6	68.6	82.9
Charlotte, Douglas............................	CLT	81.1	77.5	75.5	85.4	81.0	75.6	71.4	83.3
Chicago, Midway Intl..........................	MDW	80.0	76.8	74.4	83.4	74.0	68.9	66.3	78.4
Chicago, O'Hare..............................	ORD	77.7	78.3	75.4	86.3	78.8	77.5	74.4	85.7
Dallas-Fort Worth Intl.........................	DFW	74.1	74.6	77.7	82.6	74.3	71.4	73.3	82.4
Denver Intl.....................................	DEN	76.0	73.0	74.1	85.7	70.1	67.9	68.8	80.7
Detroit, Metro Wayne County..................	DTW	80.0	82.0	79.3	88.7	79.4	81.7	78.0	88.5
Fort Lauderdale-Hollywood Intl...............	FLL	72.8	63.9	67.3	76.8	69.7	61.3	62.1	71.4
Houston, George Bush Intercontinental.....	IAH	75.4	72.8	77.9	86.0	75.6	69.7	75.5	85.0
Las Vegas, Harry Reid Intl....................	LAS	69.5	68.4	71.3	82.6	70.3	68.1	69.4	80.1
Los Angeles Intl...............................	LAX	73.5	78.0	77.5	84.7	77.6	79.2	78.8	85.0
Miami Intl......................................	MIA	77.2	70.5	70.5	81.3	75.3	68.8	67.7	80.9
Minneapolis-St. Paul Intl......................	MSP	80.0	83.9	83.0	89.2	79.5	83.4	81.4	88.6
New York, JFK Intl.............................	JFK	75.1	72.3	67.2	82.8	75.5	74.4	68.3	82.9
New York, LaGuardia..........................	LGA	75.7	77.4	73.1	87.7	78.6	78.4	73.2	86.4
Newark Liberty Intl.............................	EWR	76.0	70.3	70.4	88.1	75.6	68.1	68.3	86.9
Orlando Intl....................................	MCO	72.5	67.1	65.6	80.5	72.0	66.9	64.3	79.1
Philadelphia Intl...............................	PHL	79.6	75.2	71.7	83.6	84.0	78.1	73.2	84.2
Phoenix, Sky Harbor Intl......................	PHX	75.2	79.2	78.7	84.4	76.7	77.9	77.6	83.8
Portland Intl...................................	PDX	77.7	80.4	79.4	85.9	82.7	84.4	83.1	88.6
Salt Lake City Intl.............................	SLC	78.3	83.8	83.6	90.0	77.4	82.8	82.2	89.8
San Diego Intl.................................	SAN	72.8	75.4	74.6	83.5	77.4	78.6	77.9	84.2
San Francisco Intl.............................	SFO	69.2	75.8	76.5	82.3	74.7	78.9	79.1	83.6
Seattle-Tacoma Intl...........................	SEA	81.6	82.5	81.0	86.0	81.9	81.6	79.9	85.0
Tampa, Tampa Intl.............................	TPA	74.9	71.3	69.1	81.7	78.8	75.7	72.3	84.1
Washington, Reagan National.................	DCA	81.0	79.7	74.7	85.1	84.1	80.8	76.0	85.8
Washington Dulles Intl........................	IAD	81.6	77.0	77.8	87.7	84.7	78.6	76.0	88.3

X Not applicable. [1] Includes other airports not shown separately.

Source: U.S. Department of Transportation, Bureau of Transportation Statistics, TranStats, "Airline On-Time Performance Data, Reporting Carrier On-Time Performance," <transtats.bts.gov>, accessed September 2024.

Table 1106. Airline Fuel Consumption and Fuel Costs: 2000 to 2023

[20,373 represents 20,373,000,000. Data shown are aggregated for scheduled and unscheduled service on U.S. carriers with over $20 million in revenue per year]

Year	Total fuel consumption (million gallons)	Total fuel cost (million dollars)	Cost per gallon (dollars)	Domestic service			International service		
				Consumption (million gallons)	Cost (million dollars)	Cost per gallon (dollars)	Consumption (million gallons)	Cost (million dollars)	Cost per gallon (dollars)
2000........	20,373	16,448	0.81	14,865	11,708	0.79	5,508	4,739	0.86
2010........	17,298	39,350	2.27	11,257	25,571	2.27	6,042	13,779	2.28
2015........	17,349	32,196	1.86	10,929	20,006	1.83	6,421	12,190	1.90
2018........	18,750	40,490	2.16	12,151	26,108	2.15	6,599	14,382	2.18
2019........	19,205	38,534	2.01	12,541	25,133	2.00	6,663	13,401	2.01
2020........	11,481	16,463	1.43	7,643	10,955	1.43	3,838	5,509	1.44
2021........	15,126	29,943	1.98	10,380	20,677	1.99	4,746	9,266	1.95
2022........	17,933	60,424	3.37	11,869	39,936	3.36	6,065	20,488	3.38
2023........	19,731	56,472	2.86	12,821	36,817	2.87	6,910	19,655	2.84

Source: U.S. Bureau of Transportation Statistics, "Airline Fuel Cost and Consumption," <transtats.bts.gov/fuel.asp>, accessed April 2024.

Table 1107. Top 50 Airports in 2023—Passengers Enplaned: 2022 and 2023

[In thousands (847,595 represents 847,595,000), except rank. For calendar year. Airports ranked by total passengers enplaned on U.S. carrier scheduled domestic and international service and foreign carrier scheduled international service from the U.S.]

Airport city and code	2022 Rank	2022 Total	2023 Rank	2023 Total	Airport city and code	2022 Rank	2022 Total	2023 Rank	2023 Total
All U.S. airports....................	(X)	847,595	(X)	939,709	San Diego, CA (SAN)..............	24	11,162	25	12,190
Total, top 50 [1]	(X)	706,882	(X)	785,236	Washington Dulles, DC (IAD).....	28	10,277	26	12,073
Atlanta, GA (ATL)......................	1	45,397	1	50,950	Tampa, FL (TPA)......................	26	10,539	27	11,677
Dallas/Fort Worth, TX (DFW)......	2	35,346	2	39,246	Nashville, TN (BNA).................	29	9,830	28	11,227
Denver, CO (DEN)....................	3	33,774	3	37,864	Austin, TX (AUS).....................	27	10,383	29	10,833
Los Angeles, CA (LAX).............	5	32,337	4	36,677	Chicago, IL (MDW)..................	30	9,650	30	10,659
Chicago, IL (ORD)...................	4	33,145	5	35,843	Honolulu, HI (HNL)..................	31	8,820	31	10,143
New York, NY (JFK).................	6	27,000	6	30,494	Dallas, TX (DAL).....................	32	7,819	32	8,559
Orlando, FL (MCO)..................	8	24,478	7	28,033	Portland, OR (PDX)..................	33	7,242	33	8,123
Las Vegas, NV (LAS)...............	7	25,412	8	27,816	St. Louis, MO (STL).................	34	6,709	34	7,307
Charlotte-Douglas, NC (CLT)......	10	23,106	9	25,896	Raleigh/Durham, NC (RDU).......	38	5,850	35	7,118
Miami, FL (MIA)......................	9	23,950	10	24,717	Houston, TX (HOU)..................	35	6,463	36	6,800
Seattle-Tacoma, WA (SEA)........	11	22,158	11	24,594	Sacramento, CA (SMF).............	36	6,041	37	6,372
Newark, NJ (EWR)..................	13	21,687	12	24,506	New Orleans, LA (MSY)............	37	5,933	38	6,309
San Francisco, CA (SFO)..........	14	20,411	13	24,191	San Jose, CA (SJC).................	39	5,590	39	5,959
Phoenix, AZ (PHX)..................	12	21,852	14	23,880	San Juan, PR (SJU).................	43	5,040	40	5,954
Houston, TX (IAH)...................	15	19,814	15	22,229	Santa Ana, CA (SNA)...............	40	5,536	41	5,706
Boston, MA (BOS)...................	16	17,444	16	19,961	Kansas City, MO (MCI)............	44	4,798	42	5,654
Fort Lauderdale, FL (FLL)..........	17	15,389	17	17,043	Oakland, CA (OAK).................	41	5,506	43	5,521
Minneapolis-St. Paul, MN (MSP)....	18	15,243	18	17,019	San Antonio, TX (SAT).............	45	4,753	44	5,337
New York, NY (LGA)................	19	14,369	19	16,173	Fort Myers, FL (RSW)..............	42	5,133	45	4,963
Detroit, MI (DTW)...................	20	13,756	20	15,379	Cleveland, OH (CLE)...............	46	4,240	46	4,804
Philadelphia, PA (PHL).............	21	12,424	21	13,656	Indianapolis, IN (IND)..............	47	4,220	47	4,788
Salt Lake City, UT (SLC)..........	22	12,384	22	12,905	Pittsburgh, PA (PIT).................	49	3,930	48	4,493
Baltimore, MD (BWI)...............	25	11,151	23	12,849	Cincinnati, OH (CVG)..............	50	3,707	49	4,288
Washington, DC (DCA).............	23	11,560	24	12,365	Columbus, OH (CMH)..............	51	3,626	50	4,095

X Not applicable. [1] The 2022 totals for the top 50 airports will not sum to total top 50 because some top 50 airports in 2023 were not in the top 50 in 2022.

Source: U.S. Bureau of Transportation Statistics, "National Transportation Statistics," <www.bts.gov/topics/national-transportation-statistics>, accessed May 2024.

Table 1108. Consumer Complaints Filed Against U.S. Airlines: 2000 to 2022

[Calendar year data. Represents complaints filed by consumers to the U.S. Department of Transportation (DOT), Aviation Consumer Protection Division, regarding service problems with air carriers. See source for data on individual airlines]

Complaint category	2000	2010	2015	2016	2017	2018	2019	2020	2021	2022
Total.................	20,564	10,988	20,175	17,908	18,156	15,544	15,342	102,560	49,991	77,656
Flight problems [1].........	8,698	3,337	6,434	6,179	6,078	4,517	4,757	1,498	6,316	24,647
Baggage..................	2,753	1,938	3,133	2,770	2,745	2,728	2,565	1,047	1,996	12,007
Ticketing/boarding [2]......	1,405	1,510	2,695	2,115	2,194	1,908	1,824	4,449	4,032	7,744
Customer service [3]......	4,074	1,345	2,276	1,934	1,781	1,618	1,705	1,484	1,903	2,912
Refunds..................	803	730	1,573	1,361	1,359	1,329	1,574	89,511	29,523	19,983
Fares [4].................	708	465	1,813	1,363	2,022	1,542	1,033	3,303	4,077	6,030
Disability [5].............	612	572	944	865	850	827	905	541	1,397	2,095
Oversales [6].............	759	544	648	597	511	409	376	132	286	1,336
Discrimination [7]..........	(NA)	143	65	95	98	97	107	49	134	178
Advertising................	42	77	163	124	80	57	61	25	45	125
Animals..................	1	8	3	1	1	2	2	1	1	0
Other [8]..................	709	319	428	504	437	510	433	520	281	599

NA Not available. [1] Cancellations, delays, and other deviations from schedule. [2] Errors in reservations and ticketing; and problems in making reservations, obtaining tickets, and boarding (except oversales). Prior to 1998, includes disability complaints. [3] Unhelpful employees, inadequate meals or cabin service, treatment of delayed passengers. [4] Incorrect or incomplete information about fares, discount fare conditions, and availability, etc. [5] Civil rights complaints by air travelers with disabilities. Prior to 2000, included in ticketing/boarding. [6] All bumping problems, whether or not airline complied with DOT regulations. [7] Civil rights complaints by air travelers (other than disability) based on factors such as race, religion, national origin or sex. [8] Frequent flyer, smoking, tours credit, cargo problems, security, airport facilities, claims for bodily injury, and others not classified above.

Source: U.S. Department of Transportation, Aviation Consumer Protection Division, *Air Travel Consumer Report*, February 2023, and earlier reports. See also <www.transportation.gov/airconsumer>.

Table 1109. U.S. Airline Carrier Delays, Cancellations, and Diversions: 2000 to 2023

[In thousands (5,683.0 represents 5,683,000), except percent. For calendar year. See headnote, Table 1105]

Item	2000	2010	2015	2017	2018	2019	2020	2021	2022	2023
Total operations	**5,683.0**	**6,450.1**	**5,819.1**	**5,674.6**	**7,206.2**	**7,422.0**	**4,688.4**	**5,995.4**	**6,729.1**	**6,847.9**
NUMBER										
Delayed departures [1]	1,131.7	1,111.9	1,055.5	1,012.5	1,303.8	1,359.6	400.8	1,023.5	1,396.1	1,386.4
Delayed arrivals [2]	1,356.0	1,174.9	1,063.4	1,029.5	1,352.2	1,389.3	431.9	1,010.1	1,376.8	1,386.7
Cancellations [3]	187.5	113.3	89.9	82.7	116.5	134.9	281.0	103.1	181.3	87.9
Diversions [4]	14.3	15.5	15.2	12.5	17.8	18.9	7.7	14.1	15.8	16.6
PERCENT										
Delayed departures [1]	19.9	17.2	18.1	17.8	18.1	18.3	8.5	17.1	20.7	20.2
Delayed arrivals [2]	23.9	18.2	18.3	18.1	18.8	18.7	9.2	16.9	20.5	20.2
Cancellations [3]	3.3	1.8	1.5	1.5	1.6	1.8	6.0	1.7	2.7	1.3
Diversions [4]	0.3	0.2	0.3	0.2	0.2	0.3	0.2	0.2	0.2	0.2

[1] Late departures departed 15 minutes or more after the scheduled departure time. [2] Late arrivals arrived 15 minutes or more after the scheduled arrival time. [3] A cancelled flight is one that was not operated but was listed in a carrier's computer reservation system within seven days of the scheduled departure. [4] A diverted flight is one that left from the scheduled departure airport but flew to a destination point other than the scheduled destination point.

Source: U.S. Bureau of Transportation Statistics, "National Transportation Statistics," <www.bts.gov/topics/national-transportation-statistics>, accessed July 2024.

Table 1110. U.S. Air Carrier Aircraft Accidents: 2000 to 2022

[For years ending December 31. U.S. air carriers operating under 14 CFR Part 135 were previously referred to as Scheduled and Nonscheduled Services. Current tables now refer to these same air carriers as Commuter Operations and On-Demand Operations, respectively. See source for more details]

Item	Unit	2000	2010	2015	2017	2018	2019	2020	2021	2022
Air carrier accidents, all services	Number	56	30	28	33	31	40	15	23	20
Fatal accidents	Number	3	1	–	–	1	2	–	–	1
Fatalities	Number	92	2	–	–	1	4	–	–	1
Aboard	Number	92	2	–	–	1	4	–	–	–
Rates per 100,000 flight hours:										
Accidents	Rate	0.31	0.17	0.16	0.18	0.16	0.20	0.13	0.14	0.11
Fatal accidents	Rate	0.02	0.01	–	–	–	0.01	–	–	0.01
Commuter air carrier accidents	Number	12	6	4	6	2	9	5	9	7
Fatal accidents	Number	1	–	1	–	–	1	1	–	1
Fatalities	Number	5	–	1	–	–	2	5	–	10
Aboard	Number	5	–	1	–	–	2	5	–	10
Rates per 100,000 flight hours:										
Accidents	Rate	3.25	1.91	1.11	1.53	0.47	1.94	1.60	2.23	1.65
Fatal accidents	Rate	0.27	–	0.28	–	–	0.22	0.32	–	0.24
On-demand air taxi accidents	Number	80	30	39	44	40	33	39	34	45
Fatal accidents	Number	22	6	7	8	7	12	6	9	4
Fatalities	Number	71	17	27	16	16	32	21	27	8
Aboard	Number	68	17	27	16	16	32	20	26	8
Rates per 100,000 flight hours:										
Accidents	Rate	2.04	0.96	1.09	1.25	1.04	0.88	1.28	0.76	1.02
Fatal accidents	Rate	0.56	0.19	0.20	0.23	0.18	0.32	0.20	0.20	0.09
General aviation accidents [1]	Number	1,837	1,441	1,211	1,234	1,275	1,221	1,086	1,154	1,205
Fatal accidents	Number	345	271	230	203	224	234	203	211	214
Fatalities	Number	596	458	378	331	379	416	329	346	339
Aboard	Number	585	455	375	331	376	408	319	343	339
Rates per 100,000 flight hours:										
Accidents	Rate	6.57	6.63	5.85	5.68	5.87	5.59	5.58	5.24	5.34
Fatal accidents	Rate	1.21	1.24	1.10	0.94	1.02	1.07	1.04	0.96	0.94

– Represents or rounds to zero. [1] U.S. civil registered aircraft not operated under 14 CFR 121 or 135.

Source: U.S. National Transportation Safety Board, Safety Research-Statistical Reviews, "US Civil Aviation Accident Statistics," <www.ntsb.gov/safety/Pages/research.aspx>, accessed April 2024.

Table 1111. Worldwide Airline Accidents and Fatalities by World Region: 2022

[Covers scheduled commercial air transport operations involving the transportation of passengers, cargo and mail for remuneration. Regions are Regional Aviation Safety Group (RASG) regions]

Region	Departures	Accidents	Accident rates [1]	Fatal accidents	Fatalities
World	**31,206,331**	**64**	**2.05**	**7**	**160**
Asia and Pacific (APAC)	9,445,233	15	1.59	2	133
Eastern and Southern African (ESAF)	710,630	4	5.63	1	19
European and North Atlantic (EUR/NAT) [2]	7,838,023	8	1.02	–	–
Middle East (MID)	1,163,085	2	1.72	–	–
North American, Central American and Caribbean (NACC)	10,100,395	28	2.77	1	1
South American (SAM)	1,687,796	5	2.96	1	2
Western and Central African (WACAF)	261,169	2	7.66	2	5

– Represents zero. [1] Number of accidents per million departures of scheduled commercial air transport operations. [2] RASG EUR/NAT includes Algeria, Morocco, and Tunisia.

Source: International Civil Aviation Organization, Montreal, Canada, *ICAO Safety Report 2023 Edition* ©, <www.icao.int/safety/Pages/Safety-Report.aspx>.

Table 1112. Airports, Aircraft, and Airmen: 1990 to 2022

[As of December 31 or for years ending December 31]

Item	1990	2000	2010	2018	2019	2020	2021	2022
AIRPORTS								
Airports, total [1]	**17,490**	**19,281**	**19,802**	**19,627**	**19,636**	**19,919**	**20,061**	**19,969**
Public use [1]	5,589	5,317	5,175	5,099	5,080	5,217	5,211	5,193
Percent with lighted runways	71.4	75.9	(NA)	(NA)	(NA)	(NA)	(NA)	(NA)
Percent with paved runways	70.7	74.3	(NA)	(NA)	(NA)	(NA)	(NA)	(NA)
Private use	11,901	13,964	14,353	14,528	14,556	14,702	14,850	14,776
Percent with lighted runways	7.0	7.2	(NA)	(NA)	(NA)	(NA)	(NA)	(NA)
Percent with paved runways	31.5	32.0	(NA)	(NA)	(NA)	(NA)	(NA)	(NA)
Military owned	(NA)	(NA)	274	305	308	312	313	313
Certificated [2]	680	651	551	523	522	519	519	517
General aviation	16,810	18,630	19,251	19,116	19,114	19,400	19,542	19,452
AIRCRAFT								
Active air carrier fleet [3]	**6,083**	**7,826**	**7,185**	**7,475**	**7,628**	**5,884**	**5,815**	**6,852**
Fixed wing	6,072	8,010	(NA)	(NA)	(NA)	(NA)	(NA)	(NA)
Helicopter [4]	11	39	(NA)	(NA)	(NA)	(NA)	(NA)	(NA)
General aviation fleet [5]	**198,000**	**217,533**	**223,370**	**211,749**	**210,981**	**204,138**	**209,195**	**209,540**
Fixed-wing	184,500	183,276	176,272	167,560	166,525	161,638	164,282	164,567
Turbojet	4,100	7,001	11,484	14,596	14,888	15,316	15,270	16,126
Turboprop	5,300	5,762	9,369	9,925	10,242	10,317	10,391	10,713
Piston	175,200	170,513	155,419	143,040	141,396	136,006	138,621	137,728
Rotorcraft	6,900	7,150	10,102	9,990	10,199	9,745	10,032	9,769
Other	6,600	6,700	5,684	4,114	4,133	3,818	4,271	4,476
Gliders	(X)	2,041	1,899	1,772	1,517	1,519	1,717	1,628
Lighter than air	(X)	4,660	3,785	2,343	2,617	2,299	2,554	2,848
Experimental	(X)	20,407	29,662	27,531	27,449	26,367	27,960	28,062
AIRMAN CERTIFICATES HELD								
Pilot, total	**702,659**	**625,581**	**627,588**	**633,317**	**664,565**	**691,691**	**720,605**	**756,928**
Female	40,515	36,757	42,218	46,463	52,740	58,541	64,979	72,428
Student [6]	128,663	93,064	119,119	167,804	197,665	222,629	250,197	280,582
Recreational	87	340	212	144	127	105	85	79
Sport	(X)	(X)	3,682	6,246	6,467	6,643	6,801	6,957
Airplane:								
Private	299,111	251,561	202,020	163,695	161,105	160,860	161,459	164,090
Commercial	149,666	121,858	123,705	99,880	100,863	103,879	104,610	104,498
Air transport	107,732	141,596	142,198	162,145	164,947	164,193	163,934	166,738
Rotorcraft only	9,567	7,775	15,377	15,033	14,248	13,629	13,191	13,180
Glider only	7,833	9,387	21,275	18,370	19,143	19,753	20,328	20,804
Flight instructor certificates	63,775	80,931	96,473	108,564	113,445	117,558	121,270	125,075
Instrument ratings [7]	297,073	311,944	318,001	311,017	314,168	316,651	317,169	321,217
Remote pilots [7]	(X)	(X)	(X)	106,321	160,302	206,322	254,587	304,256
Nonpilot [8]	**492,237**	**547,453**	**686,717**	**688,002**	**714,201**	**724,307**	**733,127**	**737,582**
Mechanic	344,282	344,434	331,989	292,002	301,087	306,301	313,093	320,042
Repairmen	(X)	38,208	41,267	35,382	36,294	36,741	37,261	37,861
Parachute rigger	10,094	10,477	8,407	6,430	6,800	7,014	7,230	7,495
Ground instructor	66,882	72,326	75,205	67,784	69,991	71,991	74,105	76,109
Dispatcher	11,002	16,340	20,691	21,465	22,598	23,286	23,835	24,526
Flight navigator	1,290	570	174	58	40	36	30	29
Flight attendant	(NA)	(NA)	159,946	231,335	245,699	248,742	249,043	246,195
Flight engineer	58,687	65,098	49,038	33,526	31,692	30,196	28,530	25,325

NA Not available. X Not applicable. [1] Includes civil and joint-use civil-military airports, heliports, STOL (short takeoff and landing) ports, and seaplane bases in the U.S. and its territories. Sole-use military airports are included beginning in 2007. [2] Certificated airports serve scheduled air carrier operations in aircraft designed for more than 9 passenger seats but less than 31 passenger seats. As of 2005, the Federal Aviation Administration (FAA) no longer certificates military airports. [3] Air-carrier aircraft carry passengers or cargo for hire under 14 CFR 121 (large aircraft—more than 30 seats) and 14 CFR 135 (small aircraft—30 seats or fewer). Beginning in 2000, the number of aircraft is the monthly average reported in use for the last three months of the year. Prior to 1990, it was the number of aircraft reported in use during December of a given year. [4] 2000 change in helicopters due to estimating methods. [5] Beginning 1995, excludes commuters. [6] Beginning 2010, duration of validity for student pilot certificates for pilots under age 40 increased from 36 to 60 months. Starting with April 2016, there is no expiration date on the new student pilot certificates, which generates a cumulative increase in the numbers. [7] Remote pilot certification started in August 2016. These numbers are not included in the pilot totals. [8] All certificates on record. No medical examination required.

Source: Prior to 2000: *FAA Statistical Handbook of Aviation*, annual. Thereafter: U.S. Bureau of Transportation Statistics, "National Transportation Statistics," <www.bts.gov/topics/national-transportation-statistics>, accessed June 2024. U.S. Federal Aviation Administration, "U.S. Civil Airmen Statistics," <www.faa.gov/data_research/aviation_data_statistics/>, accessed June 2024.

Table 1113. Passenger Airline Revenues from Fares, Fees, and Services; and Expenses and Profits: 2015 to 2022

[In millions of dollars (169,057 represents $169,057,000,000). Data shown for U.S. scheduled passenger airlines. Data for 2015, 2021, and 2022 are compiled from 25 airlines; data for 2016, 2017, and 2020 are compiled from 23 reporting airlines; 2018 and 2019 data are compiled from 21 airlines]

Item	2015	2017	2018	2019	2020	2021	2022 (P)
Total operating revenue [1]	**169,057**	**175,337**	**187,474**	**196,478**	**77,297**	**129,993**	**211,171**
Passenger fares, scheduled/charter	127,061	130,491	138,982	145,437	49,887	86,671	155,123
Cargo	2,890	2,985	3,522	3,196	3,412	5,203	5,005
Baggage fees	3,814	4,576	5,072	5,801	2,842	5,310	6,758
Reservation change fees	3,012	2,856	2,858	2,886	898	698	1,004
Transport-related [2]	27,385	28,694	28,474	29,382	13,897	23,194	30,688
Other [3]	4,895	5,735	8,566	9,776	6,361	8,918	12,593
Total operating expenses	**141,070**	**153,893**	**169,828**	**175,733**	**123,786**	**147,329**	**203,271**
Fuel	26,979	26,241	34,460	32,814	12,149	22,978	49,121
Labor	45,487	53,556	56,104	60,460	49,106	52,577	63,978
Rentals	8,632	8,887	9,098	9,786	9,733	11,313	11,223
Depreciation and amortization	7,513	9,051	9,495	10,058	10,251	9,843	10,048
Landing fees	2,853	3,056	3,211	3,340	2,107	3,600	3,801
Maintenance materials	2,521	2,438	2,208	2,487	1,829	2,475	3,363
Transport-related [2]	18,173	19,009	21,493	22,463	14,527	17,226	22,839
Other [4]	28,913	31,656	33,760	34,325	24,084	27,318	38,896
Operating profit	**27,987**	**21,444**	**17,646**	**20,746**	**-46,488**	**-17,336**	**7,899**
Operating margin (percent) [5]	17	12	9	11	-60	-13	4
Nonoperating income/expense [6]	-4,109	-2,298	-2,483	-1,549	1,258	13,991	-5,425
Pre-tax income	23,877	19,146	15,163	19,196	-45,231	-3,345	2,474
Income tax benefit/expense	911	-3,851	-3,388	-4,458	10,185	573	-884
Other income/expense	–	–	–	–	–	3	–
Net income	24,788	15,295	11,775	14,738	-35,045	-2,769	1,590
Net margin (percent) [7]	15	9	6	8	-45	-2	1

P Preliminary. – Represents or rounds to zero. [1] Based on U.S. Department of Transportation accounting standards. Total operating revenues are overstated by code share revenues, which are included in both mainline transport-related revenues and code share passenger revenues. Code share revenues are expensed out in the mainline transport-related expense to allow a true operating profit (loss). Reporting may understate all components of operating revenue, including passenger revenue, as a percent of total operating revenue. [2] Includes in-flight onboard sales, code share revenues, and revenues and expenses from associated businesses (aircraft maintenance, fuel sales, restaurants, vending machines). [3] Includes pet transportation, sale of frequent flyer award miles to airline business partners, standby passenger fees, and public service revenues subsidy. [4] Includes purchase of materials such as passenger food; and services such as advertising, communication, insurance, outside flight equipment maintenance, and traffic commissions. [5] Operating profit or loss as a percent of operating revenue. [6] Interest on long-term debt and capital leases, other interest expense, foreign exchange gains and losses, capital gains and losses, and other income and expenses. [7] Net income or loss as a percent of operating revenue.

Source: U.S. Department of Transportation, Bureau of Transportation Statistics, "Airline Financials Tables 4Q 2022," and earlier releases, <www.bts.gov/statistical-releases>, accessed May 2023.

Table 1114. Ferry System Summary: 2010 to 2021

[In units as indicated (118.1 represents $118,100,000). Excludes international, rural, rural interstate, island, and urban park ferries]

Item	Unit	2010	2015	2016	2017	2018	2019	2020	2021
Systems	Number	32	41	42	47	44	46	(NA)	(NA)
Vehicles	Number	196	201	187	214	228	246	(NA)	(NA)
Employees	Number	4,273	4,786	4,825	5,585	6,548	6,751	4,983	4,839
Passenger operating revenues	Mil. dol.	118.1	190.2	194.9	200.8	253.4	268.9	198.9	162.4
Operating expenses	Mil. dol.	487.3	640.9	675.0	642.1	786.9	828.1	831.2	815.2
Average passenger revenue per passenger-mile	Dollars	0.30	0.42	0.40	0.41	0.49	0.49	0.48	0.61
Average passenger fare, per unlinked trip	Dollars	1.91	2.66	2.59	2.64	3.12	3.14	3.44	4.05
Vehicle-miles	Millions	3.3	3.8	3.9	4.0	4.9	5.4	4.6	4.3
Unlinked passenger trips	Millions	62	71	75	76	81	86	58	40
Passenger-miles	Millions	389	451	489	486	520	547	411	268
Average trip length	Miles	6.29	6.31	6.50	6.39	6.39	6.38	7.10	6.69
Average vehicle speed	Miles per hour	9.0	8.5	8.7	8.1	8.6	9.3	(NA)	(NA)
Energy consumption, diesel	Mil. gallons	32.8	36.9	37.8	38.7	42.3	44.2	40.7	38.4

NA Not available.

Source: U.S. Bureau of Transportation Statistics, "National Transportation Statistics," <www.bts.gov/topics/national-transportationstatistics>, accessed February 2024.

Table 1115. Freight Carried on Major U.S. Waterways: 2000 to 2022

[In millions of short tons (3.1 represents 3,100,000). One short ton equals 2,000 pounds]

Waterway	2000	2005	2010	2015	2017	2018	2019	2020	2021	2022
Atlantic Intracoastal Waterway	3.1	2.7	2.9	2.6	2.3	2.4	2.1	1.7	2.2	1.9
Great Lakes	187.5	169.4	129.5	123.7	125.4	122.2	122.0	101.8	117.6	101.0
Gulf Intracoastal Waterway	113.8	116.1	116.2	118.9	111.2	110.4	110.5	101.2	99.0	108.4
Mississippi River system [1]	715.5	678.0	663.2	684.4	702.1	692.3	631.6	588.5	595.8	588.5
Mississippi River main stem [2]	515.6	464.6	483.2	521.1	552.3	557.6	495.9	473.7	485.4	480.5
Ohio River system [3]	274.4	280.1	245.2	223.1	202.1	198.0	194.0	165.7	172.1	168.5
Columbia River	55.2	51.5	54.7	54.7	63.4	67.1	60.0	62.5	65.9	59.7
Snake River	6.7	5.3	3.4	3.6	3.5	3.9	3.9	4.2	4.2	3.6

[1] Main channels and all tributaries of the Mississippi, Illinois, Missouri, and Ohio Rivers. [2] Minneapolis, MN to Mouth of Passes. [3] Main channels and all navigable tributaries and embayments of the Ohio, Tennessee, and Cumberland Rivers.

Source: U.S. Army Corps of Engineers, Institute for Water Resources, *Waterborne Commerce of the United States, 2017*, December 2018, and earlier reports; and Commerce Data, "Ports and Waterways Webtool," <ndc.ops.usace.army.mil/wcsc/webpub/#/>, accessed April 2024.

Table 1116. Water Transportation System Summary: 2000 to 2020

[33,333 represents 33,333,000,000. Data compiled from various U.S. Army Corps of Engineers, U.S. Coast Guard, U.S. Census Bureau, Bureau of Labor Statistics, U.S. Department of Energy, and U.S. Department of Transportation surveys and publications; see source for details]

Item or characteristic	Unit	2000	2010	2015	2017	2018	2019	2020
REVENUE								
Operating revenues	**Mil. dol.**	**33,333**	**37,559**	**44,373**	**43,010**	**46,042**	**48,902**	**29,653**
Domestic freight	Mil. dol.	6,930	13,133	15,924	13,420	14,146	14,690	12,932
Coastal and Great Lakes	Mil. dol.	2,373	6,254	8,166	7,557	7,901	8,102	7,103
Inland waterways	Mil. dol.	2,960	6,879	7,758	5,863	6,245	6,588	5,829
International freight	Mil. dol.	21,740	9,281	8,656	6,455	5,921	6,388	6,316
Passenger	Mil. dol.	4,663	14,978	19,793	23,135	25,975	27,824	(NA)
Domestic passenger	Mil. dol.	156	585	876	1,100	1,229	1,322	(NA)
International passenger [1]	Mil. dol.	4,507	14,393	18,917	22,035	24,746	26,502	9,497
U.S. commercial fishing fleet domestic landings	**Mil. dol.**	**3,550**	**4,520**	**5,203**	**5,421**	**5,571**	**5,478**	**4,645**
INVENTORY								
Ship and boat building employees [2]	Number	154,100	124,600	138,300	134,500	138,700	142,500	139,800
Water transportation employees [2]	Number	152,700	152,900	163,400	156,800	159,900	160,100	146,700
Number of vessels	**Number**	**49,958**	**49,501**	**40,791**	**42,152**	**43,170**	**43,257**	**44,500**
Total nonself-propelled	Number	40,665	39,883	31,748	32,808	33,266	33,329	34,167
Dry cargo	Number	33,584	19,548	19,224	19,910	20,221	20,196	20,783
Deck barges	Number	5,558	4,179	7,550	7,765	7,784	7,753	7,736
Tankers	Number	3,230	6,538	4,974	5,133	5,261	5,380	5,648
Total self-propelled	Number	9,293	9,618	9,043	9,344	9,904	9,928	10,333
Dry cargo	Number	282	273	208	220	222	217	152
Offshore supply	Number	1,895	1,988	1,752	1,717	1,714	1,711	1,846
Ferries and Passenger	Number	1,528	1,580	1,416	1,501	1,713	1,721	1,804
Tankers	Number	137	93	66	79	79	76	76
Towboats/tugs	Number	5,451	5,684	5,601	5,827	6,176	6,203	6,385
U.S. flag merchant fleet (over 1,000 gross tons):								
Total U.S. privately-owned fleet	Number	282	221	168	176	182	182	185
Freighters [3]	Number	142	138	112	111	112	114	117
Bulk carriers	Number	23	21	8	5	5	5	5
Tankers	Number	117	62	50	60	65	63	63
Number of recreational boats	**1,000s**	**12,782**	**12,439**	**11,867**	**11,962**	**11,853**	**11,879**	**11,838**
CARGO SHIP PERFORMANCE								
Domestic water freight (ton-miles) [4]	**Millions**	**645,799**	**502,273**	**490,493**	**489,031**	**491,823**	**456,380**	**439,199**
Coastwise	Millions	283,872	192,348	175,603	176,048	173,604	164,042	157,675
Internal	Millions	302,558	263,292	267,197	264,176	270,160	244,173	243,215
Lakewise	Millions	57,879	45,346	46,436	47,466	46,932	47,098	37,382
Intraport	Millions	1,490	1,287	1,256	1,341	1,127	1,067	927
Tons of freight hauled	**1,000 tons**	**2,424,589**	**2,334,548**	**2,278,974**	**2,387,032**	**2,437,690**	**2,363,374**	**2,226,442**
Domestic, total	1,000 tons	1,069,798	893,610	904,822	873,060	848,681	818,055	743,330
Coastwise	1,000 tons	226,938	164,457	175,067	163,990	160,190	154,141	136,910
Internal [5]	1,000 tons	628,445	564,995	563,323	535,558	524,587	502,253	466,900
Lakewise	1,000 tons	114,352	80,543	83,931	81,839	80,215	82,134	66,359
Intraport [5]	1,000 tons	94,558	78,972	80,924	90,894	83,324	78,458	71,930
Intraterritory	1,000 tons	5,505	4,643	1,577	778	366	1,070	1,230
Exports, total	1,000 tons	415,042	557,840	622,517	746,105	822,496	848,116	845,511
Great Lakes ports	1,000 tons	40,131	23,217	13,907	20,608	17,369	16,586	15,143
Coastal ports	1,000 tons	374,911	534,623	608,610	725,497	805,127	831,530	830,369
Imports, total	1,000 tons	939,749	883,097	751,636	767,868	766,513	697,202	637,601
Great Lakes ports	1,000 tons	23,917	16,763	18,310	14,544	16,756	18,028	15,729
Coastal ports	1,000 tons	915,832	866,334	733,326	753,323	749,757	679,174	621,872
Average haul, domestic system: [4]								
Coastwise	Miles	1,251	1,170	1,003	1,074	1,084	1,064	1,152
Internal	Miles	481	466	474	493	515	486	521
Lakewise	Miles	506	563	553	580	585	573	563
Cargo capacity:								
Total nonself-propelled	1,000 sh. tons	52,923	71,800	64,397	68,347	69,872	70,242	73,300
Dry cargo	1,000 sh. tons	36,094	34,185	34,518	36,757	37,602	37,636	39,333
Deck barges	1,000 sh. tons	7,146	9,567	12,985	13,558	13,623	13,583	13,459
Tankers	1,000 sh. tons	9,682	13,825	16,894	18,031	18,647	19,023	20,189
Total self-propelled	1,000 sh. tons	14,757	14,222	11,336	11,318	11,479	10,893	11,767
Dry cargo	1,000 sh. tons	6,928	7,958	5,738	5,459	5,497	5,145	2,532
Offshore supply	1,000 sh. tons	713	1,112	1,410	1,402	1,430	1,423	1,550
Ferries and Passenger	1,000 sh. tons	94	139	83	127	128	128	235
Tankers	1,000 sh. tons	6,944	4,909	3,965	4,159	4,171	3,911	3,911
Towboats/tugs	1,000 sh. tons	78	103	139	171	252	286	327
Fuel consumption:								
Residual fuel oil	Mil. gal.	6,410	5,143	3,358	2,579	2,687	2,189	1,457
Distillate/diesel fuel oil	Mil. gal.	2,261	2,003	2,417	2,186	2,213	2,042	1,817
Gasoline	Mil. gal.	1,124	1,167	2,066	2,323	2,090	2,128	2,326

NA Not available. [1] Revenues paid by American travelers to U.S. and foreign flag carriers. [2] Data is based on NAICS classifications. Data for water transportation includes NAICS 483100, 483200, and 488300. Data for ships, boat building, and repairing is based on NAICS 336600. [3] Freighters include containerships, general cargo vessels and roll on-roll off vessels. Prior to 1983, includes data for bulk carriers. [4] Does not include intra-territorial traffic (traffic between ports in Puerto Rico and the Virgin Islands, which are considered a single unit). [5] Beginning in 1996, fish are excluded from internal and intraport tons of freight hauled.

Source: U.S. Bureau of Transportation Statistics, "National Transportation Statistics," <www.bts.gov/topics/national-transportationstatistics>, accessed February 2023.

Table 1117. Top 30 U.S. Ports by Tons of Traffic: 2022

[In thousands of short tons (293,834 represents 293,834,000). One short ton equals 2,000 lbs. For calendar year. Represents tons of cargo shipped from or received by the specified port. Excludes cargo carried on general ferries; coal and petroleum products loaded from shore facilities directly onto bunkers of vessels for fuel; and amounts of less than 100 tons of government-owned equipment in support of Corps of Engineers projects]

Port name	Total	Domestic	Foreign		
			Total	Inbound	Outbound
Houston Port Authority, TX..................	293,834	84,185	209,649	140,889	68,759
South Louisiana, LA, Port of................	226,188	115,788	110,400	79,160	31,240
Corpus Christi, TX........................	174,327	25,710	148,618	131,403	17,215
New York, NY & NJ........................	141,290	40,542	100,748	15,226	85,522
Port of Long Beach, CA....................	92,959	13,234	79,724	21,802	57,923
New Orleans, LA..........................	83,254	43,756	39,498	22,608	16,889
Beaumont, TX............................	74,343	21,301	53,042	39,293	13,748
Port of Greater Baton Rouge, LA...........	73,372	45,832	27,540	21,684	5,855
Virginia, VA, Port of......................	69,434	4,899	64,535	47,543	16,991
Lake Charles Harbor District, LA...........	64,107	29,338	34,769	31,883	2,886
Port of Los Angeles, CA...................	59,819	3,345	56,475	14,847	41,628
Plaquemines Port District, LA..............	55,371	30,040	25,330	19,526	5,805
Port of Savannah, GA.....................	53,693	1,560	52,133	19,757	32,376
Mobile, AL...............................	50,520	16,672	33,848	15,146	18,703
Port Arthur, TX...........................	47,506	16,263	31,243	21,247	9,996
Baltimore, MD............................	40,602	4,175	36,427	20,915	15,512
Texas City, TX...........................	32,855	13,125	19,730	15,213	4,518
Philadelphia Regional Port, PA.............	31,791	12,939	18,851	7,282	11,570
Port Freeport, TX.........................	31,550	6,249	25,301	20,038	5,263
Duluth-Superior, MN and WI................	29,632	22,868	6,764	5,878	886
Tampa Port Authority, FL..................	27,980	17,596	10,384	2,267	8,116
Southern Indiana District, IN...............	27,718	27,718	–	–	–
Port of Charleston, SC....................	27,715	1,590	26,124	7,032	19,092
Port Everglades, FL.......................	25,559	14,097	11,462	2,960	8,502
Northern Indiana District, IN...............	25,447	25,087	360	71	289
Valdez, AK...............................	25,058	24,781	276	276	–
Port of Pascagoula, MS...................	24,077	11,445	12,633	6,694	5,939
Richmond, CA............................	23,578	8,692	14,886	3,792	11,094
Port of Portland, OR......................	22,868	10,090	12,778	9,347	3,431
South Jersey Port Corp, NJ...............	20,130	8,188	11,942	999	10,943

– Represents or rounds to zero.

Source: U.S. Army Corps of Engineers, Waterborne Commerce Statistics Center, Ports & State Data, "Waterborne Tonnage for Principal U.S. Ports and all 50 States and the U.S. Territories," <iwr.usace.army.mil/About/Technical-Centers/WCSC-Waterborne-Commerce-Statistics-Center-2/WCSC-Waterborne-Commerce/>, accessed April 2024.

Table 1118. Top 30 U.S. Ports/Waterways Ranked by Container Traffic: 2022

[In thousands of twenty-foot equivalent units (TEUs) (47,746.5 represents 47,746,500). For calendar year. For the 30 leading ports/waterways in total TEUs. A TEU is a measure of containerized cargo capacity equal to one standard 20-foot length by 8-foot width by 8-foot, 6 inch height container. Does not include empty foreign containers]

Port/waterway name	Total loaded	Domestic loaded			Foreign loaded		
		Total [1]	Inbound	Outbound	Total	Inbound	Outbound
Total U.S. [2]............................	**45,746.5**	**6,146.7**	**2,275.0**	**2,345.7**	**41,125.7**	**30,185.0**	**10,940.7**
Port Authority of New York and New Jersey, NY & NJ..................	6,660.3	65.5	28.1	28.1	6,604.2	5,352.1	1,252.1
Port of Los Ángeles, CA...................	6,424.3	–	–	–	6,424.3	5,231.6	1,192.8
Port of Long Beach, CA...................	6,092.0	381.0	39.7	319.7	5,732.6	4,675.7	1,056.9
Port of Savannah, GA.....................	4,329.9	–	–	–	4,329.9	3,012.7	1,317.2
Port of Houston Authority of Harris County, TX......	3,252.6	1.4	0.8	–	3,251.8	2,034.8	1,217.0
Port of Virginia, VA.......................	2,861.9	79.0	32.1	36.4	2,793.3	1,810.0	983.4
Port of Charleston, SC....................	2,126.3	–	–	–	2,126.3	1,492.0	634.3
Port of Oakland, CA......................	1,791.2	144.2	18.6	85.1	1,687.5	1,032.5	655.0
Tacoma, WA..............................	1,519.2	645.3	109.2	369.4	1,040.7	677.7	363.0
Port of Seattle, WA.......................	1,085.2	297.7	62.6	109.2	913.3	705.9	207.4
Jacksonville, FL..........................	902.6	726.8	91.0	501.4	310.2	212.2	98.0
PortMiami, FL............................	889.0	–	–	–	889.0	578.2	310.8
San Juan, PR............................	832.0	715.7	429.6	129.2	273.3	217.3	55.9
Honolulu, O'ahu, HI.......................	828.8	1,066.8	485.0	301.7	42.0	33.9	8.2
Baltimore, MD............................	790.9	66.2	36.0	23.1	731.8	521.7	210.0
Port Everglades, FL.......................	758.5	–	–	–	758.5	407.0	351.5
Philadelphia Regional Port Authority, PA............	728.5	70.3	23.2	31.8	673.5	535.8	137.7
Mobile, AL...............................	440.4	–	–	–	440.4	293.0	147.5
Port of Alaska, AK........................	419.8	556.7	323.6	96.1	–	–	–
Port of New Orleans, LA...................	352.7	1.2	0.1	0.8	351.8	126.8	225.0
Wilmington, NC...........................	237.2	–	–	–	237.2	121.0	116.2
Wilmington, DE...........................	204.4	–	–	–	204.4	187.5	16.8
Oxnard Harbor District, CA.................	197.8	–	–	–	197.8	135.7	62.1
South Jersey Port Corporation, NJ..........	163.1	110.5	38.2	48.8	76.1	70.1	6.1
Port of Gulfport, MS......................	152.0	–	–	–	152.0	94.1	57.9
Port of Boston, MA.......................	130.7	–	–	–	130.7	97.7	33.0
Port of Palm Beach District, FL.............	122.1	–	–	–	122.1	29.0	93.0
Guaynabo, PR............................	120.6	121.7	120.6	–	–	–	–
Juneau, AK..............................	111.4	161.5	84.8	26.6	–	–	–
Port of Portland, OR......................	110.6	–	–	–	110.6	79.5	31.0

– Represents or rounds to zero. [1] Includes empty TEUs, not shown separately. [2] Includes other ports/waterways not shown separately.

Source: U.S. Army Corps of Engineers, Waterborne Commerce Statistics Center, "Annual U.S. Waterborne Container Traffic by Port/Waterway," <www.iwr.usace.army.mil/About/Technical-Centers/WCSC-Waterborne-Commerce-Statistics-Center-2/WCSC-Waterborne-Commerce/>, accessed April 2024.

Table 1119. Highway Mileage—Urban and Rural by Ownership: 1990 to 2022

[In thousands (3,880 represents 3,880,000). As of December 31. Includes Puerto Rico beginning 2000]

Type and control of roadways	1990	2000	2010	2015	2018	2019	2020	2021	2022
Total mileage [1]...............	**3,880**	**3,951**	**4,084**	**4,171**	**4,195**	**4,189**	**4,192**	**4,207**	**4,217**
Urban mileage........................	757	859	1,103	1,223	1,241	1,254	1,254	1,267	1,268
Under state control................	96	112	(NA)	174	173	173	174	(NA)	174
Under local control [1]..............	661	746	(NA)	1,042	1,060	1,073	1,072	(NA)	1,089
Under federal control [2]...........	(NA)	(NA)	(NA)	7	8	8	8	(NA)	5
Rural mileage........................	3,123	3,092	2,980	2,949	2,955	2,936	2,939	2,940	2,949
Under state control................	703	664	(NA)	612	612	612	613	(NA)	614
Under local control [1]..............	2,242	2,311	(NA)	2,198	2,184	2,175	2,190	(NA)	2,186
Under federal control [2]...........	178	117	(NA)	139	159	149	136	(NA)	148

NA Not available. [1] Includes state park, state toll, other state agency, other local agency, and other roadways not identified by ownership. [2] Includes roadways in federal parks, forest, and reservations that are not part of the state and local highway system.

Source: U.S. Federal Highway Administration, "Highway Statistics 2022," and earlier reports, <www.fhwa.dot.gov/policyinformation/statistics.cfm>, accessed February 2024.

Table 1120. Highway Mileage—Functional Systems and Urban/Rural Status by State: 2022

[As of December 31. For definition of functional systems, see text, this section]

State	Total	Functional systems					Urban	Rural
		Interstate	Other freeways and expressways	Arterial	Collector	Local		
Total [1]...............	**4,217,423**	**48,890**	**18,859**	**405,750**	**822,945**	**2,920,980**	**1,268,062**	**2,949,361**
Alabama...............	98,632	1,004	33	9,666	21,339	66,589	30,462	68,170
Alaska.................	17,637	1,080	–	1,570	3,298	11,688	3,148	14,488
Arizona...............	74,507	1,169	273	6,846	11,780	54,440	31,548	42,959
Arkansas..............	99,087	768	169	7,399	20,975	69,777	17,222	81,865
California.............	182,103	2,455	1,888	26,911	33,140	117,709	103,148	78,955
Colorado..............	89,551	952	354	8,918	16,211	63,117	21,213	68,338
Connecticut...........	21,368	346	279	2,724	3,421	14,597	15,811	5,556
Delaware..............	6,575	41	68	628	1,131	4,707	3,696	2,879
District of Columbia..	1,520	12	16	271	155	1,066	1,520	–
Florida.................	123,817	1,495	778	13,000	15,578	92,965	87,421	36,396
Georgia...............	125,762	1,254	176	14,254	22,816	87,262	50,672	75,090
Hawaii.................	4,524	55	34	796	757	2,882	2,861	1,663
Idaho..................	58,428	622	84	4,786	10,477	42,459	8,808	49,620
Illinois.................	146,010	2,185	166	14,228	22,768	106,663	49,814	96,196
Indiana................	97,190	1,304	303	8,943	22,794	63,846	28,814	68,377
Iowa...................	114,970	788	–	9,941	31,587	72,654	12,964	102,006
Kansas................	139,011	877	597	8,554	34,092	94,891	13,722	125,289
Kentucky..............	79,705	944	462	5,576	17,017	55,706	14,805	64,901
Louisiana.............	65,955	944	151	5,841	11,858	47,161	22,948	43,007
Maine..................	22,843	366	19	2,106	5,939	14,412	3,240	19,603
Maryland..............	32,572	478	380	3,640	5,401	22,673	19,267	13,305
Massachusetts.......	36,799	568	335	6,356	4,545	24,995	30,627	6,173
Michigan..............	122,038	1,239	698	14,323	24,662	81,116	38,064	83,974
Minnesota............	143,217	914	254	13,188	31,854	97,008	24,068	119,149
Mississippi............	77,741	832	64	7,578	15,841	53,426	13,177	64,563
Missouri...............	132,647	1,385	1,618	8,917	25,266	95,461	24,810	107,836
Montana...............	74,502	1,193	–	6,170	16,161	50,978	4,909	69,593
Nebraska..............	95,552	484	462	7,728	20,833	66,046	8,158	87,395
Nevada................	47,348	618	55	3,510	6,002	37,163	10,610	36,738
New Hampshire......	16,247	225	83	1,662	2,647	11,629	5,102	11,145
New Jersey...........	38,783	432	488	5,897	4,436	27,530	33,424	5,358
New Mexico..........	72,161	999	12	5,628	8,820	56,701	11,267	60,893
New York.............	114,424	1,742	995	13,610	20,723	77,354	50,148	64,277
North Carolina.......	108,285	1,395	855	10,111	17,359	78,565	42,294	65,991
North Dakota.........	88,416	571	–	5,984	12,553	69,308	2,928	85,487
Ohio...................	122,884	1,580	922	10,612	23,283	86,487	47,791	75,093
Oklahoma.............	115,430	933	237	8,368	25,752	80,141	19,216	96,214
Oregon................	79,146	730	69	7,024	18,821	52,503	15,157	63,989
Pennsylvania.........	121,885	1,863	930	12,974	20,019	86,098	48,442	73,443
Rhode Island.........	6,531	70	92	852	900	4,617	4,954	1,576
South Carolina.......	77,208	851	128	7,369	14,942	53,918	24,425	52,782
South Dakota........	81,744	679	313	6,132	18,984	55,635	3,295	78,449
Tennessee............	96,406	1,202	205	9,270	18,187	67,542	32,049	64,357
Texas..................	323,364	3,476	1,617	33,129	67,330	217,812	115,320	208,044
Utah...................	49,008	938	69	3,854	8,408	35,740	12,753	36,255
Vermont...............	14,223	320	16	1,340	3,155	9,392	1,475	12,748
Virginia................	75,508	1,119	458	8,875	15,723	49,334	26,876	48,632
Washington...........	79,508	764	1,035	7,610	17,339	52,761	24,680	54,828
West Virginia........	38,843	556	15	3,509	8,653	26,110	6,691	32,152
Wisconsin.............	115,765	879	546	12,297	23,496	78,547	24,160	91,605
Wyoming..............	30,070	913	3	3,681	12,054	13,419	2,798	27,272
Puerto Rico...........	19,977	285	54	1,592	1,661	16,384	15,288	4,689

– Represents zero. [1] Total includes 50 states, DC, and Puerto Rico.

Source: U.S. Federal Highway Administration, "Highway Statistics 2022," <www.fhwa.dot.gov/policyinformation/statistics.cfm>, accessed February 2024.

Table 1121. Bridge Inventory—Total, Area, and Condition: 2012 to 2023, and by State, 2023

[Based on the National Bridge Inventory program; for details, see source]

State and year	Number of bridges	Bridge deck area (square meters)	Bridge condition [1] Number Good	Fair	Poor	Percent Good	Fair	Poor
2012........................	607,380	358,547,072	287,194	262,878	57,049	47.3	43.3	9.4
2013........................	607,751	362,428,004	287,581	265,456	54,492	47.3	43.7	9.0
2014........................	610,749	365,542,771	287,701	269,734	52,905	47.1	44.2	8.7
2015........................	611,845	369,109,088	289,158	271,690	50,917	47.3	44.4	8.3
2016........................	614,387	371,463,919	291,412	274,306	48,559	47.4	44.6	7.9
2017........................	615,002	374,362,285	288,030	279,270	47,619	46.8	45.4	7.7
2018........................	616,096	390,438,601	283,316	285,676	47,054	46.0	46.4	7.6
2019........................	617,084	393,265,002	279,582	291,339	46,163	45.3	47.2	7.5
2020........................	618,456	396,244,439	278,433	294,992	45,031	45.0	47.7	7.3
2021........................	619,622	398,580,883	278,128	297,908	43,586	44.9	48.1	7.0
2022........................	620,669	401,007,279	276,309	301,394	42,966	44.5	48.6	6.9
U.S. total, 2023.........	**621,581**	**403,488,432**	**275,117**	**304,060**	**42,404**	**44.3**	**48.9**	**6.8**
Alabama.....................	16,176	10,063,756	6,174	9,443	559	38.2	58.4	3.5
Alaska......................	1,675	772,722	750	789	136	44.8	47.1	8.1
Arizona.....................	8,544	6,158,502	5,430	3,019	95	63.6	35.3	1.1
Arkansas....................	12,962	6,924,464	6,042	6,223	697	46.6	48.0	5.4
California..................	25,818	30,462,032	11,907	12,320	1,591	46.1	47.7	6.2
Colorado....................	8,954	5,181,719	3,147	5,370	437	35.1	60.0	4.9
Connecticut................	4,362	3,407,390	1,235	2,908	219	28.3	66.7	5.0
Delaware....................	874	1,026,976	323	540	11	37.0	61.8	1.3
District of Columbia......	252	574,116	86	162	4	34.1	64.3	1.6
Florida.....................	12,881	18,533,368	7,771	4,661	449	60.3	36.2	3.5
Georgia.....................	15,058	10,661,087	11,362	3,457	239	75.5	23.0	1.6
Hawaii......................	1,190	1,438,953	350	760	80	29.4	63.9	6.7
Idaho.......................	4,588	1,811,962	1,325	3,028	235	28.9	66.0	5.1
Illinois....................	26,873	13,709,208	12,480	11,921	2,472	46.4	44.4	9.2
Indiana.....................	19,381	8,395,967	8,031	10,332	1,018	41.4	53.3	5.3
Iowa........................	23,720	8,975,321	9,244	9,918	4,558	39.0	41.8	19.2
Kansas......................	24,907	9,015,053	13,171	10,431	1,305	52.9	41.9	5.2
Kentucky....................	14,493	6,683,580	3,758	9,723	1,012	25.9	67.1	7.0
Louisiana...................	12,717	16,736,655	5,131	6,041	1,545	40.3	47.5	12.1
Maine.......................	2,521	1,278,501	645	1,504	372	25.6	59.7	14.8
Maryland....................	5,473	5,497,546	1,778	3,443	252	32.5	62.9	4.6
Massachusetts..............	5,281	4,167,326	1,339	3,492	450	25.4	66.1	8.5
Michigan....................	11,341	6,401,228	3,881	6,168	1,292	34.2	54.4	11.4
Minnesota...................	13,502	7,137,426	7,746	5,174	582	57.4	38.3	4.3
Mississippi.................	16,756	9,923,891	9,399	6,304	1,053	56.1	37.6	6.3
Missouri....................	24,617	10,891,626	9,373	13,031	2,213	38.1	52.9	9.0
Montana.....................	5,218	2,093,317	1,604	3,256	358	30.7	62.4	6.9
Nebraska....................	15,348	4,398,474	7,994	6,141	1,213	52.1	40.0	7.9
Nevada......................	2,090	1,963,298	1,229	836	25	58.8	40.0	1.2
New Hampshire..............	2,537	1,160,070	1,322	1,022	193	52.1	40.3	7.6
New Jersey.................	6,820	7,555,172	1,766	4,612	442	25.9	67.6	6.5
New Mexico.................	4,037	2,103,465	1,420	2,416	201	35.2	59.8	5.0
New York....................	17,573	13,377,401	6,294	9,701	1,578	35.8	55.2	9.0
North Carolina............	18,817	10,763,450	7,715	9,766	1,336	41.0	51.9	7.1
North Dakota..............	4,280	1,334,610	1,891	1,934	455	44.2	45.2	10.6
Ohio........................	26,960	14,124,814	16,504	9,205	1,251	61.2	34.1	4.6
Oklahoma....................	22,872	9,197,899	9,728	11,329	1,815	42.5	49.5	7.9
Oregon......................	8,292	5,119,667	2,821	5,070	401	34.0	61.1	4.8
Pennsylvania...............	23,257	13,462,310	7,880	12,355	3,022	33.9	53.1	13.0
Rhode Island..............	782	753,906	177	485	120	22.6	62.0	15.3
South Carolina...........	9,481	7,209,493	3,852	5,102	527	40.6	53.8	5.6
South Dakota..............	5,889	1,862,204	1,965	2,939	985	33.4	49.9	16.7
Tennessee..................	20,373	10,493,384	8,632	10,843	898	42.4	53.2	4.4
Texas.......................	56,313	55,452,627	28,772	26,833	708	51.1	47.6	1.3
Utah........................	3,109	2,026,750	766	2,268	75	24.6	72.9	2.4
Vermont.....................	2,856	947,638	1,494	1,287	75	52.3	45.1	2.6
Virginia....................	14,068	10,428,986	4,669	8,901	498	33.2	63.3	3.5
Washington.................	8,421	7,124,396	4,251	3,714	456	50.5	44.1	5.4
West Virginia.............	7,323	3,887,288	1,727	4,154	1,442	23.6	56.7	19.7
Wisconsin...................	14,412	7,242,135	7,358	6,111	943	51.1	42.4	6.5
Wyoming.....................	3,131	1,329,979	966	1,961	204	30.9	62.6	6.5
Guam........................	47	17,022	20	21	6	42.6	44.7	12.8
Puerto Rico................	2,335	2,223,321	418	1,623	294	17.9	69.5	12.6
Virgin Islands............	24	4,978	4	13	7	16.7	54.2	29.2

[1] Good: pavement and bridge infrastructure that is free of significant defects, and has a condition that does not adversely affect its performance. Fair: pavement and bridge infrastructure that has isolated surface defects or functional deficiencies on pavements; or minor deterioration of bridge elements. Poor: pavement and bridge infrastructure that is exhibiting advanced deterioration and conditions that impact structural capacity.

Source: U.S. Federal Highway Administration, Office of Bridges and Structures, "Bridge Condition by Highway System," <www.fhwa.dot.gov/bridge/britab.cfm>, accessed April 2024.

Table 1122. Funding for Highways and Disposition of Highway–User Revenue: 1990 to 2022

[In millions of dollars (75,444 represents $75,444,000,000). Data compiled from reports of state and local authorities]

Type	1990	2000	2010	2015	2018	2019	2020	2021	2022
Total receipts	**75,444**	**131,115**	**220,977**	**241,063**	**237,833**	**260,822**	**257,016**	**272,404**	**364,462**
Current income	69,880	119,815	187,960	218,812	216,154	238,027	231,258	245,673	343,728
Highway-user revenues	44,346	81,335	93,830	113,454	121,325	135,293	127,545	125,575	136,112
Other taxes and fees	19,827	31,137	80,220	85,434	72,859	80,313	82,099	97,542	180,588
Investment income, other receipts	5,707	7,342	13,910	19,924	21,970	22,420	21,615	22,557	27,027
Bond issue proceeds [1]	5,564	11,301	33,017	22,251	21,679	22,795	25,758	26,731	20,735
Funds drawn from or placed in reserves [2,3]	-36	-8,418	-15,664	-5,868	6,666	-2,767	4,464	-11,710	-99,199
Total funds available	75,408	122,697	205,313	235,195	244,498	258,055	261,480	260,694	265,263
Total disbursements	**75,408**	**122,697**	**205,313**	**235,195**	**244,498**	**258,055**	**261,480**	**260,694**	**265,263**
Current disbursements	72,457	117,592	193,034	207,537	228,609	236,932	244,193	244,613	248,517
Capital outlay	35,151	61,323	100,175	106,539	117,025	120,934	127,716	128,950	127,841
Maintenance and traffic services	20,365	30,636	48,773	51,817	59,139	61,503	61,346	61,622	64,158
Administration and research	6,501	10,020	16,165	16,930	19,437	20,605	20,238	20,052	22,441
Highway law enforcement and safety	7,235	11,031	18,080	20,165	21,205	21,918	22,118	23,107	22,899
Interest on debt	3,205	4,583	9,842	12,087	11,802	11,972	12,776	10,881	11,177
Bond retirement [1]	2,951	5,105	12,279	27,658	15,890	21,123	17,287	16,081	16,746

[1] Amounts shown represent Federal payments to territories, and Federal expenditures in territories for highways and mass transit. [2] Proceeds and redemptions of short-term notes and refunding issues are excluded. [3] Negative numbers indicate that funds were placed in reserves.

Source: U.S. Federal Highway Administration, "Highway Statistics 2022," and earlier reports, <www.fhwa.dot.gov/policyinformation/statistics.cfm>, accessed April 2024.

Table 1123. State Motor Fuel Tax and Related Receipts, 2019 to 2022; and Gasoline Tax Rates, 2022

[654 represents $654,000,000. Federal tax rate is 18.4 cents a gallon. This table includes revenues from state taxes on all motor-vehicle fuels and related receipts due to motor-fuel taxation and administration. In many states, however, the tax on special fuels (fuels other than gasoline and gasohol) is applicable only to the amount used on the highways. For the states that apply the tax to all fuel sold, the revenue and refunds covering the nonhighway portion of these special fuels have been excluded]

State	Adjusted total receipts (million dollars)				Tax rate,[1] 2022	State	Adjusted total receipts (million dollars)				Tax rate,[1] 2022
	2019	2020	2021	2022			2019	2020	2021	2022	
AL	654	814	920	986	28.00	MO	707	693	674	735	22.00
AK	30	29	28	29	8.00	MT	242	240	254	264	33.25
AZ	742	725	747	788	18.00	NE	391	398	420	381	24.80
AR	486	532	577	595	24.60	NV	731	698	734	788	23.81
CA	7,285	7,383	7,449	8,049	53.90	NH	190	178	170	181	23.83
CO	673	629	659	668	23.69	NJ	529	469	460	489	37.10
CT	787	644	719	760	25.00	NM	313	152	322	337	17.00
DE	143	136	125	134	23.00	NY	1,705	1,686	1,384	203	25.35
DC	81	22	23	23	23.50	NC	2,091	1,934	2,103	2,182	38.50
FL	2,858	2,809	2,749	3,057	38.08	ND	198	191	172	178	23.00
GA [2]	1,838	1,873	1,782	1,602	29.10	OH	1,861	2,488	2,551	2,627	38.50
HI	82	76	66	75	16.00	OK	564	569	555	589	20.00
ID	345	344	368	372	33.00	OR	620	567	591	617	38.00
IL	1,237	2,269	2,312	2,455	40.30	PA	3,841	3,575	3,483	3,657	57.60
IN	1,834	1,527	1,569	1,785	33.00	RI	166	146	141	151	35.00
IA	651	694	659	658	31.00	SC	742	787	870	961	28.00
KS	470	437	455	466	24.00	SD	186	183	197	194	30.00
KY	771	740	746	773	24.60	TN	1,171	1,216	1,220	1,267	26.00
LA	604	549	612	603	20.00	TX	3,738	3,389	3,678	3,781	20.00
ME	250	237	227	241	30.00	UT	514	504	546	573	31.00
MD	1,117	1,062	1,012	1,098	42.70	VT	120	109	103	113	30.46
MA	775	707	662	722	24.00	VA	932	887	1,057	1,354	28.00
MI	1,436	1,297	1,332	1,332	27.20	WA	1,655	1,585	1,470	1,580	49.40
MN	922	854	850	906	28.50	WV	424	392	372	385	35.70
MS	423	412	428	441	18.40	WI	1,054	1,019	1,032	1,076	30.90
						WY	175	163	168	168	24.00

[1] Effective dates vary by state. Data shown are latest rates in effect during 2022. Includes other miscellaneous tax (environmental, etc.). [2] Beginning 2014, Georgia receipts includes special fuel and use tax.

Source: U.S. Federal Highway Administration, "Highway Statistics 2022," and earlier reports, <www.fhwa.dot.gov/policyinformation/statistics.cfm>, accessed April 2024.

Table 1124. Public Obligations for Highways—Changes in Indebtedness During the Year: 2000 to 2022

[In millions of dollars (56,264 represents $56,264,000,000). Table summarizes state indebtedness from all state bond issues, including the toll facility issues and the state issues for local roads. This table is compiled from reports of state authorities. Table also summarizes the change in status of the highway obligations of local governments, including toll authorities]

Item	2000	2010	2015	2018	2019	2020	2021	2022
STATE GOVERNMENT								
Obligations outstanding, beginning of year.........	56,264	138,798	211,692	139,481	224,515	227,820	225,215	232,987
Obligations issued.................................	9,067	26,895	29,155	26,394	23,268	29,963	26,692	22,191
Obligations retired................................	3,897	11,143	22,909	11,334	25,170	24,488	18,795	20,272
Obligations outstanding, end of year...............	61,434	154,550	217,938	154,541	222,613	233,296	233,113	234,906
LOCAL GOVERNMENT [1,2]								
Obligations outstanding, beginning of year.........	34,904	65,679	51,377	80,313	156,261	138,132	103,764	(NA)
Bonds outstanding, beginning of year.............	34,229	63,891	48,262	76,584	150,973	132,468	97,218	(NA)
Bonds outstanding, end of year.................	34,949	67,707	49,189	71,380	153,505	134,579	99,361	(NA)
Obligations outstanding, end of year.............	35,557	69,794	52,579	77,037	161,015	143,721	107,599	(NA)

NA Not available. [1] Short-term notes data not shown. The data are included in beginning and ending year obligations. [2] Local government reporting is on a biennial basis with even-numbered years optional; therefore, data for some states is estimated in non-reporting years.

Source: U.S. Federal Highway Administration, "Highway Statistics 2022," and earlier reports, <www.fhwa.dot.gov/policyinformation/statistics.cfm>, accessed February 2024.

Table 1125. State Disbursements for Highways by State: 2000 to 2022

[In millions of dollars (89,832 represents $89,832,000,000). Comprises disbursements from current revenues or loans for construction, maintenance, interest and principal payments on highway bonds, transfers to local units, and miscellaneous. Includes transactions by state toll authorities. Data exclude amounts allocated for collection expenses, nonhighway purposes, and mass transit]

State	2000	2010	2015	2018	2019	2020	2021	2022
United States.............	**89,832**	**145,944**	**168,242**	**177,582**	**184,543**	**189,346**	**184,669**	**191,722**
Alabama.....................	1,246	1,781	2,281	2,273	2,285	2,167	1,988	3,549
Alaska......................	501	756	1,185	1,122	1,159	1,031	1,079	1,058
Arizona.....................	2,040	2,663	3,388	2,765	3,047	3,250	2,577	2,747
Arkansas....................	817	1,376	1,473	1,860	1,591	1,725	2,464	2,273
California..................	6,750	19,961	12,162	15,837	16,502	17,356	17,092	17,869
Colorado....................	1,392	2,249	2,632	2,225	2,333	2,650	2,209	3,177
Connecticut.................	1,304	1,761	2,097	1,947	2,117	2,117	2,128	2,427
Delaware....................	595	1,353	984	1,702	1,780	1,660	1,992	1,711
District of Columbia........	244	582	413	571	597	724	685	878
Florida.....................	4,208	7,867	9,635	11,356	11,517	11,214	12,256	11,609
Georgia.....................	1,567	2,926	3,017	4,450	3,781	3,650	3,854	4,514
Hawaii......................	272	460	568	385	415	474	302	428
Idaho.......................	492	959	853	1,025	1,097	1,037	1,285	1,288
Illinois....................	3,447	(NA)	6,783	6,317	5,761	6,830	7,615	7,480
Indiana.....................	1,932	2,839	2,636	3,072	3,495	3,245	4,197	3,962
Iowa........................	1,494	1,888	2,183	2,404	2,337	2,545	2,594	2,564
Kansas......................	1,206	1,571	1,806	1,333	1,481	1,559	1,743	2,110
Kentucky....................	1,651	2,528	3,013	2,565	2,594	2,645	2,551	2,978
Louisiana...................	1,301	2,457	2,698	2,293	1,725	1,847	2,656	3,374
Maine.......................	488	684	988	1,164	1,190	1,278	1,207	1,254
Maryland....................	1,599	2,255	3,395	4,380	3,441	3,316	3,459	3,719
Massachusetts...............	3,524	2,923	(NA)	(NA)	3,730	(NA)	3,609	4,260
Michigan....................	2,748	3,484	3,111	3,794	4,225	4,384	4,769	5,202
Minnesota...................	1,692	2,625	3,486	3,316	3,506	3,657	4,004	3,551
Mississippi.................	1,039	1,345	1,200	1,245	1,328	1,325	1,368	1,277
Missouri....................	1,818	2,814	2,364	2,446	2,542	2,497	2,581	2,708
Montana.....................	474	778	783	712	814	883	860	770
Nebraska....................	745	1,409	1,595	1,793	1,803	1,388	1,367	1,424
Nevada......................	651	1,007	867	1,273	1,216	1,078	1,156	1,241
New Hampshire...............	387	793	858	658	650	708	602	688
New Jersey..................	4,503	5,201	7,146	6,834	10,008	9,147	6,393	6,095
New Mexico..................	1,162	1,163	1,142	1,442	1,038	1,139	1,302	1,346
New York....................	5,307	7,711	9,821	9,597	15,290	10,103	9,364	8,818
North Carolina.............	2,621	3,646	4,324	6,128	7,289	6,330	5,673	6,358
North Dakota................	385	559	950	493	629	619	614	674
Ohio........................	3,351	4,520	5,838	5,345	5,496	6,367	5,996	5,826
Oklahoma....................	1,417	2,040	2,669	2,783	2,787	3,122	3,109	3,591
Oregon......................	1,010	1,522	2,265	(NA)	(NA)	2,567	2,871	2,621
Pennsylvania................	4,517	8,835	8,592	11,529	9,641	10,285	8,980	8,583
Rhode Island................	256	540	(NA)	488	645	824	724	680
South Carolina.............	970	1,899	1,555	2,082	2,632	2,864	2,219	2,558
South Dakota...............	466	532	625	509	565	780	827	840
Tennessee...................	1,440	2,076	1,879	2,235	2,323	2,512	2,441	2,605
Texas.......................	5,665	9,365	21,222	13,866	15,541	20,921	17,635	18,122
Utah........................	1,072	2,303	1,622	2,006	2,007	2,415	2,506	2,427
Vermont.....................	287	436	568	568	565	598	599	652
Virginia....................	2,678	3,334	5,235	7,449	5,569	5,639	6,219	6,795
Washington..................	1,871	4,149	5,489	4,981	4,562	5,019	5,698	5,157
West Virginia...............	1,170	1,327	1,227	2,315	1,489	2,219	1,449	1,942
Wisconsin...................	1,663	2,702	3,547	3,200	3,275	3,295	3,235	3,324
Wyoming.....................	396	605	635	513	564	612	563	617

NA Not available.

Source: U.S. Federal Highway Administration, "Highway Statistics 2022," and earlier reports, <www.fhwa.dot.gov/policyinformation/statistics.cfm>, accessed February 2024.

Table 1126. Federal Highway Trust Fund—Receipts, Expenditures, and Balance: 1960 to 2022

[In thousands of dollars (2,535,815 represents $2,535,815,000). For fiscal year ending September 30. Established as part of the Federal Aid Highway Act of 1956]

Year	Receipts	Expend-itures	Balance	Year	Receipts	Expend-itures	Balance
1960.............	2,535,815	2,940,251	119,221	2013.............	37,704,153	42,917,222	3,771,061
1970.............	5,469,037	4,378,253	2,611,611	2014.............	52,503,506	43,791,139	11,375,577
1980.............	7,647,310	9,212,311	10,999,460	2015.............	41,833,840	42,951,543	9,040,358
1990.............	13,453,149	14,375,194	9,628,954	2016.............	88,273,866	44,787,377	51,435,286
2000.............	30,347,117	26,999,828	22,553,544	2017.............	36,107,910	44,977,292	41,443,049
2005.............	32,908,563	33,121,424	10,592,258	2018.............	37,928,360	45,132,339	32,605,372
2009.............	37,317,479	37,571,317	8,881,338	2019.............	38,985,056	45,607,442	24,651,555
2010.............	44,892,516	32,006,716	20,743,290	2020.............	37,710,546	48,265,140	12,540,879
2011.............	32,009,947	37,324,658	14,322,539	2021.............	48,445,057	45,716,936	14,264,103
2012.............	37,641,127	41,149,827	9,730,745	2022 [1]........	131,611,420	46,350,451	98,913,138

[1] Large increase in FY 2022 due to transfers directed by the Infrastructure Investment and Jobs Act (IIJA).

Source: U.S. Federal Highway Administration, "Highway Statistics 2022," <www.fhwa.dot.gov/policyinformation/statistics.cfm>, accessed April 2024.

Table 1127. Federal Highway Trust Fund Receipts from Highway Users by State: 2022

[In thousands of dollars (46,631,466 represents $46,631,466,000). For fiscal year ending September 30. Federal Highway Trust Fund receipts are reported by the U.S. Department of the Treasury. Payments into the Fund attributable to highway users in each state are estimated by the Federal Highway Administration]

State	Total	Highway account						Mass transit account	
		Motor fuel			Other				
		Motor fuel, total	Gasoline	Special fuels	Federal use tax	Trucks and trailers	Tires	Gasoline	Special fuels
Total.............	46,631,466	33,961,570	23,201,753	10,759,817	1,585,391	4,623,251	712,991	4,317,356	1,430,907
Alabama.............	1,074,573	788,727	553,074	235,653	34,722	101,255	15,615	102,915	31,339
Alaska.............	100,231	70,382	41,999	28,383	4,182	12,196	1,881	7,815	3,775
Arizona.............	1,049,879	757,840	501,954	255,886	37,703	109,948	16,956	93,403	34,029
Arkansas.............	614,458	430,688	255,103	175,585	25,871	75,445	11,635	47,469	23,350
California.............	4,158,113	3,107,121	2,305,988	801,133	118,042	344,229	53,086	429,096	106,539
Colorado.............	760,310	556,992	388,109	168,883	24,884	72,565	11,191	72,219	22,459
Connecticut.........	409,271	308,762	235,813	72,949	10,749	31,345	4,834	43,880	9,701
Delaware.............	132,762	102,448	83,387	19,061	2,809	8,190	1,263	15,517	2,535
Dist. of Columbia. . .	26,601	20,935	17,937	2,998	442	1,288	199	3,338	399
Florida.............	2,559,358	1,934,368	1,485,286	449,082	66,169	192,961	29,758	276,380	59,722
Georgia.............	1,593,481	1,168,107	815,657	352,450	51,931	151,440	23,355	151,777	46,871
Hawaii.............	103,085	81,279	69,956	11,323	1,668	4,865	750	13,017	1,506
Idaho.............	319,365	225,176	136,579	88,597	13,054	38,068	5,871	25,414	11,782
Illinois.............	1,506,159	1,086,727	718,685	368,042	54,229	158,139	24,388	133,732	48,944
Indiana.............	1,200,446	853,134	533,640	319,494	47,075	137,279	21,171	99,299	42,488
Iowa.............	633,937	444,890	264,845	180,045	26,529	77,361	11,931	49,282	23,944
Kansas.............	479,707	342,001	216,504	125,497	18,491	53,923	8,316	40,287	16,689
Kentucky.............	805,826	577,695	373,298	204,397	30,117	87,825	13,544	69,463	27,182
Louisiana.............	768,963	555,402	368,662	186,740	27,515	80,238	12,374	68,600	24,834
Maine.............	200,910	148,971	107,936	41,035	6,046	17,632	2,719	20,085	5,457
Maryland.............	737,953	556,873	425,632	131,241	19,338	56,391	8,697	79,201	17,453
Massachusetts......	697,073	534,681	428,108	106,573	15,703	45,792	7,062	79,662	14,173
Michigan.............	1,275,203	960,585	730,366	230,219	33,921	98,920	15,255	135,906	30,616
Minnesota.............	790,925	576,542	395,075	181,467	26,738	77,972	12,025	73,515	24,133
Mississippi.........	664,220	473,114	298,476	174,638	25,732	75,038	11,572	55,540	23,224
Missouri.............	1,102,680	800,240	540,102	260,138	38,330	111,775	17,238	100,502	34,595
Montana.............	238,400	164,441	90,975	73,466	10,825	31,567	4,868	16,929	9,770
Nebraska.............	405,833	279,444	153,398	126,046	18,572	54,159	8,352	28,544	16,762
Nevada.............	418,583	302,790	202,060	100,730	14,842	43,281	6,675	37,599	13,396
New Hampshire. . . .	186,687	142,094	111,338	30,756	4,532	13,215	2,038	20,718	4,090
New Jersey.........	1,046,302	788,735	600,999	187,736	27,662	80,666	12,440	111,833	24,966
New Mexico.........	516,067	348,935	175,766	173,169	25,515	74,407	11,475	32,706	23,029
New York.............	1,662,432	1,230,561	886,792	343,769	50,652	147,710	22,780	165,013	45,716
North Carolina......	1,503,302	1,119,982	823,612	296,370	43,668	127,343	19,639	153,257	39,413
North Dakota.......	198,459	134,731	69,230	65,501	9,651	28,144	4,340	12,882	8,711
Ohio.............	1,666,823	1,205,342	803,452	401,890	59,216	172,683	26,631	149,505	53,446
Oklahoma.............	785,394	548,162	319,032	229,130	33,761	98,452	15,183	59,365	30,471
Oregon.............	577,630	409,926	255,019	154,907	22,825	66,560	10,265	47,454	20,600
Pennsylvania.......	1,599,374	1,160,029	781,359	378,670	55,795	162,706	25,092	145,394	50,358
Rhode Island........	103,345	78,032	59,747	18,285	2,694	7,857	1,212	11,118	2,432
South Carolina......	942,946	684,408	462,135	222,273	32,750	95,506	14,729	85,994	29,559
South Dakota.......	210,638	146,495	84,002	62,493	9,208	26,852	4,141	15,631	8,311
Tennessee.............	1,174,907	854,128	579,906	274,222	40,405	117,827	18,171	107,908	36,468
Texas.............	5,431,956	3,874,287	2,456,535	1,417,752	208,897	609,176	93,946	457,109	188,541
Utah.............	474,478	336,883	209,963	126,920	18,701	54,535	8,410	39,070	16,879
Vermont.............	82,911	62,379	47,256	15,123	2,228	6,498	1,002	8,793	2,011
Virginia.............	1,318,092	970,490	687,509	282,981	41,695	121,591	18,752	127,931	37,633
Washington.........	837,536	616,311	435,790	180,521	26,599	77,566	11,962	81,091	24,007
West Virginia.......	375,746	257,378	137,967	119,411	17,594	51,308	7,913	25,673	15,880
Wisconsin.............	890,957	642,052	422,745	219,307	32,313	94,231	14,532	78,664	29,165
Wyoming.............	217,179	139,875	52,995	86,880	12,801	37,331	5,757	9,861	11,554

Source: U.S. Federal Highway Administration, "Highway Statistics 2022," <www.fhwa.dot.gov/policyinformation/statistics.cfm>, accessed February 2024.

Table 1128. Motor Vehicle Distance Traveled by Type of Vehicle: 1970 to 2022

[1,110 represents 1,110,000,000,000. The travel data by vehicle type and stratification of trucks are estimated by the Federal Highway Administration (FHWA)]

Year	Vehicle miles of travel (bil.) [1]					Average miles traveled per vehicle [1]				
	Total [2]	Light duty vehicle short WB [3]	Buses [4]	Light duty vehicle long WB [3]	Trucks [5,6]	Total [2]	Light duty vehicle short WB [3]	Buses [4]	Light duty vehicle long WB [3]	Trucks [5,6]
1970.........	1,110	920	4.5	123	62	9,976.0	9,989.0	12,035.0	8,676.0	13,565.0
1975.........	1,328	1,040	6.1	201	81	9,627.0	9,309.0	13,102.0	9,829.0	15,167.0
1980.........	1,527	1,122	6.1	291	108	9,458.0	8,813.0	11,458.0	10,437.0	18,736.0
1985.........	1,775	1,256	4.5	391	124	10,020.0	9,419.0	7,545.0	10,506.0	20,597.0
1990.........	2,144	1,418	5.7	575	146	11,107.0	10,277.0	9,133.0	11,902.0	23,603.0
1995.........	2,423	1,438	6.4	790	178	11,793.0	11,203.0	9,365.0	12,018.0	26,514.0
2000.........	2,747	1,967	14.8	491	262	12,164.2	11,043.9	19,843.2	14,603.9	29,120.2
2001.........	2,796	1,987	13.0	512	272	11,879.5	10,723.3	17,319.4	14,654.3	28,850.8
2002.........	2,856	2,036	13.3	520	276	12,170.6	11,115.5	17,530.6	14,304.5	29,379.4
2003.........	2,890	2,051	13.4	528	286	12,207.4	11,062.3	17,231.5	14,769.6	30,291.9
2004.........	2,965	2,083	13.5	569	284	12,199.6	10,992.4	17,004.6	15,221.2	29,685.5
2005.........	2,989	2,096	13.2	581	285	12,082.4	10,963.2	16,297.7	14,797.0	28,819.3
2006.........	3,014	2,048	14.0	633	301	12,016.9	10,540.4	17,079.0	16,339.8	29,092.4
2007.........	3,031	2,104	14.5	587	304	11,914.7	10,710.0	17,395.8	14,969.7	28,290.3
2008.........	2,977	2,025	14.8	605	311	11,630.8	10,290.3	17,577.8	15,256.5	28,572.8
2009.........	2,957	2,016	14.4	617	288	11,618.2	10,379.6	17,052.2	15,252.0	26,273.6
2010.........	2,967	2,026	13.8	623	287	11,865.7	10,650.4	16,275.1	15,474.3	26,604.1
2011.........	2,950	2,046	13.8	604	268	11,651.7	11,150.0	20,729.8	12,007.0	26,054.2
2012.........	2,969	2,063	14.8	601	269	11,707.3	11,261.7	19,334.0	11,884.7	25,255.4
2013.........	2,988	2,074	15.2	603	275	11,678.6	11,243.6	17,543.2	11,711.8	25,951.5
2014.........	3,026	2,072	16.0	638	279	11,621.5	11,047.8	18,346.8	12,138.4	25,594.4
2015.........	3,095	2,148	16.2	632	280	11,742.2	11,327.2	18,258.2	11,854.9	24,978.9
2016.........	3,174	2,192	16.3	658	288	11,809.6	11,369.6	16,748.8	11,991.0	25,037.5
2017.........	3,212	2,221	17.2	657	298	11,789.3	11,466.8	17,521.2	11,543.0	24,334.6
2018.........	3,240	2,233	18.3	664	305	11,843.2	11,576.4	18,448.2	11,485.8	23,036.6
2019.........	3,262	2,254	18.0	670	300	11,797.0	11,599.3	18,069.7	11,262.8	22,929.7
2020.........	2,904	1,935	15.0	638	298	10,522.8	9,927.7	14,883.4	10,855.2	23,074.7
2021.........	3,132	2,084	16.7	685	327	11,099.4	10,573.2	17,829.9	11,318.2	23,601.1
2022.........	3,196	2,138	18.5	685	331	11,278.0	10,847.4	19,379.3	11,142.3	23,111.2

[1] Beginning with 2000 data, FHWA updated data using an enhanced methodology implemented in March 2011. Prior to 2000, "Light Duty Vehicles Short WB" were categorized as "Cars"; and "Light Duty Vehicles Long WB" were categorized as "Vans, pickups, sport utility vehicles." [2] Motorcycles included with "Light Duty Vehicles Short WB" through 1994; thereafter in total, not shown separately. [3] Light Duty Vehicles Short WB—passenger cars, light trucks, vans and sport utility vehicles with a wheelbase (WB) equal to or less than 121 inches. Light Duty Vehicles Long WB—large passenger cars, vans, pickup trucks, and sport/utility vehicles with WB larger than 121 inches. [4] Includes school buses. [5] Includes combination trucks. [6] Beginning in 2000: Single-Unit—single frame trucks that have 2-axles and at least 6 tires or a gross vehicle weight rating exceeding 10,000 lbs.

Source: U.S. Federal Highway Administration, "Highway Statistics 2022," and earlier reports, <www.fhwa.dot.gov/policyinformation/statistics.cfm>, accessed February 2024.

Table 1129. Licensed Drivers, Total and as a Percent of Age Group, by Age: 2000 to 2022

[Licensed drivers in thousands (190,625 represents 190,625,000). Percentages are computed using Census Bureau data]

Age or range	Licensed drivers (1,000)							Licensed drivers as percent of age group [1]		
	2000	2010	2018	2019	2020	2021	2022	2010	2020	2022
Total..................	190,625	210,115	227,558	228,680	228,196	232,782	235,086	83.5	83.9	70.5
Under 16 years old [2].....	27	398	43	44	62	111	118	4.7	0.7	0.2
16 years old............	1,470	1,213	1,066	1,088	1,042	1,091	1,077	28.1	25.1	24.9
17 years old............	2,331	2,028	1,976	1,957	1,852	1,826	1,844	46.1	44.7	43.0
18 years old............	2,839	2,731	2,630	2,621	2,467	2,561	2,587	60.7	58.0	59.8
19 years old............	3,077	3,187	3,040	3,072	2,930	2,918	2,951	69.5	67.7	68.7
20 to 24 years old.......	15,966	17,468	17,519	17,478	17,278	17,436	17,492	80.9	79.9	77.0
20 years old............	3,140	3,426	3,249	3,254	3,237	3,234	3,203	75.8	75.8	72.2
21 years old............	3,172	3,474	3,355	3,360	3,346	3,450	3,426	79.8	78.2	72.5
22 years old............	3,182	3,483	3,506	3,508	3,444	3,457	3,521	81.7	80.1	75.5
23 years old............	3,247	3,515	3,645	3,624	3,558	3,585	3,607	83.7	81.9	80.4
24 years old............	3,225	3,571	3,764	3,733	3,694	3,709	3,736	84.0	83.1	85.0
25 to 29 years old.......	17,586	18,431	20,186	20,117	19,714	19,796	19,694	87.3	83.9	88.7
30 to 34 years old.......	19,155	17,849	19,979	20,182	20,186	20,859	21,123	89.4	90.0	90.6
35 to 39 years old.......	21,059	18,161	19,603	19,743	19,743	20,304	20,465	90.0	90.8	91.9
40 to 44 years old.......	21,093	19,178	18,043	18,247	18,465	19,239	19,636	91.8	92.7	91.6
45 to 49 years old.......	19,154	20,814	19,198	18,919	18,355	18,108	18,103	91.7	90.0	92.2
50 to 54 years old.......	16,868	20,628	19,445	19,174	19,018	19,336	19,257	92.5	92.9	92.5
55 to 59 years old.......	12,760	18,440	20,539	20,497	20,123	19,916	19,498	93.8	92.0	93.0
60 to 64 years old.......	9,915	15,858	19,042	19,243	19,294	19,697	19,718	94.3	93.8	93.4
65 to 69 years old.......	8,386	11,468	15,942	16,242	16,575	17,105	17,495	92.2	95.0	93.9
70 to 74 years old.......	7,468	8,231	12,252	12,763	13,297	13,927	14,064	88.7	94.8	92.8
75 to 79 years old.......	5,911	6,158	8,054	8,346	8,635	9,041	9,894	84.1	89.5	91.1
80 to 84 years old.......	3,511	4,464	4,936	4,880	5,169	5,380	5,755	77.7	81.8	86.4
85 and over..............	2,050	3,411	4,065	4,067	3,992	4,130	4,316	62.1	59.0	66.5

[1] Calculated based on Census Bureau population estimates for the population aged 14 and over. [2] Percent of age group data based on Census Bureau population estimates for 14- and 15-year olds.

Source: U.S. Federal Highway Administration, "Highway Statistics 2022," and earlier reports, <www.fhwa.dot.gov/policyinformation/statistics.cfm>, accessed February 2024.

Table 1130. State Motor Vehicle Registrations, 1990 to 2022; and Motorcycle Registrations and Licensed Drivers, 2022

[In thousands (188,798 represents 188,798,000). Motor vehicle registrations cover publicly, privately, and commercially owned vehicles. Some states did not provide complete current registration data. Table displays estimates by FHWA, transaction data, or previous year data; see source and earlier editions for more information. For uniformity, data have been adjusted to a calendar-year basis as registration years in states differ; figures represent net numbers where possible. See also Table 1131]

| State | Motor vehicle registrations [1] | | | | | | 2022 | | Motor-cycle registra-tions [2], in 2022 | Licensed drivers in 2022 |
	1990	2000	2010	2015	2020	2021	Total	Auto-mobile		
U.S.	188,798	221,475	242,061	255,009	267,607	272,474	273,833	99,947	9,535	235,086
AL.	3,744	3,960	4,654	5,285	5,205	5,341	5,339	1,996	126	4,088
AK.	477	594	710	783	766	660	653	134	26	521
AZ.	2,825	3,795	4,320	5,470	5,933	5,784	5,811	2,201	278	5,848
AR.	1,448	1,840	2,073	2,680	2,744	3,118	3,118	929	452	2,307
CA.	21,926	27,698	31,014	28,595	29,613	30,536	30,317	13,796	789	27,632
CO.	3,155	3,626	4,180	4,814	5,172	4,916	4,937	1,442	180	4,477
CT.	2,623	2,853	3,082	2,755	2,787	2,673	2,705	1,101	85	2,629
DE.	526	630	799	936	1,002	448	443	170	25	862
DC.	262	242	212	319	353	360	376	201	4	511
FL.	10,950	11,781	14,373	15,532	17,844	18,543	19,013	7,763	647	16,496
GA.	5,489	7,155	7,702	7,937	8,622	8,930	8,936	3,412	218	7,361
HI.	771	738	904	1,209	1,230	1,210	1,218	445	25	937
ID.	1,054	1,178	1,325	1,788	1,858	1,928	1,968	555	63	1,393
IL.	7,873	8,973	10,079	10,249	10,307	10,691	10,043	3,730	291	8,509
IN.	4,366	5,571	5,698	5,822	5,990	6,015	6,040	1,993	216	4,654
IA.	2,632	3,106	3,313	3,447	3,595	3,645	3,584	1,066	195	2,354
KS.	2,012	2,296	2,436	2,539	2,513	2,516	2,499	826	89	2,052
KY.	2,909	2,826	3,589	4,041	4,363	4,309	4,185	1,479	107	2,994
LA.	2,995	3,557	4,086	3,787	3,760	3,762	4,484	1,486	109	3,402
ME.	977	1,024	1,054	1,049	1,083	1,328	1,244	373	50	1,060
MD.	3,607	3,848	4,557	4,009	4,099	4,806	4,815	2,025	104	4,399
MA.	3,726	5,265	5,334	4,902	4,899	5,060	5,038	1,897	145	4,889
MI.	7,209	8,436	9,286	8,037	8,216	9,301	9,147	2,717	256	7,777
MN.	3,508	4,630	4,848	5,033	5,447	5,288	5,449	1,690	224	4,118
MS.	1,875	2,289	2,016	2,041	2,028	2,353	2,267	837	32	2,047
MO.	3,905	4,580	5,153	5,406	5,460	5,468	5,239	1,762	135	4,290
MT.	783	1,026	926	1,448	1,597	1,763	1,850	474	400	871
NE.	1,384	1,619	1,802	1,925	1,885	1,882	1,916	595	51	1,450
NV.	853	1,220	1,362	2,242	2,480	2,598	2,594	1,020	77	2,211
NH.	946	1,052	1,203	1,222	1,279	1,333	1,350	443	87	1,175
NJ.	5,652	6,390	6,628	5,786	5,885	6,090	5,851	2,351	149	6,634
NM.	1,301	1,529	1,612	1,760	1,728	1,806	1,813	604	57	1,509
NY.	10,196	10,235	10,255	10,284	10,940	8,439	8,375	2,968	736	12,085
NC.	5,162	6,223	5,743	7,740	8,550	8,518	8,796	3,276	200	7,980
ND.	630	694	736	852	863	888	1,047	239	46	563
OH.	8,410	10,467	9,801	10,152	10,212	10,478	10,604	3,986	424	8,406
OK.	2,649	3,014	3,357	2,859	3,596	3,178	3,193	1,030	152	2,557
OR.	2,445	3,022	3,050	3,479	3,972	3,876	3,998	1,355	141	3,105
PA.	7,971	9,260	9,991	10,205	10,330	10,556	10,497	3,739	371	9,124
RI.	672	760	782	843	843	777	782	327	24	760
SC.	2,521	3,095	3,661	4,046	4,447	4,972	5,123	1,922	122	4,092
SD.	704	793	926	986	1,165	1,210	1,224	307	140	680
TN.	4,444	4,820	5,114	5,446	5,678	6,517	6,629	2,312	198	5,061
TX.	12,800	14,070	17,194	21,478	22,091	22,670	22,949	7,674	340	18,739
UT.	1,206	1,628	2,655	2,150	2,356	2,708	2,734	966	142	2,253
VT.	462	515	567	624	579	583	592	173	34	478
VA.	4,938	6,046	6,149	7,046	7,422	7,464	7,571	2,939	191	5,837
WA.	4,257	5,116	4,683	6,489	7,036	7,721	7,609	2,833	226	5,956
WV.	1,225	1,442	1,436	1,555	1,614	1,171	1,604	474	48	1,148
WI.	3,815	4,366	4,968	5,142	5,340	5,445	5,401	1,730	280	4,375
WY.	528	586	663	784	833	842	862	184	29	432

[1] Automobiles, trucks, and buses. Excludes motorocycles, and vehicles owned by military services. [2] Private and commercial, excluding publicly-owned.

Source: U.S. Federal Highway Administration, "Highway Statistics 2022," and earlier reports, <www.fhwa.dot.gov/policyinformation/statistics.cfm>, accessed February 2024.

Table 1131. State Motor Vehicle Registrations: 2000 to 2022

[In thousands (221,475 represents 221,475,000). Information obtained from state authorities; see source. For motorcycles, see Table 1130]

Type	2000	2010	2015	2018	2019	2020	2021	2022
All motor vehicles.	221,475	242,061	255,009	264,936	267,895	267,607	272,474	273,833
Private and commercial.	217,567	237,784	250,967	260,788	263,836	263,535	268,201	269,336
Publicly owned.	3,908	4,277	4,042	4,148	4,059	4,072	4,272	4,498
Automobiles.	133,621	130,892	112,864	111,242	108,548	105,144	102,974	99,947
Private and commercial.	132,247	129,434	111,412	109,814	107,181	103,805	101,601	98,574
Publicly owned.	1,374	1,458	1,453	1,429	1,367	1,339	1,373	1,373
Buses.	746	846	889	992	995	1,006	939	954
Private and commercial.	314	347	466	576	575	569	521	522
Publicly owned.	432	499	423	417	420	438	419	432
Trucks [1].	87,108	110,322	141,256	152,702	158,352	161,457	168,560	172,932
Private and commercial.	85,005	108,003	139,090	150,398	156,080	159,161	166,079	170,239
Publicly owned.	2,103	2,319	2,166	2,303	2,272	2,296	2,481	2,693

[1] Includes panel, delivery, personal, passenger vans, minivans, pickups, and utility vehicles.

Source: U.S. Federal Highway Administration, "Highway Statistics 2022," <www.fhwa.dot.gov/policyinformation/statistics.cfm>, accessed February 2024 and earlier reports.

Table 1132. Domestic Motor Fuel Consumption by Type of Vehicle: 1970 to 2022

[Consumption in billions (92.3 represents 92,300,000,000 gallons). Comprises all fuel types used for propulsion of vehicles under state motor fuels laws. Excludes federal purchases for military use. Minus sign (-) indicates decrease]

Year	Annual fuel consumption (bil. gal.) [1]						Average miles per gallon [1]				
	All vehi-cles [2]	Annual percent change [3]	Light duty vehicle short WB [4]	Buses [5]	Light duty vehicle long WB [4]	Trucks [6,7]	All vehi-cles [2]	Light duty vehicle short WB [4]	Buses [5]	Light duty vehicle long WB [4]	Trucks [6,7]
1970......	92.3	4.8	67.8	0.8	12.3	11.3	12.0	13.5	5.5	10.0	5.5
1980......	115.0	-5.9	70.2	1.0	23.8	20.0	13.3	16.0	6.0	12.2	5.4
1990......	130.8	-0.8	69.8	0.9	35.6	24.5	16.4	20.3	6.4	16.1	6.0
2000......	162.5	0.7	88.9	2.2	28.9	42.0	16.9	22.1	6.7	17.0	6.2
2001......	163.5	0.6	87.8	1.9	30.1	43.0	17.1	22.6	6.8	17.0	6.3
2002......	168.7	3.2	91.5	1.9	30.8	43.3	17.0	22.3	6.9	16.9	6.4
2003......	170.0	0.8	91.6	1.9	31.3	44.8	17.0	22.4	7.1	16.9	6.4
2004......	173.5	2.1	93.4	1.9	33.8	44.4	17.1	22.3	7.1	16.9	6.4
2005......	174.8	0.7	93.2	1.9	34.4	44.5	17.2	22.5	7.1	16.9	6.4
2006......	175.0	0.1	88.6	2.0	37.0	46.4	17.2	23.1	7.1	17.1	6.5
2007......	176.2	0.7	89.6	2.0	36.9	47.2	17.2	22.9	7.2	17.1	6.4
2008......	170.8	-3.1	85.6	2.1	34.9	47.7	17.4	23.7	7.2	17.3	6.5
2009......	168.1	-1.6	85.7	2.0	35.7	44.3	17.6	23.5	7.2	17.3	6.5
2010......	170.4	1.4	86.8	1.9	36.3	45.0	17.4	23.3	7.2	17.2	6.4
2011......	168.5	-1.1	88.4	1.9	35.3	42.4	17.5	23.2	7.1	17.1	6.3
2012......	168.6	0.1	88.6	2.1	35.1	42.4	17.6	23.3	7.2	17.1	6.4
2013......	169.7	0.6	88.6	2.1	35.2	46.8	17.6	23.4	7.2	17.2	6.4
2014......	173.3	2.2	89.3	2.2	37.3	44.0	17.5	23.2	7.2	17.1	6.3
2015......	172.9	-0.2	90.0	2.2	36.4	43.7	17.9	23.9	7.3	17.3	6.4
2016......	176.9	2.3	91.5	2.2	37.8	44.9	17.9	24.0	7.3	17.4	6.4
2017......	178.0	0.6	91.7	2.4	37.5	46.0	18.1	24.2	7.3	17.5	6.5
2018......	178.1	0.1	91.6	2.5	37.2	46.4	18.2	24.4	7.3	17.9	6.6
2019......	180.0	1.0	93.4	2.5	38.0	45.6	18.1	24.1	7.3	17.6	6.6
2020......	159.2	-11.6	76.5	2.0	35.4	44.8	18.2	25.3	7.3	18.0	6.6
2021......	174.1	9.4	85.3	2.3	38.5	47.6	18.0	24.4	7.4	17.8	6.9
2022......	172.4	-1.0	86.0	2.5	37.9	45.4	18.5	24.8	7.4	18.1	7.3

[1] See footnote 1, Table 1128. [2] Motorcycles included with Light Duty Vehicles Short WB through 1994; thereafter in total, not shown separately. [3] Change from immediate prior year. [4] Light Duty Vehicles Short WB—passenger cars, light trucks, vans and sport utility vehicles with a wheelbase (WB) equal to or less than 121 inches. Light Duty Vehicles Long WB—large passenger cars, vans, pickup trucks, and sport/utility vehicles with WB larger than 121 inches. [5] Includes school buses. [6] Includes combination trucks. [7] Beginning 2000: Single-Unit—single frame trucks that have 2-axles and at least 6 tires or a gross vehicle weight rating over 10,000 lbs.

Source: U.S. Federal Highway Administration, "Highway Statistics 2022," and earlier reports, <www.fhwa.dot.gov/policyinformation/statistics.cfm>, accessed February 2024.

Table 1133. Alternative Fuel Vehicles—Models Available and Refueling Stations by Vehicle Fuel Type: 1995 to 2021

[Data gathered as close to September 30 as possible. The Energy Policy Act of 1992 defines alternative fuels and allows the U.S. Department of Energy (DOE) to add to the list of alternative fuels if the fuel is substantially nonpetroleum, yields substantial energy security benefits, and offers substantial environmental benefits]

Fuel type	1995	2000	2005	2010	2015	2019	2020	2021
MODELS AVAILABLE								
Total................................	**13**	**37**	**29**	**36**	**141**	**130**	**130**	**(NA)**
Propane [1]............................	–	2	–	–	10	7	8	(NA)
Compressed natural gas (CNG) [1].............	10	15	5	1	17	7	10	(NA)
Ethanol (E85).........................	–	8	24	34	84	40	25	(NA)
Methanol (M85)........................	2	–	–	–	–	–	–	(NA)
Electric vehicle [2].....................	1	12	–	1	27	72	83	(NA)
Hydrogen.............................	–	–	–	–	3	4	4	(NA)
REFUELING STATIONS								
Total................................	**4,677**	**5,205**	**5,164**	**7,111**	**22,929**	**36,290**	**41,070**	**56,528**
Propane..............................	3,299	3,268	2,995	2,604	3,749	3,176	2,956	2,869
Compressed Natural Gas (CNG)..............	1,065	1,217	787	869	1,607	1,576	1,549	1,532
LNG (Liquid Natural Gas)...................	(NA)	44	40	43	117	118	106	102
Biodiesel [3]...........................	–	2	304	615	713	611	712	722
Ethanol (E85).........................	37	113	436	2,296	3,012	3,786	3,946	4,196
Methanol (M85)........................	88	3	–	–	–	–	–	–
Electric vehicle [4].....................	188	558	588	626	13,696	26,959	31,738	47,040
Hydrogen.............................	(NA)	(NA)	14	58	35	64	63	67

– Represents zero. NA Not available. [1] Dedicated and bi-fuel vehicles. [2] Electric vehicles include plug-in hybrid-electric vehicles but do not include neighborhood electric vehicles, low-speed electric vehicles, or two-wheeled electric vehicles. [3] Stations selling biodiesel blends less than B20 are only included in the 2005-2007 station counts. [4] Electric vehicle station is one geographic location where electric vehicles can charge.

Source: U.S. Department of Energy, Office of Energy Efficiency and Renewable Energy, *Transportation Energy Data Book*, Edition 40, February 2022. See also <tedb.ornl.gov>.

Table 1134. Traffic Fatalities—Number and Rate by State: 2010 to 2022

[For deaths within 30 days of the accident]

State	2010	2020	2021	2022	Fatality rate [1] 2010	Fatality rate [1] 2022	State	2010	2020	2021	2022	Fatality rate [1] 2010	Fatality rate [1] 2022
U.S.	**32,999**	**39,007**	**43,230**	**42,514**	**1.11**	**1.33**	MO	821	987	1,016	1,057	1.16	1.33
AL	862	934	983	988	1.34	1.38	MT	189	213	239	213	1.69	1.58
AK	56	64	70	82	1.17	1.50	NE	190	233	221	244	0.98	1.15
AZ	759	1,053	1,192	1,302	1.27	1.71	NV	257	333	385	416	1.16	1.50
AR	571	651	692	643	1.70	1.67	NH	128	104	118	146	0.98	1.10
CA	2,720	3,980	4,513	4,428	0.84	1.40	NJ	556	586	692	685	0.76	0.91
CO	450	622	691	764	0.96	1.42	NM	349	398	483	466	1.38	1.74
CT	320	299	303	359	1.02	1.21	NY	1,201	1,045	1,156	1,175	0.92	1.02
DE	101	116	136	162	1.13	1.64	NC	1,320	1,538	1,693	1,630	1.29	1.37
DC	24	36	41	32	0.67	0.94	ND	105	100	101	98	1.27	1.07
FL	2,444	3,329	3,741	3,530	1.25	1.55	OH	1,080	1,230	1,354	1,275	0.97	1.15
GA	1,247	1,658	1,809	1,797	1.12	1.39	OK	668	653	762	710	1.40	1.59
HI	113	85	94	116	1.13	1.13	OR	317	507	599	601	0.94	1.64
ID	209	214	273	215	1.32	1.12	PA	1,324	1,129	1,230	1,179	1.32	1.18
IL	927	1,193	1,334	1,268	0.88	1.22	RI	67	67	63	52	0.81	0.69
IN	754	897	932	949	1.00	0.99	SC	809	1,066	1,198	1,094	1.65	1.85
IA	390	343	356	338	1.24	1.03	SD	140	141	148	137	1.58	1.35
KS	431	426	423	410	1.44	1.31	TN	1,032	1,217	1,327	1,314	1.47	1.58
KY	760	780	806	744	1.58	1.55	TX	3,023	3,876	4,500	4,408	1.29	1.52
LA	721	828	971	906	1.59	1.60	UT	253	276	332	319	0.95	0.93
ME	161	164	153	182	1.11	1.24	VT	71	62	74	76	0.98	1.07
MD	496	573	563	564	0.88	0.99	VA	740	850	973	1,008	0.90	1.23
MA	347	343	413	434	0.64	0.76	WA	460	574	674	733	0.80	1.25
MI	942	1,086	1,137	1,124	0.97	1.17	WV	315	267	282	264	1.64	1.72
MN	411	394	488	444	0.73	0.77	WI	572	612	620	596	0.96	0.90
MS	641	748	766	703	1.61	1.76	WY	155	127	110	134	1.66	1.44

[1] Deaths per 100 million vehicle miles traveled.

Source: U.S. National Highway Traffic Safety Administration, "Traffic Safety Facts Annual Report Tables," <cdan.dot.gov/>, and "Fatality Analysis Reporting System," <www.nhtsa.gov/research-data/fatality-analysis-reporting-system-fars>; accessed August 2024.

Table 1135. Motor Vehicle Occupants and Nonoccupants Killed and Injured: 1990 to 2022

[Injuries in thousands (3,206 represents 3,206,000). For deaths within 30 days of the accident. Data on fatalities are derived from the Fatality Analysis Reporting System (FARS) and represent actual counts. Data on injuries are from the National Automotive Sampling System General Estimates System (NASS GES) and the Crash Report Sampling System (CRSS), which both produce estimates based on a nationally representative sample of police crash reports. In 2016, the CRSS replaced the NASS GES; for details, see <crashstats.nhtsa.dot.gov/Api/Public/ViewPublication/812509>]

Year	Total	Occupants by vehicle type Total	Passenger cars	Light trucks [1]	Large trucks [1]	Buses	Other/unknown [2]	Motorcycle occupants [3]	Nonoccupants Total	Pedestrian	Pedalcyclist	Other/unknown [2]
KILLED												
1990	44,599	33,890	24,092	8,601	705	32	460	3,244	7,465	6,482	859	124
2000	41,945	33,451	20,699	11,526	754	22	450	2,897	5,597	4,763	693	141
2005	43,510	33,070	18,512	13,037	804	58	659	4,576	5,864	4,892	786	186
2010	32,999	23,371	12,491	9,782	530	44	524	4,518	5,110	4,302	623	185
2013	32,893	22,483	12,037	9,186	695	54	511	4,692	5,718	4,779	749	190
2014	32,744	22,307	11,947	9,103	656	44	557	4,594	5,843	4,910	729	204
2015	35,484	23,899	12,763	9,878	665	49	544	5,029	6,556	5,494	829	233
2016	37,806	25,276	13,508	10,279	815	64	610	5,337	7,193	6,080	853	260
2017	37,473	25,130	13,477	10,186	878	43	546	5,226	7,117	6,075	806	236
2018	36,835	24,332	12,888	9,957	890	44	553	5,038	7,465	6,374	871	220
2019	36,355	23,891	12,355	10,017	893	35	591	5,044	7,420	6,272	859	289
2020 [5]	39,007	25,617	12,628	11,286	822	19	862	5,620	7,770	6,565	948	257
2021 [5]	43,230	28,339	13,618	12,847	1,011	15	848	6,143	8,748	7,470	976	302
2022 [5, 6]	42,514	27,344	12,691	12,729	1,097	26	801	6,218	8,952	7,522	1,105	325
INJURED (1,000)												
1990	3,206	2,935	2,360	499	40	33	4	84	186	105	75	7
2000	3,194	3,001	2,057	886	31	17	10	58	135	78	51	6
2005	2,709	2,504	1,580	874	28	12	10	88	118	65	45	8
2010	2,248	2,036	1,256	737	20	18	5	82	130	70	52	8
2013	2,319	2,105	1,299	753	25	24	5	89	125	66	48	11
2014	2,343	2,125	1,294	784	27	14	6	92	125	65	50	10
2015	2,455	2,241	1,382	809	30	12	8	89	125	70	45	10
2016 [4]	3,062	2,791	1,690	1,035	36	25	5	104	166	86	64	16
2017 [4]	2,745	2,523	1,529	937	40	12	5	89	133	71	50	12
2018 [4]	2,710	2,492	1,511	921	39	15	5	82	137	75	47	15
2019 [4]	2,740	2,516	1,498	950	46	15	7	84	140	76	49	16
2020 [4, 5]	2,282	2,095	1,023	884	42	8	139	81	106	55	39	13
2021 [4, 5]	2,498	2,296	1,109	984	42	12	149	85	117	61	42	15
2022 [4, 5, 6]	2,383	2,169	970	931	42	11	216	83	131	67	46	17

[1] Light trucks have 10,000 pounds gross vehicle weight rating or less, and include pickups, vans, truck-based station wagons, and utility vehicles. Large trucks have over 10,000 pounds gross vehicle weight rating, and include single unit trucks and truck tractors. [2] Includes combination trucks. [3] Includes mopeds, three wheel motorcycles, off-road motorcycles, etc. [4] Beginning 2016, data are not comparable to previous years due to a new data collection system. [5] Beginning 2020, data are not comparable to previous years, due to a change in vehicle type classifications. [6] Beginning in 2022, people on motorized bicycles are classified as pedalcyclists instead of motorcyclists.

Source: U.S. National Highway Traffic Safety Administration, "Traffic Safety Facts Annual Report Tables," <cdan.dot.gov/>, accessed August 2024. See also <www.nhtsa.gov/research>.

Table 1136. Fatal Motor Vehicle Accidents—National Summary: 2000 to 2022

[Based on data from the Fatality Analysis Reporting System (FARS). FARS gathers data on accidents that result in loss of human life. FARS is operated and maintained by National Highway Traffic Safety Administration's (NHTSA), National Center for Statistics and Analysis (NCSA). FARS data are gathered on motor vehicle accidents that occurred on a roadway customarily open to the public, resulting in the death of a person within 30 days of the accident. Collection of these data depend on the use of police, hospital, medical examiner/coroner, and Emergency Medical Services reports; state vehicle registration, driver licensing, and highway department files; and vital statistics documents and death certificates. See source for further detail. BAC is blood alcohol concentration. VMT is vehicle miles traveled]

Item	2000	2010	2015	2018	2019	2020	2021	2022
Fatal crashes, total	**37,526**	**30,296**	**32,538**	**33,919**	**33,487**	**35,935**	**39,785**	**39,221**
One vehicle involved	21,117	18,221	18,902	19,263	19,041	20,837	22,302	22,178
Two or more vehicles involved	16,409	12,075	13,636	14,656	14,446	15,098	17,483	17,043
Occupants involved	94,325	69,418	74,624	76,479	75,061	78,207	88,337	86,318
Drivers involved	57,280	44,599	49,163	51,905	51,302	54,165	61,379	60,048
Persons killed in fatal crashes [1,2]	**41,945**	**32,999**	**35,484**	**36,835**	**36,355**	**39,007**	**43,230**	**42,514**
Occupants	33,451	23,371	23,899	24,332	23,891	25,617	28,339	27,344
Drivers	22,914	16,864	17,615	18,321	17,984	19,552	21,716	20,908
Passengers	10,451	6,451	6,213	5,962	5,846	6,011	6,580	6,393
Other	86	56	71	49	61	54	43	43
Motorcyclists [3]	2,897	4,518	5,029	5,038	5,044	5,620	6,143	6,218
Nonoccupants	5,597	5,110	6,556	7,465	7,420	7,770	8,748	8,952
Pedestrians	4,763	4,302	5,494	6,374	6,272	6,565	7,470	7,522
Pedalcyclists [3]	693	623	829	871	859	948	976	1,105
Other	141	185	233	220	289	257	302	325
Occupants killed by vehicle type: [2]								
Passenger cars	20,699	12,491	12,763	12,888	12,355	12,628	13,618	12,691
Motorcycles and other motorized cycles [3]	2,897	4,518	5,029	5,038	5,044	5,620	6,143	6,218
Motorcycles	2,783	4,281	4,696	4,589	4,589	4,988	5,395	5,557
Other motorized cycles	114	237	333	449	455	632	748	661
Light trucks [4]	11,526	9,782	9,878	9,957	10,017	11,286	12,847	12,729
Pickup	6,003	4,486	4,471	4,267	4,213	4,321	4,770	4,572
Utility	3,358	3,942	4,213	4,554	4,727	6,015	6,990	7,103
Van	2,129	1,346	1,128	1,081	1,025	938	1,084	1,047
Other	36	8	66	55	52	12	3	7
Large trucks [5]	754	530	665	890	893	822	1,011	1,097
Buses	22	44	49	44	35	19	15	26
Other/unknown vehicles	450	524	544	553	591	862	848	801
Persons killed, and % distribution by highest driver BAC in the crash [6]	41,945	32,999	35,484	36,835	36,355	39,007	43,230	42,514
0.00 percent	62	64	65	66	67	64	63	63
0.01 to 0.07 percent	6	5	5	5	5	5	5	5
0.08 percent and over	32	31	29	29	28	30	31	32
Drivers in fatal crashes by BAC [6]	57,280	44,599	49,163	51,905	51,302	54,165	61,379	60,048
0.00 percent	42,643	33,190	37,529	39,735	39,762	40,920	45,930	44,624
0.01 to 0.07 percent	2,376	1,812	1,964	1,911	1,911	2,122	2,439	2,469
0.08 percent and over	12,261	9,598	9,670	10,259	9,629	11,123	13,011	12,955
Fatalities per 100,000 resident population:								
Under 5 years old	3.70	2.00	1.90	1.78	1.64	1.65	1.92	1.91
5 to 9 years old	3.55	1.74	1.73	1.65	1.61	1.54	1.83	1.56
10 to 15 years old	5.65	2.71	1.99	1.74	2.01	2.23	[8] 2.24	[8] 2.21
16 to 20 years old	29.38	15.44	13.16	12.09	11.30	12.62	[9] 13.82	[9] 13.17
21 to 24 years old	27.02	19.49	18.89	18.39	17.18	19.10	19.73	18.17
25 to 34 years old	17.29	13.47	14.39	14.90	14.34	16.98	18.73	17.81
35 to 44 years old	15.08	11.09	11.64	12.17	12.37	13.72	15.64	15.34
45 to 54 years old	13.79	11.32	12.33	12.48	12.21	12.80	14.34	14.07
55 to 64 years old	13.61	10.94	11.92	12.87	12.69	13.14	14.21	14.18
65 to 74 years old	15.29	10.96	11.42	11.64	11.67	10.96	12.20	12.70
75 years old and over	23.29	16.80	15.36	15.64	15.90	13.52	15.14	15.33
Fatalities per 100 million VMT	1.53	1.11	1.15	1.14	1.11	1.34	1.38	1.33
Fatalities per 100,000 licensed drivers	22.00	15.71	16.27	16.19	15.88	17.09	18.57	18.08
VMT per registered vehicle	12,657	11,532	10,984	10,909	10,899	9,773	10,351	10,530
Fatalities per 100,000 registered vehicles	19.33	12.82	12.61	12.40	12.15	13.13	14.28	14.01
Fatal crashes per 100 million VMT	1.37	1.02	1.05	1.05	1.03	1.24	1.27	1.23
Fatalities per 100,000 resident population	14.87	10.67	11.06	11.27	11.07	11.77	13.02	12.76
Vehicle miles traveled (billion)	2,747	2,967	3,090	3,240	3,262	2,904	3,132	3,196
Licensed drivers (1,000)	190,625	210,115	218,084	227,558	228,916	228,196	232,782	235,086
Registered vehicles (1,000) [7]	217,028	257,312	281,312	297,036	299,267	297,101	302,634	303,529

[1] Deaths within 30 days of the crash. [2] Due to a change in vehicle type classifications in 2020, 2019 and earlier year data are not comparable to 2020 and later year data. [3] Starting in 2022, people on motorized bicycles are classified as pedalcyclists instead of motorcyclists. [4] Trucks with a gross vehicle weight rating of 10,000 pounds or less, including pickups, vans, truck-based station wagons, and utility vehicles. [5] Trucks with a gross vehicle weight rating of over 10,000 pounds. [6] NHTSA estimates alcohol involvement when test results are unknown. Includes crashes in which there was no driver present. [7] Data on motor vehicle registrations for 2011 and beyond are not strictly comparable to data for prior years due to methodology changes. See source for details. [8] Data are for age group 10 to 14. [9] Data are for age group 15 to 20.

Source: National Highway Traffic Safety Administration, *Traffic Safety Facts, 2017*, and earlier reports; and "Traffic Safety Facts Annual Report Tables," <cdan.dot.gov/> and "Fatality Analysis Reporting System," <www-fars.nhtsa.dot.gov/Main/index.aspx>, accessed August 2024. See also <www.nhtsa.gov/research>.

Table 1137. Vehicles Involved in Crashes by Vehicle Type, Rollover Occurrence, and Crash Severity: 2022

[Excludes motorcycles. Beginning 2016, data for injury and property damage only crashes are not comparable to previous years due to a new data collection system. The National Automotive Sampling System (NASS) General Estimates System (GES) was replaced with the Crash Report Sampling System (CRSS). For details, see <crashstats.nhtsa.dot.gov/Api/Public/ViewPublication/812509>]

Crash severity by vehicle type	Total	Rollover occurrence			
		Yes		No	
	Number	Number	Percent	Number	Percent
Vehicles involved in all crashes [1]	**10,426,128**	**213,840**	**2.1**	**10,212,288**	**97.9**
Passenger cars	4,015,818	61,817	1.5	3,954,001	98.5
Light trucks: [2]					
Pickup	1,298,847	39,637	3.1	1,259,209	96.9
Utility	2,838,001	70,515	2.5	2,767,486	97.5
Van	411,191	7,597	1.8	403,594	98.2
Other	817	3	0.4	814	99.6
Large truck [3]	536,424	21,031	3.9	515,393	96.1
Bus	53,230	5	(Z)	53,225	100.0
Other/unknown	1,271,799	13,234	1.0	1,258,565	99.0
Fatal crashes	**54,142**	**8,625**	**15.9**	**45,517**	**84.1**
Passenger cars	20,049	2,567	12.8	17,482	87.2
Light trucks: [2]					
Pickup	9,627	2,006	20.8	7,621	79.2
Utility	14,117	2,671	18.9	11,446	81.1
Van	2,048	242	11.8	1,806	88.2
Other	15	3	20.0	12	80.0
Large truck [3]	5,837	749	12.8	5,088	87.2
Bus	213	5	2.3	208	97.7
Other/unknown	2,236	382	17.1	1,854	82.9
Injury crashes	**2,973,214**	**126,726**	**4.3**	**2,846,488**	**95.7**
Passenger cars	1,207,127	37,242	3.1	1,169,885	96.9
Light trucks: [2]					
Pickup	351,737	21,925	6.2	329,812	93.8
Utility	820,386	44,577	5.4	775,809	94.6
Van	117,452	4,065	3.5	113,387	96.5
Other	191	–	–	191	100.0
Large truck [3]	120,190	11,116	9.2	109,074	90.8
Bus	10,398	–	–	10,398	100.0
Other/unknown	345,733	7,802	2.3	337,932	97.7

– Represents zero. Z less than 500 or 0.05 percent. [1] Includes property-only crashes, not shown separately. [2] Light trucks of 10,000 pounds gross vehicle weight rating or less, including pickups, vans, truck-based station wagons and sport utility vehicles. [3] Large trucks over 10,000 pounds gross vehicle weight rating.

Source: U.S. National Highway Traffic Safety Administration, "Traffic Safety Facts Annual Report Tables," <cdan.dot.gov>, accessed August 2024. See also <www.nhtsa.gov/research>.

Table 1138. Distracted Drivers—Crashes, Road Fatalities, and Injuries: 2010 to 2022

["Distraction" is defined as a specific type of inattention that occurs when drivers divert their attention from the driving task to focus on some other activity instead. "Distraction" is a subset of "inattention" (which also includes fatigue and physical and emotional conditions of the driver). For more information, including revision in coding of "distracted driving," see appendix in source report]

Description	2010	2015	2018	2019	2020	2021	2022
FATAL CRASHES [1]							
Total	30,296	32,538	33,919	33,487	35,935	39,785	39,221
Drivers involved	44,599	49,163	51,905	51,302	54,165	61,379	60,048
Fatalities	32,999	35,484	36,835	36,355	39,007	43,230	42,514
Crashes involving driver distraction [2]	**2,993**	**3,242**	**2,645**	**2,872**	**2,889**	**3,214**	**3,047**
Percent	10	10	8	9	8	8	8
Involving cell phone use	366	453	356	395	355	390	368
Percent	12	14	13	14	12	12	12
Drivers involved	3,064	3,313	2,704	2,979	2,977	3,348	3,124
Percent	7	7	5	6	5	5	5
Fatalities	3,267	3,526	2,858	3,119	3,154	3,521	3,308
Percent	10	10	8	9	8	8	8
INJURY CRASHES [3] (ESTIMATED)							
Total	1,542,000	1,715,000	1,893,704	1,916,344	1,593,390	1,727,608	1,664,598
People injured	2,248,000	2,455,000	2,710,059	2,740,141	2,282,209	2,497,869	2,382,771
In crashes involving driver distraction	416,000	393,000	400,303	423,847	324,663	362,405	289,310
Percent of total	19	16	15	15	14	15	12
In crashes involving cell phone use	24,000	30,000	32,632	28,300	30,000	29,000	26,151
Percent of total distracted	6	8	8	7	9	8	9

[1] Data from NHTSA's Fatality Analysis Reporting System (FARS). [2] For multiple-vehicle crashes, the crash was reported as a distracted-driving crash if at least one driver was reported as distracted. In some of these multiple-vehicle crashes, multiple drivers were reported as distracted. [3] Data for 2010 to 2015 are from the National Automotive Sampling System (NASS) General Estimates System (GES). Beginning 2016, data are from the Crash Report Sampling System (CRSS). CRSS estimates and NASS GES estimates are not comparable due to different sample designs. See <www.nhtsa.gov/crash-data-systems/crash-report-sampling-system> for details.

Source: U.S. National Highway Traffic Safety Administration, *Distracted Driving, 2022*, April 2024, and earlier reports. See also <www-fars.nhtsa.dot.gov/> and <nhtsa.gov/risky-driving/distracted-driving>.

Table 1139. Traffic Fatalities by State and Highest Driver Blood Alcohol Concentration (BAC) in the Crash: 2022

[A crash is a police-reported event that produces injury and/or property damage, involves a vehicle in transport, and occurs on a trafficway or while the vehicle is in motion after running off the trafficway. A positive blood alcohol concentration (BAC level of .01 grams per deciliter and higher) indicates that alcohol was consumed by the person tested, and the incident is alcohol related or alcohol involved; a BAC level of .08 g/dL or more indicates that the person was alcohol impaired]

State	Traffic fatalities, total [1]	Traffic fatalities not involving alcohol (BAC=.00)		Alcohol involved driving fatalities (BAC=.01–.07)		Alcohol impaired driving fatalities (BAC=.08 or more)		Total fatalities involving alcohol (BAC=.01 or more)	
		Number	Percent	Number	Percent	Number	Percent	Number	Percent
United States [2]....	42,514	26,580	63	2,337	5	13,524	32	15,861	37
Alabama..............	988	661	67	46	5	281	28	326	33
Alaska................	82	61	75	1	2	20	24	21	25
Arizona..............	1,302	780	60	67	5	450	35	518	40
Arkansas.............	643	443	69	48	7	153	24	200	31
California............	4,428	2,717	61	224	5	1,479	33	1,703	38
Colorado.............	764	447	59	54	7	260	34	314	41
Connecticut...........	359	208	58	24	7	127	35	151	42
Delaware.............	162	104	64	9	6	49	30	58	36
District of Columbia...	32	18	56	2	5	12	39	14	44
Florida................	3,530	2,430	69	154	4	940	27	1,094	31
Georgia..............	1,797	1,197	67	92	5	507	28	599	33
Hawaii................	116	69	60	10	9	37	31	47	40
Idaho................	215	136	63	10	5	69	32	79	37
Illinois................	1,268	716	56	80	6	471	37	551	43
Indiana..............	949	624	66	51	5	274	29	325	34
Iowa.................	338	195	58	22	6	116	34	138	41
Kansas...............	410	274	67	26	6	109	27	135	33
Kentucky.............	744	539	73	28	4	176	24	204	27
Louisiana.............	906	582	64	57	6	267	29	324	36
Maine................	182	103	56	17	9	62	34	79	43
Maryland.............	564	337	60	20	3	207	37	227	40
Massachusetts........	434	289	67	22	5	123	28	144	33
Michigan.............	1,124	763	68	56	5	305	27	361	32
Minnesota............	444	291	66	23	5	130	29	153	34
Mississippi............	703	512	73	23	3	168	24	191	27
Missouri..............	1,057	689	65	77	7	290	27	367	35
Montana..............	213	129	61	11	5	71	34	83	39
Nebraska.............	244	155	64	21	9	67	28	89	36
Nevada...............	416	246	59	30	7	140	34	170	41
New Hampshire.......	146	88	61	6	4	52	36	58	39
New Jersey...........	685	470	69	34	5	177	26	211	31
New Mexico...........	466	287	62	27	6	152	33	179	38
New York.............	1,175	731	62	74	6	371	32	444	38
North Carolina........	1,630	1,100	68	68	4	460	28	528	32
North Dakota..........	98	57	58	8	8	34	34	42	42
Ohio.................	1,275	709	56	88	7	471	37	559	44
Oklahoma.............	710	492	69	31	4	186	26	216	30
Oregon...............	601	330	55	39	6	232	39	271	45
Pennsylvania..........	1,179	785	67	53	4	338	29	390	33
Rhode Island..........	52	24	46	6	12	22	43	28	54
South Carolina........	1,094	558	51	61	6	474	43	535	49
South Dakota.........	137	83	61	10	7	44	32	54	39
Tennessee............	1,314	878	67	70	5	364	28	435	33
Texas................	4,408	2,249	51	283	6	1,869	42	2,152	49
Utah.................	319	231	72	17	5	71	22	88	28
Vermont..............	76	42	55	9	11	26	34	34	45
Virginia...............	1,008	660	65	49	5	298	30	346	34
Washington...........	733	422	58	50	7	256	35	306	42
West Virginia..........	264	184	70	20	7	60	23	80	30
Wisconsin.............	596	398	67	26	4	171	29	197	33
Wyoming.............	134	85	64	9	7	40	30	49	36
Puerto Rico...........	271	161	59	17	6	91	34	108	40

[1] Total fatalities include those in which there was no driver or motorcycle rider present. [2] U.S. total excludes Puerto Rico.

Source: U.S. National Highway Traffic Safety Administration, "Traffic Safety Facts Annual Report Tables," <cdan.dot.gov/>, accessed August 2024. See also <www.nhtsa.gov/research>.

Table 1140. Alcohol Involvement for Drivers in Fatal Crashes: 2000 to 2022

[BAC = blood alcohol concentration. See headnote, Table 1139. NHTSA estimates alcohol involvement when alcohol test results are unknown; see source for more information]

Age, sex, and vehicle type	2000 Total drivers in fatal crashes	2000 Percent with .08% BAC or greater	2010 Total drivers in fatal crashes	2010 Percent with .08% BAC or greater	2020 Total drivers in fatal crashes	2020 Percent with .08% BAC or greater	2021 Total drivers in fatal crashes	2021 Percent with .08% BAC or greater	2022 Total drivers in fatal crashes	2022 Percent with .08% BAC or greater
Total drivers involved in fatal crashes [1]	**57,280**	**21**	**44,599**	**22**	**54,165**	**21**	**61,379**	**21**	**60,048**	**22**
Drivers by age group:										
Under 15 years old	120	12	61	4	88	11	96	9	87	11
15 to 20 years old	8,224	18	4,603	17	4,588	17	5,137	17	4,856	19
21 to 24 years old	5,950	32	4,608	34	4,911	26	5,568	27	5,279	29
25 to 34 years old	11,739	28	8,567	30	12,011	26	13,309	27	12,611	28
35 to 44 years old	11,132	26	7,333	25	8,956	22	10,370	24	10,344	24
45 to 54 years old	8,234	18	7,517	21	7,778	19	8,828	20	8,619	20
55 to 64 years old	4,766	12	5,577	14	7,316	16	8,146	16	7,899	17
65 to 74 years old	3,134	8	2,902	8	4,129	12	4,785	12	5,053	12
75 years old and over	3,147	4	2,688	4	2,824	7	3,280	7	3,445	8
Drivers by sex:										
Male	41,795	24	32,079	24	39,594	21	44,359	22	43,582	23
Female	14,790	13	11,859	15	13,111	16	15,260	17	14,719	17
Drivers by vehicle type: [2]										
Passenger cars	27,661	24	17,710	24	19,063	24	21,172	24	19,889	25
Light trucks [3]	20,393	22	17,385	22	22,266	19	25,689	20	25,613	21
Large trucks [4]	4,948	1	3,456	1	4,755	3	5,668	3	5,760	3
Motorcycles [5]	2,971	32	4,647	28	5,754	26	6,297	28	6,349	28

[1] Includes age and sex unknown, and other and unknown types of vehicles. [2] Beginning in 2020, due to a change in vehicle type classifications, data are not comparable to prior years. [3] Trucks of 10,000 pounds gross vehicle weight rating or less, including pickups, vans, truck-based station wagons. and utility vehicles. [4] Trucks over 10,000 pounds gross vehicle weight rating. [5] Starting in 2022, motorcycles exclude motorized bicycles. Prior to 2022, motorized bicycles were considered motor vehicles and were classified as motorcycles.

Source: U.S. National Highway Traffic Safety Administration, "Traffic Safety Facts Annual Report Tables," <cdan.dot.gov/>, accessed August 2024. See also <www.nhtsa.gov/research>.

Table 1141. Fatalities by Highest Driver Blood Alcohol Concentration (BAC) in the Crash: 1990 to 2022

[A motor vehicle crash is alcohol impaired if at least one driver involved in the crash is determined to have a BAC of .08 gram per deciliter (g/dl) or higher. Thus, any fatality that occurs in an alcohol impaired crash is considered an alcohol impaired driving fatality. A person is considered to be legally impaired with a BAC of .08 g/dl or more. See source for more information]

Item	1990	2000	2005	2010	2015	2019	2020	2021	2022
Total fatalities [1]	**44,599**	**41,945**	**43,510**	**32,999**	**35,484**	**36,355**	**39,007**	**43,230**	**42,514**
BAC=.00									
Number	23,823	26,082	27,423	21,005	23,165	24,251	25,121	27,229	26,580
Percent	53.4	62.2	63.0	63.7	65.3	66.7	64.4	63.0	62.5
BAC=.01–.07									
Number	2,901	2,422	2,404	1,771	1,930	1,834	2,073	2,324	2,337
Percent	6.5	5.8	5.5	5.4	5.4	5.0	5.3	5.4	5.5
Alcohol impaired driving fatalities: BAC=.08 or more									
Number	17,705	13,324	13,582	10,136	10,280	10,196	11,727	13,617	13,524
Percent	39.7	31.8	31.2	30.7	29.0	28.0	30.1	31.5	31.8

[1] Total fatalities include those in which there was no driver or motorcycle rider present.

Source: U.S. National Highway Traffic Safety Administration, "Traffic Safety Facts Annual Report Tables," <cdan.dot.gov/>, accessed August 2024. See also <www.nhtsa.gov/research>.

Table 1142. Motor Vehicle Crashes by Crash Severity: 2000 to 2022

[6,394 represents 6,394,000. A crash is a police-reported event that produces injury and/or property damage, involves a vehicle in transport, and occurs on a trafficway or while the vehicle is in motion after running off the trafficway. A fatal crash involves at least 1 person dying within 30 days of the crash. Data involving fatalities are derived from the Fatality Analysis Reporting System (FARS) and represent actual counts. Data involving injuries and property damage are from the National Automotive Sampling System General Estimates System (NASS GES) and the Crash Report Sampling System (CRSS), which both produce estimates based on a nationally representative sample of police crash reports. In 2016, the CRSS replaced the NASS GES; for details, see <crashstats.nhtsa.dot.gov/Api/ Public/ViewPublication/812509>]

Item	2000	2010	2015	2017 [1]	2018 [1]	2019 [1]	2020 [1]	2021 [1]	2022 [1]
Crashes (1,000)	**6,394**	**5,419**	**6,296**	**6,453**	**6,735**	**6,756**	**5,251**	**6,103**	**5,930**
Fatal	37.5	30.3	32.5	34.6	33.9	33.5	35.9	39.8	39.2
Nonfatal injury	2,070	1,542	1,715	1,889	1,894	1,916	1,593	1,728	1,665
Property damage only	4,286	3,847	4,548	4,530	4,807	4,806	3,622	4,336	4,227
Percent of total crashes:									
Fatal	0.6	0.6	0.5	0.5	0.5	0.5	0.7	0.7	0.7
Nonfatal injury	32.4	28.5	27.2	29.3	28.1	28.4	30.3	28.3	28.1
Property damage only	67.0	71.0	72.2	70.2	71.4	71.1	69.0	71.0	71.3

[1] Beginning 2016, injury and property damage only data are not comparable to previous years due to a new data collection system.

Source: U.S. National Highway Traffic Safety Administration, "Traffic Safety Facts Annual Report Tables," <cdan.dot.gov/>, accessed August 2024. See also <www.nhtsa.gov/research>.

Table 1143. Motor Vehicle Crashes—Number and Deaths: 2000 to 2022

[6,394 represents 6,394,000 Data on fatal crashes and fatalities are derived from the Fatality Analysis Reporting System (FARS) and represent actual counts. Data involving injuries and property damage are from the National Automotive Sampling System General Estimates System (NASS GES) and the Crash Report Sampling System (CRSS), which both produce estimates based on a nationally representative sample of police crash reports. In 2016, the CRSS replaced the NASS GES; for details, see <crashstats.nhtsa.dot.gov/Api/Public/ViewPublication/812509>]

Item	Unit	2000	2010	2015	2018	2019	2020	2021	2022
CRASHES									
Total [1,2]	1,000	6,394	5,419	6,296	6,735	6,756	5,251	6,103	5,930
Fatal	1,000	38	30	33	34	33	36	40	39
Injury [2]	1,000	2,070	1,542	1,715	1,894	1,916	1,593	1,728	1,665
Property damage only [2]	1,000	4,286	3,847	4,548	4,807	4,806	3,622	4,336	4,227
DEATHS									
Deaths within 30 days of crash	Number	41,945	32,999	35,484	36,835	36,355	39,007	43,230	42,514
Occupants [3]	Number	33,451	23,371	23,899	24,332	23,891	25,617	28,339	27,344
Passenger cars	Number	20,699	12,491	12,763	12,888	12,355	12,628	13,618	12,691
Light trucks [4]	Number	11,526	9,782	9,878	9,957	10,017	11,286	12,847	12,729
Large trucks [4]	Number	754	530	665	890	893	822	1,011	1,097
Buses	Number	22	44	49	44	35	19	15	26
Other/unknown	Number	450	524	544	553	591	862	848	801
Motorcycle riders [5]	Number	2,897	4,518	5,029	5,038	5,044	5,620	6,143	6,218
Nonoccupants	Number	5,597	5,110	6,556	7,465	7,420	7,770	8,748	8,952
Pedestrians	Number	4,763	4,302	5,494	6,374	6,272	6,565	7,470	7,522
Pedalcyclist	Number	693	623	829	871	859	948	976	1,105
Other/unknown	Number	141	185	233	220	289	257	302	325
TRAFFIC DEATH RATES [6]									
Per 100 million vehicle miles	Rate	1.5	1.1	1.2	1.1	1.1	1.3	1.4	1.3
Per 100,000 licensed drivers	Rate	22.0	15.7	16.3	16.2	15.9	17.1	18.6	18.1
Per 100,000 registered vehicles	Rate	19.3	12.8	12.6	12.4	12.2	13.1	14.3	14.0
Per 100,000 resident population	Rate	14.9	10.7	11.1	11.3	11.1	11.8	13.0	12.8

[1] Covers police-reported accidents in which at least one person dies within 30 days of the crash; or no one dies but at least one person is injured; or no one is injured but property damage has occurred. [2] Beginning 2016, injury and property damage only data are not comparable to previous years due to a new data collection system. [3] Beginning 2020, data not comparable to previous years due to a change in vehicle type classifications. [4] Light trucks of 10,000 pounds gross vehicle weight rating or less, including pickups, vans, truck-based station wagons and utility vehicles. Large trucks over 10,000 pounds gross vehicle weight rating. [5] Includes motor scooters, minibikes, and mopeds. Beginning 2022, excludes people on motorized bicycles. [6] Based on 30-day definition of traffic deaths.

Source: U.S. National Highway Traffic Safety Administration, "Traffic Safety Facts Annual Report Tables," <cdan.dot.gov/>, accessed August 2024. See also <www.nhtsa.gov/research>.

Table 1144. Licensed Drivers and Number in Fatal Accidents by Age and Sex: 2022

[235,086 represents 235,086,000]

Age group	Licensed drivers (1,000)			Drivers in fatal accidents			Accident rates per 100,000 drivers [1]	
	Total	Male	Female	Total [2]	Male	Female	Male	Female
Total	235,086	116,122	118,964	60,033	43,582	14,719	37.5	12.4
19 years old and under	8,576	4,391	4,186	3,702	2,691	1,006	61.3	24.0
Under 16 years old	118	59	59	211	158	52	266.3	88.7
16 years old	1,077	538	539	474	324	149	60.2	27.7
17 years old	1,844	932	912	764	540	223	57.9	24.5
18 years old	2,587	1,334	1,253	1,038	763	275	57.2	21.9
19 years old	2,951	1,528	1,423	1,215	906	307	59.3	21.6
20 to 24 years old	17,492	8,958	8,533	6,520	4,826	1,688	53.9	19.8
20 years old	3,203	1,646	1,557	1,241	920	321	55.9	20.6
21 years old	3,426	1,760	1,666	1,287	966	319	54.9	19.2
22 years old	3,521	1,804	1,717	1,382	1,019	359	56.5	20.9
23 years old	3,607	1,845	1,762	1,312	970	342	52.6	19.4
24 years old	3,736	1,904	1,832	1,298	951	347	49.9	18.9
25 to 29 years old	19,694	9,946	9,748	6,339	4,715	1,613	47.4	16.5
30 to 34 years old	21,123	10,550	10,573	6,271	4,654	1,609	44.1	15.2
35 to 39 years old	20,465	10,191	10,275	5,443	4,085	1,351	40.1	13.1
40 to 44 years old	19,636	9,738	9,898	4,901	3,749	1,147	38.5	11.6
45 to 49 years old	18,103	8,972	9,131	4,327	3,303	1,023	36.8	11.2
50 to 54 years old	19,257	9,540	9,717	4,291	3,271	1,019	34.3	10.5
55 to 59 years old	19,498	9,612	9,886	4,164	3,149	1,012	32.8	10.2
60 to 64 years old	19,718	9,635	10,083	3,735	2,880	854	29.9	8.5
65 to 69 years old	17,495	8,449	9,046	2,846	2,147	696	25.4	7.7
70 to 74 years old	14,064	6,729	7,334	2,206	1,598	605	23.7	8.2
75 to 79 years old	9,894	4,712	5,183	1,608	1,126	480	23.9	9.3
80 to 84 years old	5,755	2,702	3,052	1,000	668	329	24.7	10.8
85 and over	4,316	1,997	2,319	837	582	254	29.1	11.0

[1] Per 100,000 male or female licensed drivers. Rates for drivers 19 years old and under are likely overstated because of a higher proportion of unlicensed drivers. [2] Total includes unknown/unreported instances.

Source: U.S. Federal Highway Administration, "Highway Statistics 2022," <www.fhwa.dot.gov/policyinformation/statistics.cfm>; and National Highway Traffic Safety Administration, "Fatality and Injury Reporting System Tool," <cdan.dot.gov/query>; accessed August 2024.

Table 1145. Speeding-Related Traffic Fatalities by Road Type and State: 2022

[Speeding consists of exceeding the posted speed limit or driving too fast for the road conditions or any speed-related violation charged (racing, driving above speed limit, speed greater than reasonable, exceeding special speed limit)]

State	Traffic fatalities, total	Speeding-related fatalities by roadway function class							
		Total [2]	Interstate		Non-interstate				
			Rural	Urban	Freeway and expressway	Other principal arterial	Minor arterial	Collector	Local
United States [1]	**42,514**	**12,151**	**530**	**1,042**	**632**	**3,114**	**2,613**	**2,601**	**1,545**
Alabama	988	240	14	11	–	35	61	83	35
Alaska	82	31	5	5	–	10	1	9	1
Arizona	1,302	431	41	40	28	93	140	62	19
Arkansas	643	143	8	15	1	29	33	37	20
California	4,428	1,403	44	182	160	389	316	197	112
Colorado	764	291	17	21	20	98	59	47	29
Connecticut	359	115	–	18	10	24	36	14	13
Delaware	162	55	–	7	2	16	6	16	8
District of Columbia	32	13	–	2	–	2	8	1	–
Florida	3,530	385	9	18	10	133	90	73	51
Georgia	1,797	422	3	29	15	90	103	98	84
Hawaii	116	48	–	2	–	33	13	–	–
Idaho	215	47	7	5	–	7	7	12	9
Illinois	1,268	414	11	65	5	103	104	76	49
Indiana	949	290	19	27	1	94	41	64	44
Iowa	338	74	3	7	–	24	12	16	12
Kansas	410	95	3	10	7	6	27	26	15
Kentucky	744	131	6	10	2	21	20	29	43
Louisiana	906	210	9	18	2	43	62	36	38
Maine	182	53	3	2	–	8	7	25	8
Maryland	564	176	2	18	23	62	26	34	8
Massachusetts	434	116	–	20	10	27	26	16	15
Michigan	1,124	302	7	23	14	80	66	71	41
Minnesota	444	131	2	7	7	21	48	26	20
Mississippi	703	139	9	7	–	41	23	31	13
Missouri	1,057	375	14	33	23	81	82	91	28
Montana	213	69	6	2	–	27	12	12	8
Nebraska	244	48	1	2	2	13	14	13	3
Nevada	416	105	7	8	3	27	30	19	11
New Hampshire	146	53	1	5	2	8	12	13	12
New Jersey	685	173	4	5	10	71	40	27	15
New Mexico	466	185	33	7	–	41	36	40	28
New York	1,175	402	–	41	59	87	56	80	79
North Carolina	1,630	660	29	23	32	104	132	170	169
North Dakota	98	27	3	1	1	13	–	7	2
Ohio	1,275	271	15	20	9	52	63	67	44
Oklahoma	710	159	8	12	1	37	31	44	26
Oregon	601	215	6	6	2	81	50	58	12
Pennsylvania	1,179	457	23	33	20	115	90	80	95
Rhode Island	52	25	1	6	4	6	2	4	2
South Carolina	1,094	401	28	17	1	108	48	135	64
South Dakota	137	47	6	–	1	17	8	10	5
Tennessee	1,314	219	3	12	1	61	52	53	37
Texas	4,408	1,521	60	156	108	401	297	379	116
Utah	319	112	9	11	–	35	20	26	11
Vermont	76	20	–	1	–	1	5	7	6
Virginia	1,008	299	18	31	5	120	58	32	33
Washington	733	250	9	23	26	55	63	57	16
West Virginia	264	72	9	1	–	11	15	25	11
Wisconsin	596	171	4	13	5	41	50	41	17
Wyoming	134	60	11	4	–	12	12	12	8
Puerto Rico	271	88	10	14	–	28	21	12	3

– Represents zero. [1] U.S. totals do not include Puerto Rico. [2] Includes fatalities that occurred on roads for which the type was unknown.

Source: U.S. National Highway Traffic Safety Administration, "Traffic Safety Facts Annual Report Tables," <cdan.dot.gov/>, accessed August 2024. See also <www.nhtsa.gov/research>.

Table 1146. Roadway Traffic Congestion by Urbanized Area: 2022

[16,320 represents 16,320,000. Various federal, state, and local information sources were used to develop the database with the primary source being the Federal Highway Administration's Highway Performance Monitoring System]

Urbanized area	Daily vehicle miles of travel (1,000)		Annual person hours of delay		Annual congestion cost [1]		
	Freeway	Arterial streets	Total hours (1,000)	Per auto commuter [2]	Delay and fuel cost (million dollars)	Per person (dollars) [2]	Fuel wasted (gal. per person) [2]
101 urban areas, average [3]	**16,320**	**14,764**	**70,914**	**67**	**1,875**	**1,561**	**26**
Albuquerque, NM	5,806	7,553	19,417	44	508	1,065	18
Atlanta, GA	55,164	53,117	232,272	82	5,982	1,953	23
Austin, TX	17,988	14,768	67,840	62	1,792	1,533	24
Baltimore, MD	29,288	18,021	83,763	54	2,179	1,145	19
Baton Rouge, LA	5,561	8,732	26,723	65	755	1,458	30
Birmingham, AL	12,388	9,202	29,520	54	780	1,291	22
Boston, MA-NH-RI	41,604	40,962	165,890	73	4,303	1,664	30
Bridgeport-Stamford, CT-NY	10,528	5,553	42,523	66	1,147	1,346	25
Buffalo, NY	5,696	8,379	23,837	44	614	1,012	20
Cape Coral, FL	2,469	8,403	15,674	33	405	742	12
Charleston-North, Charleston, SC	4,398	7,891	25,978	63	665	1,324	24
Charlotte, NC-SC	16,092	14,250	44,957	48	1,162	1,226	20
Chicago, IL-IN	53,610	71,477	306,001	72	8,264	1,675	29
Cincinnati, OH-KY-IN	18,400	13,506	52,750	49	1,419	1,257	23
Cleveland, OH	18,118	13,384	51,997	48	1,340	1,125	18
Colorado Springs, CO	5,766	5,568	21,162	53	548	1,101	21
Columbus OH	16,193	12,905	47,611	53	1,270	1,316	23
Dallas-Fort, Worth-Arlington, TX	78,644	48,570	217,105	68	5,785	1,523	28
Denver-Aurora, CO	27,524	22,997	110,908	66	2,881	1,454	25
Detroit, MI	30,050	45,029	151,205	61	3,932	1,277	23
El Paso, TX-NM	6,819	6,527	20,767	38	564	903	17
Fresno, CA	4,720	4,063	19,022	40	518	917	19
Grand Rapids, MI	5,743	7,756	16,521	41	436	822	16
Hartford, CT	10,975	7,059	28,475	55	769	1,150	24
Honolulu, HI	5,997	3,048	37,456	67	1,051	1,741	30
Houston, TX	62,393	46,379	233,366	69	6,204	1,645	30
Indianapolis, IN	15,321	15,893	45,367	51	1,275	1,067	24
Jacksonville, FL	13,897	9,438	41,318	54	1,067	1,217	18
Kansas City, MO-KS	24,016	13,881	52,696	54	1,434	1,156	17
Knoxville, TN	6,752	8,862	17,016	43	442	926	16
Las Vegas -Henderson, NV	12,874	16,667	60,080	50	1,643	1,103	21
Little Rock, AR	9,564	5,505	21,802	51	607	1,014	15
Los Angeles-Long Beach-Anaheim, CA	129,226	92,228	905,556	122	24,103	3,214	35
Louisville-Jefferson Co., KY-IN	12,299	8,654	33,204	54	905	1,017	22
McAllen, TX	3,822	6,940	21,501	40	572	886	15
Memphis, TN-MS-AR	10,649	16,939	33,115	58	906	926	22
Miami, FL	47,390	51,513	315,984	79	8,127	1,852	37
Milwaukee, WI	12,114	15,787	42,607	54	1,133	1,163	24
Minneapolis-St Paul, MN-WI	30,197	23,505	103,024	59	2,701	1,208	23
Nashville-Davidson, TN	21,047	14,323	61,536	72	1,613	1,685	30
New Haven, CT	7,461	3,745	16,566	50	449	1,021	21
New Orleans, LA	5,628	9,706	49,631	53	1,504	1,422	30
New York-Newark, NY-NJ-CT	113,812	95,867	781,553	92	20,387	2,239	36
Oklahoma City, OK	11,186	9,464	43,749	52	1,159	1,026	21
Omaha, NE-IA	6,738	6,913	23,559	48	600	977	18
Orlando, FL	17,007	18,308	68,736	62	1,793	1,392	25
Philadelphia, PA-NJ-DE-MD	40,413	47,041	176,742	68	4,653	1,528	28
Phoenix-Mesa, AZ	36,157	45,610	178,541	69	4,766	1,441	28
Pittsburgh, PA	12,267	16,109	43,830	47	1,163	1,082	21
Portland, OR-WA	14,389	14,742	76,232	70	2,082	1,616	30
Providence, RI-MA	8,501	9,738	34,831	45	895	883	17
Raleigh, NC	10,630	12,710	22,473	37	575	818	15
Richmond, VA	12,814	10,704	22,642	35	582	746	18
Riverside-San Bernardino, CA	28,601	12,958	107,279	70	2,908	1,559	22
Rochester, NY	4,927	6,010	15,026	39	384	841	17
Sacramento, CA	16,759	13,581	73,841	61	1,972	1,403	28
Salt Lake City-West Valley City, UT	9,937	10,021	31,614	52	896	1,169	25
San Antonio, TX	26,939	17,392	64,395	48	1,721	1,078	23
San Diego, CA	38,082	18,700	142,070	66	3,718	1,927	35
San Francisco-Oakland, CA	34,806	17,157	248,889	109	6,492	3,148	37
San Jose, CA	15,849	11,766	100,700	77	2,637	1,790	31
San Juan, Puerto Rico	9,784	8,993	72,679	56	1,894	1,419	27
Sarasota-Bradenton, FL	3,609	7,458	14,976	31	389	651	14
Seattle, WA	28,920	24,354	168,916	82	4,475	1,874	31
St Louis, MO-IL	31,603	18,018	71,765	49	1,983	1,152	21
Tampa-St Petersburg, FL	17,683	31,140	101,021	57	2,624	1,285	22
Tucson, AZ	4,411	9,747	23,388	39	634	741	14
Tulsa, OK	7,031	7,679	20,658	41	547	756	15
Virginia Beach, VA	12,736	12,599	36,300	42	918	798	14
Washington, DC-VA-MD	41,029	39,955	188,563	85	4,854	1,903	31

[1] Value of extra time (delay) and the extra fuel consumed by vehicles traveling at slower speeds. Fuel cost per gallon is the average price for each state. [2] Per auto commuter data are based on estimated commuters in the urban area. [3] Includes additional areas not shown below.

Source: Texas A&M Transportation Institute, College Station, Texas, *Urban Mobility Report 2023*, June 2024 ©. See also <mobility.tamu.edu>.

Table 1147. Commuting to Work by Transportation Method and State: 2022

[In percent, except as indicated. Workers in thousands (160,578 represents 160,578,000). For workers 16 years old and over. The American Community Survey universe includes the household population and the population living in institutions, college dormitories, and other group quarters. Based on a sample and subject to sampling variability; see Appendix III]

State	Total workers (1,000)	Percent of workers who commuted to work by—						Percent who worked at home	Mean travel time to work (minutes)
		Car, truck, or van		Public transportation [1]	Bicycle	Walking	Taxi, motorcycle, or other means		
		Drove alone	Car-pooled						
U.S.	**160,578**	**68.7**	**8.6**	**3.1**	**0.5**	**2.4**	**1.5**	**15.2**	**26.4**
Alabama	2,260	80.5	7.9	0.3	0.1	1.2	1.1	8.9	25.4
Alaska	360	64.2	12.3	1.2	0.4	7.3	5.2	9.5	19.4
Arizona	3,403	66.1	9.8	0.8	0.5	1.7	1.9	19.2	24.9
Arkansas	1,320	79.8	8.3	0.3	0.1	1.5	1.2	8.8	22.4
California	18,612	65.5	9.8	2.7	0.7	2.4	1.7	17.2	28.3
Colorado	3,122	64.7	7.9	1.6	1.0	2.5	1.1	21.2	25.0
Connecticut	1,828	69.0	7.7	3.3	0.2	2.7	1.3	15.9	26.8
Delaware	492	72.8	7.1	1.4	0.4	2.1	1.1	15.1	26.1
District of Columbia	374	28.4	3.8	18.7	3.0	9.7	2.7	33.8	30.1
Florida	10,376	69.7	9.0	1.2	0.5	1.4	1.9	16.4	28.0
Georgia	5,215	70.5	9.0	1.1	0.2	1.3	1.6	16.3	28.2
Hawaii	699	64.1	15.0	3.5	0.9	4.5	2.5	9.5	26.1
Idaho	912	72.4	8.8	0.6	0.7	2.9	1.4	13.1	22.1
Illinois	6,192	66.1	7.9	5.6	0.6	2.6	1.4	15.8	27.9
Indiana	3,288	75.7	9.7	0.7	0.4	1.9	1.1	10.5	24.1
Iowa	1,631	76.1	8.0	0.8	0.4	2.9	0.9	11.0	19.7
Kansas	1,452	75.3	8.3	0.5	0.3	2.2	1.3	12.1	19.6
Kentucky	2,035	76.0	9.9	0.5	0.1	1.9	1.2	10.5	24.1
Louisiana	2,019	78.5	8.5	0.8	0.3	2.1	1.6	8.2	25.6
Maine	683	70.0	8.2	0.5	0.5	3.8	1.4	15.7	24.7
Maryland	3,143	65.1	7.9	4.0	0.3	1.8	1.7	19.2	30.8
Massachusetts	3,637	61.5	7.1	6.2	0.8	4.0	1.9	18.4	28.6
Michigan	4,706	74.0	7.9	0.8	0.4	2.0	1.2	13.7	24.2
Minnesota	2,960	69.3	7.7	1.6	0.5	2.6	1.2	17.2	22.8
Mississippi	1,251	81.9	9.6	0.3	0.1	1.5	1.2	5.5	25.5
Missouri	2,955	75.4	7.9	0.8	0.2	1.6	1.1	12.9	23.7
Montana	552	69.4	10.9	0.5	1.0	4.4	1.3	12.6	19.0
Nebraska	1,016	76.5	8.7	0.4	0.3	2.3	1.0	10.8	18.8
Nevada	1,506	70.0	11.2	2.2	0.3	1.4	2.7	12.2	24.5
New Hampshire	738	71.1	7.9	0.3	0.3	2.1	1.1	17.3	26.7
New Jersey	4,615	61.5	8.3	8.0	0.3	3.0	2.2	16.7	30.3
New Mexico	938	73.3	10.1	0.7	0.5	2.2	1.3	12.0	23.7
New York	9,400	49.0	6.5	21.5	0.8	5.6	2.1	14.5	33.0
North Carolina	5,131	71.2	8.5	0.5	0.2	1.6	1.2	16.8	25.1
North Dakota	410	78.8	8.8	0.3	0.3	3.4	0.8	7.6	18.3
Ohio	5,660	74.8	7.8	1.0	0.3	1.9	1.2	13.0	23.5
Oklahoma	1,829	77.8	9.4	0.3	0.2	1.7	1.2	9.4	22.7
Oregon	2,055	64.1	8.6	2.1	1.3	3.6	1.4	19.0	22.8
Pennsylvania	6,284	68.8	7.5	3.4	0.5	3.2	1.5	15.2	26.4
Rhode Island	550	72.4	7.7	1.4	0.4	2.9	1.7	13.4	25.4
South Carolina	2,448	76.4	8.5	0.4	0.2	1.6	1.5	11.4	25.6
South Dakota	460	78.5	7.1	0.5	0.2	2.5	1.2	9.9	18.2
Tennessee	3,362	75.0	8.6	0.4	0.1	1.2	1.4	13.3	25.5
Texas	14,448	71.2	10.0	0.8	0.2	1.5	1.7	14.5	26.7
Utah	1,715	67.4	9.9	1.4	0.5	1.8	1.0	18.0	21.6
Vermont	338	69.8	7.3	0.6	0.7	4.2	0.8	16.5	23.2
Virginia	4,350	67.9	8.0	1.9	0.3	2.2	1.5	18.2	27.1
Washington	3,844	62.9	8.7	3.1	0.6	3.1	1.1	20.5	26.3
West Virginia	727	78.3	8.3	0.6	0.1	2.4	1.3	9.1	26.9
Wisconsin	2,992	73.9	7.8	1.1	0.5	2.7	1.1	13.0	22.2
Wyoming	287	76.2	8.2	1.0	0.9	3.5	1.1	9.1	18.0
Puerto Rico	1,129	82.7	6.2	0.7	0.1	2.5	1.8	5.9	28.1

[1] Excluding taxicabs.

Source: U.S. Census Bureau, 2022 American Community Survey, B08006, "Sex of Workers by Means of Transportation to Work," and DP03, "Selected Economic Characteristics," <data.census.gov>, accessed November 2023.

Table 1148. Passenger Transit Industry—Summary: 2000 to 2021

[24,243 represents $24,243,000,000. Includes Puerto Rico. Includes aggregate information for all transit systems in the United States. Excludes nontransit services such as taxicab, school bus, unregulated jitney (a small bus or automobile that transports passengers on a route for a small fare), sightseeing bus, intercity bus, and special application mass transportation systems (e.g., amusement parks, airports, island, and urban park ferries). Includes active vehicles only]

Item	Unit	2000	2010	2015	2018	2019	2020	2021
Operating systems.	Number	6,000	7,088	6,752	6,704	6,782	6,804	6,710
Motor bus systems.	Number	2,262	1,206	1,163	1,241	1,240	1,233	1,182
Revenue vehicles, available.	Number	131,089	174,425	183,601	181,541	185,732	184,635	180,927
Motor bus.	Number	75,013	66,239	72,075	71,743	72,665	72,241	71,449
Trolley bus.	Number	652	571	611	571	572	633	563
Demand response [1].	Number	33,080	68,621	71,299	70,093	73,155	72,051	73,029
Commuter rail.	Number	5,498	6,927	7,216	7,184	7,209	7,685	7,706
Heavy rail.	Number	10,311	11,510	10,737	10,763	11,198	11,064	10,942
Surface rail (light rail, street car).	Number	1,327	2,104	2,423	2,663	2,716	2,704	2,764
Other.	Number	5,208	18,453	19,240	18,524	18,215	18,257	14,474
Operating funding, total.	Mil. dol.	24,243	39,117	48,367	52,278	55,099	54,955	53,743
Agency funds.	Mil. dol.	11,004	14,675	18,105	18,845	18,740	11,391	8,322
Passenger funding.	Mil. dol.	8,746	12,556	15,727	16,031	16,271	9,124	6,368
Other.	Mil. dol.	2,258	2,119	2,378	2,814	2,470	2,267	1,954
Government funds [2].	Mil. dol.	13,239	24,442	30,262	33,433	36,358	43,564	45,421
Directly generated [3].	Mil. dol.	1,959	2,549	3,242	3,196	4,502	3,367	3,565
Local.	Mil. dol.	5,319	8,458	11,812	13,857	14,851	12,953	10,903
State.	Mil. dol.	4,967	9,761	11,197	11,867	12,639	12,685	11,066
Federal.	Mil. dol.	994	3,675	4,011	4,513	4,366	14,559	19,886
Operating expense.	Mil. dol.	22,646	37,755	45,353	49,482	51,786	50,533	50,556
Vehicle operations.	Mil. dol.	10,111	17,009	19,388	20,760	21,526	21,019	20,480
Maintenance.	Mil. dol.	6,445	9,797	12,237	13,404	13,919	13,441	13,954
General administration.	Mil. dol.	3,329	5,731	7,300	8,154	8,582	8,428	8,909
Purchased transportation.	Mil. dol.	2,761	5,218	6,427	7,165	7,759	7,644	7,212
Capital expenditures.	Mil. dol.	9,587	17,824	19,696	21,772	24,286	23,718	24,400
Vehicle-miles operated.	Million	4,081	5,455	5,509	5,719	5,692	4,904	4,526
Motor bus.	Million	2,315	2,413	2,428	2,532	2,555	2,290	2,181
Trolley bus.	Million	15	12	11	11	10	9	9
Demand response [1].	Million	759	1,694	1,617	1,702	1,629	1,305	1,123
Commuter rail.	Million	271	345	374	377	382	316	306
Heavy rail.	Million	595	666	695	705	719	663	640
Surface rail (light rail, street car).	Million	53	94	114	128	131	115	108
Other.	Million	74	232	271	264	266	205	160
Trips taken.	Million	9,363	10,218	10,599	9,953	9,969	5,971	4,493
Motor bus.	Million	5,678	5,256	5,199	4,707	4,660	3,246	2,327
Trolley bus.	Million	122	99	90	77	76	55	30
Demand response [1].	Million	105	190	223	204	201	137	105
Commuter rail.	Million	413	464	495	505	511	262	149
Heavy rail.	Million	2,632	3,550	3,860	3,724	3,790	1,778	1,607
Surface rail (light rail, street car).	Million	320	457	529	543	532	369	193
Other.	Million	93	202	204	192	199	125	81
Avg. fare per trip.	Dollars	0.93	1.23	1.50	1.62	1.63	1.53	1.42
Employees, number.	1,000	360	394	433	436	448	430	415
Salaries and wages, employee.	Mil. dol.	10,400	14,286	15,913	16,947	17,512	17,132	17,191
Fringe benefits, employee.	Mil. dol.	5,413	10,342	11,992	13,477	14,042	14,176	14,262

[1] This operation (also called paratransit or dial-a-ride) is comprised of passenger cars, vans or small buses operating in response to calls from passengers or their agents to the transit operator, who then dispatches a vehicle to pick up the passengers and transport them to their destinations. [2] Represents the sum of federal, state, and local assistance, and that portion of directly generated funds that accrue from tax collections, toll transfers from other sectors of operations, and bond proceeds. [3] These are any funds generated by or donated directly to the transit agency, including passenger fare revenues, advertising revenues, concessions, donations, bond proceeds, parking revenues, toll revenues, and taxes.

Source: American Public Transportation Association, Washington, DC, *Public Transportation Fact Book*, annual ©. See also <www.apta.com/research-technical-resources/research-reports>.

Table 1149. Top Twenty Cities—Public Transit Savings for Daily Commuters: 2023

[Individuals who use public transportation for their daily commute can save on average $13,218 annually based on the costs of owning and operating a motor vehicle (including the costs to purchase and finance automobiles, and gasoline prices) and downtown parking fees. On a per month basis, transit riders can save on average $1,102 per month versus driving. See source report and other monthly "Transit Savings" releases for information and methodology on how savings are calculated. The cities with the highest transit ridership are ranked in order of their transit savings based on the purchase of a monthly public transit pass and factoring in local gas prices and the local monthly unreserved parking rate]

City	Savings (dollars)		City	Savings (dollars)	
	Monthly	Annual		Monthly	Annual
San Francisco.	1,403	16,837	Houston.	1,127	13,522
New York.	1,377	16,527	Minneapolis.	1,120	13,441
Boston.	1,310	15,714	Baltimore.	1,110	13,319
Seattle.	1,265	15,181	Washington, DC.	1,101	13,217
San Diego.	1,244	14,929	Denver.	1,084	13,010
Chicago.	1,219	14,631	Miami.	1,083	13,000
Los Angeles.	1,219	14,629	Phoenix.	1,046	12,552
Honolulu.	1,218	14,612	Las Vegas.	1,035	12,422
Philadelphia.	1,198	14,380	Dallas.	1,028	12,334
Portland, OR.	1,192	14,298	Atlanta.	1,026	12,306

Source: American Public Transportation Association, Media Center, Press Releases ©. See also <www.apta.com/research-technical-resources/research-reports>.

Table 1150. Characteristics of Rail Transit by Transit Authority: 2022

[5,043.8 represents $5,043,800,000. Due to the impacts of the COVID-19 pandemic, use caution when comparing data to previous years]

Mode and transit agency	Metro area served	Number of stations	Number of ADA accessible stations [1]	Fare revenues earned (mil. dol.)	Total operating expenses (mil. dol.)	Unlinked passenger trips (million)
Total [2]	(X)	**3,792**	**2,846**	**5,043.8**	**19,955.6**	**2,819.7**
Heavy rail	(X)	**1,055**	**620**	**3,129.7**	**9,695.8**	**2,261.1**
Chicago Transit Authority	Chicago	145	103	137.1	623.6	103.5
Greater Cleveland Regional Transit Authority	Cleveland	18	18	3.4	36.0	2.8
Los Angeles County Metropolitan Transportation Authority, Metro	Los Angeles	16	16	7.2	175.3	25.1
Maryland Transit Administration	Baltimore	14	14	5.7	76.0	2.3
Massachusetts Bay Transportation Authority	Boston	52	51	125.1	333.8	78.9
Metropolitan Atlanta Rapid Transit Authority	Atlanta	38	38	35.9	223.4	26.1
Miami-Dade Transit	Miami	23	23	11.6	107.0	11.4
MTA New York City Transit	New York	472	135	2,326.8	5,349.8	1,788.4
Port Authority Trans-Hudson Corporation	New York	13	9	113.5	481.2	46.6
Port Authority Transit Corporation	Philadelphia	13	11	11.5	57.5	4.9
San Francisco Bay Area Rapid Transit District	San Francisco	48	48	130.2	659.5	36.8
Southeastern Pennsylvania Transportation Authority	Philadelphia	75	42	53.6	212.2	52.5
Staten Island Rapid Transit Operating Authority, MTA Staten Island Railway	New York	21	5	3.3	69.9	3.8
Washington Metropolitan Area Transit Authority	Washington	91	91	161.6	1,222.0	76.1
Alternativa de Transporte Integrado ATI	San Juan, PR	16	16	3.1	68.7	2.1
Light rail	(X)	**1,055**	**966**	**239.0**	**2,582.4**	**262.3**
Missouri-Illinois Metropolitan District Metro	St. Louis	38	38	8.2	92.3	6.5
Central Puget Sound Regional Transit Authority	Seattle	19	19	29.4	195.8	23.6
Charlotte Area Transit System	Charlotte	26	26	4.6	38.7	3.9
Greater Cleveland Regional Transit Authority	Cleveland	34	18	1.2	10.3	0.7
Dallas Area Rapid Transit	Dallas	65	65	13.4	198.9	17.7
Denver Regional Transportation District	Denver	57	57	16.6	144.2	13.6
Los Angeles County Metropolitan Transportation Authority, Metro	Los Angeles	78	78	8.7	410.8	30.7
Maryland Transit Administration (MTA)	Baltimore	33	33	3.4	52.6	2.9
Massachusetts Bay Transportation Authority	Boston	73	42	47.1	199.2	31.3
Metro Transit	Minneapolis	37	37	10.9	84.3	12.4
Harris County, Texas (Metro)	Houston	61	61	2.4	102.0	11.6
New Jersey Transit Corporation	Newark	41	37	10.4	126.9	14.3
Niagara Frontier Transportation Authority	Buffalo	19	19	2.8	28.0	2.1
Port Authority of Allegheny County	Pittsburgh	88	50	3.3	73.6	2.2
Sacramento Regional Transit District	Sacramento	44	44	5.5	78.6	4.6
San Diego Metropolitan Transit System	San Diego	63	63	25.5	102.6	29.7
San Francisco Municipal Railway	San Francisco	9	9	7.0	202.0	14.0
Santa Clara Valley Transportation Authority	San Jose	62	62	2.8	116.6	2.3
Hampton Roads Transit	Hampton	11	11	0.9	12.9	0.7
Metropolitan Transportation District of Oregon	Portland	95	95	19.2	159.5	18.6
Utah Transit Authority	Salt Lake City	59	59	10.6	97.5	10.7
Valley Metro Rail, Inc.	Phoenix	43	43	5.2	55.3	8.3
Commuter rail [3]	(X)	**1,323**	**958**	**1,650.3**	**7,291.7**	**263.8**
Alaska Railroad Corporation	Anchorage	8	8	33.7	56.6	0.2
Altamont Corridor Express	San Jose	10	10	2.7	25.7	0.3
Central Florida Commuter Rail	Orlando	16	16	1.9	63.1	0.9
Central Puget Sound Regional Transit Authority	Seattle	12	12	4.1	64.0	1.3
Connecticut Department of Transportation	Hartford	9	8	0.9	26.8	0.2
Dallas Area Rapid Transit	Dallas	10	10	2.8	42.1	1.1
Denver Regional Transportation District	Denver	23	23	20.0	103.0	7.9
Fort Worth Transportation Authority	Ft. Worth	12	12	1.4	28.8	0.5
Maryland Transit Administration	Baltimore	42	26	13.8	167.2	2.3
Massachusetts Bay Transportation Authority	Boston	142	110	80.7	474.3	14.3
Metro Transit	Minneapolis	7	7	0.3	11.6	0.1
MTA Metro-North Railroad	New York	112	47	448.2	1,353.5	54.5
MTA Long Island Rail Road	New York	125	109	457.6	1,601.9	81.6
New Jersey Transit Corporation	New York	166	78	277.8	1,270.8	40.1
North County Transit District	San Diego	8	8	2.4	33.8	0.6
Northeast Illinois Regional Commuter Railroad Corporation	Chicago	242	190	126.6	822.5	23.8
Northern Indiana Commuter Transport District	Chicago	19	13	9.2	58.8	1.4
Northern New England Passenger Rail Authority	Boston	12	12	8.1	22.2	0.4
Peninsula Corridor Joint Powers Board: Caltrain	San Francisco	31	26	33.2	155.3	4.1
Pennsylvania Department of Transportation	Philadelphia	12	8	14.6	24.9	0.4
Regional Transportation Authority	Nashville	7	7	0.3	4.3	0.1
Rio Metro Regional Transit District	Albuquerque	15	15	0.8	38.1	0.3
Sonoma-Marin Area Rail Transit District	Bay Area, CA	12	12	1.3	27.8	0.4
South Florida Regional Transportation Authority	Miami	18	18	8.9	112.6	3.0
Southeastern Pennsylvania Transportation Authority	Philadelphia	155	75	56.4	309.4	16.3
Southern California Regional Rail Authority	Los Angeles	62	62	28.2	245.7	3.8
Utah Transit Authority	Salt Lake City	17	17	4.0	64.4	3.2
Virginia Railway Express	Washington	19	19	10.5	82.3	0.8

X Not applicable. [1] Number of stations that comply with the American with Disabilities Act of 1992 (ADA). Stations may be wheelchair accessible but not comply with other provisions of the ADA. [2] Includes hybrid and streetcar rail, not shown separately. [3] Excludes commuter-type services operated independently by Amtrak.

Source: U.S. Department of Transportation, Federal Transit Administration, National Transit Database, Annual Data Tables and Annual Database, "Metrics," and "Transit Stations," <transit.dot.gov/ntd/ntd-data>, accessed September 2024.

Table 1151. Commuters by Commuting Time to Work for Top Metropolitan Statistical Areas: 2022

[136,196 represents 136,196,000. For workers 16 years and over who did not work at home. Covers any mode of travel. Based on a sample, subject to sampling variability]

Metropolitan statistical area	Total commuters (1,000)	Less than 10 minutes	10 to 14 minutes	15 to 19 minutes	20 to 24 minutes	25 to 29 minutes	30 to 34 minutes	35 to 44 minutes	45 to 59 minutes	60 or more minutes
United States	**136,196**	**17,202**	**18,169**	**21,030**	**19,596**	**9,443**	**18,757**	**9,653**	**10,749**	**11,597**
Atlanta-Sandy Springs-Alpharetta, GA	2,487	197	237	332	314	173	400	238	303	295
Baltimore-Columbia-Towson, MD	1,187	93	123	172	176	97	188	106	116	117
Boston-Cambridge-Newton, MA-NH	2,085	200	213	261	264	139	329	195	233	248
Charlotte-Concord-Gastonia, NC-SC	1,092	105	130	180	162	88	173	83	103	69
Chicago-Naperville-Elgin, IL-IN-WI	3,924	352	418	486	490	273	620	372	453	460
Dallas-Fort Worth-Arlington, TX	3,336	302	376	480	487	253	547	279	342	270
Denver-Aurora-Lakewood, CO	1,277	111	139	191	203	106	221	114	110	82
Detroit-Warren-Dearborn, MI	1,713	181	214	255	268	144	259	146	143	105
Houston-The Woodlands-Sugar Land, TX	3,068	238	269	415	423	204	580	279	343	317
Los Angeles-Long Beach-Anaheim, CA	5,250	395	580	752	773	337	918	423	494	579
Miami-Fort Lauderdale-Pompano Beach, FL	2,578	179	250	341	416	185	467	223	264	254
Minneapolis-St. Paul-Bloomington, MN-WI	1,559	176	213	267	264	135	218	118	97	72
New York-Newark-Jersey City, NY-NJ-PA	8,023	598	708	831	912	450	1,146	751	981	1,645
Orlando-Kissimmee-Sanford, FL	1,120	81	131	148	167	95	202	96	107	94
Philadelphia-Camden-Wilmington, PA-NJ-DE-MD	2,545	254	290	357	342	188	377	231	255	251
Phoenix-Mesa-Chandler, AZ	1,913	195	227	280	305	165	310	152	167	112
Portland-Vancouver-Hillsboro, OR-WA	1,000	115	131	173	165	76	142	71	67	60
Riverside-San Bernardino-Ontario, CA	1,858	171	207	261	253	100	264	121	167	316
St. Louis, MO-IL	1,165	146	141	180	186	96	174	102	81	59
San Antonio-New Braunfels, TX	1,091	101	121	172	173	96	176	79	93	78
San Diego-Chula Vista-Carlsbad, CA	1,351	118	168	228	237	105	226	99	89	80
San Francisco-Oakland-Berkeley, CA	1,719	135	202	237	227	98	265	152	182	221
Seattle-Tacoma-Bellevue, WA	1,586	146	181	215	217	126	249	143	157	153
Tampa-St. Petersburg-Clearwater, FL	1,242	118	143	183	184	85	188	103	124	116
Washington-Arlington-Alexandria, DC-VA-MD-WV	2,545	178	230	304	313	175	402	260	325	358

Source: U.S. Census Bureau, 2022 American Community Survey, B08134, "Means of Transportation to Work by Travel Time to Work," <data.census.gov>, accessed November 2023.

Table 1152. Household Travel Trips and Length by Trip Purpose: 1983 to 2022

[Data based on the National Household Travel Survey (NHTS), which asks each participating household to report all travel by household members on a randomly assigned 24-hour single travel day using any mode of transportation including walking. NHTS survey methods, sampling frames, and technologies used for data collection have undergone significant changes over the years and caution should be used in comparing data between years. Notably, trip distance for 1969 through 2009 was self-reported by respondents; beginning 2017, trip distance is calculated for the shortest path between origin and destination using a Google application programming interface (API). See source for details]

Trip characteristic	1983	1990	1995	2001	2009	2009 Adj. [1]	2017	2022
Daily person trips per person	2.9	3.8	4.3	4.1	3.8	(NA)	3.4	2.3
Daily person miles of travel (PMT) per person	25.1	34.9	38.7	36.9	36.1	33.1	36.1	28.6
Daily vehicle trips per driver	2.4	3.3	3.6	3.4	3.0	(NA)	2.7	1.9
Daily vehicle miles of travel (VMT) per driver	18.7	28.5	32.1	32.7	29.0	26.3	25.8	21.8
Average person trip length (miles)	8.7	9.5	9.1	10.0	9.8	8.9	10.7	12.6
Average vehicle trip length (miles)	7.9	8.9	9.1	9.9	9.7	8.8	9.6	11.5
Average annual person trips per household:								
All purposes [2]	2,628	3,262	3,828	3,581	3,466	(NA)	3,140	1,990
To and from work	537	539	676	565	541	(NA)	546	366
Work related business	62	38	100	109	106	(NA)	51	70
Shopping	474	630	775	707	725	(NA)	580	337
Other family/personal errands	456	854	981	863	748	(NA)	628	364
School/church	310	304	337	351	333	(NA)	341	225
Social/recreation	728	874	953	952	952	(NA)	866	588
Average person trip length (miles):								
All purposes [2]	8.7	9.5	9.1	10.0	9.7	8.9	10.7	12.6
To and from work	8.5	10.7	11.6	12.1	11.8	11.0	11.5	13.4
Work related business	21.8	28.2	20.3	28.3	20.0	18.3	25.9	20.7
Shopping	5.4	5.4	6.1	7.0	6.5	5.9	7.1	5.8
Other family/personal errands	7.3	8.6	7.6	7.8	7.0	6.3	7.1	8.6
School/church	4.9	5.4	6.0	6.0	6.3	5.8	6.4	6.2
Social/recreation	12.3	13.2	11.3	11.4	10.7	9.7	10.4	17.1
Average annual vehicle trips per household:								
All purposes	1,486	2,077	2,321	2,171	2,068	(NA)	1,865	1,262
To and from work	414	448	553	479	457	(NA)	450	324
Shopping	297	431	501	459	468	(NA)	372	229
Other family/personal errands	272	579	626	537	500	(NA)	434	258
Social/recreation	335	460	427	441	436	(NA)	410	326
Average vehicle trip length (miles)								
All purposes	7.9	8.9	9.1	9.9	9.7	8.8	9.6	11.5
To and from work	8.6	11.0	11.8	12.1	12.2	11.3	12.0	13.5
Shopping	5.3	5.1	5.6	6.7	6.4	5.8	7.0	5.8
Other family/personal errands	6.7	7.4	6.9	7.5	7.1	6.4	6.9	8.7
Social/recreation	10.6	11.8	11.2	11.9	11.2	10.1	10.6	14.0

NA Not available. [1] Through 2009, respondents were asked to self-report travel. Beginning in 2017, distance was calculated using the shortest path routes between reported origins and destinations. 2009 data were forward-adjusted to provide a three-survey comparison of trip length trends using the now standard method of calculating distance traveled. [2] Includes other trips not shown separately.

Source: U.S. Department of Transportation, Federal Highway Administration, *Summary of Travel Trends: 2022 National Household Travel Survey*, January 2024. See also <nhts.ornl.gov/>.

Table 1153. Federal Transit Administration (FTA) Funding Allocations by State: 2020 to 2024

[In millions of dollars (13,607.7 represents $13,607,700,000). For fiscal years ending September 30. Data shown are apportionments and allocations for formula and discretionary programs]

State	2020	2021	2022	2023	2024
Total [1]	13,607.7	13,001.2	21,125.9	21,581.8	14,000.6
AL	78.0	65.8	104.0	92.3	80.2
AK	81.2	60.8	94.2	370.6	83.4
AZ	314.9	283.8	498.0	240.5	194.0
AR	37.3	43.3	48.6	48.5	48.4
CA	2,112.9	2,870.7	3,948.4	4,057.1	2,012.0
CO	169.4	143.8	309.6	211.8	200.6
CT	198.3	212.2	282.5	313.7	257.7
DE	32.1	38.3	64.2	45.5	36.7
DC	368.4	362.7	590.3	569.9	459.2
FL	589.8	411.3	609.3	686.7	638.7
GA	234.4	216.2	331.9	330.1	284.8
HI	69.9	53.0	142.3	82.3	65.8
ID	34.5	32.5	56.9	38.4	43.7
IL	765.2	728.7	1,314.9	1,389.9	854.6
IN	335.8	256.7	457.2	168.6	138.2
IO	83.1	50.1	96.3	105.0	63.1
KS	64.0	43.0	56.6	58.4	50.9
KY	84.2	62.7	89.5	88.1	77.3
LA	107.0	77.6	107.0	169.6	94.6
ME	54.4	37.7	55.9	89.9	49.6
MD	402.6	400.3	490.3	426.9	353.4
MA	565.0	503.9	785.3	660.9	555.5
MI	201.0	161.2	238.3	226.5	194.3
MN	141.4	328.7	664.7	461.8	173.1
MS	52.5	36.9	52.4	52.0	42.2
MO	175.4	206.7	180.2	251.6	146.5
MT	30.2	28.5	50.4	71.6	35.7
NE	50.3	32.2	37.6	38.3	40.4
NV	86.2	77.3	102.1	257.5	102.1
NH	20.9	19.5	32.1	25.0	24.5
NJ	950.2	657.7	1,065.7	1,357.7	859.0
NM	70.3	62.5	95.7	102.1	77.4
NY	1,641.4	1,544.0	3,127.1	2,993.5	2,301.3
NC	175.8	176.7	222.4	251.1	185.7
ND	32.9	17.3	30.4	21.9	23.6
OH	223.5	198.6	405.6	516.4	270.5
OK	80.0	55.4	88.2	86.9	72.0
OR	234.7	123.0	188.6	181.4	162.1
PA	570.9	452.1	817.6	789.8	617.8
RI	68.2	48.0	56.0	60.9	60.1
SC	74.9	59.7	80.1	120.2	79.5
SD	23.0	20.3	26.0	28.2	26.3
TN	115.1	101.4	212.9	209.1	131.8
TX	562.5	528.9	1,019.4	1,021.4	699.0
UT	176.9	112.1	135.9	399.5	140.4
VT	13.7	13.8	27.6	38.4	15.9
VA	192.7	190.5	299.8	323.4	229.5
WA	555.3	577.0	923.7	1,105.0	377.8
WV	35.5	29.4	38.7	39.2	41.3
WI	152.4	90.9	238.6	173.9	121.1
WY	19.0	15.8	18.0	19.2	18.8

[1] Includes data for Island Areas of the U.S. and unallocated funds, not shown separately. Does not include oversight funds.

Source: U.S. Department of Transportation, Federal Transit Administration, Apportionment Resources, Funding by State, "FTA Allocations for Formula and Discretionary Programs by State FY1998-2024," <www.transit.dot.gov/funding/grants/fta-allocations-formula-and-discretionary-programs-state-fy-1998-2024>, accessed April 2024.

Table 1154. Pipelines—Mileage and Incident Summary: 2005 to 2022

[In miles except where indicated (1,245,463 represents $1,245,463,000)]

Year	Pipeline mileage								Pipeline incidents [2]	
	Natural gas systems			Hazardous liquid or carbon dioxide systems					Number of incidents	Total cost as reported ($1,000)
	Distri-bution [1]	Trans-mission	Gathering	Total [3]	Petro-leum/ refined products	Highly volatile liquids	Crude oil	CO2 or other		
2005	1,962,351	300,468	23,754	166,760	62,899	51,284	48,732	3,846	719	1,245,463
2006	2,022,474	300,324	20,898	166,719	61,905	52,533	48,453	3,827	639	151,984
2007	2,025,731	301,066	20,042	169,846	62,091	54,382	49,488	3,884	610	153,772
2008	2,075,191	303,181	20,663	173,789	61,599	57,024	50,963	4,203	659	564,831
2009	2,086,689	304,560	20,376	175,965	61,803	57,233	52,737	4,192	627	179,070
2010	2,102,483	304,808	19,650	181,836	64,742	57,887	54,631	4,560	586	1,692,502
2011	2,121,355	305,059	19,277	183,575	64,122	58,601	56,100	4,735	588	426,330
2012	2,138,000	303,382	16,532	186,411	64,040	59,863	57,653	4,840	572	229,848
2013	2,149,819	302,869	17,377	192,602	63,349	62,770	61,277	5,190	617	368,992
2014	2,169,375	301,824	17,530	199,985	61,766	65,794	67,133	5,276	706	321,376
2015	2,190,257	301,166	17,783	208,812	62,632	67,678	73,247	5,241	712	351,417
2016	2,211,526	300,353	17,865	212,354	62,459	68,731	75,954	5,195	632	376,497
2017	2,226,199	300,737	18,097	216,237	62,362	69,165	79,458	5,237	646	340,126
2018	2,239,223	301,628	17,916	219,327	62,719	70,308	81,079	5,206	634	2,228,210
2019	2,264,522	302,340	17,767	225,380	63,107	72,634	84,475	5,147	657	350,575
2020	2,284,705	301,673	17,534	229,390	64,111	74,819	85,293	5,150	574	385,094
2021	2,300,983	301,529	17,123	229,976	64,200	75,601	84,819	5,339	633	229,499
2022	2,321,510	300,931	112,034	229,450	64,082	75,456	84,508	5,385	629	1,109,415

[1] Includes main and estimated service mileage. [2] Includes serious and significant incidents. Serious incidents include a fatality or injury requiring in-patient hospitalization. Significant incidents include serious incidents; those with $122,000 or more in total costs; highly volatile liquid releases of 5 barrels or more, or other liquid releases of 50 barrels or more; and liquid releases resulting in an unintentional fire or explosion. [3] Beginning 2010, includes fuel grade ethanol, not shown separately.

Source: U.S. Department of Transportation, Pipeline and Hazardous Materials Safety Administration, "Pipeline Mileage and Facilities" and "Pipeline Incidents: 20 Year Trends," <www.phmsa.dot.gov/data-and-statistics/pipeline/data-and-statistics-overview>, accessed December 2023.

Table 1155. Crude Oil, Fuel Ethanol and Biodiesel Movements by Rail: 2010 to 2023

[In thousands of barrels (23,788 represents 23,788,000). Crude oil movements on railroads to and from Canada, within the 50 States and the District of Columbia (including interstate and intrastate). Estimates based on data from the Surface Transportation Board and other information]

Item	2010	2015	2016	2017	2018	2019	2020	2021	2022	2023
Crude oil	23,788	317,446	175,701	139,389	201,208	251,224	157,141	126,064	97,985	97,329
Intra-U.S. movements	23,712	275,218	142,587	87,053	114,004	141,015	94,844	65,070	52,079	65,191
U.S. exports to Canada	55	4,414	–	102	180	–	369	–	–	–
U.S. imports from Canada	21	37,814	33,114	52,234	87,023	110,209	61,929	60,994	45,906	32,139
Fuel ethanol	208,061	220,877	237,259	253,874	258,954	247,752	224,196	240,723	240,003	258,357
Biodiesel	2,606	8,332	12,226	11,706	13,668	13,061	18,578	16,293	15,962	14,894

– Represents zero.

Source: U.S. Energy Information Administration, Petroleum & Other Liquids, "Movements of Crude Oil and Selected Products by Rail," <www.eia.gov/petroleum/data.php>, accessed August 2024.

Table 1156. Truck Inventory—Personal and Commercial Vehicles by Selected Feature: 2021

[171,163.1 represents 171,163,100. Data are shown for privately-owned and commercial vehicles registered with motor vehicle departments in all states (excluding New Hampshire) and the District of Columbia. Includes currently operated Class 1 through 8 trucks as classified by vehicle manufacturers: trucks, minivans, vans, and sport utility vehicles (SUVs). Excludes government-owned vehicles, ambulances, buses, motor homes, farm tractors, unpowered trailer units, and trucks reported to have been disposed of prior to January 1 of the survey year. Data are from the Vehicle Inventory and Use Survey (VIUS), which is a joint effort by the Bureau of Transportation Statistics and Census Bureau, in partnership with the Federal Highway Administration and the U.S. Department of Energy]

Feature	Pickups, minivans, other light vans, and SUVs (light vehicles)			Trucks and truck tractors (heavy vehicles)		
	Number of vehicles (1,000s)	Vehicle miles traveled (millions)	Average miles per vehicle (1,000s)	Number of vehicles (1,000s)	Vehicle miles traveled (millions)	Average miles per vehicle (1,000s)
Total [1]	**171,163.1**	**1,673,806**	**9.8**	**8,903.6**	**223,189**	**25.1**
Standard:						
Air bags	157,670.6	1,631,089	10.3	4,284.4	130,552	30.5
Anti-lock brake system	147,198.7	1,516,756	10.3	5,008.1	154,518	30.9
Cruise control	148,507.2	1,529,357	10.3	4,431.4	149,073	33.6
Driver-facing camera	26,999.9	310,012	11.5	602.2	26,212	43.5
Global Positioning System for fleet transportation use only (no navigational aid)	10,480.3	133,573	12.7	1,632.9	72,401	44.3
Global Positioning System, with navigation	47,182.4	526,501	11.2	711.1	42,610	59.9
Internet access	20,908.0	248,558	11.9	270.5	15,622	57.7
Rollover protection	19,916.1	216,372	10.9	684.7	40,996	59.9
Driving control assistance:						
Adaptive cruise control	39,717.4	447,480	11.3	753.3	45,789	60.8
Active driving assistance	17,427.0	189,260	10.9	152.5	9,497	62.3
Lane keeping assistance	29,860.5	339,503	11.4	244.8	19,934	81.4
Platooning capabilities	5,363.7	61,392	11.4	20.5	1,509	73.4
Vehicle-to-vehicle, vehicle-to-infrastructure, and/or vehicle-to-everything communications	1,556.6	21,494	13.8	34.3	2,329	68.0
Collision warning:						
Blind spot warning	43,246.7	492,287	11.4	305.1	18,263	59.9
Forward collision warning	33,913.7	394,845	11.6	537.4	39,766	74.0
Lane departure warning	30,846.8	352,284	11.4	469.5	35,706	76.0
Parking obstruction warning	35,199.1	406,393	11.5	87.1	2,897	33.3
Rear cross traffic warning	29,380.2	338,842	11.5	62.0	2,432	39.2
Collision intervention:						
Automatic emergency braking	24,609.5	274,096	11.1	553.1	39,734	71.8
Automatic emergency steering	16,495.3	190,943	11.6	855.7	46,611	54.5
Rear automatic emergency braking	8,247.5	91,640	11.1	113.7	6,036	53.1
Parking assistance:						
Active parking assistance	10,185.2	115,780	11.4	23.6	1,019	43.1
Remote parking	744.7	6,124	8.2	0.7	18	24.1
Fuel economy:						
Aerodynamic bumper	14,431.0	148,049	10.3	1,016.9	57,486	56.5
Aerodynamic hood	16,186.1	164,979	10.2	1,211.9	62,706	51.7
Aerodynamic mirrors	15,629.6	158,979	10.2	1,366.9	73,652	53.9
Automatic engine shutoff technology	16,495.3	190,943	11.6	855.7	46,611	54.5
Automatic tire inflation system	2,899.4	30,890	10.7	143.4	10,861	75.7
Fairings	(X)	(X)	(X)	680.6	47,357	69.6
Fuel tank covers	(X)	(X)	(X)	816.6	45,727	56.0
Gap reducers	(X)	(X)	(X)	281.0	21,894	77.9
Hybrid-electric drivetrain (no plug)	1,805.8	21,682	12.0	6.8	262	38.4
Idle-reducing technology	2,682.2	29,451	11.0	384.5	26,810	69.7
Low rolling resistance tires	2,467.5	26,214	10.6	469.0	31,895	68.0
Nose cone	(X)	(X)	(X)	52.3	2,305	44.1
Plug-in hybrid-electric drivetrain	620.0	6,759	10.9	3.0	(S)	70.5
Side skirts	(X)	(X)	(X)	794.7	48,085	60.5

X Not applicable. S Estimate does not meet publication standards because of high sampling variability, poor response quality, or other concerns about the estimate quality. [1] Includes vehicles with none of the listed features and with features not reported.

Source: U.S. Census Bureau, 2021 Vehicle Inventory and Use Survey, VIUS211A, "All Vehicles by Registration State, Vehicle Type, and Trailer Configuration for the U.S. (excluding New Hampshire) and States: 2021," <data.census.gov>, accessed July 2024.

Table 1157. Truck Inventory—Personal and Commercial Vehicles by Body and Trailer Type: 2021

[180,066.7 represents 180,066,700. Data are shown for privately-owned and commercial vehicles registered with motor vehicle departments in all states (excluding New Hampshire) and the District of Columbia. Includes currently operated Class 1 through 8 trucks as classified by vehicle manufacturers: trucks, minivans, vans, and sport utility vehicles (SUVs). Excludes government-owned vehicles, ambulances, buses, motor homes, farm tractors, unpowered trailer units, and trucks reported to have been disposed of prior to January 1 of the survey year. Data are from the Vehicle Inventory and Use Survey (VIUS), which is a joint effort by the Bureau of Transportation Statistics and Census Bureau, in partnership with the Federal Highway Administration and the U.S. Department of Energy]

Body and trailer type	Number of vehicles (1,000s)	Vehicle miles traveled (millions)	Body and trailer type	Number of vehicles (1,000s)	Vehicle miles traveled (millions)
Total	**180,066.7**	**1,896,995**	Van, walk-in	273.5	3,189
LIGHT VEHICLES			Van, other	335.8	8,044
Pickups, minivans, other light vans, and SUVs	**171,163.1**	**1,673,806**	Wood chipper	13.4	125
Pickups	57,336.0	511,942	Other	223.3	2,353
Minivans	11,270.8	108,963	Not reported	291.7	2,537
Other light vans	6,689.9	75,528	Trailer type:		
SUVs	95,866.4	977,374	Auto carrier, stinger-steered	16.7	1,131
			Auto carrier (conventional rack above cab)	4.1	260
HEAVY VEHICLES			Auto carrier (high mount)	4.1	313
Trucks and truck tractors	**8,903.6**	**223,189**	Beverage or bay	17.7	322
Body type:			Container	93.6	5,535
Armored	10.3	56	Curtainside	11.7	785
Beverage or bay	20.0	289	Dump	252.2	8,461
Box truck	1,314.9	24,812	Flatbed, platform	286.3	12,906
Concrete mixer	86.8	1,163	Intermodal chassis	15.5	900
Concrete pumper	5.6	74	Livestock	22.7	995
Conveyor bed	8.9	77	Logging	39.4	1,839
Crane	53.5	503	Low boy	84.3	2,272
Dump	877.7	9,408	Mobile home toter	1.4	29
Flatbed, stake, or platform	1,128.6	11,548	Open top	155.0	3,706
Hooklift/roll-off	55.5	1,242	Tank, dry bulk	54.7	2,930
Logging	15.8	172	Tank, liquids or gases	140.5	8,933
Service, utility	371.9	3,975	Van, basic enclosed	584.7	43,635
Service, other	439.0	5,827	Van, drop frame	11.5	656
Street sweeper	18.7	252	Van, insulated nonrefrigerated	24.5	1,848
Tank, liquids or gases	193.6	2,488	Van, insulated refrigerated	187.6	15,885
Tow/wrecker	124.8	2,058	Other	42.7	1,317
Trash, garbage, or recycling	98.4	1,806	Not reported	848.0	26,011
Vacuum	42.8	528			

Source: U.S. Census Bureau, 2021 Vehicle Inventory and Use Survey, VIUS211A, "All Vehicles by Registration State, Vehicle Type, and Trailer Configuration for the U.S. (excluding New Hampshire) and States: 2021," <data.census.gov>, accessed July 2024.

Table 1158. Truck Transportation—Revenue and Equipment Inventory: 2017 to 2022

[In millions of dollars (290,532 represents $290,532,000,000), except where noted. For all employer firms regardless of tax status. Covers NAICS 484. Data are based on the 2012 North American Industry Classification System (NAICS); see text, this section and Section 15]

Item	2017	2018	2019	2020	2021	2022
Total operating revenue	**290,532**	**313,809**	**320,817**	**318,602**	**376,903**	**445,509**
Total motor carrier revenue	270,154	293,789	300,108	296,864	351,099	414,693
Revenue by commodities handled:						
Agricultural products	30,191	32,957	34,309	34,114	39,502	51,042
Grains, alcohol, and tobacco products	10,665	10,907	11,173	10,650	12,802	16,697
Stone, nonmetallic minerals, and metallic ores	20,951	23,222	24,552	22,825	25,425	30,075
Coal and petroleum products	14,849	15,237	16,217	14,454	15,977	19,183
Pharmaceutical and chemical products	13,577	13,545	13,925	13,673	14,554	(S)
Wood products, textiles, and leathers	19,625	21,519	21,711	21,487	26,032	29,406
Base metal and machinery	25,255	27,404	28,224	25,534	29,094	33,888
Electronic and precision instruments, motorized vehicles	14,071	15,574	15,929	15,749	20,177	21,936
Used household and office goods	13,601	14,573	14,806	14,896	17,079	18,371
New furniture and miscellaneous manufactured products	19,737	22,128	22,003	22,854	29,889	35,964
Other goods	87,632	96,723	97,259	100,628	120,568	140,127
Hazardous materials	17,068	18,134	19,137	18,547	19,894	21,588
Inventory of revenue-generating equipment (1,000):						
Trucks	200	213	217	209	226	251
Owned and/or leased with drivers	182	192	192	185	202	225
Leased without drivers	18	21	25	24	24	26
Truck-tractors	664	681	715	684	743	791
Owned and/or leased with drivers	577	582	617	587	642	683
Leased without drivers	87	99	98	97	101	108
Trailers	1,593	1,698	1,736	1,635	1,765	1,915
Owned and/or leased with drivers	1,448	1,545	1,578	1,476	1,592	1,714
Leased without drivers	145	153	158	159	173	201

S Estimate does not meet publication standards.

Source: U.S. Census Bureau, Service Annual Survey, "Service Annual Survey Latest Data (NAICS-basis): 2022," <www.census.gov/programs-surveys/sas/data/tables.html>, accessed February 2024.

Table 1159. U.S. Postal Service—Summary: 1990 to 2023

[In units as indicated (166,301 represents 166,301,000,000). For years ending September 30. Includes Puerto Rico and all Island Areas]

Item	1990	2000	2010	2020	2021	2022	2023
Offices, stations, and branches (number)	**40,067**	**38,060**	**36,222**	**34,451**	**34,223**	**33,641**	**33,493**
Post offices	28,959	27,876	27,077	26,362	26,362	26,269	26,261
Stations and branches	11,108	10,184	9,145	8,089	7,861	7,372	7,232
Delivery points (mil.)	**(NA)**	**135.9**	**150.9**	**161.4**	**163.1**	**164.9**	**166.6**
Residential	(NA)	123.9	137.5	148.6	150.4	152.2	154.0
City	(NA)	76.1	80.5	84.2	84.8	85.4	86.0
P.O. Box	(NA)	15.9	15.7	16.0	16.0	16.1	16.2
Rural/highway contract	(NA)	31.9	41.2	48.4	49.6	50.7	51.7
Business	(NA)	12.1	13.3	12.8	12.8	12.7	12.6
Pieces of mail handled (mil.)	**166,301**	**207,882**	**170,859**	**129,171**	**128,842**	**127,444**	**116,146**
First-class mail [1,2]	89,270	103,526	77,592	52,628	50,664	48,960	45,979
Periodicals (formerly 2nd class)	10,680	10,365	7,269	4,006	3,679	3,400	2,993
Marketing Mail (formerly Standard A) [2]	63,725	90,057	81,841	64,004	66,198	67,092	59,410
U.S. Postal Service	538	363	438	441	279	386	365
Free for the blind	35	47	68	25	20	19	20
Shipping and package services [2,3,6]	(X)	(X)	3,057	7,325	7,585	7,232	7,057
Express mail [2,3,5]	59	71	43	24	29	27	24
Package services (formerly Standard B)	663	1,128	657	571	517	475	435
Priority mail [2,3,4]	518	1,223	779	1,274	1,405	1,202	1,079
International economy mail (surface) [3]	166	79	(3)	(3)	(3)	(3)	(3)
International, airmail or total [3,7]	632	1,021	594	742	417	355	322
Employees, total (1,000)	**843**	**901**	**672**	**644**	**653**	**635**	**640**
Career	**761**	**788**	**584**	**496**	**517**	**517**	**525**
Headquarters	2	2	3	3	6	7	8
Headquarters support	6	6	5	3	3	2	3
Inspection Service	4	4	2	2	2	2	2
Inspector General	(X)	1	1	1	1	1	1
Field Career	749	775	573	486	504	504	512
Postmasters	27	26	23	14	13	14	14
Supervisors/managers	43	39	28	25	23	24	27
Professional, administrative, and technical	10	10	6	5	2	2	2
Clerks	290	282	157	119	129	128	127
Mail handlers	51	61	49	37	47	47	45
City carriers	236	241	192	168	173	170	175
Motor vehicle operators	7	9	7	9	9	10	11
Rural carriers	42	57	67	74	75	77	78
Special delivery messengers	2	(X)	(X)	(X)	(X)	(X)	(X)
Building and equipment maintenance	33	42	37	29	28	27	28
Vehicle maintenance	5	6	5	5	5	5	5
Other [8]	1	2	(X)	(X)	(X)	(X)	(X)
Pre-career	**83**	**114**	**88**	**148**	**137**	**119**	**115**
Casuals	27	30	7	10	(Z)	(Z)	(Z)
Transitional	(X)	13	16	–	–	–	–
Rural part-time	43	58	52	59	54	47	49
Relief/leave replacements	12	12	11	2	2	2	2
Non-bargaining temporary	(Z)	1	2	(Z)	(Z)	(Z)	(Z)
Compensation and employee benefits (mil. dol.)	34,214	49,532	48,909	48,730	50,085	51,520	52,853
Avg. salary per employee (dol.) [9]	37,570	50,103	72,099	(NA)	(NA)	(NA)	(NA)
Pieces of mail per employee (1,000)	197	231	254	201	197	201	181
Operating postal revenue (million dollars)	**39,201**	**64,476**	**67,052**	**73,123**	**77,009**	**78,507**	**78,186**
Mail revenue	**37,891**	**62,285**	**63,262**	**69,651**	**73,005**	**73,970**	**73,711**
First-class mail [1,2]	24,023	35,516	32,111	23,781	23,264	23,990	24,505
Periodicals (formerly 2nd class)	1,509	2,171	1,879	1,024	942	955	918
Marketing Mail (formerly Standard A) [2]	8,082	15,193	16,728	13,909	14,589	15,996	15,076
Shipping and Package Services [2,3,6]	(X)	(X)	10,156	28,529	32,008	31,317	31,641
Express mail [2,3,5]	630	996	829	697	820	767	713
Package Services (formerly Standard B)	919	1,912	1,531	832	834	859	893
Priority mail [2,3,4]	1,555	4,837	5,455	11,831	13,511	12,330	11,252
International economy mail (surface) [3]	222	180	(3)	(3)	(3)	(3)	(3)
International, airmail or total [3,7]	941	1,477	2,388	2,408	2,202	1,712	1,571
Service revenue	**1,310**	**2,191**	**3,790**	**3,472**	**4,004**	**4,537**	**4,475**
Certified [10]	310	385	791	598	615	624	664
Insurance [10]	47	109	128	93	105	88	69
Money orders	155	235	182	146	147	167	186
Other [10]	592	1,342	2,635	2,635	3,137	3,658	3,556
Operating expenses (million dollars) [11]	**40,490**	**62,992**	**75,426**	**82,401**	**81,844**	**79,570**	**85,387**

– Represents zero. NA Not available. X Not applicable. Z Fewer than 500. [1] Items mailed at 1st class rates and weighing 11 ounces or less. [2] Beginning 2010, Express Mail, Priority Mail, First-Class Parcels, and Standard Parcels are not included in Mail categories but are reclassified under Shipping and Package Services. [3] "Volume" and "Mailing & Shipping Revenue" restructured for the "Postal Accountability and Enhancement Act (PAEA) of 2006." Some categories eliminated. [4] Provides 2- to 3-day delivery service. [5] Overnight delivery of packages weighing up to 70 pounds. [6] Beginning 2010, also includes Package Services. [7] Airmail only, for 2005 and earlier. Beginning 2010, total international, including all international revenues and pieces formerly included in First-Class Mail, Standard Mail, and Package Services. [8] Includes discontinued operations, area offices, and nurses. Beginning 2010, nurses are included with clerks. [9] For career bargaining unit employees. Includes fringe benefits. [10] Beginning 2000, return receipt revenue broken out from registry, certified, and insurance and included in "other." [11] Shown in year in which obligation was incurred.

Source: U.S. Postal Service, *FY2023 Annual Report to Congress*, 2023, and earlier reports, and unpublished data. See also <about.usps.com/strategic-planning/future-postal-service/publications.htm>.

Table 1160. U.S. Postal Service Rates for Letters and Postcards: 1991 to 2024

[In dollars. For 1st class retail mail. Prior to 2013, international rates exclude Canada and Mexico]

Domestic mail date of rate change	Letters First ounce	Letters Each added ounce	Post-cards	Express mail—first 1/2 pound [1]	International air mail date of rate change	Letters	Post-cards
1991 (Feb. 3)............	0.29	0.23	0.19	9.95	**First 1/2 ounce**		
1995 (Jan. 1)............	0.32	0.23	0.20	10.75	1991 (Feb. 3)........................	0.50	0.40
1999 (Jan. 10)..........	0.33	0.22	0.20	11.75	1995 (July 9)........................	0.60	0.40
2001 (Jan. 7)...........	0.34	0.21	0.20	12.25	1999 (Jan. 10).......................	0.60	0.50
2001 (July 1)...........	0.34	0.23	0.21	12.45	**First ounce** [2]		
2002 (June 30).........	0.37	0.23	0.23	13.65	2001 (Jan. 7)........................	0.80	0.70
2006 (Jan. 8)...........	0.39	0.24	0.24	14.40	2006 (Jan. 8)........................	0.84	0.75
2007 (May 14)..........	0.41	0.17	0.26	16.25	2007 (May 14).......................	0.90	0.90
2008 (May 12)..........	0.42	0.17	0.27	12.60 to 19.50	2008 (May 12).......................	0.94	0.94
2009 (May 11)..........	0.44	0.17	0.28	13.05 to 21.20	2009 (May 11).......................	0.98	0.98
2010 (Jan. 4)..........	0.44	0.17	0.28	13.65 to 22.20	2010 (no change)....................	0.98	0.98
2011 (Apr. 17).........	0.44	0.20	0.29	13.25 to 26.65	2011 (no change)....................	0.98	0.98
2012 (Jan. 22).........	0.45	0.20	0.32	12.95 to 28.00	2012 (Jan. 22)......................	1.05	1.05
2013 (Jan. 27).........	0.46	0.20	0.33	14.10 to 30.60	2013 (Jan. 27)......................	1.10	1.10
2014 (Jan. 26).........	0.49	0.21	0.34	16.95 to 38.05	2014 (Jan. 26)......................	1.15	1.15
2015 (May 31).........	0.49	0.22	0.35	16.95 to 38.05	2015 (May 31)......................	1.20	1.20
2016 (Apr. 10).........	0.47	0.21	0.34	22.95 to 38.05	2016 (Apr. 10).....................	1.15	1.15
2017 (Jan. 22).........	0.49	0.21	0.34	23.75 to 39.40	2017 (no change)...................	1.15	1.15
2018 (Jan. 21).........	0.50	0.21	0.35	24.70 to 40.95	2018 (no change)...................	1.15	1.15
2019 (Jan. 27).........	0.55	0.15	0.35	25.50 to 47.70	2019 (no change)...................	1.15	1.15
2020 (Jan. 26).........	0.55	0.15	0.35	26.35 to 50.60	2020 (Jan. 26).....................	1.20	1.20
2021 (Jan. 24).........	0.55	0.20	0.36	26.35 to 53.10	2021 (Jan. 24).....................	1.20	1.20
2021 (Aug. 29).........	0.58	0.20	0.40	26.35 to 53.10	2021 (Aug. 29).....................	1.30	1.30
2022 (Jan. 9)..........	0.58	0.20	0.40	26.95 to 56.00	2022 (Jan. 9)......................	1.30	1.30
2022 (Jul. 10).........	0.60	0.24	0.44	26.95 to 56.00	2022 (Jul. 10).....................	1.40	1.40
2022 (Oct. 2)..........	0.60	0.24	0.44	27.25 to 57.00	2022 (Oct. 2)......................	1.40	1.40
2023 (Jan. 22).........	0.63	0.24	0.48	28.75 to 56.00	2023 (Jan. 22).....................	1.45	1.45
2023 (July 9)..........	0.66	0.24	0.51	28.75 to 56.00	2023 (July 9)......................	1.50	1.50
2024 (Jan 21)..........	0.68	0.24	0.53	30.45 to 61.60	2024 (Jan 21)......................	1.55	1.55
2024 (July 14).........	0.73	0.28	0.56	30.45 to 61.60	2024 (July 14).....................	1.65	1.65

[1] On May 12, 2008, the Postal Service initiated a zoned pricing structure for Express Mail. Price range reflects starting retail price from Zones 1 and 2 to Zone 8 and, beginning 2014, to Zone 9. [2] International letter prices after the first ounce vary according to the price group that is applicable to each destination country.

Source: U.S. Postal Service, *Domestic Rate History*, July 2009; and "Price List Notice 123," <pe.usps.com/text/dmm300/Notice123.htm>, accessed July 2024.

Information and Communications

This section presents statistics on the various information and communications media: publishing, including newspapers, periodicals, books, and software; motion pictures, sound recordings, and broadcasting; telecommunications; computers, and internet access and use; and information services, such as libraries.

Information industry—The U.S. Census Bureau's *Service Annual Survey* provides estimates of revenues and expenses of firms in the information sector. Data are based on the North American Industry Classification System (NAICS). The information sector comprises establishments engaged in the following: (1) producing and distributing information and cultural products, (2) providing the means to transmit or distribute these products as well as data or communications, and (3) processing data.

The main components of the information sector include the publishing industries, including software publishing, and both traditional publishing and publishing exclusively on the internet; the motion picture and sound recording industries; the broadcasting industries, including traditional broadcasting and broadcasting over the internet (streaming); the telecommunications industries; and web search portals, data processing industries, and information services.

Telecommunications encompasses wired (including broadband internet service), wireless (including mobile), and satellite telecommunications. Broadcasting covers radio, television, and cable and other subscription programming. Internet publishing and broadcasting and web search portals are grouped together.

The NAICS is periodically updated. The information sector in particular has been subject to changes to reflect developments in communications and other technology. Major revisions in many communications industries affect the comparability of these data over time. For detailed information about NAICS, see <www.census.gov/naics/>. See also the text in Section 15, Business Enterprise.

The 1997 Economic Census was the first to cover the new information sector of the economy. The Economic Census is conducted every 5 years for the years ending in "2" and "7," and provides information on the number of establishments, receipts, payroll, and paid employees for the United States and various geographic levels in the U.S., including the U.S. territories. Data in this section are from the 2017 Economic Census. Data from the 2022 Economic Census are being released on a flow basis between January 2024 and March 2026.

In 2018, the Bureau of Economic Analysis began producing statistics to measure the digital economy. The BEA developed a digital economy satellite account to provide economic measures on the infrastructure that enables a digital economy, electronic commerce transactions, priced digital services (computing and communication services performed for a fee charged to the consumer), and federal nondefense digital services (the annual budget for federal nondefense government agencies whose services are directly

related to supporting the digital economy). The digital economy satellite account covers goods and services that are primarily digital, and the digital portion of goods and services categories that include a mix of both digital and nondigital goods and services. Please note that BEA's digital economy satellite account has been discontinued following the last update released in December 2023.

The Federal Communications Commission (FCC), established in 1934, regulates interstate and international communications by radio, television, wireline and wireless technologies, satellite, and cable across the entire U.S. Providers and carriers that provide telecommunications services are required to file annual financial reports, which are publicly available. The FCC has jurisdiction over interstate and foreign communication services but not over intrastate or local services. The gross operating revenues of the telephone carriers reporting publicly available data annually to the FCC are estimated to cover about 90 percent of the revenues of all U.S. telephone companies. Data are not comparable with Census Bureau's *Service Annual Survey* because of coverage and different accounting practices for those telephone companies which report to the FCC.

Reports filed by the broadcasting industry cover all radio and television stations operating in the United States. Private radio services represent the largest and most diverse group of licensees regulated by the FCC. These services provide voice, data communications, point-to-point, and point-to-multipoint radio communications for fixed and mobile communicators. Major users of these services are small businesses, the aviation industry, the maritime trades, the land transportation industry, the manufacturing industry, state and local public safety and governmental authorities, emergency medical service providers, amateur radio operators, and personal radio operations (CB and the General Mobile Radio Service). The FCC also licenses entities as private and common carriers. Private and common carriers provide fixed and land mobile communications service on a for-profit basis.

Statistics on publishing are available from the Census Bureau and various private agencies. Data on public libraries are from the Institute of Museums and Library Services. The Pew Research Center in Washington D.C. collects data on media use, including the internet and social media, and of mobile electronic devices, among the general public. MRI-Simmons (launched as a joint venture under GfK in 2019) also collects data on internet use, and use of other traditional media.

Statistical reliability—For a discussion of statistical collection and estimation, sampling procedures, and measures of statistical reliability applicable to Census Bureau data, see Appendix III.

Table 1161. Information Industries—Type of Establishment, Employees, and Payroll: 2022

[Employees in thousands (3,634 represents 3,634,000); payroll in millions of dollars (515,681 represents $515,681,000,000). Excludes self-employed individuals, employees of private households, railroad employees, agricultural production employees, and most government employees. For more information, see source and Appendix III]

Industry	NAICS code [1]	Establishments				Employees [6] (1,000)	Annual payroll (mil. dol.)
		Total [2]	Corpora- tions [3]	Partner- ships [4]	Non- profits [5]		
Information industries.....................	**51**	**160,946**	**130,494**	**19,140**	**5,343**	**3,634**	**515,681**
Publishing industries (except internet)...............	511	32,109	26,583	3,126	774	1,153	194,390
Newspaper, periodical, book, and directory........	5111	14,671	11,402	1,526	730	278	21,616
Newspaper publishers...............................	51111	6,096	4,810	655	173	112	6,556
Periodical publishers................................	51112	4,175	3,164	467	299	66	6,674
Book publishers.....................................	51113	2,440	1,833	195	206	68	6,309
Directory and mailing list publishers...............	51114	526	447	54	5	12	1,063
Other publishers....................................	51119	1,434	1,148	155	47	20	1,014
Greeting card publishers.........................	511191	113	95	12	(NA)	13	427
All other publishers..............................	511199	1,321	1,053	143	47	7	587
Software publishers..................................	5112	17,438	15,181	1,600	44	875	172,774
Motion picture and sound recording industries.......	512	30,371	25,040	3,227	647	308	21,819
Motion picture and video industries................	5121	25,913	21,535	2,696	574	283	18,787
Motion picture and video production..............	51211	17,683	15,136	1,560	267	140	13,657
Motion picture and video distribution..............	51212	480	373	58	21	3	324
Motion picture and video exhibition..............	51213	4,390	3,035	841	271	110	2,004
Motion picture theaters (except drive-ins)........	512131	4,158	2,921	793	269	109	1,971
Drive-in motion picture theaters.................	512132	232	114	48	(NA)	1	33
Postproduction and other motion picture and video industries...........................	51219	3,360	2,991	237	15	30	2,801
Teleproduction and other post- production services............................	512191	3,079	2,755	213	10	29	2,694
Other motion picture and video industries........	512199	281	236	24	5	1	107
Sound recording industries.........................	5122	4,458	3,505	531	73	26	3,033
Music publishers..................................	51223	886	686	112	9	6	603
Sound recording studios...........................	51224	2,117	1,697	231	14	6	469
Record production and distribution................	51225	880	677	133	11	12	1,785
Other sound recording industries..................	51229	575	445	55	39	2	176
Broadcasting (except internet).......................	515	7,746	5,294	1,095	1,069	272	28,043
Radio and television broadcasting..................	5151	7,010	4,807	1,022	916	218	19,950
Radio broadcasting................................	51511	4,804	3,221	728	660	71	5,473
Radio networks.................................	515111	600	396	48	133	9	1,070
Radio stations.................................	515112	4,204	2,825	680	527	62	4,404
Television broadcasting...........................	51512	2,206	1,586	294	256	147	14,477
Cable and other subscription programming........	5152	736	487	73	153	54	8,093
Telecommunications.................................	517	60,182	49,862	8,826	253	940	81,795
Wired and wireless telecommunications carriers...	5173	54,556	45,724	7,610	242	864	74,632
Wired telecommunications carriers................	517311	28,758	27,569	729	231	604	55,667
Wireless telecommunications carriers (except satellite)...............................	517312	25,798	18,155	6,881	11	260	18,965
Satellite telecommunications.........................	5174	460	389	43	3	9	1,147
Other telecommunications..........................	5179	5,166	3,749	1,173	8	67	6,016
Telecommunications resellers....................	517911	3,264	2,277	909	(NA)	36	2,376
All other telecommunications....................	517919	1,902	1,472	264	7	31	3,639
Data processing, hosting, and related services.....	518	17,539	14,957	1,761	143	570	83,194
Other information services..........................	519	12,999	8,758	1,105	2,457	391	106,439
News syndicates...................................	51911	355	291	13	41	6	746
Libraries and archives..............................	51912	2,299	164	15	2,075	24	972
Internet publishing and broadcasting and web search portals............................	51913	9,180	7,380	970	287	349	103,453
All other information services.......................	51919	1,165	923	107	54	11	1,269

NA Not available. [1] 2017 North American Industry Classification System; see text, this section and Section 15. [2] Includes other types of establishments not shown separately. [3] Includes C- and S-Corporations. [4] An unincorporated business where two or more persons join to carry on a trade or business with each having a shared financial interest in the business. [5] An organization that does not distribute surplus funds to its owners or shareholders, but instead uses surplus funds to help pursue its goals. Most non-profit organizations are exempt from income taxes. [6] For employees on the payroll for the pay period including March 12.

Source: U.S. Census Bureau, County Business Patterns, "County Business Patterns, including ZIP Code Business Patterns, by Legal Form of Organization and Employment Size Class for the U.S., States, and Selected Geographies: 2022," <data.census.gov/>, accessed June 2024. See also <www.census.gov/programs-surveys/cbp.html>.

Table 1162. Information Industries—Establishments, Revenue, Payroll, and Employees by Kind of Business: 2017

[1,582,098 represents $1,582,098,000,000. For establishments with payroll. Based on the 2017 Economic Census; see Appendix III]

Kind of business	2017 NAICS code [1]	Establish-ments	Receipts [2] (mil. dol.)	Annual payroll (mil. dol.)	Paid employees (1,000)
Information.................	**51**	**153,928**	**1,582,098**	**360,580**	**3,565**
Publishing industries (except internet) [3]...............	511	29,755	368,107	124,857	1,016
Newspaper publishers.............	51111	7,230	26,012	7,799	174
Periodical publishers.............	51112	5,283	26,733	6,803	87
Book publishers.............	51113	2,462	29,116	5,647	75
Software publishers.............	5112	13,371	276,234	102,415	647
Motion picture & sound recording industries.............	512	25,818	102,088	18,134	341
Motion picture & video industries.............	5121	22,118	88,587	15,795	317
Sound recording industries [3].............	5122	3,700	13,501	2,339	24
Music publishers.............	51223	709	4,653	535	6
Sound recording studios.............	51224	1,863	922	294	5
Record production and distribution.............	51225	690	7,344	1,323	9
Broadcasting (except internet).............	515	8,269	165,970	23,339	262
Radio broadcasting.............	51511	5,440	20,627	5,479	91
Television broadcasting.............	51512	2,123	56,242	10,597	118
Cable & other subscription programming.............	5152	706	89,101	7,262	52
Telecommunications.............	517	60,474	616,800	82,025	1,085
Wired telecommunications carriers.............	517311	30,332	320,758	56,657	707
Wireless telecommunications carriers (except satellite).............	517312	25,736	254,082	19,776	312
Satellite telecommunications.............	5174	441	5,742	900	9
Other telecommunications.............	5179	3,965	36,218	4,692	57
Data processing, hosting, and related services.............	518	17,693	157,477	53,787	553
Other information services [3].............	519	11,919	171,655	58,437	309
Internet publishing & broadcasting and web search portals.............	51913	8,136	165,430	56,351	267

[1] North American Industry Classification System, 2017; see text, this section and Section 15. [2] Includes value of sales, shipments, receipts, or revenue. [3] Includes other kinds of businesses not shown separately.

Source: U.S. Census Bureau, 2017 Economic Census, "EC1751BASIC: Information: Summary Statistics for the U.S., States, and Selected Geographies: 2017," <data.census.gov/>, accessed February 2021.

Table 1163. Information Industries—Establishments, Payroll, and Employees by State and Island Area: 2022

[Annual payroll in millions of dollars (515,681 represents $515,681,000,000). Based on Census Bureau's County Business Patterns program. Data based on 2017 North American Industry Classification System (NAICS) code 51]

State and Island area	Establish-ments	Annual payroll (mil. dol.)	Paid employees [1]	State and Island area	Establish-ments	Annual payroll (mil. dol.)	Paid employees [1]
United States.......	**160,946**	**515,681**	**3,634,012**	Montana.............	711	509	7,626
Alabama.............	1,868	2,174	29,246	Nebraska.............	972	1,867	23,211
Alaska.............	429	577	7,054	Nevada.............	1,645	1,953	20,408
Arizona.............	2,718	4,753	54,214	New Hampshire.......	757	1,643	13,907
Arkansas.............	1,180	1,454	18,858	New Jersey.............	3,786	10,135	83,133
California.............	27,835	176,082	794,947	New Mexico.............	881	571	8,994
Colorado.............	3,823	11,829	94,785	New York.............	12,452	49,973	328,753
Connecticut.............	1,756	4,281	35,704	North Carolina.........	4,083	9,624	90,079
Delaware.............	930	897	7,711	North Dakota...........	379	480	6,581
District of Columbia...	848	3,842	26,867	Ohio.............	4,305	6,860	88,774
Florida.............	10,345	17,810	171,894	Oklahoma.............	1,583	1,506	23,371
Georgia.............	5,100	14,741	125,853	Oregon.............	2,425	3,942	37,511
Hawaii.............	582	573	7,614	Pennsylvania.........	5,535	10,763	108,508
Idaho.............	928	1,739	18,325	Rhode Island.........	456	564	6,674
Illinois.............	5,639	13,485	115,210	South Carolina.......	1,748	2,559	32,995
Indiana.............	2,314	3,397	37,950	South Dakota.........	471	355	5,951
Iowa.............	1,620	1,927	31,619	Tennessee.............	2,973	3,780	47,691
Kansas.............	1,447	2,282	25,316	Texas.............	11,517	29,154	269,488
Kentucky.............	1,964	1,611	26,676	Utah.............	2,028	7,212	63,419
Louisiana.............	1,589	1,207	18,880	Vermont.............	491	539	6,396
Maine.............	817	717	9,538	Virginia.............	3,929	11,483	92,833
Maryland.............	2,471	5,108	48,719	Washington.............	4,051	46,032	184,141
Massachusetts........	3,645	20,726	130,330	West Virginia.........	664	439	7,105
Michigan.............	3,999	5,506	60,995	Wisconsin.............	2,429	5,436	52,150
Minnesota.............	2,632	5,964	57,880	Wyoming.............	531	238	4,054
Mississippi.............	1,048	630	10,836	Guam.............	52	75	1,725
Missouri.............	2,617	4,752	53,238	Puerto Rico.............	746	783	16,062

[1] Number of paid employees for pay period including March 12.

Source: U.S. Census Bureau, County Business Patterns, "All Sectors: County Business Patterns, including ZIP Code Business Patterns, by Legal Form of Organization and Employment Size Class for the U.S., States, and Selected Geographies: 2022," <data.census.gov/>, accessed June 2024.

Table 1164. Digital Economy—Value Added, Gross Output, Employment, and Compensation by Industry: 2020 and 2022

[In billions of dollars (2,180.1 represents $2,180,100,000,000), except as noted. Estimates are based on goods and services that are primarily digital and partially digital (mix of digital and nondigital components—only the digital portion is covered). BEA includes in its definition of the digital economy: (1) infrastructure, primarily information and communications technology (ICT) goods and services that support computer networks and the digital economy; (2) electronic commerce (e-commerce), the sale of goods and services over computer networks; (3) priced digital services, computing and communication services performed for a fee charged to the consumer; and (4) federal nondefense digital services, which represents the annual budget for federal government agencies whose services are directly related to supporting the digital economy. Industries are based on 2017 North American Classification System (NAICS). For more information, see <www.bea.gov/data/special-topics/digital-economy>]

Industry	Value added (bil. dol.) [1]		Gross output (bil. dol.) [1]		Employees (1,000)		Employee compensation (bil. dol.)	
	2020	2022	2020	2022	2020	2022	2020	2022
All industries	**2,180.1**	**2,569.5**	**3,460.3**	**4,269.6**	**8,021**	**8,857**	**1,050.3**	**1,264.3**
Private industries	**2,169.8**	**2,559.1**	**3,449.4**	**4,258.5**	**7,967**	**8,808**	**1,045.3**	**1,259.6**
Mining	0.5	0.5	0.6	0.6	1	1	0.1	0.1
Utilities	0.6	0.7	0.7	0.9	1	1	0.1	0.1
Construction	0.4	0.4	0.4	0.4	2	1	0.1	0.1
Manufacturing	193.8	219.3	255.1	303.5	774	798	111.6	123.9
Durable goods [2]	182.7	206.3	242.6	288.3	753	776	109.7	121.8
Machinery	8.0	10.7	11.4	15.4	30	35	5.0	6.7
Computer and electronic products	163.3	182.3	213.8	251.0	677	692	100.5	110.5
Electrical equipment, appliances, and components	5.2	6.1	10.7	13.8	24	26	2.3	2.5
Nondurable goods	11.1	13.0	12.5	15.1	21	22	1.9	2.2
Wholesale trade	431.2	502.2	756.0	967.5	1,838	1,981	203.2	243.9
Retail trade	169.3	193.3	280.3	361.8	613	675	42.1	48.1
Transportation and warehousing	8.2	11.5	14.5	22.0	55	61	4.1	5.0
Information	853.2	1,024.2	1,429.8	1,735.3	1,733	1,977	284.5	352.4
Publishing, except internet (includes software)	240.3	295.6	334.4	438.9	598	598	101.4	130.7
Motion picture and sound recording	25.8	34.8	51.2	69.1	91	134	13.0	18.5
Broadcasting and telecommunications	406.4	430.9	726.1	778.0	728	701	89.3	92.8
Data processing, internet publishing, and other information services	180.9	262.9	318.2	449.3	317	543	80.9	110.3
Finance, insurance, real estate, rental, and leasing	6.8	7.0	6.8	7.0	16	15	2.0	2.1
Professional and business services [2]	482.6	575.9	674.6	825.8	2,687	3,044	382.0	468.1
Computer systems design & related svcs	381.0	445.5	533.0	647.4	2,124	2,393	314.7	384.8
Educational services	10.4	11.8	14.7	16.8	127	133	8.1	8.9
Health care and social assistance	3.9	4.3	3.9	4.4	24	24	2.0	2.1
Arts, entertainment, recreation, accommodation, and food services	0.6	0.8	0.6	1.0	5	7	0.2	0.3
Other services, except government	8.3	7.0	11.1	11.3	93	91	5.1	4.4
Government	**10.3**	**10.4**	**10.9**	**11.1**	**54**	**48**	**4.9**	**4.7**
Federal	4.9	4.8	5.1	5.0	19	16	2.1	2.0
State and local	5.4	5.6	5.8	6.2	35	33	2.8	2.7

[1] Estimates are based on data valued in purchasers' prices (instead of producers' prices), which include wholesale and retail trade margins and transportation costs, and sales and excise taxes collected and remitted by producers. [2] Includes other industries not shown separately.

Source: U.S. Bureau of Economic Analysis, Special Topics: Digital Economy, "Data: 2017-2022," December 2023, <www.bea.gov/data/special-topics/digital-economy>.

Table 1165. Digital Economy—Value Added and Gross Output by Commodity: 2019 to 2022

[In billions of dollars (2,062.1 represents $2,062,100,000,000). Estimates cover goods and services that are primarily digital, and the digital portion of partially digital goods and services. See headnote, Table 1164]

Commodity	Value added (GDP) [1,2]				Gross output [2]			
	2019	2020	2021	2022	2019	2020	2021	2022
Digital economy, total	**2,062.1**	**2,180.1**	**2,398.4**	**2,569.5**	**3,303.6**	**3,460.3**	**3,885.2**	**4,269.6**
Digital-enabling infrastructure	708.0	755.8	841.5	901.1	1,005.5	1,053.6	1,187.0	1,322.7
Hardware	245.3	254.9	275.6	293.9	380.9	385.9	430.7	476.5
Software	462.7	500.8	565.9	607.2	624.7	667.7	756.3	846.2
E-commerce	458.4	516.0	552.3	599.7	820.9	888.4	1,024.2	1,141.4
Business-to-business	336.1	355.3	371.3	413.5	617.7	617.6	704.7	788.9
Business-to-consumer	122.3	160.7	181.0	186.2	203.1	270.8	319.4	352.6
Priced digital services	895.3	908.0	1,004.3	1,068.5	1,476.8	1,517.9	1,673.5	1,805.0
Cloud services	95.7	118.6	154.8	191.9	159.2	194.4	243.0	303.7
Telecommunications services	450.5	430.0	449.3	464.8	779.6	776.2	816.9	847.5
Internet and data services	129.4	129.9	154.8	154.3	217.4	215.1	250.7	259.1
All other priced digital services	219.6	229.4	245.4	257.5	320.6	332.1	362.8	394.7
Federal nondefense digital services	0.3	0.3	0.3	0.3	0.4	0.4	0.4	0.5

[1] Value added by commodity is prepared by (1) calculating ratios of commodity output to total industry output for each industry and digital commodity, (2) applying these ratios to each industry's value added, and (3) aggregating the result by digital commodity. [2] These estimates are based on data valued in purchasers' prices (instead of producers' prices), which include wholesale and retail trade margins and transportation costs, and sales and excise taxes collected and remitted by producers.

Source: U.S. Bureau of Economic Analysis, Special Topics: Digital Economy, "Data: 2017-2022," December 2023, <www.bea.gov/data/special-topics/digital-economy>.

Table 1166. Information Sector Services—Estimated Revenue and Expenses: 2020 to 2022

[In millions of dollars (1,799,807 represents $1,799,807,000,000). For all employer firms regardless of tax status. Data are based on the 2012 North American Industry Classification System (NAICS). Estimates have been adjusted using results of the 2017 Economic Census where applicable. Based on the Service Annual Survey and administrative data; see Appendix III]

Industry	NAICS code	Operating revenue			Operating expenses		
		2020	2021	2022	2020	2021	2022
Information industries................	**51**	**1,799,807**	**2,034,704**	**2,186,845**	**1,300,227**	**1,472,592**	**1,560,820**
Publishing industries (except internet)......................	511	430,547	486,814	541,742	292,258	342,711	391,459
Newspaper publishers...........................	51111	22,149	22,208	23,195	21,465	20,690	21,967
Periodical publishers...........................	51112	24,030	26,013	27,592	18,900	20,050	21,194
Book publishers.............................	51113	25,552	27,558	28,935	16,076	16,521	17,863
Directory and mailing list publishers......................	51114	4,409	4,368	4,582	3,704	(S)	3,184
Greeting card publishers........................	511191	2,931	2,927	2,601	1,772	1,543	1,499
All other publishers...........................	511199	1,340	1,350	1,288	768	877	747
Software publishers.............................	5112	350,136	402,390	453,549	229,573	279,723	325,005
Motion picture and sound recording industries............	512	96,895	115,379	133,855	72,832	79,941	90,114
Motion picture and video production and distribution [1]....	5121x	71,056	82,151	92,891	48,151	52,658	58,666
Motion picture and video exhibition........................	51213	4,722	9,102	14,033	8,435	9,582	11,724
Teleproduction and other postproduction services.......	512191	4,153	4,468	4,882	3,324	3,633	4,168
Other motion picture and video industries...............	512199	277	371	426	159	196	244
Record production..........................	51221	319	451	552	237	284	361
Integrated record production/distribution...................	51222	8,987	10,768	11,776	8,702	9,330	10,268
Music publishers............................	51223	5,729	6,129	7,124	2,672	2,979	3,244
Sound recording studios........................	51224	1,133	1,295	1,423	809	911	999
Other sound recording industries..................	51229	519	644	748	343	368	440
Broadcasting (except internet)............................	515	170,800	186,820	189,942	121,746	137,332	139,115
Radio networks...............................	515111	9,773	10,051	10,877	9,691	10,422	10,751
Radio stations................................	515112	10,896	11,927	12,265	9,921	9,888	10,442
Television broadcasting........................	51512	63,882	71,352	74,383	50,786	58,940	60,078
Cable and other subscription programming...............	5152	86,249	93,490	92,417	51,348	58,082	57,844
Telecommunications...................................	517	629,396	655,524	666,715	471,304	499,445	497,226
Wired telecommunications carriers......................	5171	305,900	311,742	309,311	256,479	260,295	248,448
Wireless telecommunications carriers (except satellite)...	5172	278,868	295,280	308,153	181,153	205,565	213,827
Satellite telecommunications............................	5174	5,680	6,149	6,310	4,492	4,624	4,731
Telecommunications resellers......................	517911	19,129	20,507	19,864	11,945	12,394	12,528
All other telecommunications.....................	517919	19,819	21,846	23,077	17,235	16,567	17,692
Data processing, hosting, and related services.............	518	219,948	271,238	308,328	160,024	184,700	197,163
Other information services..................................	519	252,221	318,929	346,263	182,063	228,463	245,743
News syndicates..............................	51911	1,466	1,606	1,710	1,135	1,228	1,353
Libraries and archives.........................	51912	2,289	2,453	2,380	2,059	2,042	2,110
Internet publishing and broadcasting, and Web search portals...................	51913	245,601	311,658	338,743	176,611	222,734	239,799
Other information services.....................	51919	2,865	3,212	3,430	2,258	2,459	2,481

S Estimate does not meet publication standards. [1] Includes NAICS 51211 (Motion Picture and Video Production) and NAICS 51212 (Motion Picture and Video Distribution).

Source: U.S. Census Bureau, Service Annual Survey, "Service Annual Survey Latest Data (NAICS-basis): 2022," <www.census.gov/programs-surveys/sas/data/tables.html>, accessed February 2024.

Table 1167. Audience Use of Media by Type and Selected Characteristic: 2024

[In percent, except total population (257,420 represents 257,420,000). As of Spring 2024. For persons age 18 and over. Represents the percent of persons using each media type during an average week, except as noted. Based on a sample and subject to sampling error]

Audience characteristic	Total population (1,000)	Magazine reading [1]	Newspaper reading [2]	Radio/ audio listening	TV prime time viewing [3]	Spanish language TV network viewing	Internet use	Social media use
Total.....................	**257,420**	**73.7**	**19.9**	**79.0**	**80.6**	**8.3**	**93.8**	**81.3**
18 to 24 years old..........	29,519	71.7	11.7	72.8	66.6	11.1	94.1	90.8
25 to 34 years old..........	44,921	68.4	13.0	77.5	74.1	10.7	94.2	89.8
35 to 44 years old..........	43,505	70.1	15.3	81.9	77.0	10.0	95.3	88.4
45 to 54 years old..........	40,326	72.9	18.8	84.5	82.5	9.0	94.7	84.8
55 to 64 years old..........	42,219	75.6	22.6	81.5	87.0	6.7	94.1	77.4
65 years old and over......	56,931	80.9	31.8	75.3	89.5	4.2	91.5	64.4
Male........................	125,222	70.9	19.9	79.3	79.2	8.3	93.4	78.5
Female......................	132,198	76.4	19.9	78.6	81.9	8.2	94.2	83.9
White only..................	184,737	73.6	20.2	79.3	82.1	5.9	95.0	81.1
Black only..................	31,688	75.8	23.0	80.2	82.4	2.5	89.7	79.7
Other/multiple categories...	40,996	72.6	16.4	76.5	72.3	23.4	91.7	82.9
Employed:								
Full time...................	125,270	70.6	16.2	81.6	79.5	7.8	95.9	86.9
Part time...................	33,498	75.4	21.2	79.9	76.5	10.4	95.0	85.2
Not employed..............	98,652	77.1	24.1	75.3	83.4	8.1	90.8	72.7
Household income:								
Less than $50,000........	72,240	72.3	23.0	75.9	78.2	14.1	88.1	76.1
$50,000 to $74,999......	40,510	71.8	19.4	78.8	80.3	10.0	94.4	81.1
$75,000 to $149,999......	80,408	73.7	18.8	80.4	82.0	6.0	96.2	82.8
$150,000 or more.........	64,262	76.5	18.0	80.8	81.7	3.5	97.0	85.2

[1] One or more issues in a month. [2] One or more issues over a 28-day period. [3] Includes broadcast and cable TV.

Source: © MRI-Simmons Spring 2024 USA Study. Courtesy of MRI-Simmons. See also <www.mrisimmons.com/>.

Table 1168. Utilization and Number of Selected Media: 2000 to 2022

[100.2 represents 100,200,000]

Media	Unit	2000	2005	2010	2015	2017	2018	2019	2020	2021	2022
Households with—											
Telephones [1]	Millions	100.2	107.0	114.0	122.2	122.1	124.2	125.2	127.23	128.4	128.3
Telephone service [1]	Percent	94.1	92.9	95.5	96.3	95.8	96.0	95.8	97.2	96.7	96.7
Landline households with											
wireless telephone [2]	Percent	(X)	42.4	58.1	41.6	37.8	36.3	37.2	34.3	29.3	27.1
Wireless only [2]	Percent	(X)	7.3	26.6	47.4	52.5	54.9	59.2	62.5	68.0	70.7
Total broadcast stations [3, 4]	Number	(NA)	27,354	30,630	31,032	33,006	33,342	33,513	33,564	33,467	33,517
Radio stations	Number	(NA)	13,660	14,619	15,480	15,503	15,508	15,500	15,445	15,389	15,377
AM stations	Number	4,685	4,757	4,782	4,684	4,639	4,619	4,593	4,551	4,509	4,484
FM commercial	Number	5,892	6,231	6,526	6,701	6,744	6,754	6,772	6,699	6,676	6,686
FM educational	Number	(NA)	2,672	3,311	4,095	4,120	4,135	4,135	4,195	4,204	4,207
Television stations [3]	Number	1,663	1,750	1,781	1,782	1,767	1,761	1,762	1,758	1,758	1,758
Commercial	Number	1,288	1,370	1,390	1,387	1,377	1,373	1,374	1,371	1,373	1,375
UHF TV band	Number	721	782	1,022	1,031	1,013	1,006	1,004	994	999	1,006
VHF TV band	Number	567	588	368	356	364	367	370	377	374	369
Educational	Number	(NA)	380	391	395	390	388	388	387	385	383
UHF TV band	Number	(NA)	254	284	289	276	270	270	267	266	263
VHF TV band	Number	(NA)	126	107	106	114	118	118	120	119	120
Broadband internet connections: [5]											
Total fixed broadband [6]	Millions	6.8	47.8	84.5	102.1	108.1	110.8	114.3	121.3	125.8	126.4
25 Mbps/3 Mbps [7]	Millions	(NA)	(NA)	(NA)	54.3	73.9	83.0	90.5	101.6	110.6	113.1
Mobile wireless [8]	Millions	(NA)	(NA)	97.5	273.7	312.8	340.3	352.0	369.6	384.4	390.7
Residential fixed broadband [6]	Millions	5.2	44.0	76.9	93.4	98.8	101.4	104.7	111.6	115.8	116.6
25 Mbps/3 Mbps [7]	Millions	(NA)	(NA)	(NA)	51.8	69.4	76.9	83.7	94.5	102.8	105.0
Residential mobile wireless	Millions	(NA)	(NA)	72.5	229.1	253.1	276.9	283.6	296.0	320.8	325.1

NA Not available. X Not applicable. [1] As of November. Based on Current Population Survey. Source: Federal Communications Commission, prior to 2011, *Telephone Subscribership in the United States*, December 2011, and earlier reports. Beginning 2012, *Universal Service Monitoring Report, 2023*, annual. See also <www.fcc.gov/general/federal-state-joint-board-monitoring-reports>. [2] January to June. Based on National Health Interview Survey. For families living in the same housing unit. Source: U.S. National Center for Health Statistics, *Wireless Substitution: Early Release of Estimates From the National Health Interview Survey, January–June 2022*, December 2022, and earlier reports. [3] As of December 31. Source: Federal Communications Commission, "Broadcast Station Totals," <www.fcc.gov/media/broadcast-station-totals>, accessed June 2024. [4] Includes Class A UHF and VHF, UHF and VHF Low Power TV, UHF and VHF Translators, FM Translators and Boosters, and Low Power FM stations. [5] As of December, except data for 2022 are as of June 30. Internet access over 200 kilobits per second in at least one direction. Based on FCC Form 477. Source: Federal Communications Commission, Wireline Competition Bureau, *Internet Access Services: Status as of December 31, 2021*, August 2023 and previous reports; and *Internet Access Services: Status as of June 30, 2022*, May 2024. [6] Excludes terrestrial mobile wireless technologies. [7] Internet download and upload speeds, measured in megabits per second (Mbps). [8] Data prior to 2008 not shown due to reporting instruction changes on FCC Form 477.

Source: Compiled from sources mentioned in footnotes.

Table 1169. Publishing Industries—Estimated Revenue by Media Type and Source of Revenue: 2017 to 2022

[In millions of dollars (368,107 represents $368,107,000,000). Data are based on the 2012 North American Industry Classification System (NAICS). Estimates have been adjusted using results of the 2017 Economic Census where applicable. Based on the Service Annual Survey; see text, this section and Section 15, and Appendix III]

Media type and source of revenue	2017	2018	2019	2020	2021	2022
Publishing industries (except software), NAICS 511 [1]	**368,107**	**384,398**	**404,700**	**430,547**	**486,814**	**541,742**
Newspaper publishers, NAICS 51111	26,012	25,436	23,618	22,149	22,208	23,195
Subscription and sales	9,158	9,258	8,850	8,795	8,862	(S)
Advertising space	13,788	12,788	11,603	10,221	10,254	(S)
Printing services	1,153	1,163	1,185	1,066	1,022	1,170
Distribution services	544	455	436	411	362	368
All other operating revenue	1,369	1,772	1,544	1,656	1,708	(S)
Print newspapers	17,679	16,985	14,679	13,642	12,824	(S)
Online newspapers	5,207	5,011	5,723	5,332	6,244	(S)
Other media newspapers	60	(S)	(S)	(S)	(S)	(S)
Periodical publishers, NAICS 51112 [1]	26,733	25,795	26,409	24,030	26,013	27,592
Subscription and sales	9,194	8,513	9,766	9,168	9,731	(S)
Advertising space	12,787	11,034	9,949	8,967	8,604	9,326
Print periodicals	14,929	12,657	12,477	10,922	10,297	(S)
Online periodicals	6,237	6,673	7,087	7,080	7,828	(S)
Book publishers, NAICS 51113 [1]	29,116	27,978	27,056	25,552	27,558	28,935
Textbooks	10,240	9,135	8,389	7,849	(S)	8,835
Children's books	3,085	3,067	2,840	(S)	2,952	(S)
General reference books	340	265	287	250	272	(S)
Professional, technical, and scholarly books	(S)	(S)	(S)	(S)	(S)	(S)
Adult trade books	5,578	5,379	5,242	5,253	6,081	6,203
Print books	16,752	14,390	13,594	12,136	13,166	13,812
Online books	(S)	(S)	(S)	(S)	(S)	(S)
Other media books	(S)	1,439	939	1,034	1,091	(S)
Directory and mailing list publishers, NAICS 51114 [1]	4,968	5,090	4,623	4,409	4,368	4,582
Subscription and sales [2]	1,653	2,432	2,480	2,038	1,840	1,854
Advertising space [2]	2,770	2,066	1,618	1,781	(S)	(S)
Print directories, databases, and other information collections	1,759	1,582	1,238	1,717	(S)	(S)
Online directories, databases, and other information collections	2,332	2,716	2,791	1,979	(S)	(S)
Greeting card publishers operating revenue, NAICS 511191	3,732	3,552	3,004	2,931	2,927	2,601

S Figure does not meet publication standards. [1] Includes other industries or revenue sources not shown separately. [2] For directories, databases, and other collections of information.

Source: U.S. Census Bureau, Service Annual Survey, "Service Annual Survey Latest Data (NAICS-basis): 2022," <www.census.gov/programs-surveys/sas/data/tables.html>, accessed February 2024.

Table 1170. Software Publishers—Estimated Revenue, Expenses, and Inventories by Type: 2017 to 2022

[In millions of dollars (276,234 represents $276,234,000,000). For all employer firms regardless of tax status. Data are based on the 2012 North American Industry Classification System (NAICS), and cover NAICS 5112. Estimates have been adjusted using results of the 2017 Economic Census where applicable. Based on the Service Annual Survey; see text, this section, and Section 15, Business Enterprise. See also Appendix III]

Item	2017	2018	2019	2020	2021	2022
Operating revenue	**276,234**	**295,225**	**318,622**	**350,136**	**402,390**	**453,549**
System software publishing [1]	70,086	84,027	69,386	96,093	91,004	94,697
Operating system software	24,768	27,272	26,890	35,554	25,656	29,830
Network software	17,539	23,130	22,316	26,552	27,535	26,068
Database management software	16,662	17,072	17,765	18,968	24,681	26,259
Development tools and programming languages software	(S)	2,601	2,415	3,078	3,239	2,100
Application software publishing [1]	118,703	132,909	151,722	159,830	196,948	234,282
General business productivity and home use applications	58,389	64,879	83,752	89,140	102,918	130,519
Cross-industry application software	30,982	34,271	31,954	31,161	45,602	47,678
Vertical market application software	16,048	17,262	15,786	21,523	25,332	28,014
Utilities application software	2,953	4,057	4,428	(S)	7,257	8,298
Other services: [1]						
Custom application design and development	4,461	(S)	[2] 7,066	8,537	11,675	16,525
Information technology technical consulting services	11,300	11,502	11,933	18,070	24,224	28,859
Resale of computer hardware and software	9,784	10,917	14,940	13,892	14,972	16,320
Information technology-related training services	3,997	3,937	3,911	3,957	3,910	4,048
By software sales type:						
System software	72,632	84,027	83,402	96,093	91,004	94,697
Personal computer software	18,610	18,022	18,323	26,712	18,997	19,937
Enterprise or network software	34,312	44,536	42,136	45,741	46,921	46,987
Mainframe computer software	13,375	14,303	14,959	14,334	14,098	17,913
Other system software	6,335	7,166	7,984	9,306	10,988	9,860
Application software	118,703	132,909	151,722	164,954	196,948	234,282
Personal computer software	30,579	36,275	43,779	42,178	57,496	72,484
Enterprise or network software	58,013	65,528	78,054	86,859	96,148	111,581
Mainframe computer software	5,309	(S)	(S)	(S)	(S)	(S)
Other application software	24,802	29,513	28,198	34,086	41,823	(S)
Operating expenses, total [1]	**190,980**	**206,554**	**225,406**	**229,573**	**279,723**	**325,005**
Gross annual payroll	(NA)	(NA)	(NA)	104,674	124,066	142,863
Employer's cost for fringe benefits	(NA)	(NA)	(NA)	23,257	26,981	30,926
Temporary staff and leased employee expense	(NA)	(NA)	(NA)	5,035	5,742	7,926
Expensed purchases of software	(NA)	(NA)	(NA)	4,172	5,400	6,676
Data processing and other purchased computer services	(NA)	(NA)	(NA)	4,186	6,975	10,091
Purchased advertising and promotional services	(NA)	(NA)	(NA)	9,817	13,861	16,040
Purchased professional and technical services	(NA)	(NA)	(NA)	8,332	10,546	12,395
Depreciation and amortization charges	(NA)	(NA)	(NA)	18,294	24,967	(S)
Inventories at end of year, total	**3,988**	**4,607**	**5,673**	**9,574**	**4,912**	**5,592**
Finished goods	2,494	3,456	4,829	8,333	3,052	3,758
Works-in-process	1,091	913	(S)	(S)	(S)	(S)
Materials, supplies, fuel, etc	403	238	652	1,038	1,656	1,637

NA Not available. S Data do not meet publication standards. [1] Includes other sources of revenue and types of expenses not shown separately. [2] Estimated coefficient of variation is between 30 and 40 percent.

Source: U.S. Census Bureau, Service Annual Survey, "Service Annual Survey Latest Data (NAICS-basis): 2022," <www.census.gov/programs-surveys/sas/data/tables.html>, accessed February 2024.

Table 1171. Internet Publishing and Broadcasting, and Web Search Portals—Estimated Revenue and Expenses: 2017 to 2022

[In millions of dollars (165,430 represents $165,430,000,000). For all employer firms regardless of tax status. Data are based on the 2012 North American Industry Classification System (NAICS). Covers NAICS 51913. See headnote, Table 1170. See text, Section 15, and Appendix III]

Item	2017	2018	2019	2020	2021	2022
Operating revenue	**165,430**	**193,119**	**218,580**	**245,601**	**311,658**	**338,743**
Source of revenue:						
Publishing and broadcasting of content on the internet	44,212	50,889	51,312	57,339	67,953	72,463
Licensing of rights to use intellectual property	(S)	(S)	4,840	(S)	4,814	(S)
Online advertising space	106,605	126,000	145,922	166,255	218,856	239,025
All other operating revenue	11,268	12,717	16,506	17,609	20,035	(S)
Revenue by type of customer:						
Household consumers and individual users	49,392	58,035	57,478	(S)	64,036	64,377
Business firms, nonprofit organizations, and government	116,038	(S)	(S)	(S)	247,622	(S)
Operating expenses	**125,810**	**136,653**	**148,193**	**176,611**	**222,734**	**239,799**

S Data do not meet publication standards.

Source: U.S. Census Bureau, Service Annual Survey, "Service Annual Survey Latest Data (NAICS-basis): 2022," <www.census.gov/programs-surveys/sas/data/tables.html>, accessed February 2024.

Table 1172. Motion Picture and Sound Recording Industries—Estimated Revenue and Sources of Revenue: 2017 to 2022

[In millions of dollars (102,088 represents $102,088,000,000). For all employer firms regardless of tax status. Data are based on the 2012 North American Industry Classification System (NAICS). Covers NAICS 512. See headnote, Table 1170. See also Appendix III]

Kind of business and revenue source	2017	2018	2019	2020	2021	2022
Total revenue, NAICS 512	**102,088**	**111,365**	**113,385**	**96,895**	**115,379**	**133,855**
Motion picture and video production and distribution, NAICS 5121X [1,2]	67,300	73,951	74,923	71,056	82,151	92,891
Domestic licensing of rights to motion picture films	13,541	12,941	12,484	10,714	10,233	12,567
Domestic licensing of rights to television programs	14,123	16,170	17,071	17,833	21,980	23,425
International licensing of rights to motion picture films	6,614	6,646	6,902	(S)	(S)	(S)
International licensing of rights to television programs	3,602	3,573	(S)	(S)	(S)	5,043
Contract production of audiovisual works	6,035	6,087	7,054	6,041	8,702	9,386
Sale of audiovisual works for wholesale, retail, and rental markets	6,157	6,009	4,803	(S)	3,871	(S)
Motion picture and video exhibition, NAICS 51213 [1]	15,967	17,577	17,375	4,722	9,102	14,033
Admissions to feature film exhibitions	9,666	10,317	9,903	2,441	4,503	7,073
Food and beverage sales	5,085	5,625	5,690	1,434	3,099	4,939
Postproduction services and other motion picture and video industries, NAICS 51219 [1]	5,319	5,124	4,976	4,430	4,839	5,308
Audiovisual postproduction services	3,070	3,210	3,091	2,732	3,088	3,295
Motion picture film laboratory services	69	(S)	(S)	59	80	80
Integrated record production and distribution, NAICS 51222 [1]	7,048	7,715	8,467	8,987	10,768	11,776
Licensing revenue	550	601	548	604	692	850
Sales of recordings	5,607	6,165	6,879	7,295	8,764	9,532
Music publishers, NAICS 51223 [1]	4,653	5,035	5,476	5,729	6,129	7,124
Licensing of rights to use musical compositions	3,754	4,045	4,488	4,704	4,964	5,841
Sale of recordings	(S)	168	176	197	250	293
Print music	243	208	195	157	185	194
Sound recording studios, NAICS 51224 [1]	922	1,027	1,206	1,133	1,295	1,423
Studio recording	561	546	633	588	613	662

S Data do not meet publication standards. [1] Includes other sources of revenue not shown separately. [2] Includes NAICS 51211 (Motion Picture and Video Production) and NAICS 51212 (Motion Picture and Video Distribution).

Source: U.S. Census Bureau, Service Annual Survey, "Service Annual Survey Latest Data (NAICS-basis): 2022," <www.census.gov/programs-surveys/sas/data/tables.html>, accessed February 2024.

Table 1173. Recorded Music Industry—Estimated Retail Volume and Value: 2000 to 2023

[1,079.2 represents 1,079,200,000. Data are net after returns. Formats with no retail value equivalent included at wholesale value. Based on reports of Recording Industry Association of America member companies who distribute about 85 percent of the music sold in the U.S.]

Format	2000	2005	2010	2015	2019	2020	2021	2022	2023
VOLUME (million units)									
Total [1]	**1,079.2**	**1,301.9**	**1,739.5**	**1,255.5**	**442.4**	**356.0**	**342.0**	**282.1**	**249.0**
Physical [2]	**1,079.2**	**748.8**	**267.7**	**135.1**	**69.5**	**58.1**	**83.8**	**79.8**	**81.7**
Compact disk, album [3]	942.5	705.4	253.0	117.1	48.0	31.0	44.9	37.7	37.0
Compact disk, single	34.2	2.8	1.0	0.4	(Z)	(Z)	(Z)	0.4	(NA)
Vinyl LP/EP (long play/extended play)	2.2	1.0	4.2	13.7	19.8	25.6	36.7	40.5	43.2
Music video [4]	18.2	33.8	9.1	3.1	1.3	1.0	1.3	0.8	0.6
Digital [2]	**(NA)**	**554.4**	**1,473.3**	**1,131.2**	**433.3**	**373.4**	**342.2**	**293.9**	**264.1**
Download single	(NA)	366.9	1,177.4	986.3	325.3	255.2	219.4	172.5	142.0
Download album	(NA)	13.6	85.8	106.8	37.5	33.1	31.1	24.5	20.5
Mobile [5]	(NA)	170.0	188.5	21.9	8.3	8.1	6.3	4.4	4.1
Paid subscription [6]	(NA)	1.3	1.5	10.8	60.4	75.5	84.0	91.6	96.8
VALUE (million dollars) [12]									
Total	**14,323.7**	**12,289.9**	**7,013.8**	**6,710.8**	**11,116.2**	**12,168.7**	**15,023.4**	**15,893.2**	**17,115.1**
Physical [2]	**14,323.7**	**11,195.0**	**3,663.7**	**1,862.2**	**1,187.2**	**1,206.4**	**1,706.0**	**1,731.0**	**1,912.0**
Compact disk, album [3]	13,214.5	10,520.2	3,389.4	1,445.0	636.7	473.9	585.8	482.6	537.1
Vinyl LP/EP (long play/extended play)	27.7	14.2	88.9	333.4	515.5	696.4	1,086.3	1,224.4	1,350.2
Vinyl single	26.3	13.2	2.3	5.8	6.7	6.3	7.9	5.6	8.4
Music video [4]	281.9	602.2	177.6	70.4	26.6	27.4	19.9	11.3	10.7
Digital [2]	**(NA)**	**1,094.9**	**3,161.4**	**4,645.7**	**9,647.9**	**10,697.0**	**13,010.9**	**13,779.7**	**14,792.2**
Permanent download	(NA)	925.3	2,699.8	2,314.4	817.1	671.8	621.6	494.7	434.1
Download single	(NA)	363.3	1,336.4	1,185.2	403.0	310.4	268.9	214.1	190.8
Download album	(NA)	135.7	872.4	1,064.4	368.5	319.3	303.3	241.9	204.7
Mobile [5]	(NA)	421.6	448.0	54.6	20.6	20.2	15.7	11.0	10.5
Subscription and streaming	(NA)	169.6	461.6	2,331.3	8,830.8	10,025.2	12,389.3	13,285.0	14,358.1
Paid subscription [6]	(NA)	149.2	212.4	1,156.7	6,074.6	6,952.1	8,562.8	9,179.0	10,149.7
Limited tier paid subscription [7]	(NA)	(NA)	(NA)	(NA)	634.1	717.9	897.0	1,063.0	1,021.4
SoundExchange distributions [8]	(NA)	20.4	249.2	802.6	908.2	947.4	992.5	959.4	1,004.8
On-demand streaming [9]	(NA)	(NA)	(NA)	372.0	1,006.6	1,196.6	1,733.4	1,822.1	1,864.5
Other ad-supported streaming [10]	(NA)	(NA)	(NA)	(NA)	207.3	211.2	203.5	261.5	317.7
Synchronization royalties [11]	**(NA)**	**(NA)**	**188.7**	**202.9**	**281.1**	**265.2**	**306.5**	**382.5**	**410.9**

Z Represents less than 50,000. NA Not available. [1] Total volume excludes paid digital subscriptions. [2] Includes other media or digital formats not shown separately. [3] Prior to 2006, includes DualDisc. [4] Includes DVD video. [5] Master ringtones and ringbacks; prior to 2013, also included music videos, full length downloads, and other mobile. [6] Streaming, tethered, and other paid subscription services not operating under statutory licenses. Volume is annual average number of subscribers. [7] Includes streaming services with interactivity limitations by availability, device restriction, catalog limitations, on demand access, or other factors. [8] SoundExchange is a nonprofit organization that collects and distributes digital performance royalties on behalf of recording artists and master rights owners. [9] Advertising supported audio and music video services not operating under statutory licenses. [10] Includes revenues from services paid directly that are not distributed by SoundExchange and not included in other streaming categories. [11] Include fees and royalties from synchronization of sound recordings with other media. [12] In 2016, accounting standards updated.

Source: Recording Industry Association of America, Washington, D.C., Facts & Research, *Year-End 2023 RIAA Revenue Statistics* ©, Spring 2024, <www.riaa.com/reports/>.

Table 1174. Radio and Television Broadcasting—Estimated Revenue and Expenses: 2017 to 2022

[In millions of dollars (61,695 represents $61,695,000,000). For all employer firms regardless of tax status. Based on the 2012 North American Industry Classification System (NAICS). Estimates have been adjusted using results of the 2017 Economic Census where applicable. Based on the Service Annual Survey; see text, this section, and Section 15, Business Enterprise]

Item	2017	2018	2019	2020	2021	2022
RADIO AND TELEVISION BROADCASTING (NAICS 5151)						
Operating expenses, total	**61,695**	**66,293**	**70,103**	**70,398**	**79,250**	**81,271**
Gross annual payroll	(NA)	(NA)	(NA)	14,259	15,158	17,419
Employer's cost for fringe benefits	(NA)	(NA)	(NA)	2,465	2,242	2,577
Broadcast rights and music license fees	(NA)	(NA)	(NA)	12,235	13,697	15,756
Network compensation fees (networks only)	(NA)	(NA)	(NA)	3,320	3,272	3,688
RADIO NETWORKS (NAICS 515111)						
Total operating revenue	**7,922**	**8,361**	**8,910**	**9,773**	**10,051**	**10,877**
National/regional/local air time	1,851	1,991	2,347	2,933	2,766	3,246
Public and non-commercial programming services	431	465	458	503	428	442
All other operating revenue	5,640	5,905	6,105	6,337	6,857	7,189
Operating expenses, total	**5,822**	**6,194**	**7,908**	**9,691**	**10,422**	**10,751**
RADIO STATIONS (NAICS 515112)						
Total operating revenue	**12,705**	**12,787**	**12,622**	**10,896**	**11,927**	**12,265**
National/regional/local air time	10,832	10,804	10,658	8,587	9,181	9,431
Public and non-commercial programming services	795	805	782	788	921	964
All other operating revenue	1,078	1,178	1,182	1,521	1,825	1,870
Operating expenses, total	**10,903**	**11,323**	**11,368**	**9,921**	**9,888**	**10,442**
TELEVISION BROADCASTING (NAICS 51512)						
Total operating revenue	**56,242**	**61,322**	**62,421**	**63,882**	**71,352**	**74,383**
National/regional/local air time	36,064	39,816	40,426	40,041	43,956	45,231
Public and non-commercial programming services	1,980	2,225	2,240	3,587	3,946	3,851
All other operating revenue	18,198	19,281	19,755	20,254	23,450	25,301
Operating expenses, total	**44,970**	**48,776**	**50,827**	**50,786**	**58,940**	**60,078**

NA Not available.

Source: U.S. Census Bureau, Service Annual Survey, "Service Annual Survey Latest Data (NAICS-basis): 2022," <www.census.gov/programs-surveys/sas/data/tables.html>, accessed February 2024.

Table 1175. Cable and Other Subscription Programming—Estimated Revenue and Expenses: 2017 to 2022

[In millions of dollars (89,101 represents $89,101,000,000). For all employer firms regardless of tax status. Based on the 2012 North American Industry Classification System. Covers NAICS 5152. See headnote, Table 1174. See text, this section and Section 15, and Appendix III]

Item	2017	2018	2019	2020	2021	2022
Operating revenue, total	**89,101**	**91,424**	**84,740**	**86,249**	**93,490**	**92,417**
Advertising and program revenue [1]	55,775	58,248	53,253	54,925	58,559	57,175
Air time	28,771	27,379	26,057	25,260	29,050	28,768
All other operating services revenue	4,555	5,797	5,430	6,064	5,881	6,474
Operating expenses, total [2]	**53,111**	**55,006**	**50,965**	**51,348**	**58,082**	**57,844**

[1] Licensing of rights to broadcast specialty programming protected by copyright.

Source: U.S. Census Bureau, Service Annual Survey, "Service Annual Survey Latest Data (NAICS-basis): 2022," <www.census.gov/programs-surveys/sas/data/tables.html>, accessed February 2024.

Table 1176. Telecommunications Industry Revenue by Service Type: 2010 to 2022

[Revenue in millions of dollars (446,386 represents $446,386,000,000). Data are based on carrier Form 499-A filings to the Federal Communications Commission, and are the basis for establishing Universal Service Fund (USF) program collections]

Category	Revenue (mil. dol.)						
	2010	2017	2018	2019	2020	2021	2022
Total reported revenue	446,386	504,516	507,474	511,692	512,497	545,482	561,341
Non-telecommunications revenue	173,228	321,597	337,212	361,245	379,509	422,670	443,356
Total telecommunications revenue	**273,158**	**182,918**	**170,262**	**150,447**	**132,989**	**122,812**	**117,985**
Local service and payphone revenue	**102,847**	**83,572**	**77,048**	**72,964**	**65,576**	**61,847**	**59,907**
Local exchange	43,878	23,208	20,771	18,806	16,115	14,995	13,382
Pay telephone	197	269	265	280	286	311	268
Local private line	26,809	30,272	26,906	25,560	21,608	19,619	19,995
Voice over internet protocol (VoIP) local	8,234	14,428	14,503	14,355	14,317	13,722	13,229
Other local	3,032	1,749	1,710	1,265	1,164	1,117	1,090
Federal and State USF support	4,880	5,904	5,994	6,422	6,484	7,349	7,779
Subscriber line charges	7,481	4,431	4,049	3,700	3,345	2,940	2,557
Access	8,336	3,312	2,850	2,575	2,257	1,793	1,607
Mobile service revenue	**111,643**	**56,952**	**52,890**	**39,631**	**33,379**	**28,688**	**28,840**
Toll service revenue	**50,006**	**34,075**	**31,885**	**29,405**	**25,975**	**23,151**	**21,443**
Operator	3,585	1,844	1,810	1,711	1,464	1,481	1,330
VoIP toll	1,943	3,768	3,925	3,518	2,491	2,373	2,332
Non-operator switched toll	25,189	11,841	11,068	9,913	9,054	7,749	7,126
Long distance private line	14,344	13,316	12,850	11,991	10,698	9,709	9,000
Other long distance	4,945	3,306	2,233	2,273	2,268	1,838	1,654
Universal service surcharges	**8,662**	**8,319**	**8,438**	**8,447**	**8,059**	**9,126**	**7,796**

Source: U.S. Federal Communications Commission, *Universal Service Monitoring Report, 2023*, March 2024. See also <www.fcc.gov/general/federal-state-joint-board-monitoring-reports>.

Table 1177. Wired and Wireless Telecommunications Carriers—Estimated Revenue: 2015 to 2022

[In millions of dollars (309,484 represents $309,484,000,000). For all employer firms regardless of tax status. Covers NAICS 5171 Wired Telecommunications Carriers and NAICS 5172 Wireless Telecommunications Carriers (except satellite). Data are based on the 2012 North American Industry Classification System. Estimates have been adjusted using results of the 2017 Economic Census where applicable. Based on the Service Annual Survey; see text, this section and Section 15, and Appendix III]

Revenue source	2015	2016	2017	2018	2019	2020	2021	2022
Wired telecommunications carriers operating revenue	**309,484**	**330,435**	**320,758**	**309,186**	**311,592**	**305,900**	**311,742**	**309,311**
Fixed local telephony	18,977	19,648	17,375	15,037	13,377	12,477	12,915	13,369
Fixed long-distance telephony	(S)	19,058	(S)	19,848	19,061	16,702	(S)	(S)
Fixed all distance	2,023	1,977	1,614	2,121	2,854	2,597	(S)	4,059
Carrier services	21,719	17,040	13,495	13,447	13,256	13,418	13,310	17,777
Private network services	17,648	17,848	10,606	5,517	5,794	5,168	5,285	7,275
Internet access services	79,136	88,395	93,256	96,461	99,077	102,893	107,610	115,758
Internet telephony	11,825	11,437	10,417	9,469	9,751	9,230	(S)	10,145
Telecommunications network installation services	906	829	856	1,278	[2] 1,695	1,653	[2] 1,781	1,715
Reselling services for telecommunications equipment, retail	1,644	1,496	1,490	697	1,746	1,724	2,464	1,972
Rental of telecommunications equipment	569	1,724	4,533	7,039	7,312	8,494	8,963	9,023
Repair and maintenance services for telecommunications equipment	984	(S)	873	(S)	(S)	(S)	(S)	632
Subscriber line charges	3,262	3,265	2,945	2,175	1,632	1,496	1,680	2,208
Basic programming package	61,699	64,492	61,757	61,339	61,589	61,114	58,780	50,704
Premium programming package	23,490	24,713	23,366	22,554	22,838	20,065	(S)	13,571
Pay-per-view	2,922	2,936	2,829	2,020	1,629	1,400	1,400	835
Air time (advertising and program content)	5,779	6,427	5,701	6,560	5,884	5,837	6,317	5,906
Rental and reselling services for program distribution equipment	14,362	14,042	12,252	11,186	10,599	10,769	11,479	7,764
Installation services for connections to program distribution networks	(S)	(S)	(S)	[2] 1,557	[2] 1,670	[2] 1,383	[2] 1,498	769
Website hosting services	574	[2] 430	(S)	(S)	(S)	145	163	93
All other operating revenue	20,989	31,700	35,145	29,432	30,600	28,684	26,941	27,696
Wireless telecommunications carrier operating revenue [1]	**252,264**	**256,298**	**254,082**	**270,220**	**276,114**	**278,868**	**295,280**	**308,153**
Messaging (paging) services	3,691	2,928	(S)	2,185	(S)	(S)	(S)	(S)
Mobile telephony	46,089	(S)	5,458	6,335	5,755	6,567	6,904	(S)
Mobile long distance	2,891	2,418	2,494	2,448	2,585	1,971	4,109	3,197
Mobile all distance	46,696	(S)	(S)	81,992	82,536	86,778	85,216	(S)
Internet access services	90,177	96,397	94,877	89,647	92,179	96,949	108,575	113,132
Telecommunications network installation services	205	239	189	185	195	267	379	515
Reselling services for telecommunications equipment, retail	41,022	43,956	46,096	56,902	58,217	56,276	62,370	64,648
Rental of telecommunications equipment	(S)	(S)	4,646	6,671	6,643	6,954	5,114	(S)
Repair and maintenance services for telecommunications equipment	2,289	2,316	1,834	1,660	1,694	(S)	[2] 285	[2] 254
All other operating revenue	15,691	16,700	17,833	22,195	24,052	20,402	20,019	25,834

S Data do not meet publication standards. [1] Excludes satellite telecommunications. [2] Estimated coefficient of variation is between 30 and 40 percent.

Source: U.S. Census Bureau, Service Annual Survey, "Service Annual Survey Latest Data (NAICS-basis): 2022," <www.census.gov/programs-surveys/sas/data/tables.html>, accessed February 2024.

Table 1178. Data Processing, Hosting, and Related Services—Estimated Revenue and Expenses: 2017 to 2022

[In millions of dollars (157,477 represents $157,477,000,000). For all employer firms regardless of tax status. Data are based on the 2012 North American Industry Classification System (NAICS), and cover NAICS 518. Estimates have been adjusted using results of the 2017 Economic Census where applicable. Based on the Service Annual Survey and administrative data; see text, Section 15, and Appendix III]

Item	2017	2018	2019	2020	2021	2022
Total operating revenue	**157,477**	**182,660**	**201,552**	**219,948**	**271,238**	**308,328**
Data processing, information technology infrastructure provisioning, and hosting services	110,172	131,435	141,903	155,645	(S)	(S)
Information technology design and development services	(S)	(S)	(S)	(S)	8,289	(S)
Information technology technical support services	5,176	5,761	6,398	6,530	6,320	(S)
Information technology technical consulting services	4,685	(S)	(S)	(S)	(S)	(S)
Information and document transformation services	2,787	(S)	(S)	(S)	(S)	(S)
Software publishing	3,700	4,562	6,554	7,531	8,523	(S)
Resale of computer hardware and software	3,330	3,786	3,602	(S)	(S)	(S)
All other operating revenue	21,546	22,311	28,955	33,398	47,978	49,032
Total operating expenses	**127,398**	**146,709**	**152,543**	**160,024**	**184,700**	**197,163**

S Data do not meet publication standards.

Source: U.S. Census Bureau, Service Annual Survey, "Service Annual Survey Latest Data (NAICS-basis): 2022," <www.census.gov/programs-surveys/sas/data/tables.html>, accessed February 2024.

Table 1179. Mobile Wireless Cellular Telecommunications Industry: 2000 to 2023

[In units as indicated (109.5 represents 109,500,000). Calendar year data, except as noted. Based on a survey sent to facilities-based commercial mobile radio service providers, including cellular, personal communications services, advanced wireless service, mobile WiMAX, and enhanced special mobile radio (ESMR) systems. Beginning 2000, the number of operational systems differs from that reported for previous periods as a result of the consolidated operation of ESMR systems in a broader service area instead of by a city-to-city basis]

Item	Unit	2000	2005	2010	2015	2020	2021	2022	2023
Wireless subscriber connections [1]	Millions	109.5	207.9	296.3	377.9	468.9	498.9	523.0	558.1
Wireless penetration [2]	Percent	38.0	69.0	94.2	115.7	139.7	148.5	155.4	164.5
Cell sites [3]	Number	104,288	183,689	253,086	307,626	417,215	418,887	414,571	432,469
Employees	Number	184,449	233,067	250,393	235,818	179,460	171,955	162,974	147,888
Service revenue	Mil. dol.	52,466	113,538	159,930	191,949	189,912	204,214	208,683	214,472
Capital investment [4]	Mil. dol.	89,624	199,025	310,015	462,605	601,018	635,759	674,487	704,635
Average monthly revenue per unit [5]	Dollars	48.55	50.65	47.53	44.65	35.31	35.74	34.56	33.56
Voice minutes, annual reported	Billions	258.9	1,495.5	2,241.3	2,881.0	2,928.0	2,361.3	2,474.1	2,415.7
Voice minutes, monthly [6]	Minutes	248.0	716.0	683.0	670.0	544.0	413.0	410.0	378.0
Wireless data usage (megabytes), annual	Billions	(NA)	(NA)	388.0	9,649.9	42,205.0	53,356.0	73,689.8	100,095.4
Number of text messages [7]	Billions	(Z)	9.8	187.7	156.7	140.0	137.2	137.6	152.4
Number of MMS [7,8]	Billions	(NA)	0.2	4.3	19.8	45.4	43.8	45.4	45.1

NA Not available. Z Entry less than half the unit of measurement shown. [1] Number of active wireless devices. Does not represent individual subscribers. [2] Number of active wireless devices divided by total U.S. population (including U.S. territories). [3] The basic geographic unit for wireless telecommunications coverage. [4] Beginning 2005, cumulative capital investment figure reached by summing the incremental capital investment in year shown with cumulative capital investment of prior year. [5] As of December 31. [6] Derived, based on minutes divided by reported devices. [7] Number of messages in final month of survey (December). [8] Multimedia Messaging Service.

Source: CTIA-The Wireless Association, Washington, DC, *Annual Wireless Industry Survey* ©.

Table 1180. Landline and Wireless Telephone Status of Adults by Selected Characteristics: 2010 to 2023

[In percent. For 2010 to 2022, data cover the 6-month period from January to June; for 2023, data cover the 6-month period from July to December. Estimates are preliminary. Based on interviews of a sample of the civilian noninstitutionalized population conducted for the National Health Interview Survey (NHIS). The 2016 NHIS implemented a new sample design. The 2019 NHIS implemented a redesigned questionnaire and changes in weighting methodology, both of which may impact comparisons between estimates for 2019 and earlier years. See source for details]

Telephone status and characteristics	2010	2015	2017	2018	2019	2020 [5]	2021 [6]	2022	2023
Adults by household telephone status:									
Wireless only	24.9	46.7	52.0	55.2	59.2	62.5	68.0	70.7	76.0
Landline with wireless	62.2	43.9	39.6	37.4	37.2	34.3	29.3	27.1	22.2
Landline only (no wireless)	10.9	6.2	4.8	4.1	2.5	2.3	1.9	1.6	1.3
Without any telephone	1.7	3.1	3.4	3.2	1.0	0.7	0.5	0.4	0.5
Other [1]	0.3	0.1	0.1	0.1	0.1	0.2	0.1	0.1	0.0
Children in wireless telephone only households	29.0	55.3	62.3	64.9	70.5	73.6	79.1	81.7	86.8
ADULTS IN WIRELESS ONLY HOUSEHOLDS [2]									
Total	(NA)	(NA)	(NA)	(NA)	58.4	61.8	67.2	69.8	75.2
Sex:									
Male	26.2	48.2	53.2	56.4	59.6	62.7	69.3	71.2	75.5
Female	23.7	45.3	51.0	54.1	57.4	61.0	65.1	68.4	74.8
Age:									
18 to 24 years	39.9	59.4	64.2	65.0	66.5	72.6	75.9	76.0	81.3
25 to 29 years	51.3	71.3	73.3	77.3	80.2	80.4	85.0	89.0	87.3
30 to 34 years	40.4	67.8	74.4	77.3	78.3	83.0	86.1	87.3	90.1
35 to 44 years	27.0	56.6	63.9	65.7	70.9	74.5	79.1	83.4	86.7
45 to 64 years	16.9	40.8	47.1	50.7	55.6	58.5	65.9	67.6	74.2
65 and over years	5.4	19.3	23.9	29.2	30.9	35.0	40.8	45.4	54.6
Race/ethnicity:									
Asian only, non-Hispanic	18.8	47.9	53.1	53.8	55.5	62.5	68.7	67.3	76.0
Black only, non-Hispanic	28.5	48.1	52.5	55.6	54.3	58.6	64.3	69.9	70.8
White only, non-Hispanic	22.7	43.2	48.0	51.6	56.0	58.7	64.5	66.9	73.2
Other race or multiple race, non-Hispanic	(NA)	(NA)	(NA)	(NA)	64.3	69.4	74.3	74.5	79.4
Hispanic or Latino, any race	34.7	59.2	66.3	69.1	71.2	74.8	77.4	80.2	83.9
Education:									
Some high school or less	28.6	49.0	54.8	58.7	58.1	63.4	67.1	68.7	75.7
High school graduate or GED [3]	23.6	46.7	51.5	56.5	57.2	58.4	66.3	67.8	73.1
Some post-high school, no degree	26.5	49.0	55.1	56.0	60.1	63.4	67.3	71.9	76.2
4-year college degree or higher	22.7	43.5	48.6	51.9	58.1	62.6	68.0	69.9	75.7
Family poverty status: [4]									
Less than 100%	39.3	59.3	67.5	67.1	67.1	69.7	73.9	74.0	80.0
100% to less than 200%	32.9	54.4	61.6	62.8	62.2	66.8	68.3	74.3	75.3
200% or greater	21.7	45.7	50.3	53.4	57.4	61.1	67.1	69.1	75.1
Home ownership status:									
Owned or home being bought	15.5	37.2	42.9	46.8	50.2	54.4	60.7	63.8	70.8
Renting	47.1	67.0	70.7	74.4	75.1	78.7	81.9	84.5	86.2
Other arrangement	34.9	52.8	64.8	60.0	61.6	57.8	66.6	67.2	70.3

NA Not available. [1] Other includes unknown cellular telephone or unknown landline status. [2] Through 2018, data are for adults who live in households without a landline telephone. Beginning 2019, data are for "wireless only adults" who have their own wireless cellular telephone and who live in a household without a landline telephone. [3] GED is General Educational Development high school equivalency diploma. [4] Family income relative to the federal poverty threshold, based on the U.S. Census Bureau's poverty thresholds by household income and size. [5] Due to the coronavirus disease 2019 (COVID-19) pandemic, on March 19, 2020, the NHIS switched to a telephone-only survey mode. This resulted in lower response rates and differences in respondent characteristics during 2nd quarter 2020. Differences observed in estimates between 1st half 2020 and earlier years, particularly estimates of persons living in households without any telephone, may be attributable to the change in survey mode. [6] The majority of interviews for the January-June 2021 period were conducted by telephone.

Source: U.S. National Center for Health Statistics, *Wireless Substitution: Early Release of Estimates From the National Health Interview Survey, July-December 2023*, June 2024, and earlier reports. See also <www.cdc.gov/nchs/nhis/erwirelesssubs.htm>.

Table 1181. Average Annual Telephone Service Expenditures by All Consumer Units: 2001 to 2022

[In dollars except percent distribution. Based on the Consumer Expenditure Survey. Expenditures reported are direct out-of-pocket expenditures. A consumer unit is defined as members of a household related by blood, marriage, adoption, or some other legal arrangement; a single person living alone, or sharing a household with others but who is financially independent; or two or more persons living together who share responsibility for at least two out of the three major types of expenses: food, housing, and other expenses]

Year	Average annual expenditures (dollars)				Percent distribution			
	Total telephone services	Residential and other telephone services [1]	Cellular phone service	Other services [2]	Total telephone services	Residential and other telephone services [1]	Cellular phone service	Other services [2]
2001	914	686	210	19	100.0	75.1	23.0	2.1
2002	957	641	294	22	100.0	67.0	30.7	2.3
2003	956	620	316	20	100.0	64.9	33.1	2.1
2004	990	592	378	20	100.0	59.8	38.2	2.0
2005	1,048	570	455	23	100.0	54.4	43.4	2.2
2006	1,087	542	524	21	100.0	49.9	48.2	1.9
2007	1,110	482	608	20	100.0	43.4	54.8	1.8
2008	1,127	467	643	17	100.0	41.4	57.0	1.5
2009	1,162	434	712	17	100.0	37.3	61.2	1.4
2010	1,178	401	760	17	100.0	34.1	64.5	1.4
2011	1,226	381	826	20	100.0	31.1	67.3	1.6
2012	1,239	359	862	19	100.0	28.9	69.6	1.5
2013	1,271	358	913	(NA)	100.0	28.2	71.8	(NA)
2014	1,315	353	963	(NA)	100.0	26.8	73.2	(NA)
2015	1,347	324	1,023	(NA)	100.0	24.1	75.9	(NA)
2016	1,431	307	1,124	(NA)	100.0	21.5	78.5	(NA)
2017	1,356	238	1,118	(NA)	100.0	17.6	82.4	(NA)
2018	1,407	220	1,188	(NA)	100.0	15.6	84.4	(NA)
2019	1,409	191	1,218	(NA)	100.0	13.6	86.4	(NA)
2020	1,441	188	1,253	(NA)	100.0	13.0	87.0	(NA)
2021	1,409	165	1,244	(NA)	100.0	11.7	88.3	(NA)
2022	1,431	147	1,284	(NA)	100.0	10.3	89.7	(NA)

NA Not available. [1] Beginning 2013, data are shown for residential telephone, phone cards, VoIP (Voice over Internet Protocol), and pay phone services combined. Prior to 2013, data are shown for residential and pay telephone services only. [2] Phone cards, pager services, and for 2007-2012, VoIP.

Source: U.S. Bureau of Labor Statistics, Consumer Expenditure Surveys, CE Tables, "Top line means tables," <www.bls.gov/cex/tables. htm>, accessed November 2023; prior to 2013, unpublished data.

Table 1182. Home Internet Access—Broadband and Smartphone Only Service by Selected Characteristic: 2018 to 2023

[In percent. Data for 2018 to 2021 are from surveys of approximately 1,500 to 2,000 adults conducted on landline and cellular telephones in January and/or February of each year. Data for 2023 are based on responses from 5,733 adults participating in a survey conducted via the internet and postal mail, May 19 to September 5, 2023 (margin of error for total sample at 95% confidence level is plus or minus 1.8 percentage points). All surveys were conducted in English and Spanish]

Characteristic	Internet broadband service in the home				Internet via smartphone only [1]			
	2018	2019	2021	2023	2018	2019	2021	2023
Total adults	**65**	**73**	**77**	**80**	**20**	**17**	**15**	**15**
SEX								
Male	66	73	77	79	20	17	14	15
Female	64	73	77	80	19	16	15	14
RACE/ETHNICITY								
White, non-Hispanic	72	79	80	83	14	12	12	12
Black, non-Hispanic	57	66	71	68	24	23	17	21
Hispanic	47	61	65	75	35	25	25	20
Asian [2]	(NA)	(NA)	(NA)	84	(NA)	(NA)	(NA)	14
AGE								
18 to 29 years	67	77	70	78	28	22	28	20
30 to 49 years	70	77	86	87	24	18	11	11
50 to 64 years	68	79	79	81	16	14	13	14
65 years and older	50	59	64	70	10	12	12	16
EDUCATION								
Less than high school graduate	24	46	(NA)	(NA)	39	32	(NA)	(NA)
High school graduate	56	59	(NA)	(NA)	22	24	(NA)	(NA)
High school graduate or less	(NA)	(NA)	59	65	(NA)	(NA)	23	24
Some college	68	77	80	83	21	16	15	13
College graduate	85	93	94	92	10	4	4	6
METRO STATUS								
Urban	67	75	77	77	22	17	16	17
Suburban	70	79	79	86	17	13	12	11
Rural	58	63	72	73	17	20	17	18

NA Not available. [1] Persons without traditional home broadband internet service who own a smartphone that can access the internet. [2] Estimates for Asian adults represent English speakers only.

Source: Pew Research Center ©, Internet & Tech, "Internet, Broadband Fact Sheet," <www.pewresearch.org/internet/fact-sheet/internet-broadband/>, accessed March 2024. See also "Mobile Technology and Home Broadband 2021," <www.pewresearch.org/internet/2021/06/03/mobile-technology-and-home-broadband-2021/>; and "Americans' Use of Mobile Technology and Home Broadband," <www.pewresearch.org/internet/2024/01/31/americans-use-of-mobile-technology-and-home-broadband/>.

Table 1183. Computer and Internet Use by Selected Characteristics: 2022

[In thousands (302,101 represents 302,101,000), except percent. Based on the American Community Survey. Data are based on a sample and are subject to sampling variability. Due to changes in the ACS questionnaire, use caution when comparing data on computer and internet use before and after 2016. For more information, see <www.census.gov/programs-surveys/acs/methodology/content-test.html>]

| Characteristic | Population with computer in household [1] | | | | No computer in household | |
| | With broadband internet subscription [2] | | No internet subscription [3] | | | |
	Number	Percent	Number	Percent	Number	Percent
Total population in households	**302,101**	**92.9**	**14,019**	**4.3**	**8,705**	**2.7**
AGE						
Under 18 years	68,884	95.4	2,350	3.3	914	1.3
18 to 64 years	185,656	94.3	7,882	4.0	3,212	1.6
65 years and over	47,560	84.8	3,788	6.8	4,579	8.2
RACE AND ETHNICITY						
White alone	184,812	93.3	7,528	3.8	5,496	2.8
Black or African American alone	35,127	90.2	2,384	6.1	1,393	3.6
American Indian and Alaska Native alone	2,721	87.6	242	7.8	140	4.5
Asian alone	18,515	96.1	524	2.7	213	1.1
Native Hawaiian/Other Pacific Islander alone	585	90.5	40	6.2	21	3.2
Some other race alone	21,947	91.2	1,438	6.0	675	2.8
Two or more races	38,393	93.5	1,863	4.5	768	1.9
Hispanic or Latino origin [4]	57,700	92.4	3,284	5.3	1,399	2.2
White alone, not Hispanic or Latino	175,039	93.3	7,067	3.8	5,280	2.8
EDUCATIONAL ATTAINMENT						
Household population age 25 and over	206,917	92.0	10,357	4.6	7,477	3.3
Less than high school graduate	18,332	81.0	2,117	9.4	2,154	9.5
High school graduate or some college [5]	109,923	90.8	6,386	5.3	4,514	3.7
Bachelor's degree or higher	78,662	96.7	1,854	2.3	808	1.0
EMPLOYMENT STATUS						
Civilian population age 16 and over	240,370	92.3	11,908	4.6	7,870	3.0
In labor force	159,993	95.1	5,994	3.6	2,197	1.3
Employed	153,434	95.2	5,619	3.5	2,047	1.3
Unemployed	6,559	92.5	375	5.3	150	2.1
Not in labor force	80,377	87.2	5,914	6.4	5,673	6.2

[1] Includes desktop or laptop; smartphone; tablet or other portable wireless computer; or some other type of computer. [2] Paid internet access services via cable, fiber optic, or DSL; a cellular data plan (smartphone or mobile phone); satellite; or a fixed wireless subscription. [3] Includes those who accessed the internet without a paid subscription and also those with no internet access at all. [4] Persons of Hispanic or Latino origin may be of any race. [5] Includes persons with high school equivalency, or with associate's degree.

Source: U.S. Census Bureau, 2022 American Community Survey, S2802 "Types of Internet Subscriptions by Selected Characteristics," <data.census.gov>, accessed November 2023.

Table 1184. Percent of Households with a Computer and Paid Internet Subscription by State: 2022

[In percent. Data are based on the American Community Survey (ACS). Survey respondents could select more than one type of computer and more than one type of internet subscription. Household computer can include desktop or laptop; smartphone; tablet or other portable wireless computer; or some other type of computer. Please note that although the ACS includes people living in group quarters, computer and internet use data were not collected from group quarters. See also headnote Table 1183]

| State | Total households with computer | Type of internet subscription | | | State | Total households with computer | Type of internet subscription | | |
		Dial-up internet service	Broadband internet service [1]	No paid internet service [2]			Dial-up internet service	Broadband internet service [1]	No paid internet service [2]
U.S.	**95.7**	**0.1**	**94.2**	**5.7**	MO	95.1	0.2	93.1	6.7
AL	94.0	0.2	91.7	8.1	MT	94.6	0.2	93.5	6.3
AK	97.3	0.3	93.8	5.9	NE	95.6	0.2	93.6	6.3
AZ	96.4	0.1	93.9	6.0	NV	97.0	0.1	93.7	6.2
AR	94.0	0.1	91.3	8.6	NH	96.9	0.2	96.1	3.7
CA	97.0	0.1	95.6	4.3	NJ	96.1	0.1	95.7	4.2
CO	97.3	0.1	95.2	4.6	NM	93.9	0.2	91.4	8.4
CT	95.6	0.1	95.2	4.7	NY	94.8	0.1	94.2	5.6
DE	96.2	0.2	95.5	4.4	NC	95.4	0.1	93.9	6.0
DC	96.8	0.1	94.6	5.2	ND	95.4	0.1	92.7	7.2
FL	96.9	0.1	93.9	6.0	OH	94.5	0.2	94.6	5.2
GA	96.2	0.1	94.0	5.9	OK	95.0	0.1	92.3	7.6
HI	96.2	(Z)	94.3	5.7	OR	96.8	0.1	94.9	5.0
ID	96.8	0.1	94.4	5.5	PA	94.2	0.2	94.5	5.3
IL	95.5	0.1	94.2	5.7	RI	94.6	0.1	95.7	4.3
IN	94.9	0.1	93.9	6.0	SC	94.6	0.1	93.2	6.7
IA	95.3	0.2	93.3	6.5	SD	94.4	0.2	94.5	5.3
KS	96.2	0.2	93.6	6.2	TN	94.9	0.1	93.5	6.4
KY	94.0	0.1	93.6	6.3	TX	96.4	0.1	94.0	5.9
LA	93.4	0.1	90.3	9.6	UT	98.2	0.1	94.9	4.9
ME	95.2	0.4	94.4	5.3	VT	95.4	0.6	94.1	5.3
MD	96.7	0.1	94.8	5.1	VA	95.5	0.2	94.3	5.5
MA	95.9	0.1	95.8	4.1	WA	97.3	0.1	95.6	4.3
MI	95.5	0.2	94.0	5.8	WV	91.7	0.3	92.6	7.1
MN	96.1	0.2	95.1	4.7	WI	94.9	0.3	94.7	5.0
MS	93.3	0.1	89.1	10.8	WY	95.7	0.4	92.7	6.9

Z less than .05%. [1] Broadband internet service includes access via cable, fiber optic, or DSL; a cellular data plan; satellite; or a fixed wireless subscription. [2] Includes households accessing the internet without a paid subscription and also households with no internet access.

Source: U.S. Census Bureau, 2022 American Community Survey, B28003, "Presence of a Computer and Type of Internet Subscription in Household," <data.census.gov/>, accessed November 2023.

Table 1185. Internet Access by Location and Selected User Characteristics: 2024

[In percent, except as noted (257,420 represents 257,420,000). For persons aged 18 and over. As of Spring 2024. Based on a sample and subject to sampling error]

Characteristic	Total adults (1,000)	Accessed the internet (percent)					Wireless internet connection from home [1] (percent)
		At home	At work	At school or library	At another place	Using a cellphone or smartphone	
Total adults [2]	**257,420**	**92.1**	**43.2**	**10.0**	**40.3**	**86.9**	**87.1**
Age:							
18 to 34 years old	74,440	90.6	53.0	19.1	47.4	89.6	85.7
35 to 54 years old	83,831	92.7	56.9	9.0	42.4	90.8	88.6
55 years old and over	99,149	92.7	24.3	4.0	33.3	81.5	86.8
Sex:							
Male	125,222	92.1	46.1	9.3	40.1	86.5	87.2
Female	132,198	92.1	40.4	10.7	40.5	87.2	86.9
Census region: [3]							
Northeast	45,263	92.7	43.9	9.9	40.3	85.8	86.8
South	98,986	91.3	42.2	9.6	38.7	86.8	86.8
Midwest	53,344	92.4	45.0	9.9	41.4	87.2	87.8
West	59,827	92.7	42.6	11.0	42.1	87.6	87.0
Household size:							
1 to 2 persons	124,790	91.9	36.9	6.0	38.6	83.8	85.6
3 to 4 persons	88,346	93.1	51.2	13.4	43.3	90.2	89.5
5 or more persons	44,285	90.8	45.0	14.4	39.2	89.0	86.3
Presence of child in household	86,783	91.9	49.9	13.1	41.2	90.0	87.6
Marital status:							
Never married	78,966	90.4	49.4	17.9	45.0	87.9	84.1
Married	132,677	94.1	43.3	6.8	40.5	88.1	90.2
Other [4]	55,555	89.4	36.6	6.6	34.1	83.0	83.5
Education:							
Graduated college	90,017	96.8	56.3	10.9	52.7	92.2	93.4
Attended college	68,023	93.8	44.5	10.5	40.4	88.8	89.0
Did not attend college	99,380	86.7	30.5	8.9	29.1	80.7	80.0
Employment status:							
Employed full-time	125,270	93.4	73.3	8.3	43.7	91.8	89.9
Employed part-time	33,498	92.7	52.0	19.5	45.0	88.7	87.2
Occupation of employed:							
Professional	39,891	97.0	80.1	15.5	53.9	94.6	93.9
Management/business/financial	30,572	95.6	79.0	7.5	50.6	93.6	93.0
Sales/office	29,340	92.0	69.3	10.2	40.7	89.7	88.7
Natural resources/construction/maintenance	14,102	90.4	57.4	6.1	35.8	88.4	84.0
Other	44,863	90.0	55.2	10.2	35.5	88.2	85.0
Sector of employment:							
Business	46,109	95.1	75.7	7.8	49.0	93.5	92.1
Government	21,766	93.9	77.9	14.2	43.1	91.3	90.6
Other	74,688	91.6	59.6	10.4	39.9	89.0	86.8
Household income:							
Less than $50,000	72,240	85.1	22.4	10.4	28.1	77.1	76.6
$50,000 to $74,999	40,510	92.7	36.5	8.8	35.4	86.7	86.7
$75,000 to $149,999	80,408	94.9	49.9	9.2	43.6	90.7	91.3
$150,000 or more	64,262	96.1	62.4	11.4	53.1	93.2	93.7

[1] Excludes cellphone access. [2] Includes other labor force status and employment categories not shown separately. [3] For composition of regions, see map inside front cover. [4] Includes separated, divorced, and widowed, and persons engaged to be married.

Source: © MRI-Simmons Spring 2024 USA Study. Courtesy of MRI-Simmons. See also <www.mrisimmons.com/>.

Table 1186. Internet Activities by Sex and Age: 2023

[In percent. Covers population age 15 and over. Based on the November 2023 Computer and Internet Use supplement to the Current Population Survey, for the National Telecommunications and Information Administration's Digital Nation research project]

Activity conducted online or via the internet	Total	By sex		By age			
		Male	Female	15 to 24 years old	25 to 44 years old	45 to 64 years old	65 years and over
Uses the internet, any location	**84.9**	**84.8**	**85.0**	**88.5**	**87.5**	**86.0**	**76.8**
Interact with household equipment	26.7	27.6	25.8	19.0	34.1	28.3	18.1
Offer services for sale	8.5	9.2	7.9	8.3	11.1	8.4	4.5
Video or voice calls, or conferencing	66.1	64.3	67.8	74.6	75.3	64.2	46.3
Post or upload blog posts, videos, or other original content	16.8	16.4	17.1	27.8	20.2	13.5	6.6
Request services provided by other people	45.9	45.8	46.0	50.0	59.7	42.4	24.3
Search for a job	20.1	20.0	20.3	34.3	26.5	15.3	4.5
Shop, make travel reservations, or use other consumer services	75.8	73.9	77.6	73.8	82.3	77.0	64.7
Stream or download music, radio, podcasts, etc.	62.1	63.7	60.6	80.0	73.9	56.7	35.1
Take class or participate in job training	24.6	23.6	25.4	37.7	29.8	21.9	8.5
Telecommute	27.2	28.8	25.7	13.0	39.3	33.6	8.7
Use email	92.4	91.5	93.3	93.1	95.0	93.0	86.5
Use financial services such as banking, investing, paying bills	76.1	75.9	76.3	69.7	85.4	77.8	63.2
Use social networks	76.4	72.9	79.7	86.7	85.1	73.3	57.4
Use text messaging or instant messaging	95.1	94.7	95.5	97.5	98.0	95.9	86.7
Use internet to sell goods	10.0	10.8	9.2	8.2	12.8	10.0	6.5
Watch videos	72.8	74.5	71.2	86.2	82.7	69.0	50.6

Source: U.S. Department of Commerce, National Telecommunications and Information Administration, Data Central, "NTIA Data Explorer," <www.ntia.doc.gov/category/data-central>, accessed June 2024.

Table 1187. Teen Electronic Device Ownership and Social Media Use by Selected Characteristics: 2023

[In percent. Based on responses from 1,453 teenagers age 13 to 17 participating in a survey conducted by Ipsos Public Affairs, September 26 to October 23, 2023. The margin of sampling error is plus or minus 3.2 percentage points. Research was reviewed and approved by an external institutional review board, Advarra. Teenage respondents were recruited via their parents who were part of Ipsos's KnowledgePanel]

Characteristic	Device ownership			Social media platform use						
	Smart-phone	Desktop or laptop computer	Gaming console	Face-book	Insta-gram	Snap-chat	TikTok	Twitter (X)[1]	Whats-App	YouTube
Total[2]	**95**	**90**	**83**	**33**	**59**	**60**	**63**	**20**	**21**	**93**
Sex:										
Male	94	89	91	29	53	56	59	21	21	96
Female	97	91	75	36	66	65	68	19	21	91
Race and ethnicity:										
White, non-Hispanic	95	90	85	34	56	62	57	18	14	92
Black, non-Hispanic	94	91	83	37	69	66	80	28	20	94
Hispanic[3]	96	89	82	31	62	59	70	19	28	96
Age:										
13 to 14 years	92	86	84	24	45	49	58	12	20	94
15 to 17 years	97	92	82	38	68	67	67	25	21	92
Household income:										
Less than $30,000	94	72	78	45	60	65	71	19	20	93
$30,000 to $74,999	92	87	80	41	59	58	66	22	25	93
$75,000 and over	96	94	85	27	59	60	61	19	19	93

[1] Twitter was rebranded as "X" in July 2023. [2] Includes teenagers of other races, such as Asian American, not shown separately. [3] Persons of Hispanic origin may be of any race.

Source: Pew Research Center, *Teens, Social Media and Technology 2023,* December 2023; and "Teens and Social Media Fact Sheet," January 2024 ©. See also <www.pewresearch.org/topic/internet-technology/>.

Table 1188. Households Using Electronics, Internet Devices, and Cell Phones by Type and Household Income: 2020

[In millions (123.5 represents 123,500,000). Based on the Residential Energy Consumption Survey. Includes single-family homes, units in multifamily buildings, and mobile homes. Excludes secondary homes, vacant, seasonal and vacation homes, group quarters, and common areas of apartment buildings. Data may not sum to totals due to rounding]

Item		Households by income (millions)							
	Total	Less than $5,000	$5,000 to $9,999	$10,000 to $19,999	$20,000 to $39,999	$40,000 to $59,999	$60,000 to $99,999	$100,000 to $149,999	$150,000 or more
Total households	**123.5**	**4.5**	**4.0**	**10.3**	**24.1**	**19.6**	**27.7**	**16.5**	**16.9**
TELEVISION AND VIDEO									
Number of televisions:									
0	3.8	0.3	0.3	0.6	0.7	0.6	0.7	0.4	0.3
1	33.8	1.6	1.5	4.0	7.5	5.4	7.1	3.6	3.2
2	41.1	1.5	1.3	3.7	8.9	6.9	8.9	5.2	4.9
3 or more	44.8	1.2	0.9	2.1	7.1	6.7	11.0	7.4	8.5
Hours TV used per weekday:[1]									
Less than 1 hour	4.5	0.3	0.2	0.4	0.8	0.7	0.9	0.6	0.7
1 to 3 hours	29.6	0.6	0.7	1.4	4.0	4.2	7.1	5.0	6.5
4 to 6 hours	41.7	1.3	0.9	2.3	7.7	6.6	10.4	6.4	6.0
7 to 10 hours	24.8	1.0	0.8	2.9	5.8	4.2	5.3	2.6	2.2
More than 10 hours	19.2	1.0	1.0	2.7	5.1	3.4	3.3	1.6	1.1
Hours TV used per weekend day:[1]									
Less than 1 hour	4.1	0.3	0.3	0.5	0.8	0.6	0.8	0.4	0.5
1 to 3 hours	20.6	0.5	0.6	1.3	3.1	3.1	4.8	3.0	4.2
4 to 6 hours	39.6	1.2	0.8	2.2	6.9	5.8	9.7	6.5	6.5
7 to 10 hours	32.2	1.1	1.0	3.0	6.7	5.5	7.3	3.9	3.6
More than 10 hours	23.3	1.0	1.0	2.8	5.9	4.1	4.4	2.4	1.7
Cable or satellite TV boxes:[2]									
1	25.6	0.6	0.4	1.6	4.5	4.2	6.2	3.7	4.3
2 or more	16.4	0.2	0.3	0.6	2.5	2.4	4.1	2.8	3.5
Internet streaming devices:									
1	34.7	1.3	1.0	2.3	6.8	5.6	8.2	5.0	4.6
2 or more	34.6	0.7	0.7	1.6	4.9	5.2	8.5	5.9	7.2
COMPUTERS AND PHONES									
Desktop computers:									
1	39.9	0.7	0.6	2.0	7.2	6.6	10.3	6.3	6.3
2 or more	10.5	0.2	(NA)	0.4	1.3	1.3	2.7	1.9	2.5
Laptop computers:									
1	44.7	1.3	1.2	3.2	9.5	8.7	11.4	5.6	4.0
2	28.2	0.6	0.5	1.3	3.6	4.0	7.3	5.4	5.5
3 or more	19.3	0.4	0.4	0.6	1.6	1.8	4.2	3.9	6.3
Tablets and e-readers:									
1	39.9	1.0	1.1	2.5	7.5	6.5	10.3	5.8	5.1
2	22.3	0.3	0.3	0.8	3.0	3.1	5.9	4.0	4.9
3 or more	11.4	0.3	0.2	0.3	1.1	1.2	2.5	2.3	3.5
Smartphones:									
1	31.0	1.3	1.2	3.6	8.1	6.3	6.6	2.3	1.5
2	46.1	1.1	0.9	2.1	6.8	7.1	12.4	7.9	7.9
3 or more	31.7	1.0	0.8	1.5	4.5	4.1	7.1	5.7	7.1

[1] Data shown for primary television. [2] Cable and satellite boxes with digital video recorder (DVR).

Source: U.S. Energy Information Administration, Residential Energy Consumption Survey—2020 Data, "Housing characteristics tables: Table HC4.5 Electronics in U.S. homes, by household income, 2020," <www.eia.gov/consumption/residential/index.php>, accessed May 2022.

Table 1189. Social Media—Use of Social Networking Sites Among Adult Internet Users: 2023

[In percent. Based on responses from 5,733 adults participating in a May 19 to September 5, 2023 survey conducted in English and Spanish via the internet (2,217 responses) and postal mail (3,516 responses). Margin of error for the total sample at 95% level of confidence is plus or minus 1.8 percentage points]

Characteristic	Social media platform								
	Facebook	Instagram	LinkedIn	Twitter (X) [1]	Pinterest	Snapchat	YouTube	WhatsApp	TikTok
Total............................	**68**	**47**	**30**	**22**	**35**	**27**	**83**	**29**	**33**
SEX									
Male...........................	59	39	31	26	19	21	82	27	25
Female.........................	76	54	29	19	50	32	83	31	40
RACE/ETHNICITY									
White, non-Hispanic............	69	43	30	20	36	25	81	20	28
Black, non-Hispanic............	64	46	29	23	28	25	82	31	39
Asian, non-Hispanic [2].........	67	57	45	37	30	25	93	51	29
Hispanic origin [3].............	66	58	23	25	32	35	86	54	49
AGE									
18 to 29 years..................	67	78	32	42	45	65	93	32	62
30 to 49 years..................	75	59	40	27	40	30	92	38	39
50 to 64 years..................	69	35	31	17	33	13	83	29	24
65 years and over..............	58	15	12	6	21	4	60	16	10
EDUCATION									
High school graduate or less...	63	37	10	15	26	26	74	25	35
Some college...................	71	50	28	24	42	32	85	23	38
College graduate or higher.....	70	55	53	29	38	23	89	39	26
INCOME									
Under $30,000..................	63	37	13	18	27	27	73	26	36
$30,000 to $69,999............	70	46	19	21	34	30	83	26	37
$70,000 to $99,999............	74	49	34	20	35	26	86	33	34
$100,000 and over.............	68	54	53	29	41	25	89	34	27
METRO STATUS									
Urban..........................	66	53	31	25	31	29	85	38	36
Suburban.......................	68	49	36	26	36	26	85	30	31
Rural..........................	70	38	18	13	36	27	77	20	33

[1] Twitter was rebranded as "X" in July 2023. [2] Estimates for Asian adults represent English speakers only. [3] Persons of Hispanic origin may be of any race.

Source: Pew Research Center ©, Internet & Technology, "Americans' Social Media Use," January 2024, <www.pewresearch.org/internet/2024/01/31/americans-social-media-use/>.

Table 1190. Public Libraries—Selected Characteristics: 2021

[Total operating income in thousands of dollars (14,967,386 represents $14,967,386,000). Data are generally for the fiscal year ending in June; see source for reporting periods. Based on a census of all public libraries in the 50 states and the District of Columbia. See source for details]

Population of service area	Number of—		Operating income			Paid staff [4]		Avg. number of public use internet computers per stationary outlet [6]
	Public libraries [1]	Stationary outlets [2]	Total [3] ($1,000)	Source (percent)		Total FTE	Librarians with ALA-MLS [5]	
				State government	Local government			
Total...................	**9,021**	**16,543**	**14,967,386**	**6.9**	**86.4**	**138,500**	**33,704**	**15.9**
Less than 1,000........	930	933	42,619	7.6	72.1	769	38	5.5
1,000 to 2,499.........	1,462	1,476	146,382	5.3	77.8	2,152	191	5.6
2,500 to 4,999.........	1,242	1,276	241,370	5.9	81.4	3,249	393	7.4
5,000 to 9,999.........	1,506	1,665	557,377	7.0	81.8	6,727	1,322	9.5
10,000 to 24,999......	1,731	2,213	1,432,080	6.5	86.6	16,207	4,060	13.0
25,000 to 49,999......	993	1,738	1,738,176	6.7	87.4	17,227	4,613	15.8
50,000 to 99,999......	578	1,566	1,771,561	8.1	86.1	17,312	4,517	18.6
100,000 to 249,999....	367	1,982	2,243,445	7.7	87.2	21,507	5,131	20.4
250,000 to 499,999....	118	1,220	1,863,253	7.1	88.5	16,531	4,013	24.9
500,000 to 999,999....	57	1,060	2,202,916	7.3	87.2	17,797	4,149	28.1
1,000,000 or more.....	37	1,414	2,728,208	5.6	85.0	19,024	5,277	26.8

[1] A public library is the administrative entity, the agency, that provides public library services. Of the 9,021 public libraries in the 50 States and DC, 81.0 percent were single-outlet libraries. There are 8,847 central library outlets, 7,696 branch library outlets, and 668 bookmobiles. [2] The sum of central and branch libraries. [3] Total includes income from the federal government (0.8%) and other sources (5.9%), not shown separately. [4] Full-time equivalents. Forty hours per week equals 1 FTE. [5] Librarians with master's degrees from a graduate library education program accredited by the American Library Association (ALA). Total librarians, including those without ALA-MLS, is 50,769. [6] The average per stationary outlet was calculated by dividing the total number of public use internet computers in central and branch outlets by the total number of such outlets.

Source: Institute of Museum and Library Services, Public Library Survey, "PLS Benchmarking Tables," <www.imls.gov/research-tools/data-collection>, accessed April 2024. See also <www.imls.gov/research-evaluation/data-collection/public-libraries-survey>.

Table 1191. Number of Public Libraries and Library Services by State: 2021

[416,959 represents 416,959,000. Data are generally for the fiscal year ending in June; see source documentation for reporting periods. Based on a census of all public libraries that meet the definition of a Federal State Cooperative System (FSCS) Public Library, which can have one or more outlets (central, branch, bookmobile, or books-by-mail-only) that provide direct service to the public]

State	Number of public libraries [1]	Visits		Circulation [3]				Average number of public use internet computers [4]
		Library visits (1,000s)	Per capita visits [2]	Total circulation (1,000s)	Per capita circulation of materials [2]	Children's circulation (1,000s)	Children's circulation as percent of total circulation	
United States........	9,021	416,959	1.3	1,553,716	4.9	509,968	32.8	15.9
Alabama...............	215	6,411	1.4	16,920	3.6	5,666	33.5	15.6
Alaska.................	63	895	1.4	2,748	4.3	952	34.6	8.5
Arizona................	87	4,431	0.6	27,919	3.8	6,976	25.0	20.6
Arkansas..............	58	4,193	1.5	11,913	4.3	2,936	24.7	11.5
California..............	184	22,126	0.6	131,404	3.3	39,255	29.9	18.0
Colorado..............	112	13,294	2.3	51,449	9.1	17,405	33.8	25.9
Connecticut...........	181	4,909	1.5	15,678	4.7	5,142	32.8	13.9
Delaware..............	21	594	0.6	2,779	2.8	675	24.3	31.6
District of Columbia....	1	902	1.4	5,043	7.5	1,506	29.9	38.5
Florida................	78	29,079	1.3	76,678	3.5	22,774	29.7	31.7
Georgia...............	61	7,873	0.7	24,666	2.3	9,743	39.5	25.8
Hawaii.................	1	713	0.5	3,645	2.6	1,898	52.1	7.0
Idaho..................	103	3,779	2.4	13,041	8.1	4,842	37.1	19.4
Illinois.................	623	17,991	1.5	77,941	6.6	26,648	34.2	19.0
Indiana................	236	15,277	2.5	45,603	7.5	16,521	36.2	16.7
Iowa...................	534	5,625	1.8	16,989	5.5	5,756	33.9	7.6
Kansas................	318	6,620	2.6	20,075	8.0	8,018	39.9	9.5
Kentucky..............	120	4,976	1.1	18,362	4.1	4,930	26.9	21.6
Louisiana..............	67	7,661	1.7	17,591	3.8	3,665	20.8	16.3
Maine..................	230	2,394	2.0	5,253	4.4	2,033	38.7	6.4
Maryland..............	25	2,414	0.4	33,970	5.6	12,035	35.4	23.3
Massachusetts........	366	5,988	0.9	37,917	5.5	12,137	32.0	12.4
Michigan..............	396	13,738	1.4	51,358	5.1	14,587	28.4	16.7
Minnesota.............	136	9,762	1.7	43,282	7.6	16,729	38.7	11.5
Mississippi............	53	2,828	1.0	4,377	1.5	1,398	31.9	11.4
Missouri...............	149	8,653	1.6	39,996	7.3	10,900	27.3	12.5
Montana...............	81	1,662	1.7	4,184	4.2	1,330	31.8	8.2
Nebraska..............	235	3,692	2.3	11,460	7.2	5,303	46.3	9.4
Nevada................	20	3,952	1.3	12,337	3.9	2,853	23.1	19.4
New Hampshire........	216	2,427	1.8	7,086	5.2	2,217	31.3	5.9
New Jersey............	295	15,672	1.8	40,110	4.6	15,344	38.3	16.4
New Mexico...........	89	1,515	1.0	6,400	4.3	1,344	21.0	15.8
New York..............	754	34,531	1.8	74,343	3.9	20,584	27.7	14.6
North Carolina.........	84	8,973	0.9	35,343	3.4	13,668	38.7	18.7
North Dakota..........	72	1,161	1.7	2,899	4.2	1,096	37.8	7.9
Ohio...................	251	30,548	2.6	132,787	11.4	41,110	31.0	15.9
Oklahoma.............	119	4,668	1.4	18,042	5.6	5,960	33.0	14.5
Oregon................	134	4,858	1.3	33,309	8.8	9,928	29.8	12.9
Pennsylvania..........	445	15,035	1.2	47,550	3.7	16,632	35.0	10.8
Rhode Island..........	48	1,963	1.8	5,333	4.9	1,660	31.1	19.5
South Carolina........	42	4,997	1.0	17,722	3.5	5,297	29.9	18.3
South Dakota..........	106	2,031	2.6	5,016	6.4	2,040	40.7	7.1
Tennessee.............	185	5,696	0.9	21,350	3.2	6,861	32.1	19.3
Texas..................	540	23,258	0.9	89,281	3.3	38,077	42.7	19.1
Utah...................	70	8,104	2.6	30,859	10.0	13,789	44.7	16.4
Vermont...............	165	959	1.6	3,044	5.2	1,032	33.9	5.1
Virginia................	94	10,041	1.2	45,104	5.3	14,533	32.2	20.0
Washington............	59	10,764	1.4	64,361	8.4	16,950	26.3	17.1
West Virginia..........	96	1,713	0.9	4,228	2.3	846	20.0	6.7
Wisconsin.............	380	13,838	2.4	41,092	7.0	14,882	36.2	12.1
Wyoming..............	23	1,776	3.1	3,880	6.7	1,504	38.8	9.7

[1] A public library is the administrative entity, the agency, that provides public library services. Of the 9,021 public libraries in the 50 States and DC, 81.0 percent were single-outlet libraries. There are 8,847 central library outlets, 7,696 branch library outlets, and 668 bookmobiles. Excludes 190 libraries that do not meet the criteria in the FSCS public library definition but that qualify as public libraries under state law. [2] Per capita rate based on total unduplicated population of legal service area determined by the state library agency of each state. [3] Total circulation includes physical and electronic materials. Children's circulation includes materials in all formats, including renewals. [4] The average per stationary outlet was calculated by dividing the total number of public use Internet computers in central and branch outlets by the total number of such outlets.

Source: Institute of Museum and Library Services, Public Library Survey, "PLS Benchmarking Tables," <www.imls.gov/research-tools/data-collection>, accessed April 2024. See also <www.imls.gov/research-evaluation/data-collection/public-libraries-survey>.

Table 1192. Public Library Holdings by Type by State: 2021

[In thousands (657,928 represents 657,928,000), except as noted. Data are generally for the fiscal year ending in June; see source for reporting periods. Based on a census of all public libraries conducted by Institute of Museum and Library Services. Covers only libraries that meet the definition of a Federal State Cooperative System (FSCS) public library. State data comparisons should be made with caution because of differences in reporting periods and adherence to survey definitions. Data are not subject to sampling error; census results may contain nonsampling error]

State	Print — Print materials [1]	Electronic materials — Electronic books [2]	Electronic materials — Electronic books, per capita	Electronic materials — Electronic collections [3]	Audio — Physical units	Audio — Downloadable units [4]	Video — Physical units	Video — Downloadable units [4]
United States..........	657,928	1,042,735	3.26	484.5	37,450	508,267	66,353	44,770
Alabama.................	8,333	8,502	1.83	25.4	496	3,104	708	336
Alaska...................	1,875	1,598	2.50	3.3	106	931	282	60
Arizona..................	7,440	13,024	1.79	2.9	491	9,375	1,149	645
Arkansas................	5,690	7,823	2.84	5.3	227	3,768	621	268
California................	51,954	48,538	1.23	4.8	2,706	26,206	4,867	4,668
Colorado................	9,205	8,736	1.54	2.0	682	5,007	1,235	1,280
Connecticut.............	11,769	2,619	0.78	8.7	700	1,079	1,109	28
Delaware................	1,438	673	0.68	0.2	116	269	168	21
District of Columbia.....	1,028	85	0.13	0.1	16	40	85	106
Florida..................	23,355	18,192	0.83	5.1	1,449	39,448	3,170	1,198
Georgia.................	13,975	2,614	0.24	3.9	448	1,865	1,120	127
Hawaii..................	2,795	137	0.10	0.1	108	30	176	–
Idaho...................	4,119	2,701	1.68	1.5	204	1,039	384	62
Illinois..................	36,890	51,243	4.36	16.7	2,483	25,751	3,811	2,624
Indiana.................	21,069	21,929	3.59	25.7	1,190	6,301	2,358	482
Iowa...................	11,255	26,726	8.72	21.9	602	14,236	1,178	78
Kansas.................	8,300	205,680	82.05	25.5	405	52,410	947	3,680
Kentucky...............	8,982	19,138	4.28	8.9	494	5,377	1,001	282
Louisiana...............	10,709	6,873	1.50	4.6	467	3,034	1,361	750
Maine..................	5,887	6,744	5.64	18.9	235	3,865	442	495
Maryland...............	9,778	3,459	0.57	1.1	634	1,934	962	610
Massachusetts..........	28,030	27,975	4.06	18.5	1,405	11,142	2,138	630
Michigan...............	25,608	30,035	2.99	2.9	1,743	14,055	2,698	2,016
Minnesota..............	13,188	5,776	1.01	8.7	734	1,390	1,083	8
Mississippi.............	5,121	259	0.09	2.8	172	227	425	26
Missouri................	14,771	7,852	1.44	3.9	857	2,756	1,366	508
Montana................	2,402	3,399	3.44	0.2	115	3,055	237	186
Nebraska...............	5,477	6,087	3.83	6.4	224	3,813	427	43
Nevada.................	3,117	1,242	0.40	1.2	194	757	494	123
New Hampshire..........	5,272	9,774	7.19	4.7	265	8,132	520	1,036
New Jersey.............	24,135	42,209	4.85	10.4	1,656	24,297	2,352	5,108
New Mexico.............	3,798	1,752	1.17	4.7	178	1,433	365	149
New York...............	62,845	52,530	2.72	23.0	2,440	26,813	5,207	1,287
North Carolina...........	14,870	15,529	1.48	7.7	591	3,494	927	377
North Dakota............	2,002	1,665	2.41	3.8	82	858	144	106
Ohio....................	37,251	155,008	13.32	18.2	3,728	75,307	5,304	6,266
Oklahoma...............	5,785	8,153	2.52	5.7	315	3,320	595	250
Oregon.................	8,606	12,147	3.21	4.1	576	5,441	991	826
Pennsylvania............	23,923	19,221	1.51	53.4	1,200	7,876	2,105	765
Rhode Island............	3,039	6,448	5.88	2.0	141	2,332	287	90
South Carolina...........	7,998	5,941	1.16	2.7	377	3,784	788	452
South Dakota............	2,647	2,823	3.58	6.7	108	1,245	174	6
Tennessee...............	10,122	29,972	4.46	12.5	469	15,387	797	647
Texas..................	33,352	19,813	0.74	35.7	1,607	6,681	3,299	1,188
Utah...................	6,344	7,477	2.42	4.0	563	12,835	710	526
Vermont................	2,686	1,823	3.12	9.9	125	1,532	238	–
Virginia.................	14,655	26,366	3.10	5.7	793	14,038	1,311	2,484
Washington.............	11,135	5,661	0.74	3.9	795	3,643	1,259	531
West Virginia............	4,532	10,085	5.44	2.0	187	20,575	377	899
Wisconsin...............	17,296	66,527	11.28	30.6	1,403	26,238	2,318	322
Wyoming................	2,076	2,153	3.73	1.8	146	743	285	118

– Represents zero. [1] Includes books and non-serial government documents. [2] E-books include digital documents digitized by the library, licensed or not; and non-serial government documents. [3] An electronic collection is a collection of electronically stored data or unit records (facts, bibliographic data, abstracts, texts, photographs, music, video, etc.) with a common user interface and software for the retrieval and use of the data. Electronic collections do not have a circulation period. [4] Downloadable units are items for which permanent or temporary access rights have been acquired. For items with a finite number of simultaneous users, the number of units equals the number of simultaneous users (equivalent to purchasing multiple copies of a single title). For items with unlimited simultaneous users, the number of units equals the number of titles acquired.

Source: Institute of Museum and Library Services, Public Library Survey, "PLS Benchmarking Tables," <www.imls.gov/research-tools/data-collection>, accessed April 2024. See also <www.imls.gov/research-evaluation/data-collection/public-libraries-survey>.

This section presents data on the nation's finances, various types of financial institutions, money and credit, securities, insurance, and real estate. The primary sources of these data are publications of several departments of the federal government, especially the U.S. Treasury Department, and independent agencies such as the Federal Deposit Insurance Corporation, the Board of Governors of the Federal Reserve System, and the Securities and Exchange Commission. National data on insurance are available primarily from private organizations, such as the American Council of Life Insurers.

Financial Accounts of the United States—The Federal Reserve Board brings together statistics on all of the major forms of financial instruments to present an economy-wide view of asset and liability relationships in the Financial Accounts of the United States. The accounts relate borrowing and lending to one another and to the nonfinancial activities that generate income and production. Each claim outstanding is included simultaneously as an asset of the lender and as a liability of the debtor. The accounts also indicate the balance between asset totals and liability totals over the economy as a whole. Several publications of the Federal Reserve Board contain information on these financial accounts: Summary data on flows and outstandings in the statistical release *Financial Accounts of the United States* (quarterly); and concepts and organization of the accounts in *Financial Accounts Guide* <federalreserve.gov/apps/fof/>. Data are also available on the Federal Reserve Board's website at <federalreserve.gov/releases/z1/>.

Survey of Consumer Finances (SCF)—The Federal Reserve Board, in cooperation with the Treasury Department, sponsors this survey, which is conducted every 3 years to provide detailed information on the finances of U.S. families. Among the topics covered are the balance sheet, pension, income, and other demographic characteristics of U.S. families. The survey also gathers information on the use of financial institutions. Since 1992, data for the SCF have been collected by NORC at the University of Chicago. Information on the survey is available on the Federal Reserve Board's website at <federalreserve.gov/econres/scfindex.htm>.

Banking system—Banks in this country are organized under the laws of both the states and the federal government and are regulated by several bank supervisory agencies. National banks are supervised by the Comptroller of the Currency. *Reports of Condition and Income*, commonly known as call reports, have been collected from national banks since 1863. Summaries of these reports are published in the Comptroller's *Annual Report*, which also presents data on the structure of the national banking system.

The Federal Reserve System was established in 1913 to exercise central banking functions, some of which are shared with the U.S. Treasury. It includes national banks and state banks that voluntarily join the system. Statements of state bank members are consolidated by the Federal Reserve Board with data for national banks collected by the Comptroller of the Currency into totals for all member banks of the system.

Balance sheet data for member banks and other commercial banks are available on the Federal Reserve Board's website at <federalreserve.gov/data.htm>.

The Federal Deposit Insurance Corporation (FDIC), established in 1933, insures each depositor up to $250,000. Major item balance sheet and income data for all insured financial institutions are published in the *FDIC Quarterly Banking Profile*. This publication is also available on the internet at <fdic.gov/analysis/quarterly-banking-profile/>. Quarterly financial information for individual institutions is available through the FDIC and Federal Financial Institutions Examination Council websites at <fdic.gov> and <ffiec.gov>.

Credit unions—Federally chartered credit unions are under the supervision of the National Credit Union Administration (NCUA), <ncua.gov/>. State-chartered credit unions are supervised by the respective state supervisory authorities. The NCUA publishes comprehensive program and statistical information on all federal and federally insured state credit unions in the *Annual Report of the National Credit Union Administration*.

Other credit agencies—Insurance companies, finance companies dealing primarily in installment sales financing, and personal loan companies represent important sources of funds for the credit market. Statistics on loans, investments, cash, etc., of life insurance companies are published principally by the American Council of Life Insurers in its *Life Insurers Fact Book*. Consumer credit data are available on the Federal Reserve Board's website at <federalreserve.gov/data.htm>. Government corporations and credit agencies make available credit of specified types or to specified groups of private borrowers, either by lending directly or by insuring or guaranteeing loans made by private lending institutions. Data on operations of government credit agencies, along with other government corporations, are available in reports of individual agencies.

Securities—The Securities and Exchange Commission (SEC) was established in 1934 to protect the interests of the public and investors against malpractices in the securities and financial markets and to provide the fullest possible disclosure of information regarding securities to the investing public.

Data on the securities industry and securities transactions are also available from a number of private sources. The Securities Industry and Financial Markets Association (SIFMA), New York, NY, <sifma.org/>, publishes the *SIFMA Fact Book*. The Investment Company Institute, Washington, DC, <ici.org/>, publishes a reference book, research newsletters, and a variety of research reports that examine the industry, its shareholders, or industry issues. Their annual *Investment Company Fact Book* is a guide to trends and statistics observed in the investment company industry. Institute research reports provide a detailed examination of shareholder demographics and other aspects of fund ownership.

Among the many sources of data on stock and bond prices and sales are the New York Stock Exchange, New York, NY, <nyse.com/>; NASDAQ, Washington,

DC, <nasdaq.com/>; and Global Financial Data, Los Angeles, CA, <globalfinancialdata.com/>.

Insurance—Insuring companies, which are regulated by the various states or the District of Columbia, are classified as either life or property. Both life and property insurance companies may underwrite health insurance. Insuring companies, other than those classified as life, are permitted to underwrite one or more property lines provided they are so licensed and have the necessary capital or surplus. There are a number of published sources for statistics on the various classes of insurance—life, health, fire, marine, and casualty. Organizations representing certain classes of insurers publish reports for these classes. The American Council of Life Insurers publishes statistics on life insurance purchases, ownership, benefit payments, and assets in its *Life Insurers Fact Book*.

Statistical reliability—For a discussion of statistical collection, estimation, and sampling procedures and measures of reliability applicable to data from the Census Bureau and the Federal Reserve Board's Survey of Consumer Finances, see Appendix III.

Table 1193. Gross Domestic Product in Finance, Insurance, Real Estate, and Rental and Leasing Industries in Current and Chained (2017) Dollars: 2010 to 2023

[In billions of dollars, except percent (993 represents $993,000,000,000). Represents value added by industry. For definition of gross domestic product and explanation of chained dollars, see text, Section 13, Income]

Industry	2012 NAICS code [1]	Current dollars				Chained (2017) dollars			
		2010	2020	2022	2023	2010	2020	2022	2023
Finance & insurance, total...............	52	**993**	**1,709**	**1,933**	**1,988**	**1,344**	**1,542**	**1,592**	**1,547**
Percent of gross domestic product......	(X)	6.6	8.0	7.5	7.3	8.0	7.6	7.3	6.9
Federal Reserve banks, credit inter- mediation, and related activities...........	521, 522	420	768	857	874	636	693	644	602
Securities, commodity contracts, & investments.................	523	197	310	361	386	330	264	304	332
Insurance carriers & related activities......	524	373	629	687	691	400	583	635	606
Funds, trusts, & other financial vehicles. ..	525	4	1	28	37	3	1	20	18
Real estate & rental & leasing, total....	53	**1,997**	**2,898**	**3,397**	**3,668**	**2,301**	**2,676**	**2,962**	**2,999**
Percent of gross domestic product......	(X)	13.3	13.6	13.2	13.4	13.7	13.2	13.6	13.4
Real estate...................	531	1,837	2,653	3,080	3,326	2,143	2,436	2,689	2,720
Rental & leasing services and lessors of intangible assets...............	532, 533	160	245	317	343	161	240	273	280

X Not applicable. [1] Data based on the North American Industry Classification System (NAICS). See text, Section 15.

Source: U.S. Bureau of Economic Analysis, Industry Economic Accounts, GDP by Industry, "Value Added by Industry" and "Real Value Added by Industry," <www.bea.gov/data/gdp/gdp-industry>, accessed July 2024.

Table 1194. Finance, Insurance, Real Estate, and Rental and Leasing—Establishments, Revenue, Payroll, and Employees by Kind of Business: 2022

[5,677 represents $5,677,000,000,000. For establishments with payroll. Based on the 2022 Economic Censuses; see Appendix III]

Industry	2022 NAICS code [1]	Establishments (number)	Value of shipments (bil. dol.)	Annual payroll (bil. dol.)	Paid employees [2] (1,000)
Finance & insurance [2]........................	52	**479,320**	**5,677**	**825**	**7,478**
Monetary authorities—central bank............	521	58	170	3	21
Credit intermediation & related activities...................	522	183,549	1,573	292	3,277
Security, commodity contracts, & like activity..............	523	114,081	788	255	1,205
Insurance carriers & related activities......................	524	181,632	3,146	275	2,975
Real estate & rental & leasing...........................	53	**468,848**	**960**	**161**	**2,630**
Real estate..................................	531	414,970	690	122	2,017
Rental & leasing services..................................	532	51,175	210	33	569
Lessors of other nonfinancial intangible assets............	533	2,703	60	6	45

[1] Based on the North American Industry Classification System (NAICS); see text, Section 15. [2] Total does not include NAICS 525, Funds, trusts, and other financial vehicles.

Source: U.S. Census Bureau, 2022 Economic Census of the United States, Table EC2200BASIC, "All Sectors: Summary Statistics for the U.S.: 2022," <data.census.gov>, accessed August 2024.

Table 1195. Finance and Insurance—Nonemployer Establishments and Receipts by Kind of Business: 2010 to 2021

[716.8 represents 716,800. Includes only firms subject to federal income tax. Nonemployers are businesses with no paid employees. Data originate chiefly from administrative records of the Internal Revenue Service; see Appendix III]

Kind of business	NAICS code [1]	Establishments (1,000)			Receipts (mil. dol.)		
		2010	2020	2021	2010	2020	2021
Finance and insurance.........................	52	**716.8**	**758.2**	**760.9**	**50,626**	**69,235**	**78,099**
Credit intermediation & related activities........................	522	53.3	48.3	49.5	2,790	3,800	4,122
Depository credit intermediation................................	5221	6.2	5.8	6.0	181	240	263
Nondepository credit intermediation..........................	5222	21.8	23.1	23.3	1,554	2,052	2,204
Activities related to credit intermediation.......................	5223	25.3	19.5	20.3	1,056	1,508	1,655
Securities, commodity contracts, & related activities...........	523	273.4	296.5	299.6	29,202	40,951	47,978
Securities & commodity contracts intermediation and brokerage........	5231	29.8	26.7	30.1	4,969	6,553	7,580
Investment banking and securities dealing..................	52311	7.2	7.9	8.0	1,748	2,446	2,571
Securities brokerage..........................	52312	18.6	15.2	14.8	2,589	3,562	4,323
Commodity contracts dealing..........................	52313	1.1	1.7	5.5	236	250	361
Commodity contracts brokerage............................	52314	2.9	1.9	1.8	397	295	324
Securities & commodity exchanges............................	5232	1.9	2.0	2.4	660	714	1,153
Other financial investment activities............................	5239	241.7	267.7	267.2	23,573	33,683	39,245
Insurance carriers & related activities............................	524	390.1	413.4	411.7	18,634	24,484	25,999
Insurance carriers................................	5241	2.7	2.0	1.9	185	196	206
Agencies & other insurance-related activities.................	5242	387.4	411.4	409.8	18,449	24,288	25,793
Insurance agencies & brokerages..........................	52421	270.5	299.1	299.5	13,854	18,315	19,449
Other insurance related activities............................	52429	116.9	112.3	110.3	4,595	5,973	6,344

[1] Data for 2010 are based on 2007 North American Industry Classification System (NAICS); 2020 and 2021 data based on 2017 NAICS. For more information, see text, Section 15.

Source: U.S. Census Bureau, Nonemployer Statistics, "All Sectors: Nonemployer Statistics by Legal Form of Organization and Receipts Size Class for the U.S., States, and Selected Geographies: 2021," <data.census.gov>, accessed March 2024.

Table 1196. Finance and Insurance—Establishments, Employees, and Payroll: 2021 and 2022

[478.9 represents 478,900. Covers establishments with payroll. Employees are for the week including March 12. Excludes most government employees, railroad employees, and self-employed persons. For statement on methodology, see Appendix III]

Kind of business	NAICS code [1]	Establishments (1,000)		Employees (1,000)		Payroll (bil. dol.)	
		2021	2022	2021	2022	2021	2022
Finance & insurance, total [2]	**52**	**478.9**	**480.5**	**6,738**	**6,832**	**824.9**	**845.1**
Monetary authorities—central bank	521	0.1	0.1	21	21	2.9	3.0
Credit intermediation & related activities	522	186.8	184.8	2,969	2,941	308.2	297.5
Depository credit intermediation [2]	5221	111.3	109.8	1,950	1,928	182.9	186.8
Commercial banking	52211	85.1	83.3	1,526	1,497	152.0	154.2
Savings institutions	52212	7.0	6.9	104	100	9.4	9.3
Credit unions	52213	19.1	19.6	317	328	21.1	23.0
Nondepository credit intermediation [2]	5222	46.2	46.9	695	[3] 687	83.2	74.1
Real estate credit	522292	17.0	18.6	361	353	49.5	37.4
Activities related to credit intermediation	5223	29.3	28.1	324	327	42.1	36.6
Securities, commodity contracts & like activity [2]	523	108.7	112.8	942	994	252.8	268.1
Securities & commodity contracts intermediation & brokerage [2]	5231	28.0	28.8	356	367	101.6	108.8
Securities brokerage	52312	22.4	23.0	253	257	57.6	58.9
Other financial investment activities [2]	5239	80.7	84.0	580	620	149.7	157.7
Portfolio management	52392	42.4	43.2	363	383	110.6	114.6
Insurance carriers & related activities	524	181.5	181.0	2,799	2,867	259.6	274.8
Insurance carriers [2]	5241	29.7	30.6	1,551	1,544	160.7	167.2
Direct life insurance carriers	524113	6.8	6.4	323	311	39.1	42.3
Direct health & medical insurance carriers	524114	5.6	6.2	539	545	51.4	52.6
Direct property & casualty insurance carriers	524126	12.2	12.7	595	595	58.9	61.2
Agencies & other insurance-related activities [2]	5242	151.8	150.4	1,248	1,322	98.9	107.6
Insurance agencies & brokerages	52421	135.9	135.1	770	808	62.0	68.0

[1] North American Industry Classification System (NAICS). Data based on NAICS 2017. See text, Section 15. [2] Includes other kinds of businesses, not shown separately. [3] High noise; cell value was changed by 5 percent or more by the application of noise to avoid disclosure.

Source: U.S. Census Bureau, County Business Patterns, "All Sectors: County Business Patterns, including ZIP Code Business Patterns, by Legal Form of Organization and Employment Size Class for the U.S., States, and Selected Geographies: 2022," <data.census.gov>, accessed June 2024. See also <www.census.gov/programs-surveys/cbp.html>.

Table 1197. Revenues of Finance and Insurance Industries: 2010 to 2022

[In billions of dollars (3,495.7 represents $3,495,700,000,000). Covers taxable employer firms only. Based on Service Annual Survey. Estimates have been adjusted to the results of the 2017 Economic Census. See Appendix III]

Kind of business	NAICS code [1]	2010	2018	2019	2020	2021	2022
Finance & insurance, total	**52**	**3,495.7**	**4,614.5**	**4,858.8**	**4,981.9**	**5,292.3**	**5,647.0**
Monetary authorities—central bank	521	88.2	113.1	103.8	105.0	122.4	170.4
Credit intermediation & related activities	522	1,161.3	1,403.5	1,488.2	1,461.2	1,459.8	1,572.9
Commercial banking	52211	407.9	518.0	540.7	518.1	512.1	566.9
Savings institutions	52212	48.2	42.5	45.9	45.5	43.1	46.1
Credit unions	52213	47.7	73.2	81.9	84.0	85.3	95.7
Other depository credit intermediation	52219	0.9	1.1	1.1	1.0	1.1	1.2
Credit card issuing	52221	81.5	139.9	150.2	135.3	134.7	160.6
Sales financing	52222	89.5	123.7	130.9	127.3	131.9	131.9
Other nondepository credit intermediation	52229	416.6	391.9	420.8	427.6	406.4	418.2
Mortgage & nonmortgage loan brokers	52231	6.3	10.3	12.1	16.6	19.5	13.4
Financial transactions processing, reserve, and clearinghouse activities	52232	52.7	83.2	84.9	85.7	103.4	115.4
Other activities related to credit intermediation	52239	9.8	19.7	19.7	20.1	22.4	23.5
Securities, commodity contracts, and other financial investment activities	523	497.6	616.6	651.8	688.7	786.0	791.7
Investment banking and securities dealing	52311	119.6	108.1	112.4	119.8	135.2	137.6
Securities brokerage	52312	114.8	131.2	139.8	142.2	159.2	158.5
Commodity contracts dealing	52313	6.9	7.8	8.3	9.2	10.2	11.2
Commodity contracts brokerage	52314	6.2	5.5	5.7	6.2	7.2	8.6
Securities and commodity exchanges	5232	10.1	12.8	13.4	15.2	15.5	16.4
Miscellaneous intermediation	52391	17.2	34.3	38.2	43.1	55.6	58.4
Portfolio management	52392	172.3	248.1	260.5	275.1	314.2	309.0
Investment advice	52393	25.7	43.2	46.6	49.8	59.1	60.8
All other financial investment activities	52399	24.9	25.7	26.9	28.1	29.7	31.2
Insurance carriers & related activities	524	1,748.6	2,481.2	2,615.0	2,727.0	2,924.1	3,112.0
Direct life, health, medical insurance carriers	52411	1,060.7	1,443.9	1,520.0	1,583.7	1,699.4	1,830.5
Other direct insurance carriers	52412	441.6	616.7	649.7	671.3	713.7	736.2
Reinsurance carriers	52413	45.7	73.2	80.0	84.4	93.5	96.0
Insurance agencies & brokerages	52421	98.4	145.1	152.1	160.4	176.1	191.1
Other insurance-related activities	52429	102.1	202.3	213.1	227.2	241.4	258.2

[1] Data for 2010 are based on the 2007 North American Industry Classification System (NAICS); beginning 2013, data are based on 2012 NAICS. See text, this section and Section 15 for more information.

Source: U.S. Census Bureau, Service Annual Survey, "Service Annual Survey Latest Data (NAICS-basis): 2022" and "Service Annual Survey Historical Survey Tables," <www.census.gov/programs-surveys/sas/data/tables.html>, accessed February 2024.

Table 1198. Financial Accounts of the United States—Financial Assets of Nonfinancial and Financial Institutions by Holder Sector: 2000 to 2023

[In billions of dollars (97,850 represents $97,850,000,000,000). As of Dec. 31]

Sector	2000	2010	2015	2017	2018	2019	2020	2021	2022	2023
All sectors	**97,850**	**165,673**	**213,867**	**244,697**	**243,160**	**273,881**	**309,266**	**345,479**	**319,770**	**349,328**
DOMESTIC NONFINANCIAL										
Households [1]	34,456	54,514	72,855	83,375	82,455	93,628	104,999	117,865	108,953	118,832
Nonfinancial business	12,569	16,412	21,277	25,309	25,564	30,022	32,220	35,944	35,050	37,717
Nonfinancial corporations	11,096	13,205	16,736	19,771	19,718	24,049	25,209	28,235	27,001	29,532
Nonfinancial noncorporate	1,473	3,207	4,541	5,537	5,845	5,972	7,010	7,709	8,048	8,186
Federal government	479	1,585	2,049	2,404	2,721	2,737	4,519	3,438	3,621	3,771
State and local government	1,673	2,798	2,933	3,245	3,269	3,425	3,865	4,440	4,493	4,751
DOMESTIC FINANCIAL										
Monetary authority	636	2,452	4,632	4,572	4,096	4,379	7,657	8,911	7,503	6,724
Private depository institutions	7,501	13,654	17,315	18,861	19,221	20,089	23,482	25,639	25,615	26,159
U.S.-chartered depository institutions	6,329	11,453	14,126	15,327	15,641	16,339	19,422	21,125	20,659	20,967
Foreign banking offices in U.S.	691	1,244	1,900	2,085	2,051	2,094	2,103	2,339	2,704	2,810
Banks in U.S.-affiliated areas	62	82	122	107	109	122	134	134	129	163
Credit unions	421	876	1,166	1,342	1,419	1,534	1,823	2,041	2,124	2,220
Property-casualty insurance companies	1,059	1,868	2,143	2,388	2,412	2,688	2,879	3,100	2,978	3,306
Life insurance companies	3,324	5,754	7,057	7,935	7,749	8,718	9,614	10,066	9,048	9,820
Private pension funds	4,283	6,604	8,649	10,019	9,695	11,060	12,042	13,165	11,689	12,892
Defined benefit plans	1,785	2,835	3,399	3,479	3,495	3,633	3,629	3,676	3,726	3,755
Defined contribution plans	2,497	3,768	5,250	6,541	6,200	7,427	8,413	9,489	7,964	9,136
Federal government retirement funds	2,028	3,144	3,709	3,925	4,013	4,196	4,383	4,560	4,530	4,724
State and local government employee retirement funds	3,301	6,169	8,054	8,703	8,929	9,193	9,477	9,723	8,846	9,246
Money market mutual funds [2]	1,845	3,034	3,078	3,121	3,290	4,002	4,766	5,205	5,223	6,358
Mutual funds [2]	5,119	9,030	12,897	15,899	14,670	17,660	19,563	22,209	17,333	19,600
Closed-end funds	143	239	263	277	252	279	282	310	252	256
Exchange-traded funds	66	992	2,101	3,401	3,371	4,396	5,449	7,191	6,477	8,085
Government-sponsored enterprises (GSE) [3]	1,965	6,687	6,503	6,820	6,927	7,130	7,730	8,292	9,188	9,324
Agency- and GSE-backed mortgage pools [4]	2,493	1,147	1,775	2,126	2,292	2,406	2,428	2,502	2,688	2,871
Asset-backed securities issuers	1,509	2,346	1,320	1,122	1,121	1,175	1,226	1,388	1,469	1,506
Finance companies [5]	1,316	1,984	1,758	1,665	1,631	1,685	1,730	2,471	2,414	2,654
Real estate investment trusts	35	208	495	537	612	681	515	533	524	551
Security brokers and dealers	2,522	4,133	3,599	3,573	3,811	3,945	4,199	4,380	4,373	4,876
Holding companies [6]	906	3,218	3,834	4,122	4,091	4,301	4,606	4,797	4,754	4,980
Other financial business [7]	1,000	629	436	690	779	783	1,127	1,355	1,278	1,353
Rest of the world	7,621	17,072	25,138	30,609	30,187	35,302	40,507	47,995	41,473	48,973

[1] Includes nonprofit organizations. [2] Open-end investment companies including variable annuity money market funds or mutual funds. [3] Federal Home Loan Banks, Federal National Mortgage Association (Fannie Mae), Federal Home Loan Mortgage Corporation (Freddie Mac), Federal Agriculture Mortgage Corporation, Farm Credit System, the Financing Corporation, and the Resolution Funding Corporation. The Student Loan Marketing Association (Sallie Mae), was included until it was fully privatized in 2004. [4] Government National Mortgage Association, Federal National Mortgage Association, Federal Home Loan Mortgage Corporation, Federal Agriculture Mortgage Corporation, and Farmers Home Administration pools. Also includes agency- and GSE-backed mortgage pool securities that are used as collateral for agency- and GSE-backed collateralized mortgage obligations (CMOs) and privately issued CMOs. Excludes Federal Financing Bank holdings of pool securities, which are included with federal government mortgages and other loans and advances. [5] Includes retail captive finance companies and mortgage companies. [6] Parent-only bank holding companies, savings and loan holding companies and security holding companies that file Federal Reserve Board form FR Y-9LP, FR Y-9SP, or FR 2320. [7] Includes funding subsidiaries, custodial accounts for reinvested collateral of securities lending operations, Federal Reserve funding, credit, and liquidity special purpose vehicles created in response to the 2008 Financial Crisis and COVID-19 pandemic, and U.S. central clearing parties.

Source: Board of Governors of the Federal Reserve System, "Financial Accounts of the United States, Z.1," <www.federalreserve.gov/data.htm>, accessed March 2024.

Table 1199. Financial Accounts of the United States—Debt Securities and Debt Loans Outstanding By Sector: 2000 to 2023

[In billions of dollars (28,638 represents $28,638,000,000,000). As of December 31. Represents credit market debt owed by sectors shown. Some sectors only borrow/lend through debt securities or loans, but not both]

Item	2000	2010	2015	2017	2018	2019	2020	2021	2022	2023
Total debt outstanding...............	28,638	54,902	63,313	68,620	71,703	74,907	82,925	89,204	94,260	98,373
Total debt securities [1]..................	15,240	31,753	37,479	40,483	42,088	44,180	50,374	53,800	55,882	59,196
Domestic nonfinancial..................	7,050	16,404	22,344	24,324	25,581	26,954	32,048	33,976	35,289	37,930
Nonprofit and household sector..............	138	269	220	218	216	213	204	203	202	204
Nonfinancial corporate business.............	2,751	4,088	5,819	6,503	6,672	6,988	7,684	7,933	8,012	8,249
Federal government.....................	2,972	8,847	13,194	14,459	15,589	16,650	20,966	22,577	23,865	26,247
State and local governments [2].................	1,189	3,199	3,112	3,144	3,104	3,102	3,194	3,263	3,210	3,231
Financial sectors.....................	7,486	13,272	12,512	12,973	13,212	13,668	14,572	15,606	16,880	17,369
U.S.-chartered depository institutions.........	99	585	416	323	288	328	437	312	466	471
Foreign banking offices in U.S.............	2	88	66	63	50	71	65	54	112	157
Government-sponsored enterprises (GSE)...	1,826	6,435	6,369	6,716	6,797	7,002	7,638	8,178	8,971	9,069
Agency- and GSE-backed mortgage pools...	2,493	1,147	1,775	2,126	2,292	2,406	2,428	2,502	2,688	2,871
Asset-backed securities issuers...........	1,515	2,346	1,320	1,122	1,121	1,175	1,226	1,388	1,469	1,506
Finance companies.....................	743	1,188	953	835	879	835	815	1,085	1,062	1,158
Real estate investment trusts..............	14	37	153	133	147	180	180	204	217	217
Securities brokers and dealers.............	41	130	131	186	184	174	184	218	236	236
Holding companies.....................	250	1,150	1,195	1,326	1,301	1,350	1,480	1,545	1,542	1,556
Other financial business.................	503	167	134	142	151	146	118	121	117	128
Rest of the world.......................	703	2,076	2,623	3,186	3,295	3,558	3,754	4,218	3,713	3,897
Total loans [3]......................	13,398	23,150	25,834	28,137	29,615	30,727	32,551	35,404	38,377	39,177
Domestic nonfinancial..................	12,255	21,529	23,566	25,718	27,141	28,221	29,928	32,483	34,987	35,878
Financial sectors.....................	1,009	1,450	1,790	1,876	1,878	1,816	1,869	2,119	2,467	2,316
Rest of the world.......................	134	171	478	544	596	690	755	802	924	983

[1] Includes open market paper, Treasury securities, agency- and GSE-backed securities, municipal securities, and corporate and foreign bonds. [2] Excludes employee retirement funds. [3] Includes depository loans not elsewhere classified, other loans and advances, mortgages, and consumer credit.

Source: Board of Governors of the Federal Reserve System, "Financial Accounts of the United States, Z.1," <www.federalreserve.gov/data.htm>, accessed April 2024.

Table 1200. Financial Accounts of the United States—Financial Assets and Liabilities of Foreign Sector: 2000 to 2023

[In billions of dollars (7,621 represents $7,621,000,000,000). As of December 31. Minus sign (-) indicates loss]

Type of instrument	2000	2010	2015	2018	2019	2020	2021	2022	2023
Total financial assets.................	7,621	17,072	25,138	30,187	35,302	40,507	47,995	41,473	48,973
Special Drawing Rights allocations..............	6	54	49	49	49	51	161	153	154
Net interbank assets.......................	49	-55	198	207	124	153	223	416	571
U.S. checkable deposits and currency..............	236	390	707	928	987	1,143	1,210	1,223	1,244
U.S. time deposits.......................	226	308	480	602	600	665	694	681	698
Money market fund shares.................	11	70	108	111	118	137	165	174	183
Security repurchase agreements..............	91	641	903	972	1,066	1,084	1,367	1,416	1,759
Debt securities, excluding negotiable certificates of deposit.................	2,335	8,252	10,337	11,186	12,368	13,254	13,652	12,603	13,910
Open market (commercial) paper............	114	102	104	125	130	86	138	191	180
Treasury securities.....................	1,021	4,459	6,146	6,270	6,918	7,292	7,740	7,319	8,018
Agency- and GSE-backed securities [1].........	348	1,096	916	1,087	1,231	1,276	1,253	1,261	1,429
Municipal securities.....................	8	72	91	102	110	118	119	108	120
U.S. corporate bonds.................	843	2,523	3,080	3,603	3,979	4,482	4,402	3,724	4,165
Other loans and advances.................	135	161	191	779	857	891	1,037	1,130	1,093
Foreign direct investment in U.S.: intercompany debt [2]...........................	334	495	621	601	568	498	485	513	517
U.S. corporate equities.................	1,483	3,213	5,501	6,630	8,279	10,673	13,898	10,822	13,525
Foreign direct investment in U.S.: equity [2]............	2,449	2,928	5,110	6,746	8,791	10,263	13,163	10,477	13,207
Mutual fund shares.......................	149	263	601	799	900	1,024	1,188	1,059	1,201
Life insurance reserves.................	(Z)	6	6	10	11	2	(Z)	(Z)	(Z)
Pension entitlements.................	(Z)	1	3	15	16	2	1	1	1
Trade receivables.................	70	203	247	333	349	430	511	555	590
Miscellaneous assets.................	46	142	76	220	221	237	241	248	321
Total liabilities.................	1,987	4,894	5,217	6,614	7,013	7,444	7,955	7,687	8,409
U.S. official reserve assets [3].................	57	121	106	115	118	134	240	233	234
U.S. private deposits.................	803	1,304	591	824	764	837	837	915	817
Security repurchase agreements.................	–	664	789	990	1,224	1,279	1,173	1,161	1,689
Debt securities.................	703	2,076	2,623	3,295	3,558	3,754	4,218	3,713	3,897
Commercial paper.................	121	173	196	310	291	218	422	332	301
Bonds.................	582	1,903	2,427	2,985	3,267	3,536	3,797	3,381	3,596
Loans.................	134	171	478	596	690	755	802	924	983
Depository institution loans n.e.c. [4].................	84	149	441	546	633	699	748	860	954
Other loans and advances.................	50	22	37	51	58	56	54	63	29
U.S. direct investment abroad [2].................	148	189	247	232	87	41	-36	-72	-58
Life insurance reserves.................	22	68	51	67	68	84	105	96	97
Pension entitlements.................	6	33	21	78	81	128	170	256	267
Trade payables.................	47	65	66	79	82	82	85	82	84
Miscellaneous liabilities.................	68	203	244	339	341	351	361	378	399

– Represents or rounds to zero. Z Less than $500,000,000. [1] GSE = Government-sponsored enterprises. [2] Direct investment is valued on a market value basis. [3] Excludes monetary gold. [4] N.e.c. = not elsewhere classified.

Source: Board of Governors of the Federal Reserve System, "Financial Accounts of the United States, Z.1," <www.federalreserve.gov/data.htm>, accessed March 2024.

Table 1201. Financial Accounts of the United States—Assets of Households and Nonprofit Organizations: 2000 to 2023

[In billions of dollars (34,456 represents $34,456,000,000,000). As of December 31. See also Table 758]

Type of instrument	Total (billion dollars)							Percent distribution		
	2000	2010	2015	2020	2021	2022	2023	2010	2020	2023
Total financial assets	**34,456**	**54,514**	**72,855**	**104,999**	**117,865**	**108,953**	**118,832**	**100.0**	**100.0**	**100.0**
Foreign deposits	48	67	32	48	48	52	46	0.1	–	–
Checkable deposits and currency	397	526	1,198	3,181	4,145	4,534	4,341	1.0	3.0	3.7
Time and savings deposits	3,032	6,136	7,984	10,300	11,064	10,271	9,838	11.3	9.8	8.3
Money market fund shares	1,296	1,790	1,724	2,691	2,804	3,082	3,806	3.3	2.6	3.2
Debt securities	1,663	4,046	3,580	3,825	2,986	4,434	5,671	7.4	3.6	4.8
Treasury securities	257	679	601	1,148	436	1,462	2,321	1.2	1.1	2.0
Agency and GSE-backed securities [1]	533	345	615	486	452	1,071	1,273	0.6	0.5	1.1
Municipal securities	475	1,901	1,934	1,941	1,808	1,621	1,766	3.5	1.8	1.5
Corporate and foreign bonds	397	1,121	430	250	290	281	311	2.1	0.2	0.3
Loans [2]	831	1,257	1,360	1,377	1,467	1,417	1,346	2.3	1.3	1.1
Mortgages	96	132	99	81	87	78	74	0.2	0.1	0.1
Consumer credit (student loans)	–	71	45	24	22	19	17	0.1	–	–
Corporate equities [3]	7,107	8,683	13,822	26,006	31,656	26,419	31,996	15.9	24.8	26.9
Mutual fund shares	2,557	4,730	6,998	10,996	12,830	9,759	11,005	8.7	10.5	9.3
Life insurance reserves	858	1,308	1,557	1,922	2,000	1,987	2,090	2.4	1.8	1.8
Pension entitlements [4]	11,055	18,339	23,485	29,789	31,560	28,921	30,964	33.6	28.4	26.1
Trade receivables	124	184	241	287	299	312	326	0.3	0.3	0.3
Miscellaneous assets	440	908	1,089	1,377	1,433	1,527	1,635	1.7	1.3	1.4

– Represents or rounds to zero. [1] GSE = government-sponsored enterprises. [2] Includes other instruments not shown separately. [3] Directly held corporate equities, including closed-end fund, exchange-traded fund, and real estate investment trust shares. [4] Includes public and private defined benefit and defined contribution plans and annuities, including those in IRAs and at life insurance companies. Excludes social security.

Source: Board of Governors of the Federal Reserve System, "Financial Accounts of the United States, Z.1," <www.federalreserve.gov/data. htm>, accessed April 2024.

Table 1202. Financial Assets Held by Families by Type of Asset: 2019 and 2022

[Median value in thousands of constant 2022 dollars (29.8 represents $29,800). All dollar figures are adjusted to 2022 dollars using the "current methods" version of the consumer price index for all urban consumers published by U.S. Bureau of Labor Statistics. Families include one-person units; for definition of family, see text, Section 1. Based on Survey of Consumer Finances; see Appendix III]

Age of family head and family income	Any financial asset [1]	Trans-action accounts [2]	Certifi-cates of deposit	Savings bonds	Stocks [3]	Pooled invest-ment funds [4]	Retire-ment accounts [5]	Life insur-ance [6]	Other man-aged [7]
PERCENT OF FAMILIES OWNING ASSET									
2019, total	98.7	98.2	7.7	7.5	15.2	9.0	50.5	19.0	5.9
2022, total	**99.0**	**98.6**	**6.5**	**6.4**	**21.0**	**11.5**	**54.3**	**16.1**	**6.2**
Under 35 years old	98.5	98.2	(B)	2.9	23.1	8.2	49.6	5.6	2.4
35 to 44 years old	98.9	98.4	4.4	6.5	20.6	10.3	61.5	12.4	1.1
45 to 54 years old	99.5	98.9	5.1	6.8	22.7	11.4	62.2	14.2	2.9
55 to 64 years old	98.7	98.3	6.6	8.5	19.2	13.3	57.0	18.2	7.9
65 to 74 years old	99.4	98.8	11.4	8.2	20.4	13.1	51.0	25.3	13.0
75 years old and over	99.8	99.8	12.4	6.2	19.0	14.1	41.8	25.7	12.5
Percentiles of income: [8]									
Less than 20	96.6	95.5	3.8	2.0	7.1	1.9	13.1	10.8	1.5
20 to 39.9	98.8	97.9	4.6	3.5	10.9	4.5	35.6	13.3	4.5
40 to 59.9	99.8	99.8	6.1	6.7	17.2	8.4	56.5	13.0	6.2
60 to 79.9	100.0	99.9	7.4	7.7	21.4	12.6	75.4	17.6	7.1
80 to 89.9	100.0	100.0	11.0	12.4	40.3	20.8	89.4	26.1	8.2
90 to 100	100.0	100.0	9.9	12.2	56.4	39.3	92.9	25.4	15.0
MEDIAN VALUE [9]									
2019, total	29.8	6.1	29.0	0.9	29.0	127.5	75.3	10.4	133.3
2022, total	**39.0**	**8.0**	**26.0**	**2.0**	**15.0**	**150.0**	**86.9**	**9.7**	**140.0**
Under 35 years old	12.8	5.4	(B)	1.3	2.5	24.0	18.6	5.0	60.0
35 to 44 years old	33.2	7.5	10.0	0.8	12.0	80.0	45.0	6.2	150.0
45 to 54 years old	55.0	8.8	14.1	1.8	10.8	175.0	115.0	10.0	200.0
55 to 64 years old	69.8	7.9	25.0	3.0	30.0	300.0	185.0	16.0	185.0
65 to 74 years old	119.7	13.5	53.0	10.0	65.0	250.0	199.6	12.0	150.0
75 years old and over	50.2	10.0	33.0	2.0	100.0	356.0	129.5	7.0	97.2

B Base figure too small to meet statistical standards of reliability. [1] Includes other types of financial assets, not shown separately. [2] Checking, savings, and money market deposit accounts, money market mutual funds, call or cash accounts at brokerages, and prepaid debit cards. [3] Covers only publicly traded stocks that are directly held by families—that is, corporate equities not held as part of a managed investment account or mutual fund. [4] Excludes money market mutual funds and indirectly held mutual funds and includes all other types of directly held pooled investment funds, such as traditional open-ended and closed-end mutual funds, real estate investment trusts, and hedge funds. [5] The tax-deferred retirement accounts consist of IRAs, Keogh accounts, and certain employer-sponsored accounts. Employer-sponsored accounts include 401(k), 403(b), and thrift saving accounts from current or past jobs; other current job plans from which loans or withdrawals can be made; and accounts from past jobs from which the family expects to receive the account balance in the future. [6] The value of such policies according to their current cash value, not their death benefit. [7] Includes personal annuities and trusts with an equity interest and managed investment accounts. [8] Percentiles of income distribution in 2022 dollars: 20th: $34,600; 40th: $59,500; 60th: $91,900; 80th: $153,100; 90th: $245,400. Percentile: A value on a scale of zero to 100 that indicates the percent of a distribution that is equal to or below it. [9] Median value of financial asset for families holding such assets.

Source: Board of Governors of the Federal Reserve System, 2022 Survey of Consumer Finances, *Changes in U.S. Family Finances From 2019 to 2022: Evidence from the Survey of Consumer Finances*, October 2023. See also <www.federalreserve.gov/econres/scfindex.htm>.

Table 1203. Financial Accounts of the United States—Liabilities of Households and Nonprofit Organizations: 2000 to 2023

[In billions of dollars (7,430 represents $7,430,000,000,000). As of December 31. Minus sign (-) indicates decrease. See also Table 758]

Type of instrument	Total (billion dollars)							Percent distribution		
	2000	2010	2015	2020	2021	2022	2023	2010	2020	2023
Total liabilities	**7,430**	**14,104**	**14,506**	**17,206**	**18,851**	**19,969**	**20,529**	**100.0**	**100.0**	**100.0**
Debt securities (municipal securities)	138	269	220	204	203	202	204	1.9	1.2	1.0
Loans	7,125	13,536	13,915	16,527	18,140	19,228	19,751	96.0	96.1	96.2
Home mortgages [1]	4,817	9,993	9,494	10,865	11,927	12,697	13,053	70.9	63.1	63.6
Consumer credit	1,741	2,647	3,400	4,185	4,549	4,894	5,020	18.8	24.3	24.5
Depository institution loans, not elsewhere classified [2]	61	214	281	371	423	495	474	1.5	2.2	2.3
Other loans and advances	376	484	501	717	831	706	736	3.4	4.2	3.6
Commercial mortgages	129	198	239	389	411	436	469	1.4	2.3	2.3
Trade payables	147	273	339	438	470	503	534	1.9	2.5	2.6
Deferred and unpaid life insurance premiums	20	26	32	37	38	37	40	0.2	0.2	0.2

[1] Includes loans made under home equity lines of credit and home equity loans secured by junior liens. [2] Includes loans extended by the Federal Reserve to financial institutions such as domestic hedge funds through the Term Asset-Backed Securities Loan Facility (TALF).

Source: Board of Governors of the Federal Reserve System, "Financial Accounts of the United States, Z.1," <www.federalreserve.gov/data. htm>, accessed March 2024.

Table 1204. Financial Debt Held by Families by Type of Debt: 2019 and 2022

[Median debt in thousands of constant 2022 dollars (75.1 represents $75,100). See headnote, Table 1202]

Age and race of family head and family income	Any debt	Secured by residential property		Installment loans [2]	Credit card balances [3]	Lines of credit not secured by residential property	Other [4]
		Primary residence [1]	Other				
PERCENT OF FAMILIES HOLDING DEBT							
2019, total	76.6	42.1	4.7	51.5	45.4	1.5	5.2
2022, total	**77.4**	**42.2**	**4.4**	**53.0**	**45.2**	**1.6**	**5.1**
Under 35 years old	86.1	33.1	3.2	71.4	48.5	3.3	4.8
35 to 44 years old	87.3	53.0	4.1	64.9	52.6	1.5	6.1
45 to 54 years old	86.9	55.7	5.8	62.3	57.0	1.0	7.5
55 to 64 years old	77.2	48.4	7.0	49.2	44.3	1.8	4.9
65 to 74 years old	64.8	32.2	4.0	35.4	33.9	0.4	4.0
75 years old and over	53.4	27.6	1.2	22.5	29.8	(B)	2.5
White, non-Hispanic	76.9	45.5	4.8	51.4	42.2	1.7	4.7
Black, non-Hispanic	81.3	33.0	2.1	62.6	56.3	1.6	7.9
Hispanic or Latino	75.9	34.0	2.5	50.5	55.8	(B)	4.2
Other or multiple race	77.8	38.8	5.9	54.9	43.3	1.6	5.4
Percentiles of income: [5]							
Less than 20	57.4	12.5	(B)	35.8	33.5	1.5	3.3
20 to 39.9	75.9	26.5	1.7	52.4	46.1	1.3	4.6
40 to 59.9	83.8	46.2	4.1	60.2	57.1	2.1	5.4
60 to 79.9	86.7	60.0	3.5	63.3	54.4	1.5	7.0
80 to 89.9	85.9	66.3	9.2	62.2	44.4	(B)	4.8
90 to 100	80.7	65.0	15.4	45.0	25.7	1.7	5.6
MEDIAN DEBT [6]							
2019, total	75.1	156.3	141.4	20.8	3.1	2.3	5.8
2022, total	**80.2**	**155.6**	**122.0**	**20.0**	**2.7**	**3.0**	**4.3**
Under 35 years old	42.8	176.4	108.8	18.2	1.7	1.8	4.0
35 to 44 years old	138.7	190.0	150.0	24.4	2.9	10.9	3.0
45 to 54 years old	140.3	190.0	92.0	24.4	3.0	7.0	7.0
55 to 64 years old	90.1	125.0	100.0	19.6	3.5	7.0	3.9
65 to 74 years old	45.0	110.0	158.0	15.9	3.5	13.0	15.0
75 years old and over	35.6	90.0	248.5	11.6	1.7	(B)	7.0
White, non-Hispanic	94.4	153.0	127.0	20.0	3.0	6.2	4.3
Black, non-Hispanic	44.3	110.2	69.4	20.1	1.7	0.3	3.5
Hispanic or Latino	40.0	175.4	135.0	16.8	1.8	(B)	4.0
Other or multiple race	84.5	200.0	107.8	20.0	3.0	1.7	9.5

B Base figure too small to meet statistical standards for reliability. [1] Debt secured by residential property consists of first-lien and junior-lien mortgages and home equity lines of credit secured by the primary residence. [2] Consumer loans that typically have fixed payments and a fixed term. Examples are automobile loans, student loans, and loans for furniture, appliances, and other durable consumer goods. [3] Balances exclude purchases made after the most recent bill was paid. [4] Includes loans on insurance policies, loans against pension accounts, borrowing on margin accounts, and unclassified loans. [5] See footnote 8, Table 1202. [6] Median amount of financial debt for families holding such debts.

Source: Board of Governors of the Federal Reserve System, 2022 Survey of Consumer Finances, *Changes in U.S. Family Finances From 2019 to 2022: Evidence from the Survey of Consumer Finances*, October 2023. See also <www.federalreserve.gov/econres/scfindex.htm>.

Table 1205. Debt Held by Families—Percent Distribution by Type and Purpose of Debt: 2010 to 2022

[See headnote, Table 1202]

Type and purpose of debt	2010	2019	2022	Type and purpose of debt	2010	2019	2022
TYPE OF DEBT				PURPOSE OF DEBT			
Total..........................	**100.0**	**100.0**	**100.0**	Total..........................	**100.0**	**100.0**	**100.0**
Secured by residential property:				Primary residence:			
Primary residence.................	74.1	70.6	70.7	Purchase........................	69.5	68.8	69.9
Other...............................	9.8	8.9	8.4	Improvement...................	1.9	1.2	1.2
Lines of credit not secured				Other residential property..........	10.5	9.2	8.9
by residential property.............	1.0	0.6	1.6	Investments, except real estate.....	2.0	1.5	1.7
Installment loans.....................	11.1	16.1	15.3	Vehicles...........................	4.7	6.1	6.0
Credit card balances.................	2.9	2.6	2.2	Goods and services................	5.7	4.6	3.7
Other................................	1.1	1.2	1.8	Education.........................	5.2	8.2	8.0
				Other..............................	0.4	0.5	0.7

Source: Board of Governors of the Federal Reserve System, 2022 Survey of Consumer Finances, *Changes in U.S. Family Finances From 2019 to 2022: Evidence from the Survey of Consumer Finances*, October 2023. See also <www.federalreserve.gov/econres/scfindex.htm>.

Table 1206. Ratios of Debt Payments to Family Income: 2010 to 2022

[In percent. See headnote, Table 1202]

Family characteristic	Ratio of debt payments to family income						Percent of debtors with—					
	Aggregate [1]			Median for debtors [2]			Ratios above 40 percent			Any payment 60 days or more past due		
	2010	2019	2022	2010	2019	2022	2010	2019	2022	2010	2019	2022
All families................	**14.7**	**11.8**	**9.9**	**18.2**	**15.3**	**13.4**	**13.9**	**9.7**	**8.4**	**10.8**	**6.0**	**6.3**
Under 35 years old..........	17.0	14.3	13.1	16.4	14.7	11.3	11.6	8.6	7.1	10.4	8.6	9.1
35 to 44 years old...........	18.4	15.9	10.9	20.9	16.5	14.5	16.4	10.3	9.4	15.7	8.0	6.6
45 to 54 years old...........	16.2	12.5	11.5	19.2	16.2	15.0	15.6	10.4	5.8	12.6	7.2	6.5
55 to 64 years old...........	12.5	10.3	9.3	17.6	15.5	14.6	13.1	9.6	10.6	8.4	3.9	6.2
65 to 74 years old...........	11.3	8.6	7.6	17.0	13.6	11.7	12.1	9.6	9.8	6.1	2.5	3.6
75 years old and over.......	6.8	7.3	5.4	14.1	13.9	10.8	11.9	9.9	8.5	3.2	2.6	2.6
Percentiles of income: [3]												
Less than 20................	23.5	16.2	18.0	16.3	13.9	10.8	26.1	20.9	23.1	21.2	11.1	16.1
20 to 39.9..................	16.9	15.9	14.2	17.5	15.6	13.6	18.7	15.6	11.3	15.2	9.4	8.1
40 to 59.9..................	19.5	16.3	16.0	20.0	16.0	16.0	15.5	11.0	7.5	10.2	6.7	5.6
60 to 79.9..................	19.3	16.4	14.8	20.4	17.3	16.0	11.0	4.9	3.1	8.8	3.8	4.4
80 to 89.9..................	18.1	15.1	12.9	19.3	16.6	12.9	5.4	1.9	3.4	5.4	3.0	1.0
90 to 100...................	9.4	7.0	5.3	13.1	11.0	8.4	2.9	1.2	0.7	2.1	0.2	0.2
Percentiles of net worth: [3]												
Less than 25................	19.2	14.0	11.5	13.6	11.8	7.9	14.9	10.4	6.0	22.2	13.8	14.8
25 to 49.9..................	19.3	16.5	17.3	21.3	18.2	17.8	15.4	11.2	12.1	13.3	7.3	7.3
50 to 74.9..................	19.2	17.5	15.1	20.8	18.7	16.8	14.1	11.2	9.3	6.8	2.8	2.8
75 to 89.9..................	15.9	13.0	11.7	16.7	14.8	12.8	11.0	6.6	6.3	2.0	1.6	0.7
90 to 100...................	8.8	6.5	4.8	13.4	10.0	8.4	11.0	4.5	4.7	1.2	0.4	0.3
Owner occupied.............	16.1	12.8	10.7	22.2	19.2	17.0	17.1	11.9	10.5	8.7	3.3	3.8
Renter occupied or other. ..	7.0	6.9	5.9	6.8	7.4	6.3	5.0	4.7	3.8	16.6	12.3	11.9

[1] The aggregate measure is the ratio of total debt payments to total income for all families. [2] The median is the median of the distribution of ratios calculated for individual families with debt. [3] Percentiles of income distribution in 2022 dollars: 20th: $34,600; 40th: $59,500; 60th: $91,900; 80th: $153,100; 90th: $245,400. Percentiles of distribution of net worth in 2022 dollars: 25th: $27,100; 50th: $192,900; 75th: $658,900; 90th: $1,938,000.

Source: Board of Governors of the Federal Reserve System, 2022 Survey of Consumer Finances, *Changes in U.S. Family Finances From 2019 to 2022: Evidence from the Survey of Consumer Finances*, October 2023. See also <www.federalreserve.gov/econres/scfindex.htm>.

Table 1207. Household Debt-Service Payments and Financial Obligations as a Percent of Disposable Personal Income: 2000 to 2023

[As of end of year (4th quarter), seasonally adjusted. Mortgage debt service ratio (DSR) is defined as the total quarterly required mortgage payments divided by total quarterly disposable personal income. The consumer DSR is defined as the total quarterly required consumer debt payments divided by total quarterly disposable personal income. The financial obligations ratio adds automobile lease payments, rental payments on tenant-occupied property, homeowners' insurance, and property tax payments to the debt service ratio]

Year	Financial obligations ratio	Household debt service ratio			Year	Financial obligations ratio	Household debt service ratio		
		Total	Mortgage	Consumer			Total	Mortgage	Consumer
2000...........	17.07	12.07	5.73	6.35	2017...........	14.91	10.03	4.28	5.76
2010...........	15.96	10.99	5.96	5.03	2018...........	14.71	9.93	4.21	5.72
2012...........	14.88	9.90	4.98	4.92	2019...........	14.71	9.97	4.15	5.83
2013...........	15.38	10.17	4.90	5.27	2020...........	13.96	9.37	3.94	5.44
2014...........	15.07	9.99	4.60	5.38	2021...........	14.01	9.49	3.87	5.62
2015...........	15.14	10.04	4.53	5.52	2022...........	14.40	9.89	4.01	5.88
2016...........	15.18	10.13	4.41	5.72	2023...........	([1])	9.83	4.03	5.81

[1] Financial Obligations Ratio data have been discontinued after publication of data for the third quarter of 2023.

Source: Board of Governors of the Federal Reserve System, "Household Debt Service and Financial Obligations Ratios," <www.federalreserve.gov/data.htm>, accessed July 2024.

Table 1208. FDIC-Insured Financial Institutions—Number and Assets by State and Island Area: 2023

[In billions of dollars, except as indicated (23,778.1 represents $23,778,100,000,000). As of December 31. Includes data from U.S. banks and U.S. branches of foreign banks that have insured deposits. Information is obtained primarily from the Federal Financial Institutions Examination Council (FFIEC) Call Reports and the Office of Thrift Supervision's Thrift Financial Reports. Data are based on the location of each reporting institution's main office. Reported data may include assets located outside of the reporting institution's home state]

State or Island Area	Number of institutions	Assets by asset size of bank				State or Island Area	Number of institutions	Assets by asset size of bank			
		Total	Less than $100 mil.	$100 mil. to $1 bil.	Greater than $1 bil.			Total	Less than $100 mil.	$100 mil. to $1 bil.	Greater than $1 bil.
Total.......	4,596	23,778.1	43.0	1,096.5	22,638.6	NE..........	149	105.6	2.6	31.3	71.7
AL..........	96	215.5	0.6	23.6	191.3	NV..........	16	51.8	–	2.9	48.9
AK..........	5	10.5	–	2.0	8.5	NH..........	19	17.1	0.2	5.8	11.1
AZ..........	14	74.8	0.3	3.7	70.9	NJ..........	53	192.3	–	14.2	178.1
AR..........	82	168.7	0.5	20.9	147.4	NM..........	30	15.4	–	10.9	4.5
CA..........	129	559.5	0.4	26.6	532.5	NY..........	124	1,770.2	0.3	26.5	1,743.3
CO..........	71	106.9	0.3	16.8	89.8	NC..........	42	3,335.6	0.3	8.0	3,327.2
CT..........	29	114.0	0.1	6.3	107.7	ND..........	63	57.0	1.0	12.5	43.5
DE..........	17	1,284.9	0.1	3.2	1,281.6	OH..........	168	4,781.6	2.3	30.0	4,749.3
DC..........	4	3.1	–	1.7	1.4	OK..........	178	189.6	2.8	41.1	145.7
FL..........	86	291.2	0.3	22.2	268.7	OR..........	15	61.0	–	6.7	54.3
GA..........	143	153.2	1.1	36.4	115.8	PA..........	124	317.8	0.5	33.8	283.5
HI..........	7	69.6	–	1.5	68.2	RI..........	7	237.9	–	0.4	237.5
ID..........	11	11.4	–	2.2	9.2	SC..........	45	58.5	0.4	15.0	43.2
IL..........	359	719.3	4.6	77.0	637.7	SD..........	56	3,469.8	0.8	7.3	3,461.8
IN..........	92	182.8	0.3	26.2	156.2	TN..........	121	226.9	0.4	36.6	189.8
IA..........	240	123.3	2.5	55.2	65.6	TX..........	382	1,048.3	3.5	95.5	949.3
KS..........	204	94.3	3.9	38.2	52.2	UT..........	41	1,037.2	0.1	7.8	1,029.3
KY..........	122	76.4	1.1	31.2	44.1	VT..........	12	8.0	0.1	3.9	4.1
LA..........	109	75.3	0.9	29.7	44.6	VA..........	61	772.0	0.3	12.1	759.7
ME..........	23	42.1	0.1	2.1	39.9	WA..........	39	99.0	0.4	9.2	89.5
MD..........	30	59.8	0.1	10.9	48.8	WV..........	46	45.1	0.3	13.1	31.7
MA..........	100	502.6	0.2	26.2	476.2	WI..........	161	152.5	1.0	47.7	103.7
MI..........	78	64.9	0.6	22.8	41.5	WY..........	26	10.3	0.2	8.7	1.3
MN..........	251	126.4	4.7	49.6	72.1	GU..........	3	2.8	–	0.2	2.5
MS..........	62	170.9	0.3	18.1	152.4	FM..........	1	0.2	–	0.2	–
MO..........	208	248.9	2.0	53.4	193.5	PR..........	4	87.1	–	0.1	87.0
MT..........	37	76.7	0.6	6.8	69.3	VI..........	1	0.5	–	0.5	–

– Represents or rounds to zero. GU—Guam, FM—Federated States of Micronesia, PR—Puerto Rico, VI—Virgin Islands.

Source: U.S. Federal Deposit Insurance Corporation, "BankFind Suite," <banks.data.fdic.gov/bankfind-suite/>, accessed April 2024.

Table 1209. FDIC-Insured Financial Institutions—Income and Selected Measures of Financial Condition: 2000 to 2023

[In billions of dollars, except as indicated (511.9 represents $511,900,000,000). Includes Island Areas. Includes foreign branches of U.S. banks. Minus sign (-) indicates decrease]

Item	2000	2010	2015	2018	2019	2020	2021	2022	2023
INCOME									
Interest income.................................	511.9	536.9	478.5	661.1	705.4	603.8	563.6	750.9	1,150.0
Interest expense...............................	276.6	106.9	46.9	119.8	158.7	77.1	36.1	117.6	451.8
Net interest income.......................	235.3	430.0	431.6	541.3	546.7	526.7	527.4	633.3	698.2
Provisions for loan losses.....................	32.1	158.0	37.1	50.0	55.1	132.3	-31.0	51.6	86.6
Noninterest income............................	165.6	235.7	253.3	266.1	264.4	280.2	300.4	290.8	305.4
Noninterest expense..........................	242.3	391.8	416.9	459.3	466.1	499.0	510.2	538.1	592.7
Income taxes..................................	43.6	38.4	70.6	61.0	60.9	36.3	72.4	67.3	59.1
Net income attributable to bank..................	81.5	85.5	163.4	236.8	232.8	147.1	279.1	262.8	254.1
PERFORMANCE RATIOS									
Return on assets (percent) [1]....................	1.14	0.65	1.04	1.35	1.29	0.72	1.23	1.11	1.10
Return on equity (percent) [2]...................	13.53	5.85	9.29	11.98	11.38	6.85	12.21	11.82	11.50
Net interest margin (percent) [3]................	3.77	3.76	3.08	3.40	3.36	2.82	2.54	2.95	3.30
Net charge-offs (bil. dol.) [4]...................	26.32	187.64	37.28	47.50	52.16	54.11	27.36	31.46	63.02
Net charge-offs to loans and leases, total (percent)...................................	0.59	2.55	0.44	0.48	0.52	0.50	0.25	0.27	0.52
Net charge-off rate, credit card loans (percent)...................................	4.36	10.08	2.92	3.75	3.82	3.48	2.17	2.09	3.56
CONDITION RATIOS									
Equity capital to assets (percent)................	8.49	11.15	11.24	11.25	11.32	10.17	9.94	9.34	9.69
Noncurrent assets plus other real estate owned to assets (percent) [5]	0.71	3.11	0.97	0.60	0.55	0.61	0.44	0.39	0.47

[1] Net income (including securities transactions and nonrecurring items) as a percentage of average total assets. [2] Net income as a percentage of average total equity capital. [3] Interest income less interest expense as a percentage of average earning assets (i.e. the profit margin a bank earns on its loans and investments). [4] Total loans and leases charged off (removed from balance sheet because of uncollectibility), less amounts recovered on loans and leases previously charged off. [5] Noncurrent assets: the sum of loans, leases, debt securities and other assets that are 90 days or more past due, or in nonaccrual status, plus other real estate owned, primarily foreclosed property.

Source: U.S. Federal Deposit Insurance Corporation, *Quarterly Banking Profile*, Second Quarter 2024, and earlier reports; and "QBP Time Series Spreadsheets, Annual Income," <www.fdic.gov/quarterly-banking-profile/>, accessed September 2024.

Table 1210. FDIC-Insured Financial Institutions—Assets and Liabilities: 2000 to 2023

[In billions of dollars, except as indicated (7,463 represents $7,463,000,000,000). As of December 31. Includes Island Areas. Excludes insured branches of foreign banks. Includes foreign branches of U.S. banks]

Item	2000	2010	2015	2018	2019	2020	2021	2022	2023
Number of financial institutions reporting......	**9,904**	**7,658**	**6,182**	**5,406**	**5,177**	**5,002**	**4,839**	**4,706**	**4,587**
Assets, total [1]......	**7,463**	**13,319**	**15,968**	**17,943**	**18,646**	**21,869**	**23,720**	**23,595**	**23,666**
Net loans and leases [1]......	4,572	7,144	8,721	10,027	10,394	10,627	11,069	12,031	12,234
Real estate loans [1]......	2,396	4,267	4,375	4,887	5,049	5,118	5,260	5,766	5,928
1-4 family residential mortgages......	1,340	1,900	1,904	2,119	2,202	2,211	2,259	2,480	2,565
Nonfarm nonresidential......	525	1,071	1,232	1,444	1,516	1,569	1,647	1,778	1,816
Construction and development......	197	321	275	350	362	386	402	467	500
Home equity loans......	151	637	465	376	342	300	265	273	272
Multifamily residential real estate......	117	213	344	431	459	479	513	599	611
Commercial and industrial loans......	1,086	1,184	1,837	2,164	2,208	2,441	2,309	2,530	2,478
Loans to individuals [1]......	672	1,316	1,498	1,743	1,838	1,744	1,882	2,071	2,136
Credit cards......	266	702	756	903	942	822	871	1,009	1,117
Other loans to individuals......	406	614	741	839	896	922	1,011	1,061	1,019
Auto loans......	(NA)	(NA)	415	455	484	492	538	548	530
Loans to depository institutions......	118	109	98	84	75	60	85	64	59
Lease financing receivables......	167	102	116	133	132	124	118	114	117
Less: Reserve for losses......	71	231	119	125	124	237	178	195	218
Securities......	1,361	2,668	3,354	3,723	3,982	5,112	6,246	5,884	5,435
Domestic office assets......	6,702	11,693	14,408	16,150	16,840	19,709	21,486	21,324	21,468
Foreign office assets......	760	1,626	1,560	1,793	1,806	2,160	2,234	2,271	2,199
Liabilities and capital, total [1]......	**7,463**	**13,319**	**15,968**	**17,943**	**18,646**	**21,869**	**23,720**	**23,595**	**23,666**
Deposits......	4,915	9,423	12,190	13,866	14,536	17,824	19,702	19,215	18,814
Foreign office deposits......	707	1,550	1,282	1,253	1,315	1,534	1,512	1,489	1,468
Domestic office deposits......	4,208	7,873	10,908	12,613	13,221	16,290	18,190	17,726	17,346
Interest-bearing deposits......	3,437	6,184	7,908	9,478	10,060	11,683	12,673	12,898	13,363
Noninterest-bearing deposits......	771	1,689	3,000	3,135	3,161	4,607	5,516	4,828	3,983
Equity capital......	633	1,511	1,801	2,023	2,114	2,227	2,360	2,206	2,294

NA Not available. [1] Includes other items not shown separately.

Source: U.S. Federal Deposit Insurance Corporation, "QBP Time Series Spreadsheets, Balance Sheet," <www.fdic.gov/quarterly-banking-profile/>, accessed September 2024.

Table 1211. FDIC-Insured Financial Institutions by Asset Size: 2023

[22,452.2 represents $22,452,200,000,000. Includes Island Areas. Includes foreign branches of U.S. banks]

Item	Unit	Total	Less than $100 mil.	$100 mil. to $1 bil.	$1 bil. to $10 bil.	Greater than $10 bil.
COMMERCIAL BANKS						
Institutions reporting......	Number	4,026	611	2,574	698	143
Assets, total......	Billion dollars	22,452.2	37.9	963.8	2,005.5	19,445.0
Deposits......	Billion dollars	17,830.9	31.7	819.2	1,649.9	15,330.1
Net income......	Billion dollars	248.0	0.4	10.3	23.6	213.8
Percentage of banks losing money......	Percent	3.75	9.33	2.87	2.15	3.50
Return on assets......	Percent	1.12	0.96	1.09	1.21	1.11
Return on equity......	Percent	11.60	8.11	11.93	12.46	11.51
Net charge-offs to loans and leases......	Percent	0.50	0.08	0.10	0.28	0.55
Noncurrent assets plus other real estate owned to assets......	Percent	0.46	0.46	0.38	0.51	0.46
Equity capital to assets......	Percent	9.76	12.25	9.57	10.08	9.73
SAVINGS INSTITUTIONS						
Institutions reporting......	Number	561	88	325	133	15
Assets, total......	Billion dollars	1,216.6	5.1	132.7	331.3	747.5
Deposits......	Billion dollars	982.4	3.8	105.2	257.7	615.7
Net income......	Billion dollars	8.9	(Z)	1.4	2.2	5.3
Percentage of banks losing money......	Percent	15.69	31.82	16.00	5.26	6.67
Return on assets......	Percent	0.73	0.54	1.11	0.66	0.69
Return on equity......	Percent	9.35	2.88	9.24	6.53	11.56
Net charge-offs to loans and leases......	Percent	0.89	0.08	0.05	0.10	1.74
Noncurrent assets plus other real estate owned to assets......	Percent	0.66	0.64	0.46	0.36	0.83
Equity capital to assets......	Percent	8.51	18.64	12.18	10.45	6.93

Z Less than $50 million.

Source: U.S. Federal Deposit Insurance Corporation, "BankFind Suite: Peer Group Comparisons," <banks.data.fdic.gov/bankfind-suite/peergroup>, accessed April 2024.

Table 1212. FDIC-Insured Financial Institutions—Deposit Insurance Fund (DIF) Indicators: 2010 to 2023

[In billions of dollars, except as indicated (7,873 represents $7,873,000,000,000). As of December 31. Includes Island Areas. Includes insured branches of foreign banks]

Item	2010	2015	2016	2017	2018	2019	2020	2021	2022	2023
Number of institutions reporting.........	7,658	6,182	5,913	5,670	5,406	5,177	5,002	4,839	4,706	4,587
Domestic deposits, total [1]...............	7,873	10,908	11,649	12,081	12,613	13,221	16,290	18,190	17,725	17,345
Estimated insured deposits [2]...........	6,302	6,519	6,916	7,157	7,517	7,810	9,102	9,902	10,251	10,621
DIF balance............................	-7	73	83	93	103	110	118	123	128	122
Reserve ratio [3].........................	-0.12	1.11	1.20	1.30	1.37	1.41	1.30	1.24	1.25	1.15
Number of problem institutions..........	884	183	123	95	60	51	56	44	39	52
Assets of problem institutions...........	390.0	47.0	28.0	13.9	48.5	46.2	56.0	170.0	47.0	66.3
Number of failed institutions.............	157	8	5	8	–	4	4	–	–	5
Assets of failed institutions..............	92.1	6.7	0.3	5.1	–	0.2	0.5	–	–	532.3

– Represents zero. [1] Excludes foreign office deposits, which are uninsured. [2] In general, insured deposits are total domestic deposits minus estimated uninsured deposits. Prior to September 30, 2009, insured deposits included deposits in accounts of $100,000 or less. Beginning September 30, 2009, insured deposits include deposits in accounts of $100,000 to $250,000 that are covered by a temporary increase in the FDIC's standard maximum deposit insurance amount. The Dodd-Frank Wall Street Reform and Consumer Protection Act of July 21, 2010 (Dodd-Frank) made permanent the standard maximum deposit insurance amount of $250,000. The Dodd-Frank Act also provided unlimited coverage for noninterest bearing transaction accounts for two years beginning December 31, 2010, and ending December 31, 2012. [3] DIF balance as percent of DIF-insured deposits.

Source: U.S. Federal Deposit Insurance Corporation, Quarterly Banking Profile, "Statistics at a Glance," December 2023, <www.fdic.gov/analysis/quarterly-banking-profile>, accessed April 2024.

Table 1213. FDIC-Insured Financial Institutions—Number of Offices and Deposits by State: 2023

[17,270 represents $17,270,000,000,000. As of June 30. Includes insured U.S. branches of foreign banks. The term "offices" includes both main offices and branches. "Banking office" is defined to include all offices and facilities that actually hold deposits, and does not include loan production offices, computer centers, and other nondeposit installations such as automated teller machines (ATMs). Several institutions have designated home offices that do not accept deposits; these have been included to provide a more complete listing of all offices. The figures for each geographical area only include deposits of offices located within that area. Based on the Summary of Deposits survey]

State	Number of offices	Total deposits (bil. dol.)	State	Number of offices	Total deposits (bil. dol.)	State	Number of offices	Total deposits (bil. dol.)
Total [1].....	77,770	17,270	IA..............	1,446	121	NC.............	2,003	606
			KS..............	1,364	99	ND.............	411	40
U.S...........	77,448	17,170	KY..............	1,477	114	OH.............	3,106	548
AL............	1,358	135	LA..............	1,330	136	OK.............	1,293	132
AK............	113	15	ME.............	441	43	OR.............	747	105
AZ............	989	209	MD.............	1,213	194	PA.............	3,443	563
AR............	1,286	97	MA.............	1,945	556	RI..............	235	42
CA............	5,768	1,822	MI..............	2,018	293	SC.............	1,141	125
CO............	1,360	187	MN.............	1,616	299	SD.............	434	797
CT............	975	167	MS.............	1,071	77	TN.............	1,919	222
DE............	247	501	MO.............	2,127	250	TX.............	6,232	1,515
DC............	196	62	MT.............	374	36	UT.............	506	944
FL............	4,279	834	NE.............	1,042	87	VT.............	227	18
GA............	2,043	342	NV.............	420	118	VA.............	1,860	303
HI............	219	58	NH.............	393	48	WA.............	1,439	214
ID............	417	39	NJ.............	2,382	445	WV.............	564	45
IL............	3,715	667	NM.............	411	44	WI.............	1,702	196
IN............	1,758	200	NY.............	4,176	2,440	WY.............	217	21

[1] Includes outlying areas not shown separately.

Source: U.S. Federal Deposit Insurance Corporation, "Summary of Deposits, Reference Tables," <www7.fdic.gov/sod/sodSummary. asp?barItem=3>, accessed September 2024.

Table 1214. U.S. Banking Offices of Foreign Banks—Summary: 2000 to 2023

[In billions of dollars (1,358 represents $1,358,000,000,000), except as indicated. As of December. The U.S. offices of foreign banking organizations consist of U.S. branches and agencies of foreign banks and bank subsidiaries of foreign banking organizations. Foreign-owned institutions are those owned by a bank located outside of the United States and its affiliated insular areas. Bank subsidiaries of foreign banking organizations are U.S. commercial banks of which more than 25 percent are owned by a foreign banking organization or where the relationship is reported as being a controlling relationship by the filer of the FR Y-10 (Report of Changes in Organizational Structure) report form. Covers the U.S. offices of foreign banking organizations that are located in the 50 states and the District of Columbia; excludes offices located in Puerto Rico, American Samoa, Guam, the Virgin Islands and other U.S.-affiliated insular areas]

Item	2000	2010	2015	2019	2020	2021	2022	2023	Share [1] 2010	Share [1] 2020	Share [1] 2023
Assets.....................	1,358	2,838	3,539	3,849	4,036	4,244	4,312	4,412	20.4	17.3	17.1
Loans, total................	557	960	1,416	1,589	1,614	1,644	1,802	1,835	13.7	14.6	14.2
Business loans...........	308	326	580	601	619	611	689	679	25.1	23.6	24.0
Deposits..................	770	1,752	2,029	2,174	2,406	2,453	2,371	2,302	18.3	13.3	12.0

[1] Foreign owned banks plus U.S. branches and offices of foreign banks as percent of all banks in the United States.

Source: Board of Governors of the Federal Reserve System, "Structure and Share Data for U.S. Banking Offices of Foreign Entities," <www.federalreserve.gov/releases/iba/default.htm>, accessed September 2024.

Table 1215. Federal and State–Chartered Credit Unions—Summary: 2000 to 2023

[43,883 represents 43,883,000. As of December 31. Federal data include District of Columbia, Puerto Rico, Guam, and Virgin Islands. Excludes state-insured, privately insured, and noninsured state-chartered credit unions and corporate central credit unions, which have mainly other credit unions as members]

Year	Operating credit unions		Number of failed institu- tions [1]	Members (1,000)		Assets (mil. dol.)		Loans outstanding (mil. dol.)		Savings (mil. dol.)	
	Federal	State		Federal	State	Federal	State	Federal	State	Federal	State
2000.......	6,336	3,980	29	43,883	33,705	242,881	195,363	163,851	137,485	210,188	169,053
2010.......	4,589	2,750	29	50,081	40,447	500,075	414,395	306,276	258,555	427,603	358,877
2011.......	4,447	2,647	16	50,743	41,093	525,633	436,121	308,845	262,640	449,316	378,093
2012.......	4,272	2,547	22	51,797	42,043	557,119	464,612	322,675	275,066	474,903	402,948
2013.......	4,105	2,449	17	52,499	43,762	571,326	490,588	343,780	301,440	485,500	424,587
2014.......	3,927	2,346	15	53,355	45,870	596,145	525,942	373,387	338,938	499,683	451,107
2015.......	3,764	2,257	16	54,284	48,369	628,012	576,266	404,729	382,288	522,109	493,892
2016.......	3,608	2,177	14	56,598	50,205	670,124	622,354	444,516	424,591	559,825	532,759
2017.......	3,499	2,074	10	59,036	52,261	718,287	660,530	490,115	467,175	594,662	564,807
2018.......	3,376	1,999	8	61,272	54,891	753,546	699,853	532,693	510,860	625,464	594,269
2019.......	3,283	1,953	2	63,080	57,283	802,993	763,706	561,192	546,766	670,912	648,837
2020.......	3,185	1,914	1	64,861	59,452	931,190	913,333	583,311	579,326	794,937	792,664
2021.......	3,100	1,842	7	68,117	61,344	1,039,738	1,020,613	632,108	623,088	893,622	895,010
2022.......	2,980	1,780	6	71,228	64,017	1,083,324	1,084,365	749,201	757,388	921,766	928,114
2023.......	2,880	1,724	3	73,682	65,595	1,131,315	1,124,502	802,738	800,004	946,947	934,154

[1] A failed institution is defined as a credit union that has ceased operation because it was involuntarily liquidated or merged with assistance from the National Credit Union Share Insurance Fund.

Source: National Credit Union Administration, *National Credit Union Administration 2023 Annual Report,* February 2024, and earlier reports; and "5300 Call Report Aggregate Financial Performance Report," December 2023, <www.ncua.gov/analysis/credit-union-corporate-call-report-data>. See also <www.ncua.gov/news/annual-reports>.

Table 1216. Noncash Payments by Method of Payment: 2015 to 2021

[143.6 represents 143,600,000,000. Estimates are based on survey data from the Federal Reserve Payments Survey, which is conducted every three years and updated with a smaller supplemental annual data collection between the triennial studies. The Study combines information gathered in three related survey efforts. Some estimates are based on data collected in the Depository and Financial Institutions Payments Survey (DFIPS), which is sent to a nationally representative, stratified random sample of depository and financial institutions. Other estimates are based on data collected in the Networks, Processors, and Issuers Payments Surveys (NPIPS) of payment organizations such as card networks, issuers and processors of card and alternative payment methods and services. Finally, some estimates are from data collected in the Check Sample Survey (CSS), which are based on the information from a random sample of checks processed by a selected number of large commercial banks. ATM withdrawals are excluded here]

Method of payment [1]	Transactions (billions)			Value (trillion dollars)			Average value per transaction (dollars)		
	2015	2018	2021	2015	2018	2021	2015	2018	2021
Total noncash payments.............	**143.6**	**173.7**	**204.5**	**86.8**	**98.0**	**128.5**	**604**	**564**	**628**
Total card payments.....................	**101.5**	**131.2**	**157.0**	**5.5**	**7.1**	**9.4**	**54**	**54**	**60**
Debit cards.............................	67.8	86.4	106.0	2.5	3.1	4.5	36	36	43
Non-prepaid............................	56.6	72.7	87.8	2.2	2.7	3.9	38	38	45
Prepaid.................................	11.2	13.8	18.1	0.3	0.3	0.6	26	25	34
General purpose [2].....................	4.3	6.0	8.9	0.1	0.2	0.4	35	32	42
Private label [3]........................	4.4	5.5	5.1	0.1	0.1	0.1	16	18	16
Electronic benefits transfer (EBT). ..	2.6	2.2	4.0	0.1	0.1	0.2	29	26	39
Credit cards..............................	33.7	44.7	51.1	3.1	4.0	4.9	91	89	96
General purpose [2].....................	31.0	40.9	47.8	2.8	3.6	4.5	90	89	95
Private label [3]........................	2.7	3.8	3.3	0.2	0.3	0.4	93	89	108
Automated clearinghouse (ACH) [4]....	**23.9**	**28.5**	**36.2**	**52.1**	**64.2**	**91.8**	**2,177**	**2,250**	**2,536**
Network [5]...............................	19.3	22.9	29.1	41.6	51.3	72.6	2,159	2,234	2,497
Credit transfers.........................	8.0	9.5	12.7	26.8	33.4	47.3	3,333	3,512	3,714
Debit transfers..........................	11.3	13.4	16.4	14.9	17.8	25.4	1,321	1,328	1,551
On-us [6].................................	4.6	5.6	7.1	10.4	12.9	19.2	2,249	2,315	2,695
Credit transfers.........................	2.0	2.4	3.2	5.7	7.5	11.4	2,922	3,154	3,591
Debit transfers..........................	2.7	3.2	4.0	4.7	5.5	7.8	1,761	1,697	1,977
Checks [7]................................	**18.1**	**14.0**	**11.2**	**29.2**	**26.8**	**27.2**	**1,609**	**1,908**	**2,430**
Interbank.................................	13.6	10.9	8.6	21.3	20.3	19.7	1,564	1,865	2,280
On-us [6].................................	4.5	3.1	2.6	7.9	6.5	7.6	1,746	2,058	2,930

[1] ATM withdrawals are not included in the data. [2] Cards issued by depository institutions and processed over card networks. They carry a network brand from one of the four major card networks or from smaller or regional networks and can be used wherever that network card is accepted, regardless of merchant or merchant type. [3] Cards issued by merchants and processed over proprietary networks. They are accepted only by the sponsoring merchant. [4] The Automated Clearing House (ACH) is an electronic funds transfer system that processes financial transactions for consumers, businesses, and governments. The ACH provides many payment services, including payroll, direct deposit, tax payments and refunds, and consumer bills. [5] Network ACH payments are mainly passed between two depository institutions (interbank payments). Some depository institutions send all ACH transfers to ACH operators; ACH network payments also include a small portion of payments that are received by the same depository institution that sent them. [6] Payments processed by a depository institution between their own customers internally. [7] Excludes checks converted to ACH, where the check is used as a source document to initiate the ACH payment.

Source: Board of Governors of the Federal Reserve System, "The Federal Reserve Payments Study: 2022 Triennial Initial Data Release," <www.federalreserve.gov/paymentsystems/fr-payments-study.htm>, accessed April 2023.

Table 1217. Consumer Credit by Type of Holder: 2000 to 2023

[In billions of dollars (1,741 represents $1,741,000,000,000). As of December 31. Not seasonally adjusted]

Type of holder	2000	2010	2015	2016	2017	2018	2019	2020	2021	2022	2023
Total	**1,741**	**2,647**	**3,400**	**3,636**	**3,831**	**4,007**	**4,192**	**4,185**	**4,549**	**4,894**	**5,020**
Nonprofit organizations [1]	–	71	45	41	35	31	27	24	22	19	17
Nonfinancial corporate business	81	44	37	38	36	36	36	36	36	36	36
Federal government [2]	60	364	950	1,049	1,146	1,236	1,319	1,381	1,436	1,487	1,460
U.S.-chartered depository institutions	616	1,186	1,428	1,532	1,612	1,682	1,771	1,686	1,826	2,030	2,101
Credit unions	184	226	353	397	439	481	498	505	532	637	663
Government-sponsored enterprises	37	–	–	–	–	–	–	–	–	–	–
Asset-backed securities issuers	528	50	26	30	21	5	3	2	1	3	16
Finance companies	234	705	561	548	541	534	538	551	695	683	727
Memo:											
Credit card loans [3]	702	839	898	960	1,017	1,054	1,092	975	1,054	1,213	1,319
Auto loans	581	713	990	1,062	1,102	1,140	1,184	1,224	1,393	1,499	1,556
Student loans [4]	–	855	1,320	1,405	1,489	1,567	1,638	1,694	1,733	1,764	1,727
Other consumer credit [5]	458	239	192	209	223	247	278	292	369	418	418

– Represents or rounds to zero. [1] Student loans originated under the Federal Family Education Loan Program. Asset of the households and nonprofit organizations sector. [2] Includes loans originated by the Department of Education under the Federal Direct Loan Program and Perkins Loans, as well as Federal Family Education Loan Program loans that the government purchased from depository institutions, finance companies, and nonprofit and educational institutions, and loans in default. [3] Revolving credit that also includes overdraft plans on checking accounts and other loans without a fixed repayment schedule. [4] Includes student loans held by nonprofit organizations, the federal government, depository institutions, and finance companies. Data begin in 2006. [5] Prior to 2006, includes student loans.

Source: Board of Governors of the Federal Reserve System, "Financial Accounts of the United States, Z.1," <www.federalreserve.gov/data.htm>, accessed April 2024.

Table 1218. Consumer Credit Outstanding and Finance Rates: 2000 to 2023

[In billions of dollars (1,717 represents $1,717,000,000,000), except percent. Covers most short- and intermediate-term credit extended to individuals, excluding loans secured by real estate. Estimated amounts of seasonally adjusted credit outstanding as of end of year; finance rates are annual averages]

Type of credit	2000	2010	2015	2017	2018	2019	2020	2021	2022	2023
Total	**1,717**	**2,647**	**3,400**	**3,831**	**4,007**	**4,192**	**4,185**	**4,549**	**4,894**	**5,024**
Revolving	683	839	898	1,017	1,054	1,092	975	1,054	1,213	1,319
Nonrevolving [1]	1,034	1,808	2,502	2,814	2,953	3,100	3,210	3,495	3,682	3,705
FINANCE RATES (percent)										
Commercial banks:										
New automobiles, 60-month loans	(NA)	6.28	4.20	4.33	5.02	5.31	5.02	4.82	5.36	7.83
New automobiles, 72-month loans	(NA)	(NA)	(NA)	4.50	5.13	5.36	5.21	4.82	5.50	7.89
Personal loans, 24-months loans	13.90	10.87	9.75	10.13	10.32	10.32	9.51	9.38	9.87	11.87
Credit card plans, all accounts	15.78	13.78	12.09	12.89	14.22	15.05	14.71	14.60	16.26	20.90
Credit card plans, accounts assessed interest	14.92	14.26	13.66	14.44	16.05	16.98	16.28	16.45	17.91	22.15
Finance companies:										
New automobiles [2]	(NA)	4.70	5.13	5.36	6.13	6.41	5.25	4.64	5.23	6.68

NA Not available. [1] Includes motor vehicle loans and all other loans not included in revolving credit, such as loans for mobile homes, education, boats, trailers, or vacations. These loans may be secured or unsecured. [2] Covers most of the captive and non-captive finance companies. Amount of finance weighted.

Source: Board of Governors of the Federal Reserve System, Data Releases, Household Finances, "Consumer Credit-G.19," <www.federalreserve.gov/econresdata/statisticsdata.htm>, accessed September 2024.

Table 1219. Mortgage Debt Outstanding by Type and Holder: 2000 to 2023

[In billions of dollars (6,773 represents $6,773,000,000,000). As of December 31]

Type of property and holder	2000	2010	2015	2017	2018	2019	2020	2021	2022	2023
MORTGAGES BY TYPE										
Total	**6,773**	**13,902**	**13,896**	**14,928**	**15,481**	**16,054**	**16,805**	**18,331**	**19,608**	**20,237**
Home [1]	5,125	10,524	10,077	10,598	10,900	11,183	11,654	12,787	13,618	13,994
Multifamily residential	405	864	1,122	1,368	1,494	1,628	1,762	1,918	2,084	2,199
Commercial	1,158	2,359	2,488	2,725	2,842	2,975	3,102	3,301	3,571	3,689
Farm	85	154	209	236	246	268	289	324	335	355
Total liabilities	**6,773**	**13,902**	**13,896**	**14,928**	**15,481**	**16,054**	**16,805**	**18,331**	**19,608**	**20,237**
Household sector	4,947	10,191	9,733	10,190	10,462	10,834	11,254	12,338	13,133	13,522
Nonfinancial business	1,827	3,710	4,163	4,738	5,019	5,220	5,551	5,993	6,475	6,715
Nonfinancial corporate business	445	858	816	793	869	983	987	1,089	1,259	1,317
Nonfinancial noncorporate business	1,381	2,853	3,348	3,945	4,150	4,237	4,564	4,904	5,216	5,398
Total assets	**6,773**	**13,902**	**13,896**	**14,928**	**15,481**	**16,054**	**16,805**	**18,331**	**19,608**	**20,237**
Household sector	96	132	99	90	84	82	81	87	78	74
Nonfinancial corporate business	49	44	78	65	62	67	82	113	149	171
Nonfinancial noncorporate business	23	42	42	48	49	51	53	52	55	56
Federal government	76	101	116	120	123	124	127	133	168	176
State and local governments	136	222	231	257	259	257	261	269	277	285
Private depository institutions	2,503	4,589	4,779	5,283	5,443	5,655	5,741	5,953	6,490	6,745
Property-casualty insurance companies	2	4	13	18	20	23	24	28	30	32
Life insurance companies	243	328	443	523	586	639	662	710	779	829
Private pension funds	12	26	22	27	24	23	24	25	26	27
State and local government retirement funds	22	11	8	7	12	8	7	7	7	5
Government-sponsored enterprises (GSE)	264	5,021	4,920	5,194	5,334	5,511	6,142	6,924	7,324	7,427
Agency- and GSE-backed mortgage pools	2,493	1,147	1,775	2,126	2,292	2,406	2,428	2,502	2,688	2,871
Asset-backed securities issuers	604	1,962	1,018	845	851	849	833	889	900	923
Finance companies	238	244	159	124	115	117	110	353	341	332
Real estate investment trusts	12	29	192	202	228	243	228	288	296	284
HOME MORTGAGES [1]										
Total liabilities	**5,125**	**10,524**	**10,077**	**10,598**	**10,900**	**11,183**	**11,654**	**12,787**	**13,618**	**13,994**
Household sector	4,817	9,993	9,494	9,931	10,207	10,479	10,865	11,927	12,697	13,053
Nonfinancial corporate business	14	14	13	16	17	17	17	19	22	21
Nonfinancial noncorporate business	294	518	570	651	676	687	772	842	900	921
Total assets	**5,125**	**10,524**	**10,077**	**10,598**	**10,900**	**11,183**	**11,654**	**12,787**	**13,618**	**13,994**
Household sector	87	124	91	79	75	72	68	65	61	58
Nonfinancial corporate business	22	17	32	20	21	22	27	33	40	48
Nonfinancial noncorporate business	9	15	15	17	18	18	19	19	20	21
Federal government	16	21	28	29	29	29	30	33	63	66
State and local governments	69	115	119	132	133	132	134	137	141	145
U.S.-chartered depository institutions	1,556	2,618	2,434	2,557	2,586	2,638	2,581	2,606	2,853	2,926
Foreign banking offices in U.S.	–	1	2	1	2	1	1	1	1	1
Banks in U.S.-affiliated areas	9	20	16	15	14	13	13	12	11	12
Credit unions	120	317	405	481	523	565	610	668	671	722
Life insurance companies	8	10	20	26	33	40	40	51	67	72
Private pension funds	8	2	1	2	2	1	2	2	2	2
State and local government retirement funds	7	4	3	2	4	3	3	2	2	2
Government-sponsored enterprises (GSE)	210	4,691	4,571	4,776	4,884	5,016	5,575	6,313	6,661	6,713
Agency- and GSE-backed mortgage pools	2,426	1,075	1,569	1,826	1,949	2,025	2,009	2,044	2,223	2,397
Asset-backed securities issuers	385	1,315	603	474	468	446	410	412	424	433
Finance companies	187	170	123	95	87	85	77	311	301	296
Real estate investment trusts	8	9	46	65	72	76	53	79	78	83
Memo:										
Home equity loans included above [2]	408	929	642	570	533	501	442	446	478	512

– Represents zero. [1] Mortgages on one- to four-family properties, including mortgages on farm houses. [2] Loans made under home equity lines of credit and home equity loans secured by junior liens. Excludes home equity loans held by individuals.

Source: Board of Governors of the Federal Reserve System, "Financial Accounts of the United States, Z.1," <www.federalreserve.gov/data. htm>, accessed April 2024.

Table 1220. Mortgage Originations and Delinquency and Foreclosure Rates: 2000 to 2023

[In percent, except as indicated (1,139 represents $1,139,000,000,000). Covers one- to four-family residential nonfarm mortgage loans. Mortgage origination is the making of a new mortgage, including all steps taken by a lender to attract and qualify a borrower, process the mortgage loan, and place it on the lender's books. Based on the National Delinquency Survey, which covers 45 million loans on one- to four-unit properties, representing between 80 to 85 percent of all 'first-lien' residential mortgage loans outstanding. Loans surveyed were reported by approximately 120 lenders, including mortgage bankers, commercial banks, and thrifts]

Item	2000	2010	2015	2017	2018	2019	2020	2021	2022	2023
MORTGAGE ORIGINATIONS										
Total (bil. dol.)	**1,139**	**1,698**	**1,679**	**1,710**	**1,250**	**2,173**	**3,828**	**3,991**	**2,305**	**1,639**
Purchase (bil. dol.)	905	530	903	1,110	873	1,272	1,433	1,646	1,619	1,325
Refinance (bil. dol.)	234	1,168	776	600	377	901	2,395	2,345	686	314
DELINQUENCY RATES [1]										
Total	**4.4**	**9.3**	**5.1**	**4.8**	**4.4**	**4.2**	**6.7**	**5.3**	**3.8**	**3.6**
Conventional loans [2]	(NA)	8.8	4.4	3.9	3.5	3.2	5.2	3.9	2.7	2.5
Prime conventional loans	2.3	6.5	3.0	(NA)	(NA)	(NA)	(NA)	(NA)	(NA)	(NA)
Subprime conventional loans	11.9	25.9	16.5	(NA)	(NA)	(NA)	(NA)	(NA)	(NA)	(NA)
Federal Housing Administration loans	9.1	12.8	9.0	9.0	8.8	8.7	13.8	12.3	9.4	9.6
Veterans Administration loans	6.8	7.5	4.5	4.1	4.0	4.0	7.0	6.2	4.2	3.9
FORECLOSURE RATES										
Total loans in foreclosure process [3]	**1.2**	**4.6**	**2.0**	**1.3**	**1.0**	**0.9**	**0.6**	**0.5**	**0.6**	**0.5**
Conventional loans [2]	(NA)	4.8	1.9	1.2	0.9	0.7	0.5	0.4	0.5	0.4
Prime conventional loans	0.4	3.5	1.2	(NA)	(NA)	(NA)	(NA)	(NA)	(NA)	(NA)
Subprime conventional loans	9.4	14.5	8.3	(NA)	(NA)	(NA)	(NA)	(NA)	(NA)	(NA)
Federal Housing Administration loans	1.7	3.5	2.6	1.8	1.7	1.6	1.1	0.8	1.1	1.0
Veterans Administration loans	1.2	2.4	1.4	1.0	0.9	0.9	0.6	0.4	0.7	0.8
Loans entering foreclosure process [4]	**1.5**	**5.0**	**1.6**	**1.1**	**1.0**	**0.9**	**0.3**	**0.2**	**0.7**	**0.6**
Conventional loans [2]	(NA)	5.1	1.4	0.9	0.8	0.7	0.2	0.1	0.5	0.4
Prime conventional loans	0.6	4.0	1.0	(NA)	(NA)	(NA)	(NA)	(NA)	(NA)	(NA)
Subprime conventional loans	9.2	12.9	5.2	(NA)	(NA)	(NA)	(NA)	(NA)	(NA)	(NA)
Federal Housing Administration loans	2.3	4.7	2.5	1.9	2.0	1.8	0.5	0.2	1.7	1.5
Veterans Administration loans	1.5	3.3	1.4	1.1	1.1	1.0	0.3	0.1	1.0	0.9

NA Not available. [1] Number of loans delinquent 30 days or more as a percent of mortgage loans serviced in survey. Annual average of quarterly figures, not seasonally adjusted. Delinquency rate does not include loans in the process of foreclosure. [2] Conventional loans include any non-government (FHA or VA) loans. The prime and subprime criteria used in the National Delinquency Survey are based on survey participants' reporting of what they consider to be their prime or subprime servicing portfolio, since internal servicing guidelines vary. Participants who service both prime and subprime loans report the results of each separately for maximum precision in the classification. [3] Percent of loans in the foreclosure process at year-end, not seasonally adjusted. [4] Percent of loans entering foreclosure process at year-end, not seasonally adjusted.

Source: Mortgage Bankers Association of America, Washington, DC, "MBA Mortgage Originations Estimates," and National Delinquency Survey, <mba.org/>, and unpublished data ©.

Table 1221. Delinquency Rates and Charge-Off Rates on Loans at Insured Commercial Banks: 2000 to 2023

[In percent. Annual averages of quarterly figures, not seasonally adjusted. Delinquent loans are those past due 30 days or more and still accruing interest as well as those in nonaccrual status. They are measured as a percentage of end-of-period loans. Charge-offs, which are the value of loans removed from the books and charged against loss reserves, are measured, net of recoveries, as a percentage of average loans and annualized. Includes only U.S.-chartered commercial banks]

Type of loan	2000	2010	2015	2018	2019	2020	2021	2022	2023
DELINQUENCY RATES									
Total loans	**2.20**	**6.96**	**2.34**	**1.62**	**1.48**	**1.56**	**1.35**	**1.22**	**1.30**
Real estate	1.87	9.69	3.62	1.97	1.63	1.82	1.64	1.29	1.32
Residential [1, 2]	2.08	10.81	5.64	3.12	2.51	2.63	2.42	1.92	1.73
Commercial [2, 3]	1.48	8.53	1.23	0.72	0.68	0.97	0.90	0.70	0.96
Consumer	3.55	4.15	2.00	2.29	2.34	2.05	1.57	1.87	2.44
Credit cards	4.51	4.90	2.14	2.52	2.58	2.31	1.65	1.96	2.82
Other	2.98	3.32	1.88	2.07	2.10	1.83	1.51	1.79	2.07
Leases	1.62	1.89	0.77	1.01	1.18	1.42	1.26	0.99	0.99
Business	2.30	3.46	0.87	1.03	1.11	1.24	1.09	1.06	0.99
Agricultural production	2.54	3.04	0.84	1.70	1.87	2.01	1.44	1.00	0.79
Farmland [2]	2.30	3.57	1.55	2.15	2.29	2.46	1.78	1.15	0.95
CHARGE-OFF RATES									
Total loans	**0.66**	**2.66**	**0.42**	**0.46**	**0.49**	**0.49**	**0.25**	**0.26**	**0.49**
Real estate	0.09	2.15	0.13	0.01	0.01	0.04	(Z)	-0.01	0.08
Residential [1, 2]	0.12	2.11	0.21	(-Z)	-0.01	-0.02	-0.04	-0.03	(-Z)
Commercial [2, 3]	0.05	2.34	0.04	0.01	0.03	0.09	0.04	0.01	0.16
Consumer	2.32	5.90	1.75	2.24	2.28	2.00	1.16	1.25	2.21
Credit cards	4.30	9.43	2.93	3.64	3.70	3.46	2.18	2.04	3.49
Other	1.13	2.05	0.68	0.88	0.91	0.73	0.38	0.61	1.01
Leases	0.31	0.72	0.18	0.17	0.21	0.52	0.15	0.12	0.15
Business	0.76	1.71	0.24	0.28	0.36	0.52	0.19	0.17	0.35
Agricultural production	0.27	0.77	0.05	0.24	0.23	0.25	0.05	0.03	0.08
Farmland [2]	0.04	0.43	0.01	0.04	0.08	0.06	0.02	0.01	0.01

Z Represents less than .005%. [1] Residential real estate loans include loans secured by one- to four-family properties, including home equity lines of credit. [2] Booked in domestic offices only. [3] Commercial real estate loans include construction and land development loans, loans secured by multifamily residences, and loans secured by nonfarm, nonresidential real estate, only.

Source: Board of Governors of the Federal Reserve, Data Releases, Bank Assets and Liabilities, "Charge-Off and Delinquency Rates on Loans and Leases at Commercial Banks," <www.federalreserve.gov/releases/chargeoff/>, accessed March 2024.

Table 1222. Banked Households by Primary Method of Accessing Bank Account and Selected Characteristics: 2015 to 2021

[In percent, except as indicated (127,538 represents 127,538,000). Data cover banked households that have accessed their accounts in the past 12 months. A "banked" household is one in which at least one member of the household has a checking or savings account. Data collected through a Federal Deposit Insurance Corporation (FDIC)-sponsored supplement to the Current Population Survey; see source for more information]

Characteristic of householder	Total households (1,000)	Banked households						
		Total (1,000)	Primary method used to access bank account (percent)					
			Bank teller	ATM/ Kiosk	Telephone banking	Online banking	Mobile banking	Other/ unknown
2015...............	127,538	113,315	28.2	21.0	3.0	36.9	9.5	1.5
2017...............	129,276	115,040	24.3	19.9	2.9	36.0	15.6	1.3
2019...............	131,248	120,847	21.0	19.5	2.4	22.8	34.0	0.3
2021, total...............	**132,517**	**124,385**	**14.9**	**16.0**	**2.9**	**22.0**	**43.5**	**0.7**
AGE								
15 to 24 years...............	5,881	5,468	4.1	14.4	1.1	6.3	74.1	0.0
25 to 34 years...............	21,513	20,299	4.8	11.7	0.9	12.9	69.4	0.3
35 to 44 years...............	22,665	21,383	6.3	13.3	1.3	18.4	60.5	0.2
45 to 54 years...............	22,249	20,878	9.9	16.1	1.8	22.8	49.1	0.3
55 to 64 years...............	24,582	23,053	16.5	19.5	3.0	27.3	33.2	0.5
65 years or more...............	35,627	33,304	30.5	18.3	6.2	28.2	15.3	1.5
EDUCATION								
No high school diploma............	10,492	8,004	33.4	27.9	6.6	6.5	24.3	1.3
High school diploma...............	32,235	29,123	22.0	21.2	4.3	13.6	38.0	0.9
Some college...............	36,886	35,247	14.5	16.4	3.1	19.8	45.6	0.6
College degree...............	52,904	52,011	8.4	11.1	1.5	30.5	48.0	0.5
FAMILY INCOME								
Less than $15,000...............	12,547	9,498	24.9	22.7	6.9	9.9	33.9	1.7
$15,000 to $30,000...............	17,889	15,659	24.8	22.0	5.6	13.0	33.4	1.2
$30,000 to $50,000...............	24,617	23,074	19.5	19.3	3.8	17.4	39.4	0.6
$50,000 to $75,000...............	24,563	23,837	14.5	17.3	2.4	20.3	44.9	0.6
At least $75,000...............	52,900	52,317	8.3	11.1	1.3	29.7	49.3	0.3
EMPLOYMENT STATUS								
Employed...............	80,133	77,532	9.1	13.9	1.4	21.3	53.9	0.4
Unemployed...............	4,903	4,261	11.8	19.8	3.0	16.2	48.7	0.5
Not in labor force...............	47,481	42,592	25.8	19.6	5.7	23.7	23.9	1.3

Source: Federal Deposit Insurance Corporation, 2021 FDIC National Survey of Unbanked and Underbanked Households, "Custom Data Table Tool," <household-survey.fdic.gov/custom-data>, accessed January 2023.

Table 1223. Households Using Nonbank Financial Transaction Services by Type of Service and Household Characteristics: 2021

[Percent, except households (132,517 represents 132,517,000). Percent of households using nonbank financial services during the last 12 months. These services can also be used to receive payments, including income. Data collected through a Federal Deposit Insurance Corporation (FDIC)-sponsored supplement to the Current Population Survey; see source for more information]

Characteristic of householder	Total households (1,000)	Nonbank financial transaction service use (percent)				
		Money order	Check cashing	International remittance	Prepaid card [1]	Online payment service [2]
Total households...............	**132,517**	**9.7**	**3.2**	**2.8**	**6.9**	**46.4**
BANK ACCOUNT OWNERSHIP [3]						
Unbanked...............	5,907	32.3	21.8	4.7	32.8	18.1
Banked...............	126,610	8.7	2.3	2.7	5.7	47.7
FAMILY INCOME						
Less than $15,000...............	12,547	19.4	6.9	2.9	13.4	26.5
$15,000 to $30,000...............	17,889	15.4	6.0	3.2	8.8	28.5
$30,000 to $50,000...............	24,617	11.9	3.8	3.2	7.6	35.8
$50,000 to $75,000...............	24,563	8.5	2.4	2.8	6.2	46.4
At least $75,000...............	52,900	5.1	1.4	2.4	4.7	62.1
EDUCATION						
No high school diploma...............	10,492	21.5	9.2	6.8	11.8	18.3
High school diploma...............	32,235	12.4	4.4	2.7	8.5	32.5
Some college...............	36,886	10.4	3.1	1.9	7.2	46.3
College degree...............	52,904	5.3	1.3	2.6	4.7	60.6
EMPLOYMENT STATUS						
Employed...............	80,133	9.3	3.1	3.5	6.3	57.7
Unemployed...............	4,903	15.7	7.7	3.5	15.1	48.4
Not in labor force...............	47,481	9.8	2.9	1.5	7.0	27.1
HOUSING TENURE						
Homeowner...............	86,172	5.7	1.7	1.9	5.2	46.4
Non-homeowner...............	46,345	17.2	5.9	4.3	10.1	46.5

[1] General purpose reloadable prepaid cards. Consumers can obtain prepaid cards from banks, retail stores, websites, employers, government agencies, and other sources. [2] Online payment services to friends or family. Includes online payment services only from nonbank providers. An online payment service is use of a website or app to send, receive, and store money in the account. Examples are PayPal, Venmo, and CashApp. To conduct online payments, households typically must have access to the internet with either a smartphone or a computer. [3] A household is 'unbanked' if no one in the household has a checking or savings account at an insured bank. A 'banked' household has at least one member of the household has a checking or savings account.

Source: Federal Deposit Insurance Corporation, 2021 FDIC National Survey of Unbanked and Underbanked Households, October 2022. See also <www.fdic.gov/analysis/household-survey/>.

Table 1224. Money Stock: 2010 to 2023

[In billions of dollars (1,837 represents $1,837,000,000,000). As of December. Seasonally adjusted averages of daily figures]

Item	2010	2015	2016	2017	2018	2019	2020	2021	2022	2023
M1, total [1]	**1,837**	**3,104**	**3,345**	**3,613**	**3,764**	**4,008**	**17,803**	**20,436**	**19,765**	**18,012**
Currency [2]	919	1,340	1,421	1,525	1,625	1,712	1,974	2,131	2,211	2,250
Travelers' checks [3]	4.7	2.5	2.2	1.9	1.7	(NA)	(NA)	(NA)	(NA)	(NA)
Demand deposits [4]	517	1,247	1,375	1,493	1,508	1,621	3,315	4,766	5,111	5,009
Other checkable deposits [5]	397	515	547	594	630	675	(NA)	(NA)	(NA)	(NA)
Other liquid deposits [6]	(NA)	(NA)	(NA)	(NA)	(NA)	(NA)	12,514	13,540	12,444	10,754
M2, total	**8,802**	**12,351**	**13,213**	**13,853**	**14,355**	**15,314**	**19,097**	**21,501**	**21,309**	**20,752**
M1	1,837	3,104	3,345	3,613	3,764	4,008	17,803	20,436	19,765	18,012
Non-M1 components of M2	6,965	9,247	9,868	10,240	10,591	11,305	1,294	1,064	1,544	2,740
Retail money funds	700	665	697	713	805	975	1,043	974	1,154	1,657
Savings deposits (including money market deposit accounts) [6]	5,331	8,155	8,801	9,093	9,231	9,724	(X)	(X)	(X)	(X)
Commercial banks	4,412	7,014	7,544	7,799	7,905	8,401	(X)	(X)	(X)	(X)
Thrift institutions	919	1,144	1,259	1,298	1,332	1,333	(X)	(X)	(X)	(X)
Small-denomination time deposits [7]	934	427	369	434	555	606	252	91	390	1,083
Commercial banks	664	315	267	322	449	485	201	(NA)	(NA)	(NA)
Thrift institutions	270	110	102	112	108	122	51	(NA)	(NA)	(NA)

NA Not available. X Not applicable. [1] As of May 2020, M1 consists of currency outside the U.S. Treasury, Federal Reserve Banks, and vaults of depository institutions; demand deposits at commercial banks; and other liquid deposits, consisting of other checkable deposits (OCDs), and savings deposits (including money market deposit accounts). Prior to May 2020, savings deposits were not included as a type of transaction account and not included in M1. See source for more information. [2] Currency outside U.S. Treasury, Federal Reserve Banks and the vaults of depository institutions. [3] Outstanding amount of U.S. dollar-denominated travelers' checks of nonbank issuers. Travelers' checks issued by depository institutions are included in demand deposits. [4] Demand deposits at domestically chartered commercial banks, U.S. branches and agencies of foreign banks, and Edge Act corporations (excluding those amounts held by depository institutions, the U.S. government, and foreign banks and official institutions) less cash items in the process of collection and Federal Reserve float. [5] Other checkable deposits consist of negotiable order of withdrawal (NOW) and automatic transfer service (ATS) balances at depository institutions, share draft accounts at credit unions, and demand deposits at thrift institutions. Beginning 2020, data are included in other liquid deposits. [6] Beginning May 2020, savings deposits were reclassified as transaction accounts and were combined with other checkable deposits, with the sum being reported as "other liquid assets." [7] Small-denomination time deposits are those issued in amounts of less than $100,000. All Individual Retirement Account (IRA) and Keogh account balances at commercial banks and thrift institutions are subtracted from small-denomination time deposits.

Source: Board of Governors of the Federal Reserve System, Data Releases, Money Stock and Reserve Balances, "Money Stock Measures – H.6 Release," <www.federalreserve.gov/releases/h6/>, accessed September 2024.

Table 1225. Volume of Debt Markets by Type of Security: 2000 to 2023

[In billions of dollars (2,604 represents $2,604,000,000,000). Covers fixed income securities as represented by the source]

Type of security	2000	2010	2015	2019	2020	2021	2022	2023
NEW ISSUE VOLUME [1]								
Total	**2,604**	**7,342**	**6,823**	**8,322**	**12,483**	**13,443**	**8,882**	**8,268**
Municipal	198	433	405	426	485	483	391	385
U.S. Treasury securities [2]	313	2,320	2,123	2,935	3,896	5,139	3,827	3,518
Federal agency debt [3]	447	1,362	645	989	1,251	693	846	1,338
Mortgage-backed securities [4]	780	2,013	1,801	2,119	4,271	4,584	2,146	1,312
Asset-backed securities [5]	240	126	333	435	304	582	303	270
Corporate debt [6]	626	1,089	1,516	1,417	2,275	1,961	1,370	1,445
AVERAGE DAILY TRADING VOLUME								
Total	**284.8**	**889.6**	**728.6**	**895.4**	**954.3**	**955.2**	**913.2**	**1,075.9**
Municipal	8.8	13.3	8.6	11.5	12.0	8.8	14.1	13.2
U.S. Treasury securities [7]	206.5	523.8	490.0	593.6	603.2	624.1	614.3	760.5
Federal agency debt [3]	(NA)	11.5	5.2	4.2	5.3	3.2	2.8	3.9
Mortgage-backed securities [4, 8]	69.5	320.6	192.3	249.0	291.1	279.3	240.6	254.7
Non-agency mortgaged-back securities [5, 9]	(NA)	(NA)	3.1	1.4	1.9	1.4	1.4	1.3
Corporate [10]	(NA)	20.5	27.9	34.3	38.9	37.0	38.3	40.5
Asset-backed securities [11]	(NA)	(NA)	1.4	1.5	1.9	1.4	1.6	1.7
VOLUME OF SECURITIES OUTSTANDING								
Total	**16,123**	**33,388**	**37,988**	**44,120**	**50,218**	**53,258**	**(NA)**	**(NA)**
Municipal [12]	1,481	3,982	3,882	3,919	4,008	4,087	4,036	4,057
U.S. Treasury securities [2]	2,952	8,853	13,192	16,673	20,973	22,584	23,934	26,366
Federal agency debt [3]	1,854	2,538	1,995	1,726	1,689	1,433	1,936	1,955
Mortgage-backed securities [4]	4,119	9,258	8,895	10,229	11,214	12,202	(NA)	(NA)
Asset-backed securities [5]	702	1,508	1,377	1,663	1,535	1,585	(NA)	(NA)
Money market instruments [13]	1,614	1,058	941	1,045	987	1,014	1,166	1,182
Corporate debt [6]	3,401	6,193	7,706	8,863	9,812	10,352	10,443	10,744

NA Not available. [1] Covers only long-term issuance. [2] Long-term only, interest bearing marketable coupon public debt. Includes floating rate notes. [3] Agency debt of Federal National Mortgage Association (Fannie Mae), Federal Home Loan Mortgage Corporation (Freddie Mac), Federal Agricultural Mortgage Corporation (Farmer Mac), Federal Home Loan Banks (FHLB), the Farm Credit System, and federal budget agencies (e.g., TVA). Beginning 2004, Sallie Mae is excluded due to privatization. [4] Includes Government National Mortgage Association (Ginnie Mae), Fannie Mae, and Freddie Mac mortgage-backed securities (MBS), and collateralized mortgage obligations (CMOs) and private-label MBS/CMOs. [5] Excludes mortgage-backed assets. Includes auto, credit card, home equity loans, manufacturing, student loan and other. Collateralized debt obligations are also included. [6] Debt obligations of U.S. financial and nonfinancial corporations including bonds, notes, debentures, mandatory convertible securities, long-term debt, private mortgage-backed securities, and unsecured debt. Includes nonconvertible corporate debt, Yankee bonds, and MTNs (Medium-Term Notes). Excludes federal agency debt, certificates of deposit and bonds issued in foreign countries by foreign subsidiaries of U.S. corporations. Recorded at book value. [7] Primary dealer reporting, includes double counting of some trades. [8] Primary dealer trading volume through May 2011. After that date, data from FINRA (Financial Industry Regulatory Authority). [9] Includes mortgage securities issued by private institutions, such as subsidiaries of investment banks, banks, financial institutions, non-bank mortgage lenders, and home builders. After October 2017, incudes Commercial mortgages backed securities. [10] Includes nonconvertible bonds only. [11] Includes collateralized debt obligations and other trading volumes. Prior to October 2017, includes Commercial mortgage backed securities figures. [12] Due to the change in underlying source data, municipal securities outstanding has been restated from 2004 onward and revised. [13] Commercial paper, bankers acceptances, and large time deposits.

Source: The Securities Industry and Financial Markets Association, New York, NY. © Based on data supplied by Bloomberg, Dealogic, Refinitiv, U.S. Treasury, Fannie Mae, Freddie Mac, Ginnie Mae, Farmer Mac, Farm Credit, FHLB, Federal Reserve Bank of New York, Municipal Securities Rulemaking Board, and FINRA Trace (Financial Industry Regulatory Authority Trade Reporting and Compliance Engine).

Table 1226. New Security Issues of Corporations by Type of Offering: 2010 to 2023

[In billions of dollars (1,025 represents $1,025,000,000,000). Represents gross proceeds of issues maturing in more than one year. Figures are the principal amount or the number of units multiplied by the offering price. Excludes secondary offerings, employee stock plans, investment companies other than closed-end, intracorporate transactions, Yankee bonds, and private placements listed. Stock data include ownership securities issued by limited partnerships]

Type of offering	2010	2020	2022	2023	Type of offering	2010	2020	2022	2023
Total [1]	**1,025**	**2,392**	**1,465**	**1,436**	Nonfinancial	498	1,364	551	619
					Financial	396	950	901	763
Bonds, total	894	2,313	1,452	1,383	Stocks, total [2]	131	335	71	64
Sold in the U.S.	880	2,257	1,414	1,362	Nonfinancial	61	187	33	45
Sold abroad	14	57	38	21	Financial	70	148	38	20

[1] Total reflects the sum of the gross issuance of bonds and the gross proceeds of stocks in the domestic market. [2] Gross proceeds of stocks in all markets.

Source: Board of Governors of the Federal Reserve System, "New Security Issues, U.S. Corporations," <www.federalreserve.gov/data/corpsecure/current.htm>, accessed July 2024.

Table 1227. Equities, Corporate Bonds, and Municipal and Treasury Securities—Holdings and Net Purchases by Type of Investor: 2010 to 2023

[In billions of dollars (8,714 represents $8,714,000,000,000). Holdings as of December 31. Minus sign (-) indicates net sales]

Type of investor	Holdings					Net purchases				
	2010	2015	2020	2022	2023	2010	2015	2020	2022	2023
TREASURY SECURITIES										
Total [1]	**8,714**	**13,146**	**21,953**	**21,649**	**24,413**	**1,590.0**	**688.1**	**4,317.3**	**1,287.4**	**2,381.6**
Household sector [2]	679	601	1,148	1,462	2,321	265.9	331.3	-329.3	1,112.0	817.6
State and local governments	438	579	996	1,463	1,589	37.5	58.1	253.3	309.9	94.3
Monetary authority	1,021	2,676	5,255	5,056	4,416	244.9	-15.6	2,554.3	-188.2	-739.7
U.S.-chartered depository institutions	218	435	1,044	1,389	1,329	93.0	14.8	327.8	8.8	-90.1
Life insurance companies	165	212	247	183	193	21.2	7.5	6.2	-5.2	6.7
Private pension funds	202	287	461	508	614	46.0	-13.1	1.3	74.4	94.3
Federal government retirement funds	20	26	24	18	19	(-Z)	1.6	(Z)	-1.9	1.2
State and local governments retirement funds	154	175	354	327	421	3.4	-22.2	4.3	-27.6	84.6
Money market funds	381	530	2,466	1,064	2,269	-72.4	45.6	1,343.3	-750.7	1,205.5
Mutual funds	417	827	1,316	1,350	1,388	129.8	155.3	1.3	-25.5	9.5
Rest of the world [3]	4,459	6,146	7,292	7,319	8,018	740.4	42.7	67.0	417.6	596.8
MUNICIPAL SECURITIES [4]										
Total [1]	**3,810**	**4,105**	**4,422**	**3,886**	**4,022**	**118.5**	**21.2**	**87.3**	**-52.6**	**20.9**
Household sector [2]	1,901	1,934	1,941	1,621	1,766	78.5	-36.0	-27.5	29.7	93.3
U.S.-chartered depository institutions	255	508	584	580	532	30.3	45.4	69.0	4.8	-64.7
Property-casualty insurance companies	370	358	298	246	224	-24.0	10.2	3.0	-7.7	-29.3
Money market funds	410	247	125	118	130	-53.1	-28.1	-14.0	7.0	11.7
Mutual funds	490	604	891	746	764	33.0	16.2	49.7	-130.9	-4.4
CORPORATE & FOREIGN BONDS										
Total [1]	**10,148**	**11,005**	**15,197**	**13,581**	**14,774**	**-6.7**	**291.2**	**1,039.7**	**388.6**	**507.9**
Household sector [2]	1,121	430	250	281	311	-191.9	-265.0	54.0	-303.6	3.8
U.S.-chartered depository institutions	551	507	511	779	718	-98.2	-12.0	8.3	107.7	-74.4
Foreign banking offices in U.S.	238	173	153	160	135	-9.4	-10.8	6.8	42.2	-32.8
Property-casualty insurance companies	348	452	661	649	730	24.3	19.2	47.1	38.9	46.6
Life insurance companies	2,129	2,495	3,649	3,233	3,520	89.0	95.0	187.9	224.4	124.5
Private pension funds	446	691	978	876	975	27.6	5.8	58.3	51.4	54.0
State and local government retirement funds	427	558	541	539	566	12.0	37.2	58.5	83.0	-18.8
Mutual funds	1,264	1,692	2,608	2,129	2,295	211.1	80.2	266.6	-77.5	56.0
Exchange-traded funds	78.0	241	708	754	867	21.0	36.8	149.3	61.6	88.5
Rest of the world [3]	2,523	3,080	4,482	3,724	4,165	-36.8	334.9	213.4	173.9	243.5
EQUITIES [5]										
Total [1]	**24,196**	**37,262**	**65,493**	**64,703**	**78,053**	**190.7**	**-50.8**	**766.0**	**138.3**	**-123.1**
Household sector [2]	8,683	13,822	26,006	26,419	31,996	-55.0	-50.1	624.6	590.2	-57.2
State and local governments	105	148	250	239	293	-3.4	-3.4	-3.4	-3.4	-3.4
Property-casualty insurance companies	224	334	519	533	621	-5.2	-1.5	-21.8	38.5	-31.8
Life insurance companies	430	579	771	660	750	46.2	28.0	-0.9	-3.3	-28.9
Private pension funds	1,778	2,220	3,379	2,933	3,463	38.7	-29.3	-112.4	-133.8	-160.5
Federal government retirement funds	145	240	419	419	534	6.1	(Z)	-23.9	-6.0	11.8
State and local government retirement funds	1,723	2,250	2,906	3,007	3,348	-67.4	22.6	-28.8	-43.6	-42.0
Mutual funds	5,873	8,625	13,391	11,867	13,789	69.0	57.9	-481.3	-388.3	-319.3
Exchange-traded funds	753	1,709	4,229	5,059	6,426	79.8	173.6	260.2	416.2	393.3
Brokers and dealers	117	167	214	170	283	-23.0	-18.4	6.8	-13.7	63.6
Rest of the world [3]	3,213	5,501	10,673	10,822	13,525	129.6	-191.4	669.3	-176.7	179.1

Z Less than $500 million. [1] Includes other types not shown separately. [2] Includes nonprofit organizations. [3] Holdings and net purchases of U.S. issues by foreign residents. [4] Includes loans. [5] Includes shares of exchange-traded funds, closed-end funds, and real estate investment trusts. Excludes mutual fund shares of open-end investment companies; see Table 1234.

Source: Board of Governors of the Federal Reserve System, "Financial Accounts of the United States, Z.1," <www.federalreserve.gov/data.htm>, accessed May 2024.

Table 1228. Foreign Securities Held by U.S. Residents: 2010 to 2022

[In billions of dollars (6,763 represents $6,763,000,000,000). Estimates for end of calendar year]

Country	Total			Equities			Long-term and short-term debt		
	2010	2020	2022	2010	2020	2022	2010	2020	2022
Total holdings [1]	**6,763**	**14,387**	**14,009**	**4,647**	**10,615**	**10,280**	**2,116**	**3,772**	**3,730**
Australia	323	378	424	150	227	254	174	151	170
Belgium	35	64	59	29	54	47	7	11	12
Bermuda	160	283	249	134	240	203	25	44	47
Brazil	235	168	157	194	144	135	41	24	22
Canada	695	1,168	1,242	409	683	731	287	484	510
Cayman Islands	366	2,565	2,658	166	2,027	1,925	200	539	732
China [2]	102	287	243	101	251	226	2	35	17
Curacao [3]	(NA)	23	53	(NA)	21	52	(NA)	2	1
France	366	698	696	244	479	506	122	220	190
Germany	299	535	454	207	422	358	92	113	96
Hong Kong	135	166	127	133	158	121	2	8	7
India	91	234	287	86	223	278	5	11	9
Ireland	132	698	777	101	608	678	31	90	98
Israel	64	94	87	45	71	68	19	23	19
Italy	66	148	124	51	96	81	14	52	43
Japan	519	1,296	1,090	450	1,013	845	69	283	245
Jersey	42	138	162	21	126	135	21	11	27
Korea, South	148	300	205	122	277	180	26	23	24
Luxembourg	100	198	201	33	131	144	68	67	56
Mexico	109	153	145	77	64	73	32	89	72
Netherlands	233	628	582	120	423	415	112	205	168
Norway	56	72	86	23	37	50	33	34	37
Russia	62	74	30	56	57	26	7	17	4
Singapore	64	92	111	56	58	72	8	34	40
South Africa	78	79	65	70	65	51	8	14	14
Spain	87	163	142	66	113	101	22	49	42
Sweden	122	196	180	63	155	131	59	42	49
Switzerland	327	632	591	319	590	549	8	42	42
Taiwan	95	304	232	94	304	231	(Z)	(Z)	1
United Kingdom	1,001	1,395	1,397	626	919	975	375	476	422

NA Not available. Z Less than $500 million. [1] Includes other countries, not shown separately. [2] Excludes Hong Kong, Macau, and Taiwan. [3] Separate reporting for Curacao began with the 2013 survey. In previous years, data were reported as part of Netherlands Antilles.

Source: U.S. Department of Treasury, "U.S. Residents' Portfolio Holdings of Foreign Securities," <home.treasury.gov/data/treasury-international-capital-tic-system>, accessed November 2023.

Table 1229. U.S. Securities Held by Foreign Residents by Country: 2020 and 2023

[In billions of dollars (21,954 represents $21,954,000,000,000). Estimates as of June. Long-term securities include all forms of equity and all debt securities with an original term-to-maturity of over one year]

Country	U.S. securities, total [1]		U.S. equities [2]		U.S Treasury long-term securities		Long-term corporate debt	
	2020	2023	2020	2023	2020	2023	2020	2023
Total [3]	**21,954**	**26,872**	**9,168**	**13,719**	**6,005**	**6,639**	**4,331**	**4,059**
Australia	352	571	267	474	33	44	37	34
Belgium	852	980	59	85	175	259	565	552
Bermuda	367	364	111	131	39	42	157	124
Brazil	276	246	8	17	248	223	1	1
British Virgin Islands	170	220	106	135	31	34	24	26
Canada	1,335	2,055	971	1,458	102	248	210	213
Cayman Islands	1,903	2,365	1,059	1,575	114	155	567	477
China, mainland [4]	1,569	1,432	233	309	1,040	829	23	19
Denmark	157	204	115	171	14	11	25	18
France	399	679	192	363	119	196	61	78
Germany	421	623	210	412	67	83	127	110
Hong Kong	455	434	126	168	236	169	51	59
India	189	248	6	12	151	233	(Z)	1
Ireland	1,182	1,476	517	842	201	202	241	248
Israel	138	170	80	106	41	47	7	9
Italy	107	127	45	64	39	44	18	16
Japan	2,553	2,494	667	837	1,194	1,035	312	300
Korea, South	414	585	187	387	118	103	63	47
Kuwait	304	375	211	279	35	40	24	27
Luxembourg	1,777	2,094	731	1,088	182	255	694	584
Netherlands	425	478	264	320	67	72	78	66
Norway	467	693	325	511	88	126	52	56
Saudi Arabia	279	306	133	184	89	100	19	8
Singapore	377	674	169	408	139	178	42	71
Sweden	238	365	194	315	38	42	6	8
Switzerland	854	1,087	496	683	214	242	99	91
Taiwan	699	717	79	112	200	236	147	154
Thailand	111	98	16	20	74	46	3	2
United Arab Emirates	162	220	127	147	15	45	8	4
United Kingdom	1,988	2,627	1,019	1,457	370	580	478	435

Z Less than $500 million. [1] Includes short-term debt and other long-term debt. [2] Includes common and preferred stock, all types of investment company shares (open-end funds, closed-end funds, money market mutual funds, and hedge funds), interests in limited partnerships, and other equity interests that may not involve stocks or shares. [3] Includes other countries not shown separately. [4] Excludes Hong Kong, Macau, and Taiwan.

Source: U.S. Department of Treasury, "U.S. International Portfolio Investment: Foreign Residents' Portfolio Holdings of U.S. Securities," <home.treasury.gov/data/treasury-international-capital-tic-system>, accessed August 2024.

Table 1230. Stock Prices and Yields: 2000 to 2023

[Closing values as of end of December, except as noted]

Index	2000	2010	2015	2019	2020	2021	2022	2023
STOCK PRICES								
Standard & Poor's indices: [1]								
S&P 500 Composite Return Index (Jan. 4, 1988 = 255.94)	1,837	2,114	3,822	6,554	7,759	9,987	8,178	10,328
S&P 500 composite (1941–43 = 10)	1,320	1,257	2,044	3,231	3,756	4,766	3,840	4,770
S&P 400 MidCap Index (1982 = 100)	517	907	1,399	2,063	2,307	2,842	2,430	2,782
S&P 600 SmallCap Index (Dec. 31, 1993 = 100)	220	416	672	1,021	1,119	1,402	1,158	1,318
S&P 500 Citigroup Value Index (Dec. 31, 1974 = 35)	636	590	876	1,286	1,267	1,548	1,435	1,718
S&P 500 Citigroup Growth Index (Dec. 31, 1974 = 35)	688	659	1,164	1,953	2,577	3,377	2,361	3,030
Russell indices: [2]								
Russell 1000 (Dec. 31, 1986 = 130)	700	697	1,132	1,784	2,121	2,646	2,217	2,622
Russell 2000 (Dec. 31, 1986 = 135)	484	784	1,136	1,668	1,975	2,245	1,761	2,027
Russell 3000 (Dec. 31, 1986 = 140)	726	749	1,206	1,892	2,248	2,788	2,106	2,748
N.Y. Stock Exchange (NYSE) common stock index:								
Composite (Dec. 31, 2002 = 5000)	6,946	7,964	10,143	13,913	14,525	17,164	15,184	16,853
Yearly high	7,165	7,983	11,255	13,944	14,533	17,443	17,443	16,934
Yearly low	6,095	6,356	9,510	11,190	8,665	13,989	13,279	14,471
NYSE American Stock Exchange Composite Index (Dec. 29, 1995 = 550)	898	2,208	2,149	2,553	2,361	3,427	4,135	4,594
NASDAQ Composite Index (Feb. 5, 1971 = 100)	2,471	2,653	5,007	8,973	12,888	15,645	10,466	15,011
Nasdaq-100 (Jan. 31, 1985 = 125)	2,342	2,218	4,593	8,733	12,888	16,320	10,940	16,826
Industrial (Feb. 5, 1971 = 100)	1,483	2,184	4,101	6,808	10,397	11,313	7,348	9,474
Banks (Feb. 5, 1971 = 100)	1,939	1,847	2,853	3,969	3,547	4,955	4,045	3,775
Computers (Oct. 29, 1993 = 200)	1,295	1,372	2,606	5,879	8,818	12,156	7,807	12,996
Transportation (Feb. 5, 1971 = 100)	1,160	2,562	3,334	5,292	5,526	6,692	5,357	6,606
Telecommunications (Oct. 29, 1993 = 200)	463	226	251	389	474	497	371	417
Biotech (Oct. 29, 1993 = 200)	1,085	970	3,540	3,787	4,759	4,729	4,213	4,371
Dow Jones Averages:								
Composite (65 stocks)	3,317	4,033	5,978	9,386	10,109	12,267	10,963	12,250
Industrial (30 stocks)	10,787	11,578	17,425	28,538	30,606	36,338	33,147	37,690
Transportation (20 stocks)	2,947	5,107	7,509	10,901	12,507	16,478	13,392	15,899
Utility (15 stocks)	412	405	578	879	865	981	967	882
COMMON STOCK YIELDS (percent)								
Standard & Poor's Composite Index (500 stocks): [3]								
Dividend-price ratio [4]	1.15	1.98	2.20	1.87	1.52	1.31	1.77	1.51
Earnings-price ratio [5]	3.63	6.04	4.64	4.19	2.64	3.36	5.01	3.80

[1] Standard & Poor's Indices are market-value weighted and are chosen for market size, liquidity, and industry group representation. The S&P 500 index represents 500 large publicly-traded companies. The S&P MidCap Index tracks mid-cap companies. The S&P SmallCap Index consists of 600 domestic small-cap stocks. [2] The Russell 1000 and 3000 indices show respectively the 1000 and 3000 largest capitalization stocks in the United States. The Russell 2000 index shows the 2000 largest capitalization stocks in the United States after the first 1000. [3] Source: U.S. Council of Economic Advisors, *Economic Indicators*, monthly. [4] Aggregate cash dividends (based on latest known annual rate) divided by aggregate market value based on Wednesday closing prices. Averages of monthly figures. [5] Averages of quarterly ratios which are ratio of earnings (after taxes) for 4 quarters ending with particular quarter- to-price index for last day of that quarter.

Source: Except as noted, Global Financial Data, Los Angeles, CA, <www.globalfinancialdata.com/> ©.

Table 1231. Stock Ownership by Age of Head of Family and Family Income: 2010 to 2022

[Median value in thousands of constant (2022) dollars (39.6 represents $39,600). All dollar figures are adjusted to 2022 dollars using the "current methods" version of the consumer price index for all urban consumers published by U.S. Bureau of Labor Statistics. Families include one-person units; for definition of family, see text, Section 1. Based on Survey of Consumer Finance; see Appendix III. For definition of median, see Guide to Tabular Presentation]

Age of family head and family income	Families having direct or indirect stock holdings [1] (percent)			Median value among families with holdings			Stock holdings share of group's financial assets (percent)		
	2010	2019	2022	2010	2019	2022	2010	2019	2022
All families	**49.9**	**52.6**	**58.0**	**39.6**	**46.4**	**52.0**	**47.0**	**54.7**	**56.3**
Under 35 years old	39.8	47.8	54.4	9.6	8.4	12.0	39.3	38.1	50.8
35 to 44 years old	50.1	56.1	63.6	27.0	36.6	30.0	50.5	58.0	52.9
45 to 54 years old	58.0	57.5	63.4	51.6	59.4	68.1	48.6	56.4	55.7
55 to 64 years old	59.7	54.9	59.4	76.5	83.8	110.0	48.3	53.8	59.1
65 to 74 years old	45.6	51.5	55.8	105.0	127.5	160.0	44.2	54.6	52.8
75 years old and over	42.0	47.0	49.4	75.1	97.4	116.4	44.6	55.5	60.3
Percentiles of income: [2]									
Less than 20	12.5	14.5	17.0	7.3	8.0	8.3	40.5	35.2	41.9
20 to 39.9	30.5	34.2	40.1	9.7	10.1	10.0	31.3	35.2	33.0
40 to 59.9	51.7	55.8	60.2	16.4	17.4	24.0	37.5	43.5	47.6
60 to 79.9	68.1	71.0	78.7	30.4	39.1	42.7	41.6	46.4	46.8
80 to 89.9	82.6	83.3	91.7	79.1	101.1	127.9	44.4	53.5	51.3
90 to 100	90.6	92.3	96.4	365.4	492.9	607.1	50.9	58.9	60.9

[1] Indirect holdings are those in pooled investment trusts, retirement accounts and other managed assets. [2] Percentiles of income distribution in 2022 dollars: 20th: $34,600; 40th: $59,500; 60th: $91,900; 80th: $153,100; 90th: $245,400. Percentiles of distribution of net worth in 2022 dollars: 25th: $27,100; 50th: $192,900; 75th: $658,900; 90th: $1,938,000. Percentile: A value on a scale of zero to 100 that indicates the percent of a distribution that is equal to or below it.

Source: Board of Governors of the Federal Reserve System, 2022 Survey of Consumer Finances, *Changes in U.S. Family Finances From 2019 to 2022: Evidence from the Survey of Consumer Finances*, October 2023. See also <www.federalreserve.gov/econres/scfindex.htm>.

Table 1232. Bond Yields: 2000 to 2023

[Percent per year. Annual averages of daily figures]

Type	2000	2010	2015	2017	2018	2019	2020	2021	2022	2023
U.S. Treasury, constant maturities: [1]										
1-year...........................	6.11	0.32	0.32	1.20	2.33	2.05	0.37	0.10	2.80	5.08
2-year...........................	6.26	0.70	0.69	1.40	2.53	1.97	0.39	0.27	2.99	4.58
3-year...........................	6.22	1.11	1.02	1.58	2.63	1.94	0.42	0.46	3.05	4.30
5-year...........................	6.16	1.93	1.53	1.91	2.75	1.95	0.53	0.86	3.00	4.06
7-year...........................	6.20	2.62	1.89	2.16	2.85	2.05	0.72	1.20	3.01	4.03
10-year..........................	6.03	3.22	2.14	2.33	2.91	2.14	0.89	1.45	2.95	3.96
20-year..........................	6.23	4.03	2.55	2.65	3.02	2.40	1.35	1.98	3.30	4.26
High-grade municipal bonds (Standard & Poor's) [2]........................	5.77	4.16	3.48	3.36	3.53	3.38	2.41	2.00	3.85	4.31

[1] Yields on actively traded non-inflation-indexed issues adjusted to constant maturities. Yields are based on closing indicative prices quoted by secondary market participants. [2] Source: U.S. Council of Economic Advisors, *Economic Indicators*, monthly, <www.govinfo.gov/app/collection/econi>, accessed July 2024.

Source: Except as noted, Board of Governors of the Federal Reserve System, "H15, Selected Interest Rates," <www.federalreserve.gov/releases/h15/>, accessed July 2024.

Table 1233. Total Returns of Stocks, Bonds, and Treasury Bills: 1980 to 2023

[Average annual percent change. Stock return data are based on the Standard & Poor's 500 index. Minus sign (-) indicates loss]

Period	Stocks				Treasury bills, total return	Bonds (10-year), total return
	Total return before inflation	Capital gains	Dividends and reinvestment	Total return after inflation		
1980 to 1989..........	17.55	12.59	4.40	11.85	9.13	13.01
1990 to 1999..........	18.21	15.31	2.51	14.85	4.95	8.02
2000 to 2009..........	-0.45	-2.73	2.27	-3.39	2.74	6.63
2001...................	-11.89	-13.04	1.32	-13.68	3.32	5.53
2002...................	-22.10	-23.37	1.65	-23.91	1.61	15.37
2003...................	28.68	26.38	1.82	26.31	1.03	0.46
2004...................	10.88	8.99	1.73	7.38	1.43	4.61
2005...................	4.91	3.00	1.85	1.45	3.30	3.09
2006...................	15.80	13.62	1.91	11.97	4.97	2.21
2007...................	5.49	3.53	1.89	1.35	4.52	10.54
2008...................	-37.00	-38.49	1.88	-37.10	1.24	20.23
2009...................	26.25	23.45	2.44	23.11	0.15	-9.50
2010...................	15.06	12.78	2.02	13.36	0.03	7.26
2011...................	2.96	–	2.96	0.83	0.06	16.89
2012...................	16.00	13.41	2.29	14.02	0.08	2.77
2013...................	32.39	29.60	2.15	30.43	0.05	-8.56
2014...................	13.69	11.39	2.06	12.83	0.03	10.74
2015...................	1.32	-0.73	2.05	0.58	0.06	11.27
2016...................	11.96	9.53	2.22	9.68	0.33	-5.40
2017...................	21.83	19.41	2.03	19.30	0.95	2.81
2018...................	-4.38	-6.24	1.98	-6.37	2.00	0.34
2019...................	31.49	28.88	2.02	28.55	2.09	9.28
2020...................	18.40	16.26	1.02	16.81	0.32	10.35
2021...................	28.71	26.89	1.43	20.24	0.04	-3.97
2022...................	-19.44	-18.11	1.65	-23.08	-3.97	-22.01
2023...................	26.29	24.23	1.66	22.20	5.43	4.35

– Represents or rounds to zero.

Source: Global Financial Data, Los Angeles, CA, "GFD Guide to Total Returns," <www.globalfinancialdata.com>, and unpublished data ©.

Table 1234. Mutual Fund Shares—Holdings and Net Purchases by Type of Investor: 2010 to 2023

[In billions of dollars (9,029.8 represents $9,029,800,000,000). Holdings as of Dec. 31. A mutual fund is an open-end investment company that continuously issues and redeems shares that represent an interest in a pool of financial assets. Excludes money market funds and exchange-traded funds. Minus sign (-) indicates net sales]

Type of investor	Holdings					Net purchases				
	2010	2020	2021	2022	2023	2010	2020	2021	2022	2023
Total...........................	9,029.8	19,562.6	22,208.8	17,333.4	19,599.7	395.8	-230.4	215.1	-800.5	-299.7
Households, nonprofit organizations........	4,730.1	10,996.3	12,829.6	9,759.4	11,005.1	260.5	-159.5	542.2	-724.1	-164.2
Nonfinancial corporate business.............	185.7	375.7	444.4	358.5	407.2	7.5	9.9	22.0	-4.4	-4.4
State and local governments.................	50.4	112.8	128.0	105.6	122.6	1.2	1.2	1.2	1.2	1.2
U.S.-chartered depository institutions.......	14.1	11.5	14.9	10.1	10.5	-5.8	1.5	2.0	-2.3	-1.0
Credit unions.................................	1.5	4.8	7.1	4.2	4.1	-0.3	0.9	1.6	-1.4	-0.7
Property-casualty insurance companies....	11.4	29.7	36.2	30.8	34.3	-0.7	0.9	-1.0	-0.6	-1.3
Life insurance companies....................	1,115.5	1,694.6	1,832.3	1,413.5	1,535.3	27.5	-101.2	-138.9	-88.3	-107.1
Private pension funds.........................	2,220.2	4,900.4	5,430.1	4,385.0	5,038.1	55.4	19.7	-83.4	-43.2	-16.1
State and local government retirement funds..................................	438.4	412.5	298.3	207.6	241.8	-6.1	-3.1	-162.3	-35.2	10.1
Rest of the world.............................	262.5	1,024.3	1,187.9	1,058.6	1,200.7	56.5	-0.8	31.8	97.7	-16.4

Source: Board of Governors of the Federal Reserve System, "Financial Accounts of the United States, Z.1," <www.federalreserve.gov/data.htm>, accessed April 2024.

Table 1235. Household Ownership of Mutual Funds by Age and Income: 2013 and 2023

[In percent. In 2023, an estimated 68.7 million households own mutual funds. Includes money market, stock, bond, and hybrid mutual funds, variable annuities, and funds owned through individual retirement accounts (IRAs) and employer-sponsored retirement plans. A mutual fund is an open-end investment company that continuously issues and redeems shares that represent an interest in a pool of financial assets. Based on the source's Annual Mutual Fund Shareholder Tracking Survey. Prior to 2014, the survey was conducted via landline telephone. In 2014, the survey added a cellular telephone sampling frame. Beginning 2022, the survey switched to a self-administered online survey fielded on the KnowledgePanel®, and includes a revised sampling and weighting methodology and an increased sample size; see source for details. Use caution comparing trends over time]

Age of household head [1]	Percent distribution of all households owning mutual funds, 2023	Percent of households owning mutual funds within each group		Household income [2]	Percent distribution of all households owning mutual funds, 2023	Percent of households owning mutual funds within each group	
		2013	2023			2013	2023
Total.........................	100	46	52	Less than $25,000......	5	12	17
Less than 35 years old......	17	31	43	$25,000 to $34,999....	4	27	25
35 to 44 years old............	16	49	49	$35,000 to $49,999....	8	39	38
45 to 54 years old............	17	60	56	$50,000 to $74,999....	16	55	51
55 to 64 years old............	19	58	56	$75,000 to $99,999....	15	67	64
65 years old and over........	31	37	57	$100,000 and over.....	52	81	73

[1] Age is based on the sole or co-decision maker for household saving and investing. [2] Total reported is household income before taxes in prior year.

Source: Investment Company Institute. Holden, Sarah, Daniel Schrass, and Michael Bogdan. 2023. "Ownership of Mutual Funds and Shareholder Sentiment, 2023." ICI Research Perspective 29, no. 9 (October) ©. See also <www.ici.org/files/2023/per29-10.pdf>.

Table 1236. Characteristics of Mutual Fund Owners: 2023

[In percent, except as indicated. Mutual fund ownership includes holdings of money market, stock, bond, and hybrid mutual funds; and funds owned through variable annuities, Individual Retirement Accounts (IRAs), Keoghs, and employer-sponsored retirement plans. A mutual fund is an open-end investment company that continuously issues and redeems shares that represent an interest in a pool of financial assets. The 2023 data are based on a survey of 6,073 households; 3,176 households owned mutual funds. Beginning 2022, the survey switched to a self-administered online survey fielded on the KnowledgePanel®, and includes a revised sampling and weighting methodology and an increased sample size; see source for details. For definition of median, see Guide to Tabular Presentation]

Characteristic	Total	Age [1]				Household income [2]			
		Under 35 years	35 to 54 years	55 to 64 years	65 years and over	Less than $50,000	$50,000 to $99,000	$100,000 to $149,000	$150,000 or more
Median age [1] (years)...........................	54	30	45	60	73	60	55	52	53
Median household income [2] (dol.)............	100,000	90,000	125,000	120,000	87,500	32,500	72,000	125,000	200,000
Median household financial assets [3] (dol.)...	225,000	87,500	200,000	375,000	456,000	62,500	125,000	250,000	500,000
Own an IRA..	66	60	59	66	78	59	60	68	76
Household with defined contribution retirement plan(s) [4]...........................	82	92	92	88	61	71	78	86	88
401(k) plan......................................	69	83	81	75	44	60	65	71	76
403(b), state, local, or federal government plan.............................	33	26	35	36	32	24	31	39	36
Median mutual fund assets (dol.)..............	125,000	45,000	90,000	200,000	200,000	35,000	62,500	135,000	375,000
Own:									
Equity funds....................................	79	73	76	82	84	67	76	80	88
Bond funds.....................................	34	22	29	36	45	24	30	35	42

[1] See Table 1235, footnote 1. [2] See Table 1235, footnote 2. [3] Includes assets in employer-sponsored retirement plans but excludes value of primary residence. [4] For definition of defined contribution plan, see headnote, Table 585.

Source: Investment Company Institute. Schrass, Daniel, and Michael Bogdan. 2023. "Profile of Mutual Fund Shareholders, 2023." ICI Research Report (December) ©. See also <www.ici.org/system/files/2023-12/23-rpt-profiles.pdf>.

Table 1237. Mutual Funds—Summary: 2000 to 2023

[6,956 represents $6,956,000,000,000. Number of funds and assets as of December 31. A mutual fund is an open-end investment company that continuously issues and redeems shares that represent an interest in a pool of financial assets. Excludes data for funds that invest in other mutual funds. Minus sign (-) indicates net redemptions]

Type of fund	Unit	2000	2005	2010	2015	2019	2020	2021	2022	2023
Number of funds, total.....................	**Number**	**8,134**	**7,967**	**7,540**	**8,115**	**7,957**	**7,644**	**7,500**	**7,421**	**7,222**
Equity funds.....................................	Number	4,359	4,566	4,508	4,762	4,655	4,469	4,396	4,391	4,290
Hybrid funds.....................................	Number	506	480	489	721	781	719	699	662	636
Bond funds.......................................	Number	2,232	2,052	1,891	2,151	2,157	2,116	2,100	2,077	2,021
Money market funds, taxable [1]..............	Number	703	592	442	336	284	265	245	236	229
Money market funds, tax-exempt [2]..........	Number	334	277	210	145	80	75	60	55	46
Net assets, total...........................	**Bil. dol.**	**6,956**	**8,889**	**11,831**	**15,648**	**21,276**	**23,831**	**26,899**	**22,107**	**25,519**
Equity funds.....................................	Bil. dol.	3,933	4,885	5,596	8,140	11,362	12,715	14,713	11,353	13,305
Hybrid funds.....................................	Bil. dol.	361	621	842	1,341	1,577	1,569	1,805	1,485	1,550
Bond funds.......................................	Bil. dol.	817	1,356	2,589	3,412	4,704	5,214	5,625	4,492	4,744
Money market funds, taxable [1]..............	Bil. dol.	1,611	1,690	2,474	2,500	3,494	4,228	4,669	4,664	5,796
Money market funds, tax-exempt [2]..........	Bil. dol.	234	336	330	255	138	105	87	112	124
Net new cash flow:...........................	**Bil. dol.**	**390**	**254**	**-282**	**-98**	**453**	**202**	**357**	**-1,130**	**292**
Equity funds.....................................	Bil. dol.	315	124	-24	-76	-362	-645	-436	-471	-518
Hybrid funds.....................................	Bil. dol.	-37	43	35	-19	-50	-88	-19	-104	-108
Bond funds.......................................	Bil. dol.	-48	25	232	-25	312	244	389	-542	-38
Money market funds............................	Bil. dol.	159	62	-525	21	553	691	422	-13	957

[1] Invested in short-term, high-grade securities sold in the money market. [2] Invested in municipal securities with relatively short maturities.

Source: Investment Company Institute. 2024. Investment Company Fact Book: A Review of Trends and Activities in the U.S. Investment Company Industry. © Washington, DC: Investment Company Institute. See also <www.icifactbook.org>.

Table 1238. Retirement Assets by Type of Asset: 2000 to 2023

[In billions of dollars, except as indicated (11,581 represents $11,581,000,000,000). As of December 31]

Item	2000	2005	2010	2015	2019	2020	2021	2022	2023
Retirement assets, total	**11,581**	**14,413**	**17,984**	**24,040**	**32,176**	**35,808**	**39,727**	**34,163**	**38,268**
IRA assets [1]	2,629	3,425	5,029	7,477	10,949	12,661	14,460	11,950	13,556
Bank and thrift deposits [2]	250	278	461	523	558	685	676	643	544
Life insurance companies [3]	202	301	314	385	470	521	554	560	614
Mutual funds	1,262	1,780	2,418	3,493	4,820	5,459	6,222	5,055	5,838
Other assets [1,4]	916	1,067	1,837	3,077	5,101	5,997	7,008	5,692	6,561
Traditional [1]	2,407	3,034	4,340	6,387	9,297	10,722	12,215	10,100	11,441
Roth [1]	78	156	355	625	1,014	1,233	1,445	1,210	1,405
SEP and SAR-SEP [1,5]	134	193	265	364	491	537	605	480	530
SIMPLE [1,6]	10	42	69	101	146	169	195	160	180
Defined contribution plans	2,958	3,739	4,770	6,457	8,927	9,968	11,129	9,219	10,567
401(k) plans	1,738	2,393	3,119	4,377	6,256	7,033	7,899	6,435	7,410
Other private-sector defined contribution plans [7]	500	413	464	483	588	612	670	530	595
403(b) plans	519	622	727	876	1,092	1,204	1,289	1,144	1,289
Thrift Savings Plan [8]	92	168	272	458	639	735	827	725	843
457 plans	110	143	189	263	351	384	445	385	430
Private-sector defined benefit plans	2,020	2,262	2,481	2,861	3,313	3,476	3,518	2,926	3,208
State and local government defined benefit plans	2,341	2,761	2,947	3,680	4,721	5,214	5,880	5,427	5,909
Federal defined benefit plans [9]	705	912	1,168	1,519	1,910	2,011	2,182	2,414	2,668
Annuities [10]	929	1,314	1,588	2,045	2,357	2,476	2,559	2,227	2,360
Memo:									
Mutual fund retirement assets	2,545	3,656	4,920	7,121	9,933	11,127	12,590	10,190	11,881
Percent of total retirement assets	22	25	27	30	31	31	32	30	31
Percent of all mutual funds	37	41	42	46	47	47	47	46	47

[1] Data for 2021, 2022, and 2023 are estimated. [2] Includes Keogh deposits. [3] Annuities held by IRAs, excluding variable annuity mutual fund IRA assets, which are included in mutual funds. [4] Excludes mutual fund assets held through brokerage accounts, which are included in mutual funds. [5] Simplified Employee Pension (SEP) IRAs and salary reduction (SAR) IRAs. [6] Savings Incentive Match Plan for Employees (SIMPLE) IRAs. [7] Includes Keoghs and other defined contribution plans (profit-sharing, thrift-savings, stock bonus, and money purchase) without 401(k) features. [8] Federal Employees Retirement System (FERS) Thrift Savings Plan (TSP) as reported by the Federal Reserve Board. [9] Federal pension plans include U.S. Treasury security holdings of the civil service retirement and disability fund, the military retirement fund, the judicial retirement funds, the Railroad Retirement Board, and the foreign service retirement and disability fund. These plans also include securities held in the National Railroad Retirement Investment Trust. [10] Annuities include all fixed and variable annuities held outside of retirement plans and IRAs.

Source: Investment Company Institute. 2024. "The US Retirement Market, First Quarter 2024" (June) ©. For the most up-to-date figures about the fund industry, please visit <www.ici.org/statistics>.

Table 1239. Pension Funds—Summary: 2010 to 2023

[In billions of dollars (15,916 represents $15,916,000,000,000). As of end of year. Covers private pension funds, state and local government employee retirement funds, and federal government retirement funds in defined benefit plans and defined contribution plans (including 401(k) type plans). Excludes social security trust funds; see Table 580]

Item	2010	2015	2016	2017	2018	2019	2020	2021	2022	2023
Total financial assets [1]	**15,916**	**20,412**	**21,238**	**22,648**	**22,638**	**24,449**	**25,902**	**27,447**	**25,065**	**26,862**
Money market fund shares	195	208	223	221	218	204	228	239	249	260
Debt securities [1]	1,670	2,104	2,171	2,393	2,436	2,582	2,867	3,066	2,762	3,103
Treasury securities [2]	376	487	547	664	762	797	840	944	853	1,054
Agency- and GSE (government-sponsored enterprises)-backed securities	334	268	277	312	356	404	441	470	426	435
Corporate and foreign bonds	881	1,262	1,249	1,317	1,225	1,334	1,536	1,590	1,428	1,554
Corporate equities	3,646	4,711	4,912	5,744	5,219	5,888	6,703	7,768	6,358	7,346
Mutual fund shares	2,659	3,552	3,770	4,368	4,041	4,693	5,313	5,728	4,593	5,280
Miscellaneous assets [1]	6,377	8,019	8,234	7,931	8,585	8,835	8,391	8,060	8,246	7,745
Unallocated insurance contracts [3]	626	723	768	805	788	826	875	915	871	903
Contributions receivable	91	91	100	119	85	80	77	71	69	66
Claims of pension fund on sponsor [4]	4,995	6,415	6,512	6,035	6,748	6,221	5,694	5,140	5,316	4,610
Pension entitlements (liabilities) [5]	**16,060**	**20,590**	**21,387**	**22,771**	**22,745**	**24,631**	**26,078**	**27,661**	**25,327**	**27,063**
Memo:										
Defined benefit plan funded status:										
Pension entitlements, total	**11,545**	**14,442**	**14,824**	**15,206**	**15,569**	**16,108**	**16,458**	**16,863**	**16,201**	**16,611**
Funded by assets [6]	6,550	8,026	8,312	9,170	8,821	9,887	10,764	11,723	10,885	12,001
Unfunded	4,995	6,415	6,512	6,035	6,748	6,221	5,694	5,140	5,316	4,610
Household retirement assets, total [7]	**22,970**	**30,452**	**31,856**	**34,843**	**34,490**	**38,459**	**41,868**	**45,438**	**40,361**	**(NA)**
Defined benefit plans	11,545	14,442	14,824	15,206	15,569	16,108	16,458	16,863	16,201	16,611
Defined contribution plans	4,515	6,149	6,562	7,565	7,176	8,522	9,620	10,798	9,125	10,452
Individual retirement plans (IRAs) [8]	5,029	7,477	8,015	9,439	9,135	10,949	12,661	14,460	11,950	(NA)
Annuities at life insurance companies [9]	1,881	2,385	2,455	2,633	2,610	2,879	3,129	3,317	3,084	(NA)

NA Not available. [1] Includes other types of assets not shown separately. [2] Includes both marketable and nonmarketable government securities. [3] Assets of pension plans held at life insurance companies. [4] Unfunded defined benefit pension entitlements. [5] Actuarial value of accrued pension entitlements in defined benefit plans and assets of defined contribution plans. These liabilities are assets of the household sector. [6] Total defined benefit financial assets plus nonfinancial assets less claims of pension fund on sponsor. [7] Households' retirement assets in tax-deferred accounts, including employer sponsored pension plans, individual retirement accounts (IRAs), Roth IRAs, and annuities. [8] IRA assets are not included in above assets or entitlements. [9] Excludes annuities held in IRAs at life insurance companies.

Source: Board of Governors of the Federal Reserve System, "Financial Accounts of the United States, Z.1," <www.federalreserve.gov/data.htm>, accessed May 2024.

Table 1240. Private Pension Fund Assets by Type, and Liabilities: 2000 to 2023

[In billions of dollars (4,283 represents $4,283,000,000,000). As of December 31. Covers private defined benefit plans and defined contribution plans (including 401(k) type plans). Minus sign (-) indicates overfunding]

Type of instrument	2000	2010	2015	2018	2019	2020	2021	2022	2023
Total financial assets [1]	**4,283**	**6,604**	**8,649**	**9,695**	**11,060**	**12,042**	**13,165**	**11,689**	**12,892**
Money market fund shares	84	142	154	158	180	205	212	226	240
Debt securities [1]	596	867	1,176	1,416	1,566	1,715	1,821	1,679	1,909
Treasury securities	111	202	287	372	440	461	508	508	614
Agency and GSE-backed securities [2]	194	181	158	205	224	235	259	251	274
Corporate and foreign bonds	263	446	691	802	867	978	1,012	876	975
Corporate equities	1,823	1,778	2,220	2,448	2,962	3,379	3,870	2,933	3,463
Mutual fund shares	1,246	2,220	3,128	3,595	4,320	4,900	5,430	4,385	5,038
Miscellaneous assets [1]	387	1,524	1,894	2,005	1,955	1,764	1,746	2,378	2,150
Unallocated insurance contracts [3]	362	466	527	556	580	620	640	593	614
Pension entitlements (liabilities) [4]	**4,323**	**6,641**	**8,686**	**9,732**	**11,097**	**12,079**	**13,203**	**11,729**	**12,932**
Funded status of defined benefit plans:									
Pension entitlements	1,826	2,872	3,436	3,532	3,671	3,666	3,714	3,765	3,796
Funded by assets [5]	2,020	2,435	2,828	2,931	3,257	3,538	3,661	3,045	3,338
Unfunded	-194	437	608	601	414	128	53	720	458
Defined benefit plan assets	1,785	2,835	3,399	3,495	3,633	3,629	3,676	3,726	3,755
Defined contribution plan assets	2,497	3,768	5,250	6,200	7,427	8,413	9,489	7,964	9,136

[1] Includes other types of assets not shown separately. [2] GSE=Government-sponsored enterprises. [3] Assets of private pension plans held at life insurance companies (e.g., GICs, variable annuities). [4] Actuarial value of accrued pension entitlements in defined benefit plans and assets of defined contribution plans. [5] Total defined benefit financial assets plus nonfinancial assets less claims of pension fund on sponsor.

Source: Board of Governors of the Federal Reserve System, "Financial Accounts of the United States, Z.1," <www.federalreserve.gov/data.htm>, accessed April 2024.

Table 1241. Public Employee Retirement Systems—Assets and Liabilities: 2000 to 2023

[In billions of dollars (3,301 represents $3,301,000,000,000). As of December 31. Includes claims of sponsor (unfunded pension entitlements). Minus sign (-) indicates overfunding]

Type of instrument	2000	2010	2015	2018	2019	2020	2021	2022	2023
STATE AND LOCAL GOVERNMENT EMPLOYEE RETIREMENT PLANS									
Total financial assets [1]	**3,301**	**6,169**	**8,054**	**8,929**	**9,193**	**9,477**	**9,723**	**8,846**	**9,246**
Debt securities [1]	721	765	881	976	967	1,098	1,196	1,043	1,151
Treasury securities	179	154	175	368	333	354	414	327	421
Agency and GSE-backed securities [2]	179	144	101	142	169	194	199	166	151
Corporate and foreign bonds	314	427	558	410	452	541	562	539	566
Corporate equities	1,299	1,723	2,250	2,479	2,555	2,906	3,374	3,007	3,348
Mutual fund shares	363	438	424	447	373	413	298	208	242
Miscellaneous assets [1]	825	3,150	4,392	4,921	5,233	4,990	4,763	4,478	4,381
Claims of pension fund on sponsor [3]	717	2,854	4,075	4,488	4,161	3,929	3,536	3,205	2,939
Pension entitlements (liabilities) [4]	**3,348**	**6,275**	**8,195**	**8,999**	**9,337**	**9,616**	**9,898**	**9,068**	**9,406**
Funded status of defined benefit plans:									
Pension entitlements	3,058	5,801	7,754	8,582	8,881	9,144	9,416	8,632	8,934
Funded by assets [5]	2,341	2,947	3,680	4,094	4,721	5,214	5,880	5,427	5,995
Unfunded [3]	717	2,854	4,075	4,488	4,161	3,929	3,536	3,205	2,939
Defined benefit plan assets	3,010	5,694	7,613	8,512	8,737	9,005	9,241	8,410	8,774
Defined contribution plan assets	291	474	441	417	456	472	482	436	472
FEDERAL GOVERNMENT EMPLOYEE RETIREMENT FUNDS									
Total financial assets [1]	**2,028**	**3,144**	**3,709**	**4,013**	**4,196**	**4,383**	**4,560**	**4,530**	**4,724**
Debt securities [1]	18	37	47	44	49	53	49	40	43
Treasury securities [6]	16	20	26	22	23	24	22	18	19
Corporate equities	57	145	240	292	371	419	524	419	534
Claims of pension fund on sponsor [7]	1,231	1,703	1,732	1,659	1,647	1,637	1,551	1,391	1,213
Pension entitlements (liabilities) [8]	**2,028**	**3,144**	**3,709**	**4,013**	**4,196**	**4,383**	**4,560**	**4,530**	**4,724**
Funded status of defined benefit plans:									
Pension entitlements	1,936	2,871	3,251	3,455	3,557	3,649	3,733	3,804	3,881
Funded by assets [9]	705	1,168	1,519	1,796	1,910	2,011	2,182	2,414	2,668
Unfunded [7]	1,231	1,703	1,732	1,659	1,647	1,637	1,551	1,391	1,213
Defined benefit plan assets [10]	1,936	2,871	3,251	3,455	3,557	3,649	3,733	3,804	3,881
Defined contribution plan assets [11]	92	272	458	559	639	735	827	725	843

[1] Includes other types of instruments not shown separately. [2] GSE=Government sponsored enterprises. [3] Unfunded defined benefit pension entitlements. [4] Actuarial value of projected pension entitlements. These liabilities are assets of the household sector. [5] Total defined benefit financial assets plus nonfinancial assets less claims of pension fund on sponsor. [6] Comprised primarily of nonmarketable Treasury securities. [7] Unfunded defined benefit pension entitlements. [8] Actuarial value of projected pension entitlements in defined benefit plans and assets of defined contribution plans. These liabilities are assets of the household sector. [9] Total defined benefit financial assets less defined benefit claims of pension fund on sponsor. [10] Includes the Civil Service Retirement and Disability Fund, Railroad Retirement Board, judicial retirement fund, Military Retirement Fund, Foreign Service Retirement and Disability Fund, and National Railroad Retirement Investment Trust. [11] Thrift Savings Plan.

Source: Board of Governors of the Federal Reserve System, "Financial Accounts of the United States, Z.1," <www.federalreserve.gov/data.htm>, accessed April 2024.

Table 1242. Life Insurance in Force and Purchases in the United States—Summary: 2000 to 2023

[369 represents 369,000,000. As of December 31 or calendar year, as applicable. Covers life insurance with life insurance companies, and beginning in 2003, also with fraternal benefit societies. Data represent all life insurance in force on lives of U.S. residents whether issued by U.S. or foreign companies]

Year	Number of policies, total (millions)	Life insurance in force			Life insurance purchases [1]					
		Value (bil. dol.)			Number (1,000)			Amount (bil. dol.)		
		Total [2]	Individual	Group	Total	Individual	Group	Total	Individual	Group
2000........	369	15,953	9,376	6,376	34,882	13,345	21,537	2,515	1,594	921
2010........	284	18,426	10,484	7,831	28,621	10,123	18,498	2,809	1,673	1,135
2013........	275	19,662	11,365	8,215	25,264	9,929	15,336	2,779	1,640	1,139
2014........	278	20,115	11,826	8,209	27,147	9,440	17,707	2,759	1,590	1,168
2015........	281	20,779	12,342	8,361	28,315	10,305	18,010	2,877	1,647	1,229
2016........	291	20,316	11,992	8,246	27,523	11,005	16,518	2,874	1,685	1,190
2017........	289	20,416	11,927	8,411	28,035	10,478	17,557	3,027	1,712	1,316
2018........	267	19,571	12,120	7,367	27,748	10,289	17,459	2,972	1,728	1,244
2019........	259	19,834	12,388	7,358	31,356	10,118	21,238	3,042	1,803	1,239
2020........	255	20,426	12,850	7,478	35,433	10,088	25,345	3,293	1,854	1,440
2021........	261	21,188	13,569	7,524	34,428	10,401	24,027	3,243	1,974	1,268
2022........	259	21,806	14,018	7,692	34,972	9,499	25,473	3,298	1,871	1,427
2023........	260	22,163	13,974	8,097	36,980	9,586	27,394	3,589	1,972	1,617

[1] Excludes revivals, increases, dividend additions, and reinsurance acquired. Includes long-term credit insurance (life insurance on loans of more than 10 years' duration). [2] Includes other types of policies not shown separately such as credit.

Source: American Council of Life Insurers, Washington, DC, *Life Insurers Fact Book*, annual ©.

Table 1243. U.S. Life Insurance Companies—Summary: 2000 to 2023

[811.5 represents $811,500,000,000. As of December 31 or calendar year, as applicable. Covers domestic and foreign business of U.S. companies. Includes annual statement data for companies that primarily are health insurance companies. Beginning in 2005, includes also fraternal benefit societies]

Item	Unit	2000	2010	2015	2018	2019	2020	2021	2022	2023
U.S. companies [1]............	**Number**	**1,269**	**917**	**814**	**773**	**761**	**747**	**737**	**727**	**719**
Income [2]......................	**Bil. dol.**	**811.5**	**862.6**	**1,064.7**	**1,008.2**	**1,094.4**	**1,020.2**	**1,086.5**	**1,163.7**	**1,123.2**
Life insurance premiums..................	Bil. dol.	130.6	104.6	155.9	150.2	156.6	148.0	164.6	170.2	122.2
Annuity considerations [3]....................	Bil. dol.	306.7	293.6	333.0	279.3	347.5	301.3	290.6	350.8	360.9
Health insurance premiums...............	Bil. dol.	105.6	172.7	159.9	185.4	188.1	186.3	192.0	189.9	202.9
Investment and other [4].....................	Bil. dol.	268.5	291.6	416.0	393.3	402.2	384.6	439.2	452.9	437.3
Payments under life insurance and annuity contracts....................	Bil. dol.	375.2	365.6	447.7	536.9	530.3	529.1	584.3	561.2	632.7
Payments to life insurance beneficiaries.............................	Bil. dol.	44.1	58.4	74.3	79.7	78.4	90.4	100.2	91.7	89.1
Surrender values under life insurance [5]............................	Bil. dol.	27.2	35.8	28.8	35.3	34.1	30.4	28.3	29.9	41.6
Surrender values under annuity contracts [5, 6]........................	Bil. dol.	214.0	184.1	247.2	319.1	310.4	297.5	339.1	323.1	374.7
Policyholder dividends......................	Bil. dol.	20.0	15.9	18.5	18.4	18.2	18.1	17.8	19.7	22.2
Annuity payments [6].....................	Bil. dol.	68.7	70.1	77.8	83.4	88.1	91.6	97.7	95.5	104.1
Matured endowments......................	Bil. dol.	0.6	0.6	0.4	0.4	0.4	0.5	0.5	0.6	0.5
Other payments...........................	Bil. dol.	0.6	0.7	0.7	0.7	0.7	0.7	0.7	0.7	0.6
Health insurance benefit payments..............................	Bil. dol.	78.8	122.5	115.3	132.2	141.6	137.7	147.2	139.4	153.4
BALANCE SHEET										
Assets...................................	**Bil. dol.**	**3,182**	**5,311**	**6,478**	**6,993**	**7,567**	**8,150**	**8,671**	**8,275**	**8,743**
Mortgage-backed securities...............	Bil. dol.	(NA)	631.0	556	576	564	549	520	510	518
Government bonds.........................	Bil. dol.	364	413	496	475	485	501	524	490	477
Corporate securities.......................	Bil. dol.	2,238	3,271	4,150	4,441	4,887	5,291	5,697	5,240	5,513
Bonds................................	Bil. dol.	1,241	1,700	2,150	2,441	2,589	2,820	3,008	3,143	3,216
Stocks................................	Bil. dol.	997	1,570	2,001	2,000	2,298	2,471	2,689	2,097	2,298
Mortgages................................	Bil. dol.	237	327	437	565	615	641	691	756	807
Real estate...............................	Bil. dol.	36	28	44	39	42	41	39	40	38
Policy loans..............................	Bil. dol.	102	127	135	137	134	133	131	131	138
Other....................................	Bil. dol.	204	515	659	760	841	994	1,069	1,108	1,251
Interest earned on assets [7]..................	Percent	7.05	4.33	4.81	4.72	4.57	3.93	4.28	4.52	4.12
Obligations and surplus funds [8].............	Bil. dol.	3,182	5,311	6,478	6,993	7,567	8,150	8,671	8,275	8,743
Policy reserves......................	**Bil. dol.**	**2,712**	**4,098**	**5,025**	**5,375**	**5,788**	**6,104**	**6,388**	**6,019**	**6,295**
Annuities [9]...............................	Bil. dol.	1,875	2,660	3,320	3,554	3,880	4,103	4,286	3,919	4,154
Group................................	Bil. dol.	960	863	1,022	1,079	1,179	1,274	1,324	1,220	1,261
Individual.............................	Bil. dol.	881	1,780	2,276	2,449	2,675	2,802	2,935	2,672	2,866
Supplementary contracts [10]..............	Bil. dol.	34	17	23	25	26	27	28	27	27
Life insurance...........................	Bil. dol.	742	1,224	1,463	1,574	1,650	1,738	1,831	1,819	1,850
Health insurance.........................	Bil. dol.	96	214	242	247	257	264	271	280	290
Liabilities for deposit-type contracts [11]............................	Bil. dol.	21	420	470	524	572	626	702	698	750
Capital and surplus.......................	Bil. dol.	188	319	383	419	441	454	497	488	512

NA Not available. [1] Includes life insurance companies that sell accident and health insurance. [2] Premiums are net of reinsurance business and fluctuate with reinsurance activities as well as sale changes. [3] Beginning 2005, excludes certain deposit-type funds from income due to codification. [4] Investment represents gross investment income. [5] "Surrender values" include annuity withdrawals of funds. [6] Beginning 2005, excludes payments under deposit-type contracts. [7] Net rate. [8] Includes other obligations not shown separately. [9] Beginning 2005, excludes reserves for guaranteed interest contracts (GICs). [10] Data for 2000 include reserves for contracts with and without life contingencies; beginning 2005, includes only reserves for contracts with life contingencies. [11] Policyholder dividend accumulations for all years. Beginning 2005, also includes liabilities for guaranteed interest contracts, supplementary contracts without life contingencies, and premium and other deposits.

Source: American Council of Life Insurers, Washington, DC, *Life Insurers Fact Book*, annual ©.

Table 1244. Real Estate and Rental and Leasing—Nonemployer Establishments and Receipts by Kind of Business: 2010 to 2021

[2,343.1 represents 2,343,100. Includes only firms subject to federal income tax. Nonemployers are businesses with no paid employees. Data originate chiefly from administrative records of the Internal Revenue Service; see Appendix III]

Kind of business	NAICS code [1]	Establishments (1,000)			Receipts (mil. dol.)		
		2010	2020	2021	2010	2020	2021
Real estate & rental & leasing, total...............	53	**2,343.1**	**2,988.4**	**3,074.5**	**209,549**	**309,053**	**336,213**
Real estate...	531	2,262.2	2,902.8	2,976.3	203,065	301,123	327,331
Lessors of real estate...............................	5311	989.3	1,256.4	1,278.9	135,015	178,545	187,346
Offices of real estate agents & brokers...........	5312	641.6	843.1	883.9	25,502	52,922	65,230
Activities related to real estate.....................	5313	631.3	803.3	813.5	42,549	69,656	74,755
Rental & leasing services.............................	532	78.9	82.8	95.5	6,288	7,625	8,554
Automotive equipment rental & leasing...........	5321	18.3	21.6	29.6	990	1,368	1,671
Consumer goods rental...............................	5322	18.3	19.2	23.0	779	892	1,150
General rental centers...............................	5323	4.8	7.3	8.0	409	611	710
Commercial & industrial equipment rental & leasing...........	5324	37.5	34.8	34.9	4,109	4,754	5,023
Lessors of other nonfinancial intangible assets..................	533	2.0	2.8	2.7	197	304	328

[1] Data for 2010 based on 2007 North American Industry Classification System (NAICS); data for 2020 and 2021 based on 2017 NAICS.

Source: U.S. Census Bureau, Nonemployer Statistics, "All Sectors: Nonemployer Statistics by Legal Form of Organization and Receipts Size Class for the U.S., States, and Selected Geographies: 2021," <data.census.gov>, accessed March 2024.

Table 1245. Real Estate and Rental and Leasing—Establishments, Employees, and Payroll: 2021 and 2022

[456.2 represents 456,200. Covers establishments with payroll. Data based on the North American Industry Classification System (NAICS) 2017; see text, section 15, Business Enterprise. Employees are for the week including March 12. Most government employees are excluded]

Kind of business	NAICS code	Establishments (1,000)		Employees (1,000)		Payroll (bil. dol.)	
		2021	2022	2021	2022	2021	2022
Real estate & rental & leasing, total...................	53	**456.2**	**466.7**	**2,180.6**	**2,333.1**	**145.6**	**162.1**
Real estate...	531	402.8	412.9	1,709.9	1,801.5	113.4	124.9
Lessors of real estate...............................	5311	136.4	136.4	579.7	600.7	33.6	36.4
Offices of real estate agents & brokers...........	5312	158.9	165.6	383.5	416.5	31.5	34.3
Activities related to real estate [1].................	5313	107.4	110.9	746.7	784.2	48.3	54.2
Residential property managers..................	531311	55.3	57.4	485.3	507.4	25.6	29.4
Rental & leasing services.............................	532	50.8	51.0	433.6	492.1	27.1	31.9
Automotive equipment rental & leasing...........	5321	15.6	16.4	142.1	166.2	7.6	9.5
Passenger car rental & leasing.................	53211	9.7	10.1	[2] 71.2	[2] 86.9	3.7	4.9
Truck, utility trailer & RV rental & leasing..........	53212	6.0	6.3	70.9	79.3	3.9	4.7
Consumer goods rental [1]...........................	5322	16.4	15.8	97.1	110.6	4.9	5.6
Consumer electronics and appliances rental..............	53221	5.2	4.9	24.0	23.1	1.2	1.1
Other consumer goods rental....................	53228	11.2	10.9	73.1	87.5	3.8	4.5
Video tape & disc rental.......................	532282	1.2	0.4	[2] 4.9	3.4	0.2	0.2
Home health equipment rental.................	532283	1.9	1.9	23.6	24.8	1.3	1.4
Recreational goods rental.....................	532284	2.7	2.9	12.8	15.4	0.6	0.7
General rental centers...............................	5323	2.8	2.8	17.9	19.1	0.9	1.0
Commercial/industrial equipment rental & leasing [1]..........	5324	16.0	16.0	176.6	196.2	13.7	15.8
Construction, transportation, mining & forestry equipment..	53241	5.8	5.7	67.7	71.4	5.8	6.6
Lessors of other nonfinancial intangible assets..................	533	2.6	2.7	37.1	39.5	5.1	5.3

[1] Includes industries not shown separately. [2] High noise; cell value was changed by 5 percent or more to avoid disclosure.

Source: U.S. Census Bureau, County Business Patterns, "All Sectors: County Business Patterns, including ZIP Code Business Patterns, by Legal Form of Organization and Employment Size Class for the U.S., States, and Selected Geographies: 2022," <data.census.gov>, accessed June 2024.

Table 1246. Real Estate and Rental and Leasing Services—Revenue by Kind of Business: 2010 to 2022

[In millions of dollars (427,687 represents $427,687,000,000). Covers taxable and tax-exempt employer firms. Estimates for 2010 are based on the 2007 North American Industry Classification System (NAICS); beginning 2013, estimates are based on the 2012 NAICS. See text, this section and Section 15. Estimates have been adjusted using the results of the 2017 Economic Census. Based on the Service Annual Survey]

Kind of business	NAICS code	2010	2018	2019	2020	2021	2022
Real estate and rental and leasing, total................	53	**427,687**	**712,020**	**755,022**	**738,029**	**844,438**	**935,393**
Real estate [1]...	531	289,294	492,243	523,772	528,475	602,446	665,943
Lessors of residential buildings and dwellings..............	53111	73,899	121,841	130,624	129,870	134,661	153,542
Lessors of nonresidential buildings (excl. miniwarehouses)...	53112	86,933	126,202	131,935	124,815	134,862	155,073
Offices of real estate agents and brokers.....................	5312	55,966	121,174	129,863	137,922	180,206	185,487
Real estate property managers..............................	53131	43,659	76,665	81,529	84,876	94,267	105,235
Offices of real estate appraisers...........................	53132	5,225	6,219	6,570	7,342	8,542	8,362
Rental and leasing services [1]...............................	532	108,491	168,236	178,258	160,478	186,528	210,584
Passenger car rental..	532111	22,534	30,843	33,655	24,699	32,968	40,430
Passenger car leasing......................................	532112	6,063	11,995	12,990	12,177	13,060	15,099
Truck, trailer, and recreational vehicle rental and leasing.....	53212	13,941	25,306	26,326	26,222	30,250	32,211
Consumer electronics and appliances rental.................	53221	5,253	7,263	7,496	7,925	10,305	9,661
Construction/transportation/mining/forestry equipment rental and leasing...........................	53241	19,483	38,495	40,445	37,302	40,233	45,447
Lessors of other nonfinancial intangible assets..................	533	29,902	51,541	52,992	49,076	55,464	58,866

[1] Includes other kinds of business, not shown separately.

Source: U.S. Census Bureau, Service Annual Survey, "Service Annual Survey Latest Data (NAICS-basis): 2022" and "Service Annual Survey Historical Survey Tables," <www.census.gov/programs-surveys/sas/data.html>, accessed February 2024.

Arts, Recreation, and Travel

This section presents data on the arts, entertainment, and recreation economic sector of the economy, and personal recreational activities, the arts and humanities, and domestic and foreign travel.

Arts, entertainment, and recreation industry—The U.S. Census Bureau surveys which provide data on the arts, entertainment, and recreation sector include County Business Patterns, the Economic Census, Nonemployer Statistics, and, through 2021, the Service Annual Survey. County Business Patterns' annual data include number of establishments, number of employees, first quarter and annual payrolls, and number of establishments by employment size class. The Economic Census, conducted every five years for the years ending in '2' and '7', provides information on the number of establishments, receipts, payroll, and paid employees for the United States and various geographic levels. Nonemployer Statistics is an annual tabulation of economic data by industry for active businesses that are subject to federal income tax and that do not have paid employees. The Service Annual Survey provides estimates of operating revenue of taxable firms and revenues and expenses of firms exempt from federal taxes for industries in this sector of the economy. See Appendix III for more details.

Recreation and leisure activities—Data on the participation in various recreation and leisure time activities are based on several sample surveys. Data on the public's involvement with arts events and activities are published by the National Endowment for Arts (NEA). The NEA's Survey of Public Participation in the Arts remains the largest periodic study of arts

participation in the United States. The most recent data are from the 2022 survey. Data on participation in fishing, hunting, and other forms of wildlife associated recreation are published periodically by the U.S. Department of Interior, Fish and Wildlife Service and the U.S. Census Bureau in *The National Survey of Fishing, Hunting, and Wildlife-Associated Recreation*. The most recent data are from the 2022 survey. MRI-Simmons, launched as joint venture under GfK in 2019, also conducts periodic surveys on sports and leisure activities, as well as other topics.

Parks and recreation—The Department of the Interior has responsibility for administering the national parks. Data regarding acreage and visits for each area administered by the service can be found in the National Park Service Visitor Use Statistics portal at <irma.nps.gov/STATS>. Statistics for state parks are compiled by the National Association of State Park Directors in its annual *Statistical Report of State Park Operations*.

Travel—Statistics on arrivals and departures to the United States, cities and states visited by overseas travelers, and tourism sales and employment are reported by the International Trade Administration (ITA), Office of Travel & Tourism Industries (OTTI). Data on domestic travel and travel expenditures are published by the research department of the U.S. Travel Association. Other data on household transportation characteristics are in Section 23, Transportation.

Statistical reliability—For a discussion of statistical collection and estimation, sampling procedures, and measures of statistical reliability applicable to Census Bureau data, see Appendix III.

Table 1247. Arts, Entertainment, and Recreation—Revenue: 2010 to 2022

[In millions of dollars (188,116 represents $188,116,000,000). For taxable and tax-exempt employer firms. Data for 2010 are based on the 2007 North American Industry Classification System (NAICS); beginning 2013, data are based on 2012 NAICS. Selected estimates have been adjusted using the results of the 2017 Economic Census. Based on the Service Annual Survey, see Appendix III]

Kind of business	NAICS Code	2010	2015	2019	2020	2021	2022
Arts, entertainment, and recreation	**71**	**188,116**	**236,317**	**297,425**	**210,246**	**281,848**	**350,099**
Performing arts, spectator sports, and related	711	80,446	104,744	135,680	90,435	116,556	155,457
Performing arts companies	7111	13,799	14,761	17,601	9,797	11,144	16,234
Sports teams and clubs	711211	21,442	28,576	37,083	26,552	32,939	41,613
Racetracks	711212	6,951	7,470	8,828	6,137	7,503	8,193
Other spectator sports	711219	3,344	3,556	3,948	3,728	4,175	4,894
Promoters of performing arts, sports, and similar events	7113	16,312	25,484	34,838	18,648	26,295	41,634
Agents and managers for artists, athletes, entertainers and other public figures	7114	5,358	7,198	9,298	6,668	9,452	11,134
Independent artists, writers, and performers	7115	13,240	17,699	24,084	18,905	25,048	31,755
Museums, historical sites, and similar institutions	712	14,255	16,536	21,554	16,688	22,824	22,099
Amusement, gambling, and recreation industries	713	93,415	115,037	140,191	103,123	142,468	172,543
Amusement and theme parks	71311	10,205	16,184	20,090	7,427	17,769	25,755
Amusement arcades	71312	1,627	2,345	4,362	2,696	4,366	5,318
Casinos (except casino hotels)	71321	15,367	16,279	17,638	14,071	17,721	19,831
Other gambling industries	71329	8,065	8,395	11,183	8,662	12,929	15,569
Golf courses and country clubs	71391	19,788	22,009	24,118	23,532	28,546	31,522
Skiing facilities	71392	2,265	2,394	3,370	3,102	3,423	3,665
Marinas	71393	3,604	4,253	5,174	5,266	5,941	6,417
Fitness and recreational sports centers	71394	22,311	28,836	35,947	25,057	31,333	38,684
Bowling centers	71395	3,007	3,386	4,109	2,209	3,396	4,287
All other amusement and recreation industries	71399	7,176	10,956	14,200	11,101	17,044	21,495

Source: U.S. Census Bureau, Service Annual Survey, "Service Annual Survey Latest Data (NAICS-basis): 2022," <www.census.gov/programs-surveys/sas/data.html>, accessed February 2024.

Table 1248. Arts, Entertainment, and Recreation—Establishments, Revenue, Payroll, and Employees by Kind of Business: 2012 and 2017

[201,193 represents $201,193,000,000. For establishments with payroll only. Definition of paid employees varies among NAICS sectors. Data are based on the 2012 and 2017 Economic Censuses which are subject to nonsampling error. See Appendix III]

Kind of business	2012 NAICS code [1]	Number of establishments		Revenue (mil. dol.)		Annual payroll (mil. dol.)		Paid employees (1,000)	
		2012	2017	2012	2017	2012	2017	2012	2017
Arts, entertainment, and recreation, total	**71**	**124,591**	**142,938**	**201,193**	**265,620**	**64,052**	**82,256**	**2,082**	**2,390**
Performing arts, spectator sports, and related industries [2]	711	45,612	53,613	86,421	119,507	31,545	41,237	434	489
Performing arts companies	7111	8,508	8,836	13,857	16,157	3,950	4,552	119	121
Spectator sports	7112	4,164	3,900	33,298	46,201	16,653	21,624	118	130
Promoters of performing arts, sports and similar events	7113	6,846	8,072	18,474	29,367	3,211	4,984	137	167
Agents and managers for artists, athletes, entertainers and other public figures	7114	3,716	4,111	5,832	7,868	1,886	2,408	18	22
Independent artists, writers, and performers	7115	22,378	28,694	14,960	19,914	5,844	7,669	41	49
Museums, historical sites, and similar institutions	712	7,319	7,557	13,726	19,631	4,197	5,414	135	158
Amusement, gambling, and recreation [2]	713	71,660	81,768	101,046	126,481	28,310	35,605	1,513	1,743
Amusement parks and arcades	7131	3,299	4,317	14,302	21,392	3,386	5,140	155	226
Gambling industries	7132	2,886	3,038	24,385	25,584	4,272	4,469	149	135

[1] Based on 2012 North American Industry Classification System (NAICS). [2] Includes other industries not shown separately.

Source: U.S. Census Bureau, 2017 Economic Census, EC1700COMP, "All Sectors: Comparative Statistics for the U.S., States, and Selected Geographies (2012 NAICS Basis): 2017 and 2012," <data.census.gov/>, accessed December 2021.

Table 1249. Artists by Occupation and Selected Characteristics: 2015 to 2019

[164,465 represents 164,465,000. Data are aggregate for the 2015 to 2019 period. Based on data from the American Community Survey]

Occupation	Number in labor force (1,000s)	Percent						Median earnings (dollars) [4]
		Non-white or Hispanic	Female	With a disability	Self-employed	Working full-year full-time [2]	Bachelor's degree or higher [3]	
Total labor force	164,465	37.9	47.2	6.2	9.3	66.0	37.3	48,305
All employed artists	**2,404**	**26.5**	**47.6**	**5.3**	**33.6**	**59.8**	**64.4**	**58,005**
Architects [1]	208	25.1	27.6	3.2	23.6	82.3	90.7	83,195
Fine artists, art directors, animators	232	24.6	46.1	7.3	53.8	56.1	58.3	50,505
Designers	933	27.6	55.3	4.6	23.3	68.3	59.9	55,560
Actors	61	33.2	45.4	5.5	37.8	23.5	61.4	41,060
Producers and directors	171	25.2	37.6	3.3	22.7	72.3	74.9	69,605
Dancers and choreographers	23	44.1	77.4	6.6	23.1	36.8	31.4	36,365
Musicians	216	28.9	33.6	7.4	45.0	32.6	57.0	45,875
Entertainers	49	31.7	45.7	7.8	45.9	37.5	44.5	41,260
Announcers	72	36.1	28.8	7.6	25.6	52.6	46.0	51,675
Writers and authors	248	17.3	59.8	6.1	41.8	55.1	83.2	60,115
Photographers	190	26.1	47.6	5.2	56.8	46.5	51.2	42,940

[1] Includes landscape architects. [2] Full-year full-time is defined as working at least 50 weeks out of the year for 35 hours or more. [3] For workers aged 25 years and older. [4] For those working full-year full-time. Earnings estimates were rounded to the nearest multiple of 5.

Source: National Endowment for the Arts, "Artists in the Workforce: National and State Estimates for 2015-2019," <www.arts.gov/impact/research/arts-data-profile-series/adp-31>, accessed February 2023.

Table 1250. Arts, Entertainment, and Recreation—Nonemployer Establishments and Receipts by Kind of Business (NAICS Basis): 2015 to 2021

[Firms in thousands (1,342 represents 1,342,000); receipts in millions of dollars (34,549 represents $34,549,000,000). Includes only firms subject to federal income tax. Nonemployers are businesses with no paid employees but with annual receipts of $1,000 or more]

Kind of business	NAICS code [1]	Firms (1,000)			Receipts (mil. dol.)		
		2015	2020	2021	2015	2020	2021
Arts, entertainment, and recreation	**71**	**1,342**	**1,339**	**1,514**	**34,549**	**35,411**	**45,131**
Performing arts, spectator sports, and related industries	711	1,177	1,205	1,365	27,590	29,400	37,194
Performing arts companies	7111	94	69	79	1,832	1,520	1,954
Spectator sports	7112	170	170	210	3,242	3,523	4,411
Promoters of performing arts, sports, and similar events	7113	56	57	67	2,467	2,050	2,932
Agents/managers for artists, athletes, and other public figures	7114	39	34	37	1,678	1,633	2,081
Independent artists, writers, and performers	7115	819	874	972	18,371	20,674	25,816
Museums, historical sites, and similar institutions	712	6	4	5	122	108	119
Amusement, gambling, and recreation industries	713	158	130	144	6,837	5,902	7,818
Amusement parks and arcades	7131	4	4	4	248	170	232
Gambling industries	7132	10	11	13	1,325	1,244	1,963
Other amusement and recreation services	7139	143	116	127	5,265	4,488	5,623

[1] Data for 2015 are based on the 2012 NAICS; data for 2020 and 2021 are based on the 2017 NAICS. See text, Section 15.

Source: U.S. Census Bureau, Nonemployer Statistics, "All Sectors: Nonemployer Statistics by Legal Form of Organization and Receipts Size Class for the U.S., States, and Selected Geographies: 2021," <data.census.gov>, accessed March 2024.

Table 1251. Arts, Entertainment, and Recreation—Establishments, Employees, and Payroll by Kind of Business (NAICS Basis): 2020 and 2022

[Employees in thousands (2,505.0 represents 2,505,000); payroll in millions of dollars (78,615 represents $78,615,000,000). Covers establishments with paid employees. Excludes self-employed individuals, employees of private households, railroad employees, agricultural production employees, and most government employees. For statement on methodology, see Appendix III]

Kind of business	NAICS code [1]	Establishments		Employees [2] (1,000)		Payroll (mil. dol.)	
		2020	2022	2020	2022	2020	2022
Arts, entertainment, & recreation	**71**	**151,881**	**162,960**	**2,505.0**	**2,318.4**	**78,615**	**110,036**
Performing arts, spectator sports	711	59,909	67,356	539.5	505.2	40,141	57,217
Performing arts companies	7111	9,341	10,260	124.6	117.3	3,206	5,333
Theater companies & dinner theaters	71111	3,239	3,503	69.4	63.4	1,420	2,512
Dance companies	71112	751	849	11.1	11.3	268	378
Musical groups & artists	71113	5,061	5,477	37.1	38.1	1,363	2,204
Other performing arts companies	71119	290	431	6.9	4.5	156	240
Spectator sports	7112	4,401	5,034	138.0	127.4	21,194	29,355
Sports teams & clubs	711211	1,041	1,372	83.8	79.2	19,161	26,785
Racetracks	711212	525	562	37.4	31.9	1,055	1,409
Other spectator sports	711219	2,835	3,100	16.8	16.3	977	1,160
Promoters of performing arts, sports, & similar events	7113	8,175	9,120	195.2	173.9	4,720	7,139
Promoters of performing arts, sports, & similar events with facilities	71131	3,757	4,178	159.0	137.8	3,258	4,909
Promoters of performing arts, sports, & similar events without facilities	71132	4,418	4,942	36.2	36.1	1,462	2,230
Agents & managers for artists, athletes, and other public figures	7114	4,523	4,878	25.2	24.5	2,539	3,899
Independent artists, writers, & performers	7115	33,469	38,064	56.6	62.0	8,483	11,490
Museums, historical sites, & similar institutions	712	7,710	8,142	160.6	143.0	5,268	6,343
Museums	71211	5,210	5,442	97.7	84.9	3,327	3,851
Historical sites	71212	1,112	1,122	12.7	10.9	333	432
Zoos & botanical gardens	71213	681	833	42.1	39.0	1,323	1,692
Nature parks & other similar institutions	71219	707	745	8.1	8.2	284	368
Amusement, gambling, & recreation industries	713	84,262	87,462	1,804.9	1,670.2	33,206	46,477
Amusement parks & arcades	7131	3,917	4,079	229.3	227.6	4,354	6,548
Amusement & theme parks	71311	567	687	162.6	166.1	3,604	5,059
Amusement arcades	71312	3,350	3,392	66.7	61.5	750	1,489
Gambling industries	7132	3,130	3,411	138.5	130.6	4,545	6,427
Casinos (except casino hotels)	71321	311	342	87.4	76.0	2,861	3,627
Other gambling industries	71329	2,819	3,069	51.1	54.6	1,685	2,799
Other amusement & recreation services	7139	77,215	79,972	1,437.1	1,312.0	24,307	33,502
Golf courses & country clubs	71391	10,261	10,076	299.8	305.0	9,291	12,005
Skiing facilities	71392	346	350	69.4	68.2	961	1,232
Marinas	71393	3,714	3,766	28.7	31.0	1,203	1,474
Fitness & recreational sports centers	71394	39,562	40,786	786.9	650.0	8,941	12,091
Bowling centers	71395	3,370	3,305	69.6	66.3	776	1,387
All other amusement & recreation industries	71399	19,962	21,689	182.8	191.4	3,135	5,313

[1] Data are based on 2017 North American Industry Classification System (NAICS) see text, this section and Section 15. [2] For employees on the payroll for the period including March 12.

Source: U.S. Census Bureau, County Business Patterns, "All Sectors: County Business Patterns, including ZIP Code Business Patterns, by Legal Form of Organization and Employment Size Class for the U.S., States, and Selected Geographies: 2022," <data.census.gov>, accessed June 2024.

Table 1252. Arts and Culture Production—Gross Output and Employment by Industry: 2017 to 2022

[Output in millions of current dollars (1,407,338 represents $1,407,338,000,000); employment in thousands (5,093 represents 5,093,000). Arts and cultural production is defined narrowly to include creative artistic activity; the goods and services produced by it; the goods and services produced in the support of it; and the construction of buildings in which it is taking place]

Industry	2017	2018	2019	2020	2021	2022
GROSS OUTPUT (million dollars)						
Total	**1,407,338**	**1,493,482**	**1,550,668**	**1,513,690**	**1,729,140**	**1,918,427**
Core arts and cultural production	**285,419**	**305,767**	**325,028**	**273,974**	**322,073**	**397,717**
Performing arts	111,229	120,134	128,384	84,499	110,517	156,775
Performing arts companies	27,114	28,128	29,430	20,531	21,150	34,416
Promoters of performing arts and similar events	33,040	35,663	38,792	21,664	30,018	47,612
Agents/managers for artists	5,486	5,937	6,319	4,483	6,356	8,658
Independent artists, writers, and performers	45,589	50,407	53,843	37,821	52,993	66,089
Museums	19,210	19,894	21,117	18,506	19,891	21,025
Design services [1]	140,753	150,706	159,639	156,348	176,098	202,280
Advertising	51,548	56,524	60,317	60,383	67,114	77,907
Architectural services	30,787	32,884	34,934	34,074	37,613	43,827
Landscape architectural services	5,694	6,055	6,240	6,392	6,756	7,878
Interior design services	18,273	19,985	21,053	21,866	26,646	30,146
Industrial design services	2,636	2,705	2,961	3,308	3,734	4,223
Graphic design services	12,310	12,228	13,079	12,826	14,833	16,789
Computer systems design	3,076	3,242	3,379	3,322	3,291	4,814
Photography and photofinishing services	14,779	15,410	15,898	12,628	14,196	14,520
Fine arts education	6,524	7,312	7,934	6,513	7,501	8,519
Education services	7,702	7,721	7,954	8,109	8,067	9,118
Supporting arts and cultural production	**1,083,532**	**1,147,682**	**1,184,435**	**1,200,120**	**1,362,630**	**1,470,623**
Art support services [1]	156,898	164,265	172,877	177,809	190,117	209,219
Rental and leasing	10,057	10,658	10,952	9,730	10,749	12,768
Grant-making and giving services	1,389	1,412	1,584	1,346	1,741	1,873
Unions	1,186	1,201	1,269	1,303	1,336	1,354
Government	142,690	149,231	157,180	164,408	174,877	191,221
Information services [1]	719,695	766,637	792,414	802,644	918,115	985,169
Publishing	137,807	139,521	142,502	145,553	162,121	175,658
Motion pictures	130,430	140,278	142,094	122,237	138,678	162,732
Sound recording	18,238	19,861	21,816	22,878	26,107	30,980
Broadcasting	274,272	282,487	277,858	278,608	296,448	303,917
Manufacturing [1]	37,957	37,463	36,138	33,170	36,080	40,162
Jewelry and silverware	7,445	7,223	7,022	6,134	7,361	8,182
Printed goods	13,366	12,815	11,975	10,425	10,790	12,016
Musical instruments	1,922	1,998	2,055	1,953	2,280	2,454
Custom architectural woodwork & metalwork	9,158	9,057	8,629	8,135	8,605	10,020
Construction	26,702	28,970	29,929	28,446	28,435	28,622
Wholesale and transportation industries	76,210	80,203	81,795	80,581	95,581	107,215
Retail industries	66,071	70,144	71,283	77,471	94,303	100,236
EMPLOYMENT (1,000s)						
Total	**5,093**	**5,122**	**5,165**	**4,686**	**4,865**	**5,176**
Core arts and cultural production	**1,244**	**1,273**	**1,302**	**1,070**	**1,130**	**1,293**
Performing arts	300	313	321	200	231	313
Performing arts companies	122	125	128	77	85	122
Promoters of performing arts and similar events	113	121	125	67	82	118
Agents/managers for artists	14	15	15	13	13	15
Independent artists, writers, and performers	51	52	53	43	50	59
Museums	152	157	160	126	128	146
Design services [1]	597	600	604	547	564	612
Advertising	208	208	208	187	191	209
Architectural services	139	142	145	140	140	149
Landscape architectural services	31	31	32	31	32	33
Interior design services	44	46	48	45	48	54
Industrial design services	19	19	19	18	22	18
Graphic design services	63	62	60	55	56	59
Computer systems design	17	17	17	16	15	21
Photography and photofinishing services	66	64	64	45	50	57
Fine arts education	122	132	143	119	130	141
Education services	74	73	74	79	78	79
Supporting arts and cultural production	**3,694**	**3,693**	**3,705**	**3,469**	**3,583**	**3,722**
Art support services [1]	1,262	1,257	1,275	1,219	1,201	1,232
Rental and leasing	22	22	22	17	17	19
Grant-making and giving services	9	8	9	8	9	10
Unions	10	9	10	10	10	9
Government	1,215	1,212	1,228	1,180	1,161	1,189
Information services [1]	1,320	1,321	1,329	1,179	1,273	1,371
Publishing	312	312	317	311	326	271
Motion pictures	405	399	410	275	342	413
Sound recording	17	18	19	18	18	20
Broadcasting	418	412	391	373	368	370
Manufacturing [1]	179	173	167	149	149	155
Jewelry and silverware	24	22	21	17	19	21
Printed goods	70	66	63	53	51	52
Musical instruments	10	10	10	9	10	11
Custom architectural woodwork & metalwork	44	43	41	38	36	39
Construction	126	132	137	129	137	142
Wholesale and transportation industries	235	231	232	236	236	244
Retail industries	572	578	565	557	588	578

[1] Includes other services or goods manufacturing, not shown separately.

Source: U.S. Bureau of Economic Analysis, "Arts and Cultural Production Satellite Account," <www.bea.gov/data/special-topics/arts-and-culture>, accessed June 2024.

Table 1253. Arts and Cultural Production—Summary by State: 2022

[In millions of dollars (1,102,085 represents $1,102,085,000,000), except employment (5,176 represents 5,176,000). Arts and cultural production is defined narrowly to include creative artistic activity; the goods and services produced by it; the goods and services produced in the support of it; and the construction of buildings in which it is taking place]

State	Total arts and cultural production industries [1]			Core arts and cultural production industries			Supporting arts and cultural production industries		
	Value added (mil. dol.) [2]	Employment (1,000)	Compensation (mil. dol.)	Value added (mil. dol.) [2]	Employment (1,000)	Compensation (mil. dol.)	Value added (mil. dol.) [2]	Employment (1,000)	Compensation (mil. dol.)
Total..............	1,102,085	5,176	540,851	249,042	1,293	115,938	825,640	3,722	410,989
Alabama...........	6,369	49	3,266	1,051	9	518	4,997	39	2,593
Alaska.............	1,468	12	1,076	164	2	93	1,252	10	957
Arizona...........	14,204	84	7,105	3,231	22	1,477	10,493	59	5,358
Arkansas..........	3,490	33	1,886	853	7	430	2,427	25	1,361
California.........	290,287	848	141,340	65,881	200	27,048	221,181	629	112,451
Colorado..........	18,083	104	10,101	4,884	(D)	(D)	12,640	72	7,514
Connecticut.......	12,770	55	5,998	2,535	(D)	(D)	9,875	37	4,543
Delaware..........	1,142	9	641	286	3	146	759	6	450
Dist. of Columbia...	13,848	57	9,475	4,139	15	2,223	9,596	41	7,175
Florida............	45,361	269	22,497	13,094	74	5,503	30,523	184	16,169
Georgia...........	31,574	159	15,226	6,747	34	3,045	23,952	120	11,759
Hawaii.............	3,263	21	1,720	948	7	443	2,229	14	1,230
Idaho..............	2,646	22	1,549	526	4	253	2,001	17	1,236
Illinois............	36,150	216	20,047	9,739	(D)	(D)	25,224	152	14,583
Indiana............	9,270	83	5,226	1,969	(D)	(D)	6,684	63	4,023
Iowa...............	4,972	42	2,677	885	9	464	3,810	31	2,091
Kansas............	4,627	42	2,793	823	8	429	3,556	33	2,255
Kentucky..........	6,490	51	3,188	1,141	9	533	5,042	39	2,500
Louisiana..........	6,978	55	3,547	1,397	(D)	(D)	5,237	42	2,764
Maine.............	2,197	19	1,213	668	5	287	1,428	13	876
Maryland..........	12,869	80	7,292	2,498	(D)	(D)	9,893	59	5,718
Massachusetts.....	28,572	134	15,640	6,725	44	3,762	21,082	86	11,448
Michigan...........	18,394	121	10,355	4,887	32	3,051	12,714	84	6,911
Minnesota.........	13,779	90	7,522	3,439	25	1,739	9,791	62	5,503
Mississippi........	2,571	27	1,469	335	3	170	2,065	23	1,227
Missouri...........	11,460	94	6,336	3,131	(D)	(D)	7,832	66	4,528
Montana...........	2,238	17	1,229	539	4	242	1,629	12	953
Nebraska..........	3,643	31	2,106	822	8	432	2,652	22	1,599
Nevada............	10,876	43	3,948	2,942	12	1,071	7,725	29	2,751
New Hampshire. ..	3,354	21	1,851	670	5	350	2,551	15	1,433
New Jersey........	27,331	139	14,460	5,418	34	2,595	21,063	100	11,411
New Mexico........	3,381	26	1,881	509	5	260	2,749	21	1,564
New York..........	151,066	461	62,335	40,226	(D)	(D)	108,991	292	42,481
North Carolina.....	22,030	134	11,333	4,706	32	2,322	16,578	97	8,613
North Dakota.......	1,613	13	885	207	2	108	1,334	10	743
Ohio...............	24,981	158	11,299	5,312	(D)	(D)	18,672	111	8,002
Oklahoma..........	4,831	42	2,666	1,136	9	495	3,387	32	2,056
Oregon............	9,518	62	5,343	2,399	(D)	(D)	6,803	43	3,932
Pennsylvania......	30,071	176	15,041	6,674	(D)	(D)	22,236	118	10,952
Rhode Island.......	2,368	18	1,281	567	5	305	1,691	13	935
South Carolina.....	8,569	61	4,318	1,857	13	821	6,293	45	3,334
South Dakota......	1,401	15	903	250	3	128	1,086	11	742
Tennessee........	18,718	96	8,023	5,259	(D)	(D)	12,917	67	5,431
Texas..............	59,322	383	30,184	14,178	87	6,829	42,677	282	22,103
Utah...............	8,469	68	4,649	1,920	17	906	6,317	49	3,620
Vermont...........	1,165	11	709	364	3	193	756	7	493
Virginia...........	19,348	119	10,027	4,200	(D)	(D)	14,447	88	7,558
Washington........	70,242	191	28,700	4,159	28	2,146	65,486	160	26,203
West Virginia......	1,469	16	958	156	2	87	1,208	13	824
Wisconsin.........	11,933	89	6,636	2,370	(D)	(D)	9,066	66	5,249
Wyoming..........	1,315	12	902	228	2	98	1,045	10	785

D Withheld to avoid disclosing data on individual companies. [1] Total arts and cultural production industries includes core industries, supporting industries, and, not shown separately, industries with secondary production that is designated as artistic and cultural. [2] Nominal.

Source: U.S. Bureau of Economic Analysis, "Arts and Cultural Production Satellite Account," <www.bea.gov/data/special-topics/arts-and-culture>, accessed April 2024.

Table 1254. Broadway Shows and Tours—Selected Data: 2010 to 2024

[In units, as indicated (1,020 represents $1,020,000,000). For season ending in year shown]

Item	Unit	2010	2015	2017	2018	2019	2020	2021	2022 [5]	2023 [6]	2024
Broadway shows:											
New productions....................	Number	39	37	45	33	38	33	(4)	39	40	39
Attendance......................	Millions	11.9	13.1	13.3	13.8	14.8	11.1	(4)	6.7	12.3	12.3
Playing weeks [1, 2].................	Number	1,464	1,626	1,580	1,624	1,737	1,282	(4)	946	1,474	1,471
Gross ticket sales................	Mil. dol.	1,020	1,365	1,449	1,697	1,829	1,358	(4)	845	1,577	1,539
Broadway road tours: [3]											
Attendance......................	Millions	15.9	13.7	13.9	17.0	18.5	(NA)	(4)	(NA)	(NA)	(NA)
Playing weeks....................	Number	1,250	953	983	1,125	1,188	(NA)	(4)	(NA)	(NA)	(NA)
Gross ticket sales................	Mil. dol.	947	957	1,007	1,416	1,633	(NA)	(4)	(NA)	(NA)	(NA)

NA Not available. [1] All shows (new productions and holdovers from previous seasons). [2] Eight performances constitute one playing week. [3] North American Tours include U.S. and Canadian companies. [4] Due to the COVID-19 pandemic, there were no Broadway or Touring Broadway performances during the 2020-21 season. [5] The 2021-22 season marked the return of Broadway. However, the start of the season was delayed by 10 weeks; re-openings were staggered; and there were numerous COVID-related cancellations of performances, including during the December and New Year's holidays. [6] The 2022-23 season was the first full season since Broadway came back from the COVID-19 pandemic shutdown.

Source: The Broadway League, New York, NY ©. See also <www.broadwayleague.com>.

Table 1255. Arts and Humanities—Selected Federal Aid Programs: 1990 to 2022

[In millions of dollars (170.8 represents $170,800,000), except as indicated. For fiscal year ending September 30. FY2010 includes funds from the American Recovery and Reinvestment Act. FY2020 includes funding provided under the Coronavirus Aid, Relief, and Economic Security (CARES) Act of 2020. FY2021 and FY2022 include funds provided under the American Rescue Plan (ARP) Act of 2021]

Type of fund and program	1990	2000	2010	2015	2018	2019	2020	2021	2022
National Endowment for the Arts:									
Funds available [1]	170.8	85.2	153.1	127.1	124.3	128.1	210.6	269.5	230.9
Program appropriation [2]	152.3	79.6	138.7	116.6	120.7	122.9	203.9	264.2	145.2
Grants awarded (number) [3]	4,252.0	1,906.0	2,731.0	2,346.0	2,306.0	2,381.0	3,335.0	2,551.0	3,459.0
Funds obligated [4,5]	157.6	83.5	141.1	118.4	121.7	122.9	207.4	186.1	226.0
National Endowment for the Humanities:									
Funds available [1]	140.6	102.6	146.6	129.8	134.4	145.0	225.4	292.6	216.8
Program appropriation	114.2	82.7	125.7	108.1	113.4	115.0	195.5	255.8	129.4
Matching funds [6]	26.3	15.1	14.3	10.9	11.3	11.3	12.5	15.0	15.6
Grants awarded (number)	2,195.0	1,230.0	1,204.0	822.0	836.0	849.0	1,207.0	1,020.0	1,018.0
Funds obligated [4]	141.0	100.0	142.7	121.5	116.1	126.1	197.6	202.0	195.3
Education programs	16.3	13.0	16.0	13.8	10.3	11.7	25.9	12.8	29.4
State partnership	29.6	30.6	49.1	42.6	47.2	48.7	81.4	105.0	55.8
Research grants	22.5	6.9	12.5	10.1	9.4	10.3	8.9	29.8	19.1
Fellowships	15.3	6.1	6.8	7.0	5.9	6.2	7.1	7.5	7.6
Challenge [7]	14.6	10.8	10.5	7.8	4.8	12.1	8.8	7.2	6.4
Public programs	25.4	11.8	19.4	17.6	13.4	12.8	29.5	15.0	26.1
Digital Humanities	(X)	(X)	4.9	4.7	4.8	4.9	8.4	5.0	11.9
A More Perfect Union initiative	(X)	(X)	(X)	(X)	(X)	(X)	2.7	6.0	5.5
Preservation and access	17.5	20.7	22.6	17.1	20.3	19.4	24.9	19.7	33.5

X Not applicable. [1] Includes other program funds not shown separately. Excludes administrative funds. FY2020 includes grants awarded using funding provided under the CARES Act. [2] FY1990-1996 include Regular Program Funds, Treasury Funds, Challenge Grant Funds, and Policy, Planning, and Research Funds. FY1998-FY2000 includes Regular Program Funds and Matching Grant Funds. FY2020 includes funds provided under the CARES Act. [3] Excludes cooperative agreements and interagency agreements. FY2020 includes grants awarded using funding provided under the CARES Act. FY2021 includes grants amended with funding provided under the CARES Act and the ARP Act. FY2022 includes funding provided under the ARP Act. [4] Includes obligations for new grants, supplemental awards on previous years' grants, cooperative agreements, and interagency agreements. Excludes obligations funded with administrative funds. FY2020 includes obligation of funding provided under the CARES Act. FY2021 and FY2022 include obligation of funding provided under the ARP Act. [5] Beginning with 1997 data, the grantmaking structure changed from discipline-based categories to thematic ones. [6] Represents federal funds obligated only upon receipt or certification by endowment of matching nonfederal gifts. Funds for matching grants are not allocated by program area because they are awarded on a grant-by-grant basis. [7] Program designed to stimulate new sources and higher levels of giving to institutions for the purpose of guaranteeing long-term stability and financial independence; currently requires a match of at least 3 private dollars to each federal dollar.

Source: U.S. National Endowment for the Arts, unpublished data; and U.S. National Endowment for the Humanities, unpublished data.

Table 1256. State Arts Agency Legislative Appropriations: 2023 and 2024

[In thousands of dollars (974,851 represents $974,851,000). For fiscal year ending June 30 in most states. The National Assembly of State Arts Agencies is the membership organization of the nations' state and jurisdictional arts agencies. Legislative appropriations include funds designated to state arts agency by state legislatures. These include line items that are passed through state arts agency budgets and designated for specific entities and projects. State arts agencies also receive monies from other sources including other state funds, the federal government (primarily the National Endowment for the Arts), private funds, and legislative earmarks. Minus sign (-) indicates decrease]

State	Legislative appropriations including line items 2023, revised	Legislative appropriations including line items 2024, enacted	Percent change, 2023 to 2024	State	Legislative appropriations including line items 2023, revised	Legislative appropriations including line items 2024, enacted	Percent change, 2023 to 2024	State	Legislative appropriations including line items 2023, revised	Legislative appropriations including line items 2024, enacted	Percent change, 2023 to 2024
Total...	974,851	740,914	-24.0	LA.	2,140	2,112	-1.3	OR.	11,207	6,179	-44.9
AL.	7,631	7,806	2.3	ME.	1,028	1,109	7.8	PA.	10,583	10,660	0.7
AK.	745	947	27.2	MD.	27,777	34,548	24.4	RI.	2,200	2,293	4.2
AZ [1]	5,000	5,000	–	MA.	23,377	25,895	10.8	SC.	13,929	13,124	-5.8
AR.	1,373	1,426	3.9	MI.	11,850	8,850	-25.3	SD.	940	1,108	17.8
CA [2]	135,962	39,344	-71.1	MN.	43,551	55,195	26.7	TN [11]	11,545	11,697	1.3
CO.	2,023	2,023	–	MS [6]	5,913	10,496	77.5	TX.	10,165	14,310	40.8
CT [12]	37,635	8,215	-78.2	MO [7]	18,617	29,386	57.8	UT.	9,451	7,946	-15.9
DE.	3,870	4,879	26.1	MT [12]	1,004	1,116	11.2	VT.	859	969	12.7
DC.	47,695	50,077	5.0	NE [8,12]	10,102	2,600	-74.3	VA [12]	4,596	4,596	–
FL [3]	83,582	55,652	-33.4	NV.	2,102	2,261	7.6	WA.	5,262	6,826	29.7
GA [4]	1,556	1,566	0.7	NH.	839	1,407	67.7	WV.	954	997	4.5
HI.	7,277	10,331	42.0	NJ.	40,780	45,730	12.1	WI.	955	1,078	12.9
ID.	906	983	8.5	NM.	1,593	1,718	7.9	WY.	898	898	–
IL.	63,665	65,480	2.9	NY [9]	241,447	110,105	-54.4	AS.	154	167	8.8
IN.	3,632	5,198	43.1	NC [10]	9,146	12,396	35.5	GU.	586	586	–
IA [12]	1,467	1,550	5.6	ND [12]	855	1,299	51.8	MP.	224	280	25.2
KS [5]	509	1,009	98.2	OH.	20,086	25,502	27.0	PR.	18,176	18,043	-0.7
KY.	1,797	1,840	2.4	OK.	3,243	3,730	15.0	VI.	392	374	-4.5

– Represents zero. [1] The Arizona Commission on the Arts received a $5 million one-time appropriation from the state legislature. [2] During FY2022, the California Arts Council was allocated a one-time, $100 million general fund allocation for creative workforce and youth development. [3] The Florida Division of Arts and Culture's FY2023 appropriation included over $23.2 million in line items, including $15 million to the African-American Cultural and Historical grant program. [4] All state departments received budget increases to finance pay raises for state employees. [5] The Kansas Department of Commerce added $500,000 to fund Kansas Creative Arts Industries Commission to expand workforce development and entrepreneurship in the creative sector. [6] The state allocated over $5 million from the Capital Expense Fund for the Mississippi Arts Commission and a $1 million pass-through for the Mississippi Museum of Art. [7] The state budget includes a pass-through of $19 million for various organizations. [8] Nebraska Arts Council's appropriation in FY2023 included a $7.5 million one-time appropriation for state arts museum renovation. [9] In FY2023, the New York State Council on the Arts received a $140 million appropriation that included $50 million in recovery funds and $50 million in capital projects support, in addition to the agency's base grant-making budget of $40 million. In FY2024, the arts council received $40 million for its core grant-making activities and $20 million for another year of capital projects funding. [10] The North Carolina Arts Council received $15 million in federal ARP Act funding from the state legislature in FY2022, to be spent over FY2023 and FY2024. [11] The Tennessee Arts Commission received a multiyear $1 million grant from the state's Department of Health Civil Monetary Penalty Fund for the period of February 1, 2019, to June 30, 2023. In FY2023, the Tennessee General Assembly authorized $350,000 in expenditures. [12] Figure reflects state arts agency appropriation only and does not include appropriation to the state's cultural endowment.

Source: National Assembly of State Arts Agencies, *State Arts Agency Revenues, Fiscal Year 2024* ©, March 2024.

Table 1257. Attendance/Participation Rates for Various Arts Activities by Selected Characteristics: 2022

[In percent. For persons 18 years old and over. Represents attendance at least once in the prior twelve months. Excludes elementary and secondary school performances. Data are from the Survey of Public Participation in the Arts, a supplement to the Census Bureau's Current Population Survey, conducted for the National Endowment for the Arts. Data are subject to sampling error; see source]

Characteristic	Adult population	Jazz concert	Classical music concert	Musicals	Non-musical plays	Art museums/ galleries	Craft/ visual art festivals	Parks/ historic buildings [1]
Total	**100.0**	**6.3**	**4.6**	**10.3**	**4.5**	**17.7**	**17.1**	**26.0**
Sex:								
Male	48.6	6.1	4.0	9.0	3.9	15.7	13.7	24.7
Female	51.4	6.4	5.2	11.5	5.1	19.5	20.4	27.1
Race and ethnicity:								
Hispanic	17.2	4.2	2.2	5.1	2.9	13.6	8.3	19.6
White	61.9	6.8	5.5	12.9	5.3	20.0	22.2	30.3
African American	11.9	8.9	3.5	6.6	5.2	10.9	8.2	16.6
Asian	6.2	1.7	4.9	8.4	1.8	17.0	8.8	20.8
Other	2.7	7.9	2.9	5.0	3.5	23.1	18.4	21.3
Age:								
18 to 24 years old	11.5	5.8	4.5	10.4	2.7	18.6	15.8	27.7
25 to 34 years old	17.3	8.3	4.9	12.4	5.2	22.2	20.0	29.5
35 to 44 years old	16.8	7.0	5.7	10.1	6.1	21.3	20.9	30.4
45 to 54 years old	15.7	5.7	4.8	11.6	4.4	18.1	16.5	29.5
55 to 64 years old	16.5	5.7	3.3	8.9	3.8	15.0	15.5	23.7
65 to 74 years old	13.3	6.8	5.1	9.6	5.2	16.5	16.9	21.2
75 years old and older	8.9	2.8	3.7	7.4	3.4	7.1	10.4	13.8
Education:								
Grade school	3.6	1.0	0.0	0.0	1.5	2.1	1.3	7.8
Some high school	5.8	0.5	0.3	1.9	0.6	4.4	4.5	9.2
High school graduate	29.0	3.0	1.8	4.6	1.6	8.1	9.3	15.7
Some college	27.0	6.4	3.1	9.2	4.0	14.4	15.9	23.2
College graduate	22.2	9.5	7.9	17.1	7.5	28.9	27.5	40.0
Graduate school	12.5	12.1	12.1	20.9	10.1	38.3	30.2	43.9

[1] Visiting historic parks or monuments or touring buildings or neighborhoods for the historic or design value.

Source: U.S. National Endowment for the Arts, *Arts Participation Patterns in 2022: Highlights from the Survey of Public Participation in the Arts*, October 2023. See also <www.arts.gov/impact/research/publications/arts-participation-patterns-2022-highlights-survey-public-participation-arts>.

Table 1258. Personal Participation in Reading by Selected Characteristics: 2022

[In percent. For persons 18 years old and over. Represents participation in the last 12 months. Data are from the Survey of Public Participation in the Arts, a supplement to the Census Bureau's Current Population Survey, conducted for the National Endowment for the Arts. Data are subject to sampling error; see source]

Characteristics	Reading [1]				Listened to audiobooks
	Books	Novels or short stories	Poetry	Plays	
Total	**48.5**	**37.6**	**9.2**	**2.4**	**18.5**
Sex:					
Male	40.0	27.7	6.5	1.9	(NA)
Female	56.6	46.9	11.8	2.9	(NA)
Race and ethnicity:					
Hispanic	32.8	24.4	6.5	2.1	(NA)
White	54.9	43.6	10.0	2.6	(NA)
African American	42.1	29.4	8.3	2.6	(NA)
Asian	42.4	28.0	9.8	1.3	(NA)
Other	46.8	43.1	10.2	2.9	(NA)
Age:					
18 to 24 years old	47.4	35.3	9.0	2.5	(NA)
25 to 34 years old	52.6	43.2	11.9	3.8	(NA)
35 to 44 years old	51.0	37.5	10.0	2.3	(NA)
45 to 54 years old	48.1	39.1	7.7	2.2	(NA)
55 to 64 years old	43.6	34.3	7.9	2.0	(NA)
65 to 74 years old	49.6	37.1	9.6	1.9	(NA)
75 years old and older	45.8	35.6	7.1	1.8	(NA)

NA Not available. [1] Respondents may have included listening to books and other literary works via audiobook, streaming, broadcast, or recording although the questions did not reference these media formats specifically. Book reading excludes books for work and school.

Source: U.S. National Endowment for the Arts, *Arts Participation Patterns in 2022: Highlights from the Survey of Public Participation in the Arts*, October 2023. See also <www.arts.gov/impact/research/publications/arts-participation-patterns-2022-highlights-survey-public-participation-arts>.

Table 1259. Outdoor Recreation Sector Gross Output by Activity: 2017 to 2022

[In millions of current dollars (819,950 represents $819,950,000,000)]

Activity	2017	2018	2019	2020	2021	2022
Total outdoor recreation..........................	**819,950**	**869,079**	**890,389**	**668,903**	**908,197**	**1,078,521**
Total core outdoor recreation.....................	**427,304**	**443,627**	**452,542**	**413,592**	**516,584**	**578,997**
Conventional outdoor recreation....................	268,279	275,168	277,202	278,092	341,620	369,572
Bicycling....................................	3,174	2,958	3,244	3,718	4,283	4,322
Boating/fishing.............................	46,910	47,654	49,163	64,321	58,475	60,860
Canoeing................................	84	75	91	127	210	164
Kayaking................................	786	800	801	786	989	908
Fishing (excludes boating).................	10,235	10,411	10,258	9,377	12,794	12,453
Sailing..................................	2,259	2,301	2,573	1,801	2,383	2,848
Other boating............................	33,546	34,067	35,440	52,231	42,099	44,487
Climbing/hiking/tent camping................	6,618	6,203	6,431	8,460	8,790	10,171
Equestrian.................................	8,679	9,049	9,237	10,127	9,565	10,161
Hunting/shooting/trapping...................	13,711	13,424	13,733	15,634	17,922	18,780
Motorcycling/ATVing........................	14,205	14,106	12,958	12,645	17,144	18,460
Recreational flying.........................	3,234	3,208	2,996	2,494	3,155	6,474
RVing......................................	42,195	45,863	44,427	44,219	63,774	70,759
Snow activities.............................	7,997	8,382	8,667	7,978	9,505	13,201
Skiing...................................	3,077	3,205	3,381	2,425	3,049	3,745
Snowboarding............................	2,770	2,904	3,056	2,141	2,709	3,294
Other snow activities [1].................	2,149	2,272	2,231	3,411	3,747	6,163
Other conventional outdoor recreation activities...	19,627	20,569	22,227	24,541	31,077	30,870
Multi-use apparel and accessories (conventional) [2]............	101,931	103,751	104,120	83,955	117,932	125,514
Other outdoor recreation........................	159,024	168,459	175,340	135,500	174,964	209,426
Amusement parks/water parks................	20,150	22,838	24,376	15,875	25,061	29,870
Festivals/sporting events/concerts...........	28,908	30,355	30,827	18,901	26,476	33,733
Field sports...............................	6,501	6,797	7,267	6,833	8,336	9,328
Game areas (includes golfing and tennis).......	36,144	37,467	39,704	29,068	36,918	44,352
Guided tours/outfitted travel.................	31,282	34,356	35,258	27,504	33,852	42,248
Productive activities (includes gardening)........	13,138	14,029	14,591	17,490	20,332	22,798
Other outdoor recreation activities [3].......	15,373	15,509	16,219	13,025	15,878	18,758
Multi-use apparel and accessories (other) [2]......	7,529	7,109	7,098	6,804	8,110	8,338
Supporting outdoor recreation...................	**392,647**	**425,452**	**437,847**	**255,311**	**391,613**	**499,523**
Construction..................................	10,425	11,127	11,897	11,634	11,003	11,803
Local trips [4]................................	80,532	89,376	89,891	51,113	87,040	108,906
Travel and tourism [5]..........................	263,977	285,241	295,688	150,452	248,539	330,414
Food and beverages.......................	41,911	42,997	42,315	23,433	44,902	51,404
Lodging...................................	60,097	63,465	65,098	39,794	54,007	71,051
Shopping and souvenirs....................	37,450	39,025	39,789	40,804	46,113	50,627
Transportation............................	124,519	139,753	148,487	46,421	103,517	157,333
Government expenditures.....................	37,713	39,708	40,371	42,112	45,030	48,400
Federal government........................	4,313	4,661	3,391	3,207	3,528	3,207
State and local government.................	33,400	35,047	36,981	38,905	41,502	45,193

[1] Dog mushing, sleighing, snowmobiling, snow shoeing, and snow tubing. [2] Backpacks, bug spray, coolers, general outdoor clothing, GPS equipment, hydration equipment, lighting, sports racks, sunscreen, watches, and other miscellaneous gear and equipment. [3] Agritourism, augmented reality games, beachgoing, disc golf, hot springs soaking, kite flying, model airplane/rocket/UAV, paintball, photography, stargazing/astronomy, swimming, therapeutic programs, water polo, and yard sports. [4] Trip expenses less than 50 miles away from home, including food and beverages, lodging, shopping and souvenirs, and transportation. [5] Expenses for travel at least 50 miles away from home.

Source: U.S. Bureau of Economic Analysis, Satellite Accounts, *Outdoor Recreation Satellite Account, U.S. and States, 2022*, November 2023. See also <www.bea.gov/data/special-topics/outdoor-recreation>.

Table 1260. Personal Consumption Expenditures for Recreation: 2000 to 2022

[In billions of current dollars (633.7 represents $633,700,000,000), except percent. Represents market value of purchases of goods and services by individuals and nonprofit institutions]

Type of product or service	2000	2010	2015	2019	2020	2021	2022
Total recreation expenditures................	**633.7**	**884.4**	**1,059.4**	**1,289.7**	**1,284.0**	**1,537.8**	**1,707.1**
Percent of total personal consumption [1]................	9.4	8.6	8.6	8.9	9.0	9.6	9.7
Video and audio equipment, computers, and related services....	181.2	275.5	311.8	384.9	430.8	497.0	535.1
Video and audio equipment...................	79.9	83.2	68.9	69.2	67.5	81.2	85.7
Information processing equipment.............	44.1	95.0	119.6	180.6	225.5	268.3	295.2
Services related to video and audio goods and computers......	57.2	97.3	123.3	135.1	137.9	147.5	154.2
Sports and recreational goods and related services..............	146.0	177.4	234.3	278.1	334.3	399.0	433.0
Sports and recreational vehicles.............	34.9	35.8	57.7	74.3	87.0	107.6	113.8
Other sporting and recreational goods............	106.8	137.2	171.2	197.8	241.3	284.4	311.8
Maintenance and repair of recreational vehicles and sports equipment...........................	4.2	4.4	5.4	5.9	6.0	6.9	7.4
Membership clubs, sports centers, parks, theaters, and museums.................................	91.9	146.1	183.5	233.1	133.1	179.6	230.4
Membership clubs and participant sports centers.................	26.4	40.9	50.5	60.8	43.5	57.0	64.9
Amusement parks, campgrounds, and related services..........	31.1	40.1	56.7	75.3	45.7	59.4	74.9
Admissions to specified spectator amusements...................	30.6	58.7	66.7	84.4	34.7	51.3	77.3
Motion picture theaters.....................	8.6	12.3	13.4	13.6	3.3	5.4	8.8
Live entertainment, excluding sports...........	10.4	26.7	29.9	39.4	17.8	25.2	37.9
Spectator sports..........................	11.6	19.7	23.4	31.4	13.5	20.7	30.6
Museums and libraries.......................	3.8	6.5	9.6	12.7	9.3	11.8	13.4
Magazines, newspapers, books, and stationery.................	81.0	74.8	75.0	91.7	105.8	121.5	134.1
Gambling...................................	67.6	109.4	129.8	147.8	125.4	161.5	172.2
Pets, pet products, and related services............	39.7	76.2	99.3	122.3	134.9	156.3	172.0
Photographic goods and services............	19.7	15.2	14.0	13.6	11.8	13.4	14.3
Package tours [2]...........................	6.7	9.8	11.8	18.1	7.9	9.6	16.0

[1] See Table 716. [2] Consists of tour operators' and travel agents' margins. Purchases of travel and accommodations included in tours are accounted for separately in other personal consumption expenditures categories.

Source: U.S. Bureau of Economic Analysis, National Income and Product Accounts Tables, "Table 2.5.5. Personal Consumption Expenditures by Function," <www.bea.gov/iTable/index_nipa.cfm>, accessed November 2023.

Table 1261. Expenditures for Entertainment and Reading: 2000 to 2022

[Data are annual averages per consumer unit. In dollars, except as indicated. Based on the Consumer Expenditure Survey (CES)]

Year and characteristic	Entertainment and reading		Entertainment				Reading
	Total	Percent of total expenditures	Total	Fees and admissions	Audio & visual equipment & services	Other supplies, equipment & services [1]	
2000	2,009	5.3	1,863	515	622	727	146
2010	2,604	5.4	2,504	581	954	970	100
2020	3,026	4.9	2,912	425	1,049	1,438	114
2021	3,682	5.5	3,568	654	1,020	1,894	114
2022, total	**3,575**	**4.9**	**3,458**	**833**	**1,020**	**1,606**	**117**
Age of reference person:							
Under 25 years old	(NA)	(NA)	2,075	374	573	(B)	(B)
25 to 34 years old	2,984	4.4	2,884	711	770	(NA)	100
35 to 44 years old	4,468	5.2	4,361	1,262	1,050	(NA)	107
45 to 54 years old	4,586	5.0	4,481	1,259	1,119	2,104	105
55 to 64 years old	3,806	4.9	3,698	714	1,204	1,780	108
65 years old and older	2,824	4.9	2,672	531	1,037	(NA)	152
Hispanic or Latino origin of reference person:							
Hispanic	2,396	3.7	2,329	451	914	964	67
Non-Hispanic	3,777	5.1	3,652	898	1,038	1,716	125
Race of reference person:							
White, and all other races [2]	3,896	5.2	3,772	882	1,060	1,831	124
Asian	2,707	3.1	2,599	1,136	748	715	108
Black	1,954	3.4	1,880	398	890	593	74
Region of residence:							
Northeast	3,661	4.6	3,509	1,049	1,092	1,367	152
Midwest	3,810	5.5	3,701	862	980	1,859	109
South	2,911	4.4	2,831	637	967	1,227	80
West	4,422	5.3	4,262	974	1,095	(NA)	160
Size of consumer unit:							
One person	2,019	4.6	1,918	384	806	728	101
Two or more persons	4,272	5.0	4,148	1,034	1,117	1,998	124
Two persons	3,973	5.2	3,839	798	1,054	(NA)	134
Three persons	4,178	4.8	4,068	916	1,148	2,003	110
Four persons	4,882	4.8	4,752	1,614	1,229	1,909	130
Five persons or more	4,642	4.8	4,541	1,271	1,139	(NA)	101
Income before taxes:							
Quintiles of income:							
Lowest 20 percent	1,304	4.0	1,233	139	591	503	71
Second 20 percent	2,051	4.3	1,972	272	801	(NA)	79
Third 20 percent	3,023	4.9	2,932	524	908	(NA)	91
Fourth 20 percent	3,889	4.7	3,765	899	1,222	1,644	124
Highest 20 percent	7,607	5.4	7,389	2,328	1,580	3,481	218
Education:							
Less than a high school graduate	(NA)	(NA)	(B)	75	557	(B)	(B)
High school graduate	1,923	4.2	1,879	195	803	(NA)	44
High school graduate with some college	2,474	4.4	2,392	349	909	(NA)	82
Associate's degree	(NA)	(NA)	3,028	507	981	1,540	(B)
Bachelor's degree	4,440	5.1	4,309	1,128	1,200	1,980	131
Master's, professional, or doctoral degree	5,659	5.2	5,433	1,835	1,234	2,364	226

B Data are suppressed due to the relative standard error (RSE) being equal to or greater than 25 percent. NA Not available. [1] Includes pets, toys, hobbies, and playground equipment, and other entertainment supplies, equipment, and services. [2] All other races includes Native Hawaiian or other Pacific Islander, American Indian or Alaska Native, and approximately 2 percent reporting more than one race.

Source: U.S. Bureau of Labor Statistics, Consumer Expenditure Survey, "Calendar year and midyear means tables by demographic characteristics," <www.bls.gov/cex/tables.htm>, accessed December 2023.

Table 1262. Households with Pets by Age of Householder: 2021

[In thousands (128,504 represents 128,504,000). Based on the American Housing Survey, a sample survey. Total households estimated using the full sample, whereas data on pets were collected from half of the sample; see source for details]

Pets	Total	Under 25 years old	25 to 29 years old	30 to 34 years old	35 to 44 years old	45 to 54 years old	55 to 64 years old	65 to 74 years old	75 years old & over
Total households	128,504	4,316	8,102	10,930	22,595	22,224	25,615	19,913	14,809
Total households with pets [1]	**63,775**	**1,913**	**4,106**	**5,371**	**12,185**	**12,658**	**13,694**	**9,101**	**4,746**
Dogs	48,963	1,256	2,840	3,967	9,896	10,358	10,735	6,682	3,230
1 dog	29,975	899	1,612	2,614	5,910	6,100	6,316	4,306	2,217
2 dogs	13,588	308	846	929	3,045	2,924	3,040	1,775	720
3 dogs	3,516	(S)	246	311	681	816	890	353	193
4 or more dogs	1,884	(S)	136	113	261	517	488	247	99
Cats	28,187	968	1,878	2,377	4,843	5,520	6,017	4,274	2,311
1 cat	14,110	555	1,081	1,225	2,326	2,562	2,969	2,085	1,305
2 cats	9,460	311	545	849	1,810	1,870	1,994	1,442	639
3 cats	2,255	(S)	187	179	397	598	483	228	111
4 or more cats	2,361	(S)	(S)	123	310	489	570	519	256
Small mammals	2,688	76	201	259	838	732	333	183	(S)
Fish	4,857	148	327	388	1,285	1,170	877	451	212
Birds	2,750	(S)	92	264	542	581	611	452	183
Reptiles	2,530	111	145	279	697	656	438	129	(S)
No pets	62,029	2,290	4,023	5,225	10,005	8,858	11,423	10,551	9,654
Pets not reported	2,700	58	103	267	516	406	706	341	304

S Estimate does not meet publication standards or withheld to avoid disclosure. [1] Includes foster pets, but excludes service animals and livestock such as cows, horses, and pigs. Figures may not add to total because more than one category may apply.

Source: U.S. Census Bureau, "American Housing Survey: AHS Table Creator," <www.census.gov/programs-surveys/ahs/data.html>, accessed April 2023.

Table 1263. Adult Participation in Selected Leisure Activities by Frequency: 2024

[In thousands (29,267 represents 29,267,000), except percent. As of Spring 2024. Percent is based on total projected population of 257,420,000. Based on sample and subject to sampling error; see source]

| Activity | Participated in the last 12 months [1] | | Frequency of participation | | | | | | | |
| | | | Two or more times a week | | Once a week | | Two to three times a month | | Once a month | |
	Number (1,000)	Percent	Number (1,000)	Percent	Number (1,000)	Percent	Number (1,000)	Percent	Number (1,000)	Percent
Adult education courses	29,267	11.4	5,654	2.2	2,573	1.0	2,093	0.8	2,228	0.9
Antique shopping	26,941	10.5	518	0.2	526	0.2	1,563	0.6	3,044	1.2
Aquarium attendance	21,333	8.3	168	0.1	182	0.1	127	0.1	572	0.2
Attend a food/beverage festival	35,328	13.7	130	0.1	261	0.1	384	0.2	2,520	1.0
Attend a state or county fair	37,067	14.4	301	0.1	264	0.1	191	0.1	1,039	0.4
Attend a virtual/online event	23,567	9.2	810	0.3	966	0.4	1,543	0.6	3,143	1.2
Attend art galleries or shows	28,797	11.2	88	(Z)	369	0.1	650	0.3	2,959	1.2
Attend auto shows	16,146	6.3	126	0.1	143	0.1	410	0.2	924	0.4
Attend country music performances	16,285	6.3	64	(Z)	47	(Z)	286	0.1	721	0.3
Attend music festival	16,586	6.4	86	(Z)	140	(Z)	254	0.1	845	0.3
Attend rock music performances	28,962	11.3	91	(Z)	154	0.1	589	0.2	1,999	0.8
Attend/coach youth sports event	27,932	10.9	5,639	2.2	4,089	1.6	4,232	1.6	2,512	1.0
Baking	74,270	28.9	8,295	3.2	9,613	3.7	16,218	6.3	15,724	6.1
Barbecuing	77,609	30.2	6,632	2.6	9,888	3.8	17,021	6.6	14,011	5.4
Billiards/pool	15,752	6.1	721	0.3	731	0.3	898	0.4	1,492	0.6
Birdwatching	18,896	7.3	7,540	2.9	1,864	0.7	1,605	0.6	1,817	0.7
Board games	58,685	22.8	3,266	1.3	4,169	1.6	8,833	3.4	12,095	4.7
Cooking for fun	72,036	28.0	25,494	9.9	11,773	4.6	11,106	4.3	7,626	3.0
Creating social media content (memes, videos, etc.)	20,140	7.8	4,180	1.6	2,904	1.1	2,952	1.2	2,303	0.9
Crossword puzzles	35,010	13.6	14,483	5.6	3,675	1.4	3,789	1.5	3,202	1.2
Dance/go dancing	21,431	8.3	2,066	0.8	1,516	0.6	2,020	0.8	2,565	1.0
Dining out	140,777	54.7	20,526	8.0	29,682	11.5	35,384	13.8	22,762	8.8
Entertain friends or relatives at home	92,197	35.8	4,758	1.9	9,447	3.7	17,026	6.6	21,060	8.2
Fantasy sports league	12,656	4.9	2,685	1.0	2,483	1.0	840	0.3	807	0.3
Go to bars/night clubs	51,437	20.0	2,263	0.9	4,683	1.8	7,799	3.0	9,257	3.6
Go to beach	74,405	28.9	2,385	0.9	1,957	0.8	4,990	1.9	7,016	2.7
Go to coffee shop	65,905	25.6	7,684	3.0	9,329	3.6	11,921	4.6	11,939	4.6
Go to comedy club or stand-up comedy show	18,340	7.1	146	0.1	195	0.1	365	0.1	1,187	0.5
Go to live theater	30,921	12.0	135	0.1	229	0.1	904	0.4	3,621	1.4
Go to museums	40,927	15.9	756	0.3	420	0.2	1,462	0.6	4,326	1.7
Home decoration and furnishing	36,450	14.2	1,497	0.6	1,684	0.7	3,434	1.3	6,943	2.7
Indoor gardening & plants	45,467	17.7	11,795	4.6	11,548	4.5	5,604	2.2	4,461	1.7
Listening to music	136,220	52.9	108,695	42.2	6,929	2.7	4,634	1.8	1,772	0.7
Painting, drawing, sculpting	26,725	10.4	5,130	2.0	2,874	1.1	3,327	1.3	3,354	1.3
PC/computer games (play offline with software)	20,927	8.1	10,273	4.0	2,157	0.8	1,624	0.6	1,417	0.6
PC/computer games (play online)	36,692	14.3	22,059	8.6	3,198	1.2	2,225	0.9	1,558	0.6
Photography	28,447	11.1	8,582	3.3	4,111	1.6	4,757	1.9	3,091	1.2
Picnic	21,917	8.5	336	0.1	379	0.2	1,297	0.5	2,633	1.0
Play bingo	14,292	5.6	708	0.3	865	0.3	1,070	0.4	1,478	0.6
Play cards	44,303	17.2	4,991	1.9	4,169	1.6	5,497	2.1	7,351	2.9
Play musical instrument	20,196	7.9	7,319	2.8	2,187	0.9	2,016	0.8	1,613	0.6
Reading books	96,945	37.7	53,491	20.8	9,667	3.8	8,901	3.5	7,062	2.7
Stargazing	18,391	7.1	2,728	1.1	1,552	0.6	1,854	0.7	2,727	1.1
Sudoku puzzles	25,497	9.9	9,226	3.6	2,814	1.1	2,819	1.1	2,635	1.0
Trivia games	21,592	8.4	3,619	1.4	2,102	0.8	1,998	0.8	3,123	1.2
Video/electronic games (console)	33,331	13.0	13,875	5.4	4,271	1.7	3,514	1.4	2,464	1.0
Video/electronic games (portable)	19,048	7.4	8,359	3.3	2,055	0.8	1,797	0.7	1,215	0.5
Wine tasting	20,244	7.9	397	0.2	497	0.2	1,095	0.4	2,452	1.0
Woodworking	13,442	5.2	1,744	0.7	968	0.4	1,926	0.8	2,095	0.8
Zoo attendance	36,734	14.3	74	(Z)	250	0.1	745	0.3	1,919	0.8

Z Represents less than 0.05. [1] Includes those participating less than once a month, not shown separately.

Source: © MRI-Simmons Spring 2024 USA Study. Courtesy of MRI-Simmons. See also <www.mrisimmons.com/>.

Table 1264. Selected Recreational Activities: 1990 to 2023

[18,719 represents 18,719,000]

Activity	Unit	1990	2000	2005	2010	2015	2020	2021	2022	2023
Golf facilities [1]	Number	12,846	15,489	16,052	15,890	15,204	14,145 [5]	14,000 [5]	14,000	13,963
Tennis players: [2]	1,000	(NA)	(NA)	(NA)	18,719	17,963	21,642	22,617	(NA)	23,835
Skiing: [3]										
Skier & snowboarder visits [4]	Million	50.0	52.2	56.9	59.8	53.6	51.1	59.0	60.7	65.4
Operating resorts	Number	591	503	492	471	470	470	462	473	480

NA Not available. [1] Source: National Golf Foundation, Jupiter, FL. [2] Source: Tennis Industry Association, Hilton Head Island, SC. Based on a nationwide telephone survey of households, in which all household members ages 6 and up are enumerated, with data on tennis participation collected for each person. Data prior to 2007 are not available due to new methodology being implemented after 2007. [3] Source: National Ski Areas Association, Lakewood, CO. ©. [4] Represents one person visiting a ski area for all or any part of a day or night, and includes full-and half-day, night, complimentary, adult, child, season, and other types of tickets. Data are estimated and are for the season ending in the year shown. [5] Rounded estimate.

Source: Compiled from sources listed in footnotes.

Table 1265. Amusement Park Attendance at Top U.S. Facilities: 2015 to 2023

[In thousands (20,492 represents 20,492,000). Covers gated (entry ticket required) commercial theme and amusement parks. 2020 attendance declines were largely due to agency restrictions limiting operating days and capacities during the COVID-19 pandemic. Excludes water parks]

Park name	Location	Attendance					
		2015	2019	2020	2021	2022	2023
Magic Kingdom, Walt Disney World	Lake Buena Vista, FL	20,492	20,963	6,941	12,691	17,133	17,720
Disneyland Park	Anaheim, CA	18,278	18,666	3,674	8,573	16,881	17,250
EPCOT, Walt Disney World	Lake Buena Vista, FL	11,798	12,444	4,044	7,752	10,000	11,980
Disney's Hollywood Studios	Lake Buena Vista, FL	10,828	11,483	3,675	8,589	10,900	10,300
Universal's Islands of Adventure	Orlando, FL	8,792	10,375	4,005	9,077	11,025	10,000
Disney California Adventure Park	Anaheim, CA	9,383	9,861	1,919	4,977	9,000	10,000
Universal Studios Florida	Orlando, FL	9,585	10,922	4,096	8,987	10,750	9,750
Universal Studios Hollywood	Universal City, CA	7,097	9,147	1,299	5,505	8,400	9,660
Disney's Animal Kingdom	Lake Buena Vista, FL	10,922	13,888	4,166	7,194	9,027	8,770
SeaWorld Orlando	Orlando, FL	4,777	4,640	1,598	3,051	4,454	4,342
Knott's Berry Farm	Buena Park, CA	3,867	4,238	811	3,681	3,899	4,228
Cedar Point	Sandusky, OH	3,507	3,610	1,020	3,327	3,444	4,050
Busch Gardens Tampa Bay	Tampa, FL	4,252	4,180	1,288	3,210	4,051	4,000
SeaWorld San Diego	San Diego, CA	3,528	3,731	1,139	2,800	3,507	3,990
Kings Island	Kings Island, OH	3,335	3,485	1,626	3,181	3,340	3,488

Source: Themed Entertainment Association and AECOM, *2023 Theme Index and Museum Index: The Global Attractions Attendance Report* ©, and previous reports. See also <aecom.com/theme-index/> and <teaconnect.org>.

Table 1266. Reading in Print, Electronic, and Audio Formats Among Adults: 2019 and 2021

[In percent. Data shown for adults aged 18 years and older who read at least one book in the formats shown during the previous 12 months. Based on telephone surveys conducted January 8-February 7, 2019 among a nationally representative sample of 1,502 adults, and January 25-February 8, 2021 among a nationally representative sample of 1,502 adults]

Characteristic	2019				2021			
	Total	Print	E-book	Audio-book	Total	Print	E-book	Audio-book
Total	**72**	**65**	**25**	**20**	**75**	**65**	**30**	**23**
GENDER								
Male	67	60	24	17	73	62	29	22
Female	76	70	27	22	78	67	31	25
RACE/ETHNICITY								
White, non-Hispanic	76	70	27	22	78	69	31	25
Black, non-Hispanic	65	58	19	13	74	62	34	26
Hispanic	59	54	20	15	60	48	18	19
AGE								
18 to 29 years	81	73	34	23	83	68	42	30
30 to 49 years	72	76	28	27	77	67	32	27
50 to 64 years	67	74	22	16	72	62	28	22
65 years and older	68	65	17	8	68	61	18	12
EDUCATION								
High school or less [1]	(NA)	(NA)	(NA)	(NA)	59	51	17	13
Some college	75	70	26	17	81	66	36	28
College graduate	90	82	41	34	88	80	39	32
HOUSEHOLD INCOME								
Less than $30,000	62	56	18	14	67	53	23	22
$30,000 to $49,000	67	63	19	13	71	65	23	15
$50,000 to $74,999	78	71	28	27	77	68	32	23
$75,000 and higher	86	78	38	30	85	74	36	33
METRO STATUS								
Urban	75	68	27	23	81	67	33	28
Suburban	74	68	27	19	74	65	28	23
Rural	66	58	20	18	69	62	26	16

NA Not available. [1] Includes both "Less than high school" and "High school graduate."

Source: Pew Research Center, *Three-in-ten Americans now read e-books*, January 2022 ©; and unpublished data. See also <www.pewinternet.org/>.

Table 1267. Leisure Time Use on Weekends and Holidays by Type of Activity and Selected Demographic Characteristics: 2023

[Data are based on interviews of approximately 8,500 individuals age 15 years and over who reported their activities for a single 24-hour period. Respondents engaging in more than one activity at a time reported only their primary activity; except for child care, secondary activities were not reported]

Selected characteristics	Average hours per day spent on all leisure and sports activities			Percent distribution of leisure time on weekends and holidays						
	All days (hours)	Weekdays (hours)	Weekends and holidays (hours)	Sports, exercise, recreation	Socializing, communicating	Watching TV	Reading	Relaxing, thinking	Playing games, using computer for leisure	Other [1]
Total, 15 years old and over	**5.15**	**4.60**	**6.43**	**5.4**	**14.2**	**51.6**	**4.4**	**5.9**	**10.4**	**8.1**
Sex:										
Men	5.56	4.97	6.95	6.3	12.7	51.2	3.3	5.3	12.9	8.1
Women	4.76	4.24	5.94	4.5	15.8	52.0	5.6	6.4	7.4	8.1
Age:										
15 to 19 years	5.46	5.17	6.18	8.6	17.3	31.2	1.9	(S)	27.2	8.1
20 to 24 years	5.36	4.92	6.32	6.6	19.3	34.2	(S)	(S)	18.7	9.8
25 to 34 years	4.29	3.59	5.91	4.9	16.1	46.4	3.0	4.1	16.1	9.3
35 to 44 years	3.87	3.16	5.55	8.1	17.8	46.8	2.3	7.6	8.1	9.0
45 to 54 years	4.40	3.57	6.30	4.1	13.7	59.0	3.3	5.2	7.3	7.3
55 to 64 years	5.18	4.64	6.40	6.3	12.7	59.1	4.5	5.5	4.8	7.3
65 to 74 years	6.71	6.33	7.58	3.8	10.8	59.1	6.2	6.6	5.3	8.0
75 years and over	7.57	7.43	7.90	2.8	9.0	61.1	8.7	6.2	6.6	5.6
Race/ethnicity:										
White	5.17	4.57	6.50	5.5	14.6	51.1	4.8	5.7	10.3	8.3
Black	5.51	5.08	6.49	4.3	11.1	59.3	2.3	7.7	9.6	5.5
Asian	4.34	3.90	5.47	7.3	15.9	45.5	5.9	5.3	11.3	9.0
Hispanic origin [2]	4.42	3.90	5.62	5.2	15.7	51.6	2.0	7.3	10.7	7.7
Employment status:										
Employed	4.22	3.51	5.89	5.8	16.5	48.7	3.4	5.6	11.5	8.7
Full-time workers	3.99	3.23	5.84	6.0	15.9	50.3	3.4	5.7	10.4	8.2
Part-time workers	5.15	4.68	6.09	5.4	18.7	42.5	3.0	5.1	15.1	10.2
Not employed	6.86	6.63	7.38	5.0	11.0	56.0	6.0	6.2	8.8	7.0
Weekly earnings: [3]										
$0 to $800	4.29	3.66	5.78	2.4	15.6	53.6	3.3	4.3	13.0	8.0
$801 to $1,200	3.92	3.18	5.82	4.8	16.5	49.0	2.7	6.7	12.7	7.6
$1,201 to $1,875	4.18	3.26	6.31	6.8	15.5	50.7	4.0	5.7	10.5	6.8
$1,876 and higher	3.94	2.99	6.04	9.9	16.6	46.9	4.6	4.3	7.8	9.9
Presence and age of children:										
No household children under age 18	5.70	5.16	6.98	4.9	12.2	54.6	5.0	5.9	10.0	7.4
Household children under age 18	4.05	3.47	5.36	6.7	19.2	44.4	3.2	5.8	11.2	9.5
Children age 13 to 17, none younger	4.85	4.21	6.11	5.1	18.2	42.2	4.6	7.0	15.9	7.2
Children age 6 to 12, none younger	3.99	3.40	5.32	7.9	16.9	46.6	3.0	4.9	8.5	12.0
Youngest child under age 6	3.55	3.03	4.78	7.5	22.8	44.1	1.7	5.2	9.2	9.2
Educational attainment, age 25 and over:										
Less than a high school diploma	5.71	5.28	6.71	2.4	11.5	63.0	1.2	11.5	5.5	4.9
High school graduates, no college	5.54	5.03	6.68	3.3	11.5	62.4	2.4	6.6	7.3	6.6
Some college or associate degree	5.10	4.50	6.57	4.1	12.9	57.5	4.3	4.9	9.3	6.8
Bachelor's degree and higher	4.69	4.02	6.22	7.4	15.6	46.8	6.9	4.7	8.5	9.8

S Estimate does not meet publication standards. [1] Includes other leisure and sports activities, not elsewhere classified, and travel related to leisure and sports activities. [2] People of Hispanic origin may be of any race. [3] These values are based on usual weekly earnings. The earnings data are limited to wage and salary workers (both incorporated and unincorporated self-employed workers are excluded). Each earnings range represents approximately 25 percent of full-time wage and salary workers who held only one job.

Source: U.S. Bureau of Labor Statistics, *American Time Use Survey—2023 Results*, USDL 24-1208, June 2024. See also <www.bls.gov/tus/>.

Table 1268. Characteristics of Selected Spectator Sports: 1990 to 2023

[54,824 represents 54,824,000. For baseball, hockey, and rodeo, the year in which the season ends; for basketball and football, the year in which the season begins]

Sport	Unit	1990	2000	2010	2015	2019	2020 [8]	2021 [8]	2022	2023
Baseball, major leagues: [1]										
Regular season attendance........	1,000	54,824	72,749	73,054	73,760	68,495	([9])	45,305	64,557	70,747
National League.................	1,000	24,492	39,851	40,890	38,903	37,902	([9])	25,364	35,452	38,261
American League.................	1,000	30,332	32,898	32,164	34,857	30,593	([9])	19,940	29,104	32,487
Playoffs attendance [2]...............	1,000	479	1,314	1,210	1,420	1,345	[9] 76	1,268	1,500	1,453
World Series attendance...........	1,000	209	277	244	215	305	[9] 69	258	266	230
Basketball: [3, 4]										
NCAA—Men's college:										
Teams..........................	Number	796	937	1,027	1,067	1,080	1,082	1,079	1,074	(NA)
Attendance.....................	1,000	29,250	28,949	32,632	32,382	30,268	(NA)	26,999	29,421	(NA)
NCAA—Women's college:										
Teams..........................	Number	806	958	1,048	1,084	1,097	1,092	1,078	1,079	(NA)
Attendance [5]...................	1,000	3,407	8,825	11,160	11,367	11,058	(NA)	8,902	11,179	(NA)
NCAA—Men's college football: [4]										
Teams..........................	Number	534	624	644	666	669	669	(NA)	(NA)	(NA)
Attendance.....................	1,000	35,330	39,059	49,671	49,058	47,538	(NA)	(NA)	(NA)	(NA)
National Hockey League: [6]										
Regular season attendance........	1,000	12,580	18,800	20,996	21,533	22,187	18,835	1,005	20,784	22,437
Playoffs attendance.................	1,000	1,356	1,525	1,702	1,701	1,575	–	769	1,656	1,616
Professional rodeo: [7]										
Rodeos..........................	Number	754	688	570	624	(NA)	(NA)	(NA)	(NA)	(NA)
Performances......................	Number	2,159	2,081	1,671	1,663	(NA)	(NA)	(NA)	(NA)	(NA)

– Represents zero. NA Not available. [1] Source: Major League Baseball, New York, NY, National League Green Book ©; and The American League of Professional Baseball Clubs, New York, NY, American League Red Book ©. [2] Beginning 1995, two rounds of playoffs were played. Prior years had one round. [3] Season beginning in year shown. [4] Source: National Collegiate Athletic Association, Indianapolis, IN ©. [5] Attendance for women's basketball includes doubleheaders with men's teams beginning with the 1997 season, if attendance was taken by halftime of the women's game. [6] For season ending in year shown. Source: National Hockey League, Montreal, Quebec ©. [7] Source: Professional Rodeo Cowboys Association, Colorado Springs, CO, ©. [8] Due to the COVID-19 pandemic, sports attendance was drastically impacted. Numbers not comparable to prior years. [9] Due to the COVID-19 pandemic, fans were not hosted during the regular season. Fans were hosted in limited capacities during the National League Championship Series and the World Series.

Source: Compiled from sources listed in footnotes.

Table 1269. Adult Attendance at Sports Events by Frequency: 2024

[In thousands (209 represents 209,000), except percent. For Spring 2024. Percent is based on total projected population of 257,420,000. Data not comparable to previous years. Based on a survey and subject to sampling error; see source]

Event	Attend regularly Number (1,000)	Attend regularly Per-cent	Attend on occasion [1] Number (1,000)	Attend on occasion [1] Per-cent	Event	Attend regularly Number (1,000)	Attend regularly Per-cent	Attend on occasion [1] Number (1,000)	Attend on occasion [1] Per-cent
Alpine skiing and ski jumping...	209	0.08	448	0.17	Other golf......................	163	0.06	445	0.17
Auto racing – NASCAR.........	395	0.15	1,648	0.64	Gymnastics....................	247	0.10	737	0.29
Auto racing – other.............	661	0.26	2,081	0.81	High school sports............	6,485	2.52	12,669	4.92
Baseball:					Horse racing (track or OTB)...	353	0.14	1,795	0.70
College........................	625	0.24	2,017	0.78	Ice hockey:				
Pro (MLB) regular season. . .	1,811	0.70	15,949	6.20	NHL regular season..........	741	0.29	4788	1.86
Pro (MLB) playoffs/					NHL playoffs and Stanley				
World Series.................	413	0.16	1,798	0.70	Cup finals...................	357	0.14	983	0.38
Minor League..................	1,086	0.42	5,343	2.08	Lacrosse......................	586	0.23	1042	0.40
Basketball:					Marathon, triathlon & other				
College........................	1,265	0.49	4,198	1.63	obstacle events..............	242	0.09	1,064	0.41
NBA regular season..........	523	0.20	4,674	1.82	Mixed martial arts (other)......	149	0.06	385	0.15
NBA playoffs..................	329	0.13	878	0.34	Monster truck racing..........	181	0.07	1,102	0.43
NCAA tournament.............	321	0.12	966	0.38	Motorcycle racing.............	293	0.11	731	0.28
WNBA.........................	253	0.10	521	0.20	Olympics – Summer...........	176	0.07	253	0.10
Bicycle racing..................	283	0.11	608	0.24	Olympics – Winter............	183	0.07	254	0.10
Bowling........................	393	0.15	1,067	0.41	Poker.........................	265	0.10	465	0.18
Boxing.........................	351	0.14	719	0.28	Rodeo.........................	356	0.14	2,254	0.88
Bull riding (Pro)..................	182	0.07	848	0.33	Soccer:				
Cheerleading...................	565	0.22	996	0.39	MLS.........................	653	0.25	2,702	1.05
Esports........................	231	0.09	446	0.17	World Cup....................	175	0.07	460	0.18
Extreme sports – Summer.....	118	0.05	200	0.08	Men's national team..........	164	0.06	530	0.21
Extreme sports – Winter.......	114	0.04	242	0.09	Women's national team......	155	0.06	451	0.18
Figure skating..................	137	0.05	291	0.11	International..................	159	0.06	865	0.34
Fishing........................	676	0.26	1,628	0.63	Tennis:				
Football:					Men's........................	314	0.12	1,083	0.42
College regular season........	2,167	0.84	7,708	2.99	Women's.....................	302	0.12	917	0.36
College playoffs/National					Track & field....................	615	0.24	1459	0.57
Championship.................	349	0.14	1,086	0.42	Truck and tractor				
NFL Monday, Thursday					pull/mud racing..............	184	0.07	609	0.24
or Sunday night games......	888	0.34	3,968	1.54	Ultimate Fighting				
NFL weekend games...........	1,242	0.48	4,519	1.76	Championship (UFC).........	144	0.06	291	0.11
NFL playoffs/Super Bowl......	444	0.17	1,096	0.43	Volleyball (Pro beach)........	116	0.04	243	0.09
Golf:					Wrestling:				
PGA...........................	249	0.10	1,080	0.42	WWE.........................	261	0.10	1,005	0.39
LPGA..........................	135	0.05	374	0.15	Other Pro....................	296	0.12	817	0.32

[1] Attended at least once during last 12 months.

Source: © MRI-Simmons Spring 2024 USA Study. Courtesy of MRI-Simmons. See also <www.mrisimmons.com>.

Table 1270. Participation in NCAA Sports by Sex: 2022 to 2023

[For the academic year ending in 2023]

Sport	Males			Females		
	Teams	Athletes	Average squad	Teams	Athletes	Average squad
Total.............................	**9,388**	**301,568**	**(X)**	**10,932**	**230,951**	**(X)**
Acrobat and tumbling [3]............	(X)	(X)	(X)	37	967	26.1
Baseball............................	943	38,849	41.2	(X)	(X)	(X)
Basketball..........................	1,077	19,213	17.8	1,087	16,668	15.3
Beach volleyball....................	(X)	(X)	(X)	91	1,615	17.7
Bowling [2].........................	7	71	10.1	99	889	9.0
Cross country [1]...................	992	14,787	14.9	1,056	14,621	13.8
Equestrian [1,2,3].................	3	7	2.3	48	1,443	30.1
Esport [2,3].......................	17	448	26.4	15	70	4.7
Fencing [1]........................	34	638	18.8	44	763	17.3
Field hockey.......................	(X)	(X)	(X)	286	6,456	22.6
Football...........................	666	77,204	115.9	(X)	(X)	(X)
Golf [1]...........................	809	8,602	10.6	704	5,733	8.1
Gymnastics.........................	15	304	20.3	83	1,715	20.7
Ice hockey.........................	151	4,388	29.1	113	2,888	25.6
Lacrosse...........................	395	16,030	40.6	522	13,481	25.8
Rifle [1]..........................	22	115	5.2	26	168	6.5
Rowing [2].........................	57	2,243	39.4	146	6,707	45.9
Rugby [2,3]........................	8	337	42.1	29	845	29.1
Sailing [1,2]......................	23	435	18.9	(X)	(X)	(X)
Skiing [1].........................	34	450	13.2	35	408	11.7
Soccer.............................	826	27,284	33.0	1,035	29,959	28.9
Softball...........................	(X)	(X)	(X)	986	21,646	22.0
Squash [2,3].......................	32	456	14.3	31	403	13.0
Stunt [3]..........................	(X)	(X)	(X)	2	77	38.5
Swimming/diving....................	449	9,945	22.1	560	13,259	23.7
Synchronized swimming [3]..........	(X)	(X)	(X)	3	37	12.3
Tennis.............................	701	7,549	10.8	858	8,343	9.7
Track, indoor......................	772	28,537	37.0	870	29,391	33.8
Track, outdoor [1].................	864	31,278	36.2	957	31,475	32.9
Triathlon [3]......................	(X)	(X)	(X)	34	249	7.3
Volleyball.........................	173	2,933	17.0	1,058	18,569	17.6
Water polo.........................	51	1,156	22.7	66	1,337	20.3
Wrestling [3]......................	267	8,309	31.1	51	769	15.1

X Not applicable. [1] Co-ed sport. [2] Sport recognized by the NCAA but does not have an NCAA men's championship. [3] Sport recognized by the NCAA as an emerging or other sport for women.

Source: The National Collegiate Athletic Association (NCAA), Indianapolis, IN, *NCAA Sports Sponsorship and Participation Rates Report* ©, September 2023. See also <www.ncaapublications.com>.

Table 1271. Participation in High School Athletic Programs by Sex: 1980 to 2023

[For academic years. Data based on number of state associations reporting and may underrepresent the number of schools with and participants in athletic programs]

Year	Participants [1]		Sex and sport	Most popular sports, 2022–2023 [2]	
	Males	Females		Schools	Participants
1980 to 1981.....................	3,503,124	1,853,789	MALE		
1990 to 1991.....................	3,406,355	1,892,316	Football (11-player)...............	13,670	1,028,761
1995 to 1996.....................	3,634,052	2,367,936	Track & field (outdoor)............	17,038	604,983
2000 to 2001.....................	3,921,069	2,784,154	Basketball.........................	18,369	537,438
2003 to 2004.....................	4,038,253	2,865,299	Baseball...........................	15,978	478,451
2004 to 2005.....................	4,110,319	2,908,390	Soccer.............................	12,484	450,455
2005 to 2006.....................	4,206,549	2,953,355	Wrestling..........................	10,962	259,431
2006 to 2007.....................	4,321,103	3,021,807	Cross country......................	15,867	240,201
2007 to 2008.....................	4,372,115	3,057,266	Tennis.............................	7,673	158,306
2008 to 2009.....................	4,422,662	3,114,091	Golf...............................	13,505	150,175
2009 to 2010.....................	4,455,740	3,172,637	Swimming & diving..................	7,831	116,741
2010 to 2011.....................	4,494,406	3,173,549			
2011 to 2012.....................	4,484,987	3,207,533	FEMALE		
2012 to 2013.....................	4,490,854	3,222,723	Track & field (outdoor)............	16,997	486,355
2013 to 2014.....................	4,527,994	3,267,664	Volleyball.........................	16,610	470,488
2014 to 2015.....................	4,519,312	3,287,735	Soccer.............................	12,100	377,838
2015 to 2016.....................	4,541,959	3,324,306	Basketball.........................	17,881	373,366
2016 to 2017.....................	4,563,238	3,400,297	Softball (fast pitch)..............	15,406	344,952
2017 to 2018.....................	4,565,580	3,415,306	Cross country......................	15,551	197,630
2018 to 2019.....................	4,534,758	3,402,733	Tennis.............................	10,564	191,036
2019 to 2020.....................	(3)	(3)	Competitive spirit squads.........	7,216	149,694
2020 to 2021.....................	(3)	(3)	Swimming & diving..................	7,937	140,711
2021 to 2022.....................	4,376,582	3,241,472	Lacrosse...........................	3,164	98,014
2022 to 2023.....................	4,529,795	3,318,184			

[1] Participants are counted in each sport in which they participate. [2] Ten most popular sports for each gender, ranked by number of participants. [3] Unavailable due to the COVID-19 pandemic.

Source: National Federation of State High School Associations, Indianapolis, IN, *The 2022-23 High School Athletics Participation Survey* ©. Reprinted with permission of the National Federation of State High School Associations. See also <www.nfhs.org/>.

Table 1272. National Park Service—Summary: 1990 to 2023

[In units as indicated (986 represents $986,000,000). For year ending September 30, except as noted. Covers all States, the District of Columbia, and the U.S. territories of American Samoa, Guam, Puerto Rico, and the U.S. Virgin Islands]

Item	1990	2000	2010	2015	2020	2021	2022	2023
FINANCES (mil. dol.): [1]								
Expenditures reported	986	1,833	3,239	2,949	(NA)	(NA)	(NA)	(NA)
Salaries and wages	459	799	1,237	1,167	(NA)	(NA)	(NA)	(NA)
Improvements, maintenance	160	299	531	532	(NA)	(NA)	(NA)	(NA)
Construction	109	215	443	184	(NA)	(NA)	(NA)	(NA)
Other	259	520	1,028	1,066	(NA)	(NA)	(NA)	(NA)
Funds available	1,506	3,316	5,402	5,161	(NA)	(NA)	(NA)	(NA)
Appropriations	1,053	1,881	2,848	2,967	(NA)	(NA)	(NA)	(NA)
Other [2]	453	1,435	2,554	2,194	(NA)	(NA)	(NA)	(NA)
Revenue from operations	79	234	387	589	(NA)	(NA)	(NA)	(NA)
RECREATION VISITS (millions): [3]								
All areas	**258.7**	**285.9**	**281.3**	**307.2**	**237.1**	**297.1**	**312.0**	**325.5**
National parks [4]	57.7	66.1	64.6	75.3	67.9	92.3	88.7	92.4
National monuments	23.9	23.8	23.0	24.9	9.0	13.8	19.1	19.8
National historical, commemorative, archaeological [5]	57.5	72.2	80.0	93.9	52.4	73.2	87.3	90.6
National parkways	29.1	34.0	28.6	29.6	27.8	30.8	30.7	32.3
National recreation areas [4]	47.2	50.0	49.0	46.2	48.2	50.4	50.2	51.4
National seashores and lakeshores	23.3	22.5	22.2	22.8	21.2	25.1	23.5	25.8
National Capital Parks [6]	7.5	4.1	2.5	3.1	1.6	1.9	2.2	2.3
Recreation overnight stays [7]	17.6	15.4	14.4	14.9	8.0	12.7	13.2	13.0
In commercial lodgings	4.7	4.7	4.7	4.8	2.3	3.7	4.2	4.2
In Park Service campgrounds	7.9	5.9	5.5	5.9	3.3	5.7	5.8	5.7
In backcountry	1.7	1.9	1.8	2.0	1.4	2.0	1.9	1.8
Miscellaneous overnight stays	3.4	2.9	2.4	2.2	0.9	1.4	1.4	1.3
LAND (1,000 acres): [8]								
Total	76,362	78,153	80,527	80,603	81,098	81,104	81,140	81,160
National Parks	46,089	49,785	50,662	50,737	50,947	50,947	50,977	50,978
Recreation areas	3,344	3,388	3,418	3,421	3,425	3,425	3,425	3,426
Other	26,929	24,980	26,447	26,445	26,726	26,732	26,737	26,756
Acquisition, net	21	186	23	127	8	7	36	20

[1] Financial data are those associated with the National Park System. Certain other functions of the National Park Service (principally the activities absorbed from the former Heritage Conservation and Recreation Service in 1981) are excluded. [2] Includes funds carried over from prior years. [3] For calendar year. Includes other types of areas, not shown separately. [4] For 1990, combined data for North Cascades National Park and two adjacent National Recreation Areas are included in National Parks total. [5] Includes National Battlefields, National Battlefield Parks, National Historic Sites, National Historical Parks, National Memorials, National Military Parks, National Preserves, and National Reserves. [6] For 1990 to 1996, data are for National Capital Parks combined. Beginning 1997, data are summed for National Capital Parks East and National Capital Parks Central (also known as National Mall and Memorial Parks). [7] Data may not sum due to rounding. [8] Federal land only, as of December 31. Federal land acreages, in addition to National Park Service administered lands, also include lands within national park system area boundaries but under the administration of other agencies. Year-to-year changes in the federal lands figures includes changes in the acreages of these other lands and hence often differ from "net acquisition."

Source: U.S. National Park Service, through 2018, *National Park Statistical Abstract* and unpublished data. Thereafter, "National Park Service Visitor Use Statistics, National Reports," <irma.nps.gov/STATS/Reports/National>, and "National Park Service Acreage Reports," <www.nps.gov/subjects/lwcf/acreagereports.htm>; accessed April 2024.

Table 1273. National Park Service (NPS) Visits and Acreage by Type of Area: 2023

[Includes data for five areas in Virgin Islands, and one area in each Puerto Rico, American Samoa, and Guam]

Type of area	Recreation visits [1]	Gross area acres	Federal land			Non-federal land	
			NPS fee acres [2]	NPS less than fee acres [3]	Other federal fee acres [4]	Other public acres [5]	Private acres
Total	**325,498,646**	**85,155,967**	**80,095,880**	**348,974**	**714,818**	**1,379,789**	**2,616,507**
International historic site	12,432	7	7	–	–	–	–
National battlefield parks	1,890,443	16,173	11,386	45	1	20	4,720
National battlefield sites	(NA)	1	1	–	–	–	–
National battlefields	2,486,063	21,817	12,238	984	226	198	8,170
National historic sites	8,077,283	31,832	23,558	833	8	378	7,055
National historical parks	27,648,920	199,720	145,072	4,601	306	29,618	20,123
National lakeshores	2,756,354	213,932	135,062	672	46	53,172	24,979
National memorials	41,152,084	10,500	9,599	3	46	60	792
National military parks	4,191,917	47,019	41,561	690	(Z)	167	4,601
National monuments	19,768,521	1,993,636	1,827,662	14,707	23,474	8,567	119,226
National parks	92,390,204	52,448,593	50,709,376	222,549	45,617	572,961	898,091
National parkways	32,316,093	183,953	162,670	9,197	125	350	11,611
National preserves	5,076,077	24,656,517	22,984,364	9,430	274,832	336,589	1,051,303
National recreation areas	51,443,904	3,710,771	3,155,729	24,674	245,815	114,347	170,207
National reserves	92,059	33,846	10,809	2,094	–	708	20,235
National rivers	3,944,304	352,559	258,493	12,533	–	17,015	64,518
National scenic trails	(NA)	255,178	110,556	12,630	60,621	48,960	22,411
National seashores	23,006,887	596,867	404,263	14,943	62,052	106,283	9,326
National wild & scenic rivers	1,625,998	344,158	59,120	15,578	1,649	90,199	177,612
Parks (other)	7,619,103	38,889	34,353	2,811	–	196	1,529

– Represents zero. Z Less than .05 acres. NA Not available. [1] Recreation visit represents the entry of a person onto lands or waters administered by the NPS for recreational purposes, excluding government personnel, through traffic, tradespeople, and persons residing within park boundaries. [2] Complete Federal ownership of all rights in the land. [3] Federal ownership of some rights in the land. [4] Tracts under the administration of another federal agency (e.g., U.S. Forest Service, Department of the Army, etc.). Bureau of Land Management tracts are also identified as Other Fee (Federal) until they are withdrawn for NPS use; then status changes to Fee (Federal). [5] Non-federal tracts owned by the state, county, and/or other municipalities, including quasi-public entities.

Source: U.S. National Park Service, Public Use Statistics Office, "National Park Service Visitor Use Statistics, National Reports," <irma.nps.gov/STATS/Reports/National>; and Land and Water Conservation Fund, "National Park Service Acreage Reports," <www.nps.gov/subjects/lwcf/acreagereports.htm>; accessed March 2024.

Table 1274. National Park Service (NPS) Visits and Acreage by State: 2023

[Includes data for five areas in Virgin Islands, and one area each in American Samoa, Guam, and Puerto Rico]

State	Recreation visits [1]	Gross area acres	Federal land — NPS fee acres [2]	Federal land — NPS less than fee acres [3]	Federal land — Other federal fee acres [4]	Nonfederal land — Other public acres [5]	Nonfederal land — Private acres
Total [6,7].............	325,498,650	85,155,967	80,095,880	348,974	714,818	1,379,789	2,616,507
Alabama.................	1,287,291	22,747	17,540	203	13	3,288	1,702
Alaska..................	3,254,809	54,653,962	52,456,455	103,094	8	372,384	1,722,022
Arizona.................	10,809,520	2,948,393	2,658,489	94	75,949	57,054	156,807
Arkansas...............	4,447,751	105,130	100,723	3,497	20	454	437
California..............	36,211,847	8,211,587	7,654,786	22,375	12,458	352,604	169,364
Colorado...............	7,280,581	738,704	678,410	4,252	42,479	302	13,260
Connecticut............	36,313	7,782	5,846	1,055	–	874	6
Delaware...............	126414	904	890	6	–	2	6
District of Columbia.....	41,101,341	8,628	8,479	8	6	134	2
Florida..................	13,309,146	2,638,605	2,491,692	20	45,816	87,628	13,449
Georgia................	6,781,837	68,770	41,231	167	1,461	18,400	7,511
Hawaii.................	4,808,385	390,925	379,534	9	22	11,228	132
Idaho..................	769,552	806,403	512,086	1,231	273,488	9,058	10,539
Illinois.................	188,138	239	13	1	–	22	203
Indiana.................	3,040,462	15,734	10,843	538	–	3,444	909
Iowa...................	171,523	2,713	2,670	–	–	42	1
Kansas.................	106,700	11,630	465	271	–	57	10,838
Kentucky...............	1,975,537	117,082	95,182	137	–	839	20,925
Louisiana..............	300,411	27,000	21,145	(Z)	–	2,779	3,075
Maine..................	3,930,777	183,818	157,743	11,204	22	10,646	4,202
Maryland...............	6,305,729	74,058	41,848	5,902	418	23,485	2,405
Massachusetts..........	8,732,682	59,797	33,530	1,030	53	22,591	2,592
Michigan...............	2,820,169	718,339	632,443	672	46	58,515	26,662
Minnesota..............	1,090,134	301,369	139,841	3,193	143	98,659	59,533
Mississippi.............	9,065,256	119,923	105,710	5,229	–	72	8,911
Missouri...............	4,170,417	83,603	54,742	9,029	–	14,071	5,760
Montana...............	5,656,615	1,274,134	1,214,870	1,795	6,192	1,464	49,812
Nebraska..............	314,896	66,557	6,462	485	845	435	58,330
Nevada................	4,552,350	801,212	797,690	–	2,508	44	971
New Hampshire.........	30,537	21,190	13,696	522	6,806	162	5
New Jersey.............	5,195,546	99,598	35,815	141	3,208	59,046	1,388
New Mexico............	2,265,573	483,731	472,743	9	25	4,667	6,286
New York...............	17,197,344	97,451	34,111	3,921	148	19,988	39,283
North Carolina..........	20,893,207	412,153	367,584	12,272	20,790	3,289	8,217
North Dakota...........	767,938	72,570	71,359	242	–	122	847
Ohio...................	3,195,784	34,580	20,491	1,461	84	8,502	4,041
Oklahoma..............	2,094,232	10,241	10,011	9	189	5	27
Oregon.................	1,045,772	203,472	196,271	1,410	4,976	295	520
Pennsylvania...........	8,300,004	117,130	53,876	3,045	387	19,586	40,235
Rhode Island...........	37,707	1,168	8	85	–	–	1,075
South Carolina.........	1,281,602	32,778	32,556	60	16	51	96
South Dakota...........	4,423,548	296,584	148,022	122,326	–	78	26,157
Tennessee..............	10,545,649	389,206	360,344	1,682	9,698	3,320	14,162
Texas..................	5,339,503	1,260,178	1,204,923	1,133	1,932	11,161	41,028
Utah...................	15,678,158	2,117,689	2,098,061	833	1,142	12,819	4,834
Vermont................	71,799	23,866	10,465	3,755	8,981	544	120
Virginia................	23,263,466	373,649	307,343	6,347	26,782	6,761	26,416
Washington.............	8,294,749	1,967,467	1,834,685	2,427	100,190	12,802	17,362
West Virginia...........	2,343,355	92,819	67,219	310	118	6,893	18,279
Wisconsin..............	650,296	134,118	62,392	11,302	802	47,473	12,148
Wyoming...............	7,683,017	2,396,431	2,345,691	177	48,462	497	1,604

– Represents zero. Z Less than 0.5 acres. [1] Represents the entry of a person onto lands or waters administered by the National Park Service (NPS) for recreational purposes, excluding government personnel, through traffic (commuters), tradespeople, and persons residing within park boundaries. [2] Fee represents complete Federal ownership of all rights in the land. [3] Represents Federal ownership of some rights in the land. [4] Tracts under the administration of another federal agency (e.g., U.S. Forest Service, Department of the Army, Coast Guard, etc.). Bureau of Land Management tracts are also identified as Other Fee (Federal) until they are withdrawn for NPS use; then status changes to Fee (Federal). [5] Non-federal tracts owned by the state, county, and/or other municipalities, including quasi-public entities. [6] Includes Island Areas of the U.S., not shown separately. [7] Differs slightly from data shown in other tables due to rounding.

Source: U.S. National Park Service, Public Use Statistics Office, "National Park Service Visitor Use Statistics, National Reports," <irma.nps.gov/STATS/Reports/National>; and Land and Water Conservation Fund, "National Park Service Acreage Reports," <www.nps.gov/subjects/lwcf/acreagereports.htm>; accessed March 2024.

Table 1275. State Parks and Recreation Areas by State: 2020

[In units as indicated (19,041 represents 19,041,000). For year ending June 30. Data are shown as reported by state park directors. In some states, the park agency has forests, fish and wildlife areas, and/or other areas under its control. In other states, the park agency is responsible for state parks only]

State	Acreage (1,000)	Visitors (1,000) [1]	Total revenue generated ($1,000)	Operating expenditures ($1,000)	Revenue share of operating expenditures
United States	**19,041**	**786,136**	**1,128,374**	**3,412,038**	**33.1**
Alabama	48	6,412	38,012	41,049	92.6
Alaska	3,387	40	4,749	13,667	34.7
Arizona	62	2,972	15,763	26,708	59.0
Arkansas	55	6,549	21,719	70,160	31.0
California	1,649	68,166	126,202	782,312	16.1
Colorado	1,468	17,066	(NA)	76,216	(NA)
Connecticut	212	12,968	14,896	17,896	83.2
Delaware	29	6,238	19,513	29,993	65.1
Florida	723	24,838	54,251	144,654	37.5
Georgia	83	10,294	40,962	55,016	74.5
Hawaii	33	8,354	6,515	14,280	45.6
Idaho	59	6,519	8,438	18,841	44.8
Illinois	265	34,392	14,300	157,300	9.1
Indiana	172	15,046	56,611	68,214	83.0
Iowa	116	16,069	5,025	19,768	25.4
Kansas	165	7,313	11,505	18,904	60.9
Kentucky	48	1,277	37,971	86,083	44.1
Louisiana	32	1,292	715	31,539	2.3
Maine	99	3,647	(NA)	9,254	(NA)
Maryland	141	17,490	10,445	45,492	23.0
Massachusetts	354	26,786	14,660	101,020	14.5
Michigan	304	38,183	52,981	65,618	80.7
Minnesota	289	11,128	25,742	113,508	22.7
Mississippi	24	1,281	6,543	10,428	62.7
Missouri	160	19,321	6,844	58,165	11.8
Montana	44	3,317	4,537	10,621	42.7
Nebraska	169	8,114	21,210	29,064	73.0
Nevada	151	3,698	5,462	21,046	26.0
New Hampshire	232	1,091	23,210	23,210	100.0
New Jersey	812	14,084	6,486	45,754	14.2
New Mexico	192	4,030	6,585	16,317	40.4
New York	4,349	79,152	89,450	227,454	39.3
North Carolina	249	17,413	10,580	49,753	21.3
North Dakota	35	1,329	4,739	14,596	32.5
Ohio	175	40,604	28,943	73,901	39.2
Oklahoma	62	11,525	25,250	38,525	65.5
Oregon	123	44,236	21,601	70,433	30.7
Pennsylvania	304	40,715	26,000	114,393	22.7
Rhode Island	9	8,386	(NA)	14,015	(NA)
South Carolina	82	8,219	30,860	34,772	88.7
South Dakota	102	8,381	18,611	26,588	70.0
Tennessee	217	36,121	38,765	90,872	42.7
Texas	637	7,317	16,204	82,492	19.6
Utah	154	12,080	19,780	139,780	14.2
Vermont	74	863	6,168	10,777	57.2
Virginia	80	7,066	22,699	42,934	52.9
Washington	111	34,718	54,950	76,824	71.5
West Virginia	151	6,354	26,844	46,248	58.0
Wisconsin	447	18,674	21,936	22,439	97.8
Wyoming	102	5,007	3,143	13,144	23.9

NA Not available. [1] Includes day and overnight visitors.

Source: National Association of State Park Directors, Raleigh NC, *Statistical Report of State Park Operations: 2019-2020, Annual Information Exchange for the Period of July 1, 2019 through June 30, 2020* ©, May 2022. See also <www.stateparks.org>.

Table 1276. Participation in Wildlife-Related Recreation Activities: 2022

[In units as indicated. 39,935 represents 39,953,000. For persons 16 years old and over engaging in activity at least once in the year of the survey. Data may not sum due to multiple responses or nonresponse. Results from the 2022 survey should not be directly compared with results from previous surveys because of changes in methodology. Data are subject to sampling error. See source for details]

Activity	Participants		Days of participation		Trips	
	Number (1,000s)	Percent	Number (1,000s)	Percent	Number (1,000s)	Percent
Fishing	39,935	100	785,226	(X)	462,733	100
Freshwater	35,069	88	559,006	71	359,052	78
Saltwater	12,705	32	123,111	16	103,682	22
Hunting	14,375	100	240,752	(X)	165,002	100
Big game	11,522	80	134,684	56	91,610	56
Small game	5,290	37	38,056	16	33,997	21
Migratory birds	2,812	20	22,861	9	19,786	12
Other animals	2,300	16	19,903	8	19,609	12
Wildlife watching [1]	148,280	100	12,993,937	(X)	1,075,753	100
Away from home [2]	73,334	49	2,443,885	19	1,075,753	100
Around the home [3]	146,503	99	10,550,052	81	(X)	(X)

X Not applicable. [1] Observing, photographing, or feeding wildlife; maintaining natural areas of at least 1/4 acre or plantings for the benefit of wildlife; and visiting public parks and areas to view wildlife. [2] Activity at least 1 mile away from home. Trips to zoos, circuses, aquariums, and museums are not included. [3] Activity within 1 mile of home.

Source: U.S. Fish and Wildlife Service, *2022 National Survey of Fishing, Hunting, and Wildlife Associated Recreation*, September 2023. See also <www.fws.gov/program/national-survey-fishing-hunting-and-wildlife-associated-recreation-fhwar>.

Table 1277. Expenditures for Wildlife-Related Recreation Activities: 2022

[In units as indicated (99,422 represents $99,422,000,000). For persons 16 years and older. Data may not sum due to multiple responses. Results from the 2022 survey should not be directly compared with results from previous surveys because of changes in methodology. Data are subject to sampling error. See source for more information on methodology changes and measures of accuracy]

Item	Total, all items	Trip-related expenditures [1]	Primary equipment	Auxiliary equipment [2]	Special equipment [3]	Other expenditures
FISHING						
Expenditures, total (million dollars)	99,422	36,604	8,660	4,327	27,748	22,083
Average per angler (dollars)	2,490	917	217	108	695	553
Spenders:						
Percent of anglers	97	94	73	37	20	73
Average per spender (dollars)	2,558	980	297	293	3,509	754
HUNTING						
Expenditures, total (million dollars)	45,221	12,323	7,904	3,948	7,743	13,304
Average per hunter (dollars)	3,146	857	550	275	539	926
Spenders:						
Percent of hunters	96	85	73	59	23	82
Average per spender (dollars)	3,264	1,011	749	468	2,310	1,134
WILDLIFE WATCHING						
Expenditures, total (million dollars)	250,199	42,059	24,636	8,911	85,097	89,495
Average per watcher (dollars)	1,687	284	166	60	574	604
Spenders:						
Percent of watchers	77	24	60	24	14	49
Average per spender (dollars)	2,188	1,205	277	247	4,087	1,235

[1] Trip-related expenditure items include food, drink, refreshments, lodging, public and private transportation, airfare, charter, guide, package, and pack trips, public and private land use, heating and cooking fuel, equipment rental, and boating expenses. [2] Auxiliary equipment includes sleeping bags, packs, duffel bags, tents, traps, binoculars and field glasses, special clothing, boots and waders, maintenance and repair of equipment, processing and taxidermy costs, and electronic auxiliary equipment such as global positioning systems. [3] Special equipment includes boats, campers, trail bikes, 4x4 vehicles, all-terrain vehicles (ATVs), 4-wheelers, snowmobiles, pickup trucks, vans, travel and tent trailers, motor homes, house trailers, and recreational vehicles.

Source: U.S. Fish and Wildlife Service, *2022 National Survey of Fishing, Hunting, and Wildlife Associated Recreation*, September 2023. See also <www.fws.gov/program/national-survey-fishing-hunting-and-wildlife-associated-recreation-fhwar>.

Table 1278. Tribal Gaming Operations and Revenues: 2010 to 2022

[Revenue in millions of dollars (26,503 represents $26,503,000,000). For year ending September 30]

Region	2010		2015		2020		2021		2022	
	Operations (number)	Revenue	Operations (number)	Revenue	Operations (number)	Revenue	Operations (number)	Revenue	Operations (number)	Revenue
Total [1]	**422**	**26,503**	**474**	**29,882**	**524**	**27,832**	**510**	**39,026**	**519**	**40,938**
Portland	50	2,655	52	3,022	57	3,116	56	4,441	55	4,484
Sacramento	62	6,794	71	7,881	77	8,399	78	11,927	87	11,759
Phoenix	48	2,539	53	2,808	52	2,358	50	3,218	51	3,723
St. Paul [2]	119	4,452	134	4,829	103	3,730	99	4,787	96	4,951
Rapid City [3]	(X)	(X)	(X)	(X)	42	239	41	372	43	406
Tulsa	65	1,769	68	2,207	76	2,104	74	3,155	74	3,489
Oklahoma City	51	1,583	65	2,142	74	2,064	70	3,027	72	3,149
Washington DC	27	6,711	31	6,994	43	5,823	42	8,098	41	8,977

X Not applicable. [1] Regions formerly were numbered I to VI, as follows: Portland (Region I): Alaska, Idaho, Oregon, and Washington. Sacramento (Region II): California, and Northern Nevada. Phoenix (Region III): Arizona, Colorado, New Mexico, and Southern Nevada. St. Paul (Region IV): Iowa, Michigan, Minnesota, Montana, North Dakota, Nebraska, South Dakota, Wisconsin, and Wyoming. Tulsa (Eastern part of Region V): Kansas, and Eastern Oklahoma. Oklahoma City (Western part of Region V): Western Oklahoma and Texas. Washington (Region VI): Alabama, Connecticut, Florida, Louisiana, Mississippi, North Carolina, and New York. See footnote 2 regarding St. Paul region and footnote 3 regarding Rapid City region. [2] Through FY2015, St. Paul region covers Iowa, Michigan, Minnesota, Montana, North Dakota, Nebraska, South Dakota, Wisconsin, and Wyoming. Beginning FY2016, St. Paul region covers Indiana, Iowa, Michigan, Minnesota, Nebraska, and Wisconsin. Also known as Region IV. [3] Rapid City region data begins with data for FY2016, and covers North Dakota, South Dakota, Montana, and Wyoming.

Source: National Indian Gaming Commission, *Gross Gaming Revenues 2017-2021*, December 2022, and earlier reports; and *FY2022 Gross Gaming Revenue Report*, December 2023, and earlier reports.

Table 1279. Tourism Output in Current and Chained (2017) Dollars by Commodity: 2019 to 2022

[In millions of dollars (1,261,502 represents $1,261,502,000,000)]

Tourism commodity	Direct output (current dollars)				Real output (chained 2017 dollars)			
	2019	2020	2021	2022	2019	2020	2021	2022
Total.............................	**1,261,502**	**608,777**	**999,427**	**1,356,711**	**1,206,045**	**611,143**	**938,531**	**1,135,666**
Traveler accommodations.........................	236,794	151,067	196,860	242,851	228,066	156,596	189,312	213,951
Food and beverage services....................	167,739	78,740	171,407	200,188	158,567	71,767	147,701	160,053
Domestic passenger air transportation services...	183,286	79,430	132,603	214,828	174,103	84,368	141,232	186,752
International passenger air transportation services.............................	109,601	33,959	45,089	91,933	104,901	34,222	46,426	84,881
Passenger rail transportation services............	235	77	72	112	243	78	69	108
Passenger water transportation services..........	20,457	6,873	4,839	8,313	20,532	7,184	4,757	8,255
Intercity bus transportation services...............	1,722	1,057	1,298	1,526	1,727	1,108	1,276	1,515
Intercity charter bus transportation services.......	2,648	1,300	1,739	2,604	2,658	1,355	1,710	2,583
Local bus and other transportation services.......	13,594	3,104	10,684	13,142	13,213	3,061	10,339	12,282
Taxicab services................................	7,379	3,127	5,763	6,689	7,180	3,099	5,583	6,260
Scenic and sightseeing transportation services...	4,364	2,020	3,549	4,109	4,166	1,900	3,294	3,678
Automotive rental and leasing....................	35,855	22,230	31,775	34,014	35,246	23,264	25,721	25,956
Other vehicle rental and leasing..................	730	578	700	849	733	573	470	560
Automotive repair services.......................	10,320	9,827	9,062	11,329	9,804	9,040	8,008	9,276
Parking...	2,933	1,459	2,685	2,804	2,790	1,378	2,450	2,489
Highway tolls...................................	1,836	837	1,877	1,965	1,746	790	1,713	1,744
Travel arrangement and reservation services.....	63,698	32,880	44,788	65,501	62,077	34,596	46,925	65,960
Motion pictures and performing arts..............	36,551	21,344	31,162	32,720	35,150	20,247	28,449	28,405
Spectator sports................................	6,509	3,805	5,406	6,077	6,266	3,546	5,208	6,112
Participant sports...............................	20,659	9,964	17,088	22,156	19,569	9,311	15,823	19,789
Gambling.......................................	60,947	47,681	63,658	67,729	58,437	45,104	57,563	56,729
All other recreation and entertainment............	7,042	2,542	9,333	13,876	6,853	2,462	8,881	12,604
Gasoline.......................................	117,077	40,853	86,211	173,810	106,969	43,966	68,973	105,989
Shopping.......................................	149,524	54,025	121,778	137,586	146,804	53,418	115,073	118,358

Source: U.S. Bureau of Economic Analysis, "Travel Satellite Accounts Data," <www.bea.gov/data/special-topics/travel-and-tourism>, accessed May 2024.

Table 1280. Tourism Industry Chain-Type Price Indexes by Commodity: 2017 to 2022

[Index numbers, 2017=100. For explanation of chain-type price indexes, see text, Section 13]

Tourism commodity	2017	2018	2019	2020	2021	2022
All tourism goods and services.............................	**100.0**	**103.2**	**104.6**	**99.6**	**106.5**	**119.5**
Traveler accommodations.........................	100.0	101.0	103.8	96.5	104.0	113.5
Food and beverage services.....................	100.0	102.6	105.8	109.7	116.1	125.1
Domestic passenger air transportation services................	100.0	101.8	105.3	94.1	93.9	115.0
International passenger air transportation services.............	100.0	104.5	104.5	99.2	97.1	108.3
Passenger rail transportation services........................	100.0	101.6	96.5	98.6	105.1	104.1
Passenger water transportation services......................	100.0	100.3	99.6	95.7	101.7	100.7
Intercity bus transportation services..........................	100.0	100.3	99.7	95.4	101.7	100.8
Intercity charter bus transportation services..................	100.0	100.3	99.6	95.9	101.7	100.8
Local bus and other transportation services..................	100.0	101.8	102.9	101.4	103.3	107.0
Taxicab services..	100.0	101.7	102.8	100.9	103.2	106.9
Scenic and sightseeing transportation services..............	100.0	102.3	104.7	106.3	107.7	111.7
Automotive rental and leasing...............................	100.0	102.2	101.7	95.6	123.5	131.0
Other vehicle rental and leasing.............................	100.0	99.0	99.5	100.9	149.1	151.5
Automotive repair services..................................	100.0	101.9	105.3	108.7	113.2	122.1
Parking...	100.0	102.3	105.1	105.9	109.6	112.6
Highway tolls...	100.0	102.3	105.1	105.9	109.6	112.6
Travel arrangement and reservation services................	100.0	100.5	102.6	95.0	95.4	99.3
Motion pictures and performing arts.........................	100.0	102.1	104.0	105.4	109.5	115.2
Spectator sports..	100.0	101.8	103.9	107.3	103.8	99.4
Participant sports...	100.0	102.9	105.6	107.0	108.0	112.0
Gambling...	100.0	102.4	104.3	105.7	110.6	119.4
All other recreation and entertainment......................	100.0	101.2	102.8	103.2	105.1	110.1
Gasoline...	100.0	113.5	109.5	92.9	125.0	164.0
Shopping...	100.0	101.9	101.9	101.1	105.8	116.2

Source: U.S. Bureau of Economic Analysis, "Travel Satellite Accounts Data," <www.bea.gov/data/special-topics/travel-and-tourism>, accessed May 2024.

Table 1281. Travel Forecast Summary: 2020 to 2026

[In units as indicated (722 represents $722,000,000,000). Data for 2023 to 2026 are forecast]

Indicator	Unit	2020	2021	2022	2023	2024	2025	2026
Consumer price index (CPI) [1]............	Percent	259	271	293	306	315	321	328
Travel price index (TPI) [1]....................	Percent	275	300	341	344	351	357	364
Total travel expenditures in U.S...........	Bil. dol.	722	909	1,020	1,090	1,150	1,180	1,200
U.S. residents..............................	Bil. dol.	682	868	918	960	989	1,010	1,020
International visitors [2]......................	Bil. dol.	41	41	99	133	158	168	185
Total international visitors to the U.S.......	Millions	19	22	51	67	79	88	92
Total domestic person trips [3]...............	Millions	1,580	2,020	2,250	2,320	2,410	2,490	2,550
Business...................................	Millions	1,400	1,770	1,880	1,910	1,970	2,020	2,060
Leisure....................................	Millions	181	250	371	414	447	469	483

[1] 1982-1984=100. [2] Includes general travel spending and passenger fares; excludes international traveler spending on medical, educational, and cross-border/seasonal work-related activities. [3] One person on one trip 50 miles or more, one way, away from home or including one or more nights away from home.

Source: U.S. Travel Association, *Travel Forecast Summary Table*, June 2023 ©. See also <www.ustravel.org/research>.

Arts, Recreation, and Travel   803

Table 1282. Tourism Sales and Employment by Industry Component: 2017 to 2022

[Sales in millions of dollars (1,088,053 represents $1,088,053,000,000); employment in thousands (5,975 represents 5,975,000). Direct tourism-related sales comprise all output purchased directly by visitors (e.g., traveler accommodations, passenger air transportation, souvenirs). Direct tourism-related employment comprises all jobs where the workers are engaged in the production of direct tourism-related sales (output), such as hotel staff, airline pilots, and souvenir sellers]

Industry component	2017	2018	2019	2020	2021	2022
DIRECT TOURISM SALES (OUTPUT) (mil. dol.)						
All tourism goods and services [1]	1,088,053	1,198,878	1,261,502	608,777	999,427	1,356,711
Traveler accommodations	218,791	229,901	236,794	151,067	196,860	242,851
Food and beverage services	143,255	151,011	167,739	78,740	171,407	200,188
Domestic passenger air transportation services	154,786	167,849	183,286	79,430	132,603	214,828
Gasoline	111,911	145,129	117,077	40,853	86,211	173,810
Shopping	103,673	126,687	149,524	54,025	121,778	137,586
DIRECT TOURISM EMPLOYMENT (1,000)						
All tourism goods and services [1]	5,975	6,589	7,283	4,362	5,625	6,647
Traveler accommodations	1,515	1,581	1,615	1,031	1,076	1,320
Vacation home rentals	13	16	16	16	13	13
Food services and drinking places	1,700	1,837	1,943	877	1,607	1,820
Air transportation services	550	577	603	430	479	571
Rail transportation services	8	8	9	3	4	5
Water transportation services	41	44	46	19	11	16
Interurban bus transportation	17	17	17	12	12	13
Interurban charter bus transportation	19	20	19	10	12	14
Urban transit systems and other transportation	67	90	100	29	75	91
Taxi service	10	7	7	4	5	5
Scenic and sightseeing transportation services	31	31	32	18	22	27
Automotive equipment rental and leasing	18	22	24	17	18	20
Automotive repair services	79	87	86	84	62	88
Parking lots and garages	34	37	40	18	28	32
Toll highways	6	8	9	3	8	8
Travel arrangement and reservation services	200	202	201	144	130	161
Motion pictures and performing arts	31	30	35	19	18	38
Spectator sports	42	43	47	30	38	66
Participant sports	261	273	304	142	233	267
Gambling	121	134	123	36	45	48
All other recreation and entertainment	68	63	49	16	45	52
Petroleum refineries	9	10	11	5	7	8
Wholesale trade and transportation services	142	149	194	94	155	159
Gasoline service stations	165	183	190	97	136	174
Retail trade services, excluding gasoline service stations	227	307	454	235	291	498
All other industries	507	698	918	875	908	977

[1] Includes other goods and services not shown separately.

Source: U.S. Bureau of Economic Analysis, "Tourism Satellite Accounts Data," <www.bea.gov/data/special-topics/travel-and-tourism>, accessed May 2024.

Table 1283. Overseas Travelers to the U.S. Ranked by State and Island Area Visited: 2019 to 2022

[40,393 represents 40,393,000. Excludes visitors from Canada and Mexico. Ranked for the most current year. Data shown only for states and island areas meeting statistical criteria in any given year; see source for details]

State and area	2019	2020	2021	2022	State and area	2019	2020	2021	2022
Total [1]	40,393	7,594	9,175	23,953	Indiana	226	33	69	168
					Oregon	323	40	72	168
Florida	9,610	2,299	4,092	7,145	Minnesota	287	34	56	163
New York	10,518	1,638	2,099	7,133	South Carolina	246	28	72	163
California	8,050	1,335	1,113	4,455	Missouri	170	38	51	139
Nevada	3,058	383	292	1,722	Maine	149	9	19	101
Texas	1,745	419	621	1,289	Oklahoma	101	8	18	81
Illinois	1,555	199	300	1,135	Kentucky	97	30	34	79
Hawaii	3,296	590	87	953	Puerto Rico	(NA)	25	23	77
New Jersey	1,159	226	490	867	Alabama	141	26	25	74
Massachusetts	1,745	204	239	807	New Mexico	153	7	18	69
Arizona	1,196	144	105	663	Alaska	109	3	17	62
Pennsylvania	1,054	126	236	592	Kansas	(NA)	17	26	62
Washington	925	134	136	467	Wyoming	246	8	14	62
Georgia	868	159	242	465	Idaho	(NA)	5	10	57
Virginia	529	74	134	438	Mississippi	(NA)	5	7	57
Utah	739	79	70	412	New Hampshire	105	11	15	57
North Carolina	452	67	157	340	Rhode Island	113	9	19	57
Maryland	408	68	121	326	Iowa	105	8	19	50
Colorado	509	104	106	321	Vermont	(NA)	8	10	46
Louisiana	501	81	71	314	South Dakota	(NA)	2	6	36
Guam	1,842	346	15	304	Delaware	(NA)	5	19	34
Tennessee	372	64	75	292	Montana	(NA)	11	6	34
Ohio	448	82	95	273	West Virginia	(NA)	5	6	34
Michigan	428	74	96	261	Arkansas	(NA)	10	14	31
Connecticut	323	60	94	225	Nebraska	(NA)	7	12	26
Wisconsin	234	27	40	175	North Dakota	(NA)	2	3	22

NA Not available. [1] Includes travelers to other states and territories, not shown separately. A person is counted in each area visited but only once in the total.

Source: U.S. Department of Commerce, International Trade Administration, National Travel and Tourism Office, "NTTO Visual Data Tools, U.S. States & Cities Visited Monitor" and "SIAT Inbound Survey Monitor," <www.trade.gov/travel-and-tourism-research>, accessed May 2024 and earlier reports.

Table 1284. Overseas Travelers to the U.S. Ranked for Top Cities and Metro Areas Visited: 2020 to 2022

[7,594 represents 7,594,000. Excludes visitors from Canada and Mexico. Ranked for the most current year. Data shown only for cities and metro areas meeting statistical criteria in any given year; see source for details]

Metro area	2020	2021	2022	Metro area	2020	2021	2022
Total[1]	**7,594**	**9,175**	**23,953**	West Palm Beach, FL[3]	80	169	254
New York-White Plains-Wayne, NY-NJ	1,604	2,032	6,992	Riverside-San Bernardino-Ontario, CA	72	57	220
Miami-Miami Beach-Kendall, FL	1,462	2,759	4,086	Phoenix-Mesa-Glendale, AZ	59	53	216
Orlando-Kissimmee-Sanford, FL	982	1,223	2,920	Salinas, CA	32	17	211
Los Angeles-Long Beach-Glendale, CA	785	708	2,750	Buffalo-Niagara Falls, NY	19	56	208
San Francisco-San Mateo-Redwood City, CA	401	243	1,739	Key West, FL	108	47	201
Las Vegas-Paradise, NV	368	281	1,660	Denver-Aurora-Broomfield, CO	59	68	199
Washington (DC Metro Area), DC-MD-VA	255	305	1,167	San Jose-Sunnyvale-Santa Clara, CA	87	37	187
Chicago-Joliet-Naperville, IL	179	285	1,061	Newark-Union, NJ-PA	56	79	184
Boston-Quincy, MA	182	204	738	Palm Bay-Melbourne-Titusville, FL	22	30	175
Honolulu, HI	503	45	711	Nashville, TN[4]	39	31	170
Fort Lauderdale, FL[2]	185	506	675	Austin-Round Rock-San Marcos, TX	47	74	160
Houston-Sugar Land-Baytown, TX	207	317	596	Santa Barbara-Santa Maria-Goleta, CA	48	28	160
San Diego-Carlsbad-San Marcos, CA	154	117	558	Detroit-Warren-Livonia, MI	36	51	139
Dallas-Plano-Irving, TX	126	193	453	Jacksonville, FL	27	70	139
Seattle-Bellevue-Everett, WA	122	117	412	Sacramento, CA[5]	19	24	137
Flagstaff, AZ	71	35	400	Baltimore-Towson, MD	30	45	132
Santa Ana-Anaheim-Irvine, CA	109	68	395	St. George, UT	18	10	132
Atlanta-Sandy Springs-Marietta, GA	143	195	362	Salt Lake City, UT	34	34	129
Tampa-St. Petersburg-Clearwater, FL	143	190	340	Minneapolis, MN-WI[6]	27	37	122
Philadelphia, PA	74	117	326	Kahului-Wailuku (Maui), HI	30	8	120

[1] Includes travelers to other cities and metro areas, not shown separately. A person is counted in each area visited but only once in the total. [2] Fort Lauderdale-Pompano Beach-Deerfield Beach, FL. [3] West Palm Beach-Boca Raton-Boynton Beach, FL. [4] Nashville-Davidson-Murfreesboro-Franklin, TN. [5] Sacramento-Arden-Arcade-Roseville, CA. [6] Minneapolis-St. Paul-Bloomington, MN-WI.

Source: U.S. Department of Commerce, International Trade Administration, National Travel and Tourism Office, "NTTO Visual Data Tools, U.S. States & Cities Visited Monitor" and "SIAT Inbound Survey Monitor," <www.trade.gov/travel-and-tourism-research>, accessed May 2024 and earlier reports.

Table 1285. International Travel: 2010 to 2023

[In thousands (60,271 represents 60,271,000). U.S. travelers cover residents of the United States, its territories and possessions. International travelers to the U.S. include travelers for business and pleasure, and excludes travel by international personnel and international businessmen employed in the United States. Some traveler data revised since originally issued]

Item and world region	2010	2015	2017	2018	2019	2020	2021	2022	2023
U.S. TRAVELERS TO FOREIGN COUNTRIES BY WORLD REGION OF DESTINATION[1]									
Total	**60,271**	**74,191**	**87,555**	**92,587**	**99,270**	**33,160**	**48,711**	**80,847**	**98,457**
Canada	11,749	12,669	14,280	14,440	15,005	1,929	2,093	9,088	12,788
Mexico	20,015	28,733	34,947	36,373	39,458	21,390	28,403	33,668	36,706
Total overseas[2]	28,507	32,789	38,327	41,774	44,808	9,841	18,214	38,101	48,963
Europe	11,104	12,599	15,793	17,742	19,049	2,582	5,238	15,822	20,059
Caribbean	5,716	7,648	8,321	8,702	9,368	3,098	6,399	9,208	10,741
Asia	4,861	4,843	5,771	6,253	6,546	1,114	626	2,653	5,579
South America	2,129	1,869	1,925	2,104	2,338	772	1,401	2,506	3,038
Central America	2,263	2,791	3,032	3,237	3,451	1,104	2,585	3,702	4,355
Oceania	687	643	776	861	958	247	63	461	822
Middle East	1,339	2,045	2,306	2,443	2,545	737	1,516	3,120	3,592
Africa	408	351	403	432	552	187	385	630	777
INTERNATIONAL TRAVELERS TO U.S. BY VISITOR REGION OF RESIDENCE									
Total	**60,010**	**77,774**	**77,187**	**79,746**	**79,442**	**19,212**	**22,280**	**50,771**	**66,482**
Canada	20,176	20,699	20,493	21,475	20,720	4,809	2,529	14,382	20,514
Mexico	13,472	18,374	17,788	18,387	18,328	6,800	10,576	12,436	14,499
Total overseas[2]	26,363	38,700	38,906	39,883	40,393	7,594	9,175	23,953	31,468
Europe	11,985	15,790	14,974	15,424	15,706	2,469	1,962	11,046	13,160
Caribbean	1,201	1,479	1,671	1,793	1,921	511	990	1,352	1,654
Asia	7,020	10,946	12,137	11,874	12,250	2,165	1,289	4,124	7,549
South America	3,250	5,699	5,556	6,027	5,733	1,433	3,019	4,214	4,833
Central America	760	1,077	1,168	1,283	1,360	391	1,181	1,192	1,473
Oceania	1,095	1,768	1,632	1,687	1,641	257	67	798	1,233
Middle East	736	1,369	1,182	1,197	1,216	262	513	861	1,035
Africa	316	573	586	598	567	107	154	367	531

[1] A person is counted in each area visited but only once in the total. [2] "Overseas" excludes Canada and Mexico.

Source: U.S. Department of Commerce, International Trade Administration, National Travel and Tourism Office, "Annual Arrivals 2000 to Present - Country of Residence (COR)," <www.trade.gov/i-94-arrivals-program>, and "US Outbound Travel to World Regions," <www.trade.gov/us-international-air-travel-statistics-i-92-data>; accessed May 2024.

Table 1286. Inbound Crossings for Top 5 U.S.-Canadian and U.S.-Mexican Border Land Passenger Gateways: 2023

[20,608 represents 20,608,000. Data reflect all personal vehicles and buses, passengers, and pedestrians entering the U.S.-Canadian border and U.S.-Mexican border, regardless of nationality]

Item and gateway	Entering the U.S. (1,000)	Item and gateway	Entering the U.S. (1,000)
ALL U.S.-CANADIAN LAND GATEWAYS		**ALL U.S.-MEXICAN LAND GATEWAYS**	
Personal vehicles................................	20,608	Personal vehicles................................	75,892
Personal vehicle passengers...................	40,619	Personal vehicle passengers...................	134,928
Buses..	48	Buses..	119
Bus passengers...................................	958	Bus passengers...................................	2,454
Train passengers.................................	246	Train passengers.................................	5
Pedestrians..	216	Pedestrians..	39,422
Top five gateways:		**Top five gateways:**	
Personal vehicles:		Personal vehicles:	
Buffalo Niagara Falls, NY.........................	3,958	San Ysidro, CA......................................	15,846
Detroit, MI...	3,426	El Paso, TX..	8,221
Blaine, WA...	2,990	Otay Mesa, CA......................................	5,754
Port Huron, MI......................................	968	Calexico, CA...	5,015
Champlain Rouses Point, NY......................	910	Laredo, TX...	4,908
Personal vehicle passengers:		Personal vehicle passengers:	
Buffalo Niagara Falls, NY.........................	8,761	San Ysidro, CA......................................	25,820
Detroit, MI...	6,093	El Paso, TX..	14,026
Blaine, WA...	5,950	Laredo, TX...	9,513
Champlain Rouses Point, NY......................	2,141	Hidalgo, TX..	9,390
Port Huron, MI......................................	1,994	Otay Mesa, CA......................................	9,371
Pedestrians:		Pedestrians:	
Buffalo Niagara Falls, NY.........................	125	San Ysidro, CA......................................	6,848
Blaine, WA...	27	El Paso, TX..	4,248
Sumas, WA..	22	Nogales, AZ..	2,934
Point Roberts, WA.................................	10	Brownsville, TX......................................	2,838
International Falls, MN............................	5	Calexico, CA...	2,815

Source: U.S. Department of Transportation, Bureau of Transportation Statistics, "Border Crossing / Entry Data," <data.bts.gov/stories/s/Data-Visualizations/pbt9-k67k>, accessed July 2024.

Table 1287. Foreign Tourists Admitted by Country of Citizenship: 2019 to 2022

[In thousands (64,865 represents 64,865,000). For years ending September 30. Represents non-U.S. citizens admitted to the country for a temporary period of time, for pleasure (tourists). Includes nonimmigrant admission classes B2 (temporary visitors for pleasure), GMT (Commonwealth of the Northern Marianas Islands visa waiver program–temporary visitors for pleasure, Guam or Northern Mariana Islands), and WT (visa waiver program–temporary visitors for pleasure)]

Country	2019	2020	2021	2022	Country	2019	2020	2021	2022
All countries [1]...........	**64,865**	**28,732**	**9,055**	**34,946**	Israel.............................	323	146	135	277
Argentina.......................	816	316	215	488	Italy..............................	1,173	426	100	704
Australia........................	1,228	475	23	430	Jamaica.........................	300	130	135	203
Austria..........................	177	67	7	111	Japan............................	3,256	1,445	40	284
Bahamas, The.................	284	129	110	197	Korea, South...................	1,990	941	75	586
Belgium.........................	244	86	9	168	Mexico [2]......................	18,803	9,148	2,743	11,036
Bolivia..........................	69	29	46	57	Netherlands [4]................	680	261	49	431
Brazil...........................	2,056	918	78	890	New Zealand...................	311	111	8	100
Canada [2].....................	10,523	5,011	840	4,869	Nicaragua.......................	65	31	31	51
Chile............................	407	177	154	462	Nigeria...........................	141	48	28	51
China [3].......................	2,048	619	32	206	Norway..........................	236	85	3	101
Colombia.......................	941	391	853	1,002	Pakistan.........................	88	37	32	61
Costa Rica.....................	309	164	196	250	Panama..........................	149	72	63	105
Czechia.........................	116	45	4	70	Peru..............................	311	150	305	309
Denmark........................	267	103	5	153	Philippines......................	321	132	35	147
Dominican Republic..........	458	239	338	418	Poland...........................	188	88	10	192
Ecuador.........................	443	202	332	357	Portugal.........................	182	75	12	126
Egypt............................	72	34	28	42	Russia...........................	215	105	65	51
El Salvador.....................	213	95	151	217	Saudi Arabia...................	90	24	14	38
Finland..........................	122	59	2	55	Singapore.......................	106	47	4	52
France [4]......................	1,895	765	69	1,260	South Africa....................	100	43	9	48
Germany........................	1,738	689	66	1,117	Spain............................	1,029	401	135	748
Greece..........................	76	35	3	51	Sweden..........................	404	177	8	179
Guatemala......................	259	131	199	241	Switzerland.....................	352	131	18	201
Haiti.............................	125	61	71	61	Taiwan...........................	388	146	25	69
Honduras.......................	206	100	192	226	Thailand.........................	80	30	11	42
Hungary.........................	98	43	3	51	Trinidad and Tobago.........	181	75	13	102
Iceland..........................	62	25	1	33	Turkey...........................	123	60	40	86
India............................	1,108	393	169	893	United Kingdom [4]...........	4,270	1,702	129	2,607
Indonesia.......................	92	41	13	55	Uruguay.........................	72	24	19	48
Ireland..........................	502	208	9	337	Venezuela.......................	435	161	191	227

[1] Total includes visitors of unknown country of citizenship and those withheld from country totals in order to avoid disclosure. [2] The majority of short-term admissions from Canada and Mexico are excluded. [3] Data for China includes Hong Kong and Macau. [4] Includes overseas territories; see source for details.

Source: U.S. Department of Homeland Security, Office of Homeland Security Statistics, "2022 Yearbook of Immigration Statistics," and earlier reports, <www.dhs.gov/ohss/topics/immigration/yearbook>, accessed February 2024.

Table 1288. Top 20 U.S. Gateway Airports for Nonstop International Air Travel Passengers: 2023

[237,345 represents 237,345,000. International passengers are residents of any country traveling nonstop to and from the United States on U.S. and foreign carriers. The data cover all passengers arriving and departing from U.S. airports on nonstop commercial international flights with 60 seats or more]

Gateway airport	Airport code	Passengers (1,000)	Gateway airport	Airport code	Passengers (1,000)
Total, all airports.............	**(X)**	**237,345**	Dallas-Fort Worth, TX................	DFW	10,866
Total, top 20 airports................	(X)	210,551	Washington, DC (Dulles).............	IAD	9,235
Top 20, percentage of total.............	(X)	88.7	Boston, MA.............................	BOS	7,763
			Fort Lauderdale, FL...................	FLL	7,511
New York, NY...........................	JFK	32,934	Orlando, FL.............................	MCO	6,793
Miami, FL...............................	MIA	21,765	Seattle, WA............................	SEA	5,579
Los Angeles, CA.......................	LAX	21,686	Charlotte, NC..........................	CLT	4,189
Newark, NJ.............................	EWR	14,460	Denver, CO............................	DEN	3,972
San Francisco, CA....................	SFO	13,811	Philadelphia, PA.......................	PHL	3,555
Chicago, IL.............................	ORD	13,164	Las Vegas, NV.........................	LAS	3,220
Atlanta, GA.............................	ATL	12,479	Honolulu, HI............................	HNL	3,191
Houston, TX............................	IAH	11,337	Detroit, MI..............................	DTW	3,041

X Not applicable.

Source: U.S. Department of Transportation, Research and Innovative Technology Administration, Bureau of Transportation Statistics, Office of Airline Information, "T-100 International Segment data," <www.transtats.bts.gov/Fields.asp?gnoyr_VQ=FJE>, accessed June 2024.

Table 1289. Average Cost of Airfare for Domestic Routes: 1995 to 2023

[In dollars, except percent. Fares based on domestic itinerary fares. Itinerary fares consist of round-trip fares unless the customer does not purchase a return trip. In that case, the one-way fare is included. Fares are based on the total ticket value, which consists of the price charged by the airlines plus any additional taxes and fees levied by an outside entity at the time of purchase. Fares include only the price paid at the time of the ticket purchase and do not include other fees paid at the airport or onboard the aircraft. Averages do not include frequent-flyer or "zero fares"]

Year	Current dollars			Constant (2023) dollars [1]		
		Percent change			Percent change	
	Average fare	From previous year	Cumulative from 1995	Average fare	From previous year	Cumulative from 1995
1995........................	292	(NA)	(NA)	584	(NA)	(NA)
1996........................	277	-5.3	-5.3	537	-8.0	-8.0
1997........................	287	3.8	-1.7	545	1.5	-6.7
1998........................	309	7.6	5.8	578	6.0	-1.1
1999........................	324	4.7	10.8	592	2.5	1.4
2000........................	339	4.7	16.0	600	1.3	2.7
2001........................	321	-5.4	9.7	552	-8.0	-5.6
2002........................	312	-2.6	6.9	529	-4.1	-9.4
2003........................	315	1.0	7.9	522	-1.3	-10.6
2004........................	305	-3.2	4.5	493	-5.7	-15.7
2005........................	307	0.6	5.2	479	-2.7	-17.9
2006........................	329	6.9	12.4	497	3.6	-15.0
2007........................	325	-1.0	11.3	478	-3.7	-18.2
2008........................	346	6.5	18.5	490	2.6	-16.1
2009........................	310	-10.4	6.2	441	-10.1	-24.6
2010........................	336	8.3	15.0	470	6.5	-19.6
2011........................	364	8.3	24.5	493	4.9	-15.6
2012........................	375	3.0	28.3	497	0.9	-14.9
2013........................	384	2.5	31.5	503	1.0	-14.0
2014........................	396	3.2	35.7	510	1.5	-12.7
2015........................	379	-4.3	29.8	488	-4.4	-16.6
2016........................	355	-6.5	21.3	450	-7.7	-23.0
2017........................	347	-2.1	18.8	431	-4.2	-26.2
2018........................	350	0.7	19.6	424	-1.7	-27.4
2019........................	352	0.8	20.6	420	-1.0	-28.1
2020........................	292	-17.0	–	344	-18.0	-41.1
2021........................	307	5.0	5.1	345	0.3	-40.9
2022........................	378	23.2	29.4	394	14.1	-32.6
2023........................	382	0.9	30.6	382	-3.1	-34.7

NA Not available. – Represents or rounds to zero. [1] Rate calculated using Bureau of Labor Statistics Consumer Price Index.

Source: U.S. Department of Transportation, Bureau of Transportation Statistics, Air Fares, "National Level Fares since 1995—Annual," <www.bts.gov/air-fares>, accessed May 2024.

Table 1290. International Travel Payments, Receipts, and Balance of Trade: 2000 to 2023

[In millions of dollars (85,490 represents $85,490,000,000)]

Year	Travel and passenger fare (mil. dol.)						U.S. net travel and passenger receipts (mil. dol.)
	Payments by U.S. travelers abroad			Receipts from international visitors			
	Total	Travel payments [1,2]	Air transport [3]	Total	Travel receipts [1,2]	Air transport [3]	
2000................	85,490	64,174	21,316	118,317	96,872	21,445	32,827
2001................	82,185	60,525	21,660	105,453	86,408	19,045	23,268
2002................	79,362	59,017	20,345	97,416	79,625	17,791	18,054
2003................	81,708	61,244	20,464	94,817	76,983	17,834	13,109
2004................	93,342	70,332	23,010	107,210	85,648	21,562	13,868
2005................	98,695	74,112	24,583	116,682	93,423	23,259	17,987
2006................	105,404	78,375	27,029	121,029	96,148	24,881	15,625
2007................	112,930	82,606	30,324	134,800	106,918	27,882	21,870
2008................	119,133	84,317	34,816	149,095	117,030	32,065	29,962
2009................	115,126	82,512	32,614	137,114	110,757	26,357	21,988
2010................	123,833	85,166	38,667	161,821	130,315	31,506	37,988
2011................	130,607	86,623	43,984	178,935	142,197	36,738	48,328
2012................	138,167	90,340	47,827	195,114	153,921	41,193	56,947
2013................	132,324	91,119	41,205	213,103	170,979	42,124	80,779
2014................	140,228	96,248	43,980	222,747	180,265	42,482	82,519
2015................	144,667	102,664	42,003	230,574	192,602	37,972	85,907
2016................	147,639	109,155	38,484	228,551	192,868	35,683	80,912
2017................	164,885	117,931	46,954	233,759	196,469	37,290	68,874
2018................	176,395	125,717	50,678	241,985	200,724	41,261	65,590
2019................	184,785	131,990	52,795	239,064	198,982	40,082	54,279
2020................	47,075	33,704	13,371	84,296	72,479	11,817	37,221
2021................	74,544	56,697	17,847	84,169	71,411	12,758	9,625
2022................	161,941	115,312	46,629	165,460	136,869	28,591	3,519
2023, preliminary........	215,411	149,984	65,427	213,089	175,855	37,234	-2,322

[1] Covers purchases of goods and services by U.S. persons traveling abroad and by foreign travelers in the United States for business or personal reasons. These goods and services include food, lodging, recreation, gifts, entertainment, local transportation in the country of travel, and other items incidental to a foreign visit. [2] Covers business travel, including expenditures by border, seasonal, and other short-term workers; and personal travel, including health-related and education-related travel, along with spending on day-trips (less than one night). [3] Fares received for the transport of nonresidents by U.S. air carriers between the United States and foreign countries and between two foreign points, and the transport of U.S. residents by foreign air carriers between the United States and foreign countries.

Source: U.S. Department of Commerce, International Trade Administration, National Travel and Tourism Office, "Annual International Visitor Spending in the United States," <www.trade.gov/travel-and-tourism-research>, accessed May 2024.

Section 27
Accommodation, Food Services, and Other Services

This section presents statistics relating to services other than those covered in the previous sections on wholesale and retail trade, transportation, communications, financial services, and recreation services. Data shown for services are classified by kind of business and cover sales or receipts, establishments, employees, payrolls, and other items.

The principal sources of these data are from the U.S. Census Bureau and include the Economic Census, Service Annual Survey, and the County Business Patterns program.

Data on these services also appear in several other sections. For instance, employment and earnings data appear in Section 12, Labor Force, Employment, and Earnings; gross domestic product of the industry (Table 708) appears in Section 13, Income, Expenditures, Poverty, and Wealth; and financial data from the quarterly *Statistics of Income Bulletin*, published by the Internal Revenue Service, appear in Section 15, Business Enterprise.

Censuses—Limited coverage of the service industries started in 1933. Beginning with the 1967 Economic Census, legislation provides for a census to be conducted every 5 years (for years ending in "2" and "7"). For more information on the most current census, see the Census Bureau's Economic Census website at <www.census.gov/programs-surveys/economic-census.html>. The industries covered in the censuses and surveys of business are defined in the North American Industry Classification System (NAICS). For information on NAICS, see the Census website at <www.census.gov/naics/>.

In general, the 2012 and 2017 Economic Censuses have three series of publications for these sectors: 1) subject series with reports such as product lines, and establishment and firm sizes, 2) geographic reports with individual reports for each state, and 3) industry series with individual reports for industry groups. Data from the 2022 Economic Census are being released on a flow basis between January 2024 and March 2026.

Current surveys—The Service Annual Survey provides annual estimates of nationwide receipts for selected personal, business, leasing and repair, amusement and entertainment, social and health, and other professional service industries in the United States. For selected social, health, and other professional service industries, separate estimates are developed for receipts of taxable firms and revenue and expenses for firms and organizations exempt from federal income taxes. Several service sectors included in the survey are covered in other sections of this publication. The estimates for tax exempt firms in these industries are derived from a sample of employer firms only. Estimates obtained from annual and monthly surveys are based on sample data and are not expected to agree exactly with results that would be obtained from a complete census of all establishments. Data include estimates for sampling units not reporting. Data are released in the *Annual Services Report* at <www.census.gov/programs-surveys/sas.html>. The *Quarterly Services Report* is a principal economic indicator that produces, for selected service industries, quarterly estimates of total operating revenue and the percentage of revenue by class of customer (government, business, household consumers/individual users). Data can be found at <www.census.gov/services/index.html>.

Statistical reliability—For a discussion of statistical collection and estimation, sampling procedures, and measures of statistical reliability applicable to Census Bureau data, see Appendix III.

Table 1291. Selected Service-Related Industries—Establishments, Sales, Payroll, and Employees by Kind of Business: 2022

[2,807,043,811 represents $2,807,043,811,000. Covers only establishments with payroll. Based on the 2022 Economic Census; for statement on methodology, see Appendix III]

Kind of business	NAICS code [1]	Establish-ments, (number)	Sales or receipts ($1,000)	Annual payroll ($1,000)	Paid employees [2] (number)
Professional, scientific, and technical services................	54	976,264	2,807,043,811	1,054,227,072	11,569,939
Management of companies and enterprises....................	55	54,225	(S)	486,949,803	4,492,037
Administrative and support and waste management and remediation services...	56	455,718	1,470,962,350	672,352,679	14,349,374
Administrative and support services..........................	561	426,554	1,332,540,047	640,685,192	13,817,470
Waste management and remediation services..............	562	29,164	138,422,303	31,667,487	531,904
Accommodation and food services............................	72	770,895	1,227,364,148	339,888,325	14,091,274
Accommodation...	721	70,306	301,023,093	66,084,814	1,824,371
Food services and drinking places............................	722	700,589	926,341,055	273,803,511	12,266,903
Other services (except public administration) [3]................	81	595,822	715,750,643	174,450,084	3,997,373
Repair and maintenance..	811	225,446	248,309,018	68,828,443	1,453,795
Personal and laundry services.................................	812	265,282	145,534,463	47,223,837	1,579,123
Religious, grantmaking, civic, professional, and similar organizations......................................	813	105,094	321,907,162	58,397,804	964,455

S Data do not meet publication standards. [1] North American Industrial Classification System, 2022; see text, Section 15. [2] For employees on the payroll during the pay period including March 12. [3] Excludes Religious Organizations (NAICS 8131), Labor Unions and Similar Labor Organizations (NAICS 81393), Political Organizations (NAICS 81394), and Private Households (NAICS 814).

Source: U.S. Census Bureau, 2022 Economic Census, "EC2200BASIC: All Sectors: Summary Statistics for the U.S.: 2022," <data.census.gov>, accessed June 2024.

Table 1292. Selected Service-Related Industries—Nonemployer Establishments and Receipts by Kind of Business: 2019 to 2021

[3,773 represents 3,773,000. Includes only firms subject to federal income tax. Nonemployers are businesses with no paid employees. Data originate chiefly from administrative records of the Internal Revenue Service; see Appendix III]

Kind of business	NAICS code [1]	Firms (1,000)			Receipts (mil. dol.)		
		2019	2020	2021	2019	2020	2021
Professional, scientific, and technical services...............	**54**	**3,773**	**3,690**	**3,832**	**185,148**	**178,993**	**201,674**
Professional, scientific, and technical services [2]................	541	3,773	3,690	3,832	185,148	178,993	201,674
Legal services...	5411	290	285	287	21,791	20,324	21,775
Accounting, tax preparation, bookkeeping, and payroll services..	5412	385	378	381	11,437	11,259	12,043
Architectural, engineering, and related services..............	5413	232	226	230	12,790	12,276	13,209
Specialized design services...................................	5414	254	254	269	10,339	9,787	11,718
Computer systems design and related services..............	5415	339	324	339	16,931	17,033	18,458
Management, scientific and technical consulting..............	5416	920	915	979	46,161	45,896	53,325
Scientific research and development services................	5417	53	48	54	1,804	1,734	1,969
Advertising, public relations, and related services............	5418	172	168	181	9,649	9,273	10,659
Administrative and support and waste management and remediation services..	**56**	**2,596**	**2,555**	**2,608**	**62,643**	**60,882**	**68,089**
Administrative and support services [2]...........................	561	2,577	2,534	2,586	60,883	59,062	66,126
Office administrative services.................................	5611	302	299	317	5,673	5,573	6,323
Business support services....................................	5614	233	230	237	6,995	6,637	7,293
Services to buildings and dwellings..........................	5617	1,633	1,641	1,645	36,288	36,968	40,944
Waste management and remediation services................	562	19	20	22	1,760	1,819	1,964
Accommodation and food services............................	**72**	**497**	**492**	**571**	**19,481**	**17,343**	**21,294**
Accommodation...	721	113	79	83	4,533	3,830	4,506
Food services and drinking places............................	722	384	413	488	14,948	13,513	16,788
Special food services..	7223	248	277	346	6,567	6,090	8,276
Drinking places (alcoholic beverages)........................	7224	27	23	25	1,650	1,194	1,498
Restaurants and other eating places.........................	7225	109	113	117	6,730	6,229	7,014
Full-service restaurants....................................	722511	49	50	51	3,185	2,975	3,265
Limited-service eating places...............................	722513	36	39	40	2,720	2,462	2,750
Other services (except public administration)...............	**81**	**2,852**	**2,812**	**2,936**	**90,930**	**81,192**	**98,420**
Repair and maintenance [2]..	811	551	554	554	25,625	25,534	27,539
Automotive repair and maintenance...........................	8111	323	334	339	15,522	15,665	16,899
Personal and household goods repair and maintenance.....	8114	161	155	151	6,520	6,384	6,986
Personal and laundry services [2].................................	812	2,111	2,087	2,205	62,047	52,580	67,698
Personal care services..	8121	1,307	1,277	1,341	37,103	29,387	40,098
Hair, nail, and skin care services..........................	81211	1,140	1,119	1,175	32,267	25,527	34,930
Beauty salons..	812112	758	740	774	19,640	15,914	21,145
Death care services...	8122	15	15	15	885	939	951
Drycleaning and laundry services............................	8123	24	23	23	1,651	1,366	1,510
Other personal services.......................................	8129	764	771	826	22,408	20,888	25,139
Religious, grantmaking, civic, professional, and similar organizations...	813	190	171	177	3,258	3,078	3,183

[1] Based on North American Industry Classification System (NAICS), 2017. See text, Section 15. [2] Includes other kinds of business not shown separately.

Source: U.S. Census Bureau, Nonemployer Statistics, "All Sectors: Nonemployer Statistics by Legal Form of Organization and Receipts Size Class for the U.S., States, and Selected Geographies: 2021," and previous releases, <data.census.gov>, accessed March 2024.

Table 1293. Selected Service-Related Industries—Establishments, Employees, and Payroll by Industry: 2021 and 2022

[In thousands (962.5 represents 962,500); payroll in billions of dollars (981.4 represents $981,400,000,000). Covers establishments with paid employees. Excludes self-employed individuals, employees of private households, railroad employees, agricultural production employees, and most government employees; see source for NAICS and other exclusions. For statement on methodology, see Appendix III]

Industry	NAICS code [1]	Establishments (1,000)		Employees [2] (1,000)		Annual payroll (bil. dol.)	
		2021	2022	2021	2022	2021	2022
Professional, scientific, & technical services...............	**54**	**962.5**	**974.3**	**9,531.5**	**10,152.1**	**981.4**	**1,067.8**
Professional, scientific, & technical services...................	541	962.5	974.3	9,531.5	10,152.1	981.4	1,067.8
Legal services..	5411	182.5	181.9	1,144.3	1,183.6	129.4	138.1
Offices of lawyers...	54111	168.0	167.0	1,045.1	1,078.1	122.3	130.7
Accounting, tax preparation, bookkeeping, and payroll services.......................................	5412	140.0	136.0	1,174.1	1,231.0	83.6	93.1
Offices of certified public accountants.....................	541211	55.3	55.6	535.3	572.9	49.5	56.1
Tax preparation services..................................	541213	33.3	28.4	154.3	131.6	2.7	3.2
Architectural, engineering, & related services [3].............	5413	116.3	117.1	1,585.9	1,663.0	150.3	164.6
Architectural services....................................	54131	22.2	22.6	171.3	182.1	15.8	17.5
Engineering services.....................................	54133	62.5	62.6	1,146.3	1,199.6	115.9	126.9
Specialized design services [3]..............................	5414	35.9	37.3	117.7	129.4	8.1	9.1
Graphic design services..................................	54143	15.9	15.9	49.0	51.4	3.1	3.4
Computer systems design & related services [3]............	5415	144.3	145.2	2,019.0	2,126.6	247.7	261.7
Custom computer programming services.................	541511	67.3	68.0	944.6	1,044.5	121.5	132.7
Computer systems design services....................	541512	59.2	58.3	830.9	815.8	100.5	98.2
Management, scientific, & technical consulting services [3]......................................	5416	206.5	215.7	1,486.7	1,625.1	150.4	169.6
Management consulting services......................	54161	170.9	178.4	1,242.9	1,368.0	128.5	145.8
Environmental consulting services....................	54162	10.3	10.1	93.4	96.2	7.4	7.8
Scientific research & development services.................	5417	21.3	22.2	871.9	950.9	131.8	142.6
Research & development in the physical engineering & life sciences......................................	54171	19.2	20.1	827.4	902.9	128.2	138.5
Advertising & related services [3].............................	5418	38.2	38.7	432.4	467.2	38.3	42.2
Advertising agencies.....................................	54181	14.6	15.0	176.9	195.3	18.8	20.5
Public relations agencies.................................	54182	8.6	8.6	54.7	62.4	6.6	7.4
Other professional, scientific, & technical services..........	5419	77.5	80.3	699.4	775.4	41.6	47.0
Veterinary services.......................................	54194	32.6	34.0	420.2	468.6	19.6	22.7
Management of companies and enterprises...............	**55**	**52.1**	**51.2**	**3,484.2**	**3,662.0**	**434.6**	**464.5**
Administrative and support and waste management and remediation services...................................	**56**	**447.5**	**450.5**	**12,509.6**	**13,578.7**	**672.9**	**764.3**
Administrative & support services [3]........................	561	419.9	421.9	12,054.2	13,100.3	643.3	731.5
Employment services.....................................	5613	58.1	56.8	7,090.8	7,961.9	417.2	483.8
Temporary help services.............................	56132	41.2	39.4	3,497.2	3,929.0	152.9	177.0
Business support services [3]..............................	5614	32.3	31.0	781.2	763.8	35.9	36.6
Telephone call centers...............................	56142	4.9	4.5	455.0	436.6	15.1	15.5
Collection agencies..................................	56144	3.3	3.1	114.6	106.2	5.5	5.4
Travel arrangement & reservation services.................	5615	15.4	15.6	155.6	169.7	13.6	16.0
Travel agencies..	56151	9.3	9.4	74.7	77.6	6.6	7.2
Investigation & security services...........................	5616	26.8	26.5	962.5	976.6	34.0	36.5
Investigation, guard, & armored car services...........	56161	15.2	15.5	821.3	834.4	25.2	27.2
Security systems services............................	56162	11.6	11.0	141.1	142.2	8.8	9.3
Services to buildings & dwellings [3]........................	5617	221.1	225.0	2,014.3	2,106.8	74.2	81.9
Landscaping services....................................	56173	115.2	117.1	741.3	774.0	35.2	38.5
Waste management & remediation services.................	562	27.6	28.6	455.4	478.4	29.5	32.8
Waste collection...	5621	12.4	12.7	240.6	249.0	15.2	16.8
Waste treatment & disposal...............................	5622	3.1	3.2	61.6	62.8	4.5	4.7
Remediation & other waste management services.........	5629	12.2	12.7	153.2	166.7	9.8	11.2
Accommodation & food services..........................	**72**	**745.9**	**771.9**	**12,142.3**	**13,793.5**	**298.8**	**353.1**
Accommodation..	721	70.8	71.4	1,515.6	1,793.8	54.8	68.4
Traveler accommodation [3]................................	7211	61.3	61.8	1,464.3	1,735.3	52.7	65.9
Hotels (except casino hotels) & motels....................	72111	56.5	56.9	1,131.3	1,366.5	38.5	48.9
RV (recreational vehicle) parks & recreational camps......	7212	7.8	8.0	43.2	49.0	1.9	2.2
Food services & drinking places............................	722	675.1	700.5	10,626.7	11,999.7	244.0	284.7
Special food services....................................	7223	52.4	54.1	623.1	730.3	17.5	21.2
Drinking places (alcoholic beverages)....................	7224	38.4	40.3	282.5	401.4	7.7	10.0
Restaurants & other eating places........................	7225	584.3	606.1	9,721.1	10,868.0	218.8	253.5
Full-service restaurants..............................	722511	250.2	257.3	4,361.9	5,208.9	118.3	140.1
Limited-service restaurants...........................	722513	256.4	265.2	4,490.3	4,711.8	84.3	94.0
Cafeterias, grill buffets, & buffets....................	722514	4.8	4.8	55.4	71.0	1.3	1.5
Snack & nonalcoholic beverage bars..................	722515	73.0	78.9	813.5	876.4	14.9	17.9
Other services (except public administration).............	**81**	**781.4**	**797.8**	**5,105.1**	**5,472.0**	**206.3**	**228.2**
Repair & maintenance [3]...................................	811	220.0	223.8	1,280.4	1,351.0	61.9	68.9
Automotive repair & maintenance.........................	8111	165.0	167.9	904.3	958.9	39.4	44.2
Personal & household goods repair & maintenance........	8114	21.5	22.1	73.1	77.2	3.0	3.3
Personal & laundry services [3].............................	812	254.4	266.0	1,344.8	1,495.2	43.1	48.0
Personal care services...................................	8121	148.0	156.6	676.1	743.5	18.9	21.7
Death care services.....................................	8122	20.5	20.5	132.7	143.2	5.9	6.3
Drycleaning & laundry services...........................	8123	30.0	29.6	230.7	247.5	8.0	8.7
Religious/grantmaking/civic/professional [4]..................	813	307.0	308.0	2,480.0	2,625.8	101.4	111.3
Religious organizations..................................	8131	185.7	185.6	1,481.4	1,538.2	39.2	42.3
Grantmaking & giving services...........................	8132	21.6	21.9	192.7	207.7	14.9	16.6
Social advocacy organizations...........................	8133	19.2	20.3	186.9	204.1	11.2	12.8
Civic & social organizations..............................	8134	24.5	24.8	167.0	203.8	5.2	6.2
Business/professional/labor/political [4].....................	8139	56.0	55.5	452.0	471.9	30.9	33.5
Labor unions [4]..	81393	13.0	12.8	126.5	131.6	6.2	6.6

[1] Data based on North American Industry Classification System (NAICS) 2017. See text, section 15. [2] Includes employees on the payroll for the pay period including March 12. [3] Includes other kinds of business, not shown separately. [4] Also includes other similar organizations.

Source: U.S. Census Bureau, County Business Patterns, "County Business Patterns, including ZIP Code Business Patterns, by Legal Form of Organization and Employment Size Class for the U.S., States, and Selected Geographies: 2022," <data.census.gov>, accessed June 2024.

Table 1294. Employed Persons in Service Industries by Sex, Race, and Hispanic Origin and by Industry: 2023

[20,735 represents 20,735,000. Civilian noninstitutionalized population 16 years and older. Based on the Current Population Survey (CPS); see text, Section 1, and Appendix III. For information on employees in other sectors, see Table 647 and Table 665]

Industry	Total employed (1,000)	Percent of total				
		Female	White [1]	Black [1]	Asian [1]	Hispanic or Latino [2]
Professional and business services....................................	**20,735**	**42.2**	**75.5**	**10.9**	**10.0**	**17.6**
Professional and technical services...................................	**13,726**	**42.7**	**75.1**	**8.5**	**13.3**	**10.3**
Legal services..	1,738	57.9	82.7	9.8	4.7	11.8
Accounting, tax preparation, bookkeeping, and payroll services....................................	1,236	60.0	77.9	9.2	11.0	10.1
Architectural, engineering, and related services....................	1,883	26.3	82.7	6.5	7.6	10.3
Specialized design services..	454	60.2	80.1	7.9	9.1	13.2
Computer systems design and related services...................	4,107	27.8	64.4	8.5	24.0	8.4
Management, scientific, and technical consulting services............	2,002	43.8	76.9	9.3	10.8	9.2
Scientific research and development services........................	831	48.5	68.2	8.9	17.6	11.7
Advertising, public relations, and related services....................	617	52.9	78.9	11.2	7.3	11.9
Veterinary services..	436	82.5	89.6	2.7	2.7	12.9
Other professional, scientific, and technical services..................	422	54.3	83.1	6.9	6.0	17.8
Management, administrative, and waste services....................	**7,009**	**41.4**	**76.4**	**15.7**	**3.5**	**31.8**
Management of companies and enterprises..........................	91	46.6	72.5	10.6	9.3	22.4
Administrative and support services................................	6,344	43.1	76.2	16.0	3.6	32.7
Employment services..	866	61.0	70.8	18.7	7.1	20.7
Business support services......................................	605	68.1	71.6	21.3	3.8	20.4
Travel arrangement and reservation services......................	349	60.3	77.4	11.4	7.8	17.7
Investigations and security services.............................	896	26.7	59.0	31.4	4.7	18.6
Services to buildings and dwellings.............................	1,680	57.0	80.9	12.9	1.9	45.8
Landscaping services..	1,491	10.7	85.7	8.1	1.5	46.5
Other administrative and support services........................	457	49.1	77.2	14.1	3.9	17.6
Waste management and remediation services........................	573	21.7	79.3	13.6	2.3	23.8
Accommodation and food services.................................	**10,759**	**53.0**	**73.3**	**12.8**	**8.0**	**29.0**
Accommodation..	1,279	58.7	68.6	16.3	8.9	30.5
Traveler accommodation..	1,186	59.3	67.3	17.0	9.3	32.4
Recreational vehicle parks and camps, and rooming and board houses...............................	93	51.7	85.3	7.3	3.3	6.4
Food services and drinking places.................................	9,479	52.3	73.9	12.3	7.8	28.8
Restaurants and other food services.............................	9,270	52.2	73.7	12.3	7.9	28.9
Drinking places, alcoholic beverages............................	209	53.9	83.2	10.1	3.0	21.6
Other services...	**7,605**	**53.3**	**77.8**	**10.9**	**7.8**	**21.7**
Other services (except private households)...........................	6,932	49.6	77.4	10.8	8.2	19.5
Repair and maintenance..	2,155	13.2	84.9	8.0	3.3	27.9
Automotive repair and maintenance.............................	1,353	12.3	85.3	7.3	3.5	29.5
Car washes..	209	20.6	78.3	16.9	1.8	37.7
Electronic and precision equipment repair and maintenance..	89	19.1	80.9	6.1	8.0	16.0
Commercial and industrial machinery and equipment repair and maintenance..	325	5.9	87.4	8.4	1.3	22.0
Personal and household goods repair and maintenance..	178	21.8	87.0	3.0	4.5	21.2
Personal and laundry services....................................	2,746	73.2	69.7	11.8	14.8	19.4
Barber shops..	164	33.9	64.2	29.9	3.3	40.6
Beauty salons...	1,008	89.2	74.2	13.3	10.0	17.3
Nail salons and other personal care services......................	625	77.2	49.9	6.3	39.0	15.7
Drycleaning and laundry services................................	232	52.4	68.1	14.6	15.5	35.1
Funeral homes, cemeteries, and crematories......................	129	38.2	73.8	15.9	0.0	15.3
Other personal services..	588	68.2	84.5	8.1	3.5	15.6
Membership associations and organizations..........................	2,031	56.2	80.0	12.4	4.4	10.6
Religious organizations..	987	48.6	82.3	10.6	4.7	9.3
Civic, social, advocacy organizations, grantmaking and giving services..	805	66.9	75.3	16.0	4.1	11.8
Labor unions..	94	36.7	86.4	8.9	1.6	19.2
Business, professional, political, and similar organizations.......................................	145	61.5	86.3	6.1	5.2	6.6
Other services, private households.................................	673	92.0	81.8	11.9	3.9	44.8

[1] The Current Population Survey (CPS) allows respondents to choose more than one race. Data represent persons who selected this race group only and exclude persons reporting more than one race. See also comments on race in text for Section 1. [2] Persons of Hispanic origin may be of any race.

Source: U.S. Bureau of Labor Statistics, CPS Tables, "Employed persons by detailed industry, sex, race, and Hispanic or Latino ethnicity," <www.bls.gov/cps/tables.htm>, accessed March 2024.

Table 1295. Selected Service-Related Industries—Establishments, Employees, and Annual Payroll by State: 2022

[Employees in thousands (10,152 represents 10,152,000); payroll in millions of dollars (1,067,844 represents $1,067,844,000,000). Covers establishments with paid employees. Excludes most government employees, railroad employees, and self-employed persons. Data are from Census Bureau's County Business Patterns program. For statement on methodology, see Appendix III]

State	Professional, scientific, and technical services (NAICS 54) [1]			Administrative and support and waste management and remediation services (NAICS 56) [1]			Accommodation and food services (NAICS 72) [1]		
	Establish- ments	Employ- ees [2] (1,000)	Annual payroll (mil. dol.)	Establish- ments	Employ- ees [2] (1,000)	Annual payroll (mil. dol.)	Establish- ments	Employ- ees [2] (1,000)	Annual payroll (mil. dol.)
United States.........	974,303	10,152	1,067,844	450,481	13,579	764,277	771,856	13,793	353,090
Alabama...............	9,682	117	10,229	5,111	168	6,868	9,911	182	3,707
Alaska.................	1,973	20	1,724	1,262	20	1,158	2,268	27	943
Arizona................	20,330	191	16,099	9,474	296	14,243	14,565	320	8,339
Arkansas..............	6,177	40	2,627	3,081	81	3,015	6,457	110	2,232
California.............	142,540	1,431	188,864	48,607	1,780	128,457	94,672	1,700	51,294
Colorado..............	28,086	237	25,091	9,799	221	12,393	15,108	292	8,410
Connecticut...........	9,102	112	12,875	5,482	89	5,197	8,964	134	3,769
Delaware..............	4,094	38	4,609	1,734	33	1,607	2,370	43	1,027
District of Columbia.....	5,703	114	17,940	1,063	32	1,839	2,762	62	2,333
Florida................	92,313	603	53,125	42,040	2,324	132,724	47,658	992	26,416
Georgia...............	32,446	331	31,652	14,412	445	21,826	23,980	446	9,873
Hawaii................	3,417	25	2,002	1,900	67	3,097	3,969	92	3,512
Idaho.................	5,724	43	3,310	3,243	49	2,416	4,521	78	1,592
Illinois................	38,012	451	52,719	17,253	495	25,347	29,808	493	12,709
Indiana................	13,212	145	12,573	8,230	230	9,315	14,536	277	5,652
Iowa..................	6,461	64	4,709	4,053	100	4,267	7,433	120	2,408
Kansas................	7,136	73	5,847	3,835	97	4,960	6,537	117	2,333
Kentucky..............	8,270	76	5,321	4,411	116	4,391	8,608	173	3,445
Louisiana..............	12,400	99	7,687	5,134	106	4,936	10,522	195	4,448
Maine.................	3,662	32	2,671	2,460	24	1,066	4,351	51	1,684
Maryland..............	21,432	299	31,993	8,648	278	13,578	12,550	228	5,866
Massachusetts.........	21,931	360	52,074	11,808	236	14,617	17,837	288	8,942
Michigan..............	22,097	307	29,191	13,542	366	15,871	21,364	373	8,380
Minnesota.............	16,161	190	17,584	7,956	172	9,138	12,302	228	5,401
Mississippi............	4,620	33	2,071	2,491	57	1,800	6,229	130	2,698
Missouri...............	13,768	177	15,451	7,820	173	8,361	13,586	254	5,670
Montana...............	4,233	22	1,542	2,200	22	798	3,850	55	1,294
Nebraska..............	4,738	42	3,162	2,941	97	6,651	4,832	78	1,548
Nevada................	10,537	70	5,719	5,118	124	5,344	7,757	293	10,738
New Hampshire.........	3,752	39	3,979	2,596	62	3,716	3,886	59	1,624
New Jersey............	28,935	339	37,766	14,590	389	20,428	22,256	313	8,899
New Mexico............	4,589	59	5,207	2,041	38	1,535	4,623	92	2,146
New York..............	61,831	674	81,400	27,425	809	76,382	54,598	736	24,149
North Carolina.........	27,428	273	25,816	14,745	308	13,985	23,624	446	9,770
North Dakota..........	1,887	17	1,252	1164	14	629	2,157	33	724
Ohio..................	23,623	271	23,337	14,185	433	20,634	25,606	474	9,532
Oklahoma.............	9,944	84	6,141	4,765	123	6,601	8,910	163	3,322
Oregon................	13,188	108	10,165	6,398	113	5,444	12,293	177	4,785
Pennsylvania...........	30,244	359	35,355	16,748	348	17,223	29,051	454	10,140
Rhode Island...........	3,077	25	2,016	1,935	26	1,397	3,231	51	1,408
South Carolina.........	12,226	108	8,538	6,872	308	14,613	11,875	232	5,188
South Dakota..........	2,165	14	924	1,331	12	552	2,656	41	893
Tennessee.............	12,334	137	11,635	8,013	289	12,090	15,199	303	7,023
Texas.................	81,011	839	85,747	32,532	1,145	58,867	64,929	1,269	29,314
Utah..................	13,166	113	8,992	5,419	185	9,371	6,740	135	2,959
Vermont...............	2,081	14	1,118	1,250	10	399	1,968	31	823
Virginia...............	31,844	541	58,676	11,667	275	14,698	19,204	347	8,190
Washington............	23,454	241	26,556	10,866	175	10,537	18,798	286	8,728
West Virginia..........	2,637	24	1,552	1,526	32	1,256	3,658	64	1,262
Wisconsin..............	11,562	121	10,310	8,044	179	8,287	15,405	233	4,794
Wyoming..............	3,068	12	904	1,261	8	355	1,882	28	755

[1] North American Industry Classification System, 2017. See text, section 15. [2] For employees on the payroll for the pay period including March 12.

Source: U.S. Census Bureau, County Business Patterns, CB2200CBP, "County Business Patterns, including ZIP Code Business Patterns, by Legal Form of Organization and Employment Size Class for the U.S., States, and Selected Geographies: 2022," <data.census.gov>, accessed June 2024.

Table 1296. Professional, Scientific, and Technical Services—Estimated Revenue by Kind of Business: 2017 to 2022

[In millions of dollars (1,806,506 represents $1,806,506,000,000). For taxable employer firms. Estimates have been adjusted to the results of the 2017 Economic Census. Based on the Service Annual Survey and administrative data; see Appendix III]

Kind of business	NAICS code [1]	2017	2018	2019	2020	2021	2022
Professional, scientific, and technical services (except notaries) [2]	54	1,806,506	1,912,658	2,019,304	2,070,612	2,309,706	2,548,675
Offices of lawyers	54111	279,613	280,229	288,889	290,435	315,836	337,392
Other legal services	54119	14,269	15,016	16,392	18,866	21,739	20,289
Offices of certified public accountants	541211	103,314	108,169	113,381	116,187	122,350	132,248
Tax preparation services	541213	7,053	7,375	7,715	7,550	8,620	9,388
Payroll services	541214	21,946	21,794	23,929	24,637	26,729	27,589
Other accounting services	541219	20,067	20,273	21,950	23,096	26,976	29,644
Architectural services	54131	37,805	40,516	43,237	42,182	46,529	51,413
Landscape architectural services	54132	4,144	4,427	4,574	4,738	5,056	5,778
Engineering services	54133	237,304	249,085	264,653	259,888	274,912	305,233
Drafting services	54134	1,140	1,232	1,276	1,325	1,345	1,416
Building inspection services	54135	2,741	3,013	3,386	3,679	4,045	4,502
Surveying and mapping services [3]	5413z	8,809	9,693	10,546	9,769	10,244	11,745
Testing laboratories	54138	20,551	21,426	23,115	24,010	24,790	27,518
Drafting, building inspection, and mapping services [4]	5413x	12,690	13,938	15,208	14,773	15,634	17,663
Interior design services	54141	12,203	12,753	13,591	14,067	17,073	19,278
Industrial design services	54142	2,162	2,261	2,498	2,842	3,216	3,404
Graphic design services	54143	8,551	8,597	9,342	9,521	11,044	12,610
Other specialized design services	54149	1,966	1,905	2,051	1,829	2,256	2,890
All other design services [5]	5414y	4,128	4,166	4,549	4,671	5,472	6,294
Computer systems design and related services	5415	442,827	485,246	495,843	516,726	582,597	648,805
Management consulting services	54161	214,126	224,169	236,012	241,827	275,554	307,310
Environmental consulting services	54162	15,590	17,084	17,189	17,081	17,494	20,680
Other scientific and technical consulting services	54169	29,116	30,575	34,300	34,074	39,091	45,622
Research and development in physical, engineering and life sciences	54171	112,693	123,778	143,835	159,848	195,188	217,187
Research and development in social sciences and humanities	54172	2,294	2,611	2,763	2,947	3,370	3,918
Advertising agencies	54181	46,241	50,220	51,186	50,796	56,078	63,832
Public relations agencies	54182	12,505	13,813	14,066	14,536	16,551	19,688
Media buying agencies	54183	8,780	9,316	10,063	9,659	11,204	11,937
Media representatives	54184	14,137	19,330	25,214	29,055	32,538	32,263
Outdoor advertising	54185	7,979	7,820	8,231	6,554	7,547	8,782
Direct mail advertising	54186	9,598	9,511	9,818	9,470	9,980	11,739
Advertising material distribution services	54187	3,611	3,516	3,499	3,526	4,232	4,976
Other services related to advertising	54189	14,767	15,414	15,856	14,525	15,274	17,742
All other advertising [6]	5418y	18,378	18,930	19,355	18,051	19,506	22,718
Marketing research and public opinion polling	54191	19,830	20,928	23,174	23,433	24,461	29,106
Photography studios, portrait	541921	4,153	4,246	4,465	3,284	3,855	4,762
Commercial photography	541922	2,131	2,310	2,250	1,867	2,266	2,849
Translation and interpretation services	54193	4,449	4,973	5,307	5,748	6,181	6,560
Veterinary services	54194	41,693	42,087	45,763	50,736	58,925	59,182
All other professional, scientific, and technical services	54199	16,348	17,947	19,945	20,299	24,560	29,398

[1] Data are based on the 2012 North American Industry Classification System (NAICS). See text Section 15 for more information. [2] Excludes NAICS 54112 (Offices of Notaries). [3] Includes NAICS 54136 (Geophysical Surveying and Mapping Services) and NAICS 54137 (Surveying and Mapping Services, except Geophysical Services). [4] Includes NAICS 54134 (Drafting Services), NAICS 54135 (Building Inspection Services), NAICS 54136 (Geophysical Surveying and Mapping Services), and NAICS 54137 (Surveying and Mapping (except Geophysical) Services). [5] Includes NAICS 54142 (Industrial Design Services) and NAICS 54149 (Other Specialized Design Services). [6] Includes NAICS 54187 (Advertising Material Distribution Services) and NAICS 54189 (Other Services Related to Advertising).

Source: U.S. Census Bureau, Service Annual Survey, "Service Annual Survey Latest Data (NAICS-basis): 2022," <www.census.gov/programs-surveys/sas/data.html>, accessed February 2024.

Table 1297. Administrative and Support and Waste Management and Remediation Services—Estimated Revenue by Kind of Business: 2017 to 2022

[In millions of dollars (950,896 represents $950,896,000,000). For taxable and tax-exempt employer firms. Estimates have been adjusted to results of the 2017 Economic Census. Based on the Service Annual Survey and administrative data; see Appendix III]

Kind of business	NAICS code [1]	2017	2018	2019	2020	2021	2022
Administrative and support and waste management and remediation services.........	**56**	**950,896**	**1,022,728**	**1,087,967**	**1,030,128**	**1,187,247**	**1,327,554**
Administrative and support services...............	**561**	**851,306**	**915,903**	**976,918**	**918,523**	**1,062,928**	**1,190,880**
Office administrative services............................	5611	58,930	60,887	63,159	63,910	66,930	79,573
Facilities support services................................	5612	28,571	32,074	33,514	29,266	27,458	31,163
Employment placement agencies & executive search services............................	56131	19,313	22,353	23,803	23,985	38,116	39,668
Temporary help services................................	56132	180,118	188,685	195,135	184,266	231,056	277,443
Professional employer organizations...................	56133	177,827	191,600	209,786	200,148	(S)	220,095
Document preparation services........................	56141	3,285	3,320	3,403	3,537	3,461	3,727
Telephone answering services.........................	561421	2,226	2,333	2,368	2,196	2,436	2,555
Telemarketing bureaus and other contact centers....	561422	19,486	21,737	20,099	20,459	23,764	22,618
Private mail centers.......................................	561431	2,829	2,981	3,018	3,270	4,048	5,067
Other business service centers (including copy shops)...	561439	6,243	5,948	7,718	8,074	7,836	(S)
Collection agencies.......................................	56144	15,171	15,325	16,280	15,269	14,247	12,587
Credit bureaus...	56145	10,152	10,613	11,082	12,647	15,419	15,581
Repossession services..................................	561491	998	1,014	1,081	921	983	1,160
Court reporting and stenotype services...............	561492	2,426	2,530	2,799	2,384	2,977	3,653
All other business support services...................	561499	8,939	9,539	9,718	9,345	9,431	10,330
Travel agencies...	56151	27,512	31,089	32,959	17,178	23,516	35,264
Tour operators...	56152	8,425	9,653	9,892	3,726	3,799	8,736
Convention and visitors bureaus......................	561591	2,239	2,396	2,513	1,908	1,943	2,717
All other travel arrangement and reservation services......................................	561599	16,996	17,951	20,392	11,426	17,259	25,137
Investigation services....................................	561611	5,893	6,325	6,247	6,088	7,229	7,850
Security guards and patrol services...................	561612	29,617	28,724	32,002	30,610	29,492	32,222
Armored car services....................................	561613	3,110	3,260	3,464	3,419	3,712	4,162
Security systems services (except locksmiths)........	561621	22,268	23,433	25,983	25,016	26,045	28,295
Locksmiths...	561622	2,016	2,131	2,380	2,351	2,579	2,701
Exterminating and pest control services...............	56171	13,089	14,886	16,390	17,612	20,442	21,466
Janitorial services..	56172	49,680	55,336	59,049	60,911	65,197	72,795
Landscaping services....................................	56173	77,034	87,008	95,387	98,637	112,671	130,672
Carpet and upholstery cleaning services..............	56174	3,426	3,529	3,764	4,032	4,710	4,906
Other services to buildings and dwellings..............	56179	7,891	8,827	9,807	9,916	11,926	13,533
Packaging and labeling services........................	56191	7,299	7,958	8,304	9,003	10,222	14,009
Convention and trade show organizers................	56192	16,361	17,256	18,606	10,129	10,546	17,175
All other support services...............................	56199	21,936	25,202	26,816	26,884	31,538	35,554
Waste management and remediation services. ..	**562**	**99,590**	**106,825**	**111,049**	**111,605**	**124,319**	**136,674**
Solid waste collection....................................	562111	49,228	53,455	56,534	55,036	61,199	66,944
Hazardous waste collection............................	562112	2,100	2,074	2,063	(S)	2,507	(S)
Other waste collection...................................	562119	1,926	2,286	2,578	2,962	3,722	4,244
Hazardous waste treatment and disposal..............	562211	8,712	8,579	8,749	8,548	8,978	8,876
Solid waste landfill..	562212	7,535	7,791	8,479	8,496	9,212	11,239
Solid waste combustors and incinerators..............	562213	1,275	1,314	1,180	1,148	(S)	(S)
Other nonhazardous waste treatment and disposal...	562219	815	958	1,048	1,010	1,202	1,347
Remediation services....................................	56291	16,076	17,486	17,014	18,354	20,405	22,102
Materials recovery facilities.............................	56292	5,940	6,420	6,514	6,947	7,720	8,053
Septic tank and related services.......................	562991	3,920	4,376	4,645	4,736	5,475	6,348
All other miscellaneous waste management services..................................	562998	2,063	2,086	2,245	2,143	2,693	3,058

S Figure does not meet publication standards. [1] Data are based on the 2012 North American Industry Classification System (NAICS). See text Section 15 for more information.

Source: U.S. Census Bureau, Service Annual Survey, "Service Annual Survey Latest Data (NAICS-basis): 2022," <www.census.gov/programs-surveys/sas/data.html>, accessed February 2024.

Table 1298. Selected Service Industries Revenue—Total and from Electronic Sources: 2021 and 2022

[18,784,631 represents $18,784,631,000,000. Data shown for service businesses with paid employees. Revenues from electronic sources include revenues from customers entering orders directly on a firm's website or mobile application, entering orders directly on third party websites or mobile applications, and entering orders via any other electronic system (such as private networks, dedicated lines, kiosks, etc.). Based on the Service Annual Survey, see Appendix III]

Kind of business	NAICS code [1]	Total revenue (million dollars)		Electronic sources revenue (million dollars)		Electronic sources revenue as a percent of total revenue	
		2021	2022	2021	2022	2021	2022
Selected service industries, total............	(X)	18,784,631	20,604,523	1,649,606	1,773,900	8.8	8.6
Utilities [2]...............................	22	642,908	755,516	(S)	(S)	(S)	(S)
Selected transportation and warehousing [3]............	4849y	1,167,343	1,429,998	191,000	231,254	16.4	16.2
Air transportation...............	481	167,354	254,631	78,792	115,114	47.1	45.2
Water transportation...............	483	27,527	50,732	(S)	12,849	(S)	25.3
Truck transportation...............	484	376,903	445,509	36,704	39,193	9.7	8.8
Transit and ground passenger transportation...........	485	45,771	61,192	(S)	(S)	(S)	(S)
Pipeline transportation...............	486	62,906	68,450	(S)	(S)	(S)	(S)
Scenic and sightseeing transportation...........	487	3,489	4,474	1,237	1,546	35.5	34.6
Support activities for transportation...........	488	295,919	346,520	38,999	41,581	13.2	12.0
Information...............	51	2,034,704	2,186,845	601,165	588,612	29.5	26.9
Publishing industries (except internet)............	511	486,814	541,742	164,549	186,599	33.8	34.4
Motion picture and sound recording industries...........	512	115,379	133,855	13,020	13,701	11.3	10.2
Broadcasting (except internet)...............	515	186,820	189,942	2,888	4,033	1.5	2.1
Telecommunications...............	517	655,524	666,715	158,706	140,939	24.2	21.1
Data processing, hosting, and related services...........	518	271,238	308,328	39,059	53,190	14.4	17.3
Other information services...............	519	318,929	346,263	222,943	(S)	69.9	(S)
Finance and insurance [4]...............	52	5,292,263	5,646,954	290,331	306,017	5.5	5.4
Activities related to credit intermediation...........	5223	145,210	152,286	45,716	55,439	31.5	36.4
Securities and commodity contracts intermediation and brokerage...............	5231	311,837	315,918	15,727	16,039	5.0	5.1
Real estate and rental and leasing...............	53	844,438	935,393	66,276	81,759	7.8	8.7
Rental and leasing services...............	532	186,528	210,584	34,651	47,200	18.6	22.4
Selected professional, scientific, and technical services [5]..	54	2,375,859	2,610,968	138,325	141,154	5.8	5.4
Computer systems design and related services...........	5415	582,597	648,805	41,089	44,660	7.1	6.9
Administrative and support and waste management and remediation services...........	56	1,187,247	1,327,554	70,809	95,082	6.0	7.2
Travel arrangement and reservation services...........	5615	46,517	71,854	24,369	31,184	52.4	43.4
Educational services [6]...............	61	78,418	91,629	15,311	17,718	19.5	19.3
Health care and social assistance...............	62	3,099,433	3,263,306	19,130	18,893	0.6	0.6
Arts, entertainment, and recreation..	71	281,848	350,099	37,438	56,734	13.3	16.2
Accommodation and food services [7]............	72	1,067,502	1,266,469	175,453	190,762	16.4	15.1
Other services (except public administration) [8]............	81	712,668	739,792	44,310	45,798	6.2	6.2
Repair and maintenance...............	811	214,530	243,385	3,028	3,317	1.4	1.4
Personal and laundry services...............	812	132,439	153,211	12,630	(S)	9.5	(S)
Religious, grantmaking, civic, professional, and similar organizations...............	813	365,699	343,196	28,652	28,256	7.8	8.2

X Not applicable. S Data do not meet publication standards. [1] North American Industry Classification System (NAICS), 2012; see text Section 15. [2] Excludes government owned utilities. [3] Excludes NAICS 482 (Rail Transportation) and NAICS 491 (Postal Service). [4] Excludes NAICS 525 (Funds, Trusts, and Other Financial Vehicles). [5] Excludes NAICS 54112 (Offices of Notaries). [6] Excludes NAICS 6111 (Elementary and Secondary Schools), NAICS 6112 (Junior Colleges), and NAICS 6113 (Colleges, Universities, and Professional Schools). [7] Prior to 2016, NAICS sector 72 was collected and published by the Annual Retail Trade Report. [8] Excludes NAICS 81311 (Religious Organizations), NAICS 81393 (Labor Unions and Similar Labor Organizations), NAICS 81394 (Political Organizations), and NAICS 814 (Private Households).

Source: U.S. Census Bureau, Service Annual Survey, "Service Annual Survey Latest Data (NAICS-basis): 2022," <www.census.gov/programs-surveys/sas/data.html>, accessed February 2024.

Table 1299. Accommodation and Food Services Revenue by Kind of Business: 2017 to 2022

[In millions of dollars (938,236 represents $938,236,000,000). Based on data from the Service Annual Survey, see headnote Table 1297. Prior to 2016, data were collected and published by the Annual Retail Trade Report]

Kind of business	NAICS code [1]	2017	2018	2019	2020	2021	2022
Accommodation and food services, total.....	72	938,236	988,201	1,038,711	808,089	1,067,502	1,266,469
Accommodation...............	721	260,089	271,287	281,369	167,595	241,794	309,025
Hotels (except casino hotels) and motels..........	72111	184,411	193,160	200,643	115,947	164,840	221,036
Casino hotels...............	72112	65,659	67,351	69,433	42,640	64,521	74,000
Other traveler accommodations...............	72119	1,937	2,115	2,013	1,603	2,340	2,556
RV (recreation vehicle) parks and recreational camps...............	7212	6,337	6,731	7,125	5,496	7,884	8,599
Rooming and boarding houses...............	7213	1,745	1,930	2,155	1,909	2,209	2,834
Food services and drinking places...............	722	678,147	716,914	757,342	640,494	825,708	957,444
Food services contractors...............	72231	45,317	46,476	49,369	35,840	34,474	47,203
Caterers...............	72232	10,934	11,535	11,994	6,906	9,595	12,528
Mobile food services...............	72233	1,179	1,394	1,673	1,729	2,798	3,516
Drinking places (alcoholic beverages)...............	7224	23,936	25,538	26,987	16,335	26,951	32,097
Full-service restaurants...............	722511	298,164	314,226	329,916	252,131	362,934	424,412
Limited-service restaurants...............	722513	253,349	269,097	284,140	280,687	328,087	367,222
Cafeterias, grill buffets, and buffets...............	722514	6,457	6,893	7,275	3,622	5,160	6,503
Snack and nonalcoholic beverage bars...............	722515	38,811	41,755	45,988	43,244	55,709	63,963

[1] North American Industry Classification System (NAICS), 2012; see text, Section 15.

Source: U.S. Census Bureau, Service Annual Survey, "Service Annual Survey Latest Data (NAICS-basis): 2022," <www.census.gov/programs-surveys/sas/data.html>, accessed February 2024.

Table 1300. Other Services—Estimated Revenue for Employer Firms by Kind of Business: 2018 to 2022

[In millions of dollars (569,495 represents $569,495,000,000). For taxable and tax exempt employer firms. Estimates have been adjusted to results of the 2017 Economic Census. Based on the Service Annual Survey; see Appendix III]

Kind of business	NAICS code [1]	2018	2019	2020	2021	2022
Other services (except public administration) [2]	**81**	**569,495**	**597,215**	**581,131**	**712,668**	**739,792**
Repair and maintenance	811	190,473	198,739	189,093	214,530	243,385
General automotive repair	811111	52,971	54,975	51,122	58,246	62,630
Automotive exhaust system repair	811112	625	665	668	832	907
Automotive transmission repair	811113	2,351	2,460	2,576	2,951	3,235
Other automotive mechanical and electrical repair and maintenance	811118	1,985	2,001	1,937	2,192	2,424
Automotive body, paint, interior repair and maintenance	811121	39,602	41,582	39,297	45,368	54,348
Automotive glass replacement shops	811122	4,591	5,111	5,351	6,220	7,440
Automotive oil change and lubrication shops	811191	5,918	6,587	6,834	8,492	10,088
Car washes	811192	10,935	11,487	11,401	14,678	16,268
All other automotive repair and maintenance	811198	2,326	2,440	2,464	2,858	3,278
Consumer electronics repair and maintenance	811211	1,449	1,502	1,622	1,575	1,695
Computer and office machine repair and maintenance	811212	4,436	4,489	4,506	4,568	4,822
Communication equipment repair and maintenance	811213	3,008	3,266	3,272	3,472	3,745
Other electronic and precision equipment repair and maintenance	811219	8,742	8,954	7,894	7,901	8,375
Commercial and industrial machinery and equipment (except automotive and electronic) repair and maintenance	8113	41,937	43,456	40,591	44,060	51,656
Home and garden equipment and appliance repair and maintenance	81141	3,937	3,621	3,754	4,015	4,377
Reupholstery and furniture repair	81142	1,167	1,148	1,023	1,179	1,311
Footwear and leather goods repair	81143	207	204	130	147	178
Other personal and household goods repair and maintenance	81149	4,286	4,791	4,651	5,776	6,608
Personal and laundry services	812	117,465	122,704	107,072	132,439	153,211
Barber shops	812111	1,207	1,452	1,132	1,471	1,819
Beauty shops	812112	24,000	24,865	18,212	22,993	27,035
Nail salons	812113	7,257	8,200	6,408	10,889	12,853
Diet and weight reducing centers	812191	2,002	1,898	1,734	1,764	1,749
Other personal care services	812199	8,971	9,685	8,273	12,070	14,269
Funeral homes and funeral services	81221	14,362	14,430	15,624	17,162	16,940
Cemeteries and crematories	81222	4,319	4,279	4,579	5,809	5,679
Coin-operated laundries and drycleaners	81231	4,560	4,508	4,241	4,842	5,442
Dry-cleaning and laundry services (except coin-operated)	81232	8,139	8,130	5,622	6,582	7,847
Linen supply	812331	4,573	5,002	3,999	4,397	5,221
Industrial launders	812332	9,989	10,983	11,664	11,423	12,405
Pet care (except veterinary) services	81291	6,143	6,666	5,961	8,041	9,973
Photofinishing	81292	1,255	1,218	1,080	1,074	991
Parking lots and garages	81293	9,893	9,861	7,027	8,534	11,295
All other personal services	81299	10,795	11,527	11,516	15,388	19,693
Religious, grantmaking, civic, professional, and similar organizations [3]	813	261,557	275,772	284,966	365,699	343,196
Grantmaking and giving services	8132	125,335	133,735	147,404	211,952	177,865
Social advocacy organizations	8133	36,983	38,928	41,855	48,543	50,677
Civic and social organizations	8134	18,363	19,361	16,935	19,892	23,278
Business, professional, labor, political, and similar organizations [4]	8139	80,876	83,748	78,772	85,312	91,376

[1] Data based on 2012 NAICS. See section 15, Business Enterprise. [2] Excludes NAICS 8131 (Religious Organizations), NAICS 81393 (Labor Unions and Similar Labor Organizations), NAICS 81394 (Political Organizations), and NAICS 814 (Private Households). [3] Excludes NAICS 8131 (Religious Organizations), NAICS 81393 (Labor Unions and Similar Labor Organizations), and NAICS 81394 (Political Organizations). [4] Excludes NAICS 81393 (Labor Unions and Similar Labor Organizations) and NAICS 81394 (Political Organizations).

Source: U.S. Census Bureau, Service Annual Survey, "Service Annual Survey Latest Data (NAICS-basis): 2022," <www.census.gov/programs-surveys/sas/data.html>, accessed February 2024.

Table 1301. National Nonprofit Associations—Number by Type: 1980 to 2024

[Data compiled during last few months of year previous to year shown and the beginning months of year shown]

Type	1980	1990	2000	2010 [1]	2015	2020	2022	2023	2024
Total	**14,726**	**22,289**	**21,840**	**23,983**	**23,891**	**24,414**	**25,225**	**26,749**	**27,417**
Trade, business, commercial	3,118	3,918	3,880	3,761	3,487	3,670	3,780	4,847	4,874
Agriculture and environment	677	940	1,103	1,442	1,421	1,484	1,501	1,529	1,563
Legal, governmental, public admin., military	529	792	790	913	894	977	1,044	1,059	1,075
Scientific, engineering, technical	1,039	1,417	1,302	1,563	1,507	1,564	1,592	1,613	1,614
Educational	[2] 2,376	1,291	1,297	1,444	1,344	1,438	1,447	1,501	1,539
Cultural	([2])	1,886	1,786	1,717	1,610	1,657	1,708	1,714	1,718
Social welfare	994	1,705	1,829	2,673	3,166	2,979	3,243	3,294	3,731
Health, medical	1,413	2,227	2,495	3,481	4,069	4,293	4,271	4,348	4,398
Public affairs	1,068	2,249	1,776	1,734	1,601	1,463	1,655	1,685	1,699
Fraternal, nationality, ethnic	435	573	525	461	398	398	393	409	409
Religious	797	1,172	1,123	1,056	964	1,000	1,003	1,088	1,126
Veteran, hereditary, patriotic	208	462	835	585	545	566	562	608	623
Hobby, avocational	910	1,475	1,330	1,374	1,287	1,341	1,347	1,368	1,362
Athletic sports	504	840	717	946	899	904	965	976	977
Labor unions	235	253	232	188	162	168	206	207	207
Chambers of Commerce [3]	105	168	143	142	125	105	101	102	102
Greek and non-Greek letter societies	318	340	296	305	294	313	313	309	309
Fan clubs	(NA)	581	381	198	118	94	94	92	91

NA Not available. [1] Beginning in 2007, there was an increase in the number of associations due to an increase in newly discovered and established associations. [2] Data for cultural associations included with educational associations. [3] National and binational. Includes trade and tourism organizations.

Source: Gale, Cengage Group. *Encyclopedia of Associations: National Organizations* © 2025 Gale, a part of Cengage, Inc. Reproduced by permission. See <www.cengage.com/permissions>.

Section 28
Foreign Commerce and Aid

This section presents data on the flow of goods, services, and capital between the United States and other countries; changes in official reserve assets of the United States; international investments; and foreign assistance programs.

The Bureau of Economic Analysis publishes current figures on U.S. international transactions and the U.S. international investment position in its monthly *Survey of Current Business* and in an interactive database on the internet at <apps.bea.gov/iTable/>. Statistics for the foreign aid programs are presented by the Agency for International Development (USAID) in its annual *U.S. Overseas Loans and Grants.*

The principal source of merchandise import and export data is the U.S. Census Bureau. Current data are presented monthly in *U.S. International Trade in Goods and Services Report* Series FT 900, as well as in the "USA Trade Online" database at <usatrade.census.gov/>. The *Guide to International Trade Statistics*, found on the Census Bureau website at <census.gov/foreign-trade/guide/index.html>, lists the Census Bureau's monthly and annual products and services in this field. In addition, the International Trade Administration and the Bureau of Economic Analysis present summary as well as selected commodity and country data for U.S. foreign trade on their websites: <trade.gov/trade-data-analysis> and <bea.gov/data/economic-accounts/international>. The merchandise trade data published by the Bureau of Economic Analysis in the *Survey of Current Business* and on the web include balance of payments adjustments to the Census Bureau data. The U.S. Treasury Department's *Monthly Treasury Statement of Receipts and Outlays of the United States Government* contains information on import duties. Various reports and specialized products on U.S. trade are released by the International Trade Commission, U.S. Department of Agriculture (agricultural products), U.S. Department of Energy (mineral fuels, like petroleum and coal), and the U.S. Geological Survey (minerals).

International accounts—The international transactions tables (Tables 1302, 1305, and 1306) show, for given time periods, the transfer of goods, services, grants, and financial assets and liabilities between the United States and the rest of the world. The international investment position table (Table 1304) presents, for specific dates, the value of U.S. investments abroad and of foreign investments in the United States. The movement of foreign and U.S. capital as presented in the balance of payments is not the only factor affecting the total value of foreign investments. Among the other factors are changes in the valuation of assets or liabilities, including changes in prices of securities, defaults, expropriations, and write-offs.

Direct investment abroad means the ownership or control, directly or indirectly, by one person of 10 percent or more of the voting securities of an incorporated business enterprise or an equivalent interest in an unincorporated business enterprise in another country. Direct investment position is the value of U.S. parents' claims on the equity of and receivables due from foreign affiliates, less foreign affiliates' receivables due from their U.S. parents.

Income consists of parents' shares in the earnings of their affiliates plus net interest received by parents on intercompany accounts, less withholding taxes on dividends and interest.

Foreign aid—Foreign assistance is divided into three major categories—grants (military supplies and services and other grants), credits, and other assistance (through net accumulation of foreign currency claims from the sale of agricultural commodities). *Grants* are transfers for which no payment is expected (other than a limited percentage of the foreign currency "counterpart" funds generated by the grant), or which at most involve an obligation on the part of the receiver to extend aid to the United States or other countries to achieve a common objective. *Credits* are loan disbursements or transfers under other agreements which give rise to specific obligations to repay, over a period of years, usually with interest. All known returns to the U.S. government stemming from grants and credits (reverse grants, returns of grants, and payments of principal) are taken into account in net grants and net credits, but no allowance is made for interest or commissions. *Other assistance* represents the transfer of U.S. farm products in exchange for foreign currencies (plus, since enactment of Public Law 87-128, currency claims from principal and interest collected on credits extended under the farm products program), less the government's disbursements of the currencies as grants, credits, or for purchases. The net acquisition of currencies represents net transfers of resources to foreign countries under the agricultural programs, in addition to those classified as grants or credits.

Exports—Export statistics consist of goods valued at more than $2,500 per commodity shipped by individuals and organizations (including exporters, freight forwarders, and carriers) from the U.S. to other countries. The Census Bureau compiles export data primarily from three sources: Shipper's Export Declaration documents filed with Customs and Border Protection and sent to the Census Bureau; data in electronic form submitted directly by exporters and their agents; and special computer tapes from Canada for U.S. exports to Canada. Estimates are made for low-value exports by country of destination, and based on bilateral trade patterns. They include U.S. exports under mutual security programs and exclude shipments to U.S. Armed Forces for their own use.

The value reported in the export statistics is generally equivalent to a free alongside ship (f.a.s.) value at the U.S. port of export, based on the transaction price, including inland freight, insurance, and other charges incurred in placing the merchandise alongside the carrier at the U.S. port of exportation. This value, as defined, excludes the cost of loading merchandise aboard the exporting carrier and also excludes freight, insurance, and any other charges or transportation and other costs beyond the U.S. port of exportation. The country of destination is defined as the country of ultimate destination or country where the merchandise is to be consumed, further processed, or manufactured, as known to the shipper at the time of exportation. When ultimate destination is not known, the shipment is statistically credited to the last country to which the shipper knows the merchandise will be shipped in the same form as exported.

Statistics for U.S. exports to Canada are based on import documents filed with Canadian agencies and forwarded to the U.S. Census Bureau under a 1987 data exchange agreement. Under this agreement, each country eliminated most cross-border export documents; maintains detailed statistics on cross-border imports; exchanges monthly files of cross-border import statistics; and publishes exchanged statistics in place of previously compiled export statistics.

Prior to 1989, exports were based on Schedule B, Statistical Classification of Domestic and Foreign Commodities Exported from the United States. Beginning in 1989, Schedule B classifications are based on the Harmonized System and coincide with the Standard International Trade Classification, Revision 3.

Imports—Import statistics consist of goods valued at more than $2,000 per commodity shipped by individuals and organizations (including importers and customs brokers) into the U.S. from other countries. The Census Bureau compiles import data from records filed with Customs and Border Protection, usually within 10 days after the merchandise enters the United States. Estimates are made for low-value shipments by country of origin, based on previous bilateral trade patterns and periodically updated. Country of origin is defined as the country where the merchandise was grown, mined, or manufactured. If country of origin is unknown, country of shipment is reported. Statistics for over 95 percent of all commodity transactions are compiled from records filed electronically with Customs and forwarded as computer tape files to the U.S. Census Bureau. Statistics for other transactions are compiled from

hard-copy documents filed with Customs and forwarded on a flow basis for U.S. Census Bureau processing.

Data on import values are presented on two valuations bases in this section: the c.i.f. (cost, insurance, and freight) and the customs import value (as appraised by the U.S. Customs Service in accordance with legal requirements of the Tariff Act of 1930, as amended). This latter valuation, primarily used for collection of import duties, frequently does not reflect the actual transaction value.

Imports are classified either as "General imports" or "Imports for consumption." *General imports* are a combination of entries for immediate consumption, entries into customs bonded warehouses, and entries into U.S. Foreign Trade Zones, thus generally reflecting total arrivals of merchandise. *Imports for consumption* are a combination of entries for immediate consumption, withdrawals from warehouses for consumption, and entries of merchandise into U.S. customs territory from U.S. Foreign Trade Zones, thus generally reflecting the total of the commodities entered into U.S. consumption channels.

Beginning in 1989, import statistics are based on the Harmonized Tariff Schedule of the United States, which coincides with import Standard International Trade Classification, Revision 3.

Area coverage—Except as noted, the geographic area covered by the export and import trade statistics is the United States Customs area (includes the 50 states, the District of Columbia, and Puerto Rico), the U.S. Virgin Islands (effective January 1981), and U.S. Foreign Trade Zones (effective July 1982).

Statistical reliability—For a discussion of statistical collection and estimation, sampling procedures, and measures of statistical reliability applicable to Census Bureau data, see Appendix III.

Table 1302. U.S. International Transactions by Type of Transaction: 2000 to 2023

[In millions of dollars (1,486,120 represents $1,486,120,000,000). Minus sign (-) indicates debits. N.i.e. is not included elsewhere]

Type of transaction	2000	2010	2015	2017	2018	2019	2020	2021	2022	2023
Exports of goods and services and income receipts	**1,486,120**	**2,687,457**	**3,238,571**	**3,550,432**	**3,794,005**	**3,842,238**	**3,281,367**	**3,794,561**	**4,412,523**	**4,645,183**
Exports of goods and services	1,082,963	1,872,320	2,280,778	2,394,476	2,542,462	2,546,276	2,160,147	2,570,802	3,039,405	3,071,816
Goods	784,940	1,290,279	1,511,381	1,557,003	1,676,913	1,655,098	1,433,852	1,765,853	2,090,339	2,045,221
General merchandise	778,718	1,271,972	1,489,795	1,535,249	1,654,629	1,635,273	1,408,999	1,733,045	2,048,474	2,006,057
Foods, feeds, and beverages	47,871	107,719	127,721	132,761	133,144	130,988	139,281	164,493	179,866	161,887
Industrial supplies and materials	171,108	388,561	418,141	459,380	536,866	526,431	451,077	617,641	810,945	719,559
Capital goods except automotive	357,000	447,839	539,805	533,696	563,438	550,749	463,351	521,473	573,183	602,636
Automotive vehicles, parts, and engines	80,356	112,008	151,894	157,867	158,833	163,075	129,378	146,410	162,978	180,039
Consumer goods except food and automotive	89,305	164,909	197,318	197,190	205,513	204,982	174,159	221,802	244,446	259,027
Other general merchandise	33,078	50,938	54,917	54,357	56,835	59,048	51,754	61,226	77,055	82,910
Net exports of goods under merchanting	159	411	261	210	338	474	825	1,336	1,116	1,150
Nonmonetary gold	6,063	17,896	21,325	21,544	21,947	19,351	24,028	31,471	40,749	38,014
Services	298,023	582,041	769,397	837,474	865,549	891,177	726,296	804,948	949,065	1,026,596
Manufacturing services on physical inputs owned by others	(NA)	(NA)	(NA)	(NA)	(NA)	(NA)	(NA)	(NA)	(NA)	(NA)
Maintenance and repair services n.i.e.	4,423	13,111	19,847	23,239	28,036	27,671	13,288	12,569	14,416	15,948
Transport [1]	49,462	76,357	84,434	86,342	93,107	91,058	57,471	66,798	92,405	97,779
Travel (for all purposes including education) [2]	96,872	130,315	192,602	196,469	200,724	198,982	72,479	71,746	142,909	189,134
Construction	1,993	2,951	2,759	2,053	2,842	3,161	2,370	2,957	1,948	1,529
Insurance services	3,631	14,854	15,763	18,976	19,118	18,579	20,023	23,011	23,987	24,985
Financial services	29,192	86,512	115,688	131,733	136,273	142,546	150,838	171,530	167,445	175,461
Charges for the use of intellectual property n.i.e.	43,476	94,968	111,151	118,147	114,819	122,533	115,936	131,079	137,833	134,442
Telecommunications, computer, and information services	12,250	26,556	41,427	47,657	49,245	55,742	56,071	57,984	64,717	70,629
Other business services	38,217	99,595	141,421	167,270	176,540	186,178	195,133	220,451	246,416	253,190
Personal, cultural, and recreational services [3]	9,351	17,612	24,220	25,664	22,715	22,192	20,710	23,906	27,711	30,732
Government goods and services n.i.e. [4,5]	9,156	19,210	20,087	19,924	22,131	22,535	21,976	22,916	29,279	32,767
Primary income receipts	365,612	723,223	824,929	995,442	1,102,964	1,139,310	954,005	1,048,567	1,184,423	1,376,721
Investment income	361,217	717,292	818,351	989,095	1,096,023	1,132,261	947,179	1,041,475	1,177,016	1,368,986
Compensation of employees	4,395	5,931	6,578	6,347	6,941	7,050	6,826	7,092	7,407	7,735
Secondary income (current transfer) receipts [6]	37,545	91,915	132,864	160,514	148,579	156,652	167,214	175,192	188,696	196,646
Imports of goods and services and income payments	**1,888,038**	**3,119,466**	**3,647,025**	**3,918,048**	**4,233,855**	**4,283,989**	**3,882,567**	**4,662,540**	**5,424,621**	**5,550,559**
Imports of goods and services	1,452,650	2,375,407	2,771,554	2,911,415	3,121,057	3,105,670	2,813,838	3,418,871	3,984,167	3,856,707
Goods	1,231,722	1,938,950	2,273,249	2,356,345	2,555,662	2,512,358	2,346,727	2,849,043	3,270,281	3,108,509
General merchandise	1,225,780	1,924,446	2,260,659	2,343,660	2,544,465	2,500,408	2,285,065	2,823,302	3,244,147	3,077,158
Foods, feeds, and beverages	46,489	92,492	128,762	138,825	148,257	151,555	155,441	183,301	209,533	201,474
Industrial supplies and materials	303,768	610,268	492,483	508,645	580,206	525,275	429,242	640,920	808,406	668,395
Capital goods except automotive	347,706	450,406	607,160	642,864	694,229	679,133	647,053	763,579	870,068	865,034
Automotive vehicles, parts, and engines	194,954	225,641	350,049	359,118	372,009	375,320	309,877	346,301	398,974	459,404
Consumer goods except food and automotive	284,634	485,121	596,417	603,470	647,659	655,293	640,726	768,085	839,085	757,458
Other general merchandise	48,229	60,519	85,789	90,739	102,104	113,833	102,727	121,116	118,081	125,392
Nonmonetary gold	5,942	14,504	12,590	12,685	11,197	11,950	61,662	25,741	26,133	31,351
Services	220,927	436,456	498,305	555,070	565,395	593,313	467,111	569,829	713,886	748,198
Manufacturing services on physical inputs owned by others	(NA)	(NA)	(NA)	(NA)	(NA)	(NA)	(NA)	(NA)	(NA)	(NA)
Maintenance and repair services n.i.e.	2,316	5,857	8,084	6,796	7,354	8,716	5,084	4,868	5,453	6,470
Transport [1]	58,526	88,394	99,557	103,109	110,441	112,813	72,954	106,797	157,711	142,874
Travel (for all purposes including education) [2]	64,174	85,166	102,664	117,931	125,717	131,990	34,399	58,998	118,623	158,678
Construction	1,447	2,578	3,012	1,950	3,077	1,361	1,008	2,326	2,146	1,594
Insurance services	11,284	63,452	50,300	53,267	43,797	51,219	57,743	59,760	62,305	64,607
Financial services	16,445	27,215	32,686	37,952	41,336	44,360	45,696	50,947	57,479	62,691
Charges for the use of intellectual property n.i.e.	16,139	31,116	35,178	44,405	42,736	42,273	45,025	50,530	60,988	47,537
Telecommunications, computer, and information services	14,128	29,421	38,815	43,091	41,701	42,768	43,612	51,853	55,107	60,142
Other business services	20,306	65,903	95,119	106,991	107,435	112,496	112,652	129,977	138,765	145,074
Personal, cultural, and recreational services [3]	1,645	5,393	11,358	17,530	18,825	21,316	24,384	28,412	29,761	33,013
Government goods and services n.i.e. [4,7]	14,516	31,960	21,531	22,047	22,975	24,000	24,553	25,360	25,547	25,517
Primary income payments	350,980	553,311	639,724	737,501	847,689	891,911	776,288	929,509	1,068,464	1,309,692
Investment income	339,107	539,783	623,031	720,549	830,466	873,002	761,857	911,235	1,043,677	1,282,578
Compensation of employees	11,873	13,528	16,693	16,952	17,223	18,908	14,431	18,274	24,786	27,114
Secondary income (current transfer) payments [6]	84,408	190,749	235,747	269,132	265,109	286,408	292,441	314,160	371,990	384,160
Capital transfer receipts and other credits	**42**	**9**	**67**	**19,200**	**3,281**	**71**	**372**	**3,864**	**8,397**	**82**

See footnotes at end of table.

Table 1302. U.S. International Transactions by Type of Transaction: 2000 to 2023-Continued.

See headnote on page 821.

Type of transaction	2000	2010	2015	2017	2018	2019	2020	2021	2022	2023
Capital transfer payments and other debits	4,259	6,900	8,006	6,805	7,541	6,527	5,982	5,287	8,578	6,402
Net U.S. acquisition of financial assets [8]	587,682	958,737	144,104	1,161,984	429,710	315,580	954,808	1,191,028	747,109	978,604
Direct investment assets	186,371	349,829	302,072	409,413	-130,720	114,924	282,333	341,955	388,510	454,085
Equity	170,011	338,294	292,455	392,467	-219,334	171,905	297,237	321,806	378,952	359,956
Debt instruments	16,360	11,535	9,618	16,947	88,613	-56,981	-14,904	20,148	9,558	94,129
Portfolio investment assets	159,713	199,620	107,154	540,728	381,863	-11,453	406,368	711,540	322,719	81,562
Equity and investment fund shares	106,714	79,150	196,922	139,940	171,300	-25,304	395,995	197,255	159,463	-4,691
Debt securities [9]	52,999	120,469	-89,767	400,788	210,562	13,851	10,373	514,285	163,255	86,253
Other investment assets	241,308	407,454	-258,831	213,533	173,578	207,450	257,133	23,541	30,066	442,916
Other equity	1,438	1,907	2,098	1,506	1,329	1,367	1,847	1,206	2,370	1,848
Currency and deposits	(NA)	150,249	-191,472	170,890	106,125	130,517	92,767	-44,169	146,765	31,359
Loans	(NA)	249,255	-67,754	35,715	64,945	74,404	170,830	64,588	-112,056	407,397
Insurance technical reserves	(NA)	(NA)	(NA)	(NA)	(NA)	(NA)	(NA)	(NA)	(NA)	(NA)
Trade credit and advances	680	6,043	-1,702	5,422	1,179	1,163	-8,311	1,915	-7,012	2,312
Reserve assets	290	1,835	-6,292	-1,690	4,989	4,659	8,974	113,993	5,814	41
Special drawing rights	722	31	9	78	156	237	81	113,685	4,966	4,624
Reserve position in the International Monetary Fund	-2,308	1,293	-6,485	-1,812	4,824	4,271	8,814	460	820	-4,931
Other reserve assets	1,876	511	185	44	10	150	78	-153	28	349
Net U.S. incurrence of liabilities [8]	1,066,074	1,391,042	503,468	1,559,219	712,178	832,266	1,621,666	1,975,626	1,535,516	1,887,085
Direct investment liabilities	349,124	264,039	511,434	380,823	214,716	315,983	137,068	475,803	408,982	348,784
Equity	258,438	207,842	426,321	333,318	318,946	276,977	173,646	410,279	333,472	306,282
Debt instruments	90,686	56,197	85,114	47,505	-104,230	39,005	-36,578	65,524	75,510	42,502
Portfolio investment liabilities	441,966	820,434	213,910	790,810	303,075	233,469	946,560	614,103	760,384	1,231,011
Equity and investment fund shares	193,600	178,952	-187,306	149,633	156,916	-291,427	687,417	-53,068	2,585	133,014
Debt securities [9]	248,366	641,481	401,216	641,177	146,159	524,896	259,144	667,171	757,799	1,098,063
Other investment liabilities [9]	274,984	306,569	-221,876	387,586	194,387	282,814	538,038	885,720	366,150	307,224
Financial derivatives, net [10]	(NA)	-14,076	-27,035	23,998	-20,404	-41,670	-5,107	-39,028	-80,698	-15,642
Statistical discrepancy [11]	-72,257	-7,481	29,993	-18,016	141,238	-110,149	-65,154	45,778	143,174	-12,427
Balance on current account (exports less imports)	-401,918	-432,009	-408,453	-367,616	-439,849	-441,751	-601,201	-867,980	-1,012,098	-905,376
Balance on goods and services	-369,686	-503,087	-490,776	-516,939	-578,749	-559,395	-653,691	-848,070	-944,762	-784,890
Balance on goods	-446,783	-648,671	-761,868	-799,343	-878,749	-857,260	-912,875	-1,083,190	-1,179,941	-1,063,288
Balance on services	77,096	145,584	271,092	282,404	300,155	297,865	259,185	235,120	235,179	278,398
Balance on primary income	14,632	169,911	185,205	257,942	255,275	247,865	177,717	119,058	115,959	67,029
Balance on secondary income	-46,863	-98,834	-102,882	-108,618	-116,530	-129,756	-125,227	-138,968	-183,295	-187,515
Balance on capital account	-4,217	-6,891	-7,940	12,394	-4,261	-6,456	-5,610	-1,423	-181	-6,320
Net lending/borrowing from current- and capital-account transactions [12]	-406,135	-438,900	-416,393	-355,221	-444,110	-448,207	-606,811	-869,403	-1,012,279	-911,696
Net lending/borrowing from financial-account transactions [12]	-478,392	-446,381	-386,400	-373,237	-302,872	-558,356	-671,965	-823,625	-869,105	-924,123

NA Not available. [1] Includes passenger fares. [2] All travel purposes include 1) business travel, including expenditures by border, seasonal, and other short-term workers and 2) personal travel, including health-related and education-related travel. [3] Includes audiovisual services, artistic-related services, educational and health services including those provided remotely, and services associated with museums and other cultural, sporting, gambling, and recreational activities, except those acquired by customers traveling outside their country of residence. [4] Includes goods and services supplied by and to embassies, consulates, and military bases; goods and services acquired from the host economy by diplomatic and military personnel; and services supplied by and to governments that are not included in other service categories. [5] Includes transfers under U.S. military sales contracts. [6] Secondary income (current transfer) receipts and payments include U.S. government and private transfers, such as U.S. government grants and pensions, fines and penalties, withholding taxes, personal transfers (remittances), insurance-related transfers, and other current transfers. [7] Includes direct defense expenditures. [8] Excluding financial derivatives. [9] Includes transactions in U.S. Treasury and other U.S. securities. [10] Transactions for financial derivatives are only available as a net value equal to transactions for assets less transactions for liabilities. A positive value represents net U.S. cash payments arising from derivatives contracts, and a negative value represents net U.S. cash receipts. [11] The statistical discrepancy is the difference between total debits and total credits recorded in the current, capital, and financial accounts. In the current and capital accounts, credits and debits are labeled in the table. In the financial account, an acquisition of an asset or a repayment of a liability is a debit, and an incurrence of a liability or a disposal of an asset is a credit. [12] Net lending means that U.S. residents are net suppliers of funds to foreign residents, and net borrowing means the opposite. Net lending or net borrowing can be computed from current- and capital-account transactions or from financial-account transactions. The two amounts differ by the statistical discrepancy.

Source: U.S. Bureau of Economic Analysis, International Economic Accounts, "Table 1.2. U.S. International Transactions, Expanded Detail." <www.bea.gov/data/economic-accounts/international>, accessed August 2024.

Table 1303. U.S. Government Reserve Assets: 2000 to 2023

[In billions of dollars (67.6 represents $67,600,000,000). As of end of year]

Type	2000	2010	2014	2015	2016	2017	2018	2019	2020	2021	2022	2023
Total	**67.6**	**132.4**	**130.1**	**117.6**	**117.3**	**123.3**	**125.8**	**129.5**	**144.9**	**251.2**	**243.8**	**245.2**
Gold stock	11.0	11.0	11.0	11.0	11.0	11.0	11.0	11.0	11.0	11.0	11.0	11.0
Special drawing rights	10.5	56.8	51.9	49.7	48.9	51.9	50.8	50.7	52.9	163.6	160.5	166.5
Reserve position in IMF [1]	14.8	12.5	25.2	17.6	18.4	17.6	22.0	26.2	36.4	35.8	35.0	30.3
Foreign currencies	31.2	52.1	41.9	39.2	39.0	42.8	41.9	41.5	44.5	40.7	37.2	37.3

[1] International Monetary Fund.

Source: Data prior to 2005, U.S. Department of the Treasury, *Treasury Bulletin*. Beginning in 2005, Board of Governors of the Federal Reserve System, "International Summary Statistics," August 2024 and earlier releases, <www.federalreserve.gov/data.htm>.

Table 1304. U.S. International Investment Position by Type of Investment: 2010 to 2023

[In billions of dollars (-2,511 represents -$2,511,000,000,000). Estimates as of end of 4th quarter. Minus sign (-) indicates loss or deficit]

Type of investment	2010	2015	2019	2020	2021	2022	2023
U.S. net international investment position	**-2,511**	**-7,590**	**-11,666**	**-14,721**	**-18,833**	**-16,264**	**-19,853**
Net international investment position excluding financial derivatives	-2,621	-7,645	-11,687	-14,714	-18,855	-16,333	-19,848
Financial derivatives other than reserves, net	110	54	20	-7	22	69	-5
U.S. assets	**21,769**	**23,302**	**28,845**	**32,023**	**34,943**	**31,440**	**34,400**
Assets excluding financial derivatives	18,116	20,858	27,055	29,477	32,960	28,897	32,197
Financial derivatives other than reserves, gross positive fair value	3,652	2,443	1,790	2,546	1,983	2,543	2,203
By functional category:							
Direct investment at market value	5,486	7,057	8,669	9,349	10,848	9,150	10,607
Equity	4,621	5,812	7,486	8,194	9,665	7,943	9,295
Debt instruments	866	1,245	1,183	1,156	1,183	1,208	1,312
Portfolio investment	7,160	9,440	13,124	14,399	16,314	14,024	15,334
Equity and investment fund shares	4,900	6,756	9,478	10,615	12,061	10,280	11,483
Debt securities	2,260	2,684	3,646	3,784	4,253	3,744	3,852
Financial derivatives other than reserves, gross positive fair value	3,652	2,443	1,790	2,546	1,983	2,543	2,203
Over-the-counter contracts	3,622	2,400	1,755	2,492	1,923	2,466	2,138
Exchange-traded contracts	31	44	35	54	60	78	65
Other investment [1]	4,981	3,978	4,747	5,101	5,086	5,016	5,478
Currency and deposits	2,767	1,633	2,059	2,192	2,131	2,231	2,266
Loans	2,110	2,238	2,567	2,794	2,837	2,672	3,095
Trade credit and advances	51	45	54	46	47	40	42
Reserve assets	489	384	514	627	712	707	777
Monetary gold	368	277	396	494	472	474	543
Special drawing rights	57	50	51	53	164	161	166
Reserve position in the International Monetary Fund	12	18	26	36	36	35	30
Other reserve assets	52	39	41	44	41	37	37
U.S. liabilities	**24,280**	**30,892**	**40,512**	**46,744**	**53,775**	**47,704**	**54,253**
Liabilities excluding financial derivatives	20,738	28,503	38,741	44,192	51,815	45,230	52,045
Financial derivatives other than reserves, gross negative fair value	3,542	2,389	1,770	2,553	1,961	2,474	2,208
By functional category:							
Direct investment at market value	4,099	6,729	10,455	11,876	14,866	12,235	14,809
Equity	2,928	5,110	8,791	10,263	13,164	10,467	12,979
Debt instruments	1,171	1,619	1,664	1,613	1,702	1,768	1,830
Portfolio investment	11,869	16,646	21,764	25,172	28,972	24,715	28,617
Equity and investment fund shares	3,546	6,209	9,296	11,835	15,251	12,127	14,737
Debt securities	8,323	10,437	12,467	13,337	13,721	12,588	13,880
Financial derivatives other than reserves, gross negative fair value	3,542	2,389	1,770	2,553	1,961	2,474	2,208
Over-the-counter contracts	3,512	2,346	1,738	2,501	1,896	2,402	2,142
Exchange-traded contracts	30	43	32	51	65	72	67
Other investment	4,769	5,128	6,523	7,144	7,977	8,280	8,619
Currency and deposits	2,365	2,947	3,475	3,820	4,167	4,299	4,534
Loans	2,238	1,970	2,793	3,057	3,413	3,577	3,654
Trade credit and advances	112	162	206	216	236	252	276
Special drawing rights allocations	54	49	49	51	161	153	154

[1] Includes value of other equity, not shown separately.

Source: U.S. Bureau of Economic Analysis, International Economic Accounts, International Investment Position, "Table 1.2 U.S. Net International Investment Position at the End of the Period, Expanded Detail," <www.bea.gov/data/economic-accounts/international>, accessed August 2024.

Table 1305. International Service Transactions by Selected Type of Service and Selected Country: 2010 to 2023

[In millions of dollars (582,041 represents $582,041,000,000). Country data are based on information available from U.S. reporting sources. In some instances, the statistics may not necessarily reflect the ultimate foreign transactor. With the June 2020 data release, the Bureau of Economic Analysis has revised all International Transactions data to incorporate a number of changes, including new services categories, new classifications, and improved methodologies. For details, see <apps.bea.gov/scb/2020/04-april/0420-international-annual-revision-preview. htm>. N.i.e. is not included elsewhere]

Type of service and country	Exports				Imports			
	2010	2020	2022	2023	2010	2020	2022	2023
Services, total	**582,041**	**726,296**	**949,065**	**1,026,596**	**436,456**	**467,111**	**713,886**	**748,198**
TYPE OF SERVICE								
Maintenance and repair services n.i.e. [1]	13,111	13,288	14,416	15,948	5,857	5,084	5,453	6,470
Transport [2]	76,357	57,471	92,405	97,779	88,394	72,954	157,711	142,874
Sea transport	16,308	17,997	22,162	19,790	28,022	34,349	76,084	44,397
Air transport [2]	55,877	34,792	65,025	72,764	56,617	35,062	77,296	94,273
Passenger	31,506	11,817	29,177	36,747	38,667	13,371	46,777	65,349
Travel [2]	130,315	72,479	142,909	189,134	85,166	34,399	118,623	158,678
Business	38,171	11,963	29,485	37,912	19,115	4,836	12,375	16,562
Personal	92,145	60,516	113,425	151,223	66,051	29,562	106,248	142,116
Health related	879	267	483	920	366	235	612	1,085
Education related	18,365	38,710	39,816	50,197	5,957	5,479	8,709	11,158
Construction	2,951	2,370	1,948	1,529	2,578	1,008	2,146	1,594
Insurance services	14,854	20,023	23,987	24,985	63,452	57,743	62,305	64,607
Direct insurance	4,348	1,736	2,175	2,526	4,470	5,373	6,821	8,671
Reinsurance	9,046	15,891	18,514	19,318	57,511	50,158	53,188	53,535
Financial services [2]	86,512	150,838	167,445	175,461	27,215	45,696	57,479	62,691
Explicitly charged and other financial services [2]	79,295	131,886	144,849	148,911	17,067	38,248	46,306	51,137
Credit card and credit-related services	10,569	23,927	32,803	38,070	3,862	8,697	12,956	14,846
Financial management services	23,889	61,317	64,748	61,973	3,112	14,043	16,580	16,228
Charges for the use of intellectual property n.i.e. [2]	94,968	115,936	137,833	134,442	31,116	45,025	60,988	47,537
Franchises and trademarks licensing fees	19,349	23,700	27,110	27,935	4,757	4,792	7,075	7,147
License to use outcomes of research & development [3]	37,561	52,408	68,084	64,132	19,422	26,687	36,363	23,715
License to reproduce/distribute computer software	35,906	34,650	38,260	36,888	5,192	12,045	12,877	12,642
License to reproduce/distribute audiovisual products	2,152	5,177	4,380	5,487	1,745	1,503	4,672	4,034
Telecommunications, computer, and information services	26,556	56,071	64,717	70,629	29,421	43,612	55,107	60,142
Telecommunications services	10,921	7,842	7,971	9,329	8,077	5,129	5,923	7,095
Computer services	10,124	41,909	46,969	50,328	19,665	35,411	44,697	47,272
Information services	5,510	6,320	9,777	10,972	1,680	3,072	4,487	5,775
Other business services	99,595	195,133	246,416	253,190	65,903	112,652	138,765	145,074
Research and development services	22,165	44,840	56,835	54,758	22,593	29,398	34,352	33,559
Professional and management consulting services	48,657	112,666	145,554	150,444	29,380	56,776	66,868	74,051
Technical, trade-related, and other business services [4]	28,774	37,628	44,026	47,988	13,930	26,479	37,545	37,465
Personal, cultural, and recreational services [5]	17,612	20,710	27,711	30,732	5,393	24,384	29,761	33,013
Government goods and services n.i.e. [6]	19,210	21,976	29,279	32,767	31,960	24,553	25,547	25,517
AREA AND COUNTRY								
Canada	57,288	52,708	76,640	85,980	28,518	33,399	47,377	54,278
Europe [7]	221,283	300,272	410,350	432,644	178,884	196,935	302,074	316,998
European Union [7, 8]	184,990	182,450	246,854	261,661	150,251	108,824	171,482	185,141
Euro Area [7, 9]	114,783	164,451	223,067	235,312	95,907	94,276	148,657	165,275
France	17,926	15,579	22,089	24,060	17,746	13,513	26,459	27,301
Germany	26,541	29,864	39,910	42,030	31,356	31,118	42,687	45,796
Italy	8,394	5,845	9,364	11,105	8,982	4,500	11,350	13,750
Netherlands	13,569	21,080	33,420	35,497	8,846	11,154	14,231	15,490
United Kingdom	55,811	61,699	82,197	90,826	44,481	54,946	74,694	86,044
Latin America, other Western Hemisphere [7]	113,715	134,926	178,048	188,811	102,534	89,778	148,152	159,909
Brazil	18,418	14,964	21,983	25,186	5,895	4,797	6,084	6,833
Mexico	23,730	23,461	38,415	44,050	15,891	17,799	38,766	44,772
Africa	11,875	11,075	14,450	16,873	7,745	5,338	10,490	12,565
Middle East	21,531	28,284	32,038	34,624	18,011	13,126	24,085	24,742
Asia and Pacific [7]	153,674	196,484	234,241	264,985	99,659	128,479	179,908	179,633
Australia	16,096	15,056	21,351	24,477	6,073	6,046	8,800	10,161
China	20,518	41,166	41,456	46,715	11,493	16,070	26,585	20,143
Hong Kong	5,836	12,527	13,125	13,375	7,381	9,888	12,634	12,643
India	9,898	16,317	26,539	33,999	15,257	26,225	33,034	36,406
Japan	43,519	37,853	38,306	43,623	25,064	32,498	39,575	37,897
Korea, South	16,618	17,714	22,589	24,860	9,530	9,801	15,197	14,643
Singapore	10,664	26,505	34,559	37,335	5,214	9,379	10,299	11,254
Taiwan	9,921	9,299	10,477	11,900	5,724	6,321	14,322	12,103
International organizations and unallocated	2,674	2,547	3,299	2,678	1,105	57	1,800	74

[1] Covers maintenance and repair services by residents of country on goods owned by residents of another country. Excludes transportation equipment, construction, and computer maintenance and repair. [2] Includes types not shown separately. [3] Includes patents, industrial processes, and trade secrets. [4] Includes construction, architectural and engineering services, waste treatment, operational leasing, trade-related, and other business services. [5] Includes audiovisual services, artistic-related services, educational services delivered online, remotely provided telemedicine services, and services associated with museums and other cultural, sporting, gambling, and recreational activities, except those acquired by customers traveling outside their country of residence. [6] See footnote 4, Table 1302. Exports include transfers under U.S. military sales contracts; imports include direct defense expenditures. [7] Includes countries not shown separately. [8] Only those countries that are members of the European Union in a given year are included in the data for that year. [9] Euro area refers to European Union member countries that have adopted the Euro as the common currency. Data for each year cover only member countries in that year.

Source: U.S. Bureau of Economic Analysis, International Economic Accounts, International Services, "Table 2.1. U.S. Trade in Services, by Type of Service," and "Table 2.2. U.S. Trade in Services by Type of Service and by Country or Affiliation," <www.bea.gov/data/economic-accounts/international>, accessed August 2024.

Table 1306. U.S. Balances on International Transactions by Area and Selected Country: 2022 and 2023

[In millions of dollars (-1,012,098 represents -$1,012,098,000,000). Country data are based on information available from U.S. reporting sources. In some instances, the statistics may not necessarily reflect the ultimate foreign transactor. With the June 2020 data release, the Bureau of Economic Analysis revised all International Transactions data to incorporate a number of changes, including new services categories, new classification of certain services and transactions, and improved methodologies. See source for details. Minus sign (-) indicates debits]

Area or country	2022, balance on—				2023, balance on—			
	Current account	Goods	Services	Primary income[1]	Current account	Goods	Services	Primary income[1]
All areas	-1,012,098	-1,179,941	235,179	115,959	-905,376	-1,063,288	278,398	67,029
Canada	-56,556	-86,827	29,262	3,163	-45,742	-72,329	31,702	-1,618
Europe	-96,214	-228,078	108,275	52,582	-89,658	-217,037	115,646	50,388
European Union[2]	-68,518	-204,401	75,372	55,251	-89,614	-201,645	76,519	32,953
Euro Area[3]	-36,391	-176,029	74,410	60,687	-71,574	-177,903	70,038	33,322
Germany	-87,411	-74,367	-2,777	-10,370	-101,249	-83,234	-3,766	-15,499
Italy	-42,703	-41,945	-1,986	1,981	-46,354	-44,451	-2,645	1,852
Netherlands	111,232	37,919	19,190	54,367	111,253	42,491	20,006	48,915
United Kingdom	24,913	11,804	7,503	3,872	47,433	9,692	4,782	32,551
Latin America, other Western Hemisphere	-21,144	-61,433	29,896	69,164	-88,614	-108,108	28,903	43,103
Brazil	34,919	14,692	15,899	6,256	28,468	5,284	18,354	6,634
Mexico	-159,733	-135,764	-351	-6,217	-185,453	-161,382	-722	-4,719
Africa	-28,595	-11,239	3,961	6,583	-30,239	-10,111	4,309	4,205
Middle East	-17,835	-12,774	7,953	-8,167	-6,852	8,829	9,882	-15,930
Asia and Pacific	-791,498	-780,706	54,333	-24,754	-652,185	-665,682	85,352	-31,184
Australia	40,168	14,351	12,551	13,523	42,288	17,569	14,315	10,214
China	-393,326	-381,068	14,872	-21,398	-278,774	-278,716	26,572	-20,180
Hong Kong	26,422	21,637	491	3,793	27,194	24,120	732	1,558
India	-48,248	-38,612	-6,495	6,845	-50,127	-43,233	-2,407	6,693
Japan	-112,585	-67,642	-1,269	-43,418	-114,396	-71,878	5,726	-47,106
Singapore	73,248	14,481	24,260	33,688	65,030	1,576	26,081	35,751
Korea, South	-43,894	-43,101	7,392	-7,504	-45,748	-50,996	10,217	-4,815
Taiwan	-65,332	-46,962	-3,845	-12,777	-62,947	-47,328	-203	-13,696
International organizations and unallocated	-255	1,116	1,499	17,388	7,913	1,150	2,604	18,066

[1] Primary income consists of investment income and compensation of employees. [2] Data for the European Union (EU) reflect the EU membership during the reference period. In 2022 and 2023, the EU was composed of Austria, Belgium, Bulgaria, Croatia, Cyprus, Czechia, Denmark, Estonia, Finland, France, Germany, Greece, Hungary, Ireland, Italy, Latvia, Lithuania, Luxembourg, Malta, Netherlands, Poland, Portugal, Romania, Slovakia, Slovenia, Spain, and Sweden. [3] Euro area refers to European Union member countries that have adopted the Euro as the common currency. Data here cover Austria, Belgium, Cyprus, Estonia, Finland, France, Germany, Greece, Ireland, Italy, Latvia, Lithuania, Luxembourg, Malta, Netherlands, Portugal, Slovakia, Slovenia, and Spain.

Source: U.S. Bureau of Economic Analysis, International Transactions, "Table 1.3. U.S. International Transactions, Expanded Detail by Area and Country," <www.bea.gov/data/economic-accounts/international>, accessed August 2024.

Table 1307. Employment of Majority-Owned U.S. Affiliates of Foreign Companies by State: 2010 to 2021

[In thousands (5,435.4 represents 5,435,400). Covers full-time and part-time employees on the payroll, generally at the end of the fiscal year. A U.S. majority-owned affiliate is a U.S. business enterprise in which a foreign entity has a direct or indirect voting interest greater than 50 percent]

State and other area	2010	2015	2020	2021	State and other area	2010	2015	2020	2021
Total	**5,435.4**	**6,822.8**	**7,714.0**	**7,940.2**	Montana	6.3	6.8	10.1	9.8
					Nebraska	23.9	31.4	37.0	38.6
Alabama	81.9	104.6	115.1	120.0	Nevada	39.0	47.8	59.1	60.8
Alaska	14.1	16.3	13.4	13.6	New Hampshire	39.3	41.2	49.3	50.6
Arizona	77.0	104.4	126.5	140.6	New Jersey	222.9	270.7	279.0	292.5
Arkansas	35.9	46.1	47.7	59.1	New Mexico	15.3	16.9	17.7	18.7
California	584.0	734.2	813.1	816.4	New York	398.9	477.9	505.7	509.2
Colorado	80.9	105.0	120.3	123.2	North Carolina	194.7	252.6	291.2	303.6
Connecticut	100.9	102.6	107.6	112.1	North Dakota	11.5	13.0	15.6	16.4
Delaware	26.7	25.2	27.1	29.2	Ohio	210.2	257.7	291.5	300.1
District of Columbia	22.4	23.5	20.4	20.8	Oklahoma	38.6	49.6	61.2	64.2
Florida	232.9	331.2	342.1	358.2	Oregon	43.0	60.6	69.9	70.3
Georgia	189.5	228.9	272.2	281.8	Pennsylvania	261.3	291.4	326.4	333.5
Hawaii	26.8	36.7	41.7	40.3	Rhode Island	26.1	25.5	30.9	31.4
Idaho	13.4	15.6	19.4	20.5	South Carolina	108.4	134.6	161.7	170.9
Illinois	252.7	321.7	368.8	376.7	South Dakota	7.2	11.9	14.1	14.5
Indiana	136.0	189.7	204.4	209.1	Tennessee	117.2	164.2	199.7	202.3
Iowa	44.9	59.9	62.6	66.7	Texas	451.4	588.5	664.7	660.5
Kansas	54.5	56.1	68.8	74.6	Utah	31.4	42.6	52.8	62.8
Kentucky	89.2	120.2	139.4	140.2	Vermont	11.1	11.0	14.6	14.2
Louisiana	56.1	67.5	76.7	78.4	Virginia	147.8	180.6	195.7	200.7
Maine	30.3	34.3	37.7	37.3	Washington	94.4	113.3	139.5	143.7
Maryland	101.6	116.9	110.2	117.8	West Virginia	28.7	29.4	28.1	28.4
Massachusetts	187.3	203.0	217.8	228.0	Wisconsin	77.5	97.3	126.2	130.2
Michigan	145.4	243.3	311.6	321.9	Wyoming	7.8	7.2	8.1	8.1
Minnesota	90.7	113.9	153.6	157.4	Puerto Rico	21.9	24.0	22.0	22.6
Mississippi	26.8	37.4	46.4	46.7	Other U.S. areas	13.9	24.2	28.4	34.1
Missouri	81.7	109.8	141.6	148.8	Foreign	2.3	([1])	7.9	8.0

[1] 2,500 to 4,999 employees.

Source: U.S. Bureau of Economic Analysis, International Economic Accounts, "Direct Investment and Multinational Enterprises (MNEs)," <www.bea.gov/data/economic-accounts/international>, accessed November 2023.

Table 1308. New Foreign Direct Investment in the U.S. by Industry of U.S. Business Enterprise and Country of Ultimate Beneficial Owner: 2022 and 2023

[In millions of dollars (206,216 represents $206,216,000,000). Data shown are first year expenditures by foreign direct investors to acquire, establish, or expand U.S. businesses. First year expenditures include those expenditures in the calendar year in which the transaction occurred. A U.S. business enterprise is categorized as "acquired" if a foreign entity acquired a 10 percent or more voting interest in an incorporated U.S. business, or an equivalent interest of an unincorporated U.S. business, either directly or indirectly through an existing U.S. affiliate. A U.S. business enterprise is categorized as "established" if a foreign entity or existing U.S. affiliate of a foreign entity establishes a new legal entity in the U.S. in which the foreign entity owns 10 percent or more of the new business enterprise's voting interest, or an equivalent interest if unincorporated. An existing U.S. affiliate is categorized as "expanded" if it expands its operations to include a new facility where business is conducted and the expansion has a projected total cost of more than $3 million]

Industry and country	2022				2023			
	Total	U.S. businesses acquired	U.S. businesses established	U.S. businesses expanded	Total	U.S. businesses acquired	U.S. businesses established	U.S. businesses expanded
Total [1]	**206,216**	**193,093**	**5,174**	**7,949**	**148,843**	**136,456**	**7,407**	**4,980**
INDUSTRY [2]								
Manufacturing	63,891	53,669	3,261	6,962	42,897	33,973	4,242	4,682
Wholesale trade	5,554	5,464	67	24	(D)	(D)	(D)	(D)
Retail trade	4,068	3,944	105	18	(D)	(D)	(D)	(D)
Information	39,398	39,263	135	–	7,307	7,132	175	1
Finance and insurance	15,889	15,828	62	–	12,792	12,737	(D)	(D)
Real estate and rental and leasing	10,903	10,310	589	3	4,186	3,894	278	14
Professional, scientific, and technical services	19,991	19,322	521	149	16,032	14,440	(D)	(D)
Other industries	46,522	45,294	434	793	(D)	(D)	406	(D)
COUNTRY [3]								
Canada	41,140	(D)	1,353	(D)	53,434	52,844	180	410
Europe [1]	117,669	113,936	2,029	1,704	50,345	48,242	1,617	486
France	21,865	(D)	(D)	(D)	6,932	6,797	46	89
Germany	8,599	8,224	126	250	5,689	5,587	(D)	(D)
Ireland	6,578	6,404	1	172	2,778	2,743	(D)	(D)
Netherlands	422	385	36	–	1,997	1,966	31	–
Switzerland	5,875	(D)	14	(D)	6,456	(D)	(D)	(D)
United Kingdom	41,098	40,665	174	1	7,199	7,063	132	4
Latin America/other Western Hemisphere	9,220	9,046	129	1	1,205	423	(D)	(D)
South and Central America	1,611	1,482	45	–	757	9	(D)	(D)
Other Western Hemisphere [1]	7,609	7,564	(D)	–	449	415	30	4
Bermuda	6,221	(D)	34	–	9	5	4	–
Caribbean Islands (British)	1,255	1,221	(D)	–	417	410	4	–
Africa	186	(D)	(D)	–	(D)	5	(D)	–
Middle East	7,570	7,035	(D)	(D)	8,228	8,171	57	(D)
Asia and Pacific [1]	27,508	20,328	(D)	(D)	35,512	26,748	4,684	4,080
Australia	3,495	(D)	(D)	(D)	2,432	2,391	41	–
China	531	(D)	(D)	(D)	621	(D)	(D)	1
Hong Kong	14	(D)	(D)	–	21	17	5	–
Japan	8,722	7,342	532	848	14,628	(D)	(D)	(D)
Singapore	5,217	5,215	(D)	(D)	(D)	(D)	6	–
South Korea	8,377	3,418	(D)	(D)	8,080	3,995	(D)	(D)

– Represents or rounds to zero. D Suppressed to avoid disclosure of data of individual companies. [1] Includes other countries not shown separately. [2] Based on 2012 North American Industry Classification System (NAICS); see text, Section 15. [3] Country of ultimate beneficial owner (UBO). The UBO is the entity proceeding up a U.S. affiliate's ownership chain, beginning with the foreign parents, which is not owned more than 50 percent by another entity.

Source: U.S. Bureau of Economic Analysis, International Economic Accounts, New Foreign Direct Investment in the United States, "Activities of U.S. Multinational Enterprises," <www.bea.gov/data/economic-accounts/international>, accessed August 2024.

Table 1309. Foreign Direct Investment Position in the United States on a Historical-Cost Basis: by Selected Country, 2010 to 2023, and by Industry, 2023

[In millions of dollars (2,280,044 represents $2,280,044,000,000). Foreign direct investment is defined as the ownership or control, directly or indirectly, by one foreign entity of 10 percent or more of the voting interest of a U.S. business enterprise. As used here, "entity" is synonymous with "person," used in a broad legal sense that includes any individual, branch, partnership, association, trust, corporation, or government. Data are based on surveys of U.S. affiliates of foreign companies]

Country	All industries total				2023			
	2010	2015	2020	2022	Total [1]	Manufac-turing	Wholesale trade	Finance and insurance [2]
All countries.....................	**2,280,044**	**3,354,907**	**4,613,481**	**5,167,142**	**5,394,095**	**2,223,555**	**541,203**	**573,833**
Canada.............................	192,463	323,207	487,449	575,626	671,671	81,141	82,608	119,931
Europe [3]...........................	1,659,774	2,306,254	2,980,117	3,376,582	3,462,655	1,707,717	235,370	312,293
Austria.............................	4,532	7,159	15,346	17,446	19,076	7,808	2,061	1
Belgium...........................	69,565	88,121	66,093	71,298	73,485	61,919	2,698	7
Denmark..........................	7,772	14,509	30,173	39,567	44,990	14,770	15,001	-105
Finland............................	4,943	6,471	8,082	9,798	10,096	5,989	2,234	(D)
France.............................	189,763	233,547	282,257	246,004	243,470	118,730	11,889	22,950
Germany..........................	203,077	281,295	347,509	413,930	472,851	177,796	68,967	53,656
Ireland............................	24,097	55,861	249,295	313,815	322,614	127,174	5,548	22,567
Italy................................	20,142	27,709	31,294	41,087	42,828	22,273	4,879	369
Luxembourg......................	170,309	350,772	316,922	228,167	246,908	159,162	4,713	6,278
Netherlands......................	234,408	298,782	554,720	700,747	717,467	410,567	36,565	30,419
Norway............................	10,478	20,641	30,362	36,650	42,436	1,656	(D)	(D)
Spain..............................	43,095	67,349	84,571	75,416	81,386	14,238	-42	(D)
Sweden...........................	38,780	44,961	59,964	93,364	104,853	52,596	23,241	(D)
Switzerland......................	180,642	241,008	293,461	336,233	351,539	201,275	(D)	(D)
United Kingdom.................	400,435	522,954	535,715	683,382	630,551	312,235	26,398	65,224
Latin America and other Western Hemisphere....................	62,130	123,846	209,774	206,894	210,923	36,973	8,892	24,480
South and Central America [3].....	17,943	25,261	44,165	64,161	61,633	18,016	5,770	795
Brazil............................	1,357	142	4,480	4,813	6,514	1,059	-13	382
Mexico...........................	10,970	15,262	20,646	33,463	38,385	10,101	4,695	290
Venezuela.......................	3,122	4,186	1,381	3,054	(D)	(D)	23	(Z)
Other Western Hemisphere [3]....	44,187	98,585	165,610	142,733	149,290	18,956	3,123	23,684
Bermuda.........................	365	-7,323	52,021	34,958	41,578	6,575	-788	-10,281
Curacao..........................	(X)	1,630	1,193	2,198	2,189	(D)	(D)	(D)
U.K. Islands, Caribbean.........	38,477	101,725	99,194	98,904	99,204	11,646	2,811	(D)
Africa [3]............................	2,265	4,310	9,875	10,349	10,053	7,828	105	-2
Middle East [3].....................	16,808	17,582	41,336	49,044	50,043	27,998	6,421	215
Israel.............................	8,714	6,865	10,487	10,616	10,327	2,126	(D)	46
Asia and Pacific [3].................	346,605	579,708	884,928	948,646	988,749	361,898	207,807	116,916
Australia..........................	35,632	65,259	85,809	106,701	110,908	27,471	3,043	7,610
China.............................	3300	14,714	36,738	29,907	28,043	7,179	1,558	448
Hong Kong.......................	4,440	10,981	14,212	17,007	18,054	8,226	1,171	(D)
India..............................	4102	9,639	1,658	3,830	4,664	2,465	319	(D)
Japan.............................	255,012	401,835	632,079	663,427	688,054	282,695	140,361	92,439
Singapore........................	21,517	21,585	28,486	37,452	37,468	10,694	3,233	(D)
South Korea......................	15,746	39,784	60,548	65,009	76,689	10,255	56,309	2,747
Taiwan............................	4,642	6,889	17,974	15,739	15,643	9,638	217	(D)

D Suppressed to avoid disclosure of data of individual companies. X Not applicable. Z Between -$500,000 and +$500,000. [1] Includes other industries, not shown separately. [2] Excludes depository institutions. [3] Includes other countries, not shown separately.

Source: U.S. Bureau of Economic Analysis, International Economic Accounts, New Foreign Direct Investment in the United States, "Direct Investment and Multinational Enterprises," <www.bea.gov/data/economic-accounts/international>, accessed August 2024.

Table 1310. U.S. Majority-Owned Affiliates of Foreign Companies—Assets, Sales, Employment, Value, Exports, and Imports by Industry of Affiliate: 2020

[In billions of dollars (16,359 represents $16,359,000,000,000); except employment in thousands (7,714 represents 7,714,000). A majority-owned U.S. affiliate is a U.S. business enterprise in which a foreign entity ("entity" is used here in a broad legal sense including any individual, branch, partnership, association, trust, corporation, or government) has a direct or indirect voting interest greater than 50 percent]

Industry	NAICS code [2]	Total assets	Sales	Employ-ment (1,000)	Employee compen-sation	Gross property, plant, and equipment	Mer-chandise exports	Mer-chandise imports
All industries.................................	**(X)**	**16,359**	**4,632**	**7,714**	**653**	**2,902**	**354**	**675**
Manufacturing [1]................................	31-33	3,256	1,941	2,761	260	1,225	223	333
Petroleum and coal products...................	324	273	219	88	13	261	18	24
Chemicals..	325	976	389	403	58	276	48	61
Machinery..	333	146	112	239	20	36	18	15
Transportation equipment.......................	336	493	504	599	46	253	56	149
Wholesale trade.................................	42	1,036	1,077	659	61	419	115	317
Retail trade.......................................	44-45	207	275	920	40	108	3	18
Information.......................................	51	487	188	325	32	142	1	1
Finance and insurance..........................	52	9,255	462	418	80	140	(D)	–
Real estate and rental and leasing..............	53	345	47	82	7	208	–	(D)
Professional, scientific, and technical services.....................................	54	367	168	509	58	34	1	1
Other industries.................................	(X)	1,406	474	2,041	116	626	(D)	(D)

X Not applicable. D Suppressed to avoid disclosure of data of individual companies. – Represents or rounds to zero. [1] Includes other industries not shown separately. [2] Based on the North American Industry Classification System (NAICS); see text, Section 15.

Source: U.S. Bureau of Economic Analysis, International Economic Accounts, "Foreign Direct Investment in the United States: Activities of U.S. Affiliates of Foreign Multinational Enterprises," <www.bea.gov/international/di1fdiop.htm>, accessed November 2023.

Table 1311. U.S. Direct Investment Position Abroad, Capital Outflows, and Income by Industry of Foreign Affiliates: 2010 to 2023

[In millions of dollars (3,741,910 represents $3,741,910,000,000). U.S. investment abroad is the ownership or control by one U.S. person (in the broad legal sense to include any individual, partnership, corporation, or other form of organization) of 10 percent or more of the voting securities of an incorporated foreign business enterprise or an equivalent interest in an unincorporated foreign business enterprise]

Industry	2010	2015	2019	2020	2021	2022	2023
DIRECT INVESTMENT POSITION ON A HISTORICAL-COST BASIS							
All industries, total [1]	**3,741,910**	**5,289,071**	**5,836,983**	**6,063,288**	**6,229,992**	**6,312,525**	**6,676,478**
Mining	172,819	180,418	155,027	127,921	130,767	141,340	151,498
Manufacturing [1]	518,321	693,847	805,439	906,793	966,249	995,947	994,789
Food	47,704	81,914	74,614	97,091	87,690	78,191	83,672
Chemicals	111,327	151,369	212,489	248,007	279,924	279,290	248,159
Primary and fabricated metals	18,674	34,506	47,142	42,484	46,952	54,338	53,652
Machinery	41,285	45,932	44,396	42,914	46,728	45,232	47,827
Computer and electronic products	72,935	97,641	125,732	131,974	155,300	178,754	188,289
Electrical equipment, appliances, and components	19,941	17,591	13,883	21,197	21,965	23,598	27,745
Transportation equipment	49,636	62,087	86,108	86,737	91,686	100,993	104,341
Wholesale trade	168,722	225,217	237,549	253,140	245,790	257,154	281,590
Information	126,063	198,689	269,375	222,928	272,192	337,745	373,937
Depository institutions (banking)	118,585	118,271	144,506	117,188	128,396	137,413	149,006
Finance and insurance	734,859	719,608	931,367	926,938	964,473	862,123	908,635
Professional, scientific, and technical services	81,874	117,646	152,175	133,864	139,815	163,605	175,947
Holding companies (nonbank)	1,584,903	2,686,477	2,720,512	2,934,527	3,016,058	3,055,492	3,255,221
FINANCIAL OUTFLOWS [INFLOWS(-)] WITHOUT CURRENT-COST ADJUSTMENT							
All industries, total [1]	**277,779**	**264,359**	**31,863**	**226,851**	**239,486**	**302,162**	**363,144**
Mining	11,884	416	-9,084	-2,903	-1,340	14,214	10,314
Manufacturing [1]	33,320	43,502	66,976	84,542	47,245	84,821	42,021
Food	5,341	4,449	1,846	2,491	991	7,619	3,868
Chemicals	7,614	6,470	29,875	62,003	15,164	7,724	10,258
Primary and fabricated metals	546	503	3,549	2,027	400	9,179	-851
Machinery	4,229	3,110	3,458	-361	3,882	2,907	3,399
Computer and electronic products	6,772	6,440	15,218	8,183	9,973	28,047	16,629
Electrical equipment, appliances, and components	1,743	1,545	1,036	7,647	3,096	2,480	4,505
Transportation equipment	-380	11,282	6,121	-2,699	1,343	11,295	4,241
Wholesale trade	15,487	9,495	19,913	19,094	22,739	5,436	26,960
Information	8,777	13,488	8,709	-9,414	34,976	62,978	40,931
Depository institutions	-4,811	-6,448	639	-6,105	1,103	-4,051	-1,079
Finance and insurance	21,887	15,632	-29,969	-33,011	45,080	17,559	39,133
Professional, scientific, and technical services	2,774	5,121	7,297	12,021	14,470	23,800	11,337
Holding companies (nonbank)	169,743	161,310	-74,165	153,706	54,073	79,271	180,019
INCOME WITHOUT CURRENT-COST ADJUSTMENT							
All industries, total [1]	**417,605**	**433,333**	**543,450**	**449,789**	**545,474**	**564,479**	**577,232**
Mining	29,138	3,541	9,707	4,174	15,777	25,969	17,058
Manufacturing [1]	61,240	67,102	74,585	57,251	82,839	82,765	83,887
Food	4,322	4,149	3,560	2,144	3,479	3,598	3,208
Chemicals	14,088	18,114	25,355	15,894	23,429	21,959	22,146
Primary and fabricated metals	1,349	1,721	2,502	2,526	2,436	1,939	2,157
Machinery	4,465	3,495	3,513	2,587	4,668	3,920	4,351
Computer and electronic products	11,440	10,868	15,481	15,849	21,537	21,246	19,233
Electrical equipment, appliances, and components	1,653	1,461	1,133	1,145	1,675	2,516	4,987
Transportation equipment	6,471	10,632	6,939	5,315	6,194	8,483	9,450
Wholesale trade	24,538	19,129	23,542	22,052	28,136	27,954	29,930
Information	12,229	14,756	20,851	9,874	20,516	21,506	31,887
Depository institutions	1,328	3,521	4,593	702	3,272	2,871	6,315
Finance and insurance	35,143	45,760	53,927	47,184	63,069	64,968	68,356
Professional, scientific, and technical services	8,856	11,145	16,291	12,788	20,377	22,027	20,312
Holding companies (nonbank)	220,101	233,272	292,579	264,245	283,903	282,417	283,972

[1] Includes other industries, not shown separately.

Source: U.S. Bureau of Economic Analysis, International Economic Accounts, Direct Investment by Country and Industry, "Direct Investment and Multinational Enterprises," <www.bea.gov/data/economic-accounts/international>, accessed August 2024.

Table 1312. U.S. Direct Investment Position Abroad on a Historical-Cost Basis by Selected Country: 2010 to 2023

[In millions of dollars (3,741,910 represents $3,741,910,000,000). U.S. investment abroad is the ownership or control by one U.S. person (in the broad legal sense to include any individual, partnership, corporation, or other form of organization) of 10 percent or more of the voting securities of an incorporated foreign business enterprise or an equivalent interest in an unincorporated foreign business enterprise. Negative position can occur when a U.S. parent company's liabilities to the foreign affiliate are greater than its equity in and loans to the foreign affiliate]

Country	2010	2015	2018	2019	2020	2021	2022	2023
All countries...............	3,741,910	5,289,071	5,792,290	5,836,983	6,063,288	6,229,992	6,312,525	6,676,478
Canada.............................	295,206	361,954	373,604	363,895	366,880	398,107	432,486	451,555
Europe [1].............................	2,034,559	3,075,567	3,413,031	3,447,083	3,606,804	3,711,460	3,803,047	3,950,153
Austria.............................	11,485	6,508	6,848	5,876	4,296	4,571	5,779	6,093
Belgium.............................	43,975	48,096	59,397	61,076	65,733	63,466	61,371	66,529
Czechia.............................	5,268	6,343	5,253	5,311	5,025	5,040	4,701	4,644
Denmark.............................	11,802	15,794	10,692	12,568	15,376	13,701	10,472	12,845
Finland.............................	1,597	1,258	4,063	2,788	3,617	4,588	6,065	5,527
France.............................	78,320	81,274	67,548	88,615	106,517	101,991	93,907	100,909
Germany.............................	103,319	120,519	134,794	139,457	152,278	162,114	178,597	193,179
Greece.............................	1,775	1,007	431	320	481	759	1,754	1,824
Hungary.............................	4,237	7,625	5,283	11,714	13,866	14,131	15,999	16,037
Ireland.............................	158,851	337,831	444,037	355,778	379,886	455,878	448,324	491,246
Italy.............................	27,137	30,869	32,842	25,376	27,459	25,432	25,537	29,025
Luxembourg.............................	272,206	599,001	720,628	724,642	654,941	575,401	526,780	532,465
Netherlands.............................	514,689	829,693	809,663	811,377	827,419	835,378	944,332	980,403
Norway.............................	28,541	31,697	25,905	22,922	13,627	16,176	15,281	15,358
Poland.............................	13,152	11,872	11,870	9,550	11,956	12,109	13,674	15,773
Portugal.............................	2,612	1,971	2,504	2,367	1,905	1,812	3,743	2,937
Russia.............................	10,040	10,259	12,779	14,169	12,874	12,054	8,231	7,669
Spain.............................	52,390	36,075	31,916	35,669	37,238	36,097	36,796	37,850
Sweden.............................	23,275	32,593	43,521	41,111	55,608	58,710	55,348	56,197
Switzerland.............................	119,891	171,342	210,800	205,916	236,767	209,802	201,606	238,228
Turkey.............................	4,155	3,798	4,193	3,572	6,223	5,998	6,048	6,254
United Kingdom.............................	501,247	632,327	754,139	852,540	944,908	1,022,826	1,069,237	1,057,592
Latin America and other Western Hemisphere..........	752,788	902,642	1,000,673	976,705	1,024,534	1,009,307	972,807	1,065,761
South America [1].................	136,598	129,303	134,707	139,045	147,949	154,570	163,240	181,410
Argentina.............................	11,747	14,624	8,907	11,373	13,325	12,701	11,887	14,514
Brazil.............................	66,963	56,847	78,963	74,483	69,086	71,664	77,377	87,909
Chile.............................	30,747	28,134	25,660	29,431	27,152	27,806	29,490	32,034
Colombia.............................	6,181	7,750	7,236	6,399	6,452	6,632	7,095	8,438
Ecuador.............................	1,283	913	781	1,429	929	846	820	906
Peru.............................	7,196	7,573	5,455	6,397	7,222	6,489	6,605	6,646
Venezuela.............................	10,255	9,825	2,338	3,311	3,106	3,162	3,089	3,268
Central America [1].................	97,752	112,690	107,381	121,015	121,016	129,746	141,447	156,428
Costa Rica.............................	1,827	1,642	1,589	3,125	3,066	2,861	3,324	3,810
Honduras.............................	936	1,274	1,202	1,484	894	939	1,242	1,391
Mexico.............................	85,751	101,326	95,543	106,433	110,753	119,947	130,794	144,507
Panama.............................	5,156	4,447	5,206	5,516	3,500	3,518	3,801	4,512
Other Western Hemisphere [1].....	518,438	660,650	758,586	716,645	755,569	724,991	668,121	727,923
Barbados.............................	7,524	14,084	40,015	42,439	57,819	43,692	46,178	45,499
Bermuda.............................	265,524	303,244	339,399	300,719	288,011	225,962	182,354	219,608
Dominican Republic.............	1,432	1,079	2,101	2,753	2,567	2,055	1,993	1,893
U.K. Islands, Caribbean.........	191,680	303,438	304,716	310,510	350,988	398,143	380,220	398,939
Africa [1].............................	54,816	52,004	48,069	45,404	43,808	46,991	48,901	56,291
Egypt.............................	12,599	14,068	11,028	10,680	10,665	11,536	11,477	13,691
Nigeria.............................	5,058	5,872	4,504	6,608	6,786	5,699	6,190	6,533
South Africa.............................	6,017	6,926	9,088	7,761	6,748	6,715	6,881	7,969
Middle East [1].........................	34,431	49,802	76,945	81,393	80,790	78,437	76,089	80,530
Israel.............................	9,464	10,251	28,997	34,100	41,329	43,074	41,832	45,910
Saudi Arabia.............................	7,436	10,025	10,807	11,002	11,188	11,241	11,022	11,311
United Arab Emirates.............	4,935	16,205	18,055	15,741	16,054	15,000	15,831	16,106
Asia and Pacific [1].................	570,111	847,102	879,968	922,502	940,473	985,690	979,194	1,072,188
Australia.............................	125,421	160,061	166,269	159,404	178,223	170,683	176,097	193,340
China.............................	58,996	92,150	107,557	109,348	116,508	116,003	122,205	126,908
Hong Kong.............................	41,264	69,367	81,215	97,788	94,495	92,664	85,917	90,564
India.............................	24,666	35,361	42,197	40,692	42,291	43,967	46,055	49,563
Indonesia.............................	10,558	15,717	19,886	19,918	12,158	12,831	13,497	15,937
Japan.............................	113,523	106,932	108,933	120,010	118,453	106,066	54,164	63,369
Malaysia.............................	11,791	15,765	10,385	12,673	13,788	11,349	12,508	10,926
New Zealand.............................	6,724	11,427	11,379	11,615	11,701	11,792	9,323	8,547
Philippines.............................	5,399	5,992	5,562	6,378	5,037	4,997	6,232	6,359
Singapore.............................	102,778	253,277	232,940	251,384	264,188	333,672	374,546	424,214
South Korea.............................	26,233	38,608	37,282	37,992	37,550	38,181	33,083	35,642
Taiwan.............................	22,188	15,295	27,479	25,406	18,569	17,040	17,772	19,327
Thailand.............................	12,999	17,942	16,415	17,134	15,484	15,755	16,467	15,138

[1] Includes other countries, not shown separately.

Source: U.S. Bureau of Economic Analysis, International Economic Accounts, Direct Investment by Country and Industry, "Direct Investment and Multinational Enterprises," <www.bea.gov/data/economic-accounts/international>, accessed August 2024.

Table 1313. U.S. Foreign Economic and Military Aid by Major Recipient Country: 2000 to 2020

[In millions of dollars (17,111.9 represents $17,111,900,000). For years ending September 30. Annual figures are for obligations. Total aid may not add due to rounding]

Region/country	2000	2010	2015	2019	2020 Total	2020 Economic aid	2020 Military aid
Total [1]	**17,111.9**	**48,356.8**	**49,946.2**	**48,176.4**	**51,058.0**	**39,417.2**	**11,640.8**
Middle East & North Africa [1]	**6,799.2**	**8,827.9**	**10,697.8**	**11,993.9**	**12,151.7**	**5,428.5**	**6,723.2**
Egypt	2,076.1	1,602.8	1,568.3	1,467.0	1,471.1	169.1	1,302.0
Iraq	1.2	2,091.8	1,550.6	959.3	1,180.5	632.4	548.1
Israel	3,863.4	2,837.6	3,293.6	3,308.5	3,310.9	10.9	3,300.0
Jordan	448.3	765.7	1,512.5	1,723.3	2,594.0	2,090.0	504.0
Lebanon	35.0	158.7	507.7	791.0	830.6	586.1	244.5
Morocco	51.1	56.1	116.5	67.0	64.0	39.8	24.3
Syria	–	22.4	913.5	653.7	837.1	837.1	(Z)
Tunisia	7.1	21.2	122.9	202.2	277.3	175.2	102.1
West Bank/Gaza [2]	122.0	686.9	556.8	28.0	18.3	18.3	–
Yemen	57.2	122.4	176.8	809.8	556.5	555.4	1.2
Sub-Saharan Africa [1]	**2,025.1**	**8,422.2**	**11,417.0**	**13,129.6**	**13,810.3**	**13,394.9**	**415.4**
Angola	105.4	99.9	58.3	50.4	62.6	62.3	0.4
Botswana	0.9	51.1	42.5	63.0	75.1	74.8	0.4
Burkina Faso	18.1	33.3	33.0	100.8	212.8	211.9	1.0
Chad	4.1	184.4	108.7	154.9	139.6	137.2	2.4
Congo, Democratic Republic of	32.6	366.2	469.7	790.7	964.6	959.5	5.1
Ethiopia	277.6	831.2	809.7	966.9	1,213.2	1,209.4	3.8
Ghana	66.8	109.4	290.3	140.6	-63.8	-68.1	4.3
Kenya	93.5	569.0	939.6	823.2	830.5	826.4	4.1
Lesotho	2.1	33.0	29.2	92.6	104.5	104.5	(Z)
Liberia	22.4	179.9	771.8	159.7	146.2	145.3	0.9
Madagascar	27.4	58.2	156.5	108.6	129.6	128.6	0.9
Malawi	44.4	172.9	244.2	344.2	367.4	366.8	0.5
Mali	43.7	125.1	206.5	220.7	213.2	211.9	1.4
Mozambique	82.1	298.6	338.3	579.6	567.7	566.5	1.2
Namibia	15.5	88.7	43.7	71.0	81.8	81.7	0.1
Nigeria	112.6	408.5	591.5	863.6	1,114.8	1,104.9	9.9
Rwanda	39.0	173.1	246.0	202.7	234.4	232.9	1.5
Senegal	37.4	656.6	121.1	217.4	160.3	158.5	1.7
Somalia	13.9	156.2	252.7	665.4	689.6	551.2	138.4
South Africa	56.8	466.6	354.6	624.1	1,114.2	1,114.0	0.2
South Sudan [3]	–	–	848.9	685.7	759.7	739.2	20.5
Sudan	51.0	894.2	233.5	373.3	375.1	374.1	1.0
Tanzania	44.5	421.9	592.9	574.5	622.3	620.8	1.5
Uganda	76.2	422.8	591.7	913.7	800.4	797.6	2.8
Zambia	35.4	263.6	244.5	405.4	451.3	450.9	0.3
Zimbabwe	20.9	217.4	188.4	316.7	340.2	340.2	–
Latin America & Caribbean [1]	**2,301.2**	**4,347.3**	**3,942.7**	**3,093.5**	**3,122.3**	**2,950.3**	**171.9**
Bolivia	241.1	91.7	56.0	3.2	13.2	13.2	–
Colombia	1,168.6	794.5	839.6	800.7	812.6	745.0	67.5
El Salvador	34.9	62.1	332.1	85.4	92.1	89.4	2.7
Guatemala	71.8	154.8	138.2	157.2	125.0	115.3	9.7
Haiti	84.5	1,366.5	493.4	293.0	265.6	265.5	0.2
Honduras	41.8	39.7	133.6	70.8	125.4	121.4	4.0
Mexico	43.9	718.1	583.6	444.7	270.7	250.8	19.9
Peru	204.2	203.4	304.7	182.5	223.8	219.5	4.3
Asia [1]	**1,163.2**	**15,170.6**	**11,462.1**	**8,358.7**	**6,917.9**	**3,765.7**	**3,152.2**
Afghanistan	54.1	10,873.6	8,263.3	4,888.8	3,946.3	1,184.8	2,761.5
Bangladesh	78.3	184.8	228.3	448.3	559.1	542.2	16.9
Cambodia	27.5	72.3	96.0	105.3	128.0	127.5	0.5
India	188.0	115.2	117.7	100.8	160.1	158.4	1.7
Indonesia	242.3	309.4	220.5	263.0	177.8	153.7	24.2
Mongolia	25.8	38.0	12.3	26.8	36.9	25.9	11.0
Nepal	22.6	67.6	264.9	174.2	124.5	123.2	1.2
Pakistan	23.8	2,681.1	1,141.5	684.8	197.0	158.9	38.1
Philippines	82.2	200.3	265.2	428.3	387.4	222.4	165.1
Sri Lanka	10.5	81.5	30.7	61.5	78.0	72.3	5.7
Oceania [1]	**164.7**	**209.7**	**231.3**	**289.0**	**336.2**	**317.3**	**18.9**
Micronesia, Federated States of	81.0	90.1	112.8	135.8	146.6	138.9	7.8
Central Asia [1]	**1,461.9**	**2,141.1**	**1,141.0**	**1,111.0**	**1,289.7**	**870.7**	**419.0**
Armenia	104.2	53.4	50.3	41.1	66.7	64.0	2.7
Georgia	112.4	229.2	109.1	124.8	169.8	89.0	80.8
Kazakhstan	53.4	331.2	106.3	49.8	60.8	32.8	28.1
Kyrgyzstan	47.3	128.2	61.4	43.1	45.9	45.8	(Z)
Moldova	48.6	294.0	47.1	66.8	49.3	44.9	4.5
Russia	708.6	505.1	314.9	6.8	10.3	10.3	–
Ukraine	199.5	314.3	269.1	592.8	677.9	393.9	284.0
Eastern Europe [1]	**1,045.3**	**706.8**	**316.5**	**643.8**	**793.3**	**263.0**	**530.4**
Kosovo	–	35.0	52.2	72.9	57.4	46.6	10.8
Poland	84.8	220.8	11.1	14.9	12.1	(Z)	12.1
Western Europe	**24.0**	**77.5**	**202.6**	**201.3**	**263.6**	**233.2**	**30.4**

– Represents zero. Z Less than $50,000. [1] Includes other countries, not shown separately, and aid not assigned to specific countries within their parent regions. [2] See footnote 3, Table 1356. [3] South Sudan seceded from Sudan in July 2011.

Source: U.S. Agency for International Development, *U.S. Overseas Loans and Grants: Obligations and Loan Authorizations, July 1, 1945–September 30, 2020*, and earlier reports. See also <foreignassistance.gov/reports>.

Table 1314. U.S. Foreign Economic and Military Aid Programs: 1990 to 2020

[In millions of dollars (16,003 represents $16,003,000,000). For years ending September 30. Total foreign aid programs are the sum of economic and military assistance. Major components in recent years include U.S. Agency for International Development (USAID), U.S. Department of Agriculture (USDA), U.S. Department of State, and U.S. Department of Treasury. Annual figures are in obligations]

Year and world region	Total foreign assistance	Military assistance	Economic assistance, by funding agency					
			Total	USAID	USDA	State Depart-ment	Treasury Depart-ment	Other U.S. agencies
1990	16,003	4,959	11,044	6,964	1,643	590	1,469	377
2000	17,112	5,149	11,963	5,907	1,936	2,278	1,110	731
2005	35,461	9,071	26,390	14,160	2,208	4,674	1,240	4,108
2007	39,726	13,973	25,754	10,371	1,806	5,594	1,476	6,507
2008	46,745	16,457	30,288	9,800	2,755	8,967	1,217	7,550
2009	46,641	14,801	31,840	11,810	2,614	11,261	1,638	4,518
2010	48,357	14,853	33,504	12,053	2,562	11,538	2,245	5,106
2011	49,145	18,668	30,476	10,553	1,999	10,577	2,034	5,313
2012	50,502	17,861	32,641	11,282	2,028	13,085	2,829	3,418
2013	46,065	13,808	32,257	11,779	1,675	11,548	2,672	4,582
2014	43,949	11,073	32,876	10,871	1,728	14,232	2,735	3,310
2015	49,946	15,097	34,849	13,398	1,679	13,423	2,642	3,708
2016	49,473	14,814	34,659	12,577	1,981	14,071	2,286	3,744
2017	48,120	12,753	35,368	14,469	2,072	13,627	1,846	3,353
2018	47,973	14,662	33,311	13,537	2,206	13,200	1,558	2,810
2019	48,176	14,082	34,095	14,525	2,024	13,687	1,552	2,306
2020, total	**51,058**	**11,641**	**39,417**	**16,166**	**1,235**	**18,479**	**1,874**	**1,662**
Asia	6,918	3,152	3,766	2,235	15	1,260	51	204
Eurasia	1,290	419	871	514	1	273	1	82
Eastern Europe	793	530	263	159	(Z)	84	(Z)	20
Latin America and Caribbean	3,122	172	2,950	1,314	17	1,473	8	137
Middle East and North Africa	12,152	6,723	5,429	3,814	226	1,308	–	81
Oceania	336	19	317	62	(Z)	19	(Z)	235
Sub-Saharan Africa	13,810	415	13,395	4,746	893	7,407	178	171
Western Europe	264	30	233	37	(Z)	185	–	12
Canada	35	(Z)	35	(Z)	–	–	–	35
World, not specified [1]	12,338	179	12,158	3,286	83	6,470	1,635	685

– Represents zero. Z indicates a value less than $50,000. [1] Includes U.S. Government loan and grant assistance not assigned to a specific country nor region, including assistance to international financial institutions, international organizations and global programs.

Source: U.S. Agency for International Development, *U.S. Overseas Loans and Grants: Obligations and Loan Authorizations, July 1, 1945–September 30, 2020*, and earlier reports. See also <foreignassistance.gov/reports>.

Table 1315. U.S. International Trade in Goods by Related Parties: 2010 to 2023

[In millions of dollars (1,900,587 represents $1,900,587,000,000). "Related party trade" is trade by U.S. companies with their subsidiaries abroad as well as trade by U.S. subsidiaries of foreign companies with their parent companies]

Country and commodity	NAICS code [2]	2010	2015	2020	2021	2022	2023
IMPORTS FOR CONSUMPTION							
Total imports	(X)	1,900,587	2,227,237	2,330,555	2,817,858	3,223,568	3,072,514
Related party trade, imports, total [1]	(X)	922,340	1,113,211	1,115,501	1,304,541	1,501,370	1,514,145
Mexico	(X)	135,989	207,923	214,007	248,842	287,958	308,323
Canada	(X)	138,210	148,471	130,319	169,393	220,093	214,982
Japan	(X)	94,001	101,753	94,012	105,600	114,938	117,845
Germany	(X)	54,005	83,616	78,585	91,435	100,775	109,405
China	(X)	107,007	131,390	79,056	90,737	98,533	83,676
Ireland	(X)	27,980	35,350	53,118	59,127	65,668	71,910
Transportation equipment	336	179,675	276,328	246,159	265,527	302,058	362,627
Chemicals	325	134,018	152,484	195,043	215,058	243,041	248,150
Computer & electronic products	334	203,829	221,761	187,059	223,617	242,705	220,905
Machinery, except electrical	333	53,722	81,871	85,807	104,981	118,315	122,671
Oil & gas	211	80,046	53,351	44,459	74,948	118,302	94,184
Electrical equipment, appliances & components	335	33,496	50,007	57,494	67,152	74,523	79,475
Primary metal manufacturing	331	26,738	29,629	48,133	44,877	52,448	45,865
EXPORTS							
Total exports	(X)	1,122,567	1,286,172	1,205,387	1,481,182	1,745,689	1,689,093
Related party trade, domestic exports, total [1]	(X)	311,693	382,910	397,831	477,011	579,185	566,110
Canada	(X)	85,861	91,863	81,457	99,557	120,200	119,222
Mexico	(X)	49,612	78,123	64,436	80,521	97,449	98,078
Netherlands	(X)	15,032	17,309	21,590	23,885	34,106	39,763
China	(X)	13,396	22,196	32,485	33,584	32,464	28,934
Germany	(X)	12,571	15,557	19,281	21,437	25,285	26,697
Japan	(X)	16,690	17,702	20,179	24,753	27,762	22,949
Chemicals	325	64,361	79,695	82,433	101,893	113,073	116,336
Transportation equipment	336	55,466	86,973	77,495	85,368	96,723	106,443
Oil & gas	211	4,316	5,362	32,380	46,883	84,962	66,500
Petroleum & coal products	324	23,367	24,271	19,542	29,356	56,328	50,100
Machinery, except electrical	333	32,318	34,338	35,210	42,353	45,597	46,339
Computer & electronic products	334	42,795	38,524	40,666	42,645	42,228	42,775

X Not applicable. [1] Includes other countries and other commodities not shown separately. [2] Based on the North American Industry Classification System (NAICS); see text, Section 15.

Source: U.S. Census Bureau, "Imports and Exports by Related Parties," <www.census.gov/foreign-trade/Press-Release/related_party/index.html>, accessed August 2024.

Table 1316. U.S. International Trade in Goods and Services: 2000 to 2023

[In millions of dollars (-369,686 represents -$369,686,000,000). Data are presented on a balance of payments basis and will not agree with the following merchandise trade tables in this section. Additionally, all data were revised due to updates to classifications and change in methodology and will not necessarily be comparable with data previously presented. See source for more information. Minus sign (-) indicates deficit]

Category	2000	2010	2015	2020	2021	2022	2023
TRADE BALANCE							
Total	**-369,686**	**-503,087**	**-490,776**	**-653,691**	**-848,070**	**-944,762**	**-784,890**
Goods	-446,783	-648,671	-761,868	-912,875	-1,083,190	-1,179,941	-1,063,288
Services	77,096	145,584	271,092	259,185	235,120	235,179	278,398
Maintenance and repair services, n.i.e. [1]	2,107	7,254	11,763	8,204	7,701	8,963	9,478
Transport [2]	-9,064	-12,037	-15,123	-15,483	-39,999	-65,306	-45,095
Travel for all purposes [3]	32,698	45,149	89,938	38,080	12,748	24,286	30,456
Construction [4]	546	373	-253	1,362	631	-198	-65
Insurance services	-7,653	-48,598	-34,537	-37,720	-36,749	-38,318	-39,622
Financial services	12,747	59,297	83,002	105,142	120,583	109,966	112,770
Charges for the use of intellectual property, n.i.e. [1,5]	27,337	63,852	75,973	70,911	80,549	76,845	86,905
Telecommunications, computer, and information services	-1,878	-2,865	2,612	12,459	6,131	9,610	10,487
Other business services [6]	17,911	33,692	46,302	82,481	90,474	107,651	108,116
Personal, cultural, recreational services [7]	7,706	12,219	12,862	-3,674	-4,506	-2,050	-2,281
Government goods and services, n.i.e. [1,8]	-5,360	-12,750	-1,444	-2,577	-2,444	3,732	7,250
EXPORTS							
Total	**1,082,963**	**1,872,320**	**2,280,778**	**2,160,147**	**2,570,802**	**3,039,405**	**3,071,816**
Goods	784,940	1,290,279	1,511,381	1,433,852	1,765,853	2,090,339	2,045,221
Services	298,023	582,041	769,397	726,296	804,948	949,065	1,026,596
Maintenance and repair services, n.i.e. [1]	4,423	13,111	19,847	13,288	12,569	14,416	15,948
Transport [2]	49,462	76,357	84,434	57,471	66,798	92,405	97,779
Travel for all purposes [3]	96,872	130,315	192,602	72,479	71,746	142,909	189,134
Construction [4]	1,993	2,951	2,759	2,370	2,957	1,948	1,529
Insurance services	3,631	14,854	15,763	20,023	23,011	23,987	24,985
Financial services	29,192	86,512	115,688	150,838	171,530	167,445	175,461
Charges for the use of intellectual property, n.i.e. [1,5]	43,476	94,968	111,151	115,936	131,079	137,833	134,442
Telecommunications, computer, and information services	12,250	26,556	41,427	56,071	57,984	64,717	70,629
Other business services [6]	38,217	99,595	141,421	195,133	220,451	246,416	253,190
Personal, cultural, recreational services [7]	9,351	17,612	24,220	20,710	23,906	27,711	30,732
Government goods and services, n.i.e. [1,8]	9,156	19,210	20,087	21,976	22,916	29,279	32,767
IMPORTS							
Total	**1,452,650**	**2,375,407**	**2,771,554**	**2,813,838**	**3,418,871**	**3,984,167**	**3,856,707**
Goods	1,231,722	1,938,950	2,273,249	2,346,727	2,849,043	3,270,281	3,108,509
Services	220,927	436,456	498,305	467,111	569,829	713,886	748,198
Maintenance and repair services, n.i.e. [1]	2,316	5,857	8,084	5,084	4,868	5,453	6,470
Transport [2]	58,526	88,394	99,557	72,954	106,797	157,711	142,874
Travel for all purposes [3]	64,174	85,166	102,664	34,399	58,998	118,623	158,678
Construction [4]	1,447	2,578	3,012	1,008	2,326	2,146	1,594
Insurance services	11,284	63,452	50,300	57,743	59,760	62,305	64,607
Financial services	16,445	27,215	32,686	45,696	50,947	57,479	62,691
Charges for the use of intellectual property, n.i.e. [1,5]	16,139	31,116	35,178	45,025	50,530	60,988	47,537
Telecommunications, computer, and information services	14,128	29,421	38,815	43,612	51,853	55,107	60,142
Other business services [6]	20,306	65,903	95,119	112,652	129,977	138,765	145,074
Personal, cultural, recreational services [7]	1,645	5,393	11,358	24,384	28,412	29,761	33,013
Government goods and services, n.i.e. [1,8]	14,516	31,960	21,531	24,553	25,360	25,547	25,517

[1] N.i.e. means not included elsewhere. [2] Covers transactions associated with moving people and freight, and related supporting and auxiliary services. [3] All travel purposes include 1) business travel, including expenditures by border, seasonal, and other short-term workers and 2) personal travel, including health-related and education-related travel. Excludes air passenger services for travel between countries, which are included in transport. [4] Construction covers the services provided to create, renovate, repair, or extend buildings, land improvements, and civil engineering constructions, such as roads and bridges. Construction exports exclude inputs purchased by foreign contractors for projects in the U.S. Construction imports include inputs purchased abroad by U.S. contractors. See source for more detail. [5] Includes charges for the use of proprietary rights, such as patents, trademarks, copyrights, and franchises, and charges for licenses to reproduce and/or distribute intellectual property. [6] Consists of research and development services, professional and management consulting services (including advertising and market research), and technical, trade-related, and other business services. [7] Covers three subcategories: 1) Audiovisual services, which covers production of audiovisual content, end-user rights to use audiovisual content, and outright sales and purchases of audiovisual originals; 2) artistic-related services, which includes the services provided by performing artists, authors, composers, and other visual artists; set, costume, and lighting design; presentation and promotion of performing arts and other live entertainment events; and fees to artists and athletes for performances, sporting events, and similar events; and 3) other personal, cultural, and recreational services, which includes services such as education services delivered online, telemedicine, and services associated with museum and other cultural, sporting gambling, and recreational activities, except those acquired by customers traveling outside their country of residence. See source for more information. [8] Includes goods and services supplied by and to embassies, military bases, and international organizations; goods and services acquired by diplomatic and military personnel in the host economy; and services supplied by and to governments not included in other categories of services.

Source: U.S. Bureau of Economic Analysis, "International Economic Accounts: Trade in Goods and Services," <www.bea.gov/data/economic-accounts/international#trade>, accessed August 2024.

Table 1317. U.S. Freight Gateways—Value of Shipments: 2023

[In billions of dollars (5,098.2 represents $5,098,200,000,000), except as indicated. For the top 40 gateways ranked by value of total shipments]

Port	Rank	Total trade	Exports	Imports	Exports as a percent of total
Total U.S. merchandise trade [1]	(X)	5,098.2	2,018.1	3,080.2	39.6
Top 40 gateways	(X)	4,033.3	1,514.4	2,518.9	37.5
As a percent of total	(X)	79.1	75.0	81.8	(X)
Laredo, TX	1	319.9	123.0	196.9	38.5
Chicago, IL	2	310.4	74.2	236.3	23.9
Los Angeles, CA	3	292.2	32.8	259.4	11.2
JFK International Airport, NY	4	247.8	112.5	135.3	45.4
Newark, NJ	5	238.8	21.6	217.2	9.1
Houston, TX	6	227.4	124.4	102.9	54.7
Detroit, MI	7	173.3	88.5	84.8	51.1
New Orleans, LA	8	155.1	88.8	66.4	57.2
Los Angeles International Airport, CA	9	132.5	59.3	73.2	44.7
Savannah, GA	10	128.3	32.9	95.4	25.6
Port Huron, MI	11	126.7	59.3	67.4	46.8
Long Beach, CA	12	107.9	26.4	81.4	24.5
Norfolk-Newport News, VA	13	107.7	38.6	69.1	35.8
Charleston, SC	14	101.6	32.8	68.8	32.3
Buffalo-Niagara Falls, NY	15	98.9	51.8	47.1	52.4
Cleveland, OH	16	86.0	48.8	37.2	56.8
Corpus Christi, TX	17	85.8	80.4	5.4	93.7
Baltimore, MD	18	80.6	21.8	58.8	27.0
Ysleta, TX	19	76.4	25.8	50.6	33.7
Miami International Airport, FL	20	74.6	43.6	31.0	58.5
Atlanta, GA	21	72.9	22.1	50.9	30.3
San Francisco International Airport, CA	22	66.3	30.3	36.1	45.6
Dallas-Fort Worth, TX	23	64.7	27.6	37.1	42.6
Otay Mesa, CA	24	63.1	22.2	40.8	35.3
Anchorage, AK	25	59.4	22.9	36.5	38.6
Oakland, CA	26	48.8	18.7	30.1	38.3
Tacoma, WA	27	48.8	7.6	41.2	15.5
Hidalgo, TX	28	45.9	16.9	28.9	36.9
New York, NY	29	39.9	29.9	10.0	75.0
Philadelphia, PA	30	38.6	6.2	32.5	16.0
Eagle Pass, TX	31	37.2	11.6	25.6	31.1
Pembina, ND	32	34.4	17.9	16.5	52.1
Brunswick, GA	33	32.4	12.1	20.3	37.4
Nogales, AZ	34	32.4	10.4	21.9	32.2
Miami, FL	35	31.8	10.8	20.9	34.1
Champlain-Rouses Point, NY	36	30.8	10.9	19.9	35.4
Blaine, WA	37	30.1	15.8	14.2	52.7
Jacksonville, FL	38	28.7	8.4	20.3	29.1
Santa Teresa, NM	39	27.7	9.9	17.8	35.6
Port Everglades, FL	40	27.7	14.9	12.8	53.7

X Not applicable. [1] Includes ports not shown separately, as well as low value and mail shipments.

Source: U.S. Census Bureau, Foreign Trade Division, "USA Trade Online," <usatrade.census.gov>, accessed June 2024.

Table 1318. U.S. Agricultural Exports by State: 2000 to 2022

[In millions of dollars (55,011 represents $55,011,000,000). Calendar year. Export estimates based on U.S. farm cash receipts. Export values are calibrated such that the sum of state export estimates for a commodity equals the total U.S. export value for the commodity]

State	2000	2010	2020	2021	2022	State	2000	2010	2020	2021	2022
U.S.	55,011	116,229	144,782	171,120	188,857	MO	1,364	3,555	4,499	5,252	6,147
						MT	501	1,068	1,455	1,473	1,469
AL	569	1,133	1,380	1,551	1,703	NE	2,298	5,378	7,264	9,294	9,977
AK	6	12	17	21	21	NV	65	112	138	172	190
AZ	485	1,082	1,280	1,382	1,704	NH	32	69	74	74	79
AR	1,315	3,238	3,536	3,837	4,336	NJ	245	418	637	705	687
CA	6,800	14,405	22,379	23,885	24,743	NM	319	688	718	868	948
CO	885	1,455	1,784	2,169	2,155	NY	498	1,259	1,594	1,863	2,044
CT	148	233	262	285	286	NC	3,297	3,633	3,731	4,376	4,499
DE	130	245	296	324	354	ND	1,194	3,510	4,344	4,983	5,875
FL	1,895	3,018	3,383	3,442	3,533	OH	1,503	3,482	4,098	5,062	6,082
GA	1,521	2,517	2,975	3,202	3,864	OK	812	1,546	1,892	2,172	2,371
HI	149	330	304	372	350	OR	780	1,388	1,957	2,355	2,375
ID	712	1,492	2,267	2,578	2,896	PA	708	1,675	2,144	2,412	2,591
IL	3,115	7,579	8,757	11,220	13,690	RI	12	32	28	33	33
IN	1,748	4,387	5,220	6,659	7,402	SC	684	838	816	989	1,162
IA	3,479	9,466	11,316	14,282	16,515	SD	1,205	2,950	3,753	4,895	5,433
KS	1,950	4,476	5,815	7,033	7,231	TN	899	1,309	1,793	1,944	2,173
KY	2,488	1,686	2,344	3,131	3,289	TX	2,667	6,393	5,899	7,169	8,540
LA	613	1,591	1,705	1,860	1,908	UT	162	321	473	539	600
ME	149	254	266	331	329	VT	48	146	182	218	256
MD	362	581	775	893	935	VA	765	947	1,212	1,337	1,465
MA	119	213	223	244	226	WA	1,304	2,833	3,801	3,804	4,119
MI	903	2,406	2,980	3,951	4,313	WV	65	119	161	181	183
MN	2,199	6,208	7,130	9,383	10,039	WI	928	2,485	3,184	3,953	4,675
MS	767	1,845	2,202	2,547	2,655	WY	146	225	339	415	410

Source: U.S. Department of Agriculture, Economic Research Service, "State Agricultural Trade Data," <www.ers.usda.gov/data-products/state-agricultural-trade-data/>, accessed November 2023.

[In billions of dollars (1,278.5 represents $1,278,500,000,000). Exports are f.a.s. (free alongside ship) value basis; imports are on customs-value basis. General imports are a combination of entries for immediate consumption, entries into customs bonded warehouses, and entries into U.S. Foreign Trade Zones. These data may differ from those in Table 1315, Table 1322, and Table 1323. For methodology, see Foreign Trade Statistics in Appendix III]

Customs district	Exports					General imports				
	2010	2020	2021	2022	2023	2010	2020	2021	2022	2023
Total [1]	1,278.5	1,430.0	1,757.7	2,066.5	2,018.1	1,913.9	2,331.5	2,828.5	3,239.9	3,080.2
Anchorage, AK	14.5	19.6	25.8	26.1	23.4	16.2	15.2	20.2	23.6	16.6
Baltimore, MD	14.7	12.9	17.4	19.8	22.1	28.8	37.5	45.4	57.0	60.2
Boston, MA	8.2	6.2	8.7	9.2	9.3	19.2	18.9	22.1	26.6	25.4
Buffalo, NY	40.6	36.8	43.1	48.6	51.9	39.2	34.2	41.6	48.8	48.3
Charleston, SC	19.5	30.6	30.3	29.2	34.1	29.4	47.1	59.5	69.8	67.3
Chicago, IL	35.8	53.7	65.6	71.7	75.4	125.6	214.9	277.7	316.2	289.6
Cleveland, OH	25.4	48.4	52.1	60.0	60.6	69.2	100.9	116.0	127.1	112.9
Columbia-Snake, OR	12.3	13.2	19.2	20.3	16.1	12.2	11.9	13.7	15.7	14.1
Dallas-Fort Worth, TX	18.1	23.1	27.0	29.8	29.4	38.4	45.4	57.1	60.4	59.8
Detroit, MI	113.2	110.8	129.1	147.7	151.1	106.0	116.3	138.5	155.6	164.9
Duluth, MN	2.6	3.6	4.9	6.1	5.6	6.8	8.1	11.5	13.9	10.5
El Paso, TX	29.3	39.2	48.9	56.3	51.0	44.1	62.8	74.8	86.4	83.7
Great Falls, MT	17.4	16.5	19.0	20.2	20.8	26.9	24.3	34.5	42.2	37.3
Honolulu, HI	7.4	1.4	2.1	3.1	4.0	4.6	6.1	10.8	9.6	4.9
Houston-Galveston, TX	94.5	127.2	177.7	256.1	238.3	116.9	67.3	96.0	133.6	124.8
Laredo, TX	81.4	110.7	142.4	160.4	167.5	104.2	180.7	212.2	250.9	268.9
Los Angeles, CA	105.1	107.6	113.4	121.9	119.7	242.7	296.9	364.9	402.1	348.0
Miami, FL	58.9	51.0	64.9	74.2	73.3	36.6	45.7	55.3	62.4	63.8
Milwaukee, WI	0.1	0.2	0.3	0.3	0.8	0.9	0.9	1.8	2.9	1.4
Minneapolis, MN	2.6	1.2	1.7	1.8	2.2	13.6	12.7	15.8	22.9	20.4
Mobile, AL	8.7	7.5	10.6	14.2	12.2	20.8	20.3	27.7	33.6	33.3
New Orleans, LA	69.1	95.9	118.1	160.6	144.5	125.3	98.3	110.3	119.4	116.8
New York, NY	136.3	124.8	156.0	171.1	164.4	190.6	270.4	310.1	349.8	319.9
Nogales, AZ	8.9	11.1	13.2	13.5	13.7	17.4	21.5	22.6	26.3	29.7
Norfolk, VA	21.1	24.6	30.6	35.5	38.7	23.9	32.4	42.3	49.2	44.0
Ogdensburg, NY	16.2	16.7	19.4	21.7	20.9	27.8	28.0	36.5	39.6	38.7
Pembina, ND	21.3	23.5	28.8	37.5	36.7	14.7	17.5	22.8	26.9	26.8
Philadelphia, PA	14.3	14.6	18.1	21.7	20.9	56.9	54.0	60.2	69.8	68.9
Port Arthur, TX	6.5	19.7	36.8	58.7	42.5	26.4	6.7	11.9	18.2	14.9
Portland, ME	4.4	3.9	5.6	7.3	7.2	9.8	11.7	16.0	16.3	13.6
Providence, RI	0.3	0.2	0.3	0.3	0.4	5.8	7.3	7.0	8.3	9.2
San Diego, CA	16.2	22.2	28.3	32.2	33.1	32.4	45.8	55.0	61.1	63.9
San Francisco, CA	47.1	61.9	65.7	62.1	55.2	60.6	71.0	79.0	91.3	89.6
San Juan, PR	19.7	12.5	13.9	16.0	18.3	19.4	20.9	22.3	27.6	26.7
Savannah, GA	41.0	50.6	60.8	64.9	67.0	68.0	119.9	139.9	161.2	153.1
Seattle, WA	58.5	48.3	58.5	66.8	64.4	52.6	62.9	82.1	90.6	81.9
St. Albans, VT	3.3	1.8	2.0	2.1	2.2	6.9	7.6	7.9	9.5	9.5
St. Louis, MO	1.0	0.3	0.5	0.6	0.8	11.5	15.4	17.7	21.9	19.2
Tampa, FL	14.4	8.5	10.1	12.9	13.1	16.4	29.9	33.6	40.6	40.9
Virgin Islands, U.S.	1.9	0.7	2.0	2.5	3.4	10.5	0.8	1.4	0.8	0.4
Washington, DC	6.0	4.5	7.3	6.3	5.7	8.2	8.4	10.2	12.1	8.4
Wilmington, NC	5.3	4.6	5.6	7.4	7.3	12.8	15.6	23.0	16.8	24.6

[1] Totals include the following special districts, not shown separately: vessels under their own power or afloat, low valued imports and exports, and mail shipments. Totals may also include data for two or more Customs Districts that have been combined and published under an arbitrary designation, as a solution to disclosure situations.

Source: U.S. Census Bureau, U.S. Foreign Trade Division, "USA Trade Online," <usatrade.census.gov/>, accessed June 2024.

Table 1320. U.S. Exports of Goods by State of Origin: 2010 to 2023

[In millions of dollars (1,278,495 represents $1,278,495,000,000), except as indicated. Data are on a Census Basis. Exports are on a f.a.s. (free alongside ship) value basis and are based on origin of movement]

State	2010	2014	2015	2016	2017	2018	2019	2020	2021	2022	2023 Total	2023 Rank
Total¹	1,278,495	1,621,874	1,503,328	1,451,460	1,547,195	1,665,787	1,645,940	1,429,995	1,757,744	2,066,454	2,018,059	(X)
United States	1,208,081	1,551,164	1,436,224	1,385,513	1,481,701	1,595,168	1,572,598	1,366,827	1,682,975	1,977,862	1,923,244	(X)
Alabama	15,495	19,450	19,322	20,471	21,798	21,416	20,796	17,392	20,927	25,729	27,440	22
Alaska	4,155	5,111	4,620	4,350	4,941	4,834	4,989	4,611	5,989	5,574	5,264	40
Arizona	15,721	21,247	22,654	22,004	20,918	22,516	24,966	20,216	24,083	27,185	28,877	19
Arkansas	5,219	6,866	5,871	5,722	6,234	6,449	6,231	5,193	5,585	5,908	6,457	38
California	143,208	173,869	165,360	163,261	171,920	178,175	173,755	155,919	174,810	186,162	178,844	2
Colorado	6,726	8,364	7,950	7,569	8,054	8,332	8,097	8,174	9,095	10,293	10,401	32
Connecticut	16,029	15,963	15,242	14,394	14,792	17,403	16,231	13,827	14,548	15,352	15,846	29
Delaware	4,945	5,267	5,408	4,517	4,565	4,704	4,406	3,912	4,727	5,239	4,936	42
District of Columbia	1,483	940	1,088	1,331	1,483	2,724	3,689	2,770	1,535	1,531	1,746	50
Florida	55,399	58,439	53,903	52,036	54,897	57,252	55,989	45,765	55,758	67,739	68,908	6
Georgia	28,899	39,413	38,596	35,673	37,222	40,619	41,260	38,618	42,426	47,374	49,906	12
Hawaii	684	1,447	1,896	795	952	659	460	329	321	433	572	51
Idaho	5,157	5,138	4,302	4,877	3,863	4,028	3,433	3,407	3,751	4,083	4,006	43
Illinois	50,061	68,394	63,369	59,862	65,288	65,468	59,767	53,272	66,130	78,952	78,849	5
Indiana	28,764	35,589	33,819	34,653	37,747	39,320	39,422	35,585	41,373	45,453	54,246	10
Iowa	10,880	15,112	13,238	12,330	13,422	14,370	13,225	12,640	15,751	18,051	18,400	26
Kansas	9,900	12,022	10,689	10,155	11,244	11,582	11,681	10,410	12,549	14,018	14,085	31
Kentucky	19,346	27,757	27,637	29,192	30,919	31,808	33,007	24,618	29,802	34,929	40,246	15
Louisiana	41,371	64,770	48,679	48,367	56,865	67,233	63,878	58,600	76,561	122,012	99,371	4
Maine	3,162	2,811	2,762	2,863	2,712	2,836	2,724	2,356	3,113	3,462	2,969	45
Maryland	10,167	12,228	10,052	9,656	9,317	12,105	13,051	12,674	16,391	17,825	18,452	25
Massachusetts	26,305	27,384	25,289	25,893	27,561	27,160	26,132	24,908	32,391	32,664	35,300	18
Michigan	44,851	57,573	53,945	54,752	59,921	58,007	55,988	44,874	56,795	62,765	65,136	7
Minnesota	18,904	21,398	20,013	19,201	20,692	22,681	22,188	20,197	23,454	27,143	24,936	23
Mississippi	8,224	11,485	10,849	10,505	10,985	11,586	11,833	10,289	12,808	15,942	14,222	30
Missouri	12,925	14,190	13,647	13,935	14,289	14,512	13,490	12,870	15,682	16,662	17,879	27
Montana	1,393	1,545	1,404	1,360	1,616	1,666	1,697	1,468	1,975	1,967	2,237	47
Nebraska	5,821	7,890	6,664	6,381	7,210	7,947	7,460	6,993	7,964	8,901	7,975	35
Nevada	5,913	7,692	8,667	9,766	12,162	11,138	9,101	10,359	10,544	10,113	9,538	33
New Hampshire	4,368	4,233	4,001	4,143	5,148	5,306	5,827	5,463	6,374	7,347	7,620	36
New Jersey	32,131	36,587	32,063	31,164	34,258	35,305	35,699	38,005	49,362	46,236	43,266	13
New Mexico	1,543	3,802	3,782	3,616	3,696	3,899	4,679	3,688	5,472	4,813	4,957	41
New York	69,685	88,834	83,125	76,691	78,190	84,734	75,607	65,651	90,234	109,246	100,055	3
North Carolina	24,918	31,420	30,202	30,183	32,620	32,765	34,333	28,482	33,488	40,206	42,203	14
North Dakota	2,532	5,513	4,027	5,294	6,148	7,800	6,971	5,171	5,176	5,246	8,779	34
Ohio	41,505	52,641	51,262	49,330	50,071	54,393	53,225	45,246	50,841	56,901	56,150	9
Oklahoma	5,354	6,308	5,251	5,046	5,363	6,112	6,151	5,400	6,244	6,817	6,513	37
Oregon	17,684	20,889	20,057	21,772	21,894	22,332	25,880	26,588	30,012	34,373	27,744	21
Pennsylvania	34,943	40,411	39,439	36,453	38,640	41,150	42,731	37,458	44,786	49,866	52,923	11
Rhode Island	1,949	2,388	2,133	2,278	2,391	2,405	2,675	2,358	2,950	2,890	3,012	44
South Carolina	20,336	29,773	31,021	31,324	32,202	34,627	41,461	30,294	29,623	31,508	37,343	17
South Dakota	1,259	1,578	1,421	1,218	1,356	1,430	1,356	1,389	1,858	2,354	2,401	46
Tennessee	25,948	33,251	32,617	31,476	33,233	32,717	31,116	28,191	34,762	38,277	38,249	16
Texas	206,992	285,559	248,780	231,527	265,068	315,843	328,585	277,377	377,987	486,021	446,214	1
Utah	13,808	12,224	13,308	12,078	11,583	14,390	17,367	17,689	18,105	16,591	17,370	28
Vermont	4,278	3,670	3,176	2,993	2,776	2,920	2,842	2,358	2,505	2,505	1,994	49
Virginia	17,169	19,391	17,801	16,311	16,508	18,336	17,826	16,411	20,014	24,884	22,472	24
Washington	53,345	90,558	86,375	79,562	76,351	77,868	60,336	41,133	53,687	61,234	61,069	8
West Virginia	6,443	7,597	5,833	5,045	7,110	8,233	5,949	4,566	6,341	7,803	5,669	39
Wisconsin	19,800	23,426	22,442	21,036	22,305	22,716	21,668	20,501	24,806	27,426	28,049	20
Wyoming	983	1,757	1,175	1,099	1,196	1,357	1,367	1,164	1,429	1,857	2,150	48

X Not applicable. ¹ Includes other areas, not shown separately, and exports with an unknown state or area of origin.

Source: U.S. Census Bureau, Foreign Trade Division, "USA Trade Online," <usatrade.census.gov/>, accessed June 2024. See also <www.census.gov/foreign-trade/data/index.html>.

Table 1321. Value of State Exports to Top Trading Countries by State: 2023

[In millions of dollars (2,018,059 represents $2,018,059,000,000). Data are on a f.a.s. (free alongside ship) value basis. Exports are based on origin of movement]

	Total	Canada	China	Germany	Japan	Korea, South	Mexico	Nether-lands	United Kingdom
United States [1]......	**2,018,059**	**354,356**	**147,778**	**76,698**	**75,683**	**65,056**	**322,742**	**81,310**	**74,315**
Alabama...............	27,440	4,011	3,742	5,059	955	1,193	3,184	283	387
Alaska.................	5,264	596	1,169	103	715	718	47	298	35
Arizona...............	28,877	2,850	1,603	743	932	559	7,979	1,662	1,372
Arkansas.............	6,457	1,641	348	78	388	67	1,106	118	219
California.............	178,844	19,386	16,866	5,903	10,602	9,386	33,254	6,119	5,676
Colorado.............	10,401	1,866	895	233	448	732	1,606	365	214
Connecticut..........	15,846	2,117	990	2,099	475	478	1,074	1,147	1,098
Delaware.............	4,936	868	417	244	212	367	333	120	166
District of Columbia...	1,746	4	1	2	1	1	8	1	337
Florida................	68,908	5,226	1,659	2,028	1,124	949	4,254	1,377	3,245
Georgia...............	49,906	7,835	3,930	2,650	1,546	1,051	4,881	1,798	1,161
Hawaii................	572	16	16	9	128	18	3	21	4
Idaho.................	4,006	1,496	181	28	234	94	284	87	56
Illinois................	78,849	20,753	4,412	4,490	2,590	1,412	12,917	2,425	2,689
Indiana...............	54,246	15,050	4,876	3,854	2,392	1,055	7,178	1,599	1,815
Iowa..................	18,400	5,506	1,122	856	974	343	3,241	505	421
Kansas...............	14,085	2,669	873	524	939	501	2,828	187	404
Kentucky.............	40,246	9,182	2,858	1,140	1,192	797	3,733	1,479	3,844
Louisiana.............	99,371	4,799	13,936	5,136	4,269	2,947	7,018	6,682	4,893
Maine.................	2,969	1,446	123	74	91	67	100	81	53
Maryland..............	18,452	2,382	1,019	1,267	1,201	843	525	1,389	656
Massachusetts........	35,300	3,320	3,325	2,290	1,546	1,395	2,737	1,949	1,611
Michigan..............	65,136	27,962	2,447	1,986	1,558	1,005	14,854	621	692
Minnesota............	24,936	7,048	2,166	884	998	632	3,338	699	509
Mississippi............	14,222	2,211	778	235	600	118	1,959	790	139
Missouri...............	17,879	6,545	594	737	475	291	3,873	367	306
Montana...............	2,237	1,020	112	18	130	189	61	26	58
Nebraska..............	7,975	1,706	666	140	700	568	1,458	165	72
Nevada................	9,538	1,937	787	199	224	251	853	155	208
New Hampshire.......	7,620	1,441	350	1,291	314	77	699	338	190
New Jersey...........	43,266	8,794	2,280	1,936	2,427	1,424	3,264	1,592	1,999
New Mexico...........	4,957	188	262	46	32	58	3,461	17	76
New York.............	100,055	21,741	3,838	4,105	1,687	1,601	3,482	1,528	4,767
North Carolina........	42,203	7,769	5,753	965	1,098	731	5,368	1,188	1,071
North Dakota.........	8,779	7,172	33	59	41	16	539	18	28
Ohio..................	56,150	21,832	2,767	1,387	2,052	1,037	8,278	997	1,902
Oklahoma.............	6,513	1,872	221	594	262	127	629	322	210
Oregon................	27,744	3,492	4,032	437	1,193	1,138	6,568	319	205
Pennsylvania..........	52,923	14,415	3,055	2,033	2,274	919	5,377	3,217	2,074
Rhode Island.........	3,012	489	94	147	126	41	220	36	52
South Carolina........	37,343	4,559	3,880	4,718	1,024	1,480	3,038	553	1,315
South Dakota.........	2,401	1,067	147	43	113	60	509	61	16
Tennessee............	38,249	8,914	2,963	1,381	2,113	590	6,088	2,346	929
Texas.................	446,214	36,072	26,708	8,009	13,117	21,303	129,598	25,990	13,499
Utah..................	17,370	1,709	1,220	397	782	387	1,351	565	7,157
Vermont...............	1,994	683	150	112	24	87	85	60	76
Virginia...............	22,472	3,562	1,975	949	642	344	1,237	992	785
Washington...........	61,069	9,623	10,906	1,281	4,338	3,050	3,511	1,003	1,651
West Virginia..........	5,669	2,157	528	156	393	121	246	303	149
Wisconsin.............	28,049	8,480	1,493	959	643	658	4,326	741	898
Wyoming..............	2,150	381	85	10	92	143	67	3	24

[1] Total includes data for Puerto Rico and the Virgin Islands, not shown separately. Total also includes exports to unknown partners and to countries not shown separately.

Source: U.S. Census Bureau, Foreign Trade Division, "USA Trade Online," <usatrade.census.gov/>, accessed August 2024. See also <www.census.gov/foreign-trade/statistics/state/index.html>.

Table 1322. U.S. Exports, Imports, and Trade Balance by Country: 2010 to 2023

[In millions of dollars (1,278,495 represents $1,278,495,000,000). Data reflect trade between foreign countries and the U.S., Puerto Rico, the U.S. Virgin Islands, and U.S. Foreign Trade Zones. Data are shown on a Census Basis. Country totals include exports of special category commodities, if any. Minus sign (-) denotes an excess of imports over exports]

Country	Exports, domestic and foreign					General imports					Merchandise trade balance				
	2010	2015	2020	2022	2023	2010	2015	2020	2022	2023	2010	2015	2020	2022	2023
Total [1]	1,278,495	1,503,328	1,429,995	2,066,454	2,018,059	1,913,857	2,248,811	2,331,477	3,239,873	3,080,170	-635,362	-745,483	-901,482	-1,173,419	-1,062,111
Afghanistan	2,151	479	673	22	50	85	24	18	22	20	2,066	455	655	-1	30
Algeria	1,194	1,876	735	1,198	1,201	14,518	3,372	488	3,009	3,029	-13,324	-1,496	247	-1,811	-1,828
Angola	1,293	1,166	470	651	599	11,940	2,806	472	1,598	1,161	-10,646	-1,640	-2	-947	-562
Antigua and Barbuda	158	678	291	1,057	973	5	7	5	9	13	153	671	286	1,048	960
Argentina	7,392	9,362	5,952	12,816	11,396	3,803	3,951	4,195	6,931	6,426	3,589	5,411	1,757	5,885	4,970
Armenia	113	50	28	195	189	75	62	68	81	133	38	-12	-40	114	56
Aruba	540	1,168	309	643	633	19	55	34	15	15	521	1,113	274	629	618
Australia	21,805	25,032	23,375	30,571	33,568	8,583	10,886	14,416	16,148	15,940	13,222	14,147	8,958	14,369	17,628
Austria	2,429	4,024	3,430	4,770	5,525	6,835	11,312	11,617	17,812	19,147	-4,407	-7,288	-8,187	-13,042	-13,622
Azerbaijan	253	478	162	186	542	1,989	507	38	174	69	-1,736	-29	124	13	472
Bahamas, The	3,178	2,387	2,805	5,472	5,464	815	453	276	1,721	1,824	2,363	1,934	2,530	3,750	3,641
Bahrain	1,235	1,271	885	950	1,676	420	902	634	1,955	1,166	815	368	251	-1,005	510
Bangladesh	576	943	1,852	2,947	2,248	4,294	5,990	6,065	11,151	8,276	-3,718	-5,048	-4,213	-8,204	-6,029
Barbados	397	595	505	820	715	43	68	48	52	48	355	527	457	767	667
Belarus	133	122	40	40	17	175	158	333	209	47	-41	-99	-211	-169	-30
Belgium	25,458	34,174	27,578	35,773	38,818	15,552	19,487	21,029	26,607	22,826	9,906	14,687	6,550	9,166	15,992
Belize	289	285	395	508	646	120	75	51	61	55	169	210	344	447	591
Benin	463	631	197	286	241	(Z)	5	6	4	13	462	626	191	282	228
Bermuda	637	601	459	648	568	22	109	24	14	25	614	492	435	634	543
Bolivia	508	932	448	494	504	680	1,006	380	644	411	-172	-75	68	-150	93
Botswana	48	39	49	45	68	170	212	175	455	490	-121	-173	-126	-410	-422
Brazil	35,418	31,641	34,592	54,245	44,639	23,958	27,474	23,364	38,909	39,066	11,460	4,167	11,228	15,335	5,572
British Virgin Islands	146	260	284	485	441	19	16	8	4	19	127	243	275	481	422
Brunei	124	133	146	114	142	12	19	83	90	255	112	114	64	23	-114
Bulgaria	171	289	375	531	511	260	598	847	1,509	1,571	-89	-308	-472	-978	-1,059
Cambodia	154	391	344	446	307	2,301	3,026	6,551	12,210	11,588	-2,147	-2,635	-6,206	-11,764	-11,281
Cameroon	132	225	187	192	219	297	132	470	102	128	-165	93	-283	90	91
Canada	249,256	280,855	256,212	359,237	354,356	277,637	296,305	270,026	437,429	418,619	-28,380	-15,450	-13,813	-78,193	-64,263
Chad	90	56	88	88	84	2,044	1,303	46	5	137	-1,954	-1,247	43	83	-53
Chile	10,907	15,449	12,462	22,332	18,774	7,017	8,777	10,100	15,567	15,589	3,889	6,672	2,362	6,765	3,185
China	91,911	115,873	124,582	154,125	147,778	364,953	483,202	432,548	536,259	426,885	-273,042	-367,328	-307,967	-382,134	-279,107
Colombia	12,068	16,302	11,932	20,917	17,680	15,659	14,079	10,780	18,479	16,115	-3,592	2,223	1,152	2,438	1,565
Congo, Rep. of	254	249	180	148	201	3,316	304	132	144	297	-3,062	-55	48	4	-96
Congo, Dem. Rep. of	93	136	152	148	187	528	154	30	183	275	-434	-18	122	-35	-88
Costa Rica	5,178	6,045	5,671	8,898	8,982	8,697	4,489	5,349	8,738	10,464	-3,519	1,556	321	160	-1,482
Cote d'Ivoire	163	266	506	506	516	1,177	1,028	881	1,055	948	-1,014	-761	-662	-549	-432
Croatia	312	332	316	1,466	1,020	336	577	601	860	901	-24	-245	-285	605	120
Cuba	363	186	177	372	404	(Z)	(Z)	15	6	4	363	186	162	366	400
Curacao [2]	(X)	521	350	521	510	(X)	335	28	48	39	(X)	186	322	474	471
Cyprus	134	103	103	120	188	11	32	59	73	53	123	70	44	48	135
Czechia	1,411	1,977	2,973	3,801	4,599	2,450	4,489	5,533	7,492	7,491	-1,039	-2,512	-2,560	-3,691	-2,892
Denmark	2,132	2,203	2,942	4,596	5,222	6,012	7,760	11,626	12,966	11,615	-3,879	-5,557	-8,684	-8,370	-6,392
Djibouti	123	145	185	172	177	3	41	35	42	47	120	109	144	130	129
Dominican Republic	6,579	7,115	7,501	13,960	13,009	3,672	4,668	5,159	6,895	7,057	2,908	2,447	2,341	7,066	5,951
Ecuador	5,409	5,818	4,134	7,850	7,977	7,451	7,467	5,939	10,398	8,599	-2,042	-1,649	-1,805	-2,548	-622
Egypt	6,833	4,759	4,705	6,316	4,480	2,238	1,406	2,180	2,803	2,387	4,594	3,353	2,526	3,512	2,093
El Salvador	2,434	3,249	2,584	4,889	4,289	2,206	2,532	1,922	2,896	2,454	228	717	663	1,994	1,835
Equatorial Guinea	272	162	94	71	99	2,214	163	135	223	285	-1,942	-1	-41	-152	-186
Ethiopia	773	1,555	911	1,084	1,220	128	310	524	718	490	645	1,245	386	366	730
Fiji	44	57	40	63	101	179	203	59	288	259	-135	-146	-184	-224	-159
Finland	2,180	1,560	1,595	2,649	2,963	3,884	4,510	4,926	8,707	7,311	-1,704	-2,951	-3,331	-6,058	-4,348
France	26,970	30,026	27,312	45,878	43,878	38,355	47,809	42,970	57,231	57,624	-11,386	-17,782	-15,658	-11,353	-13,746
French Polynesia	122	120	126	148	164	53	43	20	42	42	69	77	106	106	122
Gabon	243	204	92	133	180	2,212	337	76	220	80	-1,969	-133	16	-87	100

See footnotes at end of table.

Table 1322. U.S. Exports, Imports, and Trade Balance by Country: 2010 to 2023-Continued.

See headnote on page 837.

Country	Exports, domestic and foreign 2010	2015	2020	2022	2023	General imports 2010	2015	2020	2022	2023	Merchandise trade balance 2010	2015	2020	2022	2023
Georgia	301	340	436	1,237	1,512	198	181	149	341	113	103	159	287	895	1,400
Germany	48,155	49,979	58,002	72,871	76,698	82,450	124,888	114,897	146,612	159,272	-34,295	-74,909	-56,895	-73,741	-82,574
Ghana	989	950	829	975	861	273	309	717	2,768	1,627	716	641	112	-1,793	-766
Gibraltar	1,494	1,979	828	274	280	1	1	22	2	1	1,493	1,978	806	272	279
Greece	1,106	726	1,403	2,381	1,752	798	1,357	1,301	2,278	2,057	309	-631	102	104	-304
Grenada	71	90	99	168	202	8	9	13	17	15	64	81	86	151	187
Guatemala	4,477	5,821	5,844	10,135	9,725	3,523	4,121	3,843	5,309	4,836	954	1,700	2,002	4,826	4,889
Guyana	291	368	655	1,181	1,360	299	431	748	2,818	3,272	-8	-63	-94	-1,637	-1,912
Haiti	1,209	1,141	1,399	1,378	1,296	551	950	827	1,042	819	658	190	571	336	477
Honduras	4,606	5,216	4,193	7,827	6,782	3,933	4,760	3,841	6,053	5,561	673	457	352	1,774	1,221
Hong Kong	26,570	37,183	23,826	25,832	27,792	4,296	6,802	7,919	4,519	4,082	22,274	30,381	15,906	21,313	23,710
Hungary	1,290	1,715	2,111	2,872	3,120	2,491	5,719	5,277	7,694	10,861	-1,201	-4,004	-3,166	-4,822	-7,741
Iceland	325	415	292	634	328	201	317	424	755	674	124	99	-132	-121	-346
India	19,249	21,453	27,082	46,948	40,375	29,533	44,783	51,255	85,525	83,686	-10,284	-23,330	-24,173	-38,577	-43,311
Indonesia	6,948	7,118	7,383	9,836	9,838	16,478	19,605	20,198	34,543	26,798	-9,530	-12,487	-12,815	-24,707	-16,960
Iran	211	282	36	45	59	94	11	4	11	2	117	271	32	34	57
Iraq	1,643	1,973	770	899	2,256	12,143	4,353	3,100	10,038	8,450	-10,500	-2,380	-2,330	-9,139	-6,194
Ireland	7,276	8,931	10,668	15,947	16,781	33,848	39,351	66,053	82,595	82,334	-26,572	-30,421	-55,385	-66,648	-65,554
Israel	11,295	13,539	11,224	14,184	13,978	20,985	24,495	15,261	21,429	20,817	-9,690	-10,956	-4,037	-7,244	-6,838
Italy	14,220	16,212	19,949	27,491	28,860	28,514	44,221	49,448	69,040	72,921	-14,294	-28,008	-29,499	-41,548	-44,061
Jamaica	1,661	1,716	1,662	2,566	2,633	328	306	384	350	389	1,334	1,410	1,279	2,216	2,243
Japan	60,472	62,388	64,030	80,222	75,683	120,552	131,445	119,507	147,999	147,238	-60,080	-69,058	-55,476	-67,777	-71,555
Jordan	1,172	1,360	1,319	1,579	1,551	974	1,492	1,869	2,987	2,916	198	-132	-550	-1,409	-1,365
Kazakhstan	730	510	509	1,082	1,161	1,872	816	904	2,705	2,231	-1,142	-306	-395	-1,623	-1,070
Kenya	375	943	372	571	485	311	573	568	876	894	64	370	-196	-305	-409
Korea, South	38,821	43,484	50,978	72,089	65,056	48,875	71,775	76,011	115,315	116,154	-10,055	-28,291	-25,033	-43,226	-51,098
Kuwait	2,775	2,741	2,207	3,394	2,829	5,382	4,685	714	2,039	1,684	-2,607	-1,944	1,492	1,355	1,145
Kyrgyzstan	79	32	32	61	141	4	16	6	9	13	76	16	27	52	129
Laos	13	25	25	41	46	59	45	107	273	305	-46	-21	-82	-232	-259
Latvia	345	267	306	418	1,012	193	303	520	748	620	152	-36	-214	-330	392
Lebanon	2,009	1,286	678	766	536	84	93	195	211	198	1,925	1,193	483	555	338
Liberia	191	136	93	261	251	180	45	45	81	58	11	91	48	180	194
Libya	666	231	290	291	446	2,117	155	215	2,204	1,536	-1,451	76	75	-1,913	-1,090
Liechtenstein	29	35	40	81	86	213	310	287	267	254	-183	-274	-247	-186	-168
Lithuania	628	528	1,032	2,601	2,944	637	1,060	1,341	2,584	2,095	-9	-532	-309	18	850
Luxembourg	1,440	1,394	1,352	1,648	2,366	451	639	493	734	690	989	755	859	914	1,676
Macau	225	542	183	250	526	141	122	101	162	135	84	420	82	88	391
Madagascar	116	55	36	85	62	108	320	614	913	721	8	-265	-578	-828	-660
Malawi	37	37	13	36	18	72	61	43	54	45	-35	-24	-30	-18	-27
Malaysia	14,079	12,278	12,296	18,224	19,358	25,901	33,972	44,098	54,078	46,191	-11,821	-21,694	-31,802	-35,854	-26,833
Malta	457	491	138	268	424	262	241	172	259	226	196	249	-33	9	198
Marshall Islands	91	54	120	207	73	12	29	28	17	17	79	25	92	191	56
Martinique	297	133	118	287	385	23	37	2	9	6	274	95	116	278	379
Mauritania	84	126	128	154	167	53	1	6	6	14	31	125	122	148	153
Mexico	163,665	236,460	212,513	324,207	322,742	229,986	296,433	323,477	452,032	475,216	-66,321	-59,973	-110,964	-127,825	-152,473
Mongolia	116	69	118	149	168	12	17	12	27	31	104	52	106	121	137
Morocco	1,948	1,625	2,301	3,701	3,838	686	1,012	1,048	1,694	1,697	1,262	613	1,252	2,007	2,141
Mozambique	224	264	127	235	190	65	96	108	177	209	159	168	19	58	-19
Namibia	110	128	60	226	177	195	85	90	249	133	-85	42	-30	-23	44
Nepal	28	36	94	259	63	61	87	86	132	135	-32	-51	7	127	-72
Netherlands	34,740	40,212	44,824	72,724	81,310	19,055	16,844	27,381	34,521	38,526	15,685	23,368	17,443	38,204	42,783
New Zealand	2,820	3,631	3,196	4,167	4,352	2,764	4,293	4,207	5,372	5,537	57	-662	-1,011	-1,205	-1,185
Nicaragua	981	1,267	1,426	2,647	2,365	2,008	3,189	3,543	5,689	4,718	-1,026	-1,921	-2,117	-3,042	-2,353
Niger	49	72	145	96	78	27	5	79	74	47	22	67	66	22	31
Nigeria	4,061	3,431	2,801	3,412	2,587	30,516	1,916	1,485	4,783	5,692	-26,455	1,516	1,316	-1,371	-3,106
North Macedonia	33	31	44	49	58	37	203	159	227	287	-4	-173	-116	-178	-229
Norway	3,100	3,570	2,774	4,634	5,022	6,950	4,763	3,943	6,651	6,114	-3,850	-1,192	-1,169	-2,018	-1,093

See footnotes at end of table.

Table 1322. U.S. Exports, Imports, and Trade Balance by Country: 2010 to 2023 -Continued.

See headnote on page 837.

Country	Exports, domestic and foreign					General imports					Merchandise trade balance				
	2010	2015	2020	2022	2023	2010	2015	2020	2022	2023	2010	2015	2020	2022	2023
Oman	1,105	2,355	1,130	1,487	1,859	773	907	813	2,709	1,655	332	1,448	316	-1,222	205
Pakistan	1,901	1,838	2,912	3,155	2,044	3,509	3,701	3,899	5,994	4,885	-1,608	-1,863	-987	-2,840	-2,841
Panama	6,066	7,669	5,655	11,853	11,067	381	408	707	523	526	5,685	7,261	4,948	11,330	10,540
Papua New Guinea	186	208	63	116	129	97	91	86	74	78	89	117	-24	42	51
Paraguay	1,810	1,492	1,267	2,116	2,765	62	163	150	270	258	1,748	1,329	1,118	1,846	2,507
Peru	6,750	8,724	7,587	13,831	11,861	5,243	5,056	5,520	8,623	8,732	1,506	3,668	2,067	5,209	3,128
Philippines	7,377	7,903	7,723	9,259	9,259	7,982	10,232	11,122	16,155	13,266	-605	-2,329	-3,398	-6,896	-4,007
Poland	2,983	3,715	5,047	11,468	10,993	2,964	5,611	8,601	11,848	13,160	19	-1,896	-3,554	-380	-2,167
Portugal	1,058	942	1,663	2,907	2,379	2,142	3,271	3,776	6,147	6,510	-1,084	-2,328	-2,113	-3,240	-4,131
Qatar	3,160	4,222	3,410	3,666	4,655	466	1,354	1,181	2,908	2,045	2,693	2,868	2,230	757	2,611
Romania	730	754	923	1,350	1,305	1,008	2,150	2,126	3,774	3,996	-278	-1,396	-1,203	-2,424	-2,691
Russia	5,994	7,087	4,889	1,656	600	25,691	16,372	16,902	14,437	4,571	-19,697	-9,286	-12,013	-12,781	-3,971
Rwanda	31	14	27	65	38	21	46	33	57	38	9	-31	-5	8	(Z)
Saudi Arabia	11,506	19,792	11,131	11,393	13,847	31,413	22,083	8,994	23,278	15,897	-19,907	-2,292	2,137	-11,885	-2,050
Senegal	219	199	281	359	348	5	72	101	504	159	214	127	180	-144	189
Serbia	104	126	142	247	239	164	273	436	700	731	-60	-146	-294	-454	-492
Sierra Leone	61	77	74	106	104	29	40	32	18	22	32	38	42	88	82
Singapore	29,009	28,481	26,924	45,620	42,447	17,428	18,272	30,775	31,600	40,924	11,581	10,209	-3,851	14,020	1,523
Sint Maarten [2]	(X)	741	335	699	847	(X)	47	47	80	90	(X)	690	288	619	757
Slovakia	256	380	333	375	427	1,073	2,300	4,998	6,581	8,334	-817	-1,920	-4,664	-6,206	-7,907
Slovenia	328	346	298	396	363	465	678	1,192	2,995	3,907	-137	-332	-893	-2,598	-3,544
South Africa	5,632	5,457	4,375	6,497	7,125	8,220	7,323	11,361	14,571	13,976	-2,589	-1,866	-6,986	-8,073	-6,851
Spain	10,355	10,310	13,060	26,778	25,161	8,554	14,133	15,297	22,982	23,122	1,802	-3,823	-2,237	3,797	2,039
Sri Lanka	179	362	359	337	351	1,748	2,891	2,453	3,411	2,842	-1,569	-2,529	-2,094	-3,074	-2,491
Suriname	362	444	267	532	483	191	146	180	76	76	171	297	87	456	407
Sweden	4,740	3,939	4,772	7,778	8,635	10,497	9,910	12,279	17,079	18,371	-5,757	-5,971	-7,507	-9,301	-9,737
Switzerland	20,704	22,154	18,064	36,720	27,780	19,137	31,431	74,929	59,466	52,296	1,567	-9,277	-56,865	-22,746	-24,517
Syria	503	3	26	9	14	429	7	10	9	11	74	-3	16	0	3
Taiwan	26,050	25,826	30,214	43,960	39,957	35,847	40,911	60,430	91,719	87,767	-9,797	-15,085	-30,216	-47,759	-47,811
Tajikistan	57	8	8	124	118	1	20	1	2	1	56	-12	7	122	117
Tanzania	163	173	243	260	445	42	105	121	164	192	121	68	122	96	253
Thailand	8,976	11,229	11,266	15,733	15,557	22,694	28,622	37,555	58,626	56,282	-13,717	-17,393	-26,289	-42,893	-40,725
Togo	158	312	310	388	393	9	14	20	84	83	149	298	291	304	310
Trinidad and Tobago	1,925	2,512	2,401	3,634	2,269	6,613	4,320	2,478	5,457	3,159	-4,688	-1,808	-78	-1,824	-890
Tunisia	573	602	429	552	553	405	546	569	748	862	167	56	-139	-197	-309
Turkey	10,538	9,520	9,988	15,172	14,580	4,207	7,886	10,971	18,796	15,473	6,331	1,633	-983	-3,624	-893
Turkmenistan	40	81	33	49	56	48	56	14	35	2	-8	25	19	14	54
Uganda	94	88	95	166	121	58	64	83	174	115	36	24	12	-8	6
Ukraine	1,349	862	1,908	1,428	1,048	1,078	852	1,305	1,497	1,320	271	11	603	-68	-273
United Arab Emirates	11,662	23,001	14,744	20,836	24,849	1,145	2,474	3,114	6,863	6,620	10,517	20,527	11,630	13,973	18,230
United Kingdom	48,410	56,095	58,533	76,248	74,315	49,805	58,057	50,280	63,921	64,217	-1,395	-1,962	8,253	12,327	10,098
Uruguay	975	1,295	1,217	2,904	1,880	235	605	550	905	870	740	690	666	1,998	1,010
Uzbekistan	101	138	181	271	343	68	10	81	59	95	33	128	100	212	248
Venezuela	10,645	8,344	1,130	2,188	2,494	32,707	15,564	167	413	3,594	-22,063	-7,221	963	1,775	-1,099
Vietnam	3,706	7,101	9,915	11,344	9,843	14,868	38,015	79,582	127,512	114,426	-11,162	-30,914	-69,667	-116,168	-104,583
Yemen	398	158	329	378	192	181	48	4	31	7	216	110	325	347	185
Zambia	56	84	72	135	94	30	47	40	135	153	27	37	31	-1	-59
Zimbabwe	68	38	46	39	40	59	67	37	86	115	9	-29	9	-47	-75

X Not applicable. Z Less than $500,000. [1] Includes additional countries, not shown separately. [2] The Netherlands Antilles dissolved on October 10, 2010. Curacao and Sint Maarten became autonomous territories of the Kingdom of the Netherlands.

Source: U.S. Census Bureau, "USA Trade Online," <usatrade.census.gov>, accessed June 2024. See also U.S. International Trade in Goods and Services, Series FT-900, <www.census.gov/foreign-trade/Press-Release/ft900_index.html>.

Table 1323. U.S. Exports and General Imports by Selected Commodity Groups: 2021 to 2023

[In millions of dollars (1,757,744 represents $1,757,744,000,000). All data are presented on a Census basis. For methodology, see Foreign Trade Statistics in Appendix III]

Selected commodity	Exports			General imports		
	2021	2022	2023	2021	2022	2023
Total [1]	**1,757,744**	**2,066,454**	**2,018,059**	**2,828,515**	**3,239,873**	**3,080,170**
Manufactured goods [2]	1,138,063	1,298,148	1,290,332	2,458,208	2,784,313	2,667,667
Agricultural commodities [2]	176,631	195,680	174,172	171,096	199,293	195,859
Food and live animals [3]	124,519	132,002	121,236	140,737	160,706	156,260
Live animals other than fish	1,220	1,134	1,124	3,300	3,635	4,016
Meat and preparations	23,921	25,433	23,724	13,196	14,306	13,752
Cereals and preparations	34,613	36,089	28,197	12,728	16,277	17,520
Vegetables and fruits	22,510	22,739	23,031	43,820	48,851	50,139
Coffee, tea, cocoa, and spices	3,013	3,302	3,370	15,473	19,056	17,444
Feeding stuff for animals	14,836	16,690	16,715	4,530	5,433	5,096
Crude materials except fuels [3]	95,872	108,157	91,439	49,103	50,971	39,553
Hides, skins, and furskins, raw	1,169	1,112	981	51	36	28
Oil seeds and oleaginous fruits	29,564	36,346	30,387	1,237	1,715	1,471
Crude rubber	2,492	2,897	2,487	3,450	4,013	2,753
Cork and wood	7,159	7,572	6,835	15,942	15,012	9,392
Pulp and waste paper	9,328	10,657	8,542	4,021	4,976	3,905
Textile fibers including waste	7,624	11,042	8,141	1,440	1,571	1,321
Crude fertilizers	2,847	3,309	3,101	3,280	3,727	3,319
Metalliferous ores and metal scrap	32,323	31,745	27,668	12,321	11,872	9,820
Mineral fuels and lubricants [3]	236,233	372,488	317,057	215,734	310,358	251,865
Coal, coke, and briquettes	10,309	18,559	16,125	1,069	1,281	1,134
Petroleum products and preparations	157,530	257,113	233,356	198,648	283,233	235,236
Gas, natural and manufactured	67,890	96,085	66,389	13,380	21,416	12,336
Animal and vegetable oils [3]	3,548	3,366	1,917	9,708	13,811	14,901
Animal oil and fat	1,032	780	599	703	1,286	1,551
Fixed vegetable fats and oil, crude	1,813	1,929	917	8,664	11,641	11,481
Chemicals and related products [3]	249,408	279,159	269,024	322,296	373,154	361,745
Organic chemicals	42,649	50,960	47,604	56,523	66,496	54,119
Inorganic chemicals	12,569	15,921	14,202	12,450	17,686	16,189
Dyeing, tanning, and coloring materials	7,624	8,347	7,674	5,023	5,664	4,780
Medicinal and pharmaceutical products	69,556	70,982	77,247	157,791	174,061	190,392
Fertilizers	3,303	6,549	4,093	9,547	12,443	9,053
Plastics in primary forms	41,220	46,848	41,718	21,770	23,988	18,013
Plastics in nonprimary forms	14,763	15,900	15,491	14,423	16,607	14,481
Manufactured goods by material	107,852	119,567	118,661	325,738	366,053	310,449
Leather and leather manufactures	771	707	627	1,541	1,571	1,176
Rubber manufactures	8,829	9,748	10,180	24,127	28,904	27,878
Cork and wood manufactures	2,246	2,543	2,370	17,908	18,849	13,326
Paper and paperboard	14,888	16,399	14,459	17,274	21,564	19,115
Textile yarn, fabric	11,388	12,269	10,899	36,697	36,170	30,308
Nonmetallic mineral manufactures	11,754	13,482	15,235	48,605	55,186	48,531
Iron and steel	13,946	16,789	17,222	43,141	54,892	43,384
Nonferrous metals	18,512	18,797	17,527	66,879	70,627	57,065
Manufactures of metals	25,518	28,833	30,142	69,566	78,292	69,667
Machinery and transport equipment	462,551	505,034	545,289	1,119,163	1,269,958	1,312,443
Power generating machinery	34,182	37,376	40,087	68,583	77,858	83,198
Specialized industrial machinery	52,109	54,572	52,709	61,549	75,814	79,657
Metalworking machinery	4,434	4,891	5,436	10,557	12,006	12,872
General industrial machinery	58,596	65,624	69,050	119,399	134,225	137,517
Office machinery	18,484	19,303	19,957	162,450	172,302	149,699
Telecommunications equipment	17,464	18,648	21,411	170,571	187,097	173,778
Electrical machinery	83,188	86,117	87,893	225,957	264,639	273,173
Road vehicles	113,451	125,555	137,716	270,611	313,601	366,600
Transport equipment	80,643	92,950	111,029	29,487	32,416	35,949
Miscellaneous manufactured articles [3]	120,085	131,938	134,135	476,486	529,817	456,383
Prefabricated buildings	2,207	2,418	2,247	14,807	15,248	12,899
Furniture	5,092	5,520	5,617	59,976	63,843	53,038
Travel goods	588	699	706	10,748	13,622	11,267
Apparel and clothing accessories	3,296	3,741	3,245	100,989	110,341	85,973
Footwear	816	899	913	26,897	35,883	25,728
Scientific and controlling equipment	50,531	54,896	56,528	70,668	76,756	80,352
Photographic equipment	6,481	6,297	6,019	17,244	18,294	17,440
Miscellaneous commodities [4]	75,033	87,447	83,699	137,966	131,249	144,965
Re-exports	**276,562**	**320,765**	**328,966**	**(X)**	**(X)**	**(X)**

X Not applicable. [1] Total exports including re-exports (exports of foreign merchandise). [2] Manufactured goods is based on the North American Industry Classification System (NAICS) and Agricultural commodities is based on the Harmonized System commodities specified by the U.S. Department of Agriculture definition. All other commodity detail is based on Standard International Trade Classification (SITC). [3] Includes other commodities not shown separately. [4] Includes special transactions, coin, nonmonetary gold, and the low value estimate.

Source: U.S. Census Bureau, *U.S. International Trade in Goods and Services, Annual Revision for 2023*, Series FT-900, June 2024. See also <www.census.gov/foreign-trade/Press-Release/ft900_index.html>.

Table 1324. Domestic Exports and Imports for Consumption of Merchandise by Selected NAICS Product Category: 2010 to 2023

[In millions of dollars (1,122,567 represents $1,122,567,000,000). Includes nonmonetary gold. For methodology, see Foreign Trade Statistics in Appendix III. NAICS = North American Industry Classification System; see text, Section 15. N.e.c. = Not elsewhere classified]

Product category	2010	2015	2020	2021	2022	2023
Domestic exports, total.................................	**1,122,567**	**1,286,172**	**1,205,387**	**1,481,182**	**1,745,689**	**1,689,093**
Agricultural, forestry, and fishery products.................	65,753	69,766	77,751	93,052	103,555	85,242
Agricultural products, total............................	58,023	60,200	69,945	83,526	94,609	76,797
Livestock and livestock products.......................	1,539	2,032	1,842	2,315	1,973	1,912
Forestry products, n.e.c................................	2,181	2,354	1,895	2,381	2,212	1,851
Fish, fresh or chilled, and other marine products.........	4,011	5,180	4,069	4,830	4,762	4,682
Mining, total..	26,394	34,188	96,564	154,702	237,288	204,009
Oil and gas..	9,248	19,802	82,472	134,556	208,726	178,153
Minerals and ores.....................................	17,146	14,386	14,092	20,146	28,562	25,856
Manufacturing, total....................................	952,360	1,110,979	957,050	1,138,063	1,298,148	1,290,332
Food and kindred products.............................	50,902	61,982	65,577	76,129	82,531	79,133
Beverages and tobacco products.......................	5,339	8,476	6,955	8,122	8,914	8,809
Textiles and fabrics...................................	7,833	9,001	6,700	7,818	8,470	7,527
Textile mill products..................................	2,583	2,793	2,517	2,780	2,795	2,557
Apparel and accessories..............................	3,070	3,104	2,263	3,002	3,405	2,921
Leather and allied products............................	2,421	3,041	2,072	2,436	2,394	2,352
Wood products.......................................	5,075	6,812	6,030	7,734	8,600	7,983
Paper products.......................................	22,962	23,321	20,854	23,938	26,944	23,694
Printed, publishing, & similar products.................	6,021	5,088	3,985	4,682	4,852	4,597
Petroleum and coal products..........................	61,010	78,168	61,436	91,426	150,191	127,252
Chemicals...	171,365	182,411	183,841	233,827	258,707	248,239
Plastics and rubber products [1].......................	24,262	29,970	27,776	32,324	35,759	35,526
Nonmetallic mineral products [1].......................	9,226	10,699	9,447	11,123	11,165	11,109
Primary metal products................................	49,725	51,694	45,713	59,493	66,323	55,866
Fabricated metal products.............................	32,690	41,602	35,340	39,625	45,200	47,526
Machinery, except electrical...........................	126,023	123,736	106,776	125,454	138,089	139,415
Computers and electronic products [1].................	121,121	119,879	107,035	116,306	118,180	118,225
Electrical equipment, appliances, and components [1]....	31,035	46,671	39,968	43,512	45,170	50,851
Transportation equipment [1]............................	176,337	252,299	179,386	199,952	227,944	259,923
Furniture and fixtures.................................	3,979	4,960	3,813	4,218	3,855	3,934
Miscellaneous manufactured commodities..............	39,381	45,271	39,565	44,161	48,658	52,893
Newspapers, books, & other published matter, n.e.c.....	851	(NA)	(NA)	(NA)	(NA)	(NA)
Special classification provisions...........................	77,210	71,239	74,023	95,365	106,387	109,209
Waste and scrap......................................	29,420	17,548	20,983	31,129	30,014	26,337
Used or second-hand merchandise.....................	4,711	12,432	11,626	14,325	16,359	17,549
Goods returned or reimported.........................	30	32	64	21	33	31
Special classification provision, n.e.c...................	43,049	41,228	41,349	49,889	59,980	65,293
Imports for consumption, total........................	**1,900,587**	**2,227,237**	**2,330,555**	**2,817,858**	**3,223,568**	**3,072,514**
Agricultural, forestry, and fishery products.................	42,686	56,308	63,549	76,293	82,578	77,450
Agricultural products, total............................	24,017	33,435	39,115	44,187	49,566	49,016
Livestock and livestock products.......................	4,116	6,124	6,253	11,187	13,948	13,408
Forestry products, n.e.c................................	3,356	2,380	2,466	3,297	3,427	2,501
Fish, fresh or chilled, and other marine products.........	11,198	14,369	15,714	17,622	15,637	12,525
Mining, total..	235,401	115,949	82,717	143,689	215,284	174,561
Oil and gas..	228,066	109,006	78,300	137,784	208,371	168,229
Minerals and ores.....................................	7,335	6,943	4,417	5,904	6,914	6,332
Manufacturing, total....................................	1,550,204	1,948,837	2,067,015	2,455,213	2,777,148	2,666,493
Food and kindred products.............................	41,039	58,434	72,925	86,888	105,652	105,901
Beverages and tobacco products.......................	15,515	21,201	26,125	30,545	32,344	30,188
Textiles and fabrics...................................	6,525	8,570	8,246	9,746	10,160	8,628
Textile mill products..................................	15,825	20,752	36,905	29,977	26,998	22,311
Apparel and accessories..............................	75,411	89,281	72,526	87,226	103,624	82,328
Leather and allied products............................	30,859	40,163	30,215	39,728	50,742	39,066
Wood products.......................................	11,364	17,107	21,505	33,967	35,774	24,308
Paper products.......................................	21,029	20,304	19,317	22,563	28,005	24,463
Printed, publishing, & similar products.................	5,324	5,532	4,906	5,927	6,296	5,725
Petroleum and coal products..........................	102,169	67,950	42,468	72,672	97,505	82,962
Chemicals...	187,576	217,099	269,388	310,773	358,248	347,244
Plastics and rubber products..........................	34,364	49,836	59,632	72,634	80,532	72,086
Nonmetallic mineral products..........................	16,075	21,799	21,782	27,837	31,278	27,809
Primary metal products................................	79,617	85,118	128,076	134,907	152,483	129,721
Fabricated metal products.............................	46,712	67,397	69,585	86,944	100,397	91,899
Machinery, except electrical...........................	104,832	156,908	168,852	206,147	233,078	239,234
Computers and electronic products....................	324,379	372,260	390,817	459,329	507,678	475,517
Electrical equipment, appliances, and components......	68,465	101,912	124,202	151,472	172,678	174,050
Transportation equipment.............................	239,870	375,354	335,817	365,630	414,561	481,169
Furniture and fixtures.................................	25,702	36,874	42,582	52,056	52,902	42,118
Miscellaneous manufactured commodities..............	97,554	114,987	121,145	168,246	176,213	159,767
Newspapers, books, & other published matter, n.e.c.....	35	(NA)	(NA)	(NA)	(NA)	(NA)
Special classification provisions...........................	72,261	106,143	117,274	142,663	148,431	153,902
Waste and scrap......................................	5,261	5,089	6,869	10,279	9,090	7,678
Used or second-hand merchandise.....................	6,403	13,159	6,551	10,374	17,276	16,440
Goods returned or reimported.........................	40,992	66,960	82,264	96,809	92,354	100,319
Special classification provision, n.e.c...................	19,605	20,935	21,590	25,201	29,711	29,465

NA Not available. [1] Beginning 2009, export statistics for certain commodity classifications related to the aircraft industry are subject to suppression and have been aggregated in a manner that prevents the disclosure of confidential information.

Source: U.S. Census Bureau, Foreign Trade Division, "USA Trade Online," <usatrade.census.gov/>, accessed August 2024. See also *U.S. International Trade in Goods and Services, Series FT-900*, <www.census.gov/foreign-trade/data/index.html>.

Table 1325. Knowledge- and Technology-Intensive Products Exports and Imports by World Region and Country: 2005 to 2018

[In billions of dollars (4,759.9 represents $4,759,900,000,000). Knowledge- and technology-intensive products include high research and development (R&D) intensive and medium-high R&D intensive products classified by the Organisation for Economic Co-operation and Development. High R&D intensive products include aircraft; pharmaceuticals; and computer, electronic, and optical products. Medium-high R&D intensive products include weapons and ammunition; motor vehicles; medical and dental instruments; machinery and equipment; chemicals and chemical products; electrical equipment; and railroad, military vehicles, and transport. World exports do not equal imports due to statistical errors in reporting of trade data and lack of trade data for sub-Sahara African countries. Data are primarily from Oxford Economics, special tabulations (2019) of Global Trade Databank]

Region and country	2005	2010	2011	2012	2013	2014	2015	2016	2017	2018
EXPORTS										
World [1]	**4,759.9**	**6,582.7**	**7,491.7**	**7,499.6**	**7,707.6**	**7,955.3**	**7,377.7**	**7,318.8**	**8,058.9**	**8,587.8**
North America	791.9	995.1	1,103.3	1,161.3	1,173.9	1,219.9	1,190.2	1,154.2	1,208.1	1,271.8
Canada	146.0	136.9	151.9	159.4	155.6	159.7	156.4	154.2	153.6	159.9
Mexico	125.4	182.8	203.4	222.7	234.6	254.5	257.9	252.9	276.3	302.7
United States	**520.4**	**675.4**	**748.0**	**779.1**	**783.7**	**805.7**	**775.9**	**747.0**	**778.2**	**809.3**
Central & South America [2]	59.8	81.7	97.9	97.6	102.3	88.3	78.4	78.1	84.6	87.0
Brazil	38.1	46.3	54.4	53.8	58.9	46.8	43.3	46.3	49.8	53.3
Europe	2,351.3	2,922.9	3,391.3	3,247.5	3,396.8	3,499.0	3,142.6	3,183.2	3,475.0	3,670.6
European Union [2,3]	2,198.4	2,694.0	3,116.9	2,966.2	3,110.9	3,209.3	2,877.7	2,920.5	3,186.3	3,359.2
France	254.3	296.6	327.5	317.8	323.9	323.9	287.5	288.8	310.4	336.4
Germany	640.9	793.0	933.5	900.4	927.1	961.6	865.8	872.8	955.5	1,023.8
United Kingdom	212.1	206.5	233.9	228.6	232.2	257.7	245.5	234.4	244.7	252.8
Other Europe	152.9	228.9	274.3	281.3	285.9	289.7	264.9	262.8	288.7	311.4
Middle East	50.4	106.0	125.1	172.7	185.1	191.2	135.1	124.1	168.8	119.0
Asia [2]	1,486.9	2,453.1	2,746.9	2,791.8	2,822.8	2,930.7	2,807.7	2,755.4	3,098.5	3,414.1
China [4]	394.0	832.7	966.7	1,006.3	1,046.1	1,131.1	1,112.8	1,062.6	1,196.2	1,344.7
India	22.4	56.2	74.0	75.0	86.5	86.7	80.3	81.1	91.1	108.3
Indonesia	18.2	27.9	33.5	33.6	33.3	33.2	28.5	29.6	31.5	34.1
Japan	443.2	550.0	580.9	570.6	504.1	487.1	442.6	461.9	495.7	525.1
Malaysia	85.1	100.9	104.2	102.5	103.5	108.5	99.9	97.9	112.4	132.3
Philippines	31.3	24.5	22.0	33.3	34.3	38.3	40.2	38.2	47.2	47.5
Singapore	93.5	222.0	242.2	243.3	245.4	245.7	229.4	221.8	238.5	258.7
South Korea	210.6	344.5	390.2	378.8	399.5	410.3	393.6	369.1	428.1	444.0
Taiwan	123.1	174.0	193.6	187.1	193.3	203.4	190.1	191.0	219.5	230.6
Thailand	58.5	100.0	109.4	117.0	120.7	123.8	117.1	118.6	130.9	140.0
Vietnam	3.7	13.5	22.0	34.8	47.2	53.3	65.1	75.1	98.4	139.1
Oceania [2]	19.5	23.9	27.2	28.6	26.8	26.2	23.7	23.7	23.9	25.3
Australia	15.6	19.8	22.3	23.6	21.9	21.2	18.9	19.1	19.3	20.7
IMPORTS										
World [1]	**4,880.0**	**6,677.7**	**7,621.8**	**7,652.6**	**7,864.3**	**8,093.1**	**7,580.8**	**7,669.4**	**8,416.0**	**9,046.2**
North America	1,127.7	1,322.3	1,479.9	1,580.6	1,608.8	1,686.7	1,719.7	1,693.5	1,798.8	1,936.5
Canada	178.0	207.3	231.7	242.2	243.5	244.7	231.9	225.7	241.8	254.8
Mexico	134.0	181.9	204.5	219.7	230.1	240.1	242.7	238.0	250.3	271.6
United States	**815.6**	**933.1**	**1,043.7**	**1,118.7**	**1,135.2**	**1,201.9**	**1,245.1**	**1,229.7**	**1,306.7**	**1,410.1**
Central & South America [2]	132.8	269.0	333.8	342.9	348.2	326.0	284.0	245.7	263.6	290.4
Brazil	43.6	107.2	130.8	130.1	138.7	130.8	103.9	87.0	90.5	111.9
Europe	2,200.4	2,759.1	3,177.3	2,970.2	3,074.2	3,172.1	2,850.2	2,918.9	3,217.4	3,388.5
European Union [2,3]	1,961.4	2,379.4	2,696.9	2,474.9	2,570.1	2,694.7	2,465.4	2,524.0	2,762.4	2,923.9
France	237.5	295.2	341.6	316.4	318.9	318.9	288.1	297.4	318.3	333.1
Germany	389.8	507.1	586.5	542.1	552.2	580.2	529.4	537.7	603.0	660.1
United Kingdom	256.7	267.8	295.4	270.7	283.0	328.0	313.5	305.6	312.0	319.8
Other Europe [2]	239.0	379.6	480.4	495.3	504.1	477.4	384.9	394.9	455.0	464.6
Middle East	130.2	222.4	253.4	309.2	334.7	360.3	307.6	286.1	408.7	367.3
Asia [2]	1,204.2	1,987.7	2,246.1	2,304.6	2,365.0	2,416.0	2,297.5	2,405.0	2,586.4	2,921.6
China [4]	461.8	812.6	924.6	931.1	989.1	1,025.7	950.9	1,045.2	1,061.2	1,207.5
India	42.6	100.1	121.1	125.9	122.9	125.4	129.9	127.7	148.8	209.8
Indonesia	23.5	64.1	78.8	87.8	80.9	75.9	67.4	65.3	72.8	87.2
Japan	178.4	232.0	264.3	275.2	264.5	268.8	249.3	253.4	269.9	294.8
Malaysia	75.3	97.9	103.2	105.6	108.2	109.3	95.8	95.1	108.0	119.3
Philippines	32.3	33.3	25.0	34.5	35.0	35.4	41.8	51.2	57.8	64.4
Singapore	71.1	166.9	177.7	183.5	183.7	180.3	166.7	165.6	180.3	203.7
South Korea	110.2	170.0	187.4	181.2	187.1	195.2	195.2	191.5	219.7	229.6
Taiwan	102.1	130.1	139.9	128.9	131.9	135.2	126.6	132.7	146.1	158.3
Thailand	57.4	85.0	99.5	116.0	111.4	104.4	99.4	99.3	107.9	115.3
Vietnam	14.7	37.7	47.2	55.6	68.2	75.3	91.1	97.0	120.9	133.0
Oceania [2]	84.8	117.2	131.3	145.1	133.3	132.1	121.7	120.2	141.2	141.8
Australia	70.8	103.2	114.8	127.5	114.6	111.0	102.7	101.2	120.0	119.6

[1] World total does not include all countries and economies due to limitations in data availability. [2] Includes other countries not shown separately. [3] Data are not available for EU member Luxembourg. [4] Includes Hong Kong but, excludes bilateral flows between mainland China and Hong Kong.

Source: National Science Foundation, *Science and Engineering Indicators 2020, Production and Trade of Knowledge- and Technology-Intensive Industries, Supplemental Tables*, NSB-2020-5, January 2020. See also <ncses.nsf.gov/pubs/nsb20205/data#supplemental-tables>.

Table 1326. Exporting Firms and Revenue, Employees, and Payroll by Country and Area of Export Destination: 2021

[44,008,897 represents $44,008,897,000,000. Covers nonfarm employer firms. A company or firm is a business consisting of one or more domestic establishments that the reporting firm specified under its ownership or control. Data were compiled from two Census Bureau data products, the 2020-2021 Profile of U.S. Importing and Exporting Companies and the 2022 Annual Business Survey. Excludes firms without reported sales, payroll, and employment; non-employer firms; firms operating primarily in out of scope industries, such as crop and animal production; and firms located in the U.S. Island Areas]

Export destination	Firms (number)	Receipts (mil. dol.)	Value of exports (mil. dol.)	Paid employees (1,000)	Annual payroll (mil. dol.)
All firms with and without exports	5,893,425	44,008,897	1,304,747	123,935	8,004,674
Firms with exports [1]	**160,697**	**25,474,093**	**1,304,747**	**48,094**	**3,873,303**
Australia	22,166	11,533,094	20,220	17,468	1,655,903
Belgium	7,618	8,627,958	29,853	11,641	1,146,456
Brazil	11,591	10,300,836	32,586	14,318	1,398,569
Canada	67,761	19,865,553	208,260	34,362	2,794,949
Chile	10,243	10,271,452	12,365	14,718	1,363,208
China	23,639	12,510,793	119,625	18,967	1,752,350
Colombia	8,899	10,051,680	13,605	14,454	1,315,940
France	15,131	10,069,451	22,148	15,887	1,523,061
Germany	22,501	12,118,080	54,660	18,635	1,796,448
Hong Kong	14,370	10,300,962	19,545	14,732	1,487,571
India	14,037	10,732,095	26,697	16,769	1,601,230
Ireland	5,955	7,546,982	12,019	10,809	1,100,247
Italy	13,676	9,695,365	16,700	13,915	1,377,021
Japan	19,160	12,322,795	60,114	17,966	1,797,719
Korea, South	17,266	10,969,218	49,681	15,215	1,486,192
Malaysia	9,583	8,719,176	13,054	12,950	1,203,270
Mexico	37,186	16,142,350	207,814	26,244	2,138,938
Netherlands	14,146	11,241,056	40,060	16,174	1,577,967
Philippines	5,617	8,619,960	12,344	13,257	1,211,407
Singapore	14,144	10,708,685	27,553	15,743	1,580,370
Spain	9,058	9,214,598	11,818	13,778	1,341,678
Taiwan	13,658	10,279,614	29,330	14,438	1,425,606
United Arab Emirates	11,561	9,181,684	12,084	13,278	1,272,498
United Kingdom	28,941	13,563,675	46,722	22,237	2,108,797
Vietnam	6,341	7,515,796	11,239	10,311	1,002,045
APEC (Asia-Pacific Economic Cooperation)	121,881	23,655,810	826,219	43,129	3,516,655
ASEAN (Association of Southeast Asian Nations)	27,982	14,114,784	82,340	22,607	2,062,727
European Union	52,502	16,868,055	215,200	28,428	2,542,054
LAFTA (Latin American Free Trade Area)	51,951	17,938,692	287,623	30,123	2,481,167
OECD [2]	129,367	24,108,520	852,764	44,456	3,615,500

[1] Includes other countries, not shown separately. [2] Organisation for Economic Cooperation and Development.

Source: U.S. Census Bureau, Annual Business Survey, "U.S. Exporting Firms by Demographics: 2022 Tables (Employer Businesses)," <www.census.gov/data/tables/2021/econ/abs/2021-abs-exporting-firms.html>, accessed August 2024.

Table 1327. U.S. Exporting and Importing Companies by Employment-Size Class: 2020 and 2022

[Value of exports and imports in millions of dollars (1,276,856 represents $1,276,856,000,000). Data include all companies that can be linked to import and/or export transactions. Trade values are taken from the transactions used to compile the official U.S. Trade statistics; company information is taken from the Census Bureau Business Register. For information on data limitations, see Explanatory Notes in source]

Employment-size class and company type	Number 2020	Number 2022	Known value [1] (mil. dol.) 2020	Known value [1] (mil. dol.) 2022	Percent of— Number 2020	Percent of— Number 2022	Percent of— Known value 2020	Percent of— Known value 2022
EXPORTERS								
All companies, total	**272,571**	**279,115**	**1,276,856**	**1,814,965**	**100.0**	**100.0**	**100.0**	**100.0**
By employment-size:								
1 to 19 employees	93,112	94,975	67,658	91,889	34.2	34.0	5.3	5.1
20 to 49 employees	27,129	26,964	38,974	51,958	10.0	9.7	3.1	2.9
50 to 99 employees	14,072	14,200	38,033	50,918	5.2	5.1	3.0	2.8
100 to 249 employees	11,673	11,633	95,710	112,347	4.3	4.2	7.5	6.2
250 to 499 employees	4,774	4,961	62,734	120,944	1.8	1.8	4.9	6.7
500 or more employees	7,354	7,724	854,073	1,166,438	2.7	2.8	66.9	64.3
Unknown [2]	114,457	118,658	119,676	220,472	42.0	42.5	9.4	12.1
IMPORTERS								
All companies, total	**221,580**	**234,074**	**2,024,454**	**2,809,327**	**100.0**	**100.0**	**100.0**	**100.0**
By employment-size:								
1 to 19 employees	88,095	92,357	126,744	175,347	39.8	39.5	6.3	6.2
20 to 49 employees	20,857	21,900	76,640	97,959	9.4	9.4	3.8	3.5
50 to 99 employees	10,683	11,385	69,192	100,533	4.8	4.9	3.4	3.6
100 to 249 employees	9,205	9,581	109,104	150,665	4.2	4.1	5.4	5.4
250 to 499 employees	3,857	4,084	86,919	130,644	1.7	1.7	4.3	4.7
500 or more employees	6,077	6,261	1,373,661	1,862,838	2.7	2.7	67.9	66.3
Unknown [2]	82,806	88,506	182,194	291,341	37.4	37.8	9.0	10.4

[1] Known value is defined as the portion of U.S. total exports and general imports that could be matched to specific companies. Export values are on f.a.s. or "free alongside ship" basis. [2] Includes missing employment data, nonemployers, and companies that reported annual payroll but did not report any employees on their payroll.

Source: U.S. Census Bureau, *Profile of U.S. Importing and Exporting Companies 2021-2022*, April 2024, and earlier reports. See also <www.census.gov/foreign-trade/statistics/press-release/>.

Table 1328. Export and Import Value Indexes—Selected Countries: 2017 to 2021

[Indexes in U.S. dollars, 2015=100. Values are the current value of exports/imports converted to U.S. dollars and expressed as a percentage of the average for the base period]

Country	Export value index					Import value index				
	2017	2018	2019	2020	2021	2017	2018	2019	2020	2021
United States	**102.9**	**110.7**	**109.4**	**94.8**	**116.8**	**104.0**	**112.9**	**110.9**	**104.0**	**126.8**
Australia	123.1	137.0	144.4	133.6	183.7	109.7	112.9	106.3	101.6	125.3
Belgium	108.3	118.0	112.6	106.4	137.4	109.0	121.2	114.2	105.8	135.9
Canada	102.6	110.3	109.4	95.3	123.8	103.1	109.1	107.6	97.7	117.2
France	105.7	115.0	112.8	96.5	115.5	108.5	118.5	114.7	101.8	125.1
Germany	109.2	117.7	112.3	104.2	123.1	110.6	122.2	117.4	111.5	135.1
Greece	114.3	138.3	132.8	123.3	165.2	114.3	136.5	133.3	119.5	162.1
Ireland	111.3	133.6	137.5	146.0	154.3	121.1	139.9	131.3	129.7	155.2
Italy	111.0	120.2	117.7	109.4	133.5	110.3	122.5	115.6	103.9	135.7
Japan	111.7	118.1	112.9	102.6	121.0	103.7	115.5	111.2	98.0	118.6
Korea, South	108.9	114.8	102.9	97.3	122.3	109.6	122.6	115.3	107.1	140.9
Netherlands	114.3	127.4	124.2	118.3	146.6	112.2	126.0	124.1	116.2	148.0
Norway	97.2	117.2	98.9	81.3	154.1	106.3	113.3	111.6	105.3	127.9
Spain	113.2	122.8	118.3	109.2	135.7	112.9	125.2	119.5	104.6	134.1
Sweden	109.2	118.5	114.7	111.0	135.5	111.4	123.3	114.9	108.4	135.0
United Kingdom	94.7	104.4	98.7	85.8	100.5	101.7	106.7	110.5	101.3	110.1

Source: World Bank, "World Development Indicators" database ©, <data.worldbank.org/>, accessed August 2024.

Table 1329. U.S. Trade with China—Leading Commodity Imports and Exports: 2010 to 2023

[In billions of dollars (365.0 represents $365,000,000,000), except as noted]

Commodity	NAICS code [1]	2010	2015	2020	2022	2023	2022-2023 percent change
IMPORTS FROM CHINA [2]							
Total imports [3]	(X)	**365.0**	**483.2**	**432.5**	**536.2**	**426.8**	**-20.4**
Communications equipment	3342	33.0	67.4	55.4	65.6	56.2	-14.3
Computer equipment	3341	57.2	57.8	59.2	63.8	45.4	-28.8
Plastics products	3261	7.2	12.1	17.8	19.8	15.8	-20.2
Apparel	3152	26.6	27.9	13.2	19.3	14.6	-24.6
Motor vehicle parts	3363	6.7	13.3	10.2	13.8	12.2	-11.7
Semiconductors and other electronic components	3344	18.3	19.6	10.9	14.3	12.1	-15.5
Household and institutional furniture and kitchen cabinets	3371	11.6	15.9	13.0	15.1	10.6	-29.7
Audio and video equipment	3343	19.5	15.0	10.9	11.5	9.4	-18.4
Footwear	3162	15.7	17.1	8.2	13.6	9.4	-31.0
Basic chemicals	3251	5.2	7.4	7.7	14.0	8.4	-39.6
EXPORTS TO CHINA							
Total exports [3]	(X)	**91.9**	**115.9**	**124.6**	**154.1**	**147.8**	**-4.1**
Oilseeds and grains	1111	11.3	13.0	17.1	25.4	18.3	-27.7
Oil and gas	2111	(Z)	1.0	9.3	11.2	17.8	59.2
Pharmaceuticals and medicines	3254	0.8	2.5	5.9	10.9	11.3	3.5
Semiconductors and other electronic components	3344	7.6	6.7	12.0	11.2	6.8	-39.4
Aerospace products and parts	3364	5.8	15.4	4.4	5.5	6.8	23.2
Navigational, measuring, electromedical, and control instruments	3345	3.7	5.4	6.0	6.5	6.8	4.3
Basic chemicals	3251	4.2	4.5	4.5	6.8	6.6	-2.3
Motor vehicles	3361	3.5	8.4	6.0	5.1	6.1	20.4
Resin, synthetic rubber, artificial/synthetic fibers	3252	4.3	3.8	3.8	4.7	5.5	16.6
Industrial machinery	3332	2.2	2.2	5.6	5.6	4.9	-12.2

X Not applicable. Z Less than $50 million. [1] Based on the North American Industry Classification System (NAICS); see text, Section 15. [2] Imports classified as general imports. For definition of General Imports, see Text, this section. [3] Includes items not shown separately.

Source: U.S. International Trade Commission, "Interactive Tariff and Trade DataWeb," <dataweb.usitc.gov/>, accessed August 2024.

Table 1330. U.S. Trade with Canada and Mexico—Leading Commodity Imports and Exports: 2010 to 2023

[In billions of dollars (277.6 represents $277,600,000,000), except as noted]

Commodity	NAICS code [1]	2010	2015	2020	2022	2023	2022-2023 percent change
IMPORTS FROM CANADA [2]							
Total imports [3]............................	(X)	**277.6**	**296.3**	**270.0**	**437.4**	**418.6**	**-4.3**
Oil and gas................................	2111	66.3	55.0	48.3	132.8	103.2	-22.3
Motor vehicles.............................	3361	36.5	43.4	30.3	29.6	41.1	38.5
Nonferrous metal (except aluminum) production and processing............	3314	10.3	9.4	11.0	11.8	17.6	49.2
Motor vehicle parts......................	3363	12.1	14.4	11.4	14.9	16.2	8.3
Petroleum and coal products..........	3241	14.5	12.0	7.9	18.9	15.7	-17.0
Aerospace products and parts........	3364	6.4	10.7	8.5	10.3	13.4	30.0
Basic chemicals..........................	3251	7.4	6.4	5.7	9.0	9.3	3.3
Alumina and aluminum and processing........	3313	6.2	5.9	5.6	11.0	9.3	-15.7
Grain and oilseed milling products....	3112	2.4	3.9	4.2	7.8	8.8	12.9
Iron and steel and ferroalloy...........	3311	5.4	4.7	4.0	9.2	8.2	-11.4
EXPORTS TO CANADA							
Total exports [3]............................	(X)	**249.3**	**280.9**	**256.2**	**359.2**	**354.4**	**-1.4**
Motor vehicles.............................	3361	21.7	25.4	22.8	34.6	34.0	-1.6
Motor vehicle parts......................	3363	22.1	19.9	14.4	16.6	21.0	26.4
Petroleum and coal products..........	3241	6.3	10.3	7.7	17.5	15.0	-14.1
Agriculture, construction, and mining machinery.......	3331	9.1	8.9	7.5	12.4	13.8	11.6
Oil and gas................................	2111	5.6	10.7	8.1	16.3	12.7	-22.5
Basic chemicals..........................	3251	7.0	7.3	7.1	11.9	11.3	-5.0
Aerospace products and parts........	3364	5.7	8.3	7.0	9.3	9.6	2.8
Computer equipment....................	3341	8.3	8.1	8.3	9.0	8.6	-4.1
Plastics products........................	3261	5.2	6.4	6.7	8.9	8.3	-6.6
Motor vehicle bodies and trailers.....	3362	2.5	7.1	5.4	7.7	7.6	-1.8
IMPORTS FROM MEXICO [2]							
Total imports [3]............................	(X)	**230.0**	**296.4**	**323.5**	**452.0**	**475.2**	**5.1**
Motor vehicles.............................	3361	27.5	50.0	56.2	72.0	85.0	18.1
Motor vehicle parts......................	3363	23.6	43.9	43.3	58.3	66.2	13.4
Computer and peripheral equipment....	3341	13.2	17.1	27.0	37.2	28.6	-23.2
Oil and gas................................	2111	29.7	12.5	8.7	20.7	19.8	-4.6
Electrical equipment....................	3353	6.8	10.5	11.6	15.9	18.7	17.7
Audio and video equipment............	3343	16.5	14.5	12.7	14.6	13.9	-4.7
Navigational, measuring, electromedical, and control instruments........	3345	5.0	8.4	8.1	10.2	12.1	18.9
Medical equipment and supplies.......	3391	4.5	5.2	7.0	9.3	11.6	24.3
Beverages.................................	3121	2.6	4.2	7.6	11.4	11.6	1.1
Communications equipment............	3342	14.1	13.3	8.8	10.9	11.4	4.8
EXPORTS TO MEXICO							
Total exports [3]............................	(X)	**163.7**	**236.5**	**212.5**	**324.2**	**322.7**	**-0.5**
Petroleum and coal products..........	3241	12.0	15.4	17.3	41.1	36.9	-10.3
Motor vehicle parts......................	3363	14.0	20.8	16.3	21.1	24.8	17.6
Semiconductors and other electronic components.....	3344	12.1	11.4	15.3	18.7	17.8	-5.0
Basic chemicals..........................	3251	7.1	8.5	8.9	14.6	12.8	-12.3
Computer and peripheral equipment....	3341	9.9	16.2	11.5	14.3	11.7	-17.9
Resin, synthetic rubber, artificial and synthetic fibers and filaments.......	3252	6.3	8.2	7.2	11.8	10.5	-10.7
Oilseeds and grains.....................	1111	4.5	4.9	5.8	10.6	9.9	-6.8
Plastics products........................	3261	4.5	7.4	6.8	8.7	9.5	10.2
Oil and gas................................	2111	2.0	3.0	5.9	15.0	8.3	-45.0
Electrical equipment....................	3353	3.4	6.0	5.1	6.8	7.8	14.9

X Not applicable. [1] Based on the North American Industry Classification System (NAICS); see text, Section 15. [2] Imports classified as general imports. For definition of general imports, see Text, this section. [3] Includes items not shown separately.

Source: U.S. International Trade Commission, "Interactive Tariff and Trade DataWeb," <dataweb.usitc.gov/>, accessed August 2024.

Table 1331. U.S. Trade in Processed Foods By Commodity: 2000 to 2023

[Units as indicated. Includes Puerto Rico, U.S. territories, and shipments under foreign aid programs. Metric ton = 1.102 short tons or .984 long tons. In January 2021, the U.S. Department of Agriculture adopted the World Trade Organization (WTO) definitions of agricultural products and revised historical data to reflect the new definitions; therefore, data here may not be comparable to data presented in previous editions. See source for details]

Product category	Units	2000	2010	2020	2022	2023
Processed foods imports, total [1,2]	**Metric tons**	**11,119,084**	**16,945,432**	**25,356,964**	**30,152,405**	**30,977,533**
Chocolate and confectionery [2]	Metric tons	858,136	1,362,569	1,715,866	2,068,618	1,937,219
Chocolate	Metric tons	525,437	820,017	1,014,791	1,169,804	1,069,828
Sugar confectionery	Metric tons	293,105	499,236	673,415	865,784	834,314
Condiments and sauces	Metric tons	351,000	569,652	1,003,851	1,228,450	1,189,649
Fats and oils [2]	Metric tons	1,687,235	3,497,902	5,151,701	6,366,171	8,168,209
Olive oil	Metric tons	203,960	275,435	408,032	421,725	359,524
Soybean oil	1,000 kilograms	35,949	53,697	134,498	126,825	193,905
Vegetable oils (excl. soybean)	Metric tons	1,427,711	3,075,082	4,382,119	5,250,854	6,078,974
Food preparations [2]	Metric tons	1,122,644	2,101,102	3,127,309	3,563,624	3,306,387
Baking inputs, mixes, and doughs [3]	Metric tons	682,340	1,097,081	1,835,663	2,016,469	1,833,381
Non-alcoholic beverages [2]	Kiloliters	3,689,991	5,552,744	6,381,276	8,210,912	7,758,070
Bottled drinks [4]	Kiloliters	555,954	1,222,531	2,400,803	2,516,458	2,557,663
Juices	Kiloliters	3,134,037	4,330,213	3,980,473	5,694,455	5,200,407
Alcoholic beverages	Kiloliters	2,818,882	4,115,172	5,775,543	6,391,300	6,106,680
Beer	Kiloliters	2,331,185	3,146,395	4,262,093	4,751,171	4,703,796
Wine	Kiloliters	439,989	932,137	1,219,713	1,422,361	1,217,148
Pasta and processed cereals [2]	Metric tons	517,471	881,572	1,681,166	1,821,053	1,717,952
Breakfast cereals and other breakfast products	Metric tons	113,024	277,763	684,757	824,408	752,350
Pasta	Metric tons	316,886	367,974	658,824	665,234	647,038
Prepared/preserved meats	Metric tons	197,083	143,248	219,758	271,232	262,644
Prepared/preserved seafood	Metric tons	889,804	1,306,813	1,559,694	1,714,980	1,653,128
Processed fruit	Metric tons	865,350	1,422,793	2,012,225	2,368,631	2,154,118
Processed vegetables and pulses [2]	Metric tons	1,695,961	2,455,785	3,567,168	4,173,257	4,036,565
Frozen potato products [5]	Metric tons	527,642	725,033	1,134,344	1,432,650	1,512,965
Processed/prepared dairy products [2]	Metric tons	245,530	230,269	366,448	456,917	458,515
Cheese	Metric tons	188,707	138,539	165,970	188,392	192,504
Cream & powdered/condensed milk	Metric tons	18,897	33,250	49,441	54,912	53,724
Ice cream	Metric tons	9,151	30,263	41,013	89,727	76,212
Yogurt and dairy drinks	Liters	23,060	11,197	693,032	883,905	1,043,827
Snack foods	Metric tons	627,030	1,126,307	2,156,209	2,690,914	2,726,601
Baked snack foods [6]	Metric tons	480,515	899,781	1,939,009	2,425,486	2,466,854
Mixes of nuts and fruit [7]	Metric tons	92,782	156,182	107,830	144,136	131,956
Potato chips	Metric tons	23,758	40,569	64,723	70,571	78,017
Prepared peanuts and peanut butter	Metric tons	29,976	29,774	44,647	50,720	49,774
Spices	Metric tons	243,766	360,962	538,747	555,401	547,113
Syrups and sweeteners [2]	Metric tons	1,106,543	866,613	1,107,885	1,197,250	1,335,063
Fructose and fructose syrup	Metric tons	66,513	92,496	99,489	125,383	114,687
Glucose and glucose syrup	Metric tons	113,647	217,058	268,731	353,523	326,797
Processed foods exports, total [2]	**Metric tons**	**10,941,839**	**17,796,644**	**19,957,346**	**20,117,485**	**19,511,704**
Chocolate and confectionery [2]	Metric tons	302,600	420,212	442,862	508,538	506,543
Chocolate	Metric tons	192,742	303,757	321,128	362,619	349,970
Sugar confectionery	Metric tons	98,043	108,527	117,682	140,794	149,810
Condiments and sauces	Metric tons	363,963	638,943	914,649	1,031,009	1,041,816
Fats and oils [2]	Metric tons	1,932,014	3,280,825	2,463,602	1,739,782	952,984
Soybean oil	1,000 kilograms	586,786	1,656,926	1,237,220	633,412	149,944
Vegetable oils (excl. soybean)	Metric tons	1,044,199	1,066,611	595,446	479,563	354,554
Food preparations [2]	Metric tons	2,523,203	3,472,334	5,150,026	4,315,396	5,219,775
Baking inputs, mixes, and doughs [3]	Metric tons	1,904,460	2,280,017	3,981,800	3,179,035	4,105,436
Non-alcoholic beverages [2]	Kiloliters	1,661,547	1,617,263	1,090,152	1,061,256	1,032,576
Bottled drinks [4]	Kiloliters	487,448	636,964	639,022	646,888	665,748
Juices	Kiloliters	1,174,098	980,299	451,129	414,368	366,828
Alcoholic beverages	Kiloliters	550,712	727,964	740,376	672,671	456,287
Beer	Kiloliters	262,305	320,694	366,148	380,479	237,696
Wine	Kiloliters	264,523	383,301	353,694	268,894	197,375
Pasta and processed cereals [2]	Metric tons	683,017	983,674	819,217	861,319	800,852
Breakfast cereals and other breakfast products	Metric tons	265,399	568,666	458,122	474,622	421,426
Pasta	Metric tons	102,295	181,765	194,595	209,736	211,555
Prepared/preserved meats	Metric tons	313,841	643,614	614,689	693,948	616,337
Prepared/preserved seafood	Metric tons	501,314	533,726	426,845	425,236	451,139
Processed fruit	Metric tons	388,844	571,165	456,946	459,524	415,481
Processed vegetables and pulses [2]	Metric tons	1,272,076	1,679,157	2,152,782	2,237,612	2,123,586
Frozen potato products [5]	Metric tons	568,709	790,607	970,716	1,074,472	986,123
Processed/prepared dairy products [2]	Metric tons	398,655	1,179,545	1,826,261	2,117,183	1,902,405
Cheese	Metric tons	47,760	173,327	355,511	450,886	433,107
Cream & powdered/condensed milk	Metric tons	114,847	466,853	859,542	892,844	856,338
Ice cream	Metric tons	41,652	35,680	72,195	72,819	67,545
Snack foods	Metric tons	490,079	784,168	960,956	1,052,986	1,062,045
Baked snack foods [6]	Metric tons	274,577	476,137	653,547	703,971	708,913
Mixes of nuts and fruit [7]	Metric tons	72,748	160,303	141,190	181,351	167,764
Potato chips	Metric tons	106,040	86,510	93,168	97,091	106,216
Prepared peanuts and peanut butter	Metric tons	36,713	61,218	73,051	70,573	79,152
Soups	1,000 kilograms	97,212	140,420	310,469	277,086	288,475
Syrups and sweeteners [2]	Metric tons	726,427	2,525,583	2,050,454	2,233,680	2,336,635
Fructose and fructose syrup	Metric tons	322,904	1,395,278	1,178,210	1,102,817	1,188,304
Glucose and glucose syrup	Metric tons	209,686	738,966	382,920	545,443	539,526
Molasses	Kiloliters	199,070	203,841	61,582	34,452	10,626

[1] Imports for consumption. Excludes merchandise entered into bonded warehouses of Foreign Trade Zones under Customs custody; see source for details. [2] Includes commodities not shown separately. [3] Includes pudding. [4] Includes soda, juice mixes, beer, milk-based drinks, etc. [5] Includes French fries. [6] Pastries, pretzels, corn chips, etc. [7] Includes packaged and microwaveable popcorn.

Source: U.S. Department of Agriculture, Foreign Agricultural Service, "Global Agricultural Trade System," <apps.fas.usda.gov/gats/>, accessed August 2024.

Section 29
Puerto Rico and the Island Areas

The U.S. has twelve unincorporated territories, also known as possessions, and two commonwealths. This section presents summary economic and social statistics for the major possessions, American Samoa, Guam, and the U.S. Virgin Islands; and the major commonwealths of Puerto Rico and the Northern Marianas. Primary sources include the decennial censuses of population and housing and the annual Puerto Rico Community Survey conducted by the U.S. Census Bureau; County Business Patterns and other Census Bureau publications and databases; and the *National Vital Statistics Reports* (NSVR) series, issued by the National Center for Health Statistics. The *Informe Económico al Gobernadora/Economic Report to the Governor issued by the Gobierno De Puerto Rico, Junta de Planificación [Puerto Rico Planning Board]*, <jp.pr.gov/informe-economico-al-gobernador/>, provides more detailed data for Puerto Rico.

Jurisdiction—The United States gained jurisdiction over these areas as follows: the islands of Puerto Rico and Guam, surrendered by Spain in December 1898, were ceded to the United States by the Treaty of Paris, ratified in 1899. Puerto Rico became a commonwealth on July 25, 1952, thereby achieving a high degree of local autonomy under its own constitution. The U.S. Virgin Islands, comprising approximately 50 islands and cays, was purchased by the United States from Denmark in 1917. American Samoa, a group of seven islands, was acquired in accordance with a convention among the United States, Great Britain, and Germany, ratified in 1900 (Swains Island was annexed in 1925). By an agreement approved by the United Nations Security Council and the United States, the Northern Mariana Islands, previously under Japanese mandate, was administered by the United States between 1947 and 1986 under the United Nations trusteeship system. The Northern Mariana Islands became a U.S. commonwealth in 1986. The residents of all of these places are full U.S. citizens, with the exception of those on American Samoa who are U.S. nationals, but not citizens.

Censuses—Because characteristics of Puerto Rico and the Island Areas differ, the presentation of census data for them is not uniform. The 1960 Census of Population covered all the territories listed above except the Northern Mariana Islands (their census was conducted in April 1958 by the Office of the High Commissioner of the Trust Territory of the Pacific Islands), while the 1960 Census of Housing excluded American Samoa. The 1970, 1980, 1990, 2000, and 2010 censuses of population and housing covered all five areas. Beginning in 1967, Congress authorized the Economic Censuses, to be taken at 5-year intervals, for years ending in "2" and "7." Prior economic censuses were conducted in Puerto Rico for 1949, 1954, 1958, and 1963 and in Guam and the U.S. Virgin Islands for 1958 and 1963. In 1967, the census of construction industries was added for the first time in Puerto Rico; in 1972, the U.S. Virgin Islands and Guam were covered; and in 1982, the Economic Census was taken for the first time for the Northern Mariana Islands. Agricultural censuses have been conducted with increasing regularity in Puerto Rico since 1910, in the U.S. Virgin Islands since 1917, and in Guam and American Samoa since 1920; the first agricultural census in the Northern Mariana Islands was conducted in 1970.

Puerto Rico Community Survey—The Puerto Rico Community Survey (PRCS) began in 2005 and was an important element in the Census Bureau's re-engineered 2010 census plan. The PRCS is a part of the American Community Survey (ACS) provides information on many topics for the United States (the 50 states and District of Columbia); more information is available at <www.census.gov/programs-surveys/acs/about.html>. The PRCS collects and produces population and housing information every year instead of every 10 years. About 36,000 households are surveyed each year from across every municipio in Puerto Rico.

Information in other sections—In addition to the statistics presented in this section, other data on Puerto Rico and the island areas are included in many tables showing distribution by states in various sections of the *Abstract*. See "Puerto Rico" and "Island Areas of the U.S." in the Index.

Table 1332. Estimated and Projected Resident Population of Puerto Rico and Island Areas: 2000 to 2050

[In thousands (57.7 represents 57,700). Population as of July 1. Population data generally are de facto figures for the present territory. For details of methodology, coverage, and reliability, see source]

Area	2000	2010	2015	2020	2021	2022	2023	Projected 2030	Projected 2040	Projected 2050
American Samoa..............	57.7	55.5	52.3	47.4	46.4	45.4	44.6	40.5	35.5	31.3
Guam.........................	155.3	163.3	166.4	168.5	168.8	169.1	169.3	169.9	166.9	159.5
Northern Mariana Islands.....	69.7	55.1	52.9	51.9	51.7	51.5	51.3	50.2	48.4	45.3
Puerto Rico....................	3,810.6	3,721.5	3,472.9	3,190.4	3,142.8	3,098.4	3,057.3	2,818.3	2,469.3	2,163.7
Virgin Islands.................	108.6	108.4	107.7	106.3	105.9	105.4	104.9	100.3	91.6	82.3

Source: U.S. Census Bureau, "International Data Base (IDB)," <www.census.gov/data-tools/demo/idb/>, accessed August 2024.

Table 1333. Births, Deaths, and Infant Deaths for Puerto Rico and the Island Areas: 2000 to 2022

[Births, deaths, and infant deaths by place of residence. Rates for Census years based on population enumerated as of April 1; for other years, on population estimated as of July 1]

Area and year	Births Number	Births Rate [1]	Deaths Number	Deaths Rate [2]	Infant deaths Number	Infant deaths Rate [3]
Puerto Rico:						
2000.............................	59,333	15.6	28,365	7.4	574	9.7
2010.............................	42,153	11.3	29,153	7.8	341	8.1
2015.............................	31,157	9.0	28,085	8.1	218	7.0
2020.............................	18,933	6.0	32,008	10.1	138	7.3
2021.............................	19,304	5.9	(NA)	(NA)	134	6.9
2022.............................	19,112	5.9	(NA)	(NA)	141	7.4
Guam:						
2000.............................	3,766	24.2	648	4.2	22	5.8
2010.............................	3,416	21.4	857	5.4	48	14.1
2015.............................	3,366	20.8	985	6.1	47	14.0
2020.............................	2,935	17.4	1,167	6.9	24	8.2
2021.............................	2,623	15.5	(NA)	(NA)	41	15.6
2022.............................	2,518	14.9	(NA)	(NA)	27	10.7
Virgin Islands:						
2000.............................	1,564	14.4	641	5.9	21	13.4
2010.............................	1,600	15.1	715	6.7	13	(B)
2015.............................	1,325	12.8	673	6.5	4	(B)
2020.............................	876	8.2	701	6.6	4	(B)
2021.............................	903	8.5	(NA)	(NA)	(NA)	(NA)
2022.............................	868	8.2	(NA)	(NA)	(NA)	(NA)
American Samoa:						
2000.............................	1,731	30.0	219	3.8	11	(B)
2010.............................	1,234	22.2	224	4.0	14	(B)
2015.............................	1,078	19.8	303	5.6	10	(B)
2020.............................	(NA)	(NA)	(NA)	(NA)	(NA)	(NA)
2021.............................	(NA)	(NA)	(NA)	(NA)	(NA)	(NA)
2022.............................	(NA)	(NA)	(NA)	(NA)	(NA)	(NA)
Northern Marianas:						
2000.............................	1,431	20.5	136	2.0	11	(B)
2010.............................	1,072	20.0	174	3.3	4	(B)
2015.............................	427	8.2	223	4.3	5	(B)
2020.............................	628	12.1	219	4.2	5	(B)
2021.............................	570	11.0	(NA)	(NA)	(NA)	(NA)
2022.............................	467	9.1	(NA)	(NA)	(NA)	(NA)

NA Not available. B Base figure too small to meet statistical standards of reliability. [1] Birth rates are births per 1,000 women of child-bearing age. [2] Death rates are deaths per 1,000 population. [3] Infant death rates are infant deaths (under 1 year old) per 1,000 live births.

Source: U.S. National Center for Health Statistics, National Vital Statistics Reports (NVSR), *Births: Final Data for 2022*, Vol. 73, No. 2, April 2024, and earlier reports; *Infant Mortality in the United States, 2022: Data From the Period Linked Birth/Infant Death File*, Vol. 73, No. 5, July 2024, and earlier reports; and *Deaths: Final Data for 2020*, Vol. 72, No. 10, September 2023, and earlier reports. See also <www.cdc.gov/nchs/nvss/index.htm>.

Table 1334. Public Elementary and Secondary Education by Island Area: 2021

[Enrollment and staff are for Fall of year shown. Revenues and expenditures are for school year ending in year shown]

Item	Puerto Rico	Guam	U.S. Virgin Islands	American Samoa	Northern Marianas
Enrollment................................	259,535	28,402	10,234	(NA)	9,491
Elementary (pre-kindergarten to grade 8 and ungraded).......	172,920	19,142	6,917	(NA)	6,347
Secondary (grades 9 to 12 and ungraded)......................	86,615	9,260	3,317	(NA)	3,144
Total staff.................................	39,964	3,513	1,968	(NA)	1,113
School district staff.......................	1,531	317	152	(NA)	165
School staff..............................	26,865	2,951	1,324	(NA)	881
Teachers..............................	23,348	1,767	916	(NA)	507
Student support staff.....................	5,429	116	31	(NA)	35
Other support services staff..............	6,139	129	461	(NA)	32
Revenues, total [1] ($1,000)................	2,383,989	346,872	383,175	77,985	97,733
Current expenditures [2] ($1,000)...................	2,103,412	348,421	180,024	77,342	93,376
Per pupil [2] (dollars)........................	7,610	12,671	16,376	7,548	(NA)

NA Not available. [1] Includes federal, territorial, local, and private revenues. [2] Includes current expenditures only, and excludes capital expenditures, interest on school debt, community services, private school programs, adult education, and other expenditures not directly allocable to public school operations.

Source: U.S. National Center for Education Statistics, *Digest of Education Statistics*, "Latest version of all Digest tables," <nces.ed.gov/programs/digest>, accessed February 2024.

Table 1335. Puerto Rico—Selected Social, Demographic, and Housing Characteristics: 2021 and 2022

[The Puerto Rico Community Survey universe includes the household population and the population living in institutions, college dormitories, and other group quarters. Based on a sample and subject to sampling variability; see text, this section and Appendix III]

Characteristic	2021 Number	2021 Percent	2022 Number	2022 Percent
Total population	**3,263,584**	**100.0**	**3,221,789**	**100.0**
SEX				
Male	1,543,991	47.3	1,528,789	47.5
Female	1,719,593	52.7	1,693,000	52.5
AGE				
Under 5 years	103,841	3.2	99,432	3.1
5 to 9 years	150,197	4.6	133,195	4.1
10 to 14 years	176,442	5.4	170,757	5.3
15 to 19 years	205,814	6.3	197,196	6.1
20 to 24 years	225,881	6.9	216,771	6.7
25 to 34 years	402,204	12.3	405,834	12.6
35 to 44 years	400,607	12.3	398,749	12.4
45 to 54 years	415,974	12.7	404,722	12.6
55 to 59 years	220,356	6.8	215,212	6.7
60 to 64 years	221,782	6.8	223,075	6.9
65 to 74 years	384,163	11.8	383,979	11.9
75 to 84 years	259,065	7.9	275,913	8.6
85 years and over	97,258	3.0	96,954	3.0
MARITAL STATUS				
Males 15 years and over	**1,328,039**	**100.0**	**1,320,346**	**100.0**
Never married	631,091	47.5	596,651	45.2
Married, not separated	442,244	33.3	489,467	37.1
Separated	27,877	2.1	23,283	1.8
Widowed	52,261	3.9	46,903	3.6
Divorced	174,566	13.1	164,042	12.4
Females 15 years and over	**1,505,065**	**100.0**	**1,498,059**	**100.0**
Never married	593,773	39.5	574,817	38.4
Married, not separated	460,979	30.6	488,826	32.6
Separated	32,756	2.2	32,286	2.2
Widowed	175,926	11.7	167,368	11.2
Divorced	241,631	16.1	234,762	15.7
HOUSEHOLDS				
Total households	**1,165,982**	**100.0**	**1,289,311**	**100.0**
Married-couple families	401,781	34.5	449,853	34.9
With own children under 18 years	90,099	7.7	104,163	8.1
Cohabiting couple household	127,278	10.9	143,552	11.1
With own children under 18 years	54,099	4.6	62,602	4.9
Male householder, no spouse/partner present	199,065	17.1	217,544	16.9
With own children under 18 years	7,950	0.7	8,064	0.6
Female householder, no spouse/partner present	437,858	37.6	478,362	37.1
With own children under 18 years	80,867	6.9	93,196	7.2
Householder living alone	365,185	31.3	400,857	31.1
65 years and over	190,228	16.3	203,836	15.9
Average household size	2.77	(X)	2.47	(X)
Average family size	3.56	(X)	3.10	(X)
DISABILITY STATUS				
Total civilian noninstitutionalized population	**3,237,924**	**100.0**	**3,194,807**	**100.0**
With a disability	712,517	22.0	784,567	24.6

X Not applicable.

Source: U.S. Census Bureau, Puerto Rico Community Survey, DP02PR, "Selected Social Characteristics in Puerto Rico," and DP05, "Demographic and Housing Estimates," <data.census.gov>, accessed October 2023. See also <www.census.gov/programs-surveys/acs/about /puerto-rico-community-survey.html>.

Table 1336. Puerto Rico—Owner and Renter Occupied Housing by Household Type: 2022

[The Puerto Rico Community Survey universe includes the household population and the population living in institutions, college dormitories, and other group quarters. Based on a sample and subject to sampling variability; see text, this section and Appendix III]

Household type	Owner occupied	Renter occupied	Household type	Owner occupied	Renter occupied
Total households	**869,635**	**419,676**	Householder age 15 to 34	10,632	45,631
Family households	**586,620**	**234,168**	Householder age 35 to 64	85,212	72,760
Married-couple family	377,579	72,274	Householder age 65 and over	57,368	10,874
Householder age 15 to 34	13,896	16,120	**Nonfamily households**	**283,015**	**185,508**
Householder age 35 to 64	205,332	41,767	Householder living alone	245,438	155,419
Householder age 65 and over	158,351	14,387	Householder age 15 to 34	8,729	25,416
Other family	209,041	161,894	Householder age 35 to 64	87,856	75,020
Male householder, no spouse present	55,829	32,629	Householder age 65 and over	148,853	54,983
Householder age 15 to 34	7,889	12,012	Householder not living alone	37,577	30,089
Householder age 35 to 64	30,592	16,725	Householder age 15 to 34	3,035	14,473
Householder age 65 and over	17,348	3,892	Householder age 35 to 64	21,583	11,254
Female householder, no spouse present	153,212	129,265	Householder age 65 and over	12,959	4,362

Source: U.S. Census Bureau, 2022 Puerto Rico Community Survey, B25011, "Tenure by Household Type and Age of Householder," <data.census.gov/>, accessed October 2023. See also <www.census.gov/programs-surveys/acs/about/puerto-rico-community-survey.html>.

Table 1337. Puerto Rico—Socioeconomic Summary: 2015 to 2023

[3,504 represents 3,504,000. Data are for fiscal years]

Item	Unit	2015	2017	2018	2019	2020	2021	2022	2023 (P)
POPULATION									
Total [1]	1,000	3,504	3,366	3,259	3,194	3,238	3,272	3,241	3,213
Persons per family	Number	2.9	2.8	2.7	2.7	2.7	2.6	2.6	2.6
LABOR FORCE									
Total [2]	1,000	1,121	1,111	1,080	1,087	1,086	1,136	1,197	1,187
Employed [3]	1,000	977	983	968	995	994	1,039	1,114	1,116
Agriculture [4]	1,000	16	18	16	14	16	15	16	17
Manufacturing	1,000	81	79	88	100	101	102	100	100
Trade	1,000	237	228	237	244	235	247	281	275
Services	1,000	330	348	324	333	350	362	393	399
Government	1,000	197	197	191	175	169	175	176	175
Unemployed	1,000	144	128	111	92	92	97	82	71
Unemployment rate [5]	Rate	12.8	11.5	10.3	8.4	8.5	8.6	6.9	6.0
Compensation of employees	Mil. dol.	28,874	28,484	27,694	27,671	27,264	28,795	30,734	32,662
Average compensation	Dollar	29,554	28,976	28,609	27,810	27,428	27,714	27,589	29,267
Salary and wages	Mil. dol.	24,768	24,287	23,813	24,069	23,716	24,321	26,878	28,584
INCOME									
Personal income:									
Current dollars	Mil. dol.	63,756	64,863	71,873	67,732	73,875	80,643	83,330	86,984
Constant (2017) dollars	Mil. dol.	64,206	64,863	70,741	65,951	71,793	78,522	77,879	78,933
Disposable personal income:									
Current dollars	Mil. dol.	61,238	62,656	69,669	65,126	71,707	77,880	80,137	83,717
Constant (2017) dollars	Mil. dol.	61,670	62,656	68,572	63,413	69,686	75,833	74,895	75,968
Average family income:									
Current dollars	Dollar	52,766	53,956	59,545	57,256	60,923	64,080	66,078	69,576
Constant (2017) dollars	Dollar	53,138	53,956	58,607	55,751	59,206	62,396	61,755	63,137
TOURISM									
Number of visitors	1,000	5,051	4,927	4,260	4,930	3,882	2,755	4,596	6,226
Visitor expenditures	Mil. dol.	3,825	3,868	3,303	3,612	2,921	2,787	4,567	5,368
Average per visitor	Dollar	757	785	775	733	752	1,012	994	862

P Preliminary. [1] Average of population estimates at the beginning and end of the fiscal year. Intercensal data released July 2019 and Decennial Census 2020 (U.S. Bureau of the Census, Population Division, Population Estimates, Vintage 2019 and 2020-apportionment-data). Data gathered from <www.census.gov>. [2] For population 16 years old and over. [3] Includes employment in other industries, not shown separately. [4] Includes forestry and fisheries. [5] Unemployed as percent of the labor force.

Source: Puerto Rico Planning Board, San Juan, PR, *Informe Económico al Gobernador Puerto Rico 2023 / Economic Report for the Governor 2023*, May 2024, and earlier reports. See also <jp.pr.gov/informe-economico-al-gobernador/>.

Table 1338. Puerto Rico—School Enrollment and Educational Attainment by Level: 2010 to 2022

[The Puerto Rico Community Survey universe includes the household population and the population living in institutions, college dormitories, and other group quarters. Based on a sample and subject to sampling variability; see text, this section and Appendix III]

Item	2010	2015	2017	2018	2019	2021	2022
EDUCATIONAL ENROLLMENT							
Population 3 years and over enrolled in school	995,743	892,872	804,711	742,847	747,920	707,157	672,468
Nursery school, preschool	55,298	52,792	45,061	35,928	34,961	27,940	31,183
Kindergarten	45,366	37,989	33,751	27,389	26,301	25,330	23,457
Elementary school (grades 1-8)	414,233	340,580	307,128	289,314	279,078	265,224	246,747
High school (grades 9-12)	213,581	189,446	168,446	153,451	154,094	148,693	149,962
College or graduate school	267,265	272,065	250,325	236,765	253,486	239,970	221,119
EDUCATIONAL ATTAINMENT							
Population 25 years and over	2,444,933	2,382,526	2,343,675	2,288,030	2,301,735	2,401,409	2,404,438
Less than 9th grade	484,138	391,558	370,702	336,242	320,083	309,413	282,929
9th to 12th grade, no diploma	262,682	210,220	188,871	178,663	168,325	179,367	157,638
High school graduate (includes equivalency)	623,709	647,581	653,789	644,702	648,146	671,940	671,662
Some college, no degree	317,797	314,431	285,018	276,042	279,696	276,439	289,890
Associate's degree	212,186	228,508	242,776	241,678	258,905	280,356	284,600
Bachelor's degree	389,954	424,255	428,558	430,692	443,589	493,356	503,506
Graduate or professional degree	154,467	165,973	173,961	180,011	182,991	190,538	214,213
Percent high school graduate or higher	69.5	74.7	76.1	77.5	78.8	79.6	81.7
Percent bachelor's degree or higher	22.3	24.8	25.7	26.7	27.2	28.5	29.8

Source: U.S. Census Bureau, Puerto Rico Community Survey, DP02PR, "Selected Social Characteristics in Puerto Rico," <data.census.gov>, accessed October 2023, and earlier releases. See also <census.gov/programs-surveys/acs/about/puerto-rico-community-survey.html>.

Table 1339. Puerto Rico—Gross Product and Net Income: 2010 to 2023

[In millions of dollars (64,295 represents $64,295,000,000). For fiscal years ending June 30. Minus sign (-) indicates decrease]

Item	2010	2015	2017	2018	2019	2020	2021	2022	2023 (P)
Gross product [1]	**64,295**	**69,602**	**69,050**	**67,601**	**70,765**	**70,353**	**73,357**	**78,477**	**81,551**
Manufacturing	46,577	49,520	48,966	47,892	50,084	49,265	50,572	52,392	53,769
Wholesale trade	2,993	2,794	2,665	2,691	2,749	2,706	3,123	3,244	3,393
Retail trade	4,473	4,908	5,452	5,594	5,732	5,618	6,351	7,144	7,616
Information	2,646	2,699	1,985	1,762	1,703	1,984	2,526	2,606	2,679
Finance and insurance	5,241	4,617	4,371	4,034	3,909	4,662	3,205	3,620	3,715
Real estate and rental	13,785	15,301	15,987	16,555	17,046	17,321	17,281	18,035	19,023
Health care and social services	3,294	3,828	3,894	3,791	3,995	4,125	4,575	4,940	5,231
Government	8,350	7,264	7,175	6,343	5,861	5,309	5,129	5,144	5,552
Commonwealth	6,862	5,741	5,626	4,946	4,597	4,038	3,858	3,835	4,187
Municipalities	1,488	1,523	1,549	1,397	1,264	1,271	1,271	1,309	1,365
Rest of the world	-34,087	-33,774	-34,396	-33,357	-34,361	-32,778	-33,069	-35,090	-36,352
Statistical discrepancy	-294	371	529	-457	725	-575	-280	433	-364
Net income [1]	**50,246**	**55,995**	**54,284**	**54,061**	**55,626**	**57,009**	**58,427**	**62,016**	**65,426**
Manufacturing	43,292	45,893	45,119	44,105	46,184	45,625	46,501	48,086	49,367
Wholesale trade	2,352	2,238	2,316	2,313	2,342	2,333	2,720	2,809	2,951
Retail trade	3,803	4,260	4,697	4,836	4,971	4,965	5,665	6,407	6,859
Information	1,244	1,340	503	594	571	918	1,161	1,173	1,235
Finance and insurance	2,410	3,074	3,008	2,739	2,621	3,393	2,390	2,845	2,799
Real estate and rental	10,689	12,251	12,343	12,774	12,965	13,373	12,781	13,338	14,072
Health care and social services	2,775	3,320	3,352	3,263	3,458	3,607	4,024	4,344	4,612
Government	8,350	7,264	7,175	6,343	5,861	5,309	5,129	5,144	5,552
Commonwealth	6,862	5,741	5,626	4,946	4,597	4,038	3,858	3,835	4,187
Municipalities	1,488	1,523	1,549	1,397	1,264	1,271	1,271	1,309	1,365
Rest of the world	-34,087	-33,774	-34,396	-33,357	-34,361	-32,778	-33,069	-35,090	-36,352

P Preliminary. [1] Includes all other industries not elsewhere classified.

Source: Puerto Rico Planning Board, San Juan, PR, *Informe Económico al Gobernador 2023 / Economic Report to the Governor 2023*, May 2024, and earlier reports. See also <jp.pr.gov/informe-economico-al-gobernador/>.

Table 1340. Puerto Rico—Transfer Payments: 2010 to 2023

[16,504 represents $16,504,000,000. Data represent transfer payments between federal and state governments and other nonresidents]

Item	2010	2015	2019	2020	2021	2022	2023 (P)
Total receipts	**16,504**	**18,017**	**20,743**	**30,201**	**33,980**	**34,072**	**33,862**
Federal government	15,585	17,091	19,626	28,282	33,401	33,471	33,121
Transfers to individuals [1]	15,352	16,863	19,340	28,035	33,100	33,170	32,808
Veterans benefits	733	1,416	1,297	1,590	1,409	1,772	1,500
Medicare	2,529	4,467	5,298	6,501	6,381	7,934	7,458
Social security	7,074	7,718	7,569	9,257	8,613	9,842	9,837
Nutritional assistance	1,605	1,846	2,728	2,831	2,921	3,210	3,343
Industry subsidies	233	228	285	247	301	302	313
U.S. state governments	29	34	22	17	70	22	78
Other nonresidents	890	892	1,095	1,903	510	578	664
Total payments	**3,804**	**3,961**	**4,576**	**4,558**	**5,382**	**5,062**	**5,501**
Federal government	3,586	3,844	4,348	4,194	5,189	4,900	5,357
Transfers from individuals [1]	1,862	1,984	2,145	2,144	2,249	2,165	2,363
Contribution to Medicare	392	464	535	535	676	625	753
Employee contributions to social security systems	1,467	1,516	1,607	1,606	1,570	1,536	1,607
Transfers from industries	93	133	216	233	215	217	237
Unemployment insurance	207	248	419	464	540	615	690
Employer contributions to social security systems	1,424	1,479	1,568	1,353	2,186	1,903	2,068
Other nonresidents [2]	215	114	142	362	190	161	142
Net balance	**12,700**	**14,056**	**16,252**	**25,644**	**28,599**	**29,010**	**28,361**
Federal government	11,999	13,247	15,278	24,088	28,212	28,571	27,764
U.S. state governments	26	31	21	15	67	21	76
Other nonresidents	675	778	954	1,541	320	418	522

P Preliminary. [1] Includes other receipts and payments not shown separately. [2] Includes U.S. state governments.

Source: Puerto Rico Planning Board, San Juan, PR, *Informe Económico al Gobernador 2023 / Economic Report to the Governor 2023*, May 2024, and earlier reports. See also <jp.pr.gov/informe-economico-al-gobernador/>.

Table 1341. Puerto Rico—Exports, Imports, and Trade Balance: 2000 to 2023

[In millions of dollars (38,466 represents $38,466,000,000). Data are for fiscal years]

Item	2000	2010	2015	2016	2017	2018	2019	2020	2021	2022	2023 (P)
Exports [1]	38,466	61,657	69,463	71,740	71,092	60,528	63,684	62,237	57,910	59,715	63,579
To U.S.	33,764	41,989	51,433	54,593	55,257	48,480	48,236	47,266	45,087	44,621	45,669
To foreign countries	4,639	19,526	17,750	16,804	15,539	11,834	15,173	14,734	12,613	14,772	17,497
To Virgin Islands	64	142	281	344	295	215	276	237	210	322	413
Imports	27,043	40,810	43,093	43,316	45,938	46,488	49,402	44,513	45,051	52,150	56,359
From U.S.	15,080	20,896	22,334	24,076	24,589	25,104	24,661	22,643	25,434	27,951	32,053
From foreign countries	11,310	18,341	20,744	19,239	21,113	21,213	24,625	21,740	19,482	23,835	23,767
From Virgin Islands	653	1,573	15	1	236	171	115	131	135	364	539
Trace balance [2]	11,423	20,847	26,370	28,424	25,154	14,040	14,283	17,725	12,859	7,565	7,220
With U.S.	18,684	21,094	29,099	30,516	30,668	23,376	23,575	24,624	19,653	16,670	13,617
With foreign countries	-6,671	1,185	-2,994	-2,435	-5,574	-9,379	-9,453	-7,005	6,869	9,063	-6,271
With Virgin Islands	-590	-1,431	265	343	59	43	160	106	76	-42	-126

P Preliminary. [1] The majority of exports originate from the manufacturing sector. For 2023, the value of manufacturing exports is $61,235.6 million and is 96 percent of the total export values. [2] Trade balance is the value of imports minus exports and includes a number of adjustments. The items that are added (+) or subtracted (-) include: unregistered merchandise (+), postal parcels (+), items for display such as paintings and antiques (-), taxes on shipments of rum and tobacco (+), and others.

Source: Puerto Rico Planning Board, San Juan, PR, *Informe Económico al Gobernador 2023 / Economic Report to the Governor 2023*, May 2024, and earlier reports. See also <jp.pr.gov/informe-economico-al-gobernador/>.

Table 1342. Puerto Rico—Exports and Imports of Goods and Services by Type of Product: 2015 to 2022

[In millions of current dollars (84,477 represents $84,477,000,000). Detail may not add to total because of rounding]

Type of product	2015	2016	2017	2018	2019	2020	2021	2022 (P)
Exports of goods and services........	**84,477**	**86,612**	**78,577**	**77,055**	**78,788**	**70,672**	**70,626**	**72,741**
Exports of goods.........................	70,826	72,273	64,266	62,645	64,461	59,660	57,730	61,208
Foods, feeds, and beverages.........	4,565	4,654	4,028	1,055	1,084	1,050	1,100	1,096
Pharmaceuticals and organic chemicals [1]...................	52,453	53,921	47,801	46,961	49,679	47,307	44,710	46,808
Consumer goods, except food, automotive, and pharmaceuticals. ..	6,284	5,507	4,918	5,690	5,445	4,332	3,936	4,240
Capital goods, including parts.........	5,411	5,811	5,400	6,486	6,215	5,124	5,844	6,200
All other.................................	2,113	2,379	2,118	2,451	2,038	1,846	2,140	2,863
Exports of services......................	13,651	14,339	14,311	14,410	14,327	11,013	12,896	11,533
Travel [2].................................	3,662	3,709	3,288	3,287	3,758	1,781	4,284	5,575
All other [3].............................	9,990	10,630	11,023	11,123	10,569	9,232	8,612	5,958
Imports of goods and services........	**47,956**	**51,818**	**47,537**	**59,363**	**54,468**	**50,814**	**55,174**	**64,064**
Imports of goods.........................	42,212	45,989	41,523	52,604	47,266	44,158	48,429	57,344
Foods, feeds, and beverages.........	4,636	4,412	4,471	4,571	4,400	4,652	5,566	5,964
Pharmaceuticals and organic chemicals [1]...................	18,321	23,887	18,355	25,120	22,289	20,059	18,773	23,462
Petroleum and other energy products...............	4,066	3,237	3,884	4,468	4,198	2,896	3,726	5,061
Transportation equipment.............	2,148	2,389	2,755	3,556	3,151	2,941	4,228	4,518
Capital goods, except transportation equipment, including parts...........	4,808	4,125	4,296	5,134	4,636	4,761	5,367	6,214
All other.................................	8,233	7,939	7,763	9,755	8,593	8,849	10,770	12,124
Imports of services......................	5,744	5,829	6,014	6,759	7,201	6,656	6,746	6,720
Travel [2].................................	1,039	1,037	1,059	1,125	1,144	396	1,012	1,290
All other.................................	4,705	4,792	4,955	5,634	6,057	6,260	5,733	5,430
Addendum: Exports of medical and scientific equipment and appliances [4]...........	7,737	7,164	6,638	7,804	7,465	5,729	5,274	5,664

P Preliminary. [1] Includes medicinal and dental products. [2] For all purposes including education, business, and medical. Includes spending by nonresidents on travel and tourism, including passenger transportation services provided by domestic establishments. Other transportation services, such as freight charges on goods, are included in "all other" exports of services. [3] Includes computer services, such as software. [4] Includes consumer medical appliances embedded in "Consumer goods, except food, automotive, and pharmaceuticals"; and lab testing and control instruments and other scientific, medical, and hospital equipment embedded in "Capital goods, including parts."

Source: U.S. Bureau of Economic Analysis, "Gross Domestic Product for Puerto Rico, 2022," <www.bea.gov/data/gdp/gdp-puerto-rico>, accessed August 2024.

Table 1343. Puerto Rico—Gross Domestic Product: 2015 to 2022

[In millions of current dollars (117,752 represents $117,752,000,000). For definition of gross domestic product, see text, Section 13. Detail may not add to total because of rounding]

Item	2015	2016	2017	2018	2019	2020	2021	2022 (P)
Gross domestic product..............	**117,752**	**116,268**	**111,776**	**109,635**	**111,901**	**105,880**	**111,084**	**113,188**
Personal consumption expenditures......	55,700	55,755	55,466	58,219	58,719	57,095	65,186	71,860
Goods.........................	23,395	23,706	24,013	26,044	25,196	24,828	30,181	32,371
Durable goods...........................	6,227	6,378	6,379	7,871	7,493	7,406	9,790	10,213
Nondurable goods......................	17,168	17,327	17,635	18,173	17,703	17,422	20,391	22,158
Services..................................	35,044	34,837	33,796	34,463	36,267	33,694	38,389	43,921
Net foreign travel.......................	-2,739	-2,787	-2,344	-2,287	-2,744	-1,427	-3,385	-4,433
Gross private domestic investment.......	10,390	10,919	9,953	16,255	13,573	13,878	14,877	15,809
Fixed investment.........................	10,378	10,380	11,137	13,365	13,515	13,448	14,462	14,710
Structures...............................	1,912	1,786	1,697	2,518	2,678	2,425	3,233	3,752
Residential...........................	664	605	559	743	694	607	856	1,008
Nonresidential.......................	1,248	1,180	1,139	1,775	1,984	1,818	2,378	2,744
Equipment..............................	4,836	4,779	5,295	6,257	5,758	5,775	6,956	7,644
Intellectual property products...........	3,630	3,816	4,145	4,590	5,079	5,248	4,273	3,313
Change in private inventories...........	12	539	-1,184	2,890	58	430	415	1,099
Net exports of goods and services........	36,522	34,794	31,040	17,692	24,321	19,858	15,452	8,677
Exports....................................	84,477	86,612	78,577	77,055	78,788	70,672	70,626	72,741
Goods..................................	70,826	72,273	64,266	62,645	64,461	59,660	57,730	61,208
Services...............................	13,651	14,339	14,311	14,410	14,327	11,013	12,896	11,533
Imports...................................	47,956	51,818	47,537	59,363	54,468	50,814	55,174	64,064
Goods..................................	42,212	45,989	41,523	52,604	47,266	44,158	48,429	57,344
Services...............................	5,744	5,829	6,014	6,759	7,201	6,656	6,746	6,720
Government consumption expenditures and gross investment.....................	15,140	14,800	15,318	17,469	15,288	15,049	15,570	16,842
Federal [1].................................	2,399	2,486	3,235	3,996	3,434	3,354	3,385	3,629
Central [2].................................	9,869	9,455	9,405	10,836	9,303	9,210	9,658	10,562
Municipal.................................	2,872	2,860	2,678	2,637	2,550	2,484	2,526	2,650

P Preliminary. [1] U.S. federal government spending in Puerto Rico. [2] Spending by the Commonwealth Government of Puerto Rico and its components.

Source: U.S. Bureau of Economic Analysis, "Gross Domestic Product for Puerto Rico, 2022," accessed August 2024. See also <www.bea.gov/data/gdp/gdp-puerto-rico>.

Table 1344. Puerto Rico—Agricultural Summary: 1998 to 2022

[1 cuerda = 0.97 acre]

All farms	Unit	1998	2002	2007	2012	2018	2022
Farms...............................	Number	19,951	17,659	15,745	13,159	8,230	7,602
Farm land.........................	Cuerdas	865,478	690,687	557,530	584,988	487,775	494,481
Average size of farm............	Cuerdas	43.4	39.1	35.4	44.5	59.3	65.0
Approximate land area............	Cuerdas	2,254,365	2,254,365	2,254,365	2,254,365	2,254,365	2,256,575
Proportion in farms..............	Percent	38.4	30.6	24.7	25.9	21.6	21.9
Farms by size:							
Less than 10 cuerdas...........	Number	7,759	7,943	7,502	5,129	2,213	2,258
10 to 19 cuerdas.................	Number	4,473	3,847	3,545	2,859	1,853	1,741
20 to 49 cuerdas.................	Number	4,023	3,228	2,680	2,872	1,950	1,676
50 to 99 cuerdas.................	Number	1,792	1,282	865	940	952	762
100 to 174 cuerdas..............	Number	809	590	524	563	579	500
175 to 259 cuerdas..............	Number	421	281	207	401	330	268
260 cuerdas or more............	Number	674	488	422	395	353	397
Tenure of operator:							
Operators...........................	Number	19,951	17,659	15,745	13,159	8,230	7,602
Full owners......................	Number	15,620	13,693	11,402	9,362	5,474	5,166
Part owners.....................	Number	2,207	2,330	1,918	1,069	948	855
Tenants...........................	Number	2,124	1,636	2,425	2,728	1,808	1,581
Average size of farm by operator:							
Full owners......................	Cuerdas	29	27	25	29	41	41
Part owners.....................	Cuerdas	112	96	83	134	115	154
Tenants...........................	Cuerdas	76	61	46	61	87	94
Farms by type of organization:							
Individual or family..............	Number	17,887	15,843	13,958	11,938	6,886	5,835
Partnership......................	Number	211	162	49	117	77	188
Corporation......................	Number	437	595	575	738	1,147	1,399
Other.............................	Number	1,416	1,059	1,163	366	120	180
Farms by value of sales:							
Less than $1,000................	Number	3,307	3,977	4,442	2,973	2,885	1,474
$1,000 to $2,499.................	Number	3,633	3,471	2,771	2,015	814	690
$2,500 to $4,499.................	Number	3,900	3,044	2,428	1,986	778	810
$5,000 to $7,499.................	Number	2,408	1,575	1,206	1,209	621	589
$7,500 to $9,999.................	Number	1,233	1,087	882	771	403	466
$10,000 to $19,999..............	Number	2,366	1,781	1,497	1,521	781	1,232
$20,000 to $39,999..............	Number	1,247	1,062	1,030	968	648	761
$40,000 to $59,999..............	Number	405	375	281	394	303	319
$60,000 or more.................	Number	1,452	1,287	1,208	1,322	997	1,261

Source: U.S. Department of Agriculture, National Agricultural Statistics Service (NASS), *2022 Census of Agriculture: Puerto Rico Island and Regional Data*, Geographic Area Series, Volume 1: Part 52, July 2024. See also <nass.usda.gov/AgCensus/>.

Table 1345. Puerto Rico—Farms and Market Value of Agricultural Products Sold: 2022

[Market value in thousands (703,255 represents $703,255,000)]

Type of product	Number of farms	Market value ($1,000)	Average value per farm (dol.)	Type of product	Number of farms	Market value ($1,000)	Average value per farm (dol.)
Total...........................	**7,602**	**703,255**	**92,509**	Vegetables and melons [1]...........	934	42,497	45,500
				Horticultural specialties [2]............	376	47,511	126,358
Crops...........................	**5,206**	**353,469**	**(NA)**	Grasses, except lawn grass........	462	17,469	37,812
Coffee............................	2,449	18,165	7,417	**Livestock, poultry, and products...**	**2,375**	**349,786**	**147,278**
Pineapples......................	134	10,974	81,894	Cattle and calves....................	1,574	35,954	22,842
Plantains........................	1,978	56,345	28,486	Poultry and poultry products........	301	111,153	369,278
Bananas.........................	1,149	27,678	24,089	Dairy products.......................	315	173,001	549,208
Grains...........................	533	74,039	138,910	Hogs and pigs........................	199	7,731	38,850
Root crops or tubers..........	857	8,975	10,472	Aquaculture..........................	18	92	5,128
Fruits and coconuts...........	1,270	49,818	39,227	Other................................	617	21,856	35,423

NA Not available. [1] Includes hydroponic crops. [2] Nursery and greenhouse crops, floriculture, and sod.

Source: U.S. Department of Agriculture, National Agricultural Statistics Service (NASS), *2022 Census of Agriculture: Puerto Rico, Island and Regional Data*, Geographic Area Series, Volume 1: Part 52, July 2024. See also <www.nass.usda.gov/AgCensus/index.php>.

Table 1346. Puerto Rico—Business Summary by Industry: 2021 and 2022

[Payroll in millions of dollars (19,730.2 represents $19,730,200,000). Covers establishments with payroll. Excludes self-employed individuals, employees of private households, railroad employees, agricultural production employees, and most government employees. For statement on methodology, see Appendix III]

Industry	NAICS code [1]	Establishments 2021	Establishments 2022	Paid employees [2] 2021	Paid employees [2] 2022	Annual payroll (mil. dol.) 2021	Annual payroll (mil. dol.) 2022
Total, all industries	(X)	**47,081**	**49,356**	**660,654**	**716,341**	**19,730.2**	**22,238.7**
Agriculture, forestry, fishing and hunting	11	14	12	55	[3] 78	0.9	1.6
Mining, quarrying, and oil and gas extraction	21	39	38	610	655	16.5	17.6
Utilities	22	36	38	359	380	24.6	29.1
Construction	23	2,418	2,595	26,989	32,775	797.1	1,034.9
Manufacturing	31–33	1,879	1,968	74,759	77,504	2,991.7	3,235.4
Wholesale trade	42	2,082	2,155	31,033	33,064	1,286.5	1,405.6
Retail trade	44–45	9,558	9,971	126,048	130,120	2,791.9	3,032.6
Transportation and warehousing	48–49	1,064	1,109	14,921	18,098	522.1	609.1
Information	51	768	746	15,568	16,062	760.9	783.4
Finance and insurance	52	1,821	1,877	30,243	31,435	1,619.7	1,881.2
Real estate and rental and leasing	53	1,704	1,771	12,010	13,221	345.8	382.0
Professional, scientific, and technical services	54	5,358	5,730	37,190	41,249	1,645.4	1,920.8
Management of companies and enterprises	55	108	104	7,073	7,349	394.5	445.6
Administrative and support & waste management and remediation services	56	2,112	2,100	78,138	87,150	1,699.8	1,938.7
Educational services	61	846	872	30,617	32,332	754.9	804.0
Health care and social assistance	62	7,708	8,062	84,376	89,095	2,388.7	2,677.6
Arts, entertainment, and recreation	71	483	535	3,575	4,440	89.0	118.7
Accommodation and food services	72	5,273	5,726	70,125	82,472	1,208.1	1,486.2
Other services (except public administration)	81	3,411	3,556	16,350	18,266	364.8	412.5
Industries not classified	99	399	391	615	596	27.2	22.2

X Not applicable. [1] Data based on the North American Industry Classification System (NAICS) 2017. See text, Section 15. [2] Covers full- and part-time employees who are on the payroll in the pay period including March 12. [3] Data flagged for high noise; the value was changed by 5 percent or more to avoid disclosure of data for individual businesses.

Source: U.S. Census Bureau, County Business Patterns, "All Sectors: County Business Patterns, including ZIP Code Business Patterns, by Legal Form of Organization and Employment Size Class for the U.S., States, and Selected Geographies: 2022," <data.census.gov>, accessed June 2024. See also <www.census.gov/programs-surveys/cbp.html>.

Table 1347. Guam, Virgin Islands, Northern Mariana Islands, and American Samoa—Gross Domestic Product (GDP) and Components: 2002 to 2022

[In millions of current dollars (512 represents $512,000,000), except percent. Data are estimated by the Bureau of Economic Analysis using the same approach used to calculate GDP for the United States but adapted for each territory based on the economic structure and availability of source data; see <www.bea.gov/resources/methodologies/gdp-methodology-for-american-samoa-cnmi-guam-usvi> for more details]

Year and component	Gross domestic product (mil. dol.) American Samoa	Guam	Northern Mariana Islands	Virgin Islands	Percent change from preceding year American Samoa	Guam	Northern Mariana Islands	Virgin Islands
2002	512	3,394	1,284	3,262	(NA)	(NA)	(NA)	(NA)
2003	524	3,569	1,239	3,443	2.5	5.2	-3.5	5.5
2004	509	3,869	1,210	3,797	-2.9	8.4	-2.3	10.3
2005	500	4,213	1,061	4,428	-1.7	8.9	-12.3	16.6
2006	493	4,238	990	4,484	-1.5	0.6	-6.7	1.3
2007	518	4,397	938	4,784	5.0	3.8	-5.2	6.7
2008	560	4,658	939	4,244	8.2	5.9	0.1	-11.3
2009	675	4,828	795	4,201	20.6	3.6	-15.3	-1.0
2010	573	4,949	799	4,324	-15.2	2.5	0.4	2.9
2011	570	4,984	729	4,223	-0.6	0.7	-8.7	-2.3
2012	640	5,265	746	4,089	12.4	5.6	2.3	-3.2
2013	638	5,399	772	3,738	-0.4	2.5	3.5	-8.6
2014	643	5,610	832	3,565	0.9	3.9	7.8	-4.6
2015	673	5,799	910	3,663	4.5	3.4	9.4	2.7
2016	671	5,901	1,230	3,798	-0.2	1.8	35.2	3.7
2017	612	6,013	1,560	3,794	-8.8	1.9	26.9	-0.1
2018	639	6,051	1,301	3,923	4.5	0.6	-16.6	3.4
2019	647	6,355	1,181	4,121	1.2	5.0	-9.2	5.1
2020	721	5,916	858	4,229	11.4	-6.9	-27.4	2.6
2021	750	6,234	(NA)	4,507	3.9	5.4	(NA)	6.6
2022 (Preliminary)								
Gross domestic product	**871**	**6,910**	**(NA)**	**4,672**	**16.2**	**10.8**	**(NA)**	**3.6**
Personal consumption expenditures	621	4,140	(NA)	3,221	3.2	8.1	(NA)	9.1
Private fixed investment	53	2,013	(NA)	448	-32.6	26.7	(NA)	-10.3
Change in private inventories	-29	(NA)	(NA)	-95	[1]	(NA)	(NA)	[1]
Net exports of goods and services	-268	-3,876	(NA)	-509	[1]	[1]	(NA)	[1]
Exports	409	545	(NA)	4,549	23.1	182.4	(NA)	11.8
Exports of goods	399	76	(NA)	3,257	21.5	-7.1	(NA)	10.6
Exports of services	10	470	(NA)	1,292	150.3	320.5	(NA)	14.9
Imports	677	4,421	(NA)	5,058	-2.5	20.7	(NA)	24.7
Imports of goods	590	3,105	(NA)	4,697	-3.0	18.9	(NA)	27.4
Imports of services	87	1,316	(NA)	360	1.7	25.3	(NA)	-2.3
Government consumption expenditures and gross investment	495	4,633	(NA)	1,606	15.5	8.1	(NA)	5.1

NA Not available. [1] Not meaningful.

Source: U.S. Bureau of Economic Analysis, Regional GDP & Personal Income, "TASUMMARY1: Summary of GDP and components for U.S. territories, current dollars," <www.bea.gov/itable/regional-gdp-and-personal-income>, accessed June 2024. See also <www.bea.gov/data/by-place-states-territories>.

Table 1348. Guam, Virgin Islands, Northern Mariana Islands, and American Samoa—Economic Summary by Sector: 2022

[Sales and payroll in millions of dollars (1,440 represents $1,440,000,000). Data cover establishments with annual payroll. Based on the Economic Censuses; see Appendix III]

Kind of business	American Samoa	Guam	Northern Mariana Islands	Virgin Islands	Kind of business	American Samoa	Guam	Northern Mariana Islands	Virgin Islands
Total: [1]					Paid employees [2]	341	2,876	906	1,229
Establishments	593	3,412	1,523	2,300	Retail trade:				
Sales	1,440	10,349	1,771	7,140	Establishments	200	639	296	407
Annual payroll	164	1,770	338	1,145	Sales	393	1,815	340	1,519
Paid employees [2]	8,999	54,351	14,488	26,536	Annual payroll	26	207	38	153
Construction:					Paid employees [2]	1,670	8,447	2,068	5,287
Establishments	48	394	95	150	Professional, scientific,				
Sales	97	1,463	154	408	& technical services:				
Annual payroll	15	271	27	87	Establishments	25	249	106	270
Paid employees [2]	656	6,774	1,176	1,607	Sales	11	401	51	567
Manufacturing:					Annual payroll	3	109	15	80
Establishments	38	59	39	61	Paid employees [2]	107	2,324	462	1,093
Sales	403	103	63	139	Accommodation				
Annual payroll	33	25	16	27	& food services:				
Paid employees [2]	2,463	931	668	556	Establishments	66	546	184	293
Wholesale trade:					Sales	59	763	138	536
Establishments	32	212	89	68	Annual payroll	11	225	37	137
Sales	203	1,545	350	596	Paid employees [2]	922	11,996	2,319	5,140
Annual payroll	6	97	18	79					

[1] Includes other industries, not shown separately. [2] For pay period including March 12.

Source: U.S. Census Bureau, Economic Census of the Island Areas, Table IA2200BASIC01, "Geographic Area Series: Summary Statistics for American Samoa, Commonwealth of the Northern Mariana Islands, Guam, Puerto Rico, and U.S. Virgin Islands: 2022," <data.census.gov/>, accessed July 2024.

Table 1349. Occupational Employment and Average Annual Wages in Guam, Puerto Rico, and Virgin Islands: 2023

[Wages in dollars. The Occupational Employment Survey (OES) program conducts a semiannual survey designed to produce estimates of employment and wages for specific occupations. Excludes self-employed persons. For more details on the survey, see <www.bls.gov/oes/oes_emp.htm>]

Selected occupation	SOC code [1]	Guam Employ-ment	Guam Average annual wages [2]	Puerto Rico Employ-ment	Puerto Rico Average annual wages [2]	Virgin Islands Employ-ment	Virgin Islands Average annual wages [2]
Total, all occupations [3]	(X)	**64,680**	**42,210**	**928,240**	**34,120**	**33,700**	**50,620**
Management occupations	11	5,580	76,430	39,130	88,990	2,820	94,820
Business and financial operations	13	2,930	60,650	54,590	46,690	2,040	65,970
Computer and mathematical occupations	15	790	54,080	12,910	50,720	350	73,880
Architecture and engineering	17	1,120	69,080	13,670	63,300	130	71,440
Life, physical, and social sciences	19	680	59,790	7,390	54,010	300	62,210
Community and social services	21	850	48,570	16,060	35,270	450	51,220
Legal occupations	23	330	90,180	5,300	68,780	340	103,840
Educational instruction and library occupations	25	3,580	52,420	57,420	40,340	2,220	52,840
Arts, design, entertainment, sports, and media	27	460	41,010	8,780	41,830	180	51,370
Healthcare practitioner and technical occupations	29	2,100	80,590	55,370	43,860	1,450	81,340
Healthcare support	31	1,080	31,580	17,190	23,050	580	36,880
Protective service occupations	33	3,840	42,410	53,490	31,130	2,290	43,650
Food preparation and serving related occupations	35	7,040	22,940	76,270	23,020	4,350	37,110
Buildings and grounds cleaning and maintenance	37	2,530	23,890	45,730	21,860	1,610	32,350
Personal care and service occupations	39	1,140	24,720	8,350	23,990	500	33,850
Sales and related occupations	41	4,790	26,760	106,400	26,680	3,290	35,650
Office and administrative support	43	9,110	33,870	146,820	29,370	4,500	42,340
Farming, fishing, and forestry	45	40	37,100	2,130	24,640	40	36,960
Construction and extraction	47	7,110	38,060	35,440	27,380	1,570	50,870
Installation, maintenance, and repair	49	3,380	40,130	34,250	29,590	1,530	48,900
Production occupations	51	1,620	35,160	63,830	27,190	710	44,130
Transportation and material moving	53	4,580	37,110	67,720	25,670	2,450	40,840

X Not applicable. [1] Office of Management and Budget's Standard Occupational Classification (SOC) is used to define occupations. SOC categorizes workers into one of approximately 800 detailed occupations, which are classified into 23 major occupational groups. [2] Annual wages have been calculated by multiplying the hourly mean wage by a "year-round, full-time" hours figure of 2,080 hours; for those occupations where there is not an hourly mean wage published, the annual wage has been directly calculated from the reported survey data. [3] Estimates do not sum to the total because the total may include data for occupations not shown separately. See source for more information.

Source: U.S. Bureau of Labor Statistics, "Occupational Employment and Wage Statistics," <www.bls.gov/oes/tables.htm>, accessed July 2024.

Table 1350. Virgin Islands—Business Summary by Industry: 2021 and 2022

[Payroll in thousands of dollars (1,051,545 represents $1,051,545,000). Covers establishments with payroll. Excludes self-employed individuals, employees of private households, railroad employees, agricultural production employees, and most government employees. For statement on methodology, see Appendix III]

Industry	NAICS code [1]	Establishments		Paid employees [2]		Annual payroll ($1,000)	
		2021	2022	2021	2022	2021	2022
Total, all industries	(X)	**2,319**	**2,382**	**25,652**	**25,683**	**1,051,545**	**1,095,155**
Agriculture, forestry, fishing and hunting	11	(NA)	(NA)	(NA)	(NA)	(NA)	(NA)
Mining, quarrying, and oil and gas extraction	21	3	3	[3] 36	[3] 57	2,334	[3] 3,513
Utilities	22	5	5	38	41	3,077	3,125
Construction	23	163	157	2,530	1,735	114,318	95,831
Manufacturing	31-33	47	46	549	655	29,086	44,831
Wholesale trade	42	59	64	1,025	792	51,767	45,619
Retail trade	44-45	427	421	5,152	5,433	141,927	162,790
Transportation and warehousing	48-49	101	107	1,422	1,498	49,108	56,583
Information	51	30	34	[3] 399	[3] 414	[3] 22,266	[3] 25,807
Finance and insurance	52	100	101	1,017	926	83,122	74,204
Real estate and rental and leasing	53	181	197	867	931	36,975	41,267
Professional, scientific, and technical services	54	257	266	1,041	1,056	73,027	73,626
Management of companies and enterprises	55	5	6	[3] 14	[3] 15	[3] 1,218	1,378
Administrative and support & waste management and remediation services	56	142	146	1,583	1,532	60,069	57,449
Educational services	61	35	36	538	547	18,239	19,833
Health care and social assistance	62	201	209	2,860	2,879	159,041	162,156
Arts, entertainment, and recreation	71	49	50	585	743	19,678	24,143
Accommodation and food services	72	293	301	4,883	5,505	145,360	169,849
Other services (except public administration)	81	203	212	1,081	901	39,068	30,076
Industries not classified	99	17	20	30	[3] 21	1,805	3,018

X Not applicable. NA Not available. [1] Data based on the North American Industry Classification System (NAICS) 2017. See text, Section 15. [2] Covers full- and part-time employees who are on the payroll in the pay period including March 12. [3] Data flagged for high noise; the value was changed to avoid disclosure of data for individual businesses.

Source: U.S. Census Bureau, County Business Patterns, "All Sectors: County Business Patterns, including ZIP Code Business Patterns, by Legal Form of Organization and Employment Size Class for the U.S., States, and Selected Geographies: 2022," <data.census.gov>, accessed June 2024. See also <www.census.gov/programs-surveys/cbp.html>.

Table 1351. Guam—Business Summary by Industry: 2021 and 2022

[Payroll in thousands of dollars (1,508,500 represents $1,508,500,000). Covers establishments with payroll. Excludes self-employed individuals, employees of private households, railroad employees, agricultural production employees, and most government employees. For statement on methodology, see Appendix III]

Industry	NAICS code [1]	Establishments		Paid employees [2]		Annual payroll ($1,000)	
		2021	2022	2021	2022	2021	2022
Total, all industries	(X)	**3,353**	**3,477**	**49,876**	**53,941**	**1,508,500**	**1,713,400**
Agriculture, forestry, fishing and hunting	11	(NA)	(NA)	(NA)	(NA)	(NA)	(NA)
Mining, quarrying, and oil and gas extraction	21	(NA)	(NA)	(NA)	(NA)	(NA)	(NA)
Utilities	22	3	4	[3] 55	60	3,046	3,204
Construction	23	371	381	5,949	5,796	215,113	229,440
Manufacturing	31-33	56	52	722	700	19,418	20,026
Wholesale trade	42	216	217	2,709	2,937	90,218	102,806
Retail trade	44-45	611	632	8,591	9,215	199,886	228,266
Transportation and warehousing	48-49	85	95	1,849	2,711	75,978	134,052
Information	51	52	52	1,516	1,725	69,046	74,982
Finance and insurance	52	123	117	2,145	2,067	102,531	97,643
Real estate and rental and leasing	53	272	272	1,813	1,873	50,014	53,652
Professional, scientific, and technical services	54	234	244	2,439	2,338	111,016	114,015
Management of companies and enterprises	55	11	10	101	110	4,910	6,106
Administrative and support & waste management and remediation services	56	161	159	3,508	3,672	83,376	88,310
Educational services	61	56	59	982	1,054	23,303	25,714
Health care and social assistance	62	202	219	4,540	4,965	217,407	239,127
Arts, entertainment, and recreation	71	59	67	498	721	13,771	16,471
Accommodation and food services	72	509	550	10,195	11,734	174,991	219,967
Other services (except public administration)	81	249	262	1,902	1,884	46,343	49,796
Industries not classified	99	80	83	352	370	8,012	9,606

X Not applicable. NA Not available. [1] Data based on NAICS 2017. See text, Section 15. [2] Covers full- and part-time employees who are on the payroll in the pay period including March 12. [3] Data flagged for high noise; the value was changed by 5 percent or more to avoid disclosure of data for individual businesses.

Source: U.S. Census Bureau, County Business Patterns, "All Sectors: County Business Patterns, including ZIP Code Business Patterns, by Legal Form of Organization and Employment Size Class for the U.S., States, and Selected Geographies: 2022," <data.census.gov>, accessed June 2024. See also <www.census.gov/programs-surveys/cbp.html>.

Table 1352. Northern Marianas—Business Summary by Industry: 2021 and 2022

[Payroll in thousands of dollars (302,224 represents $302,224,000). Covers establishments with payroll. Excludes self-employed individuals, employees of private households, railroad employees, agricultural production employees, and most government employees. For statement on methodology, see Appendix III]

Industry	NAICS code [1]	Establishments 2021	Establishments 2022	Paid employees [2] 2021	Paid employees [2] 2022	Annual payroll ($1,000) 2021	Annual payroll ($1,000) 2022
Total, all industries	(X)	**1,490**	**1,559**	**12,763**	**14,202**	**302,224**	**337,274**
Agriculture, forestry, fishing and hunting	11	3	(NA)	4	(NA)	[3]101	(NA)
Mining, quarrying, and oil and gas extraction	21	(NA)	(NA)	(NA)	(NA)	(NA)	(NA)
Utilities	22	3	3	[3]457	[3]495	[3]12,804	[3]15,763
Construction	23	99	106	994	1,107	21,248	24,814
Manufacturing	31-33	33	36	409	532	10,368	11,524
Wholesale trade	42	84	88	767	898	15,361	18,467
Retail trade	44-45	289	309	1,799	2,065	31,917	39,259
Transportation and warehousing	48-49	44	42	[3]840	[3]955	[3]19,447	[3]22,157
Information	51	18	17	346	321	11,657	10,309
Finance and insurance	52	49	51	269	277	8,065	8,772
Real estate and rental and leasing	53	133	137	577	626	9,953	11,718
Professional, scientific, and technical services	54	89	92	442	460	14,105	15,017
Management of companies and enterprises	55	6	7	85	[3]137	1,664	2,423
Administrative and support & waste management and remediation services	56	129	128	1,114	967	14,141	14,738
Educational services	61	40	39	271	269	6,188	6,685
Health care and social assistance	62	43	47	1,186	1,555	70,368	73,998
Arts, entertainment, and recreation	71	34	36	249	278	4,703	5,011
Accommodation and food services	72	183	185	2,160	2,476	35,278	41,018
Other services (except public administration)	81	140	161	511	548	10,558	11,322
Industries not classified	99	69	71	240	183	3,353	3,122

X Not applicable. NA Not available. [1] Data based on North American Industry Classification System (NAICS) 2017. See text, Section 15. [2] Covers full- and part-time employees who are on the payroll in the pay period including March 12. [3] Data flagged for high noise; the value was changed to avoid disclosure of data for individual businesses.

Source: U.S. Census Bureau, County Business Patterns, "All Sectors: County Business Patterns, including ZIP Code Business Patterns, by Legal Form of Organization and Employment Size Class for the U.S., States, and Selected Geographies: 2022," <data.census.gov>, accessed June 2024. See also <www.census.gov/programs-surveys/cbp.html>.

Table 1353. American Samoa—Business Summary by Industry: 2021 and 2022

[Payroll in thousands of dollars (144,014 represents $144,014,000). Covers establishments with payroll. Excludes self-employed individuals, employees of private households, railroad employees, agricultural production employees, and most government employees. For statement on methodology, see Appendix III]

Industry	NAICS code [1]	Establishments 2021	Establishments 2022	Paid employees [2] 2021	Paid employees [2] 2022	Annual payroll ($1,000) 2021	Annual payroll ($1,000) 2022
Total, all industries	(X)	**581**	**600**	**7,808**	**6,955**	**144,014**	**154,126**
Agriculture, forestry, fishing and hunting	11	(NA)	(NA)	(NA)	(NA)	(NA)	(NA)
Mining, quarrying, and oil and gas extraction	21	(NA)	(NA)	(NA)	(NA)	(NA)	(NA)
Utilities	22	(NA)	(NA)	(NA)	(NA)	(NA)	(NA)
Construction	23	41	47	577	617	12,377	13,827
Manufacturing	31-33	37	37	[3]2,202	[3]1,206	[3]38,239	[3]38,540
Wholesale trade	42	27	25	[3]261	272	5,314	5,749
Retail trade	44-45	183	190	1,518	1,641	24,331	25,548
Transportation and warehousing	48-49	28	32	266	305	4,059	4,319
Information	51	5	5	[3]133	[3]121	[3]3,992	[3]4,236
Finance and insurance	52	13	15	95	[3]89	2,477	[3]3,087
Real estate and rental and leasing	53	22	22	98	[3]95	1,586	1,571
Professional, scientific, and technical services	54	29	26	105	96	2,471	3,671
Management of companies and enterprises	55	(NA)	(NA)	(NA)	(NA)	(NA)	(NA)
Administrative and support & waste management and remediation services	56	29	31	202	247	3,576	3,618
Educational services	61	6	5	158	141	2,264	2,070
Health care and social assistance	62	31	32	[3]990	933	[3]27,023	31,190
Arts, entertainment, and recreation	71	3	4	13	8	127	129
Accommodation and food services	72	65	64	767	775	9,964	10,481
Other services (except public administration)	81	44	46	319	343	4,514	5,012
Industries not classified	99	16	17	91	57	1,377	895

X Not applicable. NA Not available. [1] Data based on the North American Industry Classification System (NAICS) 2017. See text, Section 15. [2] Covers full- and part-time employees who are on the payroll in the pay period including March 12. [3] Data flagged for high noise; the value was changed to avoid disclosure of data for individual businesses.

Source U.S. Census Bureau, County Business Patterns, "All Sectors: County Business Patterns, including ZIP Code Business Patterns, by Legal Form of Organization and Employment Size Class for the U.S., States, and Selected Geographies: 2022," <data.census.gov>, accessed June 2024. See also <www.census.gov/programs-surveys/cbp.html>.

International Statistics

This section presents statistics for the world as a whole and for many countries on a comparative basis with the United States. Data are shown for population, births and deaths, social and economic indicators, finances, agriculture, energy, climate, science and technology, communications, and military affairs.

Statistics for individual countries may be found primarily in official national publications, generally in the form of yearbooks, issued by most countries in their own national languages and expressed in their own customary units of measure. For a listing of selected publications, see Appendix I table under international statistical abstracts from a foreign agency.

For international comparisons, the United Nations Statistics Division compiles data as submitted by member countries and issues a number of summary publications, generally in English and French. Among these are the annual *Statistical Yearbook, Demographic Yearbook, Population and Vital Statistics Report, International Trade Statistics Yearbook, Energy Statistics Yearbook, National Accounts Statistics,* and the *Monthly Bulletin of Statistics.* Specialized agencies of the United Nations also issue international summary publications on various topics, including agricultural, labor, health, and trade statistics. Among these are *Food Outlook* and the *World Food and Agriculture - Statistical Yearbook* issued by the Food and Agriculture Organization (FAO); *World Employment and Social Outlook* issued by the International Labor Organization (ILO); *World Health Statistics* issued by the World Health Organization (WHO); and the *Handbook of Statistics* issued by the Conference on Trade and Development (UNCTAD).

The U.S. Census Bureau publishes estimates and projections of key demographic measures for countries and regions of the world in its International Data Base at <www.census.gov/programs-surveys/international-programs.html>.

The International Monetary Fund (IMF), the World Bank, and the Organisation for Economic Co-operation and Development (OECD) also compile international statistics. The IMF publishes a series of reports related to financial data. These include *World Economic Outlook, Global Financial Stability Report,* and *Fiscal Monitor.* The World Bank publishes many reports on a wide range of topics related to international development. Three of their flagship statistical publications are *World Development Report, World Development Indicators,* and *Global Economic Prospects.* The OECD also produces numerous statistical publications in fields including economics, health, and education. Among these are the *Economic Outlook; National Accounts of OECD Countries; Science, Technology and Innovation Outlook; International Migration Outlook; Employment Outlook;* and *Education at a Glance.*

Statistical coverage and country classifications—
Problems of space and availability of data limit the number of countries and the extent of statistical coverage shown. The lists of countries and territories included in individual tables are generally based on source publications and databases, as cited.

In the last four decades several important changes took place in the status of the world's nations. In 1991, the Soviet Union broke up into 15 independent countries: Armenia, Azerbaijan, Belarus, Estonia, Georgia, Kazakhstan, Kyrgyzstan, Latvia, Lithuania, Moldova, Russia, Tajikistan, Turkmenistan, Ukraine, and Uzbekistan.

Germany was reunified in 1990, when the German Democratic Republic (former East Germany) joined the Federal Republic of Germany (former West Germany) to form a single country. On January 1, 1993, Czechoslovakia was succeeded by two independent countries: the Czech Republic, now known as Czechia, and Slovakia.

Following the breakup of the Socialist Federal Republic of Yugoslavia in 1992, the United States recognized Bosnia and Herzegovina, Croatia, Slovenia, and Macedonia as independent countries. Serbia and Montenegro, both former republics of Yugoslavia, became independent of one another on May 31, 2006. This separation is reflected in the population estimates of Table 1356. On February 17, 2008, Kosovo declared its independence from Serbia. In 2019, Macedonia formally adopted the name Republic of North Macedonia.

The Treaty of Maastricht created the European Union (EU) in 1992 with 12 member countries. The EU is not a state intended to replace existing states, but it is more than just an international organization. Its member states have set up common institutions to which they delegate some of their sovereignty so that decisions on specific matters of joint interest can be made democratically at a European level. This pooling of sovereignty is also called "European integration." The EU has grown in size with successive waves of accessions in 1995, 2004, 2007, and 2013. The 27 current members of the EU are: Austria, Belgium, Bulgaria, Croatia, Cyprus, Czechia, Denmark, Estonia, Finland, France, Germany, Greece, Hungary, Ireland, Italy, Latvia, Lithuania, Luxembourg, Malta, the Netherlands, Poland, Portugal, Romania, Slovakia, Slovenia, Spain, and Sweden. In June 2016, the electorate of the United Kingdom voted to withdraw from the EU. The withdrawal became official in January of 2020.

In 1992, the EU decided to establish an economic and monetary union (EMU), with the introduction of a single European currency managed by a European Central Bank. The single currency—the euro—became a reality on January 1, 2002, when euro notes and coins replaced national currencies in 12 of the then 15 countries of the European Union (Austria, Belgium, Finland, France, Germany, Greece, Ireland, Italy, Luxembourg, the Netherlands, Portugal, and Spain). Since then, 13 additional countries have acceded to EU membership, but Croatia, Cyprus, Estonia, Latvia, Lithuania, Malta, Slovakia, and Slovenia have been the only new members of the EU to adopt the euro as the national currency. In total, the euro is the official currency of 20 of the 27 EU member countries.

Elsewhere in the world, Eritrea announced its independence from Ethiopia in April 1993 and was subsequently recognized as an independent nation by the United States. In the South Pacific, the Marshall Islands, Micronesia, and Palau gained independence from the United States in 1991. In May of 2002, Timor-Leste won independence from Indonesia. The Netherlands Antilles dissolved on October 10, 2010. As a result, Curaçao and Sint Maarten became autonomous territories of the Netherlands. As of July 2011, Sudan and South Sudan became separate countries. And, in 2018, Swaziland was officially renamed Eswatini.

The population estimates and projections used in Tables 1354 through 1357, 1359, and 1360 were prepared by the U.S. Census Bureau. For each country, available data on population by age and sex, fertility, mortality, and international migration were evaluated and, where necessary, adjusted for inconsistencies and errors in the data. Comprehensive population projections were made by the cohort-component method based on an assessment of probable future trends.

Economic associations—The Organisation for European Economic Co-operation (OEEC) was originally a regional grouping of Western European countries established in 1948 for the purpose of harmonizing national economic policies and conditions. It was succeeded on September 30, 1961 by the Organisation for Economic Co-operation and Development (OECD). As of 2024, the 38 member nations of the OECD are Australia, Austria, Belgium, Canada, Chile, Colombia, Costa Rica, Czechia, Denmark, Estonia, Finland, France, Germany, Greece, Hungary, Iceland, Ireland, Israel, Italy, Japan, Latvia, Lithuania, Luxembourg, Mexico, the Netherlands, New Zealand, Norway, Poland, Portugal, Slovakia, Slovenia, South Korea, Spain, Sweden, Switzerland, Turkey, the United Kingdom, and the United States.

Quality and comparability of the data—The quality and comparability of the data presented here are affected by a number of factors:

1 The year for which data are presented may not be the same for all subjects for a particular country or for a given subject for different countries, though the data shown are the most recent available. All such variations have been noted. The data shown are for calendar years except as otherwise specified.

2 The statistical bases, methods of estimating, methods of data collection, extent of coverage, precision of definition, scope of territory, and margins of error may vary for different items within a particular country, and for like items for different countries. Footnotes and headnotes to the tables describe some of the major coverage qualifications attached to the figures; considerably more detail is presented in the source publications. Many of the measures shown are merely rough indicators of magnitude.

3 Figures shown in this section for the United States may not always agree with figures shown in the preceding sections. Discrepancies may be attributable to the use of differing original sources, differences in the definition of geographic limits (the 50 states, continental U.S. only, or the U.S. including certain outlying areas and possessions), or to possible adjustments made to the U.S. figures in order to make them more comparable with figures from other countries.

International comparisons of national accounts data—To compare national accounts data for different countries, it is necessary to convert each country's data into a common unit of currency, usually the U.S. dollar. The market exchange rates, which often are used in converting national currencies, do not necessarily reflect the relative purchasing power in the various countries. It is necessary that the goods and services produced in different countries be valued consistently if the differences observed are meant to reflect real differences in the volumes of goods and services produced. The use of purchasing power parities (see Tables 1368, 1369, and 1373) instead of exchange rates is intended to achieve this objective.

The method used to present the data shown in Table 1373 is to construct volume measures directly by revaluing the goods and services sold in different countries at a common set of international prices. By dividing the ratio of the gross domestic products of two countries expressed in their own national currencies by the corresponding ratio calculated at constant international prices, it is possible to derive the implied purchasing power parity (PPP) between the two currencies concerned. PPPs show how many units of currency are needed in one country to buy the same amount of goods and services that one unit of currency will buy in the other country. For further information, see *National Accounts of OECD Countries, Main Aggregates*, issued annually by the Organisation for Economic Co-operation and Development (OECD).

International Standard Industrial Classification—The original version of the International Standard Industrial Classification of All Economic Activities (ISIC) was adopted in 1948. A number of countries have utilized ISIC as the basis for devising their industrial classification schemes. Substantial comparability has been attained among the industrial classification schemes of many countries, including the United States, by ensuring that national classification categories correspond to ISIC categories. The United Nations, the International Labour Organization, the Food and Agriculture Organization, and other international bodies use ISIC in publishing and analyzing statistical data. Revisions of ISIC were issued in 1958, 1968, 1989, 2002, and 2008. A fifth comprehensive revision was endorsed by the United Nations Statistics Division in 2023 but is not currently in use.

Table 1354. Total World Population and Population Projections: 1950 to 2050

[2,558.02 represents 2,558,020,000. As of midyear]

Year	Population (mil.)	Population change [1] Percent	Population change [1] Number (mil.)	Year	Population (mil.)	Population change [1] Percent	Population change [1] Number (mil.)
1950............	2,558.02	(NA)	(NA)	2016............	7,441.69	1.12	82.72
1955............	2,782.97	1.89	51.59	2017............	7,523.96	1.11	82.27
1960............	3,043.72	1.41	42.29	2018............	7,605.03	1.08	81.07
1965............	3,351.45	2.11	69.30	2019............	7,685.59	1.06	80.56
1970............	3,714.26	2.07	75.38	2020............	7,764.97	1.03	79.38
1975............	4,089.90	1.78	71.61	2021............	7,837.65	0.94	72.68
1980............	4,446.02	1.61	70.56	2022............	7,906.70	0.88	69.06
1985............	4,860.69	1.78	84.80	2023............	7,982.02	0.95	75.32
1989............	5,218.86	1.76	90.49	2024............	8,057.24	0.94	75.22
1990............	5,311.09	1.77	92.23	2025............	8,131.90	0.93	74.66
1991............	5,398.25	1.64	87.15	2026............	8,205.74	0.91	73.84
1992............	5,484.86	1.60	86.61	2027............	8,279.10	0.89	73.36
1993............	5,568.56	1.53	83.70	2028............	8,351.88	0.88	72.79
1994............	5,650.43	1.47	81.87	2029............	8,424.04	0.86	72.16
1995............	5,733.48	1.47	83.05	2030............	8,495.47	0.85	71.43
1996............	5,815.63	1.43	82.15	2031............	8,566.35	0.83	70.89
1997............	5,896.16	1.38	80.53	2032............	8,636.77	0.82	70.41
1998............	5,975.54	1.35	79.38	2033............	8,706.44	0.81	69.67
1999............	6,054.37	1.32	78.84	2034............	8,775.32	0.79	68.87
2000............	6,133.01	1.30	78.63	2035............	8,843.34	0.78	68.02
2001............	6,211.82	1.29	78.82	2036............	8,910.60	0.76	67.26
2002............	6,290.90	1.27	79.08	2037............	8,977.19	0.75	66.59
2003............	6,369.90	1.26	79.00	2038............	9,042.98	0.73	65.78
2004............	6,449.06	1.24	79.17	2039............	9,107.85	0.72	64.88
2005............	6,528.03	1.22	78.97	2040............	9,171.77	0.70	63.92
2006............	6,608.49	1.23	80.46	2041............	9,234.81	0.69	63.04
2007............	6,690.68	1.24	82.19	2042............	9,297.05	0.67	62.24
2008............	6,774.89	1.26	84.21	2043............	9,358.29	0.66	61.24
2009............	6,859.06	1.24	84.16	2044............	9,418.39	0.64	60.10
2010............	6,942.15	1.21	83.09	2045............	9,477.33	0.63	58.94
2011............	7,024.89	1.19	82.74	2046............	9,535.18	0.61	57.85
2012............	7,108.24	1.19	83.35	2047............	9,591.98	0.60	56.80
2013............	7,192.34	1.18	84.10	2048............	9,647.56	0.58	55.58
2014............	7,276.12	1.16	83.78	2049............	9,701.84	0.56	54.28
2015............	7,358.97	1.14	82.85	2050............	9,754.84	0.55	53.00

NA Not available. [1] Represents change from year shown to immediate preceding year.

Source: U.S. Census Bureau, "International Data Base (IDB)," <www.census.gov/programs-surveys/international-programs/about/idb.html>, accessed August 2023.

Table 1355. World Population by World Region: 1950 to 2050

[In millions, except percent (2,558.0 represents 2,558,000,000). As of midyear. Based on United Nations geographic regions (M49 standard)]

Year	World	Africa	North America [1]	Latin America and the Caribbean [2]	Asia	Europe	Oceania
1950............	2,558.0	229.0	166.3	165.4	1,437.6	547.1	12.5
1960............	3,043.7	285.8	199.0	217.2	1,720.5	605.6	15.6
1970............	3,714.3	366.8	226.9	284.2	2,159.2	657.9	19.2
1980............	4,446.0	479.1	251.9	359.4	2,637.8	695.2	22.6
1990............	5,311.1	631.8	277.5	443.0	3,209.0	723.1	26.5
2000............	6,133.0	808.1	313.4	521.7	3,727.4	731.6	30.8
2010............	6,942.1	1,045.0	343.7	590.1	4,186.5	740.5	36.3
2020............	7,765.0	1,349.1	369.3	647.7	4,605.1	750.8	43.0
2023............	**7,982.0**	**1,450.6**	**378.3**	**661.9**	**4,704.3**	**742.0**	**44.9**
2030............	8,495.5	1,703.4	395.6	694.4	4,913.5	739.6	49.0
2040............	9,171.8	2,102.0	416.0	730.7	5,139.4	729.2	54.5
2050............	9,754.8	2,529.6	433.1	752.0	5,265.7	715.1	59.4
PERCENT DISTRIBUTION							
1950............	100.0	9.0	6.5	6.5	56.2	21.4	0.5
1960............	100.0	9.4	6.5	7.1	56.5	19.9	0.5
1970............	100.0	9.9	6.1	7.7	58.1	17.7	0.5
1980............	100.0	10.8	5.7	8.1	59.3	15.6	0.5
1990............	100.0	11.9	5.2	8.3	60.4	13.6	0.5
2000............	100.0	13.2	5.1	8.5	60.8	11.9	0.5
2010............	100.0	15.1	5.0	8.5	60.3	10.7	0.5
2020............	100.0	17.4	4.8	8.3	59.3	9.7	0.6
2023............	**100.0**	**18.2**	**4.7**	**8.3**	**58.9**	**9.3**	**0.6**
2030............	100.0	20.1	4.7	8.2	57.8	8.7	0.6
2040............	100.0	22.9	4.5	8.0	56.0	8.0	0.6
2050............	100.0	25.9	4.4	7.7	54.0	7.3	0.6

[1] Data for North America include Bermuda, Canada, Greenland, Saint Pierre and Miquelon, and the United States. [2] Latin American includes Mexico and Central and South America.

Source: U.S. Census Bureau, "International Data Base (IDB)," <www.census.gov/programs-surveys/international-programs/about/idb.html>, accessed August 2023.

Table 1356. Population and Land Area by Country or Territory: 2010 to 2023 and Projected 2030

[6,942,149 represents 6,942,149,000. Covers 227 countries or territories with populations of 5,000 or more in 2023. Population estimates were derived from information available as of August 2023. See text of this section for general comments concerning the data. For details of methodology, coverage, and reliability, see source. Minus sign (-) indicates decrease]

Country or territory	Mid-year population (1,000)				Population rank, 2023	Population percent change, 2020 to 2023	Population per sq. km, 2023	Land area, (sq. km)
	2010	2020	2023	2030 (P)				
World....................	6,942,149	7,764,965	7,982,019	8,495,468	(X)	2.8	61	131,793,164
Afghanistan............................	29,117	36,595	39,232	45,503	36	7.2	60	652,230
Albania................................	2,989	3,081	3,102	3,116	137	0.7	113	27,398
Algeria................................	35,949	43,957	46,286	51,068	34	5.3	19	2,381,740
Andorra................................	85	86	85	85	199	-0.3	183	468
Angola................................	22,641	32,522	35,981	45,369	40	10.6	29	1,246,700
Antigua and Barbuda..................	87	98	101	109	194	3.5	229	443
Argentina..............................	41,358	45,480	46,622	49,142	33	2.5	17	2,736,690
Armenia................................	3,072	3,021	2,989	2,892	139	-1.1	106	28,203
Australia..............................	21,840	25,468	26,461	28,467	54	3.9	3	7,682,300
Austria................................	8,448	8,856	8,941	9,111	99	1.0	108	82,445
Azerbaijan............................	9,332	10,465	10,605	10,901	88	1.3	128	82,629
Bahamas, The..........................	349	395	407	438	176	3.0	41	10,010
Bahrain................................	1,180	1,505	1,554	1,639	155	3.3	2,045	760
Bangladesh............................	146,554	162,533	167,184	177,171	8	2.9	1,284	130,170
Barbados..............................	290	301	303	307	180	0.8	706	430
Belarus................................	9,680	9,636	9,540	9,251	96	-1.0	47	202,900
Belgium................................	10,866	11,708	11,914	12,310	82	1.8	394	30,278
Belize................................	324	392	410	453	175	4.4	18	22,806
Benin................................	9,178	12,861	14,220	17,818	74	10.6	129	110,622
Bhutan................................	759	851	876	933	165	3.0	23	38,394
Bolivia................................	10,024	11,775	12,186	13,011	79	3.5	11	1,083,301
Bosnia and Herzegovina..............	3,885	3,833	3,808	3,730	131	-0.7	74	51,187
Botswana..............................	1,978	2,317	2,418	2,643	145	4.3	4	566,730
Brazil................................	197,855	214,752	218,690	227,310	7	1.8	26	8,358,140
Brunei................................	395	464	485	532	173	4.5	92	5,265
Bulgaria..............................	7,391	6,965	6,828	6,521	107	-2.0	63	108,489
Burkina Faso..........................	15,634	20,833	22,489	26,350	59	7.9	82	273,800
Burma................................	51,401	55,911	57,114	59,793	26	2.2	87	653,508
Burundi................................	9,140	11,846	13,163	16,039	77	11.1	513	25,680
Cabo Verde............................	508	582	604	651	171	3.7	150	4,033
Cambodia..............................	14,327	16,337	16,891	17,987	72	3.4	96	176,515
Cameroon..............................	20,900	27,744	30,136	36,269	51	8.6	64	472,710
Canada................................	34,201	37,650	38,517	40,326	38	2.3	4	9,093,507
Central African Republic..............	4,683	5,263	5,552	6,257	119	5.5	9	622,984
Chad................................	11,989	16,876	18,523	22,767	66	9.8	15	1,259,200
Chile................................	16,760	18,182	18,549	19,263	65	2.0	25	743,812
China................................	1,340,789	1,404,032	1,413,143	1,424,439	1	0.6	152	9,326,410
Colombia..............................	43,821	48,420	49,336	50,908	29	1.9	48	1,038,700
Comoros................................	710	852	888	969	164	4.3	398	2,235
Congo, Rep. of (Brazzaville).........	4,278	5,522	5,954	7,010	114	7.8	17	341,500
Congo, Dem. Rep. of (Kinshasa)....	72,742	101,769	111,860	138,708	14	9.9	49	2,267,048
Costa Rica............................	4,524	5,123	5,227	5,501	123	2.0	102	51,060
Cote d'Ivoire..........................	21,718	27,470	29,345	33,889	52	6.8	92	318,003
Croatia................................	4,417	4,230	4,169	4,037	129	-1.4	75	55,974
Cuba................................	11,262	11,059	10,986	10,843	85	-0.7	100	109,820
Cyprus................................	1,103	1,267	1,308	1,381	159	3.2	142	9,241
Czechia................................	10,551	10,779	10,830	10,808	86	0.5	140	77,247
Denmark................................	5,547	5,869	5,947	6,119	115	1.3	140	42,434
Djibouti................................	739	920	976	1,105	162	6.1	42	23,180
Dominica..............................	73	75	75	74	201	0.2	99	751
Dominican Republic..................	9,459	10,516	10,736	11,301	87	2.1	222	48,320
Ecuador................................	14,963	17,551	18,134	19,326	69	3.3	73	248,360
Egypt................................	81,571	103,995	109,547	120,413	15	5.3	110	995,450
El Salvador............................	5,967	6,481	6,602	6,697	110	1.9	319	20,721
Equatorial Guinea....................	986	1,561	1,738	2,135	154	11.3	62	28,051
Eritrea................................	5,369	6,089	6,275	6,837	111	3.1	62	101,000
Estonia................................	1,303	1,228	1,203	1,138	160	-2.1	28	42,388
Eswatini..............................	1,019	1,105	1,130	1,182	161	2.3	66	17,204
Ethiopia..............................	82,066	107,883	115,757	135,878	13	7.3	106	1,096,570
Fiji................................	876	935	948	972	163	1.3	52	18,274
Finland................................	5,355	5,572	5,615	5,669	117	0.8	19	303,815
France................................	64,972	67,792	68,236	69,223	21	0.7	107	640,427
Gabon................................	1,628	2,230	2,397	2,818	146	7.5	9	257,667
Gambia, The..........................	1,750	2,302	2,469	2,844	144	7.2	244	10,120
Georgia................................	4,903	4,998	4,927	4,792	126	-1.4	71	69,700
Germany................................	81,751	84,498	84,220	83,392	18	-0.3	242	348,672
Ghana................................	24,609	31,643	33,846	39,139	45	7.0	149	227,533
Greece................................	11,040	10,605	10,498	10,243	90	-1.0	80	130,647
Grenada................................	108	113	114	116	190	1.0	332	344
Guatemala..............................	14,212	17,140	17,981	19,842	70	4.9	168	107,159
Guinea................................	9,571	12,527	13,607	16,465	75	8.6	55	245,717
Guinea-Bissau..........................	1,516	1,927	2,079	2,484	151	7.9	74	28,120
Guyana................................	787	787	792	814	166	0.6	4	196,849
Haiti................................	9,570	11,173	11,611	12,607	83	3.9	421	27,560
Honduras..............................	7,991	9,100	9,408	10,258	97	3.4	84	111,890
Hungary................................	10,000	10,027	9,886	9,673	94	-1.4	110	89,608
Iceland................................	318	351	361	381	178	2.9	4	100,250
India................................	1,220,719	1,369,541	1,399,180	1,472,251	2	2.2	471	2,973,193
Indonesia..............................	246,257	272,856	279,476	293,085	4	2.4	154	1,811,569

See footnotes at end of table.

Country or territory	Mid-year population (1,000)				Population rank, 2023	Population percent change, 2020 to 2023	Population per sq. km, 2023	Land area, (sq. km)
	2010	2020	2023	2030 (P)				
Iran	75,035	84,983	87,591	92,448	17	3.1	57	1,531,595
Iraq	29,073	38,829	41,266	47,088	35	6.3	94	437,367
Ireland	4,610	5,030	5,181	5,482	124	3.0	75	68,883
Israel	7,382	8,829	9,256	10,314	98	4.8	431	21,497
Italy	60,786	61,338	61,022	60,840	24	-0.5	208	294,140
Jamaica	2,839	2,815	2,821	2,846	140	0.2	261	10,831
Japan	127,646	125,136	123,719	119,732	11	-1.1	339	364,485
Jordan	6,800	10,820	11,087	12,264	84	2.5	125	88,802
Kazakhstan	17,090	19,514	20,082	21,260	64	2.9	7	2,699,700
Kenya	41,761	53,514	57,052	65,582	27	6.6	100	569,140
Kiribati	100	112	115	123	189	3.2	142	811
Korea, North	24,378	25,829	26,195	26,857	55	1.4	218	120,408
Korea, South	49,258	51,577	51,967	52,579	28	0.8	536	96,920
Kosovo	1,815	1,932	1,964	2,060	152	1.7	180	10,887
Kuwait	2,543	2,995	3,104	3,337	136	3.6	174	17,818
Kyrgyzstan	5,410	5,964	6,123	6,438	112	2.7	32	191,801
Laos	6,393	7,540	7,852	8,520	103	4.1	34	230,800
Latvia	2,115	1,883	1,822	1,680	153	-3.3	29	62,249
Lebanon	4,489	5,464	5,331	5,540	121	-2.4	521	10,230
Lesotho	1,994	2,162	2,211	2,333	147	2.2	73	30,355
Liberia	3,759	4,934	5,311	6,201	122	7.7	55	96,320
Libya	6,367	6,891	7,253	7,922	106	5.3	4	1,759,540
Liechtenstein	36	39	40	42	212	2.2	250	160
Lithuania	3,089	2,740	2,656	2,468	142	-3.1	42	62,680
Luxembourg	509	629	661	728	168	5.1	256	2,586
Madagascar	20,808	26,899	28,812	33,282	53	7.1	50	581,540
Malawi	15,016	19,823	21,280	24,645	62	7.3	226	94,080
Malaysia	29,063	33,164	34,220	36,520	44	3.2	104	328,657
Maldives	396	391	390	401	177	-0.4	1,307	298
Mali	14,514	19,553	21,360	26,038	61	9.2	18	1,220,190
Malta	417	457	467	480	174	2.2	1,478	316
Marshall Islands	66	78	81	88	200	4.1	447	181
Mauritania	3,203	3,997	4,245	4,830	128	6.2	4	1,030,700
Mauritius	1,282	1,305	1,309	1,312	158	0.3	645	2,030
Mexico	114,222	128,093	129,876	137,038	10	1.4	67	1,943,945
Micronesia, Federated States of	107	102	100	95	196	-2.0	143	702
Moldova	3,920	3,587	3,620	3,476	132	0.9	110	32,891
Monaco	31	31	32	33	216	1.7	15,799	2
Mongolia	2,783	3,169	3,255	3,411	134	2.7	2	1,553,556
Montenegro	623	610	602	582	172	-1.2	45	13,452
Morocco	32,267	36,055	37,067	39,141	39	2.8	52	716,550
Mozambique	23,012	30,098	32,514	38,879	46	8.0	41	786,380
Namibia	2,183	2,627	2,757	3,105	141	4.9	3	823,290
Nauru	9	10	10	10	222	1.3	469	21
Nepal	26,663	30,175	30,899	32,341	49	2.4	216	143,351
Netherlands	16,574	17,401	17,695	18,101	71	1.7	522	33,893
New Zealand	4,269	4,925	5,110	5,412	125	3.7	19	264,537
Nicaragua	5,653	6,419	6,613	7,030	109	3.0	55	119,990
Niger	15,613	22,760	25,397	32,731	56	11.6	20	1,266,700
Nigeria	165,891	213,986	230,843	275,155	6	7.9	254	910,768
North Macedonia	2,080	2,125	2,133	2,142	148	0.4	84	25,433
Norway	4,891	5,382	5,477	5,698	120	1.8	18	304,282
Oman	2,963	3,625	3,833	4,294	130	5.8	12	309,500
Pakistan	188,341	233,431	247,654	280,266	5	6.1	321	770,875
Palau	21	22	22	22	218	1.1	47	459
Panama	3,481	4,210	4,404	4,846	127	4.6	59	74,340
Papua New Guinea	7,064	9,146	9,819	11,422	95	7.4	22	452,860
Paraguay	6,372	7,189	7,440	7,985	104	3.5	19	397,302
Peru	29,348	31,867	32,440	33,867	47	1.8	25	1,279,996
Philippines	93,746	110,462	116,434	129,001	12	5.4	391	298,170
Poland	38,616	38,375	39,142	36,950	37	2.0	129	304,255
Portugal	10,650	10,288	10,223	10,140	91	-0.6	112	91,470
Qatar	1,720	2,447	2,532	2,605	143	3.5	219	11,586
Romania	20,533	18,986	18,326	17,338	68	-3.5	80	229,891
Russia	143,493	143,488	141,505	136,781	9	-1.4	9	16,377,742
Rwanda	9,923	12,709	13,401	14,973	76	5.4	543	24,668
Saint Kitts and Nevis	50	54	55	57	207	1.9	210	261
Saint Lucia	161	166	168	170	186	0.9	277	606
Saint Vincent and the Grenadines	104	101	101	100	195	-0.5	259	389
Samoa	192	204	208	217	184	1.9	74	2,821
San Marino	31	34	35	36	214	1.9	572	61
Sao Tome and Principe	176	211	220	243	183	4.6	229	964
Saudi Arabia	27,963	34,224	35,940	40,070	42	5.0	17	2,149,690
Senegal	12,667	17,005	18,385	21,631	67	8.1	96	192,530
Serbia	7,233	6,857	6,693	6,424	108	-2.4	86	77,474
Seychelles	88	96	98	101	197	2.0	215	455
Sierra Leone	6,122	8,256	8,908	10,372	100	7.9	124	71,620
Singapore	5,190	5,810	5,975	6,325	113	2.8	8,428	709
Slovakia	5,426	5,492	5,569	5,523	118	1.4	116	48,105
Slovenia	2,084	2,102	2,100	2,079	149	-0.1	104	20,151
Solomon Islands	555	678	715	798	167	5.3	26	27,986
Somalia	9,787	11,819	12,694	15,139	78	7.4	20	627,337

See footnotes at end of table.

Table 1356. Population and Land Area by Country or Territory: 2010 to 2023 and Projected 2030-Continued.

See headnote on page 862.

Country or territory	Mid-year population (1,000)				Population rank, 2023	Population percent change, 2020 to 2023	Population per sq. km, 2023	Land area, (sq. km)
	2010	2020	2023	2030 (P)				
South Africa	51,839	58,013	59,796	64,098	25	3.1	49	1,214,470
South Sudan [1]	9,765	10,561	12,118	15,309	80	14.7	19	644,329
Spain	46,412	47,041	47,223	47,592	32	0.4	95	498,980
Sri Lanka	20,687	21,368	21,878	22,264	60	2.4	339	64,630
Sudan [1]	34,984	45,544	49,198	58,882	30	8.0	26	1,861,484
Suriname	535	618	640	686	170	3.5	4	156,000
Sweden	9,432	10,383	10,536	10,893	89	1.5	26	410,335
Switzerland	7,937	8,586	8,793	9,231	101	2.4	220	39,997
Syria	22,223	19,392	22,934	26,206	58	18.3	123	185,887
Taiwan	23,111	23,563	23,589	23,602	57	0.1	731	32,260
Tajikistan	7,477	9,603	10,195	11,595	92	6.2	72	141,510
Tanzania	44,521	60,363	65,643	79,023	23	8.7	74	885,800
Thailand	66,271	69,292	69,795	70,281	20	0.7	137	510,890
Timor-Leste	1,088	1,383	1,476	1,686	156	6.7	99	14,874
Togo	6,178	8,077	8,704	10,255	102	7.8	160	54,385
Tonga	106	106	105	102	191	-0.7	147	717
Trinidad and Tobago	1,321	1,401	1,407	1,412	157	0.5	275	5,128
Tunisia	10,526	11,719	11,976	12,372	81	2.2	77	155,360
Turkey	74,647	82,009	83,593	86,893	19	1.9	109	769,632
Turkmenistan	4,940	5,523	5,691	6,028	116	3.0	12	469,930
Tuvalu	10	11	12	12	221	2.5	448	26
Uganda	31,002	43,250	47,730	59,136	31	10.4	242	197,100
Ukraine	45,768	43,508	34,831	37,536	43	-19.9	60	579,330
United Arab Emirates	8,021	9,792	9,973	10,479	93	1.9	119	83,600
United Kingdom	62,502	67,023	68,138	70,089	22	1.7	282	241,930
United States	**309,327**	**331,512**	**339,665**	**355,101**	**3**	**2.5**	**37**	**9,151,125**
Uruguay	3,302	3,389	3,416	3,475	133	0.8	20	175,015
Uzbekistan	28,678	34,015	35,971	39,189	41	5.8	85	425,400
Vanuatu	245	298	313	347	179	5.1	26	12,189
Venezuela	28,663	28,612	30,518	33,060	50	6.7	35	882,050
Vietnam	90,459	101,745	104,799	110,901	16	3.0	338	310,070
Yemen	23,195	29,811	31,566	35,493	48	5.9	60	527,968
Zambia	13,647	18,523	20,216	24,494	63	9.1	27	743,398
Zimbabwe	13,223	15,788	16,820	19,070	73	6.5	44	386,847
TERRITORIES AND DEPENDENCIES								
American Samoa	56	47	45	40	211	-5.8	225	198
Anguilla	15	18	19	21	219	5.6	210	91
Aruba	105	119	124	133	188	3.5	687	180
Bermuda	68	72	73	74	202	1.1	1,344	54
Cayman Islands	50	62	65	73	204	5.7	248	264
Cook Islands	11	9	8	7	223	-7.0	34	236
Curacao [2]	143	151	153	155	187	1.0	344	444
Faroe Islands	49	52	53	55	208	1.9	38	1,393
French Polynesia	269	295	301	314	181	2.2	79	3,827
Gaza Strip [3]	1,510	1,972	2,098	2,400	150	6.4	5,829	360
Gibraltar	29	29	30	30	217	0.6	4,233	7
Greenland	58	58	58	57	206	(-Z)	(Z)	2,166,086
Guam	163	168	169	170	185	0.5	311	544
Guernsey	65	67	68	68	203	0.7	867	78
Hong Kong	7,029	7,248	7,288	7,315	105	0.6	6,792	1,073
Isle of Man	84	90	92	94	198	1.6	161	572
Jersey	93	101	103	106	193	2.0	886	116
Macau	569	625	640	667	169	2.3	22,856	28
Montserrat	5	5	5	6	226	1.5	53	102
New Caledonia	252	290	301	324	182	3.7	17	18,275
Northern Mariana Islands	55	52	51	50	209	-1.1	109	472
Puerto Rico	3,722	3,190	3,057	2,818	138	-4.2	345	8,869
Saint Barthelemy	7	7	7	7	225	-0.5	284	25
Saint Helena, Ascension, and Tristan da Cunha	8	8	8	8	224	0.4	20	394
Saint Martin	30	33	33	34	215	1.0	609	54
Saint Pierre and Miquelon	6	5	5	5	227	-3.5	22	242
Sint Maarten [2]	38	44	46	49	210	3.8	1,343	34
Turks and Caicos Islands	43	56	59	67	205	5.8	63	948
Virgin Islands, British	30	37	39	44	213	6.0	261	151
Virgin Islands, U.S.	108	106	105	100	192	-1.3	302	348
Wallis and Futuna	15	16	16	16	220	0.8	112	142
West Bank [3]	2,409	2,984	3,177	3,642	135	6.5	563	5,640

P Projected. X Not applicable. Z Less than 0.05 percent or less than 1 person per square kilometer. [1] Sudan and South Sudan became separate countries in July 2011. [2] The Netherlands Antilles dissolved on October 10, 2010. Curacao and Sint Maarten became autonomous territories of the Kingdom of the Netherlands. [3] The Gaza Strip and West Bank are Israeli occupied with interim status subject to Israeli/Palestinian negotiations. The final status is yet to be determined.

Source: U.S. Census Bureau, "International Data Base (IDB)," <www.census.gov/programs-surveys/international-programs/about/idb.html>, accessed August 2023.

Table 1357. Net Migration Rate by Country: 1990 to 2022

[Net migration is the difference between the number of migrants entering and those leaving a country in a year, per 1,000 midyear population. A positive figure is known as net immigration and a negative figure as net emigration]

Country	1990	2000	2005	2010	2015	2016	2017	2018	2019	2020	2021	2022
Afghanistan	-51.23	-45.30	9.43	-3.25	-1.51	-1.20	-0.90	-0.62	-0.35	-0.10	-0.10	-0.10
Algeria	-0.22	-0.55	-3.38	-0.92	-0.98	-1.01	-0.95	-0.92	-1.02	-0.25	-0.19	-0.30
Angola	-0.31	-5.05	1.89	1.52	0.53	0.32	0.22	0.13	0.04	-0.21	-0.20	-0.19
Argentina	0.60	-0.44	-0.64	-0.12	-0.10	-0.10	-0.10	-0.09	-0.09	-0.09	-0.08	-0.08
Australia	7.45	5.70	6.18	7.88	7.66	10.17	9.92	9.28	8.66	8.07	7.49	6.93
Bangladesh	-2.19	-4.79	-4.87	-4.14	-3.89	-3.08	-3.05	-3.02	-2.99	-2.96	-2.93	-2.90
Belgium	(NA)	2.45	4.38	6.37	5.87	5.64	5.42	5.21	4.99	4.79	4.58	4.38
Benin	0.81	0.50	3.89	0.43	0.31	0.34	0.32	0.28	0.27	0.26	0.25	0.24
Bolivia	(NA)	-1.47	-1.27	-1.15	-1.06	-1.05	-1.03	-1.02	-0.52	-1.00	-0.99	-0.98
Brazil	0.16	0.03	-0.04	0.03	0.10	-0.13	-0.11	-0.02	0.14	-0.05	-0.12	-0.19
Burkina Faso	(NA)	-6.42	-5.40	-3.18	-1.03	-0.88	-0.69	-0.67	-0.66	-0.64	-0.62	-0.61
Burma	-0.25	-1.46	-3.12	-2.97	-1.32	-2.22	-13.46	-1.11	-0.35	-1.93	-2.78	-1.39
Burundi	-8.82	-6.88	2.39	0.83	-22.45	-11.01	-6.61	-4.60	-2.67	-0.84	7.35	7.09
Cambodia	3.91	-3.61	-4.10	-8.83	-2.11	-2.07	-2.04	-2.01	-2.39	-2.76	-2.73	-2.70
Cameroon	-0.69	-1.34	-1.53	-0.18	2.54	0.72	-2.31	-0.35	-0.34	-0.33	-0.32	-0.31
Canada	(NA)	5.31	4.83	7.41	5.87	6.22	5.87	5.85	5.75	5.65	5.55	5.46
Chad	(NA)	-0.76	1.71	0.68	-3.57	1.30	-0.15	-0.14	-0.14	-0.14	-0.13	-0.13
Chile	1.38	0.40	0.38	0.36	0.34	0.34	0.34	0.33	0.33	0.33	0.33	0.33
China	-0.14	-0.26	-0.21	-0.17	-0.15	-0.14	-0.14	-0.13	-0.13	–	–	-0.11
Colombia	(NA)	-9.58	-3.10	-5.67	-5.43	-4.80	-2.64	21.52	6.83	-1.58	-1.31	-1.58
Congo, Dem. Rep. of	1.73	-1.24	0.76	-0.60	0.33	0.75	-0.58	-1.04	-0.95	-0.87	-0.78	-0.71
Cote d'Ivoire	56.15	-0.01	-0.93	0.17	1.42	2.30	1.32	1.29	1.26	1.24	1.21	1.18
Ecuador	-5.12	-8.03	15.63	-0.60	-2.52	-2.78	-1.35	11.42	5.25	0.96	-0.67	-0.81
Egypt	(NA)	-0.36	-0.46	-0.44	-0.56	-0.29	-0.16	-0.16	-0.28	-0.34	-0.32	-0.31
Ethiopia	3.90	-1.30	-0.64	0.05	0.62	0.41	0.77	-0.07	-1.78	-0.05	-0.24	-0.13
France	1.43	1.20	1.49	1.14	0.58	0.94	2.28	1.27	1.26	1.08	1.07	1.07
Germany	(NA)	2.03	0.96	1.85	14.83	5.92	4.24	4.19	3.67	1.78	1.78	1.78
Ghana	0.11	0.11	1.76	1.02	0.24	0.33	0.30	0.12	-0.06	-0.17	-0.17	-0.16
Guatemala	-4.36	-11.47	-0.14	-1.49	-2.75	-3.18	-2.79	-2.42	-2.06	-1.71	-1.69	-1.66
Guinea	55.97	-9.55	-8.93	-0.13	0.01	-0.34	–	–	–	–	–	–
India	(NA)	-0.12	-0.27	-0.42	-0.20	-0.19	-0.20	-0.20	-0.20	0.39	0.20	0.16
Indonesia	-0.47	-1.58	-1.32	-1.20	-1.13	-1.05	-0.97	-0.88	-0.80	-0.72	-0.72	-0.71
Iran	22.04	-1.87	-1.48	-0.27	-0.13	-0.13	-0.16	-0.21	-0.26	-0.31	-0.30	-0.30
Iraq	-58.60	–	1.90	3.19	-0.60	-2.95	-0.64	-0.37	-0.35	-0.52	-0.68	-0.83
Italy	(NA)	2.95	4.41	6.25	2.16	2.34	3.06	2.85	2.49	2.67	2.85	3.02
Japan	0.02	0.30	-0.41	–	0.75	0.75	0.75	0.75	0.75	0.75	0.75	0.74
Kazakhstan	-7.80	-3.23	1.41	0.91	-0.73	-1.14	-1.18	-1.53	-1.71	-0.91	-0.41	-0.41
Kenya	0.24	-0.77	0.32	1.05	0.05	-2.10	-0.38	-0.21	-0.20	-0.20	-0.20	-0.19
Korea, North	(NA)	1.63	0.14	-0.04	-0.04	-0.04	-0.04	-0.04	-0.04	-0.04	-0.04	-0.04
Korea, South	0.77	0.17	-1.97	1.67	2.78	2.76	2.73	2.71	2.69	2.67	2.65	2.63
Malawi	7.96	-3.29	-2.11	-1.20	-0.52	-0.40	-0.29	-0.19	-0.09	–	–	–
Malaysia	2.46	10.92	7.82	7.06	1.60	1.58	1.56	1.54	1.52	1.51	1.49	1.48
Mali	-7.88	-7.75	-4.93	-3.76	-4.57	-4.09	-3.86	-3.86	-3.86	-3.86	-3.17	-3.08
Mexico	-4.82	-5.19	-4.31	-0.36	-0.82	-0.79	-0.75	-0.72	-0.73	-0.74	-0.75	-0.76
Morocco	-0.90	-3.95	-2.49	-2.34	-1.88	-1.87	-1.83	-1.81	-1.77	-1.77	-1.76	-1.74
Mozambique	-9.04	-5.00	-4.60	-4.02	-1.84	-2.09	-1.84	-1.55	-1.61	-1.66	-1.62	-1.58
Nepal	-0.20	-6.56	-10.94	-2.44	-2.43	-2.49	-2.88	-3.27	-3.66	-4.04	-4.12	-4.21
Netherlands	(NA)	3.38	-1.68	2.00	3.26	4.66	4.72	5.02	6.24	3.93	6.19	5.12
Niger	-1.83	-1.39	-1.28	-1.05	1.59	1.30	-0.87	-0.18	-0.72	-0.69	-0.66	-0.64
Nigeria	-0.10	-0.02	-0.19	-0.32	-1.36	-1.73	-0.21	-0.21	-0.21	-0.21	-0.21	-0.21
Pakistan	0.91	8.41	-3.63	-0.49	-2.09	-3.49	-0.95	-0.77	-0.82	-0.87	-0.92	-0.96
Peru	(NA)	-1.80	-3.94	-11.12	-10.59	-10.36	-9.33	14.73	3.53	3.23	-0.62	-0.75
Philippines	-1.10	-1.33	-1.71	-2.55	-1.14	-3.61	-1.07	-0.43	0.15	3.60	0.31	0.13
Poland	-0.41	-0.51	-0.28	-0.05	-0.41	0.04	0.04	0.09	0.16	0.12	0.12	38.70
Romania	(NA)	-5.66	-5.89	-4.45	-4.80	-5.06	-6.71	-6.35	-6.70	-5.32	-4.85	-4.36
Russia	3.92	2.20	1.14	1.68	1.47	0.87	1.98	0.74	1.98	0.74	0.75	0.75
Rwanda	-4.68	-21.77	-11.59	-2.35	-12.29	0.89	0.17	-0.51	-1.16	-3.33	-3.27	-3.21
Saudi Arabia	(NA)	0.59	-1.84	16.26	4.97	4.39	3.93	4.07	4.30	4.63	5.04	5.52
Senegal	-5.62	-3.93	-2.40	-1.74	-0.81	-0.71	-0.08	-1.93	-0.90	-0.80	-0.73	-0.71
Somalia	-38.47	6.59	-0.70	-11.97	-8.46	-7.47	-6.51	-5.58	-4.68	-3.81	-2.98	-2.18
South Africa	-0.47	0.76	3.80	-3.40	-1.20	-1.91	-1.38	-1.31	-1.17	-0.67	-0.53	-0.41
South Sudan	(NA)	(NA)	(NA)	30.66	-14.35	-59.89	-64.21	-29.19	0.20	0.20	22.04	20.97
Spain	(NA)	9.60	14.55	-0.92	-0.04	1.89	3.53	7.19	9.70	4.60	4.47	4.35
Sri Lanka	(NA)	(NA)	-2.57	-9.05	1.88	-8.79	-10.21	2.19	-6.10	0.93	1.62	0.03
Sudan	(NA)	(NA)	(NA)	-9.94	1.18	1.67	4.20	1.86	-0.45	-0.44	-1.71	-1.67
Syria	(NA)	(NA)	0.72	-2.45	-69.67	-32.77	-42.46	36.62	18.83	27.07	34.34	40.58
Taiwan	0.29	0.25	0.68	0.95	0.37	0.50	0.37	0.38	0.54	0.65	0.75	0.85
Tanzania	-1.57	1.75	-1.38	-0.21	2.38	1.30	0.49	-0.53	-0.50	-0.47	-0.44	-0.41
Thailand	-1.82	1.37	1.65	1.06	0.53	0.22	0.27	0.20	0.13	0.06	-0.03	-0.13
Tunisia	(NA)	-1.00	-2.14	-2.04	-1.97	-1.84	-1.71	-1.59	-1.47	-1.35	-1.34	-1.33
Turkey	-0.50	-1.34	-1.82	-1.72	2.17	-1.15	-4.53	-4.45	-4.38	-4.30	-1.55	-1.54
Uganda	-0.75	-2.28	-9.97	-8.47	-4.74	5.58	4.05	-10.37	-4.07	-3.48	-3.37	-3.26
Ukraine	1.54	-2.36	0.10	0.35	-2.25	–	–	4.57	4.58	2.30	-0.27	-205.86
United Kingdom	(NA)	2.69	3.39	4.03	5.12	3.80	4.33	3.92	4.69	4.32	3.95	3.59
United States	**(NA)**	**(NA)**	**(NA)**	**(NA)**	**3.20**	**3.20**	**2.50**	**2.00**	**1.80**	**(NA)**	**2.10**	**3.00**
Uzbekistan	-3.58	-2.66	-3.68	-1.39	-0.94	-0.83	-0.58	-0.45	-0.40	-0.37	-0.53	-0.73
Venezuela	-0.99	-1.71	-1.68	-1.35	-2.80	-6.24	-26.29	-66.09	-21.29	-3.44	14.22	13.88
Vietnam	-1.14	-0.38	-0.42	-0.36	-0.30	-0.29	-0.27	-0.26	-0.25	-0.24	-0.23	-0.22
Yemen	(NA)	-1.73	-0.48	0.97	1.01	0.67	0.35	0.05	-0.20	-0.20	-0.19	-0.19
Zambia	0.11	4.38	-1.56	-0.64	0.06	0.25	0.79	0.41	0.52	0.42	0.33	0.24
Zimbabwe	0.76	-1.29	-20.47	-20.26	-6.05	-0.52	0.25	-1.16	-1.10	-1.41	-1.95	-2.43

– Represents or rounds to zero. NA Not available.

Source: U.S. Census Bureau, "International Data Base (IDB)," <www.census.gov/programs-surveys/international-programs/about/idb.html>, accessed August 2023.

Table 1358. Foreign or Foreign-Born Population in Selected OECD Countries: 2000 to 2022

[30,273 represents 30,273,000. In Australia, Chile, Israel, and the United States, the data refer to residents who are foreign born. In the European countries, Japan, and South Korea, data represent the legal nationality or citizenship status of residents. Data are based on censuses, population registers, and residence permits. For details about data methodology for individual countries, see source]

Country	2000	2005	2010	2015	2018	2019	2020	2021	2022
United States	30,273	35,770	39,917	43,290	44,729	44,933	44,258	45,273	46,600
Australia	4,412	4,877	5,881	6,730	7,333	7,533	7,654	7,502	(NA)
Austria	694	774	884	1,146	1,396	1,439	1,486	1,531	1,587
Belgium	897	871	1,058	1,277	1,376	1,414	1,479	1,489	1,515
Chile	(NA)	236	352	465	(NA)	1,299	1,448	1,460	1,482
Czechia	229	254	433	449	524	564	593	633	659
Denmark	259	268	330	423	506	526	537	539	562
France	3,259	(NA)	3,821	4,431	4,951	4,995	5,137	5,215	5,315
Germany	7,344	6,717	6,695	8,153	10,624	10,915	11,228	11,432	11,818
Ireland	(NA)	(NA)	575	606	594	623	644	646	801
Israel [1]	1,944	1,961	1,878	1,817	1,811	1,809	1,812	1,797	1,793
Italy	1,341	2,402	3,648	5,014	5,144	4,996	5,040	5,172	5,031
Japan	1,556	1,974	2,185	2,122	2,562	2,731	2,933	2,887	2,761
Korea, South	169	491	1,010	1,489	1,750	1,951	2,025	1,889	1,830
Netherlands	652	699	735	847	1,041	1,111	1,192	1,203	1,256
Norway	179	213	334	512	568	584	605	602	586
Portugal	191	449	454	395	422	480	590	662	699
Spain	924	3,731	5,403	4,454	4,563	4,840	5,227	5,368	5,407
Sweden	482	481	603	739	897	932	941	905	881
Switzerland	1,369	1,495	1,680	1,947	2,054	2,081	2,111	2,152	2,242
Turkey	(NA)	(NA)	167	518	919	1,211	1,531	1,792	1,824
United Kingdom	2,208	2,857	4,524	5,592	5,991	6,227	(NA)	6,013	(NA)

NA Not available. [1] See footnote 1, Table 1361.

Source: Organisation for Economic Co-operation and Development (OECD), 2024, OECD Data Explorer, Society: Migration, "International migration database" and "International migration database - stocks of foreign-born population" ©, <data-explorer.oecd.org/>, accessed July 2024.

Table 1359. Youth and Elderly Population Distribution by Country: 2023 and Projected 2030

[Percent of total population, as of mid-year. Covers countries with 12 million or more population in 2023]

Country	2023 Under 15 years old	2023 65 years old and over	2030 (P) Under 15 years old	2030 (P) 65 years old and over	Country	2023 Under 15 years old	2023 65 years old and over	2030 (P) Under 15 years old	2030 (P) 65 years old and over
Afghanistan	39.8	2.9	37.7	3.2	Malawi	38.5	3.8	33.5	4.4
Algeria	31.0	6.7	28.0	8.7	Malaysia	22.5	8.1	20.6	10.3
Angola	47.2	2.3	45.1	2.6	Mali	47.1	3.1	44.7	3.2
Argentina	23.5	12.7	21.8	13.8	Mexico	23.8	8.0	20.7	9.8
Australia	18.4	16.7	17.5	18.6	Morocco	26.0	8.1	23.6	10.5
Bangladesh	25.4	7.5	23.7	9.4	Mozambique	45.0	2.9	42.3	2.9
Benin	45.4	2.5	44.3	2.5	Nepal	26.3	6.2	23.2	7.6
Bolivia	29.1	6.8	24.8	8.2	Netherlands	15.2	20.4	15.3	23.0
Brazil	19.8	10.5	18.7	13.3	Niger	49.7	2.7	48.4	2.7
Burkina Faso	42.2	3.2	37.9	3.4	Nigeria	40.7	3.4	39.1	3.6
Burma	24.8	6.8	22.2	9.0	Pakistan	34.8	4.8	31.8	5.7
Burundi	42.7	3.3	40.4	3.7	Peru	26.0	8.0	23.7	8.9
Cambodia	29.5	5.1	25.2	7.2	Philippines	30.5	5.4	29.0	6.3
Cameroon	41.7	3.2	40.2	3.4	Poland	14.3	19.3	13.0	22.2
Canada	15.6	20.5	15.0	23.9	Romania	15.6	22.2	14.4	23.0
Chad	46.2	2.5	43.4	2.6	Russia	16.8	17.2	14.2	20.5
Chile	19.3	13.1	18.0	17.0	Rwanda	37.9	3.0	32.8	3.7
China	16.5	14.1	14.8	17.8	Saudi Arabia	23.5	4.2	20.0	5.9
Colombia	22.5	10.9	21.1	13.6	Senegal	41.2	3.3	37.2	4.0
Congo, Dem. Rep	46.0	2.5	43.8	2.6	Somalia	41.5	2.7	40.1	3.6
Cote d'Ivoire	36.6	3.0	33.7	3.1	South Africa	27.4	7.3	24.8	8.9
Ecuador	27.2	9.0	24.7	10.2	South Sudan	41.9	2.6	40.8	3.0
Egypt	34.4	5.4	28.6	6.9	Spain	13.4	20.5	11.6	23.8
Ethiopia	39.0	3.3	36.3	3.8	Sri Lanka	23.0	12.1	21.1	14.7
France	17.5	21.7	16.4	23.9	Sudan	40.5	3.2	38.5	3.8
Germany	13.7	23.3	13.9	27.0	Syria	33.3	4.1	29.7	5.3
Ghana	37.7	4.4	34.6	4.9	Taiwan	12.2	18.1	11.4	23.5
Guatemala	32.0	5.2	28.3	6.3	Tanzania	41.5	3.4	39.0	3.8
Guinea	41.0	4.0	40.5	4.2	Thailand	16.0	14.5	14.9	19.4
India	24.8	6.8	22.6	7.8	Turkey	22.1	9.3	19.8	12.0
Indonesia	24.2	7.7	21.3	9.7	Uganda	47.3	2.4	45.2	2.6
Iran	23.5	6.7	20.9	8.9	Ukraine	11.9	20.0	12.5	20.5
Iraq	35.2	3.6	31.1	4.4	United Kingdom	16.9	19.1	15.9	21.4
Italy	12.1	23.3	11.1	26.3	United States	18.2	18.1	17.8	20.6
Japan	12.3	29.2	11.3	30.8	Uzbekistan	29.7	6.4	27.9	8.7
Kazakhstan	27.9	9.3	25.3	11.3	Venezuela	25.1	8.9	23.1	11.0
Kenya	36.5	3.3	32.6	4.0	Vietnam	23.4	7.9	21.3	11.0
Korea, North	19.9	11.0	19.1	13.5	Yemen	35.1	3.3	30.3	4.1
Korea, South	11.5	18.4	10.2	24.5	Zambia	42.5	2.7	40.1	3.1
Madagascar	37.5	3.8	34.2	4.6	Zimbabwe	38.5	3.9	35.6	4.2

P Projected.

Source: U.S. Census Bureau, "International Data Base (IDB)," <www.census.gov/programs-surveys/international-programs/about/idb.html>, accessed August 2023.

Table 1360. Births, Deaths, and Life Expectancy by Country or Territory: 2023 and Projected 2030

[Covers countries with 13 million or more population in 2023]

Country or territory	Crude birth rate [1] 2023	Crude birth rate [1] 2030 (P)	Crude death rate [2] 2023	Crude death rate [2] 2030 (P)	Expectation of life at birth (years) 2023	Expectation of life at birth (years) 2030 (P)	Infant mortality rate [3] 2023	Infant mortality rate [3] 2030 (P)	Total fertility rate per woman [4] 2023	Total fertility rate per woman [4] 2030 (P)
Afghanistan	34.8	30.3	12.1	10.6	54.1	56.8	103.1	90.8	4.53	3.90
Algeria	20.9	17.5	4.4	4.5	77.8	79.3	18.8	17.4	2.97	2.76
Angola	41.4	39.2	7.8	6.5	62.5	65.3	57.2	46.5	5.76	5.29
Argentina	15.4	14.3	7.3	7.2	78.6	80.2	9.1	7.9	2.17	2.07
Australia	12.2	11.5	6.8	7.0	83.3	84.6	3.0	2.7	1.73	1.72
Bangladesh	17.5	15.9	5.5	5.8	75.0	76.8	29.6	24.6	2.08	2.04
Benin	40.7	37.8	7.8	6.6	62.6	65.2	54.3	45.1	5.39	5.09
Brazil	13.4	12.4	6.9	7.4	76.1	77.7	13.1	11.4	1.75	1.73
Burkina Faso	32.7	27.7	7.5	6.4	63.8	66.4	48.2	40.0	4.14	3.38
Burma	16.1	14.2	7.4	7.2	69.8	72.6	33.4	26.6	2.00	1.87
Burundi	34.9	32.9	5.9	5.2	67.8	70.1	36.8	29.7	4.96	4.48
Cambodia	18.8	15.9	5.7	5.6	71.0	73.6	28.8	23.5	2.20	2.01
Cameroon	35.1	32.2	7.5	6.4	63.7	66.7	47.4	38.9	4.50	4.12
Canada	10.1	9.5	8.2	8.7	84.0	85.3	4.3	3.9	1.57	1.61
Chad	39.9	36.5	9.2	7.8	59.6	62.4	64.0	54.1	5.35	4.71
Chile	12.6	11.3	6.6	7.1	80.0	81.6	6.4	5.6	1.75	1.73
China	9.7	8.5	7.8	8.4	78.2	80.3	6.5	5.4	1.45	1.52
Colombia	15.1	13.8	7.8	7.1	74.9	78.2	11.7	11.5	1.94	1.92
Congo, Dem. Rep	39.6	37.0	7.7	6.6	62.2	64.9	59.1	48.0	5.56	5.07
Cote d'Ivoire	27.9	25.1	7.5	6.7	62.7	65.7	54.0	43.6	3.47	3.04
Ecuador	18.0	16.2	7.1	5.6	74.9	80.1	11.2	11.2	2.24	2.03
Egypt	20.5	16.7	4.3	4.5	74.7	76.5	17.3	14.5	2.76	2.22
Ethiopia	30.1	26.8	6.0	4.9	67.1	70.8	33.9	25.7	3.92	3.43
France	10.9	10.9	9.9	9.8	82.5	83.8	3.1	2.9	1.90	1.88
Germany	9.0	8.5	12.0	12.0	81.7	83.1	3.1	2.8	1.58	1.61
Ghana	28.0	25.2	6.0	5.3	69.7	72.0	31.9	27.2	3.61	3.27
Guatemala	21.9	19.3	4.9	4.9	73.2	75.1	25.6	21.6	2.57	2.30
Guinea	35.5	34.0	8.0	7.0	64.3	66.7	48.3	39.8	4.82	4.59
India	16.5	14.7	9.7	7.4	67.7	71.3	30.4	30.7	2.07	1.91
Indonesia	15.1	13.8	6.8	7.0	73.3	75.2	19.3	16.4	1.99	1.84
Iran	14.8	12.3	5.2	5.6	75.4	77.1	14.6	12.4	1.92	1.86
Iraq	24.2	21.6	3.9	3.9	73.5	75.3	19.2	16.3	3.17	2.74
Italy	7.0	7.6	11.3	11.2	82.8	84.1	3.1	2.8	1.24	1.36
Japan	6.9	6.9	11.7	12.8	85.0	86.2	1.9	1.7	1.39	1.45
Kazakhstan	17.6	16.2	8.2	8.0	73.0	74.7	8.1	7.3	2.59	2.53
Kenya	26.0	23.8	5.0	4.7	70.0	72.3	26.9	21.4	3.23	2.82
Korea, North	13.4	12.1	9.5	9.2	72.9	75.4	16.2	13.1	1.82	1.78
Korea, South	7.0	6.8	7.3	8.5	83.2	84.5	2.8	2.6	1.11	1.19
Madagascar	28.1	24.5	5.9	5.5	68.5	70.5	38.3	33.3	3.55	3.04
Malawi	27.3	23.4	4.5	4.1	72.7	74.7	32.7	28.0	3.30	2.69
Malaysia	14.4	13.1	5.7	6.1	76.4	78.1	6.5	5.8	1.74	1.71
Mali	40.5	36.7	8.3	7.0	62.8	65.5	59.0	48.4	5.45	4.78
Mexico	14.0	13.9	7.1	6.1	73.5	76.9	12.0	11.1	1.73	1.80
Morocco	17.1	15.4	6.6	6.9	74.0	75.8	18.7	15.8	2.27	2.17
Mozambique	36.9	35.1	9.9	8.1	57.7	61.7	59.8	49.5	4.74	4.35
Nepal	17.3	15.4	5.6	5.7	72.7	74.6	24.6	20.8	1.88	1.75
Netherlands	10.5	10.8	9.7	9.9	81.7	83.1	3.7	3.3	1.61	1.64
Niger	46.9	44.3	9.7	8.2	60.5	63.1	65.5	57.1	6.73	6.10
Nigeria	34.0	32.4	8.5	7.4	61.8	64.7	55.2	45.5	4.57	4.22
Pakistan	26.0	22.9	5.9	5.6	70.0	71.9	52.7	44.7	3.39	2.94
Peru	17.0	15.2	11.0	6.2	68.9	75.8	10.8	10.4	2.18	2.01
Philippines	22.2	21.1	6.3	6.7	70.5	70.9	22.1	22.0	2.77	2.67
Poland	8.7	7.1	12.9	12.0	75.8	78.9	5.1	4.2	1.31	1.36
Romania	8.6	8.4	14.9	14.3	76.3	78.6	5.7	4.9	1.63	1.63
Russia	8.5	8.4	14.1	14.0	72.0	73.9	6.6	6.0	1.51	1.54
Rwanda	25.7	22.0	5.8	5.4	66.2	68.6	25.6	20.9	3.23	2.67
Saudi Arabia	13.9	12.7	3.5	3.7	76.9	78.6	12.0	10.1	1.89	1.78
Senegal	30.8	26.5	5.0	4.6	70.3	72.3	31.8	27.3	4.17	3.45
South Africa	18.3	15.2	7.2	6.5	71.0	74.7	24.4	16.5	2.31	2.08
Spain	7.1	7.5	10.1	9.9	82.8	84.1	2.4	2.2	1.29	1.40
Sri Lanka	14.6	14.0	7.4	8.0	76.6	78.1	6.8	6.4	2.14	2.07
Sudan	33.3	30.9	6.2	5.6	67.5	69.7	41.4	35.8	4.54	4.01
Syria	22.2	19.5	4.1	4.0	74.6	76.4	15.5	13.0	2.74	2.44
Taiwan	7.3	6.9	8.0	8.9	81.4	82.8	3.9	3.5	1.09	1.17
Tanzania	32.9	30.4	5.0	4.6	70.5	72.5	30.3	26.1	4.33	3.93
Thailand	10.0	9.2	7.9	8.7	77.9	79.6	6.4	5.7	1.54	1.56
Turkey	14.0	12.7	6.1	6.6	76.5	78.2	18.9	15.7	1.91	1.83
Uganda	40.3	35.5	4.9	4.1	69.3	71.8	29.4	23.3	5.26	4.62
Ukraine	5.8	7.0	19.8	17.6	69.8	71.3	9.0	8.3	1.22	1.28
United Kingdom	10.8	10.5	9.1	9.3	82.1	83.3	3.8	3.5	1.63	1.65
United States	**12.2**	**11.7**	**8.4**	**8.9**	**80.8**	**81.8**	**5.1**	**4.8**	**1.84**	**1.84**
Uzbekistan	22.2	16.8	5.2	5.0	75.8	77.9	18.9	15.7	2.92	2.46
Venezuela	17.0	15.2	6.6	6.8	74.3	76.1	14.1	12.4	2.20	2.07
Vietnam	15.3	13.2	5.8	6.1	75.8	77.6	14.4	12.3	2.04	1.95
Yemen	24.1	20.8	5.5	5.3	67.8	70.0	45.5	39.1	2.91	2.41
Zambia	34.5	31.6	6.0	5.4	66.6	68.9	36.3	31.4	4.49	4.02
Zimbabwe	29.4	25.9	6.7	5.8	66.8	69.7	34.0	29.1	3.51	3.20

P Projection. [1] Number of births per 1,000 persons, based on midyear population. [2] Number of deaths per 1,000 persons, based on midyear population. [3] Number of deaths of children under 1 year of age per 1,000 live births in a calendar year. [4] Average number of children that would be born if all women lived to the end of childbearing age, based on birth rates for each specified year.

Source: U.S. Census Bureau, "International Data Base (IDB)," <www.census.gov/programs-surveys/international-programs/about/idb.html>, accessed August 2023.

Table 1361. Life Expectancy at Birth and at Age 65 by Sex—Selected Countries: 2020 and 2022

Country	Life expectancy at birth (years)				Life expectancy at age 65 (years)			
	Females		Males		Females		Males	
	2020	2022	2020	2022	2020	2022	2020	2022
United States............	**79.9**	**(NA)**	**74.2**	**(NA)**	**19.8**	**(NA)**	**17.0**	**(NA)**
Australia..................	85.3	85.3	81.2	81.2	23.0	22.8	20.3	20.2
Austria....................	83.6	83.6	78.9	79.1	21.0	21.1	17.9	18.0
Belgium..................	83.0	83.9	78.5	79.7	20.8	21.6	17.6	18.7
Bulgaria.................	77.5	77.9	70.0	70.6	17.1	17.3	12.9	13.2
Costa Rica..............	83.2	83.5	78.1	78.3	21.4	21.5	18.8	18.9
Croatia...................	80.7	80.8	74.5	74.6	18.7	18.6	15.1	15.2
Czechia..................	81.3	81.9	75.2	76.1	19.1	19.8	15.2	16.0
Denmark.................	83.6	83.2	79.7	79.5	21.2	20.7	18.4	18.2
Estonia...................	83.0	82.3	74.4	73.6	21.1	20.5	15.9	15.2
Finland...................	84.8	83.8	79.2	78.7	22.2	21.3	18.8	18.0
France....................	85.3	85.1	79.2	79.3	23.1	23.0	19.0	19.2
Germany.................	83.5	83.0	78.7	78.3	21.2	20.8	18.0	17.6
Greece....................	83.9	83.4	78.8	78.3	21.4	20.9	18.5	17.8
Hungary.................	79.0	79.3	72.3	72.6	17.9	18.1	14.0	14.2
Iceland...................	84.6	83.4	81.6	80.9	22.0	20.7	20.3	19.4
Ireland...................	84.4	84.2	80.8	80.9	21.9	21.6	19.4	19.4
Israel [1].................	84.8	84.8	80.6	80.7	22.0	22.0	19.2	19.3
Italy......................	84.5	84.8	80.0	80.7	21.7	21.9	18.3	19.0
Japan.....................	87.7	87.1	81.6	81.1	24.9	24.3	20.0	19.4
Latvia....................	80.0	79.4	70.6	69.4	19.1	18.6	14.0	13.7
Lithuania...............	80.1	80.1	70.1	71.4	19.1	19.0	13.6	14.1
Netherlands............	83.1	83.1	79.7	80.2	20.7	20.8	18.2	18.7
Poland...................	80.6	81.1	72.4	73.4	19.1	19.6	14.5	15.4
Portugal.................	84.1	84.5	78.0	78.9	21.6	22.1	17.8	18.7
Romania................	78.3	79.2	70.4	71.3	17.7	18.1	13.4	14.0
Slovakia.................	80.4	80.5	73.5	73.6	18.9	18.8	14.8	15.0
Slovenia.................	83.4	84.1	77.8	78.6	20.6	21.5	16.9	17.8
Spain.....................	85.2	85.9	79.6	80.5	22.4	23.2	18.4	19.2
Sweden..................	84.2	84.8	80.6	81.4	21.4	21.9	18.9	19.6
Switzerland.............	85.1	85.5	81.0	81.8	22.2	22.6	19.3	20.0

NA Not available. [1] The statistical data for Israel are supplied by and under the responsibility of the relevant Israeli authorities. The use of such data by the OECD is without prejudice to the status of the Golan Heights, East Jerusalem and Israeli settlements in the West Bank under the terms of international law.

Source: Organisation for Economic Co-operation and Development (OECD), OECD Data Explorer, 2024, Health: Health status, "Life expectancy" ©, <data-explorer.oecd.org/>, accessed July 2024.

Table 1362. Percent of the Adult Population Considered to Be Obese by Selected Country: 2000 to 2022

[Obesity rates are defined as the percentage of the population with a Body Mass Index (BMI) over 30 kg/m^2. The BMI is a single number that evaluates an individual's weight status in relation to height (weight/height^2). Obesity estimates derived from health examinations are generally higher and more reliable than those coming from self-reports because they preclude any misreporting of people's height and weight; however, health examinations are only conducted regularly in a few countries. For more information on methods, see source]

Country	2000	2005	2010	2015	2019	2020	2021	2022
OBESITY, MEASURED								
United States.................	**30.9**	**(NA)**	**36.1**	**(NA)**	**(NA)**	**(NA)**	**(NA)**	**(NA)**
Australia..........................	(NA)	(NA)	(NA)	(NA)	(NA)	(NA)	(NA)	30.7
Brazil.............................	(NA)	(NA)	(NA)	(NA)	[1] 25.9	(NA)	(NA)	(NA)
Canada...........................	(NA)	23.7	(NA)	[1] 28.1	24.3	(NA)	(NA)	(NA)
Finland...........................	22.5	(NA)	(NA)	(NA)	(NA)	(NA)	(NA)	30.2
Hungary.........................	(NA)	(NA)	(NA)	(NA)	33.2	(NA)	(NA)	(NA)
Ireland...........................	(NA)	(NA)	(NA)	23.0	23.0	(NA)	(NA)	(NA)
Japan.............................	2.9	3.9	3.5	3.7	4.6	(NA)	(NA)	(NA)
Korea.............................	(NA)	3.5	4.1	5.3	5.9	7.4	7.0	(NA)
Latvia............................	(NA)	(NA)	(NA)	(NA)	(NA)	23.9	(NA)	23.3
Mexico...........................	24.2	30.2	(NA)	(NA)	(NA)	36.0	(NA)	(NA)
New Zealand....................	(NA)	(NA)	(NA)	30.9	31.3	31.2	34.3	(NA)
United Kingdom................	21.2	23.2	26.1	26.9	28.0	(NA)	(NA)	(NA)
OBESITY, SELF-REPORTED								
United States.................	**21.8**	**25.1**	**28.2**	**30.2**	**32.6**	**33.6**	**33.5**	**(NA)**
Brazil.............................	(NA)	(NA)	15.0	17.0	20.3	21.5	22.4	(NA)
Canada...........................	(NA)	15.2	17.5	[1] 19.2	20.4	21.0	21.6	22.4
Chile..............................	2.5	(NA)	(NA)	10.1	(NA)	(NA)	26.4	(NA)
Denmark.........................	9.5	11.4	13.4	(NA)	(NA)	(NA)	18.5	(NA)
Estonia...........................	14.1	(NA)	16.9	(NA)	(NA)	20.5	(NA)	21.0
Finland...........................	11.2	14.1	15.6	[1] 18.8	21.0	[1] 23.0	(NA)	[1] 24.0
Germany.........................	(NA)	13.6	(NA)	(NA)	(NA)	(NA)	16.7	(NA)
Ireland...........................	(NA)	(NA)	(NA)	18.0	26.0	(NA)	(NA)	21.0
Israel [2]........................	(NA)	(NA)	15.7	(NA)	17.7	17.0	(NA)	(NA)
Italy..............................	8.6	9.9	10.3	9.8	11.0	11.5	12.0	(NA)
Lithuania........................	(NA)	15.1	(NA)	(NA)	18.3	(NA)	(NA)	20.3
Netherlands.....................	9.4	10.7	11.4	12.8	14.1	13.4	13.9	14.6
Norway...........................	(NA)	9.0	(NA)	12.0	13.0	(NA)	(NA)	[1] 16.0
Sweden..........................	9.2	10.9	11.3	12.3	13.7	14.4	15.3	16.1
Turkey............................	(NA)	(NA)	16.9	(NA)	21.1	(NA)	(NA)	20.2

NA Not available. [1] Break in series or difference in methodology. [2] See footnote 1, Table 1361.

Source: Organisation for Economic Co-operation and Development (OECD), 2024, OECD Data Explorer, Health: Risk factors for health, "Body weight" ©, <data-explorer.oecd.org>, accessed July 2024.

Table 1363. Daily Tobacco Consumption by Sex and Country: 2010 to 2023

[Daily smokers as percent of population aged over 15. Covers only tobacco consumed by smoking. Data may be estimated]

Country	Total				Females				Males			
	2010	2020	2022	2023	2010	2020	2022	2023	2010	2020	2022	2023
United States.......	15.1	9.4	8.9	(NA)	13.6	8.6	7.9	(NA)	16.7	10.3	9.9	(NA)
Australia [1]...........	15.3	(NA)	8.5	(NA)	14.1	(NA)	7.8	(NA)	16.6	(NA)	9.1	(NA)
Canada.............	16.3	9.4	9.4	(NA)	13.7	7.6	8.3	(NA)	19.0	11.3	10.5	(NA)
Costa Rica [1]........	14.4	8.4	5.6	6.2	9.3	4.6	2.3	3.2	19.4	12.2	8.8	9.5
Czechia.............	22.8	16.6	16.2	(NA)	16.5	12.2	12.0	(NA)	29.3	21.2	20.6	(NA)
Denmark [1].........	20.9	(NA)	(NA)	11.7	19.3	(NA)	(NA)	10.5	22.7	(NA)	(NA)	12.9
Estonia.............	26.2	17.9	15.9	(NA)	18.7	12.6	12.1	(NA)	36.8	25.7	21.0	(NA)
Finland [1]..........	19.0	12.4	11.3	(NA)	15.7	11.3	10.6	(NA)	23.2	13.5	12.0	(NA)
France..............	29.7	25.5	(NA)	(NA)	26.6	22.0	(NA)	(NA)	33.1	29.1	(NA)	(NA)
Iceland [1]..........	14.2	7.3	6.2	5.7	13.9	7.9	6.4	5.5	14.5	6.7	6.0	5.9
Ireland.............	(NA)	(NA)	14.0	14.0	(NA)	(NA)	12.0	12.0	(NA)	(NA)	17.0	16.0
Israel [2]............	18.5	(NA)	(NA)	16.9	12.6	(NA)	(NA)	9.1	24.8	(NA)	(NA)	23.4
Italy................	23.1	18.8	19.8	(NA)	17.1	15.4	15.8	(NA)	29.6	22.5	24.1	(NA)
Korea, South........	22.9	15.9	14.7	(NA)	5.2	3.9	3.7	(NA)	40.8	27.8	25.8	(NA)
Luxembourg.........	18.3	16.9	20.3	18.1	15.7	16.1	19.4	17.1	20.9	17.7	21.2	19.2
Netherlands [1].......	20.9	14.4	12.7	(NA)	18.8	13.1	10.5	(NA)	23.1	15.7	15.0	(NA)
New Zealand........	(NA)	11.9	8.6	6.8	(NA)	11.3	8.0	6.4	(NA)	12.5	9.3	7.2
Norway.............	19.0	9.0	8.0	7.0	19.0	9.0	8.0	7.0	19.0	9.0	8.0	8.0
Sweden.............	13.6	9.5	8.7	(NA)	12.5	8.7	8.5	(NA)	14.7	10.2	8.8	(NA)
United Kingdom.....	20.3	14.5	11.2	(NA)	19.8	13.7	10.0	(NA)	20.9	15.3	12.5	(NA)

NA Not available. [1] Break in series or difference in methodology for all or selected years shown, see source for details. [2] See footnote 1, Table 1361.

Source: Organisation for Economic Co-operation and Development (OECD), 2024, OECD Data Explorer, Health: Risk factors for health, "Tobacco consumption" ©, <data-explorer.oecd.org>, accessed July 2024.

Table 1364. Road Traffic Fatalities by Country: 2000 to 2022

[Fatalities include any person killed immediately or dying within 30 days as a result of an injury accident. For countries that do not apply the threshold of 30 days, conversion coefficients are estimated so that comparisons on the basis of the 30 day-definition can be made]

Country	2000	2010	2020	2021	2022	Country	2000	2010	2020	2021	2022
United States....	41,945	32,999	39,007	42,939	(NA)	Italy.................	7,061	4,114	2,395	2,875	3,159
Albania............	280	353	181	197	164	Japan................	10,410	5,828	3,416	3,205	3,216
Armenia...........	214	294	348	368	321	Korea, South........	10,236	5,505	3,081	2,916	2,735
Australia..........	1,817	1,349	1,094	1,116	1,188	Latvia...............	588	218	141	146	112
Austria............	976	552	344	362	370	Lithuania............	641	299	176	147	120
Azerbaijan.........	596	925	696	706	834	Mexico..............	5,224	4,966	2,722	(NA)	(NA)
Belgium...........	1,470	850	499	516	540	Moldova.............	406	452	245	257	217
Bulgaria...........	1,012	776	463	561	531	Netherlands........	1,166	640	610	582	745
Canada...........	2,904	2,238	1,746	1,768	(NA)	New Zealand........	462	375	320	318	375
Chile..............	2,207	2,070	1,794	2,052	2,131	North Macedonia. ..	162	162	125	116	124
Croatia............	655	426	237	292	275	Norway..............	341	208	93	80	116
Czechia...........	1,486	802	518	532	528	Poland..............	6,294	3,907	2,491	2,245	1,896
Denmark..........	498	255	163	130	(NA)	Portugal............	1,857	937	536	561	(NA)
Finland............	396	272	223	225	196	Russia..............	29,594	26,567	16,152	(NA)	(NA)
France............	8,079	3,992	2,541	2,944	3,267	Serbia..............	1,048	656	492	521	553
Georgia...........	500	685	450	449	430	Slovakia............	648	353	247	247	266
Germany..........	7,503	3,648	2,719	2,562	2,788	Spain...............	5,776	2,478	1,370	1,533	(NA)
Greece............	2,037	1,258	584	624	640	Sweden.............	591	266	204	210	227
Hungary...........	1,200	740	460	544	537	Switzerland.........	592	327	227	200	241
Ireland.............	415	212	147	136	155	Turkey..............	5,510	4,045	4,866	5,362	5,229
Israel [1]...........	516	375	305	364	(NA)	United Kingdom.....	3,580	1,905	1,516	1,608	1,750

NA Not available. [1] See footnote 1, Table 1361.

Source: International Transport Forum (ITF) / Organisation for Economic Co-operation and Development (OECD), 2024, OECD Data Explorer, "Annual road fatalities, injured, injury crashes" ©, <data-explorer.oecd.org>, accessed June 2024. See also <itf-oecd.org/>.

Table 1365. Suicide Rates by Sex and Country: 2020 and 2021

[For 2021 except as noted. Deaths due to intentional self-harm per 100,000 persons. Rates are standardized]

Country	Total	Females	Males	Country	Total	Females	Males
United States...............	14.7	5.9	23.9	Hungary......................	14.9	6.1	25.9
Argentina....................	6.5	2.5	11.3	Iceland.......................	10.2	6.5	13.6
Australia.....................	12.5	6.2	19.1	Ireland [1]....................	9.4	5.1	13.9
Austria.......................	11.0	4.3	19.0	Israel [2].....................	5.1	2.4	8.0
Brazil........................	7.6	3.2	12.5	Italy [1]......................	5.4	2.2	9.0
Bulgaria......................	7.3	3.0	12.5	Japan........................	15.6	10.2	21.2
Canada.......................	9.7	4.9	14.6	Korea, South.................	24.3	15.2	34.9
Chile.........................	8.1	3.0	13.7	Latvia........................	12.7	3.2	24.6
Colombia.....................	6.2	2.1	10.7	Lithuania.....................	18.5	7.1	33.1
Costa Rica [1]................	7.1	2.8	11.5	Luxembourg..................	5.4	2.7	8.3
Croatia.......................	13.4	5.3	23.2	Mexico.......................	6.6	2.1	11.5
Czechia......................	11.1	4.6	18.4	Netherlands..................	10.2	6.1	14.5
Denmark......................	8.5	4.6	12.8	Poland.......................	11.8	3.2	21.2
Estonia.......................	13.6	5.1	23.9	Slovakia......................	6.9	2.1	12.5
Finland.......................	13.2	8.0	18.9	Spain........................	7.6	3.8	11.9
France [1]....................	12.5	5.9	20.2	Sweden......................	11.7	6.7	16.7
Germany [1]..................	9.7	4.6	15.4	Switzerland..................	10.8	6.0	16.0
Greece [1]...................	3.9	1.5	6.7	United Kingdom [1]...........	8.4	4.0	12.9

[1] 2020 data. [2] See footnote 1, Table 1361.

Source: Organisation for Economic Co-operation and Development (OECD), 2024, OECD Data Explorer, Health: Health status, "Causes of mortality" ©, <data-explorer.oecd.org>, accessed July 2024.

Table 1366. Health Expenditures by Country: 2010 to 2023

[In percent. GDP = gross domestic product. Data may be estimated or provisional and subject to breaks in data series or difference in methodology; see source for details]

Country	Total expenditures on health (percent of GDP)					Public (government) expenditures on health (percent of total)				
	2010	2020	2021	2022	2023[1]	2010	2020	2021	2022	2023[1]
United States.............	16.2	18.6	17.3	16.5	(NA)	48.7	84.5	83.4	83.6	(NA)
Australia..................	8.4	10.7	10.4	9.8	(NA)	68.6	72.0	74.5	72.6	(NA)
Austria.....................	10.2	11.3	12.2	11.2	11.0	74.6	76.9	78.2	77.6	77.1
Belgium....................	10.2	11.3	11.0	10.8	(NA)	76.2	78.0	76.6	75.1	(NA)
Canada.....................	10.7	13.0	12.4	11.2	11.2	69.9	73.8	73.0	71.2	70.5
Chile.......................	6.8	9.7	9.7	10.2	10.0	59.0	65.3	60.5	58.4	58.2
Colombia..................	7.1	8.7	9.0	7.6	7.7	74.8	77.4	78.4	76.9	76.7
Czechia....................	7.6	9.2	9.5	8.8	8.5	84.9	87.7	86.4	85.3	85.0
Denmark...................	10.6	10.7	10.7	9.5	9.4	84.2	84.3	85.1	84.6	83.5
Estonia....................	6.6	7.6	7.5	7.0	7.6	75.4	77.1	76.1	74.8	76.1
France.....................	11.2	12.1	12.3	11.9	(NA)	76.3	84.6	85.0	84.7	(NA)
Germany...................	11.1	12.7	12.9	12.6	11.8	83.2	85.3	85.5	86.7	85.9
Greece.....................	9.6	9.5	9.2	8.5	(NA)	68.9	61.8	62.1	62.0	(NA)
Hungary...................	7.4	7.3	7.4	6.7	6.4	67.1	70.8	72.5	72.6	71.5
Iceland....................	8.4	9.6	9.7	9.1	9.0	79.9	83.4	83.8	84.7	84.0
Ireland....................	10.5	7.1	6.6	6.1	6.6	76.2	78.0	77.4	77.4	77.4
Israel[2]..................	6.9	7.7	7.7	7.3	(NA)	62.8	67.9	67.3	66.5	(NA)
Italy.......................	8.9	9.6	9.3	9.0	8.4	78.5	75.9	74.4	74.4	74.0
Japan......................	9.1	11.2	11.2	11.4	(NA)	81.9	85.2	85.2	86.0	(NA)
Korea, South..............	6.0	8.4	9.0	9.4	9.9	57.0	60.9	62.0	64.1	63.2
Lithuania..................	6.8	7.5	7.8	7.2	7.3	71.7	70.2	68.8	66.5	66.5
Luxembourg...............	6.7	5.8	5.7	5.6	5.8	84.9	86.5	86.2	86.1	85.9
Mexico.....................	5.5	6.1	5.9	5.7	(NA)	50.2	52.9	50.2	51.9	(NA)
Netherlands...............	10.2	11.2	11.1	10.1	(NA)	83.4	85.0	84.9	84.2	(NA)
New Zealand..............	9.6	9.7	10.2	11.3	(NA)	81.2	79.6	79.4	80.8	(NA)
Portugal...................	10.0	10.5	11.1	10.5	10.0	66.6	64.3	62.8	62.5	61.7
Spain......................	9.1	10.7	10.3	9.7	(NA)	74.4	73.2	73.7	74.0	(NA)
Sweden....................	8.3	11.3	11.1	10.5	10.9	82.5	86.2	86.1	86.0	86.2
Switzerland...............	10.0	12.0	12.0	11.7	(NA)	65.0	69.6	68.7	68.5	(NA)
Turkey.....................	5.0	4.6	4.6	3.7	(NA)	78.0	78.8	78.8	75.2	(NA)
United Kingdom...........	9.8	12.0	12.0	11.1	10.9	81.7	84.4	83.7	82.4	81.9

NA Not available. [1] Data are estimated or provisional. [2] See footnote 1, Table 1367.

Source: Organisation for Economic Co-operation and Development (OECD), 2024, OECD Data Explorer, Health: Health expenditure and financing, "Health expenditure and financing" ©, <data-explorer.oecd.org>, accessed July 2024.

Table 1367. Physicians and Inpatient Hospital Care—Selected Countries: 2000 to 2022

[Data may be estimated or provisional and subject to breaks in data series or difference in methodology. See source for details]

Country	Practicing physicians per 1,000 population				Hospital beds per 1,000 population				Average length of stay (days)			
	2000	2010	2020	2022	2000	2010	2020	2022	2000	2010	2020	2022
United States.........	2.3	2.4	2.6	2.7	3.5	3.1	2.8	2.8	5.8	5.4	5.7	6.0
Australia................	2.5	(NA)	3.9	4.1	4.0	3.8	(NA)	(NA)	6.1	5.0	4.6	(NA)
Austria..................	3.9	4.8	5.3	5.4	8.0	7.7	7.1	6.7	7.8	6.6	6.4	6.2
Belgium.................	2.8	2.9	3.5	3.6	6.7	6.1	5.6	5.5	8.2	7.2	6.7	6.0
Bulgaria................	3.4	3.8	4.3	4.5	7.4	6.6	7.8	8.2	(NA)	(NA)	4.9	4.7
Canada..................	2.0	2.3	2.7	2.8	3.8	2.8	2.6	2.5	7.2	7.7	7.7	8.0
Croatia..................	2.3	2.9	3.5	4.0	5.9	5.8	5.7	5.8	9.2	7.2	6.6	6.3
Czechia.................	3.4	3.6	4.1	4.3	7.8	7.3	6.5	6.5	7.9	6.7	5.8	5.7
Estonia.................	2.9	3.2	3.5	3.5	7.0	5.3	4.5	4.2	7.3	5.5	6.1	6.2
France...................	3.0	3.0	3.2	3.2	8.0	6.4	5.7	5.5	5.6	5.8	5.7	5.6
Germany................	3.3	3.7	4.5	4.6	9.1	8.3	7.8	7.7	10.1	8.1	7.4	7.5
Hungary.................	2.7	2.9	3.1	3.5	8.2	7.2	6.8	6.7	7.1	5.8	5.3	5.1
Iceland..................	3.4	3.6	4.3	4.4	(NA)	3.6	2.8	(NA)	(NA)	5.4	5.6	5.6
Ireland..................	(NA)	(NA)	3.5	3.4	(NA)	2.7	2.9	2.9	6.4	6.0	5.7	6.0
Israel[1]................	3.5	3.0	3.3	3.5	3.8	3.2	2.9	3.0	5.4	5.0	4.9	4.8
Italy.....................	3.4	3.8	4.0	4.2	4.7	3.6	3.2	3.1	7.0	6.7	7.5	7.2
Japan....................	1.9	2.2	2.6	2.7	14.7	13.5	12.6	12.6	24.8	18.2	16.4	16.1
Korea, South..........	1.3	2.0	2.5	2.6	4.7	8.7	12.7	12.8	11.0	10.0	7.8	7.2
Latvia...................	2.9	3.1	3.3	3.4	8.8	5.7	5.3	5.0	8.5	6.2	5.9	5.8
Lithuania...............	3.6	4.0	4.5	4.4	8.8	7.2	6.0	5.7	9.2	7.1	6.7	6.3
Mexico..................	1.6	2.0	2.4	2.6	1.1	1.1	1.0	1.0	(NA)	(NA)	(NA)	(NA)
Netherlands...........	(NA)	(NA)	3.9	3.9	4.9	4.1	2.9	2.5	9.0	5.6	5.2	(NA)
New Zealand.........	2.2	2.6	3.4	3.6	(NA)	2.8	2.5	2.6	4.4	6.1	4.6	(NA)
Norway..................	3.4	4.1	4.7	4.9	(NA)	4.3	3.4	3.4	6.0	6.3	6.0	5.9
Poland...................	2.2	2.2	3.3	3.5	(NA)	6.5	6.1	6.1	(NA)	7.3	6.8	6.4
Romania................	1.9	2.5	3.3	3.7	7.7	6.7	7.1	7.3	(NA)	6.5	6.2	5.6
Slovenia................	2.2	2.4	3.3	3.4	5.4	4.6	4.3	4.1	7.1	5.5	6.6	6.4
Spain....................	3.1	3.8	4.6	4.3	3.7	3.1	3.0	3.0	7.1	6.4	6.4	6.3
Sweden.................	3.0	3.8	4.3	(NA)	3.6	2.7	2.1	1.9	6.6	5.8	5.3	5.5
Switzerland...........	(NA)	3.8	4.4	4.5	6.3	5.2	4.5	4.4	9.3	8.0	7.1	6.9
United Kingdom.......	2.0	2.7	3.0	3.2	4.1	2.9	2.4	2.5	(NA)	6.1	6.5	7.5

NA Not available. [1] The statistical data for Israel are supplied by and under the responsibility of the relevant Israeli authorities. The use of such data by the OECD is without prejudice as to the status of the Golan Heights, East Jerusalem and Israeli settlements in the West Bank under the terms of international law.

Source: Organisation for Economic Co-Operation and Development (OECD), 2024, OECD Data Explorer, Health: Healthcare use and Healthcare resources and equipment, "Physicians," "Healthcare utilisation," and "Hospital beds by function of healthcare" ©, <data-explorer.oecd.org>; accessed July 2024.

Table 1368. Gross National Income (GNI) by Country: 2022 and 2023

[102,463,117 represents $102,463,117,000,000. GNI is the sum of value added by all resident producers, plus any product taxes (less subsidies) not included in the valuation of output, plus net receipts of primary income from abroad]

Country	Gross national income [1]				GNI on purchasing power parity basis [2]			
	Total (mil. dol.)		Per capita (dol.)		Total (mil. dol.)		Per capita (dol.)	
	2022	2023	2022	2023	2022	2023	2022	2023
World [3]	**102,463,117**	**106,025,026**	**12,886**	**13,212**	**171,145,613**	**183,412,501**	**21,523**	**22,855**
United States	**25,526,912**	**26,894,543**	**76,590**	**80,300**	**25,926,000**	**27,525,100**	**77,790**	**82,190**
Algeria	201,445	226,263	4,490	4,960	702,938	765,521	15,650	16,790
Angola	66,533	78,319	1,870	2,130	260,439	268,199	7,320	7,310
Argentina	535,914	584,110	11,590	12,520	1,317,042	1,339,423	28,490	28,710
Australia	1,582,214	1,681,999	60,820	63,140	1,636,205	1,764,943	62,900	66,260
Austria	503,844	502,931	55,720	55,070	641,336	671,450	70,930	73,520
Bangladesh	483,371	493,932	2,820	2,860	1,486,874	1,630,532	8,690	9,430
Belgium	629,745	644,688	53,890	54,530	809,917	851,159	69,310	71,990
Brazil	1,774,307	1,962,339	8,240	9,070	4,055,711	4,325,589	18,840	19,990
Bulgaria	86,292	92,955	13,350	14,460	221,776	240,389	34,300	37,380
Canada	2,075,404	2,162,633	53,300	53,930	2,384,385	2,433,892	61,230	60,700
Chile	302,413	310,628	15,430	15,820	589,663	620,096	30,080	31,590
China	18,206,073	18,899,260	12,890	13,400	31,576,043	34,388,534	22,360	24,380
Colombia	343,773	357,640	6,630	6,870	1,068,671	1,115,520	20,600	21,420
Croatia	75,750	79,659	19,650	20,670	163,887	177,056	42,510	45,950
Czechia	278,991	294,826	26,140	27,110	526,672	558,628	49,350	51,370
Denmark	434,002	436,283	73,520	73,360	475,382	472,114	80,530	79,390
Dominican Republic	101,864	109,970	9,070	9,700	263,190	277,248	23,440	24,460
Ecuador	117,439	118,390	6,520	6,510	267,765	282,205	14,880	15,510
Egypt	455,137	439,247	4,100	3,900	1,906,999	2,028,160	17,180	17,990
Ethiopia	126,125	142,605	1,020	1,130	354,799	392,414	2,880	3,100
Finland	304,106	298,118	54,730	53,390	351,043	362,670	63,180	64,940
France	3,078,221	3,072,464	45,290	45,070	3,984,079	4,235,079	58,610	62,130
Germany	4,527,641	4,559,133	54,030	53,970	5,799,414	6,092,387	69,210	72,110
Ghana	79,663	79,823	2,380	2,340	234,680	251,598	7,010	7,370
Greece	227,407	233,935	21,810	22,580	401,630	423,606	38,520	40,880
Guatemala	92,770	98,165	5,340	5,580	225,999	243,226	13,020	13,820
Hong Kong, China	396,683	415,973	54,000	55,200	536,859	586,896	73,080	77,880
Hungary	183,691	190,074	19,050	19,820	408,116	428,173	42,320	44,650
India	3,394,542	3,630,237	2,400	2,540	12,858,238	14,324,038	9,070	10,030
Indonesia	1,260,912	1,352,588	4,580	4,870	3,870,444	4,221,517	14,050	15,210
Iran	352,567	417,389	3,980	4,680	1,466,983	1,596,261	16,570	17,900
Iraq	242,086	254,601	5,440	5,600	629,742	638,811	14,150	14,040
Ireland	408,767	423,059	79,730	80,390	492,740	519,143	96,100	98,650
Israel	527,023	536,858	55,140	55,020	493,986	520,397	51,690	53,340
Italy	2,261,746	2,244,585	38,370	38,200	3,324,775	3,446,469	56,410	58,650
Japan	5,324,575	4,859,878	42,550	39,030	6,254,021	6,554,254	49,980	52,640
Kazakhstan	188,688	217,778	9,610	10,940	637,245	704,870	32,450	35,420
Kenya	117,313	116,406	2,170	2,110	313,981	342,703	5,810	6,220
Korea, South	1,868,327	1,835,476	36,160	35,490	2,706,619	2,846,253	52,380	55,040
Kuwait	173,890	198,885	40,730	46,140	273,945	291,933	64,170	67,730
Malaysia	401,461	410,754	11,830	11,970	1,149,763	1,239,317	33,880	36,120
Mexico	1,378,549	1,554,336	10,810	12,100	2,972,064	3,207,460	23,310	24,970
Morocco	139,595	142,289	3,670	3,700	345,133	368,785	9,070	9,600
Netherlands	1,066,103	1,084,790	60,230	60,670	1,307,176	1,390,099	73,850	77,750
New Zealand	248,327	253,874	48,530	48,610	259,817	275,518	50,770	52,750
Nigeria	471,252	432,497	2,160	1,930	1,290,242	1,386,820	5,900	6,200
Norway	528,089	565,538	96,770	102,460	698,614	600,502	128,020	108,790
Oman	91,616	100,047	20,020	21,540	181,921	191,738	39,750	41,280
Pakistan	369,102	360,729	1,570	1,500	1,421,254	1,468,453	6,030	6,110
Panama	75,145	80,480	17,050	18,010	153,153	170,288	34,740	38,110
Peru	231,758	240,295	6,810	6,990	519,360	544,903	15,250	15,860
Philippines	456,997	496,166	3,950	4,230	1,221,448	1,400,619	10,570	11,940
Poland	698,084	723,682	18,960	19,730	1,652,620	1,738,300	44,880	47,380
Portugal	270,087	276,490	25,950	26,270	456,708	503,638	43,870	47,850
Puerto Rico	79,715	80,926	24,760	25,240	101,376	105,765	31,480	32,990
Romania	295,020	317,743	15,490	16,670	793,992	888,342	41,690	46,620
Russia	1,879,408	2,084,758	12,810	14,250	5,884,375	6,366,121	40,110	43,510
Saudi Arabia	1,001,225	1,059,856	27,500	28,690	1,992,358	2,042,886	54,720	55,290
Singapore	377,485	417,722	66,970	70,590	646,129	702,498	114,620	118,710
Slovakia	119,958	123,676	22,080	22,790	219,305	236,046	40,370	43,500
South Africa	406,039	407,576	6,780	6,750	899,050	944,348	15,010	15,630
Spain	1,533,031	1,556,447	32,090	32,180	2,337,161	2,535,604	48,920	52,420
Sri Lanka	80,336	77,923	3,620	3,540	306,326	308,229	13,810	13,990
Sweden	670,158	649,620	63,900	61,650	747,021	769,090	71,230	72,990
Switzerland	837,997	842,132	95,490	95,160	780,283	797,154	88,910	90,080
Tanzania	75,955	79,293	1,200	1,210	234,112	255,069	3,690	3,900
Thailand	518,837	515,549	7,240	7,180	1,546,858	1,642,525	21,570	22,880
Turkey	903,983	994,012	10,640	11,650	3,227,873	3,729,107	37,980	43,700
Ukraine	151,668	174,919	4,280	5,070	599,043	640,411	16,920	18,560
United Arab Emirates	464,105	507,149	49,160	53,290	741,392	797,034	78,530	83,750
United Kingdom	3,297,427	3,266,990	48,640	47,800	3,866,883	3,974,003	57,040	58,140
Uzbekistan	78,380	86,005	2,200	2,360	325,930	351,135	9,140	9,640
Vietnam	394,875	412,944	4,020	4,180	1,312,689	1,423,576	13,370	14,400

[1] Gross national income calculated using the World Bank Atlas conversion factor; for details, see source. [2] For explanation of purchasing power parity (PPP), see headnote, Table 1369. [3] Includes other countries not shown separately.

Source: The World Bank, Washington, DC, "World Development Indicators" database ©, <databank.worldbank.org/source/world-development-indicators>, accessed August 2024.

Table 1369. Real Gross Domestic Product (GDP) Per Capita and Per Employed Person by Country: 1960 to 2023

[U.S. figures based on the System of National Income and Product Accounts (NIPA) from the Bureau of Economic Analysis. Data for all other countries are based on the 1993 or 2008 United Nations System of National Accounts (SNA). Per capita data based on total resident population. Real GDP is a macroeconomic measure of the size of an economy adjusted for price changes and inflation. Employment data include people serving in the armed forces. Real dollars are calculated based on 2023 Purchasing Power Parities (PPPs). PPPs are currency conversion rates used to convert GDP expressed in different currencies to a common value (U.S. dollars in this case). A PPP for a given country is the number of national currency units needed to buy the specific basket of goods and services that one dollar will buy in the United States. See text, this section]

Country	1960	1970	1980	1990	2000	2010	2015	2017	2018	2019	2020	2021	2022	2023
REAL GDP PER CAPITA (2023 U.S. dollars)														
United States	23,780	31,868	39,053	49,253	61,084	66,368	71,668	73,758	75,547	77,059	74,627	78,831	80,062	81,695
Canada	20,329	28,169	36,919	42,352	50,644	54,997	58,245	59,237	60,009	60,282	56,633	59,285	60,438	60,313
Australia	21,011	28,407	32,743	38,879	48,744	57,054	60,434	61,567	62,378	62,574	60,464	63,761	65,456	63,932
Japan	8,090	19,712	27,743	40,038	44,294	46,459	49,319	50,593	50,987	50,860	48,909	50,418	51,127	52,594
South Korea	2,183	3,857	7,322	15,492	28,108	42,100	47,528	50,134	51,368	52,338	51,896	54,225	55,768	56,651
Singapore	7,086	13,727	27,376	45,658	75,624	115,588	139,014	148,107	152,222	153,047	146,469	162,975	165,641	166,335
Austria	17,691	26,455	37,343	45,561	56,828	63,417	64,758	66,267	67,547	68,218	63,413	65,845	68,237	67,076
Belgium	17,610	26,878	36,647	43,561	52,786	58,854	60,678	61,887	62,710	63,769	60,125	64,029	65,429	65,871
Czechia	(NA)	17,779	25,070	28,816	30,762	41,142	44,636	47,922	49,294	50,583	47,662	49,368	50,574	50,335
Denmark	22,440	32,305	39,064	47,859	59,981	62,322	64,866	67,870	68,874	69,626	67,787	72,129	73,447	74,306
Finland	14,823	22,784	30,807	40,283	48,789	56,102	55,112	58,176	58,754	59,415	57,920	59,448	60,075	59,141
France	16,894	26,057	34,211	41,407	48,797	51,768	53,200	54,576	55,320	56,085	51,668	54,804	55,963	56,160
Germany	21,866	30,759	40,053	45,203	53,288	58,881	62,922	65,275	65,717	66,274	63,686	65,673	66,379	65,598
Ireland	10,479	15,171	20,900	28,935	44,793	45,837	50,506	52,588	55,003	56,570	53,092	55,451	57,457	57,607
Italy	16,296	26,770	36,220	44,935	52,879	51,926	49,844	51,525	52,111	52,492	48,015	52,492	54,468	55,125
Netherlands	21,068	30,811	37,963	44,792	58,255	63,923	65,077	67,676	68,868	69,757	66,674	70,434	72,786	72,145
Norway	19,607	27,292	40,935	50,822	69,040	74,089	76,106	77,588	77,716	78,060	76,618	79,186	80,834	80,003
Spain	8,307	17,090	24,888	32,602	42,032	45,129	45,240	47,874	48,763	49,333	43,592	46,407	48,793	49,384
Sweden	20,965	31,025	35,806	42,400	50,429	59,324	63,219	64,484	64,982	65,604	63,718	67,230	68,553	68,096
United Kingdom	18,821	23,961	29,254	37,932	47,218	51,334	54,552	56,273	56,723	57,343	51,184	55,670	57,853	57,448
REAL GDP PER EMPLOYED PERSON (2023 U.S. dollars)														
United States	61,629	78,420	86,755	100,714	123,871	145,397	152,183	153,918	156,348	157,881	163,679	167,300	165,795	168,599
Canada	55,642	74,620	82,662	89,940	105,665	110,638	116,288	117,972	119,641	119,377	119,616	119,926	119,770	118,194
Australia	52,179	65,472	74,954	82,546	101,857	111,785	120,126	121,813	121,515	120,963	117,920	123,818	124,546	123,395
Japan	15,971	37,593	53,984	76,568	85,638	90,694	95,614	96,023	94,972	93,751	90,324	92,714	93,458	94,877
South Korea	7,968	12,860	20,289	36,519	62,112	86,807	92,622	96,351	98,792	99,889	99,986	102,882	102,502	102,784
Singapore	23,960	43,846	60,400	96,038	130,517	159,004	166,367	178,634	183,613	183,167	179,810	200,751	199,002	191,807
Austria	36,478	60,900	80,920	99,474	121,960	130,142	131,166	132,859	133,821	134,325	127,438	130,211	132,990	130,666
Belgium	45,919	69,507	95,559	112,893	131,690	142,755	148,181	148,276	148,754	149,692	141,659	148,624	149,989	150,832
Czechia	(NA)	34,692	49,671	55,037	64,697	85,120	90,348	94,442	96,200	98,873	95,063	98,064	98,893	97,844
Denmark	48,706	65,757	79,565	93,407	116,232	124,026	130,307	134,042	134,715	134,784	132,576	138,381	136,955	137,530
Finland	29,815	45,974	62,389	81,377	109,810	120,615	119,677	125,086	123,414	123,121	122,657	123,453	120,906	119,003
France	39,051	63,466	83,271	101,919	115,905	125,174	129,122	131,181	132,313	133,153	123,134	127,470	127,233	126,771
Germany	42,741	63,446	81,009	90,359	108,579	115,145	119,177	121,909	121,417	121,612	117,898	121,976	120,712	120,712
Ireland	24,056	36,348	52,585	74,822	96,228	108,761	115,573	115,397	118,824	120,316	117,462	116,580	115,466	113,735
Italy	38,971	71,844	95,364	112,416	130,807	125,388	122,504	123,036	123,034	122,986	114,407	122,827	125,473	124,361
Netherlands	52,598	71,813	88,760	98,465	113,102	120,979	125,160	126,609	126,141	125,734	121,340	126,361	126,847	125,073
Norway	46,339	65,100	86,387	105,266	133,966	141,970	145,786	149,028	147,896	147,237	147,646	151,679	150,380	149,170
Spain	20,608	43,050	73,737	91,035	103,316	109,084	114,979	116,387	116,480	115,735	107,293	111,615	114,974	114,212
Sweden	43,356	63,759	70,256	79,736	105,206	125,358	130,366	130,793	131,224	133,051	131,944	138,463	138,393	136,153
United Kingdom	40,777	53,652	65,669	81,157	101,622	110,716	113,934	116,336	116,619	117,216	106,018	115,348	118,767	118,217

NA Not available.

Source: The Conference Board, New York, NY, "Total Economy Database™," May 2024 ©. Reproduced with permission from The Conference Board, Inc. © 2024, The Conference Board, Inc.

Table 1370. Sectoral Contributions to Gross Value Added by Selected Country: 2021 and 2022

[In percent. According to the 2008 System of National Accounts (SNA) and the International Standard Industrial Classification (ISIC), Revision 4 (2008), with some exceptions, value added is estimated at basic prices and includes financial intermediation services indirectly measured (FISIM). Value added represents an industry's contribution to national GDP and is calculated as the difference between production and intermediate inputs. Value added comprises labor costs, consumption of fixed capital, indirect taxes less subsidies, and net operating surplus and mixed income. Selected data are estimated or provisional; see source for details]

Country	Agriculture [1]		Industry [2]				Services	
			Total		Manufacturing			
	2021	2022	2021	2022	2021	2022	2021	2022
United States [3]	1.0	(NA)	14.4	(NA)	11.1	(NA)	80.5	(NA)
Austria	1.4	1.5	22.1	21.9	18.9	17.7	69.5	69.3
Belgium	0.7	0.7	16.3	17.1	13.5	14.1	77.6	76.9
Chile [4]	3.9	3.9	28.1	28.4	9.5	10.6	61.5	61.3
China [4]	7.6	7.7	32.6	32.8	(NA)	(NA)	53.0	52.8
Czechia	1.9	2.3	25.9	26.6	21.5	21.3	66.8	65.6
Denmark	1.1	0.9	17.4	18.7	14.6	14.6	76.2	75.5
Finland	2.8	2.7	20.6	22.0	16.9	18.0	69.5	68.4
France	1.7	2.0	12.5	12.7	10.3	10.7	80.1	79.9
Germany	0.8	1.0	24.6	24.0	20.9	20.4	69.4	69.3
Greece	4.2	4.3	15.5	17.2	10.0	10.4	78.5	76.6
Hungary	4.1	3.7	22.4	22.5	19.8	20.1	67.3	67.3
Indonesia	13.8	13.0	30.7	33.1	20.1	19.2	44.6	43.7
Ireland	1.0	1.2	38.0	40.1	36.6	38.9	58.5	56.3
Italy	2.1	2.1	20.6	20.8	17.3	17.3	72.1	71.7
Japan [5]	1.0	1.0	23.8	21.9	21.0	19.4	69.5	71.9
Korea, South	2.0	1.8	30.0	29.0	28.0	28.0	62.4	63.5
Mexico	4.0	4.1	28.1	28.7	22.3	22.7	61.8	60.8
Netherlands	1.9	1.8	14.7	15.9	12.1	11.6	78.2	77.3
Norway	1.8	1.8	36.2	48.4	6.2	5.3	56.1	45.1
Poland	2.6	3.1	25.9	26.4	19.9	20.0	65.1	64.3
Portugal	2.5	2.1	17.6	17.1	14.3	14.1	75.3	76.3
Slovakia	2.0	2.1	25.3	22.1	21.6	20.3	65.9	68.4
Spain	3.0	2.6	16.8	17.4	12.5	12.5	74.5	74.6
Sweden	1.3	1.2	19.4	20.4	15.2	15.8	72.8	71.8
Switzerland	0.6	0.6	21.3	20.7	19.7	18.9	73.0	73.8
Turkey	6.2	7.2	29.2	29.5	24.9	24.7	59.0	57.8
United Kingdom	0.8	0.9	12.7	12.4	9.7	9.3	80.7	80.5

NA Not available. [1] Includes forestry, fishing, and hunting sectors. [2] Includes energy; does not include construction. [3] Value added is estimated at factor cost for U.S. [4] Value added is estimated at producer's prices. [5] Value added is estimated approximately at market prices for Japan. According to 1993 System of National Accounts (SNA).

Source: Organisation for Economic Co-operation and Development (OECD), 2024, OECD Data Explorer, Economy: National Accounts, "NAAG Chapter 4: Production" ©, <data-explorer.oecd.org>, accessed July 2024.

Table 1371. Index of Industrial Production by Country: 2000 to 2023

[Annual averages of monthly data. Industrial production indexes generally measure output in the manufacturing, mining, electric, gas, and water utilities sectors. Excludes construction. Minus sign (-) indicates decrease]

Country	Index (2015=100)								Annual percent change			
	2000	2010	2018	2019	2020	2021	2022	2023	2019 to 2020	2020 to 2021	2021 to 2022	2022 to 2023
United States	91.7	90.8	102.3	101.6	94.3	98.5	101.8	102.0	-7.2	4.4	3.4	0.2
Australia	67.2	82.8	108.9	111.7	110.6	110.3	109.5	110.3	-0.9	-0.3	-0.8	0.7
Belgium	71.2	97.0	108.7	114.0	110.0	138.1	137.0	126.8	-3.5	25.6	-0.8	-7.5
Brazil	83.8	112.2	96.9	95.8	91.5	95.1	94.5	94.6	-4.5	3.9	-0.7	0.1
Canada	96.8	89.9	107.0	107.0	98.7	103.5	107.5	107.5	-7.7	4.9	3.9	-0.1
Colombia	77.5	93.4	106.5	107.9	99.2	115.2	127.3	121.4	-8.1	16.2	10.5	-4.7
Croatia	85.6	105.1	105.7	106.3	103.4	109.9	111.2	110.9	-2.7	6.2	1.2	-0.3
Czechia	60.5	87.1	113.5	113.2	105.1	112.4	115.2	114.3	-7.2	6.9	2.5	-0.8
Denmark	106.8	96.8	107.6	110.5	104.6	115.0	129.3	140.8	-5.3	9.9	12.4	8.9
Estonia	45.5	76.0	112.7	120.5	116.9	132.4	134.8	118.2	-3.0	13.3	1.8	-12.3
France	108.5	99.9	103.4	103.8	92.9	98.1	97.8	98.0	-10.5	5.6	-0.2	0.2
Germany	82.7	91.4	105.0	101.6	91.8	96.0	95.8	93.9	-8.8	4.7	-0.4	-2.3
Greece	140.2	113.2	108.8	107.9	105.8	116.8	119.8	122.4	-2.0	10.4	2.5	2.3
Hungary	58.1	82.2	109.8	116.0	108.1	118.5	125.4	119.3	-6.9	9.7	5.8	-4.9
India	42.9	87.9	114.5	115.3	102.7	115.7	121.0	128.0	-11.0	12.7	4.6	5.8
Ireland	43.5	63.8	97.0	103.2	119.5	153.2	179.9	168.3	15.7	28.3	17.4	-6.4
Israel [1]	70.1	91.6	104.0	108.1	110.8	114.8	127.3	125.6	2.5	3.6	10.8	-1.3
Netherlands	95.9	106.9	103.1	102.4	99.0	103.6	105.9	98.1	-3.3	4.7	2.2	-7.4
New Zealand	87.2	97.2	104.7	106.2	101.6	104.6	100.8	97.6	-4.3	3.0	-3.6	-3.2
Norway	121.6	102.5	96.7	92.5	99.3	101.4	101.0	101.3	7.4	2.1	-0.4	0.3
Poland	47.5	83.4	116.1	120.9	119.4	136.8	150.8	149.0	-1.3	14.5	10.3	-1.2
Portugal	117.0	102.1	104.2	101.8	93.6	97.3	97.5	94.4	-8.0	3.9	0.2	-3.2
Slovakia	34.4	81.8	103.2	96.6	88.1	97.5	93.1	94.5	-8.8	10.7	-4.5	1.5
Slovenia	78.3	93.4	120.7	124.5	117.9	130.0	131.5	124.1	-5.2	10.2	1.2	-5.6
Spain	124.5	106.3	105.4	105.8	96.0	103.0	105.5	104.1	-9.3	7.3	2.5	-1.4
Sweden	101.2	103.1	108.9	111.5	106.6	114.4	116.7	116.5	-4.3	7.3	2.0	-0.2
Switzerland	83.1	95.6	111.9	116.8	113.0	123.3	130.4	131.5	-3.2	9.1	5.7	0.9
Turkey	43.8	69.4	114.0	113.3	115.8	134.9	141.6	143.9	2.2	16.5	5.0	1.6
United Kingdom	98.1	95.8	103.5	105.3	107.8	103.6	100.0	99.6	2.3	-3.9	-3.4	-0.4

[1] See footnote 1, Table 1367.

Source: Organisation for Economic Co-operation and Development (OECD), 2024, OECD Data Explorer, Economy: Short-term economic statistics, "Key short-term economic indicators" ©, <data-explorer.oecd.org>, accessed July 2024.

Table 1372. Annual Percent Change in Labor Productivity and Hours Worked by Country: 2010 to 2023

[Annual percent change for period shown. Labor productivity growth refers to the growth in gross domestic product (GDP) per hour worked. Data are derived from The Conference Board Total Economy Database. Regional labor productivity growth rates are aggregated using shares in nominal Purchasing Power Parities (PPP) converted GDP; regional hours growth is weighted using total hours shares. Growth rates are the averages of yearly growth rates. Minus sign (-) indicates decrease]

Country	Labor productivity					Total hours worked				
	2010 to 2019	2020	2021	2022	2023	2010 to 2019	2020	2021	2022	2023
Advanced economies [1]	1.3	2.5	1.4	0.0	0.4	0.8	-6.4	4.2	2.7	1.2
United States	**1.0**	**5.0**	**1.1**	**-1.2**	**1.0**	**1.0**	**-6.8**	**4.6**	**3.2**	**1.5**
Japan	1.1	-1.2	2.4	0.7	1.7	1.1	-3.0	0.2	0.3	0.2
European Union (EU-14, old) [2]	0.9	1.6	-0.4	-0.1	-0.6	0.4	-7.9	6.1	3.4	1.3
Austria	0.7	2.3	-0.5	2.3	-1.7	0.7	-8.7	4.7	2.5	0.9
Belgium	0.6	3.2	-0.9	-1.3	0.2	0.6	-8.3	7.9	4.4	1.2
Denmark	1.6	0.6	0.7	-1.3	1.4	1.6	-3.0	6.1	4.1	0.5
Finland	0.9	0.1	0.8	-1.2	-0.6	0.9	-2.4	2.0	2.6	-0.5
France	0.9	0.3	-1.7	-1.9	-0.3	0.9	-7.8	8.3	4.5	1.0
Germany	1.2	1.2	0.6	0.5	-0.7	1.2	-4.9	2.6	1.3	0.4
Greece	-1.7	2.8	0.0	1.6	0.3	-1.7	-11.8	8.4	3.9	1.7
Ireland	1.0	5.0	-1.2	-2.7	0.0	1.0	-9.7	6.6	8.6	3.8
Italy	0.4	3.1	-1.7	-0.2	-1.4	0.4	-11.7	10.2	4.2	2.3
Luxembourg	-0.1	3.2	0.0	-1.4	-3.5	-0.1	-4.0	7.2	2.8	2.5
Netherlands	0.4	0.1	2.8	0.4	-1.0	0.4	-4.0	3.3	3.9	1.1
Portugal	0.8	0.3	3.0	3.1	1.1	0.8	-8.6	2.6	3.7	1.2
Spain	1.0	-0.2	-0.8	1.8	0.6	1.0	-11.0	7.2	3.9	1.9
Sweden	1.1	1.1	3.5	0.4	-1.4	1.1	-3.2	2.6	2.3	1.2
European Union (EU-13, new) [3]	2.9	0.4	2.3	1.8	0.7	0.2	-3.9	4.1	2.6	-0.1
Bulgaria	2.7	0.8	6.5	4.4	0.8	2.7	-4.7	1.1	-0.5	1.0
Croatia	1.9	-7.2	11.6	4.5	0.9	1.9	-1.4	1.3	2.4	2.2
Cyprus	0.8	3.1	1.9	0.9	0.7	0.8	-6.3	7.8	4.1	1.7
Czechia	1.8	2.4	0.4	-2.1	-0.6	1.8	-7.7	3.1	4.6	0.3
Estonia	2.6	5.3	-0.8	-5.0	-4.5	2.6	-6.0	8.1	4.8	1.6
Hungary	1.3	0.5	3.8	2.4	0.2	1.3	-5.0	3.1	2.1	-1.1
Latvia	2.8	2.2	7.9	-1.8	0.0	2.8	-5.6	-1.1	4.9	-0.3
Lithuania	3.1	6.1	3.4	-2.7	-2.8	3.1	-5.7	2.8	5.3	2.5
Malta	2.0	-3.3	9.2	4.1	1.4	2.0	-5.0	3.0	3.9	4.2
Poland	3.6	-1.3	0.9	2.4	0.7	3.6	-0.8	6.0	3.1	-0.5
Romania	3.6	1.0	1.1	3.8	3.1	3.6	-4.6	4.6	0.3	-0.9
Slovakia	2.5	6.1	4.7	-1.7	0.6	2.5	-8.8	0.0	3.6	1.0
Slovenia	1.8	0.8	2.8	-1.5	0.0	1.8	-5.0	5.3	4.0	1.6
European Union (EU-27, enlarged) [4]	1.2	1.0	0.2	0.3	-0.3	0.4	-6.9	5.6	3.2	0.9
Addenda:										
Other advanced economies	2.2	4.1	2.7	0.8	-0.6	0.9	-5.7	3.0	2.1	2.1
Australia	1.2	-0.6	5.2	1.2	-0.8	1.2	-1.6	0.3	2.6	2.9
Canada	1.0	7.9	-4.9	-0.8	-2.4	1.0	-12.0	10.7	4.6	3.5
Hong Kong	2.3	1.5	4.8	-1.9	1.8	2.3	-7.9	1.6	-1.9	1.4
Iceland	1.0	-1.3	4.1	1.7	0.0	1.0	-5.8	1.1	7.1	4.1
Israel	1.9	6.8	2.0	-0.7	0.1	1.9	-7.8	7.2	7.2	3.0
New Zealand	0.8	-0.4	5.4	-1.3	-2.2	0.8	-0.8	0.6	3.6	3.0
Norway	0.5	0.9	1.6	-0.8	-0.3	0.5	-2.2	2.3	3.9	0.8
Singapore	2.9	2.6	7.5	-0.7	-2.4	2.9	-6.3	2.0	4.6	3.6
South Korea	2.9	3.2	2.5	1.2	0.4	2.9	-3.8	1.8	1.4	1.0
Switzerland	1.2	1.7	2.6	1.2	-1.5	1.2	-3.7	2.8	1.3	2.3
Taiwan	3.2	8.2	8.1	3.9	-0.1	3.2	-4.5	-1.4	-1.5	0.9
United Kingdom	0.6	0.2	1.7	0.0	0.0	0.6	-10.5	6.8	4.0	0.1

[1] "Advanced" includes the U.S., EU-27, Japan, and "other advanced" economies. [2] Referring to membership of the European Union until April 30, 2004 (excluding the United Kingdom). [3] Referring to new membership of the European Union as of January 1, 2007. [4] Referring to all 27 current members of the European Union. See text, this section.

Source: The Conference Board, "Total Economy Database™," May 2024 ©. Reproduced with permission from The Conference Board, Inc. © 2024, The Conference Board, Inc.

Table 1373. Comparative Price Levels—Selected OECD Countries: May 2024

[Purchasing power parities (PPPs) are rates of currency conversion that eliminate the differences in price levels between countries. Comparative price levels are defined as the ratios of PPPs for private final consumption to exchange rates. The PPPs are given in national currency units per U.S. dollar. This table should be read vertically. Each column shows the number of specified monetary units needed in each of the countries listed to buy the same representative basket of consumer goods and services. In each case the representative basket costs a hundred units in the country whose currency is specified. For example, in May 2024, an item that costs $1.00 in the United States would cost $0.96 (U.S. dollars) in Australia]

Country	United States (USD)	Australia (AUD)	Canada (CAD)	Chile (Chilean peso)	France (EUR)	Germany (EUR)	Italy (EUR)	Japan (JPY)	Korea, South (KRW)	Mexico (MXN)	Spain (EUR)	Turkey (TRY)	United Kingdom (GBP)
United States.	100	104	111	182	126	126	139	151	149	154	145	303	106
Australia [1]	96	100	107	175	120	121	133	145	143	148	139	291	101
Austria.	82	85	91	149	103	103	114	123	122	126	118	248	86
Belgium.	83	86	92	151	104	104	115	125	124	128	120	251	87
Canada.	90	94	100	164	113	113	125	136	134	138	130	272	95
Chile.	55	57	61	100	69	69	76	83	82	84	79	166	58
Colombia.	44	46	49	81	56	56	62	67	66	68	64	135	47
Costa Rica.	66	69	74	121	83	83	92	100	99	102	96	201	70
Czechia.	63	66	71	116	80	80	88	96	95	98	92	192	67
Denmark.	104	108	116	189	130	131	144	157	155	160	150	315	110
Estonia.	74	77	82	135	93	93	103	112	110	114	107	224	78
Finland.	91	95	102	166	115	115	127	138	136	141	132	277	96
France.	80	83	89	145	100	100	111	120	119	123	115	242	84
Germany.	79	83	88	145	100	100	110	120	118	122	115	241	84
Greece.	63	66	70	115	79	79	87	95	94	97	91	191	66
Hungary.	56	58	62	101	70	70	77	84	83	86	81	169	59
Iceland.	119	124	132	216	149	150	165	179	177	183	172	360	125
Ireland.	104	108	116	190	131	131	144	157	155	160	151	315	110
Israel [2]	103	108	115	188	130	130	144	156	154	159	150	314	109
Italy.	72	75	80	131	90	91	100	109	107	111	104	218	76
Japan.	66	69	74	121	83	83	92	100	99	102	96	201	70
Korea, South.	67	70	75	122	84	84	93	101	100	103	97	203	71
Latvia.	63	66	71	115	80	80	88	96	95	98	92	192	67
Lithuania.	58	61	65	106	73	73	81	88	87	90	84	177	61
Luxembourg.	98	102	109	178	123	123	136	148	146	151	142	297	103
Mexico.	65	68	72	118	82	82	90	98	97	100	94	197	69
Netherlands.	84	87	93	152	105	105	116	126	125	129	121	253	88
New Zealand [1]	92	96	103	168	116	116	128	139	137	142	133	280	97
Norway.	91	95	101	165	114	114	126	137	135	140	131	275	96
Poland.	51	53	57	93	64	65	71	77	76	79	74	156	54
Portugal.	64	66	71	116	80	80	88	96	95	98	92	193	67
Slovakia.	66	69	73	120	83	83	91	99	98	101	95	199	69
Slovenia.	66	69	73	120	83	83	91	99	98	101	95	200	69
Spain.	69	72	77	126	87	87	96	104	103	106	100	210	73
Sweden.	84	88	93	153	105	106	117	127	125	129	122	255	89
Switzerland.	124	130	138	227	156	157	173	188	185	191	180	377	131
Turkey.	33	34	37	60	41	42	46	50	49	51	48	100	35
United Kingdom.	95	99	106	173	119	119	132	143	141	146	137	288	100

[1] Estimates based on quarterly consumer prices. [2] The statistical data for Israel are supplied by and under the responsibility of the relevant Israeli authorities. The use of such data by the OECD is without prejudice to the status of the Golan Heights, East Jerusalem and Israeli settlements in the West Bank under the terms of international law.

Source: Organisation for Economic Co-operation and Development (OECD), 2024, OECD Data Explorer, Economy: Prices, "Monthly comparative price levels" ©, <data-explorer.oecd.org>, accessed July 2024.

Table 1374. Percent of Consumer Expenditures Spent on Food, Alcohol, and Tobacco Consumed at Home by Selected Country: 2022

Country/territory	Food [1]	Alcoholic beverages and tobacco	Country/territory	Food [1]	Alcoholic beverages and tobacco	Country/territory	Food [1]	Alcoholic beverages and tobacco
United States	**6.7**	**1.8**	Georgia	32.1	3.4	Nigeria	59.0	1.0
Algeria	37.1	1.0	Germany	11.8	3.5	Norway	12.4	4.0
Argentina	23.1	1.9	Ghana	38.3	0.6	Pakistan	39.1	1.2
Australia	10.4	4.2	Greece	18.8	5.0	Peru	26.6	2.4
Austria	10.8	3.7	Honduras	31.6	4.9	Philippines	37.9	2.0
Bahrain	13.0	0.4	Hong Kong	11.7	0.8	Poland	19.4	6.4
Bangladesh	52.7	2.1	Hungary	17.6	7.6	Portugal	17.6	3.4
Belarus	31.7	7.7	India	32.0	2.1	Romania	25.1	5.5
Belgium	13.5	3.9	Indonesia	33.7	7.4	Russia	28.9	7.3
Bolivia	29.0	2.1	Iran	28.4	0.5	Saudi Arabia	20.4	0.7
Bosnia-Herzegovina	29.2	8.3	Iraq	28.8	4.3	Serbia	22.9	8.4
Brazil	16.2	1.7	Ireland	8.2	5.6	Singapore	7.0	1.9
Bulgaria	19.1	5.3	Israel	16.0	2.8	Slovakia	20.0	5.0
Cambodia	41.4	1.9	Italy	14.6	4.2	Slovenia	14.1	4.5
Canada	9.5	3.7	Japan	16.3	2.7	South Africa	21.6	5.0
Chile	18.0	3.3	Jordan	26.1	4.5	South Korea	12.1	1.8
China	20.1	3.0	Kazakhstan	49.1	2.4	Spain	15.4	4.3
Colombia	18.5	3.5	Kenya	56.7	3.7	Sweden	12.5	3.1
Croatia	19.3	7.7	Kuwait	19.2	0.1	Switzerland	9.3	3.5
Czechia	16.4	8.2	Laos	50.5	10.8	Taiwan	14.2	2.4
Denmark	11.7	4.0	Latvia	19.1	7.4	Thailand	26.8	3.0
Dominican Republic	26.6	3.8	Lebanon	20.7	1.1	Tunisia	23.1	3.3
Ecuador	26.4	0.8	Lithuania	19.8	5.8	Turkey	25.4	3.3
Egypt	37.1	4.6	Malaysia	24.5	1.8	Ukraine	42.7	6.9
El Salvador	26.5	0.5	Mexico	25.7	3.6	United Arab Emirates	13.5	0.4
Ethiopia	39.7	3.1	Morocco	33.9	1.4	United Kingdom	8.5	3.4
Finland	11.9	5.1	Netherlands	11.8	3.0	Uruguay	18.6	1.3
France	13.6	4.1	New Zealand	12.5	4.9	Vietnam	31.1	2.1

[1] Food includes nonalcoholic beverages.

Source: U.S. Department of Agriculture, Economic Research Service, International Consumer and Food Industry Trends, "Data on expenditures on food and alcoholic beverages in selected countries," <www.ers.usda.gov/topics/international-markets-us-trade/international-consumer-and-food-industry-trends/>, accessed June 2024.

Table 1375. Gross Government Assets and Liabilities as a Percent of GDP by Country: 2010 to 2025

[Percent of nominal gross domestic product. The general government sector is a consolidation of accounts for the central, state, and local governments plus social security]

Country	General government gross financial assets as a percent of GDP				General government gross financial liabilities as a percent of GDP			
	2010	2020	2024	2025 (P)	2010	2020	2024	2025 (P)
United States	**24.7**	**33.9**	**24.8**	**24.8**	**94.9**	**131.8**	**125.4**	**129.4**
Australia	44.3	60.7	54.8	54.8	24.6	65.0	57.0	58.6
Austria	44.9	51.2	40.1	39.6	96.4	111.6	84.5	84.9
Belgium	26.8	40.3	31.5	31.5	108.8	141.4	106.7	108.3
Canada	55.8	102.1	94.3	94.3	89.6	128.8	103.9	104.1
Czechia	38.2	32.4	34.1	34.1	44.6	47.0	52.0	53.1
Denmark	56.7	71.0	53.7	55.8	53.4	59.0	32.7	33.8
Estonia	46.4	42.1	41.1	41.1	11.9	24.8	32.3	36.4
Finland	122.7	154.9	137.8	133.8	58.9	90.8	86.7	87.9
France	45.5	54.0	43.8	43.8	101.4	144.6	120.1	122.1
Germany	41.5	46.2	38.5	38.5	87.8	81.7	65.8	65.9
Greece	37.4	61.2	50.8	50.8	130.9	242.4	178.5	173.3
Hungary	25.7	35.5	29.9	29.9	86.6	97.2	82.4	82.8
Ireland	36.8	24.5	21.1	21.1	83.5	71.3	44.3	41.3
Israel [1]	5.8	4.1	3.4	3.4	69.2	70.9	66.4	67.7
Italy	25.8	32.7	26.7	26.7	125.7	185.1	153.2	154.1
Japan	79.8	113.9	123.5	123.5	181.5	240.4	239.2	238.0
Latvia	40.8	39.5	36.5	36.5	53.7	57.0	56.8	58.3
Lithuania	32.7	34.7	30.0	30.0	45.5	55.2	41.9	43.6
Luxembourg	75.4	83.1	75.0	72.0	27.2	32.9	32.1	32.6
Netherlands	35.5	35.2	27.3	27.3	69.4	70.2	51.4	51.1
New Zealand	35.3	38.5	40.8	40.8	38.7	45.9	59.2	61.8
Poland	34.6	32.2	26.0	26.0	62.3	77.7	63.2	64.2
Portugal	33.4	44.8	32.7	32.7	106.7	157.5	102.4	99.2
Slovakia	19.1	27.9	25.0	24.0	48.3	79.1	65.8	67.7
Slovenia	48.9	71.1	50.5	48.8	48.3	109.8	73.6	73.2
Spain	28.8	40.6	35.7	35.7	67.6	148.0	113.6	113.2
Sweden	70.4	91.4	78.0	75.9	47.3	53.4	41.8	41.7
Switzerland	36.9	61.6	42.0	42.0	43.1	43.9	37.0	36.8
United Kingdom	36.8	40.3	34.7	34.7	75.9	105.8	103.9	105.4

P Projected. [1] See footnote 2, Table 1373.

Source: Organisation for Economic Co-operation and Development (OECD), 2024, OECD Data Explorer, Economy: Economic outlook, "Economic Outlook 115" ©, <data-explorer.oecd.org/>, accessed August 2024.

Table 1376. Percent Distribution of Tax Receipts by Tax Type by Country: 2020 and 2022

Country	Total [1]	Taxes on income and profits [2]			Social security contributions			Taxes on goods and services [5]		
		Total [3]	Individual	Corporate	Total [4]	Employees	Employers	Total [3]	General consumption taxes [6]	Taxes on specific goods, services [7]
United States:										
2020............	100.0	46.1	41.0	5.1	24.5	11.2	12.0	17.1	8.2	6.7
2022 [8]...........	100.0	51.8	45.3	6.5	21.9	10.0	10.7	15.7	7.6	6.2
Canada:										
2020............	100.0	51.0	37.4	12.6	14.0	5.8	7.7	20.9	13.2	6.4
2022 [8]...........	100.0	50.9	36.9	12.6	14.3	6.0	7.7	21.9	13.6	6.8
Chile:										
2020............	100.0	32.3	10.2	24.3	8.0	7.7	0.3	54.8	41.1	9.4
2022 [8]...........	100.0	43.7	10.5	23.7	4.1	3.9	0.2	47.8	39.0	5.7
Czechia:										
2020............	100.0	22.9	13.5	9.4	45.4	9.5	28.9	31.0	21.3	8.4
2022 [8]...........	100.0	20.9	9.2	11.7	46.6	9.3	28.7	32.0	23.3	7.5
France:										
2020............	100.0	26.2	21.1	5.1	32.7	7.9	22.2	27.1	17.3	8.8
2022 [8]...........	100.0	27.9	21.6	6.3	32.5	7.9	22.0	26.5	17.6	8.2
Germany:										
2020............	100.0	31.3	27.0	4.3	39.7	16.8	19.0	25.7	17.2	6.9
2022 [8]...........	100.0	33.3	27.1	6.2	37.2	16.2	17.5	26.7	18.8	5.9
Greece:										
2020............	100.0	20.4	16.3	3.1	33.2	18.1	15.1	38.5	20.2	12.6
2022 [8]...........	100.0	20.3	(NA)	(NA)	29.5	(NA)	(NA)	42.3	(NA)	0.6
Italy:										
2020............	100.0	32.8	26.8	4.8	31.8	5.8	21.2	27.0	14.1	9.2
2022 [8]...........	100.0	32.8	25.5	6.7	30.6	5.7	20.5	27.5	16.6	7.2
Japan:										
2020............	100.0	30.4	18.7	11.7	40.4	18.0	18.7	20.9	14.9	4.5
2021 [9]...........	100.0	31.9	18.9	13.1	39.2	17.4	18.3	20.8	14.9	4.4
Korea, South:										
2020............	100.0	30.9	18.8	12.1	28.0	12.1	12.6	24.4	15.1	7.8
2022 [8]...........	100.0	37.4	20.5	16.8	25.6	11.2	11.7	22.7	15.3	6.3
Turkey:										
2020............	100.0	21.9	13.2	8.7	29.7	11.4	16.9	42.9	19.2	22.4
2022 [8]...........	100.0	27.7	11.4	16.3	23.8	9.2	13.6	43.9	24.2	18.9
United Kingdom:										
2020............	100.0	36.0	28.7	7.3	20.8	8.1	12.0	31.3	20.3	9.7
2022 [8]...........	100.0	37.6	28.8	8.8	20.1	7.4	12.1	30.7	20.9	8.0

NA Not available. [1] Includes property taxes, employer payroll taxes other than social security contributions, and miscellaneous taxes, not shown separately. [2] Includes taxes on capital gains. [3] Includes other taxes, not shown separately. [4] Includes contributions of self-employed persons, not shown separately. [5] Taxes on the production, extraction, sale, transfer, leasing or delivery of goods, and the rendering of services. [6] Primarily value-added and sales taxes. [7] For example, excise taxes on alcohol, tobacco, and gasoline. [8] Data are provisional/estimates. [9] Data for 2022 are not available.

Source: Organisation for Economic Co-operation and Development (OECD), 2024, "Revenue Statistics: Comparative tables," OECD Tax Statistics (database) ©, <dx.doi.org/10.1787/data-00262-en>, accessed June 2024.

Table 1377. Household Tax Burden by Country: 2023

[As percent of gross wage earnings of the average worker. The tax burden reflects income tax plus employee social security contributions less cash benefits]

Country	Single person without children	One-earner married couple with two children	Country	Single person without children	One-earner married couple with two children
OECD average [1]............	24.94	19.89	Israel [3]...................	18.81	15.69
			Italy....................	27.72	25.60
United States..................	**24.25**	**13.17**	Japan....................	22.56	21.20
Australia......................	24.93	24.93	Korea, South.............	16.24	14.58
Austria.......................	32.94	24.69	Latvia...................	27.14	20.67
Belgium.......................	39.94	28.27	Lithuania................	37.81	37.81
Canada.......................	25.57	22.37	Luxembourg..............	33.21	20.91
Chile.........................	7.15	7.00	Mexico...................	10.96	10.96
Colombia.....................	(NA)	(NA)	Netherlands..............	27.35	27.35
Costa Rica....................	10.67	10.67	New Zealand.............	21.05	21.05
Czechia.......................	20.01	4.55	Norway..................	28.10	28.10
Denmark......................	35.99	32.34	Poland...................	23.56	16.77
Estonia.......................	18.85	15.14	Portugal.................	28.55	19.21
Finland.......................	31.58	31.58	Slovakia.................	24.30	-0.74
France [2].....................	27.53	20.84	Slovenia.................	34.20	26.57
Germany......................	37.43	19.69	Spain....................	22.06	15.90
Greece.......................	24.77	25.65	Sweden..................	23.90	23.90
Hungary......................	33.50	26.79	Switzerland..............	18.57	12.00
Iceland.......................	27.39	20.92	Turkey...................	27.60	27.60
Ireland.......................	27.96	19.15	United Kingdom.........	23.65	23.13

NA Not available. [1] As of 2023, the Organisation for Economic Co-operation and Development (OECD) is comprised of the 38 member countries shown. See text, this section. [2] Figures correspond to tax calculations that are based on the tax legislation relating to the income earned in the selected year. [3] See footnote 2, Table 1373.

Source: Organisation for Economic Co-operation and Development (OECD), 2024, OECD Data Explorer, Taxation: Personal and property tax, "Labour taxation - OECD comparative indicators" ©, <data-explorer.oecd.org>, accessed August 2024.

Table 1378. Household Net Saving Rates by Country: 2000 to 2022

[As a percentage of household disposable income. Household savings are estimated by subtracting household consumption expenditure from household disposable income, plus the change in net equity of households in pension funds. Households include households plus nonprofit institutions serving households. Net saving rates are measured after deducting consumption of fixed capital (depreciation), with respect to assets used in enterprises operated by households, as well as owner-occupied dwellings. The household saving rate is calculated as the ratio of household savings to household disposable income (plus the change in net equity of households in pension funds). Minus sign (-) indicates an excess of expenditures over income]

Country	2000	2005	2010	2015	2017	2018	2019	2020	2021	2022
United States.	4.47	2.33	6.14	6.04	5.96	6.68	7.63	15.86	11.67	3.43
Australia [1]	1.59	-0.83	7.36	6.10	4.87	5.71	12.22	15.33	13.03	(NA)
Austria.	10.63	11.14	9.59	6.74	7.52	7.73	7.89	13.23	11.17	9.25
Belgium.	11.45	10.18	9.26	5.53	5.37	4.66	5.54	14.05	10.46	[2] 5.75
Canada.	5.05	1.53	4.27	4.07	1.85	0.67	2.04	14.12	10.34	5.36
Chile.	(NA)	11.43	9.42	9.79	8.88	8.94	11.61	11.48	7.54	-0.98
Denmark.	-5.69	-4.27	1.84	3.91	6.03	5.42	4.28	5.70	2.55	6.82
Finland.	2.63	0.51	3.27	-0.46	-0.93	-0.84	0.39	4.61	2.61	-1.64
France.	8.67	8.50	10.45	8.33	8.37	8.62	9.17	15.19	[2] 13.06	[2] 11.20
Germany.	9.33	10.56	10.31	10.06	10.64	11.29	[2] 10.86	[2] 16.52	[2] 14.92	[2] 11.14
Greece.	(NA)	(NA)	[3] -4.12	-11.55	-14.20	-14.70	-9.97	[2] -6.26	[2] -4.95	[2] -11.31
Hungary.	4.50	7.56	5.99	7.34	8.10	10.86	10.48	11.04	12.63	[2] 9.90
Ireland.	-2.84	2.60	8.83	3.55	5.54	4.35	5.24	20.09	15.70	7.70
Italy.	7.36	8.90	3.93	2.89	2.56	2.54	2.38	10.21	7.90	1.58
Japan.	8.07	2.69	3.31	0.13	1.60	1.78	3.36	11.28	7.29	4.02
Korea, South.	(NA)	4.61	3.18	9.63	7.54	7.17	8.13	14.68	12.62	[2] 10.81
Latvia.	-9.76	-5.23	-1.87	-5.75	-3.20	-1.63	-0.03	5.55	1.94	-7.23
Luxembourg.	5.85	5.18	5.49	7.39	7.41	6.56	8.80	20.64	12.20	11.61
Mexico.	(NA)	-3.54	3.55	6.96	6.11	4.14	8.41	12.51	11.06	2.73
New Zealand [1]	-2.57	-5.79	2.12	-0.30	-0.14	0.81	3.06	9.26	[2] 3.56	(NA)
Norway.	3.84	9.33	3.75	9.77	6.57	5.93	7.06	12.88	12.75	4.19
Poland.	10.15	2.13	4.13	2.17	1.89	1.39	2.52	9.46	2.00	-2.89
Portugal.	6.08	2.76	1.57	-1.19	-2.24	-2.47	-2.17	2.10	0.36	[2] -4.92
Slovakia.	4.58	0.81	3.20	3.23	2.11	4.68	3.91	5.49	4.24	-1.70
Spain.	6.60	4.27	5.06	3.17	1.65	1.42	4.16	13.66	9.65	2.95
Sweden.	0.44	2.88	9.83	12.09	12.17	13.66	15.57	16.99	15.52	13.00
United Kingdom.	4.06	2.22	6.84	4.41	-0.59	-0.64	-0.51	11.21	6.70	2.28

NA Not available. [1] Data refer to fiscal year. [2] Data are estimates. [3] Break in series.

Source: Organisation for Economic Co-operation and Development (OECD), 2024, "National Accounts at a Glance," OECD National Accounts Statistics (database) ©, <dx.doi.org/10.1787/data-00369-en>, accessed June 2024.

Table 1379. Insurance and Pensions by Country: 2021

[106,613 represents $106,613,000,000]

Country	Insurance					Pensions [2]	
	Investment assets (mil. U.S. dollars) [1]	Direct gross premiums (percent of GDP)	Total gross premiums (mil. U.S. dollars)		Gross claims payments (mil. U.S. dollars)	Investment assets (mil. U.S. dollars)	Benefits paid (percent of GDP)
			Life	Non-life			
United States.	(NA)	12.4	1,382,902	1,859,813	1,793,955	40,027,760	(NA)
Australia.	106,613	3.3	23,499	43,224	46,796	2,291,929	6.2
Belgium.	392,814	6.2	18,472	22,599	32,368	(NA)	(NA)
Chile.	60,645	3.6	6,655	4,934	9,756	167,556	2.4
Colombia.	18,371	3.0	4,781	4,857	5,355	91,806	(NA)
Costa Rica.	3,543	2.2	238	1,212	727	24,906	0.8
Czechia.	17,442	2.9	2,408	5,857	4,916	26,183	0.5
Denmark.	664,696	11.5	34,271	12,500	32,088	889,945	0.7
Finland.	94,937	2.0	6,051	(NA)	4,604	197,173	1.7
Germany.	2,277,016	6.7	118,632	278,086	279,786	325,103	0.2
Greece.	21,807	2.4	2,874	2,455	(NA)	2,083	(NA)
Hungary.	9,845	2.4	1,988	2,398	2,339	8,844	0.1
Iceland.	1,388	2.5	57	577	433	54,207	6.4
Israel [3]	219,171	4.5	11,595	10,183	16,613	360,569	(NA)
Italy.	1,086,822	7.9	125,497	42,974	119,739	254,454	0.5
Korea, South.	1,055,408	11.0	103,896	105,572	126,414	551,075	2.9
Latvia.	1,613	2.6	305	699	640	7,638	0.1
Lithuania.	1,644	1.9	378	854	647	6,944	0.1
Luxembourg.	318,381	38.0	30,494	4,302	21,381	2,187	0.2
Mexico.	78,840	2.5	14,880	18,204	17,658	(NA)	0.5
Norway.	243,934	5.7	16,006	11,527	17,553	(NA)	0.2
Poland.	33,815	2.5	5,728	12,195	11,490	57,321	–
Portugal.	55,610	5.9	8,785	6,789	13,488	52,539	0.4
Slovakia.	6,668	2.4	1,250	1,481	1,473	17,469	0.2
Slovenia.	8,628	4.8	676	2,725	2,086	4,624	0.2
Spain.	352,659	4.9	28,209	48,264	60,603	194,509	0.3
Sweden.	756,402	11.2	58,754	14,343	29,071	705,712	(NA)
Switzerland.	483,975	7.1	25,829	45,100	57,508	(NA)	5.6
Turkey.	10,516	1.4	2,364	10,061	5,583	(NA)	0.1
United Kingdom.	3,114,035	11.3	313,983	131,449	429,176	3,751,713	2.9

NA Not available or not applicable. – Represents or rounds to zero. [1] Includes total investment assets of direct insurance companies (excludes re-insurance). [2] Includes public and private autonomous pension funds of all types (occupational and personal, mandatory and voluntary). [3] See footnote 2, Table 1373.

Source: Organisation for Economic Co-operation and Development (OECD), 2023, "Outstanding investment by direct insurance companies," OECD Insurance Statistics (database) ©, <dx.doi.org/10.1787/data-00326-en>; "Insurance activity indicators," OECD Insurance Statistics (database) ©, <dx.doi.org/10.1787/data-00333-en>; "Gross Claims payments," OECD Insurance Statistics (database) ©, <doi.org/10.1787/data-00328-en>; "Pensions statistics," OECD Pensions Statistics (database) ©, <dx.doi.org/10.1787/data-00517-en>; and "Pensions indicators," OECD Pensions Statistics (database) ©, <dx.doi.org/10.1787/data-00518-en>; accessed August 2023.

Table 1380. Inflation—Annual Percent Change in Consumer Prices by Selected Country: 2019 to 2023

[Percent change from previous year. Inflation as measured by the consumer price index reflects the annual percent change in the cost to the average consumer of acquiring a basket of goods and services that may be fixed or adjusted at specified intervals, such as yearly. For general comments concerning the data, see text, this section. For additional qualifications of the data for individual countries, see source. Minus sign (-) indicates decrease]

Country	2019	2020	2021	2022	2023	Country	2019	2020	2021	2022	2023
World [1]	**2.2**	**1.9**	**3.4**	**8.0**	**5.8**	Kenya	5.2	5.4	6.1	7.7	7.7
United States	**1.8**	**1.2**	**4.7**	**8.0**	**4.1**	Korea, South	0.4	0.5	2.5	5.1	3.6
Algeria	2.0	2.4	7.2	9.3	9.3	Lebanon	3.0	84.9	154.8	171.2	221.3
Angola	17.1	22.3	25.8	21.4	13.6	Malawi	9.4	8.6	9.3	21.0	28.8
Australia	1.6	0.8	2.9	6.6	5.6	Malaysia	0.7	-1.1	2.5	3.4	2.5
Bangladesh	5.6	5.7	5.5	7.7	9.9	Mali	-1.7	0.4	3.9	9.6	2.1
Belgium	1.4	0.7	2.4	9.6	4.0	Mexico	3.6	3.4	5.7	7.9	5.5
Brazil	3.7	3.2	8.3	9.3	4.6	Morocco	0.3	0.7	1.4	6.7	6.1
Burkina Faso	-3.2	1.9	3.7	14.3	0.7	Mozambique	2.8	3.5	6.4	10.3	7.1
Canada	1.9	0.7	3.4	6.8	3.9	Nepal	5.6	5.1	4.1	7.7	7.1
Chad	-1.0	4.5	-0.8	5.8	10.8	Netherlands	2.6	1.3	2.7	10.0	3.8
Chile	2.6	3.0	4.5	11.6	7.6	New Zealand	1.6	1.7	3.9	7.2	5.7
China	2.9	2.4	1.0	2.0	0.2	Nigeria	11.4	13.2	17.0	18.8	24.7
Colombia	3.5	2.5	3.5	10.2	11.7	Pakistan	10.6	9.7	9.5	19.9	30.8
Czechia	2.8	3.2	3.8	15.1	10.7	Peru	2.3	2.0	4.3	8.3	6.5
Egypt	9.2	5.0	5.2	13.9	33.9	Philippines	2.4	2.4	3.9	5.8	6.0
Ethiopia	15.8	20.4	26.8	33.9	30.2	Poland	2.2	3.4	5.1	14.4	11.5
France	1.1	0.5	1.6	5.2	4.9	Romania	3.8	2.6	5.1	13.8	10.4
Germany	1.4	0.1	3.1	6.9	5.9	Saudi Arabia	-2.1	3.4	3.1	2.5	2.3
Ghana	7.1	9.9	10.0	31.3	38.1	South Africa	4.1	3.2	4.6	7.0	6.1
Greece	0.3	-1.2	1.2	9.6	3.5	Spain	0.7	-0.3	3.1	8.4	3.5
Haiti	18.7	22.8	16.8	34.0	36.8	Sri Lanka	3.5	6.2	7.0	49.7	16.5
India	3.7	6.6	5.1	6.7	5.6	Tanzania	3.5	3.3	3.7	4.4	3.8
Indonesia	3.0	1.9	1.6	4.2	3.7	Thailand	0.7	-0.8	1.2	6.1	1.2
Iran	39.9	30.6	43.4	43.5	44.6	Turkey	15.2	12.3	19.6	72.3	53.9
Ireland	0.9	-0.3	2.3	7.8	6.3	Uganda	2.9	3.3	2.2	7.2	5.4
Israel	0.8	-0.6	1.5	4.4	4.2	Ukraine	7.9	2.7	9.4	20.2	12.8
Italy	0.6	-0.1	1.9	8.2	5.6	United Kingdom	1.7	1.0	2.5	7.9	6.8
Japan	0.5	0.0	-0.2	2.5	3.3	Vietnam	2.8	3.2	1.8	3.2	3.3
Kazakhstan	5.3	6.7	8.0	15.0	14.7	Zambia	9.2	15.7	22.0	11.0	10.9

[1] Includes other countries not shown separately.

Source: The World Bank, Washington, DC, World Development Indicators database, "Inflation, consumer prices (annual %)" ©, <databank.worldbank.org/source/world-development-indicators>, accessed July 2024.

Table 1381. Unemployment Rates by Country: 2010 to 2023

[Annual averages. The standardized unemployment rates shown here are calculated as the number of unemployed persons as a percentage of the civilian labor force. The unemployed are persons of working age who, in the reference period, are without work, are available for work, and have taken specific steps to find work. Selected data are estimated or subject to a break in series, see source for details]

Country	2010	2015	2016	2017	2018	2019	2020	2021	2022	2023
OECD, total [1]	8.5	6.9	6.5	5.9	5.5	5.4	7.1	6.2	5.0	4.8
EU-27 [2]	9.8	10.0	9.1	8.1	7.3	6.7	7.1	7.0	6.2	6.0
United States	**9.6**	**5.3**	**4.9**	**4.4**	**3.9**	**3.7**	**8.1**	**5.4**	**3.7**	**3.6**
Australia	5.2	6.1	5.7	5.6	5.3	5.2	6.4	5.1	3.7	3.7
Austria	4.8	5.7	6.0	5.5	4.8	4.5	5.4	6.2	4.7	5.1
Belgium	8.3	8.5	7.8	7.1	5.9	5.4	5.5	6.3	5.6	5.5
Canada	8.2	6.9	7.0	6.4	5.8	5.7	9.7	7.5	5.3	5.4
Chile	8.2	6.3	6.7	7.0	7.4	7.2	10.8	8.9	7.9	8.7
Czechia	7.3	5.0	4.0	2.9	2.2	2.0	2.5	2.8	2.3	2.6
Denmark	7.7	6.3	6.0	5.8	5.1	5.0	5.6	5.1	4.4	5.1
Estonia	16.7	6.2	6.8	5.8	5.4	4.4	6.8	6.2	5.6	6.4
Finland	8.4	9.4	8.8	8.6	7.4	6.7	7.8	7.6	6.7	7.1
France	8.9	10.4	10.0	9.4	9.0	8.4	8.0	7.9	7.3	7.3
Germany	7.0	4.6	4.1	3.7	3.4	3.1	3.8	3.6	3.1	3.0
Greece	12.7	24.9	23.5	21.5	19.3	17.3	16.3	14.8	12.4	11.1
Hungary	11.2	6.8	5.1	4.2	3.7	3.4	4.3	4.0	3.6	4.1
Ireland	14.5	9.9	8.4	6.7	5.7	5.0	5.6	6.2	4.5	4.3
Israel [3]	6.6	5.2	4.8	4.2	4.0	3.8	4.3	5.0	3.8	3.4
Italy	8.4	11.9	11.7	11.2	10.6	10.0	9.2	9.5	8.1	7.6
Japan	5.1	3.4	3.1	2.8	2.4	2.4	2.8	2.8	2.6	2.6
Korea	3.7	3.6	3.7	3.7	3.8	3.8	3.9	3.7	2.9	2.7
Latvia	19.5	9.9	9.6	8.7	7.4	6.3	8.1	7.5	6.8	6.5
Lithuania	17.8	9.1	7.9	7.1	6.2	6.3	8.5	7.1	6.0	6.8
Luxembourg	4.4	6.7	6.3	5.5	5.6	5.6	6.8	5.2	4.6	5.2
Mexico	5.3	4.3	3.9	3.4	3.3	3.5	4.5	4.1	3.3	2.8
Netherlands	5.0	6.9	6.0	4.8	3.8	3.4	3.8	4.2	3.5	3.5
New Zealand	6.2	5.4	5.1	4.7	4.3	4.1	4.6	3.8	3.3	3.7
Norway	3.5	4.3	4.7	4.2	3.8	3.7	4.4	4.4	3.2	3.6
Poland	9.6	7.5	6.2	4.9	3.8	3.3	3.2	3.4	2.9	2.8
Portugal	10.8	12.4	11.1	8.9	7.0	6.5	6.8	6.7	6.1	6.5
Slovakia	14.4	11.5	9.7	8.1	6.5	5.8	6.7	6.8	6.1	5.8
Spain	19.9	22.1	19.6	17.2	15.3	14.1	15.5	14.8	12.9	12.1
Sweden	8.6	7.4	7.0	6.7	6.4	6.8	8.3	8.7	7.4	7.6
Switzerland	4.8	4.8	4.9	4.8	4.7	4.4	4.8	5.1	4.3	4.1
Turkey	10.7	10.2	10.8	10.8	10.9	13.7	13.1	12.0	10.5	9.4
United Kingdom	7.9	5.4	4.9	4.4	4.1	3.8	4.6	4.5	3.8	4.0

[1] For OECD membership listing, see Section 30 introduction. [2] European Union as of February 1, 2020. [3] See footnote 2, Table 1373.

Source: Organisation for Economic Co-operation and Development (OECD), 2024, OECD Data Explorer, Employment: Unemployment indicators, "Annual labour force survey, summary tables" ©, <data-explorer.oecd.org/>, accessed August 2024.

Table 1382. Youth Educational Enrollment and Employment Status by Country, Age Group, and Education Attainment: 2022

[Percent of total youth population for selected age group. Upper secondary education refers to stronger specialization than at lower secondary level and programs offered are differentiated by whether general or vocational and have a typical duration of three years. Post-secondary non-tertiary education serves to broaden rather than deepen the knowledge, skills and competencies gained in upper secondary level and is usually vocationally oriented]

Country	18 to 24 year olds			25 to 29 year olds by educational attainment								
				Upper secondary or post-secondary non-tertiary (general)			Upper secondary or post-secondary non-tertiary (vocational)			Tertiary		
	In education, total	Not in education		In education, total	Not in education		In education, total	Not in education		In education, total	Not in education	
		Employed	Not employed		Employed	Not employed		Employed	Not employed		Employed	Not employed
OECD average.....	54.2	31.2	14.7	28.6	54.6	17.1	9.3	75.2	17.1	18.9	71.6	9.9
United States.......	**44.8**	**39.7**	**15.5**	[1] **8.7**	[1] **68.3**	[1] **23.1**	**([1])**	**([1])**	**([1])**	**14.3**	**76.3**	**9.4**
Australia.......	48.2	41.2	10.6	20.0	61.8	18.2	14.2	71.2	14.6	17.4	75.2	7.4
Austria.........	49.3	40.3	10.5	50.9	42.6	6.5	3.4	84.9	11.8	28.5	64.0	7.5
Canada.......	50.0	38.0	11.9	12.8	65.8	21.4	4.9	82.4	12.7	14.8	76.3	8.9
Costa Rica....	49.8	27.1	23.1	17.3	51.1	31.7	27.0	43.2	29.8	41.5	46.8	11.7
Czechia........	58.2	10.9	30.9	23.1	62.4	14.5	3.8	77.9	18.3	15.7	71.4	13.0
Denmark.......	58.0	31.6	10.4	55.0	37.6	7.4	12.6	80.2	7.1	22.3	67.0	10.7
Estonia........	58.0	27.0	15.0	16.9	74.8	8.3	7.4	79.6	13.0	17.9	74.8	7.4
Finland........	59.0	30.1	10.9	53.8	30.8	15.4	19.0	66.2	14.8	28.9	66.1	5.0
France........	55.6	29.0	15.4	21.9	56.3	21.8	4.3	76.6	19.1	12.0	78.4	9.6
Germany......	61.6	29.9	8.6	57.2	30.4	12.3	10.8	81.1	8.1	25.1	69.4	5.5
Greece........	66.1	17.0	17.0	34.7	44.5	20.8	1.2	65.5	33.3	16.1	63.2	20.7
Hungary.......	50.2	36.3	13.5	17.6	72.8	9.6	2.4	88.9	8.7	12.0	83.4	4.6
Italy..........	53.0	22.9	24.1	34.8	40.5	24.7	7.1	66.7	26.2	28.5	55.2	16.3
Mexico........	38.9	41.2	20.0	13.3	63.5	23.1	4.6	71.2	24.2	11.9	73.6	14.5
Netherlands...	70.5	25.3	4.1	55.4	39.1	5.4	18.0	76.1	5.9	22.9	72.6	4.5
New Zealand..	28.4	57.4	14.3	13.2	69.7	17.1	11.7	74.7	13.5	13.7	81.3	4.9
Poland........	57.1	30.2	12.6	12.6	65.9	21.5	2.4	81.3	16.3	8.5	82.9	8.6
Portugal.......	62.4	26.3	11.4	19.5	66.1	14.4	8.7	77.8	13.6	15.0	75.1	9.8
Slovakia.......	60.6	26.4	13.0	14.4	68.9	16.7	1.8	83.4	14.8	13.0	77.8	9.2
Spain.........	61.2	21.6	17.2	31.9	47.8	20.3	8.5	65.2	26.3	19.5	64.3	16.3
Switzerland....	53.3	34.3	12.4	52.7	37.0	10.3	13.8	77.1	9.0	21.6	73.7	4.7
Turkey........	32.9	33.6	33.5	20.9	45.8	33.3	14.3	58.9	26.8	17.8	56.5	25.6
United Kingdom.....	45.2	43.1	11.8	12.3	75.5	12.2	9.3	78.1	12.6	15.9	79.4	4.7

[1] Data for vocational included with general.

Source: Organisation for Economic Co-operation and Development (OECD), 2024, "Indicator A2: Transition from education to work: Where are today's youth?" *Education at a Glance 2023: OECD Indicators,* OECD Publishing ©, <doi.org/10.1787/9117e379-en>, accessed August 2024.

Table 1383. Educational Performance and Attainment by Country: 2022

| Country | Student mean proficiency scores [1] | | | Educational attainment of adults age 25 to 64 (percent) | | |
	Reading scale	Mathematics scale	Science scale	Below upper secondary	Upper secondary and vocational	Tertiary [2]
United States [3]....................	**503.9**	**464.9**	**499.4**	**8.2**	**41.8**	**50.0**
Australia [3].......................	498.1	487.1	507.0	14.8	33.7	51.5
Austria........................	480.4	487.3	491.3	14.1	50.4	35.6
Belgium........................	478.9	489.5	490.6	17.6	36.7	45.8
Canada [3].......................	507.1	496.9	515.0	6.8	30.4	62.7
Colombia.......................	408.7	382.7	411.1	37.9	33.9	28.3
Czechia........................	488.6	487.0	497.7	5.6	67.8	26.7
France.........................	473.9	473.9	487.2	16.7	41.7	41.6
Germany.......................	479.8	474.8	492.4	16.5	51.0	32.5
Greece.........................	438.4	430.1	440.8	19.7	45.2	35.1
Ireland [3].......................	516.0	491.6	503.8	12.4	33.2	54.4
Israel [4]........................	473.8	457.9	464.8	11.8	37.6	50.6
Italy...........................	481.6	471.3	477.5	37.0	42.7	20.3
Japan..........................	515.9	535.6	546.6	(NA)	(NA)	56.1
Korea, South...................	515.4	527.3	527.8	8.8	38.4	52.8
Mexico.........................	415.4	395.0	409.9	56.2	23.1	20.6
Netherlands [3]...................	459.2	492.7	488.3	18.8	36.6	44.7
Norway.........................	476.5	468.4	478.2	17.4	34.5	48.1
Poland.........................	488.7	489.0	499.2	6.5	59.6	33.9
Portugal........................	476.6	471.9	484.4	39.7	28.9	31.5
Spain..........................	474.3	473.1	484.5	35.8	23.1	41.1
Sweden........................	487.0	481.8	493.5	14.4	37.1	48.5
Switzerland.....................	483.3	508.0	502.5	13.9	41.4	44.7
Turkey.........................	456.1	453.2	475.9	53.3	21.7	25.0
United Kingdom [3]................	494.4	489.0	499.7	18.6	30.1	51.3

NA Not available. [1] Proficiency scores are based on the Program for International Student Assessment (PISA), an international standardized test which takes place in three-year cycles. PISA tests are administered to a nationally representative sample of fifteen-year-old students in each country. [2] Tertiary education entails completion of an advanced course of study or research program leading to an associate's, bachelor's, master's, or doctorate degree, usually 2 years or longer in duration. [3] For proficiency scores, interpret data with caution; some sampling standards were not met. [4] See footnote 2, Table 1373.

Source: Organisation for Economic Co-operation and Development (OECD), 2023, "Adult education level" (indicator) ©, <dx.doi.org/10.1787/36bce3fe-en>; and "How did countries perform in PISA 2022? Chapter 2 tables" in *PISA 2022 Results (Volume 1): The State of Learning and Equity in Education*, PISA, OECD Publishing, Paris, <doi.org/10.1787/53f23881-en>, accessed August 2024.

Table 1384. World Supply and Utilization of Major Crops and Livestock: 2017 to 2024

[In millions of units (222.5 represents 222,500,000). For major crops, data are for marketing or trade year ending in year shown, unless otherwise indicated. For livestock and dairy, data are for calendar year]

Commodity	2017	2018	2019	2020	2021	2022	2023	2024 (P)
Wheat:								
Area harvested (hectares)................	222.5	217.9	214.7	215.2	220.2	221.6	219.6	222.8
Production (metric tons)................	757.3	760.3	729.8	759.3	772.7	780.4	789.0	789.0
Exports (metric tons)................	185.7	187.0	178.1	195.1	199.6	205.2	216.6	223.8
Consumption (metric tons)................	734.2	739.5	731.2	739.5	777.2	788.8	782.6	797.2
Ending stocks (metric tons)................	268.0	287.6	284.0	297.6	284.2	273.3	271.0	261.0
Corn:								
Area harvested (hectares)................	197.2	194.2	193.2	194.1	199.6	206.8	200.7	203.1
Production (metric tons)................	1,129.2	1,087.1	1,132.8	1,125.6	1,131.9	1,217.7	1,159.6	1,225.5
Exports (metric tons)................	143.6	154.1	173.5	175.8	184.0	193.4	180.9	198.0
Consumption (metric tons)................	1,068.2	1,099.0	1,132.7	1,133.9	1,151.5	1,178.0	1,164.1	1,206.1
Ending stocks (metric tons)................	350.6	342.1	326.0	313.1	295.7	313.7	302.3	309.1
Rice, milled:								
Area harvested (hectares)................	164.0	163.7	163.1	161.3	164.9	165.6	165.5	165.7
Production (metric tons)................	492.1	494.8	498.4	498.6	509.3	513.8	515.8	520.9
Exports (metric tons)................	48.7	48.3	43.9	45.4	52.7	56.8	53.3	55.1
Consumption (metric tons)................	478.4	481.4	485.3	492.4	498.4	516.0	522.0	520.6
Ending stocks (metric tons)................	150.8	163.6	176.8	182.2	188.3	183.7	179.4	177.2
Coarse grains: [1]								
Area harvested (hectares)................	338.7	330.8	331.2	334.0	345.1	343.7	336.4	336.7
Production (metric tons)................	1,419.8	1,366.4	1,404.5	1,422.5	1,445.0	1,502.6	1,451.5	1,500.2
Exports (metric tons)................	184.8	191.7	206.9	214.8	235.1	236.7	221.5	240.8
Consumption (metric tons)................	1,383.9	1,377.8	1,423.0	1,434.4	1,461.6	1,487.4	1,459.5	1,495.8
Ending stocks (metric tons)................	384.9	373.4	355.0	343.0	326.4	341.6	333.6	337.9
Oilseeds:								
Area harvested (hectares)................	270.6	281.9	282.9	281.3	288.0	296.7	304.2	307.8
Production (metric tons)................	577.3	583.8	601.5	582.1	610.1	611.6	637.8	657.2
Exports (metric tons)................	171.6	177.5	172.1	191.7	192.3	179.6	201.4	201.4
Consumption (metric tons)................	556.3	574.9	582.1	602.1	607.2	611.5	626.6	644.2
Ending stocks (metric tons)................	110.7	118.6	134.0	112.2	113.8	111.8	119.1	128.3
Coffee, green:								
Production (60 kg bags)................	161.1	159.8	175.9	169.0	176.6	165.0	164.4	169.2
Exports (60 kg bags)................	133.3	134.0	143.3	138.9	144.8	143.5	134.5	141.5
Consumption (60 kg bags)................	155.8	160.9	166.1	162.5	162.2	167.9	169.2	167.5
Ending stocks (60 kg bags)................	36.5	32.0	36.9	35.8	37.5	31.9	26.6	23.9
Sugar, centrifugal:								
Production (metric tons)................	172.1	194.2	179.2	166.6	180.2	180.6	179.5	183.5
Exports (metric tons)................	60.0	65.9	58.3	53.5	64.1	64.8	62.2	68.2
Consumption (metric tons)................	169.1	173.3	172.0	171.5	171.1	173.9	176.8	177.3
Ending stocks (metric tons)................	42.0	51.6	52.8	47.8	50.3	47.7	46.0	40.2
Cotton:								
Area harvested (hectares)................	29.9	33.4	32.7	34.5	31.7	32.3	31.8	31.4
Production (480 lb. bales)................	106.3	122.1	114.5	119.1	114.0	114.4	116.4	113.7
Exports (480 lb. bales)................	38.1	41.6	41.6	41.2	49.0	43.3	37.1	44.2
Domestic use (480 lb. bales)................	116.6	123.0	119.4	105.5	124.4	116.1	112.4	113.3
Ending stocks (480 lb. bales)................	78.0	77.0	73.0	86.3	75.7	74.2	79.5	79.3
Beef:								
Beef cow beginning stocks (head)................	200.5	202.1	203.3	202.8	202.3	204.8	207.0	206.1
Production (metric tons) [2]................	56.4	57.7	58.5	57.6	58.4	59.3	60.0	60.7
Exports (metric tons) [2]................	10.1	10.6	11.4	11.2	11.4	12.0	12.2	12.9
Consumption (metric tons) [2]................	54.0	55.4	56.2	56.0	56.9	57.5	58.2	58.8
Ending stocks (metric tons) [2]................	0.5	0.5	0.5	0.6	0.5	0.6	0.5	0.5
Pork:								
Sow beginning stocks (head)................	73.6	72.7	66.1	60.4	68.6	70.8	71.4	69.9
Production (metric tons) [2]................	111.5	112.4	101.5	96.1	108.0	114.6	116.3	116.3
Exports (metric tons) [2]................	9.2	9.4	10.4	12.6	12.2	11.0	10.1	10.4
Consumption (metric tons) [2]................	110.7	111.4	100.2	95.3	107.3	113.3	115.5	115.1
Ending stocks (metric tons) [2]................	0.7	0.7	0.9	0.8	0.7	0.9	0.8	0.8
Chicken (meat): [3]								
Beginning stocks (metric tons)................	0.7	0.8	0.8	0.8	0.8	0.7	0.8	0.8
Production (metric tons)................	91.0	92.6	97.2	99.7	101.2	102.1	103.7	105.3
Exports (metric tons)................	12.1	12.5	13.1	13.1	13.3	13.5	13.5	13.8
Consumption (metric tons)................	88.8	90.2	94.8	97.3	98.8	99.6	101.4	102.6
Ending stocks (metric tons)................	0.8	0.8	0.8	0.8	0.7	0.8	0.8	0.8
Dairy:								
Dairy cows beginning stocks (head)................	233.5	236.0	238.2	239.3	239.6	239.3	239.6	239.3
Milk production (metric tons) [4]................	511.6	522.6	527.7	539.7	545.2	545.1	551.0	552.0
Milk exports (metric tons) [4]................	2.9	3.0	3.2	3.3	3.5	3.2	2.9	2.9
Milk consumption (metric tons) [4]................	612.4	628.9	634.5	648.8	656.2	658.7	667.0	670.7

P Preliminary. [1] Coarse grains include corn, barley, sorghum, oats, rye, millet, and mixed grains but exclude trade in barley malt, millet, and mixed grains. [2] Carcass weight equivalent (CWE). [3] Weight in ready-to-eat equivalent meat. [4] Cow's milk only.

Source: U.S. Department of Agriculture, Foreign Agricultural Service, "Production, Supply and Distribution Online," <apps.fas.usda.gov/psdonline/app/index.html#/app/home>, accessed August 2024.

Table 1385. World Crop Production Summary: 2022 to 2024

[In millions of metric tons (789.0 represents 789,000,000). Data are for marketing or trade year. Data for 2023-2024 are preliminary]

Country	Wheat 2022–2023	Wheat 2023–2024	Coarse grains [1] 2022–2023	Coarse grains [1] 2023–2024	Rice (milled) 2022–2023	Rice (milled) 2023–2024	Oilseeds [2] 2022–2023	Oilseeds [2] 2023–2024	Cotton 2022–2023	Cotton 2023–2024
World	**789.0**	**789.0**	**1,451.5**	**1,500.2**	**515.8**	**520.9**	**637.8**	**657.2**	**116.4**	**113.7**
Total foreign	744.1	739.6	1,095.1	1,097.3	510.7	513.9	512.0	535.0	101.9	101.6
United States	**44.9**	**49.3**	**356.4**	**402.9**	**5.1**	**6.9**	**125.8**	**122.2**	**14.5**	**12.1**
Canada	34.3	32.0	30.5	27.2	–	–	25.3	25.9	–	–
Mexico	3.6	3.5	33.9	27.8	0.1	0.2	0.9	0.6	1.6	0.9
Russia	92.0	91.5	44.1	42.5	0.6	0.7	26.6	28.1	–	–
Ukraine	21.5	23.0	33.9	38.3	–	–	19.8	24.5	–	–
European Union	(3)	(3)	(3)	(3)	(3)	(3)	(3)	(3)	1.6	1.1
China	137.7	136.6	285.7	297.1	145.9	144.6	67.9	69.1	30.7	27.5
India	104.0	110.6	56.8	56.0	135.8	137.0	42.3	41.7	26.3	26.2
Indonesia	–	–	12.4	12.7	33.9	33.0	15.0	15.1	–	–
Pakistan	26.2	28.2	11.5	10.4	7.3	9.9	2.7	3.7	3.9	6.7
Thailand	–	–	5.3	5.4	20.9	20.0	1.0	1.0	–	–
Argentina	12.6	15.9	42.9	60.4	0.8	0.8	31.5	55.6	1.2	1.5
Brazil	10.6	8.1	143.5	128.5	6.8	7.0	166.9	158.8	11.7	14.6
Australia	40.5	26.0	18.8	14.5	0.4	0.4	9.8	7.0	5.8	5.0
South Africa	2.1	2.1	17.5	14.5	–	–	3.8	2.8	0.1	0.1
Turkey	17.3	21.0	14.8	17.0	0.6	0.5	4.0	3.1	4.9	3.2
All others	241.7	241.4	343.4	344.9	157.6	159.8	94.6	98.0	14.2	15.0

– Represents zero. [1] Includes corn, barley, sorghum, oats, rye, millet, and mixed grains. [2] Includes soybean, cottonseed, peanut (in shell), sunflower seed, and rapeseed for individual countries. Copra and palm kernel are added to world totals. [3] Indicates no reported or insignificant production.

Source: U.S. Department of Agriculture, Foreign Agricultural Service, Data Publications, *World Agricultural Production*, July 2024. See also <apps.fas.usda.gov/psdonline/app/index.html#/app/downloads>.

Table 1386. Meat Production by Type and Country: 2022 and 2023

[In thousands of metric tons (59,324 represents 59,324,000). Carcass weight equivalent basis for beef, veal, and pork. Chicken weight based on ready-to-cook equivalent meat]

Country	Beef and veal [1] 2022	Beef and veal [1] 2023	Country	Pork 2022	Pork 2023	Country	Chicken [2] 2022	Chicken [2] 2023
World	**59,324**	**59,963**	**World**	**114,642**	**116,311**	**World**	**102,086**	**103,655**
United States	**12,890**	**12,286**	China	55,410	57,940	**United States**	**20,993**	**21,082**
Brazil	10,350	10,950	EU-27 [3]	22,277	20,800	Brazil	14,465	14,900
China	7,180	7,530	**United States**	**12,252**	**12,391**	China	14,300	14,800
EU-27 [3]	6,722	6,460	Brazil	4,350	4,450	EU-27 [3]	10,880	11,060
India	4,350	4,470	Russia	3,910	4,000	Russia	4,800	4,875
Argentina	3,140	3,300	Vietnam	3,313	3,555	Mexico	3,763	3,888
Australia	1,878	2,224	Canada	2,078	2,106	Thailand	3,300	3,450
Mexico	2,177	2,215	Mexico	1,530	1,557	Argentina	2,319	2,330
Russia	1,350	1,365	Korea, South	1,419	1,435	Turkey	2,418	2,330
Canada	1,412	1,326	Japan	1,293	1,294	Egypt	2,000	1,850
Others	7,875	7,837	Others	6,810	6,783	Others	22,848	23,090

[1] May include meat of other bovines. [2] Excludes chicken paws. [3] See footnote 3, Table 1387.

Source: U.S. Department of Agriculture, Foreign Agricultural Service, "Production, Supply and Distribution Online," <apps.fas.usda.gov/psdonline/app/index.html#/app/home>, accessed August 2024.

Table 1387. Meat Consumption by Type and Country: 2022 and 2023

[In thousands of metric tons (57,486 represents 57,486,000). Carcass weight equivalent basis for beef, veal, and pork. Chicken weight based on ready-to-cook equivalent meat]

Country	Beef and veal [1] 2022	Beef and veal [1] 2023	Country	Pork 2022	Pork 2023	Country	Chicken [2] 2022	Chicken [2] 2023
World	**57,486**	**58,209**	**World**	**113,332**	**115,488**	**World**	**99,572**	**101,385**
United States	**12,799**	**12,637**	China	57,434	59,741	**United States**	**17,676**	**17,866**
China	10,662	11,089	EU-27 [3]	18,220	17,782	China	14,401	15,002
Brazil	7,524	8,108	**United States**	**9,957**	**9,829**	Brazil	10,023	10,135
EU-27 [3]	6,468	6,200	Russia	3,758	3,815	EU-27 [3]	9,881	10,133
India	2,908	2,918	Vietnam	3,413	3,657	Russia	4,750	4,915
Argentina	2,324	2,421	Brazil	3,033	3,038	Mexico	4,666	4,890
Mexico	1,945	2,080	Japan	2,765	2,740	Japan	2,877	2,843
Russia	1,597	1,592	Mexico	2,544	2,653	Thailand	2,310	2,333
Japan	1,228	1,227	Korea, South	2,072	2,109	Argentina	2,138	2,192
Canada	1,043	1,001	Philippines	1,545	1,522	Philippines	1,917	1,942
Others	8,988	8,936	Others	8,591	8,602	Others	28,933	29,134

[1] May include meat of other bovines. [2] Excludes chicken paws. [3] European Union-27: Austria, Belgium, Bulgaria, Croatia, Cyprus, Czech Republic, Denmark, Estonia, Finland, France, Germany, Greece, Hungary, Ireland, Italy, Latvia, Lithuania, Luxembourg, Malta, Netherlands, Poland, Portugal, Romania, Slovakia, Slovenia, Spain, and Sweden.

Source: U.S. Department of Agriculture, Foreign Agricultural Service, "Production, Supply and Distribution Online," <apps.fas.usda.gov/psdonline/app/index.html#/app/home>, accessed August 2024.

Table 1388. Wheat, Rice, and Corn—Exports and Imports of Leading Countries: 2022 to 2024

[In thousands of metric tons (33,000 represents 33,000,000). Wheat data represent trade years ending in June of year shown; corn data represent trade years ending in September of year shown; rice data represent trade years ending in December of year shown]

Leading country	Exports			Leading country	Imports		
	2022	2023	2024 (P)		2022	2023	2024 (P)
WHEAT				**WHEAT**			
Russia..............	33,000	49,000	55,500	China.................	9,568	13,282	13,635
European Union [1]......	31,927	35,079	37,500	Indonesia.............	11,271	9,446	13,015
Canada...............	15,010	25,334	25,664	European Union [1]......	4,631	12,193	13,000
Australia.............	25,958	32,329	22,515	Egypt.................	11,256	11,221	12,000
United States.........	**21,347**	**20,279**	**19,594**	Algeria...............	8,500	8,700	9,200
Ukraine..............	18,844	17,122	18,400	Turkey................	9,555	12,500	8,922
Turkey...............	6,646	6,953	9,991	Bangladesh...........	6,340	5,120	6,500
Kazakhstan...........	8,455	9,862	8,500	Philippines............	6,886	5,743	6,500
Argentina.............	17,651	4,681	7,282	Morocco..............	4,726	5,770	6,000
Uruguay..............	661	533	1,491	Brazil.................	6,582	4,985	5,921
RICE				**RICE**			
India.................	22,122	17,733	17,000	Philippines.............	3,800	3,900	4,600
Thailand.............	7,682	8,736	8,800	Indonesia.............	740	3,500	3,500
Vietnam..............	7,054	8,225	8,300	Vietnam...............	2,350	2,750	2,600
Pakistan.............	4,562	4,528	6,100	European Union.......	2,490	2,170	2,200
United States.........	**2,190**	**2,397**	**3,170**	Iraq..................	2,124	1,845	2,200
Burma...............	2,335	1,577	2,000	Nigeria...............	2,400	2,000	2,000
China................	2,172	1,602	1,500	China.................	6,155	2,597	1,600
Brazil................	1,445	1,208	1,000	Malaysia..............	1,240	1,410	1,600
Uruguay..............	982	991	875	Saudi Arabia...........	1,324	1,487	1,600
Guyana..............	338	399	465	Cote d'Ivoire..........	1,560	1,313	1,450
CORN				**CORN**			
United States.........	**62,903**	**42,844**	**57,000**	China.................	21,884	18,711	23,000
Brazil...............	31,921	53,285	51,000	Mexico...............	17,584	19,392	22,500
Argentina.............	38,853	25,740	33,000	European Union [1]......	19,735	23,188	19,500
Ukraine..............	26,980	27,122	29,500	Japan.................	15,003	14,927	15,500
European Union [1]......	6,027	4,196	4,400	Vietnam...............	9,100	9,500	11,500
Paraguay.............	3,187	3,968	3,100	Korea, South...........	11,510	11,099	11,300
South Africa...........	3,830	3,619	2,600	Iran..................	8,600	6,700	8,500
Turkey...............	458	1,160	2,100	Egypt.................	9,763	6,215	7,500
Burma...............	2,300	2,000	1,800	Colombia..............	6,512	6,343	6,500
Canada...............	2,200	2,839	1,800	Algeria...............	3,273	4,069	4,900

P Preliminary. [1] Beginning May 2021 with the release of 2021-2022 data, field crops Production, Supply, and Distribution (PSD) datasets reflect EU-27 (shown in the PSD system as "European Union") and UK separately. See footnote 3, Table 1387 for list of EU-27 countries.

Source: U.S. Department of Agriculture, Foreign Agricultural Service, "Production, Supply and Distribution Online," <www.fas.usda.gov/psdonline>, accessed September 2024.

Table 1389. World Production of Major Mineral Commodities: 2019 to 2022

[Units are as noted. Th. represents thousand, mil. represents million, and bil. represents billion]

Commodity	Unit	2019	2020	2021	2022	Leading producers, 2022
MINERAL FUELS						
Coal.........................	mil. short tons	8,902	8,486	8,900	9,064	China, India, Indonesia
Dry natural gas...............	bil. cubic feet	141,817	138,292	144,184	145,068	United States, Russia, Iran
Natural gas plant liquids........	mil. barrels [1]	4,276	4,355	4,485	4,688	United States, Saudi Arabia, Canada
Petroleum, crude..............	mil. barrels [1]	29,975	27,735	28,167	29,525	United States, Saudi Arabia, Russia
NONMETALLIC MINERALS						
Barite........................	th. metric tons	8,500	5,910	6,640	8,160	India, China, Morocco
Cement, hydraulic.............	mil. metric tons	4,200	4,220	4,350	4,140	China, India, Vietnam
Fluorspar....................	th. metric tons	8,610	8,530	8,680	8,320	China, Mexico, Mongolia
Nitrogen in ammonia...........	mil. metric tons	145	150	149	145	China, Russia, United States
Phosphate rock, marketable.....	mil. metric tons	224	221	238	228	China, Morocco, United States
Potash, marketable............	mil. metric tons	42	45	46	40	Canada, Russia, China
Salt........................	mil. metric tons	310	282	269	270	China, United States, India
Sulfur.......................	mil. metric tons	84	80	81	82	China, United States, Russia
METALS						
Aluminum, metal content........	mil. metric tons	63	65	68	68	China, India, Russia
Bauxite, gross weight..........	mil. metric tons	388	393	384	400	Australia, Guinea, China
Chromium (chromite), gross weight. . .	th. metric tons	46,100	35,300	42,900	41,900	South Africa, Kazakhstan, Turkey
Cobalt [2]......................	th. metric tons	153	147	162	197	Congo, Dem. Rep. of; Indonesia: Russia
Copper, metal content [2].........	th. metric tons	20,400	20,600	21,200	21,900	Chile; Peru; Congo, Dem. Rep. of
Gold, metal content...........	metric tons	3,260	3,050	3,120	3,160	China, Australia, Russia
Iron ore, gross weight [3].........	mil. metric tons	2,450	2,470	2,680	2,500	Australia, Brazil, China
Lead, metal content [2]...........	th. metric tons	4,650	4,440	4,550	4,460	China, Australia, United States, Mexico
Magnesium [4]..................	th. metric tons	1,080	1,080	1,030	1,050	China, Kazakhstan, Brazil
Manganese ore, metal content........	th. metric tons	20,700	19,500	20,200	20,100	South Africa, Gabon, Australia
Nickel, metal content [2]..........	th. metric tons	2,610	2,510	2,730	3,270	Indonesia, Philippines, Russia
Steel, raw....................	mil. metric tons	1,870	1,880	1,950	1,880	China, India, Japan
Tantalum concentrates [2]........	metric tons	1,750	1,840	1,830	1,990	Congo, Dem. Rep. of; Brazil; Rwanda
Tin, metal content [2]............	th. metric tons	294	276	305	307	China, Indonesia, Burma
Titanium (Ilmenite concentrate) [2, 5]...	th. metric tons	10,600	11,100	8,900	8,800	China, Mozambique, South Africa
Tungsten [2, 6].................	th. metric tons	82	78	84	80	China, Vietnam, Russia
Zinc, metal content [2]..................	th. metric tons	12,800	12,200	12,800	12,500	China, Peru, Australia

[1] 42-gallon barrels. [2] Mine output. [3] Includes iron ore concentrates and agglomerates. [4] Primary production; excludes U.S. production. [5] World production includes U.S. production of rutile and ilmenite. [6] Content of ore and concentrate.

Source: Mineral fuels, U.S. Energy Information Administration, "International Energy Statistics," <www.eia.gov/international/data/world>, accessed August 2024. Nonmetallic minerals and metals, U.S. Geological Survey, *Mineral Commodity Summaries*, annual; and "Minerals Yearbook - Metals and Minerals," <www.usgs.gov/centers/nmic/minerals-yearbook-metals-and-minerals>, accessed August 2024.

Table 1390. Net Electricity Generation by Energy Source and Country: 2022

[28,626.4 represents 28,626,400,000,000. kWh = kilowatt hours. Ranked for top 40 countries]

Country	Total [1] (bil. kWh)	Amount				Percent distribution			
		Fossil fuels [2]	Hydro-electricity	Nuclear	Non-hydro renew-ables [3]	Fossil fuels [2]	Hydro-electricity	Nuclear	Non-hydro renew-ables [3]
World, total [4].........	**28,626.4**	**17,523.2**	**4,352.6**	**2,588.9**	**4,206.7**	**61.2**	**15.2**	**9.0**	**14.7**
China..................	8,881.9	5,761.2	1,354.5	417.8	1,362.6	64.9	15.2	4.7	15.3
United States..........	**4,292.0**	**2,553.2**	**254.8**	**771.5**	**718.4**	**59.5**	**5.9**	**18.0**	**16.7**
India.................	1,760.3	1,338.8	173.4	46.2	201.8	76.1	9.9	2.6	11.5
Russia................	1,138.4	687.0	219.0	223.4	9.7	60.3	19.2	19.6	0.9
Japan.................	991.4	711.0	71.8	51.7	161.0	71.7	7.2	5.2	16.2
Brazil................	674.3	66.9	427.1	14.6	165.7	9.9	63.3	2.2	24.6
Canada...............	638.0	109.9	392.5	82.3	53.5	17.2	61.5	12.9	8.4
Korea, South...........	606.8	394.9	3.5	167.3	42.1	65.1	0.6	27.6	6.9
Germany..............	560.8	274.0	17.4	31.9	240.6	48.9	3.1	5.7	42.9
France...............	446.3	54.2	44.6	279.0	70.5	12.1	10.0	62.5	15.8
Saudi Arabia...........	431.9	430.6	–	–	1.3	99.7	–	–	0.3
Iran..................	360.7	337.4	15.9	6.0	1.4	93.5	4.4	1.7	0.4
Indonesia.............	337.2	269.4	27.3	–	40.5	79.9	8.1	–	12.0
Mexico...............	333.1	249.9	33.8	10.5	38.8	75.0	10.2	3.2	11.7
United Kingdom.........	318.6	132.2	6.1	43.3	137.6	41.5	1.9	13.6	43.2
Turkey................	308.2	179.5	66.7	–	62.0	58.2	21.7	–	20.1
Taiwan...............	283.6	237.5	5.8	22.9	18.0	83.7	2.1	8.1	6.3
Spain.................	278.7	105.3	17.1	56.0	101.8	37.8	6.1	20.1	36.5
Italy.................	274.2	174.6	28.3	–	72.0	63.7	10.3	–	26.3
Vietnam..............	267.7	152.0	79.1	–	36.6	56.8	29.6	–	13.7
Australia..............	261.5	171.2	16.8	–	73.9	65.5	6.4	–	28.2
South Africa...........	229.5	201.5	3.1	10.1	16.3	87.8	1.4	4.4	7.1
Egypt................	215.8	191.0	13.5	–	11.3	88.5	6.2	–	5.2
Malaysia..............	194.3	158.2	32.7	–	3.3	81.4	16.9	–	1.7
Thailand..............	181.9	149.3	6.8	–	25.8	82.1	3.7	–	14.2
Sweden...............	173.8	1.7	72.8	50.1	49.3	1.0	41.9	28.8	28.3
United Arab Emirates...	169.2	143.2	–	19.3	6.7	84.6	–	11.4	4.0
Pakistan..............	168.5	105.3	34.6	22.3	6.4	62.5	20.5	13.2	3.8
Poland................	167.2	131.1	1.8	–	34.8	78.4	1.1	–	20.8
Argentina.............	145.0	94.6	24.0	7.5	19.2	65.3	16.5	5.2	13.2
Norway...............	143.4	0.8	127.6	–	15.5	0.5	89.0	–	10.8
Netherlands...........	120.8	66.8	0.1	3.9	50.0	55.3	(Z)	3.3	41.4
Kazakhstan............	118.9	105.9	9.5	–	3.5	89.0	8.0	–	3.0
Iraq..................	115.6	112.9	2.7	–	0.1	97.7	2.3	–	(Z)
Philippines............	113.0	88.3	9.1	–	15.6	78.2	8.0	–	13.8
Ukraine...............	112.2	36.6	7.3	61.1	7.2	32.6	6.5	54.5	6.4
Bangladesh............	102.0	100.7	0.8	–	0.5	98.7	0.8	–	0.5
Chile.................	90.9	39.5	23.0	–	28.4	43.4	25.3	–	31.2
Belgium..............	90.9	26.4	0.2	41.6	23.1	29.0	0.2	45.8	25.4
Algeria...............	88.2	87.5	(Z)	–	0.7	99.2	(Z)	–	0.8

– Represents zero. Z Less than 50 million or .05%. [1] Electricity generated from fossil fuels, and hydroelectric, nuclear, geothermal, solar, wind, tidal, biomass, and waste energy resources. Includes negative values from hydroelectric pumped storage. [2] Electricity generated from coal, oil, and gas resources. [3] Electricity generated from geothermal, solar, wind, tidal and wave, biomass, and waste resources. [4] Includes countries not shown separately.

Source: U.S. Energy Information Administration, "International Energy Statistics," <www.eia.gov/international/data/world>, accessed April 2024.

Table 1391. World Primary Energy Production by Region and Type: 1995 to 2022

[In quadrillion Btu (350.7 represents 350,700,000,000,000,000). Btu = British thermal unit. For Btu conversion factors, see source]

Region and type	1995	2000	2005	2010	2015	2018	2019	2020	2021	2022
World total........................	**350.7**	**377.9**	**439.7**	**493.8**	**539.0**	**566.0**	**576.0**	**552.2**	**571.0**	**598.7**
REGION										
North America.....................	90.3	93.1	92.7	97.1	111.3	119.2	124.1	117.7	120.5	126.0
United States [1]......................	**68.9**	**69.3**	**67.4**	**72.5**	**85.4**	**92.0**	**97.6**	**91.9**	**93.8**	**98.5**
Central and South America..............	18.3	22.0	24.8	26.9	29.5	27.4	26.6	24.0	24.0	25.2
Europe...........................	46.8	47.5	45.6	41.2	37.7	36.9	35.6	34.0	34.3	33.0
Eurasia..........................	53.1	53.8	66.8	70.8	75.2	81.2	82.1	76.9	81.2	77.7
Middle East.......................	48.4	56.1	65.5	70.2	83.0	89.2	86.7	83.0	84.6	91.4
Africa............................	23.1	26.0	32.9	36.0	32.0	33.7	33.6	29.8	31.3	31.0
Asia and Oceania...................	70.9	79.4	111.4	151.7	170.1	178.4	187.3	186.8	195.0	214.3
TYPE OF FUEL										
Petroleum [2].......................	141.3	152.9	168.4	171.0	187.5	193.3	192.2	179.5	181.9	189.9
Dry natural gas....................	80.3	89.3	102.1	116.9	129.6	143.9	148.6	144.8	151.0	151.9
Coal............................	93.2	96.5	126.1	156.4	168.2	168.8	172.7	165.1	172.6	189.6
Nuclear, renewables, and other.........	36.0	39.2	43.1	49.5	53.6	60.1	62.6	62.8	65.5	67.3

[1] Includes biomass, geothermal, and solar energy produced in the United States and not used for generating electricity. [2] Includes crude oil, lease condensate, and natural gas plant liquids.

Source: U.S. Energy Information Administration, "International Energy Statistics," <www.eia.gov/international/data/world>, accessed August 2024.

Table 1392. World Primary Energy Consumption by Region and Type: 1980 to 2022

[In quadrillion Btu (281.0 represents 281,000,000,000,000,000). Btu = British thermal unit. For Btu conversion factors, see source]

Region and type	1980	1990	2000	2010	2015	2019	2020	2021	2022
World, total................	**281.0**	**338.1**	**383.8**	**503.3**	**537.6**	**567.7**	**542.3**	**569.8**	**600.6**
REGION									
North America........................	87.7	95.5	113.1	113.9	114.4	117.0	107.5	112.3	114.6
United States [1].................	**76.0**	**82.3**	**96.7**	**95.1**	**94.5**	**96.6**	**88.9**	**93.4**	**94.8**
Central and South America.............	9.7	12.0	17.2	22.5	25.1	24.0	21.5	23.2	24.1
Europe............................	72.2	76.5	78.3	80.1	74.8	75.1	68.3	72.5	69.4
Eurasia [2]........................	50.3	61.3	38.2	42.7	43.0	44.3	42.5	45.3	44.3
Middle East.........................	5.8	11.0	17.7	30.8	34.5	38.3	35.3	38.7	40.7
Africa............................	6.2	9.3	11.6	16.2	18.5	20.1	19.1	19.9	20.7
Asia and Oceania.......................	49.2	72.5	107.8	197.0	227.3	248.9	248.0	257.9	286.9
TYPE OF FUEL									
Petroleum [3]........................	132.1	136.1	156.7	179.0	188.5	196.8	178.5	189.7	194.8
Dry natural gas.......................	53.9	75.1	89.6	119.4	130.1	146.2	143.9	149.7	148.7
Coal............................	78.9	95.9	98.7	157.9	168.5	166.3	161.0	169.0	194.0
Nuclear, renewables, and other........	16.2	31.0	38.8	48.0	51.7	59.8	60.1	62.8	64.4

[1] Includes biomass, geothermal, and solar energy consumed in the United States and not used for generating electricity. [2] Prior to 1992, data were for the former U.S.S.R. [3] Includes all refined petroleum products.

Source: U.S. Energy Information Administration, "International Energy Statistics," <www.eia.gov/international/data/world>, accessed April 2024.

Table 1393. Energy Consumption by Country: 2010 to 2022

[In quadrillion Btu (503.25 represents 503,250,000,000,000,000). Btu = British thermal units. Total primary energy consumption includes the consumption of petroleum, dry natural gas, coal, and net nuclear, hydroelectric, and non-hydroelectric renewable electricity. For data qualifications for countries and Btu conversion factors, see source]

Country	Total (quad. Btu)				Country	Total (quad. Btu)			
	2010	2015	2020	2022		2010	2015	2020	2022
World, total [1]........	**503.25**	**537.62**	**542.27**	**600.60**	Kuwait....................	1.40	1.68	1.47	1.72
United States..........	**95.14**	**94.48**	**88.85**	**94.79**	Libya.....................	0.90	0.61	0.64	0.80
Algeria.................	1.78	2.35	2.48	2.63	Malaysia.................	2.94	3.24	3.53	3.95
Argentina...............	3.41	3.68	2.99	3.45	Mexico...................	7.34	7.53	6.96	7.56
Australia................	5.43	5.48	5.59	6.17	Morocco.................	0.70	0.78	0.81	0.93
Austria.................	1.25	1.19	1.14	1.11	Netherlands.............	4.27	3.77	3.56	3.31
Azerbaijan...............	0.57	0.61	0.62	0.64	New Zealand.............	0.64	0.69	0.65	0.62
Bahrain.................	0.59	0.69	0.79	0.80	Nigeria..................	0.82	1.60	1.76	1.87
Bangladesh...............	0.96	1.33	1.55	1.66	Norway..................	1.14	1.13	1.13	1.10
Belarus.................	1.12	0.95	0.92	0.95	Oman.....................	0.89	1.18	1.22	1.41
Belgium.................	2.81	2.44	2.35	2.39	Pakistan.................	2.40	2.76	3.08	3.51
Brazil..................	8.88	10.34	9.41	10.77	Paraguay.................	0.10	0.14	0.17	0.19
Bulgaria.................	0.68	0.74	0.65	0.74	Peru.....................	0.74	0.90	0.81	0.85
Burma..................	0.21	0.33	0.51	0.50	Philippines..............	1.10	1.49	1.65	1.80
Canada.................	11.44	12.32	11.68	12.27	Poland...................	4.08	4.05	3.99	4.05
Chile..................	1.12	1.24	1.30	1.37	Portugal.................	0.95	0.91	0.79	0.83
China..................	107.25	129.11	145.35	173.96	Qatar....................	1.25	2.06	2.15	2.20
Colombia.................	1.04	1.36	1.20	1.34	Romania.................	1.32	1.21	1.18	1.15
Czechia.................	1.76	1.68	1.57	1.62	Russia...................	29.24	29.97	30.01	32.54
Denmark.................	0.78	0.64	0.56	0.59	Saudi Arabia.............	9.86	9.86	9.07	11.43
Ecuador.................	0.54	0.61	0.51	0.54	Serbia...................	0.61	0.58	0.60	0.59
Egypt..................	3.41	3.64	3.60	4.05	Singapore...............	2.93	3.29	3.30	3.71
Finland.................	1.21	1.08	1.01	1.01	Slovakia.................	0.73	0.68	0.66	0.51
France.................	10.52	9.91	8.47	8.29	South Africa.............	5.61	5.56	5.54	5.72
Germany.................	13.70	12.84	11.13	11.09	Spain....................	5.63	5.07	4.61	5.05
Greece.................	1.29	1.05	0.91	0.98	Sweden..................	1.79	1.61	1.50	1.58
Hong Kong..............	1.34	1.28	0.96	1.26	Switzerland.............	1.07	0.97	0.89	0.90
Hungary.................	1.04	0.97	1.02	1.00	Syria....................	1.01	0.41	0.39	0.40
India..................	21.41	27.07	30.13	35.26	Taiwan...................	4.63	4.66	4.56	4.92
Indonesia................	6.02	6.56	7.12	9.10	Thailand.................	4.38	5.11	4.95	5.02
Iran....................	8.97	10.57	11.98	13.50	Trinidad and Tobago. ..	0.96	0.98	0.66	0.65
Iraq....................	1.33	1.41	2.06	2.57	Turkey...................	4.16	5.28	5.64	6.02
Ireland.................	0.61	0.54	0.56	0.61	Turkmenistan............	1.03	1.76	1.80	1.82
Israel..................	0.94	1.01	0.95	1.03	Ukraine..................	5.08	3.81	3.36	2.19
Italy..................	7.25	6.25	5.54	5.81	United Arab Emirates...	3.64	4.70	4.34	4.69
Japan..................	20.98	18.69	16.96	16.89	United Kingdom........	9.10	8.04	6.65	6.74
Kazakhstan..............	3.14	3.27	3.27	3.42	Uzbekistan..............	1.89	1.96	1.78	1.85
Korea, North...........	0.75	0.42	0.74	0.67	Venezuela...............	2.63	2.62	1.45	1.62
Korea, South...........	10.83	11.86	11.98	12.20	Vietnam.................	1.72	2.50	3.65	3.84

[1] Includes countries not shown separately.

Source: U.S. Energy Information Administration, "International Energy Statistics," <www.eia.gov/international/data/world>, accessed April 2024.

Table 1394. World Energy Consumption by World Region and Energy Source: 2022, and Projections, 2025 to 2050

[In quadrillion Btu (637.8 represents 637,800,000,000,000,000). Btu = British thermal units. For Btu conversion factors, see source]

Region and energy source	2022	Projections 2025	2030	2035	2040	2045	2050	Average annual percent change 2022-2050
World	**637.8**	**661.4**	**698.2**	**736.4**	**772.2**	**813.6**	**854.7**	**1.05**
Americas	152.6	152.3	155.8	160.3	165.0	171.2	178.7	0.57
United States	**98.9**	**97.3**	**97.4**	**98.3**	**99.4**	**101.9**	**105.1**	**0.22**
Canada	14.7	14.7	15.5	16.4	17.5	18.7	20.1	1.14
Mexico	7.7	7.8	8.4	8.9	9.3	9.9	10.5	1.10
Brazil	14.9	15.6	16.5	17.4	17.9	18.3	18.8	0.82
Other Americas	16.4	16.8	18.0	19.3	20.8	22.4	24.2	1.40
Europe and Eurasia	130.1	132.9	134.3	138.1	143.1	148.3	154.4	0.61
Western Europe	84.2	86.1	86.9	88.7	91.2	93.6	96.7	0.49
Russia	33.5	33.9	34.1	35.3	36.4	37.8	39.2	0.56
Eastern Europe and Eurasia	12.3	12.8	13.3	14.2	15.4	16.8	18.5	1.46
Asia Pacific	292.6	309.4	336.6	360.5	381.1	403.7	424.1	1.33
Japan	18.6	18.6	17.1	16.5	16.2	15.9	15.8	-0.58
South Korea	13.0	13.5	13.8	14.1	14.2	14.2	14.3	0.34
Australia and New Zealand	7.2	7.2	7.7	8.0	8.4	8.8	9.2	0.92
China	172.5	179.7	187.2	191.4	192.8	194.9	195.4	0.45
India	38.3	43.5	56.2	69.4	82.5	96.7	110.4	3.85
Other Asia Pacific	43.1	46.9	54.5	61.1	67.1	73.2	78.9	2.18
Africa and Middle East	62.5	66.9	71.4	77.4	83.1	90.4	97.6	1.60
Africa	24.3	26.0	29.5	33.6	37.2	42.5	47.8	2.44
Middle East	38.2	40.8	42.0	43.9	45.9	47.9	49.8	0.95
Liquid fuels	190.4	198.2	202.0	207.3	214.0	222.8	231.9	0.71
Natural gas	153.3	155.4	161.4	167.4	176.4	186.5	197.0	0.90
Coal	166.0	163.8	166.1	170.4	169.3	170.5	172.1	0.13
Nuclear	27.7	29.3	31.9	33.4	33.6	33.9	34.7	0.81
Other	100.5	114.8	136.8	157.9	178.9	199.9	219.0	2.82

Source: U.S. Energy Information Administration, *International Energy Outlook 2023*, October 2023. See also <www.eia.gov/outlooks/ieo/>.

Table 1395. Energy Consumption Per Capita by Country: 2010 to 2022

[Million Btu per person (72.2 represents 72,200,000. Btu = British thermal unit. Total energy consumption includes the consumption of petroleum, dry natural gas, coal, and net nuclear, hydroelectric, and non–hydroelectric renewable electricity. For data qualifications for countries and Btu conversion factors, see source]

Country	2010	2015	2020	2022	Country	2010	2015	2020	2022
World, total [1]	**72.2**	**72.4**	**69.2**	**75.3**	Korea, South	221.8	232.4	231.0	235.3
United States	**307.6**	**293.8**	**268.1**	**284.6**	Madagascar	1.4	2.1	1.4	1.9
Afghanistan	3.9	3.1	2.3	2.7	Malaysia	102.2	104.3	106.2	116.5
Algeria	49.5	59.5	57.0	58.5	Mali	2.1	2.9	3.7	4.5
Angola	11.2	13.2	10.1	9.6	Mexico	65.2	62.7	55.2	59.3
Argentina	82.9	85.2	66.3	75.7	Morocco	21.5	22.5	22.0	24.9
Australia	246.2	229.5	218.1	236.7	Mozambique	3.5	6.7	5.0	5.4
Bangladesh	6.5	8.4	9.3	9.7	Nepal	2.2	2.6	4.6	5.9
Brazil	45.2	50.4	44.2	50.0	Niger	1.4	1.8	1.5	1.4
Burkina Faso	1.7	2.8	3.0	3.4	Nigeria	5.1	8.7	8.5	8.6
Burma	4.2	6.4	9.6	9.2	Pakistan	12.3	13.1	13.6	14.9
Cameroon	5.1	5.3	5.0	4.7	Peru	25.3	29.4	24.3	24.9
Canada	337.0	345.2	307.4	315.6	Philippines	11.6	14.4	14.7	15.6
China	79.5	92.6	102.0	122.0	Poland	107.2	106.5	105.4	106.2
Colombia	23.2	28.9	23.5	25.8	Russia	204.1	207.1	206.1	225.2
Congo, Dem. Rep.	0.8	1.0	0.9	1.0	Saudi Arabia	335.2	301.0	252.1	313.9
Cote d'Ivoire	5.7	7.0	7.1	7.7	South Africa	108.3	99.5	94.2	95.5
Egypt	39.1	37.2	33.5	36.5	Spain	120.8	109.2	97.4	106.0
Ethiopia	1.2	1.8	2.3	2.3	Sudan	7.7	6.9	7.0	6.3
France	162.1	148.8	125.3	121.9	Taiwan	199.9	198.4	193.2	208.3
Germany	170.5	156.9	133.8	132.3	Tanzania	2.5	3.2	2.8	3.2
Ghana	5.6	8.5	10.7	11.4	Thailand	64.1	72.7	69.3	70.0
India	17.2	20.4	21.6	24.8	Turkey	56.8	66.3	67.0	70.6
Indonesia	24.7	25.3	26.2	33.0	Uganda	1.8	2.1	2.1	2.2
Iran	119.0	129.3	137.2	152.5	Ukraine	110.5	88.7	80.3	53.3
Iraq	42.6	37.2	48.3	57.7	United Kingdom	144.8	123.4	99.2	99.4
Italy	122.3	102.9	93.3	98.5	Uzbekistan	66.0	63.4	53.0	53.5
Japan	163.9	146.9	135.5	136.1	Venezuela	91.5	86.0	50.8	57.3
Kenya	4.9	5.7	5.5	5.7	Vietnam	19.6	27.1	37.8	39.1
Korea, North	30.4	16.5	28.7	25.9	Yemen	13.8	6.2	3.6	3.9

[1] Includes countries not shown separately.

Source: U.S. Energy Information Administration, "International Energy Statistics," <www.eia.gov/international/data/world>, accessed May 2024.

Table 1396. World Dry Natural Gas Production by Major Producing Country: 1980 to 2022

[In billions of cubic feet (53,361 represents 53,361,000,000,000). Ranked for top 30 countries, as of most recent year]

Country	Dry natural gas production								
	1980	1990	2000	2010	2015	2019	2020	2021	2022 (P)
World, total [1]	**53,361**	**73,379**	**86,770**	**113,787**	**125,641**	**141,817**	**138,292**	**144,184**	**145,068**
United States	**19,403**	**17,810**	**19,182**	**21,316**	**27,065**	**33,899**	**33,811**	**34,529**	**36,353**
Russia	(X)	(X)	19,335	21,458	21,531	23,938	22,501	24,775	21,818
Iran	250	818	2,127	5,161	6,526	8,273	8,860	9,116	9,298
China	505	508	962	3,278	4,632	6,333	6,908	7,486	7,958
Canada	2,759	3,849	6,470	5,876	6,165	6,068	5,960	6,196	6,628
Qatar	184	222	1,028	4,121	5,794	5,914	5,883	5,936	5,989
Australia	313	723	1,159	1,859	2,546	5,125	5,112	5,196	5,431
Norway	917	976	1,867	3,756	4,139	4,068	3,964	4,070	4,369
Saudi Arabia	334	1,077	1,759	3,096	3,614	3,982	4,018	4,082	4,304
Algeria	411	1,787	2,940	2,988	2,933	3,145	2,978	3,682	3,557
Turkmenistan	(X)	(X)	1,642	1,466	2,831	2,953	2,813	2,850	3,054
Malaysia	56	501	1,465	2,171	2,240	2,539	2,291	2,501	2,665
Egypt	30	286	646	2,166	1,565	2,355	2,105	2,408	2,289
Indonesia	654	1,602	2,237	2,917	2,571	2,369	2,090	2,082	2,027
United Arab Emirates	200	780	1,355	1,811	2,125	2,007	2,006	1,985	2,002
Uzbekistan	(X)	(X)	1,992	2,123	1,967	1,975	1,622	1,755	1,677
Argentina	280	630	1,321	1,416	1,285	1,544	1,416	1,428	1,528
Oman	28	99	322	957	1,057	1,281	1,253	1,354	1,439
Nigeria	38	131	440	1,024	1,594	1,635	1,644	1,529	1,411
United Kingdom	1,323	1,754	3,826	2,111	1,428	1,390	1,392	1,150	1,333
Pakistan	286	482	856	1,400	1,349	1,211	1,281	1,331	1,304
Azerbaijan	(X)	(X)	200	552	636	815	868	1,108	1,207
India	51	399	719	1,848	1,103	1,106	979	1,146	1,171
Mexico	900	903	1,297	1,769	1,426	1,027	1,036	1,050	1,110
Thailand	–	208	658	1,278	1,406	1,353	1,217	1,199	1,088
Kazakhstan	(X)	(X)	314	621	749	819	749	945	954
Trinidad and Tobago	81	177	493	1,499	1,306	1,259	1,091	908	945
Bangladesh	50	162	343	711	892	966	887	882	869
Israel	5	1	(Z)	55	300	363	595	731	808
Brazil	42	97	257	523	829	897	844	848	801

P Preliminary. X Not applicable. – Represents zero. Z Less than 500 million cubic feet. [1] Includes countries not shown separately.

Source: U.S. Energy Information Administration, "International Energy Statistics," <www.eia.gov/international/data/world>, accessed April 2024.

Table 1397. World Coal Production by Major Producing Country: 1980 to 2022

[In thousands of short tons (4,154,789 represents 4,154,789,000). Coal includes anthracite, bituminous, subbituminous, metallurgical and lignite. Ranked for top 30 countries, as of most recent year]

Country	Coal production								
	1980	1990	2000	2010	2015	2019	2020	2021	2022
World, total [1]	**4,154,789**	**5,186,572**	**5,134,299**	**8,208,186**	**8,706,618**	**8,901,840**	**8,486,367**	**8,899,735**	**9,435,569**
China	683,587	1,189,725	1,525,800	3,779,212	4,129,849	4,239,848	4,300,747	4,548,131	4,766,784
India	121,502	241,899	362,804	578,216	696,349	805,053	793,418	839,963	1,040,500
Indonesia	627	13,165	93,736	397,343	508,789	679,199	621,403	676,808	726,817
United States	**829,700**	**1,029,076**	**1,073,612**	**1,084,368**	**896,941**	**706,307**	**535,434**	**577,361**	**593,608**
Australia	115,196	226,347	338,999	486,341	574,181	564,027	550,889	514,937	510,991
Russia	(X)	(X)	264,912	329,258	409,701	481,701	442,475	479,800	508,541
South Africa	126,898	189,479	247,917	280,796	282,334	284,234	272,392	259,844	269,292
Germany	(X)	(X)	226,047	202,286	203,612	144,749	118,363	139,174	144,183
Kazakhstan	(X)	(X)	82,548	122,278	118,299	115,216	113,920	98,214	127,438
Poland	253,517	237,082	178,247	146,257	149,147	123,406	110,638	118,346	119,269
Turkey	20,531	52,280	69,741	80,908	64,390	95,999	82,356	94,394	92,546
Colombia	4,590	22,562	42,044	82,021	94,300	92,972	54,378	61,948	59,884
Vietnam	5,732	5,100	12,797	49,422	45,927	50,361	48,386	52,740	48,076
Canada	40,442	75,323	76,239	74,840	68,722	58,605	49,918	52,318	45,352
Bulgaria	33,304	34,916	29,136	32,413	39,528	30,865	24,580	31,184	39,150
Serbia	(X)	(X)	(X)	41,861	41,696	42,858	43,732	40,143	38,723
Czechia	(X)	(X)	71,829	60,857	51,168	45,088	34,809	34,677	38,659
Mongolia	5,818	7,889	5,715	27,736	26,682	61,508	48,331	38,157	31,097
Korea, North	33,367	36,542	32,786	28,109	33,345	29,966	28,176	23,134	23,866
Romania	38,762	42,090	32,281	34,312	28,101	23,868	16,537	19,547	20,018
Laos	–	3	252	809	5,284	17,003	16,189	15,781	16,364
Philippines	363	1,370	1,491	7,330	8,133	16,836	14,624	15,849	15,965
Greece	25,571	57,205	70,423	62,303	50,977	30,176	15,491	13,333	15,105
Thailand	1,681	13,711	19,605	20,126	16,701	15,518	14,607	15,677	15,038
Bosnia & Herzegovina	(X)	(X)	8,200	7,047	6,666	7,228	6,815	7,363	14,652
Pakistan	1,905	3,249	3,492	3,803	4,566	9,629	9,584	9,306	14,012
Kosovo	(X)	(X)	(X)	9,534	9,084	8,888	9,239	9,409	10,003
Mozambique	–	–	26	79	7,276	11,991	8,211	11,695	9,937
Mexico	6,349	9,873	13,251	19,018	11,769	9,843	9,703	9,786	7,344
Brazil	5,778	5,065	7,502	5,969	8,850	5,963	6,149	7,347	6,835

– Represents zero. X Not applicable. [1] Includes other countries not shown separately.

Source: U.S. Energy Information Administration, "International Energy Statistics," <www.eia.gov/international/data/world>, accessed April 2024.

Table 1398. World Daily Crude Oil Production by Major Producing Country: 1990 to 2023

[In thousands of barrels per day (60,498 barrels represents 60,498,000 barrels). Includes lease condensate. Ranked for top 40 countries, as of most recent year]

Country	1990	1995	2000	2005	2010	2015	2020	2021	2022	2023
World, total [1]	60,498	61,569	66,359	74,028	74,408	80,965	76,027	77,210	80,825	81,804
United States	7,355	6,560	5,822	5,184	5,484	9,446	11,308	11,268	11,911	12,933
Russia	(X)	6,166	6,477	9,491	9,694	10,253	9,865	10,112	10,314	10,124
Saudi Arabia	6,258	7,937	7,997	9,780	8,417	10,336	9,406	9,313	10,644	9,733
Canada	1,342	1,535	1,696	1,831	2,741	3,677	4,180	4,439	4,543	4,592
Iraq	2,005	550	2,567	1,816	2,399	4,055	4,088	4,085	4,471	4,341
China	2,768	3,000	3,259	3,594	4,078	4,278	3,889	3,988	4,090	4,183
Iran	3,098	3,652	3,685	4,068	4,080	3,293	2,644	3,110	3,293	3,623
Brazil	631	686	1,231	1,639	2,055	2,437	2,940	2,905	3,022	3,402
United Arab Emirates	2,117	2,486	2,238	2,723	2,570	3,149	3,138	3,091	3,468	3,394
Kuwait	1,048	1,837	1,765	2,423	2,300	2,859	2,545	2,527	2,826	2,710
Mexico	2,548	2,617	3,012	3,333	2,621	2,302	1,723	1,780	1,843	1,936
Kazakhstan	(X)	422	717	1,269	1,525	1,653	1,757	1,761	1,727	1,854
Norway	1,621	2,756	3,207	2,690	1,871	1,610	1,713	1,776	1,704	1,814
Nigeria	1,750	1,932	2,039	2,469	2,408	2,171	1,775	1,523	1,291	1,442
Qatar	403	449	688	959	1,297	1,356	1,274	1,304	1,321	1,322
Libya	1,349	1,405	1,411	1,680	1,710	464	408	1,238	1,058	1,225
Algeria	755	763	806	1,650	1,540	1,429	1,122	1,134	1,212	1,183
Angola	476	639	745	1,243	1,909	1,802	1,243	1,112	1,153	1,144
Oman	676	857	956	774	865	981	949	971	1,063	1,048
Colombia	440	585	684	526	785	1,003	781	736	754	777
Venezuela	2,098	2,752	2,894	2,840	2,410	2,489	527	595	704	751
United Kingdom	1,825	2,558	2,480	1,652	1,233	893	951	809	745	663
Argentina	483	721	801	665	613	532	480	514	583	635
Azerbaijan	(X)	185	281	448	1,035	848	695	711	667	617
Indonesia	1,281	1,431	1,278	1,061	945	786	708	659	611	608
India	673	717	659	663	751	761	627	611	613	604
Egypt	874	910	689	618	636	682	587	561	568	564
Malaysia	622	705	663	726	638	654	556	509	505	501
Ecuador	290	381	401	532	486	543	479	473	481	475
Guyana	(NA)	(NA)	(NA)	–	–	–	75	117	290	391
Australia	577	514	721	419	479	322	351	334	311	280
Congo, Republic of	156	180	256	239	340	238	283	266	275	262
Gabon	269	369	276	270	246	213	174	175	196	204
Turkmenistan	(X)	70	144	190	196	243	187	196	195	191
Bahrain	42	182	187	187	182	202	171	175	188	180
Vietnam	52	153	325	358	299	333	193	184	179	173
Ghana	(NA)	6	7	6	7	102	199	180	165	160
South Sudan	(X)	(X)	(X)	(X)	(X)	153	163	157	155	146
Thailand	42	61	120	183	242	248	202	177	143	136
Chad	(NA)	(NA)	(NA)	170	123	123	123	106	110	124

– Represents zero or rounds to zero. X Not applicable. NA Not available. [1] Includes countries not shown separately.

Source: U.S. Energy Information Administration, "International Energy Statistics," <www.eia.gov/international/data/world>, accessed April 2024.

Table 1399. Carbon Dioxide Emissions From Consumption of Fossil Fuels by Country: 1980 to 2022

[In millions of metric tons of carbon dioxide (18,722 represents 18,722,000,000). Ranked for top 25 countries, as of most recent year shown. Includes carbon dioxide emissions from the consumption of petroleum, natural gas, and coal]

Country	1980	1990	2000	2010	2015	2018	2019	2020	2021	2022
World, total [1]	18,722	22,150	24,266	32,531	34,836	35,663	35,764	33,848	35,720	38,502
China	1,597	2,417	3,483	9,004	10,427	10,602	10,729	10,850	11,466	13,506
United States	4,756	5,038	5,889	5,594	5,262	5,278	5,147	4,584	4,905	4,941
India	270	541	886	1,648	2,145	2,383	2,462	2,339	2,392	2,805
Russia	(X)	(X)	1,540	1,661	1,690	1,763	1,754	1,676	1,845	1,840
Japan	872	1,109	1,233	1,197	1,215	1,159	1,119	1,052	1,041	1,049
Iran	102	195	303	537	613	643	649	653	681	750
Indonesia	72	149	256	409	461	529	563	538	584	685
Germany	(X)	(X)	872	822	788	782	721	631	675	668
Korea, South	139	264	466	612	662	703	687	657	679	643
Saudi Arabia	107	199	290	497	621	568	561	525	599	638
Canada	426	439	515	565	592	615	605	542	555	573
Brazil	188	243	327	410	500	453	530	496	533	517
South Africa	229	329	393	479	474	456	482	469	441	477
Mexico	206	280	382	457	465	454	474	411	421	454
Australia	221	268	339	392	382	402	409	376	384	415
Turkey	62	128	207	268	351	398	392	372	404	392
United Kingdom	613	606	570	542	451	409	393	331	346	353
Italy	337	421	452	416	349	340	332	288	321	317
France	472	385	409	388	347	344	339	288	316	312
Thailand	34	84	158	258	296	304	311	287	281	308
Taiwan	70	119	238	272	273	283	293	285	301	306
Vietnam	10	13	42	127	193	244	292	291	283	298
Poland	399	365	303	315	305	320	304	284	297	293
United Arab Emirates	16	77	128	219	283	248	265	262	268	268
Spain	189	236	316	305	284	294	281	231	250	266

X Not applicable. [1] Includes other countries not shown separately.

Source: U.S. Energy Information Administration, "International Energy Statistics," <www.eia.gov/international/data/world>, accessed April 2024.

Table 1400. Telephones, Mobile Cellular Phones, and Internet Use by Country: 2022

[Data are from the International Telecommunication Union. Data are for 2022 except as noted. For data qualifications for individual countries, see source]

Country	Fixed telephone subscriptions per 100 people [1]	Cellphone subscriptions per 100 people [2]	Internet users as percent of population [3]	Country	Fixed telephone subscriptions per 100 people [1]	Cellphone subscriptions per 100 people [2]	Internet users as percent of population [3]
World....................	**11.4**	**108.0**	[4] 63.1	Italy........................	33.8	133.0	85.1
United States............	**27.1**	**110.2**	[4] 91.8	Japan.......................	49.0	167.5	[4] 82.9
Albania......................	6.2	97.9	82.6	Kazakhstan..............	14.9	130.4	92.3
Argentina..................	16.7	132.4	88.4	Kenya......................	0.1	121.7	[4] 28.8
Australia...................	24.5	107.0	[4] 96.2	Korea, South............	44.0	148.6	97.2
Austria......................	39.6	123.4	93.6	Latvia......................	9.4	117.1	91.0
Belarus.....................	44.4	123.4	89.5	Lithuania.................	9.1	139.1	87.7
Belgium....................	25.3	101.9	94.0	Malaysia..................	24.9	141.3	97.4
Bosnia & Herzegovina...	20.1	117.9	78.8	Malta.......................	48.6	131.6	91.5
Brazil.......................	12.7	98.9	80.5	Mexico....................	21.3	100.3	[4] 75.6
Bulgaria....................	10.2	117.4	79.1	Montenegro.............	30.4	203.2	88.2
Canada....................	29.4	91.2	[4] 92.8	Netherlands.............	26.0	118.1	92.5
China.......................	12.6	124.9	75.6	Nigeria....................	0.0	101.7	[4] 55.4
Colombia..................	14.6	155.8	72.8	Norway....................	2.6	110.7	99.0
Costa Rica................	9.5	152.0	82.6	Pakistan..................	1.2	81.7	[4] 21.0
Cote d'Ivoire.............	0.9	174.0	35.5	Paraguay.................	2.5	127.7	76.3
Croatia.....................	30.6	111.2	82.1	Peru........................	5.3	122.0	74.7
Cuba........................	14.0	67.8	[4] 71.1	Poland.....................	13.2	131.9	86.9
Czechia....................	11.6	128.4	84.5	Portugal..................	52.9	124.5	84.5
Denmark...................	12.1	126.5	97.9	Romania..................	11.3	118.1	85.5
Ecuador....................	9.1	97.2	69.7	Russia.....................	[4] 16.4	[4] 169.0	90.4
Egypt.......................	10.5	93.2	72.2	Saudi Arabia............	18.6	132.4	100.0
Estonia.....................	20.1	155.0	91.0	Singapore................	31.9	156.5	96.0
Finland.....................	3.4	128.7	93.0	Slovenia..................	31.9	126.2	88.9
France......................	58.4	118.8	85.3	South Africa.............	2.2	167.4	[4] 72.3
Georgia....................	8.0	156.1	78.7	Spain......................	39.3	124.1	94.5
Germany..................	46.3	125.2	91.6	Sweden...................	[4] 12.0	125.1	95.0
Greece.....................	47.3	109.1	83.2	Thailand..................	6.1	176.3	88.0
Hong Kong, China.......	49.1	291.9	95.6	Tunisia....................	14.5	129.3	[4] 81.4
Hungary...................	28.5	104.1	90.5	Turkey.....................	13.1	105.8	83.4
India........................	1.9	80.6	[4] 46.3	United Arab Emirates...	24.2	212.2	100.0
Indonesia..................	3.1	114.9	66.5	United Kingdom.........	44.1	120.8	[4] 96.7
Iran.........................	33.1	164.5	[4] 78.6	Uruguay..................	36.8	138.5	89.9
Iraq.........................	5.4	98.2	78.7	Vietnam..................	2.4	139.9	78.6

[1] Refers to the sum of active number of analogue fixed telephone lines, voice-over-IP (VoIP) subscriptions, fixed wireless local loop (WLL) subscriptions, ISDN voice-channel equivalents and fixed public payphones. [2] Subscriptions to a public mobile telephone service that provides access to the public switched telephone network (PSTN) using cellular technology. Includes number of postpaid subscriptions and active prepaid accounts. Applies to all mobile cellular subscriptions that offer voice communications. Excludes subscriptions via data cards or USB modems, subscriptions to public mobile data services, private trunked mobile radio, telepoint, radio paging, and telemetry services. [3] Internet users are individuals who have used the internet (from any location) in the last 3 months. The internet can be used via a computer, mobile phone, personal digital assistant, electronic game device, digital TV etc. [4] Data for 2021.

Source: The World Bank, Washington, DC, "World Development Indicators" database ©, <databank.worldbank.org/source/world-development-indicators>, accessed August 2024.

Table 1401. Global Telecommunications Indicators: 2000 to 2022

[975 represents 975,000,000. Data are from the International Telecommunication Union]

Indicator	2000	2005	2010	2015	2017	2018	2019	2020	2021	2022
NUMBER (million)										
Fixed telephone subscriptions [1]..................	975	1,244	1,229	1,046	984	948	925	903	892	841
Mobile cellular subscriptions [2].....................	738	2,206	5,296	7,132	7,696	7,852	8,214	8,269	8,490	8,361
Fixed broadband internet subscriptions [3]........	(NA)	220	532	840	1,026	1,069	1,141	1,230	1,328	1,411
PERCENT OF POPULATION										
Internet users [4].................................	6.7	15.7	28.8	40.3	45.5	49.2	53.8	59.6	63.1	(NA)
PER 100 INHABITANTS										
Fixed telephone subscriptions [1]..................	15.9	19.3	17.6	14.1	13.0	12.7	12.0	11.6	11.3	11.4
Mobile cellular subscriptions [2].....................	12.1	33.7	75.9	96.1	101.4	104.7	105.9	105.6	107.4	108.0
Fixed broadband internet subscriptions [3]........	(NA)	3.7	7.8	11.5	13.7	14.5	14.8	15.8	16.9	18.4

NA Not available. [1] Refers to the sum of active number of analogue fixed telephone lines, voice-over-IP (VoIP) subscriptions, fixed wireless local loop (WLL) subscriptions, ISDN voice-channel equivalents and fixed public payphones. [2] Subscriptions to a public mobile telephone service that provides access to the public switched telephone network (PSTN) using cellular technology. Includes number of postpaid subscriptions and active prepaid accounts. Applies to all mobile cellular subscriptions that offer voice communications. Excludes subscriptions via data cards or USB modems, subscriptions to public mobile data services, private trunked mobile radio, telepoint, radio paging, and telemetry services. [3] Refers to fixed subscriptions to high-speed access to the public internet (a TCP/IP connection), at downstream speeds equal to, or greater than, 256 kbit/s. Includes cable modem, DSL, fiber-to-the-home/building, other fixed (wired)-broadband subscriptions, satellite broadband, and terrestrial fixed wireless broadband. Excludes subscriptions that have access to data communications (including the internet) via mobile-cellular networks. [4] Internet users are individuals who have used the internet (from any location) in the last 3 months. The internet can be used via a computer, mobile phone, personal digital assistant, electronic game device, digital TV etc.

Source: The World Bank, Washington, DC, "World Development Indicators" database ©, <databank.worldbank.org/source/world-development-indicators>, accessed August 2024.

Table 1402. Patents Issued to Residents of Foreign Countries by Country of Residence: 2013 to 2023

[Data are shown for fiscal years ending September 30. Each patent grant is listed under only one country of residence. Includes utility, design, plant, and reissue patents. Countries are in rank order for top 30 countries in 2023]

Country	2013	2014	2015	2016	2017	2018	2019	2020	2021	2022	2023 (P)
Total...................	150,014	167,937	168,049	173,656	180,287	177,550	193,373	210,695	201,862	198,382	184,583
Japan....................	53,359	56,639	54,487	53,044	51,741	50,012	53,172	55,899	49,668	46,937	40,055
China...................	6,181	7,715	8,598	10,993	14,154	16,315	20,836	26,176	29,947	35,193	33,524
Korea, South............	15,058	17,815	19,615	21,867	22,689	22,054	22,427	24,218	23,489	23,014	23,148
Germany.................	15,798	17,926	17,485	17,569	17,994	17,434	18,758	19,799	18,219	16,949	14,988
Taiwan..................	12,168	12,271	12,317	12,735	12,535	11,424	11,857	13,390	12,922	12,268	12,063
United Kingdom.........	6,292	7,232	7,143	7,289	7,636	7,549	8,494	8,834	8,328	7,528	7,200
Canada..................	6,915	7,922	7,487	7,260	7,539	7,225	7,790	8,179	7,794	6,951	7,069
India...................	2,222	2,937	3,328	3,685	4,207	4,248	5,075	5,888	6,198	6,132	6,373
France..................	6,245	7,144	7,034	6,907	7,365	6,991	7,532	7,981	7,079	6,781	6,027
Israel..................	2,948	3,561	3,839	3,820	4,304	4,168	4,630	5,011	4,822	4,510	4,619
Italy...................	2,834	3,043	3,060	3,158	3,209	3,247	3,718	3,913	3,582	3,339	3,007
Sweden..................	2,309	2,905	2,828	3,044	3,327	3,164	3,321	3,495	3,308	3,197	2,998
Switzerland.............	2,278	2,660	2,745	2,905	3,024	2,893	3,197	3,394	3,102	3,013	2,943
Netherlands.............	2,391	2,883	2,732	2,941	3,132	3,215	3,340	3,552	3,135	2,950	2,358
Australia...............	1,878	2,062	1,937	1,888	1,964	1,966	2,136	2,298	2,348	2,208	1,975
Saudi Arabia............	206	273	339	442	541	608	871	1,007	1,245	1,333	1,380
Finland.................	1,205	1,499	1,437	1,605	1,730	1,601	1,545	1,641	1,415	1,441	1,282
Denmark.................	1,009	1,309	1,186	1,221	1,249	1,270	1,320	1,425	1,400	1,379	1,277
Austria.................	1,065	1,296	1,248	1,416	1,615	1,528	1,618	1,650	1,530	1,426	1,273
Belgium.................	1,111	1,267	1,234	1,315	1,358	1,408	1,447	1,537	1,453	1,418	1,263
Singapore...............	840	963	1,074	1,019	1,046	1,071	1,103	1,191	1,100	1,082	1,150
Spain...................	739	862	857	940	926	965	1,058	1,187	1,137	1,148	982
Ireland.................	435	486	523	570	611	628	754	930	934	913	887
Hong Kong...............	734	828	805	824	892	973	1,073	1,071	938	946	821
Norway..................	510	601	625	720	628	636	676	759	699	660	589
Russia..................	409	438	457	542	569	536	615	711	731	655	559
Brazil..................	265	352	372	399	396	442	432	547	520	523	458
New Zealand.............	285	308	342	349	374	376	435	494	495	478	409
Poland..................	101	172	201	265	281	291	337	439	445	371	406
Czechia.................	174	196	197	219	263	350	383	380	315	293	278
Other countries.........	2,050	2,372	2,517	2,705	2,988	2,962	3,423	3,699	3,564	3,346	3,222

P Preliminary.

Source: U.S. Patent and Trademark Office, USTPO Annual Reports, "FY2023 Workload Tables," <www.uspto.gov/about-us/performance-and-planning/uspto-annual-reports>, accessed March 2024.

Table 1403. Foreign Currency Exchange Rates by Country: 2017 to 2023

[Foreign currency units per U.S. dollar. Data are yearly averages]

Country	Currency	2017	2018	2019	2020	2021	2022	2023
Afghanistan.............	Afghani	71.09	73.60	77.58	76.65	83.48	90.08	82.64
Algeria.................	Dinar	115.88	117.41	119.40	126.74	135.01	142.12	135.93
Argentina...............	Peso	17.23	28.17	48.19	70.64	95.10	130.79	296.15
Australia...............	Dollar	1.36	1.34	1.44	1.45	1.33	1.44	1.51
Bahrain.................	Dinar	0.40	0.40	0.38	0.38	0.38	0.38	0.38
Brazil..................	Real	3.32	3.66	3.95	5.15	5.40	5.17	4.99
Canada..................	Dollar	1.35	1.30	1.33	1.34	1.25	1.30	1.35
Cayman Islands.........	Dollar	0.88	0.83	0.83	0.83	0.83	0.83	0.83
China...................	Yuan	7.03	6.62	6.91	6.90	6.45	6.73	7.08
Denmark.................	Krone	6.86	6.32	6.67	6.54	6.29	7.08	6.89
Egypt...................	Pound	18.59	17.81	16.81	15.81	15.70	19.21	30.65
Euro Zone...............	Euro	0.92	0.85	0.89	0.88	0.85	0.95	0.92
Hong Kong...............	Dollar	8.11	7.84	7.84	7.76	7.77	7.83	7.83
Hungary.................	Forint	285.58	270.44	290.71	307.77	303.29	372.78	353.02
Iceland.................	Krona	111.23	116.38	122.57	135.35	126.99	135.30	137.86
India...................	Rupee	67.81	68.42	70.39	74.10	73.94	78.60	82.57
Iraq....................	Dinar	1,241.68	1,193.48	1,191.25	1,197.50	1,460.13	1,459.75	1,376.53
Israel..................	New Shekel	3.75	3.60	3.56	3.44	3.23	3.36	3.69
Japan...................	Yen	116.67	110.42	109.01	106.73	109.82	131.45	140.51
Lebanon.................	Pound	1,593.97	1,511.68	1,510.29	1,510.68	1,519.23	1,515.67	1,370.99
Mexico..................	Peso	19.68	19.23	19.25	21.47	20.28	20.11	17.73
Morocco.................	Dirham	10.23	9.39	9.61	9.50	9.00	10.28	10.13
New Zealand.............	Dollar	1.47	1.45	1.52	1.54	1.42	1.58	1.63
Norway..................	Kroner	8.61	8.14	8.80	9.41	8.60	9.62	10.56
Qatar...................	Rial	3.85	3.64	3.64	3.64	3.64	3.64	3.64
Russia..................	Ruble	60.69	62.85	64.69	72.30	73.69	69.90	85.51
Saudi Arabia............	Riyal	3.90	3.75	3.75	3.75	3.75	3.76	3.75
Singapore...............	Dollar	1.44	1.35	1.36	1.38	1.34	1.38	1.34
South Africa...........	Rand	13.86	13.26	14.45	16.46	14.79	16.38	18.46
South Korean...........	Won	1,178.59	1,100.59	1,165.70	1,179.20	1,144.88	1,291.73	1,306.69
Sweden..................	Krona	8.89	8.70	9.46	9.21	8.58	10.12	10.61
Switzerland.............	Franc	1.02	0.98	0.99	0.94	0.91	0.96	0.90
Taiwan..................	Dollar	31.68	30.15	30.90	29.46	27.93	29.81	31.16
Thailand................	Baht	35.37	32.32	31.03	31.27	32.00	35.04	34.80
Tunisia.................	Dinar	2.51	2.71	2.93	2.84	2.78	3.08	3.10
Turkey..................	New Lira	3.79	4.85	5.69	7.03	8.90	16.57	23.82
United Arab Emirates...	Dirham	3.82	3.67	3.67	3.67	3.67	3.67	3.67
United Kingdom.........	Pound	0.81	0.75	0.78	0.78	0.73	0.81	0.80

Source: U.S. Internal Revenue Service, "Yearly Average Currency Exchange Rates," <www.irs.gov/individuals/international-taxpayers/yearly-average-currency-exchange-rates>, accessed February 2024.

Table 1404. Foreign Stock Market Indices: 2000 to 2023

[As of year end. The DAX-40 index is a total return index that includes dividends, whereas the other foreign indices are price indices that exclude dividends]

Year	London FTSE 100	Tokyo Nikkei 225	Hong Kong Hang Seng	Germany DAX-40	Paris CAC-40	Dow Jones Europe STOXX 50
2000	6,223	13,786	15,096	6,434	5,926	4,557
2005	5,619	16,111	14,876	5,408	4,715	3,349
2006	6,221	17,226	19,965	6,597	5,542	3,697
2007	6,457	15,308	27,813	8,067	5,614	3,684
2008	4,434	8,860	14,388	4,810	3,218	2,065
2009	5,413	10,546	21,873	5,957	3,936	2,579
2010	5,900	10,229	23,035	6,914	3,805	2,586
2011	5,572	8,455	18,434	5,898	3,160	2,370
2012	5,898	10,395	22,657	7,612	3,641	2,578
2013	6,749	16,291	23,306	9,552	4,296	2,919
2014	6,566	17,451	23,605	9,806	4,273	3,004
2015	6,242	19,034	21,914	10,743	4,637	3,100
2016	7,143	19,114	22,001	11,481	4,862	3,011
2017	7,688	22,765	29,919	12,918	5,313	3,178
2018	6,728	20,015	25,846	10,559	4,731	2,760
2019	7,542	23,657	28,190	13,249	5,978	3,403
2020	6,461	27,444	27,231	13,719	5,551	3,108
2021	7,385	28,792	23,398	15,885	7,153	3,818
2022	7,452	26,095	19,781	13,924	6,474	3,652
2023	7,733	33,464	17,047	16,752	7,543	4,093

Source: Global Financial Data, Los Angeles, CA ©, <www.globalfinancialdata.com>.

Table 1405. Research and Development (R&D) Expenditures by Sector and Country: 2022

[Total expenditures in millions of dollars (2,105,943 represents $2,105,943,000,000). Gross domestic expenditure on R&D (GERD) may include financing from abroad. Selected data are preliminary or estimated. For methodological information for individual countries, see source. GDP = gross domestic product]

Country	Gross domestic expenditure on R&D (GERD)			Percent of GERD performed by:			
	Total (million current PPP U.S. dollars) [1]	Per capita (current PPP U.S. dollars) [1]	Percent of GDP	Business enterprise sector	Higher education sector	Government sector	Private non-profit sector
OECD total [2]	2,105,943	1,527	2.7	73.8	15.6	8.5	2.1
EU-27 [2]	542,119	1,208	2.1	65.8	21.9	10.8	1.4
United States	**923,243**	**2,768**	**3.6**	**79.0**	**9.9**	**8.2**	**3.0**
Argentina	7,377	160	0.5	39.4	20.7	38.5	1.5
Austria	20,539	2,269	3.2	68.9	23.1	7.5	0.5
Belgium	27,170	2,326	3.4	73.6	17.1	8.9	0.5
Bulgaria	1,730	268	0.8	67.8	6.3	25.4	0.5
Canada	41,351	1,062	1.7	58.6	34.9	6.1	0.4
China	811,862	575	2.6	77.6	7.8	14.6	(NA)
Croatia	2,294	587	1.4	54.3	27.8	17.5	0.3
Czechia	10,838	1,014	2.0	64.2	19.4	16.0	0.3
Denmark	13,301	2,252	2.9	61.5	35.2	3.0	0.3
Estonia	1,152	865	1.8	56.2	33.0	10.2	0.7
Finland	10,311	1,856	3.0	68.0	24.0	7.3	0.7
France	85,167	1,244	2.2	65.8	20.6	11.6	2.0
Germany	174,857	2,087	3.1	67.4	18.1	12.1	2.4
Greece	6,059	573	1.5	49.1	29.4	21.0	0.6
Hungary	5,861	605	1.4	71.9	15.3	12.2	(NA)
Iceland	730	1,972	2.6	72.3	24.9	2.8	(NA)
Ireland	6,605	1,291	1.0	79.8	16.6	3.7	(NA)
Israel [3]	29,992	3,140	6.0	92.3	6.1	1.0	0.7
Italy	43,507	737	1.3	58.6	24.6	14.8	2.0
Japan	200,770	1,607	3.4	79.4	11.5	7.9	1.2
Korea, South	138,995	2,692	5.2	79.4	9.1	9.4	2.1
Latvia	589	312	0.8	36.0	46.5	17.5	(NA)
Lithuania	1,479	522	1.0	48.5	36.4	15.1	(NA)
Luxembourg	934	1,425	1.0	50.8	24.9	24.3	(NA)
Netherlands	30,298	1,712	2.3	68.0	27.3	4.7	(Z)
Norway	10,561	1,935	1.6	55.3	32.8	11.9	(Z)
Poland	25,011	661	1.5	65.9	32.0	1.9	0.2
Portugal	7,880	765	1.7	62.2	31.1	4.3	2.4
Romania	3,756	197	0.5	62.2	9.6	27.9	0.3
Slovakia	2,184	398	1.0	57.2	25.6	17.2	(Z)
Slovenia	2,283	1,082	2.1	70.4	12.9	15.7	1.0
Spain	33,387	698	1.4	56.4	26.0	17.2	0.3
Sweden	24,336	2,321	3.4	73.7	22.0	4.2	0.1
Taiwan	63,972	2,742	4.0	85.5	6.5	7.9	0.1
Turkey	43,136	508	1.3	61.4	33.8	4.8	(NA)

NA Not available or not applicable. Z Less than .05%. [1] Purchasing power parities (PPPs) are currency conversion rates used to convert different currencies to a common value (U.S. dollars in this case). See introductory text, this section. [2] For full membership listing of the Organisation for Economic Co-operation and Development (OECD) and the European Union-27, see introductory text, this section. [3] The statistical data for Israel are supplied by and under the responsibility of the relevant Israeli authorities. The use of such data by the OECD is without prejudice to the status of the Golan Heights, East Jerusalem and Israeli settlements in the West Bank under the terms of international law.

Source: Organisation for Economic Co-operation and Development (OECD), 2024, OECD Data Explorer, Science, Technology, and Innovation: Research & development (R&D), "Main Science and Technology Indicators (MSTI database)" ©, <data-explorer.oecd.org/>, accessed August 2024.

Table 1406. Development Assistance Outlays by Donor Country: 2021 to 2023

[In millions of current U.S. dollars (184,948.4 represents $184,948,400,000), except percent. Official development assistance (ODA) includes concessional loans and grants made by donor governments to developing countries and to multilateral institutions such as the United Nations or the World Bank]

Country	2021			2022			2023 (Preliminary)	
	ODA net disburse-ments	Multi-lateral ODA	Net private grants	ODA net disburse-ments	Multi-lateral ODA	Net private grants	ODA net disburse-ments	Multi-lateral ODA
DAC countries total [1]...	**184,948.4**	**55,583.4**	**11,839.4**	**213,359.5**	**50,308.0**	**55,980.3**	**222,163.6**	**55,184.3**
United States..............	**47,528.2**	**9,298.9**	**5,150.7**	**60,328.7**	**8,326.7**	**48,000.8**	**65,886.7**	**6,845.6**
Australia.....................	3,546.4	477.9	(NA)	3,078.8	456.3	(NA)	3,220.5	531.0
Austria......................	1,492.2	783.4	202.5	1,836.1	767.3	224.4	1,826.5	925.9
Belgium.....................	2,649.2	1,297.2	(NA)	2,687.5	1,376.8	(NA)	2,885.7	1,484.5
Canada......................	6,257.7	1,372.4	2,848.4	9,274.1	2,190.0	3,343.2	9,197.2	1,955.5
Czechia......................	366.1	277.6	(NA)	1,051.3	316.4	(NA)	788.1	303.9
Denmark....................	2,913.7	907.5	188.7	2,764.3	757.5	272.6	3,014.1	936.0
Finland......................	1,497.6	795.4	(NA)	1,615.1	596.1	(NA)	1,626.8	747.1
France......................	16,721.9	6,409.7	(NA)	17,558.9	7,025.5	(NA)	16,679.3	6,555.3
Germany....................	32,455.6	8,496.4	1,512.6	36,444.7	7,321.8	1,811.3	35,191.7	8,393.3
Hungary.....................	435.1	181.8	(NA)	371.3	77.0	(NA)	304.3	74.0
Ireland......................	1,154.9	532.8	(NA)	2,410.2	585.7	173.8	2,815.2	674.5
Italy.........................	6,271.8	3,782.6	57.8	6,705.9	3,319.8	592.1	5,908.5	3,368.8
Japan.......................	15,767.0	4,144.7	636.1	16,747.4	2,622.4	750.1	18,662.4	3,709.2
Korea, South...............	2,997.9	704.4	555.1	2,906.3	588.5	(NA)	3,267.3	835.1
Luxembourg................	539.4	175.0	16.1	530.1	156.9	49.5	580.1	162.1
Netherlands................	5,265.9	1,497.8	(NA)	6,450.2	2,166.6	(NA)	7,281.4	2,277.4
New Zealand...............	685.3	106.1	116.4	515.2	99.8	137.4	746.4	122.8
Norway......................	4,673.0	1,181.5	(NA)	5,161.0	1,042.6	(NA)	5,292.9	1,020.6
Poland......................	971.2	687.3	(NA)	3,481.3	833.1	(NA)	2,594.5	859.4
Portugal....................	447.0	291.6	29.3	439.6	311.5	35.0	450.0	310.8
Spain........................	3,358.5	2,187.8	2.0	4,046.5	2,069.0	1.3	3,596.4	2,299.9
Sweden.....................	5,934.2	2,014.7	(NA)	5,458.0	1,969.3	(NA)	5,466.2	2,261.1
Switzerland................	3,911.4	958.8	523.8	4,496.4	811.2	588.7	5,141.3	1,005.0
United Kingdom...........	16,277.8	6,449.3	(NA)	15,761.3	3,878.2	(NA)	18,661.7	6,800.6

NA Not available. [1] Development Assistance Committee (DAC) of the Organisation for Economic Co-operation and Development (OECD). Includes additional countries and European Union institutions, not shown separately.

Source: Organisation for Economic Co-operation and Development (OECD), 2024, OECD Data Explorer, Development: Official Development Assistance (ODA), "DAC1: Flows by donor (ODA+OOF+Private)" ©, <data-explorer.oecd.org/>, accessed August 2024.

Table 1407. Net Flow of Financial Resources to Developing Countries and Multilateral Organizations by Donor Country: 2018 to 2022

[297,731 represents $297,731,000,000. Net flow covers official and private loans, grants, development assistance, and technical assistance, minus amortization on loans. Military flows are excluded. GNI = gross national income. Minus sign (-) indicates net inflow]

Country	Amount (million dollars)					Percent of GNI				
	2018	2019	2020	2021	2022	2018	2019	2020	2021	2022
DAC countries total [1]........	**297,731**	**408,426**	**206,417**	**468,229**	**500,093**	**0.59**	**0.80**	**0.41**	**0.84**	**0.88**
United States....................	**50,784**	**148,083**	**4,809**	**238,682**	**228,696**	**0.24**	**0.68**	**0.02**	**1.00**	**0.89**
Australia.........................	398	5,032	2,894	3,546	3,150	0.03	0.37	0.22	0.22	0.19
Austria..........................	2,585	2,741	-91	2,138	3,230	0.57	0.61	-0.02	0.45	0.69
Belgium.........................	3,896	4,316	4,220	5,536	5,045	0.73	0.81	0.86	0.92	0.86
Canada..........................	8,886	4,620	2,742	10,009	27,671	0.53	0.27	0.17	0.51	1.31
Czechia.........................	129	285	428	442	928	0.06	0.12	0.18	0.16	0.34
Denmark........................	5,724	3,121	3,523	3,858	2,734	1.59	0.88	0.96	0.94	0.66
Estonia..........................	49	48	50	60	201	0.16	0.16	0.17	0.16	0.54
Finland..........................	2,297	2,247	2,612	3,349	2,160	0.84	0.83	0.96	1.10	0.77
France...........................	12,632	21,848	20,721	19,036	25,665	0.44	0.79	0.78	0.63	0.90
Germany........................	51,983	42,193	44,701	69,197	55,471	1.27	1.07	1.14	1.59	1.32
Greece..........................	261	369	449	165	290	0.12	0.18	0.24	0.08	0.13
Hungary.........................	1,100	12,264	3,473	6,334	1,247	0.81	8.35	2.25	4.09	0.87
Iceland..........................	77	119	58	71	94	0.30	0.48	0.27	0.28	0.34
Ireland..........................	1,368	1,149	1,123	1,155	2,584	0.46	0.37	0.35	0.30	0.68
Italy.............................	7,378	6,613	6,529	11,963	10,284	0.35	0.33	0.34	0.56	0.51
Japan............................	53,667	55,519	32,472	38,496	54,238	1.05	1.04	0.62	0.73	1.20
Korea, South...................	12,615	12,162	12,201	14,814	15,703	0.73	0.73	0.74	0.81	0.92
Lithuania.......................	65	68	72	86	216	0.12	0.13	0.13	0.14	0.32
Luxembourg....................	473	472	452	555	580	0.98	1.03	1.03	1.02	1.09
Netherlands....................	14,696	27,456	13,229	-8,239	6,424	1.61	3.04	1.46	-0.82	0.66
New Zealand...................	556	752	688	884	725	0.28	0.37	0.34	0.36	0.31
Norway..........................	4,262	4,548	4,188	6,138	9,418	0.94	1.09	1.11	1.22	1.58
Poland...........................	976	961	958	971	3,482	0.17	0.17	0.17	0.15	0.53
Portugal........................	1,569	472	-442	498	1,295	0.68	0.20	-0.20	0.20	0.52
Slovakia........................	138	110	164	167	172	0.13	0.11	0.16	0.15	0.15
Slovenia........................	236	147	600	386	606	0.44	0.28	1.15	0.63	1.03
Spain............................	14,452	13,561	13,878	7,401	7,624	1.01	0.96	1.08	0.52	0.54
Sweden..........................	6,639	7,101	7,058	10,480	8,189	1.19	1.30	1.27	1.60	1.34
Switzerland.....................	18,902	11,107	3,258	3,903	5,911	2.68	1.57	0.45	0.50	0.74
United Kingdom................	18,937	18,944	19,399	16,146	16,059	0.68	0.69	0.73	0.52	0.52

[1] The Development Assistance Committee (DAC) of the Organisation for Economic Co-operation and Development (OECD) is comprised of the above-listed member countries, and European Union institutions, not shown separately.

Source: Organisation for Economic Co-operation and Development (OECD), 2024, OECD Data Explorer, Development: Official Development Assistance (ODA), "DAC1: Flows by donor (ODA+OOF+Private)" ©, <data-explorer.oecd.org/>, accessed August 2024.

Table 1408. External Debt by Developing Country: 2010 to 2022

[In millions of U.S. dollars (26,796 represents $26,796,000,000). Total external debt is debt owed to nonresidents repayable in foreign currency, goods, or services. Total external debt is the sum of public, publicly guaranteed, and private nonguaranteed long-term debt, use of International Monetary Fund (IMF) credit, and short-term debt. Short-term debt includes all debt having an original maturity of one year or less and interest in arrears on long-term debt]

Country	2010	2015	2020	2022
Angola	26,796	48,772	65,387	60,107
Argentina	126,642	177,185	255,558	247,681
Bangladesh	26,572	38,705	73,551	97,012
Belarus	28,412	38,258	41,792	39,794
Brazil	352,364	543,397	549,300	578,599
Cambodia	4,010	9,439	17,594	22,471
China	742,737	1,333,769	2,326,233	2,388,742
Colombia	64,432	113,362	155,728	184,118
Costa Rica	8,154	23,589	31,269	38,946
Cote d'Ivoire	11,703	11,388	25,246	31,960
Dominican Republic	13,499	26,727	40,560	48,243
Ecuador	15,377	28,393	56,423	60,685
Egypt	36,804	49,874	132,572	163,104
El Salvador	11,496	15,570	18,479	21,299
Ethiopia	7,287	20,444	30,364	28,610
Georgia	8,790	14,875	20,089	23,982
Ghana	17,985	31,269	40,647	44,840
Guatemala	15,043	20,378	24,813	24,992
India	290,428	478,831	564,979	616,863
Indonesia	198,278	307,850	417,183	396,235
Iraq	(NA)	19,136	26,388	22,588
Jamaica	14,193	14,075	15,914	17,560
Jordan	16,894	25,598	38,038	41,204
Kazakhstan	119,151	153,470	161,455	161,721
Kenya	8,885	19,784	38,038	41,563
Laos	6,554	11,642	20,504	18,710
Lebanon	47,819	68,219	68,874	67,109
Mauritius	7,929	10,302	12,402	17,365
Mexico	306,835	530,515	602,686	600,423
Mongolia	5,928	21,953	32,360	33,765
Morocco	27,296	44,388	65,712	64,713
Mozambique	11,231	38,032	58,708	64,028
Nigeria	28,262	41,541	82,833	98,335
Pakistan	63,483	68,750	118,049	126,942
Papua New Guinea	5,987	20,387	18,047	18,700
Paraguay	16,123	17,298	20,727	24,515
Peru	42,154	67,186	73,549	88,084
Philippines	65,346	76,266	98,498	111,217
Senegal	4,650	10,479	23,286	32,126
Serbia	32,907	30,261	38,041	44,160
South Africa	115,322	127,741	175,417	172,133
Sri Lanka	21,684	43,925	56,874	58,713
Sudan	22,593	21,658	23,811	22,433
Tanzania	8,937	18,160	25,546	30,170
Thailand	107,166	132,367	197,234	192,078
Tunisia	22,666	27,487	41,117	39,652
Turkey	316,657	399,580	429,422	458,699
Uganda	2,975	9,571	17,207	19,488
Ukraine	124,527	118,566	132,410	139,331
Uzbekistan	7,981	13,386	33,711	49,099
Vietnam	45,022	81,825	129,479	146,627
Zambia	4,373	12,623	29,987	28,701

Source: The World Bank, Washington, DC, "External debt stocks, total," World Development Indicators (database) ©, <databank.worldbank.org/home.aspx>, accessed August 2024.

Table 1409. Foreign Direct Investment Flows in Selected Countries: 2019 to 2023

[In millions of dollars (256,687 represents $256,687,000,000). Data are converted to U.S. dollars using the yearly average exchange rate]

Country	Inflows					Outflows				
	2019	2020	2021	2022	2023	2019	2020	2021	2022	2023
United States	**256,687**	**113,177**	**410,778**	**364,040**	**341,407**	**55,630**	**261,476**	**311,760**	**402,214**	**441,586**
Australia	38,880	13,579	20,894	61,624	(NA)	9,958	6,033	3,401	116,552	(NA)
Austria	-22,439	-12,841	18,621	10,150	4,392	-17,234	519	29,662	8,323	10,062
Belgium	9,547	2,415	12,391	9,641	22,154	4,910	8,149	38,129	22,848	12,602
Brazil	65,386	28,322	50,651	73,352	63,619	19,031	-13,415	20,450	32,100	29,919
Canada	50,535	25,594	60,400	46,169	50,348	77,480	43,666	104,909	83,003	89,623
Chile	14,403	11,292	12,627	16,882	21,027	11,169	6,242	12,024	11,852	5,567
Costa Rica	2,812	1,757	3,360	3,418	4,122	117	112	214	358	288
Czechia	10,109	9,411	9,049	9,251	7,786	4,128	2,989	7,733	5,677	7,053
Denmark	-12,869	-983	6,712	8,108	7,147	-2,733	7,274	24,543	6,227	11,671
Estonia	3,166	3,588	264	909	4,565	1,971	251	-636	838	1,492
Finland	13,455	-1,576	13,290	5,787	7,923	4,864	5,844	9,154	13,257	10,943
France	13,100	11,334	30,881	36,365	29,798	43,812	21,561	44,667	47,962	75,388
Germany	52,682	69,795	51,211	27,374	36,699	151,322	38,612	147,585	145,333	101,258
Greece	5,019	3,205	6,327	8,440	5,430	642	547	1,109	3,194	3,952
Hungary	70,569	94,047	20,527	7,878	-38,685	70,323	91,023	15,969	2,761	-42,286
Iceland	-225	-927	519	846	390	479	-427	3	-118	81
Indonesia	23,883	18,591	21,131	25,390	21,628	3,352	4,448	3,845	7,322	7,070
Ireland	158,489	82,122	15,926	1,488	-9,346	34,442	-46,482	62,229	5,332	-7,449
Italy	22,720	-18,534	-2,951	32,134	18,219	24,361	2,922	26,412	16,521	13,015
Japan	13,751	11,770	33,925	32,526	21,431	232,550	99,720	209,233	161,556	184,003
Korea, South	12,548	6,837	14,662	(NA)	(NA)	50,984	36,879	79,179	(NA)	(NA)
Latvia	928	1,002	3,305	1,402	1,213	-104	259	2,326	113	583
Lithuania	3,022	3,510	2,798	2,161	1,908	1,746	2,868	1,323	366	1,044
Luxembourg	-203,870	18,602	-209,136	-486,682	-281,533	-139,637	25,532	-45,723	-401,880	-234,240
Netherlands	-14,090	-234,090	-180,064	-134,399	-309,428	-15,193	-311,966	-33,756	2,876	-301,002
New Zealand	4,296	3,998	4,116	7,900	3,568	-168	658	-1,451	746	-807
Norway	17,354	-4,269	3,508	8,985	(NA)	12,973	3,581	13,225	13,431	(NA)
Poland	13,326	15,274	29,826	31,095	24,638	1,674	1,151	3,827	6,047	6,282
Portugal	12,360	7,838	9,620	8,411	7,301	3,638	2,230	963	2,593	3,621
Russia	32,076	10,410	38,639	-15,203	8,364	22,024	6,778	64,072	11,510	29,110
Slovakia	2,511	-2,398	1,820	2,898	180	43	347	297	432	89
Slovenia	1,463	219	1,846	2,037	1,103	610	518	1,356	682	540
Spain	18,526	14,210	33,063	42,835	34,377	27,426	32,311	12,941	42,099	30,208
Sweden	9,991	19,088	21,558	46,276	29,437	16,266	23,081	30,389	61,909	47,530
Switzerland	-97,862	-159,701	-145,168	-59,835	-11,070	-47,954	-27,238	-125,778	-72,952	84,105
Turkey	9,470	7,649	11,352	13,410	10,417	2,977	3,234	5,041	4,712	5,780
United Kingdom	53,908	58,260	-71,180	14,914	-89,927	11,715	-78,170	84,926	95,364	2,007

NA Not available.

Source: Organisation for Economic Co-operation and Development (OECD), 2024, OECD Data Explorer, "FDI flows main aggregates, BMD4" ©, <data-explorer.oecd.org>, accessed June 2024.

Table 1410. International Transaction Balances, Reserve Assets, and Trade in Relation to Gross Domestic Product (GDP) by Country: 2022 and 2023

[In millions of U.S. dollars (-971,594 represents -$971,594,000,000), except as noted. Minus sign (-) indicates deficit]

Country	Current account balance		Reserve assets [1]		Goods and services trade balance		Exports as percent of GDP		Imports as percent of GDP	
	2022	2023	2022	2023	2022	2023	2022	2023	2022	2023
United States.........	-971,594	-818,822	232,717	234,111	-971,119	(NA)	11.6	(NA)	15.4	(NA)
Algeria................	19,448	5,424	61,739	69,709	24,930	9,930	31.5	25.2	20.4	21.0
Angola................	11,763	4,210	13,655	13,942	19,941	11,193	44.4	39.9	25.3	26.7
Argentina.............	-4,290	-21,494	41,198	18,987	5,987	-7,258	16.3	12.9	15.4	14.1
Australia..............	17,741	21,384	53,385	56,605	96,795	92,419	25.4	26.7	19.7	21.4
Austria................	-1,290	13,686	16,763	12,647	2,265	14,631	62.1	59.5	61.6	56.6
Azerbaijan...........	23,478	8,329	11,338	13,749	26,000	10,471	60.0	49.1	27.0	34.6
Bangladesh..........	-14,438	4,388	32,930	20,928	-36,882	-20,421	12.9	13.2	20.9	17.8
Belgium..............	-5,304	-6,205	28,023	25,735	-9,505	-5,896	95.7	86.7	97.3	87.6
Bolivia................	939	-1,247	1,275	241	-1,115	-1,967	32.6	27.3	35.1	31.6
Brazil.................	-48,253	-30,828	317,119	346,424	8,695	51,442	19.6	18.1	19.2	15.7
Cambodia............	-7,582	553	14,738	(NA)	3,978	10,409	68.3	73.2	54.9	40.4
Canada...............	-7,622	-13,255	106,952	117,551	2,836	-8,355	33.9	33.5	33.7	33.9
Chile.................	-26,162	-11,899	39,088	46,361	-11,956	4,383	35.5	31.1	39.5	29.8
China................	443,374	252,987	3,189,689	3,301,320	577,847	386,035	20.8	19.7	17.6	17.6
Colombia............	-21,367	-9,715	56,432	58,731	-26,277	-18,045	20.2	17.8	27.8	22.7
Czechia..............	-17,366	1,281	139,284	146,345	2,852	16,865	76.5	72.0	75.5	66.9
Denmark.............	53,067	44,195	92,195	104,958	44,399	38,668	70.0	69.0	58.9	59.4
Dominican Republic...	-6,549	-4,376	14,490	15,509	-11,474	-8,911	22.1	21.1	32.2	28.5
Ecuador..............	2,133	2,291	6,491	2,699	-57	336	30.8	29.1	30.8	28.8
Egypt................	-10,537	(NA)	24,824	24,696	-32,462	-8,862	15.1	19.1	21.9	21.3
Ethiopia..............	-5,160	-4,788	(NA)	(NA)	-12,814	-12,113	8.2	6.6	18.4	14.0
France................	-56,672	-22,792	100,429	79,201	-107,747	-67,233	34.7	32.7	38.6	34.9
Germany.............	174,831	262,723	98,414	100,392	80,323	185,460	50.9	47.1	49.0	43.0
Ghana...............	-1,517	(NA)	4,696	3,044	-585	-736	34.7	34.0	35.5	35.0
Greece...............	-22,623	-15,056	5,405	6,023	-21,156	-11,737	49.1	44.9	58.9	49.8
Guatemala...........	1,197	3,281	20,013	20,854	-15,807	-16,071	19.0	17.2	35.7	32.9
Honduras............	-2,063	-1,335	8,370	7,497	-8,743	-8,233	42.4	37.0	70.3	60.9
Hong Kong, China....	36,525	35,366	423,904	425,415	14,677	3,211	194.5	176.2	190.4	175.4
Hungary.............	-14,470	624	35,713	39,453	-7,860	10,858	90.4	81.2	94.9	76.1
India.................	-79,051	-32,336	521,419	574,509	-119,529	-73,506	23.2	21.9	26.8	24.0
Indonesia............	13,215	-1,880	132,644	141,149	46,716	29,857	24.5	21.8	21.0	19.6
Iraq..................	58,010	(NA)	89,415	102,779	(NA)	(NA)	(NA)	(NA)	(NA)	(NA)
Ireland...............	57,807	53,997	12,338	12,107	212,767	182,916	137.1	134.1	97.2	100.6
Israel................	20,340	25,089	194,231	204,661	15,500	19,018	31.7	30.9	28.8	27.1
Italy..................	-32,783	11,552	81,715	84,819	-33,687	31,147	36.5	35.1	38.1	33.7
Japan................	90,277	150,991	1,178,279	1,238,541	-160,053	(NA)	21.5	(NA)	25.3	(NA)
Jordan...............	-4,159	(NA)	(NA)	(NA)	(NA)	(NA)	(NA)	(NA)	(NA)	(NA)
Kazakhstan...........	7,054	-8,658	14,585	16,455	34,837	(NA)	41.8	(NA)	26.3	(NA)
Kenya................	-5,766	(NA)	7,968	7,341	-10,547	-9,393	12.2	11.8	21.5	20.6
Korea, South.........	25,829	35,488	417,280	414,004	119	885	48.3	44.0	48.3	43.9
Lebanon..............	-7,265	-5,643	15,799	(NA)	-9,495	-6,524	34.8	46.1	80.1	82.5
Malaysia.............	12,271	(NA)	112,393	110,860	29,455	19,956	77.0	68.4	69.7	63.4
Mexico...............	-17,667	-5,716	194,125	206,351	-42,823	-30,692	42.8	36.2	45.7	37.9
Morocco..............	-4,775	(NA)	31,026	34,861	-15,050	-11,717	44.8	44.0	56.3	52.3
Mozambique..........	-6,880	-2,426	2,709	3,254	-5,609	(NA)	52.5	(NA)	83.0	(NA)
Nepal................	-2,518	939	8,854	11,926	-14,648	-11,343	6.7	7.0	42.3	34.7
Netherlands..........	93,836	112,952	27,666	29,219	108,941	124,217	93.8	85.0	83.0	73.9
New Zealand.........	-21,627	-16,982	14,400	15,487	-13,070	(NA)	24.4	(NA)	29.7	(NA)
Niger.................	-2,500	(NA)	(NA)	(NA)	-2,205	-2,148	8.5	8.8	22.8	21.6
Nigeria...............	1,019	-806	35,564	(NA)	(NA)	(NA)	(NA)	(NA)	(NA)	(NA)
Norway..............	177,149	86,368	72,077	80,459	168,113	71,415	55.5	47.2	27.2	32.5
Pakistan.............	-12,216	-350	6,159	9,443	-44,800	-24,796	10.5	10.4	22.5	17.7
Peru.................	-9,743	2,219	70,308	69,095	1,375	8,745	28.9	27.1	28.4	23.8
Philippines...........	-18,261	-11,206	86,850	93,196	-63,301	-61,591	28.4	26.7	44.0	40.7
Poland...............	-16,697	12,689	153,340	169,999	12,245	49,408	62.9	57.8	61.1	51.7
Portugal..............	-3,108	3,974	9,940	9,871	-6,143	2,390	49.6	47.4	52.0	46.6
Romania.............	-27,326	-24,487	49,772	66,129	-19,967	-16,787	43.3	39.1	50.0	43.9
Russia...............	237,678	50,224	445,784	442,537	289,887	87,679	28.0	23.1	15.2	18.8
Rwanda..............	-1,246	-1,654	1,726	1,834	-2,156	-2,135	22.5	25.4	38.7	40.6
Saudi Arabia.........	151,519	34,070	459,407	436,527	187,669	78,696	40.2	34.8	23.3	27.4
Singapore............	89,701	99,128	287,670	344,581	192,076	187,333	185.8	174.3	147.2	136.9
South Africa.........	-1,698	-6,160	53,248	54,176	8,171	1,223	33.5	33.0	31.5	32.7
Spain................	8,095	41,094	76,498	84,418	17,178	65,180	40.9	39.0	39.7	34.8
Sri Lanka.............	-1,448	1,559	(NA)	(NA)	-2,642	-1,260	21.6	20.4	25.1	21.9
Sweden..............	31,881	40,073	56,963	52,527	16,142	26,089	52.9	54.0	50.1	49.6
Switzerland...........	77,245	67,821	863,028	794,931	112,138	110,058	76.9	75.3	63.2	62.9
Tajikistan.............	1,635	584	3,355	(NA)	-3,506	(NA)	16.4	(NA)	49.1	(NA)
Tanzania.............	-5,384	(NA)	(NA)	(NA)	-3,164	-1,712	15.4	17.8	19.6	20.0
Thailand.............	-15,742	7,002	202,274	208,281	-10,560	8,956	65.4	65.5	67.5	63.7
Tunisia...............	-4,018	(NA)	7,696	8,786	-6,178	-3,389	51.4	51.1	65.3	58.1
Turkey...............	-45,799	-44,961	77,889	92,694	-36,300	-26,870	38.6	32.3	42.6	34.7
Uganda..............	-4,172	(NA)	(NA)	(NA)	-4,767	-5,150	12.0	13.4	22.5	23.8
Ukraine..............	7,972	-9,209	26,929	38,716	-26,738	-37,407	35.5	28.6	52.0	49.5
United Kingdom.......	-100,436	-110,393	158,330	157,341	-82,371	-41,486	33.4	32.2	36.1	33.4
Uzbekistan...........	-618	-7,788	12,703	9,932	-13,699	-17,268	27.0	26.5	43.9	45.5
Vietnam..............	1,402	25,090	86,540	(NA)	15,731	(NA)	93.8	(NA)	90.0	(NA)

NA Not available. [1] Reserve assets are comprised of special drawing rights and reserve position in International Monetary Fund (IMF), and foreign exchange holdings. Gold holdings are excluded.

Source: The World Bank, Washington, DC, "World Development Indicators" database ©, <data.worldbank.org/data-catalog/world-development-indicators>, accessed August 2024.

Table 1411. Military Expenditures as a Percent of GDP by Country: 2019 to 2024

[Military expenditures compares spending on defense programs for the most recent year available as a percent of gross domestic product (GDP), calculated on an exchange rate basis. Includes countries not shown separately]

Country	Data as of year	Percent of GDP	Rank [1]	Country	Data as of year	Percent of GDP	Rank [1]
United States	**2024**	**3.4**	**24**	Kosovo	2023	1.3	111
Afghanistan	2019	3.3	26	Kuwait	2023	5.0	10
Albania	2024	2.0	68	Kyrgyzstan	2022	1.5	96
Algeria	2023	9.0	2	Latvia	2024	3.2	28
Angola	2023	1.3	104	Lebanon	2021	3.2	27
Armenia	2023	5.3	7	Lesotho	2023	1.5	88
Australia	2023	2.0	72	Lithuania	2024	2.9	36
Austria	2024	1.0	124	Luxembourg	2024	1.3	112
Azerbaijan	2023	4.5	12	Malaysia	2023	0.9	133
Bahrain	2023	3.1	29	Mali	2023	4.0	18
Bangladesh	2023	1.0	126	Mauritania	2023	2.5	44
Belarus	2023	1.5	89	Mexico	2023	0.6	157
Belgium	2024	1.3	107	Montenegro	2024	2.0	70
Bolivia	2023	1.2	118	Morocco	2023	4.0	16
Botswana	2023	2.6	41	Mozambique	2023	1.5	94
Brazil	2023	1.1	119	Namibia	2023	2.8	38
Brunei	2023	3.0	31	Nepal	2023	1.0	129
Bulgaria	2024	2.2	57	Netherlands	2024	2.1	64
Burkina Faso	2023	4.0	17	New Zealand	2023	1.3	106
Burma	2023	3.9	22	Niger	2023	2.0	67
Burundi	2022	2.3	49	North Macedonia	2024	2.2	56
Cambodia	2022	2.1	61	Norway	2024	2.2	54
Cameroon	2023	1.0	123	Oman	2023	5.5	6
Canada	2024	1.4	100	Pakistan	2023	3.0	33
Central African Republic	2023	1.8	78	Panama	2023	1.1	121
Chad	2023	2.9	34	Peru	2023	1.0	125
Chile	2023	1.5	91	Philippines	2023	1.5	87
China	2023	1.5	90	Poland	2024	4.1	15
Colombia	2023	2.9	35	Portugal	2024	1.6	85
Congo, Dem. Rep. of the	2023	1.2	113	Qatar	2023	4.0	20
Congo, Rep. of the	2023	2.0	71	Romania	2024	2.3	51
Croatia	2024	1.8	77	Russia	2023	5.0	9
Cuba	2020	4.2	14	Rwanda	2023	1.4	97
Cyprus	2023	1.8	79	Saudi Arabia	2023	7.0	3
Czechia	2024	2.1	63	Senegal	2023	1.5	93
Denmark	2024	2.4	48	Serbia	2023	2.4	46
Djibouti	2019	3.5	23	Seychelles	2023	1.6	83
Ecuador	2023	2.0	74	Singapore	2023	2.7	39
Egypt	2023	1.0	131	Slovakia	2024	2.0	69
El Salvador	2023	1.2	114	Slovenia	2024	1.3	108
Equatorial Guinea	2023	1.6	86	Somalia	2021	6.0	5
Eritrea	2019	10.0	1	South Africa	2023	0.7	145
Estonia	2024	3.4	25	South Sudan	2022	2.5	42
Eswatini	2023	1.6	81	Spain	2024	1.3	102
Ethiopia	2023	1.0	128	Sri Lanka	2023	1.6	84
Fiji	2023	1.1	120	Sudan	2021	1.0	132
Finland	2024	2.4	47	Suriname	2019	1.2	115
France	2024	2.1	65	Sweden	2024	2.1	59
Gabon	2023	1.3	110	Syria	2019	6.5	4
Georgia	2023	1.7	80	Taiwan	2023	2.4	45
Germany	2024	2.1	66	Tajikistan	2023	1.2	117
Greece	2024	3.1	30	Tanzania	2023	1.3	103
Guinea	2023	2.2	53	Thailand	2023	1.3	105
Guinea-Bissau	2023	1.4	98	Timor-Leste	2023	1.3	109
Honduras	2023	1.5	92	Togo	2023	2.2	55
Hungary	2024	2.1	58	Tonga	2023	1.6	82
India	2023	2.3	50	Trinidad and Tobago	2023	1.0	127
Indonesia	2023	0.8	137	Tunisia	2023	2.5	43
Iran	2023	2.1	62	Turkey	2024	2.1	60
Iraq	2023	3.0	32	Turkmenistan	2019	1.9	75
Ireland	2023	0.2	165	Uganda	2023	2.0	73
Israel	2023	4.5	13	Ukraine	2021	4.0	19
Italy	2024	1.5	95	United Arab Emirates	2023	4.0	21
Jamaica	2023	1.2	116	United Kingdom	2024	2.3	52
Japan	2024	1.4	101	Uzbekistan	2019	2.8	37
Jordan	2023	4.5	11	Venezuela	2019	5.2	8
Kenya	2023	1.0	122	Vietnam	2023	1.8	76
Korea, South	2023	2.7	40	Zambia	2023	1.4	99

[1] Based on a list of 166 countries for which data are available. Not all countries are shown.

Source: Central Intelligence Agency, The World Factbook, "Country Comparisons, Military and Security," <www.cia.gov/the-world-factbook/references/guide-to-country-comparisons/>, accessed August 2024.

Guide to Sources of Statistics, State Statistical Abstracts, and Foreign Statistical Abstracts

Alphabetically arranged, this guide contains references to important primary sources of statistical information for the United States and other countries. Secondary sources have been included if the information contained in them is presented in a particularly convenient form or if primary sources are not readily available. Nonrecurrent publications presenting compilations or estimates for years later than 2015, or types of data not available in regular series, are also included. Data are also available in press releases.

Valuable information may also be found in state reports and foreign statistical abstracts, which are included at the end of this appendix, and in reports for particular commodities, industries, or similar segments of our economic and social structures, many of which are not included here.

Publications listed under each subject are divided into two main groups: "U.S. Government" and "Nongovernment." The location of the publisher of each report is given except for federal agencies located in Washington, DC. Most federal publications may be purchased from the Superintendent of Documents, U.S. Government Printing Office, Washington, DC, tel. 1-866-512-1800, or at <bookstore.gpo.gov>. In some cases, federal publications may be obtained from the issuing agency.

"Quad." represents "quadrennial," or every four years. "Quin." represents "quinquennial," or every five years. Examples of other internet formats include ebooks, digital maps, XML files, and other kinds of digital files.

Appendix I Table: Sources of Statistics, State Statistical Abstracts, and Foreign Statistical Abstracts

Title	Frequency	Paper	Internet				
			PDF	Excel	HTML	Database *or API*	Other
U.S. GOVERNMENT							
Administrative Office of the United States Courts							
www.uscourts.gov							
Calendar Year Reports on Authorized Wiretaps (state and federal)	Annual			X	X		
Federal Court Management Statistics	Quarterly		X	X	X		
Federal Judicial Caseload Statistics	Annual			X	X		
Judicial Business of the United States Courts	Annual		X		X		
Statistical Tables for the Federal Judiciary	Semiannual			X			
Agency for International Development							
foreignassistance.gov							
U.S. Overseas Loans and Grants: Obligations and Loan Authorizations	Annual		X	X		X	X
Army Corps of Engineers Institute for Water Resources							
www.iwr.usace.army.mil							
Waterborne Commerce of the United States Waterways and Harbors	Annual		X	X		X	X
Board of Governors of the Federal Reserve System							
www.federalreserve.gov							
Assets and Liabilities of Commercial Banks in the United States H.8	Weekly		X	X	X	X	X
Consumer Credit G.19	Monthly		X	X	X	X	X
Federal Reserve Bulletin	Periodic	X	X		X		X
Financial Accounts of the United States Z.1	Quarterly		X		X	X	X
Foreign Exchange Rates H.10	Weekly			X	X	X	X
Industrial Production and Capacity Utilization G.17	Monthly		X	X	X	X	X
Money Stock Measures H.6	Monthly			X	X	X	X
Survey of Consumer Finances	Triennial		X	X		X	X
Bureau of Economic Analysis							
www.bea.gov							
Arts and Cultural Production Satellite Accounts	Ongoing		X	X	X	X	
Digital Economy Satellite Account	Ongoing		X	X		X	
Health Care Satellite Account	Ongoing		X	X			
International Economic Accounts	Ongoing		X	X	X	X	
National Economic Accounts	Ongoing		X	X	X	X	
Regional Economic Accounts	Ongoing		X	X	X	X	
Survey of Current Business	Monthly		X		X	X	
Travel and Tourism Satellite Accounts	Ongoing		X	X	X		
Bureau of Justice Statistics							
www.bjs.ojp.gov							
Background Checks for Firearm Transfers	Periodic		X	X			
Capital Punishment	Annual		X	X			
Census of Problem-Solving Courts	Periodic		X	X			
Census of Publicly Funded Forensic Crime Laboratories	Periodic		X	X			
Census of State and Federal Adult Correctional Facilities	Periodic		X	X			
Federal Justice Statistics	Periodic		X	X			
Criminal Victimization	Annual		X	X			
Federal Law Enforcement Officers	Periodic		X	X			
HIV in Prison and Jail	Periodic		X	X			
Indicators of School Crime and Safety	Annual		X	X			
Prison and Jail Inmates at Midyear	Annual		X	X			

See footnotes at end of table.

Appendix I Table: Sources of Statistics, State Statistical Abstracts, and Foreign Statistical Abstracts-Continued.

See headnote on page 897.

Title	Frequency	Paper	PDF	Excel	HTML	Database or API	Other
Jails in Indian Country	Annual		X	X			
Justice Expenditure and Employment Extract Series	Annual		X	X			
Local Police Departments	Periodic		X	X			
Prisoners	Annual		X	X			
Probation and Parole in the United States	Annual		X	X			
Recidivism of Prisoners Released	Periodic		X	X			
Sheriffs' Offices	Periodic		X	X			
Survey of State Criminal History Information Systems	Biennial		X				
Tribal Crime Data Collection Activities	Annual		X	X			
Victims of Identity Theft	Periodic		X	X			
Bureau of Labor Statistics							
www.bls.gov							
College Enrollment and Work Activity of High School Graduates	Annual		X		X		
Consumer Expenditure Surveys	Annual		X	X	X		X
Consumer Price Index (CPI) Databases	Monthly			X		X	X
Consumer Price Index (CPI) Detailed Report	Monthly		X				
Contingent and Alternative Employment Arrangements	Periodic		X		X		
Employer Costs for Employee Compensation	Quarterly		X		X		X
Employment and Earnings	Monthly				X		
Quarterly Census of Employment and Wages	Quarterly			X	X	X	X
Employment Characteristics of Families	Annual		X		X		
Employment Cost Index	Quarterly		X	X	X	X	X
The Employment Situation	Monthly		X		X		
Geographic Profile of Employment and Unemployment	Annual			X	X		
Metropolitan Area Employment and Unemployment	Monthly		X		X		
Monthly Labor Review	Monthly		X		X		
National Compensation Survey	Annual		X	X	X	X	
Occupational Employment and Wages	Annual		X	X	X		
Occupational Injuries and Illnesses	Annual		X	X	X	X	
Occupational Employment Projections Data	Biennial			X	X	X	
Producer Price Index (PPI) Detailed Report	Monthly		X	X			
Productivity and Costs by Industry	Annual		X		X		
Real Earnings	Monthly		X		X		
Regional and State Employment and Unemployment	Monthly		X		X		
Relative Importance of Components in the Consumer Price Indexes	Annual				X		
U.S. Import and Export Price Indexes	Monthly		X	X	X	X	
Union Membership	Annual		X		X		
Usual Weekly Earnings of Wage and Salary Workers	Quarterly		X		X		
Work Experience of the Population	Annual		X		X		
Bureau of Land Management							
www.blm.gov							
Public Land Statistics	Annual		X				
Census Bureau							
www.census.gov							
America's Families and Living Arrangements	Annual			X			
American Housing Survey for Selected Metropolitan Areas, H170	Biennial			X		X	
American Housing Survey for the United States, H150	Biennial			X		X	
Annual Business Survey	Annual			X		X	
Annual Revision of Monthly Retail and Food Services: Sales and Inventories	Annual		X	X			X
Annual Revision of Monthly Wholesale Distributors: Sales and Inventories	Annual		X	X			X
Annual Survey of Entrepreneurs	Annual			X		X	
Annual Survey of Manufactures	Annual		X	X		X	
Census of Governments	Quin.		X	X			
Census of Population and Housing Decennial (2020, most recent)	Decennial		X	X		X	
Computer and Internet Access in the United States: 2021	Biennial		X				
Consumer Income and Poverty, P60	Periodic		X	X			
County Business Patterns	Annual			X		X	
Current Construction Reports: New Residential Construction and New Residential Sales	Monthly		X	X	X		
Current Construction Reports: Value of Construction Put in Place, C30	Monthly		X	X	X		
Current Population Reports (Series P20 and P23)	Periodic		X	X		X	
Economic Census	Quin.			X	X	X	
Economic Census of Island Areas	Quin.			X			
Fertility of American Women in the United States	Annual		X	X			
Health Insurance Coverage in the United States	Annual		X	X			
Household Economic Studies, P70	Periodic		X				
Housing Vacancies and Homeownership, H111	Quarterly		X	X	X		
Income in the United States	Annual		X	X			
International Database	Annual			X		X	
International Population Reports (Series P95)	Periodic		X				
Manufacturing and International Trade Report	Periodic		X	X			
Manufacturer's Shipments, Inventories, and Orders	Monthly		X	X			
National Survey of Fishing, Hunting, and Wildlife Associated Recreation	Quin.		X				
New York City Housing and Vacancy Survey	Triennial			X			
Nonemployer Statistics	Annual			X		X	
Population Estimates and Projections	Annual			X		X	
Quarterly Financial Report for Manufacturing, Mining, and Trade Corporations	Quarterly		X	X			
Service Annual Survey Report	Annual			X			

See footnotes at end of table.

Appendix I Table: Sources of Statistics, State Statistical Abstracts, and Foreign Statistical Abstracts-Continued.

See headnote on page 897.

Title	Frequency	Paper	Internet PDF	Excel	HTML	Database or API	Other
Survey of Market Absorption of New Multifamily Units (SOMA)	Quarterly		X	X		X	
Survey of Plant Capacity Utilization	Quarterly			X			
U.S. International Trade in Goods and Services (FT900)	Monthly		X	X			
U.S. Trade with Puerto Rico and U.S. Possessions (FT895)	Annual		X				
Centers for Disease Control and Prevention, Atlanta, Georgia www.cdc.gov							
Morbidity and Mortality Weekly Report	Weekly		X		X		
National Immunization Survey (NIS) – Children (19-35 months)	Annual		X	X		X	X
Surveillance for Foodborne Disease Outbreaks	Annual		X				
Centers for Medicare and Medicaid Services (CMS) www.cms.gov							
CMS Program Statistics	Annual		X	X			
Trustees Report	Annual		X	X			
Central Intelligence Agency www.cia.gov							
World Factbook	Annual		X		X		X
Coast Guard (See Department of Homeland Security)							
Council of Economic Advisers www.whitehouse.gov/cea							
Economic Indicators	Monthly	X	X	X			X
Economic Report of the President	Annual	X	X				
Department of Agriculture, Economic Research Service www.ers.usda.gov							
Amber Waves	Monthly				X		
America's Diverse Family Farms	Annual		X				
Cotton and Wool Yearbook	Annual			X			
Feed Grains Yearbook	Annual			X			
Food Availability (Per Capita) Data System	Ongoing			X			
Food Expenditures	Annual			X			
Fruit and Tree Nut Yearbook	Annual			X			
Household Food Security in the United States	Annual		X				
Oil Crops Yearbook	Annual			X			
Rice Yearbook	Annual			X			
Situation and Outlook Reports. Issued for: agricultural exports, feed, fruit and tree nuts, livestock and poultry, oil crops, rice, sugar and sweeteners, vegetables, wheat, and world agriculture	Periodic	X	X	X			
Sugar and Sweeteners Yearbook	Annual			X			
Vegetable and Pulses Yearbook	Annual			X			
World Agricultural Supply and Demand Estimates	Monthly		X	X		X	X
Department of Agriculture, Food and Nutrition Service www.fns.usda.gov							
Characteristics of Supplemental Nutrition Assistance Program Households	Annual		X				
WIC Participant and Program Characteristics	Biennial		X	X		X	
Department of Agriculture, Foreign Agricultural Service www.fas.usda.gov							
Livestock and Poultry: World Markets and Trade	Quarterly		X				
Department of Agriculture, National Agricultural Statistics Service www.nass.usda.gov							
Agricultural Chemical Usage	Periodic		X	X		X	
Agricultural Land Values	Annual			X		X	
Agricultural Statistics	Annual		X				
Catfish Production	Semiannual		X	X		X	
Cattle	Semiannual		X	X			X
Census of Agriculture	Quin.		X	X		X	X
Census of Agriculture: Organic Survey	Periodic		X	X			X
Cherry Production	Annual		X	X			X
Chickens and Eggs	Monthly		X	X		X	X
Citrus Fruits	Annual		X	X			X
Cranberries	Annual		X	X			X
Crop Production	Monthly		X	X			X
Crop Progress	Weekly		X	X		X	X
Crop Values	Annual		X	X			X
Dairy Products	Monthly		X	X		X	X
Farm Labor	Semiannual		X	X		X	X
Farms and Land in Farms	Annual		X	X			X
Floriculture Crops	Annual		X			X	X
Livestock Slaughter	Monthly		X	X		X	X
Meat Animals Production, Disposition, and Income	Annual		X	X			X
Milk Production	Monthly		X	X		X	X
Milk Production, Disposition, and Income	Annual		X	X			X
Noncitrus Fruits and Nuts	Semiannual		X	X			X
Stock Reports. Stocks of grain, peanuts, potatoes, and rice	Periodic		X	X			X
Trout Production	Annual		X	X			
Turkey Hatchery	Monthly		X	X		X	X
Turkeys Raised	Annual		X	X		X	X
Vegetables Annual Summary	Annual		X	X		X	
Weekly Weather and Crop Bulletin	Weekly		X				
Winter Wheat and Canola Seedlings	Annual		X	X			X

See footnotes at end of table.

Appendix I Table: Sources of Statistics, State Statistical Abstracts, and Foreign Statistical Abstracts-Continued.

See headnote on page 897.

Title	Frequency	Paper	Internet PDF	Internet Excel	Internet HTML	Internet Database or API	Internet Other
Winter Wheat Seedlings	Annual		X	X			X
Department of Agriculture, Natural Resources Conservation Service www.nrcs.usda.gov							
National Resources Inventory	Periodic		X	X		X	
Department of Defense, Acquisition & Sustainment Office www.acq.osd.mil							
Base Structure Report: A Summary of the Real Property Inventory	Annual		X	X			
Department of Defense, Defense Manpower Data Center dwp.dmdc.osd.mil/dwp/app/dod-data-reports/workforce-reports							
Personnel Statistics	Periodic		X	X			X
Department of Defense, Defense Security Cooperation Agency www.dsca.mil/resources/dsca-historical-sales-book							
Historical Sales Book	Annual		X				
Department of Defense, Military OneSource www.militaryonesource.mil							
Demographics Report	Annual		X			X	
Department of Education www2.ed.gov							
Annual Report for Federal Student Aid	Annual		X				
Federal Campus-Based Programs Data Book	Annual			X			
Federal Pell Grant Program, End of Year Report	Annual			X			X
Department of Energy, Oak Ridge National Laboratory tedb.ornl.gov							
Transportation Energy Data Book	Annual		X	X			
Department of Health and Human Services, Administration for Community Living acl.gov							
Profile of Older Americans	Annual		X	X			X
Department of Health and Human Services, Office of Inspector General oig.hhs.gov							
Health Care Fraud and Abuse Control Program Annual Report	Annual		X				
Department of Homeland Security www.dhs.gov							
Budget in Brief	Annual		X				
Entry/Exit Overstay Report	Annual		X				
Department of Homeland Security, Coast Guard www.uscg.mil							
State of the Coast Guard	Annual		X				X
Department of Homeland Security, Office of Immigration Statistics www.dhs.gov/immigration-statistics							
Yearbook of Immigration Statistics	Annual		X	X			
Department of Housing and Urban Development www.hud.gov							
National Housing Market Summary	Quarterly		X		X		X
Department of Justice www.justice.gov							
Asset Forfeiture Fund Report to Congress	Annual		X				
Department of Justice, Bureau of Alcohol, Tobacco, Firearms and Explosives www.atf.gov							
Firearms Commerce in the United States: Annual Statistical Update	Annual		X				
Firearms Trace Data (by State)	Annual			X	X		
Department of Labor www.dol.gov							
Agency Financial Report	Annual		X				
Annual Performance Report	Annual		X				
Health Insurance Coverage Bulletin	Annual		X				
Retirement Bulletins	Periodic		X	X			X
Department of Labor, Employment and Training Administration oui.doleta.gov/unemploy/claims.asp							
Unemployment Insurance Weekly Claims	Weekly			X	X	X	
Department of State www.state.gov							
Country Reports on Terrorism	Annual		X		X		
United States Contributions to International Organizations	Annual		X	X			
Department of Transportation www.dot.gov							
Air Travel Consumer Report	Monthly		X				
Annual U.S Domestic Average Itinerary Fare in Current and Constant Dollars	Annual			X			
National Transportation Statistics	Quarterly	X	X	X			

See footnotes at end of table.

Title	Frequency	Paper	Internet				
			PDF	Excel	HTML	Database or API	Other
Transportation Statistics Annual Report	Annual		X				
U.S. International Air Passenger and Freight Statistics	Quarterly		X	X		X	X
Department of the Treasury, Alcohol and Tobacco Tax and Trade Bureau							
www.ttb.gov							
Tobacco Products Monthly Statistical Releases	Monthly			X			
Department of the Treasury, Bureau of the Fiscal Service							
www.fiscal.treasury.gov							
Combined Statement of Receipts, Outlays, and Balances of the United States Government	Annual	X	X	X			
Financial Report of the United States Government	Annual	X	X		X		
Monthly Statement of the Public Debt of the United States	Monthly		X	X		X	X
Monthly Treasury Statement of Receipts and Outlays of the United States Government	Monthly		X	X			
Treasury Bulletin	Quarterly	X	X				X
Department of Veterans Affairs							
www.va.gov							
Annual Benefits Report	Annual		X				
Annual Performance Plan and Report	Annual		X				
Geographic Distribution of VA Expenditures	Annual		X	X			
Energy Information Administration							
www.eia.gov							
Annual Coal Report	Annual		X	X			
Annual Energy Outlook	Annual		X	X		X	X
Electric Power Annual	Annual		X	X			
Electric Power Monthly	Monthly		X	X			
Electric Sales, Revenue and Average Price	Annual		X	X			
International Energy Outlook	Annual		X	X			
International Energy Statistics	Ongoing			X		X	
Monthly Energy Review	Monthly		X	X			
Petroleum Marketing Monthly	Monthly		X				
Petroleum Supply Annual	Annual		X	X			
Petroleum Supply Monthly	Monthly		X	X			
Quarterly Coal Report	Quarterly		X	X			
Residential Energy Consumption Survey	Quad.		X	X			
State Electricity Profiles	Annual			X	X		
State Energy Data System Reports	Annual		X	X	X		
U.S. Crude Oil and Natural Gas Proved Reserves	Annual		X	X			
Weekly Coal Production	Weekly		X	X		X	X
Environmental Protection Agency							
www.epa.gov							
Air Quality Statistics Report	Annual				X		
Clean Watersheds Needs Survey	Periodic		X	X		X	
Drinking Water Infrastructure Needs Survey and Assessment	Quad.		X			X	
National Water Quality Inventory Report to Congress	Periodic		X				
Toxics Release Inventory National Analysis	Annual		X	X		X	
UST Performance Measures	Semiannual		X				
Export-Import Bank of the United States							
www.exim.gov							
Annual Report	Annual		X				
Report to the U.S. Congress on Global Export Credit Competition	Annual		X				
Farm Credit Administration							
www.fca.gov							
Annual Report on the Farm Credit System	Annual		X				
Federal Bureau of Investigation							
www.fbi.gov/how-we-can-help-you/ more-fbi-services-and-information/ucr							
Crime in the United States	Annual			X	X	X	
Hate Crime Statistics	Annual		X	X		X	
Law Enforcement Officers Killed and Assaulted	Annual			X	X		
Federal Communications Commission							
www.fcc.gov							
Annual Assessment of the Status of Competition in the Market for the Delivery of Video Programming	Annual		X				X
International Telecommunications Traffic and Revenue Data Report	Periodically		X	X			
Internet Access Services	Semiannual		X				X
Report on Cable Industry Prices	Periodically		X				
Voice Telephone Services Report	Semiannual		X	X			X
Federal Deposit Insurance Corporation							
www.fdic.gov							
Annual Report	Annual		X				
FDIC Survey of Unbanked and Underbanked Households	Biennial		X	X	X	X	
FDIC Quarterly	Quarterly		X				
Historical Bank Data	Annual			X		X	
Quarterly Banking Profile	Quarterly		X	X	X		X
Statistics at a Glance	Quarterly		X	X			
Summary of Deposits	Annual			X	X	X	
Federal Highway Administration							
www.fhwa.dot.gov/							

See footnotes at end of table.

Title	Frequency	Paper	Internet PDF	Internet Excel	Internet HTML	Internet Database or API	Internet Other
Highway Statistics	Annual		X	X			
Federal Railroad Administration							
data.transportation.gov/stories/s/FRA-Safety-Data/dakf-i7zd							
Railroad Safety Statistics	Annual		X	X	X		X
Forest Service							
www.fs.usda.gov							
Land Areas of the National Forest System	Annual		X	X	X		
RPA Assessment Tables	Periodic		X	X			
U.S. Timber Production, Trade, Consumption, and Price Statistics	Periodic		X				
General Services Administration							
www.gsa.gov							
Federal Real Property Profile	Annual			X			
Geological Survey							
www.usgs.gov							
Estimated Use of Water in the United States	Quin.		X	X			X
Mineral Commodity Summaries	Annual		X	X			
Mineral Industry Surveys	Periodic		X	X			
Minerals Yearbook	Annual	X	X	X			
Internal Revenue Service							
www.irs.gov/statistics							
Corporation Income Tax Returns	Annual		X	X			
Individual Income Tax Returns	Annual		X	X			
IRS Data Book	Annual		X	X			
Statistics of Income Bulletin	Quarterly		X	X			
International Trade Administration, National Travel and Tourism Office							
www.trade.gov/national-travel-and-tourism-office							
U.S. Travel and Tourism Statistics	Annual	X		X		X	X
International Trade Commission							
www.usitc.gov							
Interactive Tariff and Trade Dataweb	Ongoing			X		X	X
Recent Trends in U.S. Services Trade	Annual		X			X	X
Library of Congress							
www.loc.gov							
Annual Report	Annual		X				
Maritime Administration							
www.maritime.dot.gov							
U.S. Waterborne Foreign Trade	Annual			X			
Vessel Calls	Annual			X			
Mine Safety and Health Administration							
www.msha.gov							
Mine Injuries and Worktime	Quarterly		X				
National Aeronautics and Space Administration							
www.nasa.gov							
Annual Procurement Report	Annual		X				
National Center for Education Statistics							
www.nces.ed.gov							
After the Post-9/11 GI Bill: A Profile of Military Service Members and Veterans Enrolled in Undergraduate and Graduate Education	Periodic		X				
Career and Technical Education Programs in Public School Districts	Periodic		X				
Characteristics of Private Schools in the United States	Semiannual		X				
The Condition of Education	Annual		X	X	X		
Digest of Education Statistics	Annual		X	X	X		
Indicators of School Crime and Safety	Annual		X				
National Teacher and Principal Survey	Periodic		X	X	X		
Profile and Financial Aid Estimates of Graduate Students	Quad.		X			X	X
Programs and Services for High School English Learners in Public School Districts	Periodic		X				
The Nation's Report Card	Periodic		X	X		X	
Trends in Undergraduate Nonfederal Grant and Scholarship Aid by Demographic and Enrollment Characteristics	Quad.		X			X	X
Trends in Pell Grant Receipt and the Characteristics of Pell Grant Recipients	Quad.		X			X	X
Projections of Education Statistics	Annual		X	X	X		
Status and Trends in the Education of Racial and Ethnic Groups	Irregular		X		X		X
Trends in High School Dropout and Completion Rates in the United States	Annual		X	X	X		X
National Center for Health Statistics							
www.cdc.gov/nchs							
Health, United States	Annual		X	X			
National Health and Nutrition Examination Survey	Ongoing		X	X			X
National Health Interview Survey	Ongoing		X	X			X
National Health Statistics Reports	Periodic		X				
National Vital Statistics Reports	Periodic		X				
Vital and Health Statistics Series	Periodic		X				
National Credit Union Administration							
www.ncua.gov							

See footnotes at end of table.

Title	Frequency	Paper	Internet PDF	Internet Excel	Internet HTML	Internet Database or API	Internet Other
Annual Report	Annual		X				
Call Report Quarterly Summary Reports	Quarterly		X				X
National Endowment for the Arts							
www.arts.gov							
Annual Report	Annual		X				
Appropriations Request	Annual		X				
National Endowment for the Humanities							
www.neh.gov							
Annual Report	Annual		X				
Appropriations Request	Annual		X				
National Guard Bureau							
www.nationalguard.mil							
Posture Statement	Annual		X		X		
National Highway Traffic Safety Administration							
www.nhtsa.gov							
Traffic Safety Facts	Annual		X	X	X		
National Oceanic and Atmospheric Administration							
www.noaa.gov							
Climatic Data for the World	Monthly		X	X		X	
Comparative Climatic Data	Annual						X
Fisheries of the United States	Annual		X	X		X	
Storm Data	Monthly		X	X		X	
Storm Prediction Center	Ongoing				X	X	X
U.S. Climate Normals	Decennial	X	X	X		X	
National Park Service							
www.nps.gov							
Social Science Program	Annual		X	X	X	X	
National Science Foundation							
nsf.gov/home							
Academic Institutional Profiles	Annual			X	X		
Business and Industry R&D	Periodic		X	X	X		
Characteristics of Scientists and Engineers with U.S. Doctorates	Biennial		X	X	X		
Diversity and STEM: Women, Minorities, and Persons with Disabilities	Biennial		X	X			X
Doctorate Recipients from U.S. Universities	Annual		X	X			
Federal Funds for Research and Development	Annual		X	X			X
Federal Research and Development Funding by Budget Function	Annual		X				
Federal Science and Engineering Support to Universities, Colleges, and Nonprofit Institutions	Annual		X	X		X	X
Graduate Students and Postdoctorates in Science and Engineering	Annual		X	X		X	X
Higher Education in Science and Engineering	Annual		X	X			
National Patterns of Research and Development Resources	Annual		X	X	X		X
Science and Engineering Degrees, by Race/Ethnicity of Recipients	Periodic			X	X	X	
Science and Engineering State Profiles	Annual			X	X	X	X
Scientific and Engineering Research Facilities	Biennial		X	X		X	X
The State of U.S. Science and Engineering	Biennial		X	X		X	X
National Transportation Safety Board							
www.ntsb.gov							
Annual Summary of US Civil Aviation Accidents	Annual			X	X		
Office of Juvenile Justice and Delinquency Prevention							
www.ojjdp.gov							
Juvenile Arrests	Annual		X				
Office of Management and Budget							
www.whitehouse.gov/omb							
The Budget of the United States Government	Annual	X	X	X			
Office of Personnel Management							
www.opm.gov							
Common Characteristics of the Government	Annual		X				
Retirement Age & Trend Analysis of the Executive Branch	Periodic		X				
Office of the Clerk, U.S. House of Representatives							
www.clerk.house.gov							
Statistics of the Presidential and Congressional Election	Biennial		X				
Patent and Trademark Office							
www.uspto.gov							
Open Data Portal	Ongoing					X	X
Railroad Retirement Board							
www.rrb.gov							
Annual Report	Annual		X				
Quarterly Benefit Statistics	Quarterly		X				
Securities and Exchange Commission							
www.sec.gov							
SEC and Markets Data	Annual		X	X			
Small Business Administration							
www.sba.gov							
Economic Bulletin	Semiannual		X				
Loan Program Performance Reports	Annual		X		X		
Small Business Economic Bulletin	Monthly		X				

See footnotes at end of table.

Appendix I Table: Sources of Statistics, State Statistical Abstracts, and Foreign Statistical Abstracts-Continued.

See headnote on page 897.

Title	Frequency	Paper	Internet PDF	Internet Excel	Internet HTML	Internet Database or API	Internet Other
Small Business Lending in the United States	Annual		X	X			
Small Business Profiles for States and Territories	Annual		X				
Social Security Administration							
www.ssa.gov							
Annual Statistical Report on the Social Security Disability Insurance Program	Annual		X	X	X		
Annual Statistical Supplement to the Social Security Bulletin	Annual		X	X	X		
Congressional Statistics	Annual		X	X	X		
Fast Facts & Figures about Social Security	Annual		X		X		
OASDI Beneficiaries by State and County	Annual		X	X	X		
Social Security Bulletin	Quarterly		X		X		
SSI Annual Statistical Report	Annual		X	X	X		
SSI Recipients by State and County	Annual		X	X	X		
Substance Abuse and Mental Health Services Administration							
www.samhsa.gov							
Behavioral Health Barometer, United States	Annual		X				
National Mental Health Services Survey (N-MHSS)	Annual		X				
National Survey on Drug Use and Health (NSDUH)	Annual		X		X		X
National Survey on Substance Abuse Treatment Services (N-SSATS)	Annual		X				
U.S. Copyright Office							
www.copyright.gov							
Annual Report	Annual		X				
U.S. Equal Employment Opportunity Commission							
www.eeoc.gov							
Enforcement and Litigation Statistics	Ongoing		X	X		X	X
U.S. Health Resources & Services Administration							
www.hrsa.gov							
Health Center Program Uniform Data System	Ongoing		X	X	X	X	
U.S. Sentencing Commission							
www.ussc.gov							
Sourcebook of Federal Sentencing Statistics	Annual		X	X	X	X	X
NONGOVERNMENT							
Aerospace Industries Association, Arlington, VA							
www.aia-aerospace.org							
Facts & Figures: U.S. Aerospace & Defense	Annual		X				
Airlines for America, Washington, DC							
www.airlines.org							
American Council of Life Insurers, Washington, DC							
www.acli.com							
Life Insurers Fact Book	Annual		X				
American Dental Association, Chicago, IL							
www.ada.org							
Survey of Dental Practice	Annual		X	X			
American Forest and Paper Association, Washington, DC							
www.afandpa.org							
Monthly Exports/Imports Report	Monthly		X				
Paper Industry Annual Capacity and Fiber Consumption	Annual		X				
Paper Industry Annual Statistical Summary	Annual		X				
American Gas Association, Washington, DC							
www.aga.org							
Gas Facts	Annual		X		X		
American Iron and Steel Institute, Washington, DC							
www.steel.org							
Annual Statistical Report	Annual	X	X				
American Osteopathic Association, Chicago, IL							
www.osteopathic.org							
Osteopathic Medical Profession Report	Annual		X				
American Public Transportation Association, Washington, DC							
www.apta.com							
Public Transportation Fact Book	Annual		X	X			
American Society for Aesthetic Plastic Surgery							
www.theaestheticsociety.org							
Aesthetic Plastic Surgery Statistics	Annual		X				
Association of American Medical Colleges							
www.aamc.org							
Physician Specialty Data Report	Biennial		X		X		
State Physician Workforce Data Report	Biennial		X				
U.S. Physician Workforce Data Dashboard	Ongoing		X			X	X
Association of American Railroads, Washington, DC							
www.aar.org							
Freight Commodity Statistics	Annual		X	X			
Berman Jewish Data Bank, Storrs, CT							
www.jewishdatabank.org							
AJC Survey of American Jewish Opinion	Annual		X				X
American Muslim Poll	Annual		X				X

See footnotes at end of table.

Appendix I Table: Sources of Statistics, State Statistical Abstracts, and Foreign Statistical Abstracts-Continued.

See headnote on page 897.

Title	Frequency	Paper	Internet				
			PDF	Excel	HTML	Database or API	Other
Bloomberg BNA, Washington, DC www.bloombergindustry.com							
BNA's Labor and Employment Outlook Report	Annual		X				
BNA's Job Absence and Turnover Report	Quarterly		X				
Directory of U.S. Labor Organizations	Annual	X					
Source Book on Collective Bargaining	Annual	X					
Brookings Institution, Washington, DC www.brookings.edu							
Vital Statistics on Congress	Biennial		X	X			
Chronicle of Higher Education, Inc., Washington, DC www.chronicle.com							
Almanac of Higher Education	Annual	X	X				
College Board, New York, NY www.collegeboard.org							
SAT Suite Annual Report	Annual		X				
cmdty® by barchart, Chicago, IL www.barchart.com/cmdty							
Commodity Index Report	Monthly						
Commodity Indexes	Ongoing		X	X			
cmdty Yearbook®	Annual	X					
End of Day Data	Daily			X			
Conference Board, New York, NY www.conference-board.org							
Business Cycle Indicators	Monthly		X			X	X
International Comparisons of Hourly Compensation Costs for Production Workers in Manufacturing	Annual		X				X
International Comparisons of Manufacturing Productivity and Unit Labor Cost Trends	Annual		X				X
Congressional Quarterly (CQ) Press, Washington, DC cqpress.sagepub.com/							
America Votes	Biennial	X					X
Council of State Governments, Lexington, KY www.csg.org							
Book of the States	Annual		X				
Dodge Data & Analytics, New York, NY www.construction.com							
Construction Outlook	Semiannual						X
Dow Jones and Company, New York, NY www.dowjones.com							
Wall Street Journal	Daily	X					X
Curated Experiences Group, Fountain Valley, CA www.editorandpublisher.com							
Editor and Publisher	Monthly	X					X
News Media Databook	Annual	X		X		X	
Edison Electric Institute, Washington, DC www.eei.org							
Statistical Yearbook of the Electric Power Industry	Annual		X				
Euromonitor International, London, England www.euromonitor.com							
Consumer Lifestyles in the US	Annual						X
Federal National Mortgage Association, Washington, DC www.fanniemae.com							
Annual Report on Form 10-K	Annual		X				
Food and Agriculture Organization of the United Nations, Rome, Italy www.fao.org							
World Fertilizer Trends and Outlook	Annual		X				
The State Of Food and Agriculture	Annual		X		X		X
The State of Food Security and Nutrition in the World	Annual		X		X		X
The State of World Fisheries and Aquaculture	Annual		X		X		X
The State of the World's Forests	Annual		X		X		X
General Aviation Manufacturers Association, Washington, DC www.gama.aero							
Annual Data	Annual			X	X		
General Aviation Aircraft Shipment Report	Quarterly		X				
Giving USA Foundation, Chicago, IL www.givingusa.org							
Annual Survey on State Laws	Annual		X				
Guttmacher Institute, New York, NY www.guttmacher.org							
Data Center	Ongoing			X		X	
Health Forum, an American Hospital Association Company, Chicago, IL www.ahadata.com							
AHA Annual Survey Data Base	Annual					X	X
AHA Dataquery	Annual					X	X

See footnotes at end of table.

Appendix I Table: Sources of Statistics, State Statistical Abstracts, and Foreign Statistical Abstracts-Continued.

See headnote on page 897.

Title	Frequency	Paper	Internet				
			PDF	Excel	HTML	Database or API	Other
IHS Global, Inc., Englewood, CO							
www.janes.com							
IHS Jane's All the World's Aircraft: Development & Production	Annual	X					X
IHS Jane's C4ISR & Mission Systems	Annual	X					X
IHS Jane's Fighting Ships	Annual	X					X
IHS Jane's Flight Avionics	Annual	X					X
IHS Jane's Land Warfare Platforms: Armoured Fighting Vehicles—Tracked	Annual	X					X
IHS Jane's Land Warfare Platforms: Logistics, Support & Unmanned	Annual	X					X
IHS Jane's Simulation & Training Systems	Annual	X					X
IHS Jane's Space Systems & Industry	Annual	X					X
IHS Jane's Weapons: Air-Launched	Annual	X					X
IHS Jane's Weapons: Infantry	Annual	X					X
Independent Petroleum Association of America, Washington, DC							
www.ipaa.org							
The Economic Contribution of Independent Operators in the United States	Irregular		X				
IPAA Oil & Gas Producing Industry in Your State	Annual	X	X				
Information Today, Inc., Medford, NJ							
informationtodayinc.com/							
American Library Directory	Annual	X					X
Library and Book Trade Almanac (formerly The Bowker Annual)	Annual	X			X		
Institute for Criminal Justice Ethics, New York, NY							
new.jjay.cuny.edu/							
Criminal Justice Ethics	Triannual	X	X				
Insurance Information Institute, New York, NY							
www.iii.org							
Triple-I Insurance Facts	Annual		X				
Inter-American Development Bank, Washington, DC							
www.iadb.org							
Development Effectiveness Overview	Annual		X				
Inter-American Development Bank Annual Report	Annual		X				
International Air Transport Association, Montreal, Canada and Geneva, Switzerland							
www.iata.org							
Annual Review	Annual		X				
World Air Transport Statistics	Annual	X	X				X
International City Management Association, Washington, DC							
www.icma.org							
ICMA Chief Administrative Officers Salary & Compensation Survey	Annual		X				
International Labour Organization, Geneva, Switzerland							
www.ilo.org							
World Employment and Social Outlook	Annual		X				
International Monetary Fund, Washington, DC							
data.imf.org							
Balance of Payments and International Investment Position Statistics	Monthly		X	X		X	X
Direction of Trade Statistics	Quarterly		X	X		X	X
Government Finance Statistics	Annual			X		X	X
IEO Annual Report	Annual		X				X
International Financial Statistics	Monthly		X	X		X	X
International Telecommunication Union, Geneva, Switzerland							
www.itu.int/home/index.html							
ITU DataHub	Annual			X		X	
ITU Yearbook of Statistics	Annual		X				
Investment Company Institute, Washington, DC							
www.ici.org							
Investment Company Fact Book	Annual		X	X			X
Joint Center for Housing Studies of Harvard University, Cambridge, MA							
www.jchs.harvard.edu							
The State of the Nation's Housing	Annual		X	X			X
Media Source, Inc., New York, NY							
www.mediasourceinc.com							
Library Journal	Biweekly	X			X		X
School Library Journal	Monthly	X			X		X
National Academy of Social Insurance, Washington, DC							
www.nasi.org							
Workers Compensation: Benefits, Coverage, and Costs	Annual		X				
National Association of Home Builders, Washington, DC							
www.nahb.org							
HousingEconomics.com (online subscription)	Ongoing				X		X
National Association of Latino Elected and Appointed Officials, Los Angeles, CA							
www.naleo.org							
National Directory of Latino Elected Officials	Annual		X				
National Association of Realtors, Chicago, IL							

See footnotes at end of table.

Title	Frequency	Paper	PDF	Excel	HTML	Database or API	Other
www.nar.realtor							
Economist's Outlook	Daily				X		X
NAR Member Profile	Annual		X				
NAR Profile of Home Buyer and Sellers	Annual		X				
National Association of State Budget Officers, Washington, DC							
www.nasbo.org							
Fiscal Survey of the States	Semiannual	X	X	X			X
State Expenditure Report	Annual	X	X	X			X
National Association of State Park Directors, Raleigh, NC							
www.stateparks.org							
Statistical Report of State Park Operations: Annual Information Exchange	Annual	X	X	X			X
National Catholic Educational Association, Arlington, VA							
www.ncea.org							
The Annual Financial Report	Annual	X	X				
U.S. Catholic Elementary and Secondary Schools: The Annual Statistical Report on Schools, Enrollment and Staffing	Biennial	X	X				
National Education Association, Washington, DC							
www.nea.org							
Rankings & Estimates: Rankings of the States and Estimates of School Statistics	Annual		X				
National Fire Protection Association, Quincy, MA							
www.nfpa.org							
National Fire Protection Association (NFPA) Journal	Quarterly				X		X
National Golf Foundation, Jupiter, FL							
www.ngf.org							
Golf Facilities in the U.S.	Annual						X
National Restaurant Association, Washington, DC							
www.restaurant.org							
Restaurant Industry 2030	Recurring		X				
Restaurant Operations Data Abstract	Recurring	X	X				
Restaurant Performance Index	Monthly		X				
Restaurant Trendmapper (online subscription)	Ongoing				X		
State of the Industry	Annual		X				X
National Safety Council, Itasca, IL							
injuryfacts.nsc.org							
Injury Facts	Annual		X	X	X		
National Sporting Goods Association, Mount Prospect, IL							
www.nsga.org							
Sports Participation in the U.S.	Annual		X				
Organisation for Economic Cooperation and Development, Paris, France							
www.oecd-ilibrary.org							
CO2 Emissions From Fuel Combustion	Annual		X				
Coal Information	Annual		X				
Digital Economy Outlook	Biennial		X	X	X		X
Education at a Glance: OECD Indicators	Annual		X	X	X		X
Electricity Information	Annual		X				
Energy Prices and Taxes	Quarterly		X				
Geographical Distribution of Financial Flows to Developing Countries	Annual		X				X
International Trade by Commodity Statistics	Ongoing		X	X		X	
ITF Transport Outlook	Biennial		X	X	X		X
Main Economic Indicators	Monthly		X	X		X	
Main Science and Technology Indicators	Semiannual		X	X			
National Accounts of OECD Countries							
Issue 1: Main Aggregates	Annual		X	X			
Issue 2: Detailed Tables	Annual		X	X			
National Accounts of OECD Countries, Financial Accounts	Annual		X	X			
National Accounts of OECD Countries, Financial Balance Sheets	Annual		X	X			
National Accounts of OECD Countries, General Government Accounts	Annual		X	X			
Natural Gas Information	Annual		X				
Nuclear Energy Data	Annual		X				
OECD Economic Outlook	Semiannual		X	X	X	X	X
OECD Economic Surveys	Periodic		X		X		X
OECD Education Statistics	Annual		X	X	X	X	
OECD Employment and Labour Market Statistics	Annual		X	X	X	X	
OECD Employment Outlook	Annual		X	X	X		X
OECD Environment Statistics	Annual		X	X		X	
OECD-FAO Agricultural Outlook	Annual		X	X	X		X
OECD Health Statistics	Annual		X	X	X	X	X
OECD Insurance Statistics	Annual		X	X		X	
OECD International Development Statistics	Annual		X	X	X	X	X
OECD International Migration Statistics	Annual		X	X	X	X	X
OECD Patent Statistics	Annual			X		X	
OECD Pensions at a Glance	Biennial		X	X	X		X
OECD Productivity Statistics	Annual		X	X	X	X	
OECD Quarterly International Trade Statistics	Quarterly		X	X			X
OECD Regional Statistics	Annual		X	X	X	X	X
OECD Review of Fisheries	Annual		X	X	X		X

Appendix I Table: Sources of Statistics, State Statistical Abstracts, and Foreign Statistical Abstracts-Continued.

See headnote on page 897.

Title	Frequency	Paper	Internet PDF	Internet Excel	Internet HTML	Internet Database or API	Internet Other
OECD Science, Technology, and Innovation Outlook	Biennial		X	X	X		X
OECD Science, Technology and R&D Statistics	Annual		X	X	X	X	X
OECD Social and Welfare Statistics	Annual		X	X	X	X	X
OECD Telecommunications and Internet Statistics	Biennial		X	X	X	X	X
OECD Territorial Reviews	Periodic		X		X		X
OECD Tourism Statistics	Annual		X	X		X	
Oil Information	Annual		X				
Oil, Gas, Coal, and Electricity Quarterly Statistics	Quarterly		X				
PISA (OECD Programme for International Student Assessment)	Periodic		X	X	X		X
Quarterly National Accounts	Quarterly		X	X			
Revenue Statistics	Annual		X	X	X		X
Society at a Glance	Biennial		X	X	X		X
Taxing Wages	Annual		X	X	X		X
Uranium: Resources, Production, and Demand	Biennial		X				
World Energy Balances	Annual		X				
World Energy Outlook	Annual		X				
World Energy Statistics	Annual		X				
Pew Research Center www.pewinternet.org							
Book Reading	Periodic		X				X
Home Broadband	Periodic		X				X
Libraries and Learning	Periodic		X				X
Social Media Update	Periodic		X				X
Technology Device Ownership	Periodic		X				X
Teens, Social Media & Technology	Periodic		X				X
PWxyz, LLC, New York, NY www.publishersweekly.com							
Publishers Weekly	Weekly	X					X
Radio Advertising Bureau, Dallas, TX www.rab.com							
Why Radio: Fact Sheets	Ongoing				X		
Regional Airline Association, Washington, DC www.raa.org							
Regional Airlines Association Annual Report	Annual						X
Securities Industry and Financial Markets Association, New York, NY www.sifma.org							
Capital Markets Fact Book	Annual		X	X			
U.S. Foreign Activity Report	Semiannual		X	X			
Skyhorse Publishing, New York, NY www.skyhorsepublishing.com							
The World Almanac and Book of Facts	Annual	X					X
Standard and Poor's Financial Services LLC, New York, NY www.spglobal.com/ratings							
Analyst's Handbook	Annual	X					
Corporation Records: Corporate Description	Monthly						X
Corporation Records: Daily News	Daily						X
Daily Stock Price Records	Quarterly						X
United Nations Conference on Trade and Development, Geneva, Switzerland hunctad.org							
Development and Globalization: Facts and Figures	Periodic		X		X	X	
Handbook of Statistics	Annual		X				
United Nations Statistics Division, New York, NY unstats.un.org/UNSDWebsite							
Demographic Yearbook (Series R)	Annual		X	X			
Energy Balances	Annual	X	X				
Energy Statistics Yearbook (Series J)	Annual	X	X				
Industrial Commodity Statistics Yearbook	Annual	X	X				
International Trade Statistics Yearbook (Series G)	Annual	X	X				
Monthly Bulletin of Statistics (Series Q)	Monthly	X	X	X		X	X
National Accounts Statistics: Analysis of Main Aggregates	Annual	X					
National Accounts Statistics: Main Aggregates and Detailed Tables (Series X)	Annual	X					
Population and Vital Statistics Report (Series A)	Annual		X				
Statistical Yearbook	Annual		X				
World Statistics Pocketbook (Series V)	Annual	X	X				
The World's Women	Quin.		X	X		X	X
World Bank Group, Washington, DC www.worldbank.org							
International Debt Report	Annual		X	X		X	X
The Little Data Book	Annual		X	X		X	
World Development Indicators	Annual			X		X	X
World Health Organization, Geneva, Switzerland www.who.int							
World Health Statistics Report	Annual		X	X	X		
World Trade Organization, Geneva, Switzerland www.wto.org							

See footnotes at end of table.

Title	Frequency	Paper	Internet				
			PDF	Excel	HTML	Database or API	Other
World Trade Statistical Review	Annual	X	X	X			
STATE STATISTICAL ABSTRACTS FROM UNIVERSITIES							
Iowa State University: Iowa Community Indicators Program, Ames, IA www.icip.iastate.edu Iowa Community Indicators Program	Ongoing		X	X	X		
State University of New York: Nelson A. Rockefeller Institute of Government, Albany, NY www.rockinst.org/nys-statistical-yearbook/ New York State Statistical Yearbook	Annual		X	X		X	X
University of Alabama, Center for Business and Economic Research, Tuscaloosa, AL cber.culverhouse.ua.edu/ Alabama Economic Outlook	Annual		X				
University of Georgia: Selig Center for Economic Growth, Athens, GA www.terry.uga.edu/selig Georgia Economic Outlook	Annual		X				
University of Idaho Extension, Moscow, ID indicatorsidaho.org/ Indicators Idaho	Ongoing		X	X	X		
University of Kansas: Institute for Policy and Social Research, Lawrence, KS ipsr.ku.edu/ksdata/ksah/ Kansas Statistical Abstract	Annual		X	X			
University of Missouri-Columbia: Economic and Policy Analysis Research Center, Columbia, MO mcdc.missouri.edu/ Missouri Census Data Center	Ongoing		X	X	X		
STATE STATISTICAL ABSTRACT FROM AN ASSOCIATION							
Texas State Historical Association, Austin, TX texasalmanac.com Texas Almanac	Biennial	X	X				X
INTERNATIONAL STATISTICAL ABSTRACTS FROM A FOREIGN AGENCY							
Austria **Statistik Austria, Vienna** www.statistik.at/en Statistisches Jahrbuch Osterreichs	Annual	X		X		X	
Belgium **Statistics Belgium, Brussels** statbel.fgov.be/en Key Figures	Annual		X	X		X	
Brazil **Instituto Brasileiro de Geografia e Estatística, Rio de Janeiro** anuario.ibge.gov.br/index.php Statistical Yearbook of Brazil	Annual	X	X	X		X	
Canada **Statistics Canada, Ottawa** www.statcan.gc.ca/en/start Canada at a Glance	Annual	X	X		X		
China **National Bureau of Statistics China, Beijing** www.stats.gov.cn/english/ China Statistical Yearbook	Annual	X			X		X
Czechia **Czech Statistical Office, Praha** csu.gov.cz Demographic Yearbook of the Czech Republic	Annual		X	X			X
European Union **Eurostat, Luxembourg** ec.europa.eu/eurostat Eurostat Regional Yearbook	Annual	X	X				
Key Figures on Europe	Annual	X	X				
Finland **Statistics Finland, Helsinki** www.stat.fi/index_en.html Statistical Yearbook of Finland	Annual	X	X				
France **National Institute of Statistics and Economic Studies, Paris** www.insee.fr/en/accueil Tableau de Bord de l'Économie Française	Annual			X		X	
Greece							

See footnotes at end of table.

Appendix I Table: Sources of Statistics, State Statistical Abstracts, and Foreign Statistical Abstracts-Continued.

See headnote on page 897.

Title	Frequency	Paper	Internet PDF	Internet Excel	Internet HTML	Internet Database or API	Internet Other
Hellenic Statistical Authority, Pireus www.statistics.gr/en/home Greece in Figures	Quarterly		X				
Hungary **Hungarian Central Statistical Office, Budapest** www.ksh.hu/?lang=en Statistical Yearbook of Hungary	Annual	X	X	X			
Ireland **Central Statistics Office, Cork** www.cso.ie/en Ireland: The Year in Numbers	Annual			X	X		X
Italy **Italian National Institute of Statistics, Rome** www.istat.it/en Annuario Statistico Italiano	Annual	X	X	X			
Japan **Statistics Bureau, Ministry of Internal Affairs and Communications, Tokyo** www.stat.go.jp/english/data/index.html Japan Statistical Yearbook	Annual			X	X		
Korea, South **Statistics Korea, Daejeon** kosis.kr/eng/ Korean Statistical Information Service	Ongoing			X		X	X
Luxembourg **Service Central de la Statistique et des Etudes Economiques, Luxembourg** statistiques.public.lu/en.html Luxembourg in Figures	Annual		X				
Mexico **Instituto Nacional de Estadística y Geografía, Aguascalientes** en.www.inegi.org.mx Anuario Estadístico y Geográfico por Entidad Ferderativa	Annual		X	X			
Netherlands **Statistics Netherlands, The Hague** www.cbs.nl/en-gb The Netherlands in Numbers	Annual		X	X	X		
Poland **Central Statistical Office of Poland, Warsaw** www.stat.gov.pl/en/intrastat Concise Statistical Yearbook of Poland Statistical Yearbook of the Republic of Poland	Annual Annual	X X	X X				
Portugal **Statistics Portugal, Lisbon** www.ine.pt Statistical Yearbook of Portugal	Annual	X	X	X			
Russia **Russian Federation Federal State Statistics Service, Moscow** rosstat.gov.ru Russian Statistical Yearbook	Annual		X				X
Slovakia **Statistical Office of the Slovak Republic, Bratislava** slovak.statistics.sk Statistical Yearbook of the Slovak Republic	Annual	X	X	X			X
Spain **Instituto Nacional de Estadística, Madrid** www.ine.es/en/index.htm Statistical Yearbook of Spain	Annual	X	X	X	X	X	X
Switzerland **Federal Statistical Office, Neuchâtel** www.bfs.admin.ch/bfs/en/home.html La Suisse en Chiffres—Annuaire Statistique Die Schweiz in Zahlen—Statistiches Jahrbuch	Annual Annual	X X	X X				
Turkey **Turkish Statistical Institute, Ankara** www.tuik.gov.tr/Home/Index Türkiye's Statistics Türkiye in Statistics	Annual Annual		X X				

Source: ProQuest research.

Guide to State Statistical Abstracts

This bibliography includes the most recent statistical abstracts for states and island areas published since 2015. For some states, a near equivalent has been listed in substitution for, or in addition to, a statistical abstract. All sources contain statistical tables on a variety of subjects for the state as a whole, its component parts, or both. Internet sites also contain statistical data.

Alabama

University of Alabama, Center for Business and Economic Research, P.O. Box 870221, Tuscaloosa, AL 35487-0221. 205-348-6191. Fax: 205-348-2951. Internet site <cber.culverhouse.ua.edu/>.
Alabama Economic Outlook. Annual. Online.

Alaska

Department of Labor and Workforce Development, P.O. Box 111149, Juneau, AK 99811. 907-465-4500. Fax: 907-308-2824. Internet site <live.laborstats.alaska.gov>.
Alaska Economic Trends. Monthly. Online.

Arizona

University of Arizona, Eller College of Management, 1130 East Helen Street, McClelland Hall, P.O. Box 210108, Tucson, AZ 85721-0108. 520-621-2155. Internet site <www.azeconomy.org>.
Arizona's Economy. Quarterly. Online.

Arkansas

University of Arkansas at Little Rock, Arkansas Economic Development Institute, 2801 South University Avenue, Little Rock, AR 72204. 501-916-3519. Internet site <www.youraedi.com>.
Arkansas Data Center Online. Online.

California

Government Operations Agency, 1304 O Street, Suite 300, Sacramento, CA 95814. 916-651-9011. Fax: 916-651-9011. Internet site <data.ca.gov>.
California Open Data. Online.

Colorado

State Demography Office, 1313 Sherman Street, Suite 521, Denver, CO 80203. 303-864-7720. Internet site <demography.dola.colorado.gov>.
State Demography Office Publications and Reports. Online.

Connecticut

CTD Data Collaborative, 2389 Main Street, Glastonbury, CT 06033. 860-500-1983. Internet site <profiles.ctdata.org>.
Connecticut Town Profiles. Recurring. Online.

Delaware

Open Data Council, 801 Silver Lake Boulevard, Dover, DE 19904. 302-739-9500. Internet site <data.delaware.gov>.
Delaware Open Data. Online.

District of Columbia

Office of the Chief Technology Officer, 200 I Street SE, Washington, DC 20003. 202-727-2277. Fax: 202-727-6857. Internet site <opendata.dc.gov>.
Open Data DC. Online.

Florida

Office of Economic and Demographic Research, 111 West Madison Street, Suite 574, Tallahassee, FL 32399-6588. 850-487-1402. Fax: 850-922-6436. Internet site <www.edr.state.fl.us/Content/>.
State Data Center. Online.

Florida Geographic Information Office, 3900 Commonwealth Boulevard, Tallahassee, FL 32399-3000. 850-245-2118. Internet site <geodata.floridagio.gov/>.
Florida's Geospatial Open Data. Online.

Georgia

University of Georgia, Terry College of Business, Selig Center for Economic Growth, E201 Ivester Hall, 650 S. Lumpkin Street, Athens, GA 30602. 678-646-9782. Internet site <www.terry.uga.edu/faculty-and-research/research-centers/selig/>.
Georgia Economic Outlook. Annual. Online.

University of Georgia, Carl Vinson Institute of Government, 201 North Milledge Avenue, Athens, GA 30602. 706-542-2736. Fax: 706-542-9301. Internet site <georgiadata.org/data/data-tables>.
Georgia Data. Online.

Hawaii

Hawaii State Department of Business, Economic Development and Tourism, Research and Economic Analysis Division, P.O. Box 2359, Honolulu, HI 96804. 808-586-2355. Internet site <www.dbedt.hawaii.gov/economic/databook>.
State of Hawaii Data Book. Annual. Online.

Idaho

University of Idaho Extension, 875 Perimeter Drive, MS 2331, Moscow, ID 83844-2331. 208-885-6111. Internet site <indicatorsidaho.org/>.
Indicators Idaho. Online.

Illinois

Office of the Governor, 207 State House, Springfield, IL 62706. 217-782-6830, 217-782-6831. Internet site <data.illinois.gov>.
State of Illinois Data Portal. Online.

Indiana

Indiana University, Kelley School of Business, Indiana Business Research Center, 1309 E. Tenth Street, Bloomington, IN 47405. 812-855-5507. Internet site <www.stats.indiana.edu>.
STATS Indiana. Online.

Iowa

Iowa State University of Science and Technology, Community Indicators Program, 260 Heady Hall, 518 Farm House Lane, Ames, IA 50011. 515-294-2954. Internet site <www.icip.iastate.edu>.
Iowa Community Indicators Program. Online.

State Library of Iowa, 1112 East Grand, Des Moines, IA 50319. 800-248-4483. Internet site <www.iowadatacenter.org>.
State Data Center. Online.

Kansas

University of Kansas, Institute for Policy and Social Research, 1541 Lilac Lane, 607 Blake Hall, Lawrence, KS 66045-3129. 785-864-3701. Fax: 785-864-3683. Internet site <ksdata.ku.edu/>.
Kansas Statistical Abstract. Annual. Online.
Kansas State Data Center. Online.

Kentucky

Kentucky Cabinet for Economic Development, Old Capitol Annex, 300 West Broadway, Frankfort, KY 40601. 502-654-7670. Internet site <www.selectkentucky.com>.

Louisiana

Louisiana State Census Data Center, 1201 N. Third Street, Baton Rouge, LA 70802. 225-342-7105. Fax: 225-219-9465. Internet site <www.louisiana.gov/demographics-and-geography>.
Select Current Statistics for Louisiana. Online.

Maine

Department of Administrative and Financial Services, 78 State House Station, Augusta, ME 04333. 207-624-7800. Internet site <www.maine.gov/portal/about_me/statistics.html>.

Maryland

Maryland State Data and Analysis Center, 120 E. Baltimore Street, 20th Floor, Baltimore, MD 21202. 410-767-4500. Internet site <www.planning.maryland.gov/MSDC/Pages/default.aspx>.
Maryland Statistical Handbook. Annual. Online.

Massachusetts

University of Massachusetts Donahue Institute, Massachusetts State Data Center, 100 Venture Way, Suite 9, Hadley, MA 01035. 413-545-0001. Internet site <www.donahue.umass.edu/business-groups/economic-public-policy-research/massbenchmarks>.
MassBenchmarks. Online.

Michigan

Office of the Governor, P.O. Box 30013, Lansing, MI 48909. 517-335-7858. Internet site <data.michigan.gov>.
Michigan's Open Data Portal. Online.

Minnesota

Minnesota Department of Employment and Economic Development, 180 E. 5th Street, Suite 1200, Saint Paul, MN 55101. 651-259-7384. Internet site <www.mn.gov/deed/data>.
Data Center. Online.

Minnesota State Demographic Center, 203 Administration Building, 50 Sherburne Avenue, Saint Paul, MN 55155. 651-201-2472. Internet site <mn.gov/admin/demography>.

Mississippi

Mississippi Secretary of State, Publications, 401 Mississippi Street, Jackson, MS 39201. 601-359-6344. Fax: 601-576-2541. Internet site <www.sos.ms.gov/communications-publications/2020-2024-mississippi-blue-book>.
Mississippi Blue Book. Quadrennial. Print and online.

Missouri

Missouri State Library, 600 West Main Street, Jefferson City, MO 65101. 573-751-4936. Internet site <mcdc.missouri.edu/>.
Missouri State Data Center. Online.

Montana

Montana Department of Commerce, Census and Economic Information Center, 301 S. Park Avenue, Helena, MT 59620. 406-841-2700. Internet site <ceic.mt.gov>.

Nebraska

Nebraska Library Commission, 1200 N. Street, Suite 120, Lincoln, NE 68508-2023. 402-471-2083. Internet site <www.nebraska.gov/government/open-data/>.
Open Data. Online.

Nevada

Nevada Governor's Office of Economic Development, 808 West Nye Lane, Carson City, NV 89703. 775-687-9900. Fax: 775-687-9924. Internet site <goed.nv.gov/why-nevada/data-portal/>.
Nevada Dashboard. Online.

New Hampshire

New Hampshire Office of Planning and Development, 100 North Main Street, Concord, NH 03301. 603-271-1773. Internet site <www.nheconomy.com/office-of-planning-and-development/what-we-do/state-data-center-(census-data)>.
State Data Center. Online.

New Jersey

State of New Jersey Office of Information Technology, P.O. Box 212, Trenton, NJ 08625. 1-800-622-4357. Internet site <data.nj.gov/>.
NJOIT Open Data Center. Online.

New Mexico

University of New Mexico, Bureau of Business and Economic Research, 400 Cornell Drive NE, Albuquerque, NM 87131-0001. 505-277-6626. Internet site <bber.unm.edu/data>.

New York

Nelson A. Rockefeller Institute of Government, 411 State Street, Albany, NY 12203. 518-443-4150. Internet site <www.rockinst.org/nys-statistical-yearbook/>.
New York State Statistical Yearbook. Annual. Print and Online.

North Carolina

Office of State Budget and Management, MSC 20320, Raleigh, NC 27699-0320. 984-236-0600. Internet site <linc.osbm.nc.gov/pages/home>.
LINC. Online.

North Dakota

Geographic Information Systems, 4201 Normandy Street, Bismark, ND 58203-1324. 701-328-4470. Internet site <www.gis.nd.gov>.
GIS Hub. Online.

Ohio

Ohio Development Services Agency, Office of Research, 77 South High Street, 29th floor, Columbus, OH 43215. 800-848-1300. Internet site <devresearch.ohio.gov>.
Reports and Reseach. Online.
InnovateOhio, 77 South High Street, 30th floor, Columbus, OH 43215. 614-644-4357. Internet site <data.ohio.gov>.
DataOhio. Online.

Oklahoma

Oklahoma State Capitol, 2300 N. Lincoln Boulevard, Oklahoma City, OK 73105. Internet site <data.ok.gov>.
Oklahoma's Open Data. Online.

Oregon

Oregon State Archives, 800 Summer Street NE, Salem, OR 97310. 503-373-0701. Internet site <sos.oregon.gov/blue-book/Pages/default.aspx>.
Oregon Blue Book. Biennial. Online.

Pennsylvania

Pennsylvania State Data Center, 777 West Harrisburg Pike, Middletown, PA 17057-4898. 717-948-6336. Fax: 717-948-6754. Internet site <pasdc.hbg.psu.edu>.

Rhode Island

Rhode Island Department of Labor and Training, 1511 Pontiac Avenue, Cranston, RI 02920. 401-462-8740. Internet site <dlt.ri.gov/labor-market-information/data-center>.
Data Center. Online.

South Carolina

South Carolina Revenue and Fiscal Affairs Offices, 1000 Assembly Street, Rembert Dennis Building, Suite 421, Columbia, SC 29201. 803-734-3793. Internet site <rfa.sc.gov/data-research>.
Data and Research. Online.

South Dakota

South Dakota State University Census Data Center, 1015 Campanile Avenue, Brookings, SD 57007. 605-688-4322. Internet site <www.sdstate.edu/school-psychology-sociology-and-rural-studies/census-data-center>.

Tennessee

The University of Tennessee, Knoxville, Boyd Center for Business and Economic Research, 2280 Sutherland Avenue, Suite 228, Knoxville, TN 37919. 865-974-6070. Internet site <tndata.utk.edu>.
Tennessee State Data Center. Online.

Texas

Texas State Historical Association, P.O. Box 5428, 3001 Lake Austin Boulevard, Austin, TX 78703. 512-471-2600. Internet site <texasalmanac.com>.
Texas Almanac. Biennial. Print and online.

Texas Demographic Center, One USTA Circle, San Antonio, TX 78249. 210-458-6543. Internet site <demographics.texas.gov>.

Utah

The University of Utah, Gardner Policy Institute, 411 East South Temple Street, Salt Lake City, UT 84111. 801-585-5618. Internet site <gardner.utah.edu/economics-and-public-policy/economic-report-to-the-governor/>.
Economic Report to the Governor. Annual. Online.

Vermont

Vermont Department of Labor, Economic and Labor Market Information, P.O. Box 488, Montpelier, VT 05601-0488. 802-828-4157. Fax: 802-828-4050. Internet site <www.vtlmi.info/>.
Vermont Economic and Demographic Profile. Annual. Online.

Virginia

Office of Data Governance and Analytics, P.O. Box 1475, Richmond, VA 23218. 804-786-1201. Internet site <data.virginia.gov>.
Virginia Open Data Portal. Online.

Washington

Washington State Library, P.O. Box 40220, Olympia, WA 98504-0220. 360-704-5221. Internet site <data.wa.gov>.
Data.WA. Online.

West Virginia

West Virginia University, John Chambers College of Business and Economics, Bureau of Business and Economic Research, P.O. Box 6527, Morgantown, WV 26506. 304-293-7831. Internet site <business.wvu.edu/research-outreach/bureau-of-business-and-economic-research>.
West Virginia County Data Profiles. Annual. Online.
West Virginia Economic Outlook. Annual. Online.

Wisconsin

Wisconsin Legislative Reference Bureau, 1 East Main Street, Suite 200, Madison, WI 53703. 608-504-5801. Internet site <legis.wisconsin.gov/lrb>.
Wisconsin Blue Book. Biennial. Print and Online.

Wyoming

Department of Administration and Information, Economic Analysis Division, 2800 Central Avenue, Cheyenne, WY 82002-0060. 307-777-7504. Internet site <eadiv.state.wy.us>.
Wyoming and County Profiles. Annual. Online.

American Samoa

Department of Commerce, A.P. Lutali Executive Building, 2nd Floor, Pago Pago, AS 96799. 684-633-5155. Internet site <www.doc.as.gov/resource-center>.
Statistical Yearbook. Online.

Guam

Bureau of Statistics and Plans, Planning and Information Program, P.O. Box 2950, Hagatna, GU 96932. 671-472-4201. Internet site <bsp.guam.gov/planning-information-program-2/>.
Guam Statistical Yearbook. Online.
Guam Facts and Figures at a Glance. Online.

Northern Mariana Islands

Department of Commerce, Central Statistics Division, P.O. Box 5795 CHRB, Saipan, MP 96950. 670-664-3023. Internet site <ver1.cnmicommerce.com/divisions/central-statistics/report-hub/>.
CSD Report Hub. Online.

Puerto Rico

Junta de Planificación. P.O. Box 41119, San Juan, PR 00940-1119. 787-723-6200. Internet site <jp.pr.gov>.
Economic Report to the Governor. Online.

U.S. Virgin Islands

Department of Labor, Bureau of Labor Statistics, 2353 Kronprindsens Gade, St. Thomas, VI 00802. 340-776-3700. Fax: 340-715-5743. Internet site <www.vidol.gov/labor-statistics/>.
Labor Market Information. Online.

Appendix II
Metropolitan and Micropolitan Statistical Areas: Concepts, Components, and Population

The United States Office of Management and Budget (OMB) defines metropolitan and micropolitan statistical areas according to published standards that are applied to U.S. Census Bureau data. The general concept of a metropolitan or micropolitan statistical area is that of a core area containing a substantial population nucleus, together with adjacent communities having a high degree of economic and social integration with that core. The metropolitan and micropolitan statistical areas appearing in this edition of the *Statistical Abstract* are based on 2020 standards published in the Federal Register July 16, 2021, and adhere to delineations of statistical areas issued by the OMB effective July 2023.

Standard definitions of metropolitan areas were first issued in 1949 by the then Bureau of the Budget, under the designation "standard metropolitan area" (SMA). The term was changed to "standard metropolitan statistical area" (SMSA) in 1959 and to "metropolitan statistical area" (MSA) in 1983. The term "metropolitan area" (MA) was adopted in 1990 and referred collectively to metropolitan statistical areas (MSAs), consolidated metropolitan statistical areas (CMSAs), and primary metropolitan statistical areas (PMSAs). The term "core-based statistical area" (CBSA) became effective in 2000 and refers collectively to metropolitan and micropolitan statistical areas.

OMB has been responsible for the official metropolitan areas since they were first defined, except for 1977-1981, when they were the responsibility of the Office of Federal Statistical Policy and Standards, U.S. Department of Commerce. The standards for defining metropolitan areas were modified in 1958, 1971, 1975, 1980, 1990, 2000, 2010, and 2021.

Defining Metropolitan and Micropolitan Statistical Areas—The standards provide that each CBSA must contain at least one urban area of 10,000 or more population. Each metropolitan statistical area must have at least one urbanized area of 50,000 or more inhabitants. Each micropolitan statistical area must have at least one urban cluster of at least 10,000 but less than 50,000 population.

Under the standards, the county (or counties) in which at least 50 percent of the population resides within urban areas of 10,000 or more population, or that contain at least 5,000 people residing within a single urban area of 10,000 or more population, is identified as a "central county" (counties). Additional "outlying counties" are included in the CBSA if they meet specific requirements of commuting to or from the central counties. Counties or equivalent entities form the geographic "building blocks" for metropolitan and micropolitan statistical areas throughout the United States and Puerto Rico.

If specific criteria are met, a metropolitan statistical area containing a single core with a population of 2.5 million or more may be subdivided to form smaller groupings of counties referred to as "metropolitan divisions."

Under the July 2023 OMB delineations, there are 387 metropolitan statistical areas and 538 micropolitan statistical areas in the United States. Additionally, there are 6 metropolitan and 4 micropolitan statistical areas in Puerto Rico.

Principal Cities and Metropolitan and Micropolitan Statistical Area Titles—The largest city in each metropolitan or micropolitan statistical area is designated a "principal city." Additional cities qualify if specific requirements are met concerning population size and employment. The title of each metropolitan or micropolitan statistical area consists of the names of up to three of its principal cities in order of descending population size and the name of each state into which the metropolitan or micropolitan statistical area extends. Titles of metropolitan divisions also typically are based on principal city names, but in certain cases consist of county names.

New England City and Town Areas—Cities and towns are the primary units of local government in the six New England states, where counties have little or no official governmental functions. The New England city and town areas (NECTAs) are defined using the same criteria as metropolitan and micropolitan statistical areas and are identified as either metropolitan or micropolitan, based, respectively, on the presence of either an urbanized area of 50,000 or more population or an urban cluster of at least 10,000 but less than 50,000 population. If the specific criteria are met, a NECTA containing a single core with a population of at least 2.5 million may be subdivided to form smaller groupings of cities and towns referred to as New England city and town area divisions.

Changes in Definitions Over Time—Changes in the definitions of these statistical areas since the 1950 census have consisted chiefly of (1) the recognition of new areas as they reached the minimum required city or urbanized area population and (2) the addition of counties (or cities and towns in New England) to existing areas as new decennial census data showed them to qualify. In some instances, formerly separate areas have been merged, components of an area have been transferred from one area to another, or components have been dropped from an area. The large majority of changes are based on decennial census data; however, Census Bureau data serve as the basis for intercensal updates in specific circumstances.

Because of these historical changes in geographic definitions, users must be cautious in comparing data for these statistical areas from different dates. For some purposes, comparisons of data for areas as defined at given dates may be appropriate; for other purposes, it may be preferable to maintain consistent area definitions. Historical statistical area delineations are available for selected years from 1950 to 2020.

See the Census Bureau website at <www.census.gov/programs-surveys/metro-micro.html> for information on historical delineations and component counties.

Table A. Metropolitan Statistical Areas and Components—Population: 2023

[In thousands (182 represents 182,000). Population as of July 2023. Metropolitan Statistical Areas delineated by the U.S. Office of Management and Budget as of July 2023. The estimates are developed from a base that incorporates the 2020 Census, Vintage 2020 estimates, and 2020 Demographic Analysis estimates. All Metropolitan Statistical Areas are arranged alphabetically]

Metropolitan Statistical Area ~~Metropolitan Division ~~~~Component county	Population, 2023 (1,000)
Abilene, TX	**182**
Callahan County, TX	14
Jones County, TX	20
Taylor County, TX	147
Akron, OH	**698**
Portage County, OH	163
Summit County, OH	536
Albany, GA	**146**
Dougherty County, GA	83
Lee County, GA	34
Terrell County, GA	9
Worth County, GA	20
Albany, OR	**131**
Linn County, OR	131
Albany-Schenectady-Troy, NY	**905**
Albany County, NY	317
Rensselaer County, NY	159
Saratoga County, NY	239
Schenectady County, NY	160
Schoharie County, NY	30
Albuquerque, NM	**922**
Bernalillo County, NM	672
Sandoval County, NM	156
Torrance County, NM	16
Valencia County, NM	79
Alexandria, LA	**148**
Grant Parish, LA	22
Rapides Parish, LA	126
Allentown-Bethlehem-Easton, PA-NJ	**874**
Warren County, NJ	111
Carbon County, PA	65
Lehigh County, PA	378
Northampton County, PA	319
Altoona, PA	**120**
Blair County, PA	120
Amarillo, TX	**272**
Armstrong County, TX	2
Carson County, TX	6
Oldham County, TX	2
Potter County, TX	115
Randall County, TX	148
Ames, IA	**125**
Boone County, IA	27
Story County, IA	99
Amherst Town-Northampton, MA	**163**
Hampshire County, MA	163
Anchorage, AK	**401**
Anchorage Municipality, AK	286
Matanuska-Susitna Borough, AK	115
Ann Arbor, MI	**366**
Washtenaw County, MI	366
Anniston-Oxford, AL	**116**
Calhoun County, AL	116
Appleton, WI	**246**
Calumet County, WI	53
Outagamie County, WI	193
Asheville, NC	**417**
Buncombe County, NC	276
Henderson County, NC	119
Madison County, NC	22
Athens-Clarke County, GA	**222**
Clarke County, GA	130
Madison County, GA	32
Oconee County, GA	44
Oglethorpe County, GA	16
Atlanta-Sandy Springs-Roswell, GA	**6,307**
Atlanta-Sandy Springs-Roswell, GA	**4,914**
Barrow County, GA	93
Butts County, GA	27
Carroll County, GA	127
Clayton County, GA	298
Coweta County, GA	156
Dawson County, GA	32

Metropolitan Statistical Area ~~Metropolitan Division ~~~~Component county	Population, 2023 (1,000)
DeKalb County, GA	763
Douglas County, GA	149
Fayette County, GA	123
Forsyth County, GA	273
Fulton County, GA	1,079
Gwinnett County, GA	984
Heard County, GA	12
Henry County, GA	255
Jasper County, GA	16
Lumpkin County, GA	35
Meriwether County, GA	21
Morgan County, GA	21
Newton County, GA	120
Pickens County, GA	36
Pike County, GA	20
Rockdale County, GA	96
Spalding County, GA	70
Walton County, GA	107
Marietta, GA	**1,394**
Bartow County, GA	115
Cherokee County, GA	287
Cobb County, GA	777
Haralson County, GA	32
Paulding County, GA	183
Atlantic City-Hammonton, NJ	**370**
Atlantic County, NJ	275
Cape May County, NJ	95
Auburn-Opelika, AL	**202**
Lee County, AL	183
Macon County, AL	18
Augusta-Richmond County, GA-SC	**629**
Burke County, GA	24
Columbia County, GA	165
Lincoln County, GA	8
McDuffie County, GA	22
Richmond County, GA	205
Aiken County, SC	177
Edgefield County, SC	28
Austin-Round Rock-San Marcos, TX	**2,473**
Bastrop County, TX	111
Caldwell County, TX	50
Hays County, TX	280
Travis County, TX	1,335
Williamson County, TX	697
Bakersfield-Delano, CA	**914**
Kern County, CA	914
Baltimore-Columbia-Towson, MD	**2,834**
Anne Arundel County, MD	595
Baltimore County, MD	845
Carroll County, MD	177
Harford County, MD	265
Howard County, MD	336
Queen Anne's County, MD	53
Baltimore city, MD	565
Bangor, ME	**155**
Penobscot County, ME	155
Barnstable Town, MA	**232**
Barnstable County, MA	232
Baton Rouge, LA	**874**
Ascension Parish, LA	132
Assumption Parish, LA	20
East Baton Rouge Parish, LA	448
East Feliciana Parish, LA	19
Iberville Parish, LA	30
Livingston Parish, LA	150
Pointe Coupee Parish, LA	20
St. Helena Parish, LA	11
West Baton Rouge Parish, LA	28
West Feliciana Parish, LA	15
Battle Creek, MI	**133**
Calhoun County, MI	133
Bay City, MI	**103**
Bay County, MI	103
Beaumont-Port Arthur, TX	**395**
Hardin County, TX	58

Metropolitan Statistical Area ~~Metropolitan Division ~~~~Component county	Population, 2023 (1,000)
Jefferson County, TX	251
Orange County, TX	86
Beckley, WV	**111**
Fayette County, WV	39
Raleigh County, WV	72
Bellingham, WA	**232**
Whatcom County, WA	232
Bend, OR	**261**
Crook County, OR	27
Deschutes County, OR	209
Jefferson County, OR	25
Billings, MT	**191**
Carbon County, MT	11
Stillwater County, MT	9
Yellowstone County, MT	171
Binghamton, NY	**244**
Broome County, NY	196
Tioga County, NY	48
Birmingham, AL	**1,184**
Bibb County, AL	22
Blount County, AL	60
Chilton County, AL	46
Jefferson County, AL	663
St. Clair County, AL	96
Shelby County, AL	233
Walker County, AL	65
Bismarck, ND	**136**
Burleigh County, ND	100
Morton County, ND	34
Oliver County, ND	2
Blacksburg-Christiansburg-Radford, VA	**181**
Floyd County, VA	16
Giles County, VA	16
Montgomery County, VA	99
Pulaski County, VA	34
Radford city, VA	17
Bloomington, IL	**170**
McLean County, IL	170
Bloomington, IN	**161**
Monroe County, IN	139
Owen County, IN	22
Boise City, ID	**825**
Ada County, ID	525
Boise County, ID	9
Canyon County, ID	258
Gem County, ID	21
Owyhee County, ID	13
Boston-Cambridge-Newton, MA-NH	**4,919**
Boston, MA	**2,031**
Norfolk County, MA	727
Plymouth County, MA	535
Suffolk County, MA	768
Cambridge-Newton-Framingham, MA	**2,434**
Essex County, MA	810
Middlesex County, MA	1,624
Rockingham County-Strafford County, NH	**454**
Rockingham County, NH	321
Strafford County, NH	133
Boulder, CO	**327**
Boulder County, CO	327
Bowling Green, KY	**189**
Allen County, KY	22
Butler County, KY	12
Edmonson County, KY	12
Warren County, KY	142
Bozeman, MT	**126**
Gallatin County, MT	126
Bremerton-Silverdale-Port Orchard, WA	**278**
Kitsap County, WA	278
Bridgeport-Stamford-Danbury, CT	**952**
Greater Bridgeport Planning Region, CT	328

See footnotes at end of table.

Table A. Metropolitan Statistical Areas and Components—Population: 2023-Continued.

See headnote on page 916.

Metropolitan Statistical Area ~~Metropolitan Division ~~~~Component county	Population, 2023 (1,000)
Western Connecticut Planning Region, CT	624
Brownsville-Harlingen, TX	**427**
Cameron County, TX	427
Brunswick-St. Simons, GA	**116**
Brantley County, GA	18
Glynn County, GA	86
McIntosh County, GA	12
Buffalo-Cheektowaga, NY	**1,156**
Erie County, NY	946
Niagara County, NY	209
Burlington, NC	**179**
Alamance County, NC	179
Burlington-South Burlington, VT	**228**
Chittenden County, VT	169
Franklin County, VT	51
Grand Isle County, VT	7
Canton-Massillon, OH	**399**
Carroll County, OH	27
Stark County, OH	373
Cape Coral-Fort Myers, FL	**835**
Lee County, FL	835
Cape Girardeau, MO-IL	**98**
Alexander County, IL	5
Bollinger County, MO	11
Cape Girardeau County, MO	83
Carson City, NV	**58**
Carson City, NV	58
Casper, WY	**80**
Natrona County, WY	80
Cedar Rapids, IA	**276**
Benton County, IA	26
Jones County, IA	21
Linn County, IA	229
Chambersburg, PA	**158**
Franklin County, PA	158
Champaign-Urbana, IL	**236**
Champaign County, IL	206
Ford County, IL	13
Piatt County, IL	17
Charleston, WV	**203**
Boone County, WV	21
Clay County, WV	8
Kanawha County, WV	175
Charleston-North Charleston, SC	**849**
Berkeley County, SC	255
Charleston County, SC	424
Dorchester County, SC	170
Charlotte-Concord-Gastonia, NC-SC	**2,805**
Anson County, NC	22
Cabarrus County, NC	240
Gaston County, NC	237
Iredell County, NC	200
Lincoln County, NC	96
Mecklenburg County, NC	1,164
Rowan County, NC	152
Union County, NC	256
Chester County, SC	32
Lancaster County, SC	108
York County, SC	298
Charlottesville, VA	**225**
Albemarle County, VA	116
Fluvanna County, VA	28
Greene County, VA	21
Nelson County, VA	15
Charlottesville city, VA	45
Chattanooga, TN-GA	**581**
Catoosa County, GA	69
Dade County, GA	16
Walker County, GA	69
Hamilton County, TN	380
Marion County, TN	29
Sequatchie County, TN	17
Cheyenne, WY	**101**

Metropolitan Statistical Area ~~Metropolitan Division ~~~~Component county	Population, 2023 (1,000)
Laramie County, WY	101
Chicago-Naperville-Elgin, IL-IN	**9,263**
Chicago-Naperville-Schaumburg, IL	**7,075**
Cook County, IL	5,087
DuPage County, IL	921
Grundy County, IL	54
McHenry County, IL	313
Will County, IL	701
Elgin, IL	**755**
DeKalb County, IL	100
Kane County, IL	515
Kendall County, IL	140
Lake County, IL	**709**
Lake County, IL	709
Lake County-Porter County-Jasper County, IN	**723**
Jasper County, IN	34
Lake County, IN	501
Newton County, IN	14
Porter County, IN	175
Chico, CA	**207**
Butte County, CA	207
Cincinnati, OH-KY-IN	**2,271**
Dearborn County, IN	51
Franklin County, IN	23
Ohio County, IN	6
Boone County, KY	140
Bracken County, KY	8
Campbell County, KY	94
Gallatin County, KY	9
Grant County, KY	26
Kenton County, KY	171
Pendleton County, KY	15
Brown County, OH	44
Butler County, OH	393
Clermont County, OH	212
Hamilton County, OH	827
Warren County, OH	252
Clarksville, TN-KY	**340**
Christian County, KY	72
Trigg County, KY	14
Montgomery County, TN	240
Stewart County, TN	14
Cleveland, OH	**2,159**
Ashtabula County, OH	97
Cuyahoga County, OH	1,233
Geauga County, OH	95
Lake County, OH	232
Lorain County, OH	318
Medina County, OH	184
Cleveland, TN	**130**
Bradley County, TN	112
Polk County, TN	18
Coeur d'Alene, ID	**185**
Kootenai County, ID	185
College Station-Bryan, TX	**281**
Brazos County, TX	245
Burleson County, TX	19
Robertson County, TX	17
Colorado Springs, CO	**769**
El Paso County, CO	744
Teller County, CO	25
Columbia, MO	**217**
Boone County, MO	189
Cooper County, MO	17
Howard County, MO	10
Columbia, SC	**858**
Calhoun County, SC	14
Fairfield County, SC	20
Kershaw County, SC	70
Lexington County, SC	310
Richland County, SC	425
Saluda County, SC	19
Columbus, GA-AL	**324**
Russell County, AL	59

Metropolitan Statistical Area ~~Metropolitan Division ~~~~Component county	Population, 2023 (1,000)
Chattahoochee County, GA	9
Harris County, GA	37
Marion County, GA	7
Muscogee County, GA	202
Stewart County, GA	5
Talbot County, GA	6
Columbus, IN	**84**
Bartholomew County, IN	84
Columbus, OH	**2,180**
Delaware County, OH	232
Fairfield County, OH	165
Franklin County, OH	1,326
Hocking County, OH	28
Licking County, OH	183
Madison County, OH	45
Morrow County, OH	36
Perry County, OH	36
Pickaway County, OH	61
Union County, OH	70
Corpus Christi, TX	**448**
Aransas County, TX	25
Nueces County, TX	352
San Patricio County, TX	71
Corvallis, OR	**98**
Benton County, OR	98
Crestview-Fort Walton Beach-Destin, FL	**305**
Okaloosa County, FL	218
Walton County, FL	86
Dallas-Fort Worth-Arlington, TX	**8,100**
Dallas-Plano-Irving, TX	**5,463**
Collin County, TX	1,195
Dallas County, TX	2,606
Denton County, TX	1,008
Ellis County, TX	223
Hunt County, TX	113
Kaufman County, TX	186
Rockwall County, TX	131
Fort Worth-Arlington-Grapevine, TX	**2,637**
Johnson County, TX	203
Parker County, TX	173
Tarrant County, TX	2,183
Wise County, TX	78
Dalton, GA	**145**
Murray County, GA	41
Whitfield County, GA	104
Daphne-Fairhope-Foley, AL	**254**
Baldwin County, AL	254
Davenport-Moline-Rock Island, IA-IL	**379**
Henry County, IL	48
Mercer County, IL	15
Rock Island County, IL	141
Scott County, IA	174
Dayton-Kettering-Beavercreek, OH	**814**
Greene County, OH	170
Miami County, OH	111
Montgomery County, OH	534
Decatur, AL	**159**
Lawrence County, AL	34
Morgan County, AL	125
Decatur, IL	**101**
Macon County, IL	101
Deltona-Daytona Beach-Ormond Beach, FL	**722**
Flagler County, FL	131
Volusia County, FL	590
Denver-Aurora-Centennial, CO	**3,005**
Adams County, CO	533
Arapahoe County, CO	656
Broomfield County, CO	77
Clear Creek County, CO	9
Denver County, CO	717

Table A. Metropolitan Statistical Areas and Components—Population: 2023-Continued.

See headnote on page 916.

Metropolitan Statistical Area ~~Metropolitan Division ~~~~Component county	Population, 2023 (1,000)
Douglas County, CO.	384
Elbert County, CO.	29
Gilpin County, CO.	6
Jefferson County, CO.	576
Park County, CO.	18
Des Moines-West Des Moines, IA.	**737**
Dallas County, IA.	111
Guthrie County, IA.	11
Jasper County, IA.	38
Madison County, IA.	17
Polk County, IA.	505
Warren County, IA.	55
Detroit-Warren-Dearborn, MI.	**4,342**
Detroit-Dearborn-Livonia, MI.	**1,751**
Wayne County, MI.	1,751
Warren-Troy-Farmington Hills, MI.	**2,591**
Lapeer County, MI.	89
Livingston County, MI.	197
Macomb County, MI.	875
Oakland County, MI.	1,270
St. Clair County, MI.	160
Dothan, AL.	**153**
Geneva County, AL.	27
Henry County, AL.	18
Houston County, AL.	108
Dover, DE.	**190**
Kent County, DE.	190
Dubuque, IA.	**99**
Dubuque County, IA.	99
Duluth, MN-WI.	**282**
Carlton County, MN.	37
St. Louis County, MN.	201
Douglas County, WI.	44
Durham-Chapel Hill, NC.	**609**
Chatham County, NC.	82
Durham County, NC.	337
Orange County, NC.	151
Person County, NC.	40
Eagle Pass, TX.	**58**
Maverick County, TX.	58
Eau Claire, WI.	**175**
Chippewa County, WI.	67
Eau Claire County, WI.	108
El Centro, CA.	**179**
Imperial County, CA.	179
Elizabethtown, KY.	**128**
Hardin County, KY.	112
Larue County, KY.	15
Elkhart-Goshen, IN.	**206**
Elkhart County, IN.	206
Elmira, NY.	**81**
Chemung County, NY.	81
El Paso, TX.	**873**
El Paso County, TX.	870
Hudspeth County, TX.	3
Enid, OK.	**62**
Garfield County, OK.	62
Erie, PA.	**268**
Erie County, PA.	268
Eugene-Springfield, OR.	**381**
Lane County, OR.	381
Evansville, IN.	**271**
Posey County, IN.	25
Vanderburgh County, IN.	180
Warrick County, IN.	66
Fairbanks-College, AK.	**95**
Fairbanks North Star Borough, AK.	95
Fargo, ND-MN.	**263**
Clay County, MN.	66
Cass County, ND.	196
Farmington, NM.	**121**
San Juan County, NM.	121
Fayetteville, NC.	**392**
Cumberland County, NC.	338
Hoke County, NC.	54
Fayetteville-Springdale-Rogers, AR.	**590**
Benton County, AR.	311

Metropolitan Statistical Area ~~Metropolitan Division ~~~~Component county	Population, 2023 (1,000)
Madison County, AR.	18
Washington County, AR.	262
Flagstaff, AZ.	**144**
Coconino County, AZ.	144
Flint, MI.	**402**
Genesee County, MI.	402
Florence, SC.	**200**
Darlington County, SC.	62
Florence County, SC.	137
Florence-Muscle Shoals, AL.	**155**
Colbert County, AL.	58
Lauderdale County, AL.	97
Fond du Lac, WI.	**104**
Fond du Lac County, WI.	104
Fort Collins-Loveland, CO.	**371**
Larimer County, CO.	371
Fort Smith, AR-OK.	**231**
Crawford County, AR.	62
Sebastian County, AR.	129
Sequoyah County, OK.	40
Fort Wayne, IN.	**458**
Allen County, IN.	395
Wells County, IN.	29
Whitley County, IN.	35
Fresno, CA.	**1,180**
Fresno County, CA.	1,017
Madera County, CA.	163
Gadsden, AL.	**103**
Etowah County, AL.	103
Gainesville, FL.	**352**
Alachua County, FL.	286
Gilchrist County, FL.	20
Levy County, FL.	47
Gainesville, GA.	**217**
Hall County, GA.	217
Gettysburg, PA.	**107**
Adams County, PA.	107
Glens Falls, NY.	**125**
Warren County, NY.	65
Washington County, NY.	60
Goldsboro, NC.	**119**
Wayne County, NC.	119
Grand Forks, ND-MN.	**103**
Polk County, MN.	30
Grand Forks County, ND.	73
Grand Island, NE.	**76**
Hall County, NE.	62
Howard County, NE.	7
Merrick County, NE.	8
Grand Junction, CO.	**160**
Mesa County, CO.	160
Grand Rapids-Wyoming-Kentwood, MI.	**1,163**
Barry County, MI.	64
Ionia County, MI.	66
Kent County, MI.	661
Montcalm County, MI.	68
Ottawa County, MI.	303
Grants Pass, OR.	**88**
Josephine County, OR.	88
Great Falls, MT.	**85**
Cascade County, MT.	85
Greeley, CO.	**359**
Weld County, CO.	359
Green Bay, WI.	**332**
Brown County, WI.	271
Kewaunee County, WI.	21
Oconto County, WI.	40
Greensboro-High Point, NC.	**790**
Guilford County, NC.	550
Randolph County, NC.	147
Rockingham County, NC.	93
Greenville, NC.	**175**
Pitt County, NC.	175
Greenville-Anderson-Greer, SC.	**975**
Anderson County, SC.	213
Greenville County, SC.	558
Laurens County, SC.	69

Metropolitan Statistical Area ~~Metropolitan Division ~~~~Component county	Population, 2023 (1,000)
Pickens County, SC.	135
Gulfport-Biloxi, MS.	**422**
Hancock County, MS.	46
Harrison County, MS.	211
Jackson County, MS.	146
Stone County, MS.	19
Hagerstown-Martinsburg, MD-WV.	**306**
Washington County, MD.	156
Berkeley County, WV.	132
Morgan County, WV.	18
Hammond, LA.	**138**
Tangipahoa Parish, LA.	138
Hanford-Corcoran, CA.	**153**
Kings County, CA.	153
Harrisburg-Carlisle, PA.	**606**
Cumberland County, PA.	271
Dauphin County, PA.	289
Perry County, PA.	46
Harrisonburg, VA.	**138**
Rockingham County, VA.	87
Harrisonburg city, VA.	51
Hartford-West Hartford-East Hartford, CT.	**1,152**
Capitol Planning Region, CT.	975
Lower Connecticut River Valley Planning Region, CT.	176
Hattiesburg, MS.	**156**
Forrest County, MS.	78
Lamar County, MS.	66
Perry County, MS.	11
Helena, MT.	**96**
Broadwater County, MT.	8
Jefferson County, MT.	13
Lewis and Clark County, MT.	75
Hickory-Lenoir-Morganton, NC.	**370**
Alexander County, NC.	36
Burke County, NC.	88
Caldwell County, NC.	81
Catawba County, NC.	165
Hilton Head Island-Bluffton-Port Royal, SC.	**233**
Beaufort County, SC.	199
Jasper County, SC.	34
Hinesville, GA.	**89**
Liberty County, GA.	69
Long County, GA.	20
Homosassa Springs, FL.	**167**
Citrus County, FL.	167
Hot Springs, AR.	**100**
Garland County, AR.	100
Houma-Bayou Cane-Thibodaux, LA.	**199**
Lafourche Parish, LA.	95
Terrebonne Parish, LA.	104
Houston-Pasadena-The Woodlands, TX.	**7,510**
Austin County, TX.	32
Brazoria County, TX.	399
Chambers County, TX.	54
Fort Bend County, TX.	917
Galveston County, TX.	362
Harris County, TX.	4,835
Liberty County, TX.	108
Montgomery County, TX.	711
San Jacinto County, TX.	29
Waller County, TX.	64
Huntington-Ashland, WV-KY-OH.	**368**
Boyd County, KY.	48
Carter County, KY.	26
Greenup County, KY.	35
Lawrence County, KY.	16
Lawrence County, OH.	56
Cabell County, WV.	92
Putnam County, WV.	57

See footnotes at end of table.

Metropolitan Statistical Area ~~Metropolitan Division ~~~~Component county	Population, 2023 (1,000)
Wayne County, WV	38
Huntsville, AL	**527**
Limestone County, AL	115
Madison County, AL	413
Idaho Falls, ID	**168**
Bonneville County, ID	131
Butte County, ID	3
Jefferson County, ID	34
Indianapolis-Carmel-Greenwood, IN	**2,138**
Boone County, IN	76
Brown County, IN	16
Hamilton County, IN	372
Hancock County, IN	86
Hendricks County, IN	186
Johnson County, IN	168
Madison County, IN	133
Marion County, IN	968
Morgan County, IN	73
Shelby County, IN	45
Tipton County, IN	15
Iowa City, IA	**180**
Johnson County, IA	158
Washington County, IA	23
Ithaca, NY	**104**
Tompkins County, NY	104
Jackson, MI	**159**
Jackson County, MI	159
Jackson, MS	**610**
Copiah County, MS	28
Hinds County, MS	215
Holmes County, MS	16
Madison County, MS	113
Rankin County, MS	160
Scott County, MS	28
Simpson County, MS	26
Yazoo County, MS	26
Jackson, TN	**182**
Chester County, TN	18
Crockett County, TN	14
Gibson County, TN	51
Madison County, TN	99
Jacksonville, FL	**1,713**
Baker County, FL	28
Clay County, FL	232
Duval County, FL	1,031
Nassau County, FL	102
St. Johns County, FL	320
Jacksonville, NC	**214**
Onslow County, NC	214
Janesville-Beloit, WI	**164**
Rock County, WI	164
Jefferson City, MO	**151**
Callaway County, MO	45
Cole County, MO	77
Moniteau County, MO	15
Osage County, MO	13
Johnson City, TN	**213**
Carter County, TN	57
Unicoi County, TN	18
Washington County, TN	138
Johnstown, PA	**131**
Cambria County, PA	131
Jonesboro, AR	**136**
Craighead County, AR	114
Poinsett County, AR	22
Joplin, MO-KS	**205**
Cherokee County, KS	19
Jasper County, MO	125
Newton County, MO	61
Kahului-Wailuku, HI	**164**
Kalawao County, HI	0
Maui County, HI	164
Kalamazoo-Portage, MI	**262**
Kalamazoo County, MI	262
Kankakee, IL	**106**
Kankakee County, IL	106
Kansas City, MO-KS	**2,221**

Metropolitan Statistical Area ~~Metropolitan Division ~~~~Component county	Population, 2023 (1,000)
Johnson County, KS	622
Leavenworth County, KS	84
Linn County, KS	10
Miami County, KS	35
Wyandotte County, KS	165
Bates County, MO	16
Caldwell County, MO	9
Cass County, MO	112
Clay County, MO	260
Clinton County, MO	22
Jackson County, MO	719
Lafayette County, MO	33
Platte County, MO	112
Ray County, MO	23
Kennewick-Richland, WA	**314**
Benton County, WA	215
Franklin County, WA	99
Kenosha, WI	**167**
Kenosha County, WI	167
Killeen-Temple, TX	**501**
Bell County, TX	393
Coryell County, TX	85
Lampasas County, TX	23
Kingsport-Bristol, TN-VA	**313**
Hawkins County, TN	59
Sullivan County, TN	162
Scott County, VA	21
Washington County, VA	54
Bristol city, VA	17
Kingston, NY	**182**
Ulster County, NY	182
Kiryas Joel-Poughkeepsie-Newburgh, NY	**705**
Dutchess County, NY	297
Orange County, NY	407
Knoxville, TN	**946**
Anderson County, TN	80
Blount County, TN	141
Campbell County, TN	40
Grainger County, TN	25
Knox County, TN	501
Loudon County, TN	61
Morgan County, TN	22
Roane County, TN	56
Union County, TN	21
Kokomo, IN	**84**
Howard County, IN	84
La Crosse-Onalaska, WI-MN	**170**
Houston County, MN	19
La Crosse County, WI	120
Vernon County, WI	31
Lafayette, LA	**414**
Acadia Parish, LA	56
Lafayette Parish, LA	250
St. Martin Parish, LA	51
Vermilion Parish, LA	57
Lafayette-West Lafayette, IN	**227**
Benton County, IN	9
Carroll County, IN	21
Tippecanoe County, IN	189
Warren County, IN	9
Lake Charles, LA	**240**
Calcasieu Parish, LA	204
Cameron Parish, LA	5
Jefferson Davis Parish, LA	32
Lake Havasu City-Kingman, AZ	**224**
Mohave County, AZ	224
Lakeland-Winter Haven, FL	**818**
Polk County, FL	818
Lancaster, PA	**559**
Lancaster County, PA	559
Lansing-East Lansing, MI	**473**
Clinton County, MI	80
Eaton County, MI	109
Ingham County, MI	285
Laredo, TX	**269**
Webb County, TX	269

Metropolitan Statistical Area ~~Metropolitan Division ~~~~Component county	Population, 2023 (1,000)
Las Cruces, NM	**225**
Doña Ana County, NM	225
Las Vegas-Henderson-North Las Vegas, NV	**2,337**
Clark County, NV	2,337
Lawrence, KS	**121**
Douglas County, KS	121
Lawton, OK	**127**
Comanche County, OK	122
Cotton County, OK	5
Lebanon, PA	**144**
Lebanon County, PA	144
Lewiston, ID-WA	**66**
Nez Perce County, ID	43
Asotin County, WA	23
Lewiston-Auburn, ME	**114**
Androscoggin County, ME	114
Lexington-Fayette, KY	**520**
Bourbon County, KY	20
Clark County, KY	37
Fayette County, KY	320
Jessamine County, KY	55
Scott County, KY	60
Woodford County, KY	27
Lexington Park, MD	**210**
Calvert County, MD	95
St. Mary's County, MD	115
Lima, OH	**101**
Allen County, OH	101
Lincoln, NE	**344**
Lancaster County, NE	327
Seward County, NE	18
Little Rock-North Little Rock-Conway, AR	**764**
Faulkner County, AR	130
Grant County, AR	18
Lonoke County, AR	76
Perry County, AR	10
Pulaski County, AR	400
Saline County, AR	130
Logan, UT-ID	**158**
Franklin County, ID	15
Cache County, UT	142
Longview, TX	**293**
Gregg County, TX	126
Harrison County, TX	71
Rusk County, TX	53
Upshur County, TX	43
Longview-Kelso, WA	**113**
Cowlitz County, WA	113
Los Angeles-Long Beach-Anaheim, CA	**12,799**
Anaheim-Santa Ana-Irvine, CA	**3,136**
Orange County, CA	3,136
Los Angeles-Long Beach-Glendale, CA	**9,663**
Los Angeles County, CA	9,663
Louisville/Jefferson County, KY-IN	**1,366**
Clark County, IN	125
Floyd County, IN	81
Harrison County, IN	40
Washington County, IN	28
Bullitt County, KY	85
Henry County, KY	16
Jefferson County, KY	772
Meade County, KY	30
Nelson County, KY	48
Oldham County, KY	70
Shelby County, KY	50
Spencer County, KY	21
Lubbock, TX	**360**
Cochran County, TX	3
Crosby County, TX	5
Garza County, TX	5
Hockley County, TX	21
Lubbock County, TX	321

See footnotes at end of table.

Table A. Metropolitan Statistical Areas and Components—Population:
2023-Continued.

See headnote on page 916.

Metropolitan Statistical Area ~~Metropolitan Division ~~~~Component county	Population, 2023 (1,000)
Lynn County, TX.............	6
Lynchburg, VA......................	**265**
Amherst County, VA.............	31
Appomattox County, VA..........	17
Bedford County, VA.............	82
Campbell County, VA.............	55
Lynchburg city, VA.............	80
Macon-Bibb County, GA..........	**236**
Bibb County, GA.............	157
Crawford County, GA.............	12
Jones County, GA.............	29
Monroe County, GA.............	31
Twiggs County, GA.............	8
Madison, WI......................	**694**
Columbia County, WI.............	58
Dane County, WI.............	575
Green County, WI.............	37
Iowa County, WI.............	24
Manchester-Nashua, NH............	**427**
Hillsborough County, NH.........	427
Manhattan, KS...................	**133**
Geary County, KS.............	35
Pottawatomie County, KS.......	26
Riley County, KS.............	71
Mankato, MN.....................	**104**
Blue Earth County, MN.............	70
Nicollet County, MN.............	34
Mansfield, OH...................	**125**
Richland County, OH.............	125
McAllen-Edinburg-Mission, TX.....	**898**
Hidalgo County, TX.............	898
Medford, OR.....................	**221**
Jackson County, OR.............	221
Memphis, TN-MS-AR................	**1,336**
Crittenden County, AR.............	47
Benton County, MS.............	7
DeSoto County, MS.............	193
Marshall County, MS.............	34
Tate County, MS.............	28
Tunica County, MS.............	9
Fayette County, TN.............	44
Shelby County, TN.............	910
Tipton County, TN.............	62
Merced, CA......................	**292**
Merced County, CA.............	292
Miami-Fort Lauderdale-West Palm Beach, FL.............	**6,183**
Fort Lauderdale-Pompano Beach-Sunrise, FL............	**1,963**
Broward County, FL.............	1,963
Miami-Miami Beach-Kendall, FL.............	**2,687**
Miami-Dade County, FL..........	2,687
West Palm Beach-Boca Raton-Delray Beach, FL.......	**1,534**
Palm Beach County, FL.........	1,534
Michigan City-La Porte, IN......	**112**
LaPorte County, IN.............	112
Midland, MI.....................	**84**
Midland County, MI.............	84
Midland, TX.....................	**182**
Martin County, TX.............	5
Midland County, TX.............	177
Milwaukee-Waukesha, WI........	**1,560**
Milwaukee County, WI.............	916
Ozaukee County, WI.............	93
Washington County, WI.........	138
Waukesha County, WI...........	413
Minneapolis-St. Paul-Bloomington, MN-WI.....	**3,712**
Anoka County, MN.............	372
Carver County, MN.............	111
Chisago County, MN.............	59
Dakota County, MN.............	447
Hennepin County, MN.............	1,259
Isanti County, MN.............	43
Le Sueur County, MN.............	29
Mille Lacs County, MN.............	27
Ramsey County, MN.............	536
Scott County, MN.............	156

Metropolitan Statistical Area ~~Metropolitan Division ~~~~Component county	Population, 2023 (1,000)
Sherburne County, MN..........	102
Washington County, MN.........	279
Wright County, MN.............	151
Pierce County, WI.............	43
St. Croix County, WI.............	97
Minot, ND......................	**76**
McHenry County, ND.............	5
Renville County, ND.............	2
Ward County, ND.............	68
Missoula, MT...................	**127**
Mineral County, MT.............	5
Missoula County, MT.............	122
Mobile, AL......................	**412**
Mobile County, AL.............	412
Modesto, CA....................	**551**
Stanislaus County, CA..........	551
Monroe, LA.....................	**222**
Morehouse Parish, LA.............	24
Ouachita Parish, LA.............	158
Richland Parish, LA.............	20
Union Parish, LA.............	21
Monroe, MI.....................	**155**
Monroe County, MI.............	155
Montgomery, AL.................	**385**
Autauga County, AL.............	60
Elmore County, AL.............	90
Lowndes County, AL.............	10
Montgomery County, AL.........	225
Morgantown, WV.................	**142**
Monongalia County, WV.........	108
Preston County, WV.............	34
Morristown, TN.................	**124**
Hamblen County, TN.............	66
Jefferson County, TN.............	58
Mount Vernon-Anacortes, WA...	**131**
Skagit County, WA.............	131
Muncie, IN.....................	**112**
Delaware County, IN.............	112
Muskegon-Norton Shores, MI...	**177**
Muskegon County, MI.............	177
Myrtle Beach-Conway-North Myrtle Beach, SC............	**397**
Horry County, SC.............	397
Napa, CA.......................	**133**
Napa County, CA.............	133
Naples-Marco Island, FL........	**404**
Collier County, FL.............	404
Nashville-Davidson-- Murfreesboro--Franklin, TN...	**2,103**
Cannon County, TN.............	15
Cheatham County, TN.............	42
Davidson County, TN.............	712
Dickson County, TN.............	57
Hickman County, TN.............	26
Macon County, TN.............	27
Maury County, TN.............	111
Robertson County, TN.............	77
Rutherford County, TN.............	367
Smith County, TN.............	21
Sumner County, TN.............	208
Trousdale County, TN.............	12
Williamson County, TN.........	264
Wilson County, TN.............	164
New Haven, CT.................	**568**
South Central Connecticut Planning Region, CT.............	568
New Orleans-Metairie, LA.......	**962**
Jefferson Parish, LA.............	422
Orleans Parish, LA.............	364
Plaquemines Parish, LA..........	22
St. Bernard Parish, LA.............	44
St. Charles Parish, LA.............	51
St. James Parish, LA.............	19
St. John the Baptist Parish, LA...	40
New York-Newark-Jersey City, NY-NJ......................	**19,498**
Lakewood-New Brunswick, NJ......................	**2,514**
Middlesex County, NJ.............	864

Metropolitan Statistical Area ~~Metropolitan Division ~~~~Component county	Population, 2023 (1,000)
Monmouth County, NJ.............	643
Ocean County, NJ.............	659
Somerset County, NJ.............	349
Nassau County-Suffolk County, NY.............	**2,905**
Nassau County, NY.............	1,382
Suffolk County, NY.............	1,523
Newark, NJ.....................	**2,215**
Essex County, NJ.............	851
Hunterdon County, NJ.............	130
Morris County, NJ.............	514
Sussex County, NJ.............	146
Union County, NJ.............	573
New York-Jersey City-White Plains, NY-NJ.................	**11,864**
Bergen County, NJ.............	958
Hudson County, NJ.............	705
Passaic County, NJ.............	513
Bronx County, NY.............	1,356
Kings County, NY.............	2,561
New York County, NY.............	1,597
Putnam County, NY.............	98
Queens County, NY.............	2,252
Richmond County, NY.............	491
Rockland County, NY.............	341
Westchester County, NY.........	991
Niles, MI......................	**152**
Berrien County, MI.............	152
North Port-Bradenton-Sarasota, FL.............	**910**
Manatee County, FL.............	441
Sarasota County, FL.............	469
Norwich-New London-Willimantic, CT........	**280**
Southeastern Connecticut Planning Region, CT.............	280
Ocala, FL......................	**410**
Marion County, FL.............	410
Odessa, TX.....................	**164**
Ector County, TX.............	164
Ogden, UT......................	**658**
Davis County, UT.............	373
Morgan County, UT.............	13
Weber County, UT.............	272
Oklahoma City, OK................	**1,478**
Canadian County, OK.............	176
Cleveland County, OK.............	301
Grady County, OK.............	57
Lincoln County, OK.............	35
Logan County, OK.............	53
McClain County, OK.............	47
Oklahoma County, OK..........	809
Olympia-Lacey-Tumwater, WA...	**299**
Thurston County, WA.............	299
Omaha, NE-IA...................	**984**
Harrison County, IA.............	15
Mills County, IA.............	15
Pottawattamie County, IA.........	93
Cass County, NE.............	27
Douglas County, NE.............	590
Sarpy County, NE.............	200
Saunders County, NE.............	23
Washington County, NE..........	21
Orlando-Kissimmee-Sanford, FL.............	**2,818**
Lake County, FL.............	424
Orange County, FL.............	1,471
Osceola County, FL.............	438
Seminole County, FL.............	484
Oshkosh-Neenah, WI.............	**172**
Winnebago County, WI..........	172
Owensboro, KY.................	**113**
Daviess County, KY.............	103
McLean County, KY.............	9
Oxnard-Thousand Oaks-Ventura, CA.............	**830**
Ventura County, CA.............	830
Paducah, KY-IL.................	**102**
Massac County, IL.............	14

See headnote on page 916.

Metropolitan Statistical Area ~~Metropolitan Division ~~~~Component county	Population, 2023 (1,000)
Ballard County, KY	8
Carlisle County, KY	5
Livingston County, KY	9
McCracken County, KY	67
Palm Bay-Melbourne-Titusville, FL	**644**
Brevard County, FL	644
Panama City-Panama City Beach, FL	**216**
Bay County, FL	191
Washington County, FL	26
Parkersburg-Vienna, WV	**88**
Wirt County, WV	5
Wood County, WV	83
Pensacola-Ferry Pass-Brent, FL	**530**
Escambia County, FL	327
Santa Rosa County, FL	203
Peoria, IL	**362**
Marshall County, IL	12
Peoria County, IL	178
Stark County, IL	5
Tazewell County, IL	130
Woodford County, IL	38
Philadelphia-Camden-Wilmington, PA-NJ-DE-MD	**6,246**
Camden, NJ	**1,305**
Burlington County, NJ	469
Camden County, NJ	527
Gloucester County, NJ	308
Montgomery County-Bucks County-Chester County, PA	**2,065**
Bucks County, PA	646
Chester County, PA	550
Montgomery County, PA	869
Philadelphia, PA	**2,127**
Delaware County, PA	577
Philadelphia County, PA	1,551
Wilmington, DE-MD-NJ	**750**
New Castle County, DE	579
Cecil County, MD	106
Salem County, NJ	65
Phoenix-Mesa-Chandler, AZ	**5,070**
Maricopa County, AZ	4,586
Pinal County, AZ	484
Pinehurst-Southern Pines, NC	**107**
Moore County, NC	107
Pittsburgh, PA	**2,423**
Allegheny County, PA	1,225
Armstrong County, PA	64
Beaver County, PA	166
Butler County, PA	198
Fayette County, PA	124
Lawrence County, PA	84
Washington County, PA	210
Westmoreland County, PA	351
Pittsfield, MA	**127**
Berkshire County, MA	127
Pocatello, ID	**90**
Bannock County, ID	90
Portland-South Portland, ME	**566**
Cumberland County, ME	310
Sagadahoc County, ME	38
York County, ME	219
Portland-Vancouver-Hillsboro, OR-WA	**2,508**
Clackamas County, OR	423
Columbia County, OR	54
Multnomah County, OR	790
Washington County, OR	599
Yamhill County, OR	109
Clark County, WA	521
Skamania County, WA	13
Port St. Lucie, FL	**537**
Martin County, FL	163
St. Lucie County, FL	374
Prescott Valley-Prescott, AZ	**249**
Yavapai County, AZ	249

Metropolitan Statistical Area ~~Metropolitan Division ~~~~Component county	Population, 2023 (1,000)
Providence-Warwick, RI-MA	**1,678**
Bristol County, MA	582
Bristol County, RI	50
Kent County, RI	171
Newport County, RI	84
Providence County, RI	661
Washington County, RI	130
Provo-Orem-Lehi, UT	**732**
Juab County, UT	13
Utah County, UT	719
Pueblo, CO	**169**
Pueblo County, CO	169
Punta Gorda, FL	**206**
Charlotte County, FL	206
Racine-Mount Pleasant, WI	**197**
Racine County, WI	197
Raleigh-Cary, NC	**1,509**
Franklin County, NC	77
Johnston County, NC	242
Wake County, NC	1,190
Rapid City, SD	**156**
Custer County, SD	9
Meade County, SD	31
Pennington County, SD	116
Reading, PA	**433**
Berks County, PA	433
Redding, CA	**180**
Shasta County, CA	180
Reno, NV	**565**
Lyon County, NV	63
Storey County, NV	4
Washoe County, NV	498
Richmond, VA	**1,350**
Amelia County, VA	13
Charles City County, VA	7
Chesterfield County, VA	384
Dinwiddie County, VA	28
Goochland County, VA	27
Hanover County, VA	114
Henrico County, VA	335
King and Queen County, VA	7
King William County, VA	19
New Kent County, VA	26
Powhatan County, VA	32
Prince George County, VA	43
Sussex County, VA	11
Colonial Heights city, VA	18
Hopewell city, VA	23
Petersburg city, VA	33
Richmond city, VA	229
Riverside-San Bernardino-Ontario, CA	**4,688**
Riverside County, CA	2,492
San Bernardino County, CA	2,196
Roanoke, VA	**314**
Botetourt County, VA	34
Craig County, VA	5
Franklin County, VA	56
Roanoke County, VA	97
Roanoke city, VA	97
Salem city, VA	26
Rochester, MN	**229**
Dodge County, MN	21
Fillmore County, MN	22
Olmsted County, MN	165
Wabasha County, MN	22
Rochester, NY	**1,052**
Livingston County, NY	61
Monroe County, NY	748
Ontario County, NY	112
Orleans County, NY	39
Wayne County, NY	91
Rockford, IL	**334**
Boone County, IL	53
Winnebago County, IL	281
Rocky Mount, NC	**145**
Edgecombe County, NC	49
Nash County, NC	97

Metropolitan Statistical Area ~~Metropolitan Division ~~~~Component county	Population, 2023 (1,000)
Rome, GA	**100**
Floyd County, GA	100
Sacramento-Roseville-Folsom, CA	**2,421**
El Dorado County, CA	192
Placer County, CA	424
Sacramento County, CA	1,584
Yolo County, CA	221
Saginaw, MI	**188**
Saginaw County, MI	188
St. Cloud, MN	**203**
Benton County, MN	42
Stearns County, MN	161
St. George, UT	**202**
Washington County, UT	202
St. Joseph, MO-KS	**118**
Doniphan County, KS	7
Andrew County, MO	18
Buchanan County, MO	83
DeKalb County, MO	10
St. Louis, MO-IL [1]	**2,797**
Bond County, IL	16
Calhoun County, IL	4
Clinton County, IL	37
Jersey County, IL	21
Macoupin County, IL	44
Madison County, IL	263
Monroe County, IL	35
St. Clair County, IL	251
Franklin County, MO	106
Jefferson County, MO	231
Lincoln County, MO	65
St. Charles County, MO	417
St. Louis County, MO	987
Warren County, MO	38
St. Louis city, MO	282
Salem, OR	**437**
Marion County, OR	347
Polk County, OR	90
Salinas, CA	**431**
Monterey County, CA	431
Salisbury, MD	**130**
Somerset County, MD	25
Wicomico County, MD	105
Salt Lake City-Murray, UT	**1,268**
Salt Lake County, UT	1,186
Tooele County, UT	82
San Angelo, TX	**121**
Irion County, TX	2
Tom Green County, TX	119
San Antonio-New Braunfels, TX	**2,704**
Atascosa County, TX	52
Bandera County, TX	23
Bexar County, TX	2,088
Comal County, TX	194
Guadalupe County, TX	188
Kendall County, TX	51
Medina County, TX	55
Wilson County, TX	54
San Diego-Chula Vista-Carlsbad, CA	**3,270**
San Diego County, CA	3,270
Sandusky, OH	**114**
Erie County, OH	74
Ottawa County, OH	40
San Francisco-Oakland-Fremont, CA	**4,567**
Oakland-Fremont-Berkeley, CA	**2,777**
Alameda County, CA	1,622
Contra Costa County, CA	1,155
San Francisco-San Mateo-Redwood City, CA	**1,535**
San Francisco County, CA	809
San Mateo County, CA	726
San Rafael, CA	**254**
Marin County, CA	254

Metropolitan Statistical Area ~~Metropolitan Division ~~~~Component county	Population, 2023 (1,000)
San Jose-Sunnyvale-Santa Clara, CA	**1,946**
San Benito County, CA	68
Santa Clara County, CA	1,878
San Luis Obispo-Paso Robles, CA	**282**
San Luis Obispo County, CA	282
Santa Cruz-Watsonville, CA	**262**
Santa Cruz County, CA	262
Santa Fe, NM	**156**
Santa Fe County, NM	156
Santa Maria-Santa Barbara, CA	**441**
Santa Barbara County, CA	441
Santa Rosa-Petaluma, CA	**482**
Sonoma County, CA	482
Savannah, GA	**425**
Bryan County, GA	50
Chatham County, GA	304
Effingham County, GA	72
Scranton--Wilkes-Barre, PA	**569**
Lackawanna County, PA	216
Luzerne County, PA	327
Wyoming County, PA	26
Seattle-Tacoma-Bellevue, WA	**4,045**
Everett, WA	**845**
Snohomish County, WA	845
Seattle-Bellevue-Kent, WA	**2,271**
King County, WA	2,271
Tacoma-Lakewood, WA	**929**
Pierce County, WA	929
Sebastian-Vero Beach-West Vero Corridor, FL	**170**
Indian River County, FL	170
Sebring, FL	**108**
Highlands County, FL	108
Sheboygan, WI	**118**
Sheboygan County, WI	118
Sherman-Denison, TX	**147**
Grayson County, TX	147
Shreveport-Bossier City, LA	**383**
Bossier Parish, LA	130
Caddo Parish, LA	226
De Soto Parish, LA	27
Sierra Vista-Douglas, AZ	**125**
Cochise County, AZ	125
Sioux City, IA-NE-SD	**144**
Woodbury County, IA	106
Dakota County, NE	21
Union County, SD	17
Sioux Falls, SD-MN	**305**
Rock County, MN	10
Lincoln County, SD	73
McCook County, SD	6
Minnehaha County, SD	207
Turner County, SD	9
Slidell-Mandeville-Covington, LA	**276**
St. Tammany Parish, LA	276
South Bend-Mishawaka, IN-MI	**324**
St. Joseph County, IN	273
Cass County, MI	52
Spartanburg, SC	**383**
Spartanburg County, SC	357
Union County, SC	27
Spokane-Spokane Valley, WA	**600**
Spokane County, WA	551
Stevens County, WA	49
Springfield, IL	**205**
Menard County, IL	12
Sangamon County, IL	193
Springfield, MA	**460**
Hampden County, MA	460
Springfield, MO	**491**
Christian County, MO	94
Dallas County, MO	18
Greene County, MO	305
Polk County, MO	33
Webster County, MO	41
Springfield, OH	**135**
Clark County, OH	135

Metropolitan Statistical Area ~~Metropolitan Division ~~~~Component county	Population, 2023 (1,000)
State College, PA	**158**
Centre County, PA	158
Staunton-Stuarts Draft, VA	**127**
Augusta County, VA	78
Staunton city, VA	26
Waynesboro city, VA	23
Stockton-Lodi, CA	**801**
San Joaquin County, CA	801
Sumter, SC	**104**
Sumter County, SC	104
Syracuse, NY	**653**
Madison County, NY	67
Onondaga County, NY	468
Oswego County, NY	118
Tallahassee, FL	**393**
Gadsden County, FL	44
Jefferson County, FL	15
Leon County, FL	297
Wakulla County, FL	36
Tampa-St. Petersburg-Clearwater, FL	**3,343**
St. Petersburg-Clearwater-Largo, FL	**962**
Pinellas County, FL	962
Tampa, FL	**2,381**
Hernando County, FL	213
Hillsborough County, FL	1,536
Pasco County, FL	633
Terre Haute, IN	**169**
Clay County, IN	26
Sullivan County, IN	21
Vermillion County, IN	15
Vigo County, IN	106
Texarkana, TX-AR	**146**
Little River County, AR	12
Miller County, AR	42
Bowie County, TX	92
Toledo, OH	**600**
Fulton County, OH	42
Lucas County, OH	425
Wood County, OH	133
Topeka, KS	**232**
Jackson County, KS	13
Jefferson County, KS	18
Osage County, KS	16
Shawnee County, KS	178
Wabaunsee County, KS	7
Traverse City, MI	**156**
Benzie County, MI	18
Grand Traverse County, MI	96
Kalkaska County, MI	18
Leelanau County, MI	23
Trenton-Princeton, NJ	**382**
Mercer County, NJ	382
Tucson, AZ	**1,063**
Pima County, AZ	1,063
Tulsa, OK	**1,045**
Creek County, OK	73
Okmulgee County, OK	37
Osage County, OK	46
Pawnee County, OK	16
Rogers County, OK	100
Tulsa County, OK	683
Wagoner County, OK	89
Tuscaloosa, AL	**278**
Greene County, AL	7
Hale County, AL	15
Pickens County, AL	19
Tuscaloosa County, AL	237
Twin Falls, ID	**121**
Jerome County, ID	25
Twin Falls County, ID	95
Tyler, TX	**245**
Smith County, TX	245
Urban Honolulu, HI	**989**
Honolulu County, HI	989
Utica-Rome, NY	**287**
Herkimer County, NY	59
Oneida County, NY	228

Metropolitan Statistical Area ~~Metropolitan Division ~~~~Component county	Population, 2023 (1,000)
Valdosta, GA	**151**
Brooks County, GA	16
Echols County, GA	4
Lanier County, GA	10
Lowndes County, GA	121
Vallejo, CA	**449**
Solano County, CA	449
Victoria, TX	**99**
Goliad County, TX	7
Victoria County, TX	92
Vineland, NJ	**152**
Cumberland County, NJ	152
Virginia Beach-Chesapeake-Norfolk, VA-NC	**1,787**
Camden County, NC	11
Currituck County, NC	32
Gates County, NC	10
Gloucester County, VA	40
Isle of Wight County, VA	41
James City County, VA	83
Mathews County, VA	9
Surry County, VA	7
York County, VA	71
Chesapeake city, VA	254
Hampton city, VA	137
Newport News city, VA	183
Norfolk city, VA	231
Poquoson city, VA	13
Portsmouth city, VA	97
Suffolk city, VA	101
Virginia Beach city, VA	454
Williamsburg city, VA	16
Visalia, CA	**479**
Tulare County, CA	479
Waco, TX	**305**
Bosque County, TX	19
Falls County, TX	17
McLennan County, TX	269
Walla Walla, WA	**62**
Walla Walla County, WA	62
Warner Robins, GA	**201**
Houston County, GA	172
Peach County, GA	29
Washington-Arlington-Alexandria, DC-VA-MD-WV	**6,305**
Arlington-Alexandria-Reston, VA-WV	**3,155**
Arlington County, VA	234
Clarke County, VA	15
Culpeper County, VA	55
Fairfax County, VA	1,142
Fauquier County, VA	75
Loudoun County, VA	436
Prince William County, VA	490
Rappahannock County, VA	7
Spotsylvania County, VA	150
Stafford County, VA	165
Warren County, VA	42
Alexandria city, VA	155
Fairfax city, VA	25
Falls Church city, VA	15
Fredericksburg city, VA	29
Manassas city, VA	43
Manassas Park city, VA	16
Jefferson County, WV	60
Frederick-Gaithersburg-Bethesda, MD	**1,352**
Frederick County, MD	293
Montgomery County, MD	1,058
Washington, DC-MD	**1,798**
District of Columbia, DC	679
Charles County, MD	172
Prince George's County, MD	947
Waterbury-Shelton, CT	**456**
Naugatuck Valley Planning Region, CT	456
Waterloo-Cedar Falls, IA	**168**
Black Hawk County, IA	130

See footnotes at end of table.

Table A. Metropolitan Statistical Areas and Components—Population: 2023-Continued.

See headnote on page 916.

Metropolitan Statistical Area ~~Metropolitan Division ~~~~Component county	Population, 2023 (1,000)	Metropolitan Statistical Area ~~Metropolitan Division ~~~~Component county	Population, 2023 (1,000)	Metropolitan Statistical Area ~~Metropolitan Division ~~~~Component county	Population, 2023 (1,000)
Bremer County, IA	25	Harvey County, KS	34	Davidson County, NC	175
Grundy County, IA	12	Sedgwick County, KS	528	Davie County, NC	45
Watertown-Fort Drum, NY	**115**	Sumner County, KS	22	Forsyth County, NC	393
Jefferson County, NY	115	**Wichita Falls, TX**	**150**	Stokes County, NC	46
Wausau, WI	**139**	Archer County, TX	9	Yadkin County, NC	38
Marathon County, WI	139	Clay County, TX	11	**Worcester, MA**	**867**
Weirton-Steubenville, WV-OH	**114**	Wichita County, TX	130	Worcester County, MA	867
Jefferson County, OH	64	**Wildwood-The Villages, FL**	**152**	**Yakima, WA**	**257**
Brooke County, WV	21	Sumter County, FL	152	Yakima County, WA	257
Hancock County, WV	28	**Williamsport, PA**	**113**	**York-Hanover, PA**	**465**
Wenatchee-East Wenatchee, WA	**125**	Lycoming County, PA	113	York County, PA	465
Chelan County, WA	80	**Wilmington, NC**	**467**	**Youngstown-Warren, OH**	**426**
Douglas County, WA	45	Brunswick County, NC	160	Mahoning County, OH	226
Wheeling, WV-OH	**136**	New Hanover County, NC	239	Trumbull County, OH	200
Belmont County, OH	65	Pender County, NC	69	**Yuba City, CA**	**184**
Marshall County, WV	29	**Winchester, VA-WV**	**147**	Sutter County, CA	98
Ohio County, WV	41	Frederick County, VA	96	Yuba County, CA	86
Wichita, KS	**653**	Winchester city, VA	28	**Yuma, AZ**	**213**
Butler County, KS	69	Hampshire County, WV	24	Yuma County, AZ	213
		Winston-Salem, NC	**696**		

[1] The portion of Sullivan city in Crawford County, Missouri, is legally part of the St. Louis, MO-IL Metropolitan Statistical Area.

Source: U.S. Census Bureau, "Metropolitan and Micropolitan Statistical Areas Totals: 2020-2023," <www.census.gov/programs-surveys/popest/data/data-sets.html>.

Table B. Micropolitan Statistical Areas and Components—Population: 2023

[In thousands (42 represents 42,000). Population as of July 2023. Micropolitan Statistical Areas delineated by the U.S. Office of Management and Budget as of July 2023. The estimates are developed from a base that incorporates the 2020 Census, Vintage 2020 estimates, and 2020 Demographic Analysis estimates. All Micropolitan Statistical Areas are arranged alphabetically]

Micropolitan Statistical Area ~~Component county	Population, 2023 (1,000)	Micropolitan Statistical Area ~~Component county	Population, 2023 (1,000)	Micropolitan Statistical Area ~~Component county	Population, 2023 (1,000)
Aberdeen, SD	**42**	**Baraboo, WI**	**66**	Cassia County, ID	26
Brown County, SD	38	Sauk County, WI	66	Minidoka County, ID	22
Edmunds County, SD	4	**Barre, VT**	**60**	**Burlington, IA-IL**	**44**
Aberdeen, WA	**77**	Washington County, VT	60	Henderson County, IL	6
Grays Harbor County, WA	77	**Bartlesville, OK**	**54**	Des Moines County, IA	38
Ada, OK	**38**	Washington County, OK	54	**Butte-Silver Bow, MT**	**36**
Pontotoc County, OK	38	**Batavia, NY**	**58**	Silver Bow County, MT	36
Adrian, MI	**98**	Genesee County, NY	58	**Cadillac, MI**	**49**
Lenawee County, MI	98	**Batesville, AR**	**38**	Missaukee County, MI	15
Alamogordo, NM	**69**	Independence County, AR	38	Wexford County, MI	34
Otero County, NM	69	**Bay City, TX**	**36**	**Calhoun, GA**	**60**
Alamosa, CO	**28**	Matagorda County, TX	36	Gordon County, GA	60
Alamosa County, CO	17	**Beatrice, NE**	**22**	**Cambridge, MD**	**33**
Conejos County, CO	8	Gage County, NE	22	Dorchester County, MD	33
Costilla County, CO	4	**Beaver Dam, WI**	**88**	**Cambridge, OH**	**38**
Albemarle, NC	**66**	Dodge County, WI	88	Guernsey County, OH	38
Stanly County, NC	66	**Bedford, IN**	**45**	**Camden, AR**	**26**
Albert Lea, MN	**31**	Lawrence County, IN	45	Calhoun County, AR	5
Freeborn County, MN	31	**Beeville, TX**	**31**	Ouachita County, AR	22
Albertville, AL	**101**	Bee County, TX	31	**Campbellsville, KY**	**38**
Marshall County, AL	101	**Bellefontaine, OH**	**46**	Green County, KY	11
Alexander City, AL	**41**	Logan County, OH	46	Taylor County, KY	26
Tallapoosa County, AL	41	**Bemidji, MN**	**47**	**Cañon City, CO**	**50**
Alexandria, MN	**40**	Beltrami County, MN	47	Fremont County, CO	50
Douglas County, MN	40	**Bennington, VT**	**37**	**Canton, IL**	**33**
Alice, TX	**46**	Bennington County, VT	37	Fulton County, IL	33
Brooks County, TX	7	**Big Rapids, MI**	**41**	**Carbondale, IL**	**52**
Jim Wells County, TX	39	Mecosta County, MI	41	Jackson County, IL	52
Alma, MI	**41**	**Big Spring, TX**	**31**	**Carlsbad-Artesia, NM**	**60**
Gratiot County, MI	41	Howard County, TX	31	Eddy County, NM	60
Alpena, MI	**29**	**Bishop, CA**	**19**	**Carroll, IA**	**21**
Alpena County, MI	29	Inyo County, CA	19	Carroll County, IA	21
Altus, OK	**25**	**Blackfoot, ID**	**50**	**Cedar City, UT**	**64**
Jackson County, OK	25	Bingham County, ID	50	Iron County, UT	64
Americus, GA	**33**	**Bloomsburg-Berwick, PA**	**65**	**Cedartown, GA**	**44**
Schley County, GA	5	Columbia County, PA	65	Polk County, GA	44
Sumter County, GA	29	**Bluefield, WV-VA**	**97**	**Celina, OH**	**42**
Amsterdam, NY	**49**	Tazewell County, VA	39	Mercer County, OH	42
Montgomery County, NY	49	Mercer County, WV	58	**Centralia, IL**	**37**
Anderson Creek, NC	**141**	**Blytheville, AR**	**39**	Marion County, IL	37
Harnett County, NC	141	Mississippi County, AR	39	**Centralia, WA**	**86**
Andrews, TX	**19**	**Bogalusa, LA**	**45**	Lewis County, WA	86
Andrews County, TX	19	Washington Parish, LA	45	**Charleston-Mattoon, IL**	**46**
Angola, IN	**35**	**Bonham, TX**	**38**	Coles County, IL	46
Steuben County, IN	35	Fannin County, TX	38	**Chillicothe, OH**	**77**
Arcadia, FL	**36**	**Boone, NC**	**55**	Ross County, OH	77
DeSoto County, FL	36	Watauga County, NC	55	**Clarksburg, WV**	**89**
Ardmore, OK	**49**	**Borger, TX**	**20**	Doddridge County, WV	8
Carter County, OK	49	Hutchinson County, TX	20	Harrison County, WV	65
Arkadelphia, AR	**21**	**Bradford, PA**	**40**	Taylor County, WV	16
Clark County, AR	21	McKean County, PA	40	**Clarksdale, MS**	**20**
Arkansas City-Winfield, KS	**34**	**Brainerd, MN**	**100**	Coahoma County, MS	20
Cowley County, KS	34	Cass County, MN	31	**Clearlake, CA**	**68**
Ashland, OH	**52**	Crow Wing County, MN	68	Lake County, CA	68
Ashland County, OH	52	**Branson, MO**	**57**	**Cleveland, MS**	**29**
Astoria, OR	**41**	Taney County, MO	57	Bolivar County, MS	29
Clatsop County, OR	41	**Brattleboro, VT**	**46**	**Clewiston, FL**	**56**
Atchison, KS	**16**	Windham County, VT	46	Glades County, FL	13
Atchison County, KS	16	**Breckenridge, CO**	**38**	Hendry County, FL	43
Athens, OH	**63**	Lake County, CO	7	**Clinton, IA**	**46**
Athens County, OH	63	Summit County, CO	30	Clinton County, IA	46
Athens, TN	**69**	**Brenham, TX**	**37**	**Clovis, NM**	**66**
McMinn County, TN	56	Washington County, TX	37	Curry County, NM	47
Meigs County, TN	14	**Brevard, NC**	**34**	Roosevelt County, NM	19
Athens, TX	**86**	Transylvania County, NC	34	**Cody, WY**	**31**
Henderson County, TX	86	**Brigham City, UT-ID**	**68**	Park County, WY	31
Auburn, IN	**44**	Oneida County, ID	5	**Coldwater, MI**	**45**
DeKalb County, IN	44	Box Elder County, UT	63	Branch County, MI	45
Auburn, NY	**74**	**Brookhaven, MS**	**35**	**Columbus, MS**	**67**
Cayuga County, NY	74	Lincoln County, MS	35	Lowndes County, MS	57
Augusta-Waterville, ME	**127**	**Brookings, OR**	**23**	Noxubee County, MS	10
Kennebec County, ME	127	Curry County, OR	23	**Columbus, NE**	**45**
Austin, MN	**40**	**Brookings, SD**	**36**	Colfax County, NE	11
Mower County, MN	40	Brookings County, SD	36	Platte County, NE	35
Bainbridge, GA	**29**	**Brownwood, TX**	**39**	**Concord, NH**	**157**
Decatur County, GA	29	Brown County, TX	39	Merrimack County, NH	157
Baker City, OR	**17**	**Bucyrus, OH**	**42**	**Connersville, IN**	**23**
Baker County, OR	17	Crawford County, OH	42	Fayette County, IN	23
		Burley, ID	**48**	**Cookeville, TN**	**148**

See footnotes at end of table.

Table B. Micropolitan Statistical Areas and Components—Population: 2023-Continued.

See headnote on page 924.

Micropolitan Statistical Area ~~Component county	Population, 2023 (1,000)
Jackson County, TN.	12
Overton County, TN.	23
Putnam County, TN.	84
White County, TN.	29
Coos Bay-North Bend, OR.	**64**
Coos County, OR.	64
Corbin, KY.	**150**
Clay County, KY.	20
Knox County, KY.	30
Laurel County, KY.	63
Whitley County, KY.	37
Cordele, GA.	**20**
Crisp County, GA.	20
Corinth, MS.	**34**
Alcorn County, MS.	34
Cornelia, GA.	**49**
Habersham County, GA.	49
Corning, NY.	**92**
Steuben County, NY.	92
Corsicana, TX.	**56**
Navarro County, TX.	56
Cortland, NY.	**46**
Cortland County, NY.	46
Coshocton, OH.	**37**
Coshocton County, OH.	37
Crawfordsville, IN.	**39**
Montgomery County, IN.	39
Crescent City, CA.	**27**
Del Norte County, CA.	27
Crossville, TN.	**65**
Cumberland County, TN.	65
Cullman, AL.	**92**
Cullman County, AL.	92
Cumberland, MD-WV.	**94**
Allegany County, MD.	67
Mineral County, WV.	27
Danville, IL.	**72**
Vermilion County, IL.	72
Danville, KY.	**56**
Boyle County, KY.	31
Lincoln County, KY.	25
Danville, VA.	**101**
Pittsylvania County, VA.	60
Danville city, VA.	42
Decatur, IN.	**36**
Adams County, IN.	36
Defiance, OH.	**38**
Defiance County, OH.	38
Del Rio, TX.	**48**
Val Verde County, TX.	48
Deming, NM.	**25**
Luna County, NM.	25
DeRidder, LA.	**37**
Beauregard Parish, LA.	37
Detroit Lakes, MN.	**35**
Becker County, MN.	35
Dickinson, ND.	**38**
Billings County, ND.	1
Dunn County, ND.	4
Stark County, ND.	33
Dixon, IL.	**34**
Lee County, IL.	34
Dodge City, KS.	**34**
Ford County, KS.	34
Douglas, GA.	**52**
Atkinson County, GA.	8
Coffee County, GA.	43
Dublin, GA.	**59**
Johnson County, GA.	9
Laurens County, GA.	50
DuBois, PA.	**77**
Clearfield County, PA.	77
Dumas, TX.	**21**
Moore County, TX.	21
Duncan, OK.	**44**
Stephens County, OK.	44
Durango, CO.	**56**
La Plata County, CO.	56
Durant, OK.	**49**

Micropolitan Statistical Area ~~Component county	Population, 2023 (1,000)
Bryan County, OK.	49
Dyersburg, TN.	**36**
Dyer County, TN.	36
Easton, MD.	**38**
Talbot County, MD.	38
East Stroudsburg, PA.	**166**
Monroe County, PA.	166
Edwards, CO.	**54**
Eagle County, CO.	54
Effingham, IL.	**45**
Cumberland County, IL.	10
Effingham County, IL.	34
El Campo, TX.	**42**
Wharton County, TX.	42
El Dorado, AR.	**37**
Union County, AR.	37
Elizabeth City, NC.	**41**
Pasquotank County, NC.	41
Elk City, OK.	**22**
Beckham County, OK.	22
Elkins, WV.	**27**
Randolph County, WV.	27
Elko, NV.	**56**
Elko County, NV.	54
Eureka County, NV.	2
Ellensburg, WA.	**46**
Kittitas County, WA.	46
Emporia, KS.	**35**
Chase County, KS.	3
Lyon County, KS.	32
Enterprise, AL.	**56**
Coffee County, AL.	56
Escanaba, MI.	**37**
Delta County, MI.	37
Española, NM.	**40**
Rio Arriba County, NM.	40
Eufaula, AL-GA.	**27**
Barbour County, AL.	25
Quitman County, GA.	2
Eureka-Arcata, CA.	**134**
Humboldt County, CA.	134
Evanston, WY-UT.	**23**
Rich County, UT.	3
Uinta County, WY.	21
Fairmont, MN.	**20**
Martin County, MN.	20
Fairmont, WV.	**56**
Marion County, WV.	56
Fallon, NV.	**26**
Churchill County, NV.	26
Faribault-Northfield, MN.	**68**
Rice County, MN.	68
Farmington, MO.	**67**
St. Francois County, MO.	67
Fergus Falls, TN.	**36**
Lincoln County, TN.	36
Fergus Falls, MN.	**61**
Otter Tail County, MN.	61
Findlay, OH.	**75**
Hancock County, OH.	75
Fitzgerald, GA.	**17**
Ben Hill County, GA.	17
Forest City, NC.	**66**
Rutherford County, NC.	66
Forrest City, AR.	**22**
St. Francis County, AR.	22
Fort Dodge, IA.	**36**
Webster County, IA.	36
Fort Leonard Wood, MO.	**54**
Pulaski County, MO.	54
Fort Madison, IA.	**33**
Lee County, IA.	33
Fort Morgan, CO.	**30**
Morgan County, CO.	30
Fort Payne, AL.	**73**
DeKalb County, AL.	73
Frankfort, IN.	**33**
Clinton County, IN.	33
Frankfort, KY.	**76**

Micropolitan Statistical Area ~~Component county	Population, 2023 (1,000)
Anderson County, KY.	25
Franklin County, KY.	52
Franklin, KY.	**20**
Simpson County, KY.	20
Fredericksburg, TX.	**28**
Gillespie County, TX.	28
Freeport, IL.	**43**
Stephenson County, IL.	43
Fremont, NE.	**37**
Dodge County, NE.	37
Fremont, OH.	**59**
Sandusky County, OH.	59
Gaffney, SC.	**57**
Cherokee County, SC.	57
Gainesville, TX.	**44**
Cooke County, TX.	44
Galesburg, IL.	**48**
Knox County, IL.	48
Gallipolis, OH.	**29**
Gallia County, OH.	29
Gallup, NM.	**69**
McKinley County, NM.	69
Garden City, KS.	**37**
Finney County, KS.	37
Gardnerville Ranchos, NV-CA.	**51**
Alpine County, CA.	1
Douglas County, NV.	50
Gillette, WY.	**47**
Campbell County, WY.	47
Glasgow, KY.	**55**
Barren County, KY.	45
Metcalfe County, KY.	10
Gloversville, NY.	**52**
Fulton County, NY.	52
Granbury, TX.	**68**
Hood County, TX.	68
Grand Rapids, MN.	**45**
Itasca County, MN.	45
Great Bend, KS.	**25**
Barton County, KS.	25
Greencastle, IN.	**38**
Putnam County, IN.	38
Greeneville, TN.	**73**
Greene County, TN.	73
Greenfield, MA.	**71**
Franklin County, MA.	71
Greensburg, IN.	**26**
Decatur County, IN.	26
Greenville, MS.	**42**
Washington County, MS.	42
Greenville, OH.	**51**
Darke County, OH.	51
Greenwood, MS.	**36**
Carroll County, MS.	10
Leflore County, MS.	26
Greenwood, SC.	**94**
Abbeville County, SC.	24
Greenwood County, SC.	69
Grenada, MS.	**31**
Grenada County, MS.	21
Montgomery County, MS.	10
Guymon, OK.	**20**
Texas County, OK.	20
Hailey, ID.	**32**
Blaine County, ID.	25
Camas County, ID.	1
Lincoln County, ID.	5
Hannibal, MO.	**39**
Marion County, MO.	28
Ralls County, MO.	10
Harrison, AR.	**46**
Boone County, AR.	39
Newton County, AR.	7
Hastings, NE.	**40**
Adams County, NE.	31
Clay County, NE.	6
Webster County, NE.	3

See footnotes at end of table.

Table B. Micropolitan Statistical Areas and Components—Population: 2023-Continued.

See headnote on page 924.

Micropolitan Statistical Area ~~Component county	Population, 2023 (1,000)
Hays, KS	**29**
Ellis County, KS	29
Heber, UT	**80**
Summit County, UT	43
Wasatch County, UT	37
Hemlock Farms, PA	**61**
Pike County, PA	61
Henderson, KY	**57**
Henderson County, KY	44
Webster County, KY	13
Henderson, NC	**42**
Vance County, NC	42
Hereford, TX	**18**
Deaf Smith County, TX	18
Hermiston-Pendleton, OR	**92**
Morrow County, OR	12
Umatilla County, OR	80
Hermitage, PA	**109**
Mercer County, PA	109
Hillsdale, MI	**46**
Hillsdale County, MI	46
Hilo-Kailua, HI	**208**
Hawaii County, HI	208
Hobbs, NM	**72**
Lea County, NM	72
Holland, MI	**122**
Allegan County, MI	122
Hood River, OR	**24**
Hood River County, OR	24
Houghton, MI	**40**
Houghton County, MI	38
Keweenaw County, MI	2
Hudson, NY	**60**
Columbia County, NY	60
Huntingdon, PA	**44**
Huntingdon County, PA	44
Huntington, IN	**37**
Huntington County, IN	37
Huntsville, TX	**81**
Walker County, TX	81
Huron, SD	**20**
Beadle County, SD	20
Hutchinson, KS	**61**
Reno County, KS	61
Hutchinson, MN	**37**
McLeod County, MN	37
Indiana, PA	**83**
Indiana County, PA	83
Iron Mountain, MI-WI	**31**
Dickinson County, MI	26
Florence County, WI	5
Jackson, WY-ID	**36**
Teton County, ID	13
Teton County, WY	23
Jacksonville, IL	**37**
Morgan County, IL	32
Scott County, IL	5
Jacksonville, TX	**52**
Cherokee County, TX	52
Jamestown, ND	**21**
Stutsman County, ND	21
Jamestown-Dunkirk, NY	**125**
Chautauqua County, NY	125
Jasper, IN	**44**
Dubois County, IN	44
Jefferson, GA	**89**
Jackson County, GA	89
Jesup, GA	**31**
Wayne County, GA	31
Juneau, AK	**32**
Juneau City and Borough, AK	32
Kalispell, MT	**114**
Flathead County, MT	114
Kapaa, HI	**74**
Kauai County, HI	74
Kearney, NE	**57**
Buffalo County, NE	51
Kearney County, NE	7
Keene, NH	**78**
Cheshire County, NH	78

Micropolitan Statistical Area ~~Component county	Population, 2023 (1,000)
Kendallville, IN	**47**
Noble County, IN	47
Kennett, MO	**27**
Dunklin County, MO	27
Kerrville, TX	**54**
Kerr County, TX	54
Ketchikan, AK	**14**
Ketchikan Gateway Borough, AK	14
Key West-Key Largo, FL	**81**
Monroe County, FL	81
Kill Devil Hills, NC	**38**
Dare County, NC	38
Kingsland, GA	**58**
Camden County, GA	58
Kingsville, TX	**30**
Kleberg County, TX	30
Kinston, NC	**55**
Lenoir County, NC	55
Kirksville, MO	**29**
Adair County, MO	25
Schuyler County, MO	4
Klamath Falls, OR	**70**
Klamath County, OR	70
Laconia, NH	**65**
Belknap County, NH	65
La Grande, OR	**26**
Union County, OR	26
LaGrange, GA-AL	**105**
Chambers County, AL	34
Troup County, GA	71
Lake City, FL	**73**
Columbia County, FL	73
Lake of the Woods, VA	**39**
Orange County, VA	39
Laramie, WY	**38**
Albany County, WY	38
Las Vegas, NM	**31**
Mora County, NM	4
San Miguel County, NM	27
Laurel, MS	**82**
Jasper County, MS	16
Jones County, MS	66
Laurinburg, NC	**34**
Scotland County, NC	34
Lawrenceburg, TN	**46**
Lawrence County, TN	46
Lebanon, MO	**37**
Laclede County, MO	37
Lebanon-Claremont, NH-VT	**225**
Grafton County, NH	93
Sullivan County, NH	44
Orange County, VT	30
Windsor County, VT	58
Le Mars, IA	**26**
Plymouth County, IA	26
Lewisburg, PA	**42**
Union County, PA	42
Lewisburg, TN	**37**
Marshall County, TN	37
Lewistown, PA	**46**
Mifflin County, PA	46
Lexington, NE	**26**
Dawson County, NE	24
Gosper County, NE	2
Liberal, KS	**21**
Seward County, KS	21
Lincoln, IL	**28**
Logan County, IL	28
Lock Haven, PA	**38**
Clinton County, PA	38
Logansport, IN	**38**
Cass County, IN	38
Los Alamos, NM	**19**
Los Alamos County, NM	19
Ludington, MI	**29**
Mason County, MI	29
Lufkin, TX	**87**
Angelina County, TX	87

Micropolitan Statistical Area ~~Component county	Population, 2023 (1,000)
Lumberton, NC	**117**
Robeson County, NC	117
Macomb, IL	**27**
McDonough County, IL	27
Madison, IN	**33**
Jefferson County, IN	33
Madisonville, KY	**45**
Hopkins County, KY	45
Magnolia, AR	**22**
Columbia County, AR	22
Malvern, AR	**33**
Hot Spring County, AR	33
Manitowoc, WI	**81**
Manitowoc County, WI	81
Marietta, OH	**59**
Washington County, OH	59
Marinette, WI-MI	**65**
Menominee County, MI	23
Marinette County, WI	42
Marion, IN	**66**
Grant County, IN	66
Marion, NC	**45**
McDowell County, NC	45
Marion, OH	**65**
Marion County, OH	65
Marion-Herrin, IL	**67**
Williamson County, IL	67
Marquette, MI	**67**
Marquette County, MI	67
Marshall, MN	**25**
Lyon County, MN	25
Marshall, MO	**23**
Saline County, MO	23
Marshalltown, IA	**40**
Marshall County, IA	40
Martin, TN	**33**
Weakley County, TN	33
Martinsville, VA	**63**
Henry County, VA	50
Martinsville city, VA	14
Maryville, MO	**21**
Nodaway County, MO	21
Mason City, IA	**50**
Cerro Gordo County, IA	42
Worth County, IA	7
Massena-Ogdensburg, NY	**107**
St. Lawrence County, NY	107
Mayfield, KY	**36**
Graves County, KY	36
McAlester, OK	**43**
Pittsburg County, OK	43
McComb, MS	**53**
Pike County, MS	39
Walthall County, MS	14
McMinnville, TN	**43**
Warren County, TN	43
McPherson, KS	**30**
McPherson County, KS	30
Meadville, PA	**82**
Crawford County, PA	82
Menomonie, WI	**46**
Dunn County, WI	46
Meridian, MS	**86**
Clarke County, MS	15
Lauderdale County, MS	71
Mexico, MO	**24**
Audrain County, MO	24
Miami, OK	**30**
Ottawa County, OK	30
Middlesborough, KY	**23**
Bell County, KY	23
Milledgeville, GA	**43**
Baldwin County, GA	43
Minden, LA	**35**
Webster Parish, LA	35
Mineral Wells, TX	**30**
Palo Pinto County, TX	30
Mitchell, SD	**26**
Davison County, SD	20

See footnotes at end of table.

Microplitan Statistical Area ~~Component county	Popu-lation, 2023 (1,000)
Hanson County, SD.	3
Sanborn County, SD.	2
Moberly, MO.	**24**
Randolph County, MO.	24
Monticello, IN.	**25**
White County, IN.	25
Monticello, NY.	**80**
Sullivan County, NY.	80
Montrose, CO.	**44**
Montrose County, CO.	44
Morehead City, NC.	**70**
Carteret County, NC.	70
Morgan City, LA.	**47**
St. Mary Parish, LA.	47
Moscow, ID.	**41**
Latah County, ID.	41
Moses Lake, WA.	**103**
Grant County, WA.	103
Moultrie, GA.	**46**
Colquitt County, GA.	46
Mountain Home, AR.	**43**
Baxter County, AR.	43
Mountain Home, ID.	**30**
Elmore County, ID.	30
Mount Airy, NC.	**71**
Surry County, NC.	71
Mount Pleasant, MI.	**64**
Isabella County, MI.	64
Mount Pleasant, TX.	**56**
Camp County, TX.	13
Morris County, TX.	12
Titus County, TX.	31
Mount Sterling, KY.	**48**
Bath County, KY.	13
Menifee County, KY.	6
Montgomery County, KY.	29
Mount Vernon, IL.	**36**
Jefferson County, IL.	36
Mount Vernon, OH.	**63**
Knox County, OH.	63
Murray, KY.	**38**
Calloway County, KY.	38
Murrells Inlet, SC.	**66**
Georgetown County, SC.	66
Muscatine, IA.	**42**
Muscatine County, IA.	42
Muskogee, OK.	**67**
Muskogee County, OK.	67
Nacogdoches, TX.	**65**
Nacogdoches County, TX.	65
Nantucket, MA.	**14**
Nantucket County, MA.	14
Natchez, MS-LA.	**53**
Concordia Parish, LA.	18
Adams County, MS.	29
Jefferson County, MS.	7
Natchitoches, LA.	**36**
Natchitoches Parish, LA.	36
New Bern, NC.	**124**
Craven County, NC.	102
Jones County, NC.	9
Pamlico County, NC.	12
Newberry, SC.	**39**
Newberry County, SC.	39
New Castle, IN.	**49**
Henry County, IN.	49
New Iberia, LA.	**68**
Iberia Parish, LA.	68
New Philadelphia-Dover, OH.	**92**
Tuscarawas County, OH.	92
Newport, OR.	**51**
Lincoln County, OR.	51
Newport, TN.	**37**
Cocke County, TN.	37
New Ulm, MN.	**26**
Brown County, MN.	26
Nogales, AZ.	**49**
Santa Cruz County, AZ.	49
Norfolk, NE.	**49**

Microplitan Statistical Area ~~Component county	Popu-lation, 2023 (1,000)
Madison County, NE.	36
Pierce County, NE.	7
Stanton County, NE.	6
North Platte, NE.	**34**
Lincoln County, NE.	33
Logan County, NE.	1
North Wilkesboro, NC.	**66**
Wilkes County, NC.	66
Norwalk, OH.	**58**
Huron County, OH.	58
Oak Harbor, WA.	**86**
Island County, WA.	86
Ocean Pines, MD.	**54**
Worcester County, MD.	54
Oil City, PA.	**49**
Venango County, PA.	49
Okeechobee, FL.	**41**
Okeechobee County, FL.	41
Olean, NY.	**76**
Cattaraugus County, NY.	76
Oneonta, NY.	**60**
Otsego County, NY.	60
Ontario, OR-ID.	**59**
Payette County, ID.	27
Malheur County, OR.	32
Opelousas, LA.	**81**
St. Landry Parish, LA.	81
Orangeburg, SC.	**83**
Orangeburg County, SC.	83
Oskaloosa, IA.	**22**
Mahaska County, IA.	22
Othello, WA.	**21**
Adams County, WA.	21
Ottawa, IL.	**147**
Bureau County, IL.	33
LaSalle County, IL.	108
Putnam County, IL.	6
Ottawa, KS.	**26**
Franklin County, KS.	26
Ottumwa, IA.	**35**
Wapello County, IA.	35
Owatonna, MN.	**37**
Steele County, MN.	37
Owosso, MI.	**68**
Shiawassee County, MI.	68
Oxford, MS.	**71**
Lafayette County, MS.	58
Yalobusha County, MS.	12
Ozark, AL.	**50**
Dale County, AL.	50
Pahrump, NV.	**56**
Nye County, NV.	56
Palatka, FL.	**76**
Putnam County, FL.	76
Palestine, TX.	**58**
Anderson County, TX.	58
Pampa, TX.	**22**
Gray County, TX.	21
Roberts County, TX.	1
Paragould, AR.	**47**
Greene County, AR.	47
Paris, TN.	**33**
Henry County, TN.	33
Paris, TX.	**63**
Lamar County, TX.	51
Red River County, TX.	12
Payson, AZ.	**54**
Gila County, AZ.	54
Pella, IA.	**34**
Marion County, IA.	34
Peru, IN.	**35**
Miami County, IN.	35
Petoskey, MI.	**34**
Emmet County, MI.	34
Picayune, MS.	**58**
Pearl River County, MS.	58
Pierre, SD.	**21**
Hughes County, SD.	18
Stanley County, SD.	3

Microplitan Statistical Area ~~Component county	Popu-lation, 2023 (1,000)
Pikeville, KY.	**90**
Floyd County, KY.	34
Pike County, KY.	56
Pine Bluff, AR.	**71**
Cleveland County, AR.	7
Jefferson County, AR.	64
Pittsburg, KS.	**39**
Crawford County, KS.	39
Plainview, TX.	**37**
Floyd County, TX.	5
Hale County, TX.	32
Platteville, WI.	**51**
Grant County, WI.	51
Plattsburgh, NY.	**78**
Clinton County, NY.	78
Plymouth, IN.	**46**
Marshall County, IN.	46
Ponca City, OK.	**44**
Kay County, OK.	44
Pontiac, IL.	**35**
Livingston County, IL.	35
Poplar Bluff, MO.	**42**
Butler County, MO.	42
Port Angeles, WA.	**78**
Clallam County, WA.	78
Port Lavaca, TX.	**20**
Calhoun County, TX.	20
Portsmouth, OH.	**72**
Scioto County, OH.	72
Port Townsend, WA.	**34**
Jefferson County, WA.	34
Pottsville, PA.	**144**
Schuylkill County, PA.	144
Price, UT.	**21**
Carbon County, UT.	21
Pullman, WA.	**48**
Whitman County, WA.	48
Putnam, CT.	**97**
Northeastern Connecticut Planning Region, CT.	97
Quincy, IL-MO.	**74**
Adams County, IL.	64
Lewis County, MO.	10
Raymondville, TX.	**20**
Willacy County, TX.	20
Red Bluff, CA.	**65**
Tehama County, CA.	65
Red Wing, MN.	**48**
Goodhue County, MN.	48
Rexburg, ID.	**69**
Fremont County, ID.	14
Madison County, ID.	55
Rice Lake, WI.	**47**
Barron County, WI.	47
Richmond, IN.	**66**
Wayne County, IN.	66
Richmond-Berea, KY.	**127**
Estill County, KY.	14
Madison County, KY.	97
Rockcastle County, KY.	16
Rifle, CO.	**79**
Garfield County, CO.	63
Pitkin County, CO.	17
Rio Grande City-Roma, TX.	**66**
Starr County, TX.	66
Riverton, WY.	**40**
Fremont County, WY.	40
Roanoke Rapids, NC.	**64**
Halifax County, NC.	47
Northampton County, NC.	17
Rochelle, IL.	**51**
Ogle County, IL.	51
Rockingham, NC.	**42**
Richmond County, NC.	42
Rock Springs, WY.	**41**
Sweetwater County, WY.	41
Rolla, MO.	**45**
Phelps County, MO.	45

See footnotes at end of table.

Micropolitan Statistical Area ~~Component county	Popu- lation, 2023 (1,000)
Roseburg, OR.	**112**
Douglas County, OR.	112
Roswell, NM.	**64**
Chaves County, NM.	64
Ruidoso, NM.	**20**
Lincoln County, NM.	20
Russellville, AL.	**32**
Franklin County, AL.	32
Russellville, AR.	**85**
Pope County, AR.	65
Yell County, AR.	20
Ruston, LA.	**48**
Lincoln Parish, LA.	48
Rutland, VT.	**60**
Rutland County, VT.	60
Safford, AZ.	**40**
Graham County, AZ.	40
St. Marys, PA.	**30**
Elk County, PA.	30
Salem, OH.	**100**
Columbiana County, OH.	100
Salina, KS.	**59**
Ottawa County, KS.	6
Saline County, KS.	53
Sandpoint, ID.	**53**
Bonner County, ID.	53
Sanford, NC.	**67**
Lee County, NC.	67
Sault Ste. Marie, MI.	**36**
Chippewa County, MI.	36
Sayre, PA.	**60**
Bradford County, PA.	60
Scottsbluff, NE.	**36**
Banner County, NE.	1
Scotts Bluff County, NE.	36
Scottsboro, AL.	**53**
Jackson County, AL.	53
Seaford, DE.	**264**
Sussex County, DE.	264
Searcy, AR.	**78**
White County, AR.	78
Sedalia, MO.	**44**
Pettis County, MO.	44
Selinsgrove, PA.	**40**
Snyder County, PA.	40
Selma, AL.	**36**
Dallas County, AL.	36
Seneca, SC.	**81**
Oconee County, SC.	81
Seneca Falls, NY.	**32**
Seneca County, NY.	32
Sevierville, TN.	**99**
Sevier County, TN.	99
Seymour, IN.	**46**
Jackson County, IN.	46
Shawano, WI.	**45**
Menominee County, WI.	4
Shawano County, WI.	41
Shawnee, OK.	**74**
Pottawatomie County, OK.	74
Shelby-Kings Mountain, NC.	**101**
Cleveland County, NC.	101
Shelbyville, TN.	**53**
Bedford County, TN.	53
Shelton, WA.	**68**
Mason County, WA.	68
Sheridan, WY.	**33**
Sheridan County, WY.	33
Show Low, AZ.	**109**
Navajo County, AZ.	109
Sidney, OH.	**48**
Shelby County, OH.	48
Sikeston, MO.	**50**
Mississippi County, MO.	12
Scott County, MO.	38
Silver City, NM.	**27**
Grant County, NM.	27
Snyder, TX.	**16**
Scurry County, TX.	16
Somerset, KY.	**66**
Pulaski County, KY.	66

Micropolitan Statistical Area ~~Component county	Popu- lation, 2023 (1,000)
Somerset, PA.	**72**
Somerset County, PA.	72
Sonora, CA.	**54**
Tuolumne County, CA.	54
Sparta, WI.	**46**
Monroe County, WI.	46
Spearfish, SD.	**28**
Lawrence County, SD.	28
Spencer, IA.	**17**
Clay County, IA.	17
Spirit Lake, IA.	**18**
Dickinson County, IA.	18
Starkville, MS.	**61**
Oktibbeha County, MS.	51
Webster County, MS.	10
Statesboro, GA.	**95**
Bulloch County, GA.	84
Evans County, GA.	11
Steamboat Springs, CO.	**38**
Moffat County, CO.	13
Routt County, CO.	25
Stephenville, TX.	**44**
Erath County, TX.	44
Sterling, CO.	**21**
Logan County, CO.	21
Sterling, IL.	**54**
Whiteside County, IL.	54
Stevens Point-Plover, WI.	**71**
Portage County, WI.	71
Stillwater, OK.	**83**
Payne County, OK.	83
Storm Lake, IA.	**21**
Buena Vista County, IA.	21
Sturgis, MI.	**61**
St. Joseph County, MI.	61
Sulphur Springs, TX.	**38**
Hopkins County, TX.	38
Summerville, GA.	**25**
Chattooga County, GA.	25
Sunbury, PA.	**108**
Montour County, PA.	18
Northumberland County, PA.	90
Susanville, CA.	**29**
Lassen County, CA.	29
Sweetwater, TX.	**14**
Nolan County, TX.	14
Tahlequah, OK.	**48**
Cherokee County, OK.	48
Talladega-Sylacauga, AL.	**91**
Coosa County, AL.	10
Talladega County, AL.	81
Taos, NM.	**34**
Taos County, NM.	34
Taylorville, IL.	**33**
Christian County, IL.	33
The Dalles, OR.	**26**
Wasco County, OR.	26
Thomaston, GA.	**28**
Upson County, GA.	28
Thomasville, GA.	**72**
Grady County, GA.	26
Thomas County, GA.	46
Tiffin, OH.	**55**
Seneca County, OH.	55
Tifton, GA.	**50**
Tift County, GA.	42
Turner County, GA.	9
Toccoa, GA.	**27**
Stephens County, GA.	27
Torrington, CT.	**113**
Northwest Hills Planning Region, CT.	113
Town of Pecos, TX.	**12**
Reeves County, TX.	12
Troy, AL.	**33**
Pike County, AL.	33
Truckee-Grass Valley, CA.	**102**
Nevada County, CA.	102
Tullahoma-Manchester, TN.	**67**

Micropolitan Statistical Area ~~Component county	Popu- lation, 2023 (1,000)
Coffee County, TN.	61
Moore County, TN.	7
Tupelo, MS.	**132**
Itawamba County, MS.	24
Lee County, MS.	83
Prentiss County, MS.	25
Ukiah, CA.	**89**
Mendocino County, CA.	89
Union City, TN.	**30**
Obion County, TN.	30
Urbana, OH.	**39**
Champaign County, OH.	39
Uvalde, TX.	**25**
Uvalde County, TX.	25
Van Wert, OH.	**29**
Van Wert County, OH.	29
Vermillion, SD.	**15**
Clay County, SD.	15
Vernal, UT.	**38**
Uintah County, UT.	38
Vernon, TX.	**13**
Wilbarger County, TX.	13
Vicksburg, MS.	**42**
Warren County, MS.	42
Vidalia, GA.	**36**
Montgomery County, GA.	9
Toombs County, GA.	27
Vincennes, IN.	**36**
Knox County, IN.	36
Vineyard Haven, MA.	**21**
Dukes County, MA.	21
Wabash, IN.	**31**
Wabash County, IN.	31
Wahpeton, ND-MN.	**23**
Wilkin County, MN.	6
Richland County, ND.	17
Wapakoneta, OH.	**46**
Auglaize County, OH.	46
Warren, PA.	**38**
Warren County, PA.	38
Warrensburg, MO.	**55**
Johnson County, MO.	55
Warsaw, IN.	**80**
Kosciusko County, IN.	80
Washington, IN.	**34**
Daviess County, IN.	34
Washington, NC.	**44**
Beaufort County, NC.	44
Washington Court House, OH.	**29**
Fayette County, OH.	29
Watertown, SD.	**29**
Codington County, SD.	29
Watertown-Fort Atkinson, WI.	**86**
Jefferson County, WI.	86
Waycross, GA.	**57**
Pierce County, GA.	20
Ware County, GA.	36
Waynesville, NC.	**63**
Haywood County, NC.	63
Weatherford, OK.	**39**
Custer County, OK.	28
Washita County, OK.	11
West Plains, MO.	**41**
Howell County, MO.	41
Whitewater-Elkhorn, WI.	**106**
Walworth County, WI.	106
Williston, ND.	**39**
Williams County, ND.	39
Willmar, MN.	**44**
Kandiyohi County, MN.	44
Wilmington, OH.	**42**
Clinton County, OH.	42
Wilson, NC.	**79**
Wilson County, NC.	79
Winchester, TN.	**45**
Franklin County, TN.	45
Winnemucca, NV.	**17**

See footnotes at end of table.

Table B. Micropolitan Statistical Areas and Components—Population: 2023-Continued.

See headnote on page 924.

Micropolitan Statistical Area ~~Component county	Popu-lation, 2023 (1,000)
Humboldt County, NV	17
Winona, MN	**50**
Winona County, MN	50
Wisconsin	
Rapids-Marshfield, WI	**74**
Wood County, WI	74

Micropolitan Statistical Area ~~Component county	Popu-lation, 2023 (1,000)
Woodward, OK	**20**
Woodward County, OK	20
Wooster, OH	**117**
Wayne County, OH	117
Worthington, MN	**22**
Nobles County, MN	22

Micropolitan Statistical Area ~~Component county	Popu-lation, 2023 (1,000)
Yankton, SD	**24**
Yankton County, SD	24
Zanesville, OH	**86**
Muskingum County, OH	86
Zapata, TX	**14**
Zapata County, TX	14

Source: U.S. Census Bureau, "Metropolitan and Micropolitan Statistical Areas Totals: 2020-2023," <www.census.gov/programs-surveys/popest/data/data-sets.html>.

Introduction—The data presented in this *Statistical Abstract* come from not only federal statistical bureaus and other organizations that collect and issue statistics as their principal activity, but also government administrative and regulatory agencies, private research organizations, trade associations, insurance companies, and health associations. Consequently, the data vary considerably as to reference periods, definitions of terms, and for ongoing series, the number and frequency of time periods for which data are available.

The statistics presented were obtained and tabulated by various methods. Some statistics are based on complete enumerations or censuses, while others are based on samples. Some information is extracted from records kept for administrative or regulatory purposes (such as school enrollment, hospital records, securities registration, financial accounts, social security records, and income tax returns), while other information is obtained explicitly for statistical purposes through surveys.

Each set of data relates to a group of individuals or units of interest referred to as the *target universe,* or *target population*, or simply as the *universe* or *population*. Tables may present data obtained for all population units, *a census*, or data obtained for only a portion, or *sample*, of the population units.

Prior to data collection, the target universe is clearly defined. For example, if data are to be collected for the universe of households in the United States, it is necessary to define a "household." The target universe may not be completely tractable. Cost and other considerations may restrict data collection to a *survey universe* based on an available list. This list is called a *survey frame, sampling frame,* or *survey sample.*

When data are based on a sample, the sample is usually a scientifically selected *probability sample.* This is a sample selected from a list or sampling frame in such a way that every possible sample has a known chance of selection and usually each unit selected can be assigned a number, greater than zero and less than or equal to one, representing its likelihood or probability of selection.

For large-scale sample surveys, the probability sample of units is often selected as a multistage sample. The first stage of a multistage sample is the selection of a probability sample of large groups of population members, referred to as primary sampling units (PSUs). For example, in a national multistage household sample, PSUs are often counties or groups of counties. The second stage of a multistage sample is the selection, within each PSU selected at the first stage, of smaller groups of population units, referred to as secondary sampling units. In subsequent stages of selection, smaller and smaller nested groups are chosen until the ultimate sample of population units is obtained. To qualify a multistage sample as a probability sample, all stages of sampling must be carried out using probability sampling methods.

Prior to selection at each stage of a multistage (or a single stage) sample, a list of the sampling units or sampling frame for that stage must be obtained. For example, for the first stage of selection of a national household sample, a list of the counties and county groups that form the PSUs must be compiled. For the final stage of selection, lists of households, and sometimes persons within the households, have to be compiled in the field. For surveys of economic entities and for the economic censuses, the U.S. Census Bureau generally uses a frame constructed from the Bureau's Business Register. The Business Register contains all establishments with payroll in the United States, including small single-establishment firms as well as larger firms with multiple establishments.

Wherever the quantities in a table refer to an entire universe but are constructed from data collected in a sample survey, the table quantities are referred to as *sample estimates.* In constructing a sample estimate, an attempt is made to come as close as is feasible to the corresponding universe quantity that would be obtained from a complete census of the universe. Estimates based on a sample will, however, generally differ from the hypothetical census figures. Two classifications of errors are associated with estimates based on sample surveys:

1 *Sampling error*—the error arising from the use of a sample, rather than a census, to estimate population quantities.

2 *Nonsampling error*—those errors arising from nonsampling sources, which can be numerous and varied, depending on the type of survey. Nonsampling errors can include mistakes made in data collection or data processing, misunderstandings of the interviewer or the respondent, and data entry errors.

The particular sample used in a survey is only one of a large number of possible samples of the same size which could have been selected using the same sampling procedure. Estimates derived from the different samples would, in general, differ from each other. The *standard error* (SE) is a measure of the variation among the estimates derived from all possible samples. The standard error is the most commonly used measure of the sampling error of an estimate. Valid estimates of the standard errors of survey estimates can usually be calculated from the data collected in a probability sample. For convenience, the standard error is sometimes expressed as a percent of the estimate and is called the relative standard error (RSE) or *coefficient of variation* (CV). For example, an estimate of 200 units with an estimated standard error of 10 units has an estimated CV of 5 percent.

A sample estimate and an estimate of its standard error or CV can be used to construct interval estimates that have a prescribed confidence that the interval includes the average of the estimates derived from all possible samples with a known probability. If all possible samples were selected under essentially the same general conditions, and using the same sample design, and if an estimate and its estimated standard error were calculated from each sample, then: 1) approximately 68 percent of the intervals from one standard error below the estimate to one standard error above the estimate would include the average estimate derived from all possible samples; 2) approximately 90 percent of the intervals from 1.6 standard errors below the estimate to 1.6 standard errors above the estimate would include the average estimate derived from all possible samples; and 3) approximately 95 percent of the intervals from two standard errors below the estimate to two standard errors above the estimate would include the average estimate derived from all possible samples.

Thus, for a particular sample, one can say with the appropriate level of confidence (e.g., 90 percent or 95 percent) that the average of all possible samples is included in the constructed interval. Example of a confidence interval: an estimate is 200 units with a standard error of 10 units. An approximately 90 percent confidence interval (plus or minus 1.6 standard errors) is from 184 to 216.

All surveys and censuses are subject to nonsampling errors. Nonsampling errors arise from a variety of factors, including total nonresponse (no usable data obtained for a sampled unit), partial or item nonresponse (only a portion of a response may be usable), survey respondents who are unable or unwilling to provide correct information or who have difficulty understanding questions, mistakes in recording, editing and transferring data, errors of collection or processing, and coverage problems (overcoverage and undercoverage of the target universe). Nonresponse errors usually, but not always, result in an understatement of sampling errors and thus an overstatement of the precision of survey estimates. Estimating the magnitude of nonsampling errors would require special experiments or access to independent data. Organizations seldom attempt to measure nonsampling errors. The surveys and censuses described in this appendix are subject to nonsampling error.

Nearly all types of nonsampling errors that affect surveys also occur in complete censuses. Since surveys can be conducted on a smaller scale than censuses, nonsampling errors can presumably be controlled more tightly. Relatively more funds and effort can perhaps be expended toward eliciting responses, detecting and correcting response error, and reducing processing errors. As a result, survey results can sometimes be more accurate than census results.

To reduce nonsampling errors, most surveys use computer-assisted telephone or personal interviewing (CATI or CAPI), or a computer-assisted self-interview online. The computer-assisted data collection method employs computer software and programs that guide the interviewer through the questionnaire to keep the survey consistent across all respondents, and can automatically route the interviewer to appropriate questions based on answers to previous questions. Computer programs can determine if responses are within an allowable range and check for consistency against other data collected during the interview or even with data from a previous interview. Capturing a survey on a computer also aids in the complete and accurate transfer of data to the organization's data system. Once collected, survey organizations run automated reviews and edits of data, and impute and weight data items. Other steps to reduce nonsampling

errors can include designing questionnaires that are easy to understand and have clear instructions, training personnel in data collection and processing, and conducting audits and other quality control measures. The surveys described below have detailed documentation available online that describes sources of nonsampling error and the many and various efforts they take to reduce nonsampling errors.

Imputations are adjustments of sample estimates, generally made in the absence of data (nonresponse), to provide for a complete set of survey data. Imputation for total nonresponse is usually made by substituting the "average" questionnaire responses of the respondents. These imputations usually are made separately within various groups of sample members, formed by attempting to place respondents and nonrespondents together that have similar characteristics. Imputation for item nonresponse is usually made by substituting for a missing item the response to that item of a respondent having characteristics that are similar to those of the nonrespondent.

For an estimate calculated from a sample survey, the *total error* in the estimate is composed of the sampling error, which can usually be estimated from the sample, and the nonsampling error, which usually cannot be estimated from the sample. The total error present in a population quantity obtained from a complete census is composed of only nonsampling errors. Ideally, estimates of the total error associated with data presented in the *Statistical Abstract* tables would be available; however, due to the unavailability of estimates of nonsampling errors, only estimates of the levels of sampling errors, in terms of estimated standard errors or coefficients of variation, are available. To obtain estimates of the estimated standard errors from the sample of interest, see the source cited at the end of each table.

Source of Additional Material: The Federal Committee on Statistical Methodology (FCSM) is an interagency committee dedicated to improving the quality of federal statistics, online at <www.fcsm.gov/>. See also information available on the Census Bureau website at <www.census.gov/quality/>.

Special Note: Please note that the coronavirus 2019 (COVID-19) pandemic impacted data collection and survey results for many of the sources described below. The COVID-19 public health emergency in the U.S. was in effect from January 31, 2020 to May 11, 2023. Users should exercise caution in their use of data collected during the COVID-19 pandemic. See each source's website for more information.

Principal data sources—Beginning below are brief descriptions of over 30 of the sample surveys and censuses that provide a substantial portion of the data contained in this *Statistical Abstract.*

U.S. DEPARTMENT OF AGRICULTURE, National Agricultural Statistics Service

Census of Agriculture

Universes, Frequency, and Types of Data: Complete count of U.S. farms and ranches conducted once every 5 years, with data at the national, state, and county level. The survey includes any place from which $1,000 or more of agricultural products were produced and sold, or normally would have been sold, during the census year. The census collects data on all commodities produced in the U.S. as well as detailed information on land use and ownership, operator characteristics (such as race, gender, age, tenure on farm, and operating arrangement), production practices, and income and expenditures.

Data Collection: The NASS mails out questionnaires to all farmers and ranchers. Producers can return their forms by mail or utilize a census form online. For nonrespondents, NASS sends reminder notices and attempts to contact those producers for a personal interview over the telephone or in-person. Personal interviewing is conducted for special classes of records in the census operations. Response to the Census of Agriculture is required by federal law. The response rate for the 2022 Census is 60.1 percent; the response rates for the 2017 Census is 71.8 percent, and for the 2012 Census, 74.6 percent.

Data Editing and Imputation: Captured data go through a computer editing process that validates various aspects of the record and determines whether to accept the value for each data item or to take corrective action. Imputation is conducted for unreasonable and missing data. NASS may contact a producer to verify information or compare information to existing known data, to ensure the most accurate information. See *Appendix A Census of Agriculture Methodology* for detailed imputation methods.

Methodology: NASS uses capture-recapture methodology, an accepted statistical methodology, to account for undercoverage (farms not reached in the original mailing), nonresponse (people not returning their census questionnaires), and misclassification (whether an operation is correctly classified as a farm or not). Details are in *Appendix A Census of Agriculture Methodology*. The uncertainty these adjustments introduce causes the exact numbers to be unknown; however, the uncertainty can be quantified. This measure of relative reliability is known as the coefficient of variation. Estimates of reliability are available from NASS.

Sources of Additional Material: U.S. Department of Agriculture (NASS), 2017 Census of Agriculture, *Appendix A Census of Agriculture Methodology*, and *Appendix B General Explanation and Census of Agriculture Report Form*, online at <www.nass.usda.gov/AgCensus/>. See also <www.nass.usda.gov/AgCensus/FAQ/2022/index.php>.

June Area Survey

Universe, Frequency, and Types of Data: Conducted annually, the June Area survey utilizes an area sampling frame and is designed to account for every acre of land, all agricultural activities, and land uses within segment boundaries. Data are collected from all states except Alaska, on crop acreage, grain stocks, cattle inventory, hog inventory, sheep and goat inventory, land values, farm numbers, sales, and technology use. The survey also serves to measure list incompleteness and is subsampled for multiple frame surveys.

Data Collection and Imputation: A sample of over 9,000 segments, smaller units of a PSU measuring roughly one square mile, is selected from each land use stratum for data collection. All farm operators operating within the boundaries of the selected segments are interviewed. In a given year, approximately 70,000 agricultural and non-agricultural land use tracts are identified within the sampled segments. From that identification, over 30,000 detailed interviews are conducted with farmers operating farms inside the segment boundaries or that have the potential to qualify as a farm. Historically, data collection for the June Area survey was completed entirely by personal interview. Currently, data from operators are collected by mail, internet, telephone, or personal interview. Operators in selected segments are identified, and an information packet, including an aerial photograph and sample questionnaire, is mailed to each prospective respondent. This information packet helps identify tracts of land operated within the segment boundary. Imputation is based on enumerator observation or data reported by respondents having similar agricultural characteristics.

Data Reliability: The National Agricultural Statistics Service publishes *Methodology and Quality Measures* reports by subject, available at the website given below.

Sources of Additional Material: U.S. Department of Agriculture, National Agricultural Statistics Service, *Area Frame Design for Agricultural Surveys*, June 2009, online at <www.nass.usda.gov/Publications/Methodology_and_Data_Quality/>; and <www.nass.usda.gov/Surveys/Guide_to_NASS_Surveys/June_Area/>.

Objective Yield Surveys

Universe, Frequency, and Types of Data: The Objective Yield surveys provide data for monthly forecasts and end-of-season estimates of planted and harvested acres, yield, and production of winter wheat, corn for grain, soybeans, fall potatoes, and upland cotton. All acres for harvest as grain in the leading producing states are eligible for this survey. Survey samples are selected from participants in the March and June Crops/Stocks Survey or the June Area Survey, and include only the top producing states that together produce the majority of a given crop in the U.S.

Data Collection: Field work begins April 25 for winter wheat and July 25 for all the other crops. Sample units are visited at the end of each month during the growing season. Enumerators count and measure plant characteristics in sample fields. Sample fruit (ears, pods, bolls, heads, or tubers) is sent to a lab to determine fruit weight, threshed grain weight, and moisture content. A post harvest visit is made to glean fruit left in some sample fields. Production is measured from plots at harvest. Harvest loss is measured from post harvest gleanings. Detailed methods are available in the sources cited below.

Data Reliability: Reliability measures at the national level are provided in reports presenting data from the Objective Yield Surveys.

Sources of Additional Material: U.S. Department of Agriculture, National Agricultural Statistics Service, Statistical Methods Branch, *The Yield Forecasting Program of NASS*, May 2012, online at <www.nass.usda.gov/Publications/Methodology_and_Data_Quality/> and

<www.nass.usda.gov/Surveys/ Guide_to_NASS_Surveys/Objective_Yield/index. php>.

U.S. BUREAU OF JUSTICE STATISTICS (BJS)

National Crime Victimization Survey (NCVS)

Universe, Frequency, and Types of Data: The NCVS is an annual survey of U.S. household members age 12 and older and is the primary source for information on criminal victimization. Data are obtained from a nationally representative sample of about 240,000 persons in about 150,000 households. Survey excludes victimizations occurring outside of the U.S. The NCVS covers nonfatal personal crime and household property crime victimization, and the characteristics of crimes and victims. Nonfatal personal crimes include rape or sexual assault, robbery, aggravated and simple assault, and personal larceny (purse-snatching, pick-pocketing). Household property crimes include burglary and trespassing, motor vehicle theft, and other types of theft. The survey covers crimes that are both reported and not reported to the police. The survey excludes homicide, arson, and commercial crimes.

Data Collection and Weighting: Eligible household members age 12 and older are interviewed every 6 months for a total of 7 interviews. Households stay in the sample for about 3 1/2 years. New households rotate into the sample on an ongoing basis. Personal interviews are used in the first interview; subsequent interviews are conducted either in person or by telephone. Survey respondents provide information about their crime victimization experiences during the past 6 months, and their personal characteristics. NCVS data include both person and household weights to provide estimates of the population and households represented by each person and each household in the sample. Weights are designed to adjust data to known population totals and to compensate for survey nonresponse and other aspects of the complex sample design. Please note that the 2017 NCVS utilized new household weighting adjustments that resulted in 2017 NCVS household estimates being about 8 percent lower than the previous year. Users should exercise caution when comparing trends in household property crimes over time.

Data Reliability: The *Criminal Victimization* report discusses different methods BJS uses to produce standard errors, including the use of a specialized version of a Balanced Repeated Replication estimation (a type of direct replication variance estimation) using Fay's method, and the use of generalized variance function parameters produced by the Census Bureau for BJS. Estimates and standard errors are also presented in the report, available online; see sources cited below. Detailed documentation is also available online.

Sources of Additional Material: U.S. Bureau of Justice Statistics, *Criminal Victimization,* and the National Crime Victimization Survey website at <bjs.ojp.gov/data-collection/ncvs>.

U.S. BUREAU OF LABOR STATISTICS

Consumer Expenditure Survey (CE)

Universe, Frequency and Types of Data: The Consumer Expenditure Survey (CE) is a nationwide household survey on expenditures for goods and services. The CE also collects information on amount and sources of household income, changes in assets and liabilities, and demographic and economic characteristics of family members. The CE has two components: a quarterly interview survey and a 2-week diary survey. Estimates covering 12-month periods are released annually. Samples are national probability samples of households that are representative of the civilian noninstitutional population. Prior to 2020, sample sizes were 12,000 addresses per calendar quarter for the Interview Survey and 12,000 addresses per year for the Diary Survey. Beginning 2020, the Interview Survey contacts 13,000 addresses per quarter; usable interviews are obtained from about 5,000 households each quarter. The Diary Survey sample is approximately 18,000 addresses per year; usable diaries come from about 6,700 households.

Data Collection: Both the Interview Survey and the Diary Survey are conducted primarily by personal visit, with some telephone interviewing. The measurement unit is the set of eligible individuals constituting a consumer unit (CU). The CU is defined as 1) all members in a housing unit who make up a family (includes foster children); 2) a person living alone or sharing a household with others, or living as a roomer in a private home or other lodging (includes hotel or motel), but who is financially independent; or 3) two or more unrelated persons living together who pool their income to make joint expenditure decisions. Students living in university-sponsored housing are also included in the sample as separate consumer units. For the Interview Survey, consumer units are interviewed every three months, for 4 quarters. The Interview Survey collects expenditure data for large and recurring items that respondents can recall for 3 months or longer, such as property, automobiles, major appliances, rent, and insurance. The Diary Survey collects expenditure data for smaller and frequently purchased items such as food and beverages, and household and personal care products and services. Consumer units report expenses for two consecutive 1-week periods. Data for the Interview Survey and the Diary Survey are collected and processed separately.

Data Reliability: BLS adjusts data using various imputation and allocation methods. Detailed discussion of imputation and allocation methods are available at the source cited below. Consumer Expenditure tables include estimates of standard errors and coefficients of variation or relative standard errors for expenditure data.

Sources of Additional Material: Bureau of Labor Statistics website <www.bls.gov/cex/>; and "BLS Handbook of Methods," <www.bls.gov/opub/hom/ cex/home.htm>.

Consumer Price Index (CPI)

Universe, Frequency, and Types of Data: The Consumer Price Index (CPI) is a measure of the average change over time in the prices paid by urban consumers for a market basket of consumer goods and services. The CPI is derived from a monthly survey. The CPI reflects spending patterns of two population groups: all urban consumers (CPI-U), and urban wage earners and clerical workers (CPI-W). The all urban consumer group represents over 90 percent of the total U.S. population. The CPI-W population represents about 30 percent of the total U.S. population and is a subset of the CPI-U population. Not included in the CPI are the spending patterns of people living in rural non-metropolitan areas, farm families, Armed Forces personnel, and those in institutions such as prisons and mental hospitals. The BLS calculates CPI indexes for the U.S., the census regions and divisions, urban areas by population size, and selected metropolitan and local areas. The CPI covers over 200 item categories of consumer purchases in eight major groups: food and beverages, housing, apparel, transportation, medical care, recreation, education and communication, and other goods and services. Includes user fees (such as water and sewer services) and sales and excise taxes. The index measures price change from a designed reference date. For most of the CPI-U and the CPI-W, the reference base is 1982-84 equals 100.

Data Collection: Approximately two-thirds of price data collection is done by personal visits to brick-and-mortar stores; the remaining data are collected via telephone or the internet (including business websites and applications). Prices are collected either every month or every other month, depending on the item and its location, for approximately 80,000 goods and services in 75 urban areas across the country from about 6,000 housing units and approximately 23,000 retail and service establishments. The BLS collects rent information every 6 months from about 50,000 landlords or tenants.

Data Adjustment and Imputation: To account for products disappearing, products replaced with new versions, and new products, the BLS uses a CPI item replacement procedure, making adjustments as necessary. The CPI also uses imputation for missing data. See source cited below for more detailed discussion of these methods and other calculations.

Data Reliability: The CPI is a statistical estimate that is subject to sampling error because it is based upon a sample of retail prices and not the complete universe of all prices. BLS calculates and publishes estimates of the 1-month, 2-month, 6-month, and 12-month percent change standard errors annually for the CPI-U by expenditure item. These standard error estimates can be used to construct confidence intervals for hypothesis testing. For the latest data, including information on how to use the estimates of standard error, see source cited below and <www.bls.gov/cpi/tables/variance-estimates/home. htm>.

Sources of Additional Material: U.S. Bureau of Labor Statistics, <www.bls.gov/cpi/overview.htm>; and "BLS Handbook of Methods," <www.bls.gov/opub/ hom/cpi/>.

Current Employment Statistics (CES) Program

Universe, Frequency, and Types of Data: Monthly survey of approximately 119,000 businesses and government agencies representing about 629,000

worksites drawn from a sampling frame of Unemployment Insurance (UI) tax accounts covering over 11 million establishments, which is about 97 percent of all employment within the scope of the CES. The active CES sample includes approximately one-third of all nonfarm payroll employees in the 50 states and the District of Columbia. An update is performed each summer to select units from the population of business openings and other units not previously eligible for selection. The CES collects data on employment, hours, and earnings at detailed industry levels. The CES series are estimates of nonfarm wage and salary jobs, not of employed persons; an individual with 2 jobs is counted twice by the payroll survey. The CES excludes employees in agriculture and private households, and the self-employed.

Data Collection: The BLS uses various collection techniques. Data collection centers (DCCs) perform initial enrollment of each firm via telephone, collect the data for several months, and, where possible, have respondents switch to reporting data online. Very large, multi-establishment firms are often enrolled via personal visit, and thereafter report data via electronic data interchange (EDI). These firms provide electronic files to BLS that include data from all their worksites. When firms are rotated into the sample, they are retained for 2 years or more. Each month, respondents extract the employment, hours, and earnings data from their payroll records and submit them to the BLS. Data are collected for the pay period that includes the 12th of each month. BLS staff prepare national estimates of employment, hours, and earnings. State agencies cooperate with the BLS to develop state and metropolitan area estimates.

Editing and Microdata Review: All reported data, regardless of method of collection, are edited by BLS to ensure the information is correctly reported and consistent with the data reported by the establishment in earlier months. The data are further edited to detect processing and reporting errors that might have been missed during collection. When questionable reports are discovered, BLS contacts the respondent for clarification or correction. The CES program tests all respondent data, collectively known as microdata. These tests, also called microdata screening tests, compare all new data reported by survey respondents to the respondent's historically reported data. Data that fail these microdata screening tests are then reviewed by analysts to determine whether the microdata should be used in the estimation of employment, hours, and earnings. Detailed information is available online at <www.bls.gov/web/empsit/cestn.htm>.

Data Reliability: The magnitude of sampling error, or variance, is directly related to the size of the sample and the percentage of universe coverage achieved by the sample. The establishment survey sample covers over one-third of total universe employment; this yields a relatively small variance on the total nonfarm estimates. Information on measurements of error associated with sample estimates are available online under "Technical Notes for the Current Employment Statistics Survey" at <www.bls.gov/web/empsit/cestn.htm>.

Total Error: The benchmark error is used as a proxy measure of total error for the CES survey, and it represents the difference between two employment estimates derived from separate statistical processes (the CES sample process and the Unemployment Insurance administrative process), and thus reflects the sum of the errors present in each program. Historically, benchmark revisions have been very small for total nonfarm employment, averaging 0.1 percent over the past 10 years.

Sources of Additional Material: U.S. Bureau of Labor Statistics, "BLS Handbook of Methods," Chapter 2, <www.bls.gov/opub/hom/pdf/ces-20110307.pdf>; and Current Employment Statistics, "Technical Notes," <www.bls.gov/web/empsit/cestn.htm>.

National Compensation Survey (NCS)

Universe, Frequency, and Types of Data: The NCS is a voluntary establishment-based survey that provides comprehensive measures of: 1) employer costs for employee compensation, including wages and salaries, and benefits, 2) compensation trends, and 3) the availability of and/or employee participation in employer-provided benefits, with an emphasis on health insurance and retirement benefits. The NCS includes establishments in private industry and in state and local government; major exclusions are workers in federal and quasi-federal agencies, military personnel, agricultural workers, workers in private households, the self-employed, and unpaid workers. The NCS releases data through the quarterly Employment Cost Index and the Employer Costs for Employee Compensation, and annual reports on employee benefits, with data shown by various employer and/or employee characteristics, including industry, occupational group, labor union status, and other characteristics.

Sample Selection: The total sample is selected in two stages: one for establishments, and one for occupations within the sample of establishments. The establishment sample has three rotation groups: one for private industry, one for state and local government, and one for the aerospace industry. Government establishments are rotated approximately every 10 years, and all others are rotated every 3 years (except during the government rotation year). Field economists use a probability selection of occupations method to select jobs to sample, then match employees with those jobs, and classify workers according to their duties rather than specific job title. NCS data releases include the number of establishments and occupations covered in the survey.

Data Collection and Adjustments: BLS field economists use personal visits, mail, telephone, and email to obtain data from NCS survey respondents; they do not use paper and online surveys, but rather use conversational interviews and descriptive documents. Updated data are collected quarterly. Discussion of weight adjustments and imputation for the various types of data collected is available online at the source cited below.

Data Reliability: NCS uses standard errors to evaluate published series. A discussion of sampling and nonsampling errors, as well as web-based links to more detailed data on the reliability of estimates from the NCS, are available online at <www.bls.gov/opub/hom/ncs/calculation.htm>. Each data product produced using NCS data also provides information on where to access data on measures of reliability.

Sources of Additional Material: Bureau of Labor Statistics, Handbook of Methods, "National Compensation Measures," <www.bls.gov/opub/hom/ncs/home.htm>.

Producer Price Index (PPI)

Universe, Frequency, and Types of Data: The Producer Price Index (PPI) is a family of indexes that measures the average change over time in prices received (price changes) by producers for domestically produced goods, services, and construction. Producer price indexes (PPIs) measure price change from the perspective of the seller. The monthly survey covers nearly all industries in the goods-producing sectors (including agriculture, fishing, forestry, mining, and manufacturing), and approximately 70 percent of the service sector's output as measured by revenue reported in the 2017 Economic Census. Domestic production of goods for the military is included, as are goods shipped between establishments owned by the same company. The PPI sample includes over 16,000 establishments providing approximately 64,000 price quotations per month supplemented with data from other sources for some areas. The BLS releases each month about 10,000 PPIs for individual products and groups of products. PPIs are organized into three main sets: 1) Final demand-Intermediate demand (FD-ID) indexes, 2) commodity indexes, and 3) indexes for the net output of industries and their products.

Data Collection: PPIs are constructed using selling prices reported by establishments of all sizes, selected by probability sampling, with the probability of selection proportionate to size. Individual items and transaction terms also are chosen by probability proportionate to size. BLS encourages cooperating companies to supply actual transaction prices at the time of shipment to minimize the use of list prices. Prices submitted by survey respondents are effective on the Tuesday of the week containing the 13th day of the month. The survey is conducted online via the BLS Internet Data Collection Facility. Participation in the survey is voluntary. BLS publishes price indexes, not actual prices. All PPIs are subject to monthly revisions up to 4 months after original publication to reflect the availability of late reports and corrections by respondents.

Reference Base: The current standard base period for most commodity-oriented PPI series is 1982, but many indexes that began after 1982 are based on the month of their introduction. The FD-ID indexes typically have a reference base of November 2009 = 100.

Weights, Adjustments, and Variance Estimates: BLS provides extensive documentation for the PPI, including descriptions of PPI weights, quality adjustments for products that change over time, seasonal adjustments, and methodologies for selected industries. Please see sources cited below. The PPI program also began publishing variance estimates in 2016 based on data for 2015. The median absolute value of the percent change is provided as the reference statistic and the corresponding median standard error is provided as the measure of variance. Reports on variance methodology and estimates are available online at <www.bls.gov/ppi/variances/>.

Sources of Additional Material: U.S. Bureau of Labor Statistics, PPI overview available online at <www.bls.gov/ppi/overview.htm>, and documentation online at <www.bls.gov/ppi/methods-overview.htm>. Technical notes are also available at <www.bls.gov/news.release/ppi.tn.htm>.

BOARD OF GOVERNORS OF THE FEDERAL RESERVE SYSTEM

Survey of Consumer Finances (SCF)

Universe, Frequency, and Types of Data: The Survey of Consumer Finances has been conducted every three years since 1989, and collects data on family income, net worth, asset and debt holdings, and use of credit, and other experiences and relationships with financial services and institutions. The 2022 Survey of Consumer Finances is the most recent survey available for coverage in this *Statistical Abstract*. Data include detail by respondent demographic characteristics. In this survey a given household is divided into a primary economic unit (the family), and everyone else in the household. The primary economic unit is the economically dominant single person or couple (married or cohabiting) and all other persons in the household who are financially interdependent with the economically dominant person or couple. The primary economic unit is used as the reference family. The survey instrument remains generally consistent over the years, but the SCF periodically updates questions and adds new questions to accommodate developments in financial behaviors and related topics.

Sample Design: The SCF employs a sample design consisting of two parts: a standard area-probability sample (a geographically based random sample), and a special list sample that oversamples relatively wealthy families under strict rules to provide confidentiality and give potential respondents the right to refuse participation. For the 2022 survey, the standard geographically based sample was redesigned to oversample households predicted to be Black, Asian, and Hispanic. Weights are used to combine information from the two samples to make estimates for the full population. The 2019 survey interviewed 5,783 families, 4,291 from the area-probability sample and 1,492 from the list sample; the 2022 survey interviewed 4,602 families, 3,298 from the area-probability sample and 1,304 from the list sample.

Data Collection and Imputation: National Opinion Research Center (NORC) at the University of Chicago has collected data for the survey since 1992. The majority of interviews for the SCF had been conducted in person; interviews were conducted via telephone if more convenient for respondents. The 2022 survey, for the first time, conducted the majority of interviews over the telephone. The SCF uses weighting to adjust for differential nonresponse to the survey. To address missing information on individual questions within the interview, the SCF uses statistical methods to impute missing data; the technique makes multiple estimates of missing data to allow for an estimate of the uncertainty attributable to this type of nonresponse.

Data Reliability: Sampling error is estimated using replication methods. Replication methods draw samples, called replicates, from the set of actual respondents, and compute weights for all cases in each of the replicates. Please see source website for documentation regarding calculating standard errors.

Sources of Additional Material: Board of Governors of the Federal Reserve System, "Changes in U.S. Family Finances from 2019 to 2022: Evidence from the Survey of Consumer Finances," October 2023; and other files and documentation; <www.federalreserve.gov/econres/scfindex.htm>.

U.S. CENSUS BUREAU

Economic Census

Universe, Frequency, and Types of Data: The Economic Census (EC) is conducted every 5 years to obtain data on number of establishments, number of employees, payroll, measure of output (sales, shipments, receipts, or revenue), and other industry-specific statistics from approximately 4.2 million businesses of all sizes. Data are shown by North American Industry Classification code. The universe is all establishments with paid employees in most industries (exclusions include agriculture, forestry, fishing and hunting, rail transportation, postal service, schools and colleges, religious organizations, private households, and public administration). The sample frame comes from the Census Bureau's Business Register. All establishments of multi-establishment firms are included; single-establishment firms are included based on certain criteria. (Nonemployer Statistics covers establishments without paid employees; see below.) This edition of the *Statistical Abstract* includes data from the 2017 and the 2022 Economic Censuses. The Census Bureau is scheduled to release data from the 2022 EC on a flow basis from January 2024 to March 2026. Businesses included in the Economic Census are required by law under Title 13 (sections 131, 224, and 225) to respond to the survey. Section 9 of the same law makes the information collected confidential. The survey is conducted in the 50 states, District of Columbia, and the 5 Island Areas (American Samoa, Commonwealth of the Northern Mariana Islands, Guam, Puerto Rico, and U.S. Virgin Islands).

Data Collection: Beginning with the 2017 EC, businesses use a secure online portal to respond to the survey. Businesses are mailed instructions for completing the survey online. Businesses with multiple locations can download and upload data spreadsheets. Paper surveys are available for establishments in U.S. territories. The Economic Census uses hundreds of different surveys that are tailored for particular business activities, industries, and industry groups. The EC also includes a non-sampled component; data for selected small single-establishment firms are collected from administrative data from the Census Bureau and other government agencies.

Data Edits and Imputation: Data edits detect and validate data by considering factors such as proper classification for a given record, historical reporting for the record, and industry and geographic ratios and averages. Imputation is used for replacing missing data due to nonresponse. The primary sources for obtaining or deriving data for imputation are administrative data, other data that are either reported or administrative, and data from the previous Economic Census or another Census Bureau survey. The most common source of imputed data is from the Internal Revenue Service.

Data Reliability: Estimates of basic data items, such as receipts, sales, payroll, employment, and inventories, included in the Economic Census First Look and Geographic Area Series publications are computed from all in-scope establishments in the country and therefore are not subject to sampling error. For those establishments that were not sampled or did not respond, missing data items were either imputed or filled in with administrative data from other government agencies. Data tables include information on percent of data imputed.

Sources of Additional Material: U.S. Census Bureau, Economic Census, <www.census.gov/programs-surveys/economic-census.html>.

American Community Survey (ACS)

Universe, Frequency, and Types of Data: The American Community Survey is conducted every month, every year. Annually, the survey is sent to a sample of about 3.54 million households in the U.S. and 36,000 households in Puerto Rico to obtain data about demographic, social, economic, and housing characteristics of housing units and the people residing in them. The ACS was fully implemented in 2005 and replaced the long form of the Decennial Census that collected more detailed data about the population. Initially, the ACS covered only households; beginning in 2006, the ACS included the group quarters population living in correctional facilities, skilled-nursing homes, military barracks, college residence halls, and other group quarters. Sampling frames are drawn from the Census Bureau's Master Address File.

Sample Selection: Detailed descriptions of the sample design and selection are available in the *American Community Survey and Puerto Rico Community Survey Design and Methodology* report, available online at <www.census.gov/programs-surveys/acs/methodology.html>.

Data Collection: The data collection operation for housing units (HUs) consists of four modes: internet, mail, telephone, and personal visit. For most housing units, the first phase includes a mailed request to respond by internet, followed later by an option to complete a paper questionnaire and return it by mail. If no response is received by mail or internet, the Census Bureau follows up with telephone interviewing when a telephone number is available. If a telephone interview is not successful, then the ACS attempts a personal visit and interview. Mailable addresses with neither a response to the mail-out nor a telephone interview are sampled at a rate of 1 in 2, 2 in 5, or 1 in 3 based on the expected rate of completed interviews at the tract level. Unmailable addresses are sampled at a rate of 2 in 3. Those addresses selected through this process are assigned to field representatives (FRs) who visit the addresses, verify their existence, determine their occupancy status, and conduct interviews.

Group quarters: The group quarter data collection operation is conducted in two phases. First, U.S. Census Bureau field representatives (FRs) conduct interviews with the group quarter facility contact person or the administrator of the selected group quarter (referred to as the group quarter level

interview), and second, the FR conducts interviews with a sample of individuals from the facility (referred to as the person- or resident-level interview). Each year FRs conduct data collection at approximately 20,000 individual group quarter facilities, and collect data from approximately 170,000 sample residents. The ultimate sampling units are the residents, not the facilities. Field representatives' methods for collecting data include completing the questionnaire while speaking to the resident in person or over the telephone, or leaving paper questionnaires for residents to complete for themselves and then pick up later. This last option is used for data collection in federal prisons. If needed, a personal interview can be conducted with a proxy such as a relative or guardian.

Imputation: The Census Bureau employs a complex set of procedures to edit erroneous data and impute values when data are missing. The Census Bureau uses two principal methods to impute missing or inconsistent data: assignment and allocation. Assignment involves looking at other data as reported by the respondent to fill in missing responses. For example, if sex is unknown but the respondent reported giving birth, the assignment is female. Hot-deck allocation uses a statistical method to supply missing or inconsistent responses from other housing units or survey respondents with similar characteristics.

Data Reliability: All ACS estimates are accompanied by margins of errors or confidence intervals to assist users.

Special Note for 2020 ACS 1-Year Experimental Estimates: Due to the impacts of the coronavirus 2019 (COVID-19) pandemic on data collection, the Census Bureau did not release standard 1-year estimates from the 2020 American Community Survey. The standard 2020 ACS 1-year estimates did not meet statistical quality standards. The ACS collected only two-thirds of the responses that it normally collects, and respondents had significantly different social, economic, and housing characteristics compared to nonrespondents. The Census Bureau released experimental 1-year estimates from the 2020 ACS; users should exercise caution in using these data. For more information, see <www.census.gov/programs-surveys/acs/data/experimental-data.html>.

Sources of Additional Material: U.S. Census Bureau, American Community Survey, online at <www.census.gov/programs-surveys/acs/>; and American Community Survey Accuracy of the Data documents available on the internet at <www.census.gov/programs-surveys/acs/methodology.html>.

American Housing Survey (AHS)

Universe, Frequency, and Types of Data: The American Housing Survey is sponsored by the Department of Housing and Urban Development (HUD) and is conducted biennially in odd-numbered years by the Census Bureau to collect data on occupied or vacant housing units in the United States (group quarters are excluded). The AHS provides information on a range of core housing subjects, including size and composition of the nation's housing inventory, vacancies, fuel usage, physical condition of housing units, characteristics of occupants, equipment breakdowns, home improvements, mortgages and other housing costs, persons eligible for and beneficiaries of assisted housing, home values, and characteristics of recent movers. Beginning 2011, the AHS includes topical supplements that rotate in and out of the survey. The integrated national longitudinal sample includes national cases representing the U.S., an oversample of housing units in top 15 metropolitan areas, and housing units that are part of a HUD-assisted renter oversample. The integrated metropolitan longitudinal sample represents an additional ten metropolitan areas. The 2021 AHS sample includes 93,000 eligible housing units, including 6,907 HUD-assisted housing units; 28,859 did not yield interviews for an overall response rate of 68.8 percent.

Data Collection: Census Bureau interviewers visit or telephone the household occupying each housing unit in the sample. For unoccupied units, they obtain information from landlords, rental agents, or neighbors. Housing units participating in the AHS are scientifically selected to represent a cross section of all housing in the nation. The same basic sample of housing units is interviewed every two years until a new sample is selected. The U.S. Census Bureau updates the sample by adding newly constructed housing units and units discovered through coverage improvement efforts.

Data Reliability: The AHS provides documentation for users to use to calculate sampling errors. See source website under Technical Documentation, "Accuracy of the Data." The AHS data tool online also provides margins of error along with estimates.

Sources of Additional Material: U.S. Census Bureau, American Housing Survey, Technical Documentation, <www.census.gov/programs-surveys/ahs/tech-documentation.html> and <www.census.gov/programs-surveys/ahs/about/methodology.html>.

Annual Survey of Public Employment and Payroll, and Census of Governments

Universe, Frequency, and Types of Data: A sample survey is conducted annually except in years ending in '2' and '7', when a census of all state and local governments takes place. Covers employees of all agencies of the 50 state governments, the District of Columbia, and about 91,800 local governments (i.e., counties, municipalities, townships, special districts, and school districts). For the annual survey, a sample is selected from the Census of Governments. The typical annual sample contains approximately 11,500 state and local governments; the 2023 sample contains approximately 11,200 state and local governments. The 2022 Census of Governments, Survey of Public Employment and Payroll covers 79,300 governments. The survey measures the number of state and local government employees and their gross payrolls for the pay period including March 12. The survey provides state and local government data on full-time and part-time employment, full-time equivalent employment, and payroll statistics by governmental function. The census obtains data on how governments are organized, employment and payroll, and government finances. Through 2014, the survey also collected data for federal government employees.

Data Collection: Most state governments provide data from central payroll records for all or most of their

agencies and institutions. Data for agencies and institutions for the remaining state governments and all local governments are obtained by an online collection instrument. Some elementary and secondary school system data are supplied by special arrangements with the state government.

Data Editing: Edits are built into the internet data collection instrument and the data entry programs. Post collection edits consist primarily of two types: consistency, and a ratio of the current year's reported value to the value from other years.

Imputation: For general purpose governments, school districts, and special districts not responding to the survey, imputations were based on recent historical data from either a prior year annual survey or the most recent Census of Governments, as available. These data were adjusted by a growth rate that was determined by the growth of units that were similar (in size, geography, and type of government) to the nonrespondent. If no recent historical data were available, imputations were based on the data from a randomly selected donor that was similar to the nonrespondent.

Data Reliability: Census data are not subject to sampling and do not contain sampling error. Data from the annual survey are subject to sampling error. The estimated coefficients of variation (CVs), which are provided for each estimate in data tables containing local government data, are an estimate of this sampling variability. The CVs are expressed as percentages. The CV is the ratio of the standard error to the expectation of the estimate. State government employment and payroll data are not subject to sampling error. Consequently, state and local government aggregates for individual states are more reliable statistically than the local government only estimates.

Sources of Additional Material: Census Bureau, Annual Survey of Public Employment and Payroll (ASPEP), <www.census.gov/programs-surveys/apes/technical-documentation.html>.

Annual Survey of State and Local Government Finances

Universe, Frequency, and Types of Data: In the years ending in "2" and "7," the Census Bureau conducts a census of the entire universe of all 50 state governments, the District of Columbia, and approximately 90,000 local governments (counties, cities, townships, special districts, and school districts). In intervening years, the Bureau conducts an annual survey of a sample of state and local governments. The survey collects data on government revenue (including taxes, charges, interest, and other earnings), expenditures by function and accounting category, debt, and financial assets by type. Data are published about 20 months after data collection. Revisions are made for the next 2 years.

Data Collection: Data are collected via mail canvass, internet, and central collection from State sources. Collection methods vary by state and type of government. Reviews of government accounting records provide data for most state government agencies and some of the largest and most complex county and municipal governments. Data for local governments in about 27 states are consolidated and submitted by state agencies (central collections), usually as electronic transmissions or mutually developed questionnaires. In some cases, data could be obtained from state Annual Comprehensive Financial Reports.

Data Editing: Edits are built into the internet data collection instrument and the data entry programs; edits also occur after data collection. Data edits primarily include consistency checks, historical ratio edits, current year ratio edits, and balance checks.

Imputation: Imputations for nonresponding general purpose governments are based on recently reported historical data from either a prior year annual survey or the most recent census, adjusted by a growth rate. If no historical data are available, or the unit has not responded in over five years, data from a randomly selected similar unit are adjusted by the ratio of the populations of the nonresponding and randomly selected donor governments. The imputations for nonresponding special districts are done similarly. If prior year reported data are available, the prior year data for the nonrespondent are adjusted by a growth rate that is determined from reporting units that are similar to the nonrespondent.

Data Reliability: State government financial statistics result from a complete canvass of all state government agencies and do not have an associated measure of sampling error. Data from local governments come from a sample of local governments and are subject to sampling variability. Data files include the coefficients of variation along with the data.

Sources of Additional Material: Census Bureau, State and Local Government Finances, <www.census.gov/programs-surveys/gov-finances/technical-documentation/methodology.html>.

Annual Survey of Manufactures (ASM)

Universe, Frequency, and Types of Data: The Annual Survey of Manufactures is a sample survey of approximately 50,000 manufacturing establishments conducted annually, except for years ending in '2' and '7' when the survey is included in the Economic Census, for all manufacturing establishments having one or more paid employees. The sample is drawn from the manufacturing portion of the most recent Economic Census available, and, for new establishments, from the Census Bureau's Business Register. The ASM collects data on employment, payroll, worker hours, payroll supplements, cost of materials, select operating expenses, value added by manufacturing, capital expenditures, inventories, and energy consumption. The ASM also covers the value of shipments for approximately 3,500 products.

Data Collection: The ASM mails out instructions for responding to the survey via an online tool. Firms not responding receive follow up mailings and telephone calls. Response is required by law.

Data Editing and Imputation: Data editing first verifies whether an establishment's kind of business or industry classification is valid, then survey responses are evaluated for consistency and validity. The primary sources for imputing data missing due to nonresponse are administrative data, other data reported by the establishment, and data reported in previous surveys or other census

surveys. Sampled establishments that did not report product data are assigned products in a hot-deck imputation process. In this process the products from a similar establishment (called the donor) are assigned to the establishment missing the product data (the recipient).

Data Reliability: Statistics include estimated relative standard errors. Relative standard errors vary by industry and product category.

Special Note: Please note that the Annual Survey of Manufactures is discontinued after the 2021 survey year. The data formerly collected by the ASM will now be collected as part of the Annual Integrated Economic Survey (AIES) for 2023, which began data collection in 2024. Information on the AEIS is online at <www.census.gov/programs-surveys/aies.html>.

Sources of Additional Material: Census Bureau, Annual Survey of Manufactures Methodology, <www.census.gov/programs-surveys/asm/technical-documentation/methodology.html>.

Decennial Census of Population and Housing

Universe, Frequency, and Types of Data: Mandated by the U.S. Constitution, the Decennial Census has made a complete count of the U.S. population every 10 years since 1790. The data collected by the decennial census are used to apportion the number of seats each state has in the U.S. House of Representatives, as well as to realign congressional districts and determine allocation of federal funding. The Census obtains data on the number and characteristics of people in the United States and its outlying territories, and also counts Federally affiliated Americans overseas. The 2010 and 2020 Censuses asked information on name, gender, age, race, ethnicity, relationship to householder, and whether the respondent owns or rents their home.

Data Collection: Up until 2020, the Decennial Census was conducted by mail. For the 2020 Census, the Census Bureau mailed out invitations to households to complete the census by mail, telephone, or the internet. The 2020 Census incorporates design changes in four key areas: new methodologies to conduct address canvassing, including using geographic information systems and aerial imagery to add new addresses (formerly, Census workers physically walked neighborhoods); encouraging the public to respond using the internet; using administrative data that the public has already provided to the government and data from commercial sources; and using sophisticated operational control systems to send Census workers to follow up with nonresponding housing units. See source for more information on these methods. Prior to 2010, the Census used 2 forms of questionnaires; all households had to answer questions on the short form, and a portion of households would receive the long form seeking more detailed information. Beginning 2010, the Census uses a single questionnaire that contains about 9 to 10 questions, with several questions repeated for each member of a household. Detailed information that was asked on the long form questionnaire was moved to the annual American Community Survey.

Disclosure Avoidance: For the 2020 Census results, the Census Bureau is using a mathematical approach that inserts a small amount of "noise" into the data to protect the privacy of individual respondents. This is essentially adding or subtracting a small amount of statistical noise to the data. The Census Bureau is providing metrics to help users understand how much statistical noise is in data products; metrics include the mean absolute error, which indicates how close a data point is to the enumerated count on average, and mean error, which indicates how much higher or lower published data are to the enumerated count. Technical documentation with detailed information are available on the Census Bureau's website.

Imputation: For missing data, the 2010 Census employed count imputation using three general procedures: assignment, allocation, and substitution. For the 2020 Census, the Census Bureau is using imputation procedures for missing characteristics (demographic and housing data) and counts of people. See source given below for technical documentation and Census news releases and blog posts for more information on imputation.

Coverage Measurement: The Census Bureau uses several methods to assess the quality of data and to provide data on net coverage errors. One principal method is the demographic analysis. The demographic analysis collects data from other sources, including vital statistics records, migration data, and Medicare records, to estimate the population size for comparison with official census data. Net coverage error is calculated as the percent difference between the census count and the demographic analysis estimate. Another method to assess coverage is a post-enumeration survey, an independent survey to measure how many people and housing units were counted correctly and erroneously, or missed by the Decennial Census. Detailed documentation and data from these data quality operations are available through links at the source cited below.

Sources of Additional Material: U.S. Census Bureau's Decennial Census webpage has links to numerous documents, <www.census.gov/programs-surveys/decennial-census.html>. Information is organized by type and by decade. See also <www.census.gov/programs-surveys/decennial-census/technical-documentation/complete-technical-documents.2020.html#dhc-and-dp>.

County Business Patterns

Universe, Frequency, and Types of Data: County Business Patterns is an annual series that contains data on number of establishments, employment during the week of March 12, and first quarter and annual payrolls, by detailed geography and industry level, for the U.S., Puerto Rico, and Island Areas (Guam, American Samoa, the Commonwealth of the Northern Mariana Islands, and the U.S. Virgin Islands). Data cover over 6 million single-unit establishments and 2 million multi-unit establishments, and are available by geographic area (state, county, and metropolitan areas), 6-digit NAICS industry, legal form of organization (U.S. and state only), and employment size class. Most industries are covered; excluded are crop and animal production; rail transportation; U.S. Postal Service; pension, health, welfare, and other insurance funds; trusts, estates, and agency accounts; private households; and public

administration. CBP also excludes most establishments reporting government employees.

Data Collection: Most basic data items are extracted from the Census Bureau's Business Register, a database of all known employer companies. The Census Bureau's Report of Organization, formerly the Company Organization Survey, provides individual establishment data for companies that operate 2 or more units (multi-establishment companies). Data for single establishment companies are obtained from various Census Bureau programs such as the Economic Census, Annual Survey of Manufactures, and Current Business Surveys, as well as from administrative records of the Internal Revenue Service, the Social Security Administration, and the Bureau of Labor Statistics.

Data Reliability: Payroll and employment data are obtained from administrative records for single-unit companies and a combination of administrative records and survey-collected data for multi-unit companies. They are not subject to sampling error. Missing employment and payroll data are imputed using averages, or by examing patterns for various time periods.

Noise Infusion: Since reference year 2007, County Business Patterns has used noise infusion to protect the confidentiality of respondent data. Noise infusion is a method of avoiding disclosure in which data values for each establishment are perturbed prior to table creation by applying a random noise multiplier to the magnitude data (i.e., characteristics such as first-quarter payroll, annual payroll, and number of employees) for each establishment. This results in a relatively small change in the vast majority of cell values. See source below for more information.

Sources of Additional Material: U.S. Census Bureau, County Business Patterns, online at <www.census.gov/programs-surveys/cbp/about.html> and <www.census.gov/programs-surveys/cbp/technical-documentation/methodology.html>.

Current Population Survey (CPS)

Universe, Frequency, and Types of Data: Nationwide monthly sample of approximately 60,000 households designed primarily to produce national and state estimates of labor force and other characteristics of the civilian noninstitutionalized population 15 years of age and older. The CPS also includes supplements that focus on a variety of topics and are sponsored by various public and private organizations. The March CPS includes the Annual Social and Economic Supplement (ASEC), which covers family characteristics, household composition, marital status, education attainment, health insurance coverage, foreign-born population, previous year's income from all sources, work experience, receipt of noncash benefits, poverty, program participation, and geographic mobility.

Data Collection: The CPS uses a multistage probability sample that currently includes 60,000 households from 824 sample areas. A continual sample rotation system is used. Households are in the sample for 4 months, out for 8 months, and in for 4 more. Census Bureau field representatives administer the CPS questionnaire across the country through both personal and telephone interviews; a personal visit interview is required for the first time households participate unless the respondent requests a telephone interview. One person, usually the person who owns or rents the housing unit, generally responds for all eligible members in a household regarding activities during the prior week (the week including the 12th of the month). Participation is voluntary.

Imputation: The CPS makes imputations for missing data items, including data items that were eliminated due to probems such as being illogical or out-of-range. The CPS uses 3 imputation methods for item nonresponse: relational imputation, which infers the missing value from other characteristics on the person's record or within the household; longitudinal edits (using response from the previous month) for most of the labor force edits, as appropriate; and "hot deck" allocation, a method of assigning a missing value from a record with similar characteristics, which is the hot deck. Hot decks are defined by variables such as age, race, and sex.

Sampling: Sufficient sample is allocated to maintain, at most, a 1.9 percent coefficient of variation on national monthly estimates of unemployment, assuming a 6 percent unemployment rate. This translates into a change of 0.2 percentage point in the unemployment rate being significant at a 90 percent confidence level. For each of the 50 States and for the District of Columbia, the design maintains a coefficient of variation of at most 8 percent on the annual average estimate of unemployment, assuming a 6 percent unemployment rate.

Sources of Additional Material: U.S. Census Bureau, Current Population Survey, <www.census.gov/ programs-surveys/cps/technical-documentation/ methodology.html> and <www.census.gov/ programs-surveys/cps/technical-documentation/ complete.html>.

Foreign Trade—Export Statistics

Universe, Frequency, and Types of Data: Export statistics cover goods valued at more than $2,500 per commodity shipped by individuals and organizations (including exporters, freight forwarders, and carriers) from the U.S. to other countries. Data are compiled in terms of commodity classification, quantities, values, shipping weights, method of transportation (air or vessel), state of (movement) origin, customs district, customs port, country of destination, and whether contents are domestic goods or reexports. Transactions are classified under approximately 8,000 different products leaving the United States. Data cover over 200 U.S. trading partners. Data are continuously compiled and processed. Documents are collected as shipments depart and processed on a flow basis. Reports summarize shipments made during calendar months, quarters, and years. Statistics are reported monthly approximately 35 days after the end of the reference month and on a year-to-date basis.

Data Collection: Data consist of a full compilation (i.e., a census) of commodity exports, plus U.S. Census Bureau estimates of low-valued exports and Bureau of Economic Analysis (BEA) estimates of trade in services. Data on U.S. exports of merchandise from the U.S. to all countries, except Canada, are compiled from the Electronic Export Information (EEI) filed by the U.S. Principal Party in Interest (USPPI, the seller, manufacturer, order party, or

whoever receives the primary benefit from an export transaction) or their agents through the Automated Export System (AES). The AES is the central point through which export shipment data are filed electronically and transmitted to U.S. Customs and Border Protection and the Census Bureau. Each EEI represents a shipment of one or more kinds of merchandise from one exporter to one foreign importer on a single carrier. Filing the EEI is mandatory under Chapter 9, Title 13, United States Code. Estimates are made for low-value exports by country of destination and based on bilateral trade patterns. Statistics for U.S. exports to Canada are based on import documents filed with Canadian agencies and forwarded to the U.S. Census Bureau under a 1987 data exchange agreement. Under this agreement, each country eliminated most cross-border export documents; maintains detailed statistics on cross-border imports; exchanges monthly files of cross-border import statistics; and publishes exchanged statistics in place of previously compiled export statistics. Department of Defense Military Assistance Program Grant-Aid shipments being transported as Department of Defense cargo are reported directly to the U.S. Census Bureau by the Department of Defense.

Data Reliability: The goods data are a complete enumeration of electronic export information (EEI) reported in the automated export system (AES) and are not subject to sampling errors, but they are subject to several types of nonsampling errors. The most significant of these include reporting errors, undocumented shipments, timeliness, data capture errors, and errors in the estimation of low-valued transactions. Other quality issues are described in the source cited below.

Sources of Additional Material: U.S. Census Bureau, Foreign Trade, Guide to the U.S. International Trade Statistical Program, <www.census.gov/foreign-trade /guide/sec2.html>.

Foreign Trade—Import Statistics

Universe, Frequency, and Types of Data: The import statistics cover goods valued at more than $2,000 per commodity shipped by individuals and organizations (including importers and customs brokers) into the U.S. from other countries. Data are compiled in terms of commodity classification, quantities, values, shipping weights, methods of transportation (air or vessel), duties collected, unit prices, and market share, country of origin, customs district, customs port, and import charges and duties. Commodities are compiled under the Harmonized Tariff Schedule of the United States containing approximately 14,000 commodity classifications. Data cover over 200 U.S. trading partners. Data are continuously compiled and processed. Documents are collected as shipments arrive and processed on a flow basis. Reports summarize shipments made during calendar months and years. Statistics are reported monthly approximately 35 days after the end of the reference month and on a year-to-date basis.

Data Collection: A full compilation (i.e., a census) is taken of import shipments, plus U.S. Census Bureau estimates of low-valued imports and Bureau of Economic Analysis (BEA) estimates of trade in services. Statistics for imported goods shipments are compiled from the records filed with Customs and Border Protection (CBP), usually within 10 days after the merchandise enters the United States. Estimates are made for low-value shipments by country of origin based on previous bilateral trade patterns and periodically updated. Statistics for over 95 percent of all commodity transactions are compiled from records filed electronically with CBP and forwarded to the U.S. Census Bureau. Statistics for other transactions are compiled from hard-copy documents filed with CBP and forwarded on a flow basis for U.S. Census Bureau processing.

Data Reliability: The goods data are a complete enumeration of documents collected by the U.S. Customs and Border Protection and are not subject to sampling errors, but they are subject to several types of nonsampling errors. The most significant of these include reporting errors, undocumented shipments, timeliness, data capture errors, and errors in the estimation of low-valued transactions. Other quality issues are described in the source cited below.

Sources of Additional Material: U.S. Census Bureau, Foreign Trade, Guide to the U.S. International Trade Statistical Program, <www.census.gov/foreign-trade /guide/sec2.html>.

Monthly and Annual Retail Trade Survey

Universe, Frequency, and Types of Data: The size of the Monthly Retail Trade Survey (MRTS) sample is approximately 13,000 employer firms. Data cover retail store and food service sales, and inventories held by retail stores. Monthly retail trade data are available at the national level only. The Annual Retail Trade Survey (ARTS) uses a sample of approximately 16,500 employer firms in the retail trade sector and electronic commerce sales, and requests data on sales, sales taxes, inventories, purchases, operating expenses, and other financial items. Annual data are also available at the national level only, and are published at the industry level using the North American Industry Classifcation System.

Data Collection and Imputation: Firms for the retail trade surveys come from the Economic Census and the Census Bureau's Business Register. Data are collected by mail questionnaire and the internet, with telephone follow-ups for nonrespondents. Imputation is made for each nonresponse item and each item failing edit checks. For both unit and item nonresponse, a missing value is replaced by a predicted value obtained from an appropriate model for nonresponse. This imputation uses survey data and administrative data as input. In any given month, about a third of monthly retail trade data is imputed. For the annual survey, imputed data amount to about 11.6 percent for sales and about 14 percent for inventories. Additional information about the imputation rates for published estimates are available upon request.

Data Reliability: Estimated CVs and standard errors are released with monthly reports. Annual data releases include measures of sampling variability.

Special Note: Please note that 2022 represents the last data collection for the Annual Retail Trade Survey. The Annual Retail Trade Survey (ARTS) has transitioned to the Annual Integrated Economic Survey (AIES). The data formerly collected for the ARTS will now be collected as part of the AIES, which began data collection in 2024. Information

on the AEIS is online at <www.census.gov/ programs-surveys/aies.html>.

Sources of Additional Material: Census Bureau, Monthly and Annual Retail Trade, <www.census.gov/retail/mrts/ how_surveys_are_collected.html> and <www.census.gov/programs-surveys/arts/technical-documentation/methodology.html>.

Survey of Construction

Universe, Frequency, and Types of Data: The Survey of Construction provides current national and regional statistics on starts, completions, and characteristics of new, privately-owned single-family and multifamily housing units and on sales of new single-family houses. Data collected include start and completion dates, sales date, sales price (single-family houses only), and the physical characteristics of housing units. Survey data are available monthly and annually for housing starts since 1959, for new home sales since 1963, and for completions since 1968. Reported data are for building or sales activity taking place during the applicable reference period. Monthly data collection begins the first day after the reference month and continues through the 7th working day.

Survey Design: The Survey of Construction includes two parts: the Survey of Use of Permits (SUP), which covers new construction in areas that require a building permit, and the Non-Permit Survey (NP), which covers new construction in areas that do not require a building permit. Less than 2 percent of all new construction takes place in non-permit areas. A multistage probability sample of approximately 900 permit-issuing jurisdictions in the U.S. is selected. Each month in each of these permit offices, field representatives list and select a sample of permits for which to collect data. To obtain data in non-permit areas, a multistage probability sample of over 80 land areas (census tracts or subsections of census tracts) is selected. All roads in these areas are canvassed and data are collected on all new residential construction found. Sampled buildings are followed up until they are completed (and sold, if for sale), or abandoned. Permits for 1- to 4-unit buildings are sampled at an overall rate of 1 in 50. All permits authorizing buildings with 5 or more housing units in the sampled permit offices are selected.

Data Collection and Processing: Data from both parts of SOC are collected by Census field representatives in person or by telephone. For the SUP, Census representatives visit a sample of permit offices and select a sample of permits issued for new housing. These permits are then followed through to see when they are started and completed, and when they are sold for single-family units that are built to be sold. Each project is also surveyed to collect information on characteristics of the structure. For the Non-Permit Survey, roads in sampled non-permit land areas are driven at least once every 3 months to see if there is any new construction. Once new residential construction is found, it is followed up the same as in SUP. Each month, interviews are required for about half of the buildings currently being followed up. Nonresponse/undercoverage adjustment factors are used to account for late reported data. Each month, housing starts, completions, and sales estimates derived from this survey are adjusted by the total numbers of authorized housing units (obtained from the Building Permits Survey) to develop national and regional estimates. Estimates are adjusted to reflect variations by region and type of construction, and to account for late reports and houses started or sold before a permit has been issued. Reported data are seasonally adjusted.

Data Reliability: Data are subject to sampling errors. Estimates of the standard errors have been computed from the sample data for selected statistics. They are presented in the source tables in the form of average relative standard errors (RSEs).

Sources of Additional Material: Census Bureau, Survey of Construction, online at <www.census.gov/construction/nrc/how_the_data_are_collected/soc.html>.

Nonemployer Statistics

Universe, Frequency, and Types of Data: Nonemployer statistics are an annual tabulation of economic data by industry for active businesses without paid employees or payroll, that are subject to federal income taxes, and that have receipts of $1,000 or more ($1 or more for the construction sector). Excluded are corporations and partnerships with over $1 million in receipts (except for service-type industries, maximum is $2 million). Maximum receipts for sole proprietorships depends on industry classification. Most nonemployers are self-employed individuals operating unincorporated businesses (known as sole proprietorships). Data showing the number of firms and receipts by industry are available for the U.S., states, counties, and metropolitan areas. Most types of businesses covered by the Census Bureau's economic statistics programs are included in the nonemployer statistics. Nonemployer statistics exclude crop and animal production; investment funds, trusts, and other financial vehicles; management of companies and enterprises; and public administration.

Data Collection and Processing: The universe of nonemployer firms is created annually in conjunction with identifying the Census Bureau's employer universe. If a business is active but without paid employees, then it becomes part of the potential nonemployer universe. The data are primarily from business income tax returns filed with the Internal Revenue Service and maintained in the Census Bureau's Business Register. The potential nonemployer universe undergoes an analytical review to distinguish nonemployers from employers.

Data Reliability: Data are tabulated from administrative records and are not subject to sampling error. Data are subject to nonsampling errors. The improper inclusion of possible employer establishments in the nonemployer universe is the primary source of nonsampling error.

Noise Infusion: Since reference year 2005, the noise infusion data protection method has been applied to prevent disclosure of receipt cell values. Noise infusion is a method of disclosure avoidance in which values are perturbed prior to table creation by applying a random noise multiplier to the magnitude data (in this case, receipts) independently for each business. Disclosure protection is accomplished in a manner that results in a relatively small change for the vast majority of cell values.

Sources of Additional Material: U. S. Census Bureau, Nonemployer Statistics, <www.census.gov/programs-surveys/nonemployer-statistics/technical-documentation.html>.

Service Annual Survey (SAS)

Universe, Frequency, and Types of Data: The U.S. Census Bureau conducts the Service Annual Survey (SAS) to provide nationwide estimates of revenues and expenses for most traditional service industries. Estimates are summarized by industry classification based on the North American Industry Classification System (NAICS). Service industries covered by the Service Annual Survey include all or part of the following NAICS sectors: Utilities (NAICS 22); Transportation and Warehousing (NAICS 48-49); Information (NAICS 51); Finance and Insurance (NAICS 52); Real Estate and Rental and Leasing (NAICS 53); Professional, Scientific, and Technical Services (NAICS 54); Administrative and Support and Waste Management and Remediation Services (NAICS 56); Educational Services (NAICS 61); Health Care and Social Assistance (NAICS 62); Arts, Entertainment, and Recreation (NAICS 71); Accommodation and Food Services (NAICS 72); and Other Services except Public Administration (NAICS 81). The SAS includes firms of all sizes and covers both taxable firms and firms exempt from federal income taxes.

Data Collection: The Service Annual Survey estimates are developed from a probability sample of approximately 78,000 employer firms, and administrative records for nonemployers. Service Annual Survey uses a probability sample that is periodically reselected from a universe of firms having paid employees. Updates to the sample are made on a quarterly basis to account for new and closed businesses. Firms without paid employees, or nonemployers, are included in the estimates through imputation and/or administrative records data provided by other federal agencies.

Data Reliability: Estimates are based on a sample and subject to sampling error. The most recent Service Annual Survey results, including coefficients of variations (CVs), can be found on the internet at <www.census.gov/programs-surveys/sas/data/tables.html>. Additional information regarding sampling error may also be found online at <www.census.gov/programs-surveys/sas/technical-documentation/methodology.html>. To address the potential bias due to nonresponse, for both unit and item nonresponse a missing value is replaced by a predicted value obtained from an appropriate model for nonresponse. This imputation uses survey data and administrative data as input.

Special Note: Please note that 2022 represents the last data collection for the Service Annual Survey (SAS). The SAS has transitioned to the Annual Integrated Economic Survey (AIES). The data formerly collected for the SAS will now be collected as part of the AIES, which began data collection in 2024. Information on the AEIS is online at <www.census.gov/programs-surveys/aies.html>.

Sources of Additional Material: U.S. Census Bureau, Service Annual Survey, <www.census.gov/programs-surveys/sas/technical-documentation/methodology.html>.

Annual Business Survey (ABS)

Universe, Frequency, and Types of Data: The survey is conducted by the U.S. Census Bureau and the National Science Foundation's National Center for

Science and Engineering Statistics. The survey began in 2017 and replaces several surveys, including the Census Bureau's Survey of Business Owners, and the Annual Survey of Entrepreneurs. The survey covers all nonfarm employers filing 941, 944, or 1120 tax forms with receipts of $1,000 or more. The ABS samples approximately 850,000 employer businesses every 5 years and approximately 300,000 employer businesses annually. The survey collects data on the number of employer firms, sales and receipts, payroll, industry, and employment by sex, race, ethnicity, and veteran status. Data are tabulated by business owner sex, race, ethnicity, and veteran status. The survey also collects data on research and development, innovation, and technology, and new topics relevant to the business community. Data are available for the U.S. and by state, metropolitan statistical area, and county, and economic place levels.

Data Collection: Businesses selected for the survey receive an initial letter about the survey and instructions for accessing the survey on the internet. Survey response is required by law. Additional data are collected electronically from the Economic Census and government administrative records, and are combined with survey data. Data results are available by business owner characteristics. Business ownership is defined as more than 50 percent of the stock or equity in the business and is categorized by sex, race, ethnicity, and veteran status, and firms unclassifiable by sex, race, ethnicity, and veteran status. Businesses can be tabulated in more than one racial group. Historical data and imputation methods were used to adjust for nonresponse.

Noise Infusion: The Annual Business Survey uses noise infusion as the primary method of disclosure avoidance. Noise infusion perturbs data values prior to tabulation by applying a random noise multiplier to all data. For this reason, detailed estimates may not sum to the total for estimates of firm counts. Disclosure protection is accomplished in a manner that causes the vast majority of cell values to be perturbed by, at most, a few percentage points.

Data Reliability: The estimated relative standard errors and estimated standard errors presented in ABS data tables estimate the sampling variability, and thus measure the precision with which an estimate from the particular sample selected for this survey approximates the average result of all possible samples. Relative standard errors and standard errors are applicable only to those published cells in which sample cases are tabulated. A relative standard error is an expression of the standard error as a percent of the quantity being estimated. For the *Characteristics of Businesses* and *Characteristics of Business Owners* datasets, some data are expressed as percentages with standard errors rather than relative standard errors.

Sources of Additional Materials: U.S. Census Bureau, Annual Business Survey, <www.census.gov/

programs-surveys/abs.html> and <www.census.gov/programs-surveys/abs/technical-documentation/methodology.html>

U.S. DEPARTMENT OF EDUCATION, National Center for Education Statistics

Integrated Postsecondary Education Data Survey (IPEDS)

Universe, Frequency, and Types of Data: The IPEDS annually collects institution-level data from postsecondary institutions across the U.S. on tuition and fees, number and types of degrees and certificates conferred, number of students applying and enrolled, number of employees, financial statistics, graduation rates, student outcomes, student financial aid, and academic libraries. The survey consists of 12 components that are administered across the fall, winter, and spring reporting seasons. Submission of data to IPEDS is mandatory for any institution that participates in or is an applicant for participation in any federal financial assistance program authorized by Title IV of the Higher Education Act of 1965. IPEDS response rates for each component are nearly 100 percent. Close to 7,000 institutions participate in the survey each year.

Data Collection: The IPEDS collects data via the internet. As respondents enter data online, the data collection system automatically calculates totals, averages, and percentages, and compares the responses with the previous year's submission for the same institution to ensure the data are consistent. The system also compares data with other related values to ensure consistency of reporting within each survey component and across the data collection program. If data are still missing, analysts conduct imputations to complete the database.

Imputation: Missing data are imputed by using data of similar institutions. With the exception of the Institutional Characteristics component, all items collected in each component were eligible for imputation. Within the Institutional Characteristics component, only cost of attendance and other institutional charges data are eligible for imputation. IPEDS may apply one of three imputation methods for both unit and item nonresponse, depending on the data available. Carry Forward uses data from previous years to substitute for current data, with adjustments to account for yearly changes. The Nearest Neighbor procedure identifies data related to the key statistics of interest for each component (the distance measure), then uses those data to identify a responding institution similar to the nonresponding institution and uses the respondent's data as a substitute for the nonrespondent's missing items. Lastly, for data that cannot be imputed by carry forward or nearest neighbor methods, the Group Median method identifies the median institution that provides values that are missing for another institution.

Edit Procedures: The internet-based survey instrument conducts edit checks to detect major reporting errors. The system can prompt survey respondents to correct errors as they are found. If accurate data fails the edit checks, survey respondents either confirm the response or explain why the data appear to be out of the expected data range. The system requires all edit checks to be confirmed or explained. In some cases, respondents could contact IPEDS for assistance. IPEDS staff also review data for additional errors and contact respondents for verification.

Data Reliability: Data are not subject to sampling error. Data are subject to such nonsampling errors as errors of design, reporting, processing, nonresponse, and imputation.

Sources of Additional Material: U.S. Department of Education, National Center for Education Statistics, IPEDS Survey Methodology, online at <nces.ed.gov/ipeds/ReportYourData/IpedsSurveyMethodology>.

National Household Education Surveys (NHES) Program

Universe, Frequency, and Types of Data: The National Household Education Surveys Program is a system of surveys of the noninstitutionalized civilian population of the United States. NHES surveys have been conducted periodically since 1991 and have varying universes of interest depending on the particular survey. Some surveys are recurring; others are fielded as 1-time surveys. Currently, the NHES surveys cover young children's care and education before kindergarten, and parent and family involvement in their children's education, which also encompasses home schooling. A list of past surveys and their collection years are available online at <nces.ed.gov/nhes>. The most recent surveys covered in this *Statistical Abstract* were fielded in 2016 and 2019, and include:

1 Early Childhood Program Participation—Surveys of parents of a representative sample of children age 6 and younger not yet enrolled in kindergarten.

2 Parent and Family Involvement in Education—Surveys of parents of a representative sample of children age 3 to 20 who were enrolled in kindergarten through grade 12. Separate questionnaires are administered for children enrolled in public and private schools, and for children who are home schooled.

Data Collection: NHES typically fields 2 to 3 topical surveys at a time, although the number has varied across its administration. Surveys are administered in English and in Spanish. From 1991 to 2007, the NHES used telephone interviews to collect data. In 2012, the NHES switched to a mail survey, and samples were developed using household address information for all 50 states and the District of Columbia. The 2016 survey included use of the internet for a small portion of the sample. In 2019, the NHES mailed invitations to participate in the survey and provide responses either by mail or the internet. Both of the 2016 and 2019 NHES samples were selected using a 2-stage address-based sampling frame. Black and Hispanic American households were sampled at a higher rate than other households.

Data Reliability: Reports presenting NHES data include tables on standard errors. Efforts to prevent nonsampling errors include cognitive interviews to assess respondents' knowledge of the survey topics, their comprehension of questions and terms, and the sensitivity of items.

Sources of Additional Material: Please see the NHES website at <nces.ed.gov/nhes>; and technical notes and related methodological information in individual NHES reports available online at <nces.ed.gov/pubsearch/getpubcats.asp?sid=004>.

U.S. DEPARTMENT OF JUSTICE, FEDERAL BUREAU OF INVESTIGATION

Uniform Crime Reporting (UCR) Program

Overview: The Uniform Crime Reporting (UCR) Program encompasses several data collections, including the National Incident Based Reporting System (NIBRS), Hate Crime Statistics data collection, and Law Enforcement Officers Killed and Assaulted (LEOKA) data collection. The UCR Program includes data from city, university and college, county, state, tribal, and federal law enforcement agencies. Agencies participate voluntarily and submit their crime data either through a state UCR program or directly to the FBI's UCR Program. The NIBRS collects data for 52 offenses, plus another 10 offenses for which only arrests are reported. The NIBRS also captures details on each single crime incident and the separate offenses within the same incident. The additional details provide context and circumstances of the incident, including time, victim types, relationships of victims to offenders and offenses, demographic details, location of incident, property descriptions, involvement of drugs and alcohol, and the involvement of gang activity. Prior to Jan 1, 2021, the Uniform Crime Reporting (UCR) Program collected crime data through its Summary Reporting System (SRS), which was narrower in scope. The SRS used a hierarchy rule that counted only the most serious crime within a criminal incident and led to an undercount of crimes. The NIBRS eliminates the hierarchy rule and counts up to 10 offenses within a single incident.

Data Collection: State UCR programs streamline the collection of NIBRS data from the local law enforcement agencies (LEAs) under their administration, ensure consistency and comparability of data, and provide quality service to the law enforcement community. Local enforcement agencies report data on offenses based on reports of crime received from victims, law enforcement officers, and other sources on a monthly basis to the FBI through the state UCR program or directly. The NIBRS submissions also include an indication of whether an offense was motivated by an offender's bias regarding race, ethnicity, ancestry, religion, sexual orientation, disability, gender, or gender identity, and information on law enforcement officers killed or assaulted. Data must be prepared in accordance to UCR standards. Beginning with the 2013 data collections, all data must be submitted electronically.

Data Quality Procedures: The UCR program examines each NIBRS submission for accuracy and deviations in crime data on a monthly and annual basis. UCR personnel compare aggregated data from agencies of similar population size to detect any unusual fluctuations in an agency's crime counts and study monthly data to evaluate periodic trends. Deviations are brought back to the state UCR program or reporting agency for verification or correction as needed. The accuracy of statistics depends primarily on program participants' adherence to standards of reporting.

Estimates of Sampling Error: Not applicable.

Sources of Additional Material: U.S. Department of Justice, Federal Bureau of Investigation, <www.fbi.gov/how-we-can-help-you/more-fbi-services-and-information/ucr>; data and reports available on FBI's Crime Data Explorer include methodologies, online at <cde.ucr.cjis.gov/LATEST/webapp/#/pages/home>.

U.S. INTERNAL REVENUE SERVICE, Statistics of Income (SOI)

Corporation Income Tax Returns

Universe, Frequency, and Types of Data: Annual study of unaudited income tax returns filed by corporations or businesses legally defined as corporations. The IRS Statistics of Income (SOI) Division produces estimates of corporate assets, liabilities, receipts, deductions, net income, income tax liability, tax credits, and other financial data. Data are presented with detail by industry, asset size, business receipts size, and other categories. SOI aggregates these data for corporations and passthrough entities, such as S corporations. The target population consists of all returns of active corporations organized for profit that are required to file one of the 1120 forms that are part of the SOI study. The survey universe generally consists of over 6 million active corporate returns from which the IRS chooses a sample of about 120,000 returns to produce statistical estimates. Tax returns are allocated to sample classes based on type of return, and either size of total assets alone or both size of total assets and a measure of income. Sampling rates for sample classes varied from 0.25 percent to 100 percent. Please note that changes in tax laws affect comparability of data from year to year.

Data Collection and Imputation: Corporate tax returns are posted to the IRS business master file (BMF). The sampling period spans 24 months to accommodate various accounting periods and extensions of filing deadlines. Data processing for SOI begins with information already extracted for IRS administrative purposes; over 100 items available from the Business Master File system are checked and corrected as necessary. SOI extracts some 2,500 additional data items from corporate tax returns during processing. After data capture, data go through hundreds of tests for consistency and error resolution. The SOI addresses missing data items and identifies returns to be excluded from the study. For missing balance sheet items, as of tax year 2012, only the largest returns with incomplete balance sheets are subject to a balance sheet imputation procedure. The IRS's Statistics of Income (SOI) division performs imputation on an ad hoc basis only. For other items, SOI uses various methods to impute data for some certainty returns

unavailable for editing, depending on the information available. The data completion process includes identifying returns not eligible for the sample (duplicates and other out-of-scope returns).

Measures of Variability: Estimated coefficients of variation for selected data are published in the Statistics of Income, *Corporation Complete Report*, and are also available with data tables online.

Sources of Additional Material: U.S. Internal Revenue Service, Statistics of Income, *Corporation Income Tax Returns*, <www.irs.gov/statistics/soi-tax-stats-corporation-tax-statistics>.

Individual Income Tax Returns

Universe, Frequency, and Types of Data: Annual study of unaudited individual income tax returns, Forms 1040, 1040A, and 1040EZ, filed by U.S. citizens and residents. Beginning tax year 2019, also included is form 1040-SR, for taxpayers born before January 2, 1955. The IRS compiles data on sources of income, adjusted gross income, exemptions, deductions, taxable income, income tax, modified income tax, tax credits, self-employment tax, and tax payments. Data include detail by size of adjustable income and other items. Please note that changes in tax laws affect comparability of data from year to year.

Data Collection and Processing: Data are collected for returns processed during the most recent year available, which mostly includes returns for a single tax year but can also include returns for earlier tax years that were filed and processed during the year of processing. Thus, returns processed in 2022 include mostly returns filed for tax year 2021 but also a few returns for earlier tax years. All returns processed during the year of coverage are subject to sampling except tentative and amended returns. Tax returns are classified into one of 4 subpopulations, strata, and each strata are sampled at a rate of 0.10 percent to 100 percent. Data are captured and processed electronically. The administrative data and controlling information for each record designated for the sample are loaded into an online submission processing database. Computer data for the selected administrative records are then used to identify inconsistencies, questionable values, and missing values, as well as any additional variables that an editor needs to extract for each record. After the submission processing center review, data are further validated, tested, and balanced. Adjustments and imputations are made for selected items based on prior-year data and other available information.

Measures of Variability: Coefficients of variation and confidence intervals are provided along with selected data tables in the report and online at the website, both indicated below.

Sources of Additional Material: U.S. Internal Revenue Service, Statistics of Income, *Individual Income Tax Returns* (Publication 1304), annual, <www.irs.gov/statistics/soi-tax-stats-individual-income-tax-returns-complete-report-publication-1304>, and <www.irs.gov/statistics/soi-tax-stats-individual-income-tax-return-form-1040-statistics>.

U.S. NATIONAL CENTER FOR HEALTH STATISTICS (NCHS)

National Health Interview Survey (NHIS)

Universe, Frequency, and Types of Data: Since 1957, the NHIS has been a continuous data collection covering the civilian noninstitutional population in the 50 states and the District of Columbia to obtain information on health indicators by demographic and socioeconomic characteristics. The NHIS universe includes residents of households and noninstitutional group quarters (e.g., homeless shelters, group homes). Persons excluded from the universe are those with no fixed household address (e.g., homeless and/or transient persons not residing in shelters), active duty military personnel and civilians living on military bases, persons in long-term care institutions (e.g., nursing homes for the elderly), persons in correctional facilities, and U.S. nationals living in foreign countries. Civilians residing with Armed Forces personnel in non-military housing are eligible to be sampled. The sampling plan is redesigned after every decennial census. A new sampling plan for the 2016–2025 NHIS was designed with results of the 2010 decennial census. Commercial address lists are used as the main source of addresses, supplemented by field listing. Beginning in 2019, the sample is expected to yield 30,000 sample adult and 9,000 sample child completed interviews. The annual sample size can be reduced or increased as needed. Every year the survey collects data on demographic characteristics and selected health topics, including health insurance coverage, chronic conditions, health care access and use, health-related behaviors, and functioning and disability. Additional topics are covered on a rotating basis, including mental health, preventive services, chronic pain, sleep, physical activity, and other topics. Please note that the content and structure of the NHIS were redesigned and updated in 2019. Details of the NHIS redesign are available online at <www.cdc.gov/nchs/nhis/about_nhis. htm> and <www.cdc.gov/nchs/nhis/ 2019_quest_redesign.htm>.

Data Collection: The U.S. Census Bureau collects data for the NHIS. Several hundred interviewers across the country conduct personal face-to-face interviews in respondents' homes; follow-up interviews may be conducted by telephone. Telephone interviews are also used at the request of the respondent, or when travel conditions are difficult. The interview begins with a household roster to ask basic demographic information for everyone in the household. One sample adult from each household is randomly selected to answer detailed questions about his or her health. One sample child, if present, is also randomly selected from each household and an adult knowledgeable and responsible for the child's health answers questions about the child's health. Prior to the 2019 NHIS, the survey also included a separate family questionnaire; questions at the family level are now included in the sample adult and sample child surveys.

Data Reliability: NHIS Adult and Child Summary Health Statistics contain estimates and confidence intervals for all data items. All estimates shown meet the NCHS standards of reliability as specified in *National Center for Health Statistics Data Presentation Standards for Proportions*. Detailed and technical documentation are available online.

Special Note: Due to the coronavirus disease 2019 (COVID-19) pandemic, NHIS data collection switched to a telephone-only mode beginning March 19, 2020. Personal visits resumed in all areas in September 2020 but cases were still attempted by telephone first through April 2021. Starting in May 2021, interviewers were instructed to return to regular survey interviewing procedures, whereby first contact attempts to households were made in person, with follow-up allowed by telephone. Changes to 2020 NHIS data collection resulted in lower response rates and differences in respondent characteristics for April–December 2020. Differences observed in estimates between 2020 and other time periods may be impacted by these changes.

Sources of Additional Material: National Center for Health Statistics, National Health Interview Survey, online at <www.cdc.gov/nchs/nhis/shs.htm>, with additional information at <www.cdc.gov/nchs/nhis/ about_nhis.htm>. Technical documentation, including survey description documents organizationed by year are online at <www.cdc.gov/nchs/nhis/data-questionnaires- documentation.htm>.

National Survey of Family Growth (NSFG)

Universe, Frequency, and Types of Data: The National Survey of Family Growth (NSFG) gathers information on pregnancy and births, marriage and cohabitation, infertility, use of contraception, and general and reproductive health. The NSFG also collects data on sexual behavior and attraction, and sexual orientation. The NSFG began in 1973 as a periodic survey of ever-married women age 15-44 among the civilian noninstitutionalized population. In 1982, the survey covered all women regardless of marital status; in 2002, men were included in the survey; and in 2015 the age range expanded to cover people age 15-49. Periodic surveys were conducted 1973 to 2002. Beginning in 2006, the survey employed continuous interviewing. The most recent NSFG data available for coverage come from the 2011 to 2019 interviewing period, which gathered data in 2-year increments and overall completed approximately 23,000 interviews with women and 19,000 interviews with men. Overall weighted response rate for the 2011-2019 period is 67.7 percent.

Data Collection: Survey participation is voluntary. Only one person is interviewed in a selected household. Signed consent is required for minors age 15-17. The NSFG collects data by employing female interviewers to conduct personal interviews using computer-assisted personal interviewing (CAPI). Selected data items are also collected using audio computer-assisted self-interviewing (ACASI). In ACASI, the respondent listens to the questions through headphones, reads them on the screen, or both, and enters the response directly into the computer. This method avoids asking the respondent to give his or her answers to the interviewer and it has been found to yield more complete reporting of sensitive behaviors.

Imputation: In the NSFG, item imputation is performed on a number of "recoded variables," or "recodes," rather than all of the thousands of variables in the data set. For the 2017-2019 NSFG, most missing recode values were assigned using regression imputation software in which multiple regression was used to predict a value for the case using other variables in the data set as predictors. For each variable with missing data, a regression model was estimated to predict the values for the missing data. In some cases, recodes were imputed using logical imputation, which involved having a subject-matter expert at NCHS examine variables related to the variable in question, and assign a value that was consistent with those other variables. Logical imputation is an educated guess of the true value when there is any ambiguity.

Data Quality: Data releases generally include standard errors. The NSFG utilizes the following to maintain high quality data: 1) questionnaire design work, 2) consistency checks built into the interview to enable the interviewer to resolve problems in the field, 3) evaluation of monthly data files to find and correct survey instrument problems, and 4) extensive interviewer training. The NSFG website provides detailed documentation that cover survey design and methods, variance estimation examples, and survey instruments. See "Questionnaires, Datasets, and Related Documentation" for each cycle of the NSFG online at <www.cdc.gov/nchs/ nsfg/nsfg_questionnaires.htm>.

Sources of Additional Material: National Center for Health Statistics, National Survey of Family Growth, online at <www.cdc.gov/nchs/nsfg/about_nsfg. htm>.

National Vital Statistics System

Universe, Frequency, and Types of Data: Vital statistics for the United States are obtained from the official records of live births, deaths, fetal deaths, marriages, divorces, and annulments. The official recording of these events is the responsibility of the individual States, the District of Columbia, New York City, and 5 territories (Puerto Rico, the Virgin Islands, Guam, American Samoa, and the Commonwealth of the Northern Mariana Islands) in which the event occurs. The Federal Government obtains use of the records for statistical purposes through a cooperative arrangement with the responsible agency in each State and area. Data are published annually.

Data Collection: Jurisdictions record vital events. Through its Vital Statistics Cooperative Program, NCHS cooperates with state vital statistics offices to develop and recommend standard forms for data collection, model regulations, and procedures to ensure uniform reporting of the events. The National Vital Statistics System uses electronic systems to collect data, including an electronic death reporting system. NVSS is working with states to modernize systems to improve the timeliness and quality of vital statistics data.

Data Reliability: Currently, there is no sampling for these files; the files are based on 100 percent of certificates registered. Generally more than 99 percent of the births and deaths occurring in this country are registered. Reports presenting vital statistics data include technical notes with further information on data sources and where to find information on methods and data reliability.

Sources of Additional Material: U.S. National Center for Health Statistics, National Vital Statistics System,

<www.cdc.gov/nchs/nvss/about_nvss.htm>; and individual reports and technical documentation for data of interest available via the NVSS website, <www.cdc.gov/nchs/nvss/index.htm>.

National Highway Traffic Safety Administration (NHTSA)

Fatality Analysis Reporting System (FARS)

Universe, Frequency, and Types of Data: FARS is a census of all fatal motor vehicle traffic crashes that occur throughout the United States, including the District of Columbia and Puerto Rico, on roadways customarily open to the public. The crash must be reported to the state/jurisdiction, and is classified as fatal if a directly related fatality occurs within thirty days of the crash. The FARS database contains descriptions, in a standardized format, of each fatal crash reported. Each crash has over 140 different coded elements that characterize the crash, the vehicles, and the people involved. The specific data elements may be modified slightly each year to conform to changing user needs, vehicle characteristics, and highway safety emphasis areas. Data are in two versions of annual files, with the second report for the year being the final file with additional cases or updates.

Data Collection and Imputation: NHTSA has a cooperative agreement with an agency in each State government to provide specific information in a standard format on fatal crashes occurring in the State. State analysts extract data from state documents and enter the data into a standardized electronic database. State documents include police crash reports, death certificates, state vehicle registration files, coroner/medical examiner reports, emergency medical service reports, and other types of files and records. Each analyst interprets and codes data directly into an electronic data file. The data are automatically checked when entered for acceptable range values and for consistency, enabling the analyst to make corrections immediately. Several programs continually monitor and improve the completeness and accuracy of the data. The FARS incorporates a sophisticated mathematical multiple imputation procedure to develop a probability distribution of missing blood alcohol concentration (BAC) levels in the database for drivers, pedestrians, and pedalcyclists.

Data Reliability: Since this is census data, there are no sampling errors. Data are dependent on the accuracy of police crash reports and other reports, which may contain errors or omissions that go undetected.

Sources of Additional Material: Fatality Analysis Reporting System (FARS), online at <www.nhtsa.gov/research-data/fatality-analysis-reporting-system-fars>; and *Fatality Analysis Reporting System Analytical User's Manual, 1975-2022,* online at <crashstats.nhtsa.dot.gov/#!/ DocumentTypeList/23>.

Appendix IV
Weights and Measures

U.S. Customary/Metric Conversion Table

[Conversions provided in the table are approximate]

Symbol	When you know U.S. customary	Multiply by	To find metric	Symbol
in	inches	2.54	centimeters	cm
ft	feet	30.48	centimeters	cm
yd	yards	0.91	meters	m
mi	miles	1.61	kilometers	km
in^2	square inches	6.45	square centimeters	cm^2
ft^2	square feet	0.09	square meters	m^2
yd^2	square yards	0.84	square meters	m^2
mi^2	square miles	2.59	square kilometers	km^2
	acre	0.41	hectare	ha
oz	ounces	28.35	grams	g
lb	pounds	0.45	kilograms	kg
oz (troy)	troy ounces	31.1	grams	g
	short tons (2,000 lb)	0.91	metric tons	t
	long tons (2,240 lb)	1.02	metric tons	t
fl oz	fluid ounces	29.57	mililiters	mL
c	cups	0.24	liters	L
pt	pints	0.47	liters	L
qt	quarts	0.95	liters	L
gal	gallons	3.79	liters	L
ft^3	cubic feet	0.03	cubic meters	m^3
yd^3	cubic yards	0.76	cubic meters	m^3
°F	degrees Fahrenheit (subtract 32)	0.55	degrees Celsius	°C

Symbol	When you know metric	Multiply by	To find U.S. customary	Symbol
cm	centimeters	0.39	inches	in
cm	centimeters	0.03	feet	ft
m	meters	1.09	yards	yd
km	kilometers	0.62	miles	mi
cm^2	square centimeters	0.16	square inches	in^2
cm^2	square centimeters	10.76	square feet	ft^2
m^2	square meters	1.2	square yards	yd^2
km^2	square kilometers	0.39	square miles	mi^2
ha	hectare	2.47	acre	
g	grams	0.04	ounces	oz
kg	kilograms	2.20	pounds	lb
g	grams	0.04	troy ounces	oz (troy)
t	metric tons	1.1	short tons (2,000 lb)	
t	metric tons	0.98	long tons (2,240 lb)	
mL	mililiters	0.03	fluid ounces	fl oz
L	liters	4.23	cups	c
L	liters	2.11	pints	pt
L	liters	1.06	quarts	qt
L	liters	0.26	gallons	gal
m^3	cubic meters	35.31	cubic feet	ft^3
m^3	cubic meters	1.31	cubic yards	yd^3
°C	degrees Celsius (after multiplying, add 32)	1.8	degrees Fahrenheit	°F

Source: National Institute of Standards and Technology (NIST), Office of Weights and Measures. See <www.nist.gov/pml/owm/metric-si/unit-conversion>

Index

[NOTE: Index citations refer to **table** numbers, not **page** numbers]

Note: Index citations refer to **table** numbers, not **page** numbers

Note: Index citations refer to **table** numbers, not **page** numbers

Grandparents living with grandchildren, 69
Health and dental care visits, 181, 192, 223
Heart disease, deaths, 118, 123
Housing, 36, 1048
Income, 36
Internet access and use, 1183
Jail inmates, 391
Life expectancy, 107
Marital status, 72
Occupation, 36
Poverty, 36, 755
Public assistance, 609
States, 20
Suicides, death, 118, 128
Teachers, 272, 273
Tribes, 43
Veterans, 558
Weapons in school, 333
American Samoa. (See Island areas of the U.S.)
American Sign Language, 303
American Stock Exchange, 1230
Amusement, gambling, and recreation industry:
Capital, 817
Earnings, 665, 791, 1251
Employees, 665, 791, 1248, 1251
Establishments, 791, 1248, 1250, 1251
Gaming revenue, 1278
Gross domestic product, 708
Nonemployer establishments, 1250
Productivity, 673
Receipts, revenue, 791, 1247, 1248, 1250
Amusement parks, 1009, 1247, 1248, 1250, 1251, 1265
Ancestry, 54
Andorra. (See Foreign countries.)
Anemia, deaths, 119
Anesthesiologists, 171
Angola. (See Foreign countries.)
Animal oils and fats. (See Oils, animal.)
Animal slaughtering and processing industry, 665, 673, 917, 918
Animals, domestic (see also individual classes):
Livestock, 860, 913, 915
Pets, 665, 1262, 1300
Annuities. (See Pensions and retirement benefits.)
Antigua and Barbuda. (See Foreign countries.)
Antimony, 950
Anxiety, 207
Apparel goods (see also Clothing and accessory stores):
Consumer expenditures, 716, 725, 729, 730
Foreign trade, 1323, 1324, 1329
Prices, 764, 765, 766, 775, 776
Sales, 1077, 1088
Apparel manufacturing:
Capital, 817
Earnings, 665, 1057, 1063
Employees, 665, 1055, 1057, 1059, 1063
Establishments, 1055, 1057
Foreign trade, 1324
Gross domestic product, 708, 1054
Industrial production index, 826
Productivity, 673
Shipments, 1057, 1065, 1066

Toxic chemical releases, 428
Appeals Courts, U.S., 379, 381
Apples, 238, 771, 884, 908, 912
Appliances, household:
Consumer expenditures, 716, 729, 730
Homes with, 1032, 1042, 1043
Injuries associated, 209
Price indexes, 766, 775
Sales and shipments, 1088
Appliances (household) manufacturing:
Inventories, 1066
Shipments, 1066
Apricots, 908
Aquaculture, (see also Fisheries and fish products under Natural resources), 417, 884, 945
Architects, 323, 324, 326, 647, 1249
Architectural services. (See Engineering and architectural services.)
Area of:
Developed land, 413, 414
Foreign countries, 1356
Forest land, 413, 414, 415, 929
Horticultural crops, 903
Island areas of the U.S., 404
Lakes, 405, 406, 407
Parks, 1272, 1273, 1274, 1275
States, 404
Timberland, 929
United States, 1, 404, 1356
Water, 1, 404, 413, 414, 416
World, 1356
Argentina. (See Foreign countries.)
Arizona. (See State data.)
Arkansas. (See State data.)
Armed Forces, 544, 545, 546, 547, 549
Armenia. (See Foreign countries.)
Army, personnel, 545
Arrests. (See Law enforcement.)
Arson, 369, 370, 403
Artists, employed, 647, 1249
Arts and humanities:
Aid to, 1255
Appropriations by state, 1256
Attendance, 1254, 1257
Charitable contributions, 617
Federal aid, 1255
Participation, 1258
States, 1256
Arts, entertainment, and recreation:
Capital, 817, 819
Earnings, 663, 665, 676, 791, 806, 807, 808, 809, 810, 811
Electronic commerce, 1298
Employees, 654, 663, 665, 671, 791, 794, 806, 807, 808, 809, 810, 811, 1248, 1249, 1251, 1252, 1253
Establishments, 671, 791, 792, 794, 795, 805, 806, 807, 808, 809, 810, 811, 1248, 1250, 1251
Finances, 785, 1247
Gaming, 1278
Gross domestic product, 708
Hires and separations, 669, 670
Hours, 663

Note: Index citations refer to **table** numbers, not **page** numbers

Note: Index citations refer to **table** numbers, not **page** numbers

(Births and birth rates, continued)
  Black, African American population, 80, 81, 82, 83,
    85, 86, 87, 90, 91, 92, 93
  Cesarean section deliveries, 83
  Characteristics of mother, 80, 82, 83, 85, 86, 87,
    89, 90, 91, 92, 93, 94, 95, 96
  Delivery characteristics, 83, 84, 88, 89, 90
  Education, 91, 94, 95
  First births, 93
  Foreign countries, 1360
  Hispanic population, 80, 81, 82, 83, 85, 86, 87,
    90, 91, 92, 93
  Household income, 96
  Induction of labor, 89
  Island areas of the U.S., 81, 1333
  Life expectancy, 103, 104, 105, 106, 107, 1361
  Native Hawaiian, Other Pacific Islander, 80, 81, 85,
    86, 87, 91
  Nativity, 91, 95
  Poverty, 91, 95
  Premature, 90
  Race, 80, 81, 82, 83, 85, 86, 87, 90, 91, 92, 93
  States, 16, 81, 88, 95
  Twin and multiple, 82
Births, businesses, 803
Bismuth, 950
Black, African American population, 6, 8, 9, 12, 13,
  20, 36, 40
  Adoption, 607
  Age and/or sex, 6, 8, 9, 12
  AIDS and/or HIV, 198, 199
  Birth and birth rates, 80, 81, 82, 83, 85, 86, 87,
    90, 91, 92
  Body weight, 220, 221
  Bullying, 335, 336
  Business owners, 809
  Cancer, 193, 195
  Child care, 604, 608
  Children, 8, 9, 12, 68
    Obesity, 234
    Poverty, 750, 751
  Cigarette smoking and tobacco use, 212, 237
  Congress, members of, 463
  Consumer expenditures, 729
  Contraceptive use, 97, 101
  Criminal victimizations, 344, 345, 346, 349, 352,
    358
  Deaths and death rates, 108, 109, 110, 114, 115,
    116, 118, 123, 126, 127, 128, 132, 344
  Degrees conferred, 294, 322, 850
  Disabled persons, 202, 301
  Educational attainment, 36, 252, 253, 254, 255
  Elderly, 8, 9, 12, 751
  Families, characteristics, 36, 66
  Food stamp participants, 576, 603
  Foster care, 607
  Grandparents living with grandchildren, 66, 69
  Hate crimes, 352
  Health and dental care visits, 181, 184, 192, 223
  Health insurance coverage, 162, 163, 164
  Heart disease, deaths, 118, 123
  Homeschooled, 279
  Homicides, 118, 344, 346
  Households, characteristics, 61, 72

Housing, 36, 1035, 1039, 1045, 1048, 1050, 1051
Immunization of children, 232
Income, 36, 574, 575, 731, 732, 734, 736, 737,
  738, 741, 744, 745
Infant deaths, 114, 115
Internet access and use, 1182, 1183, 1189
Jail inmates, 391, 392
Job search, 656
Labor force, 621, 622, 623, 627, 630, 635, 680,
  702
  Displaced workers, 644
  Earnings, 255, 504, 680, 685, 688
  Educational attainment, 627, 630, 641, 653, 660
  Employed, 504, 622, 623, 639, 641, 642, 647,
    653, 654
  Industry, 654, 1294
  Multiple job holders, 639
  Unemployed, 622, 623, 630, 655, 656, 660
Leisure time use, 1267
Life expectancy, 103, 104, 107
Living arrangements, 68
Marital status, 58, 62, 72
Maternal mortality, 116
Minimum wage workers, 685
Nurses, 647
Occupations, 36, 271, 647, 653
Poverty, 36, 749, 750, 751, 753, 754, 755
Property owners, 1035, 1039, 1045, 1050, 1051
Public assistance, 574, 575, 576, 603, 609
Recreation activities, 1257, 1258
Schools and education:
  College enrollment, 266, 286, 293, 294, 295,
    297, 298, 299, 305
  Degrees conferred, 850
  Enrollment, 249, 258, 266, 286, 293, 294, 297,
    298, 299, 630
  High school dropouts, 266, 286, 288, 289
  High school graduates, 266, 286, 295
  Historically Black Colleges and Universities, 294
  Parent participation, 265
  Teachers, 271, 272, 273, 274, 275, 647
  Weapons in school, 333
Sexual activity, 97, 101
States, 20
Suicides, 118, 128
Union membership, 702
Veterans, 558
Voter registration and turnout, 450, 452
Black lung benefit program, 513, 514, 572, 592, 593
Blast furnace and basic steel products. (See Iron and
  steel products.)
Blind persons, 228, 594
Blood alcohol concentration, 1136, 1139, 1140,
  1141
Blood poisoning (See Septicemia.)
Blueberries, 238, 884, 908, 912
Boats and boating (see also Ships), 1100, 1104,
  1116
Body Mass Index (BMI), 221
Bolivia. (See Foreign countries.)
Bolts, nuts, etc. (See Iron and steel products.)
Bonds:
  Foreign, 1228

Note: Index citations refer to **table** numbers, not **page** numbers

ProQuest Statistical Abstract of the United States: 2025

Note: Index citations refer to **table** numbers, not **page** numbers

---

Note: Index citations refer to **table** numbers, not **page** numbers

Note: Index citations refer to **table** numbers, not **page** numbers

Note: Index citations refer to **table** numbers, not **page** numbers

Note: Index citations refer to **table** numbers, not **page** numbers

Note: Index citations refer to **table** numbers, not **page** numbers

---

Note: Index citations refer to **table** numbers, not **page** numbers

Note: Index citations refer to **table** numbers, not **page** numbers

Manufacturing, 665, 925, 1057, 1062
Mineral industries, 946
Minimum wage workers, 684, 685
Minority-owned businesses, 807
Nonprofit employees, 671
Occupations, 649, 680, 682, 683, 686, 687, 1249
Personal income, 574, 575, 717, 719, 720, 721, 722
Private employer firms, 677, 678
Retail industries, 665, 1082
School teachers, 261, 270, 272, 275
States, 679
Union members, 702
Women, 680, 681, 686, 687, 689, 806
Earth sciences, degrees conferred, 851
Eating and drinking places. (See Food services and drinking places.)
E-commerce. (See Electronic commerce.)
Economic aid, foreign, 1313, 1314
Ecuador. (See Foreign countries.)
Education:
American College Testing (ACT) Program, 290
Attainment, 33, 36, 252, 253, 254, 256, 265, 1383
American Indian, Alaska Native population, 36, 288
Asian and Pacific Islander population, 252, 253
Asian population, 36, 252, 253, 254, 255, 288, 653
Black, African American population, 36, 252, 253, 254, 255, 286, 288, 289, 653
Earnings, 255, 681
Elderly, 33, 254
Families with children, 65
Foreign born, 40, 41
Foreign countries, 1383
Hispanic origin population, 36, 37, 252, 253, 254, 255, 286, 288, 289, 653
Income, 733, 739, 742
Internet access and use, 1182, 1183, 1185
Island areas of the U.S., 1334, 1338
Labor force status, 254, 305, 627, 660
Leisure time use, 1267
Native Hawaiian, Other Pacific Islander population, 36, 288
Occupation, 653
Race, 36, 286, 288
Recreation activities, 1257, 1267
States, 256
Student loan debt, 310
Women, 253, 254, 286, 288
Average class size, 280
Bullying, 332, 335, 336
Career and technical education (CTE), 287
Catholic schools, 268
Charitable contributions, 617
Charter schools, 281, 282, 283
College freshman, 306
Construction, value, 1009, 1010
Crime incidents, 330, 331, 333, 335
Degrees conferred, 321, 322, 323, 324, 325, 326, 327, 846, 847, 849, 850, 851
Earnings, 689
Nonresident, foreign students, 322
Salary offers, 320

Disabled students, 228, 229, 288, 301
Disciplinary problems, 332
Dress code, 334
Employment, state and local government, 505, 507
Enrollment, 245, 246, 247, 248, 249, 250, 251, 258, 261, 262, 263, 264, 266, 267, 269, 281, 292, 293, 295, 296, 297, 298, 299, 302, 303, 848
Catholic schools, 268
Disabled, 288, 301
Foreign, nonresident, 293, 297, 302
Homeschooling, 279
Island areas of the U.S., 1334, 1338
Preprimary schools, 250, 258, 266
States, 264, 293, 306
Expenditures:
Consumer expenditures, 716, 725, 729, 730, 776
Control, 244
Local government, 502
State and local government, 483, 484, 485, 491, 497, 500, 502, 517
Farm to school programs, 875
Federal aid, 243, 308, 312, 313, 314, 482, 512, 513, 571, 572, 573, 574, 575, 835, 837, 843, 844
Foreign countries, 1383
Fundraising, 265
Handicapped students, 228, 229, 301
Higher education institutions:
Admissions, 300
Campus crime, 330
Costs, 307, 309
Degrees conferred, 246, 321, 322, 323, 324, 325, 326, 327, 846, 847, 849, 850, 851
Distance education, 328
Dormitory charges, 307, 309
Employees, 318
Enrollment, 245, 246, 247, 250, 251, 292, 293, 295, 296, 297, 298, 299, 302, 303, 315, 328, 848
Expenditures, 244
Faculty, 292, 317, 318, 319
Federal funding, 243, 512
Finances, 244, 315
Financial aid, 308, 311, 312, 313, 314
Foreign languages, 303
Libraries, 329
Number, 292, 293, 300
Online course enrollment, 328
Price indexes, 316, 766
Research and development, 835, 837, 842, 843, 844, 1405
Salary offers, college graduates, 320
State appropriations, 315
Tuition and fees, 307, 309
Voluntary financial support, 311, 313, 314
High school dropouts, 266, 286, 288, 289
Homeschooling, 279
Island areas of the U.S., 1334, 1338
Language spoken at home, 257, 265
Literacy, 1383
Loans and grants, federal government, 308, 312, 313, 314

Note: Index citations refer to **table** numbers, not **page** numbers

Note: Index citations refer to **table** numbers, not **page** numbers

Note: Index citations refer to **table** numbers, not **page** numbers

Note: Index citations refer to **table** numbers, not **page** numbers

Productivity, 673
Shipments, 1057, 1065, 1066
Toxic chemical releases, 428
Fabrics. (See Textile mill products.)
Falls, accidental deaths, 119, 120
Families. (See Households.)
Family and consumer sciences, degrees conferred, 323, 324, 325, 326
Family farms, 863, 865, 871, 872
Farm loans, 1219, 1221
Farms:
  Acreage, 860, 861, 862, 863, 864, 865, 866, 867, 869, 872, 877
    Cropland, 413, 415, 860, 864, 901
    Crops harvested (see also individual crops), 901, 902, 904, 905, 906, 907, 1384
    Farm type, 863, 865, 872
  Agrichemicals, 882, 887, 892
  Agricultural products:
    Exports, 1388
    Foreign countries, production, 1385, 1386
    Market value, 860
    Prices. (See Prices received by farmers.)
    World production, 1384, 1385, 1386
  Assets and liabilities, 880
  Corporate, 863, 866, 872
  Crops (see also individual crops):
    Acreage, 860, 901, 902, 912, 1344
    Fruits and nuts, 908, 909, 912, 1331, 1345
    Income, 884, 885, 886, 1344
    Production, 896, 901, 902, 912, 1384, 1385
    Vegetables, 907, 911, 912
  Debt, 880, 1219
  Expenses, 879, 882
  Family or individual, 863, 865, 871, 1344
  Farm land and buildings value, 865, 866, 867, 880
  Farm operators, farmers, 870
  Farm products sold, marketing receipts, 865, 866, 867, 868, 869, 874, 876, 877, 881, 882, 884, 885, 886
  Farm to school programs, 875
  Fertilizers:
    Farm expenditures for, 882
    Foreign trade, 892, 1323
    Prices, 775, 887
  Government payments to farmers (subsidies), 868, 881, 882, 883, 889
  Gross farm value added, 708, 881
  Housing, rental value, 882
  Income, 871, 872, 881, 882, 883, 884, 886
  Inventories, change in, 881
  Labor expenses, 882
  Machinery and motor vehicles, 880, 882
  Mortgage loans, 1219
  Number of farms, 860, 861, 862, 863, 864, 865, 867, 868, 869, 876, 877
  Organic, 876, 877, 912, 913
  Parity ratio, 887
  Partnerships, 863, 865, 1344
  Prices, 887, 902, 915
  Renewable energy systems, 873
  Sales direct to consumers, 874, 876
  Taxes, 881, 887
  Value of land and buildings, 865, 866, 867, 880

Water use, 417
Farmers, characteristics, 870
Fat, consumption, 240, 241
Fatalities. (See Accidents and fatalities.)
Federal aid to education, 243, 482
  Elementary and secondary education, 243
  Higher education institutions, 243
  Research and development, 835, 837, 844
  Science and engineering, 843
Federal aid to state and local government, 481, 482, 483
Federal budget. (See Expenditures of U.S. government.)
Federal debt, 509, 1225
Federal employee's retirement trust fund. (See under Government.)
Federal government. (See Government.)
Federal government finances. (See Expenditures of U.S. government; and Receipts.)
Federal Highway Trust Fund, 1126, 1127
Federal Housing Administration, mortgage loans, 1220
Federal Transit Administration, 1153
Federal trust funds, 514, 515
Feed. (See Grain.)
Feedstock, 976
Feldspar, 949, 950
Female householders. (See Households or families.)
Female population. (See Women.)
Fencing, sport, 1270
Fentanyl, 131, 560
Ferry system, 1114
Fertility rates, 80, 81, 85, 1360
Fertilizers:
  Farm expenditures for, 882
  Foreign trade, 892, 1323
  Prices, 775, 887
Fetal deaths (neonatal), 113, 114
Fiber, dietary, 240, 241
Fiber, textiles, 773, 775
Field hockey, 1270
Fiji. (See Foreign countries.)
Filberts (hazelnuts), 908, 909
Filling stations. (See Gasoline stations.)
Finance and insurance industry:
  Capital, 817, 819, 1226
  Earnings, 663, 665, 676, 677, 791, 806, 807, 808, 809, 810, 811, 1194, 1196, 1197
  Electronic commerce, 1298
  Employees, 654, 663, 664, 665, 671, 791, 794, 799, 806, 807, 808, 809, 810, 811, 1194, 1196
  Establishments, 671, 791, 792, 794, 795, 799, 805, 806, 807, 808, 809, 810, 811, 1194, 1195, 1196
  Finances, 785, 1198, 1199, 1311, 1339
  Foreign investments in U.S., 1308, 1309
  Gross domestic product, 708, 712, 1339
  Hires and separations, 669, 670
  Hours worked, 663
  Multinational companies, 831, 833, 834, 1311
  Nonemployers, 792, 1195
  Occupational safety, 697, 699
  Profits, 829, 830

Note: Index citations refer to **table** numbers, not **page** numbers

Note: Index citations refer to **table** numbers, not **page** numbers

Note: Index citations refer to **table** numbers, not **page** numbers

Note: Index citations refer to **table** numbers, not **page** numbers

Construction, value, 1009, 1010
Coverage, 162
Dental care visits, 192, 207, 223
Expenditures, 138, 139, 140, 141, 143, 144, 145,
    147, 148, 159, 483, 484, 491, 497, 500, 502,
    512, 716, 725, 726, 728, 729, 730, 776, 1366
Government employment and payrolls, 505, 507
Government, federal expenditures, 144, 145, 149,
    482, 512, 513
Hospitals, 185, 187, 188, 189, 190
Industry, 167, 168, 170, 665, 817
Long-term care facilities, 175
Medicaid, 139, 140, 142, 145, 149, 153, 156, 158,
    159, 162, 482, 513
Medicare, 139, 140, 142, 145, 149, 150, 151, 152,
    153, 154, 155, 160, 162, 185, 512, 513
Mental health treatment, 176, 177, 178, 185, 224,
    227
Nursing homes, 138, 140, 141, 145, 152, 175,
    185, 186
Occupations, 170, 173, 180, 647, 853, 856
Price indexes, 146, 766
Salary, 856
Security breaches, 169
Substance abuse treatment, 179, 214
Veterans' health care, 139, 142, 149, 177
Heart disease, 123, 205
    Deaths, 117, 118, 119, 120, 121, 122, 123
Heating and plumbing equipment, 1012, 1032, 1044
Heating oil, 768
HVAC and commercial refrigeration equipment
    manufacturing, 665
Heavy and civil engineering construction, 665, 1004,
    1005
Height, average, 219
Helium, 949
Hepatitis, 119, 197, 231, 232
Heroin, 130, 131, 215, 375
Higher education institutions:
    Admissions, 300
    Campus crime, 330
    Coronavirus disease 2019 (COVID-19), impact, 304
    Costs, 307, 309
    Degrees conferred, 246, 294, 321, 322, 323, 324,
        325, 326, 327, 846, 847, 849, 850, 851
    Distance education, 328
    Dormitory charges, 307, 309
    Employment, 318, 505, 507
    Enrollment, 245, 246, 247, 250, 251, 292, 293,
        294, 295, 296, 297, 298, 299, 302, 303, 315,
        848
    Expenditures, 244, 294
    Faculty, 292, 317, 318, 319
    Federal funding, 243
    Finances, 244, 294, 315
    Financial aid, 308, 311, 312, 313, 314
    Foreign-born students, 297, 302, 846, 848
    Foreign languages, 303
    Historically Black Colleges and Universities, 294
    Housing population, 70
    Libraries, 329
    Number, 292, 293, 294, 300
    Online course enrollment, 328
    Price indexes, 316, 766

Research and development, 835, 837, 843, 844,
    1405
Salary offers, college graduates, 320
State appropriations, 315
Tuition and fees, 307, 309
Voluntary financial support, 311, 313, 314
Highways:
    Accidents, 1104, 1134, 1135, 1136, 1137, 1138,
        1140, 1142, 1143, 1144, 1145
    Bridge inventory and condition, 1121
    Debt, state and local government, 1124
    Distracted driving, 1138
    Employees, government, 505, 507
    Expenditures:
        Local government, 485, 486, 502
        State and local government, 483, 484, 485, 486,
            491, 517
        State government, 485, 486, 497, 500
        U.S. government, 482, 517
    Funding, 1122, 1126, 1127
    Interstate highways, 1120
    Mileage, 1099, 1119, 1120
    Motor fuel consumption, 971, 1132
    Motor fuel tax, 1123, 1127
    Transit savings, 1149
    Types of roads, 1119, 1120
    Value of new construction, 1009, 1010
Hispanic or Latino origin population, 6, 8, 9, 12, 13,
    19, 36, 37, 42
    Adoption, 607
    Age and/or sex, 6, 8, 9, 12, 37
    AIDS and/or HIV, 198, 199
    Births and birth rates, 80, 81, 82, 83, 85, 86, 87,
        90, 91, 92, 93
    Body weight, 220, 221
    Bullying, student, 335, 336
    Business owners, 808
    Cancer, 193
    Child care, 604, 608
    Children, 8, 9, 12, 37, 68, 234
    College enrollment, 266, 286, 293, 295, 297, 298,
        299, 305
    Congress, members of, 463
    Consumer expenditure, 729
    Contraceptive use, 97, 101
    Criminal victimizations, 346, 349, 352, 358
    Deaths, 108, 110, 116, 118, 123, 126, 127, 128,
        132
    Degrees conferred, 322, 850
    Dental care visits, 192, 223
    Disability status, 202, 301
    Educational attainment, 36, 37, 252, 253, 254,
        255, 286, 295
    Elderly, 8, 9, 12, 751
    Elected officials, 463, 472
    Elections, voter registration and turnout, 450
    Families, characteristics, 36, 37, 66, 72
    Food stamp participants, 576, 603
    Foreign-born populations, 37, 41, 42, 623
    Foster care, 607
    Grandparents living with grandchildren, 66, 69
    Hate crimes, 352
    Health and dental care visits, 181, 184, 192
    Health insurance coverage, 162, 163, 164

Note: Index citations refer to **table** numbers, not **page** numbers

---

Note: Index citations refer to **table** numbers, not **page** numbers

---

Note: Index citations refer to **table** numbers, not **page** numbers

Note: Index citations refer to **table** numbers, not **page** numbers

---

Note: Index citations refer to **table** numbers, not **page** numbers

---

Note: Index citations refer to **table** numbers, not **page** numbers

L

Laboratories, medical and dental, 167, 170
Labor force (see also individual industries or
   occupations):
  Accidents and fatalities, 696, 697, 698, 699, 700
  Average pay, states, 679
  Back wages, 690
  Certification and license status, 688
  Civilian labor force:
    Age, 623, 625, 626, 631, 634, 642, 648, 655,
      656
    Asian and Pacific Islander population, 622
    Asian population, 36, 622, 623, 627, 630, 635,
      639, 642, 647, 653, 654, 655, 656, 660,
      680, 685, 688, 702
    Black, African American population, 36, 504,
      621, 622, 623, 627, 630, 635, 639, 642,
      647, 653, 654, 655, 656, 660, 680, 685,
      688, 702
    Displaced workers, 644
    Educational attainment, 623, 627, 641, 653,
      660, 675
    Employed, 620, 622, 623, 628, 630, 633, 634,
      635, 636, 639, 641, 643, 653, 654
    Females, 504, 622, 623, 626, 627, 628, 630,
      631, 632, 633, 635, 639, 642, 647, 660,
      685, 688, 702, 1294
    Foreign-born population, 623
    Hispanic origin population, 36, 37, 504, 621,
      622, 623, 627, 630, 635, 639, 642, 647,
      653, 654, 655, 656, 660, 680, 685, 688,
      702
    Hours worked, 634, 636, 675, 733
    Married couples with children, 633, 646
    Metropolitan areas, 629
    Minimum wage workers, 685
    Multiple job holders, 639, 675
    Native Hawaiian, Other Pacific Islander
      population, 36
    Not at work, 637
    Part-time, 643, 675, 685
    Participation rates, 621, 622, 627, 628, 631,
      632, 635
    Projections, 621, 651, 652
    Race, 36, 621, 622, 627, 630, 635, 647, 660,
      1294
    Reason not in, 645
    School enrollment, 305, 630
    Self-employed workers, 634, 638
    States, 628
    Unemployed, 620, 622, 623, 625, 628, 629,
      630, 655, 656, 657, 658, 659, 660, 661,
      662
    Women who had a birth in previous year, 94
  Commuting to work, 1147, 1151
  Contract employees, 648
  Disabled persons, 535, 625
  Displaced workers, 644
  Earnings, 663, 665, 676, 677, 678, 679, 680, 681,
    682, 686, 687, 688, 689
  Educational attainment, 254, 255, 627, 660, 688, 689
  Elderly, 33, 621, 623, 626, 631, 634, 639

Employee benefits, 165, 166, 503, 581, 584, 585,
   588, 675, 692, 694, 695
Employees, 504, 648, 663, 664, 665, 678, 803, 1059
Employer costs, 693
Employment cost index, 683, 772
Employment taxes and contributions, 514
  Females, 504, 621, 622, 626, 627, 628, 630, 631,
    632, 635, 642, 646, 647, 654, 655, 656, 657,
    658, 659, 660, 661, 666, 680, 682, 685, 688,
    702
Firm sizes, 845
Flexible schedules, 695
Foreign countries, 1372, 1381
Foreign-owned firms, 1307, 1310
Government. (See Government: Employees.)
Hires and separations, 669, 670
Hours, 636, 643, 663, 675, 1372
Indexes of compensation, 674
Internet access, 1167, 1183, 1185
Job creation, 802, 803
Job gains/losses, 667, 668, 669, 670, 802
Labor law compliance, 690
Labor strikes, 704
Marital status, 631, 632, 634, 635, 639
Metropolitan areas, 629
Minimum wage workers, 685
Mobility (geographic) status, 29
Occupational groups. (See Occupations, and
   individual occupations.)
Occupational safety, 696, 697, 698, 699, 700
On-call workers, 648
Parents, 633, 646
Part-time work, 643, 648, 675, 694, 695
Poverty status, 640, 752
Production workers, 1057, 1058, 1060, 1062, 1070
Productivity, 672, 673, 674, 1372
Projections, 621, 651, 652
Self-employed, 638, 854
Social insurance coverage, 577
State data, 628, 650, 662, 679
Telecommuting, 675, 695, 796, 801, 1186
Temporary nonimmigrant workers, 45
Tenure with employer, 642
Unemployed workers:
  Age, 623, 655, 656
  Asian and Pacific Islander population, 622, 655
  Asian population, 622, 623, 630, 655, 656, 660
  Black, African American population, 622, 623,
    630, 655, 656, 660
  Educational attainment, 254, 623, 630, 660
  Foreign countries, 1381
  Foreign-born population, 623
  Hispanic origin population, 37, 622, 623, 630,
    655, 656, 660
  Industry, 658
  Job search activities, 656
  Occupation, 659
  Race, 622, 623, 630, 655, 656, 660
  Reason, 645, 657, 661
  Sex, 622, 623, 628, 630, 655, 656, 657, 658,
    659, 660, 661
  States, 628, 662
Union membership, 701, 702, 703
Veterans, 535, 624

Note: Index citations refer to **table** numbers, not **page** numbers

---

Note: Index citations refer to **table** numbers, not **page** numbers

---

Note: Index citations refer to **table** numbers, not **page** numbers

Meditation, 206
Melons, 238, 907
Membership organizations:
  Earnings, 665
  Employees, 665, 1293, 1294
  Establishments, 1293
  Revenue, 1300
Meningitis, 197
Mental disorders and illness, 224, 227, 228, 230, 363, 700
Mental health hospitals and facilities, 167, 170, 176, 177, 178, 188, 189
Mercury, 950
Metal detectors, in public schools, 334
Metal ore mining industry, 946, 947, 948
Metals, 949, 950, 953
  Foreign trade, 950, 953, 1323, 1324
  Prices, 775, 779, 780, 950, 951
  Production and value, 948, 949, 950
  Recycling, 425
  Spot market price indexes, 773
  World production, 1389
Metalworking manufacturing, 665, 673, 1057, 1059
Methamphetamine (see also Drugs, illegal), 131, 215, 375, 560
Methane emissions, 422
Metropolitan statistical areas:
  Air quality index, 424
  Airline markets, 1105, 1107
  Civilian labor force, 629
  Commuting, 1151
  Components of change, 22
  Consumer expenditures, 726
  Consumer price index, 765
  Crime, 340
  Housing, 1021, 1031
  Migration, 22
  Personal income, 722
  Population, 21, 22, 23
  Science and engineering employment, 855
  States, 23
  Unemployment rate, 629
  Vacancy rates, housing, 1031
Mexican-origin population, 37
  Body weight, 221, 234
  Educational attainment, 37
  Labor force, 37, 622
Mexico. (See Foreign countries.)
Mica:
  Foreign trade (sheet), 950, 953
  Production and value, 949, 950
Michigan. (See State data.)
Micronesia, Federated States of. (See Foreign countries.)
Migration, 3, 4, 5, 16, 22, 28, 29, 30, 31, 32, 1357
Military assistance, 552, 1313, 1314
Military expenditures outlays, 541, 543, 1411
Military manpower, 544, 545, 546, 549
Military sciences, degrees conferred, 324, 325
Military services and personnel:
  Casualties, 548
  Pay grades, 546
  Personnel, 544, 545, 546, 549
  Retirement system, 547

Sexual assault, 551
Suicide, 548, 550
Milk, cream, and other dairy products:
  Consumption, 239, 921
  Prices, 771, 775, 921
  Production, 919, 920, 921
  Sales, 874, 885, 920
Mine safety, 947
Mineral fuels, 779, 780, 949, 951, 1323
Minerals and mineral products (see also Mining industry, and individual minerals):
  Foreign trade, 950, 953
  Imports as percent of consumption, 953
  Price indexes, 779, 780
  Prices, 950
  Production and value, 949, 950, 952, 1389
  World production, 1389
Minimum wage, 684, 685
Mining industry (see also Minerals and mineral products, and individual minerals):
  Capital, 817, 819
  Earnings, 665, 676, 791, 806, 807, 808, 809, 810, 811, 924, 925, 946
  Employees, 654, 665, 791, 794, 806, 807, 808, 809, 810, 811, 854, 924, 925, 946
  Establishments, 791, 792, 794, 795, 805, 806, 807, 808, 809, 810, 811, 924, 925
  Finances, 785
  Gross domestic product, 708, 926
  Industrial production index, 826
  Multinational companies, 831, 833, 834, 1311
  Nonemployers, 792
  Occupational safety, 697, 699, 947
  Productivity, 673
  Profits, 830
  Research and development, 841
  Sales and receipts, 785, 791, 792, 806, 807, 808, 809, 810, 811, 925
  Union membership, 702
Mining machinery, manufacturing, 665, 1057
Minnesota. (See State data.)
Missing persons, 376
Mississippi. (See State data.)
Mississippi River, freight, 1115
Missouri. (See State data.)
Mobile homes, 1019, 1032, 1033
Mobility (geographic) status of population, 27, 28, 29, 30, 31, 32
Moldova. (See Foreign countries.)
Molybdenum, 949, 950
Monaco. (See Foreign countries.)
Monetary authorities, 1196, 1197, 1198, 1227
Money market accounts, funds, 786, 787, 1198, 1200, 1201, 1202, 1225, 1237
Money orders, 1159
Money supply (stock), 1224
Mongolia. (See Foreign countries.)
Montana. (See State data.)
Montenegro. (See Foreign countries.)
Morocco. (See Foreign countries.)
Mortgage pools and trusts, 1198, 1199, 1219
Mortgages. (See Loans and mortgages.)
Motels. (See Hotels.)

Note: Index citations refer to **table** numbers, not **page** numbers

Motion picture and sound recording industry:
  Capital, 817
  Earnings, 665, 791, 1161, 1162
  Employees, 665, 791, 1161, 1162
  Establishments, 791, 1161, 1162
  Finances, 1166, 1173
  Gross domestic product, 708
  Productivity, 665
  Receipts, revenue, 791, 1162, 1166, 1172, 1298
Motor freight transportation and warehousing. (See
    Truck transportation industry, and Warehousing
    and storage industry.)
Motor fuel taxes, 1123
Motor vehicle alternative fuel stations, 1133
Motor vehicle and parts dealers, retail:
  Earnings, 665, 791, 797, 1082, 1089
  Electronic commerce, 1077, 1087
  Employees, 665, 791, 797, 1074, 1080, 1082, 1089
  Establishments, 791, 797, 1074, 1080, 1081, 1089
  Finances, 1089
  Franchises, 1089
  Inventories, 1086, 1089
  Nonemployers, 1081
  Price indexes, 766, 775, 776
  Profits, 1089
  Sales, 791, 1074, 1077, 1081, 1083, 1085, 1086,
    1087, 1089, 1091
Motor vehicle manufacturing:
  Capital, 817
  Earnings, 665, 1057, 1063
  Employees, 665, 1057, 1059, 1063, 1070, 1071
  Foreign trade, 1324, 1329, 1330
  Gross domestic product, 708, 1053
  Industrial production index, 826
  Inventories, 1067
  Productivity, 673
  Sales, 1057, 1067, 1070, 1071
  State data, 1071
Motor vehicles:
  Accidents/deaths, 119, 120, 122, 1104, 1134, 1135,
    1136, 1137, 1138, 1139, 1142, 1143
  Air pollutant emissions, 421
  Alternative fuel, 1133
  Buses, 971, 1100, 1128, 1131, 1132, 1286
  Common carriers, 1148
  Consumer expenditures, 716, 725, 726, 729, 730
  Crashes, 1137, 1138, 1142
  Distracted driving, 1138
  Drivers' licenses, 1129, 1130, 1144
  Electric vehicles and fueling stations, 1091, 1133
  Features, 1156, 1157
  Foreign trade, 779, 780, 1323
  Fuel consumed, 971, 1132, 1133
  Imports, 1090
  Injuries, 208
  Miles of travel, 1128, 1152, 1156, 1157
  Number, 1100
  Price indexes, 766, 775, 776, 779, 780
  Production, 1090
  Registrations, 1130, 1131
  Safety features, 1156
  Sales, 1089, 1090, 1091
  Service and repair shops. (See Automotive repair and
    maintenance service.)

Taxes, licenses and motor fuel, 484, 499
Theft, 330, 339, 340, 341, 342, 343, 348, 354
Traffic fatalities, 1134, 1135, 1136, 1138, 1139,
    1140, 1141, 1143, 1144, 1145
Trucks, 971, 1100, 1128, 1131, 1132, 1136, 1143,
    1156, 1157
Motorcycles, 1100, 1130, 1143
  Accidents and deaths, 1104, 1135, 1136, 1143
  Racing, 1269
Movie theaters, 1172
Mozambique. (See Foreign countries.)
Multinational companies, 831, 832, 833, 834, 1311
Multiple births, 82
Multiple job holders, 639, 675
Mumps, 197
Municipal and state bonds, 786, 787, 788, 1201,
    1232, 1233
Municipal waste, 425, 986
Municipalities. (See Cities and Metropolitan areas.)
Murders, 330, 339, 340, 343, 346, 347
Museums, 1252, 1257
Museums, historical sites:
  Earnings, 665, 791
  Employees, 665, 671, 791, 1248, 1251
  Establishments, 671, 791, 1248, 1250, 1251
  Federal aid, 1255
  Nonemployers, 1250
  Receipts, revenue, 791, 1247, 1248, 1250
Mushrooms, 238, 884
Music:
  Electronic commerce sales, 1088, 1173
  Industry shipments and value, 1173
  Listening to, 1257
Musicians and composers, 647, 1249
Mutton (see also Meat and meat products), 914
Mutual funds, 787, 788, 1198, 1200, 1201, 1202,
    1227, 1234, 1235, 1236, 1237, 1238

N

National Association of Securities Dealers (NASDAQ)
    stock prices, 1230
National College Athletic Association (NCAA) sports
    participation, 1270
National debt. (See Debt.)
National forests. (See Forests.)
National health expenditures, 138, 139, 140, 141,
    142, 143, 144, 145
National income (see also Gross domestic product),
    705, 706, 707, 709, 718
National Park Service, 1272, 1273, 1274
National Security. (See Defense, Department of;
    Homeland Security, Department of; and
    individual military services.)
Native Hawaiian, Other Pacific Islander, 6, 8, 9, 12, 13,
    20, 72
  Age and/or sex, 6, 8, 9, 12
  AIDS and/or HIV, 198, 199
  Births, 80, 81, 85, 86, 91
  Children, 8, 9, 12
  Deaths, 108, 109, 123, 126, 127, 128
  Educational attainment, 36, 288

Note: Index citations refer to **table** numbers, not **page** numbers

ProQuest Statistical Abstract of the United States: 2025

Elderly, 8, 9, 12
Grandparents, living with grandchildren, 69
Health and dental care visits, 181
Housing, 36, 1048
Income, 36, 72
Internet access and use, 1183
Marital status, 72
Occupation, 36
Poverty, 36
Suicide, 128
Teachers, 272, 273
Veterans, 558
Weapons in school, 333
Natural disasters. (See Disasters, natural.)
Natural gas:
  Consumption, 960, 968, 969, 971, 973, 989
    World, 1392, 1394
  Electricity generation, 990, 992
  Emissions, 423
  Expenditures, 975
  Foreign trade, 956, 969, 978, 979, 1323
  Pipelines, 1154
  Prices, 766, 768, 951, 960
  Production, 949, 956, 957, 958, 960, 961, 968, 969
    World, 960, 1389, 1391, 1396
  Reserves, 959, 960, 961
  Shale gas, 961
  Vehicles and fuel stations, 1133
Natural gas distribution industry, 665, 673, 826,
  966, 967
Natural gas plant liquids, 955, 956, 957, 961
Natural resources (see also Forest products, Minerals
  and mineral products, Paper and paperboard
  products, Timber, Wood products manufacturing,
  and individual resources and minerals):
  Federal outlays, 512, 839
  Fisheries and fish products (see also Aquaculture),
    940, 941, 942, 943, 944, 945
  Forests and timberland, 929, 930, 931, 932
  Governmental finances, 483, 484
    Aid to state and local governments, 482
    Government employment and payrolls, 507
    Governmental revenue, 484
    State and local governments, 483, 484, 485, 491
    State governments, 497
  Minerals, 951
    Coal, 962, 963, 964
    Employment, 946, 950
    Mining, 947, 948
    Natural gas, 955, 957, 958, 959, 960, 961
    Petroleum, 955, 958, 959
    Price, 950, 951
    Production, 949, 950, 952, 1389
    Products, 951
    Trade, 950, 953
    Uranium, 965, 985
  Paper products, 934, 936, 937, 938
  Wood products, 933, 934, 935, 936, 937
Natural resource-related industry (see also Mining
  industry, Oil and gas extraction, and individual
  industries):
  Employment, 507, 665, 669, 670, 677, 924, 925
  Establishments, 924, 925
  Gross domestic product, 926

Mineral industry, 946
  Oil and gas extraction, 946, 954
  Payroll and earnings, 665, 924, 925
  Petroleum industry, 955
  Sales and revenue, 925
  Timber-related industry, 927, 928
Naturalized citizens, 37, 40, 42, 46, 48, 452
Nauru. (See Foreign countries.)
Navy, personnel, 545
Nebraska. (See State data.)
Nectarines, 238, 908
Neonatal deaths (see also Deaths and death rates),
  114
Nepal. (See Foreign countries.)
Nephritis, nephrotic syndrome, and nephrosis (see
  also Kidney disease), 117, 118, 119, 120, 121
Netherlands. (See Foreign countries.)
Neurologists, 171
Nevada. (See State data.)
New Hampshire. (See State data.)
New Jersey. (See State data.)
New Mexico. (See State data.)
New York. (See State data.)
New York Stock Exchange, 1230
New Zealand. (See Foreign countries.)
Newspaper, book, and directory publishers:
  Earnings, 665, 1161
  Employees, 665, 1161, 1162
  Establishments, 1161, 1162
  Finances, 1166, 1169
  Productivity, 673
  Revenue, 1162, 1166, 1169
Newspapers (see also Publishing industry):
  Reading, 1167
Newsprint, 937, 938
Nicaragua. (See Foreign countries.)
Nickel:
  Consumption, 950
  Employment, 950
  Foreign trade, 950, 953
  Prices, 950, 951
  Production and value, 949, 950
  World production, 1389
Niger. (See Foreign countries.)
Nigeria. (See Foreign countries.)
Niobium, 950, 953
Nitrogen in ammonia, 950, 1389
Nonalcoholic beverages, 729, 730
Nonemployer establishments, 610, 792, 1075, 1081,
  1098, 1195, 1244, 1250, 1292
Nonimmigrant admissions, 45
Nonmetallic mineral mining and quarrying, except
  fuels, 817, 924, 946
Nonmetallic mineral product manufacturing (see also
  Metals and metal products):
  Earnings, 665, 1057, 1063
  Employees, 665, 1055, 1057, 1059, 1063
  Establishments, 1055
  Foreign trade, 1323, 1324
  Gross domestic product, 708, 1053
  Productivity, 673, 826
  Shipments, receipts, 1057, 1065, 1066
  Toxic chemical releases, 428

Note: Index citations refer to **table** numbers, not **page** numbers

Nonprofit organizations, 614, 618, 665, 671, 1300, 1301
North Carolina. (See State data.)
North Dakota. (See State data.)
North Korea. (See Foreign countries.)
Northern Mariana Islands. (See Island areas of the U.S.)
Norway. (See Foreign countries.)
Notifiable diseases, 197
Nuclear power, 983, 984, 985, 989, 990
    Capacity, 983, 984
    Consumption, 968, 969, 973, 1394
    Production, 968, 969, 983, 984, 989, 990, 992, 1390, 1391
    Reactors, 983, 984
    State data, 984, 992
Nursing and residential care facilities:
    Capital, 817
    Earnings, 665, 791
    Employees, 170, 665, 791
    Establishments, 185, 186, 791
    Expenditures, 138, 140, 141, 142, 145, 148
    Gross domestic product, 708
    Medicare utilization, 152
    Population, 70, 186
    Receipts, 167, 168, 791
Nursing personnel, 173, 180, 647, 649, 651
Nutrients and nutritional intake, 240, 241
Nutritional deficiencies, deaths, 119
Nuts, 239, 884, 897, 899, 908, 909

O

Obesity, 221, 222, 234, 1362
Obstetricians (see also Physicians), 171, 180
Occupational safety, 696, 697, 699, 947
Occupations (see also individual occupations):
    American Indian, Alaska Native population, 36
    Artists, 1249
    Asian population, 36, 647, 653
    Black, African American population, 36, 647, 653
    Earnings, 649, 680, 682, 687, 689
    Employment, 36, 647, 649, 650, 653, 682
    Employment cost index, 683, 772
    Hispanic origin population, 36, 647, 653
    Island areas of the U.S., 1349
    Mobility (geographic) status, 29
    Native Hawaiian, Other Pacific Islander population, 36
    Retirement and health plan benefits, 694
    Self-employed, 638
    Science and engineering, 852, 853, 854, 856
    Women, 647, 687, 689
Office buildings. (See Commercial buildings.)
Office equipment, 1088
Office supplies, stationery, and gift stores, 665, 673, 1080, 1081, 1082, 1083
Ohio. (See State data.)
Oil. (See Petroleum and products.)
Oil and gas extraction industry:
    Capital, 817
    Earnings, 665, 791, 924, 925, 946
    Employees, 651, 665, 791, 924, 925, 946, 954
    Establishments, 791, 924, 925, 954

Gross domestic product, 708, 926
Output, 948
Payroll, 954
Production indexes, 948
Productivity, 673
Shipments, receipts, 791, 925
Oil crops, 882, 887, 890, 891, 894
Oil spills, 432
Oils:
    Animal oils and fats, 1323
    Prices, 775
    Vegetable, 891, 897, 899, 1323
Oilseeds, 779, 884, 891, 897, 1323, 1384, 1385
Oklahoma. (See State data.)
Old-age pensions. (See Pensions.)
Old-age, survivors, disability, and health insurance. (See Social insurance.)
Olives, 908
Oman. (See Foreign countries.)
Onions, 238, 884, 907, 912
Online. (See Internet access and use.)
Operations. (See Surgical procedures.)
Ophthalmologists, 171
Opioid/opiate drugs, 130, 131, 132, 179, 217, 375, 560
Opioid addiction treatment, 179, 214
Optometrists, 167
Oranges, 238, 771, 884, 908, 912
Oregon. (See State data.)
Ores, crude (see also individual ores), 1323
Organ transplants, 201
Organic agriculture, 876, 877, 912, 913
Osteopathic physicians, 171, 172
Outdoor, recreation activities (see also Recreation, and specific forms of recreation), 1259, 1276
Outlays, federal budget (see also Expenditures of U.S. government), 149, 508, 510, 511, 512, 513, 857
Outpatient care centers, 167, 168, 170, 176, 177, 178, 180, 185, 652, 665
Outpatient hospital visits, 184, 189, 190
Overweight persons, 220, 221, 222, 1362
Oxycodone, 131
Oysters, 941, 942

P

Pakistan. (See Foreign countries.)
Palau. (See Foreign countries.)
Panama. (See Foreign countries.)
Papayas, 238
Paper and paperboard products:
    Foreign trade, 779, 780, 1323
    Prices, 775, 779, 780, 937
    Production, 936, 938
    Recycling, 425
Paper products, manufacturing:
    Capital, 817
    Earnings, 665, 924, 925, 928, 1057, 1063
    Employees, 665, 924, 925, 927, 928, 1055, 1057, 1059, 1063
    Establishments, 924, 925, 927, 1055

Note: Index citations refer to **table** numbers, not **page** numbers

Foreign trade, 1323, 1324
Gross domestic product, 708, 926, 1053
Industrial production index, 826
Output, 938
Productivity, 673
Sales, 925, 927, 928, 1057, 1065, 1066
Toxic chemical releases, 428
Papua New Guinea. (See Foreign countries.)
Paraguay. (See Foreign countries.)
Pardons, presidential, 372
Parent-Teacher Association/Organization (PTA/PTO), 265
Parent-teacher conferences, 265
Paris CAC-40 stock market index, 1404
Parkinson's disease, deaths, 119, 120
Parks, 491, 500, 502, 505, 507, 1272, 1273, 1274, 1275
Parolees (see also Correctional institutions, and Prisoners), 397, 398
Parties, political. (See Political parties.)
Partnerships, establishments and finances, 781, 782, 784, 785, 790
Passenger transit industry (see also Passengers), 665, 776, 971, 1114, 1148, 1149
Passengers (see also Passenger transit industry, and various transportation modes):
  Arriving from overseas, 1283, 1284, 1285, 1287, 1290
  Border crossings, 1286
  Carrier operation, summary, 1148
  Ferry system, 1114
  Screenings, 570
Patents and trademarks, 814, 815, 1402
Paycheck Protection Program, 822
Payrolls. (See Earnings, and individual industries.)
Peaches, 238, 884, 908, 912
Peanuts, 239, 771, 884, 1331
Pears, 238, 771, 884, 908, 912
Peas, green, 907
Peat, 949, 950
Pecans, 908, 909
Pedestrians, killed and injured, 1104, 1135, 1136, 1143
Pediatricians (see also Physicians), 171, 180
Pennsylvania. (See State data.)
Pensions and retirement benefits (see also Social insurance):
  Annuities, 1238, 1243
  Expenditures, 693, 725, 728, 729, 730
  Foreign countries, 1379
  Funds (flow of funds), 1198, 1201, 1239
  Government employees, 574, 575, 583, 1241
  Plans, 581, 584, 585, 694, 1227, 1234, 1238, 1239, 1240, 1241
  Veterans, 547, 555, 556, 574
Pentanes plus, 957
Peppers, 238, 771, 884, 907, 912
Performing arts, 1247, 1250, 1251, 1252, 1254, 1257
Performing arts, spectator sports industry:
  Capital, 817
  Earnings, 665, 791
  Employees, 665, 791, 1248, 1251, 1252, 1253
  Establishments, 791, 1248, 1250, 1251

Nonemployers, 1250
  Receipts, revenue, 791, 1247, 1248, 1250
  Valued added, 1253
Periodical publishing, 1161, 1166, 1169
Perlite, 949, 950
Personal and laundry services:
  Earnings, 665, 791
  Employees, 665, 791, 1293, 1294
  Establishments, 791, 1292, 1293
  Productivity, 673
  Receipts, 791, 1292, 1298, 1300
Personal care, 209, 647, 725, 729, 730, 766
Personal computers (PCs). (See Computers.)
Personal consumption expenditures, 705, 706, 716, 718, 727, 776, 777, 1261
Personal health care expenditures, 141, 142, 143, 144
Personal income, 717, 719, 720, 721, 722
Personal savings, 710, 714, 717
Peru. (See Foreign countries.)
Pesticides, 882
Petroleum and coal product manufacturing:
  Capital, 817
  Earnings, 665, 925, 1057, 1063
  Employees, 665, 925, 1055, 1057, 1059, 1063
  Establishments, 925, 1055
  Finances, 982
  Foreign trade, 1324, 1330
  Gross domestic product, 708, 1053
  Industrial production index, 826
  Multinational companies, 833, 834
  Productivity, 673
  Profits, 982
  Sales, shipments, 925, 1057, 1065, 1066
  Toxic chemical releases, 428
Petroleum and natural gas extraction, 954
Petroleum and products:
  Consumption, 968, 969, 973, 989, 1392
  Disposition, 956
  Electricity generation, 990, 992
  Emissions, 423
  Expenditures, 975, 977
  Foreign trade, 955, 956, 969, 978, 979, 980, 981, 1315, 1323, 1324, 1330
  Oil spills, 432
  Pipelines, 1154
  Prices, 768, 775, 778, 779, 951, 955, 969
  Production, 949, 954, 955, 956, 958, 968, 969
    World, 1389, 1391, 1398
  Refineries, 955, 956, 981
  Reserves, 955, 959, 981
  Stocks, 956, 981
  Strategic reserve, 981
  Value, 955, 958
Pets, 766, 1080, 1260, 1262
Pharmaceutical and medicine manufacturing, 665, 673, 833, 834, 841, 1057, 1059
Pharmacies and drug stores, 1080, 1082, 1083
Pharmacists, 647
Philanthropy, 614, 618, 619
Philippines. (See Foreign countries.)
Phosphate rock, 949, 950, 1389
Photographic equipment and supplies, 1260, 1323
Physical activity, 235

Note: Index citations refer to **table** numbers, not **page** numbers

---

Note: Index citations refer to **table** numbers, not **page** numbers

---

Note: Index citations refer to **table** numbers, not **page** numbers

Note: Index citations refer to **table** numbers, not **page** numbers

Program participation of household, 576
   Recipients, 574, 575, 594, 595, 596, 597
Public domain. (See Public lands.)
Public lands (see also Forests):
   Area, 413, 415, 929, 1273, 1274
   National forests, 929, 930
   National park system, 1272, 1273, 1274
   Ownership, 929
   Recreation, 1272, 1273, 1274
   States, 930, 1274, 1275
Public officials, prosecutions, 377
Public roads. (See Highways.)
Public safety (see also Law enforcement):
   Employment, 647
      Fire protection, 400, 505, 507
      Police protection and correction, 364, 365, 505,
         507
   Expenditures:
      Construction, value, 1009, 1010
      State and local government, 366, 483, 484, 491
      State government, 497, 500, 502
Public schools. (See Education.)
Public transportation, 725, 729, 730, 766
Public utilities, 967, 1000, 1001, 1002, 1003
Publishing (see also Books, and Newspapers):
   Books, 775, 1161, 1166, 1169
   Directory and mailing list, 1161, 1166, 1169
   Newspapers, 1161, 1166, 1169
   Periodicals, 1161, 1166, 1169
Publishing industry:
   Capital, 817
   Earnings, 665, 791, 1057, 1063, 1161, 1162
   Employees, 665, 791, 1055, 1057, 1059, 1063, 1161,
      1162
   Establishments, 791, 1055, 1161, 1162
   Finances, 1166, 1169
   Gross domestic product, 708, 1053
   Industrial production index, 826
   Multinational companies, 833, 834
   Receipts, revenue, 791, 1162, 1166, 1169, 1298
   Shipments, 1057, 1065, 1066
Puerto Rican population (see also Hispanic origin
      population):
   Agriculture, 1344, 1345
   Births, 16, 1333
   Deaths, 16, 115, 1333
   Educational attainment and enrollment, 37, 1334,
      1338
   Households, 37, 1335, 1336
   Housing tenure, 1336
   Labor force, 37, 622, 1337
   Population, 16, 37, 1332, 1333, 1335, 1337
   Summary, 1335, 1337
Puerto Rico. (See Island areas of the U.S.)
Pulmonary diseases (see also Respiratory diseases),
      117, 118, 119, 120, 121, 122, 197
Pulp manufacturing, 924, 927, 928
Pulpwood, 932, 933, 934, 936
Pumice and pumicite, 949, 950
Purchasing power of the dollar, 763

Q

Qatar. (See Foreign countries.)
Quarries. (See Mining industries.)
Quicksilver (mercury), 950

R

Rabies, 197
Race. (See individual race categories.)
Radio broadcasting industry (see also Broadcasting,
      and Telecommunications):
   Earnings, 665, 1161, 1162
   Employees, 665, 1161, 1162
   Establishments, 1161, 1162
   Finances, 1166, 1174
   Productivity, 673
   Revenue, 1162, 1166, 1174
   Stations, 1168
Radio listening, 1167
Radiologists, 171
Rail transportation industry (see also Railroads):
   Capital, 817
   Earnings, 665
   Employees, 665, 1094, 1095
   Establishments, 1095
   Foreign trade, 1101
   Gross domestic product, 708
   Shipments, 1101, 1102, 1155
Railroad employees' retirement funds, 513, 514,
      515, 572
Railroads:
   Amtrak, 1099, 1100
   Energy consumption, 971
   Mileage owned and operated, 1099
   Occupational safety, 1104
   Passenger traffic and revenue, 1150, 1286
   Shipments, 1101, 1102, 1155
   Vehicles, 1100
Rankings:
   Airport traffic, 1107, 1288
   Amusement parks, 1265
   Cities:
      Population, 21, 24, 39
      Residential property tax, 493
      Science and engineering employment, 855
   Countries:
      Agricultural exports and imports, 1388
      Consumption of beef, pork, poultry, 1387
      Military expenditures, 1411
      Population, 1356
   Federal R&D obligations to higher education, 844
   Freight gateways, 1317
   Port traffic, 1117, 1118
   State:
      Exports, 1320
      Farm marketings, 886
      Foreign trade, 1320
      Immigrants, 46
      Population, 15
      Public elementary/secondary school finances, 260

Note: Index citations refer to **table** numbers, not **page** numbers

---

Note: Index citations refer to **table** numbers, not **page** numbers

Note: Index citations refer to **table** numbers, not **page** numbers

Note: Index citations refer to **table** numbers, not **page** numbers

Note: Index citations refer to **table** numbers, not **page** numbers

Note: Index citations refer to **table** numbers, not **page** numbers

Note: Index citations refer to **table** numbers, not **page** numbers

Note: Index citations refer to **table** numbers, not **page** numbers

---

Note: Index citations refer to **table** numbers, not **page** numbers

V

Vacancy rates, housing, 1025, 1027, 1028, 1030, 1031, 1034
Vaccination, 200, 231, 232
Vanadium, 949, 953
Vanuatu. (See Foreign countries.)
Vaping (Electronic cigarette use), 207, 237
Veal (see also Beef, and Meat and meat products), 239, 775, 914, 1386, 1387
Vegetable oils. (See Oils.)
Vegetables (see also individual commodities):
  Acreage, 907, 912
  Consumer expenditures, 725, 729, 730
  Consumption, 238, 911
  Farm marketings, sales, 874, 882, 884, 912
  Foreign trade, 890, 891, 894, 897, 899, 911, 1323, 1331
  Organic, 912
  Prices, 766, 775, 779, 780, 887
  Production, 907, 911, 912
Vehicles. (See Motor vehicles.)
Veneer, wood products, 924, 927, 928, 937
Venezuela. (See Foreign countries.)
Vermiculite, 949, 950
Vermont. (See State data.)
Vessels. (See Ships.)
Veterans:
  Characteristics, 554, 557, 558, 612
  Employment, 535, 624
  Medical care, 149
  Number, 553, 554, 556
  Pensions and other benefits:
    Beneficiaries, 555, 556, 574
    Service-connected compensation, 555, 556
      Disbursements, 541, 556, 572, 573
      Federal aid to state and local governments, 482
      Federal payments, 512, 513, 571, 572, 573
Veterans Affairs, Dept. of:
  Expenditures, 139, 145, 555, 556, 571, 572, 573
  Home loans, 1220
  Mental health treatment facilities, 176, 177
Veterinary services, 1293, 1294, 1296
Vetoed bills, Congressional, 466
Victimizations, criminal, 348, 349, 350, 351, 352, 353, 354, 355, 358, 359, 360
Vietnam. (See Foreign countries.)
Violent crime, (see also Crime), 330, 339, 340, 341, 342, 343, 344, 345, 346, 347, 348, 358, 359, 360, 369, 370
Virgin Islands. (See Island areas of the U.S.)
Virginia. (See State data.)
Virtual schools, 281
Visa holders, doctorates, 846
Visa overstays, 565
Visual and performing arts, degrees, 323, 324, 325, 326
Vital statistics. (See Births and birth rates, Deaths and death rates, Divorces, and Marriages.)
Vitamins, 240
Vocational rehabilitation, 139, 611
Volleyball, 1269, 1270, 1271
Volunteer activities, 265, 615, 616

Votes:
  Congressional, 447, 449, 457, 458, 459
  Early voting, 448
  Gubernatorial, 468
  Presidential, 447, 449, 453, 454, 455, 456
Votes cast, 447, 448, 449, 450, 451, 452, 468
Voting-age population, 447, 449, 450, 451

W

Wage earners. (See Labor force, and individual industries.)
Wages and wage rates. (See Earnings.)
Walnuts, 884, 908, 909, 912
Warehouse clubs and superstores, 1080, 1083
Warehousing and storage industry:
  Capital, 817
  Earnings, 665, 1097
  Employees, 665, 1094, 1095, 1097
  Establishments, 1095, 1097, 1098
  Gross domestic product, 708
  Revenue, 1096, 1098
Washing machines, homes with, 1032, 1042, 1043
Washington. (See State data.)
Waste management & remediation services, 426, 791, 817, 1292, 1293, 1294, 1297
Wastepaper, 775, 937
Wastewater treatment, 426, 966, 967, 1003
Watches. (See Clocks and watches.)
Water (see also Wastewater treatment, and Water transportation industry):
  Area, 1, 404, 413
  Consumption, 417
  Freight, 1115, 1116, 1317
  Lakes, 405, 406, 407
  Pollution, 427, 432
  Public supply, 417, 1032
  Vessels, 1100, 1116
Water polo, 1270
Water, sewage and other systems, 486, 665, 966, 967, 1003
Water transportation industry:
  Accidents and deaths, 1104
  Capital, 817
  Earnings, 665, 1097
  Employees, 507, 665, 1094, 1095, 1097, 1114
  Establishments, 1095, 1097, 1098
  Ferry system, 1114
  Foreign trade, 1101, 1117, 1118
  Freight, 1115, 1116, 1117, 1118, 1317
  Fuel consumption, 971, 1116
  Gross domestic product, 708
  Outlays, 512
  Shipments, 1101, 1102, 1116
  Revenue, 1096, 1098, 1114, 1116, 1298
Water utility, 486, 729, 730, 766, 966, 967
Waterborne commerce, 1115, 1116, 1117, 1118
Watermelons, 238, 884, 907, 912
Waterways, 1099, 1115, 1116
Wealth:
  Business, 759
  Families, 756, 757
  Family farms, 871
  Government, 759

Note: Index citations refer to **table** numbers, not **page** numbers

Note: Index citations refer to **table** numbers, not **page** numbers